45th Edition

CAMRA's GOOD BEER GUIDE 2018

Edited by Roger Protz

Head of Publishing Simon Hall
Project Manager Emma Haines
Assistant Editors Ione Brown, Simon Tuite
Project Assistance Katie Button, Julie Hudson, Callum Allaway-North
Sales & Marketing Marilyn O'Donoghue

CAMRA

BOOKS

Clachaig Inn, Glencoe, Highlands, p656 (Photo: Ed Daynes)

Special thanks to 188,000 CAMRA members who carried out research for the pub entries; the Campaign's Regional Directors and Area Organisers, who co-ordinated the pub entries; the Campaign's Brewery Liaison Co-ordinators and Brewery Liaison Officers, who carried out research for the brewery entries; Rick Pickup and Andy Shaw for assistance co-ordinating the brewery entries; Iain Barker and Christine Beatty at AMA Dataset; Michael Slaughter for advising on heritage pubs; Alex Presland for technical support; all CAMRA's staff and CAMRA's National Executive for their help and support.

Thanks also to the publicans, breweries and others who have kindly contributed their photographs.

Photo credits: [Key: t = top; b = bottom; c=centre; l = left; r = right] Cover: (l&c) Cath Harries, (r) Plunkett Foundation; P4 Cath Harries; p12 Roger Protz; p1026 (b) Roger Protz; p470 Brian North.

Design: Colour pages design: Keith Holmes, Thames Street Studio; cover design: Dale Tomlinson. *Typeset in Guardian Sans and Dax.*

Maps & illustrations: Pubs section maps: David and Morag Perrot, PerroCarto; illustrations Hannah Moore.

Production: Database, typesetting of listings and indexes: AMA Dataset Ltd, Preston.

Printing: Printed and bound in the UK by CPI William Clowes, Beccles, Suffolk.

Published by the Campaign for Real Ale Ltd, 230 Hatfield Road, St Albans, Herts, AL1 4LW. www.camra.org.uk

Contents

All of the papers used in this book are recyclable and made from wood grown in managed, sustainable forests. They are manufactured at mills certified to ISO 14001 and/or EMAS.

PEFC
BMT-PEFC-0026

About the Good Beer Guide

Your independent guide to pubs and beer

The *Good Beer Guide*, first and foremost, will take you to great pubs serving great beer. But that's only one part of its role. It also directs you to breweries and their ales, as well as to the essential outlets in towns and rural areas where you can enjoy them.

A unique guide of different parts

Pubs are the central core of the Guide, the essential outlets for real ale. But the *Good Beer Guide* has always played a dual role, with its Breweries section complementing the pub listings by detailing all the producers of cask beer and their regular ales. As well as listing some 4,500 of the finest outlets for real ale and the ever-growing number of breweries, we also look at the campaigns to save pubs, curtail the powers of giant pub companies and the threats posed by takeovers by global brewers: see the Introduction on pages 6–9 and also pages 686–687. Other pages contain lively and informative consumer features on beer, pubs and brewing.

Comprehensive Breweries section

The *Good Beer Guide* includes a comprehensive listing of all British breweries and their core beers. Breweries are monitored on a regular basis and each brewery is visited by CAMRA members, who speak to the brewer and check on the beers being produced before reporting to the Guide. When a new brewery comes on stream, a liaison officer will be appointed to ensure the Breweries section of the Guide is accurate and up to date.

Democratically selected entries

The way in which pubs are chosen is equally meticulous. Much of CAMRA's 188,000 membership is involved and those members who cannot be active or attend regular meetings are invited to recommend pubs via email or branch websites. Branch areas are broken down into local sections so pubs can be monitored regularly. The quality of beer in each pub is checked using a national beer scoring system. Special branch meetings are convened once a year where short-lists are presented and then members vote on the final selection for the Guide.

Regular inspections

The entries in most pub guides are chosen either by small editorial teams or by members of the public, whose recommendations are not necessarily checked. However, every pub that appears in this Guide has been visited regularly, often weekly, by CAMRA members. We offer full entries, with no unchecked 'lucky dip' sections of pubs sent in at random. Readers' recommendations are passed to local CAMRA branches, who take this feedback into account during their survey work.

It's not only about quality beer

The key driving force of the Guide – beer quality – has not changed over 45 years. However, the Guide also takes account of the history and architecture of pubs and such important aspects as food, family and disabled facilities, gardens, special events such as mini-beer festivals, and even the standard of the toilets. CAMRA volunteers are called on to be minor essayists, describing in detail all aspects of the pubs they choose. We know, from the feedback we receive, that users of the Guide need full information about pubs before embarking on journeys to visit them.

Town & country pubs

In addition to full descriptions, users want a good spread of pubs. Unlike some guides that concentrate on rural pubs, we recognise that most people live in towns and cities and expect a good selection of pubs in those areas. But we don't neglect suburban and country pubs: on the contrary, CAMRA campaigns for the survival of rural pubs that are often hubs of their communities.

We strive hard to ensure that all areas of the country are covered. Each county or region has an allocation of pubs based on a scientific calculation

Southampton Arms, Kentish Town, London

of its population, number of licensed premises and levels of tourism. As a result, the *Good Beer Guide's* reach is unparalleled.

Proudly independent

Unlike with many of our competitors, all entries in our guide are free. CAMRA is a proudly independent organisation and there are no hidden costs of appearing in the *Good Beer Guide*. Guides that charge for entries restrict consumer choice as not all publicans can afford the fees demanded. CAMRA is a broad church and the Guide reflects that by choosing pubs across a wide spectrum that will appeal to people from all walks of life, regardless of income and background.

Keeping up to date

The Campaign has more than 200 branches. Each branch surveys the pubs in its area and monitors not only the quality of the cask beer in each one but also watches for change of ownership or management that could affect the range of ale on offer and the overall standard of the pub. In addition, branch officers liaise frequently with breweries in their areas and keep a close eye on the local brewing scene. Thanks to modern technology, the Guide is checked and re-checked many times before publication.

Checking doesn't stop there: both CAMRA's national website and its monthly newspaper *What's Brewing* publish regular information about, and updates to the Guide, including pubs that have closed or where beer quality has declined. These changes are also reflected in the *Good Beer Guide* mobile app that, alongside an e-book and sat-nav POI file, give readers access to the Guide in many different formats (see page 1029).

An all-new Good Beer Guide app was launched in August 2017, taking the Guide to a growing digital audience

Such rigorously updated information provides CAMRA and the *Good Beer Guide* with an unrivalled electronic storehouse of information about Britain's pubs and breweries.

Additional resources

There are limits to the size of the *Good Beer Guide*. We believe – thanks to our members' efforts and the recommendations sent in by readers – that we offer a choice of the very best pubs throughout the country. But the Guide is complemented by other resources, including local pub guides produced by CAMRA branches which are available at beer festivals and local outlets, and the online **www.whatpub.com** – CAMRA's official guide to all known real ale outlets in the country.

CAMRA also produces a constantly expanding range of other books on the subjects of beer, pubs and brewing. Some of the latest are highlighted on pages 1027–1028. The full list of CAMRA books can be found at **www. camra.org.uk/books**.

National Beer Scoring System

Pubs are selected for the Guide by CAMRA branches who use the scores submitted by members to help them identify places that serve consistently good beer. The system uses a 0–5 scale that can be submitted online. Any CAMRA member can submit a beer score by going to CAMRA's online pub guide **www.whatpub.com**, logging in as a member and selecting 'Submit Beer Scores'.

Updates, reader feedback & readers' survey

You can keep your copy of the Guide up to date by visiting the *Good Beer Guide* area of the CAMRA website: **www.camra.org.uk/gbg**. Click on 'Updates to GBG 2018' where you will find information about changes to pubs and breweries.

The Guide is keen to hear from readers. If you wish to recommend a pub or feel that one you have visited fell below your expectations, then we would like to know. Please use the Readers' recommendations form at the back of the book or contact the editor at **gbgeditor@camra.org.uk**.

Additionally, in this 45th-anniversary year, **we are undertaking an online survey of our readers**. We would like as many of our readers as possible to take part and give us their views. For more details, please see page 1032 and visit **www.camra.org.uk/gbg2018survey**.

Introduction

Real ale booms but pubs and beer threatened

From Shetland to the Scilly Isles, breweries and beer are booming. This is the 45th edition of the *Good Beer Guide* and it's an opportunity to take stock and marvel at the changes that have transformed the pleasure of beer drinking over that period. On page 10 we look back at the first edition of the Guide, 96 pages in length. Just two pages were devoted to breweries that concentrated in the main on two types of beer, mild and bitter. Pubs serving real ale were thin on the ground. This was the result of the awesome power of national brewers who had phased out cask ale and massively promoted fizzy keg beers that would be laughed to scorn today.

How the beer world has changed! Today, in spite of closures, a growing number of pubs clamber to offer the best-possible range of real ales. They present them with special events such as mini beer festivals, beer tastings and discussions about matching food and beer. Such initiatives are boosted by CAMRA beer festivals that offer drinkers a wide choice of beers from all parts of Britain and beyond. The beer festivals section (pages 17–19) lists the vast range of events in towns, cities and rural areas. It spotlights those that have been flying the flag for good beer for 40 years and more and helped put real ale back on the bar during the dog days of national brewers and keg beer in the 1970s.

Breweries carry on opening to meet the insatiable demand for real ale. You might think from studying the media that the British are enjoying a love affair with gin, English sparkling wine and 'craft keg' beer. But as the Breweries section in this edition proves, real ale is the drink of the moment. As well as 261 new breweries, others repeat the same messages, entry upon entry: 'installing new equipment... moving to bigger premises... doubling capacity'. Many brewers are using such innovations as crowd funding to invest in their plants and many are also buying one or two pubs that act as shop windows for their beer.

Ups and downs

Since the 2017 edition of the Guide was published there have been significant developments in both brewing and retailing that offer both hope and concern. In the continuing battle to save the Great British Pub, undoubtedly the most significant victory was the one that now stops pubs being demolished or turned into shops without planning permission. It was a curious anomaly of English planning laws that pubs were uniquely able to be flattened or converted to convenience stores without first gaining local authority permission through the usual planning application process.

Thanks to a long-running campaign led by CAMRA and parliamentarians, in Spring 2017 Lord Roy Kennedy won support in the House of Lords for a change to the law that will prevent 'change of use' or demolition of a pub without planning permission. The Lords' decision was adopted by the Government and gives the battered and endangered British pub the kiss of life. See pages 11–13 for fuller details of this decision.

Pubs Code and MRO

The power of the major national pub companies, Enterprise Inns – renamed Ei Group – and Punch Taverns was at long last challenged in 2016. The pubcos often impose high rents on their tenants, charge inflated prices for beer to those tenants and restrict the choice of beers for pubgoers. This led to a long-running campaign by CAMRA, MPs and tied publicans for a root-and-branch investigation of the pub trade. The result in 2016 was a Government decision to introduce both a Pubs Code and a new post of Pubs Adjudicator who will intervene when there is a dispute between a tenant and the pub owner.

A central element of the Pubs Code – one that was a key part of CAMRA's campaigning – was the right of tenants whose pub companies own more than 500 pubs to apply for a market rent option, MRO for short, whereby rent is paid for the building only. This means that in return for negotiating a fair market rent, tenants would

CAMRA campaigned to get General Election candidates signed up to their beer and pubs manifesto

be free to choose beers and not be tied to the pubcos' lists. MRO was fiercely opposed by the big pubcos who put every road block in the way of giving both publicans and drinkers better choice. The pubcos are determined to enforce 'the tie' that determines the beers a tenant can sell. This is because the pubcos have sweetheart deals with big national and global brewers to buy their beers at substantial discounts.

A year on from the introduction of the Pubs Code, CAMRA is assessing how effective the Adjudicator has been. The fact that to date more than 120 cases have been to the Adjudicator proves how right the campaign for a Pubs Code was and highlights the stubborn refusal of the pubcos to meet the demands of both tenants and customers.

In July 2017, a group of pub operators called the Pubs Code Adjudicator a 'rabbit in the headlights' for his alleged slowness and inaction over MRO applications. They said the PCA's inertia and slow progress had already costs three of the operators around £50,000 in professional service fees. The PCA responded by saying his methods 'reduced risk'.

MRO currently only applies in England and Wales but CAMRA in Scotland is working with Members of the Scottish Parliament (MSPs) to ensure that Scottish publicans can also benefit from the market rent only option.

Punch sale

The driving force for the way in which Ei and Punch operate is their astonishing levels of debt: Ei's stands at £2.2bn and at one stage Punch had to be restructured to avoid administration. This parlous state of affairs was the result of a buying-spree of pubs at the turn of the century that was holed below the water line by the economic crash of 2008.

In order to reduce their debts, both companies sell pubs – often perfectly successful ones – and charge inflated rents and prices to their tenants. In 2015 Punch sold 158 pubs for £53.5 million to a retail property company called New River Retail that has a track record of turning pubs into convenience stores. As a result of discussions with CAMRA, New River Retail has made it clear that its intention is to minimise pub closures and instead focus on developing pub sites so they host both a convenience store and a pub.

But the sale by Punch to New River was dwarfed in 2017 by the disposal of 1,900 of its 3,000 pubs to Heineken UK for £300 million. Heineken is Britain's biggest brewer as a result of buying the Scottish & Newcastle group in 2008: as well as major beer brands, the sale gave the global Dutch group 1,049 pubs branded Star Bars & Pubs. The estate will more than doubled with the acquisition of a large tranche of Punch pubs.

This could be a case of better the devil you know... Pub tenants in Scotland who have first-hand experience of Heineken have expressed concern that the group will impose a tight regime and will flood the former Punch pubs with its own products. Heineken has denied this but the Competition and Market Authority (CMA) told Heineken it must resolve local monopolies by selling pubs in 33 areas where the brewery's holdings are considered to be anti-competitive. In July 2017 the CMA gave provisional clearance to the Heineken/Punch sale and Heineken said it would sell 30 pubs as part of the deal.

Rates bombshell

The pub sector was dealt another major blow with a Government re-assessment of business rates that at first threatened some pubs with rises of 70 per cent. Many publicans said such swingeing increases would force them to close. Here was another anomaly: while pubs account for 0.5 per cent of the total economy they pay 2.8 per cent of total business rates. See pages 11-13 for more on business rates.

The uproar caused by the increases forced the Government to back track and to offer some help to pubs. CAMRA has called for a £5,000 business rates discount for pubs and has also called for a major review of the crippling level of business rates for pubs in recognition of the social welfare benefits they provide for their local communities and for society as a whole.

In the summer of 2017, the Association of Licensed Multiple Retailers said a number of pubs had already closed as a result of the increased level of business rates imposed on them.

Stealth tax

In the March 2017 Budget, the Chancellor, Philip Hammond, was cheered when he said he was freezing beer duty. It quickly transpired that this was a sleight-of-hand piece of

Cut the tax burden on pubs: CAMRA calls for business rate relief for pubs

accounting and in fact all alcohol duties were increasing using the Retail Price Index (RPI). Far from being frozen, beer duty increased, with the price of a pint going up by some two pence.

This was yet another hammer blow for the pub. While supermarkets can absorb duty increases as a result of the deep discounts they demand from suppliers, most publicans have to pay the full list price for their beer and are forced to pass on duty increases.

Beer duty increases brought in by the last Labour government did terrible harm to beer and pubs by increasing duty every year in the Budget without debate in parliament. When the duty escalator was scrapped by the Coalition Government it was estimated this prevented:

- 1,000 pubs from closing
- 750 million more pints of beer a year were sold as a result.

CAMRA has joined forces with other key players in brewing and retailing including the British Beer & Pub Association, the Association of Licensed Multiple Retailers, the Society of Independent Brewers, the Pub is the Hub, and the British Institute of Innkeeping. These bodies will collectively lobby the Government on beer duty and business rates. Lobbying may be difficult at a time of political uncertainty following the June 2017 general election but the priority is to emphasise the important contribution that brewing and retailing make to the economy, accounting for:

- 90,000 jobs and
- £23.1 billion in taxes and duty.

While the number of pub closures has declined and there are also many new openings, it requires vigilance to ensure that as many pubs as possible remain as beacons of community activity in towns, cities and villages.

Impact of Brexit
The decision to leave the European Union will give this country more freedom to decide how to levy taxes and duties on alcohol. CAMRA will argue strongly for draught beer sold in pubs to have lower rates of duty, which is contrary to EU legislation. At present pubs are at a disadvantage as the 'off trade' – supermarkets and other licensed retail outlets – sell beer at substantial discounts. Lower duty rates for draught beer would create more of a level playing field and attract drinkers away from the sofa and back into the pub.

Pubs and well-being
Pubs are about more than drinking. They are at the heart of communities and welcome people from all social backgrounds. As well as enjoying good beer, pub-goers can meet for a chat or a serious discussion, and can read a newspaper or a book while eating and drinking. Crucially, the pub helps break down the isolation that many people feel in our modern, fragmented society.

In 2016 CAMRA commissioned an in-depth report called Friends on Tap that highlighted the role of pubs at the heart of the community: see pages 11-13.

Standing up for beer
The Campaign was highly critical of the severe restrictions recommended by the Chief Medical Officers in England, Scotland, Wales and Northern Ireland in 2016. The recommendations replaced the former suggested limits of 21 units of alcohol a week for men and 14 for women with a new limit of 14 units for both sexes.

CAMRA and the Good Beer Guide believe in the moderate and sensible consumption of alcohol but we were unimpressed by the poor science that underpinned the recommendations. CAMRA pointed out that several countries not known for their wild or profligate drinking behaviour have higher recommended units:

- Ireland and Denmark: 21 units.
- US and Canada: 25 units.
- France: 17.5 units.
- Italy: 21 units.
- Spain: 34 units.

Spain in particular is famous for its healthy 'Mediterranean diet' based on fresh vegetables, olive oil and fish, accompanied by wine and beer: the craft beer sector is growing appreciably there.

CAMRA was critical of the fact that the Chief Medical Officers were disproportionately influenced by temperance organisations, including the Temperance Movement of the United States that campaigned for total Prohibition in the 20th century. The medical officers also took advice from the Alcohol Health Alliance that claimed the consumption of alcohol had increased in recent years. In fact statistics accumulated by HM Revenue & Customs, which collects all the duties and taxes levied on alcohol, show that consumption has fallen by close to 20 per cent over the past decade.

There is a wealth of evidence compiled by universities in the UK, United States, Europe and Scandinavia proving that a moderate intake of

AB InBev

The world's biggest brewer now accounts for 30 per cent of beer production

alcohol can help prevent heart attacks, strokes, diabetes, dementia and gall stones. Research is being conducted in both the US and Germany into how the natural chemicals in the hop plant – resins, oils and tannins – can ward off certain types of cancer.

The Guide's recommendation is quite simple: enjoy beer in moderation and choose beer made with the finest natural ingredients.

Big brewers on the march

While the growth of the craft or artisan brewing sector is encouraging, we cannot ignore the worrying trend to concentrate brewing power into fewer hands. The sale in 2016 of the world's second biggest brewer SABMiller to world giant AB InBev gave the American-Brazilian-Belgian colossus control of 30 per cent of world beer production. AB InBev is using its wealth and muscle to buy craft breweries, including Camden Town in the UK and Goose Island in the US.

In July 2017, Carlsberg announced it was buying the London Fields Brewery in East London. At the same time, AB InBev opened a much bigger brewery for Camden Town in Enfield. In August 2017, the iconic Anchor Brewing Co. of San Francisco was bought by Sapporo of Japan.

Equally worrying is the increasing domination of three national brewers: Greene King, Marston's and Molson Coors. In the past two years Marston's has bought two large regional breweries, Thwaites and, more recently in May 2017, Charles Wells. This gives the Burton-based group not only a large portfolio of brands but also gives the impression to drinkers that the likes of Thwaites Bitter and Wells Bombardier still come from their original family breweries.

Whether they are brewed by global or large national brewers, beers change under new ownership. Long-term contracts with grain and hop suppliers means that recipes, flavours and character will alter. Production methods can also be speeded up to get beer to pubs and bars faster in order to brew more and maximise profits – again with often profound changes to the taste of the end product. This trend is discussed in greater depth in the Breweries section starting on page 685.

CAMRA looks to the future

Since 2016, CAMRA has been engaged in an exhaustive review of its role in recognition of the profound changes taking place in the beer world. The initial stage of the review, known as the Revitalisation Project, was run by a steering group independent of the Campaign's ruling National Executive.

The group ran a series of meetings throughout the country at which CAMRA members were able to voice their opinions on the future direction of the Campaign. The 188,000-strong membership was also encouraged to take part in a series of surveys in which members were asked to give their opinions on whether CAMRA should stick to its founding beliefs or widen its scope. The steering group also took wider soundings, with advice from brewers, cider makers, publicans and pub owners, MPs and peers, and journalists.

The message came back loud and clear from CAMRA members that the organisation should continue to campaign for real ale, cider and perry, and should support pubs as the hubs of their communities. But when asked if the Campaign should recognise different types of quality beer, 61 per cent voted in the affirmative.

A final report from the Steering Group has gone to the Campaign's National Executive, which will make recommendations to the annual Members' Weekend in 2018.

Whatever the outcome, it is crystal clear – like a glass of the finest cask beer – that real ale will remain central to CAMRA's aims and activities. It is vital to reach out to all beer lovers, including the welcome growth in the number of women drinkers, by offering the widest choice of beer in pubs and at beer festivals.

But while much has changed since the *Good Beer Guide* was first published 45 years ago, both the first and the 45th editions are linked by a passionate belief in real ale. We happen to believe that beer should be made from the finest malts and hops and allowed to brew and ferment naturally without any chemical help. It should be neither filtered nor pasteurised in the brewery and then allowed to enjoy a second fermentation in its cask in the pub cellar.

Served cool and refreshing, it is the pinnacle of the brewers' art – a Pint of the Best.

Cheers!

Looking back over 45 years...

The 1974 *Good Beer Guide* was a call to arms for beer lovers. The introduction railed against 'two major developments threatening to kill off good ale once and for all: the large-scale promotion of characterless keg and tank beers at an advertising cost of millions of pounds a year; and the transfer from traditional methods of serving draught beer to pumps using carbon dioxide pressure, which makes ale gassy and sickly.'

The Guide was published at a time when the brewing industry had changed out of all recognition as a result of a merger frenzy that had created six large national brewing groups. They owned more than half the country's pubs and flooded them with pressurised keg beer.

The marketing power of the Big Six rubbed off on family and regional brewers who thought they should go down the keg route to survive. It's fascinating to find in the breweries listing such modern icons of cask beer as Fuller's and Harvey's described as the first having 'only a handful of draught houses' and the second as running pubs where it was 'difficult to find real ale'.

It was the influence of CAMRA and the Guide that encouraged the likes of Fuller's and Harvey's to rejoin the path of bibulous righteousness.

But it was a hard path at first. CAMRA was a fledgling organisation. Membership was patchy and the editor John Hanscomb admitted that some areas were covered inadequately. The 96-page guide cost 75 pence and listed around 1,500 pubs. There was not a single entry for Scotland, the result of there being few CAMRA members on the ground and the lack of real ale from the two breweries that dominated the country, Scottish & Newcastle and Tennent Caledonian.

The pubs listed reflected the breweries that still offered good beer. Leeds had just five pubs, the result of the major brewery in the city, Tetley, busily converting to keg. York fared better as both John Smith and Samuel Smith were still committed to cask. Liverpool and Manchester had nine and 13 entries respectively as both cities still enjoyed a clutch of local breweries. But the entire county of Norfolk had just eight entries – the result of the London brewer Watney buying all three breweries in Norwich. It eventually closed them along with many pubs in the county it considered to be 'uneconomic' and supplied the remainder with keg beer.

London had 120 pubs. Fuller's might have been retreating from real ale but many of its pubs still sported handpumps while the legendary Young's of Wandsworth never turned its back on cask beer. And Bass Charrington was then a major presence in the capital and offered Charrington IPA and Draught Bass in many of its pubs.

Pub descriptions were rudimentary, such as 'near airport' for one Manchester entry. Some pubs had no descriptions at all while an entry in Preston –'working-class pub but clean and courteous' – would be considered politically incorrect today.

It's the breweries section that emphasises the enormous change that has taken place over the following 45 years. It runs to just two pages and lists 105 brewing companies, though Bass with nine subsidiaries and Whitbread with 14 added to the tally while indicating their growing dominance as a result of takeovers.

The entry for Watney has gone down in CAMRA history. The Guide was printed by John Waddington in Leeds. The owner was a keen real ale drinker and was happy to offer CAMRA a good printing deal. But he was horrified to find, as the first copies were printed, that the description for Watney – responsible for the abysmal Red Barrel keg beer – advised readers to avoid the brewery's products 'like the plague'. Fearing a libel writ, the Guide was hastily reprinted, with drinkers now told that Watney should be 'avoided at all costs'.

Of equal interest is the beer range available in 1974 – mild and bitter, with a smattering of winter and Christmas ales. Compare that with the plethora of beer styles – old and new – listed in the 45th edition.

But both guides are linked by a common cause – a passion for traditional draught ale that has to be protected from the manufacturers of factory beer at national and global levels. It should hold us in good stead for the next 45 years.

The great British pub

Meeting new challenges from government & supermarkets

The British pub is unique. Other countries have bars, taverns, drinking shops and what Australians quaintly called 'hotels' (accommodation optional). The British pub is different. It's rooted in our island's history, dating from Roman and Saxon times, with names that commemorate monarchs and tradesmen, lords and ladies and their coats of arms, battles, ships, planes, games, and literary and sporting heroes.

Pub is shorthand for public house. It welcomes all-comers, regardless of background and income. There's no better place for people to meet, enjoy a beer, strike up a conversation, make new friends and put the world to rights.

Most importantly, the pub is the glue that holds communities together. Close a pub in a village or suburb and the community withers and dies.

And above all, the British pub, ancient and modern, has character and atmosphere. You can buy beer in a supermarket but you can't enjoy it there. The pub on the other hand offers theatre: the welcome from 'the guv'nor' or the landlady, the buzz of conversation and the drama of a pump being pulled and delivering a glass of refreshing beer topped by a tempting collar of foam.

But the pub is under threat as never before. When CAMRA was formed in the early 1970s, Britain had 80,000 pubs. The number is now fewer than 50,000 and more beer is drunk at home than in the pub.

There are complex reasons for this. Giant pub companies dispose of perfectly successful outlets to ease their dire financial problems. The pub once stood proud on the high street, the centre of town or village life. Now coffee shops, bakeries, restaurants offering a vast range of food styles, and fast food outlets compete for the 'leisure pound'. And multi-channel television and other forms of home entertainment encourage people to stay on the sofa.

There are signs of hope, however. The number of weekly closures has fallen from 29 to 21. As we report in the Introduction to this edition, a major victory was achieved in 2017 when new Government legislation laid down that English pubs can no longer be demolished or have a change of retail use without planning permission. This was the result of a long campaign waged by CAMRA, the Parliamentary Pubs Group and other campaigners, and was successfully steered through the House of Lords by Lord Roy Kennedy. The Lords' decision was swiftly endorsed by the Commons where MPs Nigel Adams, Charlotte Leslie and Greg Mulholland championed the need for this change.

This important decision means that winning Asset of Community Value (ACV) status for a pub is no longer necessary. ACV is a type of listing, the local government equivalent of Grade II national listing. Some 1,500 pubs now have ACV status but it will become an increasing rarity as an ACV listing is no longer a precondition for a pub to be given full planning protection.

London leads the fight-back

A report compiled by CAMRA in April 2017 into the number of pub closures in London prompted a swift response by the Mayor, Sadiq Khan. He had appointed a Night Tsar, Amy Lamé, to promote the capital's night-time cultural life and an important element of her work will be to boost the fortunes of London's pubs.

The Mayor was reacting to the stark figures in the CAMRA report. It showed that in 2001 there were 4,835 pubs in London and the number had fallen to 3,615 by 2016, a loss of 1,200.

Two London boroughs – Barking & Dagenham and neighbouring Newham – reported the loss of more than half their pubs, with drops of 56 per cent in the former and 52 per cent in the latter. Other badly-affected boroughs include Croydon (45 per cent drop), Waltham Forest (44 per cent), Hounslow (42 per cent) and Lewisham (41 per cent). Hackney was the only London borough to report an increase in the number of pubs opening.

Sadiq Khan said: 'I am shocked at the rate of closure highlighted by these statistics and that's why we have partnered with CAMRA, to ensure we track the number of pubs open in the capital and redouble our efforts to stem the rate of closures.

'The Great British Pub is at the heart of the capital's culture. From traditional working men's clubs to cutting-edge micro-breweries, London's locals are as diverse and eclectic as the people who frequent them.'

The Mayor, with his Night Time Commission and Night Tsar, will carry out an annual audit of London's pubs. He believes that a key reason for the decline in pub numbers is the steep rise in business rates.

Rates time bomb

New business rates announced for pubs in 2017 could have a devastating impact on the sector. Some of the increases, due to be phased in over a five-year period, are eye-watering. The Baum in Rochdale, CAMRA's National Pub of the Year 2012, and on the site of the Rochdale Pioneers' first co-op in the 19th century, will see its rateable value increase by 377 per cent. Sandford Park Alehouse in Cheltenham, National Pub of the Year 2015, faces an increase of 181 per cent.

In CAMRA's home base of St Albans, which has the biggest number of pubs per square mile of any town or city in the country, the planned rises are astronomical. Sean Hughes, who runs the 15th-century, *Good Beer Guide*-listed Boot, says his rates will eventually go up from £14,000 to £53,000, an increase of 280 per cent. Twenty-nine pubs in St Albans face a combined increase of £70,000 a year and Sean Hughes thinks several of them would be forced to close.

In neighbouring Old Hatfield, Andy Parish at the Eight Bells says his business is on the 'cliff edge' as a result of the increases. The pub, close to historic Hatfield House, is Grade II listed and is an ancient coaching inn on the Great North Road visited by Dick Turpin and Charles Dickens.

The outcry caused by the increases led to the government announcing a £300 million rescue package that will be handled by local authorities. In addition the majority of pubs in England will receive a £1,000 discount on their business rates bill. As stated in the Introduction, CAMRA has called for affected pubs to be given an annual relief reduction of £5,000 each. CAMRA will lobby the government for both rate relief and a root-and-branch review of the way in which business rates are levied for the pub sector, which pays a disproportionately high level compared to other businesses. Significantly, when the new rates were announced, many out-of-town supermarkets and stores based on industrial estates saw their rates decreased. It's town-centre pubs that face the brunt of the increases, which can only fuel the rate and level of closures.

'Wet pubs' under threat

A number of pub groups and breweries announced welcome 'new build' pubs in 2017. JD Wetherspoon plans to open 15 new pubs, including one in Edinburgh's main Waverley railway station.

The Stonegate pub company, which enjoys a good reputation for beer choice in its pubs, has opened several new outlets. In 2017 it bought from Wetherspoon the 90 year-old Tally Ho at Tally Ho Corner in Finchley, North London. The Enfield & Barnet branch of CAMRA campaigned to save the pub when Wetherspoon put it up for sale and set about gaining ACV status for the three-storey building, originally built by London brewer Charrington. It's named after a 19th-century coaching company on the Great North Road.

In the event, it was bought by Stonegate, which spent £750,000 on a refit. This includes opening up the second storey that was once used as an office by Wetherspoon founder Tim Martin when he started to build his pub chain.

Greene King and Marston's, the UK's biggest brewery and pubs groups, have opened new pubs. Welcome though this is, the new outlets tend to be restaurant-style pubs, some with accommodation as well. The Guide has no complaints about pubs offering food as this creates the opportunity to organise beer-and-food matching events and menus that recommend beers to accompany particular dishes. But by concentrating on food-led pubs, breweries and pub companies have turned their backs on traditional 'wet-led' outlets where beer is the main consideration.

Not everyone wants to go to a pub to eat. Many people enjoy the ability to have a couple of pints after work or to meet friends and enjoy a beer or two. It's possible to just drink in a restaurant-style pub but many people find them off-putting, with all available space set aside for dining, with table numbers and menus.

Local CAMRA branches have criticised Marston's in particular for closing many wet-led pubs. But the group's chief executive Ralph Findlay told the Guide that this policy is being reconsidered in the light of its growing and revamped beer range that, he says, has created great interest among

Tally Ho in Finchley, North London: an historic pub rescued by Stoneygate

younger drinkers. In defence of some closures, Mr Findlay added that the pubs in question had become unviable, based in areas that failed to attract custom.

The Craft Union pub company has launched a major drive to build an estate of wet-led pubs. Operations director Frazer Grimbleby said he was 'flying the flag for wet-led pubs' and planned to open 170 sites during 2017.

While the sale of Thwaites' and Charles Wells's breweries is a cause for regret, both companies will use the income from the sale to invest in new pubs. Charles Wells, which sold its Bedford brewery and key brands to Marston's for £55 million in May 2017, has said it plans to expand its 200-strong pub estate, some of which will be run on a franchise basis. Its chain of pubs in France will continue to offer real ale to French drinkers.

In sharp distinction to traditional pubs, the micropub or pop-up pub phenomenon continues to grow. These are outlets based in redundant shops or in railway stations or arches in former industrial areas. As the name implies, they are small with a focus on beer, real ale predominating. There are now close to 300 micropubs throughout the country, supported by the Micropub Association (**www.micropubassociation.co.uk**) and backed by a micropub guide book.

Saving pubs

Don't lose your locals! If a pub is under threat, contact your local CAMRA branch: **www.camra. org.uk/branches**. Set up an action group or steering group and lobby your local council to deny planning permission for change of use.

The Localism Act of 2011 gave much greater powers to local authorities to protect local amenities from closure or unwarranted change of use. For details of how to use the Act go to www. gov.uk and follow the links to a 'A Plain English Guide to the Localism Act'.

Seek help, advice and possible funding from the Plunkett Foundation: **www.plunkett.co.uk**; Co-operative & Mutual Solutions: **www.cms.coop**, and the Pub is the Hub: **www.pubisthehub.org.uk**.

Why going to the pub is good for you

The traditional British pub offers more than just a good pint, it also provides the ideal environment for meeting old and new friends.

This is one of the key findings from a special report, commissioned by CAMRA in 2016, 'Friends on Tap – the role of pubs at the heart of the community'. The report and analysis, carried out by Professor Robin Dunbar and a team from the Department of Experimental Psychology at the University of Oxford, said nothing is more significant, both to people's lives and to the national economy, than health and happiness: 'The more friends you have, the happier and healthier you are.'

And health and happiness are enhanced by having a local pub and visiting it regularly, Professor Dunbar found. 'People who said they have a "local" or those who patronise small community pubs have more close friends on whom they can depend for support, are more satisfied with their lives and feel more embedded in their local communities than those who said they do not have a local pub,' he added.

A key part of the research for the report was a special poll conducted by YouGov on behalf of CAMRA in which adults were asked about their use of pubs and their overall sense of health and wellbeing. The poll showed that people were most likely to drink alcohol at home with friends (57%), with the second most common location being in a pub with food – 41% of drinkers say the pub is the place where they regularly drink alcohol.

Significantly, the people polled regarded the pub as a relatively safe place to drink and to avoid binge drinking, as well as the best place to socialise with friends after their own or friend's homes.

The report added that 'a limited alcohol intake improves wellbeing and some (though not all) social skills... These findings suggest that pubs in general, and local community pubs in particular, may have unseen social benefits.

'Being more engaged with your local community and being involved more frequently in conversations with other individuals can have substantial benefits by reducing loneliness, which in turn is likely to have significant health and wellbeing benefits... Pubs serve an important hub function, by providing a venue at which people can meet.'

The full report can be read at **www.camra.org/pubs-wellbeing**.

Award winning pubs & clubs

Pub of the Year

A village pub in Yorkshire's Swaledale that was saved by the local community was named CAMRA's National Pub of the Year in 2017. It now plans to expand with its own micro-brewery.

Stuart Miller, landlord of the **George & Dragon in Hudswell**, near Richmond, North Yorkshire (see page 534) is looking at possible sites in the village or close by to install his kit. Stuart has been on an intensive course at Brewlab in Sunderland to learn the brewing skills. Keith Thomas, who runs Brewlab, lives in Richmond and has planted Cascade, Fuggles and Goldings hops in the garden behind the pub that can be used in Stuart's beers.

The George & Dragon closed in 2008 when its owners were declared bankrupt during the recession. But the pub's regulars – including then local MP William Hague – formed a co-operative to buy and refurbish it. The Hudswell Community Pub Group raised £220,000 to restore the George & Dragon, which re-opened in 2010.

Today the pub is a hub of the community. It has a library, allotments and a convenience shop selling milk, eggs and newspapers. 'The George & Dragon is a great example of how a pub has been resurrected as a true community asset,' said Paul Ainsworth, CAMRA coordinator for the Pub of the Year competition. 'To go from closed doors to winning National Pub of the Year in just a few short years is a fantastic achievement for any pub – and all the more impressive for one that is cooperatively owned.'

Members of the Hudswell co-operative that rescued the George & Dragon

Stuart Miller added: 'Since we took over the George & Dragon in 2014 we've strived to achieve our vision for the pub. To be appreciated for these goals by our customers and CAMRA is extremely satisfying and makes all the hard work worthwhile.'

Pubs entered for the Pub of the Year Award are judged by CAMRA on atmosphere, level of service, value for money and community focus, but extra weighting is, of course, given to the quality of the real ale, cider and perry. In the case of the George & Dragon, judges also praised Stuart Miller's 'great passion' for quality beer. Stuart sources most of his beers from Yorkshire breweries, including Rudgate and Wensleydale.

Stuart Miller, landlord of National Pub of the Year, the George & Dragon.

The three other finalists in the Pub of the Year competition were:

Swan with Two Necks, Pendleton, Lancashire (see page 248):

Dating from 1772, as a licensed farm, the Swan With Two Necks sits beside the stream in the heart of the village of Pendleton. The landlords have been in charge for 30 years and are renowned for their welcome and hospitality. National CAMRA Pub of the Year in 2013, you will find five beers here (including a mild) and a changing cider on

---

CAMRA's National Pub of the Year competition considers all the criteria that make for a good pub. The competition is judged by the Campaign's 188,000-plus members. Each branch selects its top pub. The branch winners are entered into 16 regional competitions, with the regional winners battling it out to reach the final stages of the competition. Look out for the ♥ symbol against pub entries in the Guide and see 'Award-winning pubs' on pages 1022–1023 for the winning branch pubs.

the bar. CAMRA members receive a discount. Home-cooked, locally-sourced food is served daily; booking is essential at weekends, especially for the Sunday roast.

Salutation Inn, Ham,
Gloucestershire (see page 178):

Local CAMRA Branch Pub of the Year and former National Pub of the Year 2014, this cracking rural freehouse/brewpub is within walking distance of the Jenner Museum and Berkeley Castle. The enthusiastic landlord has turned brewer (Tiley's), keeping an inspired selection of ales and eight real ciders and perries. The pub has two cosy bars, a woodburner and a function room with a skittles alley. Food is served at lunchtimes and on occasional evenings. Live folk music and piano sing-alongs occur fairly regularly.

Stanford Arms, Lowestoft,
Suffolk (see page 439):

The spacious open-plan bar at the Stanford Arms has a large array of handpumps serving mainly local beers – it is a rare outlet for Redwell brewery. A fine collection of beer trays adorns the walls. To the rear is a courtyard garden with its own wood-fired pizza oven (Friday night is pizza night) and a small aviary. A food night is held most Wednesdays (booking required) and a dish of the day is available late Saturday afternoons. Live music features on most Saturday evenings and on Sunday afternoons.

Club of the Year

A Cheltenham club that caters to motor enthusiasts won the prestigious CAMRA Club of the Year award for a second time in 2017.

The **Cheltenham Motor Club in Cheltenham**, Gloucestershire (see page 175) first won the award in 2013. Since then, it has made significant improvements, demonstrating a clear commitment to improving the experience of their members and guests alike.

The friendly and welcoming club, formed in 1906, usually has six real ales and three real ciders on tap, alongside its new bottled beer bar and a Belgian draught beer. It runs two beer festivals a year and is decorated with motoring paraphernalia and a collection of pump clips.

John Holland, chairman of CAMRA's Clubs Working Group, said: 'While the other finalists in

the competition are great examples of well-run and welcoming clubs, Cheltenham Motor Club really sets itself apart. Rather than resting on its laurels, the committee has taken huge steps to improve the bar area and beer selection.

'It's clear that the local community passionately supports Cheltenham Motor Club and that the club is a pivotal fixture in that community.'

Neil Way, Cheltenham Motor Club manager, added: 'As a long-time member of CAMRA, I am overwhelmed and honoured to win Club of the Year for a second time. I am lucky to have a very supportive wife and committee, along with a hard-working, motivated and loyal bar team. The locals are tremendous, too!'

Cheltenham Motor Club manager Neil Way receiving his award from local MP Alex Chalk

The other finalists in the Club of the Year competition were:

The Albatross Club (RAFA), Bexhill,
East Sussex (see page 453):

The Albatross Club won Club of the Year last year, and has won multiple other CAMRA awards. It always serves at least one local ale, often from the likes of Franklins or Rother Valley. They have four handpumps and a comprehensive range of upcoming beers is listed on a blackboard behind the bar. The club holds regular beer festivals in April and September in its large function room as well as many social events such as jazz nights, quizzes and folk evenings. It is popular among its members and CAMRA members are always welcome. The club boasts an interesting collection of RAF memorabilia.

The Club of the Year competition is run by CAMRA in conjunction with the journal *Club Mirror* to find the best real ale clubs in the country. One of the criteria for entry into the competition is that clubs must admit CAMRA members, both men and women. A number of the best real ale clubs feature in the *Good Beer Guide* alongside recommended pubs. As well as admitting CAMRA members, many will also admit non-members carrying a copy of this book. See individual entries for more information.

Dartford Working Men's Club,
Kent (see page 220):

This Club & Institute Union (CIU) club boasts a selection of fifteen real ales on handpump as well as ciders on gravity. The ales come from various micro and regional breweries, with over 500 different beers being served each year. The club is home to the BBC award winning Dartford Folk Club meeting on Tuesday evenings and there is live music every Saturday night and a popular quiz night on the first Wednesday of each month. Up to four beer festivals are held each year and CAMRA members are welcome as guests.

Leyton Orient FC Supporters' Club,
East London (see page 288):

A previous Club of the Year award winner, the Leyton Orient FC Supporters' Club is very friendly and welcoming. It boasts a fantastic range of high quality beers and knowledgeable staff. Serving real ale since 1995, the club usually offers a range of seven ales, along with one or two ciders and perries, with bar snacks and rolls available.

The club usually closes during matches but reopens afterwards – and it only regularly opens when Leyton Orient FC are playing at home. It is a busy club with a loyal and mixed clientele. The club hosts two beer festivals each season as well as several special brewery-themed nights. Free entry is permitted with a CAMRA membership card or a copy of the *Good Beer Guide*. It has previously shared the national CAMRA Club of the Year award.

Pub Design Awards

When CAMRA unveiled the best pub design awards for 2017 the winners included a former strippers' pub, a 300-plus-year old public house and a stunning Edwardian street-corner local.

The Scottish Stores in London's King's Cross won this year's Conservation Award. The Scottish Stores, a Grade II-listed building, was designed between 1900 and 1901 when joints of deer meat used to hang from the bar to be bought by visiting Scotsmen. In the 1980s, it was restyled and was renowned as one of the last remaining strippers' pubs in London. In 2015 it was restored back to its Jacobean-style woodwork and was praised as a splendid example of how to bring a much-loved, urban landmark back to life.

Two other CAMRA pub design awards, The Refurbishment and Joe Goodwin Awards, have both gone to the **Tim Bobbin in Burnley,** Lancashire. This handsome stone building dates back to 1701, but was insensitively restored in the 1960s, leading it to look tired and jaded by the 1990s. Now Samuel Smith's in-house architects have rescued this prominent pub through an excellent refurbishment.

The Ship Inn in Shalesmoor, Sheffield (see page 550), was commended in the Refurbishment category of the awards. The pub's interior was allowed to deteriorate after its surrounding community was bulldozed and it found itself perched on the edge of a busy road. It was shut for many years but the pub has now been restored to its former Edwardian glitz and glitter.

Sean Murphy, CAMRA's Pub Design Awards coordinator, said: 'The judges have singled out three buildings – all of which, in their own way, point to a bright future for the traditional British pub. All three show the huge potential for restoring and preserving much-loved heritage pubs to their former glory, even after decades of change.'

The Scottish Stores in King's Cross, London, was the winner of CAMRA's 2017 Conservation Award

CAMRA's Pub Design Awards aim to find the most stunningly designed pubs in the UK. The awards, held in association with Historic England, recognise high standards of architecture in the refurbishment and the conservation of existing pubs. See **www.camra.org.uk/pub-design-awards**.

CAMRA beer festivals

Showcasing our ale heritage

CAMRA beer festivals play a key role in spreading the message about good beer in Britain. Pubs frequently stage their own festivals but they are limited by the size of their cellars. If they are tied to a brewery or a pub company they may be restricted in the range of beers they can offer.

Festivals have no such restraints and they serve to pinpoint the astonishing range and variety of beer available today. They have also played an important role in the long campaign to roll back the power of giant breweries and offer a wider choice of beer for consumers. In the early days of CAMRA, festivals proved that good beer was still alive and well... and available.

As we celebrate the 45th edition of this Guide, we also salute the CAMRA festivals that date from the days when real ale had to be rescued as a tidal wave of heavily promoted keg beers rolled over the nation's pubs. It's significant that a number of the early festivals were staged in towns and cities that had lost or were about to lose independent breweries as a result of the takeover frenzy of the 1960s and 70s. Without CAMRA's festivals in Norwich, Sheffield, Newcastle and Derby, for example, beer lovers would have been denied the opportunity to enjoy a decent pint.

Today there are around 200 CAMRA festivals – local, regional and national – held throughout the country. They are accompanied by festivals run by other organisations: the Campaign welcomes all events that attract beer lovers but it feels its festivals have something special to offer.

It's not difficult to run a beer event that offers just pale and golden ales. But Britain has a rich beer heritage and CAMRA festivals stress that heritage by also featuring such styles as dark mild, porter, stout and barley wine. Darker beers come into their own in the colder parts of the year and many festivals feature autumn and winter events, culminating in the Great British Beer Festival - Winter, currently held in Norwich in February.

CAMRA's festivals also feature innovative new styles of beer, including those aged in wood or made with the addition of fruit, herbs and spices. A number of festivals also make available beers suitable for vegans and vegetarians as well as beers that are gluten-free. And just about every festival will also feature cider and perry, drinks growing fast in popularity and which CAMRA has supported for many years.

There's no hard sell at CAMRA festivals. The atmosphere is relaxed and many events will offer small tasters of beer so visitors can sample before buying. Prices for both entry and beer are kept as low as possible. Wherever possible, there will be ample seating provided along with family rooms for visitors with children. Beer's diversity is stressed by talks and tastings while live entertainment ranges from jazz, folk and blues to light classical.

Food is a key element of most festivals, ranging from light snacks to bigger offerings, often including 'street food' and food made by local artisans who share the ideals of craft brewers.

It's food – and beer – for thought. On the following pages you will find a festival near you. Come and raise a glass to the best of British.

Packing them in... Beer festivals such as this one in Cambridge attract large crowds

CAMRA beer festivals through the year

Beer festivals come in all shapes and sizes but offer a wide choice for discerning drinkers. Some festivals feature beers for such seasons as harvest time and winter but all offer a warm welcome with good food and, in many cases, live entertainment and family facilities. The listing below shows all the planned CAMRA beer festivals for 2018, although please note that some festivals, dates and details are to be confirmed. For more information visit **www.camra.org.uk/events**.

January
Cambridge – Winter
Ely – Winter
Exeter – Winter
Manchester
Salisbury – Winter

February
Norwich – Great British (Winter)
Atherton – Bent & Bongs
   Beer Bash
Bradford
Chappel – Winter
Chelmsford – Winter
Chesterfield
Colchester – Winter
Darlington – Spring
Dorchester
Dover – White Cliffs Winter
Fleetwood
Gosport – Winter
Hucknall
Jersey – Winter
Liverpool
Luton
Pendle
Redditch
Stevenage
Stockton – Ale & Arty
Tewkesbury – Winter

March
Brighton – Sussex
Bristol
Bromley

Burton upon Trent
Coventry
Horsham – Equinox
Leicester
London Drinker
Loughborough
Rugby
Seascale
St Neots – Booze on the Ouse
Walsall
Wantage
Wigan
Winchester

April
Bolton
Bury St Edmunds –
   East Anglian
Chippenham
Doncaster
Farnham
Glenrothes – Kingdom of Fife
Gloucester
Hull
Isle of Man
Larbert – Falkirk
Maldon
New Mills
Newcastle upon Tyne
Oldham
Paisley
Thanet

May
Banbury

Barnsley
Bexley
Cambridge
Colchester
Eastbourne – Beer & Cider
   by the Sea
Kidderminster
Kingston
Lincoln
Macclesfield
Newark
Newport – Tredegar House
   Folk Festival
Reading
Stourbridge
Wrexham –
   North Wales
Yapton
Yaxley

June
Braintree
Bromsgrove
Glasgow
Hitchin
Leeds
Lewes – South Downs
Nuneaton & Bedworth
Old Harlow – Gibberd Garden
Salisbury
Skipton
Stockport
Stratford-Upon-Avon
Tenterden – Kent & East
   Sussex Railway

Thurrock
Wolverhampton

July
Bishop's Stortford
Canterbury – Kent
Chelmsford – Summer
Chorlton
Derby
Devizes
Ealing
Edinburgh – Scottish
Hereford – Beer on the Wye
Market Bosworth – Rail Ale
Southampton
Stafford
Stowmarket – Summer
Winchcombe – Cotswold
Woodcote – Veteran
    Transport Rally
Wyke Regis – Wykefest

August
London – Great British
Clacton-on-Sea
Darlington
Durham
Grantham
Peterborough
Swansea
Worcester

September
Barnsley
Belper – Amber Valley
Bridgnorth – Severn Valley
Bromley
Burnley
Calderdale
Cannock
Cardiff – Great Welsh
Chappel
Crewe – Rail Ale

East Malling (Kent)
Faversham – Hop
Harbury
Hinckley
Jersey
Melton Mowbray
Moreton-in Marsh –
North Cotswolds
Nottingham
Plymouth
Scunthorpe
Shrewsbury
St Albans
St Helens
Tamworth
Ulverston
Westmorland
Woolston – Southampton
York

October
Alloa
Ascot
Basingstoke – OctoberFest
Bedford
Birmingham
Carmarthen
Chesterfield – Market
Egremont (Cumbria)
Falmouth
Gainsborough
Huddersfield – Oktoberfest
Kendal – Westmorland
Louth
Lytham
Maidenhead
Matlock
Milton Keynes –
    Concrete Pint
Norwich
Poole
Richmond (North Yorkshire)

Sheffield – Steel City
Solihull
South Woodham Ferrers
Southport
Spa Valley Railway
(West Kent)
St Ives (Cambs) –
    Booze on the Ouse
Stoke-on-Trent – Potteries
Sunderland
Swindon
Troon – Ayrshire
Twickenham
Wakefield
Weymouth
Worthing

November
Bath
Belfast
Cambridge – Winter
Carlisle
Chester – Cheshire
Dudley
Grimsby
Harwich & Parkeston
Heathrow
Normanton
Oxford
Redhill
Rochdale
Rochford
Saltburn
Shifnal
Uttoxeter
Watford
Woking

December
London – Pig's Ear

Cask Marque

Champions of beer quality

Cask Marque are delighted to be sponsoring CAMRA's *Good Beer Guide 2018*, a definitive and informative guide to the best real ale pubs throughout the UK.

For beer drinkers, the *Good Beer Guide* is their beer bible, and we congratulate all the pubs who have made it into this year's Guide, many of them Cask Marque accredited. These are denoted by a tick symbol (✔) so please look out for them.

This year, Cask Marque hit the magic number: over 10,000 pubs are now Cask Marque accredited, a massive achievement, and reflective of how cask beer quality in the UK is better than ever. But we continually strive to identify where improvement can be made, not only in pubs, but also at breweries, in the supply chain, and in pub cellars to ensure the final product is 'best in glass'. Take a look at some our projects and initiatives from the past twelve months...

What is Cask Marque?

Founded in 1998, Cask Marque is a not-for-profit organisation set up to promote cask beer, and particularly beer quality. With a team of over 50 beer inspectors, mainly brewers and trade quality technicians, we make over 20,000 visits to pubs and test in excess of 65,000 samples of beer a year. Every pub which applies for the prestigious Cask Marque Award is visited twice a year at least, unannounced, by one of our assessors. They check the temperature, appearance, aroma and taste of each of the cask ales on sale at the time of the visit. A minimum score has to be achieved to gain the Award, and if just one beer fails the test, the pub will fail the whole inspection.

It doesn't matter whether the pub has just one cask ale on sale or a dozen: we look for quality over quantity. So seeing a Cask Marque plaque outside a pub provides drinkers with the reassurance that they can expect a great pint. We have produced a series of short informative films showing what happens during an inspection, how we test the beer, and what else we do, and these can be viewed by visiting **www.cask-marque.co.uk**

We also now inspect the cellars where the beer is stored to ensure perfection behind the scenes. We launched the Scores on the

Cellar Doors scheme in 2016, and to date over 2,000 cellars have been inspected and rated. Each pub is given a rating of between 1 and 5 stars and those achieving 4 or 5 stars can be seen at **www.sotcd.co.uk**

We strive for excellence in the quality of cask ale, and always appreciate CAMRA members providing feedback. Please do tell us about your beer experiences in any Cask Marque-accredited pubs, both good and bad, by contacting us at **info@cask-marque.co.uk**

CaskFinder app

One of the major success stories over the past few years has been the free CaskFinder app which enables drinkers to find a Cask Marque accredited pub anywhere in the UK. Over 160,000 users have downloaded the app, and we have continually upgraded and updated the functions CaskFinder offers to embrace the needs of cask ale drinkers.

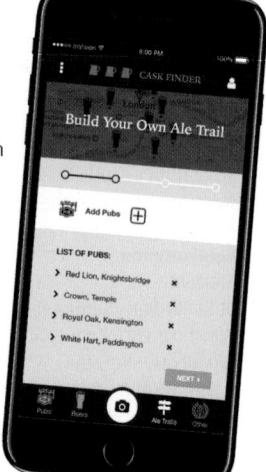

Cask Marque's free CaskFinder app

The World's Biggest Ale Trail goes from strength to strength, with over 30,000 'Ale Trailers' taking part. For those of you who haven't come across this facility, click on the Ale Trail button on CaskFinder, fill in a short registration form and you're ready to go. Each time you visit a Cask Marque pub, look for the framed 'Certificate of Excellence' and scan the QR code in the bottom left hand corner. Each code is unique to the pub and this will record your visit, and you can see a list of the pubs you have visited. The more certificates you scan, the more prizes you will gain from Cask Marque, which include bottle openers, polo shirts, fleeces, and branded

BEER CELLAR RATING

1ᴾ 2ᴾ 3ᴾ 4ᴾ 5ᴾ

Valid to: 31st Dec 2017   GOOD

A ratings scheme assesses standards of cellarmanship

glasses. Hit 500 scans and you will automatically become an Ale Ambassador and be invited to a brewery for an engaging and informative day out, testing beer, learning about what Cask Marque does and touring the brewery. Take a look at our Ale Trail leader board at **www.cask-marque.co.uk/leaderboard** and see if you can beat the current record!

As well as the Ale Trail, the CaskFinder app also has many other great features such as where to find beer festivals, tasting notes for over 8,000 beers, and what facilities each Cask Marque accredited pub offers. New for this year are a couple of great developments: firstly, a pump clip recognition scanner. Simply hold your device in front of the pump clip, and within seconds tasting notes of the beer appear on the phone as well as allergens in the beer, units of alcohol, calories, a beer and food matching suggestion from the brewer and more. It's great fun and it's also a brilliant training aid for staff particularly if there are a large number of guest beers.

On top of this, an additional new feature allows drinkers, breweries, and pub groups to create their own individual ale trails tailored specifically for friends or customers alike.

A Cask Marque beer assessor on a pub inspection

Cask Marque and Cyclops Beer

Cask Marque are proud to announce ownership of the Cyclops Beer scheme which has become the industry standard for educating, engaging and enthusing both drinkers and bar staff alike.

Cyclops Beer is a scheme which was launched by the industry to de-mystify and simplify some of the flavour profiles of cask ale, for both consumers and publicans. Using easy to understand language and symbols, it describes the colour, aroma and taste of over 2,500 beers in the UK, boasting tasting notes from more than 300 breweries. Cyclops notes are increasingly found on pump clips, bottle labels, websites and phone apps to navigate the sometimes bewildering array of beers available. Cyclops Beer notes can also be printed off and used on cask containers at beer festivals.

Robinsons
Trooper
IPA
ABV 4.8 %

AMBER

SEE — Amber
SMELL — sweet malt, zesty hop
TASTE — bitter, strong roasted malt

BITTER
SWEET

A Cyclops Beer note

Beer Education

To ensure pubs reach the exacting standards Cask Marque demands, we are the industry's leading supplier of training courses in how to handle beer. From bespoke one-to-one courses delivered at a publican's site, to full day Cellar Management courses held at breweries, we are proud to state we have trained over 15,000 people in the skill and art of handling cask ale.

We have however realised that there is great appetite (and a need) for a nationally recognised beer training scheme which encompasses all styles of beer, not just for pubs, but also for the off-trade and consumers. Our aims are to offer a 'one-stop shop' for beer education using a blended approach of e-learning, traditional classroom-based training and distance learning. The wine and spirits industry has a similar programme which has been running successfully for over 40 years, and we believe beer deserves the same investment. A working party, provisionally named the Beer Education Alliance, is currently developing the tools, resources and framework to deliver this to the industry during 2018. The Beer Education Alliance's primary objective is to educate and enthuse drinkers and those working in the business and to build on the positive momentum of consumer interest in beer.

A FINAL WORD
To find out more about Cask Marque, please do visit our website at **www.cask-marque.co.uk** and we hope you will join with us in championing beer quality in the glass to make sure you get served the perfect pint every time.

All about beer

....

Ever greater choice for drinkers

As we celebrate 45 editions of the *Good Beer Guide*, we can also marvel at the profound changes that have taken place in British brewing over that long period.

In the 1970s, most brewers concentrated on two main types of beer, mild and bitter. Today the number of styles rivals those of our bibulous neighbour Belgium. Bitter remains the most popular type of draught beer but it's been joined by India Pale Ale, porter, stout, barley wine, beers aged in wood or made with the addition of fruit, herbs, spices, coffee and chocolate.

There has never been greater choice for beer drinkers. It's clear from the attendance at festivals that younger people are now enjoying good beer in greater numbers and are no longer drinking the mass-advertised products of giant brewers.

Since the last edition of the Guide, the often passionate and occasionally angry debate about the merits of 'craft beer' and real ale has diminished. CAMRA believes cask-conditioned ale is craft beer. At the same time, it appreciates that not all outlets are suitable for storing and serving cask beer – though the problems can be exaggerated – and there is room in the market for new types of keg beer.

Modern keg beers have little in common with the risible beers of the 1970s, such as Double Diamond and Red Barrel, which encouraged the founding of CAMRA and its rapid growth and influence. Today's keg beers are not always filtered and are usually unpasteurised and served with only light gas pressure. In effect, they are identical to the draught beers produced by thousands of independent breweries in the United States, Australia and other countries.

Several new beer festivals offer just craft keg, others have a mix of cask and keg. Any events that welcome people to the pleasures of good beer are to be welcomed. But in spite of the sound and fury produced by some craft keg brewers, it's important to keep the sector in perspective. It's a niche and the big success story in recent years has been the increased demand for real ale. As the Breweries section of the Guide proves, most new breweries are committed to producing cask beer.

The *Good Beer Guide* remains devoted to real ale not because we're living in an age of cloth caps and whippets but because we believe that it's not only rooted in Britain's heritage and traditions but also offers the finest drinking experience for pub-goers. It's the beer of the moment, not the past.

Importance of 'terroir'

The popularity of real ale is driven to a growing extent by the concerns many consumers have with eating and drinking products made from natural ingredients. It's perfectly legal to make something called beer that comes from a factory controlled by computers and is produced with rice, corn starch, industrial enzymes and hop oil. However, artisan brewers eschew the cost cutting of the global brewers. Many have adopted the term *terroir* from French wine makers, meaning using the finest ingredients made possible by soil, sun and rain, and avoiding fertilisers and 'agrichemicals'.

This concern for quality is underscored by the growing use of Maris Otter malting barley, grown predominantly in England's 'grain basket' of Norfolk with its rich alluvial soil. Maris Otter was de-listed by big grain farmers and replaced by new 'high yielding' varieties that produce more grain per acre. Artisan brewers have remained loyal to Maris Otter and are prepared to pay a premium for a barley variety that creates delightful honey and biscuit flavours.

The quality of Maris Otter is highlighted by the fact that the majority of winners of CAMRA's Champion Beer of Britain competition use it.

Hops clamber back

Modern interpretations of IPA and pale ale are called 'hop forward' beers by artisan brewers and in Britain there has been a major move to import hops from the United States and New Zealand that deliver rich citrus notes as well as bitterness. This clamour for hops from abroad created a crisis for British hop growers whose varieties offer a more muted fruit character.

Prized Maris Otter barley growing in Norfolk

But with true British grit, the growers have not rested on their traditional hop bines but have developed new varieties such as Endeavour and Jester that deliver more of the fruitiness demanded by brewers and drinkers. The American Cascade hop is being grown under trial in Britain and it will be interesting to see how it adapts to an environment with less hot sun than the Pacific North-west of the US.

Cloudy or clear?

A growing number of brewers are responding to modern consumer concerns by producing beers that are cloudy in the glass. In some cases, the beers have just a slight haze but others are opaque. Traditionally, cask-conditioned beers have been cleared of yeast and protein by the addition of isinglass, made from fish bladders.

The increase in the number of vegetarians and vegans has encouraged brewers to avoid isinglass and, if they are keen to produce beers that are bright rather than hazy, to look at alternative fining agents. Some brewers use Irish Moss while experts at Nottingham University are analysing a new role for the hop plant as a clearing agent for beer – cask ale in particular. They are looking at whether used or 'spent' hops from brewing can be re-cycled to attract yeast.

It's not only non-meat and fish eaters that object to the use of isinglass. Justin Hawke, who owns the prize-winning Moor Beer brewery in Bristol, avoids isinglass as he believes it strips some of the flavour from beer. His beers are naturally cloudy and he says he has not encountered any consumer resistance to them.

Scarborough Fair IPA is one of a growing number of gluten free beers

But it's important to stress that when beers are fined with isinglass, there's no fish in the pint. Isinglass attracts yeast and protein in the cask by a natural chemical reaction that drags them to the base of the vessel below the serving tap.

Brewers have also responded to the needs of people who have an allergy to gluten. Gluten is present in grain, though levels vary from one grain to another. Wheat has the highest level of gluten and a number of brewers now avoid using it. As Wold Top's Scarborough Fair IPA proves (see Top 10 Beers, page 31), gluten-free beers do not lack flavour.

India Pale Ale – the return voyage

India Pale Ale – IPA – was first brewed in London and most famously in Burton-on-Trent during the 19th century for export to the Raj. Today, it is brewed the world over.

Several decades before the first golden lager was produced in Central Europe, IPA was the original pale beer and its lower strength domestic version, Pale Ale, challenged the popularity of darker mild, porter and stout.

Punitive levels of tax on beer in World War One sent IPA into steep decline but a century later brewers in both the UK and the US rediscovered the style and restored its popularity. The revival of IPA is phenomenal. It's now the most popular beer style among more than 5,000 craft brewers in the US and is the biggest category at the Great American Beer Festival.

There are several hundred interpretations of IPA brewed in Britain and it can be found Down Under in Australia and New Zealand and in such unlikely countries as Belgium, China, Japan, France, Italy, Spain, Switzerland, Denmark and Mexico.

The world-wide interest in IPA has prompted the question: how true to the original are modern versions? The answer came in research conducted by brewing historian Ron Pattinson who discovered that Bass and other Burton brewers stored oak casks of beer for a full year in their brewery before they were despatched to India. This research suggests that many modern versions of IPA – clear, sparkling and packed with aromatic hops – are quite different to their forebears. But knowledge of what Victorian IPAs tasted like has encouraged a growing number of brewers to age their versions in wood.

Brewers on both sides of the Atlantic are also brewing what they dub 'sour beers', based on the lambic and gueuze styles in Belgium. Wild Beer in Somerset is based on a farm and specialises in barrel-ageing. It captured wild yeast from surrounding cider apple orchards to give their beers a funky and fruity character.

A beer style called Saison brewed in the French-speaking Wallonia region of Belgium has also been taken up by a number of brewers in the UK and US. The beer was originally brewed by farmers to refresh their labourers during harvest time but they have now become regular commercial brews. In sharp distinction to IPA and sour beers, Saison has a rich malt backbone and comparatively modest hop bitterness.

How beer is brewed

Barley is beer's building block. Other grain can be used and many brewers blend in small amounts of wheat or oats and even rye, but barley is the preferred grain because it works in perfect harmony with hops and yeast.

British barley enjoys a world-wide reputation: the finest varieties are known as 'maritime barley' as they grow close to the coast. Norfolk, with its rich alluvial soil, grows some of the best barley, such as Maris Otter, suitable for brewing. Scotland also enjoys a good reputation for its barley, where the Golden Promise variety is prized.

But barley has to be turned into malt before brewing can begin. Once it's harvested, the grain is taken to a maltings where it's steeped in water to absorb moisture before being spread on heated floors or inside rotating drums where it starts to germinate. Once germination is under way, the grain is transferred to an oven known as a kiln. Heat dries the grain and, depending on the temperature, produces pale or darker malts.

All beer, regardless of colour, is made mainly from pale malt as it has the highest level of enzymes – natural chemical catalysts – that can convert starch within the grain into fermentable sugars crucial to the brewing process. Higher malting temperatures produce brown, black and chocolate malts, which are used for colour and flavour in darker beers.

Roasted barley, which is not malted, is often featured in stouts while a method similar to toffee-making produces specialist crystal malts used for colour and flavour. Depending on the mix of malts the brewer chooses, the grain will contribute aromas and flavours similar to Horlicks, Ovaltine, oatmeal biscuits, Ryvita, almonds and other nuts, as well as notes of honey, butterscotch, caramel, tobacco and vanilla.

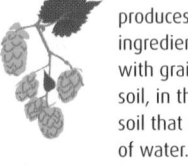

The annual harvest also produces beer's other key ingredient: hops. In common with grain, hops need good soil, in this case loamy or sandy soil that retains a good supply of water. Kent, Herefordshire and Worcestershire are the main hop-growing counties of England.

Hops grow at great speed in the spring and summer and once harvested they are dried by warm air in special sheds or oast houses. Hops contain acids, oils and resins that deliver bitterness to beer along with fragrant aromas of spice, pepper, grass, cedar wood and citrus fruit. The oils and tannins in the plant help stabilise beer and prevent infection. English hops are prized for their spice and pepper notes. Fuggles and Goldings are the best known traditional varieties but new hops have been introduced in recent years, including First Gold, Boadicea, Endeavour and Jester: the last two have been bred to give the aromas and flavours of grapefruit, mango and tropical fruits demanded by many modern brewers.

The brewing process

When malt reaches the brewery, it's ground in a mill into a powder called grist. Grist and pure hot water flow into the mash tun, where the porridge-like mixture of grain and water starts the brewing process.

Pure water can come from springs, bore holes or from the public supply. It will be filtered and brewers often add such sulphates as gypsum and magnesium to enhance the flavours of malt and hops.

The mixture is left to stand in the mash tun for some two hours and during that time enzymes in the malt convert the remaining starch into fermentable sugar. When starch conversion is complete, the brewer and his team will run the sweet extract, called wort, to a second vessel, the copper, where it's vigorously boiled with hops.

The copper boil lasts between 1½ and 2 hours. The hopped wort is passed through a cooler to lower the temperature and is then pumped to fermenting vessels. These can be open or closed, upright or horizontal, but it's here that the liquid starts the conversion of malt sugars to alcohol with the aid of yeast.

Yeast is a fungus that feeds on sugary liquids. Every brewery will have its own yeast culture that's carefully guarded and stored, as it gives its own important 'house character' to the beer.

Ale fermentation is rapid and lasts for a week – it's a method known as 'warm fermentation' to distinguish it from the cold fermentation method used to make genuine lager. Yeast converts malt sugar into alcohol and carbon dioxide and creates a dense, rocky blanket on top of the liquid. It also produces natural chemical compounds called esters that give off aromas reminiscent of apples, oranges, pear drops, banana, liquorice, molasses and, in especially strong beers, fresh leather. These add to the complexity of the finished beer.

The brewing process

Beer is made from just four natural ingredients:

1 HOPS:

Hops can be used either as whole flowers or ground and compressed into pellets.

2 WATER:

The water used for brewing is called 'liquor'.

3 MALT:

The mix of malts used contribute to the colour, flavour and strength of a beer.

4 YEAST:

Every brewery has its own 'house' yeast culture that is carefully guarded.

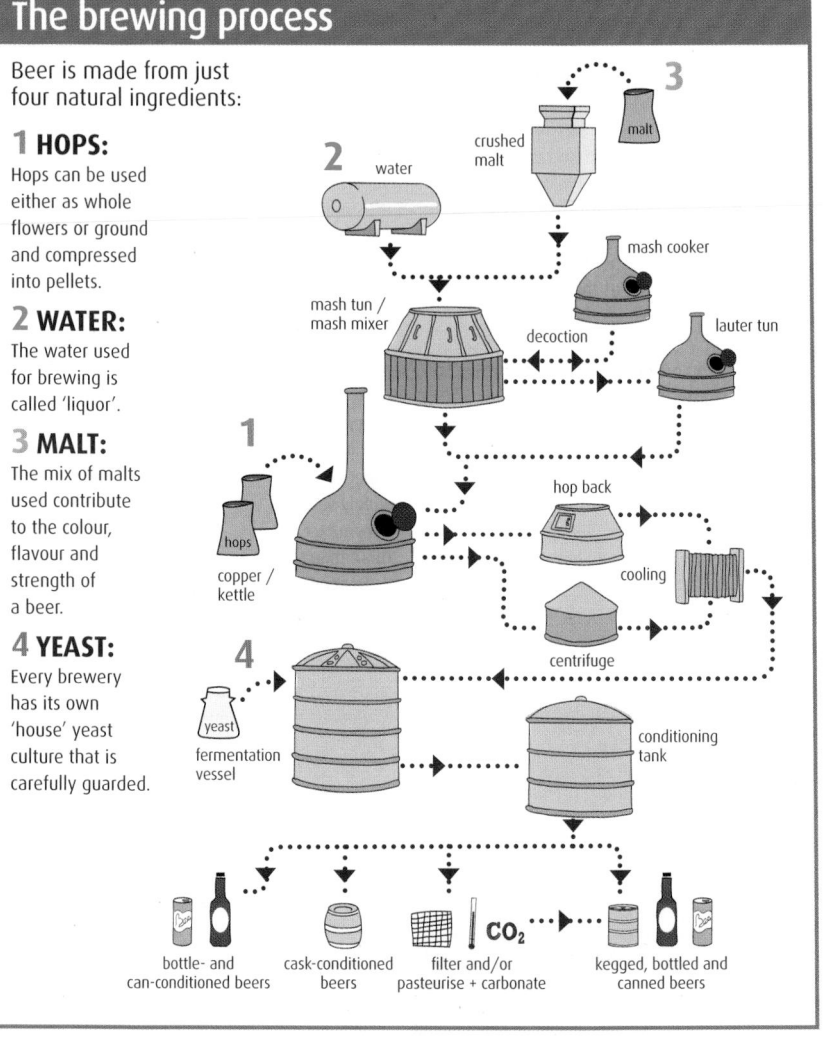

Eventually the yeast will be overcome by the alcohol it has created and the yeast blanket is skimmed from the vessel. The beer will rest for several days in conditioning tanks to mature and to purge unwanted rough alcohols and esters.

Then comes the major divide in the world of brewing. One route leads to brewery-conditioned beer that is filtered, pasteurised and carbonated. The other creates Britain's great contribution to the world of beer: cask-conditioned ale.

Cask ale is unique as it's not finished in the brewery but in the pub cellar. From conditioning tanks, it's racked into casks. Finings may be added to clear the beer and additional hops may be placed in the casks for extra aroma and flavour. Brewing sugar can be added to encourage a strong secondary fermentation. The beer that reaches the pub cellar is said to be 'still working' as remaining yeast turns the final sugars into alcohol and CO_2.

Casks have to be vented to allow some of the natural gas to escape. A cask has two openings: a bung at the flat end where a tap is inserted to serve the beer; and a shive hole on top. A soft porous peg of wood, known as a spile or peg, is knocked into the shive, enabling some of the CO_2 to escape. As fermentation dies down, the soft spile is replaced after 24 hours by a hard one that leaves some gas in the cask: this gives the beer its natural sparkle, known as 'condition'.

Inside the cask, finings sink to the floor, attracting yeast in suspension. When the publican is satisfied that the beer has 'dropped bright', plastic tubes or 'lines' are attached to the tap and the beer is drawn by a suction pump activated by a handpump on the bar.

Beer appreciation

We can increase our appreciation of beer by sampling and tasting. Gently swirl the liquid in the glass to release the aroma or the 'nose' and discover the malt, hop and fruit notes that emerge. Allow the beer to trickle over the tongue, which picks up bitterness, sweetness and salt, and enjoy the palate or 'mouthfeel' as the beer coats the cheeks. Finally, the beer passes down the back of the throat in what is known as the 'finish'.

On the nose you may find a rich biscuit or Ovaltine-like malt character. Hops will add their own distinctive note. English hops deliver a restrained spicy, peppery, earthy, wood and resinous note. American hops are renowned for their profound citrus notes, with grapefruit to the fore. German hops are called 'noble' varieties and offer cedar wood, mint, pine kernels and lemon zest. New Zealand hops have a vinous fruit character. One leading variety, Nelson Sauvin, is so called as a result of flavours similar to Sauvignon wine.

Fruit may be detected and this comes from both hops and yeast. A sulphur or salty note is derived from the water, which may have been treated to improve its brewing qualities.

In the mouth, the malt may have a delicious juicy note while hop bitterness will build, balancing any fruitiness. Finally the finish should combine all the elements of malt, hops and fruit into a satisfying, dry finale. The flavour characteristics of

a particular beer will depend on its style: see the British beer styles section that follows.

Tasting beer can be carried out in the home but greater appreciation will emerge if a group of people take part – and there's no better place to do it than in a pub. Many pubs now stage regular beer festivals, with a wide choice of beers available. If festivals are not held in your local but it has a good range on the bar, ask whether a room or part of the bar could be set aside for a tasting event.

Glasses should be either half-pint beer glasses or the large ones used for red wine. You will need fresh water and a supply of crackers to allow tasters to clean their palates between beers. Scoring sheets add to the enjoyment of the event, especially if you want to name a 'best beer'. The sheets should be divided into marks out of 10 for appearance, aroma, palate and finish. Usually, not more than six beers are judged in a single event.

Depending on the availability of beer, you could base a tasting round just one style, such as Mild, Bitter or Porter & Stout. However, it's unlikely that many pubs would have six versions of a single style, so it's best to have a mixed event. It's advisable to work up from the lowest strength: it would be difficult to judge a Mild after a Barley Wine.

Marks for appearance will be based on the clarity of the beer when the glass is held up to the light. Does it have a good head of foam, which indicates the beer has what brewers call 'condition'. The absence of foam means the beer is flat. Some beers, such as wheat beers, are designed to have a cloudy appearance, and this should be borne in mind when marking.

Marks for aroma will be based on the appeal of the beer as it's sniffed. Is there a good balance of malt, hops and fruit or is the beer overly malty or, conversely, too bitter? If you are judging bitter beers, including IPA, then expect to find the balance tilted towards hops and bitterness. Palate is based on the appeal of the beer in the mouth: you would mark down for cloying sweetness or harsh bitterness, and give higher marks when both characteristics are in balance. Finally, the finish: is the beer harmonious as it passes over the back of the tongue and down the throat, well-balanced between malt, hops and fruit, ending neither too malty nor too bitter. Again, marks in this section will be guided by the style of beer: you would expect a roasted grain character from a Stout or Porter.

If it's not possible to organise a tasting event of your own, bear in mind that many CAMRA festivals stage beer tastings, often hosted by experts in the field. Monitor the festivals listed in this Guide (see pages 18–19).

The many colours and flavours of beer can be appreciated at a tasting event

Beer packaging

Real ale traditionally is served by handpumps and beer engines that draw beer from casks in pub cellars. In some small pubs that don't have cellars, beer can be served direct from casks either behind or close to the bar.

In recent years, however, new systems have been introduced to deliver beer to the drinker's glass. A number of pubs that brew their own beer use a method of dispense similar to the one used by the Zerodegrees group (see Breweries section). The beer is stored in large tanks under bags of air that drive the beer to the bar.

A number of breweries use one-trip key kegs that take up little space and can be kept close to the bar if the temperature is controlled. There is no need for breweries to pick up the empties.

As the name suggests, a key keg is designed for modern keg beers. It's made up of a plastic container inside which is a sterile bag that holds the beer. The kegs are connected to gas cylinders at the point of delivery: the gas replaces the beer as it's served.

As a result of small venues asking for real ale, key kegs now have a variant called a key cask. The principle is the same, with the beer inside a bag in the container. But the gas – either carbon dioxide or oxygen – lies in a second bag on top of the beer. When the serving tap is turned, the bag pushes down on the beer. As the gas does not come into contact with the beer, which is neither filtered nor pasteurised and contains live yeast, key casks are acceptable to CAMRA.

Justin Hawke at Moor Beer, who are successfully putting real ale in cans

Since its founding years, CAMRA has supported bottle-conditioned beers that contain live yeast and have a secondary fermentation in bottle. It has published several editions of Jeff Evans's best-selling *Good Bottled Beer Guide*. For years canned beers were dismissed as inferior products as a result of the poor quality of the liquid and the metallic flavour imparted by the metal.

But technology has changed perceptions of canned beer. Cans have a lining that keeps the beer from contact with the container and as a result better quality beers are now available in cans.

Moor Beer in Bristol not only produces canned beer but has won approval for it from CAMRA. The cans contain live yeast and, so, the beer enjoys a secondary fermentation.

Cans have an important advantage over bottles: the beer can't be 'light struck', a fault that imparts a stale, oxidised, cardboard flavour.

Insist on quality beer

Real ale, when it's conditioned with care, should be bright, sparkling, with a lively head and served cool and refreshing (though some beers, such as wheat beers, may be intentionally cloudy). As a consumer, forking out a high price for beer, don't be afraid to take your pint back to the bar if it is not in good condition. Bar staff should replace it and might not be aware of an issue unless you tell them.

Take your pint back to the bar if:

- Your beer is served either too warm or too cold. Real ale should be served cool – around 11–12°C. It's a myth that it should be served at room temperature. Warm beer tastes bad. But bear in mind that some Golden Ales are meant to be served cooler than other styles.

- Your beer smells of acetone, vinegar or stale bread.

- The pint has no head, is totally flat and out of condition.

- It's not only flat but hazy and has yeast particles or protein floating in the liquid.

National Beer Scoring System

Pubs are selected for the Guide by CAMRA branches who use beer scores submitted by members to help them identify places that serve consistently good real ale. The system uses a 0–5 scale that can be submitted online. Any CAMRA member can submit a beer score by going to CAMRA's online pub guide **www.whatpub.com**, logging in as a member and selecting 'Submit Beer Scores'.

British beer styles

Britain may be embarking on a new relationship with the rest of Europe but it will not be immune to beer styles from the continent. Many brewers in the UK are now producing their interpretations of such styles as Belgian lambic and saison, along with German wheat beers.

But our own distinctive beer styles are far from ignored or forgotten. Bitter remains the most popular style and Mild ale still enjoys support, particularly in the West Midlands, South Wales and Merseyside. Golden Ale has become enormously popular and most breweries now have at least one version in their portfolios. Brewers are also becoming more adventurous and are adding to beer's pleasure with versions that are aged in wood or which use such ingredients as herbs, spices, coffee, chocolate and fruit.

Brewers are also digging deep in to the rich treasure trove of older styles. Porters and stouts from the 18th century are now widely available. But undoubtedly the most dramatic revival comes in the shape of India Pale Ale or IPA, a great style of the 19th century that almost disappeared in the 20th but has now been restored to its place of honour in the ale pantheon.

A number of brewers are producing 'sour beers' based on the traditional Belgian style known as lambic. Such beers do not use conventional brewers' yeast but allow wild yeasts in the atmosphere to turn malt sugars into alcohol. These beers have a tart and acidic character and offer a fascinating glimpse of what the earliest beers tasted like many centuries ago.

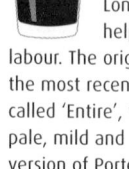

PORTER & STOUT

Porter was a London beer that created the first commercial brewing industry in the world in the early 18th century. Its name came from its popularity with London porters who needed calories to help sustain them in their hard manual labour. The origins of the beer are disputed but the most recent research suggests Porter, first called 'Entire', was blended in the brewery from pale, mild and aged or 'stale' beer. The strongest version of Porter was called Stout Porter, later shortened to just Stout.

Porter and Stout were exported from London to the rest of the British Isles and, as a result, Arthur Guinness built his own Porter brewery in Dublin. During World War One, when the British government restricted the use of malt, heavily roasted versions in particular, in order to divert

grain and energy to bread making and the arms industry, Guinness and other Irish brewers came to dominate the market. In recent years, Porter and Stout have returned to popularity in Britain, the United States and Australasia, with brewers digging into old recipes books to create genuine versions of the style.

Look for a jet-black colour and expect a dark and roasted grain character with burnt fruit, espresso or cappuccino coffee, liquorice and molasses. The beer should have a deep bitterness to balance the richness of malt and fruit. Milk Stout, made by a few brewers, uses lactose or 'milk sugar' to give a creamy character to the beer.

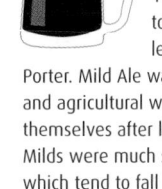

MILD

Mild developed in the 18th and 19th centuries as drinkers started to demand a slightly sweeter and less aggressively hopped beer than Porter. Mild Ale was drunk primarily by industrial and agricultural workers who needed to refresh themselves after long hours of arduous labour. Early Milds were much stronger than modern versions, which tend to fall into the 3% to 3.5% category though a number of brewers are bringing strength back to the style. Mild is usually dark brown in colour, due to the use of well-roasted malts or roasted barley, though there are paler versions such as Banks's Mild and Timothy Taylor's Golden Best. Look for a rich malty aroma and flavour, with hints of dark fruit, chocolate, coffee and caramel, with a gentle underpinning of hop bitterness.

OLD ALE

Old Ale is another style from the 18th century, stored for many months or even years in wooden vessels where the beer picked up some lactic sourness from wild yeasts and tannins in the wood. As a result of the sour taste, it was dubbed 'stale' by drinkers and the beer was one of the components of the early Porters. In recent years, Old Ale has made a return to popularity, due primarily to the success of such beers as Theakston's Old Peculier and Gales' Prize Old Ale. Contrary to expectations, Old Ales do not have to be especially strong and can be no more than 4% alcohol. Neither do they have to be dark: Old Ale can be pale and bursting with lush malt, tart fruit and spicy hops. Darker versions will have a more profound malt character, with powerful hints of roasted grain, dark fruit, polished leather and fresh tobacco. The hallmark of the style is a lengthy period of maturation, often in bottle rather than cask.

BARLEY WINE

Barley Wine dates from the 18th and 19th centuries when England was often at war with France and it was the duty of patriots, usually from the upper classes, to drink ale rather than French claret. Barley Wine had to be strong – often between 10% and 12% – and was stored for as long as 18 months or two years. Fuller's Vintage Ale (8.5%) is a bottle-conditioned version of its Golden Pride and is brewed with four different varieties of malts and hops every year. Expect massive sweet malt and ripe fruit of the pear drop, mandarin orange and lemon type, with chocolate and coffee if darker malts are used. Hop rates are generous and produce bitterness and peppery, grassy and floral notes.

BITTER

At the turn of the 19th and 20th centuries, brewers built large estate of 'tied' pubs and they moved away from beers stored for months or years and developed 'running beers' that could be served after a few days of conditioning in pub cellars. Bitter was a new type of running beer: it developed from Pale Ale but was usually copper coloured or deep bronze due to the use of slightly darker malts, such as crystal, that gave the beer fullness of palate. Best is a stronger version of Bitter but there is considerable crossover. Bitter falls into the 3.4% to 3.9% band while Best Bitter is 4% upwards, though a number of brewers call their ordinary Bitter 'best'. A further development of the style comes in the shape of Strong Bitter of 5% or more: Fuller's ESB and Greene King Abbot are well-known examples. With ordinary Bitter, look for spicy, peppery and grassy hop character, a powerful bitterness, tangy fruit and juicy/nutty malt. With best and strong Bitters, malt and fruit character will tend to dominate but hop aroma and bitterness are still crucial to the style, often achieved by 'late hopping' during the copper boil or by adding additional hops to casks as they leave the brewery.

BURTON ALE

As the name suggests, the origins of Burton Ale lie in Burton-on-Trent, but the style became so popular in the 18th and 19th centuries that most brewers had 'a Burton' in their portfolio and the expression 'gone for a Burton' entered the English language. Bass in Burton at one time had six different versions of the beer, ranging from 6% to 11.5%: the strongest versions were exported to Russia and the Baltic States. In the 20th century, Burton was overtaken in popularity by Pale Ale and Bitter but it was revived with great success in the late 1970s with the launch of Ind Coope Draught Burton Ale. When Allied Breweries broke up, the beer was owned by Carlsberg, who stopped production in 2015. But the style has been recreated by Burton Bridge Brewery in its home town. Other versions of the style exist under different names: Young's Winter Warmer was originally called Burton. Bass No 1, brewed occasionally, is called a barley wine but is in fact the last remaining version of a Bass Burton Ale. Look for a bright amber colour, a rich malt and fruit character underscored by a solid resinous and cedar wood hop note.

PALE ALE

According to a legend in the 19th century, when a sailing ship bound for India with a cargo of IPA foundered off the coast at Liverpool, the casks were brought ashore and news of both the colour and taste of Pale Ale spread throughout the country. IPAs were brewed for the domestic market as a result but the Burton brewers were keen to produce versions with lower alcohol and hop rates that didn't require months to mature. The spread of the railway system allowed brewers in Burton to move beer around the country at speed and Pale Ale was dubbed 'the beer of the railway age' as a result. The clamour for Pale Ale was so great that brewers from London, Liverpool and Manchester opened second breweries in Burton to make use of the mineral-rich water to make their own versions of the style. From the early 20th century, Bitter began to overtake Pale Ale in popularity and a result Pale Ale became mainly a bottled product. A true pale ale should be different to Bitter, similar in colour and style to IPA and brewed without the addition of coloured malts. It should have a spicy/resinous aroma and palate with biscuit malt and tart fruit from the hops. Many beers called Bitter today should properly be labelled Pale Ale.

IPA

India Pale Ale changed the face of brewing in the 19th century. The new technologies of the Industrial Revolution enabled brewers to use pale malts to design beers that were pale bronze in colour. The first 'India Ales' were brewed in London and were probably based on October Beers that were matured for many months and were ideally suited to a long sea journey to India. But London was soon eclipsed by Burton-on-Trent with its spring waters rich in minerals that brought out the fullest flavours of malt and hops. 19th century IPAs were high in both alcohol and hops to keep them in good condition during the journey to the colonies. Its life span was brief, driven out of Africa and India by German lager beer. But the style has made a big comeback in recent years and is now made in abundance throughout the world. Look for a big peppery hop aroma and palate balanced by juicy malt and tart citrus fruit.

GOLDEN ALE

Golden Ales have become so popular with both drinkers and brewers that the style now has its own category in the annual Champion Beer of Britain competition. Exmoor Gold, Hop Back Summer Lightning and Rooster's Yankee started the trend in the early 1980s and other brewers quickly followed in a rush to wean younger drinkers from mass-produced lager to the pleasures of cask ale. The style is different to Pale Ale in two critical ways: Golden Ale is paler, often brewed with lager malt or specially produced low colour ale malt and, as a result, hops are allowed to give full expression, balancing sappy malt with luscious fruit, floral, herbal, spicy and resinous notes. While brewers of Pale Ale tend to use such traditional English hop varieties as Fuggles and Goldings, imported hops from North America, the Czech Republic, Germany, Slovenia and New Zealand give radically different notes to Golden Ale. As a result these beers offer a new and exciting drinking experience. They are often served colder than draught Bitter and some brewers, such as Fuller's, have installed special cooling devices to ensure the beer reaches the glass at an acceptably refreshing temperature.

SCOTTISH BEERS

Historically, Scottish beers tend to be darker and maltier than beers south of the border, the reflection of a colder climate where beer needs to be nourishing. It's an urban myth, though, that Scottish beers are less heavily hopped than English ones. The classic traditional styles are Light, Heavy and Export, which are not dissimilar to Mild, Bitter and IPA. They are also known as 60, 70 and 80 Shilling ales from a 19th century system of invoicing beers according to strength. A 'Wee Heavy' or 90 Shilling Ale, now rare, is the Scottish equivalent of barley wine. Many of the newer brewers in Scotland are producing beers lighter in colour and with pronounced hop character.

WHEAT BEER

Wheat beer is a style closely associated with Bavaria and Belgium and its popularity in Britain has encouraged many brewers to add wheat beers to their portfolios. The title is something of a misnomer as all 'wheat beers' are a blend of malted barley as well as wheat, as the latter grain is difficult to brew with and needs the addition of barley, which acts as a natural filter during the mashing stage. But wheat, if used with special yeast cultures developed for brewing the style, gives distinctive aromas and flavours, such as clove, banana and bubblegum, that make it a complex and refreshing beer. The Belgian version of wheat beer often has the addition of herbs and spices, such as milled coriander seeds and orange peel – a habit that dates back to medieval times.

FRUIT/SPECIALITY BEERS

Brewers endlessly search for new flavours to reach out to a wider audience for their beers. The popularity in Britain of Belgian fruit beers has not gone unnoticed and now many domestic brewers are using fruit in their beer. Others have gone the extra mile and add honey, herbs, heather, spice and even spirits – brandy and rum feature in a number of speciality beers, while beers matured in Bourbon, whisky and Cognac casks have become a major development in both this country and the U.S. It's important to dispel the belief that fruit and honey beers are sweet: the ingredients add new dimensions to the brewing process and are highly fermentable, with the result that beers that use the likes of cherries or raspberries are dry and quenching rather than cloying.

SOUR BEER

Also known simply as 'Sours', this is a style brewed in both the UK and US by brewers fascinated by Belgian lambic beer, made by 'wild' or spontaneous fermentation. Instead of carefully cultivated brewer's yeast, lambic is left open to the atmosphere to allow wild yeasts to attack the sugars in the extract known as wort and begin the fermentation process. Elgood's brewery in Wisbech, Cambridgeshire, makes a fine example of lambic as it has the 'cool ships' or open cooling trays that enable the wort to be attacked by passing yeasts. Following the first fermentation, true lambics are stored in wooden casks for a year or more. The main wild yeast, *Brettanomyces*, is used by modern brewers to inoculate their worts and gain the required sour or acidic character. Other good examples of British sours come from Wild Beer, Kernel and Burning Sky.

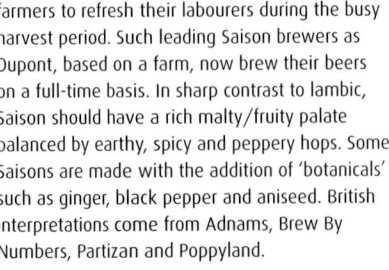

SAISON

Saison is another Belgian beer style now finding favour in Britain and other countries. It originates in Wallonia, the French-speaking region of Belgium, and was a seasonal beer brewed by farmers to refresh their labourers during the busy harvest period. Such leading Saison brewers as Dupont, based on a farm, now brew their beers on a full-time basis. In sharp contrast to lambic, Saison should have a rich malty/fruity palate balanced by earthy, spicy and peppery hops. Some Saisons are made with the addition of 'botanicals' such as ginger, black pepper and aniseed. British interpretations come from Adnams, Brew By Numbers, Partizan and Poppyland.

Ten of the best

Roger Protz selects some of the best interpretations of British beer styles

MILD: Rutland Panther

Brewed by Grainstore, the beer has a modest strength of 3.4% but is packed with rich grain character from brown and chocolate malts with Challenger and Fuggles English hops.

BITTER: Lacons Encore

Winner of a gold medal in the International Brewing Awards 2017, this classic bitter from a reborn Yarmouth brewery is a fine balance of Maris Otter malt and American fruity Centennial and Citra hops.

BEST BITTER: Sambrook's Junction

Duncan Sambrook brought brewing pride back to South London following the closure of Young's. This classic 'best' balances juicy malt with a powerful punch of bitter and spicy hops.

GOLDEN ALE: Phipps Midsummer Meadow

Another famous name restored to brewing, this time in Northampton. The tart and quenching beer balances the honey notes of Maris Otter with four hops: two English and two American.

STRONG BITTER: Adnams Ghost Ship

A sumptuous beer from Adnams that is a complex blend of pale malt, rye crystal and caramalt and hopped with American Citra and Chinook, plus the New Zealand variety Motueka. It offers citrus fruit along with deep malt notes.

PORTER & STOUT: Five Points Railway Porter

Five Points are fittingly based close to Hackney Downs train station in East London, the area where porter was first brewed in the 18th century. Railway Porter has roasted malt and liquorice notes balanced by dark fruit and peppery hops.

IPA: Wold Top Scarborough Fair

At 6%, this is an IPA with the strength of a Victorian original. It's a wonderfully refreshing beer with a big punch of hops balancing lightly toasted malt from barley grown on the brewer's farm. It's gluten-free but lacks nothing in taste and aroma.

BARLEY WINE: Moor Old Freddy Walker

Named Champion Winter Beer of Britain by CAMRA in 2017, this is a complex, rich, warming ale with a burnt fruit – raisins and sultanas – Dundee cake character from roasted malts but with a good balance of spicy hops.

SPECIALITY: Saltaire Triple Chocoholic

Just the beer for chocolate lovers, this is a mouth-filling stout that uses chocolate malt but also has an addition of cocoa nibs and chocolate essence. Roasted grain and Fuggles and Goldings hops add balance and prevent any cloying sweetness.

SCOTTISH: Fyne Jarl

This beer has a modest strength of 3.8% but is bursting with honey malt alongside fruity and spicy hops. It's a fine, refreshing beer with great depth, a good example of modern craft beers in Scotland. Jarl is an old name for earl.

CAMRA's Beers of the Year

The beers listed below are CAMRA's Beers of the Year. They were short-listed for the 2017 Champion Beer of Britain competition, held at the Great British Beer Festival in August, or the Champion Winter Beer of Britain competition, held in February that year. Each beer was found by a panel of trained CAMRA judges to be consistently outstanding in its category and they all receive a ◙ against their entry in the Breweries section. In the Champion Beer of Britain finals, the best beers from each category in both competitions are judged together to decide the overall national winner. For the full results visit **www.camra.org.uk/cbob**.

GOLDEN ALES
Abbeydale, Moonshine
Alechemy, Secret Citra
Blue Monkey, Infinity
Brewster's, Hophead
Dark Star, Hophead
Exe Valley, It's Phil's Ale
Flowerpots, Goodens Gold
Fyne Ales, Jarl
Goose Eye, Chinook
Grain, ThreeOneSix
Grey Trees, Diggers Gold
Hawkshead, Windermere Pale
Heavy Industry, Nelson's Eye
Kinver, Noble
Ludlow, Gold
Oakham, Citra
Okell, MPA
St Austell, Proper Job

BITTERS
Acorn, Barnsley Bitter
Adnams, Southwold Bitter
Barngates, Cracker
Bateman's, XB
Bishop Nick, Ridley's Rite
Born in the Borders, Game Bird
Butcombe, Original
Church End, Goat's Milk
Exeter, Avocet
Heavy Industry, Electric Mountain
Hobsons, Best
Isle of Skye, Young Pretender
Monty's, Old Jailhouse
Sambrooks, Wandle Ale
Thornbridge, Wild Swan
Triple fff, Alton's Pride
Yates, Golden
York, Guzzler

MILDS
Arran, Dark
Batham's, Mild
Blue Monkey, 99 Red Baboons
Brecon Brewing, Dark Beacons
Exe Valley, Darkest Devon
Foxfield, Dark Mild
Rudgate, Ruby Mild
West Berkshire,
    Maggs Magnificent Mild
Winter's, Mild

BEST BITTERS
Barngates, Tag Lag
Blackedge, Pike
Brentwood, Best
Castle Rock, Elsie Mo

Dancing Duck, Ay Up
Exmoor, Gold
Kelburn, Misty Law
Mantle, Moho
Milton, Sparta
Mordue, Workie Ticket
Salopian, Darwin's Origin
Skinner's, Cornish Knocker
Surrey Hills, Shere Drop
Swannay, Scapa Special
Timothy Taylor, Landlord
Tiny Rebel, Cwtch
West Berkshire,
    Good Old Boy
Wye Valley, HPA

PORTERS
Batemans, Salem Porter
Cambridge Brew House,
    Night Porter
Dunham Massey,
    Dunham Massey Porter
Elland, 1872 Porter
North Cotswold, Hung,
    Drawn 'N' Portered
Sulwath,
    Black Galloway
Tavy Ales, Tavy Porter
Tudor, Black Rock
Vibrant Forest,
    Black Forest Porter

STRONG BITTERS
3 Brewers of St Albans,
    Special English Ale
Barngates, Red Bull Terrier
Blue Monkey, Ape Ale
Cromarty, Rogue Wave
Grey Trees, Afghan Pale Ale
Kelham Island, Pale Rider
Otter, Head
Ramsgate, Gadds No 3
    Kent Pale Ale
Salopian, Automaton

STRONG MILDS
& OLD ALES
Adnams, Old Ale
Daleside, Monkey Wrench
Grainstore, Rutland Beast
Heavy Industry, Collaborator
Kelburn, Dark Moor
Old Dairy, Snow Top
Sarah Hughes,
    Dark Ruby Mild
Tintagel, Gwaf Tan
Watermill, Shih Tzu

STOUTS
Barngates, Goodhew's Dry Stout
Beowulf, Dragon Smoke Stout
Boss, Black
Castle Rock, Sherwood Reserve
London Brewing Co, Oyster Stout
Loch Lomond, Silkie Stout
Magic Rock, Dark Arts
Milton, Marcus Aurelius
Penzance, Scilly Stout

BARLEY WINES
& STRONG OLD ALES
Brass Castle, Wallop
Downland,
    Vintage Black Seven Four
Grainstore, Nip
Green Jack, Ripper Tripel
Moor, Old Freddy Walker
Montys, Magnitude
Kinver, Over the Edge
Orkney, Skull Splitter
Robinson's, Old Tom

SPECIALITY BEERS
Blackedge, Black Port Porter
Bristol Beer Factory, Independence
Canterbury Brewers, Red Rye
Cromarty, Red Rocker
Derventio, Cleopatra
Moonshine, Chocolate Orange Stout
Purple Moose, Ysgawen
Salopian, Lemon Dream
Saltaire, Triple Chocoholic

**CHAMPION
WINTER BEER
OF BRITAIN**
Moor,
    Old Freddy Walker

**CHAMPION BEER
OF BRITAIN 2017**
Church End,
    Goat's Milk

The Pubs

Cod & Lobster Inn, Staithes, North Yorkshire, p541 (Photo: Daniel Neilson)

SHETLAND

NORTHERN
ISLES

HIGHLANDS
&
WESTERN ISLES

ABERDEEN
& GRAMPIAN

TAYSIDE

ARGYLL &
THE ISLES

LOCH LOMOND,
STIRLING
& THE
TROSSACHS

FIFE

EDINBURGH & LOTHIANS

GREATER
GLASGOW &
CLYDE

BORDERS

AYRSHIRE
& ARRAN

DUMFRIES &
GALLOWAY

NORTHERN
IRELAND

NORTHUMBERLAND

TYNE &
WEAR

CUMBRIA

DURHAM

ISLE OF
MAN

NORTH
YORKSHIRE

LANCASHIRE

MERSEYSIDE

WEST
YORKS

EAST
YORKS

GREATER
MANCHESTER

SOUTH
YORKS

NW
WALES

NE
WALES

CHESHIRE

DERBYSHIRE

NOTTINGHAM-
SHIRE

LINCOLNSHIRE

STAFFORD-
SHIRE

LEICESTERSHIRE

SHROPSHIRE

WEST
MIDLANDS

RUTLAND

NORFOLK

MID
WALES

WORCESTER-
SHIRE

WARWICK-
SHIRE

NORTHAMPTON-
SHIRE

CAMBRIDGE-
SHIRE

SUFFOLK

HEREFORD-
SHIRE

BUCKINGHAM-
SHIRE

BEDFORD-
SHIRE

HERTFORD-
SHIRE

ESSEX

WEST
WALES

GWENT

GLOUCS &
BRISTOL

OXFORD-
SHIRE

GREATER
LONDON

GLAMORGAN

WILTSHIRE

BERKSHIRE

SURREY

KENT

SOMERSET

HAMPSHIRE

WEST
SUSSEX

EAST
SUSSEX

CHANNEL
ISLANDS

DEVON

DORSET

ISLE OF
WIGHT

CORNWALL

England

BEDFORDSHIRE

Ampthill

Albion 🅛
36 Dunstable Street, MK45 2JT
🕙 11.30-11 (midnight Fri & Sat); 12-10.30 Sun
☎ (01525) 634857
B&T Shefford Bitter, Golden Fox, Dragon Slayer; Everards Tiger; 8 changing beers 🅗
A proper, narrow-fronted Victorian pub with one large bar and 12 handpumps serving a range of the local B&T beers as well as Everards Tiger and eight constantly changing ales mainly from microbreweries. Two regular real ciders and a guest cider are also served. Beer and cider festivals are held at least annually. There are a meeting room and a secluded patio garden towards the rear. English music nights feature once a month on Wednesday evenings. Twice Bedfordshire CAMRA Pub of the Year. 🛏️🞠♣🐾🔊🐾

Arlesey

Vicar's Inn 🅛
68 Church Lane, SG15 6UX
🕙 5-midnight; 12-4, 7-midnight Sat; 12-4, 7-11 Sun
☎ (01462) 731215
Wells Eagle IPA; 1 changing beer (sourced nationally) 🅗
Quiet local pub opposite St Peter's Church and just a five-minute walk from the station. Access is through a wooden door from the street. A short corridor leads directly to a large lounge area with

the entrance to the public bar on the left. Both rooms offer simple furniture with red upholstery. On both bars you will often find complementary cheese and biscuits. 🅠🛏️🞠Å🚆♣P🚃 (72,97)

Bedford

Brewhouse & Kitchen 🅛 ✅
115 High Street, MK40 1NU
🕙 11-11 (midnight Fri & Sat); 12-10 Sun ☎ (01234) 342931
🌐 brewhouseandkitchen.com/bedford
Brewhouse & Kitchen Banker's Draught, Intrepid, Night Fever, Sprinter, Invarsity; 1 changing beer (sourced locally) 🅗
A former bank and Wetherspoon pub relaunched by the Brewhouse & Kitchen Group in 2016. A microbrewery is located within the main bar area, which is further sectioned into different seating areas by half-height dividers that are features in themselves. Orders can be placed at the table or at the bar – the menu offers an extensive list of different styles of drink as well as good food. Occasional special ales are available, made to the brewer's own recipes. 🛏️🞠🍽️🛒♣🚃🛜

Castle
17 Newnham Street, MK40 3JR
🕙 12-11 (midnight Thu); 11.30-midnight Fri; 11-midnight Sat
☎ (01234) 353295 🌐 castlebedford.co.uk
Courage Directors; Wells Eagle IPA; Young's Bitter, London Gold, Special; 3 changing beers (sourced nationally) 🅗

A recently refurbished two-bar pub with a pleasant walled patio garden. Lunches are served daily and evening meals on weekdays only. Current guest beers with tasting notes are listed on the website. Peacock's Auction Rooms and Bedford Rugby Club are close by. A guest house behind the pub provides five en-suite letting bedrooms. Local CAMRA Pub of the Year 2016. 🌞🍴⊜⌁🌛⊘🕆🅿🔲🌂🏵

Devonshire Arms 🄻 ✅
32 Dudley Street, MK40 3TB (1 mile E of town centre S of A4280)
🕐 5-11; 4-midnight Fri; 12-midnight Sat; 12-10.30 Sun
☎ (01234) 301170 ⊕ devonshirearmsbedford.co.uk
Courage Directors; Wells Eagle IPA; Young's London Gold, Special; 2 changing beers (sourced regionally) Ⓗ
Pleasant Victorian LocAle pub in a residential area. Guest and seasonal ales are mainly from Charles Wells, the two ciders and perry are from Westons. Beer festivals are held each year. The front bar has bare floorboards and an open fire, while there is a separate rear bar. The garden has a gazebo for smokers and a no-smoking paved area. A good range of wines is sold by the glass or bottle.
Q🌞🍴🏵🔲(4)🌂🏵

King's Arms
24 St Mary's Street, MK42 0AS
🕐 11-11; 12-midnight Fri & Sat; 2-9 Sun ☎ (01234) 354494
⊕ thekingsarmsbedford.com
Greene King IPA; 3 changing beers (sourced nationally) Ⓗ
A busy former coaching inn which has been a public house since 1230. It has several interconnecting rooms and a conservatory providing a quiet area. There is a quiz on Monday evening, free pool on Tuesday, TV poker on Thursday and live performances by top local bands every Saturday evening. A selection of real bottled beers is available. No food at weekends.
🌞🅱⌁⊜(St Johns)🍴🅿🔲🏵

Three Cups 🍴 🄻 ✅
45 Newnham Street, MK40 3JR (200yds S of A4280 near rugby ground)
🕐 12-11; 11-11.30 Fri & Sat; 12-10.30 Sun
☎ (01234) 352153 ⊕ threecupsbedford.co.uk
Greene King IPA; Morland Old Speckled Hen; 5 changing beers Ⓗ
Comfortable inn dating from the 1770s, now a Greene King Local Hero pub offering local microbrewery beers. Seven real ales are always available, including at least two from White Park Brewery, which holds the lease. Tasting thirds are available for all beers. Locally sourced home-cooked lunches are served. Old wood panelling helps retain some of the pub's original character. Five minutes from the town centre and close to Bedford Blues rugby ground. Local CAMRA Pub of the Year 2017. 🌞🍴🍴⊜🍴🅿🔲🌂🏵

Wellington Arms 🄻
40-42 Wellington Street, MK40 2JX (off A6 N of town centre)
🕐 12-11 (10.30 Sun) ☎ (01234) 308033
⊕ thewelly.wix.com/bedford
Adnams Southwold Bitter; B&T Shefford Bitter; 10 changing beers (sourced nationally) Ⓗ
This street-corner local retains a traditional style and offers a wide selection of ever-changing regional and microbrewery beers from 12 handpumps. Real ciders are served from two

further handpumps. Draught continental beers plus a range of bottled Belgian beers are also available. There is a courtyard for drinkers and smokers. A friendly pub with a mixed clientele, it can get very busy on Friday and Saturday evenings. 🌞🍴

Biggleswade

Golden Pheasant 🄻 ✅
71 High Street, SG18 0JH
🕐 12-midnight (1am Fri & Sat); 12-11.30 Sun
☎ (01767) 313653 ⊕ goldenpheasantpub.co.uk
Wells Eagle IPA; 5 changing beers (sourced nationally) Ⓗ
Traditional double-fronted Charles Wells Speciality Beer House featuring six handpumps and four changing ciders. Located in the centre of town, the single bar's seating area, overlooking the street, has dark wood furnishings and red cushioned chairs. Regulars congregate around the bar and community groups often hold meetings here. The pub occasionally hosts charity fundraising events with live music which, if the weather is fine, are held on the spacious patio. Q🌞🍴⌁🌛🍴🔲🌂🏵

New Inn Ale House & Kitchen 🍴 🄻 ✅
Market Square, SG18 8AS
🕐 10-11.30 (midnight Thu); 9am-1am Fri & Sat
☎ (01767) 222938 ⊕ thenewinnalehouseandkitchen.co.uk
Greene King XX Mild, IPA; 6 changing beers (sourced nationally) Ⓗ
A short walk from the train station, this comfortably furnished hostelry is the local CAMRA Pub of the Year for 2017. A chalkboard lists up to four beers from the new on-site brewery, four Greene King beers, five guest ales plus three rotating real ciders. Food is served daily – the regular Sunday lunch carvery is especially popular. Two large-screen TVs show mainly muted news or rugby. Mini beer festivals are held from time to time. Q🌞🍴🌛⌁⊜🍴🔲🏵

Bolnhurst

Plough 🄻
Kimbolton Road, MK44 2EX (on W side of B660 S of turning to Thurleigh) TL088587
🕐 closed Mon; 12-3, 6.30-11; 12-3 Sun ☎ (01234) 376274
⊕ bolnhurst.com
3 changing beers (sourced regionally; often Adnams) Ⓗ
Award-winning pub restaurant dating back to Tudor times, serving excellent food and beer. The main bar has a wood-burning stove and a second room is used for diners and functions. There is a large garden with decking beside a small pond. The pub has no prominent signage, just a modest hanging sign on a post by the road entrance. Closed from Christmas until the second week of January each year. Q🌞🍴🌛⌁🅿🌂🏵

REAL ALE BREWERIES
Ampthill Ampthill
B&T Shefford
Biggleswade 🍺 Biggleswade (NEW)
Brewhouse & Kitchen 🍺 Bedford
Leighton Buzzard Leighton Buzzard
Rockhopper Luton (NEW)
Wells Bedford
White Park Cranfield

Broom

Cock ★ Ⓛ
23 High Street, SG18 9NA
✪ 12-11 (10 Sun) ☎ (01767) 314411
🌐 thecockatbroom.co.uk
Greene King Abbot; 4 changing beers (sourced nationally) Ⓖ
Step through the front door and enter a time capsule – a games room with Northamptonshire skittles and darts, two cosy rooms with benches, tables and chairs, a separate restaurant plus an open drinking area with a door to the garden. Ale and cider are served at the top of the steps leading down to the cellar. Good beer and food, fortnightly quizzes, live music including two days of Broomstock, occasional beer festivals and Civil War re-enactments add to the atmosphere of this unique pub. Q🏠🐾⊘◑Å♣♠P🐾🛜

Carlton

Fox Ⓛ
High Street, MK43 7LA (off Turvey Rd S of village centre)
✪ 12-11 (10.30 Sun) ☎ (01234) 720235
🌐 thefoxatcarlton.pub
Fuller's London Pride; Wells Eagle IPA; 2 changing beers (sourced regionally) Ⓗ
Charming thatched community pub with a warm welcome and an attractive garden popular with families. Guest beers are often from local microbreweries. Good-value, home-cooked lunches (daily except Monday) and evening meals Wednesday to Saturday are served. There is a regular quiz on Thursday evenings, occasional themed food events and spring and summer bank holiday beer and cider festivals, using an outhouse in the garden as an additional bar. Local CAMRA Country Pub of the Year 2016 and 2017.
Q🏠🐾⊘◑&♣P🚃(25)🐾🛜

Clifton

Admiral
1 Broad Street, SG17 5RJ
✪ 3-11; 11-1am Fri & Sat; 11-11 Sun ☎ (01462) 811069
4 changing beers (sourced nationally) Ⓗ
An original beerhouse with an L-shaped bar offering excellent service and four ales, often featuring Adnams, Courage and Robinsons. A real cider is available in spring and summer. A wood-burning stove adds to the cosy atmosphere, amid maritime pictures, model ships and a collection of books and games. There is a weekly meat raffle, monthly quiz and regular live music events. Friday evening fish and chips is very popular (booking essential), plus weekend big breakfasts and a Sunday roast. 🏠🐾◑♣♠🚃(71,72)🐾🛜

Clophill

Stone Jug Ⓛ
10 Back Street, MK45 4BY (500yds off A6 at N end of village) TL083381
✪ 12-3.30 (not Mon), 6-11; 12-midnight Fri & Sat; 12-10.30 Sun ☎ (01525) 860526 🌐 stonejug.co.uk
Otter Amber; St Austell Trelawny; 2 changing beers (sourced nationally; often B&T) Ⓗ
Originally three 16th-century cottages, this popular village local has an L-shaped bar serving two drinking areas and a family/function room. Excellent home-made lunches are available

Tuesday to Saturday. The two guest beers are often from local microbreweries, the cider is Westons. Picnic benches at the front and a rear patio garden offer space for outdoor drinking in fine weather. Parking can be difficult at busy times. A good pit-stop for the Greensand Ridge Walk.
Q🏠🐾⊘◑♣♠P🚃(44,81)🐾

Cople

Five Bells
1 Northill Road, MK44 3TU
✪ closed Mon; 12-3, 5-11.30; 12-11.30 Fri-Sun
☎ (01234) 831330 🌐 thefivebellsatcople.com
Greene King IPA; 2 changing beers (sourced regionally) Ⓗ
A 17th-century building with colour-washed rough cast walls over a timber frame, listed for its special architectural and historic interest. The main bar has low beams and a side snug with an even lower ceiling. A second smaller bar, which can be hired for private functions, and a small room at the rear are used for dining. A large garden opens on to fields at the rear. 🏠🐾◑P🚃(74)🐾🛜

Dunstable

Gary Cooper ✔
Grove Park, Court Drive, LU5 4GP
✪ 8am-midnight (1am Fri & Sat) ☎ (01582) 471452
Greene King Abbot; Ruddles Best Bitter; Sharp's Doom Bar; 7 changing beers Ⓗ
A large modern Wetherspoon bar serving a selection of up to seven guest ales, often local. Situated in Grove Park leisure area, its patio overlooks the Grove House gardens with many bus routes stopping outside. The pub is named after the famous Hollywood star who attended the local grammar school between 1910 and 1913. Busy on Friday and Saturday nights. 🏠◑&♠🚃🛜

Globe Ⓛ
43 Winfield Street, LU6 1LS
✪ 12-11 (midnight Fri & Sat); 12-10.30 Sun
☎ (01582) 512300
B&T Shefford Bitter, Black Dragon Mild, Edwin Taylor's Extra Stout, SOD; 5 changing beers Ⓗ
Popular beer destination and community local where 13 handpumps dispense a good range of regular B&T beers, five ever-changing microbrewery beers, a real cider and perry. Over 20 Belgian beers are also available. Bare boards, bar stools, breweriana and a famous plank at the end of the bar create a traditional town pub atmosphere buzzing with conversation. Tuesday is acoustic music night. Beer festivals feature regularly. A former county and local CAMRA Pub of the Year. Q🏠&♣♠🚃(70)🐾

Pheasant Inn Ⓛ
208 West Street, LU6 1NX
✪ 11-11 (11.30 Fri & Sat); 12-11 Sun ☎ (01582) 662706
🌐 the-pheasant-inn-dunstable.co.uk
Sharp's Doom Bar; Young's Bitter; 4 changing beers Ⓗ
A just-out-of-town-centre pub on a bus route which doubles as a hotel/B&B. The large main bar and function room offers six real ales and two real ciders. TVs show all major sports and traditional pub games are played. Outside are a covered and heated front smoking area, rear garden, large umbrellas and a car park. Free curry is served on Friday and free pizza on Saturday evening (drinks

must be purchased). The pub hosts an annual beer festival and live music on occasion.
ちゃ★①&♣☻P呂☺≈

Dunton

March Hare 🄻
34 High Street, SG18 8RN
☼ 6-11 (midnight Thu); 3-midnight Fri; 12 (3 winter)-midnight Sat; 12-10.30 Sun ☎ (01767) 448093
⊕ themarchharedunton.co.uk
5 changing beers (sourced nationally) Ⓗ
Built in 1840, this pub is at the heart of the village community, hosting quiz, cribbage and games nights. It also provides the bar for regular folk music gigs in the church next door. An eclectic range of ales is usually available and two beer festivals are held each year. An open fire creates a cosy atmosphere in the winter and the garden is a pleasant spot when the weather is fine. Framed brewery-related jigsaws adorn the walls.
Qちゃ♣●☝呂(188)☺≈

Eversholt

Green Man
Church End, MK17 9DU
☼ closed Mon; 12-3, 6-11; 12-11 Sat; 12-6 Sun
☎ (01525) 288111 ⊕ greenmaneversholt.com
Sharp's Doom Bar; Tring Side Pocket for a Toad; 1 changing beer (sourced nationally) Ⓗ
A genuine free house in Church End, one of the many Ends that make up the village of Eversholt. It features flagstone floors, exposed brick fireplaces and a large patio/garden. Freshly prepared, good-quality food, mainly seafood plus an award-winning Sunday lunch, is served in the bar and the separate restaurant (not Sun eve). Conveniently placed for the nearby and popular tourist attractions of Woburn. ちゃ★①&P☺≈

Felmersham

Sun 🄻
Grange Road, MK43 7EU
☼ 4-11 (10 Mon); 3.30-11 Fri; 12-11 Sat; 12-10 Sun
☎ (01234) 781355
Wells Eagle IPA; 2 changing beers (sourced regionally) Ⓗ
Pretty, thatched community local reopened as a family-owned free house in 2013. The guest beer range changes weekly and often includes at least one from a local microbrewery. Home-made pie-on-a-plate snacks are available at most times. The pub has a family-friendly rear garden and is convenient for visits to the historic parish church and a nature reserve just across the river. There is a quiz on the first Wednesday of the month and occasional beer festivals are held.
ちゃ★♣P呂(50)☺≈

Flitwick

Crown ✅
Station Road, MK45 1LA
☼ 11.30-3, 5.30-11; 11.30-midnight Fri & Sat; 12-10.30 Sun
☎ (01525) 713737 ⊕ crownflitwick.co.uk
Sharp's Doom Bar; 3 changing beers (sourced nationally) Ⓗ
Large and very tidy, thriving estate pub, successfully rescued by the current tenants who are keen on their real ales – interesting guests from

the Punch Finest Cask list are often to be found. There is a games room with TV, jukebox and pool. The Saturday music nights are popular. Outside is a large garden with patio and children's play area. Traditional pub food is served lunchtimes daily and evenings Monday to Saturday.
ちゃ★①≠♣P呂(42,C2)☺≈

Swan 🄻 ✅
1 Dunstable Road, MK45 1HP
☼ 10-midnight (1.30am Fri & Sat); 12-midnight Sun
☎ (01525) 754777
Wells Bombardier; Young's Bitter; 1 changing beer Ⓗ
A handsome, traditional, red-bricked pub right alongside Flitwick station. The two regular beers are from Marston's Charles Wells brewery with a third handpump serving a guest. The two bars offer different experiences catering for all comers, and there is ample and pleasant outside seating. Food served daily includes breakfasts from 10am to 3pm. An annual beer festival is held over the August bank holiday weekend.
ちゃ★①&≠♣P呂(42,44)☺≈

Harlington

Carpenters Arms
Sundon Road, LU5 6LS
☼ 12-3, 6-11.30; 12-midnight Fri & Sat; 12-11 Sun
☎ (01525) 872384 ⊕ thecarpentersarmsharlington.com
Greene King IPA; Marston's Wainwright; Woodforde's Wherry; 1 changing beer (sourced nationally; often Purity) Ⓗ
Situated in the heart of Harlington, this low-beamed watch-your-head traditional village pub was first licensed in 1790 and has listings of landlords from then until the present. Three regular ales and one changing guest are available. Food is reasonably priced with good helpings – Monday is burger night. The railway station and bus service along with a range of country walks make this a popular stop-off. Qちゃ★①&≠♣P呂(42)☺≈

Old Sun
34 Sundon Road, LU5 6LS
☼ 12-11.30 ☎ (01582) 526208
Adnams Ghost Ship; St Austell Trelawny; 2 changing beers (sourced nationally; often St Austell, Timothy Taylor) Ⓗ
Traditional half-timbered pub dating back to 1785 and the building to the 1740s. There are two separate bars plus a side room, and outdoor seating with a children's play area. Sport TVs feature in both bars. Two regular ales and two guests are served and two beer festivals held on the May and August bank holidays. Situated just a short walk from the mainline rail station.
Qちゃ★≠P呂(X42)≈

Heath & Reach

Axe & Compass 🄻
Leighton Road, LU7 0AA
☼ 12-midnight ☎ (01525) 237394
⊕ theaxeandcompass.pub
3 changing beers Ⓗ
This village community pub has been a free house since 2014. The older front bar, with its low beams, is a lounge and dining area, while the rear public bar has gaming machines, a pool table and a TV screen. The large garden includes a children's play area. Guest beers often come from local breweries

such as Hornes, Tring and Leighton Buzzard. Accommodation is available in a separate lodge. ⛅❄♿◑♣P🖪(150)🐾🛜

Henlow

Engineers Arms L ✅
68 High Street, SG16 6AA
🌀 12-midnight (1am Fri & Sat); 12-10.30 Sun
☎ (01462) 812284 🌐 engineersarms.co.uk
10 changing beers (sourced nationally) Ⓗ
Award-winning free house serving 10 rotating ales and six ciders from local and national producers. The front bar houses collections of jugs and bottles, books and local photographs while the back bar, with walls adorned with pictures of sporting heroes, has two large TV screens to keep sports fans happy. The rear patio is popular in summer and used for beer and cider festivals. Regular comedy nights, live music evenings and discos are also held. ⛅❄🅰♣◑🖪(71,188)🐾🛜

Old Transporter Ale House L
300 Hitchin Road, SG16 6DP
🌀 closed Mon; 12 (3 winter)-10.30; 12-11 Fri & Sat; 12-9 Sun
☎ (01462) 817410 🌐 theoldtransporter.co.uk
6 changing beers (sourced nationally) Ⓖ
Small single-room bar located near to RAF Henlow operating as a beer house with many transport-themed pictures and artefacts. Six or more ales are offered direct from the cask, often from local and regional brewers, together with a range of real ciders mostly from Lilley's. Regular events include live music, darts, quizzes and raffles. Seasonal mini beer festivals featuring dark ales are always popular. ⛅♣◑🖪(71,188)🐾🛜

Leighton Buzzard

Bald Buzzard Alehouse L
6 Hockliffe Street, LU7 1HJ
🌀 12-9 (10 Fri & Sat); closed Sun & Mon ☎ 07581 146491
🌐 baldbuzzard.co.uk
Leighton Buzzard Restoration Ale; 7 changing beers (sourced locally; often Blue Monkey, Chiltern, Dark Star) Ⓖ
This award-winning micropub opened its doors in July 2015. It is a small but perfectly formed premises with a clever bespoke chiller room with sliding glass doors behind the bar containing 12 casks on stillage and three or four ciders. Ales from the local Leighton Buzzard Brewing Co and Oakham Brewery are regulars. The generous pork pies and cheeseboard are popular. As well as the cask ales and ciders there is a selection of bottled beers, wheat beer, wines and more.
Q⛅❄◑♿♣◑🖪(70,150)🐾

Black Lion 🍷
20 High Street, LU7 1EA
🌀 12-11 (midnight Fri & Sat); 12-10.30 Sun
☎ (01525) 853725
Draught Bass; Nethergate Growler Bitter; Oakham Bishops Farewell; 5 changing beers (sourced nationally) Ⓗ
A traditional alehouse with 17th-century origins, featuring exposed beams, wooden floors and an open fire. Eight handpumps showcase beers from Hook Norton, North Cotswold and local microbreweries such as Hornes and XT. Eight changing real ciders are also available and an impressive bottled beer menu lists over 100

continental and British beers. There is a large paved garden. Bar snacks are served and BYO cold lunches are welcome. Local CAMRA Pub of the Year 2015 to 2017. Q❄◑♣◑🖪(70,150)🐾

Red Lion
1 North Street, LU7 1EF
🌀 10-11 (midnight Fri & Sat); 11-11 Sun ☎ (01525) 374350
Black Sheep Ale; Greene King Abbot; 1 changing beer Ⓗ
A town-centre institution, this is an old-fashioned 17th-century pub with old-fashioned values – a warm welcome from the manager of over 20 years is assured. The public bar has all the traditional pub games and the main bar resembles a living room with comfy chairs, a large fish tank, TV and the pub dog wandering around. As well as the well-kept ales there is Westons Old Rosie real cider plus a selection of Irish and Scottish single malt whiskies. ♣◑🖪(70,150)🐾🛜

Swan Hotel ✅
50 High Street, LU7 1EA
🌀 6 (7 Mon)-midnight; 7-midnight Sat; 7-11.30 Sun
☎ (01525) 380170
Greene King Abbot; Ruddles Best Bitter; Sharp's Doom Bar; 7 changing beers (sourced nationally) Ⓗ
Dating from the 17th-century, this former coaching inn was renovated by Wetherspoon. With good-value food and 39 guest rooms, the Swan is busy and bustling for much of the week. Friendly staff operate one long bar serving two rooms, a conservatory and a courtyard. Guest beers may come from local microbreweries such as Tring and Vale, and real cider is kept in the summer months. Families are welcome until 10pm. Events include beer festivals twice a year.
Q⛅❄♿◑♿♣◑🖪(70,150)🛜

Luton

Black Horse L
23 Hastings Street, LU1 5BE
🌀 1-11 (midnight Sat) ☎ (01582) 965290
4 changing beers (sourced nationally; often Leighton Buzzard, Oakham, Tring) Ⓗ
A back-street pub not far from Luton town centre serving between two and four ever-changing ales, often from local breweries. A refurbishment in 2016 saw the addition of sports TV, a dartboard and a stage for live music to complement the popular jukebox and pool table. There is a covered, outdoor seating area for smokers. Food is served every afternoon, including Sunday. ⛅◑♻♣P🖪🐾

Bricklayers Arms
High Town Road, LU2 0DD
🌀 12-11 (midnight Fri & Sat); 12-10.30 Sun
☎ (01582) 611017 🌐 bricklayersarmsluton.co.uk
Batemans XB; 5 changing beers (sourced nationally; often Oakham) Ⓗ
Six handpumps serve over 10 guest beers a week from national breweries, with a choice of light, amber and often a mild alongside an Oakham brew. Two changing real ciders and draught Belgian beers are also available. This quirky High Town area pub has been run by the same landlady for over 30 years and is a favourite with Hatters fans on match days. There are TVs in both bars and a very popular quiz night on Monday.
❄♻♣🐾🐾🛜

Melchbourne

St John's Arms

Knotting Road, MK44 1BG (at jct with Yelden-Swineshead road) TL030662
☼ 4-11 (10 Mon & Tue); 3-11 Sat; 12-8 Sun
☎ (01234) 708238 ⊕ stjohnsmelchbourne.co.uk
Greene King IPA Ⓗ, Abbot Ⓖ; 1 changing beer (sourced regionally) Ⓗ

A truly rural pub, once a hunting lodge on the Melchbourne estate and named after the former family owners. The L-shaped bar opens into a conservatory and large garden. A second room is used mainly for dining. There is a games room to the rear with skittles and darts, and camping facilities in the field behind the pub. Home-cooked food is served, including traditional roast lunch on Sunday. ⏱☺Ⓓ▲♣P❀❄🐾🛜

Moggerhanger

Guinea Ⓛ ✅

Bedford Road, MK44 3RG
☼ 12-11 (midnight Fri & Sat); 12-10.30 Sun
☎ (01767) 640388 ⊕ guineamoggerhanger.co.uk
Courage Directors; Wells Eagle IPA; Young's Bitter; 1 changing beer (sourced regionally) Ⓗ

Large 18th-century village pub with beamed ceilings in a prominent position at the heart of the village. There is a garden at the front and car parks at the side and rear. The main bar has a drinking area and two areas beyond for diners. A separate games bar has hood skittles and darts. Quiz night is every Thursday. Freshly prepared food is available daily (not Sun eve). Q⏱☺Ⓓ&♣P🖦(73,188)🐾🛜

Odell

Bell

Horsefair Lane, MK43 7AS
☼ 11.30-11; 12-10.30 Sun ☎ (01234) 910850
⊕ thebellinodell.com
Greene King IPA, Abbot; 3 changing beers (sourced nationally) Ⓗ

Handsome thatched village pub with a large garden near the River Great Ouse. With the Harrold-Odell Country Park just down the lane, this is a popular stop for walkers. Sympathetic refurbishment and a series of linked but distinct seating areas help retain a traditional pub atmosphere. Good-value, quality food includes a Sunday roast, steak and chips night Monday and pie and chips night Tuesday. Local CAMRA Most Improved Pub 2016. Q⏱☺ⒹP🖦(25,26)🐾🛜

Renhold

Polhill Arms ✅

25 Wilden Road, MK41 0JP (at Salph End)
☼ 12 (4.30 Mon)-11; 12-10.30 Sun ☎ (01234) 771398
⊕ polhillarms.co.uk
Hardys & Hansons Bitter; 5 changing beers (sourced nationally) Ⓗ

Family-friendly village local with a welcoming atmosphere and a large garden, play area and restaurant. An interesting collection of pub and brewery artefacts and airship memorabilia is displayed. Traditional pub food is served, including fish and chips (not Sun or Mon eves). There are regular quiz nights, live music, and darts and skittles games. Two real ciders are kept in the

winter months, four in summer. Local CAMRA Cider Pub of the Year 2016 and 2017.
⏱☺Ⓓ♣🖦P🖦(27)🐾🛜

Sandy

Sir William Peel Ⓛ ✅

39 High Street, SG19 1AG
☼ 12-11 ☎ (01767) 680607 ⊕ sirwilliampeel.webs.com
Batemans XB; 3 changing beers Ⓗ

An open-plan pub offering a U-shaped bar, with a digital jukebox and library to the right and a seating area to the left leading to the patio and old stables, home to April beer and July cider festivals and an annual music fest in aid of Clic Sargent. Quiz night is the first Wednesday of the month, disco and karaoke on the last Saturday. There is also outdoor seating at the front.
⏱☺≈♣🖦P🖦(73,188)🐾🛜

Sharnbrook

Swan with Two Nicks Ⓛ

High Street, MK44 1PF
☼ 12-3, 6 (5 Fri & Sat)-11; 12-3, 12-5 Sun ☎ (01234) 781585
⊕ swanwith2nicks.co.uk
Wells Eagle IPA; Young's London Gold; 2 changing beers (sourced regionally) Ⓗ

Friendly village pub with a rear courtyard and patio garden. Home-cooked quality lunches and evening meals meals are served, using locally sourced ingredients where possible and including daily specials, pies and fresh fish. A selection of award-winning wines is also available by the glass or bottle. There is a live music session every other week. This is a good base for local walks, with nature reserves near the River Great Ouse.
⏱☺ⒹP🖦🐾🛜

Shefford

Brewery Tap Ⓛ

14 North Bridge Street, SG17 5DH
☼ 11.30-11; 12-10.30 Sun ☎ (01462) 628448
B&T Shefford Bitter, Shefford Dark Mild, Dragon Slayer; Everards Tiger; 2 changing beers (sourced nationally) Ⓗ

Renamed by the nearby B&T Brewery in 1996, the Tap is primarily a drinkers' pub, offering four regular beers plus two, usually stronger guest ales. Breweriana decorate an open-plan interior divided into two distinct areas with a family room at the rear. Lunchtime pies and rolls are available. Darts, dominoes and cribbage teams are supported, as is a golf society. The rear patio garden is heated on cool evenings. Car park access is through the archway beside the pub. ⏱☺♣P🖦(71,72)🐾

Souldrop

Bedford Arms Ⓛ

High Street, MK44 1EY (½ mile W of A6)
☼ closed Mon; 12-3, 5-11; 12-midnight Fri & Sat; 12-10 Sun
☎ (01234) 781384
Black Sheep Best Bitter; Greene King IPA; 3 changing beers (sourced nationally; often Phipps NBC) Ⓗ

Large village pub created partly from a 17th-century hop and ale house. Guest beers are often from local microbreweries. The restaurant has a central open fireplace and offers traditional, hearty pub favourites with daily specials and a roast on Sunday. A games room with skittles runs off the

41

main bar. The spacious garden with pétanque is popular with families in summer. A former local CAMRA Country Pub of the Year.
ॐ☺◑&♣P⊒(26)❀☎

Stanbridge

Five Bells
Station Road, LU7 9JF
☼ 11-11 (11.30 Sat); 12-10.30 Sun ☎ (01525) 210224
⊕ fivebellsstanbridge.co.uk
Fuller's London Pride; Gale's Seafarers Ale; 2 changing beers ℍ
A Fuller's-owned country pub with wooden floors, two real fires, a cosy snug and mind-your-head beams. A separate 80-seat restaurant in the 18th-century wing offers good-quality food and can be used for weddings and functions. The pub is set in extensive and attractive grounds. It is named after the nearby church which originally had five bells (although it subsequently acquired one more). Guest ales are usually from Fuller's/Gale's but may occasionally include one from a local microbrewery. ॐ☺◑&♣P⊒(70)❀☎

Toddington

Cuckoo 🗇
Market Square, LU5 6QJ
☼ 5 (4 Fri)-11; 1-11 Sat; closed Sun ☎ (01525) 877780
⊕ thecuckootoddington.co.uk
House beer (by Leighton Buzzard); 7 changing beers (sourced nationally) ℍ
Located in the old town hall, a 15th-century Grade II-listed building, the pub has a main bar, separate lounge with comfy chairs and an upstairs function room with separate bar. A selection of real ales and ciders with a strong local leaning is offered. There is no TV and no music, just convivial conversation. A small range of quality pub snacks is available.
Q♣●⊒(42,E)❀

Oddfellows Arms
2 Congar Lane, LU5 6BP
☼ 5 (1 Sat & Sun)-11 ☎ (01525) 872021
Adnams Broadside; Fuller's London Pride; 2 changing beers ℍ
Attractive 700-year-old two-bar pub facing the village green with a heavily beamed bar featuring a vast collection of pumpclips, and a games room with a pool table. With two regular real ales and a wide selection on the two guest handpumps, there is always plenty of choice. The regular real cider is Westons Old Rosie and there is often an alternative. The patio garden is popular in summer and has shelter for smokers. ♣●⊒(42,E)❀☎

Whipsnade

Old Hunters Lodge
The Crossroads, LU6 2LN
☼ 12-2.30 (3 Fri & Sat), 6-11; 12-11 Sun ☎ (01582) 872228
⊕ oldhunterslodge.co.uk
Greene King Abbot; 2 changing beers ℍ
A beautiful 15th-century thatched inn set on the outskirts of Whipsnade village close to the world-renowned Whipsnade Zoo. The cosy main bar, warmed by a log fire, offers comfortable seating as well as traditional dining tables. The side bar has kept many original features including the inglenook fireplace. Separate restaurant areas may be used as function rooms. The picturesque front garden makes a lovely area for summer dining and drinking. Six guest rooms include a bridal suite.
Q ॐ☺⇆◑P⊒(X31)❀☎

Wingfield

Plough
Tebworth Road, LU7 9QH
☼ 12-3, 5.30-midnight; 12-10.30 Sun ☎ (01525) 873077
⊕ theploughinn.com
Fuller's London Pride; Gale's HSB; 2 changing beers (often Fuller's) ℍ
Charming thatched village inn dating from the 17th century, decorated with paintings of rural scenes and ploughs. Beware the low beams! Good home-cooked food is served daily except on Sunday evening when a fortnightly quiz is held. To the rear is a conservatory which can be booked for functions. There are tables outside at the front and at the back a lovely garden. ॐ☺◑♣P☎

Woburn

Woburn Ale House 🗇
11 Market Place, MK17 9PZ
☼ 12 (5 Mon)-11 ☎ (01525) 290142
⊕ woburnalehouse.com
Hornes Triple Goat Porter; Leighton Buzzard Restoration Ale; 4 changing beers (sourced locally; often Hornes, Tring) ℍ
This charming bar in a former flower shop has six handpumps for cask ales and two for varying ciders and perries. Local beers feature heavily, in particular from Hornes Brewery and Leighton Buzzard Brewing Company. Sausage rolls and pork pies complement the beers and ciders. There are no TVs or music to distract from the buzz of conversation. Q&●⊒(49)❀☎

Wrestlingworth

Chequers 🗇
43 High Street, SG19 2EP
☼ 12-3 (not Mon), 5-11; 12-midnight Fri & Sat; 12-10.30 Sun
☎ (01767) 631818 ⊕ chequersfreehouse.co.uk
Adnams Southwold Bitter; Black Sheep Best Bitter; Woodforde's Wherry; 3 changing beers (sourced regionally) ℍ
Attractive cream-coloured Grade I-listed building on a large plot with four to six real ales and one or two Westons ciders. The drinking area extends the length of the pub's frontage and shares with a dining area (no food Mon). This is a popular meeting place for local groups and is home to darts and pétanque teams. Occasional beer festivals are held outside where there is a south-facing patio. Local CAMRA Rural Pub of the Year 2017.
ॐ☺◑♣●P⊒(188)❀☎

Public transport information

Leave the car behind and travel to the pub by bus, train, tram or even ferry...

Using public transport is an excellent way to get to the pub, but many people use it irregularly, and systems can be slightly different from place to place. So, below are some useful websites and phone numbers where you can find all the information you might need.

Combined travel information

The national **Traveline** system gives information on all rail and local bus services throughout England, Scotland and Wales. Calls are put through to a local call centre and if necessary your call will be switched through to a more relevant one. There are also services for mobiles, including a next-bus text service and smart-phone app. The website offers other services including timetables and a journey planner with mapping:

- 0871 200 22 33
  www.traveline.org.uk

LONDON

In London use Traveline or **Transport for London (TfL)** travel services. TfL provides information and route planning for all of London's transport networks, including London Underground and Overground, Docklands Light Railway, National Rail, buses, River Buses, Tramlink, Barclays Cycles and cycle routes. Detailed ticketing information helps you find the most cost-effective ways to travel in London. There are also live departure boards, service and traffic updates; mobile services and more:

- 020 7222 1234
  www.tfl.gov.uk

Train travel

National Rail Enquiries covers the whole of Great Britain's rail network and provides service information, ticketing, online journey planning and other information.

- 08457 48 49 50
  www.nationalrail.co.uk

Coach travel

The two main UK coach companies are **National Express** and **Scottish Citylink**. Between them, they serve everywhere from Cornwall to the Highlands. Their websites offer timetables, journey planning, ticketing, route mapping, and other useful information. CAMRA members can benefit from 20% off travel with National Express*. See **www.camra.org.uk/benefits**.

- National Express: 08717 81 81 81
  www.nationalexpress.com

- Scottish Citylink: 08705 50 50 50
  www.citylink.co.uk

Scottish ferries

Caledonian MacBrayne (CalMac) operate throughout Scotland's Hebridean and Clyde islands, stretching from Arran in the south to Lewis in the north. They run 475 sailings per day in summer and around 350 per day in winter.

- 0800 066 5000
  www.calmac.co.uk

Northern Ireland & islands

For travel outside mainland Britain but within the area of this Guide, information is available from the following companies:

NORTHERN IRELAND
- Translink: 028 9066 6630
  www.translink.co.uk

ISLE OF MAN
- Isle of Man Transport: 01624 662 525
  www.iombusandrail.info

JERSEY
- Liberty Bus: 01534 828 555
  www.libertybus.je

GUERNSEY
- Island Coachways: 01481 720 210
  www.buses.gg

Public transport symbols in the Guide

Pub entries in the Guide include helpful symbols to show if there are stations and/ or bus routes close to a pub. There are symbols for railway stations (≫); tram or light rail stations (Ⓠ); London Underground, Overground or DLR stations (⊖); and bus routes (🚍). See the 'Key to symbols' on the inside front cover for more details.

Membership benefits are subject to change.

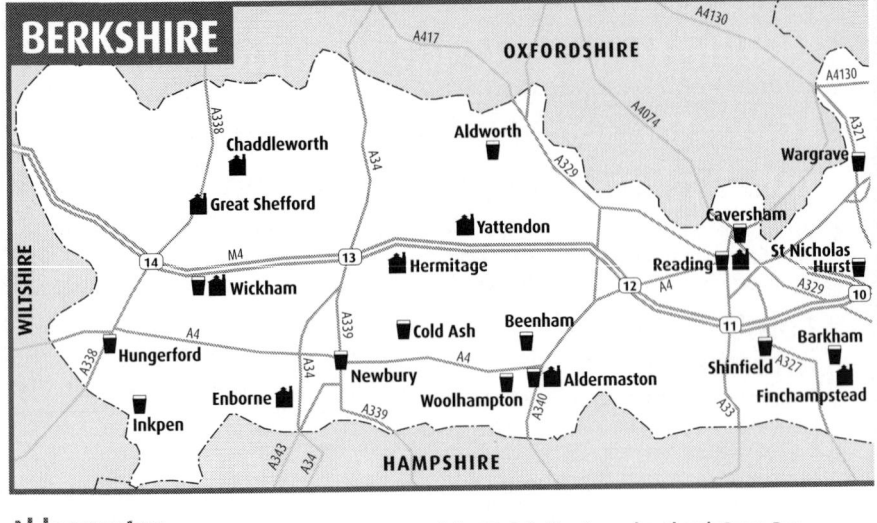

Aldermaston

Butt Inn
Station Road, RG7 4LA
☼ 11.30-11; 12-10.30 Sun ☎ (0118) 971 3309
⊕ thebuttinn.biz
Sharp's Doom Bar; 3 changing beers (sourced nationally; often Indigenous, West Berkshire, Wild Weather Ales) Ⓗ
The pub is easily reached by train, canal and road. It is loved by walkers and welcomes dogs. It has a bar with a roaring fire, comfortable seating in the snug area and a dining area where food is served all day. Tuesday is curry night and on Thursday there is a quiz. Outside, the garden is complete with a large sun shade and a pizza oven in use in the summer. ⊛⇦◑⇌P🎵

Aldworth

Bell Inn ★ Ⓛ
Bell Lane, RG8 9SE (250yds off B4009)
☼ closed Mon; 11-3, 6-11; 12-3, 7-10.30 Sun
☎ (01635) 578272
Arkell's 3B, Kingsdown; house beer (by West Berkshire); 2 changing beers (sourced locally; often Loose Cannon, Rebellion, West Berkshire) Ⓗ
This village inn was built in 1340 – its name refers to the bells that were part of the coat of arms of the landowners. It has been run by the same family for over 120 years. Popular with walkers enjoying the nearby Ridgeway, it is famed for a range of hot filled rolls, scrumptious desserts, excellent beers and its historic interior. Local ciders are from Tutts Clump and Red Dog, plus Lilley's from Somerset. The spacious garden is a delight in summer. A former national, regional and branch CAMRA Pub of the Year. Q🚋⊛◑♣♠P🌸

Barkham

Bull Ⓛ
Barkham Road, RG41 4TL (on B3349 jct with Barkham St)
☼ 12-11; 12-7 Sun ☎ (0118) 976 2816
⊕ thebullbarkham.com

Gale's HSB; Rebellion Smuggler; Sharp's Doom Bar; Timothy Taylor Landlord; 2 changing beers (sourced locally; often Rebellion) Ⓗ
Community village pub and restaurant. The building is Grade II listed with etched-glass windows and an inglenook with a real fire. Formerly it was a smithy and the forge remains. The relaxing bar area offers up to six ales including some from local breweries. Food is freshly prepared from ingredients mostly sourced locally. The authentic Thai dishes are always a treat. The well-kept garden hosts regular beer festivals and other events. Q⊛⊛◑P🖳(3)🌸

Beenham

Six Bells Ⓛ
The Green, RG7 5NX (at Bucklebury end of main road through village)
☼ 12-2.30 (not Mon), 6-11; 12-2.30, 6.30-11 Sat; 12-3 Sun
☎ (0118) 971 3368 ⊕ thesixbells.co.uk
West Berkshire Good Old Boy; 2 changing beers (sourced locally; often Loddon) Ⓗ
A welcoming and comfortable two-bar village local. The name commemorates the recasting of the parish church bells following a 1794 fire. This LocAle pub offers Good Old Boy alongside two guest ales, usually from Loddon and Loose Canon. Enjoy a home-cooked meal, or play a range of board games in front of the open fire. Accommodation is in four bedrooms, and a separate room is available for local club and community meetings. Q⊛⇦◑Å♠P🖳(104)🎵

Binfield

Binfield Club
Forest Road, RG42 4HP (at mini roundabout jct with Terrace Rd South)
☼ 11-11; 12-10.30 Sun ☎ (01344) 420690
⊕ binfieldclub.com
Sharp's Doom Bar; Shepherd Neame Spitfire; Wells Bombardier; 1 changing beer (sourced nationally; often Fuller's) Ⓗ
A long-established club at the heart of the village, serving good-value food and drink to the many groups who meet here. The club supports local good causes and holds regular charity nights. The

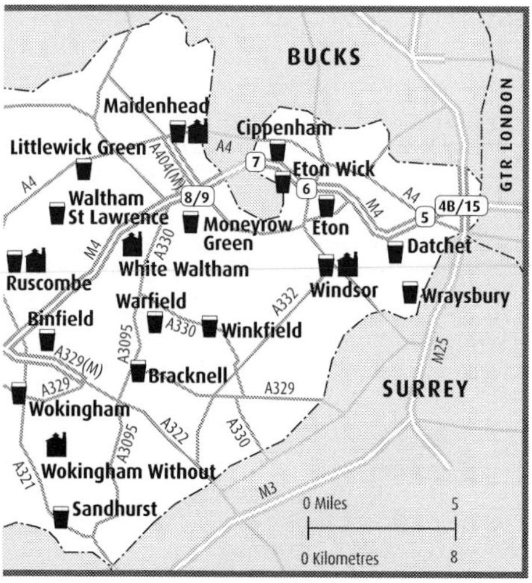

Caversham

Fox & Hounds ⓛ
51 Gosbrook Road, RG4 8BN
✪ 12-midnight; 12-11 Sun ☎ 07540 816293
8 changing beers (often Dark Star, Oakham, Surrey Hills) Ⓗ
Local CAMRA Pub of the Year for the past two years, the Fox & Hounds recently underwent a major refurbishment and now sports a more contemporary style. Situated in the heart of Caversham, this pub has become a lively community hub and extends a friendly welcome to all visitors. Thursday quiz nights are always well attended – they are almost as popular as the excellent Sunday roasts. ⓑ⊛◑♣●P�“Ⓡ

Griffin ✅
10/12 Church Road, RG4 7AD
✪ 11-11 (midnight Fri); 11-10.30 Sun ☎ (0118) 947 5018
Brains Rev James; Greene King IPA; 4 changing beers Ⓗ
There has been a hostelry on this site since the 1800s (when eels were fished in the nearby River Thames and sold in the inn). The current pub was built in 1916 and offers good food and ale with numerous specials on chalkboards and regular themed produce weeks. The spacious interior and heated rear patio garden offer plenty of choice for a quiet drink or a big family meal. ⓑ⊛◑♣●P�“Ⓡ

Cippenham

Barleycorn ⓛ
151 Lower Cippenham Lane, SL1 5DS
✪ 12-midnight (12.30am Fri & Sat); 12-11.30 Sun ☎ (01628) 603115
6 changing beers (sourced nationally) Ⓗ
A traditional single-bar pub, recently refurbished, with seating on one side and a pool table on the other, catering for a strong local following. Around the walls is a large collection of bottles and jugs. Of the six guest ales there is always one from Rebellion and a strong ale. The remaining four guests come from around the country. There are a couple of TVs for sport, and occasional live music. A free public car park is nearby. Q⊛♣P�“(5)Ⓡ

Cold Ash

Castle Inn ⓛ ✅
Cold Ash Hill, RG18 9PS

facilities are excellent, with snooker, pool, darts plus live sports TV. Four real ales are available including three club favourites and a rotating guest beer. Although a private club, CAMRA members are welcome on production of a membership card. ⓑ◑♿♣P�“(150,151)Ⓡ

Bracknell

Cannie Man ⓛ ✅
Bywood, Hanworth, RG12 7RF
✪ 12-11 (11.30 Fri & Sat); 12-10.30 Sun ☎ (01344) 307620
Fuller's London Pride; Sharp's Doom Bar; West Berkshire Good Old Boy; 3 changing beers (sourced nationally; often Brains, Hogs Back, Rebellion) Ⓗ
Excellent modern community estate pub with a strong local trade and friendly to visitors. Four of the six handpumps are mostly in use serving well-kept ales from national and local breweries. Two large TVs show sporting events and there is live music most Saturdays. The pub hosts darts, pool and a local football team, and is a keen sponsor of local community and charitable events. Children are welcome until the early evening. A former CAMRA branch Most Improved Pub of the Year winner. ⊛♣P�“(171,172)Ⓡ

Old Manor ⓛ ✅
Grenville Place, RG12 1BP (at Met Office/College roundabout jct with Church Rd)
✪ 8am-midnight (1am Fri & Sat) ☎ (01344) 304490
Greene King Abbot; Ruddles Best Bitter; 6 changing beers (sourced nationally; often Loddon, Rebellion, Titanic) Ⓗ
A perennial favourite, this Wetherspoon pub has featured in every edition of the Guide since 2000. The 17th-century listed former manor house is divided into a number of distinct areas including a snug and the Monks Room, popular for meals, functions and meetings. A genuine community pub, popular with a mixed clientele, it offers eight real ales including six constantly changing guests and at least two real ciders. Outside is a pleasant walled garden and two paved terrace areas. Working dogs only are allowed throughout. Qⓑ⊛◑♿♣PᚋᏚⓇ

✪ 11.30-11.30 (midnight Fri & Sat); 12-11 Sun
☎ (01635) 863232 ⊕ thecastleatcoldash.co.uk
Courage Best Bitter; Fuller's London Pride; Sharp's Atlantic; West Berkshire Good Old Boy; 2 changing beers (sourced nationally) ⊞
This welcoming 19th-century village inn has been in the same family for 24 years and retains a traditional pub feel. It is known for its good-quality, reasonably priced food including Sunday roasts. Regular beers include one from West Berkshire brewery. Rotating guest beers and a real cider are also offered. Monday is quiz night (no meals served) and a meat raffle is held on Friday. Darts and other traditional pub games are played and there is occasional live music.
ಶ☺◑♣♦P🚻(101)🐾🐾🛜

Datchet

Royal Stag 🄻 ✅
The Green, SL3 9JH
✪ 11-midnight ☎ (01753) 584231
Fuller's London Pride; Windsor & Eton Knight of the Garter, Guardsman; 1 changing beer (sourced locally) ⊞
Next to the church, the pub is reputed to be the oldest village house – ring-counting of roof timbers dates it to 1494. It may have been an ale house in the 1500s called the Five Bells, changed to the Royal Stag in 1796. Three regular beers are supplemented by Windsor & Eton seasonals/specials. The front part of the pub is for drinking and the restaurant to the rear, serving home-made food. Outside is a large patio-style seating area. Quiz and bingo are played.
Qಶ☺◑≈♦P🚻(10)🐾🛜

Eton

George 🄻
77 High Street, SL4 6AF
✪ 8am-11; 8am-10 Sun ☎ (01753) 861797
⊕ georgeinn-eton.co.uk
Windsor & Eton ParkLife, Windsor Knot, Guardsman, Conqueror; 2 changing beers (sourced locally) ⊞
Windsor & Eton Brewery's first pub faces Eton Bridge. Recent refurbishment includes a new bar which hosts six ales all from the brewery. Wooden floors and lighting by carriage lamps and candles create a warm atmosphere. The range of Windsor & Eton beers can change depending on the number of specials/seasonals available. The Hop House is available for private parties. Real cider is on offer in the summer months. Breakfast is served 8-10am.
Q☺🛏◑≈♦P🚻(10)🐾🛜

Waterman's Arms 🄻 ✅
Brocas Street, SL4 6BW
✪ 12-11.30; 12-11 Sun ☎ (01753) 861001
⊕ watermans-eton.com
Adnams Ghost Ship; Brakspear Bitter; Skinner's Cornish Knocker; Windsor & Eton Knight of the Garter; Wychwood Hobgoblin; house beer (by Caledonian); 2 changing beers ⊞
Located a few yards from Eton Bridge, this welcoming, cosy pub dates back to 1682. Popular with a good mix of locals and tourists, the interior features rowing memorabilia and murals. The Sunday carvery is recommended. Quiz night is Thursday and salsa night Wednesday. A function room is available free of charge. A good selection of books is on sale in aid of the local Swan Support charity. ☺◑≈♣♦🚻(10)🐾🛜

Eton Wick

Greyhound
The Walk, 16 Common Road, SL4 6JE
✪ 12-11; 11.30-midnight Fri & Sat; 11.30-10 Sun
☎ (01753) 868633 ⊕ greyhoundetonwick.co.uk
Fuller's London Pride; Rebellion IPA; Windsor & Eton Knight of the Garter ⊞
A proper locals' pub with a clean contemporary air and a friendly welcome. A free house, it sells only local real ales. Food is served Monday to Friday lunchtimes. Unusual for this part of the country is the skittle alley, available to hire. Live music features regularly and karaoke on the second Saturday of the month. ಶ☺◑♣P🚻(10)🐾🛜

Hungerford

Hungerford Club ✅
3 The Croft, RG17 0HY (on foot via Church Lane)
✪ 12-3, 7-11; 12-5 Sun ☎ (01488) 682357
⊕ hungerford-club.co.uk
Fuller's London Pride; 1 changing beer (sourced nationally) ⊞
Facing the Croft, a village green just yards from the busy main street, visitors are warmly welcomed at this social and sports club. The changing guest ale is usually sourced from a smaller brewery countrywide, often chosen by the club members themselves. Barbecues and other events are held including a beer festival over the August bank holiday. Show your CAMRA membership card or this Guide to gain admission. Qಶ☺≈♣P🚻🐾🛜

John o' Gaunt 🄻 ✅
21 Bridge Street, RG17 0EG (30yds N of canal bridge)
✪ 11-11 (midnight Fri & Sat); 12-10.30 Sun
☎ (01488) 683535 ⊕ john-o-gaunt-hungerford.co.uk
6 changing beers (sourced regionally; often INNformal) ⊞
The welcoming smell of a real fire greets you as you enter this listed building, just north of the canal bridge in a charming small town, well served by the Great Western Railway. Six real ales are available, usually including two INNformal beers brewed at sister pub the Five Bells at nearby Wickham. Real cider is also offered along with a wide selection of bottled beers. The seasonal, locally sourced food is highly regarded.
Qಶ☺◑≈♣♦P🚻🐾🛜

Inkpen

Swan Inn 🄻
Craven Road, Lower Green, RG17 9DX
✪ closed Mon & Tue; 12-2.30, 7-11 Wed-Fri; 12-11 Sat; 12-4 Sun ☎ (01488) 668326 ⊕ theswaninn-organics.co.uk
Butts Jester, Traditional; 1 changing beer (sourced locally; often Butts) ⊞
An attractive 17th-century village inn situated in an area popular with walkers and cyclists. Open fires, old beams and a flagstone darts room add character. Good quality organic food features prominently on the menu, served in both the bar and the award-winning restaurant. Butts organic beers are always available on handpump. Quiz and darts nights alternate every Thursday and there is occasional live music. The garden and terraces offer delightful outdoor seating.
Qಶ☺🛏◑🅳♣P🚻(3)🐾🛜

Littlewick Green

Cricketers
Coronation Road, SL6 3RA
☼ 12-11 ☎ (01628) 822888 ⊕ cricketers-berkshire.co.uk
Hall & Woodhouse Badger First Call; 1 changing beer H
This pub is in a quintessential British pub location next to the village green and cricket pitch that featured in Midsomer Murders. The refurbished terrace area at the front overlooks this idyllic setting. In winter wood-burning stoves keep the pub cosy. Hall & Woodhouse seasonal beers are sometimes available. A traditional menu offers a range of freshly prepared pub food.
Q🛏️🏡🍴◑🚆🚪(4,127)🐾🛜

Maidenhead

Craufurd Arms L
15 Gringer Hill, SL6 7LY
☼ 12-midnight (1am Fri & Sat) ☎ (01628) 675410
⊕ cacgmaidenhead.com
Rebellion IPA, Smuggler; 2 changing beers (sourced locally; often West Berkshire, Windsor & Eton) H
The pub was registered as an Asset of Community Value and is now owned by the community. The building dates back to the late-1800s and was close to Craufurd College, a private school for boys, hence the unusual spelling. The cosy single bar hosts a multitude of activities – crib on Monday, ladies' darts Tuesday, gents' darts Wednesday and quiz night on Thursday. Two large screens show Sky and BT sport. Live music features on occasion.
🛏️🏡🚆🍴🚪(5,8)🐾🛜

Grenfell Arms L ✓
22 Oldfield Road, SL6 1TW
☼ 10-11.30 (1am Fri & Sat); 11-10.30 Sun ☎ (01628) 620705
⊕ grenfellarmsmaidenhead.com
Greene King IPA, IPA Gold; 6 changing beers H
A welcoming wood-panelled two-room pub situated a short walk from the town centre and the Thames, with eight bedrooms. There are eight handpumps on the bar – four Greene King, including a seasonal, and four rotating guests from local micros. Two real ciders are offered, normally Orchard Pig and Hogan's. Breakfast is available from 10am followed by traditional pub food lunchtimes and evenings. The garden has had a makeover and is pleasant for the summer.
Q🛏️🏡🍴◑🍴🚪(4,53)🐾🛜

Maidenhead Conservative Club ✓
32 York Road, SL6 1SF
☼ 11-11 (11.45 Fri & Sat); 12-11 Sun ☎ (01628) 620579
⊕ maidenheadconclub.com
Fuller's London Pride; 4 changing beers H
Friendly real ale outlet close to the station and local CAMRA branch Club of the Year 2017. The four guests ales come from mainly local independent breweries, and a selection of bottle-conditioned beers is available. Crib, pool and snooker nights are held during the week and a quiz night on the last Wednesday of the month. The TV lounge has been recently refurbished. Your CAMRA membership card allows entry for a minimal fee. Public parking is nearby. 🛏️◑♿🚆🚪(4)🛜

Moneyrow Green

White Hart L
SL6 2ND

☼ 12-11 (10 Mon; 11.30 Fri); 12-9 Sun ☎ (01628) 621460
⊕ thewhitehartholyport.co.uk
Greene King IPA; 3 changing beers H
A welcoming, traditional pub half-a-mile south of the village. The guest beers include one LocAle and two non-Greene King ales. The wood-panelled lounge features leather sofas and log fires in winter. The larger public bar has wooden flooring, a TV and traditional pub games including bar billiards. There is a weekly quiz night on a Monday and open mic on the second Tuesday of the month. Outside is a large, fenced beer garden with a pétanque pitch and children's play area.
🛏️🏡◑♣🚪(53)🐾🛜

Newbury

Catherine Wheel L
35 Cheap Street, RG14 5DB
☼ 12-11.30 (1am Thu); 10-2am Fri & Sat; 10-11 Sun
☎ (01635) 33627 ⊕ thecatherinewheel.com
West Berkshire Good Old Boy; house beer (by Longdog); 4 changing beers (often Binghams, Siren, Wild Weather Ales) H
Following an extensive refurbishment in 2014, the spacious single-bar pub offers a good selection of local ales on six handpulls, complemented by a range of bottles from across the world. A large selection of real cider is also available. Pieminister pies and bar snacks are served. A covered courtyard provides additional seating and there is occasional live music. 🛏️◑🚆♣🍴🚪🐾🛜

Cow & Cask L
1 Inches Yard, Market Street, RG14 5DP
☼ 12-2 (not Tue & Wed), 5-9; 12-2, 4.30-10 Fri; 12-9 Sat; closed Sun & Mon ☎ 07517 658071 ⊕ cowandcask.co.uk
3 changing beers (sourced regionally; often Indigenous, Longdog, Ramsbury) G
Housed in a former shop near the bus and train stations, Berkshire's first micropub has dispensed well over 300 different beers since it opened in November 2014. The small bar is set in the corner of the room, serving up to four ales, often from Berkshire and the surrounding counties, along with two ciders. Friendly conversation is the order of the day, and traditional pub games such as crib are popular. Q🚆♣🍴🚪🐾

King Charles Tavern L ✓
54 Cheap Street, RG14 5BX
☼ 11.30-midnight (1am Thu-Sat) ☎ (01635) 36695
⊕ kctavern.com
West Berkshire Good Old Boy; house beer (by Greene King); 6 changing beers (sourced nationally; often Butts, Oakham, St Austell) H
Known locally as the KC, this historic family-friendly town-centre pub is run by a landlord passionate about real ale. A former CAMRA branch Pub of the Year, it offers a choice of six beers from across the country. A warm welcome is assured from the knowledgeable bar staff. Two front bars with real fires are complemented by a rear dining area, leading to a small patio. Situated between the station and marketplace, the pub is ideal for locals and visitors alike. 🛏️🏡◑🚆🐾🛜

Reading

Alehouse L
2 Broad Street, RG1 2BH

✪ 11-11; 12-10.30 Sun ☎ (0118) 950 8119
⊕ the-alehouse-reading.co.uk
9 changing beers Ⓗ
One of Reading's quirkiest pubs, the Alehouse always leaves an impression on visitors. As a champion of microbreweries, both local and from further afield, rare and unusual ales are frequently to be found on the pumps. Often busy around the bar area, those wishing for a more peaceful drink can take advantage of the secluded cubbyholes at the back of the pub. ≈●🖥️🚃♿

Allied Arms 🅛
57 St Mary's Butts, RG1 2LG
✪ 12 (5 Mon)-11; closed Sun ☎ (0118) 958 3323
⊕ allied-arms.co.uk
Loddon Hullabaloo; 4 changing beers Ⓗ
A family-run, town-centre pub dating from around 1828, with two cosy bars – enter via the side passage, not the front door. The large, walled garden is a popular refuge from the chaos of town with patio heaters for those colder nights. A wide and interesting selection of songs is available on the jukebox. An enhanced range of 10 ales is available from Wed-Sat on the last weekend of each month. Regular charity pub quiz. Closed Sundays. 🛏️❀≈●🚃♿🛜

Butler 🅛
85-91 Chatham Street, RG1 7DS
✪ 10.30-11.30 (1am Fri); 12-2am Sat; 12-11 Sun
☎ (0118) 959 5500 ⊕ thebutlerreading.co.uk
6 changing beers Ⓗ
Very much a local in the heart of town, the pub was recently taken over by a local consortium and is in the process of being upgraded both inside and out. Formerly a Fuller's pub, it was named after Butler's Wine Merchants, who operated from these premises many years ago. Ales are sourced from regionals and larger micros – often unusual choices for Reading. A secluded patio caters for smokers. 🛏️◑≈♣●P🚃(17)♿

Castle Tap 🅛
120 Castle Street, RG1 7RJ
✪ 11-11.30 (midnight Fri & Sat); 11-10.30 Sun
☎ (0118) 958 0473 ⊕ thecastletap.co.uk
4 changing beers Ⓗ
Alongside its ever-changing selection of real ales and ciders, the Castle Tap offers an excellent range of bottled beers. The pub maintains a friendly local atmosphere while offering a warm welcome to visiting real ale aficionados. Entertainment includes frequent live music and other events, and is well worth checking out. For those feeling peckish, cheeseboards are available. The back room can be booked for functions. 🛏️❀♣●P🚃♿

Fisherman's Cottage
224 Kennet Side, RG1 3DW
✪ closed Mon; 12-11.30 (midnight Fri & Sat); 12-8 Sun
☎ (0118) 956 0432 ⊕ thefishermanscottagereading.co.uk
4 changing beers Ⓗ
Reopened in 2016 under new management who have a good pedigree from other local pubs. Four handpumps are complemented by a large selection of bottled beers, all well sourced and offering a varied selection. The menu is based around tapas and paella, cooked by the I Love Paella company, including a good selection of vegetarian and vegan dishes. Roast dinners are also served on Sunday from opening time until they run out. 🛏️❀◑♣P🚃(17)♿🛜

Foresters Arms ✓
79-81 Brunswick Street, RG1 6NY
✪ 4-11; 12-midnight Sat; 12-11 Sun
2 changing beers Ⓗ
Identified by CAMRA as having an historic pub interior of some regional importance, this traditional back-street local has two bars linked by a side corridor. The carpeted front bar is a home-from-home, with a proper fire and sports TV. The rear room, with a pool table and darts, leads to a recently renovated garden, ideal for a sunny evening pint. The current licensees and staff are enthusiastic about cask and happy to advise on beer choice. No food is served but there is an impressive array of snacks. 🛏️❀≈♣🚃♿🛜

Greyfriar
53 Greyfriars Road, RG1 1PA
✪ 12-11 (midnight Fri & Sat); 12-6 Sun ☎ (0118) 958 0560
⊕ thegreyfriarreading.co.uk
6 changing beers Ⓗ
A local success story – the Greyfriar has thrived since coming back from a long period of closure a few years ago and was shortlisted for the local CAMRA branch's Pub of the Year in 2017. Six real ales and a variety of craft gins are on offer, and the pub hosts occaional tap takeovers. Quiz night is every other Monday. Darts is played here. CAMRA members receive 10 per cent off the price of a pint of real ale. There is easy access from the newly rebuilt station entrance. 🛏️◑≈♣●🖥️🚃♿🛜

Hop Leaf
163-165 Southampton Street, RG1 2QZ
✪ 12-11.30 (12.30am Fri & Sat) ☎ (0118) 931 4700
Downton New Forest Ale; Hop Back GFB, Citra, Crop Circle, Summer Lightning; 2 changing beers Ⓗ
A traditional local with pub games such as bar billiards, crib and backgammon (featuring regular competitions in each), as well as a pinball machine. The pub stocks six Hop Back beers plus a selection of ciders and perries. A variety of pub snacks is available. Fans of classic rock will enjoy the landlord's choice in music. A good range of daily newspapers is provided. 🛏️♣●🚃♿

Nag's Head 🍺 🅛
5 Russell Street, RG1 7XD
✪ 12-11 (midnight Fri); 11-midnight Sat ☎ 07765 880137
⊕ nagsheadreading.com
12 changing beers Ⓗ
With a wide range of real ales, ciders and perries, visitors can be sure to find something to their taste at the Nag's Head. Its dedication to quality has made it a multiple winner of local CAMRA Pub of the Year and Cider Pub of the Year awards. A selection of board games is available for those wanting to while away a few hours. Gets busy on Reading FC match days. 🛏️❀◑≈♣●P🚃♿🛜

Purple Turtle ✓
9 Gun Street, RG1 2JR
✪ 11-3am ☎ (0118) 959 7196 ⊕ purpleturtlebar.com
4 changing beers Ⓗ
Celebrating its 25th year in 2015, the Purple Turtle is Reading's longest-running independent pub. While many people will associate the pub with the trappings of noisy misspent youth, it underwent a major overhaul in 2013/14. The revitalised bar offers real ale and cider as well as its infamous late opening. Beer choice is eclectic – you never know what you will get from one week to the next. ❀◑♿≈●🚃🛜

Retreat

8 St John's Street, RG1 4EH
✪ 4.30-11; 12-11.30 Fri & Sat; 12-10.30 Sun
☎ (0118) 9376 9159 ⊕ theretreatpub.co.uk
6 changing beers Ⓗ
Arguably one of Reading's best-loved back-street pubs, the Retreat has always been a favourite for fans of unusual beers. But it spent a few years in the wilderness until a new landlord took over in 2014, returning the pub to stability. A good range of real ale is squeezed into the small bar. The pub is locally renowned for regular live music and hosting community events. Q☺৬♣♠❄✿

Ruscombe

Royal Oak Ⓛ

Ruscombe Lane, RG10 9JN (on B3024 E out of Twyford)
✪ 12-3 Mon, 12-3, 6-11; 12-4 Sun ☎ (0118) 934 5190
⊕ burattas.co.uk
Fuller's London Pride; 2 changing beers Ⓗ
The pub's spacious open-plan area is naturally divided between cosy seating areas and a dining space. Through the restaurant is a bright conservatory overlooking a beautifully kept garden, excellent for families in summer. The interior is comfortably furnished and decorated with quirky objects and antiques (many are for sale). Also known as Buratta's, the pub is noted for its food, but welcomes drinkers with up to three real ales and a fine range of wines.
Q☺☺❄♠❄(127)✿

St Nicholas Hurst

Wheelwright's Arms ✪

Davis Way, RG10 0TR (off B3030 opp entrance to Dinton Pastures)
✪ 12-3, 5.30-11 Mon-Wed; 12-11 ☎ (0118) 934 4100
⊕ thewheelwrightsarms.co.uk
Wadworth IPA, Horizon, 6X, Bishops Tipple, Swordfish; 2 changing beers (sourced nationally; often Hogs Back, Tomos Watkin) Ⓗ
Refurbished in late 2016, this historic wheelwright's shop is now a vibrant village pub. It has two interconnecting bars with an eclectic mix of furniture and low beams creating an olde-worlde atmosphere. There are five permanent Wadworth's ales and two real ciders on draught. The restaurant has been extended and the garden improved to provide more space for beer and food lovers alike. Bikers, walkers and their dogs are all welcome in this friendly, family-run country pub.
Q☺☺❄৬♠❄(128)✿

Sandhurst

Rose & Crown Ⓛ ✪

108 High Street, GU47 8HA (on A321, 7 mins' walk W of Sandhurst railway station)
✪ 12-11 (midnight Fri & Sat); 12-10 Sun ☎ (01252) 878938
⊕ roseandcrownsandhurst.info
Otter Bitter; 6 changing beers (sourced nationally; often Binghams, Hammerpot, Redemption) Ⓗ
Lively community local close to the Blackwater Valley Path, hosting an array of events including Easter and Halloween beer festivals with up to 20 real ales and legendary decorations. Beer is at the heart of the pub, with six changing guest handpumps including at least one LocAle, often from Bond Brews, Binghams or Ascot Ales. Pub food is served throughout, with the Sunday roast a

very popular choice (no food Mon). A former CAMRA branch Pub of the Year.
☺☺❄≠♣♠❄(194)✿✿

Shinfield

Bell & Bottle Ⓛ

37 School Green, RG2 9EE
✪ 12-11 ☎ (0118) 988 3563
Plain Sheep Dip; 3 changing beers Ⓗ
Spacious yet cosy free house facing the village green with a real community feel. Although primarily a drinkers' pub, a good range of pub grub is served lunchtimes and evenings (until 4pm Sun). A local ale is always available. A games area hosts pool and darts, and Monday is poker night. There is a garden for fine weather and a real fire if it is cold. The interior is fully accessible, with a disabled toilet. Children and dogs are welcome.
☺☺❄৬♠❄(3,10)✿✿

Waltham St Lawrence

Bell Ⓛ

The Street, RG10 0JJ
✪ 12-3, 5-11; 12-11 Sat; 12-10.30 Sun ☎ (0118) 934 1788
⊕ thebellwalthamstlawrence.co.uk
Loddon Hoppit; 4 changing beers Ⓗ
A relaxed and unfussy 14th-century pub, bequeathed to the village in 1608, which continues to serve as the village local. Managed by brothers since 2004, the pub is proud to promote real ales and ciders from small independent brewers. The food menu offers bar snacks as well as quality meals, using locally sourced ingredients where possible. Fresh bread is baked daily. You will also find log fires in winter and a good-sized beer garden for those sunny summer days.
Q☺☺❄♣♠❄(4)✿✿

Warfield

New Leathern Bottle Ⓛ

Jealotts Hill, RG42 6ET (on A3095 Maidenhead Rd 100yds N of Tickleback Row)
✪ 12-10.30 (11 Fri & Sat) ☎ (01344) 421282
3 changing beers (sourced nationally; often Malt the Brewery, Rebellion, St Austell) Ⓗ
Seventeenth-century Grade II-listed pub with welcoming staff. Three changing beers are available, at least one from a local brewery, plus one or two real ciders. Wholesome home-made food is served daily at competitive prices, with Friday steak night a highlight. Annual events include the Warfield Pumpkin Show in September and Steam Up in October, with full size traction and miniature steam engines on show. A large play area is available for children and ample outside seating. ☺☺❄★♣♠❄(53)✿✿

Wargrave

Wargrave & District Snooker Club

Woodclyffe Hostel, Church Street, RG10 8EP
✪ 7-11; closed Sat & Sun ⊕ wargravesnooker.co.uk
2 changing beers Ⓗ
The club opens weekday evenings and shares the building with the local library. The regularly changing beers reflect members' recommendations, with two on in the winter months and one in the summer. Bar billiards, darts, chess, cards and books are available. The TV's

default is off. Visitors may show this Guide or CAMRA membership card for entry (£3 fee to use the snooker tables). Winner of CAMRA branch Club of the Year for several years. ≈♣🖳(850)🐾

Wickham

Five Bells 🕒 ✔
Baydon Road, RG20 8HH
✪ 12-3, 5-11; 12-11 Sat; 12-10.30 Sun ☎ (01488) 657300
⊕ fivebellswickham.co.uk
INNformal INNHouse Bitter, INNDeep, San FrINNcisco; 7 changing beers (sourced regionally; often Vale, Wild Weather Ales, XT) 🄷
Characterful country inn with a thatched roof, exposed beams and an open log fire creating a traditional feel. It offers nine regional cask ales and eight ciders, and is the brewery tap for the on-site INNformal brewery. Live acoustic music plays occasionally on Saturday afternoons. The large garden to the rear is popular during the summer months. With quality food and friendly staff, the pub is a winner of several CAMRA branch awards. Q🏵🕗🐾🖐🅿🐾🛈

Windsor

Acre 🕒 ✔
Donnelly House, Victoria Street, SL4 1EN
✪ 11-11 (midnight Fri & Sat); 12-10.30 Sun
☎ (01753) 841083 ⊕ theacrewindsor.com
Windsor & Eton Guardsman; 2 changing beers 🄷
Formerly the Liberal Club, now a free house open to all. The name refers to the adjacent Bachelors Acre. Three ales are on offer, with Windsor & Eton's Guardsman a permanent feature and two regularly changing guests, often from local breweries. Live music is hosted every Saturday night plus an open mic night on the first Monday of the month. Two screens show live sporting events and there are excellent facilities for darts. Two function rooms are available for hire. 🐾≈♣🖳(2)🛈

Queen Charlotte 🕒 ✔
6 Church Lane, SL4 1PA
✪ 12-11 (midnight Fri & Sat); 12-10.30 Sun
☎ (01753) 859268 ⊕ queencharlottewindsor.co.uk
6 changing beers 🄷
This pub in the lanes close to the castle has undergone a major refurbishment, including a name change, and is under new management. It now has a contemporary feel to it, with the bar on the left and separate seating areas on the right including a conservatory. Two private rooms are available for hire. An extensive drinks menu features six constantly changing cask beers, including several from local breweries. Q🖐🕗≈🖳🛈

Vansittart Arms 🕒
105 Vansittart Road, SL4 5DD
✪ 12-11 (11.30 Thu; midnight Fri); 10.30-midnight Sat; 10.30-11 Sun ☎ (01753) 865988
⊕ vansittartarmswindsor.co.uk
Fuller's Oliver's Island, London Pride, ESB; Gale's Seafarers Ale; 1 changing beer (sourced regionally) 🄷
Known to all as the Vanni, this popular and well-run Fuller's pub is well worth the 10-minute walk from the town centre. The ale range includes the current Fuller's seasonal beer or a non-Fuller's guest. There is a separate pool room which has a small book swap library, and a good selection of

daily newspapers is available. The large garden is ideal for summer barbecues and can be hired for functions. Breakfast is served weekends, 10.30am-1pm. A car park is nearby.
Q🐾🕗🖐🕘≈♣🖳(2,702)🐾🛈

Winkfield

Squirrels Bar & Restaurant 🕒
North Street, SL4 4TF (on B3022 100yds W of jct with Drift Rd)
✪ 12-11 (1am Fri & Sat) ☎ (01344) 882205
⊕ squirrelsbar.co.uk
Rebellion IPA, Smuggler; 1 changing beer (sourced nationally; often Sharp's) 🄷
Close to Legoland Windsor, this friendly family-run pub has a large bar area, a restaurant to the left and an adjacent snug for informal dining (try Debbie's home-made steak and ale pie). At the other end is a pool table and sports TV. Three handpumps serve the real ales, with at least one locally supplied. The large garden provides seating, barbecue, children's play area and camping by prior arrangement. Dogs are welcome except in the restaurant. 🐾🕗🕘🅿🖳(4,702)🐾🛈

Wokingham

Crispin 🕒
45 Denmark Street, RG40 2AY (opp library)
✪ 12-11; 12-10.30 Sun ☎ (0118) 978 0309
⊕ crispinpub.co.uk
5 changing beers (sourced nationally; often Hogs Back, Loddon, Sharp's) 🄷
One of the oldest pubs in Wokingham. This centre-of-town pub is free of tie and offers up to five changing local and national real ales plus two real ciders. No food is served but you can bring in your own takeaway to eat with a drink purchased from the bar. There is a TV and jukebox. Seasonal beer and cider festivals are held. The garden area has seating for warmer days. Aunt Sally is played here. 🕗≈♣🖐🖳(4,4X)🛈

Hope & Anchor ✔
Station Road, RG40 2AD (jct with Shute End)
✪ 12-11 (midnight Fri; 1am Sat); 12-10 Sun
☎ (0118) 978 0918 ⊕ hopeanchor.co.uk
Brakspear Bitter; 4 changing beers (sourced nationally; often Caledonian, Wychwood) 🄷
Seventeenth-century pub, built originally from former ships' timbers. Welcoming staff and wood beams, panelling and floorboards contribute to the old-fashioned ambience, and outside is a spacious, pretty garden with a heated smoking shelter and barbecue, well used in summer. Four changing real ales, mainly from the Brakspear range, always include one from a local brewery. There is a quiz night on Thursday and live music on Saturday. Regular events are held, some for charity. Three en-suite bedrooms are available. 🐾🕗🖐🕭≈🖳(4)🐾🛈

Queen's Head 🍷 🕒 ✔
23 The Terrace, RG40 1BP
✪ 12-11 (12.30am Fri & Sat); 12-10.30 Sun
☎ (0118) 978 1221 ⊕ queensheadwokingham.co.uk
Greene King London Glory, Abbot; house beer (by Hardys & Hansons); 3 changing beers (sourced locally; often Binghams, Loddon) 🄷
Originally a 15th-century timber cruck-framed building, this historic pub sits in one of the oldest

parts of town. A Greene King Local Heroes pub, three local ales accompany three from the GK stable. Beer paddles with three third-pint glasses are available to sample a selection of ales. The refurbished rear garden with its covered area is home to the pub's Aunt Sally team. Local CAMRA branch and county Pub of the Year 2015 and 2016. ⏳❀✿➔♣🖵(4)🐾🔊

Woolhampton

Rowbarge ♈
Station Road, RG7 5SH
✪ 11-11; 11-10.30 Sun ☎ (0118) 971 2213
Brunning & Price Original; 5 changing beers (sourced regionally; often Indigenous, Red Cat, Vale) Ⓗ
A popular Brunning & Price pub-restaurant, in an idyllic location alongside the River Kennet. The bar serves a changing selection of beers including several local ales. Regular Meet the Brewer events are held throughout the year, as well as a beer festival outdoors in summer. The interior has many areas to drink and dine, warmed by a real fire in the winter. In the warmer months, an outdoor

barbecue complements the usual good food menu (booking advisable at weekends). There are regular rail and bus services nearby.
⏳❀◑⅃♣♣🅿🖵🐾🔊

Wraysbury

Perseverance ✅
2 High Street, TW19 5DB
✪ 12-11; 12-9.30 Sun ☎ (01784) 482375 ⊕ thepercy.co.uk
Otter Ale; 3 changing beers (sourced nationally) Ⓗ
Comfortable pub with several seating areas. The larger front room has soft sofas, a piano and a large inglenook fireplace with a real log fire. Another seating area, again with an open fire, leads through to the rear dining area, which has well-stocked bookshelves. To the rear of the building is a delightful garden. Three guest ales are always varied and sourced from some of the more interesting breweries around the country. Regular beer festivals are held. Quiz night is Thursday and live music plays on Sunday afternoon.
Q⏳❀◑♣🔴🅿🖵(10,305)🐾🔊

Swan Inn, Inkpen

BUCKINGHAMSHIRE

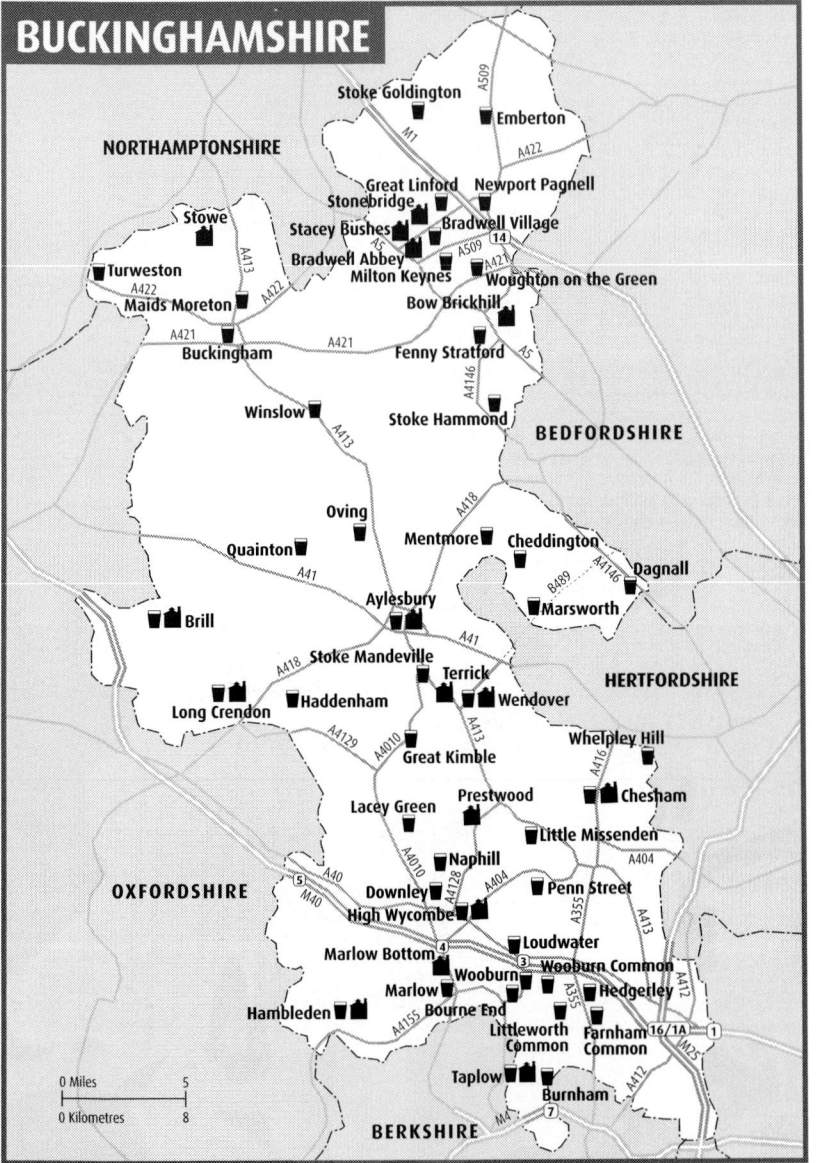

Aylesbury

Hop Pole Inn 𝕃
83 Bicester Road, HP19 9AZ
☼ 4-10 Mon; 12-2.30, 4.30-11; 12-midnight Fri & Sat;
12-10.30 Sun ☎ (01296) 482129
⊕ aylesburybrewhouse.co.uk
Vale Best IPA, Gravitas; 7 changing beers ⊞
'Aylesbury's Permanent Beer Festival' is home to the Aylesbury Brewhouse and shop which opened in 2011. The individual brews feature regularly in the pub, but may not last very long. This is Vale's sister brewery – the pub is the brewery's main outlet, featuring beers from them plus a selection of other small brewers. A friendly ambience as well as good food (no food Mon) add to the attraction. Children welcome until 9pm if dining. ❀◑●❑♣

King's Head 𝕃
Market Square, HP20 2RW
☼ 11-11; 12-10.30 Sun ☎ (01296) 718812
⊕ farmersbar.co.uk
Chiltern Pale Ale, Beechwood Bitter; 2 changing beers ⊞
When Chiltern Brewery took over the running of the Farmers' Bar at the King's Head for the National Trust it became the first bar in the country to be no-smoking and free from piped music. Dating from circa 1455, this is the oldest courtyard inn in England and was donated by the Rothschild family in 1924. Ales are often used in cooking – lunches are made from ingredients freshly sourced from local suppliers. A former local CAMRA Pub of the Year. Q❀⛃◑&≠●❑�

Old Millwrights Arms ✅

83 Walton Road, HP21 7SN

✪ 12-11 (midnight Fri); 9am-midnight Sat

☎ (01296) 488161

Greene King IPA, Abbot; 6 changing beers Ⓗ

Nine handpumps greet you as you enter this recently refurbished pub, featuring four ales from the Greene King stables and, as part of the Local Heroes scheme, five mainly locally brewed real ales. There are also regular pump takeovers from one of many local breweries. The open-plan pub has three distinct areas and excellent food is served throughout, as well as in the pleasant outside space to the rear. ✿◑▶≒Pᴪ☀

Bourne End

Garibaldi Ⓛ ✅

Hedsor Road, SL8 5EE

✪ 12-3, 6-midnight; 12-midnight Fri & Sat; 12-11 Sun

☎ (01628) 522092 ⊕ garibaldipub.co.uk

Rebellion IPA; 2 changing beers Ⓗ

A warm welcome awaits at this traditional pub, saved from closure when it was bought by the local community in 2013. A mixture of comfortable settees and tables and chairs adorns the L-shaped bar room, as well as a real fire, TV screen and dartboard. Beer from the nearby Rebellion Brewery is available on at least one of the three handpumps. A small outside terrace provides views across fields at the rear. ✿◑≒♣Pᴪ(37)☀ 🛜

Bradwell Village

Victoria Inn

Vicarage Road, MK13 9AQ

✪ 3-11; 12-11 Sat & Sun ☎ (01908) 312769

4 changing beers (sourced regionally; often Everards, Hart Family Brewers, Tring) Ⓗ

A stone-built pub with a tiled roof. As you enter, the bar, with its four handpumps, is directly in front of you. To the right is a room with a pool table and dartboard, to the left is a room on two levels with tables and chairs and an open fireplace. Exposed beams and low ceilings help to create a comfortable and relaxed atmosphere. Behind the pub is a large beer garden with children's swings. ✿♣Pᴪ☀ 🛜

Brill

Pointer Ⓛ ✅

27 Church Street, HP18 9RT

✪ closed Mon; 12-11 (midnight Fri & Sat); 12-10 Sun

☎ (01844) 238339 ⊕ thepointerbrill.co.uk

Vale Best IPA; house beer (by XT); 2 changing beers Ⓗ

This free house has become a destination ale house as well as a gastro-pub, thanks to the skilled cellarwoman. The always reliable selection of beers on four handpumps includes XT Pointer from five miles away and Vale VPA from Brill itself, complemented by a stout or porter and another guest ale. The pub supports the Brill beer festival in August. An open kitchen serves wonderful locally sourced food to the separate vaulted dining room. Q✿◑♣ᴪ☀ 🛜

Buckingham

Mitre

2 Mitre Street, MK18 1DW

✪ 5-11 (midnight Fri); 12-midnight Sat; 12-10.30 Sun

☎ (01280) 813080 ⊕ themitre.org.uk

5 changing beers (sourced regionally; often Banks's, Oakham, Tring) Ⓗ

A short walk from the centre of Buckingham takes you to the town's oldest pub. Its cosy atmosphere is enhanced by a real open fire in winter. Board games and books can be borrowed from the lending shelf. As you would expect from a free house, the Mitre has changing and interesting beers, often featuring guests from Animal Brewing and specials from Oakham. Major sporting events are shown on five large-screen TVs, including one in the garden. Parking is on the street. ✿♣P☀ 🛜

Burnham

Bee

1 Britwell Road, SL1 8AG

✪ 11-midnight (1.30am Fri & Sat); 11-11.30 Sun

☎ (01628) 665789

Brakspear Bitter; Wychwood Hobgoblin; 1 changing beer (sourced nationally) Ⓗ

A friendly Grade II-listed pub on a corner at the top of Burnham High Street. It has a large L-shaped bar and outside a popular decked area with tables at the front, where you can watch the world go by. The guest ale is from the Marston's stable. Entertainment includes open mic on Tuesday, quiz night on Thursday and live music on Saturday. A cider festival features in July. Q♿🐕❀♿Pᴪ(53,68)☀ 🛜

Cheddington

Old Swan

58 High Street, LU7 0RQ

✪ 12-11 ☎ (01296) 662171

⊕ theoldswancheddington.co.uk

Fuller's London Pride; Young's Bitter; 2 changing beers (sourced locally) Ⓗ

You are assured of a warm welcome at this pretty thatched Grade II-listed free house which dates back some 400 years. In the hands of a new landlord since January 2015, the pub has been recently refurbished, keeping its low beams and fireplaces. A 10-minute walk from the Grand Union Canal and close to the Ridgeway Path and Ashridge Estate, it is popular with walkers and their dogs. Four real ales are available, some from local breweries. 🐕✿◑≒Pᴪ(164)☀ 🛜

REAL ALE BREWERIES

Aylesbury 🍺 Aylesbury
Blackened Sun Milton Keynes: Stacey Bushes (NEW)
Blackpit Stowe (NEW)
Bootlegger 🍺 High Wycombe
Bucks Star Milton Keynes: Stonebridge
Chiltern Terrick
Concrete Cow Bradwell Abbey
Fisher's High Wycombe
Haresfoot Chesham
Hillfire Aylesbury
Hope Springs Wendover (NEW)
Hornes Bow Brickhill
Malt Prestwood
moogBREW Taplow
Old Luxters Hambleden
Rebellion Marlow Bottom
Vale Brill
XT Long Crendon

Chesham

Black Cat ✓
Lycrome Road, Lye Green, HP5 3LF (off A416)
☼ 9am-2.30, 5-11 (7 Mon); 11-11 Sat; 12-10.30 Sun
☎ (01494) 773966 ⊕ blackcatchesham.co.uk
Timothy Taylor Landlord; Young's Bitter; 1 changing
beer (sourced nationally) ⊞
A cosy, welcoming pub, run by a family who care,
at the heart of the village community and a regular
in the Guide. It serves generous home-cooked food
and a small range of well-kept quality beer,
concentrating on the basics. Pub entertainment
includes darts, cribbage, dominoes and quiz nights.
The large garden has children's games and a
woodland walk. Dogs are welcome on a lead
outside mealtimes. Sunday roasts are a highlight
and breakfast is served 9am-noon weekdays.
රු֍ⓓ♣PⱤ(730)🐾♿

Dagnall

Red Lion
21 Main Road North, HP4 1QZ
☼ 12-11 (10.30 Sun) ☎ (01442) 843020
⊕ theredliondagnall.co.uk
Sharp's Doom Bar; 2 changing beers (sourced
regionally) ⊞
Dating from 1740, this is a well-run free house
offering a warm welcome and well-kept beers.
Warmed by an open fire and a wood-burning
stove, it is popular with locals and walkers alike.
Home-made, good-value food using fresh
ingredients is available all week. Local watercolour
views by a village artist hang on the dining room
walls. The pub hosts quiz nights and has a darts
team, and local interest groups meet here
regularly. Dogs (in the bar) and children are
welcome. ඇ֍ⓓ♣PⱤⱤ🐾♿

Downley

De Spencer Arms ✓
The Common, HP13 5YQ (across common from village
on flint track beyond end of Plomer Green Lane)
☼ 12-11 (midnight Fri & Sat); 11.30-10 Sun
☎ (01494) 535317 ⊕ ledespencersarms.co.uk
Fuller's London Pride, ESB; 2 changing beers (sourced
nationally) ⊞
Named after Francis Dashwood, the notorious 15th
Baron le Despencer, whose family still owns the
surrounding estate, this traditional village pub
offers four real ales, as well as good wines and
home-cooked food. It is popular with walkers and
cyclists and just a quarter of a mile by road or
across the common from the village hall bus stop.
Quiz nights, music nights, beer and food events
add to the attraction of this cosy flint pub on
Downley Common. ඇ֍ⓓ♣PⱤ🐾♿

Emberton

Bell & Bear 🅛
12 High Street, MK46 5DH
☼ 5-10 Mon; 12-2.30, 5-11 Tue-Thu; 12-11 Fri & Sat; 12-8 Sun
☎ (01234) 711565 ⊕ bellandbear.net
4 changing beers (sourced regionally; often Banks's,
Leighton Buzzard, Marston's) ⊞
A stone-built pub with a slate roof. It serves a
variety of interesting beers and real ciders, always
including at least one local beer and a local cider
from Virtual Orchard. The old building houses a

long narrow bar with a Northamptonshire skittles
table in the far corner. There is a separate popular
restaurant for fine dining – booking in advance is
recommended (closed Sun eve-Tue lunchtime).
Parking is on the street outside.
Q֍ⓓ▲♣PⱤ(21)🐾♿

Farnham Common

Stag & Hounds 🅛 ✓
18 The Broadway, SL2 3QQ
☼ 12-midnight (1am Fri & Sat) ☎ (01753) 647716
10 changing beers ⊞
Cosy one-room pub with comfy sofas and beer
casks as stools. The cellar can be viewed through a
window near the side entrance. Ten changing
beers are generally available, five from local and
national microbreweries and five from the Greene
King stable. A good selection of ciders is also on
offer, and bottled beers from around the world. A
beer bat serves three third-pint glasses, allowing a
good number of ales to be tasted. The TV is only
turned on for major sporting events.
Qඇ֍ⓓ♣♣PⱤ(X74)🐾♿

Fenny Stratford

Red Lion ✓
11 Lock View Lane, Simpson Road, MK1 1BY
☼ 12-11 (midnight Fri & Sat); 12-10.30 Sun
☎ (01908) 372317
3 changing beers (sourced nationally; often
Camerons, Gale's, Woodforde's) ⊞
A popular lockside pub on the Grand Union Canal.
The landlord is a real ale enthusiast and offers a
rolling choice of up to three ales, selected to
contrast in style and strength. Up to five real ciders
are also available including Old Rosie, Rosie's Pig,
Thatchers Cheddar Valley and Heritage. There is a
quiet room as you enter and beyond is the main
bar with TV and pool table. Through the bar a
corridor leads to the canalside garden. CAMRA
branch Cider Pub of the Year 2016 and 2017.
֍⇄♣●PⱤ(18)🐾♿

Great Kimble

Swan 🅛
Lower Icknield Way, HP17 9TR
☼ 12-3, 5-10 (11 Thu-Sat); 12-8 Sun ☎ (01844) 275288
⊕ kimbleswan.co.uk
3 changing beers (sourced locally; often Loddon,
Tring, XT) ⊞
An authentic, family-owned free house on the
village green, catering for both locals and the many
hikers, cyclists and equestrians who come to enjoy
the beautiful surroundings of the Chiltern Hills Area
of Outstanding Natural Beauty. The pub, which
dates back to the 18th century, is an enthusiastic
supporter of nearby breweries, with two or three
LocAles usually available. Closing time may vary,
especially in the winter.
֍ⓗⓓ♿⇄♣●PⱤ(300)🐾♿

Great Linford

Black Horse ✓
Wolverton Road, MK14 5AJ
☼ 11-11 (10.30 Sun) ☎ (01908) 398461
⊕ theblackhorsegreatlinford.co.uk
Brakspear Oxford Gold; Sharp's Doom Bar; 1 changing
beer (sourced nationally) ⊞

A popular canalside pub with extensive beer gardens. The focus is mainly on food but drinkers are welcome. Rooms are on several levels – the highest level being adjacent to the Grand Union Canal. There is wooden decking alongside the canal towpath with steps down to the large garden and an inside staircase down to the bar. ✪❍♿P🅿🛜

Haddenham

Green Dragon L
Church End, HP17 8AA (near church and duckpond)
✪ 11-11; 12-10 Sun ☎ (01844) 292826
🌐 greendragonhaddenham.co.uk
Black Sheep Best Bitter; Hook Norton Hooky; Tring Side Pocket for a Toad; 1 changing beer (sourced locally) Ⓗ
Attractive flint-stone building which is essentially a restaurant. The pleasantly decorated L-shaped bar has space for drinkers as you enter, while areas to the left and right and a room at the back are all for dining. At least one local cask ale is almost always available. It has a cosy, relaxed atmosphere and offers a warm welcome to one and all.
Q✿✪❍P🚍(280)🐾🛜

Rising Sun L ✔
9 Thame Road, HP17 8EN
✪ 12-2.30, 5-11; 12-midnight Fri & Sat; 12-10.30 Sun
☎ (01844) 291744
XT Four; 5 changing beers (sourced locally) Ⓗ
The new landlords have already celebrated their first year at the Rising Sun. This bustling village pub boasts six real ales on handpump, with favourites from XT Brewing as well as unusual ales from Animal Brewing Co, plus an ever-changing selection of guest ales and ciders. With a newly landscaped garden, and treats on tap for canine companions, this family- and pooch-friendly pub blends the best of old and new.
Q✿✪🚍(280)🐾🛜

Hambleden

Stag & Huntsman L
RG9 6RP
✪ 11-10.30 (11.30 Fri & Sat); 11-6 Sun ☎ (01491) 571227
🌐 thestagandhuntsman.co.uk
Rebellion IPA, Roasted Nuts; 2 changing beers Ⓗ
Historic pub in this beautiful unspoilt village, recently refurbished while keeping its old-fashioned charm. It serves four hand-drawn real ales including Rebellion IPA plus a wide variety of changing local beers. Nestled in the Chilterns, midway between Marlow and Henley, just up from the River Thames, the pub often featured in Midsomer Murders. The present name was reportedly changed in 1820 from the Dog & Badger – now a pub in nearby Medmenham.
Q✿✪🛏❍♿P🐾🛜

Hedgerley

White Horse 🏆 L
Village Lane, SL2 3UY (in old village, near church)
✪ 11-2.30, 5-11; 11-11 Sun; 12-10.30 Sun ☎ (01753) 643225
🌐 thewhitehorsehedgerley.co.uk
Rebellion IPA; 7 changing beers (often Mallinson's, Mighty Oak, Oakham) Ⓖ
CAMRA branch Pub of the Year on numerous occasions, including two years ago, this village local has an impressive range of real ales. New

breweries are a feature, as well as favourites from Oakham, Mallinson's and Mighty Oak. A draught Belgian beer and three real ciders are also available. This classic pub has a well-tended garden and a heated, covered patio area. Regular beer festivals are held – the largest is over the Whitsun weekend and is a must for real ale enthusiasts.
Q✿✪❍♣🐾P🐾🛜

High Wycombe

Belle Vue ✔
45 Gordon Road, HP13 6EQ
✪ 4.30-11; 3.30-midnight Fri; 12-1am Sat; 12-10.30 Sun
☎ (01494) 524728 🌐 thebv.pub
Adnams Broadside; Sharp's Doom Bar; 4 changing beers Ⓗ
Near the railway station, the pub is a friendly traditional community venue and a regular in the Guide for over 10 years. It has six ales, four ciders and a real fire, and holds occasional beer festivals. There is live music, regular quiz nights, a literary society, knitting circle, ukulele club, vinyl night, folk sessions, occasional charity events, film nights and even Christmas carol 'shouting'! There is also a permanent art exhibition. The ciders are from Westons. ✪🛏≈♣●🚍🐾🛜

Bootlegger L
Amersham Hill, HP13 6NQ
✪ 12-midnight (1am Fri & Sat); 12-11 Sun
☎ (01494) 525457 🌐 thebootleggerpub.co.uk
10 changing beers (sourced locally; often Chiltern, Rebellion, Vale) Ⓗ
Spacious, stylish alehouse opposite the railway station with a small corner room offering a degree of privacy. Ten handpumps stand in a row along the bar. There is a comprehensive beer menu with tasting notes for 300 speciality beers and ciders sourced worldwide. Bottled beers are in glass-fronted chiller cabinets. Live music is hosted and live sport shown on screen. The large garden with decking and a lawn has plenty of seating plus a wood-burning stove. ✪♿≈●🚍🐾🛜

Lacey Green

Black Horse ✔
Main Road, HP27 0QU
✪ 12-3 (not Mon), 5-11; 12-11 Thu; 12-midnight Fri & Sat; 12-11 Sun ☎ (01844) 345195 🌐 blackhorse-pub.co.uk
Brakspear Bitter; 3 changing beers (sourced nationally) Ⓗ
This friendly village pub, located in the heart of the Chilterns, offers four draught ales, three changing regularly, plus a good selection of bottled beers and one regularly changing real cider. Excellent home-cooked and freshly prepared food is available including a traditional Sunday lunch (children under six eat free). Pub games are a feature. Walkers, cyclists and children are welcome and there is a play area in the garden. Full English breakfast is served Tuesday-Saturday.
Q✪❍♿♣●P🚍🐾🛜

Pink & Lily L ✔
Pink Road, Parslows Hillock, HP27 0RJ
✪ 12-11.30 ☎ (01494) 489857 🌐 pink-lily.com
Sharp's Doom Bar; 3 changing beers (sourced locally) Ⓗ
This 300-year-old historic pub, where World War I poet Rupert Brooke was a regular, has thrived since

reopening in 2013. It is a free house offering fine food and four real ales, including three guests from local breweries. The garden includes a heated outdoor dining space, a barbecue and a children's play area. A games room is available for adults and children. Muddy boots and (well-behaved) dogs are welcome. Q ➣ ⊛ ➊ ⅃ ♣ P ✿ ➤ ☎

Whip Inn ℂ
Pink Road, HP27 0PG
✪ 11-11; 12-10.30 Sun ☎ (01844) 344060
⊕ thewhipinn.co.uk
6 changing beers (sourced nationally) Ⓗ
High in the Chilterns, easily accessible by bus, and popular with real ale fans, ramblers and cyclists, this pub is renowned for its variety of ales. It has six handpumps serving more than 900 different beers per annum, some from local breweries and others from micros and nationals. It also offers three real ciders and holds regular beer festivals. An excellent range of reasonably priced food is on offer. There is an attractive enclosed garden overlooking Lacey Green Windmill.
⊛ ➊ ♣ ◗ P ◻ (300) ✿ ➤

Little Missenden

Crown Inn
HP7 0RD (off A413, between Amersham and Gt Missenden)
✪ 11-2.30, 6-11; 12-3, 7-10.30 Sun ☎ (01494) 862571
⊕ thecrownlittlemissenden.co.uk
St Austell Tribute; Young's Bitter; 2 changing beers (sourced nationally; often Oakham, Otter) Ⓗ
A lovely old village pub, the Crown is a Guide regular and was CAMRA branch Pub of the Year in 2016. The same family has run this establishment for nearly 100 years and a warm welcome awaits. A real log fire adds to the ambience in winter and four real ales and four real ciders are on handpump. There is a large garden and the pub is popular with walkers. Three double en-suite rooms are available. Q ➣ ⊛ ⊗ ➊ ◗ P ✿ ➤

Littleworth Common

Blackwood Arms
Common Lane, SL1 8PP SU937863
✪ closed Mon; 12-11; 12-7.30 Sun ☎ (01753) 645672
⊕ theblackwoodarms.net
Brakspear Bitter, Oxford Gold; Wychwood Hobgoblin; 3 changing beers Ⓗ
A delightful Victorian country pub brought back to life by an enthusiastic couple after a long period of closure. Close to Burnham Beeches and popular with walkers and diners, it has a roaring fire in winter and an attractive garden with plenty of seating for the summer. Three guest ales are on offer – one from the Marston's group plus two free of tie. Dog- and horse-friendly, hay is provided. Cider is available in the summer only.
Q ➣ ⊛ ➊ ♣ ◗ P ✿ ➤

Long Crendon

Eight Bells ℂ ✪
51 High Street, HP18 9AL
✪ 12 (10 Sat & Sun)-11 ☎ (01844) 208244 ⊕ 8bellspub.com
Ringwood Boondoggle; XT Four; 2 changing beers Ⓗ
The Eight Bells was refurbished internally in 2014, but retains the charm and character of a village pub. It is renowned for slaking the thirst of ale

aficionados – XT Four from less than a mile away and Ringwood Bitter are permanent fixtures on two of the four handpumps, joined by guest ales from across the country. Long Crendon cider is also an attraction, and diners can enjoy good food featuring local produce. Beer festivals are held over the Easter weekend and August bank holiday.
Q ⊛ ➊ ♣ ◗ P ◻ (110) ✿ ➤

Loudwater

Derehams Inn
5 Derehams Lane, HP10 9RH
✪ 11.30-3.30, 5.30-11; 11-midnight Fri & Sat; 12-11 Sun
☎ (01494) 530965 ⊕ derehamsinn.co.uk
5 changing beers Ⓗ
Hidden away up a lane just off the London Road, this cosily furnished L-shaped pub is listed as an asset of community value. Traditional pub food is served daily, with a full roast on Sunday lunchtime. The annual Fag & Firkin beer festival is a real treat. The pub runs a darts team and cribbage team, and has a pool table outside. Quiz night is Tuesday.
Q ⊛ ➊ P ◻ ✿

General Havelock
114 Kingsmead Road, HP11 1HZ
✪ 12-2.30, 5.30-11; 12-11 Fri & Sat; 12-10.30 Sun
☎ (01494) 520391 ⊕ generalhavelock.co.uk
Fuller's London Pride, ESB; Gale's Seafarers Ale; 3 changing beers Ⓗ
A regular in the Guide and run by the same family since Fuller's acquired it in 1986, the General Havelock remains popular with all ages. The interior has an eclectic selection of bric-a-brac and antiques. Six ales are available at all times including a range of seasonals and guests. Meals are served lunchtimes (not Sat) and Friday evenings. The pub has a cosy feel in winter while the garden makes for a peaceful haven in summer.
⊛ ➊ ♣ P ◻ (35) ✿ ➤

Maids Moreton

Wheatsheaf
Main Street, MK18 1QR
✪ closed Mon; 12-11; 12-10.30 Sun ☎ (01280) 822903
⊕ thewheatsheafmaidsmoreton.com
Shepherd Neame Spitfire; Tring Side Pocket for a Toad; 2 changing beers (sourced nationally; often Binghams, Rooster's, Twickenham) Ⓗ
A family-run, traditional village inn, full of character with a thatched roof, low ceilings and exposed beams. In the bar there is an inglenook fireplace with a wood-burning stove. Food is available in the bar and restaurant – à la carte is offered Tuesday to Saturday, roast lunches only on Sunday. There is a large garden at the rear. The restaurant can be hired for private parties. CAMRA branch Pub of the Year in 2016.
Q ⊛ ➊ ♣ P ◻ (60) ✿ ➤

Marlow

Royal British Legion ℂ ✪
Station Approach, SL7 1NT (near train station)
✪ 7-11 (midnight Fri); 11-3, 7-midnight Sat; 11-4 Sun
☎ (01628) 486659 ⊕ rblmarlow.co.uk
Jennings Bitter; 5 changing beers Ⓗ
Effectively a free house, this friendly RBL members' club offers four handpumped ales from four independent breweries, with a Derbyshire beer

usually among the selection. Home of the Marlow Jazz Club, music features regularly on Saturday nights. Pool, darts and crib are encouraged. The recently refurbished hall is for hire. Show a CAMRA membership card or copy of the Guide for entry. A regular CAMRA branch award winner and Regional Club of the Year in 2016. ✪&≠♣♠P✿🖵🛜

Three Horseshoes 🅛 ✪
Burroughs Grove Hill, SL7 3RA
✪ 11.30-11; 12-6 Sun ☎ (0800) 612 5564
Rebellion IPA, Mutiny, Roasted Nuts; 1 changing beer Ⓗ
A large open-plan pub a short bus ride from both High Wycombe and Marlow, offering good food including an extensive specials board, open fires and a pleasant garden. Diners and drinkers are all made welcome (as are well-behaved children and dogs). Close proximity to the Rebellion Beer Company means that the six Rebellion ales are always in excellent condition.
Q✿🌓P🖵(800,850)✿

Marsworth

Red Lion 🅛 ✪
90 Vicarage Road, HP23 4LU (opp church)
✪ 11-3, 5-11; 11-11 Sat; 12-10.30 Sun ☎ (01296) 668366
⊕ redlionmarsworth.co.uk
Fuller's London Pride; 5 changing beers (sourced locally) Ⓗ
An excellent 17th-century traditional village pub close to the Grand Union Canal, with one regular beer, London Pride, and four or five guest beers mostly from local breweries. Regular mini-fests are held offering up to 10 beers. Good home-cooked food is served in the public bar, where there is a real fire, and upstairs restaurant area. Pub games include bar billiards, shove-ha'penny and darts. Outside, there is a seating area at the front and a beautiful garden to the rear.
Q⟆✿🌓♣♠P🖵(164)✿🛜

Mentmore

Stag ✪
The Green, LU7 0QF
✪ closed Mon; 12-2, 6-11; 12-11 Sat; 12-5 Sun
☎ (01296) 660602 ⊕ stagmentmore.co.uk
Wells Bombardier; Young's Bitter; 1 changing beer (sourced locally; often Wells) Ⓗ
A spacious pub in the village with three bars – Froggy's Bar with a real log fire and nostalgic pictures, the cocktail bar with a piano, and the restaurant serving fresh food, including veggies from the large garden. There is a bar menu as well as a more formal menu. Traditional pub games such as cribbage and dominoes are played.
⟆✿🌓&♣P✿

Milton Keynes: Central

Wetherspoons 🍷 🅛 ✪
201 Midsummer Boulvard, MK9 1EA
✪ 7am-midnight (1am Fri & Sat) ☎ (01908) 606074
Greene King Abbot; Ruddles Best Bitter; Sharp's Doom Bar; 9 changing beers Ⓗ
Unbeatable for price and beer range, with 12 handpumps, including several dispensing local beers, this is a popular meeting place for local CAMRA members. A beer shop was introduced in 2016 and a wide range of bottled beers is available

to take away. The usual Wetherspoon food menu is served from early morning until late evening. Local CAMRA Pub of the Year 2017. ✪🌓&≠P🖵🛜

Naphill

Wheel ✪
100 Main Road, HP14 4QA
✪ 12 (4.30 Mon)-11; 12-10.30 Sun ☎ (01494) 562210
⊕ thewheelnaphill.com
Greene King IPA Reserve; Ruddles Best Bitter; 2 changing beers Ⓗ
A traditional 18th-century village pub in the heart of the Chilterns. It offers four excellent cask ales including two regularly changing guests and good-quality, home-cooked pub meals. Two bars and a large dining area are available for all – walkers, cyclists, families – and dogs and muddy boots are welcome too. There is a large garden to the front and a secluded, smoker-friendly courtyard at the rear. Two large beer festivals are held each year.
Q✿🌓🛏♣P🖵✿🛜

Newport Pagnell

Cannon
50 High Street, MK16 8AQ
✪ 11-11 (midnight Fri & Sat) ☎ (01908) 211495
Banks's Amber Ale; Marston's Pedigree; 2 changing beers (often Ringwood, Wychwood) Ⓗ
A family-run town-centre free house with one bar and four handpumps. There is a heated smoking area outside and a large car park to the rear, accessed from Union Street which runs behind the pub and the High Street. A room in an outbuilding is used for regular events such as open mic night and is available to hire. ✿P🖵

Oving

Black Boy 🅛
Church Lane, HP22 4HN
✪ 12-11 (6 Sun) ☎ (01296) 641258
⊕ theblackboyoving.co.uk
3 changing beers (sourced locally) Ⓗ
A pleasure to visit, this 17th-century pub has a cosy interior with flagstone floors, wooden beams and a roaring fire. The carpeted restaurant opposite the bar is divided from the drinking area by a wooden mesh around an archway. Good food is served. There are wonderful views across the countryside from the huge beer garden. ⟆✿🌓♠P✿🛜

Penn Street

Squirrel 🅛 ✪
HP7 0PX
✪ 12 (4 Mon)-11; 12-1am Fri; 12-10.30 Sun
☎ (01494) 711291 ⊕ thesquirrelpub.co.uk
5 changing beers (sourced locally; often Rebellion, Vale) Ⓗ
This is a delightful pub by the village green which has improved greatly over the past few years due to the hardworking licensees. The bar area has a log fire and comfortable armchairs, and serves four to five real ales plus a real cider. Good pub food including a traditional Sunday roast is available. An outdoor decked heated area with comfy chairs is to the back of the pub and the garden is ideal for families. Themed quiz nights plus home-made food feature monthly on a Monday.
Q⟆✿🌓♣♠P🖵(1)✿🛜

Quainton

George & Dragon L ✔
32 The Green, HP22 4AR
✪ closed Mon; 12-2.30, 5-11; 12-11.30 Sat; 12-3, 6-10.30 Sun
☎ (01296) 655436 ⊕ georgeanddragonquainton.co.uk
6 changing beers (sourced locally) Ⓗ
Free house always offering LocAles from Vale and XT plus two guests. Parts of this well-maintained and delightful pub date back to the 1700s, with traditional English features such as inglenook fireplaces, beams and a quarry-tiled floor. The friendly public bar offers darts, a jukebox and TV while the saloon bar is dedicated to dining, although home-cooked food is served throughout. Regular beer festivals are held overlooking the green in summer. ᏠꙨᏋᎧ&♣♠P⛽(16)🐾🛜

Stoke Goldington

Lamb L
Main Street, MK16 8NR
✪ 12 (5 Mon)-11; 12-7 Sun ☎ (01908) 551233
⊕ thelambatstokegoldington.co.uk
Tring Brock Bitter, Death or Glory; 2 changing beers (sourced regionally) Ⓗ
Situated in the village a few miles from Milton Keynes and Northampton on the B526. The bar area has a dartboard and a Northamptonshire skittles table. Home-cooked food is served featuring local seasonal produce (no food Mon). The cider is typically Old Rosie. The garden has a stage for music events. The Lamb has ample parking and encourages walking groups to park early and order food before their walk, so they can return later to enjoy a drink and their meal.
Q🤍🚃🍽️♣P🐾

Stoke Hammond

Three Locks L ✔
Leighton Road, MK17 9DD
✪ 11.30-11 (10.30 Sun) ☎ (01525) 270214
⊕ thethreelocks.co.uk
Sharp's Doom Bar; 4 changing beers (sourced regionally; often Concrete Cow, Leighton Buzzard, Tring) Ⓗ
Popular canalside hostelry that likes to support breweries in the area, with three out of the four changing beers usually local. The cider can come from nearby producer Virtual Orchard, or may be sourced from traditional producers around the country. A beer festival is held over the late May bank holiday. The pub is particularly popular in summer, with customers arriving by road and narrowboat. Inland Waterways Association members receive a 10 per cent discount on food. The long narrow building has the bar at one end and the restaurant at the other. There is plenty of outdoor seating alongside the locks.
🤍🍽️&♠P⛽(70)🐾🛜

Stoke Mandeville

Bull
5 Risborough Road, HP22 5UP
✪ 12-11 (midnight Fri & Sat) ☎ (01296) 613632
Greene King IPA; Sharp's Doom Bar Ⓗ
Reopened in May 2012 as a free house, this small two-bar, family-run village pub, situated on a main road, is well served by buses and trains. The public bar at the front is popular with locals, who gather

to watch football on TV. The comfortable lounge bar at the back tends to be quieter and leads out to a large secure garden at the rear, which can be busy in summer. Q🤍🍽️🚃♣P⛽(300)🐾🛜

Taplow

Oak & Saw L
Rectory Road, SL6 0ET
✪ 4-9.30 Mon; 12-11 (midnight Fri); 12-10.30 Sun
☎ (01628) 604074 ⊕ oakandsaw.co.uk
Brakspear Bitter; Sharp's Doom Bar; 1 changing beer (sourced locally) Ⓗ
Situated opposite the village green and church in an idyllic setting, this pub offers good pub food and three real ales including the Rebellion monthly. The food is home made and features local produce, with the meat, including venison, coming from a farm and butchery just 20 miles away. A large decked patio to the rear, with a covered area for smokers, is popular in the summer. Dogs are permitted in the non-dining area. Q🏠🤍🍽️P🐾🛜

Turweston

Stratton Arms
Main Street, NN13 5JX
✪ 12-2.30, 4-10; 12-midnight Fri & Sat; 12-10 Sun
☎ (01280) 704956
Sharp's Doom Bar; Timothy Taylor Golden Best, Landlord; 2 changing beers (sourced nationally; often Adnams, Otter, Shepherd Neame) Ⓗ
A stone-built pub with a slate roof set in a quiet village with five real ales on handpump. Major sports fixtures are shown on TV but the volume is low enough for conversation. Food is available Friday to Sunday (booking advisable). Outside there are extensive lawns often used for barbecues and functions in summer. Q🤍🍽️♣P🐾🛜

Wendover

Pack Horse
29 Tring Road, HP22 6NR
✪ 12-11 (midnight Fri & Sat) ☎ (01296) 622075
Fuller's London Pride; 1 changing beer (often Fuller's) Ⓗ
A varied range of beers from the wider Fuller's portfolio is served at this small, friendly village pub. The building, dating from 1769, is situated at the end of a terrace of thatched cottages named after Anne Boleyn – reportedly a gift from Henry VIII. The place has been owned by the same family for over 50 years – they also run the White Swan, another Fuller's establishment in the village that deserves a visit. The pub is on the Ridgeway Path and has connections with nearby RAF Halton.
🚃♣♠🖥️

Whelpley Hill

White Hart L
White Hill Road, HP5 3RL
✪ 12-11 (10.30 Sun) ☎ (01442) 833367
⊕ hartonthehill.tumblr.com
2 changing beers (sourced locally) Ⓗ
Situated on the Herts/Bucks border, this village free house offers a warm welcome to all. It has gained an excellent reputation for its beers, supplied by local breweries, and also for an interesting food menu that uses locally sourced ingredients. Two log fires add to the warm, cosy

atmosphere in winter months, while the garden at the rear is ideal in summer. An annual beer festival and regular charity events also feature. ☻❀❶◗❖⚓AP🚶(730)

Winslow

George Inn 🄻
16 Market Square, MK18 3AB
🕑 2 (12 Thu)-11; 12-midnight Fri & Sat; 12-10.30 Sun
Vale Best IPA, Gravitas; 5 changing beers (sourced nationally; often Milton, Scarborough, Vale) 🄷
A 200-year-old listed building standing at one corner of the old Market Square. The main bar has tables and chairs and a red leather curved bench seat in the bay window. There is another room leading from the bar, also with red leather bench seating. Both rooms have a real fire. A beer shop offers three cask ales for sale in two-, four- or six-pint containers, and American, Belgian, German and Vale bottled beers. The cider is typically Old Rosie or Rosie's Pig. Q♣♠P🚶(X60,50)❖

Wooburn

Queen & Albert 🄻
24 The Green, HP10 0EJ
🕑 12-11 (midnight Fri & Sat); 12-10.30 Sun
☎ (01628) 523098
Rebellion IPA, Roasted Nuts; 2 changing beers 🄷
Wonderful little pub overlooking Wooburn Green. Recently refurbished, the front half is a traditional drinkers' bar, complete with a fire in cooler months. A large room to the rear provides ample space for dining, and can be booked for functions. A family-run pub, children are welcome, with games in the garden in the summer. The Sunday roast lunches are recommended. ☻❀❷◗▣🚶❖

Wooburn Common

Royal Standard 🄻
Wooburn Common Lane, HP10 0JS (follow signs to Odds Farm)
🕑 12-11 (10.30 Sun) ☎ (01628) 521121
⊕ theroyalstandard.biz
Caledonian Deuchars IPA 🄷; **Hop Back Summer Lightning** 🄶; **St Austell Tribute; 7 changing beers** 🄷
Ever-popular semi-rural pub with a congenial ambience in the bar, catering for diners and discerning drinkers alike. Ten real ales, five direct from the cask, alongside many real ciders, make this venue an important flagship pub in the area. There is always at least one dark beer on offer – either a stout, porter or dark mild. Two beer festivals are held, one over the May Day weekend, the other on the last weekend in October. Quiz night is the second Monday of the month. Q❀❶◗❖♠P❖♠🛜

Woughton on the Green

Olde Swan ✅
Newport Road, MK6 3BS
🕑 12-11 (10.30 Sun) ☎ (01908) 679489
Greene King IPA, Abbot; Morland Old Speckled Hen; 1 changing beer (sourced nationally; often Sharp's) 🄷
A period building dating from Tudor times, with a crooked roof, low ceilings and exposed beams. Extended over the centuries, it has seating on different levels. Most of the pub is given over to dining, but there is a small but comfortable bar area to one side. Four handpumps offer ales from the Greene King range. The large garden backing on to the village green is very popular in the summer. ❀◗❖♣P🚶(18)❖🛜

Food for thought

Ale is an enemy to idlenesse, it will worke and bee working in the braine as well as in the Barrel; if it be abused by any man, it will trip up his heeles, and give him either a faire or fowle fall, if hee bee the strongest, stowtest, and skilfullest Wrastler either in Cornwall or Christendome. But if Ale bee moderately, mildly, and friendly dealt withall it will appease, qualifie, mitigate, and quench all striffe and contention, it wil lay anger asleepe, and give a furious man or woman a gentle Nap, and therefore it was rightly called Nappy ALE, by our Learned and Reverend Fore-fathers.

Besides it is very medicinable, (as the best Physitians doe affirme) for Beere is seldom used or applyed to any inward or outward maladies, except sometimes it bee warmed with a little Butter to wash the galled feete, or toes of a weary Traveller; but you shall never knowe or heare of a usuall drinker of ALE, to bee troubled with the Hippocondra, with Hiopocondragacall obstructions or convulsions, nor are they vexed (as others are) with severall paines of sundry sorts of Gowts, such as are the Gonogra, Podegra, Chirocgra, and the lame Hop-halting Sciatica, or with the intollerable griefe of the Stone in the Reines, Kidneys, or Bladder.

Beere is a dutch Boorish Liquor, a thing not knowne in England, till of late dayes an Alien to our Nation, till such time as Hops and Heresies came amongst us, it is a sawcy intruder into this Land, and it's sold by usurpation; for the houses that doe sell Beere onely, are nickname Ale-houses; marke beloved, an Ale-house is never called a Beere-house, but a Beere-House would have but small custom, if it did not falsely carry the name of an Ale-house; also it is common to say a Stand of Ale, it is not onely a Stand, but it will make a man understand, or stand under; but Beere is often called a Hogshead, which all rational men doe knowe is but a swinish expression.

John Taylor (1580-1653), Ale ale-vated into the Ale-titude, 1651

CAMBRIDGESHIRE

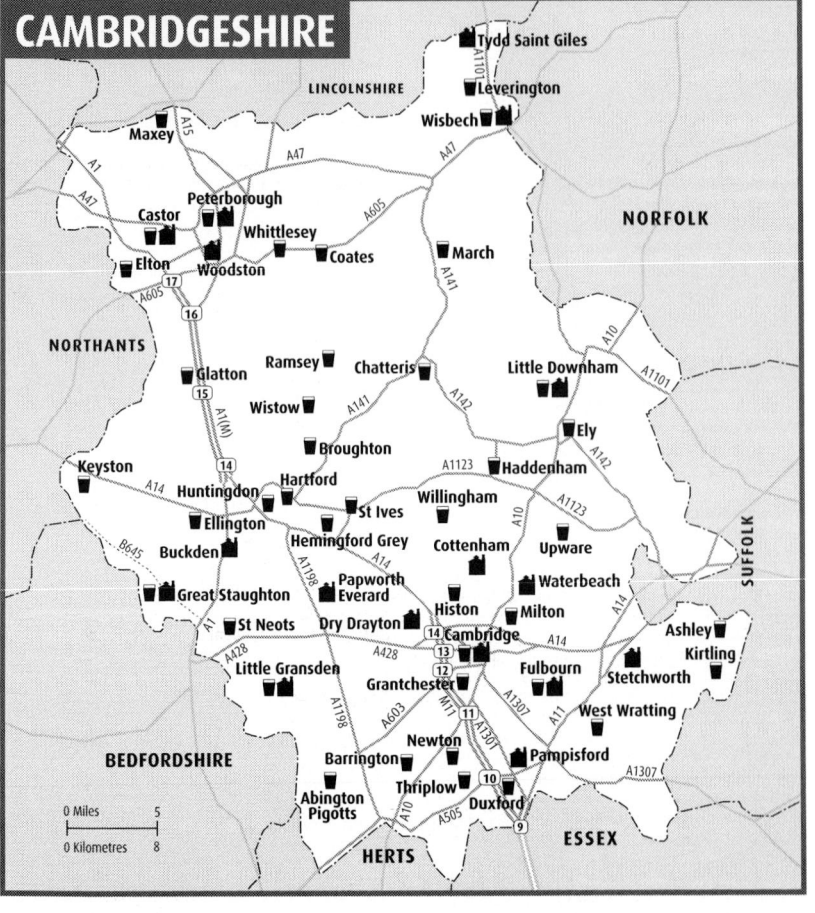

LINCOLNSHIRE

NORFOLK

NORTHANTS

SUFFOLK

BEDFORDSHIRE

HERTS

ESSEX

Tydd Saint Giles
Leverington
Wisbech
Maxey
Peterborough
Castor
Whittlesey
March
Elton
Woodston
Coates
Glatton
Ramsey
Chatteris
Little Downham
Wistow
Ely
Broughton
Keyston
Haddenham
Hartford
Willingham
Huntingdon
St Ives
Ellington
Hemingford Grey
Cottenham
Upware
Buckden
Waterbeach
Great Staughton
Papworth
Everard
Histon
Milton
St Neots
Dry Drayton
Ashley
Cambridge
Kirtling
Little Gransden
Fulbourn
Stetchworth
Grantchester
West Wratting
Newton
Barrington
Pampisford
Thriplow
Abington
Pigotts
Duxford

0 Miles 5
0 Kilometres 8

Abington Pigotts

Pig & Abbot

High Street, SG8 0SD (off A505 through Litlington)
✪ 12-3, 6-11; 12-11 Sat; 12-10.30 Sun ☎ (01763) 853515
⊕ pigandabbot.co.uk
Adnams Southwold Bitter; Fuller's London Pride; 2 changing beers (sourced regionally; often Humpty Dumpty, Mighty Oak, Woodforde's) ⊞
Located in a surprisingly remote part of the south Cambridgeshire countryside, this Queen Anne period pub offers a warm welcome. The interior has exposed oak beams and two fires, including a large inglenook featuring a wood-burning stove. A comfortable restaurant offers home-made traditional pub food, specialising in fresh fish and chips, steak and kidney puddings and pies. Two guest beers are stocked, often from Burton Bridge, Humpty Dumpty, Mighty Oak, Timothy Taylor or Woodforde's. A former CAMRA branch Pub of the Year. Q✿⟲❀⊕♿♣P✿

Ashley

Crown Inn

24 Newmarket Road, CB8 9DR
✪ 3-11 (9 Mon); 12-11 Sat; 12-10 Sun ☎ (01638) 730117
⊕ thecrowninnashley.co.uk
Mighty Oak IPA; 3 changing beers ⊞

This family- and dog-friendly community hub was first recorded as a pub in 1712 though parts of the building predate this. Until recently owned by Greene King, the Crown became free of tie in January 2014. Mighty Oak IPA features regularly alongside up to three guest ales. Real ciders, direct from the box, are also available. Pub games include darts, pool and pétanque. Local CAMRA Pub of the Year 2016.
✿♿⟲❀♣♠P☐(47,901,902)✿ 🛜

Barrington

Royal Oak Ⓛ

31 West Green, CB22 7RZ
✪ 12-2.30, 6-11; 12-3, 6-10.30 Sun ☎ (01223) 870791
⊕ royaloakbarrington.co.uk
4 changing beers (sourced locally; often Adnams) ⊞
Large thatched village pub dating from the 16th century, overlooking the 22 acre green – claimed as the longest in England. Around the bar and to the right is the drinking area, with the main dining area to the left through the former fireplace, leading to the rear conservatory. Four changing ales are on offer, including at least one from Adnams, and up to eight mostly local real ciders. Food is very important and is of high quality. Local CAMRA Most Improved Rural Pub of the Year 2017.
Q✿♿⟲❀♿♣P✿ 🛜

Broughton

Crown Inn
Bridge Road, PE28 3AY
✪ 11.30-3, 6.30-11; 11.30-6 Sun ☎ (01487) 824428
⊕ thecrowninnrestaurant.co.uk
Mauldons Moletrap Bitter; 2 changing beers (sourced locally) ℍ
An idyllic early-19th-century pub next to the village church, in a conservation area. The decor is modern yet comfortable, with scrubbed pine tables and a stone floor. The pub can seat up to 40 diners, with a bar and à la carte menu, but retains a sociable drinking area. A separate area is available for private use. Q❀❀❀◑P❀❀❖

Cambridge

Calverley's Brewery Tap
23A Hooper Street, CB1 2NZ
✪ 6-10.30 Thu & Fri; 11-10.30 Sat; closed Sun-Wed
☎ (01223) 312370 ⊕ calverleys.com
House beer (by Calverley's); 4 changing beers Ⓖ
Close to Mill Road, the brewery was established in September 2013. Calverley's is now open for on-sales on Thursday and Friday evenings and all day Saturday. Up to four of its ales are served direct from the cask. The bar is in the same room as the brewing equipment with tables in a side room and others outside. Additional seating is in one of the outbuildings. Gourmet food vans or stalls are always present. Q❀❀❀◑❀

Cambridge Blue
85-87 Gwydir Street, CB1 2LG
✪ 12-11 (10.30 Sun) ☎ (01223) 471680 ⊕ cambridge.pub/the-blue
Dark Star Hophead, American Pale Ale; Woodforde's Wherry ℍ**; changing beers** ℍ**/**Ⓖ
Ever-popular side-street pub close to Mill Road. A large rear extension leads to the garden which frequently has a marquee. Breweriana and pumpclips provide much of the decoration. Up to 14 beers, sourced from microbreweries nationwide, are dispensed by handpump or by gravity from the taproom. A number of ciders and perries and a large selection of international bottled beers is also available. The main beer festival is held in June. Local CAMRA Cider Pub of the Year 2016. ❀❀❀◑❀❀❀❀❀❀

Devonshire Arms Ⓛ
1 Devonshire Road, CB1 2BH
✪ 12-11 (midnight Fri & Sat); 12-10.30 Sun
☎ (01223) 316610
Milton Cyclops; 6 changing beers (sourced nationally) ℍ
Milton Brewery's first Cambridge pub. Just off Mill Road, it attracts a mix of characters for beer, food and conversation. Deceptively large inside, tall front windows and a high ceiling makes the front area light while the rear section is darker. Outside are small patio areas front and back. Five Milton cask ales are available, including at least one dark beer, with a further three guests from other micros. There are also bottled beers, including Moravka unpasteurised lager, plus ciders. ❀❀❀◑❀❀❀❀❀

Elm Tree
16a Orchard Street, CB1 1JT
✪ 11-11; 12-10.30 Sun ☎ (01223) 502632
⊕ theelmtreecambridge.co.uk

Changing beers (sourced nationally) ℍ
Back-street pub close to Parker's Piece, decorated with breweriana, quirky bric-a-brac, photos and Belgian flags. The bar is near the entrance with a long seating area extending to the back. Ten handpumps dispense three beers from B&T and Wells plus changing guest ales. A cider or perry is also served. Complementing these is a menu of around 100 bottled Belgian beers – the landlord has written a book on the subject and is happy to advise. Regular live music features.
❀❀❀❀❀(PR3,X5)❀

Flying Pig Ⓛ
106 Hills Road, CB2 1LQ
✪ 12-11 (midnight Fri); 7-11 Sat & Sun ☎ (01223) 354623
Crouch Vale Brewers Gold; Dark Star Hophead; 4 changing beers ℍ
Much-loved, cosy and friendly pub with a local feel that defies its main road location. A beer and music venue, its walls and ceiling are adorned with an eclectic collection of old posters and pig paraphernalia. In the evenings the intimate lighting is enhanced by candles. Ales often come from local breweries. Basic pub grub is served weekday lunchtimes only. Live music plays on most Tuesday and Thursday evenings and some Saturdays. The pub hosts an annual Pigfest charity music and beer festival. ❀❀❀◑❀❀❀❀❀

Free Press
7 Prospect Row, CB1 1DU
✪ 12-11 (midnight Fri & Sat) ☎ (01223) 368337
⊕ freepresspub.com
Greene King XX Mild, IPA, Abbot; 4 changing beers (often Greene King) ℍ
Close to Parker's Piece, this intimate, friendly pub serves high-quality food and great beer, including the rare Greene King XX Mild, and Greene King seasonals and guests. A pub for over 120 years, it just survived the 1970s Kite area redevelopment, with only the tiny snug remaining unchanged. It is identified by CAMRA as having a regionally important historic pub interior. A walled garden is at the rear. The pub was named after a temperance movement newspaper that lasted for just one edition. Q❀❀❀◑❀❀❀❀❖

Geldart ✔

1 Ainsworth Street, CB1 2PF (off Mill Road)

✪ closed Mon; 5-11.30 (1am Fri); 1-1am Sat; 12-midnight Sun
☎ (01223) 314264 ⊕ the-geldart.co.uk

Caledonian Deuchars IPA; Oakham Citra; St Austell Tribute; Young's Special; 4 changing beers (sourced nationally) Ⓗ

Large two-bar back-street corner pub, decorated throughout with film and music memorabilia, with an enclosed patio garden behind. It has a good reputation for both food and drink. To the left of the entrance is the drinkers' side with eight ales, always including a dark beer among the guests. Oakham Citra has proved popular and is now one of the regulars. A wide selection of malt whiskies and rums is also offered. Good home-made food including 'hot rocks' is available in both bars. Frequent live music is hosted. ⏚⊛◑♣☙🖵☎

Haymakers 🗓

54 High Street, CB4 1NG

✪ 12-11 (midnight Fri & Sat); 12-10.30 Sun
☎ (01223) 311077

Milton Pegasus; 7 changing beers (often Milton) Ⓗ

Milton Brewery's second of three Cambridge pubs, popular with locals and employees from the nearby science park. There are several drinking areas – one either side of the door, a snug (with bar access), and another room to one side. Dark wood and warm colours abound. Eight real ales and four real ciders or perries are on offer. Outside is a good-sized beer garden. The car park has the largest pub cycle park in Cambridge, leaving few spaces for cars. Local CAMRA Community City Pub of the Year 2017. ⏚⊛◑♣☙🅿🖵☙☎

Kingston Arms ✔

33 Kingston Street, CB1 2NU

✪ 12-3 (not Tue & Wed), 5-11; 12-midnight Fri; 11-midnight Sat; 11-11 Sun ☎ (01223) 319414 ⊕ kingston-arms.co.uk

Crouch Vale Brewers Gold; Hop Back Summer Lightning; Oakham JHB; Thornbridge Jaipur IPA; Timothy Taylor Landlord; Woodforde's Wherry; 4 changing beers Ⓗ

A classic, cosy, side-street pub close to Mill Road, equally popular with drinkers and diners. Windows and mirrors keep the interior light and welcoming. The walled garden behind has canopies and heaters and is popular all year round. Twelve handpumps offer regular and changing beers, at least one dark ale, as well as two changing ciders or perries. A selection of Belgian and other bottled beers is also stocked. Home-cooked food is available at all sessions including breakfast at the weekend. Q⏚⊛◑♣♣🖵☙☎

Live & Let Live

40 Mawson Road, CB1 2EA

✪ 11.30-2.30 (not Wed & Thu), 5.30-11; 11.30-2.30, 6-11 Sat; 12-2.30, 7-11 Sun ☎ (01223) 460261

Nethergate Umbel Ale; Oakham Citra; 3 changing beers Ⓗ

A discreet corner local, just off Mill Road, with a single bar and a small snug to the rear, furnished with simple tables and chairs plus a few bar stools. Wood panelling and railway and beer memorabilia add to the atmosphere. It is a pub for contemplation, conversation and ale and cider consumption. Five ales cover a range of styles and strengths, alongside three changing ciders or perries. The Live has won several CAMRA branch awards, including local CAMRA Cider Pub of the Year in 2015. Q♣♣🖵🖵☙

Maypole 🗓

20a Portugal Place, CB5 8AF

✪ 11.30-midnight (1am Fri & Sat); 12-11.30 Sun
☎ (01223) 352999 ⊕ maypolefreehouse.co.uk

Changing beers Ⓗ

The Maypole has been in the capable hands of the Castiglione family since 1982, initially as tenants, latterly as owners. The landlord's dedication to quality beers won him the CAMRA branch's first Real Ale Champion award. Up to 16 ever-changing ales are kept, including LocAles, more during festivals, often sourced from micros. It has a busy front bar and quieter back bar downstairs plus a function room upstairs. There is a large patio to one side. Food focuses on home-cooked Italian dishes and English pub classics. Local CAMRA Dark Beer Pub of the Year 2016. ⊛◑&🖵☙☎

Mill 🗓 ✔

14 Mill Lane, CB2 1RX

✪ 11-11 (midnight Thu-Sat) ☎ (01223) 311829
⊕ themillpubcambridge.co.uk

7 changing beers (sourced locally; often Cambridge Brewing Company) Ⓗ

Set in a honeypot riverside location across from Laundress Green, the building has been refurbished – improvements include an especially attractive wood-panelled side room. A vintage radiogram is used for playing vinyl records. The curved wooden bar has eight handpumps, including one for cider. Free of tie, there is a strong commitment to local beers, including those brewed at sister pub the Cambridge Brew House. Tasty food is cooked on the premises using locally sourced ingredients wherever possible. Local CAMRA branch Pub of the Year 2015 and City LocAle Pub of the Year 2017. ⏚◑♣☙☎

Pint Shop

10 Peas Hill, CB2 3PN

✪ 12-11; 12-midnight Fri; 11-midnight Sat; 11-11 Sun
☎ (01223) 352293 ⊕ pintshop.co.uk

6 changing beers Ⓗ

Located close to the market square, this impressive Georgian townhouse was formerly Cambridge University's pensions office. It features multiple rooms across two floors providing several drinking and dining areas. There is also a terraced patio garden for outdoor eating and drinking. Food is upmarket, but homemade cold bar snacks are available at all times if you do not fancy a full meal. ⏚⊛◑&🖵

Queen Edith 🗓

Wulfstan Way, CB1 8QN

✪ 12-11 (midnight Fri & Sat); 12-10.30 Sun
☎ (01223) 244536

Milton Pegasus; 7 changing beers (often Milton) Ⓗ

The first new-build pub in Cambridge for around 30 years, after the demolition of a pub of the same name at the rear of the site, and the third Milton Brewery pub in the city. The style is mock-Georgian inside and out. The larger bar to the left of the entrance has large windows on two sides and a wood-burning stove. The second bar has wooden booths down one side. Regular and changing Milton ales are complemented by changing guests. Q⏚⊛◑&♣🅿🖵☙☎

Castor

Prince of Wales Feathers ⓛ
38 Peterborough Road, PE5 7AL
🕐 12-11.30 (1am Fri & Sat); 12-midnight Sun
☎ (01733) 380222 🌐 princeofwalesfeathers.co.uk
6 changing beers 🅗/🅖
This corner village inn is about 300 years old and built of stone with stained-glass windows. Originally a boot and shoe shop, it has one main bar area, divided in two by the fireplace, and there are two smaller rooms for pool and darts. Dominoes and crib are also played. Entertainment includes Sky Sports on TV, live music every Saturday and a quiz on Sunday. Away football fans visiting Peterborough United are warmly welcomed. There are two drinking areas outside with benches and parasols. ⓩ🛏🌂❄♣🚲🍴🚃🐾

Royal Oak ⓛ
24 Peterborough Road, PE5 7AX
🕐 12-2 (not Mon), 5.30-11; 12-2, 5.30-midnight Fri; 12-11 Sat; 12-10.30 Sun ☎ (01733) 380217
St Austell Tribute; Timothy Taylor Landlord; 2 changing beers 🅗
Seventeenth-century, stone-built, Grade II-listed thatched inn with three drinking lounges, all with real fires, and many old photographs on the walls. Lunch is served daily except Monday. Traditional pub games including darts, dominoes and cribbage are played. The pub is on the Peterborough Green Wheel sustainable transport network and is popular with cyclists and ramblers. Free from jukebox and gaming machines, this is a quiet pub with friendly locals. Q🌂❄♣🚃

Chatteris

Ship
34 Bridge Street, PE16 6RN
🕐 12-2.30, 6.30-11; 12-3, 7-10 Sun ☎ 07880 326263
Fuller's London Pride; Sharp's Doom Bar; 2 changing beers (often Deeside, Tydd Steam) 🅗
A low-ceilinged, wood-beamed community free house dating from the 1850s. It was called Walk The Dog from the early 1990s to 2011 but after a period of closure reopened in August 2012 as the Ship, its former name. The L-shaped interior is adorned with many maritime memorabilia. Games include scrabble, chess, darts, dominoes and crib, with a pool table in the small back room. A quiz is held once a month. The pub supports two charities, Macmillan and the Stroke Association, and a local cricket team. Q🌂♣🚃(33)🐾🛜

Coates

Vine ⓛ
4 South Green, PE7 2BJ
🕐 4-11; 12-midnight Fri; 9am-11 Sat; 12-11 Sun
☎ (01733) 840343
Grainstore Ten Fifty; 2 changing beers 🅗
Lively bar and lounge with a separate restaurant with its own bar. In the summer of 2013 a private investor secured ownership of the pub from Charles Wells to make it officially a free house, now fully refurbished, including a new kitchen. Meals are served lunchtimes and evenings, and breakfast on Saturdays. The varying beer list includes a LocAle. The large outdoor area has nine pétanque terrains and a children's play area. Local buses pass in front of the building. Winter opening times vary.
Q⏸🌂❄🐕♣🚃(33)🐾🛜

Duxford

Plough
57 St Peter's Street, CB22 4RP
🕐 11-11 ☎ (01223) 833170 🌐 theduxfordplough.co.uk
Adnams Southwold Bitter; Everards Tiger; 3 changing beers 🅗
Thatched building first recorded as a pub in the 1820s. A single bar is divided into two distinct areas, one side for diners, the other for drinkers. Food is served daily. A range of regular and changing ales is kept, more than 500 in recent years, often including local beers, alongside four changing ciders and perries. Close to Duxford Airfield and the Imperial War Museum, the pub is home to Duxford United football club, local badminton players and three darts teams. Local CAMRA Cider Pub of the Year 2017.
⏸🌂❄🐕♿♣🐕🚃(7)🐾🛜

Ellington

Mermaid
High Street, PE28 0AB
🕐 closed Mon; 12-3, 5.30-11; 12-11 Sat; 12-10.30 Sun
☎ (01480) 891106 🌐 themermaidellington.co.uk
3 changing beers (sourced locally; often Digfield, Nobby's, Oakham) 🅗
Quintessential English village pub, dating mainly from the early 17th century but going back to around the 13th century in parts. The oak-beamed bar has a welcoming atmosphere, with a fire in winter months. There is a separate upper snug with a wood-burning stove. In warmer weather, the garden offers an idyllic setting near the village church and has a pétanque pitch. Quality bar food is served, with a choice of eight hand-made dishes, alongside a full à la carte menu. Q⏸🌂❄🐕♣🐾🛜

Elton

Crown ⓛ ✅
8 Duck Street, PE8 6RQ
🕐 12-11 ☎ (01832) 280232 🌐 crowninnelton.co.uk
Greene King IPA; Oakham JHB; house beer (by King's Cliffe); 2 changing beers 🅗
Thatched 16th-century stone pub with one main bar, a small dining area to the front and a restaurant to the rear. Six real ales are usually on offer including the house beer, Crown Bitter. There is a dedicated handpump for real cider. No bar food is served Saturday evening or Sunday. Look for the unusual cartoons and drawings on the walls around the toilets. Five-star B&B accommodation is available. 🌂🛏🐕🐕♣🚃(24,X4)🐾🛜

Ely

Drayman's Son 🍺 ⓛ
29a Forehill, CB7 4AA
🕐 5.30-10.30; 11-11 Thu-Sat; 12-10.30 Sun
☎ (01353) 662920
Changing beers (sourced nationally) 🅖
Micropub nostalgically themed with old signs, posters and musical scores. Ten real ales are usually available, mostly sourced from local microbreweries. A large range of 20 or more ciders is also sold, many local. The pub is a supporter of local produce including the Ely Gin Co. The cellar is in a temperature-controlled back room and service is direct to your table. Quiz nights and music nights are regular features. ♿🚆♣🐕🚃🐾🛜

Prince Albert 🗟 ✅

62 Silver Street, CB7 4JF (opp cathedral car park)
✪ 11-11.30; 12-10.30 Sun ☎ (01353) 663494
Greene King XX Mild, IPA, Abbot; 5 changing beers (sourced nationally; often Milton, Purity, Timothy Taylor) 🖽

A pub with two distinct characters – the front is a music-free drinkers' bar with a friendly atmosphere and a mixture of bench seating, stools and regulars (who are almost part of the furniture). The rear area is a recently renovated restaurant serving meals and snacks (booking advisable on Sundays). Outside is a secluded garden perfect for summer days. The pub is a short walk from Ely's cathedral and approximately two-thirds of a mile from the railway station. Q🌑🐕🍴👌🆑⇄🍺🖨🐾🛜

Fulbourn

Six Bells ✅

9 High Street, CB21 5DH
✪ 11.30-2.30, 5-midnight; 11.30-2am Fri; 12-2am Sat; 12-11 Sun ☎ (01223) 880244 ⊕ thesixbellsfulbourn.co.uk
Adnams Southwold Bitter, Broadside; Greene King IPA; Woodforde's Wherry; 2 changing beers 🖽
Traditional thatched village pub and former coaching inn. Beyond the rear car park is one of the largest beer gardens in the area. The main bar has low ceilings, a real fire and many cosy corners. The second bar is smaller. Beers come from the Punch Finest list. Home-cooked, locally sourced food is served in the bar and separate dining room. The function room hosts a trad jazz club twice a month. A regular in this Guide. 🌑🐕🍴👌♣🍺🖨🐾🛜

Glatton

Addison Arms 🗟

Sawtry Road, PE28 5RZ
✪ 11-3, 5-11; 11-11 Fri-Sun ☎ (01487) 830410
⊕ addisonarms.co.uk
Adnams Broadside; house beer (by Digfield) 🖽; **2 changing beers (sourced locally; often Grainstore, Nene Valley)** 🖽/🅖
Grade II-listed pub built at the start of the 18th century and named after the playwright and politician Joseph Addison (co-founder of The Spectator), who was a relative of the first landlord. The pub offers at least three real ales and a real cider, with a focus on local producers. Food prepared from fresh locally sourced supplies is a popular attraction, and there is a thriving Sunday night quiz. The house beer Addison Ale is Digfield Shacklebush. Q🌑🐕🍴👌🅰♣🍺🖨(46)🐾🛜

Grantchester

Green Man 🗟 ✅

59 High Street, CB3 9NF (in village centre)
✪ 11-11; 12-10.30 Sun ☎ (01223) 844669
⊕ thegreenmangrantchester.co.uk
Adnams Southwold Bitter; Oakham Citra 🖽; **3 changing beers** 🖽/🅖
A 17th-, possibly 16th-century building, the Green Man was first recorded as a pub in 1847. Complete with low ceilings and oak beams, it has a single L-shaped bar with various seating areas and a separate restaurant area off to the right. Outside is a pretty, sheltered seating area and a long, narrow garden reaching down to Grantchester meadows and the river, making the pub accessible by punt. Q🌑🐕🍴👌🍺🖨(18)🐾

Great Staughton

White Hart

56 The Highway, PE19 5DA (on B645)
✪ 12-2.30, 4-11 (midnight Fri); 12-11 Sat & Sun
☎ (01480) 861131 ⊕ whitehartgreatstaughton.co.uk
Batemans XB, XXXB; 1 changing beer 🖽
Passing through the narrow entrance to this fine small former coaching inn takes you back to the days of horse-drawn coaches. The building dates from 1630 and although it has been extended and altered, still warrants a Grade II listing. It has one main bar, a small pool room at the front and a restaurant to the rear. Traditional pub food is served 12-2.30pm and 6-9pm Thursday-Saturday and 12-3pm Sunday. Q🌑🐕🍴👌🍺🖨🐾🛜

Haddenham

Three Kings 🗟 ✅

1 Station Road, CB6 3XD
✪ 11-11; 11.30-10 Sun ☎ (01353) 749080
⊕ threekingsely.co.uk
Greene King IPA; 2 changing beers (sourced nationally) 🖽
Although updated over time, this 17th-century village inn retains its rustic framework and charm with plenty of exposed old beams, cosy areas and an inglenook fireplace. While the pub focuses on fine food, it is also keen to promote high-quality ales and ciders, and is well supported by local drinkers. At the rear is a relaxing courtyard drinking area and a large car park. Q🌑🐕🍴👌🍺🖨🐾🛜

Hartford

King of the Belgians 🍷 🗟

27 Main Street, PE29 1XU (on old village high street parallel to B1514)
✪ 11-11 (midnight Fri & Sat); 12-10.30 Sun
☎ (01480) 52030 ⊕ kingofthebelgians.com
4 changing beers (sourced locally; often Elgood's, Great Oakley, Nene Valley)
A 16th-century inn in a picturesque setting. This genuine community pub actively and generously supports local charities. It hosts an annual beer festival in May and a mini festival in late August. An ever-changing selection of four real ales and ciders is available alongside good-value food including Sunday roasts and takeaway pizza. Oak beams and a copper-topped bar characterise the public bar. There is a separate quiet dining area. Entertainment includes regular quizzes, games nights and an open mic night on the first Monday of the month. 🌑🐕♣🍺🖨🐾🛜

Hemingford Grey

Cock 🗟

47 High Street, PE28 9BJ (off A14 SE of Huntingdon)
✪ 11.30-3, 6 (5 Fri)-11; 11.30-11 Sat; 12-10.30 Sun
☎ (01480) 463609 ⊕ cambscuisine.com
Brewsters Hophead; Elgood's Cambridge Bitter; Great Oakley Wagtail; 1 changing beer 🖽
This village pub and restaurant has won local, regional and national awards. The cosy interior has recently been refurbished to provide more comfortable facilities and is popular with locals who enjoy the well kept locally sourced beers and real Cromwell cider made in the village. The separate restaurant features an extensive selection of fish, meat, game and excellent home-made

sausages (booking essential at all times). During the summer, occasional beer festivals are held in the garden. Q❄①⑥&▲P♖(5)❀ 🛜

Histon

Red Lion ▼
27 High Street, CB24 9JD
🕓 10.30-11 (midnight Fri); 12-11 Sun ☎ (01223) 564437
🌐 theredlionhiston.co.uk

Adnams Ghost Ship; Tring Side Pocket for a Toad; 7 changing beers (often Batemans, Lacons, Oakham) Ⓗ
The two bars of this free house are adorned with a wonderful collection of breweriana and historical photos. The bar on the left features the TV, while the nine handpumps are in the quieter and child-free bar on the right. Guest beers always include a mild. There are also Belgian and German beers on draught, a range of continental bottled beers, two ciders and a perry. Two beer festivals are held each year – the Easter aperitif and the main event in September. Local CAMRA Pub of the Year 2017.
❀🖾①⑥♣♖P♖ 🛜

Huntingdon

Falcon Ⓛ
Market Hill, PE29 3NR
🕓 11-midnight (1am Fri & Sat); 12-midnight Sun
☎ (01480) 457416 🌐 falconhuntingdon.co.uk

Elgood's Black Dog; J Church Gold Testament; Potbelly Best; 14 changing beers (often Great Oakley, Marston's, Nobby's) Ⓗ
An established venue steeped in local history. This former coaching inn used to be Oliver Cromwell's recruiting station and the gates from the market square were once the entrance to Huntingdon Prison. The ever-changing selection of beers includes ones from the landlord's own J Church Brewery and many more from Northamptonshire breweries. Choose from up to 18 handpumps, along with a range of real ciders. Good value food is available every day. Local branch and Cambridgeshire Pub of the Year 2016.
Q🗢❀①≈♣♖🖾❀

Old Bridge Hotel Ⓛ ✅
1 High Street, PE29 3TQ (at S end of High St on ring road by river)
🕓 11-11 (10.30 Sun) ☎ (01480) 424300 🌐 huntsbridge.com

3 changing beers (sourced locally; often Hart Family Brewers, Nene Valley) Ⓗ
A handsome ivy-clad hotel in an 18th-century former private bank at the southern end of the High Street. It has a prominent position on the bank of the River Great Ouse close to riverside footpaths. Imaginative and high-quality food is served in the Terrace Restaurant, or outside on the covered patio and in the garden. Drinkers can also relax in the bar and lounge. The award-winning Old Bridge Wine Shop offers wine tasting as a diversion and there is an emphasis on local and regional beers. The bus station is a short walk away.
Q🗢❀🖾①⑥&▲P🖾❀ 🛜

Keyston

Pheasant Ⓛ
Loop Road, PE28 0RE (on B663, 1 mile S of A14, E of Thrapston)
🕓 closed Mon; 12-3, 6-11; 12-11 Fri & Sat; 12-5 Sun
☎ (01832) 710241 🌐 thepheasant-keyston.co.uk

Adnams Southwold Bitter; 2 changing beers Ⓗ
The village is named after Ketil's Stone, probably an Anglo-Saxon boundary marker. Created from a row of thatched cottages in an idyllic setting, the pub offers high-quality food, fine wines and well-kept cask ales. There is a splendid lounge bar and three dining areas. Regularly changing guest beers are offered, usually from Nene Valley or Digfield. Food is served 12-2pm and 6.30-9.30pm Tuesday to Saturday, 12-3.30pm on Sunday. One of the few pubs included in the first edition of the Good Beer Guide in 1972. Q🗢❀①P❀ 🛜

Kirtling

Red Lion
214 The Street, CB8 9PD
🕓 closed Mon & Tue; 12-3, 6-11 (midnight Fri & Sat); 12-6 Sun
☎ (01638) 731976 🌐 kirtlingredlion.co.uk

Adnams Southwold Bitter; 1 changing beer Ⓗ
The last of three pubs in the village, this two-bar local has a main bar with a traditional clay-tiled floor. It is one of several former Greene King pubs in the area now privately owned. Home-made food using locally sourced ingredients is available lunchtimes and evenings, cooked to order. Plenty of family-friendly community events are held including monthly quiz nights to raise money for local charities. Walkers and dogs are welcome.
🗢❀①♣P🖾❀ 🛜

Leverington

Rising Sun Inn Ⓛ
Dowgate Road, PE13 5DH
🕓 12-2, 6-11; 12-11 Fri; 12-4 Sun ☎ (01945) 583754

Elgood's Cambridge Bitter; 2 changing beers (often Elgood's) Ⓗ
Comfortably furnished village local with an enclosed garden. Dating back to at least 1872, the pub was refurbished a few years ago but the bar retains the feel of a true village local. Cambridge Bitter and two changing beers are served including Elgood's seasonals and guest beers. Renowned for good-value, quality food, the restaurant hosts regular themed nights including Wednesday steak night. Dogs and children are welcome. Closing time may be earlier if there is no trade. A CAMRA branch Gold Award winner in 2016. ❀①♣P❀

Little Downham

Plough
106 Main Street, CB6 2SX (W end of village)
🕓 12-3 (not Mon), 6-11; 12-midnight Fri & Sat; 12-3, 6-10.30 Sun ☎ (01353) 698297

2 changing beers (sourced regionally) Ⓗ
An early-Victorian Grade II-listed pub, well preserved in character and charm, with a good community spirit. At least two changing regional cask ales are normally on offer. An annual beer festival is held in early-September. Excellent Thai cuisine is available to eat in or take away. The venue supports traditional pub games and local customs. Children are welcome until 9pm.
❀①♣P🖾(125)

Little Gransden

Chequers Ⓛ
71 Main Road, SG19 3DW

✪ 12-2, 7-11; 12-11 Fri & Sat; 12-6, 7-10.30 Sun
☎ (01767) 677348 ⊕ chequersgransden.co.uk
4 changing beers (sourced locally) Ⓗ
Village pub owned and run by the same family for over 60 years and in this Guide for more than 20. The unspoilt middle bar, with its wooden benches and roaring fire, is a favourite spot to catch up on the local gossip. The pub's Son of Sid brewhouse supplies the pub and local beer festivals. Fish and chips are a highlight on Friday night (booking essential). Pickled Pig cider is nearly always available. Winner of numerous CAMRA awards.
Q❁🕭🛦🍴P🖵🔌🐾🛜

March

Rose & Crown ⓁⓋ
41 St Peters Road, PE15 9NA
✪ 12-11 (midnight Fri & Sat) ☎ (01354) 652077
St Austell Cornish Best Bitter; 5 changing beers (often Oakham, Tydd Steam, Wells) Ⓗ
Traditional rural free house, over 150 years old, with low-beamed ceilings in both rooms and a real fire in the main bar. The beer range includes up to six ales, mainly from micros, with regular West Country beers and an occasional LocAle. Perry is permanently on handpump and up to four ciders. Good-quality food is served lunchtimes and evenings. A family-run community pub, it hosts a popular quiz night on Thursday. A beer festival is held at Easter. Q❁🕭🍴P🖵(33,46)

Ship Inn Ⓛ
1 Nene Parade, PE15 8TD
✪ 12-11 Mon & Tue; 9am-midnight Wed & Thu;
9am-12.30am Fri & Sat; 9am-10.30 Sun ☎ (01354) 607878
Woodforde's Wherry; 4 changing beers (often Church End, Timothy Taylor, Tydd Steam) Ⓗ
Thatched Grade II-listed riverside pub built in 1680, with extensive riverside moorings. The unusual carved beams are said to have 'fallen off a barge' during the building of Ely Cathedral. A quaint wobbly floor and wall lead to the toilets and a small games room. Reopened in March 2010 as a free house, after a major refit, the pub has a friendly and welcoming atmosphere and displays a large collection of pumpclips. A reglar in the Guide, it is a former CAMRA Gold Award winner. Breakfast is available Wednesday to Sunday.
Q🛥❁🍴♣🖵(33,46.)🐾🛜

Maxey

Blue Bell Ⓛ
39 High Street, PE6 9EE
✪ 5.30-11.30; 1-11.30 Sat; 12-6 Sun ☎ (01778) 348182
Abbeydale Absolution; Fuller's London Pride, ESB; Oakham Bishops Farewell; 5 changing beers (sourced regionally; often Grainstore, Oakham, Woodforde's) Ⓗ
Originally a limestone barn, the building was converted many years ago and reflects the rural setting in which it is found. Paraphernalia of country life adorn the stone walls and shelves of the two-roomed interior. Nine handpumps dispense a range of quality ales from large and small breweries far and wide. It is a popular meeting place for groups including birdwatchers and golfers. A former local CAMRA Pub of the Year and Gold Award winner. Q❁♣P🖵(22,413)🐾🛜

Milton

White Horse
22 High Street, CB24 6AJ
✪ 11-11 (midnight Fri & Sat); 12-10.30 Sun
☎ (01223) 860327 ⊕ whitehorsemilton.co.uk
Greene King Abbot; Sharp's Doom Bar; 4 changing beers (sourced regionally) Ⓗ
This local CAMRA Rural Community Pub of the Year 2016 has a small bar/dining area that leads to a conservatory and then on to a large garden and children's play area. An area to the rear of the fireplace can be used as a function room. A separate public bar has pool and darts. There is a large car park to the rear, offering good disabled parking, with access to the pub through the dining area. 🛥❁🕭🏃♣🍴P🖵(9)🐾🛜

Newton

Queen's Head
CB22 7PG
✪ 11.30-2.30, 6-11; 12-2.30, 7-10.30 Sun ☎ (01223) 870436
Adnams Southwold Bitter, Broadside; 2 changing beers Ⓖ
This village local is one of a handful of pubs to have appeared in every edition of this Guide. The list of landlords since 1729, displayed on the wall in the simply furnished public bar, has just 18 entries. The cosy lounge has a welcoming fire in the colder months. Guest beers are often Adnams seasonals. Simple but excellent food centres on soup and sandwiches. The King and Kaiser are reputed to have stopped here for a pint in the early 1900s.
Q🕭🛦♣🍴P🖵(31)

Peterborough

Bumble Inn
46 Westgate, PE1 1RE
✪ 12-10 (8 Mon); 12-11 Fri & Sat; 12-6 Sun
⊕ thebimbleinn.wordpress.com
5 changing beers (often Axholme, North Riding, Tyne Bank) Ⓗ
A new micropub opened on 13 June 2016 in what was a chemist's shop. Minimalist in style, it has five handpumps dispensing quality ales from far and wide – expect the unusual. Rare bottled beers are also available, as well as tea, coffee and soft drinks. Home-made snacks include pasties, pies and Scotch eggs. 🚆🍴🖵

Charters Ⓛ Ⓥ
Town Bridge, PE1 1FP (down steps at Town Bridge)
✪ 12-11 (midnight Fri & Sat); 12-10.30 Sun
☎ (01733) 315700 ⊕ charters-bar.com
Oakham JHB, Inferno, Citra, Bishops Farewell; 6 changing beers Ⓗ/Ⓖ
The converted Dutch grain barge from circa 1907 sits on the River Nene near the city centre. An oriental restaurant is on the upper deck and food is also served in the bar. Up to 12 beers are on offer plus cider. The large garden with a marquee, bar and landing stage for boats is popular in summer. Live music plays some weekends and in summer outside the pub. It gets busy on football match days. Close to the Nene Valley Railway.
❁🕭🍴♣🍴P🖵🐾🛜

Coalheavers Arms
5 Park Street, Woodston, PE2 9BH
✪ 12-2 (not Mon-Wed), 5-11; 12-11 Fri & Sat; 12-10.30 Sun
☎ (01733) 565664 ⊕ individualpubs.co.uk/coalheavers

Milton Justinian, Sparta; 4 changing beers ⊞
Friendly back-street one-room community pub
dating back to the 1850s. Up to four guest ales plus
cider, Belgian bottled beers, and an English
unpasteurised lager are stocked. Bombers Drop,
the house beer, is brewed by Milton. Home-made
pies are available all week, with fresh rolls on
Friday. Beer festivals are held in spring and autumn
and the large garden is popular in the summer with
families. A free quiz is held on Sunday night. Very
busy on football match days. Q✿❀♣●🛏🖭🐾🛜

Draper's Arms 🗕 ✅
29-31 Cowgate, PE1 1LZ
☀ 8am-midnight (1am Fri & Sat) ☎ (01733) 847570
**Courage Directors; Greene King Abbot; Ruddles Best
Bitter; Sharp's Doom Bar; Woodforde's Wherry; 5
changing beers (often Oakham, Xtreme Ales)** ⊞
A converted former draper's shop, built circa 1899,
this is one of two Wetherspoon pubs in the city.
The large interior is broken up with wood-panelled
intimate spaces and dividers. The beer range, with
many from local microbreweries, is dispensed
through 10 handpumps. Food is served all day and
regular beer and wine festivals are held throughout
the year. Quiz night is Wednesday. A regular top
10-listed real ale pub within the company's chain.
Close to bus and rail stations. Q🕭🕜&🛲➡🖭🛜

Hand & Heart ★ 🗕
12 Highbury Street, PE1 3BE
☀ 3-11.30 (midnight Fri); 12-midnight Sat; 12-11.30 Sun
☎ (01733) 564653 ⊕ thehandandheart.com
**5 changing beers (sourced regionally; often
Brewsters, Dark Star, Tydd Steam)** ⊞
This 1930s back-street pub is on CAMRA's National
Inventory of Historic Pub Interiors for its unspoilt
character. There is a main bar to the front and a
quiet room to the rear connected by a drinking
corridor. It became free of tie in 2016 and its five
handpumps often feature some hard-to-find real
ales. Live music plays on the second Thursday of
the month. The large garden has an outside bar
and stage used for beer festivals and music events.
Home-made rolls are usually available. A former
local CAMRA Pub of the Year. Q✿♣●🖭(1)🐾🛜

Ostrich Inn 🗕
17 North Street, PE1 2RA
☀ 12-11; 11-1am Fri & Sat ☎ (01733) 746370
**House beer (by King's Cliffe); 4 changing beers
(sourced locally; often Tydd Steam)** ⊞
Refurbished in 2009, the pub reopened with its
original name restored. A relaxing one-room side-
street pub off the main drag, it has a U-shaped bar
and displays many pictures and posters of bygone
breweries and famous acts who appeared in the
city. Up to five regularly changing beers are on
offer, many from local breweries. Live music plays
most weekends. The small enclosed patio is a
suntrap at the rear. 🕭✿&🛲♣●🖭🐾

Palmerston Arms 🗕
82 Oundle Road, PE2 9PA (on main A605 road S of city
centre)
☀ 3 (12 Fri & Sat)-midnight; 12-11.30 Sun ☎ (01733) 565865
**Batemans Gold, XXXB 🗔; Castle Rock Harvest Pale;
Oakham Citra ⊞/🗔; 10 changing beers (sourced
regionally)** 🗔
Popular 400-year-old listed stone-built locals' pub.
Owned by Batemans, three of its beers are rotated
alongside nine or more different ales, including
some from Oakham Ales. Traditional cider, perry

and an extensive range of malt whiskies are also
available. Most beers are served straight from the
cellar which can be seen through a large glass
screen. Rolls and a variety of snacks tempt
customers. Live music features most weekends and
occasional philosophy nights. Busy on football
match days. ✿♣●🖭(1,24)🐾🛜

Ploughman 🗕
1 Staniland Way, Werrington, PE4 6NA
☀ 4-11; 2-11.30 Fri; 12-11.30 Sat & Sun ☎ (01733) 327696
⊕ theploughman-werrington.co.uk
10 changing beers (sourced regionally) ⊞
A rejuvenated two-roomed community pub,
brought to the forefront of the city's real ale outlets
by the enthusiastic licensee. Ten handpumps serve
beers from both local breweries and from afar. An
annual beer festival features early in July. Many
activities are held including charity events and live
music at weekends. A two-times local CAMRA
branch Pub of the Year. ✿♣●P🖭(1,22)

Ramsey

Jolly Sailor 🗕 ✅
43 Great Whyte, PE26 1HH
☀ 11-11 ☎ (01487) 813388 ⊕ jollysailorramsey.co.uk
**Greene King Abbot; St Austell Tribute; Wells
Bombardier; 2 changing beers (often Dark Star,
Digfield)** ⊞
This Grade II-listed building has been a pub for over
400 years. Three linked rooms on slightly different
levels feature wooden beams dating from different
periods as the pub has been extended over the
years. On the walls are pictures and artefacts
depicting Ramsey history. Friendly and welcoming,
it attracts a varied clientele of all ages, and hosts
occasional charity nights plus acoustic music
sessions on the first Thursday of the month. Crib,
darts and dominoes are played. Guest beers are
available at the weekend. Good-value home-
cooked food is served every day.
Q🕭✿🕜●P🖭(31)🛜

St Ives

Nelson's Head 🗕 ✅
Merryland, PE27 5ED
☀ 11.30-11 (midnight Fri & Sat); 12-9 Sun
☎ (01480) 494454 ⊕ nelsonsheadstives.pub
**Greene King IPA; 5 changing beers (often Moonshine,
Nene Valley, Oakham)** ⊞
Situated in a picturesque narrow street in the
centre of town, this is a Greene King Local Heroes
pub. In addition to the Greene King range, three
beers from local breweries can be found. Local
Cromwell Cider is also available. The pub is popular
with a young clientele in the evenings and busy for
food at lunchtimes. The name provides an unusual
local reference to the maritime hero, more
common around his Norfolk birthplace. Live music
features every Sunday afternoon. ✿🕜●🖭🐾🛜

Oliver Cromwell 🗕
13 Wellington Street, PE27 5AZ
☀ 11-11 (11.30 Thu; 12.30am Fri & Sat); 12-11 Sun
☎ (01480) 465601 ⊕ theolivercromwell.co.uk
**Adnams Southwold Bitter; Oakham JHB; Woodforde's
Wherry; 3 changing beers (often Nene Valley,
Nethergate)** ⊞
A popular pub near the town quay and old town
bridge and chapel. A true free house, it offers three

regular and three rotating beers, often from local breweries. A selection of Belgian bottled beers complements the cask beers and local Cromwell cider is always available. Lunchtime meals are freshly prepared and use local ingredients. Live music plays every Thursday evening. A quiz is hosted on the first Tuesday of the month. The rear patio is a suntrap in the summer. An annual beer festival is held in June. ❀◑🚲🐾

Royal Oak L ✔

13 Crown Street, PE27 5EB
❀ 11-11 (2am Fri & Sat); 12-midnight Sun ☎ (01480) 462586
Oakham Inferno; 4 changing beers (often Nobby's, Oakham, Tydd Steam) H
Busy town-centre pub, one of a number of historic listed pubs in St Ives, whose most famous inhabitant was Oliver Cromwell. Despite the date 1502 over the door, most of the building is 18th century. The room layout and character were happily preserved in a sensitive renovation in the 1990s. A changing choice of four beers is offered, often from local breweries, plus several ciders – this is also a rare local outlet for perry. Live music plays on Saturday evenings. 🛏❀♿♣🍴🚲🐾🛜

St Neots

Olde Sun L

11 Huntingdon Street, PE19 1BL
❀ 12-11 ☎ (01480) 216863 🌐 yeoldesun.moonfruit.com
Woodforde's Wherry; 5 changing beers (often Adnams, Elgood's, Woodforde's) H
Low-beamed and cosy traditional town-centre pub with two large inglenook fireplaces, three bar areas, a dining area and a secluded patio. The jukebox is zoned allowing quiet areas for conversation. Shove-ha'penny and bar billiards are played. Five constantly changing guest beers come from various regional breweries including Adnams, Elgood's, Marston's, Thwaites and Woodforde's. A mild and other dark beers are usually among the range. Good home-cooked food includes a menu of traditional pub fare and blackboard specials. ❀◑♣🚲(X5)🐾

Pig 'n' Falcon L

9 New Street, PE19 1AE (behind Barretts department store)
❀ closed Mon; 11.30 (11 Thu)-midnight; 11-2.30am Fri & Sat; 11-midnight Sun ☎ 07951 785678 🌐 pignfalcon.co.uk
Greene King IPA H**, Abbot** G**; Potbelly Best** H**; 5 changing beers (often Potbelly)** G
This busy town-centre free house has up to eight real ales and six real ciders, focusing on microbreweries and unusual beers including milds, porters and stouts. A good range of bottled ciders, UK and foreign bottled beers includes Belgian Trappist ales. Live blues and rock nights are hosted on Wednesday, Friday and Saturday. Thursday is quiz night. Outside is a large, imaginatively created, covered and heated beer garden. 🛏❀♣🍴🚲(X5)🐾🛜

Thriplow

Green Man ✔

2 Lower Street, SG8 7RJ
❀ closed Mon; 11-11; 12-7 Sun ☎ (01763) 208855
🌐 thegreenmanthriplow.co.uk
4 changing beers (sourced regionally) H

Purchased by villagers in 2013, the welcoming pub has a light interior divided in two. To the left is a relaxed area complete with armchairs and an open fire, and to the right a larger area mostly for dining. The pub has a reputation for good food. The beers tend to come from smaller regional breweries. There is outside seating both on the green in front and in the pleasant garden. Local CAMRA Most Improved Rural Pub 2016. Q🛏❀◑▶⚂P🚲(31)🐾🛜

Upware

Five Miles Inn

Old School Lane, CB7 5ZR
❀ 11-11 (midnight Fri & Sat) ☎ (01353) 721654
🌐 fivemilesinn.com
Morland Old Speckled Hen; 3 changing beers (sourced nationally) H
Located off the beaten track, next to the River Cam, the pub's full name is the Five Miles From Anywhere No Hurry Inn. Four ales are on handpump with an occasional fifth beer from the cask during the summer, along with one real cider. A selection of food is available in the bar and separate restaurant, with a recent extension to the building. Visitor moorings and services are provided for narrowboats/motor cruisers, and there is a large car park for those arriving by land. 🛏❀◑♿⚂♣🍴P🐾🛜

West Wratting

Chestnut Tree

1 Mill Road, CB21 5LT
❀ 12-3 (not Mon), 5.30-11.30; 12-midnight Fri & Sat; 12-10.30 Sun ☎ (01223) 290384 🌐 chestnuttreepub.co.uk
Greene King IPA; 3 changing beers H
Impressive two-bar Victorian-style pub, with modern extensions creating a roomy, comfortable interior. On the left is a nicely furnished public bar with a pool table and on the right a lounge bar mainly for dining. The pub hosts darts, pool and pétanque teams, and a small lending library. Originally a Greene King pub, it has been free of tie since the present owners bought it in 2012. Greene King IPA is regularly available, with three guest beers mainly from micros. Q🛏❀◑♣🍴P🚲(19)🐾

Whittlesey

Boat Inn L

2 Ramsey Road, PE7 1DR
❀ 4 (11 Fri-Sun)-midnight ☎ (01733) 202488
🌐 quinnboatinn.wordpress.com
Elgood's Cambridge Bitter, Golden Newt H**; 2 changing beers** H/G
This 11th-century inn is mentioned in the Domesday Book. It attracts locals, anglers and visitors, who all receive a warm welcome. The bar in the lounge is an unusual boat shape. Up to seven ciders and perries supplement the real ales, some of which are served direct from the cask. A whisky club meets on the second Friday of every month. Open mic music nights feature on some Tuesdays and Fridays. Outside is a pétanque terrain. Good-value accommodation is offered. Closing times can be flexible. 🛏❀🛌♿♣🍴P🚲(31)🐾🛜

Hubs Place

No.1, 12 Market Place, PE7 1AB
❀ closed Mon; 12-2, 5-midnight; 12-1am Fri & Sat; 12-11 Sun
☎ (01733) 204199 🌐 hubs-place.co.uk

Fuller's London Pride; 1 changing beer Ⓗ
Pleasant and comfortable bar opened by a lottery winner in November 2010. A former solicitors' offices, it has three rooms, refurbished with a cream and red colour scheme but retaining some original wood panelling. A large patio is to the rear. The guest ale is usually from Woodforde's. Other real ales may be available on special occasions such as the Whittlesey Straw Bear Festival. Closed Monday plus Tuesday and Wednesday afternoons in winter. ✿&♣P➡(31,33)🛜

Letter B 🍷 ⓛ

53-57 Church Street, PE7 1DE
🕐 5-11; 3.30-midnight Fri; 12-midnight Sat; 12-11 Sun
☎ (01733) 206975 ⊕ theletterb.co.uk
Sharp's Doom Bar; 4 changing beers (often Tydd Steam) Ⓗ
A friendly and welcoming community pub over 200 years old. It is said to be named the Letter B because there were so many pubs in Whittlesey they ran out of names. A beer festival takes place in January on Straw Bear weekend. Between five and 10 ciders and perries are always available. Quiz nights are held on alternate Tuesdays and Sundays, and popular charity events are hosted. A former winner of CAMRA Gold Awards, County Pub of the Year and branch and county Cider Pub of the Year. Q➦✿⇄♣♠➡(31,33)🐾🛜

Willingham

Bank Micropub

High Street, CB24 5ES
🕐 5.30-10 (11 Thu-Sat); closed Sun & Mon
☎ (01954) 200045 ⊕ thebankmicropub.co.uk
6 changing beers Ⓖ
Formerly a village bank, this micropub opened in late 2012. The single room has a short bar rescued from a closed Cambridge pub. The walls are decorated with photos of local interest. Up to six real ales are available direct from the cask, with regional and local beers featuring strongly. The

Bank offers a warm welcome and the casual visitor is certain to be included in local conversation. Q♦➡🐾

Wisbech

Red Lion ⓛ

32 North Brink, PE13 1JR
🕐 11.30-3, 6 (5 Fri)-11; 11.30-3, 7-midnight Sat; 12-11 Sun
☎ (01945) 582022
Elgood's Cambridge Bitter; 2 changing beers Ⓗ
This is the nearest Elgood's pub to the brewery and is very comfortable, with a pleasant, relaxed atmosphere. Drinkers and diners are well catered for with quality ales and excellent food seven days a week in the revamped split-level restaurant. There is always a specials board and a Wednesday mid-week roast offer. The main access is via a side passage which links the North Brink road to the rear car park and patio. Baby changing facilities have been added. The outdoor drinking area is popular on sunny days. Q➦✿①&P➡(X1)🛜

Wistow

Three Horseshoes ✓

Mill Road, PE28 2QQ
🕐 6-10 Mon; 12-3, 6-11; 12-10 Sat; 12-4 Sun
☎ (01487) 822270
Adnams Southwold Bitter, Ghost Ship Ⓗ
Multi-roomed brick and thatch 18th-century inn opposite the village church. Thought to have always been a pub, the building has evolved over time – part was once a blacksmith's and it provided accommodation for workers employed in church rebuilding work in the 18th century. Traditional pub food is available daily. A quiz is held once a month. Families are welcome in both bars and there is a covered smoking area outside. ➦✿①&♣P⛟➡(30)🛜

Three Kings, Haddenham (Photo: Bruce Pattern)

CHESHIRE

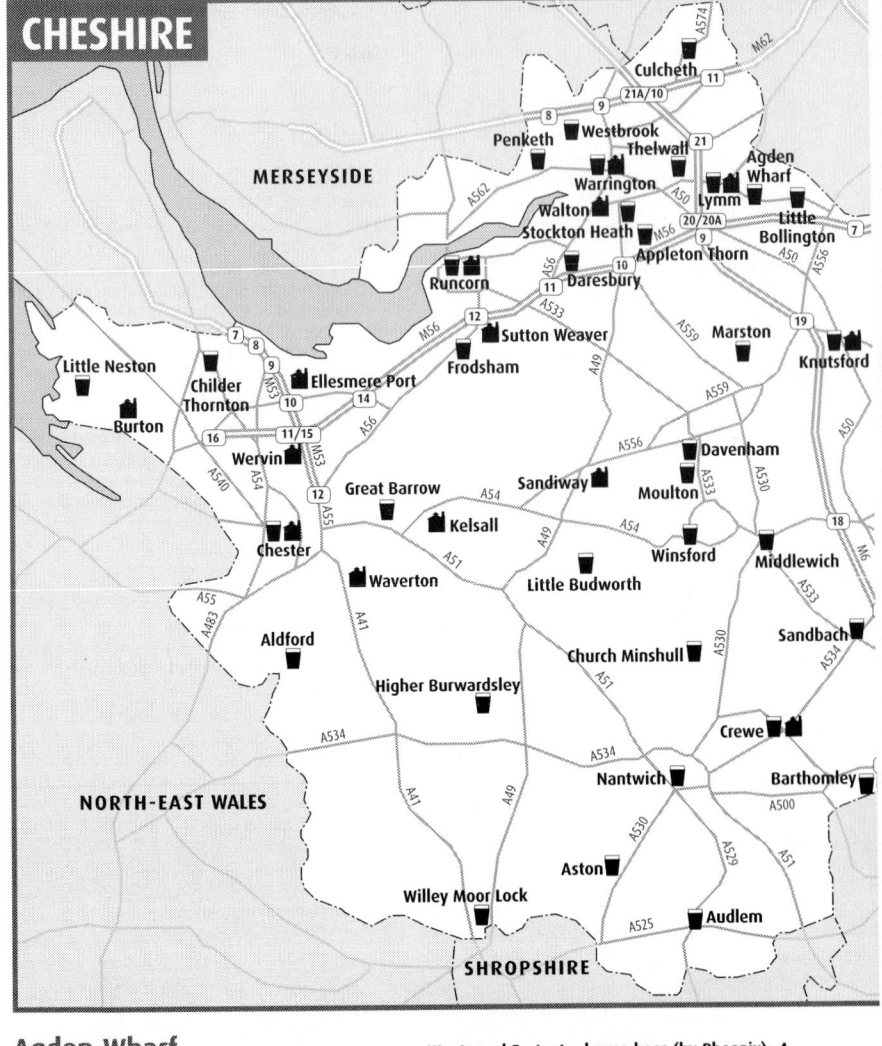

Agden Wharf

Barn Owl 🅛
Warrington Lane, WA13 0SW (on Bridgewater Canal)
☼ 12-11 ☎ (01925) 752020 ⊕ thebarnowlinn.co.uk
Marston's Wainwright, Lancaster Bomber; Thwaites Original; 3 changing beers (sourced regionally; often Pictish, Storm) 🅗
This place offers fine views across the Cheshire countryside and a canalside patio for the summer months. The three regular beers are joined by up to three guest ales, mainly from independent breweries, including at least one LocAle. Renowned for its freshly cooked meals featuring mainly local produce, the pub can be busy at mealtimes. ⛵❀◑🚹P🐾🛜

Aldford

Grosvenor Arms 🅛
Chester Road, CH3 6HJ (on B5130)
☼ 12-11 (10.30 Sun) ☎ (01244) 620228
⊕ grosvenorarms-aldford.co.uk

Weetwood Eastgate; house beer (by Phoenix); 4 changing beers (sourced nationally) 🅗
Spacious and stylish countryside pub. The multi-roomed interior is full of character with a modern-traditional decor featuring lots of bare wood, bookcases, pictures and chalkboards. A pleasant garden room leads to a terrace and lawn with picnic tables. Four ever-changing guest beers complement the regular Weetwood Eastgate and Brunning & Price house beer (brewed by Phoenix). High-quality food from an imaginative menu is very popular and served all day until 9.30pm (10pm Sat). Q⛵❀◑🚹&♣P🚃(C56)🐾🛜

Allgreave

Rose & Crown 🅛 ✅
Buxton Road, SK11 0BJ (on A54)
☼ closed Mon; 11-11 ☎ (01260) 227232
⊕ roseandcrownallgreave.co.uk
5 changing beers (sourced regionally) 🅗
Cosy pub nestled against the hillside in the beautiful Peak District overlooking Shutlingsloe – Cheshire's Matterhorn. It offers up to five often

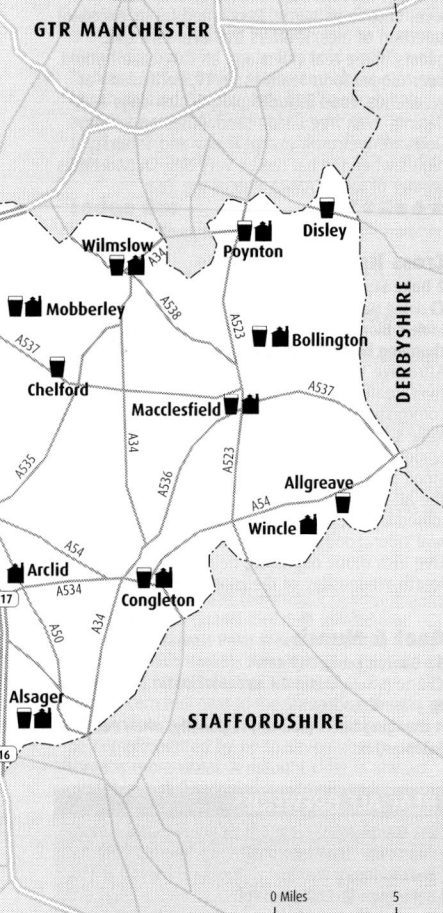

Appleton Thorn

Appleton Thorn Village Hall
Stretton Road, WA4 4RT
🕑 closed Mon-Wed; 7.30-11.30 Thu-Sat; 1-4, 7.30-10.30 Sun
☎ (01925) 261187 ⊕ appletonthornvillagehall.co.uk
7 changing beers (sourced nationally) Ⓗ
The bar serves a cosy lounge and a larger function room with a pool room off. Stained glass fringes the lounge while the function room is adorned with period agricultural implements. Welcoming staff will give tasters of the seven regularly changing ales, together with ciders and perries. Sunday lunches are popular, as is the new gin bar.
Q✕🛏🕮◑🎋🍴♿🅿🚐(8E)🐾🛜

Aston

Bhurtpore 🏆 ⓛ
Wrenbury Road, CW5 8DQ (just off A530)
🕑 12-11.30 (midnight Fri & Sat); 12-11 Sun
☎ (01270) 780917 ⊕ bhurtpore.co.uk
11 changing beers (sourced nationally) Ⓗ
This friendly country pub can now boast that it has been in the Guide for 25 consecutive years. It has a quiet, timeless atmosphere in the main bar area, with two further rooms, one with a pool table and TV. There is also a restaurant serving locally sourced food and excellent curries. Star of the show is the superb range of 11 changing ales from breweries all over, plus two ciders and Belgian beers.
Q✕🛏🕮◑♿▲⇆♿🅿🚐(72)🐾🛜

Audlem

Lord Combermere ⓛ ✅
The Square, CW3 0AQ
🕑 12-midnight ☎ (01270) 812277
⊕ thelordcombermere.co.uk
Greene King IPA; Salopian Darwins Origin; Timothy Taylor Landlord; 3 changing beers (sourced locally) Ⓗ
Very much a local but where visitors are always assured of a warm welcome. The main verandah entrance leads to the convivial bar, serving six real ales plus one real cider. There are alcoved seating areas to the left and right, including a good mixture of drinking and dining areas. Beer choice is a good mix, from national and local breweries. The excellent food menu features gluten-free meals as a speciality. ✕🛏◑♿🅿🚐(73)🐾🛜

Barthomley

White Lion ★ ✅
Audley Road, CW2 5PF (opp St Bertoline's Church)
🕑 12-11 (10.30 Sun) ☎ (01270) 882242
⊕ whitelionbarthomley.co.uk
Banks's Amber Ale, Sunbeam; Jennings Cocker Hoop, Sneck Lifter; Marston's 61 Deep, Pedigree Ⓗ
The three-roomed thatched building with its rustic charm and beamed ceilings is at the hub of this beautiful historic Cheshire village. The hard-working and friendly staff have one thing on their agenda and that is the comfort and happiness of the customer. Extremely popular with locals, walkers and cyclists. Q✕🛏◑🅿🐾🛜

Bollington

Poachers Inn ⓛ
95 Ingersley Road, SK10 5RE (edge of village)

local ales together with a highly regarded food menu. Accommodation makes this a destination pub and a great base for walking in the area. Part of the Langley 11 walk in May, taking in 11 pubs over 15 miles. ✕🛏◑◑ ▲🅿🐾🛜

Alsager

Lodge ⓛ
88 Crewe Road, ST7 2JA (jct Crewe Rd/Station Rd)
🕑 4-11 (midnight Fri); 2-midnight Sat; 2-11 Sun
☎ (01270) 873669
House beer (by Marston's); 7 changing beers (sourced nationally; often Dark Star, Oakham) Ⓗ
Community pub with an on-site two-and-a-half barrel plant, occasionally producing brews. The real ale selection comprises a good variety of styles and reflects the owners' preference for supporting local breweries. A range of continental beers on draught and in bottle is also on offer alongside up to three real ciders from smaller producers. Occasional events are hosted, otherwise this is usually a quiet pub for conversation. There is a large beer garden to the rear. Q✕🛏🕮⇆♿🅿🚐(3)🐾

Situated in an impressive street-corner location, this well-stocked bottled beer specialist is also a micropub. Three handpumps dispense predominantly local beers, with local cider available in bottles. The bottled beer selection focuses on British beers but there is a well-chosen selection of foreign beers too. A discount scheme offers a free pint/bottle for every 10 purchased. Occasional Meet the Brewer events are held, and Pie and Pint every Friday and Saturday. Closing time may vary according to demand.
Q ঌ ▸ ♠ ➍ (38,42) ❀ ☞

Prince of Wales L
4-6 Lawton Street, CW12 1RP
✪ 4 (12 Wed & Thu)-11; 12-midnight Fri & Sat; 12-10.30 Sun
☎ (01260) 280714
Joule's Pale Ale, Blonde, Slumbering Monk; 3 changing beers (sourced regionally; often Joule's) Ⓗ
A good revitalised pub for the town owned by Joule's Brewery. It sells three Joule's beers plus three guests, one often local. The pub has been divided into three areas, creating snug corners, warmed by a real fire. There is a good-sized outside drinking area behind the pub.
ঌ ❀ ◑ ♠ ➍ (250) ❀ ☞

Queen's Head Hotel
Park Lane, CW12 3DE
✪ 12-midnight (1am Fri & Sat) ☎ (01260) 272546
⊕ queensheadhotel.org.uk
Draught Bass; Black Sheep Best Bitter; Greene King Abbot; Joule's Pale Ale; 3 changing beers (sourced regionally) Ⓗ
Independent free house next to the railway station and canal. It does good-quality food without being a restaurant. Pub games include darts, pool, crib and, in summer, boules. A quiz is held on Monday, pool on Wednesday, and a Yappy hour on the last Sunday of the month. There is a large beer garden with a separate children's play area, a large undercover smoking area and a patio.
ঌ ❀ ➍ ◑ ▸ ➔ ♠ ➍ P ➍ (94) ❀ ☞

Young Pretender L
30-34 Lawton Street, CW12 1RS
✪ 4-11; 12-1am Fri & Sat; 12-11 Sun ☎ (01260) 273277
⊕ youngpretenderbeerparlour.co.uk
5 changing beers (sourced locally) Ⓗ
Modern, town-centre bar set within a part Grade II-listed building, with a strong community base, offering an ever-changing range of five real ales plus one real cider. The large single-room interior divides into smaller areas. Bonnie Prince Charlie allegedly slept here, hence the name. The real ales always come from Manchester and East Cheshire. Regular Meet the Brewer evenings, Sunday quizzes, film nights and pub games feature and the bar is a meeting point for local groups.
ঌ ❀ ◑ ▸ ዬ ♠ P ➍ ❀ ☞

Crewe

Borough Arms L
33 Earle Street, CW1 2BG (on Earle St railway bridge, with entrance up steps in adjoining Thomas St)
✪ 5-11; 12-midnight Fri & Sat; 12-11 Sun
10 changing beers (sourced nationally; often Fyne Ales, Oakham, Salopian) Ⓗ
Within sight of Crewe Municipal Square, 10 handpumps here serve constantly changing real ales, with two more dispensing real ciders. Nineteen dispensers and cold cabinets offer a wide range of continental draught and bottled beers. The L-shaped bar has three distinct seating areas on split levels. Downstairs, a larger seating area has doors opening onto a secluded walled beer garden and smoking area. The Borough Arms Brewery is located here, brewing occasionally.
ঌ ❀ ♠ ◑ P ➍ ☞

Hop Pole ✅
140 Wistaston Road, CW2 7RQ
✪ 1-11 (midnight Fri); 1-12.30am Sat ☎ 07912 796032
⊕ hoppolecrewe.co.uk
Sharp's Doom Bar; 3 changing beers (sourced nationally) Ⓗ
Friendly two-room community pub retaining some of its Victorian past. The separate semicircular bar is full of character with the original sash window. To the back of the pub is a south-facing patio and verandah overlooking its own Crown bowling green, one of few still left in Crewe. A covered external area to the rear allows access, via a side drive, to double doors opening into the open-plan lounge area. ❀ ዬ ♠ ➍ (42) ❀ ☞

Hops L
Prince Albert Street, CW1 2DF (opp Lifestyle Centre)
✪ 11 (5 Mon)-11.30; 12-11.30 Sun ☎ (01270) 211100
6 changing beers (sourced nationally) Ⓗ
Family-run, friendly, Belgian-style café-bar, free from brewery tie, popular with all ages and a wide clientele. Real ales come from local and interesting micro and regional brewers. A row of six handpumps has stronger beers to the left, session beers to the right, with stout or porter always available. A superb range of bottled Belgian beers is also stocked. Up to six real ciders and perries are also available. Q ঌ ❀ ◑ ዬ ♠ ◑ ➍ ❀ ☞

Culcheth

Cherry Tree ✅
35 Common Lane, WA3 4EX (on B5207, 400yds from A574)
✪ 12-11 (1am Fri & Sat) ☎ (01925) 762624
⊕ thecherrytreewarrington.co.uk
Greene King Abbot; Tetley Bitter; 4 changing beers (sourced nationally) Ⓗ
Large open-plan pub near the village centre with a family-oriented emphasis. Part of Mitchells & Butlers Oak Tree pub chain, excellent-value food is served all day including meal deals and offers. The beer range includes two regulars plus four changing guests from the pubco's list. All major sports fixtures are shown on TV. Quiz night is Wednesday. The car park fee is refunded against purchases at the bar. A former local CAMRA Community Pub of the Year. ঌ ❀ ዬ ♠ P ➍ ☞

Daresbury

Ring o' Bells L ✅
Chester Road, WA4 4AJ (centre of village)
✪ 11.30-11 (10.30 Sun) ☎ (01925) 740256
⊕ ringobells-daresbury.co.uk
Greene King IPA; 4 changing beers (sourced locally; often Weetwood) Ⓗ
Once the village courthouse, this 19th-century pub retains many original features including a listed horse trough. Although food oriented, the Chef & Brewer pub has four handpumps usually serving local ales from breweries such as Weetwood and Spitting Feathers. The pub is close to All Saints

Church which was once officiated over by Rev Charles Dodgson, better known by his pen name Lewis Carroll. ⓢ☺◑&P⊒(X30)☻

Davenham

Davenham Cricket Club 🄻
Butchers' Stile, Hartford Road, CW9 8JG
☼ 4.30-8.30; 4-11 Fri & Sat ☎ (01606) 48922
⊕ davenham.play-cricket.com
4 changing beers (sourced locally; often Beartown, Brimstage, Mobberley) Ⓗ
This is a welcoming community club in an idyllic village setting. There is a newly refurbished main lounge and a sports bar. Four handpumps serve real ale mainly sourced from local breweries. Extensive seating in front of the pavilion makes this a perfect place to enjoy beer, cricket and the summer warmth. Other sporting groups also share the club facilities including table tennis, football and cycling. During the cricket season the opening hours are extended. ⓢ☺&P⊒☻♥

Disley

White Lion 🄻
135 Buxton Road, SK12 2HA (on A6 towards E end of village, near Bridge 26 of Peak Forest Canal)
☼ 12 (6.30 Mon)-11; 12-12.30am Fri & Sat
☎ (01663) 762800
9 changing beers (often Adnams, Ossett, Purity) Ⓗ
Originally the red house that gave the name to the adjacent side road, this multi award-winning pub is now painted white. Nine ever-changing real ales are on offer, many from micros and all selected from SIBA member breweries. The contemporary interior is open plan apart from a separate dog room. ☺◑P⊒(199)☻♥

Frodsham

Helter Skelter 🄻
31 Church Street, WA6 6PN
☼ 11-11.30 (midnight Fri & Sat); 12-11 Sun
☎ (01928) 733361 ⊕ thehelterskelter.net
Oakham Bishops Farewell; Salopian Oracle; Weetwood Bitter; 7 changing beers (sourced nationally; often Liverpool Organic, Ossett, Thornbridge) Ⓗ
A regular local CAMRA branch award winner, this single-room bar offers three regular cask ales alongside seven more handpumps serving a range of guest beers, mainly from local and national micros. Two rotating guest ciders and a selection of imported bottled beers are also available. The relaxed atmosphere attracts both locals and travellers. Excellent home-cooked food is served in the bar and upstairs restaurant. An informal folk band plays music upstairs on Sunday evenings. ◑�🍴⊒(48,X30)☻♥

Great Barrow

White Horse 🄻
Main Street, CH3 7HX (100yds E of B5132 in centre of village)
☼ 4-11.30 (12.30am Fri); 12-12.30am Sat; 12-11.30 Sun
☎ (01829) 741633 ⊕ whitehorsebarrow.co.uk
3 changing beers (sourced regionally; often Big Hand, Purple Moose, Weetwood) Ⓗ
Welcoming family-run village free house. The split-level interior has a small raised front room with a

pool table, dartboard and large-screen TV. The bar room has Indian stone flooring and a real fire. Outside, there is a small patio to the front and a beer garden to the rear. Up to three real ales are on handpump, regularly from local breweries. Pizzas are served Thursday and Friday evenings. Excellent accommodation is available with disabled facilities. BT Sport is on TV and occasional live music plays. ⓢ☺╱◑Å♣P☻♥

Higher Burwardsley

Pheasant Inn 🄻
Barracks Lane, CH3 9PF
☼ 11 (12 Sun)-11 ☎ (01829) 770434
⊕ thepheasantinn.co.uk
Weetwood Bitter; house beer (by Cheshire Brew Brothers); 2 changing beers (sourced locally; often Weetwood) Ⓗ
Charming 300-year-old inn nestled high in the Peckforton Hills with stunning views over the Cheshire plain to the Welsh hills. It is popular with walkers on the Sandstone Trail and visitors to the nearby candle workshops. Up to three changing beers are on offer plus a house beer from Cheshire Brew Brothers. High-quality food is served in both the bar and separate dining room. Accommodation is in 12 en-suite rooms. Well-behaved children and dogs are welcome. Qⓢ☺╱◑&P☻♥

Knutsford

Tap & Bottle 🍷 🄻
15 Minshull Street, WA16 6HG
☼ 3 (12 Fri & Sat)-midnight; 12-10.30 Sun
☎ (01565) 228269 ⊕ tapandbottle.co.uk
5 changing beers (sourced locally; often Tatton) Ⓗ
Independently owned bar offering six real ales in casks, one regularly from Tatton Brewery, with the others from nearby and further afield. There is an extensive range of bottled beers, usually including Belgian fruit beers and a few gluten-free ones. Mass branded products are avoided, even for spirits. The upstairs area is spacious, comfortable, light and airy, with a modern decor, while downstairs is more compact. ⇌●⊒☻♥

Little Bollington

Swan with Two Nicks 🄻 ✅
Park Lane, WA14 4TJ (signed off A56)
☼ 12-11 (10.30 Sun) ☎ (0161) 928 2914
⊕ swanwithtwonicks.co.uk
Black Sheep Best Bitter; Dunham Massey Big Tree Bitter; Timothy Taylor Landlord; house beer (by Coach House); 2 changing beers (sourced locally) Ⓗ
Large, traditional-style country pub popular with walkers and canal boaters. The house beer, Swan with Two Nicks, is typically accompanied by at least two local beers, often from Dunham Massey brewery, and two nationally sourced ales. There is a varied food offering available all day until 9pm (8pm Sun), served in the pub rooms and the restaurant, with gluten-free dishes on the menu. ⓢ☺◑P⊒(5,35)☻♥

Little Budworth

Egerton Arms 🍷 🄻 ✅
Pinfold Lane, CW6 9BS

✪ closed Mon (except bank hols); 3-11 Tue-Thu; 12-Midnight Fri & Sat; 12-11 Sun ☎ (01829) 760424
🌐 egerton-arms.co.uk
Thwaites Original; house beer (by Deva Craft); 5 changing beers (sourced locally; often Brimstage, Howard Town, Storm) Ⓗ
Unspoilt pub with friendly staff. In addition to the cask ales, a range of continental lagers and bottled world beers is available. The food range includes pub favourites, pizzas on Thursday and specials. Relax and warm yourself by the woodburner in winter and catch the sun watching cricket in the beer garden in summer. Regular live music, themed events and beer festivals are held. Local CAMRA Pub of the Year 2017. ⛵🕮🍴▲♣♥P🐾☀🛜

Little Neston

Harp Ⓛ ✅
19 Quayside, CH64 0TB (turn left at bottom of Marshlands Rd, pub is 300yds on left overlooking marshes)
✪ 12-midnight (12.30am Fri & Sat); 12-11 Sun
☎ (0151) 336 6980
Holt Bitter; Peerless Triple Blonde; Timothy Taylor Landlord; 2 changing beers (sourced nationally) Ⓗ
A former coal miners' inn converted from two cottages, it has a public bar with a real fire in winter and a basic lounge. It holds a popular curry night on Tuesday evenings. In a glorious location on the Deeside to Neston (NCN 568) part of the national cycle network, the pub overlooks the Dee Marshes and North Wales, with a garden and a drinking area abutting the edge of the marshes.
Q⛵🕮♣P🚆(22,487)🐾🛜

Lymm

Brewery Tap Ⓛ
18 Bridgewater Street, WA13 0AB (near canal)
✪ 12-11 (midnight Fri & Sat); 12-10.30 Sun
☎ (01925) 755451 🌐 lymmbrewing.co.uk
Lymm Bitter, Bridgewater Blonde; 5 changing beers (sourced locally; often Dunham Massey, Lymm) Ⓗ
In the red-brick former post office, its well-lit bar is complemented by a tastefully decorated front room with subdued lighting, comfy armchairs and a wood-fired stove. Five guest ales are often either from the microbrewery under the pub or nearby Dunham Massey, and one rotating real cider is available. Free newspapers are on offer.
⛵🕮&♣♥🚆🐾🛜

Bull's Head Ⓛ ✅
32 The Cross, WA13 0HU (in village centre)
✪ 12-midnight (1am Fri & Sat) ☎ (01925) 753614
Hydes Original, Lowry; 3 changing beers (sourced regionally) Ⓗ
Situated by the Bridgewater Canal next to the humpback bridge leading out of the village, this unspoilt pub with a thriving local trade is well worth a visit. A comfortable lounge, with real fire, is at the front, while the public bar is at the rear. Hydes Original Bitter is offered alongside Lowry, and three changing beers from the Hydes seasonal and Beer Studio ranges and the Hydes guest list.
⛵🕮♣🚆(5,35)🐾🛜

Macclesfield

Park Tavern Ⓛ ✅
158 Park Lane, SK11 6UB

✪ 4-11; 12-midnight Fri & Sat; 12-11 Sun ☎ (01625) 667846
🌐 park-tavern.co.uk
Bollington Long Hop, Best; 4 changing beers (sourced locally; often Bollington) Ⓗ
Bollington Brewery-owned community local close to the town centre. Guest beers and ciders are also available. It has an L-shaped main room and bar, a room downstairs and a function room upstairs which doubles as a small cinema showing a range of films for all ages. Quiz nights and SciBar science talks also feature regularly. Food is available Thursday to Saturday. ⛵🕮🍴➔♣♥🚆🐾🛜

RedWillow Ⓛ
32A Park Green, SK11 7NA
✪ closed Mon; 4-11 Tue & Wed (midnight Thu); 3-midnight Fri; 12-midnight Sat; 12-10.30 Sun ☎ (01625) 503253
🌐 redwillowbar.com
RedWillow Headless; 4 changing beers (sourced regionally) Ⓗ
Former shop, sensitively converted to a smart, open-plan town-centre bar with a wide range of locally brewed RedWillow beers, plus interesting guests from other UK microbreweries, a regularly changing real cider and a wide selection of gins. Food is in the form of cheese and charcuterie boards and pizza. ⛵🕮&➔♥🚆🐾🛜

Treacle Tap Ⓛ
43 Sunderland Street, SK11 6JL
✪ 4-11; 12-midnight Fri & Sat; 12-11 Sun ☎ (01625) 615938
🌐 thetreacletap.co.uk
3 changing beers (sourced locally) Ⓗ
Small, welcoming, stylish bar where three handpumps serve a range of cask beers plus a selection of bottled beers from around the world. Despite its small size, this is a very active community pub, home to local clubs and special interest groups. Food is served every day, including the renowned locally made pies. Q⛵🕮➔🚆🐾🛜

Waters Green Tavern Ⓛ
96 Waters Green, SK11 6LH (close to town centre)
✪ 12-3, 5-11; 12-4, 7-11 Sat; 12-4, 7-10.30 Sun
☎ (01625) 422653
7 changing beers (sourced regionally; often Abbeydale, Elland, Acorn) Ⓗ
Celebrating over 20 consecutive years in the Guide, this superbly run free house has up to seven changing beers and is also a CAMRA award-winning real cider pub. A friendly, traditional community inn, it has an open-plan interior with two distinct seating areas and a separate room with a pool table. Good-value home-cooked food is served every lunchtime except Sunday. Ideally placed for train and bus stations.
⛵🕮➔♣♥🚆🐾🛜

Wharf Ⓛ
107 Brook Street, SK11 7AW
✪ 4 (12 Mon)-11.30; 12-midnight Fri & Sat; 12-11.30 Sun
☎ (01625) 261879 🌐 thewharfmacc.co.uk
Everards Tiger; 4 changing beers (sourced locally; often Pictish) Ⓗ
A former Cheshire CAMRA Pub of the Year, this popular traditional venue offers a warm welcome to all. The open bar area serves a range of traditional cask ales. It has a pool table and a cosy snug with a stove, books and games. A rare remaining example of a wet-led community local, with pub games teams and regular music at the weekends, it is well worth the trip up the hill from the town centre. ⛵🕮➔♣♥🚆(1,58)🐾🛜

Marston

Salt Barge ⓛ
Ollershaw Lane, CW9 6ES (opp Lion Salt Works)
☼ 12-3, 5-11; 12-11 Thu; 12-midnight Fri; 12-11.30 Sat; 12-11 Sun ☎ (01606) 43064 ⊕ thesaltbargemarston.co.uk
Tatton Best; 2 changing beers (sourced locally) Ⓗ
Multi-roomed pub built in 1861 offering a friendly welcome to all, with a focus on local ales and ciders and home-cooked food. Quiz nights are monthly and music events every other Friday. The pub is popular with walkers, situated near Marbury country park, as well as the Trent and Mersey Canal and not far from the Anderton Boat Lift.
ᵜ⚅🛏️◑ᵔ♣🐾P🐾🐾

Middlewich

White Bear Hotel ⓛ
Wheelock Street, CW10 9AG (close to church and canal)
☼ 11-11 (midnight Fri & Sat); 12-10.30 Sun
☎ (01606) 837666 ⊕ thewhitebearmiddlewich.co.uk
4 changing beers (sourced locally) Ⓗ
Free house dating from 1625, with a rotating range of four real ales and a traditional cider on handpull. The licensee supports the LocAle scheme and sources unusual micro-beers. This is welcoming pub both for locals and visitors. There are four distinct drinking areas, all very comfortably furnished. Excellent, good-value food is served in the restaurant. Real ale is discounted on Monday nights from 5pm. ᵜ⚅🛏️◑ᵔP🚌(37,42)🐾🐾

Mobberley

Bull's Head ⓛ ✓
Mill Lane, WA16 7HX
☼ 12-10.30 (midnight Fri & Sat) ☎ (01565) 873395
⊕ thebullsheadpub.co.uk
Weetwood Cheshire Cat; 7 changing beers (sourced regionally) Ⓗ
Excellent country inn with cobbles outside, three open fires, stone floor, candlelit tables, low beams, exposed brick and an old back-to-back fireplace. Food and beer are often sourced locally, with the house beer supplied by Weetwood. Each beer has tasting notes and tasters are available in tiny pots. Dogs are welcome in the snug.
ᵜ⚅◑ᵔ♣P🚌(88)🐾🐾

Moulton

Lion Hotel ⓛ
74 Main Road, CW9 8PB
☼ 5-11; 4-midnight Fri; 2-midnight Sat; 2-10.30 Sun
☎ (01606) 606049
Wychwood Hobgoblin; 4 changing beers (sourced locally; often Cheshire Brewhouse, RedWillow, Tatton) Ⓗ
A welcoming community focused pub and former local CAMRA Pub of the Year. Located in the centre of the village, six handpumps dispense quality ales and ciders mainly from local breweries. Quiz nights and themed music events are always very popular. A complementary cheeseboard is offered on Friday evening. A beer garden to the side and decking to the front enable customers to take advantage of the warm summer months. ᵜ⚅🅰️♣P🚌🐾🐾

Nantwich

Vine Inn ✓
42 Hospital Street, CW5 5RP (near St Mary's Church)
☼ 12 (11.30 Sat)-midnight ☎ (01270) 619055
⊕ vineinnnantwich.co.uk
Hydes Original; 3 changing beers Ⓗ
Traditional 17th-century building with its ground floor below street level, open plan with three distinct levels rising towards the rear of the pub. Refurbished in 2015, it now serves good-value food until 8pm. Beers are from the Hydes range, including the Beer Studio, plus two guest ales sourced nationally. Ales are discounted on Mondays. Silent Sky Sports and BT Sport are screened. ᵜ⚅◑⚲♣🚌(84)🐾🐾

Penketh

Ferry Tavern
Station Road, WA5 2UJ (near yacht marina)
☼ 5.30-10 Mon; 12-3, 5.30-11 (midnight Fri); 12-midnight Sat; 12-10.30 Sun ☎ (01925) 791117 ⊕ theferrytavern.com
Jennings Cumberland Ale; 5 changing beers (sourced nationally) Ⓗ
The ancient Ferry Tavern is a thriving community pub as well as a picturesque venue between the Mersey and the St Helens Canal. The large beer garden is a welcome stop-off for cyclists and walkers enjoying the Transpennine Trail. One regular beer is complemented by up to five guests from far and wide. There is an historic selection of pictures of the local area including the seven floods that have engulfed the pub. ᵜ⚅◑ᵔP🚌(32)🐾🐾

Poynton

Cask Tavern ⓛ
42 Park Lane, SK12 1RE
☼ 4-11; 12-midnight Fri & Sat; 12-10.30 Sun
☎ (01625) 875157 ⊕ casktavern.co.uk
Bollington Long Hop, Best, Dinner Ale, Eastern Nights; 2 changing beers (sourced regionally) Ⓗ
One of three Bollington Brewery taps in Cheshire. It is a mecca for real ale drinkers with national brands conspicuous by their absence. The one-roomed pub has comfortable seating areas including two outside. A regular clientele has developed but a warm welcome is assured to all visitors.
Q⚅ᵔ♣🐾🐾🐾

Runcorn

Ferry Boat ✓
10 Church Street, WA7 1LR
☼ 8am-midnight (1am Fri & Sat) ☎ (01928) 583380
Greene King Abbot; Ruddles Best Bitter; Sharp's Doom Bar Ⓗ; **2 changing beers** Ⓗ/Ⓖ
Large, busy Wetherspoon venue on a corner plot in the town centre. The pub has a community focus and a changing clientele, from diners to office workers to those on a night out. It is also frequented by shoppers and visitors to the Brindley Theatre. The dining area is to the rear. The pub's name derives from the town's maritime heritage, with the Mersey, Manchester Ship Canal and Bridgwater Canal nearby. ᵜ⚅◑ᵔ⚲♣P🚌🐾

Norton Arms
125-127 Main Street, WA7 2AD
☼ 12-11 (midnight Fri & Sat); 12-10.30 Sun
☎ (01928) 567642 ⊕ thenortonarms.co.uk

4 changing beers (sourced nationally) ⊞
Another year in the Guide for this two-roomed, Grade II-listed, oak-beamed pub in the centre of Halton village. Although dominated by football on three TV screens, this hostelry is still a nice find and it can get very busy at weekends. Ales are on four handpumps, with third-pint taster glasses available. Due to the age of the pub, disabled access is difficult – the door is up a flight of stone steps. Quiz nights, live music and open mic nights are hosted. ⏰❀◖◗ᕼ♣ᕒ🖵🐾🛜

Prospect 🛴
70 Weston Road, WA7 4LD
✪ 12-11 (10.30 Sun) ☎ (01928) 561280
⊕ folkattheprospect.co.uk
Adnams Broadside; Timothy Taylor Landlord; 2 changing beers ⊞
This traditional inn has ale on three handpumps plus one dedicated to cider. The lounge is decorated with local memorabilia and warmed by a real fire. The pub prides itself on sourcing local produce for its home-cooked meals and commits to local businesses whenever possible. Situated high above the Rivers Mersey and Weaver, it has views reaching from Liverpool to North Wales. A winner of numerous awards including local CAMRA Pub of the Year 2015. ⏰❀◖◗ᕼ♣🖵🐾

Royal Oak
Lambsickle Lane, WA7 4QZ
✪ 11.30 (11 Sun)-11 ☎ (01928) 580908
Wychwood Hobgoblin ⊞**; 2 changing beers** Ⓐ
Refurbished in 2016, the pub offers a clean, balanced decor that is easy on the eye, with a comfortable drinking atmosphere. It has two changing beers on draught and one regular draught cider. The imaginative jukebox provides separate music levels in three discrete areas. There is a pool table. Food is served 2-9pm Tuesday to Friday and all day Sunday. The pub has a positive, upbeat feel. ⏰❀♣🖵🐾

Sandbach
Beer Emporium 🛴
8 Welles Street, CW11 1GT (off Hightown roundabout, down one-way street)
✪ 12-8 (10 Thu-Sat) ☎ (01270) 760113
⊕ thebeeremporium.com
Merlin Dark Magic; 4 changing beers ⊞
This former butcher's shop has been transformed into a thriving micropub. It started up as a bottle shop and has a vast range of British and European beers. Five handpumps have been added, dispensing a revolving range from small breweries, one usually from Merlin plus regulars from Oakham, Hawkshead and Vocation. There is seating in the front window and a small rear room. The pub's choir is the only source of music, with friendly conversation the order of the day.
Q⏰🖵(37,38)🐾🛜

Stockton Heath
Costello's Bar 🛴
23 Walton Road, WA4 6NJ
✪ 12-11 (midnight Fri & Sat); 12-10.30 Sun
☎ (01925) 600910 ⊕ costellosbar.co.uk
Dunham Massey Big Tree Bitter; Lymm Bridgewater Blonde; 5 changing beers (sourced locally; often Dunham Massey, Lymm) ⊞

Friendly real ale bar owned and run by Dunham Massey Brewing. There are seven handpumps for cask ale, five beers on rotation and two mainstays. One or more dark beer, mild and strong ale are always among the range. All cask ale is provided by Dunham Massey and Lymm Brewing. Real cider is also always offered. ⏰❀◖♣🖵🐾🛜

Thelwall
Little Manor 🛴
Bell Lane, WA4 2SX
✪ 10.30-11 (10.30 Sun) ☎ (01925) 212070
⊕ littlemanor-thelwall.co.uk
Coach House Cromwells Best Bitter; house beer (by Phoenix); 6 changing beers (sourced locally) ⊞
A large upmarket food-based pub with an interesting and changing range of local cask ales. The pub is tastefully furnished and has attractive garden areas for dining alfresco in the summer. The building has graced Thelwall since 1660 and the pub sign uses the crest of the Percival family, the original owners. Q⏰❀◖◗ᕼ♣🖵(5,6)🐾🛜

Warrington
Looking Glass 🛴 ✅
41-43 Buttermarket Street, WA1 2LY
✪ 8am-midnight (1am Fri & Sat) ☎ (01925) 405030
Greene King Abbot; Ruddles Best Bitter; Sharp's Doom Bar; Theakston Old Peculier; house beer (by Coach House); 5 changing beers (sourced nationally; often Kelham Island, Peerless, Thornbridge) ⊞
Located on the edge of the town centre and originally converted from a cinema, this Wetherspoon pub is on two levels with a small bar upstairs. There is always an interesting selection of guest ales. Jabberwocky is brewed for the pub by local brewery Coach House. The patio area in front opens out onto the pedestrianised town centre. Guest ales often include high ABV beers sourced nationally. Q⏰❀◖◗ᕼ⇄🖵🛜

Lower Angel 🛴
27 Buttermarket Street, WA1 2LY (in pedestrianised town centre)
✪ 11-11 (midnight Sat); 12-10 Sun ☎ (01925) 653326
Weetwood Bitter; 6 changing beers (sourced nationally) ⊞
Enjoy a step back in time here, with a traditional vault and lounge layout and sheltered beer garden. Memorabilia from the former Walker's Brewery and stained-glass windows remain. The summer room to the rear is adorned with hundreds of pumpclips. The pub supports local charities and a visit at Halloween or Christmas is a must to see the decorations. The six changing beers are mainly from independent breweries. ❀⇄♣🖵🐾🛜

Tavern 🛴
25 Church Street, WA1 2SS
✪ 12 (4 Mon & Tue; 3 Wed & Thu)-midnight ☎ 07747 668817
4T's Pale Ale; 8 changing beers (sourced nationally) ⊞
A popular sports bar on the edge of the town centre. The brewery tap for 4T's, it serves up to four of the brewery's beers plus up to four guests generally from micros around the country. Three or four mini beer festivals are held throughout the year. Very busy when Rugby League is showing on TV or when Warrington Wolves are at home. ❀⇄♣🖵🐾🛜

Westbrook

Seven Woods
Westbrook Crescent, WA5 8TE
🌓 11-11 (midnight Fri & Sat); 12-11 Sun ☎ (01925) 241036
🌐 sevenwoodspub.co.uk
Wychwood Hobgoblin; 5 changing beers (sourced
nationally; often Brakspear, Jennings, Ringwood) Ⓗ
Single-room, new-town pub with a focus on food.
There are large gardens at the rear with a
children's play area and an enclosed smoking area
at the front. Poker night is Tuesday and quiz night
Sunday. Occasional live entertainment is hosted on
a Saturday evening. One regular and up to five
changing beers from the Marston's group are
available. 🎴🐾🅿️🖐️🅿️🚌(17,18)🛜

Willey Moor Lock

Willey Moor Lock Tavern
Tarporley Road, SY13 4HF (400yds off A49, around 1½
miles N of Whitchurch)
🌓 12-2.30, 6-10.30; 12-3, 6-11 Sat; 12-3, 6-10.30 Sun
☎ (01948) 663274 🌐 willeymoorlock.co.uk
6 changing beers (sourced nationally) Ⓗ
This family-run free house is a former lock-keeper's
cottage, reached from the car park by a footbridge
over the Llangollen Canal. The pub is popular with
boaters and walkers on the Sandstone Trail,
especially in summer. Good-value meals are
served lunchtimes and evenings. Three changing
beers, many from local brewers, increase to six in
summer. Outside seating is available by the canal
and in the attractive beer garden. There is a
campsite close by. Q🎴🐾🅿️🖐️AP🐾🛜

Wilmslow

Coach & Four Ⓛ ✅
69-71 Alderley Road, SK9 1PA
🌓 11.30-11 (midnight Thu-Sat); 12-11 Sun
☎ (01625) 525046 🌐 thecoachandfour.co.uk
Hydes Original, 1863, Lowry; 3 changing beers
(sourced locally; often Hydes) Ⓗ
Large, comfortable old coaching house close to the
centre of Wilmslow, catering to a wide clientele.
The spacious single room is divided into secluded
alcoves, with a separate restaurant. Three Hydes
and Beer Studio beers are available plus one or two
rotating guests and a real cider. Food is served all
day in both the restaurant and bar area. Quiz
nights, music and comedy all feature, as well as
charity and community events. There is a covered
and heated patio for smokers and lodge-style
accommodation.
🎴🐾🅿️🖐️🐾🖐️🅿️🚌(130,88)🐾🛜

Old Dancer Ⓛ
16 Grove Street, SK9 1DR (on pedestrianised shopping
street)
🌓 12-midnight (1am Fri & Sat) ☎ (01625) 530775
🌐 theolddancer.co.uk
5 changing beers (sourced locally) Ⓗ
Lively café-bar furnished mainly with simple
wooden tables set on boarded floors. The walls are
decorated with striking hand-painted murals with a
dance theme. Six handpumps serve an interesting
range of beers including LocAles and a cask cider.
Tea, coffee and food are available until 10pm
including snacks, cakes and a selection of award-
winning pies. The bar hosts weekly live music, film,
science and quiz nights, and a writers' group and
book club. 🎴🐾🅿️🖐️🐾🖐️🅿️🐾🛜

Winsford

No.4 Bar
Over Square, CW7 2LS (on roundabout at S end of
Delamere St)
🌓 12-midnight Fri & Sat; 12-11 Sun ☎ (01606) 550835
🌐 no4pub.com
4 changing beers (sourced regionally) Ⓗ
A unique bar in Winsford, No.4 prides itself on its
four ever-changing cask beers sourced from
regional and microbreweries throughout the
country. Victorian awnings to the front provide
shelter over an outside area that is popular all year.
An upstairs seating area offers a quieter
environment when occasional live music plays
downstairs. Mirrors, lighting and background music
enhance a pleasant atmosphere. Complementary
bar snacks are available for both customers and
dogs on request. 🐾🖐️🅿️(31,31A)🐾🛜

Queen's Arms ✅
Dene Drive, CW7 1AT (opp Winsford Cross shopping
centre)
🌓 8am-midnight (1am Fri & Sat); 9am-11 Sun
☎ (01606) 595350
Greene King Abbot; Ruddles Best Bitter; 4 changing
beers (sourced regionally) Ⓗ
Open-plan Wetherspoon pub in the town centre,
with muted TV screens at both ends. The pub has a
large number of local regulars and can get very
busy. The patio area with decking out front proves
popular in summer. As well as the Wetherspoon
national beer festivals, Queen's hosts monthly
Meet the Brewer sessions and an annual Battle of
the Brewers challenge. A good range of ever-
changing beers is on offer, both local and national.
Close to a bus stop and taxi rank.
Q🎴🐾🅿️🖐️🅿️🚌(31,31A)🛜

Ale conner

The official ale-tester wore leather breeches. He would enter an inn without warning,
draw a glass of ale, pour it on a wooden bench, and then sit down in the puddle he had
made. He would sit for half an hour and would not change his position. At the end of the
half hour, he would make as if to rise, and this was the test of the ale; for if the ale was
impure, if it had sugar in it, the tester's leather breeches would stick fast to the bench, but
if there was no sugar in the liquor, no impression would be present – in other words, the
tester would not stick to the seat.

**17th-century description of the work of the ale conner, a public official who
inspected inns, taverns and ale houses to test the quality of the beer. William
Shakespeare's father was an ale conner**

CORNWALL

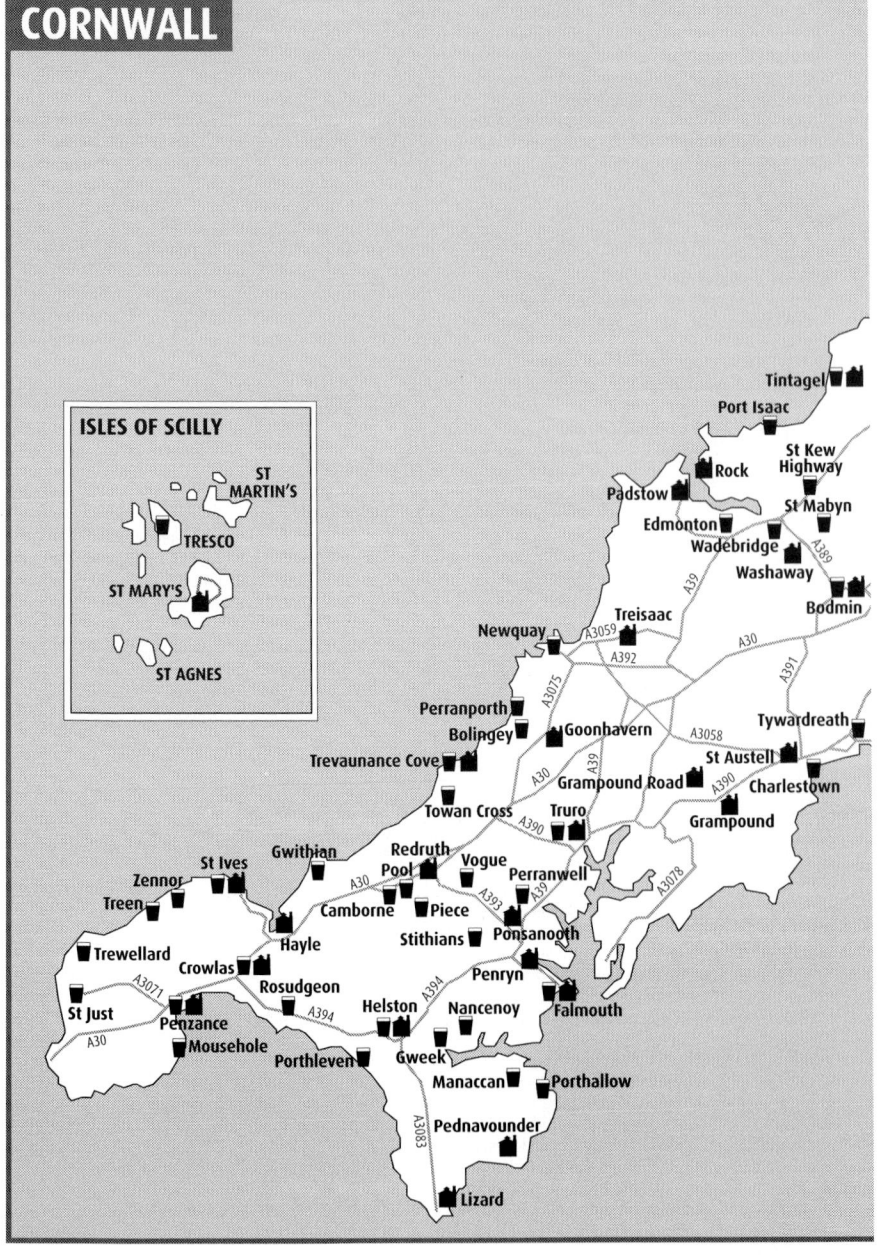

ISLES OF SCILLY

ST MARTIN'S

TRESCO

ST MARY'S

ST AGNES

Tintagel
Port Isaac
St Kew Highway
Rock
Padstow
Edmonton
Wadebridge
Washaway
Bodmin
St Mabyn
Treisaac
Newquay
A3059
A392
A30
A391
A39
A388
Perranporth
Bolingey
Goonhavern
A3058
Tywardreath
Trevaunance Cove
St Austell
Charlestown
Towan Cross
Grampound Road
Truro
Grampound
A30
A39
A390
A3075
A3078
Gwithian
Redruth
Vogue
St Ives
Pool
Perranwell
Zennor
Camborne
Piece
A30
A393
A39
Treen
Stithians
Ponsanooth
Trewellard
Hayle
Crowlas
Penryn
Rosudgeon
A3071
St Just
Helston
Nancenoy
Falmouth
Penzance
A394
A394
Mousehole
Porthleven
Gweek
Manaccan
Porthallow
A30
Pednavounder
A3083
Lizard

Bodmin

Chapel an Gansblydhen ⬡ ✅

Fore Street, PL31 2HR (near top of main street)

🕐 9am-midnight; 9am-10.30 Sun ☎ (01208) 261730

Greene King Abbot; Ruddles Best Bitter; Sharp's Doom Bar; 4 changing beers (often Cornish Crown, Harbour, Tintagel) Ⓗ

This busy town-centre pub has been beautifully converted from a former Methodist chapel, with many original features restored or retained. Seven real ales are on offer, several from Cornish microbreweries, with two draught ciders also

available. The pub supports the popular CAMRA pub guide that covers the Bodmin district, and outings to local breweries are run from time to time. Two beer festivals and a real cider festival are held annually, and a quiz night each Sunday.
Q ☸ 🐕 ◗ Å ♣ ♠ ➡ 🛜

Hole in the Wall ⬡ ✅

16 Crockwell Street, PL31 2DS (entrance from town car park)

🕐 12-11; 12-10.30 Sun ☎ (01208) 72397

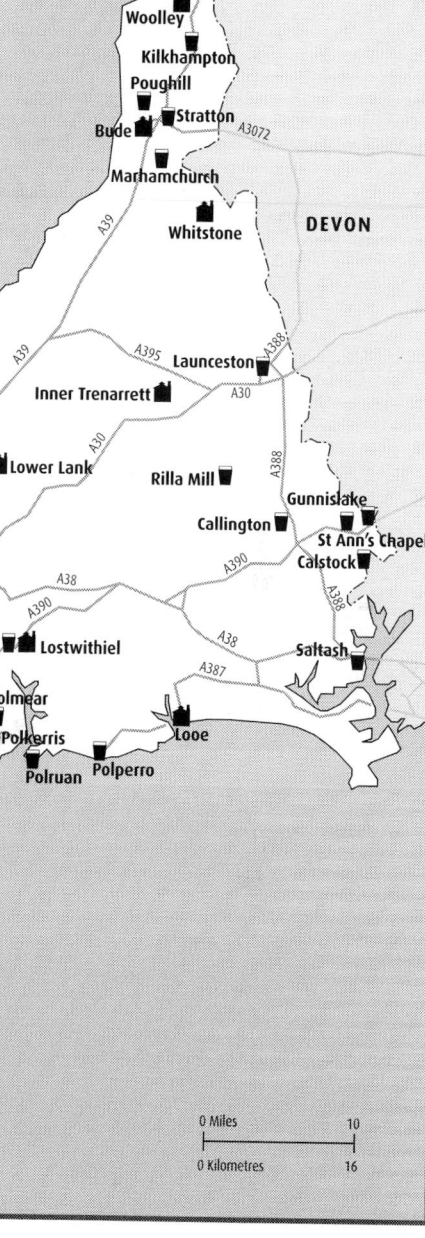

Bolingey

Bolingey Inn L ✓
Penwartha Road, TR6 0DH (near B3284) SW763531
🕐 11-midnight; 12-11 Sun ☎ (01872) 571626
Sharp's Doom Bar; 3 changing beers (sourced nationally; often Greene King, St Austell, Wadworth) Ⓗ
Tucked away in a small hamlet, this quaint 17th-century pub is reached by narrow, hilly lanes. Small but attractive, it has limited parking – but is equipped with a hitching rail for horses. The regular beer is supplemented by up to three regularly varying brews from the Punch Taverns lists. The bar area has a wooden floor and an open fire; a separate restaurant offers locally sourced food, proudly advertised. Music events and twice-yearly 'bangers and ale' festivals are held.
Q☆🏠🛢️Å♣🅿️🐾🛜

Callington

Bull's Head
38 Fore Street, PL17 7AQ
🕐 10.30-midnight; 11-11 Sun ☎ (01579) 383387
🌐 thebullsheadatcallington.co.uk
Sharp's Doom Bar; 3 changing beers (sourced locally; often Dartmoor, St Austell) Ⓗ
Friendly and sociable locals' drinking house dating from the 15th century. The comfortable lounge has a vast stone fireplace, low oak beams, latticed windows and a profusion of brass. The pub supports darts teams and there is live music every Friday. Meals are to a traditional pub food format and home cooked – a barbecue may be held outside in the summer months. Occasional beer festivals are hosted. There is disabled access and nappy-changing facilities. Parking is limited.
☆🏠🛢️♿♣🍴🅿️🚌🐾🛜

Calstock

Tamar Inn ✓
The Quay, PL18 9QA SX436686
🕐 12-midnight summer; 12-2.30, 4.30-11; 12-midnight Fri & Sat; 12-10.30 Sun winter ☎ (01822) 832487
Sharp's Doom Bar; 4 changing beers (sourced regionally; often Exeter, Tintagel) Ⓗ
Split-level village pub beside the River Tamar, built in granite and other materials. The beamed interior is divided into distinct drinking areas with well-worn floorboards and slate flagstones underfoot, and decorated with a few framed paintings. A small bookshelf provides an additional service for the locals. The rear bar is airy and leads to the courtyard. Beers are usually from Cornwall and Devon, the cider is Westons Old Rosie. Live entertainment plays on Friday or Saturday evenings. ☆🏠🛢️Å⇄♣🍴🚌(79)🐾

Camborne

John Francis Basset ✓
21 Commercial Street, TR14 8JZ
🕐 9am-midnight (1am Fri & Sat) ☎ (01209) 721720
Greene King Abbot; Ruddles Best Bitter; Sharp's Doom Bar; 5 changing beers Ⓗ
This Wetherspoon pub in the town centre is in the former market house built by architect William Bond in 1866. Previous uses of the building have included a cinema, night club and pub, the Corn Exchange. Named after a prominent former mine

Dartmoor Jail Ale; Draught Bass; Sharp's Doom Bar; 2 changing beers (sourced nationally; often Butcombe) Ⓗ
Popular locals' pub built in the 18th century as a debtors' prison. The building can be accessed directly from the public car park or through a secluded, leafy garden containing its own hop bine and stream, and presided over by a bleached stuffed lion. The single bar, which is subdivided by archways, displays a large and eclectic collection of antiques and military memorabilia. Upstairs is a separate function room. Cornwall CAMRA Pub of the Year 2015 and 2016. Q☆🏠🛢️♿⇄♣🍴🚌🐾🛜

owner, it is a large, airy, open-plan venue with high ceilings, tall windows and a single long bar. It offers an impressive selection of guest beers and a wide variety of meals served all day 7am-11pm. Q☺❄🍴◖◗&🚲🚪🛲📶

Charlestown

Rashleigh Arms ✿
Quay Road, PL25 3NX
🕐 11-11 (midnight Fri & Sat) ☎ (01726) 73635
🌐 rashleigharms.co.uk
Bath Ales Gem; St Austell Tribute, Proper Job; Skinner's Betty Stogs; 4 changing beers (sourced locally; often St Austell) ⊞
Near the South-West Coast Path, this large, welcoming inn comprises two spacious comfortable bars and a restaurant, with a patio for alfresco dining and drinking. The pub hosts live music including jazz a couple of times a month, and offers eight en-suite bedrooms with further accommodation nearby. Charlestown is a historic port, a popular location with film-makers, often with large sailing ships in the harbour. The pub car park has the only Grade I listed cobbles in Britain.
☺❄🍴◖◗&🅿🚪(24,25)♥📶

Crowlas

Star Inn 🅛
TR20 8DX (on A30, 3 miles E of Penzance)
🕐 11.30-11; 12-10.30 Sun ☎ (01736) 740375
Penzance Mild, Crowlas Bitter, Potion No.9; 4 changing beers (sourced nationally; often Coastal) ⊞
Roadside free house and former Cornwall CAMRA Pub of the Year, home to the Penzance Brewery. The long U-shaped bar features real ales from the pub's own brewhouse and two or three from other microbreweries. There is a pool table to the right, a comfy raised seating area, a cosy lounge area with leather sofas and chairs, and an adjacent meeting room. This is essentially a beer-drinkers' local where conversation is the main entertainment, with no noisy machines to distract. ❄♣♠🅿🚪♥

Edmonton

Quarryman Inn 🅛
PL27 7JA (just off A39 near Royal Cornwall showground)
🕐 12-11; 12-10.30 Sun ☎ (01208) 816444
🌐 thequarryman.co.uk
Otter Bitter; 3 changing beers (sourced regionally; often Padstow, Skinner's) ⊞
A diversion to this ever-popular gem rewards the effort. Frequented by locals and tourists alike, conversation and banter thrive in this characterful and convivial free house, where mobile phone use is prohibited. The quiet, comfortable interior divides into a public bar and a large lounge with dining area, local art featuring among the somewhat eclectic decor. The changing beer menu offers up to four ales, and the pub is known for quality food. Q☺❄◖◗🅿🚪(11A,95)♥📶

Falmouth

'Front 🅛
Custom House Quay, TR11 3JT
🕐 11-11 (midnight Fri & Sat); 11-10.30 Sun ☎ 07977 813494
Sharp's Special; 9 changing beers (sourced regionally; often Atlantic, Skinner's, Tintagel) ⊞

A warm welcome awaits at this quayside cellar-style bar. Friendly, knowledgeable staff are on hand to serve from 14 handpumps arranged along the bar, 10 dedicated to real ales and four to ciders. Cornish breweries are well represented, and there are regular brewery showcase sessions which can be local or regional. A popular Sunday quiz is hosted and other evening entertainment. No food is available but you may bring your own. The pub offers a 10 per cent discount on real ales and ciders before 6pm. Q☺❄&🚲♥🐾♥

Beerwolf Books
3-4 Bells Court, TR11 3AZ (up a side alley off main street)
🕐 10-midnight; 12-11 Sun ☎ (01326) 618474
🌐 beerwolfbooks.com
7 changing beers (sourced nationally; often Marble, Penzance, Shiny) ⊞
Pub or bookshop? Actually, it is both. Popular with all ages, this former maritime storage loft and pleasant outside courtyard is tucked away off Market Street. It is accessed via a steep flight of stairs – at the top is the bookshop, to the right is the bar with seven handpumps dispensing an adventurous selection of constantly changing beers. Four more handpumps ensure that cider lovers are not forgotten. There is no food, but you may bring your own. Q☺❄♣♥🚪♥📶

Boathouse 🅛
Trevethan Hill, TR11 2AG (top of High St)
🕐 12-11 (midnight Fri & Sat) summer; 4-11; 12-midnight Fri & Sat; 12-11 Sun winter ☎ (01326) 315425
🌐 theboathousefalmouth.co.uk

REAL ALE BREWERIES

Ales of Scilly St Mary's: Isles of Scilly
Altarnun Inner Trenarrett
Atlantic Treisaac
Black Flag Goonhavern
Black Rock Falmouth
Blue Anchor ❸ Helston
Bude Bude
Castle Lostwithiel
Coastal Redruth
Cornish Chough Lizard
Cornish Crown Penzance
Dowr Kammel Lower Lank (NEW)
Driftwood ❸ Trevaunance Cove
Dynamite Valley Ponsanooth
Fish Key Looe
Forge Woolley
Fowey Lostwithiel (NEW)
Granite Rock Penryn
Harbour Bodmin
Keltek Redruth
Leafy Hollow Washaway
Lizard Ales Pednavounder
Longhill Whitstone
Padstow Padstow
Paradise ❸ Hayle
Penzance ❸ Crowlas
Rebel Penryn
Sharp's Rock
Skinner's Truro
St Austell St Austell
St Ives St Ives
Tintagel Tintagel
Tremethick Grampound
Wooden Hand Grampound Road
Woodman's Ponsanooth (NEW)

4 changing beers (sourced regionally; often Black Rock, Skinner's) H
This two-storey pub can be found up a short but steep hill on the edge of the town centre. The interior is modern, with distinct drinking and dining areas. The upstairs bar and decked drinking balcony afford spectacular views across the river towards Flushing. Four handpumps dispense regularly changing regional and local brews, often including a Black Rock Brewery beer. Food is locally sourced where possible and freshly cooked (booking advisable for the popular Sunday lunch).
🛇🌑◑♣●🖵🐾🛜

Seven Stars ★ 🅛
The Moor, TR11 3QA
🕒 11-11; 12-10.30 Sun ☎ (01326) 312111
Draught Bass; Sharp's Atlantic, Special; 2 changing beers (sourced locally) G
This timeless and unspoilt town-centre local has been in the same family for 165 years and features on CAMRA's National Inventory of Historic Pub Interiors. It has a lively narrow taproom and a quiet snug at the back. The old bottle and jug hatch is still in use for outdoor drinkers. Beers are served on gravity from a unique, eccentrically designed stillage. Bass is ever-present, as are beers from Sharp's Brewery. A real gem not to be missed.
Q🛇🌑●🖵🐾🛜

Gunnislake

Rising Sun Inn
Calstock Road, PL18 9BX (off A390) SX432711
🕒 12-11 (midnight Fri & Sat) ☎ (01822) 832201
🌐 rising-sun-inn.co.uk
Dartmoor Jail Ale; 5 changing beers (sourced regionally) H
Friendly, oak-beamed country inn dating from the 17th century, lying in a conservation area in a rural setting off the beaten track. It has much charm and character, with exposed stone walls and wooden beams home to an extensive display of chinaware. A good choice of up to six ever-changing real ales is served, usually from Cornish or other West-Country breweries. The beautiful terraced garden affords views of the Tamar Valley. Food is available daily (except Mon and Tue in winter).
Q🛇🌑◑➥♣●P🖵(79)🐾🛜

Gweek

Black Swan ✅
TR12 6TU
🕒 11-11 (midnight Fri & Sat); 12-11.30 Sun
☎ (01326) 221502 🌐 blackswangweek.co.uk
Draught Bass; St Austell Tribute; Sharp's Doom Bar; Skinner's Betty Stogs, Lushingtons; 2 changing beers (sourced locally) H
Welcoming and lively pub situated in an old port on the Helford River. The interior walls are half clad with wood, with exposed stonework above; an airy slate-floored dining room adjoins up a few steps. The bar is furnished with ample seating and warmed by a stove in winter, a bay window affords views to the harbour. The rightward end of the bar room hosts a pool table. Parking is up a flight of steps to the rear. 🛇🌑🚲◑♣●P🖵(35)🐾🛜

Gwithian

Red River Inn 🅛
1 Prosper Hill, TR27 5BW
🕒 12-11 summer; closed Mon; 12-2, 5.30-11; 12-11 Sat & Sun winter ☎ (01736) 753223 🌐 red-river-inn.com
Sharp's Sea Fury; 4 changing beers (sourced locally) H
This popular, community-oriented free house, where the ambience is quiet and relaxing and conversation and banter thrive, is well worth seeking out. Close to Gwithian Towans (sand dunes), it gets its name from the nearby river. Wood furnishings dominate an attractive single bar which accommodates both drinking and dining, a wood-burning stove adding winter warmth. The ever-changing beer menu offers up to five beers, generally Cornish. Meals using local produce are served daily. Live music is hosted each Saturday evening. Q🛇🌑◑&🖵A♣P🖵(515,57)🐾🛜

Helston

Blue Anchor
50 Coinagehall Street, TR13 8EL
🕒 10-midnight (1am Fri & Sat) ☎ (01326) 562821
🌐 spingoales.com
Blue Anchor Jubilee IPA, Middle H, Special H/G
A former monks' rest, this 15th-century brewpub is one of the oldest in Britain, changing little over the years and retaining much of its original character. Two small bars are to the right of the central passageway, one with an open fire, and two sitting rooms to the left, all with slate floors. To the rear are a skittle alley and partly covered garden area with a separate bar and barbecue. An anchor is visible on the thatched roof. Q🛇🌑🚲♣●🖵🐾

Coinage Hall ✅
9-11 Coinagehall Street, TR13 8ER
🕒 8am-midnight (1am Fri & Sat) ☎ (01326) 565344
Ruddles Best Bitter; Sharp's Doom Bar; 4 changing beers (sourced regionally; often St Ives, Skinner's) H
This pub in a former furniture store takes its name from when locally mined tin was assayed in the coinage hall. Surprisingly large and deep inside, it spans four separate levels, with steps between them and a number of distinct drinking and dining spaces throughout. The single long bar usually offers up to four changing local microbrewery beers. The lowest level at the rear leads out to a patio for outside drinking. There is also a roof terrace. Q🛇🌑◑&●🖵🐾🛜

Kilkhampton

New Inn
EX23 9QN
🕒 11-11 (midnight Fri & Sat); 12-11.30 Sun
☎ (01288) 321488 🌐 newinncornwall.com
Sharp's Original; 2 changing beers (sourced regionally) H
Spacious 15th-century village pub on three levels – a quiet front bar where conversation dominates, a busy middle bar with dartboard and TV, and an old skittle alley deep in the back. The interior makes extensive use of recycled materials and is furnished with wooden tables, settles and other pew-style seating. The bar itself is constructed of old bricks and timber beams with a polished wooden top. The changing beers are usually from Devon, cider is sourced from all over.
Q🛇🌑🚲◑A♣●P🖵🛜

Launceston

Bell Inn
1 Tower Street, PL15 8BQ
✿ 12-11; 12-10.30 Sun ☎ (01566) 779970
6 changing beers Ⓗ
Cosy 14th-century town pub originally built to house stonemasons erecting the nearby church. Conversation rules at this locals' pub, which offers an ever-changing range of mostly local beers and two ciders, although the selection may be reduced out of season. A separate family room, available for local groups, has some ancient frescoes uncovered when previous owners stripped away decades of modernisation. Pub games include chess and other board games. Food is limited to a pasty or pork pie. Q ➳ ❀ ♣ ♦ 🖵 ╤

Lostwithiel

Globe Inn Ⓛ
3 North Street, PL22 0EG (near railway station, town side of river bridge)
✿ 12-11 (midnight Fri & Sat) ☎ (01208) 872501
⊕ globeinn.com
Sharp's Original; Skinner's Betty Stogs; 2 changing beers (sourced regionally) Ⓗ
Cosy 13th-century pub in the narrow streets of an old stannary town, close to the medieval bridge. The welcoming, rather rambling interior accommodates a single bar with several drinking and dining spaces, a restaurant, and suntrap patio at the rear. An extensive home-cooked menu features fish and game; the beer range increases to four in summer. The pub is named after a ship in a sea battle in 1813, where a member of the then-owner's family was killed.
Q ➳ ❀ ♯ ◖ Å ✦ ♣ 🖵 ❀ ╤

Manaccan

New Inn
Churchtown, TR12 6HA (on Lizard Peninsula, near Helford village) SW763249
✿ 12-3, 6 (5 Fri)-11; 12-11 Sat; 12-10 Sun
☎ (01326) 231301 ⊕ thenewinnmanaccan.co.uk
Sharp's Cornish Coaster; 3 changing beers (sourced locally) Ⓗ
Although hard to find, this traditional thatched village pub, owned by the locals, is well worth seeking out. The cosy bar has a beamed ceiling and partly planked walls, even squeezing a table into the former inglenook fireplace. An adjoining room provides further seating and dining space, and a new garden room is being added to the rear. Lunchtime food is limited to sandwiches and pasties. Q ➳ ❀ ◖ P ❀ ╤

Marhamchurch

Buller's Arms Hotel
Helebridge Road, EX23 0HB (off A39 S of Bude)
✿ 12-11 summer; closed Mon; 12-11 (10 Sun) winter
☎ (01288) 361277 ⊕ thebullersarmshotel.com
Greene King Abbot; St Austell Cornish Best Bitter; Sharp's Atlantic; Tintagel Arthur's Ale; house beer (by Tintagel); 1 changing beer (sourced locally; often Longhill) Ⓗ
Large, community-oriented village pub/hotel with a spacious beamed and slate-flagged bar room. Decorative bric-a-brac includes buffalo horns and a stuffed fox and badger at one end of the room; the other end is home to a dartboard, pool table and an upright piano 'for adult use only'. The beers may vary occasionally but are generally from local breweries. The pub holds quiz nights and monthly live weekend entertainment. An under-fives soft play area is available most afternoons and birthday parties are hosted on Saturday.
Q ➳ ❀ ♯ ◖ & Å ✦ 🖵 (218) ❀ ╤

Mousehole

Old Coastguard Hotel
The Parade, TR19 6PR
✿ 10.30-11.30 ☎ (01736) 731222
⊕ oldcoastguardhotel.co.uk
3 changing beers (sourced locally) Ⓗ
This interesting hotel and former coastguard station is located at the top of Mousehole, on the cliffside slopes. Its elegant single-bar interior has several stepped levels, with wooden floors and furnishings, and numerous drinking and dining areas affording stunning views over St Clement's Isle and Mount's Bay. A patio terrace overlooks a large tropical-style palmed garden. Local microbreweries supply a varying range of beers, with an attractive daily food menu also available. Parking is limited to an adjoining public car park.
Q ➳ ❀ ♯ ◖ Å ✦ 🖵 (6) ❀ ╤

Nancenoy

Trengilly Wartha Inn Ⓛ
TR11 5RP (off B3291 near Constantine) SW732283
✿ 11-3.15, 6-11; 12-midnight Sat summer
☎ (01326) 340332 ⊕ trengilly.co.uk
Penzance Potion No.9; Sharp's Original; 2 changing beers (sourced locally) Ⓗ
Versatile inn in extensive grounds including a lake, set in an isolated steeply wooded valley – the pub's name means 'settlement above the trees'. Originally a farmhouse, it has a variety of furniture and rooms, the wood-beamed bar displaying pictures by local artists. A conservatory extension serves as a family room. The real ales are mainly from local microbreweries. The Trengilly offers a wide-ranging and imaginative food menu using mostly fresh local produce from named suppliers.
Q ➳ ❀ ♯ ◖ ✦ P ❀ ╤

Newquay

Red Lion ✪
North Quay Hill, TR7 1HE (NW of town centre, overlooking harbour)
✿ 11-11 (midnight Fri & Sat) ☎ (01637) 872195
⊕ redlionnewquay.co.uk
Sharp's Doom Bar, Atlantic, Special; Skinner's Betty Stogs, Cornish Knocker, Porthleven; 2 changing beers (sourced nationally; often Exmoor, Timothy Taylor, Titanic) Ⓗ
This deceptively large open-plan pub has picture windows affording panoramic views. It offers eight cask ales and a range of ciders, and food is available all day. Live music is popular at weekends, as are open mic nights and a mid-week quiz, all warmed by a log fire in winter. The pub is within easy walking distance of the town centre towards the famous Fistral Beach. CAMRA Cornish Cider Pub of the Year in 2016, CAMRA members are offered a discount on ales and ciders.
➳ ❀ ◖ & ✦ ♣ ♦ P 🖵 ❀ ╤

Penzance

Crown ⃝L
Victoria Square, TR18 2EP
☼ 12-11 (midnight Fri & Sat); 12-10.30 Sun
☎ (01736) 351070 ⊕ thecrownpenzance.co.uk
4 changing beers (sourced locally; often Cornish Crown) Ⓗ
Close to the railway and bus stations, this small traditional community local is tucked away behind the main shopping street. Offering a relaxing, friendly atmosphere, it has a tidily furnished bar with upholstered window seats and a huge mirror covering one wall; a cosy two-table snug is at the rear. The tap for Cornish Crown, the real ales are usually from the brewery although an occasional guest may appear. You are welcome to bring your own food (plates provided). Q⌂❀⇌♣🖵🐾🔊

Perranporth

Perranporth Inn ✔
36 St Pirans Road, TR6 0BJ
☼ 12-midnight summer; 2-11 (midnight Fri); 12-midnight Sat; 12-11 Sun winter ☎ (01872) 573266
⊕ perranporthinn.com
St Austell Tribute; Sharp's Doom Bar; Skinner's Porthleven; 1 changing beer (sourced nationally; often Timothy Taylor) Ⓗ
This lively sports-oriented pub, popular with all ages, was once part of a hotel. It is dominated by large screens showing a number of live sporting events. The L-shaped layout extends deep into the rear of the building, leading to a pool table and dartboard. The red-brick central bar also hosts quizzes, poker nights and live music, and has even been known to stage the occasional boxing match. The regular locally sourced ales are usually supplemented by another guest in summer.
⌂🕭🖵🅿🚌(86,87)🐾🔊

Perranwell

Royal Oak ⃝L
TR3 7PX
☼ 11-3, 6 (5 Fri)-midnight; 11-midnight Sat; 12-11.30 Sun
☎ (01872) 863175 ⊕ theroyaloakperranwellstation.co.uk
Sharp's Doom Bar; 3 changing beers (sourced locally; often Bath Ales, Skinner's) Ⓗ
Small 18th-century cottage-style village community pub with an emphasis on good food – most of the tables are set for meals but drinkers are equally welcome. Booking for meals is advisable, however, especially in the evening. The beers vary frequently and are often from local breweries. The pub holds monthly quiz nights and frequent fundraising events for local charities. Bus services stop close by; the railway station is about 15 minutes' walk away.
Q⌂❀🕭⇌♣🖵🅿🖵(36,46)🐾🔊

Piece

Countryman Inn
TR16 6SG (on Four Lanes to Pool road) SW679398
☼ 11-11 (midnight Sat); 12-11 Sun ☎ (01209) 215960
Courage Best Bitter, Directors; St Austell Tribute; Skinner's Betty Stogs, Hops 'n' Honey; Theakston Old Peculier; 1 changing beer (sourced nationally) Ⓗ
Once a grocery shop for miners, this is now a lively community pub set high among old copper mines near the distinctive landmark of Carn Brea. The

larger of the two bars is dominated by a granite fireplace and massive cast-iron coal-fired cooking range; the smaller room is more of a public bar in style and welcomes families. The pub hosts entertainment most nights, and a raffle in support of local charities on Sunday lunchtime.
⌂❀🕭🖤A♣🖵🖵(442)🐾🔊

Polkerris

Rashleigh Inn ⃝L
PL24 2TL (off A3082 Par to Fowey road) SX093521
☼ 11-11 ☎ (01726) 813991
⊕ therashleighinnpolkerris.co.uk
Skinner's Porthleven; Tintagel Harbour Special; 4 changing beers (sourced regionally; often Otter) Ⓗ
This former 18th-century pilchard boathouse is now an excellent family-run free house beside a sheltered beach near the Saints' Way footpath, and on the South-West Coast Path. The atmospheric interior features exposed stonework, wooden flooring, a beamed ceiling, open fires and a splendid slate-topped bar. Up to six ales are available and quality meals are served in the bar and restaurant. The bar bay windows and sheltered terrace offer panoramic views of St Austell Bay.
Q⌂❀🕭♣🅿🐾🔊

Polmear

Ship Inn
Polmear Hill, PL24 2AR (on A3082)
☼ 11.30-midnight ☎ (01726) 812540 ⊕ theshipinnpar.com
Fuller's London Pride; Sharp's Doom Bar; Skinner's Lushingtons; 1 changing beer Ⓗ
Cosy free house, very popular with both locals and summer visitors, close to Par beach and coastal footpath; boats used to tie up at the quay behind the pub. There are several drinking and dining areas, with wagon wheels forming an unusual partition. An ideal family pub, it boasts a large garden and play area, a function room upstairs, and a big car park. Occasional beer festivals are held, and the pub runs unusual competitions for charity.
⌂❀🕭🖤♣A♣🖤🖵(25)🐾🔊

Polperro

Blue Peter Inn ⃝L
Quay Road, PL13 2QZ (W side of harbour)
☼ 8.30am-11; 8.30am-10.30 Sun ☎ (01503) 272743
⊕ thebluepeterinn.yolasite.com
St Austell Tribute; 4 changing beers (often Bays, Cornish Crown, Harbour) Ⓗ
Named after the naval flag, this friendly inn is reached up a flight of steps near the quay, and is the only pub with a sea view in the village. In summer it offers up to five ales from Cornwall and Devon, and a varied menu of home-cooked dishes including breakfast. Featuring low beams, wooden floors, unusual souvenirs and work by local artists, the pub is popular with locals, fishermen and visitors – and their dogs. ⌂🕭A🐾🔊

Polruan

Lugger ✔
The Quay, PL23 1PA (on quayside)
☼ 12-11; closed Mon winter ☎ (01726) 870007
⊕ luggerinnpolruan.co.uk

St Austell Cornish Best Bitter, Tribute, Proper Job, HSD; 1 changing beer (sourced locally; often Fish Key) H
Quaint, welcoming pub close to the foot ferry to Fowey. Popular with locals and family-friendly, the Lugger first opened as a pub in 1794 in a building that has also housed sail lofts and fish cellars; the large main room with the bar has a period fireplace. Interestingly, a beer from the local small brewery Fish Key may sometimes be available; HSD is added in summer only, and occasionally a St Austell seasonal ale. ☎◑▲♣☐➥♦🐾

Pool

Plume of Feathers
Fore Street, TR15 3PF
☼ 11.30-11.30; 12-midnight Sat; 12-10.30 Sun
☎ (01209) 713513
3 changing beers (sourced nationally; often Adnams, Sharp's, Tintagel) H
Cosy old granite inn with low beams and several drinking areas around a central bar. There is a separate restaurant and a sandwich takeaway bar. The ever-changing beers come mainly from Cornish and South-West microbreweries, with three brews always available. Family-friendly, with an outdoor play area and a patio, it is also a meeting place for clubs. Once used as a mortuary for a local mining disaster, the pub is reputedly home to two ghosts. No food on Tuesday or Sunday evenings.
Q☎❀◑♣☐➥(T1,T2)🐾♦

Port Isaac

Golden Lion ✔
13 Fore Street, PL29 3RB
☼ 12-11; 12-midnight Fri; 12-10.30 Sun ☎ (01208) 880336
⊕ thegoldenlionportisaac.co.uk
St Austell Trelawny, Tribute, Proper Job, HSD H
This fine old 18th-century pub in the heart of Port Isaac has several drinking areas and a small balcony overlooking the harbour. Its three-room layout and old fittings earn the pub recognition in CAMRA's Regional Inventory of Historic Pub Interiors and it has slightly uneven bare-boarded floors. The games room downstairs was originally the Bloody Bones locals' bar, and boasts a smugglers' tunnel down to a causeway on the beach. There is a small flagstoned courtyard at the rear for alfresco drinking. ☎❀◑♣➥(96)🐾♦

Porthallow

Five Pilchards Inn
TR12 6PP (down narrow lanes, NNE of St Keverne) SW797232
☼ 12-11 summer; 12-3 (not Mon), 6-11; 12-11 Sun winter
☎ (01326) 280256 ⊕ thefivepilchards.co.uk
4 changing beers (sourced regionally; often Bays, Cornish Chough) H
In an isolated beachside location, this popular community local is well worth finding. Its open-plan layout has distinct drinking and dining areas, furnished with wooden settles, tables and chairs. The bar area with its wood-planked floor and beamed ceiling is festooned with nautical bric-a-brac of all kinds, including enormous scale models of local harbour tugs and a lifeboat. Up to four real ales are offered, frequently changing but often including a Bays brew, and a locally made cider.
Q☎❀◸◑♣♦🐾

Porthleven

Ship Inn
Mount Pleasant Road, TR13 9JS (SW corner of harbour)
☼ 11-11.30; 11-12.30am Fri-Sun ☎ (01326) 564204
⊕ theshipinnporthleven.co.uk
Sharp's Cornish Coaster, Doom Bar; Skinner's Porthleven; Tintagel Harbour Special; 2 changing beers (sourced locally; often Bude) H
Seventeenth-century fishermen's inn accessed via a steep flight of steps. With the pub's commanding view you can sit comfortably and watch the rough seas on stormy days. The open, if rambling, split-level interior has wooden floors and beams decorated with an eclectic mix of coins, banknotes, beermats and brass artefacts, and sketches of local characters. A large log fire adds warmth in winter.
☎❀◑➥(2,2A)🐾

Poughill

Preston Gate Inn
Poughill Road, EX23 9ET (just outside Bude, on Sandymouth Bay road) SS224077
☼ 11-11 ☎ (01288) 354017 ⊕ prestongateinn.co.uk
Dartmoor Jail Ale; Skinner's Lushingtons; 2 changing beers (sourced locally; often Holsworthy Ales, Tintagel) H
Originally two cottages, this cosy 16th-century building became the village pub in 1983. The spacious U-shaped room has a dartboard at one end of the bar; the other, roomier end offers more seating and a roaring log fire in winter. Conversation rules here, and the pub supports darts and quiz teams. Meals include monthly themed nights (booking is advised). The beer range may be reduced in winter; the cider varies. The name Preston comes from the Cornish word for priest.
Q☎❀◑▲♣♦➥(128)🐾♦

Rilla Mill

Manor House Inn
PL17 7NT (NE of Liskeard off B3254)
☼ 12-3, 5-11; 12-11 Sat & Sun ☎ (01579) 362354
⊕ manorhouserilla.co.uk
Draught Bass; Sharp's Original; 1 changing beer (sourced locally) H
Comfortable, traditional 17th-century inn and restaurant in the upper Lynher Valley, on the edge of Bodmin Moor, allegedly haunted by three ghosts. It has three main rooms, one with a slated and carpeted floor, the other two comprising the restaurant areas. The changing beer varies frequently but is usually sourced from a local brewery; meals also feature local produce. The pub is situated near the Sterts open-air theatre and a dairy that makes Cornish cheeses.
Q☎❀◑♣➥(236)🐾

Rosudgeon

Falmouth Packet L
TR20 9QE (on A394 Penzance-Helston road)
☼ 12-11 summer; 12-3, 5.30-11; 12-7 Sun winter
☎ (01736) 762240 ⊕ falmouthpacketinn.co.uk
4 changing beers (often Penzance, St Austell) H
This vibrant family-owned pub welcomes regulars and visitors alike. It has a single L-shaped bar room with distinct drinking and dining areas warmed by a large fire. A separate conservatory houses a pool table. With its reputation for good beer and high-

quality meals, the pub has won several food awards. Two of its changing beers are usually from Penzance Brewery, the other two are also from Cornish brewers. A one-bedroom cottage is available to rent. Q♣☺✿☕⌖◑&♠♣⬤P🖵(2)☻☞

St Ann's Chapel

Rifle Volunteer Inn
PL18 9HL (on A390)
☼ 11.30-11 ☎ (01822) 833038 ⊕ theriflevolunteer.co.uk
St Austell Tribute; 2 changing beers (sourced regionally) Ⓗ
Former mine captain's house, converted to a coaching inn during the mid-19th century. The main bar has been extended to accommodate a conservatory, popular with diners for the view over the garden. Meals are made with locally sourced ingredients. A separate public bar caters for more dedicated drinkers and houses a pool table and dartboard. The changing beer is usually from a local brewery. The pub offers panoramic views across the Tamar Valley and is in good walking country. Q♣✿☕◑&♣⬤P🖵(79)☞

St Ives

Castle Inn
16 Fore Street, TR26 1AB
☼ 11-11; 12-11 Sun ☎ (01736) 796833
⊕ castleinn-stives.co.uk
Sharp's Special; Skinner's Betty Stogs Ⓗ**; 5 changing beers (sourced nationally)** Ⓗ/Ⓖ
This pub has had a chequered history, being by turns accommodation for men building Tregenna Castle, a brothel, and a shipping office for the former Union Castle line. Now a thriving town-centre local, loved by locals and visitors alike, its emphasis is on an ever-varying real ale menu. The single bar sports an eye-catching stained-glass window at the front, and the walls are adorned with various items of nautical bric-a-brac. A fun quiz is held on Monday night.
Q♣✿◑⌖♣⇄♣🖵☻☞

Hain Line ✔
Tregenna Place, TR26 1SB
☼ 9am-midnight; 8am-1am Fri & Sat; 8am-midnight Sun
☎ (01736) 792920
Greene King Abbot; Ruddles Best Bitter; 4 changing beers (sourced nationally; often St Ives) Ⓗ
Named after a shipping company that operated here in the early-20th century, this former nightclub has been extended into a former shop since opening in 2012, brightening up the ground floor. Beers vary, with local microbreweries usually represented. There are two bars, although the upstairs bar has a limited beer range and piped music. Inspiration has been taken from the local artistic community for some of the fittings, and local artists' works are displayed on the walls. Q♣◑&⌖⇄♣🖵☻☞

St Just

Star Inn ✔
1 Fore Street, TR19 7LL
☼ 11.30-midnight; 11.30-11.30 Sun ☎ (01736) 788767
⊕ thestarinn-stjust.co.uk
St Austell Cornish Best Bitter, Tribute, Proper Job; 2 changing beers (sourced locally; often St Austell) Ⓗ

A proper drinkers' pub, this 18th-century inn is a timeless place where the emphasis is on good ale and conversation. The decor in the atmospheric bar reflects a long association with former local mining and maritime activities, and Celtic flags adorn the beamed ceiling. Wooden furnishings and an open fire enhance the ambience. A separate snug functions as a meeting and family room. Up to five St Austell ales are offered, but no food. Live music features on Monday, Thursday and Saturday nights. Q♣✿☺&♣⬤🖵(10,300)☻

St Kew Highway

Red Lion Inn Ⓛ
PL30 3DN
☼ 12-3 (not Mon-Wed), 5.30-11; 12-11 Sun summer; 12-3 (not Mon-Thu), 5.30-11; 12-5 Sun winter ☎ (01208) 841271
⊕ redlionstkew.com
St Austell Tribute; 2 changing beers (sourced regionally; often Padstow) Ⓗ
This welcoming 17th-century community pub has an L-shaped interior with a small dining area at the front, the main bar extending down the longer arm, and a larger room with stone walls and its own bar at the rear, used for live entertainment and functions. Furnishings include a mix of sofas and wooden chairs and tables. The pub offers up to three real ales from local microbreweries and is known locally for its good food. Q♣✿☕◑ A P🖵(95)☻☞

St Mabyn

St Mabyn Inn
Churchtown, PL30 3BA (near church)
☼ 12-midnight; 12-11 Sun ☎ (01208) 841266
⊕ stmabyninn.com
Sharp's Doom Bar, Special; Tintagel Cornwall's Pride; 1 changing beer (sourced locally) Ⓗ
Conversation thrives at this village local, a popular, attractive, 17th-century free house, with four quality ales and an ever-changing menu specialising in local produce. It has a single bar and adjoining snug, games room and a stylish well-appointed restaurant. Open fires, wood furnishings including settles, stained-glass partitions and windows add character, supplemented by an interesting collection of Toby jugs, horse brasses and vintage advertising. At the rear is an attractive beer garden. Q♣✿☕◑&♣⬤P🖵(55)☻☞

Saltash

Union Inn
Tamar Street, PL12 4EL (on waterfront, beneath Tamar bridges)
☼ 11-11; 12-10.30 Sun ☎ (01752) 844770
Dartmoor Legend, Jail Ale; Sharp's Doom Bar Ⓗ**; 1 changing beer (sourced locally; often Bays)** Ⓖ
The frontage of this riverside local is strikingly painted as a union flag. The single bar offers a selection of real ales and an ever-changing guest beer, usually on gravity from the cellar. The draught cider is Sam's Devon Dry. Tables outside overlook the river. Live music features on Tuesday and weekend evenings. Tamar Street used to be known as Pickle Cock Alley, as shellfish were sold through open windows. Q♣✿⇄♣⬤P🖵☻☞

Stithians

Seven Stars Inn
Church Road, TR3 7DH
✆ 12-11 (midnight Fri & Sat) ☎ (01209) 860003
⏚ sevenstarsstithians.net
St Austell Trelawny, Tribute; 1 changing beer (sourced nationally; often Bath Ales) Ⓗ
Lively cottage-style village local, used by a broad cross-section of the community and supportive of local events and sports teams. The pub was purpose-built as a farmhouse extension to serve the drinking needs of tin miners at the end of the 19th century. The original bar and lounge (note the adjacent twin front doors) have been merged into one L-shaped drinking/dining area, with a later extension added towards the rear. The ever-changing guest beer is usually from a microbrewery. Q☺⛵☯◑♣🚌(36,442)🐾⧖

Stratton

King's Arms ⓛ
Howells Road, EX23 9BX (on A3072)
✆ 12-11 ☎ (01288) 352396
Sharp's Atlantic; Tintagel Cornwall's Pride; 2 changing beers (often Forge, Tintagel) Ⓗ
Popular locals' local in the heart of this ancient market town, a 17th-century former coaching inn whose name reflects the town's loyalties after the Civil War. The pub has many original features including two simply furnished bars, with well-worn Delabole slate flagstone and wooden floors. During renovation work, a small bread oven was exposed in the lounge. The two changing beers usually include one from a Cornish brewery and one from Devon. Four letting rooms are available, one of them en-suite. Q☯🛌◑♿Å♣🚶🚌🐾

Tintagel

King Arthur's Arms
Fore Street, PL34 0DA
✆ 9am-midnight ☎ (01840) 770628
⏚ kingarthursarms.co.uk
St Austell Tribute; Sharp's Doom Bar; Tintagel Cornwall's Pride, Arthur's Ale, Merlins Muddle; 3 changing beers (sourced locally; often Skinner's, Tintagel) Ⓗ
Directly opposite Tintagel Old Post Office, this 14th-century inn with beamed ceilings and thick granite walls has been extensively refurbished. The larger bar is open plan with a pool table, and designed to cope with large numbers of summer visitors. It hosts occasional entertainment including discos. A smaller bar is favoured by locals. Up to eight real ales in summer include a broad selection from Tintagel Brewery. Food is available daily 9am-9pm. Adjacent parking is Pay & Display.
⛵☯🛌◑♿Å♣🚶🚌(95,96)🐾⧖

Towan Cross

Victory Inn ⓛ
TR4 8BN
✆ 12-11 ☎ (01209) 890359
St Austell Tribute; Skinner's Betty Stogs, Lushingtons; 1 changing beer (sourced locally) Ⓗ
Originally built to serve local miners, this convivial family-run 16th-century inn sits atop the cliffs above Porthtowan. The spacious single bar interior is open plan with separate drinking and dining areas including the adjoining conservatory. Family-friendly, the pub is quiet and relaxing with comfortable furnishings, wood-burning stoves and nautical decor. The guest ale is generally from a local brewery and the high-quality food menu offers fresh local produce. A large beer garden adjoins the car park. Local buses stop outside. Q☺☯◑Å♣🚌(304,315)🐾⧖

Treen

Gurnard's Head Hotel ⓛ
TR26 3DE (on B3306, Lands End-St Ives coast road near Zennor)
✆ 10-11.30 ☎ (01736) 796928 ⏚ gurnardshead.co.uk
St Austell Tribute; 3 changing beers (sourced locally) Ⓗ
Named after the nearby headland, this strikingly coloured inn stands near the coastal path. Its wood-floored interior comprises a large bar, cosy snug and stylish restaurant. Wood furnishings, comfy sofas and open fires create a relaxed atmosphere, with local art adorning the walls. The varying beer range mainly showcases Cornish microbreweries, and the food menu changes daily, reflecting the availability of local produce. Community-oriented, the pub holds weekly Cornish cultural evenings. Events are also staged in the large lawned gardens. Q☺⛵🛌◑♿♣🚶🚌(7,16A)🐾⧖

Tresco (Isles of Scilly)

New Inn
Townshill, TR24 0QG
✆ 11-11 summer; 11-3, 6-11 winter ☎ (01720) 422844
Sharp's Doom Bar; 3 changing beers (sourced locally; often Ales of Scilly, St Austell, Skinner's) Ⓗ
Excellent old pub near New Grimsby harbour, a haven between demanding coastal walks and the boat to St Mary's. Extensions to the garden and provision of a covered pavilion have added to the attractions of this popular real ale outlet. The varying beers are mostly from Cornish breweries, usually including a brew from Skinner's and St Austell, with local brewer Ales of Scilly often represented. Beer festivals are held over the spring and late summer bank holidays. Q☺⛵🛌◑♣🚶🐾⧖

Trevaunance Cove

Driftwood Spars ⓛ ✅
Quay Road, TR5 0RT
✆ 11-11 (midnight Fri & Sat) ☎ (01872) 552428
⏚ driftwoodspars.com
Sharp's Doom Bar; 5 changing beers (sourced locally; often Driftwood) Ⓗ
A magnet for ale drinkers, this outstanding free house is a must-visit. Atmospheric and nautically themed with three bars, the pub also offers a sea-view restaurant with sun terrace, two separate beer gardens, and ample parking. As the Driftwood Brewery tap, the brewery's ales dominate the ever-changing beer selection – an imaginative food menu is also available. The pub is community-oriented and stages regular live music and occasional theatre, plus beer festivals in March, May and October. It is also a popular wedding venue. Q☺⛵🛌◑♿♣🚶🚌(57,87)🐾⧖

Trewellard

Trewellard Arms 🅛
Trewellard Road, TR19 7TA (on B3318/B3306 jct)
🕐 12-11 (midnight Sat); 12-10.30 Sun ☎ (01736) 788634
6 changing beers (sourced regionally; often Bays, Tintagel) ℍ
A warm welcome is assured at this award-winning, family-run free house, once the Geevor mine owner's residence. Its cosy interior accommodates a spacious open-beamed single bar, pleasant restaurant, a secluded cellar space, and a patio outside. The homely atmosphere is enhanced by open fires. Good value home-cooked food is available. A varied beer menu features up to six ales and two ciders, with a beer festival held each May. The pub is easily accessed by bus and there is ample parking. 🛏🏵🍴◑🅰♣👜P🚍🐾🛜

Truro

Old Ale House 🍺 ✅
7 Quay Street, TR1 2HD (near bus station)
🕐 11-11 (midnight Mon & Fri); 11-1am Sat; 12-10.30 Sun
☎ (01872) 271122 ⊕ old-ale-house.co.uk
Skinner's Betty Stogs, River Cottage EPA, Lushingtons, Cornish Knocker, Porthleven ℍ; **5 changing beers (sourced regionally; often Skinner's)** ℍ/🅖
This lively two-storey city-centre pub is Skinner's brewery tap. The lower floor is an atmospheric main bar dominated by wood flooring, furnishings, pillars and beamed ceilings; old artefacts add to the character and relaxed ambience. Up to 13 ales and eight ciders are on offer, plus bar meals and free monkey nuts. Upstairs, the more intimate Hop Store restaurant and bar serves an interesting and fuller menu. Live music plays on Friday and Saturday evenings. Q◑♣👜🐾🛜

Rising Sun ✅
Mitchell Hill, TR1 1ED
🕐 11.30 (12 Sun)-midnight summer; closed Mon winter
☎ (01872) 240003 ⊕ risingsuntruro.co.uk
Fuller's London Pride; Skinner's Betty Stogs; 2 changing beers (sourced locally; often Skinner's) 🅖
Up a steep hill near the city centre, this award-winning pub's narrow frontage belies a spacious interior accommodating a small public bar with adjacent dining area, a lounge bar, and raised restaurant area. Comfortably furnished throughout, the decor includes old Truro scenes. Up to four ever-changing ales are dispensed straight from casks, and locally sourced food is also popular (booking advised). Outside is a sheltered patio where periodic beer festivals are held.
Q🛏🏵◑♣P🚍🐾🛜

Tywardreath

New Inn 🅛
Fore Street, PL24 2QP
🕐 12-11 ☎ (01726) 813901
Draught Bass 🅖; **St Austell Trelawny, Tribute, Proper Job; 1 changing beer** ℍ
This classic pub is a perfect example of a community local, built in the mid-18th century by mine owners. Although tied to a brewery, the landlord serves a guest beer, as well as Draught Bass, which the pub is covenanted to sell in

perpetuity. Pub games, good conversation and regular live music provide the entertainment. Groups meet here regularly and fêtes are held in the extensive gardens. The pub is a former Cornwall CAMRA rural Pub of the Year.
Q🛏🏵◑♣P🚍(24)🐾🛜

Vogue

Star Inn 🅛 ✅
St Day Road, TR16 5NP (on Redruth-St Day road)
🕐 12-midnight (1am Fri & Sat); 11-11.30 Sun
☎ (01209) 820242 ⊕ starinnvogue.biz
4 changing beers ℍ
'The pub is the hub' well describes this community-oriented village inn acting as a meeting place hosting a library branch and hairdressing salon. Welcoming and family-friendly, its relaxed interior accommodates a busy bar with an interesting range of beers, a quiet lounge and a separate restaurant. The wooden furnishings and open fire add character. Home-cooked food is available daily, Sunday lunch being particularly popular. Live entertainment features at weekends, and a charity beer and music festival is held in June.
🛏🏵◑🅰♣👜P🚍(47)🐾🛜

Wadebridge

Ship Inn 🅛
Gonvena Hill, PL27 6DF (across bridge from town centre)
🕐 12-2, 5-11; 12-10 (6 winter) Sun ☎ (01208) 813845
⊕ shipinnwadebridge.co.uk
Sharp's Doom Bar, Atlantic; 3 changing beers (sourced locally; often Harbour, Padstow) ℍ
Award-winning pub enjoying a growing reputation for quality ales and cuisine. Over the bridge from the town centre, its extensive, stylish interior has a comfortable bar adjoining a split-level well-appointed restaurant, leading in turn to suntrap decking and courtyard seating at the rear. Wood and upholstered furnishings, open fires and beamed ceilings enhanced by the contemporary nautical decor create a relaxed ambience. Local produce features in daily-changing cuisine. The varying beer is usually from a Cornish microbrewery. Q🛏🏵◑🅰♣👜P🚍🐾🛜

Zennor

Tinner's Arms ✅
TR26 3BY (off B3306 St Ives-St Just coast road)
🕐 11.30-11; 12-11 Sun ☎ (01736) 796927
House beer (by St Austell); 2 changing beers (sourced locally; often Skinner's) ℍ
On the Penwith north coast, this ancient village free house is popular with walkers and tourists. Its atmospheric single-bar interior accommodates a separate lounge area and adjacent restaurant. Exposed granite walls, wood beams, wall panels and furnishings create a cosy ambience; a sheltered beer garden is pleasant for alfresco drinking. The interesting food menu features local produce. St Austell Trelawny is rebadged as Tinners Ale and Sharp's Special as Zennor Mermaid – check the mermaid legend at the nearby museum.
Q🛏🏵🍴◑🔥🅰♣👜P🚍🐾🛜

I never drink water. I'm afraid it will become habit-forming. **W C Fields**

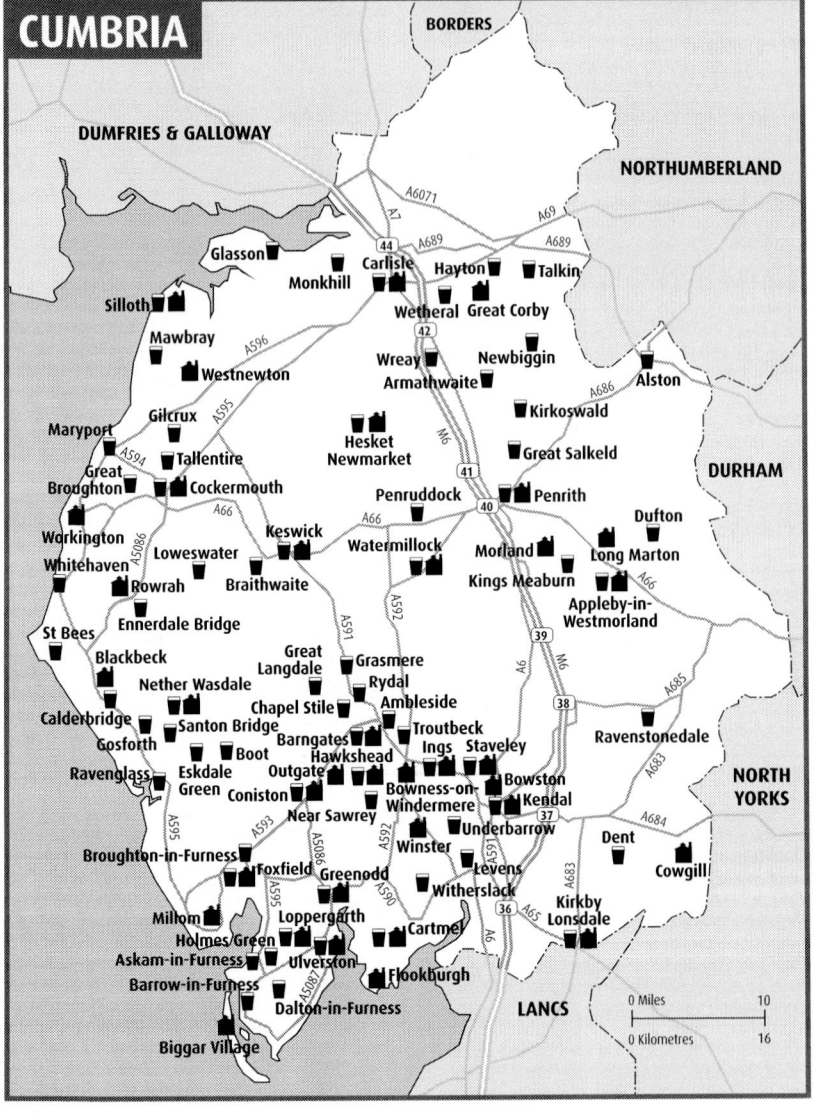

CUMBRIA

BORDERS

DUMFRIES & GALLOWAY

NORTHUMBERLAND

Glasson
Carlisle Hayton Talkin
Monkhill
Silloth
Wetheral Great Corby
Mawbray
Newbiggin
Westnewton Wreay
Armathwaite Alston
Gilcrux Kirkoswald
Maryport
Hesket
Tallentire Newmarket Great Salkeld
Great
Broughton Cockermouth DURHAM
Penruddock Penrith
Workington Dufton
Loweswater Keswick
Whitehaven Watermillock Long Marton
Rowrah Braithwaite Morland
Kings Meaburn Appleby-in-
St Bees Ennerdale Bridge Westmorland
Blackbeck Great
Langdale Grasmere
Nether Wasdale Rydal
Calderbridge Chapel Stile Ambleside NORTH
Santon Bridge Troubeck YORKS
Gosforth Barngates Ings Staveley Ravenstonedale
Boot Hawkshead
Ravenglass Eskdale Outgate Bowston
Green Coniston Bowness-on- Kendal
Near Sawrey Windermere Dent
Winster Underbarrow Cowgill
Broughton-in-Furness Levens
Foxfield Greenodd
Witherslack Kirkby
Millom Lonsdale
Loppergarth Cartmel
Holmes/Green
Askam-in-Furness Ulverston LANCS
Barrow-in-Furness Flookburgh
Dalton-in-Furness

Biggar Village

0 Miles 10
0 Kilometres 16

Alston

Cumberland Inn 🅛
Townfoot, CA9 3HX
☺ 12-11 ☎ (01434) 381875 ⊕ alstoncumberlandhotel.co.uk
Yates Bitter; 3 changing beers Ⓗ
A family-run 19th-century inn overlooking the South Tyne river. Close to the Coast-to-Coast cycle route and Pennine Way, it is an ideal base to explore the highest market town in England. Guest beers come from Hesket Newmarket, Allendale, High House Farm, Mordue breweries and further afield. Old Rosie and occasional Cumbrian ciders and perry are stocked. Q✿❀🛏◑🐾P🖩✿🛜

Ambleside

Lily Bar 🅛
12-14 Lake Road, LA22 0AD (just a two-minute walk from local bus stops)

☺ 12-11 (midnight Fri & Sat) ☎ (015394) 33175
⊕ thelilybar.co.uk
Cumbrian Legendary Ales Loweswater Gold; 3 changing beers Ⓗ
Popular former wine bar with local students making up a large percentage of the clientele. Four local beers are always on, plus a selection of bottled beers and an extensive list of cocktails. Live music features on most weekend nights, with regular soul and funk sessions and a monthly open mic, and occasional comedy nights. ◑🛗🚌🐾🛜

Appleby-in-Westmorland

Midland Hotel 🅛
25 Clifford Street, CA16 6TS (adjacent to town station on Settle and Carlisle railway)
☺ closed Mon; 11.30 (5.30 Tue)-11 ☎ (017683) 51524
⊕ themidlandhotelappleby.co.uk
3 changing beers Ⓗ

The Midland is in the beautiful Eden Valley between the Lake District National Park and the Yorkshire Dales National Park. It has been extensively refurbished and much improved, now having a light modern feel. The three handpumps offer beers from local microbreweries, often Appleby and Eden breweries. Real cider and perry are frequently available. ✪🏠🍴♿⇄P🚌(563)🐾🐾📶

Armathwaite

Fox & Pheasant ✓
CA4 9PY
🕐 11-11 ☎ (016974) 72162 ⊕ foxandpheasantinn.co.uk
Robinsons Dizzy Blonde, Cumbria Way, Unicorn; 1 changing beer (sourced nationally; often Robinsons) Ⓗ
Atmospheric 17th-century coaching inn overlooking the River Eden. The main bar has a flagstone floor and inglenook fireplace. The former stables have been converted into a bar and eating area. Original wooden beams, exposed stonework and stable stalls all add to the friendly ambience. Booking is recommended if dining. The guest beer is the Robinsons seasonal beer. 🛏️✪🏠🍴♣P🐾📶

Askam-in-Furness

Railway Inn Ⓛ
24 Ireleth Road, LA16 7DJ (short walk from station)
🕐 7-midnight; 3-1am Fri; 12-1am Sat; 12-midnight Sun
☎ (01229) 467366
Cumbrian Legendary Ales Loweswater Gold; 2 changing beers (sourced nationally) Ⓗ
This welcoming refurbished pub has two separate rooms – a public bar containing the dartboard and TVs for Sky and BT Sport, plus a lounge bar which has some very comfortable seating and a pool table. Main sporting events are also shown in the lounge on a large screen. Food is served Saturday and Sunday only. Three real ales are stocked, of which two are from local breweries.
Q🛏️✪🍴♿👟♣🚌(7)🐾📶

Barngates

Drunken Duck Inn Ⓛ
LA22 0NG (signed off B5286 Hawkshead to Ambleside road)
🕐 11.30-11; 12-10.30 Sun ☎ (015394) 36347
⊕ drunkenduckinn.co.uk
Barngates Cat Nap, Cracker, Tag Lag; 3 changing beers (sourced locally) Ⓗ
The Drunken Duck stands high above Ambleside, a traditional Lakeland dwelling reflecting the simplicity, beauty and longevity of its natural environment. From the fells the on-site Barngates Brewery draws the water for its beers. The bar has six handpumps and serves all of the Barngates beers on rotation. The outside seating area at the front offers commanding dramatic views of the fells to the north-east. Dogs are allowed except in the dining room. Q🛏️✪🏠🍴♿👟♣P🐾📶

Barrow-in-Furness

Duke of Edinburgh Ⓛ ✓
Abbey Road, LA14 5QR
🕐 11-midnight ☎ (01229) 821039
⊕ dukeofedinburghhotel.co.uk
Lancaster Amber, Blonde, Red; Marston's Wainwright; 4 changing beers (sourced nationally) Ⓗ

On the edge of the town centre near the station, the Duke does not get as noisy as similar bars in the town. The bar has an airy feel with modern, comfortable furniture and a fine open fire. Paintings by local artists are displayed. Good-quality, reasonably priced bar meals are served. There is a separate restaurant and large function room. Beers are mainly from Lancaster, alongside four guest ales. 🛏️🏠🍴♿⇄P🚌📶

King's Arms 🍷 Ⓛ
Quarry Brow, Hawcoat, LA14 4HY
🕐 5.30-11; 4-midnight Fri; 12.30-midnight Sat; 1-midnight Sun ☎ (01229) 828137
Barngates Cracker; Copper Dragon Best Bitter; Cumbrian Legendary Ales Loweswater Gold; 6 changing beers (sourced locally) Ⓗ
Popular local pub selling ales mainly from nearby micros. A beer menu on a chalkboard lists forthcoming attractions. The pub, which has been on these premises since the 1860s, has been extensively extended and renovated, and features an open bar with adjacent separate rooms. The friendly staff give a warm welcome. Well-behaved dogs are allowed in one of the rooms. Local CAMRA Pub of the Year 2017. Q🛏️♿♣🚌🐾📶

Boot

Hardknott Bar & Café @ the Woolpack Inn ⃝L

CA19 1TH (¾ mile E of Boot village on approach to Hardknott Pass)
☼ 8am-11 ☎ (019467) 2328 ⊕ woolpack.co.uk
Barngates Goodhew's Dry Stout; Bowness Bay Amazon Amber; 10 changing beers ⃝H
Iconic Lakeland inn on the approach to Hardknott Pass and surrounded by the stunning scenery of Eskdale Valley. This popular tourist pub serves food, cask ales and draught ciders – it has 10 handpumps. The lounge and walkers' bar offer an attractive mix of traditional and modern styles, with wood-burning stoves in both areas. It participates in the annual Boot Beer Festival in June, has its own own cider festival in April, and hosts live music and quiz nights.
🌄😊🍴◐Å♣♦P🐾🐶🏠

Braithwaite

Middle Ruddings Country Inn ⃝L

CA12 5RY (W end of Braithwaite at Thornthwaite/Gallery turn on A66)
☼ 10.30-11 ☎ (017687) 78436 ⊕ middle-ruddings.co.uk
3 changing beers ⃝H
Comfortable country inn run by a family who are passionate about food and real ales usually brewed in Cumbria. The bar comprises two rooms and a lounge. A separate conservatory restaurant serves home-made food using locally sourced produce. Well-behaved dogs are allowed in the bar areas. It serves real ciders and an increasing range of bottle-conditioned ales, and hosts an annual beer-lovers dinner. Winner of a number of CAMRA awards. Q🌄😊🍴◐🚶Å♦P🍴🖥(X5)🐶🏠

Broughton-in-Furness

Manor Arms ⃝L

The Square, LA20 6HY
☼ 12-11.30 (midnight Fri & Sat); 12-11 Sun
☎ (01229) 716286 ⊕ manorarmsthesquare.co.uk
Cumberland Corby Blonde; Hawkshead Windermere Pale; Yates Bitter; 5 changing beers ⃝H
An outstanding free house owned by the Varty family for more than 27 years. Its awards include local CAMRA Pub of the Year 2015. A comprehensive, frequently changing choice of up to eight real ales is served with a range to suit all tastes. Six traditional ciders and perries are also available. Q🌄😊♣♦🍴🖥🐶🏠

Calderbridge

Stanley Arms Hotel

CA20 1DN (on A595)
☼ 12-11 ☎ (01946) 841235 ⊕ stanleyarmshotel.com
4 changing beers ⃝H
At the southern edge of this small village, this is a welcoming late-Georgian hostelry with an extensive beer garden, sitting beside a bend in the River Calder (with full fishing rights) and at the gateway to Ennerdale. Locally sourced produce features in the meals served in the two-room bar and restaurant. In addition to the Cumbrian ales offered, Titanic Plum Porter is a regular.
Q🌄😊🍴◐♣♦P🖥(X6)🐶🏠

Carlisle

Crown & Thistle

53 Church Street, CA3 9DS
☼ 10-midnight ☎ (01228) 532965
2 changing beers (sourced nationally) ⃝H
A popular community local at the centre of Stanwix village and close to the route of Hadrian's Wall. This friendly hostelry comprises a bar, lounge and outdoor drinking area. There is a popular quiz night every Thursday. It serves Sharp's Atlantic and one changing nationally sourced real ale. This is a pub of great character and great characters.
🌄😊♣P🖥🐶🏠

Howard Arms ✅

107 Lowther Street, CA3 8ED
☼ 11-11 (11.30 Fri & Sat); 12-10.30 Sun ☎ (01228) 532926
Robinsons Dizzy Blonde; Theakston Best Bitter; 1 changing beer (often Morland) ⃝H
Like all Carlisle hostelries over 30 years old, the Howard Arms is an ex-state management pub. The front rooms have changed little in character since those days. The city's late-lamented theatre was situated opposite the pub, and old photos and posters on the walls remind us of past links with the theatre. The building has a superb tiled exterior which pre-dates its state management days. It has a big screen for sports events and a heated patio for smokers. 🌄😊◐🚶🖥🐶🏠

Joiners Arms

Church Street, Caldewgate, CA2 5TF (five minutes' walk from Carlisle castle)
☼ 11-midnight (1am Fri; 2am Sat); 12-midnight Sun
☎ (01228) 534275 ⊕ joiners-arms.co.uk
Theakston Best Bitter; Wells Bombardier; 1 changing beer (sourced nationally) ⃝H
Old-fashioned pub completely refurbished after the 2015 Carlisle floods. It retains community focus and continues to host many sports teams including football and darts. Also flooded in 2005, this survivor has plaques near the entrance comparing the heights of the waters that inundated it. Inside, ask the staff to explain the story of Blue Lugs.
◐♣🖥🐶

King's Head Inn ⃝L

Fisher Street, CA3 8RF
☼ 10-11; 11-midnight Sat; 12-11 Sun
⊕ kingsheadcarlisle.co.uk
Yates Bitter; 3 changing beers ⃝H
An excellent city-centre pub and winner of many CAMRA awards. It serves Yates Bitter and a range of guest ales from four handpumps. Pictures of old Carlisle adorn the internal walls and outside is an explanation of why the city is not in the Domesday Book. Good-value meals are served at lunchtime. Children and dogs are not allowed. The spacious covered outdoor courtyard has a large-screen TV and regularly features live music. CAMRA City Pub of the Year 2015. 😊◐🚶♣🖥🐶🏠

Spinners Arms ⃝L

Cummersdale, CA2 6BD
☼ 6 (5 Fri)-midnight; 12-midnight Sat & Sun
☎ (01228) 532928 ⊕ thespinnersarms.org.uk
Carlisle Spun Gold, Flaxen, Magic Number, Oatmeal Stout; 1 changing beer (sourced locally; often Carlisle) ⃝H
Cosy family-friendly hostelry, an original Redfern pub with unique features. Situated less than half a mile from Carlisle's south-western boundary, it is

close to the Cumbrian Way and National Cycle Route 7, which run alongside the picturesque River Caldew. There is regular live music, with Irish music sessions every first and third Wednesday. Children are welcome until 9pm and well-behaved dogs are permitted. The pub is the brewery tap for Carlisle Brewing Co, showcasing its beer on five pumps. ⛲🌞♿♣🅿🚪(75)🌸

Woodrow Wilson 🅛 ✅

48 Botchergate, CA1 1QS
🕐 8am-midnight (1am Fri & Sat) ☎ (01228) 819942
Cumberland Corby Ale; Greene King Abbot; Jennings Sneck Lifter; Marston's Old Empire; Ruddles Best Bitter; Sharp's Doom Bar; 6 changing beers (sourced nationally) 🅗
Wetherspoon pub in a refurbished Co-op building named after the former US president, whose mother was born in Carlisle. Up to 12 handpumps offer the largest range of real ales to be found in Carlisle, usually including many LocAle beers. Food is served all day till 10pm. At the rear there is a spacious outdoor seating area, heated patio and smokers' area. Children are welcome in some areas until 8pm. Five minutes' walk from the railway station and city centre. ⛲🌞🕐♿🍽♦🅿🚪📶

Cartmel

Royal Oak Inn 🅛

The Square, LA11 6QB
🕐 11-midnight ☎ (015395) 36259
🌐 theroyaloakinncartmel.com
Cumbrian Legendary Ales Loweswater Gold; Hawkshead Windermere Pale, Bitter; Unsworth's Yard Sir Edgar Harrington's Last Wolf; 1 changing beer (sourced locally) 🅗
A traditional village inn, under the flagship of the adjacent King's Arms, in the village square within five minutes' walk of the famous Priory and racecourse. A firm favourite with locals and tourists alike, the meals, decor and atmosphere are all excellent. A welcoming log fire and oak beams (some so low as to carry headroom warnings) give a rustic appeal. The extensive enclosed riverside garden at the rear is an attraction for families. Q⛲🌞🕐♦🅰🚪(530,532)🌸📶

Chapel Stile

Wainwrights Inn ✅

LA22 9JH
🕐 11.30-11; 12-11 Sun ☎ (015394) 38088
🌐 langdale.co.uk/wainwrights-inn.html
Jennings Cumberland Ale, Sneck Lifter; Marston's Wainwright; 4 changing beers 🅗
Originally a farmhouse near the former gunpowder works before becoming a hotel, it was converted in the late '80s to a pub that is well known for its location in one of the most popular Lakeland valleys, for its quality of service and its variety of real ales. The stone-flagged bar area, where customers with dogs are welcome, has the regular beers plus four guests, usually from Cumbrian or small northern breweries. ⛲🌞🕐♿🅰🅿🚪(516)🌸📶

Cockermouth

Castle Bar

14 Market Place, CA13 9NQ
🕐 11-11 (midnight Fri & Sat); 12-11 Sun ☎ (01900) 829904
🌐 cockermouth.org.uk/castlebar
Cumbrian Legendary Ales Loweswater Gold; Jennings Bitter, Cumberland Ale; Titanic Plum Porter; 2 changing beers 🅗
A 16th-century building that has been tastefully refurbished to showcase original features such as a spiral staircase. The middle floor is reserved for dining and the upper floor has a lounge, the ground floor has a number of TV screens that show sporting events, and the back bar has a row of cinema seats. An outside patio area is particularly popular with families and offers a suntrap. Jars on the bar display the beers available. ⛲🌞🕐♦🍽🚪🌸

New Cock & Bull

7 South Street, CA13 9RT (centre of town opp Sainsbury's)
🕐 12-11.30 (midnight Fri & Sat); 12-10.30 Sun
☎ (01900) 827999 🌐 thenewcockandbull.co.uk
Coniston Bluebird Bitter; Cumberland Corby Blonde; 5 changing beers 🅗
Situated a five-minute walk from Cockermouth main street, this pub has a varied clientele helping to create a welcoming atmosphere. Recently a fifth handpump was introduced, extending the beer choice, with Cumbrian beers still featuring heavily. An extensive beer garden with table and sunshades makes this pub particularly popular when the weather is good. A wide range of whiskies is available. ⛲🌞🚪🌸📶

Swan Inn 🅛

52-56 Kirkgate, CA13 9PH
🕐 5.30-11.30 (midnight Fri); 12-11 Sat & Sun
☎ (01900) 822425 🌐 swaninncockermouth.com
Jennings Bitter, Cumberland Ale, Cocker Hoop; 3 changing beers 🅗
A traditional inn with a number of distinctive areas, just a few minutes' walk from Cockermouth town centre. The back bar has a sports-bar feel with a large-screen TV, but this does not impinge on the rest of the pub. There is a community ambience, with a number of organisations using the pub as a meeting place. An informal music session is held on the second Wednesday of the month, and a folk night the following Wednesday. Q⛲♣🚪🌸📶

Coniston

Black Bull Inn & Hotel 🅛

LA21 8DU
🕐 8.30am-11 (10.30 winter) ☎ (015394) 41335
🌐 blackbullconiston.co.uk
Coniston Oliver's Light Ale, Bluebird Bitter, Bluebird Premium XB, Old Man Ale, Special Oatmeal Stout, No.9 Barley Wine; 3 changing beers (sourced locally) 🅗
This 16th-century coaching inn serves good food in traditional, comfortable surroundings. It is the tap house for the on-site Coniston Brewing Company and offers six regular beers supplemented by others from the brewery on a rotation basis. The spacious bar and lounge are well frequented by tourists in this hugely popular area. Outside seating is perfect for the summer months, in a spectacular location near Coniston Old Man. Dogs are not allowed in the restaurant. Alcohol is served from 11am. ⛲🌞🕐♿♣🅿🚪(X12,505)🌸📶

Yewdale Inn 🅛

2 Yewdale Road, LA21 8DU
🕐 12-11 ☎ (015394) 41280 🌐 yewdaleinn.com

Barngates Tag Lag; Cumbrian Legendary Ales
Loweswater Gold; Theakston Old Peculier; 2 changing
beers (sourced nationally) ⓗ
A welcoming village inn, in the centre of Coniston,
for locals and visitors alike. In winter a cosy fire and
jovial atmosphere prevail. In summer enjoy a drink
on the terrace with stunning views of the Old Man
of Coniston and surrounding fells and Church Beck,
a babbling brook that runs through the village.
Opening hours and the availability of food are
reduced in winter. ⬛🏠🍴◑🛏▲🚒🚌(505,X12)💐🐾🛜

Dalton-in-Furness

Brown Cow ⓛ
10 Goose Green, LA15 8AQ
🕐 11.30-midnight ☎ (01229) 462553
Barngates Tag Lag; Black Sheep Best Bitter; 5
changing beers (sourced nationally) ⓗ
A warm and friendly atmosphere awaits visitors to
this 400-year-old coaching house, which has
retained many original features including beams,
brasses, local prints and an open fire. A winner of
many awards for its six real ales, the pub also
serves excellent food from a full and varied menu.
Meals can be enjoyed in the large dining room or,
on warmer days, on the charming patio with
heating and lighting. ⬛🏠🍴◑P🚌(6,X6)🛜

Dent

Sun Inn ⓛ
Main Street, LA10 5QL
🕐 11-11; 12-10.30 Sun ☎ (015396) 25208
🌐 sunninndent.co.uk
Kirkby Lonsdale Ruskins Bitter, Monumental Blonde;
3 changing beers ⓗ
A typical Dales village inn at the top of Dent's
cobbled main street. This 300-year-old hostelry has
no modern distractions but offers a warm welcome
and open fires. There is one main bar with original
coin-studded beams and interesting small rooms
leading off. It is the focal point for local events and
acoustic music performances. A traditional roast
can be had every Sunday and good home-made
meals are served throughout the week, including
the pub's own Cumberland sausage.
Q⬛🏠🍴◑▲🚒P💐🛜

Dufton

Stag Inn ⓛ
CA16 6DB
🕐 12-3 (not Mon & Tue), 6-11; 12-3, 6-midnight Fri; 12-11 Sat
& Sun ☎ (017683) 51608 🌐 thestagdufton.co.uk
3 changing beers ⓗ
Standing on the green of this picturesque village
on the Pennine Way, this pub is a beacon for locals,
walkers and cyclists. The bar has an open range
and a side room with a woodburner, ideal for long
cold evenings, and a separate dining room to the
rear. A changing range of beers and good hearty
meals are the order of the day. There are
spectacular views from the beer garden, which
hosts the August beer festival.
Q⬛🏠◑▲🚒P💐🛜

Ennerdale Bridge

Fox & Hounds Inn ⓛ
CA23 3AR

🕐 12-11; 11-11.30 Fri & Sat ☎ (01946) 861373
🌐 foxandhoundsinn.org
Jennings Bitter; Ennerdale Blonde, Darkest; 1
changing beer ⓗ
Traditional community-owned rural pub in a
picturesque setting on the Coast-to-Coast route. Its
stone-flagged floors, exposed beams, cosy
inglenook and real fires add to a friendly
atmosphere. It has a large beer garden, and offers
locally sourced food. It is used by the community as
a meeting place for local groups, including a
monthly book club. Q⬛🏠🍴◑🛏&▲🚒🚌P🚌💐🛜

Eskdale Green

King George IV ⓛ
CA19 1TS (400yds E of Outward Bound Centre, Eskdale
Green)
🕐 11-midnight (1am Fri & Sat) ☎ (019467) 23470
🌐 kinggeorge-eskdale.co.uk
6 changing beers ⓗ
Traditional Lakeland pub with oak beams, flagged
floors, open fires and a number of rooms. Set at the
entrance to the glorious Eskdale Valley, this pub is
renowned for its food and cask ales, and is popular
with tourists and locals alike. Up to nine beers are
on tap in the main season, during which time
Mountain Goat buses run past. It offers a range of
accommodation from B&B to an apartment.
Q⬛🏠🍴◑▲🚉P🚌💐🛜

Foxfield

Prince of Wales ⓛ
LA20 6BX
🕐 closed Mon & Tue; 2.45-11 Wed & Thu; 11.45-11 Fri & Sat;
12-10.30 Sun ☎ (01229) 716238
🌐 princeofwalesfoxfield.co.uk
6 changing beers (sourced nationally) ⓗ
This splendid pub is testament to what is
achievable through passion and hard work;
numerous awards have been presented to hosts
Stuart and Lynda over the years. Guest ales come
from the pub's two house breweries, Foxfield and
Tigertops, and from carefully selected nationwide
breweries. The range will always include a mild.
Various events are organised throughout the year.
Excellent accommodation includes superb
breakfast. The railway stops outside. A cash-only
pub, no card payments. Q⬛🏠🍴&🚉♣🚒P🚌💐🛜

Gilcrux

Barn Bistro ⓛ
CA7 2QX (4 miles S of Aspatria via A596, 5 miles N of
Cockermouth via A5086, near A594 and A595) NY114380
🕐 closed Mon; 12 (5 Tue)-11 ☎ (016973) 23289
🌐 barnbistro.co.uk
Jennings Bitter; 2 changing beers ⓗ
Next to the Beeches caravan park in the village of
Gilcrux, this restaurant-bar always has Jennings
Bitter as it is the landlord's favourite. Two more
handpumps showcase Cumbria's many other
breweries, with over 300 different local brews
having being served in the Barn's seven years. It
also offers 35 malt whiskies plus a gin menu and
has a great reputation for its locally sourced food. It
is aiming to add a fourth handpump, and holds a
beer festival in July. Q⬛🏠◑P💐

Glasson

Highland Laddie
Water Street, CA7 5DT
🌐 12-midnight ☎ (016973) 25007
🌐 highlandladdieinnglasson.co.uk
Greene King IPA; Morland Old Speckled Hen; 1 changing beer Ⓗ
Popular village local close to the Solway Firth and a bird reserve, and the only pub in the area open all day for people walking the Hadrian's Wall route. Meetings are held here for the fishermen who follow the ancient occupation of haaf net fishing, unique to the Solway. The licensee has gained a reputation for providing excellent food, locally sourced, including delicacies such as sea salmon, sea bass and sea trout. Three ales are usually available. Q🏠🛏🕮🌂♣🐾🗢

Gosforth

Gosforth Hall Inn ▼ Ⓛ
Wasdale Road, CA20 1AZ (from A595 follow road signed to Wasdale)
🌐 12-midnight ☎ (019467) 25322 🌐 gosforthhall.co.uk
Yates Golden Ale; 3 changing beers Ⓗ
A mid 17th-century Grade II-listed building in attractive surroundings at the edge of this west Lakeland village close to Wasdale, and next to St Mary's Church with its Viking cross. The lounge reputedly has the widest spanning hearth in England. In winter there are real fires in both the bar and lounge. Accommodation in the main building has recently been extensively refurbished. The menu always features a selection of the landlord's home-made pies.
Q🏠🕮🕮🕀♣🌂P🗢🐾🗢

Grasmere

Tweedies Bar (Dale Lodge Hotel)
Langdale Road, LA22 9SW
🌐 12-11 (midnight Fri & Sat) ☎ (015394) 35300
🌐 dalelodgehotel.co.uk
8 changing beers Ⓗ
Busy hotel in the centre of Grasmere. The stone-flagged bar is warm and welcoming, with an adjacent side room, and a large garden with picnic benches. An interesting menu is available. Local beers are mixed with those from further afield, along with changing ciders. A popular beer festival, The Grasmere Guzzler, takes place in a marquee on the lawn in early September.
🏠🕮🕮🌂P🗢(555,599)🐾🗢

Great Broughton

Punch Bowl Inn
19 Main Street, CA13 0YJ
🌐 closed Mon-Wed; 8-11 Thu; 6-11 Fri; 5-11 Sat; 12-3, 6-11 Sun ☎ (01900) 267070
2 changing beers Ⓗ
Originally a coaching inn, this 17th-century venue is now a community pub. Very much aimed at drinkers, it is run by a committee that includes a number of CAMRA members. It has two handpumps serving beer from a choice of Cumbrian breweries (usually one light and one dark), and the bar is adorned with sporting memorabilia and a selection of water jugs. It offers darts, dominoes and quizzes. Q🏠♣🐾🗢

Great Langdale

Old Dungeon Ghyll Hotel Ⓛ ✅
LA22 9JY
🌐 11-11; 11-10.30 Sun ☎ (015394) 37272 🌐 odg.co.uk
Cumbrian Legendary Ales Esthwaite Bitter; Jennings Cumberland Ale; Theakston Old Peculier; Yates Bitter; 3 changing beers Ⓗ
A legendary climbers' and walkers' bar at the end of the Great Langdale Valley enjoying excellent views from the terrace with an open fire in the range in the bar. Hearty meals are served including a varied specials board. The pub hosts regular music nights as well as folk festivals. A must-visit bar in the heart of the Lake District.
Q🏠🕮🕮🕮🌂P🗢(516)🐾🗢

Great Salkeld

Highland Drove Ⓛ
CA11 9NA
🌐 12-2.30 (not Mon), 6-11; 12-midnight Sat
☎ (01768) 898349
Theakston Black Bull Bitter; house beer (by Eden); 1 changing beer Ⓗ
Just off the main road through this attractive village, everything here is of a high standard. Entering the exceptionally well-stocked bar, there is a lounge and games room either side with the award-winning Kyloes restaurant upstairs, all with well-chosen decor featuring exposed timber and brickwork embellished with Highland-style soft furnishings, brass and copper ornaments. Excellent food can be enjoyed every day, and themed nights have recently been introduced. Watch out for the Highland cows! 🏠🕮🕮🕀🌂♣🐾🗢

Greenodd

Ship Ⓛ
Main Street, LA12 7QZ
🌐 closed Mon; 5-11 (midnight Fri); 2-midnight Sat; 2-10.30 Sun ☎ (01229) 861553
Greenodd Kiln, Citra, Roundabout, Coal Wharf; 1 changing beer (sourced locally) Ⓗ
A traditional village inn attracting a good mix of locals and visitors. Beers on five handpumps are sold from a range of over 20 brewed by Greenodd Brewery at the back of the building. The pub has recently been refurbished and its open-plan interior features slate floors, stone walls, exposed beams and open fires, with a separate quiet room to the rear. Not all X6 buses stop at Greenodd.
🏠♣P🗢(X6)🐾🗢

Hawkshead

King's Arms Hotel Ⓛ
The Square, LA22 0NZ
🌐 11-midnight ☎ (015394) 36372
🌐 kingsarmshawkshead.co.uk
Cumbrian Legendary Ales Loweswater Gold; Hawkshead Bitter; 2 changing beers (sourced locally) Ⓗ
Characterful 500-year-old village inn on the square of this historic settlement. The traditional interior features beamed ceilings, an open fire and a hand-carved king in the bar supporting the floor above. Good food is available in the bar and dining area. The patio is south facing on the edge of the square. Frequent live music and twice-yearly beer festivals take place. Family friendly, dogs are welcome in

the bar area. There is plenty of parking available in the village. Winter hours vary.
Q❀🅰️◗♣🖥️(505,525)🐾

Red Lion 🅛

Main Street, LA22 0NS
✪ 12-11; 12-10.30 Sun ☎ (015394) 36213
🌐 redlionhawkshead.co.uk
Cumbrian Legendary Ales Esthwaite Bitter; Hawkshead Bitter; Tarn Hows Pigling Blonde; house beer (by Hawkshead); 1 changing beer (sourced locally) 🅷
A 15th-century coaching inn set in one of the prettiest villages in the Lake District with links to Wordsworth and Beatrix Potter. Excellent beers include some from the wood. The food is honestly priced, sourced locally and on offer all day. There is a warm and friendly informal atmosphere; dogs and wet boots are welcome and it is a great place to relax. The attractive paved patio area has plenty of tables for summer dining and drinking. Comfortably priced rooms are available.
🛏️❀🅰️◗🅰️♣🖥️(505,525)🐾🛜

Hayton

Stone Inn

CA8 9HR
✪ 12-2, 5.30-11 (midnight Fri); 11-midnight Sat; 12-10.30 Sun ☎ (01228) 670896 🌐 stoneinnhayton.co.uk
Thwaites Original; 2 changing beers (often Hadrian Border) 🅷
A traditional family-run community pub in the village of Hayton, home to the local leek club. There is an upstairs dining room which can be hired for small gatherings. A fine pair of 1904 Christ Church boat club oars adorn one wall, and ask to see the CAMRA mirror. There are two changing ales, often from a local brewery, as well as the regular Thwaites Original bitter. 🛏️◗♣P🐾🛜

Hesket Newmarket

Old Crown 🅛 ✔️

CA7 8JG
✪ 5.30-11; 12-3, 5-11 Fri; 12-11 Sat; 12-10.30 Sun
☎ (016974) 78288 🌐 theoldcrownpub.com
Hesket Newmarket Haystacks, Black Sail, Helvellyn Gold, High Pike, Doris' 90th Birthday Ale, Brim Fell; 4 changing beers (sourced locally; often Hesket Newmarket) 🅷
Sitting in the heart of this lovely fell-side village, the Old Crown is a showcase for the Hesket Newmarket Brewery, which is immediately behind the inn. It is well known as the first co-operatively owned pub in the country and is popular with locals and visitors alike, with Prince Charles and Sir Chris Bonington among its supporters. Closed Monday to Thursday afternoons in winter, with no meals on winter Mondays. Q🛏️❀◗♣🐾🛜

Holmes Green

Black Dog Inn 🅛

Broughton Road, LA15 8JP (from Dalton 1 mile past South Lakes Safari Zoo) SD233761
✪ closed Mon; 4 (3 Fri & Sat)-midnight; 2-9 Sun
☎ (01229) 462975
Abbeydale Moonshine; Cumbrian Legendary Ales Loweswater Gold; 3 changing beers (sourced regionally) 🅷

A warm welcome awaits here from the landlord and locals alike. This former coaching inn with two real fires, quarry-tiled floor and rustic beams has plenty of character. Live music features most Saturdays, plus open mic nights and music festivals. With five real ales on offer, it is supportive of local microbreweries. Outside, it has a decked seating area. Home-made burgers are served on Friday evening. Q🛏️❀◗P🐾🛜

Ings

Watermill Inn 🅛

LA8 9PY
✪ 11-11; 11-10.30 Sun ☎ (01539) 821309
🌐 lakelandpub.co.uk
Watermill Collie Wobbles, A Bit 'er Ruff, Isle of Dogs, Wruff Night, Dogth Vader, Shih Tzu Faced; 8 changing beers 🅷
A consistent award winner, this pub and brewery tap has a relaxed atmosphere. Up to 11 ales are available including those brewed on site. Recently refurbished, this mecca for real ale serves a wide selection of home-made meals daily until 9pm. Drinkers of the four-legged variety are not forgotten, with biscuits and water provided.
Q🛏️❀🅰️◗♿♣🐶P🖥️(555)🐾🛜

Kendal

Factory Tap 🍷 🅛

5 Aynam Road, LA9 7DE
✪ closed Mon & Tue; 4 (3 Fri)-9; 12-9 Sun ☎ (015394) 82541
🌐 thefactorytap.co.uk
Bowness Bay Swan Blonde; 7 changing beers 🅷
Opened as the Bowness Bay tap in 2015, the range now includes many breweries (predominantly Cumbrian). Sited in converted cottages on a former carpet factory complex, its bare limestone walls and tables made from barrel ends on old cable drums make for a fascinating interior. Upstairs, exposed beams create an atmospheric space, sometimes hired out for private functions. From its opening the tap has been popular with locals and visitors to the south lakes. Q🛏️❀♿⇌P🐾

Rifleman's Arms 🅛 ✔️

4 Greenside, LA9 4LD
✪ 6.30-midnight; 12-midnight Sat & Sun ☎ (01539) 723224
Greene King Abbot; 4 changing beers 🅷
A true community pub on the edge of town with the Vaux motif still etched on the windows. Numerous local groups meet here, with popular live folk music sessions on Thursdays. It has a quiet atmosphere, with a Sunday quiz and traditional pub games. There are always five real ales on the bar, including local beers. The pub looks out onto a pleasant green and is often involved with events taking place there. Q🛏️♣🖥️(44,48)🐾

Ring o' Bells

37-39 Kirkland, LA9 5AF
✪ 12 (6 Thu)-11 ☎ (01539) 720326
🌐 ringobellskendal.webs.com
Coniston Bluebird Bitter; Thwaites Nutty Black; 1 changing beer 🅷
A heartening example of a true community inn, where nothing is too much trouble. The family welcome is equalled by the warmth of the roaring fire. Set on consecrated ground, it has the parish church to the rear. A well-maintained original cellar ensures consistently good local ales, and home-

made family food is available. Regular live music includes a folk session on Monday. The last remaining pub in Kirkland, it has a regionally important historic interior. Q☆🐕🌜◐🛍⬤🚍❀

Keswick

Pheasant Inn 🅻 ⊘
Crosthwaite Road, CA12 5PP
☎ 11.45-11; 12-11 Sun ☎ (017687) 72219
⊕ pheasantinnkeswick.co.uk
Jennings Bitter, Cumberland Ale, Cocker Hoop, Sneck Lifter; 1 changing beer Ⓗ
This traditional yet upmarket pub on the outskirts of town delivers a selection of Marston's beers from five handpumps, with four from Jennings. Food is available lunchtimes and evenings, while Sunday lunch (served 12-3pm) come in standard, small and child sizes. It has a real fire inside, with outdoor seating at the front near the road and at the rear, up steps, providing good views, partially under shelter. 🐕🌜🖨◐🚍

Wainwright 🅻
Lake Road, CA12 5BZ
☎ 11.30-11.30 (midnight Fri & Sat) ☎ (017687) 44927
⊕ thewainwright.pub
Marston's Wainwright; 8 changing beers Ⓗ
A traditional pub in the town centre which provides a relaxing atmosphere for the casual tourist as well as the committed fell walker. There are large-screen TVs, with sound turned off, showing Wainwright walks. Eight real ales from all over Cumbria are on the bar, with the occasional offering from further afield. Dogs are welcome except in the dining area during mealtimes. Q🐕◐⬤🚍❀

Kings Meaburn

White Horse Inn 🅻
CA10 3BU
☎ 5 (12 Sat)-11; 12-10.30 Sun ☎ (01931) 714256
3 changing beers Ⓗ
A 400-year-old pub in a peaceful corner of Westmorland, offering a warm welcome, good craic and well-kept ales. It is now the unofficial outlet for the nearby Appleby Brewery, with one of its beers always on. A locals' pub, it runs the annual beer and music festival on a nearby farm, an annual pie-making competition and the post office. All food is home made and sourced locally. Q🐕🌜◐♣♠❀

Kirkby Lonsdale

Orange Tree 🅻
9 Fairbank, LA6 2BD (turn left past churchyard, and the hotel is on your right)
☎ 11-11 (midnight Fri & Sat) ☎ (015242) 71716
⊕ theorangetreehotel.co.uk
Kirkby Lonsdale Ruskins Bitter, Radical Red, Monumental Blonde, Jubilee Stout Ⓗ
This local establishment, formerly the Fleece, was renamed after a pub near Twickenham and the walls are adorned with rugby memorabilia. It is the tap for Kirkby Lonsdale Brewery, and always has five of its beers on plus a guest and a real cider. There is a separate dining area to the rear serving good wholesome food. A worthy local CAMRA Pub of the Year winner on several occasions. 🐕🖨◐♣⬤🚍(567)❀🛜

Kirkoswald

Fetherston Arms
The Square, CA10 1DQ
☎ 4-11; 12-midnight Sat & Sun ☎ (01768) 898284
⊕ fetherston-arms.co.uk
Theakston Best Bitter; 3 changing beers (often Allendale, Hesket Newmarket) Ⓗ
The Fethers is in the centre of this historic village. Extensive alterations and the friendly enthusiasm of the family owners have helped convert it into a truly outstanding pub, and it has a deservedly excellent reputation for its food. Three changing real ales are sold from breweries such as Allendale and Hesket Newmarket. Although the village is not on a bus route, it is a 20-minute stroll from Lazonby station on the Carlisle-Settle line. Check opening hours in winter. Q🐕🌜◐⬤❀🛜

Levens

Hare & Hounds Inn
LA8 8PN
☎ 12-11; 12-10.30 Sun ☎ (015395) 60004
⊕ hareandhoundslevens.co.uk
Bowness Bay Swan Blonde; 4 changing beers Ⓗ
Recently extended, this thriving pub is everything a village hostelry should be. A free house, it serves up to five real ales, aiming to showcase the best in Cumbria. A good range of international bottled beers is also available. The fare is mostly of the quality comfort food variety – the pizzas are a must. Q🐕🌜◐♿P🚍❀🛜

Loppergarth

Wellington Inn 🅻
Main Street, LA12 0JL (1 mile from A590 between Lindal and Pennington)
☎ 6-11 (midnight Fri & Sat); closed Sun & Mon
☎ (01229) 582388
Healey's Golden, Blonde, Best; 2 changing beers (sourced locally) Ⓗ
Superb village local with its own microbrewery – Healey's – a custom-made stainless steel plant which can be viewed from the games room. Four handpumps, occasionally five, primarily dispense Healey's beers. These include an award-winning blonde, a golden bitter, a traditional darker best bitter, a superb mild and occasional specials. Wood-burning stoves make this a cosy pub, with games, books and good conversation. There is a quiz on alternate Saturdays. Well-behaved dogs on leads are welcome. 🐕🌜♣⬤❀🛜

Loweswater

Kirkstile Inn 🅻
CA13 0RU (off B5289) NY140210
☎ 11-11; 12-10.30 Sun ☎ (01900) 85219 ⊕ kirkstile.com
Cumbrian Legendary Esthwaite Bitter, Langdale, Grasmoor Dark Ale, Loweswater Gold; 2 changing beers Ⓗ
A 16th-century inn that lies a short stroll from the waters of Crummock and Loweswater. It is the brewery tap for Cumbrian Legendary Ales – creator of a former Champion Golden Ale of Britain, Loweswater Gold – with six handpumps. It has four seating areas including a separate restaurant, and can be very busy at meal times. A consistent winner and finalist for local CAMRA Pub of the Year since the early 2000s. Q🐕🌜🖨◐♿♣P🚍❀🛜

Maryport

Lifeboat 🄻

Shipping Brow, Senhouse Street, CA15 6AB
🌣 11.30-midnight ☎ (01900) 814636
Cumbrian Legendary Ales Langdale, Loweswater Gold; 1 changing beer Ⓗ
A Grade II-listed building close to the harbour, there has been a pub on this site since 1751. It is a popular venue offering a cosy atmosphere and a friendly welcome. Two local beers are always available and home-cooked food is offered. The owner is the current holder of the World's Biggest Liar title. 🛏🐾🎭🍺&⚒♿🚆🏠🐾

Mawbray

Lowther 🄻

CA15 6QT
🌣 6-11; closed Tue; 5-midnight Fri & Sat; 12-11 Sun
☎ (01900) 881750 ⏣ mawbraypub.co.uk
Derwent Parsons Pledge; 2 changing beers Ⓗ
A traditional 19th-century inn with a contemporary feel set in a village close to the Solway Coast. It has two rooms plus a conservatory, attracts customers from the wider local area, supports village events and holds a quiz night on Monday. Food is served in the evening and Sunday lunchtime. Two of the three beers are brewed close to the pub.
Q🛏🐾🎭🍺♣P🐾🛜

Monkhill

Drovers Rest 🏆

CA5 6DB
🌣 12-2, 5-11; 12-11 Thu-Sun ☎ (01228) 576141
4 changing beers Ⓗ
A traditional country pub close to the popular Hadrian's Wall path with a strong community focus. Although opened up, the interior still has the feel of three distinct rooms. The bar area is cosy and welcoming, with a roaring fire in winter. Some interesting historical State Management Scheme documents adorn the walls. The Drovers is an oasis for many different and sometimes obscure (for the area) real ales. Winner of the CAMRA super regional Pub of the Year award.
🛏🐾🍺Å♣P🚆(93)🐾

Near Sawrey

Tower Bank Arms 🄻

LA22 0LF (on B5285 2 miles S of Hawkshead)
🌣 12-11; 12-10.30 Sun ☎ (015394) 36334
⏣ towerbankarms.co.uk
Barngates Tag Lag; Cumbrian Legendary Ales Loweswater Gold; Hawkshead Bitter; 2 changing beers (sourced locally) Ⓗ
A 17th-century Lakeland inn with slate floors, oak beams and a cast-iron range with open fire. It is next to the National Trust's Hill Top (Beatrix Potter's home). Delivering great local flavours in food, beer and atmosphere, its five handpumps serve local beer, and it has cider and perry. Families and dogs are welcomed. There is a seasonal bus service connecting to the Windermere ferry and Hawkshead. Phone to check winter hours.
Q🛏🐾🖾🍺♣♦P🚆🐾

Nether Wasdale

Strands Inn 🄻

CA20 1ET
🌣 12-11; 12-10.30 Sun ☎ (019467) 26237
⏣ thestrandsinn.com
Strands Pied Piper, Green Bullet, Brown Bitter, Low Flyer, Irresponsibly, T'errmmm-inator; 6 changing beers Ⓗ
Along narrow, wooded and gently hilly lanes, this picturesque village is a delightful surprise, with its view of the highest mountains in England just a few miles away. One of three real ale pubs, Strands has its own brewery, with any six of around 30 beers on the bar (and more in bottles). Try them all in May at the festival of beers. There is no mobile phone reception in the valley but the pub does have free Wi-Fi. Awarded local CAMRA branch Pub of the Year for 2016. Q🛏🐾🖾🍺Å♣P🐾🛜

Newbiggin

Blue Bell Inn 🄻

Heads Nook, CA8 9DH (8 miles S of Brampton in small village just off B6413)
🌣 6 (7 Mon)-midnight; 6-1am Fri; 12-3, 6-1am Sat; 12-3, 6-midnight Sun ☎ (01768) 896615
⏣ bluebellinnnewbiggin.co.uk
1 changing beer (sourced locally; often Cumberland, Eden, Tirril) Ⓗ
Nestled in the North Pennines Area of Outstanding Natural Beauty, this small country pub is used mainly by locals. It is also popular with holidaymakers and walkers needing refreshment, with food served every evening and lunchtime at weekends. Try the renowned home-made chips. Traditional pub games – darts and pool – can be enjoyed. It stocks one real ale from a local brewery. Winter hours may vary. Look out for the naughty gnomes! 🐾🍺&♣P

Penrith

Agricultural Hotel 🄻 ✅

Castlegate, CA11 7JE
🌣 11-11 (midnight Fri & Sat); 12-10.30 Sun
☎ (01768) 862622
Jennings Bitter, Cumberland Ale, Sneck Lifter; 3 changing beers Ⓗ
The hotel is built from local sandstone and the bar and dining room are open plan, with steps from one to the other. There is also a small reception area. The Victorian shuttered sash screen bar has six handpumps selling Jennings and guest beers. Food is served in the large dining area, as well as in the bar at quiet times. It is convenient for the railway station and nearby bus stops. A former CAMRA branch Pub of the Year.
🛏🐾🖾🍺&🚆♣P🚆

Dockray Hall

Great Dockray, CA11 7DE
🌣 10.30-11; 12-10.30 Sun ☎ (01768) 210676
⏣ dockrayhall.com
Cumbrian Legendary Ales Loweswater Pale Ale, Grasmoor Dark Ale, Loweswater Gold, American Invasion Ⓗ
Grade I-listed 16th-century inn with many original features including three large fireplaces, fully refurbished in 2016. The future Richard III stayed during his exploits in the area and there used to be a tunnel between the hall and nearby Penrith Castle. It sells a range of beers from Cumbria

Legendary Ales, and is the sister pub to the Kirkstile Inn, Loweswater. Good food using local produce is available all week. ⑂❀◧➡♣P⊟

Penruddock

Herdwick Inn 𝕃
CA11 0QU
❁ 4-11; 12-2.30, 5-midnight Sat; 12-2.30, 5-11 Sun
☎ (017684) 83007 ⊕ herdwickinn.com
3 changing beers (sourced nationally; often Banks's, Brakspear) ⊞
A modernised country pub with a large log fire during the colder winter months and a separate dining room. A beer patio is available for smokers and non-smokers alike. Good food is served, with senior citizens' specials throughout the week. It has a large hops display in the bar and hosts the village shop for tourists and locals. Dogs are welcome. A sister pub to the Punchbowl, Askham.
Q⑂❀◧◑⑂♣A▲P⊟❀❖

Ravenglass

Inn at Ravenglass 𝕃
Main Street, CA18 1SQ (at N end, overlooking Irish Sea)
❁ 12-11; 11-11 Sun ☎ (01229) 717230
⊕ theinnatravenglass.co.uk
Bowness Bay Swan Blonde; Ulverston Laughing Gravy; 2 changing beers ⊞
A 17th-century inn in this National Park coastal hamlet that was once a Roman port. The dining room has a reputation for fresh seafood from the local catch of the day. The choice of real ales is particularly enjoyable after a day in the fells, or messing about in boats. The pub offers great sunset views over the estuary. Close to Ravenglass stations for mainline and Ravenglass & Eskdale valley railway (La'al Ratty), it offers easy access to the Western Lakes valleys.
Q⑂❀◧◑▲➡♣♣P⊟(6)❀❖

Ravenstonedale

Black Swan Hotel ●
CA17 4NG
❁ 11-midnight (1am Fri & Sat); 12-midnight Sun
☎ (015396) 23204 ⊕ blackswanhotel.com
Black Sheep Best Bitter, Baa Baa; Timothy Taylor Boltmaker; 2 changing beers ⊞
A Victorian inn, rebuilt in 1899, in a tranquil conservation village in the Eden valley. This small hotel offers a varied range of real ale. The bar has TV and darts, while the lounge has adjoining dining rooms. Across the road is an extensive well-maintained garden and stream.
Q⑂❀◧◑⑂P⊟(564)❀

Rydal

Badger Bar (Glen Rothay Hotel) 𝕃
LA22 9LR
❁ 10-11; 10-10.30 Sun ☎ (015394) 34500
⊕ theglenrothay.co.uk
Barngates Goodhew's Dry Stout; 4 changing beers ⊞
A quirky pub opposite Rydal Water and adjacent to Rydal Mount, once the home of William Wordsworth. There are lots of walking options, from easy to challenging, close by. The pub is notable for its badger cam of setts in the grounds, and toilets with local stone features. It is on the popular summer open top bus route from Bowness

to Grasmere. There are comfortable rooms and good-quality food available.
Q⑂❀◧◑▲P⊟(555,599)❀❖

St Bees

Manor ●
Main Street, CA27 0DE (100yds from station)
❁ 12-11 ☎ (01946) 820587 ⊕ manorinnstbees.co.uk
St Austell Tribute; 3 changing beers ⊞
A Grade I-listed hotel, one of four pubs on the main street offering real ale, popular with tourists and locals alike for its food and the three different real ales. The pub boasts a sports bar, lounge bar, dining areas, garden and a pleasant outside drinking area. It is on the picturesque Carlisle to Barrow train line and is near the start of the Coast-to-Coast walk. ⑂❀◧◑➡P⊟(6)❀❖

Santon Bridge

Bridge Inn 𝕃 ●
CA19 1UX (on road from Gosforth to Eskdale)
❁ 11-11 ☎ (019467) 26221 ⊕ santonbridgeinn.com
Jennings Cumberland Ale; 6 changing beers ⊞
Once a modest mail coach halt, this hotel, with low beams and creaking floors, is in a beautiful and scenic location close to major tourist spots, such as the Eskdale steam railway, Wastwater and Muncaster Castle. The clientele is a mix of tourists and locals. It offers a range of beers, including a couple of guest beers from Marston's, and is the home to the World's Biggest Liar competition. Food is served daily. Q⑂❀◧◑▲P❀❖

Silloth

Albion 𝕃
Eden Street, CA7 4AS
❁ closed Mon-Wed; 12 (7 Thu; 2 Fri)-11.30 ☎ (016973) 3121
Derwent Parsons Pledge; 1 changing beer (sourced locally; often Derwent) ⊞
Traditional one-bar pub with a separate family room containing a pool table and TV, well supported by locals and summer visitors. Pictures of old Silloth decorate the walls, along with two models of whaling trawlers. There are numerous photos celebrating the Isle of Man TT races; the local motorcycle club meets here on the first Sunday of each month and welcomes visitors. The nearby Derwent Brewery often tries out new beers at this hostelry. ⑂❀▲♣P⊟❀❖

Staveley

Beer Hall 𝕃 ●
Mill Yard, LA8 9LR
❁ 12-6 (5 Mon; 11 Fri & Sat); 12-8 Sun ☎ (01539) 825260
⊕ hawksheadbrewery.co.uk
Hawkshead Windermere Pale, Bitter, Red, Lakeland Gold, Brodie's Prime, Cumbrian Five Hop; 3 changing beers ⊞
The brewery tap next door to the brewery, a busy and an unusual two-storey pub in the vibrant mill yard complex of local and artisan businesses, with lots of walking and cycle routes nearby. The pub serves hearty beer tapas alongside larger meals. Popular beer festivals take place in March and July each year. Local CAMRA Pub of the Year 2016.
Q⑂❀◑⑂▲➡♣P⊟(555)❀❖

Eagle & Child Hotel

Kendal Road, LA8 9LP

✪ 11-11; 12-10.30 Sun ☎ (01539) 821320
⊕ eaglechildinn.co.uk

5 changing beers Ⓗ

A welcoming and popular destination in this busy village between Kendal and Windermere. The pub has a varied menu with alternating daily specials. Two beer gardens and an open fire, along with interesting pictures and artefacts adorning the walls, make this a must-visit. A well-attended pub quiz takes place weekly. Q❄️☕◑≈♣P🚏(555)🐾🛜

Talkin

Blacksmiths Arms Ⓛ

CA8 1LE

✪ 12-midnight ☎ (016977) 3452 ⊕ blacksmithstalkin.co.uk

Black Sheep Ale; Yates Bitter; 2 changing beers Ⓗ

Since taking over in 1997, the present owners have made this probably the most popular pub in the vicinity. The winning formula includes four real ales, a superbly stocked bar, friendly and efficient staff, no TV and meticulous attention to detail. With a golf course and country park within two miles and plenty of other outdoor activities locally, it attracts visitors from far outside north Cumbria to this Area of Outstanding Natural Beauty. Q🛏️❄️☕◑&♣P🛜

Tallentire

Bush Inn ✪

CA13 0PT

✪ closed Mon; 5.30-midnight ☎ (01900) 823707

3 changing beers Ⓗ

An old-fashioned pub that usually serves at least one ale from a Cumbrian brewery. This hub of the community and home of the cricket team hosts a traditional music session on the last Wednesday of the month. In addition to its exposed beams, stone floor and wood-burning stove, the pub also has an exterior sensitive to the character of the village. Well-behaved dogs are welcome. Food is served in a separate restaurant Thursday to Saturday evenings. Q◑🐾🛜

Troutbeck

Mortal Man Ⓛ

LA23 1PL

✪ 10.30-midnight ☎ (015394) 33193
⊕ themortalman.co.uk

Coniston Bluebird Bitter; Cumbrian Legendary Ales Loweswater Gold; Hawkshead Bitter; Hesket Newmarket Haystacks; 1 changing beer Ⓗ

A 4-star hotel with a main bar serving local ales including a changing guest beer. Several smaller rooms are off this, where meals are served all day, along with a large function room. The extensive garden seating area offers spectacular views of the surrounding fells and Windermere in the distance. A popular beer festival is staged in the summer, and local folk nights and quizzes take place throughout the year. 🛏️❄️☕◑▲♣P🐾🛜

Ulverston

Devonshire Arms Ⓛ

Braddyll Terrace, Victoria Road, LA12 0DH (next to railway bridge in town centre)

✪ 4-11 (10.30 Mon); 12-midnight Fri & Sat; 12-10.30 Sun ☎ (01229) 582537

Abbeydale Deception, Moonshine, Absolution; Bank Top Flat Cap; Saltaire Blonde; 2 changing beers (sourced nationally) Ⓗ

Conveniently situated between the bus and train station, the Dev is a real locals' pub with a welcoming atmosphere. Four TVs provide comprehensive sports coverage, while there is still plenty of room for banter around the bar or more intimate conversation in the comfortable seating areas. Outside tables are popular, especially in summer, and solar panels provide supplementary power. A pool table and two dartboards add to the entertainment. 🛏️❄️☕&▲≈♣♠P🚏🐾🛜

Mill Ⓛ ✪

Mill Street, LA12 7EB

✪ 11-11 (1am Fri & Sat); 11-10.30 Sun ☎ (01229) 581384
⊕ mill-at-ulverston.co.uk

Lancaster Amber, Blonde, Black, Red; 6 changing beers (sourced nationally) Ⓗ

Town-centre converted flour mill with an interesting layout. The original waterwheel is central to the ground floor, fed from the stream channelled alongside the first-floor outdoor terrace. Food is served in both the bar and, on weekends, in the upstairs restaurant (booking recommended). Tuesday is quiz night and the open mic session is Wednesday. A recently opened loft bar/function suite serves wine and cocktails on Friday and Saturday evenings. Dogs are welcome in the bar area. 🛏️❄️◑&▲≈🐾🛜

Old Friends Ⓛ

49 Soutergate, LA12 7ES

✪ 4 (2 Thu)-11; 2-midnight Fri; 12-midnight Sat; 12-10.30 Sun ☎ (01229) 208195 ⊕ oldfriendsulverston.co.uk

Old School Blackboard; Stringers Plan B; 6 changing beers (sourced locally) Ⓗ

Welcoming old-fashioned locals' pub about 200 yards uphill from the town centre. There is a cosy snug in front of the bar with an open fire; another seating area with TV is separated by a passageway with a hatch to the bar. Beers are mostly from local brewers. A popular quiz night is held every Tuesday and there is a wonderful beer garden, with heating in the winter, at the back. 🛏️❄️▲≈♣🚏🐾🛜

Stan Laurel Inn Ⓛ

31 The Ellers, LA12 0AB

✪ 7-11 Mon; 12-2.30, 6-11 (midnight Fri & Sat); 12-11.30 Sun ☎ (01229) 582814 ⊕ thestanlaurel.co.uk

Thwaites Original; 5 changing beers (sourced locally) Ⓗ

Just off the centre of Stan Laurel's home town, the Stan offers a warm welcome to locals and visitors alike. Six handpulls serve a variety of mainly locally brewed beers. Excellent-value quality food is available throughout the week (no food Mon). Adjacent to the bar is a large room with pool and darts and a smaller room primarily used by diners. In winter a log-burning stove adds to the pub's comfortable ambience. Well-behaved dogs are welcome in the bar. Q🛏️❄️☕◑▲≈♣P🚏(6,6A)🐾🛜

Sun Inn 🅛
Market Street, LA12 7AY
✪ 11-1am (3am Thu-Sat); 12-1am Sun ☎ (01229) 585044
Theakston Best Bitter; house beer (by Theakston); 5 changing beers (sourced regionally) 🅗
Tastefully refurbished Grade II-listed coaching inn situated in the heart of Ulverston town centre. The bar carries a selection of six guest beers, ranging from ales from small local breweries to the larger more well-known brands. Along with a warm welcome, you can expect a number of screens for watching sport, a large heated beer garden, en-suite hotel rooms and delicious food served daily.
🛏️🏵️🛤️🕽️🍴🚻🚆P🚃(6,X6)🐾🛜

Swan Inn 🅛
Swan Street, LA12 7JX (on edge of town centre overlooking A590)
✪ 3.30-11; 2-midnight Fri; 12-midnight Sat; 12-11 Sun
☎ (01229) 582519
9 changing beers (sourced nationally) 🅗
The pub has an open-plan feel yet there are three distinct drinking areas for darts, TV or just good conversation by the fire. Live music features occasionally, while a jukebox allows all genres of music to be played. All Premier League football and major sporting events are screened, and a Sunday night quiz rounds off the entertainment. A large beer garden behind the pub is popular in summer.
🏵️🚻🍴🚶🚃(6,X6)🐾🛜

Underbarrow
Black Labrador 🅛
LA8 8HQ
✪ 12-3, 6-11; closed Tue; 12-11 Sat & Sun
☎ (015395) 68234 ⊕ theblacklabrador.co.uk
3 changing beers 🅗
Formerly the Punchbowl, this traditional village inn has been recently extended to include disabled access and facilities. The outstanding new lounge area opens into a semi outdoor space in summer. The pub's beer festival, once held in a marquee, will now use this area. The original flagstone-floored bar remains, along with an attractive upstairs dining room. On a picturesque route between Kendal and Bowness, it is popular both with visitors and locals. Transport home is provided for local diners. Q🛏️🏵️🕽️🍴🚶P🐾🛜

Watermillock
Brackenrigg Inn 🅛
CA11 0LP (on A592)
✪ 12-11; 12-10.30 Sun ☎ (017684) 86206
⊕ brackenrigginn.co.uk
Brack 'n' Brew Bitter, Blonde; 4 changing beers 🅗
An imposing roadside inn with stunning views over Ullswater and the northern fells. It has a large bar with a welcoming open fire and a separate dining room. Superb local fare accompanies the ales from the brewery at the rear of the pub. A laid-back atmosphere is a tribute to the friendly staff. The pub is on the new Ullswater circular path.
Q🛏️🏵️🛏️🕽️🍴🚶P🚃(108)🐾🛜

Wetheral
Wheatsheaf Inn 🅛 ✅
CA4 8HD
✪ 12-11 (midnight Fri & Sat); 12-11.30 Sun
☎ (01228) 560686 ⊕ wheatsheafwetheral.co.uk
Cumberland Corby Ale; 2 changing beers 🅗
An early 19th-century village pub, just a few minutes' walk from the village green and railway station, deservedly popular with locals and visitors, and a former local CAMRA award winner. Along with Corby Ale from the local Cumberland Brewery, there are two changing ales from local and national breweries. Good-value bar meals are served Wednesday to Sunday (booking advisable at weekends). The regular Tuesday quiz night is well supported. 🛏️🏵️🕽️🚶🍴P🚃(75)🐾🛜

Whitehaven
Vagabond 🅛
9 Marlborough Street, CA28 7LL
✪ 5-11; 4-midnight Fri; 12-midnight Sat; 12-9 Sun
☎ (01946) 66653 ⊕ thevagabondpub.co.uk
4 changing beers 🅗
This quaint, traditional pub is tucked just off the historic harbourside in this Georgian west-coast town. The wood-floored pub is on two storeys and offers real ales, good food – including stone-baked pizzas – and a welcoming atmosphere. Beers are constantly changing, with varied choices and styles from local, national and Scottish breweries.
Q🛏️🕽️🍴🚶🚃🛜

Witherslack
Derby Arms Hotel ✅
LA11 6RH
✪ 12-11 ☎ (015395) 52207 ⊕ thederbyarms.co.uk
Bowness Bay Swan Blonde; 5 changing beers 🅗
Reopened by the Witherslack community land trust, this local hub includes a community shop. A large room with open fires is entered from the front door, with dining spaces in adjoining rooms, and a snug with games room at the rear. The eclectic furniture is in the style of a faded stately home. The pub is a popular stop-off for cyclists and walkers to enjoy hearty local food and good company. The house beer, Jolly Boys, is brewed by Cumbrian Legendary Ales. 🛏️🏵️🛏️🕽️🍴P🚃(X6)🐾

Wreay
Plough Inn 🅛
CA4 0RL
✪ 7-11 Mon; closed Tue; 12-3, 5.30-11 ☎ (016974) 75770
⊕ theploughwreay.co.uk
Hawkshead Lakeland Gold; 2 changing beers (sourced locally) 🅗
Tastefully modernised pub dating back to 1786, located in the heart of this picturesque village, just five miles south of Carlisle. Locally sourced, excellent food is served in the split-level bar and dining area, with two cask ales from Cumbrian breweries usually on the bar. The village guardians continue to use it as their meeting place – a display of their clay pipes can be seen inside. Quiz night is Monday. Q🛏️🏵️🕽️P🐾

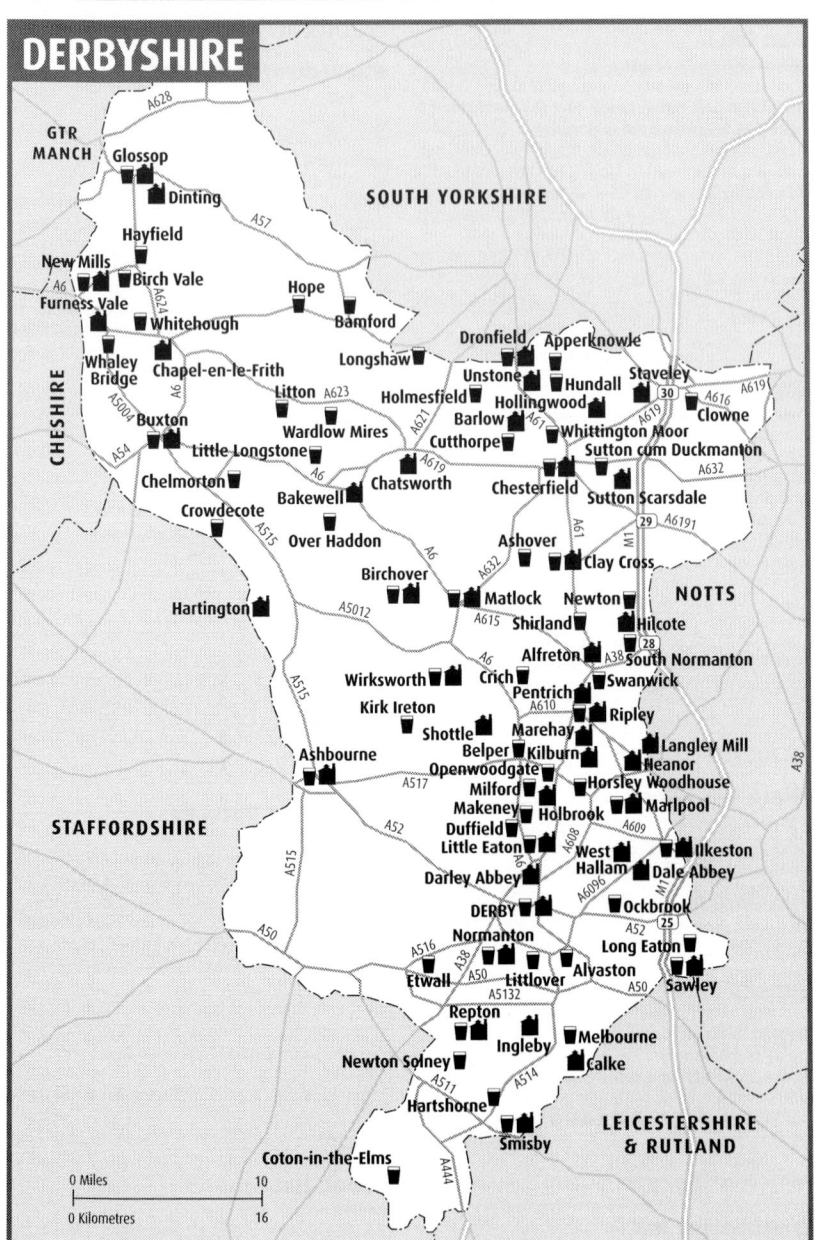

DERBYSHIRE

GTR MANCH

Glossop
Dinting
Hayfield
New Mills
Birch Vale
Furness Vale
Whitehough
Whaley Bridge
Chapel-en-le-Frith
Litton
Buxton
Wardlow Mires
Little Longstone
Chelmorton
Bakewell
Crowdecote
Over Haddon
Hartington

SOUTH YORKSHIRE

Hope
Bamford
Longshaw
Dronfield
Apperknowle
Unstone
Hundall
Staveley
Holmesfield
Hollingwood
Clowne
Barlow
Whittington Moor
Cutthorpe
Sutton cum Duckmanton
Chatsworth
Chesterfield
Sutton Scarsdale

CHESHIRE

Birchover
Matlock
Newton
Clay Cross
Ashover
Shirland
Hilcote
Alfreton
South Normanton
Wirksworth
Crich
Swanwick
Kirk Ireton
Pentrich
Ripley
Shottle
Marehay
Langley Mill
Ashbourne
Belper
Kilburn
Heanor
Openwoodgate
Horsley Woodhouse
Milford
Marlpool
Makeney
Holbrook
Duffield
Little Eaton
West Hallam
Ilkeston
Darley Abbey
Dale Abbey
DERBY
Ockbrook
Normanton
Long Eaton
Etwall
Alvaston
Littlover
Sawley
Repton
Ingleby
Melbourne
Newton Solney
Calke
Hartshorne
Coton-in-the-Elms
Smisby

NOTTS

STAFFORDSHIRE

LEICESTERSHIRE & RUTLAND

0 Miles 10
0 Kilometres 16

Apperknowle

Traveller's Rest

High Street, S18 4BD SK384782

🕏 12-11 ☎ (01246) 460169

🌐 travellersrestapperknowle.co.uk

John Smith's Bitter; Neepsend Blonde; Timothy Taylor Landlord Ⓗ; 3 changing beers (sourced nationally; often Church End, Coastal, Welbeck Abbey) Ⓗ/Ⓖ
The Traveller's Rest, a regular winner of CAMRA branch awards, is a traditional country pub at the edge of the village, serving a good range of beers, ciders and perries. The outdoor drinking area provides sweeping views over the Drone Valley –

one of the best views in Derbyshire. Good-quality food is available at all times, with the cheese platters and pork pies particularly popular. Live music features strongly, with jazz every Monday night. Q🕏🏠🎅🍴▲♣●P🚪🐾🐕🛜

Ashbourne

Artisan 🏆

33 St John Street, DE6 1GP

🕏 closed Mon; 11-10; 12-6 Sun ☎ (01335) 300110

St Austell Tribute; 3 changing beers (often Welbeck Abbey, Wild Weather Ales, Wolf) Ⓗ

Bar, café and bottle shop opened June 2016, housed in a former restaurant, previously the Green Dragon pub. An ancient building, with a low-ceilinged bar, it has four handpumps. A huge range of bottled beers is on offer to take home or crack open on the spot, and it has an interesting and creative menu of cold food offerings, meat, cheese and veggie platters, plus many varieties of Scotch egg. Closing time may be later on Sunday evenings when live music sessions are hosted. Local CAMRA Pub of the Year 2017. Q🕮🏠🍴🕹🚃🐾🛜

Smith's Tavern ●
36 St John Street, DE6 1GH
☼ 12-11 (midnight Fri & Sat) ☎ (01335) 300809
Banks's Sunbeam; Jennings Bitter; Marston's Pedigree; Ringwood Fortyniner; 4 changing beers (often Jennings, Marston's) Ⓗ
Small, highly traditional town-centre pub, with as many as seven real ales on, mostly from the Marston's portfolio of beers, from which the landlord selects the widest possible choice; he is also allowed one free choice guest ale, served at weekends, always from a local brewery. Local CAMRA Pub of the Year three times in succession in recent years. Q🕮🌳🚗🚃🐾🛜

Ashover

Old Poets' Corner Ⓛ
Butts Road, S45 0EW (downhill from church)
☼ 12-11 ☎ (01246) 590888 ⊕ oldpoets.co.uk
Ashover Poets Tipple, Butts Pale Ale; changing beers Ⓗ
Home of the award-winning Ashover Brewery, this large Brewers' Tudor pub is a frequent CAMRA award winner. The staff welcome walkers and dogs and provide excellent food and beer. Choose from up to 10 ales, including Ashover's, along with a range of guest beers, traditional ciders, bottled Belgian beers and country wines. The pub hosts three beer festivals a year, weekly quizzes and live music. Q🌳🏠🕹🛏🚗🐾🚃(63,64)🐾🛜

Bamford

Anglers Rest Ⓛ
Main Road, S33 0DY
☼ 11-11 (midnight Fri & Sat); 12-11 Sun ☎ (01433) 659317
⊕ anglers.rest
Acorn Barnsley Bitter; Black Sheep Best Bitter; 3 changing beers (sourced locally; often Abbeydale) Ⓗ
At the heart of Bamford and not far from Ladybower Reservoir, this is a community hub in every sense, where the locals have been running the pub (and associated shop and café) since 2013. The main bar is the focal point and is extremely popular with families, walkers and, particularly, cyclists, who have access to dedicated cycle parking and a DIY repair shop. There is also a quieter snug. Good-value, rustic bar food is served Wednesday to Sunday.
Q🕮🌳🕹🛏🚗🐾P🚃(273,274)🐾🛜

Belper

Angels Micro Pub
Market Place, DE56 1FZ (top right-hand side of Market Place)
☼ closed Mon-Wed; 12-10
Oakham Citra; Thornbridge Jaipur IPA; Titanic Plum Porter; 5 changing beers (sourced nationally) Ⓖ

A small, friendly bar offering real ales, an excellent choice of real ciders, wines, gin and juices. A full selection of beers (up to 16 at times) from Thursday gradually decreases as Sunday approaches and the beer is drunk! Locally sourced pork pies and cheeses are served. Live artists perform most Sunday afternoons. 🚃🚌🐾

REAL ALE BREWERIES

Abstract Jungle Langley Mill
Amber Ripley
Ashleyhay 🍺 Wirksworth (brewing suspended)
Ashover Clay Cross
Aurora Ilkeston (NEW)
Bad Bunny Derby (NEW)
Barlow Barlow
Birchover 🍺 Birchover
Boot 🍺 Repton
Bottle Brook Kilburn
Brampton Chesterfield
Brunswick 🍺 Derby
Buxton Buxton
Chapel-en-le-Frith Chapel-en-le-Frith (NEW)
Dancing Duck Derby
Derby Derby
Derventio Darley Abbey
Draycott Dale Abbey
Drone Valley Unstone
Falstaff 🍺 Derby: Normanton
Gaol Wirksworth
Globe 🍺 Glossop
Grasshopper Langley Mill (NEW)
Hairy Brewers Holbrook
Hartshorns Derby
Haywood Bad Ram Ashbourne
High Peak Chapel-en-le-Frith
Hopjacker Dronfield
Howard Town Glossop
Instant Karma 🍺 Clay Cross
John Thompson 🍺 Ingleby
Landlocked 🍺 Alfreton
Leadmill Heanor
Leatherbritches 🍺 Smisby
Little Bush 🍺 Marehay
Littleover Derby
Marlpool Marlpool
Matlock Wolds Farm Matlock
Middle Earth Derby
Moody Fox Hilcote (NEW)
Mouselow Farm Dinting
Mr Grundy's 🍺 Derby
Muirhouse Ilkeston
Nutbrook West Hallam
Old Sawley 🍺 Sawley
Peak Chatsworth
Pentrich Pentrich
Pigeon Fishers Hollingwood
Raw Staveley
Rock Mill New Mills
Rowditch 🍺 Derby
Shiny 🍺 Little Eaton
Shottle Farm Shottle
Spire Sutton Scarsdale
Thorley & Sons Ilkeston
Thornbridge Bakewell
Tollgate Calke
Torrside New Mills
Townes 🍺 Staveley
Urban Chicken Ilkeston (NEW)
Whaley Bridge Furness Vale
Whim Hartington

night on Tuesday with free food. The centre is well cared for, with a relaxed and friendly atmosphere, and it has a beer festival in May. There is a Timothy Taylor changing house beer, plus guests. Ample car parking is available. ⑤❀⟪PⓅ⊟

Coton-in-the-Elms
Black Horse
17 Burton Road, DE12 8HJ (centre of village)
✪ 4-11 (midnight Fri); 1-midnight Sat; 12-10.30 Sun
☎ (01283) 762947 ⊕ theblackhorsederbyshire.co.uk
Draught Bass; Joule's Pale Ale; Marston's Pedigree; 1 changing beer (sourced regionally) Ⓗ
Lively and popular free house, owned by the licensee, with a bright and airy main room divided into bar and lounge areas by glass-topped wood partitions. A small snug, served through a hatch, features a bar billiards table. The guest beer is usually from a microbrewery. Up to 15 ciders/perries are available from varying sources. A free cheeseboard is offered weekday evenings and weekend lunchtimes. Quiz night is Tuesday, and live music is played monthly on a Sunday. Accommodation is a two-person self-catering holiday flat. Q❀⟪Å♣♠PⓅ(22)❀ 🕏

Crich
Black Swan Ⓛ
6 Bowns Hill, DE4 5DG
✪ 12-11 (11.30 Fri & Sat) ☎ (01773) 856406
8 changing beers (often Ashover, Oakham) Ⓗ
A recent addition to Ashover Brewery's portfolio, this distinctive 19th-century Tudor-style pub has a large bar area with wood-burning stove, and is canine-friendly and walker-welcoming. The eight handpumps usually dispense four to six Ashover ales and a couple of guests. For serious sampling try three third-pint measures. The stables have been converted into the Old Drinking Trough bar, which is open every weekend and provides four further cask ales and traditional ciders. Q⑤❀⟪⟭♣Å♠⊟

Crowdecote
Pack Horse Inn Ⓛ
SK17 0DB (about 8 miles from Buxton)
✪ closed Mon & Tue; 12-3, 6-11; 12-3, 6-10.30 Sun
☎ (01298) 83618 ⊕ thepack-horseinn.co.uk
4 changing beers Ⓗ
Friendly and welcoming pub on the side of the hill in the Upper Dove Valley. The knowledgeable landlord keeps his beers in fine condition. Separate drinking areas in the main bar create a cosy feel and there is a dining room and pool room on the lower level. Open on bank holiday Mondays, but may close early weekday evenings. A remote pub, but well worth the effort. ⑤❀⟪♣♠❀

Cutthorpe
Gate Inn Ⓛ
Overgreen, S42 7BA
✪ 11.30-11; 12-11 Sun ☎ (01246) 276923
Black Sheep Best Bitter; Fuller's London Pride; 4 changing beers Ⓗ
In a great scenic location, with views overlooking two counties, the pub has large dining areas to the left and rear of the main bar area, where meals are served all day until 9pm. Usually two beers are

available from local breweries such as Peak, Bradfield and Thornbridge. Although in a remote location, it is only a 10-minute walk from the nearest bus stop at Linacre Reservoir. Q❀⟪⟭♿Å P

Derby
Alexandra Hotel Ⓛ
203 Siddals Road, DE1 2QE
✪ 12-11 (midnight Fri); 11-midnight Sat ☎ (01332) 293993
⊕ alexandrahotelderby.co.uk
Castle Rock Harvest Pale; 6 changing beers (sourced nationally) Ⓗ
The Alexandra is a Castle Rock pub, serving two or three of its beers and up to five guest ales, including a mild and a stout/porter. There are also more than 50 UK and continental bottled beers of varying styles. The bar is adorned with railway memorabilia and the lounge with breweriana. A Class 37 locomotive cab resides in the car park. This venue was the birthplace of Derby CAMRA in 1974. Q⑤❀⟪⟭♿≈♣♠PⓅ❀🕏

Babington Arms Ⓛ ✔
11-13 Babington Lane, DE1 1TA
✪ 8am-midnight ☎ (01332) 383647
Draught Bass; Greene King Abbot; Marston's Pedigree; Ruddles Best Bitter; Small World Thunderbridge Stout, Twin Falls; 11 changing beers (sourced nationally) Ⓗ
This Wetherspoon pub is a converted furniture showroom close to the city centre. It boasts a huge range of real ales, many from local microbreweries, and typically has six ciders on handpump or gravity dispense. The back end of the large bar has some half-partitioned banquette seating and caters for family dining. At the front of the pub there is a small fenced-off area where outdoor drinkers can smoke. Local CAMRA Cider Pub of the Year 2017. ⑤❀⟪⟭♿♠⊟🕏

Brunswick Inn ☙ Ⓛ
1 Railway Terrace, DE1 2RU
✪ 11-11 (11.30 Fri & Sat); 12-10.30 Sun ☎ (01332) 290677
⊕ brunswickderby.co.uk
Brunswick White Feather, Triple Hop, The Usual; Everards Beacon Hill, Tiger; Timothy Taylor Landlord; 10 changing beers (sourced nationally) Ⓗ
Originally part of the railway village, this multi-roomed pub was restored and opened as Derby's first multiple choice real ale house in 1987. The purpose-built Brunswick Brewery was added in 1991 and the pub has since become one of the best-known free houses in the country. Owned by Everards, the range of up to 16 real ales includes at least six from Brunswick. It gets busy on Derby County match days. Local CAMRA City and overall Pub of the Year 2017. Q⑤❀⟪⟭♿≈♣♠PⓅ❀🕏

Exeter Arms Ⓛ ✔
13 Exeter Place, DE1 2EU
✪ 12-11 (11.30 Wed & Thu; midnight Fri & Sat); 12-10.30 Sun
☎ (01332) 605323 ⊕ exeterarms.co.uk
Dancing Duck Ay Up, Dark Drake; Marston's Pedigree; 4 changing beers Ⓗ
A joint venture between Dancing Duck Brewery and a local food and drink entrepreneur has resulted in a fine range of beers and an excellent dining experience, all put together in a pub with old-world charm. The small bar has an open fire and leads to several other rooms, including a wooden-settled snug with an old-fashioned range. The adjoining atmospheric cottage dating from

about 1815 has now been incorporated into the pub. There is a popular and quirky quiz on Monday evenings. ▭❀◑♣●P▭❀🛜

Five Lamps ⓛ ✅
25 Duffield Road, DE1 3BH
🕓 12-11 (midnight Fri & Sat) ☎ (01332) 348730
🌐 fivelampsderby.co.uk
Draught Bass; Everards Tiger; Peak Ales Chatsworth Gold; St Austell Proper Job; Thornbridge Jaipur IPA; house beer (by Derby); 8 changing beers (sourced regionally) Ⓗ
Since it reopened in 2010 the pub has gone from strength to strength, thanks to the dedication of the licensees and staff. Fourteen handpumps showcase many local ales from breweries such as Derby, Peak and Whim. The Lamps is essentially open plan, but has many little nooks and crannies, giving it a homely feel. It has been tastefully refurbished with wood panelling and leather seating in a traditional style. ❀◑&●P▭❀🛜

Flowerpot ⓛ
23-25 King Street, DE1 3DZ
🕓 12-11 (11.30 Wed & Thu; 12.30am Fri & Sat)
☎ (01332) 204955 🌐 flowerpotderby.co.uk
Marston's Pedigree; Oakham Bishops Farewell; Sharp's Doom Bar Ⓗ**; Whim Hartington IPA** Ⓗ/Ⓖ**, Flower Power** Ⓗ**; 9 changing beers (sourced nationally)** Ⓗ/Ⓖ
Dating from around 1800 but much expanded from its original premises, this vibrant pub reaches back from the roadside frontage and divides into several interlinking rooms. One room provides the stage for regular live bands; another has a glass cellar wall revealing rows of stillaged firkins. Up to 14 real ales and two ciders are offered. Good en-suite accommodation is available. ▭❀🚐&♣●▭❀🛜

Furnace Inn ⓛ
Duke Street, DE1 3BX
🕓 2-11; 11-midnight Fri & Sat; 11-11 Sun ☎ (01332) 385981
8 changing beers (sourced nationally) Ⓗ
Since it reopened in 2012 the pub has been transformed into a real ale mecca. A former Hardys and Hansons pub, it is now the tap for the Shiny Brewing Company. Up to eight real ales and three ciders/perries are served plus guest beers from all over. There are two distinct open-plan rooms with a central bar. Poker and cheese nights feature, with regular beer festivals held throughout the year. ▭❀&♣●P❀🛜

Golden Eagle ⓛ
55 Agard Street, DE1 1DZ
🕓 12-11.30; 12-11 Sun
Morland Old Golden Hen; Titanic Plum Porter; 3 changing beers (sourced nationally) Ⓗ
Completely refurbished by the Titan Brewery, this is now its brewery tap, and its original name has been restored. A mural on the outside pays homage to Derby history. Inside, the single room has a wooden floor throughout. It is comfortable and welcoming, with a table next to the bar for newspapers and local interest books. The upstairs function room hosts a poker night on Sunday and there is live acoustic music every Thursday evening. ▭❀♣●P❀🛜

Horse & Groom
48 Elms Street, DE1 3HN
🕓 12-11 🌐 horseandgroomderby.co.uk

Draught Bass; 3 changing beers (sourced nationally) Ⓗ
A traditional community pub that has morphed from a small corner house into a larger establishment by knocking through into two adjoining properties. In the heart of Derby's West End, this family-owned, family-run free house is noted for its regular Draught Bass and interesting range of three guest beers. Free live music is staged at the weekend, open mic on Thursday evening and jazz the last Wednesday of the month. ▭❀♣●P▭❀🛜

Last Post ⓛ
1 Uttoxeter Old Road, DE1 1GA
🕓 11-11 (8 Mon-Wed) ☎ (01332) 296737
🌐 thelastpostderby.pub
4 changing beers (sourced nationally) Ⓗ
This former post office was Derby's second micropub. At least one of the four changing beers is from Muirhouse and one is usually dark. A warm welcome is guaranteed from staff and locals in this intimate venue where live acoustic music can be heard every evening Thursday to Sunday. The small rear yard is a dedicated smoking area. Beer festivals coincide with those of the local CAMRA branch. ▭♣●▭(8)❀🛜

Little Chester Ale House ⓛ
4a Chester Green Road, DE1 3SF
🕓 3-10.30; 12-11 Fri & Sat; 12-10.30 Sun
Hartshorns Ignite; 3 changing beers (sourced nationally) Ⓗ
Derby's first micropub. On the edge of a tree-lined conservation area, it is in the historic Little Chester part of the city, site of Roman Derventio, where two ancient wells can still been seen. This former shop has one small main room with a passageway leading to a tiny rear room. It has four changing beers, including three from local Hartshorns Brewery, the pub's owner. Q▭&♣●▭❀🛜

Peacock Inn ⓛ
87 Nottingham Road, DE1 3QS
🕓 11 (3 Mon)-11; 11-midnight Fri & Sat; 12-10.30 Sun
☎ (01332) 583308
Draught Bass; Marston's Pedigree; Whim Arbor Light, Hartington IPA; house beer (by Leatherbritches); 4 changing beers (sourced nationally) Ⓗ
An attractive 18th-century stone-built roadside pub that used to be a staging post on the main coach road out of Derby, which ran alongside the old Derby Canal. Two rooms on different levels are divided by a central bar, with wooden floors, photos of old Derby and Derby County memorabilia. Up to nine real ales and two ciders and/or perries feature; beer festivals are held in the covered garden area to the rear. Q▭❀◑&●●

Rowditch Inn
246 Uttoxeter New Road, DE22 3LL
🕓 7-11; 12-2, 7-11 Sat & Sun ☎ (01332) 343123
Marston's Pedigree; 2 changing beers Ⓗ
A welcoming roadside hostelry with an unexpectedly deep interior which divides into two bar areas and a small snug. There is a display cabinet of pub memorabilia, and the pumpclips adorning the walls testify to the myriad of guest ales. Downstairs, at the rear, the garden is a peaceful haven. The output of the pub's brewery is almost exclusively consumed on the premises. Well worth the walk or the five-minute bus trip from the city centre. Q❀♣●▭❀🛜

Silk Mill Cider & Ale House 🅛

19 Full Street, DE1 3AF
🕑 12-11 (midnight Fri & Sat); 12-10.30 Sun
☎ (01332) 349160 🌐 thesilkmillderby.co.uk
Dancing Duck Ay Up; Draught Bass; 5 changing beers Ⓗ

Handsome stone-faced building named after the historic silk mill nearby, which marks the start of the Derwent Valley World Heritage Trail. To the right of the entrance is the Offilers' Lounge with a cosy real fire, ideal for drinkers. There is a dedicated dining area to the rear of the pub – booking is recommended at peak times. The central bar has nine handpumps shared between real ales and ciders. Quirky decorative ornaments and fittings are used throughout. 🌝🕮🕪🌡P🛜

Derby: Alvaston

Coronation

Baker Street, DE24 8SL
🕑 11.30-11; 12-10.30 Sun ☎ (01332) 913140
Steamin' Billy Tipsy Fisherman, Bitter, 1485; 1 changing beer (sourced regionally) Ⓗ

Built in the 1920s but renamed the Coronation in 1937, it is now in the hands of the Steamin' Billy Brewing Company. There is a comfortably furnished and separate bar area to one side. The other side has a spacious main lounge which is subtly split, one side being dominated by the pizza oven and featuring table seating. There is a large garden area to the back of the pub. Real ale is provided by Steamin' Billy but supplemented by one or two guest beers. 🌝🕮🕪🕭🌡P🛜(4)🌸🛜

Derby: Littleover

White Swan 🅛 ✔

Shepherd Street, DE23 6GA
🕑 12-11.30 (midnight Fri-Sun) ☎ (01332) 766481
🌐 thewhiteswanlittleover.co.uk
Castle Rock Harvest Pale; Greene King IPA, Abbot; Marston's Pedigree; 5 changing beers (sourced regionally) Ⓗ

This community-based local has two rooms, each with a bar and TV screen; the rear room, in which children are welcome, is used mainly for dining. More seating is available at tables outside at the back, and there is a covered and heated smoking area. There is a weekly quiz, a resident darts team, and other pub games are played. It stocks a good and varying range of well-kept guest beers, mainly from local breweries. 🌝🕮🕪🕭🌡P🛜

Derby: Normanton

Falstaff 🅛

74 Silverhill Road, DE23 6UJ
🕑 12-11 (midnight Fri & Sat) ☎ (01332) 342902
🌐 falstaffbrewery.co.uk
Falstaff Fist Full of Hops, Phoenix, Smiling Assassin; 1 changing beer Ⓗ

A 20-minute walk from the city centre rewards you with this atmospheric and reputedly haunted free house. Originally a coaching inn before the neighbourhood was built up, it is now the Falstaff Brewery tap and has long been the best real ale house in the Normanton area of Derby. The rear lounge is a shrine to Offilers' Brewery, with a display of memorabilia. Other collectables can be viewed throughout the games room and second bar room. Q🌝🕮🌡🛜

Dronfield

Coach & Horses 🅛

Sheffield Road, S18 2GD
🕑 4-10.30 Mon; 12-11 (midnight Fri & Sat); 12-10.30 Sun
☎ (01246) 413269 🌐 mycoachandhorses.co.uk
6 changing beers (sourced nationally; often Drone Valley, Mallinson's, Spire) Ⓗ

Next to Sheffield FC's ground on the northern edge of Dronfield, this pub is operated by Thornbridge Brewery and showcases a good range of its beers, with guest ales across a wide variety of beer styles. The large outdoor drinking area is particularly popular. Good-value meals are served from Chariot's Kitchen (no food Sun or Mon). The pub hosts a quiz night on Sunday and an open mic acoustic night on Monday evening. A 'buy nine pints, get the tenth free' loyalty card is popular. Q🌝🕮🕪🌡🛜(43)🌸

Duffield

Town Street Tap 🅛

17 Town Street, DE56 4EH
🕑 closed Mon; 4-10; 12-10.30 Fri & Sat; 12-5 Sun ☎ 07925 461706 🌐 thetownstreettap.co.uk
6 changing beers (sourced nationally) Ⓖ

This new micropub for Tollgate Brewery has been converted into a modern uncluttered drinking space with table service. Of the six changing real ales, two are from the Tollgate range and at least one is dark. Four ciders are also available, and take-outs come in containers or from the Bottle Shop. Walkers with boots are welcome. Pork pies and Scotch eggs are available for the hungry, and free tea and coffee for drivers. Q➿🕭🌡P🛜🌸

Etwall

Hawk & Buckle

46 Main Street, DE65 6LP
🕑 12-11 (12.30am Fri & Sat) ☎ (01283) 733460
Draught Bass; Marston's Pedigree; 4 changing beers (sourced nationally) Ⓗ

A roadside pub with the name dating back to at least 1804. It has the bar on the left and the lounge on the right, both served by a central bar. Outside, the covered smoking area is separated from the grassed seating area by an old stable block. Three changing beers are offered, mainly from local breweries. There is a quiz on Monday evening, dominoes is played on Wednesday evening, and on the first Thursday of the month there is a jam/open mic night. 🌝🕮🕪🕭🛜(V1,V2)🌸🛜

Glossop

Crown Inn ★

142 Victoria Street, SK13 8JF (on Hayfield road out of town centre)
🕑 5 (12 Fri & Sat)-11; 12-10.30 Sun ☎ (01457) 862824
Samuel Smith Old Brewery Bitter Ⓗ

Stone built end-of-terrace locals' pub, a few minutes from the town centre and railway station, built in 1846 and acquired by the brewery in 1977. The interior of the pub is listed by CAMRA as of Outstanding National Historic Importance. A curved bar serves two snugs, each with a real fire in winter, and a pool/games room. Pictures of bygone Glossop add to the traditional character. An enclosed outdoor drinking area is provided in the rear yard. Q🕮🕭➿🌡🛜(390)🌸

Queen's Arms 🍷

1 Shepley Street, SK13 7RZ
🌐 10.30-midnight ☎ (01457) 853005
⊕ queens-arms-hotel-old-glossop.co.uk
Holt Bitter; Marston's Wainwright; Morland Old Speckled Hen; Thornbridge Jaipur IPA; 3 changing beers (sourced locally) ℍ
Situated in the Old Glossop part of the town, below the Bleaklow hills, a pleasant 15-minute walk from Glossop centre through Manor Park. Popular with locals, visitors and hikers, it serves breakfast from 10.30am. A standard pub menu is available downstairs, while the Queen Spice Indian restaurant is on the first floor. Live entertainment features on Tuesday and Saturday, Thursday is quiz night. Local CAMRA branch Derbyshire Pub of the Year 2017. 🚫🏮🛏️🍴◑♿🚌🚇(390)🐾🐕📶

Star Inn ✅

2 Howard Street, SK13 7DD (next to railway station)
🌐 2-11 (midnight Fri); 12-midnight Sat; 12-10.30 Sun
☎ (01457) 853072
Timothy Taylor Landlord; 4 changing beers (sourced regionally; often Abbeydale, Howard Town, Pictish) ℍ
A popular town-centre pub, run by a dedicated CAMRA member. A large, comfortable main room, where conversation predominates, features wood panelling. A smaller room is to the rear. Guest beers are mainly from local microbreweries and real draught cider is available. Regular beer and cider festivals are held throughout the year. Situated close to the railway station, the pub is an ideal starting/finishing point for walking within the Dark Peak area. Q🅰️🚉♿🚇🐾🐕📶

Hartshorne

Admiral Rodney Inn

65 Main Street, DE11 7ES (on A514)
🌐 5 (11 Sat)-11; 12-11 Sun ☎ (01283) 227771
Exmoor Gold; 3 changing beers (sourced nationally) ℍ
A friendly village pub dating back to the early 19th century, but rebuilt and extended in the late 20th century to provide an open-plan L-shaped drinking area while retaining the original oak beams in the former snug. There is also a secluded raised area tucked away behind the bar. An additional two guest beers usually feature at weekends. It has a cheese tasting on the first Monday of the month, a quiz night on Sunday, and occasional live music. The grounds include a cricket pitch, home of Hartshorne Cricket Club. 🚫🏮♿♣🚇(2)🐾🐕📶

Hayfield

George Hotel

14 Church Street, SK22 2JE (close to Hayfield bus station)
🌐 11.45-11 (11.30 Fri & Sat); 12-11 Sun ☎ (01663) 743691
⊕ georgehotelhayfield.co.uk
Banks's Amber Ale; Ringwood Boondoggle; 2 changing beers (sourced nationally) ℍ
Rambling stone-built 16th-century pub in the centre of the village. Originally a mail house, the Derby Militia was formed here in 1808. In addition to the handpulled ales, Thatchers Heritage cider is available. Two comfortable lounges, a cosy bar area, and a separate dining room await the visitor. The interior includes stained-glass mullioned windows and a magnificent cast-iron range

fireplace incorporating a real fire in winter. Hikers and cyclists are very welcome. 🚫🏮🛏️🍴◑♿🅰️♿🚇🐾🐕📶

Royal Hotel

Market Street, SK22 2EP
🌐 11-11 ☎ (01663) 742721 ⊕ theroyalhayfield.co.uk
Marston's Lancaster Bomber; house beer (by Happy Valley); 3 changing beers (sourced locally) ℍ
An imposing stone pub, built as a coaching inn in the 18th century, close to the church, cricket ground and River Sett. The interior boasts oak panels and pews, creating a relaxing atmosphere, with real fires in winter. Guest beers from local micros are always available. A restaurant and function room complete the facilities (food is served all day in summer). The village is the base for many leisure activities in the Dark Peak and was the birthplace of actor Arthur Lowe.
Q🚫🏮🛏️🍴◑♿🅰️🚇🐾🐕📶

Holmesfield

Rutland Arms 🄻

96 Main Road, S18 7WT
🌐 12-11.30 ☎ (0114) 289 0374
Black Sheep Best Bitter; Bradfield Farmers Blonde; Castle Rock Harvest Pale; Theakston Best Bitter; 2 changing beers (often Bradfield, Everards, Pheasantry) ℍ
An extremely popular traditional country pub with open fires and low wooden beams which offers a relaxing, warm and snug atmosphere. The beer range has increased steadily over the years to six handpulled cask ales. The extensive outdoor seating area with grassed children's play area is idyllic in late spring and summer. A collection of books and magazines of local interest is available for the entertainment and enlightenment of customers. Q🚫🏮◑♣♿🚇(15)🐾📶

Hope

Cheshire Cheese Inn

Edale Road, S33 6ZF
🌐 closed Mon; 12-3, 6-11; 12-11 Sat; 12-9 Sun
☎ (01433) 620381 ⊕ thecheshirecheeseinn.co.uk
Bradfield Farmers Blonde; Peak Ales Bakewell Best Bitter; 3 changing beers (sourced locally; often Bradfield, Peak Ales) ℍ
A cosy country inn dating from 1578 with an open-plan bar area and a smaller room at a lower level, probably originally used to house animals, but now mainly used as a dining area. Home-cooked meals using local produce are served lunchtimes and evenings. It is in good walking country but the parking is limited as the road outside is narrow. Q🚫🏮🛏️◑🚇🐾📶

Horsley Woodhouse

Old Oak Inn

176 Main Street, DE7 6AW
🌐 4 (3 Thu & Fri; 12 Sat)-11; 12-10.30 Sun ☎ (01332) 881299
Changing beers (sourced nationally; often Bottle Brook, Leadmill) ℍ
The taphouse for the Leadmill Brewery, the Old Oak features an extensive variety of Leadmill beers, plus a couple of guests. This traditional pub boasts four rooms of differing character, some with open fires. At weekends drinkers can enjoy the RuRAD bar – effectively a mini beer festival offering

gravity-dispensed ales from brewers near and far alongside the more local Leadmill and Bottle Brook beers. Local CAMRA and East Midlands Pub of the Year 2016. Q❧☺☺P🚪🚐❀

Hundall

Miners Arms 🏆
Hundall Lane, S18 4BP
☼ 12-midnight ☎ (01246) 414505
Drone Valley Dronny Bottom Bitter; Pictish Alchemists Ale; 3 changing beers (sourced nationally; often Church End, Drone Valley, Welbeck Abbey) Ⓗ
On the high ridge above Unstone, this traditional village local has thrived since its change of ownership in 2015. The beer garden to the rear provides an excellent space in which to enjoy the wide range of beers and ciders always available. The Miners operates a Monday Club, when real ales are £2 a pint. Local CAMRA Cider Pub of the Year 2015 and Pub of the Year 2016 and 2017.
Q❧☺◑▲♣●P🚪🚐❀🛜

Ilkeston

Burnt Pig 🏆 Ⓛ
53 Market Street, DE7 5RB
☼ closed Mon-Wed; 11-11 ☎ 07538 723722
5 changing beers Ⓗ/Ⓖ
A short walk from the marketplace will bring you to what was a long-closed corner shop. It is now a busy and popular micropub run by its very enthusiastic owner, Simon. It dispenses five varying beers and a good selection of real ciders and continental bottled beers. It has a multi-roomed, cosy interior and is famous for its pork scratchings. Q♣●🚐❀

Dewdrop Ⓛ
24 Station Road, DE7 5TE
☼ 4 (3 Fri)-11; 12-11 Sat; 12-10.30 Sun ☎ (0115) 932 9684
Oakham Bishops Farewell, Green Devil IPA; changing beers (often Acorn, Blue Monkey, Castle Rock) Ⓗ
Award-winning Victorian pub on the outskirts of town. The large lobby features a plaque commemorating the wartime visit of bouncing bomb inventor Barnes Wallis. Conversation thrives in the friendly lounge featuring a large woodburner. A pool table and classics jukebox dominate the bar. Lastly, there is a quiet family room. A dark beer is usually served. Westons Old Rosie and Wyld Wood are the permanent ciders. Hearty cobs are made to order.
Q❧☺◑♣●🚐(27)❀

Observatory ✅
14A Market Place, DE7 5QA
☼ 8am-midnight ☎ (0115) 932 8040
Greene King Abbot; Ruddles Best Bitter; Sharp's Doom Bar; 4 changing beers (often Exmoor) Ⓗ
This glass-fronted edifice with its astronomical theme commemorates John Flamsteed, the first Astronomer Royal. It is on the east side of the marketplace. A large bar dispenses seven cask beers and there are ground floor toilets and a drinking area. Upstairs is a smaller eating and drinking area and an outside terrace. It is a short walk to Wharncliffe Road for all bus routes.
Q❧☺◑♿●🚐❀🛜

Kirk Ireton

Barley Mow Inn
Main Street, DE6 3JP (off B5023) SK266501
☼ 12-2, 7-11; 12-2, 7-10.30 Sun ☎ (01335) 370306
Whim Hartington IPA; 3 changing beers Ⓖ
In a charming village overlooking Ecclesbourne Valley, this gabled Jacobean building is home to an old-fashioned down-to-earth pub, of the type that is increasingly hard to find. Several interconnecting rooms of different character have low beams, mullioned windows and well-worn woodwork, and there is a welcoming open fire in the main bar. A small serving hatch reveals a stillage with up to six gravity beers. Local breweries such as Blue Monkey, Dancing Duck, Burton Bridge, Thornbridge and Peak Ales often feature. Q☺🛏♣●P❀

Little Eaton

Queen's Head Ⓛ
131 Alfreton Road, DE21 5DF
☼ 12-11 (midnight Fri); 11-midnight Sat; 11-11 Sun
☎ (01332) 986065 ⊕ queenshead-dbc.co.uk
Derby Business As Usual, Dashingly Dark; Everards Tiger; 4 changing beers Ⓗ
An Everards Project William pub operated by Derby Brewing Company. This stone-built Grade II-listed building has been renovated inside, giving the pub a modern feel. Outside, a patio area offers seating for warm summer days. Up to five real ales from Derby Brewing, at least one guest and a real cider are available. Good-quality home-cooked food, some locally sourced, is served. ❧☺◑●P🚐❀🛜

Little Longstone

Packhorse Inn
Main Street, DE45 1NN
☼ 12-3, 5-11; 12-11 Sat & Sun ☎ (01629) 640471
⊕ packhorselongstone.co.uk
Black Sheep Best Bitter; Thornbridge Wild Swan, Lord Marples, Jaipur IPA; 2 changing beers (often Thornbridge) Ⓗ
This small pub, which began life as two miners' cottages, has been welcoming drinkers since 1787. Situated just a short stroll from stunning views of Monsal Head, dogs and walkers are welcome. Fresh local produce is a passion, an ethos also extended to the beers, which always include a choice from the nearby Thornbridge Brewery. There is a pleasant beer garden, and food is available all day at weekends.
❧☺◑▲♣🚐(173)❀🛜

Litton

Red Lion Ⓛ ✅
Church Lane, SK17 8QU
☼ 12-11 (midnight Fri & Sat); 12-10.30 Sun
☎ (01298) 871458 ⊕ theredlionlitton.co.uk
Abbeydale Absolution; Peak Ales Bakewell Best Bitter; 2 changing beers (sourced locally) Ⓗ
Nestling on the green and the only pub in the village, the Red Lion is a welcome refuge for locals and visitors alike. There is a large fireplace serving several rooms off a central passageway. Not to be missed, the annual wakes week is at the end of June with events including a well dressing on the village green, during which the pub holds a beer festival. Fresh food is served all day, every day.
❧☺🛏◑♣🚐(65,173)❀🛜

Long Eaton

Hole in the Wall ℒ
Regent Street, NG10 1JX
🕒 2-11.30; 11-12.30am Fri & Sat; 12-11.30 Sun
☎ (0115) 973 4920 ⊕ holeinthewallpub.weebly.com
Draught Bass; Nottingham Extra Pale Ale; Oakham Citra, Bishops Farewell; 1 changing beer Ⓗ
A welcome return to the Guide for this Dutch gabled back-street local, a true free house with a good range of beers. Split into two distinct areas, it has a raised lounge to the left and a breweriana-filled bar to the right. Note the old-style serving hatch in between. The landlord here is the longest serving in Long Eaton, with nearly 30 years in situ. Close to local bus services and with a large public car park opposite. Q🕏♿♣🍴�🚲

York Chambers ℒ
40 Market Place, NG10 1LT
🕒 1 (4 Mon)-10; 11-11 Fri & Sat; 12-10 Sun
☎ (0115) 946 0999
6 changing beers (sourced nationally) Ⓗ
Opened December 2015 in a Grade II-listed building, the interior is little changed apart from the installation of a temperature-controlled cool room cellar. It serves six real ales straight from the cask and a range of ciders and quality wines. It is located next to Long Eaton Green, with regular buses to Derby, Nottingham and Loughborough. A sister pub to the Chequered Flag in Castle Donington. Q♿🍴🚲🚲🏠

Longshaw

Grouse
S11 7TZ
🕒 12-3, 6-11; 12-11 Sat & Sun ☎ (01433) 630423
⊕ thegrouseinn-derbyshire.co.uk
Banks's Amber Ale; Marston's EPA, Pedigree; 1 changing beer Ⓗ
In the same family for the past 52 years, this free house stands in isolation on moorland south-west of Sheffield, and is a welcome refuge for walkers as well as climbers from the nearby Froggatt Edge. The comfortable lounge and bar are at the front, with a separate room at the rear reached through the conservatory in which vines manage to grow. No food Monday evening. Q🕏🕏🍴♿P🚲🏠

Makeney

Holly Bush ★ ✅
Holly Bush Lane, DE56 0RX
🕒 12-11; 12-10.30 Sun ☎ (01332) 841729
⊕ hollybushinnmakeney.co.uk
Fuller's London Pride; Greene King Abbot; Marston's Pedigree; Timothy Taylor Landlord; 3 changing beers (sourced nationally) Ⓗ
The Holly Bush is an excellent late 17th-century Grade II-listed pub with character. Once a farmhouse and brewery on the Strutt Estate, the inn stood on the main Derby turnpike before the new road opened in 1818. Dick Turpin reputedly drank here. The pub has nationally important, historic interior features throughout its various hideaway, stone-flagged rooms, with welcoming fires in winter. Bar snacks are always available. Regular beer festivals are held, and walkers, families and dogs are all welcome. Local CAMRA 2015 Pub of the Year. Q🕏🕏🍴♣P🚲🏠

Marlpool

Marlpool Ale House ℒ
5 Breach Road, DE75 7NJ
🕒 closed Mon-Thu; 2-11 Fri; 12-11 Sat; 12-10 Sun ☎ 07963 511855 ⊕ marlpoolbrewing.co.uk
Marlpool Blind Boris, Otters Pocket, Scratty Ratty Ⓗ; **5 changing beers (sourced regionally; often Marlpool)** Ⓗ/Ⓖ
One of the smallest alehouses in Derbyshire. Originally a butcher's shop, it has been transformed into a cosy place, with friendly, informative staff. Divided as two main rooms, the rear room has a wood-burning stove, and the bar is an old Methodist chapel pulpit. Beers are on handpump or from the cellar, and a two-barrel brewery is in the rear yard. Impromptu acoustic sessions and beer festivals take place during the year. Q🕏🍴🚲🏠

Matlock

Crown ℒ ✅
Crown Square, Derwent House, DE4 3AT
🕒 8am-midnight ☎ (01629) 56458
10 changing beers (sourced nationally; often Greene King, Thornbridge) Ⓗ
A popular town-centre Wetherspoon ideally located within a few minutes' walk of Matlock train station and both bus terminals. The pub takes its name from the former Crown Hotel which was once close by and gave Crown Square its name. Typical Wetherspoon's food is served until 11pm daily. It is busy all year round with tourists, walkers and locals, and home and away supporters are welcomed on Matlock Town FC match days. Q🕏🕕♿🚆🍴🚲🏠

Thorn Tree Inn
48 Jackson Road, DE4 3JQ (up Bank Rd, left into Smedley St, 2nd right up Smith Rd, 1st left)
🕒 12-2 (not Mon), 5-11.30; 12-midnight Fri & Sat; 12-11.30 Sun ☎ (01629) 580295 ⊕ thorntreeatmatlock.co.uk
Draught Bass; Nottingham Extra Pale Ale; Timothy Taylor Landlord; 4 changing beers (sourced nationally; often Castle Rock, Oakham, Thornbridge) Ⓗ
Perched high above Matlock town, this two-roomed but compact pub enjoys beautiful views from the heated patio area. Children and dogs are welcome. Regulars, ramblers and real ale enthusiasts convene in the lounge to enjoy the atmosphere. Three permanent real ales are complemented by four guests. Home-made food is available Tuesday-Friday lunchtimes, bar snacks all day, pie night is Wednesday 6-8pm, and Sunday lunch is served until 5pm. Q🕏🍴♣🚆🚲🏠

Twenty Ten ℒ
16 Dale Road, DE4 3LT (near railway station)
🕒 closed Mon; 12-10 (1am Fri & Sat) ☎ 07710 427442 ⊕ twentytenmatlock.co.uk
4 changing beers (sourced locally; often Matlock Wolds Farm) Ⓗ
Twenty Ten nestles among the antique shops on Matlock's historic Dale Road. Bare floorboards and French chic furnishing lend the place a style not often encountered. Focusing on LocAle, the establishment is the only dedicated outlet for Matlock Wolds Farm ales. Children and dogs are welcome, and food is served throughout the day. Often quiet early doors, things liven up considerably on Friday and Saturday evenings, with live music laid on. 🕏🕕♿🚆🚲🏠

Melbourne

Chip & Pin 🄻
8-10 High Street, DE73 8GN
🌐 closed Mon; 4.30 (12 Fri & Sat)-9.30; 12-2.30
Sun ☎ 07957 806454 ⊕ chipandpinpub.com
4 changing beers 🄶
A micropub centrally located in Melbourne's old
Midland Bank premises. It is owned by a group of
local real ale enthusiasts who serve you at your
table. The building has been sympathetically
restored and has two rooms – a main drinking area
and a meeting room for local groups. Real ales are
available in third-pint taster racks. Real cider, wine,
soft drinks and snacks are also on sale.
Q●🍴🚃(2)🐾

Milford

King William
The Bridge, DE56 0RR (on A6 between Derby and
Belper)
🌐 5-11.30; 12.30-11.30 Sat & Sun ☎ (01332) 840842
Draught Bass 🄶; **Greene King Abbot** 🄷/🄶; **Sharp's
Doom Bar; Timothy Taylor Landlord; 2 changing beers
(sourced nationally)** 🄷
A stone-built Georgian inn dramatically situated at
the foot of sandstone cliffs. An open fire at one end
of the elongated bar adds to the ambience of the
cosy pub interior. Original period furniture and
quarry-tiled flooring date from the time it was
built. Regular beer festivals and live music are
added attractions at this popular, comfortable
hostelry. Q🍴🚃🐾

New Mills

Beehive
67 Albion Road, SK22 3EY
🌐 5-midnight; 4-1am Fri; 2-1am Sat; 3-midnight Sun
☎ (01663) 742087
**Marston's EPA; 3 changing beers (sourced
nationally)** 🄷
An interesting triangular building, this friendly free
house features three guest beers from far and
wide, alongside the regular Marston's ale, and is a
frequent outlet for the local Rock Mill Brewery.
Upstairs is a well-furnished cocktail and whisky bar
with a single handpump. Recently renovated, the
pub features a logburner, hosts community events
and live music, and welcomes walkers and dogs. A
beer festival is held on the late spring bank holiday
weekend. 🛏🏵🍴🚆♣🚃🐾📶

Newton

New Inn 🄻
80 Main Street, DE55 5TE
🌐 closed Mon; 4-midnight (1am Fri); 12-1am Sat;
12-midnight Sun ☎ (01773) 873944
**Dukeries IPA, Farmers Branch; 1 changing beer
(sourced locally)** 🄷
Four handpulls here offer two beers from the
Dukeries range and one guest, as well as one real
rotating cider. Traditional Sunday lunch is served
12-4pm, Thursday is steak night, followed by a quiz
and 13-card bingo. Karaoke is every other Friday,
while live music is a feature most Saturdays. Third-
pint taster batons are available for the price of a
pint. The L-shaped bar has comfortable seating
with a real fire. Q🛏🏵🍴🍽♣🍴🚃📶

Newton Solney

Brickmakers Arms
9-11 Main Street, DE15 0SJ (opp jct with Trent Lane)
🌐 5 (4 Fri)-11; 12-11 Sat & Sun ☎ 07525 220103
⊕ brickmakersarms.pub
**Burton Bridge Golden Delicious, Bitter, Porter,
Stairway to Heaven; 1 changing beer (sourced
regionally)** 🄷
A cosy local at the end of an 18th-century terrace
of cottages; it was converted into a pub in the early
19th century for workers at a nearby brickworks.
Internally, it features a narrow central bar leading
at one end to a room served through a hatch, and
at the other to an impressive oak-panelled room.
There is also a function/meeting room. Quiz night
is Monday, bingo Tuesday, and poker Tuesday and
Thursday. Q🛏🏵♣🍴🚃(V3)🐾📶

Ockbrook

Cross Keys ✅
Green Lane, DE72 3SE
🌐 12-midnight; 12-11.30 Sun ☎ (01332) 662308
⊕ crosskeys-ockbrook.co.uk
**Marston's Pedigree; Sharp's Doom Bar; Tetley Mild; 2
changing beers** 🄷
A traditional village pub with a quirky character and
a selection of five real ales and one real cider. The
bar has a low-beamed ceiling, several screens for
sports TV and a woodburner for the winter months.
Events include darts, karaoke, quizzes and theme
nights. Home-made food features stone-baked
pizza. Outside there is a small terrace at the front
and an enclosed garden and play area to the side.
🛏🏵🌙♣🍴🚃(9,9A)🐾📶

Royal Oak 🄻
55 Green Lane, DE72 3SE
🌐 11.30-3, 5-11.30; 11.30-11.30 Sat; 12-11.30 Sun
☎ (01332) 662378 ⊕ royaloakockbrook.com
Draught Bass; 4 changing beers 🄷
Attractive 18th-century pub with a number of small
rooms. Run by the Wilson family since 1953, they
have brought about many improvements while
retaining the original character and features.
Excellent home-cooked food is served Monday to
Saturday lunchtimes and early evenings, plus
Sunday lunch. The pub hosts many community and
public events including live music and open mic
nights. It has two pleasant gardens, one with an
enclosed play area for children. Local CAMRA
Country Pub of the Year 2015-2017.
Q🛏🏵🌙🚻♣🍴🚃(9,9A)🐾📶

Openwoodgate

Black Bull's Head
2 Kilburn Lane, DE56 0SF
🌐 12-11; 12-10.30 Sun ☎ 07860 757741
⊕ blackbullshead.com
**Draught Bass; Greene King Abbot; Oakham Bishops
Farewell; 6 changing beers (sourced nationally; often
Blue Monkey, Castle Rock, Dancing Duck)** 🄷
A two-roomed former Greene King pub, now a free
house, offering a warm welcome in comfortable
surroundings. Walls are adorned with historic
photographs and newspaper clippings of local and
national interest, with one wall dedicated to the
RAF. A wide range of real ales and ciders is served,
with more available in the separate Bedlam Bar,
open Friday to Sunday. Q♣🍴🚃(6.4,6.X)🐾

Over Haddon

Lathkil Hotel 🅛
School Lane, DE45 1JE
☼ 11-11; 12-10.30 Sun ☎ (01629) 812501 ⏀ lathkil.co.uk
Everards Ascalon; 4 changing beers ⊞
This pub overlooks a masterpiece of Peak District scenery, marvellous in any weather. One side is an old-fashioned bar room with a real fire and oak beams, while the larger room opposite is where diners enjoy superb home-cooked meals, again with a log fire. The beer garden is the perfect place to while away summer evenings. Dogs are welcome in the bar, but walkers should remove their boots at the door. Q☼♿️🛏🍽️🅿🚃🐾🅟❄🛜

Repton

Boot 🅛 ✅
12 Boot Hill, DE65 6FT
☼ 11-11.45 ☎ (01283) 346047 ⏀ thebootatrepton.co.uk
Boot Repton Cross, Clod Hopper, Tuffer's Old, IPA, Beast of Bloodstock; 1 changing beer (sourced locally) ⊞
Close to the Repton Cross at the centre of the village, this pub has been brought back to life by the local Bespoke pub company with a recent refurbishment and the addition of an on-site microbrewery supplying all the real ales. Boot Brewery beers are also to be found in Bespoke sister pubs in the neighbouring villages of Willington and Melbourne, the Dragon and Harpur's respectively. 🛏🍽️🅿(V3)❄🛜

Ripley

Red Lion ✅
Market Place, DE5 3BS
☼ 8am-midnight (1am Fri & Sat) ☎ (01773) 512875
Greene King Abbot; Ruddles Best Bitter; Sharp's Doom Bar; 6 changing beers (sourced nationally; often Exmoor, Thornbridge) ⊞
A former Home Brewery pub built in the 1960s and easily identified by the large red lion rampant on the pub frontage, it faces the Victorian town hall and marketplace at the centre of a vibrant, well-pubbed market town. A busy Wetherspoon outlet, it serves a large selection of guest beers and all-day food. 🛏❄🅿🚃🛜

Talbot
1 Butterley Hill, DE5 3LT
☼ 12-10.30 (11.30 Fri & Sat) ☎ (01773) 742382
5 changing beers (sourced nationally) ⊞
A traditional Victorian flat iron-shaped former Shipstone's and, more recently, Amber Ales taphouse, the Talbot is blissfully free of music, instead preferring the sounds of conversation, laughter and traditional games. It offers an excellent selection of real ales pulled from casks stored on the original stone stillage. Locally turned pump handles add to the delights of this welcoming, friendly pub. Q🛏🅿🚃

Sawley

White Lion 🅛
Tamworth Road, NG10 3AT
☼ 2-midnight; 12-1am Fri & Sat; 12-midnight Sun
☎ (0115) 946 3061
Draught Bass; Old Sawley Gold, Little Jack, Tollbridge Porter; 4 changing beers ⊞

There are normally five real ales on offer in this traditional pub, with two rooms separated by a central bar. One of the rooms has a cosy wood fire and the ceilings are decorated with hop vines. There is a large beer garden and ample parking. A small on-site microbrewery supplies Old Sawley beers on a regular basis. Q🛏❄🅿🚃🐾❄🛜

Shirland

Shoulder of Mutton 🅛
Hallfieldgate Lane, DE55 6AA (on B6013)
☼ 5-11 Mon, Wed & Thu; closed Tue; 12-11 Fri & Sat; 12-10.30 Sun ☎ (01773) 834992
3 changing beers ⊞
Eclectic, 16th-century traditional drinking den, nestling on the edge of Amber Valley. The beer garden offers spectacular views and sunsets. It is a true free house where real people enjoy real ale from small breweries; there is no beer list because the ales change daily. Customers are drawn from far and wide, fuelling the unique, easy atmosphere created by the licensees. Q❄🅰🐾🅟❄🛜

Smisby

Tap House
Annwell Lane, LE65 2TA (on jct with Burton Rd)
☼ 11-11 (midnight Fri & Sat) ☎ (01530) 413604
⏀ taphousesmisby.co.uk
Marston's Pedigree; house beer (by Leatherbritches); 5 changing beers (sourced locally; often Sharp's) ⊞
Friendly 19th-century local. The main beamed bar is at the front, with the restaurant beyond featuring a popular carvery. One changing beer is usually from Sharp's, the others badged as Tap House from Leatherbritches Brewery, or sometimes from another microbrewery. Pie night is Wednesday, with occasional live music on Friday evening. Beer festivals are held on the spring and August bank holidays. The garden has a play area. 🛏❄🍽️🅰🅿(9)❄🛜

South Normanton

Clock Inn ✅
107 Market Street, DE55 2AA
☼ 4-11 (midnight Fri); 12-midnight Sat; 12-11 Sun
☎ (01773) 811396 ⏀ theclockinn.co.uk
Everards Tiger; Peak Swift Nick; 1 changing beer ⊞
Multi-room pub with a lounge and public bar area served from a central bar. Up to three beers are sold – the house beer is usually from Peak Ales. Outside is a nice lawn and garden with seating and a covered smoking space. Sky Sports and BT Sport feature on large projection screens. Look out for the Clocktober Fest. 🛏❄🅿🚃(9.1)❄🛜

Devonshire Arms
137 Market Street, DE55 2AA
☼ 12-midnight ☎ (01773) 810748
Sarah Hughes Dark Ruby Mild; 4 changing beers (often Oldershaw, Thornbridge) ⊞
Genuine free house offering up to five real ales and three real ciders or perries. Home-cooked food is served until 9pm every day except Sunday, when a popular carvery is offered. Vegetarians, vegans and coeliacs are catered for, and there are daily specials. Sky Sports is shown on three big screens, one outside in the smoking area. A winner of many CAMRA awards over the past 10 years. 🛏🍽️🐾🅿🚃(9.1)❄🛜

Sutton cum Duckmanton

Arkwright Arms ▼ 🏠
Chesterfield Road, S44 5JG (on A632 between Chesterfield and Bolsover)
🕐 11-11 (midnight Fri & Sat); 11-10.30 Sun
☎ (01246) 232053
Greene King Abbot; Whim Arbor Light; changing beers 🅷
Brewers' Tudor-fronted free house. A range of 10 different guest ales, many from local micros, is complemented by 12 ciders and four perries. Beer festivals are held at Easter and bank holidays, with mini events throughout the year. Quality food is served until 8pm (3pm Sun). The spacious beer garden has play equipment for children. A winner of numerous CAMRA awards, including East Midlands Cider Pub of the Year and local CAMRA Pub of the Year. ⌂❀🅓🍴🅐♣🐾P🖵✿

Swanwick

Steampacket Inn
Derby Road, DE55 1AB
🕐 2.30-11; 2-midnight Fri; 12-midnight Sat; 12-11 Sun
☎ (01773) 607771
5 changing beers (sourced nationally; often Blue Monkey, Derby, Nottingham) 🅷
A friendly ex-Shipstone's local in the centre of Swanwick and a popular Pub People Company establishment, the Steampacket boasts an excellent and changing range of well-kept real ales and ciders, many sourced from local microbreweries. A lively pub with live music at the weekend, quiz nights during the week, a fire in winter and tables outside in summer. Local CAMRA 2015 Cider Pub of the Year. Q⌂♣🐾P🖵✿🛜

Wardlow Mires

Three Stags' Heads ★
Mires Lane, SK17 8RW (jct A623/B6465)
🕐 closed Mon-Thu; 7-11 Fri; 11-11 Sat; 12-10.30 Sun
☎ (01298) 872268
Abbeydale Daily Bread, Absolution; house beer (by Abbeydale); 1 changing beer (sourced regionally) 🅷
A quaint 300-year-old pub with two small rooms, stone-flagged floors and low ceilings. Unspoilt, it is one of the few pubs in the area on CAMRA's National Inventory of Historic Pub Interiors. An ancient range warms the bar and the house dogs, one of which gave the name to the house beer, Black Lurcher. Traditional cider is available only in summer. Q❀🅐P🖵(173)✿🛜

Whaley Bridge

Shepherds Arms
7 Old Road, SK23 7HR
🕐 3 (2 Sat)-midnight; 2-11.30 Sun ☎ (01663) 732384
Marston's 61 Deep, Pedigree; 3 changing beers 🅷
This little gem of a pub nestling close to the centre of the village is an attractive, whitewashed

building which has been preserved unspoilt, conveying the feel of the farmhouse it once was. The taproom is a delight, with an open fire, flagged floor and scrubbed table tops. The comfortable lounge also has an open fire. Changing guest beers are selected from the Marston's range. In walking country, hikers are welcome. Q❀🚲♣P🖵(199,61)

Whitehough

Old Hall Inn 🏠
Chinley, SK23 6EJ (village is 750yds off B6062)
🕐 12-11 ☎ (01663) 750529 🌐 old-hall-inn.co.uk
Marston's 61 Deep; changing beers 🅷
The 14th-century Whitehough Hall forms part of this quintessential country inn, which has won the Great British Pub award for best cask pub in the region for several years and is a regular entry in this Guide. Eight ales, including seven changing guests from quality local micros, complement those available at the adjacent Paper Mill Inn (under the same ownership). A well-attended beer festival runs in September. ⌂❀🅗🍴🅐🚲♣P🖵(189,190)✿🛜

Whittington Moor

Derby Tup 🏠
387 Sheffield Road, S41 8LS
🕐 5-11; 12-11.30 Fri & Sat; 2-11 Sun ☎ (01246) 269835
Castle Rock Harvest Pale; Timothy Taylor Landlord; house beer (by Pigeon Fishers); 6 changing beers 🅷
Ten handpumps offer beers from near and far, with a dark ale usually available. The main bar has a real fire, a variety of wooden settles and etched-glass windows, dating from its original incarnation as the Brunswick Hotel. There is also a small snug. The pub is the brewery tap for the Pigeon Fishers Brewery, serving House Pale and IPA. Live music features three times a month, usually on Saturday. Q❀♣🐾🖵(43,50)✿🛜

Wirksworth

Royal Oak 🏠
North End, DE4 4FG
🕐 8-11.30 (midnight Fri & Sat); 12-4, 8-midnight Sun
☎ (01629) 823000
Draught Bass; Timothy Taylor Landlord; Whim Hartington IPA; 2 changing beers 🅷
This excellent, ultra-traditional local near the marketplace is highlighted at night by rows of fairy lights. The bar features old pictures of local interest and there is also a pool room and smoking grotto. The Oak enjoys a long-standing reputation for Draught Bass, and always serves at least five ales, including a LocAle. The pub is set in a former lead-mining town with much to interest the historian. Q⌂❀♣🖵✿🛜

Sick note

Me and some of the fellers decided to cook up a batch of home brew and the instructions on the yeast said 'Add one packet and wait three days' so we added three packets and waited one day. Well, we drank all that brew right up the very next day. Never been sicker in my life. **American home brewer during Prohibition**

Many entries in the Guide refer to pubs' support for CAMRA's LocAle scheme. The ℃ symbol is used where a pub has LocAle accreditation. The aim of the scheme is to get publicans to stock at least one cask beer that comes from a local brewery no further than 20 miles away. It also encourages publicans to use the Beerflex scheme run by SIBA, the Society of Independent Brewers. SIBA members deliver direct to pubs in their localities instead of going through the central warehouses of pub-owning companies.

The aim is a simple one: to cut down on 'beer miles'. Research by CAMRA shows that food and drink transport accounts for 25 per cent of all HGV vehicle miles in Britain. Taking into account the miles that ingredients have travelled on top of distribution journeys, an imported lager produced by a multi-national brewery could have notched up more than 24,000 'beer miles' by the time it reaches a pub.

Supporters of LocAle point out that £10 spent on locally-supplied goods generates £25 for the local economy. Keeping trade local helps enterprises, creates more economic activity and jobs, and makes other services more viable. The scheme also generates consumer support for local breweries.

Support for LocAle has grown at a rapid pace since it was created in 2007. It's been embraced by pubs and CAMRA branches throughout England and has now crossed the borders into Scotland and Wales.

For more information, see the CAMRA website www.camra.org.uk and type 'locale' into the search window.

What is CAMRA LocAle?

- An initiative that promotes pubs which sell locally-brewed real ale
- The scheme builds on a growing consumer demand for quality local produce and an increased awareness of 'green' issues.

Everyone benefits from local pubs stocking locally brewed real ale...

- Public houses, as stocking local real ales can increase pub visits
- Consumers, who enjoy greater beer choice and locally brewed beer
- Local brewers, who gain from increased sales and get better feedback from consumers
- The local economy, because more money is spent and retained in the local economy
- The environment, due to fewer 'beer miles' resulting in less road congestion and pollution
- Tourism, due to an increased sense of local identity and pride – let's celebrate what makes our locality different.

DEVON

Lynton • Lynmouth
Ilfracombe
Lee Bay
Heddon Valley
Brendon
Bradiford
Braunton
Barnstaple
Yarde Down
Abbotsham
Yelland
Chittlehampton
South Molton
Bideford
Kings Nympton
High Bickington
Roborough
Portsmouth Arms
Sutcombe
Chulmleigh
Tiverton
Petrockstow
Butterleigh
Cullompton
Iddesleigh
Lapford
Bradninch
Hatherleigh
Exbourne
Sandford
Silverton
Clawton
North Tawton
Crediton
Broadclyst
Okehampton
Spreyton
Newton St Cyres
Cowley Bridge
St Giles on the Heath
Sticklepath
Half Moon Village
Exeter
Woodbury Salterton
South Zeal
Drewsteignton
Ide
Topsham
Lewdown
Lydford
Chagford
Bridford
Lympstone
Horndon
Manaton
Christow
Cockwood
Liddaton
Mary Tavy
Postbridge
Chudleigh
Dawlish
Exmouth
Peter Tavy
Bovey Tracey
Holcombe
Tavistock
Widecombe-in-the-Moor
Bishopsteignton
Teignmouth
CORNWALL
Princetown
Ashburton
Ringmore
Buckland Monachorum
Dousland
Buckfastleigh
Newton Abbot
Shaldon
Bere Alston
Meavy
Ipplepen
Yelverton
Littlehempston
Torquay
Bere Ferrers
South Brent
Totnes
Paignton
Plympton
Lee Mill
Avonwick
Stoke Gabriel
Plymouth
Ashprington
Brixham
Billacombe
Bittaford
Ashburton
Kingswear
Turnchapel
Brixton
Dartmouth
Wembury
Ledstone
Slapton
Stokenham
Salcombe
East Prawle

Ashburton

Exeter Inn 🅛

26 West Street, TQ13 7DU (on main road through centre of Ashburton opp church)
🕐 11-2.30, 5-11 (midnight Fri & Sat); 12-3, 7-10.30 Sun
☎ (01364) 652013
Dartmoor IPA, Legend 🅷
This friendly local, the oldest in Ashburton, was built in 1131, with additions in the 17th century. Its original purpose was to house the workers building the nearby church. There are seated drinking areas either side of the entrance, leading to an L-shaped, rustic, wood-panelled bar to the right which includes a canopy. There is also a small serving counter for the seated area in the rear bar. A lovely secluded walled garden is out at the back. Local Thompstone's cider is on sale.
Q🍽🕮🅾♣🖶🖺(88)🐾🛜

Ashill

Ashill Inn 🅛

EX15 3NL ST086113
🕐 12-2.30 (not Mon), 5.30-11; 12-4, 6.30-10.30 Sun
☎ (01884) 840506 🌐 ashillinndevon.co.uk
3 changing beers (sourced regionally) 🅷
A Grade II-listed pub, built in 1835, down narrow lanes in the Culm Valley. It is a charming small venue with a cosy bar and a recently extended restaurant area to one side, with large windows overlooking the beer garden. The comfortable bar serves changing local South-West brewery ales – selected to offer a range of ABVs in low, medium and higher strengths – and Orchard Pig Navel Gazer real cider. Good-value food is available, with produce mainly from local farms. Live music and special events are often featured.
Q🕮🅾♣🖤P🐾🛜

Avonwick

Turtley Corn Mill ⓛ

TQ10 9ES (off A38, follow signs for South Brent &
Avonwick)
🕔 8.30am-11; 8.30am-10.30 Sun ☎ (01364) 646100
🌐 turtleycornmill.com
**Otter Ale; St Austell Tribute; Summerskills Start Point;
1 changing beer (sourced locally; often Salcombe,
South Hams, Tavy Ales)** Ⓗ
This former roadside restaurant stands by its own
river and lakeside grounds. The three regular ales
are supplemented by up to two rotating local guest
ales. Reverting to its former name to reflect its
origins, it encompasses the ethos of its owners by
supplying local beers and locally sourced food. Old
photos of the area adorn the walls, including a rare
print of a Plymouth brewery now demolished.
Children are welcome, as are well-behaved dogs.
Q🕏🏡🕮🕭🕯🐾🐕🎵🛜

Axminster

Axminster Inn ⓔ

Silver Street, EX13 5AH
🕔 10.30-1am (midnight Mon); 10-1am Thu; 11-1am Sun
☎ (01297) 34947 🌐 axminsterinn.pub
**Palmers Copper Ale, Best Bitter, Dorset Gold, 200,
Tally Ho!; 1 changing beer** Ⓗ
A friendly traditional pub, lying just off the town
centre, with a real log fire and lovely enclosed beer
garden. It offers a good range of Palmers ales.
Good-value home-cooked food, often locally
sourced, is served lunchtimes Thursday to Sunday,
including roasts on Sunday. Breakfast is available
8am-1pm. There is free Wi-Fi, a skittle alley and
dartboard, and live music is featured. Children are
welcome, and the pub is dog-friendly. The real
cider is from Sheppy's. 🕏🕮🕭🕯🐾🐕🛜

Bere Ferrers

Olde Plough Inn ⓛ

Fore Street, PL20 7JG (close to church and river)
🕔 11-3, 6-11; 12-11 Sun ☎ (01822) 840358
🌐 theoldeploughinn.co.uk
**Sharp's Doom Bar; 3 changing beers (sourced locally;
often Dartmoor, Noss Beer Works, Summerskills)** Ⓗ
A friendly 16th-century pub, just a 15-minute walk
from the station, and only 18 minutes from
Plymouth on the Tamar Valley line. Up to four real
ales are on tap, featuring local Devon breweries,
and a real cider in summer. Inside, there are real
fires, exposed stonework, flagstone floors and a
warm welcome. From the beer garden, there are
spectacular views over the River Tavy. Food is
served to suit all ages, tastes and appetites,
including vegetarian. Opening hours are extended
in summer. Q🕏🕮🕭🕯🐾🐕🚌(87)🐕🛜

Bideford

Appledore Inn ⓛ

Chingswell Street, EX39 2NF
🕔 11-11; 12-10.30 Sun ☎ (01237) 476956
🌐 appledoreinnbideford.co.uk
**Jollyboat Grenville's Renown; Sharp's Doom Bar,
Special; 1 changing beer (sourced nationally)** Ⓗ
Dating from the 15th century and one of the oldest
inns in Bideford, this friendly family-run pub lies
close to Bideford football ground. There is a single
bar, with a restaurant area to the side and a paved

Ashprington

Durant Arms

TQ9 7UP (exit Totnes on A381; left turn signposted after
1,500yds)
🕔 closed Mon; 12-3, 6-10 (11 Thu); 12-3, 5-11 Fri; 12-11 Sat;
12-5 Sun ☎ (01803) 732240 🌐 durantarms.co.uk
Noss Beer Works Church Ledge Ⓗ; **2 changing beers
(sourced regionally)** Ⓗ/Ⓖ
Sitting in the heart of a pretty village, this pub is a
true country hostelry, with wood-burning fires,
slate floors and traditional furnishings. Family-run,
it has built up a good reputation for beer and food
quality, and there are two dining areas. Outside
seating at the front overlooks the war memorial
and village centre, and there is a pretty courtyard
at the back. Both family and dog friendly, it is
popular with walkers and cyclists. B&B
accommodation is offered in three rooms. Close to
Sharpham Vineyard and the River Dart. The pub is
open on Bank Holiday Mondays but closed the day
after. Q🕏🕮🕭🕯🐕🛜

SOMERSET
DORSET

Ashill Luppitt
Honiton Axminster
Kilmington
Ottery St Mary
Newton Poppleford Colyton
Branscombe
Sidmouth
East Budleigh

0 Miles 10
0 Kilometres 16

beer garden at the rear. Four real ales are generally available, sometimes joined by a fifth served from the cask. The pub is renowned for high-quality authentic Thai food served daily from noon-9pm. Q❀◑❸⎶❀🛜

Lacey's Ale & Cider House L
36 Mill Street, EX39 2JJ
❀ 12 (4 Mon-Wed)-11 ☎ (01237) 470280
Country Life Old Appledore, Reef Break, Shore Break; 2 changing beers (sourced nationally) 🅗
Lively town-centre bar, originally set up by Country Life Brewery as its brewery tap, but run independently since November 2012. The two regular real ales still come from Country Life and the pub offers a real ale discount club. Large double doors open on to the street in the summer. A quiz night is held every Sunday and live music sessions are hosted monthly. No food is served. ❀🌢♣⎶❀🛜

Bittaford

Horse & Groom L
Exeter Road, PL21 0EL
❀ 12-11 (midnight Fri & Sat) ☎ (01752) 892358
Dartmoor Jail Ale; house beer (by Hunters); 4 changing beers (sourced locally; often Dartmoor, Hunters, Summerskills) 🅗
A family-owned pub run by a keen real ale enthusiast. It features good home-cooked food and six pumps, two dedicated to real cider. The other pumps predominantly offer ales from local breweries in south Devon and Cornwall. The pub has a long bar and separate dining area, with pictures of the former Moorhaven Hospital on the wall. A monthly quiz night is held. One beer festival, and a cider and sausage festival, are staged, supporting local charities. Third-pint tapas are available. Q❀❀◑🅐♣●P⎶(X38,Gold)❀🛜

Bovey Tracey

Cromwell Arms ✓
Fore Street, TQ13 9AE
❀ 11-11 (11.30 Fri & Sat); 12-11 Sun ☎ (01626) 833473
⊕ thecromwellarms.co.uk
St Austell Tribute; house beer (by St Austell); 3 changing beers (sourced nationally) 🅗
Centrally located 17th-century pub with a frontage on the main square. Five constantly rotating beers, including seasonals and guests, cater for a convivial mix of both locals and tourists, given its access to Dartmoor. One large bar area is separated into two, and there is also a dining area and separate restaurant where children are welcome. To the rear is an unusual wisteria-covered smokers' area leading to a quiet garden next to the car park. Fourteen letting rooms are available. Q❀❀🛏◑&♣P⎶❀🛜

Bradiford

Windsor Arms L
55 Bradiford, EX31 4AD (on main road through village, approximately ½ mile N of Pilton)
❀ 12-2.30 (not Mon), 5-11; 12-11.30 Fri & Sat; 12-10.30 Sun ☎ (01271) 343583 ⊕ windsorarms.co.uk
Adnams Broadside; Fuller's London Pride; 1 changing beer (sourced nationally) 🅗
A friendly welcome is assured to all who visit this community-oriented village pub. Three handpumps

offer a wide range of guest ales, which usually include London Pride, Broadside or Abbot Ale. Good, freshly-cooked and locally sourced food is served every evening and on Sunday and Wednesday lunchtimes in the separate lounge bar. A function room, with skittle alley, pool table, and dartboard lies to the rear of the pub. ❀❀◑♣⎶❀🛜

Bradninch

Olde White Lion
26 High Street, EX5 4QL
❀ 4-midnight; 12-1am Fri & Sat; 12-midnight Sun ☎ (01392) 881263
Butcombe Adam Henson's Rare Breed; Dartmoor Jail Ale; Otter Ale; 1 changing beer (sourced regionally; often Otter) 🅗
A friendly family-run locals' pub that caters for everyone. It offers up to four real ales and one real cider. Food is served Tuesday to Sunday from a

REAL ALE BREWERIES

Art Brew Sutcombe
Bale Liddaton (NEW)
Barum 🍺 Barnstaple
Bays Paignton
Beer Engine 🍺 Newton St Cyres
Bere Bere Alston (NEW)
Black Tor Christow
Branscombe Vale Branscombe
Bridgetown 🍺 Totnes
Checkstone 🍺 Exmouth
Clearwater Bideford
Country Life Abbotsham
Crossed Anchors 🍺 Exmouth
Dartmoor Princetown
Devon Earth Buckfastleigh
Exe Valley Silverton
Exeter Exeter
Fat Belly 🍺 Lynton (NEW)
Fat Pig 🍺 Exeter
Grampus 🍺 Lee Bay
GT Braunton
Hanlons Half Moon Village
Holsworthy Clawton
Hunters Ipplepen
Isca Holcombe
Jollyboat Bideford
Madrigal Lynmouth
Moonchild Petrockstow
Moorstone Horndon
New Lion Totnes
Noss Beer Works Lee Mill
Occasional Silverton (brewing suspended)
Otter Luppitt
Platform 5 Newton Abbot
Powderkeg Woodbury Salterton
Red Rock Bishopsteignton
Riviera Stoke Gabriel
Salcombe Ledstone
South Hams Stokenham
Stannary Tavistock (NEW)
Summerskills Billacombe
Tally Ho! 🍺 Hatherleigh
Tavy Plymouth
Teignworthy Newton Abbot
Topsham 🍺 Topsham (brewing suspended)
Totnes 🍺 Totnes
Two Beach Shaldon
Woodbury Woodbury Salterton (NEW)
Yelland Manor Yelland

selected menu including a Sunday roast. It has many dark-oak beams, plus a wood-burning stove under a stone alcove, and stages regular and varied music nights, with a folk club on the first Tuesday of the month. The pub is involved with the annual music festival in June. Darts, skittles and pool are played. Q🕮🖙♪♣🚻P🖭🐾🛜

Branscombe

Fountain Head Inn 🄻

EX12 3BG (in main street 1 mile S of A3052)
🕓 11-3, 6-11; 12-10.30 Sun ☎ (01297) 680359
🌐 fountainheadinn.com
Branscombe Vale Branoc, Golden Fiddle, Summa That; 1 changing beer (sourced locally) 🄷
Popular with walkers, this neat 500-year-old pub is at the west end of this long straggly village in a beautiful coastal valley. It retains wood-panelled walls and flagstone floors, with an inglenook fireplace. A beer festival is held on the nearest weekend to the longest day. The guest beer is from Branscombe Vale or another local brewery, and the cider is Branscombe Vale Pip. Good-value home-cooked food is served. Dogs are welcome, as are children (but not in the bar).
Q🕮🏵🕽&🅰♣🚻P🖭(899)🐾

Braunton

Ebrington Arms 🄻

Winsham Road, Knowle, EX33 2LW
🕓 11-11 ☎ (01271) 812166 🌐 ebringtonarmsdevon.co.uk
Exmoor Ale; Otter Ale; 2 changing beers (sourced nationally) 🄷
The Ebrington Arms is one of the oldest buildings in the village. Inside, it is a mixture of old and new, with comfortable bar areas, a restaurant and a separate games room with skittle alley. At least three real ales are usually available, together with good pub food all year round. It is a Devon village pub in the old style. Outside there is a pleasant seating area, a large car park, and an excellent bus service within easy distance.
Q🕮🏵🕽&🅰♣🚻P🖭🐾🛜

Brendon

Staghunters Inn 🄻

EX35 6PS SS767481
🕓 12-11 ☎ (01598) 741222 🌐 staghunters.com
Exmoor Ale; St Austell Proper Job; 2 changing beers (sourced nationally) 🄶
Set deep in the Lyn Valley within Exmoor National Park, this family-owned and run inn provides an ideal base for those exploring the local area. It has 14 well-appointed rooms and dogs can stay overnight for a nominal charge. Up to four real ales are served on gravity, with the regular Exmoor and St Austell ales often joined by guests from other local breweries. Good locally sourced food can be enjoyed in the attractive restaurant.
Q🕮🏵🛏🕽🅰♣🚻P🐾🛜

Bridford

Bridford Inn 🄻 ✅

EX6 7HT
🕓 12-11 (midnight Fri & Sat) ☎ (01647) 252250
🌐 bridfordinn.co.uk
Dartmoor Jail Ale; 3 changing beers (sourced regionally) 🄷

A 17th-century Devon longhouse, within the Dartmoor National Park, that was converted to a pub in 1968 and now houses a village shop. It has a spacious open-plan interior both for drinkers and diners, with old oak beams, and an inglenook fireplace complete with bread oven and a woodburner. Freshly home-cooked quality food is served to order. Outside there is a beer garden with picnic tables and stunning views. Traditional ciders from Devon and Somerset producers are always on sale. Q🕮🏵🕽&♣🚻P🖭(360,361)🐾🛜

Brixham

Queen's Arms 🄻 ✅

31 Station Hill, TQ5 8BN (from Brixham Library go up Church Hill East, then Station Hill)
🕓 4-11; 2-midnight Fri; 12-midnight Sat; 12-11 Sun
☎ (01803) 852074 🌐 thequeensarmsbrixham.co.uk
House beer (by Teignworthy); 5 changing beers (sourced nationally) 🄷
A single-bar end-of-terrace pub that has gained a well deserved reputation for the quality of its six varied beers, one of which is always priced at £2.60. Up to three real ciders are offered. The friendly one-room bar is made cosy by wood-burning fires, and the strong community ethos is complemented by live music at weekends, an annual charity beer festival, good-value Sunday lunches and Monday suppers. Local CAMRA Pub of the Year 2016. 🖙🏵🕽♣🚻P🖭

Brixton

Foxhound Inn 🍺 🄻

Kingsbridge Road, PL8 2AH
🕓 11-11 (midnight Fri & Sat); 12-11 Sun ☎ (01752) 880271
🌐 foxhoundinn.co.uk
Courage Directors; house beer (by Summerskills); 3 changing beers (sourced nationally; often Caledonian, Courage, Summerskills) 🄷
This 18th-century coaching house is in a rural village just east of Plymouth, where it is well served by a frequent daytime bus service. The pub has two separate bars and a small restaurant. Traditional English meals are offered daily, using locally sourced ingredients. Look out for Red Coat, an ale crafted by the landlord, among four guest ales. A monthly charity quiz night is held. Local CAMRA Country Pub of the Year 2017.
Q🕮🏵🕽🅰♣🚻P🖭🐾

Broadclyst

New Inn 🄻

Whimple Road, EX5 3BX (½ mile E of village)
🕓 11-11 ☎ (01392) 461312 🌐 newinn-exeter.co.uk
Dartmoor Jail Ale; Hanlons Yellowhammer; Otter Bitter; Sharp's Doom Bar 🄷
Large, traditional 17th-century inn, with a recently extended car park to the rear, and a two-acre beer garden and play area. The spacious grounds host the village Year Seven football club. Freshly cooked food is served lunchtimes and evenings. There are three secluded rooms and the skittle alley can double as a function room. Regular events are held, plus an annual bonfire night.
Q🕮🖙🏵🕽♣🚻P🛜

Buckland Monachorum

Drake Manor Inn L ✓
The Village, PL20 7NA
⚙ 11-2.30, 6.30-11; 11.30-11.30 Fri & Sat; 12-11 Sun
☎ (01822) 853892 ⊕ drakemanorinn.co.uk
**Dartmoor Jail Ale; Sharp's Doom Bar; 1 changing beer
(sourced regionally; often Otter)** H
The longstanding landlady ensures a warm
welcome at this 16th-century inn, nestled in a
quaint Devon village. The well-kept beer range will
often include an ale from Otter Brewery. The pub is
divided into the friendly and cosy drinking area,
and the formal, though relaxed, dining room. A
weekly curry night, monthly open mic sessions,
luxurious upstairs accommodation and a lovely rear
garden complete the scene. The pub enjoys a loyal
local following, and has a good reputation for food.
Q ⚑ 🛏 ⚙ ◑ ♣ 🍴 🚍 (55) 🐾 📶

Butterleigh

Butterleigh Inn L
The Green, EX15 1PN (opp church) SS9746108212
⚙ 12-2.30 (not Mon), 6-11; 12-2.30, 6-midnight Fri & Sat;
12-3 Sun ☎ (01884) 855433 ⊕ butterleighinn.co.uk
**Cotleigh Tawny Owl; Dartmoor Jail Ale; Otter Ale; 1
changing beer** H
Situated in this small, quaint village, the
Butterleigh is an excellent country pub with a
mixed clientele creating a great atmosphere with
diverse conversation. Good-value home-cooked
food is served lunchtimes and evenings Tuesday to
Saturday, with a carvery Sunday lunchtime. There is
always a choice of four real ales, one a LocAle, plus
Sandford Orchards Devon Scrumpy, Winkleigh
Sam's Medium and a rotating guest cider. There is
a main bar, lounge and a modern dining room.
Q ⚑ 🛏 ⚙ ◑ & ♣ 🍴 P 🐾 📶

Chagford

Globe Inn L ✓
9 High Street, TQ13 8AJ
⚙ 11-11.30 (midnight Fri & Sat); 12-11 Sun
☎ (01647) 433485 ⊕ theglobeinnchagford.co.uk
Dartmoor IPA; Otter Bitter; 1 changing beer H
Formerly a coaching inn and coopery, the Globe
overlooks the parish church and has evolved into a
focal point of this historic town, providing good
food, music evenings, a cinema club and numerous
other events. There is a splendid public bar and a
separate lounge bar and restaurant, both with
large open fires. A small courtyard garden is at the
rear and parking is nearby. The ciders are Westons
Old Rosie and Sam's. ⚑ 🛏 ⚙ ◑ 🍴 🚍 (173,178) 🐾 📶

Chittlehampton

Bell Inn L
The Square, EX37 9QL (opp St Hieritha's parish church)
SS636254
⚙ 11-3, 6-midnight; 11-midnight Fri & Sat; 12-11 Sun
☎ (01769) 540368 ⊕ thebellatchittlehampton.co.uk
**Exmoor Ale; Otter Ale; 5 changing beers (sourced
nationally)** H
Owned and run by the same family for more than
30 years, the Bell celebrated 20 continuous years
of Guide inclusion in 2016. There is always a good
selection of real ales, with four on handpump and
up to four more regularly available on gravity. The
bar area is notable for its sporting memorabilia,

and good-value home-cooked food is served both
here and in the adjoining restaurant. Well-behaved
children and dogs are welcome.
⚑ 🛏 ⚙ ◑ & 🅰 ♣ 🍴 P 🚍 (658,859) 🐾 📶

Christow

Artichoke Inn ✓
Village Road, EX6 7NF
⚙ 9-11.20; 12-10.50 Sun ☎ (01647) 252387
⊕ theartichokeinn.co.uk
Dartmoor Legend, Jail Ale; 1 changing beer H
Lovely 12th-century thatched pub in the centre of
this tranquil Teign Valley village, where thatched
properties abound. It offers a warm welcome and a
comfortable interior, with a woodburner in the
winter months and a pleasant beer garden to enjoy
in the summer. Breakfasts are served weekday
mornings, and a good range of menu options is
available at lunchtimes, evenings and all day
Sunday. Q ⚑ 🛏 ⚙ ◑ & ♣ P 🚍 (360,361) 🐾 📶

Chudleigh

Bishop Lacy Inn L
Fore Street, TQ13 0HY
⚙ 12-midnight (1am Fri & Sat) ☎ (01626) 854585
3 changing beers (sourced regionally) H
Grade II-listed pub where you are likely to be
greeted warmly by the ebullient landlady, to
whom the witch dolls adorning the bar ironically
refer. The left-hand bar is dominated by a massive
fireplace that was once used to cure ham, and a TV
screen for sport, while the right-hand bar is more
food-oriented. The rotating beers are often from
local breweries including Black Tor, Hanlons and
Exeter. Excellent home-cooked food is served, and
children and dogs are welcome.
Q ⚑ 🛏 ⚙ ◑ & 🅰 ♣ P 🚍 (39,182) 🐾 📶

Chulmleigh

Old Court House
South Molton Street, EX18 7BW
⚙ 11-11 ☎ (01769) 580045 ⊕ oldcourthouseinn.co.uk
**Butcombe Original; Dartmoor IPA; Exmoor Ale; 1
changing beer (sourced nationally)** H
Charles I stayed in this traditional pub in 1634 and
the pub dates from long before this. A bedroom
still contains an original Royal House of Stuart coat
of arms, and a replica hangs above the fireplace in
the main bar. There are three, more likely four, real
ales on offer together with a local cider. Good
home-cooked food is served in the separate
restaurant. 🛏 ⚙ ◑ & ♣ 🍴 🚍 (377) 🐾 📶

Cockwood

Anchor Inn L ✓
EX6 8RA (just off A379, outside Starcross, next to
harbour) SX9756480692
⚙ 11-11; 11.30-10.30 Sun ☎ (01626) 890203
⊕ anchorinncockwood.com
Otter Ale; 3 changing beers (often Dartmoor) H
On picturesque Cockwood harbour, this 450-year-
old inn and former seaman's mission has many old
settles, timber panelling, low beams and snugs,
with an impressive display of old nautical
memorabilia. It has an extensive award-winning
seafood menu, with mussels a speciality. Four ales
are usually served in winter, up to six at other
times. Haunted by a friendly ghost and his dog, this

is a really atmospheric Devon gem. Close to the main GWR line, it is a steam train-spotters' paradise. It has limited parking, and a bus stop over the bridge. Q✿⏵❀⏺❖⎶⚲⏸♣▲✦♋🅿🚲(2)🐾

Ship Inn 🅛 ✅

Church Road, EX6 8NU (just off A379, outside Starcross, close to harbour)
🕐 11-11; 12-10.30 Sun ☎ (01626) 890373
🌐 shipinncockwood.co.uk
Dartmoor Jail Ale; Hanlons Yellowhammer; Otter Bitter; St Austell Tribute; 1 changing beer Ⓗ
A busy family-run pub, close to the picturesque harbour at Cockwood, with a large beer garden with views of the estuary, and a log fire in winter. Popular with drinkers and diners alike, it offers a choice of four regular ales and usually one rotating guest, and has an excellent food menu. Meals are prepared with local produce where possible including a varied choice of locally caught fish. The bus stops 100 yards across the bridge.
Q⏵❀⏺▲♣♋🅿🚲(2)🐾

Colyton

Gerrard Arms 🅛

St Andrew's Square, EX24 6JN
🕐 12-3, 5.30-11 (1am Fri); 12-3, 6-midnight Sat; 12-3, 7-10.30 Sun ☎ (01297) 552588 🌐 thegerrardarms.co.uk
Branscombe Vale Branoc; Draught Bass; Otter Ale; 1 changing beer Ⓗ
Busy one-bar pub dating back to 1506 and next to the church, in this delightful little town with lots of lovely old cottages and tangled narrow streets and alleyways. There is a safe courtyard at the back, now with disabled access. The home-made food menu is good value but only served Friday and Saturday, plus a traditional roast lunch on Sunday. In summer the lunchtime session may run on. Colyton station on the Seaton Tramway is a level walk. Q⏵❀⏺❖⎶⚲♣▲✦🅿🚲🐾

Cowley Bridge

New Inn 🅛

Cowley Bridge Hill, EX4 5BX
🕐 11-11 ☎ (01392) 431010
🌐 thenewinncowleybridge.co.uk
Brains Rev James; Exeter Avocet Ⓗ**; 1 changing beer (often Hanlons)** Ⓖ
This friendly free house is found on the outskirts of Exeter beside the railway and the junction of the A377 and A396. Formerly the Cowley Bridge Inn, the pub reopened in 2014 after several years as a Chinese restaurant. Delicious home-cooked food (including gluten-free and vegetarian dishes) is served all week except Sunday and Monday evenings. A games room with a free pool table leads to a pleasant garden, where BBQ's and beer with music festivals are held.
⏵❀⏺❖⚲♣▲✦🅿🚲🐾

Crediton

Crediton Inn 🅛

28a Mill Street, EX17 1EZ (opp Mole Avon)
🕐 10-11; 12-3, 7-10.30 Sun ☎ (01363) 772882
🌐 crediton-inn.co.uk
5 changing beers Ⓗ
The framed deeds date this inn to 1878, with windows etched with the ancient town seal. It is a genuine free house, well supported by the locals.

The handpumps have increased to 10, served by local breweries, with an ale festival in November. The skittle alley doubles as a function room. Good home-cooked food is available at weekends, with snacks and renowned Scotch eggs at other times. The welcoming owner is the longest-serving landlady in Crediton. ❀⏺🚆♣▲♋🅿🚲(5)🐾🐾🛜

Mitre

9 High Street, EX17 3AE (on A377 in town centre opp Co-op)
🕐 1-1am; 12-1am Sat & Sun ☎ (01363) 772508
4 changing beers (sourced regionally) Ⓗ
A Grade II-listed free house, fondly known by older locals as Number Nine, located on the high street. It has interesting pub decor, with beer-originated curios and other knick-knacks, and is well supported by local rugby, football and dart teams. Live music features every Saturday 9.30-11.30pm. The terraced garden, which is south-facing, is great for warmer months, and serves as the smoking area in all weathers. You can always depend on well-kept ales and good conversation here.
⏵❀⚲♣🅿🚲🐾🛜

Cullompton

Pony & Trap 🅛 ✅

10 Exeter Hill, EX15 1DJ (on B3181 S of town)
🕐 12-3, 5-11; 12-midnight Fri; 12-3, 5-midnight Sat; 12-5, 8-11 Sun ☎ (01884) 34182 🌐 ponyandtrapcullompton.co.uk
Dartmoor Jail Ale; Draught Bass; Exmoor Ale, Gold; 4 changing beers Ⓗ
A traditional local with a good atmosphere and a mixed clientele. It has a smart interior featuring a logburner, making it cosy in winter; flowers and ornaments add a homely feel. Up to eight real ales could be on offer, plus four real ciders. Home-cooked food is available Friday, Saturday and Sunday lunchtimes only. There is a garden and seating area. Live music features once a month and pub games are played. Q❀⏺♣♋🅿🚲(1)🐾

Dartmouth

Cherub Inn ✅

13 Higher Street, TQ6 9RB
🕐 11-11; 12-10.30 Sun ☎ (01803) 832571
🌐 the-cherub.co.uk
Exeter Ferryman; St Austell Proper Job; South Hams Devon Pride; house beer (by St Austell); 1 changing beer (sourced locally) Ⓗ
Probably the oldest house in Dartmouth, this belonged to a merchant in the 14th century and is Grade II listed. Behind the Tudor façade, the small bar has dark wooden seating and a comfortable atmosphere. It has beams made from ships' timbers and a spiral wooden staircase to the restaurant and rest rooms. Locally sourced fish and steaks are among the choices on the lunchtime and evening menus; food is served in the first floor restaurant and the bar area. Q⏵⏺▲🅿🚲(3,X64)🐾

Dawlish

Marine Tavern

2 Marine Parade, EX7 9DJ
🕐 11-11.30 ☎ (01626) 865245 🌐 marinetaverndawlish.com
Dartmoor Best; Otter Ale; Sharp's Doom Bar; 1 changing beer (sourced nationally) Ⓗ
Traditional seaside pub with a suntrap patio at the front, and a sea view balcony which is also a great

lookout post for passing steam train specials. Good-value food is served all day in the peak summer season, and lunch and evenings at other times. Accommodation consists of four rooms, and children are welcome in an area away from the bar. Dogs are also welcome. Occasional live music is hosted, and there are interesting local photos to admire. ⛪🏠🛏️🍴🚲(2)🐾🐕📶

Dousland

Burrator Inn 🅛 ✅
PL20 6NP
🕐 12-11 (12.30am Sat) ☎ (01822) 853121
🌐 theburratorinn.com
Dartmoor Jail Ale; Otter Amber; St Austell Tribute; Sharp's Doom Bar Ⓗ
This substantial pub, on the road between Yelverton, Burrator Reservoir and Princetown, has a large bar area with space for a pool table and two dart boards, along with various other rooms including a separate dining room. Food is served all day. Outside there is ample parking and a garden incorporating a children's play area. A beer festival is held annually in September. Live music features on Saturday evenings, a quiz on Sunday plus other regular entertainment. Q⛪🏠🛏️🍴♿♣P🚲🐾🐕📶

Drewsteignton

Drewe Arms ★
EX6 6QN
🕐 12-3, 5-11 (midnight Fri); 12-5 Sun ☎ (01647) 281409
🌐 thedrewearmsinn.co.uk
Dartmoor Jail Ale Ⓗ/Ⓖ; **Otter Ale** Ⓗ; **4 changing beers** Ⓖ
A thatched, white-walled village pub in front of the parish church in a picturesque village square. This unmistakably English drinking hostelry has a historic interior and rustic charm. The venue is most famous for Aunt Mabel, who held the record as the longest-serving landlady, running the place for 75 years before retiring at 99. The pub serves excellent food using locally sourced ingredients and prides itself on maintaining the ales from cask to glass, just as Mabel did. Q⛪🏠🛏️🍴♿♣P🚲(173)🐾🐕📶

East Budleigh

Sir Walter Raleigh Inn 🅛
22 High Street, EX9 7ED (off B3178 opp Hayes Lane)
🕐 12-3, 6-11; 12-3, 7-10.30 Sun ☎ (01395) 442510
4 changing beers (sourced regionally) Ⓗ
Set in the middle of a delightful village, the birthplace of Sir Walter Raleigh, this free house is a truly welcoming 16th-century country inn. Good-quality local pub food is served lunchtimes and evenings in addition to four varying real ales, and up to six real ciders. Originally two cottages, the buildings were converted into a Jacobean-style pub, retaining the original wooden beams throughout. This gem is well worth a visit for good-quality real ale, cider, traditional pub food and friendly service. Q⛪🏠🍴♣🚲(157)🐾

East Prawle

Pig's Nose Inn 🅛
TQ7 2BY
🕐 12-3, 6-11 ☎ (01548) 511209 🌐 pigsnoseinn.co.uk

Otter Bitter Ⓖ; **South Hams Devon Pride** Ⓗ/Ⓖ, **Eddystone; 1 changing beer** Ⓖ
A much-loved 500-year-old smugglers' inn on the village green that attracts birdwatchers and coast path walkers. The maritime-themed interior is cluttered and quirky. Gravity beers are racked behind the bar, and home-cooked locally sourced food is served. Children and dogs are welcome and have their own menus. Occasional live music events are held in a hall adjoining the pub. Children's games are available, as is knitting for adults. Closed Sunday evenings as in winter. Q⛪🏠🛏️🍴⛺♣🚲🐾🐕📶

Exbourne

Red Lion 🍺 🅛 ✅
High Street, EX20 3RY (200yds N of jct with A3072)
SS602018
🕐 4-11; 12-11 Fri-Sun ☎ (01837) 851551
Exmoor Fox; Sharp's Original; 1 changing beer (sourced nationally) Ⓖ
Village local dating from the 16th century with no handpumps of any description, as the landlord refuses to serve draught lager. Casks are set on stillage at the end of the L-shaped bar, along with Sam's cider from nearby Winkleigh. Good food, much of which is sourced locally, is available Wednesday to Sunday. Regular beer festivals are held and live music features monthly. Local CAMRA Pub of the Year in 2015 and again in 2017. Q⛪🏠🍴♣P🚲🐾🐕📶

Exeter

Fat Pig 🅛
2 John Street, EX1 1BL (behind Fore St)
🕐 5 (12 Sat)-11; 12-5 Sun ☎ (01392) 437217
🌐 fatpig-exeter.co.uk
3 changing beers (sourced locally) Ⓗ
Formerly the Coachmakers Arms, this Victorian corner local has been brought back to life as a traditional pub, featuring a range of locally sourced food, including brewery-fed pork and sausages from a herd of rare-breed pigs. In addition to making its own cider, it is also a brewpub producing a wide range of styles for its three pubs. There are malt whisky evenings, a Monday quiz night and home-brew competitions. Various spirits are now being made. Q🍴≈♣🚲📶

George's Meeting House ✅
38 South Street, EX1 1ED
🕐 8am-midnight (1am Fri & Sat) ☎ (01392) 454250
Dartmoor Jail Ale; Greene King Abbot; Ruddles Best Bitter; Sharp's Doom Bar; 6 changing beers (sourced nationally) Ⓗ
This Wetherspoon opened in January 2005, having been sympathetically converted from a Unitarian Chapel dating from 1760. Many of the original features remain unaltered including two upstairs galleries, a pulpit and stained-glass windows. A range of national, regional and local real ales, and five real ciders are served. Food is available throughout the day until 10pm. A newer extension, at the rear of the main building, leads to more seating outdoors. Q⛪🏠🍴♿≈♣🚲🐾📶

Hour Glass Inn
21 Melbourne Street, St Leonard's, EX2 4AU (approx 300yds from Exeter quayside)

5-10.30 Mon; 12-2.30, 5-11 (midnight Fri); 12-midnight Sat; 12-10.30 Sun ☎ (01392) 258722 ⊕ hourglassexeter.co.uk
Changing beers Ⓗ
A traditional hostelry in the back streets of Exeter, established 1848, in the hub of the local area close to the quay and about five minutes' walk from the main city centre. The pub has two restaurants and a bar, serving contemporary and continental food. It is very traditional in its features, with a mixture of live entertainment including light theatre and music, which has proved popular with its eclectic group of customers. Five handpumps offer constantly changing real ales. Q◖Ⓓ♣🚲🚌🛏️🐾

Thatched House Inn ✅
Exwick Road, Exwick, EX4 2BQ
🕑 12-11 (11.30 Fri & Sat); 12-10 Sun ☎ (01392) 272920 ⊕ thatchedhouse.net
Greene King Abbot; 5 changing beers (sourced locally; often Dartmoor, Hanlons, Hunters) Ⓗ
This thatched building dates from the 1600s and is a community pub next to the Exwick playing fields, opposite the Exeter College Sports Hub. It is close to the river, convenient for dog walkers, cyclists and sightseers. Seven real ales and one real cider are usually on sale, with great-value home-cooked food sourced from local ingredients and producers. On-street parking is available nearby, and the pub is on the Stagecoach F1 and F2 bus route.
Q🕑🐕🏠◖Ⓓ♿🚲🚌🐾🛜

Exmouth

Bicton Inn Ⓛ
5 Bicton Street, EX8 2RU
🕑 11-midnight ☎ (01395) 272589 ⊕ bictoninn.co.uk
Branscombe Vale Branoc; Dartmoor Jail Ale; Wadworth 6X; 5 changing beers Ⓗ
A friendly and popular back-street local, offering good beer and chat. A community hub, traditional games are played such as darts, pool and euchre, and regular live music events are featured. Up to eight real ales and one cider are normally on offer, usually including several LocAles. The snug is available for small gatherings and meetings. There is a logburner in the main bar. Three beer festivals are held throughout the year. 🏠🚲♣🛏️🐾🛜

First & Last Inn Ⓛ
10 Church Street, EX8 1PE (off B3178 Rolle St)
🕑 11-11 (11.30 Sat); 12-10.30 Sun ☎ (01395) 263275
Courage Directors; Otter Ale; Teignworthy Neap Tide Ⓗ**; 2 changing beers (sourced locally; often Checkstone)** Ⓖ
Victorian pub near the town centre with a public car park opposite. It is a genuine free house, with three distinct areas and a courtyard patio with heated awnings. The Checkstone Brewery started here in 2016 and supplies the pub with changing ales from an increasing range. Games include pool and darts, and there is a skittle alley. Televised sport is prominent and there is regular live music. Up to nine ciders are on sale including Westons Old Rosie and Thatchers Traditional.
🏠♿🚲♣🛏️(57)🐾

Grapevine
2 Victoria Road, EX8 1DL
🕑 4-11; 12-midnight Fri & Sat; 12-11 Sun ☎ (01395) 222208
6 changing beers (often Butcombe, Crossed Anchors) Ⓗ

The Grapevine brewhouse is a stylish Victorian free house in the centre of Exmouth. It is home to Crossed Anchors Brewing and Ruby Diner burger specialists. As well as serving up to four Crossed Anchors beers there is always a wide selection of guest ales and Green Valley Cyder. You will find a pub quiz on Mondays, live music at the weekends and a good selection of board games.
🏠🐕◖Ⓓ♿🚲🛏️(57)🐾🛜

Heddon Valley

Hunters Inn Ⓛ
Heddon Valley, EX31 4PY (signed from A39 N of Parracombe; keep going down this country lane for what seems like a few miles) SS655481
🕑 10-11 ☎ (01598) 763230 ⊕ thehuntersinnexmoor.co.uk
Exmoor Ale, Beast, Stag; 3 changing beers (sourced nationally) Ⓗ
A hidden gem in a valley on the edge of Exmoor, this large country inn is particularly popular with walkers. There are two bars in which to enjoy almost the entire range of Exmoor beers, together with the Heddon Ales brewed especially for the pub. Both light bites and an extensive à la carte menu are available, while regularly held theme nights also offer excellent value. A large beer and music festival is held in September.
Q🕑🐕🏠◖Ⓓ♿🅰️♣🛏️🐾🛜

High Bickington

Golden Lion Ⓛ
North Road, EX37 9BB (on B3217) SS600205
🕑 12 (4.30 Mon & Tue)-11; 12-10.30 Sun ☎ (01769) 561006
Forge Litehouse; 1 changing beer (sourced nationally) Ⓗ
On the main road through the village and dating from the 19th century, this traditional Devon village pub is a genuine hub of the community. The single bar has an adjacent skittle alley which converts into a pleasant dining area. Good-value home-cooked food is served throughout most of the opening hours. Two competitively priced local real ales are usually on the bar, together with a good choice of real ciders. Well-behaved children and dogs are welcome.
Q🕑🐕◖Ⓓ♿♣🛏️P🚌(325)🐾🛜

Honiton

Holt Ⓛ
178 High Street, EX14 1LA
🕑 11-3, 5.30-11; closed Sun & Mon ☎ (01404) 47707 ⊕ theholt-honiton.com
Otter Bitter, Amber, Bright, Ale, Head; 1 changing beer (sourced locally) Ⓗ
A former wine bar that was converted 11 years ago. It has a cosy bar at street level, with a fine dining restaurant upstairs. The kitchen is in full view of the clientele. A lunch menu of tapas and home-smoked food is served in the bar. Independently owned by two sons of the Otter Brewery family, the Holt has won Gastro-Pub of the Year, and is a past winner of Taste of the West. Seasonal music festivals are held.
Q🕑◖Ⓓ♿🚲♣🛏️🐾

Iddesleigh

Duke of York
EX19 8BG (off B3217 next to church) SS570083

✪ 11-11; 12-10.30 Sun ☎ (01837) 810253
⊕ dukeofyorkdevon.co.uk
Adnams Broadside; Bays Topsail; 1 changing beer (sourced nationally) Ⓖ
This traditional village inn was where local resident Michael Morpurgo was inspired to write his famous War Horse story. Close to the Tarka Trail, it is popular with cyclists and has seven en-suite rooms. The pub itself is a thatched 15th-century cob building with a welcoming open fire in the bar. A beer festival is held on the August bank holiday. A free courtesy bus service is available to pick up groups wishing to dine here.
Q ⅀ ☀ 🚞 ◖ ⅄ 🖙 ♣ ♠ 🖳 ❀ 🕾

Ide

Poachers Inn Ⓛ
55 High Street, EX2 9RW (3 miles from M5 jct 31, via A30)
✪ 12-midnight (1am Fri & Sat) ☎ (01392) 273847
⊕ poachersinn.co.uk
Branscombe Vale Branoc; Exeter Lighterman; 5 changing beers (sourced regionally; often Exeter, Palmers, Sharp's) Ⓗ
A busy, friendly local at the top of the village street. The Poachers has a history of serving beer since the 18th century. Five ales are usually on tap, and a varied, locally sourced menu is offered all day, plus excellent-value fish and chips on Wednesday evening. The bar is comfortably furnished with old sofas and chairs, heated by a log fire, and decorated with an interesting collection of hats and ties. There is a lovely garden with countryside views. Q ⅀ ☀ 🚞 ◖ ⅄ P 🖳 (360) ❀ 🕾

Ilfracombe

Admiral Collingwood ✅
Wilder Road, EX34 9AP
✪ 8am-midnight (1am Fri & Sat); 8-11 Sun
☎ (01271) 862373
Greene King Abbot; Ruddles Best Bitter; Sharp's Doom Bar; 3 changing beers (sourced nationally) Ⓗ
Built on the site of the old Collingwood Hotel, this purpose-built Wetherspoon was awarded best new-build at the National Pub Design Awards in 2015. On Ilfracombe's seafront, it has stunning views from the roof terrace, which is open March to October. Since opening its doors it has earned a well-deserved reputation for its range of well-kept ales, many of which are from local breweries.
⅀ ☀ ◖ ⅃ ♠ P 🖳 (21A) 🕾

Kilmington

New Inn Ⓛ ✅
The Hill, EX13 7SF (in village, S of A35)
✪ 12-3 (not Mon), 6-11; 12-8 Sun ☎ (01297) 33376
⊕ newinnkilmington.com
Palmers Copper Ale, Best Bitter, 200 Ⓗ
Thatched Devon longhouse that became a pub in the early 1800s. It was rebuilt after a major fire in 2004, retaining a welcoming atmosphere and gaining excellent toilets with disabled access. There is a large, safe garden, and a well-used skittle alley. A quiz night is held monthly on the first Sunday, with other events that maintain the pub's position as an important part of village life. A meat draw is held on Friday. Q ☀ ◖ ⅃ ♣ ♠ P 🖳 ❀ 🕾

Old Inn Ⓛ ✅
EX13 7RB
✪ 8am-11 ☎ (01297) 32096 ⊕ oldinnkilmington.co.uk
Branscombe Vale Branoc; Otter Bitter; 2 changing beers Ⓗ
Thatched 16th-century inn on the A35. The Cricketers' bar, a lounge with a log fire, and a restaurant area are complemented by a suntrap patio and a raised lawn. Food, served lunchtimes and evenings (except Sun eve), is sourced locally, including good mussels, and the many specials are changed daily. Beer festivals are held at the end of May, in August, on bonfire night in November, and there are regular themed nights. The pub opens at 8am for breakfast (alcohol is served from 11am).
Q ⅀ ☀ ◖ ⅄ ♣ P 🖳 (4) ❀ 🕾

Kings Nympton

Grove Inn Ⓛ
EX37 9ST (in centre of village) SS683194
✪ closed Mon; 12-3, 6-11; 12-4, 7-10 Sun ☎ (01769) 580406
⊕ thegroveinn.co.uk
Exmoor Ale Ⓖ**; 3 changing beers (sourced nationally)** Ⓗ
Attractive to locals and visitors alike, this 17th-century thatched village inn has flagstone floors and log fires, together with a pretty enclosed terrace to enjoy in summer. Four real ales are normally on tap, alongside a good range of local ciders. Award-winning food is served in the dining area, which is adjacent to the bar. Local CAMRA Pub of the Year 2016 and Cider Pub of the Year 2017.
Q ⅀ ☀ 🚞 ◖ ♣ ♠ P ❀ 🕾

Kingswear

Ship Inn Ⓛ ✅
Higher Street, TQ6 0AG
✪ 12-3, 6-midnight; 12-midnight Sat & Sun
☎ (01803) 752348 ⊕ theshipinnkingswear.com
Adnams Southwold Bitter; Exmoor Ale; Otter Ale; 3 changing beers (sourced regionally) Ⓗ
A family-run pub which has been in the Guide for 12 years, it has a horseshoe-shaped bar with a nautical theme. It serves six ales in summer and four in winter, while the kitchen has a well-deserved reputation for fish and seafood. The building is 15th century and overlooks Dartmouth and the Dart estuary with lovely views from the patio, and there are open fires in winter. Dartmouth food and sailing festivals are celebrated by the pub holding beer festivals.
Q ⅀ ☀ ◖ ⅃ ⇌ ♣ 🖳 ❀ 🕾

Lapford

Old Malt Scoop Inn Ⓛ
EX17 6PZ
✪ 12-midnight (2am Fri & Sat); 12-11.30 Sun
☎ (01363) 83330 ⊕ oldmaltscoopinn.com
St Austell Tribute; house beer (by Beer Engine); 2 changing beers (often Dartmoor, Exeter, Hanlons) Ⓗ
In the village centre, this is an old coaching inn dating back to the 16th century. Previously a run-down tied house, it is now an excellent free house with four handpumps at the bar, three usually serving LocAle beers. The pub offers good-quality home-cooked food lunchtimes and evenings, including a traditional Sunday roast. Occasional live music events take place. Families and dogs are welcome. ⅀ ☀ ◖ ⅃ ⇌ P 🖳 (5C) ❀ 🕾

Lewdown

Blue Lion Inn 🄻

EX20 4DL

🕙 5 (6 Tue & Thu)-11; 12-midnight Sat; 12-3.30 Sun

☎ (01566) 783238

Dartmoor Jail Ale; Otter Amber; Sharp's Doom Bar; 1 changing beer (sourced nationally) 🄷

This family-owned and run pub has grown around a 17th-century farmhouse and is an interesting building with beautiful views of the surrounding countryside. Extended and developed in the early-20th century as part of the Lewtrenchard Estate, it is home to numerous local groups and supports several pub teams. Predominantly wet sales-oriented, it is also dog-friendly. An annual beer and music festival is held in late-July/early-August.
🐕⊛🖾⊅🕭♣♠P🖃🌣🛜

Littlehempston

Tally Ho 🄻

TQ9 6LY SX813627

🕙 closed Mon; 11-3, 5.30-11; 12-10.30 Sun

☎ (01803) 862316 🌐 tallyhoinn.co.uk

Dartmoor Legend; 2 changing beers (sourced locally) 🄷

A charming 14th-century stone-built pub saved by the local community from closure in 2014. The timber-beamed single-roomed bar furnished with pews and wooden settles has a cosy feel enhanced by two woodburners. The pub hosts numerous events including an annual beer festival, occasional local live music and a regular Sunday night quiz. Guest beers are from local breweries including Hunters and New Lion. The enclosed beer garden is to the rear. CAMRA branch Pub of the Year runner-up 2017. Q🐕⊛🕭 AP🖃(X64,177)🌣🛜

Lydford

Castle Inn ⊘

School Road, EX20 4BH

🕙 11-11; 11-10.30 Sun ☎ (01822) 820241

🌐 castleinnlydford.com

St Austell Trelawny, Tribute, Proper Job; 2 changing beers (sourced locally) 🄷

Comfortable and welcoming 16th-century pub, open from 8am for breakfast. The 12th-century Lydford Castle is adjacent, and St Petroc's Church and Lydford Gorge (National Trust) are close by. The pub is on the NCN27 Devon Coast-Coast, Dartmoor Way and West Devon Way cycle/walking routes. Up to three St Austell ales are served, complemented by two guest beers, usually from Devon. A quiz night is held every Wednesday in aid of the local school. 🕭P🖃(46)🛜

Lympstone

Redwing Bar & Dining

Church Road, EX8 5JT

🕙 11.30-3, 5.30-11; 11.30-11 Fri-Sun ☎ (01395) 222156

🌐 redwingbar-dining.co.uk

Bath Ales Gem; Branscombe Vale Branoc; St Austell Proper Job 🄷 🄶

Formerly the Redwing, this delightful pub is set in a charming riverside village. The tastefully decorated accommodation comprises a long bar with some soft furnishings, a conservatory and an upstairs function room. Outside is a large garden at the back and parking at the side. Excellent fresh food is served lunchtimes and evenings, with a separate lunch menu Monday to Friday. Dogs are welcome in the bar. Q🐕⊛🕭🕹⊅P🌣🛜

Lynmouth

Blue Ball Inn 🄻

Countisbury Hill, Countisbury, EX35 6NE (on A39, 1 mile east of Lynmouth) SS747496

🕙 11-11 ☎ (01598) 741263 🌐 blueballinn.com

St Austell Tribute; Exmoor Gold; 2 changing beers (sourced nationally) 🄷

Dog friendly and ever popular with walkers and hikers, this privately owned and run 13th-century inn lies on the old coaching route from Porlock to Lynmouth. The unspoilt interior has low ceilings, blackened beams and stone fireplaces. Four real ales are usually available, including a good house beer and at least one guest. Food is served all day from an extensive menu, either in the bar or the large dining area. Q🐕⊛🖾⊅🕭 A♣P🖃(300)🌣🛜

Lynton

Sandrock Hotel 🄻

Longmead, EX35 6DH

🕙 11-11 (midnight Fri & Sat); 12-11 Sun ☎ (01598) 752000

🌐 sandrockhotel.co.uk

Draught Bass; Exmoor Stag; 2 changing beers (sourced nationally) 🄷

Edwardian hotel and pub nestled between the wildly rugged Valley of the Rocks and the picturesque village of Lynton. Many of the original features have been retained and the large wood-burning stove adds to the cosy and welcoming atmosphere in the bar. There is also a pleasant beer garden to enjoy in summer and three recently refurbished rooms for accommodation. Four real ales are usually available and good-quality, reasonably priced food is served.
Q🐕⊛🖾🕭🕹⊅♣🐾P🖃🌣🛜

Manaton

Kestor Inn 🄻

TQ13 9UF (on main road through village)

🕙 11-11 ☎ (01647) 221626 🌐 kestorinn.com

Dartmoor Legend 🄷; Otter Bitter 🄷/🄶; 1 changing beer (sourced locally) 🄷

Spacious local village inn, within the Dartmoor National Park, with a warm welcome and friendly atmosphere. The pub has a large open-plan L-shaped bar with plenty of seating. In addition it has a long, separate dining room, which can also be used for functions. There is a selection of local real ales on offer. The lobby area of the pub has become a small shop selling basic items, and a book exchange scheme is in operation. Sam's Medium Cider is sold.
Q🐕⊛🕭🕹⊅♣🐾P🖃(271,671)🌣🛜

Mary Tavy

Mary Tavy Inn 🄻

Lane Head, PL19 9PN

🕙 12-2.30, 6-11 (5-midnight Fri); 12-11 Sat & Sun

☎ (01822) 810326 🌐 themarytavyinn.com

Dartmoor IPA, Jail Ale; St Austell Proper Job; 2 changing beers (sourced nationally; often Exeter, Moorstone) 🄷

A traditional roadside inn where families, visitors and locals are welcome. The popular bar area

accommodates pool, darts, TV and a large fire, with up to four real ales on offer. This is complemented by a spacious restaurant and garden with views to Dartmoor. Music nights, charity events, a Sunday carvery and a bank holiday beer festival feature among the pub's attractions. Modern B&B accommodation is available in an adjacent building. The pub closes on Monday and weekend afternoons in winter.
Q�✿✍◑♣●P🚪(46)🐾🛜

Meavy

Royal Oak Inn 🅛
PL20 6PJ (on village green)
🕙 11-11; 11-10.30 Sun ☎ (01822) 852944
⊕ royaloakinn.org.uk
Dartmoor IPA, Jail Ale; house beer (by Dartmoor); 1 changing beer (sourced regionally) 🅗
An iconic English village inn, dating from the 16th century, next to the church and overlooking the green, where the eponymous tree stands. The lounge has a restaurant serving home-cooked food, complemented by an eclectic wine list. Up to four local ales figure prominently. The public bar provides a return to its history and agricultural roots, with a flagstone floor, large open fire and photos of times past. It has a good cider range. Local CAMRA Country Pub of the Year runner-up 2016. Q☎✿◑🛆●🚪(56)🐾🛜

Newton Abbot

Teign Cellars 🅛
67 East Street, TQ12 2JR
🕙 10.30-11 (midnight Fri & Sat); 11-11 Sun
☎ (01626) 332991
4 changing beers (sourced nationally) 🅗/🅖
Once an annexe to the workhouse, this is now a rejuvenated pub presenting an excellent range of real ales and local ciders. There is one central bar, a lower drinking area with 170 bottled beers for sale and, to the front, a dining area. Four handpumped beers, often unusual for the area, and one competitively priced local ale, are sold. Food is excellent, but you will need to book, especially at weekends when diners are likely to dominate.
Q✿◑≉●🚪🐾🛜

Newton Poppleford

Cannon Inn ✅
High Street, EX10 0DW
🕙 11-2.30, 5.30-11 (midnight Thu & Fri); 11-midnight Sat; 12-11 Sun ☎ (01395) 568266 ⊕ pubindevon.com
Exmoor Gold; 2 changing beers (sourced nationally) 🅖
Cheery, welcoming, two-bar pub with tables for dining in the lounge bar, and a restaurant area. Real ales are served by gravity from stillage behind the bar. This is a friendly locals' pub with busy passing trade. Good-value home-cooked food, served lunchtimes and evenings, covers most traditional pub favourites and, locals say, is of a very tasty standard. Well-behaved dogs are allowed. There are two large gardens, and a skittle alley. The only pub in the village, and a community hub. Q☎map✿◑🛆♣●P🚪(52,157)🐾🛜

Newton St Cyres

Beer Engine 🅛
EX5 5AX (beside railway station N of A377)
🕙 11-11; 12-10.30 Sun ☎ (01392) 851282
⊕ thebeerengine.co.uk
Beer Engine Rail Ale, Silver Bullet, Piston Bitter, Sleeper Heavy 🅗
Victorian pub, built in 1850, on the Exeter to Barnstaple Tarka Line, half-a-mile north of the A377. Popular with drinkers and diners alike, it is well frequented by locals, visitors and its own cricket team. Home-cooked food is served lunchtimes and evenings using locally sourced produce. The pub brews its own ales including four regulars and a seasonal ale which, like the village pictures and old pub signs, reflect a railway theme. Q☎✿◑🛆●P🚪🐾

North Tawton

Railway Inn 🅛
Whiddon Down Road, EX20 2BE (1 mile S of town, just off A3124 and next to old North Tawton railway station, closed 1971) SS666000
🕙 12-3, 6-11; 12-3, 7-10.30 Sun ☎ (01837) 82789
⊕ therailwaynorthtawton.co.uk
Teignworthy Reel Ale; 1 changing beer (sourced nationally) 🅗
Family-run local where there is always a warm welcome and good value to be found. The Railway has now deservedly achieved 20 consecutive appearances in the Guide. Reel Ale from Teignworthy is normally joined by a guest ale from one of the other West Country breweries, together with a real cider in summer. The dining room is popular in the evening (no food Thu), with light meals served at lunchtime. No dogs allowed except guide dogs. Q☎✿◑♣●P🚪🛜

Okehampton

Plymouth Inn 🅛
26 West Street, EX20 1HH (W end of town near West Okement Bridge)
🕙 11-11 (midnight Fri & Sat) ☎ (01837) 53633
⊕ plymouthinn.co.uk
Black Tor Pride of Dartmoor; 2 changing beers (sourced nationally) 🅗
Former coaching inn dating back to the 17th century, a friendly place that brings the welcome and atmosphere of a village pub to an old market town. The ales are usually from West Country brewers, at least one local cider is kept, and reasonably priced locally sourced food is served. Two popular beer festivals take place each May and October. ☎✿◑♣●P🐾🛜

Ottery St Mary

London Inn
4 Gold Street, EX11 1DG
🕙 12 (4 Mon)-11; 12-midnight Fri & Sat; 12-10 Sun
☎ (01404) 812045 ⊕ londoninn.net
Sharp's Doom Bar; 5 changing beers (sourced regionally) 🅗
A 17th-century coaching inn, which is close to the historic 14th-century parish church. Good-value home-cooked food, using local ingredients where possible, is served lunchtimes and evenings, plus traditional roast on Sunday. It is a typical locals' pub, offering one regional real ale, and up to five

guests. Four B&B rooms are available. Dogs are allowed in the bottom bar.
Q❀☺☕🍴🅍♿♣🅿🚍(4)🐾🛜

Volunteer Inn
Broad Street, EX11 1BZ
🕐 12-midnight; 12-11 Sun ☎ (01404) 814060
🌐 volunteerinnottery.co.uk
Otter Bitter, Ale; 2 changing beers (sourced regionally) 🅖
The pub has been part of Ottery St Mary's history since 1810, when it opened as a dwelling, hostelry and recruitment centre for the Napoleonic War. In the centre of the town, it is popular with a broad clientele. The front bar has been kept traditional and the rear bar is more modern. All real ales, mainly from local breweries, are delivered by gravity. Food is served seven days a week, including traditional Sunday roast, in the recently refurbished restaurant. ☕🍴🅍♿♣🍺🚍(4)🐾🛜

Paignton

Henry's Bar 🗺 ✅
53 Torbay Road, TQ4 6AJ
🕐 11-11 (midnight Fri & Sat) ☎ (01803) 551190
🌐 henrysbarpaignton.co.uk
Dartmoor IPA; Sharp's Doom Bar; 2 changing beers (sourced nationally; often Exmoor) 🅗
Traditional-style town pub on the main street, minutes from the bus and railway stations and only moments from the beach. This welcoming, warm venue boasts excellent beers that are reasonably priced. On handpump there are three regular beers, one guest beer and Sam's traditional cider, plus various polyboxes and bottles. Wholesome fairly priced home-cooked food is served throughout the day until 9pm; there is a highly rated roast on Sundays. Families are welcome until 10pm, there is free Wi-Fi, and it is dog-friendly.
☕🍴🅍🚍🐾🛜

Peter Tavy

Peter Tavy Inn
Lane Head, PL19 9NN
🕐 12-11; 12-10.30 Sun summer; 12-3, 6-11; 12-3, 6.30-10.30 Sun winter ☎ (01822) 810348 🌐 petertavyinn.com
Dartmoor Jail Ale; Tavy Ales Ideal Pale Ale; 3 changing beers (sourced regionally; often Branscombe Vale, Dartmoor, Moorstone) 🅗
In a quiet village on the edge of Dartmoor, a varying range of up to five local beers can be found in the pub's small central bar. Traditionally attired throughout, there are also two larger rooms, one for families. A patio and hidden garden are added attractions. The pub is renowned for its food, but drinkers are made welcome. The inn is on the No.27 cycle route, near a caravan and camping site. Open all day in summer.
Q❀☺🅍🍴♣🅿(46,95)🐾🛜

Plymouth

Artillery Arms 🗺
6 Pound Street, Stonehouse, PL1 3RH (behind Stonehouse Barracks and Millbay Docks)
🕐 12 (4 Mon & Tue)-midnight ☎ (01752) 262515
Draught Bass; 2 changing beers (sourced locally; often Dartmoor, Summerskills) 🅗
Cracking back-street local tucked away in the old quarter of Stonehouse, close to the magnificent

Grade I-listed Royal William Yard, and maintaining the area's military connections. Good, home-cooked food is served (no food Mon & Tue). Two South-West guest beers and Thatchers Heritage cider are normally on sale. An out-of-season beach party takes place on the last weekend of February, and charity monkey racing also features. This pub is a real find and is popular with local hockey teams.
❀🅍🍴🚍(34,34A)🐾🛜

Dolphin Hotel ✅
14 The Barbican, Barbican, PL1 2LS
🕐 10-11 (midnight Thu-Sat); 11-11 Sun ☎ (01752) 660876
Dartmoor Jail Ale; Draught Bass; Otter Ale; St Austell Tribute; Sharp's Doom Bar; Skinner's Betty Stogs; 2 changing beers (sourced regionally; often St Austell, Sharp's) 🅖
A Plymouth institution, this unpretentious hostelry is steeped in history. The character of this establishment is charming, with tiled floors, well-used wooden benches and a traditional open fire, all creating the perfect ambience. The walls are adorned with paintings by a local artist, the late Beryl Cook, who painted many of the characters she encountered in the Dolphin. Up to eight ales are all dispensed by gravity from the cask. Local CAMRA City Pub of the Year runner-up 2016.
🍺🚍(25)🐾

Fawn Private Members Club 🗺
39 Prospect Street, Greenbank, PL4 8NY
🕐 3 (2 Fri)-11; 12-11 Sat & Sun ☎ (01752) 226385
Bays Topsail; 4 changing beers (sourced regionally; often Cotleigh, St Austell, Teignworthy) 🅗
This mid 19th-century establishment was originally the Fawn Inn/Hotel, prior to converting to a club. CAMRA members are welcome with a valid membership card; regular visitors will be required to join. Four guest ales from the area are generally available, as well as a rotating range of local ciders from Countryman. The club is popular for rugby and other televised sports, and supports multiple darts and euchre teams. Local CAMRA branch Club of the Year 2017. ❄♣🍺🚍🐾

Ferry House Inn
888 Wolesley Road, Saltash Passage, PL5 1LA
🕐 12-midnight ☎ (01752) 361063 🌐 ferryhouseinn.com
Dartmoor Jail Ale; Sharp's Doom Bar, Atlantic; 1 changing beer (sourced regionally) 🅗
A warm welcome awaits you from the landlord and locals at this picturesque riverside pub on the River Tamar. Three regular West Country ales are served, as well as good home-cooked food. A decking area on the edge of the river gives spectacular views of Brunel's iconic 1859 railway bridge, and the bars display photos of his bridge dating from the turn of the 20th century, as well as photos of the pub and the Saltash foot ferry. Accommodation is also available.
☕❀☺🅍♿🚆(St Budeaux Victoria Road)🍺🚍(13)🐾

Fisherman's Arms 🗺
31 Lambhay Street, Barbican, PL1 2NN
🕐 11-midnight (1am Fri & Sat) ☎ (01752) 268243
🌐 fishermansarms.co.uk
Dartmoor Jail Ale; house beer (by Summerskills); 1 changing beer (often Otter) 🅗
Owner Donna, her partner Lee, and his family have returned this former St Austell pub into a traditional free house. The interior is welcoming with several distinctly decorated areas. The dartboard has made

a comeback and a variety of games and puzzles is available. Ale and cider festivals are held twice a year. Traditional pub grub at affordable prices is supplemented by specials; on Sunday only the famous roast is available. ➤◑♣⊕🖶(25)🐾🐕?

Fortescue Hotel ⓛ ⊘
37 Mutley Plain, PL4 6JQ
🕓 11-midnight; 12-11 Sun ☎ (01752) 660673
Bays Devon Dumpling; St Austell Proper Job; Skinner's Betty Stogs; 6 changing beers (sourced nationally; often Cornish Crown, Hunters, South Hams) Ⓗ
The landlord is a real ale enthusiast and the bar has nine handpumps, plus one dedicated to a real cider. The rest serve a constantly changing range of ales, usually from Devon and Cornwall, but they can be from further afield, and up to seven real ciders/perries. There is a long main bar, a cellar bar and a covered beer garden. Traditional roasts are served on Sundays only, washed down with Spingo beer. Local CAMRA City Pub of the Year 2017.
➤🐾◑◁≉♣⊕🖶🐕?

Lord High Admiral
33 Stonehouse Street, PL1 3PE
🕓 11-11; 12-10.30 Sun ☎ (01752) 256881
St Austell Tribute, HSD; 1 changing beer (sourced regionally) Ⓗ
A friendly community pub not far off Union Street in an area undergoing regeneration. It is close to Millbay ferry port, not far from Plymouth Albion's Brickfields rugby ground and across the road from a highly rated restaurant. Diners having a drink before or after their meal mix happily with locals. On entering, customers are offered free tapas. It is advisable to book for Sunday lunch. Large-screen TVs show major sports. A woodburner keeps you warm in winter. ➤🐾◑♣🖶(21,21A)

Lounge
7 Stopford Place, Devonport, PL1 4QT
🕓 11.30-3 (not Mon), 6-11; 11.30-3, 5.30-midnight Fri; 11.30-11 Sat; 12-11 Sun ☎ (01752) 561330
Draught Bass; 2 changing beers (sourced regionally; often Cotleigh, Hunters, Skinner's) Ⓗ
Located in a quiet residential area, this street-corner local is near to Devonport Park, and offers you a warm welcome. The wood-panelled bar is comfortable and relaxing, although may be busy at times with Plymouth Albion RFC's ground nearby. One weaker, one stronger than the regular Bass is the rule for guest beers, with lighter and darker brews also alternating. A secluded garden at the front offers a retreat for smokers. Food is available at lunchtimes. Q➤🐾◑◁≉♣⊕🖶(32,34)🐕

Minerva Inn ⓛ
31 Looe Street, Barbican, PL4 0EA
🕓 11.30-11.30 (midnight Wed; 12.30am Thu & Fri); 12-12.30am Sat; 1-10.30 Sun ☎ (01752) 223047
⊕ minervainn.co.uk
St Austell Trelawny, Tribute; 2 changing beers (sourced nationally) Ⓗ
Plymouth's oldest inn, dating from circa 1540, within easy walking distance of the city centre and the historic Barbican. It has a long and narrow bar, leading through to a cosy seating area at the rear. Two guest beers are available, plus beer festivals in spring and autumn where beer could, and does, come from all over the country. Live music takes place Thursday to Sunday evenings and Sunday lunchtime. The pub benefits from a varied clientele. ➤🐾♣⊕🖶🐕?

Prince Maurice ⓛ ⊘
3 Church Hill, Eggbuckland, PL6 5RJ
🕓 11-3, 6-11; 11-11 Fri & Sat; 12-10.30 Sun
☎ (01752) 771515
Dartmoor Jail Ale; Hanlons Stormstay; St Austell Tribute, Proper Job; Sharp's Doom Bar; Summerskills Best Bitter; 2 changing beers (sourced locally; often Hunters, St Austell, Tavy Ales) Ⓗ
There is very much a village feel to this four-times local CAMRA Pub of the Year, which sits between the church and village green. The seven regular ales are supplemented by a changing guest ale. It is named after the Royalist general, the King's nephew, who had his headquarters nearby during the siege of Plymouth in the Civil War. The two log fires keep you warm in winter, adding to the ambience. Food is not available at weekends.
➤🐾◑♣⊕P🖶(28A)🐕

Stoke Inn ⓛ ⊘
43 Devonport Road, Stoke, PL3 4DL
🕓 12-midnight (1am Fri & Sat) ☎ (01752) 515749
⊕ stokeinnplymouth.co.uk
Skinner's Betty Stogs; 5 changing beers (sourced nationally; often Bays, Summerskills, Wadworth) Ⓗ
Traditional pub in the village suburb of Stoke, close to the city centre and has a large garden. Six beers and at least three ciders are on tap, with the range being chosen from the national pubco list. Good-value food is served (no food Sun, Mon or Tue eves). Live sport is shown on TV, with occasional live music events held in the garden. Two function rooms are available for hire, with parking for motorhomes by prior arrangement.
🐾◑◁≉♣⊕P🖶(32,34)🐕?

Waterloo Inn ⓛ
30 Waterloo Street, Stoke, PL1 5RS
🕓 10-midnight; 11-11 Sun ☎ (01752) 550090
Sharp's Atlantic; 1 changing beer (sourced regionally; often Hunters, St Austell, Summerskills) Ⓗ
Situated in the western part of the city, the inn lies between Stoke Village and Plymouth Albion's Brickfields rugby ground. The building dates back to about 1890. Sharp's Atlantic is usually on offer, supplemented by a changing regional guest ale. There are two main seating areas within the open-plan pub, which has a large conservatory and a covered beer garden. Traditional games are played, with teams for darts, pool and euchre. Full wheelchair access is via the garden – please ring ahead. ➤🐾&≉♣⊕🖶(32,32A)🐕?

Plympton

Union Inn ⓛ
17 Underwood Road, PL7 1SY
🕓 4-11 (11.30 Fri); 2-midnight Sat; 12-11 Sun
☎ (01752) 336756 ⊕ unioninnplympton.com
4 changing beers (sourced regionally; often Exeter, Summerskills, Tintagel) Ⓗ
Family-run community pub with a warm welcome for all who enter the traditional, cosy, early 19th-century venue. The landlord's passion for ale is evident, with up to four varying West Country beers providing a year-round beer festival. There are also five real ciders served on gravity. All meals are freshly prepared using local produce, and booking is advisable. Lunchtime meals are only available on Sunday. Dogs on leads are welcome.
Q➤🐾◑♣⊕P🖶🐕?

Portsmouth Arms

Portsmouth Arms

EX37 9ND (on A377 approx 4 miles S of Umberleigh)
✪ 4-11; 12-11 Fri-Sun ☎ (01769) 561117
⊕ the-portsmouth-arms-hotel.co.uk
Otter Bitter Ⓗ; 1 changing beer (sourced nationally) Ⓖ
Set in the heart of the Taw Valley, this traditional coaching inn is an ideal base for walkers, fishermen and those exploring the local area. There is a comfortable lounge bar with a wood-burning stove, a restaurant serving hearty home-cooked food, a public bar with pool table and an attractive patio garden at the rear with views across the river. The regular Otter Bitter is joined by a rotating guest ale, which is invariably served straight from the cask. Q ➲ ❀ ✪ ⊕ ➤ ♣ P ❀ ☎

Postbridge

Warren House Inn Ⓛ

PL20 6TA (on B3212 between Postbridge and Bennett's Cross)
✪ 11-10 (3 Mon & Tue); 12-10.30 Sun ☎ (01822) 880208
⊕ warrenhouseinn.co.uk
Otter Ale; 3 changing beers (sourced regionally; often Black Tor, Butcombe, Summerskills) Ⓗ
Isolated and exposed at 1,425 feet above sea level, this is one of the highest pubs in England. The interior features exposed beams, wood panelling, rustic benches and tables, and the famous fire. All food menus offer home-cooked dishes using locally sourced ingredients. There is a large family room, and tables outside give breathtaking views over the moors. Countryman cider is available; guest beers, usually from Devon, vary. The pub is open all day in summer. Q ➲ ❀ ⊕ ▲ ♣ P ☎ (98) ❀

Princetown

Plume of Feathers Inn Ⓛ ✔

Plymouth Hill, PL20 6QQ
✪ 10.30-11 (midnight Fri & Sat) ☎ (01822) 890240
⊕ theplumeoffeathersdartmoor.co.uk
Dartmoor Jail Ale; St Austell Tribute; Sharp's Doom Bar; 3 changing beers (sourced regionally; often Bays, Otter, Tavy Ales) Ⓗ
The Plume, in this historic town, is always busy with tourists, walkers and locals. However, with its various distinct areas, there is usually a seat to be found. Dating from 1785, the interior is comfortable, with tasteful decor and rustic charm aided by wooden beams, slate floors and welcoming fires. The beer is always in great condition, supplemented with cider, especially in summer. Other features include the bunkhouse, camping and breakfast opportunities, B&B and a garden with a play area.
Q ➲ ❀ ✪ ⊕ ♿ ▲ ♣ P ☎ (98) ❀

Ringmore

Journey's End Inn Ⓛ

TQ7 4HL
✪ closed Mon; 12-3, 6-11; 12-11 Sat & Sun
☎ (01548) 810205 ⊕ journeysendinn.co.uk
House beer (by Red Rock); 3 changing beers (sourced locally; often Exeter, South Hams, Teignworthy) Ⓖ
The 13th-century inn takes its name from RC Sherriff's famous play, Journey's End, which he started writing while staying here. Up to four

Devon beers on gravity behind the bar are served in summer, and three in winter. Real cider is available in summer. The dining room is now the games room. The car park is 200 yards away opposite All Hallows church. Beer festivals are held in March and September. ➲ ❀ ✪ ⊕ ♣ ♥ P ☎ (875) ❀

Roborough

New Inn Ⓛ

West Road, EX19 8SY (100yds W of parish church) SS575170
✪ 12-3 (not Mon & Tue), 5-11; 12-11 Fri-Sun
☎ (01805) 603247 ⊕ thenewinnroborough.co.uk
Black Tor Pride of Dartmoor; 2 changing beers (sourced nationally) Ⓗ
Thatched village inn dating from the 16th century, where locals and visitors alike are assured of a warm welcome. Three real ales are usually on the bar, together with an outstanding range of ciders and perries. The pub also keeps an impressive selection of up to a dozen different gins. The interesting menu is based on locally sourced ingredients and attracts diners from several miles around. Dogs are made particularly welcome. Local CAMRA Cider Pub of the Year in 2015 and 2016.
Q ➲ ❀ ⊕ ♿ ♣ ♥ P ☎ ❀ ☎

St Giles on the Heath

Pint & Post

PL15 9SA (just off main road through village)
✪ 12-3 (not Mon), 6-11; 12-3, 6-midnight Fri & Sat; 12-6 Sun
☎ (01566) 779933
Holsworthy Ales Muck 'n' Straw; 1 changing beer (sourced nationally) Ⓗ
Close to the Devon and Cornwall county border, this was once the village post office before becoming a pub containing the post office, thereby acquiring its name. Today, although the post office has gone, this friendly family-run pub remains at the heart of the community, with skittles and darts teams and a fortnightly local charity quiz night. The regular Muck 'n' Straw from Holsworthy is usually joined by another local guest ale.
Q ➲ ❀ ⊕ ▲ ♣ P ❀ ☎

Salcombe

Victoria Inn ✔

Fore Street, TQ8 8BU
✪ 11-11 ☎ (01548) 842604 ⊕ victoriainn-salcombe.co.uk
St Austell Tribute, Proper Job; house beer (by St Austell); 1 changing beer (sourced regionally) Ⓗ
A long cottage-style building hides a large pub and restaurant which is extremely popular for food and has won many prestigious awards. The bar has a slate floor, an open fire and three to four handpumps. Upstairs there is a large garden, patio and play area for children and an airy addition to the restaurant. The pub is highly family-oriented with toys for children and menus for dogs. Staff members are young, friendly and enthusiastic.
Q ➲ ❀ ✪ ⊕ ♣ ☎ (606) ❀ ☎

Sandford

Lamb Inn

The Square, EX17 4LW
✪ 10.30-11 ☎ (01363) 773676 ⊕ lambinnsandford.co.uk
Otter Ale; 4 changing beers (sourced regionally; often Dartmoor, Powderkeg, Teignworthy) Ⓗ

A traditional 16th-century free house in the village centre with a warm, welcoming atmosphere. It is well supported by locals and visitors alike, offering award-winning food, West Country ales and Sandford Orchards cider. Skittles is played four nights a week in the alley-cum-cinema-cum-conference venue. There are open mic music and comedy evenings. Accommodation is available and children and dogs are welcome. It is frequented by the village football, squash and cricket teams.
Q❧❀✿⌀◑❺♣✿P⊒(369)❀✿

Shaldon

London Inn 🗓

The Green, TQ14 0DN
❂ 11-11.30 ☎ (01626) 872453
Otter Bitter; St Austell Proper Job; 1 changing beer ⊞
Opposite the bowling green and close to the beach in a quaint estuary-side village, this is a well established gastro-pub offering a quiet, relaxed and informal atmosphere popular with locals and visitors alike. Three local ales feature, with a comfortable bar area with stools, seating and a sofa. It is also accessible by foot ferry across the river from Teignmouth. With other pubs in close proximity, the London Inn makes an ideal lunch stop when visiting the area.
Q❧❀◑❺P⊒(22)❀✿

Shaldon Conservative Club 🗓

Dagmar Street, TQ14 0DU
❂ 12-3, 5-11; 12-11 Sat & Sun ☎ (01626) 873667
Teignworthy Reel Ale; 2 changing beers (sourced nationally) ⊞
On a side street in the heart of the village, this friendly club is well patronised by all ages and offers three real ales and a cider. The large, comfortable single-bar room hosts a snooker table, darts, euchre, bingo and a weekly meat draw. Televised rugby and football and regular Saturday night live entertainment are popular, as is the August mini beer festival. Card-carrying CAMRA members are welcome. ❺♣✿⊟⊒(22)✿

Sidmouth

Marine

The Esplanade, EX10 8BB
❂ 11-midnight; 12-midnight Sun ☎ (01395) 513145
⊕ themarinesidmouth.com
Exeter Lighterman; 2 changing beers (sourced regionally; often Exeter, Hanlons, Tanners) ⊞
The only pub on the seafront in Sidmouth, with a small drinking area outside with tables and chairs for customers to enjoy the view of the sea. There is a large room on two levels with one bar. Sports fans are well catered for with several screens around the room. This is a family-run pub, and this is reflected in the friendly atmosphere. The pub attracts an eclectic clientele of all ages.
❧❀◑⌀❀✿

Slapton

Queen's Arms 🗓

TQ7 2PN
❂ 12-3, 5.30-11; 12-3, 6-10.30 Sun ☎ (01548) 580800
⊕ queensarmsslapton.co.uk
Dartmoor Jail Ale; Otter Bright, Ale; 1 changing beer (sourced regionally) ⊞

Splendid 14th-century village pub at the heart of the community boasting a flower-filled garden in the summer months, with patios to the rear and an open fire in the winter. Numerous WWII evacuation photographs adorn the walls, depicting local life and history. An extensive menu is served with daily specials; the chef is known for his home-made pies in winter, and Sunday roasts are popular (booking advisable). A takeaway food service is available. Children and dogs are welcome.
Q❧❀◑◑♣✿P⊒(3)❀✿

South Brent

Oak

Station Road, TQ10 9BE
❂ 4-11 Mon & Tue; 12-2, 4-11 Wed & Thu; 12-2, 4-midnight Fri; 12-midnight Sat; 12-10.30 Sun ☎ (01364) 72133
⊕ oakonline.net
Dartmoor IPA; Teignworthy Gun Dog; 2 changing beers (sourced locally) ⊞
Village-centre pub on the edge of Dartmoor. The wood-panelled, L-shaped bar is surrounded by a large open-plan area on both sides with plenty of seating. An excellent range of real ales is available in a friendly atmosphere. At the rear a restaurant serves good-quality food, and a new function room can be found upstairs, which is available for meetings. There is a no-smoking courtyard outside and good quality accommodation is offered.
Q❧❀✿⌀P⊒(X38,Gold)❀✿

South Molton

Town Arms Hotel 🗓 ✓

124 East Street, EX36 3BU (100yds E of town square)
❂ 11-midnight (1am Fri) ☎ (01769) 572531
Sharp's Doom Bar; Exmoor Ale; 1 changing beer (sourced nationally) ⊞
Main-street local near the centre of this small, historic market town which is ideally situated for exploring Exmoor and North Devon. Popular with locals and particularly busy on market day (Thursday), there is a strong commitment to real ale. Although no cooked food is served, good-value filled rolls are usually available. The single main bar has an open fire and pool table, while there is also a quieter back room and four rooms for accommodation. ❀⌀❺▲♣✿P⊒(X7,155)❀✿

South Zeal

King's Arms 🗓

EX20 2JP (centre of village) SX649936
❂ 12-11 ☎ (01837) 840300 ⊕ thekingsarmssouthzeal.com
Dartmoor IPA, Legend; 1 changing beer (sourced nationally) ⊞
Thatched 14th-century village local that was once a cider house and is now the hub of the village community. The long single bar has two regular Dartmoor beers, together with a changing guest ale from another local brewery and a local cider. Good food is served lunchtimes and evenings every day. Regular live music sessions are held throughout the year and the pub plays a central role during the Dartmoor Folk Festival in August.
Q❧❀◑❺▲♣✿P⊒❀✿

Oxenham Arms 🗓

EX20 2JT (on main road through village at lower end)
❂ 11-11; 11-10.30 Sun ☎ (01837) 840244
⊕ theoxenhamarms.com

4 changing beers (sourced nationally) H
Originally built as a 12th-century monastery, the
Oxenham was later an imposing manor house. It
now has the unspoilt atmosphere of an old country
inn, with low beams, flagstone floors and open
fires. Two guest beers, usually from local
breweries, join the regular Oxy Ale and Merry
Monk house beers. Good food can be enjoyed both
in the bar and the separate AA-starred restaurant.
During January and February the pub closes 3-6pm.
Q❄️✿🍴◑♿👶🅿🚌(178)🐕🛜

Spreyton

Tom Cobley Tavern 🍷 L
EX17 5AL (off A3124 in village) SX6986096761
⏲ 6.30-10.30 Mon; 12-3, 6-11; 12-4, 7-10.30 Sun
☎ (01647) 231314 ⊕ tomcobleytavern.co.uk
Changing beers (sourced locally) H/G
Here you have a choice of up to 14 West Country
real ales, depending on season, plus 18-30 real
ciders and perries. It also offers an extensive food
menu plus a wide range of bar snacks. There is an
eye-catching display of CAMRA certificates from
National Pub of the Year 2006 onwards, covering
local, regional and national awards. A true village
community pub, it hosts darts, quizzes and social
events, run by always-cheery family and staff.
Dogs and children are welcome. There is a
delightful garden and five en-suite guest rooms.
Q❄️✿🍴◑♿🅿🐕🛜

Sticklepath

Devonshire Inn L
EX20 2NW (in centre of village)
⏲ 12-3 (not Tue), 6-11; 11-11 Fri & Sat; 12-3 Sun
☎ (01837) 840626
Dartmoor IPA; Holsworthy Ales Sunshine, Muck 'n'
Straw; 1 changing beer (sourced nationally) G
An atmospheric step back in time. This unspoilt
thatched local, with low ceilings and an open fire,
was originally at the end of a terrace of Elizabethan
cottages in this Dartmoor village. There is a leat
running past the rear wall of the pub which helps
cool the three real ales on stillage, as well as
powering the waterwheel of the Finch Foundry
Museum (NT) next door. Q❄️✿🍴◑♿🅿🚌🐕

Taw River Inn L
EX20 2NW (on main road – old A30 – going through
village) SX642941
⏲ 12-midnight; 12-11 Sun ☎ (01837) 840377
⊕ tawriver.co.uk
Dartmoor Jail Ale; St Austell Tribute; Sharp's Doom
Bar; 1 changing beer (sourced nationally) H
A former 17th-century manor house, this oak-
beamed pub on the edge of Dartmoor is popular
with locals and visitors alike. The real ales are
attractively priced, while the cider is made in the
village. Good-value pub food is served in both the
bar area and adjacent dining room. There is a TV in
the large single bar, where numerous sports and
pub games are played by friendly locals. Well-
behaved children and dogs are welcome.
❄️✿🍴◑♿🅿🚌🐕🛜

Teignmouth

Blue Anchor Inn L
Teign Street, TQ14 8EG
⏲ 12-midnight (11 Mon-Wed) ☎ (01626) 772741

6 changing beers (sourced nationally; often Bays,
Teignworthy) H
Friendly, single-bar Grade II-listed pub on the edge
of the town's shopping centre. Eight handpumps
serve six changing beers and two ciders, with beer
and cider festivals held over Easter and the August
bank holiday. The pool table, dartboard and
jukebox are popular and most major televised
sporting events are shown. Well-kept outside areas
to the side and rear are a floral explosion in spring
and summer and a winter wonderland at
Christmas. Locally made sausage rolls and Scotch
eggs are usually available. Q✿♿🚲🐕🅿🚌(2,22)🐕

Brass Monkey L ✔
Hollands Road, TQ14 8SR
⏲ 11-midnight; 12-11 Sun ☎ (01626) 773961
St Austell Tribute, HSD H
A lovely, small and simple one-bar community pub
for locals and in marked contrast to some of the
other more bustling establishments nearby. It
serves as the unofficial public transport waiting
room for Teignmouth, being near to the bus bays
and only a short distance from the railway station.
It is capable of being either very quiet enabling a
newspaper to be read, or relatively lively at the
weekend while the fun karaoke is in operation.
Q♿🚲🐕🚌(2,22)🐕

Tiverton

Courtenay's
10 Newport Street, EX16 6NH
⏲ closed Mon; 1.30-11; 12.30-midnight Fri & Sat; 1-4
Sun ☎ 07967 125185
4 changing beers (sourced regionally) G
A micropub that opened in 2012 in a former street-
corner pet shop and named after the family who
lived in the nearby Tiverton Castle. The old curved
windows now contain some fine etched glass.
There are four cask ales from South-West regional
breweries, plus six real ciders, set up behind the
compact wooden bar. Local suppliers are preferred.
A small carpeted seating area is off to one side of
the bar. Toilet facilities are limited. Q🐕🅿🚌🛜

Topsham

Bridge Inn ★ L
Bridge Hill, EX3 0QQ
⏲ 12-2, 6-10.30 (11 Fri & Sat); 12-2, 7-10.30 Sun
☎ (01392) 873862 ⊕ cheffers.co.uk/bridge.html
Branscombe Vale Branoc; changing beers G
Historic, cosy, 16th-century inn run by six
generations of the same family since 1897, with a
varying range of ales from local breweries and
further afield. This hostelry is a delight for fans of
real ale, in a traditional setting overlooking the
banks of the River Clyst. The inn was visited by the
Queen in 1998. Nine beers are usually on tap, all
dispensed by gravity straight from the cellar.
Wholesome traditional pub lunches, such as
ploughman's, sandwiches and pasties, are offered.
Q✿◑🚲🅿🚌(57,T)🐕

Exeter Inn L
68 High Street, EX3 0DY
⏲ 11-11 (midnight Fri & Sat); 12-10.30 Sun
☎ (01392) 873131
Sharp's Special; Teignworthy Beachcomber; 1
changing beer (sourced regionally) H

A pub since at least 1860, some of this partially thatched building dates from the 17th century when it was part of a farm. The Exeter is a friendly local serving three real ales and two ciders, plus snacks such as rolls. Three TVs show various sports, while the front area is devoted to pool and darts. There is a small sheltered garden and smoking area at the side. Dogs are welcome, and there is occasional live music. ♿ ❄ ♣ � (57) ☼ 📶

Passage House Inn ✔
Ferry Road, EX3 0JN
🕐 10-11; 10-10.30 Sun ☎ (01392) 873653
🌐 passagehouseinntopsham.co.uk
Dartmoor Jail Ale; Otter Bitter, Amber; St Austell Tribute; 1 changing beer (sourced nationally) Ⓗ
A picturesque building in this historic port with a plaque dated 1788, sitting above the River Exe opposite the ferry point. The cosy interior is divided into three areas with a central fireplace. Good-value food using local produce, with an ever-changing menu, is served all day, every day. Theme nights, such as fish and chips with a pint, are a feature. The garden by the river is a popular suntrap in summer. ♿ ☼ ❄ ♣ ♠ P ☕ (57) ☼ 📶

Torquay

Crown & Sceptre
2 Petitor Road, St Marychurch, TQ1 4QA
🕐 12 (1 Mon & Tue)-4, 6-11; 12-11 Sat; 12-4, 7-11 Sun
☎ (01803) 328290
Butcombe Adam Henson's Rare Breed; Courage Best Bitter, Directors; Dartmoor Jail Ale; Hanlons Yellowhammer; Otter Bitter; 2 changing beers (sourced nationally) Ⓗ
Welcoming two-bar local at the end of the St Marychurch shopping precinct, which has been in the same family for over 40 years, with eight handpumped beers serving mainly West Country beers. Interesting artefacts include a large number of chamber pots suspended from the ceiling, a giant cockerel and a large Whitbread sign. Music is well represented, with jazz on Tuesday, folk on Friday and Appalachian mountain music every other week. Do not ignore the pleasant garden. ♿ ☼ ❄ ♣ P ☕ ☼ 📶

Hole in the Wall Ⓛ
6 Park Lane, TQ1 2AU
🕐 12-midnight ☎ (01803) 200755
🌐 holeinthewalltorquay.co.uk
Butcombe Adam Henson's Rare Breed; Otter Ale; Sharp's Doom Bar; Shepherd Neame Spitfire; 4 changing beers (sourced regionally) Ⓗ
Torquay's oldest pub (circa 1540) and an oasis of solace, very much in contrast to the nearby youth-oriented establishments of the town centre. The approach is up some steps from the harbour/clock tower area and via an attractive flower-covered passageway. It has one large atmospheric L-shaped bar with some separate drinking areas and eight handpumped beers, including four rotating guests. A cobbled floor and low-beamed ceilings create an intimate atmosphere throughout, with a separate restaurant serving high-quality food. ♿ ☼ ❄ ♣ P ☕ ☼ 📶

Totnes

Albert Inn Ⓛ
32 Bridgetown, TQ9 5AD

🕐 12-11 (midnight Fri & Sat) ☎ (01803) 863214
🌐 albertinntotnes.com
Bridgetown Bitter, Albert Ale, Shark Island Stout Ⓗ
Named after the scientist Albert Einstein, this welcoming traditional community pub is on the far side of the Dart Bridge from the town centre in the Bridgetown district. It hosts live music, darts, quiz and culinary nights. Holding three beer festivals, it is also the home of the Bridgetown Brewery. It is noted for an excellent sheltered beer garden to the rear, with views over the River Dart. Q ♿ ☼ ❄ ◑ Å ♣ ♠ P ☕ ☼ 📶

Bay Horse Inn Ⓛ
8 Cistern Street, TQ9 5SP
🕐 12-11.30 ☎ (01803) 862088 🌐 bayhorsetotnes.com
New Lion Mane Event, Totnes Stout, Pandit IPA; 3 changing beers (sourced regionally; often Noss Beer Works, Otter, Teignworthy) Ⓗ
At the top of the main shopping street, this friendly, traditional community pub hosts Easter and August bank holiday beer festivals, and regular live music (jazz, folk and acoustic) and quiz nights. It is a 15th-century Grade II-listed coaching inn with three interconnecting rooms; the front features a woodburner and the rear is like a snug. Outside is a large semi-covered courtyard garden. The pub is the brewery tap for the town's New Lion Brewery. Q ♿ ☼ ❄ ◑ ❄ ♣ ♠ P ☕ (X64,164) ☼ 📶

Royal Seven Stars Hotel Ⓛ
The Plains, TQ9 5DD
🕐 8am-11; 9am-11.30 Fri & Sat ☎ (01803) 862125
🌐 royalsevenstars.co.uk
Dartmoor Jail Ale; Sharp's Doom Bar; 2 changing beers (sourced locally) Ⓗ
A former coaching inn with parts dating back to the 17th century at the bottom of Fore Street and close to the River Dart. Family-owned, it has two bars, one traditional with timber beams and an open fire in winter, the other contemporary with a south-facing alfresco terrace. There are also two function rooms and an à la carte restaurant in the old stables. Live music plays every Friday, and it has 21 en-suite bedrooms. ♿ ☼ ❄ ◑ ♣ ❄ P ☕ ☼ 📶

Totnes Brewing Company
59a High Street, TQ9 5PB (at top of High St by market square)
🕐 5 (12 Fri & Sat)-midnight; 12-11.30 Sun
🌐 thetotnesbrewingco.co.uk
7 changing beers (sourced nationally; often Totnes) Ⓗ
The small quirky bar interconnects with the pub next door, allowing for more space and seating. All the staff members are enthusiastic and knowledgeable about beer. The range, which is constantly changing, generally includes at least one of the ales brewed on the premises along with a selection of guest ales on up to seven handpumps. Takeaway food may be brought in. Q ♿ ☼ ❄ Å ❄ ♠ ☼ 📶

Turnchapel

Clovelly Bay Inn Ⓛ
1 Boringdon Road, PL9 9TB
🕐 6-11; 12-3, 6-11 Fri & Sat; 12-4, 7-10.30 Sun
☎ (01752) 402765 🌐 clovellybayinn.co.uk
5 changing beers (sourced nationally; often Bays, Skinner's) Ⓗ/Ⓖ
This family-run freehouse is nestled in a picturesque village on the South West Coastal Path.

It has an enthusiastic landlord with a passion for real ales and ciders, with up to five available. Guest ales and ciders are usually sourced locally, but can come from further afield. It holds a variety of festivals throughout the year, with an emphasis on local produce. It is also renowned for its wonderful food. ⟡◑👌♣🍴🖨(2,2A)😋

Wembury

Odd Wheel 🅛
Knighton Road, PL9 0JD
✪ 12-3, 5-midnight; 12-midnight Sat & Sun
☎ (01752) 863052 🌐 theoddwheel.co.uk
Dartmoor Jail Ale; St Austell Tribute; Sharp's Doom Bar; 3 changing beers (sourced regionally) Ⓗ
Friendly country pub which was tastefully refurbished several years ago, situated at the northern end of this picturesque village. The three regular beers are supplemented by up to three guests, mainly from Devon and Cornwall. Regular beer festivals are held. It is only a short distance from many walking routes, including the South-West Coast Path. Food is served daily, with ingredients from local suppliers. Outside, there is a terraced garden and play area for children.
⟡🌼◑👌♣🖨(48)😋🛜

Widecombe-in-the-Moor

Rugglestone Inn 🏆 🅛
TQ13 7TF (¼ mile from centre of village)
✪ 11.30-3, 6-11.30 (5-midnight Fri); 11.30-midnight Sat; 12-11 Sun ☎ (01364) 621327 🌐 rugglestoneinn.co.uk
Dartmoor Legend; house beer (by Teignworthy); 2 changing beers (sourced regionally) Ⓖ
The name comes from a local logan stone – the pub is a Grade II-listed unspoilt Dartmoor building converted to an inn in 1832. There is a cosy bar with a woodburner and two further rooms, one with an open fire. Beer is also served through a hatch in the passageway. A wide selection of home-cooked food is available. Across the stream is a large grassed seating area, with the car park just down the road. Local farm Ashridge cider is sold. Q⟡🌼🖨◑♣🖨P😋

Yarde Down

Poltimore Arms 🅛 ✅
EX36 3HA (2 miles E of Brayford on jct with unclassified road from South Molton to Simonsbath) SS725356
✪ 11-11 ☎ (01598) 710381 🌐 poltimorearms.co.uk
Exmoor Ale; Otter Bitter; 1 changing beer (sourced nationally) Ⓖ
Dating from the 13th century, this old coaching inn lies in a remote area of glorious Exmoor countryside. It has no mains electricity and is still powered by generator. The Poltimore is an atmospheric and welcoming locals' pub, which retains many interesting and original features including, it is said, a friendly ghost. The emphasis here is very much on the real ale, with a choice of two and often three available.
Q⟡🌼◑🅰♣P😋🛜

Yelverton

Rock Inn
PL20 6DS
✪ 11-11 (midnight Fri & Sat); 11-10.30 Sun
☎ (01822) 852022 🌐 therockinnyelverton.pub
Dartmoor Jail Ale; St Austell Tribute; Sharp's Doom Bar; 1 changing beer (sourced regionally; often Otter) Ⓗ
A pub since 1888, this popular hostelry is on the edge of Dartmoor. It has three rooms – the lounge caters for tourists and families, the farmers bar for locals, the back bar for those looking for music, darts, pool and sport. The three regular ales are supplemented by a guest ale from a South-West brewery. There is plenty of outside seating and a large car park. Q⟡🌼◑👌♣P🖨😋🛜

Tom Cobley Tavern, Spreyton (Photo: Ian Packham)

DORSET

Bourton
Gillingham
WILTSHIRE
Buckhorn Weston
Motcombe
West/Stour
Shaftesbury
SOMERSET
Trent
Stourton
Caundle
Stalbridge
Sherborne
Manston
Longburton
Bishops
Caundle
Child Okeford
Farnham
Cranborne
HANTS
Thorncombe
Chetnole
Gussage All Saints
Corscombe
Blandford St Mary
Pamphill
Whitchurch
Canonicorum
Cerne Abbas
Spetisbury
Wimborne
West Parley
Sydling St Nicholas
Uploders
Piddlehinton
Christchurch
Bridport
Askerswell
Stratton
Upper Parkstone
Winton
Lyme
Regis
Burton Bradstock
Dorchester
Crossways
Poole
Lower
Parkstone
Southbourne
Bournemouth
Preston
Wool
Wareham
Weymouth
East Chaldon
Corfe Castle
Studland
Wyke Regis
West Lulworth
Swanage
Portland
Worth
Matravers
Langton Matravers

0 Miles 10
0 Kilometres 16

Askerswell

Spyway Inn 🄻
DT2 9EP (on road to Eggardon hill fort)
⏱ 12-3, 6-11 ☎ (01308) 485250 ⊕ spyway-inn.co.uk
Otter Bitter, Ale 🄶
Family-friendly 16th-century smugglers' inn
perched on a hill outside Askerswell. There is a
selection of local ciders as well as the Otter beers
on gravity. The lounge bar has beams and a
woodburner; a further bar has tables for dining. The
menu features dishes made with locally produced
ingredients. The garden is popular with locals,
walkers and dog owners. Q☕❀🄻🄸🄰🅿🤶

Bishops Caundle

White Hart
DT9 5ND
⏱ closed Mon; 12-2.30, 6-11; 12-2.30 Sun ☎ (01963) 23301
⊕ whitehartbishopscaundle.com
**3 changing beers (sourced regionally; often
Butcombe, Cerne Abbas, St Austell)** 🄷
A warm welcome awaits you at this Grade II-listed
17th-century inn. It comprises a cosy bar with
logburner and a restaurant with a rustic feel.
Outside, lovely gardens overlook beautiful
countryside. This popular pub is known for its three
ever-changing local and regional ales and quality
home-made food made with fresh local produce.
There is also a skittle alley and dartboard. In
summer, Sherborne cider is available and the pub
opens on Sunday evenings. ☕❀🄸🄻🄰🅿🤶🤶

Bournemouth

Cricketers ✅
41 Windham Road, BH1 4RN
⏱ 11-11; 12-10.30 Sun ☎ (01202) 551589
**Fuller's London Pride; 2 changing beers (sourced
nationally)** 🄷
Bournemouth's oldest public house, dating from
1847, has two bar areas rich in mahogany and

stained-glass windows. The vaulted upper section
of the main bar was converted from the gym
where world champion boxer Freddie Mills once
trained. This friendly community pub offers two
varying guest beers and Westons cider, and hosts
an annual beer festival in October. There is
occasional live entertainment and lunches are
served at weekends. Away fans are welcome
when AFC Bournemouth are playing.
☕❀🄸❧♣🄻🅿(P2,P3)🤶🤶

Firkin Shed
279 Holdenhurst Road, BH8 8BZ
⏱ 4-11 (9 Mon); 12-midnight Fri & Sat; 12-9 Sun
☎ (01202) 302340
**9 changing beers (sourced nationally; often Cerne
Abbas, Siren, Vibrant Forest)** 🄶
A friendly, family-run micropub. Tables and
benches hug the walls and a shed is used as the
bar, offering changing beers and more than 20
ciders from around the country. Beers are served
straight from the cellar, viewable through the
window in the rear corridor. There is occasional
acoustic music with instruments provided by the
landlord. The pub is a mobile-free zone with fines
payable to charity. ❀❧♣🄻(P2,P3)🤶

Bourton

White Lion
High Street, SP8 5AT (set back from B3081)
⏱ 11.30-11; 12-10.30 Sun ☎ (01747) 840866
⊕ whitelionbourton.co.uk
Otter Amber; 1 changing beer 🄷
A traditional inn dating from 1763. Originally
separate rooms, the cosy bar with stone-flagged
floor has been opened out but there is always a
quiet corner to be found. It has a cosy, intimate
restaurant and a large beer garden. Either
Thatchers Original or Rich's Cider is served on
handpump. The pub has parking opposite as well
as in the car park. Q❀🄸🄻🄰🅿(158)🤶

134

Bridport

Oddfellows Arms L ✓
172 North Allington, DT6 5EB
✪ 11-2.30, 6.30-11 ☎ (01308) 422665
Palmers Copper Ale, Best Bitter Ⓗ
A small, unpretentious local, plain but welcoming, in an old Victorian building to the north of this West Dorset market town centre. This pub concentrates on serving local Palmers beers in top condition – no food is available. A quiz, run by the regulars, takes place every Sunday evening. Outside, there is a big garden and smoking area to the rear. Opening hours can be uncertain – check ahead.
Q✿♣🖵(40,73)❀

Ropemakers Arms L ✓
36 West Street, DT6 3QP
✪ 10-11 (12.30am Fri & Sat); 12-4 Sun ☎ (01308) 421255
⊕ theropemakers.com
Palmers Copper Ale, Best Bitter, Dorset Gold, 200, Tally Ho!; 1 changing beer (often Palmers) Ⓗ
Deceptively large pub situated in the centre of town serving the full Palmers range of beers. The interior is divided into separate themed areas decorated with memorabilia and local history. There is a large partially covered courtyard at the rear and disabled access via the back door. Quality home-cooked food is from local suppliers. Music features on Friday and Saturday evenings. The pub closes around 4pm on Sundays in winter (later on bank holiday weekends or if there is live music).
➸✿🕪🅰♣🖤🖵❀🛜

Tiger Inn ✓
14-16 Barrack Street, DT6 3LY
✪ 12-11 (midnight Fri & Sat) ☎ (01308) 427543
⊕ tigerinnbridport.co.uk
6 changing beers (sourced regionally; often Gyle 59, Hop Back, Sharp's) Ⓗ
A busy and popular Victorian pub tucked away near the town centre. The Tiger offers six changing real ales including occasional beers brewed on-site by the Stripey Cat Craft Brewery. The single bar has two distinct areas, with TV for major sporting events and pub games including darts and cribbage. There are two outdoor seating areas. Look for the rare Groves Brewery etched window and collection of old fishing rods on the ceilings. B&B is offered in seven en-suite rooms.
➸✿🛏♣🖤🖵❀🛜

Buckhorn Weston

Stapleton Arms
Church Hill, SP8 5HS (between A303 and A30)
ST75652462
✪ 11-3, 6-11; 11-11 Sat & Sun ☎ (01963) 370396
⊕ thestapletonarms.com
Sharp's Doom Bar; 3 changing beers (often Plain Ales) Ⓗ
Imposing village pub with a large car park and secluded garden. Two changing beers are usually from Plain Ales and the cider is often Thatchers Cheddar Valley. Excellent food is served as well as classic bar snacks such as hand-made pork pies, Scotch eggs and chutney. Children, dogs and muddy boots are welcome. Four individually designed bedrooms complete the Drink, Eat, Sleep motto. Q➸✿🛏🕪🖤P❀🛜

Burton Bradstock

Anchor Inn ✓
High Street, DT6 4QF
✪ 12-3, 6-11; 12-11 Fri-Sun ☎ (01308) 897228
⊕ anchorinnburtonbradstock.co.uk
4 changing beers (sourced regionally) Ⓗ
One of just a few free houses in this part of Dorset. Inside, the Stables Bar has a traditional pub feel and serves bar food – there is a larger restaurant area offering an extensive menu. Local shellfish and seafood is the speciality. The beers vary but will always be four from Dartmoor Jail Ale, Dorset Jurassic, Exmoor Gold, Sharp's Cornish Coaster/ Doom Bar and St Austell Tribute. Accommodation is offered in two recently refurbished rooms.
Q➸✿🛏🕪🅰♣P🖵(X53)❀

Three Horseshoes L ✓
Mill Street, DT6 4QZ
✪ 12-3, 5-11; 12-11 Sat; 12-10.30 Sun ☎ (01308) 897259
⊕ threehorseshoesburtonbradstock.co.uk
Palmers Copper Ale, Best Bitter, Dorset Gold, 200, Tally Ho!; 1 changing beer (often Palmers) Ⓗ
Three-hundred-year-old thatched pub and restaurant with suntrap seating outside at the front and in the beer garden. It serves good home-cooked food and is popular with families using the beach. The full Palmers range is available plus a Palmers seasonal beer or Dorset Orchards First Press cider. Open all day and serving food throughout April to September, Easter and summer school holidays and bank holidays. Dogs are welcome in the bar area.
➸✿🕪🅰♣🖤P🖵(210,X53)❀🛜

Cerne Abbas

New Inn L ✓
14 Long Street, DT2 7JF
✪ 12-11 ☎ (01300) 341274 ⊕ thenewinncerneabbas.co.uk
Palmers Copper Ale, Best Bitter, Dorset Gold Ⓗ
A stone and flint coaching inn, with friendly, welcoming staff, which has been extensively

REAL ALE BREWERIES
Blackmore Stourton Caundle
Bournemouth Poole
Brew Shack Wimborne Minster
Brewhouse & Kitchen 🍺 Bournemouth (NEW)
Brewhouse & Kitchen 🍺 Dorchester
Brewhouse & Kitchen 🍺 Poole
Brewhouse & Kitchen 🍺 Southbourne
Cerne Abbas Cerne Abbas
Dorset Crossways
Drop The Anchor Christchurch (NEW)
Eight Arch Wimborne
Gyle 59 Thorncombe
Hall & Woodhouse (Badger) Blandford St Mary
Hattie Brown's Swanage
Isle of Purbeck 🍺 Studland
King Alfred Bourton
Lyme Regis Lyme Regis
Palmers Bridport
Piddle Piddlehinton
Sixpenny Cranborne
Small Paul's Gillingham
Southbourne Bournemouth
Stripey Cat 🍺 Bridport (NEW)
Way Outback Bournemouth (NEW)
Wriggle Valley Stalbridge

refurbished to a very high standard over the last few years and has 10 well-equipped luxury rooms named after local rivers. Quality food is served in a separate dining room featuring seasonal local produce. Outside to the rear is a secluded courtyard. Dorset Orchards First Press cider is available in the summer. The pub may close early on quiet evenings. Q ⁂❀⏧◖ⅅⅉ▲◖P⊟(X11)⌖❄

Royal Oak Inn Ⅼ
23 Long Street, DT2 7JG
✪ 12-3, 5-11; 12-11 Fri-Sun ☎ (01300) 341797
⊕ theroyaloakcerne.com
3 changing beers (sourced nationally; often Cerne Abbas, Greene King, St Austell) Ⓗ
A delightful thatched pub in the heart of the village. It was built in 1540 using stone and other building materials from the abbey, which was largely destroyed following the Dissolution of the Monasteries. The interior, comprising three interconnecting rooms, has a cosy feel. One of the beers is usually from Cerne Abbas Brewery. Good wholesome food is served lunchtimes and evenings with daily specials. The pub may open all day during the summer but is closed Tuesdays in winter – check ahead. Q ⁂❀◖◖🍴⊟(X11)⌖❄

Chetnole

Chetnole Inn Ⅼ ⊘
DT9 6NU
✪ 11.30-3, 6-11.30; 11.30-11.30 Sat; 12-4 Sun
☎ 872337 ⊕ thechetnoleinn.co.uk
Yeovil Lynx Wildcat; 3 changing beers (sourced regionally; often Butcombe, Cerne Abbas) Ⓗ
Flagstone floors and a wood-burning stove help this inn blend the modern with the traditional. There are three bar areas and a beautiful garden. One regular beer is served and two or three guest ales – the selection is often led by customer recommendation and changes on a weekly basis. The cider is Burrow Hill. Award-winning food is served 12-2pm and 6.30-9pm. B&B accommodation comprises three large rooms. Q ⁂❀⏧◖≠♣●P⊟(212)⌖❄

Child Okeford

Saxon Inn
Gold Hill, DT11 8HD
✪ 12-3, 6-11 ☎ (01258) 860310 ⊕ saxoninn.co.uk
Butcombe Gold; Otter Bitter; 1 changing beer (sourced regionally; often Palmers) Ⓗ
Local CAMRA Rural Pub of the Year 2015, this 300-year-old inn retains rustic charm. The bar area is cosy with tables and chairs around a log fire. There are two distinct dining areas, and a garden for alfresco refreshment, where a September beer festival is held. A varied menu of quality home-cooked food is available. The pub also offers B&B. Q ⁂❀⏧◖⏧♣●⌖❄

Christchurch

Saxon Bear Ale House
5 The Saxon Centre, Fountain Way, BH23 1QN
✪ 4-10; 12-11 Thu-Sat; 12-10.30 Sun ☎ (01202) 488931
⊕ bearbeerfamily.co.uk/the-saxon-bear
5 changing beers (sourced regionally) Ⓖ
Cousin to Southbourne's Wight Bear, this friendly single-room micropub has perimeter seating and

high tables at which beer handlers will help you select from a variety of well-chosen ales and ciders. The walls are adorned with musical instruments, records, maps and interesting beer information posters. Hops, bottles and the occasional bear hang from the ceiling. Speciality snacks and local gin are also available. The Carlsbog urinal is not to be missed. Q ≠●🖳

Thomas Tripp ⊘
10 Wick Lane, BH23 1HX
✪ 11-11.30 (midnight Fri & Sat); 12-11.30 Sun
☎ (01202) 490498 ⊕ thomastripp.co.uk
Ringwood Razorback, Fortyniner; 2 changing beers (sourced nationally; often Vibrant Forest) Ⓗ
Historic inn named after a legendary local smuggler, recently refurbished by the enthusiastic landlord. Live music plays several nights a week. Bar food is available lunchtimes and all day at weekends, with speciality fish dishes served in the Seafood Shack. There is a barbecue in summertime on the extensive patio. A covered area for smokers is provided. Situated just off the high street, near the Priory, Quay and preserved trolley bus turntable. ⁂❀◖◖♣🖳⌖❄

Corfe Castle

Bankes Arms Hotel ⊘
23 East Street, BH20 5ED
✪ 10.30-11 ☎ (01929) 288188 ⊕ bankesarmshotel.co.uk
4 changing beers (sourced nationally) Ⓗ
Historic 16th-century hotel, owned by the National Trust and run by an enthusiastic landlord. A recent refurbishment has kept the original features including the front drinkers' bar. The restaurant to the rear serves excellent home-cooked food. A large garden overlooks Swanage Steam Railway and Corfe Castle station and enjoys views of the Purbeck Hills. Palmers beers are often available as well as beers recreated by the Dead Brewery Society, brewed by Barnet. Occasional beer festivals are held. ❀⏧◖≠●P⊟(40)⌖❄

Royal British Legion Club
70 East Street, BH20 5EQ (off A351)
✪ 12-2.30, 6-11; 12-11 Sat & Sun ☎ (01929) 480591
Ringwood Razorback; Timothy Taylor Landlord; 1 changing beer (sourced nationally) Ⓗ
Welcoming club in the village centre, formerly a school and built in Purbeck stone. The main bar has upholstered bench seating, TV for major sporting events, and darts and shove-ha'penny. An upstairs room has a pool table and can be hired for meetings. Filled rolls are available all day. The spectacular garden boasts a boules court and views over the Purbeck Hills. Convenient for the castle and steam railway, visitors can show a CAMRA membership card or copy of the Guide for entry. ❀≠♣P⊟(40)❄

Corscombe

Fox Inn Ⅼ
DT2 0NS
✪ closed Mon & Tue; 12-2, 7-11; 12-8.30 Sun
☎ (01935) 892381 ⊕ foxinncorscombe.com
3 changing beers (sourced regionally; often Dorset, Otter, St Austell) Ⓗ
Traditional family-run free house in ramblers' countryside with a thatched roof and an unspoilt interior including a slate bar, flagstone floors and

lovely old inglenook fireplaces. Three changing guest beers are offered along with a real cider from West Milton. Food menus appeal to all ages and offer local seasonal produce, served in the conservatory. The pub hosts many events including regular live music. Q❄️☕🍴◑❿💰♣◑🐾💷📶

Dorchester

Bakers Arms ✿
140 Monmouth Road, DT1 2DH
✿ 6-11 Mon; 12-2.30, 5-11; 12-11 Sat & Sun
☎ (01305) 264382
Ringwood Razorback, Fortyniner; 2 changing beers (sourced nationally; often Marston's) 🅷
Traditional and friendly local in a residential area within 10 minutes' walk of the town centre with a good mixed clientele of all ages. Look for the original baker's ovens which are still in situ. In addition to the Ringwood beers, there are normally two guest beers from Marston's guest ales list. No food is served Saturday, Sunday and Monday. ☕◑≠(South)P🐾

Blue Raddle 🅻
9 Church Street, DT1 1JN
✿ 11.30-3 (not Mon), 6.30-11; 12-3, 7-10.30 Sun
☎ (01305) 267762 ⊕ blueraddle.co.uk
Otter Bitter; St Austell Tribute; 2 changing beers (sourced locally; often Cerne Abbas, Eight Arch) 🅷
Popular, genuine, town-centre free house with friendly staff and an enthusiastic landlord. The regular beers are complemented by guest ales and local ciders. Good locally sourced food is served lunchtimes Wednesday to Saturday and evenings Thursday to Saturday. The pub takes part in local events and hosts regular folk music sessions. Amusing covers from Private Eye are displayed in the conveniences. No children permitted, but dogs are welcome. ◑≠(West)◑🐾📶

Bull's Head
92 High Street, Fordington, DT1 1LD
✿ 5-10 Mon; 12-2, 5-11 Tue-Thu; 12-11 Fri & Sat; 12-10 Sun
☎ (01305) 257353
St Austell Tribute; 3 changing beers (sourced nationally) 🅷
Recently reopened as a free house, the pub is a spacious local nestled within the heart of Fordington. It sports an ever-varying selection of ales from local, regional and national breweries. Home to local skittles, cribbage and darts teams, it also has a pool table. Events such as live music, a weekly quiz and frequent raffles are hosted. There is a large car park and garden to the rear. ☕☕♣◑🐾📶

Royal Oak ✿
20 High West Street, DT1 1UW
✿ 8am-midnight (1am Fri & Sat); 8am-11 Sun
☎ (01305) 755910
Greene King Abbot; Ruddles Best Bitter; 6 changing beers (sourced nationally; often Butcombe, Dorset, Otter) 🅷
A busy town-centre Wetherspoon pub offering a wide selection of frequently changing local and national ales on handpump, with regular beer festivals adding to the range. The pub offers a full food menu and is open for breakfast daily, welcoming children and families. To the rear is a sunny patio area with disabled access to the main internal area. Q❄️☕◑🕹️≠(West)◑🔲📶

East Chaldon

Sailor's Return 🅻
DT2 8DN
✿ closed Mon; 12-2.30, 6-11; 12-11 Sat; 12-10.30 Sun
☎ (01305) 854441 ⊕ sailorsreturnpub.com
Otter Ale; Palmers Copper Ale; 2 changing beers (sourced locally; often Cerne Abbas, Flack Manor) 🅷
Historic thatched inn situated on the fringe of a small tranquil hamlet, a few miles from the Jurassic Coast. The pub dates from the 1860s and has a number of distinct areas of different shapes and sizes, with flagstone floors throughout – however, the main bar retains the feel of a local village pub. Food is popular and comes mainly from local suppliers with many seasonal variations and a pie night every Wednesday. Up to four local ciders are available. Q❄️☕◑◑🐾💷📶

Farnham

Museum 🅻 ✿
DT11 8DE (off A354)
✿ 12-11 ☎ (01725) 516261 ⊕ museuminn.co.uk
Sixpenny 6d Best Bitter; 2 changing beers (sourced locally) 🅷
Set in tranquil Dorset countryside, this 17th-century, part-thatched country inn has a cosy, intimate feel. Refurbished in 2012, the interior is open plan but divided into four distinct areas. Some original features have been retained including the flagstone floor in the bar area, large inglenook and window seat. The pub is predominantly food-oriented but welcoming to those who just want a drink. Excellent, locally sourced food is served all day from a good varied menu. Q❄️☕🍴◑P🐾📶

Gillingham

Phoenix
High Street, SP8 4AY
✿ 10-11; 11-midnight Sat; 11-11 Sun ☎ (01747) 823277
Sharp's Doom Bar; 1 changing beer (often Brains, Exmoor) 🅷
Originally built in the 15th century as a coaching inn, when it had its own brewery and stables, it was rebuilt and renamed in the 17th century following a fire. It has an open-plan layout with a dining area to one side. There are two public car parks within walking distance and a small car park to the rear. Good-value pub grub includes senior citizen specials and traditional Sunday lunch. ◑≠P🔲(158)🐾📶

Gussage All Saints

Drovers Inn
Bowerswain Hollow, BH21 5ET
✿ closed Mon; 11-11 (9 Sun) ☎ (01258) 840550
⊕ thedroversinn-gussage.co.uk
5 changing beers (sourced regionally) 🅷
Located in a picturesque village in the heart of rural Dorset, this pub was saved from redevelopment and won CAMRA's inaugural Community Pub Saving award in 2016. Cosy and welcoming, it serves between three and five regional ales including the locally brewed house beer Drovers Ale, plus Cranborne Chase cider. Providing camper-van parking with electric hook-ups, and gardens to the front and rear, this is an excellent destination all year round. Opening times are seasonal so check ahead. Q❄️☕◑◑▲◑🐾📶

Langton Matravers

King's Arms ✅
27 High Street, BH19 3HA
☼ 12-11 ☎ (01929) 422979
Ringwood Razorback, Fortyniner; 2 changing beers (sourced nationally) ℍ
Dating back to 1743, this Purbeck-stone built pub, with original flagstone floors, has many quirky little rooms off a central bar area, and a suntrap rear garden. The seaside town of Swanage with its steam railway is close by, as are many fine walks where you can explore the Purbecks and the South-West Coast Path. A dog- and family-friendly pub serving fine pub food and well-chosen ales, it is a magnet both for locals and visitors.
Q🚲🕮🅿◑Å♣●🚃(40)🐾🛜

Longburton

Rose & Crown
DT9 5PD
☼ closed Mon; 12-3, 6-11; 12-4 Sun ☎ (01963) 210202
⊕ roseandcrownlongburton.co.uk
5 changing beers (sourced regionally) ℍ
A lovely old thatched 17th-century former coaching inn which is now the hub of village life. The interior is a fascinating blend of traditional beams, stone flags and open fireplaces, set off by contemporary decor. A free house, it offers one beer from Sharp's and four constantly rotating regional and local beers. Traditional pub food is served in the bar and restaurant. Outside, there is a large beer garden, car park, plus two B&B rooms in a separate building. Real cider is available in summer.
Q🚲🕮🅿◑&♣●🅿🚃(X11)

Lower Parkstone

Bermuda Triangle
10 Parr Street, BH14 0JY
☼ 12-3, 5-11; 12-midnight Fri & Sat; 12-11 Sun
☎ (01202) 748047 ⊕ bermudatrianglepub.com
4 changing beers (sourced nationally; often Dark Star, Goddards, Sharp's) ℍ
This busy pub is decorated to reflect the Bermuda Triangle story. The single-room bar is on three levels. The walls and ceiling display a range of artefacts relating to ships and planes including maps and ship and aircraft fittings. The bar has four handpumps offering an ever-changing range of ales sourced locally and throughout the UK as well as speciality lagers and foreign beers. There is a covered patio area, occasionally used for barbecues and street seating. 🕮≈●🅿🚃(M1,R2)🐾

Poole Ex-Servicemen's (RBL) Club
66 North Road, BH14 0LY
☼ 12-3 (not Mon & Tue), 6-11; 12-11 Fri-Sun
☎ (01202) 744515
4 changing beers (sourced nationally) ℍ
A regular local CAMRA Club of the Year winner and featuring in the top four of the national competition, this friendly social club is affiliated to the Royal British Legion. It stocks four ever-changing, well-chosen ales and two real ciders. The club has a large main room, meeting rooms and beer garden. Numerous dartboards, a pool table, upstairs snooker room and a varied jukebox add to the bustle of this popular venue. Beer festivals are held summer and winter. Visitors are welcome with a CAMRA membership card or copy of this Guide. 🚲🕮◑&≈♣●🅿🛒🚃(M2)🛜

Lyme Regis

Cellar 59 🄻
57/58 Broad Street, DT7 3QF
☼ closed Mon; 12-11 (8.30 Sun) ☎ (01297) 445086
⊕ cellar59.co.uk
4 changing beers (sourced nationally; often Eight Arch, Gyle 59, Vibrant Forest) ℍ
Atmospheric cellar bar and brewery tap for the Gyle 59 brewery, situated 10 miles away. It aims to supply half the ales from its own range, and prefers to offer unfined beers, sourced nationally. Check the website for tasting events and the weekly beer list. There is a bottle shop on site selling beers sourced from around the world. The bar stays open longer when busy and may open on Mondays in the summer. Children are welcome before 7pm.
🚲🕮♣●🛒🚃🐾🛜

Nag's Head 🄻
32 Silver Street, DT7 3HS
☼ 11-midnight ☎ (01297) 442312
⊕ nagsheadlymeregis.co.uk
Otter Bitter, Ale; 2 changing beers (sourced nationally) ℍ
Popular locals' pub away from the seafront serving two Otter beers and two changing guest beers from a variety of breweries across the UK. A woodburner makes it cosy in the winter, and the large patio and garden make it busy in the summer. Live music is hosted most Saturdays, and a big screen shows most major sporting events on Sky and terrestrial TV. 🚲🕮🅿Å♣🚃(X51,X53)🐾

Manston

Plough Inn
Shaftesbury Road, DT10 1HB (on B3091 2 miles NE of Sturmister Newton) ST81351611
☼ 11.30-2.30, 6-11; 12-6 Sun ☎ (01258) 472484
⊕ ploughmanston.co.uk
Fuller's London Pride; Palmers Copper Ale; Sharp's Doom Bar; Timothy Taylor Landlord; 1 changing beer ℍ
This 450-year-old stone-built country inn has a single large bar with oak beams and unique plaster decorations to the ceiling and bar front, thought to be harvest fertility symbols. There is a large conservatory dining area, a covered patio, a large garden complete with pétanque rink and a campsite. Live music features every Saturday night. An annual beer festival is in May.
🚲🕮◑&Å♣🅿🚃(309)🐾

Motcombe

Coppleridge Inn ✅
Elm Hill, SP7 9HW
☼ 10 (12 Sun)-11 ☎ (01747) 851980 ⊕ coppleridge.com
Butcombe Bitter; 2 changing beers ℍ
Family-run country inn and restaurant. The main building is a converted farmhouse set in 15 acres of woodland, meadows and gardens. There is a cosy wood-panelled bar and a number of separate dining areas. Local produce is sourced for the excellent meals and there are occasional themed nights. Two guest beers are offered, often quite unusual to the area. Accommodation is provided in converted stables around a courtyard. Function and conference facilities are available and the pub is licensed for weddings. Q🚲🕮🅿◑&🅿🐾🛜

Pamphill

Vine Inn ★
Vine Hill, BH21 4EE (off B3082)
🕓 11-3, 7-10.30 (11 Thu-Sat); 12-3, 7-10.30 Sun
☎ (01202) 882259
2 changing beers (sourced regionally) Ⓗ/Ⓖ
Former bakery, now owned by the National Trust and run by the same family for 117 years – the current landlady has been here for 30 years. The pub has two small bars plus an upstairs room, outside there is a large suntrap patio and garden. Two changing beers are served from local and regional breweries. At lunchtime there is a choice of ploughman's or toasties. This rural gem is popular with walkers and cyclists, has won many local CAMRA awards and is listed in the National Inventory of Historic Pub Interiors.
Q🌳🕸🍴♣🐾PⓉ🐱

Poole

Brewhouse
68 High Street, BH15 1DA
🕓 11 (11.30 Sun)-11 ☎ (01202) 685288
Milk Street Same Again, Beer; 2 changing beers (sourced nationally; often Dark Star, Milk Street, Oakham) Ⓗ
A long-established feature of Poole High Street, this multi award-winning pub is a reliably good source of interesting ales from Milk Street Brewery and well-chosen nationally sourced ales from microbreweries. Entering from the High Street, you find tables in the window, and past the busy bar area a space for pool and darts. This no-frills traditional community pub offers a warm welcome to locals, visitors and their dogs alike.
🕸🍺♣🐾🚆🐱🛜

Drift 🍷 Ⓛ
9 The Quay, BH15 1HJ
🕓 12-11 (1am Fri & Sat)
4 changing beers (sourced nationally; often Eight Arch, Siren, Vibrant Forest) Ⓗ
A small quayside microbar, formerly part of the adjoining Italian restaurant. Modern styles of cask ale predominate. Live rugby is screened and live music features on some weekends. The upstairs bar has commanding views over the waterfront and serves specialist gins. There is seating outside close to the harbour. Winner of local CAMRA Pub of the Year 2016. 🕸🍺🐾🚆(8)🐱

King Charles Inn Ⓛ ✅
Thames Street, BH15 1JN
🕓 11-11 (midnight Thu-Sat) ☎ (01202) 672518
⊕ kingcharlespoole.co.uk
Timothy Taylor Landlord; Young's Bitter Ⓗ**; 2 changing beers (sourced locally; often Eight Arch)** Ⓗ/Ⓖ
An historic and allegedly haunted 14th-century pub just off Poole Quay retaining many original features. The long main bar area offers comfortable seating, darts and bar billiards, and shows live sport. The unique adjoining medieval King's Banquet Hall is constructed from original oak ship beams and hosts live music every weekend. There is an excellent menu of home-cooked food and a carvery on Sunday. Two regular beers are complemented by two well-chosen guests usually sourced from local breweries. ◖🍺♣🐾🚆(8)🐱🛜

Portland

New Star Inn
115 Fortuneswell, DT5 1LU
🕓 11-midnight ☎ (01305) 822477
2 changing beers (sourced nationally; often Caledonian, Castle Rock, Lees) Ⓗ
Basic single-bar pub serving two ales on handpump, sourced both locally and nationally, with an area at the back for a pool table and dartboard. The pub gets particularly busy with locals at the weekend as it shows all the major sporting events from Sky, BT and ESPN, and features live music on occasion. There is a bus stop directly opposite and a small car park for up to four cars at the rear. Closing time may be later at weekends. ♣P🚆🛜

Royal British Legion
3 High Street, Fortuneswell, DT5 1JQ
🕓 12-3, 7-11; 11.30-3, 6.30-11.15 Fri; 11-11.30 Sat; 12-4, 7.30-11 Sun ☎ (01305) 821207
⊕ royalbritishlegionportland.co.uk
Exmoor Ale; 2 changing beers (sourced nationally; often Cerne Abbas, St Austell, Wadworth) Ⓗ
Popular members' club with a large downstairs bar serving three ales on handpump. There is a pool table, snooker table and skittle alley. All major sporting events on Sky and BT are screened. The upstairs function room is available for hire. Live music features some weekends, plus meat and alcohol raffles on Sunday lunchtime. Show your CAMRA membership card to be signed in as a guest. ♣P🚆🛜

Preston

Spiceship Inn
240 Preston Road, DT3 6BJ
🕓 12-11 ☎ (01305) 834651 ⊕ spiceship.co.uk
Ringwood Razorback; Sharp's Doom Bar; Timothy Taylor Landlord; 1 changing beer (sourced nationally; often Brains, St Austell, Sharp's) Ⓗ
Family-friendly Grade II-listed coaching house with wood panelling, low beams and a central bar separating the restaurant from the bar, where screens show televised sport. The restaurant, which serves good quality food from an à la carte menu, adjoins a covered, elevated patio overlooking a large beer garden. Thursday is curry night and live music plays most Fridays. Wheelchair access is available using the road entrance to the bar and restaurant, and a toilet with access has been installed. Q🌳🕸🛏◖🧼🦽Å♣P🚆(4A,X54)🐱🛜

Shaftesbury

Ship Inn ✅
24 Bleke Street, SP7 8JZ
🕓 1-midnight (1am Fri); 12-1am Sat; 12-midnight Sun ☎ (01747) 853219
Butcombe Bitter; 3 changing beers Ⓗ
Stone-built town pub at the top of the very steep Tout Hill. The single bar serves four different areas – the main bar, a games room with pool, darts, fruit machine and jukebox, a snug with an open fire, and a newly refurbished lounge bar. Outside there is a sunny patio and covered smoking area. No cooked food is available but you can order from local takeaways or bring your own and eat it on the premises. 🕸🐾🚆🐱🛜

Sherborne

Digby Tap ✔

Cooks Lane, DT9 3NS

⏲ 11 (12 Sun)-11 ☎ (01935) 813148 🌐 digbytap.co.uk

4 changing beers (sourced regionally; often Cottage, Hop Back, Plain Ales) 🄷

An institution in West Dorset, hidden away between the railway station and beautiful Abbey church. The owners of 19 years have retained the old character and atmosphere, with four separate drinking areas, pine panelling, flagstone floors, old beams, settles and three fireplaces. Four beers, mostly from the West Country, offer superb value, as does the excellent lunchtime pub food. **Q❀◐♿⇌♣🚌🐾**

Southbourne

Wight Bear Ale House

65 Southbourne Grove, BH6 3QU

⏲ 12 (4 Mon)-11; 12-10.30 Sun ☎ (01202) 433733 🌐 thewightbear.co.uk

6 changing beers (sourced nationally) 🄶

This popular, friendly, high-street micropub opened in a former card shop in 2015. Knowledgeable beer handlers serve you at high benches and tables surrounding the open-plan room, where convivial conversation rules in a mobile-free zone. A blackboard details the six ever-changing ales, of varying styles from across the country, which are dispensed straight from the cask in the windowed cellar, along with five ciders and perries. A wide range of traditional bar snacks is available. **Q🍎🚌🐾**

Spetisbury

Woodpecker 🄻

High Street, DT11 9DJ (on A350)

⏲ closed Mon; 12-3, 6-11; 12-3, 7-10.30 Sun ☎ (01258) 452658 🌐 woodpeckerspetisbury.co.uk

4 changing beers (sourced regionally; often Hop Back, Isle of Purbeck, Palmers) 🄷

An imposing free house in the heart of a picturesque village on the River Stour. This comfortable open-plan pub offers four changing ales and up to seven real ciders and perries. Excellent locally sourced food is served. Traditional games such as bar billiards and shove-ha'penny can be played. The spacious garden hosts an annual cider festival in May and morris dancing on St George's Day. **Q🐴❀◐♿⛺♣🍎P🚌**(X8)**🐾📶**

Stourton Caundle

Trooper

Golden Hill, DT10 2JW (1½ miles E of A357) ST71491495

⏲ closed Mon; 12-2 (2.40 Sat), 7-11; 12-3.30, 7-11 Sun ☎ (01963) 362405 🌐 thetrooperinn.co.uk

3 changing beers 🄷

Stone-built, single-room community pub with a separate function room/skittle alley. There is an attached camping and caravan site and children's play area next to the beer garden. Good food is available lunchtimes and early evenings including a popular Friday fish and chips night. The on-site microbrewery occasionally supplies one of the three ales. There is also a farmhouse cider. An annual beer festival is held in spring. Dogs and walkers are welcome. A former CAMRA regional Pub of the Year. **Q❀◐⛺♣🍎P🐾**

Stratton

Saxon Arms 🏆

20 The Square, DT2 9WG

⏲ 11-2.30, 5.30-11; 11-midnight Fri & Sat; 12-midnight Sun ☎ (01305) 260020 🌐 thesaxon-stratton.co.uk

Butcombe Original; Timothy Taylor Landlord; 2 changing beers (sourced nationally; often Greene King, St Austell) 🄷

A thatched, stone and flint country pub built in 2001 overlooking the village hall and green. This welcoming and homely free house offers four real ales and a changing cider, and serves good locally sourced food (booking recommended). The pub supports the local community and is popular with visitors from further afield. Staff are friendly and knowledgeable. Dogs are welcome, but not in the main restaurant area. Local CAMRA Pub of the Year 2017. **Q🐴❀◐⛺♣🍎P🚌**(212)**🐾📶**

Sydling St Nicholas

Greyhound Inn 🄻

26 High Street, DT2 9PD

⏲ 11-3, 5.30-11.30; 11-11.30 Sat; 12-10 Sun ☎ (01300) 341303 🌐 dorsetgreyhound.co.uk

3 changing beers (sourced nationally; often St Austell, Timothy Taylor) 🄷

Large refurbished pub in a picturesque village with a separate restaurant serving food to a high standard. The flagstoned bar has a woodburner; an adjoining carpeted area with tables has a small open fire. There is one changing cider, usually from Weymouth Cider or Purbeck Cider, and three changing beers from breweries such as St Austell and Timothy Taylor, although local breweries such as Cerne Abbas, Dorset Brewing Company and Piddle Brewery frequently feature. The pub is popular with locals, and dogs are welcome in bar areas. **🐴❀🛏◐♿⛺🍎P🐾📶**

Trent

Rose & Crown

DT9 4SL

⏲ 11-11 daily ☎ (01935) 850776 🌐 theroseandcrowntrent.co.uk

Wadworth IPA, Horizon, 6X; 2 changing beers (sourced nationally; often Wadworth, Westgate) 🄷

Originally built in the 14th century to house the spire workers of the neighbouring St Andrew's Church, the pub retains many period features. The main bar has five handpumps offering three regular and one changing Wadworth beer plus one guest. There are dining areas inside and out, three B&B rooms, and a log fire in winter. Enjoy the views of the countryside from the garden and conservatory. **Q🐴❀🛏◐♿♣P🐾📶**

Uploders

Crown Inn 🄻 ✔

New Road, DT6 4NU

⏲ closed Mon; 11.30-2.30, 6.30-11 (11.30 Fri & Sat); 12-3, 7-10.30 Sun ☎ (01308) 485356 🌐 crownuploders.co.uk

Palmers Copper Ale, Best Bitter, Dorset Gold 🄷

Traditional country pub with flagstone flooring and a large log fire in winter. It is well supported by locals, walkers, cyclists and holidaymakers from the nearby cottage lets and acts as a focal point for village activities such as the scarecrow trail. It is also one of five pubs on the annual walk, cycle or horseback trek held in August. The pub has a separate area that is used for family gatherings such as wedding parties. Q☺⛲☕◖▮P☖(73)☕❀ 🛜

Upper Parkstone

Smuggler's Run ⓛ

184 Ashley Road, BH14 9BY

☯ 12 (5 Mon)-11 ☎ (01202) 385399

8 changing beers (sourced nationally; often Bournemouth, Oakham, Vibrant Forest) ⓗ

Formerly a Chinese restaurant, this award-winning Artisan Ale House offers an interesting range of ales from local and national microbreweries. Bournemouth Brewery beers always feature, alongside numerous well-chosen guests and real ciders. The bustling open-plan main bar offers comfortable seating for conversation and Monday quiz-goers. Occasional live music is hosted. A rear games room doubles as a function room. Customers are welcome to dine on site from the Chinese takeaway next door. ⛲⇌(Branksome)♣●▮❀🛜

Wareham

King's Arms ✅

41 North Street, BH20 4AD

☯ 12-11 (10.30 Sun) ☎ (01929) 552503

⊕ kingsarmswareham.co.uk

5 changing beers (sourced regionally; often Otter, St Austell, Skinner's) ⓗ

Award-winning traditional thatched inn that has its roots in the 1500s and survived the great fire of 1762. This multi-roomed establishment has a flagstone-floored public bar, real fire, a drinking corridor and one room exclusively for dining, with an excellent range of home-cooked food on offer. To the rear is a large garden with a covered area for smokers. The five guest beers are usually from the West Country and there is occasional live music at weekends. Q☺⛲☕◖⇌●P☖(40,X54)❀

West Lulworth

Castle Inn ⓛ ✅

Main Road, BH20 5RN

☯ 12-10 ☎ (01929) 400311

⊕ thecastleinn-lulworthcove.co.uk

5 changing beers (sourced regionally) ⓗ/ⓖ

This enchanting 16th-century thatched inn close to Lulworth Cove has two comfortable bars, one with a low ceiling, both beamed. Up to six mostly local ales and 45 ciders and perries are served alongside an extensive menu of good-value home-made dishes in generous portions. At the rear is a tiered garden with a giant chess set. Board games are available inside. The inn has 15 bedrooms, 14 en-suite, and is dog-friendly. A former CAMRA Cider Pub of the Year. Q☺⛲☕◖◖Å♣●P❀🛜

West Parley

Owls Nest ⓛ

196 Christchuch Road, BH22 8SS

☯ 12-3 (not Mon), 5-11; 11.30-3, 6-midnight Sat; 12-3, 6-10 Sun ☎ (01202) 572793 ⊕ theowlsnest-westparley.com

Otter Bitter; 3 changing beers (sourced regionally; often Eight Arch, Flack Manor, Hop Back) ⓗ

Charming and welcoming, this Tudor-style building with beamed ceilings and a woodburner provides a comfortable ambience. Decorated with numerous adornments, owls feature heavily among miniatures, jugs and plates. Four handpumps dispense well-chosen local and regional ales. A beer and home-made pie festival has become an early-in-the-year favourite. There is occasional live music with an Irish session on the first Thursday of the month. Very popular for its excellent home-made food, booking is recommended for diners. Q☺◖☕👤●P☖❀🛜

West Stour

Ship Inn

on A30, SP8 5RP

☯ 12-3, 6-11; 12-11 Sun ☎ (01747) 838640

⊕ shipinn-dorset.com

3 changing beers ⓗ

Once a coaching inn, this popular roadside pub has views across the Blackmore Vale. The public bar features a flagstone floor, the separate light and airy restaurant area has stripped oak floorboards. There is a patio and large garden at the rear. This friendly pub is renowned for superb home-cooked food (no meals Sun eve) and comfortable accommodation. A choice of six local ciders usually accompanies the three ales. Dogs are welcome in the bar. A beer festival is held in July. Q☺⛲◖◖♣●P❀

Weymouth

Globe Inn

24 East Street, DT4 8BN

☯ 11-1am ☎ (01305) 786061

Dartmoor Jail Ale; St Austell Cornish Best Bitter, Proper Job; Sharp's Doom Bar; 2 changing beers (sourced regionally; often Cerne Abbas, Milk Street, Palmers) ⓗ

Free house with a friendly welcome, tucked away on a street corner, just 30 yards from the iconic harbourside. The Globe is only a short distance from the town centre, the beach and the esplanade, and offers a distinct change from the packed waterside. There is a jukebox and a separate games room with pool table, darts and pub games. A fun quiz is held on Sunday afternoon. Guest ales are not always available in the low season. The cider is Thatchers Cheddar Valley. ⛲♣●❀🛜

Whitchurch Canonicorum

Five Bells Inn ⓛ ✅

DT6 6RH

☯ closed Mon; 12-3 (not Tue & Wed), 6.30-11; 12-3, 7-11 Sun ☎ (01297) 489262 ⊕ thefivebellsinn.co.uk

Palmers Copper Ale, Best Bitter, seasonal beer ⓗ

A hidden gem nestled in the stunning Marshwood Vale. The pub serves traditional food prepared using locally sourced produce and is children- and dog-friendly, with a large beer garden and a seven-acre campsite with shower and toilet block. The winter opening times are listed above, but the pub opens all day every day in the summer. However, times can vary so please call ahead. Q☺⛲◖Å♣P❀🛜

Wimborne

Green Man ✅

1 Victoria Road, BH21 1EN

⚙ 10-11.30 (11 Mon); 10-midnight Fri & Sat
☎ (01202) 881021 ⊕ greenmanwimborne.com
Wadworth IPA, 6X, Swordfish; 1 changing beer (often Wadworth) ⓗ
An 18th-century one-bar inn with open-plan drinking areas, a cosy woodburner and a separate restaurant. Excellent food, including breakfast, is served until 4pm, with a roast on Sunday. The garden has a marvellous floral display in summer, guarded by the green man in his red telephone box. A partially covered patio leads to the barn where pool and pub games are played. Live music features at weekends and the ghost of Nelly and her dog may appear on occasion.
Q✿❀⑩♣●P🖵❀⚡

Taphouse ✔
11 West Borough, BH21 1LT
⚙ 11-11.30 ☎ (01202) 911200
⊕ thetaphousewimborne.com
Sharp's Doom Bar; 6 changing beers (sourced nationally; often Brew Shack, Eight Arch, Sixpenny) ⒼCQ
Close to the town centre, the centrepiece of this narrow wood-panelled pub is the long hardwood bar, with beer displayed on a stillage behind. The pub offers seven well-chosen real ales from local and national microbreweries as well as some popular favourites. Always a bustling community pub full of atmosphere, with cosy window seating, conversation rules, although there is live acoustic music on Sundays. For warmer days there is a suntrap area outside. A former winner of local CAMRA Pub of the Year. Q✿♣●🖵❀

Winton
Micro Moose
326 Wimborne Road, BH9 2HH
⚙ 4 (12 Fri & Sat)-11; 1-6 Sun ☎ (01202) 538542
⊕ micromoose.co.uk
4 changing beers ⓗ/Ⓖ
Established when the Canadian owner decided to convert her coffee shop into a micropub, advertising 'great British ales with Canadian hospitality'. This friendly and cosy bar offers a selection of local and regional ales served either on handpump or gravity. The bottled beer selection is Canadian-themed, as is the decor, complete with fluffy moose head. In common with other micropubs, sharing tables is encouraged. Local cider is available as well as a good selection of bar snacks. Q●🖵❀

Silverback Alehouse
518 Wimborne Road, BH9 2EX
⚙ 12-11 (10 Sun) ☎ 07999 586730
⊕ silverbackalehouse.co.uk
5 changing beers (sourced nationally; often Brew Shack, Cerne Abbas, Eight Arch) Ⓖ
Set among the busy shops of Winton high street, this micropub offers a welcome respite from the weekly shop. Five carefully chosen real ales from both local and regional breweries are served on gravity. Four ciders are also available, sourced from small independent cider makers. Benches and tables surround the perimeter of the pub, with

beer brought to you by the friendly staff. The Silverback has a relaxed and welcoming atmosphere, making it popular with locals and visitors alike. Q✿●🖵❀⚡

Wool
Black Bear Inn ✔
High Street, BH20 6BP
⚙ 10.30-11 (midnight Fri & Sat); 10.30-10.30 Sun
☎ (01929) 405541 ⊕ blackbear.website
House beer (by Flack Manor); 3 changing beers (sourced nationally) ⓗ
This thriving free house was recently awarded local CAMRA Rural Pub of the Year, and is close to the many attractions of the Purbecks. Offering five real ales, mostly regional, the front bar area caters for drinkers and diners, but there is a dedicated restaurant to the rear. The extensive menu offers reasonably priced home-cooked food including vegetarian options. This real community pub regularly hosts curry nights, quizzes, pub walks and a breakfast club. Q✿❀⑩➔P🖵(X54)❀⚡

Worth Matravers
Square & Compass ★ ⓛ
Weston Road, BH19 3LF (off B3069)
⚙ 12-11 ☎ (01929) 439229 ⊕ squareandcompasspub.co.uk
4 changing beers (sourced regionally; often Hattie Brown's) Ⓖ
On CAMRA's National Inventory of Historic Pub Interiors, this multi award-winning gem has appeared in every edition of the Guide and has been in the same family since 1907. Two rooms either side of a serving hatch convey an impression that little has changed. The sea-facing garden offers fantastic views across the Purbecks and fossils are displayed in the small adjacent museum. Pasties are available along with home-made cider. Two of the beers are from Hattie Brown's. Beer and cider festivals are held in October and November respectively. In winter the pub closes in the afternoon. Q✿❀&●🖵(44)❀

Wyke Regis
Wyke Smugglers ✔
76 Portland Road, DT4 9AB
⚙ 11-11; 12-midnight Thu; 12-1am Fri & Sat; 12-midnight Sun
☎ (01305) 760010 ⊕ thewykesmugglers.com
St Austell Proper Job; 2 changing beers (sourced regionally) ⓗ
A large, lively local hosting many community pastimes. Regional guest beers often come from breweries in SIBA's south-west region, and there is an occasional local cider. Good food is served in the main dining area next to the woodburner, and the large skittle alley doubles as a function room, with cyclists benefiting from the bike racks outside. Separate beer and cider festivals are held in July and the autumn, and live music features at weekends. ✿❀⑩&▲♣●P🖵❀⚡

'What is your best – your very best – ale a glass?' 'Twopence-halfpenny,' says the landlord, 'is the price of the Genuine Stunning Ale.' 'Then,' says I, producing the money, 'Just draw me a glass of the Genuine Stunning, if you please, with a good head to it.'
Charles Dickens, David Copperfield

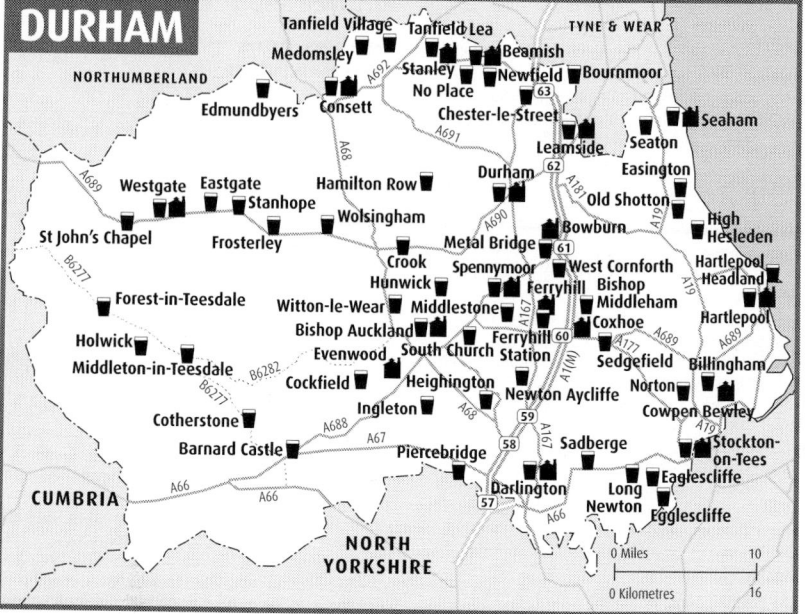

DURHAM

Tanfield Village Tanfield Lea TYNE & WEAR
Medomsley   Beamish
NORTHUMBERLAND   Stanley Newfield Bournmoor
No Place   63
Edmundbyers Consett   Chester-le-Street
Seaham
Leamside Seaton
Westgate Eastgate Hamilton Row Durham 62 Easington
Stanhope   Old Shotton
St John's Chapel Wolsingham Metal Bridge 61 High Hesleden
Frosterley Bowburn
Crook Spennymoor West Cornforth Hartlepool
Hunwick Ferryhill Bishop Headland
Forest-in-Teesdale Witton-le-Wear Middlestone Middleham Hartlepool
Bishop Auckland Ferryhill 60 Coxhoe
Holwick Evenwood South Church Station Sedgefield Billingham
Middleton-in-Teesdale Cockfield Heighington Norton
Cotherstone Ingleton 59 Newton Aycliffe Cowpen Bewley
Barnard Castle Piercebridge 58 Sadberge Stockton-on-Tees
CUMBRIA A66 Darlington 57 Long Newton Eaglescliffe
NORTH YORKSHIRE Egglescliffe

Co Durham incorporates part of the former county of Cleveland

Barnard Castle

Golden Lion
30 Market Place, DL12 8NB
12-11 (midnight Fri & Sat) ☎ (01833) 690295
Marston's 61 Deep, Pedigree; Wychwood Hobgoblin; 1 changing beer ⊞
Tall chequered-front building built partly into the castle ditch, dating back to 1679, making it the town's oldest pub. It has a quirky layout with a central bar serving two rooms, one with an open fire. A friendly and welcoming Marston's pub, it offers good-value food, and real ale and cider at £2.50 a pint to CAMRA members. An annual beer and sausage festival is held. Local CAMRA Town Pub of the Year 2017. ☎☺◑♿♠☐(75,76)♣☎

Old Well Inn ⓛ ✓
21 The Bank, DL12 8PH
12-11 ☎ (01833) 690130 ⊕ theoldwellinn.co.uk
Timothy Taylor Landlord; 5 changing beers ⊞
The boundary of this 17th-century town-centre inn incorporates part of the medieval castle wall. The pub has a cosy front bar and a comfortable lounge, a separate restaurant and an airy conservatory, plus an enclosed beer garden. At least five well-kept beers are available including four guests from local micros. (On Mon & Wed 6-8pm CAMRA members get a buy two, get one free offer). Food is served daily, and there is accommodation in 10 rooms. Five-day beer festivals are held at Easter and in October. Q☎☺◑♿♠☐(75,76)♣☎

Beamish

Stables Bar & Restaurant ⓛ
Beamish Hall Country House Hotel, DH9 0YB
11-11 (midnight Fri & Sat); 11-10.30 Sun
☎ (01207) 288750

Stables Beamish Burn, Beamish Hall Best Bitter, Bell Tower, Bobby Dazzler, Old Miner Tommy, Silver Buckles; 1 changing beer ⊞
Attached to Beamish Hall Country House Hotel, it has its own microbrewery. Stone floors, old beams and crackling log fires in winter help to create a relaxing environment. An extensive menu of locally produced food is served. Outside is a courtyard seating area, a play area, and Beamish Wild high ropes course is just yards away. Beer festivals are hosted in September and January. A popular live music venue. Q☎☺♿◑♿♠P

Billingham

Green Hops Real Ale Bar ⓛ
55 The Green, TS23 1EW (on village green in Old Billingham)
12-10.30 (12.30am Fri & Sat) ☎ (01642) 205025
4 changing beers ⊞
The town's first micropub was opened by two enthusiasts who noticed a gap in the local market. Four interesting beers are available, and four ciders and two perries add to an eclectic mix – some well known, some more uncommon, and some quite strong. Third-pint beer and cider bats are available. Quiz night is Monday and live music features on Wednesday fortnightly. Local CAMRA branch Cider Pub of the Year 2017. ☎☒♣♠☐(36,X9)♣☎

Greenholme Catholic Club ⓛ
37 Wolviston Road, TS23 2RU (on E side of old A19, just S of Roseberry Rd roundabout, next to bus stop)
7-midnight (12.30am Fri); 12.30-1am Sat; 12-midnight Sun
☎ (01642) 901143 ⊕ billinghamcatholicclub.webs.com
3 changing beers ⊞
This Victorian mansion and former school is a friendly members' club, renowned locally for its vibrant R&B/rock scene, and where a genuine welcome awaits CAMRA members. Dedicated and enthusiastic volunteers ensure that the club's

reputation for serving 150 different beers annually continues. Three beers, two ciders and a perry are normally served, with up to eight beers available during regular beer/music festivals, held during bank holiday weekends. Regular quiz and open mic nights also take place. Local CAMRA Club of the Year 2017. ⊕♿♣●P🚲🚃(35,36)☻

Bishop Auckland

Green Tree
Cockton Hill Road, DL14 6EN
✪ 4-midnight (1am Thu); 12-1am Fri & Sat; 12-midnight Sun
☎ (01388) 663249
Greene King IPA; house beer (by Greene King); 1 changing beer 🅗
Large pub at the south end of the shopping street, with a spacious lounge and a bar with a pool table area. Recent refurbishment has added a disabled toilet – the layout has remained unchanged but the interior has a new, bright decor. Paintings, interesting football and music memorabilia adorn the walls. A large garden patio with a covered smoking area is to the rear. Popular for TV sport and a Tuesday quiz. ⊕♿🚃♣🚃☻

Pollards
104 Etherley Lane, DL14 6TU
✪ 12-2, 5.30-11; 12-3, 6-11 Sun ☎ (01388) 603539
⊕ thepollardsinn.co.uk
Jennings Cumberland Ale; Marston's Pedigree; 5 changing beers 🅗
Towards the western edge of town, this comfortable and busy establishment is a great combination of traditional pub and pleasant eatery. Open fires feature in two of the four original areas, including the bar, with a spacious restaurant to the rear, where the famous Sunday carvery can be enjoyed. There is a quiz on Sunday evening, while good conversation and seven well-kept ales top things off. Q🚲⊕🕀♿🚃♣P☻

Bishop Middleham

Cross Keys 🅛
9 High Street, DL17 9AR (1 mile from A177)
✪ 12 (2.30 Mon)-11 ☎ (01740) 651231 ⊕ crosskeysbm.com
3 changing beers 🅗
A busy family-run village inn with a good reputation for food. It has a bar with a real fire, a lounge and a large restaurant at the back. The village has a series of walks through beautiful countryside and to the ruins of Bishop Middleham Castle. Q🚲⊕🕀♣🚃☻

Bournmoor

Dun Cow 🅛
Primrose Hill, DH4 6DY
✪ 12-midnight (11 Sun) ☎ (0191) 385 2631
⊕ theduncowbournmoor.co.uk
3 changing beers 🅗
Welcoming 18th-century pub, reputedly haunted by an oft-seen Grey Lady ghost. A varying range of ales is offered, one of which is always local. Good-value pub food is served in the lounge and bar, which has a welcoming open fire, and an à la carte menu in the Lambton restaurant. There is also a large function room. The pub is family-friendly with extensive gardens and a children's play area. Music festivals in June and September feature local folk and rock bands. 🚲⊕🕀P☻🛜

Chester-le-Street

Butchers Arms
Middle Chare, DH3 3QD (off Front St)
✪ 11-11 (midnight Fri & Sat) ☎ (0191) 388 3605
⊕ butchersarms.org.uk
Jennings Cumberland Ale; Marston's Pedigree; 5 changing beers 🅗
A cosy pub acknowledged for the quality and quantity of its beers, selling seven cask ales from the Marston's range. The pub is also noted for its food, with home-cooking a speciality; Sunday lunches are popular and good value. Teas and coffees are also served. Dogs are welcome and it is convenient for the railway station and all buses through the town. Quiz night is Tuesday. Q🚲⊕🕀🛏♿♣🚃☻

Lambton Worm 🅛 ✔
North Road, DH3 4AJ
✪ 11.30-11 (midnight Fri & Sat); 12-10.30 Sun
☎ (0191) 387 1162 ⊕ thelambton.com
Sonnet 43 Abolition, Seraphim, The Raven, The Aurora, Impressment; 1 changing beer 🅗
A bar at the front and gastro restaurant at the back offering traditional English food. Relaxed surroundings, friendly staff, a spacious bar area and plenty of tucked away seating areas add to the ambience. Experimental and limited edition Sonnet 43 beers are available alongside the core range of five. There is a patio drinking area to the rear, a weekly quiz on Tuesday, buskers' night on Wednesday and live music on Friday. Accommodation is in 14 boutique B&B rooms. 🚲⊕🛏🕀P🚃(21)🛜

Smiths Arms 🍺 🅛
Forge Lane, Castle Dene, DH3 4HE NZ299507
✪ 4-11; 12-midnight Fri & Sat; 12-11 Sun ☎ (0191) 385 7559
12 changing beers 🅗
Somewhat off the beaten track, this traditional pub has a recently extended small cosy bar with an open fire, a room for pool and darts, and a larger lounge also with an open fire. The beers are sourced by the landlord, including up to 12 real ales, with LocAle always featured. Food is available. The pub is reputed to be haunted. Beer

festivals are held in May and December. Voted local CAMRA branch Country Pub of the Year 2017. ➤🍴♣🍺P🚪(71,78)🐾☕

Cockfield

Queen's Head
106 Front Street, DL13 5AA
♣ 5 (11 Sat)-11; 12-11 Sun ☎ (01388) 710981
2 changing beers Ⓗ
This cosy, welcoming and popular pub is close to the bus stop at the north end of the village, and serves two constantly changing beers from the Marston's range. It is open plan but with various seating areas, as well as tables outside at the front. Bar staff will happily ask your opinion of the beers, and chat about which ones have proved popular. A proper community local, close to the historic Cockfield Fell and associated industrial archaeology. Q🐾♣P🚪(6,8)

Consett

Company Row ⒧ ✓
Victoria Road, DH8 5BQ
♣ 8am-midnight ☎ (01207) 585600
Greene King Abbot; Ruddles Best Bitter; 5 changing beers Ⓗ
Modern pub named after the rows of houses built by the Derwent Iron Company for its workers, which were mostly demolished in the mid-1920s. The spacious and well-decorated Wetherspoon establishment is a real asset to Consett town centre. An excellent beer selection and good food make this social pub popular with a clientele of all ages. Alcohol is served from 9am.
➤🐾🍴&♣🍺🚪☕

Grey Horse ⒧ ✓
115 Sherburn Terrace, DH8 6NE
♣ 12-midnight (12.30am Wed-Sat) ☎ (01207) 502585
⊕ thegreyhorse.co.uk
Consett Red Dust, Steel Town Bitter, White Hot; 4 changing beers Ⓗ
Traditional pub dating back to 1848. The interior comprises a lounge and L-shaped bar, with a wood-beamed ceiling. Consett Ale Works Brewery is located at the rear. Beer festivals are held twice a year, live entertainment is hosted on Thursday and a quiz on Wednesday. The coast-to-coast cycle route is close by. There is some bench seating outside at the front of the pub. 🐾&🍺🚪🐾☕

Cotherstone

Red Lion ⒧
Main Street, DL12 9QE
♣ 6-10.30 (closed Tue & Thu); 2-10.30 Sat & Sun
☎ (01833) 650236 ⊕ theredlionhotel.blogspot.com
3 changing beers Ⓗ
An 18th-century Grade II-listed coaching inn, built in stone and set in an idyllic village. Simply furnished, this homely local with two open fires has changed little since the '60s. There is no TV, jukebox or one-armed bandit, just good beer and conversation. Children, dogs and clean boots are welcome. Local CAMRA Community Pub of the Year, the venue is used by various local clubs, and the small garden is a suntrap. The house beer, Rowantree, is brewed by Yorkshire Dales, and guest beers regularly come from Mithril Ales.
➤🐾♣🐾☕

Crook

Horse Shoe ⒧ ✓
4 Church Street, DL15 9BG
♣ 8am-midnight (1am Fri & Sat) ☎ (01388) 744980
Greene King Abbot; Maxim Double Maxim; Ruddles Best Bitter; 6 changing beers Ⓗ
Formerly a pub and butcher's shop, with a nod to its previous use in the metal bar top. This busy and tasteful Wetherspoon refurbishment has four interlinked drinking areas making up the main part of the pub, with a pleasant patio to the side. Local history is reflected in the decor. ➤🐾🍴🍺🚪(1)☕

Darlington

Britannia ⒧ ✓
1 Archer Street, DL3 6LR (next to ring road W of town centre)
♣ 12-11 (9 Sun) ☎ (01325) 463787
Camerons Strongarm; John Smith's Bitter; 3 changing beers Ⓗ
Friendly, popular local CAMRA award-winning inn – a bastion of cask beer since 1859. The comfortable traditional pub retains much of the appearance and layout of the private house it once was. A modestly enlarged bar and small parlour sit either side of a central corridor. Listed for its historic associations, it was the birthplace of teetotal 19th-century publisher JM Dent. Three guest ales are complemented by three regular ales. ➤♣🍺P🐾☕

Darlington Snooker Club ⒧
1 Corporation Road, DL3 6AE (corner of Northgate)
♣ 12-11; 11-1am Sat; 12-11 Sun ☎ (01325) 241388
4 changing beers Ⓗ
A warm welcome is assured at this first-floor, family-run and family-oriented private snooker club which celebrated its centenary in 2015. Four guest beers from micros countrywide are stocked. A cosy, comfortable TV lounge is available for those not playing on one of the 10 top-quality snooker tables. Twice-yearly, the club plays host to a professional celebrity, and two beer festivals are held annually. Frequently voted CAMRA Regional Club of the Year, it welcomes CAMRA members on production of a membership card or a copy of this Guide. ➤🍴➤🍺

Half Moon ⒧
130 Northgate, DL1 1QS
♣ 12 (5 Wed)-11 ☎ (01325) 469965 ⊕ thecraftypint.co.uk
7 changing beers Ⓗ
Across the ring road from the town centre, this relaxed and welcoming local reopened in 2013 as a real ale pub following a long period of closure. Seven guest beers include brews from micros unusual for the area as well as from the on-site Crafty Pint Nano Brewery. You have a choice of two ciders. It has a library for reading in the pub or to borrow. ➤🐾&♣🐾☕

Number Twenty 2 ⒧ ✓
22 Coniscliffe Road, DL3 7RG
♣ 12-11 (9 Mon); closed Sun ☎ (01325) 354590
Village Bull, Old Raby, White Boar; 7 changing beers Ⓗ
Town-centre ale house with a passion for cask beer and a winner of many CAMRA awards. Ales are dispensed from 16 handpumps, including a stout or porter, plus two real ciders and 10 draught European beers. Huge curved windows, stained glass panels and a high ceiling give the interior an

airy, spacious feel. To the rear is the in-house nano distillery and microbrewery producing gin, vodka and fine ale. Sandwiches and snacks are available throughout the day. Home of Village Brewer beers, commissioned from Hambleton by the licensee. Q⑦⏚◖⏛&♿♠🌶

Old Vic 🅛

95a Victoria Road, DL1 5JQ (200yds from Victoria Rd train station entrance)
🕒 11.30 (1 Sun)-11 ☎ 07984 574332
🌐 theoldvicdarlington.co.uk
4 changing beers Ⓗ
This upstairs pub was formerly the Victoria Social Club, situated on the corner of Victoria Road and Backhouse Street, and perfect for a pint on the way to or from the train station. Once you have negotiated the stairs you are welcomed by an enthusiastic landlady. Up to four real ales in a good range of styles are sourced from local breweries, always including one from Mithril – the house beer is Mithril The Quaker. Up to five real ciders are also offered. Quiz night is every Tuesday. CAMRA branch Town Cider Pub winner in 2015, 2016 and 2017. Q➳♣●🖂(14,14A)🌶🌐

Old Yard Tapas Bar

98 Bondgate, DL3 7JY
🕒 11-11; 12-10.30 Sun ☎ (01325) 467385 🌐 tapasbar.co.uk
John Smith's Bitter; 5 changing beers Ⓗ
Interesting mixture of a bar and Mediterranean taverna offering real ales alongside a fascinating blend of international wines and spirits in a friendly setting. Five guest beers from local micros and countrywide are stocked, with an extra two from Thursday onwards. Although this is a thriving restaurant you are more than welcome to pop in for a pint and tapas. The pavement café is popular in good weather. TV is for sport only. Food is served lunchtimes and evenings Sunday to Friday and all day Saturday. Q❀◖⏛&🌐

Quakerhouse 🍷 🅛

2 Mechanics Yard, DL3 7QF (off High Row)
🕒 11-11 (midnight Fri & Sat) ☎ (01325) 245052
🌐 quakerhouse.co.uk
7 changing beers Ⓗ
Fifteen times local CAMRA Town Pub of the Year and North-East Pub of the Year 2015, this gem is in one of the town's historic Yards. The lively bar offers 10 handpulled guest beers from local and regional breweries, usually including one from the in-house brewery, The Mad Scientist. It also sells three ciders. A popular music venue, with live music every Wednesday and other nights too, it caters for all tastes from acoustic to rock. Entry is free to all music events. ❀&♣●🅟🖂🌶🌐

Tanners Hall ✅

63-64 Skinnergate, DL3 7LL
🕒 8am-midnight (1am Sat) ☎ (01325) 369939
Greene King Abbot; Ruddles Best Bitter; 7 changing beers Ⓗ
A popular Wetherspoon town pub named after the local 18th-century leather trade that dominated the town. Its 12 handpumps provide a good selection of real ales including up to nine guests, often from local micros. The spacious interior makes it an ideal venue for holding its own beer festivals and Meet the Brewer nights as well as the chain's national events. Reasonably priced food is served until 11pm with a 20 per cent discount for CAMRA members. Q⑦❀◖●🌐

Durham

Colpitts Hotel

Colpitts Terrace, DH1 4EG
🕒 2 (12 Thu-Sat)-11; 12-10.30 Sun ☎ (0191) 386 9913
Samuel Smith Old Brewery Bitter Ⓗ
Step back in time into this late-Victorian pub which has changed little since it was first built. Like all Samuel Smith pubs, the noise comes from the chatter of conversation rather than from a jukebox or TV. The unusual A-shaped building comprises a cosy snug, a pool room and the main bar area partially divided by a fireplace. A quiz is hosted on Tuesday evening. Q⑦⏚➳♣🖂🌶

Court Inn 🅛

Court Lane, DH1 3AW
🕒 11-11 (midnight Fri & Sat) ☎ (0191) 384 7350
🌐 courtinn.co.uk
Timothy Taylor Landlord; 5 changing beers Ⓗ
A popular pub with decor that reflects the location near the city's Crown Courts. Up to six real ales are on offer here at any one time as well as two real ciders. A wide selection of food is served until 10.15pm daily. The pub is popular with students and prison staff, but offers a warm welcome to all visitors to the area. ⏚❀◖●🖂(6)🌶🌐

Dun Cow 🅛 ✅

37 Old Elvet, DH1 3HN
🕒 11-11.30; 12-11 Sun ☎ (0191) 386 9219
Black Sheep Best Bitter; Camerons Castle Eden Ale; Moorhouse's White Witch Ⓗ
In 995AD Lindisfarne monks were searching for a resting place for the body of St Cuthbert when they came across a milkmaid looking for her lost cow. She directed them to Dun Holm (Durham). This Grade II-listed pub, dating back to the 15th century in parts, is named after the historic animal. There is a friendly front snug and a larger lounge to the rear. Q⏚◖🖂(58,59)🌶🌐

Half Moon Inn 🅛 ✅

86 New Elvet, DH1 3AQ
🕒 11-11 (midnight Fri & Sat); 12-11 Sun ☎ (0191) 374 1918
🌐 thehalfmooninndurham.co.uk
Draught Bass; Durham White Gold; Greene King IPA; Timothy Taylor Landlord; 2 changing beers Ⓗ
Named after the crescent-shaped bar that runs from the front room through to the lounge area, this is a busy city-centre inn with a large beer garden next to the river. It has traditional decor throughout, with photos of the pub at the beginning of the 20th century, including many from the Miners' Gala. A friendly venue with a relaxed atmosphere, it offers a good selection of ales to locals and visitors to the city. ❀&🖂(6)🌶🌐

Head of Steam 🅛

Reform Place, DH1 4RZ (through archway from North Rd)
🕒 12-11 (midnight Fri & Sat) ☎ (0191) 383 2173
4 changing beers Ⓗ
A popular pub that attracts beer lovers of all ages. As well as the four changing real ales, it offers an extensive choice of bottled beers from around the world and a range of real ciders. Excellent, good-value food is prepared on the premises, and the pub often holds tasting events featuring a wide choice of ales and ciders. During the day families are welcome and it gets busy at weekends. Local CAMRA branch Town Cider Pub of the Year runner-up 2016. ⏚❀◖&➳●🌐

Market Tavern ⓛ ✅
27 Market Place, DH1 3NJ
⊕ 11-midnight (12.30am Sat); 11-11 Sun ☎ (0191) 386 2069
5 changing beers Ⓗ
Occupying a central location in Durham's historic market place, this single-roomed, L-shaped bar offers a good selection of five local and national cask ales and one real cider. Despite recent refurbishments, the pub has managed to keep its traditional wooden alehouse appearance and offers a warm welcome to locals and visitors to the city. Good food based on pub classics is served up to 9.30pm. Quiz night is Thursday.
ᗜ❀◑≉♠🖵🛜

Newton Grange
Finchale Road, Brasside, DH1 5SA
⊕ 11-11 (10.30 Sun) ☎ (0191) 384 4708
⊕ newtongrangepub.co.uk
6 changing beers Ⓗ
Large Marston's pub on the edge of Newton Hall housing estate with a busy yet friendly and very welcoming atmosphere. There is a strong emphasis on food, including a pizza bar offering freshly made pizzas, complemented by six real ales from the Marston's stable. Families are welcome and there is an indoor children's play area. Wednesday is quiz night. ᗜ❀◑👥🖵(62)❀🛜

Old Elm Tree ⓛ
12 Crossgate, DH1 4PS
⊕ 11.30-11 (midnight Fri & Sat) ☎ (0191) 386 4621
6 changing beers Ⓗ
One of Durham's oldest inns, dating back to at least 1600, this pub is reputed to have two ghosts. The interior comprises an L-shaped bar and a top room linked by stairs, with a friendly atmosphere attracting a good mix of locals, students and visitors to the city. A good range of ales and home-cooked food is available. The pub hosts a Wednesday quiz (arrive early) and a folk group on Monday and Tuesday. Local CAMRA branch Town Pub of the Year in 2015 and 2016.
ᗜ❀◑≉♠P🖵❀🛜

Station House ⓛ
North Road, DH1 4SE
⊕ closed Mon; 4-10.30 Tue-Thu; 12-11 Fri & Sat; 2-10.30 Sun
⊕ stationhousedurham.co.uk
4 changing beers Ⓖ
Durham city's first micropub offers a good selection of ever-changing local and national real ales as well as ciders straight from the cask. Customers are served through a hatch directly from the cold room. The absence of music or TV allows a back to basics approach, with an emphasis on conversation. The two rocking chairs by the window in the main room are highly sought after. This is a quirky and friendly pub, welcoming both locals and visitors to the city. Local CAMRA Town Cider Pub of the Year 2017. Q ᗜ≉♠🛢🖵❀🛜

Tap & Spile ⓛ
Front Street, Framwellgate Moor, DH1 5EE
⊕ 12-3 (not Mon-Fri), 6-11; 12-3, 7-10.30 Sun
☎ (0191) 386 5451
8 changing beers (sourced nationally) Ⓗ
A local CAMRA award winner in 2016, this popular drinkers' pub offers a wide range of eight constantly changing real ales. There are two bars at one side while the other side can be partitioned into two – families are welcome in the side room until 9pm. Folk music night is hosted on Thursday

and a quiz on Wednesday. The atmosphere is relaxed and locals and visitors from further afield are given a warm welcome. ᗜ♠P🖵(21)❀

Victoria Inn 🍷 ★ ⓛ
86 Hallgarth Street, DH1 3AS
⊕ 11.45-11; 12-10.30 Sun ☎ (0191) 386 5269
⊕ victoriainn-durhamcity.co.uk
Big Lamp Bitter; Wylam Gold Tankard; 3 changing beers Ⓗ
The quaint decor, coal fires, cosy snug and genuine Victorian cash drawer help create the old-world feel of this family-run Grade II-listed Victorian pub, which has remained almost unchanged since it was built in 1899. Ales are mainly from local breweries and a wide selection of single malt whiskies and whiskeys is on offer. No meals are served but toasties are available. Voted local CAMRA Town Pub of the Year for the ninth time in 2017, it is popular with locals, students and visitors to the city.
Q ᗜ🛏♣♠🖵(6,PR2)❀🛜

Woodman Inn ⓛ
23 Gilesgate, DH1 1QW
⊕ 12-11.30 (12.30am Fri & Sat); 12-9.30 Sun; winter 5-11; 12-12.30am Fri & Sat; 3-10 Sun ☎ (0191) 386 5515
⊕ woodmaninn.co.uk
Maxim Double Maxim; 2 changing beers Ⓗ
This traditional-style pub serves three real ales and a good selection of lagers as well as a great selection of spirits including gin and malt whisky. The pub has a pool table, dartboard and various other games, and popular karaoke on Saturday evening. Bar food is available throughout the day. There is a large, attractive beer garden with plenty of seating to the rear. ᗜ❀◑♣♠🖵❀🛜

Eaglescliffe

Cleveland Bay ⓛ
718 Yarm Road, TS16 0JE (jct of A67 and A135, N of Tees bridge)
⊕ 11-1am ☎ (01642) 780275 ⊕ clevelandbay.co.uk
Camerons Strongarm; Marston's Wainwright; Timothy Taylor Landlord; 1 changing beer Ⓗ
Popular locals' pub under the stewardship of an enthusiastic licensee with an enviable reputation for serving a fine range of premium bitters, dispensed in the pub's own oversized glasses, as well as serving a free Sunday lunch. The main bar, with four handpumps, has two sports TVs. There is also a lounge and a function room where live bands play on Friday evenings. Third-pint glasses and tasting notes are available. A former CAMRA branch Community Pub of the Year.
Q ❀👥♠P🖵(7,17)❀🛜

Easington

Half Moon
The Green, SR8 3AZ (at top of village green)
⊕ 11-3, 5-11; 11-midnight Fri & Sat; 11.30-midnight Sun
☎ (0191) 527 0203 ⊕ halfmoonuk.com
Sharp's Doom Bar; 1 changing beer Ⓗ
A welcoming, good-sized former Vaux Brewery hostelry in a prominent position at the head of the pleasant village green. Meals can be enjoyed in the bar or the restaurant lounge, with all the meats locally sourced. Two well-kept beers are always on offer. The pub's history can be traced back to the early 19th century when its was an inn owned by the church until 1866. ᗜ❀◑👥♣♠P🖵(208)❀🛜

Eastgate

Cross Keys ⎣
DL13 2HW
☼ 5 (12 Sat & Sun)-midnight; closed Mon winter
☎ (01388) 517234 ⊕ crosskeyseastgate.co.uk
Allendale Wagtail Best Bitter; 1 changing beer Ⓗ
Ancient building with a pleasant interior right next
to the main road up Weardale. Popular with
holidaymakers and locals, a restaurant provides
relaxed dining, while the bar is comfortable and
welcoming, and there is a beer garden to the rear.
The ceiling is adorned with tankards, and there are
tables to the front of the pub. A second Allendale
beer is usually available.
Q⏾❀✄◑♿▲♣P🚌(101)🐾

Edmundbyers

Punch Bowl ⎣
DH8 9NL (2½ miles W of A68)
☼ 11-11; 12-10.30 Sun ☎ (01207) 255545
⊕ thepunchbowlinn.info
3 changing beers Ⓗ
Set in a lovely rural location close to Derwent
Reservoir, three handpumps dispense a wide range
of local ales. The three comfortable rooms are
smartly furnished with roaring log fires in the
winter months. A full menu is offered all day
featuring home-cooked food using local
ingredients with a changing specials board. Great
for walkers, accommodation is available for
extending your stay to explore the area. Quiz night
is Thursday. Q⏾❀✄◑♿P🚌(773)🐾🛜

Egglescliffe

Pot & Glass ⎣ ✔
Church Road, TS16 9DQ (300yds E of A167, opp parish
church)
☼ 12-2.30 (not Mon), 6-11; 12-2.30, 5.30-midnight Fri;
12-midnight Sat; 12-11 Sun ☎ (01642) 651009
**Black Sheep Best Bitter; Caledonian Deuchars IPA;
Greene King IPA, Abbot; Wychwood Hobgoblin; 2
changing beers** Ⓗ
A local CAMRA branch multi-award winner, this
classic, old-fashioned and ever-popular multi-
roomed 17th-century village local is situated in a
quiet cul-de-sac. Former licensee and cabinet
maker Charlie Abbey, whose last resting place
overlooks the pub, fashioned the ornate bar fronts
from old country furniture. Tasting notes are
available for the seven handpumps, which include
two guest beers. Themed food evenings
complement the good-value home-cooked food.
Outside is a large, sometimes sunny, south-facing
garden. Q⏾❀◑♿⇄♣P🚌(7,17)

Ferryhill Station

Surtees Arms ⎣ ✔
Chilton Lane, DL17 0DH
☼ closed Mon; 4-11; 12-midnight Sat; 12-11 Sun
☎ (01740) 655724 ⊕ thesurteesarms.co.uk
**Yard of Ale Black as Owt Stout, One Foot in the Yard,
Surtees Gold; 2 changing beers** Ⓗ
Traditional pub serving locally and nationally
sourced ales and ciders as well as beers from the
on-site Yard of Ale Brewery (est 2008). Annual
beer festivals are held in the summer and at
Halloween. Live music and charity nights are
regular events. Lunches are served on Sunday only.

A 60-seat function room is available. A former
regional CAMRA Pub of the Year and local branch
Country Pub of the Year 2015. Q⏾❀◑♿P🚌🐾🛜

Forest-in-Teesdale

Langdon Beck Hotel ✔
DL12 0XP (on B6277, 8 miles NW of Middleton-in-
Teesdale)
☼ 11-10.30; 12-10.30 Sun; closed Mon winter
☎ (01833) 622267 ⊕ langdonbeckhotel.com
**Black Sheep Best Bitter; house beer (by Great North
Eastern); 1 changing beer** Ⓗ
Known as the Sportsman's Rest in the early 1800s,
this pub is situated in the North Pennines, three
miles from the spectacular High Force and Cauldron
Snout waterfalls and close to the Pennine Way. The
welcoming inn has long been a destination for
walkers, fishermen and those seeking hospitality in
scenic and peaceful surroundings, whether staying
overnight or just long enough to enjoy the
excellent food and drink. A beer festival is held
over the late May bank holiday weekend.
Q⏾❀✄◑♿▲♣P🐾

Frosterley

Black Bull ⎣
Bridge End, DL13 2SL
☼ closed Mon-Wed; 11-11 Thu-Sat; 11-5 Sun
☎ (01388) 527784 ⊕ blackbullfrosterley.com
4 changing beers Ⓗ
A truly unique, family-run pub next to the
Weardale Railway and river, with four guest ales
usually from local brewers, and up to four ciders
and perries. Bare boards, stone flags featuring
Frosterley marble, all manner of artefacts and
antique furniture create a wonderful ambience. It
offers high-quality, locally sourced food, and music,
plays and story-telling. The outbuilding houses a
peal of bells, visited by enthusiasts from far and
wide. Local CAMRA Country Cider Pub of the Year
runner-up 2015-17. Q⏾◑♿♣♣P🚌(101)🐾

Hamilton Row

Black Horse ⎣
DH7 9AU
☼ 2-11.30; 12-midnight Sat; 12-11.30 Sun
☎ (0191) 373 4576
3 changing beers Ⓗ
A friendly local with an open fire at one end and a
glass-fronted fire at the other helping to create a
warm, cosy atmosphere. Three well-kept real ales
include one invariably from a local brewery. Good-
value Sunday lunches are served and there is a
pool table. An excellent pub for walkers as it is
handily situated adjacent to the Deerness Valley
Way. Q⏾◑♣P🚌(52,725)🐾🛜

Hartlepool

Brewery Tap ⎣
Stockton Street, TS24 7QY (on A689, in front of
Camerons Brewery)
☼ 11 (12 Sat)-4; closed Sun ☎ (01429) 852000
⊕ cameronsbrewery.com
Camerons Strongarm; 2 changing beers Ⓗ
When Camerons discovered that it owned a derelict
pub, the former Stranton's future was secured – it is
now in its 14th successful year. A strengthened
marketing department has resulted in there now

being 16 'monthly' specials, one of which is always available, together with Strongarm and another of its regular beers – IPA or Gold Bullion. Brewery tours start from here. Meetings and conferences, evening opening and other social events, as well as superb buffets, can all be arranged. ♿≑Pⓓ⌂(1,36)♣

Causeway 🄻
Vicarage Gardens, Stranton, TS24 7QT (beside Camerons Brewery)
✪ 11.30-11 (11.30 Thu; midnight Fri & Sat); 11-11 Sun
☎ (01429) 263000
Camerons Strongarm; 3 changing beers Ⓗ
Marvellous multi-roomed, red-brick Victorian building, dating from 1862, and Camerons' unofficial brewery tap for more than a century. The Causeway is now owned by Marston's, though the sales of banked Strongarm remain huge. The licensees host an eclectic mix of live music most evenings, while Tuesday is quiz night. Guest beers are from Marston's. Good-value bar snacks are available. A former local CAMRA branch multi-award winner. ⏴♿≑ⓓ⌂(1,36)♣

King John's Tavern 🅥
1 South Road, TS26 9HD (at NW corner of market)
✪ 8am-midnight (1am Fri & Sat) ☎ (01429) 274388
7 changing beers Ⓗ
Converted from a marketplace furniture shop, this Wetherspoon outlet is named after King John who, in 1201, granted the town the right to hold markets. The pub offers the chain's nationally contracted beers and ciders, alongside regionally sourced guest beers. Beer festivals, Meet the Brewer, a January sale and celebrations of saints' days are hosted. There is a large sunny patio; however, with onshore north-easterly winds, it is advisable to wrap up really well, even in the middle of summer. ⏴✿❶♿≑●⌂ ᗧ

Rat Race Ale House
Hartlepool Railway Station, Station Approach, TS24 7ED (on Platform 1)
✪ 12.02-2.15, 4.02-8.15; 12.02-9 Sat; closed Sun & Mon ☎ 07903 479378 🌐 ratracealehouse.co.uk
4 changing beers Ⓗ
A former CAMRA Regional Cider Pub of the Year and branch multi-award winner, the station's newsagent is now a drinkers' paradise, offering a wide choice of beers, cider and perry, and bottled Belgian beers. Its opening/closing times coincide with the arrival/departure of the coast trains. No fizzy lager/beer, no spirits/alcopops, no TV/jukebox, no one-arm bandit, no bar! During the last nine years, more than 1,500 different beers, sourced from 500 different breweries, have been served direct to the table by the landlord himself. Q♿≑♣●ⓓ⌂

Hartlepool Headland

Fisherman's Arms 🅥
Southgate, TS24 0JJ (on headland close to Fish Quay in Old Hartlepool)
✪ closed Mon; 7-11.30 Tue (11 Wed & Thu; midnight Fri & Sat); 5.30-11 Sun ☎ 07847 208598
5 changing beers Ⓗ
The Fish, a recent local CAMRA branch Community Pub of the Year and branch multi award-winner, is a typical friendly, family-run, one-room locals' establishment. Now free of tie, five beers and Westons Rosie's Pig are served. 'Keeping music

alive' is the theme, with popular music and open-mic nights well supported, while a quiz is held on Sunday. Third-pint beer bats are available. Two beer festivals are hosted annually. Q●ⓓ⌂(7)♣ ᗧ

Globe 🄻
26 Northgate, TS24 0LJ (on Headland, towards the Fish Quay in Old Hartlepool)
✪ 11.30 (11 Sun)-11 ☎ (01429) 860097
Camerons Strongarm Ⓗ
Opposite the port that was once bustling with ship building, fishing boats, coal staithes and pit props, this recent CAMRA Community Pub of the Year is under the stewardship of a friendly and experienced licensee with over 25 years of service to the trade. The price of Strongarm (ask for a Hartlepool Head) still represents remarkable value, reflecting the pub's freehold status, with savings negotiated with Camerons passed on to customers. Q♿♣ⓓ⌂(7)

Heighington

Bay Horse Inn 🅥
28 West Green, DL5 6PE
✪ 11-11; 12-10.30 Sun ☎ (01325) 312312
🌐 bayhorseheighington.co.uk
Black Sheep Best Bitter; Camerons Strongarm; Copper Dragon Best Bitter; John Smith's Bitter; Timothy Taylor Landlord; 2 changing beers Ⓗ
Picturesque, historic, 300-year-old pub overlooking the award-winning village's largest green. Its traditional interior with exposed beams and stone walls is partitioned into distinct drinking and dining areas, with a large restaurant extending from the lounge. Food plays a prominent role, with home-cooked meals available as well as bar snacks. However, the bar area allows drinkers to enjoy the good beer range, including two guest ales, in the evening. ⏴✿❶♿⌂

High Hesleden

Ship Inn 🄻
Mickle Hill Road, TS27 4QD (signed from B1281, between A19 and Blackhall)
✪ closed Mon; 12-3 (not Tue-Fri), 6-11; 12-8 Sun
☎ (01429) 836453 🌐 theshipinn.net
7 changing beers Ⓗ
Now in its 17th year of family ownership, satisfaction is guaranteed at this rural gem. The landlord serves seven beers, some locally sourced, as well as real cider. His wife runs the superb restaurant offering top-quality food at reasonable prices, including mid-week early-doors two-course specials. Six motel-style chalets provide good-value accommodation. There are stupendous coastal views from the well-kept gardens. The pub closes during the owners' annual holidays, so check before making a long journey. A recent CAMRA Regional Pub of the Year. Q⏴✿➤❶♿●P⌂(206)

Holwick

Strathmore Arms 🄻
DL12 0NJ (off B6277 just outside Middleton-in-Teesdale)
✪ 12-midnight; closed Tue ☎ (01833) 640362
🌐 strathmoregold.co.uk
Marston's Wainwright; Mithril A66; 3 changing beers Ⓗ

This 17th-century stone and buttressed roadside pub has a welcoming bar with a stone flag floor, beams and real fire, a separate lounge with tiled floor and pool table, and a beer garden. It offers a house beer from Mithril, Strathmore Gold, four guest ales (six in summer) and up to 16 ciders. A beer festival is held at the end of July and a cider festival in Cider Month, October. Food is served during all sessions. Regular live music plays on Fridays. Four en-suite letting rooms are available. CAMRA Country Cider Pub 2016 and 2017.
🛏️🍴🚐🕽️♣️🚶P🌭🐾🛜

Hunwick

Joiners Arms
13 South View, DL15 0JW
🍺 5-11; closed Tue; 12-11 Sat; 11.30-11 Sun
☎ (01388) 605131 ⊕ thejoinersarms.webnode.com
Theakston Best Bitter; 2 changing beers ⊞
A friendly bar which also has a restaurant, small snug and covered yard/pool room. Three handpumps feature a varied selection, occasionally including cider or perry. Quality locally sourced food is offered Wednesday to Saturday evenings, and Sunday lunchtimes in the restaurant. Cheese night is Monday evening in the bar.
🍴🕽️♣️P🛒(108,109)🛜

Ingleton

Black Horse 🅛
Front Street, DL2 3HS
🍺 5 (12 Sat & Sun)-11 ☎ (01325) 730374
⊕ blackhorseingleton.co.uk
Camerons Strongarm; 3 changing beers ⊞
Village free house and restaurant with a large car park set back from the road. This is a popular community hostelry with a relaxed atmosphere serving excellent locally sourced food. The friendly bar extends into the dining area. Three guest ales come from local micros within a 30-mile radius of the pub. The restaurant menu is served Wednesday to Sunday. Local darts teams are supported. The weekly quiz night is on a Sunday.
Q🛏️🛖🍴🕽️♣️P🛒(84)🌭🛜

Leamside

Three Horseshoes 🅛
Pit House Lane, DH4 6QQ (½ mile N of A690, just outside West Rainton)
🍺 11-11 ☎ (0191) 584 2394
⊕ threehorseshoesleamside.co.uk
Timothy Taylor Landlord; 5 changing beers ⊞
A country pub with an excellent restaurant, the Back Room (booking advisable). The traditional bar has open fires in winter and a large TV for sport. The attached Working Hand Brewery provides up to four real ales with names all linked to characters from the pub with a story to tell. Timothy Taylor Landlord is always available. The pub is home to a local cycle club and hosts a quiz on Sunday evening. Q🛏️🛖🕽️♣️P🌭🛜

Long Newton

Vane Arms 🅛 ✅
Darlington Road, TS21 1DB (at W end of village, close to A66 jct)
🍺 12-2 (not Mon), 5-11; 12-2, 5-midnight Fri & Sat; 12-11 Sun
☎ (01642) 580401 ⊕ thevaneatlongnewton.com

Black Sheep Best Bitter; 2 changing beers ⊞
This picturesque village inn is fast becoming the benchmark for country pubs – offering a warm welcome, real beer, real food and first class B&B. The pub's reputation for serving interesting guest beers in the locals' bar, together with home-made, reasonably priced, top-quality restaurant meals, has now spread far and wide. Accommodation is in four well appointed en-suite bedrooms. The large, sunny, south-facing outdoor drinking facilities can only enhance the experience.
Q🛏️🚐🕽️♣️P🛒(88)🌭🛜

Medomsley

Royal Oak 🅛
7 Manor Road, DH8 6QN
🍺 11.30-3, 5.30-11; 11-11 Sat; 12-11 Sun ☎ (01207) 560336
Hadrian Border Tyneside Blonde; 2 changing beers ⊞
The Royal Oak is a traditional country-style pub which has been refurbished to create a warm, welcoming ambience. It has a large bar with a selection of seating including soft sofas and leather chairs, and plenty of dining space. Outside, there is a large, attractive garden at the back and ample parking at the front. An excellent, friendly local, it offers a rotation of quality beers as well as good food. Quiz night is Sunday. Q🛏️🛖🕽️♣️P🛒🌭🛜

Metal Bridge

Old Mill 🅛
Thinford Road, DH6 5NX (off A1M jct 61, follow signs on A177)
🍺 12-11 (10.30 Sun) ☎ (01740) 652928
⊕ oldmilldurham.co.uk
4 changing beers ⊞
Originally a paper mill in 1813, it offers good-quality food and well-kept ales – four handpumps serve a diverse range, with local breweries supplying at least one of the beers. The food menu is extensive, with daily specials written on a board above the bar. Larger groups are welcome in the conservatory. Accommodation is of a high standard, with all rooms en-suite. Q🛏️🚐🕽️P

Middlestone

Ship Inn 🅛
Low Road, DL14 8AB (between Coundon and Kirk Merrington)
🍺 4-11.30 (10 Tue); 12-11.30 Fri & Sat; 12-10 Sun
☎ (01388) 810904
6 changing beers ⊞
Regular drinkers come from far and wide to the Ship. It has a bar divided into three areas with an open fire, and a large function room upstairs which is the location for occasional beer festivals. The rooftop patio has spectacular views, and there is always an event either taking place or imminent. Various pieces of Vaux memorabilia are on display – one of the many subjects of conversation. Sunday lunches are popular. Local CAMRA Country Pub runner-up in 2015. Q🛏️🛖🕽️♣️🚶P🛒(56)🌭

Middleton-in-Teesdale

Cafe 1618
16 Market Place, DL12 0QG
🍺 closed Mon; 11-midnight ☎ (01833) 640300
⊕ cafe1618.com
2 changing beers ⊞

The bar serves visitors and locals a wide range of freshly cooked local food, which can also be enjoyed at street tables or in the extensive beer garden. Two beers come from near and far, with beer festivals on the May and August bank holidays and Carnival (first weekend in August). The pub is a Northumberland in Bloom winner. The area, one of natural beauty, attracts walkers, cyclists and many bikers. Please ring to check if open.
🛏🏠🍴◗◖♿🖂(95)🐾♣🛜

Newfield

Newfield Inn 🅛
Front Street, DH2 2SP
🕓 6 (12 Sat & Sun)-11.30 ☎ (0191) 370 0565
Maxim Ward's Best Bitter; 2 changing beers 🅗
A friendly two-roomed pub in the centre of the village known locally simply as The Inn, owned by Maxim Brewery from nearby Houghton-le-Spring, with two of its beers and a guest on the bar. The pub offers accommodation, monthly live music, a regular Tuesday night quiz and football on TV. Families are welcome and there is a pleasant beer garden. Occasional beer festivals are held.
🛏🏠♿P🖂(78)

Newton Aycliffe

Turbinia 🅛
Parsons Centre, Sid Chaplin Drive, DL5 7PA
🕓 12.30-midnight; 12-1am Fri & Sat ☎ (01325) 313034
🌐 turbiniapub.co.uk
4 changing beers 🅗
Named after the famous Tyneside ship, this friendly free house comprises a large lounge and function room with traditional pub decor, featuring a pictorial history of the Turbinia throughout. This local favourite serves an ever-changing variety of light and dark beers sourced locally and nationally, and hosts its own beer and cider festival twice yearly. Darts, dominoes and pool can be found in the main bar during the week and live music at the weekend. 🛏♿♣P🖂(7)🛜

No Place

Beamish Mary Inn 🅛
DH9 0QH (follow signs to No Place off A693 from Chester-le-Street to Stanley)
🕓 12-11 (10.30 Sun) ☎ (0191) 370 0237
🌐 beamishmaryinn.com
Big Lamp Sunny Daze, Lamplight Bitter; Consett White Hot, Red Dust; 5 changing beers 🅗
Full of character, this pub is well respected for its warm atmosphere, generously portioned pub grub and ample selection of well-kept real ale. The location is handy for visitors to the nearby world-renowned Beamish Open Air Museum. Consett Ale Works and Big Lamp beers are usually among the range of LocAles on offer. Accommodation is available including twin, double and family rooms.
Q🛏🏠◗◖♿♥P🖂(8,78)🐾🛜

Norton

George & Dragon
109 High Street, TS20 1AA (80yds S of duck pond)
🕓 3-11; 12-midnight Fri & Sat; 12-11 Sun ☎ (01642) 554150
3 changing beers 🅗
Traditional, ornate and unobtrusive, this three-roomed locals' pub has been described as 'how

pubs used to be and how pubs ought to be'. It comprises a bar, where locals sit on leather benches and muse over wise quotations and photographs of yesteryear, together with two lounges, a pool room and sheltered outdoor drinkers/smokers' area. The three beers are always stronger premium bitters and include a dark brew, all chosen by the regulars themselves. A recent CAMRA branch Community Pub of the Year.
🛏🏠♣🖂(35,37)🐾

Old Shotton

Royal George 🅛
The Village, SR8 2ND
🕓 11-11 (midnight Fri & Sat); 11-10.30 Sun
☎ (0191) 586 6500 🌐 royalgeorgeoldshotton.co.uk
Timothy Taylor Landlord; 3 changing beers 🅗
Pub and restaurant situated on the old village green, reopened after a major refurbishment of a virtually derelict establishment in 2014. The bar has been reinstated as well as a larger lounge and restaurant area. Owned by Working Hand Brewery, its beers are among the changing range of ales. Handpulled cider is always on offer. Traditional pub grub and bar snacks are available. Dogs are welcome with complementary treats on the bar.
Q🛏◗◖♥P🐾🛜

Piercebridge

Fox Hole 🅛
Carlbury, DL2 3SJ (on B6275)
🕓 11-11; 12-10.30 Sun ☎ (01325) 374286
🌐 the-foxhole.co.uk
3 changing beers 🅗
Set in what was a Roman village, the pub sits almost centrally between the towns of Darlington, Barnard Castle, Bishop Auckland and Richmond. From the welcoming Wellie bar through to the relaxed yet elegant dining room and alfresco dining terrace, the emphasis is on high-quality, carefully sourced local food and drink, combined with traditional pub values. A warm welcome and friendly service, along with three beers from nearby micros including Mithril three miles away, make this pub a must-visit. A beer festival is staged over the May Day weekend.
🏠◗◖♿P🖂(75,76)🐾🛜

Sadberge

Buck Inn 🅛
Middleton Road, DL2 1RR
🕓 12-11 (10 Sun winter) ☎ (01325) 401283
🌐 thebuckinnsadberge.co.uk
Mithril A66; 2 changing beers 🅗
Friendly traditional English pub overlooking the green in an attractive village setting, with two bars, one mainly for dining. It is named after George Buck, a benevolent 18th-century landowner. There is a beer garden to the rear and benches and tables at the front. A supporter of local micros, it always has one beer from Mithril and another often from Stockton. A variety of good food is served lunchtimes and evenings – try the tapas and parmos. The village sits atop a hill in a popular walking area. 🛏🏠◗◖♿P🖂(20)🛜

St John's Chapel

Blue Bell Inn 🅛

Hood Street, DL13 1QJ (on A689)

✪ 5 (12 Sat & Sun)-1am ☎ (01388) 537256

2 changing beers Ⓗ

Originally a pair of terraced cottages, the Blue Bell is a friendly and cosy pub with a bar across the front of the building leading to a small pool room, and a garden to the rear. It serves the local community and those who holiday in Upper Weardale. Pub games are popular and there are plenty of books to choose from.
Q🛏🏠🕏🚆(101)🛜

Seaham

Hat & Feathers 🅛 ✅

57-59 Church Street, SR7 7HF

✪ 8am-midnight (1am Fri & Sat); 8am-11 Sun

☎ (0191) 513 3040

Greene King Abbot; Sharp's Doom Bar; 3 changing beers Ⓗ

This Wetherspoon pub gets its name from the Doggarts store that occupied the site from the 1920s to the 1980s and had a department selling hats and feathers. Upstairs are old photographs depicting the headgear of the best-dressed ladies of the time. Other interesting pictures show the past history of Seaham. The furnishings are a mix of modern and traditional styles, including comfortable settees. Outside is a plaque displaying a history of the building. 🛏🏠🕏🏮🛏🚆🛜

Seaton

Dun Cow 🅛

The Village, SR7 0NA

✪ 4 (winter 5)-midnight; 12-midnight Fri-Sun

☎ (0191) 513 1133

4 changing beers Ⓗ

Excellent, friendly, unspoilt inn on the village green with public bar and lounge areas. A pub for good conversation or a game of darts, the TV is only turned on for special events. No meals are served but toasties are available. The guest beer selection changes but usually comprises two light and two dark beers to satisfy all tastes. Regular busker and acoustic music nights feature. CAMRA branch Country Pub of the Year 2016. 🛏🏠🕏🏮🚆(238)🏠

Sedgefield

Dun Cow 🅛

43 Front Street, TS21 3AT

✪ 11-3, 6-11; 11-11 Sat; 12-10.30 Sun ☎ (01740) 620894

🌐 duncowinn.co.uk

Black Sheep Best Bitter; Theakston Best Bitter; 2 changing beers Ⓗ

Run by the same landlord for over 40 years, this large and comfortable 18th-century inn has an excellent county-wide reputation for good food using locally sourced produce as much as possible. It was the scene of a historic George Bush and Tony Blair lunch in 2003. There are three bars including a farmers' bar-cum-snug and restaurant. Four real ales are always available, with at least one local beer. Q🛏🏠🕏🏮🕏P🚆

South Church

Red Alligator

Auckland Road, DL14 6SP (nr St Andrew's church)

✪ 12-2.30, 5.30-10.30 (11.30 Sat); 11.30-3 Sun

☎ (01388) 605644

3 changing beers Ⓗ

A mile from the centre of Bishop Auckland, this smart local has a bright feel and a good reputation for food. There is a spacious L-shaped bar across the front and a small dining room/snug to the rear. The eponymous Grand National winner was trained just across the road. Closed on some Mondays.
Q🕏🕏P🚆(1,5)

Spennymoor

Frog & Ferret 🅛

Coulson Street, DL16 7RS

✪ 2-11; 12-midnight Thu-Sat; 12-8 Sun ☎ (01388) 815840

🌐 thefrogandferretspennymoor.co.uk

5 changing beers Ⓗ

Friendly, traditional, family-run free house offering five constantly changing real ales, sourced from far and wide, with local and northern microbreweries well represented. The comfortably furnished lounge has a three-sided bar, with brick, stone and wood cladding and a solid-fuel burner. Sports TV is featured and children are welcome until 9pm. Live music is hosted on a Saturday night. Sunday lunch is served 12-3pm. 🛏🏮🚆(21)🏠

Grand Electric Hall 🅛 ✅

Cheapside, DL16 6DJ

✪ 8am-midnight (1am Fri & Sat) ☎ (01388) 825470

Greene King Abbot; Ruddles Best Bitter; 6 changing beers Ⓗ

Formerly a cinema and bingo hall, this is a bright and airy Wetherspoon conversion, with a film-themed decor and fittings. The main area is spacious with a high ceiling, and there is a smaller room on a lower level. Set in the centre of town, it boasts a large patio drinking area to the front which can be quite a suntrap in the summer. Alcohol is served from 9am. 🛏🏠🕏🕏🚆(6,21)🛜

Stanhope

Grey Bull

17 West Terrace, DL13 2PB

✪ 12 (11.45 Sat)-midnight ☎ (01388) 529428

3 changing beers Ⓗ

At the foot of Crawleyside Bank at the west end of town, the pub has a busy bar area across the front and a lounge to the rear, served by a central bar. A community-focused hostelry with a warm welcome, it is also convenient for the coast-to-coast cycle route. The tables to the front are popular in good weather. Q🕏🕏🏮🚆(101)🏠 🛜

Stockton-on-Tees

Golden Smog 🍷

1 Hambletonian Yard, TS18 1DS (in a ginnel between High St and West Row)

✪ 2-10 ☎ (01642) 385022

4 changing beers Ⓗ

The town's first micropub, and CAMRA branch 2016 and 2017 Pub of the Year, located in a ginnel, leading west off the main road. Four real beers and two real ciders are served alongside a hugely impressive range of Belgian beers, some familiar,

most not so familiar, but all served in matching glasses in the continental way. Third-pint glasses and tasting tables are available.
Q✦✷(Stockton/Thornaby)●🚃♣

Wasp's Nest 🅛
Wasp's Nest Yard, 1 Calvert's Square, TS18 1TB (E of High St towards river)
✿ 11-11 (midnight Fri & Sat); 12-11 Sun ☎ 07789 277364
3 changing beers 🅷
Tucked away in a small square, between the Grade II-listed Georgian Theatre and the River Tees, this bright, modern and lively micropub is one of several newer outlets in the town, serving a selection of locally sourced beers, real cider and perry. The pub's claim to fame is that it has the town's only outdoor courtyard drinking area.
Q✷&✦●🚃♣

Tanfield Lea

Tanfield Lea Working Mens Club
West Street, DH9 9NA
✿ 2-4, 7-11; 12-11.30 Fri & Sat; 12-2, 7-11 Sun
☎ (01207) 238783
2 changing beers 🅷
The village has no pub, reflecting its strong Methodist history, but guests are most welcome in this CIU-affiliated club, which has become something of a flagship for real ale in the area after a diet of keg beer for many years. TV sport is shown in the bar and there is a comfortable, quiet lounge. Traditional club activities such as bingo take place and there is usually a live act on Sunday when nibbles are provided on the bar. Local CAMRA Club of the Year 2016 and 2017. ☎&♣P🚃(V7,V8)📶

Tanfield Village

Peacock
Front Street, DH9 9PX
✿ 4.30-10.30 Mon; 3-11; 12-midnight Sat & Sun
☎ (01207) 232720
Black Sheep Best Bitter; 1 changing beer 🅷
A warm welcome is guaranteed at this friendly, traditional two-bar pub in a pretty village, popular with locals and visitors alike – including bell-ringers from the church opposite. Lovely home-cooked meals are available Thursday to Saturday evenings and Sunday lunchtime – the portions are generous and great value for money. There is a small beer garden and ample parking. Black Sheep is always available plus a changing guest beer.
Q☎✷◐♣P🚃(V8)

West Cornforth

Square & Compass 🅛
7 The Green, DL17 9JQ (off Coxhoe-W Cornforth road)
✿ 5 (4 Fri)-11; 12-11 Sat & Sun ☎ (01740) 653050
3 changing beers 🅷
A proper drinking pub and friendly local on the village green in the old part of Doggy (the village's local nickname). It has sold real ale for over 30 years and always offers at least one local beer among its three guests. It is home to darts, dominoes and chess clubs. The pub has good views over to Wear Valley and Durham City.
Q☎✷♣P🚃(56)♣

Westgate

Hare & Hounds 🅛
24 Front Street, DL13 1RX
✿ closed Mon; 6.30 (5.30 Fri)-11; 3-11 Sat; 12-3, 6.30-9.30 Sun ☎ (01388) 517212
🌐 hareandhoundswestgate.blogspot.co.uk
Weard'ALE Challenger, Gold, Fell Over, Chilled Nights, Dark Nights; 1 changing beer 🅷
On the A689 up Weardale, with the Wear at the bottom of the garden. The spacious stone-flagged bar is partially fitted out with furniture and other items salvaged from the former village chapel, and the restaurant has a patio overlooking the river. Catch up on the local news over a pint brewed only a few feet below you. Food, including the famous Sunday carvery, is locally sourced. Local CAMRA Country Pub of the Year runner-up in 2015.
Q☎✷◐&▲♣P🚃(101)

Witton-le-Wear

Dun Cow
19 High Street, DL14 0AY
✿ 6 (1 Sat)-11; 12-11 Sun ☎ (01388) 488294
3 changing beers 🅷
Dating from 1799, this comfortable and welcoming pub is set back from the road through the village. The single room has an open fire at both ends, one guarded by a sleeping fox who always seems to have just closed his eyes, and the other by an impressive set of horns. There are benches to the left of the bar, and seating outside offering pleasant views over the Wear valley. The decor includes some interesting football memorabilia.
Q✷♣P

Wolsingham

Black Lion 🅛
21 Meadhope Street, DL13 3EN (50yds N of marketplace)
✿ 6.30 (6 Fri)-11; 12-11 Sat; 12-10.30 Sun
☎ (01388) 527772
4 changing beers 🅷
Nationally recognised for its commitment to real cider, the Lion is hidden away a minute from the Market Place. A welcoming, comfortable gem, it is a great place to relax. An open fire warms the single, open-plan room, with a pool table to the rear and a bar with TV sport to the front. Local charities benefit from the efforts of the pub. Six or more ciders can be on offer. North-East Region Cider Pub of the Year 2016, and local branch Country Cider Pub of the Year 2013-2017.
Q✷&♣●🚃(101)♣📶

There is not a brewer who doesn't doctor his beer with something or other. Really something is in it. Four glasses made a Brooklyn man shoot down Dr Duggan in cold blood. Beer made a New York husband put a hole through his wife with a 22-calibre defender. Murder is in it. Who drinks lager beer is too apt to swallow the murder with it.
Elisha Chenery MD, 1889

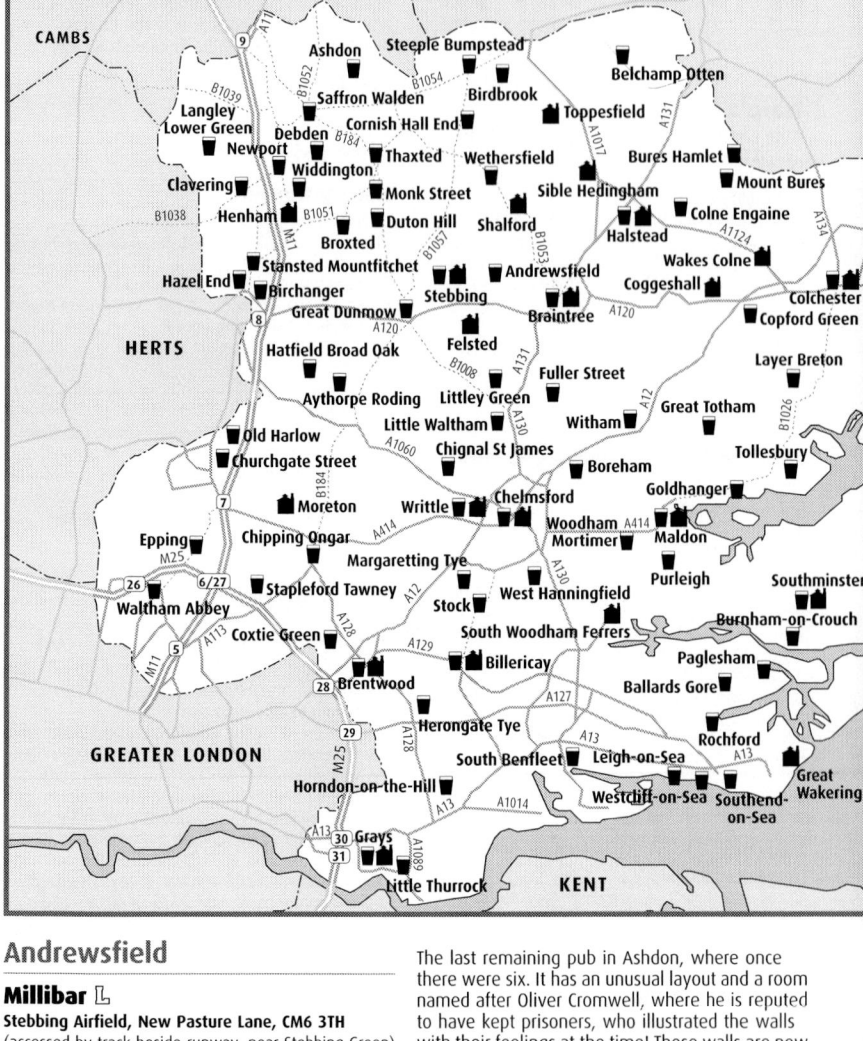

Andrewsfield

Millibar L

Stebbing Airfield, New Pasture Lane, CM6 3TH
(accessed by track beside runway, near Stebbing Green)
TL689248
☼ 11-9 ☎ (01371) 856744 ⊕ andrewsfield.com/
andrewsfield-millibar
Bishop Nick Ridley's Rite H

Local private pilots' airfield with a small grass strip and clubhouse. Also a flying school, it offers trial lessons up to a commercial pilot's licence, and is dominated by single-engined Cessna aircraft, a Mustang III and B17 Meteor IIIs. The bar manager is keen on local supply and has installed Ridley's Rite from Bishop Nick Brewery as his sole ale. There is also a range of bottled beers from Bishop Nick. The public are welcome here and the bar stays open until 11pm if there are customers. Q☺◑P❀❄

Ashdon

Rose & Crown

Crown Hill, CB10 2HA
☼ closed Mon; 12-2.30, 5.30 (5 Fri)-11; 12-11 Sat; 12-7 Sun
☎ (01799) 584337
Woodforde's Wherry; 4 changing beers (sourced nationally) H

The last remaining pub in Ashdon, where once there were six. It has an unusual layout and a room named after Oliver Cromwell, where he is reputed to have kept prisoners, who illustrated the walls with their feelings at the time! These walls are now hidden behind removable panels. Guest beers often come from Nethergate and other Essex breweries. The pub is the focus of village social activities. ☜☺◑P❀

Aythorpe Roding

Axe & Compasses L

Dunmow Road, CM6 1PP (on B184 5 miles SW of Dunmow) TL594154
☼ 9am-11 (midnight Fri & Sat) ☎ (01279) 876648
⊕ theaxeandcompasses.co.uk
Adnams Broadside; Sharp's Doom Bar H**; 3 changing beers (sourced regionally)** G

Surrounded by beautiful countryside, the Axe is an 18th-century building. An award-winning dining pub, those who just wish to drink are also very welcome. A mixed clientele of locals and farming folk enjoys the well-kept selection of beers and ciders. The restaurant offers pub classics with a modern twist, all locally sourced, and the service is efficient and friendly. Quizzes and food theme nights are hosted. Q☺◑●P♪(17,18)❀❄

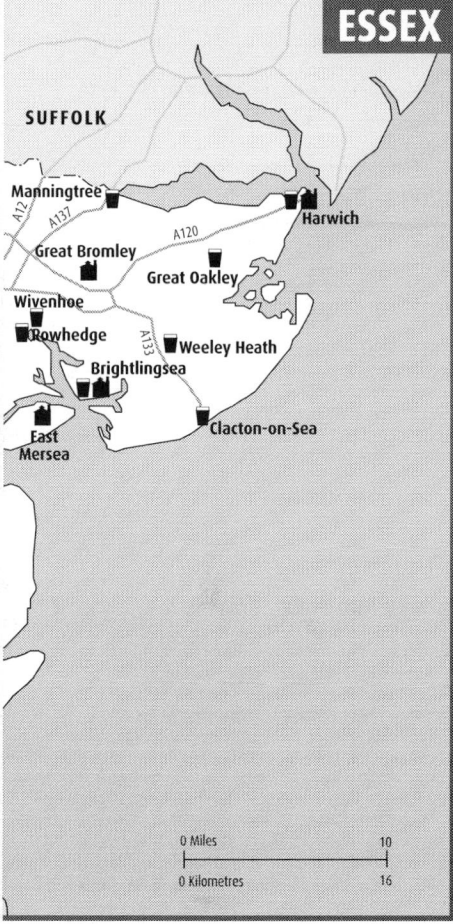

Lovely local inn, hidden away in the smallest of the Belchamps. The owner provides a warm welcome, with an open fire in winter. The pub has darts and a pool table, and runs occasional events. There are excellent views, good walks and cycle rides from here. Food is not currently served but there are delivery arrangements with local takeaway restaurants. A friendly labrador welcomes you on arrival. Local CAMRA Pub of the Year 2017. ▷❀♣♠P❀♿🛜

Billericay

Billericay Brewing Co Shop & Micropub

52 Chapel Street, CM12 9LS

🕙 10-6; 9am-9 Thu-Sat; 11-5 Sun ☎ (01277) 500121

⊕ billericaybrewing.co.uk

Billericay Zeppelin, Blonde, Dickie; 4 changing beers (sourced locally; often Billericay) Ⓖ

Brewery tap micropub next door to the Billericay Brewery, which can be viewed while drinking. It serves up to six ales, five from Billericay, with usually one gold, amber, dark and strong ale available on gravity. The micropub is also a beer shop where bottle-conditioned ales are sold from Billericay, Essex and London breweries plus foreign beers. Beer festivals are held during the year, in March, June, September and December.

Q▷❀≉♣♠🚃(100,222)❀

Coach & Horses Ⓛ

36 Chapel Street, CM12 9LU

🕙 11 (10 Sat)-11; 12-10 Sun ☎ (01277) 622873

⊕ thecoachandhorses.org

Sharp's Doom Bar; Skinner's Betty Stogs; Wibblers Dengie IPA; 2 changing beers (sourced nationally) Ⓗ

Close to the high street, this welcoming one-bar pub with an inviting atmosphere is a regular in the Guide. Five ales are served, with one always from

Ballards Gore

Shepherd & Dog

Gore Road, SS4 2DA (between Rochford and Paglesham)

🕙 12-11; 12-10.30 Sun ☎ (01702) 258658

⊕ sdpub.wordpress.com

6 changing beers (sourced locally; often George's) Ⓗ

The Shepherd & Dog reopened in 2015 with new owners, and has since won local CAMRA Country Pub of the Year twice. It is a traditional hostelry with beams throughout and a real fire. It delivers up to six changing real ales – two from the local George's Brewery – and a range of real ciders, including the local Buffoon's. The restaurant serves home-cooked food using local produce. There is seating outside at the front, and a beer garden to the rear. ▷❀◑♣♠P🚃(60)❀

Belchamp Otten

Red Lion 🍺 Ⓛ

Fowes Lane, CO10 7BQ (on very small single track lane, signed by duck pond) TL799415

🕙 12-3, 5.30-11; closed Tue; 12-6 Sun ☎ (01787) 278301

⊕ ottenredlion.co.uk

Adnams Southwold Bitter; 2 changing beers (sourced nationally) Ⓗ

REAL ALE BREWERIES

Billericay 🍺 Billericay
Bishop Nick Braintree
Brentwood Brentwood
Colchester Wakes Colne
Crouch Vale South Woodham Ferrers
Deverell's Grays
Dominion Moreton
Fallen Angel Writtle
Famous Railway Tavern 🍺 Brightlingsea
Felstar Felsted
George's/Hop Monster Great Wakering
Hart of Stebbing 🍺 Stebbing
Harwich Town Harwich
Hope Grays
Maldon 🍺 Maldon
Mersea Island East Mersea
Mighty Oak Maldon
Moody Goose 🍺 Braintree
Mr Majolica Grays
Pumphouse 🍺 Toppesfield
Red Fox Coggeshall
Round Tower Chelmsford
Saffron Henham
Shalford Shalford
Silks Sible Hedingham
Sticklegs Great Bromley
Watson's Colchester (NEW)
White Hart 🍺 Halstead (NEW)
Wibblers Southminster

Oakham. Good-quality, home-made food is available lunchtimes and evenings, with curry night on Wednesday (including Thai and Goan). The bar and food service is efficient and friendly. The walls are adorned with prints and decorative plates, and a collection of jugs and tankards hangs from the ceiling. BT Sport shows rugby and football matches. Q✤❁❶❶&≠♦P🖩(100)❁📶

Railway 🅛
1 High Street, CM12 9BE
🌟 12-11 (midnight Fri & Sat) ☎ (01277) 652173
Wibblers Dengie IPA; Woodforde's Wherry; 3 changing beers (sourced regionally) 🄷
Friendly pub in the heart of the community, adjacent to the railway station. Since taking over, the current licensees have transformed the pub into a thriving local, with an emphasis on real ales – over 500 different beers have been on offer in the past few years, mainly local but often from further afield, such as the West Country. A changing cider is sourced from around the UK. Live music from an extensive range of genres plays twice a month. ➽❁&≠♦P🖩❁📶

Birchanger

Birchanger Sports & Social Club
229 Birchanger Lane, CM23 5QJ
🌟 7-11 Mon & Tue; 12-2.30, 6-11 Wed; 7-11 Thu; 12-11 Fri & Sat; 12-10.30 Sun ☎ (01279) 813441 ⊕ birchangerclub.com
Greene King IPA; 3 changing beers (sourced nationally) 🄷
A friendly local social club where CAMRA members are welcome to drink as guests. Many matches and events are held here so it can get very busy. Beers change frequently as the turnover is high. The club has football, cricket, bowls, darts, crib and snooker teams, regular quizzes plus bingo and bottle draws. It has won CAMRA branch Club of the Year on several occasions. ➽❁❶&♣P🖩(7,7A)📶

Birdbrook

Plough 🅛
The Street, CO9 4BJ
🌟 5-11; 4-midnight Fri; 12-midnight Sat; 12-11 Sun
☎ (01440) 788066
Greene King IPA; 2 changing beers (sourced locally) 🄷
The Plough is the central focus of the village. With very low ceilings, it has been divided into three rooms: a games room, the bar area and a restaurant. The owners have extended the building, adding new toilets at the back that replaced the outside loos. The roof has been rethatched and the pub is once again a flourishing, successful business. ➽❁❶♣P📶

Boreham

Queen's Head
Church Road, CM3 3EG
🌟 3-midnight Mon; 3-10 Tue; 12-midnight
☎ (01245) 467298
Greene King IPA; 5 changing beers (sourced nationally) 🄷
In the same family for over 20 years, this friendly pub, dating from the 16th century, is tucked away behind houses just past the church. It has two contrasting bars, one with bench seating, where darts, dominoes and crib are played, the other for

dining. In the warmer months the garden is a lovely area to sit at one of the picnic benches and enjoy drinks and food in a tranquil setting in sight of the village church. Home-cooked food is served Wednesday to Sunday. ➽❁❶♣P🖩(71,71C)📶

Braintree

King William IV 🅛
114 London Road, CM77 7PU
🌟 3-11; 12-midnight Fri-Sun ☎ (01376) 567755
⊕ kingwilliamiv.co.uk
4 changing beers (sourced nationally) 🄖
Friendly free house, serving a changing range of real ales, usually featuring Essex microbreweries and at least one from the Moody Goose Brewery, located in the grounds of the pub. It also serves an interesting selection of ciders. There is a main bar and a small back bar with a dartboard. A large patio area with picnic tables and extensive gardens are used to host beer festivals and other events. This is a traditional drinking pub that does not offer cooked meals. Q❁♣♦P🖩(70,352)❁📶

Brentwood

Rising Sun 🅛 ✅
144 Ongar Road, CM15 9DJ (on A128, at Western Rd jct)
🌟 3-11.30 (midnight Fri); 12-midnight Sat; 12-10.30 Sun ☎ 07828 738549 ⊕ rising-sun-brentwood.co.uk
Fuller's London Pride; Sharp's Cornish Coaster; Timothy Taylor Landlord; 2 changing beers 🄷
Superb community local with five real ales. A charity quiz is held on Monday evening, there are frequent darts matches in the public bar, and occasional chess evenings. Five handpumps in the saloon bar dispense three regular ales plus two guests, one of which is usually from Brentwood Brewery while the other is from anywhere. Framed prints of the local area decorate the walls. Outside is a covered and heated smokers' area and a patio. ➽❁♣P🖩(21,71)❁

Spread Eagle ✅
88 Queens Road, CM14 4HD (on B186)
🌟 11-11 (midnight Fri & Sat) ☎ (01277) 232485
⊕ spreadeaglebrentwood.co.uk
Adnams Broadside; Fuller's London Pride; Sharp's Doom Bar; 1 changing beer (sourced nationally) 🄷
Much improved and refurbished, this wedge-shaped community pub has a focus on real ale. The menu includes Southern States style barbecue food; the pub has a food smoker. Live music features open mic on Sunday evening and acoustic bands. Events range from charity rock and roll bingo to Elvis nights. There is a courtyard patio. ➽❁❶&⊖♣🖩(498)❁📶

Victoria Arms
50 Ongar Road, CM15 9AX (on A128)
🌟 11-11; 12-10.30 Sun ☎ (01277) 223371
Adnams Broadside; Harvey's IPA, Sussex Best Bitter; 3 changing beers 🄷
Pleasant and comfortable Gray & Sons pub with a friendly atmosphere. Unusually for the area, there are normally two Harvey's beers available, as well as Broadside and three changing beers. There are several TV screens, mostly showing sport, and an outside smoking area. ❁❶P🖩(498)

Brightlingsea

Railway Tavern ⃝L
58 Station Road, CO7 0DT
☼ 4 (5 winter)-10; 3-11 Fri; 12-11 Sat; 12-3, 7-10.30 Sun
⊕ thefamousrailwaytavern.co.uk
Crouch Vale Essex Boys Best Bitter; 2 changing beers (sourced nationally) ⊞
This basic but friendly pub has been a regular feature in the Guide. While it may not be to everyone's taste, it will appeal to the many who like a good pint (often a dark, vegetarian one, brewed on the premises) in a quirky atmosphere. It stages an annual cider and perry festival and live music nights. Children are not allowed. Q ❀ ♠ ♣ ♨ ✿

Broxted

Prince of Wales ⃝L ✔
Brick End, CM6 2BJ
☼ closed Mon; 11.30-11 (midnight Fri & Sat); 12-11 Sun
☎ (01279) 850256 ⊕ princeofwalesbroxted.co.uk
Greene King IPA; 5 changing beers (sourced nationally) ⊞
Former Charrington's pub transformed into a welcoming community venue after the current landlords took over in late 2011. It has a comfortable split-level bar, an adjoining room with two woodburners and a conservatory seating up to 50. Generously portioned pub grub, mostly locally sourced, will satisfy the most demanding appetite. A small garden is to the rear. Up to five guest beers are available, with LocAle from Bishop Nick.
🐕 ❀ ◐ P ☐ (6) ♣ ✿

Bures Hamlet

Eight Bells
6 Colchester Road, CO8 5AE
☼ 12-3, 5-11.30; 12-11 Sat & Sun ☎ (01787) 227354
Greene King Abbot, IPA; 4 changing beers (sourced nationally) ⊞
The four changing beers sourced both nationally and locally include Bishop Nick, Colchester and Nethergate. This pleasant pub in the village has one bar serving three large drinking and dining areas. The landlord has been here 36 years, with a regular local clientele. Traditional pub food is served, including specials and excellent Sunday roasts. One of the drinking areas can be used for functions, and a monthly open mic night is hosted. The pub is popular with walkers. Q ❀ ◐ & ⇌ P ☐

Burnham-on-Crouch

Queen's Head
26 Providence, CM0 8JU
☼ 2 (4 Mon)-11; 12-11 Fri-Sun ☎ (01621) 784825
Dark Star Hophead; Wibblers Dengie IPA; 2 changing beers (sourced nationally; often Green Jack, Harvey's, Mighty Oak) ⊞
A little less than a mile from the railway station is this friendly, welcoming Gray's house. It is tucked away in a narrow side street opposite the clock tower on Burnham's high street. Four cask beers are always on tap, complemented by Westons Old Rosie cider. A wood-fired stove, bare floorboards and an absence of meals make this a true drinkers' pub. There is a pool table and dogs are welcome. Outside, there is a sheltered beer garden.
🐕 ❀ ♣ ♠ ☐ ☐ (31X) ♣ ✿

Chelmsford

Ale House ⃝L
24-26 Viaduct Road, CM1 1TS
☼ 11-11 (midnight Fri & Sat); 12-10.30 Sun
☎ (01245) 260535 ⊕ the-ale-house-chelmsford.co.uk
12 changing beers (sourced nationally) ⊞
In the style of a continental alehouse, this pub is in three railway arches beneath Chelmsford station. There are 12 real ales, with the changing range always including dark and stronger beers, plus 12 real ciders. There are also imported German lagers on tap and a wide range of bottled beers from around the world. No food is served, but customers are welcome to bring their own. Mini beer festivals are held throughout the year. & ⇌ ♠ ☐ ✿

Hop Beer Shop ♟ ⃝L
173 Moulsham Street, CM2 0LD
☼ 12-9; closed Sun & Mon ☎ (01245) 353570
4 changing beers (sourced nationally) ⃝G
Essex's first micropub. Four beers are served by gravity, always including local brews as well as interesting beers from around the country, often a stout, porter and a golden beer. In addition there are around 100 bottled beers from local and international breweries, and bottled cider, which may be drunk here or purchased to take home. The atmosphere is one of a traditional pub where people can meet and talk. Local CAMRA Pub of the Year 2016 and 2017. Q ♠ ☐

Orange Tree ⃝L
6 Lower Anchor Street, CM2 0AS
☼ 12-11 (11.30 Fri & Sat) ☎ (01245) 262664 ⊕ the-ot.com
Dark Star Hophead; Mighty Oak Oscar Wilde; Plain Sheep Dip; 5 changing beers (sourced nationally) ⊞
The Orange Tree is one of the best real ale pubs in Chelmsford and was local CAMRA Pub of the Year in 2015. It is a place for conversation and meeting friends, with separate public and saloon bars. If rugby is your sport, this is the pub for you, as the landlord loves the game. A great range of beers is on tap. Lunchtime food is served, including Sunday roasts, with a steak and curry night on Thursday.
Q 🐕 ❀ ◐ & ♠ P ☐ ♣ ✿

Queen's Head ⃝L
30 Lower Anchor Street, CM2 0AS
☼ 12-11 (11.30 Fri & Sat) ☎ (01245) 265181
⊕ queensheadchelmsford.co.uk
Crouch Vale Brewers Gold, Essex Boys Best Bitter; 5 changing beers (sourced nationally) ⊞
Crouch Vale Brewery's first pub, this venue sells three of its beers permanently, with four guests which may include a Crouch Vale seasonal and always include a dark beer. The Victorian L-shaped pub has bare-board flooring and comfortable bench seating. Two fires make it cosy in winter. This popular local can be busy when there is a match at the nearby county cricket ground. The Essex Beard Club meets here once a year in February.
Q ❀ ◐ ♣ P ☐ ♣ ✿

Railway Tavern ⃝L
63 Duke Street, CM1 1LW
☼ 10-11 (11.30 Fri & Sat); 12-8 Sun ☎ (01245) 280679
Greene King Abbot; Red Fox IPA; Sharp's Special; 5 changing beers (sourced nationally) ⊞
A Tardis-like corner pub right outside Chelmsford station, more visible now due to nearby development. Not surprisingly, a railway theme dominates. A Gray's house, it is long and narrow,

with banks of handpumps at opposite ends of the central bar counter and seating towards the rear. There is even a small garden where you can listen to the station announcements and marvel at the ever-changing mural. It also sells more than 50 gins. May stay open later on Sunday in summer. Q🏠❄️◐⇆♣️🍴🚪😺🎵📶

Woolpack

23 Mildmay Road, CM2 0DN

✪ 12-11 (midnight Fri & Sat) ☎ (01245) 259295

🌐 thewoolpack.wix.com/woolpackchelmsford

Greene King St Edmunds; Hardys & Hansons Bitter; 6 changing beers (sourced nationally) Ⓗ

It is an easy walk from the town centre to this award-winning, friendly, Victorian local. There are three rooms, with a lounge area overlooking the garden. Darts and a pool table are in a smaller room. Pub grub is served, specialising in sausages, with light snacks until 11pm. Beer festivals are at the Easter weekend and the first weekend in September, with up to 80 beers, ciders and perries. Smaller festivals take place at Halloween and in December. Opens 4pm Monday-Thursday September to Easter. 🏠◐♣️🍴🅿️🚪📶

Chignal St James

Three Elms Ⓛ

CM1 4TZ

✪ 12-3 (not Tue), 5-11; 12-midnight Fri-Sun

☎ (01245) 443151 🌐 the-three-elms.com

4 changing beers (sourced nationally) Ⓗ

A traditional village pub with one large bar with exposed beams, a wood-burning fire and a piano. TV, darts and bar billiards are tucked away in an annexe. Outside there is a garden at the rear and benches in front. Essex CAMRA Cider Pub of the Year 2015 and 2016, it offers 16 or more ciders. Food is from local suppliers with home-made pork scratchings, pork pies and Scotch eggs. Beer and cider festivals are held in May, August and October. 🏠◐♣️🍴🅿️😺📶

Chipping Ongar

Cock Tavern Ⓛ

218 High Street, CM5 9AB

✪ 11-11 (midnight Fri & Sat) ☎ (01277) 365261

🌐 thecocktavern.com

Harvey's IPA; 3 changing beers (sourced regionally) Ⓗ

A welcoming traditional pub on the High Street, under new management from February 2016. Local real ales predominate in the selection from the four handpumps. Traditional pub food with pies and sausages is served. Handy for the Epping Ongar railway station. All bus routes stop outside the front door. Live music plays on many Friday and Saturday nights. 🚌🏠◐⇆♣️🍴🚪😺📶

Churchgate Street

Queen's Head

26 Churchgate Street, Old Harlow, CM17 0JT (from bypass follow signs to Old Harlow, then Churchgate St)

✪ 12-11; 12-9.30 Sun ☎ (01279) 427266

🌐 tqhchurchgatest.co.uk

Adnams Southwold Bitter, Ghost Ship; Lacons Encore; Woodforde's Wherry Ⓗ**, Once Bittern** Ⓗ/Ⓖ

Dating back to Tudor times, with wooden beams spanning a spacious interior, the building is

believed to have been a hostelry since 1750. It is in a pleasant village street on the outskirts of Harlow. The smaller side bar has a fire in winter and there is a beach bar and barbecue in the summer. The home-made food is known for its fresh ingredients. There are regular quizzes and special events. Monday is curry night. Q🏠◐◐♣️🅿️🚪(7)😺📶

Clacton-on-Sea

Moon & Starfish ✅

1 Marine Parade East, CO15 1PT

✪ 8am-11.30pm (1am Fri & Sat) ☎ (01255) 222998

Greene King Abbot; Ruddles Best Bitter; Sharp's Doom Bar; 6 changing beers (sourced nationally) Ⓗ

This pub occupies part of the ground floor of the Old Royal Hotel and has been a regular in the Guide since 2014. It is opposite Clacton's historic pier and Pavilion Fun Park, and the outside area offers excellent views of the Clacton Airshow and the Clacton carnival street procession. In common with other Wetherspoon pubs it holds two beer festivals and one cider festival each year. Food is available daily. Q🌞🏠◐◐♿⇆🍴🚪📶

Old Lifeboat House

39 Marine Parade East, CO15 6AD

✪ 12-10 ☎ (01255) 476799

5 changing beers (sourced nationally; often Colchester, Greene King, St Austell) Ⓗ

A regular in this Guide since 2011 and local CAMRA Cider Pub of the Year in 2015, the pub is popular with local CAMRA members and visiting darts teams. Four different meals are available on Wednesday, when real ales are discounted by 50p. The pub is home to four darts teams – two play on Monday and two on Thursday, when it can be busy. The patio offers good views of the Clacton Airshow and carnival procession. 🏠◐⇆♣️🍴🅿️🚻🚪📶

Clavering

Fox & Hounds ✅

High Street, CB11 4QR

✪ 4-11 (midnight Fri); 12-midnight Sat; 12-11 Sun

☎ (01799) 550321

Adnams Ghost Ship; Woodforde's Wherry; 1 changing beer (sourced nationally) Ⓗ

A local drinkers' pub, the oldest licensed premises remaining in Clavering. Set in the middle of the village close to the River Stort, it is a good place to start walks from. It runs events supporting the local school and charities, with a regular quiz on the second and fourth Tuesdays of the month. Excellent home-cooked and locally sourced pub meals are served including a Sunday roast. There is a large car park. 🌞🏠◐♣️🅿️😺📶

Colchester

Ale House Ⓛ

82 Butt Road, CO3 3DA

✪ 3-11; 12-midnight Fri; 12-11 Sat; 12-9.30 Sun

☎ (01206) 573464 🌐 thealehousecolchester.co.uk

10 changing beers (sourced nationally) Ⓗ

Free house with a very friendly landlady and staff. This award-winning pub offers a wide range of ales, always including at least one dark beer, served from handpump and on gravity. Quiz night is every third Wednesday, and a folk music session is usually held on the fourth Tuesday of the month. Darts, bar billiards and BT Sport are available. There

is a large, secluded walled garden at the rear and a public car park nearby in Roman Circus Walk.
🐝🍺♣👤🖵(64)🐾📶

Bricklayers
27 Bergholt Road, CO4 5AA
🕑 11-3, 5.30-11; 11-midnight Fri; 11-11 Sat; 12-7 Sun
☎ (01206) 852008
Adnams Broadside, Southwold Bitter; 7 changing beers (sourced nationally) 🅗
Large Adnams flagship pub close to the station, with up to eight ales from the brewery's regular and seasonal range, as well as a variety of guests. Up to six ciders, including Crone's, are always on. It has a traditional public bar with darts and pool, and a lounge bar with a conservatory. The large beer garden has cycle racks. Excellent home-cooked food is available lunchtimes (no food Sat), with a great-value roast on Sunday.
Q🐝🕮🍺(North)♣👤🖵📶

Britannia Gurkha Restaurant & Bar 🅛
42 Meyrick Crescent, CO2 7QY
🕑 3.30-11; 2-1am Fri; 12-11 Sat & Sun ☎ (01206) 761003
Colchester No.1, Metropolis; 2 changing beers (sourced nationally) 🅗
Large corner pub and restaurant, owned and run by a Gurkha family. The bar has lots of Gurkha memorabilia. There is a large-screen TV for major sports and a display of clocks showing times in various cities. Pool and darts are at the far end of the bar, where dogs are allowed. The separate restaurant serves delicious home-cooked Nepalese cuisine 6-9pm evenings except Tuesday (booking is recommended). Takeaways are also available.
🛏🕮♦♿♣👤P🖵🐾📶

British Grenadier 🅛
67 Military Road, CO1 2AP
🕑 5-11.45; 2-midnight Fri; 12-midnight Sat; 12-3, 7-11.45 Sun ☎ 07832 215118
4 changing beers (sourced nationally) 🅗
A welcoming local with a knowledgeable publican, which has featured in the Guide for over 10 years. A Victorian two-bar pub, it has a pool table in the small rear bar and a dartboard in the main bar, heated by an open fire in the winter months. This former Adnams tied house offers local ale and real cider, serving a changing range of local, regional and nationally sourced beers and ciders via handpump. 🐝♿🍺♣👤🖵🐾📶

Fat Cat
65 Butt Road, CO3 3BZ (near police station)
🕑 12-11 (midnight Fri); 11-midnight Sat ☎ (01206) 577990
🌐 fatcatcolchester.co.uk
Crouch Vale Yakima Gold; Fat Cat Honey Ale; Hop Back Summer Lightning; Woodforde's Wherry; 9 changing beers (sourced nationally) 🅖
Popular single-bar split-level pub, just outside the town centre. Its main feature is a taproom from which all ales are dispensed on gravity. Do not miss out on the full programme of events, including three beer festivals a year, brewery trips, crib nights, Sunday quiz night and Sunday real ale club 3-7pm. It is the ideal place for pre-match drinks before Colchester United home games, as a bus departs from the pub directly to the stadium.
🐝🕮🍺👤🖵(64,63)🐾📶

Live & Let Live 🅛
12 Millers Lane, CO3 0PS (in small lane less than 100yds from London Rd, Stanway, W of Colchester)
🕑 12-11 (midnight Fri & Sat) ☎ (01206) 574071
5 changing beers (sourced nationally) 🅗
The Live's reputation continues to grow thanks to the publicans' great pride in the condition of their real ales and their sausage/pie festivals. Family and dog friendly, it is very welcoming, appealing to a broad demographic with a quiet, homely saloon bar and a public bar offering sports TV, darts, pool and a comprehensive jukebox, as well as a beer garden. Beers are very competitively priced, as is traditional home-cooked food, served lunchtimes each day and Friday and Saturday evenings.
🛏🕮♦♿♣👤P🖵(65,70)🐾📶

New Inn 🍽 🅛
36 Chapel Street South, CO2 7AX
🕑 12-11 (midnight Fri & Sat) ☎ (01206) 575277
🌐 theoldnewinnpub.co.uk
Bishop Nick Ridley's Rite; 5 changing beers (sourced nationally) 🅗
Local CAMRA Pub of the Year 2017, offering up to six real ales and four real ciders. In this community hub with two bars and garden the saloon bar focuses on comfort and relaxation, with the public bar having music, TV sports and plenty of friendly conversation. Contemporary bar food is served until 9pm Monday-Saturday, and Sunday roasts 12-5pm. Brewery tap takeovers are regular events. Well-behaved children and dogs are welcome and a plethora of pub games is on offer.
Q🛏🕮🕮♦♿🍺(Town)♣👤P🖵(64)🐾📶

Odd One Out 🅛
28 Mersea Road, CO2 7ET
🕑 4.30-11; 12-11 Fri & Sat; 12-10.30 Sun ☎ (01206) 513958
7 changing beers (sourced nationally) 🅗
Classic pub in the Guide for a 30th year. It offers up to seven guest ales on handpump, often from local breweries, including at least one dark beer. Up to five real ciders are dispensed from the barrel and it is current local CAMRA Cider Pub of the Year. Over 50 malt whiskies are also stocked. It has two welcoming open fires. A back bar function room is available for hire and local Peldon honey is sold.
Q🐝🍺(Town)👤🖵🐾

Victoria Inn 🅛
10 North Station Road, CO1 1RB
🕑 12-11 (midnight Fri & Sat); 2-11 Sun ☎ (01206) 514510
🌐 victoriainncolchester.co.uk
5 changing beers (sourced nationally) 🅗
A proper pub serving five real ales including a house beer, Yorkshire Embassy Blonde, specified by the publicans and brewed by Colchester Brewery. Nine real ciders and a selection of bottled beers are also available. Live music is on Sunday, often accompanied by Yorkshire puddings and roast tatties. It hosts a monthly cheese club, wine clubs and a coffee morning. There is a courtyard garden with turfed outbuildings. Two annual themed beer festivals are held. A four-times local CAMRA Pub of the Year, and a previous county and regional winner. 🐝🍺(North)♣👤🖵🐾📶

Colne Engaine

Five Bells
Mill Lane, CO6 2HY
🕑 12-11 ☎ (01787) 224166 🌐 fivebells.net

Adnams Southwold Bitter; 4 changing beers (sourced nationally) ⊞
A welcome return to the Guide for this 16th-century free house which retains many of its original features. The pub has been transformed by its owners and has several small drinking and dining areas as well as a separate restaurant, where food is a cut above many traditional British pubs. There are lovely views across the Colne Valley both from inside the pub and the alfresco drinking area. Occasional beer festivals are held, and regular live music events. Q☆☜♔◑⑅♿P🖵🐾💷❄

Copford Green

Alma 🄻 🆓
School Road, CO6 1BZ (signed from London Rd, Copford)
🕐 12-3, 5-11; 12-midnight Fri & Sat; 12-11 Sun
☎ (01206) 210607 🌐 thealma.org.uk
Greene King IPA; Red Fox Hunter's Gold; 3 changing beers (sourced nationally) ⊞
In the Guide for the seventh consecutive year, this 16th-century pub is once again an award winner in the local CAMRA Rural Pub of the Year. It has old-world village charm, with an open fire, combined with Sky and BT sport, darts and pool table. Quiz night is the first Thursday of the month and it hosts occasional music nights. A beer festival each May showcases over 20 different ales. Lunchtime and evening meals are served daily, with a menu and specials board, plus roast dinners on Sunday.
Q☆☜♔◑⑅♿♣P🐾❄

Cornish Hall End

Horse & Groom 🄻 🆓
CM7 4HF (on B1057) TL683366
🕐 closed Mon, 12-11 ☎ (01799) 586306
🌐 thehorseandgroom.org
Greene King IPA; 4 changing beers (sourced nationally) ⊞
A pleasantly refurbished and redecorated village pub opposite the parish church, with a restaurant and garden. A warm and friendly venue, it is the social centre of this village, supporting many charities and hosting beer festivals and events. The pub offers frequently changing beers and good food including special lunches, carveries and regular fish and chips nights. These can be popular, so may need booking ahead. Q☆☜♔◑P🐾❄

Coxtie Green

White Horse 🄻
173 Coxtie Green Road, CM14 5PX (1 mile W of A128, at jct with Mores Lane) TQ564959
🕐 11.30-11 (midnight Fri & Sat); 12-11 Sun
☎ (01277) 372410 🌐 whitehorsebrentwood.co.uk
Fuller's London Pride; Greene King Abbot, IPA Reserve; house beer (by Brentwood); 6 changing beers ⊞
Pleasant country free house with an extended comfortable saloon bar. The 10 handpumps normally dispense four regular beers and six guests, of which two are usually from Brentwood Brewery and the rest are from anywhere. The pub is badged as the Brentwood Brewery tap. Beer festivals are held in the large garden at the end of May and in October. There is a large children's play area in the garden to keep them happy. The local bus service is limited, but reliable.
Q☆☜♔◑⑅♿♣P🖵(71,72)🐾❄

Debden

Plough 🄻
High Street, CB11 3LE
🕐 12-3 (not Tue), 5-11; 12-midnight Fri & Sat; 12-10 Sun; closed Mon ☎ (01799) 541899
Greene King IPA; 3 changing beers (sourced locally) ⊞
The sole remaining village pub, now revitalised, with a restaurant and garden. It is a warm and friendly place with an extensive food menu and an interesting and varied range of local beers. The pub runs beer festivals, events and other local celebrations. It is now a very important social centre for this village and the surrounding area, as well as a good base for walkers and cyclists. A monthly quiz night is normally held on the third Wednesday. Q☆☜♔◑P🖵(6,313)

Duton Hill

Three Horseshoes 🄻
CM6 2DX (1 mile W of B184) TL606268
🕐 12-2.30 (not Mon-Thu), 6-11; 12-3, 6-11 Sat; 12-3, 7-10.30 Sun ☎ (01371) 870681
Mighty Oak Maldon Gold; 2 changing beers (sourced nationally) ⊞
Outstanding village local with a garden, wildlife pond and terrace overlooking the Chelmer Valley and farmland. The landlord often hosts a weekend of open-air theatre in July. A Millennium beacon in the garden, breweriana and a remarkable collection of Butlin's memorabilia are pub features. A beer festival is held on the late spring bank holiday in the Duton Hill Den. Look for the pub sign depicting a famous painting, Our Blacksmith, by a former local resident, Sir George Clausen. Local and parish newspapers are available.
☜♔⑅♣P🖵(313)🐾

Epping

Forest Gate Inn
111 Bell Common, CM16 4DZ (S of town turn off main road opp Bell Motel, then 500yds on bend)
🕐 10-3, 5-11; 10-11 Sat; 12-8 Sun ☎ (01992) 572312
Adnams Southwold Bitter, Broadside; Bishop Nick Ridley's Rite ⊞; 2 changing beers ⊞
On the edge of Epping Forest, the pub dates back to the 17th century, with low ceilings and flag floors. Run by the same family for 50 years, it is popular with locals, walkers and their dogs. Hot pub meals and soups are served in the bar, as well as in Haywards Restaurant next door, with a B&B. There is a large grassed seating area. The pub is around a mile from the town centre and Underground station. Q☆☜♔◥◑⑅♿P🖵(213,541)🐾❄

Fuller Street

Square & Compasses
CM3 2BB TL748161
🕐 11.30-11; 12-midnight Sat; 12-11 Sun ☎ (01245) 361477
🌐 thesquareandcompasses.co.uk
3 changing beers (sourced nationally) 🄶
A 17th-century free house, known locally as the Stokehole. In attractive countryside and handy for the Essex Way long distance footpath, this is a small well looked after country pub. There are exposed beams throughout, with two wood-burning stoves in inglenook fireplaces. Old local woodworking tools adorn the taproom bar. Up to

three real ales and local Berties cider are served. Fresh locally sourced home-cooked food is available daily, including game from the surrounding estates (no food Sun eve). ⚜◑&♣P❀

Goldhanger

Chequers
Church Street, CM9 8AS
☼ 11-11; 12-10.30 Sun ☎ (01621) 788203
⊕ thechequersgoldhanger.co.uk
Adnams Ghost Ship; Crouch Vale Brewers Gold; St Austell Proper Job; Sharp's Atlantic; Woodforde's Wherry; 1 changing beer (sourced nationally) ⓗ
A charming 15th-century inn in an attractive village, including a snug and games room with bar billiards. The changing beer could well be a stout or a porter. Additionally, up to five real ciders are usually available. An extensive menu offers superb quality meals made with local produce. The courtyard is a real suntrap in summer and real fires in two of the bars provide warmth in winter. Extensive walks are to be enjoyed on the nearby Blackwater Estuary. Q☼⚜◑♣♣P➡(95)❀⧖

Grays

Theobald Arms
141 Argent Street, RM17 6HR (about 7 mins on foot from Grays rail and bus stations, down Kings Walk)
☼ 11-11 (midnight Fri & Sat); 12-11 Sun ☎ (01375) 372253
4 changing beers ⓗ
Genuine, traditional pub with a public bar that has an unusual hexagonal pool table. The changing selection of four guest beers features local independent breweries, and a range of British bottled beers is also stocked. Regular St George's weekend and summer beer festivals are held in the old stables and on the rear enclosed patio. Lunchtime meals are served Monday to Friday. Darts and cards are played. Local CAMRA Pub of the Year 2016. ⚜◑&≈♣P➡

White Hart ⬥ 🇱
Kings Walk, RM17 6HR (about 7 mins on foot from Grays rail and bus stations down Kings Walk)
☼ 12-11.30 (midnight Fri & Sat); 12-11 Sun
☎ (01375) 373319 ⊕ whitehartgrays.co.uk
Crouch Vale Brewers Gold; 4 changing beers ⓗ
Traditional local just outside the town centre, rejuvenated since it was taken over in 2006. The regular beer is supplemented by four guests (one usually dark) and a selection of over 30 bottled Belgian beers. Good-value meals can be had weekday lunchtimes. There is a meeting/function room and a large secluded beer garden. Live music plays on Saturday. The pub supports pool and darts teams, and sport is screened on TV. Local CAMRA Pub of the Year 2015 and 2017. ⚜🚗◑&≈♣P➡❀⧖

Great Dunmow

Boar's Head ✓
37 High Street, CM6 1AB
☼ 11-11 (1am Fri & Sat); 12-11 Sun ☎ (01371) 873630
Adnams Southwold Bitter; Fuller's London Pride; 1 changing beer (sourced nationally) ⓗ
Traditional town centre pub, dating back 400 years, also accessible from the main public car park. This is a timber-framed lath and plaster building with

beamed low ceilings and three large-screen TVs for sport. Live music is performed on Saturday evenings except in some winter months. A large decking area at the rear includes covered seating for smokers. No food is served, so you can enjoy visiting here for social drinking. ⚜P➡(42A,133)⧖

Great Oakley

Maybush Inn
Farm Road, CO12 5AL
☼ 12-11 (1am Fri & Sat); 12-10.30 Sun ☎ (01255) 880123
⊕ maybushinn.co.uk
Wells Bombardier; 3 changing beers (sourced nationally) ⓗ
Dating back to the 18th century, this is Tendring's first (and the UK's 40th) community co-operative pub. It reopened in February 2016 after the locals came together to save the last pub in their village. This two-roomed venue is currently staffed entirely by volunteers, who aim to ensure a warm welcome for all, and its appearance in the Guide for the first time is a testament to their commitment. Q☼♣♣P➡❀⧖

Great Totham

Compasses ⬥ ✓
12 Colchester Road, CM9 8BZ (on B1022)
☼ 5-11 Mon; 12-midnight; 12-8.30 Sun ☎ (01621) 332587
⊕ tothamcompasses.com
Theakston Old Peculier; Wibblers Apprentice ⓗ; 6 changing beers (sourced locally; often Colchester, Crouch Vale, Red Fox) ⓗ/ⓖ
Friendly 16th-century village pub, with a fine reputation for its wide range of local ales and numerous traditional ciders. There is an open fire, cosy armchairs and an old-fashioned feel to the public bar. Good food is served lunchtimes and evenings (no food Mon). The Sunday roast is a speciality – booking is essential. There is a restaurant and a small meeting room. CAMRA Essex Pub of the Year for 2016 and branch Pub of the Year for 2016 and 2017. ⚜◑♣♣P➡(75,505)❀⧖

Halstead

Dog Inn
37 Hedingham Road, CO9 2DB (on A1124)
☼ 4-11.30; 12-midnight Sat; 12-10.30 Sun
☎ (01787) 477774 ⊕ doginnhalstead.co.uk
4 changing beers (sourced nationally) ⓗ
Traditional welcoming inn, close to the small market town centre. The Dog makes a welcome return to the Guide under new management, with up to four ales on handpump in the two cosy bars, one with a TV, plus a large beer garden to the rear with fine views over the valley. Live music takes place two Saturdays a month, plus folk music on the first Sunday afternoon each month. B&B is available and beer festivals are planned for the future. Q☼⚜🚗➡(88)❀⧖

Harwich

Alma Inn 🇱 ✓
25 Kings Head Street, CO12 3EE
☼ 12-11 (midnight Fri & Sat) ☎ (01255) 318681
⊕ almaharwich.co.uk
Adnams Southwold Bitter, Broadside; 4 changing beers (sourced regionally) ⓗ

A mark two feet up the wall shows the height of the January 1953 floods – just one part of the history this unspoilt 16th-century building has seen. Food is available daily. The two regular ales are from Adnams, while the other four come from East Anglia. Whenever possible the two real ciders are from Herefordshire as they remind the landlord, Nick, of home. Local CAMRA Pub of the Year 2016. ⏣☺☕⏴◖⇌●🖳☻🛱

Hanover Inn
65 Church Street, CO12 3DR
⏣ 12-11 (12.30am Fri & Sat); 11.30-11 Sun
☎ (01255) 502927 ⊕ hanoverinn.co.uk
Green Jack Trawlerboys Best Bitter; 2 changing beers (sourced nationally) Ⓗ
This buzzing community pub is in the heart of Old Harwich next to the church. New owners moved in during 2016 and have sympathetically put their own stamp on the place. The cosy front bar is a place of conversation while the back bar adjoins the dining area, and a function room upstairs can be hired for events. Hearty, traditional food is served lunchtimes and evenings and one regular and two guest real ales complete the compelling line-up. ◖⏴☕♣●🖳☻🛱

New Bell Inn
Outpart Eastward, CO12 3EN
⏣ 11-3, 7-midnight; 11-midnight Fri & Sat; 12-midnight Sun
☎ (01255) 503545 ⊕ thenewbell.co.uk
Greene King IPA; Mighty Oak Oscar Wilde; 2 changing beers (sourced regionally) Ⓗ
After changing hands in 2015, the new owners have managed to maintain the pub's reputation as a destination for real ale drinkers. There are no evening meals, but cutlery and crockery are provided for takeaways from the local outlets. Two real ciders are normally available and are often chosen for the pub by one of their cider-drinking regulars – though be warned, they tend to be on the strong side, such as Black Dragon at 7% ABV. Q⏣☺◖⇌♣●P🖳☻🛱

Hatfield Broad Oak

Cock Inn
High Street, CM22 7HF
⏣ 12-11 (midnight Fri & Sat); 12-10.30 Sun
☎ (01279) 718306 ⊕ thecockinn-hatfieldbroadoak.co.uk
Adnams Southwold Bitter; Wells Bombardier; 1 changing beer (sourced regionally) Ⓗ
A Grade II-listed 16th-century coaching inn in the centre of an historic village and close to Hatfield Forest. Food is freshly made from local ingredients and served in one of the four areas, the others being the bar, the TV and darts room, and a quiet room known as the Taps Bar. The pub is close to Stansted Airport. Bus 5 runs from outside, direct to the airport until late. Q⏣◖P🖳(5)🛱

Hazel End

Three Horseshoes
CM23 1HB
⏣ 12-3, 6-11; 12-3 Sun ☎ (01279) 813429
⊕ threehorseshoeshazelend.co.uk
Adnams Southwold Bitter; Sharp's Doom Bar; 1 changing beer (sourced nationally) Ⓗ
A friendly pub, opposite the cricket green at Hazel End. This pub has been completely renovated and serves an impressive fish menu. A large extension

added after renovation has created more space to both eat and drink here comfortably. This is a good example of a once run-down premises being transformed into a thriving, successful pub. It has low ceilings, black wooden beams and two wood-burning stoves. ⏣☺◖⏴Å P☻

Herongate Tye

Olde Dog Inn Ⓛ
129 Billericay Road, CM13 3SD (E of A128) TQ641909
⏣ 11.30-11; 12-11 Sat; 12-9 Sun ☎ (01277) 810337
⊕ theolddoginn.co.uk
Crouch Vale Brewers Gold; Greene King Abbot Ⓗ; 3 changing beers Ⓖ
This 17th-century weatherboarded inn is a family-owned and run free house with traditional decor, offering a variety of real ales, with three different guest beers from microbreweries countrywide, along with more established national brands and its own Olde Dog IPA, brewed locally. A traditional cider is also available. Food is served at the bar, or in its separate restaurant area lunchtimes and evenings. Fish and chips is available as a takeaway. Dogs are welcome in the area at the end of the bar known as the Dog House. ☺◖☕●P☻🛱

Horndon-on-the-Hill

Bell Inn
High Road, SS17 8LD
⏣ 11-11; 12-10.30 Sun ☎ (01375) 642463 ⊕ bell-inn.co.uk
Crouch Vale Brewers Gold; Greene King IPA; Sharp's Doom Bar; 2 changing beers Ⓗ
Popular 15th-century coaching inn, where beamed bars feature wood panelling and carvings. Run by the same family since 1938, note the hot cross bun collection; a bun has been added every Good Friday for more than 100 years. Three regular beers plus two guests are on tap, including ales from Essex breweries. The award-winning restaurant is open daily, lunchtimes and evenings. Booking is advisable. Gourmet nights are held. Accommodation is available in 27 bedrooms. Q☺🛏◖⏴☕P🖳(265)☻🛱

Langley Lower Green

Bull
Park Lane, CB11 4SB TL437345
⏣ 5-11; 12-2, 4-11 Fri; 12-11 Sat & Sun ☎ (01279) 777307
Adnams Mosaic; Greene King IPA; 2 changing beers (sourced regionally) Ⓗ
Classic Victorian village local with original cast-iron lattice windows. Set in a tiny isolated hamlet close to both Hertfordshire and Cambridgeshire, the pub has a band of loyal local regulars. There is an aquarium in the lounge bar. An open mic night is held on the last Tuesday of the month and occasional quiz nights are hosted. An annual beer festival takes place in September. ⏣☺◖♣P☻🛱

Layer Breton

Hare & Hounds
Crayes Green, CO2 0PN
⏣ 9am-midnight (1am Fri & Sat); 9am-11 Sun
☎ (01206) 330459 ⊕ thehareandhound.co.uk
Greene King IPA; Sharp's Doom Bar; 3 changing beers (sourced nationally) Ⓗ
Friendly village community pub with a comfortable bar and welcoming real fire. The separate spacious

dining area serves a good range of quality home-cooked food. It hosts three beer festivals a year including a popular one on St George's Day. Quiz night is the first Wednesday of the month and Thursday is steak night. Occasional themed evenings include live music. The pub hosts a post office on Tuesday morning and Thursday afternoon. ▷❀✉◖❹☘✦●P🖵(92)🐾❄

Leigh-on-Sea

Crooked Billet ✅
51 High Street, SS9 2EP (nr Leigh station)
✪ 12-11 (11.30 Fri); 11-10.30 Sun ☎ (01702) 480289
Adnams Southwold Bitter; St Austell Nicholson's Pale Ale; Sharp's Doom Bar; 3 changing beers (sourced regionally) Ⓗ
In Old Leigh fishing village overlooking the Thames Estuary, this 16th-century pub has two small bars with bare floorboards and beamed ceilings. The walls are decorated with local village and fishing pictures. It has a small garden to one side and a larger seating area to the front which is shared with a seafood merchant. It offers up to six real ales, with three regulars and three guests from the Nicholson's guest list. ▷❀◖●�templP🖵(21,26)❄

Mayflower
5-6 High Street, Old Leigh, SS9 2EN
✪ 11-11 (midnight Fri & Sat); 12-11 Sun ☎ (01702) 478535
● mayfloweroldleigh.com
Crouch Vale Brewers Gold; George's Cockleboats; St Austell Proper Job; house beer (by George's); 2 changing beers (sourced regionally) Ⓗ
LocAle is available from both George's and Crouch Vale – the house beer is Bell End Bitter from George's. A dark beer should always be on tap. Food is mainly fish dishes from the attached restaurant. There is an outdoor terrace with views across the Thames Estuary. One wall depicts the Pilgrim Fathers passenger manifest of those who sailed on the Mayflower. Local CAMRA Pub of the Year 2014-2016. ▷❀◖●➕●P🖵(26)🐾❄

Little Thurrock

Traitors' Gate Ⓛ
40-42 Broadway, RM17 6EW (on A126)
✪ 12-11 (midnight Fri-Sun)
Greene King Abbot; 5 changing beers (sourced locally) Ⓗ
Since being taken over in Autumn 2013, this pub has become the tap for Deverell's Brewery. Six handpumps offer a rotating selection of Deverell's beers, plus other guest beers, with an emphasis on Essex breweries. Look out for the chalkboards above the bar listing current and forthcoming beers. Live music is played on alternate Thursdays, with live bands most Fridays and Saturdays. ▷❀☘❹🖵(22A,66)🐾❄

Little Waltham

White Hart Ⓛ
107 The Street, CM3 3NY
✪ 9am-11 (11.30 Fri & Sat); 9am-10.30 Sun
☎ (01245) 360205 ● whitehartessex.co.uk
4 changing beers (sourced nationally) Ⓗ
This village pub has had a revival as a popular gastro-pub, but those who just want a drink are welcome. Grade II listed, the outside has been attractively refurbished while inside a complete

renovation has created a modern, light and airy interior. Two areas are reserved for those having meals but the bar area is for drinkers. Five handpumps normally supply four beers and one cider, including at least one beer from Adnams and two from local breweries. Meals start at 9am for breakfast. Q▷❀◖❹☘●P🖵(70,352)🐾❄

Littley Green

Compasses Ⓛ
CM3 1BU
✪ 12-3, 5.30-11.30 Mon-Wed; 12-11.30 ☎ (01245) 362308
● compasseslittleygreen.co.uk
Bishop Nick Ridley's Rite; Crouch Vale Essex Boys Best Bitter; 3 changing beers (sourced nationally) Ⓖ
Formerly Ridley's Brewery tap, this is a picturesque Victorian country pub in a quiet hamlet. A wood-panelled bar has benches around the walls and a tiled floor. Beers are drawn directly from casks in the half-cellar. It has an interesting range of three ciders and a perry. Renowned filled huffers (giant baps) are served lunchtimes and evenings, plus other traditional dishes. There are seats and tables outside and in the large gardens. Regular beer festivals are held. Five high-quality rooms are available. Q▷❀✉◖❹☘●P🛏🐾❄

Maldon

Carpenters' Arms
33 Gate Street, CM9 5QF
✪ 11-11 ☎ (01621) 859896 ● carpentersarmsmaldon.com
Adnams Southwold Bitter; Crouch Vale Yakima Gold; 4 changing beers (sourced nationally; often Green Jack, Red Fox, Wibblers) Ⓗ
An historic, welcoming, back-street community local just yards from Maldon's bustling high street. Awarded CAMRA branch Cider Pub of the Year in 2017 for the third year running, it usually offers six real ciders, including a house cider produced at its own orchard in Normandy. A good selection of beer styles is always available to cater for all tastes. Home-baked pies, pasties and baguettes are served lunchtimes. The pub hosts darts and dominoes teams and a local golf society. ▷❀☘❹●🐾❄

Farmers Yard
140 High Street, CM9 5BX
✪ 12 (5 Mon)-10 ☎ (01621) 854202
● maldonmicropub.co.uk
4 changing beers (sourced locally) Ⓖ
This 400-year-old Grade-II listed building is home to Maldon's first micropub and bottle shop. The small public room measures just 12 feet square, with seating for a dozen people and a similar number of standing places. Conversation flows easily in the convivial, welcoming atmosphere. The complete range of Maldon Brewing Company's bottled ales is complemented by Belgian ales. Three real ciders and English mead are also available. Q▷●🖵🐾

Mighty Oak Tap Room
10 High Street, CM9 5PJ
✪ 5-10 Mon; 12-10 Tue & Wed; 12-11 Thu-Sat; 12-10 Sun
☎ (01621) 853892 ● micropubmaldon.uk
Mighty Oak Oscar Wilde, Captain Bob, Maldon Gold, Kings; 2 changing beers (sourced locally) Ⓖ
A 500-year-old beamed taproom for the Mighty Oak Brewery, showcasing its award-winning range

of beers, served direct from the cask from a cooled ground-floor cellar. The friendly atmosphere in the downstairs bar encourages conversation – there are no fruit machines, TVs or piped music. There is a quiet and relaxing reading room upstairs, furnished with comfortable sofas. Cheeseboards and locally produced pork pies are on offer. Live acoustic music sessions feature most Sundays. Q🛇🕗🍴♣🍲🚃🐾🛜

Manningtree

Red Lion
42 South Street, CO11 1BG
🕗 12-11 (midnight Fri & Sat) ☎ (01206) 391880
🌐 redlionmanningtree.co.uk
Adnams Southwold Bitter; 2 changing beers (sourced nationally; often Colchester, Maldon, Nethergate) Ⓗ
The oldest pub in Manningtree, now refurbished and extended, and appearing in the Guide for the fourth consecutive year. There are particularly unusual furnishings in the Gents toilets. Food is not available, but crockery and cutlery are provided for food from local takeaways (menus provided). Runner-up in the Observer food monthly awards Place To Drink for four years running. The large function room upstairs is often a venue for live music and other events. 🛇🕗♣🍲🚃🐾🛜

Margaretting Tye

White Hart Inn Ⓛ ✅
The Tye, CM4 9JX
🕗 11.30-3 (2.30 Mon), 6-11; 11.30-midnight Sat; 12-midnight Sun ☎ (01277) 840478 🌐 thewhitehart.uk.com
Adnams Southwold Bitter, Broadside; Mighty Oak Oscar Wilde, IPA Ⓗ; 2 changing beers (sourced nationally) Ⓖ
Slightly off the beaten track, this fine pub has its origins in the 17th century. Known for good traditional home-cooked food and quality ale, it generally offers at least two guest beers on gravity. Regular club meetings are held here for cyclists, car owners, ramblers and the Young Farmers. Very much community focused, a book stall raises money for charities, and a beer festival is held in July. Children are welcome in the conservatory or in the large garden. Accommodation is also available. Q🛇🕗🍴🅿🐾🛜

Monk Street

Farmhouse Inn Ⓛ
Thaxted, CM6 2NR (off B184) TL614288
🕗 11-11 (midnight Fri & Sat); 11-10 Sun & Mon
☎ (01371) 830864 🌐 farmhouseinn.org
Greene King IPA; 2 changing beers (sourced locally) Ⓗ
Built in the 16th century, this former Dunmow Brewery pub has been enlarged to incorporate a restaurant and accommodation; the bar is in the original part of the building. The quiet hamlet here overlooks the Chelmer Valley, two miles south of historic Thaxted. A disused well in the garden supplied the hamlet with water during World War II. The pub has a rear patio, front garden and a top field. Draught cider from Westons is usually sold. 🛇🕗🍴🅿🖦(313)🐾🛜

Mount Bures

Thatchers Arms Ⓛ ✅
Hall Road, CO8 5AT TL905318

🕗 closed Mon; 12-11; 12-9 Sun ☎ (01787) 227460
🌐 thatchersarms.co.uk
Adnams Southwold Bitter; Crouch Vale Brewers Gold; Red Fox Black Fox Porter; 2 changing beers (sourced nationally) Ⓗ
A family and dog friendly country pub on the Essex/Suffolk border, with exceptional views across the Stour Valley. A former CAMRA Pub of the Year, it offers up to five real ales and bottled beers. Excellent locally sourced and home-made food, made on the premises, is served daily. The Thatchers also boasts a bar billiards table, a piano and a cinema. It is approximately two miles from the East Anglian Railway Museum at Chappel & Wakes Colne branch line station. Q🛇🕗🍴♣🅿🐾🛜

Newport

White Horse Inn
Belmont Hill, CB11 3RF (on B1383)
🕗 12-11.30 (1am Fri & Sat) ☎ (01799) 540002
3 changing beers (sourced nationally) Ⓗ
On the main road in the middle of Newport, this is a friendly drinkers' local, serving three changing ales. It is an ex-Greene King house, transformed into a pub focused on the community, having been purchased by a local business. Extensive repair work has been done to the building, and the change of ownership, with a new real ale enthusiast licensee, has raised its popularity as a beer drinkers' pub. Meals are served Tuesday and Thursday evenings only. 🍴🚃♣🖦(301)🐾🛜

Old Harlow

Crown Ⓛ ✅
40 Market Street, CM17 0AQ
🕗 12-11 (midnight Fri & Sat); 12-10.30 Sun
☎ (01279) 301380
Greene King IPA, Abbot; 4 changing beers (sourced locally; often Greene King) Ⓗ
A 16th-century coaching inn, the pub has many original beams and an 18th-century floral wall painting preserved in the small side room. The large garden with a bar is popular in summer and the pub is a favourite meeting place for a varied clientele. Home-cooked food and snacks are served lunchtimes. The tenants pride themselves on having no TV, and host occasional acoustic afternoons. It is a short walk from Harlow Mill railway station. Three non-Greene King beers are normally on tap. 🕗♿🚃(Harlow Mill)🖦🐾🛜

Paglesham

Plough & Sail Ⓛ
East End, SS4 2EQ (5 miles E of Rochford) TQ943923
🕗 12-3, 6-11; 12-10.30 Sat & Sun ☎ (01702) 258242
🌐 theploughandsail.co.uk
George's Wallasea Wench; Mighty Oak Maldon Gold; 1 changing beer Ⓗ
A traditional pub a short walk from the River Roach, and an inn for over 300 years, with an aviary in the garden, real fires, fine ales, and a warm welcome. You are not just in good hands at the bar, you will be treated like royalty! In 1890, over 30 oyster smacks were based in Paglesham, and the pub became a meeting place for the hardworking crews. The home-cooked food is popular, so the restaurant is often busy. 🕗🍴🅿

Purleigh

Bell

The Street, CM3 6QJ

🌐 closed Mon; 11.30-3, 6-11; 12-4, 6-11 Sat; 12-5 Sun
☎ (01621) 828348 ⊕ purleighbell.co.uk

Adnams Southwold Bitter; Mighty Oak Captain Bob; 2 changing beers (sourced regionally; often Crouch Vale) Ⓗ

A friendly, traditional hilltop pub next to the village church, with fine views of the Blackwater Estuary, dating back to the 14th century. There is one large divided bar with log fires, which is attractively decorated with hop garlands. High-quality food is served, and beer drinkers are well catered for. The pub hosts a wide range of activities, including movie nights and art exhibitions. It is popular with walkers, as it is on the St Peter's Way long-distance footpath. Q❀🕭❤🅿🍴♿🎵🛜

Rochford

Golden Lion Ⓛ

35 North Street, SS4 1AB

🌐 11-midnight (1am Fri & Sat) ☎ (01702) 545487
⊕ goldenlionrochford.co.uk

Adnams Southwold Bitter; Greene King Abbot; Mighty Oak Maldon Gold; 4 changing beers (sourced nationally) Ⓗ

Long-standing Guide entry, within the town centre conservation area. This is a small, 16th-century, weatherboarded free house with stained-glass windows and a fireplace with a traditional logburner. Seven ales are always on tap, including three changing guests (one usually a dark beer) and always one from Cotleigh. Three ciders are also served, one from Essex. There is a pretty patio garden to the rear with a vintage petrol pump water feature. Two beer festivals are held each year in May and October. ❀♿🚲❤❤🅿🛒(7,8)♿🛜

Miley

1 Union Lane, SS4 1AP (behind Sainsbury's Local at end of West St and through pub courtyard)

🌐 12-midnight (1am Fri & Sat) ☎ (01702) 544229

4 changing beers (sourced nationally) Ⓗ

True community local with a genuine warm welcome, which has only ever been in one family in the 24 years since it opened. It is a live music venue all year round, with a piano, and a newly refurbished courtyard and outdoor stage for the summer months. With two dartboards, it has regular tournaments. Two annual beer festivals are held on the spring and August bank holidays. Happy hour is all day Monday. Two minutes' walk from the train station and historic town centre. ❀♿🚲❤❤🅿🛒(7,8)♿🛜

Rowhedge

Olde Albion

High Street, CO5 7ES

🌐 12-3 (not Mon), 5-11; 12-11 Thu-Sat; 12-10.30 Sun
☎ (01206) 728972

4 changing beers (sourced nationally) Ⓗ

Welcoming split-level community pub on Rowhedge waterfront with a range of well-kept beers and cider. The interior is adorned with nautical items and memorabilia. There are high tables and stools on the upper bar area while the lower level has benches, tables and chairs, plus a logburner in winter. Outside is a riverside beer garden with views over the River Colne. Beer

festivals are put on for St George's Day, Rowhedge Regatta, and another one in autumn, plus the annual Carols on the Quay. ❀♣❤🛒(66)♿🛜

Saffron Walden

King's Arms ⊘

10 Market Hill, CB10 1HQ

🌐 12-11 Mon; 12-midnight (12.30am Fri & Sat); 12-11 Sun
☎ (01799) 522768 ⊕ thekingsarmssaffronwalden.co.uk

Adnams Southwold Bitter; Oakham JHB; Woodforde's Wherry; 2 changing beers (sourced nationally) Ⓗ

Venerable wooden-beamed, multi-roomed pub, just off the market square (market days are Tuesday and Saturday). A mild or dark beer is often served in winter. There is live music at weekends, acoustic music on Thursdays and a monthly quiz. Welcoming log fires in winter and a pleasant patio for alfresco eating and drinking are particular features. Food is served at lunchtimes. Local CAMRA branch Town Pub of the Year 2017. Q🕭❀🕭🅿♿🛜

South Benfleet

South Benfleet Social Club Ⓛ

8 Vicarage Hill, SS7 1PB

🌐 12-11 (midnight Fri & Sat) ☎ (01268) 206159

5 changing beers Ⓗ/Ⓖ

A family-oriented club that gives a warm welcome to all. CAMRA members only need to show a membership card or a copy of this Guide for entry. LocAle is a feature and the bar's interest in real ale and cider is backed by regular beer festivals. TV sports, darts, pool, quiz nights and live music are part of the busy social scene, keeping this club at the centre of local activity. Three ales on handpump are complemented by two more on gravity. Four times CAMRA branch Club of the Year. 🕭❀🕭🚲≠(Benfleet)♣❤🛒🛜

Southend-on-Sea

Last Post Ⓛ ⊘

Weston Road, SS1 1AS

🌐 8am-midnight (1am Fri & Sat) ☎ (01702) 431682

Greene King Abbot; Ruddles Best Bitter; Sharp's Doom Bar; 7 changing beers (sourced nationally) Ⓗ

Large Wetherspoon pub in a Victorian post office building, built in 1896. Up to 10 real ales and up to four real ciders are sold, split across two bars. Accommodation is available and there is a pleasant outside seating area and conservatory. Beers can often be found from the local George's Brewery in addition to national and regional ales. Breakfast is served from 7am every day and food until 10pm. Q🕭❀🕭🕭♿≠(Central/Victoria)❤🛒🛜

Mawson's Micro Pub 🍷 Ⓛ

781 Southchurch Road, SS1 2PP

🌐 4-11 (12.30am Fri); 12-12.30am Sat; 12-10 Sun
☎ (01702) 601781

George's Cockleboats, Wakering Gold Ⓗ**; Harvey's Sussex Best Bitter; 3 changing beers (sourced nationally; often George's)** Ⓖ

Southend's first micropub opened in 2015, named after the owner's family and became an immediate success. The two most popular beers are from the local brewery, George's, and are served on handpump, while up to three guests are served on gravity, including more beers from George's or Hopmonster. Foreign bottled beers,

draught and bottled ciders complement the range. Local CAMRA Pub of the Year 2017.
&♿🚲🍴🚌🚃🐱📶

Olde Trout Tavern
56 London Road, SS1 1NX (opp Sainsbury's)
✪ 11-11; 12-11 Sun ☎ (01702) 337000
🌐 theoldetrout.co.uk
House beer (by Brentwood); 3 changing beers (sourced nationally) Ⓗ
Modern town centre ale bar with an eclectic mix of adornments on the walls and ceiling, including breweriana, signs and numerous clocks. Hot food and snacks are served 12-3pm. Up to three changing ales are available alongside the house beer, Trout Ale, from Brentwood Brewery, and Westons Rosie's Pig cider. A fortnightly quiz is on Sunday nights. Within walking distance of the High Street and both mainline railway stations.
◗🚉(Victoria/Central)🍴🚌🚃📶

Railway Hotel Ⓛ
32 Clifftown Road, SS1 1AJ
✪ 11 (5 Mon)-11; 12-1am Fri & Sat; 12-10 Sun
☎ (01702) 343194 🌐 railwayhotelsouthend.co.uk
Adnams Southwold Bitter, Mosaic, Ghost Ship, Broadside; Crouch Vale Brewers Gold; Woodforde's Wherry Ⓗ
This Victorian three-storey community inn has been identified by CAMRA as having an historic pub interior of some regional importance. Historical features include the counter, bar back, panelled walls and parquet floor. The Nelson Street entrance has stained-glass windows and 19th-century mosaic floors. Live bands play most nights, including blues Tuesday and jazz Wednesday. All food is vegan or vegetarian and pizzas are a speciality. Up to six ales are served and two ciders, usually from Kentish Pip.
🚲🎪◗♿🚉(Central)🚌🚃📶

Southminster

Station Arms
39 Station Road, CM0 7EW
✪ 12-2.30, 6-11; 2-11 Sat; 12-10.30 Sun ☎ (01621) 772225
🌐 thestationarms.co.uk
Adnams Southwold Bitter; George's Broadsword; 3 changing beers (sourced regionally; often Crouch Vale, Elgood's, George's) Ⓗ
This typical Essex white-weatherboarded pub is a regular in the Guide. It is a well-frequented, friendly local in the genuine pub tradition. Musicians are often to be found playing impromptu sessions and live music is hosted monthly. The comfortable, bare-boarded single bar is decorated with railway and brewery memorabilia. An attractive courtyard is a suntrap in fine weather and a barn, with wood-burning stove, provides shelter. Q🎪🚉🍴🚌🚃

Wibblers Brewery Taproom & Kitchen
Goldsands Road, CM0 7JW
✪ closed Mon-Thu; 4-10 Fri; 12-8 Sat; 12-6 Sun
☎ (01621) 772044 🌐 wibblers.co.uk
Wibblers Dengie IPA, Apprentice, Dengie Gold, Hop Black Ⓗ**, Crafty Stoat** Ⓖ**; 3 changing beers (sourced locally)** Ⓗ/Ⓖ
The Taproom, which was officially opened in January 2017, is adjacent to the beautifully restored late-medieval tithe barn which houses the

recently relocated brewery. The brewery building won the Maldon District Design and Conservation Award for Sustainability in 2016. The cosy bar is attractively furnished, and there is also outside seating to take in the rural setting. Creative home-cooked food is served, using local produce when available. Various events are held throughout the year. Q🚲🎪◗🚉🍴🚌(31X)🐱

Stansted Mountfitchet

Rose & Crown Ⓛ
31 Bentfield Green, CM24 8HX (1 mile W of B1383)
TL505256
✪ closed Mon, 12-3 (not Tue), 6-11; 12-midnight Fri & Sat; 12-9 Sun ☎ (01279) 812107
3 changing beers (sourced regionally) Ⓗ
Family-run Victorian pub near a duck pond on the edge of a small hamlet. This free house has been modernised to provide one large bar, but retains the welcoming atmosphere of an active village local. Food is home cooked and made from locally sourced produce. A large variety of gins is kept. The pub has been extended to include a new largish snug, and has an old seven-inch singles jukebox – you can bring your own records to play.
🚲🎪◗🍴🅿🚃(7,7A)🐱📶

Stapleford Tawney

Moletrap
Tawney Common, CM16 7PU (3 miles E of Epping)
TL500013
✪ 11.30-2.30, 6-11; 12-4 Sun ☎ (01992) 522394
🌐 themoletrap.co.uk
Fuller's London Pride; 3 changing beers (sourced regionally) Ⓗ
A 200-year-old pub in beautiful countryside, offering a good selection of guest ales, normally including one dark beer. Good-value home-cooked food is served (no food Sun or Mon eves). There is a cosy bar with a real fire; well-behaved children and dogs are allowed at the landlord's discretion. Extensive outdoor seating provides amazing views. In the middle of nowhere, it is difficult to locate without a sat nav, but well worth it.
Q🚲🎪◗🅿🐱📶

Stebbing

White Hart Ⓛ
High Street, CM6 3SQ
✪ 11-3, 4.30 (5.30 Mon)-11; 11-11 Fri & Sat; 12-10.30 Sun
☎ (01371) 856383
Hart of Stebbing IPA; 1 changing beer (sourced nationally) Ⓗ
A 15th-century timbered inn in a picturesque village, featuring exposed beams, an open fire, eclectic collections from chamber pots to cigarette cards, and a section of exposed lath and plaster wall behind a glass screen. The Hart of Stebbing microbrewery is in the garage producing beers currently only available here and at beer festivals. Good-value food is served daily. Outside are a patio and covered, heated gazebo.
Q🚲🎪◗🍴🅿🚃(16)🐱📶

Steeple Bumpstead

Fox & Hounds Ⓛ ✔
3 Chapel Street, CB9 7DQ

12-3, 5-11; 12-midnight Fri & Sat; 12-11 Sun
☎ (01440) 731810 ⊕ foxinsteeple.co.uk
Greene King IPA; 3 changing beers (sourced nationally) ⓗ
A 500-year-old pub with a main bar and an open fire. Two other rooms are used mainly for dining and there is a rear courtyard garden. Four beers are offered from local and national breweries. The locally sourced food includes bar snacks to a full à la carte menu. Live music plays on occasional Friday evenings, and some Sundays are quiz nights. Reduced price beer, wine and free cheese are on offer on Wednesday evening, with steak night on Thursday. Q🏃🞉🌃🔌♣️🖵(18)🐾🛜

Stock

Hoop ✅
High Street, CM4 9BD (by B1007)
11-11; 12-10.30 Sun ☎ (01277) 841137 ⊕ thehoop.co.uk
Adnams Southwold Bitter ⓗ; **4 changing beers (sourced regionally)** ⓗ/ⓖ
This 15th-century weatherboarded pub, with a beamed interior and two fires, has lots of character. A Guide regular for over 20 years, it is welcoming to drinkers and diners alike. Up to four guest ales and three real ciders are on sale, often from local suppliers. Home-made food is served in the bar weekdays lunchtime and evening, 12-5pm on Sunday. The large garden is the setting for a popular beer festival held over the spring bank holiday each May. Q🞉🔌♿♣️🖵(100)🐾

Thaxted

Maypole ✅
Orange Street, CM6 2LT
12-11 (midnight Fri & Sat); 12-10.30 Sun
☎ (01371) 831152
Greene King IPA; 2 changing beers (sourced nationally) ⓗ
A renamed ex-Ridleys pub, all in one room with games/TV area, sofas, chairs and an area with tables. There is a garden and a car park at the rear. Up to four guest ales are available. The pub holds musical events and runs beer festivals, and is a beer drinkers' hospitable local. It has a pleasant patio at the rear. 🏃🞉🔌♣️P🖵(6,312)🐾🛜

Tollesbury

King's Head
1 High Street, CM9 8RG
12-11 (midnight Fri & Sat); 12-10.30 Sun
☎ (01621) 869203
Bishop Nick Ridley's Rite; house beer (by Colchester); 3 changing beers (sourced nationally) ⓗ
A warm, welcoming free house whose landlord is knowledgeable about the fine well-kept beers he has served for more than 25 years. The pub has strong connections with the village's historic and picturesque waterside (10 minutes' walk away), and hosts the annual Old Gaffers Rally. Pool and darts are played in the public bar, and home-cooked meals are served Friday lunchtimes only. A neighbouring baker sells pies, pasties and sandwiches, which can be eaten in the pub. Q🏃🞉🔌♣️P🖵🐾

Waltham Abbey

Woodbine Inn ⓛ
Honey Lane, EN9 3QT (close to jct 26 of M25)
11.30-11 (2am Fri & Sat); 11.30-10.30 Sun
☎ (01992) 713050 ⊕ thewoodbine.co.uk
Adnams Ghost Ship; Dominion Woodbine Racer; Mighty Oak Captain Bob ⓗ; **6 changing beers (sourced locally)** ⓗ/ⓖ
Local CAMRA branch Pub of the Year 2015 and Cider Pub of the Year 2017, situated in Epping Forest. Popular with walkers, locals and motorists, it specialises in real ales and over 25 small-producer ciders. Food is home made, locally sourced and hearty, with sausages, ham and steak as specialities. The Ale Sampling Society meets monthly and there are weekly quizzes and music. The Woodbine Brewery is expected to start production shortly. 🏃🔌♣️🍺P🖵(250,251)🐾🛜

Weeley Heath

White Hart ♉
Clacton Road, CO16 9ED (on B1441) TM153208
12-2.30, 4-11 (10 Mon); 12-11 Fri & Sat; 12-8 Sun
☎ (01255) 830384
2 changing beers (sourced nationally; often Greene King, Mauldons, Woodforde's) ⓗ
This community-focused local is a regular Guide entry thanks to consistently good real ale. It has its own real ale club and hosts pool and darts teams, with pool played in the large conservatory. There is a garden with a covered patio for smokers. Sky and BT Sport on various TV screens are popular with sports fans. Local CAMRA Pub of the Year 2015 and 2017 and Cider Pub of the Year 2016.
🞉⛺♣️🍺P🖵(2,76)🛜

West Hanningfield

Three Compasses ⓛ
Church Road, CM2 8UQ
11.30-3, 6-11; 12-3, 7-10.30 Sun ☎ (01245) 400447
Bishop Nick Ridley's Rite; 1 changing beer (sourced nationally) ⓗ
A delightful small country pub dating from 1425. The timber-framed and plastered Grade II-listed building has two bars, many low beams, and bench seats in front of the windows. It is ideally situated for country walkers and cyclists, with outside seating. A free house, the landlady has been here since 1971 and her son is now joint licensee. Home-cooked food is available every lunchtime and some evenings. Q🏃🞉🔌P🖵(13,13A)🐾🛜

Westcliff-on-Sea

Cricketers
228 London Road, SS0 7JG (on A13 London Rd)
12-midnight (11 Tue & Wed); 12-1am Fri & Sat; 12-10.30 Sun ☎ (01702) 345053
Dark Star Hophead; Greene King Abbot; Mighty Oak Oscar Wilde, Maldon Gold; Sharp's Doom Bar ⓗ
A large family-run street-corner Gray & Sons hostelry close to Southend. The pub has been split into restaurant and bar areas, with home-made food served until 9.30pm and roast dinners on Sunday. Jazz night is every second Wednesday of the month, featuring Digby Fairweather, and quiz night is Monday. The Venue adjoins the premises, so this popular pub can get busy on music nights. 🏃🞉🔌♿🚆🖵🐾🛜

Wethersfield

Wethersfield Village Club
Old Mill Chase, CM7 4EB
⊕ 5-11; 3-midnight Sat; 2-8 Sun ☎ (01371) 850598
⊕ wethersfield.org.uk
Wells Eagle IPA; 2 changing beers (sourced nationally) ⊞
A friendly and hospitable club in a village with no pubs; it is spacious and was dug out of the ground after WWI. It has two full-size snooker tables, pool, darts and table tennis, a dance floor and plenty of seating. To find the club, take the cul de sac to the right of the village hall, where the entrance is down the alleyway at the end on the left. CAMRA members are welcome. ♿♣♥☎

Widdington

Fleur de Lys
High Street, CB11 3SG TL538316
⊕ 12-3 (not Mon & Tue), 6-11; 12-11.30 Fri & Sat; 12-10 Sun
☎ (01799) 543280 ⊕ thefleurdelys.co.uk
Adnams Southwold Bitter, Broadside; Woodforde's Wherry; 2 changing beers (sourced nationally) ⊞
Rumours of a ghost abound at this welcoming 400-year-old village local, which boasts a large open fireplace and beams. This was the first pub to be saved from closure by North West Essex CAMRA after the branch's formation. Quality meals are offered with fresh local ingredients. The source of the River Cam and Prior's Hall Barn, an English heritage site, are both nearby. A bridge club is held here on Monday night. ♿⊕♿♣P🚍(301)♥

Witham

Battesford Court ⓛ ✅
100-102 Newland Street, CM8 1AH
⊕ 8am-midnight (1am Fri & Sat); 8am-11 Sun
☎ (01376) 504080
Greene King Abbot; Ruddles Best Bitter; Sharp's Doom Bar; 5 changing beers (sourced locally) ⊞
Large Wetherspoon conversion of a former hotel of the same name. The 16th-century building was previously the courthouse of the manor of Battesford. It has distinct areas with wood panelling and oak beams, including a family area. Up to five regional beers are served, including something local, usually from Bishop Nick or Wibblers, plus up to two ciders and perries, usually from Westons and Gwynt y Ddraig. The standard Wetherspoon food offering is available.
Q♿♿⊕♿♥🚍☎

Woolpack Inn ⓛ
7 Church Street, CM8 2JP
⊕ 11.30-11.30 (midnight Fri & Sat); 12-10.30 Sun
☎ (01376) 511195
Greene King IPA; Witham Scruffy, No Name; 2 changing beers (sourced nationally) ⊞
A traditional local pub, it is the only regular outlet for the Witham Brewery, which is now based in Coggeshall. Set in the conservation area, the building probably dates from the 15th century. It has two rooms with low wooden beams and a real log fire during the winter. Up to two guest beers are served, always local, and real cider in summer. Bar snacks are sold Monday to Saturday.
≈♣♥🚍(40)♥☎

Wivenhoe

Black Buoy
Black Buoy Hill, CO7 9BS
⊕ 11-11; 12-10.30 Sun ☎ (01206) 822425
⊕ blackbuoy.co.uk/index.html
Adnams Southwold Bitter; 6 changing beers (sourced nationally) ⊞
Popular and welcoming community-owned pub, three-times winner of local CAMRA Rural Pub of the Year. The main bar has a real fire with high stools and tables, and there is also a second bar with separate dining, and a pleasant outdoor area which hosts a summer beer festival. Open mic and quiz evenings feature regularly. A range of good-value home-cooked food is offered, plus a specials board. Two B&B rooms are available.
♿♿♨⊕⊕≈P🚍♥☎

Horse & Groom
55 The Cross, CO7 9QL
⊕ 10.30-3, 5.30 (6 Sat)-11; 12-4.30, 7-11 Sun
☎ (01206) 824928
Adnams Southwold Bitter, Broadside; 2 changing beers (sourced nationally) ⊞
A real locals' pub, at the top end of Wivenhoe, comprising both public and lounge bars, with a range of ales from Adnams, as well as locally sourced guests. Pub games include dominoes and darts. Children and dogs are welcome throughout and there is a small play area in the beer garden. It offers a home-cooked menu with a roast lunch on Thursday and a regular curry club (no food Sun).
Q♿♿⊕♣P🚍♥

Woodham Mortimer

Hurdlemakers Arms
Post Office Road, CM9 6ST
⊕ 12-11; 12-9 Sun ☎ (01245) 225169
⊕ hurdlemakersarms.co.uk
5 changing beers (sourced locally; often Maldon, Mighty Oak, Wibblers) ⊞
Best viewed from its substantial gardens, this pretty Gray's country pub boasts an excellent selection of mainly local beers, alongside a fine range of ciders. Of its two bars, one is given over to dining, while the second, smaller bar retains a locals' feel. The good, locally sourced food makes this a popular dining venue. There is a monthly quiz and a beer festival in late June. The gardens, with plenty of seating, include a large barbecue and play area. Q♿♿♨⊕♿♣♥P🚍🚍♥☎

Writtle

Wheatsheaf ⓛ
70 The Green, CM1 3DU
⊕ 11-11.30 (midnight Fri & Sat); 12-11 Sun
☎ (01245) 420672 ⊕ thewheatsheafwrittle.co.uk
Adnams Southwold Bitter, Broadside; Maldon Drop of Nelson's Blood ⊞; Mighty Oak Oscar Wilde Ⓖ, Maldon Gold; Maldon Dengie IPA ⊞; 2 changing beers (sourced nationally) Ⓖ
Traditional village pub built in 1813, with a small public bar, an equally compact lounge, and a covered patio by the road. It is a long-time favourite of the local CAMRA branch. The atmosphere is generally quiet, with the TV switched on only for occasional sporting events. Traditional pub food is served Tuesday to Saturday lunchtimes. Q⊕♣P🚍(45)♥

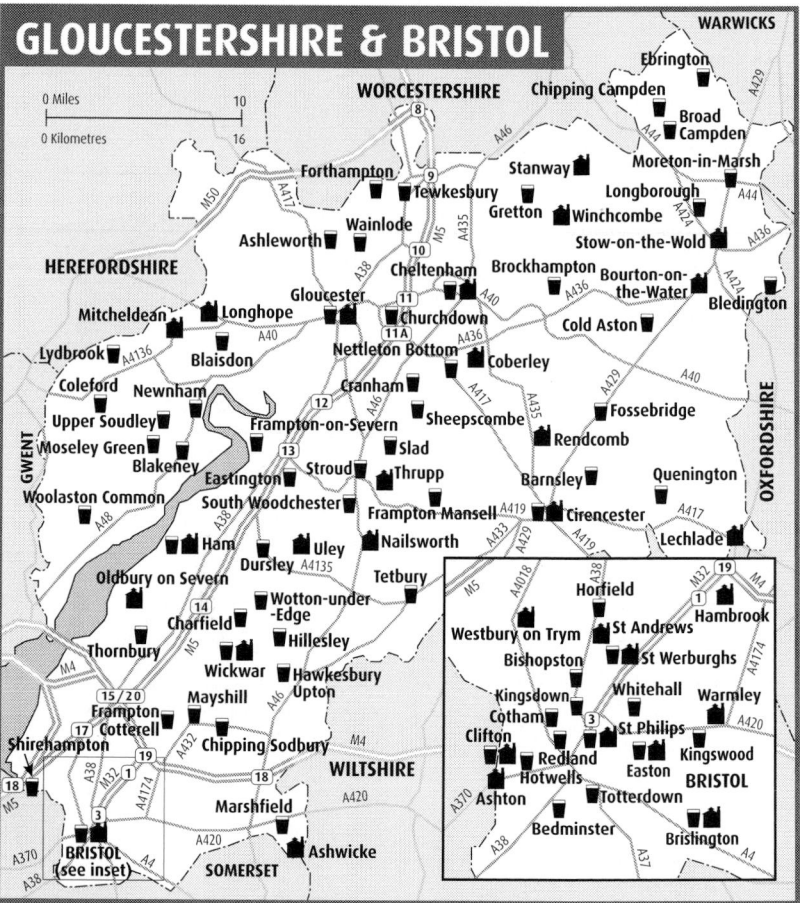

GLOUCESTERSHIRE & BRISTOL

Ashleworth

Boat Inn ⃝

The Quay, GL19 4HZ (beyond tithe barn on road to quay)
SO8187025073
☼ 12-11 (midnight Fri & Sat); 12-10.30 Sun
☎ (01452) 700272 ⊕ boatinn.wordpress.com
**6 changing beers (often Box Steam, Church End,
North Cotswold)** ⃝
This tranquil haven on the banks of the River
Severn is a real gem. It serves around six regional
brewery beers by gravity along with up to 20 real
ciders. There is a covered courtyard and a grass
area on the river edge with tables. The pub has its
own moorings and is popular in the summer. Hot
basket meals and locally produced burgers are a
speciality. Winter opening times vary.
Q ➄ ☼ ◑ ▲ ♣ ● P ⊟ (351) ♣ ☏

Barnsley

Village Pub ⃝

GL7 5EF (on B4425 in centre of village)
☼ 11-3, 6-11 ☎ (01285) 740421 ⊕ thevillagepub.co.uk
**4 changing beers (sourced locally; often North
Cotswold)** ⃝
An unashamedly upmarket dining and drinking
establishment, twinned with the luxurious hotel
down the road. This convivial 370-year-old village

inn has a comfortable, relaxed atmosphere
(although one of the bedrooms is haunted). A
symphony of wood and natural stone, the layout
reflects that of the original building, with several
dining areas, including the attractive patio. While
the emphasis is on food (reservations advised), the
keen landlord loves trying new ales, gins and
ciders from local suppliers. ☼ ⊯ ◑ P ♣ ☏

Blaisdon

Red Hart ⃝

GL17 0AH (centre of village; signed from A4136 E of
Longhope or N of A48)
☼ 12-3, 6-11; 12-3, 7-11 Sun ☎ (01452) 830477
⊕ redhartinn.co.uk
**4 changing beers (sourced nationally; often Bespoke,
Young's)** ⃝
This lovely, award-winning old inn has worn
flagstones in the bar, a welcoming fireplace and a
veritable plethora of memorabilia as decoration.
Guest ales are usually LocAle, alongside a local
cider or perry from Severn Cider. The cracking
restaurant means the pub can get very busy, so be
prepared to mix it with a rack of lamb, not to
mention free-range children, if the meals encroach
into the bar area. Families are welcome to use the
well-tended garden. ➄ ☼ ◑ ♿ ▲ ♣ ● P ☼

Blakeney

Cock Inn ✓

Nibley Hill, GL15 4DB (bottom of hill)
🌓 closed Mon; 5-10.30; 12-11 Fri & Sat; 12-8 Sun
☎ (01594) 510239 ⊕ thecockinnblakeney.com
3 changing beers (sourced regionally) Ⓗ
Over 200 years old, this attractive roadside pub retains many original features, including natural stone walling and old beams. A blazing fire in winter adds to the welcoming atmosphere in the low L-shaped bar. The chef takes great pride in adding a modern twist to the excellent menu. The three ales usually showcase a mixture of local and regional breweries, and two ciders are available. A large garden with children's play equipment offers great views. 🛏️🏠♿️◀️🍴♣🚶🐕🅿️🚌 (73)

Bledington

King's Head Ⓛ ✓

The Green, OX7 6XQ (off B4450 on village green)
🌓 11-11 ☎ (01608) 658365 ⊕ kingsheadinn.net
Flying Monk Elmers; Hook Norton Hooky; 3 changing beers (sourced regionally; often Wye Valley) Ⓗ
Delightful 16th-century stone-built inn overlooking the village green. The pub has original beams and an open inglenook log fire with high-back settles. This free house, with 12 comfortable letting rooms, is renowned for its wide range of ale and food. There are good local walks to nearby villages, with Kingham station close by. The two guest beers are selected from local brewers in Gloucestershire and Oxfordshire. CAMRA award winner and finalist Pub of the Year in 2017. Q🛏️🏠♿️◀️🍴♣🅿️

Bristol

Bank Tavern ✓

8 John Street, BS1 2HR
🌓 12-midnight (1am Thu-Sat) ☎ (0117) 930 4691
⊕ banktavern.com
4 changing beers Ⓗ
Popular compact one-bar pub, hidden away near the old city wall. The four beers are often from microbrewers from the South-West and, occasionally, further afield, and can be of any style. Two real ciders change constantly. Quirky humour and many varied events define the pub, and it is a great alternative to the more predictable establishments all around. It has a quiz on Tuesday and live music on Thursday. Look out for the summer fête and Christmas party. Quality food is served 12-4pm (booking is advisable on a Sunday). 🛏️🍴◀️♣🚶🐕🚌🚺

Beer Emporium

13-15 King Street, BS1 4EF
🌓 12-2am; 1-midnight Sun ☎ (0117) 379 0333
⊕ thebeeremporium.net
12 changing beers Ⓗ
In the beermuda triangle on King Street, this cellar bar is set in three tunnels – one containing the bar, seating and a modern stained-glass window skylight, one for seating only, and a third housing the kitchens. A lift makes it accessible to all. Up to 12 changing cask ales are served and a wide range of world bottled beers. There is also a bottle shop just inside the entrance. The food is authentic Italian pizza and pasta, with vegetarian and vegan options. ◀️♿️🍴🚶🚌🚺

Bridge Inn

16 Passage Street, BS2 0JF
🌓 12-11 (1am Fri & Sat); 2-11 Sun ☎ (0117) 929 0942
Dark Star Hophead; 3 changing beers Ⓗ
A short waterside stroll from Temple Meads station, this small and friendly pub is a good place to start your visit to Bristol. An adventurous choice of ales is served including seasonal favourites. It offers weekday lunches 12-3pm and free cheese 'n' cracker feasts on Sunday at 6pm. Musical memorabilia adorns the walls and board games are available to play. Thirty malt whiskies and selected vodkas, gins and rums are also served, together with Belgian bottled beers. The tables outside increase capacity during good weather. 🏠◀️🚶♣🚌🐕🚺🚺🚺

Commercial Rooms ✓

43-45 Corn Street, BS1 1HT
🌓 8am-midnight (1am Fri & Sat) ☎ (0117) 927 9681
Greene King Abbot; Ruddles Best Bitter; changing beers Ⓗ
This centrally located, Grade II-listed building dating from 1810 was Bristol's first Wetherspoon pub. It offers up to 10 guest beers and food served 8am-11pm. There is a quieter galleried room at the rear, but the main bar does get very busy at peak times. The interior features Greek revival-style decor, a stunning ceiling with dome, portraits and

REAL ALE BREWERIES

Arbor Bristol
Ashley Down Bristol: St Andrews
Bath Bristol: Warmley
Battledown Cheltenham
Beer Bores Ashwicke
Bespoke Mitcheldean
Bolthole Bristol: Westbury on Trym
Brewhouse & Kitchen 🍴 Bristol: Clifton
Brewhouse & Kitchen 🍴 Cheltenham
Brewhouse & Kitchen 🍴 Gloucester
Bristol Beer Factory Bristol: Ashton
Ciren 🍴 Cirencester (brewing suspended)
Cocksure Oldbury on Severn (NEW)
Corinium Cirencester
Cotswold Bourton-on-the-Water
Cotswold Lion Coberley
Dawkins Bristol: Easton
Donnington Stow-on-the-Wold
Force Cirencester
Gloucester Gloucester
Goff's Winchcombe
Good Chemistry Bristol: St Philips
Great Western Bristol: Hambrook
Halfpenny 🍴 Lechlade (brewing suspended)
Hillside Longhope
Incredible Bristol: Brislington
Keep 🍴 Nailsworth
King Street 🍴 Bristol
Left Handed Giant Bristol: St Philip's
Moor Bristol
New Bristol Bristol
Prescott Cheltenham
Stanway Stanway
Stroud Thrupp
TAP Rendcomb
Tiley's 🍴 Ham
Uley Uley
Wickwar Wickwar
Wiper and True Bristol: St Werburghs
Zerodegrees 🍴 Bristol

memorabilia from its days as a businessmen's club. Disabled access is via the side entrance in Small Street. Q🏠🅿◖♿🍴🚪🐕📶

Cornubia

142 Temple Street, BS1 6EN
🕐 12-11; 12-6 Sun ☎ (0117) 925 4415 ⊕ thecornubia.co.uk
8 changing beers Ⓗ

A cosy small pub with two linked rooms adorned with much patriotic memorabilia as well as countless pumpclips. Eight real ales are served, plus changing ciders in spring and summer. Pork pies and pasties are usually available. You can also enjoy a wide range of board games and books here. Live blues takes place on Thursday evening, when anyone can come along and jam, and live bands some Saturdays. The outside area has seating and a boules piste. 🅿🚲♣♿🍴🚪🐕📶

Famous Royal Navy Volunteer

17-18 King Street, BS1 4EF
🕐 12-midnight (1am Thu-Sat) ☎ (0117) 316 9237
⊕ navyvolunteer.co.uk
8 changing beers Ⓗ

The Volley, on historic King Street, is a much-loved part of Bristol's heritage. This listed 17th-century building has four bar areas, one of which is for dining. Its beers are available in one-third, half-pint, two-third and pint measures from unmarked pumps. The wooden boards to the right of the bar show the current selection, but be aware that only the eight ales shown on the far right of the boards are served on cask. Disabled access is at the rear entrance. 🏠🅿🚲◖♿🍴🚪🐕📶

Gryphon

41 Colston Street, BS1 5AP
🕐 4-11.30 (1am Fri); 1-1am Sat; 6-11 Sun ☎ 07894 239567
6 changing beers Ⓗ

A shrine to dark beer and great rock/heavy metal music. Posters, guitars and many pumpclips adorn the walls. Triangular in shape due to its corner plot, and just a few yards uphill from the Colston Hall, it has six handpumps dispensing rapidly changing brews, many dark and often strong. Live bands sometimes play upstairs and beer festivals are in March and September. Food is served evenings Wednesday to Saturday. It may open earlier on Sundays. Children and dogs are admitted at the licensee's discretion. ▶🚪🐕📶

Lime Kiln

17 St Georges Road, BS1 5UU
🕐 12-11; 12-10.30 Sun ☎ 07903 068256
6 changing beers Ⓗ

Cosy city-centre free house reopened in May 2015 directly behind the City Hall on College Green. The six handpumps dispense ever-changing beers in a variety of styles. Many of the breweries featured are seldom seen in Bristol, but beers from local breweries are often stocked. There is also at least one traditional cider. You are welcome to bring your own food. A St Georges Road beer festival is usually held twice a year in conjunction with the nearby Three Tuns and Bag of Nails pubs. 🏠🍴🅿🚪🐕📶

No.1 Harbourside

1 Canons Road, BS1 5UH
🕐 10-midnight (11 Mon; 1am Fri & Sat); 12-11 Sun
☎ (0117) 929 1100 ⊕ no1harbourside.co.uk
8 changing beers (often Bristol Beer Factory, Arbor) Ⓗ

Modern pub/diner on the covered walkway on the quayside of the floating harbour and handy for city-centre buses. With early opening it is ideal for morning coffee, snacking or a cheeky early beer. Five handpumps usually feature two Bristol Beer Factory beers and three guests, often from Arbor, supplemented by a selection of bottled beers and changing ciders. There are some tables outside from where you can watch the ferry boats arriving and departing. Live music features late evenings Wednesday to Saturday. 🅿◖♿🍴🚪🐕📶

Seven Stars

1 Thomas Lane, BS1 6JG (just off Victoria St)
🕐 12-11; 12-10.30 Sun ☎ (0117) 927 2845 ⊕ 7stars.co.uk
8 changing beers Ⓗ

Many who live miles away call this small free house their local. It has a pool table, a rock-oriented jukebox and outdoor seating. Eight pumps dispense a full range of styles and strengths from near and far, plus ciders and perries. Beeriodicals are held on the first Monday to Thursday of every month, with up to 20 beers from a different county each time. Anti-slavery campaigner Thomas Clarkson used this pub as a base during his research into the trade. 🅿🚲♣♿🍴🚪🐕📶

Small Bar

31 King Street, BS1 4DZ
🕐 12-12.30am (1am Fri & Sat); 12-midnight Sun
⊕ smallbar.co.uk/bristol
4 changing beers Ⓗ

Despite its name this bar, which opened in 2013, is not small – it has two rooms downstairs and one upstairs. The latter has comfortable sofas and chairs plus a small library. Around 25 beers are served on draught, of which at least four will be cask, plus an expanding selection of bottled beers. Unusually, beer is served in one-third, half and two-thirds of a pint measures only. Food consists of quality bar food, including burgers and hot dogs, available most times when open. 🅿◖🍴🚪🐕📶

Three Tuns

78 St George's Road, BS1 5UR
🕐 12-11 (midnight Thu-Sat); 12-10.30 Sun
☎ (0117) 329 4310 ⊕ the3tuns.com
Arbor Blue Sky Drinking; 6 changing beers Ⓗ

This independent pub has seven handpumps dispensing the full range of beer styles, with at least one from Arbor Brewery and the rest from top-rated British brewers, plus many unusual bottled beers and several ciders. The L-shaped interior has scrubbed wooden tables and mixed seating, plus a covered heated rear patio featuring an impressive mural by artist Silent Hobo. A small range of quality bar food is served. It hosts regular quizzes, magic shows, live Irish music, movies and more. 🅿◖🍴🚪🐕📶

Volunteer Tavern

9 New Street, BS2 9DX
🕐 4-11 (midnight Thu); 12-midnight Sat; 1-10 Sun
☎ (0117) 955 8498 ⊕ volunteertavern.co.uk
6 changing beers Ⓗ

Tucked away in a side street but extremely close to Cabot Circus shops, Old Market and its bus interchange, this popular pub dates from 1670 and is listed. There are always six changing beers including at least one dark one, plus two changing ciders. Beer festivals feature in the large paved and heated garden. Irish folk music or open mic take place every Sunday evening. Food is served every day and is hugely popular particularly on Sunday (booking advised). Local CAMRA branch Pub of the Year 2016. ✿🗲🍴♿🐾🖂

Bristol: Bedminster

Victoria Park
66 Raymend Road, BS3 4QW (250yds off St Johns Lane)
✿ 12-11 (11.30 Sat); 12-10.30 Sun ☎ (0117) 330 6043
🌐 thevictoriapark.co.uk
Wye Valley Butty Bach; 2 changing beers (often Electric Bear, Milk Street) Ⓗ
A thriving red-brick venue in a residential area, but with the feel of a cosy country pub inside. There is a large south-facing garden/patio area to the rear which features a wood-fired pizza oven and stunning views towards Dundry Hill. Three pumps serve quality beers often including a dark offering, plus there is a large selection of bottled ales. The seasonal award-winning menu is displayed on a chalkboard. Events take place throughout the week including films, book club and a quiz.
🌙✿🗲🚆♣🖂(90,91)🐾🖂

Bristol: Bishopston

Prince Of Wales
5 Gloucester Road, BS7 8AA
✿ 12 (4 Mon & Tue)-11; 12-midnight Fri & Sat
☎ (0117) 924 5552 🌐 powbristol.co.uk
Bath Ales Gem; Butcombe Gold; Otter Amber; 3 changing beers (sourced regionally) Ⓗ
The exterior of this popular local boasts a beautifully painted mural of a row of handpumps (by local artist Andrew Burns Colwill) and Victorian stained-glass windows. Inside, the U-shaped bar serves two linked drinking areas, with comfortable padded settles around the walls. There is a covered, heated outdoor area at the rear. Guest beers are locally and regionally sourced, complemented by several real ciders. A broad food menu is available. 🌙✿🗲🚆♣🖂🐾🖂

Bristol: Brislington

King's Arms ✓
1 Hollywood Road, BS4 4LF
✿ closed Mon; 12-midnight ☎ (0117) 401 5962
🌐 kingsarmsbs4.co.uk
Courage Best Bitter; 4 changing beers (sourced regionally) Ⓗ
Reopened in June 2015 after a major refurbishment by Enterprise Inns, this is a beautiful traditional inn with all you would expect from a 17th-century (reputedly haunted) pub – thick stone walls and fireplaces, oak beams and lots of cosy nooks and crannies. The beer garden is open all year. Entertainment includes a Tuesday quiz, open mic night on Thursday, and a live band once a month. Although there is wheelchair access to the bar area, there are no accessible toilets. No children after 7pm. 🌙✿🗲🍴♿P🖂🐾

Bristol: Clifton

Lansdown
8 Clifton Road, BS8 1AF
✿ 4-11; 12-midnight Fri & Sat; 12-10.30 Sun
☎ (0117) 973 4949
St Austell Proper Job; house beer (by Otter); 4 changing beers (sourced regionally; often Cheddar Ales, Great Western) Ⓗ

Traditional pub with a strong real ale offering, mainly from South-West breweries. Beers from Great Western and Cheddar Ales are often among the five or six on the bar, which change every few months, and there is usually a good mix of styles. An upstairs lounge/dining room is available for functions. Good food is served weekend lunchtimes and every evening. The courtyard garden, which is heated and covered in winter, shows rugby (Freeview) on a big screen and is the venue of occasional beer festivals. ✿🗲🍴🖂(8,9)🐾

Portcullis
3 Wellington Terrace, BS8 4LE
✿ 4 (12 Fri & Sat)-11; 12-10.30 Sun ☎ (0117) 973 0270
Dawkins Bristol Best; 4 changing beers Ⓗ
A pub since 1821, rescued by Dawkins in 2008, with a downstairs bar and an upstairs lounge (also used for functions). Of a beautifully strange design, it is in a Georgian terrace. The handpumps dispense a Dawkins beer, a range of guest ales, usually from other micros, and a traditional cider. More formal pub food is now served but not on Wednesday. Events such as quiz and comedy nights feature as well as the Eurovision Beer Contest. The rear garden is accessed from upstairs.
✿🗲🍴🖂(8,505)🐾🖂

Victoria
2 Southleigh Road, BS8 2BH (off St Pauls Rd)
✿ 4 (1 Sat)-11; 12-10.30 Sun ☎ (0117) 974 5675
Dawkins Bristol Best; 5 changing beers (often Dawkins, Tiny Rebel) Ⓗ
Small and cosy 19th-century Grade II-listed Dawkins tavern, tucked away just off the bottom of Whiteladies Road next to the Clifton Lido. Seven pumps offer changing independent beers and ciders, always including two or more from Dawkins Brewery. A changing Tiny Rebel beer is usually sold from one of the pumps, with hoppier beers more in evidence than previously. A function room is available upstairs. Parking close by can be difficult. 🚆♣🖂🐾🖂

Bristol: Cotham

Brewhouse & Kitchen ✓
31-35 Cotham Hill, BS6 6JY
✿ 11-11 (midnight Fri & Sat) ☎ (0117) 973 3793
🌐 brewhouseandkitchen.com/bristol
Brewhouse & Kitchen Crockers, Hornigold, Yankee Cabot; 3 changing beers (often Brewhouse & Kitchen) Ⓗ
Popular brewpub and dining spot within 100 yards of Clifton Down station on the other side of Whiteladies Road, opened in March 2015. The brewery is at one end of the large room and catches the eye (and nose, on brewing days) upon entry to the pub. Brewery experience days and beer masterclasses are offered throughout the year, and the pub hosts an annual beer festival. Almost all beers brewed in-house are suitable for vegetarians and vegans. A patio area is just across the road. 🌙✿🗲🚆♣🖂🐾🖂

Bristol: Easton

Greenbank
57 Bellevue Road, BS5 6DP
✿ 11 (9am Thu)-midnight; 9am-1am Fri & Sat
☎ (0117) 939 3771 🌐 thegreenbankbristol.co.uk

4 changing beers (often Arbor, Electric Bear, Wiper & True) H
Nominated as an Asset of Community Value in 2014 after a long closure, this community pub reopened in March 2014 under a management team including people from Zazu's Kitchen in Bedminster. Four changing real ales are on handpump, often local, in a range of styles and strengths, plus a selection of interesting bottled beers from suppliers including Wiper & True. Popular Sunday roasts are served all day (reservation advisable). It is family friendly, and your dog can come too. 🛏️🕯️◑♿⇌🚪😺🛜

Bristol: Horfield

Annexe
Seymour Road, BS7 9EQ (behind Sportsman pub)
🕐 11.30-3, 5-11.30; 11.30-11.30 Sat; 12-11 Sun
☎ (0117) 949 3931
Exmoor Gold; Otter Amber; Sharp's Doom Bar, Atlantic; Timothy Taylor Landlord; Wye Valley HPA; 2 changing beers H
Community pub not far from the Memorial Stadium, which means it can be busy on match days. Inside is a converted skittle alley and a large conservatory/family room to one side. Several TVs show live sport, including one on the partially covered patio outside. Good wholesome food is served, plus quality pizzas, which are available until 10.45pm (10.15pm Mon). One or two of the guest beers can be fairly adventurous. No dogs are allowed, even on the patio. 🛏️🕯️◑♿🚪🛜

Drapers Arms ♟
447 Gloucester Road, BS7 8TZ
🕐 5 (12 Sat)-9.30 ⊕ thedrapersarms.co.uk
7 changing beers G
Bristol's first micropub, opened in November 2015, close to the Memorial Stadium and county cricket ground. It has close links with the local Ashley Down Brewery, but also prides itself on an interesting changing beer selection from in and around Bristol. It offers up to seven real ales served by gravity, frequently including a dark ale, and up to three ciders. Wine and bar snacks are also available. There is no music or TV, but there is a warm welcome and a convivial, cosy atmosphere, with a focus on conversation. Local CAMRA Pub of the Year 2017. Q🕯️♿🚪😺

Bristol: Hotwells

Bag of Nails
141 St Georges Road, BS1 5UW
🕐 12-11; 12-10.30 Sun
10 changing beers H
Small terraced free house dating from the 1860s, serving up to 10 changing cask ales, mainly from microbreweries. An extensive selection of bottled beer is available along with a real cider. An eccentric list of pub policies includes no children or 'idiot pub crawls'. The interior features terracotta colours, portholes in the floor, many pub cats roaming free, and eclectic music from a proper record player. Board games for the customers and toys for the cats make the pub a fun way to spend an evening. A quiz takes place every Thursday. ♿🚪

Grain Barge
Mardyke Wharf, Hotwell Road, BS8 4RU (moored on opp bank to SS Great Britain)

🕐 12-11 (11.30 Thu-Sat) ☎ (0117) 929 9347
⊕ grainbarge.co.uk
5 changing beers (often Bristol Beer Factory) H
Easily accessed on foot, by bus or ferry, this moored boat was built in 1936 and converted into a floating pub by Bristol Beer Factory in 2007. It boasts great views of the SS Great Britain, the floating harbour and passing boats from the top deck. Food nights include Wednesday pie and a pint, Thursday steak club and Sunday roasts. Other activities include a Monday night quiz, a Tuesday open mic night and live music on Thursday in the downstairs Hold Bar. 🕯️◑♿🚪🛜

Bristol: Kingsdown

Hare on the Hill
41 Thomas Street North, BS2 8LX
🕐 closed Mon; 5-11 Tue-Thu; 5-1am Fri; 2-1am Sat; 12-8 Sun ☎ 07480 624212 ⊕ thehareonthehill.com
Bath Ales Gem; Moor Beer Nor'Hop; 3 changing beers (often Bristol Beer Factory, Butcombe, Good Chemistry) H
This small street-corner local with a traditional green-tile frontage reopened in 2015 as a free house. An array of beers from South-west microbrewers is served, usually including one dark ale. Cold platters are available every evening plus Sunday lunches featuring locally sourced ingredients. There are three simply furnished drinking areas, with wooden seating and flooring throughout, and paintings by local artists adorning the walls. Three TVs show big sporting events. ◑⇌♣🚪😺🛜

Hillgrove Porter Stores
53 Hillgrove Street North, BS2 8LT
🕐 4-midnight (1am Fri); 2-1am Sat; 2-midnight Sun
☎ (0117) 924 9818
Dawkins Bristol Blonde, Bristol Best; 12 changing beers (sourced regionally; often Dawkins) H
This excellent community pub is the second of the Dawkins Taverns, and is the brainchild of a local entrepreneur who also owns the Dawkins Brewery. The interior is horseshoe-shaped, with a lounge area hidden behind the bar, and a pleasant patio. Hundreds of pumpclips decorate the walls. Up to 10 guest ales, many regional, are served, including dark beers and rare styles, plus one or two changing traditional ciders. Pop-up kitchens from local chefs are a regular feature too, and booking is advised for the popular Sunday roast. 🕯️◑⇌♣🚪😺

Bristol: Redland

Chums
22 Chandos Road, BS6 6PF
🕐 4-10.30; 12-11 Fri & Sat; 12-10 Sun ☎ (0117) 973 1498
⊕ chumsmicropub.co.uk
6 changing beers (often Cheddar Ales, Plain, Butcombe) H
Bristol's second micropub opened in April 2016 in converted shop premises. Conversation rules here, with no TV, gaming machines or Wi-Fi – electronic communication devices should be used with discretion. Real ales are dispensed from six handpumps, three reserved for changing beers from three breweries (for those who like some consistency in the beer range). A selection of wines and spirits is available, and simple bar snacks including filled rolls and cockles. Last orders is called half an hour before closing due to licensing restrictions. Q🛏️♿⇌♣🚪😺

Bristol: St Philips

Barley Mow
39 Barton Road, BS2 0LF
☼ 12-11 (11.30 Fri & Sat); 12-10 Sun ☎ (0117) 930 4709
⊕ barleymowbristol.com
Bristol Beer Factory Nova, Seven; 6 changing beers (often Bristol Beer Factory) ⑭
A short walk from the railway station, this is Bristol Beer Factory's flagship pub. Eight handpumps offer three beers from the brewery plus five changing guests from all over the UK. There is also an extensive bottled beer selection. A small food menu changes frequently, including vegan dishes, and there is a quiz on Monday evening. Dogs are welcome in the rear beer garden, and there are benches at the front. ⌂❀◑≒♦🚌(506)☞

Bristol: St Werburghs

Duke of York
2 Jubilee Road, BS2 9RS (S side of Mina Rd park)
☼ 5-11; 3 (4 Fri)-midnight Sat; 3-11 Sun ☎ (0117) 941 3677
4 changing beers (sourced locally; often Arbor, Ashley Down, Moor Beer) ⑭
This well-hidden free house serves an eclectic clientele. Visit at night to experience the warm glow of the grotto-like interior. The decor comprises fairy lights, memorabilia, wooden floors, a refurbished skittle alley, local art and more. There are two rooms, with an extra bar upstairs offering a quite different feel. The exterior side wall features a Daliesque/'70s album cover mural depicting The Grand Old Duke of York nursery rhyme. Four handpumps serve unusual beers from local microbreweries as well as others from the South-West. ❀🅰≒♣♦🚌(5)☞

Bristol: Shirehampton

Lamplighters
Station Road, BS11 9XA
☼ 11-11 ☎ (0117) 279 3754 ⊕ thelamplighters.co.uk
Bath Ales Gem; 3 changing beers ⑭
The Friends of the Lamplighters worked hard to reopen this historic pub, which had been closed for several years. Built by a Mr Toy, a contractor for lighting half the parishes in Bristol, as his country residence, by 1810 it became the Lamplighters Hotel. In 1973 the building underwent extensive interior modernisation but the exterior remained unaltered. Spacious and comfortable, this multi-levelled pub now stocks four cask ales, usually including a dark offering. There is a pleasant garden overlooking the river and good food is served every day. ⌂❀◑&≒♣♦P🚌(X5)❀☞

Bristol: Totterdown

Oxford
120-122 Oxford Street, BS3 4RL (behind Tesco Express)
☼ 4-11 (midnight Fri); 2-midnight Sat; 12-11 Sun
☎ (0117) 907 5845
St Austell Tribute; Sharp's Doom Bar; 3 changing beers (often Arbor, Bristol Beer Factory, Tiny Rebel) ⑭
Small single-bar urban and residents' pub. To one side of the central bar is an area with a stage and TV. The guest beers are often adventurous, usually from local breweries such as Arbor and Bristol Beer Factory, but a large range of pumpclips on the walls shows a wide range of guest beers from small to medium-sized breweries in the Bristol

area and slightly farther afield. Regular live music features, including open mic, bands and jam sessions. ❀≒♣🚌❀☞

Bristol: Whitehall

Red Lion
206 Whitehall Road, BS5 9BP
☼ 2-12.30am (3am Fri); 12-3am Sat; 12-midnight Sun
☎ (0117) 329 1316
4 changing beers ⑭
Built at the beginning of the 20th century, this basic pub, which has a very late licence, has two rooms, one of which can be booked for private events. There is a pool table, dartboard, a table tennis table put up on request, plus a real fire, and a beer garden. The real ales change constantly with least three available during the week and a fourth at weekends – mostly unusual ones from microbreweries, normally including at least one dark beer, plus two real ciders. Live music features regularly. ⌂❀≒♣♦🚌(6,7)❀☞

Broad Campden

Bakers Arms ♥ Ⅼ
GL55 6UR (signed off B4081, at NW end of village)
☼ 12-3, 6-11; 12-11 Sat & Sun ☎ (01386) 840515
⊕ bakersarmscampden.com
North Cotswold Windrush Ale; Stanway Stanney Bitter; Wickwar BOB; Wye Valley HPA; 2 changing beers (sourced locally) ⑭
Fine old village local and genuine free house, first licensed as a public house in 1724. A photograph of the building in 1905 shows it as the village bakery and grain store. It boasts Cotswold stone walls, exposed beams and a fine inglenook. Excellent food is available in the bar and dining room extension and there is a large garden and children's play area. Local guest beers alongside regular ales are served from its handsome oak bar. Local CAMRA Pub of the Year 2017. Q⌂❀◑♣♦P❀☞

Brockhampton

Craven Arms Ⅼ
Kingsbury Street, GL54 5XQ
☼ 12-3, 6-11 ☎ (01242) 820410 ⊕ thecravenarms.co.uk
Butcombe Adam Henson's Rare Breed; Otter Bitter; 2 changing beers ⑭
A 17th-century free house in an attractive hillside village with outstanding views and walks. It has a cosy bar area with an open fire and a dining room separated by church-style stone windows. Four carefully selected beers are well kept by the owner/chef. This regular Guide pub is a gem managed well by a friendly family who organise functions for locals each month and a summer beer festival. Local CAMRA Pub of the Year 2016. Q⌂❀🛏◑🅰♣❀☞

Charfield

Pear Tree Micropub Ⅼ
6 Wotton Road, GL12 8TP (on B4058 1½ miles from jct 14 on M5)
☼ 2-9.30; 12-10.30 Sat; 12-9.30 Sun ☎ (01454) 260663
4 changing beers (sourced regionally) ⑤
Reinvented as a lively micropub, this cosy little one-roomed wonder is a joy to behold, from the attractively tiled flooring, the small wooden bar,

the way the ales are served (through old casks mounted in a fireplace), to the myriad humorous details among the wonderful murals covering most of the vertical surfaces. It offers up to four beers at busy times, usually from local and regional microbreweries. There is a large fenced outdoor seating area at the front. Q♣🏠P🚽🐾☀

Cheltenham

Bank House ✓
15-21 Clarence Street, GL50 3JL
🕐 7am-midnight (1am Fri & Sat) ☎ (01242) 240940
Greene King Abbot; Purity Mad Goose; Ruddles Best Bitter; 7 changing beers Ⓗ
A large town-centre Wetherspoon pub on two floors in a former bank. The building retains many fine architectural features, the upper floor taking the form of a gallery with a cosy library area and views into the floor below. Ten ales are generally on tap, with the three regular beers also available from the upper floor bar. As with many Wetherspoon pubs, the internal wall decor provides interesting facts about the building and other local history. Q🕐🍴👤🚽🐾🛜

Brewhouse & Kitchen Ⓛ ✓
The Brewery Quarter, GL50 4FA (on St Margarets Rd)
🕐 11-11 (midnight Fri & Sat); 12-10 Sun ☎ (01242) 509946
Brewhouse & Kitchen Crystal Rock, Big Chase, Tin Man, Brillig, Landed Eagle II, Colonel Jack; 2 changing beers (often Brewhouse & Kitchen) Ⓗ
Modern, large town-centre bar/restaurant in the trendy new Brewery Quarter on the site of the former Whitbread brewery. Up to seven ales are brewed on-site plus one draught cider. A brewery experience day is available at £85, or an evening beer masterclass sampling eight ales with nibbles for £20. The mezzanine area is available for private hire. 🐾🍴👤🚽🐾🛜

Charlton Kings Club
21 Church Street, Charlton Kings, GL53 8AP
🕐 12-3, 6-11; 11.30-3, 6-midnight Fri; 12-midnight Sat; 12-11 Sun ☎ (01242) 525511 🌐 charltonkingsclub.co.uk
Butcombe Blonde; 3 changing beers Ⓗ
Popular club in the heart of Charlton Kings, with a large lounge, separate sports bar and a skittle alley on the ground floor, plus a function room and snooker room upstairs. Live music is played upstairs (Vonnies Blues Club) and in the main lounge. Four beers change regularly, with guests sourced nationally. A beer festival is held in November. Card-carrying CAMRA members are admitted free for occasional visits (a small fee usually applies). Bar snacks are available. 🐾🏠♣P🚽🛜

Cheltenham Motor Club Ⓛ
Upper Park Street, GL52 6SA
🕐 6-midnight (1am Fri); 12-1am Sat; 7-midnight Sun ☎ (01242) 522590 🌐 cheltmc.com
Stroud Tom Long; 5 changing beers (often Moor Beer) Ⓗ
Visitors are welcome at this friendly club just off London Road, recently refurbished with the addition of a new snug. Five changing ales from across the country are stocked, plus regular Stroud Tom Long, four real ciders and a range of bottled Belgian beers. At least two beer festivals are held annually, plus Meet the Brewer/takeover evenings. Home to local darts and pool teams. A multiple award winner including CAMRA National Club of the Year in 2013. Q🐾🏠♣P🚽(B,51)🐾🛜

Jolly Brewmaster 🏆 Ⓛ
39 Painswick Road, GL50 2EZ (off A40 Suffolk Rd)
🕐 2.30-11; 12-11 Sat; 12-10.30 Sun ☎ (01242) 772261
7 changing beers (often Bespoke, Moor Beer) Ⓗ
Frequent local CAMRA Pub of the Year. Seven handpumps feature a changing range of ales sourced nationally, and at least six ciders. This busy and friendly community hub has original etched windows, a horseshoe bar and open fire. As a traditional drinking pub it has no food menu, but bar snacks such as pasties are generally available. The attractive courtyard garden is popular in the summer, with regular barbecues. Quiz nights are Mondays and most Wednesdays. Q🐾🏠🚽🚌(10,94U)🐾🛜

Kemble Brewery Inn Ⓛ
27 Fairview Street, GL52 2JF (look for Fairview St beside Machine Mart, pub is approx 100yds on right)
🕐 11-11 (midnight Fri & Sat); 12-11 Sun ☎ (01242) 701053
Bath Ales Gem; Wye Valley Butty Bach; 4 changing beers Ⓗ
Small, popular, back-street local, hard to find, but well worth the effort. Originally a butcher's shop in 1845, it became a pub in 1847, and was fully refurbished in January 2016. Six ales from near and far are served alongside Westons Traditional Scrumpy. There is a small, attractive walled garden where smoking is permitted. A guest chef night is arranged for Mondays 7-9pm for charity. Q🐾🏠👤♣♣

Sandford Park Alehouse Ⓛ
20 High Street, GL50 1DZ (E end of High St)
🕐 12-midnight; 12-11 Sun & Mon ☎ (01242) 574517 🌐 spalehouse.co.uk
Oakham Citra; Purity Mad Goose; Wye Valley Butty Bach; 6 changing beers Ⓗ
CAMRA National Pub of the Year 2015, this smart, contemporary alehouse has a U-shaped main area complete with bar billiards, a cosy front snug with wood-burning stove and a large south-facing patio/garden. A function room/lounge with sports TV is on the first floor. Ten handpumps feature changing ales from microbreweries sourced nationally and locally, plus a cider. Q🐾🏠👤♣🚽🐾🛜

Strand Ⓛ
40-42 High Street, GL50 1EE
🕐 12-11 (midnight Fri); 10-midnight Sat; 12-10.30 Sun ☎ (01242) 511848 🌐 strandpub.co.uk
5 changing beers (often Bespoke, Otter, Stroud) Ⓗ
Modern, wine bar-style pub, recently refurbished, at the east end of the High Street, offering five beers mainly from the region (at least one from the featured brewery of the month) and a cider. Good-value food is served daily, with a gourmet burger night on Wednesday. An upstairs function room is available for hire, along with a cellar bar, home to live comedy and music nights. A large south-facing patio/garden provides a pleasant outdoor drinking area. 🏠👤🚽🐾🛜

Chipping Campden

Eight Bells Ⓛ
Church Street, GL55 6JG
🕐 12-11; 12-10.30 Sun ☎ (01386) 840371 🌐 eightbellsinn.co.uk
Hook Norton Hooky; Purity Pure UBU; Wye Valley HPA; 2 changing beers (sourced regionally) Ⓗ

175

The Eight Bells was originally built in the 14th century to house the stonemasons that built St James' Church, and was later used to store the peal of eight bells that were hung in the church tower, hence its name. The inn was rebuilt using most of the original stone and timbers during the 17th century. What exists today is an outstanding example of a traditional Cotswolds inn, with a cobbled courtyard with underground priest passage. Changing local or regional ales are sold. Q❄️☺️🍴◑🅙&♣●🖾(21)🛜

Chipping Sodbury

Horseshoe
2 High Street, BS37 6AH
🕐 10-11 (midnight Fri & Sat) ☎ (01454) 325658
🌐 horseshoechippingsodbury.co.uk
Sharp's Doom Bar; Wye Valley Butty Bach; 5 changing beers 🅷
One of the oldest buildings in the town and with a real cellar, this former stationery shop, then briefly a wine bar, was converted into a pub at the start of 2014 by Dave and Gilly, formerly of the Grapes, almost opposite (and now closed). It serves two regular and five guest beers which can be unusual and often include dark or strong choices, as well as five traditional ciders. There are three linked rooms, with assorted furniture, and a pleasant rear garden. A selection of freshly made rolls complements the lunchtime menu.
☺️🍴◑♣●🖾🛜

Churchdown

Old Elm 🅛
Church Road, GL3 2ER
🕐 12-11 (midnight Thu & Fri); 10-midnight Sat; 10-10.30 Sun
☎ (01452) 530961 🌐 theoldelminn.co.uk
Sharp's Doom Bar; 4 changing beers (sourced locally; often Gloucester, Stroud) 🅷
Set in the heart of this village, the Old Elm was fully refurbished before reopening in November 2015. It is gaining a deserved reputation for its food (the menu features good vegetarian options), and serves five quality beers, including LocAles and some cider. Lively quiz and music nights are hosted and important rugby matches are shown in the sports bar. Families are welcome and the large garden hosts a children's play area. Five letting rooms are available. ☺️☀️🍴◑◑&♣P🖾●

Cirencester

Drillman's Arms
34 Gloucester Road, GL7 2JY
🕐 11-2.30, 5.30-11; 11-midnight Sat; 12-4.30 Sun
☎ (01285) 653892
Sharp's Doom Bar; 3 changing beers (sourced nationally) 🅷
A lively Georgian inn, perched beside a busy thoroughfare, featuring a convivial lounge with woodburner, a pub games-dominated public bar and a popular skittle alley. Graced by the same landlady for over 25 years, this excellent free house features low-beamed ceilings, horse brasses, fresh flowers and brewery pictures, alongside well priced pub food (lunchtimes only). An annual beer festival swamps the small front car park on August bank holiday weekends.
☀️◑△♣P●🛜

Marlborough Arms 🅛
1 Sheep Street, GL7 1QW
🕐 5-midnight; 12-midnight Fri-Sun
Box Steam Piston Broke; North Cotswold Windrush Ale; 6 changing beers (sourced nationally; often Corinium) 🅷
A lively real ale haven, selling eight beers from regionals and microbreweries, this wooden-floored pub lies opposite the old GWR station. Local CAMRA Cider Pub of the Year once again, it offers a plethora of interesting boxed ciders and perries. Brewery memorabilia adorn the walls, with pews and a deep-set fireplace adding character. The ceiling is disappearing behind the pumpclip collection. The rear patio is used for barbecues during beer and cider festivals. ☀️♣●●🛜

Cold Aston

Plough Inn 🅛
GL54 3BN (centre of village)
🕐 12-3 (not Mon) 6-11; 12-11 Fri-Sun ☎ (01451) 822602
🌐 coldastonplough.com
Flying Monk Elmers 🅷; **2 changing beers (sourced nationally)** 🅷/🅖
A transformed stone-flagged country pub high in the Cotswolds. The attractive village went by the name of Aston Blank in the Domesday Book. This venue was reopened in 2013 by young owners and their team; it has three letting luxury bedrooms with an innovative internal extension of the 17th-century cottage. The emphasis is on real ale and serving good, interesting food. Look out for three changing beers from award-winning brewers, two served directly from the barrel. Local CAMRA Pub of the Year finalist 2016. Q❄️☺️🍴◑◑&△♣P●

Coleford

Dog House Micropub
13-15 St John Street, GL16 8AP
🕐 5 (12 Sat)-10; 12-3 Sun ☎ 07442 787015
🌐 thedoghousemicropub.co.uk
6 changing beers (sourced locally) 🅷/🅖
Local CAMRA Pub of the Year, this friendly micropub is in an attractively fronted old chemists' shop. It offers two varying ales on handpump, plus up to four more from the barrel, a couple of them usually LocAle. A cider fridge stocks eight varying selections, plus a few Belgian beers. The pub's Facebook page highlights special events and music nights, which are invariably wonderful social occasions and are always popular, so arrive early if you want to be sure of finding a seat. Q❄️●🖾●

Cranham

Black Horse Inn 🅛
GL4 8HP (off A46 or B4070)
🕐 12-11; 12-9 Sun ☎ (01452) 812217
🌐 blackhorseinncranham.co.uk
4 changing beers (sourced regionally; often Wye Valley) 🅷
A 17th-century, stone-built free house almost hidden up a side lane in the village. A quiet, idyllic pub with no jukebox, TV or fruit machines, and with a proper fire; the lack of a reliable mobile phone signal in the village means that patrons here indulge in the traditional pursuit of conversation with friends, strangers and walkers who have explored the myriad woodland paths nearby. Well-behaved dogs are welcome. Q❄️◑♣●P●

Dursley

New Inn 🗂
82-84 Woodmancote, GL11 4AJ (on A4135)
✪ closed Mon-Wed; 2.30 (5 Thu)-11 ☎ (01453) 519288
⊕ newinnwoodmancote.co.uk
4 changing beers (sourced nationally; often Wye Valley) ⓗ
Known as a dog-friendly establishment, where the pub's labrador often helps provide the greeting, this welcoming, comfortable inn features a large L-shaped public bar with tiled floor, and a smaller lounge. Fine beers are sourced from smaller, local brewers where possible, dependent upon what the regulars request. There is a spacious suntrap of a garden at the rear, which is popular on sunny days. Food is limited to freshly made rolls. ❧❀♣️♠️P❀

Old Spot Inn 🗂
2 Hill Road, GL11 4JQ (by bus station and free car park)
✪ 12-11 ☎ (01453) 542870 ⊕ oldspotinn.co.uk
Uley Old Ric; 7 changing beers (sourced nationally) ⓗ
Excellent free house dating from 1776, serving great ales, ciders and perries. Named after the Gloucestershire Old Spot pig, a porcine theme blends with the extensive brewery memorabilia, low ceilings, wood-burning stoves and welcoming staff to create a convivial atmosphere. There is an attractive garden with a heated, covered area. Freshly prepared food is served 12-3pm (12-4pm Sun). On the Cotswold Way, it is popular with walkers, and hosts regular events in the evenings. Q❧❀❅❧♠️❀❀❀❀❀

Eastington

Old Badger Inn 🗂 ✅
Alkerton Road, GL10 3AT (on Spring Hill)
✪ 12-11; 12-10.30 Sun ☎ (01453) 822892
⊕ oldbadgerinn.co.uk
5 changing beers (sourced regionally; often St Austell, Wickwar, Wye Valley) ⓗ
Formerly the Victoria – closed by Punch Taverns in 2010 – the pub was reopened as a free house after being sympathetically renovated, modernised and extended. The large single bar features a wood-burning stove, with smaller rooms on either side plus a restaurant area. The walls are covered with brewery and other memorabilia. Outside there is a covered and heated patio and a large garden with a children's play area. Very dog-friendly. Local CAMRA Cider Pub of the Year.
Q❧❀❅❧♣️♠️P❀(61,401)❀❀

Ebrington

Ebrington Arms 🗂
GL55 6NH (off B4035; centre of village by green)
✪ 12-11 ☎ (01386) 593223 ⊕ theebringtonarms.co.uk
North Cotswold Moreton Mild; 3 changing beers (sourced regionally; often North Cotswold) ⓗ
A 17th-century Cotswold stone-built pub with a lovely open fireplace in a beautiful village with excellent walks. Of the six handpumps, three dispense the pub's own Yubby ales and two serve changing guests. An excellent range of food features ingredients from local suppliers. It is a regular Guide entry, with the same owners as the Killingworth Castle in Wotton, Oxfordshire. A family-run pub with enthusiastic staff and accommodation in five en-suite rooms, it was a 2015 and 2016 CAMRA Pub of the Year finalist.
❧❀❅❧❀❅❧♣️♠️P

Forthampton

Lower Lode Inn 🗂
GL19 4RE (signed from A438) SO8788231809
✪ 12-midnight (2am Fri & Sat) ☎ (01684) 293224
⊕ lowerlodeinn.co.uk
Sharp's Doom Bar; Wickwar BOB; 2 changing beers (often Brains, Malvern Hills) ⓗ
Blessed with views across the River Severn to Tewkesbury Abbey, this attractive 15th-century brick-built hostelry, with its three acres of lawns, is a popular stopover for boats and is a Camping and Caravanning Club site. Food is advertised as simple and wholesome, and is excellent quality and value for money. A beer festival is staged in September. A small ferry operates from the Tewkesbury side from Easter to mid-September. Day fishing is available, plus en-suite accommodation. Opening times are reduced in winter.
Q❧❅❧❀❅❧❀♣️♠️P❀

Fossebridge

Inn at Fossebridge ✅
GL54 3JS (on A429)
✪ 12-11 ☎ (01285) 720721 ⊕ fossebridgeinn.co.uk
Wadworth Horizon, 6X; 3 changing beers (sourced locally; often Wadworth) ⓗ
This hostelry is in a pretty hamlet where the Fosse Way drops into the Cotswolds valley of the River Coln, an Area of Outstanding Natural Beauty. An attractive one-bar inn, it has old timbers, a fine flagstone floor and open fires. The premises also benefit from a lovely four-acre garden with a lake and river. A selection of Wadworth ales and guests from local breweries is available in cosy surroundings. Local CAMRA runner-up for 2017 Pub of the Year. Q❧❀❅❧❀♠️P❀❀

Frampton Cotterell

Globe Inn
366 Church Road, BS36 2AB
✪ 12-11; 12-10.30 Sun ☎ (01454) 778286
⊕ theglobeframptoncotterell.co.uk
Butcombe Original; Fuller's London Pride; 3 changing beers (often St Austell) ⓗ
Independent free house on the Frome Valley walkway, which links the Cotswolds with the Avon Valley walkway. An open-plan pub, with a separate pavilion which can be hired for functions, it specialises in home-made food using local produce. The pub has an active golf society, a Tuesday quiz and caters for children with an excellent play area. Three guest beers are normally stocked, including many local brews. Moles Black Rat cider is served. ❧❀❅❧♠️P❀❀

Rising Sun
43 Ryecroft Road, BS36 2HN
✪ 11.30-11.30 (midnight Fri & Sat); 12-11 Sun
☎ (01454) 772330
Draught Bass; Great Western Maiden Voyage, Classic Gold, Moose River; 2 changing beers ⓗ
A village local with a cosy log-burning stove. There is a single bar, with slate pillars and flagstone floors, and a restaurant in the warm conservatory. An extensive menu offers lunchtime snacks and more substantial evening meals. The pub is the brewery tap for the Great Western Brewing Company, and guest beers are usually from small independent brewers. The skittle alley can be used for private functions. Q❀❅❧♣️P❀(46,82)❀❀

Frampton Mansell

Crown Inn

GL6 8JG (opp Jolly Nice farm shop)
☼ 12-11 ☎ (01285) 760601 ⊕ thecrowninn-cotswolds.co.uk
Butcombe Gold; Stroud OPA Organic Pale Ale; Uley Laurie Lee's Bitter; 2 changing beers (often Sharp's, Uley) ⊞
This thriving village local dates back to 1633, when it was a cider house with a slaughterhouse next door. The three bars feature exposed stone walls, wooden beams and open fires. The suntrap front garden offers fine views over the Golden Valley. Children are welcome and there are books available for them. The pub has a modern 12-bedroom hotel annexe with ample car parking.
🌣😺🚲🍴◑➁♿♣Ⓟ🚌(54,54A)🐾

Frampton-on-Severn

Three Horseshoes ⅃

The Green, GL2 7DY (off B4071)
☼ 11.30-2, 5.30-11 (1am Fri); 11.30-1am Sat; 11.30-10 Sun
☎ (01452) 742100 ⊕ threehorseshoespub.co.uk
Sharp's Doom Bar; Timothy Taylor Landlord; Uley Bitter ⊞
Atmospheric two-bar community pub originally built by a farrier at the south end of England's longest village green. The food is home-cooked, especially the unique 3-Shu pie, which is freshly baked to order. Both bars have coal fires, and dogs are welcome in the flagstoned public bar. Evening jamming sessions are popular (largely biased towards folk music), as are pasty baking competitions, conker contests and veggie Olympics. A double boules court hosts annual championships. Q🌣😺◑➁♿▲♣●🐾

Gloucester

Brewhouse & Kitchen ✅

Unit R1, St Anne Walk, Gloucester Quay, GL1 5SH
☼ 11-11 (midnight Fri & Sat); 11-10.30 Sun
☎ (01452) 222965
Brewhouse & Kitchen Stevedore, Shed Head; 2 changing beers (often Brewhouse & Kitchen) ⊞
Based in the bustling Gloucester Quays development, this smart bar and restaurant is part of the growing Brewhouse & Kitchen chain, brewing its own range of ales on-site. Customers can sit in comfort and enjoy a quality beer and food from a varied menu, while watching the brewing process. On a fine day you can relax in a seating area alongside the Gloucester-Sharpness Canal.
◑➁♿🚌

Pelican Inn ⅃ ✅

4 St Mary's Street, GL1 2QR (WNW of cathedral)
☼ 11-11.30 ☎ (01452) 387877
Wye Valley Bitter ⊞**, HPA** ⊞**/Ⓖ, Butty Bach; 4 changing beers (sourced regionally; often Wye Valley)** ⊞
Local CAMRA Pub of the Year, again, it was licensed as an alehouse in the 17th century. It is believed that some of its beams are from Drake's Golden Hind, which began life as the Pelican. Rescued and refurbished by Wye Valley Brewery in 2012, the pub's popularity has grown steadily, with the single bar dominated by conversation; there is a smaller room to the side and an attractive outdoor drinking area. A growing range of cider and perry increases during the summer. Q😺♿≈♣●🚌🐾

Tank ✅

12-14 Llanthony Road, GL1 2EH
☼ 12-11 ☎ (01452) 690541 ⊕ tankgloucester.com
Gloucester Mariner, Citra, Dockside Dark, American Pale; 4 changing beers (sourced nationally) ⊞
This brewery tap is a welcoming, urban warehouse-style bar with a contemporary feel, located in the heart of the Gloucester Docks redevelopment that opened in 2015. The decor utilises the building's strengths, and is well worth a look. Though primarily selling Gloucester beers, there is a wide range of guest and bottled beers and ciders. Food is available in the shape of local meats and cheeses served on platters, along with a selection of hand-made pizzas. ◑➁♿●Ⓟ🚌(10)🛜

Gretton

Royal Oak ⅃ ✅

Gretton Road, GL54 5EP (E end of village)
☼ 11-11; 12-10.30 Sun ☎ (01242) 604999
⊕ royaloakgretton.co.uk
Ringwood Fortyniner; St Austell Trelawny; Sharp's Atlantic; Wye Valley HPA, Butty Bach; 2 changing beers ⊞
A warm welcome is assured from the local owners of this popular Cotswold pub set in two acres. All the regular beers are from local breweries or Marston's. The home-cooked food can be eaten in the L-shaped bar or in the conservatory with its outstanding views across the Vale of Evesham. The Royal Oak dates from about 1830 and the large garden includes a children's play area and a tennis court. The Gloucestershire-Warwickshire railway runs past the garden. 🌣😺◑➁♿♣Ⓟ🐾

Ham

Salutation Inn 🍺 ⅃

Ham Green, GL13 9QH (take road signed to Jenner Museum)
☼ 12-2.30 (not Mon-Thu), 5-11; 12-11 Sat; 12-10.30 Sun
☎ (01453) 810284 ⊕ the-sally-at-ham.com
Butcombe Original; Tiley's Pale Ale, Best Bitter; 4 changing beers (sourced nationally) ⊞
Multi award-winning rural free house, and County CAMRA Pub of the Year again. It offers up to seven real ales, nine real ciders and perries, and a bottled beer menu. The on-site microbrewery (Tiley's) produces hop-forward pale ales and traditional bitters. There are three bars (two cosy ones share a central woodburner) and a skittles alley/function room. Food is served weekend lunchtimes and occasional evenings only, and there are folk nights and singalongs. Q🌣😺◑♿♣●Ⓟ🚌(62)🐾🛜

Hawkesbury Upton

Beaufort Arms ⅃

High Street, GL9 1AU (off A46, 6 miles N of M4 jct 18)
☼ 12-11; 12-10.30 Sun ☎ (01454) 238217
⊕ beaufortarms.com
Bath Ales Special Pale Ale; Bristol Beer Factory Seven; 3 changing beers (sourced regionally) ⊞
A wonderful Grade II-listed Cotswold stone free house, built in 1602, close to the historic Somerset Monument. It features separate public and lounge bars, a dining room and skittle alley/function room, which are required to house a veritable plethora of ancient brewery and local memorabilia. It serves up to five ales and a traditional cider on handpump, and has an attractive garden with a

barbecue used for local community activities. A great bunch of regulars assures a warm welcome. Q☕🕑🍴🍺🐾P🅿🐕🛜

Hillesley

Fleece Inn 🅛
Chapel Lane, GL12 7RD
🕐 11-11 (midnight Fri & Sat) ☎ (01453) 520003
🌐 thefleeceinnhillesley.com
Wye Valley Butty Bach; 5 changing beers 🅷
An attractive 17th-century whitewashed pub, owned by the community. It has a single bar with a separate lounge/dining room and a snug area, and offers an extensive food menu mainly sourced from local produce. The pub offers a 10 per cent discount for CAMRA members on real ales, which usually come from local micros. Thatchers Heritage is on handpump. Children are welcome and the garden has a safe play area with restricted access to the large car park. Q☕🕑🍴🍺P🅿🛜

Kingswood

King's Arms
16 High Street, BS15 4AB
🕐 12-11 (midnight Sat); 10-11 Sun ☎ 07737 794115
Cheddar Ales Gorge Best; 2 changing beers 🅷
Traditional no-frills free house thriving in an area short of real ale-friendly outlets. The pub is a Grade II-listed former coaching inn, with a recessed games area and a large patio and garden area to the rear. The young owner/landlord is a real ale enthusiast and offers interesting guest beers, including stouts, porters and milds – one or two at a time – plus bottle-conditioned beers. No food is served but you are welcome to bring in a takeaway. Pool, darts and cribbage are available. ☕🕑🍺🍴🐾🛜

Longborough

Coach & Horses
GL56 0QU (off A424 in village centre)
🕐 11-2.30, 5.30-11; 11-11 Fri-Sun ☎ (01451) 830325
🌐 coachnhorseslongborough.co.uk
Donnington BB, Gold, SBA 🅷
Dating from the 18th century, this village pub of Cotswold stone is perched on a bank overlooking a small green and war memorial. Located only one mile from the renowned Donnington Brewery, this friendly family-run, one-bar premises is the focal point of community activity in the village. Flagstone floors and an open fire greet locals and visitors, with the full range of good-value Donnington Ales on offer along with home-cooked food. Q☕🕑🍴🍺🐾🛜

Lydbrook

Royal Spring Inn
Vention Lane, GL17 9RL (off B4228 to W of village)
🕐 12-3, 7-11 ☎ (01594) 860492
Brains Rev James; Fuller's London Pride; 1 changing beer (sourced regionally; often Wye Valley) 🅷
Traditional whitewashed community free house in an attractive position up a narrow lane above the Wye. The carpeted floors in the wooden bar areas do vary in depth, but help separate the pub games from diners enjoying much-appreciated home-cooked food. A stream flows through the sloping fenced rear garden that houses a menagerie,

which is open as a playground and drinking area with some lovely views. The adjacent cottage is available to rent. ☕🕑🍴A🐾P

Marshfield

Catherine Wheel
39 High Street, SN14 8LR
🕐 12-11 ☎ (01225) 892220 🌐 thecatherinewheel.co.uk
Butcombe Original; Fuller's London Pride; 1 changing beer (sourced locally) 🅷
Impressive building with a 17th-century frontage and a much older interior in a large village on the edge of the Cotswolds, but close to Georgian Bath. Ideally situated for a number of tourist attractions in three counties and also the city of Bristol, it is an owner-run free house with several dining areas in addition to the bar. The large fire creates a cosy atmosphere in the winter months. There are also three letting rooms. Q☕🕑🛏🕑🍴🍺P🅿🐕🛜

Mayshill

New Inn 🏅
Badminton Road, BS36 2NT (on A432)
🕐 11.45-2.30, 5.30-10.30; 11.45-11 Fri & Sat; 11.45-10 Sun
☎ (01454) 773161 🌐 newinn-mayshill.co.uk
3 changing beers (sourced nationally) 🅷
Pleasantly located in the countryside, this roadside 17th-century inn is hugely popular for its food, including gluten-free options (booking is advised). The three guest beers are from far and wide, with one of them usually dark, plus a traditional cider. The main bar is warmed by a real fire in winter, and the rear area serves as a restaurant. Children are welcome until 8.45pm. The large garden, with a play area, is pleasant in summer. Q☕🕑🍴🍺🍴P🅿🐕🛜

Moreton-in-Marsh

Bell Inn 🅛 🏅
High Street, GL56 0AF (on A429)
🕐 11-11 ☎ (01608) 651688 🌐 thebellinnmoreton.co.uk
Prescott Hill Climb; Purity Pure UBU; Timothy Taylor Landlord; 2 changing beers (sourced locally; often Hook Norton, North Cotswold) 🅷
Old high-street coaching inn dating from the 18th century and now pleasantly refurbished. The interior comprises a mainly open-plan area sympathetically divided into more intimate snug sections, with a real fire and good food. A large courtyard area is found through the old arched entrance, with an enclosed garden at the rear. Famed for links with JRR Tolkien, Lord of the Rings author, it has a map of Middle Earth adorning the walls. Local and national ales are stocked. Q☕🕑🛏🍴🍺A🚲P🅿🐕🛜

Moseley Green

Rising Sun 🅛
GL15 4HN (off A48 at Blakeney towards Parkend)
🕐 12-11 (midnight Fri & Sat) ☎ (01594) 562008
Wickwar BOB; 3 changing beers (sourced nationally) 🅷
Enjoying panoramic views from its isolated position amid disused coal mines, this extended pub was built for miners in the early 1800s. Popular with cyclists, hikers, cavers and families, there are several patios, large gardens and a pond. It is hard to believe that trams and trains ran only yards from

the pub doors. There is a bar on both floors, a games room and a kids' menu in the dining areas. A local music ensemble rehearses here.
🏠⊛🛏◑♣🐾P🗒

Nettleton Bottom

Golden Heart

Birdlip, GL4 8LA (on A417)
☼ 10.30-11 ☎ (01242) 870261 ⊕ thegoldenheart.co.uk
Brakspear Bitter; 3 changing beers (sourced nationally; often Marston's) ℍ
A welcome oasis of tranquillity beside the single-carriageway section of the Gloucester to Swindon road, this 400-year-old Cotswold free house retains most of its original features, although adjoining cottages have been absorbed to create extra rooms. The small bar, almost hidden beyond a huge open fireplace, overlooks a stone-paved patio and garden abutting a cow pasture. Their menu uses the finest award-winning meats and local produce at reasonable prices. There are two en-suite guest bedrooms. Q🏠⊛🛏◑P🐾🛜

Newnham

Railway Inn

Station Road, GL14 1DA (turn off A48 at clock tower)
☼ 1-midnight; 12-midnight Sat & Sun ☎ (01594) 516317
3 changing beers (sourced nationally; often Brains, Butcombe) ℍ
County CAMRA Cider Pub of the Year for the fifth year in succession, this friendly community hub is a joy to visit, with railway memorabilia adorning the walls, flagstoned floors, warm fires and an Indian restaurant upstairs. Offering umpteen ciders and perries and 20-plus bottled real ciders, several local cider producers drink here, and love explaining their craft to visitors. Everyone wants you to find a cider or perry that you genuinely enjoy. Lively music acts are hosted most weekends.
⊛◑♣🐾🛜

Quenington

Keepers Arms

Church Road, GL7 5BL (from Fairford turn right at green)
☼ 12-3 (not Mon & Tue), 6-11; 12-3, 5.30-11 Fri; 12-3, 6-11 Sat; 12-3, 7-11 Sun ☎ (01285) 750349
⊕ thekeepersarms.co.uk
4 changing beers (sourced nationally; often Butcombe, Otter, St Austell) ℍ
Local CAMRA Pub of the Year, this wonderful community local has been transformed into a fine modern hostelry by the delightfully enthusiastic owner. Dogs, children, cricketers, cyclists, art lovers and ramblers are welcome in both the refurbished oak bar and the petite front garden. Unpretentious food menus help fill both dining areas (no food Mon and Tue), with regular theme nights and quizzes proving popular. Accommodation is available in four en-suite rooms. 🏠⊛🛏◑P🐾🛜

Sheepscombe

Butchers Arms ℓ ✓

GL6 7RH (signed off A46) SO8911610434
☼ 11.30-3, 6.30 (6 Fri)-11; 11.30-11 Sat; 12-10.30 Sun
☎ (01452) 812113 ⊕ butchers-arms.co.uk
Prescott Hill Climb; 2 changing beers (sourced regionally; often Butcombe, Otter, Wye Valley) ℍ

Handsome 17th-century Cotswold stone pub overlooking a wooded valley. Its inn sign, a painted three-dimensional carving of a butcher quaffing ale while tethered to a pig, is world famous. In 2014 the lean-to outdoor toilets metamorphosed into a new bar, seamlessly executed in reclaimed stone and Welsh oak. This complements a quality inter-war refurbishment that added the generous bay windows and porch. The forecourt tables and sloping side garden are suntraps in summer.
Q⊛⊛◑🛏♣🐾P🗒🐾🛜

Slad

Woolpack ℓ

GL6 7QA (on B4070)
☼ 12-midnight ☎ (01452) 813429 ⊕ thewoolpackslad.com
Stroud Budding; Uley Bitter, Old Spot Prize Strong Ale, Pig's Ear Strong Beer; 1 changing beer (sourced regionally; often Gloucester) ℍ
Seventeenth-century inn made famous by Cider with Rosie – its author, Laurie Lee, was a regular all his life. Only one room deep, the pub offers superb views over the Slad Valley, and has been thoughtfully restored; the built-in dark-wooden settles in the end rooms are modern. The bar runs the length of the building, extending into all four rooms. Popular with both tourists and a loyal clientele, a daily changing food menu is available, with pizza on Sunday night. Q🏠⊛◑♣🐾🛜

South Woodchester

Ram Inn ℓ

Station Road, GL5 5EL (signed off A46) SO8395202189
☼ 11-11; 12-11 Sat & Sun ☎ (01453) 873329
Butcombe Adam Henson's Rare Breed; Flying Monk Elmers; Otter Amber; St Austell Tribute; 2 changing beers (sourced regionally; often St Austell, Sharp's) ℍ
Sensitively altered and extended 400-year-old Cotswold stone inn tucked into the west flank of the Nailsworth Valley. It commands fine views towards Amberley and Minchinhampton Common on the opposite side of the valley from a suntrap front terrace. Inside, three interconnecting rooms (one with a log fire) are grouped around a long stone-built bar. Popular with locals and visitors alike, it is situated in superb walking country, with extensive car parking at the front.
Q⊛⊛◑♿♣🐾P🚌(40,63)🐾🛜

Stroud

Ale House ℓ

9 John Street, GL5 2HA (opp Cornhill farmers' market)
☼ 12-3, 5-11; 12-midnight Fri; 10.30-midnight Sat; 12-11 Sun
☎ (01453) 755447
Cotswold Lion Golden Fleece; Dark Star Hophead; Stroud Budding; 6 changing beers (sourced nationally; often Brass Castle, Burning Sky, Tiny Rebel) ℍ
Built in 1837 for the Poor Law Guardians, this Grade II-listed building is a mecca for ale lovers. The bar occupies the double-height top-lit former boardroom, where an all-year-round beer festival showcases ales from Marble, Salopian and Saltaire among others – plus a cider and perry, dispensed from handpumps. Opposite is a blazing log fire and adjoining are two smaller rooms. Local CAMRA Pub of the Year, live music nights are popular here, as are the special home-made curries.
Q🏠⊛◑♿🍴♣🐾🖩🛜

Crown & Sceptre 🄻

98 Horns Road, GL5 1EG
🌣 3 (12 Fri & Sat)-11; 12-10.30 Sun ☎ (01453) 762588
⊕ crownandsceptrestroud.com
**Stroud Budding; Uley Bitter, Pig's Ear Strong Beer; 1
changing beer (sourced regionally; often Brains)** Ⓗ
Lively back-street local at the heart of its
community – a genuine free house where Blue
Anchor Spingo beers are regular guests. The walls
display an eclectic mix of framed prints and
posters. A large oak table in a side room is popular
with local groups, including Knit and Natter. The
pub also has its own motorcycle society. Football,
rugby and cricket are screened in the back bar. A
terrace to the rear offers panoramic views over
Stroud. 🌣❀♣●P🚌(8,227)😺🛜

Prince Albert 🄻 ✅

Rodborough Hill, GL5 3SS (corner of Walkley Hill)
🌣 4-11.30 (12.30am Fri); 12-12.30am Sat; 12-10.30 Sun
☎ (01453) 755600 ⊕ theprincealbertstroud.co.uk
**Otter Bitter; Stroud Budding; Timothy Taylor Landlord;
3 changing beers (sourced nationally; often Bath
Ales, Bristol Beer Factory, Church End)** Ⓗ
Lively, cosmopolitan, Cotswold stone pub below
Rodborough Common that is simultaneously
bohemian, homely and welcoming, with a big
reputation for live music. The L-shaped bar boasts
an eclectic mix of furniture, fittings and
memorabilia, the walls covered with film and
music posters. The pub hosts a May beer festival,
exhibitions and open mic nights. Pop-up street
food is available in the yard on a Friday night, or
you can order in a takeaway (plates and cutlery
provided). 🌣❀≋♣●🚌😺🛜

Tetbury

Royal Oak 🄻 ✅

1 Cirencester Road, GL8 8EY (on B4067)
🌣 11-11 (11.30 Fri & Sat); 12-11 Sun ☎ (01666) 500021
⊕ theroyaloaktetbury.co.uk
**Moor Beer So'Hop; Stroud Tom Long; 3 changing
beers (sourced regionally; often Butcombe, Left
Handed Giant)** Ⓗ
This wonderful award-winning pub utilises clever
design to marry a traditional feel to a modern
layout. The swathe of wooden surfaces provides a
welcoming feel, with a small fireplace adding
warmth. Six handpumps include Severn Cider and a
vegan ale from Moor – chosen to match the vegan
menu option. The one-pot dish goes well,
especially on quiz nights. Upstairs dining rooms and
six letting rooms are popular, as are the lively
music and beer festivals. 🌣❀🛏🄳&♣●P😺🛜

Tewkesbury

Berkeley Arms ✅

8 Church Street, GL20 5PA (on old A38)
🌣 10-11 ☎ (01684) 290555
⊕ berkeleyarmstewkesbury.co.uk
**Wadworth IPA, 6X, Swordfish; 2 changing beers
(often Titanic, Wadworth)** Ⓗ

Half-timbered Grade II two-bar pub, just off
Tewkesbury Cross. At the rear, a barn, which is
believed to be the oldest non-ecclesiastical
building in this historic town, is used for dining in
the summer and serves as a meeting room year
round. Good-value home-cooked food is served
daily in this popular 15th-century inn, and of
particular note are the landlord's home-baked pies.
Live music is performed on Friday and Saturday
evenings. Buses to Cheltenham and Gloucester
stop close by. Q🌣❀🛏🄳&🄰♣●🚌(41)😺🛜

Nottingham Arms 🄻 ✅

129 High Street, GL20 5JU (on A38 in town centre)
🌣 11-11 ☎ (01684) 276346
**St Austell Tribute; Sharp's Doom Bar; Wye Valley HPA,
Butty Bach** Ⓗ
Fourteenth-century hostelry with two welcoming
rooms, a public bar at the front and the restaurant
behind, with timber predominating. Framed
photographs of old Tewkesbury adorn the walls.
The pub is getting noticed for its excellent, well-
priced food, served lunchtimes and evenings.
Knowledgeable staff will happily tell you about the
resident ghosts. Live music takes place most
Sunday evenings and Thursday is quiz night.
🌣🄳🄰♣●🚌😺🛜

Royal British Legion Club

50 Church Street, GL20 5SN
🌣 8-11 Mon, Wed & Thu; closed Tue; 7-11.30 Fri; 12-3,
7.30-11.30 Sat; 12-3, 7.30-11 Sun ☎ (01684) 293798
⊕ branches.britishlegion.org.uk/branches/tewkesbury
2 changing beers (often Exmoor, Ludlow) Ⓗ
Services club near the abbey in a timber-framed
building that used to be two pubs. The main lounge
area is open to non-members. The venue has a
community feel where several clubs hold their
meetings and it has a team in the local crib league.
Live music every Saturday night. Local CAMRA's
Club of the Year 2015-2017. Q🄰≋●🚌(41)😺

Royal Hop Pole Hotel 🄻 ✅

94 Church Street, GL20 5RS (between Abbey and Cross)
🌣 7am-11 ☎ (01684) 278670
**Great Western Old Higby; Greene King IPA; Hook
Norton Old Hooky; Ruddles County; 4 changing beers
(sourced locally; often Battledown, Exmoor,
Prescott)** Ⓗ
This well-known landmark is an amalgamation of
historic buildings from the 15th and 18th centuries.
It has been known as the Royal Hop Pole since a
visit in September 1891 from Princess Mary of Teck
(Queen Mary, Royal Consort of George V). The pub
is mentioned in The Pickwick Papers. Purchased by
Wetherspoon, it reopened in 2008, and is a
spacious, multi-roomed drinking establishment
with a large patio and garden area at the rear.
Q🌣❀🛏🄳&🄰P🚌🛜

Tudor House Hotel 🄻

51 High Street, GL20 5BH
🌣 11-11; 12-10 Sun ☎ (01684) 297755
**Butcombe Adam Henson's Rare Breed; 7 changing
beers (often Butcombe, Exmoor, Titanic)** Ⓗ
This delightful Tudor building oozes charm and
dignity. The bar offers a selection of eight ales,
seven constantly changing. Pub meals are served
in the bar and adjoining dining areas. Two outdoor
spaces provide a relaxing place to watch the boats
on the river behind the pub or you can enjoy a
quiet drink in the secret garden.
Q🌣❀🛏🄳&🄰P🚌🛜

White Bear 🄻

Bredon Road, GL20 5BU (off N end of High St)
✪ 10-midnight ☎ (01684) 296614
⊕ famouswhitebear.co.uk
**Salopian Oracle; 6 changing beers (sourced
nationally; often Bristol Beer Factory, Sadler's,
Uley)** 🄷
On the north-western edge of town, this good-
value, friendly pub attracts ale and cider drinkers
from far and wide. The open-plan L-shaped bar
offers room to play pool and darts; there is also a
skittle alley. Live music features every Sunday
afternoon. The seven frequently changing ales
come from local and national award-winning
breweries. At least five traditional perries and
ciders are always on sale. togo+A♣🖐PꝐ🐾☺

Thornbury

Anchor Inn 🄻 ✔

Gloucester Road, BS35 1JY
✪ 11-11 ☎ (01454) 281375 ⊕ theanchorthornbury.co.uk
Draught Bass; 5 changing beers 🄷
Licensed since 1695 and the second oldest pub in
Thornbury, this friendly, traditional inn has one
regular beer and five changing guests, mostly of
low to medium strength, with occasional milds,
plus a real cider. Good home-cooked food is served
daily. There are two large rooms, one of which has
been split to provide a function/meeting area and
is used by local artists. The pub also has its own
darts, crib, dominoes and cricket teams and an
angling syndicate. The garden includes a boules
piste and children's play area. togo🐕🍴♣🖐PꝐ🐾☺

Upper Soudley

White Horse Inn

Church Road, GL14 2UA (on B4227)
✪ 7-11 (midnight Fri); 3-midnight Sat; 12-6 Sun
☎ (01594) 825968
2 changing beers (sourced nationally) 🄷
Built as a railway hotel, next to the now defunct
Soudley Halt, it has great views across the valley
from the garden, and is close to the Blue Rock Trail
and Soudley Ponds. Run by an enthusiastic couple,
this lovely old pub has a small main bar with a
welcoming fireplace and two regularly changing
guest ales. The old dining room down the
passageway is used for functions, and leads
through to a much-loved skittle alley.
togo🐕♣🖐PꝐ(717)🐾

Wainlode

Red Lion Inn 🄻 ✔

Wainlode Hill, GL2 9LW
✪ 12-3, 5-11; 12-11 Fri; 12-11.30 Sat; 12-10.30 Sun
☎ (01452) 730935 ⊕ redlionwainlode.co.uk
**Butcombe Adam Henson's Rare Breed; Wye Valley
HPA; 1 changing beer (sourced regionally)** 🄷
On a picturesque stretch of the River Severn, this
iconic pub has been popular as a stopping-off point
since the mid-1800s. Refurbished in 2015, there is
much exposed red brickwork and wooden flooring

in its well-tended rooms. Very popular in good
weather, it has a good name for both food and
drink. It makes an ideal break for cyclists and
walkers alike, and there is a Caravan Club site
adjacent. togo🐕🍴A🖐P🐾☺

Wickwar

Buthay 🄻

15 High Street, GL12 8NE (close to traffic lights)
✪ closed Mon; 12-11 (midnight Fri & Sat); 12-9 Sun
☎ (01454) 299083 ⊕ thebuthay.co.uk
**3 changing beers (sourced regionally; often
Wickwar)** 🄷
This family-run 16th-century coaching inn attracts a
varied clientele into its welcoming single-bar main
drinking area, complete with log fire. Some lovely
internal glazing enhances a large dining room
which specialises in authentic Italian food cooked
fresh to order by chef Roberto. There is a skittles
alley/function room and to the rear is a large
enclosed garden with a well-equipped children's
play area. Well-behaved dogs are more than
welcome in the bar area. togo🐕🍴🕤♣🖐PꝐ🐾☺

Woolaston Common

Rising Sun

The Common, GL15 6NU (1 mile off A48 at Woolaston)
SO5901500924
✪ 12-2.30, 6.30-11 (midnight Sat); 12-3, 6.30-11 Sun
☎ (01594) 529282
**Butcombe Adam Henson's Rare Breed; Wye Valley
Bitter; 1 changing beer (sourced regionally)** 🄷
Off the beaten track, this comfortable 350-year-old
stone-built pub enjoys gorgeous views over the
Forest of Dean. There is a welcoming main bar with
an open fire, and a small snug, both of which
feature part of the landlord's large collection of
framed banknotes. The varied menu of good
home-cooked food is popular with ramblers (no
food Mon and Tue lunchtimes). Some great locals
help make for a very convivial atmosphere.
Q🐕🍴♣P

Wotton-under-Edge

Royal Oak Inn 🄻

3-5 Haw Street, GL12 7AG (at top end of town)
✪ 12-midnight ☎ (01453) 844366
⊕ theroyaloakwotton.com
**Fuller's London Pride; 2 changing beers (sourced
nationally)** 🄷
A large coaching inn with a friendly atmosphere,
complete with two comfortable bars, both with
open fires, plus a large dining room with wood
beams. There is a full-size snooker table upstairs
which is popular. This lively establishment supports
the local community and welcomes walkers using
the Cotswold Way. At the rear is a car park and
enclosed garden with a well-equipped children's
play area, formerly home to the stables, pigsty and
poultry house. Qtogo🐕🍴PꝐ🐾☺

'Let's have filleted steak and a bottle of Bass for dinner tonight. It will be simply exquisite.
I shall love it.' 'But my dear Nella,' he exclaimed, 'steak and beer at Felix's! It's impossible!
Moreover, young women still under twenty-three cannot be permitted to drink Bass.'
Arnold Bennett, The Grand Babylon Hotel, 1902

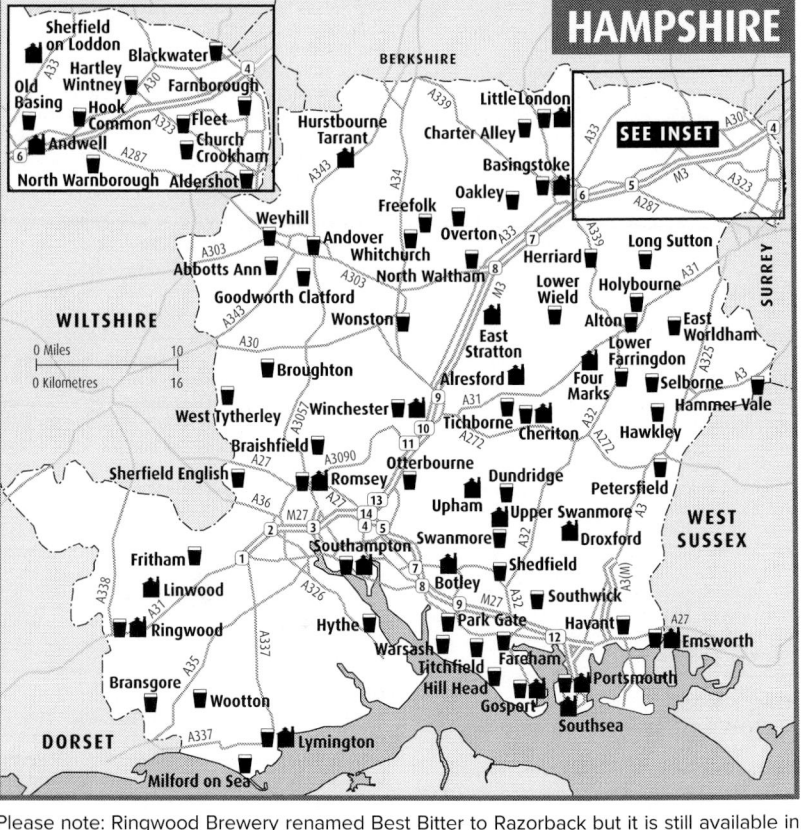

Please note: Ringwood Brewery renamed Best Bitter to Razorback but it is still available in some outlets as Best Bitter

Abbotts Ann

Eagle Inn 🗍
Duck Street, SP11 7BG
🕭 11.30-11; 12-10.30 Sun ☎ (01264) 710339
🌐 theeagleinn.wordpress.com
Bowman Wallops Wood; 3 changing beers (sourced locally) 🅷
In a picturesque village just two miles south-west of Andover, this pub is at the heart of the community. Friendly conversation rules the house. The regular Wallops Wood is supplemented by three changing beers, often from local breweries. A real cider made in the village is sometimes available. A beer and cider festival is held over the second weekend of June. The public bar has pool and there is a skittle alley at the rear. Locally sourced food features. No food Sunday and Tuesday evenings. 🏵️🍴♣️🍺P🚃(87)🐾🎅

Aldershot

Garden Gate 🗍
4 Church Lane East, GU11 3BT (½ mile S of town centre)
🕭 5-11 (midnight Thu; 1am Fri); 12-1am Sat; 12-10.30 Sun
☎ (01252) 219717
Greene King IPA; Surrey Hills Ranmore; Timothy Taylor Boltmaker; 1 changing beer (sourced nationally) 🅷
A community focused pub within easy walking distance of the railway station, the Garden Gate's

recent renaissance has seen real ale sales soar. The pub is firmly established at the heart of both the local canine and human communities, buzzing with conversation and background music. Live music, usually unamplified, features, as does the Thursday quiz. Two distinct drinking areas, a back room where darts is played, and a pleasant courtyard garden are available for use. 🏵️🚃P🚃🐾🎅

Queen Hotel ✅
1 High Street, GU11 1BH
🕭 7am-midnight (1am Thu-Sat) ☎ (01252) 361770
Greene King Abbot; Ruddles Best Bitter; Sharp's Doom Bar; 5 changing beers 🅷
A Grade II-listed hotel in the centre of this historic military town. Recently refurbished and expanded, it has a light and airy feel, slightly café bar in style, with a long single marble bar down one side and the family area boasting exposed beams. The original rooms are more intimate and have been retained, down small flights of stairs at the front of the building. Outside is an attractive patio, offering some shelter for smokers. Q🖤🏵️🛏️🍴◑🍺🎅

White Lion 🗍
20 Lower Farnham Road, GU12 4EA (200yds from A331/A323 jct)
🕭 1-11 (10.30 Mon; midnight Fri); 12-midnight Sat; 12-10.30 Sun ☎ (01252) 323832

Triple fff Alton's Pride, Moondance; 2 changing beers (sourced nationally; often Cottage, Triple fff, Weltons) Ⓗ
One of the oldest pubs in Aldershot, the White Lion retains two rooms; the main room has a real fire, while the back room tends to be quieter. There is also a well-maintained courtyard garden. The landlord has a fine reputation for the quality of his beer, usually from Triple fff Brewery. A popular quiz and rock & roll bingo alternate on Thursday evenings. Food is restricted to snacks and pizza all day. Millie is the pub dog. ❀♣🖫🐾

Alton

Eight Bells
Church Street, GU34 2DA (opp St Lawrence Church)
🕓 11.30-midnight; 12-10.30 Sun ☎ (01420) 82417
Bowman Swift One; Sharp's Doom Bar; 3 changing beers (sourced nationally; often Butcombe, Red Cat) Ⓗ
Grade II-listed free house, close to the site of the Civil War Battle of Alton. Guest beers come from far and wide but usually include at least one southern region brew. The original oak-beamed main bar is a haven for drink and conversation while the rear drinking area has a TV for major sporting events. The secluded paved garden incorporates a 17th-century well. Nigel's not-so-secret beer festival follows the late summer holiday.
Q❀⇌🖫(13,65)🐾 ᰦ

King's Head
28 Market Street, GU34 1HA (opp market sq)
🕓 10.30-1am; 12-10.30 Sun ☎ (01420) 82313
Courage Best Bitter; 3 changing beers (sourced regionally; often Itchen Valley, Longdog, Upham) Ⓗ
A welcome return to the Guide for this Grade II-listed two-bar pub. Very much a traditional local, it combines a consistently high standard in beer quality with a rapid turnover of guest ales, which are often locally sourced. The pleasant terraced garden at the rear which backs on to the community centre car park is sometimes the venue for live music on summer Sundays and otherwise provides a peaceful contrast to this bustling town centre pub. ⮩❀♣P🖫(65)🐾 ᰦ

Railway Arms Ⓛ
26 Anstey Road, GU34 2RB (opp Station Rd)
🕓 12-11; 11-midnight Fri & Sat ☎ (01420) 82218
⊕ fffrailwayarms.com
Triple fff Alton's Pride, Pressed Rat & Warthog, Moondance; 3 changing beers (sourced nationally; often Brewsters, Red Cat, Triple fff) Ⓗ
Friendly pub close to the Watercress Line and mainline station with a striking sculpture of a steam locomotive emerging from the front over outside seating. Owned by Triple fff Brewery, the six beers include guests from a host of micros and a Triple fff seasonal beer. Real cider is from Mr Whitehead's and many continental bottled beers are stocked. A function room is available for hire. The patio area at the rear, designed with a traditional railway theme, incorporates a covered smoking area. ❀⇌♣🍺🖫(13,64)🐾 ᰦ

Andover

Angel Inn Ⓥ
95 High Street, SP10 1ND
🕓 10-11 (midnight Sat); 10-8 Sun ☎ (01264) 352086

Morland Old Speckled Hen; 2 changing beers (sourced nationally) Ⓗ
The oldest building in Andover, saved when the town centre was redeveloped, this Grade II*-listed timber-framed courtyard inn was built by Winchester College in 1445-55. It has had some later modifications but is remarkably intact. There are two bars – the upper one was once used as a court. A pleasant small patio is at the rear and there is a sheltered courtyard at the front. Live music and karaoke feature as well as pool and darts. Sunday lunches are popular. Open from 10am for breakfast. ❀◖🖫🐾

Town Mills Ⓥ
20 Bridge Street, SP10 1BL
🕓 11-12.30am ☎ (01264) 332540 ⊕ thetownmills.co.uk
Wadworth IPA, 6X, Swordfish; 2 changing beers (sourced regionally; often Wadworth) Ⓗ
This is just off the town centre, in an historic mill with a working water wheel and the River Anton passing through. There are several separate areas for dining and drinking including a comfy lounge upstairs. Pub games are also played upstairs and a well-supported quiz is held on Wednesday evening. The riverside garden is popular in summer months. The changing beers are almost always from Wadworth. ⮩❀◖🖫♣P🖫🐾 ᰦ

Basingstoke

Angel Ⓛ Ⓥ
Unit R6, Lower Ground, Festival Place, RG21 7BB

🌣 8am-12.30am (2am Fri & Sat); 8am-midnight Sun
☎ (01256) 854800
**Greene King IPA, Abbot; Sharp's Doom Bar; 7
changing beers (often Longdog, Vibrant Forest, Wild
Weather Ales)** Ⓗ
Formerly a Lloyds No.1 Bar, this spacious and
modern one-bar pub is at the edge of the
restaurant quarter in the town's Festival Place
shopping centre, handy for the nearby bus station
and five minutes' walk from the rail station.
Popular with younger people, the pub can get very
busy and often noisy in the evenings, especially at
weekends. Lunchtimes attract a wider age range
and tend to be quieter. The walls are adorned with
TVs, all in silent mode. 🌣🌣🕛🕭⇌🖴🕭🛜

Basingstoke Sports & Social Club 🗸
Fairfields Road, RG21 3DR (S end of town)
🌣 12-3, 5-11; 12-11 Fri & Sat; 12-10.30 Sun
☎ (01256) 331646 🌐 basingstoke-sports-club.co.uk
**Fuller's Oliver's Island, London Pride; Gale's Seafarers
Ale; 2 changing beers (sourced nationally; often
Andwells, Little London, Longdog)** Ⓗ
While technically a club, the public has access as if
this was a public house. Founded in 1865 by local
brewery owner and entrepreneur Col. John May,
this fine venue is home to cricket, rugby, football
and squash. A widescreen TV in the bar is dedicated
to sports events. A full programme of social
activities is held throughout the year, and the
grounds can be hired – they are currently home to
the annual Hampshire OctoberFest. Opening hours
and meal times are flexible depending on the
season and sporting fixtures. 🌣🌣🕛♣🖴🕭🛜

Bounty Inn 🗸
Bounty Road, RG21 3BZ
🌣 12-11 (11.30 Fri & Sat); 12-10.30 Sun ☎ (01256) 320071
🌐 thebountyinnbasingstoke.co.uk
**3 changing beers (sourced nationally; often Brains,
Dartmoor, Red Cat)** Ⓗ
This 1830s pub is now one of Basingstoke's few
remaining historic hostelries. The present name
acknowledges a gift of land, which includes the
adjacent cricket ground, to the people of
Basingstoke by local brewer John May in 1880.
Three bars cater for a wide-ranging clientele
including those wishing to partake of the high-
quality food. There is a pleasant south-facing rear
garden. Hardy males might appreciate the last
remaining outside Gents' toilet in town.
🌣🌣🕛🖴🕭🛜

Maidenhead Inn Ⓛ 🗸
17 Winchester Street, RG21 7ED
🌣 8am-midnight (1am Fri & Sat) ☎ (01256) 316030
**Greene King Abbot; Ruddles Best Bitter; Sharp's
Doom Bar; 4 changing beers (sourced nationally)** Ⓗ
Formerly home to a building society and on the site
of an inn of the same name, this JD Wetherspoon
pub is in the sometimes lively Top of Town area,
with five pumps dispensing local and guest ales.
Beers from local breweries such as Andwell's,
Longdog, Wild Weather and Loddon regularly
feature. A dining area at the front leads to the
compact bar, with further seating to the rear over
two levels, complemented by a courtyard beer
garden to the rear. 🌣🌣🕛⇌🖴🖴🛜

Queen's Arms
Bunnian Place, RG21 7JE
🌣 11-11 (midnight Fri & Sat) ☎ (01256) 465488
🌐 thequeensarmspub.co.uk

**Courage Best Bitter; Sharp's Doom Bar; 4 changing
beers (sourced nationally)** Ⓗ
Just outside the main shopping area, this cosy pub
is handy for all transport links. It attracts a broad
clientele of all ages from all walks of life, and is a
regular port of call for rail commuters. The choice of
up to four guest beers is imaginative and the
turnaround can be swift. Good-value home-cooked
food is served lunchtimes and evenings. During
warmer weather the shady courtyard garden at the
rear is a popular attraction. Q🌣🕛⇌🖴🛜

Blackwater

Mr Bumble Ⓛ
19 London Road, GU17 9AP
🌣 12-11 (midnight Fri); 11-midnight Sat; 12-10.30 Sun
☎ (01276) 32691
**Fuller's London Pride; 3 changing beers (sourced
regionally; often Dark Star, Tillingbourne, Windsor &
Eton)** Ⓗ
Busy pub in the centre of Blackwater, near the
station, a bus route and local shops. London Pride is
the regular beer, with up to three other real ales,
including LocAles; stout and porter are popular in
the winter months. There is a large bar for drinking
and conversation; a smaller bar leads to the pool
room, with three tables, which in turn leads out to
the patio and smoking area. Live music plays on
Thursday and Saturday. ⇌♣🖴(3)🛜

Braishfield

Dog & Crook Ⓛ
Crook Hill, SO51 0QB (S edge of village)
🌣 11-11 ☎ (01794) 368530
**Marston's Wainwright; Ringwood Best Bitter
(Razorback); Sharp's Doom Bar; 1 changing beer
(sourced nationally)** Ⓗ
Well-established village inn with a restaurant, real
fire and large garden. Three regular beers and one
guest are sold, often from a local brewery.
Excellent home-cooked food and bar snacks are
available daily, lunchtimes and evenings (no food
Sun). There is no jukebox or sports TV, but sport is
sometimes shown on terrestrial TV. Cribbage and
darts are played and alternate Tuesdays are quiz
nights. A Pubs in Bloom award winner and close to
the famous Sir Harold Hillier Gardens.
Q🌣🌣🕛♣🖴🛜

Wheatsheaf Ⓛ
Braishfield Road, SO51 0QE
🌣 11.30-11; 12-10.30 Sun ☎ (01794) 368652
🌐 thewheatsheafbraishfield.co.uk
**Flack Manor Double Drop; St Austell Tribute; Sharp's
Doom Bar; 1 changing beer (sourced nationally)** Ⓗ
A welcoming village pub with a good-sized car
park. It has views over the surrounding countryside
from a large garden with a children's mini assault
course. The interior has several discrete areas,
including an extension principally used by diners
and a non-intrusive games annexe. Quality food is
on offer (pies are a speciality). Events include live
music on Thursday, occasional pie nights and
quizzes, and an annual carol service. It has a loyalty
card scheme and is dog-friendly.
🌣🌣🕛♣🖴(35)🛜

Bransgore

Three Tuns ✓
Ringwood Road, BH23 8JH (between Burley Rd and Harrow Rd)
✪ 11 (11.30 Sat)-11; 12-10.30 Sun ☎ (01425) 672232
⊕ threetunsinn.com
Otter Amber; Ringwood Best Bitter (Razorback), Fortyniner; 2 changing beers (sourced nationally) Ⓗ
A beautiful thatched pub, an early-20th-century conversion of a 17th-century farmhouse, serving award-winning food featuring local produce and much individuality. The bar area leads to a large dining area and a separate, cosy snug with woodburner and bread oven. The terrace and gardens afford views of fields, trees and sky. There is occasional live music, and a beer festival on the last weekend in September. Buses serve the village Monday to Friday only, until early afternoon. Q❄☺✺◑ᴅ♣A♣P☐(125)❀☞

Broughton

Tally Ho!
High Street, SO20 8AA (in village centre, opp church)
✪ 12-11 (midnight Fri & Sat); 12-10.30 Sun
☎ (01794) 301280 ⊕ thetallyhobroughton.co.uk
Brakspear Bitter; Ringwood Best Bitter (Razorback); 2 changing beers (sourced regionally) Ⓗ
The house beer, Tally Ho! Ale, is the tasty 3.4% ABV bitter from Brakspear (Marston's). Guest beers tend to be from the Wessex area and draught cider is also usually available in summer. A beer and cider festival is held over the August bank holiday. Upmarket pub food including takeaways is featured. The garden has play equipment for children. An ideal stopping point if walking the Clarendon Way. Dogs are welcome too.
☺✺◑♣♣P☐(16)❀☞

Charter Alley

White Hart Ⓛ
White Hart Lane, RG26 5QA (1 mile W of A340, opp turning for Little London)
✪ 7-11 Mon & Tue; 12-2.30, 5.30-11 Wed-Fri; 12-3, 6.30-11 Sat; 12-4 Sun ☎ (01256) 850048
⊕ whitehartcharteralley.com
3 changing beers (sourced locally) Ⓗ
A cosy inn, built in 1819, the epicentre of this rural village, where allcomers are assured of a friendly greeting. Welcoming features include log fires, oak beams and a capacious dining area, serving a variety of quality food and home-made pies. The breweriana-decorated main bar dispenses an array of frequently changing ales. The White Hart has been a stalwart Guide entry for the past 26 years.
Q❄✺◑P❀☞

Cheriton

Flowerpots Inn Ⓛ
Brandy Mount, SO24 0QQ (½ mile N of A272 Cheriton/ Beauworth crossroads) SU581283
✪ 12-2.30, 6-11; 12-3, 7-10.30 Sun ☎ (01962) 771318
⊕ flowerpotscheriton.co.uk
Flowerpots Perridge Pale, Bitter, Goodens Gold; 1 changing beer (sourced locally; often Flowerpots) Ⓖ
Early 19th-century two-bar village pub. The public has a large fireplace, welcoming on winter days, and a curious glass-covered well in the floor; the lounge is smaller and cosy. Home-cooked food is

available daily except Sunday evenings, Wednesday is curry night. The gravity dispensed beer travels just 50 yards from the on-site Flowerpots Brewery, now Hampshire's oldest independent. The large garden has plenty of seating and, usually, extra covered marquee space. Two double rooms are available for night stops.
Q❄☺⇄◑ᴅ♣P☐(67)❀

Church Crookham

Fox & Hounds ✓
71 Crookham Road, GU51 5NP
✪ 12-11 (midnight Fri) ☎ (01252) 663686
⊕ foxandhoundscc.co.uk
Caledonian Edinburgh Castle 80/-; Courage Best Bitter; Fuller's London Pride; 1 changing beer (sourced nationally; often Caledonian) Ⓗ
A welcoming old-style community pub, alongside a picturesque section of the Basingstoke Canal, with three seating areas. Walls are adorned with historic pub photos. Traditional home-cooked pub food is served daily, with a dining space available for dog walkers. Four cask ales are sold including Fox & Hounds Ale, which is a Caledonian beer rebadged. The garden and children's play area are busy on warmer days. Live music features on Friday and a pub quiz is held every fortnight on Tuesday.
Q❄☺◑ᴅ♣P☐(10)❀☞

Dundridge

Hampshire Bowman Ⓛ
Dundridge Lane, SO32 1GD (turn E off B3035 ½ mile N of Bishops Waltham, then 1½ miles) SU578184
✪ 12-11 (midnight Fri); 12-10.30 Sun ☎ (01489) 892940
⊕ hampshirebowman.com
Bowman Swift One; West Berkshire Good Old Boy; 4 changing beers Ⓖ
A true country pub, typically offering six mostly local beers served directly from the cask, 10 real ciders and a wide selection of bottled beers. Freshly prepared food ranges from sandwiches and traditional pub fare to an interesting specials menu. Outside, a large well-kept garden and patio area, with plenty of seating, can be busy at weekends. The pub is ideally placed for walkers, and welcomes dogs. Mobile phones are frowned upon, with a charity bottle in use for offenders.
Q❄☺◑ᴅ♣♣P❀☞

East Worldham

Three Horseshoes ✓
Cakers Lane, GU34 3AE
✪ 11.30-2.30 (not Mon), 5.30-10.30; 12-11 Sat; 12-5 Sun
☎ (01420) 83211
Fuller's London Pride; Gale's Seafarers Ale, HSB Ⓗ
Once a Gale's house and a coaching inn, part of the building dates back over 300 years and is allegedly haunted. John and Gill have rapidly gained an excellent reputation for their high-quality locally sourced food as well as their ales. Very much a community pub, it is the place to go to for details of local events. Quiz night is the last Thursday of the month. Other events include live music.
Q❄☺⇄◑ᴅ♣A♣P☐(13)❀☞

Emsworth

Blue Bell Ⓛ ✓
29 South Street, PO10 7EG

✪ 10-11 (midnight Fri & Sat); 12-11 Sun ☎ (01243) 373394 ⊕ bluebellinnemsworth.co.uk

Sharp's Doom Bar; 2 changing beers (sourced nationally; often Dark Star, Emsworth Brewhouse, Irving) ℍ

The original Blue Bell was further south and originally known as the Brewery Tap. The current pub was built in 1960, hence the rather modern-looking building for this part of town. Following the closure of the brewery, the owner at the time had it rebuilt on the current site to improve access to other properties. It has been owned by one family since 1994. Inside it has the look of a much older building and is decorated throughout with naval memorabilia. ✪◑➡🚆(700)●

Coal Exchange ✪

21 South Street, PO10 7EG

✪ 10.30-3, 5.30-11; 10.30-midnight Fri & Sat; 12-11 Sun ☎ (01243) 375866 ⊕ thecoalexchange.co.uk

Fuller's London Pride; Gale's Seafarers Ale, HSB; 3 changing beers (sourced nationally; often Butcombe) ℍ

A traditional single-bar pub close to the town square with, for a former Gale's pub, an unusual green tiled frontage. The building has seen many uses over the years including being a pork butchery and a trading place for coal delivered by sea (hence the name). The award-winning lunchtime food is popular both with locals and visitors, so it can be busy during service times. Themed evening meals are served Monday to Thursday.
🖤✪◑➡🚆(700)●

Lord Raglan ✪

35 Queen Street, PO10 7BJ

✪ 11-3, 5.30-11; 11-11 Sat; 12-11 Sun ☎ (01243) 372587

Fuller's London Pride; Gale's Seafarers Ale, HSB; 1 changing beer (sourced nationally; often Fuller's) ℍ

Dating from the 18th century, this pub was later named after the first Baron Raglan, who achieved much military success in the 19th century. It is a quintessential community pub with low ceilings and wall lighting, quiet with no machines or loud background music. The extensive pub garden backs on to the moorings of Slipper Mill Pond and in the summer plays host to barbecues and live music events. Vape-friendly. Q🖤✪◑♣🚆(700)●🛜

Fareham

Lord Arthur Lee ✪

100-108 West Street, PO16 0EP

✪ 8am-11 (midnight Fri & Sat) ☎ (01329) 280447

Greene King Abbot; Ruddles Best Bitter; Sharp's Doom Bar; 5 changing beers (often Ringwood) ℍ

This busy, spacious Wetherspoon pub has an offering of three regular beers and five guest beers, often selected from local breweries, and the standard Wetherspoon food menu. It is close to Fareham bus and railway stations. The walls are lined with photos and historic details of the pub's namesake and other locals. The family/dining area is often popular at lunchtimes. There is a small garden and smoking area to the rear.
🖤✪◑&➡●🚆🛜

Farnborough

Prince of Wales 🅻 ✪

184 Rectory Road, GU14 8AL

✪ 11.30-2.30, 5.30-11; 11.30-11 Fri & Sat; 12-10.30 Sun ☎ (01252) 545578 ⊕ theprinceinfarnborough.co.uk

Andwells Gold Muddler; Dark Star Hophead; Fuller's London Pride; Hop Back Summer Lightning; Ringwood Fortyniner; 5 changing beers (sourced nationally) ℍ

After over 30 years in the Guide and many awards, this traditional local remains a haven for real ale drinkers. Five regular beers are served along with five guests, normally including a dark beer, and two real ciders. Evening meals are only available on Monday (pie night) and Friday (fish and chips). Quiz night is the first Sunday of each month and there is occasional live entertainment. A beer festival is held every October.
✪◑🚆(North)●P🚆(41)●🛜

Swan 🅻

91 Farnborough Road, GU14 6TL (on A325 between Farnborough and North Camp, facing airfield)

✪ 11-11 (11.30 Fri & Sat); 11.30-10 Sun ☎ (01252) 510920 ⊕ swanfarnborough.com

4 changing beers (sourced nationally; often Andwells, Cottage, Triple fff) ℍ

An imposing building near Farnborough Airport, looking directly out over the runway. Inside it is one continuous space but on separate levels and with distinct drinking and dining areas separated by partitions. It caters equally for diners and drinkers, with excellent food and a selection of four ales including at least one from a local brewery. Occasional live music and a monthly quiz are hosted. 🖤✪◑&P🚆(1,42)●🛜

Tilly Shilling 🅻 ✪

Unit 2-5, Victoria Road, GU14 7PG

✪ 8am-midnight (1am Fri & Sat) ☎ (01252) 893560

Greene King Abbot; Ruddles Best Bitter; Sharp's Doom Bar; 5 changing beers (sourced nationally; often Ascot Ales, Binghams, Hogs Back) ℍ

Modern town-centre Wetherspoon pub named after a celebrated engineer at the nearby Royal Aircraft Establishment. Its aviation theme includes a row of airline seats and various Spitfire memorabilia. The large rectangular open-plan lounge features a glass frontage that opens in good weather, extending the pub on to the pavement. Ten handpumps serve regular and changing guest beers. Real cider is dispensed from polypins at the end of the bar. Alcohol is on sale from 9am.
🖤◑&➡(Main)●🚆🛜

Fleet

Prince Arthur 🅻 ✪

238 Fleet Road, GU51 4BX

✪ 8am-midnight (1am Fri & Sat) ☎ (01252) 622660

Greene King Abbot; Ruddles Best Bitter; Sharp's Doom Bar; 5 changing beers (sourced nationally; often Elusive, Langham, West Berkshire) ℍ

Wetherspoon pub with rustic charm located in a 100-year-old former grocery store, named after Prince Arthur, son of Queen Victoria, who lived in Fleet in the 1890s when commander of the nearby Aldershot garrison. Eight different cask ales, including those from some 19 local breweries, appear regularly, and a real cider is available on handpump. An annual beer festival is held, featuring LocAles and beers from further afield, in addition to the two Wetherspoon festivals.
Q🖤✪◑&●🚆(7,10)🛜

Freefolk

Watership Down Inn 🅛
Freefolk Priors, RG28 7NJ (just off B3400)
🕐 12-3, 6.30-11; 12-11.30 Fri & Sat; 12-9.30 Sun
☎ (01256) 892254 ⊕ watershipdowninn.com
5 changing beers (sourced locally) Ⓗ
In the Upper Test Valley, built in 1840, and still affectionately known locally as The Jerry, the pub has been named in honour of local author Richard Adams' book, set in the downland to the north of the pub. Outside there is an extensive garden, patio and family area. The pub is popular with walkers and cyclists in the Test Valley. Each May a beer festival is held and occasional live music evenings arranged. Close to the Laverstoke gin distillery. Local CAMRA Pub of the Year 2016.
Q🕭🏵🚲◑P🚐(76)🐾🐕🛜

Fritham

Royal Oak 🅛 ✅
SO43 7HJ (W end of village no through road)
🕐 11-3, 6-11; 11-11 Sat; 12-10.30 Sun ☎ (023) 8081 2606
Flack Manor Double Drop; Ringwood Best Bitter (Razorback); house beer (by Bowman); 4 changing beers (sourced locally; often Dancing Cows, Keystone, Stonehenge) Ⓖ
A New Forest institution. The front bar leads through (duck!) to interconnected back rooms. Throughout, bare boards, beams, log fires and wainscotted, colourwashed walls epitomise the rural inn. A haven, welcoming walkers, cyclists, equestrians and dog lovers. Seven gravity dispensed ales, in their black cooling jackets, are from small local breweries. The house beer, Royal Oak, is Bowman Wallops Wood. Excellent, simple lunches utilise much local produce. A vast garden houses three high-grade rentable shepherd's bothies and a midsummer beer festival.
Q🕭🏵🚲◑🐕

Goodworth Clatford

Clatford Arms ✅
Village Street, SP11 7RN
🕐 11.30-10.30 (11.30 Thu; midnight Fri & Sat)
☎ (01264) 363298
Flack Manor Double Drop; 3 changing beers (sourced regionally; often Longdog, Stonehenge) Ⓗ
Popular village local in a pretty village. There is a dining room at one end where good-value home-cooked food is served. At the other end is the sports area with pool table, darts and TV. Four beers are served, mostly from local breweries, alongside traditional favourites. There is a large garden to the rear with a boules pitch.
Q🕭🏵◑🦽♣P🚐(15)🐾🛜

Gosport

Junction Tavern
1 Leesland Road, Camden Town, PO12 3ND
🕐 11-12.30am (11.30 Tue & Wed); 12-10.30 Sun
☎ (023) 9258 5140
3 changing beers (sourced regionally; often Broken Bridge, Langham) Ⓗ
Relatively small pub on the site of Brockhurst Junction, on the Fareham to Gosport railway line, now a cycle track and footpath. In addition to the three real ales from independent breweries, the pub boasts up to four ciders and a perry from various suppliers, and is a mecca for cider lovers. A beer festival takes place over the Easter weekend.
🏵♣🍴🚐(E1)🐾🐕🛜

Queen's Hotel
143 Queens Road, Forton, PO12 1LG
🕐 4.45-11; 11.30-2.30, 4.45-11.30 Fri; 11.30-11.30 Sat; 12-3, 7-11 Sun ☎ 07974 031671 ⊕ queenshotelgosport.co.uk
Ringwood Fortyniner; Young's Bitter; 3 changing beers (sourced nationally; often Fallen Acorn, Newtown, Titanic) Ⓗ
No visit to Gosport is complete without a visit to this award-winning free house, with over 30 years in this Guide. The guest beer range normally includes a dark brew, and the pub is the principal outlet for the nearby Newtown Brewery. A regular beer festival takes place in October. Snacks are served on Friday lunchtime. The pub often gets crowded during major sporting events. 🏵♣🍴🚐

Hammer Vale

Prince of Wales
Hammer Lane, GU27 1QH (enter Hammer Lane from Haslemere end, due to width restriction at Liphook end)
🕐 11-11; 12-11 Sun ☎ (01428) 652600
Fuller's London Pride; Gale's HSB; 2 changing beers (often Fuller's) Ⓗ
Benefitting from a recent refurbishment which revealed previously unknown doorways dating from the 1924 construction, this pub is well worth a visit to sample the Pride, HSB and Fullers' seasonal beers and guests. It has a large outside seating area and car park and is well sited for walkers and campers. Mine hosts Nick and Heidi do excellent meals and snacks. Stories abound as to how a large roadhouse was sited away from the main road. Check out the stained-glass windows, one for Amey's of Petersfield.
Q🕭🏵◑🦽♣P🐾🛜

Hartley Wintney

Waggon & Horses
High Street, RG27 8NY
🕐 11-11 (midnight Fri & Sat); 12-11 Sun ☎ (01252) 842119
Courage Best Bitter; Gale's HSB; 3 changing beers (sourced locally) Ⓗ
The new landlord served several years behind the bar of this award-winning local before taking over. HSB and Courage Best are the regular beers, alongside changing guests, often from micros. The pub's lively public bar contrasts with a quieter lounge. Tables outside on the pavement enable customers to enjoy the atmosphere of the village, renowned for its unique shops. At the rear is a pleasant courtyard garden and a heated, covered smokers' area. Food is served lunchtimes only (not Sun). Light snacks are available afternoons and evenings, typically pies and wraps.
Q🏵◑🍴🚐(7)🐾🛜

Havant

Robin Hood
6 Homewell, PO9 1EE
🕐 11-11 (midnight Fri); 12-10.30 Sun ☎ (023) 9248 2779
Fuller's London Pride; Gale's Seafarers Ale, HSB; 1 changing beer (sourced nationally; often Fuller's) Ⓗ
Originally this pub was more like someone's front room; it has expanded considerably. The bar is divided into two areas; the front has bare

flagstones and the rear is carpeted, with comfortable seating. There is a small garden and smoking area outside. The low beams, open fireplaces and cosy interior add to the appeal of this hidden gem in the centre of town. ✿◑⇌🚐♨

Wheelwright's 🅛 ✅

27 Emsworth Road, PO9 2SN
🕓 11-11; 12-10.30 Sun ☎ (023) 9247 6502
🌐 wheelwrightshavant.co.uk
Upham Punter, Tipster; 3 changing beers (sourced locally; often Fallen Acorn, Irving, Staggeringly Good) Ⓗ

Old coaching inn on the outskirts of Havant. Six handpulls feature one cider, two Upham ales and three changing LocAles. Modern British cuisine is prepared and cooked on site using fresh local produce where possible. The bar area has a traditional, welcoming feel, with modern aesthetics, serving a variety of wines, spirits and bottled beers as well as draught real ales and cider. The pub has outside seating as well as two open fireplaces. **Q**🔥✿◑&⇌♣♨🚐(700)♨🛜

Hawkley

Hawkley Inn

Pococks Lane, GU33 6NE
🕓 12-3, 5.30-11; 12-11 Sat; 12-9 Sun ☎ (01730) 827205
🌐 hawkleyinn.co.uk
Dark Star Hophead; Palmers Copper Ale; 5 changing beers (sourced regionally; often Flowerpots, Red Cat, Triple fff) Ⓗ

A gem of a country free house welcoming to locals, walkers, passers-by and dogs. A cosy pub with a reputation for quality food, it has a steak night each Monday, and a good variety of real ales, mostly from Hampshire breweries. It boasts a good-sized garden at the back and a verandah to the front. There is a beer festival in June every year. B&B accommodation is available. 🔥✿♨🛏◑&♨🛜

Herriard

Fur & Feathers 🅛

Back Lane, RG25 2PN (on old Basingstoke to Alton road, parallel to A339)
🕓 closed Mon; 12-10; 11-11 Fri & Sat; 12-6 Sun
☎ (01256) 510510 🌐 theherriardinn.co.uk
Hogs Back TEA; Sharp's Doom Bar; 2 changing beers (sourced locally; often Flack Manor, Longdog, Red Cat) Ⓗ

Hampshire Life Food & Drink Pub of the Year 2016. This family-owned and family-run free house was built in 1880 to serve farm workers; it is now open plan with a central bar area. Four handpumps deliver beers mainly from Hampshire breweries such as Flack Manor, Longdog, Red Cat, Itchen Valley... the list is long. Two dining areas provide a pleasant atmosphere to enjoy the mouthwatering locally sourced menu that changes daily; reservations are recommended, but a quiet pint can be enjoyed at any time. A well-appointed secluded garden features partly paved and grassed areas. Winter hours vary. **Q**🔥✿◑&🚐(13X)🛜

Hill Head

Crofton ✅

48 Crofton Lane, PO14 3QF
🕓 11-11; 12-10.30 Sun ☎ (01329) 314222
🌐 thecrofton.co.uk

St Austell Proper Job; Sharp's Doom Bar; 4 changing beers (sourced nationally)** Ⓗ

A successful Punch Taverns outlet, not far from the Solent. Interesting beers from Punch are supplemented by beers from SIBA breweries, plus Westons Old Rosie cider. The function room with skittle alley gets booked up well in advance. A small beer festival takes place on St George's Day, with a larger weekend festival in November. Home-cooked food is available all day every day. 🔥✿◑&♣♨🚐(21,21A)♨🛜

Holybourne

Queen's Head ✅

20 London Road, GU34 4EG
🕓 12-11.30 (12.30am Fri & Sat); 12-11 Sun ☎ (01420) 86331
🌐 queensheadalton.co.uk
Hardys & Hansons Olde Trip; 3 changing beers (sourced nationally; often Greene King, Skinner's, Triple fff) Ⓗ

A friendly, traditional and unpretentious pub run by the same landlord and landlady for over 13 years, and a regular in this Guide. It hosts a number of activities including a monthly quiz and Thursday poker night, darts (three dartboards) and pool leagues. There are three separate drinking areas, a games room, a heated smoking refuge and an extensive family-friendly garden. Happy hour is 4.30-6pm Monday to Friday.
Q🔥✿◑♣🚐(65)♨🛜

Hook Common

Crooked Billet ✅

London Road, RG27 9EH
🕓 11.30-3, 6-11; 11.30-midnight Sat; 12-10 Sun
☎ (01256) 762118 🌐 thecrookedbilletpub.co.uk
Courage Best Bitter; Sharp's Doom Bar; 2 changing beers Ⓗ

The Crooked Billet is just outside Hook and has been a free house under the safe ownership of Richard and Sally for 31 years. In the summer you can enjoy the pleasant riverside garden or the air-conditioned bars, restaurant and snug. In winter, warm up around one of the traditional log fires. A fine selection of good food and real ales is always available. An annual beer and music festival is held over the August bank holiday weekend. Food is served until 8pm on Sunday. Quiz night is the first Monday of the month. **Q**✿◑P♨

Hythe

Ebenezers 🅛

18A Pylewell Road, SO45 6AR (100yds SW of Hythe Ferry)
🕓 11.30-2.40, 5.30-11; 11.30-11.10 Fri & Sat; 12-10.30 Sun
☎ (023) 8020 7799
Flack Manor Double Drop; Greene King Abbot; 2 changing beers (sourced locally; often Bowman, Flowerpots, Red Cat) Ⓗ

Ebenezers, or Ebz to the regulars, is a well-run pub serving four excellently kept real ales. Flack Manor's Double Drop and Greene King's Abbot Ale are the mainstays, with the two guest ales regularly rotating from various local breweries. The food is of a great standard, served lunchtimes and evenings. The interior decor has quotes from the ages adorning the walls, and the atmosphere of this quiet pub is friendly and jovial. Just a ferry ride from Southampton. **Q**✿◑&♨🚐🛜

Little London

Plough Inn
Silchester Road, RG26 5EP
☼ 12-3, 5.30 (6 Fri & Sat)-11; 12-3, 7-10.30 Sun
☎ (01256) 850628
Otter Amber; Ringwood Razorback Ⓖ; 2 changing beers (sourced regionally; often Andwells, Branscombe Vale, Little London) Ⓗ/Ⓖ
Excellent traditional village pub and recent CAMRA Regional Pub of the Year. Enjoy beer gravity fed from casks behind the bar and sit in front of a log fire or in the peaceful garden. A good range of baguettes is available (no food Sun eve). Very popular with locals and also visitors to Pamber Forest and the nearby Roman remains in Silchester.
Q ⑅ ⊛ ♣ ♠ P ⊞ (14) ☙

Long Sutton

Four Horseshoes
The Street, RG29 1TA (follow brown signs from B3349 Odiham to Alton Rd) SU748470
☼ 12-3 (not Mon & Tue), 6.30-11; 12-3 Sun
☎ (01256) 862488 ⊕ fourhorseshoes.com
2 changing beers (sourced regionally; often Andwells, Palmers, Slater's) Ⓗ
A quintessential English country pub, to the east of Long Sutton village, with fine views of the surrounding countryside. Formerly a Gale's tied house, the pub has been free of tie for many years and now offers two low-strength guest beers. The single bar is spacious yet cosy, with two real fires, exuding traditional charm. Food is simple English fare, with a popular roast on Sunday. Opening times may vary. Q ⊛ ⊯ ◑ ▶ A P ☙ 🖤

Lower Farringdon

Golden Pheasant Ⓛ
Gosport Road, GU34 3DJ (at Farringdon Crossroads on A32)
☼ 12-11 (10.30 Sun) ☎ (01420) 588255
Courage Best Bitter; Dark Star Hophead; Sharp's Doom Bar; 4 changing beers (sourced nationally) Ⓗ
The owners have run pubs in the area for over 10 years, and five years ago brought their expertise to this delightful free house. The beers are well kept, with seven handpumps serving three fixed and four guest beers. The food is freshly cooked with vegetarian options – the fish and chips warrants special mention due to the secret batter recipe used. Easily accessible down the A32 four miles from Alton, this is a pub not to be missed.
Q ⑅ ⊛ ◑ ♣ P ☙ 🖤

Lower Wield

Yew Tree Ⓛ
SO24 9RX SU636398
☼ closed Mon, 12-3, 6-11; 12-10.30 Sun ☎ (01256) 389224
⊕ the-yewtree.org.uk
House beer (by Triple fff); 1 changing beer (sourced locally; often Bowman, Itchen Valley, Stonehenge) Ⓗ
Out-of-the-way rural local set in picturesque rolling Hampshire countryside, with an old yew tree growing outside (hence the name), situated on a quiet lane opposite the local cricket pitch. The house beer is Triple fff Alton's Pride and the guest normally comes from a local brewery. All real ales are sold at very attractive prices. The pub has a separate dining area where locally renowned,

reasonably priced food is served. Cyclists, ramblers and dog walkers are very welcome.
Q ⑅ ⊛ ◑ ▶ P ☙ 🖤 ╤

Lymington

Monkey House Ⓛ
167 Southampton Road, SO41 9HA (on A337 N of town)
☼ 11-11; 12-10.30 Sun ☎ (01590) 676754
⊕ themonkeyhouse.co.uk
Dancing Cows Pony; Flack Manor Double Drop; 2 changing beers (sourced locally; often Bowman, Goddards, Vibrant Forest) Ⓗ
The Monkey House is privately owned, and is one of the last free houses in Lymington. It features home-cooked food, with daily menu specials at lunchtime and in the evening. There is an excellent changing range of ales from local breweries, log fires and welcoming friendly service. The pub is family and dog friendly, and regularly hosts live musicians from around the area. There is a good-sized garden and, now, two B&B rooms.
Q ⑅ ⊛ ⊯ ◑ ▶ & P ⊞ (6) 🖤 ╤

Six Bells Ⓛ
48 St Thomas Street, SO41 9ND (top of High St)
☼ 8am-11 (midnight Fri & Sat) ☎ (01590) 689990
Greene King Abbot; Ringwood Razorback; Sharp's Doom Bar; house beer (by Vibrant Forest); 2 changing beers (sourced nationally; often Vibrant Forest) Ⓗ
The original Six Bells stood next door to this building, which was a kitchen and hardware store, taking its current form in 2013. The ground floor has a good-sized dining area; the main bar and dining area is up half a dozen curved stone steps (lift available), with the partly covered, walled garden off at the far end. The bar offers at least six real ales, and also a good selection of real ciders, served from 20-litre boxes.
Q ⑅ ⊛ ◑ & ≠ (Town) ♠ ☙ 🖤 ╤

Milford on Sea

Red Lion
32 High Street, SO41 0QD
☼ 11.30-2.30, 6-11 (11.30 Fri); 11.30-11.30 Sat; 12-6 Sun
☎ (01590) 642236 ⊕ theredlionmilford.co.uk
House beer (by Ringwood); 2 changing beers (sourced locally; often Dancing Cows, Harvey's, Itchen Valley) Ⓗ
Popular, homely community pub in a vibrant village. It has a partial tie on ales but guest ales are usually from local breweries (maybe only one at quiet times), and it offers one real cider. Red Lion Bitter is Ringwood Razorback. Good-value, traditional pub food is served, and entertainment from local musicians is well supported. It is close to the beach, Sturt Pond nature reserve and Danestream woodland walks. The accommodation is not suitable for families, unlike the pub. Dogs and walkers are welcome.
Q ⑅ ⊛ ⊯ ◑ & ♠ ♣ ♠ P ⊞ (X1) 🖤 ╤

North Waltham

Fox Ⓛ ✅
Popham Lane, RG25 2BE (off Frog Lane, between village and A30, M3 jct 7)
☼ 11-11 (midnight Fri & Sat); 12-10.30 Sun
☎ (01256) 397288 ⊕ thefox.org

Brakspear Bitter; West Berkshire Good Old Boy; 2 changing beers (sourced locally) Ⓗ
Lovely traditional country pub on the edge of the village and overlooking extensive farmland. The pub is divided into two – a popular restaurant and a public bar where food is also served (booking advisable). Local seasonal produce is featured where possible. Outside there is an extensive beer garden and a children's adventure play area. The Ushers signage remains on the rear of the pub. Q✿ᕦⓘ⑀&P🖩♣🐾🛜

North Warnborough

Mill House Ⓛ

Hook Road, RG29 1ET (M3 jct 5; head towards Odiham)
☾ 11-11 ☎ (01256) 702953 ⊕ millhouse-hook.co.uk
Hogs Back TEA; house beer (by Phoenix); 4 changing beers (sourced regionally; often Andwells, Longdog, Triple fff) Ⓗ
Listed as one of eight mills of Odiham in the Domesday Book, current sections are 17th-century additions, and it was last used as a corn mill in 1895. Most recently a restaurant, it is now under Brunning & Price ownership. It has a central bar area, separate dining spaces and a lower-level view of the waterwheel and restaurant. The pleasant area with seating surrounding the millpond fed from the Whitewater links the function barn and parking. Q✿ᕦⓘ⑀&P🖩(13)🐾🛜

Oakley

Barley Mow Ⓛ ✪

19 Oakley Lane, RG23 7JZ
☾ 12-11 (10.30 Sun) ☎ (01256) 782591
⊕ barleymowatoakley.com
Flowerpots Goodens Gold; Sharp's Doom Bar; Wychwood Hobgoblin Gold; 1 changing beer (sourced nationally) Ⓗ
An old-fashioned local English hostelry in the heart of this picturesque village, serving well-kept traditional ales including one from a local brewer. Bar meals are cooked to order, including daily specials, and chip shop-type food is available to take away Tuesday to Saturday evenings. The family-oriented pub has a large garden with climbing frame and swings, plus a pizza oven and barbecue. It is dog friendly and a popular refreshment stop for ramblers and cyclists. Q✿ᕦⓘ♣P🖩(11)🐾🛜

Old Basing

Barton's Mill ✪

Bartons Lane, RG24 8AE (follow the signs from Bartons Lane to Basing House and car park)
☾ 11 (10 Sat)-11; 10-10.30 Sun ☎ (01256) 331153
⊕ bartonsmillpubanddining.co.uk/home
Wadworth IPA, Horizon, 6X, Swordfish; 1 changing beer Ⓗ
An attractively situated Wadworth house, once part of a still-existing water mill that overlooks the River Loddon and a water meadow. It is a short walk from the historic and picturesque ruins of Basing House and a large medieval tithe barn. The venue features traditional pub food and Wadworth cask ales, plus one rotating guest ale, served seven days a week by friendly staff. Children are welcome, as is the occasional duck from the river! Conference facilities available. ᕦⓘ⑀&P🐾🛜

Otterbourne

Otter

Boyatt Lane, SO21 2HW (on hilltop at S end of village)
☾ 11-11; 12-10.30 Sun ☎ (023) 8025 2685
⊕ theotterpub.co.uk
Otter Ale; Ringwood Razorback; Sharp's Doom Bar; Timothy Taylor Landlord Ⓗ
Atop the steep hill to the south of Otterbourne village, the Otter looks out across a grassy village green. The pub's four real ales include Devon's Otter Ale and Yorkshire's Landlord. Food features prominently, with an extensive menu including local produce, plus themed events such as burger nights and steak nights. Bar snacks are also available. Entertainment includes a Monday quiz and Sunday meat draw. An exotic range of spirits, especially gins, is featured. There is a pleasant, quiet rear garden. Q✿ⓘ♣P🖩(1,E2)🐾🛜

Overton

Red Lion Ⓛ

37 High Street, RG25 3HQ
☾ 12-3, 6-11 (midnight Fri & Sat); 12-10.30 Sun
☎ (01256) 773363 ⊕ redlion-overton.co.uk
Flowerpots Bitter; Sharp's Doom Bar; 1 changing beer (sourced locally) Ⓗ
Popular village pub that prides itself on well-kept local real ales and high-quality, freshly cooked food every day, including a range of speciality steaks. It is divided into three areas: a restaurant, main bar, and snug with wood-burning stove. Near to the new Bombay Sapphire distillery, the pub also offers an extensive gin menu. Outside there is a pleasant beer garden, a partially covered patio area, a separate function room with skittle alley available for hire, and a car park. Q✿ᕦⓘ&♣P🖩(76)🐾🛜

Park Gate

Village Inn ✪

67 Botley Road, SO31 1AZ
☾ 11.30-11; 10-midnight Fri & Sat; 10-11 Sun
☎ (01489) 573223
Black Sheep Best Bitter; Brakspear Bitter; 5 changing beers (often Bays, Harviestoun, Oakham) Ⓗ
A cosy atmospheric inn and part of Ember Inns. It offers great food alongside a selection of ales on seven handpumps, including five rotating guest beers. The pub is less than five minutes' walk from Swanwick railway station. There is metered car parking Monday to Friday until 5pm, but charges are refundable on bar purchases. ᕦⓘ&🚲(Swanwick)P🖩(28,28A)🐾🛜

Petersfield

Townhouse Ⓛ

28 High Street, GU32 3JL
☾ 10-11 (9 Mon); 10-midnight Fri & Sat; 10-9 Sun
☎ (01730) 265630 ⊕ petersfieldtownhouse.com
3 changing beers (sourced regionally; often Broken Bridge, Langham, Red Cat) Ⓗ
This is a popular bistro-style pub offering food (breakfast, lunch and dinner), local ales and ciders. It is located toward the eastern end of the High Street. There is a separate function room upstairs with its own bar, providing additional seating. Outside at the rear of the premises is the patio garden. Children and dogs are welcome. ᕦⓘ&🚲♣P🖩(67)🐾🛜

Portsmouth

Artillery Arms 🅛
Hester Road, Milton, PO4 8HB
☼ 12-11.30 (midnight Fri & Sat) ☎ (023) 9273 3610
Ringwood Fortyniner; Triple fff Alton's Pride,
Moondance; 2 changing beers (sourced locally) 🅷
Traditional split-level locals' pub serving ales both
local and from further afield, with a large garden. It
supports both darts and pool teams, and other
traditional pub games are played. Just five minutes'
walk from Fratton Park, it can get busy on match
days but is welcoming to away supporters.
🏠🌣♣🅿🍴(1,2)🐾🛜

Barley Mow 🅛 ✅
39 Castle Road, Southsea, PO5 3DE
☼ 12 (11 Sat)-midnight; 12-11 Sun ☎ (023) 9282 3492
⊕ barleymowsouthsea.com
Fuller's London Pride; Gale's HSB; 6 changing beers
(sourced nationally) 🅷
Friendly two-bar community pub offering eight
ales including a mild, stout or porter, and Westons
Old Rosie cider. The pub hosts an impressive array
of events including live music, meat raffles,
quizzes, pool, darts, golf teams, bar billiards, a
chess league, and druid moots. The garden is a real
gem and has won awards in its own right. Children
are welcome until 8pm (as are dogs on leads, but
not in the garden). 🌣♿♣🍴🐾🛜

Belle Isle
39 Osborne Road, Southsea, PO5 3LR
☼ 12-11 (midnight Thu-Sat) ☎ (023) 9282 0515
⊕ thebelleisle.co.uk
4 changing beers (sourced nationally; often Irving,
Fallen Acorn, Sharp's) 🅷
This large café bar is divided into three drinking
areas and also has some pavement seating at the
front. It has a mix of seating including comfortable
sofas and wooden chairs at kitchen-style tables.
One wall is decorated with old suitcases and
another lists some of the types of food on offer,
which include continental and American-influenced
dishes. All in all, a splendid place to relax after
trekking round the shops in the nearby precinct.
🍴🅿(1,23)🛜

Brewhouse & Kitchen 🅛 ✅
26 Guildhall Walk, Landport, PO1 2DD
☼ 11-11 (10.30 Sun) ☎ (023) 9289 1340
Brewhouse & Kitchen Sexton, Mucky Duck, Black
Swan; 2 changing beers (sourced locally; often
Brewhouse & Kitchen) 🅷
The White Swan, or Mucky Duck, as it is often
locally known, has been a constant fixture in the
Guildhall Walk area before opening in 2013 as the
first brewpub in Brewhouse & Kitchen's expanding
estate. The selection of five house ales are all
brewed onsite from the gleaming 2.5-barrel plant
which greets you as you walk in - brewery
experiences offered. Close to Portsmouth &
Southsea station, ideal for the city centre.
🏠🌣🍴🚆(Portsmouth & Southsea)♣🍴🅿(7,700)
🐾🛜

Hole in the Wall 🅛
36 Great Southsea Street, Southsea, PO5 3BY
☼ 4-11; 12-midnight Fri; 2-11 Sat & Sun ☎ (023) 9229 8085
⊕ theholeinthewallpub.co.uk
Flowerpots Goodens Gold 🅖; 5 changing beers
(sourced nationally) 🅷

The Hole may be one of the smallest pubs in
Portsmouth but, as a genuine free house, it offers a
wide and changing choice of beers from local and
national breweries. Staggeringly Good Hole in
Time, exclusively brewed for this pub, is usually on,
but other locally brewed beers may be offered
instead. Opens at noon on Saturday for Pompey
home games. No admittance after 11pm. Dogs
must be on leads. 🍴🐾🅿🚆🐾🛜

John Jacques ✅
78-82 Fratton Road, Fratton, PO1 5BZ
☼ 8am-midnight (11 Sun) ☎ (023) 9277 9742
Greene King Abbot; Ruddles Best Bitter; Sharp's
Doom Bar; 9 changing beers (sourced nationally;
often Irving, Itchen Valley) 🅷
Wetherspoon pub built on the site of the former
Portsea Island Mutual Co-operative Society
(PIMCO), and named after PIMCO's former chief
executive - who became Lord John Jacques of
Portsea Island. A good choice of guest real ales is
available at all times, as well as at least one real
cider. Modern art adorns the walls, along with
framed historical photographs. Convenient for
Fratton Road and Bridge Centre shops and the
station. 🏠🌣🍴♿🚆(Fratton)♣🍴🅿(13,18)🛜

Lawrence Arms 🅛 ✅
63 Lawrence Road, Southsea, PO5 1NU
☼ 2-11.30 (12.30am Fri); 11-12.30am Sat; 11-11 Sun
☎ (023) 9282 1280 ⊕ lawrence-arms-portsmouth.co.uk
Harvey's Sussex Best Bitter; 5 changing beers
(sourced nationally) 🅷
Dating back to 1887, this street-corner pub's
exterior retains some traditional tiles and lanterns.
The L-shaped bar faces a large lounge area. Very
much a friendly community pub, there are darts
and pool teams, weekly meat raffles, quizzes and
themed days. The bar offers a rotating selection of
five local ales, one from further afield, plus a bottle
shop. There is also a good cider selection, often
from Westons and Lilley's. Food includes tasty
gourmet toasties. 🏠🌣🍴♣🍴(18)🛜

Meat & Barrel 🅛
110-114 Palmerston Road, Southsea, PO5 3PT
☼ 11.30-11 (midnight Fri & Sat); 11.30-10 Sun
☎ (023) 9217 6291 ⊕ meatandbarrel.co.uk
6 changing beers (sourced nationally) 🅷
Opened in 2014, this modern bar has carved its
own niche in Southsea's burgeoning beer scene.
Great for groups, plenty of tables adorn the large
open-plan bar. Six rotating cask ales are featured,
alongside an expansive selection of draught ales.
The menu features British classics, steaks and
vegetarian options - burgers are a must!
🏠🍴🅿(1,7)🐾🛜

Phoenix
13 Duncan Road, Southsea, PO5 2QU
☼ 10-midnight (1am Fri & Sat); 12-midnight Sun
☎ (023) 9278 1055
Ringwood Fortyniner; 2 changing beers (sourced
nationally; often Exmoor, Irving, Urban Island) 🅷
A genuine community inn with strong connections
to the nearby Kings Theatre (see the posters and
photos in the lounge). It is one of just a few pubs in
the area that retain two bars. The public bar has a
jukebox - with just about every record you could
imagine - and posters of Portsmouth FC teams,
while the lounge has a piano and a tabletop Space
Invaders machine. A patio garden separates the
bars from the games room. 🌣♣🍴🅿(2)🐾

Rose in June 🗈 ✅
102 Milton Road, Milton, PO3 6AR
🕐 12–midnight (1am Fri & Sat) ☎ (023) 9282 4191
🌐 theroseinjune.co.uk
Ballards Midhurst Mild; Gale's HSB; Irving Frigate; Marston's Lancaster Bomber; Upham Punter; 2 changing beers ⊞
About 10 minutes' walk from Fratton Park, this two-bar pub is popular with football fans. There are plenty of events such as a Thursday quiz, pool and darts teams, occasional comedy nights and a curry night on the first Wednesday of the month. The extensive garden has a play area and hosts a well-attended summer beer festival. The annual winter festival is also enjoyable. Ciders and a perry are available. 🗈🏵️🍴P�
🚃 🎶

Rutland Arms 🗈 ✅
205 Francis Avenue, Southsea, PO4 0AH
🕐 4–11; 2–midnight Fri; 11–midnight Sat; 12–10 Sun
☎ (023) 9275 1221
Butcombe Original; 2 changing beers (sourced locally; often Irving, Bowman) ⊞
A family-run pub, with four generations involved in the business. Five minutes' walk from Fratton Park, this two-bar pub is popular with football fans. Drinks are served in plastic glasses on match days, before and after the game. Regular events include a Sunday roast, Thursday quiz night and darts. The extensive garden is popular in summer.
🗈🏵️🍴⇌(Fratton)♣P🚃(1,15)🎶

Sir Loin of Beef
152 Highland Road, Eastney, PO4 9NH
🕐 11–midnight; 12–midnight Sun ☎ (023) 9282 0115
Gale's HSB; Titanic Plum Porter; 6 changing beers (sourced nationally) ⊞
Large single-bar pub whose walls are decorated with submarine paraphernalia. A good selection of bottle-conditioned ales is stocked to supplement the ales on draught. Traditional cider is available. The pub hosts a quiz night every Thursday and live entertainment Sunday lunchtime, as well as the ever-popular meat raffle. 🖣♣🍴🚃

Thatchers 🗈 ✅
95 London Road, North End, PO2 0BN
🕐 9am–11 (1am Fri & Sat); 11.30–11 Sun ☎ (023) 9266 2146
Ringwood Fortyniner; 4 changing beers (sourced regionally; often Andwells, Hammerpot, Irving) ⊞
Originally owned by Miles Brewery, then later by Whitbread for many years, when it was a two-bar local named the Thatched House. Sensitively modernised in 2002 and renamed Thatchers, it now has an open-plan layout subdivided into three main areas: a floorboarded public space to the front (look for Elvis here), a carpeted lounge with upholstered seating, and a raised dining and drinking area in the rear extension. The walls are adorned with photographs, paintings and old metal advertisements. 🗈🏵️🍴♣🚃(3,7)🚃🎶

Wave Maiden 🗈
36 Osborne Road, Southsea, PO5 3LT
🕐 6–11; 12–midnight Fri & Sat; 12–10 Sun ☎ (023) 9217 8878
3 changing beers (sourced nationally; often Gun, Staggeringly Good, Vibrant Forest) 🗓
An independent, family-owned establishment, focusing on artisanally produced beer and cheese. Go to this premises for beer brewed for taste, not mass consumption, alongside a menu that offers delicious home-made cheese-based dishes. It is one of the few gravity stillages in the area, with a

constant rotation of local and national ales, offering a welcoming atmosphere for beer lovers from 18 to 80. 🗈🍴♿🍴🚃(1,23)🚃🎶

Winchester Arms
99 Winchester Road, Buckland, PO2 7PS
🕐 4–11; 3–midnight Fri; 12–11 Sat & Sun ☎ (023) 9266 2443
Wychwood Hobgoblin Gold; 3 changing beers (sourced regionally) ⊞
The Winch is a proper back-street local, offering one regular beer and two or three varying guests. Ciders are available during the summer. Live music is a feature on Sunday evenings, with every third Sunday of the month being open mic night with music and comedy, plus music one Saturday a month. A beer festival is held over the spring bank holiday weekend. The garden has a covered smoking shelter. It may stay open until midnight on Saturday night if busy. 🏵️🍴🚃(3,7)🚃

Wine Vaults 🗈
41-47 Albert Road, Southsea, PO5 2SF
🕐 12–11 (12.30am Fri & Sat); 12–10.30 Sun
☎ (023) 9286 4712
Fuller's London Pride, ESB; Gale's Seafarers Ale, HSB; Staggeringly Good ThaiRannoCitrus; 3 changing beers (sourced locally; often Dark Star) ⊞
On the bustling Albert Road, this sprawling establishment offers five bars over three floors. Up to eight real ales are available at any time. Food is served until 9.30pm (8pm Sun), with pizzas, scrumptious bar boards and Sunday roasts particular highlights. Live music on Thursdays and jazz on alternate Tuesdays make this a destination for partygoers or serious beer drinkers.
🗈🏵️🍴♿🚃(2)🚃🎶

Ringwood

Inn on the Furlong ✅
12 Meeting House Lane, BH24 1EY
🕐 9.30am–11 (midnight Fri & Sat); 10–10.30 Sun
☎ (01425) 475139
Ringwood Best Bitter (Razorback), Boondoggle, Fortyniner; 2 changing beers (often Marston's, Ringwood) ⊞
A convenient place in which to meet, situated on the edge of the town centre near the bus station, town car park and local shops. The bar area at the front of the pub serves several rooms which are used mainly by diners. There are three outside patio areas, and dogs are welcome (in the bar area only). Open from 9.30am for breakfast, food is served until 8pm (3pm Sun). 🗈🏵️🍴♣🚃🚃🎶

Railway Hotel 🗈
35 Hightown Road, BH24 1NQ SU152048
🕐 11.30–11; 12–10 Sun ☎ (01425) 473701 🌐 therailway.co
Ringwood Best Bitter (Razorback); 4 changing beers (sourced locally; often Downton, Sixpenny, Vibrant Forest) ⊞
Unspoilt community pub close to Ringwood Brewery. The three rotating cask ales include at least one local ale and a Ringwood seasonal plus bottled beers and a range of craft gins and rums. Food is available all day – home-made burgers, traditional breakfasts and Sunday roasts. Family and dog friendly, there is a large, secure garden with play area, pub chickens and vegetable garden. The annual beer festival is on the early May bank holiday. Q🗈🏵️🍴🖣♣P🚃🚃🎶

Romsey

Luzborough 🅛 ✅
Luzborough Lane, SO51 9AA (1½ miles E of Romsey)
✪ 11-11 ☎ (01794) 523816
Greene King IPA, Abbot; 2 changing beers (sourced locally; often Flack Manor, Itchen Valley, Longdog) Ⓗ
Grade II*-listed pub in the eastern outskirts of Romsey, just off the A27, a Greene King Old English Inn. It provides an extensive menu throughout the day. Originally a 16th-century house, it has been refurbished and extended, yet it retains some original features. There is a large walled garden at the rear, and outside tables both front and rear. The menu features pub classics, breakfasts (until noon), curry evenings, and many offers and specials. There is a weekly quiz night.
♿🕮🅓🛏👜🅿🚃🐾🛜

Old House at Home
62 Love Lane, SO51 8DE (next to Waitrose car park)
✪ 11-11 (11.30 Fri & Sat); 12-10.30 Sun ☎ (01794) 513175
🌐 theoldhouseathomeromsey.co.uk
Fuller's London Pride; Gale's Seafarers Ale, HSB; 2 changing beers (sourced nationally; often Fuller's) Ⓗ
Popular old thatched pub in the centre of Romsey. It has appeared in every Guide since 2005 and has received several Fuller's national awards. The front entrance accesses a single L-shaped bar on two levels. Food is served in the bar and in a separate dining area. Booths, wooden beams and woodburners make for cosy drinking all year round, while the large, tidy courtyard garden is a relaxing retreat on warmer days. Live folk features on Monday. 🕮🅓🚃♣🅿🐾🛜

Star Inn 🅛
13 The Horsefair, SO51 8EZ (on road to Stockbridge)
✪ 12-11 (midnight Fri & Sat) ☎ (01794) 511165
St Austell Tribute; 2 changing beers (sourced locally; often Bowman, Dancing Cows, Red Cat) Ⓗ
The 18th-century Grade II-listed Star was originally the Strong's brewery tap, standing near the former brewery site. Several local beers are often available, plus draught cider in summer. A TV is usually on silent in the large single bar, near the woodburner. There is live music every Saturday, and an informal folk session on Wednesday. League darts and poker occupy Tuesday, Friday and Thursday. The Star is indeed an inn, providing much-needed accommodation in the town.
♿🕮🅓🛏🚃♣🅿🛜

Selborne

Selborne Arms 🅛
High Street, GU34 3JR
✪ 11-3, 6-11; 11-11 Sat; 12-11 Sun ☎ (01420) 511247
🌐 selbornearms.co.uk
Bowman Swift One; Ringwood Fortyniner; 3 changing beers (sourced nationally) Ⓗ
A traditional award-winning village pub with real fires and a friendly atmosphere, at the foot of the zig-zag path carved by famous naturalist Gilbert White. Extensive menus showcase local and home-made produce, with vegetarian and gluten-free options. Up to three guest beers come from local breweries. Beer bats offer three thirds of beer for the price of a pint. The play area in the garden is popular with children, and parents should note that it is also safe. Q♿🕮🅓♣👜🅿🚃(38)🛜

Shedfield

Wheatsheaf Inn 🅛
Botley Road, SO32 2JG (on A334)
✪ 12-11 (10.30 Sun) ☎ (01329) 833024
Flowerpots Perridge Pale, Bitter, Goodens Gold; 3 changing beers (sourced locally; often CrackleRock, Goddards, Palmers) Ⓖ
Popular award-winning pub with a lively public bar, warmed by a new wood-burning stove. The back lounge was extended and refurbished in 2016, adding disabled access and a toilet. Lovely home-cooked food is served every lunchtime and Tuesday and Wednesday evenings. Beers are dispensed from the cask, mainly from the owners' Flowerpots Brewery, alongside real ciders. Live music plays most Saturday evenings. The annual beer festival is on the late May bank holiday weekend. Q🕮🅓🛏♣👜🅿(69)🐾🛜

Sherfield English

Hatchet Inn ✅
Salisbury Road, SO51 6FP
✪ 12-3, 5-11.30; 12-11.30 Fri-Sun ☎ (01794) 322487
🌐 hatchetinn.com
Dartmoor Jail Ale; St Austell Tribute; Sharp's Doom Bar; Wells Bombardier Burning Gold Ⓗ
A family-run pub, for three generations, at the edge of Hampshire, on the A27. Entering, on the right is a square public bar, and on the left a long saloon bar, laid mainly for dining. Two ladies have shared the role of landlady for six years, one of them the chef for much longer than that. An extensive choice of food, in generous portions and often home-made, makes this a popular place for mature diners. There is a beer festival every August. Q🕮🅓🗡♣🅿(X7R)🐾🛜

Southampton

Belgium & Blues ✅
180 Above Bar Street, SO14 7DW
✪ 3-11; 12-midnight Fri & Sat; 12-10.30 Sun
☎ (023) 8022 5411 🌐 belgiumandblues.co.uk
4 changing beers (sourced regionally) Ⓗ
Named for the beer and music styles favoured, but complemented by a varied range of real ales and ciders in the main cellar bar area downstairs. The bar serves at least four ever-changing real ales, a selection of Belgian bottled beer plus Belgian-style food such as moules and frites. It has several booths to accommodate groups. At ground level is a brasserie with lunchtime table service which also functions as a speciality gin bar. Q🅓🚃👜🅿🐾🛜

Bitter Virtue 🅛
70 Cambridge Road, SO14 6US (jct with Alma Rd)
✪ closed Mon, 10.30-8.30 (2 Sun) ☎ (023) 8055 4881
🌐 bittervirtue.co.uk
2 changing beers (sourced regionally; often Bowman, Flowerpots, Siren) Ⓖ
Corner shop off-licence that is a treasure trove both for beer aficionados and those who just want something good to drink at home. Over 900 bottled beers and ciders are stocked, from local staples to rare imports. Draught cider and two draught ales are usually available, at least one from a local brewery. Knowledgeable staff are always willing to give advice. Beer books, glasses and brewing merchandise are also for sale. 👜🅿🐾

Bookshop Alehouse 🍷

21 Portswood Road, SO17 2ES (60yds N from Lodge Rd)
🕲 12-11
4 changing beers (sourced locally) Ⓗ
Award-winning micropub consisting of a front room leading to a tiny, narrow upper bar with four handpumps and a fridge with four bag-in-box ciders. Converted from a bookshop in 2016, it retains that relaxing ambience, with a wall of bookshelves and tables and chairs. No food is available but you are welcome to eat here from a choice of nearby takeaways. A portable ramp allows wheelchair access from outside. Local CAMRA Pub of the Year 2017.
Q�&≠(St Denys)♣🌑🖿😺🛜

Butcher's Hook

7 Manor Farm Road, SO18 1NN (hidden by Bitterne Triangle monument)
🕲 closed Mon & Tue; 6-11 Wed & Thu; 4-11 Fri; 1-11 Sat; 2-10 Sun ☎ (023) 8178 2280 🌐 butchershookpub.com
4 changing beers (sourced nationally) Ⓖ
Southampton's first micropub, opened in 2014, in what was a Victorian butcher's shop. Look for its scaffold benches outside to avoid walking past. It serves four ever-changing, gravity dispensed, cask ales, plus a number of bottled ales. With no bar, approach one of the staff to place your order. The small interior – there is seating inside for around 25 people – makes for a lively, sociable and conversational drinking atmosphere. A hub of the local community. Friendly dogs welcome.
Q�&≠(Bitterne)🌑🖿(7)😺🛜

Dancing Man Ⓛ

Wool House, Town Quay, SO14 2AR (opp Isle of Wight ferry terminal)
🕲 11-11 (midnight Thu-Sat) ☎ (023) 8083 6666
🌐 dancingmanbrewery.co.uk
8 changing beers (sourced nationally) Ⓗ
Wool House is a Grade I-listed medieval building, and a fine example of what can be achieved within severe constraints. Since opening in 2015 the brewing equipment has had to increase its capacity twice. The mix of ancient and modern provides a fitting venue for sampling the six beers brewed on the premises and two from across the country. Food is excellent, including many vegan options (roasts only on Sunday). The first floor may be reserved for private functions, so check before planning a special visit. 🌑🌑🌑🖿😺🛜

Freemantle Arms Ⓛ

31 Albany Road, SO15 3EF
🕲 12-2.30, 5-11 (8 Mon); 12-11 Thu & Sat; 12-midnight Fri; 12-10 Sun ☎ (023) 8077 2536 🌐 thefreemantlearms.co.uk
Flowerpots Goodens Gold; Sharp's Doom Bar; house beer (by Hardys & Hansons); 2 changing beers (sourced regionally; often Flowerpots, Otter, Red Cat) Ⓗ
In a tranquil cul-de-sac in the back streets, the Freemantle Arms is an oasis in this busy city, with friendly, welcoming staff and locals. It is now a single bar, with comfortable seating and walls displaying old tools and historic vistas of the area. Five real ales are sold, two of which change. The enclosed, colourful garden has many trestle tables and makes a great, safe place for children. Two crib teams, a fortnightly quiz, darts, a beer festival, and other regular events feature.
🌑≠(Millbrook)♣🖿😺🛜

Giddy Bridge Ⓛ ✅

12-18 London Road, SO15 2AF
🕲 8am-11.30 ☎ (023) 8033 6346
Greene King Abbot; Ruddles Best Bitter; Sharp's Doom Bar; 7 changing beers (sourced nationally) Ⓗ
A former furniture shop, now a busy Wetherspoon pub, just north of the city centre. It has a large ground-floor bar with additional seating upstairs and, unusually, a secluded roof garden terrace for sunny days. There is also a covered table area outside. Food is served all day, alcohol from 9am. Twelve handpumps deliver national, regional and some local beers plus several ciders. Close to Southampton Solent University and the law courts, London Road is central to the city's evening economy. Q🌑🐦🌑🖿🛜

Guide Dog Ⓛ

38 Earl's Road, SO14 6SF (corner with Ancasta Rd)
🕲 12-11 (10.30 Sun) ☎ (023) 8063 8947
Dark Star Hophead, American Pale Ale; Flowerpots Goodens Gold; Red Cat Prowler Pale; 7 changing beers (sourced nationally; often Fuller's, Siren, XT) Ⓗ
In a residential side street, out of sight of the main roads, this two-roomed pub concentrates on a wide and interesting range of real ales from local and national breweries, and currently has 11 handpumps. The bar area is small and enjoys a friendly atmosphere, but can become crowded at peak times and when Southampton are playing at home. The pub has won a number of awards including local CAMRA branch Pub of the Year several times. Q🌑🖿(7,U6)😺🛜

Olaf's Tun

8A Portsmouth Road, SO19 9AA
🕲 closed Mon & Tue; 6-10 Wed & Thu; 4-11 Fri; 1-9.30 Sat; 1-9.30 Sun ☎ 07437 935223
4 changing beers (sourced nationally) Ⓖ
Olaf's Tun is an exciting new entrant to Southampton's real ale scene. A short walk from the River Itchen and well served by public transport, Olaf's prides itself on a frequently changing selection of quality real ale served straight from the cask. Real ciders and wine are also available. Named after the Viking name for Woolston, Olaf's is a communal, homely micropub where the customers are assured of a warm welcome. Note the opening time constraints.
Q�&≠(Woolston)♣🌑🖿😺🛜

Platform Tavern Ⓛ ✅

Town Quay, SO14 2NY
🕲 12-11 (midnight Thu); 11.30-midnight Fri; 12-midnight Sat ☎ (023) 8033 7232 🌐 platformtavern.com
Fuller's London Pride; Gale's Seafarers Ale; 3 changing beers (sourced regionally) Ⓗ
Cosy, welcoming, two-roomed pub; a restaurant area is through a ragged slate archway. Interior decoration includes African art, batik, musical instruments, and part of the ancient town walls. Three rotating guest ales add to the two regular beers. Home-cooked food is served every day. There is live music several nights each week plus Sunday lunchtime, and the pub gets extremely busy Friday and Saturday nights. Beer festivals are held throughout the year, with a cider festival at Easter. 🌑♣🌑🖿😺🛜

Rockstone Ⓛ

63 Onslow Road, SO14 0JL
🕲 12-midnight (1am Fri & Sat) ☎ (023) 8063 7256
🌐 therockstone.co.uk

7 changing beers (sourced regionally; often Dark Star, Flack Manor, Vibrant Forest) Ⓗ
A well-kept pub, growing in popularity each year, with friendly management and staff who are knowledgeable about the products sold. Nine handpumps feature, seven with changing real ales and two with ciders. The pub holds a large range of bottled beers, and a good selection of gins, rums and whiskies from around the world. As well as its drink trade, the Rockstone is gaining a reputation for some of the finest burgers in Southampton.
Ѣ ⊛ ◑ ♿ 🚆 (7,U6) ❀ 🛜

South Western Arms Ⓛ ✪
38-40 Adelaide Road, SO17 2HW (E side of St Denys station)
✪ 12-11 (midnight Fri & Sat) ☎ (023) 8032 4542
Bowman Swift One; Hop Art Hoppy Blonde; 8 changing beers (sourced nationally) Ⓗ
A single bar with a seating area on the ground floor, and pool and football tables and more seating on the upstairs gallery. Its rustic appearance, with exposed brick walls, and a range of old bottles and household objects, gives the pub character. The walled garden, with covered smoking area, is a suntrap in summer. Ten ales are usually stocked, plus one cider and up to 20 bottled beers. A couple of beer festivals are held each year. A pizza van serves outside Wednesday to Saturday.
Q Ѣ ⊛ 🚆 (St Denys) ♣ ● P🚆 (7) ❀ 🛜

Waterloo Arms Ⓛ
101 Waterloo Road, SO15 3BS
✪ 12-11 (midnight Fri & Sat) ☎ (023) 8022 0022
Downton New Forest Ale; Hop Back GFB, Crop Circle, Entire Stout, Summer Lightning; 3 changing beers (sourced nationally) Ⓗ
The Waterloo, a 1930s-built community pub, deservedly has a fan base extending well beyond the community boundary. The principal public area, an irregular T in plan, has perimeter seating and stools, and is graced by two Roman-brick fireplaces. There is also a large, modern conservatory (available for functions), beyond which is a paved garden. Beer and food are reasonably priced, and the home-made Scotch eggs are recommended. Three or four beer festivals are held each year.
⊛ ◑ 🚆 (Millbrook) ♣ 🚆 ❀ 🛜

Southwick

Golden Lion Ⓛ
High Street, PO17 6EB
✪ 12-3, 5.30-11; 12-midnight Sat; 12-7 Sun
☎ (023) 9221 0437
Suthwyk Old Dick, Skew Sunshine Ale; 4 changing beers (sourced locally; often Langham, Palmers, Triple fff) Ⓗ
A privately owned village free house with an historic brewhouse and off-licence (open Wednesday to Sunday) in the car park. The pub was used as the officer's mess for the D-Day landings and is decorated with World War II memorabilia. The real ales usually come from within 30 miles, plus real ciders. Award-winning food can be enjoyed in the bar or the separate dining room and there is a secluded garden. Live jazz music features on Tuesday night. Q Ѣ ⊛ ◑ 🚻 ♣ ● P ❀

Swanmore

Rising Sun Ⓛ
Droxford Road, SO32 2PS
✪ 12-2.30, 5.30-11; 12-7 Sun ☎ (01489) 896663
⊕ risingsunswanmore.co.uk
Flowerpots Goodens Gold; house beer (by Flack Manor); 1 changing beer (sourced locally; often Andwells, Irving, Itchen Valley) Ⓗ
Friendly 17th-century coaching inn with many interesting features, including oak beams, decorative brickwork and the Dungeon, an arch-shaped alcove, once part of the cellar but now part of the restaurant. The bar serves only Hampshire beers (house beer is Flack's Double Drop) and the popular restaurant offers freshly cooked food with a varied specials menu. Outside is a large beer garden. An Ocktoberfest is held mid-September featuring five German beers and German sausages on the barbecue. Q Ѣ ⊛ ◑ P ❀

Tichborne

Tichborne Arms
SO24 0NA (1¼ miles S from B3047 Alresford Rd jct)
SU571304
✪ 11.45-3, 6-9.30 (11 Wed & Thu; 11.30 Fri); 11.45-11.30 Sat; 12-7.30 Sun ☎ (01962) 733760 ⊕ tichbornearms.co.uk
Palmers Copper Ale; 2 changing beers (sourced locally) Ⓖ
Village pub with an old-fashioned antique-finished interior, popular with local drinkers and walkers. The guest beers tend to be from Dorset or Somerset and draught cider is usually on offer. A beer and cider festival is held over the August bank holiday. Upmarket pub food is served, but drinkers are welcome in both bars. The main bar has a piano and a logburner and there is an open fire in the smaller, panelled bar. Dogs and children welcome. Q Ѣ ⊛ ◑ ♣ ● P ❀ 🛜

Titchfield

Queen's Head Ⓛ ✪
13 High Street, PO14 4AQ
✪ 12-11 (11.30 Fri); 11-11.30 Sat; 11-11 Sun
☎ (01329) 842154 ⊕ queenshead-titchfield.co.uk
4 changing beers (sourced locally; often Bowman, Flack Manor, Irving) Ⓗ
A 17th-century pub, centrally located in the village. Four beers rotate regularly, generally from local breweries such as Bowman and Irving. An open fire is the central feature of the bar. A function room can be used for events. Home-cooked food using mainly local ingredients is served in the bar every lunchtime and evening (no food Sun eve). A separate restaurant opens Friday and Saturday evenings and Sunday lunchtimes. A quiz and meat raffle are held regularly on Sunday evenings.
Q Ѣ ⊛ ◑ P🚆 (X4) ❀ 🛜

Wheatsheaf Ⓛ
1 East Street, PO14 4AD
✪ 12-11 (midnight Fri & Sat) ☎ (01329) 842965
⊕ wheatsheaftitchfield.co.uk
Flowerpots Bitter; Palmers Best Bitter; 3 changing beers (sourced regionally; often Fallen Acorn, Hop Back, Red Cat) Ⓗ
As Titchfield's only free house, this welcoming 17th-century pub continues to gain in popularity for its excellent selection of ales and high-quality food. An intimate bar with a real fire and a cosy snug to the back add to the friendly atmosphere. Food is

available Monday to Sunday in the bar and separate restaurant – steak night is Tuesday and roasts are served every Sunday. A popular beer festival is held summer and winter.
Q ⌂ ❀ ◑ ᵬ ● P ☷ (X4) ❀

Warsash

Ferryman
2 Warsash Road, SO31 9HX
☼ 12-11 (11.30 Fri & Sat); 12-10.30 Sun ☎ (01489) 573088
4 changing beers (sourced nationally; often Adnams, Milk Street) ⊞
A warm welcome awaits visitors, and especially dogs, to this pub at the heart of the village. It has a single bar with ample seating, a restaurant area and an outside decked area. It is adjacent to the bus stops for Fareham and Southampton and a mere 600 yards from the River Hamble, of Howards Way fame. Good food is available alongside four real ales, and occasional beer festivals are hosted. Live music sometimes features.
⌂ ❀ ◑ ᵬ ● P ☷ (X5) ❀ ☍

West Tytherley

Black Horse ⌾
North Lane, SP5 1NF
☼ closed Mon & Tue; 12-3, 6-11; 12-7 Sun
☎ (01794) 340308 ⊕ theblackhorsepub.co.uk
Hop Back GFB; 3 changing beers (sourced regionally; often Bowman, Butcombe, Fuller's) ⊞
A gem of a village pub. Dating from the early 17th century and at one time a fully fledged coaching inn, the stables are now the skittle alley and function room. It is Grade II listed, with a special mention of the magnificent carved wood fireplace which dates from 1680 and was moved from the nearby Norman Court to the pub in 1830. The menu features locally sourced produce such as venison and buffalo; steak night is Thursday.
Q ⌂ ❀ ◑ ♣ ● P ☷ (37) ❀

Weyhill

Weyhill Fair ✔
Weyhill Road, SP11 0PP
☼ closed Mon; 11.30-3, 5.30-11; 11.30-11 Fri & Sat; 12-6 Sun
☎ (01264) 773631 ⊕ weyhillfair.com
Fuller's London Pride; Gale's Seafarers Ale, HSB; 2 changing beers (often Butcombe, Castle Rock, Wychwood) ⊞
Country-style pub three miles west of Andover, standing on the site of the historic Weyhill Fairground. It serves meals at every session, using locally sourced ingredients where possible. The three regular Fuller's beers are often supplemented by both a seasonal and a guest ale from the Fuller's portfolio. A popular outdoor music and beer festival is usually held in July, featuring local bands and musicians. The pub opens on Monday in summer.
⌂ ❀ ◑ A P ☷ ❀ ☍

Whitchurch

Prince Regent ⌾
104 London Road, RG28 7LT
☼ 12-11 ☎ (01256) 892179
Hop Back Summer Lightning; Young's London Gold ⊞
The pub up the hill is a single-bar local free house on the edge of this pleasant country town, overlooking the higher reaches of the Test Valley.

Local conversation takes pride of place among a mixed clientele. There is an excellent jukebox, a pool table and sports TV, with an emphasis on football matches. It is a good start for walks in the countryside. Occasional live music and quizzes are hosted. ♣ P ☷ (76) ❀

Whitchurch Sports & Social Club
Winchester Road, RG28 7RB (southern edge of town)
☼ 7-11.30; 12-11.30 Sun ☎ (01256) 892493
Fuller's London Pride; Red Cat Prowler Pale; 1 changing beer ⊞
Tucked away opposite the tranquil Millennium Meadow, this club features two large bars, open evenings and weekends. The three real ales may be locally sourced. Home to Whitchurch United FC, the venue is shared by the indoor bowling club whose impressive green can be viewed from the comfortable lounge bar. Regular events include quizzes, parties, cabarets, discos and live bands. Opens at 1pm on Saturday when Whitchurch United are at home. Local CAMRA Club of the Year 2017. ⌂ ❀ P ☷ (86) ☍

Winchester

Albion ⌾
2 Stockbridge Road, SO23 7BZ (just E of station)
☼ 12-11 (11.30 Fri & Sat); 12-10.30 Sun ☎ (01962) 867991
Flowerpots Perridge Pale, Bitter, Goodens Gold; 1 changing beer (sourced locally; often Alfred's) ⊞
Every town should have one: a small cosy pub close to the railway station. This one is at the bottom of Station Hill, going into town, on a busy road junction, ideal for people-watching. It is a smart, grey-painted, acutely angled pub in a Victorian (circa 1860) building. Owned by Cheriton's Flowerpots Brewery, expect excellent examples of its beers. Quality pork pies are generally available. A great place to take a break from any rail journey. Q ❀ ☷ ❀ ☍

Black Boy ⌾
1 Wharf Hill, SO23 9NQ (just off Chesil St, B3404)
☼ 12-11 (midnight Fri & Sat); 12-10.30 Sun
☎ (01962) 861754 ⊕ theblackboypub.com
Alfred's Saxon Bronze; Flowerpots Bitter; 3 changing beers (sourced locally; often Bowman, Hop Back, Itchen Valley) ⊞
An ancient, multi-level collection of interconnected rooms surround a central island bar here. The extraordinary decor resembles a folk museum having a psychedelic overdose. Surprises are everywhere: tradesmen's tool collections, scientific instruments, a complete farmhouse kitchen, serious taxidermy, and so forth. The beer range emphasises local small breweries. Lunches are served daily except Monday, evening food is Tuesday to Saturday but, for more formal dining, the co-owned Black Rat restaurant is opposite. Also co-owned, the attached Black Hole has 10 double en-suite B&B rooms. Q ❀ ◑ ⌂ ♣ ● ☷ (4) ❀ ☍

Eclipse Inn
25 The Square, SO23 9EX
☼ 11-11 (midnight Thu-Sat) ☎ (01962) 865676
⊕ eclipseinnwinchester.co.uk
Sharp's Doom Bar; Timothy Taylor Landlord; 2 changing beers (sourced nationally) ⊞
A Strong's brewery lamp illuminates the entrance to this small Tudor pub close to Winchester's city museum and cathedral. Inside are a beamed bar with perimeter benches and a wood-burning stove,

a small back room, and a perilously small Gents' toilet; outside there are tables on the pavement. The reasonably priced food is recommended. Lady Alice Lisle, victim of the Bloody Assizes, spent her last night here before being beheaded for giving succour to the wrong people – she reputedly still visits. Q⏰🕮🍴🚆🐾🛜

Hyde Tavern 🅛
57 Hyde Street, SO23 7DY
☼ 12.30-2 (not Mon-Wed), 5-11; 5-midnight Fri; 12-midnight Sat; 12-11 Sun ☎ (01962) 862592
Flowerpots Bitter; Harvey's Sussex Best Bitter 🅗; 4 changing beers (sourced locally; often Flowerpots, Red Cat, West Berkshire) 🅗/🅖
This is an ancient twin-gabled building, below street level – beware low ceilings and uneven floors. The main bar leads through to another, smaller, cosy back room plus a cellar room that hosts regular events such as storytelling, a writers' circle, traditional folk music and a singaround. Up to six beers, mostly local, always include a dark brew. Several real ciders are also on offer. There is no food, but takeaways may be delivered – plates and cutlery provided for a small fee. Outside is an attractive garden. Q🏡🍴🌳🍂🐾🛜

Old Vine 🅛 ✅
8 Great Minster Street, SO23 9HA (facing cathedral)
☼ 11-11 (10.30 Sun) ☎ (01962) 854616
⊕ oldvinewinchester.com
Alfred's Saxon Bronze; Timothy Taylor Landlord; 2 changing beers (sourced locally; often Bowman, Flowerpots, Longdog) 🅗
Attractive, vine-clad 18th-century inn, with stunning views across to the cathedral. Its medieval cellars are said to have two ghosts who haunt the premises. The single, cosy, oak-beamed bar has an adjoining restaurant serving home-cooked food using much local produce. There are two guest beers, with a strong LocAle emphasis. The rear courtyard has a terrace, which is smoke-free, and an inviting courtyard garden room. Superior accommodation is available in six stylish en-suite rooms. Q🏡🍴🛏🌳🚆(1,69)🐾🛜

Queen Inn ✅
28 Kingsgate Road, SO23 9PG (S Winchester, opp college sports ground)
☼ 11-midnight ☎ (01962) 853898
⊕ thequeeninnwinchester.co.uk
Greene King IPA; Morland Old Speckled Hen; 8 changing beers (sourced nationally; often Alfred's, Flowerpots, Red Cat) 🅗/🅖
Back in the Guide after many years, the Queen Inn is cosy and comfortable, appealing to a wide variety of people. Indeed, variety is the keyword for this pub: there are five Greene King and related beers plus another five, mainly local, focusing on Winchester, often with one brewed on the premises. Enthusiastic staff members organise a variety of events including a springtime beer festival. Between mealtimes, home-made snacks are available. The sheltered front patio catches the sun. 🕮🏡🍴P🚆(1,69)🐾🛜

Westgate 🅛 ✅
2 Romsey Road, SO23 8TP (opp Great Hall)
☼ 11-11.30 (midnight Fri & Sat); 11-10.30 Sun
☎ (01962) 820222 ⊕ westgatewinchester.com
Flowerpots Goodens Gold; Red Cat Prowler Pale; 2 changing beers (sourced locally; often Flack Manor, Flowerpots, Red Cat) 🅗

A prominent Grade II-listed pub in a commanding position atop the High Street, close to the city centre. Dating from circa 1877, it became the Westgate Hotel in 1894, operated by Dorset brewers Eldridge Pope. A 2016 renovation has retained the fine etched windows and provided a spacious, well-decorated bar area. A separate, raised dining area doubles as the breakfast room for hotel guests and morning visitors. Up to five beers are available, focusing on local breweries. 🕮🏡🍴🍴🌳🍂🚆🐾🛜

Wykeham Arms
75 Kingsgate Street, SO23 9PE
☼ 11-11 (10.30 Sun) ☎ (01962) 853834
Flowerpots Goodens Gold; Fuller's London Pride; Gale's Seafarers Ale, HSB; 1 changing beer 🅗
Historic Georgian inn, circa 1755, in the city's cathedral and college heritage area. Several interlinked rooms, crammed floor to ceiling with memorabilia, are served from the central bar. Nelsoniana abounds and furnishings include many old school desks. Although a Fuller's pub, a Flowerpots beer is almost always present. This civilised hostelry for conversationalists features in nearly every guide book. Accommodation comprises 14 highly-rated bedrooms. There is an extensive food service and over 20 wines are offered by the glass. Q🏡🍴🛏🚆(1,69)🐾🛜

Wonston

Wonston Arms 🏆 🅛
Stoke Charity Road, SO21 3LS
☼ closed Mon; 6-10 (10.30 Fri); 12-10 Sat; 12-8 Sun ☎ 07909 993388
4 changing beers (sourced locally; often Bowman, Flowerpots, Red Cat) 🅗
Local CAMRA Pub of the Year 2016 and 2017, in the heart of the village around a 15-minute walk from Sutton Scotney and the nearest bus stop. Four changing beers are served, often from local breweries such as Bowmans, Flowerpots and Red Cat. Although the pub does not serve food, a fish and chip van visits on Tuesday evening, while Friday is curry night, with food delivered. A fishmonger visits on Thursday 4.30-6.30pm. There is folk music on the second and fourth Wednesdays, and a pop-up café usually on the third Monday of the month 9.30am-midday. Q🏡🍂P🐾🛜

Wootton

Rising Sun 🅛 ✅
Bashley Common Road, BH25 5SF (on B3058)
☼ 10-11 (10.30 Sun) ☎ (01425) 610360
⊕ therisingsunbashley.co.uk
Flack Manor Double Drop; Morland Old Speckled Hen; 3 changing beers (sourced nationally; often Greene King, Dancing Cows, Vibrant Forest) 🅗
An impressive Victorian building, decorated with finials, gables, pillars and eyebrow windows. It borders the southern edge of the New Forest, with the A35 a good mile away to the north-west. The large interior is divided into several areas, some retaining original Victorian stained-glass windows and features. The extensive menu and adventure playground make the pub popular with families. Crop Circle gluten-free real ale is available in a bottle. 🕮🏡🍴🛏P🚆(C32,C33)🐾🛜

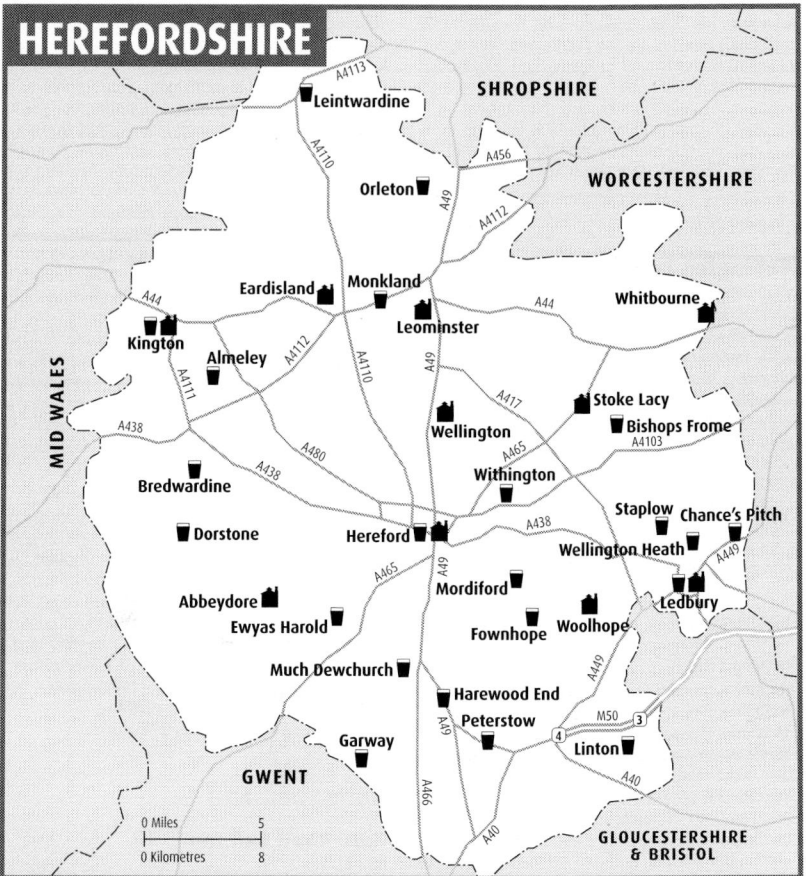

Almeley

Bells Inn ℒ

HR3 6LF (in village)
☼ 9am-midnight ☎ (01544) 327216 ⊕ almeley.net
2 changing beers (sourced locally; often Cottage, Goff's, Swan) Ⓗ
This unpretentious stone-built village pub is entered through the erstwhile jug and bottle. To the right is a large low-ceilinged bar and to the left a farm shop and delicatessen. Horses may be seen at the hitching rail in the car park. Traditional, home-prepared lunches are served, with a pensioners' special on the first Tuesday, plus a monthly steak night. The beers are mainly from local brewers. Live music plays on some Saturday evenings. ⌂❀❀⏚♣⬤P🖵🐾🐾 🛜

Bishops Frome

Green Dragon ℒ

WR6 5BP (in village, just off B4214)
☼ 5 (4.30 winter)-11; 4-11.30 Fri; 12-11.30 Sat; 12-6 Sun
☎ (01885) 490607 ⊕ thegreendragoninn.com
Otter Bright; Purple Moose Cwrw Eryri/Snowdonia Ale; Timothy Taylor Golden Best; Wye Valley Bitter; 2 changing beers (sourced locally) Ⓗ
A warren of flagstone-floored rooms, low beams and a fabulous inglenook fireplace are a treat for visitors to this 17th-century village inn, set at the heart of its community. With six handpumps offering a range of local and regional beers, plus five local ciders and perries, it is no surprise the pub is a regular award winner. Bar meals are served Tuesday to Saturday evenings and lunchtimes Saturday and Sunday.
Q⌂❀⏚⬤♣⬤P🐾 🛜

Bredwardine

Red Lion Hotel

HR3 6BU (in village on B4352)
☼ 12-2.30 (3 Sat), 6-11; 7-11 Sun; winter hours vary Sun
☎ (01981) 500303 ⊕ redlion-hotel.com
Wye Valley Butty Bach; 1 changing beer (often Hobsons, Swan, Three Tuns) Ⓗ

A large red-brick hotel overlooking the River Wye, with eight miles of fishing rights, and the Wye Valley Walk. Traditional home-cooked pub food is served March-November – snacks at lunchtime and meals in the evening. Fish and chip night is Tuesday (5-7pm) and curry night is the first Thursday of each month. Hours vary in winter 1 December-30 April. Q☺🛏️⚙️❄️◑⅋♿Å♣P🅿️🚲

Chance's Pitch

Wellington Inn ⓛ
WR13 6HW (on A449, near B4218 jct)
☼ 12-3, 6.30-11; 12-3.30 Sun ☎ (01684) 540269
⊕ thewellingtoninnmalvern.co.uk
Goff's Tournament; 2 changing beers (often Butcombe, Gloucester) Ⓗ
A landmark venue standing alone on the main Ledbury-Malvern road, this is a much-extended, multi-level pub. While majoring on food, it also caters for the drinking trade. A comfortable and plainly decorated drinkers-only bar area presents a traditional feel, with a lounge on the lower level offering views across open country. Two restaurant areas to the rear offer a wide range of often locally sourced meals. Q☺🛏️⚙️◑◑P🐾🚲

Dorstone

Pandy Inn ⓛ
HR3 6AN (signed off B4348)
☼ 12 (5 Mon)-11; 12-9 Sun; winter 5 (12 Fri & Sat)-11; 12-9 Sun ☎ (01981) 550273 ⊕ thepandyinn.co.uk
Sharp's Doom Bar; Three Tuns XXX; Wye Valley Butty Bach; 1 changing beer Ⓗ
Opposite the village green, the Pandy has a history dating back to the 12th century. Although opened out, discrete areas give a welcoming feel, with both timber-framing and exposed stone walls plus a huge fireplace. Ciders from Gwatkins and nearby Pips are available in bottles. Themed evenings are held regularly and a monthly quiz and curry night (booking advisable). Winter hours apply from the first Monday in October to the last Sunday in April. Q☺⚙️◑♣♦P🅿️🐾🚲

Ewyas Harold

Temple Bar ⓛ
HR2 0EU (in village, just off B4347)
☼ 11-3, 5-11.30; 11-1am Sat; 11-midnight Sun
☎ (01981) 240423 ⊕ thetemplebarinn.co.uk
Wye Valley Butty Bach; 2 changing beers (sourced locally) Ⓗ
Licensed in the 1850s, the Temple Bar was purchased from Enterprise Inns in 2011. It was extensively refurbished with bar, games room, restaurant, outside seating area, function room and three en-suite B&B rooms. Meals are served in the bar lunchtimes and early evenings and in the restaurant from 7pm and on Sunday lunchtimes. The restaurant menu changes weekly to include locally sourced seasonal ingredients. Q☺🛏️⚙️◑♿♣P🅿️(440)🐾🚲

Fownhope

New Inn ⓛ
HR1 4PE (in village, on B4224)
☼ 12-3, 6-midnight; 12-midnight Sat & Sun
☎ (01432) 860350 ⊕ thenewinnfownhope.co.uk

Hobsons Best; house beer (by Wye Valley); 1 changing beer (often Swan) Ⓗ
A true locals' pub at the heart of a thriving village community. A single room with exposed beams and light decor is divided into more discrete spaces by a central, bare-brick fireplace. Typical pub food is served Monday to Saturday lunchtimes, with occasional evening specials featuring fish and chips, pies, steaks and curry. A Sunday roast is served monthly. Jam sessions and quiz evenings are hosted regularly. Fownhope football team use the pub as a base. ☺⚙️◑♿Å♣P🅿️(454)🐾🚲

Garway

Garway Moon ⓛ ✅
Garway Common, HR2 8RQ SO465227
☼ 6-11 Mon & Tue; 11-2.30, 5-11 Wed-Fri; 11-11 Sat & Sun
☎ (01600) 750270 ⊕ garwaymooninn.co.uk
2 changing beers (sourced locally) Ⓗ
A remote but popular and welcoming pub overlooking the village green and cricket pitch, with a lounge and public bar plus a separate snug/family room, garden and play area. A British pub food and grill menu features specials inspired by local growers and farmers, sourced locally where possible and freshly prepared, including vegetarian options. Food evenings include Italian on Tuesday, curry on Wednesday and steak on Thursday, and roasts feature on Sundays. The last Friday of the month is open mic night and the last Sunday is quiz night. Four local ciders are available. ☺🛏️◑♿Å♣♦P🅿️(412)🐾🚲

Harewood End

Harewood End Inn ⓛ ✅
HR2 8JT (on A49)
☼ closed Mon; 12-3, 6-11; 12-3, 7-10.30 Sun
☎ (01989) 730637 ⊕ theharewoodend.com
St Austell Tribute; 2 changing beers (sourced locally; often Kelpaul, Purity, Wobbly) Ⓗ
An old roadside pub where the compact and cosy bar with pool table leads out to a beer garden and to two separate dining areas, featuring rustic-style panelling and a wealth of old enamel signs. An interesting menu of freshly prepared food is offered (booking advised at weekends). Families are welcome. The accommodation comprises five en-suite rooms. Q☺🛏️⚙️◑♣P🅿️🚲(33)🐾🚲

Hereford

Barrels ⓛ ✅
69 St Owen Street, HR1 2JQ
☼ 11-11.30 (midnight Fri & Sat); 12-11.30 Sun
☎ (01432) 274968
Wye Valley Bitter, The Hopfather, HPA, Golden Ale, Butty Bach, Wholesome Stout; 1 changing beer (often Wye Valley) Ⓗ
The Barrels enjoys a cult following. Winner of CAMRA Herefordshire Pub of the Year six times, it is first and foremost a community pub. No food, no gimmicks, but tons of character across five different bars, plus a cobbled courtyard to the rear that hosts a charity beer and music festival each August bank holiday weekend. With the TV only on for major sports events, this is a pub where lively conversation and good times always hold sway. ☺⚙️≈♣♦🅿️🐾🚲

Beer in Hand ⓛ

136 Eign Street, HR4 0AP
✆ 5-11 (10.30 Mon); 12-11 Fri & Sat; 12-10.30
Sun ☎ 07443 487124 ⊕ beerinhand.co.uk
5 changing beers (often Odyssey, Purity) Ⓖ
Herefordshire's first micropub, the Beer in Hand
was converted from a launderette in 2013. In 2015
it was named CAMRA Herefordshire Cider Pub of
the Year. With an impressive chilled racking
system, it sells up to five ales on cask (normally
including one from Odyssey Brewing Co) and 10
mainly local ciders and perries. Meals are served
Thursday to Saturday evenings. Quiz night is the
first Wednesday and jam session the last Tuesday
of each month. Q✿❄️⏺️♿️♣️🐕🚌❀

Firefly

16 King Street, HR4 9BX
✆ 3-11.30; 12-1am Fri (1.30am Sat); 12-11 Sun
☎ (01432) 358252
4 changing beers Ⓗ
Probably dating from the 17th century, it offers a
large range of widely sourced draught real ale and
local cider from Westons and Snails Bank. Modern-
style world food is available. Events include open
mic nights on alternate Thursdays and a DJ on
alternate Saturdays. ❄️⏺️🐕🚌❀🛜

Kington

Olde Tavern ★ ⓛ

22 Victoria Road, HR5 3BX
✆ 6.30-11.30; 5-midnight Fri; 12-midnight Sat; 12-11 Sun
☎ (01544) 231945
**4 changing beers (often Hobsons, Ludlow, Three
Tuns)** Ⓗ
One for the pub connoisseur, this is a real time-
warp. Once called the Railway Tavern, unlike the
long-closed railway, this is a survivor. Behind an
understated Victorian façade is a two-bar gem,
with its original entrance lobby, serving hatches,
flagstone floor and bench seating. Pub teams root
it firmly in the local community. A changing menu
of freshly prepared food is served in the Out the
Back restaurant Thursday to Saturday evenings and
Sunday lunchtime. Q✿❄️⏺️🅰️♣️🐕🚌❀

Ledbury

Lion ⓛ

38 Bye Street, HR8 2AA
✆ closed Mon; 4-9.30 (10.30 Fri); 4-10 Sat; 1-5 Sun
2 changing beers (sourced locally) Ⓖ
Opened in July 2016, this two-room micropub has a
bar at the front and a room with tables and chairs
to the rear. The two beers, served direct from the
cask, are expected to be sourced mainly from the
three counties of Gloucestershire, Worcestershire
and Herefordshire. Q🚌❀

Prince of Wales ⓛ ✔

Church Lane, HR8 1DL
✆ 11-11 (10.30 Sun) ☎ (01531) 632250 ⊕ powledbury.com
**Hobsons Best; Ledbury Dark; Wells Eagle IPA; Wye
Valley HPA, Butty Bach; 2 changing beers** Ⓗ
Hidden away in a cobbled alley leading up to the
church, this 16th-century timber-framed pub
boasts two bars, plus a discrete alcove where a folk
jam session is held each Wednesday evening.
Herefordshire CAMRA Town Pub of the Year in
2015, it is a genuine community pub – always
bustling with locals and visitors. Orchard Pig

draught cider is stocked, together with an
extensive range of foreign beers. The bar meals are
excellent value (booking advisable for the Sunday
roasts). ✿❄️⏺️♣️🐕🚌❀🛜

Talbot Hotel ⓛ ✔

14 New Street, HR8 2DX
✆ 11-11 (midnight Fri & Sat) ☎ (01531) 632963
⊕ talbotledbury.co.uk
**Wadworth IPA, 6X; Wye Valley Butty Bach; 1 changing
beer (often Wadworth)** Ⓗ
An outstanding black and white half-timbered
hotel and bar dating back to the 1590s. Various
comfortably furnished seating areas surround an
island servery facing a splendid fireplace. The
restaurant, with its superb wood panelling, offers
affordable fine cuisine featuring locally sourced
ingredients, while conventional bar snacks are also
available in the bar. The guest beer is from
Wadworth's seasonal range or Red Shoot
subsidiary. ❄️🛏️⏺️♣️🚌🛜

Leintwardine

Sun Inn ★ ⓛ

Rosemary Lane, SY7 0LP (in village, off A4113)
✆ 11-11 ☎ (01547) 540705 ⊕ suninn-leintwardine.co.uk
**Hobsons Best; 2 changing beers (sourced locally;
often Ludlow, Three Tuns)** Ⓗ
A national treasure and one of the last parlour
pubs, the building was saved in 2009 following a
CAMRA-led campaign. A red brick-tiled public bar
features bench furniture and a fireplace. The
untouched parlour is where Flossie, the landlady of
74 years, once held court. To the rear is a stylish
pavilion-style extension overlooking the garden –
the venue for the August bank holiday Sunday beer
festival. Light lunches are served or you can order
fish and chips from next door.
Q✿❄️⏺️♿️🅰️♣️🐕❀🛜

Linton

Alma Inn ⓨ ⓛ

HR9 7RY (off B4221, W of M50 jct 3) SO659255
✆ 12-3 (not Mon), 6-11; 12-3, 7-10.30 Sun
☎ (01989) 720355 ⊕ almainnlinton.co.uk
**Butcombe Adam Henson's Rare Breed; Ludlow Gold;
Malvern Hills Black Pear; Oakham JHB; 1 changing
beer (often Bespoke, Untapped)** Ⓗ
A long-standing drinkers' pub, the Alma has lost
none of its charm and atmosphere with the
introduction of meals. A convivial front bar,
complete with real fire, contrasts with a rear pool
room and a separate wood-panelled restaurant.
Hearty freshly prepared pub classics are offered,
with seasonal specials, light bites and bar snacks.
Events include the major Linton Music Festival in
June and Summer Acoustic Sessions in August –
both held in the extensive grounds, with
accompanying beer festivals. Q✿❄️⏺️♣️🅿️❀

Monkland

Monk ⓛ

HR6 9DE (W end of village, on A44)
✆ closed Mon; 11-11; 12-10.30 Sun ☎ (01568) 720464
Hobsons Best; 2 changing beers Ⓗ
After several years of closure, the Monkland Arms
was bought out of pubco ownership in 2015. A
single bar serves a drinking area and dining areas
to the side and rear. Good-quality, classic British

food is available, from local suppliers where possible. The beer garden to the rear has views across open country. The six real ciders are not on display – look for the cider menu on the bar.
🛇⊛🕽🌢♣👄P🖵(502)🐾🛜

Mordiford

Moon Inn
HR1 4LW (in village, on B4224)
🟢 12-3 (not Mon), 6-midnight; 12-midnight Sat & Sun
☎ (01432) 873067 🌐 mooninnmordiford.co.uk
Otter Amber; St Austell Proper Job; Timothy Taylor Landlord; Wells Bombardier; 1 changing beer ⊞
A half-timbered and much-altered two-bar roadside inn, the Moon started life as a farmhouse over 400 years ago. Popular among locals and with families tripping out from Hereford, it benefits from its proximity to the Mordiford Loop – a well-known local walk – as well as the Rivers Lugg and Wye. Traditional, locally sourced pub food is served. Quiz night is alternate Tuesdays. There is a children's play area in the garden, plus a camping and caravan site to the rear.
🛇⊛🕽🌢👌🌢♣👄P🖵(453)🐾🛜

Much Dewchurch

Black Swan
HR2 8DJ (in village, on B4348)
🟢 12 (11.30 Sat)-3, 5.30-11; 12-4, 6-11 Sun
☎ (01981) 540295
Timothy Taylor Landlord; 2 changing beers (often Butcombe, Slater's, Three Tuns) ⊞
Possibly the oldest pub in Herefordshire, this delightful 15th-century heavily beamed village inn comes complete with its own priest hole. A small lounge leads to a dining room with open fire, and a separate public bar with flagstone floors leads to a pool and darts room. Home-prepared, mainly locally sourced food is available every session. The guest beers are typically from regional breweries. Draught Westons cider and perry are stocked, plus Gwatkin cider. Thursday is folk night.
🛇⊛🕽🌢♣👄P🖵🐾🛜

Orleton

Baker's Arms 🅛
SY8 4JB (on B4361)
🟢 12-11 (midnight Fri & Sat) summer; 12-3.30 (not Mon), 6-11; 12-3.30, 5-11 Fri; 12-11 Sat & Sun winter
☎ (01584) 831686
Hobsons Twisted Spire, Best; Ludlow Boiling Well; Wood Shropshire Lass, Beauty; 1 changing beer (sourced locally) ⊞
A 17th-century roadside pub reopened after comprehensive refurbishment. To the left is a lounge with restaurant to the rear, while to the right is a public bar – the snug – and behind that a games room with pool and darts. Two woodburners supplement the ground-source central heating. Food includes home-baked bread from the on-site bakery. Horses are welcome, with a hitching bar and trough in the car park. Happy hour is Tuesday to Friday 5-6pm.
🛇⊛🕽🌢♣👄P🖵(490)🐾

Peterstow

Yew Tree
HR9 6JZ (in village, on A49)

🟢 12-11 ☎ (01989) 562815 🌐 rosscider.com
Hobsons Best; 2 changing beers (often Lancaster, Townhouse) ⊞
The lease of the Yew Tree was taken over in 2014 by Ross-on-Wye Cider & Perry Company. Three ales, often from distant microbreweries, and two draught ciders, are complemented by a large range of bottled ciders and perries. A quiz is held on Tuesday evening and live music on Friday. Wednesday is pie and pint night. Thursday is cider night, accompanied by local sausages and mash. A camping/caravan site adjoins the pub. Hereford-Ross bus service 32 stops nearby.
Q🛇⊛🕽🌢👌🌢👄P🖵(32)🐾🛜

Staplow

Oak Inn 🅛
HR8 1NP (on B4214)
🟢 12-11 (10.30 Sun) ☎ (01531) 640954
🌐 oakinnstaplow.co.uk
Bathams Best Bitter; Ledbury Gold; Wye Valley Bitter; 1 changing beer ⊞
A stylishly renovated roadside country inn, offering exceptional food, good beer, and quality accommodation. A contemporary public area neatly divides into three – a reception bar area with modern sofas and low tables, a snug, and a main dining area featuring an open kitchen. At the rear is a further room with scrubbed tables. Such is the reputation of the Oak that booking is essential for both food and accommodation.
Q🛇⊛🛏🕽🌢👌P🖵(417)🐾🛜

Wellington Heath

Farmers Arms 🅛
Horse Road, HR8 1LS (in village, east of B4214)
🟢 closed Mon; 12-3 (not Tue), 5.30-11; 12-11 Sat; 12-10 Sun
☎ (01531) 634776 🌐 farmersarmswellingtonheath.co.uk
Hillside Legless Cow; Otter Bitter; Wye Valley HPA, Butty Bach; 2 changing beers ⊞
The bar and main dining area are in the original 18th-century building, and on either side are more modern extensions housing a games room and a restaurant. The food covers a wide range from burgers and pub classics to steaks and speciality dishes, locally sourced where possible. Guest beers usually include one from Hillside Brewery. Eight local draught ciders are available.
🛇⊛🕽🌢👌♣👄P🖵(675)🐾🛜

Withington

Cross Keys 🅛
HR1 3NN (on A465 in Withington Marsh)
🟢 5 (12 Sat)-11; 12-10.30 Sun ☎ (01432) 820616
Otter Ale; Wye Valley Butty Bach; house beer (by Wye Valley); 1 changing beer ⊞
Run by the same landlord for over 45 years, this is drinking in the slow lane, Herefordshire style. A long single bar divides either side of a central servery into two drinking areas, with original beams, exposed stonework and comfortable bench seating along each wall, both book-ended by two woodburners. A folk jam session is held on the last Thursday of each month. Filled rolls are available on Saturdays. Q🛇⊛🕽🌢♣👄P🖵(420)🐾

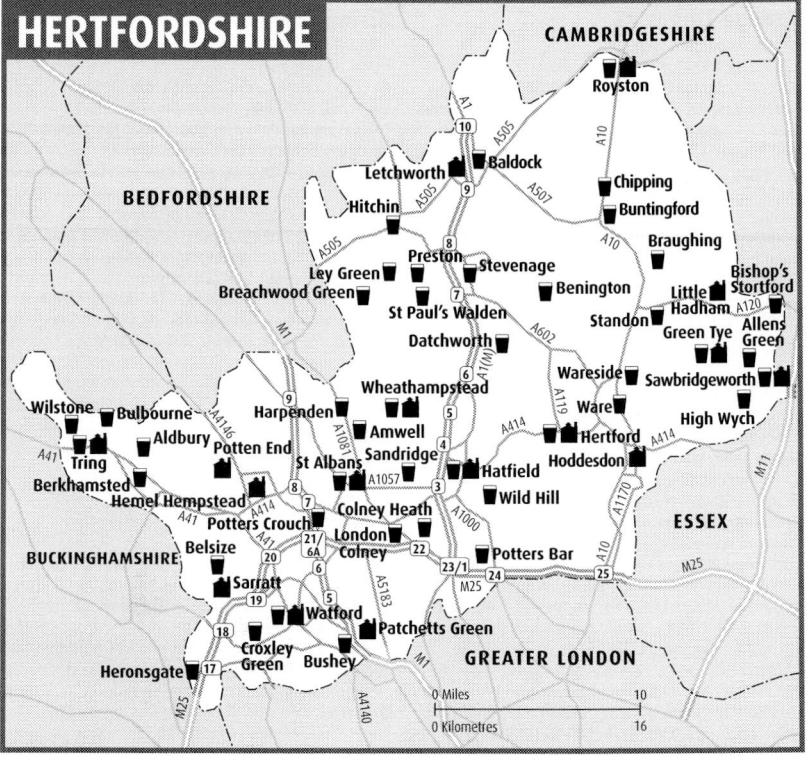

Aldbury

Valiant Trooper ▼ ⬡

Trooper Road, HP23 5RW
🕙 11 (10 Sat)-11; 10-10.30 Sun ☎ (01442) 851203
🌐 valianttrooper.co.uk
Chiltern Beechwood Bitter; Tring Side Pocket for a Toad; 3 changing beers (sourced locally) Ⓗ
Situated in the heart of the Chiltern Hills, the Trooper is a stunning 17th-century pub that retains the classic style and charm from that era. There is a lovely beer garden for the summer and a log fire for winter. It offers an outstanding selection of beers in excellent condition, from local breweries and further afield, and has a separate restaurant serving an array of classic British pub fare. Local CAMRA Pub of the Year.
Q❄🛏🏠⬤♿➡♣P🚃(30,31)🐾🛜

Allens Green

Queen's Head ⬡

CM21 0LS TL455170
🕙 12-2.30 (not Mon & Tue), 5-11; 12-11 Sat; 12-10.30 Sun
☎ (01279) 723393 🌐 qhpub.co.uk
Fuller's London Pride; Mighty Oak Maldon Gold Ⓗ; **2 changing beers (sourced locally)** Ⓗ/Ⓖ
This popular village inn is well worth seeking out for the constantly changing range of up to four beers. On the third weekend of every month and over bank holiday weekends mini beer festivals are held that use gravity stillage to bring up the number of beers to 10 or 12. Hot snacks are available unless the pub is busy. A frequent local CAMRA branch Pub of the Year. Q❄♿➡P🐾🛜

Amwell

Elephant & Castle ⬡ ✅

Amwell Lane, AL4 8EA (from Wheathampstead take left fork at top of Brewhouse Hill) TL167131
🕙 12-11 ☎ (01582) 832175 🌐 elephantcastle.co.uk
Greene King Abbot, IPA; 3 changing beers (sourced nationally) Ⓗ
Hidden away in an attractive, peaceful setting, this popular and successful rural community pub dates from 1714 and has never forsaken real ale. The terracotta-tiled front and back bar with a 200-foot well are warmed by real fires. Outside are two large gardens (one for adults only). Lunches are served daily and evening meals Tuesday to Saturday. The pub hosts Amwell Day, a charity event in June each year. Q❄🛏🏠⬤♣P🚃🐾

Baldock

Cock ✅

43 High Street, SG7 6BG
🕙 5-11.30 (midnight Thu); 4-midnight Fri; 12-3, 5-1am Sat; 12-11.30 Sun ☎ (01462) 892366
Brewsters Hophead; Greene King IPA, Abbot; Titanic Plum Porter; 2 changing beers (sourced nationally) Ⓗ
Set in an historic Roman market town, the Cock is an appealing inn dating from the 17th century with a beamed interior including a split-level drinking area and an open log fire. The popular, friendly local is full of character. An enclosed outside drinking area is pleasant in good weather. Up to five changing guest beers are served from the Greene King portfolio alongside two regular Greene King ales. Private functions can be catered for. 🏠♿➡🚃(98,635)🐾🛜

Orange Tree L ✓
Norton Road, SG7 5AW
☼ 12-2.30, 4.30-11; 12-midnight Thu-Sat; 12-10.30 Sun
☎ (01462) 892341 ⊕ theorangetreebaldock.com
Greene King XX Mild, IPA, Abbot; 10 changing beers (sourced nationally) ⓗ
The 10 guest beers are from small brewers including one from nearby Buntingford Brewery and there are five local real ciders. Entertainment includes a quiz night on Tuesday, folk music on Wednesday, and a comedy club. Good home-made locally sourced food is served. Six Nations Rugby is shown. The pub also takes part in the annual Balstock Music Festival in September as well as many other local events. Local CAMRA Cider Pub of the Year 2017. ☎🏠🛏🕪&≈♣🍴P🚌(91,98)🐾🐾📶

Belsize

Plough
Dunny Lane, WD3 4NP
☼ 12-11; 12-10.30 Sun ☎ (01923) 262261
⊕ theploughatbelsize.co.uk
Greene King IPA; St Austell Tribute; 1 changing beer (sourced nationally) ⓗ
This free house was purpose built for the Kings Langley Brewery in the 1840s. Located in the hamlet of Belsize between Chipperfield and Sarratt, it is in the style of a traditional English country pub, with open log fires, comfy settees, a pleasant garden and a large rear car park. Food is served Wednesday to Sunday lunchtimes and Wednesday to Saturday evenings. Dogs are not allowed in the restaurant area. Q☎🏠🛏🕪&♣P🚌(352)🐾📶

Benington

Lordship Arms
42 Whempstead Road, SG2 7BX
☼ closed Mon; 12-3, 6 (7 Sun)-11 ☎ (01438) 869665
⊕ lordshiparms.com
Black Sheep Best Bitter; Crouch Vale Brewers Gold; Timothy Taylor Landlord; 6 changing beers (sourced nationally) ⓗ
A regular winner of local and county CAMRA Pub of the Year competitions. The single bar is decorated with telephone memorabilia – some of the handpumps are even modelled on telephones. The superb garden features floral displays to be enjoyed in the summer. Wednesday evening curry night is popular. Lunchtime snacks are served until 2pm Monday to Saturday. There is a classic car gathering on the third Tuesday of each month April to September. Q🏠🕪🍴P🚌📶

Berkhamsted

Lamb L ✓
277 High Street, HP4 1AJ
☼ 12-11.30; 11-12.30am Fri; 11-11.30 Sat; 12-10.30 Sun
☎ (01442) 862615
Adnams Ghost Ship; Fuller's London Pride; Tring Ridgeway, Side Pocket for a Toad ⓗ
The Lamb is a friendly local pub on the edge of Berkhamsted. Over 300 years old, it retains a classic feel with some recent contemporary renovations. There is a small beer garden outside and a log fire and old town photos within. Food is available some weekday lunchtimes and evenings. Regular charity raffles and games feature. The ales are kept particularly well and the atmosphere is welcoming. 🏠🕪≈♣🍴🚌(500,501)🐾

Rising Sun L
1 Canal Side, George Street, HP4 2EG (at lock 55 on Grand Union Canal)
☼ 12-11 (midnight Thu-Sat); 12-10.30 Sun
☎ (01442) 864913 ⊕ theriserberko.net
Tring Drop Bar Pale Ale; house beer (by Tring); 3 changing beers (sourced nationally) ⓗ
The Riser is a thriving canalside pub and the recipient of many well-deserved CAMRA awards. It serves five ales and 10-20 real ciders, and boasts an excellent ploughman's. A number of popular events are hosted including a cheese club, folk music, quiz night and gastro night, with frequent ale festivals and a generous CAMRA discount. A firm favourite of local hikers, cyclists and dog walkers. ☎🏠🕪≈♣🚌(500,501)🐾📶

Bishop's Stortford

Star L ✓
7 Bridge Street, CM23 2JU
☼ 11-midnight (2am Fri); 12-2am Sat; 12-6 Sun
☎ (01279) 654211 ⊕ thestar-bishopsstortford.co.uk
3 changing beers (sourced regionally; often Adnams) ⓗ
A 17th-century town-centre pub catering for all ages. It is busy on Friday and Saturday evenings with a young crowd, and on Tuesday quiz night. A quiet pint can be enjoyed on other evenings and at lunchtimes. Very reasonably priced traditional pub food is freshly prepared throughout the day. Additionally, pizzas are made to order at any time. 🏠🕪≈🚌📶

Braughing

Brown Bear
14 The Street, SG11 2QF
☼ 3-6 Mon; 3-11 Tue; 12-11.30; 12-6 Sun ☎ (01920) 82215
⊕ brownbearbraughing.co.uk
Buntingford Twitchell; 3 changing beers (sourced nationally) ⓗ
A pub since at least 1740, the Brown Bear has a public bar and restaurant, both with impressive fireplaces. Real ale comes from local breweries including Three Brewers and Hadham, and guests from all over. The Thursday pub quiz, darts and pétanque, a large garden with pizza oven, occasional outside bar and monthly live music mean there is something for everyone here. 🏠🕪♣P🚌(331)🐾📶

REAL ALE BREWERIES
3 Brewers of St Albans Hatfield
Ash Valley 🍺 Green Tye
Buntingford Royston
Farr Brew Wheathampstead
Foragers 🍺 St Albans (NEW)
Garden City 🍺 Letchworth
Hadham Little Hadham
Mad Squirrel Potten End
McMullen Hertford
Mix Hemel Hempstead
New River Hoddesdon
Old Cross 🍺 Hertford
Paradigm Sarratt
Pope's Yard Watford
Sawbridgeworth 🍺 Sawbridgeworth
Tring Tring
Watling Street Patchetts Green
White Hart Tap 🍺 St Albans (NEW)

Breachwood Green

Red Lion ✔

16 Chapel Road, SG4 8NU

✪ 12-11; 12-midnight Sat ☎ (01438) 833123

⊕ redlionbreachwoodgreen.co.uk

Adnams Broadside; Greene King IPA; St Austell Tribute; 1 changing beer (sourced nationally) Ⓗ

The only pub in the village, the Brown Bear attracts many locals and some visitors from further afield. It serves good home-made food and guest beers often unusual for this area. There is a TV showing major sporting events and also a quiet dining area. The pub is home to darts and dominoes teams and football and cricket sides. The garden provides fine views of the countryside and is a good vantage point to view aircraft approaching Luton Airport. ኈ❀◑♣P🖫❀❖

Bulbourne

Grand Junction Arms

Bulbourne Road, HP23 5QE (adjacent to bridge 138 on Grand Union Canal)

✪ 12-11; 12-10.30 Sun ☎ (01442) 891400

⊕ grandjunctionarms.co.uk

Sharp's Doom Bar; Tring Side Pocket for a Toad; 2 changing beers (sourced locally; often Chiltern, Loose Cannon) Ⓗ

A popular canalside pub on the outskirts of Tring with displays of work by local artists for sale. The restaurant is on a raised area separate from the bar, serving traditional and interesting food lunchtimes and evenings. There is a lovely large beer garden by the canal with a children's play area. A good stopping-off point for walkers and cyclists, dogs and horses are welcome in the garden. ኈ❀◑&♣P🖫(61)❖

Buntingford

Crown

17 High Street, SG9 9AB

✪ 12 (6 Tue)-11; 12-6 Sun ☎ (01763) 271422

St Austell Trelawny; Shepherd Neame Spitfire; 1 changing beer (sourced nationally) Ⓗ

This town-centre pub on CAMRA's Regional Inventory of Historic Pub Interiors has a large front bar, cosy back bar and a function room. Outside are a covered patio and a secluded garden. Although the emphasis is on drinking, there are regular themed speciality food nights as well as traditional fish and chips on Thursday and Friday (booking required for food). Crossword fans find the large collection of dictionaries and reference books useful. An acoustic music night features on the third Monday of each month. Q❀ኈ❀◑♣🖫(331,386)❖

Bushey

Swan

25 Park Road, WD23 3EE

✪ 11-11; 12-10.30 Sun ☎ (020) 8950 2256

⊕ swanpubbushey.co.uk

Greene King Abbot; Sharp's Doom Bar; Timothy Taylor Landlord; Young's Bitter Ⓗ

Timeless, friendly local with four regular beers. A real gem, it has a long but cosy narrow bar room boasting two coal fires. Historic photos and sporting mementos adorn the walls, and the original jug and bottle window has been retained. Hot snacks,

including good-value toasties and pies, are available at all times. Pub games include darts, shut the box and board games. The ladies' loo is accessed from the garden via a side alley. ❀♣🖫(142,258)❖ 🞈

Chipping

Countryman

Ermine Street, SG9 0PG TL356319

✪ closed Mon-Thu; 12-11 Fri & Sat; 12-10.30 Sun

☎ (01763) 272721

3 changing beers (sourced nationally) Ⓗ

Built in 1663, and a pub since 1760, the Countryman has a single-room split-level interior with an impressive fireplace. The bar front boasts some well-executed carvings dating from the 1970s, and obscure agricultural implements decorate the walls. The beer range varies but three real ales (and a cider in summer) are usually available. This is a pub where social networking happens at the bar. There are chickens in the garden. Q❀ኈ❀◑♣P🖫(331)❖

Colney Heath

Crooked Billet Ⓛ

88 High Street, AL4 0NP

✪ 11-2.30, 4.30-11; 11-11 Fri; 12-11 Sat; 12-10.30 Sun

☎ (01727) 822128

Sharp's Doom Bar; Tring Side Pocket for a Toad; Young's Special Ⓗ

Popular and friendly cottage-style village pub dating back over 200 years. A genuine free house, it stocks three beers from national, regional and microbreweries. A wide selection of good-value home-made food is served lunchtimes and Friday and Saturday evenings. Saturday events and summer barbecues are held occasionally. This is a favourite stop-off for walkers on the many local footpaths. Families are welcome in the bar until 9pm and in the large garden, where there is play equipment. ኈ❀◑♣P🖫(304)❖

Croxley Green

Sportsman Ⓛ

2 Scots Hill, WD3 3AD (at A412 jct with the Green)

✪ 2 (12 Fri & Sat)-11; 12-10.30 Sun ☎ (01923) 443360

Fuller's ESB; Sharp's Doom Bar; 6 changing beers (sourced nationally) Ⓗ

Welcoming, family-run community pub with up to eight real ales. Beers are varied and usually include a dark brew, with an emphasis on microbreweries – tasting trays are available. Pub games include darts and pool. The pub hosts a popular weekly quiz and a monthly music jam on the last Sunday afternoon of the month. Community activities include a book group and a ladies' darts team. Croxley tube station is a 15-minute walk away. ❀♣P🖭🖫

Datchworth

Plough Ⓛ

5 Datchworth Green, SG3 6TL (on crossroads)

✪ 12-11; 12-10 Sun ☎ (01438) 813000

3 changing beers (sourced nationally) Ⓗ

Small single-bar free house on the edge of Datchworth Green sporting an ever-changing selection of real ales including LocAle. This is a genuine locals' pub at the hub of the village and all are made to feel welcome. The secret garden is a suntrap in the summer months and features a well-used pétanque piste. Darts and pétanque teams meet here regularly. CAMRA members receive a discount on ale. ⊛♣●P🖫(379)😼🤏

Green Tye

Prince of Wales 🗔
SG10 6JP TL444184
🕐 12-3, 5.30-11; 12-11 Sat; 12-9.30 Sun ☎ (01279) 842139
⊕ thepow.co.uk
Ash Valley Prince of Wales IPA; Wadworth 6X; 3 changing beers (sourced locally; often Ash Valley) 🖽
A traditional and welcoming village local, whether you are a walker, cyclist, dog owner or just plain thirsty. The landlord has recently established the Ash Valley Brewery at the back of the pub, making the Prince of Wales its brewery tap. Food includes sandwiches and great-value pub grub. There is a small garden for fine weather. Beer festivals with a barbecue and entertainment are held in May and September. Q🏮🕏🏵🕹🖑●P😼🤏

Harpenden

Cross Keys ✔
39 High Street, AL5 2SD (opp war memorial)
🕐 11.30-11; 12-10.30 Sun ☎ (01582) 763989
Farr Brew Our Greatest Golden; Rebellion IPA; Timothy Taylor Landlord 🖽
Tucked in among the shops in the town centre, this two-bar pub has retained its traditional charm, with a rare fine pewter bar top and flagstone floors. The original oak-beamed ceiling has tankards from past and present customers hanging from it. In spring and summer enjoy your pint in the secluded, attractive rear garden, and in autumn or winter relax in front of the saloon bar's fire. Traditional home-cooked lunches are served Monday to Saturday. Q🏮🕏🏵🕹≒♣🖫😼🤏

Hatfield

Horse & Groom
21 Park Street, AL9 5AT
🕐 11.30-11 (midnight Fri & Sat); 12-10.30 Sun
☎ (01707) 264765 ⊕ horseandgroom-oldhatfield.com
Black Sheep Best Bitter; Greene King Abbot; Oakham JHB; 3 changing beers (sourced nationally) 🖽
In the heart of Old Hatfield, this allegedly haunted, 16th-century, Grade II-listed building is thought to house a priest hole. The former timber-framed and later brick-clad pub serves up to six real ales and hosts three beer festivals every year. Tuesday is bangers and mash night and Saturday is chilli and rice night – purchase an ale for a free portion. Hatfield railway and bus stations are just a few minutes' walk away using 'Blood and Guts Alley'. Q🏮🕏🏵🕹≒♣●P🖫😼

Heronsgate

Land of Liberty, Peace & Plenty 🍸 🗔
Long Lane, WD3 5BS (off jct 17 M25) TQ023949
🕐 12-11 (midnight Fri & Sat); 12-10.30 Sun
☎ (01923) 282226 ⊕ landoflibertypub.com
8 changing beers (sourced nationally) 🖽
Welcoming, award-winning pub that is popular with walkers, cyclists, locals and real ale enthusiasts. Up to 10 microbrewery beers are offered in a range of styles and strengths. Real

ciders, a perry and a wide range of whiskies are also on offer, as are bottled beers to take away. Beer festivals, tastings and other regular events are held throughout the year. Bar snacks are available all day. There is a large outside pavilion for families. ⊛♣●P🖫🖫(R2)😼🤏

Hertford

Black Horse 🗔
29-31 West Street, SG13 8EZ
🕐 12-11.30 (1am Fri & Sat); 12-11 Sun ☎ (01992) 583630
⊕ theblackhorse.biz
6 changing beers (sourced nationally) 🖽
A community-focused, timbered free house, dating from 1642 and situated in one of Hertford's most attractive streets, near the start of the Cole Green Way. Six real ales from around Britain are on offer, including one from Hertfordshire. The well-kept garden includes a separate and safe children's area. The interesting food menu features game and the pub has its own bakery. Handy for Hertford Town FC supporters and the Black Horse has a rugby team affiliated to the RFU. 🏮🏵🕹≒♣●🖫😼🤏

Hertford Club
Lombard House, Bull Plain, SG14 1DT
🕐 12 (11 Sat)-11; 12-8 Sun ☎ (01992) 421422
⊕ thehertford.club
4 changing beers (sourced nationally) 🖽
Dating from the 15th century and with later additions, Lombard House, on the River Lea, was built as an English Hall House and is one of the oldest buildings in Hertford. It has been the home of this private members' club since 1897. CAMRA members are welcome and may be signed in on production of a membership card. You will find three or four ever-changing beers and real cider, which in summer can be enjoyed in the delightful walled garden. 🏮🏵🕹≒♣●🖫🤏

Old Barge ✔
2 The Folly, SG14 1QD (ask for Folly Island and you'll find the Old Barge)
🕐 11-11 (midnight Fri & Sat); 12-11 Sun ☎ (01992) 581871
⊕ theoldbarge.com
Woodforde's Wherry; 4 changing beers (sourced nationally) 🖽
A free house on Folly Island pleasantly situated canalside on the River Lea, offering not only a good selection of ales – often including a dark beer – but also a range of ciders and perries together with locally sourced home-cooked food served all day. There is a popular Sunday night quiz. The Spring Fling music festival takes place on the second May bank holiday Monday. Look out for the annual duck race and the children's crayfish festival held in August. 🏮🏵🕹≒♣●🖫😼🤏

Old Cross Tavern 🗔
8 St Andrew Street, SG14 1JA
🕐 4.30-11; 4-midnight Fri; 12-midnight Sat; 12-10.30 Sun
☎ (01992) 583133
Old Cross Gertcha!; Timothy Taylor Landlord; 5 changing beers (sourced nationally) 🖽
Superb town free house offering a friendly welcome. Up to six real ales, usually including a dark beer of some distinction, come from brewers large and small, including the pub's own microbrewery, and there is a fine choice of Belgian bottle-conditioned beers. Two beer festivals are held each year – one over the spring bank holiday,

the other in October. No TV or music here, just good old-fashioned conversation. Home-made pork pies are available. Runner-up local CAMRA Pub of the Year. Q❧♠🚲(395)🐾

White Horse
33 Castle Street, SG14 1HH
☼ 12-midnight ☎ 07539 373422
Castle Rock Harvest Pale; Fuller's ESB, London Pride; Gale's Seafarers Ale; 5 changing beers (sourced nationally) Ⓗ
Not to be missed if you are visiting Hertford. The charming old timber-framed building has two downstairs bars and additional rooms upstairs, one featuring bar billiards, others where children are welcome. Guest beers are from the Fuller's stable and from around Britain. There are no gaming machines to distract from the buzz of conversation. A folk music night is held every second and fourth Tuesday of the month. Listed as an asset of community value in 2015. Q❧🐶❧♠●🚲🐾🛜

High Wych

Rising Sun ♈
High Wych Road, CM21 0HZ
☼ 12-2.30 (not Tue & Thu), 5.30-11; 12-3, 6-11 Sat; 12-3, 7-10.30 Sun ☎ (01279) 724099
Courage Best Bitter; 4 changing beers (often Mighty Oak, Oakham) Ⓖ
This friendly village local has never used handpumps – a range of four or five beers is served on gravity, often from East Anglian breweries. Although refurbished, the original character has been preserved by means of a stone floor, attractive fireplace and wood panelling. Popular with locals and walkers, the pub holds a monthly quiz and an annual vegetable competition. Parking is in the village hall car park opposite. Local CAMRA Pub of the Year for the second year running. Q🏵♠P🚍(347)🐾

Hitchin

Half Moon ⓛ
57 Queen Street, SG4 9TZ
☼ 12-midnight (1am Fri & Sat); 12-11 Sun
☎ (01462) 452448 ● thehalfmoonhitchin.co.uk
Adnams Southwold Bitter; Young's Bitter; 6 changing beers (sourced nationally) Ⓗ
This split-level one-bar pub dates from 1748 and was once owned by Hitchin brewer W&S Lucas. It sells two regular and six guest beers, often from local breweries, plus two ciders, a perry and four guests. Home-prepared food including tapas is served daily. Monthly quiz and speciality food nights are popular in this friendly community pub, and cribbage is played in the summer. Local CAMRA Pub of the Year in 2016.
🐶🏵◑❧♠●P🐾🛜

Ley Green

Plough
Plough Lane, SG4 8LA (follow brown pub signs)
TL162243
☼ 4 (12 Wed)-11; 12-midnight Thu & Fri; 12-10.30 Sun
☎ (01438) 871194
Greene King IPA, Abbot; 1 changing beer (sourced nationally) Ⓗ
This has been an alehouse as far back as 1846 when it was called Godlets Hall. A warm and

friendly traditional pub hidden deep in the countryside, the garden has a large patio with gorgeous views. There is an open invite to join in the acoustic music session on a Tuesday evening. Hot and cold snacks are available throughout the week. On-site camping facilities are available for campervans and tents – please ring to confirm availability. 🐶🏵◑Å▲P🚍🐾🛜

London Colney

Bull ⓥ
Barnet Road, AL2 1QU
☼ 12-11 (midnight Thu-Sat) ☎ (01727) 823160
● thebullatlondoncolney.co.uk
Fuller's London Pride; Woodforde's Wherry; 2 changing beers (sourced nationally) Ⓗ
Lovely old 17th-century timbered building near the River Colne with a cosy lounge and original fireplace, offering a range of real ales. The large public bar features darts, pool and TV. Evening events include live music on Saturday and a quiz every second Sunday of the month. Good-value home-made meals are served Monday to Saturday lunchtimes and Tuesday to Friday nights – pizza night is Thursday, roast lunch on Sunday. There is a children's play area outside. 🏵◑♠●P🚍🐾🛜

Potters Bar

Admiral Byng ⓥ
186-192 Darkes Lane, EN6 1AF (on corner of Byng Drive)
☼ 8am-midnight (12.30am Thu-Sat) ☎ (01707) 645484
Adnams Broadside; Greene King Abbot; Ruddles Best Bitter; Sharp's Doom Bar; 5 changing beers (sourced nationally) Ⓗ
A friendly local community Wetherspoon pub with a display of two model sailing ships and other memorabilia celebrating the exploits and death of Admiral Byng, who was executed for 'failing to do his utmost' to save Minorca from falling to the French in 1756. (The family estate is located nearby between Potters Bar and Barnet.) In summer the frontage of the pub is opened onto the street with additional seating provided. There is a good choice of real cider. 🐶🏵◑👴❧♠●🚍🛜

Potters Crouch

Holly Bush ⓥ
Bedmond Lane, AL2 3NN (off B5183 at jct of Potters Crouch Lane and Ragged Hall Lane) TL116052
☼ 12-2.30, 6-11; 12-3, 7-10.30 Sun ☎ (01727) 851792
● thehollybushpub.co.uk
Fuller's ESB, London Pride; Gale's Seafarers Ale; 1 changing beer (sourced nationally) Ⓗ
Charming wisteria-covered early 17th-century pub in rural surroundings. Attractively furnished throughout, it boasts large oak tables and period chairs. Spotless, there is no jukebox, slot machine or TV to disturb the peace in any of the three drinking areas. The food menu is not extensive but is of high quality. The garden is ideal in summer and children are welcome.
Q🐶🏵◑👴P🚍(300,301)

Preston

Red Lion ♈ ⓛ
The Green, SG4 7UD

✪ 12-2.30 (3.30 Sat), 5.30-11; 12-3.30, 7-10.30 Sun
☎ (01462) 459585 ⏚ theredlionpreston.co.uk
Fuller's London Pride; Young's Bitter; 3 changing beers (sourced nationally) ⊞
The first community-owned pub in Great Britain, this attractive free house stands on the village green. It offers an ever-changing list of beers, many from small breweries. Fresh home-made food is served, with many of the ingredients sourced locally (no food Sun eve and Mon). The pub hosts village cricket teams and fundraises for charity. Local CAMRA Pub of the Year 2017.
Q🌑🏠🕽♣♠P🖵🐾🌱

Royston

Manor House ✪
14 Melbourn Street, SG8 7BZ
✪ 8am-midnight (1am Fri & Sat) ☎ (01763) 250160
Adnams Broadside; Fuller's London Pride; Sharp's Doom Bar; 6 changing beers (sourced nationally) ⊞
Thriving Wetherspoon pub, full of character and personality. The Grade II-listed former town house dates from the early 18th century, with the block on the left added late in the 19th century. Local artwork is on display. The decorative iron railings at the front were removed during World War II. Royston Manor House was the name adopted in October 1948 for what later became known as the Manor House Club. Food is served all day.
🌑🏠🕽⅙🖵(331)🌱

St Albans

Boot Inn 🅛 ✪
4 Market Place, AL3 5DG
✪ 12-midnight (12.30am Fri & Sat) ☎ (01727) 857533
⏚ thebootstalbans.com
8 changing beers (sourced nationally) ⊞
A regular in the Guide, this city-centre, Grade I-listed, one-bar pub dates back to 1422, featuring low ceilings, wood floors and a real fire. The Clock Tower is outside the front door and the Abbey and Verulamium Park are nearby. The quality of the ale is consistently high and there is a rapid turnover of beers. Food is all locally sourced and the kitchen staff are highly professional. Families are welcome until 6pm. 🌑🕽⅙⇆♠🖵🐾🌱

Garibaldi ✪
61 Albert Street, AL1 1RT
✪ 2.30-11 Mon; 12-11 Tue & Wed; 12-11.30 Thu; 12-midnight Fri & Sat; 12-10 Sun ☎ (01727) 894745
⏚ garibaldistalbans.co.uk
Fuller's ESB, London Pride; Gale's HSB, Seafarers Ale; 2 changing beers (sourced nationally) ⊞
Classic back-street Victorian local, a Tardis with ale, much bigger on the inside than it looks from the outside. Friendly management and staff provide excellent service. A superbly kept selection of beers from the Fuller's stable is available. Good home-cooked food is served – make sure you book for Sunday lunch. A genuine community pub, it supports good causes throughout the year and hosts regular quiz, music and darts nights. Winner of a Fuller's Master Cellarman award.
🌑🏠🕽⅙⇆♣🖵🐾🌱

Lower Red Lion 🅛
34-36 Fishpool Street, AL3 4RX
✪ 12-11; 12-10 Sun ☎ (01727) 855669
⏚ thelowerredlion.co.uk

5 changing beers (sourced nationally) ⊞
Both bars in this classic Grade II-listed pub have plenty of character and history. Located in a conservation area between the city centre and the site of Roman Verulamium, the pub stands in one of St Albans' most picturesque streets. The Lower Red was an early champion of CAMRA's values in the real ale revival movement, and continues to stock quality real ales. Home-made food is served lunchtimes and evenings throughout the week (no food Sun eve). Quiz night is Wednesday.
Q🌑🏠🕽♣♠P🖵🐾🌱

Mermaid 🍸
98 Hatfield Road, AL1 3RL
✪ 12-11 (11.30 Wed-Sat); 12-10.30 Sun ☎ (01727) 845700
Oakham Citra; 5 changing beers (sourced nationally) ⊞
This friendly free house is one of the few remaining bare-boards pubs in St Albans. Customers can choose from the award-winning Oakham Citra and five regularly changing ales, over a dozen ciders and perries, and a range of Belgian beers. Entertainment includes music nights on Wednesdays, regular quizzes and events held in the garden and covered areas during the spring and summer. Two beer festivals and a 50-plus cider and perry festival are held every year. Local CAMRA Pub and Cider Pub of the Year and Hertfordshire CAMRA Cider Pub of the Year 2017.
🌑🏠🕽⅙⇆♣♠P🖵🐾🌱

Olde Fighting Cocks 🅛 ✪
16 Abbey Mill Lane, AL3 4HE
✪ 12-10.30 (11.30 Fri & Sat) ☎ (01727) 869152
⏚ yeoldefightingcocks.co.uk
Farr Brew Black Listed IBA; Purity Pure UBU; 6 changing beers (sourced nationally) ⊞
The pub claims to be the oldest in England, dating from the late 8th century, though the current building was completed in 1485. Original features include low ceilings, interesting nooks and crannies, and a bread oven next to an open fireplace. The garden has a marquee and safe area for children. Popular with tourists visiting the Abbey and the nearby Roman remains in Verulamium Park, parking nearby is challenging – perhaps take a pleasant walk through the park. Runner-up local CAMRA Pub of the Year.
🌑🏠🕽⅙♣🗱🐾🌱

Robin Hood ✪
126 Victoria Street, AL1 3TG
✪ 12 (1 Sat)-11; 1-10.30 Sun ☎ (01727) 856459
⏚ robin-hood-st-albans.co.uk
Harvey's Sussex Best Bitter; 2 changing beers (sourced nationally) ⊞
A friendly community pub, handy for the City station. The large single bar has been significantly improved to provide a warm and comfortable environment. To the rear there is a large, pleasant beer garden. The recently refurbished cellar houses a constantly changing range of well-kept guest ales from around Britain. Three real ales and a real cider or perry are always available.
Q🌑🏠⅙⇆♣♠🖵🐾🌱

Six Bells 🅛 ✪
16-18 St Michael's Street, AL3 4SH
✪ 11.30-11; 11.30-midnight Fri-Sun ☎ (01727) 856945
⏚ the-six-bells.com
Oakham JHB; Timothy Taylor Landlord; Tring Ridgeway; 3 changing beers (sourced nationally) ⊞

A 16th-century timbered free house offering three regular beers and three changing guests, always including one from a Hertfordshire brewer. The pub is the only licensed premises within the walls of Roman Verulamium and is within walking distance of the city centre, Museum, Abbey and Verulamium Park. Quiz nights and live music sometimes feature. Good home-cooked food is served lunchtimes and evenings (not Sun eve). Outside is a pleasant patio area. Real cider is available during the summer. ⏰🐕🍴🅿🚭(300,301)🐾📶

White Hart Tap
4 Keyfield Terrace, AL1 1QJ
🕐 11-11; 12-11 Sun ☎ (01727) 860974
🌐 whitehearttap.co.uk
Castle Rock Harvest Pale; Oakham Citra; Sharp's Doom Bar; Timothy Taylor Landlord; 3 changing beers (sourced nationally) ⏣
Welcoming, one-bar, back-street local with four regular beers and three guests, now brewing beers on the premises with a weekly offering in a varying style. Beer festivals are held throughout the year. Good-value home-prepared food is served lunchtimes and evenings, with fish and chips on Friday and roasts on Sunday (no food Sun eve). Barbecues are held in summer. Quiz night is Wednesday. Outside is a large garden and a separate heated and covered smoking area. A public car park is opposite. ⏰🐕🍴🅿🚭📶

White Lion
91 Sopwell Lane, AL1 1RN
🕐 12-11 ☎ (01727) 850540 🌐 whitelionstalbans.co.uk
Adnams Broadside; Oakham Citra, JHB; St Austell Tribute; 3 changing beers (sourced nationally) ⏣
Pleasantly laid-out pub within a 16th-century half-timbered frame. Recently refurbished, it has a small, friendly front bar and a spacious main bar with alcoves. The large rear garden is a haven for drinkers in warm weather and boules, chess and Jenga can be played here. There is an inviting menu of quality home-made food served lunchtimes and weekday evenings. Open mic music night is Tuesday. ⏰🐕🍴(Abbey/City)🅿🚭📶

St Pauls Walden

Strathmore Arms Ⓛ
London Road, SG4 8BT TL193222
🕐 6-11 Mon; 12-2.30, 5-11 Tue-Thu; 12-11 Fri & Sat; 12-10.30 Sun ☎ (01438) 871654 🌐 thestrathmorearms.co.uk
Tring Side Pocket for a Toad; 4 changing beers (sourced nationally) ⏣
On the Bowes-Lyon estate, this pub has been serving drinkers since 1882, offering a constantly changing list of guest beers from obscure breweries. Unusual bottled beers are also available along with real ciders and perries. A regular in the Guide since 1981, the pub displays a full collection of the Good Beer Guide going back to 1976. Pizza and pasta evening is Wednesday and wild food nights are held on occasion (booking essential). Well known for fundraising locally. It has a separate snug. Q⏰🐕🍴🅿🚭📶

Sandridge

Green Man ✓
31 High Street, AL4 9DD
🕐 11-midnight; 11-11.30 Sun ☎ (01727) 854845

Cotswold Cask; Greene King Abbot; Sharp's Doom Bar Ⓖ
This family-run pub extends a warm welcome to ale and cider drinkers alike. The landlord has been in residence for over 25 years. All ales are served straight from the cask, and up to six real ciders are also kept. On the doorstep of the newly established 850 acre Heartwood Forest, the pub is an ideal place for refreshment after a stroll in the woods. Dogs are welcome in the conservatory and the garden which has a small aviary. Q⏰🐕🍴🅿🚭📶

Sawbridgeworth

Gate Ⓛ
81 London Road, CM21 9JJ
🕐 11.30-2.30, 5.30-11 Mon; 11.30-2.30 Tue & Thu; 11.30-2 Wed; 11.30-11 Fri & Sat; 12-11 Sun ☎ (01279) 722313
🌐 thegatepub.com
Sawbridgeworth Gold; 6 changing beers (often Sawbridgeworth)
A lively pub with a huge collection of pumpclips adorning the beams. It is sports-oriented with several satellite TV screens, and home to numerous darts and other pub teams. A range of up to six beers is offered, typically three from the small Sawbridgeworth Brewery at the back of the pub and three guest beers from near and far. Beer festivals are held over the Easter and August bank holiday weekends. No dogs are allowed. 🐕🍴🅿🚭

Old Bell
38 Bell Street, CM21 9AN
🕐 11-11 (1am Fri & Sat); 12-11 Sun ☎ (01279) 721050
Adnams Broadside; Woodforde's Wherry; 1 changing beer (sourced nationally) ⏣
This 16th-century timber-framed pub boasts many exposed beams in the main bar. Situated among Bell Street's traditional village shops, it is cosy and friendly. There is a side bar where food is served and in the summer a popular courtyard and sunny garden with a children's play area. A quiz is hosted on Sunday evening and ukulele jam session on Tuesday. Real cider and perry are always available. ⏰🐕🍴🅿🚭(510,509)🐾📶

Standon

Star ✓
62 High Street, SG11 1LB
🕐 12-3, 5-11; 12-11.30 Fri & Sat; 12-11 Sun
☎ (01920) 823725 🌐 star-standon.co.uk
Greene King IPA, Abbot; 2 changing beers ⏣
Traditional 17th-century pub with exposed wooden beams. It has a separate sports-themed public bar and a quiet and comfortable saloon/restaurant. Food is classic pub grub with roasts on Sunday. Two guest beers are offered, at least one sourced independently of Greene King – usually from a small local brewer. ⏰🐕🍴🅿🚭(331,386)🐾📶

Stevenage

Chequers
164 High Street, SG1 3LL
🕐 12-midnight (1am Fri & Sat); 12-10.30 Sun
☎ (01438) 488692
Greene King XX Mild, IPA, IPA Gold, IPA Reserve; 8 changing beers (sourced nationally) ⏣

Friendly locals' pub situated between the old and new towns. It is home to a ladies' darts team and Scrabble team, and a book and a bike club. There is an interesting old map of Stevenage on the wall and a newly refurbished beer garden. It hosts a weekly quiz night, and cask club every Wednesday from 5pm, with a 50p discount on a pint of guest ale. Q☺⑧◑&♣♣♥🎘

Dun Cow

Letchmore Road, SG1 3PP

❂ 3-midnight (1am Fri); 12-1am Sat; 12-midnight Sun
☎ (01438) 313268

Greene King IPA; St Austell Proper Job, Tribute; 3 changing beers (sourced nationally) ⊞

Situated in a residential area around half a mile east of Stevenage's old town High Street, this friendly local dates back to the 18th century. The pub has a wood-panelled snug and a larger public bar with pool table. It serves three regular and three changing guest beers along with a wide choice of gins and whiskies. Q☺⑧&✆♣P🎘🐾♥🎘

Our Mutual Friend ✔

Broadwater Crescent, SG2 8EH

❂ 12-11 (11.30 Fri & Sat) ☎ (01438) 312282
⊕ omfpub.co.uk

6 changing beers (sourced nationally) ⊞

Thriving community pub on the southern side of Stevenage serving an ever-changing selection of cask beers and real ciders. Since it was rescued from the cask ale graveyard back in 2002 it has featured in every edition of the Guide. The lounge bar aims to recreate the feel of the 'Old Mutual' which was demolished in the 1960s to make way for the new town. Very busy when Stevenage FC have home matches. A winner of many local CAMRA awards, members receive a discount on ales. Q☺◑✆♣♦P🎘🖥(4,5)🐾🎘

Tring

Castle 🄻

Park Road, HP23 6BN (around corner from Natural History Museum)

❂ 3-11; 12-11.30 Fri & Sat; 12-11 Sun ☎ (01442) 823552

Vale Red Kite, Wychert Ale; 1 changing beer (sourced locally; often Tring) ⊞

Just a stone's throw from Tring's popular Zoological Museum, the Castle is a hot spot for locals, offering an intimate single-room layout and TVs showing sports fixtures. Small but brimful with atmosphere, and with a welcoming, cask-savvy landlord, you are guaranteed a quality local pint at this great corner pub. The regular beers are from the owner, Vale Brewery, and Tring Brewery ales are also frequently offered. ⑧♣🖥🐾🎘

King's Arms 🄻

King Street, HP23 6BE (on corner of Queen St and King St) SP921111

❂ 12-2.30, 5.30-11.30; 12-3, 5-11.30 Fri; 12-11.30 Sat & Sun
☎ (01442) 823318 ⊕ kingsarmstring.co.uk

Tring Moongazing; 4 changing beers (sourced regionally; often Leighton Buzzard, Oakham, XT) ⊞

Affectionately known as 'the pink pub' by its regulars, the King's Arms is a classic English inn with an attached dining room, offering a variety of fine local ales and great cuisine. Situated in the centre of Tring, with a traditional interior free from music and TV, this is a great place to sample the best that local breweries have to offer in a peaceful and pleasant atmosphere. Q⑧◑♣♦🖥🎘

Robin Hood 🄻 ✔

1 Brook Street, HP23 5ED (on jct with B4635/B486)

❂ 11.30-11; 12-11.30 Sat; 12-11 Sun ☎ (01442) 824912
⊕ therobinhoodtring.co.uk

Fuller's ESB, London Pride; 4 changing beers (sourced nationally; often Fuller's) ⊞

A classic 17th-century Fuller's house offering well-kept beer and good food. On Sunday evenings you can now enjoy Tip Khao Thai cuisine, at other times a traditional pub menu is available. Characterful features including log-burning stoves, low ceilings and wooden beams add to the cosy, country pub experience. Situated at the foot of Tring's High Street, with a heated patio and conservatory area, this pub is well worth a visit. Q⑧◑&♣🐾♥🎘

Ware

Brewery Tap 🄻

83 High Street, SG12 9AD

❂ 12-midnight ☎ (01920) 468549 ⊕ brewerytapware.co.uk

Hardys & Hansons Olde Trip; 5 changing beers (sourced nationally) ⊞

A refurbished Grade II-listed town-centre pub with six handpumps featuring Greene King and more local Hertfordshire beers – the house beer Ware House Ale is brewed by Greene King. Three or four traditional ciders and perries are also available. The all-day food menu comprises a range of pies, paninis and pizzas. The long-closed cellar bar has been reopened and outside there is a heated courtyard. Old photographs and maps of Ware are an interesting distraction and look for the one penny wall. ☺⑧✆◑&✆♦🖥(331,383)🐾🎘

Crooked Billet ✔

140 Musley Hill, SG12 7NL (via New Rd from High St)

❂ 5.30-11.30 (midnight Fri); 12-midnight Sat; 12-11.30 Sun
☎ (01920) 462516

4 changing beers (sourced nationally) ⊞

Stuart and Sue have presided over the Billet for more than 20 years, stocking more than 600 different ales since the pub was acquired by Admiral Taverns. Utilising the local SIBA Direct Delivery Scheme, there is a varying range of four or five ales, always including a mild, porter or stout. Two beer and cider festivals are held annually. This gem of a community pub has two small bars featuring TV sport, pool and darts. Carlisle United and Ware FC fans are assured of a warm welcome. ☺⑧&♣🖥(395)🐾🎘

Wareside

Chequers

Ware Road, SG12 7QY (on B1004)

❂ 12-3, 6-11; 12-4, 6.30-10.30 Sun ☎ (01920) 467010

House beer (by Hadham); 2 changing beers (sourced regionally; often Adnams) ⊞

A rural free house dating from the 15th century, the Chequers was originally a coaching inn and has three distinct bars plus a restaurant. All the food is home made and reasonably priced, and there are plenty of vegetarian options. Walkers and cyclists are welcome, making this a good base for a ramble. No machines, no music, and there is a ban on swearing. Q⑧◑&♣P🖥(M3,M4)🐾

Watford

Flag ✔

Station Road, WD17 1ET

🌣 8am-11 (midnight Thu; 1am Fri & Sat); 8am-10.30 Sun
☎ (01923) 218413 ⊕ theflagwatford.co.uk
St Austell Tribute; 4 changing beers (sourced nationally) Ⓗ

The Flag is an iconic Victorian building dating back to 1860 and the advent of the current Watford Junction station. Easily accessible by rail and bus, and with a large car park, it boasts grand Victorian features as well as two garden areas. Famous for its live music weekends, and with sports on satellite TV, you are unlikely to find a friendlier and more diverse pub in the town. Winner of the 2015 Best Bar None award.
🌣🏵🕻🕭ᵭ⇌Θ(Junction)P🖵🐾🗢

West Herts Sports Club

8 Park Avenue, WD18 7HP (S of A412 near town hall)
🌣 5-11; 4-11.30 Fri; 12-11 Sat; 10-10.30 Sun
☎ (01923) 229239 ⊕ westhertssportsclub.co.uk
5 changing beers (sourced nationally) Ⓗ

This members' bar is a multiple winner of the East Anglia CAMRA Club of the Year award. Real ciders are regularly on offer. The bar is decorated with sporting memorabilia, and sporting events are shown on big screens throughout. A separate function room, home of the Watford Beer Festival, is available to hire. Show a CAMRA membership card or a copy of this Guide to gain entry up to four times a year. The club can get busy on Watford match days. 🌣🏵Θ🗢

Wheathampstead

Swan 🅥

56 High Street, AL4 8AR
🌣 11-midnight; 11-11.30 Sun ☎ (01582) 833110
⊕ theswanwheathampstead.co.uk
Greene King IPA; St Austell Tribute; 3 changing beers (sourced nationally) Ⓗ

Dating from the 16th century, this thriving and friendly traditional village inn has retained many interesting features including exposed beams and an inglenook fireplace. Popular with workers and walkers, lunches are available every day, evening meals Monday and Friday. Wednesday is quiz night and there is bingo on the last Thursday of the

month. This community pub has an upper bar with darts and sports TV. The three guest ales may come from the SIBA range. 🌣🏵🕻🕭ᵭ♣P🖵🐾🗢

Wild Hill

Woodman

45 Wildhill Road, AL9 6EA (between A1000 and B158)
TL264068
🌣 11.30-2.30, 5.30-11; 12-2.30, 7-10.30 Sun
☎ (01707) 642618
Greene King IPA, Abbot; 4 changing beers (sourced nationally) Ⓗ

An unpretentious, friendly, rural community local. This superb 90 per cent wet-led pub thrives on and is a staunch supporter of real ale, with six beers including four guests. Lined oversized glasses are available on request. The large garden is ideal in summer. Good pub grub is served lunchtimes (no food Sun). Look for God's Waiting Room. Eleven times winner of local CAMRA Pub of the Year and three times Hertfordshire CAMRA Pub of the Year.
🌣🏵🕻♣🐾P🐾🗢

Wilstone

Half Moon Ⓛ

60 Tring Road, HP23 4PD
🌣 12-11 ☎ (01442) 826410
Sharp's Doom Bar; Tring Side Pocket for a Toad; 2 changing beers (sourced locally; often Malt the Brewery, Tring, XT) Ⓗ

Lovely traditional pub in the centre of the village with a real fire, wood beams and lots of horse brasses. The walls are adorned with old pictures of the pub and village. A varied food menu is available at competitive prices. Three or four beers are offered, usually from local breweries. Scrabble night is the fourth Sunday of the month. Cribbage and dominoes teams play here and other traditional pub games are available.
Q🌣🏵🕻♣P🖵(164)🐾🗢

Old Barge, Hertford (Photo: Emma Haines)

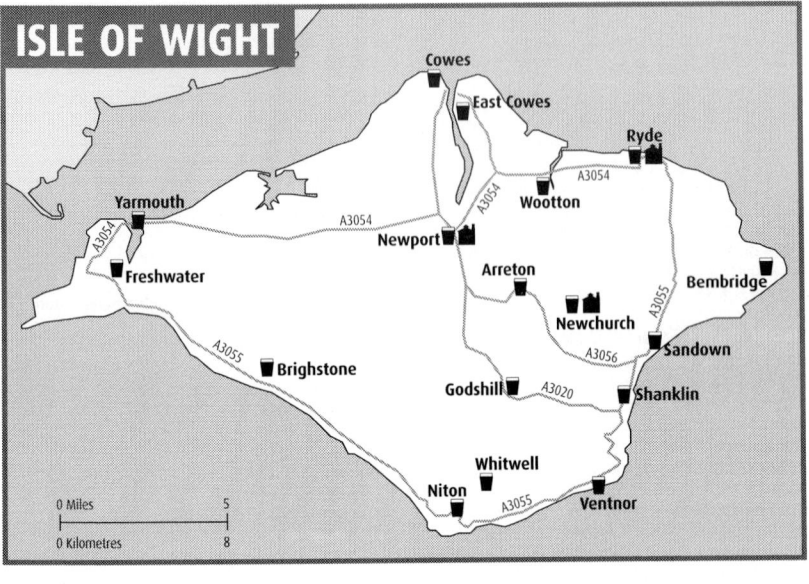

ISLE OF WIGHT

Map locations: Cowes, East Cowes, Ryde, A3054, Wootton, Yarmouth, A3054, Newport, Arreton, Bembridge, Freshwater, A3054, A3055, Newchurch, A3055, Brighstone, Godshill, A3056, Sandown, A3020, Shanklin, Whitwell, Niton, A3055, Ventnor

0 Miles 5
0 Kilometres 8

Arreton

Dairyman's Daughter 🅛
Main Road, PO30 3AA SZ53258680
🕓 10-11; 10-10.30 Sun ☎ (01983) 539361
🌐 thedairymansdaughter.com
Goddards Fuggle-Dee-Dum; Ringwood Boondoggle, Fortyniner; house beer (by Ringwood); 2 changing beers (sourced nationally; often Andwells) 🇭
A hugely popular museum, gift shop, craft and pub experience on the site of the once massive Arreton Barn. As well as a range of six ales, there is a large selection of Island bottled beers in the old brewery. A full menu is available until 9.30pm featuring locally sourced meat and vegetables. Adjacent is the 11th-century church of St George, the carp pond, the Maritime Museum and the dairyman's daughter's grave. Live entertainment features throughout the week. ⤳🏵🛈🤝P🚲(8)👶🛜

Fighting Cocks 🅛
Hale Common, PO30 3AR (opp greenhouses)
🕓 10-11 ☎ (01983) 865254 🌐 thefightingcocksiow.co.uk
Fuller's London Pride; Sharp's Doom Bar; 1 changing beer (sourced locally; often Goddards) 🇭
This pub, in a prime position on the main Newport to Sandown road, has capitalised on its location, with a combination of good service, quality food and fine beer making it a popular stop-off. Once a humble country pub, the building now has plenty of room for its customers and lots of car parking space. Families and children are catered for and there is a large, safe play area. It is one of only two pubs serving local Kemphill beef. The pub may close earlier on winter evenings.
Q⤳🏵🛈👶🅰🤝P🚲(8)👶🛜

Bembridge

Old Village Inn ✅
61 High Street, PO35 5SF (along High St towards Sandown)
🕓 12-11 (midnight Fri & Sat); 12-10.30 Sun
☎ (01983) 872616 🌐 yeoldevillageinn.co.uk

Courage Directors; Greene King Abbot; 2 changing beers (often Butcombe, St Austell, West Berkshire) 🇭
The Old Village Steak and Ale House is the latest addition to the Bembridge scene, specialising in local meat and fish dishes. A fine choice of real ales and selected wines is served in a refined and relaxed atmosphere. Food is served 12-3pm and 5-9pm. Live music plays on occasional Fridays and a popular quiz is held on the first Monday of the month. There is a patio area to the rear and a pétanque terrain. Q⤳🏵🛈🤝🅰🤝P🚲(8)👶🛜

Brighstone

Three Bishops ✅
Main Road, PO30 4AH
🕓 12-10.30 (9 Sun) ☎ (01983) 740226
🌐 threebishopspub.co.uk
Sharp's Doom Bar; Young's Bitter; 2 changing beers (often Courage, Fuller's, Greene King) 🇭
Large, food-led village-centre inn. The three bishops were once rectors of the adjacent village church and went on to become bishops. Major refurbishments in the past have turned this ordinary pub into a successful pub restaurant, yet the public bar still retains the feel of a local. Food is served all day in summer, lunchtimes and evenings in winter, including gluten-free dishes. Bottled beer is available alongside the real ale. Outside is a large car park and garden with an adventure playground for children. Closing time may vary in the winter. Q⤳🏵🛈👶🅰🤝P🚲(12)👶🛜

Cowes

Anchor Inn 🅛
1 High Street, PO31 7SA (opp Sainsbury's)
🕓 11-11 (midnight Fri & Sat); 12-10.30 Sun
☎ (01983) 292823 🌐 theanchorcowes.co.uk

REAL ALE BREWERIES

Goddards Ryde
Island Newport
Yates' Newchurch

Fuller's London Pride; Ringwood Razorback; 3 changing beers (often Adnams, Goddards, Wadworth) Ⓗ

This High Street pub, originally the Trumpeters back in 1704, is close to the Marina, tempting visiting yachtsmen for their first pint ashore. A recent conversion has integrated the stables and created a pleasant beer garden. A good selection of beer is kept, with one Island ale and two guests always available. The varied food menu is served in prodigious quantities. Live entertainment features regularly. Accommodation is in seven comfortable rooms. 🛏🏠🍴◑🚪🚆(1)🐾🐕📶

Union Inn ✓

Watch House Lane, PO31 7QH (just off the Parade)
🕐 11-midnight; 12-10.30 Sun ☎ (01983) 293163
🌐 unioninncowes.co.uk

Fuller's London Pride; Gale's HSB; 3 changing beers (often Butcombe, Fuller's) Ⓗ

A haven for yachting enthusiasts, locals and holidaymakers, one three-sided bar serves the lounge, snug, dining area and airy conservatory. A roaring fire in winter adds to the cosy atmosphere. Delicious family meals are served with portions for children and ingredients sourced from local suppliers. There is pay parking on the Parade 25 yards away, free later in the day. A popular quiz evening is held every Wednesday. Closing time may vary. Q🛏🏠◑🚪🚆(1)🐾🐕📶

East Cowes

Lifeboat ⓛ

Britannia Way, PO32 6UB (by river, well signposted)
🕐 10-11 (10.30 Sun) ☎ (01983) 292711
🌐 thelifeboatcowes.co.uk

Fuller's London Pride; Goddards Fuggle-Dee-Dum; Wadworth 6X Ⓗ

Large, comfortable, waterfront establishment, in the heart of East Cowes Marina. The modern pub is attractively decorated with much wood and bare brick. The decked patio has a superb view over the river and marina activities, and is surrounded by stylish contemporary buildings. The emphasis here is on good food, but a selection of well-kept beers is always available. In winter closing time may be earlier. Q🛏🏠◑🚪♿🅿🚆🐾🐕📶

Freshwater

Red Lion ⓛ

Church Place, PO40 9BP (leaving Freshwater towards the Bay follow Hook Hill towards the Causeway)
SZ34508738
🕐 11-11 ☎ (01983) 754925 🌐 redlion-freshwater.co.uk
4 changing beers (sourced nationally; often St Austell, Upham, West Berkshire) Ⓗ

Former three-bar coaching inn dating back to the 11th century, now converted to one large bar but still retaining much of its original character. The red-brick building is situated in the most picture postcard area of Freshwater in the church square and by the Causeway. From here splendid views of the River Yar can be had towards Yarmouth. May close earlier in winter. Q🏠◑🅿🚆(7,12)🐾🐕📶

Godshill

Taverners ⓛ ✓

High Street, PO38 3HZ

🕐 11-11 (5 Sun) ☎ (01983) 840707
🌐 thetavernersgodshill.co.uk

Sharp's Doom Bar; house beer (by Yates'); 2 changing beers (often Brains, Butcombe, Goddards) Ⓗ

Tasteful and sympathetic conversion and expansion of an old cottage abounding with beams and flagstones – it is difficult to see the join between the old and the new. The accent here is on food – the comfortable bar is sandwiched between restaurant areas but is none the worse for that. Outside is an excellent large outdoor play area for children. Locally produced cider is available. Closed for the first three weeks in January.
Q🛏🏠◑♿🍴🅿🚆(2,3)🐾

Newchurch

Pointer Inn

High Street, PO36 0NN (next to church)
🕐 11-11; 12-10.30 Sun ☎ (01983) 865202
🌐 pointernewchurch.co.uk

Fuller's London Pride; Gale's HSB; 1 changing beer (often Fuller's, Wychwood) Ⓗ

Ancient village local where families are welcome. The home-cooked food, served until 9.30pm (9pm Sun), is prepared by a chef with a vast experience of Island trade (booking is essential). A highchair and toys are available for children. The large garden has a pétanque terrain and a covered area for smokers. Awards include Fuller's Best Country/ Village Pub and a Certificate of Excellence by Trip Advisor. Q🛏🏠◑♣🅿🚆(23)🐾📶

Newport

Bargeman's Rest ⓛ

Little London Quay, PO30 5BS (signed from dual carriageway)
🕐 10.30-11 (10.30 Sun) ☎ (01983) 525828
🌐 bargemansrest.com

Goddards Fuggle-Dee-Dum; Ringwood Fortyniner; 5 changing beers (sourced nationally; often Jennings, Marston's, Ringwood) Ⓗ

This massive, locally owned pub has been an animal feed store and a sail and rigging loft for the barge fleet that used to ply the river. The huge bar provides intimate drinking areas and the nautical memorabilia, decor and ambience are all you could hope for in a traditional, well-seasoned pub. The outdoor drinking area is only a few feet from the bustling River Medina. Beer and food are consistently good and the range varied. Live entertainment features most nights.
🛏🏠◑♿🅿🚆🐾🐕📶

Newport Ale House ⓛ

24A Holyrood Street, PO30 5AZ
🕐 12-11; 11-midnight Fri & Sat; 12-10.30
Sun ☎ 07515 493460 🌐 alehousefamily.co.uk/newport-ale-house
4 changing beers (sourced nationally; often Palmers) Ⓖ

The listed building has previously traded as a hairdressers, undertakers and posting house and stables. It is the Island's smallest pub, recalling the days when there were several such establishments in Newport (though it is unlikely its predecessors sported flock wallpaper). This is a hugely popular pub with all generations, where conversation comes easy – it can get very crowded and noisy. There is live music on Sunday afternoon. No meals, but snacks include high-quality locally sourced pies, rolls and sandwiches. Q🛏🐕🚆🐾

Niton

Buddle 🅛
St Catherine's Road, Niton Undercliff, PO38 2NE
(follow signs to St Catherine's Lighthouse) SZ50207580
☼ 12-3 Mon; 12-10.30 Tue & Thu; 12-11 Wed & Sat; 12-11.30
Fri; 12-7 Sun ☎ (01983) 730243 ⊕ buddleinn.co.uk
Sharp's Doom Bar; house beer (by Timothy Taylor); 3
changing beers (sourced regionally; often Fuller's,
Goddards, Yates') Ⓗ
A 16th-century inn that was built as a farmhouse
and reputedly became a smugglers' inn during the
18th century. Extensively refurbished, it retains the
ancient flagstones and beams, inglenook fireplace
and many interesting photographs. Offering good
food (served until 9pm), it also has a strong real ale
following, with five beers in the summer and two
in the winter. A choice of ciders is also available.
Winter opening times vary. Q🖤🐾🅖🅓♣🛏🅿🖵(6)♣

Ryde

High Park Tavern 🅛
84 Marlborough Road, PO33 1AF (out of Ryde towards
Tesco)
☼ 12-11.30 (12.30am Fri & Sat) ☎ (01983) 562841
Sharp's Doom Bar; 3 changing beers (often Island,
Timothy Taylor, Wychwood) Ⓗ
Corner pub on a busy road on the outskirts of Ryde.
As a result of several makeovers in recent years,
this is now a comfortable local. The beer range
varies, but usually includes at least one local ale
and one dark ale. Live music features on Friday,
Saturday and Sunday afternoons. A large function
room has easy access for events. Breakfast is
served in the morning, plus Thursday night specials
and Sunday roasts. 🐾🅖🅓♣🛏🖵(2,3)♣🗢

S. Fowler & Co 🅛 ✅
41-43 Union Street, PO33 2LF (top of Union St)
☼ 7am-11 ☎ (01983) 812112
Adnams Broadside; Fuller's London Pride; 8 changing
beers (sourced nationally) Ⓗ
Although perhaps not the most charismatic pub in
the Wetherspoon chain, this converted drapery
store offers a varied range of well-kept beers. The
pub is in the centre of town, with a bus stop
conveniently outside. The name was the
suggestion of the local CAMRA branch – not only is
it the name of the former store, but also that of the
first local CAMRA chairman and revered early
campaigner. There is an upstairs restaurant which
is family friendly. Q🖤🅓🅖♿🛋🛏🖵🗢

Sandown

Castle Inn ⚑ 🅛
12-14 Fitzroy Street, PO36 8HY (off High St)
☼ 11-11 (midnight Fri); 10.30-midnight Sat & Sun
☎ (01983) 403169 ⊕ sandowncastle.co.uk
Wadworth Swordfish; Wychwood Hobgoblin Gold,
Hobgoblin; 3 changing beers (sourced locally; often
Island, Wadworth) Ⓗ
The Castle is an excellent town free house and
locals' pub, home to cribbage and two darts teams.
Six real ales are on offer including the best from
local breweries. Happy hour (5-7pm nightly) is
popular, as is the Sunday quiz. Beer festivals are
held twice a year, usually featuring local ales and
cider. The TV is not allowed to intrude, but is turned
on for special occasions. There is a children's room
at the back and a patio for warm weather.
Q🖤🐾🅖♿🛢♣🛏🖵(3,8)♣🗢

Culver Haven Inn 🅛
Culver Down, PO36 8QT (by monument on Culver
Down) SZ63258565
☼ closed Tue; 10.30-11 (4 Mon) ☎ (01983) 406107
⊕ culverhaven.com
3 changing beers (often Goddards, Timothy Taylor,
Wadworth) Ⓗ
Surely one of the best pub views in the whole of
Great Britain, perched on Culver Down overlooking
Sandown Bay and Bembridge Harbour. The view
back down the hill is also spectacular. Nearby is the
Culver Battery, an impressive remnant of the
Napoleonic Wars and built to protect Portsmouth
(opened regularly by the National Trust). An
excellent and varied menu of snacks and full meals
is offered in this cosy restaurant and pub. Closed
February. Q🖤🐾🅖🅓♿🅰🅿♣🗢

Shanklin

King Harry's Bar
6 Church Road, PO37 6NU (on edge of old village
towards Ventnor)
☼ 12-11 (10 Mon); 12-10.30 Sun ☎ (01983) 863119
⊕ kingharrysbar.co.uk
Fuller's ESB; 3 changing beers (often Goddards,
Shepherd Neame, Young's) Ⓗ
Charming 19th-century thatched property with two
established Tudor bars, restaurants, decked
gardens and the Chine walk, plus car parking front
and rear. Up to three guest beers are offered,
chosen for their originality. Food is served
lunchtimes and summer evenings – the long-
established Henry Vlll kitchen specialises in steaks
to die for. Function facilities, entertainment and
accommodation are provided. Winter opening
hours vary. Q🖤🐾🅖🅓🅰♣🛏🅿🖵(3,2)♣

Ventnor

Perks
46 High Street, PO38 1LT (next to Tesco Express)
☼ 9am-midnight; 10-midnight Sun ☎ (01983) 857446
⊕ perksofventnor.com
Draught Bass; 1 changing beer (sourced regionally;
often Long Man, Yates') Ⓗ
Perks is one of those gems that happens
infrequently, with good service and sensible prices.
It has one beer, plenty of wine, and a 'best of
British' theme, with a fascinating collection of
memorabilia. Owner Graham Perks has spent over
25 years running a succession of bars and knows
what the customer wants – good company and a
tipple to suit the most discerning palate. There may
be a second beer from the Yates' Brewery at the
weekend. Q🅖🅓♿♣🖵(3,6)♣

Whitwell

White Horse Inn 🅛
High Street, PO38 2PY SZ52007800
☼ 10-11 (10 Sun) ☎ (01983) 730375
⊕ whitehorseiow.co.uk
4 changing beers (often Adnams, Hop Back,
Upham) Ⓗ
Built in 1454, this ancient stone building is
considered to be the oldest established inn on the
Isle of Wight. An extension to the side adds a
family area and additional dining space. The
remainder of the building is traditional, with
intimate areas to the rear. Four handpumps serve a
changing range of beers, and the extensive food

menu is excellent. A large garden is fine for children on warmer days. Breakfast is served 10am-midday. **Q** 🍽🐾🌳🍴👍🍺♿P🚬(6)🐱🌐

Wootton

Cedars

2 Station Road, PO33 4QU (top of village by traffic lights)
🕐 11-11; 12-10.30 Sun ☎ (01983) 882593
🌐 cedarsisleofwight.co.uk
Fuller's London Pride; Gale's Seafarers Ale, HSB Ⓗ
In a prominent position at the top of Wootton High Street is this late-Victorian two-bar village local. It is a large pub, though, curiously, it has one of the smallest front doors on the Island. There is a children's room and, outside, a large garden with a play area. Smokers are spoilt – the smoking area is adapted from a beautiful Victorian outbuilding. An extensive food menu is offered and the friendly bar

staff ensure a welcoming atmosphere. Close to the steam railway station.
Q 🍽🐾🌳🍴👍♿🚊P🚬(4,9)🐱🌐

Yarmouth

King's Head Ⓛ

Quay Street, PO41 0PB (opp ferry terminal)
🕐 11-11 ☎ (01983) 760177 🌐 kingsheadyarmouth.co.uk
6 changing beers (often Adnams, Upham, Yates') Ⓗ
Ancient 16th-century town pub with a big open fire and an interesting collection of old Island prints and local photographs. Stone floors, low ceilings and cosy corners feature in abundance. Beers are from a selection of favourites, with six in summer and three in winter. A home-cooked food menu is complemented by fresh fish and daily specials. Food is served all day in summer. A handy place to wait for the Yarmouth-Lymington ferry.
🍽🐾🍴👍♿🚌(7)🐱🌐

Pointer Inn, Newchurch

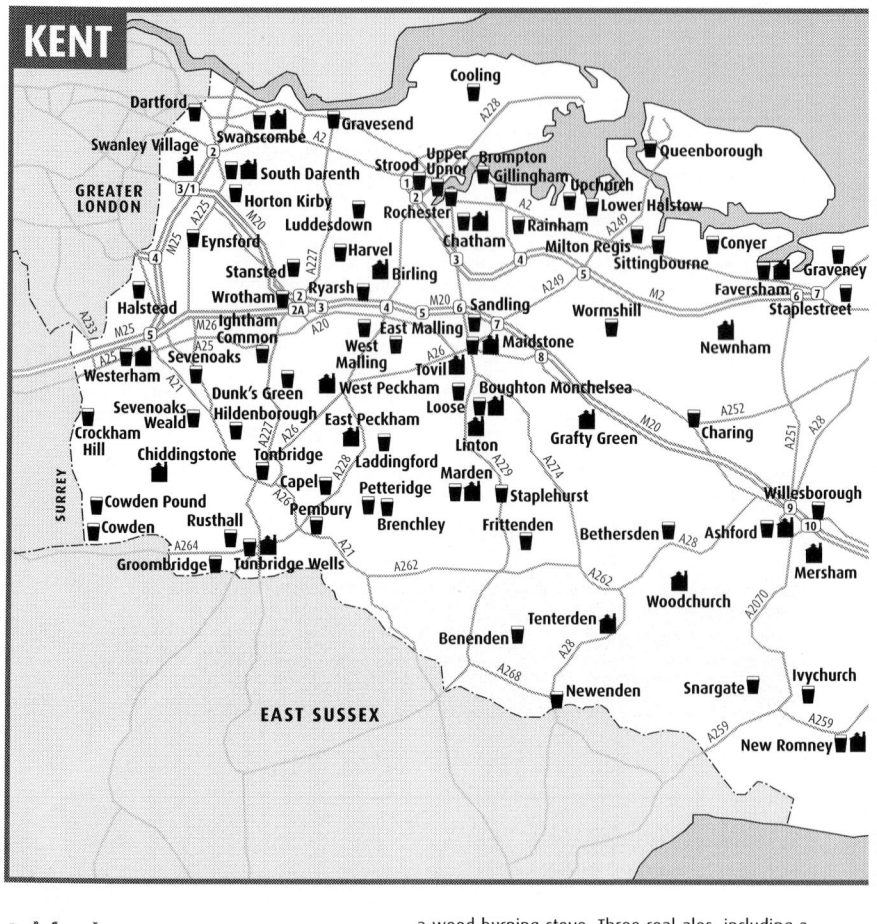

KENT

GREATER LONDON

SURREY

EAST SUSSEX

Ashford

County Hotel ✅
10 High Street, TN24 8TD (at lower end of High St)
☼ 8am-midnight (1am Fri & Sat) ☎ (01233) 646891
**Greene King Abbot; Ruddles Best Bitter; Sharp's
Doom Bar; 4 changing beers (sourced nationally)** Ⓗ
A spacious Wetherspoon pub in an 18th-century
building in the centre of town; the single bar has
three separate seating areas. Originally red brick,
the top floor and the parapet are now tile hung. Up
to two real ciders are dispensed from polypins in
the fridge. Food is served every day, and children
are allowed in the dining area until 9pm. Summer
and autumn national and international beer
festivals, plus one regional festival, and a summer
cider festival are held. Q❄☺◑⑃◔≠♠P🖵🛜

Barfrestone

Wrong Turn Ⓛ
Pie Factory Road, CT15 7JG (2½ miles from Barfrestone
jct off A2) TR261503
☼ closed Mon & Tue; 3-9 (8 Thu); 12-9 Sat; 12-8
Sun ☎ 07522 554118
**Wantsum Black Prince; 2 changing beers (sourced
locally)** Ⓖ
Rural pub with a comfortable, country-style kitchen
interior with wooden tables, chairs, sideboard and

a wood-burning stove. Three real ales, including a
mild, usually feature, primarily from Kent
microbreweries, alongside real ciders from Kentish
Pip and Westons. Snacks include pork pies, Scotch
eggs and cheeseboards. Opening times may vary
during the seasons and the pub may close early if
quiet. Outside, there is a sheltered patio and
garden. Voted as the CAMRA branch Pub of the
Year in 2016. Q❄☺&Å♣♠P🐾🛜

Benenden

Bull Ⓛ
The Street, TN17 4DE
☼ 12-midnight ☎ (01580) 240054
⊕ thebullatbenenden.co.uk
**Dark Star Hophead; Harvey's Sussex Best Bitter;
Larkins Traditional Ale; 1 changing beer (sourced
locally; often Old Dairy, Shepherd Neame)** Ⓗ
An imposing free house dating back to the 17th
century overlooking the village green. The public
bar features an inglenook fireplace with wooden
floors and exposed oak beams. A separate
restaurant/function room serves locally grown
produce, and meals can also be taken in the public
bar (no food Sun eve). Booking is advisable for the
Sunday lunchtime carvery. An acoustic music club is
held after lunch on a Sunday afternoon each
month. Q❄☺🛏◑♣♠P🖵(297)🐾🛜

Shepherd Neame Master Brew, Spitfire Gold; 2 changing beers (sourced nationally; often St Austell, Shepherd Neame) Ⓗ

A 16th-century coaching inn built to provide lodgings for Canterbury pilgrims, full of character, with oak beams and an inglenook fireplace. A large and varied menu complemented by real ales is served in both the bar and restaurant (no food Sun eve). There is a large patio area, and various board games are available. Situated near the Greensand Way, dogs and walkers are welcome.

Q ☆ ☆ ◑ ▶ P ♨ ☕

Bramling

Haywain Ⅼ

Canterbury Road, CT3 1NB

🕓 7.30-11 Mon; 12-3, 6-11; 12-4 Sun ☎ (01227) 720676

🌐 thehaywainbramling.co.uk

Fuller's London Pride; Wells Bombardier; 2 changing beers (sourced locally; often Goacher's, Ramsgate, Whitstable) Ⓗ

Classic friendly country pub which features hop bines and a cosy snug. Traditional games include darts and bat and trap. There is a Monday quiz night, a Wednesday crib night, a cheese club on the

REAL ALE BREWERIES

Amazing ⬛ Sandgate
Angels & Demons Capel-le-Ferne (NEW)
Boutilliers Faversham (NEW)
Breakwater Dover (NEW)
Brew Buddies Swanley Village
Brumaison Marden (NEW)
By The Mile Broadstairs (NEW)
Canterbury Ales Chartham
Canterbury Brewers ⬛ Canterbury
Caveman Swanscombe
Farriers Arms ⬛ Mersham
Four Candles ⬛ St Peters
G2 Ashford
Goacher's Tovil
Goody Herne
Hop Fuzz West Hythe
Hopdaemon Newnham
Isla Vale Margate
Kent Birling
Larkins Chiddingstone
Mad Cat Faversham
Maidstone Maidstone
Millis (Dartford Wobbler) South Darenth
Musket Linton
NauticAles Broadstairs (NEW)
Nelson Chatham
Old Dairy Tenterden
Pig & Porter Tunbridge Wells
Ramsgate Broadstairs
Range Lympne
Ripple Steam Sutton
Rockin' Robin Boughton Monchelsea
Romney Marsh New Romney
Samphire Folkestone (NEW)
Shepherd Neame Faversham
Stag Woodchurch (NEW)
Swan on the Green ⬛ West Peckham
Tír Dhá Ghlas ⬛ Dover
Tonbridge East Peckham
Turnstone Whitstable
Wantsum St Nicholas at Wade
Westerham Westerham
Whitstable Grafty Green

Bethersden

George

The Street, TN26 3AG (off A28 between Ashford and Tenterden in centre of village)

🕓 12-midnight ☎ (01233) 820235

Harvey's Sussex Best Bitter; Morland Old Speckled Hen; 2 changing beers (sourced nationally; often Old Dairy) Ⓗ

Two-bar free house in a pretty Kentish village decorated with pictures of local life. The public bar is a survivor of what village inns used to be like, with wood panelling, hops over the bar, a wood-burning stove, pub games, a jukebox and good conversation. The former saloon now doubles as a restaurant. Food is served daily except Monday lunchtime and Sunday evening, with a carvery on Wednesday evening and Sunday lunchtime. A beer festival is held around St George's Day.

☆ ☆ ◑ ♣ P ▤ (2) ♨ ☕

Boughton Monchelsea

Cock Inn Ⅼ ⊘

Heath Road, ME17 4JD TQ776512

🕓 11-11; 12-9 Sun ☎ (01622) 743166

🌐 cockinnmaidstone.co.uk

Map labels

Cliftonville
Westgate-on-Sea
Herne Bay — Margate
Whitstable
Tankerton — A299 — St Peter's
Herne — Broadstairs
St Nicholas A253
at Wade — Ramsgate
Ickham
A257 — Sandwich
Canterbury — Bramling
Chartham — Eastry
Petham — Finglesham
Barfrestone — Sutton — Deal
Coldred — Walmer
Hastingleigh
Temple Ewell
Dover
Lympne A259 — Folkestone
Sandgate
West Hythe
Hythe

0 Miles 5
0 Kilometres 8

last Sunday of the month, and jazz on the last Tuesday. Guest beers are usually from Kent breweries, and an annual beer festival is hosted over the Spring Bank Holiday weekend in a marquee in the attractive garden. Excellent home-cooked food, using local produce, is served. ☺⍟✉◖▶♣P🏠(13,14)♨

Brenchley

Halfway House 🅛 ⊘
Horsmonden Road, TN12 7AX (½ mile SE of village)
🕓 12-11; 12-10.30 Sun ☎ (01892) 722526
🌐 halfwayhousebrenchley.co.uk
Dark Star Hophead; Goacher's Fine Light Ale; Skinner's Betty Stogs; Westerham 1965 Special Bitter Ale; Young's Special; house beer (by Goacher's); 3 changing beers (sourced locally; often Hopdaemon, Larkins, Whitstable) 🅖
A former coaching inn with a red-brick façade, this renowned free house is outside the village on the road to Horsmonden. Seven permanent and two guest beers are served direct from cooled casks. Hops hanging from wooden beams in rooms arranged over many levels, farming and brewery memorabilia and open fires combine to provide a cosy, rustic ambience. Beer festivals are held on the Whitsun and August bank holidays in the garden which includes a separate family area. Hard to beat! Q☺⍟◖♣♥P🏠(297)♨🛜

Broadstairs

Thirty-Nine Steps Brewhouse
11-13 Charlotte Street, CT10 1LR
🕓 12-11
4 changing beers 🅖
This alehouse/brewpub has relocated to a more spacious premises a few doors down from its original location. Eight handpumps adorn the bar. The knowledgeable landlord is continuing his quest to vary the beer offerings and favours interesting and hard-to-find ales among the range. There is a bar billiards table upstairs and live music is hosted. The Broadstairs Town Brewery is in the basement. ☺⇌♥🏠(56)♨

Brompton

King George V
1 Prospect Row, ME7 5AL
🕓 12-11; 12-10.30 Sun ☎ (01634) 842418
🌐 kinggeorgevpub.co.uk
Harvey's Sussex Best Bitter; 2 changing beers (sourced nationally; often Dark Star, Oakham, Wantsum) 🅗
An 18th-century free house with three connected areas decorated with military memorabilia, and a covered and heated area outside for smokers. At least two guest ales feature, usually including a mild, plus a wide variety of Belgian beers, malt whiskies, gin and rums. Food is served every day including daily specials. Sunday roasts are recommended. A quiz night is held every third Tuesday. The pub also offers three en-suite guest rooms. ☺⍟✉◖♣♥🏠(101,182)🛜

Canterbury

Dolphin 🅛
17 St Radigund's Street, CT1 2AA
🕓 12-11 (midnight Thu-Sat) ☎ (01227) 455963
🌐 thedolphincanterbury.co.uk
Sharp's Doom Bar; Timothy Taylor Landlord; 2 changing beers (sourced locally; often Hopdaemon, Ramsgate) 🅗
Friendly local decorated with 1950-1970 memorabilia, free of TV screens but with a comprehensive collection of board games. Pub food in generous portions is served, with roasts on Sundays. The attractive verandah is popular with diners, and there is a large suntrap garden, in which Henri the H Van sells rotisserie food. One handpump dispenses cider, and there is a range of beers on other pumps. Opening hours vary from month to month. ☺⍟◖⇌♥🏠🛜

Eight Bells ⊘
34 London Road, CT2 8LN
🕓 3-11; 12-midnight Fri & Sat; 12-10.30 Sun
☎ (01227) 454794
Young's Bitter, Special 🅗
Small, traditional local dating from 1708 and rebuilt in 1902, retaining original embossed windows and decorated with memorabilia. There is live music fortnightly on Fridays, and a quiz, usually on the last Wednesday of the month. Five darts teams play every week and their trophies are on display. Food is served only on Sunday lunchtime. There is an attractive small walled garden and a comfortable heated smoking area. ⍟◖⇌(West)♣🏠♨🛜

Foundry Brew Pub 🅛
White Horse Lane, CT1 2RU (just off High St)
🕓 12-midnight (3am Fri & Sat); 12-11 Sun
☎ (01227) 455899 🌐 thefoundrycanterbury.co.uk
Canterbury Foundryman's Gold, Foundry Torpedo, Streetlight Porter; 4 changing beers (often Canterbury) 🅗
The home of Canterbury Brewers, this 19th-century foundry is on two floors. There are usually six ales, brewed on the premises, and it is producing its own ciders. The brewery's bottled ale can be bought to take away. Good-value pub food is available until 8pm (6pm Sun & Mon; 9pm Fri & Sat). A DJ plays upstairs on Friday and Saturday nights. CAMRA members receive a 10 per cent discount on the brewery's ales. There is a pleasant patio. ☺⍟◖&⇌♥🏠🛜

New Inn ♈
19 Havelock Street, CT1 1NP (off ring road near St Augustine's Abbey)
🕓 12-3, 5.30-11.30; 12-midnight Fri & Sat; 12-11.30 Sun
☎ (01227) 464584 🌐 newinncanterbury.co.uk
7 changing beers (often Dark Star, Oakham, Ramsgate) 🅗
Victorian back-street terraced house a few minutes' walk from the cathedral, St Augustine's Abbey and the bus station. The main bar has a cosy woodburner and a jukebox. At the back is a long bright conservatory with newspapers and a range of board games. Beer festivals are held on the Whitsun and August bank holiday weekends. Disabled access is through the attractive garden via Old Ruttington Lane. It has a large whisky selection and an interesting and varying range of seven cask beers. Q☺⍟&♣♥🏠♨🛜

Thomas Tallis Alehouse 🅛

48 Northgate, CT1 1BE

☼ 5-9.30 Mon; 12-11; 12-10 Sun ☎ (01227) 464952

Changing beers (often Kent, Old Dairy, Ramsgate) Ⓖ

Canterbury's first micropub-style alehouse, opened March 2016 in a lovely 15th-century half-timbered building, part of the historic Hospital of St John. Two or three different Kent beers from the cask are served, along with four or five Kentish ciders, and many national and international beers in bottles, cans and key casks. There are two front rooms, one with a log-burning stove, and a rear snug with chairs and a sofa. Generally, table service applies. Outside seating is available on the street.

Q🕭☸🌟🚶♣🚌😾🕏

Unicorn 🅛 ✔

61 St Dunstan's Street, CT2 8BS

☼ 11.30-11 (midnight Fri & Sat) ☎ (01227) 463187

⊕ unicorninn.com

Sharp's Doom Bar; Shepherd Neame Master Brew; 2 changing beers (often Hopdaemon, Ramsgate, Timothy Taylor) Ⓗ

Comfortable 1604 pub near the historic Westgate, with an attractive suntrap garden. Bar billiards is played and a quiz, set by regular customers, is held weekly on Sunday evening. One of the guest beers is usually from one of several Kent microbreweries, and beer updates are posted on Twitter. There is a bottled beer list. Food is good value, with a two-meals-for-£12 special offer on selected meals. Sporting events (not Sky) are televised unobtrusively. Q🕭☸🕪🚶♣🚌😾🕏

Capel

Dovecote Inn

Alders Road, TN12 6SU (½ mile W of A228 towards Tudeley)

☼ 12-3 (not Mon), 5.30-11; 12-10.30 Sun ☎ (01892) 835966

⊕ dovecote-capel.co.uk

Gale's HSB; Harvey's Sussex Best Bitter; 3 changing beers (sourced nationally; often Long Man, Tonbridge, Hop Back) Ⓖ

Superb rural pub close to Tonbridge. Cosy and welcoming with real fires, it has a classic beamed interior garlanded with dried hops. Several separate areas cater for diners and drinkers, and the bar is dominated by an impressive array of wall-mounted barrels dispensing four to five varying ales in top condition, along with Westons Old Rosie cider. A rear decking patio acts as a suntrap, with the local bat and trap game being played in the garden. Good food is served (no food Sun and Mon eves). Q🕭☸🕪🕭♣●P🕏

Charing

Bowl Inn

Egg Hill Road, TN27 0HG (signposted from A20 and A251)

☼ 12-11 (midnight Fri & Sat) ☎ (01233) 712256

⊕ bowlinncharing.com

Sharp's Doom Bar; 3 changing beers (sourced locally; often Hopdaemon, Wantsum, Whitstable) Ⓗ

A 16th-century free house on the top of the North Downs in an Area of Outstanding Natural Beauty. A large inglenook fire warms the bar and there is a large garden with a heated patio area. The pub is a popular stop-off point for walkers and cyclists, and offers five rooms. Camping is also available. In summer the Bowl opens from noon Monday to Saturday. An annual beer festival is held.

🕭☸🛏🕪🕭♿♠P😾🕏

Chatham

Prince of Wales ✔

1-3 Railway Street, ME4 4HU

☼ 8am-11 (1.30am Fri & Sat); 12-10.30 Sun ☎ (01634) 829190

Greene King IPA; 6 changing beers (sourced nationally; often Fuller's, Timothy Taylor, Wells) Ⓗ

The pub is in the main pedestrian part of Chatham town centre, two minutes' walk from the railway and bus stations. It is well known in the area for great-value food and drink, and sports viewing on two floors. The Cask Marque accredited outlet offers six real ales and a discount to CAMRA members, with ale sample jars and detailed tasting notes to help you choose. A large function room is available. ☸🕪♿🕭●🖳

Thomas Waghorn 🅛 ✔

14 Railway Street, ME4 4JL

☼ 8am-midnight (1am Fri & Sat) ☎ (01634) 405422

Greene King IPA, Abbot; Sharp's Doom Bar; house beer (by Rockin' Robin); 4 changing beers (sourced regionally; often Hopdaemon, Westerham, Whitstable) Ⓗ

An establishment ideally situated in the heart of Chatham, with both the railway and bus stations within easy walking distance. The manager is a cask beer enthusiast and this shows in the quality of the ale served. The house ale, Waghorn Express, has been brewed in conjunction with Rockin' Robin brewery only 12 miles away. The pub has many nooks and crannies for you to while away the hours. Q🕭☸🕪♿🕭●🖳🕏

Cliftonville

Tap Room

4 Northdown Parade, Price's Avenue, CT9 2NR

☼ 12-3, 4.30-10 (11 Sat); 12-3 Sun

4 changing beers Ⓖ

This micropub opened in April 2015 in a former takeaway food shop. The walls are adorned with various advertisements in frames and as enamels. An adventurous range of real ales is served on gravity dispense through five wall-mounted quarter-turn taps which are directly connected to casks in a temperature-controlled cellar room behind the wall. There is a bar counter and a single handpump not currently in use but which may enter service at a future date. Q♣●🖳😾🕏

Coldred

Carpenters Arms 🅛

The Green, CT15 5AJ

☼ 5-9 (11 Fri & Sat); 7-11 Sun ☎ (01304) 830190

2 changing beers Ⓗ/Ⓖ

Overlooking the village green and duck pond, this 18th-century two-roomed pub is a real gem and well worth seeking out. It has been in the Fagg family for over a century, and largely unchanged in the last 50 years. The pub is the centre of the community and conversation is king. At least two real ales are served alongside three real ciders from Kentish Pip. The pub hosts regular community events including quizzes and vegetable competitions. A beer festival is held in June. Q⌂♿❀♣💧P🐾🐶🛜

Conyer

Ship ✪
Conyer Quay, ME9 9HR
✪ 12-3, 6-11 (midnight Fri); 10-11.30 Sat; 10-9.30 Sun
☎ (01795) 520881 🌐 shipinnconyer.co.uk
Shepherd Neame Master Brew; 3 changing beers (sourced regionally; often Adnams, Old Dairy) ⊞
An 18th-century creekside pub with a nautically themed interior. Bare floorboards and scrubbed pine tables add rustic charm, and a real fire adds character. The pub is popular with walkers and cyclists and is on the Saxon Shore Way. It is a 20-minute walk from Teynham train station. Food is served in the main bar and in an upstairs dining room. Outside, a small courtyard garden overlooks the creek. Four ales are served.
Q⌂♿❀①♣P🖵(8,344)🐾🛜

Cooling

Horseshoe & Castle ⎣
Main Road, ME3 8DJ
✪ 6-11 Mon; 12-3, 6-11 Tue; 12-11 Wed-Sat; 12-10.30 Sun
☎ (01634) 221691 🌐 horseshoeandcastle.com
Shepherd Neame Master Brew; 1 changing beer (sourced locally) ⊞
This free house is in a village on the Hoo Peninsula. The pub may seem in a remote place, but in reality is only a short distance from the Medway towns. Quality accommodation is available as well as a separate restaurant where good seafood is a speciality. Friendly and welcoming, the owners are approaching three decades in charge. There is always a real ale on from one of Kent's many microbreweries. Q❀⛏🛏①♣P🐾🛜

Cowden

Fountain ✪
30 High Street, TN8 7JG (1 mile W of B2026)
✪ 12-3, 6-11; 12-11 Sun ☎ (01342) 850528
🌐 fountaincowden.com
Harvey's IPA, Sussex Best Bitter; 1 changing beer (sourced locally; often Harvey's) ⊞
An attractive and popular village pub in the west Kent countryside. On offer is a selection of Harvey's beers and good substantial food, served every day in the conservatory restaurant or in the bar. Families, walkers, dogs and all are made welcome by the friendly staff. In the winter there is the warmth of a real fire and, for the summer, there is a pleasant garden to the rear. Accessible by car, bus or rail. Q⌂❀①♣P🖵(234)🐾🛜

Cowden Pound

Queen's Arms ★ ⎣
Hartfield Road, TN8 5NP (on B2026 halfway between Edenbridge and A264)
✪ 5-7.30 (10.30 Mon & Tue; 9 Fri); 12-3 Sun
Larkins Traditional Ale ⊞; 1 changing beer (sourced locally; often Larkins) Ⓖ
Owned and operated by a local family, this is one of only three Kent pubs recognised as having a

nationally important historic interior – the public bar has remained unaltered since the Victorian era. Local Larkins Trad may be accompanied by one of its seasonal beers, enjoyed alongside friendly locals in the ambience of the pub's old-world charm, with open fires in both bars. Customers can bring in their own food to eat at the bar. Q♣P🖵🐾

Crockham Hill

Royal Oak ⎣
Main Road, TN8 6RD (on B2026 jct with B269)
✪ 11-3, 5-11; 11-11 Sat; 12-10.30 Sun ☎ (01732) 866335
🌐 royaloakcrockhamhill.co.uk
Westerham Finchcocks Original; 3 changing beers (sourced locally; often Westerham) ⊞
One of two Westerham Brewery-owned pubs offering a selection of its beers according to season, which can be served in three third-pint sampler trays. A sympathetic refurbishment of the building, parts of which date back to the 16th century including stone-mullioned and leaded windows, has been carried out. The smart and comfortable furnishings are enhanced by a log fire, and amusing Tottering cartoons adorn the walls. Walkers and cyclists are attracted to the delightful countryside and the home-cooked dishes. Q❀①♣P🖵(236)🐾🛜

Dartford

Dartford Working Men's Club ⎣
Essex Road, DA1 2AU
✪ 11-11; 12-10.30 Sun ☎ (01322) 223646
🌐 dartfordwm.club
Courage Best Bitter ⊞; 14 changing beers (sourced regionally; often Caveman, Oakham, Thornbridge) ⊞/Ⓖ
Finalist for CAMRA National Club of the Year 2017, this venue has 15 ales on handpump, plus ciders on gravity. The ales come from various micro and regional breweries, with over 500 different ales served each year. The club is home to the BBC award-winning Dartford Folk Club, meeting on Tuesday evenings, and has live music every Saturday and Sunday night. A quiz is on the first Wednesday of the month and a live tribute act the last Friday. CAMRA members are welcome as guests. ⌂❀①♿≠♣💧🖵🛜

Foresters ✪
15/16 Great Queen Street, DA1 1TJ
✪ 12-11.30; 12-11 Sun ☎ (01322) 223087
Adnams Ghost Ship; Harvey's Sussex Best Bitter; 1 changing beer (sourced regionally; often Exmoor, Wychwood, Young's) ⊞
Five minutes' walk from the town centre, this pleasant back-street local offers two regular beers plus a guest ale sourced nationally. Busy in the evenings, darts (male and female), pool and crib teams operate from here regularly. It has an L-shaped bar with a wood-burning fire at one end. In the graveyard opposite is the unmarked pauper's grave of steam pioneer Richard Trevithick, its approximate location being indicated by a plaque on the north wall. ⌂❀≠♣💧🖵🐾

Malt Shovel
3 Darenth Road, DA1 1LP
✪ 3 (12 Thu)-11; 12-midnight Fri; 12-11 Sat; 12-10.30 Sun
☎ (01322) 224381

St Austell Tribute; Young's Bitter, Special; 2 changing beers (sourced nationally) Ⓗ
This Young's-owned pub is five minutes' walk from the town centre. It has two bars – a low-ceilinged taproom featuring an 1880s Dartford Brewery mirror, and a larger bar leading to a conservatory where meals are served Thursday to Sunday lunchtimes and Friday and Saturday evenings. A large beer garden is accessed from the conservatory. Quiz night is Monday and crib night Tuesday. The Fastrack B bus stops nearby.
Q❀◑⇌P🖛

Deal

Farrier Ⓛ
90 Manor Road, CT14 9DB
🕭 12-11; 12-10.30 Sun ☎ (01304) 360080
House beer (by Ripple Steam); 2 changing beers Ⓗ
This traditional black and white beamed inn is at least 16th century, possibly older, and is reputedly the oldest pub in Deal. It has a real community feel to it, a friendly ambience, and is a relaxing place to drink and chat. There is plenty of seating and two open fires, and the background music is kept deliberately quiet. If you are peckish, light bar snacks are available. The events diary includes pool and darts, monthly quiz nights and a Sunday meat raffle. ⏃❀Å♣P🖛😺🛜

Just Reproach Ⓛ
14 King Street, CT14 6HX
🕭 12-3, 5-8 (9 Tue-Thu); 12-2, 5-11 Fri; 12-11 Sat; 12-4 Sun
4 changing beers Ⓖ
One of Kent's first micropubs, in the town centre. The welcoming ambience, high benches and table service make for a friendly, convivial atmosphere. Up to five real ales are served, with at least one from a Kent brewery. Ciders are from Kent producers, typically Kent Cider Company. Wines from the local Barnsole vineyard, and quality soft drinks, are also sold. Snacks include pork pies and local cheese. No keg, no fruit machines, no music, and do not let your mobile phone ring!
Q⏃⇌♣🖛😺

Ship Inn Ⓛ
141 Middle Street, CT14 6JZ
🕭 11-midnight; 12-midnight Sun ☎ (01304) 372222
Dark Star Hophead; Ramsgate Gadds' No.7 Bitter Ale; 3 changing beers (often Dark Star, Ramsgate) Ⓗ
Only 10 minutes' walk from the town centre, this unspoilt, traditional pub is in Deal's historic conservation area. Dark wooden floors and subdued lighting give a warm and comfortable atmosphere, complemented by the nautical theme. A wide variety of drinkers enjoy the good range of beers dispensed from the five handpumps, including beers from Ramsgate and Dark Star. There is a small cosy rear bar overlooking a large patio garden, accessed by a staircase, with a covered smoking area. ⏃❀♣🖛😺

Dover

Eight Bells Ⓛ ✅
19 Cannon Street, CT16 1BZ
🕭 8am-midnight (1am Fri & Sat) ☎ (01304) 205030
Greene King Abbot; Ruddles Best Bitter; Sharp's Doom Bar; 8 changing beers Ⓗ

The name of this popular and bustling Wetherspoon pub, situated on the precinct, is linked to the church opposite. Inside, there is a large open-plan room with a long bar and a raised restaurant area. At the front an enclosed seating area looks out onto the precinct. Twelve handpumps dispense a range of regular and guest ales, with at least two from a Kent microbrewery. There are real ale offers on Monday. The pub is close to public transport services.
Q⏃❀◑🕭⇌♦🖛🛜

Lanes 🍷 Ⓛ
15 Worthington Street, CT17 9AQ
🕭 12-11 (6 Mon); 1-10 Sun ☎ 07504 258332
5 changing beers Ⓖ
A friendly micropub, comfortably furnished and carpeted, near the pedestrian precinct. Real ales, ciders, wines, a mead and soft drinks are from Kent producers. Five real ales from microbreweries (two from Kent) and 10 or more ciders are served on gravity dispense from the temperature-controlled cellar room. There is no keg beer, lager, or piped music. Snacks can be brought in from the local deli and a feasting board is available with 48 hours' notice. Dogs on a lead are allowed, but no children.
Q♣⇌♣🍺🐾😺🛜

Louis Armstrong Ⓛ
58 Maison Dieu Road, CT16 1RA
🕭 3-11; 7-11 Sun ☎ (01304) 204759
🌐 thelouisarmstrong.com
Hopdaemon Skrimshander IPA; 3 changing beers Ⓗ
Down-to-earth pub and music venue that has featured live music for over 50 years. The large L-shaped bar and stage are surrounded by music posters, a large mirror and long bench seating. Up to four real ales are stocked, principally from Kent microbreweries, and a real cider from Dudda's Tun. On Wednesday evening, good-value food and real ales for £2.50 are served. There is a monthly charity quiz night. It has a pleasant beer garden and is easily accessible by bus. A public car park is opposite. ❀◑♣🖛😺🛜

Mash Tun Ⓛ
3 Bench Street, CT16 1JH
🕭 closed Mon & Tue; 12-10; 12-4 Sun ☎ (01304) 219590
House beer (by Westerham) Ⓐ; 2 changing beers Ⓖ
Comfortable micropub on the edge of Dover's shopping precinct. Soft armchairs, a sofa, tables and chairs give the bar a homely feel. A 200-year-old church pulpit forms the pub's bar. On offer is a varying list of ales, including a gluten-free, unrefined Pilsner-style ale from Westerham, and a large range of ciders from rare and smaller cider makers including some from Kent. There is no food, but customers are welcome to bring their own or order a takeaway. Open Monday and Tuesday by arrangement. ⏃❀◑⇌♣🖛😺🛜

Rack of Ale Ⓛ
7 Park Place, CT16 1DF
🕭 4-10; 12-1am Fri & Sat ☎ 07452 817420
5 changing beers Ⓗ/Ⓖ
Modern two-roomed pub with a simple but quirky decor. It encourages conversation, reading a paper or a book, or playing a game or two, but frowns upon the use of mobile phones. Typically five real ales, including beers from Kent microbreweries, and cider from Kentish Pip, are served, on a tasting rack if requested. Occasional beer festivals are held. Food is not available but you can bring your

own. Opening hours are flexible, depending on how busy the pub is. There is a loyalty card scheme. Q☕⇥♣●🚻🚃☼

Thirsty Scarecrow
107 High Street, CT16 1EB
✪ closed Mon; 12-10; 1-9 Sun ☎ 07454 934833
1 changing beer Ⓖ
This cider micropub opened in what was previously the Corner Café. It is rustically and brightly furnished on two levels, which are linked by a small set of stairs. The chilled cellar room is on the upper level, from which 20-25 ciders and perries and a single cask ale are served on gravity dispense. There is also a small selection of bottled beers. The ciders/perries major on Kentish cider makers, but may come from far and wide.
☕☼♣●🚻🚃☼

Dunk's Green

Kentish Rifleman Ⓛ
Roughway Lane, TN11 9RU (jct with Dunks Green Rd, 4 miles N of Tonbridge, off A227)
✪ 11.30-3, 6-11; 11.30-11 Fri-Sun ☎ (01732) 810727
⊕ thekentishrifleman.co.uk
Harvey's Sussex Best Bitter; Whitstable Native Bitter; 2 changing beers (sourced locally; often Tonbridge, Westerham) Ⓗ
A beautiful 16th-century pub in a quiet hamlet, close to Tonbridge and Sevenoaks, and a popular stop for cyclists and walkers with or without dogs. Support for local producers is reflected in the good food available in the restaurant and bar (no food Sun and Mon eve) and in the local Kentish beers. There is a pretty rear garden ideal when beer festivals are held. Internally the bar is hung with antique rifles and features an open fire.
Q☕☼🍴◑P🚃(222,404)☼☎

East Malling

King & Queen Ⓛ ✔
1 New Road, ME19 6DD
✪ 11 (12 Sat)-11; 12-6 Sun ☎ (01732) 842752
⊕ kingandqueeneastmalling.co.uk
Harvey's Sussex Best Bitter; Musket Fife and Drum; 2 changing beers (sourced nationally) Ⓗ
A 16th-century Grade II-listed inn noted for the quality of its restaurant food and traditional bar snacks available all day. The garden is pleasant in the summer and dogs are welcome here but not in the bar. Quiz nights and occasional music or comedy nights take place on Sunday evenings, for which the pub stays open later. Accommodation is available at the rear with three well-appointed rooms. Handy for the station.
Q☕☼🍴◑⇥P🚃(58)☎

Eastry

Five Bells Ⓛ ✔
The Cross, CT13 0HX
✪ 11-11.30 (1am Fri & Sat) ☎ (01304) 611188
⊕ thefivebellseastry.com
Greene King IPA; Wantsum Black Prince; 1 changing beer Ⓗ
Traditional community pub in the heart of the village, well served by local buses. It has a comfortable lounge bar and public bar. Three ales

are sold, including a mild from the Wantsum Brewery. The old fire station, with historic memorabilia, serves as a restaurant/function room. The busy calendar features live music, quiz nights and an Easter beer festival. Home-made food is served all day, plus a good-value two-course lunchtime menu Monday to Friday. The suntrap patio has a children's play area and pétanque pitch. ☕☼🍴◑▲♣P🚃☎

Eynsford

Five Bells
High Street, DA4 0AB
✪ 3 (12 Sat)-11; 12-10.30 Sun ☎ (01322) 863135
Harvey's Sussex Best Bitter; Sharp's Doom Bar; 2 changing beers (sourced nationally; often Courage, Dark Star) Ⓗ
Traditional community pub in the heart of an attractive village. The public bar retains a homely atmosphere with wooden tables and a wood-burning fire in winter. It also has a comfortable separate saloon bar. Quiz night is the third Thursday of each month. There is a pleasant garden to the rear and a small car park. Dogs are welcome in the public bar. Food is not served here but try its larger sister pub, the Malt Shovel, nearby.
Q☼♣P🚃(421)☼☎

Faversham

Bear Inn
3 Market Place, ME13 7AG
✪ 10.30-11; 11.30-11 Sun ☎ (01795) 532668
⊕ bearinnfaversham.co.uk
Shepherd Neame Master Brew; 1 changing beer (sourced locally; often Shepherd Neame) Ⓗ
A 16th-century pub in Faversham's historic market square, popular with visitors to the town and locals alike. The traditional and historic interior has three separate bar areas running the length of the building. The lunchtime menu is good, and a seasonal Shepherd Neame beer is often featured. A general knowledge quiz is held on the last Monday of the month. Tables outside at the front are busy in summer. Q◑⇥♣🚃☼☎

Elephant Ⓛ ✔
31 The Mall, ME13 8JN
✪ closed Mon; 3 (12 Sat)-11; 12-7 Sun ☎ (01795) 590157
5 changing beers (sourced regionally; often Dark Star, Mad Cat, Rother Valley) Ⓗ
A popular and characterful pub close to Faversham railway station. The five changing beers often include rarer styles such as mild, and they mainly come from microbreweries. Local real cider, often from Kent Cider Company or Dudda's Tun, is available on handpump. The pub has a log fire and a large enclosed garden. Regular music nights feature and dogs and children are welcome. A house beer is brewed by Hopdaemon or Mad Cat.
☕☼⇥♣●🚻🚃☼☎

Furlongs Ale House
6A Preston Street, ME13 8NS
✪ 4-10; 3-11 Fri; 12-11 Sat; 12-9 Sun ☎ 07747 776200
5 changing beers (sourced locally; often Canterbury Ales, Kent, Ramsgate) Ⓗ
Faversham's first micropub opened in late-2014 and is proving very popular. The beers drawn by handpump from the cellar to a small bar are mainly

from Kent microbreweries, although others from across the UK also feature. Kent wines and ciders are also served. Micropub wooden bench-style seating and solid tables predominate. It offers a CAMRA discount on ale and cider. Q❄️➹➖🍴🚪🐾

Shipwrights Arms 🅛

Hollowshore, ME13 7TU (over 1 mile N of Faversham at confluence of Faversham and Oare creeks) TR017636
🕑 closed Mon; 11-3, 6-10; 11-11 Sat; 12-10 Sun
☎ (01795) 590088 🌐 theshipwrightsathollowshore.co.uk
Goacher's Real Mild Ale, Special/House Ale, Old 1066; 3 changing beers (sourced locally; often Bexley, Kent) 🅖
Remote 300-year-old family-run free house with a jolly, welcoming, old-style landlord – a good pub to relax in after a 45-minute walk across the marshes from Faversham. The wooden-clad building's interior reflects its nautical heritage, with many associated ornaments and pictures on display or tucked into nooks and crannies. The large garden at the rear is open spring to autumn, with outside seating at the front in all seasons. Extended opening hours operate in the summer. In severe winter weather telephone to check opening times. Q❄️🕷️🍴♣️P🐾

Finglesham

Crown Inn 🅛

The Street, CT14 0NA
🕑 12-11; 12-10 Sun ☎ (01304) 612555
🌐 thecrownatfinglesham.co.uk
Dark Star Hophead; 2 changing beers 🅗
Traditional village pub with a warm welcome and a friendly atmosphere. Three to four real ales, one usually from a local microbrewery, are served, and you can get quality home-made food lunchtimes and evenings, including a roast on Sunday. Eat in the bar or the restaurant, which opens onto the pleasant garden. Occasional live music events take place, bat and trap is played in summer, and there is a children's play area. Buses are a 5-15 minutes' walk, depending on the day and time. The magnificent Kentish barn is available for functions and weddings. 🕷️🍴♣️P🚪🐾📶

Folkestone

Chambers 🅛

Radnor Chambers, Cheriton Place, CT20 2BB (off Hythe end of Sandgate Rd)
🕑 12-11 (1am Fri & Sat); closed Sun ☎ (01303) 223333
Adnams Lighthouse; 4 changing beers 🅗
A spacious cellar bar with six handpumps beneath a licensed coffee shop; beers include some from local breweries and at least two real ciders. A beer festival is held over the Easter weekend. Food including Mexican, European and daily specials is served (no food Mon and Fri eves). There is a disco on Friday, a quiz on the first Sunday of the month and live music on Thursday, usually with free admission. 🕷️🍴➹🍴🚪📶

Firkin Alehouse

18 Cheriton Place, CT20 2AZ
🕑 12-9 (10 Fri & Sat); 12-4 Sun ☎ 07894 068432
🌐 firkinalehouse.co.uk
3 changing beers 🅖
Folkestone's first micropub sells up to four cask beers, often including one from a Kent

microbrewery. No lager, alcopops or spirits are sold but there is a limited wine selection and six ciders are always available. Traditional bar snacks include pickled eggs and pickled onions. There is no music or pub games, only good company and conversation, making it a place to enjoy a nice drink. The use of mobile phones is prohibited and their usage incurs a minimum donation of £1 to charity. Q➹🍴🚪🐾

Kipps' Alehouse

11-15 Old High Street, CT20 1RL
🕑 12-10 (11 Fri & Sat) ☎ (01303) 246766
3 changing beers (sourced regionally; often Mad Cat) 🅖
Real ale is on gravity dispense from casks racked in a cooled stillage enclosed in glass. There is usually a Kentish ale, an award winner and another unusual beer from around the country. All ales are from small independent microbreweries. Several ciders are on sale from boxes on the bar counter. This micropub is unusual in that it serves a variety of bottled and draught international lagers together with a selection of international wines, gins, port and sherry. 🕷️🍴♿🍴🚪🐾📶

Frittenden

Bell & Jorrocks

Biddenden Road, TN17 2EJ TQ815412
🕑 12 (3 Mon & Tue)-11; 12-10.30 Sun ☎ (01580) 852415
🌐 thebellandjorrocks.co.uk
Harvey's Sussex Best Bitter; Woodforde's Wherry; 2 changing beers (sourced nationally; often Dark Star, Rother Valley, Tonbridge) 🅗
This charming pub is very much the centre of the local community. It was originally called the Bell and gained its current name when the other pub in the village, the John Jorrocks, closed in 1969. The pub sign celebrates both antecedents. A coaching inn dating from the early 18th century, the stables hold a beer festival in mid-April. It is a good base for circular walks in the picturesque Low Weald and for exploring the famous Frittenden Treacle Mines. Excellent food is served. 🕷️🍴▲♣️🐾📶

Gillingham

Past & Present 🍷 🅛

2 Skinner Street, ME7 1HD
🕑 12-7 (9 Thu; 11 Fri & Sat); 12-6.30 Sun ☎ 07725 072293
🌐 pastandpresentmicropub.co.uk
3 changing beers (sourced locally) 🅖
Medway's first micropub, a friendly community venue, with a minimum of three ales on gravity dispense and up to eight ciders. It has an interesting display of closed Gillingham pubs (Past) and Kent micropubs (Present). Service is friendly, with crisps and nuts available together with meals from an adjacent café. It stages an Easter cider festival and an August bank holiday ale festival. No admittance after 10pm on Friday/Saturday. Local CAMRA Pub of the Year and Cider Pub of the Year 2017. Q🕷️🕷️➹♣️🍴🐾

Will Adams

73 Saxton Street, ME7 5EG
🕑 7-11; 12.30-4, 7-11 Sat; 12.30-4, 7.30-11 Sun
☎ (01634) 575902
3 changing beers (sourced nationally; often Dark Star, Oakham, St Austell) 🅗

A back-street corner venue and a previous CAMRA branch Pub of the Year winner, it takes its name from a local seafarer and adventurer. Three ales are available, with up to five on Gillingham FC home match days. The pub also sells three cask ciders and a perry, plus, for whisky connoisseurs, up to 30 single malts. Various games are provided, a pool table is used avidly by locals, and it supports darts league teams. Sports events and football matches are screened. ⊛◁≽♣♠⍾⌨♨ ♥

Historic riverside pub near the town pier and ferry to Tilbury, with good views of the Thames from the rear terrace garden. The elegant main bar area has chandeliers and a log fire, with local photographs, and there are two upstairs function rooms. No TV or gaming machines, just background music at times. Home-cooked meals are served at lunchtimes. Up to six real ales include several from local breweries. May close early if very quiet. ♿⊛◁&≽⌨♨ ♥

Graveney

Freewheel
Head Hill Road, ME13 9DE
⊛ 9am-9 ☎ (01795) 538143 ⊕ thefreewheel.pub
3 changing beers (sourced locally; often Canterbury) Ⓗ
Reopened in April 2015, the present owners have turned this venue into a true community hub, with film and music nights. During the day it doubles as a cycle repair shop. Beers are from local breweries and the house ale comes from Canterbury Brewers. Ciders are from Kentish Pip and the Kent Cider Company. The cycle business opens at 9am and beer is served from midday.
Q♿⊛◁♣♠P⍾⌨(660)♨ ♥

Gravesend

Compass Alehouse Ⓛ
7 Manor Road, DA12 1AA
⊛ closed Mon; 12-2 (not Tue & Wed), 5-9; 12-2, 5-10 Fri; 12-10 Sat; 1-6 Sun ☎ 07873 918545
4 changing beers (sourced nationally) Ⓖ
Micropub opened in autumn 2014 in a former estate agents. There is a small front room and an even smaller room off a little courtyard to the rear. Up to four different real ales are sold, frequently from Kentish breweries. At least three ciders are available, again often from Kent producers. It has a convivial atmosphere and conversation is paramount – but talking on mobile phones is outlawed, with a fine for charity. Water is provided for dogs. Q♿⊛⍾≽♠⍾⌨♨

Jolly Drayman
1 Love Lane, Wellington Street, DA12 1JA
⊛ 12-11.30 (midnight Fri & Sat); 12-11 Sun
☎ (01474) 352355 ⊕ jollydrayman.com
Dark Star Hophead; Skinner's Betty Stogs; 3 changing beers (sourced nationally) Ⓗ
A comfortable and cosy pub with a friendly, intimate atmosphere, just to the east of the town on the site of Walker's Wellington Brewery. Three guest beers include either St Austell Tribute or Proper Job. It has quirky low ceilings and a relaxed atmosphere, with a TV that is muted and no gaming machines. Daddlums (Kentish skittles) is played on Sunday. The pub hosts men's and women's darts teams. There is live music on the first Saturday of every month.
♿⊛⍾⊠◁≽♣♠P⌨♨ ♥

Rum Puncheon Ⓛ
87 West Street, DA11 0BL (on one-way system between parish church and river)
⊛ closed Mon; 11-11 (11.30 Fri); 12-11 Sat; 12-9 Sun
☎ (01474) 353434 ⊕ rumpuncheon.co.uk
6 changing beers (sourced nationally; often Bexley, Tonbridge) Ⓗ

Three Daws Ⓛ
7 Town Pier, DA11 0BJ
⊛ 11-11 (1am Fri & Sat); 12-11 Sun ☎ (01474) 566869
⊕ threedaws.co.uk
6 changing beers (sourced locally; often Bexley, Dartford Wobbler, Tonbridge) Ⓗ
An historic inn steeped in tales of smugglers, press gangs, ghosts and secret tunnels. From the back room and terrace there are spectaclar views of the Thames and passing river traffic. The pub offers various rooms and nooks and crannies enhanced by photos and pictures of local interest. The large selection of real ales always includes some from Kent microbreweries. Meals are served until 9pm every day. Live music features on Friday, a quiz on Sunday. ♿⊛◁≽♣♠⌨♥

Groombridge

Crown Inn Ⓛ
Groombridge Hill, TN3 9QH (on village green)
⊛ 12-3, 5.30-11; 12-11 Sat; 12-10 Sun ☎ (01892) 864742
⊕ thecrowngroombridge.com
Black Cat Original; Harvey's Sussex Best Bitter; Larkins Traditional Ale Ⓗ
Proudly overlooking the village green and Groombridge Place beyond, this charming family-run pub dates back to the 16th century. A rare outlet for Black Cat beer, which may increase to a choice of two when open all day May to September. The Crown is a popular stop-off for villagers, walkers, families and rock climbers. Food from the popular restaurant can be enjoyed inside, surrounded by the pub's many original features or, in summer, outside using the front or rear seating.
Q♿⊛⊠◁♠≽♣♠P⍾(291)♨ ♥

Halstead

Rose & Crown
Otford Lane, TN14 7EA
⊛ 12-midnight ☎ (01959) 533120
Larkins Traditional Ale; 5 changing beers (sourced nationally; often Bexley, Rudgate, Tonbridge) Ⓗ
A homely Victorian brick and flint free house serving a wide choice of ales from Kentish brewers and from afar, often featuring a mild alongside local favourite Larkins Trad. A sports-orientated front bar sits between a separate restaurant or function room and an informal side bar for diners and drinkers, complete with log fire. Keenly priced home-cooked dishes are served until 3pm weekdays and 5pm weekends, along with a children's menu, and over-50s meal offers are displayed prominently on chalkboards.
♿⊛◁♣P⍾(402,R5)♨ ♥

Harvel

Amazon & Tiger 🅛
Harvel Street, DA13 0DE
🕓 4 (6 Mon)-11; 12-11 Fri & Sat; 12-10.30 Sun
☎ (01474) 814705
3 changing beers (sourced locally; often Kent, Tonbridge) 🅗
This hostelry was purpose built in 1914 in the centre of a remote village close to popular footpaths in the North Downs. It has two distinct bar areas where modern furnishings combine with flagstones and wood floors. The TV and bar billiards table are in separate areas. Food is served Friday and Saturday lunchtimes and evenings, with speciality fresh fish night on Thursday, and Sunday lunches. Real ales come mainly from West Kent and East Sussex. The large garden overlooks the village cricket ground. Q🐕🕸🍴🌓🅙▲♣P🌼�

Hastingleigh

Bowl Inn 🍷 🅛
The Street, TN25 5HU TR095449
🕓 closed Mon; 5-9 (10 Thu & Fri); 12-10 Sat; 12-9 Sun
☎ (01233) 750354 🌐 thebowlonline.co.uk
3 changing beers (sourced locally) 🅗
This lovingly restored listed village pub building retains many period features, including a taproom used for playing pool and decorated with vintage advertising material. The lovely garden has a tame European eagle owl. A beer festival is held on the August bank holiday Monday. Excellent sandwiches and baguettes are available weekends. The pub will stay open if custom warrants it or if you phone ahead. The adjacent barn is used for blues and folk music and open mic evenings. Local CAMRA Pub of the Year 2017. Q🐕🕸🌓♣🅙P

Herne

Butcher's Arms 🅛
29A Herne Street, CT6 7HL (opp church)
🕓 closed Mon; 12-1.30, 6-9; 1-3 Sun ☎ (01227) 371000
🌐 micropub.co.uk
Adnams Broadside; Dark Star Hophead; Old Dairy Copper Top; 2 changing beers (sourced locally; often Adnams, Ramsgate) 🅖
Britain's first micropub, opened in 2005, is a real ale gem and the inspiration for other micropubs. Once a butcher's shop, it still has the original chopping tables. There is seating for 12 customers and standing room for 20 – the compact drinking area ensuring lively banter. The range of ales changes frequently, and customers can also buy beer to drink at home. The pub has won many CAMRA awards and the landlord was voted one of CAMRA's top 40 campaigners. Q▲🅙🌼

Herne Bay

Bouncing Barrel 🅛
20 Bank Street, CT6 5EA
🕓 closed Mon; 12-2, 6-9; 12-11 Sat; 12-2 Sun ☎ 07777 630685
4 changing beers (often Goody Ales, Old Dairy, Ramsgate) 🅖
Welcoming micropub with bench seating for 20 customers around old workshop tables. The beer range changes regularly and is mainly from microbreweries, generally at least one from a Kent brewery. Local snacks are available. The pub is named after the bombs used in the Dam Buster raids, which were tested off the coast nearby. The pub has a mural of a bomber flying past the Reculver Towers. A small beer festival is held over the May Day weekend. Q🐕🕸♣🍴🅙🌼

Hildenborough

Plough 🅛 ✅
Leigh Road, TN11 9AJ (½ mile S of Hildenborough at Powdermills)
🕓 closed Mon & Tue; 12-11; 12-9 Sun ☎ (01732) 832149
🌐 theploughatleigh.com
Tonbridge Coppernob; 2 changing beers (sourced locally; often Musket, Old Dairy, Rockin' Robin) 🅗
A 16th-century inn clearly amalgamated from several cottages and imbued with rambling charm, close to the outskirts of Tonbridge yet quintessentially rural. Features include low beams heavily decked with hops, a stone floor, and the centrepiece – a magnificent double-sided log fire. The tenants are keen to support Kent breweries, offering a revolving range of beers. The peaceful garden sits by a meandering stream. An impressive great barn is used for functions which may close the pub at times, so it is worth checking by phone before visiting. Q🐕🕸🌓♣P🅙(210)🌼widehat

Horton Kirby

Bull 🅛 ✅
Lombard Street, DA4 9DF
🕓 12-11; 12-10.30 Sun ☎ (01322) 860341
🌐 thebullhortonkirby.com
Dark Star Hophead; 3 changing beers (sourced nationally) 🅗
Comfortable one-bar village local with a large garden affording views across the Darent Valley, a mile from Farningham Road railway station and close to the daytime 414 bus route. This friendly pub has five handpumps, with one regular and three rotating guest ales as well as one real cider. There is an open mic night on the first Friday night of each month. 🐕🕸🌓♣🍴🅙(414)🌼widehat

Hythe

Potting Shed 🅛
160A High Street, CT21 5JR
🕓 closed Mon; 12-6 Tue (7 Wed & Thu; 9 Fri & Sat); 12-4 Sun ☎ 07780 877226
4 changing beers (sourced regionally) 🅖
A former café that has been converted into a micro-alehouse, retaining the original high service counter. At the Folkestone end of Hythe High Street, this alehouse serves an interesting range of ales from around the country including at least one local Kentish beer, usually from Hop Fuzz. Ciders and ales are on gravity except for one ale which is sometimes pulled through a handpump. Limited bar snacks are available. A good place to enjoy a drink and interesting conversation. 🕸🍴🅙widehat

Three Mariners 🅛
37 Windmill Street, CT21 6BH
🕓 4-10 Mon; 12-11 (midnight Fri & Sat); 12-10.30 Sun
☎ (01303) 260406

Young's Bitter; 4 changing beers (sourced regionally) Ⓗ
Hidden away in a side street not far from the Royal Military Canal, this traditional corner two-bar pub is well worth visiting, and an ideal destination after a walk along the canal or a trip on the narrow gauge Romney Hythe & Dymchurch Railway. With no food available, customers come to enjoy the quality of the ales and cider and a friendly atmosphere. The enclosed outside area is partly heated.
🛏️⊛❄♣♠🖳🛒

Ickham

Duke William
The Street, CT3 1QP
🕐 11-11 (midnight Fri & Sat); 10-10.30 Sun
☎ (01227) 721308 ⊕ thedukewilliamickham.com
3 changing beers (sourced locally; often Timothy Taylor) Ⓗ
This attractive, busy pub in a quintessentially English village is welcoming towards locals, diners and drinkers. The guest ales are sourced mostly from local microbreweries. The pub has been recently renovated and is the latest addition to Chef of the Year 2002 and ex-Gordon Ramsay restaurant head chef Mark Sargeant's portfolio. Brunch is available 11am-noon Friday to Sunday. Events include live music, a magician on Friday night, and occasional beer festivals.
🛏️⊛🛆◑🖳(11)🐾🛜

Ightham Common

Old House ★ Ⓛ
Redwell Lane, Redwell, TN15 9EE (½ mile SW of Ightham village, between A25 and A227) TQ590558
🕐 7-11 (9 Mon & Tue); 12-3, 7-11 Sat & Sun
☎ (01732) 886077 ⊕ oldhouse.pub
6 changing beers (sourced regionally; often Harvey's, Oakham, Otter) Ⓖ
Kentish red-brick, tile-hung cottage in a narrow and isolated country lane. The public bar features a Victorian wood-panelled counter, parquet flooring and an imposing inglenook fireplace. The parlour is a quiet haven. Up to six rotating beers are dispensed by gravity from wooden casks from the chilled taproom, always including at least one bitter, a golden ale and a dark beer from a large range of local and regional breweries. On CAMRA's National Inventory of Historic Pub Interiors.
Q⊛Å♣♠P🐾🛜

Ivychurch

Bell Inn ✅
Ashford Road, TN29 0AL (signed from A2070 between Brenzett and Hamstreet, 1 mile from A259/A2070 roundabout at Brenzett) TR028275
🕐 12-11; 12-10.30 Sun ☎ (01797) 344355
⊕ thebellinnromneymarsh.co.uk
St Austell Trelawny; Sharp's Doom Bar, Atlantic; 2 changing beers Ⓗ
A pretty 16th-century free house adjacent to St George's Church with a warm welcome for allcomers. CAMRA branch Pub of the Year in 2016, its real ales and beers are also award winners. During the colder months a wood-burning stove adds to the comfortable atmosphere. The Bell Inn is well worth finding and is steeped in marshland

history – it was once the centre of smugglers known as the Romney Marsh Owlers.
🛏️⊛◑♣♠P🐾🛜

Laddingford

Chequers ✅
The Street, ME18 6BP TQ689481
🕐 12-3, 5-11; 12-11 Sat & Sun ☎ (01622) 871266
⊕ chequersladdingford.co.uk
Adnams Southwold Bitter; 3 changing beers (sourced nationally) Ⓗ
An attractive, oak-beamed pub, dating from the 15th century, that has one double letting room. It is at the heart of village life, with a variety of events held throughout the year, including a beer festival in late April. A roaring log fire keeps customers warm in winter, and the pub frontage is a sea of flowers in summer. Good food is served and, on Thursdays, a wide selection of sausage dishes is available. The large garden has children's play equipment. Buses stop outside.
Q🛏️⊛🛆◑♣P🖳(23,26)🐾🛜

Loose

Chequers Ⓛ
Old Loose Hill, ME15 0BL
🕐 12-11 (11.30 Fri & Sat); 12-10.30 Sun ☎ (01622) 743125
⊕ theloosechequers.com
Fuller's London Pride; Harvey's Sussex Best Bitter; Rockin' Robin Reliant Robin; Sharp's Doom Bar; Shepherd Neame Master Brew; 1 changing beer (often Rockin' Robin, Timothy Taylor) Ⓗ
This former 17th-century coaching inn on the old road to Hastings has been tastefully decorated to emphasise original oak beams. It lies in Loose Valley by the side of a trout stream in the shadow of a Thomas Telford viaduct. Traditional home-cooked food is served including vegetarian options. Live music is played monthly and there is an annual duck race on the river. Morris dancers feature every Boxing Day. 🛏️⊛◑♿P🖳(5,89)🐾🛜

Lower Halstow

Three Tuns Ⓛ
The Street, ME9 7DY
🕐 12-11 (midnight Fri & Sat); 12-10.30 Sun
☎ (01795) 842840 ⊕ thethreetunsrestaurant.co.uk
Goacher's Real Mild Ale; 3 changing beers (sourced locally; often Caveman, Hop Fuzz, Wantsum) Ⓗ
True family village pub with a friendly, cheerful atmosphere and lively conversation. The owners actively support real ale, offering mainly Kentish ales and several local ciders including Dudda's Tun. It has a good reputation for high-quality locally sourced food and has won many awards. A beer festival is held during the summer bank holiday and there are monthly quizzes. A log fire, sofa seating, brick walls and beams add character. It has a large garden with streamside decking.
🛏️⊛◑♿♣♠P🖳🐾🛜

Luddesdown

Cock Inn Ⓛ ✅
Henley Street, DA13 0XB TQ664672

☼ 12-11; 12-10.30 Sun ☎ (01474) 814208
⊕ cockluddesdowne.com

Adnams Lighthouse, Southwold Bitter, Broadside; Goacher's Real Mild Ale; St Austell Trelawny; Young's Bitter; 2 changing beers (sourced regionally; often Musket) ⊞

Ultra-traditional rural free house dating from 1713 and under the same ownership since 1984. It has two distinct bars, a large conservatory, a separate function room, and a comfortable heated smoking area, and is a meeting place for many local clubs and societies. Traditional pub games are played including pétanque, bar billiards and several forms of darts. There is a free quiz on Tuesday evenings devised and hosted by the landlord. Children are not allowed in the bars or garden. Q❀◐♣P✿

Maidstone

Cellars Alehouse

The Old Brewery, Buckland Road, ME16 0DZ (if front gates closed use rear via alley alongside railway)
☼ closed Mon; 4.30-9 Tue & Wed; 4.30-11 Thu; 12-11 Fri & Sat; 12-6 Sun ☎ (01622) 761045 ⊕ thecellarsalehouse.co.uk
5 changing beers (sourced nationally; often Burning Sky, Dark Star, Ramsgate) Ⓖ

Situated in what was the barley wine cellar of the old Style & Winch Brewery, access is down a flight of steps, revealing a surprisingly spacious interior. The vaulted ceiling is adorned with pumpclips. Up to five real ales from far and wide are served by gravity from the capacious cool room. Several real ciders are also stocked. Regular nights feature quiz, folk music, comedy, curry and Meet the Brewer events. Q➸♣●🚍

Flower Pot ♟ Ⓛ

96 Sandling Road, ME14 2RJ
☼ 12 (11 Sat)-11; 12-10.30 Sun ☎ (01622) 757705
⊕ flowerpotpub.com
Goacher's Gold Star Strong Ale; 8 changing beers (sourced nationally; often Dark Star, Maidstone, Oakham) ⊞

Split-level street-corner free house, a must-visit when in Maidstone. The upper bar has nine handpumps, with the ales coming mainly from microbreweries. Up to four ciders and perries are served directly from the container. The lower bar has a pool table and there are video screens showing the beers and ciders on offer and the prices. The football ground is nearby. There are music nights every other Saturday and jam nights on Tuesdays. A beer festival is held in June. ❀◐➸♣●🖥🚍(101,155)✿🛜

Olde Thirsty Pig Ⓛ ✔

4a Knightrider Street, ME15 6LP
☼ 12-1am (2am Fri; 3am Sat) ☎ (01622) 299283
⊕ thethirstypig.co.uk
4 changing beers (sourced locally; often Mad Cat, Musket, Rockin' Robin) ⊞

The Pig was built in the 15th century and may be the third-oldest building in Maidstone. Originally it was a farmhouse within the estate of the archbishop's palace. It is Grade II listed and has two storeys, with original beams, low ceilings and tucked-away rooms. Outside there is a heated and covered courtyard area. The bar contains four handpumps dispensing ales mainly from Kent microbreweries. Draught local cider is also available. Many bottled beers are stocked, including several foreign ones. ❀♣●🚍🛜

Rifle Volunteers Ⓛ

28 Wyatt Street, ME14 1EU
☼ 12-3 (not Mon), 6-11; 12-6 Sun ☎ (01622) 758891
Goacher's Real Mild Ale, Fine Light Ale, Gold Star Strong Ale; 1 changing beer (often Goacher's) ⊞

One of only two Goacher's tied houses, the Rifle was the Kent CAMRA Regional Pub of the Year 2016. A short walk away from the town centre, this Victorian stone-built single-bar pub has been recognised by CAMRA for its unspoilt interior. An absence of noisy machines ensures that it is a place for conversation or quiet drinking. A popular fun quiz open to all is held on alternate Tuesdays, with a local winter quiz league operating in other weeks. Snacks can be made to order.
Q❀➸♣●🚍✿🛜

Society Rooms ✔

Brenchley House, Week Street, ME14 1RF
☼ 7am-midnight (1am Fri & Sat) ☎ (01622) 350910
Greene King Abbot; Ruddles Best Bitter; Sharp's Doom Bar; 7 changing beers (sourced nationally; often Old Dairy, Rockin' Robin, Wantsum) ⊞

A spacious Wetherspoon pub on the site of a former local newspaper printing works situated on the ground floor of a five-storey office block. The mainly glass external walls allow panoramic views of the pedestrian shopping street alongside. A large covered outside space is split into smoking and non-smoking areas. The name is taken from William Shipley, founder of the Royal Society of Arts and the Maidstone Society for Promoting Useful Knowledge, who is buried nearby. Food is served 7am-11pm. Q🛏❀◐&➸♣🚍(101,155)🛜

Wheatsheaf

301 Loose Road, ME15 9PY (S of Maidstone at jct A229 and A274)
☼ 4-11; 12-11.30 Fri & Sat; 12-10.30 Sun ☎ (01622) 752624
⊕ thewheatsheaf-maidstone.co.uk
Courage Best Bitter; 2 changing beers (sourced nationally; often Brains, Caledonian, Theakston) ⊞

There has been a pub here since the 1600s, the current one having been built in 1830. A free house owned by the same family for 33 years, there are usually at least two guest beers including Caledonian seasonal brews. One long spacious bar shows live football, rugby and other sports. This community pub hosts a poker night every Tuesday, darts teams and a golf society. It also features a large patio area and a covered, heated smoking area. ☎❀◐♣🚍(82,89)🛜

Marden

Marden Village Club Ⓛ

Albion Road, TN12 9DT
☼ 6 (5 Fri)-11; 12-3, 7-11 Sat; 6.30-10.30 Sun
☎ (01622) 831427
Shepherd Neame Master Brew; 3 changing beers (sourced regionally; often Goacher's, Kent, Ramsgate) ⊞

Four real ales are offered at this Grade II-listed club; three change regularly and are generally from local Kent microbreweries. A community hub, many members are followers of football and rugby on the TV and are also involved in the club's snooker and darts teams; others simply enjoy the friendly ambience. Card-carrying CAMRA members are welcome but regular visitors will be required to join. Regularly voted CAMRA branch Club of the Year. &➸♣●🚍(26,27)✿🛜

Margate

Fez
40 High Street, CT9 1DS
✪ 12-10.30; 12-10 Sun
4 changing beers Ⓖ
Micropub opened in December 2015 in the former Card Centre shop premises. Eclectically furnished with a mixture of high and low tables and some raised bench seating, brewery and fairground memorabilia adorn the walls. The small bar counter at the rear has a temperature-controlled cellar room from which cask ales and ciders are served on gravity dispense. A limited wine range is sold too. Q❧☞⇚♣♿🚲(56)🐾🌳🛜

London Tavern 🍸
Addington Street, CT9 1PN
✪ closed Mon; 5-10.30; 4-11 Fri; 1-11 Sat; 12-9 Sun ☎ 07598 647753
3 changing beers Ⓗ
This 18th-century hostelry with two single-storey extensions was at one time known as the Shakespeare Tavern, then from 1858 until the early-1990s as the London Tavern, after which it was the Everybodys Inn. It is across the road from the Theatre Royal, with many famous thespians agonising over their lines in the bar. The pub was taken over in July 2015 by new owners who have reverted back to its former name, giving the pub a complete and welcoming refit. Local CAMRA Pub of the Year 2017. 🏵🍴♣♿🚲🐾

Milton Regis

Three Hats ✅
93 High Street, ME10 2AR
✪ 12-11; 12-10.30 Sun ☎ (01795) 427645
4 changing beers (sourced nationally; often Dartmoor, Purity, St Austell) Ⓗ
Popular and friendly community local in this historic village. The open-plan interior has low beams and a large back lounge bar area. The landlord serves an excellent selection of national ales. A large, attractive beer garden is popular in summer. The pub was instrumental in organising the annual Milton Regis Saffron Fair – this was once a noted saffron-producing area.
☞🏵🍴♿🚲(347)🐾🛜

New Romney

Cinque Ports Arms ✅
1 High Street, TN28 8BU (W end of High St on A259)
✪ 12-11 (midnight Fri & Sat) ☎ (01797) 361894
Greene King IPA, Abbot; 3 changing beers (sourced regionally) Ⓗ
A cosy, friendly and welcoming 16th-century public house with a wealth of oak beams. It has recently been sympathetically refurbished and extended with a new kitchen and dining area, together with the opening up of additional spaces for family use. Children under the age of 18 are not permitted in the bar area. In winter enjoy the cosy real fire, in summer relax in the enclosed beer garden and patio at the rear. Live music and beer festivals feature. ☞🏵🍴🅿Å♿🐾🛜

Smugglers' Alehouse
10 St Lawrence Court, High Street, TN28 8BU (W end of High St)
✪ 12-9 (10 Fri & Sat); 12-6 Sun ☎ 07581 230397
⊕ smugglersalehouse.co.uk
3 changing beers (sourced regionally) Ⓗ
A welcoming micropub which opened in February 2016, awarded runner-up CAMRA branch Pub of the Year 2017. You can relax, read the newspapers or join in with the varied conversations between customers and friendly staff. Well-behaved dogs are welcome. In addition to the different real ales and ciders on offer, there is a selection of wines, gin, vodka and rum. Tea and coffee are also available, as are snacks including pickled eggs.
QÅ♿🚲🐾

Newenden

White Hart Ⓛ
Rye Road, TN18 5PN (on A28 in centre of village)
TQ834273
✪ 11-11; 12-11 Sun ☎ (01797) 252166
⊕ thewhitehartnewenden.co.uk
Harvey's Sussex Best Bitter; Rother Valley Level Best; 2 changing beers Ⓗ
This historic 16th-century weatherboarded building includes old oak-beamed bars and an inglenook fireplace. The pub provides good-quality home-cooked food and has six en-suite rooms. Conveniently situated for the Kent and East Sussex Railway and several National Trust properties, it is an ideal location for exploring the Rother Valley. Pub quizzes are held on the first Monday of the month (except on bank holidays).
☞🏵🛏🍴👪Å⇚♣♿🅿🚲(2)🐾🛜

Pembury

King William IV ✅
87 Hastings Road, TN2 4HQ
✪ 3 (12 Thu-Sat)-11; 12-10.30 Sun ☎ (01892) 578550
Greene King IPA, Abbot; Morland Old Speckled Hen; house beer (by Greene King); 4 changing beers (sourced locally; often High Weald, Old Dairy, Tonbridge) Ⓗ
Welcoming refurbished community pub, reopened last year and much improved by new licensees who also run the Bedford in Tunbridge Wells. Four Greene King and four guest ales from the likes of Pig & Porter, Old Dairy or Tonbridge, and a Kent cider, are served in spacious surroundings with ample seating. Family and dog friendly, it has large rear and front patio gardens. Delicious stone-baked pizzas are served until 9.30pm. Live music is hosted, mostly on Friday nights, plus ukulele evenings, and darts and crib are played.
☞🏵🍴👪♿♣♿🅿🚲🐾🛜

Petham

Chequers Ⓛ
Stone Street, CT4 5PW
✪ 12-3 (not Mon), 6-11; 12-4, 7-10.30 Sun
☎ (01227) 700734 ⊕ thechequersinn.wordpress.com
Dark Star Hophead; Oakham Citra; 1 changing beer (often Old Dairy, St Austell, Skinner's) Ⓖ
On the Roman road from Canterbury to Hythe, the Chequers was built in 1898. The bar area has comfortable leather sofas. A spacious dining area

and restaurant are at the back, with a tempting menu including a popular carvery on Sunday lunchtime. Darts and bar billiards are played. Up to six beers are served at busy times. Mini beer festivals featuring Kent microbreweries are planned. The Canterbury Reach Retreat next door offers luxury lodge accommodation.
ﾋ田ODÅ♣●P

Petteridge

Hopbine
Petteridge Lane, TN12 7NE (1 mile W of Brenchley)
✪ 12-2.30, 5-11; 12-11 Fri-Sun ☎ (01892) 722561
⊕ thehopbine.pub
Long Man Best Bitter; Tonbridge Traditional; 2 changing beers (sourced locally; often Dark Star, Isfield) Ⓗ
Unique, compact, weatherboarded free house set in a secluded hamlet and serving four local ales and a Kentish cider from Turners. A favourite among walkers, it has a central log fire adding to the homely feel. Tasty food is available – hand-made wood-fired pizzas are the speciality (no food Mon or Tue lunchtimes). The patio decking and landscaped garden serve as a most inviting place to dine or drink in a tranquil setting during the warmer months. Q ﾋ田OD♣●P🚌(296,297)● �🛜

Queenborough

Admiral's Arm Ⓛ ✔
West Street, ME11 5AD (in Trafalgar Court, 30yds left from High St/Park Rd crossroads)
✪ 4.30-9; 12-11 Fri & Sat; 12-9 Sun ☎ (01795) 668598
⊕ admiralsarm.co.uk
4 changing beers (sourced locally; often Oakham, Pig & Porter, Ramsgate) Ⓗ/Ⓖ
In the historic heart of Queenborough, a nautical theme, including local shipping maps, adds character here. It is close to bus and rail stations and hosts regular quiz nights and cheese Sundays. Frequented by locals and visitors alike, it has a good range of beers, ciders and gins. The warm and welcoming owners will happily serve beer direct from the cask or via handpump. Mobile phone calls must be taken outside.
Q ﾋ田☀≒♣●🚌(334)

Rainham

Prince of Ales Ⓛ
121 High Street, ME8 8AN
✪ closed Mon; 5.30-9.30; 12-10 Fri & Sat; 12-3 Sun ☎ 07982 756412 ⊕ princeofales.co.uk
3 changing beers (sourced nationally; often Nelson, Romney Marsh) Ⓖ
A new and worthy addition to the Medway micropub scene, this attractive and well-planned pub offers three to five real ales on a rotating basis. The main area has wooden bench seating, with cushions available for a donation to charity. The small rear garden is a suntrap in the warmer months. Beer quality is good and wine is available by the bottle. The small bar area enjoys a friendly atmosphere at weekends. Q田⅍≒♣🚌(326)🛜

Ramsgate

Conqueror Alehouse
4c Grange Road, CT11 9LR (on corner of St Mildred's Rd)
✪ closed Mon; 11.30-2.30, 5.30-9.30; 12-3 Sun ☎ 07890 203282 ⊕ conqueror-alehouse.co.uk
3 changing beers Ⓖ
This welcoming award-winning micropub has room for about 20 customers, offering a cosy and pleasant environment with comfortable seating around high tables. Three changing real ales, mainly sourced locally, are served straight from the cask, as is a local cider. It is named after a two-funnelled paddle steamer that operated excursions from the town in the early 1900s, pictures of which adorn the walls. Q Å♣●🚌●

Hovelling Boat Inn
12 York Street, CT11 9DS
✪ 11.30-9 (10 Fri & Sat); 12-4 Sun summer; 11.30-7 (9 Wed & Thu; 10 Fri & Sat); 12-4 Sun winter ☎ 07974 613030
⊕ hovellingboatinn.co.uk
4 changing beers Ⓖ
This sympathetic shop conversion micropub in a handy town centre location was to have had another name until the landlord discovered it had originally been the Hovelling Boat pub that ceased trading in 1909. With exposed brickwork displaying breweriana, the venue offers up to four changing beers from Kent and beyond, served at customers' tables by friendly staff. Local cider, along with wine, cold snacks, tea and coffee, are also available. Q ﾋ田●🚌●

Montefiore Arms
1 Trinity Place, CT11 7HJ
✪ 12-2.30 (not Wed), 5.30-11; 12-11 Sat; 12-3, 7-10.30 Sun ☎ (01843) 593265 ⊕ montefiorearms.co.uk
Ramsgate Gadds' No.7 Bitter Ale; 4 changing beers Ⓗ
An award-winning traditional back-street local enjoying a good reputation with real ale drinkers in the Thanet area. The pub's name and sign are unique, honouring the great Jewish financier and philanthropist Sir Moses Montefiore, who lived locally for many years. Now under the personal control of Eddie Gadd of nearby Ramsgate Brewery, the pub showcases its beers along with changing guest ales and Biddenden cider. ♣●🚌🛜

NauticAles
347 Margate Road, CT12 6SG
✪ 4.30-10.30; 12-11 Sat; 12-9 Sun ☎ 07552 600919
4 changing beers Ⓖ
Micropub which opened in former office premises in the Northwood district in April 2016 after several planning delays. It has a small L-shaped bar counter behind which real ales and ciders are served on gravity dispense from a stillage in a cooled cabinet on the back wall. It serves up to four ales including at least one of the house NauticAles beers. ●🚌●🛜

Rochester

Coopers Arms
10 St Margarets Street, ME1 1TL
✪ 12-11 (midnight Fri & Sat) ☎ (01634) 404298
⊕ thecoopersarms.co.uk
Courage Best Bitter; Young's Special; 4 changing beers (sourced regionally; often Canterbury Ales, Tonbridge, Westerham) Ⓗ

A few minutes' stroll past Rochester's cathedral and castle, this charming old coal inn dates from 1199 and is one of the oldest in Kent. The front bar is of historic interest, with an impressive beamed ceiling and fireplaces. A passageway leads to a more modern back bar and on to a large, well-kept garden which is busy in the summer. Lunchtime specials and Sunday roasts are offered. There is a quiz night Tuesday and live music Sunday evening. No children allowed in the bar area. ❀◫◖➔⊟☙♔

Flippin' Frog ⓛ
318 High Street, ME1 1BT
❀ closed Mon; 3-11 Tue-Thu; 12.30-11 Fri & Sat; 12-7 Sun ☎ 07889 214000
4 changing beers (sourced locally; often Goody Ales, Old Dairy, Whitstable) Ⓖ
Brilliant pub with an offering of ales, ciders, wines and local gin. The owners and staff are welcoming and will chat with you when the pub is not too busy. The food is cooked in an open-plan area so you can see and smell the flavours you have ordered. It is a great micropub, adding to Medway's growing reputation as an excellent place to visit and drink. A rotation of ales and ciders from Kent microbreweries is sold. Q❀☙◫◖➔➕⊟♔

Good Intent
3 John Street, ME1 1YL
❀ 12-midnight ☎ (01634) 843118
3 changing beers (sourced regionally) Ⓖ
A welcoming two-bar estate community pub that has not followed the modern trends. It has a traditional pool table, darts and jukebox in the main bar. Access to the quiet back bar is via the garden, where regular beer festivals are held. The three ales on offer are served by gravity from racking behind the main bar. There is a lively, friendly atmosphere, with regular quiz nights and music events. Q❀♣➕P⊟♔☙

Man of Kent Ale House ⓛ
6-8 John Street, ME1 1YN (200yds off A2 from bottom of Star Hill)
❀ 2 (3 Mon)-11; 2-midnight Fri; 12.30-midnight Sat; 12.30-11 Sun ☎ 07772 214315
Goacher's Gold Star Strong Ale; 10 changing beers (sourced locally) Ⓗ
Great little pub a short walk from the main high street, and always very welcoming, with a resident dog who is as friendly as the locals. It offers a good selection of real ales, ciders and foreign ales, and live music during the week. It is a great place for meeting up with friends for nights out or lazy afternoons. The small garden is always full in the summer months. ❀➔♣➕⊟⊟♔

Who'd Ha' Thought It
9 Baker Street, ME1 3DN
❀ 12-midnight ☎ (01634) 830144 ⊕ whodha.co.uk
3 changing beers (sourced nationally) Ⓗ
On a side street off Maidstone Road, this welcoming pub has a spacious wood-panelled main bar and a variety of seating. The TV shows sporting matches, and a log fire is lit in winter. There is a snug bar to the rear that leads to a well-maintained garden. A selection of three varying ales is served. It has a pub quiz once a month, occasional live music, and holds charity events. Bar snacks include rolls and pizzas. ☙❀♣⊟(155)♔☙

Rusthall

Toad Rock Retreat ✔
1 Upper Street, TN4 8NX
❀ closed Mon; 3-11 Tue; 12-3.30, 5.30-11; 12-10.30 Sun
☎ (01892) 520818 ⊕ toadrockretreattunbridgewells.co.uk
Harvey's Sussex Best Bitter; 3 changing beers (sourced nationally; often Adnams, Black Sheep, Old Dairy) Ⓗ
An extensive refurbishment in February 2016 has created a bright and cheerful interior, with a separate comfy sofa area and an open wood fire on entering to welcome you on cooler days. There is a large, raised garden and a seating area to the front which is a suntrap in the summer, and from there can be seen the famous sandstone Toad Rock formation. Delicious home-cooked food from a varied menu is served lunchtimes and evenings Wednesday to Saturday, and Sunday lunchtime. ☙❀◫◖&♣P⊟(281)♔☙

Ryarsh

Duke of Wellington ⓛ ✔
The Street, ME19 5LS
❀ 11-11; 12-10.30 Sun ☎ (01732) 842318
⊕ dukeofwellingtonryarsh.com
Harvey's Sussex Best Bitter; Kent Pale; 2 changing beers (sourced nationally) Ⓗ
A 16th-century pub in the village centre, welcoming to ramblers. The main bar is to the left, and the restaurant to the right features a varied menu plus Sunday roasts. Fireplaces in both bars provide winter warmth. A covered and heated patio with tables opens on to the garden and overlooks the pétanque piste. In front, an area with tables provides additional space. A popular jazz evening is held the first Thursday of each month. Every other Sunday is quiz night. Q☙❀◫◖♣P⊟(58)♔☙

St Peter's

Four Candles Alehouse
1 Sowell Street, CT10 2AT
❀ 5-10.30 (11.30 Fri); 12-11.30 Sat; 12-3.30, 5-10.30 Sun ☎ 07947 062063 ⊕ thefourcandles.co.uk
3 changing beers Ⓖ
This former shop is now firmly cemented into the local micropub scene and is renowned for its friendly atmosphere. Seating is provided at high-bench tables, while the beer is served from a cooled cabinet in an adjacent room. The pub has its own microbrewery in the cellar which supplies excellent one-off beers to complement the offerings from other brewers. In the warmer weather benches outside provide for a superb suntrap. Q➔➕⊟(56)♔

Yard of Ale
61 Church Street, CT10 2TU
❀ 5-11; 12-11 Sat & Sun ☎ 07790 730205
3 changing beers Ⓖ
Attractive rustic stable converted into a unique micropub in a village location. It is adorned with hops and old riding equipment; seating varies from high stools to straw bales, and there is a wood-burning stove for the colder months. It is family and dog friendly and has a strong link to the community. The outside yard is a suntrap with a

large seating area, while a canopy and heaters are available for inclement weather. It offers a wide-ranging selection of ales and cider, and was a finalist for CAMRA National Pub of the Year in 2015. Q🌞🛏️❄️♣️●🚻🐾

Sandgate

Inn Doors
96 Sandgate High Street, CT20 3BY
🕑 5-10 (11 Fri); 12.30-11 Sat; 12.30-5 Sun ☎ 07958 474473
⊕ inndoorsmicropub.co.uk
4 changing beers (sourced regionally; often Four Kings) Ⓖ
A micropub at the west end of Sandgate based on a 1930s living room, comprising a small bar and two-level seating. Beers are served from a cold room visible through a window. Gary, the landlord, brews his own beers at the Four Candles Brewery in Broadstairs. Tasty snacks are served, as is a large variety of gins. Do not try and open the door in the ceiling! The pub hosts bring your own vinyl nights – played on a vintage record player – and monthly charity quiz evenings. Q🛏️♣️●🚻🐾

Ship Inn Ⓛ
65 Sandgate High Street, CT20 3AH (on A259)
🕑 11.30-11.30 (12.30am Fri & Sat) ☎ (01303) 248525
Amazing Cotter VC, Grace; Dark Star Hophead; Greene King IPA, Abbot; Hop Back Summer Lightning Ⓗ**; 3 changing beers** Ⓖ
This narrow corner pub incorporating the Amazing Brewery fronts on to the High Street and backs on to the beach. Partly dating from 1798, it has a front bar, back room, function room and a restaurant with sea views; upstairs there is a top deck for drinkers. Nautical maps and pictures featured on the walls reflect the landlord's naval and military interests. Biddenden and guest ciders are always stocked and an August bank holiday beer festival is held. 🚪🌓●🚻

Sandling

Yew Tree
Grange Lane, ME14 3DB (down Boarley Lane, bear right, and on right just before going under M20) TQ757584
🕑 closed Mon; 12-11 (midnight Fri & Sat); 12-6 Sun summer; closed Mon; 12-3.30, 5.30-11 Tue-Thu; 12-midnight Fri & Sat; 12-6 Sun winter ☎ (01622) 752882
⊕ theyewtreesandling.co.uk
Dark Star Hophead; St Austell Tribute, Proper Job; Young's Bitter; 1 changing beer Ⓗ
A former cottage dating from 1782 that lies in the shadow of the M20 and is accessed via a narrow lane. The nearest bus stop, at Ringlestone, is an easy 15-minute walk. The homely bar has red quarry tiles on the floor while the popular restaurant is carpeted (booking for the restaurant is advisable). Bar food is served all day on Friday and Saturday. The pub is open all day Tuesday to Thursday in the summer months. 🛏️🌞🌓♣️P🐾📶

Sandwich

Crispin Inn Ⓛ ✅
4 High Street, CT13 9EA
🕑 11-11 (midnight Fri & Sat); 12-10.30 Sun
☎ (01304) 621967 ⊕ sandwichpubs.co.uk

House beer (by Mad Cat); 1 changing beer (often Adnams, Sharp's) Ⓗ
Ancient public house by the medieval barbican and toll bridge. Low ceilings, wooden beams and brick walls provide a congenial ambience. Relax by the window and watch the world go by, or sit in the back courtyard overlooking the river. One or two real ales feature alongside the house ales from the Mad Cat Brewery. Real cider is from Westons or Thatchers. A range of home-made food and snacks usually features Caribbean specialities. Regular live music events are held. 🛏️🌞🌓♿👣❄️♣️●🚻🐾📶

Sevenoaks

Anchor Ⓛ
32 London Road, TN13 1AS
🕑 11-3, 6-11; 10.30-midnight Fri; 12-4, 7-10.30 Sun
☎ (01732) 454898 ⊕ anchorsevenoaks.co.uk
Harvey's Sussex Best Bitter; house beer (by Franklins); 1 changing beer (sourced locally; often Tonbridge, Westerham) Ⓗ
A friendly town-centre local, popular with all ages, run by long-serving landlord Barry, with an atmosphere of banter and fun. Good-value home-cooked food is served lunchtimes throughout the week, with bar snacks in the evening. Guest ales are from microbreweries and change weekly. Regular live evening entertainment, ranging from blues music to open mic nights and morris dancing, is enthusiastically promoted – full details are available in the pub. 🌓●♣️🚻🐾

White Hart Ⓛ
Tonbridge Road, TN13 1SG (1 mile S of town centre)
🕑 11.30-11; 12-10.30 Sun ☎ (01732) 452022
⊕ whitehart-sevenoaks.co.uk
Harvey's Sussex Best Bitter; Old Dairy Blue Top; house beer (by Phoenix); 4 changing beers (sourced nationally; often Timothy Taylor, Titanic, Tonbridge) Ⓗ
Imposing whitewashed coaching inn high up on the Greensand Ridge. The rambling wood-floored interior, full of cosy seating areas, is popular with diners, but drinkers are equally welcome.
With eight to nine ales on, taster boards are thankfully available. In winter several real fires bring cheer to customers and in summer the extensive patio and garden allows the sun to do the same. The wide range of ales is from around the UK and a varying real cider is always available. Q🛏️🌞🌓♿♣️●P🚌(402)🐾📶

Sevenoaks Weald

Windmill Ⓛ
1 Windmill Road, TN14 6PN
🕑 5-9 Mon; 12-11; 12-9 Sun ☎ (01732) 463330
Goacher's Fine Light Ale; Larkins Traditional Ale; 4 changing beers (sourced nationally; often Goddards, Rockin' Robin, Titanic) Ⓗ
Situated on the green in Weald village, the Windmill is renowned for its quality beer, food and good service. Kentish ciders sit alongside the range of ales, carefully selected to provide a choice of strengths and styles. In the restaurant there is an interesting array of dishes on the menu, both classic and house recipes (no food Mon and Sun eve). Families and dogs are welcome and there is a pleasant patio garden to the rear.
Q🛏️🌞🌓👣♣️●🚌(401,402)🐾📶

Sittingbourne

Golden Hope ✅
The Court House, 1 Park Road, ME10 1DR
☼ 8am-midnight (1am Fri & Sat) ☎ (01795) 476791
Greene King Abbot; Ruddles Best Bitter; Sharp's
Doom Bar; 5 changing beers (sourced nationally;
often Batemans, Shepherd Neame, Wantsum) Ⓗ
Opened in summer 2015, this Wetherspoon has
been converted from the old magistrates court and
police station. Some original features remain,
including the old cells which have been converted
into small dining areas. The name derives from a
Thames sailing barge built on the nearby creek. It
has one main bar area with several smaller seating
areas. There are front and rear patios; smoking is
allowed on the rear one. Disabled access is via Park
Road. Q⇄❀❀✿◑♿🚲🚌🍴🐾🛜

Paper Mill ♈ 🅛
2 Charlotte Street, ME10 2JN (almost in Milton Regis, at
the corner of Church St and Charlotte St)
☼ 12-2 (not Mon-Thu), 5-9; 12-9 Sat; 12-6
Sun ☎ 07927 073584 ⊕ thepapermillmicropub.co.uk
Goacher's Real Mild Ale; 3 changing beers (sourced
locally; often Goacher's, Kent, Wantsum) Ⓖ
A popular micropub close to Sittingbourne town
centre and north of the train station. It is a one-
room pub, with bench seating around four large
wood tables. Local beers feature alongside national
beers such as Blue Monkey and Redwillow, and
there is a range of Dudda's Tun ciders available.
Occasional events such as Meet the Brewer and
pub quizzes take place. Opening hours are flexible
with advance notice. Local CAMRA Pub of the Year
2015 and 2016. Q⇄❀♿✿◑♿🚲🚌(334,347)🐾

Red Lion
58 High Street, ME10 4PB
☼ 12-11 (1am Fri & Sat) ☎ (01795) 472706
3 changing beers (sourced nationally; often Fuller's,
St Austell, Sharp's) Ⓗ
A large and welcoming coaching inn in the High
Street. The pub is steeped in history and it is
believed that both Henry V and Henry VIII stayed
here. A large real fire separates the restaurant area
from a large bar, where dogs are welcome. It
recently changed hands and now serves excellent-
quality food at lunchtime and dinner. Up to four
beers are sold including Betty Stogs, Purity Pure
Gold and Purity UBU. ⇄❀◑♿🚲🐾🛜

Snargate

Red Lion ★ 🅛
TN29 9UQ (on B2080, 1 mile NW of Brenzett) TQ990285
☼ closed Mon; 12-3, 7-11; 12-4, 7-10.30 Sun
☎ (01797) 344648
4 changing beers Ⓖ
Multi-room 16th-century smugglers' pub which has
been in the same family for over 100 years. This
superb pub passed to the next generation in April
2016 but is still universally known as Doris's.
Decorated with posters from the 1940s and the
Women's Land Army, it is on CAMRA's National
Inventory of Historic Pub Interiors. It serves four or
five guest beers, including at least one from
Goacher's. Food is limited to basic bar snacks. A
beer festival is held in June, with a mini festival in
October. Q❀♣🅿️🚌(11B)🐾

South Darenth

Queen ♈ 🅛
58-62 New Road, DA4 9AR
☼ 2-11; 12-11.30 Sat; 12-10.30 Sun ☎ (01322) 862430
Fuller's London Pride; Greene King Abbot; Kent Black
Gold, Brewers Reserve; 1 changing beer (sourced
nationally) Ⓗ
Friendly community back-street local within
walking distance of Farningham Road railway
station. Extended in 1998 to incorporate a former
shop, it has two separate bars, one with a sports
theme adorned with memorabilia of London
football teams, the other a traditional, quieter
saloon bar. It is a genuine free house, promoting
beers from Kent breweries. The pub has a garden
and patio area and free bar food is available
Sunday lunchtime. Children are welcome until
8.30pm. Local CAMRA Pub of the Year 2017.
⇄❀◑♣♿🚌(414)🐾🛜

Stansted

Black Horse 🅛
Tumblefield Road, TN15 7PR (1 mile N of A20)
TQ606620
☼ 12-11; 12-10.30 Sun & Mon ☎ (01732) 822355
⊕ theblackhorsestansted.co.uk
Larkins Traditional Ale; Young's Bitter; 2 changing
beers (often Bexley, Tonbridge) Ⓗ
In the heart of the North Downs, this village free
house is surrounded by rolling hills and woodlands,
attracting ramblers and cyclists. Traditional English
meals are served Tuesday to Sunday until 9.30pm.
Recently refurbished, and featuring a notable Bass
& Co mirror, the pub has regular live music, card
games and quizzes. Guest real ales are normally
from local breweries. An extensive range of wines
and bottled beers is also available.
⇄❀◑♣🅿️🐾🛜

Staplehurst

Lord Raglan 🅛
Chart Hill Road, TN12 0DE (½ mile N of A229 at Cross at
Hand) TQ786472
☼ 12-3, 6.30-11; closed Sun ☎ (01622) 843747
Goacher's Fine Light Ale; Harvey's Sussex Best Bitter;
1 changing beer (sourced locally; often Musket,
Tonbridge, Westerham) Ⓗ
A long-standing entry, this popular and unspoilt
free house retains the atmosphere of a country pub
from bygone days. The bar is hung with hops and
warmed by two log fires and a stove. The large
orchard garden catches the evening sun. Excellent
snacks and full meals are always on offer. The
guest beer changes regularly and Weston's perry
and local Double Vision cider are sold. Well-
behaved children and dogs are welcome. A short
walk from the (No.5) bus stop on the A229.
Q❀◑♣🅿️🐾

Staplestreet

Three Horseshoes
46 Staple Street, ME13 9UA (follow signs from A299 for
Mount Ephraim Gardens)
☼ 12-3 (not Mon), 5-11; 12-midnight Fri & Sat; 12-4, 7-11 Sun
☎ (01227) 750842 ⊕ threehorseshoesfaversham.co.uk

Shepherd Neame Master Brew, Spitfire; 1 changing beer (sourced locally) ⓗ

Dating from 1690, this is a traditional community pub at the heart of village life. It is popular with walkers, cyclists and locals alike. It has an attractive, weatherboarded exterior with a traditional Kent peg tile roof, and inside has exposed brickwork, old oak beams and a large open fireplace. A small outdoor suntrap patio is sheltered by an ancient walnut tree. The pub serves good-quality food, and has regular music nights and an annual charity wheelie-bin race. ✿❶♿♣🅿🚌(638)❀🎵

Strood

10:50 From Victoria ⓛ
Rear of 37 North Street, ME2 4SJ
✪ 4-9; 12-10 Fri & Sat; closed Sun ☎ 07941 449137
⊕ 1050fromvictoria.co.uk
Kent Prohibition; Ripple Steam IPA; Rockin' Robin Robin Redbest; house beer (by Grainstore) Ⓖ; **5 changing beers (sourced regionally)** ⓗ/Ⓖ

Popular micropub that opened in 2015 in a railway arch at the rear of a supermarket car park. The name relates to the network rail arch number rather than a real or imagined train time. The pub is full of train memorabilia and bric-a-brac, and has bench seating plus a large outside deck area which is pleasant on nice summer days. A logburner stove keeps you warm and cosy in winter. No children are permitted either in the pub or outside area. A choice of five ales and five real ciders is always available. Q✿♿🚲♣🍴🅿🚌❀

Swanscombe

George & Dragon ⓛ
1 London Road, DA10 0LQ
✪ 12 (4 Mon & Tue)-11; 12-10.30 Sun ☎ (01322) 386440
⊕ georgedragonswanscombe.co.uk
6 changing beers (sourced nationally; often Caveman) ⓗ

Enterprising privately owned former Victorian coaching inn, now a popular destination for quality real ales and good food. A horseshoe-shaped bar supports six handpumps with changing beers and at least three local ciders, as well as a cabinet with whiskies and bottled beers from UK and international brewers. The restaurant is open Wednesday to Saturday lunchtimes and evenings, plus Sunday lunchtime for recommended roasts. At least one Caveman Brewery beer is always on sale. CAMRA branch Cider Pub of the Year 2017. Q✿🍴🚲❶♣🍴🚌❀

Tankerton

Tankerton Arms ⓛ
139B Tankerton Road, CT5 2AW
✪ closed Mon; 12-2, 5-9.30 (11 Fri); 12-11 Sat; 12-3, 5-9 Sun ☎ 07532 025626 ⊕ thetankertonarms.co.uk
4 changing beers (sourced regionally; often Kent, Ripple Steam, Tonbridge) Ⓖ

This friendly micropub, with a policy of supporting microbreweries, is situated among Tankerton's small shops. The pleasant, airy room is lined with high wooden tables which encourage conversation. The walls are adorned with hop bines, bunting, and pictures featuring Thames

sailing barges. Food is local Ashmore cheeses, and Scotch eggs from the butcher's shop opposite. There is some seating outdoors on the tree-shaded pavement. There are Italian cheese evenings and occasional quizzes. Local CAMRA branch Pub of the Year 2016. Q✿♣🚲🅿🚌❀

Temple Ewell

Fox ⓛ
14 High Street, CT16 3DU
✪ 11.30-3.30, 6-11.30; 12-4, 7-11 Sun ☎ (01304) 823598
Butcombe Adam Henson's Rare Breed; Kelham Island Pride of Sheffield; 2 changing beers ⓗ

A traditional village pub that offers a warm welcome to locals and visitors. A good range of styles and strengths of real ales is on offer, including a regular from Shepherd Neame. A variety of events, quiz nights, curry nights and occasional music evenings keep the place busy. In June a charity beer festival is organised by the local Rotary Club. There is an attractive streamside garden with skittle alley. The pub is close to Kearsney Abbey Gardens and public transport. 🚲✿❶🚲♣🅿🚌❀

Tonbridge

Humphrey Bean ✪
94 High Street, TN9 1AP (near castle and river)
✪ 9am-midnight (1am Fri & Sat) ☎ (01732) 773850
Greene King Abbot; Ruddles Best Bitter; Sharp's Doom Bar; 6 changing beers (sourced locally; often By The Horns, Long Man, Tonbridge) ⓗ

Ever-popular Wetherspoon house close to Tonbridge Castle and the River Medway, with ample space and an extensive flower-adorned garden. An interesting range of six guest beers from breweries such as Tonbridge, Long Man, Old Dairy and Dark Star illustrates the commitment to real ale, enhanced by organised brewery visits and occasional events showcasing a brewery's beers. Ask for the current choice of ciders supplementing Westons Old Rosie, kept behind the bar. Food is served until 11pm. Q🚲✿❶♿🚲♣🍴🅿🚌❀

Tunbridge Wells

Fuggles Beer Café 🏆 ✪
28 Grosvenor Road, TN1 2AP
✪ 11.30-11; 12-10.30 Sun ☎ (01892) 457739
⊕ fugglesbeercafe.co.uk
Tonbridge Coppernob; 4 changing beers (sourced nationally; often Bristol Beer Factory, Howling Hops, Kent) ⓗ

In only a little over four years since opening, Fuggles has established itself as both a firm favourite and a multi award-winner on the Tunbridge Wells social scene. With a varied range of five cask ales, a real cider and 100 bottles, this comfortable and relaxed café-style bar is a haven for quality and choice. The enthusiastic and friendly staff will help should you need guidance beyond the chalkboard information behind the bar. 🚲❶🚲♣🍴🚌❀

George ✪
29 Mount Ephraim, TN4 8AA
✪ 12-11 (midnight Thu; 1am Fri & Sat) ☎ (01892) 539492
⊕ thegeorgetw.co.uk

Long Man Best Bitter, American Pale Ale; 5 changing beers (sourced nationally; often Harbour, Purity, Thornbridge) Ⓗ
A smart, friendly free house at the top end of town and recently restored to its former 19th-century coaching inn glory, with distinct areas featuring wood flooring and panelling. There is patio seating to the front, or seek out the secret courtyard garden in which to enjoy the range of real ales, Seacider cider and other beers in fine weather. Lunchtime food is served until 3pm (4pm weekends) with a light bites bar menu available in the evening. ⌂♿🅿🍴♿♿🅿♿📶

Grove Tavern Ⓛ ✔
19 Berkeley Road, TN1 1YR
⊕ 12-midnight ☎ (01892) 526549 ⊕ grovetavern.co.uk
Harvey's Sussex Best Bitter; Timothy Taylor Landlord; 2 changing beers (sourced nationally; often Dark Star, Otter) Ⓗ
A traditional local single-bar pub, dating from the 17th century, at the top of a cobbled lane in the Grove Village area of the town. Conveniently located a few minutes' walk from the railway station and numerous bus routes, it sits between the Pantiles and main shopping area. This busy local hosts a pool table and dartboard and an open fire in winter, and is a venue for lively and topical conversation while enjoying ales from near and far. ⌂♿♿🅿♿📶

Mount Edgcumbe
The Common, TN4 8BX
⊕ 11-11 (11.30 Thu-Sat); 12-10.30 Sun ☎ (01892) 618854
⊕ themountedgcumbe.com
Harvey's Sussex Best Bitter; 3 changing beers (sourced nationally; often Canterbury, Cottage, Gun Dog Ales) Ⓗ
Less than a mile from the railway station but hidden in the middle of the common, this pub and restaurant forms the ground floor of a large Georgian house surrounded by woods. Walkers and dogs are welcome in the garden, bar and in the unusual adjacent internal cave. You will find friendly service in a relaxed atmosphere in which to enjoy changing guest ales. The patio beer garden, with play area, overlooks sandstone rock formations towards the town and is well used in the warmer months. ⌂♿🅿♿♿🅿♿📶

Royal Oak Ⓛ
92 Prospect Road, TN2 4SY
⊕ 12-11.30; 12-10.30 Sun ☎ (01892) 542546
Harvey's Sussex Best Bitter; 4 changing beers (sourced locally; often Dark Star, Larkins, Whitstable) Ⓗ
Good-sized yet homely town pub five to ten minutes' walk from the centre and the railway station. The beers are mainly from Kent and Sussex breweries such as Larkins and Dark Star, while Biddenden and Dudda's Tun ciders are often stocked. Local bands perform live most Saturday evenings, with lunchtime jazz every fourth Sunday of the month. Check for information about music and beer festival weekends. Darts and bar billiards are other popular local pastimes. ⌂♿🅿♿♿🅿(6,285)♿📶

Upchurch

Brown Jug
76 Horsham Lane, ME9 7AP

⊕ 12-10 ☎ (01634) 366543
Harvey's Sussex Best Bitter; 2 changing beers (sourced nationally; often Greene King, Harvey's, Timothy Taylor) Ⓗ
This welcoming and popular community pub is on the outskirts of the village. It is unpretentious, with good service and a friendly atmosphere. Sold off by Shepherd Neame, it is now a true free house with a strong liking for Harvey's of Lewes, whose seasonal specials also feature. The food menu is predominantly Italian but also includes British classics. There is a spacious garden with an area of decking and a large car park. The pub is particularly popular with cyclists. Q⌂♿🅿♿🅿(327)♿📶

Upper Upnor

King's Arms
2 High Street, ME2 4XG
⊕ 11.30-midnight; 12-midnight Sun ☎ (01634) 717490
⊕ kingsarmsupnor.co.uk
5 changing beers (sourced regionally; often Ringwood) Ⓗ
Close to the village car park, the pub has been a frequent winner of local CAMRA Pub of the Year. There is a good choice of five guest ales and also European bottled beers and ciders. At the opposite end of the small cobbled High Street stands Upnor Castle, which affords views over the River Medway and the old naval Historic Dockyard at Chatham. The restaurant has an excellent reputation for quality food. Q⌂♿🅿♿🅿(197)♿

Walmer

Berry Ⓛ
23 Canada Road, CT14 7EQ
⊕ 11 (2 Tue; 12 Thu)-11.30; 11.30-11 Sun
☎ (01304) 362411 ⊕ theberrywalmer.co.uk
Burning Sky Plateau; Dark Star American Pale Ale; Harvey's Sussex Best Bitter; 8 changing beers (often Oakham) Ⓗ
This multi award-winning alehouse is off Walmer seafront. The bar has a light and airy feel and at the back there is a pleasant patio. The welcome, service and quality of the ales and ciders reflect the landlord's enthusiasm. There is plenty of choice, with up to 11 cask ales and up to 10 ciders. Three ale festivals and a cider festival are hosted annually. Entertainment includes darts, pool, a monthly quiz and live music. ♿♿♿🅿♿

Freed Man Ⓛ
329 Dover Road, CT14 7NX
⊕ 12-9 (10 Tue; 11 Fri & Sat); 12-8 Sun ☎ (01304) 364457
⊕ thefreed-man.co.uk
4 changing beers (sourced locally) Ⓗ
This pub offers everything for the discerning drinker in a micropub atmosphere. The decor is cosy and warm, with nautical memorabilia covering the reclaimed-wood walls. Up to four real ales, predominantly from local breweries, are served from the Victorian beer engine. Alongside these are real ciders, wines, selected spirits and authentic draught and bottled European lagers. Food can be brought in and the staff will provide plates and cutlery. Regular events include a Thursday ladies' night and a monthly quiz night. ⌂♿♿🅿♿

West Malling

Bull L
1 High Street, ME19 6QH
✪ 12-2.30, 4-11; 12-11 Fri & Sat; 12-10.30 Sun
☎ (01732) 842753 ⊕ thebullinnwestmalling.com
Timothy Taylor Landlord; Young's Bitter; 6 changing beers (sourced nationally; often Goacher's, Musket, Tonbridge) ⊞
A welcoming village pub with wood panelling, hops on the beams and a log fire. There is a focus on local beer and cider, with the cider on handpump. A terrace at the rear offers alfresco drinking. A quiz is held on Monday evenings and live music is provided twice-monthly on Saturdays. Good pub meals are served throughout but the left-hand bar is mainly for diners.
Q ☎ ⊛ ⊲▶ ♣ ⊜ ☒ (72,151) ♣ ☂

Westerham

George & Dragon
Market Square, TN16 1AW
✪ 11.30-11 (midnight Fri & Sat); 12-11 Sun
☎ (01959) 563071
⊕ george-and-dragon-pub-in-westerham.co.uk
Fuller's London Pride; 2 changing beers (sourced locally; often Fuller's) ⊞
Warm and welcoming Grade II-listed, 16th-century pub on the market square, with oak beams, wood panelling and a wood-burning stove. Beers are sourced from the Fuller's range and an extensive food menu is available until 8pm every day. St George's Day and Australia Day are celebrated and there is an occasional Aston Martin festival. A peaceful rear terrace garden gives sanctuary from the busy main road. Sky and BT sports channels show major football and rugby games.
☎ ⊛ ⊲▶ P ☒ (246) ♣ ☂

Westgate-on-Sea

Bake & Alehouse
21 St Mildred's Road, CT8 8RE (down alleyway between Coral bookmakers and Carlton Cinema on left-hand side opp United Services club)
✪ closed Mon; 12-2, 5.30-9; 12-2 Sun ☎ 07913 368787
⊕ bakeandalehouse.co.uk
4 changing beers ⑥
Friendly micropub, an oasis for the local real ale drinker. A selection of four different beers, mainly from Kentish breweries, as well as Kentish cider, is served straight from the barrel kept in a temperature-controlled room. With seating for around 20 people, the small interior has been managed well to create a welcoming atmosphere. Locally produced cheese and pork pies are on sale.
Q ≈ ♣ ⊜ ☒ ♣

Whitstable

Black Dog L
66 High Street, CT5 1BB
✪ 12-11.30 (midnight Thu-Sat)

What care I how time advances: I am drinking ale today. **Edgar Allan Poe**

Kent Session Pale; 4 changing beers (sourced regionally; often Kent, Oakham, Triple fff) ⑥
An attractive town-centre micropub enjoying lush Victorian decor with a twist. There are five different real ales, from local and regional microbreweries, and up to 18 local ciders and perries. The five handpumps on the bar counter are for decoration only, though they do show the beers available, which are dispensed by gravity from the cooled cellar room. There is a quiz on the first Wednesday of each month, and occasional live music from local folk singers and morris dancers. Q ≈ ⊜ ☒ ♣

Handsome Sam L
3 Canterbury Road, CT5 4HJ
✪ 6-10 Mon; 12-2, 6-10.30 (11 Fri & Sat); 12-3 Sun ☎ 07931 662081
5 changing beers (often Dark Star, Mighty Oak, Rockin' Robin) ⑥
Popular micropub just outside the town centre and five minutes from the railway station. Named after the owner's pet cat who died in 2010, the high-ceilinged pub has the original exposed beams. High tables, benches and stools provide seating, and hops adorn the two bay windows. There are between four and six beers on tap, always including a pale ale, a copper ale and a stronger ale, as well as ciders, wines, champagne, spirits, tea and coffee, and pub snacks. Q ☎ ⊛ ⬥ ≈ ⊜ ☒ ☒ ♣

New Inn L
30 Woodlawn Street, CT5 1HG
✪ 3-11 (midnight Fri); 12-midnight Sat; 12-10 Sun
☎ (01227) 264746 ⊕ newinnwhitstable.co.uk
Shepherd Neame Master Brew; 1 changing beer (sourced locally; often Shepherd Neame) ⊞
Dating from 1860, this is a typical Whitstable back-street pub not far from the harbour and shopping area. The etched windows hint at the original layout of several small bars; there is now a long, narrow bar and a cosy area further back with pool, darts and a collection of board games. There is a good selection of gins and malt whiskies. A quiz is held on the first Tuesday of the month, and a jazz jam session on the last Thursday. ☎ ≈ ♣ ⊜ ☒ ♣ ☂

Ship Centurion L ✓
111 High Street, CT5 1AY
✪ 11-11 (11.30 Fri & Sat); 12-7 Sun ☎ (01227) 264740
Adnams Southwold Bitter; 4 changing beers (often Canterbury Ales, Old Dairy, Pig & Porter) ⊞
A friendly and traditional town-centre pub, and local CAMRA Pub of the Year 2015. Colourful hanging baskets add to its charm in summer. Pictures of Whitstable decorate the bar, where a Kentish beer is always available. Home-cooked bar food often includes authentic German dishes, and there is a schnitzel on Saturday (no food Sun). Live music plays on Thursday evenings (except in January). There is a summer cider festival and an October beer festival. ☎ ⊲▶ ≈ ⊜ ☒ ♣ ☂

Willesborough

Blacksmiths Arms ✓
84 The Street, TN24 0NA
✪ 12-11 (midnight Fri & Sat); 12-11.30 Sun
☎ (01233) 623975 ⊕ blacksmithsarmsashford.co.uk
Fuller's London Pride; 3 changing beers (sourced nationally) ⊞
This 18th-century Grade II-listed family-friendly pub is on the outskirts of Ashford. It offers a range

of cask ales and wines and has a changing food menu. There is a large terraced garden and children's play area. 🛏️🏵️🍴🚿♣️🍺P🖳🐾🛜

Clocks and various antique artefacts can be purchased. Dogs are allowed in the bar. Q🏵️🍴P🖳🐾🛜

Wormshill

Blacksmiths Arms
The Street, ME9 0TU TQ878571
✪ closed Mon & Tue; 7-11; 12-11 Sun ☎ (01622) 884386
3 changing beers (sourced regionally; often Arran, Westerham) Ⓗ
Grade II-listed, timber-framed, 17th-century village pub that was formerly three cottages. It is situated in rolling downland countryside near to the Pilgrims' Way. It has a cosy bar with original brick floor, and is warmed in winter by an inglenook log fire. Beers feature from near and far, with Scottish brews alongside local ales, often from Westerham Brewery. Beautifully cooked food is served in the beamed, candlelit restaurant (booking required).

Wrotham

George & Dragon
High Street, TN15 7AA
✪ 12-11; 12-10.30 Sun ☎ (01732) 884298
🌐 georgeanddragon.wrotham.net
Wells Bombardier; 4 changing beers (sourced nationally; often Harvey's, Otter) Ⓗ
A welcoming village local at the foot of the North Downs. This single-bar pub offers five real ales, which are sourced regionally and nationally. Conversation is king in this pub; however, live music is a feature on Saturday nights. In the winter, pool is played in a separate area. Thai food is served Thursday and Friday evenings, along with a roast on Sunday. Q🛏️🏵️🍴♣️🖳(308)🐾🛜

Foundry Brew Pub, Canterbury (Photo: Claire-Michelle Taverner-Pearson)

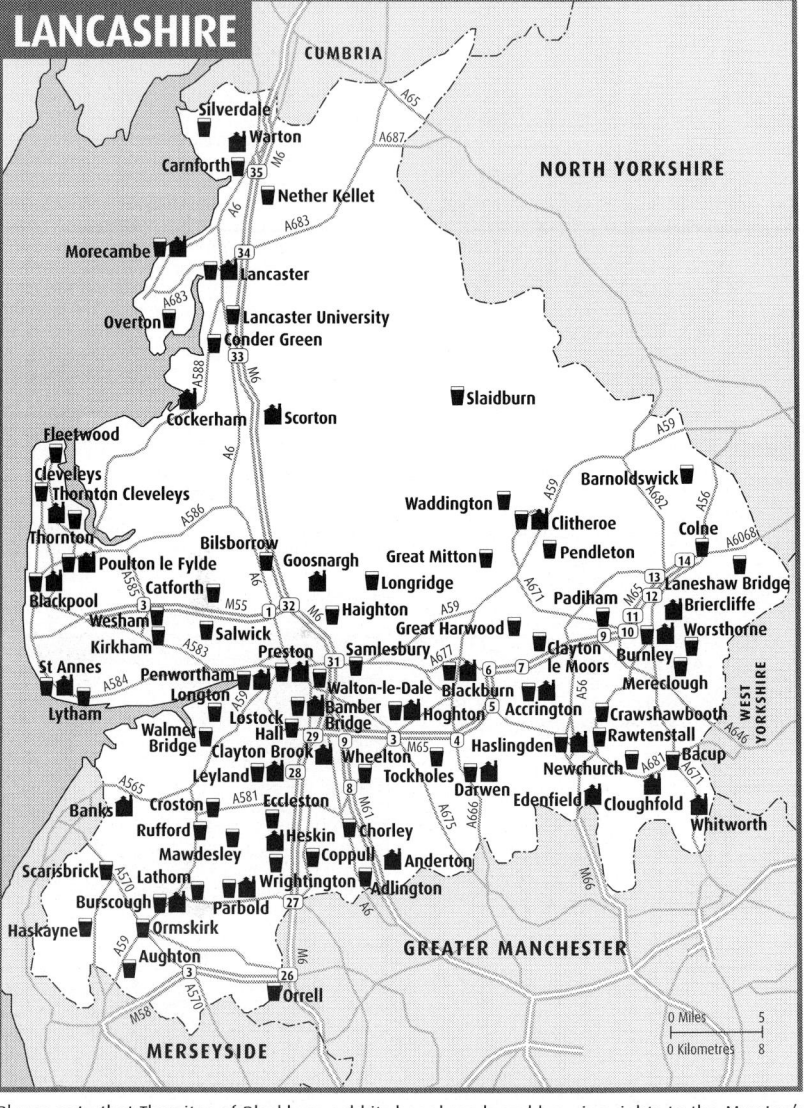

LANCASHIRE

CUMBRIA

NORTH YORKSHIRE

WEST YORKSHIRE

GREATER MANCHESTER

MERSEYSIDE

Silverdale
Warton
Carnforth 35
Nether Kellet
Morecambe 34
Lancaster
Overton
Lancaster University
Conder Green 33
Cockerham Scorton
Slaidburn
Fleetwood
Cleveleys
Thornton Cleveleys
Barnoldswick
Thornton
Waddington
Clitheroe
Colne
Bilsborrow
Poulton le Fylde Goosnargh
Great Mitton
Pendleton
14
Catforth
Longridge
Laneshaw Bridge
13
Blackpool 3
Wesham
Haighton
Padiham
12 Briercliffe
St Annes
Kirkham
Salwick
Great Harwood
11
Worsthorne
Penwortham
Samlesbury
Clayton 10
le Moors Burnley
Preston 31
6
Mereclough
Longton
Walton-le-Dale Blackburn
7
Crawshawbooth
Lytham
Lostock Bamber
Hoghton 5 Accrington
Rawtenstall
Walmer Hall Bridge
9
Bridge Clayton Brook
29
Haslingden
Bacup
Banks Leyland 28
Wheelton
Newchurch
Croston Eccleston
8
Tockholes Darwen
Edenfield Cloughfold
Rufford
Heskin Chorley
Whitworth
Mawdesley
Coppull Anderton
Scarisbrick Lathom
Wrightington Adlington
Burscough Parbold 27
Haskayne Ormskirk
Aughton
26
Orrell

0 Miles 5
0 Kilometres 8

Please note that Thwaites of Blackburn sold its beer brands and brewing rights to the Marston's group in 2015. With the exception of small-run beers brewed on Thwaites's micro plant, all the main Thwaites beers are now brewed and supplied by Marston's. See Breweries section, p705.

Accrington

Grants L

1 Manchester Road, BB5 2BQ
☼ 12-11 (midnight Fri & Sat) ☎ (01254) 393938
⊕ grantsbar.co.uk
Big Clock Pals, Dirty Blonde, Dark Knight; 8 changing beers Ⓗ
A large, imposing building on the southern edge of the town centre, close to the local college campus. Fully refurbished in 2009, the shabby-chic interior attracts an eclectic clientele. The building is home to the 6.5-barrel Big Clock Brewery, which can be viewed from the main bar. Up to eight beers from Big Clock are served alongside a range of real ciders. There is a separate smart function room upstairs for hire with catering available (no

disabled access). Weekly acoustic music nights are held. Food is limited to olives and nuts.
ⓓ✿≈●Pⴀ

Peel Park Hotel L

Turkey Street, BB5 6EW
☼ 12-11.30 ☎ (01254) 235830
Tetley Bitter; 5 changing beers (sourced nationally) Ⓗ
A true free house opposite the site of the old Accrington Stanley football ground, still used by Peel Park FC. Six beers are sold, mainly from smaller regional breweries. The welcoming main bar is divided into split-level front, side and rear sections. There is a separate small pool room, and a rear room used for functions and meetings. Outside is a pleasant garden area to the side of the pub.
ⓓ✿✿Pⴀ➡❀

Adlington

Spinners Arms 🍺
23 Church Street, PR7 4EX
✪ 12-midnight (1am Fri & Sat) ☎ (01257) 483331
Moorhouse's Pride of Pendle; Southport Dark Night; 5 changing beers (sourced regionally; often Abbeydale, George Wright, Oakham) ⊞
The pub is known as the Bottom Spinners to differentiate it from the other Spinners Arms in the village. Built in 1838, it is welcoming and friendly; a single bar serves three seating areas. There is a pleasant outdoor drinking area to the front. It has no pool table or gaming machine, just an open log fire. The bar menu offers home-cooked food, with Sunday specials. Five alternating guest beers are served, often from local breweries. Small functions are catered for. ☎✿◗≠P🚃(8A)🐾 ☺

Aughton

Derby Arms 🍺 ✪
Prescot Road, L39 6TA (on B3197 at Bowkers Green)
✪ 12-midnight (1am Fri & Sat); 12-11 Sun ☎ (01695) 422237
Tetley Bitter; 4 changing beers (often Lytham, Rudgate) ⊞
Friendly country pub with a long CAMRA award-winning heritage. The interior is intimate with many small nooks and crannies. The four guest handpumps offer a changing choice of beers from both local and national breweries. The pub holds quiz nights on Tuesday and Thursday and regular charity events. Excellent-value food is available, with breakfast served on Saturday from 9am.
Q☎✿◗P☺

Bacup

Crown Inn 🍺 ✪
19 Greave Road, OL13 9HQ
✪ 5-11; 3-midnight Fri; 12-midnight Sat; 12-11 Sun
☎ (01706) 873982
Pictish Brewers Gold; 3 changing beers ⊞
Cosy, traditional country pub with an L-shaped bar and stone-flagged floors throughout. A welcoming coal fire warms the atmosphere in the cooler months. There are always three beers available, usually local. Food is served most evenings. Quiz nights are Wednesday and Sunday. On the second floor is a function room accommodating up to 35 guests. There is a patio beer garden to the front of the pub, and beer festivals are held in July and October. ☎✿◗♣P🚃(465)☺

Bamber Bridge

Withy Arms ✪
Station Road, PR5 6QP
✪ 11-midnight (1am Fri); 10.30-1am Sat; 10.30-midnight Sun
☎ (01772) 697706 ⊕ withyarms.com
Ribble WA Bitter, Odd Job; 3 changing beers (sourced nationally) ⊞
There is a small taproom to the right of the entrance while the open-plan main bar area has a slightly continental feel. An impressive bar counter features six handpumps. The two house beers from Ribble Brewery are brewed under contract by an unnamed brewery to the pub's own recipe. The changing guest ales tend to be below 4.5% ABV and from microbreweries. There is outdoor seating on decking at the front and rear of the pub.
☎✿◗≠🍴🚃☎

Barnoldswick

Barlick Tap Ale House 🍺
8 Newtown, BB18 5UQ
✪ closed Mon & Tue; 4-9; 2-10 Fri & Sat; 2-8 Sun ☎ 07739 088846
5 changing beers (sourced nationally) ⊞
You can be sure of a warm welcome from Hazel and Steve at this friendly micropub just off the town square, two minutes from the main bus stop. The bar offers a choice of five changing cask beers, with one a dark beer. A selection of American and European bottled beers and lagers, and bottled ciders and wines is also available. A place to meet and chat over a glass or two without the intrusion of loud music. Q🚃🐾☺

Bilsborrow

Owd Nell's Canalside Tavern
Canalside, St Michael's Road, PR3 0RS (100yds off the A6)
✪ 10-1.30am; 10-1am Sun ☎ (01995) 640010
⊕ guysthatchedhamlet.co.uk
Black Sheep Best Bitter; Cross Bay Sunset Blonde, Zenith; Marston's Wainwright; 6 changing beers (sourced regionally; often Moorhouse's, Reedley Hallows) ⊞

REAL ALE BREWERIES

Beer Brothers Bamber Bridge
Big Clock 🍺 Accrington
Bishop's Crook Penwortham
Bloomfield 🍺 Blackpool (NEW)
Bluestone Whitworth
Borough Lancaster
Bowland Clitheroe
Chapel Street 🍺 Poulton-le-Fylde
Crankshaft Leyland (NEW)
Cross Bay Morecambe
Darkwave Preston
Doghouse Darwen (NEW)
Edenfield 🍺 Edenfield (brewing suspended)
Farm Yard Cockerham (NEW)
Fuzzy Duck Poulton-le-Fylde
Goosnargh 🍺 Goosnargh
Grill & Grain 🍺 Hoghton (NEW) (brewing suspended)
Hart Preston
Hop Vine 🍺 Burscough
Hopstar Darwen
Hubsters Clayton Brook (NEW)
Lancaster Lancaster
Lytham St Annes
Mighty Medicine Whitworth (NEW)
Moonstone 🍺 Burnley
Moorhouse's Burnley
Northern Whisper Cloughfold (NEW)
Old School Warton
Parker Banks
Priest Town Preston (NEW)
Problem Child 🍺 Parbold
Recoil Clitheroe (NEW)
Reedley Hallows Burnley
Rivington Anderton
Rossendale 🍺 Haslingden
Skippool Creek Thornton-Cleveleys (NEW)
Snowhill Scorton
Third Eye Heskin
Three B's 🍺 Blackburn
Thwaites Blackburn
Withnell's Bamber Bridge (NEW)
Worsthorne Briercliffe

Alongside the Lancaster Canal, this spacious pub is central to Guy's Thatched Hamlet, which was developed in the 1980s by the present owners. The hamlet also offers accommodation, shops, a restaurant and sports facilities. It spreads out from the main, stone-flagged bar area with its many festivals and family entertainments, and is a hive of activity all year round. The beer range is unusually large for Rural Fylde and strongly supports local brewers. Excellent, locally sourced food is also on offer. ➤☺🍴◖◗&♣P🚲🐾❄🛆

Blackburn

Black Bull Ⓛ

Brokenstone Road, BB3 0LL (corner of Brokenstone Rd and Heys Lane) SD666247

✪ closed Mon & Tue; 4-11 Wed & Thu (midnight Fri); 12-midnight Sat; 12-10.30 Sun ☎ (01254) 581381

⊕ threebsbrewery.co.uk

Three B's Stoker's Slake, Bobbin's Bitter, Black Bull, Knocker Up; 6 changing beers (sourced locally) Ⓗ
Brewpub on a crossroads in the hills above Blackburn, two miles from the town centre. Formerly a Thwaites establishment, it now houses the Three B's Brewery and sells the full range including the house beer, Black Bull Bitter, and a cider, usually Ribble Valley Gold. Third-pint tasters are available. It has a real coal fire, and is popular with walkers, cyclists and beer connoisseurs. With magnificent views over the hills and out towards the coast, it is an uphill walk from Golden Cup, Mill Hill and Leyburn Road bus stops.
Q➤☺&♣●P🚲🐾

Hare & Hounds Ⓛ

78 Lammack Road, BB1 8LA

✪ 4-midnight; 12.30-1.30am Sat & Sun ☎ (01254) 676724

5 changing beers (sourced regionally; often Martland Mill, Prospect, Worsthorne) Ⓗ
A former Whitbread estate pub rescued by the current landlord and backed by a passionate local community. It is adjacent to Old Blackburnians FC, and to Pleckgate and Lammack playing fields, and is a meeting place for local sports teams including women's netball and hockey. The comfortable open-plan lounge is served from a bar with five handpumps. Beer from Worsthorne is regularly available. Popular quality live entertainment features at weekends, when the pub can get busy.
➤☺&♣P🚲(5)🐾

Rising Sun Ⓞ

797 Whalley New Road, BB1 9BE

✪ 3 (2.30 Thu)-11.30; 2-midnight Fri; 12-midnight Sat; 12-11.30 Sun ☎ (01254) 248407

3 changing beers (sourced nationally) Ⓗ
Around two miles from the centre of Blackburn towards Wilpshire and the Ribble Valley, this former Matthew Brown house is a late-Victorian end-of-terrace hostelry. Friendly, comfortable and popular with locals, dominoes and card games are played here. The small public bar and larger open-plan lounge areas are served from a central bar. Handy for buses and trains from Blackburn, Whalley and Clitheroe. Q⇌♣🚲(22)

Blackpool

Bar 19

19 Queen Street, FY1 1NL

✪ 11 (10 Fri & Sat)-4am ☎ (01253) 627986

4 changing beers (often Coach House, Lees, Titanic) Ⓗ
An oasis of real ale on one of Blackpool's main party streets, this uncomplicated single-room bar is just off the Promenade and close to North Pier and Blackpool North railway station. Very much a locals' bar during the day, it becomes more of a nightclub as the night goes on. The four changing beers come from a wide variety of breweries near and far. Beer festivals are held twice a year in May and November. &⇌🚉(North Pier)🚋🛆

Blackpool Cricket Club Ⓞ

Barlow Crescent, West Park Drive, FY3 9EQ (follow signs to Stanley Park)

✪ 4.30-11; 12-midnight Sat; 12-11 Sun ☎ (01253) 393347

⊕ blackpoolcricket.co.uk

Marston's Wainwright; 4 changing beers (sourced regionally) Ⓗ
On the western edge of Stanley Park, within the cricket pavilion, this club is host to many sports teams, while several TVs show major sports fixtures. An upstairs room is available for social events. The club has its own squash courts and holds quiz and entertainment nights. There is now a ladies' cricket team. It is the many-times local CAMRA branch Club of the Year and holds an annual beer festival. Free entry to all cricket games except Lancashire's. ➤☺&P🚲(15,16)🐾🛆

Layton Rakes Ⓞ

17-25 Market Street, FY1 1ET

✪ 8am-midnight (1am Fri & Sat) ☎ (01253) 743710

Greene King Abbot; Ruddles Best Bitter; Sharp's Doom Bar; 5 changing beers Ⓗ
Just off the Promenade close to North Pier and local bus and tram connections, this multi-floored pub is popular with locals and tourists alike. With bars on each of its floors, all accessible by lift, it offers a wide range of beers changing on a regular basis, and a small range of ciders. The ground floor can get busy on Friday and Saturday evenings, although the middle floor remains fairly quiet. An open-air roof terrace tops the building.
➤☺◖◗&⇌🚉(North Pier)●🚲🛆

Pump & Truncheon Ⓨ

13 Bonny Street, FY1 5AR

✪ 11-midnight ☎ (01253) 624099

⊕ thepumpandtruncheon.co.uk

6 changing beers (sourced nationally) Ⓗ
Friendly, old-fashioned, back-street pub behind the Sealife Centre and Madame Tussauds. The wood-panelled decor has a strong police theme, inspired by the police station opposite. Up to six real ales are served along with an often large range of ciders and perries from all over the country. A roaring log fire is at one end of the pub. Local CAMRA Pub of the Year 2017. ➤◖◗♣●🚲🐾🛆

Saddle Inn Ⓞ

286 Whitegate Drive, FY3 9PH

✪ 10.30-11 (midnight Fri & Sat); 11-midnight Sun

☎ (01253) 767827 ⊕ thesaddleblackpool.co.uk

Draught Bass; 5 changing beers (sourced nationally; often Lytham) Ⓗ
This pub is a Blackpool institution, with the building dating from about 1776 when it was owned by a saddler. Real fires are situated in each of the two rooms off the main bar area, and walls covered in mostly sporting prints add to the ambience. Food is normally served until 9pm daily. Two real ciders are usually available in the summer months.
➤☺◖◗●P🚲🛆

Washington ✔

Topping Street, FY1 3AF

🕓 10.30-11 (midnight Fri & Sat); 11-11 Sun

☎ (01253) 620885

Greene King IPA; Morland Old Speckled Hen; Ruddles Best Bitter; 5 changing beers (sourced nationally) Ⓗ

A single-roomed, bustling street-corner pub between the town centre and Bickerstaff Square development. Due to its multi-level layout, however, it is possible to find a quiet corner if required. Handy for the railway station and most bus routes, it offers a changing range of beers from all over the country, often with a bias towards the North-west. Good-value food is served all day. Several TVs show sporting events, and live music features most weekends. 🐕🍽🚲♣🚌🛏�

Burnley

Bridge Bier Huis Ⓛ

2 Bank Parade, BB11 1UH

🕓 closed Mon & Tue; 12-midnight (1am Fri & Sat); 12-11 Sun

☎ (01282) 411304 🌐 thebridgebierhuis.co.uk

Moorhouse's Premier Bitter; 4 changing beers (sourced regionally) Ⓗ

An award-winning true free house with a large open-plan bar warmed by a logburner, and a small snug to one side. It offers mainly microbrewery beers alongside a changing real cider. More than 60 foreign bottled beers are sold plus seven foreign beers on tap, including rare German brews. Wednesday is quiz night and live music is hosted on occasional weekends. This welcoming pub opens at 5pm Monday or Tuesday if Burnley FC are at home. 🐕🞉🍽🚲♣Pಭ🛏

KSC 110 Club Ⓛ

1 Albert Street, BB11 3BY

🕓 7-midnight (11.30 Mon & Wed; 11 Tue); 1-midnight Sun

☎ (01282) 422571

4 changing beers (sourced regionally) Ⓗ

A club on three storeys, the award-winning Knights of St Columba is on the road to Turf Moor, the home of Burnley FC. Thursday is quiz night, and live music features Friday and Saturday nights plus Sunday afternoon. Games room and function rooms are on the upper floors. The club does get very busy before and after Burnley home matches, when it opens earlier. 🐕♣🛏(592)

Ministry of Ale

9 Trafalgar Street, BB11 1TQ

🕓 closed Mon & Tue; 5-11; 12.30-midnight Fri & Sat; 3-11 Sun

☎ (01282) 830909

Moonstone Black Star Dark, Pale Ale; 2 changing beers (sourced nationally) Ⓗ

Home of the Moonstone Brewery, which can be viewed in the front room of the pub. This small friendly local places an emphasis on excellent beer and good conversation. One Moonstone beer is generally on sale alongside three rotating guests, usually from microbreweries. A popular quiz is held every Thursday night and the pub hosts regular photo exhibitions of old Burnley pubs. Opens Monday or Tuesday evening if Burnley FC are at home. Q🞉🛏🛏

New Brew-m Ⓛ

St James Row, BB11 1DR

🕓 12-8 Mon & Wed; closed Tue; 12-10 Thu-Sat; 12-6 Sun ☎ 07902 961426

6 changing beers (sourced nationally) Ⓗ

Smart micropub in the centre of town run as the Reedley Hallows brewery tap. At least one of its own beers is always on the bar alongside five others sourced nationwide using the head brewer's contacts from years in the trade. A limited range of foreign bottled beers and bottled ciders is available. Comfortable seating around wooden hogsheads on the raised portion complements bench seating opposite the bar. It will open if Burnley FC are at home on a Tuesday night. Q🞉🛏🛏

Burscough

Hop Vine

Liverpool Road North, L40 4BY (village centre on A59)

🕓 10.30-midnight (12.30am Fri & Sat); 10.30-11 Sun

☎ (01704) 893799 🌐 thehopvine.co.uk

Hop Vine Hoppy Blonde, Bitter; Timothy Taylor Landlord; 4 changing beers (sourced regionally; often Salopian) Ⓗ

A spacious former coaching house that is now a thriving community brewpub renowned for its friendly atmosphere and popular for its exceptional ale and food. The classic country pub interior has wood panelling and characterful wood flooring throughout and is decorated with historic local maps, photographs and vintage bottled ales. The Hop Vine Brewery operates from the attractive floral courtyard at the rear. Catering for all age groups, it offers great value meals, live music, and twice-yearly beer festivals. 🐕🞉🍽🛠♣P🛏(2A,3)widehat

Carnforth

Snug

Unit 6, Carnforth Gateway Building, LA5 9TR (at N end of former mainline up platform)

🕓 closed Mon, 12-2, 5-9; 12.30-4.30 Sun ☎ (01524) 735677

🌐 thesnugmicropub.blogspot.co.uk

5 changing beers Ⓗ

The area's first micropub where the only drinks are ale, cider, wine, a few soft drinks and at least 10 good-quality gins, the only food is a few light snacks, and the only sounds are conversation and the roar of the passing trains. The decor is similarly stripped back – painted walls, bare floorboards and chunky tall tables. The eye is naturally drawn to a beautiful glazed wooden cabinet where all the drinks are stored. Parking is in the station car park (charge payable). Q🞉🛠🚲♣🛏🚌🛏🛏

Catforth

Running Pump

Catforth Road, PR4 0HH

🕓 4-7 Mon; 12-10 (1am Fri & Sat) ☎ (01772) 690265

🌐 runningpump.co.uk

Thwaites Original; house beer (by Pixie Spring/ Hopcraft); 3 changing beers (sourced nationally; often Elland, Wishbone) Ⓗ

A 300-year-old building, this traditional country pub reopened in 2015 after refurbishment. Five ales are on tap, three of which are from brewers far and wide. It is well known for offering good food, served throughout the pub, though it also has a separate dining room. The pub is in a pleasant rural area with stunning views of the Pennine Fells. There is a water trough and pump, and an old horse stop with feeding cage outside. Q🐕🞉🍽🛠♣P🛏(80)🛏widehat

Chorley

Ale Station 🅛 ✅
60 Chapel Street, PR7 1BS
❂ closed Mon; 4-11; 2-11 Thu; 2-midnight Fri & Sat; 2-11 Sun
☎ (01257) 368003
6 changing beers (sourced locally; often Rock the Boat) Ⓗ
A micropub conveniently close to both the bus and train stations. A modern-looking venue with a wine-bar feel, this inviting pub offers a full range of drinks. Five changing real ales are served, increasing to six at weekends, mainly from Northwestern microbreweries, although expect to find others from far and wide. There are also two changing real ciders. Pictures of old Chorley adorn the walls. The pub may close earlier during the week depending on custom. Q&≉●🖵😼🛜

Bob Inn
24 Market Place, PR7 1DA
❂ 10-6; closed Wed & Sun ☎ 07767 238410
3 changing beers (sourced nationally) Ⓗ
This tiny bar housed in a market stall, with an adjacent unit now used as a lounge area, is the smallest pub in the CAMRA branch area. Outside seating is available during the summer and drinkers often spill over into the market area. With three changing cask beers from smaller breweries, at least two ciders and a good selection of bottled beers, there is something for every taste. No food, but you are welcome to bring your own.
Q≉●🖵😼

Crown 🅛
46-48 Chapel Street, PR7 1BW
❂ 11-11.30 (1am Fri & Sat); 12-11 Sun ☎ 07552 092176
House beer (by Fuzzy Duck); 3 changing beers (sourced locally; often Bowland, Lancaster, Reedley Hallows) Ⓗ
Newly refurbished and reopened in February 2014 following two years of closure, this pub has an impressive bar counter and bar-back, together with contemporary seating in a mainly open-plan layout. A small area to the side of the bar and a cosy lounge area offer more privacy. Five handpumps provide a changing array of ales, sourced mainly from local microbreweries, and a changing cider. A dark beer is usually available.
🛏&≉●🖵😼🛜

Malt 'n' Hops 🍺 🅛 ✅
50-52 Friday Street, PR6 0AA
❂ 12 (3 Mon)-11; 12-midnight Sat & Sun ☎ (01257) 260074
Bank Top Dark Mild; 8 changing beers (sourced nationally; often Fernandes, Moorhouse's, Rat) Ⓗ
Converted from an old shop, the pub is handily situated for both the railway and bus stations. It has a single L-shaped bar on two levels, recently redecorated and with a bright yet traditional feel. A genuine free house, it offers up to eight guest ales usually sourced from Lancashire and Yorkshire micros, with Rat, Ossett, Elland, Lancaster and Blackedge often featuring. At least one dark beer is usually among the range. Filled rolls and pork pies are often available. Local CAMRA Pub of the Year 2016/17. 🛏😼≉🖵😼🛜

Potters Arms 🅛
42 Brooke Street, PR7 3BY (next to Morrisons)
❂ 3-11.30 (midnight Fri); 12-4, 7-midnight Sat; 12-5, 7-11
Sun ☎ (01257) 267954

Black Sheep Best Bitter; Three B's Doff Cocker; 1
changing beer (sourced nationally) Ⓗ
Small, friendly free house named after the owners, at the bottom of Brooke Street alongside the railway bridge. The central bar serves two games areas, while two comfortable lounges are popular with locals and visitors alike. The pub displays a fine selection of photographs from the world of music, as well as vintage local scenes. Regular darts and dominoes nights are well attended and the chip butties go down a treat. The smoking area is covered. ≉♣P🖵(109A)🛜

Shepherds' Hall Ale House 🅛
67 Chapel Street, PR7 1BS
❂ closed Mon; 2-10 (11 Fri); 12-11 Sat; 2-9
Sun ☎ 07412 584907
5 changing beers (sourced nationally) Ⓗ
Formerly a shop, it has been tastefully converted, utilising fittings from closed pubs in the town – the bar coming from Harry's Bar and the tables from the Tut 'n' Shive. Like most micropubs, there is no food, TV or music, and the drinks range is limited to real ale, cider, bottled beers, wine and soft drinks. The beers come mainly from microbreweries across the country, although a LocAle or two should be expected. Q≉●🖵🖵😼

Clayton le Moors

Forts Arms 🅛
1 Lower Barnes Street, BB5 5TA
❂ 4-midnight; 2-2am Fri & Sat; 2-11 Sun ☎ (01254) 433713
4 changing beers (sourced nationally; often Snaggletooth) Ⓗ
Partially opened out in a modern style, yet still retaining a separate lounge, this corner pub boasts a large rear beer garden and a two-floor function suite to the side. Beers are from local and regional breweries such as Snaggletooth, Bowland and Wishbone. It has a small library and a few games, including some for children. Folk music sessions take place weekly and music and beer festivals are held twice a year. Handy for Mercer Park and a short walk downhill from the Leeds-Liverpool Canal. Q🛏😼♣P🖵😼

Cleveleys

Jolly Tars ✅
154-158 Victoria Road, FY5 3NE
❂ 8am-11 (12.30am Thu-Sat); 8am-midnight Sun
☎ (01253) 856042
Greene King Abbot; Ruddles Best Bitter; Sharp's Doom Bar; 7 changing beers (sourced nationally) Ⓗ
A Wetherspoon conversion of a former supermarket which provides a pleasant and airy environment in which to enjoy a drink, including a number of secluded areas for a quiet pint. Regional and national beers are generally available from a range of constantly rotating guest ales, along with at least one cider. An open-air drinking area is at the front of the pub. Several works by renowned local glassmaker John Ditchfield decorate the interior. 🛏😼🕽&🖵●🖵🛜

Clitheroe

New Inn 🍺 🅛
20 Parson Lane, BB7 2JN
❂ 11-11; 12-11 Sun ☎ (01200) 423312

Coach House Gunpowder Mild, Farrier's Best Bitter; Moorhouse's Premier Bitter, White Witch, Pride of Pendle, Blond Witch; 5 changing beers (sourced regionally) ⊞
This gem of a pub can be found beneath the 12th-century castle and only a few minutes' walk from the station. Its quirky layout has a narrow corridor that leads to a cosy bar area, with four other rooms and a spacious beer garden at the rear. Guest beers are mainly from local breweries including Bowland, Prospect and Worsthorne. The back room hosts a traditional Irish music session every alternate Sunday afternoon and a number of local groups meet here regularly. Q❀▲≉⊟❀

Colne

Admiral Lord Rodney ℒ
Mill Green, BB8 0TA
🕓 4-midnight (2am Fri); 1-2am Sat; 1-midnight Sun
☎ (01282) 219759 ∰ thelordrodney.co.uk
9 changing beers (sourced regionally) ⊞
A much-loved community pub in Colne's old South Valley area, the old industrial heart of the town. The stone floor includes mosaics and there are beautiful tiles up the inner staircase. Set out in three rooms, the pub has become the meeting place for a number of clubs. Regular live entertainment takes place during the evenings, and there are local history and art displays. Recently refurbished, it has open fires and flagged floors, plus a much-improved outdoor seating area and a separate smokers' area. Q❧❀◗♣❀❀

Boyce's Barrel
7 New Market Street, BB8 9BJ
🕓 closed Mon; 4 (1 Sat)-9 ☎ 07736 900111
5 changing beers (sourced nationally) ⊞
The first micropub in Colne, it offers five real ales, no music, no lager, just a great atmosphere and plenty of banter. Tastefully styled with tall polished wooden sleeper tables, it is reminiscent of a rail staging post. Ales are rotated often, with new beers put on the bar almost as soon as a cask runs dry (all ales are from non-local breweries). One mild and one porter or stout are always included. A place that is sure to suit any real ale fan's taste. Q♿≉●⊟❀

Conder Green

Stork ✔
Corricks Lane, LA2 0AN
🕓 12-11 (midnight Fri & Sat) ☎ (01524) 751234
∰ thestorkinn.com
Black Sheep Best Bitter; Jennings Cumberland Ale; Lancaster Blonde; Timothy Taylor Golden Best, Landlord ⊞
Delightful, hospitable country inn close to the estuaries of the Lune and Conder. There is a main wood-panelled bar, a restaurant specialising in South African food, and several small rooms including a pleasant snug and a playroom for children. The hilly garden has a play area and a well. Cycle racks are provided outside, handy for the Lune estuary cycle path. The earliest record of this popular destination is from 1660 and some of the existing buildings may date back that far. A stork featured in the coat of arms of a previous owner. ❧❀⇆◗▲P⊟(89)❀❀

Coppull

Red Herring
Mill Lane, PR7 5AN
🕓 3-11; 12-11.30 Fri & Sat; 12-11 Sun ☎ (01257) 470130
5 changing beers ⊞
Real ale pub in the former offices of the next-door mill. It was converted to a pub some years ago; the bar area comprises a large single room plus an extension. Up to five beers, mainly from micros, are usually served. TV sports fans are catered for, as are anglers who use the pond opposite. The pub hosts regular music nights and barbecues, and has a large first-floor function room. ❧❀♿♣P⊟(362)❀❀

Crawshawbooth

Masons Arms ℒ ✔
6 Co-operation Street, BB4 8AG (200yds off A682)
🕓 2 (12 Fri)-11; 12-midnight Sat & Sun ☎ 07957 855012
3 changing beers (sourced locally) ⊞
Hidden away in the village centre, this is an old stone inn at the end of a row of terraced cottages. Across the road sits an interesting Friends (Quaker) meeting house. Inside the pub you will find three small rooms including one for pool and a TV room for live sport, with the bar and its three handpumps in the larger main room. ❧♿♣(X43)❀

Croston

Wheatsheaf
Town Road, PR26 9RA
🕓 12-11 (midnight Fri); 10-midnight Sat; 10-11 Sun
☎ (01772) 600370 ∰ wheatsheaf-croston.com
Robinsons Dizzy Blonde; 4 changing beers (often Hawkshead) ⊞
On the main road and overlooking the village green, this recently refurbished pub has a contemporary feel. It has a distinct area for dining as well as a comfortable drinking area with sofas and chairs. The large patio to the front is used to hold an annual beer festival in October. Up to five ales are served from the SIBA list. Live music features on Friday or Saturday nights twice a month. ❧❀◗♿⇆P⊟(113)❀❀

Darwen

Number 39 ℒ
39-41 Bridge Street, BB3 2AA
🕓 12-midnight ☎ 07531 425352
Hopstar Dizzy Danny Ale, Dark Knight, JC, Lancashire Gold; 1 changing beer (sourced locally) ⊞
The Hopstar Brewery tap, where new brews are tried out. A classic single-roomed continental-style bar, it serves a variety of Hopstar beers, a local guest ale and two ciders or perries. Bottled continental and world beers and draught Timmermans are also on offer. An eclectic range of background music plays and there are weekly live music sessions. Friday is tapas day and Sunday afternoon is apple, cheese and perry time. ❧⇆●⊟(2,X43)❀❀

Old Function Room
5 Watery Lane, BB3 2ET
🕓 2-11 (1am Thu); 12-1am Fri & Sat; 11-midnight Sun
☎ (01254) 701232
5 changing beers (sourced regionally) ⊞

Opened as a working men's club in 1846, it was known throughout the 1960s and 70s as the Barracuda Club, then for 30 years as the Craiglands Function Rooms. It has comfortable surroundings, a real fire, regular cask ale, folk and quiz nights, and live entertainment on Saturday. Meals are served on Sunday only. Five ales are on offer from local and regional breweries such as Moorhouse's, Lees and Worsthorne. ❀◖♣●🖵

Eccleston

Original Farmers Arms 🅻
Towngate, PR7 5QS
✪ 12-midnight (1am Fri & Sat) ☎ (01257) 451594
⊕ originalfarmersarms.co.uk
Lancaster Blonde; Marston's Wainwright; Moorhouse's White Witch; Sharp's Doom Bar; 2 changing beers (sourced nationally) Ⓗ
White-painted village pub that has expanded over the years into the cottage next door, adding a substantial dining area. However, the original part of the pub is still used mainly for drinking. Meals are available throughout the day, seven days a week, and there is accommodation in four good-value guest rooms. There are currently four standard beers – the Moorhouse's usually being White Witch. Two other pumps serve changing guests, one of which is free of tie.
➷❀╝◖P🖵(113,347)🛜

Fleetwood

Royal Oak Hotel
171 Lord Street, FY7 6SR
✪ 12-midnight (1am Fri & Sat) ☎ (01253) 873486
Banks's Sunbeam; house beer (by Reedley Hallows); 6 changing beers (sourced locally; often Blackedge, Bowness Bay, Cross Bay) Ⓗ
Known locally as Dead 'Uns, this pub has gone from strength to strength after being rescued from closure in 2013. It still retains many original features. Up to eight beers on tap, mainly from local brewers. Westons Old Rosie cider is also served. There is a function room available for hire. Fleetwood Rock and Blues Club have live bands on regularly. Dogs are allowed in the vaults. Away fans are welcome when playing Fleetwood Town.
➷♿🜨♣●🖵🛜

Steamer
Queens Terrace, FY7 6BT
✪ 12 (11 Tue & Thu)-midnight; 11-1am Fri; 12-1am Sat
☎ (01253) 681001
Reedley Hallows Pendleside; Wells Bombardier; 5 changing beers Ⓗ
Historic coaching inn dating from 1842 overlooking the former docks, featuring an impressive mahogany and Spanish teak bar. It is close to Fleetwood Market, a short stroll from the tram and bus stops, and a short walk from the ferry to Knott End. Up to seven beers and a changing cider are on offer. Live bands feature at weekends. Food is provided in the attached restaurant where you will often be served by comedy legend Syd Little of Little and Large.
➷◖♿🜨♣●🖵🛜

Great Harwood

Victoria ★ 🅻
St Johns Street, BB6 7EP
✪ 2-11; 12-11 Sat & Sun ☎ (01254) 885210

8 changing beers Ⓗ
A fine Edwardian multi-roomed gem featuring much original woodwork and tiling. Note the sash windows around the central horseshoe bar, the small separate snug, and the darts room with latticed seating. The large outdoor area to the rear has moorland views. Lancashire, Yorkshire and Lakeland beers predominate. It is a meeting place for numerous local societies, from running and cycling to chess and vegetable growing. A varying cider is sold in the summer months. The adjacent disused railway joins up with the Leeds-Liverpool Canal, making it an excellent destination for walkers and cyclists. Q➷❀♣●🖵(6,7)🛜

Great Mitton

Aspinall Arms
Mitton Road, BB7 9PQ
✪ 10.30-11; 10.30-10.30 Sun ☎ (01254) 826555
⊕ aspinallarmspub.co.uk
Brunning & Price Original; 5 changing beers (sourced regionally) Ⓗ
Sat atop the River Ribble, this former ferryboat house is bright, airy and welcoming. With 12 handpumps serving six cask ales, it is a haven for walkers, cyclists and anglers. Looking across to medieval All Hallows Church, with a landscaped beer garden and children's play area, it is popular on fine days, while Persian rugs and open fires provide a warm winter welcome. A favoured destination for local diners, convivial staff serve freshly prepared food all day, catering to any dietary requirements. ➷❀◖P🖵(5)🛜

Haighton

Haighton Manor
Haighton Green Lane, PR2 5SQ
✪ 11-11 (midnight Fri & Sat); 11-10.30 Sun
☎ (01772) 706350
Moorhouse's White Witch; Timothy Taylor Boltmaker; house beer (by Phoenix); 4 changing beers (often Hawkshead, Worsthorne) Ⓗ
Opened in September 2016 after major refurbishment and extension, this former country house hotel and wedding venue is now a bustling pub and dining establishment. Seven handpumps offer a varied range of beers, usually including a dark mild or stout, and a real cider. Quality locally sourced food is available as well as a selection of beer tapas. Stone walls, flagged and wooden floors, low-beamed ceilings and open fires add to the country house feel, while a new conservatory and external patio area provide views across the fields for diners and drinkers alike. Walkers and dogs welcome. ➷❀◖♿♣●P🛜

Haskayne

King's Arms Hotel
1 Delph Lane, Downholland, L39 7JJ (near bridge where Leeds-Liverpool Canal crosses A5147)
✪ 2-midnight; 12-midnight Sat & Sun ☎ (01704) 840033
Salopian Oracle; 4 changing beers (sourced regionally; often Martland Mill, Rock the Boat, Windmill) Ⓗ
A hostelry on the busy A5147 between Maghull and Scarisbrick – a real community pub with two rooms and many attractive original features. It holds a small beer festival over the August bank holiday weekend which includes a family fun day

with many quirky rural competitions. Occasional coach trips to local breweries and other interesting places are organised. ☎🏠P🚐(300)🐾

Haslingden

Griffin Inn 🅛
86 Hud Rake, BB4 5AF
🕐 2-midnight; 12-2am Fri & Sat; 12-midnight Sun
☎ (01706) 214021
Rossendale Floral Dance, Glen Top Bitter, Ale, Halo Pale, Pitch Porter, Sunshine; 1 changing beer 🅗
A traditional community pub and also the home of the Rossendale Brewery. The spacious bar area has a separate area for pub games, and the large lounge has picture windows overlooking the local hills and valleys. The brewery sits below the pub, and on the hill facing the front sits the Halo Panopticon. It is a steep uphill walk from the main road bus stops. Q&♣●🚐(464,X41)🐾 📶

Rose & Crown 🅛
276 Manchester Road, BB4 6PU
🕐 4 (3 Fri)-midnight; 12-midnight Sat; 12-11 Sun
☎ (01706) 213556
Moorhouse's Pride of Pendle; 1 changing beer (sourced nationally; often Sharp's) 🅗
Stone-built end-of-terrace pub on the busy Manchester Road, with an open-plan bar and separate pool room. There is a large beer garden to the rear. The façade of the building features the original windows advertising one-time owner Massey's Brewery of Burnley. Nowadays you will find that other Burnley brewery, Moorhouse's, on sale. Handy for local bus services. 🏠🚐

Hoghton

Royal Oak 🅛
Blackburn Old Road, Riley Green, PR5 0SL
🕐 11-11; 12-10.30 Sun ☎ (01254) 201445
🌐 chrisrawlinson.co.uk/index.htm
Marston's Wainwright, Lancaster Bomber; Thwaites Nutty Black, Original; 1 changing beer 🅗
An attractive stone-built pub on the old road between Preston and Blackburn, near Riley Green basin on the Leeds-Liverpool Canal and popular with diners and drinkers alike. Four distinct rooms including the dining area are served from the central bar, while low-beamed ceilings, bare walls and horse brasses give the pub a rustic feel. A pleasant beer garden has views of nearby Hoghton Tower. The guest beer is normally from either the Thwaites microbrewery or from the Marston's range. Q☎🏠◖●P🚐(152)🐾 📶

Kirkham

Stable Bar
48 Preston Street, PR4 2ZA
🕐 12-12.30am; 12-midnight Sun ☎ (01772) 490689
Moorhouse's Blond Witch, Pendle Witches Brew; 3 changing beers (sourced locally; often Cross Bay, Moorhouse's, Pennine) 🅗
Close to Kirkham town centre, this is a family-run pub serving five quality real ales. It has a friendly and lively atmosphere, with helpful staff, and is decorated with many photos of old Kirkham. A wide range of sport is shown live on big screens. There is a free jukebox and an interesting multi-level suntrap beer garden to the rear. ☎🏠♣P🚐(61,78)📶

Lancaster

Bobbin ✔
8 Chapel Street, LA1 1HH
🕐 11-midnight (1am Thu-Sat) ☎ (01524) 32606
🌐 thebobbinlancaster.co.uk
Coniston Bluebird XB; York Guzzler; 4 changing beers (often Abbeydale, Skinner's, York) 🅗
Large mainly Victorian pub (part 18th century), entirely open plan but still divided up by raised areas and pillars. It is frequented by a goth/metal crowd (but they are by no means the only customers), and has a vaguely Edwardian decor. The jukebox is extremely eclectic. Open mic night is Monday, and live music features Thursday and some Fridays. There is a quiz on Sunday. Handy for the bus station. 🏠&🚄♣●🚐🐾📶

Lancaster Brewery ✔
Lancaster Leisure Park, LA1 3LA
🕐 10-6 ☎ (01524) 848537 🌐 lancasterbrewery.co.uk
Lancaster Amber, Blonde, Black, Red; 5 changing beers (often Lancaster) 🅗
The brewery visitor centre is in a capacious steel shed on a leafy leisure park with various attractions. It is open to the public at the times above, and available for functions at other times. It is mainly furnished with dining tables and benches, also a few sofas. Brewery tours are 11am and 3pm. It has a retail shop with ale, clothing and souvenirs. No food is available but you can bring your own. 🏠&♣P🚐(18)🐾📶

Merchants ✔
29 Castle Hill, LA1 1YN
🕐 11.30-11 (12.30am Fri); 11-12.30am Sat ☎ (01524) 66466
🌐 merchants1688.co.uk
House beer (by Old School); 7 changing beers (sourced regionally; often Allendale, Kirkby Lonsdale, Tirril) 🅗
Converted wine-merchants' cellars built in 1688, with an extensive outdoor drinking area that creates a peaceful haven from the hubbub of the city centre. The main drinking areas are in three separate tunnels, with a fourth forming the entrance and bar area. One tunnel is now a restaurant, another is used for functions as required. Quiz night is Sunday. Look for the stoneware bottles used in the construction of the cellar walls. The house beer, Castle Blonde, is brewed by Old School. Many board games are available, and there is live music late every Saturday evening. 🏠◖🚄🚐📶

Sun
63 Church Street, LA1 1ET
🕐 11-midnight; 11.30-1am Fri & Sat; 11-11.30 Sun
☎ (01524) 66006 🌐 thesunhotelandbar.co.uk
Lancaster Amber, Blonde, Black, Red; Marston's Wainwright; 5 changing beers (often Lancaster) 🅗
Completely altered in 2004 and then extended next door in early 2005, the decor here combines a mixture of exposed stonework, wood panelling and solid furniture, with ambient candlelight in the evenings. The original pub has open space for vertical drinking; the extension is mostly furnished with old dining tables. Some original features remain, including stone fireplaces (one with a wood-burning stove) and a well. The pub is the primary outlet for Lancaster Brewery in the city. Outside is a peaceful courtyard with a heated and covered smoking area. Opens early for breakfast. ☎🏠🛏◖&🚄🚐📶

Tap House L
2 Gage Street, LA1 1UH
🕓 4 (2 Wed; 12 Thu)-midnight; 12-1am Fri & Sat; 2-11 Sun
☎ (01524) 842232 ⊕ taphouselancaster.com
**Hawkshead Windermere Pale; 3 changing beers
(often York)** Ⓗ
This place describes itself as a World Beer Shrine,
but sells plenty of British beer alongside the
imports. A small 19th-century street-corner pub, it
was completely refurbished in 2012, with some
bare brickwork, a lot of visible wood (including old
beer casks incorporated into the furnishings), high,
chunky tables, and otherwise a white and grey
decor. It holds a small beer library, and has weekly
tastings/Meet the Brewer events on Wednesdays,
and a quiz on Mondays. ♿🚆🛏🐱♿ 🛜

Three Mariners 🏆 ✅
Bridge Lane, LA1 1EE (near Parksafe car park entrance)
🕓 12-midnight (1am Fri & Sat) ☎ (01524) 388957
⊕ thethreemarinerslancaster.co.uk
Oakham Citra; Robinsons Wizard; 4 changing beers Ⓗ
Commonly claimed to be the oldest pub in
Lancaster, it certainly looks old, inside as well as
out, but has suffered some rebuilding, and it had a
comprehensive revamp in 2004. The cellar is
excavated at first-floor level. The pub is now a
popular watering hole with a thriving local
clientele. Home-cooked, reasonably priced food is
available. Bluegrass music takes place on
Wednesday, folk on the first Friday of the month.
There is limited parking. Q🏠🕏🍴♿🚆♣♥🛏🐱🛜

White Cross L ✅
Quarry Road, LA1 4XT (behind town hall, on canal
towpath)
🕓 11.30-11 (12.30am Fri & Sat); 12-11 Sun ☎ (01524) 33999
⊕ thewhitecross.co.uk
**Castle Rock Harvest Pale; Sharp's Doom Bar; Timothy
Taylor Landlord; 10 changing beers (sourced
regionally; often Allendale, Hardknott, Tirril)** Ⓗ
A modern (1988) renovation of an old canalside
warehouse with an open-plan interior and a light,
airy feel. French windows open on to extensive
canalside seating. There is a Tuesday quiz, and a
beer and pie festival each April. It stands in the
corner of an extensive complex of Victorian textile
mills, now converted to other uses. The wide open
spaces and decor make it look like a circuit pub, but
in fact much of the custom comes either from the
residential areas up the hill or from the nearby
workplaces. 🏠🕏♿♣♥🛏🐱🛜

Lancaster University
Graduate College Bar
Bailrigg, LA2 0PF (signposted, on pedestrian square in
Alexandra Park)
🕓 7-11; 5-11.30 Fri ☎ (01524) 592824 ⊕ lancaster.ac.uk/
eat/graduate.php
4 changing beers Ⓗ
The graduate college bar is much pubbier and
attracts a higher age range than the usual student
watering hole. The choice of beer is good, with
eight handpumps. There is a beer fest in June. Curry
night is Friday, and open mic alternates with live
bands on Thursday. The university bars all have
alternative names: this one is the Herdwick. It has
reduced hours in vacations. There are pork pies and
pickled eggs for sale. 🏠♿♣♥🛏(3,4)🐱🛜

Laneshaw Bridge
Emmott Arms L ✅
Keighley Road, BB8 7HX
🕓 12-10 (11 Thu; midnight Fri & Sat) ☎ (01282) 864889
⊕ the-emmott-arms.co.uk
**Lancaster Blonde; Tetley Bitter; 2 changing beers
(sourced regionally)** Ⓗ
Popular pub at the centre of the village, easily
accessible by bus from Keighley or Colne, being on
the main road between the two towns. It is named
after a local landowning family from the time of
William the Conqueror. A three-roomed pub with
open fires and a beer garden to the rear, it is set
out mainly for diners, but with a snug bar area.
Constantly changing guest beers come from local
and regional brewers. Q🏠🕏🛏♿🍴🕏🛏(25)

Lathom
Ring o' Bells L
Ring o' Bells lane, L40 5TF (about 500yds from A5209
main road between Burscough and Parbold)
🕓 11-midnight (midnight Fri & Sat) ☎ (01704) 893157
**Marston's Lancaster Bomber; Thwaites Nutty Black; 4
changing beers (often Old School, Thwaites)** Ⓗ
Impressive country pub in large rural grounds along
the Leeds-Liverpool Canal about a 20-minute walk
from Burscough village. Reopened in 2011 by a
local pubco, the huge split-level interior boasts
stone and wood floors with separate locals' and
family areas. Six handpumps serve Thwaites and
other local beers and there are two cider handpulls.
The food is well priced and beef is locally sourced.
An upstairs private room is available as well as
canal moorings. Two rotating ciders come from
Gwynt y Ddraig. 🕏🛏🍴♿🛏(3A,337)🐱🛜

Ship Inn ✅
4 Wheat Lane, L40 4BX (take School Lane from
Burscough, turn right after humpback bridge) SD452116
🕓 12-midnight; 12-11.30 Sun ☎ (01704) 893117
⊕ shipatlathom.co.uk
**House beer (by Moorhouse's); changing beers
(sourced regionally; often Black Sheep, Sharp's)** Ⓗ
A traditional country pub in an idyllic canalside
location. The cosy central bar features a real fire,
and separates the two dining areas which serve
pub classics through to interesting and changing
specials. There is a dog-friendly boot room. The pub
is popular all year, and the large beer garden gets
busy in summer. A highlight is the September Beer,
Pie and Sausage Festival with over 40 handpulled
ales. 🕏🛏🍴♿🚆🛏(337,3A)🐱🛜

Leyland
Gables ✅
2 Hough Lane, PR25 2SD
🕓 12-11.30 (midnight Fri & Sat) ☎ (01772) 493077
**Robinsons Dizzy Blonde; Sharp's Doom Bar; Timothy
Taylor Landlord; 3 changing beers (sourced
nationally)** Ⓗ
A red-brick former doctors' house in the town
centre, converted to a pub in the 1950s by the
Bolton brewer Magee Marshall. A central bar
serves two distinct drinking areas. The vault has a
pool table and TVs, while the comfortable lounge
has walls decorated with pictures, plates and a
collection of teapots. A large wooden decking area
to the front provides pleasant outside drinking in
fine weather. The three changing beers are often
from smaller breweries. 🕏🛏🍴♿🚆♣🛏🐱🛜

Golden Tap Ale House 🄻
1 Chapel Brow, PR25 3NH
☿ closed Mon; 3-10; 2-11 Fri & Sat; 2-10 Sun
☎ (01772) 431859
6 changing beers Ⓗ
Located in a former shop, this cosy one-roomed micropub (one of two in Leyland) opened its doors at the end of April 2016. Six changing cask ales are served, usually including two dark beers, from microbreweries far and wide, but normally at least one from the local region. No food is served other than a few snacks, but the pub is right in the heart of the town's fast-food and takeaway area.
Q ❧ ≈ ● ➡ (109,111) ❀ 🛜

Leyland Lion 🄻 ✅
60 Hough Lane, PR25 2SA
☿ 8am-11.30 (12.30am Fri & Sat) ☎ (01772) 643990
Hawkshead Windermere Pale; Ruddles Best Bitter; Sharp's Doom Bar; house beer (by Moorhouse's); 6 changing beers Ⓗ
Opened in 2011, this conversion of a town-centre post office is smaller than most Wetherspoon pubs. A central log fire is also unusual for this operator. The pub's name commemorates one of the buses which made this town famous and which were built a few yards up the road. Up to eight guest beers are usually available, often coming from local breweries, plus a real cider. The house beer, Leyland Lion, is brewed by Moorhouse's. Handy for the Commercial Vehicle Museum. Alcohol is served from 9am. ❧ ⊛ ◑ ᵹ ≈ ● ➡ 🛜

Market Ale House 🄻
33 Hough Lane, PR25 2SB
☿ 2-8 Mon; 2-10 Tue & Wed; 2-11 Thu; 12-11 Fri & Sat; 1-8 Sun ☎ (01772) 623363
6 changing beers (sourced locally) Ⓗ
Leyland's smallest pub opened in 2013 in former shop premises. It is the area's first micropub and is located at the entrance to the former Leyland Motors North Works, which now serves as the town's market hall. Six changing real ales come from breweries all over the country. Changing ciders, wine and a few spirits are also served. Food is limited to Lancashire cheeses and pork pies. TV and music are notable for their absence. In summer, tables are put on the wide pavement to create an outside drinking area. Q ≈ ♣ ● ➡ ❀ 🛜

Withy Arms 🄻 ✅
3 Worden Lane, PR25 3EL (opp Fox & Lion near Tesco)
☿ 11-11.45 ☎ (01772) 301969
Ribble WA Bitter, Odd Job; 4 changing beers Ⓗ
Formerly the Roebuck, the Withy Arms at Leyland is a sister pub to the Withy Arms at Bamber Bridge. It is located in the centre of historic Leyland (or what remains of it) in front of the iconic Leyland Cross and behind the 1,000-year-old parish church. This pub is noted for its many beer festivals (at least five per year) which are held in the large yard/beer garden at the rear, with open and covered areas. The Ribble Brewery house beers are brewed locally. ❧ ⊛ ◑ ➡ ❀ 🛜

Longridge

Corporation Arms 🄻
Lower Road, PR3 2YJ (near B5243/B6245 jct)
☿ 11-midnight (1am Fri & Sat); 12-10.30 Sun
☎ (01772) 782644 🌐 corporationarms.com
4 changing beers (sourced nationally) Ⓗ

A substantial 18th-century stone-built inn close to the Longridge reservoirs on the road to Ribchester, handy for local walks. This free house has a reputation for excellent ale, food, service and accommodation. Four handpumps serve beers sourced mainly from local breweries, with Bowland, Saltaire and Moorhouse's being among the favourites. Real cider is normally only available during summer months. There is an annual beer festival on the spring bank holiday weekend.
Q ❧ ⊛ ✑ ◑ ᵹ ♠ ● ➡ (5A,5B) 🛜

Towneley Arms ✅
41 Berry Lane, PR3 3JP
☿ 11-11 (1am Fri & Sat) ☎ (01772) 780335
🌐 towneleyarms.co.uk
4 changing beers (sourced nationally) Ⓗ
Large, fully refurbished pub on the main street. Food is served all day from a seasonally changing menu. The pub has a good reputation for real ale, with four handpumps offering a variety of up to 16 different ales each week. There is a quiz night on Wednesday and live music and entertainment at weekends. The Towneley has a welcoming feel about it and is family and dog friendly.
❧ ⊛ ◑ ᵹ ♣ ➡ ❀ 🛜

Longton

Dolphin
Marsh Lane, PR4 5JY
☿ 12-11; 11.30-11 Sun ☎ (01772) 612032
🌐 greencrabpubs.co.uk
4 changing beers (sourced locally) Ⓗ
An isolated country pub at the end of a lane on Longton Marsh. The handpumps are in the wood-floored public bar, and there is a restaurant in the rear conservatory. A large and varied menu covers everything from sandwiches to man v food challenges. Up to four handpulled real ales and a cider are available, part of a changing selection with an emphasis on local micros, often including a mild or dark beer. Evening closing is flexible, dependent on trade. ❧ ⊛ ◑ ᵹ ♠ ● P ❀

Lostock Hall

Anchor ✅
Croston Road, PR5 5LA (300yds from B5254 alongside Preston-Blackburn railway line)
☿ 4.30-11.30; 4-midnight Fri; 12-midnight Sat; 1-11.30 Sun
☎ (01772) 335637
5 changing beers (sourced nationally) Ⓗ
Just a short distance from the Tardy Gate shopping area, this friendly community pub offers five changing cask ales from the Heineken Discover Cask range, with LocAle beers often available. In both spring and autumn a beer festival takes place in marquees on a large grassy area adjacent to the pub. A traditional roast is served on Sundays only 3-5pm. Q ❧ ⊛ ◑ ᵹ ≈ ♣ P ➡ 🛜

Lytham

Railway Hotel ✅
Station Road, FY8 5DH (next to fire station on B5259)
☿ 8am-midnight ☎ (01253) 797250
Greene King Abbot; Moorhouse's Pendle Witches Brew; Ruddles Best Bitter; Sharp's Doom Bar; house beer (by Moorhouse's); 6 changing beers (sourced nationally) Ⓗ

When Wetherpoon acquired this pub it revived the original Victorian name. It has a bright, new-look interior on different levels, with four distinct themed areas featuring golf, railways and old photos of Lytham's halcyon days as a tourist resort. There is a small beer garden at the front with a separate smoking area and another small drinking area at the side. The C&S Ale harks back to a long-defunct local brewery. There is limited parking at the rear. Q❄️🏠🍴🚭🚆♿🚕🐕📶

Taps ✪
12 Henry Street, FY8 5LE
🕐 11-11 (midnight Fri & Sat) ☎ (01253) 736226
🌐 thetaps.net
Greene King IPA; Morland Old Speckled Hen; Robinsons Dizzy Blonde; 7 changing beers (sourced nationally) Ⓗ

A multi award-winning pub, twice CAMRA National Pub of the Year runner-up and many times branch Pub of the Year. The venue serves three permanent beers and seven guests from far and wide as well as cider. One beer is always a mild. A sympathetic refurbishment took place recently to give much-needed additional space and a pleasant outdoor drinking area. A quiz features every Monday night and several charity events take place during the year. 🏠🍴♿🚆♣🚕🐕🐾📶

Mawdesley
Red Lion ✪
68 New Street, L40 2QP (on main road in centre of village)
🕐 12-11 (midnight Fri & Sat) ☎ (01704) 822208
🌐 redlion-mawdesley.com
Moorhouse's White Witch; 3 changing beers (often Hawkshead, Moorhouse's, Salopian) Ⓗ

This small white-painted pub at the centre of the village is gaining a growing reputation for food, which is served in the attractive conservatory at the rear as well as in the lounge bar. There is a small public bar with a cosy real fire in winter. Guest beers are from the Enterprise list and change regularly. Regulars have a preference for pale and golden beers below 4% ABV and the ale selection reflects this. ❄️🏠🍴♿🅿🚕(347)🐾📶

Mereclough
Kettledrum
302 Red Lees Road, BB10 4RQ
🕐 12 (4 Mon)-midnight; 12-1am Fri & Sat ☎ (01282) 416960
Worsthorne Packhorse; 3 changing beers (sourced regionally) Ⓗ

Tastefully decorated roadside venue named after an 1861 Epsom Derby-winning thoroughbred owned by the Towneley family of nearby Towneley Hall. The pub was bought by brothers Robin and Steve and fully refurbished in 2014, and is now a thriving hostelry serving good-value food. The views across the valley from the pub and beer patio are an added bonus. 🍴🐾📶

Morecambe
Eric Bartholomew ✪
10 Euston Road, LA4 5DD
🕐 8-11 (midnight Fri & Sat) ☎ (01524) 405860
Greene King Abbot; Ruddles Best Bitter; Sharp's Doom Bar; 5 changing beers (often Cross Bay) Ⓗ

Opened in April 2004, this Wetherspoon pub is dedicated to Eric Morecambe (born Eric Bartholomew). Near the seafront, it functions on two levels, with an upstairs lounge and dining area. The long bar services an open-plan pub with pictures of 19th-century Morecambe and some artwork with a Morecambe and Wise theme. Some outside seating is at the front for smokers but no drinking is allowed. Close to shops and a public car park. Q🏠🍴♿🚆♿🚕🐕📶

King's Arms ✪
253 Marine Road Central, LA4 4BJ
🕐 10.30-10 (3 Wed & Fri); 10.30-4 Sat; 11-10 Sun
☎ (01524) 410006 🌐 thekingsfeast.co.uk/kings-arms-morecambe
3 changing beers (often Cross Bay, Wychwood) Ⓗ
A vast drinking emporium opposite the Eric Morecambe statue, with red carpet and varnished woodwork. It has two quite different faces: in the day it is part of the King's Feast chain of family dining pub-restaurants; on Wednesday, Friday and Saturday nights there are DJs, bouncers and much of the youth of Morecambe. The sports bar is upstairs. 🏠🍴♿♣🚕

Morecambe ✪
25 Lord Street, LA4 5HX
🕐 12-11 daily ☎ (01524) 415239
🌐 themorecambehotel.co.uk
Cross Bay Halo; 4 changing beers Ⓗ
Reopened in 2015 after renovation in contemporary style, the pub is light and airy with flagged floors and a variety of seating and tables. The bar is faced with unplaned wood, and has four rooms around it. Screens show videos of 20th-century Morecambe. For most of the day, food dominates. Outside is a surprisingly spacious garden. The name is not hubris: this was a coaching inn built long before there was a town called Morecambe. 🏠🚗🍴🚆♿🚕🐕🐾

Nether Kellet
Limeburners Arms
32 Main Road, LA6 1EP
🕐 closed Mon; 7.45-11; 4-11 Sun
1 changing beer Ⓗ
Once – within living memory – most country pubs were like this early 19th-century building: no food, no jukebox, plain and simply furnished. Minor improvements have not changed the character of the place. Unsurprisingly, most of the customers are locals, and the landlord himself is a local farmer whose family has run the establishment for 80 years. The old photos in the bar are a rewarding study. Local CAMRA Pub of the Year for 2016. Q🏠🅰♣🅿🚕(51)🐾

Newchurch
Boar's Head
69 Church Street, BB4 9EH
🕐 4-11 (9 Mon; 8 Tue); 1-1am Fri; 12-midnight Sat; 1-9 Sun
☎ (01706) 224751
3 changing beers Ⓗ
A large three-storey building on the corner of Church Street and Newchurch Road, near to St Nicholas Church. The stone above the door indicates the building was constructed in 1674. Once owned by Kenyon's brewery, the central bar with its four handpumps serves three drinking

areas. It is said that somewhere in the cellar was a sealed-up door to an underground passage leading to the church. ☎☀♣♠⚲(10)

Ormskirk

Cricketers ♟ Ⓛ
24 Chapel Street, L39 4QF
✪ 12-midnight; 12-11 Sun ☎ (01695) 571123
⊕ thecricketers-ormskirk.co.uk
Marston's Wainwright; Thwaites Nutty Black; 4 changing beers (sourced regionally; often Blackedge, Mobberley, Old School) Ⓗ
Close to Ormskirk town centre, the pub prides itself on both quality food and cask beers. It features six cask ales from local and regional breweries, and earned a CAMRA award in 2015. The extensive menu is served all day in its restaurant and bar area. Cricket memorabilia around its walls reflects its close relationship with Ormskirk Cricket Club, as does the successful Ormskirk Food and Drink Festival run each September, featuring over 60 cask ales. ☎☀◑♿⇌P⚲(375,385)⭑

Orrell

Delph Tavern
Tontine Road, WN5 8UJ
✪ 11.30-11.30 (12.30am Fri & Sat) ☎ (01695) 622239
House beer (by Old School); 4 changing beers (often Thwaites) Ⓗ
Recently refurbished traditional pub which attracts both locals and visitors enticed by great beer and quality, generously portioned food, including various daily specials. Meals are served in the separate dining area adjacent to the main bar. There is also a separate vault area. Activities include pool, darts, dominoes, quiz nights and TV sport on several large screens. There is an outside seating area adjacent to the large car park. Children are welcome until 8pm except in the vault. ☎☀◑♿⇌♣P⭑

Overton

Ship
9 Main Street, LA3 3HD
✪ closed Mon & Tue; 5-10 Wed & Thu; 5-11 Fri; 4-11 Sat; 3-10 Sun ☎ 07979 030196
4 changing beers Ⓗ
Restored in 2016 to Victorian basics (bar and fittings, decorative floor tiles), traces of its 20th-century alterations have almost vanished; there remain four quite distinct public rooms, one a games room. A hole between two of them is occupied by a wood-burning stove, and it has upholstered bench seating around the walls and café-style tables in the middle. The white or beige walls carry paintings for sale. There is no food except on specials nights. Upstairs are two function rooms that have just come back into use. Q☀♣♠P⚲(5)⭑

Padiham

Hare & Hounds Ⓛ ✅
58 West Street, BB12 8JD
✪ 4-11; 12-midnight Sat; 12-10.30 Sun ☎ (01282) 545308
Coach House Gunpowder Mild; 6 changing beers (sourced regionally) Ⓗ
An award-winning true free house rescued from pub company mismanagement, now thriving and

selling an excellent choice of beers alongside a changing real cider. Two rooms front the large bar, with a large separate room to one side where beer festivals are held. There are real fires in all rooms. A large beer garden to the rear and a small seating area to the front complete this warm, friendly pub. Adjacent to Padiham FC and cricket club. ☎☀♿♣●P⚲(27,152)⭑

Parbold

Railway Hotel Ⓛ ✅
1 Station Road, WN8 7NU
✪ 5-11; 12-11.30 Fri & Sat; 12-10.30 Sun ☎ (01257) 462917
⊕ railwayhotelparbold.co.uk
Tetley Bitter; 4 changing beers (sourced locally; often Hophurst, Problem Child, Prospect) Ⓗ
A traditional village pub adjacent to the railway station, with a central drinking area, two separate rooms on each side, and a welcoming real fire in winter. There is a large-screen TV, pool table, and comfy seats and sofas. Pies are sold subject to availability. A quiz is hosted every Tuesday. During the last week of each month there is open mic on Thursday, a disco on Friday and live music on Saturday. Q☎☀◑♿⇌♣P⚲⭑⭑

Wayfarer Inn Ⓛ
1-3 Alder Lane, WN8 7NL
✪ 12 (11 Fri & Sat)-midnight; 11-11 Sun ☎ (01257) 464600
⊕ wayfarerparbold.co.uk
Problem Child Dirty Bier; 4 changing beers Ⓗ
A country pub with a focus on dining – bar meals in the bar area, fine dining in the large restaurant, and Italian meals in Il Viadante bistro, which can be hired for functions. The premises incorporate the Problem Child Brewery and two of its beers feature on the bar alongside four guests. The interior has low-beamed ceilings and cosy nooks and crannies. There is outside seating with pleasant views. Popular with walkers, it is close to the Leeds-Liverpool Canal and Parbold Hill. Q☎☀◑♿⇌P⚲⭑⭑

Windmill Hotel
3 Mill Lane, WN8 7NW
✪ 12-11 (11.30 Fri & Sat); 12-10.30 Sun ☎ (01257) 462935
⊕ thewindmillparbold.co.uk
6 changing beers (sourced regionally; often Windmill) Ⓗ
A former grainstore to the adjacent windmill, parts of this building date back to 1794. Two open fires provide a warm welcome to visitors including bargees and walkers, and it is often busy with diners during the early evening. Up to five real ales on the bar include some from the Windmill Brewery. A separate snug to the right of the doorway features delightful carved animals in wooden panels. Unfortunately the pub has no disabled access due to steep stone steps. Q☎☀⇌P⚲

Pendleton

Swan with Two Necks Ⓛ
Main Street, BB7 1PT
✪ 12-2.30 (not Mon), 6-11; 12-11 Sat; 12-8 Sun
☎ (01200) 423112 ⊕ swanwithtwonecks.co.uk
5 changing beers (sourced regionally) Ⓗ
An outstanding, family-run, community pub in the Ribble Valley which has won many awards, including CAMRA National Pub of the Year 2014.

The selection of five rotating cask beers regularly includes a mild and/or strong ale and frequently some less common brews sourced nationally. A paddle of three thirds is available if you cannot make up your mind. The home-cooked food (locally bought wherever possible) is excellent. An early bird menu features mid-week 6-7pm. Q❀❂◑♣♠P☘❀

Penwortham
Black Bull Inn ✔
83 Pope Lane, PR1 9BA
✪ 11-11 (midnight Fri; 11.30 Sat); 12-11 Sun
☎ (01772) 752953 ⊕ blackbull-penwortham.co.uk/ales
Theakston Best Bitter, Lightfoot; 3 changing beers (sourced nationally; often Robinsons) ⊞
Attractive cottage-style inn dating back to the early 1800s, which has managed to retain a village pub atmosphere despite its location in a well-populated area. On entering, a narrow passageway leads through to a central bar serving a number of drinking areas including a separate public bar. This is a friendly community pub which actively supports local charities. The CAMRA discount has seen a big increase in local members. A Cask Marque Excellence award winner. Q❀♣P☖❀☘

Poulton le Fylde
Old Town Hall ✔
5 Church Street, FY6 7AP
✪ 11-midnight (1am Fri & Sat); 12-11.30 Sun
☎ (01253) 892257
5 changing beers (sourced locally; often Cross Bay, Kirkby Lonsdale, Moorhouse's) ⊞
Right in the centre of Poulton, overlooked by its historic church, this pub was originally called the Bay Horse before being used, for many years, as the town hall, hence the current name. Once multi-roomed but now open plan, it is a great asset to the local real ale scene. Live bands play most weekends. A wine bar on the first floor is open on Friday and Saturday. ☎⬥≄♣♠❀☘

Poulton Elk ✔
22 Hardhorn Road, FY6 7SR
✪ 8am-midnight (1am Fri & Sat) ☎ (01253) 895265
Greene King Abbot; Ruddles Best Bitter; 8 changing beers (sourced nationally; often Bradfield, Phoenix, Saltaire) ⊞
Named after the local discovery of a 13,000-year-old elk skeleton accompanied by two spear points, the earliest evidence that people were living in the North-west of England. Close to the town centre, with a varied clientele, it is very busy, particularly at weekends. It is mainly one room, although subdivided to avoid an open-plan feel. There is a terrace at the front and a recently added beer garden with smoking shelters overlooking a large car park at the rear. ☎❀◑⬥≄♠☘

Thatched House ⊔ ✔
30 Ball Street, FY6 7BG
✪ 11-11 (11.30 Thu; midnight Fri & Sat); 12-11 Sun
☎ (01253) 891063 ⊕ thatchedhousepoulton.co.uk
Chapel Street Brewhouse Blonde, Cream Stout, Double Hopped; 7 changing beers (sourced regionally; often Bradfield, Rooster's, Saltaire) ⊞
A popular mock-Tudor pub next to a delightful Norman church and graveyard. Ten beers are generally available, including a number that are

brewed in the microbrewery at the rear of the pub in the former stabling area. Many pictures of sporting heroes and historic Poulton decorate the wood-panelled walls. There are two wood-burning stoves and a log fire. Q❀⬥≄♣♠❀☘

Preston
Continental
South Meadow Lane, PR1 8JP
✪ 12-11 (12.30am Fri & Sat) ☎ (01772) 499425
⊕ newcontinental.net
House beer (by Marble); 6 changing beers (sourced nationally) ⊞
Beside the River Ribble, the main railway line and Miller Park, the pub has a main bar area plus a lounge with a real fire in winter and a conservatory overlooking the garden. Live music and theatre regularly feature. It has seven pumps offering up to six microbrewery beers, including the house ale from Marble and a dark beer, plus a real cider. Four handpumps are in the main bar area, the others are in the back bar. Freshly cooked meals are served daily except Monday. A two-times winner of local CAMRA Pub of the Year. Q☎❀◑⬥≄♠P☘❀☘

Guild Ale House ⊔
56 Lancaster Road, PR1 1DD
✪ 12-9.30 (10 Thu; 11 Fri & Sat); 12-10 Sun ☎ 07932 517444
House beer (by Bishop's Crook); 6 changing beers (sourced locally; often Beer Brothers, Dark Star, Phoenix) ⊞
Larger-than-usual micropub opened in February 2016, the first in Preston. The main room has a light and airy feel with high and low level seating and high ceilings, and there is a comfortable lounge upstairs. Seven changing guest beers are served, mainly local or from Yorkshire, always at least one dark beer, plus a range of Belgian bottled beers. There is no TV, food, jukebox or background music. Live jazz or blues is hosted on Sunday late afternoon. A few doors from Preston's Guildhall entertainment complex. Q☎❀≄♣♠☖☘

Moorbrook
370 North Road, PR1 1RU
✪ 12-midnight ☎ (01772) 823302 ⊕ themoorbrook.com
Thwaites Original; house beer (by Blackjack); 6 changing beers (sourced nationally) ⊞
Now privately owned, this pub is where the West Lancs CAMRA branch was formed over 40 years ago. It has a traditional-style wood-panelled bar with two rooms off, complete with William Morris wallpaper. The beer garden to the rear is a suntrap. Authentic wood-fired pizzas are now available. Up to six guest beers from all over the country plus a house beer attract people from far and wide. The house beer, Moorbrook Pale Ale, is brewed by Blackjack of Manchester. The pub gets very busy on Preston North End match days. ☎❀◑⬥♣♠❀☘

Old Vic ⊔
79 Fishergate, PR1 2UH
✪ 10-midnight; 12-midnight Sat & Sun ☎ (01772) 828519
Wells Bombardier; 6 changing beers ⊞
Opposite the railway station and on bus routes into the city, this is a popular pub and it can get busy at weekends. A number of TVs show sports events and this is a rare city-centre pub for darts enthusiasts. To the rear is an outdoor decked smoking area and a car park (available evenings and Sundays only). Seven handpumps offer a good

range of beers, with local microbreweries usually represented. Real ale carryouts and third-of-a pint taster paddles are available. CAMRA Wetherspoon vouchers are accepted. ⏱👹◑≋♣P🖫？

Princess Alice Ⓛ ✪
29-31 Cambridge Walk, PR1 7SL
🕓 4.30-11.30 (12.30am Fri); 12-12.30am Sat; 12-11.30 Sun
☎ (01772) 823737
Wells Bombardier; 3 changing beers Ⓗ
Friendly Victorian street-corner local in a redeveloped residential area. The ornate tilework reflects the former Matthew Brown brewery ownership. The interior has been modernised and opened out. A large number of TV screens show multiple (often sports) channels. The pub is only 10 minutes' walk from Deepdale Stadium and popular on match days. In autumn 2016 a cooler was installed that serves real ale at the correct temperature. Beers are normally from small Lancashire breweries, often Lancaster, Chadwicks, Snowhill and Wily Fox. 👹♣P🖫(23)？

Wheatsheaf
50 Water Lane, Ashton-on-Ribble, PR2 2NL
🕓 11-11 (11.30 Fri & Sat); 12-10.30 Sun ☎ (01772) 725917
5 changing beers (sourced nationally; often Moorhouse's) Ⓗ
Victorian local on the way to Preston marina, a mile from the city centre. Beer prices here are among the lowest in the area. Big on TV sport, live music plays Friday and Saturday nights. There is disabled access through the courtyard. Five guest beers include at least one from Moorhouse's, otherwise they come from anywhere in the country; third-pint tasting racks are available. At least two beer festivals are held a year in a marquee at the rear. 👹&♣●🖫？

Rawtenstall

Buffer Stops Ⓛ
Bury Road, BB4 6AG
🕓 11-9 Mon & Tue; 10-10 Wed; 10-11 Thu-Sat; 10-10 Sun
☎ (0161) 764 7790 ⊕ eastlancsrailway.org.uk/plan-your-day-out/food-drink.aspx
Outstanding Piston Broke; 4 changing beers Ⓗ
Located on the platform at the northern terminus of the East Lancs Railway, this unique one-roomed bar, once the station café, is small, but further seating is available in the ticket hall and waiting room and on benches and at tables on the platform. It keeps busy both with railway visitors and locals. Close to Ski Rossendale, Whitaker park and museum and the Weavers' Cottage.
Q⏱👹◑&≋●P🖫😺

Red Lion ✪
437 Newchurch Road, Cloughfold, BB4 7TG
🕓 5-11; 4-midnight Fri; 12-midnight Sat; 12-11 Sun
☎ (01706) 215631
4 changing beers Ⓗ
A double-fronted stone building on the corner of Newchurch Road and Peel Street in Higher Cloughfold. The bar is in the main room but also serves the taproom. The four real ales include offerings from Moorhouse's and Reedley Hallows, with a changing selection from other mainly North-west breweries. The pub dates from 1776 but was renovated in 1905. There is a large beer garden overlooking the picturesque Rossendale Valley. ⏱👹♣P🖫(10)😺

Rufford

Hesketh Arms
81 Liverpool Road, L40 1SB (on A59 at jct with B5246)
🕓 12-11 (midnight Fri & Sat) ☎ (01704) 821002
Moorhouse's White Witch, Pride of Pendle; 7 changing beers (sourced regionally; often Cross Bay, Phoenix, Reedley Hallows) Ⓗ
A spacious former Greenall's inn, the Hesketh is now a free house serving up to six ales, mostly from local microbreweries. Set in the charming village of Rufford, it is near to the National Trust property of Rufford Old Hall, the delightful St Mary's Marina, and the popular Mere Sands nature reserve. A large split-level venue with several dining areas, the pub serves good-quality food throughout the day. Monthly live entertainment and a Tuesday quiz attract a mixed clientele.
Q⏱👹◑&≋P🖫(2A,347)

St Annes

Fifteens at St Annes Ⓛ ✪
42 St Annes Road West, FY8 1RF
🕓 11-11 (midnight Fri & Sat); 12-11 Sun ☎ (01253) 725852
⊕ fifteensstannes.com
House beer (by Moorhouse's); 5 changing beers (sourced regionally) Ⓗ
A quirky conversion of a former bank, Fifteens provides several drinking areas, including the surprisingly cosy former bank vault and a small gallery area. Sport features on several screens, while background music is eclectic. Regular live music takes place at weekends and a popular quiz on Sundays. It is the winner of many awards and current runner-up local CAMRA branch Pub of the Year and Cider Pub of the Year. &≋♣●🖫😺？

No.10 Ale House
10 Park Road, FY8 1QX
🕓 12-11 (midnight Fri & Sat); 12-10 Sun ☎ 07809 368682
4 changing beers (sourced locally) Ⓗ
Handy for the railway station and near to the shopping in St Anne's Square, this friendly micropub serves fours beers, mainly from local brewers, and a small range of ciders. Decorated with retro Blackpool tourism posters and with no TV or food service, this pub is a little real ale haven.
Q👹&≋●🖫😺？

Victoria
Church Road, FY8 3NE
🕓 12-11 (midnight Thu-Sat) ☎ (01253) 721041
⊕ victoriahotel-lytham-stannes.co.uk
Draught Bass; Greene King IPA; 4 changing beers (sourced nationally) Ⓗ
Long-standing entry in this Guide, first appearing in 1974, it is a large traditional pub with a separate vault that underwent a significant and tasteful refurbishment in 2015. A range of six ales greets the visitor along with a small selection of foreign beer. Food is served all day. Sport is shown on two big screens; darts, pool and a full-sized snooker table are also available. A beer festival is held in a marquee at the rear of the pub in summer.
⏱👹◑&≋♣P🖫(11,68)😺？

Salwick

Hand & Dagger
Treales Road, PR4 0SA (at Station Rd jct, next to canal)
🕓 closed Mon; 12-11 ☎ (01772) 690306
⊕ handanddagger.com

2 changing beers (sourced regionally) H
Dating back to about 1800, this welcoming and attractive pub with a real fire gets its name from the coat of arms of the Clifton family which is carved in stone above the front door. It is next to Bridge 26 on the Preston to Lancaster Canal. A good range of quality food is served all day until 9pm (7pm Sun). Q ☎ ❀ ◑ ᗒ ▲ ♣ ❀ P ❀ 🛈

Samlesbury

Nabs Head ⊘
Nabs Head Lane, PR5 0UQ
⊙ 12-11 Mon; 12-3, 5-11 Tue-Thu; 5-midnight Fri; closed Sat; 12-11 Sun ☎ (01254) 851416 ⊕ thenewnabshead.co.uk
Thwaites Original, Best Cask; 2 changing beers H
Welcoming and friendly village local in a picturesque setting. The central bar, which is decorated with dried hops, serves two distinct drinking areas. There is a taproom behind the bar with bare boards. The L-shaped lounge is mainly used by diners; the walls are decorated with pictures from local photographers. An extensive menu is available, with food from local suppliers wherever possible. Quiz night is Tuesday and occasional live music features. Q ☎ ◑ ♣ P ❀ 🛈

Scarisbrick

Heatons Bridge Inn ⊘
2 Heatons Bridge Road, L40 8JG (on B5242 by Leeds-Liverpool Canal)
⊙ 12-midnight ☎ (01704) 840549
Moorhouse's Black Cat; 2 changing beers (sourced regionally; often Copper Dragon, George Wright, Wily Fox) H
Great canalside hostelry dating from 1837, when it served as offices for the Leeds and Liverpool freight services. It is a traditional pub, with separate areas and home-cooked food. Pillbox beer is often served as a memorial to WWII. There is a lookout post outside, and twice-yearly military displays and annual classic bus services are held, with themed beers for the occasion. This is a popular pub with families, walkers and cyclists, in an excellent rural setting with a garden with dining area.
☎ ❀ ◑ ᗒ ▲ ♣ 🖫 (375) ❀ 🛈

Silverdale

Woodlands
Woodlands Drive, LA5 0RU
⊙ 5-11.30; 12-midnight Sat; 12-11.30 Sun
☎ (01524) 701655
4 changing beers H
Large country house on an elevated site, dating from circa 1878 and converted to a pub with only minimal alterations. Most of the trade is provided by locals. The bar has a large fireplace as big as the counter and enjoys great views across Morecambe Bay. The beer pumps are in another room, with a list of the four available ales on the wall. Home-made sandwiches are served at weekends. The smoking area is covered and sheltered. There is a beer festival of 30 ales in October, and a quiz on the last Sunday of the month. To telephone the pub you need to ring twice. Q ☎ ❀ ♣ 🖢 P 🖫 ❀

Slaidburn

Hark to Bounty ᒪ
Townend, BB7 3EP

⊙ 8am-11; closed Tue ☎ (01200) 446246
⊕ harktobounty.co.uk
Theakston Best Bitter, Old Peculier H
Situated in the centre of the village, this traditional country inn has nine en-suite bedrooms and is well placed to enjoy the delights of the Forest of Bowland Area of Natural Beauty. The lounge, with oak beams, has a real fire and is a comfortable place to enjoy one of the four ales on offer. Meals are served from a traditional home-cooked menu with a range of daily changing specials. Brass bands play in the large beer garden during the summer. Q ☎ ❀ ㊐ ◑ ᗒ ▲ P 🖫 (10) ❀ 🛈

Thornton

Bay Horse Hotel ⊘
Station Road, FY5 5HY
⊙ 9am-11 (midnight Fri & Sat) ☎ (01253) 852324
Tetley Bitter; 4 changing beers (sourced nationally) H
Next to the level crossing on the disused Poulton to Fleetwood railway line in the centre of Thornton, this pub is little changed externally from when it was built in the late-1800s. It is a comfortable community pub with a pleasant beer garden to the side. A range of five beers is available and good-value food is served throughout the day. There are regular quiz nights and music many weekends.
☎ ❀ ◑ ᗒ ♣ P 🖫 (24,74) 🛈

Tockholes

Royal Arms ᒪ
Tockholes Road, Rydal Fold, BB3 0PA
⊙ 4-8 Mon; 12-11 ☎ (01254) 705373
4 changing beers H
Traditional free house formed from two cottages knocked together. It is small but has a great atmosphere within its four back-to-back rooms, where the original stone walls, real fires, flagged and wooden floors have been retained. Beers are from local microbreweries. In the West Pennine Moors close to Darwen Tower and adjacent Roddlesworth Visitor Centre, it looks over moors, woods and reservoirs. Friendly staff welcome walkers, cyclists, ramblers and dogs alike and offer a good menu. It may be worth checking opening times before visiting in winter. Q ☎ ❀ ◑ ♣ P ❀ 🛈

Waddington

Higher Buck
The Square, BB7 3HZ
⊙ 12-11 (midnight Fri & Sat); 12-10.30 Sun
☎ (01200) 423226 ⊕ higherbuck.com
Marston's Wainwright; Thwaites Original; 1 changing beer (sourced locally) H
Nestled beneath Waddington Fell and open moorland at the head of the picturesque Ribble Valley, this village pub dates from the 19th century when it was named the Buck in the Vine. It is now a traditional pub with modern touches. The central bar with stools and comfortable seating is flanked either side by tables and chairs, with an open fire to one side. Excellent food, much with a local and seasonal content, is served daily. Outdoor seating is available. ☎ ❀ ㊐ ◑ ᗒ P 🖫 (7) ❀ 🛈

Walmer Bridge

Walmer Bridge ⊘
Liverpool Old Road, PR4 5QE

✪ 4-midnight (1am Thu); 12.30-1am Fri & Sat; 2-11 Sun
☎ (01772) 612296
3 changing beers ⊞
Village local comprising two rooms, for either of which you have to go through four doors to reach the bar. The comfortable lounge contains photographs of bygone Walmer Bridge and Longton. The vault is popular with the sporting fraternity, while outside there is a large garden with a children's play area. Up to three changing beers are available from the Punch portfolio, with an emphasis on pale and golden ales.
🛏🕏♣️P�☐(2,2A)🕏🛜

Walton-le-Dale

White Bull �🄻
109 Victoria Road, PR5 4BA
✪ 12-11.30 (midnight Fri & Sat); 12-12.30am Sun
Marston's Wainwright; 3 changing beers (sourced locally; often Cross Bay, Hopstar, Three B's) ⊞
A true community local retaining the original multi-room layout, with a bar area and lounge at the front, a games room with pool table and dartboard, and a small lounge behind the bar. Be warned that the corridor leading to the rear rooms slopes steeply downwards. There is a small seating area on the paving at the front of the building. This cosy pub serves three guest beers, usually from local micros, and can get busy at weekends.
🛏🕏👵♣️Pᐧ🕏

Wesham

Stanley Arms
8 Garstang Road South, PR4 3BL
✪ 3 (12 Thu & Fri)-midnight; 11-midnight Sat; 10-midnight Sun ☎ (01772) 469495 ⊕ stanleyarmswesham.co.uk
Sharp's Doom Bar, Atlantic; 1 changing beer (sourced nationally) ⊞
A friendly street-corner pub close to Fox's biscuit factory and half a mile from the AFC Fylde Mill Farm complex. The open-plan layout was refurbished two years ago with a fine wooden bar at its centre. It has the longest-serving landlord in town and a benign, resident ghost. A hub for many local activities, it extends a warm welcome to all. Open for breakfast and coffee from 10am on Sunday.
🛏🕏🕪➤♣️☐🕏🛜

Wheelton

Red Lion
Blackburn Road, PR6 8EU (in centre of village opp clock tower)
✪ 11-midnight ☎ (01254) 659890
6 changing beers ⊞
Built around 1826, this authentic village pub reflects the former mill village it used to serve. Once a Matthew Brown house, the bar retains the Lion Ales windows. There is a comfortable lounge with an open fire and a second room up a few steps which is used for games and sports TV. It is a free house, with up to eight real ales, usually including a mild and a stout or porter. Beers from Coniston and Timothy Taylor often feature.
🛏🕏🕪♣️Pᐧ(24)🛜

Worsthorne

Crooked Billet �🄻
1-3 Smith Street, BB10 3NQ
✪ 7 (6 Thu)-midnight; 4.30-1am Fri; 12-1am Sat; 12-12.30am Sun ☎ 07766 230175 ⊕ crookedbilletworsthorne.co.uk
Tetley Bitter; Timothy Taylor Boltmaker, Landlord; 4 changing beers (sourced regionally) ⊞
An award-winning true free house, this well-presented village pub has a beautiful wood and glass horseshoe bar serving both the main lounge area and snug. Guest beers are mainly from local microbreweries. Quiz nights are popular as are Thai nights and soul nights. This pub is dog friendly and has a large covered outdoor drinking area where you can enjoy the flower-bedecked exterior.
Q🛏🕏🕪👵♣️Pᐧ(2)🕏🛜

Wrightington

White Lion ✅
117 Mossy Lea Road, WN6 9RE
✪ 10-11 ☎ (01257) 425977 ⊕ thewhitelionlancs.co.uk
Jennings Cumberland Ale; 7 changing beers ⊞
Popular country pub with a main bar area and separate dining room offering drinkers and diners a good selection of eight beers from the Marston's range. There is a large beach-hut themed garden area, adjacent to the car park. A breakfast menu is served 10am-noon, followed by full lunch and dinner menus. The pub is community focused, with various trips and events organised for the regulars.
Q🛏🕏🕪👵Pᐧ(113)

Kitchen of an inn

In the evening we reached a village where I had determined to pass the night. As we drove into the great gateway of the inn, I saw on one side the light of a rousing kitchen fire beaming through a window. I entered, and admired for the hundredth time that picture of convenience, neatness, and broad honest enjoyment, the kitchen of an English inn. It was of spacious dimension, hung around by copper and tin vessels, highly polished, and decorated here and there with a Christmas green. Hams, tongues, and flitches of bacon were suspended from the ceiling; a smoke-jack made its ceaseless clanking behind the fireplace, and a clock ticked in one corner. A well-scoured deal table extended along one side of the kitchen, with a cold round of beef, and other hearty viands upon it, over which two foaming tankards of ale seemed mounting guard. Travellers of inferior order were preparing to attack this stout repast, while others sat smoking or gossiping over their ale, on two high-backed oaken settles beside the fire.
Washington Irving, Travelling at Christmas, 1884

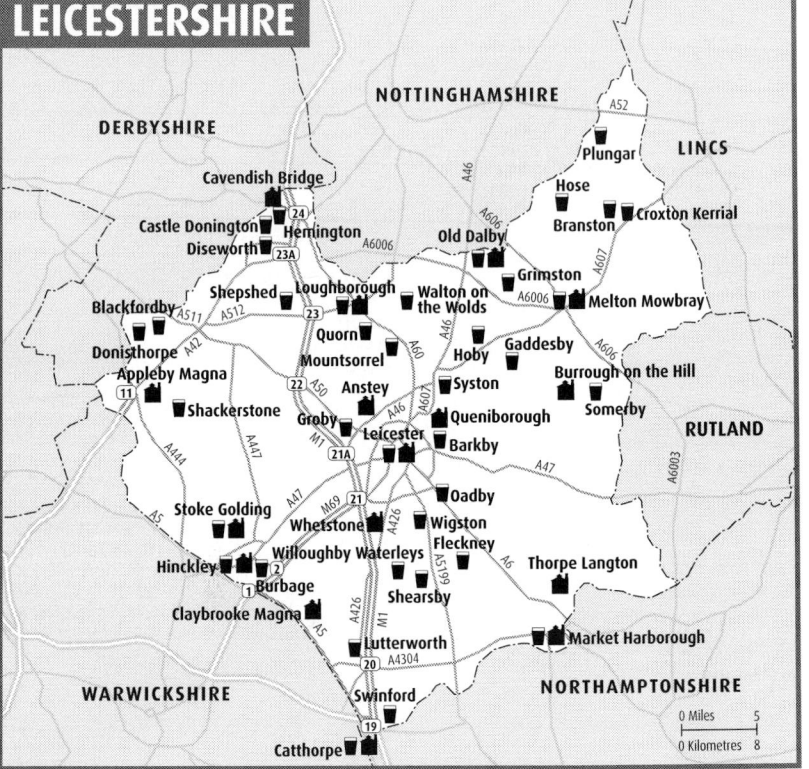

Everard's Brewery closed July 2017. Its beers are now brewed by Joules and Robinsons.

Barkby

Malt Shovel ✔

27 Main Street, LE7 3QG
🕐 11.30-2.30, 5-11.30 (11 Mon, 11.45 Fri); 11.30-11.45 Sat & Sun ☎ (0116) 269 2558 🌐 maltshovelbarkby.co.uk
Marston's Wainwright, Lancaster Bomber; Thwaites Nutty Black, Original; 3 changing beers (often Hydes, Jennings, Thwaites) ⊞
This family-friendly village pub serves good-value home-cooked food in the bar and restaurant, while offering drinkers a warm welcome. Guest beers are supplied by Thwaites, often from other North-west English breweries. A beer festival is held on the first weekend in August. There is a large garden area for the summer months.
🏠🛏🍴🛐🏧🅿🚭(100)🐾🛜

Blackfordby

Black Lion

3 Main Street, DE11 8AB
🕐 3-11 (1am Fri); 12-1am Sat; 12-11 Sun ☎ (01283) 337551
🌐 theblacklionblackfordby.com
Draught Bass; 5 changing beers (sourced locally; often Blue Monkey, Derby) ⊞
Popular local in a quiet village in north-west Leicestershire, bought from Enterprise Inns and reopened in 2013 as a free house following a substantial refurbishment. Grade II-listed with old beams and open fires, it has a lovely courtyard and covered smoking area. Guest beers are often sourced from small local breweries, and up to four ciders are on draught. A selection of tapas is available Saturday evening and Sunday afternoon. Quiz night is the first Sunday of each month, jam night the last Wednesday. Q🏠🛏🛐🏧🛜🐾🛜

Branston

Wheel Inn 🄻

Main Street, NG32 1RU
🕐 12-11; 12-8 Sun ☎ (01476) 870376
🌐 thewheelinnbranston.co.uk
Black Sheep Best Bitter; 2 changing beers ⊞
This stone-built 18th-century village pub houses a cosy bar with seating plus a larger restaurant with rustic tables and a real fire. The attractive outdoor area is quiet and relaxing in the summer months, with traditional outbuildings used for beer festivals and live music. The Wheel boasts an extensive food menu using locally sourced ingredients where possible, including produce from the Belvoir Estate. Cask cider is usually on the bar. Local CAMRA Leicestershire Pub of the Year 2015 and 2016.
Q🏠🛏🛐🏧🅿🐾🛜

Burbage

Burbage & District Constitutional Club 🄻

Church Street, LE10 2DE
🕐 11-2, 6-11; 11-11.30 Fri; 11-11.45 Sat; 12-3, 7-11 Sun
☎ (01455) 615142 🌐 burbageconclub1911.com
Greene King Abbot; Marston's Saddle Tank; 3 changing beers (often Church End, Grainstore) ⊞

Formerly the home of Prime Minister George Canning, the club was founded in 1911. The Grade II-listed building is in the heart of the village, featuring a comfortable lounge with an open fire, a function room equipped with a skittle alley, snooker and pool tables, and a garden. Darts, dominoes, crib, chess and table tennis can be played. Live music features every Saturday night. Sandwiches and cobs are available. Branch and East Midlands CAMRA Club of the Year in 2016. ⊛ & ♣ 🖳 ☎

Lime Kilns
Watling Street, LE10 3ED
✪ 12-3, 5.30-11; 12-11 Sat; 12-10.30 Sun ☎ (01455) 631158
⊕ limekilnsinn.co.uk
Jennings Cocker Hoop; Marston's Saddle Tank, Pedigree; 2 changing beers Ⓗ
Situated alongside the Ashby Canal and the A5, the pub was originally an 18th-century coaching inn. It offers garden-side moorings and a large canalside beer garden with a marquee for functions. The first-floor lounge has canal views and an open fire in winter. The guest beers change regularly alongside seven real ciders, often from Thatchers and Westons. Traditional food is served, with special deals Monday to Thursday evenings. Local CAMRA Pub of the Year 2016. Q ☎ ⊛ ⅅ ♣ 🖳 P ☎

Castle Donington

Castle Inn
High Street, DE74 2PP
✪ 11-11 (11.30 Fri & Sat); 12-11 Sun ☎ (01332) 391296
⊕ the-castle-inn.co.uk
4 changing beers (often Charnwood, Shardlow) Ⓗ
Eighteenth-century coaching inn, recently refurbished to a high standard and reopened as a family-run free house. This fine addition to the Castle Donington dining and drinking scene has a wood-burning pizza oven which can be seen in use. The separate bar is welcoming and there is also a comfortable covered outdoor courtyard. Booking for meals is recommended. Local CAMRA branch Most Improved Pub 2015. ☎ ⅅ 🖳

Chequered Flag
32 Borough Street, DE74 2LA
✪ closed Mon; 4-10.30 (11 Fri & Sat); 12-5
Sun ☎ 07841 374441
House beer (by Dancing Duck) Ⓖ; **6 changing beers** Ⓗ
A thriving micropub in a busy street in Castle Donington, serving real ales straight from the cask, visible from a temperature controlled cool-room cellar. It also serves a range of eight ciders and quality wines. Award-winning local pork pies and pickles are often available to enjoy with your beer. Bus services on the Skylink routes make it accessible from Derby, Nottingham, Loughborough and Leicester. Q ♣ ☎ ☎

Catthorpe

Cherry Tree Ⓛ
Main Street, LE17 6DB (on main road through village ½ mile from A5)
✪ 12-2.30, 5-11 Mon; 5-11 Tue-Thu; 12-2.30, 5-12.30am Fri; 12-12.30am Sat; 12-11.30 Sun ☎ (01788) 860430
Jennings Bitter; 3 changing beers (sourced nationally; often Dow Bridge, Marston's) Ⓗ
Welcoming two-roomed village free house adorned with railway and aviation memorabilia,

with a garden and patio overlooking the Avon Valley. An excellent bar menu features local produce and Sunday roasts (no food Thu and Sun eves). One beer from the local Dow Bridge brewery is usually among the range. This community pub supports skittles, draughts and dominoes teams. A small beer festival is held twice yearly, and occasional live music and quizzes are hosted. Westons cider is available. ⊛ ⅅ ▲ ♣ 🖳 P ☎ ☎

Croxton Kerrial

Geese & Fountain 🍺 Ⓛ ✅
1 School Lane, NG32 1QR
✪ 11-11; 12-10.30 Sun ☎ (01476) 870350
⊕ thegeeseandfountain.co.uk
5 changing beers Ⓗ
This village inn reopened in 2016 after a long period of closure. With wood fires, a flagstone floor and rustic seating, it has a quiet, pleasant atmosphere. Dogs, children, cyclists and walkers are all welcome. It has five handpumps with at least one of six local breweries always represented, as well as guest beers from other local micros, plus locally brewed lagers and three real ciders. Food is served every day, including breakfast. There is no jukebox or fruit machine, but occasional folk nights supplement the hum of conversation. Local CAMRA branch Leicestershire Pub of the Year 2017. Q ☎ ⊛ ⅅ & ♣ 🖳 P 🖳 ☎ ☎

Diseworth

Plough ✅
33 Hall Gate, DE74 2QJ
✪ 11.30-11 (midnight Fri & Sat); 12-10.30 Sun
☎ (01332) 810333 ⊕ theploughdiseworth.com
Draught Bass; Marston's Pedigree; Timothy Taylor Landlord; 1 changing beer (often Wadworth) Ⓗ
Situated in a village with many half-timbered buildings, this is a cosy, multi-roomed pub with parts dating back to the 13th century. Low-beamed ceilings and exposed brickwork are just some of the original features discovered during renovation work in the 1990s. There is an interesting display of old photographs of the area. Tasty home-made food is served. The spacious, well-presented beer garden is popular in summer. A former local CAMRA Village Pub of the Year. Q ⊛ ⅅ & ▲ 🖳 P 🖳 ☎

REAL ALE BREWERIES

Anstey Anstey
Beardy Monkey Melton Mowbray
Belvoir Old Dalby
Charnwood Loughborough
Co Pilot Whetstone
Dow Bridge Catthorpe
Elliswood Hinckley
Framework Leicester (NEW)
Gas Dog 🍺 Melton Mowbray
Golden Duck Appleby Magna
Langton Thorpe Langton
Market Bosworth Stoke Golding (NEW)
Market Harborough Market Harborough
O'Brien Whetstone
Parish Burrough on the Hill
Pig Pub 🍺 Claybrooke Magna
Q Queniborough
Shardlow Cavendish Bridge
West End 🍺 Leicester

Donisthorpe

Halfway House
65 Church Street, DE12 7PX
☼ 12-11 (midnight Fri & Sat) ☎ (01530) 588783
⊕ halfwayhousedonisthorpe.com
Draught Bass; Marston's Pedigree; 3 changing beers ⊞
Traditional dog-friendly village inn in the heart of Donisthorpe. Refurbished to a high standard, it comprises a public bar, lounge bar and a separate dining room, with beamed ceilings and a wood-burning fire. Home-made food is available Tuesday to Saturday. Three guest beers, one usually from Burton Bridge, can be served in a taster selection of three third-pint glasses. Local CAMRA Pub of the Year in 2015. Q✿🕭🕪🖚P🖵🐾🐱🛜

Fleckney

Golden Shield 🅛
46 Main Street, LE8 8AN
☼ 4 (12 Wed & Thu)-11; 12-midnight Fri & Sat; 11.30-11 Sun
☎ (0116) 240 2366 ⊕ goldenshieldfleckney.co.uk
Greene King IPA, Abbot; St Austell Tribute; Timothy Taylor Landlord; 2 changing beers (sourced nationally; often Bradfield, Church End, Theakston) ⊞
Village pub in the heart of Leicestershire offering six real ales, including ever-changing LocAles, microbrewery and regional beers. Home-cooked and à la carte meals are served lunchtimes and evenings Wednesday to Saturday, plus popular Sunday lunches. A pétanque court is available and BT Sport is screened regularly.
🖙✿🕭🖚P🖵(44,49)🐱🛜

Gaddesby

Cheney Arms 🅛
2 Rearsby Lane, LE7 4XE
☼ 12 (3 Mon)-11 ☎ (01664) 840260
Everards Beacon Hill, Old Original, Tiger; 1 changing beer (sourced nationally) ⊞
A pleasant and friendly village pub with a bar room on one side of the central servery for those just wanting a pint and a chat, and a popular restaurant room on the other side. Both rooms have a real fire, creating a cosy feel. A garden, patio and pétanque court to the rear make this place an ideal stop-off point for those walking the Leicestershire Round or Midshires Way in the summer months.
Q🖙✿🕭🖚P🖵🐾🐱🛜

Grimston

Black Horse
3 Main Street, LE14 3BZ
☼ 12-3, 6-11; 12-6 Sun ☎ (01664) 812358
⊕ theblackhorsegrimston.co.uk
Adnams Southwold Bitter; Marston's Pedigree; 2 changing beers (sourced nationally) ⊞
Standing prominently above the village green, the pub cannot be missed. It is divided into three areas on two separate levels, allowing space for dining or just enjoying a pint. The larger lower level has a significant amount of cricket memorabilia on the walls while the upper levels are more cosy. The pub is often busy at mealtimes, and usually has four real ales on offer. It retains the qualities that made it a former CAMRA branch Pub of the Year.
✿🕭🚌🖵

Groby

Stamford Arms 🅛
2 Leicester Road, LE6 0DJ
☼ 10-11 ☎ (0116) 287 5616 ⊕ stamfordarms.co.uk
Everards Beacon Hill, Tiger, Old Original; house beer (by Everards); 3 changing beers (sourced nationally; often Brunswick) ⊞
At the heart of Groby and home of the Everard family until 1921, the main house has become a comfortable drinking area, while an annexe is now a large restaurant. The menu includes pizzas, pasta, tapas and more traditional fare. The house ale, Lady Jane, is brewed by Everards and complements the Everards cask ales and three guest ales. Beer and cider festivals are held during the year.
🖙✿🕭🕪🖚♣🖚P🖵🐾🐱🛜

Hemington

Jolly Sailor
21 Main Street, DE74 2RB
☼ 4-11; 2-midnight Fri; 12-11 Sat & Sun ☎ (01332) 812665
Black Iris Snake Eyes; Marston's Pedigree; Oakham Bishops Farewell; 3 changing beers ⊞
Thought to have originally been a weaver's cottage, this 17th-century building has been a pub since the 19th century. It retains many original features including old timbers, open fires and a beamed ceiling – a convenient place to hang the collection of blowlamps and beer mugs. Well-filled rolls are available and there is a free cheeseboard on the bar. Recently purchased from Greene King, it has been redecorated and is returning to top form. ✿🕪P🐾🐱🛜

Hinckley

Elbow Room Ale & Cider House 🅛
26 Station Road, LE10 1AW
☼ closed Mon; 2-11 Tue-Thu; 12-11.30 Fri & Sat; 12-7 Sun ☎ 07900 191388 ⊕ elbowroomalehouse.co.uk
6 changing beers Ⓖ
Family-run micropub, decorated in an industrial style, with a welcoming and lively atmosphere. The ales and ciders are served by gravity directly from the cellar behin glass doors. High-quality wines, gins, whiskies, vodkas, world-class beers and lagers plus a range of soft drinks are available. Pork pies, sausage rolls and Scotch eggs complement the drinks. There is no TV, jukebox or gaming machine as conversation is king. Children are welcome until 8pm. You can drink outdoors on the pavement outside the bar.
Q🖙✿🕭🕪🚆♣🖚🐱🛜

New Plough Inn ✅
Leicester Road, LE10 1LS
☼ 4.45-11; 3-midnight Fri; 12-midnight Sat & Sun ☎ (01455) 615037 ⊕ thenewploughinn.co.uk
Marston's Saddle Tank, Pedigree; 3 changing beers (often Jennings, Ringwood, Wychwood) ⊞
Run by CAMRA members, this award-winning Victorian pub has old settles and a comfortable ambience. Sporting memorabilia reflect sponsorship of local cricket and rugby teams. Pub quizzes have raised £85,000 for charity. Darts, dominoes, skittles and shooting teams attract the local community. The Stables function room is available to hire. Nearby the Greyhound, Elliswood's brewery tap, is of historic interest, with a Blue Plaque honouring brewer William Butler.
🖙✿🕭♣🖵(1,159)🐾🛜

Pestle & Mortar 🅛

81 Castle Street, LE10 1DA

✪ 2 (12 Fri & Sat)-11; 12-10 Sun ☎ 07715 106876

Draught Bass; 6 changing beers (sourced locally) Ⓗ

Since opening in 2015, Hinckley's first micropub has been awarded both branch and East Midlands CAMRA Cider Pub of the Year. Up to 22 changing real ciders are available, always including Westons Old Rosie Rhubarb and Gwynt y Ddraig Farmhouse Scrumpy. Handpumps deliver up to six changing real ales from casks behind the bar. Cobs and pork pies are available. This comfortable, pleasantly quirky micropub meets a wide range of drinking tastes, with a friendly atmosphere.
Q♿🚲≠♣♠P🖰(8,X55)♣🎧📶

Queen's Head 🏆

Upper Bond Street, LE10 1RJ

✪ 5-11 (midnight Fri); 12-midnight Sat; 12-6 Sun ☎ 07887 770038

4 changing beers Ⓗ

A warm welcome awaits at this Victorian free house serving four ever-changing real ales. It has been sympathetically refurbished and features open fires and a Victorian range, helping to create a cosy atmosphere. A frequent CAMRA award winner, it has featured in this Guide since 2013. Children are not permitted. ☸♣🖰

Hoby

Blue Bell 🅛

36 Main Street, LE14 3DT

✪ 12-11 ☎ (01664) 434247 ⊕ bluebell-hoby.co.uk

Everards Beacon Hill, Old Original, Sunchaser, Tiger; 2 changing beers (sourced nationally) Ⓗ

A busy, picturesque village pub with a thatched roof and beer garden which provides fine views across the Wreake Valley. The pub was extensively and sensitively refurbished around nine years ago following a serious fire. It is an ideal stopping-off point for those walking the Leicestershire Round footpath. A skittle alley is available to hire for functions. There is always a good range of Everards beers available, including its seasonal brews, and usually a guest ale too. 🚲☸�♣P🖰♣🎧📶

Hose

Rose & Crown 🅛

Bolton Lane, LE14 4JE

✪ 5-11; 12-midnight Fri; 12-1am Sat; 12-10.30 Sun ☎ (01949) 358913 ⊕ roseathose.com

Brewster's Hophead; Pheasantry Best Bitter; changing beers Ⓗ

In the heart of the Vale of Belvoir, this 200-year-old country pub has undergone a new lease of life over the past year. Up to six cask ales are offered including at least one LocAle. The pub has a large bar and seating area, and a separate restaurant. Tuesday is gourmet pizza evening, with a varied menu the rest of the week. Outside is an attractive and spacious deck plus a paddock. Regular live music and other cultural events are held throughout the year. Q🚲☸🌭&🅰♣P🖰(24)🎧📶

Leicester

Ale Wagon

27 Rutland Street, LE1 1RE

✪ 11-11; 7-10.30 Sun ☎ (0116) 262 3330 ⊕ alewagon.co.uk

Hoskins Hob Bitter, IPA; 4 changing beers (sourced regionally; often Hoskins) Ⓗ

Run by the Hoskins family, this city-centre inn with a 1930s interior, including an original oak staircase, has two rooms with tiled and parquet floors and a central bar. There is always a selection of Hoskins Brothers ales and guests available. The pub is popular with visiting rugby fans and real ale drinkers. A function room is available to hire. Handy for the nearby Curve Theatre. ≠♣🚌🖰

Black Horse

1 Foxon Street, Braunstone Gate, LE3 5LT

✪ 12-midnight; 12-11 Sun ☎ (0116) 254 0446

Everards Beacon Hill, Sunchaser, Tiger, Old Original; 2 changing beers (sourced nationally) Ⓗ

The only remaining traditional pub in a street of youth-oriented bars, with two rooms separated by a central bar. Comfortably furnished with practical furniture and wood-panelled walls, this is a genuine community venue. The large roof terrace is popular for alfresco drinking. Live music is hosted four nights a week and Wednesday is quiz night. The guest beers are sourced through Everards and the cider is Westons Old Rosie. ☸♣♠🖰📶

Black Horse

65 Narrow Lane, Aylestone, LE2 8NA

✪ 11-11; 12-midnight Fri & Sat ☎ (0116) 283 7225 ⊕ blackhorse-aylestone.co.uk

Everards Beacon Hill, Tiger, Old Original; 4 changing beers (sourced nationally; often Brunswick, Everards, Titanic) Ⓗ

Welcoming traditional Victorian pub with a distinctive bar servery in a village conservation area on the city's edge, sympathetically refurbished in 2015. Up to eight real ales are available and home-cooked food is served noon-8.30pm daily (until 5.30pm Sun). Coaches are welcome by prior arrangement. The skittle alley and function room can be hired and live music and comedy feature regularly. Beer festivals and community events are hosted. Quiz night is Sunday. There is a large beer garden.
Q🚲☸🌭🍴♣♠🖰♣📶

Blue Boar 🅛

16 Millstone Lane, LE1 5JN

✪ 11-11 ☎ (0116) 319 6230

House beer (by Leatherbritches); 8 changing beers (sourced nationally) Ⓗ

Micropub opened in 2016 on the ground floor of a building in a conservation area, named after the Blue Boar Inn where Richard III stayed before the Battle of Bosworth Field. The light airy room has the bar opposite as you enter, and the cellar is visible through a glass partition behind the bar. The house beer is specially brewed by Leatherbritches. Guest ales from microbreweries around the country include many rare beers. This is probably the only pub in the city using lined glasses to ensure customers get a full pint. Q🌭≠♣♠🖰🚌♣📶

Bowling Green ✅

44 Oxford Street, LE1 5XW

✪ 10-midnight (1am Thu-Sat) ☎ (0116) 254 6496 ⊕ greatukpubs.co.uk/thebowlinggreenleicester

Marston's Pedigree; Wychwood Hobgoblin; 5 changing beers (sourced nationally) Ⓗ

One of the oldest pubs in Leicester, the listed building was given a makeover in late 2015 to return it to a more traditional pub, blending original features with modern facilities. Two original fireplaces were uncovered during the refurbishment and the load-bearing truss in the entrance area dates back to the 14th century. The pictures and wall displays feature scenes of Leicester and bowling. The landlord is an enthusiastic cellarman committed to serving top-class beer. ⑤❀◑ѻ≈➊▣❀🔊

Criterion
44 Millstone Lane, LE1 5JN
🕒 12-11; closed Sun ☎ (0116) 262 5418
🌐 criterionleicester.com
Changing beers (sourced nationally; often Market Harborough, Tres Bien) Ⓗ
A free house since 2003, leased to Market Harborough Brewery in 2016. The two-roomed pub offers up to 10 cask ales from microbreweries and regionals, usually including an offering from Market Harborough or Tres Bien. Beer festivals are held regularly. Darts and dominoes are played. Quiz night is Wednesday, live music plays Thursday to Saturday. The pub hosts monthly comedy events and is a venue for Leicester Comedy Festival. Pizzas are available Monday to Saturday. ⑤❀◑♣➊▣🔊

Globe
43 Silver Street, LE1 5EU
🕒 11-11 (1am Fri & Sat) ☎ (0116) 253 9492
🌐 eversosensible.com/globe
Everards Beacon Hill, Sunchaser, Tiger, Old Original; 2 changing beers (often Everards) Ⓗ
The Globe has been an inn since 1720. Ales used to be brewed using water from the well under the building. The pub has been been sympathetically renovated in recent years to create a restaurant upstairs while leaving the cosy snug downstairs. The restored gas lights are used on special occasions. It was the first Everards pub to return to real ale and now serves a good range to appeal to all tastes. ◑ѻ➊▣🔊

High Cross ✅
103-105 High Street, LE1 4JB (400yds from Clock Tower on corner of High St)
🕒 8am-midnight (1am Sat); 8am-11 Sun ☎ (0116) 251 9218
Greene King Abbot; Ruddles Best Bitter; Sharp's Doom Bar; 3 changing beers (sourced nationally; often Grainstore, Nottingham, Oakham) Ⓗ
Named after the cross marking the centre of medieval Leicester which has recently been resited nearby, this is a Wetherspoon conversion of a former shop. The large L-shaped room has some changes of level to create different areas. Guest beers often come from local breweries, and international guest brewers also feature. Beer festivals are held twice yearly as part of national company events. ⑤❀◑ѻ➊▣🔊

King's Head
36 King Street, LE1 6RL
🕒 12-midnight ☎ (0116) 254 8240
🌐 thekingsleicester.co.uk
Black Country Bradley's Finest Golden, Pig on the Wall, Fireside; 7 changing beers Ⓗ
A traditional one-room city-centre local owned by Black Country Ales. Ten handpulls serve seven regularly changing guest ales, and up to eight varying ciders are also often available, attracting real ale and cider enthusiasts. With an open fire inside and a roof terrace, it is popular whatever the time of year. Seasonal beer festivals are held. Sky and BT sports are screened. Local CAMRA Pub of the Year 2016. ❀≈➊▣❀🔊

Old Horse
198 London Road, LE2 1NE
🕒 11-11.30 (midnight Fri & Sat); 11-11 Sun
☎ (0116) 254 8384 🌐 oldhorseleicester.co.uk
Everards Beacon Hill, Sunchaser, Tiger, Old Original; 4 changing beers (sourced nationally) Ⓗ
Nineteenth-century coaching inn, handy for dog walkers, students and sports supporters. The four guest beers change monthly. The addition of a cider bar serving eight handpulled ciders earned the pub local CAMRA Cider Pub of the Year in 2015. Tasty and good-value food is served. Behind the building is the largest pub garden in town complete with children's play equipment. Regular quiz nights, karaoke and special events take place. ⑤❀◑ѻ♣➊P▣❀🔊

Real Ale Classroom 🍷 Ⓛ
22 Allandale Road, LE2 2DA
🕒 closed Mon; 4-10 (11 Fri); 12-11 Sat; 1-4 Sun
☎ (0116) 319 6998 🌐 therealaleclassroom.com
5 changing beers (sourced regionally; often Grainstore, Oakham) Ⓖ
A classroom-themed micropub set up by career-change teachers in a converted shop in a suburban shopping street. The furniture includes reclaimed desks with original graffiti and the beers are written up on a blackboard. Cask ales and ciders are served from a home-made chiller cabinet behind the high bar. A logburner warms the rear room. In both rooms seating around large tables encourages conversation between regulars and visitors. Bar snacks include local pork pies, a cheeseboard and charcuterie platter. Local CAMRA Pub of the Year 2017. Q♣➊▣❀🔊

Rutland & Derby Ⓛ
21 Millstone Lane, LE1 5JN
🕒 12-11 (1am Fri & Sat); closed Sun ☎ (0116) 262 3299
🌐 therutlandandderby.co.uk
Everards Sunchaser, Tiger; 2 changing beers (sourced nationally) Ⓗ
This pub has an open-plan interior with a contemporary ambience. The long servery bar directly faces the front entrance while off to the left is a lounge bar which leads to a restaurant area on a raised level. At the back is a block-paved courtyard with a metallic spiral staircase leading to a rooftop terrace. Good food features uncomplicated, ethically sourced ingredients. ⑤❀◑ѻ≈➊▣❀🔊

Salmon
19 Butt Close Lane, LE1 4QA
🕒 11-11 (midnight Fri & Sat) ☎ (0116) 253 2301
Black Country Bradley's Finest Golden, Pig on the Wall, Fireside; 7 changing beers (sourced nationally) Ⓗ
A small corner local with a U-shaped single-room interior, refurbished in 1992 in a bright traditional style. It has a friendly, welcoming atmosphere and a strong sports following. A Black Country Ales pub since 2016, it has 12 handpumps dispensing the brewery's ales, guest beers and two real ciders. Lunchtime meals and a Sunday carvery are complemented by cobs, pork pies and Scotch eggs available throughout the day. St Margaret's bus station is nearby. Q❀◑♣➊▣❀🔊

West End Brewery
68-70 Braunstone Gate, LE3 5LG
🕒 closed Mon; 5-11 Tue-Thu; 2-midnight Fri; 12-midnight Sat; 12-10 Sun ☎ 07875 745302 🌐 thewestendbrewery.co.uk

West End Stout, Copper, IPA; 5 changing beers ⓗ
Leicester's original brewpub opened in March 2016. The brewer aims to produce innovative beers, and plans to increase the range over time. He likes to experiment with his recipes and takes on board customers' suggestions. Four house beers are available plus at least three guests from quality local microbreweries or from further afield. The brewery is behind the pub and can be visited by customers. Live music nights are held twice a month. ⓓ♣🖤🚃🐾🎵

Western

70 Western Road, LE3 0GA
✪ 12-midnight (1am Fri & Sat) ☎ (0116) 254 5287
Steamin' Billy Tipsy Fisherman, Bitter, Skydiver; 4 changing beers (sourced regionally; often Charnwood, Everards, Leatherbritches) ⓗ
Traditional local, sympathetically refurbished in 2015, in a residential location close to football and rugby grounds on the edge of the city centre. The bar and lounge are popular with a mixed clientele of all ages. Up to four guest beers are available, mainly from microbreweries. Old pub signs decorate the pub and beer garden. There are regular music and beer festivals and the pub is home to a theatre upstairs. 🐕😺♣🖤🚃🐾🎵

Loughborough

Amber Rooms

15 The Rushes, LE11 5BE
✪ 8am-midnight (1am Fri; 2am Sat) ☎ (01509) 638570
Greene King Abbot; Ruddles Best Bitter; changing beers (often Brewster's, Langton, Nottingham) ⓗ
Family-oriented during the day and welcoming to customers who come for the great-value pub meals, served 8am-11pm. The beer range features five guest ales of high quality, always including some rarities. There are also two annual beer festivals where international brewers are showcased. A resident DJ plays Friday and Saturday 9pm-2am. ⓓ👍🖤🚃🎵

Generous Briton

85 Ashby Road, LE11 3AB
✪ 12-11 (midnight Fri & Sat) ☎ (01509) 263565
Draught Bass; Nottingham Legend; Oakham JHB; 4 changing beers (often Charnwood) ⓗ
Reopened in 2011 as a genuine free house, the GB is ideally situated between the town centre and university. The traditional bar has a dartboard and features old local photographs; the lounge has a pool table and jukebox. Satellite sport is shown throughout. A limited food menu is available but customers are welcome to bring their own food. There is an enclosed beer garden to the rear and families are welcome until 7.45pm. A former local CAMRA Town Pub and Pub of the Year. 😺♣🖤🚃(126)🎵

Needle & Pin

The Rushes, LE11 5BE
✪ closed Mon; 5 (3.30 Fri)-11; 12-11 Sat; 12-10 Sun ☎ 07973 754236
4 changing beers ⓗ
Micropub in what was the old H&R Electronics shop. Beer is served downstairs in a continental-style bar with high stools, and upstairs with a record player, board games and music. More than 50 continental beers are stocked. CAMRA Cider Pub of the Year. 🐕🖤🐾

Organ Grinder

4 Woodgate, LE11 2TY
✪ 12-11 (midnight Fri & Sat); 12-10.30 Sun ☎ (01509) 264008
Blue Monkey BG Sips, 99 Red Baboons, Infinity, Guerrilla; 4 changing beers (sourced locally; often Blue Monkey) ⓗ
Previously known as the Pack Horse and bought by Blue Monkey Brewery in 2012, the building has received a top-to-bottom renovation, uncovering lots of interesting original features. The stable bar at the back reflects the pub's past life as a coaching inn. Eight cask ales are always available alongside Belgian bottled beers and a choice of four real ciders and sometimes a perry. Bar snacks include an interesting range of pork pies. A former local CAMRA Pub of the Year. 🐕😺🖤🚃🐾🎵

Tap & Mallet

36 Nottingham Road, LE11 1EU
✪ 7 (5 Tue & Thu)-midnight; 6-midnight Sat; 3.30-midnight Sun
Marston's Pedigree; 4 changing beers (sourced regionally; often Abbeydale, Charnwood, Salopian) ⓗ
Genuine free house with a regularly changing beer range, mainly seasonal brews from the Abbeydale and Salopian breweries. The interior consists of a large single room divided into two distinct drinking areas – a public bar with pool table, darts and board games, and a quieter lounge area that can be partitioned off for functions. Outside there is a large, secluded lawned garden, patio and pets' corner. Q😺♣🖤🚃🎵

White Hart 🏆

27 Churchgate, LE11 1UD
✪ 11-midnight; 12-11 Sun ☎ (01509) 236976
Draught Bass; Timothy Taylor Landlord; 3 changing beers (sourced locally; often Charnwood, Leatherbritches, Sarah Hughes) ⓗ
Reopened in 2013 as a free house after an extensive refurbishment, the pub has a secluded patio and beer garden to the rear. Regularly changing guest beers are often from local breweries such as Leatherbritches and Charnwood, and Sarah Hughes Dark Ruby is usually available. Live music is hosted on Friday evenings and Sunday afternoons. A former local CAMRA branch Town Pub and Pub of the Year in 2016. 😺ⓓ♣🖤🚃🐾🎵

Lutterworth

Fox

34 Rugby Road, LE17 4BN (400yds from Whittle Roundabout)
✪ 12 (5 Mon)-1am ☎ (01455) 550935
🌐 fox-lutterworth.co.uk
Draught Bass; Sharp's Doom Bar; 2 changing beers (sourced nationally; often Timothy Taylor) ⓗ
Situated at the southern end of the town close to the Sir Frank Whittle jet monument, this popular 18th-century pub offers a warm welcome. An open-plan L-shaped interior is warmed by two open fires. Pub food is served lunchtimes including excellent Sunday roasts; Thai food is available in the Sawasdee restaurant in the evenings. Outside is a large landscaped award-winning garden and drinking area. Quizzes are held weekly on Tuesday evening. A function room hosts bands and private parties. 😺ⓓ🖤P🚃(84,X84)🐾🎵

Unicorn ✪

29 Church Street, LE17 4AE (near church)
✪ 10.30-11 (midnight Fri & Sat); 12-11 Sun
☎ (01455) 552486
Adnams Southwold Bitter; Draught Bass; Greene King IPA; 1 changing beer (sourced nationally; often Hobsons) Ⓗ
Traditional town-centre, street-corner local with a black-and-white frontage, built in 1919 on the site of a 19th-century coach house. The large public bar with an open fire offers TV sports coverage and hosts darts, dominoes and skittles teams. A small, comfortable, family-friendly lounge and dining area, decorated with historic local photographs, is separated from another dining room by a central fireplace. Good inexpensive lunchtime meals include vegetarian and children's options.
🛏️◗♣🅿️🚌(84,X84) 🛜

Market Harborough

Beerhouse

76 St Mary's Road, LE16 7DX
✪ closed Tue; 6-11 Mon & Wed; 12-11 Thu-Sat; 12-10 Sun
☎ (01858) 465317 ∰ beerhouses.uk
Changing beers (sourced nationally; often Hart Family Brewers, Market Harborough, Tres Bien) Ⓖ
Market Harborough's first micropub, set in a converted furniture shop behind the chip shop on St Mary's Road. The focus is very much on beer – there is no food, gaming machines or loud music. Up to 12 real ales, mostly from local microbreweries, are served by gravity from casks lined up behind the bar. Monday is quiz night and comedy nights and live music feature regularly.
♿️🚆💗🅿️🐾🛜

Melton Mowbray

Boat ♟️ ✪

57 Burton Street, LE13 1AF
✪ 11-3 (not Mon & Wed); 12-11.45; 12-11.45 Thu & Fri; 11-11.45 Sat ☎ (01664) 500969
Hook Norton Hooky; Wells Bombardier; 2 changing beers (sourced nationally) Ⓗ
This traditional single-roomed pub takes its name from a canal basin that was once adjacent. The wood-panelled walls are decorated with old pictures of the town and a map of the Melton-Oakham canal. The pub is always busy with those who enjoy good conversation with their pint. An open-range fire gives plenty of warmth and adds to the atmosphere in winter. CAMRA branch Pub of the Year in 2017. 🚆♣🅿️🐾🛜

Kettleby Cross Ⓛ ✪

Wilton Road, LE13 0UJ
✪ 7am-11.30 ☎ (01664) 485310
Greene King Abbot, IPA; 6 changing beers (sourced nationally) Ⓗ
The Kettleby Cross is a Wetherspoon new-build, opened in 2007 as a flagship eco-pub complete with a prominent wind turbine on the roof. The building stands close to the bridge over the nearby River Eye and is named after the cross that once directed travellers in the direction of Ab Kettleby. The large single-room interior is on two levels. The manager is a supporter of local breweries and local ales feature regularly. Q🛏️◗♿️🚆💗🅿️🛜

Mountsorrel

Swan

10 Loughborough Road, LE12 7AT
✪ 12-2.30, 5.30-11; 12-11 Sat; 12-10.30 Sun
☎ (0116) 230 2340
Black Sheep Best Bitter; Castle Rock Harvest Pale; 2 changing beers (often Dancing Duck, Greene King) Ⓗ
Traditional 17th-century, Grade II-listed coaching inn entered via a narrow arch into a courtyard. The split-level interior has open fires, stone floors and low ceilings, and includes a small dining area with a polished wood floor. Good-quality, interesting food is cooked to order, with the menu changing weekly, and there are regular themed events. Outside is a long secluded riverside garden with moorings. A beer festival is hosted annually.
Q🐕◗🅿️🚌🐾

Oadby

Cow & Plough

Gartree Road, LE2 2FB
✪ 11-11 ☎ (0116) 272 0852
Fuller's London Pride; Steamin' Billy Bitter, Skydiver; 4 changing beers (sourced regionally; often Abbeydale, Belvoir, Charnwood) Ⓗ
Situated in a former farm building with a conservatory, the pub is decked out with breweriana. It is home to Steamin' Billy beers, named after the owner's now departed Jack Russell who features on the logo and pumpclips. A mild is always available and real cider in the summer months. The pub holds an annual beer festival. The former dairy buildings house a renowned restaurant. Q🛏️🐕◗🍴♿️♣💗🐾

Lord Keeper of the Great Seal

96-100 The Parade, LE2 5BF
✪ 7am-midnight ☎ (0116) 272 0957
Greene King Abbot; Ruddles Best Bitter; Theakston Best Bitter; 6 changing beers (sourced regionally) Ⓗ
Named after Sir Nathan Wright, a local landowner who held this position in the 17th century, this typical Wetherspoon conversion of a row of shops stands on the former site of Sandhurst Infants School. It features pictures of old Oadby buildings and industries, and a varied library of books. Regular beer festivals and charity events are held. Families are welcome until 9pm.
🛏️🐕◗♿️💗🚌(31,31A) 🛜

Old Dalby

Belvoir Alehouse Ⓛ

Station Road, LE14 3NQ
✪ 10-9 (11 Thu-Sat); 12-6 Sun ☎ (01664) 823978
∰ belvoiralehouse.co.uk
Belvoir Dark Horse, Whippling, Star Bitter, Beaver Bitter, Oatmeal Stout, Old Dalby Ⓗ
The brick-fronted Belvoir Alehouse on the outskirts of the village incorporates a bar, function room and visitors' centre, with brewery tours available by arrangement. A range of regular and seasonal Belvoir Ales is available. The spacious interior is filled with brewing artefacts, and has a traditional bar area, with room for long-alley skittles and a bar billiards table. Large internal windows provide views into the brewery. A full food menu is served daily, with the focus on wholesome meals made with local produce. A former local CAMRA Pub of the Year. 🐕◗♿️♣🅿️🚌(23) 🛜

Plungar

Anchor ⃝L

Granby Lane, NG13 0JJ
✪ 12-3 (not Mon-Thu), 5-11; 12-11 Sat; 12-10.30 Sun
☎ (01949) 860589
House beer (by Belvoir); 2 changing beers Ⓗ
This brick building in the middle of a small Leicestershire village dates from 1774 – it was at one time the local courtroom. The pub now houses a large bar and cosy lounge area, a separate restaurant and a pool room. Outside is an attractive beer garden and pleasant seating area. The Anchor has developed a reputation for good food, using locally sourced ingredients, and serving quality cask ale – at least one but sometimes all beers are from local breweries. Q🕏❀🍴🏃♿♣P🚍(24)🐾🎵

Quorn

Manor House

Woodhouse Road, LE12 8AL
✪ 12-11 (midnight Sat); 12-10 Sun ☎ (01509) 413416
⊕ themanorhouseatquorn.co.uk
Charnwood Salvation; Draught Bass; 3 changing beers (often Batemans, Leatherbritches) Ⓗ
Built in 1899 by the Great Central Railway, the Manor House was designed to serve passengers arriving at Quorn & Woodhouse Station, which it still does today – the preserved steam- and diesel-hauled trains pass by 150 yards from the door. The building has an open-plan bar and award-winning restaurant with a separate function/meeting room available to hire. A free house, two guest beers are available during the week and three at weekends.
Q❀🍴♿🅰🚆♣P🚏🐾🐾

Royal Oak

2 High Street, LE12 8DT
✪ 5-11; 4.30-11.30 Fri; 2-11.30 Sat; 12.30-11 Sun
☎ (01509) 413506 ⊕ theroyaloakquorn.co.uk
Black Sheep Best Bitter; Charnwood Vixen; Timothy Taylor Landlord; 1 changing beer Ⓗ
Traditional inn in the centre of the village, which has recently changed hands. The building has been an inn for around 160 years. Originally three terraced cottages, the internal walls were removed long ago to open up the pub while retaining many original features including beamed ceilings, tiled floors and an open log fire. There is a sheltered, covered courtyard to the side. Draught cider is available occasionally. Q🅰♣🚍🐾🎵

White Hart

32 High Street, LE12 8DT
✪ 4-11 (midnight Fri); 2-midnight Sat; 12-10.30 Sun
☎ (01509) 732958
4 changing beers Ⓗ
The oldest pub in Quorn, dating from 1690, once had its own brewhouse. Over the years it has been modernised, including recent complete redecoration, and little remains to show its true age. The L-shaped bar and central chimney split the pub into three distinct drinking areas, each with a real fire. Outside there is an illuminated, heated seating area and pétanque court. ❀🅰P🚍

Shackerstone

Rising Sun ⃝L

Church Road, CV13 6NN
✪ 12-2.30 (not Mon), 5.30-11; 11.30-11 Sat & Sun
☎ (01827) 880215 ⊕ risingsunpub.com

Marston's Pedigree; Timothy Taylor Landlord; 2 changing beers Ⓗ
Traditional family-owned free house located in the heart of Shackerstone village near the Ashby Canal and the preserved Battlefield Railway. It has a wood-panelled bar serving traditional ales, a restaurant, pool room with Sky Sports, family-friendly conservatory and an attractive garden. The inn, popular with locals and visitors alike, is renowned for the quality and variety of its ales and serves good pub food – the ideal hub for visiting this rural part of Leicestershire.
Q🕏❀🍴♿♿🚆♣🍴P🚍🐾🎵

Shearsby

Chandlers Arms ⃝L

Fenny Lane, LE17 6PL
✪ closed Mon; 12-3 (not Tue), 6-11; 12-7 Sun
☎ (0116) 247 8384 ⊕ chandlersatshearsby.co.uk
Dow Bridge Acris; 6 changing beers (sourced regionally) Ⓗ
Quintessential village inn with a big reputation – a winner of the prestigious Leicester CAMRA Country Pub of the Year award for many years, it was the first pub in the branch to sign up to CAMRA's LocAle scheme. Microbrewery beers are always on the bar, often locally sourced. The pub's name is a reminder of the building's original use as a tallow candlemaker's business. It has a public bar, dining room and a beer garden overlooking the village green from a high vantage point. ❀🍴♣🐾🐾🎵

Shepshed

Horse

196 Ashby Road West, LE12 9EF (on A512)
✪ 12 (4 Mon)-11 ☎ (01509) 507006
⊕ thehorseshepshed.co.uk
Charnwood Salvation; Marston's Pedigree; Sharp's Doom Bar; Shepherd Neame Spitfire; 1 changing beer Ⓗ
The Horse, one of the oldest free houses in Shepshed, is traditionally built, with a restaurant and bar. In 2015 major extension work almost doubled the size of the premises, enabling a much greater emphasis on food. It has a feature fireplace with a wood-burning stove and an alfresco dining area serving fresh pizzas cooked in a wood-fired oven. A good range of beers is available and the pub takes pride in serving freshly prepared food made on the premises using produce sourced within a five mile radius of Shepshed. 🕏❀🍴P🚍

Somerby

Stilton Cheese ⃝L

High Street, LE14 2QB
✪ 12-3, 6 (7 Sun)-11 ☎ (01664) 454394
⊕ stiltoncheeseinn.co.uk
Grainstore Ten Fifty; Marston's Saddle Tank; 3 changing beers (sourced nationally) Ⓗ
Late 16th-century pub built in local ironstone, an ideal refreshment stop for walkers on the Leicestershire Round. The cosy bar and adjoining room are decorated with a large collection of objects including a stuffed pike and badger. Tall customers beware the wide range of pumpclips on the low beam above the bar. CAMRA branch Pub of the Year 2015 and 2016. Q🕏❀🍴🍴♣🐾P🚍🎵

Stoke Golding

George & Dragon L
Station Road, CV13 6EZ
☼ closed Mon; 12-3, 6-11; 12-11 Fri & Sat; 12-10.30 Sun
☎ (01455) 213268
Church End Goats Milk, Gravediggers Ale, What the Fox's Hat, Stout Coffin, Fallen Angel; 3 changing beers (sourced locally; often Church End) Ⓗ
Renowned village local serving eight real ales from the Church End range and a real cider. Good home-cooked lunches feature local produce and bar snacks, made on the premises, are always available. Steak night is the second Tuesday of the month and roast lunch is served on the last Sunday. Close to the historic Bosworth Battlefield, the pub supports a number of clubs and societies, and is popular with walkers, cyclists and boaters from the nearby Ashby Canal. Q✿▲♣♠P🖵🐾🖢

Swinford

Chequers ✪
High Street, LE17 6BL (near church)
☼ 7-11 Mon; 12-2.30 (3 Sat), 6-11; 12-3, 7-11 Sun
☎ (01788) 860318 ⊕ chequersswinford.co.uk
Adnams Southwold Bitter; 2 changing beers (sourced nationally; often Sharp's, Timothy Taylor) Ⓗ
In January 2017, the landlord celebrated 30 years at this family-run community local, where a warm welcome is assured. The food menu caters for all and includes vegetarian and children's options. The large garden and play area are popular with families in good weather. A marquee provides the venue for the annual beer festival and is available for private hire. Pub games include table skittles. Within a mile is the 18th-century Stanford Hall with a caravan park and museum. Q✿▲♣P

Syston

Queen Victoria
76 High Street, LE7 1GQ
☼ 4-11; 12-midnight Fri & Sat; 12-10.30 Sun
☎ (0116) 260 5750
Everards Beacon Hill, Sunchaser, Tiger, Old Original; 3 changing beers (sourced nationally; often Bath Ales, Brunswick, Everards) Ⓗ
A former coach house, the building is 200 years old – Everards has traded here since 1922. The pub has several small rooms and a large garden at the rear. A separate restaurant carvery is accessed via the garden. Entertainment is hosted every other Saturday and beer festivals are held at Easter and in the summer. Guest beers are sourced through Everards. Opening hours vary throughout the year. ✿◑⇌♣P🖵🐾🖢

Walton on the Wolds

Anchor ✪
2 Loughborough Road, LE12 8HT
☼ 12-2.30 (not Mon, Tue & Thu), 5.30-11; 12-3, 5.30-11 Sat; 12-10.30 Sun ☎ (01509) 880018
Adnams Southwold Bitter; Fuller's London Pride; Timothy Taylor Landlord; 1 changing beer (often Charnwood) Ⓗ
The Anchor is situated in the centre of a small village within easy reach of Leicester and Nottingham via the A46. It is a popular venue for walkers who stop for a well-earned home-cooked lunch in front of the fire. There is a menu to suit all tastes plus an extensive specials board. Outside is an elevated seating area to the front and a garden and large car park to the rear. Q✿⇌◑P🖵🐾🖢

Wigston

Horse & Trumpet
Bull Head Street, LE18 1PB
☼ 5-11; 12-midnight Fri & Sat; 12-11 Sun ☎ (0116) 288 6290
Everards Tiger, Old Original; 2 changing beers (sourced locally) Ⓗ
An old pub, converted in the 1860s from two cottages. The large elongated U-shaped room has a games section to one end and a dining area at the other, separated by a seating space in the middle. The building to the rear which houses the skittles long alley originated as a purpose-built framework knitters' shed. Outside is a large paved courtyard furnished with picnic tables. ✿◑♣P🖵🐾

Star & Garter
114 Leicester Road, LE18 1DS
☼ 12-11 (midnight Fri); 11-midnight Sat; 11.30-11.30 Sun ☎ (0116) 319 1626
Everards Beacon Hill, Tiger; 1 changing beer Ⓗ
This traditional community pub consists of a public and a lounge bar as well as a games room and skittles alley. A date stone set high in the front gable-end wall suggests the pub was built in 1879, a suggestion endorsed by a plaque hung in the lounge listing tenants since that date. Filled cobs and pork pies are available for those who are a little peckish. ✿♣♠P🖵🖢

Willoughby Waterleys

General Elliott
Main Street, LE8 6UF
☼ closed Mon; 11-2 (not Tue), 5.30-11.30; 11-2, 4.30-10.30 Fri; 11.30-11.30 Sat; 11.30-6 Sun ☎ (0116) 247 8058
Draught Bass; Theakston Best Bitter; 1 changing beer (sourced nationally) Ⓗ
The pub is named after an 18th-century British Army officer, most noted for his successful defence of the garrison during the Great Siege of Gibraltar, which lasted from 1779 to 1783. The L-shaped room has skittles and darts at one end, a public/lounge bar space in the middle and a snug area at the other end. It is conveniently situated for passing hikers on the Leicestershire Round and cyclists on Cycle Route 6. ▲♣🐾🖢

Project William

Mentions in some pub listings to Everard's Brewery's Project William refers to a scheme whereby the Leicester brewery buys or refurbishes an existing pub and leases it to a smaller brewery that can sell its own range of beers in return for stocking at least one Everard's beer.

LINCOLNSHIRE

Map of Lincolnshire showing locations including: East Yorkshire, South Yorkshire, Burton-upon-Stather, Eastoft, Winterton, Barton-upon-Humber, Crowle, Scunthorpe, Brigg, Habrough, Grimsby, East Butterwick, Melton Ross, Cleethorpes, Belton, Scawby Brook, Westwoodside, Messingham, Scawby, Scotter, Rothwell, North Thoresby, Owston Ferry, Willoughton, Snitterby, Swinhope, Ludford, Gainsborough, Louth, Sutton-on-Sea, Scampton, Little Cawthorpe, Saxilby, Langworth, Wragby, South Ormsby, Aby, Chapel St Leonards, Lincoln, Hemingby, Skendleby, Skellingthorpe, Fiskerton, Horncastle, Ingoldmells, North Hykeham, Heighington, Thimbleby, Raithby, Waddington, Harmston, Kirkby on Bain, Little Steeping, Skegness, Coleby, Tattershall Thorpe, Stickford, Wainfleet, Navenby, Ruskington, Sleaford, Boston, Ancaster, Heckington, Barkston Heath, Swineshead, The Wash, Threekingham, Bicker, Kirton, Grantham, Donington, Barrowby, Horbling, Fosdyke, Ropsley, Skillington, Haconby, Gosberton Risegate, Irnham, Spalding, Leicestershire, South Witham, Bourne, Whaplode St Catherine, Norfolk, Rutland, Barholm, Market Deeping, Stamford, Cambs

Aby

Railway Tavern
Main Road, LN13 0DR (off A16 via South Thoresby)
☼ 12-11.30 ☎ (01507) 480676
2 changing beers (sourced nationally) Ⓗ
A lovely rural venue which lies just outside this beautiful village. There is always a good selection of carefully chosen real ales and a good home-cooked food menu. A real fire adds to the homely atmosphere at this welcoming pub. It is closed on Tuesdays during November and between January and Easter. ⏱ⓓP❀

Ancaster

Ancaster Social Club
Ermine Street, NG32 3PW
☼ 7-11; 12-10.30 Sun ☎ (01400) 230896
Wells Bombardier; 2 changing beers (often Brewsters, Tom Wood's) Ⓗ
Located in the heart of the village, this club hosts various sporting events on its playing fields,

including football, cricket and rounders. Inside, darts, pool and live sports are available. It has an airy conservatory and outside seating overlooking the sports field. Local CAMRA Club of the Year for the past five years. ⏱❀&≠♣P🚌❀🐕🛜

Barholm

Five Horseshoes Ⓛ
PE9 4RA
☼ 4 (1 Sat)-11; 12-10.30 Sun ☎ (01778) 560238
Adnams Southwold Bitter; Oakham JHB; 3 changing beers (often Grainstore, Hopshackle) Ⓗ
An 18th-century stone-built country pub, comprising two bars, two side rooms and a pool room. A wood fire burns throughout the winter. Stuffed birds and enamelled adverts adorn the walls. Outside is a garden, kids' play area and car park. Barbecues and music events are held in the summer. A range of beers from local and regional breweries is served, along with real ciders. Pizzas are available Friday and Saturday. The pub supports many charities. Q⏱❀ⓓ&♣P❀🐕🛜

Barrowby

White Swan ✪

Main Street, NG32 1BH
☼ 12-midnight (1am Fri & Sat) ☎ (01476) 562375
Adnams Southwold Bitter; Sharp's Doom Bar; 2 changing beers (often Castle Rock, Sadler's) Ⓗ
Popular village pub run by the same landlord for 24 years, who is an enthusiastic CAMRA member. There is a comfortable lounge, a separate bar area and a further space where the local darts, cribbage and pool teams play. Offering two regular and two changing guest ales, it also provides locally sourced traditional home-made food Wednesday to Saturday. Outside there is a heated smoking area and a secluded garden. First Sunday of the month is quiz night. Q❄️🛏️🍴♣️P🚎🐾🛜

Barton-upon-Humber

George Inn ✪

George Street, DN18 5ES
☼ 11-11 (midnight Fri & Sat) ☎ (01652) 636303
⊕ thegeorgebarton.co.uk
4 changing beers (sourced regionally; often Black Sheep, Courage, St Austell) Ⓗ
Large 17th-century coaching inn occupying a prominent position just off the market place and offering town centre accommodation. Originally called the George & Dragon, it served Barton on the London to Hull route, but has also been used as an excise office, posting house and local government venue. The central bar serves several rooms. Quiz night is Thursday. A justifiably popular pub. Q❄️🛏️🍽️🍴♿️P🚎🐾🛜

Wheatsheaf

3 Holydyke, DN18 5PS
☼ 12-11.30 (12.30am Fri & Sat); 12-11 Sun
☎ (01652) 633292
Everards Tiger; Theakston Best Bitter; 2 changing beers (sourced nationally; often Lancaster) Ⓗ
Serving up to four real ales and real cider and occupying a prominent position on the main road through Barton, this friendly pub dates back to the 18th century, with a list of former licensees going back to 1791. It has an unspoilt, traditional atmosphere, with regulars enjoying classic bar games of dominoes and crib. There is a small snug at the rear with a front bar and seating area for diners. 🛏️🍴♣️P🚎(250,350)

White Swan 🏆

66 Fleetgate, DN18 5QD (follow signs for railway station)
☼ closed Mon; 11-11; 10-11 Sun ☎ (01652) 661222
2 changing beers (sourced regionally; often Black Sheep, Clark's) Ⓗ
The White Swan reopened in 2013 and is a large, recently renovated and modernised pub with a separate dining area. It has a large, secure beer garden to the rear and is decorated in contemporary style while retaining original pub features such as the large bay windows. Friday night activities are supported by numerous groups and societies. Good, locally sourced food is available. Adjacent to bus and rail terminuses. Q❄️🛏️🍴♿️🚆♣️P🚎🐾🛜

Belton

Crown Inn Ⓛ

Church Lane, DN9 1PA (300yds off A631 behind parish church)
☼ 1-midnight; 12-midnight Sat & Sun ☎ (01427) 872834
Bradfield Farmers Blonde; Brakspear Bitter; Jennings Cocker Hoop; Marston's Wainwright; 1 changing beer (sourced nationally; often Marston's) Ⓗ
Difficult to find but well worth the effort, this pub is a haven for the discerning drinker. The present licensees have carried on a tradition of offering a range of cask ales. Up to six are always available, as well as real cider. Quizzes, live music and occasional beer festivals are a feature of this lively community pub. 🛏️🍽️🏕️♣️♦️P🚎(399)🐾🛜

Bicker

Red Lion

Donington Road, PE20 3EF
☼ closed Mon & Tue; 12-11; 12-7 Sun ☎ (01775) 821200
⊕ redlionbicker.co.uk
Courage Directors; Greene King IPA; 1 changing beer (often Austendyke Ales) Ⓗ
A typical country inn with low beams and tiled floor, and in a pleasant setting, extensively and tastefully redecorated in 2015 and reopened after two years of closure. The welcoming multi-roomed pub has a small bar, and is a popular dining venue with a varied, extensive menu. The pub is known to date from at least 1665, the time of the Great Plague of London. The Wash would have been in closer proximity years ago. 🛏️🍽️♿️♣️P🚎(59)🛜

Boston

Eagle

144 West Street, PE21 8RE
☼ 11-midnight ☎ (01205) 361116
Castle Rock Black Gold, Harvest Pale, Preservation Fine Ale, Screech Owl; 7 changing beers Ⓗ
Part of the Castle Rock chain, the Eagle is known as the real ale pub of Boston. This two-roomed, friendly hostelry has an L-shaped bar with a large

REAL ALE BREWERIES	
8 Sail Heckington	
Austendyke Spalding	
Axholme Crowle	
Bacchus 🍺 Sutton-on-Sea	
Batemans Wainfleet	
Black Horse Louth	
Blue Bell 🍺 Whaplode St Catherine	
Brewster's Grantham	
Cheeky Imp Skellingthorpe	
Dark Tribe 🍺 East Butterwick	
Ferry Fiskerton (NEW)	
Firehouse Louth	
Fuddy Duck Kirton (NEW)	
Greg's 🍺 Scampton	
Hopshackle Market Deeping	
Horncastle 🍺 Horncastle	
Leila Cottage 🍺 Ingoldmells	
Lincolnshire 🍺 Langworth	
Newby Wyke Grantham	
Oldershaw Barkston Heath	
Poachers North Hykeham	
Rowett North Thoresby	
Tom Wood's Melton Ross	
Willy's 🍺 Cleethorpes	

TV screen for big sports events. The small cosy lounge has an open fire. The pub stocks a wide range of guest ales, and at least one cider. A function room upstairs is home to Boston Folk Club. Thursday is quiz night – allegedly the hardest in town. Q❀❅✿❆♠✿♻🚲🐾☮

Goodbarns Yard ✪

8 Wormgate, PE21 6NP
✿ 11.30-11; 12-11 Sun ☎ (01205) 355717
⊕ goodbarnsyard.co.uk
Morland Old Speckled Hen; Timothy Taylor Landlord; 1 changing beer (sourced nationally) Ⓗ
In a cobbled medieval street, which runs northwards away from the Boston Stump, parallel to the River Witham. The 700-year-old pub is popular for meals, with a busy restaurant. Old signs and pictures of Boston adorn the walls. A large garden with tables and covered patio areas overlooks the river. 🐾❀◑)♻☮

Bourne

Smith's Ⓛ

25 North Street, PE10 9AE
✿ 10-11 (midnight Fri); 8.30am-midnight Sat; 8.30am-11 Sun
☎ (01778) 426819
Fuller's London Pride; Oakham JHB; 4 changing beers (often Hopshackle) Ⓗ
A successful conversion of an old grocery store into an atmospheric pub with exposed red-brick walls throughout. The building is a warren of interconnecting rooms spanning three floors. The main front bar serves six beers, mostly from independent brewers. Six ciders are sold from all over the country. Outside there is a large patio and beer garden with a children's play area. There is an annual beer festival in summer and also an annual cider and sausage festival in August.
Q❀◑&♠✿🐾☮

Brigg

Yarborough Hunt Ⓛ

49 Bridge Street, DN20 8NS (across bridge from marketplace)
✿ 11-11 (11.30 Thu; midnight Fri); 10-midnight Sat; 11-10.30 Sun ☎ (01652) 658333
Tom Wood's Best Bitter, Lincoln Gold, Bomber County; 3 changing beers (sourced nationally; often Greene King, Morland, Timothy Taylor) Ⓗ
Former Sergeants Brewery tap built in the 1700s and retaining original rustic features. It is simply furnished, with open fires in some rooms, and an enclosed beer garden. An extensive range of wines, ciders and whisky is sold, with up to eight quality UK and continental beers on draught. Daily newspapers are available. No food is served, but customers can bring their own sandwiches and other cold food. Q🐾❀&♠✿♻(4,95)🐾☮

Burton-upon-Stather

Ferry House Inn ✪

Stather Road, DN15 9DJ (follow campsite signs through village; down hill at church)
✿ 6-11; 12-11 Sat & Sun ☎ (01724) 721783
⊕ ferryhousepub.co.uk
2 changing beers (sourced locally; often Tom Wood's) Ⓗ
Friendly village pub on the banks of the River Trent which has been in the same family for over 55

years. It has its own microbrewery (check ahead for beer availability). Real cider is sold. An annual beer festival is held on the August bank holiday weekend. It has a large outdoor children's play area and hosts occasional live music events. Food is served all day Friday, and on Saturday and Sunday lunchtimes. The pub is a popular meeting place for local heritage groups. Q🐾❀◑)♠♣✿♻P♻🐾☮

Chapel St Leonards

Admiral Benbow

The Promenade, PE24 5BQ
✿ 10-7 (10.30 Fri & Sat); 10-8 Sun ☎ (01754) 871847
⊕ admiralbenbowbeachbar.co.uk
Black Sheep Best Bitter; 2 changing beers Ⓗ
Beach bar on the promenade. Opening times and facilities are dependent on the weather and are limited in winter, but if the flag is flying it is open. Bar snacks and hot food are served, and there is an outside seating area themed as a boat deck, the Hispaniola. Picnic trays and plastic glasses to take out your favourite ale are provided for the beach. Dogs are welcome on leads. 🐾❀◑)♻🐾☮

Cleethorpes

No.1 Pub

Railway Station, DN35 8AX
✿ 12-7.30 Mon; 1-midnight; 12-midnight Sat & Sun
☎ (01472) 696221
Batemans XXXB; Draught Bass; 6 changing beers (sourced regionally) Ⓗ
Typical railway bar situated on Cleethorpes station. This popular local has a main bar, with a smaller one off it which overlooks the platform, while there is a fair-sized seating area outside the front. From the bar, customers can order quality real ales and home-cooked food. Sunday lunches are considered some of the best in the area.
❀◑)♻♠P♻🐾☮

No.2 Refreshment Room

Station Approach, DN35 8AX
✿ 7.30am-12.30am (11 Mon; 11.30 Tue & Wed); 9am-midnight Sun ☎ 07905 375587
Hancocks HB; Rudgate Ruby Mild; Sharp's Doom Bar, Atlantic; 2 changing beers (sourced nationally) Ⓗ
Multiple CAMRA award-winning local - a small and cosy pub on the scenic river front station at Cleethorpes, with a reputation for quality ale and conversation, serving both travellers and locals throughout the day. Just the place for a refresher before or after your train journey or a walk on the beach. A little gem. ❀♻♠☮

Nottingham House 🍷 ✪

7 Seaview Street, DN35 8EU
✿ 12-11; 11.30-midnight Fri; 11.30-1am Sat; 11.30-11 Sun
☎ (01472) 505150 ⊕ nottinghamhousehotel.com
Oakham Citra; Tetley Mild, Bitter; Timothy Taylor Landlord; 3 changing beers (sourced regionally) Ⓗ
An excellent example of a real English pub. Converted from two cottages built in 1856, this three-roomed venue comprises a bar, lounge and snug. In winter, open fires add to the atmosphere. Excellent food is served Wednesday to Sunday both in the bars and in an upstairs restaurant where booking is essential. Sky and BT sports are shown in the bar. Dogs welcome in the bar only. A good selection of ales and ciders completes the picture.
Q🐾❀◑)♠♣✿♻🐾☮

Signal Box Inn

Lakeside Station, King's Road, DN35 0AG

🕓 11-11 ☎ (01472) 604657 ⏣ cclr.co.uk/signalboxinn

4 changing beers (sourced nationally) Ⓗ

An original signal box, signed as the smallest pub on the planet. However, on any day with reasonable weather, the beer garden is a great location for a pint or two. Part of the Cleethorpes Coast Light Railway, the site runs some fabulous events, such as the Real Ale and Blues or the folk and cider festivals. In 2016, the pub served over 250 different real ales and ciders. Closes a week before Christmas and reopens a week before Easter. Q ☺ ◉ ♿ ▲ ♠ ➡ ✿ 🗢

Willy's ♉

17 High Cliff, DN35 8RQ

🕓 11-11 (midnight Wed & Thu; 2am Fri & Sat); 11-1am Sun

☎ (01472) 602145

Draught Bass; Willy's Original; 2 changing beers (sourced nationally) Ⓗ

A popular brewpub and longstanding Guide entry, with views across the River Humber to Spurn Point and the Yorkshire wind farms. Good beer and tasty, good-value food is dished up all year round. Dogs are not admitted during mealtimes; beers are welcome when dining until 7pm. The brewery is visible from the large open downstairs bar; the function room upstairs is often open at weekends, when the pub is popular and sometimes noisy. Local CAMRA Pub of the Year 2017.

☺ ◉ ◑ ➔ ➡ ✿

Coleby

Tempest Arms

Hill Rise, LN5 0AG

🕓 closed Mon; 12-11 (midnight Fri & Sat); 12-8 Sun

☎ (01522) 810258 ⏣ thetempestcoleby.co.uk

Brains Rev James; Dark Star Hophead; Fuller's ESB; St Austell Cornish Best Bitter; Timothy Taylor Landlord; 1 changing beer Ⓗ

A popular village pub on the ridge, with panoramic views of the Witham Valley. A major refurbishment has been carried out following the pub's purchase by a group of villagers. It is a haven for foodies, drinkers and dog walkers alike. An acoustic music session is held on the second Tuesday and a quiz on the last Thursday of each month.

Q ☺ ◉ ◑ ♿ ♠ P ➡ (1) ✿ 🗢

Donington

Black Bull

7 Market Place, PE11 4ST

🕓 10-11.30 ☎ (01775) 822228 ⏣ blackbulldonington.com

Batemans XB; Sharp's Doom Bar; 3 changing beers (often Black Sheep, Marston's) Ⓗ

Busy local just off the A52. Five handpumps feature two regular beers and three varying guest beers from small brewers as well as large regionals. The comfortable bar has low, beamed ceilings, wooden settles and a cosy fire in winter. The restaurant offers a good choice of reasonably priced evening meals; lunches are served in the bar. Tables in the car park are used for outdoor drinking. Buses run from Boston and Spalding (not Sun).

☺ ◉ ◑ ▲ ♠ P ➡ 🗢

East Butterwick

Dog & Gun Ⓛ

High Street, DN17 3AJ (off A18 at Keadby Bridge, E bank)

🕓 5-11; 12-11 Sat & Sun ☎ (01724) 782324

Dark Tribe Pieces of 8; 2 changing beers (sourced locally; often Dark Tribe) Ⓗ

Both the pub and the on-site brewery changed hands in 2016 and the new owners have retained its traditional style, alongside the River Trent. There are three rooms, with one for families. Picnic-style bench seating is set out on the riverbank as well as at the rear of the pub. Darts is popular and a weekly quiz is held on Tuesday evening. During the warmer months motorsport meetings are held for motorcycles and vintage cars. ☺ ◉ ♿ ♠ P ➡ (12) ✿

Eastoft

River Don Tavern

Sampson Street, DN17 4PQ (on A161 Goole-Gainsborough road)

🕓 3.30-11; 12-11 Sun ☎ (01724) 798040

2 changing beers (sourced regionally; often Acorn, Milestone, Rooster's) Ⓗ

Traditional village local on the main road through the village. It has two distinct drinking areas, styled with dark-wood ceiling beams, rustic furniture and framed photos showing village life through the ages. One area is used for dining and a separate restaurant is also available for the renowned Sunday carvery. Two rotating guest beers are offered, usually including one from Rooster's, plus a real cider in summer. Accommodation is in three rooms in the pub and four lodges at the rear. ☺ ◉ 🛏 ◑ ♿ ♠ ➡ P ➡ (356) ✿ 🗢

Fosdyke

Ship Inn

Moulton Washway, PE12 6LH (just outside Fosdyke when travelling from Boston on main A17 next to bridge)

🕓 11.30-10 (11 Fri & Sat) ☎ (01205) 260764

⏣ shipinnfosdyke.com

Adnams Southwold Bitter, Broadside; Batemans XB Ⓗ

As its name suggests, this former Batemans hostelry is dedicated to all things maritime; maps, photographs, charts and model ships of every description are in plentiful supply. The week's tide table is also detailed on a blackboard. The inn is near to the busy Fosdyke Marina and boaters and landlubbers are well catered for, with excellent home-cooked food and a welcome cheer.

Q ☺ ◑ P ✿ 🗢

Gainsborough

Blues Club

Northolme, North Street, DN21 2QW

🕓 7-midnight; 5-1am Fri; 12-1am Sat; 12-midnight Sun

☎ (01427) 613688

3 changing beers Ⓗ

The club has a bar area with several TVs showing sport, a quieter lounge and a large function room which hosts regular live entertainment (admission charges may apply). Two changing real ales are usually sold and details of forthcoming beers can be emailed to customers on request. CAMRA guests are always welcome on production of a membership card or a copy of the Guide.

☺ ➔ (Central) ♠ ➡ 🗢

Eight Jolly Brewers 🅛
Ship Court, DN21 2DW
⊕ 11-midnight; 12-midnight Sun ☎ 07926 797767
Dukeries A Ray of Sunshine; changing beers 🖽
The CAMRA branch's flagship real ale haven, in the Guide since 1995, based in a 300-year-old Grade II-listed building. Eight beers, at least one at a discounted price, are always on sale, many from northern micros, but new breweries from all areas feature. Real cider and continental bottled beers can also be enjoyed. Fortnightly Wednesday quiz nights take place. Customers bring in food to share on Sunday lunchtimes. Q&≠●P묘(200)

Elm Cottage 🍷 🅛 ✅
138 Church Street, DN21 2JU
⊕ 11.30-midnight; 12-11.30 Sun ☎ 07590 806584
Changing beers 🖽
The pub is close to Gainsborough Trinity's football ground and the Blues Club. There are six varying beers, some from the Marston's portfolio, but frequently from microbreweries. Good value lunchtime food is served Tuesday to Sunday and early evening meals on Thursday and Friday. The pub is popular with local amateur sports teams. Weekly live music is featured.
Q➸🕮&≠(Central)●P묘🐾☕

Sweyn Forkbeard ✅
22-24 Silver Street, DN21 2DP
⊕ 8am-midnight (1am Wed & Thu; 2am Fri & Sat)
☎ (01427) 675000
Ruddles Best Bitter; Sharp's Doom Bar; 3 changing beers 🖽
This town-centre Wetherspoon establishment is making itself one of the must-do pubs in town. A range of three rotating guest beers often includes some oddities for this part of the country; customers can ask for their favourite ale and it often appears. The pub is named after the Danish King of England in 1013, whose son Canute is rumoured to have stopped the Trent aegir (tidal bore). Really cheap, good food is on sale until 11pm. ➸🕮&≠(Central)●묘☕

Gosberton Risegate

Duke of York 🅛
106 Risegate Road, PE11 4EY
⊕ 12 (6.30 Mon)-11; 11-3, 7-10.30 Sun ☎ (01775) 840193
Batemans XB; St Austell Tribute; 1 changing beer (sourced regionally) 🖽
A friendly pub and a long-standing entry in the Guide, with a deserved reputation for value-for-money beers and food. As well as regular beers, guests come from a range of independent brewers. A wide choice of cooked food is available with portions to suit the largest appetite. Local community life is supported through charities, sports teams, and other social events. Visitors can expect an enthusiastic welcome from the two pub dogs. Q➸🐾🕮♣P

Grantham

BeerHeadZ
27 Watergate, NG31 6NS
⊕ 1-11; 12-midnight Fri & Sat; 12-10 Sun ☎ (01476) 330274
⊕ beerheadz.biz
5 changing beers 🖽
The sign 'Fancy a pint of the unusual?' greets customers outside this pub in the area of town

dominated by St Wulfram's Church spire. Grantham's long-awaited first micropub opened in 2016 and in its first year sold over 400 different cask ales. Continental beers are also available. There is a free function room and customers are welcome to bring in their own food. CAMRA Town Pub of the Year for 2017. Q♣●🕮묘🐾☕

Chequers 🅛
25 Market Place, NG31 6LR (between High St and Market Place)
⊕ 11-3, 7-midnight; 11-1am Fri & Sat; 12-midnight Sun
☎ (01476) 570149
3 changing beers (sourced regionally) 🖽
A cosmopolitan contemporary bar on a paved side street off the High Street known locally as Butchers Row. It serves LocAle beers from Brewsters and Oldershaws complemented by changing guest beers. Popular with all ages, the bar has a relaxed atmosphere during the day and comes alive in the evenings and at weekends. Q➸&●묘🐾

Lord Harrowby 🅛
65 Dudley Road, NG31 9AB
⊕ 3 (12 Sat)-11; 1-11 Sun ☎ (01476) 563515
Oldershaw Heavenly Blonde; 4 changing beers 🖽
A friendly back-street community pub, one of the few in Grantham, with a bar and lounge with a real fire as pubs used to have, a dartboard on the corner, and crib and dominoes played in leagues. There is an enclosed area at the back where at least two beer festivals with live music are held. Oldershaw's Heavenly Blonde is permanent while the landlord, a CAMRA member and real ale enthusiast, sources four changing guest beers and real cider. Q➸🐾≠♣●🐾

Nobody Inn 🅛
9 North Street, NG31 6NU (opp Asda car park)
⊕ 12-11; 12-10.30 Sun ☎ (01476) 565288
Sharp's Doom Bar; 5 changing beers (often Black Sheep, Newby Wyke) 🖽
The Nobody is famous for its hidden toilet door behind the bookcase. The pub sells beer from the award-winning Newby Wyke Brewery in Grantham. It gets lively at the weekend and when a big sporting event is taking place, but is also a pleasant place for a quiet drink, with good bar staff. There is a downstairs room for meetings. Live music is staged during the year. Watch out for the giant spider! ♣●묘🐾☕

Grimsby

Barge
Riverhead, DN31 1NH
⊕ 10-11 (2am Tue, Fri & Sat); 12-11 Sun ☎ (01472) 340911
Wells Bombardier; Wychwood Hobgoblin 🖽
This pleasant riverside pub on the edge of Freshney Place shopping precinct has two main seating areas. The first is at deck level while the second, larger area is in the boat's hold. There is also an outside area with tables and chairs. From the larger bar, customers can order quality beer and home-cooked food. A warm welcome is given both to regular and first-time visitors. A regular quiz night is on Monday. Evening meals are served until 7pm. ➸🐾🕮≠묘

Spiders Web
180 Carr Lane, DN32 8LN
⊕ 12-11 (midnight Fri & Sat) ☎ (01472) 692065
⊕ thespiderswebgy.co.uk

John Smith's Bitter; 3 changing beers (sourced nationally; often Leeds, Thwaites) Ⓗ
Friendly, family-run pub with a bar, quiet lounge and a function room which hosts folk, blues and local band nights. The rotating guest beers are chosen by the regular customers. A large, grassed area is a suntrap suitable for families and there is a separate smoking area. Traditional pub games can be played in the bar and poker (league and non-league) in the lounge. Q☆♿⚙♣P🚲(4)🐾🛜

Yarborough Hotel ✅

Bethlehem Street, DN31 1JN
🕐 7am-midnight (1am Fri & Sat) ☎ (01472) 268283
Greene King Abbot; Kelham Island Easy Rider; Ruddles Best Bitter; 12 changing beers Ⓗ
Recently refurbished, this Wetherspoon pub is one of the newer hotels in the portfolio. Over £3 million was spent on upgrading the former station hotel from a public bar back into a hotel. There are two bars —a large front bar hosting 12 handpulls, while a smaller rear bar offers a range of six handpulls. It is open plan, in keeping with the Wetherspoon style, with pictures of local history adorning the walls. Q☆♿🛏◐🚲Ⓐ🚃♿🚲

Habrough

Station Inn

Station Road, DN40 3AP
🕐 7am-11 ☎ (01469) 572896
3 changing beers (sourced regionally; often Caledonian) Ⓗ
A welcoming local pub which over the years is slowly being transformed into a country hostelry not to be missed. The village community has brought it back to a place that serves drinkers of real ale and the people of the village well. Originally the building, dating back to 1848, was a hotel built by the railway company with an eye to securing business from the nearby station. ☆⚙🚃♣P🐾

Haconby

Hare & Hounds

2 West Road, PE10 0UZ
🕐 12-2, 6-11 (10.30 Mon); 12-11 Sat; 12-10.30 Sun ☎ (01778) 570521
Marston's EPA; 1 changing beer (often Wychwood) Ⓗ
This low-beamed inn built around 1600 has soft settees in the back room and is a popular dining hostelry. Walking groups frequent the pub and there is live music on the first and second Sundays as well as the third Monday in the month. The guest ale is from the Marston's stable and changes regularly. Nearby is the Primitive Baptist Methodist Chapel built in 1867, which must be one of the smallest chapels in the land. Q☆⚙◐&♣♿P🐾

Harmston

Thorold Arms

High Street, LN5 9SN
🕐 closed Mon; 6-11; 12-3, 5-11 Fri; 12-3, 6-11 Sat; 12-11 Sun ☎ (01522) 720358 ⊕ thoroldarmssharmston.co.uk
4 changing beers (sourced nationally; often Dark Star, Oldershaw) Ⓗ
Expect a warm welcome in this 17th-century, stone-built pub in the heart of the village. The bar has an open fire with sofas and armchairs, in addition to traditional dining tables and

chairs. There is also a dining room with a full menu and weekly themed nights including pie and a pint, and fish and chips. Beers on the four handpumps are from near and far. ☆⚙◐P🚲(1)🛜

Heighington

Butcher & Beast

High Street, LN4 1JS
🕐 12-11; 12-10 Sun ☎ (01522) 790386
⊕ butcherandbeast.co.uk
Batemans XB, XXXB; 4 changing beers (often Batemans, Castle Rock, Oakham) Ⓗ
This charming, stone-built pub is in the centre of a pretty village. The refurbished restaurant is at the rear and does not impinge on the drinking pub. If you want a proper steak with good beer, this is well worth a visit. Pictures of village history adorn the walls. There is a fine selection of malt whiskies. Q☆⚙◐♣♿P🚲(2)🐾🛜

Hemingby

Coach & Horses

Church Lane, LN9 5QF (1 mile from A158 at Baumber)
🕐 6 (7 Mon & Tue)-11; 12-2.30, 6-11 Sat; 12-2.30, 7-10.30 Sun ☎ (01507) 578280 ⊕ hemingby.net/the-coach-horses
3 changing beers (sourced regionally) Ⓗ
In a picturesque Wolds village, this pub is popular with walkers and cyclists, as well as locals. It is a cosy building with low-beamed ceilings, and has been under the same ownership for nearly a quarter of a century. Home-cooked food is served and there is always an interesting selection of beers, mainly from small local and regional breweries, on the three handpumps. Camping is on the pub's two-acre campsite. Q☆⚙Ⓐ♣P🐾

Horbling

Plough Inn

4 Spring Lane, NG34 0PF
🕐 11.30-2.30 (not Mon), 6.30-11.30; 11.30-midnight Fri & Sat; 12-10.30 Sun ☎ (01529) 240263
⊕ theploughinnhorblingltd.co.uk
Marston's Wainwright; 1 changing beer (often Reunion) Ⓗ
A true community pub built in 1832 and owned by the parish, set in a quiet village. In addition to the lounge and bar, its snug is surely one of the smallest and most intimate of its kind. Beers are often from microbreweries, and change regularly. Home-cooked meals are served in the bar and restaurant. Spring wells are a feature just a few yards down the lane. It stages a beer festival in August and a cider festival in July. ☆⚙◐&♣♿P🐾🛜

Horncastle

King's Head

16 Bull Ring, LN9 5HU
🕐 12-11 ☎ (01507) 523360
Batemans XB, XXXB; 1 changing beer (sourced locally; often Batemans) Ⓗ
A comfortable and friendly pub with a single bar/lounge that, nevertheless, accommodates two separate drinking areas. Three beers from Batemans are normally stocked. Unusually for this locality, the building has a thatched roof, hence its local name, the Thatch. Reputedly the pub inspired an OO gauge Hornby model, an example of which

is displayed behind the bar. In summer the pub is bedecked with hanging baskets and has won the Batemans Floral Display competition.
🐕☀️◑💧🍽️🐾📶

Ingoldmells

Countryman Ⓛ
Chapel Road, PE25 1ND
🕐 12-midnight summer; 12-3, 7-midnight winter
☎ (01754) 872268
Leila Cottage Leila's Lazy Days, Ace Ale, Lincolnshire Life, Leila's One Off Ⓗ
The privately owned Countryman appears to be a modern building but it incorporates the early 19th-century Leila Cottage, which gives its name to the brewery behind the pub. A notorious smuggler, James Waite, used to reside here when Ingoldmells was a wild and lonely place, but he certainly would not recognise the current holiday coast, with Skegness, Butlin's and Fantasy Island nearby. Information boards give brewery, pub and beer information for visitors. 🐕☀️🚐◑♿⚓Ⓟ🚂🚌

Irnham

Griffin Inn Ⓛ
15 Bulby Road, NG33 4JG
🕐 11-3, 6-11; 12-3, 6-10.30 Sun ☎ (01476) 550201
🌐 thegriffininirnham.co.uk
Oakham JHB; 2 changing beers (often Batemans) Ⓗ
One of Lincolnshire's best-kept secrets, this fine stone building set in its own grounds in the heart of the countryside dates from the 1700s. The newly refurbished interior with its separate bar and dining areas has an atmosphere of ancient and modern. The pub's policy is to source beers and food from local suppliers, and it was a finalist for Les Routiers Country Inn of the Year 2015. Classic and vintage car enthusiasts meet on the first Wednesday of the month April to September. Q🐕☀️🚐◑Ⓟ🐾📶

Kirkby on Bain

Ebrington Arms
Main Street, LN10 6YT
🕐 12-2 (not Mon), 6-11 ☎ (01526) 354560
🌐 ebringtonarms.com
Adnams Broadside; Batemans XB; Black Sheep Golden Sheep; Sharp's Doom Bar; 2 changing beers (often Brains, Timothy Taylor) Ⓗ
Attractive country pub close to the River Bain and dating from 1610. World War II airmen used to slot coins into the ceiling beams to pay for beer when they returned from missions over Germany. Sadly, many of these coins are still in situ and make a unique memorial to the dead. The popular restaurant offers good food made with local produce (booking advised). There is a convenient caravan site within a mile of the pub. A folk club meets on Monday evenings except on the second Monday of the month, when the book club is on.
Q🐕☀️◑♿⚓Ⓟ🚌(65)🐾📶

Lincoln

Adam & Eve Tavern
25 Lindum Road, LN2 1NT
🕐 12-11 (midnight Fri & Sat) ☎ (01522) 537108
🌐 adamandevelincoln.co.uk
Castle Rock Harvest Pale; Morland Old Speckled Hen; 2 changing beers (sourced nationally) Ⓗ

With low beams and thick walls, this is reputedly the oldest tavern in Lincoln. The main bar has a number of alcoves, one with a dartboard. The front room, offering views of the medieval Pottergate and the cathedral, leads to a secluded beer garden. There are weekly music gigs and quiz nights, and sports matches are shown on two screens. The guest beers usually include a local brew, and good-value meals are available. 🐕☀️◑Ⓟ🚌🐾📶

Cardinal's Hat
268 High Street, LN2 1HW
🕐 12-11 (1am Fri & Sat) ☎ (01522) 527084
🌐 cardinalshatlincoln.co.uk
Adnams Mosaic; Bad Comfortably Numb; Tom Wood's Lincoln Gold; house beer (by Tom Wood's); 5 changing beers Ⓗ
Steeped in history, this Grade II-listed, timber-framed building was an inn from the 15th to the 19th century. Restored in 1952, it became home to the St John Ambulance. In 2015 the building was sympathetically refurbished, revealing a number of historic features. The many rooms lend themselves to a social gathering, including a choice of snugs for a quiet drink. The eight ales and four ciders can be enjoyed with a food menu of charcuterie and cheese-based platters. Q🐕☀️◑♿🍴🐾📶

Golden Eagle
21 High Street, LN5 8BD
🕐 11-11 (11.30 Fri & Sat); 12-11 Sun ☎ (01522) 521058
Castle Rock Harvest Pale; Fuller's London Pride; house beer (by Castle Rock); 8 changing beers (sourced nationally; often Newby Wyke, Oldershaw, Pheasantry) Ⓗ
This friendly two-roomed old coaching inn has up to nine real ales and at least one real cider. The bar is a pleasant room but can get busy on match days. The lounge is quiet, relaxed and cosy, with old football programmes on display. Occasional beer festivals, live music events, and whisky, port or gin tasting nights take place. Friday is quiz night. Outside is a premier beer garden with sheltered seating, lighting and heaters. Q🐕☀️🍀💧Ⓟ🚌🐾📶

Joiners Arms
4 Victoria Street, LN1 1HU
🕐 4-11; 2-midnight Fri & Sat; 4-10.30 Sun ☎ 07871 887459
5 changing beers (sourced nationally) Ⓗ
Just off the city centre, this traditional side-street pub is deceptively spacious. On entering, there is a large area with darts, pool and, unusually for Lincoln, bar billiards. Two steps lead up to the bar, and there is a small seating area to the rear. Pictures of old Lincoln are displayed. The changing beers are from small breweries across the UK.
🐕🍀💧🐾

Jolly Brewer Ⓛ
27 Broadgate, LN2 5AQ
🕐 12-11 (10 Mon; midnight Fri & Sat); 12-10 Sun
☎ (01522) 528583 🌐 jollybrewer.org
Welbeck Abbey Henrietta, Portland Black; 4 changing beers (sourced regionally) Ⓗ
A town-centre pub with an amazing Art Deco interior, a real fire, unusual red-top tables in the bar, and cinema seating in the side room. It is big on hosting live music every weekend, with an excellent jukebox and open mic on Wednesday. The impressively designed beer garden, with nice covered areas, has live music in good weather. There is a weekly quiz night. Value-for-money food is available until 7pm. 🐕☀️◑🚆🍀💧Ⓟ

Morning Star ✔

11 Greetwell Gate, LN2 4AW
🌣 11-11; 12-11 Sun ☎ (01522) 51426
⊕ morningstarlincoln.co.uk
Ruddles Best Bitter; Sharp's Doom Bar; Timothy Taylor Golden Best; Wells Bombardier; 2 changing beers (sourced regionally; often Moorhouse's, Pheasantry, Salamander) ⊞

Just a short walk from the cathedral and tourist area, this building has been a pub since 1791. With its award-winning garden and roaring winter fire, it is popular with locals all year round. Serving four regular and two changing beers, there is plenty of choice. Food is available at lunchtime. There is a Tuesday night quiz and, in the summer, a programme of live music. Q🌣❀◐♣P🖰🐾🛜

Ritz Ⓛ ✔

143-147 High Street, LN5 7PJ
🌣 8am-midnight (1am Fri & Sat) ☎ (01522) 512103
Greene King Abbot; Ruddles Best Bitter; Sharp's Doom Bar; 8 changing beers (sourced nationally) ⊞

A short walk down the High Street from the bus and rail stations stands the old Ritz cinema which was converted by JD Wetherspoon. The oak-panelled walls display photographs of bygone artists who appeared on the venue's small stage. There is plenty of seating at road level and a few steps (plus stairlift) lead to the main bar area. Monthly Meet the Brewer evenings showcase local micros. Q🌣❀◐♿⇄🖰🛜

Strugglers Inn Ⓛ ✔

83 Westgate, LN1 3BG
🌣 12-1am (11 Mon & Tue; midnight Wed); 12-11.30 Sun
☎ (01522) 535023 ⊕ strugglers-lincoln.co.uk
Greene King Abbot; St Austell Tribute; Timothy Taylor Landlord; 7 changing beers (sourced nationally; often Dukeries, Welbeck Abbey) ⊞

The Struggs stands under the castle walls. The handpumps dispense regular beers and guests from far and wide, including two dark beers, as can be seen from the pumpclips that cover the walls and ceiling. The chalkboard beer list also includes details of forthcoming ales. The sunken garden is a summer suntrap. Acoustic music most Saturday nights and Sunday teatimes is the only entertainment other than the buzz of lively conversation. Simple snack food is available. Q❀♣🖰🐾🛜

Victoria

6 Union Road, LN1 3BJ
🌣 11-midnight (1am Fri & Sat); 12-midnight Sun
☎ (01522) 541000 ⊕ victoriapub.net
Batemans XB; Castle Rock Harvest Pale; Timothy Taylor Landlord; 3 changing beers (sourced regionally; often Adnams, Oakham) ⊞

Built in the 1800s, the inn stands next to the west gate of Lincoln Castle. A long-standing Guide entry, this Batemans pub has two rooms, with helpful staff and a friendly atmosphere. It features live music on Saturday night and a fortnightly quiz. The free function room hosts many local clubs and is home to the Lincoln Steampunk Society. Outside is a pleasant seating area with views of the castle. Q❀◐🖰🐾🛜

Little Cawthorpe

Royal Oak Inn (Splash)

Watery lane, LN11 8LZ (right off main road to Legbourne then left onto Buston Lane, through ford and turn left)
🌣 11-midnight ☎ (01507) 600750 ⊕ royaloaksplash.co.uk
Black Sheep Best Bitter; Greene King IPA; 2 changing beers ⊞

Known locally as the Splash because of the picturesque ford nearby, this 400-year-old inn is located in its own large lawned gardens on the edge of the Lincolnshire Wolds near Louth. Four beers are regularly available, plus often a guest ale from a local brewery. Three restaurants cover most culinary requirements and themed evenings are popular. The en-suite rooms are often used by visitors to Cadwell Park or explorers of the Wolds. 🛏❀◐◖♿🅰♣P

Little Steeping

Eaves Inn

Main Road, PE23 5BL
🌣 closed Mon-Wed; 6.30-11; 12-4 Sun ☎ (01754) 830639
⊕ theeavesinn.com
Batemans XB ⊞

The pub is the only one remaining in the Five Parishes. It has maintained a good local feel and the bar area with a log fire and comfortable chairs is a cosy place to spend time, with the staff often joining in with the conversation. The restaurant serves good-quality, locally sourced food and attracts visitors from the surrounding area. There is a camping and caravan site attached. Q🛏❀◐◖♿🅰P🐾

Louth

Brown Cow

133 Newmarket, LN11 9EG (top of Newmarket on jct with Church St)
🌣 5-11; 12-3 Fri; 12-11 Sat & Sun ☎ (01507) 605146
Black Sheep Best Bitter; Castle Rock Harvest Pale; Courage Directors; Fuller's London Pride; 1 changing beer ⊞

Friendly town pub with a great atmosphere and, most importantly, great beer. A free quiz is held every Sunday night and the local folk club meets here on a Tuesday evening. The popular bistro serves traditional, home-cooked food, made with locally sourced products, Thursday to Sunday. Every Thursday is pie night, with a selection of different pies. The pub is a great community meeting place. Q🛏❀◐♿♣🖰🛜

Gas Lamp Lounge Ⓛ

13 Thames Street, LN11 7AD (bottom of Thames St by factories)
🌣 5-11; 12-11 Sat & Sun ☎ (01507) 607661
⊕ sales12018.wixsite.com/firehousebrewery
1 changing beer ⊞

A unique pub, and one of only 22 in the UK lit by gas lamps. You will not find music or bandits, just good pub traditions. It serves four regular beers from the upstairs brewery, plus a guest beer. Benches are set alongside the canal for enjoying a drink during the summer, while inside there is a roaring logburner for the winter months. Dogs are welcome. Q🛏♿♣🖰🐾🛜

Joseph Morton ✔

Pawnshop Passage, LN11 9EZ
🌣 8am-midnight (1am Fri & Sat) ☎ (01507) 353700

Batemans XXXB; Greene King Abbot; Ruddles County; changing beers (sourced regionally; often Black Horse, Milestone) ⊞
A JD Wetherspoon pub, which opened in May 2011, in a small alleyway just off Mercer Row in Louth town centre. The pub offers good-value food and a large selection of regional and national ales. Originally a warehouse, it was built between 1808 and 1834 with cast-iron wall plates bearing the name of the local ironmonger, Joseph Morton. ▷❀◐&♠⊞♠

Wheatsheaf
62 Westgate, LN11 9YD
✿ 11-11 ☎ (01507) 606262
Batemans XB; Black Sheep Ale; Brains Bitter; Thornbridge Jaipur IPA; 1 changing beer ⊞
This picturesque pub lies close to Louth's historic St James' Church, whose spire is visible for miles around – it is the tallest spire of any medieval parish church in England, and second only to the 19th-century Roman Catholic church of St Walburge in Preston, Lancashire. The pub offers a good selection of real ales and a tasty home-made food menu, has a lovely beer garden, and is a popular meeting place for walkers and ramblers. ▷◐&P♠

Woolpack ⓛ
Riverhead Road, LN11 0DA
✿ 11-11 ☎ (01507) 606568
Batemans XB, Gold, XXXB; 1 changing beer ⊞
Close to the theatre, this pub is popular with drinkers and diners alike. It usually offers four or five real ales on handpull. The Grade II-listed building is dog friendly and is next to the canal. It has disabled access and baby-changing facilities. There is a beer garden and ample parking. ▷❀◐&P⊞♠♠

Ludford

White Hart ♥ ⓛ
Magna Mile, LN8 4AD
✿ closed Mon & Tue; 6-11; 12-2.30, 6-11 Sat; 12-3.30 Sun
☎ (01507) 313489
4 changing beers (sourced nationally) ⊞
A flagship ale pub whose licensees do their best to feature as many ales behind the bar as possible. Formerly a coaching house dating from the 18th century, it is now a two-roomed, rural village inn. It is close to the Viking Way, popular with hikers and ramblers. Four different guest beers are offered. The licensees pride themselves on serving real ale from microbreweries. All food is home-made using ingredients from local suppliers. Meals are available lunchtimes and evenings. Q♠◐P

Market Deeping

Vine Inn ⓛ
19 Church Street, PE6 8AN
✿ 4-11; 12-11 Fri-Sun ☎ (01778) 218622
Sharp's Doom Bar; house beer (by Hopshackle); 3 changing beers (often Hopshackle) ⊞
Former Charles Wells pub which has been a small, friendly free house since 2011, and was originally a Victorian school. The bar features oak beams and stone floors, with many 20th-century prints on the walls. There is a large patio at the rear. Five handpumps dispense two regular beers, one brewed especially for the pub by Hopshackle, plus a changing range of guests. Boxed real cider is

sold. Free nibbles are provided Sunday lunchtime and early during the week. The television is only used for major sporting events. ❀♠P⊞(101)♠♠

Messingham

Horn Inn
61 High Street, DN17 3NU
✿ 12-11 ☎ (01724) 761190 ⊕ horninn.co.uk
Timothy Taylor Golden Best, Landlord; 3 changing beers (sourced regionally; often Adnams, Black Sheep, Fuller's) ⊞
Thriving village local fully refurbished in 2015 after a period of closure under another operator. The open-plan design includes a separate area for dining, and the remainder has a more traditional pub feel, with old pictures of the village and vintage brewery signs of the four real ales offered. Two from Timothy Taylor are regulars, two are rotating guest beers. An extensive food menu is available from Wednesday. There is a cask ale club and a quiz on Monday evening. Q▷◐&♠P⊞♠

Pooleys
46 High Street, DN17 3NT
✿ closed Mon; 6-11; 7-11 Sun ☎ (01724) 762220
Batemans XXXB; 4 changing beers (sourced regionally; often Batemans, Everards, Oakham) ⊞
Pooleys is a busy and popular bar for locals and visitors alike, only open in the evenings. It has three separate drinking areas with rustic furniture, real fires and wooden and flagstone floors. Five handpumps adorn the bar, offering changing real ales; a large selection of malt whiskies is also available. Q&♠♠♠

Navenby

Lion & Royal
57 High Street, LN5 0DZ
✿ 12-11 (midnight Fri & Sat); 12-10.30 Sun
☎ (01522) 810368
Greene King Abbot, IPA; 2 changing beers (sourced nationally; often Adnams, Castle Rock, Dark Star) ⊞
Walk into this welcoming village pub and find the bar fire always alight in cold weather. A flagged floor area is in front of the L-shaped bar, with a separate pool room. Saturday nights feature live music, with a quiz night on Tuesdays. Children are welcome in the bar area until 8pm. Outside is a large, enclosed garden. Viking Way walkers often pop in to enjoy the good-value food, served until 8pm. An upstairs function room is available. ▷❀◐&♣P⊞(1)♠♠

North Hykeham

Centurion ✔
Newark Road, LN6 8LB
✿ 11-11 (midnight Thu-Sat) ☎ (01522) 509814
Abbeydale Moonshine; Brakspear Bitter; Wells Bombardier; house beer (by Black Sheep); 5 changing beers (sourced nationally) ⊞
Built in the 1960s, this large pub has been through a number of incarnations and is now part of the Ember Inns chain. It is popular with diners as well as drinkers, and families are welcomed. Food is served until 10pm. The decor and furnishings are modern and the atmosphere is airy. Regular events include three quizzes per week and food theme nights. Westons cider is occasionally stocked. ▷❀◐&♣P⊞♠

Owston Ferry

Crooked Billet
Silver Street, DN9 1RN (on road out of village in direction of West Stockwith)
✪ 5-midnight; 12-midnight Sun ☎ (01427) 728262
Marston's Pedigree; Milestone Black Pearl; Sharp's Doom Bar; 1 changing beer (sourced regionally; often Milestone) Ⓗ
A friendly village local by the River Trent. The river's tidal bore, the aegir, can be observed from the pub's garden at the rear. Three cask ales are always on the bar, with the beer range representing a variety of styles. The licensee is committed to promoting cask ales in this remote part of Lincolnshire. There is usually a rotating guest ale from the Milestone Brewery. Opening hours vary on Saturdays for special events.
Q🛏️🕮🕮🕭♣️P🚃(399)🐾🌐

Raithby

Red Lion
Raithby Road, PE23 4DS
✪ closed Mon; 12-2, 7-10 ☎ (01790) 753727
Batemans XB; Black Sheep Ale Ⓗ
Cosy village pub built around 1650, with beamed low ceilings in its many small rooms that surround the bar. Pictures of outdoor pursuits and old photographs adorn the walls. The pub sits in an attractive quiet village in the Wolds and is excellent for walking and cycling. The landlord has been known to provide plastic covers for the muddy boots of CAMRA trekkers. Q🛏️🕮🕮🕭🕭♣️P🚃

Ropsley

Green Man ♆
24 High Street, NG33 4BE
✪ closed Mon; 11-11 (10.30 Sun) ☎ (01476) 585897
⊕ green-man-ropsley.co.uk
Marston's Wainwright; 3 changing beers (sourced nationally; often Caledonian, Grainstore, Theakston) Ⓗ
Newly crowned local CAMRA Pub of the Year 2017, this 17th-century village pub has a growing reputation for innovative food (including exotic meats), locally sourced game and seafood. The relaxed tearoom area is frequented by walkers and cyclists, as is the pleasant, tranquil beer garden. Themed food and drink-matching evenings are held regularly. It is also renowned for an extensive bottled range. 🛏️🕮🕭♣️P🐾🌐

Rothwell

Blacksmith's Arms
Wold View, Hill Rise, LN7 6AZ
✪ closed Mon; 12-3, 5-11.30 Sat; 12-11 Sun
☎ (01472) 371300 ⊕ blacksmiths-rothwell.co.uk
Robinsons Dizzy Blonde; 3 changing beers (sourced nationally) Ⓗ
In a quiet Wolds village three miles off the A46, the pub attracts walkers and cyclists. The Grade II-listed building housed a coaching inn and smithy; workers from the local farm estate used to take meals in the adjacent dining hall, which now hosts community events. The pub is popular for its locally sourced food; while it can be busy at mealtimes, it caters equally well for drinkers. An open fire adds extra warmth. Q🛏️🕮🕭♣️P🐾🌐

Ruskington

Shoulder of Mutton
11 Church Street, NG34 9DU
✪ 12-midnight ☎ (01526) 832220
John Smith's Bitter; Sharp's Doom Bar; Wells Bombardier; 1 changing beer (sourced regionally) Ⓗ
A popular and thriving pub in the heart of the village which attracts customers of all ages. It is one of the oldest buildings in the village and was once a butcher's shop, hence the name. A few old meat hooks can still be seen in the wooden ceiling in the bar. Although additions have been made in recent years, they have not spoiled the essential character. The pub has been East Midlands Charity Pub of the Year. 🕮🖂♣️P🚃(31)🐾🌐

Saxilby

Anglers
65 High Street, LN1 2HA
✪ 11.30-11.30 (12.30am Fri & Sat); 12-11.30 Sun
☎ (01522) 702200 ⊕ anglerspublichouse.com
Theakston Best Bitter; 3 changing beers (often Adnams, Everards, St Austell) Ⓗ
Convivial pub at the heart of the local community. Pool, dominoes, darts and two golf societies all feature, and regular poker nights are held. An outdoor boules court is much in demand in the summer. The pool table is in a room off the main bar. The lounge is decorated with many old photographs. Moorings on the Fossdyke Navigation are nearby. 🕮🖂♣️P🚃(100,105)🐾🌐

Scampton

Dambusters Inn ♆ Ⓛ
23 High Street, LN1 2SD
✪ closed Mon; 12-9.30 Tue; 12-11 Wed & Thu; 12-midnight Fri & Sat; 12-7.30 Sun ☎ (01522) 731333
⊕ dambustersinn.co.uk
Greene King Abbot; Greg's Scampton Ale, Mayson, Dambusters Ale; 3 changing beers (sourced locally; often Brewsters, Oldershaw, Pheasantry) Ⓗ
This feels like walking into a working World War II museum, full of memorabilia. The bar proudly displays seven real ales, three of which Greg brews in the on-site brewery. The pub is named after the famous RAF 617 squadron at Scampton, now home to the Red Arrows, who can often be seen flying over. An annual beer festival is held in May, commemorating the Dambuster raid; 2018 is the raid's 75th anniversary. Oh – do pop into the loos!
Q🛏️🕮🕭🖤P🚃(103)🐾🌐

Scawby

Sutton Arms
10 West Street, DN20 9AN
✪ 11.30-midnight; 11.30-11 Sun ☎ (01652) 652430
⊕ suttonarmsscawby.co.uk
Sharp's Doom Bar; Theakston Best Bitter; 2 changing beers (often Horncastle Ales, Milestone) Ⓗ
Comfortable, traditionally styled village local with a good reputation for its excellent food. A central bar serves an open-plan dining area and a separate dining room, plus a small snug to one side used mainly for drinking. It has an extensive food menu plus daily specials lunchtimes and evenings. Theakston Best Bitter is a regular beer, supplemented by two rotating guest ales. Quiz night is on Sunday evening. 🛏️🕮🕭🕭P🐾🌐

Scawby Brook

King William IV ✓
Scawby Road, DN20 9JX
🕐 12-2, 5.30-11 ☎ (01652) 657106
3 changing beers (sourced regionally; often Everards, Timothy Taylor, Wells) Ⓗ
Comfortable and well-appointed village local with a strong emphasis on food. It has an open-plan design with a dining area to the rear and a traditionally styled lounge at the front. Meals are served every day at lunchtime and in the evening, with daily specials. There are three real ales on handpump which rotate from a choice of seven.
🏴👁️◑&♿P🅿️🐕♿🌐

Scotter

Sun & Anchor
54 High Street, DN21 3RX
🕐 2 (12 Sat)-11; 12-10.30 Sun ☎ (01724) 763444
John Smith's Bitter; Sharp's Doom Bar; 1 changing beer Ⓗ
An inviting pub with a warm welcome for all. A wide selection of drinks is served as well as traditional pub food, not forgetting the popular Sunday roast. For those looking to catch up on the latest sporting action, it shows all the latest matches and events Sky and BT Sport have to offer. There is a darts and pool area and a large private beer garden with a children's play area. Whether you are looking for a few drinks with friends over a friendly game of pool or a relaxing meal with the family, the Sun & Anchor is a great pub to visit.
🏴👁️&♣P🅿️🐕🌐

White Swan
9 The Green, DN21 3UD
🕐 12-midnight; 11.30-midnight Fri-Sun ☎ (01724) 763061
🌐 whiteswanscotter.com
Black Sheep Best Bitter; Sharp's Doom Bar; 3 changing beers Ⓗ
A privately owned and run small hotel and restaurant nestled between the historic city of Lincoln and the Humber Estuary. The White Swan boasts an amazing history with images dating from before 1911, and still maintains the character and charm associated with a traditional coaching inn, while internally it has enjoyed a modern transformation. There is a main restaurant and a smaller one, the Mucky Duck. Q🏴👁️◑P🅿️🌐

Scunthorpe

Berkeley Hotel ★
Doncaster Road, DN15 7DS (½ mile from end of M181)
🕐 11.30-2.30, 5-11; 12-11 Fri & Sat; 12-10.30 Sun
☎ (01724) 842333 🌐 theberkeleyscunthorpe.co.uk
Samuel Smith Old Brewery Bitter Ⓗ
Large 1930s Samuel Smith's Art Deco pub and hotel identified by CAMRA as having a nationally important historic interior. It contains a number of drinking areas: a main bar with real fire, a restaurant lounge and separate ballroom, plus a large public bar and beer garden with its own side entrance. Eight guest rooms are available. The landscaped front entrance also has a large car park. The pub is five minutes' walk from Glanford Park football ground. Q👁️◑&♣P🅿️🌐

Blue Bell ✓
1-7 Oswald Road, DN15 7PU (at town centre crossroads)

🕐 8am-midnight (1am Sat) ☎ (01724) 863921
Greene King Abbot; Ruddles Best Bitter; Sharp's Doom Bar; 7 changing beers (sourced regionally; often Acorn, Kelham Island, Saltaire) Ⓗ
Popular Wetherspoon pub with an open-plan layout on two levels; the family area is on the top level. Outside is a patio area with seating and a heated area for smokers. Beer festivals are held regularly and the pub celebrates special events such as Burns Night and St Patrick's Day. There is a muted TV screen showing sport and news. Food is served all day up to 11pm. Q🏴👁️◑&♿🐕🌐

Malt Shovel Ⓛ
219 Ashby High Street, DN16 2JP (in Ashby Broadway shopping area)
🕐 10-11 (midnight Fri & Sat) ☎ (01724) 843318
Exmoor Gold; Tetley Bitter; 4 changing beers (sourced regionally; often Acorn, Elland, Oakham) Ⓗ
Oak-beamed, low-ceilinged, country-style pub with an attached members-only snooker club and beer garden at the front. Four rotating guest beers from regional breweries are on the bar. It gets busy at lunch and tea time, when good-quality food is served (booking is advisable). There are food offers in the week and quiz nights are Tuesday and Thursday. Real ciders and perries are served from the cellar. Q🏴👁️◑♣🐕🌐

Skegness

Seathorne Arms
Seathorne Crescent, PE25 1RP
🕐 11-midnight ☎ (01754) 767797
2 changing beers (often Belhaven, Greene King) Ⓗ
Set back from Roman Bank and 15 minutes' walk from Butlin's, the pub has a large outside seating area and a spacious interior. Inside it has partioned spaces for dining, pub games, drinking and TV watching. It has a very seasonal trade due to local caravan sites, and closes in January. The landlord operates a rotating two-beer selection. There is an extensive food menu including locally sourced meat. 🏴👁️◑&♣🐕♿

Vine Hotel
Vine Road, PE25 3DB (off Drummond Rd)
🕐 11-11 ☎ (01754) 763018
Batemans XB, XXXB; 1 changing beer (often Batemans) Ⓗ
A delightful building, one of the oldest in Skegness, dating from the 18th century and set in two acres of pleasant grounds. Inside are comfortable wood-panelled bars in which to enjoy a quiet pint or two after experiencing some of the noisier attractions and bustle of Skegness. Within striking distance of the Gibraltar Point National Nature Reserve, walking trails, beach and golf links, the inn has reputed Tennyson connections.
🏴👁️◑&♣P🅿️🌐

Skendleby

Blacksmiths Arms 🍺 Ⓛ
Main Road, PE23 4QE
🕐 12-3 (not Mon), 5.30-11; 12-4 Sun ☎ (01754) 890662
Batemans XB; house beer (by Horncastle Ales); 2 changing beers (sourced regionally) Ⓗ
A traditional country pub, dating back to the 18th century, nestling on the south-east edge of the Lincolnshire Wolds. Ducking beneath the low door lintel, fortunately well padded, you discover a gem

of a snug, complete with quarry tiles, range and settles, with the cellar visible through a glass panel behind the bar. The dining room at the rear incorporates the building's former well. There is also a separate restaurant and a conservatory. On the last Sunday in the month live music features 7pm-late. Q⌂❀◐♣P🖪(96)😺🌣

Skillington

Cross Swords
The Square, NG33 5HB
✪ closed Mon; 12-2, 7-11; 12-2 Sun ☎ (01476) 861132
🌐 thecross-swordsinn.co.uk
2 changing beers (sourced nationally) ⊞
Dating from the early to mid 18th century, this impressive stone-built pub commands a good position in the centre of the village. The current hosts have owned it since 1991. The bar area boasts a real fire. Ales are from regional and national breweries. Quality pub food is served daily (no food Mon); the menu shows allergen information. There is a patio area with outside seating, and three letting cottages are available. Q❀🛏◐P🌣

Sleaford

Carre Arms Hotel
Mareham Lane, NG34 7JP
✪ 11-11 ☎ (01529) 303156 🌐 carrearmshotel.co.uk
3 changing beers (often Marston's, Oldershaw, Springhead) ⊞
A privately run hotel previously owned by Bass, adjacent to the Bass Sleaford maltings complex which is now awaiting a regeneration scheme. It has a comfortable bar area with two rooms, and offers three regularly changing real ales sourced from both larger regional breweries and local breweries. An extensive food menu is available, served in the bar area and restaurant. There is a pleasant covered courtyard, ideal on inclement days. ⌂❀🛏◐&⇌P🖪

Packhorse Inn Ⅼ ✪
7 Northgate, NG34 7BH
✪ 8am-midnight ☎ (01529) 308730
Greene King Abbot; Ruddles Best Bitter; Sharp's Doom Bar; 4 changing beers (sourced nationally; often 8 Sail) ⊞
An 18th-century coaching inn on the London to Lincoln road that has had several names during its lifetime, reverting to the original name when taken over by Wetherspoon a few years ago. Despite being remodelled as partly open plan, it retains an intimate atmosphere. As the Lion Hotel it hosted the opening dinner for the Sleaford Railway, an event that marked the start of the decline in coaching trade. Q⌂❀◐&⇌🍴🖪🌣

Snitterby

Royal Oak
High Street, DN21 4TP (1½ miles from A15)
✪ 5 (12 Sat)-midnight; 12-9 Sun ☎ (01673) 818273
Greene King IPA; Rooster's Buckeye ⊞; **6 changing beers (sourced regionally; often Adnams, Wold Top)** ⊞/Ⓖ
Traditional family-run community pub in a village setting. It has up to eight real ales, with more on bank holidays and special occasions, which are themed either by region, beer type or event. The

comfortable, spacious interior is light and airy, with real fires. Outside, the seating area overlooks a stream and ford. Sky Sports is available in the snug. It does monthly pop-up pizzeria and jazz and jalfrezi nights. Local CAMRA Pub of the Year 2016. ⌂❀🅰♣🐾P🖪🌣

South Ormsby

Massingberd Arms
Brinkhill Road, LN11 8QS (1 mile off A16)
✪ closed Mon; 12-2.30, 6-11; 12-11 Sun ☎ (01507) 480492
Thwaites Original; 1 changing beer ⊞
A old, traditional pub set in the heart of the Lincolnshire Wolds, an Area of Outstanding Natural Beauty. There is home-cooked food, and a quiz for charity every Wednesday night. The landlord has recently upgraded the dining room and now has a woodburner. A proper country pub in a beautiful location – walkers welcome. Q⌂❀◐&P

South Witham

Angel Inn ✪
13 Church Street, NG33 5PJ
✪ 12-11 (12.30am Fri & Sat); 12-10.30 Sun
☎ (01572) 768302 🌐 angelinn.bar
Black Sheep Ale; Wells Bombardier; 1 changing beer ⊞
Nestling in the centre of South Witham, the Grade II-listed Angel Inn is adjacent to St John's Church. With two real fires and recently refurbished, you can expect a warm welcome from mine hosts Steven and Vicky. The staff are friendly, which makes this a real community pub. Live sport is shown, and the pub helps sponsor the local football team. Having worked at Buckingham Palace, head chef Shaun Mason produces food fit for a queen in the cosy restaurant. ❀◐♣P

Spalding

Drayman's Arms
44 London Road, PE11 2UE
✪ 3-11; 12-11 Sat & Sun ☎ (01775) 723755
St Austell Tribute; 1 changing beer ⊞
Early 19th-century coaching inn, now a large single-bar pub, a little over a mile to the south of the town in an area known as Little London. It is popular with local residents from the surrounding district which has lost several of its pubs in recent years. Although the main focus is wet sales, food is served on a Wednesday evening and Sunday lunchtime. ⌂❀◐♣P🖪(37)🌣

Priors Oven Ⅼ
1 Sheep Market, PE11 1BH
✪ closed Mon; 12-8 (9 Thu; midnight Fri & Sat)
6 changing beers Ⓖ
The first micropub to be opened in Lincolnshire. The pub building has quite a history – it is believed to be 800 years old and was originally the prison of the local priory. Its more recent use was as a bakery, and it became a pub in December 2013. As well as the ground floor bar with its domed ceiling, a comfortable lounge room can be reached via a stone spiral staircase. Beer can be sampled in third-pint measures. Q⇌🍴🖪

Stamford

Green Man 🅛
29 Scotgate, PE9 2YQ

☼ 11-midnight; 12-midnight Sun ☎ (01780) 753598

Castle Rock Harvest Pale; Fuller's London Pride; Stoney Ford Sheepmarket Supernova Straw; 4 changing beers (often Grainstore) Ⓗ

Dating from 1796, this stone-built former coaching inn has an L-shaped split-level bar with a real fire. Up to eight ales, complemented by a good range of European bottled beers, are available. As many as seven ciders and perries, often Moonshine and Broad Oak, are also on offer. Beer festivals are held at Easter and September on the secluded patio, which boasts a mounting block from the days of horse riding. ❀🖂≷♣🏠🚌(201)🐾🛜

Jolly Brewer 🏆 🅛
1 Foundry Road, PE9 2PP

☼ 11-midnight; 12-11.30 Sun ☎ (01780) 755141

⊕ thejollybrewer.com

Brewsters Marquis; Oakham JHB; 4 changing beers (sourced locally; often Bakers Dozen) Ⓗ

A stone-built community pub which dates from 1830, comprising an L-shaped room around the bar with a smaller adjoining dining room. Outside, there is a large patio with tables. The home-cooked food is locally sourced. It is home to pool, darts, crib and dominoes teams, and the world Push Penny Championships are held here. Six handpumps dispense a range of LocAles, national ales and its own Baker's Dozen beers. One handpump serves cider, usually Old Rosie. A good range of malt whiskies is available. Local CAMRA Pub of the Year 2017. Q❀🕪≷♣🏠🚌(9,202)🐾🛜

King's Head ✔
19 Maiden Lane, PE9 2AZ

☼ closed Mon; 12-11; 12-5 Sun ☎ (01780) 753510

⊕ kingsheadstamford.com

Adnams Southwold Bitter; 4 changing beers (sourced locally; often Grainstore) Ⓗ

Small town-centre pub, which opened in the early 19th century. It is now a single room with two areas that were once two small rooms, with a wood-burning stove and wooden beamed ceiling. A small patio area is at the rear. It sells a much-improved range of beers, from one handpump a couple of years ago but now increased to five, sourced from near and far. Q❀🕪≷🚌

Tobie Norris
12 Saint Paul's Street, PE9 2BE

☼ 10-11 (midnight Fri & Sat); 12-10.30 Sun

☎ (01780) 753800

Fuller's London Pride; Oakham JHB Ⓗ; 3 changing beers (sourced regionally; often Adnams) Ⓗ/Ⓖ

The building, parts of which date back to 1280, was bought by Tobie Norris in 1617 and used as a bell foundry. After conversion into a pub from the former RAFA Club, it was split into many small rooms with real fires, stone floors and low beams. Five handpumps serve beers from local and countrywide brewers. At least one real cider is always available. Q🛏❀🕪≷♣🏠🚌(202,203)🐾

Stickford

Red Lion Inn 🅛
Church Road, PE22 8EP

☼ closed Mon & Tue; 7-11 Wed & Thu; 4-11.30 Fri & Sat; 12-10.30 Sun ☎ (01205) 480395 ⊕ redlionstickford.co.uk

Batemans XB; 1 changing beer (sourced locally) Ⓗ

The pub name, Red Lion, the most common in England, is frequently found hereabouts because it was a heraldic emblem of 14th-century John of Gaunt, Earl of Lancaster and Lord of the Manor at nearby Bolingbroke Castle. This cosy and friendly two-bar pub produces its own range of cider and holds an annual cider festival. Food is served evenings and Sunday lunchtime using local produce, and all pies are home made. There are two en-suite letting bedrooms.

Q🛏❀🖂🕪▲♣🏠🚌(113)🐾🛜

Swineshead

Green Dragon
Market Place, PE20 3LJ

☼ 5-11; 12-midnight Fri & Sat; 12-11 Sun ☎ (01205) 821381

Batemans XB; Theakston Traditional Mild; 3 changing beers (sourced regionally) Ⓗ

Years ago the pub was called the Green Dragon. Its fortunes gradually declined, it became run down and, despite a change of name, it eventually closed. New owners brought it back to life as a vibrant and thriving village local, successfully blending old and new to recreate a genuine community pub with an emphasis on beer and traditional pub games. Another change of ownership has now seen the pub revert to its original name. ❀🕪♣🏠🚌(K59)🐾

Swinhope

Clickem Inn
Binbrook Road, LN8 6BS (2 miles N of Binbrook on B1203)

☼ 12-3 (not Mon-Wed), 5-11; 12-11.30 Fri & Sat; 12-10.30 Sun ☎ (01472) 398253 ⊕ clickem-inn.co.uk

Batemans XXXB; Timothy Taylor Landlord; house beer (by Pheasantry); 3 changing beers (sourced regionally; often Horncastle Ales, Rudgate, Springhead) Ⓗ

Set in the picturesque Lincolnshire Wolds and a popular stopping place for walkers and cyclists, this pub's name originates from the counting of sheep passing through a nearby clicking gate. Renowned for its home-cooked food served in the bar and conservatory, it also offers a choice of drinks, including six real ales and a traditional cider. The house beer is Terry's Tipple. There is pool, darts and a jukebox. Monday is quiz night. A covered, unheated area is provided for smokers.

Q❀🕪♣🏠🐾🛜

Tattershall Thorpe

Blue Bell Inn
Thorpe Road, LN4 4PE

☼ closed Mon; 12-3, 6-11; 12-4 Sun ☎ (01526) 342206

⊕ bluebell-inn.com

Tom Wood's Bomber County; 2 changing beers (sourced locally; often St Austell, Shepherd Neame) Ⓗ

This ancient building, in a delightful location, has 13th-century origins and is one of Lincolnshire's oldest inns. It has a large open fire and beamed ceilings that are covered in signatures and photographs of airmen from World War II RAF squadrons who used the pub, including the 617 Dambusters and 627 Pathfinders. King Henry VIII reputedly visited the Blue Bell and there is a ghost in residence. Q🛏❀🕪♿▲♣🏠🛜

Thimbleby

Durham Ox

Main Road, LN9 5RB
☼ 12-3, 6-11 ☎ (01507) 527152
⊕ durhamoxpubthimbleby.co.uk
Batemans XB; Black Sheep Best Bitter; 1 changing beer (often Charnwood) ⊞
Fine country inn over 200 years old and reopened in November 2013. This welcoming pub, with its beamed ceilings, cowshed bar and RAF corner, also has a large field at the rear for caravans and campers. There is an extensive menu serving local produce. The pub is named after a huge 18th-century ox which toured the country; at its largest it weighed 270 stone. ⌂✿◑▶Å♣P🖵

Threekingham

Three Kings Inn

Saltersway, NG34 0AU
☼ closed Mon; 12-3, 6-11; 12-3, 6-10.30 Sun
☎ (01529) 240249 ⊕ thethreekingsinn.com
Draught Bass; Timothy Taylor Landlord; 1 changing beer ⊞
A classic country inn with charm and character. Its bright and comfortable lounge bar, with attractive rural prints, and panelled dining room serving locally sourced food, are deservedly popular with locals and visitors. Guest beers are usually from independent brewers. There is a pleasant beer terrace and garden for summer months and a large function room. The pub's name refers to the slaying, by the Saxons, of three Danish chieftains in battle in 870 at nearby Stow; look for the effigies above the entrance. Q⌂✿◑▶ÅP✿

Waddington

Three Horseshoes 🅻

High Street, LN5 9RF
☼ 3 (11 Sat)-11; 12-11 Sun ☎ (01522) 720448
John Smith's Bitter; 5 changing beers (sourced locally; often Horncastle, Newby Wyke, Springhead) ⊞
A community pub at the heart of the village but easily accessed from Lincoln. The varied selection of five beers is often local, but smaller breweries from further afield are not ignored. Televised sport and a range of pub games provide a lively atmosphere. The smaller back room is usually quiet, unless there is a big game on. Real fires give both rooms a cosy feel. ⌂✿♣🖵(1,13)✿ 📶

Wainfleet

Batemans Brewery Visitor Centre 🅻

Salem Bridge Brewery, Mill Lane, PE24 4JE
☼ 11.30-4 May-Aug; autumn and winter hours vary
☎ (01754) 882017
Batemans XB, Gold, XXXB, Salem Porter; 2 changing beers (sourced locally; often Batemans) ⊞
Visiting Batemans Brewery provides the chance to experience its proud 140-plus years of craft brewing tradition. Mr George's Bar, within the attractive windmill, is the ideal venue to sample a range of the brewery's beers. Further entertainment is to be found with brewery tours featuring the Theatre of Beers, and in the pleasant beer garden with its games. A good range of Lincolnshire food is served 12-2pm. Tours are at 12.30pm and 2.30pm in summer, 2.30pm in winter. ⌂✿◑Å⇌♣P🖵(7)📶

Westwoodside

Carpenter's Arms

Newbigg, DN9 2AT (follow B1396; pub is in centre of village)
☼ 4 (2 Sat)-midnight; 1-midnight Sun ☎ (01427) 752416
Black Sheep Best Bitter; Caledonian Deuchars IPA; Sharp's Atlantic; 2 changing beers (sourced nationally; often Greene King, Wychwood) ⊞
This popular village local has been a regular in the Guide under the present licensees. The pub actively participates in the local community and raises significant amounts of money for charity; it also hosts a variety of community events and takes part in the local Haxey Hood game every January. Up to five cask ales are stocked, with local micros occasionally featured. ✿♣P🖵(399)✿

Willoughton

Stirrup Inn 🅻

1 Templefield Road, DN21 5RZ
☼ 5 (3 Sat)-midnight; 12-11.30 Sun ☎ (01427) 668270
Black Sheep Best Bitter; 1 changing beer ⊞
Built from local Lincolnshire limestone, this hidden gem in an out-of-the-way location is well worth seeking out, and you can be sure of a warm welcome. The pub oozes character, with a roaring log fire in winter, and is popular with locals and folk from further afield. A choice of ales is always on the bar, with Black Sheep Best Bitter a permanent fixture and two changing guests. Pub quizzes are well supported and traditional pub games are played. Q⌂✿&P✿

Winterton

George Hogg 🅻 ✔

25 Market Street, DN15 9PT
☼ 2-11 (midnight Fri); 9.30am-11 Sat & Sun
☎ (01724) 732270 ⊕ thegeorgehogg.co.uk
Draught Bass; Tom Wood's Lincoln Gold; 2 changing beers (sourced regionally) ⊞
Popular Grade II-listed marketplace pub and local CAMRA award winner. It has a large lounge/dining area and separate public bar, both with real fires. Good-value locally sourced food is served at weekends, plus home-made snacks. It opens for Sunday breakfast from 9.30am. The guest beers change regularly. It holds an annual beer festival, and is a meeting place for football teams and the local supporters' club. A further dining area is available upstairs, as are tea and coffee. The pub is Cask Marque accredited. Q⌂✿◑♣P🖵(350)✿ 📶

Wragby

Ivy 🅻

Market Place, LN8 5QU
☼ 12-11 (midnight Fri & Sat); 12-11.45 Sun
☎ (01673) 858768 ⊕ theivy.vpweb.co.uk
Batemans XB; Draught Bass; 3 changing beers (sourced nationally) ⊞
With its origins in the 17th century, the Ivy is at the heart of this small market town. The well-appointed interior houses a restaurant, lounge and bar area, and is warmed by a substantial wood-burning stove. The wide-ranging menu uses fresh local produce, and specialises in gluten-free food. Parking is available in a free car park over the road and there is a bus stop around the corner. Q⌂◑&♣🖵(6,10)📶

CAMRA's Wild Pub Walks

Daniel Neilson

CAMRA's *Wild Pub Walks* brings you some of the most beautiful walks among the hills and mountains of the British Isles, each with one or more great pubs at journey's end. The book is aimed at the large market of hill walkers who enjoy long days out followed by some refreshing beer in a welcoming pub. The areas covered are: England – the Peak District, Lake District, Yorkshire Dales and North York Moors; Scotland – the Highlands and Borders; Wales – Snowdonia, the Brecon Beacons and Mid Wales. The walks vary in the level of challenge, from long walks in lower-lying areas to Grade 1 scrambles.

RRP £11.99 ISBN 978-1-85249-340-0 **192 pages**

For this and other books on beer and pubs visit CAMRA's online bookshop at **www.camra.org.uk/books** or call **01727 867201**. Discounts are available for CAMRA members.

London index

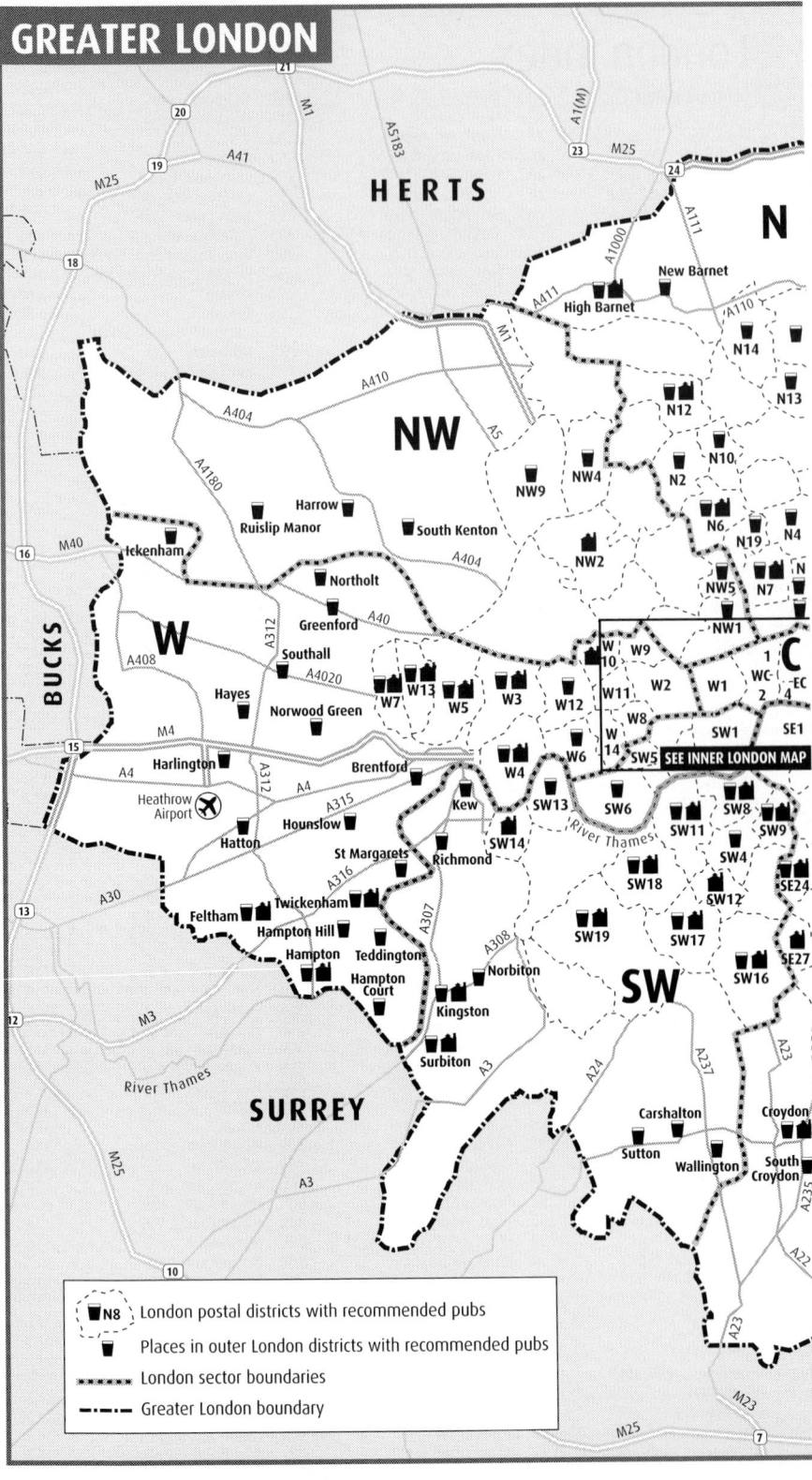

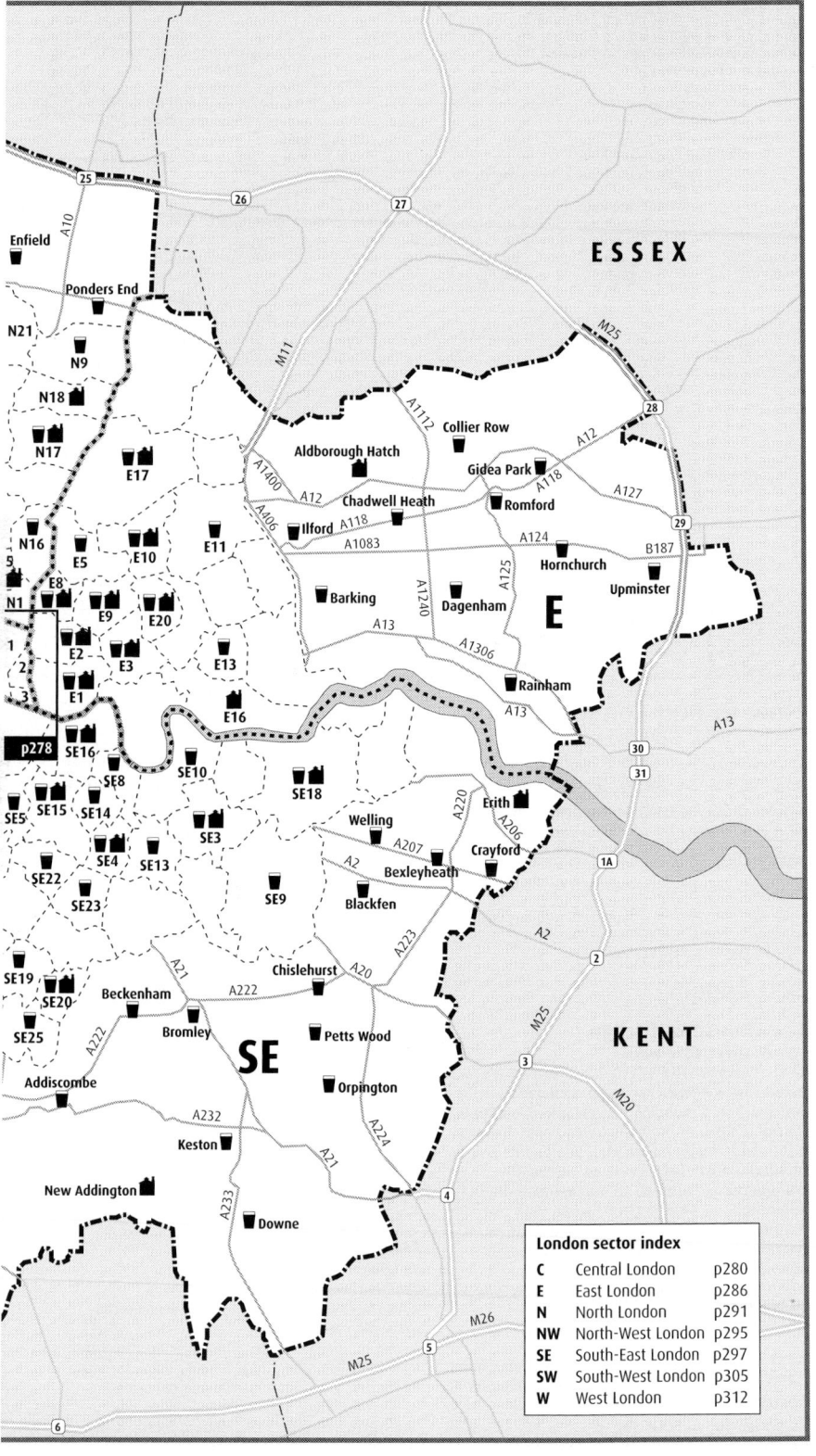

ESSEX

Enfield

Ponders End

N21

N9

N18

N17

E17

Aldborough Hatch

Collier Row

Gidea Park

Chadwell Heath

Romford

Ilford

N16

E5

E10

E11

Barking

Hornchurch

Upminster

5

E8

N1

E9

E20

E13

Dagenham

E

1

2

3

E2

E3

E1

E16

Rainham

p278

SE16

SE8

SE10

SE18

Erith

SE5

SE15

SE14

SE3

Welling

Crayford

SE22

SE4

SE13

SE9

Bexleyheath

Blackfen

SE19

SE20

SE25

Chislehurst

Beckenham

Bromley

SE

Petts Wood

Addiscombe

Orpington

Keston

New Addington

Downe

KENT

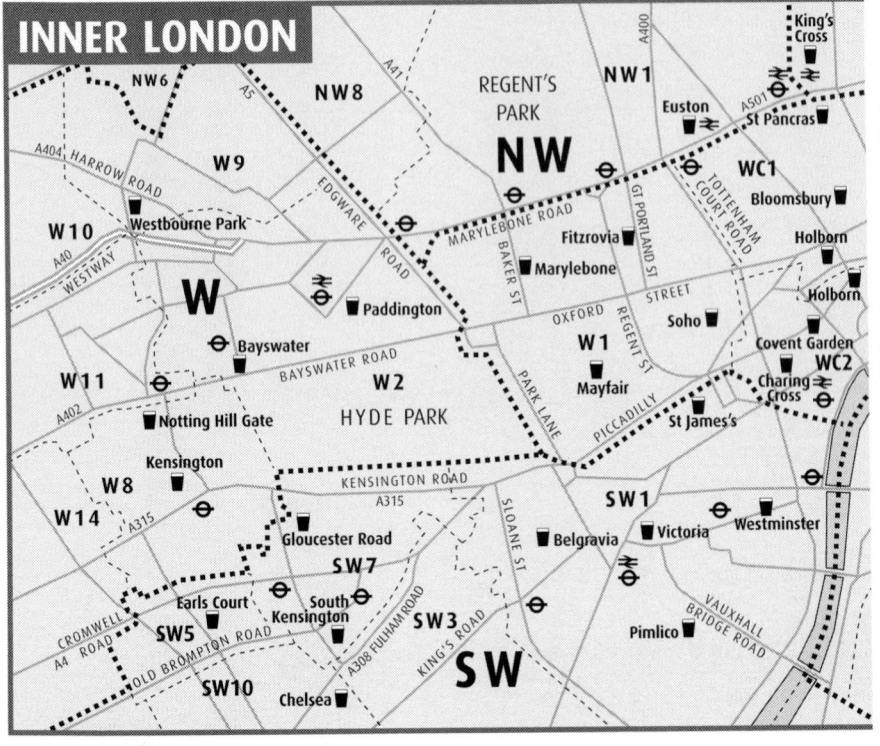

How to find London pubs

Greater London is divided into seven sectors: Central, East, North, North-West, South-East, South-West and West, reflecting postal boundaries. The Central sector includes the City (EC1 to EC4) and Holborn, Covent Garden and the Strand (WC1/2) plus W1, where pubs are listed in postal district order. In each of the other six sectors the pubs with London postcodes are listed first in postal district order (E1, E2 etc), followed by those in outer London districts, which are listed in alphabetical order (Barking, Chadwell Heath, etc) – see Greater London map. Postal district numbers can be found on every street name plate in the London postcode area.

CENTRAL LONDON

EC1: Angel

Brewhouse & Kitchen
Torrens Street, EC1V 1NQ
☼ 11-11 (midnight Fri & Sat); 12-10 Sun ☎ (020) 7837 9421
Brewhouse & Kitchen Arc Angel, Spandau B, Watchmaker; 5 changing beers (sourced locally) ⊞
Part of a chain of brewpub/restaurants, this pub has a rustic feel with wooden floorboards and furniture. Most of the beers on the eight handpumps are brewed on the premises. There is a large range of bottled beers, along with five-litre mini-casks to take away. An extensive menu is provided throughout the day. You can see the brewery in the corner of the pub. Brew masterclasses and how-to-brew days are available.
🝔❶👌➌♿🚪😸🛜

EC1: Farringdon

Jerusalem Tavern
55 Britton Street, EC1M 5UQ
☼ 11-11; closed Sat & Sun ☎ (020) 7490 4281

St Peter's Best Bitter, Mild, Golden Ale, Organic Best, Organic Ale, Grapefruit Beer Ⓐ
The name recalls the nearby headquarters of the medieval Knights of St John, but this building is not what it seems. It is a recent successor to a much older pub of the same name on a different site. Built as the outlet for St Peter's Brewery, it dispenses the ales, including seasonal beers, from taps in the wall behind the bar. There are three drinking areas. It closes at Christmas.
🝔🌂➌♿➊➌🚪😸🛜

EC1: Hatton Garden

Craft Beer Co Ⓛ
82 Leather Lane, EC1N 7TR
☼ 12-11 (10.30 Sun) ☎ (020) 7404 7049
House beer (by Kent); changing beers (sourced nationally) ⊞
A vast beer range is on offer here: up to 14 cask, over 20 other draught, and many bottles – some exotic and expensive – and two real ciders. Downstairs there are stools and tables around the walls allowing plenty of standing room (it can get very crowded), with further seating upstairs. Food

handpumps for ales and one devoted to cider, with a large range of other draught and bottled beers. ◑▣&≠⊖☻🖵🐾🐾📶

Old Fountain 🅛
3 Baldwin Street, EC1V 9NU
❁ 11 (12 Sat)-11; 12-10.30 Sun ☎ (020) 7253 2970
Fuller's London Pride; changing beers (sourced regionally) 🎋
This pub essentially consists of one bar, separated into two areas by a step (with a large fish tank on the upper level). The small Fountain Brewhouse has recently been installed in the cellar. Its beers are not always available, however there is always a good selection of draught and other beers from elsewhere – see the blackboard. There is a roof garden for smokers. Food is served all day (12-5, 6-9pm Sun). 🏠◑≠⊖♣🖵🐾📶

EC1: Smithfield

Butcher's Hook & Cleaver
60-63 West Smithfield, EC1A 9DY
❁ 10-11; closed Sat & Sun ☎ (020) 7600 9181
Fuller's Oliver's Island, London Pride, ESB; Gale's Seafarers Ale; 1 changing beer 🎋
A Fuller's pub created from a former bank and a butcher's shop. The single bar has 12 handpumps dispensing four ales – three from Fuller's and a guest – and there is a range of bottled beer. An extensive food menu is available, though the speciality is pies, with a changing house special. The pub has a traditional feel, with wooden floorboards and walls covered with pictures, murals and mirrors. A spiral staircase leads to a mezzanine floor with extra tables.
🏂◑&≠(Farringdon)⊖(Barbican)🖵📶

Old Red Cow 🅛
71-72 Long Lane, EC1A 9EJ
❁ 12-11 (midnight Fri & Sat); 12-10.30 Sun
☎ (020) 7726 2595 ⊕ theoldredcow.com
4 changing beers 🎋
Near Smithfield Market, this is part of the Local Beer House group. The focus is on a different brewery every month, but other draught beers are also sold. In addition to the small downstairs bar there is a larger room for drinking and dining upstairs, which is available for hire. Meals change seasonally – Tuesday is pie night, and roasts are served on Sunday. Food is available all day, lunchtime only on Sunday.
🏂◑≠(Farringdon)⊖(Barbican)🖵🐾📶

EC2: Bank

Green Man
1 Poultry, EC2R 8EJ
❁ 8am-11 (midnight Thu & Fri); 10-6 Sat; closed Sun
☎ (020) 7248 3529
Fuller's London Pride; Greene King Abbot; Ruddles Best Bitter; Sharp's Doom Bar; changing beers 🎋
A large two-floor Wetherspoon pub with a modern feel. The larger downstairs bar, with an entrance outside exit 9 of Bank station, has 12 handpumps including at least one for cider. There is plenty of seating, especially along the walls and outside. The upstairs bar, with an entrance on Queen Victoria Street, has eight handpumps, different guest ales and less seating. The guest ales are mainly from London breweries. Q🏂◑≠⊖♣🖵📶

is confined to Scotch eggs and pork pies. Beers aside, notable features are a huge Bass mirror and a glass ceiling. Music is played but there are no TVs.
🏂🏠≠⊖(Chancery Lane/Farringdon)●🖵🐾📶

Olde Mitre ★ 🅛
1 Ely Court, Ely Place, EC1N 6SJ
❁ 11-11; closed Sat & Sun ☎ (020) 7405 4751
Fuller's Oliver's Island, London Pride; Gale's Seafarers Ale; 3 changing beers (often Clarkshaws, Sambrook's, Windsor & Eton) 🎋
Down a passage off Hatton Garden is this gem of a pub, with parts dating to 1546, and the stump of a cherry tree that Queen Elizabeth I danced around. The small side bar has wood panelling and is an original part of the building. The lounge bar has some interesting seating. There is an upstairs room, reached by a steep staircase, with information about the pub. Snacks, toasties and pork pies are available.
Q≠(City Thameslink)⊖(Chancery Lane/Farringdon)♣●🖵🐾📶

EC1: Old Street

Draft House Old Street
The Bower, 211 Old Street, EC1V 9NR (use exit 4 at Old Street station)
❁ 12-11 (11.30 Fri & Sat) ☎ (020) 3141 9095
Sambrook's Wandle Ale; 3 changing beers 🎋
A recent addition to a growing chain. The austere feel of the glass entry gives way to comfortable seating, different on each of the three levels. The disabled toilet is on the ground floor, making the facilities available to all. Meals (changing with the seasons, and including vegan and vegetarian options) are served until 10pm. There are three

EC2: Liverpool Street

Hamilton Hall

Street-level Concourse, Unit 32, Liverpool Street Station, EC2M 7PY

✪ 7am-11.30; 9am-10.30 Sun ☎ (020) 7247 3579

Fuller's London Pride; Greene King IPA, Abbot; Sharp's Doom Bar; changing beers Ⓗ

Built as the ballroom of the Great Eastern Hotel, it takes its name from the chairman of the company at the time. Low-relief white stucco figures and gold highlighting decorate the ceiling. With an entrance in Bishopsgate, the ground floor bar has 10 handpumps selling beers from the usual Wetherspoon range; upstairs is a smaller, more comfortable bar with five. In the evening it can be busy with commuters waiting for trains and consulting the timetable display screens on the wall. Q ⎈ ✿ ⏺ ◗ ⎒ ⇌ ⊖ ● ⬚ 🖵 ☏

EC3: Gracechurch Street

Crosse Keys

7-12 Gracechurch Street, EC3V 0DR

✪ 8am-11 (midnight Fri); 9am-11 Sat; 9.30am-6 Sun
☎ (020) 7623 4824

Fuller's London Pride; Greene King IPA; Ruddles Best Bitter; Sharp's Doom Bar; changing beers Ⓗ

A palatial pub in a former bank headquarters with marble pillars. The single bar has 24 handpumps with the beers available shown on the large screens above the bar, listed by the number of the pump. Food is served throughout the day. The pub is highly popular with city workers and can get crowded. There are function rooms that can be booked at the rear. It hosts several beer festivals including the two main Wetherspoon's festivals. ⎈ ◗ ⎒ & ⇌ (Cannon St) ⊖ (Bank/Monument) ● 🖵 ☏

EC4: Cannon Street

Pelt Trader

Arch 3, Dowgate Hill, EC4N 6AP

✪ 12-11; closed Sat & Sun ☎ (020) 7160 0253
⊕ pelttrader.co.uk

6 changing beers (often Burning Sky, Dark Star, Harvey's) Ⓐ

Cask beers are served from wall-mounted taps via air pressure, alongside several other draught and bottled beers. The cask taps are the central ones, usually badged with pumpclips. The bar is furnished with high tables with alcoves off – note the mirrors. Pizza and platters are served 12-3pm and 5-9.30pm. The name relates to the Skinners' Company hall opposite. Music is played but there are no TVs. Drinkers spill out on to the pavement at busy times. ⎈ ◗ ⎒ ⇌ ⊖ 🖵 ✿ ☏

WC1: Bloomsbury

Calthorpe Arms

252 Grays Inn Road, WC1X 8JR

✪ 11 (12 Mon-Tue)-11.30; 12-10.30 Sun ☎ (020) 7278 4732

Young's Bitter, Special; 3 changing beers (sourced nationally; often Young's) Ⓗ

Unusual double doors lead into this single-bar corner local. With no music and an unobtrusive

REAL ALE BREWERIES

40FT E8: Dalston
Alphabeta ⬮ EC2: Liverpool Street
Anspach & Hobday ⬮ SE1: Bermondsey
Barnet ⬮ High Barnet
Beerblefish N18: Upper Edmonton (NEW)
Belleville SW12: Wandsworth Common
Bexley Erith
Big Smoke ⬮ Surbiton
Brew By Numbers SE16: Bermondsey
Brewheadz N17: Tottenham Hale (NEW)
Brewhouse & Kitchen ⬮ EC1: Angel
Brewhouse & Kitchen ⬮ N5: Highbury
Brick SE15: Peckham
Brixton SW9: Brixton
Brockley SE4: Brockley
Bullfinch SE24: Herne Hill
By The Horns SW17: Summerstown
Canopy SE24: Herne Hill
Clarkshaws SW9: Loughborough Junction
Crate E9: Hackney Wick
Cronx New Addington
Dragonfly ⬮ W3: Acton
East London E10: Leyton
Enfield N18: Upper Edmonton (NEW)
Essex Street ⬮ WC2: Temple
Five Points E8: Hackney Downs
Fuller's W4: Chiswick
Gipsy Hill SE27: West Norwood
Gorgeous ⬮ N6: Highgate (NEW)
Hackney E2: Haggerston
Hammerton N7: Barnsbury
Hop Stuff SE18: Woolwich
Howling Hops ⬮ E9: Hackney Wick
Husk E16: West Silvertown
Kernel SE16: Bermondsey
Kew SW14: East Sheen

Laine ⬮ E9: Victoria Park
Laine ⬮ SW11: Battersea
London Beer Factory SE27: West Norwood
London Beer Lab SW9: Brixton
London Brewing ⬮ N12: North Finchley
Long Arm ⬮ W5: South Ealing
Magic Spells E10: Leyton (NEW)
Maregade ⬮ E8: Hackney
Marko Paulo ⬮ W13: Northfields (NEW)
Moncada NW2: Dollis Hill
Mondo SW8: South Lambeth
Oddly Hampton (NEW)
One Mile End ⬮ E1: Whitechapel/N17: Tottenham
Orbit SE17: Walworth
Park Kingston
Partizan SE16: South Bermondsey
Portobello W10: North Kensington
Pressure Drop N17: Tottenham Hale
Redemption N17: Tottenham
Reunion Feltham
Rocky Head SW18: Southfields
Sambrook's SW11: Battersea
Signature Brew E10: Leyton
Solvay Society Aldborough Hatch
Southey SE20: Penge (NEW)
Southwark SE1: Bermondsey
Streatham SW16: Streatham (NEW)
Tap East ⬮ E20: Stratford Westfield
Three Sods ⬮ E2: Bethnal Green
Truman's E3: Hackney Wick
Twickenham Twickenham
Volden Croydon
Weird Beard W7: Hanwell
Wild Card E17: Walthamstow
Wimbledon SW19: Colliers Wood
Zerodegrees ⬮ SE3: Blackheath

corner TV, it is easy either to strike up a conversation from a bar stool or take one of the tables along the sides for more privacy. The upstairs dining room opens for lunch (12-2.30pm) but can be booked at other times. Evening meals are served 5.45-9.30pm. Young's bottle-conditioned beers are stocked plus a Young's seasonal and/or two guest beers. There is pavement seating outside.
🏠◑⊖(Russell Sq)●🦮❀

Lamb 🅛
94 Lambs Conduit Street, WC1N 3LZ
🕐 11-11 (midnight Thu-Sat); 12-10.30 Sun
☎ (020) 7405 0713 ⊕ thelamblondon.com
Young's Bitter, London Gold, Special; 5 changing beers (sourced locally; often Redemption, Truman's, Wimbledon) Ⓗ
Beautifully preserved, Grade II listed and with a regionally important historic pub interior, the Lamb has green upholstery, a small snug and etched-glass snob screens above the bar. The Empire Room bar and meeting room is upstairs. The glorious Victorian history of the pub and area is commemorated by a working polyphon (predecessor to the gramophone) and sepia prints of music hall players. Many of the guest beers are locally brewed, with ciders served from boxes. Behind is a small walled garden.
Q🏠◑⊖(Russell Sq)●🛏🛜

Swan 🅛 ✅
7 Cosmo Place, WC1N 3AP
🕐 12-11 (11.30 Fri & Sat); 12-10.30 Sun ☎ (020) 7837 6223
Greene King London Glory, Abbot; Taylor Walker 1730; 5 changing beers (sourced regionally) Ⓗ
Popular family-oriented pub among the tourist hotels on Southampton Row, close to Great Ormond Street Children's Hospital. There is a single long room, and tables in front on a pedestrian passage. Eight handpumps serve three regular real ales and five guests, mainly from London breweries. Real cider is on handpump during summer and festivals. Pub grub and snacks are available until 10pm. A large-screen TV shows live sports events. Q🥂🏠◑◐⊖(Russell Sq)●🛏❀🛜

WC1: Holborn

Holborn Whippet
25-29 Sicilian Avenue, WC1A 2QH
🕐 12-11.30; 12-10.30 Sun ☎ (020) 3137 9937
⊕ holbornwhippet.com
6 changing beers (sourced nationally) Ⓗ
This pub uses a flow-jet to pump the beer to the taps; a blackboard above shows what is on sale. Real ales come from the likes of Adnams, Bristol Beer Factory, Dark Star, Mighty Oak, Oakham, Redemption (and other London breweries). It has a simple menu: pizza, bratwurst, burgers - all nicely done. The decor is basic, with bare wooden floors, brown tiles and cream-painted walls; there is outside seating. 🏠◑⊖🛏

WC1: St Pancras

Mabel's Tavern ✅
9 Mabledon Place, WC1H 9AZ
🕐 11-11 (midnight Thu-Sat) ☎ (020) 7387 7739
⊕ mabelstavern.co.uk
Shepherd Neame Master Brew, Whitstable Bay Pale Ale, Spitfire, Bishops Finger; 1 changing beer Ⓗ

Originally owned by Whitbread and called the Kentish Arms (note the plaque high on the outside wall), the pub was renamed for landlady Mabel Macinelly, who is said to haunt these cosy premises. Up to the left of the bar is a snug, and a raised area at the back has a nice fireplace plus a large TV screen. Various prints and old photos adorn the walls. Food is served until 9.30pm. Handy for the British Library.
🏠◑🚆⊖(King's Cross/St Pancras)🛏❀🛜

Queen's Head 🅛
66 Acton Street, WC1X 9NB
🕐 12-midnight (11 Mon); 12-11 Sun ☎ (020) 7713 5772
⊕ queensheadlondon.com
Redemption Trinity; 2 changing beers (sourced regionally) Ⓗ
Narrow, late-Georgian premises off the Gray's Inn Road, with a single bar, a smoking patio at the rear and benches in front. The piano is used for jazz and blues on Thursdays. Guest beers from microbreweries usually include a dark one. One handpump serves cider, with three more real ciders and a range of other draught and bottled beers. Sharing platters of snacks are on offer at this comfortable pub, frequented by locals and the occasional tourist.
🏠◑🚆⊖(King's Cross/St Pancras)●🛏🛜

WC2: Chancery Lane

Seven Stars
53-54 Carey Street, WC2A 2JB
🕐 11-11; 12-10.30 Sun ☎ (020) 7242 8521
⊕ thesevenstars1602.co.uk
Adnams Broadside; Sharp's Cornish Coaster; 3 changing beers (often Adnams) Ⓗ
Dating from 1602 and formerly the League of Seven Stars, this pub has a regionally important historic interior. With its decorative Victorian bar-back, the bar occupies the narrow space between two distinctive drinking areas, one named the Wig Box (the Royal Courts of Justice are nearby). The landlady favours Adnams beers and serves good food. The pub's resident cat is now Peabody; RIP Ray Brown. Q◑⊖🛏🛜

WC2: Charing Cross

Harp 🅛 ✅
47 Chandos Place, WC2N 4HS
🕐 10.30-11 (midnight Fri & Sat); 12-10.30 Sun
☎ (020) 7836 0291
Dark Star Hophead, American Pale Ale; Fuller's London Pride; Sambrook's Wandle Ale; 6 changing beers (sourced nationally) Ⓗ
Small, friendly Fuller's pub, which became a haven for beer choice as a free house under the management of the late, legendary, Binnie Walsh. Ciders and perries complement the fine range of real ales. The narrow bar is adorned with mirrors and portraits. There is no intrusive music or TV and a cosy upstairs room provides a refuge from the busy throng. Numerous awards include the CAMRA National Pub of the Year accolade for 2010.
Q◑🚆⊖●🛏🛜

Lemon Tree ✅
4 Bedfordbury, WC2N 4BP
🕐 12-11; 12-10.30 Sun ☎ (020) 7831 1391
⊕ lemontreecoventgarden.com

Harvey's Sussex Best Bitter; Sharp's Doom Bar; 3 changing beers (often Portobello, St Austell, Timothy Taylor) Ⓗ
This one-bar pub next to the stage door of the Coliseum is a favourite among locals, musicians and theatregoers. The Thai restaurant upstairs doubles as a function room. Look out for the pub's entrance, slightly set back. There is an emphasis on London brews among the guest beers, by popular demand. ◑≈⊖🖭🛜

WC2: Covent Garden

Coach & Horses
42 Wellington Street, WC2E 7BD
✪ 11-11; 12-10.30 Sun ☎ (020) 7240 0553
Adnams Southwold Bitter; St Austell Tribute Ⓗ
A small, traditional, independent pub with a strong Irish influence, used very much by locals, to which visitors make a beeline, along with theatre- and opera-goers. It has a fantastic collection of about 70 Irish whiskeys and gins, and Scottish whiskies. There are theatre posters and photos of Gaelic football teams, and the sport of hurling also features. Note the beautiful engraved front windows. Q🏵️🍺🖭⊖🖭❀

Cross Keys ⓛ
31 Endell Street, WC2H 9BA
✪ 11-11 ☎ (020) 7836 5185 ⊕ crosskeyscoventgarden.com
Brodie's Bethnal Green Bitter; 2 changing beers (often Brodie's) Ⓗ
Built in the mid-1840s when Endell (formerly Belton) Street was widened as part of clearing the St Giles's rookery (slum), an ornate façade reveals a long, welcoming bar, subdued lighting, comfortable banquette seating and tables and chairs. Copper kettles, pans, street signs, stuffed fish, framed pictures and photos, Beatles memorabilia and a fine Truman, Hanbury, Buxton & Co mirror cover the walls. Families are welcome (over-12s only) until 7pm unless it is busy, but no dogs. 🏵️◑⊖🖭

White Swan ✅
14 New Row, WC2N 4LF
✪ 10-11 (11.30 Sat); 12-10.30 Sun ☎ (020) 3077 1129
St Austell Nicholson's Pale Ale; 7 changing beers (sourced nationally) Ⓗ
Grade II listed, once owned by the London banking firm of Hoare & Co and formerly an O'Neills, this M&B Nicholson's pub is popular with Covent Garden tourists. It has been tastefully refurbished with a small bar; there is limited seating in the bar area but more room past a partition. The first-floor dining room can be booked for functions – note its contrasting fireplaces. Breakfast is served until noon (not Sun). 🏵️◑≈(Charing Cross)⊖(Leicester Sq)🖭🛜

WC2: Holborn

Shakespeare's Head ✅
Africa House, 64-68 Kingsway, WC2B 6BG
✪ 7am-midnight (1am Fri); 8am-1am Sat; 8am-midnight Sun ☎ (020) 7404 8846
Fuller's London Pride; Greene King IPA; Sharp's Doom Bar; 6 changing beers Ⓗ
Large Wetherspoon bank conversion from 1998, named after a famous pub in the locality until the demolition of Wych Street over 100 years ago. It is usually busy with shoppers, tourists, local office workers and, during term time, students from the nearby London School of Economics. A convenient place for a couple of pints after your cultural sojourn at the British Museum. 🏵️◑🍺⊖🖭🖭🛜

W1: Fitzrovia

Draft House Charlotte ✅
43 Goodge Street, W1T 1TA
✪ 12-11 (midnight Fri & Sat); closed Sun ☎ (020) 7323 9361
3 changing beers (often By the Horns, Harbour, Sambrook's) Ⓗ
A big welcome awaits you in this small, single-bar corner pub with its bare wooden floors and simple furnishings. Changing offerings from Sambrook's and other local smaller breweries are sold in one-third and two-third pint measures as well as the usual halves and pints. Plenty of other interesting draught and bottled beers are also stocked. Cooked dishes, including speciality burgers, are served lunchtimes only during the week and until 9pm on Saturdays; bar snacks, including giant pork scratchings, are otherwise available. 🏵️❀◑⊖(Goodge St)🖭🛜

Stag's Head ⓛ
102 New Cavendish Street, W1W 6XW
✪ 11 (12 Sat)-11; 12-8 Sun ☎ (020) 7580 8313
Fuller's London Pride; Tring Side Pocket for a Toad; 1 changing beer (sourced locally; often Tring) Ⓗ
A smart, oak-panelled pub, offering a friendly welcome to regulars and visitors alike. Rebuilt in the late-1930s by brewers William Younger, it has a marvellous Art Deco exterior sporting a curved corner profile, and a regionally important historic interior. Vertical drinking is assisted by unusual peninsular shelf projections to the bar and elsewhere. Sun-lovers and smokers can relax on shaded benches outside. Traditional pub food is available lunchtimes only. 🏵️❀◑🍺⊖(Gt Portland St)🖭

W1: Marylebone

Carpenters Arms
12 Seymour Place, W1H 7NE
✪ 11-11; 11-10.30 Sun ☎ (020) 7723 1050
Harvey's Sussex Best Bitter; 5 changing beers (sourced nationally; often Adnams, Portobello) Ⓗ
A sister pub to Southwark's Market Porter, but with fewer beers, and a welcoming haven for escapees from the bustle of Oxford Street. TV sport and a dartboard add to the appeal for the regulars. A sensitive refurbishment has preserved the wall tiling and floor mosaics at the main entrance. Elsewhere is a display of woodworking tools. Pork pies are the main snacks. ❀◑⊖(Marble Arch)♣🖭❀🛜

Golden Eagle
59 Marylebone Lane, W1U 2NY
✪ 12-11 (midnight Fri & Sat); closed Sun ☎ (020) 7935 3228
Fuller's London Pride; St Austell Tribute; 2 changing beers (often Adnams, Twickenham) Ⓗ
First licensed in 1842 and rebuilt in 1890, this single-bar pub is traditional in every way: small and cosy, with smart decor, a fine etched bar-back mirror and leaded windows. Landlady Gina Vernon and her family celebrated 25 years here in 2016. Piano singalongs on Tuesday, Thursday and Friday evenings maintain the timeless atmosphere. Real ales are quality, not quantity. Q🍺⊖(Bond St)🖭

Thornbury Castle 🄻
29A Enford Street, W1H 1DN
🕐 12-11; closed Sat & Sun ☎ (020) 7402 2189
🌐 thornburycastle.uk.com
6 changing beers (sourced regionally; often Rebellion, Red Squirrel, Vale) 🄷
A small, family-run pub in a side street near Marylebone Station, with wood panelling throughout and a raised seating area at the back. There is a strong Rugby Union connection (Wasps) and the pub may open at weekends for big games on TV. Discerning drinkers will find it a worthwhile alternative to the more mainstream pubs in the area. Thai food is served. Q🕐◗⬆❂♣🚆🐾☗

W1: Mayfair

Clarence ✅
4 Dover Street, W1S 4LB
🕐 10-11.30 (midnight Fri & Sat); 10-11 Sun
☎ (020) 7491 3607
Fuller's London Pride; St Austell Nicholson's Pale Ale; Sharp's Doom Bar; 5 changing beers (sourced nationally) 🄷
Licensed in 1724 as the Coach & Horses, later named after the Duke of Clarence, who became King William IV in 1830. A smallish frontage belies a much larger area extending back, which incorporates a beer library. The atmosphere is convivial, especially since M&B Nicholson's refurbishment in 2012; it has a pleasant, quieter upstairs bar. Close to the Ritz Hotel in Piccadilly. ◗❂(Green Park)🚆☗

Windmill
6-8 Mill Street, W1S 2AZ
🕐 11.45-11; 12-5 Sun ☎ (020) 7491 8050
🌐 windmillmayfair.co.uk
Young's Bitter, Special; 6 changing beers (sourced locally; often Hackney, Wimbledon) 🄷
Created in the 1980s from adjoining buildings, this pub has a spacious bar with painted panelling, decorative ceilings and a large chandelier. To the rear is one of two pie rooms reserved for diners; the other, upstairs, has its original floor and panelling. Pies include monthly specials such as beef and stilton. There is also a roof terrace. Q🏵◗❂(Oxford Circus)🚆🐾☗

W1: Soho

Argyll Arms ★ ✅
18 Argyll Street, W1F 7TP
🕐 10-11.30 (midnight Fri & Sat); 10-11 Sun
☎ (020) 7734 6117
Fuller's London Pride; St Austell Nicholson's Pale Ale; 6 changing beers (sourced nationally) 🄷
A Victorian Grade II*-listed M&B Nicholson's house with a nationally important historic pub interior. Three snugs are separated by etched-glass partitions; note the remarkable Bass mirror. The bar back is impressive and adjacent is a rare survivor, a manager's office with more etched glazing. The magnificent saloon is decorated with ornate mirrors. Enjoy a reliable range of regular and guest ales on eight or more handpumps. ◗♿❂(Oxford Circus)🚆☗

Crown ✅
64 Brewer Street, W1F 9TP
🕐 10-11 (11.30 Fri & Sat); 10-10.30 Sun ☎ (020) 7287 8420

St Austell Nicholson's Pale Ale; Truman's Runner; 3 changing beers 🄷
A popular M&B Nicholson's pub on the site of the Hickford Rooms, London's main concert rooms in the 1740s and 50s – a notice displays the history of the pub. The main bar, with its banquettes, is a welcome retreat from the bustling street. Children are welcome in the upstairs dining room. Starting with breakfast, food is served daily until 10pm. Three changing and often unusual guest beers are on the bar. Q◗❂(Piccadilly Circus)🚆☗

Dog & Duck ★ ✅
18 Bateman Street, W1D 3AJ
🕐 11-11 (11.30 Fri & Sat); 12-10.30 Sun ☎ (020) 7494 0697
Fuller's London Pride; St Austell Nicholson's Pale Ale; Truman's Runner; 4 changing beers (often Orkney, Sambrook's) 🄷
In the heart of Soho, this Grade II-listed Nicholson's outlet, built in 1897, has a nationally important historic pub interior. An elaborate mosaic depicts dogs and ducks, and wonderful advertising mirrors adorn the walls. The upstairs Orwell Bar can be hired for functions. The pub is small and so popular, especially with media people, that it is not just smokers who have to stand outside. The bar has been extended towards the Frith Street door. ◗❂(Tottenham Court Rd)🚆☗

Lyric 🄻
37 Great Windmill Street, W1D 7LU
🕐 11-11.30 (midnight Fri & Sat); 12-10.30 Sun
☎ (020) 7434 0604 🌐 lyricsoho.co.uk
8 changing beers 🄷
A small, independently owned bar just off Shaftesbury Avenue, bay-fronted with a tiled, panelled interior, popular with local trade. Once two adjacent taverns, the Windmill and the Ham merged in the mid-18th century to form the Windmill & Ham, renamed in 1890 and rebuilt 16 years later. Cask ales may come from Big Smoke, Brodie's, Dark Star, Magic Rock, Marble, RedWillow, Redemption, Tiny Rebel or Thornbridge. ◗❂(Piccadilly Circus)🚆☗

Old Coffee House 🄻
49 Beak Street, W1F 9SF
🕐 11-11; 12-11 Sun ☎ (020) 7437 2197
Brodie's Bethnal Green Bitter, London Fields Pale, Old Street Pale Ale; 1 changing beer (often Brodie's) 🄷
A large but cosy pub, close to the buzz of Carnaby Street, with six handpumps offering a range of ales from Brodie's. First licensed as the Silver Street Coffee House, it was rebuilt in 1894 and is now Grade II listed. The long bar and dark panelling are adorned with Watneys Red Barrel signage, brewery mirrors and sundry prints, posters, pictures and brassware. At lunchtimes you will find good sized portions of pub grub, reasonably priced. ♿🏵◗❂(Piccadilly Circus)🚆🐾

Queen's Head 🄻 ✅
15 Denman Street, W1D 7HN
🕐 11-11.30 (midnight Fri & Sat); 12-10.30 Sun
☎ (020) 7437 1540 🌐 queensheadpiccadilly.com
Fuller's London Pride; Robinsons Trooper; 3 changing beers (sourced regionally; often Dark Star, Sambrook's) 🄷
A rare West End free house with plenty of vertical drinking space below and a restaurant upstairs, hosting a comedy club most Sunday evenings. The traditional feel is enhanced by an attractive bar-back and wall mirroring downstairs and an unusual

leather-fronted bar in the restaurant. With its real ales, good-value pies and other pub food, including snacks and cheeseboards at the bar, this is a popular pub pre- and post-theatre.
🛏🕪▶⊖(Piccadilly Circus)🛋🌸🛜

Star & Garter
62 Poland Street, W1F 7NX
✪ 11 (12 Sat)-11; closed Sun ☎ (020) 7437 9278
Fuller's London Pride; Greene King IPA; Shepherd Neame Spitfire Ⓗ
A pub on one of the earliest sites to be developed in Poland Street: its name appears in 1825 in the Westminster victuallers' records. Formerly a Courage house, it had previously belonged to Style & Winch of Maidstone and the windows advertised Maidstone Ales. It has a small, cosy, wood-panelled bar with matchwood ceiling. An additional bar upstairs is usually open on Thursday and Friday nights to cope with the throng.
Q&⊖(Oxford Circus)🛋

EAST LONDON
E1: Aldgate
Dispensary
19A Leman Street, E1 8EN
✪ 11.30-11; closed Sat & Sun ☎ (020) 7977 0486
⊕ thedispensarylondon.co.uk
Dark Star Hophead; 4 changing beers (sourced regionally; often Harvey's, Vale) Ⓗ
Long before the National Health Service, the local dispensary, founded in 1782, provided treatment and medicines to the poor. Moved to its present location in 1852, it closed in 1940, to be rescued from near-dereliction by the present owners. It is now known for its fine ales (up to four) and dining, for which booking is advised. There are various rooms on three floors and a small outside area for smoking. Closed Christmas and Easter.
🏵🕪≄(Fenchurch St)⊖(Aldgate/Aldgate East)🛋🌸🛜

E1: Spitalfields
Crown & Shuttle
226 Shoreditch High Street, E1 6PJ
✪ 11-11 (midnight Thu; 1am Fri); 12-1am Sat; 12-10.30 Sun
☎ (020) 7375 2905 ⊕ crownandshuttle.co.uk
6 changing beers (sourced regionally; often Redemption, Sharp's, Truman's) Ⓗ
The bar has six handpumps which dispense a changing selection of cask ales (check the blackboard) along with a variety of other draught and bottled beers. Food is available, with a separate menu on Sunday. The pub has been recently refurbished with bare floorboards and decorated with bric-a-brac. It has a large garden with ample seating, hosts a regular quiz and shows major sporting events.
🏵🕪≄(Liverpool St)⊖(Shoreditch High St)🛋🛜

King's Stores
14 Widegate Street, E1 7HP
✪ 12-11 (midnight Thu-Sat); 12-10 Sun ☎ (020) 7247 4089
⊕ kingsstores.co.uk
Greene King IPA; 4 changing beers (often Hop Stuff, London Beer Factory, Sharp's) Ⓗ
A single-bar pub that has five handpumps serving Greene King IPA and four changing guest ales mainly from London breweries. A full menu is available throughout the day. The ground floor has

two distinct areas and there are upstairs function rooms that can be hired. Sport is shown on large TVs. The site was used to store munitions in the Civil War. 🛏🕪▶&≄⊖(Liverpool St)♣🛋🌸🛜

Pride of Spitalfields
3 Heneage Street, E1 5LJ
✪ 10-1am (2am Fri & Sat); 10-midnight Sun
☎ (020) 7247 8933
Fuller's London Pride, ESB; Mighty Oak Maldon Gold; 1 changing beer (sourced locally; often Sambrook's) Ⓗ
In the midst of the curry houses of Brick Lane, a small alley opens out to this small but famous pub. It can be busy in the two bars, where the main attraction for many is the Maldon Gold, but three other beers are served. Some come to see Lennie the cat (famous for his appearance in London Pubcats), usually perched on the back of a seat next to the chimney. Food is served at lunchtime.
🛏🕪≄(Liverpool St)⊖(Aldgate East/Shoreditch High St)🛋🌸

Williams Ale & Cider House Ⓛ ✓
22-24 Artillery Lane, E1 7LS
✪ 11-11 (midnight Thu-Sat); 12-11 Sun ☎ (020) 7247 5163
⊕ williamsspitalfields.com
House beer (by Greene King); 5 changing beers (sourced locally; often Crouch Vale, Hackney, Truman's) Ⓗ
Thirteen handpumps grace the bar of this pub in a lane just off Bishopsgate. They dispense up to seven ales, mainly from London breweries, and six ciders. A selection of bottled beers is also available. Food is served throughout the day. The two distinct areas of the pub are comfortably furnished, with pictures of old Truman's pubs and brewery posters on the walls. Televised major sports events and live music performances feature.
🛏🕪≄⊖(Liverpool St)♣🌸🛋🌸🛜

E1: Whitechapel
White Hart Ⓛ
1-3 Mile End Road, E1 4TP
✪ 10.30-midnight (1am Fri) ☎ (020) 7790 2894
⊕ the-white-hart.co.uk/home
9 changing beers (sourced locally; often One Mile End) Ⓗ
The large windows give this single bar at the corner of Mile End and Cambridge Heath roads a welcoming feel. There is also a function room upstairs. Food is served 12-3, 6-10pm Monday to Friday, 12-5pm Saturday and 12-9pm Sunday. Beers are provided by the One Mile End Brewery, which has moved to Tottenham, with a small plant retained here for possible special brews.
🛏🏵🕪▶&≄⊖(Bethnal Green/Whitechapel)🌸🛋🌸🛜

E2: Bethnal Green
Camel ✓
277 Globe Road, E2 0JD
✪ 12-11; 12-10.30 Sun ☎ (020) 3620 2333
Adnams Broadside; Sambrook's Wandle Ale; 2 changing beers (often Five Points, Oakham, St Austell) Ⓗ
Convenient for the Museum of Childhood and York Hall, this small refurbished Victorian pub has a single bar and a traditional feel. Four handpumps serve two regular ales from Adnams and Sambrook's and two changing guest beers. There is

food throughout the day with a range of pies and mash, and puddings. The distinctive exterior tiling gives a clue to the original brewery – the last one when tied was Ind Coope. ♿️🏠🍽️🚭➕🚪🐾☕🛜

Carpenter's Arms

73 Cheshire Street, E2 6EG
🕐 4 (12 Thu)-11; 12-12.30am Fri & Sat; 12-11.30 Sun
☎ (020) 7739 6342 🌐 carpentersarmsfreehouse.com
Timothy Taylor Landlord; 2 changing beers (often Purity, St Peter's) Ⓗ
A former Truman's street-corner pub that has been smartly refurbished. Besides the Landlord and two changing guest ales, it offers a large range of bottled beer. An opening at the front bar leads through to the garden and smoking area. Food is served from 1pm, with a full menu most of the week and roast dinners on Sunday until they run out. Pictures on the wall show historic views of the pub and local area.
🏠🍽️(Bethnal Green/Shoreditch High St)🚪

Dundee Arms

339 Cambridge Heath Road, E2 9LH
🕐 4-11 Mon; 12-1am (midnight Tue & Wed); 12-10.30 Sun
☎ (020) 7729 6903 🌐 thedundeearms.com
3 changing beers (often Dark Star, East London Brewing, Truman's) Ⓗ
A single-bar pub that serves three real ales mainly from small, local independent brewers. It has a traditional feel with a mixture of wood panelling and brick walls. There are padded benches, stools and sofas to sit on, with a small garden to the rear of the pub. Sports TV is available, including in the garden, and music is usually played. An excellent cheese toastie is the only food offering.
♿️🏠🍽️🚪🐾☕🛜

King's Arms

11A Buckfast Street, E2 6EY
🕐 12-11.30 (midnight Fri & Sat) ☎ (020) 7729 2627
🌐 thekingsarmspub.com
4 changing beers (often Dark Star, Howling Hops, Redemption) Ⓗ
A back-street pub with a central bar and seating around. Six handpumps dispense four cask ales and two ciders; in addition about 50 bottled beers are available from the UK, US and Scandinavia. The pub does not use pumpclips but there is a beer menu on the bar, wall and tables. Cheese and meat boards are served all day.
♿️🏠🍽️(Bethnal Green/Shoreditch High St) 🚪🐾☕🛜

E3: Bow

Eleanor Arms

460 Old Ford Road, E3 5JP
🕐 4 (12 Fri-Sat)-11; 12-11 Sun ☎ (020) 8980 6992
🌐 eleanorarms.co.uk
Shepherd Neame Master Brew, Whitstable Bay Pale Ale, Spitfire Gold, Spitfire; 2 changing beers (sourced nationally) Ⓗ
This CAMRA award-winning pub has been run by the same three-person team for the last nine years, with occasional help from the customers. It is traditionally furnished, with wood panelling and an eclectic mix of pictures adorning the walls. People return again and again for the quality of the beer, along with the regular live jazz every Sunday and disco every Friday and Saturday night. There is a small beer garden at the back.
♿️🏠🍽️➕🐾🚪(8)☕🛜

E5: Clapton

Anchor & Hope Ⓛ

15 High Hill Ferry, E5 9HG (800yds N of Lea Bridge Rd, along river path)
🕐 1 (12 Sat)-11; 12-10.30 Sun ☎ (020) 8806 1730
Fuller's London Pride, ESB; 2 changing beers Ⓗ
By the River Lea, and opposite the marshes, this 1850s traditional pub with its small, single bar reminds you of days gone by. To the right there is an open fire and a TV; to the left there is a back room with a dartboard. Payment is by cash only. Customers spill out and drink on the towpath when the pub is busy in summer. Live music and quiz nights feature on occasion. ♿️🏠🐾🚪(393)🐾☕🛜

Clapton Hart Ⓛ

231 Lower Clapton Road, E5 8EG
🕐 4-11 (midnight Thu; 1am Fri); 12-1am Sat; 12-11 Sun
☎ (020) 8985 8124 🌐 claptonhart.com
Volden Session Ale, Pale Ale, Porter; changing beers (often Dark Star, Otley, Siren) Ⓗ
Brought back by Antic after many years' closure, this place has an impressive architectural frontage, while the interior is shabby-chic with eclectic furniture. A long single bar has eight handpumps for cask ales and a range of bottled beers. To the right is an open fire and table football. There is a restaurant at the rear and a large garden behind. Live music is performed at weekends, and Tuesday is quiz night. ♿️🏠🍽️♿️🍽️➕🚪🐾☕🛜

Crooked Billet Ⓛ

84 Upper Clapton Road, E5 9JP
🕐 4-11 (midnight Fri); 12-midnight Sat; 12-11 Sun
☎ (020) 3058 1166 🌐 e5crookedbillet.co.uk
Changing beers (often Hammerton, Siren, Truman's) Ⓗ
Transformed in 2013 and now a vibrant pub, where two entrances lead to a single large bar with three sides. London beers always feature on the five handpumps at the back; on the other two sides are another 21 fonts. Monday night quizzes are popular and sport is shown. Furniture is a mix of tables and chairs, with some sofas. There is a large, well-equipped garden. The kitchen, visible from the bar, produces a changing selection of food.
♿️🏠🍽️♿️🍽️➕🚪🐾☕🛜

E8: Hackney

Cock Tavern Ⓛ

315 Mare Street, E8 1EJ
🕐 12-11 (10.30 Sun)
8 changing beers (sourced locally; often Hackney, Howling Hops, Maregade) Ⓗ
Retaining its Truman's tiled exterior and wood panelling, this pub serves eight beers and eight ciders. The beers usually include offerings from Maregade (in the cellar) and Howling Hops (now in Hackney Wick) breweries along with others, often local. The interior is dimly lit and the furnishing is somewhat basic, and it has a tiny patio. Food is limited to crisps and interesting pickled eggs. Music is played, but there is no TV, and the pub is cash only. ♿️🏠🚉(Downs)🍽️(Central/Downs)🐾🚪🐾☕🛜

Pembury Tavern

90 Amhurst Road, E8 1JH
🕐 12-11 (1am Fri & Sat) ☎ (020) 8986 8597
Milton Minotaur, Pegasus, Nero, Cyclops; changing beers (sourced nationally) Ⓗ

A large, open-plan pub with bare floorboards and mostly wooden furniture, with pool and bar billiard tables. The single bar has 12 handpumps serving mainly Milton ales, with guest beers and two real ciders. Food is served during opening hours, chiefly pizza, with the addition of other dishes during lunchtime and evening sessions and roast dinners on a Sunday. A growing collection of pumpclips decorates the beams in the ceiling.
Q 🛏 🕔 🧑‍🦽 ♿ ➤ (Downs) ⊖ (Central/Downs) ♣ 🍺 🚪 🐾 🛜

E8: Haggerston

Fox
372 Kingsland Road, E8 4DA
🕔 4 (2 Fri)-midnight; midnight Sat & Sun ☎ 07807 217734 ⊕ thefoxe8.com
5 changing beers (often Dark Star, Marble, Siren) Ⓗ
A corner pub in an up-and-coming area. Independently owned, it serves up to five cask beers and two ciders. Brewery tap takeovers feature regularly. The interior has a variety of wooden furniture and there is a roof terrace. Food is served until 10.30pm Monday to Saturday and 10pm Sunday. Music is played and major sporting events including Six Nations rugby are shown.
🛏 🕔 🕔 ⊖ 🍺 🚪 🐾 🛜

E9: Hackney Wick

Crate Brewery Bar & Pizzeria Ⓛ
Unit 7, White Building, Queen's Yard, White Post Lane, E9 5EN (down steps by canal bridge or through Queen's Yard)
🕔 12-11 (midnight Fri & Sat) ☎ 07834 275687
⊕ cratebrewery.com
Crate Best Bitter, Stout; 4 changing beers (sourced regionally; often Crate) Ⓗ
Alongside the River Lea navigation, this former printworks is the tap for Crate Brewery across the yard (though this may relocate during the currency of this Guide). Four Crate and two guest beers are sold along with a range of bottles. Spirits are not available. Home-cooked pizzas are served all day. Some of the furniture was made by locals. Wheelchair access is via the waterside entrance, and outside drinking is by the river. There is music but no TVs. 🛏 🕔 🕔 🧑‍🦽 ⊖ 🚪 🐾 🛜

E9: Homerton

Adam & Eve Ⓛ
155 Homerton High Street, E9 6AS
🕔 4-11 (midnight Thu; 1am Fri); 12-midnight Sat; 12-11 Sun
☎ (020) 8985 1494 ⊕ adamandevepub.com
6 changing beers (often East London Brewing, Hackney, Siren) Ⓗ
Tile-fronted pub rebuilt in 1913, retaining some original features. Up to six beers come, mostly, from smaller breweries. It is much larger within than it looks from the outside - the bar extends to both sides of the pub, past an open kitchen and an L-shaped pool table to a rear garden. Seating is plentiful. Much of the food is from Cornwall. Quiz nights feature regularly, music is played and sport is shown on several screens. 🛏 🕔 🕔 ⊖ ♣ 🚪 🐾 🛜

Chesham Arms
15 Mehetabel Road, E9 6DU
🕔 4 (12 Sat)-11; 12-10.30 Sun ☎ (020) 8986 6717
⊕ cheshamarms.com

4 changing beers (sourced nationally) Ⓗ
A back-street pub that was reopened in 2015 after being listed as an Asset of Community Value. It was an instant success and the local CAMRA Pub of the Year. A single bar dispenses four changing cask ales and a real cider. It is split into two areas, with an attractive garden below at the back, and has a traditional feel. Food is not available but you can order pizza for delivery to the pub.
🛏 🕔 ⊖ (Hackney Central) 🍺 🚪 🐾 🛜

E9: South Hackney

People's Park Tavern
360 Victoria Park Road, E9 7BT
🕔 12-11 (1am Fri); 11-2am Sat; 11-11 Sun
☎ (020) 8533 0040 ⊕ peoplesparktavern.pub
7 changing beers (often Laine) Ⓗ
A large pub that shares the building with its own brewery, one of several operated in London by the Laine Brewing Company, and the majority of the cask ales on offer are brewed on-site. The sizeable beer garden, which overlooks Victoria Park, is ideal at any time of the year, with plenty of seating, covered in winter. Traditional pub food is served daily. Comedy, quiz, live music and DJ nights all contribute to this pub's lively feel.
🛏 🕔 🕔 🧑‍🦽 ⊖ (Homerton) 🚪 (388) 🐾 🛜

E10: Leyton

King William IV Ⓛ
816 High Road, E10 6AE
🕔 11-midnight (1am Fri & Sat); 12-midnight Sun
☎ (020) 8556 2460
Changing beers (often Brodie's) Ⓗ
Victorian street-corner pub with etched windows. The large bar area with additional seating at the back allows access to the garden, behind which was Brodie's original brewery. An impressive number of handpumps dispenses Brodie's beers; all of them are used only during the two annual festivals. A variety of food options is offered. A large mirror hangs above the open fire, football and other sports are broadcast on several screens, and live music is performed at weekends.
🕔 🕔 ⊖ (Midland Rd) ♣ 🚪 🐾 🛜

Leyton Orient Supporters Club Ⓛ
Matchroom Stadium, Oliver Road, E10 5NF
🕔 5.30-7.30, 9.30-11 Tue; 12-2.30, 5-8 Sat
☎ (020) 8988 8288 ⊕ orientsupporters.org
Mighty Oak Oscar Wilde Ⓖ; **9 changing beers** Ⓗ
Usually only open on home match days, and not during the game, this multi award-winning bar is staffed by volunteers. It gets busy but service is swift and efficient. In addition to match days it often opens for England football matches and other events, including brewery takeovers and beer festivals. A small admission charge is sometimes levied for non-club/CAMRA members. Up to 10 cask ales are served along with ciders and a small range of bottles. 🛏 🕔 🧑‍🦽 ⊖ 🍺 🚪 🐾

Leyton Technical ⦿
265B High Road, E10 5QN
🕔 4-11 (midnight Thu; 1am Fri); 12-1am Sat; 12-11 Sun
☎ (020) 8558 4759 ⊕ leytontechnical.com
Volden Session Ale; 7 changing beers (sourced nationally) Ⓗ
In the old Leyton town hall, this Antic pub has eight handpumps serving a variety of beers. There are

two main rooms and three smaller rooms, full of eclectic furniture and fittings. Wheelchair access is through the library – ask at the bar as the door is usually locked. A full menu of home-cooked food is available. The pub hosts several events. Close to Leyton Orient football ground, the pub welcomes away fans. ☺🌮🍴♿⊖🚍🐾🛜

E11: Leytonstone

North Star
24 Browning Road, E11 3AR
🕓 4 (12 Sat)-11; 12-10.30 Sun ☎ (020) 8530 3197
East London Brewing Foundation Bitter; 5 changing beers (often Oakham) Ⓗ
A small community pub in Leytonstone Village. The wooden floorboards and furniture give it a traditional feel. Six handpumps in the saloon bar dispense two regular beers and four changing guest ales; you can be served via the hatch in the public bar, though note the external door to this bar is sometimes locked. Thai food is served, with freshly made pizza Thursday and Friday evenings and at weekends. There is a quiz on Sunday evening. ☺🌮🍴⊖♣🚍🐾🛜

Northcote Arms
110 Grove Green Road, E11 4EL
🕓 2-11 (10.30 Mon; 11.30 Tue); 12.30-12.30am Fri; 12-1am Sat; 12-midnight Sun ☎ (020) 8518 7516
⊕ thenorthcotee11.com
4 changing beers (sourced nationally) Ⓗ
A family-friendly, traditional community pub with a central bar surrounded by various drinking areas. Pizza is served during food times, with occasional additional dishes. There is a drag cabaret on Sunday, a quiz on Tuesday, and other events. Within walking distance of Leyton Orient's ground, this pub also welcomes away supporters. ☺🌮🍴⊖(Leyton)♣🚍🐾

Red Lion Ⓛ ✅
640 High Road, E11 3AA
🕓 12-11 (midnight Thu; 2am Fri & Sat) ☎ (020) 8988 2929
⊕ theredlionleytonstone.com
Sharp's Atlantic; Volden Session Ale, Pale Ale; 7 changing beers Ⓗ
A single-bar Antic pub with a traditional feel, featuring wooden floorboards, eclectic furniture and a large garden. The downstairs bar serves three regular ales and seven changing guests, as well as real cider and a large selection of bottled beers. The upstairs ballroom has a bar with no handpumps and hosts films and music events. A changing menu of home-cooked food is available. ☺🌮🍴♿⊖♣🍴🚍🐾🛜

E11: Wanstead

George Ⓛ
155-159 High Street, E11 2RL
🕓 8am-midnight (12.30am Fri & Sat) ☎ (020) 8989 2921
Fuller's London Pride; Greene King Abbot; Ruddles Best Bitter; Sharp's Doom Bar; 8 changing beers (sourced regionally) Ⓗ
Though there has been a pub on this site for hundreds of years, the large two-storey Edwardian building dates from 1903 and is now a Wetherspoon free house, with etched windows and pictures of Old Wanstead and famous Georges on the walls – with the dragon hovering above the bar. The main bar, with its 12 handpumps, is at the

rear of the pub. The upstairs bar has no handpumps. The garden and car park are to the rear. Q☺🌮🍴♿⊖🚍🛜

E13: Plaistow

Black Lion ✅
59-61 High Street, E13 0AD
🕓 11-11; 12-10.30 Sun ☎ (020) 8472 2351
⊕ blacklionplaistow.co.uk
Courage Best Bitter; Mighty Oak Captain Bob; Sharp's Doom Bar; 3 changing beers Ⓗ
A coaching inn has stood on this site for over 600 years, though the current building dates from the early 18th century. The beams and wood panelling give the pub a rustic feel. There are two bars, with sports TV in both. There are always four ales on the seven handpumps, with more guest ales on when West Ham United are at home. Home-cooked food is served weekday lunchtimes and evenings and for West Ham home matches. ☺🌮🍴⊖P🚍🛜

E17: Walthamstow

Bell Ⓛ ✅
617 Forest Road, E17 4NE
🕓 12-midnight (1am Fri & Sat); 12-11 Sun & Mon
☎ (020) 8523 2277 ⊕ belle17.com
Sharp's Doom Bar; Timothy Taylor Landlord; 6 changing beers Ⓗ
This large Victorian pub is a prominent landmark at a busy junction and has been transformed in recent years into a popular hostelry, with comfortable seating on two levels. Family friendly during the day, it has a DJ on Friday and Saturday evenings, with live music once a month. A popular quiz is held each Tuesday. Look for the pinball machine. Biscuits and water are provided for dogs. ☺🌮🍴♿⊖(Central)♣🚍🐾🛜

Mirth, Marvel & Maud 🍸 Ⓛ
186 Hoe St, E17 4QH
🕓 4-11 (midnight Thu; 2am Fri); 12-2am Sat; 12-11 Sun
☎ (020) 8520 8636 ⊕ mirthmarvelandmaud.com
6 changing beers (sourced locally; often East London Brewing, Volden) Ⓗ
In 2002 this 1931 cinema closed, and in 2015 Antic reopened it as a pub. Original glass doors open into a grand foyer, where the ticket office is currently a cocktail bar. Behind is the downstairs bar serving a varying range of draught beers, boxed cider and bottles. To the left is the restored cinema and toilets, while at the rear two flights of stairs rise to a restaurant seating area. Local CAMRA Pub of the Year 2017. 🍴⊖(Central)🚍🐾🛜

Olde Rose & Crown Ⓛ ✅
53-55 Hoe Street, E17 4SA
🕓 10-11 (1am Fri & Sat); 12-11 Sun ☎ (020) 8509 3880
⊕ yeolderoseandcrowntheatrepub.co.uk
6 changing beers (sourced nationally) Ⓗ
This large Victorian pub with many original features has become a Walthamstow institution. Besides changing ales from six handpumps, cider is on one handpump and in boxes. There is often live music in the bar, and also a theatre where many events take place. Very much part of the local community, it is used by clubs and supports local street parties. The Sunday roast is highly recommended (no meals weekdays). There are pop-up food concessions outside on some evenings. ☺🌮🍴♿⊖(Central)♣🍴🚍🐾🛜

E20: Westfield Stratford City

Tap East ⓛ
7 International Square, Montfichet Road, E20 1EE
✆ 11-11; 12-10 Sun ☎ (020) 8555 4467 ⊕ tapeast.co.uk
Tap East Tonic Ale; 5 changing beers (sourced nationally; often Tap East) Ⓗ
Home-brew bar in Europe's largest indoor shopping centre. Three house and three guest beers are dispensed along with a huge range of bottles. The brewery is visible from the bar which is furnished with high tables and sofas. Basic pub grub is served all day. It gets packed when West Ham United play at home (and Boleyn Bitter is available). Major sporting events are shown and music is played occasionally. Beer festivals are also held here.
ᕦ🞉◖◗🖢🕃⊖(Stratford/Stratford Intl)🚌🐾🛜

Barking

Barking Dog ✔
61 Station Parade, IG11 8TU
✆ 8am-midnight ☎ (020) 8507 9109
Greene King Abbot; Ruddles Best Bitter; Sharp's Doom Bar; 6 changing beers Ⓗ
Busy town-centre Wetherspoon pub, close to Barking Station and many bus routes, popular with locals and passing commuters alike. An impressive 12 handpumps serve up to six different beers of varying types and strengths, plus three or four periodically changing regular beers and two or three real ciders, including Westons Old Rosie and Gwynt y Ddraig Black Dragon. Food is served until 11pm, alcoholic drinks from 9am. Muted TV screens show rolling news and occasional sport.
ᕦ◖◗🖢⊖🚌🐾🛜

Chadwell Heath

Eva Hart ✔
1128 High Road, RM6 4AH (on A118)
✆ 8am-midnight ☎ (020) 8597 1069
Adnams Broadside; Greene King Abbot; Morland Old Speckled Hen; Ruddles Best Bitter; Sharp's Doom Bar; Truman's Runner; 4 changing beers (sourced regionally) Ⓗ
Large, comfortable Wetherspoon pub in a building that used to be the local police station. It is named after a local musical personality who was one of the longest-living survivors of the Titanic disaster in 1912; photographs and memorabilia are on display around the pub. Alcoholic drinks are served from 9am, food until 10pm. Qᕦ🞉◖◗🖢⊖🚌🛜

Collier Row

Colley Rowe Inn ✔
54-56 Collier Row Road, RM5 3PA (on B174)
✆ 9am-midnight (1am Fri & Sat) ☎ (01708) 760633
Fuller's London Pride; Greene King Abbot; Ruddles Best Bitter; Sharp's Doom Bar; 3 changing beers Ⓗ
Converted from two shops, the pub is close to six bus routes, giving easy access to and from Romford. It has a changing selection of guest ales from the Wetherspoon list and also two ciders on handpump (usually Westons Old Rosie and Gwynt y Ddraig Black Dragon). It is often lively around the bar, but there are quieter alcoves at the rear. Food is served all day, every day, and Steak Night is particularly popular. Local CAMRA Pub of the Year 2016. ᕦ◖◗🖢🐾🛜

Dagenham

Eastbrook ★
835 Dagenham Road, RM10 7UP (near jct with A1112)
✆ 11-11 (midnight Fri & Sat) ☎ (020) 8592 1873
2 changing beers Ⓗ
A welcoming community local, this Grade II*-listed 1937 two-bar pub has been identified by CAMRA as having a nationally important historic interior. The main bar is the Walnut Room with extensive panelling; the Oak Room, used for functions, is in Brewers'-Tudor and can be visited if you ask. Beers are from the Brakspear range and change monthly. Football memorabilia adorn the pub; it is the local for Dagenham & Redbridge football supporters, particularly when their team is at home.
🞉🚐◗🖢P🚌(103,174)🐾🛜

Gidea Park

Ship ✔
93 Main Road, RM2 5EL (on A118)
✆ 12-11 (midnight Thu-Sat) ☎ (01708) 741571
⊕ theshipgideapark.co.uk
Courage Best Bitter; Sharp's Doom Bar; Timothy Taylor Landlord; 2 changing beers Ⓗ
More than 250 years old, this Grade II-listed split-level pub has extensive dark-wood panelling, timber beams and huge fireplaces. The building is largely unchanged and has low ceilings in places – so duck or grouse! It is a family-run business. Quiz nights are held on Thursdays and there is live music on Saturdays. Qᕦ🞉◖◗⊖P🚌🐾🛜

Hornchurch

JJ Moon's ✔
48-52 High Street, RM12 4UN (on A124)
✆ 8am-11.30 (12.30am Fri & Sat) ☎ (01708) 478410
Greene King Abbot; Ruddles Best Bitter; Sharp's Doom Bar; 6 changing beers Ⓗ
A busy Wetherspoon pub, opened in October 1993 and popular with all age groups, featuring a good variety of ales with an emphasis on breweries from London and the South-east. Watercolour paintings of local scenes provide the main decoration, with the usual local interest panels to the rear. Families are welcome until 6pm, and alcoholic drinks are served from 9am.
Qᕦ◖◗🖢⊖(Emerson Park/Hornchurch)🚲🚌🛜

Ilford

Jono's ✔
37 Cranbrook Road, IG1 4PA (on A123)
✆ 11-11 (midnight Thu; 1am Fri & Sat); 12-10.30 Sun
☎ (020) 8514 6676
Castle Rock Harvest Pale; St Austell Tribute Ⓗ
Just a couple of minutes' walk from the station, Jono's is a converted shop with an unusual style. The front of the bar is in dark wood and the rear is half-timbered with a patch of thatch over the seating and fire. There are large-screen TVs and a TV projector showing sports fixtures – it can be noisy at times. Friendly and efficient bar staff serve well-kept ales. It hosts Thursday quizzes and live music at weekends. 🖢⊖🚌🛜

Rainham

Phoenix
Broadway, RM13 9YW (on B1335)

⚙ 11-11; 12-3, 7-11 Sun ☎ (01708) 553700
🌐 the-phoenix-hotel.com
Courage Directors; Greene King Abbot; John Smith's Bitter; Wells Bombardier; 1 changing beer Ⓗ
Busy, spacious town pub close to Rainham station and convenient for the RSPB Rainham Marshes nature reserve. It has two bars: a public bar with dartboard and a saloon for dining. Poker is played on Wednesday, quizzes and live entertainment/ music alternate on Thursday; entertainment also features on Saturday and Sunday. The large garden has three aviaries, animals and a barbecue area. Family fun days are held every bank holiday Monday. ⛪🏵🍴◑🚲⚑♣🅿🚪🛜

Romford

Moon & Stars ✅
99-103 South Street, RM1 1NX
⚙ 8am-11.30 (midnight Fri & Sat) ☎ (01708) 730117
Greene King Abbot; Ruddles Best Bitter; Sharp's Doom Bar; 5 changing beers (sourced nationally) Ⓗ
A Wetherspoon pub close to Romford station and buses. Children are allowed in the raised area at the back until 6pm Friday and Saturday, later on other days. Real ciders dispensed by gravity from cooled containers behind the bar are usually Old Rosie and Black Dragon. Displays of local history are on the walls and assorted books on the shelves. It can get busy on Thursday and Friday evenings. Food is served until 11pm. Q⛪🏵◑♿🚲⊖♥🚪🛜

Upminster

Huntsman & Hounds ✅
2 Ockendon Road, Corbets Tey, RM14 2DN (on B1421)
⚙ 10-11 (midnight Fri); 11-midnight Sat; 11-11 Sun
☎ (01708) 221672
Adnams Broadside; Brakspear Bitter; Greene King Abbot; house beer (by Black Sheep); 5 changing beers Ⓗ
Refurbished and much-extended local with an increased range of real ales, including seasonal guest beers from microbreweries. There is a range of meat, seafood and vegetarian food offerings throughout the day until 10pm, as well as a set-price buffet and daily specials. A weekly quiz night is held on Wednesday at 9pm. Outside is a south-facing beer garden and large car park. ⛪🏵◑♿🅿🚪(370)🐾🛜

Upminster TapRoom 🏆
1b Sunnyside Gardens, RM14 3DT (off B187, St Mary's Lane)
⚙ closed Mon; 4 (12 Sat)-11; 12-10 Sun
Dark Star Hophead; 5 changing beers (sourced locally) Ⓖ
Upminster and East London's first micropub, opened in a converted office in November 2015 as a snack bar selling real ale, before being granted change of use. Garlands of hops adorn the walls. Real ales come straight from the casks in the cool cellar, visible from the bar. Table service is optional. There is no parking available, so please use public transport. Set mobile phones to silent or pay a fee for charity. Local CAMRA Pub of the Year 2017. Q⛪🏵♿⊖♥🚪🐾

NORTH LONDON
N1: Angel

Angel
3-5 Islington High Street, N1 9LQ (opp tube station)
⚙ 8am-midnight ☎ (020) 7837 2218
Greene King IPA; Sharp's Doom Bar; 6 changing beers (sourced nationally) Ⓗ
A large, modern, open-plan Wetherspoon conversion with some booths towards the back giving slightly more privacy. The adjacent tower was a part of the Angel (one of the first talkie cinemas) that was sadly mostly demolished. With the long-gone Philharmonic Hall (subsequently Grand Theatre), this was always a centre of popular entertainment. Its classic columns and caryatids can apparently be seen in the Museum of London. ⛪🏵◑♿⊖♥🚪🛜

N1: Hoxton

Wenlock Arms 🏆 Ⓛ
26 Wenlock Road, N1 7TA
⚙ 3-11 (midnight Thu); 12-1am Fri & Sat; 12-11 Sun
☎ (020) 7608 3406 🌐 wenlockarms.com
10 changing beers (sourced nationally) Ⓗ
Local CAMRA Pub of the Year 2017, this free house was saved from closure by a vigorous local campaign. It features beers from across the UK, concentrating on ales from small and medium sized breweries, usually including a mild and subject to regular change. With up to seven ciders and perries and a small snacks menu of toasties, Scotch eggs, sausage rolls and pickled eggs, this is a truly welcoming street-corner local with an international reputation. Jazz is played in the bar on Thursday night. ⛪◑♿🚲⊖(Old St)♣♥🚪🐾🛜

N1: Islington

New Rose Ⓛ
84-86 Essex Road, N1 8LU
⚙ 12-11 (midnight Thu); 2am Fri & Sat); 12-10.30 Sun
☎ (020) 7226 1082
5 changing beers (sourced nationally) Ⓗ
Spacious and friendly pub, traditional but quirky, in the heart of Islington. There is a changing range of five quality real ales, light through dark, many from the surrounding area, as well as American bottled beers and traditional cider. A tempting menu of pub favourites, from locally sourced ingredients, is served, including home-cooked pizzas and impressive Sunday roasts. Enjoy a pint in the small rear garden or on a bench at the front, or catch the big game on TV. 🏵◑🚲(Essex Rd)♥🚪🐾🛜

N1: King's Cross

Parcel Yard
Upper Level, King's Cross Station Concourse, N1C 4AP
⚙ 8am-11; 9am-10.30 Sun ☎ (020) 7713 7258
Butcombe Bitter; Fuller's Oliver's Island, London Pride, ESB; Gale's Seafarers Ale, HSB; 4 changing beers (sourced regionally; often Fuller's) Ⓗ
Large pub approached by stairs at the rear of the concourse, converted from the former station parcel office. It is used by local workers, commuters and for meetings; as well as bars on two levels there are semi-private rooms converted from offices (bookable) and an indoor balcony. It has no music; the decor is minimal and features

rescued furniture. Food, starting with breakfast, is served until 10pm (9pm Sun). Disabled access is by lift and there are no smoking facilities.
☎☀◑▯🚴⇌⊖(King's Cross/St Pancras)♣🚆📶

N1: Pentonville

Craft Beer Co
55 White Lion Street, N1 9PP
🌞 4-11 (1am Fri); 12-1am Sat; 12-10.30 Sun
☎ (020) 7278 0318
Kent Pale; 9 changing beers (sourced nationally) Ⓗ
Multi-room pub with a wooden bar displaying 10 handpumps, all serving beers from independent brewers. Green curtains and red carpet give some warmth to the main bar, which has two Victorian pillars, a wooden floor and raised tables and stools, all overseen by Winston Churchill. A cosy room, with settees and subtle lighting, is to the right as you enter, and there is a smaller room at the back. To the side is a small garden. ☀◑▯⊖(Angel)▯🚆

N2: East Finchley

Bald Faced Stag ✓
69 High Road, N2 8AB
🌞 12-11 (midnight Fri & Sat) ☎ (020) 8442 1201
⊕ thebaldfacedstagn2.co.uk
Greene King IPA; 3 changing beers (sourced regionally; often Adnams, Triple fff, Truman's) Ⓗ
A short walk from the underground station – look for the iconic rooftop stag emblem overlooking the High Road. The three guest ales come from a range of local and regional breweries. The pub is popular with patrons from the local Phoenix cinema and has a large dining area with a smaller second area, both of which are available for private functions. There is also a decked garden, built around an historic sycamore tree. A selection of board games can be played. ☀◑▯⊖🚆📶

N4: Stroud Green

Old Dairy ✓
1-3 Crouch Hill, N4 4AP
🌞 12-11 (midnight Thu; 1am Fri & Sat); 12-10.30 Sun
☎ (020) 7263 3337 ⊕ theolddairyn4.co.uk
Greene King IPA; house beer (by Greene King); 3 changing beers (sourced regionally; often Hop Back, Twickenham) Ⓗ
Popular in the evenings, this Greene King Metropolitan outlet was built as a dairy, and murals on Crouch Hill illustrate all of its previous dairy activities. The cavernous space is divided between a sit-down restaurant and two large rooms served by the bar. A menu of British standards is common to both; food is available all day at weekends. A real cider is offered in summer.
◑▯⊖(Crouch Hill)♣🚆📶

N5: Canonbury

Snooty Fox Ⓛ
75 Grosvenor Avenue, N5 2NN
🌞 4-11 (1am Fri); 12-1am Sat; 12-10.30 Sun
☎ (020) 7354 9532 ⊕ snootyfoxlondon.co.uk
Otter Ale; 3 changing beers (sourced nationally) Ⓗ
A vibrant community pub with 1960s icons depicted throughout, serving four real ales and a real cider. The airy bar features a 45rpm jukebox and the patio offers pleasant outside drinking. A function room is available for local groups and

private dining. The pub is well known for its ale and cider festivals, which attract people from far and wide. Its kitchen serves quality modern British food and an excellent Sunday roast. ☀◑▯⊖🚆

N5: Highbury

Brewhouse & Kitchen Ⓛ ✓
2a Corsica Street, N5 1JJ
🌞 11-11 (midnight Fri & Sat); 12-11 Sun ☎ (020) 7226 1026
Brewhouse & Kitchen Tramshed, The Goalscorer, Romford Pele, No 19, Illustrator; 1 changing beer Ⓗ
The former tram shed at Highbury Corner, refurbished and reopened with an in-house brewery. The company is continuing to expand, opening new outlets across the UK, but this location offers a lovely outdoor space at the front, a large interior to accommodate private parties, brewing classes in its academy and plenty of room to enjoy pub classics with a delicious twist. On Arsenal home match days it is open only to season ticket holders.
☎☀◑▯🚴⇌⊖(Highbury & Islington)●🚆🐾📶

N6: Highgate

Duke's Head Ⓛ
16 Highgate High Street, N6 5JG
🌞 12-midnight (1am Thu-Sat); 12-11.30 Sun
☎ (020) 8341 1310 ⊕ thedukesheadhighgate.co.uk
8 changing beers (sourced nationally) Ⓗ
Former coaching inn with a courtyard, reopened as a specialist beer house offering a large range of real ale and cider. Local brewer Hammerton is a fairly permanent presence but expect to find beers from around the country, such as Brodie's, Burning Sky, Magic Rock, Moor and Siren – usually at least a mild, a porter or stout, a pale and a best bitter are listed on a board behind the bar.
☎◑▯⊖♣●▯(210,271)🐾📶

N7: Holloway

Coronet Ⓛ ✓
338-346 Holloway Road, N7 6NJ
🌞 8am-midnight ☎ (020) 7609 5014
Fuller's London Pride; Greene King Abbot; 6 changing beers (sourced nationally) Ⓗ
Impressive Wetherspoon conversion of a cinema, the Savoy, designed by William Glen, that showed its last film in 1983 and now displays large prints of movie stars and former local entertainers, with an old projector the centrepiece of a raised dais towards the rear. Sometimes there are single brewery festivals. Expect plastic glasses and higher prices when Arsenal are playing at home. Tables (some under cover) are on the pavement and at the rear. Q☎☀◑▯🚴⊖(Holloway Rd)●🚆📶

N9: Lower Edmonton

Beehive ✓
24 Little Bury Street, N9 9JZ
🌞 12-11.30 (1am Fri & Sat); 12-11 Sun ☎ (020) 8360 4358
⊕ thebeehivebhp.co.uk
Draught Bass; Greene King Abbot; 2 changing beers (often Enfield, New River, Purity) Ⓗ
Rebuilt in 1929, this pub has been refurbished and retains its friendly community feel. Tucked away in semi-detached suburbia, it has a through bar offering pool and darts at one end and a dining area at the other, and is popular with a good mix of

local customers. Quiz night is Tuesday and live music plays most Saturday evenings. Fresh daily specials as well as good pub grub are served lunch and evening, and now Saturday breakfasts from 9am. ⛄😇🍺♣🅿🚆(329,W8)❀ 📶

N10: Muswell Hill

John Baird
122 Fortis Green Road, N10 3HN
🕐 11-11 (midnight Fri & Sat); 12-10.30 Sun
☎ (020) 8444 8830 🌐 thejohnbaird.co.uk
Sharp's Atlantic; 4 changing beers (sourced nationally) Ⓗ
A local mecca for real ale and cider fans, sporting up to six ales and a couple of ciders. One wing of this large pub is home to an excellent Thai restaurant and the other provides ample space for drinkers and those wanting to watch major sporting events in comfort. A sizeable outside smoking and drinking area is provided at the rear. Quiz night is Thursday. Children are allowed in the bar until 7pm and in the restaurant until 9pm.
⛄😇🍺♿🚆📶

Mossy Well
258 Muswell Hill Broadway, N10 3SH
🕐 8am-1am (11.30 Mon; midnight Tue & Wed)
☎ (020) 8444 2914
Fuller's London Pride; Greene King IPA, Abbot; Sharp's Doom Bar; 8 changing beers (sourced nationally) Ⓗ
A former Express Dairies tearoom and milk depot but a pub since 1984, reopened by Wetherspoon in October 2015, its name derived from the etymology of Muswell. Many internal features reflect its milky history. It is spacious inside, with a mezzanine floor and outdoor drinking areas at both front and back (closing at 9pm). Despite the size, it can be packed. Four house beers are sold plus up to eight guests and one Westons cider, served from the fridge. Q⛄😇🍺♿🚆📶

N12: North Finchley

Bohemia 🅛
762-764 High Road, N12 9QH
🕐 12-11 (midnight Thu; 1am Fri & Sat); 12-10.30 Sun
☎ (020) 8446 0294 🌐 thebohemia.co.uk
London Brewing Company Beer Street, Skyline; 3 changing beers (sourced locally; often London Brewing Company) Ⓗ
Popular brewpub near Tally Ho, hosting varied community events including salsa classes, quiz nights and Friday and Saturday boogie nights. Its own London Brewing Company real ales are brewed on site; take-home growlers are available. With strong emphasis on its own draught beers, it offers a wide range, draught and bottled, as well as real cider. An interesting food menu with a contemporary twist includes sharing platters. Comfortable lounge chairs at the front complement the relaxed atmosphere.
⛄😇🍺♿⊖(Woodside Park)♣🚆(125,263)❀ 📶

Elephant Inn
283 Ballards Lane, N12 8NR
🕐 11-11 (midnight Fri & Sat); 12-10.30 Sun
☎ (020) 8343 6110
Fuller's London Pride, ESB; 1 changing beer (sourced locally; often Fuller's) Ⓗ

Popular corner pub with fine wood panelling. The guest beer is normally a Fuller's seasonal. There are three distinct drinking areas in a U-shape: screens to the right show live sport; the left bar is TV-free for a more relaxed feel; the middle bar has raised tables and stools and the daily papers. Thai food from the restaurant upstairs can be eaten in the pub. At the front is a large patio with wooden seating and huge umbrellas.
⛄😇🍺♿⊖(West Finchley)♣🚆📶

N13: Palmers Green

Alfred Herring
316-322 Green Lanes, N13 5TT ☎ (020) 3232 1083
🕐 8am-11 (midnight Thu-Sat)
Greene King Abbot; Ruddles Best Bitter; Sharp's Doom Bar; 7 changing beers (sourced nationally; often Adnams, Redemption, Sambrook's) Ⓗ
A busy Wetherspoon shop conversion opened in 2006 in the heart of the Green Lanes shops, comprising a large open drinking and dining area with side booths. Seven of the 10 handpumps offer a varying range, with the manager regularly obtaining beers from a wide list of London breweries. There is a resident darts team. The pub is named after a local First World War soldier who was awarded the Victoria Cross for his heroic action in France in 1918. ⛄🍺⇄♣🚆📶

N14: Southgate

New Crown
80-84 Chase Side, N14 5PH
🕐 8am-11.30 (12.30am Fri & Sat) ☎ (020) 8882 8758
Greene King IPA, Abbot; Sharp's Doom Bar; 5 changing beers (sourced nationally; often Jennings, Portobello, Redemption) Ⓗ
There was an Old Crown on Chase Side until its demolition in the 1960s, hence the name. It is now one of the older Wetherspoon pubs and is close to the Underground and bus stations. Pictures of Southgate from days gone by hang on the walls of the open-plan bar, which offers a superb range of five guest real ales, two of which are from London breweries. Breakfast is served from 8am; you can enjoy a beer from 9am. Q⛄😇🍺♿⊖♣🚆📶

N16: Dalston Kingsland

Railway Tavern Ale House 🅛
2 St Jude Street, N16 8JT
🕐 4-11 (midnight Fri); 12-midnight Sat; 12-10.30 Sun
☎ (020) 3092 3344
Adnams Southwold Bitter; Five Points Railway Porter; Redemption Pale Ale; 3 changing beers (sourced nationally) Ⓗ
A gem of a pub well worth visiting, a stone's throw from bustling Dalston. It has six varied and interesting cask ales to suit all tastes, including one from Adnams and a local beer, plus exceptional bottled beers such as Kernel. A tasty Thai food menu and Sunday roasts complete the offering. It is full of quirky character, friendly, and a perfect venue to relax away from the sports crowd with good beer and good company.
⛄🍺♿⊖(Dalston Jct/Kingsland)♣🚆❀📶

N16: Stoke Newington

Jolly Butchers 🅛
204 Stoke Newington High Street, N16 7HU

✪ 4-midnight (1am Fri); 12-1am Sat; 12-11 Sun
☎ (020) 7249 9471 ⊕ jollybutchers.co.uk
6 changing beers (sourced nationally) Ⓗ
A classic Art Deco-style bar boasting elaborate ironwork and glass, with a lively modern feel and the enviable status of being a true free house. Nine handpumps offer six different real ales, usually from microbreweries, and three ciders or perries. The beers are always changing but the website provides up-to-date pouring information. The beer is complemented by great food, served lunchtimes and evenings weekdays and evenings at weekends. ⊛⊕➌❸➍➎❀☞

N17: Tottenham

Antwerp Arms Ⓛ
168-170 Church Road, N17 8AS (bus stop is Tottenham Sports Centre)
✪ 3 (12 Fri)-11; 11-midnight Sat; 11-10.30 Sun
☎ (020) 8216 9289 ⊕ antwerparms.co.uk
Redemption Pale Ale, Hopspur; 2 changing beers (sourced locally) Ⓗ
Tucked away in the historic and atmospheric Bruce Castle Park area, this is Tottenham's longest-established working pub. Serving local people since 1822, this Georgian building with beer garden faced demolition in 2013. It was saved from developers by the local community and CAMRA campaigners, and is now a community collective-owned pub and, in effect, a permanent outlet for Redemption Brewery beers. Pub food is available at weekends.
➽⊛⊕➌(White Hart Lane)♣P➍❀☞

Beehive Ⓛ
Stoneleigh Road, N17 9BQ
✪ 4-11 (1am Fri); 12-1am Sat; 12-11 Sun
☎ (020) 8808 3567 ⊕ beehiven17.com
Redemption Trinity; Sambrook's Junction Ale; Truman's Swift; 4 changing beers (sourced regionally) Ⓗ
Facing the public car park off the High Road, this fine Brewers' Tudor pub (1927) has a regionally important historic interior. It offers two bars, a games room with sports TV and a big garden with children's play equipment. Many of the changing cask and other beers come from London brewers, such as local Beavertown. Food includes Sunday lunches and summer barbecues. Live music and DJs feature at weekends, and Wednesday is quiz night.
➽⊛⊕➌❸➌(Bruce Grove)♣●➍❀☞

N19: Upper Holloway

Shaftesbury Tavern Ⓛ
534 Hornsey Road, N19 3QN
✪ 12-11 (12.30am Fri & Sat); 12-10.30 Sun
☎ (020) 7272 7950
4 changing beers (sourced nationally; often Fuller's, Hammerton) Ⓗ
A nice old pub, now comprehensively restored, with the former pool room turned into a restaurant area under a fine skylight. There is a beer garden, and outside seating at the front. Operated by Remarkable Restaurants, following a 2014 refurbishment, it initially sold beers from the Dragonfly Brewery at its pub at Acton. The range is more varied now. There is a Tuesday quiz.
➽⊛⊕➌❸➌(Crouch Hill)●➍❀☞

N21: Winchmore Hill

Dog & Duck ✔
74 Hoppers Road, N21 3LH
✪ 12-11.30 (12.30am Fri & Sat) ☎ (020) 8886 1987
Greene King IPA; Timothy Taylor Landlord; Young's Bitter; 1 changing beer (sourced nationally; often Adnams) Ⓗ
Friendly one-bar pub, popular with locals and welcoming to visitors. The guest ale is either a sport-related named beer, a seasonal ale or Adnams Ghost Ship. A large-screen TV shows sporting events. Local football teams meet here, and it hosts a golf society. Quiz night is Monday, when you can partake of a takeaway pizza. There is a pretty patio-style walled garden at the rear. This pub has been in the Guide for 14 consecutive years, 27 in total. ⊛♣➍(W9)❀☞

Orange Tree
18 Highfield Road, N21 3HA
✪ 12-midnight ☎ (020) 8360 4853
⊕ the-orange-tree-pub.co.uk
Greene King IPA; Morland Old Speckled Hen; house beer (by Hook Norton); 2 changing beers (sourced nationally; often New River, Redemption) Ⓗ
Step back in time into this back-street local just yards from the New River walk. Toby jugs, decorated plates and sporting posters adorn the walls and shelves. There is a pool table, dartboard and TVs showing news or live sport. Enjoy a summer barbecue or a hearty Sunday lunch. Add all of this to the well-kept ales and you will understand how the landlord has kept this pub in the Guide since 1995. ➽⊛⊕➌⇌♣P➍(329)☞

Enfield

Wonder Ⓛ
1 Batley Road, EN2 0JG
✪ 11-11 (midnight Fri & Sat); 12-11 Sun ☎ (020) 8363 0202
McMullen AK; 3 changing beers (sourced locally) Ⓗ
Traditional two-bar back-street local; a rare survivor for the area and registered as an Asset of Community Value since 2016. The public bar features a real fire, dartboard and piano while the lounge area is small and cosy. Football-free and with a focus on live music, you can enjoy honky tonk on Saturday evenings and Sunday afternoons and jam sessions on the last Wednesday of each month. Note that a cask breather may be used on beers other than AK.
Q➽⊛⊕➍⇌(Gordon Hill)♣P➍(191,W8)☞

High Barnet

Lord Nelson
14 West End Lane, EN5 2SA
✪ 12-11 (midnight Fri & Sat); 12-10.30 Sun
☎ (020) 8449 7249
Young's Bitter, Special; 1 changing beer (sourced regionally; often Young's) Ⓗ
A homely community pub on the fringe of High Barnet, just off Wood Street and close to the hospital. It has a lovely sunshine-style stained-glass front window. The bar is full of character, with maritime artefacts that befit its name, as well as a vast collection of cruet sets, some still used to complement home-cooked food. Autographs of Richard Burton and Elizabeth Taylor are preserved on a wall. Cribbage, dominoes and scrabble are played; the TV is used sparingly. ⊛⊕♣➍❀☞

Olde Mitre Inne ♈ ✅
58 High Street, EN5 5SJ
🕐 12-midnight (1am Fri & Sat) ☎ (020) 8449 5701
Adnams Southwold Bitter; Caledonian Deuchars IPA; Greene King Abbot; Timothy Taylor Landlord; 4 changing beers (sourced nationally; often Five Points, Redemption, Vale) Ⓗ
Popular 17th-century multi-roomed former coaching inn close to Barnet church, oozing character and charm, enhanced by recent, sensitive and barely perceptible internal alteration. Always busy, it offers efficient service from well-trained staff. Family-friendly – customers are requested to refrain from bad language – it has a large courtyard, which is heated and covered in winter months. There is live music every Sunday evening. Local CAMRA Pub of the Year 2017 and several times previously. ⥾❀⦿❸♣🍴🚌🐾�%🐾🛜

New Barnet

Railway Bell ✅
13 East Barnet Road, EN4 8RR
🕐 8am-midnight (12.30am Fri & Sat) ☎ (020) 8449 1369
Courage Directors; Greene King Abbot; Ruddles Best Bitter; Sharp's Doom Bar; 6 changing beers (sourced nationally; often Adnams, Sambrook's, Truman's) Ⓗ
Unlike many other Wetherspoon pubs, this one has been a pub since the early 1900s, soon after the railway came to Barnet. It now has a large conservatory with open kitchen; it may remind you of your school refectory, but do not let that put you off. The guest beers often include ales from London breweries selected by the keen manager. The large patio to the side and back of the pub helpfully provides a no-smoking area. ⥾❀⦿❸👍🌂🚆🚌🛜

Ponders End

Picture Palace Ⓛ ✅
Howard Hall, Lincoln Road, EN3 4AQ
🕐 9am-11 (midnight Fri & Sat) ☎ (020) 8344 9690
Caledonian Deuchars IPA; Greene King Abbot; Sharp's Doom Bar; 4 changing beers (sourced nationally; often New River, Redemption, Twickenham) Ⓗ
Retaining the management team from its previous owners, this pub maintains its enthusiasm for real ale, with London and nearby New River choices available most of the time. Some architectural features from the original 1913 cinema are preserved as well as fabulous murals of 1920s stars high above in the spacious main hall. Two smaller areas to the front and the side are quieter. There is also an outside patio. Good-value food is served throughout the day. ⥾❀⦿❸👍⦿(Southbury)P🚌🛜

NORTH-WEST LONDON
NW1: Camden Town

Constitution Ⓛ
42 St Pancras Way, NW1 0QT
🕐 11-11 (midnight Fri & Sat); 12-10.30 Sun
☎ (020) 7380 0767 🌐 conincamden.com
Dark Star Hophead; Sambrook's Junction Ale; 2 changing beers (sourced locally) Ⓗ
Founded in 1858, this dog and family friendly community pub is a welcome haven within bustling Camden and its vibrant market area. Its award-winning terraced patio garden (four times Camden in Bloom finalist) has a pleasant south-facing outlook over the Regent's Canal. The

downstairs cellar bar is host to live music and comedy events. Pool and darts are available and it has a large-screen TV. Weather permitting, there is occasional home-made street food outside. ⥾❀⦿👍⦿(Camden Rd/Town)♣🚌🐾

Prince Albert Ⓛ ✅
163 Royal College Street, NW1 0SG
🕐 12-11; 12-10.30 Sun ☎ (020) 7485 0270
🌐 princealbertcamden.com
4 changing beers (sourced nationally) Ⓗ
Following sensitive, tasteful refurbishment of a traditional Charrington tavern (1843), this comfortable, welcoming and charming pub retains many original period features including the horseshoe bar, wood panelling, leaded windows, stunning outdoor tiling and a pleasant garden. The first-floor restaurant area, or the whole pub, can be booked for private functions – check in advance if visiting on a Saturday. The pub hosts a quiz night on Tuesday and live acoustic music on Sunday, as well as twice-yearly beer festivals. Happy hour is Monday to Friday 3-6pm.
Q⥾❀⦿👍⦿(Camden Rd/Town)🍴🚌🐾🛜

Tapping the Admiral Ⓛ
77 Castle Road, NW1 8SU
🕐 12-11 (midnight Wed-Sat) ☎ (020) 7267 6118
🌐 tappingtheadmiral.co.uk
8 changing beers (sourced regionally) Ⓗ
Local CAMRA Pub of the Year in 2015, this is a popular and enjoyable community pub where friendly and knowledgable staff offer a warm welcome. Eight handpumps deliver guest ales, mainly local. The menu is great British food, including speciality home-made pies. A heated and covered beer garden is well designed and a nice feature. There is a popular Wednesday quiz and live traditional music on Thursday evening. Look out for monthly tap takeovers and pop-up events.
Q⥾❀⦿❸⦿(Kentish Town West)🍴🚌🐾🛜

NW1: Euston

Bree Louise Ⓛ ✅
69 Cobourg Street, NW1 2HH
🕐 11-11; 12-10.30 Sun ☎ (020) 7681 4930
🌐 breelouise.pub
Titanic Plum Porter Ⓗ**; 20 changing beers (sourced nationally; often Windsor & Eton)** Ⓗ/Ⓖ
One-bar corner pub, busy with locals and Euston commuters. A cooled gravity stillage of up to 11 beers, complemented by 10 handpumps, offers a wide range from London and across the UK, alongside up to 11 ciders and perries. Regular tap takeovers are held. There is no music, just conversation, with occasional TV sport (especially rugby, no football). Outdoor seating is on the pavement. Pies are a speciality of the house. Local CAMRA Pub of the Year 2016. The pub's owners were given notice to quit on 20 November 2017 as the area will be demolished to make way for HS2 but there could be appeals.
❀⦿⇌⦿(Euston/Euston Sq)🍴🚌🐾🛜

Doric Arch Ⓛ
Euston Station Colonnade, 1 Eversholt Street, NW1 2DN
🕐 11-11; 11-10.30 Sun ☎ (020) 7383 3359
Fuller's Oliver's Island, London Pride, ESB; 6 changing beers (sourced nationally) Ⓗ
Up a flight of stairs, the pub's large picture windows in a raised area afford a view of the busy

urban world below. Right next to Euston Station, it is used extensively by commuters, aided by the train times screen. The excellent staff are helpful and informative about the ales, including guest beers from London and all across the UK. Brewery and railway memorabilia adorn the walls, and food is served all day. Toilets are at basement level. ☺◑⇄⊖(Euston/Euston Sq)●🚌🏠📶

Euston Tap
East & West Lodges, 190 Euston Road, NW1 2EF
✪ 12-11.30 (10.30 Mon); 11.30-11.30 Sat; 12-10 Sun
☎ (020) 3137 8837 ⊕ eustontap.com
16 changing beers (sourced nationally) ⊞
Fronting the main station building, these impressive Grade II-listed Portland stone lodges, separated by a bus lane, are relics from the original 1830s station. Up to eight changing beers in each lodge, mostly from smaller breweries, are pumped up to taps behind the bar. Small ground floor spaces are augmented by a large outside heated drinking area as well as seating (and toilets) up the wrought-iron spiral staircases. The East Lodge has banquette seating on the ground level.
Q❀⇄⊖(Euston/Euston Sq)🚌🐾📶

Royal George ⅃ ✔
8-14 Eversholt Street, NW1 1DG
✪ 11-midnight (1am Fri); 10-1am Sat; 12.30-11.30 Sun
☎ (020) 7387 2431
Greene King IPA, London Glory; Taylor Walker 1730; 3 changing beers (sourced locally) ⊞
Large pub built in 1939, Grade II listed, arranged as interconnecting areas facing the three street frontages with a central bar. One side has an unusual fireplace with marquetry work on the surrounds. Right opposite Euston Station, it is named after HMS Royal George, a flagship vessel for the Royal Navy in the 1800s. Local London beers are augmented by regional guests or Greene King seasonal beers. ❀◑⇄⊖🚌📶

NW4: Hendon

Midland Hotel
29 Station Road, NW4 4PN
✪ 12-11 (1am Sat) ☎ (020) 3602 1320
Dark Star Hophead; 2 changing beers (sourced nationally; often Box Steam, Greene King, Portobello) ⊞
A welcome real ale addition to the area, the pub is owned by a finance company and the landlord is free from any tie, hence the varied beers on offer. Hophead has become a firm favourite and there are always two real ales on (three at weekends), mainly from London breweries. A national beer is sometimes offered. There are many seating areas, including a large garden with decking and a covered space. Classic cars are regularly displayed.
☺❀⇄♣P🚌(83,183)📶

NW5: Kentish Town

Grafton ⅃ ✔
20 Prince of Wales Road, NW5 3LG
✪ 12-11 (midnight Fri & Sat); 12-10.30 Sun
☎ (020) 7482 4466 ⊕ thegraftonnw5.co.uk
Purity Mad Goose; Sambrook's Wandle Ale; Timothy Taylor Landlord; 4 changing beers (sourced locally) ⊞
Popular pub with beautiful Victorian features, combining a traditional feel with many contemporary touches and specialising in local cask

beers. The spacious ground-floor horseshoe bar is partly tiled, with ample seating. Upstairs is a bar/function room (no real ale). It has an elegant, covered roof garden (closes 11pm). Knowledgable and friendly bar staff will serve you. Quiz night is Tuesday and there are occasional open mic evenings, as well as a piano and board games.
☺❀◑⇄⊖(Kentish Town West)●🚌🐾📶

Junction Tavern ⅃
101 Fortess Road, NW5 1AG
✪ 5-11; 12-midnight Fri & Sat; 12-11 Sun ☎ (020) 7485 9400
⊕ junctiontavern.co.uk
Adnams Broadside; Sambrook's Junction Ale; Sharp's Doom Bar; 2 changing beers (sourced regionally) ⊞
Popular real ale and gastro-pub, with the restaurant on the main road and the pub to the rear, boasting two connected drinking areas, conservatory and award-winning beer garden. The ornate interior has wood panelling and large mirrors. It has a quality food menu (book ahead for the dining area). Guest beers alternate between other Sambrook's and wider regional offerings. There is a seated and covered outside smoking area. Families and dogs are welcome.
Q☺❀◑⇄⊖(Kentish Town/Tufnell Park)🚌🐾📶

Lion & Unicorn ⅃
42 Gaisford Street, NW5 2ED
✪ 12-midnight; 10-11 Sat; 12-10.30 Sun ☎ (020) 7267 2304
Sharp's Cornish Coaster; Young's Bitter; 3 changing beers (sourced regionally) ⊞
This popular community venue is a great favourite, with its genuine homely feel, open fire and comfortable seating. Run by friendly management and staff as a Geronimo-branded gastro-pub, it offers a good-quality cask ale range featuring several local breweries. It has won local and regional awards for both front and back gardens. There are quizzes on Sunday. Above is the Lion and Unicorn Theatre; details of productions are available on the theatre's website (lionandunicorntheatre.co.uk).
Q☺❀◑⅃⇄⊖🐾📶

Pineapple ⅃
51 Leverton Street, NW5 2NX
✪ 12-11 (midnight Fri & Sat); 12-10.30 Sun
☎ (020) 7284 4631
Sharp's Doom Bar; 4 changing beers (sourced nationally) ⊞
An authentic and friendly community pub, saved from closure by the locals, Grade II listed and with a regionally important historic interior, notable for its mirrors and splendid bar-back. The front bar, with comfortable seating around tables, leads through to an informal conservatory overlooking the patio garden. The food menu is Thai kitchen cuisine. Local beers can come from across London and, the pub being free of tie, the range changes regularly. Q☺❀◑⇄⊖🐾📶

Southampton Arms
139 Highgate Road, NW5 1LE
✪ 12-11 (midnight Fri & Sat); 12-10.30 Sun
⊕ thesouthamptonarms.co.uk
10 changing beers (sourced nationally) ⊞
This pub does what it says on the sign outside: Ale, Cider, Meat. The multiple CAMRA award-winning venue has 18 handpumps on and behind the bar serving almost equal amounts of cider and different beers from microbreweries across the UK.

Snacks include pork pies, roast pork in baps, cheese and meat baps plus veggie options. Music is played on vinyl only and the piano is in regular use. At the back there is a secluded patio.
🏵🅓≖⊖(Gospel Oak/Kentish Town)●🚃🚇

NW9: Kingsbury

JJ Moon's Ⓛ ✔
551-553 Kingsbury Road, NW9 9EL
🏵 8am-midnight ☎ (020) 8204 9675
Adnams Broadside; Greene King Abbot; Sharp's Doom Bar; Theakston Old Peculier; 4 changing beers (sourced nationally) Ⓗ
Early (1988) Wetherspoon shop conversion, with silent TV screens and admitting children until 9pm. A large, one-room establishment with low ceilings, lots of wood panelling, subdued lighting and a raised section at the rear, here is a rare outlet for real ale in this part of outer London. The name plays on the George Orwell Moon Under Water theme of some of the company's earliest pubs.
Q🦽🛏🅓♿⊖🚇📶

Harrow

Castle ♈ ★
30 West Street, HA1 3EF
🏵 12-11 (midnight Fri & Sat); 10-11 Sun ☎ (020) 8422 3155
Fuller's London Pride, ESB; Gale's Seafarers Ale, HSB; 1 changing beer (often Butcombe, Fuller's) Ⓗ
A lively and friendly Fuller's house, located in the heart of historic Harrow-on-the-Hill. Built in 1901 and Grade II listed, it has a nationally important historic interior. Food is served until 9.30pm (8pm Sun); reservations are recommended for Sunday lunchtime. Three real coal fires help to keep the pub warm and cosy in the colder months, and a secluded beer garden is popular during the summer. Local CAMRA Pub of the Year 2017.
Q🦽🛏🏵🅓♿♣🚇(258,H17)🐾📶

Ruislip Manor

JJ Moon's ♈ Ⓛ ✔
12 Victoria Road, HA4 0AA
🏵 8am-midnight (1am Fri & Sat) ☎ (01895) 622373
Courage Directors; Fuller's London Pride; Greene King Abbot; Ruddles Best Bitter; Sharp's Doom Bar; 7 changing beers Ⓗ
A large Wetherspoon conversion conveniently located opposite the tube station. It is popular and often busy in the evening and at weekends. Food and beer alike are of good value, with the usual promotions. At the rear there is an elevated section for dining, leading to a small garden patio, while the front has a partitioned-off smoking area on the street. Local CAMRA Pub of the Year 2017.
Q🦽🛏🏵🅓♿⊖●🚇📶

South Kenton

Windermere ★ ✔
Windermere Avenue, HA9 8QT
🏵 12-11; 2-12.30am Thu & Fri; 11-12.30am Sat; 11-11.30 Sun
☎ (020) 3632 0020 ⊕ windermerepub.com
Courage Best Bitter; 1 changing beer (sourced nationally; often Fuller's, Young's) Ⓗ
Built in 1939 and next to South Kenton station, the Windermere has a nationally important historic interior. It is a genuine community pub with three bars, although the public one is now used only for

functions. The saloon and lounge retain many original features, including the large inner porches, bar counters, back fittings, wall panelling and fireplaces. A quiz is held on alternate Thursdays, and there is sometimes live entertainment.
🦽🏵♿⊖♣P🚇(223)📶

SOUTH-EAST LONDON
SE1: Bermondsey

Simon the Tanner Ⓛ
231 Long Lane, SE1 4PR
🏵 12 (5 Mon)-11; 12-10.30 Sun ☎ (020) 7357 8740
⊕ simonthetanner.co.uk
4 changing beers (often Redemption, Siren, Southwark) Ⓗ
In a quiet road just off busy Bermondsey Street, the Simon is a mid-terrace, modestly sized, Grade II-listed pub. A former Shepherd Neame outlet, it is now a free house. The regularly changing real ales are often from London breweries, and there is real cider. Food is along the lines of Scotch eggs and cheese and meat platters. A quiz is held on Tuesday evening. Children are permitted until 7pm.
🦽🅓≖⊖(London Bridge)●🚇🐾📶

SE1: Borough

Lord Clyde
27 Clennam Street, SE1 1ER
🏵 11 (12 Sat)-11; 12-6 Sun ☎ (020) 7407 3397
⊕ lordclyde.com
Adnams Southwold Bitter; Hogs Back TEA; Sharp's Doom Bar; Young's Bitter; 1 changing beer (often Moorhouse's) Ⓗ
A gem of a street-corner pub that has changed little since being rebuilt in 1913. It has been identified by CAMRA as having a regionally important historic pub interior with its traditional decor, comfortable seating and curtains over the doors. The exterior retains its beautiful Truman's Brewery tilework. There is one main bar and also a side room with its own serving hatch. The pub has been run by the same family for over 50 years.
🅓≖(London Bridge)⊖🚇🐾

Royal Oak ✔
44 Tabard Street, SE1 4JU
🏵 11 (12 Sat)-11; 12-9 Sun ☎ (020) 7357 7173
Harvey's Sussex XX Mild Ale, IPA, Sussex Best Bitter; 3 changing beers (often Fuller's, Gale's, Harvey's) Ⓗ
A charming back-to-basics drinkers' pub separated into two sections by the bar counter and an off-sales hatch. This is Sussex-based Harvey's Brewery's first London tied house and is renowned for friendly and attentive service. The wide range of beers includes seasonal brews and, unusually for London, a mild, plus a changing guest Fuller's beer. The inventive and extensive food menu sources many ingredients from London markets. Regulars come from miles around to spend time here.
Q🅓≖(London Bridge)⊖♣●🚇

SE1: Borough Market

Market Porter
9 Stoney Street, SE1 9AA
🏵 11 (12 Sat)-11; 12-10.30 Sun ☎ (020) 7407 2495
Harvey's Sussex Best Bitter Ⓗ**; 10 changing beers (often Cottage, Jennings, Otley)** Ⓗ/Ⓐ
A classic, rustic market pub next to the famous Borough Market, also open for the traditional 6am-

8am weekday hours. It is a Guide regular with up to 10 changing real ales plus four ciders, usually including a Westons. Adorning the walls is a vast array of pumpclips reflecting the huge range of beers offered over the years. Popular with locals and visitors alike, it can get busy, with drinkers spilling out on to the street. An upstairs restaurant serves lunches. ◑≹⊖(London Bridge)●🖪🖭

Old King's Head
King's Head Yard, 45-49 Borough High Street, SE1 1NA
✪ 11-midnight (1am Fri & Sat); 12-midnight Sun ☎ (020) 7407 1550 ● theoldkingshead.uk.com
Harvey's IPA, Sussex Best Bitter; St Austell Tribute, Proper Job; Sharp's Doom Bar; 1 changing beer (often Otter) Ⓗ
A traditional pub down a narrow, cobbled lane off Borough High Street. Stained-glass windows hint at a bygone era and the pictures adorning the walls tell the story of a pub, and an area, that has a rich history. The layout inside is simple, with an L-shaped bar in one corner usually offering six real ales on handpump. The clientele is a mix of tourists, office workers and visitors to the nearby Borough Market. ◑&≹⊖(London Bridge)🖭🖪🛜

Rake
14 Winchester Walk, SE1 9AG
✪ 12 (11 Fri; 10 Sat)-11; 12-8 Sun ☎ (020) 7407 0557
4 changing beers (sourced nationally; often Binghams, Vocation) Ⓗ
On the edge of Borough Market, this small pub prides itself on offering a high-quality, varied beer selection, and over the years has become a global destination for beer aficionados and brewers. Four handpumps are complemented by a comprehensive range of bottled beers, mainly from North America and Europe, plus a small range of wines and spirits. It holds periodic brewery tap takeovers and other themed beer selections.
Q🕸&≹⊖(London Bridge)🖪🛜

SE1: Waterloo

King's Arms 🅛
25 Roupell Street, SE1 8TB
✪ 11-11; 12-10.30 Sun ☎ (020) 7207 0784
● thekingsarmslondon.co.uk
Adnams Southwold Bitter; house beer (by Sharp's); 7 changing beers (sourced nationally) Ⓗ
Tucked away on a back street, this pub is worth seeking out although it gets busy in the early evenings. The two small rooms are separated by a central bar and drinking is also allowed outside at the front. It has been identified by CAMRA as having a regionally important historic pub interior. Nine real ales usually include two or more from London breweries and at least one dark beer. To the rear is a Thai restaurant.
🖰◑≹(Waterloo/Waterloo East)⊖🖪🛜

Waterloo Tap
Arch 147, Sutton Walk, SE1 7ES
✪ 12 (11 Sat)-midnight; 11-10 Sun ☎ (020) 3455 7436
● waterlootap.com
6 changing beers (sourced nationally; often Hammerton, Siren)
This fairly compact, modern sister pub to the Euston Tap is in a railway arch close to Waterloo Station and a short stroll from the South Bank, making it handy for visitors to the BFI IMAX and Royal Festival Hall complex. There is an extensive selection of six

cask beers, all dispensed from taps mounted on the copper bar-back. Details of the beers available are listed on a blackboard above the bar.
🖰&≹⊖🖪🐾

SE3: Blackheath

Hare & Billet ✔
1A Eliot Cottages, Hare & Billet Road, SE3 0QJ
✪ 12 (11 Sat)-11; 11-10.30 Sun ☎ (020) 8852 2352
● hareandbillet.com
Greene King IPA; house beer (by Greene King); 6 changing beers (often Dark Star, Five Points, Sharp's) Ⓗ
An inn of this name has existed on the site since at least 1732, though the current building dates from the 19th century. The decor is faux-Victorian in a contemporary style with stripped natural finish wood cladding and bare floorboards. There are usually up to eight real ales on handpump, including one from Greene King, plus Biddenden Bushels cider. In the summer plastic glasses are available for outdoor drinking overlooking the open expanse of the heath.
🖰◑&≹♣🖭🖪(380)🐾🛜

SE4: Brockley

Brockley Barge
184 Brockley Road, SE4 2RR ☎ (020) 8694 7690
✪ 8am-midnight (1am Fri & Sat)
Greene King Abbot; Ruddles Best Bitter; Sharp's Doom Bar; 5 changing beers (sourced nationally; often Jennings) Ⓗ
This former Courage pub, reopened by Wetherspoon in 2000, has flourished since the nearby railway station became part of the London Overground network. Now surrounded by a variety of artisan food outlets, it is popular with a wide range of age groups, reflecting the diversity of the local population. Several TV screens show terrestrial coverage of sporting events. The courtyard garden can become busy during the summer months. Beer festivals and Meet the Brewer events are held regularly.
Q🖰🕸◑&≹⊖●🖪🛜

Talbot 🅛
2-4 Tyrwhitt Road, SE4 1QG
✪ 12-11 (midnight Fri & Sat); 12-10.30 Sun ☎ (020) 8692 2665 ● talbotpublichouse.com
Harvey's Sussex Best Bitter; 4 changing beers (often Brockley, Theakston, Weltons) Ⓗ
A fine Victorian suburban local on two floors, popular with all ages, families and dog owners. The pub has recently been tastefully redecorated inside and out, with large windows making the interior light and airy. A series of murals, highlighted with gilt, decorates the walls. An extensive, upmarket menu also caters for vegetarians and vegans, with daily specials and meal deals on Mondays. Regular live music, seasonal events and a weekly quiz take place.
Q🖰🕸◑&≹(St Johns)⊖(Elverson Rd)🖪🐾🛜

SE5: Camberwell

Stormbird
25 Camberwell Church Street, SE5 8TR
✪ 4-midnight; 12-midnight Sat & Sun ☎ (020) 7708 4460
● thestormbirdpub.co.uk

Dark Star American Pale Ale; 3 changing beers (often Dark Star, Magic Rock) Ⓗ
The sister pub to the Hermit's Cave across the road, offering a slightly more contemporary feel and attracting a mixed but generally younger crowd. There is a huge array of beers of all types on the bar, including four real ales on handpump and an extensive bottled beer selection. This range encompasses brews from the UK, continental Europe and the US. Draught beers are available in third-pint measures. ◑▶≉⊖(Denmark Hill)🚫 🛜

SE8: Deptford

Dog & Bell ⏸ ✅
116 Prince Street, SE8 3JD
🕐 12-11 (11.30 Fri-Sun) ☎ (020) 8692 5664
Fuller's London Pride; 3 changing beers (often Clarkshaws, Dent, Old Dairy) Ⓗ
Traditional and welcoming pub down a side street close to Deptford centre. A Guide stalwart, it offers six real ales plus a selection of Belgian bottled beers, malt whiskies and simple, tasty meals. A lively bar and a real fire in winter greet a good mixed clientele including locals, cyclists and those strolling along the nearby Thames Path. A quiz is held on Sunday evening. Long-serving licensees Charlie and Eileen retired in late 2016 – the pub is now tenanted. Q🏠◑≉♣🍴🚫🐾

Job Centre
120 Deptford High Street, SE8 4NS
🕐 4-11 (midnight Thu-Fri); 11-midnight Sat; 12-11 Sun
☎ (020) 8692 6859 🌐 jobcentredeptford.com
Volden Session Ale; 3 changing beers (often Brixton, Brockley, Thornbridge) Ⓗ
A welcome addition to the fairly sparse Deptford real ale pub scene, opened by Antic in 2014 and named after a former occupier. The spacious rectangular bar area has minimalist decor, including bare concrete flooring and exposed ducts and pipework. Music is often playing from a twin-deck turntable. The beer range has a regional focus, with a variety of styles and strengths. The cider on handpump is frequently Westons. Food is varied and includes light bites and burgers. ⬥🏠◑≉⊖(Deptford Bridge)🍴🚫🛜

SE9: Eltham

Long Pond 🍸
110 Westmount Road, SE9 1UT
🕐 5-10 Mon; 11.30-2.30, 5-10 (11 Thu & Fri); 11-3, 6.30-11 Sat; 12-2.30 Sun ☎ (020) 8331 6767
House beer (by Tonbridge); 5 changing beers (sourced regionally; often Mad Cat, Old Dairy, Pig & Porter) Ⓖ
Micropub, opened in 2014, in a former plumbers' merchants and named after the pond in nearby Eltham Park North. Six real ales, including Kentish, are served on gravity dispense from a rear chilled stillage room. In true micropub tradition, no lager or spirits are served but wine and Dudda's Tun real cider/perry are, plus bar snacks. Seating is mainly high benches and tables, though the rear snug features low tables and chairs. Local CAMRA Pub of the Year 2017. Q⬥≉🍴🚫(B16)

Park Tavern ✅
45 Passey Place, SE9 5DA
🕐 12-11 ☎ (020) 8850 3216 🌐 parktaverneltham.co.uk

8 changing beers (often Otter, Sambrook's, Shepherd Neame) Ⓗ
Traditional Victorian pub with original Truman's Brewery tiled frontage and signage. The compact interior has an L-shaped bar with stylish lamps and chandeliers. The etched windows have elegant drapes, and decorative plates and pictures line the walls. Light background music is played. There is a well-kept, heated rear garden and further seating to the front and side. In addition to the changing range of real ales, an impressive selection of whiskies and wines is available. Q🏠◑≉🚫🐾

SE10: East Greenwich

Pelton Arms ✅
23-25 Pelton Road, SE10 9PQ
🕐 12-midnight (1am Fri & Sat); 12-11 Sun
☎ (020) 8858 0572 🌐 peltonarms.com
Greene King IPA; St Austell Tribute; 6 changing beers (sourced regionally; often Hop Stuff, Truman's, Westerham) Ⓗ
A popular back-street pub just over half a mile from Greenwich town centre. The L-shaped bar is surrounded by an eclectic mix of furnishings. Soft lighting also contributes to a cosy and welcoming feel. Community-oriented and spacious, it offers a range of live music four nights a week and a quiz on Tuesday. The Pelton knitters get together on Wednesday. A changing cider on handpump is often from Herefordshire. Local CAMRA Pub of the Year 2016. ⏥🏠🏠◑♿≉(Maze Hill)♣🍴🚫🐾🛜

SE10: Greenwich

Plume of Feathers ✅
19 Park Vista, SE10 9LZ
🕐 12-11; 11-midnight Fri & Sat ☎ (020) 8858 1661
🌐 plumeoffeathers-greenwich.co.uk
Harvey's Sussex Best Bitter; Sharp's Doom Bar; 2 changing beers (sourced nationally) Ⓗ
With dates dating from 1691, this cosy and quiet historic pub is near the northern entrance to Greenwich Park, close to the National Maritime Museum. The maritime location is reflected inside the bar with much memorabilia on display and interesting historical paintings. As well as bar meals, there is a separate restaurant to the rear, and also a pleasant garden area. The pub has a football team, the Plume Rockets, and a golf society. ⏥🏠◑≉(Maze Hill)⊖(Cutty Sark)🚫🐾🛜

SE11: Kennington

Mansion House ✅
48 Kennington Park Road, SE11 4RS
🕐 12-midnight (1am Fri & Sat) ☎ (020) 7582 5599
🌐 oakalondon.com
Oakham JHB, Inferno, Citra, Bishops Farewell; 1 changing beer (often Gale's, Oakham) Ⓗ
Oakham Ales' only tied outlet in London, this former cocktail lounge and piano bar was refurbished in 2014. The contemporary design includes a stylish juxtaposition of materials and textures. During the summer, the glass frontage can be opened on to the outside seating area. One guest or seasonal Oakham beer complements the permanent range. Attentive staff also serve in the attached pan-Asian Oaka restaurant. Discounted cask beers are on the bar 5-7pm every evening. ⏥◑♿≉(Elephant & Castle)⊖🚫🐾🛜

SE13: Lee

Dacre Arms ✓
11 Kingswood Place, SE13 5BU
🕐 12-11; 12-10.30 Sun ☎ (020) 8852 6779
Greene King IPA; Harvey's Sussex Best Bitter; 4 changing beers (often Brains, Sharp's, Wells) Ⓗ
Family-owned end-of-terrace back-street local somewhat hidden in between Blackheath, Lee and Lewisham. The interior is split into three large double booths with a bar on the side. The decor includes the archetypal Courage high dark-wood panelling and leaded windows, all beautifully preserved, and numerous wall decorations and trinkets. A quiet garden drinking area is accessed from the bar by grand old wooden double doors.
🎇🎇≈(Blackheath)🚐🐾🛜

SE14: New Cross

Royal Albert ✓
460 New Cross Road, SE14 6TJ
🕐 4-midnight (1am Fri); 12-1am Sat; 12-midnight Sun
☎ (020) 8692 3737 🌐 royalalbertpub.com
Dark Star Hophead; Volden Session Ale; 5 changing beers (sourced regionally; often Five Points, Gipsy Hill, Gun) Ⓗ
Grade II-listed Victorian pub with the original etched glass and bar-back. It has a convivial atmosphere and offers up to seven real ales and one real cider on handpump. The cask ales change constantly but usually include one of Antic's Volden brews. Furnishings and decor are an eclectic mix, and the food is distinctive and enticing. There is a quiz on Monday evening, a DJ on Friday and live music on Sunday. 🎇🎇🎇≈🎇♣🎇🚐🐾🛜

SE15: Nunhead

Beer Shop London
40 Nunhead Green, SE15 3QF
🕐 4-11 (11.30 Fri); 12-11.30 Sat; 12-8 Sun
☎ (020) 7732 5555 🌐 thebeershoplondon.co.uk
3 changing beers (often Hop Stuff, Moor Beer, Weird Beard) Ⓖ
Former corner shop, haberdashery, and latterly a recording studio. The knowledgable staff serve a varied selection of three real ales direct from the cask, along with an extensive range of bottled beers, plus wine, spirits and soft drinks. Boxed cider, from various producers, is also sold, as are pub snacks. It hosts occasional events such as Meet the Brewer evenings. Note that January opening hours may vary. 🎇🎇≈🎇🚐(78,P12)🐾🛜

Ivy House
40 Stuart Road, SE15 3BE
🕐 12-11 (midnight Fri & Sat); 12-10.30 Sun
☎ (020) 7277 8233 🌐 ivyhousenunhead.com
Dark Star Hophead; Truman's Runner; 6 changing beers (sourced regionally; often Brockley, Buxton, Moor Beer) Ⓗ
Large 1930s former Truman's pub with the original wood-panelled interior. The building was saved in the nick of time from conversion to flats by being Grade II listed, and the pub is now community owned. There are three bars, the largest of which features a stage hosting regular live music, continuing the venue's proud history of live entertainment. Eight varying cask ales and one real cider are sold, with one ale, usually Truman's Runner, at a discounted price.
Q🎇🎇🎇♣🎇🚐(343,484)🐾🛜

SE15: Peckham

Beer Rebellion
129 Queens Road, SE15 2ND
🕐 12-11 (12.30am Fri & Sat) ☎ (020) 7732 7552
4 changing beers (sourced locally; often Gipsy Hill, Southwark) Ⓗ
Close to Queens Road Station, this bar is in the style of a micropub, situated in former shop premises. The concrete walls and floor give a post-industrial feel. Lamps fashioned from jars, along with high tables and stools, add to the utilitarian ambience. Details of the range of varying real ales and cider are listed on a large chalkboard. There is limited outdoor seating on the pavement at the front.
🎇🎇≈Ⓞ(Queens Rd)🎇🚐🛜

SE16: Rotherhithe

Mayflower
117 Rotherhithe Street, SE16 4NF
🕐 11-11; 12-9.30 Sun ☎ (020) 7237 4088
🌐 mayflowerpub.co.uk
Greene King Abbot; 4 changing beers (often Ossett, St Austell, York) Ⓗ
A themed pub celebrating the Mayflower and its historic journey to New England. The place is bustling and you feel as if you are aboard a ship of old; indeed, the walls are adorned with various nautical objects and documents. Tables and seating are close set and contribute to a communal atmosphere, although upstairs is a more luxuriant restaurant with an ambience of fine dining. At the rear is a fantastic wooden jetty above the Thames from where the Mayflower set sail.
Q🎇🎇Ⓞ🚐(381,C10)

SE18: Plumstead Common

Old Mill
1 Old Mill Road, SE18 1QG
🕐 12-11 (11.30 Fri; midnight Sat); 12-10.30 Sun
☎ (020) 3719 1499
6 changing beers (often Bexley, Goddards, Hop Stuff) Ⓗ
On the north side of Plumstead Common, this pub was formerly an 18th-century windmill, the Grade II-listed tower of which still remains. The single L-shaped bar is sparsely furnished, including a pool table to the rear, leaving ample space for the frequent live music acts. Real ales change often, with those from local and regional independent breweries predominating. Two changing real ciders are also usually available. Lunchtime and evening meals are served except on Wednesday.
🎇🎇🎇♣🎇🚐🛜

SE18: Shooters Hill

Bull
151 Shooters Hill, SE18 3HP
🕐 1-11; 12.30-11.30 Fri & Sat; 12-10.30 Sun
☎ (020) 8856 0691
5 changing beers (often Adnams, Castle Rock, Purity) Ⓗ
On the brow of a hill, this reputedly haunted Grade II-listed pub was rebuilt in 1881. It retains separate public and saloon bars with individual street entrance doors and a central circular bar counter serving both rooms. The saloon bar is well appointed, whereas the public bar has a more basic appearance. There is a pool table and occasional

live music events are held. The licensee makes good use of his landlord's beer range.
🏠🏤♣🐾☂️

SE18: Woolwich

Taproom Ⓛ
15 Major Draper Street, SE18 6GD
🕐 4-11 (midnight Fri); 12-midnight Sat; 12-10 Sun
☎ (020) 8316 4413 🌐 taproomse18.com
7 changing beers (often Bristol Beer Factory, Hop Stuff, Thornbridge) Ⓗ
Opened in 2015 as the first bar owned by the nearby Hop Stuff Brewery, this pub has a somewhat minimalist decor of bare wood and exposed brickwork. The bar area is furnished with stools and barrel tables, with a metal spiral staircase leading to an upper floor with conventional table seating. The varying real ale range usually includes two or three from Hop Stuff plus four from other local breweries. It also serves a good-quality, changing pizza menu.
🏠🏤🍴♿️�(Woolwich Arsenal)🚌🐾

SE19: Crystal Palace

Westow House Ⓥ
79 Westow Hill, SE19 1TX
🕐 12-midnight (2am Fri & Sat) ☎ (020) 8670 0654
🌐 westowhouse.com
Dark Star Hophead; 7 changing beers (sourced nationally; often Brick, Gipsy Hill, Volden) Ⓗ
Large Victorian corner pub on the edge of the Crystal Palace triangle, with the clientele reflecting the up-and-coming nature of the area. The Antic style of vintage shabby-chic provides a warm ambience and there is a spacious outdoor seating area. Up to eight real ales are complemented by changing ciders on handpump. It hosts regular live music, particularly on Thursdays, DJs on Fridays, and a quiz on Tuesday evenings.
🏠🏤🍴🚃🚇♣🐾☂️🛜

SE19: Gipsy Hill

Beer Rebellion
126 Gipsy Hill, SE19 1PL
🕐 12-11 ☎ (020) 8670 9034
6 changing beers (sourced regionally) Ⓟ
Conveniently located opposite the railway station. Despite having the feel of a micropub in a parade of shops, this pub packs in everything you would expect in a full-sized version. The small ground-floor bar is supplemented by additional seating in the basement. Do not be put off by the keg-style taps located in a Welsh dresser; the top row dispenses cask ales and ciders pumped up from a cellar under the pavement. 🍴🚃♣🚌(322)🛜

SE20: Penge

Moon & Stars Ⓛ Ⓥ
164-166 High Street, SE20 7QS
🕐 8am-11 ☎ (020) 8776 5680
Dark Star Hophead; Greene King Abbot; Kelham Island Pale Rider; changing beers (sourced nationally) Ⓗ
This popular high-street Wetherspoon pub has a large L-shaped bar with a raised seating area at the rear and many small alcoves suitable for small groups. There are 17 handpumps, offering a variety of beer styles, usually including some beers from

London microbreweries. The pub hosts regular mini festivals and other beer-related events.
🏠🏤🍴♿️🚃(Kent House)🚉(Beckenham Rd)🐾Ｐ🚌🛜

SE22: East Dulwich

East Dulwich Tavern Ⓥ
1 Lordship Lane, SE22 8EW
🕐 12-midnight (1am Fri & Sat) ☎ (020) 8693 1316
🌐 eastdulwichtavern.com
Adnams Lighthouse; Dark Star Hophead; Harvey's Sussex Best Bitter; Sharp's Doom Bar; 5 changing beers (often Franklins, Sambrook's, Volden) Ⓗ
A proper wedge of a pub in a prominent corner position and the home of the Antic pub company. The interior is classic boozer but contemporared and alive with customers. Previously a hotel, the upper storeys are now offices, although the first-floor masonic hall with its own bar opens occasionally for music and events, including a monthly film club. There is usually real cider during summer months, and good-quality food is on offer.
🏠🏤🍴♿️♣🐾🛜

SE23: Forest Hill

Blythe Hill Tavern
319 Stanstead Road, SE23 1JB
🕐 11-11 (midnight Thu-Sat); 12-11 Sun ☎ (020) 8690 5176
🌐 blythehilltavern.org.uk
Dark Star Hophead; Harvey's Sussex Best Bitter; Sharp's Doom Bar; 2 changing beers (often Dark Star) Ⓗ
Friendly Victorian local rooted in the community, identified by CAMRA as having a regionally important historic pub interior, with an interesting three-room layout and 1920s panelling. TV screens in two of the bars often show sport. The garden includes a children's play area and is abloom in summer. A quiz night is held on Monday from September to April, and traditional Irish music on Thursday. Local CAMRA Pub of the Year and Cider Pub of the Year 2015.
Ⓠ🏠🏤🚃(Catford/Catford Bridge)🐾🚌🛜

Sylvan Post Ⓥ
24-28 Dartmouth Road, SE23 3XU
🕐 4-11 (midnight Fri); 12-midnight Sat; 12-11 Sun
☎ (020) 8291 5712 🌐 sylvanpost.com
3 changing beers (often Brixton, Gipsy Hill, Volden) Ⓗ
Various types of ambient lighting add to the quirky feel of this Antic pub, set out like a utilitarian café. A former post office, it retains many original features. The two strongrooms have been converted into intimate booths and postal memorabilia decorate the walls. Brunch is a feature of the Saturday menu. A quiz is held on Tuesday evening and a DJ spins on Friday night. Most of the guest beers are from small London breweries. 🏠🍴♿️🚃🚇♣🐾🛜

SE24: Herne Hill

Commercial Ⓥ
210-212 Railton Road, SE24 0JT
🕐 12-midnight (1am Fri); 10-1am Sat; 11-midnight Sun
☎ (020) 7733 8783 🌐 thecommercialhotelhernehill.co.uk
Sharp's Doom Bar; 3 changing beers (sourced nationally; often Black Wolf, Brains) Ⓗ
An imposing, curved-fronted hostelry opposite the railway station, with a spacious wood-panelled

interior split into two rooms. The larger room containing the bar runs the full length of the pub, is furnished with a mix of low tables and comfy chairs and has a lighter, more airy section towards the rear. The smaller second room is laid out for dining but without feeling like a restaurant. There is outdoor seating at the front and in a small back yard. ▷🕷◑⌖👌♣🚃🐾🛜

SE25: South Norwood

Joiners Arms 🗸

52 Woodside Green, SE25 5EU

🍺 12-11 (midnight Fri & Sat) ☎ (020) 8656 8180

Fuller's London Pride; Purity Mad Goose; Sharp's Doom Bar ⊞

This traditional local has one bar divided into three drinking areas: a small snug at one end, a bar area and a sitting space at the other end. The interior is filled with brassware and other artefacts, giving a rural atmosphere which has remained largely unchanged since the present tenant, now Croydon's longest serving landlady, arrived in 1972. Several screens provide sports coverage, and popular karaoke evenings are regularly held. Sunday lunchtime roast is served.
🕷◑🚃(Blackhorse Lane)🚃(197)

Shelverdine Goathouse 🗸

7-9 High Street, SE25 6EP

🍺 4-11 (midnight Thu & Fri); 12-midnight Sat; 12-11 Sun

☎ (020) 8916 1001 ⊕ shelverdinegoathouse.com

Volden Session Ale, Pale Ale; 4 changing beers (sourced nationally) ⊞

A former Wetherspoon pub now run by Antic and demonstrating its customary shabby-chic style. The establishment's name pays homage to the history of the area. Large windows on to the street give a light and airy feel. The three sections of the large bar area have differing styles of wall decor, with features including clocks, kitchen equipment and pictures. The guest beers often include some from London breweries.
◑👌≉⊖(Norwood Junction)🚃🛜

Addiscombe

Claret & Ale

5 Bingham Corner, Lower Addiscombe Road, CR0 7AA

🍺 11.30-11 (11.30 Thu; midnight Fri & Sat); 12-11 Sun

☎ (020) 8656 7452

Palmers Best Bitter; 5 changing beers (sourced nationally) ⊞

Small, privately owned free house around the corner from the tram stop, with 30 years in this Guide and well over one million pints of Palmers Best Bitter sold. A community pub where conversation is king, it received a sympathetic makeover in 2016. Five changing beers, mainly from microbreweries, come from all over the UK. See the unique board opposite the bar for beers on and coming next. Cider is fetched from the cellar.
🚃🍴🚃🛜

Beckenham

Bricklayers Arms

237 High Street, BR3 1BN

🍺 12 (11 Thu-Sat)-11; 12-10.30 Sun ☎ (020) 8402 0007

⊕ bricklayersarms.co

St Austell Tribute, Proper Job; Young's Special; 1 changing beer (sourced nationally) ⊞

A traditional local high-street pub attracting a clientele of all ages. There is an open log fire in winter and a covered outdoor seating area with heaters and even a TV screen. The changing guest ales often reflect recommendations by customers. The pub holds occasional beer festivals and in 2016 was the local branch Community Pub of the Year.
▷🕷❋◑(Junction/Clock House)🚃(Junction)
♣🍴🚃🐾🛜

Bexleyheath

Furze Wren 🗸

6 Market Place, Broadway Square, DA6 7DY

🍺 8am-midnight ☎ (020) 8298 2590

Greene King Abbot; Ruddles Best Bitter; Sharp's Doom Bar; 7 changing beers (sourced nationally; often Shepherd Neame, Twickenham, Westerham) ⊞

Spacious Wetherspoon pub named after a local bird, perhaps better known as the Dartford Warbler. At the heart of the shopping area, with a full mix of clientele, plenty of seating and large windows, this makes a great place to eat, drink and people-watch. The toilets are on the same level, a rarity for this chain. Local history panels are displayed throughout the pub. Alcoholic drinks are served from 9am, including Westons and Gwynt y Ddraig Black Dragon ciders. Q▷◑👌🍴🚃🛜

Robin Hood & Little John ⓛ

78 Lion Road, DA6 8PF

🍺 11-3, 5.30 (7 Sat)-11; 12-4, 7-10.30 Sun

☎ (020) 8303 1128 ⊕ robinhoodbexleyheath.co.uk

Adnams Southwold Bitter, Broadside; Bexley BOB; Fuller's London Pride; Harvey's Sussex Best Bitter; Sharp's Doom Bar; 2 changing beers (sourced locally; often Shepherd Neame, Westerham) ⊞

A back-street local dating from the 1830s, when it was surrounded by fields. Eight real ales are on offer, mostly from independent breweries including the Bexley Brewery. It has a good reputation for its home-cooked food at lunchtimes (no food Sun), with Italian specials, which can be eaten at tables made from old Singer sewing machines. Frequent CAMRA branch Pub of the Year and regional winner three times. Over-21s only.
Q🕷◑🚃(B13)

Wrong 'Un ⓛ 🗸

234-236 Broadway, DA6 8AS

🍺 8am-midnight ☎ (020) 8298 0439

Greene King Abbot; Ruddles Best Bitter; Sharp's Doom Bar; 5 changing beers (sourced nationally) ⊞

Bexleyheath's first Wetherspoon pub, opened in 1994 in a single-storey former furniture store. There are records of cricket being played locally since 1746 and the unusual pub name is an alternative expression for a googly. Westons Old Rosie cider is stocked. There are comfortable booths to sit in as well as an open-plan area. Alcohol is served from 9am and food until 11pm daily. Q▷◑👌♣🍴🚃🛜

Blackfen

Broken Drum ⓛ

308 Westwood Lane, DA15 9PT

🍺 3-9.30; 12-9.30 Sat; 1-3.30 Sun ☎ 07803 131678

⊕ thebrokendrum.co.uk

3 changing beers (sourced nationally) ⑄

One of Bexley's growing list of micropubs, opened in April 2015 and named after an inn in a Terry

Pratchett novel. It sells real ale and cider on gravity from a stillage in a temperature-controlled room at the rear, viewable through its glazed door. Seating is provided by a settee in each of the bay windows and a variety of tables and chairs.
Q ☺ ♣ ♠ P 🖥 🚃 (51,132) ❀

George Staples ✓
273 Blackfen Road, DA15 8PR
🕐 12-11 (midnight Thu-Sat) ☎ (020) 8850 3181
Sharp's Doom Bar; 4 changing beers (often Adnams, Shepherd Neame) ⒣
Originally the Woodman, dating from 1845 and one of the first buildings in Blackfen, this pub was demolished and rebuilt in 1931 when large-scale construction began in the area. It was refurbished in 2007 and renamed after the original landlord. It is now a large, comfortable, single-roomed pub, with plenty of outside seating. There is a buy-six, get-one-free loyalty scheme.
☺ ❀ ◑ ᕲ ♠ P 🚃 (51,132) ❀ 🔊

Bromley

Partridge
194 High Street, BR1 1HE
🕐 11-11; 10-midnight Fri & Sat; 11-10.30 Sun
☎ (020) 8464 7656
Fuller's London Pride, ESB; Gale's HSB; 2 changing beers (often Adnams, York) ⒣
A former NatWest bank, now a Fuller's Ale and Pie house, retaining many original features including the high ceilings and chandeliers. There are two small snug rooms off the main bar. It offers an extensive, upmarket food menu including vegetarian choices. Located in the centre of Bromley, the pub is popular with shoppers, sports fans for football and rugby, and for live music on Saturday nights. ☺ ❀ ◑ ᕲ ≠ (North/South) 🚃

Red Lion ✓
10 North Road, BR1 3LG
🕐 11-11; 12-11 Sun ☎ (020) 8460 2691
Greene King IPA, Abbot; Harvey's Sussex Best Bitter; 2 changing beers (often Black Sheep, Jennings, Oakham) ⒣
In the quiet back streets just north of Bromley town centre, this traditional pub has featured regularly in the Guide for many years and is well worth seeking out. It retains many original features including tiling, and has an extensive library of books dominating one wall. A range of good-value meals is available. Q ❀ ◑ ≠ (North) ♣ 🚃

Shortlands Tavern
5 Station Road, BR2 0EY
🕐 12-11.30 (midnight Fri & Sat); 12-11 Sun
☎ (020) 8466 0202 ⊕ theshortlandstavern.com
St Austell Tribute; 5 changing beers (often Brentwood, Dorking, Plain) ⒣
This gem of a pub is part of the town but is far enough away from the main road to feel quite peaceful. You can be sure of a friendly and helpful welcome whether you are after the changing range of non-mainstream real ales, the food or one of the many activities including comedy nights, live music, a book club, a knitting group, painting classes and even bingo.
Q ☺ ❀ ◑ ≠ (Shortlands) ♣ 🚃 ❀ 🔊

Chislehurst

Imperial Arms ✓
Old Hill, BR7 5LZ
🕐 12-11 (11.30 Thu; midnight Fri & Sat); 12-10.30 Sun
☎ (020) 3605 7899 ⊕ imperialarms.co.uk
Fuller's London Pride; Harvey's Sussex Best Bitter; Marston's Pedigree ⒣
A cosy and inviting hillside pub with two bars. The Catherine Bar is named after the mistress of Napoleon III who stayed here when he was exiled to Chislehurst in 1870. The management are proud of their food – lobster and steaks being specialities – but also emphasised their continuing commitment to real ale with the addition of a fourth handpump in 2016, which sometimes serves guest beers. Q ☺ ❀ ◑ ▶ ≠ 🚃 (162,269) ❀ 🔊

Crayford

Penny Farthing ▽ ⒧
3 Waterside, DA1 4JJ
🕐 closed Mon; 12-3, 5-9.30; 12-10.30 Fri & Sat; 12-3 Sun ☎ 07772 866645 ⊕ pennyfarthingcrayford.co.uk
4 changing beers (sourced nationally) ⒢
The local CAMRA branch's second micropub, opened in September 2014, a haven of real ale near the banks of the River Cray, where ale and cider are dispensed direct from the cask in a cold room with a viewing window. A charity fine is levied should your mobile phone ring. Cider is usually from Dudda's, although Westons is also often sold. CAMRA branch Pub of the Year 2015.
Q ☺ ≠ ♣ ♠ 🖥 🚃 ❀

Croydon

Cronx
Units 3 & 4, Boxpark Croydon, 99 George Street, CR0 1LD
🕐 11-10.30; 11-10 Sun ☎ (01689) 809093 ⊕ thecronx.com
Cronx Standard, Kotchin; 2 changing beers (sourced locally) ⒣
A modern micropub-sized bar located in Croydon's Boxpark development beside East Croydon Station, accessed via Dingwall Road by the bus stop. Six handpumps serve a range of Cronx beers and two varying guests. The decor is simple but stylish, employing scaffolding and adapted beer casks and fonts. Plastic glasses may be used evenings and weekends. Food is available elsewhere in Boxpark itself. ᕲ ≠ ♠ (East) 🚃 🔊

Dog & Bull
24 Surrey Street, CR0 1RG
🕐 12-11 (11.30 Fri); 11-11 Sat; 12-10.30 Sun
☎ (020) 8667 9718 ⊕ dogandbullcroydon.co.uk
Young's Bitter, Special; 2 changing beers (sourced nationally) ⒣
Historic Grade II-listed pub in the middle of Croydon's daily street market, with origins going back to the 16th century. The interior has a classic layout – an island bar with two adjoining rooms. It has an unexpected and attractive walled garden at the rear with bedding plants and seasonal baskets. During the summer there are regular barbecues with beers served from a garden bar. An upstairs function room can be hired. Local CAMRA Pub of the Year 2016.
❀ ◑ ≠ (East/West) ♠ (George St/Reeves Corner) ⊖ (West) 🚃 🔊

George 🅛 ✅

17-21 George Street, CR0 1LA

♻ 8am-midnight (1am Fri & Sat) ☎ (020) 8649 9077

Greene King IPA, Abbot; Oakham JHB; Sharp's Doom Bar; Thornbridge Jaipur IPA; 9 changing beers (often Surrey Hills, Tillingbourne, Twickenham) Ⓗ

A converted shop, this Wetherspoon pub is named after a former coaching inn in Croydon. The 17 handpumps are fully utilised. The pub has two bars, the rear one being slightly raised (a ramp allows access), with its six handpumps often showcasing three beers each from two breweries such as Burning Sky, Dark Star, Oakham and Thornbridge. The front bar has a wider mix of beers, including the Wetherspoon national range. ⌂🍽❶⛔♿⇌(East/West)⛠(George St/Reeves Corner) ⊖(West)🍴⛟🛜

Green Dragon 🅛 ✅

58 High Street, CR0 1NA

♻ 11-11 (midnight Thu; 1am Fri & Sat); 12-10.30 Sun
☎ (020) 8667 0684

6 changing beers Ⓗ

A conversion from former bank premises opposite one end of Croydon's street market, this is a large bar with six handpumps serving a rotating selection of beers, some of which are brewed locally. Up to six draught ciders are also stocked. A function room upstairs hosts open mic evenings and other events and there are also occasional beer and cider festivals. The food includes a brunch menu and Sunday roasts. ⌂🍽❶⛔♿⇌(East/West)⛠(George St/Reeves Corner) ⊖(West)♣🍴⛟🛜

Oval Tavern ✅

131 Oval Road, CR0 6BR

♻ 12-11 (midnight Fri & Sat) ☎ (020) 8686 6023

Robinsons Trooper; 3 changing beers (often St Austell, Twickenham, Wychwood) Ⓗ

Back-street family-friendly pub with a good reputation for live music, including jam sessions, acoustic acts and the occasional DJ. Tasty home-made food is served; the huge Scotch eggs and sausage rolls are especially recommended. There is a large garden and barbecue area to the rear. The decor is unusual – half-timbering creates an interesting interior with a rural atmosphere. The pub continues to improve and promote its range of cask ale. ⌂🍽❶⛔⇌⛠(East)♣🍴⛟🐾🛜

Skylark ✅

34-36 South End, CR0 1DP

♻ 8am-midnight (1am Fri & Sat) ☎ (020) 8649 9909

Fuller's London Pride; Greene King Abbot; Ruddles Best Bitter; Sharp's Doom Bar; Shepherd Neame Spitfire; 7 changing beers Ⓗ

In the restaurant quarter to the south of the town centre, this Wetherspoon pub is named after one of the well known and widely appreciated poems of former local resident Gerard Manley Hopkins. Wood-panelled walls and bookshelves in a raised seating area give a relaxed atmosphere. The internal decoration focuses in part on the history of London's first airport, at Croydon. Changing ales often come from local breweries or micros. ⌂🍽❶⛔♿⇌(South)🍴⛟🛜

Spreadeagle

39-41 Katharine Street, CR0 1NX

♻ 11-11 (midnight Fri & Sat); 12-10.30 Sun
☎ (020) 8781 1134

Fuller's Oliver's Island, London Pride, ESB; Gale's HSB; 2 changing beers Ⓗ

Large street-corner pub built in 1893 as the Croydon branch of the United Bank of London. It is spacious inside, with wood panelling, high ceilings, glass mirrors and an imposing staircase leading to two function rooms upstairs, one regularly used as a 50-seater theatre/cinema. As well as ale from six handpumps, a range of Fuller's bottled beers and quality foreign bottled beers is on offer. The pub has Fuller's Master Cellarman accreditation. Quiz night is Sunday. ⌂🍽❶⛔♿⇌(East/West)⛠(George St/Reeves Corner) ⊖(West)⛟🛜

Downe

Queen's Head 🅛 ✅

25 High Street, BR6 7US TQ432616

♻ 12-11; 12-10.30 Sun ☎ (01689) 852145
⊕ queensheaddowne.com

Harvey's Sussex Best Bitter; 3 changing beers (sourced regionally; often Fuller's, Westerham) Ⓗ

Attractive pub dating from 1565, in the centre of an historic village but less than 20 minutes by bus from Bromley or Orpington. Charles Darwin, a regular patron, lived at Down House, less than a mile away. Traditional and comfortable, with open fireplaces and several dining areas, the pub is popular with walkers and locals all year round. ⌂🍽❶♣🍴⛟(146,R8)🐾🛜

Keston

Greyhound 🍷 ✅

Commonside, BR2 6BP TQ413646

♻ 11-11; 12-10.30 Sun ☎ (01689) 856338
⊕ greyhoundkeston.co.uk

Sharp's Doom Bar; Timothy Taylor Landlord; 4 changing beers (sourced nationally) Ⓗ

Local CAMRA Pub of the Year for 2017. A popular local with an enthusiastic and welcoming landlord, it overlooks the common and is on walking routes including the London Outer Orbital Path, but is also easily accessed by bus from Bromley. It is at the heart of village life, with a crowded calendar of local events, detailed in the newsletter. Regular beer festivals are held, especially during the Easter weekend, when up to 15 non-mainstream beers are available. Q⌂🍽❶♣🍴P⛟(146,246)🐾🛜

Orpington

Orpington Liberal Club 🅛

7 Station Road, BR6 0RZ

♻ 8 (6 Fri)-11; 12-3, 7-11 Sat; 12-3, 8-10.30 Sun
☎ (01689) 820882 ⊕ orpingtonliberalclub.co.uk

4 changing beers Ⓗ

Free-of-tie club that continues to serve an eclectic range of more than 200 different real ales per year, focusing on microbreweries, with twice-yearly beer festivals. A changing range of real ciders and perries is always on offer together with a small range of local bottled and gluten-free beers. Regular live folk/blues music nights are held in a separate room. The club has won many local and regional CAMRA awards. CAMRA or NULC membership card required for entry. Q⌂🍽❶♣🍴P🚻🐾🛜

Petts Wood

One Inn the Wood 🗓️
209 Petts Wood Road, BR5 1LA

🌀 closed Mon; 12-2.30, 5-9.30 (11 Fri); 11.30-11 Sat; 12-8 Sun ☎ 07799 535982 ⊕ oneinnthewood.co.uk

House beer (by Tonbridge); 4 changing beers (sourced regionally; often Kent, Old Dairy, Rockin' Robin) 🄶

Since opening in May 2014 in former wine bar premises, this Kent-themed micropub has won various CAMRA awards including Greater London CAMRA Pub of the Year in 2015. Seating is in bench form and a large woodland scene on the left-hand wall adds to a rustic feel. Beer is served on gravity from a glass-fronted cold room. A range of snacks is available, including local cheeses.

Q🛋️🕙🗝️♿🍴🚌🐾

Sovereign of the Seas 🗓️ ✅
109-111 Queensway, BR5 1DG

🌀 9am-11 (11.30 Fri & Sat) ☎ (01689) 891606

Greene King Abbot; Ruddles Best Bitter; Sharp's Doom Bar; 7 changing beers (sourced nationally; often Kent) 🄷

Converted from a supermarket, this Wetherspoon pub in the centre of Petts Wood serves a changing selection of beers from 12 handpumps. Local historic photographs adorn the walls, including images of Petts Wood during its construction in the 1930s. Above the bar is a model of the 17th-century Royal Navy vessel after which the pub is named. Seating is in various styles, including cosy alcoves. 🛋️🕙🕙♿🕿♿🍴🚌🐾

South Croydon

Crown & Sceptre
32 Junction Road, CR2 6RB

🌀 12-11 (10.30 Sun) ☎ (020) 8688 8037

Fuller's London Pride, ESB; 2 changing beers (sourced locally; often Fuller's, Gale's) 🄷

Quiet, traditional side-street pub, with its name etched into one of the front windows. The single bar has been extended towards a patio at the rear, and the walls carry pictures of local scenes and an impressive brewery mirror. The pub participates in local community events such as the summer street carnival, and a cabinet of trophies attests to the local golfing society's successes. Beers come from the Fuller's range. Home-cooked food is served (to 6pm at weekends). 🛋️🕙🕙♿🕿♣P🚌🐾♿

Welling

Door Hinge 🗓️
11 Welling High Street, DA16 1TR

🌀 closed Mon; 3-9 (10 Fri); 12-10 Sat; 12-3 Sun ☎ 07956 845509 ⊕ thedoorhinge.co.uk

3 changing beers (sourced nationally) 🄶

A welcome breath of fresh air on the local pub scene and handy for the football ground, London's first permanent micropub opened in 2013 in part of a former electrical wholesalers. Normally at least three beers are dispensed from within a glass-fronted cold room. The cosy bar encourages conversation among previous strangers. Cider comes from various sources. Q🕙🖱️🚌🐾

SOUTH-WEST LONDON
SW1: Belgravia

Antelope
22-24 Eaton Terrace, SW1W 8EZ

🌀 12-11 (11.30 Fri); 12-10 Sun ☎ (020) 7824 8512

Fuller's London Pride, ESB; Gale's Seafarers Ale; 2 changing beers (sourced nationally) 🄷

Dating back to 1827, this Fuller's venue spent several years as a Nicholson's pub until 2005. Original preserved features include etched-glass windows, a side room used as a snug, and the central bar. This is an upmarket house and the clientele consists mainly of local professionals. The pub plays cricket matches against the Churchill Arms (Notting Hill). The upstairs bar and side room can be hired for functions.

Q🛋️🕙🕙⊖(Sloane Sq)🚌🐾

Star Tavern 🍷 🗓️
6 Belgrave Mews West, SW1X 8HT

🌀 11 (12 Sat)-11; 12-10.30 Sun ☎ (020) 7235 3019

Fuller's London Pride, ESB; 2 changing beers (often Fuller's) 🄷

Down a mews, near embassies and rich in the history of the powerful and famous, it is rumoured that the Great Train Robbery was planned here. Now it is a popular Fuller's pub where local residents, business people and embassy staff rub shoulders with casual visitors. Sometimes a special Fuller's beer can be found. Upstairs is a dining room, also bookable for functions. The pub has featured in every edition of this Guide.

Q🛋️🕙🕙⊖(Hyde Park Corner/Knightsbridge)🚌🐾🚌🐾

SW1: Pimlico

Cask Pub & Kitchen
6 Charlwood Street, SW1V 2EE

🌀 12-11; 12-10.30 Sun ☎ (020) 7630 7225

⊕ caskpubandkitchen.com

Dark Star Hophead; 9 changing beers 🄷

Formerly the Pimlico Tram, it was converted to a beer destination by owners who have since acquired and modernised several more pubs in the South-east. Ten handpumps serve real ales from many microbreweries such as Arbor Ales and Dark Star, and a vast range of bottled beers from the UK and around the world complements some unusual draught choices. Burgers feature on the weekday menu, with Sunday roasts until late afternoon. Q🕙🕙🕿(Victoria)⊖

SW1: St James's

Red Lion ★ ✅
2 Duke of York Street, SW1Y 6JP

🌀 11.30-11; closed Sun ☎ (020) 7321 0782

Fuller's Oliver's Island, London Pride, ESB; Gale's Seafarers Ale; 2 changing beers (often Fuller's) 🄷

Close to the upmarket shops in Jermyn Street, this is a deservedly celebrated little gem, worth visiting for its nationally important historic pub interior and, in particular, its spectacular Victorian etched and cut mirrors and glass. The Grade II-listed building dates from 1821 and was given a new frontage in 1871. With little space inside, visitors often spill out on to the pavement. Beware of the precipitous steps down to the toilets! Food is served 11.30-4pm (5pm Sat).

Q🛋️🕙🕙⊖(Green Park/Piccadilly Circus)🚌🐾♿

SW1: Victoria

Cask & Glass ✓
39 Palace Street, SW1E 5HN
✪ 11-11; 12-8 Sat; closed Sun ☎ (020) 7834 7630
Shepherd Neame Master Brew, Spitfire; 1 changing beer Ⓗ
First licensed in 1862 as the Duke of Cambridge, this attractive, one-room pub on the route between Buckingham Palace and Westminster Cathedral, adorned with flowers in summer, is a haven for tourists, office workers and local residents. The wood-panelled bar has pictures of local scenes and politicians. Look out on the way to the toilets for the bull's-eye windows and the two paintings of the pub. A cosy place for a pint after or instead of visiting the sights.
Q❀◗≉⊖(St James's Park/Victoria)🚇❔

Wetherspoon's ✓
Unit 5, Upper Concourse, Victoria Station, Terminus Place, SW1V 1JT
✪ 6am-midnight; 8am-11 Sun ☎ (020) 7931 0445
Fuller's London Pride; Greene King IPA; 9 changing beers (often Adnams, Windsor & Eton) Ⓗ
Overlooking the station concourse and accessed mainly by escalators, this pub has a bright café-bar atmosphere. Features include blue and cream tiling, two curved bars with marble-style tops and banquettes along the opposite side. Two sets of six handpumps dispense four regular beers and eight changing guest ales. TV screens show times of train departures. Note that British Transport police sometimes close the bar when football fans are due. Q❀◗⅊≉⊖●🚇❔

SW1: Westminster

Buckingham Arms
62 Petty France, SW1H 9EU
✪ 11-11; 11-6 Sat & Sun ☎ (020) 7222 3386
Young's Bitter, London Gold, Special; 2 changing beers (often Young's) Ⓗ
Said to have once been a hat shop, this pub opened in the 1720s as the Bell, was renamed the Black Horse in the 1740s, was rebuilt in 1898 and renamed again in 1901. Substantially renovated in recent years, it has appeared in every edition of this Guide. A mix of modern and traditional seats and tables, high and low, draws civil servants, visitors and the occasional Member of Parliament. Open 11-6pm Sunday from the end of March through the summer. ❀◗⊖(St James's Park)🚇

Speaker Ⓛ ✓
46 Great Peter Street, SW1P 2HA
✪ 12-11; closed Sat & Sun ☎ (020) 7222 1749
Sambrook's Wandle Ale; Timothy Taylor Landlord; house beer (by Adnams); 2 changing beers (sourced nationally) Ⓗ
A friendly pine-panelled one-bar local decorated with parliamentary caricatures. Dating from 1729 or earlier, the Castle, renamed the Elephant & Castle around 1800 and the Speaker from 1999, was part of the Devil's Acre, a notorious slum next to the world's first public gas works. The pub now welcomes local estate residents and office workers, not to mention the occasional MP, all of whom enjoy the attractive range of beers and the home-made food. No music, TV or children.
Q◗⊖(St James's Park)🚇❔

SW4: Clapham

Craft Beer Co
128 Clapham Manor Street, SW4 6ED
✪ 4-11 (midnight Fri); 12-midnight Sat; 12-11 Sun
☎ (020) 7622 2894
House beer (by Kent); changing beers Ⓗ
Originally the Manor Arms, and now the fifth pub in the Craft Beer Co group. Depending on the season, between six and 10 handpumps serve real ales, with a good selection of other draught and bottled beers, priced according to their strength. A central square bar has high tables and stools at the front with padded settles, tables and chairs to the sides and rear. The large garden is popular in good weather and for beer festivals.
❀◗⊖(Common/High St/North)🚇🚊❔

King & Co
100 Clapham Park Road, SW4 7BZ
✪ 4-11 (midnight Thu; 1am Fri); 12-1am Sat; 12-11 Sun
☎ (020) 7498 1971 ⊕ thekingandco.uk
House beer (by London Beer Lab); 4 changing beers (sourced nationally) Ⓗ
An innovative pub that has in no small measure contributed to the real ale renaissance in Clapham. You can expect to find an interesting selection of styles from microbreweries throughout the UK, plus a changing real cider. Regular events include Meet the Brewer nights, tap takeovers and a quiz on Mondays. Food is available from pop-up caterers who usually change over every six weeks and have provided pies, Japanese cuisine and tapas.
❀◗⊖(Common)●🐾❖❔

SW5: Earls Court

King's Head Ⓛ
17 Hogarth Place, SW5 0QT
✪ 8am-11 (10.30 Sun) ☎ (020) 7373 5239
Fuller's Oliver's Island, London Pride; Gale's Seafarers Ale; 2 changing beers (often Fuller's) Ⓗ
A 1937 rebuild of the oldest (circa 17th century) licensed premises in the area, this is a friendly corner pub off the busy Earl's Court Road. A recent major refurbishment saw a first-floor restaurant added and the bar area has been extended by relocating the toilets. Seating is a mixture of high stools around tall tables and standard tables. Quiz night is Monday.
❀◗⊖≉(West Brompton)⊖❖❔

SW6: Fulham

Durell Arms Ⓛ ✓
704 Fulham Road, SW6 5SB
✪ 12-11 (1am Fri & Sat) ☎ (020) 7736 3014
⊕ durellarmsfulham.com
Greene King IPA; 4 changing beers (often Sambrook's, Sharp's, Wychwood) Ⓗ
Making a second consecutive appearance in the Guide is this spacious GK Metropolitan corner pub with its L-shaped drinking area. The large rear room, with mouldings and mirrors giving an air of Victorian decadence, can be hired for functions. There is a big screen for sporting events. Attractive local ales complement Greene King and national guests, and it is busy on Sundays for the excellent roast. ❀❀◗⊖(Parsons Green)♣●🚇❖❔

SW6: Parsons Green

White Horse 🄻
1-3 Parsons Green, SW6 4UL
☼ 9.30am-11.30 (midnight Thu-Sat) ☎ (020) 7736 2115
⊕ whitehorsesw6.com
Harvey's Sussex Best Bitter; Oakham JHB; 6 changing beers Ⓗ
Destination Mitchells & Butlers pub that normally boasts five guest beers on handpump and an international selection of bottled beers. Regular beer and food matching events take place as well as four annual beer festivals, including the Old Ale Festival in late November when the Coach House, normally reserved for dining, has a stillage. The pub can get busy when Chelsea FC are playing at home, but the upstairs area is a good place to escape the crowds.
Q🏠🕸🕮🦽😍🚌🍽(22,424)🐾🛜

SW7: Gloucester Road

Queen's Arms ✪
30 Queen's Gate Mews, SW7 5QL
☼ 12-11; 12-10.30 Sun ☎ (020) 7823 9293
⊕ thequeensarmskensington.co.uk
Fuller's London Pride; Sharp's Doom Bar; 6 changing beers Ⓗ
Lovely corner mews pub, discreetly tucked away off Queen's Gate, that is well worth seeking out for its real ales and its large range of interesting draught and bottled beers, malt whiskies and other spirits. Note the unusual curved doors. The L-shaped room has wooden floors and panelling. The clientele reflects the location: opulent locals, students from Imperial College and musicians from, and visitors to, the nearby Royal Albert Hall. The food menu and specials are of superior quality.
Q🕮🦽😍🍽🐾🛜

SW7: South Kensington

Anglesea Arms ✪
15 Selwood Terrace, SW7 3QG
☼ 11-11; 12-10.30 Sun ☎ (020) 7373 7960
⊕ angleseaarms.com
Greene King IPA; 5 changing beers (sourced regionally; often Dark Star, Hogs Back, Sambrook's) Ⓗ
A real ale stalwart in CAMRA's early years, this hostelry was built in 1827 and was a Meux tied house for more than a century. Now a Grade II-listed Greene King Metropolitan pub, it has the air of a country inn, with outside seating and an interior featuring a diverse collection of mirrors, prints, photographs and paintings. Apart from the range of real ales, the menu offers a variety of food at reasonable prices for the area.
Q🏠🕸🕮😍🍽🐾🛜

SW8: South Lambeth

Priory Arms 🄻
83 Lansdowne Way, SW8 2PB
☼ 5 (3 Sat)-11; 3-10 Sun ☎ (020) 7622 1884
⊕ theprioryarms.com
5 changing beers (often Dark Star, Kent, Tiny Rebel) Ⓗ
Award-winning and stylish free house with a listed frontage and a modernised, split-level interior. Microbreweries are well supported here, and there is a good range of German and Belgian beers

(bottled and draught). The pub hosts a beer festival in early May and another, usually German-themed, in the autumn. The menu is Mexican. Board games are available in the bar, while at the front of the pub is a small patio for smoking and outdoor drinking. 🕸🕮⊖(Stockwell)🐾🍽🚌

SW9: Brixton

Trinity Arms
45 Trinity Gardens, SW9 8DR
☼ 11-11 (midnight Fri); 12-midnight Sat; 12-11 Sun
☎ (020) 7274 4544 ⊕ trinityarms.co.uk
Young's Bitter, London Gold, Special; 2 changing beers (often Young's) Ⓗ
Something of a hidden gem in a quiet square just off Brixton's bustling high street, this attractive pub retains its tiled Young's façade, complete with the ram logo. Inside, a recent refurbishment has created a light and open interior with photographs of old Brixton. A dining area has been provided upstairs. There is outdoor seating at the front and a pleasant patio at the rear. 🏠🕸🕮🦽�" ⊖🍽🐾🛜

SW10: Chelsea

Sporting Page
6 Camera Place, SW10 0BH
☼ 11-11; 12-10.30 Sun ☎ (020) 7349 0455
Sambrook's Wandle Ale; 4 changing beers (sourced regionally) Ⓗ
A comfortable single-bar gastro-pub with a friendly feel, now one of the small London-based Food & Fuel chain. It was previously known as the Red Anchor, built in 1974 on the site of the Odell Arms (1856-1971); the current name dates from 1989. Five handpumps serve real ales, often including local brews. An interesting wine selection complements the food offering. Sporting-themed prints and memorabilia adorn the walls.
Q🕮🍽🐾🛜

SW11: Battersea

Lighthouse 🄻
441 Battersea Park Road, SW11 4LR
☼ 12-11 (midnight Fri); 10-midnight Sat; 10-10.30 Sun
☎ (020) 7223 7721 ⊕ thelighthousebattersea.com
Sambrook's Wandle Ale; 3 changing beers (sourced nationally) Ⓗ
Smart, popular pub near the south-west entrance to Battersea Park, usually offering an interesting selection of ales for the area. Its strong emphasis on food attracts families, particularly at weekends, but drinkers are equally welcome. The rear covered patio has heaters, a big screen and two small booths for more intimate drinking. Board games are available and quiz night is Tuesday. Other regular events are steak night on Monday and pie night on Wednesday. 🏠🕸🕮🦽🍽🐾🛜

SW11: Clapham Junction

Beehive ✪
197 St John's Hill, SW11 1TH
☼ 12-midnight (1am Fri & Sat) ☎ (020) 7450 1756
Fuller's London Pride, ESB; 2 changing beers (often Fuller's) Ⓗ
Tasteful and elegant refurbishment and enthusiastic management have revitalised this classic local, Fuller's 2016 Town Pub of the Year. A roll-up TV screen shows major sporting events. The

rear area is available for functions and there is now a sheltered garden. Food, although limited, is excellent. Blankets are thoughtfully supplied for guests wishing to sit outside. Look out for the wonderful 1898 housing survey map of SW London; since then the Luftwaffe and town planners have altered things somewhat! ⏱🌔➡🚮😺📶

Eagle Ale House 🄻

104 Chatham Road, SW11 6HG
☼ 4 (3 Fri; 12 Sat)-11; 12-10.30 Sun ☎ (020) 7228 2328
⊕ eaglealehouse.com
Surrey Hills Shere Drop; changing beers (often Downton, Hackney, Pilgrim) Ⓗ
Homely, traditional pub, a short uphill walk from Northcote Road, affording lively conversation among regulars and visitors. Dogs also get a friendly welcome. In recent years it has been at the heart of the Fair Deal For Your Local campaign. Twice the local CAMRA Pub of the Year and three times the runner-up, it shows major sporting events on three TV screens, stages beer festivals and has a heated marquee in the garden.
⏱🌔🚮(319,G1)😺📶

Four Thieves

51 Lavender Gardens, SW11 1DJ
☼ 12-midnight (2am Fri & Sat); 12-10.30 Sun
☎ (020) 7223 6927 ⊕ fourthieves.pub
3 changing beers (often Laine) Ⓗ
Reopened in September 2014 by Laine Pub Company after major refurbishment and the installation of a brewery. Laine's beers, including Light, Best and Porter, are now generally brewed on the premises. The pub comprises a main bar, split over two levels, the Boat House to the right which hosts music and comedy entertainment, a massive upstairs games room, and a gin yard with heated and covered areas. 🌔🌓➡🚮📶

Powder Keg Diplomacy

147 St John's Hill, SW11 1TQ
☼ 12-11; 10-midnight Sat; 10-11 Sun ☎ (020) 7450 6457
⊕ powderkegdiplomacy.co.uk
3 changing beers (sourced nationally; often By the Horns, Five Points, Siren) Ⓗ
This gastro-pub, kitted out in a quirky colonial style, is immensely popular. Three handpumps dispense real ale from innovative microbreweries, often from London. Six draught beers, coming from the likes of Kernel, always include one stout or porter, and about 50 bottled beers are available, mainly from local breweries but also from around the world. High class but reasonably priced restaurant meals include a Sunday brunch, and are served in a glass-roofed Observatory dining area. An exemplar for the future of the British pub! ⏱🌔➡🚮😺📶

SW13: Barnes

Red Lion

2 Castelnau, SW13 9RU
☼ 11-11; 12-10.30 Sun ☎ (020) 8748 2984
Fuller's Oliver's Island, London Pride, ESB; 1 changing beer (often Fuller's) Ⓗ
A large Victorian landmark pub at the entrance to the Wetland Centre. Known as The Strugglers in 1781, it was destroyed by fire in 1835, rebuilt in its present form and renamed. The rear room has an ornate fireplace, chandeliers, dark-wood panelling and an exclusive, comfortable feel. Beyond are a no-smoking patio and a spacious garden, which is popular in the summertime. Food is served from a

varied, modern menu – the annual Great Sausage Roll-Off cooking event is renowned.
Q⏱🌔🌓➡🚮😺📶

SW16: Streatham

Railway 🄻 ✓

2 Greyhound Lane, SW16 5SD
☼ 12-11 (midnight Thu; 1am Fri & Sat) ☎ (020) 8769 9448
⊕ therailwaysw16.co.uk
Sambrook's Wandle Ale; 4 changing beers (often Belleville, Redemption, Twickenham) Ⓗ
Across the road from Streatham Common station, this busy community pub showcases beers exclusively from London microbreweries, both cask and bottled. It hosts a quiz on Tuesday, music nights, and a popular comedy night in the large room at the rear on the last Sunday of the month. There is seating outside and in the yard, where a farmers' market is held on the second and fourth Saturdays. Runner-up local CAMRA Pub of the Year in 2016. ⏱🌔🌓♿➡(Common)🚮(60,118)😺📶

SW17: Summerstown

By the Horns Brewery Tap

25 Summerstown, SW17 0BQ
☼ closed Mon; 4-10 (11 Thu); 5-11.30 Fri; 12-10 Sat; 12-9 Sun
☎ (020) 3417 7338 ⊕ bythehorns.co.uk
Changing beers (often By the Horns) Ⓗ
A brewery taproom and adjoining beer hall, open Tuesday to Sunday. Three cask beers are usually on, with other draught and bottled choices and occasional guests from small breweries. There is plenty of space in the bar and the enclosed car park outside. Major sporting events shown on large projection TVs are popular (it is often advisable to reserve your place in advance). Brewery tours and private event hire are also offered. ⏱🌔P🚮😺

SW17: Tooting

Antelope ✓

76 Mitcham Road, SW17 9NG
☼ 4-11 (midnight Thu; 1am Fri); 12-1am Sat; 12-11 Sun
☎ (020) 8672 3888 ⊕ theantelopepub.com
Sambrook's Wandle Ale; Thornbridge Jaipur IPA; Volden Pale Ale; 4 changing beers Ⓗ
A cavernous Victorian community pub close to Tooting Broadway, featuring a panelled bar at the front and green painted walls decorated with stuffed animals and china plates. The two large rooms at the rear include a dining area and at weekends the Anchor Bar (no real ale). Friendly staff serve a changing variety of ales (the Volden porter may replace the pale ale in winter). There is live music on Thursdays, and the Sunday roasts are popular. ⏱🌔🌓♿➡⊖(Broadway)🌭🚮😺📶

Wheatsheaf 🄻

2 Upper Tooting Road, SW17 7PG
☼ 12-midnight (1am Fri); 10-1am Sat; 12-11 Sun
☎ (020) 8672 2805 ⊕ thewheatsheafsw17.com
5 changing beers (often Hackney, Truman's, Wimbledon) Ⓗ
A massive late-Victorian coaching house at Tooting Bec crossroads with huge pillars, arches and fireplace. A back room is currently used as a restaurant. Seats have been added to the roadside exterior to provide respite for smokers. Now run by Urban Pubs & Bars, it promotes local cask beers alongside others from further away. As an Asset of

Community Value with two Article 4 Directions, this pub is famously protected from opportunist development activity. ☎🏠🍽🕭&♿(Bec)♣🖪

SW18: Southfields

Earl Spencer ✔

260-262 Merton Road, SW18 5JL
✪ 4-11; 11-midnight Fri & Sat; 12-10.30 Sun
☎ (020) 8870 9244 ⊕ theearlspencer.com
Fuller's London Pride; Sambrook's Wandle Ale; Wimbledon Tower SPA; 1 changing beer ⊞
Winner of the 2016 Pub of the Year in the Wandsworth Business Awards, this is a gastro-pub with a no reservations policy, a sport-free oasis with no TVs, and a quiet pub with no music. Open plan with some sofas, its walls display antique mirrors and old photographs. At the front is a large, comfortable and covered terrace. It serves a popular Sunday lunch, and excellent Cuban cigars are on sale from a humidor – for smoking on the terrace only! Q☎🏠🕭🖪(39,156)😺🕭

Pig & Whistle ⎣

479-481 Merton Road, SW18 5LD
✪ 12-midnight (11 Mon & Tue); 12-10.30 Sun
☎ (020) 8874 1061 ⊕ pigandwhistlesw18.co.uk
Young's Bitter, Special; 2 changing beers (often Sambrook's, Twickenham, Wimbledon) ⊞
Converted from retail premises in 1974, this corner local has a split-level interior decorated tastefully with old photos and posters. The larger area is flooded with natural light, thanks to the huge windows. The garden features several private chalets almost in 1950s seaside style. There is a doggie menu, including pigs' ears. Humans can enjoy light bites, platters, sides and burgers as well as main meals.
☎🏠🕭&≷(Earlsfield)⊖🖪(156)😺🕭

SW18: Wandsworth

Alma

499 Old York Road, SW18 1TF
✪ 10-midnight; 10-10.30 Sun ☎ (020) 8870 2537
⊕ almawandsworth.com
Young's Bitter, Special; 4 changing beers (often Purity, Sambrook's, Twickenham) ⊞
Imposing green-tiled Victorian corner pub opposite Wandsworth Town station, named after the Crimean battle. Identified by CAMRA as having a regionally important historic pub interior, it retains an island bar, circular mosaics and fine back-painted mirrors featuring birds in their natural habitat. The separate restaurant at the rear, renowned for fine cuisine, leads to a newly refurbished garden. Guest beers usually include at least one from Sambrook's.
☎🏠🕭&≷(Town)♣🖪😺🕭

Cat's Back ✔

86-88 Point Pleasant, SW18 1NN
✪ 12-midnight; 12-10 Sun & Mon ☎ (020) 8617 3448
⊕ thecatsback.com
Harvey's Sussex Best Bitter, Old Ale; 1 changing beer ⊞
Harvey's first south-west London pub is an elegant, restrained refurbishment of a wonderful back-street local and a welcome survivor among the mass development of luxury riverside apartments that surround it. Four of its cask beers are usually available. The pub offers occasional live music

(folk, jazz, classical) on Thursday evenings and a film show (also upstairs at 8pm) most Wednesdays. The food offering is excellent, especially Sunday lunch. ☎🏠🕭&♣🖪😺🕭

Old Sergeant ⎣

104 Garratt Lane, SW18 4DJ
✪ 12-11 (midnight Fri & Sat) ☎ (020) 8874 4099
Sambrook's Wandle Ale; Young's Bitter, Special; 2 changing beers (sourced nationally) ⊞
This friendly local has been voted the best place to bring your dog for a drink. Table menus for the excellent food include an informative beer list. The John Young Room upstairs displays treasured memorabilia of the Wandsworth brewery. The outside seating area has a splendid hidden lovers' corner and plenty of decking space for smokers. Quiz night is Monday. The pub achieved a Guinness world record in 2014 for the longest barbecue marathon. 🏠🕭&🖪(44,270)😺🕭

SW19: South Wimbledon

Sultan

78 Norman Road, SW19 1BT ☎ (020) 8544 9323
✪ 12-11 (midnight Fri & Sat)
Hop Back GFB, Summer Lightning; 3 changing beers (sourced regionally; often Downton, Hop Back) ⊞
Hop Back's only London tied house, an attractive two-bar 1950s brick building, mostly carpeted, with dark-wood walls, large tables with chairs, some fixed seating, and settees in the recently added conservatory. Westons Country Perry, Wyld Wood cider and an occasional guest cider are available, and sandwiches made to order. A Beer Club, 6-9pm Monday and Wednesday, offers a 50p a pint discount. Three-day beer festivals are held, usually in April and September. Local CAMRA Pub of the Year 2016.
🏠&≷(Haydons Rd)⊖(Colliers Wood/South Wimbledon)♣🍽🖪🕭

Trafalgar ⎣

23 High Path, SW19 2JY
✪ 12-11 (midnight Fri & Sat) ☎ (020) 8542 5342
⊕ trafalgarfreehouse.co.uk
Downton Quadhop; Surrey Hills Shere Drop; 4 changing beers (sourced nationally; often Binghams, Coastal, Downton) ⊞
A narrow, one-bar, street-corner house – the main part dates from the 1860s, the extension from 1906. It is mostly carpeted, and furnished with farmhouse chairs and tables and Nelson memorabilia. Alongside the cask choice is a variety of bottled beers and three real ciders, often Lilley's, SeaCider. Cold and hot snacks (pot meals) are served until 10pm. Regular live music is a feature. Local CAMRA Pub of the Year 2015.
🏠🖪(Morden Rd)⊖♣🍽🖪😺🕭

SW19: Wimbledon

Crooked Billet

14-15 Crooked Billet, SW19 4RQ
✪ 11-11 (midnight Fri & Sat); 12-10.30 Sun
☎ (020) 8946 4942 ⊕ thecrookedbilletwimbledon.com
Sharp's Doom Bar; Young's Bitter, Special; 3 changing beers (often Young's) ⊞
A homely late 18th-century building, extended in 1969 into an adjacent cottage, and again more recently to increase dining space. The wood-panelled walls are adorned with old prints,

photographs and local painters' works. There are flagstone and wooden floors, a variety of seating and a real fire in winter. Good food is served throughout, including the intimate restaurant room at the back. Quiz night is Monday. Plastic glasses are used outside in the summer.
⍩❀◖◗🍴(200)🐾🛜

Hand in Hand ℓ
7 Crooked Billet, SW19 4RQ
✪ 11-11 (midnight Fri & Sat); 12-11 Sun ☎ (020) 8946 5720
⊕ thehandinhandwimbledon.co.uk
Courage Directors; Young's Bitter, Special; 3 changing beers (often Adnams, Portobello, Wimbledon) ℍ
Celebrated single-bar ale house on the edge of Wimbledon Common with separate drinking areas and a variety of seating. At least three guest beers are usually sold. Children are welcome in the family room. This is a great place to eat, with beer included in several recipes. There is poker on Monday, a quiz on Tuesday and occasional beer tastings and cellar tours. Winner of the DogBuddy award for the most dog-friendly pub in the UK.
Q⍩❀◖◗♿♣🐾(200)🐾

Carshalton

Hope 🍷 ℓ
48 West Street, SM5 2PR
✪ 12-11; 12-10.30 Sun ☎ (020) 8240 1255
⊕ hopecarshalton.co.uk
Downton New Forest Ale; Windsor & Eton Knight of the Garter; 5 changing beers (often Arbor, Magic Rock, Vibrant Forest) ℍ
Traditional customer-owned village free house. Seven handpumps dispense beers from the country's best independent breweries, served in half, third, two-thirds and pint lined glasses. Frequent beer festivals are held. Free from machines and TV, the pub hosts select live music sessions and is home to interest groups covering music, dancing and other traditional activities. Lunches are served until 3pm and pot meals until 10pm. Local CAMRA Pub of the Year 2017 and regional winner in 2016.
Q⍩❀◖◗⇌♣🐾P🍴🛜

Sun ℓ
4 North Street, SM5 2HU
✪ 12-11 (midnight Fri); 11-midnight Sat; 12-10.30 Sun & Mon
☎ (020) 8773 4549 ⊕ thesuncarshalton.com
6 changing beers (sourced nationally; often Arbor, Brighton Bier, Rooster's) ℍ
This handsome and imposing Victorian pub was given a tasteful makeover several years ago and has not looked back since. Several distinct areas accommodate diners, with excellent food, and discerning drinkers, with a wide beer choice on six handpumps. In summer the large courtyard garden with its continental-style verandah is popular. The huge upstairs function room, available for hire, receives sunlight almost all day, reflecting the pub's name. ⍩❀◖◗⇌♣🐾🛜

Kew

Tap on the Line
Kew Gardens Station, Station Parade, TW9 3PZ
✪ 8.30am (8am Fri; 9am Sat)-11; 10-10.30 Sun
☎ (020) 8332 1162
Fuller's Oliver's Island; London Pride; Gale's Seafarers Ale, HSB; 1 changing beer (often Butcombe) ℍ

Located beside the line's eastbound platform, this attractive old building with oak-beamed ceilings was acquired by Fuller's in 2012 and reopened after refurbishment in 2013. Main features include an arched ornate conservatory atrium and floor-to-ceiling picture windows looking directly on to the platform. There is a popular outside seating area at the front. Food is available all day.
⍩❀◖◗⊖(Kew Gardens)🚌🐾🛜

Kingston

Albion ℓ ✅
45 Fairfield Road, KT1 2PY
✪ 11-11 (11.30 Fri & Sat); 12-10.30 Sun ☎ (020) 8541 1691
⊕ thealbionkingston.com
10 changing beers (often Big Smoke) ℍ
The L-shaped interior has cosy wood-panelled walls and wooden floors, a small seating area to the front with an open fire and a larger area to the side, leading to the patio and garden. Background music comes from traditional vinyl discs. Cask beers include at least three from Big Smoke, the rest mainly from local and national micros. Five changing ciders are also available. Home-cooked food is served. The pub overlooks Fairfield Green and is next to the sports centre. ⍩❀◖◗♿⇌🐾🚌🛜

King's Tun ℓ ✅
153-157 Clarence Street, KT1 1QT
✪ 8am-midnight (1am Fri & Sat) ☎ (020) 8547 3827
Greene King IPA, Abbot; Oakham Citra; Sharp's Doom Bar; 8 changing beers (sourced locally) ℍ
In the building that was once the Empire Theatre, this large Wetherspoon pub is named after the town where seven Saxon kings were crowned. It attracts all during the day, with a younger crowd in the evenings, particularly Friday and Saturday nights for a disco from 9pm. A long bar at the rear serves two separate seating areas. There is also a good-sized bar upstairs with lift access. Alcoholic drinks, including three changing ciders, are served from 9am. ⍩◖◗♿⇌🐾🚌🛜

Willoughby Arms ℓ
47 Willoughby Road, KT2 6LN
✪ 10.30-midnight; 12-midnight Sun ☎ (020) 8546 4236
⊕ thewilloughbyarms.com
Hop Art Hoppy Blonde; Park Killcat Pale; Surrey Hills Shere Drop; Twickenham Grandstand Bitter; Weltons Horsham Pale; 2 changing beers (sourced locally) ℍ
Friendly Victorian back-street local, divided into a sports bar with games and large-screen TV, and a quieter lounge area. All beers tend to be from small breweries within a 50-mile radius of the pub. The upstairs function room, where the Yardbirds rehearsed in the '60s, can be hired. Pizzas and pies are cooked to order. The spacious garden includes a covered, heated and lit smoking area with a large TV screen. Quiz night is Sunday.
Q⍩❀♿♣🐾🚌(371,K5)🐾🛜

Norbiton

Black Horse ℓ ✅
204 London Road, KT2 6QP
✪ 12-11 (midnight Fri); 11-midnight Sat; 12-10.30 Sun
☎ (020) 3637 6199 ⊕ blackhorsekingston.co.uk
Harvey's Sussex Best Bitter; Park Gallows Gold; Twickenham Naked Ladies; 2 changing beers (often Truman's) ℍ

A recently refurbished pub with plenty of room to meet for a drink or comfortable dining. The TV is away from the main bar and there is a games room with table football, darts and a pinball machine. The garden/sun patio is wheelchair-accessible, as is the main bar. Table tennis and Jenga can be found in the garden. The changing beers are usually local and beer festivals have been held here. ☆🌸🕪🏵️⇌P🖳🌸🛜

Richmond

Hope

115-117 Kew Road, TW9 2PN

🌐 4-11; 12-11 Thu; 12-1am Fri & Sat; 12-10.30 Sun ☎ (020) 8940 5099 ⊕ thehopeofrichmond.co.uk

Fuller's London Pride; Timothy Taylor Golden Best; Twickenham Naked Ladies; 3 changing beers (sourced nationally; often East London Brewing, Purity, Young's) 🅷

This traditional pub is dominated by the U-shaped central bar with eight handpumps, one of which is allocated to Orchard Pig cider. A good range of wines and cocktails is also stocked. To the left of the bar are some tables laid out for dining, with table service. Food is locally sourced. Outside at the back is an unusual semi-enclosed area with comfortable seating, and beyond is an open garden with trestle tables. Q☆🌸🕪⇌➊🌸🖳🛜

Mitre

20 St Mary's Grove, TW9 1UY

🌐 3 (12 Sat)-11; 12-10.30 Sun ☎ (020) 8940 1336 ⊕ themitretw9.co.uk

10 changing beers (sourced nationally; often Dark Star, Hardknott, Wild Weather Ales) 🅷

A traditional pub tucked away off Sheen Road, originally owned by Young's and now a free house. Several leaded stained-glass windows feature different colourful church mitres. Simply furnished with wood flooring, it has a decked area at the front, benches to the side and a patio at the back. Ten handpumps serve beers from independent brewers outside the M25, four dispense cider or perry. Pizzas can be ordered in from Basilico. ☆🌸⇌(North Sheen)➊🌸🖳🌸

Roebuck ✅

130 Richmond Hill, TW10 6RN

🌐 12-11 (midnight Fri); 11-midnight Sat; 12-10.30 Sun ☎ (020) 8948 2329

5 changing beers (often Downton, Purity, Surrey Hills) 🅷

Close to Richmond Park Gate, this 200-year-old pub overlooks the World Heritage view of Petersham Meadows and the River Thames. Air-conditioned and carpeted except in front of the bar, it has one or two regular beers from Greene King, four frequently rotated guest beers and one real cider on tap. In the summer another three handpumps come into use. The outside terrace across the road can also be used by patrons. Food is served until 10pm. ☆🕪🏵️🖳(371)🌸🛜

Surbiton

Antelope ♀ 🄻 ✅

87 Maple Road, KT6 4AW

🌐 12-11 (11.30 Fri & Sat); 12-10.30 Sun ☎ (020) 8399 5565 ⊕ theantelope.co.uk

7 changing beers (sourced nationally; often Big Smoke) 🅷

A spacious, split-level pub with a real fire in winter. At least three cask beers come from the Big Smoke Brewery across the covered courtyard at the back. Up to seven other real ales and five changing ciders are also usually offered. Occasional beer festivals and Meet the Brewer events are held. Home-cooked food includes Sunday roasts. Popular with locals and commuters, it can be particularly busy evenings and weekends. Local CAMRA Pub of the Year for 2016 and 2017. 🌸🕪⇌➊🌸🖳🌸🛜

Lamb 🄻

73 Brighton Road, KT6 5NF

🌐 12-11.30 (12.30am Thu-Sat) ☎ (020) 8390 9229 ⊕ lambsurbiton.co.uk

Black Sheep Best Bitter; Hop Back Summer Lightning; Surrey Hills Ranmore; 1 changing beer (sourced regionally) 🅷

Small, family-run free house at the heart of the local community. Built in 1850 and formerly four separate rooms, it retains the original horseshoe-shaped bar. The changing beer is from a micro (sometimes local) or family brewery. Specialist cheeses are available, with cheeseboards on offer all day Friday to Sunday. Live music and other events are regularly held, including pop-up street food stalls in the garden. ☆🌸⇌🖳🛜

Sutton

Cock & Bull

26-30 High Street, SM1 1HF

🌐 12-11 (midnight Fri & Sat); 12-10.30 Sun ☎ (020) 8652 9910

Fuller's Oliver's Island, London Pride, ESB; 1 changing beer 🅷

A warm and friendly Fuller's house at the top of the High Street, just a stone's throw from the station and bus stops. The building is a former bank branch, now a spacious one-bar pub with three separate drinking areas and an outdoor heated smoking area. Five plasma screens show major sporting events and there is live music on Saturdays. An extensive menu caters for all tastes, and children are welcome during food serving hours. ☆🕪🏵️⇌🌸🖳🌸🛜

Moon on the Hill ✅

5-9 Hill Road, SM1 1DZ

🌐 8am-midnight (1am Fri & Sat) ☎ (020) 8643 1202

Greene King Abbot; Ruddles Best Bitter; Sharp's Doom Bar; 7 changing beers (sourced regionally; often Dark Star, Surrey Hills) 🅷

Formerly the furniture repository of a department store, this is a popular and well-established Wetherspoon pub, conveniently situated for Sutton's main shopping area. It comprises a single bar with ample seating on three levels and a garden for those preferring to drink and eat alfresco. The guest beers are local whenever possible and mini beer festivals are held throughout the year. Draught ciders come from different parts of the country. ☆🌸🕪🏵️⇌➊🌸🖳🛜

Shinner & Sudtone

67 High Street, SM1 1DT

🌐 4-midnight (11 Mon; 2am Fri); 12-2am Sat; 12-midnight Sun ☎ (020) 8661 5327 ⊕ shinnerandsudtone.com

3 changing beers (sourced nationally) 🅷

In the shopping area of Sutton, this is a pub acquired by Antic and decorated in its familiar shabby-chic style. Its name combines a former department store nearby and an old name for

its reputation having been taken over in 2014 by the ETM Group. The Long Arm Brewery opened in an outbuilding in 2015. ⚲🍴◑▶🚪🚲(65,E3)🛜

W6: Hammersmith

Andover Arms ✪
57 Aldensley Road, W6 0DL
🕓 12-11 ☎ (020) 8748 2155 ⊕ theandoverarms.com
Fuller's London Pride; Gale's Seafarers Ale; 2 changing beers (often Fuller's) ⊞
Hidden away in the back streets of Hammersmith, this popular and welcoming local is an enduring real ale champion with a rural feel about it. The attractive panelled bar counter, with its elaborate bar-back, separates two areas furnished with an assortment of dining tables and chairs. The kitchen offers a wide range of dishes lunchtimes and evenings. Quiz night is every Sunday at 9pm.
Q⚲🍴◑▶⊖(Ravenscourt Park)🚪🐾🛜

Dove
19 Upper Mall, W6 9TA
🕓 11-11; 12-10.30 Sun ☎ (020) 8748 9474
Fuller's Oliver's Island, London Pride, ESB; 1 changing beer (often Fuller's, Gale's) ⊞
A Grade II-listed pub dating from the 1740s, with a regionally important historic interior, overlooking the Thames and hence often crowded in summer. The likes of Dylan Thomas, Ernest Hemingway and Alec Guinness have enjoyed a pint or two here. Off the main bar area, a tiny public bar holds the Guinness world record for the smallest bar area. Food service can be slow at busy times but is worth the wait.
⚲🍴◑▶⊖(Hammersmith/Ravenscourt Park)
🐾🚪🐾🛜

Swan ✪
46 Hammersmith Broadway, W6 0DZ
🕓 10-11 (midnight Fri & Sat; 10.30 Sun) ☎ (020) 8748 1043
St Austell Nicholson's Pale Ale; Sharp's Doom Bar; Truman's Runner; 5 changing beers (often Adnams, Elgood's, Thornbridge) ⊞
Claimed to be on the site of the first coaching stop after leaving the City, wood predominates in this bustling M&B Nicholson's pub, handily located opposite Hammersmith Broadway. Note the fine tessellated gables. Ornate stairs lead to a first-floor restaurant and bar (and to the toilets). It is well worth breaking your journey here to or from Heathrow Airport. ⚲◑▶⊖🚪🛜

W7: Hanwell

Fox ⅃
Green Lane, W7 2PJ
🕓 11-11; 12-10.30 Sun ☎ (020) 8567 4021
⊕ thefoxpub.co.uk
Fuller's London Pride; St Austell Trelawny, Proper Job; Timothy Taylor Landlord; 2 changing beers ⊞
Wonderful back-street free house in the welcoming multicultural town of Hanwell, as popular with walkers, cyclists and other nearby canal users as with locals. A good range of beers, with changing guest ales from independent breweries, is complemented by excellent, inexpensive food, including a popular Sunday lunch (booking recommended). Added to all this are two annual beer festivals and occasional jazz. Local CAMRA Pub of the Year on many occasions.
⚲🍴◑▶🚲♣🐾P🚪(195,E8)🐾🛜

Grosvenor ♟ ⅃
127 Oaklands Road, W7 2DT
🕓 12 (9am Fri)-11; 12-10.30 Sun ☎ (020) 8840 0007
6 changing beers (sourced locally; often Sharp's, Truman's, Weird Beard) ⊞
A traditional local dating back to 1904, refurbished in 2014 without losing its features and charm. There is a dining room section and a main bar. A good selection of real ales and bottle-conditioned beers is available, plus a wide range of other locally produced beers. Family-friendly, it has a congenial atmosphere and promotes local events. Jazz night is the second Tuesday of every month, open mic night the fourth Tuesday. Local CAMRA Pub of the Year 2017. ⚲🍴◑▶🚲♣🐾🚪🐾🛜

W8: Kensington

Elephant & Castle ✪
40 Holland Street, W8 4LT
🕓 11-11; 12-10.30 Sun ☎ (020) 7937 6382
St Austell Nicholson's Pale Ale; Sharp's Doom Bar; 3 changing beers (sourced nationally) ⊞
Licensed in 1865 as a beer house in what were two adjacent houses tucked away north-east of the town hall, this cosy, wood-panelled M&B Nicholson's pub is a welcome refuge from the hurly-burly of Kensington High Street. There are strong journalistic connections – witness the notable framed newspapers in the back bar. Food is served all day with a break 4-5pm. Note the fine Charrington's bar-back.
🍴◑▶⊖(High St Kensington)🚪🐾🛜

W8: Notting Hill Gate

Churchill Arms
119 Kensington Church Street, W8 7LN
🕓 11-11 (midnight Thu-Sat); 12-10.30 Sun
☎ (020) 7727 4242
Fuller's Oliver's Island, London Pride, ESB; Gale's Seafarers Ale; 1 changing beer (often Fuller's) ⊞
Long-serving landlord Gerry keeps standards high at this multi award-winning pub with a regionally important historic interior. Churchillian and Irish memorabilia hang from the panelled ceiling, and plaques commemorate former drinkers. The Thai restaurant in the conservatory was one of the first in a London pub. At busy times drinkers stand outside on the pavement below the hanging flower baskets. Q⚲◑▶⊖🚪🐾🛜

W9: Westbourne Park

Union Tavern ⅃
45 Woodfield Road, W9 2BA
🕓 12-11 (midnight Fri & Sat); 12-10.30 Sun
☎ (020) 7286 1886
Five Points Pale; Fuller's London Pride; 3 changing beers ⊞
A radical departure by Fuller's, this unbranded beer house offers cask ales from within only 30 miles and, with only one brewery exception, from London. The mainly young crowd enjoys reduced beer prices on Monday, a weekly quiz, and a Meet the Brewer event on the first Tuesday of the month. Good-value food is another attraction, with traditional Sunday lunches. The canalside terrace comes into its own on a warm, sunny day.
⚲🍴◑▶⊖🚪🛜

W12: Shepherds Bush

Defector's Weld L
170 Uxbridge Road, W12 8AA
☼ 12-midnight (2am Fri & Sat); 12-11 Sun
☎ (020) 8749 0008 ⊕ defectors-weld.co.uk
Young's Bitter, Special; 3 changing beers (sourced locally; often Redemption, Truman's, Twickenham) Ⓗ
Since Young's took over this pub, it has continued to rotate local guest beers. The large horseshoe-shaped main bar has a welcoming mix of sofas, tables and chairs. An upstairs bar is available for hire. DJs play music Thursday to Sunday evenings. Home fans only are admitted on Queen's Park Rangers match days, but card-carrying CAMRA members not wearing team colours are welcome.
Q❀⬤♿≉⊖(Shepherd's Bush/Market)🚌🚐❀ 🛜

W13: West Ealing

Forester ★ L ✔
2 Leighton Road, W13 9EP
☼ 11-11.30 (midnight Wed & Thu); 1am Fri & Sat); 11-11 Sun
☎ (020) 8567 1654 ⊕ theforesterealing.com
Fuller's London Pride, ESB; 4 changing beers (sourced nationally; often Fuller's, Gale's) Ⓗ
Built in 1909 from designs by Nowell Parr for the Royal Brewery of Brentford and bought by Fuller's in 2012, this pub has a nationally important historic interior. Thai and English food are available daily, except Sunday when a traditional carvery is served until 6pm. Wednesday is quiz night and on Thursday there is a poker tournament. Two guests beers are supplemented by two additional beers from Fuller's (often Gale's HSB), and two beer festivals are held annually.
♿❀🚑⬤♿≉⊖(Northfields)♣🚐(E2,E3)❀ 🛜

Brentford

Express Tavern
56 Kew Bridge Road, TW8 0EW
☼ 11-11 (midnight Fri & Sat) ☎ (020) 8560 8484
⊕ expresstavern.co.uk
Draught Bass; Haresfoot Lock Keeper's Launch Ale; 8 changing beers (sourced nationally) Ⓗ
A local landmark since the 1800s, the building still features its illuminated external Bass signage, and Draught Bass remains a fixture on the bar. It has a regionally important historic pub interior. The Chiswick Bar has 10 ale handpumps and a playable upright piano (music is also on vinyl LPs), while the Saloon and Lounge Bar has five ciders and perries on handpump. At the rear is a beer garden with a covered and heated area.
❀⬤♿≉(Kew Bridge)♣●🚐❀ 🛜

Magpie & Crown L
128 High Street, TW8 8EW
☼ 12-midnight (1am Thu-Sat) ☎ (020) 8560 4570
Butcombe Original; 5 changing beers (often Magic Rock, Marble, Oakham) Ⓗ
A traditional Brewers' Tudor free house detailing its six cask ales, one cider and one perry on a chalkboard. The range includes one golden, one dark and one bitter, usually from Manchester, Yorkshire and London breweries, and served by enthusiastic and knowledgeable staff. Kay's Kitchen serves freshly cooked food lunchtimes and evenings. The pub has a pool table. There are tables and a cycle rack in front, and a rear patio with a covered smokers' area. ❀⬤≉♣●🚐❀ 🛜

Feltham

Moon on the Square ✔
30 The Centre, High Street, TW13 4AU
☼ 8am-midnight; 8am-10.30 Sun ☎ (020) 8893 1293
Courage Best Bitter; Greene King Abbot; Ruddles Best Bitter; Wells Bombardier; changing beers (sourced regionally; often Twickenham) Ⓗ
A real ale oasis that continues to flourish. The interior is early Wetherspoon's – wood panels and glass-partitioned booths, with pictures and local history panels. Eight real ales include varying guests, often local brews, with a bar-top gravity cask on tap during beer festivals in April and October. Westons cider is sold. Food is served all day, alcoholic drinks from 9am. Families are welcome until 6pm. ♿⬤♿≉●🚐 🛜

Greenford

Black Horse
425 Oldfield Lane North, UB6 0AS
☼ 11.30-11 (midnight Thu-Sat); 12-11 Sun
☎ (020) 8578 1384
Fuller's London Pride, ESB; 1 changing beer (often Fuller's, Gale's) Ⓗ
Tastefully extended canalside pub close to mainline rail, tube and bus routes, with a landscaped garden. Bargees, cyclists and walkers are frequent visitors. Good food includes traditional Sunday roasts, available 12-3, 6-9pm Monday to Thursday, 12-9pm Friday to Sunday. There is TV, a quiz on Thursday and live music on Friday and Saturday. Q♿❀⬤♿≉⊖♣P🚐(92,395)❀ 🛜

Hare & Hounds
229 Ruislip Road, UB6 9RZ
☼ 11-11 (midnight Fri); 11-10.30 Sun ☎ (020) 8575 7240
⊕ harehoundspub.co.uk
Marston's Pedigree; 1 changing beer (sourced nationally; often Marston's, Ringwood) Ⓗ
A friendly, traditional locals' pub on the busy Ruislip Road. There are two bars, with the saloon divided into two sections, the three handpumps being at the rear. The large beer garden is completely enclosed and usually offers a bouncy castle along with the picnic tables. A welcome oasis in a real ale desert. ♿❀♿♣P🚐❀ 🛜

Hampton

Jolly Coopers
16 High Street, TW12 2SJ
☼ 11-11 (midnight Fri & Sat); 12-10.30 Sun
☎ (020) 8979 3384 ⊕ squiffysrestaurant.co.uk
Caledonian Deuchars IPA; Courage Best Bitter; Hop Back Summer Lightning; 2 changing beers (sourced locally; often Reunion) Ⓗ
A popular, traditional community pub, proud of its heritage: a wooden wall panel lists landlords from 1727 to the present owners, who took over in 1986. The small horseshoe bar features five handpumps with a local guest beer often on tap. Walls are adorned with water jugs and other memorabilia including some coopers' tools. Squiffy's restaurant serves an extensive menu of tapas and traditional food, including Sunday lunches. Weather permitting, you can eat on the sun patio outside. ♿❀⬤≉♣🚐❀

Hampton Court

Mute Swan

3 Palace Gate, KT8 9BN

🌣 11-11 (midnight Fri & Sat); 11-10.30 Sun

☎ (020) 8941 5959 ∰ muteswan.co.uk

Hogs Back TEA; house beer (by Phoenix); 4 changing beers (often Brightwater, Tillingbourne, Timothy Taylor) Ⓗ

A friendly, modern and spacious pub and restaurant opposite the palace gates. A good selection of food can be enjoyed either in the upstairs restaurant or in the main bar. Real cider is often served, as well as an extensive range of whisky and gin. Seating and tables are provided outside. There are no TV screens to spoil the civilised atmosphere of this popular addition to the area. Ⓓⷤⷮⷯⷰⷱ🐾🐕❄

Hampton Hill

Roebuck

72 Hampton Road, TW12 1JN

🌣 11-11 (11.30 Fri & Sat); 12-4, 7-10.30 Sun

☎ (020) 8255 8133 ∰ roebuck-hamptonhill.co.uk

St Austell Tribute; Sambrook's Junction Ale; Young's Bitter; 2 changing beers (sourced nationally; often Triple fff, Truman's, Windsor & Eton) Ⓗ

A comfortable Victorian street-corner pub with screens dividing the single bar into separate seating areas. Its array of bric-a-brac and other displays (framed banknotes, military memorabilia, model sea planes, cigar store Indian and the wickerwork Harley-Davidson) is amazing but does not detract from the comfort of the pub. The small award-winning garden has a gazebo for smokers and a garden room (available for hire) for cooler evenings. The real fire never goes out in winter. Q🍴🐕❄⒟ⷤ≢(Fulwell)🐾P🚌

Harlington

White Hart

158 High Street, UB3 5DP

🌣 11-11 (11.30 Thu; midnight Fri & Sat); 12-11 Sun

☎ (020) 8759 9608

Fuller's London Pride, ESB Ⓗ

Large, Grade II-listed Fuller's pub standing proud at the north end of the village. The bar provides access to an open-plan area with soft seating, leading to a seated area favoured by diners. The pub was refurbished in 2009 to improve facilities and create the open feel it has now. Local history is the theme of the wall displays, enjoyed by regulars and visitors from nearby Heathrow airport. Quiz night is Thursday. Fuller's or Gale's seasonal ales are sometimes on the bar. 🍴🐕❄⒟🚻P🚌🐾❄

Hatton

Green Man ✓

Green Man Lane, TW14 0PZ

🌣 12-11 (midnight Fri & Sat) ☎ (020) 8890 2681

∰ thegreenman-bedfont.co.uk

Greene King IPA; 2 changing beers (sourced nationally) Ⓗ

A surprisingly rural-looking pub for the area. Dating from 1640, it was recently refurbished sympathetically with several seating areas and varying floor levels; look out for low beams (though they are padded). The seating area at the front and large garden to the side provide good

views of aircraft passing directly overhead on their way in to Heathrow Airport – they can also be clearly heard. 🍴🐕❄⒟⊖(Hatton Cross)🐾🚌🚭

Hayes

Botwell Inn ✓

25-29 Coldharbour Lane, UB3 3EB

🌣 9am-midnight ☎ (020) 8848 3112

Greene King Abbot; Ruddles Best Bitter; Sharp's Doom Bar; 3 changing beers (often Adnams, Hogs Back, Windsor & Eton) Ⓗ

A large Wetherspoon pub opened in 2000 following a shop conversion from furnishers S Moore and Son, with several areas for dining and drinking. There is a fenced, paved area to the front and a patio at the rear with large parasols with heaters. At least one Westons cider is stocked. Several beer festivals are held annually. Q🍴🐕❄⒟🚻≢(Hayes & Harlington)🐾🚌🚭

Hounslow

Moon under Water ✓

84-88 Staines Road, TW3 3LF (W end of High St)

🌣 9am-12.30am (1am Fri & Sat) ☎ (020) 8572 7506

Greene King Abbot; Ruddles Best Bitter; Sharp's Doom Bar; 5 changing beers (sourced nationally) Ⓗ

A 1991 Wetherspoon shop conversion in original style, displaying local history panels and photos. It is a regular venue for the town's beer lovers, also attracting others from surrounding areas. Up to five guest ales are offered, both national and local, with more at festival times when 10 handpumps are put to work. The cider is usually Westons Old Rosie, again with more during festivals. Q🍴🐕❄⒟🚻⊖(Central)🐾🚌🚭

Ickenham

Tichenham Inn ✓

11 Swakeleys Road, UB10 8DF

🌣 8am-midnight (1am Fri & Sat) ☎ (01895) 678916

Greene King Abbot; Ruddles Best Bitter; Sharp's Doom Bar; 7 changing beers (sourced locally; often Twickenham) Ⓗ

Small and friendly Wetherspoon pub with a strong local following. Food and beers are good value, with the usual chain promotions. The pub has its own festivals with more guest ales, in conjunction with other local Wetherspoons. Gwynt y Ddraig Black Dragon cider is served from the fridge from a bag in a box. Alcohol is served from 9am. Q🍴🐕❄⒟🚻⊖🐾🚌(U1,U10)🚭

Northolt

Greenwood Hotel ✓

674 Whitton Avenue West, Wood End, UB5 4LA

🌣 7am-11 (12.30am Fri & Sat) ☎ (020) 8423 6169

Greene King Abbot; Ruddles Best Bitter; Sharp's Doom Bar; 4 changing beers Ⓗ

This 1930s former Courage roadhouse was reopened by Wetherspoon in July 2016 after six years of closure. The pub has been sensitively and impressively refurbished, honouring the Grade II-listed heritage features, including the original flooring, bar and light fittings. Twelve hotel rooms have also been added. Alcoholic drinks are served from 9am. Q🍴🐕❄⒟🚻≢🐾P🚌(487)🚭

Norwood Green

Plough ✪
Tentelow Lane, UB2 4LG
🕑 11-midnight; 12-midnight Sun ☎ (020) 8574 7473
Fuller's London Pride; Gale's Seafarers Ale; 2 changing beers (sourced nationally; often Fuller's, Gale's) 🅷
Dating back to circa 1650, this Grade II-listed building is Fuller's oldest tied house. With low, exposed beams, two real fires and a superb landlord who takes pride in both friendly service and a well-kept range of real ales and ciders, it offers traditional roasts alongside other dishes every day of the week. Musicians entertain from time to time in the pub as well as in the garden in summer. There is now patio seating at the front. ☎⊛◑♣●🖵(120)❀

St Margarets

Crown
174 Richmond Road, TW1 2NH
🕑 11-11 (11.30 Fri & Sat); 11-10.30 Sun ☎ (020) 8892 5896
⊕ crowntwickenham.co.uk
Harvey's Sussex Best Bitter; Oakham Citra; Surrey Hills Shere Drop; 2 changing beers (sourced locally; often Twickenham) 🅷
A large, spacious pub dating from about 1730 and Grade II listed, recent rerfurbishment enhancing the Georgian heritage of the building. The Victorian hall to the back of the pub has been opened up for dining and the courtyard garden attractively remodelled. Inside are various seating areas and fireplaces, one with a real fire. Food is served 12-9.30pm (10pm Fri & Sat). ☎⊛◑♿⇌P🖵❀🛜

Southall

Southall Conservative & Unionist Club 🅛
Fairlawn, High Street, UB1 3HB
🕑 11.30-2.30, 7-11; 11.30-3, 6-11 Fri & Sat; 12-3, 7-10.30 Sun ☎ (020) 8574 0261 ⊕ scuc.co.uk
Rebellion IPA; 1 changing beer (often Rebellion) 🅷
Just about the last real ale outlet in Southall, the club is to be found behind the former town hall. Access can be gained with this Guide or a CAMRA membership card. It was completely refurbished to a high standard in early 2015. Lunches are served daily except Sunday, but it is a good place to visit either before or after eating in one of the numerous Indian restaurants nearby. At quiet times only one beer may be available. ☎⊛◑⇌♣P🖵🛜

Teddington

Masons Arms ♟
41 Walpole Road, TW11 8PJ
🕑 12-11 (11.30 Fri & Sat); 12-10.30 Sun ☎ (020) 8977 6521
⊕ the-masons-arms.co.uk
Hop Back Citra; Sambrook's Junction Ale; 2 changing beers (often Andwells, Coastal, Kissingate) 🅷
Small back-street community free house with a friendly atmosphere, very much a beer drinkers' haven, as reflected in the array of bottles, pictures and pub memorabilia on display (including an infamous Watney's Party Seven). There is a log-burning stove, dartboard and a small secluded rear patio. Guest beers change frequently, sourced from independent brewers across the UK. Local CAMRA Pub of the Year 2015 and 2016. ⊛♿⇌♣●🖵

Twickenham

Sussex Arms ✪
15 Staines Road, TW2 5BG
🕑 12-11; 12-10.30 Sun ☎ (020) 8894 7468
⊕ thesussexarmstwickenham.co.uk
Changing beers (sourced nationally; often Big Smoke, Twickenham) 🅷
A traditional pub with a real fire, now a firm favourite with beer lovers. Fifteen handpumps showcase beers from independent UK breweries and six ciders and perries. Live acoustic blues and Irish music feature regularly, and music is played from vinyl LPs. Food includes Anthea's famous pies. Every 10th pint of ale is free with the pub's loyalty card. ⊛◑⇌(Strawberry Hill)♣●🖵❀🛜

White Swan ✪
Riverside, TW1 3DN
🕑 11 (10 Sat)-11; 11-10.30 Sun & Mon ☎ (020) 8744 2951
⊕ whiteswantwickenham.co.uk
Sharp's Doom Bar; Twickenham Naked Ladies; 3 changing beers (sourced locally) 🅷
A Grade II-listed building and award-winning traditional pub, built around 1690. Entry is via steps up to the first floor, with real fires and walls covered with rugby and other memorabilia. A small verandah/balcony and a triclinium (three-sided room with window seats) afford views of the river and Eel Pie Island. Directly opposite is a larger beer garden (tides permitting), right on the water's edge. A summer beer festival is held. Q☎⊛◑⇌🖵❀🛜

The Maypole

All bars are snug places, but the Maypole's was the very snuggest, cosiest and completest bar, that ever the wit of man devised. Such amazing bottles in old oaken pigeon-holes; such gleaming tankards dangling from pegs at about the same inclination as thirsty men would hold them to their lips; such sturdy little Dutch kegs ranged in rows on shelves...such closets, such presses, such drawers full of pipes, such places for putting away in hollow window-seats, all crammed to the throat with eatables, drinkables, or savoury condiments; lastly, and to crown all, as typical of the immense resources of the establishment, and its defiance to all visitors to cut and come again, such a stupendous cheese.

Charles Dickens, Barnaby Rudge, 1841. The model for the Maypole is the King's Head, Chigwell, Essex

GREATER MANCHESTER

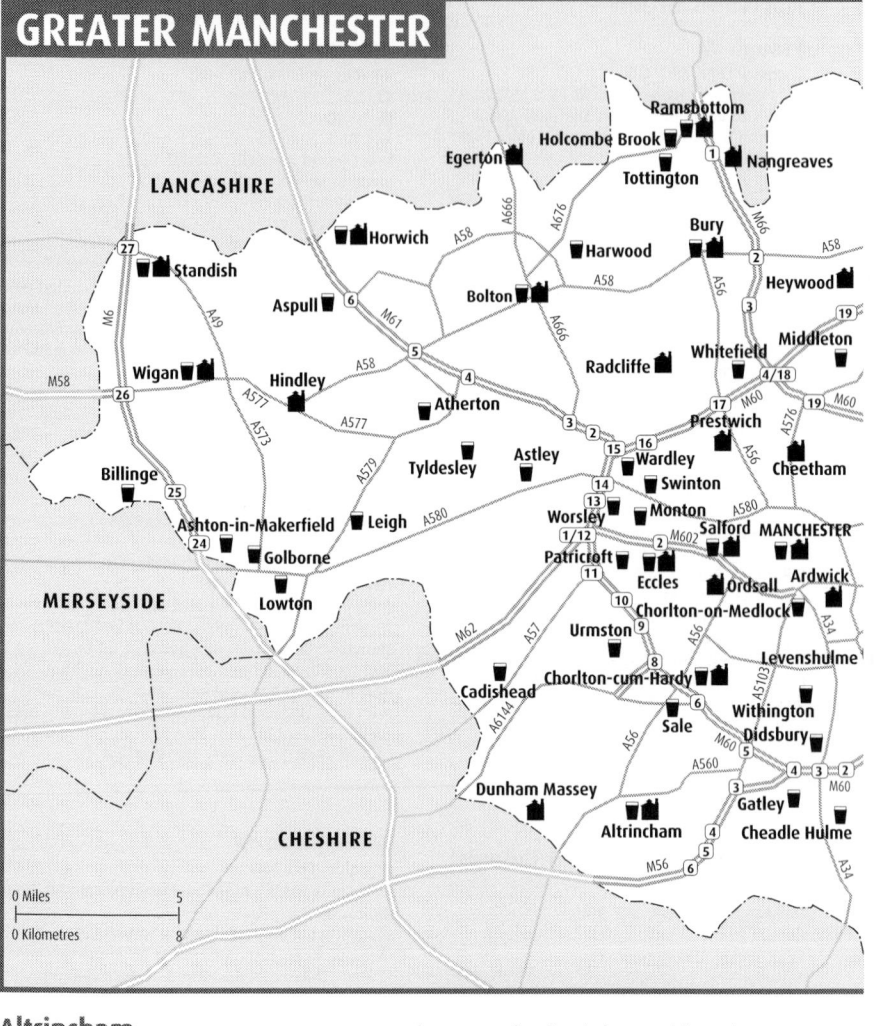

LANCASHIRE

Ramsbottom
Holcombe Brook
Egerton
Tottington
Nangreaves
Bury
Horwich
Harwood
Standish
Heywood
Aspull
Bolton
Radcliffe
Whitefield
Middleton
Wigan
Hindley
Atherton
Prestwich
Billinge
Tyldesley
Astley
Wardley
Cheetham
Ashton-in-Makerfield
Leigh
Worsley
Swinton
Monton
Salford MANCHESTER
Golborne
Patricroft
Ardwick
Lowton
Eccles
Ordsall
Chorlton-on-Medlock
Urmston
Levenshulme
Cadishead
Chorlton-cum-Hardy
Withington
Sale
Didsbury
Dunham Massey
Gatley
Altrincham
Cheadle Hulme
CHESHIRE
MERSEYSIDE

0 Miles 5
0 Kilometres 8

Altrincham

Cheshire Tap

36 Railway Street, WA14 2RE
☼ 12-midnight (1am Fri & Sat) ☎ (0161) 929 7810
4 changing beers (sourced regionally; often Poynton, RedWillow, Robinsons) Ⓗ
A long, thin bar that backs on to Kings Court. Soft lighting, a bare-brick feature wall, stainless steel bar top and bare squirrel cage filament lamps above the bar create a stylish laid-back feel. There are four real ales on handpump, mostly from Cheshire. There is also a handpump dedicated to cider. Cocktails are a speciality.

Costello's Bar

18 Goose Green, WA14 1DW (alleyway from Stamford New Rd/opp Regent Rd, adjacent to new hospital)
☼ 12-11 (midnight Fri & Sat); 12-10.30 Sun
☎ (0161) 929 0903 ⊕ costellosbar.co.uk
Dunham Massey Big Tree Bitter, Dunham Dark; 5 changing beers Ⓗ
Costello's is Dunham Massey Brewery's tap house, and only sells its beers on its seven handpumps –

the two regulars listed above and five other changing ones; the brewery has more than 25 different recipes and showcases them all here over time. The small bar has a modern feel and is popular with locals and visitors alike. Three real ciders are also sold, as well as tea and coffee. Award certificates adorn the walls.

Jack in the Box

Altrincham Market Hall, Market Street, WA14 1SA
☼ closed Mon; 12-10 (6 Sun) ☎ 07917 792060
⊕ blackjack-beers.com
Blackjack House Pale; 4 changing beers (sourced nationally) Ⓗ
A tap for Blackjack Brewery, located inside the popular Altrincham Market House, part of the town's historic market and a short walk from Altrincham Interchange. There are six handpumps on the bar. Blackjack beers are always available as well as a changing cider and guests sourced from a range of breweries such as Track and Squawk. The casks are housed in a chilled 'cellar' located behind the bar.

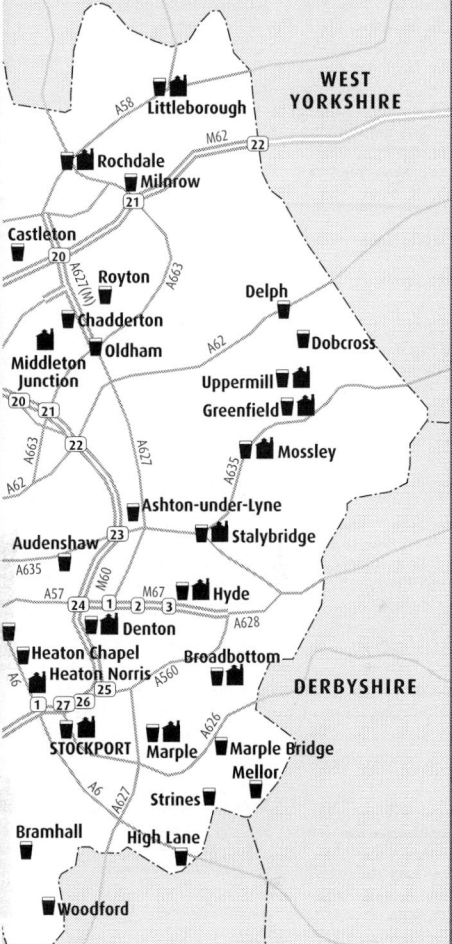

Tetley Bitter; 2 changing beers (sourced regionally) H
Large, Victorian community pub with interesting prints of old Ashton adorning the spacious open-plan lounge. A small raised area to one side is used as a stage for live music. The games room has large-screen TV and upstairs is a function room used by a variety of community groups. The pub is home to pub, pool and football teams, and hosts a popular quiz on Thursdays, open mic on Tuesdays and artists in the lounge most Saturday evenings, plus various charity nights. Q ⊗ ✤ P ₪ 🖥 ᚼ

Ashton-under-Lyne

Ash Tree ⊘
9-11 Wellington Road, OL6 6DA
🕐 8am-midnight ☎ (0161) 339 9670
Greene King Abbot; Ruddles Best Bitter; Sharp's Doom Bar; 4 changing beers (sourced regionally) H
Directly facing the Victorian Market Hall and square, this pub has become one of the premier real ale destinations in the town centre and is easily accessible by bus and train. Families are welcome in the lower level; above are the bar and lounge/dining area which leads to the rear entrance and outdoor smoking area. Wetherspoon's usual good value applies to the beers and food. Two real ale festivals are run each year. TVs operate with the sound off.
⊗ ❀ ◑ ᚼ ⇌ ₪ 🖥 ᚼ

Dog & Pheasant ⊘
528 Oldham Road, OL7 9PQ
🕐 12-11 (11.30 Fri & Sat) ☎ (0161) 330 4894
Banks's Mild; Marston's Saddle Tank, Pedigree H; 3 changing beers H/G
Known as the Top Dog, this popular, friendly local near the Medlock Valley Country Park has been a regular in the Guide since 1992. It has a large bar serving three areas, plus another room at the front. The beer range is supplemented by three guest ales from the Marston's portfolio. A menu of good-value food includes vegetarian options. Quiz night is Thursday. The pub is home to local hiking group the Bog Trotters. ❀ ◑ ᚼ P ₪ (409,419)

Aspull

Victoria
50 Haigh Road, Haigh, WN2 1YA
🕐 2-11 (midnight Fri & Sat); 12-midnight Sun
6 changing beers (sourced regionally) H
A traditional two-roomed local, adjacent to the popular Haigh Country Park, this pub is part of the local AllGates chain and features its beers alongside varying guests. The large lounge displays photographs depicting the history of Aspull and Haigh. Large-screen TVs cater for sports fans. Pool, darts, and dominoes are played. There is a covered smoking area to the rear. A small car park is available as well as on-street parking. Children are permitted until 9pm. Q ⊗ ✤ ◉ P ₪ ❀

Astley

Old Boat House
Higher Green Lane, M29 7JB
🕐 12-midnight ☎ (01942) 883300
🌐 oldboathouseeastley.co.uk
Marston's Wainwright; 3 changing beers (sourced regionally) H

Pi L
18 Shaws Road, WA14 1QU
🕐 11-11 (midnight Fri & Sat) ☎ (0161) 929 9098
🌐 abarcalledpi.com
Tatton Blonde; 2 changing beers (sourced nationally; often First Chop Brewing Arm, RedWillow, Saltaire) H
An intimate venue in a lively location. The ground floor is a compact bar with tables for dining and drinking, the first floor is a more spacious room. Outside there are pavement tables with blankets for cooler times of year. Typically, three real ales are on handpump, including Tatton Blonde and two guests which may be sourced from micros or more established breweries such as RedWillow, Saltaire and First Chop. Pieminister pies and mash are served until 10pm daily. The bar is a sibling to Pi (Chorlton). ᚼ ❀ ◑ ᚼ ⇌ ◉ ₪ ᚼ

Ashton-in-Makerfield

Caledonian Hotel
154 Bolton Road, WN4 8PF (on A58)
🕐 5.30-11.30; 3-midnight Fri; 12-1am Sat; 12.30-11.30 Sun
☎ (01942) 727875

Situated on the towpath of the Bridgewater Canal, the Old Boat House is off Higher Green Lane and was originally built as stabling for horses that pulled the barges. A major refurbishment was carried out in July 2016, opening up the pub to create more dining space. There are still areas for drinking though, particularly outside where there is plenty of seating near the canal. Live music features most weekends. ⏰❀◑▶♣P🖨(551)♣❦ 🛜

Atherton

Atherton Arms
6 Tyldesley Road, M46 9DD
☼ 11.30-11 (midnight Fri & Sat); 12-11.30 Sun
☎ (01942) 882885
Holt Mild, Bitter; 2 changing beers Ⓗ
Traditional public house with a great atmosphere and good facilities, including a full-sized snooker table and function room. The pub is known for its superb beer garden, which has TV screens and heaters. The beer is competitively priced and promotions change on a monthly basis. A wide range of events is hosted, with live entertainment at the weekends and most sport shown throughout the week. ⏰❀å♣P🖨(V2)🛜

Audenshaw

Fairfield Arms ✪
Fairfield House, 92 Manchester Road, M34 5GB
☼ 11.30 (12 Sun)-midnight ☎ (0161) 371 1331
⊕ fairfieldarmsaudenshaw.co.uk
House beer (by Black Sheep); 4 changing beers (sourced nationally) Ⓗ

Billinge

Masons Arms
99 Carr Mill Road, WN5 7TY
☼ 2-11.30; 12-midnight Sat & Sun ☎ (01744) 603572
⊕ masonsarmsbillinge.co.uk
5 changing beers Ⓗ
Built in 1779 and run by the same family for over 200 years, the pub has featured in this Guide since 2013. Five handpumps offer varying top-quality guest beers. Entertainment includes folk night on Thursday and quiz night on Wednesday. Sky Sports TV is played quietly on request. Outside is a quirky smoking shelter with a bison's head and logburner, and a pleasant beer garden overlooking fields to the rear. A popular stop-off for walkers and cyclists from the nearby Carr Mill Dam. ❀å♦P♣ 🛜

Bolton

Bank Top Brewery Tap ▼ Ⓛ
68-70 Belmont Road, Astley Bridge, BL1 7AN
☼ 12-11 (11.30 Fri & Sat) ☎ (01204) 302837
⊕ banktopbrewery.com

REAL ALE BREWERIES

AllGates Wigan (brewing suspended)
Alphabet Manchester
Bank Top Bolton
Beer Nouveau Manchester: Ardwick
Blackedge Horwich
Blackjack Manchester
Bootleg ᴇ Chorlton-cum-Hardy
Brewsmith Ramsbottom
Brightside Radcliffe
Carbon Smith Manchester
Chorlton Manchester
Cryptic Stockport
Dan's Manchester (NEW)
Deeply Vale Bury
Dunham Massey Dunham Massey
Dunscar Bolton
Epicurus Denton
First Chop Eccles
Five Oh Prestwich
Fool Hardy ᴇ Stockport: Heaton Norris
Four Kings Hyde (NEW)
Gasworks ᴇ Manchester (NEW)
Green Mill ᴇ Broadbottom
Greenfield Greenfield
Hay Rake Littleborough
Hexagon Marple
Hogarths ᴇ Bolton
Holt Cheetham
Holy Well Egerton
Hophurst Hindley
Hydes Salford
Irwell Works Ramsbottom
Lees Middleton Junction

Leyden ᴇ Nangreaves
Manchester Manchester
Marble Manchester
Martland Mill Wigan
Mayflower ᴇ Wigan
Millstone Mossley
Northern Monkey Bolton (NEW)
Origami Manchester (NEW)
Outstanding Manchester: Ordsall
Phoenix Heywood
Pictish Rochdale
Prospect Wigan
Ramsbottom Craft Ramsbottom
Remedy ᴇ Stockport
Rising Sun ᴇ Mossley
Robinsons Stockport
Runaway Manchester
Saddleworth ᴇ Uppermill (brewing suspended)
Serious Rochdale
Seven Bro7hers Salford
Silver Street Bury
Six O'Clock Manchester
Squawk Manchester: Ardwick
Stockport Stockport
Stubborn Mule Altrincham
Thirst Class Stockport
Ticketybrew Stalybridge
Track Manchester
Tweed Hyde
Watts Brewing? ᴇ Stockport
Westwood ᴇ Denton (NEW)
Wily Fox Wigan (NEW)
Windmill Standish (NEW)

Originally a private house, this rather grand Victorian building, once a Boddingtons pub, was refurbished in 2015. The central core of the building forms the main part of the pub. Around two sides are conservatories which provide light and airy spaces mainly used for dining. The drinker is not forgotten, with 10 handpulls adorning the bar counter, although these are doubled-up banks of five. Disabled access is via a lift from the side car park. ⏰❀◑▶⇌P🖨 🛜

Bank Top Dark Mild, Flat Cap, Gold Digger, Old Slapper, Pavilion Pale Ale, Port o' Call; 2 changing beers (sourced locally) ⊞
The Tap, which has won numerous local CAMRA awards, is a popular two-roomed street-corner local. There are eight handpumps supplying ales from Bank Top Brewery, plus a guest beer. Up to six real ciders are also on offer in a pleasant environment, with great service, quiet music and an absence of distractions from TV, jukebox or gaming machines. A dartboard is situated in the vault and there is a large outdoor drinking area with a covered smoking shelter. ⌂🕸🏃🍴🍺🖥🐾🐕📶

Bolton Ukrainian Social Club 🅛

99 Castle Street, BL2 1JP
✪ 3.30 (12 Sat & Sun)-11 ☎ (01204) 529258
3 changing beers (sourced locally; often Bank Top, Blackedge) ⊞
Large, imposing building to the east of town with a comfortable and well laid-out two-room bar. At least one of the three handpumps will have a beer from Bank Top or Blackedge and guests from further afield feature on the other two. The club is home to several societies including brass band, choir, chess and bagpipes. The annual Bolton CAMRA Beer Festival is held here in April. Local CAMRA Club of the Year from 2011 to 2017. Q⌂🕸🏃🍴P🖥📶

Brewhouse 🅛

987 Blackburn Road, Astley Bridge, BL1 7LG
✪ 12-11 (midnight Fri & Sat) ☎ (01204) 301372
⊕ thebrewhousebolton.co.uk
Moorhouse's White Witch; 12 changing beers (sourced regionally) ⊞
The building has recently been refurbished, with comfortable distinct seating areas including the original brewery area providing a light, airy interior. Food and accommodation are also available. The number of beers on offer at any one time varies, but most are sourced from the Northwest. There are two outdoor seating areas, both at the rear near the car park. Wednesday is quiz night. The pub opens until 'late' so closing times may vary. 🕸🏃🍴🍴P🖥(1,538)📶

Bunbury's

397 Chorley Old Road, BL1 6AH
✪ 12 (5 Mon & Tue)-10; 12-8 Sun ☎ 07952 344838
⊕ bunburys.co.uk
3 changing beers (sourced locally) ⊞
Opened on Back to the Future Day in 2015, this cosy bottle shop with a bar serves the needs of an area of Bolton bereft of good beer. Bunbury's offers three ever-changing beers on handpump from emerging local breweries such as Rivington, Holy Well and Northern Monkey, plus those from up and coming breweries further afield. It also stocks a wide range of often rare bottled beers from around the world. Q⌂🛒🐾📶

Great Ale at the Market

Stalls F14 to F16, Ashburner Street Lifestyle Hall, BL1 1TJ
✪ 9am-6.30; closed Mon, Wed & Sun ☎ 07815 058862
3 changing beers (sourced locally) ⊞
This microbar is located in the Lifestyle Hall of Bolton's award-winning indoor market. It offers a choice of three beers from a wide range of smaller breweries, as well as a selection of nearly 80 bottled beers from many countries. Sharing the same large seating area at the front of the bar is a

choice of takeaway eateries, including food from Malaysia and Cameroon alongside the more standard sandwich and pasty outlets. Local CAMRA Pub of the Year 2016. Q⌂🏃♿🍴🖥

Great Ale at The Vaults 🅛

Vaults Below Market Place, BL1 2AL
✪ 11-11 ☎ (01204) 773458 ⊕ greataleatthevaults.co.uk
4 changing beers (sourced locally) ⊞
This is the jewel in the crown of The Vaults, the below ground-level arches of the former Market Hall development – a dining and leisure venue with chain eateries, cinema and kids' play area. The long bar has four handpumps serving three guest beers and Vaults Bitter specially brewed by Outstanding Brewery using Australian hops. The beer is kept in glass-fronted chilled cupboards behind the bar. Paddles of three thirds of cask ale are available along with hot beverages and cold bar food. Q⌂🍴♿🎗P🖥📶

King's Head 🅛

52-54 Junction Road, Deane, BL3 4NA
✪ 3.30 (12 Sat & Sun)-11 ☎ (01204) 62609
Bank Top Flat Cap; Wells Bombardier ⊞
A late-18th century Grade II-listed building, extended in the mid-19th century. Located near to Deane Parish Church in the Deane Village conservation area, it is set back from the road with a two-tier car park, which is partially surrounded by woodland. The pub has three rooms, one with a cast-iron range and the others with low wooden ceiling beams. Crown Green bowling and a children's play area are available. Q⌂🕸♿🍴P🖥(715,540)🐾📶

Olde Man & Scythe 🅛

6-8 Churchgate, BL1 1HL
✪ 11-11 (12.30am Fri & Sat) ☎ (01204) 559060
Bank Top Flat Cap; Hop Back Summer Lightning; 2 changing beers (sourced locally) ⊞
The pub is reputedly the fourth oldest in the country and sits near the parish church on the historic Churchgate, site of a famous Civil War execution. The interior retains some traditional features such as wooden beams, leaded windows and stone floors, though there have been recent modifications to the layout. Nevertheless, it has a cosy snug and a separate room used for jamming and open mic nights. Only the Thatchers cider is real. 🕸🎗🍴🍺🖥🐾📶

Spinning Mule 🅿

Unit 2 Nelson Square, BL1 1JT
✪ 8am-midnight (1am Fri & Sat) ☎ (01204) 533339
Greene King Abbot; Ruddles Best Bitter; 9 changing beers (sourced nationally) ⊞
Opened in 1998, this large town-centre pub has an open-plan split level interior with a separate comfortable dining area. It is named after Samuel Crompton's mule, a revolutionary invention in cotton spinning that made Bolton famous worldwide. In 1862 a statue of Samuel Crompton was erected in the square in front of the pub. The nine guest beer handpumps serve an ever-changing range of ales from near and far. Two or three real ciders are normally available. Q⌂🍴♿🎗🍺🖥📶

Bramhall

Mounting Stone

8 Woodford Road, Stockport, SK7 1JJ

✪ 4 (2 Wed & Thu)-10.30; 12-11 Fri & Sat; 12-10.30 Sun
☎ (0161) 439 7563 ⊕ themountingstone.co.uk
Bollington Best, Long Hop; 4 changing beers (sourced locally) Ⓗ
The sister pub to Cheadle Hulme's Chiverton Tap, the Mounting Stone is a cosy, friendly micropub in the centre of Bramhall village. The former shop operates on two floors and has a small beer garden to the rear. Six cask lines dispense two beers from Bollington Brewing alongside four from local and national microbreweries, with one reserved for a dark beer. The pub has made a huge impact since opening, winning the City Life Awards 2016 best pub in Greater Manchester. Q ⊁ ⊛ ᕕ ⟳ 🚲 ➡ 🖵 ☎

Broadbottom

Harewood Arms Ⓛ ✔
2 Market Street, SK14 6AX
✪ 3-11 (midnight Fri); 2-midnight Sat; 12.30-11 Sun
☎ (01457) 762500
Green Mill Gold, Stellar, Chief, Old Git; 2 changing beers (sourced regionally) Ⓗ
This Regional CAMRA Pub of the Year has gone from strength to strength since it was bought by the current owners in 2013. Home of the Green Mill Brewery, it offers five regular Green Mill beers plus seasonals, guests and a rotating real cider. The pub has various seating areas and two real fires. For warmer days, there is a beer garden to the rear. Approximately five minutes' walk from Broadbottom railway station and on local bus routes. A real gem. ⊁ ⊛ ᕕ ⟳ Å ➡ ♣ ⟳ 🖵 ☎

Bury

Black Bull ✔
8-10 Lowercroft Road, Starling, BL8 2EY (on B6196 from Bury)
✪ 12-midnight (1am Fri & Sat) ☎ (0161) 761 5961
⊕ theblackbullbury.co.uk
Marston's Wainwright, Lancaster Bomber; Thwaites Nutty Black, Original; 1 changing beer Ⓗ
This family-run local offers a warm, friendly welcome to drinkers and diners alike. Winner of a number of Thwaites beer and cellar awards, it is also Cask Marque accredited and takes great pride in serving the perfect pint. Guest beers are from the Thwaites 1807 Cask Club range. Excellent meals are served daily, prepared using locally sourced top-quality produce. The restaurant is in a separate area from the bar. Booking is advisable as its reputation creates high demand for tables. ⊁ ⊛ ᕕ ⟳ 🖵 (486,510) ☎

Clarence Ⓛ
2 Silver Street, BL9 0EX
✪ 11 (12 Sun)-11 ☎ (0161) 464 7404 ⊕ theclarence.co.uk
Silver Street Session, One, Ruby, Ruby, Ruby; 3 changing beers (often Deeply Vale, Saltaire, Silver Street) Ⓗ
The Clarence is a gastro-pub with fine dining and four floors, serving real ale and real food. It has been lovingly and stylishly restored, to recreate the pub 'as it was'. The basement houses the Silver Street Brewery, although most of the beer is produced at its brewery at The Mill. The main bar is now restored to its former place on the ground floor, as shown by the original floor tiles. The restaurant is on the first floor and the members' cocktail bar (open Fri & Sat) on the second floor. Q ⊁ ᕕ ⟳ ➡ 🖵 ☎

Lamb Ⓛ
533 Tottington Road, Woolfold, BL8 1UB (on B6213)
✪ 4.30-11; 4-midnight Fri; 1-midnight Sat; 1-10.30 Sun
☎ (0161) 764 2714
2 changing beers (sourced locally; often Deeply Vale, Outstanding, Ramsbottom Craft) Ⓗ
Originally a coaching house built in 1831, this well-run local has an enviable reputation for being a friendly pub with a warm welcome for all. The atmosphere is enhanced by an open fire in winter months. The landlord is keen on real ale and promotes local microbreweries – mainly Deeply Vale, Ramsbottom Craft, Moorhouse's and Outstanding. Other local breweries and those from further afield are also seen on the bar. A local real cider from Red Bank is permanently on tap. A defibrillator has been installed outside.
⊁ ⊛ ♣ ⟳ P 🖵 (468,469) ☎

Robert Peel Ⓛ ✔
10 Market Place, BL9 0LD
✪ 8am-midnight (1am Fri & Sat) ☎ (0161) 764 7287
Greene King Abbot; Ruddles Best Bitter; Sharp's Doom Bar; changing beers (often Brightside) Ⓗ
Situated in Bury's cultural quarter, the Robert Peel is a well-established and popular Wetherspoon pub, named after the local mill owner and MP whose son became Prime Minister and founded the modern police force. This branch has the largest open public area in Bury, with a mixture of different-sized tables and booths. The decor celebrates other local worthies such as Richmal Crompton, author of the Just William books. Local breweries such as Brightside are featured while three handpumps dispense ever-changing ciders. ⊁ ᕕ ⟳ ➡ 🖵 ☎

Rose & Crown Ⓛ
36 Manchester Old Road, BL9 0TR
✪ 5 (3 Sat & Sun)-midnight ☎ 07845 748882
Moorhouse's Black Cat; 7 changing beers (often Bank Top, Castle Rock, Ramsbottom Craft) Ⓗ
A traditional friendly community pub just a short walk from the town centre. There is an impressive range of up to eight real ales on handpump, with flights of three thirds available for the price of a pint. On match days the pub is popular with Bury FC home fans and opens two hours before kick-off. A live acoustic night (8.45 till late) is held on the first Thursday of every month. Q ⊁ ➡ ⟳ ♣ P 🖵 ☎

Sundial ✔
312 Walmersley Road, Walmersley, BL9 6QF
✪ 12 (3.30 Mon)-11; 12-12.30am Fri; 12-midnight Sat; 9.30am-11 Sun ☎ (0161) 943 7705 ⊕ sundialbury.co.uk
Marston's Wainwright, Lancaster Bomber; 2 changing beers Ⓗ
A warm welcome awaits regulars and visitors alike to this award-winning Thwaites community pub. Situated a mile outside Bury town centre, it has an impressive red-brick exterior with an equally attractive decor, and was local CAMRA branch Most Improved Pub of 2016. Four real ales of excellent quality are on offer – two regular beers plus two ever-changing beers from the Thwaites 1807 Cask Club range, with Casque Marque accreditation. Thursday is quiz night and there is live entertainment every Friday and the last Saturday in the month. Breakfasts are served on Sunday morning. ⊁ ⟳ ♣ P 🖵 ☎

Trackside Bar ♥ Ⓛ

Bolton Street Station, BL9 0EY (Platform 2 East Lancs Railway)

🕓 12 (9am Wed & Thu)-midnight; 9am-12.30am Fri-Sun
☎ (0161) 764 6461 ⊕ eastlancsrailway.org.uk

Outstanding Piston Broke; 11 changing beers Ⓗ

Situated on Platform 2 of Bolton Street Station, the Trackside is an excellent example of combining the nostalgia of a heritage railway with great ales. The bar sells a house beer from local brewery Outstanding and 11 ever-changing guest ales. With up to 10 real ciders and perries, it was voted local CAMRA Cider Pub of the Year in 2016. The large outdoor seating area provides a lovely suntrap. There is also a covered heated space in cooler temperatures for those wanting a closer railway experience. ⏃⊛◑≷≈☐◑P➡️✿

Cadishead

Grocers

152a Liverpool Road, M44 5DD (close to Moss Lane)

🕓 closed Mon; 5-10 (10.30 Fri); 2-10 Sat; 2-9 Sun ☎ 07950 522468

3 changing beers (sourced regionally; often Cheshire, Dunham Massey, Track) Ⓖ

No TV, no jukebox, no electronic entertainment of any sort. No bar either. Just great beer brought to you by the landlord. Salford's first micropub has gone from strength to strength since opening in March 2015, including winning CAMRA branch Pub of the Year in 2016. Regular quizzes and cheese Sundays bring the punters in, as do the legendary coach trips to beery destinations. Cider drinkers will not be disappointed either. Q⊛⏃◑➡️(67,100)✿

Castleton

Blue Pits Inn

842 Manchester Road, OL11 2SP

🕓 12-midnight ☎ (01706) 632151

Lees Bitter, Dragon's Fire; 1 changing beer (sourced locally; often Lees) Ⓗ

The Blue Pits is a welcoming, friendly local in a former railway building once used as a mortuary. The building was fully refurbished by Lees in 2013 and now has three distinct drinking areas, offering a much warmer atmosphere than before. Cards and darts are played in the taproom and sport is shown on TV. There is a regular quiz night and karaoke. Of particular interest is the tiled mosaic of John Willie Lees on the outside wall. Lees' seasonal ales are featured alongside bitter and Dragon's Fire. ⏃⊛⏃≈♣P➡️(17)✿🛜

Old Post Office Ale House Ⓛ

858 Manchester Road, OL11 2SP

🕓 2-11; 12-1am Fri & Sat; 12-11 Sun ☎ 07740 837967

5 changing beers (sourced locally) Ⓗ

A community microbar, opened in 2016, free from music and TV. Quality locally brewed ales are on offer plus ciders and wines. There is no food but you are welcome to bring your own, with plates and cutlery provided. The building was converted to a bar by the owners, resulting in a unique interior, and well worth a visit. The beer garden backs on to the Rochdale Canal. The Rochdale-bound bus stops outside the door. Q≈◑➡️(17)✿🛜

Chadderton

Rose of Lancaster ✔

7 Haigh Lane, OL1 2TQ

🕓 11.30-11 (11.30 Fri & Sat); 12-11 Sun ☎ (0161) 624 3031 ⊕ roseoflancaster.co.uk

Lees Brewer's Dark, Manchester Pale Ale, Bitter; 1 changing beer (sourced locally; often Lees) Ⓗ

With a conservatory restaurant, lounge bar and thriving separate vault (in which sporting events are shown), the Rose provides a great choice for its varied clientele. Drinkers and diners mix easily in the lounge and the management ensures swift and cheerful service. Outside, a covered patio, with views to the rear of the Rochdale Canal, is popular in summer. The pub is handy for both bus and train links. Look out for the chalkboard detailing the number of pints of real ale sold each week. ⊛◑⏃≈(Mills Hill)♣P➡️(58,59)🛜

Cheadle Hulme

Chiverton Tap ♥

8 Mellor Road, SK8 5AU (off Station Rd)

🕓 4 (12 Fri-Sun)-10.30 ☎ (0161) 485 4149 ⊕ thechivertontap.co.uk

Bollington Best, Long Hop; 4 changing beers (sourced locally) Ⓗ

This friendly micropub opened in early 2015 in what was once Arthur Chiverton's draper's shop and was voted local CAMRA Pub of the Year for 2017. Note the mosaic in the doorway and framed displays of drapery tools on the wall and bar. Six handpumps dispense two regular beers plus four varying ales from small breweries both local and further afield. An ever-changing real cider is served straight from the box. Beer tapas (three third-pint measures) is available. Q⏃⏃≈◑➡️✿🛜

Chorlton-cum-Hardy

Chorlton Tap Ⓛ

533 Wilbraham Road, M21 0UE

🕓 4-11.30 (midnight Thu); 12-1am Fri & Sat; 12-11.30 Sun ☎ (0161) 861 7576 ⊕ barchorlton.co.uk

Dan's Pale Ale; 7 changing beers (sourced regionally; often Acorn, Magic Rock, Pictish) Ⓗ

A Chorlton institution specialising in cask beer for over 15 years and attracting the most diverse clientele in the area. Eight handpumps split over two sections of the bar focus on local breweries and the best micros from further afield. A choice of four ciders and perries is kept in the fridge. A full menu is offered until 10pm daily with soups, burgers, sandwiches, pub classics and a new addition, artisan cheeses. Traditional roasts are served on Sunday and Monday is quiz night. ⏃⊛◑⏃♣◑➡️🛜

Dulcimer Ⓛ

567 Wilbraham Road, M21 0AE

🕓 4-12.30am (1.30am Fri); 12-1.30am Sat; 12-11.30 Sun ☎ (0161) 860 6444 ⊕ dulcimer-bar.co.uk

Marston's Wainwright; house beer (by Outstanding); **3 changing beers** (sourced nationally; often Blackjack, Wild Beer) Ⓗ

One of Chorlton's most established specialist beer bars with five cask ales, four of which are from the best local and national micros. House branded beers are from Outstanding Beers and the bar also has its own cuckoo brewery, Oud Craft Brew, plus one or two bag-in-box ciders. The first floor regularly hosts live gigs from the local folk and

indie circuit, and there is a quiz on Monday. A beer garden/smoking area is to the rear.
♿❄️👤🔥🌳🍴🚌🐕🔊📶

Font 🅛

115-117 Manchester Road, M21 9PG
🕐 11-12.30am (1am Fri & Sat) ☎ (0161) 871 2022
🌐 thefontbar.wordpress.com
8 changing beers (sourced nationally; often RedWillow, Mallinson's, Track) 🅗
Eight ever-changing real ales are sourced from local, regional and national microbreweries including RedWillow, Track, Squawk, Blackjack, Mallinson's, Kirkstall, Arbor and more. The bar also features between four and 10 traditional ciders, varying seasonally. Simple but hearty dishes including pot meals and platters are served from the small but functional open kitchen until 10pm daily. Local CAMRA Cider Pub of the Year three years running. ♿❄️🍴🚌🐕🍴(86)🔊📶

Marble Beer House 🅛

57 Manchester Road, M21 9PW
🕐 12-11 (midnight Thu-Sun) ☎ (0161) 881 9206
Marble Manchester Bitter, Pint, Lagonda IPA, Chocolate Marble, Earl Grey IPA; 1 changing beer (sourced locally) 🅗
A Chorlton must-visit for over 17 years, the Beer House has recently become even more of a Marble tap with most beers from the brewery. Guest breweries still feature occasionally and there is also a good choice of bottled beers from Marble and others. The pub runs poker nights and homebrew demonstrations. Pop-up food offerings in the front beer garden feature from time to time. Dogs (and cats) are welcome, children until early evening.
Q♿❄️🍴🐕🍴🚌(86)🔊📶

Parlour

60 Beech Road, M21 9EG
🕐 12-11.30 (12.30am Fri & Sat); 12-11 Sun
☎ (0161) 881 3871 🌐 theparlour.info
6 changing beers (sourced locally; often RedWillow) 🅗
A winner of awards for both food and excellent ale, the Parlour has become a favourite. With a warm welcome for all, it has comfy sofas inside and an extended covered seating area facing the popular leafy Beech Road. The good British food menu features ingredients from local independent suppliers. RedWillow provides the regular beers and there is usually a dark beer among the range, as well as a real cider. ♿❄️🍴👤🔥🌳🚌🐕🔊📶

Pi 🅛

99 Manchester Road, M21 9GA
🕐 11-11 (12.30am Fri & Sat) ☎ (0161) 882 0000
🌐 abarcalledpi.com
Tatton Blonde; 3 changing beers (sourced regionally) 🅗
Small but perfectly formed, Pi is a popular bar on the increasingly crowded northern part of Manchester Road, celebrating its 10th anniversary in 2017. Four real ales and a guest cider or perry are all on handpump alongside a selection of world beers on draught and an impressive menu of bottled beers from around the world. Food is a changing selection of Pieminister pies (with or without mash, peas and gravy) served until 11pm daily. Coffee, teas and cake are also available.
♿❄️🍴👤🔥🚌🐕(86)🔊📶

Delph

Royal Oak (Th' Heights) 🅛

Broad Lane, OL3 5TX (via Thame Lane)
🕐 closed Mon; 7 (5 Thu & Fri)-11; 12-6.30 Sun
☎ (01457) 874460
House beer (by Coach House); 3 changing beers (sourced nationally; often Millstone) 🅗
Isolated, 250-year-old, stone-built pub on a packhorse route overlooking the Tame Valley. In a popular walking area, it benefits from outstanding views. The building comprises a cosy bar and three rooms, each with an open fire. The refurbished side room boasts a hand-carved stone fireplace, while the comfortable snug has exposed beams and old photos of the inn. The house beer is from Coach House and three changing beers include at least one from Millstone. A regular in the Guide for 25 consecutive years. Q❄️🔥🐕📶

Denton

Carters Arms

Stockport Road, M34 6AQ
🕐 4-11; 12-11 Sat & Sun ☎ (0161) 320 3752
Black Sheep Best Bitter; Box Steam Tunnel Vision; 2 changing beers (sourced regionally) 🅗
Friendly local with two large open-plan rooms – a lounge-style room to the left, regularly hired out for functions, and a traditional bar/games room to the right, appointed with wood panelling and dark leather seating. The pool team plays on Wednesday, quiz night is Thursday, a live artist features from 9.30pm on Friday, Saturday is karaoke and disco from 9pm. The Carters football team gathers post-match on Sunday. Accompanied children are welcome until 8pm. Disabled access is to the rear. Q♿❄️🔥🅿🚌🐕

Crown Point Tavern 🅛

16 Market Street, M34 2XW (in Civic Square)
🕐 10-10 (11 Fri & Sat) ☎ (0161) 337 9615
🌐 thecrownpointtavern.co.uk
House beer (by Tweed); 5 changing beers (sourced locally) 🅗
A micropub located on the pedestrianised Denton Civic Square near the old post office and library. The house real ale is brewed by the nearby Tweed Brewery and is complemented by five changing guests normally from breweries in Greater Manchester. A blackboard provides useful information about the ales on offer. A wide selection of bottled beers is also available. A community feel is evident, with offers for senior citizens weekdays, free nibbles on Sunday afternoons, and its own football team.
Q❄️🍴🔥🌳🚌🐕🔊📶

Lowes Arms

301 Hyde Road, M34 3FF
🕐 12-11 ☎ (0161) 336 3064 🌐 lowesarms.co.uk
4 changing beers (sourced locally; often Conwy) 🅗
Built in 1824 to serve the then new Manchester Road, this thriving local features quality beers and good-value food. Beers from Conwy, unusual for the area, are regulars alongside three others, mainly from local micros. The Westwood microbrewery is on site. Beer festivals are held in May, August and October. The lounge to the left is the main food area. The pub has teams in local darts, dominoes and pool leagues. Breakfast club is Saturdays and Sundays 10.30-12.
♿❄️🍴👤🔥🅿🚌(201)🔊

Didsbury

Fletcher Moss ✅

1 William Street, M20 6RQ (off Wilmslow Rd, A5145 via Albert Hill St)
🕐 12-11 (11.30 Thu); 12-midnight Fri & Sat
☎ (0161) 438 0073
Hydes Original; 5 changing beers (sourced nationally; often Hydes) Ⓗ
Named after the alderman who donated the nearby botanical gardens, this thriving community local is home to people of all ages and drinking tastes, usually engaged in lively conversation. The front encompasses three traditional snugs full of Hydes memorabilia and a collection of teapots, while the rear opens up into a conservatory, leading to a neat garden. There is a quiz every Tuesday, acoustic music on alternate Mondays and acoustic bands monthly. Q❀ᓍ♿ᗡ(Village)●🚃🚌🛜

Gateway ✅

882 Wilmslow Road, M20 5PG
🕐 8am-11.30 (midnight Fri & Sat); 9am-11 Sun
☎ (0161) 438 1700
Ruddles Best Bitter; Sharp's Doom Bar; house beer (by Brightside); 5 changing beers (sourced nationally) Ⓗ
This large, comfortable and extremely popular late-1930s roadhouse is conveniently located opposite the Parrs Wood leisure complex and public transport hub. It has a central island bar surrounded by various drinking areas, with quieter spaces to the rear, giving customers real choice. What makes this Wetherspoon such a deserved success, however, is the enthusiastic manager and staff who have successfully strived to create a real pub atmosphere and to provide excellent beer – long may it continue! Q🏠❀🕙⇌(East)ᗡ(East)●P🚌🛜

Dobcross

Navigation Inn Ⓛ

21-23 Wool Road, OL3 5NS
🕐 12-3, 5-11 (midnight Fri); 12-11 Sat; 12-10.30 Sun
☎ (01457) 872418 🌐 thenavigationdobcross.co.uk
Millstone Tiger Rut; 3 changing beers Ⓗ
Nestling in the idyllic rolling countryside of Saddleworth and close to the Huddersfield Narrow Canal, the Navigation was built in 1806 to serve the navvies cutting the Standedge Tunnel, and has been the destination for many a thirsty or hungry traveller for more than 200 years. A traditional family-run pub, it serves four real ales alongside mouthwatering meals using locally sourced seasonal ingredients to suit all tastes and appetites. Q🏠🕙♿P🚌(184,354)🐾🛜

Swan Inn (Top House) ✅

The Square, OL3 5AA
🕐 5-10.30 Mon; 12-3, 5-11 (midnight Fri); 12-midnight Sat; 12-10.30 Sun ☎ (01457) 873451 🌐 theswandobcross.com
Banks's Sunbeam; Marston's Wainwright, Pedigree; 2 changing beers (often Banks's, Jennings, Marston's) Ⓗ
A traditional Saddleworth pub serving five real ales and good home-cooked food. Built in 1765, it has three charming rooms, each with an open fire. The historic function room upstairs is an award-winning theatre and performance space. Quiz night is Thursday. Awards include Greater Manchester Fringe Best Theatre Venue 2015 and Saddleworth Best Illuminated Pub 2012-16.
Q🏠🕙🚌(353,354)🐾🛜

Eccles

Lamb Hotel ★

33 Regent Street, M30 0BP (opp Eccles Metrolink)
🕐 11.30-11 (11.30 Fri & Sat); 12-11 Sun ☎ 07827 850252
Holt Mild, Bitter; 1 changing beer (sourced nationally; often Fuller's, Greene King, Holt) Ⓗ
A large Grade II-listed red-brick Edwardian pub built in 1906. CAMRA recognises this pub as having a nationally important historic interior, with a central bar featuring polished mahogany and large curved etched-glass windows, and two lounges and a billiards room, also with polished wood in the panelling and fireplaces. A fourth room, front right, is an L-shaped vault. Wednesday is quiz night and karaoke is hosted on Friday night. Lunches are served on Sunday. Holts beers are 20p cheaper Monday to Thursday. ⇌🚃(Eccles)♣P🚌🛜

Gatley

Horse & Farrier ✅

144 Gatley Road, SK8 4AB (jct Church Rd)
🕐 11.30-11 (midnight Fri); 12-11 Sat & Sun
☎ (0161) 428 2080 🌐 horseandfarriergatley.co.uk
Hydes 1863, Original; house beer (by Hydes); 5 changing beers (sourced nationally; often Hydes) Ⓗ
This Hydes house was originally three cottages, with four bay windows added and the elevations later rendered to look like stone. It has a mock-Tudor upper floor. The central bar serves six different rooms and a food bar at the rear. Meals are available 12-7pm every day. A couple of seats are set cosily under the stairs leading up to the function room. There is an outside smoking area and a car park. Q🏠❀🕙♿⇌♣●P🚌🛜

Golborne

Queen Anne

14 Bridge Street, WA3 3PZ
🕐 12-11 (10.30 Sun) ☎ (01942) 726922
🌐 queenanne-golborne.co.uk
3 changing beers (sourced regionally) Ⓗ
Tucked away on Bridge Street just off the East Lancs Road, the Queen Anne is handy for Haydock Park Racecourse and caters for pre-race parties. Home-cooked food is served in the bar and a separate dining area, with early bird specials available weekdays 3.30-7, and popular Sunday roasts. The beer garden is a real suntrap in the summer. Q🏠❀🕙P🚌(360)🛜

Greenfield

King William IV Ⓛ ✅

134 Chew Valley Road, OL3 7DD
🕐 12 (2 Mon & Tue)-midnight; 12-1am Fri & Sat
☎ (01457) 873933
Black Sheep Best Bitter; Sharp's Doom Bar; Tetley Bitter; 3 changing beers (sourced locally; often Greenfield, Millstone) Ⓗ
Traditional stone-built pub featuring a central bar with a log-burning fire. Six handpumps serve the regular beers alongside three LocAles, often from Greenfield and Millstone. Traditional food is available Wednesday to Sunday. Monday is quiz night with free supper and cash prizes. The outdoor seating area to the front of the pub has recently been refurbished with a retractable awning and heaters. There is a large car park to the rear. 🕙🕙♿P🚌(180,350)🐾🛜

Wellington Inn ⓛ

29 Chew Valley Road, OL3 7AF (100yds past Tesco)
❀ 3-9 Mon; 3-11 Tue; 12-11 Wed-Sat; 12-9 Sun
Greenfield Silver Owl; Marston's Wainwright; Nook Blond; Phoenix Arizona; Salopian Lemon Dream; Thwaites Nutty Black; 1 changing beer ⊞
Friendly village end-of-terrace local which became a privately owned free house in 2011. It comprises a small bar area, an open-plan room catering for diners and a separate function/sports room with dominoes, crib and a dartboard. Good-value home-made food includes pies, puddings and real chips served all day Wednesday, Friday and Sunday, with fish specials on Friday. A guest beer is sometimes available. ⛄◑⛄⩜⩙⩙⊟(180,350)⛄ 🛜

Harwood

House Without a Name ⓛ ❂

75 Lea Gate, BL2 3ET
❀ 12-midnight (1am Fri & Sat) ☎ (01204) 433568
⊕ housewithoutaname.co.uk
Holt Bitter; Sharp's Doom Bar; 4 changing beers (sourced locally; often Holy Well, Northern Monkey) ⊞
Locally known as the No Name, this is a cosy terraced venue converted from two cottages originally built in the 1830s. It has been sensitively refurbished and modernised, retaining the flag floors and wooden beams. The main lounge has a bar servery with a blackboard beer listing, large-screen TV and a real fire, and to the left is a small bar. Simple pub food is served throughout opening hours. All premium TV sports channels are available. ⛄⛄◑⊟(480,507)⛄ 🛜

Heaton Chapel

Heaton Hops

7 School Lane, SK4 5DE (jct Manchester Rd)
❀ closed Mon; 4.30-10 Tue; 1.30-10 Wed; 1.30-10 Thu-Sat; 1.30-10 Sun ☎ (0161) 442 3541 ⊕ heatonhops.co.uk
2 changing beers (sourced regionally) ⊞
Since opening in 2015, this cosy, friendly, highly popular micropub has been collecting awards, including the CityLife Awards 2015 Best Pub and Manchester Food & Drink Craft Bar of the Year 2016. It has two small rooms on the ground floor and basement, with refectory-style bench seating and high stools. As well as cask beers, mostly sourced from local micros, and cider, it sells a large range of bottle-conditioned beers. Draught beer is available to take away alongside off-licence bottles. ⛄⛄⩙⩙⛄⊟⛄

High Lane

Royal Oak ❂

Buxton Road, SK6 8AY
❀ 12-midnight ☎ (01663) 766827
Marston's 61 Deep, Pedigree; 4 changing beers ⊞
A traditional inn situated on the main A6 as it ascends from Stockport towards the Peak District and Lyme Park. It offers four guest beers from the Marston's portfolio in addition to two regular Marston's beers. Families are welcome and a dog-friendly room is provided. Food is available lunchtimes and evenings in the week and until 6pm at weekends. The pub is home to crib, darts and pool league teams. Q⛄⛄⛄◑⩜⩙⊟⛄

Holcombe Brook

Hare & Hounds ⓛ ❂

400 Bolton Road West, BL0 9RY (on A676, jct with Longsight Rd)
❀ 12-11 (midnight Thu-Sat) ☎ (01706) 822107
⊕ hare-and-hounds-bury.co.uk
10 changing beers ⊞
This popular community pub goes from strength to strength. Its function room is used by various local groups to hold meetings and by the pub's quiz team in a local quiz league. The licensee organises two beer festivals a year, around St Patrick's Day and Halloween, with beers sourced from around the country and extra handpumps on the bar. Food is served daily until 10pm. Sports TV is shown around the bar, but there is a quiet room for talking and eating. ⛄⛄◑⛄⩜⛄P⊟(472,474)⛄ 🛜

Horwich

Bank Top Brewery Ale House ⓛ

36 Church Street, BL6 6AD
❀ 12-11 (11.30 Fri & Sat) ☎ (01204) 693793
⊕ banktopbrewery.com
Bank Top Bad to the Bone, Dark Mild, Flat Cap, Gold Digger, Old Slapper, Port o' Call; 2 changing beers (sourced locally) ⊞
The second pub opened by Bank Top Brewery, set in a conservation area opposite Horwich Parish Church and alongside 18th- and 19th-century cottages associated with the area's history of textiles. It is an immaculate pub showcasing eight beers from Bank Top, always including Dark Mild, former Champion Mild of Britain, plus one ever-changing guest ale. Alongside the beers are up to six real ciders and perries, most kept cellar cool. Walkers and their dogs are welcome. ⛄⛄⊟(125)⛄

Brewery Bar ⓛ

Moreton Mill, Hampson Street, BL6 7JH (just behind the Old Original Bay Horse)
❀ closed Mon & Tue; 4-11 Wed-Fri; 2-11 Sat; 2-7.30 Sun ☎ (01204) 692976
7 changing beers (sourced locally; often Blackedge) ⊞
An upstairs bar serving seven changing cask beers from the award-winning Blackedge Brewery plus a range of real ciders. Converted from former industrial premises and retaining some original features, comfortable settees and barrel tables with stools are spread throughout a large drinking area. The brewery is visible downstairs through large glass windows as you enter. The toilets are also on the ground floor and no lift is available. On Saturday match days the pub opens at midday. ⛄⛄P⊟ 🛜

Crown ⓛ

1 Chorley New Road, BL6 7QJ (on B6226, 200yds from A673)
❀ 11-11 (midnight Fri & Sat); 12-11.30 Sun ☎ 07827 850221
Holt Mild, IPA, Bitter, Two Hoots; 4 changing beers (sourced locally; often Bootleg) ⊞
A spacious, comfortable and popular landmark pub with a multi-room layout providing a home to many community activities. The separate pool and games room with its own bar hosts darts, dominoes and pool teams. Elsewhere are quiet drinking areas and a large sports TV. There is live entertainment on Sunday evenings and home-cooked food is served every day. The pub's location

attracts outdoor enthusiasts stopping for a pint after enjoying the beautiful countryside of the neighbouring West Pennine Moors.
Q℞🕭🌃◑&♣P🖵?

Hyde

Cheshire Cheese ✅

407 Stockport Road, Gee Cross, SK14 5RY

🕭 4 (12 Sat & Sun)-midnight ☎ (0161) 637 0233

John Smith's Bitter; Sharp's Doom Bar; 3 changing beers (sourced nationally) Ⓗ

Comfortable and welcoming pub with a loyal group of regulars. Beer is the thing here – there is no food. Three constantly changing guests (all over 4% ABV) from around the country complement the two regular ales. The pub is a member of the Ossett Beer Excellence Club so there is every chance of finding an unusual Ossett beer here. An outside seating area to the front features a retractable canopy to protect customers in wet weather. Children are welcome until 8pm.
Q℞🕭🌃&♣🖵🐾?

Cheshire Ring Hotel 🅛

72-74 Manchester Road, SK14 2BJ

🕭 4 (12 Sat)-11; 12-10.30 Sun ☎ 07917 055629

6 changing beers Ⓗ

One of the oldest pubs in Hyde and overhauled several years ago by Beartown Brewery, but now a free house. Seven handpumps offer a range of ales from micros near and far in addition to ciders, perries and continental beers. A selection of bottled beers is also stocked. Home-made curries are served on Thursday evenings, and Sunday is quiz night. Opening hours vary with the season and closing time may be earlier on Mondays and Tuesdays. ℞🕭🌃≒●P🖵(201)🐾

Godley Hall

Godley Hill, SK14 3BL (go up Kerry Way, bear left past Kerry building and turn left between terraced houses)

🕭 4 (12 Fri-Sun)-midnight ☎ (0161) 368 4415

Sharp's Atlantic; 2 changing beers Ⓗ

Not easy to find but worth the effort, with a warm and friendly welcome assured. This is a converted farmhouse built in 1718 and used as a public house since 1830. The comfortable interior retains many original features. While wheelchairs can pass through the very low main door, they cannot access the toilets as the Grade II-listed building cannot be changed. There are one or two guest beers changing weekly. Q℞🕭🌃◑≒●P🖵(201,202)

Sportsman Inn 🅛

57 Mottram Road, SK14 2NN (exit of Morrisons car park)

🕭 12-midnight ☎ (0161) 368 5000

Rossendale Floral Dance, Glen Top Bitter, Ale, Halo Pale, Pitch Porter, Sunshine Ⓗ

A regular in this Guide, with a full range of Rossendale ales plus a mild from Thwaites and real cider on a regularly changing basis. The upstairs is a Cuban restaurant, including tapas and vegetarian options. The pub is home to pool teams and also hosts matches for the local chess team. This former CAMRA Pub of the Region is popular with locals and retains its character. The rear patio includes a covered and heated smoking area.
℞🕭🌃◑≒♣●P🖵(201,202)🐾?

Leigh

George & Dragon

7 King Street, WN7 4LP

🕭 11-11 (midnight Fri & Sat); 12-11 Sun ☎ (01942) 605214

Moorhouse's Blond Witch; 2 changing beers Ⓗ

A pub with a Tudor façade in the centre of Leigh near the bus station. The smartly furnished interior is divided into two areas – the upper part is mainly for drinking while the lower level has plenty of seating. There are many TV screens showing live rugby, horse racing and football and there is a large outdoor seating area to the rear. Please note that children are not allowed. 🌃&P🖵?

Waterside Inn ✅

Canal Street, Twist Lane, WN7 4DB

🕭 11-11 (3am Thu & Fri) ☎ (01942) 605005

🌐 watersideinn-leigh.co.uk

Greene King IPA Gold; 4 changing beers Ⓗ

Not far from Leigh town centre, the inn is in a large converted warehouse situated by the canal with waterside seating. With wooden beams and themed coal fires, this is a setting that will suit most people. It attracts shoppers and office workers at lunchtime but is aimed at the 18-25 circuit trade at night, with DJs and live entertainment. ℞🌃◑&P🖵?

White Lion 🅛

6a Leigh Road, WN7 1QL

🕭 12 (2 Mon-Wed)-midnight ☎ 07814 575883

6 changing beers (sourced regionally) Ⓗ

The pub is situated opposite Leigh's historic parish church, just a few minutes' walk from the town centre. You can choose whether to enjoy the comfort of the main bar, bar games in the vault, or the quiet of the snug, in this friendly venue. Up to six handpumps dispense a selection of real ales from local and regional micros. Local CAMRA Pub of the Year three times in the past five years. Over-18s only. Q🌃&🖵(12,582)?

Levenshulme

Fred's Ale House ✅

843 Stockport Road, M19 3PW (opp Albert Rd)

🕭 4-midnight (11 Tue & Wed); 12-midnight Sat; 12-11 Sun ☎ (0161) 221 0297

Marston's Wainwright; Timothy Taylor Landlord; 4 changing beers (sourced regionally; often Blackjack) Ⓗ

Set on three floors, this is part-bar, part-coffee shop, and an art gallery. The neat yet narrow interior has the stylish bar set to the left, its size dictating that it is mostly standing room only on the ground floor apart from some seats at the front and rear. The spartan basement is a large drinking area-cum-art gallery space and can also accommodate live gigs and acoustic acts. An upstairs lounge exudes warmth and intimacy with comfortable leather sofas and mood music.
🌃◑&≒●🖵?

Littleborough

Red Lion 🅛

6 Halifax Road, OL15 0HB

🕭 2-midnight; 12.30-1am Fri & Sat; 1-midnight Sun ☎ (01706) 378195

Lees Bitter; Timothy Taylor Landlord; house beer (by Phoenix); changing beers (often Robinsons) Ⓗ

Port Street Beer House

39-41 Port Street, M1 2EQ (opp Brewer St)
🕔 4 (2 Fri)-midnight; 12-1am Sat; 12-midnight Sun
☎ (0161) 237 9949 🌐 portstreetbeerhouse.co.uk
7 changing beers (sourced nationally) Ⓗ
Opened in 2011, this bar has become a mecca for beer lovers from far and wide. Its knowledgeable staff serve seven real ales plus an extensive selection of draught and bottled beers from the US, Belgium, Holland and beyond. Local breweries Track and Squawk often feature. There is additional seating on the first floor with toilets on the second. Bottled beers can be expensive but you pay for quality. Regular Meet the Brewer events are held. 🚶🏼‍♂️🌜≅(Piccadilly)🚌(Piccadilly Gdns)♣🌭🚌🐾🛜

Rising Sun ✅

22 Queen Street, M2 5HX
🕔 12-11 (midnight Fri & Sat); closed Sun ☎ (0161) 834 1193
7 changing beers (sourced nationally) Ⓗ
Traditional, historic, city-centre pub, off Deansgate, with entrances on Queen Street and Lloyd Street (this is one of only three pubs in Manchester with entrances from two streets). Seven handpumps dispense a range of ever-changing beers and a regular real cider. Food is served lunchtimes Monday to Friday. The pub hosts regular beer festivals and Meet the Brewer evenings. An impressive refurbishment in 2012 has made a huge difference to the feel of this friendly locals' and visitors' pub. 🍴≅(Deansgate)🚌(St Peters Sq)🌭🚌🐾

Smithfield Market Tavern

37 Swan Street, M4 5JZ (corner Coop St)
🕔 4-11; 2-midnight Fri; 12-midnight Sat; 12-11 Sun
6 changing beers (sourced nationally) Ⓗ
Once a regular in this Guide, the Smithfield has had a chequered life in recent years with several changes of ownership and declining custom. Since then it has been extended into a neighbouring property and smartened up. In 2015 it was leased by Blackjack Brewery and has quickly gained a reputation for excellent cask ale, winning local CAMRA Pub of the Year in 2016. A mixture of Blackjack and guest real ales is available, supplemented by a real cider. ≅(Victoria)🚌(Shudehill)♣🌭🚌🐾🛜

Terrace

43 Thomas Street, M4 1NA (opp Kelvin St)
🕔 12-midnight; 10-2am Fri & Sat ☎ (0161) 819 2345
Thornbridge Jaipur IPA; 3 changing beers (sourced nationally) Ⓗ
This modern bar attracts an eclectic clientele. It has one long room which opens out as you go further in. Good food is served and live music plays most evenings. There is a rear entrance on Edge Street although this may not always be open. A free-to-use community space is available upstairs. 🍴≅(Victoria)🚌(Shudehill)🚌🛜

Marple

Beer Traders

113 Stockport Road, SK6 6AF
🕔 4.30-10 (11 Fri); 12-11 Sat; 12-10 Sun ☎ (0161) 427 0667
3 changing beers (sourced locally) Ⓗ
An interesting innovation for the area – this is a combined bottle shop and micropub in converted shop premises. Three handpulls serve changing beers, usually from local micros – ideally one traditional bitter, one darker beer and something

hoppy. Three bag-in-box ciders are also available. Live music often features on Saturday evenings. Opening times can vary – it may be worth checking prior to making a visit. 🏼‍♂️≅🌭🚌🐾

Samuel Oldknow 🍺

22 Market Street, SK6 7AD
🕔 1-10.30 (11 Fri); 11-11 Sat; 12-10 Sun ☎ 07766 301627
5 changing beers (sourced locally; often Brightside, Outstanding) Ⓗ
Named after a local mill owner who was responsible for much of the development of Marple and Mellor some 200 years ago, this is a somewhat quirky two-level bar in a converted shop. Six vintage-style handpulls dispense five changing real ales plus a real cider. The regular beers are from Brightside and Outstanding, complemented by guests from local micros. A range of bottled beers is also available to take away or to drink on the premises. Opening hours are subject to change. Q🏼‍♂️≅🌭🚌🐾🛜

Marple Bridge

Norfolk Arms

2 Town Street, SK6 5DS
🕔 12-11 (10.30 Sun) ☎ (0161) 427 8090
🌐 thenorfolkarms.co.uk
4 changing beers (sourced regionally; often Blackjack, Green Mill, Moorhouse's) Ⓗ
A recently refurbished stone-built pub sits in an attractive setting next to the Goyt river bridge. Comfortably furnished, it attracts a wide-ranging clientele by catering for all tastes. The beer range is a good addition to the choice in the area, with four real ales usually from micros. The atmosphere is warm and friendly, with good-value food also available. Live music plays on Thursdays and occasional beer festivals are held in the summer. Well served by public transport. Q🏼‍♂️🌜🚌🐾🛜

Spring Gardens

89 Compstall Road, SK6 5HE
🕔 12-11 (11.30 Fri & Sat) ☎ (0161) 637 5950
🌐 springgardenssk6.co.uk
Fool Hardy Ales Rendezvous #5, Rude Vagablond; 6 changing beers (sourced locally; often Fool Hardy Ales) Ⓗ
This is the sister pub to the Hope in nearby Stockport. The two regular Fool Hardy beers are joined by two rotating ales from the brewery plus four guests. The interior is smart, light and airy with interconnected spaces running off a large bar area. The bar counter features industrial-chic fittings, with eight handpulls. Food is described as 'traditional with a twist'. There is a Crown Green bowling green on site. 🏼‍♂️🌜♣🌭P🚌

Mellor

Oddfellows Arms ✅

73 Moor End Road, SK6 5PT
🕔 closed Mon; 12-11 ☎ (0161) 449 7826
🌐 oddfellowsmellor.com
Marston's Pedigree; 3 changing beers (sourced regionally) Ⓗ
This elegant stone-built pub is tucked away in a dip in the road in the old part of the village. Inside, the smart but traditional ambience is enhanced by beams and flagged floors, with blazing real fires in winter. Guest beers are often sourced from micros

such as Marble, Howard Town and Thornbridge. Sought-after food comes from a realistic menu with a gourmet twist. The 375 bus service passes the door but runs only infrequently.
❀◑ᕓ₳P☐(375)❀

Middleton

Ring o' Bells
St Leonards Square, M24 6DJ
❀ 5-midnight; 12-1am Fri & Sat; 12-midnight Sun
☎ (0161) 654 9245
Lees Manchester Pale Ale, Bitter; 1 changing beer (sourced locally; often Lees) Ⓗ
A pub since 1831, the Ringers is up a steep hill within the conservation area, just above Jubilee Park and opposite the medieval parish church. It is set in a fine, elevated location and visitors can enjoy stunning views across to Oldham and beyond, especially at night. Very much community-focused, the pub hosts an annual Maypole event on May bank holiday Monday and a unique Pace Egg play on Easter Monday. Occasional live music, Sunday lunches and quizzes add to its attraction. A covered smoking area and an attractive beer garden are to the rear. ❀◑♣P☐(17)❀ 🛜

Tandle Hill Tavern
14 Thornham Lane, M24 2SD (on unmetalled road from either A664 or A627)
❀ closed Mon & Tue; 5-10 Wed & Thu; 5-11 Fri; 12-10.30 Sat & Sun ☎ (0161) 376 4492
Lees Bitter; house beer (by Lees); 1 changing beer (sourced locally; often Lees) Ⓗ
The Tandle Hill Tavern nestles among a number of farms along an unmade, potholed lane. A one-mile walk from either end rewards the drinker with a neat little pub with a main bar, lounge area and separate quiet side room. A walled rear beer garden and benches to the front and side provide outdoor seating. Popular with walkers, farmers and locals, dogs are welcome. Food is limited to toasties. The house beer, Bumpy Lane, is dry-hopped Lees Bitter. In adverse weather, or in winter, phone ahead to check opening times.
Q❀❀

Milnrow

Waggon Inn
35 Butterworth Hall, OL16 3PE
❀ 12-11 (midnight Fri & Sat) ☎ (01706) 648313
Banks's Amber Ale; 2 changing beers Ⓗ
The Waggon, locally known as the Back Waggon, was built in 1782 and still retains many of its original features including mullioned windows. It has been sympathetically refurbished but maintains a traditional ambience. There is an excellent food menu with daily specials, tapas and a Sunday roast. The fine dining is complemented by three beers from Marston's, two of which change on a monthly basis. The pub is within easy walking distance of the Metrolink Milnrow stop and local bus services. ⧢❀◑ᕓ♣P☐ 🛜

Monton

Malt Dog
169 Monton Road, M30 9GS (opp the Park Hotel)
❀ 4 (5 Mon & Tue)-11; 1-11 Fri & Sat; 1-10.30
Sun ☎ 07541 553646 ⊕ maltdog.com

3 changing beers (sourced locally; often Blackjack, Brightside, Manchester) Ⓗ
A small but friendly community pub converted from an old shop. The ground floor is open plan and upstairs is a spacious lounge which hosts live music twice a week, mainly jazz. A range of mostly German and Belgian draught beers is available plus a good number of bottled beers. Teas and coffees are also served. A popular and thriving part of the Monton village scene. Q⧢❀❀☐❀ 🛜

Mossley

Fleece Ⓛ
53 Stamford Street, OL5 0LN
❀ 12-midnight (1am Fri & Sat) ☎ (01457) 835487
House beer (by Tatton); 6 changing beers (sourced nationally; often Brightside, Grafton, Titanic) Ⓗ
The Fleece is in Brookbottom, less than half-a-mile from the station, but much higher up. You will deserve a pint after the climb – or you could catch the bus. In 1890 the inn could accommodate three travellers, feed up to 50 and stable one horse. Today the visitor will find a tidy pub with a small vault area, an airy back room and a lounge. Cider or perry is always available. Dogs are welcome but horses perhaps less so. ⧢❀╪♣●☐(343,350) 🛜

Oldham

Ashton Arms Ⓛ
28-30 Clegg Street, OL1 1PL (opp Odeon cinema complex)
❀ 11.30-11 (11.30 Fri & Sat); 11.30-8.30 Sun
☎ (0161) 630 9709
6 changing beers (often Millstone, Pictish, Riverhead) Ⓗ
Extremely popular town-centre free house across from the new cinema complex and just 100 yards from the Metrolink Oldham Central tram stop. The bar offers an excellent range of four to six rotating beers from both new and long-established breweries, specialising in local micros and LocAles but also ales from further afield. Traditional cider or perry is always stocked, as well as a good selection of Belgian and German bottled beers. Good-value food is served weekdays until 6 (5 Friday), with pork pies and sandwiches at the weekend.
⧢◑♣●☐ 🛜

Carrion Crow ✔
271 Huddersfield Road, OL4 2RJ
❀ 12-midnight ☎ (0161) 633 4490
6 changing beers (often Banks's, Jennings, Marston's) Ⓗ
A former coaching inn dating from 1796, the Crow is an attractive, open-plan, popular community pub. Six handpumps serve a range of cask ales from the Marston's stable. Reasonably priced pub fare is available. The hostelry hosts crib, darts, dominoes, football and quiz teams, plus live music and regular beer festivals. The boozy news corner features histories of local pubs and breweries. All cask ales are discounted after 5pm on Monday. A former CAMRA branch Pub of the Year and Marston's award-winner. ⧢❀◑ᕓ♣●P☐(350)❀ 🛜

Up Steps Inn Ⓛ ✔
17-23 High Street, OL1 3AJ (between Spindles Shopping Centre and Tommyfield Market)
❀ 8am-midnight ☎ (0161) 627 5001

Greene King Abbot; Moorhouse's Blond Witch; Ruddles Best Bitter; Sharp's Doom Bar; 4 changing beers ⊞
Traditional town-centre Wetherspoon on the main shopping street close to the bus station, market and cinema. There are usually four regular real ales plus four rotating guests on offer, including beers from local breweries under the LocAle scheme. The pub hosts beer festivals throughout the year, featuring special real ales and traditional ciders. Food is available all day and families are welcome until 9pm. The cider is usually from Westons and Gwynt y Ddraig, with others at festival times. ⌂⊕&♿⬤♠⊟🚲🛜

Patricroft

Queen's Arms
Green Lane, M30 0SH (adjacent to railway station, up ramp opp James Nasmyth Way)
🕓 7 (5 Fri)-11; 12-11 Sat & Sun ☎ (0161) 789 2019
Thwaites Original; 1 changing beer (sourced nationally) ⊞
A regular in the Guide, the Grade II-listed building was built in 1828 for the arrival of the Liverpool and Manchester Railway in 1830. It was originally the Patricroft Tavern but renamed after a visit by Queen Victoria to the area. A real gem, it has three rooms served by a central bar. A two-times winner of local CAMRA Best Traditional Pub.
Q⌂⊕≈♣P⊟(67,100)🐾🛜

Ramsbottom

Irwell Works Brewery Tap ⃝
Irwell Street, BL0 9YQ
🕓 closed Mon; 12-11 ☎ (01706) 825019
⊕ irwellworksbrewery.co.uk
Irwell Works Tin Plate, Copper Plate, Costa Del Salford, Iron Plate; 5 changing beers (often Irwell Works) ⊞
This small local is situated on the first floor above the Irwell Works Brewery and serves a range of its own beers. The brewery prides itself on the production and sale of traditional-style ales, with hops and barley predominantly English. Food is now served Friday to Sunday 12-5.30. The bar is decorated with old photographs of the Ramsbottom area and is situated just a short walk from the East Lancashire Railway, the local preserved railway. ◑≈♣⬤⊟🚲⊟(472,474)🐾

Major Hotel ⃝ ✔
158 Bolton Street, BL0 9JA
🕓 12-midnight ☎ (01706) 826777
Bank Top Flat Cap; 4 changing beers ⊞
A regular in the Guide, this stone-built pub is on the main road into Ramsbottom. The building has two rooms – a central bar with TV and a main lounge featuring a large logburner. An extra handpump has been installed, increasing the range to one regular and four guest beers. Real cider is now available – Westons Old Rosie and Rosie's Pig. Good-value food is served. Live music features on the last Friday of each month.
⊕◑≈♣⬤P⊟(472,474)🐾🛜

Rochdale

Baum ⃝
35 Toad Lane, OL12 0NU

🕓 11.30-11 (midnight Fri & Sat); 11.30-10.30 Sun ☎ (01706) 352186 ⊕ thebaum.co.uk
7 changing beers ⊞
A former CAMRA National Pub of the Year with an excellent reputation. Situated just off St Mary's Gate, it is an easy 10-minute walk from the tram and bus stations. The pub is quite intimate, with bare wood floors and a traditional feel. It has a conservatory area at the back and a beer garden. Seven different real ales and one traditional cider are immaculately kept and served by knowledgeable, friendly staff. A fair selection of world bottled beers and draught continental lagers is also available. Reasonably priced, excellent-quality food is served daily. ⌂⊕⊛◑&♿⬤⊟🚲🐾🛜

Cemetery Hotel ★ ⃝ ✔
470 Bury Road, OL11 5EU (1 mile from town centre on B6222)
🕓 12-11 (1am Thu-Sat) ☎ (01706) 645635
7 changing beers (often Black Sheep, Moorhouse's, Phoenix) ⊞
The Cemetery Hotel is recognised by CAMRA as having a nationally important historic pub interior for its Grade II-listed Edwardian decor. The main bar area leads to three separate rooms – the front left room has impressive tiles and splendid mahogany seating areas. Seven real ales are available. Rochdale AFC is close by and the pub is popular on match days, with one room displaying club memorabilia. Despite its location next to Rochdale Cemetery, it has a lively atmosphere! ⌂⊕◑♣⬤P⊟(468,469)🐾🛜

Flying Horse Hotel ♥ ⃝
37 Packer Street, OL16 1NJ
🕓 11-midnight (1am Fri & Sat); 12-midnight Sun ☎ (01706) 646412 ⊕ theflyinghorsehotel.co.uk
Lees Bitter; changing beers (sourced locally; often Phoenix, Pictish) ⊞
Built in 1691 and rebuilt in 1926, this impressive stone-built free house is situated in the Town Hall square. Many original architectural features remain, including log fires. There is also accommodation, a function room for hire and a heated smokers' area outside. Seven cask ales and four cask ciders are available. Live music plays Thursdays, Fridays and Saturdays alongside live sport on TV. The home-made food menu features meat from the local butcher and pies made on the premises. Free parking is available. Local CAMRA Pub of the Year in 2017. 🛏◑≈♣⬤P⊟🐾🛜

Healey
172 Shawclough Road, OL12 6LW
🕓 11.30-11.30 (midnight Fri & Sat); 12-11.30 Sun ☎ (01706) 645453
Robinsons Dizzy Blonde, Unicorn; 4 changing beers (often Robinsons) ⊞
This always excellent pub – featuring in the Guide for 36 of the last 40 years – continues its long tradition of selling beautifully kept beers. There are three Robinsons cask beers, three changing guests and a guest cider. The indoor dining areas are complemented by a decked and covered area for alfresco dining. The beer garden has a covered smoking area plus a pétanque piste to the rear. Excellent food is served until 9pm Monday to Saturday and until 6pm Sunday. Children are welcome during food service hours.
Q⌂⊕◑♣⬤⊟(446,466)🐾🛜

Regal Moon L ⊘
The Butts, OL16 1HB
⚙ 9am-midnight (1am Fri & Sat) ☎ (01706) 657434
Elland 1872 Porter; Hawkshead Windermere Pale; Moorhouse's Blond Witch; Ossett Silver King; Ruddles Best Bitter; changing beers Ⓗ
A large and imposing former cinema in the town centre, handy for the tram and bus interchange. This is regularly the top-selling real ale establishment in the Wetherspoon estate, with 18 handpumps dispensing a wide variety of ales from local and West Yorkshire microbreweries. The ciders are usually from Westons with four rotating guests. The pub splits into discrete drinking areas in an open-plan interior. It was refurbished after the Boxing Day 2015 flood, but the mannequin organist remains on his perch above the bar. There is a patio to the rear for smokers. Q ❀ ⓓ & Ⓡ ● ⛨ ？

Royton

Puckersley Inn ⊘
22 Narrowgate Brow, OL2 6YD (off A671 via Dogford Rd & Fir Lane)
⚙ 12-midnight (1am Fri & Sat) ☎ (0161) 652 2834
Lees Supernova, Manchester Pale Ale, Bitter; 1 changing beer (sourced locally; often Lees) Ⓗ
Popular, detached, stone-fronted pub situated on the edge of the green belt, with panoramic views over Royton, Shaw and Oldham. This welcoming Lees local has a traditional vault and a comfortable lounge. The dining extension serves an excellent range of well-prepared meals, lunchtimes and evenings until 9pm (8pm on Sunday), with children welcome in this area. Cosy corners provide plenty of space to chat and chill out over a pint or two. A garden area is available for warmer weather.
❀ ❀ ⓓ & ♣ P ⛨ (408) ？

Sale

JP Joule L ⊘
2A Northenden Road, M33 3BR
⚙ 8am-midnight (1am Fri & Sat) ☎ (0161) 962 9889
Greene King Abbot; Ruddles Best Bitter; Sharp's Doom Bar; 7 changing beers (sourced nationally) Ⓗ
Named after the famous physicist, this popular Wetherspoon pub is close to the tram station and on several bus routes. Set on two floors, with a bar on each, the Cask Marque-accredited pub offers a total of 13 handpumps featuring nine real ales at any one time. Seven of these are constantly changing and sourced locally, regionally and nationally. Wetherspoon's annual real ale and cider and perry festivals are held here.
Q ❀ ❀ ⓓ & Ⓡ ● ⛨ ？

Salford

Eagle Inn
18 Collier Street, M3 7DW (opp Rolla St)
⚙ 3-11 (1am Fri); 1-1am Sat; 1-11 Sun ☎ (0161) 819 5002
⊕ eagleinn.info
Bootleg Chorlton Pale Ale; Holt Bitter, Two Hoots; 2 changing beers (sourced locally) Ⓗ
Salford's hidden gem, this Grade II-listed, 1902-built, three-roomed pub is hard to find, tucked away in an industrial estate behind ever-expanding new apartment buildings. A beautifully tiled drinking lobby and many etched windows and panels make for a truly delightful drinking experience. A neighbouring cottage has been converted into a performance venue. Note the terracotta eagle above the entrance. Close to Trinity Way and handy for the Manchester Arena. ❀ ❀ ⇌ (Central) Ⓡ ♣ ● ⛨ ❀ ？

Egerton Arms Hotel
2 Gore Street, M3 5FP (opp Central railway station)
⚙ 11-11; 12-10.30 Sun ☎ (0161) 834 7072
⊕ egerton-arms.pub
Coniston Bluebird Bitter; Holt Bitter; 4 changing beers (sourced regionally) Ⓗ
The present building dates from 1897 – the original building was demolished due to the widening of the railway viaduct. The bar is facing you as you enter, a vault with pool table is to the left. The lounge is to the right where chess and other board games are played. There is karaoke on Friday, an easy session on Sunday afternoon and live music on the first Saturday of the month. Accommodation is room only. ❀ ⊨ ⓓ ⇌ (Central) ♣ ⛨ ？

New Oxford ♜
11 Bexley Square, M3 6DB (corner of Browning St)
⚙ 12-midnight ☎ (0161) 832 7082 ⊕ thenewoxford.com
16 changing beers (sourced regionally) Ⓗ
Situated just off the A6, this well-regarded pub attracts regulars as well as visitors from far afield. A multiple CAMRA award winner, it has 16 real ale and three real cider handpumps on a central bar that serves two rooms. Beers are sourced from around the region and change regularly. The pub also keeps a wide range of Belgian bottled beers. Occasional beer festivals are held.
❀ ⓓ ⇌ (Central) ● ⛨ ❀ ？

Stalybridge

Bridge Beers L
55 Melbourne Street, SK15 2JJ
⚙ 12-7 (9 Thu); 12-10 Fri & Sat; closed Sun & Mon ☎ 07948 617145 ⊕ bridgebeers.co.uk
4 changing beers (sourced locally) Ⓖ
A combined micropub and bottle shop on the main pedestrianised shopping street in Stalybridge. Originally a hairdresser's, the interior has been restyled to satisfy the needs of its new function. A small entrance area leads to the bar which sits in front of a row of stillaged casks, of which four are generally in use. Beers are constantly changing and all locally sourced. The bottle display is opposite. Upstairs is a comfortable lounge. Last entry is one hour before closing. Q ❀ ⇌ ♣ ● ⛨ ❀

Station Buffet Bar ★
Stalybridge Railway Station, Platform 4, Rassbottom Street, SK15 1RF (access from station Platform 4)
⚙ 11 (12 Mon)-11; 11-midnight Fri & Sat ☎ (0161) 303 0007
Changing beers (sourced regionally) Ⓗ
One of the very few Victorian station buffet bars remaining and well worth missing a train for. A sympathetic refurbishment has allowed expansion of the food menu including home-cooked meals. Nine handpumps dispense a variety of beers, most of which are locally sourced, plus at least one real cider or perry. A good range of bottled beers is also available. Events include live music and Meet the Brewer nights. Monday is quiz night. On the Transpennine Real Ale Trail. Q ⓓ & ⇌ ● P Ⓡ

Wharf Tavern
77 Caroline Street, SK15 1PD
⚙ 12-2, 7-11.30; 12-midnight Fri & Sat; 12-10 Sun ☎ (0161) 338 2662

Copper Dragon Golden Pippin; Marston's Wainwright, Lancaster Bomber Ⓗ

A cosy canalside locals' pub occupying a triangular plot next to the Huddersfield Narrow Canal. Opened as a beer house in 1850, it was taken over by Gartsides Brewery in 1922 and the stained-glass windows recall that era. It has been a free house since 1981. No food is available but the fish and chip shop next door is under the same ownership and food can be brought in (Mon-Fri only). Opening hours may vary due to functions. ⊛🛏♿🚌🅿🛜

White House ⊘
1 Water Street, SK15 2AG
⊛ 12-11.30 (1am Fri & Sat); 12-11 Sun ☎ (0161) 303 2154
Hydes Original; 5 changing beers Ⓗ
Previously the Laughing Cavalier, this popular pub is semi-open plan but retains four distinct drinking areas. Up to five changing guest beers from micros and Hydes Studio complement the regular Original. Up to three real ciders are offered. A popular live music venue, folk night is Thursday and bands play on most Fridays and Saturdays. Sunday is quiz night. Food is served until 6 on Sunday. Close to both bus and rail stations. ⊛◑🍴≷♣🐾🅿🛜♿

Standish

Albion Ale House ⓁⒺ ⊘
12 High Street, WN6 0HL
⊛ closed Mon; 3-10 Tue-Thu; 2-11 Fri & Sat; 2-10 Sun
☎ (01257) 367897 🌐 albionalehouse.co.uk.
House beer (by Bank Top); 7 changing beers Ⓗ
A deceptively roomy microbar, Cask Marque and LocAle accredited, leading off the main high street with a small outdoor seating area to the rear. The interior is dominated by the pine bar towards the rear, with a stone-style tiled floor and high tables and stools. Pies and cheeseboard snacks are usually available. Live music is hosted occasionally. It is on the main bus route from both Wigan and Chorley – parking is limited in the immediate area. Equipped with a fully fitted disabled WC. ᕦ♿🍴🅿🐾

Hoot Standish
34A High Street, WN6 0HL
⊛ closed Mon & Tue; 11-11 (midnight Fri & Sat); 11-10.30 Sun
☎ (01257) 806262
7 changing beers (sourced nationally) Ⓗ
This modern café-bar, with interesting accent lighting, a slate-tiled floor and modest silent TVs, opened in January 2016. Novelty owls feature around the large one-room bar area. Varying local real ales are served alongside speciality coffees and prosecco, attracting all age groups. Qᕦ⊛♿♣🍴🅿🐾🛜

Standish Unity Club Ⓛ
Cross Street, WN6 0HQ
⊛ 7.30-11 (midnight Fri & Sat) ☎ (01257) 424007
🌐 standishunityclub.com
Sharp's Doom Bar; 4 changing beers Ⓗ
Not easily found but well worth the effort, this independent, non-profit-making club was established over a decade ago, and is a regular winner of the CAMRA branch Club of the Year award. A busy venue with music, quizzes and pool, it has a comfortably furnished bar, side lounge and separate pool/snooker room. Local beers always feature on the bar. Private functions are held in the main bar on some Saturdays. CAMRA members are welcome. Qᕦ♿♣🅿🛜

Stockport

Armoury
31 Shaw Heath, Edgeley, SK3 8BD (on B5465, jct Greek St)
⊛ 1-midnight; 11-1am Fri & Sat; 11-midnight Sun ☎ 07931 621220
Robinsons Unicorn, Dizzy Blonde; 1 changing beer (often Robinsons) Ⓗ
Comfortable, multi-roomed local with efficient, friendly service and a strong community involvement. It caters for a varied clientele from sports watchers and darts players to quiet bookworms. The lounge walls feature memorabilia of the Cheshire Regiment. Outside there is a pleasant beer garden, quite a suntrap in summer months. Handy for the train station and football ground – the pub opens at 11am when Stockport County are at home. Q⊛♿≷♣🅿🛜

Bakers Vaults ⊘
Market Place, SK1 1ES (jct Vernon St)
⊛ 12-11.30 (1.30am Fri & Sat); 12-10.30 Sun
☎ (0161) 480 9448
Robinsons Unicorn, Dizzy Blonde, Trooper, Old Tom; Titanic Plum Porter; 4 changing beers (sourced nationally; often Robinsons) Ⓗ
Grade II-listed marketplace house with high ceilings and feature arch windows. These give the gin palace-style interior a wonderfully spacious feeling, further enhanced by the well-stocked bar positioned towards the back of the room. A small lounge area with sofas is at the rear, providing a welcome retreat from the hustle and bustle of the main bar area. Live weekend jazz and blues adds to the buzz and vibrancy of this bohemian setting. ᕦ⊛◑≷♣🐾🛜

Blossoms ⊘
2 Buxton Road, Heaviley, SK2 6NU (at A6/A5102 jct)
⊛ 12 (3 Mon)-midnight; 11-midnight Sat & Sun
☎ (0161) 222 4150
Robinsons Unicorn Ⓗ**, Old Tom** Ⓖ**, Dizzy Blonde, Trooper; 1 changing beer (often Robinsons)** Ⓗ
An excellent local pub with a vault, front lounge and cosy snug around the central bar. It has been given a recent makeover by owner Robinsons, and is now one of the brewery's Ale Shrine pubs, with a striking decor and an air of elegance. At the rear, the now disused cobbled street sports benches for outside drinking, while the former outside toilet is now the smoking area. The pub offers excellent service and a warm welcome, and is well worth a visit. Q⊛◑≷(Davenport)♣🐾🅿🛜

Boar's Head
2 Vernon Street, Market Place, SK1 1TY (jct Market Pl)
⊛ 11-11; 12-6.30 Sun ☎ (0161) 480 3978
Samuel Smith Old Brewery Bitter Ⓗ
A multi-roomed hostelry with a genuine, cosy, town-centre feel. Owners Samuel Smith spent a fair sum restoring this pub to what it may have looked like in previous years. On entering, the bar runs to the left in the lobby, an open area to the right leads to a corner room, and there are two small rooms facing the bar. Beyond this is a large function room with its own bar. Outside is a small decked drinking area. Coal fires on winter days add warmth and ambience. Q⊛≷🐾

Crown ⊘
154 Heaton Lane, SK4 1AR (jct King St W under viaduct)
⊛ 12-midnight ☎ (0161) 480 5850

Oakham JHB; Salopian Shropshire Gold; 14 changing beers (sourced nationally) ⊞
Dramatically located beneath Stockport's famous viaduct, the Crown is a leading real ale destination. Four rooms with many original features including real fires radiate from the busy bar. Up to 16 beers are available, including a mild, stout/porter and up to four cask ciders. The pub presents a 'brewery tap' of around eight beers from a changing, premium brewery on the last Friday and Saturday of each month. Caribbean food and pizzas are served 12-2pm Monday to Thursday and 6-9pm Friday. Q✿❀◑≠●🚌(192)🐾🐕🛜

Hope Inn

118 Wellington Road North, Heaton Norris, SK4 2LL (N of Belmont Way)
✪ 12-11 (midnight Fri & Sat) ☎ (0161) 637 6191
⊕ thehopestockport.co.uk
Fool Hardy Ales Rou Shou, Risky Blond, Reckless Danger, Rash Dash; Outstanding 3.9; 6 changing beers (sourced nationally; often Fool Hardy Ales) ⊞
A thorough refurbishment and installation of the Fool Hardy Ales microbrewery turned a dead duck into a gem. Comprising two large rooms, to the right is the cask ale side with 11 handpumps serving at least six home-brewed beers including one regular from Outstanding plus changing guests. The left is the dog-friendly room and dedicated to foreign beers and real ciders. An extensive bottled beer range and festivals complete the picture. Q✿❀♣●P🚌🐾🛜

Magnet

51 Wellington Road North, Heaton Norris, SK4 1HJ (jct Duke Street)
✪ 4-11; 12-11 Fri-Sun ☎ (0161) 429 6287
⊕ themagnetfreehouse.co.uk
Salopian Oracle; 13 changing beers (sourced nationally) ⊞
A family-run, award-winning pub focusing on quality and choice. It sells 14 handpumped beers and a large range of foreign bottled beers. On the left is a bustling vault leading to a lower pool room and a series of rooms separated by arched doorways. Outside, there is a twin-storey beer terrace with seating. An in-house microbrewery opened in 2014. Local CAMRA Pub of the Year 2015. Q🐕✿❀≠♣P🚌🐾🛜

Olde Vic

1 Chatham Street, Edgeley, SK3 9ED (jct Shaw Heath)
✪ 5-11 ⊕ yeoldevic.pub
6 changing beers (sourced nationally) ⊞
Saved from closure in 2015 by a community buy-out, a gentle renovation is currently in progress. The interior resembles a licensed version of the Olde Curiosity Shop, containing a huge array of bric-a-brac and memorabilia, all presided over by larger-than-life host Steve. Details of the six guest beers are displayed on the 'pumpotron' TV screen. A real fire makes this a cosy haven in winter. Last entry is usually at 10.30pm. A regular in this Guide. Q✿❀≠♣●🚌🐾🛜

Railway

1 Avenue Street, Portwood, SK1 2BZ (jct Gt Portwood St A560)
✪ 12-11 (10.30 Sun) ☎ (0161) 429 6062
Outstanding Blond; Pictish Brewers Gold; Rossendale Floral Dance, Pitch Porter, Sunshine, Rossendale Ale; 6 changing beers (sourced nationally) ⊞

Bustling street-corner house showcasing Rossendale and other local micros plus guests. A changing mild and real ciders are always stocked, plus a wide selection of Belgian, German and other bottled beers. Occasional beer and cider festivals also take place. Note the model railway atop the bar canopy, and other railway-related material. A bar billiards table is well used, and the outside yard is a suntrap in summer. A former local CAMRA Pub of the Year, and local Cider Pub of the Year on numerous occasions. Q✿❀♣●🚌🐾🛜

Railway

74-76 Wellington Road North, Heaton Norris, SK4 1HF (jct Georges Road)
✪ 12-midnight ☎ (0161) 477 3680
Holt Bitter; 4 changing beers (sourced nationally) ⊞
Welcoming multi-roomed, award-winning pub on a busy main road. To the front are two lounges, one with a raised stage area for frequent and highly rated live entertainment (jazz on Sunday and Tuesday, rockabilly the last Saturday of the month, open mic on Friday). To the rear is a games room with darts (numerous teams are based here) and pool. The four guest beers usually come from micros, often breweries rarely seen in the local area. ✿❀♣🚌

Remedy Bar & Brewhouse

10-11 Market Place, SK1 1EW (jct Mealhouse Brow)
✪ closed Mon; 12-11.30 ☎ (0161) 477 1842
⊕ remedybarandbrewhouse.co.uk
6 changing beers (sourced regionally; often Remedy) ⊞
Since opening in 2015, the Remedy has been a significant addition to the regeneration of the market place and the pub scene in Stockport Old Town. It overlooks the historic Market Hall and has views of St Mary's Church. A simple but inspired conversion of two shop units into an atmospheric steampunk-style bar, it has pristine in-house brewing equipment sited behind a glazed wall, producing occasional brews. Friendly staff are always welcoming and knowledgeable. Live music often features at weekends. 🐕◑&≠●🚌(300)🐾🛜

Swan with Two Necks ★

36 Princes Street, SK1 1RY (jct Hatton St)
✪ 11-7 (11 Fri & Sat); 12-6 Sun ☎ (0161) 480 2341
Robinsons Unicorn, Old Tom; 1 changing beer (often Robinsons) ⊞
Narrow fronted with a mock-Tudor façade, the building was bought by Robinsons in 1924 and rejuvenated in 2008 by young licensees with ideas and vigour. It is impressively panelled in light oak throughout, with labelled doors to match. The front door leads to a vault, then the bustling bar-corridor, and beyond that a cosy snug with an attractive skylight. At the rear is a small lounge and diner. Outside is a compact walled drinking area-cum-beer garden. Quality lunchtime meals are served Tuesday to Saturday. The cider is Westons Old Rosie. 🐕✿❀◑≠♣●🚌(300,330)🐾

Strines

Sportsman ⓛ

105 Strines Road, SK6 7GE (2 miles out of Marple on B6101)
✪ 12-11 ☎ (0161) 427 2888 ⊕ the-sportsman-pub.co.uk
Phoenix Spotland Gold; 4 changing beers ⊞

Splendid white pub standing alone overlooking the wooded Goyt Valley, popular both with local drinkers and others. The comfortable lounge has large picture windows giving superb views to the hills beyond. A monumental fireplace accommodates log fires in winter and there is a separate taproom. Five guest beers, mainly from micros, are sold. Outside, a terrace and balcony are busy in summer. The pub is close to the Peak Forest Canal and Goyt Way Trail.
Q ➳ ✿ ◖◗ ⬥ ▲ ♣ P ⊟ (62,358) ✿

Swinton

Cock & Swine

207-209 Worsley Road, M27 5SQ (corner Partington Lane, 100yds from East Lancashire Rd)
✿ 12-11 (midnight Fri & Sat) ☎ (0161) 794 8443
4 changing beers (sourced regionally) ⊞
Formerly the Staff of Life, the pub was reborn and revamped as the Cock & Swine in 2014. Now operated by the Atwill pubco, it has undergone quite a transformation since its takeover. A changing selection of up to six handpumped ales is now on offer, kept to a high standard. Lunches and evening meals are available, traditional pub games are played and sport is screened on TV. On a bus route. ➳ ◖◗ ♣ ⊟ ⊟ ✿ 🗢

Tottington

Dungeon Inn

9 Turton Road, BL8 4AW
✿ 5-11 (12.30am Fri); 2-12.30am Sat; 2-10 Sun
☎ (01204) 887068 ⊕ thedungeontottington.co.uk
Marston's Lancaster Bomber; Thwaites Original, Best Cask; 3 changing beers ⊞
Traditional Edwardian-style pub, although built in 1835, with a quiet lounge with an open fire and a separate pool room. The pub offers six handpumped ales, fine wines and an extensive choice of over 40 gins. Live music features on Saturdays and a smartphone fun quiz on Wednesday evenings. An acoustic open mic session, from folk to soft rock, is held every Sunday. A delightful suntrap beer garden, comfortable surroundings and a great ambience complete the picture. Winner of Thwaites Best Pint 2015. Q ➳ ✿ ♣ P ⊟ ✿ 🗢

Tyldesley

Union Arms

83 Castle Street, M29 8EW
✿ 12-11 (midnight Fri & Sat); 12-10.30 Sun
☎ (01942) 870645
3 changing beers (sourced locally) ⊞
This family-friendly pub is very much part of the local community with regular charity events and occasional themed nights featuring live music. The pub is divided into a number of separate connected areas. On the left is the vault and on the right a lounge used for dining. Good-value home-cooked food is served until 8 and traditional lunch on Sundays until 6. Three to four real ales are usually available including Marston's Wainwright. Most sporting events are shown on TV.
➳ ✿ ◖◗ ♣ ⊟ (V2) ✿

Uppermill

Cross Keys Inn

Running Hill Gate, OL3 6LW (off A670 up Church Rd)
✿ 12-midnight ☎ (01457) 874626 ⊕ crosskeysinn.co.uk
Lees Brewer's Dark, Manchester Pale Ale, Bitter; 2 changing beers (sourced locally; often Lees) ⊞
Overlooking Saddleworth Church, this attractive 18th-century stone building has exposed beams throughout and was completely refurbished in January 2017. The public bar features a stone-flagged floor and Yorkshire range. Home-cooked food includes puddings, pies and real chips. Folk music is played on Wednesday and Sunday nights. Outside is a children's play area and a covered, heated smoking area on the extended patio. The Rushcart Festival in August is popular. The pub is the centre for Mountain Rescue and the Saddleworth Runners. A regular in the Guide for over 40 years. Q ➳ ✿ ◖◗ ⬥ ● P ✿ 🗢

Urmston

Flixton Conservative Club ✓

Abbotsfield, 193 Flixton Road, M41 5DF
✿ 12-3, 6-11; 12-11.30 Fri & Sat; 12-11 Sun
☎ (0161) 748 2846 ⊕ flixtonconservativeclub.co.uk
5 changing beers (sourced nationally; often Bank Top, Elland, Pictish) ⊞
With six handpumps on its main bar, this CAMRA award-winning club continues to display a genuine commitment to selling quality real ales and the occasional real cider. A further five pumps upstairs allow the club to run monthly brewery nights with a small entry fee, pie and peas included. Various other events are held including a regular quiz night. The club is home to a wide range of sports teams including snooker, bowls, darts, dominoes and chess. ➳ ✿ ⇌ (Chassen Rd) ♣ ● P ⊟ (255) 🗢

Lord Nelson

49 Stretford Road, M41 9LG
✿ 11-11 (11.30 Fri & Sat); 12-11 Sun ☎ 07827 850255
Holt Mild, Bitter, IPA, Two Hoots ⊞
The Nellie is a classic Holt's drinking pub, not so much wet-led as completely soaking. There is no food beyond crisps, nuts and pork scratchings. People go there to drink, to talk, and to watch sport on large-screen TVs. The building dates back to around 1805 and the pub is very much part of the Urmston community, raising astonishing sums of money for local charities. It was local CAMRA branch Community Pub of the Year in 2016.
✿ ⬥ ⇌ ♣ P ⊟ 🗢

Prairie Schooner Taphouse

33 Flixton Road, M41 5AW
✿ closed Mon; 3-10.30 Tue-Thu; 12-midnight Fri & Sat; 12-9 Sun ⊕ prairie-schooner-taphouse.co.uk
4 changing beers (sourced regionally) ⊞
Ostensibly a micropub but actually of a decent size, with two distinct seating areas either side of an island bar. The emphasis is on the unusual, with cask ales and bottled beers from independent British, continental and American breweries. Cider lovers are not forgotten, with real cider and perry in a box along with bottled ciders from the likes of Dunkertons and the Moss Cider Project. Bottles can be bought to take away. Q ➳ ◖◗ ⬥ ⇌ ⊟ (255) ✿ 🗢

Wardley

Morning Star
520 Manchester Road, M27 9QW (opp Bagot St)
⏱ 12-11 (11.30 Fri & Sat) ☎ 07827 850258
Holt Mild, Bitter; 2 changing beers (sourced locally) Ⓗ
Built in 1890, this imposing red-brick building is a good example of a community establishment. A smart and tidy pub, to the left is the traditional vault with darts, dominoes and TV. To the right is a small open front room leading to a much larger lounge/dining room. The three rooms are served from a central bar. The pub hosts a fortnightly Wednesday quiz night and Saturday evening entertainment. A covered outside drinking area is a real asset in summer. ✿◗≉♣P🚌(36,37)🛜

Whitefield

Eagle & Child
Higher Lane, M45 7EY
⏱ 12-11 (midnight Fri & Sat) ☎ 07827 850229
Holt Mild, IPA, Bitter, Two Hoots; 1 changing beer Ⓗ
Traditional, black-and-white timbered, double fronted pub with a central bar, spacious lounge and vault room. The separate front room is ideal for meetings/private parties (up to maximum of fifty). Family friendly with dogs allowed outside on a lead. A large floodlit bowling green, available for hire, is open from April to September. The pub hosts darts, dominoes and cribbage teams, offers live entertainment every Friday and screens live TV sports events. Q🛏✿&🅿♣P🚌(98,135)🛜

Wigan

Anvil Ⓛ ✅
Dorning Street, WN1 1ND
⏱ 11-11; 12-10.30 Sun
AllGates California; Hydes 1863; Thwaites Best Cask; 6 changing beers (sourced nationally) Ⓗ
Popular town-centre pub with seven handpumps offering beers from the nearby AllGates Brewery, various guest ales, two real ciders, six draught continental ales and a range of bottled beers. Several TV screens show sports action and the small snug features a Wall of Fame displaying numerous award certificates. There is a garden to the rear. Close to bus and railway access for the DW Stadium, the pub can be busy on match days. Over-18s only. ✿≉(Wallgate/N Western)●🚌

Berkeley ✅
27-29 Wallgate, WN1 1LD
⏱ 11-11 (1am Fri & Sat); 12-midnight Sun ☎ (01942) 242041
5 changing beers Ⓗ
A former coaching house close to both rail stations and adjacent to the infamous King Street, attracting a younger clientele at weekends. The large bar offers a range of rotating guest ales. Food is served daily 12-7pm. Children are allowed only until 2.30 when dining. Sport predominates during the day, screened on eight large-screen TVs and a massive projector. A first-floor function area can be hired. ◗≉(Wallgate)🚌

Crooke Hall Inn
Crooke Road, WN6 8LR
⏱ 12-11 ☎ (01942) 236088
12 changing beers (often AllGates) Ⓗ
CAMRA Community Pub of the Year 2014-16, located in the small canalside hamlet of Crooke just outside Wigan. This multi-roomed country-style pub, owned by AllGates Brewery, features a range of its beers alongside varying guest ales. The large garden overlooks the Leeds-Liverpool Canal. Food is available, with children welcome until 9pm. The Cellar Bar provides a separate facility, ideal for clubs and functions. Dogs are welcome, with dog food and treats on sale. Q🛏✿◗♣●P✿🛜

Doc's Symposium Ⓛ
85 Mesnes Street, WN1 1QJ
⏱ closed Mon-Wed; 12-11 Thu-Sat; 1-10.30 Sun ☎ 07462 896822
Facer's DHB; Weetwood Cheshire Cat; 2 changing beers Ⓗ
This was Wigan's first micropub. The bar has a light and airy feel, with a well-stocked deli counter and daily specials. Outside, there is some seating overlooking Mesnes Park. Five real ales are sold, including local Wigan brews, and a variety of European beers. Sporting events are shown on TV on occasion. Run by well-respected landlords, you are guaranteed a warm welcome from the staff. Q✿◗≉P🚌🛜

John Bull Chophouse ✅
2 Coopers Row, Market Place, WN1 1PQ
⏱ closed Mon; 4.30-11 Tue-Thu; 1-1am Fri & Sat; 5-11 Sun ☎ (01942) 242862 ⊕ johnbullchophousewigan.co.uk
Thwaites Best Cask; 5 changing beers Ⓗ
A vibrant and lively town-centre pub in a 300-year-old building that has been cottages, stables and a slaughterhouse in the past. It has been run by the same family for over 40 years. There are six handpumps serving Thwaites beers. The quirky pub is on two floors, with what is claimed to be the best pub jukebox in the North-west, plus a pool table. Live music is hosted on occasion. There is seating outside. The toilets are upstairs. ≉(Wallgate/N Western)🚌

Raven Hotel ✅
5 Wallgate, WN1 1LD
⏱ 11-11 ☎ (01942) 239764 ⊕ theravenwigan.com
5 changing beers Ⓗ
An early 1900s commercial hotel, virtually derelict before a tasteful renovation in 2012, retaining and restoring many original features including tiles, panelling and windows. The retro interior is typical of the local Inn The Bar pub chain, warmed by cosy real coal fires in winter and with two unobtrusive TVs. It serves a varying range of real ales and cider on handpump, alongside good home-made pub food at a reasonable price. Customer loyalty cards are used and a weekly cask critics night offers discounts on real ale. ◗≉(Wallgate/N Western)●🚌🛜

Royal Oak
111-113 Standishgate, WN1 1XL
⏱ 9am-11 (1am Sat & Sun) ☎ (01942) 820563 ⊕ theroyaloakwigan.co.uk
Thwaites Best Cask; 4 changing beers Ⓗ
The pub has four separate seating areas, decorated in the retro style favoured by the Inn The Bar pub chain. It offers four cask ales, a variety of wines and a range of speciality gins. There are daily specials as well as a regular food menu, and fresh coffee and tea. A loyalty card scheme is used and a quiz is held every Wednesday night. Outside, the large beer garden has cosy covered alcoves down one side. 🛏✿◗&🚌🛜

Tap 'n' Barrel L ✓
16 Jaxon's Court, WN1 1LR
☼ 12-10 Mon, Wed & Thu; 1-7 Tue; 12-midnight Fri; 12-1am
Sat; 1-10 Sun ☎ (01942) 386966
⊕ martlandmillbrewery.co.uk
**6 changing beers (sourced regionally; often Martland
Mill)** ⊞
Located adjacent to the bus station in a narrow
shopping mews, this micro bar is the brewery tap
for Martland Mill. The main bar area is long and
narrow, leading to a covered, heated, smoke-free
garden, which hosts live music on Sunday
afternoons and monthly comedy evenings. There is
additional seating upstairs. Four real ciders are
served from the fridge. Beers and ciders are
available in paddles of three third-pints. Occasional
beer and sausage festivals are held.
Q≠(Wallgate/N Western)●🚌🐾🎵♿

Wigan Central ♟ L
Arch No. 1 & 2, Queen Street, WN3 4DY
☼ 12-11 (midnight Fri); 11-midnight Sat; 12-10.30 Sun
☎ (01942) 246425 ⊕ wigancentral.bar
**House beer (by Prospect); 6 changing beers (sourced
nationally)** ⊞
Two-roomed pub with a railway-themed interior
and a live screen displaying arrival and departure
times from the two rail stations. The pub is owned
by the nearby Prospect Brewery but sources real
ales from all over, alongside continental bottled
beers displayed in the 'library'. Regular beer club
and beer matching events are held. Live music
plays in the Platform room on Sundays. Bar snacks
are available. Wigan CAMRA Pub of the Year and
Cider Pub of the Year 2015 and 2016.
Q&≠(Wallgate/N Western)●🚌🐾🎵♿

Withington

Victoria
438 Wilmslow Road, M20 3BW (on B5093, jct
Davenport Av)
☼ 12-11 (midnight Thu-Sat) ☎ (0161) 434 2600
**Hydes Old Indie, Original, 1863; 6 changing beers
(sourced nationally; often Hydes)** ⊞
What makes this thriving community pub so
popular is the friendliness of the licensees and
staff, plus the excellence of the beers. The period
exterior hides a large open-plan interior divided
into distinct areas, allowing you to choose what
you want from your visit – whether it is a quiet
chat, watching sport on TV, listening to the
entertainment or playing pool. You can even bring
in your own food to eat. The etched-glass windows
and tiled floor around the bar add character.
🏠🍴♿●🚌🐾🎵♿

Woodford

Davenport Arms (Thief's Neck)
550 Chester Road, SK7 1PS (on A5102, jct Church La)
☼ 11-11; 12-10.30 Sun ☎ (0161) 439 2435
⊕ davenportarms.co.uk
**Robinsons Unicorn, Dizzy Blonde, Old Tom, Wizard; 1
changing beer (often Robinsons)** ⊞
Characterful red-brick farmhouse-style pub which
received a smart refurbishment in 2014 but retains
a multi-roomed feel with real fires in winter. This is
its 31st consecutive year in the Guide, and the
licence has now been in the same family for a
mammoth 85 years. Excellent food is mostly home
made, with some adventurous specials. Outside,
the spacious forecourt and attractive garden, set
well away from the road, are popular in summer,
boasting impressive floral displays.
🏠🍴♿♣P🚌(42B)🐾🎵

Worsley

John Gilbert ✓
Worsley Brow, M28 2YA (opp St Mark's Church)
☼ 9am-11; 9am-1am Fri & Sat ☎ (0161) 703 7733
**Greene King IPA; 7 changing beers (sourced
regionally)** ⊞
Large pub close to Worsley village on Worsley Brow
adjacent to the Novotel, with a modern and clean
interior and friendly bar staff. It has ample parking
space and is on a bus route. Owned by Greene
King, IPA is always available plus up to seven guest
beers from a good variety of breweries, both local
and regional. A popular dining spot with a good
and varied menu, it now opens from 9am for
breakfast. 🏠🍴♿&♣P🚌🎵

Worsley Old Hall
Worsley Park, off Walkden Road, M28 2QT (next to
Worsley Park Marriott Hotel)
☼ 9am-11 (10.30 Sun) ☎ (0161) 703 8706
**Brunning & Price Original; house beer (by Facer's); 4
changing beers (sourced regionally)** ⊞
Seventeenth-century building refurbished in 2013
to a high standard with a country-house feel. It
offers spacious dining areas and drinking rooms
with comfortable seating and numerous pictures
for added interest. Excellent food is served for all
the family to enjoy. Cider is always available on
handpump. It has a large beer garden and is set in
open woodland adjacent to a golf course.
Q🏠🍴♿&♣●P🚌(33,34)🐾🎵

One hundred years old

I met the other day an old man, who asked me to drink. 'I am not thirsty,' said I, 'and I will
not drink with you.' 'Yes, you will,' said the old man, 'for I am this day one hundred years
old; and you will never again have the opportunity of drinking the health of a man on his
hundredth birthday.' So I broke my word and drank. 'How have you passed your time?'
said I. 'As well as I could,' said the old man, 'always enjoying a good thing when it came
honestly within my reach; not forgetting to praise God for putting it there'. 'I suppose you
were fond of a glass of good ale when you were young'. 'Yes,' said the old man, 'I was,
and so, thank God, I am still'. And he drank off a glass of ale.
George Barrow, 1857

MERSEYSIDE

Barnston

Fox & Hounds ✔

107 Barnston Road, CH61 1BW (on A551)

🕐 11-11; 12-10.30 Sun ☎ (0151) 648 7685

🌐 the-fox-hounds.co.uk

Brimstage Trappers Hat Bitter; Theakston Best Bitter, Old Peculier; Timothy Taylor Landlord; 2 changing beers (sourced nationally; often Purple Moose) Ⓗ

Village pub with a bar, lounge and snug full of bric-a-brac, local photos and other memorabilia. The lounge, converted from tea rooms, is quiet with no music or games machines. The pub retains its character with real fires in the bar and snug. The stone courtyard is a profusion of colour in the summer. Good food includes fish dish of the day, daily specials and traditional Sunday roasts (no evening meals Mon). The two real ciders are Rosie's Triple D and Black Bart.

Q ➤ ❀ ◑ ᗒ ♣ ● P ☷ (77) ❀ 🛜

Bebington

Rose & Crown

57 The Village, CH63 7PL

🕐 12-midnight (1am Fri & Sat) ☎ (0151) 643 1312

Marston's Wainwright, Lancaster Bomber; Thwaites Original; 1 changing beer (sourced nationally; often Jennings, Thwaites, Wychwood) Ⓗ

Former coaching inn built in 1732, adjacent to Mayer Park and now a thriving suburban pub with a lounge, bar and games room. Nearby is Port Sunlight Village, founded by William Hesketh Lever in 1888 to house his soap factory workers. In the village is the Lady Lever Art Gallery, home to one of the most beautiful collections of art in the country. ➤♣☷(410,487) ❀

Birkenhead

Gallaghers Pub & Barbers Ⓛ

20 Chester Street, CH41 5DQ

🕐 12 (4 Mon)-11; 12-midnight Fri & Sat ☎ (0151) 649 9095

Brimstage Trappers Hat Bitter; 5 changing beers (sourced regionally; often Hawkshead, Rat, Salopian) Ⓗ

Multiple award-winning genuine free house close to the famous Mersey ferries, rescued after closure and refurbished in 2010 as a unique pub with a barber's shop. Sadly the barber's closed in 2016. It is decorated with a fascinating range of military memorabilia and a collection of shipping images. Good-value meals are served lunchtimes Wednesday to Saturday. Several ciders are always available. Live music plays every Sunday evening. Cheese night is the last Sunday of the month – bring your own cheese.

❀◑➤(Hamilton Sq)●☷❀🛜

Crank

Red Cat
Red Cat Lane, WA11 8RU
☼ 12-11 ☎ (01744) 882422
3 changing beers (sourced nationally; often Timothy Taylor, Titanic) ⊞
Situated in the semi rural hamlet of Crank, the Red Cat offers both a comfortable lounge bar and home cooked food in the restaurant. Beers are sourced from the Punch Taverns list. From the beer garden there are good views of the Lancashire countryside and language classes are held in the snug on a Monday evening. Q◑P☐

Crosby

Corner Post 🅛
25 Bridge Road, L23 6SA
☼ closed Mon; 4 (1 Sat)-9; 1-7 Sun ☎ 07587 177453
4 changing beers (sourced locally; often Rock the Boat) ⊞
Crosby's second micropub, located in a former post office – hence the name – is easily spotted by the postbox outside. As well as real ales and cider, bottled continental beers, wine and soft drinks are available. Interesting pictures depicting the history of the building and local area adorn the walls. Close to the 53 bus route and a short walk from Blundellsands and Crosby railway station, it is also near the Iron Men attraction on Crosby beach.
Q⇌♣●☐(53)☻

Liverpool Pigeon 🅛
14 Endbutt Lane, L23 0TR
☼ closed Mon; 4 (1 Sat)-9; 1-5 Sun ☎ 07766 480329
⊕ liverpoolpigeon.co.uk
5 changing beers ⊞
Merseyside's pioneering micropub is a fine example of the type, with real ales, ciders and bottled beers available but no spirits, alcopops, keg beers or music. The cask beers will usually include a local brew and often a dark beer. Locally made pies are available at the bar. The Liverpool Pigeon is named after an extinct bird from Polynesia – long may this one live. A former Liverpool CAMRA Pub of the Year. Q&♣●☐☐☻

Stamps Bar 🅛
5 Crown Buildings, L23 5SR
☼ 12-11 (midnight Fri & Sat) ☎ (0151) 286 2662
⊕ stampsbar.co.uk
4 changing beers (often Stamps) ⊞
Stamps is a true community pub attracting a wide mix of people who visit for the great range of real ales, cider and live music. The pub supports a range of local and national charities and hosts a number of activities including art classes on Monday, a ukulele band on Tuesday and a quiz night on Wednesday. Live music features Friday to Sunday. Not sure which beer to choose? Try three different third-pints for the price of a pint. ☎&●☐☐♋

Eccleston

Griffin Inn ✅
Church Lane, WA10 5AD
☼ 12-11 (10.30 Sun) ☎ (01744) 27907 ⊕ griffininn.co.uk
3 changing beers ⊞
An independent locally owned free house with a distinctive sandstone frontage. The pub dates from 1812 and offers home-cooked food and accommodation as well as a comfortable bar area.

A large screen shows TV sport in the lounge and a quiz night is hosted on Wednesday. Beers are often sourced from the Marston's range, supplemented by ales from independent local microbreweries.
☼🛏◑P☐

Formby

Sparrowhawk
Southport Old Road, L37 0AB (adjacent to Formby bypass opp Woodvale Airfield)
☼ 10.30 (9am Sat)-11; 9am-10.30 Sun ☎ (01704) 882350
⊕ sparrowhawk-formby.co.uk
Salopian Oracle; Titanic Plum Porter; 3 changing beers (sourced regionally) ⊞
A first-rate place to eat and drink. The emphasis here is on dining but the excellent well-kept beer range is varied and interesting. Set in an old country house with gardens, it offers a relaxing oasis between the towns of Formby and Ainsdale. Weekends can get busy for food but the pleasant patio is a welcome retreat. Dogs are welcome on a lead. Q☎☼◑&♣●P☐(49,X2)☻ �🛜

Freshfield

Beer Station
3 Victoria Buildings, L37 7DB (opp railway station)
☼ 12-9 (10 Fri & Sat) ☎ (01704) 807450
3 changing beers (sourced locally; often Neptune, Red Star) ⊞
Freshfield's first micropub, with local produce given a heavy prominence. Beers are sourced to promote local brewers, with the exception of one 'foreign' beer a month from out of the region. The few spirits available also have their provenance checked. A fridge full of bottled beers adds to the variety. Food comes in the form of local pies and nuts. The walls are decorated with work by local artists. Dogs are welcome on a lead.
Q☎&⇌♣●☐☻

Freshfield 🅛 ✅
1 Massams Lane, L37 7BD
☼ 11-11 (midnight Sat); 12-11 Sun ☎ (01704) 874871
⊕ freshfield-liverpool.co.uk
Greene King IPA, Abbot; Oakham Citra; 11 changing beers (sourced regionally) ⊞
A former CAMRA National Pub of the Year finalist and multi award-winner. At its heart a community pub, it has three distinct areas – a dining-room serving quality food, a bar area dominated by a bar

full of handpumps, and 'the flags' where well-behaved dogs are allowed. Sport is shown on three large TVs. A real fire adds warmth in winter. A place to meet, talk and be with friends old and new.

Greasby

Irby Mill ✓
Mill Lane, CH49 3NT
11-11 (midnight Fri & Sat); 12-11 Sun ☎ (0151) 694 0194
irbymill.co.uk
Caledonian Deuchars IPA; Greene King Abbot; 6 changing beers (sourced nationally; often Everards, Holt, Young's) ℍ
Formerly a café, the pub was originally the house of the miller of the windmill on the site, and opened as a pub in 1982. With thick sandstone walls, low beams and a real fire, it comprises a small L-shaped, stone-floored bar and a lounge used mainly by diners. The pub has an excellent reputation for locally sourced home-made food, with a menu to suit most tastes.

Heswall

Dee View Inn
Dee View Road, CH60 0DH
12-midnight (11 Sun) ☎ (0151) 345 9165
Brains Rev James; Brimstage Trappers Hat Bitter; Timothy Taylor Landlord; 2 changing beers (sourced nationally) ℍ
Homely, traditional local built in the late 1800s. It has retained its character and friendly atmosphere, and offers a warm welcome. The pub sits on a hairpin bend by the war memorial and famous mirror, with views over the Dee Estuary and close to the Wirral Way path. A popular and entertaining quiz night is held on Tuesday and live music is a frequent attraction. Traditional home-cooked food is served (not Sat eve) and children are welcome if dining.

Jug & Bottle
13 Mount Avenue, CH60 4RH
12-11.30 ☎ (0151) 342 5535 the-jugandbottle.co.uk
Brains Rev James; Brimstage Trappers Hat Bitter; house beer (by Coach House); 3 changing beers (sourced locally) ℍ
Originally a private house built in the 1870s, hidden behind the village hall and library a short distance from the main shopping street, this smart pub reopened in December 2016 after refurbishment. Open fires and different cosy areas create a warm and friendly atmosphere, while outside the new decking gives views towards the River Dee and North Wales. The house beer 4.1% ABV Bottle Juggler is brewed by Coach House.

Huyton

Barkers Brewery ✓
Archway Road, L36 9UJ
8am-11 (midnight Fri & Sat) ☎ (0151) 482 4500
Greene King Abbot; Ruddles Best Bitter; Sharp's Doom Bar; 4 changing beers ℍ
A large, airy Wetherspoon pub with a traditional feel. A good selection of ales means at least one local and one dark beer are always available. Popular with workers and families in the early

evening, the main dining area leads to a beer garden at the rear. The building is on the site of the old Huyton Brewery, founded in 1825, and managed by the Barker family over four generations until 1925 – the sculpture is of Richard Barker. Alcohol is served from 9am, no children after 9pm. Q (10,10A)

Liscard

Lazy Landlord Ale House
56 Mill Lane, CH44 5UG
4 (2 Fri)-10.30; closed Tue; 12-10.30 Sat & Sun ☎ 07583 135616
5 changing beers (sourced regionally) ℍ
Wirral's first micropub, opened in 2014 in former shop premises, is run by the Henry brothers who are cask ale enthusiasts. Two small cosy rooms, decorated with large amounts of breweriana, local artworks and a small library, are served from the front bar. Mostly frequented by a more mature, discerning local clientele, the pub is a venue for meetings of local societies. Local CAMRA Pub of the Year 2017.

Liverpool: Aigburth

Que Pasa Cantina
94-96 Lark Lane, L17 8UU
2.30-11; 12-midnight Fri & Sat; 12-11 Sun ☎ (0151) 727 0006
2 changing beers (sourced locally) ℍ
Situated in Lark Lane, a popular hive of bespoke restaurants, bars and pubs close to Sefton Park. Currently food is no longer available, with the upstairs restaurant closed. But sales of cask beer continue to increase, with two now usually available. Beers are delivered directly from breweries, usually local, but sometimes from further afield. There is a pleasant outdoor patio.

Liverpool: Childwall

Childwall Fiveways ✓
179 Queens Drive, L15 6XS
8am-11.30 ☎ (0151) 738 2100
Fuller's London Pride; Greene King Abbot; Sharp's Doom Bar; 4 changing beers (often Titanic) ℍ
A former Higson's tied house, this large single-roomed pub opened as a Wetherspoon in 2010. Located in a leafy suburb, it has good motorway and public transport links. The refurbished interior is decorated with wood panelling, and outside there is a beer garden. A popular establishment, it can get busy, especially at weekends. The site was used for a water tank during WWII.

Liverpool: City Centre

Augustus John
Peach Street, L3 5TX (off Brownlow Hill)
11.30-11; closed Sat & Sun ☎ (0151) 794 5507
5 changing beers (sourced nationally; often Peerless, Rock the Boat) ℍ
Opened in 1968 and run by the University of Liverpool, the Augustus John is an open-plan pub popular with students, lecturers and locals. Up to five guest beers are available alongside a large number of ciders – two on handpump and many more from the cellar. Pizza is served at all times,

341

sport is shown and there is a jukebox. Closed over Christmas and the New Year. A former local and regional CAMRA Cider Pub of the Year.
🍴👌♣🚬🚪(79)🛜

Baltic Fleet 🅻

33A Wapping, L1 8DQ

🕐 12-11 (midnight Fri & Sat) ☎ (0151) 709 3116
🌐 balticfleetpubliverpool.com

Brimstage Sandpiper; 6 changing beers (sourced locally; often Big Bog, Liverpool Organic, Melwood) Ⓗ

This Grade II-listed building is located near the Albert Dock. It has a distinctive flat-iron shape and the interior is decorated with a nautical theme. Real ale and cider are dispensed from seven handpumps. Pies and home-cooked scouse are available from lunchtime until they run out. The existence of tunnels in the cellar has led to speculation that the pub's history may involve smuggling and press gangs. The previous Wapping Brewery kit was removed from the cellar in 2017.
🏴‍☠️🍴🍺👌🚬🐾🛜

Belvedere 🅻 ✓

8 Sugnall Street, L7 7EB (off Falkner St)

🕐 12-11 ☎ (0151) 709 0303 🌐 belvedereliverpool.com

4 changing beers (sourced regionally; often Melwood, Salopian) Ⓗ

Tucked away in the Georgian area of the city, close to the famous Philharmonic Hall and frequented by its orchestra members, this small two-roomed pub is a free house serving four rotating beers mainly from local microbreweries. Redeemed in 2006 from closure for housing development, this Grade II-listed building retains original fixtures and interesting etched-glass features. With a mixed local clientele, it is a pub where various small cultural groups meet and good conversation thrives. Q🏴👌🍺🚪(86,80)🐾🛜

Caledonia 🅻

22 Caledonia Street, L7 7DX (corner of Catherine St behind Philharmonic Hall)

🕐 12-midnight (1am Fri & Sat) ☎ (0151) 708 0235
🌐 thecaledonialiverpool.com

4 changing beers (often Liverpool Craft, Melwood) Ⓗ

Situated in the Georgian quarter of the city, this street-corner pub, popular with students, comprises one room on two levels and a small function room upstairs. The enterprising licensee has developed a programme of live music events and on these occasions the pub, which can be a haven for quiet conversation during the day, buzzes with atmosphere. Food includes vegetarian and vegan options (served 5-9pm Mon-Fri, 12-6pm Sat & Sun). 🍴🍺🚪(80,86)🐾🛜

Crown Hotel ★ 🅻 ✓

43 Lime Street, L1 1JQ

🕐 8am-11 (midnight Fri & Sat); 10-11 Sun
☎ (0151) 707 6027 🌐 thecrownliverpool.co.uk

Black Sheep Best Bitter; Greene King IPA; Wells Bombardier; 4 changing beers (sourced nationally) Ⓗ

Grade II-listed pub with a nationally important historic interior and ornate plasterwork ceilings. Many original features remain in the two downstairs rooms, including some impressive wood panelling and original push bells. There is also an ornate glass dome above the staircase. Breakfast is served until midday, a wide menu of good-value pub food until 10pm. Close to Lime Street station and public transport links.
🛏️🍴�🍺🛜

Dispensary 🅻

87 Renshaw Street, L1 2SP

🕐 12-11 (midnight Fri & Sat) ☎ (0151) 709 2160

George Wright Mild; changing beers (often Fyne Ales, Ossett, Titanic) Ⓗ

The licensee's impeccable attention to beer quality is renowned at this lively city pub, making it a haven for real ale drinkers of all ages. Seven handpumps serve an ever-changing choice of interesting microbrewery beers, offering a good range in terms of both style and strength. A regular local beer, Mark's Mild, commemorates the much-missed barman who died in 2012. The attractive bar area has Victorian features, and there is a raised wood-panelled area to the rear. �🚪

Excelsior 🅻 ✓

121-123 Dale Street, L2 2JH (close to Birkenhead Tunnel entrance)

🕐 11 (12 Sun)-11 ☎ (0151) 236 0079

Brains Rev James; Robinsons Dizzy Blonde; Timothy Taylor Landlord; 3 changing beers (sourced locally; often Parker, Red Star, Rock the Boat) Ⓗ

Large, comfortable corner pub on the edge of the business district. The main room has a three-sided bar with a series of distinct seating areas. There is a large room leading off with a raised seating area, available to hire for meetings or other functions. Three big-screen TVs show sports events, particularly football, but are usually silent otherwise. Tuesday is quiz night unless Liverpool or Everton are on TV. 🍴�æP🚪🛜

Fly in the Loaf 🅻

13 Hardman Street, L1 9AS

🕐 12-11 (midnight Fri & Sat) ☎ (0151) 708 0817
🌐 flyintheloaf.co.uk

Okell's Bitter; 6 changing beers (sourced nationally; often Kirkstall, Okell's) Ⓗ

A former bakery, the name comes from the slogan 'no flies in the loaf'. Owned by Isle of Man brewer Okell's, it serves its beers alongside a changing range of guests from around the country, many from microbreweries, and a good selection of foreign beers. The spacious interior, decorated with Rugby League memorabilia, has a light, airy frontage with contrasting wood-panelled areas towards the rear. There is a small, attractive on-street drinking area at the front and a function room upstairs. 🍴👌�🚪🛜

Grapes 🅻

60 Roscoe Street, L1 9DW

🕐 12 (2.30 Mon)-12.30am; 12-1.30am Fri & Sat
☎ (0151) 709 3977 🌐 thegrapesliverpool.co.uk

8 changing beers (often Liverpool Organic) Ⓗ

This corner local dates back to 1804 and retains its original Mellors signage outside. There is a total of nine handpumps, with a large number of beers coming from local microbreweries such as Mad Hatter and Liverpool Craft. Following major refurbishment in 2016, stairs now lead to a partly sheltered patio area atop the new extension. Live jazz features every Sunday night from 9pm. Home-cooked Thai and Lao food is available.
🏴🍴�🍺🚪🛜

Hard Times & Misery 🅻

2B Maryland Street, L1 9DE

🕐 closed Mon & Tue; 4-11 (midnight Fri); 2-midnight Sat; 4-9 Sun ☎ 07595 588426

4 changing beers (sourced locally; often Big Bog, Rock the Boat) Ⓖ

Cosy bar next door to the Shisha bar on Maryland Street, downhill from the Hope & Anchor. The small room upstairs has more seating. Three or four, often local, cask ales are on gravity dispense in pins, plus a selection of bottled beers. The bar also specialises in artisan gins and vodkas. Opening times may change during the year. There is 50p off the price of a pint Tuesday to Thursday. Q✤⊟♥

Lime Kiln L ✪
Fleet Street, L1 4NR
☼ 9am-midnight (1am Thu); 9am-2am Fri & Sat
☎ (0151) 702 6810
Greene King Abbot; Ruddles Best Bitter; 9 changing beers (often Peerless) ⊞
On first impression the decor and layout may not appear to offer much for the real ale drinker, but looks can be deceptive. Thanks to continued commitment by the management, real ale is well catered for, with at least one local beer usually available. Handpulls are in the downstairs bar only. Situated in the Concert Square area, the pub is a peaceful haven during the day. A Victorian warehouse, home to manufacturing chemists, occupied the site from the early 1900s to the 1950s. ⍟✤⊙ᕫ✤♥⊟♥

Lion Tavern ★
67 Moorfields, L2 2BP
☼ 11 (12 Sun)-midnight ☎ (0151) 236 1734
Adnams Broadside; Castle Rock Harvest Pale; Moorhouse's Pride of Pendle; Young's Bitter; 4 changing beers (sourced nationally; often Red Star) ⊞
Named after the locomotive that worked the Liverpool to Manchester railway, the Lion features exquisite artwork plus intricately etched and stained glass which bear testimony to its Grade II-listed status and its entry on CAMRA's National Inventory of Historic Pub Interiors. It was refurbished in 2017. Four beers are available from the SIBA list, usually including ales from local micros. The cider is from Westons. Lunchtime food is served and speciality pork pies are available at all times. ◖✤♥⊟♥

Mackenzie's
32 Rodney Street, L1 2TQ
☼ 12-11.30 ☎ 07746 577028 ⊕ mackenziesbar.co.uk
5 changing beers (sourced nationally) ⊞
Attractive, spacious bar, tastefully converted from a listed ex-HSBC bank in 2015, with up to five changing real ales, many from local breweries. It is also renowned for its worldwide collection of over 200 whiskies. Situated in a lively area of the city, with an illuminated beer garden, the bar is popular with a wide-ranging clientele. It is named after a legendary local 19th-century civil engineer whose 15-foot pyramid-shaped tombstone is along the street. Live music plays on Monday and Wednesday evenings and Sunday afternoons. ✤◖✤⊟(86)

Pen Factory L
13 Hope Street, L1 9BQ
☼ closed Mon; 12-midnight; 2-8 Sun ☎ (0151) 709 7887
⊕ pen-factory.co.uk
Titanic Plum Porter; 5 changing beers (sourced nationally; often Brimstage, Hawkshead, Liverpool Organic) ⊞
The Pen Factory opened in 2015, brought to you by innovator of the original Everyman Bistro, entrepreneur Paddy Byrne. A large open-plan bistro with a wood-burning stove and small

garden, it is a convivial place to drink and eat. Up to six handpumps include beers from smaller breweries such as Brimstage. The venue can be busy before or after productions at the nearby Everyman Theatre or Philharmonic Hall. Excellent food, not your average pub grub. ✤◖ᕫ✤♥⊟(86)♥

Peter Kavanagh's ★
2-6 Egerton Street, L8 7LY
☼ 12-midnight (1am Fri & Sat) ☎ (0151) 709 3443
Greene King Abbot; 4 changing beers (sourced nationally; often Castle Rock) ⊞
Pub with a nationally important historic interior in the Georgian area of the city. The snugs feature murals by Eric Robinson and there are fine stained-glass windows with wooden shutters. The benches have carved armrests thought to be caricatures of Peter Kavanagh, the licensee for 53 years until 1950. These features were not adversely affected when the pub was expanded, firstly in 1964 into next door, then in 1977 into next door but one. Q✤⊟✿

Richard John Blackler L ✪
Units 1 & 2 Charlotte Row, L1 1HU
☼ 8am-midnight (1am Fri & Sat) ☎ (0151) 709 4802
Greene King Abbot; Ruddles Best Bitter; Sharp's Doom Bar; Wychwood Hobgoblin; 8 changing beers ⊞
This Wetherspoon pub is the ground floor of the former Blackler's department store which opened in 1908 and finally shut in 1988. The famous rocking horse from that store is in the corner. Close to the bus station, Saint John's shopping centre and Liverpool One, it is always busy – especially when either Liverpool or Everton are playing at home – but is a good place to take a break. The Beatles' George Harrison served his electrician's apprenticeship at Blackler's. ⍟◖ᕫ✤♥⊟♥

Roscoe Head L
24 Roscoe Street, L1 2SX
☼ 11.30 (12 Sun)-midnight ☎ (0151) 709 4365
⊕ roscoehead.co.uk
Tetley Bitter; Timothy Taylor Landlord; 4 changing beers (sourced regionally; often Rock the Boat) ⊞
One of the Magnificent Five pubs in every edition of the Guide. This is a cosy four-roomed hostelry where conversation and the appreciation of real ale rule. Run by members of the same family for over 30 years, the name commemorates William Roscoe, a leading campaigner against the slave trade. Six handpumps feature national and local breweries. Home-cooked food is served Monday to Friday lunchtimes. Since its sale in 2015 there is concern over the future of the pub, with an active Save the Roscoe Head campaign. Q◖✤♣⊟(80,86)♥

Ship & Mitre L ✪
133 Dale Street, L2 2JH (by Birkenhead Tunnel)
☼ 10-11 (midnight Thu); 9am-midnight Fri & Sat
☎ (0151) 236 0859 ⊕ theshipandmitre.com
House beer (by Stamps); 15 changing beers (sourced nationally; often Big Bog, Saltaire) ⊞
A 1930s Art Deco pub, the name derives from two previous incarnations, the Flagship and the Mitre. It is partly hidden by the Queensway tunnel entrance and the Churchill Way flyover. Fifteen handpulls serve an ever-changing array of beers and real ciders, with the friendly and knowledgeable staff always willing to make a recommendation. It now brews its own beers using the plant at Stamps

Brewery in Crosby, as the Ship & Mitre brewing company. There is also an impressive range of world beers. Beer and cider festivals are hosted throughout the year. ◖▶≠♣●➌❀

Thomas Rigby's ✅
23-25 Dale Street, L2 2EZ
✪ 11.30-11 (10.30 Sun) ☎ (0151) 236 3269
Okell's Bitter, Dr Okell's IPA; 4 changing beers (sourced nationally; often Kirkstall) Ⓗ
This multi-roomed, Grade II-listed building, bearing the name of wine and spirit dealer Thomas Rigby, now supplies an extensive world beer range on draught and in bottles. The regular beers on handpump come from the pub's owner, Okell's Brewery, the rest are frequently changing guests. Good-value food including specials is served until early evening, with one room offering a friendly and efficient table service. There is a courtyard for outdoor drinking. ❀◖▶≠➌❖

Ye Hole in ye Wall Ⓛ
4 Hackins Hey, L2 2AW (off Dale St)
✪ 12-11 (10.30 Sun) ☎ (0151) 227 3809
⊕ yeholeinyewall.com
5 changing beers (sourced nationally; often Red Star) Ⓗ
A traditional side-street pub rumoured to be the oldest hostelry in the city, dating back to the start of Liverpool's maritime heyday in 1726. Wood panelling and stained glass abound. Built on the site of an old Quaker graveyard, there are tales of ghosts, and this old coaching house boasts at least two. Unusually, the beer cellar is on the first floor above the bar. Five guest beers are offered on rotation and may be from local and microbreweries. A great hidden gem. Q◖≠➌❖

Liverpool: Garston

Masonic Ⓛ
35 Gladstone Road, L19 1RR
✪ 11-midnight (1am Fri & Sat); 12-midnight Sun
☎ (0151) 280 0200
6 changing beers (sourced regionally; often Big Bog) Ⓗ
Community pub amid terraced houses with seven handpumps, one usually dispensing a cider. Beers are supplied directly by local breweries and from around the country through brewery swaps. Real ale promotions are offered on Tuesday evenings. A supporter of local sports teams, horse racing and other sport are shown on TV. Live music plays Thursday to Sunday. There is a drinking area outside in front of the pub and a covered smoking area in the yard to the side. Beer festivals are held in January, May and September. ❀🛏♣●➌❀❖

Liverpool: Kirkdale

Thomas Frost Ⓛ ✅
177-187 Walton Road, L4 4AJ
✪ 8am-11.30 ☎ (0151) 207 8210
Greene King Abbot; Ruddles Best Bitter; Sharp's Doom Bar; 4 changing beers (sourced nationally) Ⓗ
This Wetherspoon pub occupies the ground floor of a Grade II-listed building that was formerly Frost's department store. Draper Thomas Frost moved into one of six shops on this site in 1885 and, by 1910, had expanded his business into all the shops. The pub is near both Everton and Liverpool grounds and gets very busy on match days. It has a spacious

open-plan layout with a large family area. No children permitted after 9pm.
🛏◖▶♿≠●➌(20,21)❀

Liverpool: Mossley Hill

Pi
106 Rose Lane, L18 8AG
✪ 11-11 (11.30 Fri & Sat) ☎ (0151) 222 0443
⊕ pi-roselane.co.uk
Tatton Blonde; 3 changing beers (sourced regionally) Ⓗ
A café-style bar in premises that were previously a shop, near to Mossley Hill railway station. The guest beers are from smaller breweries in the region. A number of foreign beers are also on tap alongside dozens of bottled beers. A simple hot-food menu – real pies with sides – is available all day. The extension into the shop next door has provided more space. ◖▶≠●(61,80)❀

Liverpool: Old Swan

Ale House
674/676 Prescot Road, L13 5XG
✪ 4-9.30; 2-10.30 Fri & Sat; 2-9.30 Sun ☎ 07944 565323
⊕ thealehouse.pub
5 changing beers (sourced nationally) Ⓗ
This new bar opened in 2016 in a building that was previously a job centre and is therefore bigger than other micropubs in the area. It currently has six handpumps, with one dispensing cider. More ciders and perries are served from the cool room. Beers are a selection of better and lesser known brands supplied by agents and local ales supplied directly – usually including a porter or stout.
Q♿♣●➌(10)❖

Liverpool: Stoneycroft

Cask ♟ Ⓛ
438 Queens Drive, L13 0AR (near jct Queens Drive and Derby Lane)
✪ closed Mon; 4 (2 Sat & Sun)-9.30 ☎ 07747 034499
7 changing beers (sourced nationally; often Hawkshead, Offbeat) Ⓗ
Comfortable, immaculate, one-roomed micropub that opened in 2015. Located on Queens Drive, a busy dual carriageway that acts like a Liverpool circular road, near the turning to West Derby, some roadside parking is available. An interesting collection of breweriana includes some from Higsons. There are usually four beers on Tuesday and Wednesday, five on Thursday and up to seven Friday to Sunday. Cider and perry are dispensed direct from taps at the rear of the bar. Occasional special beers are kept in wooden pins.
Q♣●➌➌(60,81)

Liverpool: Woolton

Gardeners Arms ✅
101 Vale Road, L25 7RW
✪ 12-midnight (11.30 Sun) ☎ (0151) 428 1443
Fuller's London Pride; Greene King IPA; Marston's 61 Deep; Sharp's Doom Bar; 3 changing beers (sourced regionally; often Big Bog, Taylors) Ⓗ
Friendly community village pub situated over the hill from Woolton village and separated from Menlove Avenue by blocks of flats. Guest beers regularly include a local Big Bog beer and a Welsh beer from Purple Moose, Heavy Industry or Cwrw

Lal. A quiz is held on Tuesday evening. Woolton is famous as the home of the Beatles – their original name was The Quarrymen – and Eleanor Rigby's gravestone can be found in St Peter's churchyard. Q🕮🍺�"🍴(76)🐾📶

Maghull

Frank Hornby 🅛 ✅
38 Eastway, L31 6BR
🕛 8am-11.30 (midnight Fri & Sat) ☎ (0151) 520 4010
Phoenix Wobbly Bob; 9 changing beers (often Lancaster, Lytham, Moorhouse's) 🅷
This Wetherspoon establishment is named after local man Frank Hornby, famous inventor of the Hornby train set. Unsurprisingly, samples of his work are on display in the pub including Meccano and Dinky Toys. Situated in a suburban street, the bar is spacious and light inside with a decked area outside at the front. An ever-changing selection of guest ales is available including some from local microbreweries. Alcohol is served from 10am. No children after 10pm. Q🕮🍺🍴◑🅿🍴(231,310)📶

New Brighton

Magazine Hotel 🅛
7 Magazine Brow, CH45 1HP (above Egremont Promenade)
🕛 12-11 (11.30 Fri & Sat) ☎ (0151) 630 3169
🌐 the-magazine-hotel.co.uk
Brimstage Trappers Hat Bitter; Draught Bass; 3 changing beers (sourced locally; often Big Bog, Brimstage, Peerless) 🅷
This unspoilt multi-roomed, low-beamed pub with an attractive black and white frontage, dating from 1759, suffered from a fire in 2010 but has been restored without losing its unique character. Three rooms lead off the main central bar area with an open fireplace. Traditionally renowned for its Draught Bass, other beers are usually from local microbreweries. Overlooking Egremont Promenade, the pub has fine views over the River Mersey to Liverpool. Q🍺🐾♣🅿🍴(106)🐾

Stage Door Tap
Queen's Royal, Marine Promenade, CH45 2JT
🕛 11-11 (10.30 Sun) ☎ (0151) 691 0101
🌐 thequeensroyal.com
5 changing beers (sourced regionally; often Brimstage, Hawkshead, Phoenix) 🅷
A bright, airy, modern bar in the Queen's Royal Hotel, an imposing Victorian building close to the Floral Pavilion Theatre. In a seafront location overlooking Marine Promenade, Marine Lake and Fort Perch Rock, this free house is popular both with locals and day trippers. The enclosed drinking area outside affords superb views over Liverpool Bay. Good-value bar snacks and meals are served in the bar until 9pm (7pm Sun) and there is an adjoining restaurant. 🐾🍽◑🅛🍴🐾📶

Stanley's Cask ✅
212 Rake Lane, CH45 1JP
🕛 11-midnight (11 Mon & Wed); 12-midnight Sun
☎ (0151) 691 1093
5 changing beers (sourced nationally; often Brains, Caledonian, Robinsons) 🅷
This ever-popular local continues to thrive, due in no small part to the efforts of the landlady who has a track record of serving quality beer. The five guest ales on offer often include seasonal beers

from regional breweries. A traditional, single-roomed community local, it hosts various sports teams, quiz nights and regular popular live music including rock, blues and folk.
🐾🅛♣🍴(410,433)🐾📶

New Ferry

Freddie's Club 🅛
36 Stanley Road, CH62 5AS
🕛 7 (5 Fri & Sat)-11; 12-11 Sun
Brimstage Trappers Hat Bitter; 1 changing beer (sourced locally; often Brimstage) 🅷
A popular social club, formerly a Conservative Club, converted into a comfortable lounge bar with adjoining snooker room with two full-size tables. It is situated in a residential area just a short walk from New Ferry shopping centre. There is regular live entertainment. A former local CAMRA Club of the Year, show a CAMRA membership card or a current copy of the Guide for entry. Q🐾🅛🍴♣🅿🍴

John Masefield ✅
70-72 New Chester Road, CH62 5AD
🕛 8am-midnight ☎ (0151) 644 4250
Greene King Abbot; Ruddles Best Bitter; 6 changing beers (sourced nationally; often Peerless) 🅷
Comfortable open-plan Wetherspoon venue in a former bicycle shop in the main shopping area. Named after the former poet laureate, controversy surrounded the opening of the pub when locals suggested that the portrait on the sign looked more like Adolf Hitler – judge for yourself. The pub features Wetherspoon's meal deals, a Wednesday night quiz and regular vintage bus pub trips. Real cider is sometimes available. 🍺🐾◑🅛🍴🍴📶

Newton-le-Willows

Firkin
65 High Street, WA12 9SL
🕛 closed Mon-Wed; 5.30-11 Thu; 1-11.30 Fri & Sat; 1-10.30 Sun ☎ (01925) 225700 🌐 thefirkin.co.uk
8 changing beers (sourced locally) 🅷
A former shop, this small, friendly establishment dispenses a selection of eight real ales, including at least one dark beer, all sourced from micro or SIBA breweries. Two traditional ciders are also available. Small seating areas are to the front and rear, and pictures of Newton of old adorn the walls. Free of electronic noise, this is a place in which to engage in conversation with like-minded people and to make new friends. Over-18s only.
Q🍴🍴🍴(22,34)🐾📶

Oxton

Oxton Bar & Kitchen 🅛
2 Claughton Firs, CH43 5TQ
🕛 12-midnight (11 Mon); 12-1am Fri & Sat; 12-11 Sun
☎ (0151) 651 2535 🌐 oxtonbar.co.uk
3 changing beers (sourced locally; often Brimstage, Liverpool Organic, Peerless) 🅷
Situated in the centre of the attractive Oxton village among shops, bars and restaurants, this former John Smith's pub built in 1969 has been tastefully converted into a smart, comfortable, single-room lounge bar. There is a strong emphasis on quality food, ranging from sandwiches and snacks to full meals, available daily until 9.30pm (9pm Sun). Beers are usually all from local microbreweries. 🍺🐾◑🅛🅿🍴📶

Raby

Wheatsheaf Inn L
Raby Mere Road, CH63 4JH
☼ 11.30-11 (midnight Fri & Sat); 12-10.30 Sun
☎ (0151) 336 3416 ⊕ wheatsheaf-cowshed.co.uk
Brimstage Trappers Hat Bitter; Marston's Wainwright; Tetley Bitter; 6 changing beers (sourced regionally; often Brimstage, George Wright, Purple Moose) ⊞
An inn for 350 years, this is Wirral's oldest pub. The thatched building was rebuilt following a fire in 1611 and is reputed to be haunted by Charlotte, who died here. The walls are decorated with old photographs of Raby. The single bar serves three rooms and a restaurant in a converted cowshed. Lunch is served in the bar until 2pm, then snacks until 5pm. The restaurant is open evenings from 6pm Tuesday through to Saturday.
Q ☞ ✿ ◑ ⑂ P ⊟ (84,85) ✿

Rainhill

Skew Bridge Alehouse L
5 Dane Court, L35 4LU
☼ 4 (2.30 Sat)-11; 2.30-10.30 Sun ☎ (0151) 792 7906
⊕ skewbridge.co.uk
Outstanding 3.9; 5 changing beers (sourced locally; often Melwood) ⊞
A micropub in the heart of Rainhill's Dane Court Shopping Arcade. Opened by a local CAMRA member, the Skew Bridge Alehouse offers a wide selection of high-quality cask-conditioned ales and ciders from both local and national independent breweries. There are no TVs or other distractions and the art of conversation is encouraged among a varied and friendly clientele. Q ⑂ ⇌ ♣ P ⊟ ✿ ⬙

Rock Ferry

Refreshment Rooms L
Bedford Road East, CH42 1LS (off B5136, take Rock Lane East, then 4th right and over bridge)
☼ 12-11 (midnight Fri); 9am-midnight Sat; 9am-11 Sun
☎ (0151) 644 5893 ⊕ refreshmentrooms.info
House beer (by Lees); 2 changing beers (sourced locally; often Liverpool Organic, Peerless) ⊞
Refurbished and reopened in 2012 under its original name, the pub was built in the 1880s for ferry passengers to Liverpool. Although the ferry terminal is long gone, this off-the-beaten-track establishment is well worth seeking out, with excellent views over the Mersey. One central bar services two rooms. The focus is on food, with excellent-quality, reasonably priced meals served daily until 9pm. The house beer, 4% ABV HMS Conway, is from Lees and the cider is from Rosie's.
☞ ✿ ◑ ⑂ ♣ ⊟ ✿ ⬙

St Helens

Cricketers Arms 🏆 L ⊘
Peter Street, WA10 2EB
☼ 12-11 (1am Fri & Sat) ☎ (01744) 361846
13 changing beers (sourced regionally) ⊞
The Cricketers has established itself as an excellent cask ale pub, with 13 handpumps on the bar. Beers come from newer regional brewers and local microbreweries. There is also an excellent selection of real ciders. This is a friendly local community pub on the edge of the town centre, hosting darts and pool teams, and entertainment at the weekend. Beer festivals are staged several times a year. It

was 2014-17 local CAMRA and 2015 and 2016 regional CAMRA Pub of the Year.
☞ ✿ ♣ ♠ P ⊟ ☕ ✿ ⬙

News Room L
Duke Street, WA10 2JG
☼ closed Mon & Tue; 5-11 Wed & Thu; 3-midnight Fri & Sat; 3-11 Sun ☎ (01744) 322129
George Wright Pipe Dream; 6 changing beers (sourced locally; often Hawkshead, Martland Mill, Prospect) ⊞
A small, stylish bar in a developing real ale hotspot on Duke Street. With a vibrant and cosy atmosphere, it is a fairly recent convert to real ale – three beers are offered from local microbreweries, and there is a CAMRA discount of 20p a pint. It also stocks many different Belgian and foreign bottled beers. Often busy, particularly at weekends. ⊟

Sefton ⊘
Baldwin Street, WA10 2RS
☼ 11-11 Mon-Thu; 9am-11 Fri & Sat; 12-11 Sun
☎ (01744) 22065
Brains Bitter; Greene King IPA; 3 changing beers (sourced nationally; often Moorhouse's) ⊞
This town-centre local is basically one large room with a long bar down one side offering four beers, usually including one from George Wright Brewery in nearby Rainford. Real ale sales have increased significantly over recent years. There is a large function room upstairs and live bands often play at the pub. Good-value food is offered.
◑ ⇌ (Central) ⊟

Talbot Ale House L
Duke Street, WA10 2JG
☼ 12-1am (2am Fri & Sat) ☎ (01744) 607578
George Wright Drunken Duck, Cheeky Pheasant; 7 changing beers (sourced nationally; often George Wright) ⊞
Friendly town-centre pub divided into two areas – a public bar with pool and darts, and a comfortable lounge. Ten handpumps dispense local George Wright beers and quality ales from further afield, and there are up to nine real ciders. Look for the attractive stained-glass windows featuring sporting scenes. There is free Wi-Fi and daily newspapers.
♣ ♠ P ⊟ ☕ ✿ ⬙

Turk's Head L ⊘
Morley Street, WA10 2DQ
☼ 2-11; 12-11 Sat & Sun ☎ (01744) 751289
Changing beers ⊞
A short distance from town, this popular pub was a previous CAMRA National Pub of the Year runner-up. Half-timbered, with etched-glass windows, it was built in the 1870s by Ellis Warde Brewery. It offers a constantly changing beer range, with 14 handpulls in use over the weekend, six at other times. Draught and bottled continental beers are also stocked, and there are 10 different ciders. On Tuesday night there is a free quiz, Wednesday is cheese night, and Thursday is curry and jazz night. Darts and dominoes are played. ◑ ♣ ♠ ⊟ ✿

Southport

Barons Bar ⊘
239 Lord Street, PR8 1NZ
☼ 12-11 (midnight Fri & Sat) ☎ (01704) 534000
Moorhouse's Pride of Pendle; Tetley Bitter; house beer (by Moorhouse's); 6 changing beers (sourced

regionally; often Lancaster, Moorhouse's, Southport) H

An ornate baronial-style bar situated within the Scarisbrick Hotel complex, with a front lounge with chairs, tables and comfy settees overlooking the town's famous Lord Street. The bar has been championing real ale in Southport for many years and offers a varied selection of beers, both local and national. One real cider is available. ☺🌹🍴👌🚲🚆🍺☀🛜

Guest House

16 Union Street, PR9 0QE
✪ 11.30-11 (midnight Fri & Sat); 12-10.30 Sun
☎ (01704) 537660 ⊕ guesthouse-southport.blogspot.com

Adnams Best; Butcombe Original; Caledonian Deuchars IPA; Ruddles Best Bitter; house beer (by Caledonian); 4 changing beers (sourced nationally; often Phoenix, Salopian, Southport) H

Close to the station and Lord Street, this listed building has an impressive frontage and interior with three separate wood-panelled drinking rooms. The bar has 11 handpumps, one serving a local micro beer, and offers a wide range of malt whiskies. A quiet, traditional pub, attracting a mixed clientele, there is seating outside at the front and a courtyard area to the rear. Entertainment includes a Thursday night quiz and acoustic folk club on the first and third Mondays of the month. Q🌹🎵🍴🚆🍺🛜

Peaky Blinders

589 Lord Street, PR9 0AN
✪ 10-midnight (1am Fri & Sat) ☎ (01704) 651881
⊕ thepeakyblinders.com

Robinsons Cumbria Way, Double Hop; Timothy Taylor Landlord; 2 changing beers (sourced regionally; often Martland Mill, Old School, Tatton) H

Peaky Blinders, named after the popular TV programme, opened in 2015 on the north end of Lord Street in what is now known as the Northern Quarter of Southport. The bar is in an old corner shop just up Seabank Road from the promenade. It is dog-friendly and gives out doggy treats to four-legged friends. ☺🌹🍴👌🍺☀🛜

Sir Henry Segrave L ✅

93-97 Lord Street, PR8 1RH (on A565, S end of Lord Street)
✪ 8am-midnight ☎ (01704) 530217

Greene King Abbot; Marston's Wainwright; Moorhouse's Pendle Witches Brew; Phoenix Wobbly Bob; Ruddles Best Bitter; Sharp's Doom Bar; 6 changing beers (sourced regionally; often Lytham, Robinsons, Saltaire) H

Named after the former land-speed world record holder who used to race on Southport flats, this is a spacious Wetherspoon pub with an attractive 19th-century exterior. The manager is a strong supporter of real ale and runs regular beer festival trips and occasional Meet the Brewer evenings. The 12 handpumps offer the best all-round choice of microbrewery beers in Southport – regular orders are placed with Phoenix, Saltaire, Titanic and Hawkshead. There is outside seating on Lord Street. Q☺🌹🎵👌🚆🍺🛜

Tap & Bottles 🍷

19A Cambridge Walk, PR8 1EN
✪ 12-11 (midnight Fri & Sat); 12-10.30 Sun
☎ (01704) 544322
4 changing beers H

The Tap & Bottles is a micropub situated in the arcade between Chapel Street and Lord Street next to the Atkinson Centre. It has recently expanded into the next door unit. Four real ales may come from virtually any brewery, with a preference for North-west England beers. A huge range of bottles is also offered – but not all are real ale in a bottle. Pork pies and chutney are available all day. Children are welcome until 7pm. Q☺🌹🍴♣👌🚆🍺☀🛜

Willow Grove L ✅

387-389 Lord Street, PR9 0AG (on A565)
✪ 8am-midnight ☎ (01704) 517830

Greene King Abbot; Marston's Wainwright; Moorhouse's Pendle Witches Brew; Phoenix Wobbly Bob; Ruddles Best Bitter; Shepherd Neame Bishops Finger; 9 changing beers (sourced regionally; often Bank Top, Parker, Saltaire) H

The Willow Grove is a quiet Wetherspoon pub with an emphasis on real ale and food. It is situated on Lord Street opposite the impressive 1920s war memorial. The interior is L-shaped with a long bar, some cubicles and a mixture of furniture including comfy settees, chairs and tables. Ten handpumps dispense a choice of beers from breweries ranging from the local Parker to other micros to nationals. Q☺🌹🎵👌🚆🍺🛜

Southport: Birkdale

Barrel House L

42 Liverpool Road, PR8 4AY
✪ 10-9.30 ☎ (01704) 566601
2 changing beers (often Parker, Salopian, Southport) H

The Barrel House micropub opened in May 2014. A former newsagent's and still selling daily papers, it owes its existence to the Sainsbury's that opened across the road – as it could not compete, it changed business. It is an Aladdin's cave of wonderful bottled beers, wines, loose-leaf teas and speciality coffees. It also offers two real ales on handpumps, usually from local breweries such as Parker. Q☺🌹🎵👌🚆🍺🚌(49,X2)☀🛜

Southport: Hillside

Grasshopper

70 Sandon Road, PR8 4QD
✪ 4 (12 Sat & Sun)-10.30 ☎ (01704) 569794
5 changing beers (sourced regionally; often Bank Top, 3 Potts, Salopian) H

A micropub opened in 2016 in what was an old Martins Bank branch until 1978. The name is taken from the old logo of Martins Bank which featured a grasshopper. The pub is situated in the row of shops just down the road from Hillside station. Food can be ordered from a nearby takeaway and eaten in the pub. Children are welcome until 8pm. Q🌹👌🚆♣🍺🅿🚌(47)☀

Pines

3 Hillside Road, PR8 4QB
✪ 4-10.30; 12-11 Sat; closed Sun ☎ 07454 453090
2 changing beers (sourced regionally; often Red Star, Salopian, Southport) H

Newly opened, attractively decorated bar in a former hairdressers' in what was previously an area with no pubs or bars. Beers on two handpumps are dispensed alongside a good selection of bottled beers. An interesting food menu includes home-made tapas, sandwiches and breakfast. Doggy treats are available for well-behaved dogs, and there is an outside seating area at the front. ㅎ🐾&≠P➡(47)🐾🐾 🛜

Thornton Hough

Red Fox ℄
Neston Road, CH64 7TL
☼ 10.30-11 (10.30 Sun) ☎ (0151) 353 2920
House beer (by Phoenix); 5 changing beers (sourced regionally; often Conwy, Neptune, Ticketybrew) ⊞
Imposing building in its own extensive grounds dating from the 1890s, refurbished and reopened in 2014 as a smart gastropub serving quality food and well-kept beers. The front bar has the ambience of a friendly pub, with up to seven real ales and eight real ciders available. A smaller bar area at the back serves seating outside and a large lawned garden. House beers are Facer's 4% ABV Sunlight Blonde and Phoenix 3.8% ABV Brunning & Price Original Bitter. Q ㅎ🐾🐾&🐾P➡(487)🐾 🛜

Waterloo

Liver ℄ ✅
137 South Road, L22 0LT
☼ 11-11 (midnight Fri & Sat); 12-11 Sun ☎ (0151) 928 1708
⊕ theliverpub.co.uk
Robinsons Dizzy Blonde; Tetley Bitter; 2 changing beers (often Liverpool Craft, Liverpool Organic, Rock the Boat) ⊞
More than 200 years old, this is probably Waterloo's most famous pub. A former coaching inn, it is listed as being of specific historic and architectural interest. However, some years ago it was subject to a demolition order but, fortunately, a petition signed by around 1,400 patrons preserved it. The main dining area is to the rear, and outside a large beer garden, where the wall is surprisingly effective in limiting the intrusion of nearby traffic noise. ㅎ🐾🐾&≠🐾➡🛜

Stamps Too ℄
99 South Road, L22 0LR (opp Waterloo station)
☼ 12-11 (midnight Thu-Sat) ☎ (0151) 280 0035
5 changing beers (sourced locally; often Brimstage, Liverpool Organic) ⊞

A former local CAMRA branch Pub of the Year and its original accredited LocAle pub. This friendly open-plan venue, where lively banter predominates at the bar, is the haunt both of real ale enthusiasts and live music fans. Five handpumps serve mainly local beers, from Liverpool Organic, Brimstage, Southport and AllGates in particular, with occasional beers from further afield – a sixth handpump dispenses real cider. Bands and local musicians feature Thursday through to Sunday. &≠🐾➡(53,133)🐾 🛜

Volunteer Canteen ★ ℄ ✅
45 East Street, L22 8QR
☼ 2-11; 12-midnight Fri & Sat; 12-10.30 Sun ☎ 07891 407464
4 changing beers (sourced nationally) ⊞
A cosy traditional pub in a Grade II-listed terraced building, the Volly, as it is locally known, still provides table service. Nestling in the back streets of Waterloo, the pub dates back to 1871 and, until the 1980s, was owned by Higsons, evidence of which can be seen etched into its windows. Small breweries around Merseyside and north Wales often supply guest ales. Pies, pâté, olives and a variety of nuts are served at all times.
Q🐾≠♣➡(53)🐾 🛜

West Kirby

West Kirby Tap ℄
Grange Road, CH48 4DY
☼ 12-11 (11.30 Fri & Sat) ☎ (0151) 625 0350
⊕ westkirbytap.co.uk
Spitting Feathers Thirstquencher; 7 changing beers (sourced nationally) ⊞
Refurbished and reopened by Spitting Feathers brewery in 2014, this smart, modern bar features wood panelling, bare brick walls and a high ceiling. The single bar has a small raised area and some discrete spaces. It is close to West Kirby's shops and transport connections, a short walk to the beach and convenient for trekkers to Hilbre Island. Eight handpumps dispense a varying range of beers plus a changing real cider. ㅎ🐾&≠🐾➡🐾 🛜

Definitions

bivvy – beer
bumclink – inferior beer
bunker – beer
cooper – half stout, half porter
gatters – beer
shant of gatter – glass of beer
half and half – mixture of ale and porter, much favoured by medical students
humming – strong (as applied to drink)
ponge or pongelow – beer, half and half
purl – mixture of hot ale and sugar, with wormwood infused
rot-gut – bad
small beer shandy – gaffs ale and gingerbeer
shant – pot or quart (shant of bivvy – quart of beer)
swipes – soup or small beer
wobble-shop – shop where beer sold without a licence
J C Hotten, The Slang Dictionary, 1887

So You Want to Be a Beer Expert?

Jeff Evans

More people than ever are searching for an understanding of what makes a great beer, and this book meets that demand by presenting a hands-on course in beer appreciation, with sections on understanding the beer styles of the world, beer flavours, how beer is made, the ingredients, and more. Uniquely, *So You Want to Be a Beer Expert?* doesn't just relate the facts, but helps readers reach conclusions for themselves. Key to this are the interactive tastings that show readers, through their own taste buds, what beer is all about. This is the ideal book for anyone who wants to further their knowledge and enjoyment of beer.

RRP £12.99 **ISBN** 978-1-85249-322-6 **224 pages**

For this and other books on beer and pubs visit CAMRA's online bookshop at **www.camra.org.uk/books** or call **01727 867201**. Discounts are available for CAMRA members.

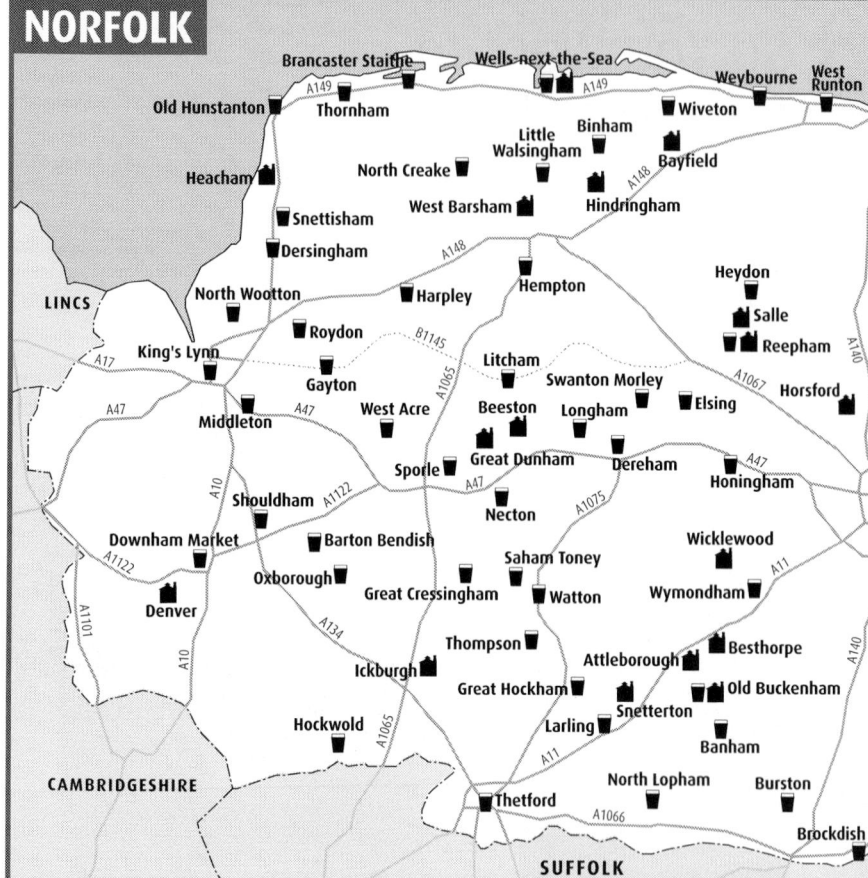

NORFOLK

Old Hunstanton
Brancaster Staithe
Wells-next-the-Sea
Weybourne West Runton
Thornham
Little Walsingham
Binham
Wiveton
North Creake
Bayfield
Heacham
West Barsham
Hindringham
Snettisham
Dersingham
Heydon
North Wootton
Harpley
Hempton
Salle
LINCS
Reepham
King's Lynn
Roydon
Litcham
Horsford
Gayton
Swanton Morley
Middleton
West Acre
Beeston
Longham
Elsing
Sporle
Great Dunham
Dereham
Honingham
Shouldham
Necton
Downham Market
Barton Bendish
Wicklewood
Oxborough
Saham Toney
Denver
Great Cressingham
Watton
Wymondham
Thompson
Besthorpe
Ickburgh
Attleborough
Old Buckenham
Great Hockham
Snetterton
Hockwold
Larling
Banham
North Lopham
Burston
CAMBRIDGESHIRE
Thetford
Brockdish
SUFFOLK

Banham

Garden House (Cider House)
Overcross, NR16 2BY (NE of Banham)
🕓 12-11; 12-10.30 Sun ☎ (01953) 860437
Adnams Southwold Bitter; Woodforde's Wherry; 2 changing beers (often Grain, Hoxne) Ⓗ
This recently refurbished pub is under new ownership and usually has four real ales on offer, as well as a local real cider. An extensive food menu includes a Man v Food challenge and eclectic American-themed meals along with matching decor. A beer festival is held during the August bank holiday. ⏰🏠🌲♣♠🐾🐾☂

Banningham

Crown Inn Ⓛ ✅
Colby Road, NR11 7DY (N of B1145, 1 mile E of A140)
🕓 12-2.30, 6-11 (12.30am Fri); 12-12.30am Sat; 12-11 Sun
☎ (01263) 733534 ⊕ banninghamcrown.co.uk
Greene King IPA, Abbot; 3 changing beers Ⓗ
Popular traditional 17th-century free house with a warm, friendly and welcoming atmosphere, overlooking the village green. The original beamed interior has a log fire in the bar area. Three guest beers (four in summer) are from regional breweries and microbreweries. With a first-class reputation for fine cuisine, using local produce, the

superb modern restaurant is open to the kitchen and chefs. The patio, garden and barbecue areas are ideal for summer alfresco dining. Regular events include quiz nights and jazz on Sundays.
Q🏠🌲♿🅰♣🅿🚲(18)🐾☂

Barton Bendish

Berney Arms
Church Road, PE33 9GF
🕓 12-11 ☎ (01366) 347995 ⊕ theberneyarms.co.uk
Adnams Southwold Bitter, Broadside; 2 changing beers Ⓗ
The food in this smart village local is a step above regular pub fare, but look out for good-value special set menus, or try the afternoon teas 2.30-6pm. The beer mostly comes from Adnams, including its seasonal range, but a guest ale is usually on offer. The decoration in the bar includes some interesting calendars, and there are also a well-appointed dining room and lovely garden as alternatives. The old stable block offers accommodation. Q🏠🛏🌲🅿🐾☂

Binham

Chequers Inn
Front Street, NR21 0AL

family and dog friendly. Brancaster beers are produced by a local brewery to the pub's recipes and at least one is always available. Food offerings include local seafood and stone-baked pizza, with the oven visible from the bar. Coasthopper buses stop outside. There is a beer and music festival every June. Closed 3-6pm weekdays in winter.
Q ☎ 🏵 🍴 ⅏ & Å ♣ P 🚌 ❀ 🐾 ☎

Brockdish

Old King's Head 🍺

50 The Street, IP21 4JY
☼ closed Mon; 10-10 (11 Fri & Sat); 10-9 Sun
☎ (01379) 668843 ⊕ kingsheadbrockdish.co.uk
Adnams Southwold Bitter, Broadside; 3 changing beers (often Barrell & Sellers, Grain, Wolf) Ⓗ
A 16th-century beamed community pub with a friendly atmosphere. The pub reopened in 2015 with an added coffee shop (open at 10am) serving delicious home-made cakes and bread at weekends. It has a family-friendly bar, and another bar with a woodburner, both serving imaginative Italian food from noon. Locally sourced meats and ingredients are used where possible, and gluten-free meals and cakes are available. Regular music events take place, usually on a Thursday. A gin club adds to the mix. Local artists display work in the bars and in the gallery. ☎ 🏵 🍴 & ♣ P 🚌 ❀

REAL ALE BREWERIES

All Day Salle
Ampersand Earsham (NEW)
Beeston Beeston
Boudicca West Barsham
Buffy's Wicklewood
Bullards Norwich
Chalk Hill 🍺 Norwich
Dancing Men 🍺 Happisburgh
Elmtree Snetterton
Fat Cat 🍺 Norwich
Fox 🍺 Heacham
Golden Triangle Norwich
Grain Alburgh
Humpty Dumpty Reedham
Iceni Ickburgh
Lacons Great Yarmouth
Neatishead 🍺 Neatishead
Norfolk Hindringham
Oakwood Wells-next-the-Sea
Opa Hay's Aldeby
Panther Reepham
People's Thorpe-next-Haddiscoe
Poppyland Cromer
Redwell Norwich
S&P Horsford
St Andrews 🍺 Norwich
Stumptail Great Dunham
Taylors 🍺 Attleborough
Tindall Seething
Tipples Salhouse
Tombstone 🍺 Great Yarmouth
Two Rivers Denver
Wagtail Old Buckenham
Waveney 🍺 Earsham
Why Not Norwich
Wildcraft Buxton (NEW)
Winter's Norwich
Wolf Besthorpe
Woodforde's Woodbastwick
Yaarbrew Hickling (NEW)
Yetman's Bayfield

☼ 12-3, 6-11; 12-11 Fri & Sat; 12-10.30 Sun
☎ (01328) 830297 ⊕ binhamchequers.co.uk
Adnams Southwold Bitter; Norfolk Brewhouse Moon Gazer Golden Ale; 3 changing beers Ⓗ
A friendly traditional brick-and-flint village pub, the Chequers is a tremendously popular place both with locals and visitors, with strong support from the surrounding community. The menu comprises a range of good wholesome fare (including vegetarian) at reasonable prices. There is an additional specials menu with regular themed evenings. One of the guests beers is from Norfolk Brewhouse, and others are sourced regionally, but often from Norfolk. In addition to the bar area, there are benches and tables both inside and outside, and a large garden to the rear.
☎ 🏵 🍴 ♣ P 🚌 (46) ❀ ☎

Brancaster Staithe

Jolly Sailors

Main Road, PE31 8BJ
☼ 12-11; 12-10.30 Sun ☎ (01485) 210314
⊕ jollysailorsbrancaster.co.uk
Brancaster Best; 1 changing beer Ⓗ
A cosy inn with several small drinking areas and two dining rooms, convenient for the Norfolk coast path and Brancaster Staithe harbour. It has a garden and play area, an ice cream hut, and is

Brooke

White Lion
49 The Street, NR15 1JW (400yds from B1332, by side of mere)
✪ 12-11 ☎ (01508) 550938
6 changing beers Ⓖ
Welcoming village pub with a long single bar on two levels, serving up to eight cask beers from small breweries throughout the UK, all on gravity. A real cider is also sold seasonally. Parts of the building date from the late-18th century. The pub faces the mere that divides the village street. There is a regular bus service from Norwich to Beccles.
✿🄍◗♣⛱P🖵(88)✿

Burston

Crown Inn
Mill Road, IP22 5TW (by crossroads in middle of village, on green)
✪ 12-11; 12-10.30 Sun ☎ (01379) 741257
🌐 burstoncrown.com
Adnams Southwold Bitter; 4 changing beers (often Adnams) Ⓗ/Ⓖ
Attractive 16th-century Grade II-listed pub featuring exposed beams, deep sofas, newspapers and a log fire blazing in the inglenook fireplace. There are two bars, one with a pool table and darts. Boules is played in the garden in summer. A small restaurant serves locally sourced freshly cooked food (no food Sun eve or Mon). The cuisine is mixed, and booking is advisable. Regular live music features at weekends, and there is an open mic night on Thursday. The village is famous for the Burston School Strike that ran from 1914 to 1939.
Q🔕🄍✿🄍◗♣P🖵🛜

Cantley

Cock Tavern
Manor Road, NR13 3JQ (1½ miles N of village centre)
✪ 11-3, 6-11.30 ☎ (01493) 700895
Adnams Southwold Bitter; 4 changing beers Ⓗ
A characterful rural roadside pub which serves a large catchment area, not just the nearby village of Cantley. Although a popular food venue (booking advisable at busy times), it retains the feel and atmosphere of a real pub, helped by the traditional decor. There are several themed food nights weekly, and a quiz night on the first and third Mondays of the month. Its wide range of reasonably priced ales makes the pub well worth the detour off the usual Broads tourist trail. Its five handpumps offer Adnams, Fuller's and Wadworths beers and more than 100 malt whiskies are stocked. 🔕◗♣P🖵(730)✿

Catfield

Crown Inn Ⓛ ✪
The Street, NR29 5AA (in centre of village, S of A149, E of Stalham)
✪ 12-2.30, 7 (5 Fri)-11; 12-3, 7-midnight Sat; 12-6, 7-10.30 Sun ☎ (01692) 580128 🌐 catfieldcrown.co.uk
Greene King IPA; 3 changing beers Ⓗ
Formerly a Lacons pub, now a free house, this 300-year-old inn with a real fire is a great focus for village life. There is an interesting selection of quality guest beers, mainly from local breweries. The food includes traditional pub offerings, with fresh local ingredients used where possible. There

is a separate function/dining room and a secluded rear garden for the summer. Accommodation is available in two self-catering holiday cottages.
Q✿🛏🄍◗♣P🖵✿🛜

Coltishall

Red Lion Ⓛ
77 Church Street, NR12 7DW
✪ 12 (4 Mon)-11 ☎ (01603) 736644
🌐 redlion-coltishall.co.uk
Sharp's Doom Bar; 2 changing beers Ⓗ
Intricate two-level establishment with a separate dining area, complemented by a café. Warm, friendly and comfortable, the Red Lion dates from the 16th century. In the cosy lower bar, with logburner, up to five real ales can be found, including some from local or regional microbreweries. The pub also presses its own bottled cider from local orchards. The varied menu features specials, and there are theme nights. Beer festivals are held at Easter and in late-summer, and the pub even has its own taxi.
Q✿🄍♣⛱P🖵(29)✿🛜

Cromer

Wellington
Garden Street, NR27 9HN
✪ 11-11 (midnight Fri & Sat); 12-10.30 Sun
☎ (01263) 511075 🌐 thewellycromer.co.uk
Adnams Southwold Bitter; 3 changing beers Ⓗ
A stone's throw from the beach, the Welly is an interesting building with one long bar. There is a good selection of pub games and a widescreen TV for live sport. It has en-suite rooms and a, recent addition, the Courtyard restaurant serving locally sourced food at good prices in a converted stable block. The house beer is from Wolf Brewery, with changing beers on handpump from Adnams and Woodforde's. Owned by the same family for over 20 years. 🔕✿🄍◖🛏♣🖵✿🛜

Dereham

Royal Standard Ⓛ
86 Baxter Row, NR19 1AY (from Market Place head E down High St; at mini roundabout outside library bear right into Baxter Row; pub is 150yds on the right)
✪ 11-midnight (1am Fri & Sat); 12-midnight Sun
☎ (01362) 690948
Batemans XB; 3 changing beers Ⓗ
A lively, cosy, two-roomed pub with a friendly and welcoming atmosphere. Two beers are typically from Batemans' guest beer range, with another usually local. Traditional pub games feature strongly, with pool, darts and cribbage all played. Live football is screened on a regular basis, and the pub has a comprehensive jukebox. It is 10 minutes' walk from the Mid-Norfolk Heritage Railway.
🔕✿♣🛗♣P🖵✿🛜

Dersingham

Coach & Horses ✪
77 Manor Road, PE31 6LN
✪ 12-11 ☎ (01485) 540391 🌐 thecoachpub.com
Woodforde's Wherry; 3 changing beers Ⓗ
Local CAMRA Pub of the Year 2015, this 19th-century carrstone inn near Sandringham serves one regular beer, three guest ales and a draught real cider at reasonable prices. Popular for home-made

traditional meals, entertainment includes quiz nights, piano, pool table and live music Friday nights and some Sundays. The large garden has a children's play area. An October beer festival offers around 20 real ales plus five real ciders. There are three en-suite B&B rooms. Dogs are welcome.
Q☕🍴◑▲♿P�⚲🐾 📶

Downham Market

Crown Hotel
12 Bridge Street, PE38 9DH
🕒 9.30am-11 ☎ (01366) 382322 ⊕ crowncoachinginn.com
Adnams Southwold Bitter; Greene King IPA, Abbot; 2 changing beers Ⓗ
An unspoilt 17th-century coaching inn at the heart of the town. After entering through a room with a lovely staircase, you will find a good selection of ales served in a bar with a beamed ceiling and large fireplace. There is a restaurant and separate function room that caters for parties and weddings, and plenty of outside seating. Accommodation is provided in 18 rooms including family suites.
Q☕🍴◑➡P🚗 📶

Earsham

Queen's Head Ⓛ
Station Road, NR35 2TS (just W of Bungay)
🕒 12-11; 12-10.30 Sun ☎ (01986) 892623
Waveney East Coast Mild, Lightweight, Welterweight; 1 changing beer (sourced locally; often Wolf) Ⓗ
On the Norfolk-Suffolk border, near Bungay, this busy 17th-century locals' pub has a large front garden overlooking the village green. The main bar has a flagstone floor, wooden beams and a large fireplace with a roaring fire in winter. It is home to the Waveney Brewing Co. There is a separate dining area serving lunchtime meals (no food Mon and Tue). The landlord has owned the pub since 2000. Usually four ales and at least one real cider are available. Q☕🐕◑ᐁ♣♿P🚗(580)⚲ 📶

Elsing

Mermaid Inn
Church Street, NR20 3EA (opp St Mary's Church)
🕒 12-3 (not Mon), 6-11; 12.30-10.30 Sun ☎ (01362) 637640
⊕ elsingmermaidinn.co.uk
Adnams Broadside; Woodforde's Wherry Ⓖ; 1 changing beer Ⓗ
Well-regarded rural pub with a restaurant comprising a large bar and a dining room, featuring a fire at one end and a pool table at the other. A good selection of ales is on offer dispensed by gravity. The menu includes the landlord's well-rated pies and curries together with several vegetarian options and a local Norfolk cheeseboard. Local groups and societies meet here regularly, while ramblers from further afield arrive via the 12-mile Wensum Way. Two outdoor seating areas provide for pleasant summer drinking.
🐕⚾◑♿♣P⚲ 📶

Gayton

Crown Inn ✅
Lynn Road, PE32 1PA
🕒 12-11 (11.30 Fri & Sat) ☎ (01553) 636252
⊕ gaytoncrown.com/index
Greene King IPA, Abbot; Morland Old Speckled Hen; 1 changing beer Ⓗ

Originating from the 13th century, the Crown Inn combines a charming historic feel with a friendly atmosphere. The regular beer range is complemented by an occasional interesting guest. There are several drinking areas and a patio outside for the summer with attractive flowerbeds. The restaurant serves locally sourced food including game dishes and a popular Sunday carvery.
Q☕🍴◑♿▲♣P🚗(48)⚲ 📶

Gorleston

Dock Tavern Ⓛ
Dock Tavern Lane, NR31 6PY (opp N side of Morrisons)
🕒 11-11; 12-11 Sun ☎ (01493) 442255
⊕ thedocktavern.com
Adnams Broadside; 4 changing beers Ⓗ
As its name suggests, this pub is close to the river, and not far from the main shopping area. It has been subject to flood damage many times and the various flood levels can be seen by the front door. The outside drinking area at the front has views of the river and docks. There is live music most weekends, and curry and quiz nights monthly, plus an annual charity music day. 🐕⚾◑♣♿P⚲ 📶

New Entertainer
80 Pier Plain, NR31 6PG
🕒 12-11 ☎ (01493) 300022
Greene King IPA; 8 changing beers Ⓗ
This traditional street-corner local with a curved frontage has an interesting design and layout. There is a varied choice of beers on offer, including up to 10 guests, many locally brewed, and five draught ciders. The customers are as widely varied as the beer. This free house is well worth seeking out – note that the main entrance is at what appears to be the back. ♣♣♿⚲ 📶

Oddfellows Arms
43 Cliff Hill, NR31 6DG
🕒 4-11 (8 Mon; midnight Fri); 2-8 Sun ☎ 07584 355161
⊕ oddiesgy.co.uk
4 changing beers Ⓗ
A well-refurbished town pub with two bars, tucked away a short distance from the harbour mouth. Jazz nights are a speciality, and there are always four beers on tap, mostly bitters/golden ales at 3.5-4.5% ABV. Free peanuts are often provided on the bar in glass carafes. It has pleasant outdoor seating for fine summer evenings, and limited parking at the rear. ⚾P⚲ 📶

Great Cressingham

Olde Windmill Inn
Water End, IP25 6NN (off A1065 S of Swaffham)
🕒 11-11 ☎ (01760) 756232 ⊕ oldewindmillinn.co.uk
Adnams Southwold Bitter, Broadside; Greene King IPA; 2 changing beers Ⓗ
Run by three generations since 1956, the Windmill is a large rural inn and hotel with the feel of a village pub despite its size. It features a rolling range of beers, often including Windy Miller, a house beer supplied by Purity. Real cider is also a popular feature. Modern hotel accommodation is provided in a separate building behind the pub. The food caters for all tastes and prices and is very popular. The varied dining areas include a large conservatory and smaller intimate rooms.
Q☕🐕➡◑♿▲♣♣P⚲

Great Hockham

Eagle 🏠 ✅
Harling Road, IP24 1NP
☼ 12-2.30, 6-11 (11.30 Thu); 12-midnight Fri & Sat; 12-10.30 Sun ☎ (01953) 498893 ⊕ hockhameagle.com
Adnams Southwold Bitter, Ghost Ship; Morland Old Speckled Hen; Woodforde's Wherry; 1 changing beer Ⓗ
Dating from the 1850s, this large family and dog friendly pub is set in a picturesque village close to Thetford Forest. Two bars divided by an open fire serve five real ales on handpump. Outdoor seating is provided at the front and in an enclosed brick-weave courtyard at the rear. The pub hosts three pool teams and a darts team in addition to a fortnightly quiz and other regular events.
⛵🕮🌙◑&♣P🚌🐾🛜

Great Yarmouth

Barking Smack 🏠
16 Marine Parade, NR30 3AH
☼ 11-11 (midnight Fri & Sat) ☎ (01493) 859752
4 changing beers Ⓗ
Named after the famous Short Blue fishing fleet (the largest in the world at the time) that moved from Barking to Gorleston in the 19th century. An ex-Lacons pub, it has an elegant carved wooden bar, a smart modern interior, with a large patio opening onto Marine Parade and the seafront. Close to the Hippodrome Circus, the pub is a refuge from the fizz of keg nearby, and serves a range of Grain beers. Barbecues are held during the season, and real cider is sold. Check opening times out of season. ⛵🕮🌙◑&♦

Mariners 🏠
69 Howard Street South, NR30 1LN (behind both Palmers and the Star Hotel)
☼ 12 (11 Sat)-midnight ☎ (01493) 331164
8 changing beers Ⓗ
Traditional two-bar pub in the town centre, with up to eight ales and eight real ciders/perries on offer. Visitors could be excused for thinking that a beer festival is always in progress, given the range and choice from all over the country. Beer festivals are in fact held throughout the year, including at Easter and in early September when the town's maritime festival is held. Most local buses stop nearby.
Q⛵🕮🌙⇌♣♦P🚌🐾

Red Herring 🏠
24-25 Havelock Road, NR30 3HQ (off St Peters St and at back of Time & Tide museum)
☼ 12-3, 7-11.30; 12-midnight Sat & Sun ☎ (01493) 853384
3 changing beers Ⓗ
This back-street corner local is close to spectacular sections of the medieval town wall. There is a nice, relaxed and comfortable atmosphere, and the pool table and television are tucked away in a room separated from the bar by folding doors. There are many photos of Old Yarmouth during the herring fishing days when the town was invaded by countless Scottish herring boats. The cider is Westons Old Rosie. 🕮♣♦

Tombstone Saloon
6 George Street, NR30 1HR (on NE corner of Hall Quay)
☼ closed Mon-Wed; 12-midnight; 12-11 Sun ☎ 07584 504444 ⊕ tombstonebrewery.co.uk
10 changing beers Ⓖ
Old West-style bar specialising in real ale and cider, operated by the local Tombstone Brewery sited at the rear of the premises. Staff are friendly and knowledgeable about beer, and there are usually up to six Tombstone real ales plus four others from local breweries. Many buses stop outside the pub. George Street was once one of the main roads into Yarmouth, and in 1870 there were 12 pubs within 100 yards. May close Monday to Wednesday in winter except December. ⇌♣♦🚌🐾

Happisburgh

Hill House 🏠
The Hill, NR12 0PW (off B1159, behind church)
☼ 12-11.30 ☎ (01692) 650004 ⊕ hillhouseinn.co.uk
6 changing beers Ⓗ
A Grade II 16th-century former coaching inn in an attractive coastal village, and a haunt of Sir Arthur Conan Doyle after whose work, The Dancing Men, the in-house brewery is named. The pub usually offers a range of up to six real ales and one cider, all from this brewery. Hot meals are served lunchtimes and evenings. The pub hosts a noteworthy beer festival each June that showcases over 120 real ales and ciders.
Q⛵🕮🌙⇌◑🅿️⚓♣♦P🐾🛜

Harpley

Rose & Crown
Nethergate Street, PE31 6TW
☼ closed Mon; 12-3.30 (not Tue), 6.30-10.30; 12-5 Sun ☎ (01485) 521807
Woodforde's Wherry; 2 changing beers Ⓗ
Just off the A148 King's Lynn to Fakenham road, this attractive 17th-century pub offers guest ales from local breweries. It features open bar areas with a stylish and comfortable feel and has log fires in winter, while outside is an enclosed beer garden for summer drinking. There is an extensive menu serving excellent food, including one of the best Sunday roasts in the area. The unspoilt village provides pleasant walks and is close to Houghton Hall. Q⛵🕮🌙◑P🚌(X8)🐾🛜

Hempton

Bell
24 The Green, NR21 7LG
☼ 11-2.30 (not Tue), 5-midnight; 11-midnight Sat; 12-midnight Sun ☎ (01328) 864579 ⊕ hemptonbell.co.uk
Sharp's Doom Bar; Woodforde's Wherry; 1 changing beer Ⓗ
A traditional family-run village pub with a relaxed, friendly atmosphere. It retains a two-bar layout little altered since the early 1970s. Pub games including dominoes, cribbage and poker dice are popular – you will be welcome to get involved. Changing guest beers are from micros or independent breweries and are typically slightly stronger than the regulars. An open mic folk session takes place on the second Tuesday of the month and regular quizzes are held. ♣P🐾

Heydon

Earle Arms ✅
The Street, NR11 6AD
☼ closed Mon; 12-3, 6 (5 Fri)-11; 12-11 Sun ☎ (01263) 587376 ⊕ theearlearms.com
Adnams Southwold Bitter; 2 changing beers Ⓗ

A delightful former coaching inn at the heart of an idyllic privately owned village. The bar, with equine memorabilia, is cosy, mainly candlelit, and has a log fire in winter. At the rear is a candlelit conservatory. There are three real ales and up to four ciders. High-quality meals, prepared to order using locally sourced ingredients, may be enjoyed in the separate restaurant or the bar. The green opposite hosts various community events. A quintessentially English gem. Q✿❀❍♣❤P🅿🐾📶

Hickling

Greyhound Inn L ✓
The Green, NR12 0YA
✿ 12-11 ☎ (01692) 598306
Adnams Ghost Ship; Woodforde's Wherry; 2 changing beers H
This is very much a cosy traditional country pub, in the middle of Hickling. It is the social hub for the community, housing a single bar with an attractive open fire and games area, a small restaurant to the side, and a large attractive rear garden. There is a further outdoor covered dining area between the bar and garden for alfresco dining. Social events are held throughout the year including live music from bands and vocalists. Dogs are welcome and Wi-Fi is available. Q✿❀❍♣❤P🐾📶

Hockwold

Red Lion
114 Main Street, IP26 4NB
✿ 11.30-3, 6 (5 Fri)-11.30; 11.30-11.30 Sat; 12-10.30 Sun
☎ (01842) 829728
3 changing beers H
Traditional, friendly village pub set on a green. It was refurbished and reopened as a free house in 2012, with a smart, but comfortable interior – see how many toby jugs you can spot. A good selection of home-made food is served all week, with a carvery Tuesday lunchtime, Thursday evening and Sunday. There are regular, well-supported quizzes and darts matches. Outside is a spacious garden with plenty of seating and a children's play area. ❀✿❍♣P🐾

Honingham

Buck L
29 The Street, NR9 5BL (centre of village)
✿ 11.30-11; 11.30-10 Sun ☎ (01603) 880393
⊕ thehoninghambuck.co.uk
Lacons Affinity, Encore, Pale Ale; 1 changing beer H
Dating back to 1789, this traditional one-bar village pub has a separate restaurant area with an emphasis on home-cooked food. It serves Lacons real ales since the brewery bought the pub in May 2015, and has slate floors, oak beams, a large fireplace and period furniture that all fit the image of a country pub. The excellent menu of unusual food, freshly cooked to order, makes it a great venue for dining. Q❀✿❍❍♣P🐾

Horsey

Nelson Head L
The Street, NR29 4AD (just off B1159, 300yds down lane N of Horsey Mill)
✿ 11-11; 12-11 Sun ☎ (01493) 393378
⊕ thenelsonhead.com

Woodforde's Wherry, Nelson's Revenge H; 1 changing beer G
This traditional, National Trust-owned country pub has a bar area with an open fire, decorated with various Nelson-related memorabilia and paintings. Quality food is served in a separate area, prepared using locally sourced ingredients. The extensive beer garden is host to festivals and events all year round. The pub is on a popular walk to access the beach and seal population. The staff are friendly, knowledgeable and eager to help if required. Q❀✿❀❍♣❤P🐾📶

King's Lynn

Live & Let Live L
18 Windsor Road, PE30 5PL (off London Rd near Catholic church)
✿ 11-10.30 (11 Fri & Sat) ☎ (01553) 764990
5 changing beers H
Popular locals' pub with two bars, a small cosy lounge and a larger public bar with a TV. Five beers are dispensed including a mild (rare for the area). Cider drinkers have a choice of four, usually including something from local producer Downham Cider Company. Live music sometimes plays in the public bar. ❤

Stuart House Hotel
35 Goodwins Road, PE30 5QX (up gravel drive off Goodwins Rd)
✿ 6-11 ☎ (01553) 772169 ⊕ stuart-house-hotel.co.uk
3 changing beers H
A long-standing entry in the Guide, the hotel bar is open to all and, despite being close to town, its large beer garden and proximity to the park give it a more rural feel. There is a regular beer festival, usually the last week in July, and events such as live music and murder mystery evenings are held here. The beers are mostly from the larger regional breweries and although the bar is open evenings only, it is often possible to arrange lunchtime opening if you get in contact. ✿❄❍≈P🐾📶

Larling

Angel
NR16 2QU (1 mile SW of Snetterton racetrack, just off A11)
✿ 10-midnight; 11-11 Sun ☎ (01953) 717963
⊕ angel-larling.co.uk
Adnams Southwold Bitter; 4 changing beers H
The Angel offers five real ales on handpump, always including a mild, one real cider, plus a huge range of whiskies. The variety of beers is eclectic to say the least. The lounge and bar have open fires and a friendly atmosphere reflecting the agricultural nature of the area. There is a dining room where the food is home-made and comes in what can only be described as farmer's portions! The pub offers B&B accommodation plus camping facilities. These are popular during the beer festival in August. Q❄✿❄❍♣🅰❤P🏳

Lessingham

Star Inn L
Star Hill, NR12 0DN (just off main B1159, corner of High Rd and Star Hill)
✿ closed Mon; 12-3, 6-11; 12-11 Sun ☎ (01692) 580510
⊕ thestarlessingham.co.uk

Adnams Southwold Bitter; Buffy's Norfolk Terrier; Woodforde's Once Bittern; 1 changing beer ⒼG
A traditional pub, just outside the village, with a friendly atmosphere and a log fire in winter. Four ales, including one guest, served from the cask, are complemented by up to five ciders. It is popular for high-quality meals made from carefully sourced ingredients, expertly cooked and served in decent portions. Meals may be enjoyed in the bar, a separate restaurant room or in the spacious beer garden. Families are welcome. A popular beer festival is staged in August. Close to the north-east Norfolk coast and the Broads, this is a gem. CAMRA branch Rural Pub of the Year 2017.
Q❀☸◑✦➊P🖵(34)❀🐾🛜

Litcham

Bull Hotel
1 Church Street, PE32 2NS (on crossroads of B1145)
✪ 5-11; 12-10.30 Sun ☎ (01328) 701340
Beeston Worth the Wait; 2 changing beers ⒽH
In the centre of a picturesque village, fronting the green, this 17th-century inn has an interior with low wooden-beamed ceilings and wooden floorboards, and a small patio drinking area at the rear. The three ales are from local microbrewer Beeston Brewery and Greene King. The pub has nine rooms, all en-suite, with some converted for disabled use. Q🐕❀☸◑❤✦P

Little Walsingham

Black Lion Hotel
Friday Market Place, NR22 6DB
✪ 11-11; 11-10.30 Sun ☎ (01328) 820235
⊕ blacklionhotelnorfolk.co.uk
Adnams Ghost Ship; Woodforde's Wherry; 1 changing beer ⒽH
This family-friendly pub with rooms, parts of which date back to the 15th century, is in the centre of Walsingham, which is a major pilgrimage centre, famed for its religious shrines in honour of the Virgin Mary. The bar is relaxed, with a slightly rustic feel, including oak beams, farm implements and old tractor seat stools. The food is all locally sourced, and prepared on site (except the pies).
Q🐕❀☸◑🖵❀🛜

Bull Inn ✅
8 Common Place, NR22 6BP
✪ 12-11 ☎ (01328) 820333 ⊕ walsinghambull.co.uk
3 changing beers ⒽH
Over 600 years old, this cosy and welcoming local is in the centre of the village, with a small yard to the front and a larger garden at the rear. Near the southern end of Wells and Walsingham light railway, the pub can be busy in pilgrimage season (there are three shrines). Three or four rotating ales are served, along with excellent home-cooked meals (including proper pies, not dishes with puff pastry on top). Q🐕❀☸◑✦P🖵❀🛜

Longham

White Horse
Wendling Road, NR19 2RD
✪ 11.30-2.30, 5-11; 11.30-3, 4.30-midnight Sat; 11-3, 5.30-10.30 Sun ☎ (01362) 687464
⊕ longhamwhitehorse.co.uk
4 changing beers ⒽH

Quiet, attractive village inn with a restaurant. The beers, which can be as many as six, usually include Oakham Bishop's Farewell and local brews such as Moongazer. The current landlord has traced his predecessors back to 1640, with names displayed on a glass panel in the bar. Beer festivals are staged, with live music in August and December. The pub has a pleasant garden and outdoor seating area. Two doubles and a family room provide B&B.
Q🐕❀☸◑✦P🐾🛜

Martham

King's Arms ✅
15 The Green, NR29 4PL
✪ 12-11 (midnight Fri & Sat); 12-10.30 Sun
☎ (01493) 749156
5 changing beers ⒽH
Previously owned by Adnams, and (well) before that by the original incarnation of Lacons, this venue, in the centre of the village by the pond, has recently become a free house, serving four or five ales from local and less-local breweries. There is also a pleasant garden at the back, and a large car park. A sloe gin competition is held annually.
🐕❀☸◑✦P🖵❀🛜

Middleton

Gate
Hill Road, Fair Green, PE32 1RW (N of A47; follow Fair Green signs)
✪ closed Mon; 12-2, 6 (5 Fri)-11; 12-11 Sat; 12-10.30 Sun
☎ (01553) 840518 ⊕ thegatemiddleton.co.uk
3 changing beers ⒽH
It is worth the short detour off the A47, east of King's Lynn, to find what is at heart still a village local. The bar has a log fire in winter and welcomes dogs. It caters for drinkers and those who come to enjoy the good-value pub food, while those who prefer more formal dining can choose the smart restaurant area. Note that the pub is closed on Mondays except bank holidays. Q🐕❀◑✦🐕P❀

Neatishead

White Horse Ⓛ
The Street, NR12 8AD
✪ 11-11; 11-10.30 Sun ☎ (01692) 630828
⊕ thewhitehorseinnneatishead.com
Woodforde's Wherry; 6 changing beers ⒽH
Local CAMRA Rural Pub of the Year 2016. A tastefully modernised, traditional village hostelry with many original features, including log fires in winter. Of the seven real ales, six change frequently and are mainly from microbreweries across the UK, including the in-house brewery. Excellent reasonably priced meals are home prepared using local produce. The restaurant area is split level and cosy. Beer festivals are held in spring and autumn. It is a short walk from the moorings to this beer lovers' haven. Q🐕❀◑✦🐕P❀🛜

Necton

Windmill Inn
15-17 Mill Street, PE37 8EN
✪ 11-3, 6-11; 11-midnight Sat; 12-11 Sun
☎ (01760) 722057 ⊕ thenectonwindmill.co.uk
Greene King IPA; 2 changing beers ⒽH
Adjacent to the ground floor remains of the former Necton Windmill, hence the name, this is a

friendly, family-run, two-bar pub with a large restaurant extension. There is a games room with a pool table. It serves regular Greene King IPA and a Beeston beer, plus a varying guest, usually from Humpty Dumpty. The pub has a large rear beer garden and paved and decked areas at the front with tables. Bar meals and a full restaurant menu are served, with an excellent local reputation. ☺✿🕪♣P

North Creake

Jolly Farmers
1 Burnham Road, NR21 9JW
✿ closed Mon & Tue; 12 (12.30 Sat)-2.30, 7-11; 12-7 Sun ☎ (01328) 738185 ⊕ jollyfarmersnorfolk.co.uk
Woodforde's Wherry, Nelson's Revenge; 1 changing beer ⑤
Comfortable chairs and pine tables, open fires and excellent food from the finest ingredients combine to create a great atmosphere in this unchanging venue. Local artwork is displayed on the walls, and you are as likely to meet locals as tourists straying from the nearby north Norfolk coast. Dogs and walkers are welcome. The friendly landlords make this a lovely pub to visit. Q☺🕪♣P✿

North Lopham

Kings Head ✅
16 The Street, IP22 2NE
✿ 5-11 Mon; 11.30-3, 5-11 Tue-Fri; 11.30-midnight Sat; 12-3, 12-10.30 Sun ☎ (01379) 688007 ⊕ lophamkingshead.co.uk
Adnams Southwold; Woodfordes Wherry; 1 changing beer ⑪
Two bar, timber-framed and thatched 16th century pub set back from the main road through the village. The public bar has a pool table and inglenook fireplace while the comfortable saloon/dining room has a woodburner. The discounted guest ale on Saturdays is popular. Food is served Wednesday to Saturday plus Sunday lunchtime. The pub has a crazy golf course with free club and ball hire. Q✿🕪♣P✿

North Wootton

Red Cat Hotel
Station Road, PE30 3QH (road is opp All Saints church, at jct of N end of Nursery Rd and W end of Manor Rd)
✿ 5-11; 12-2, 7-11 Sun ☎ (01553) 631244 ⊕ redcathotel.com
Adnams Southwold Bitter; 1 changing beer ⑪
Village local with a reputation for well-kept beer, albeit in a limited range. It has a nicely decorated bar in a quiet location. Look for and ask the history of the namesake red cat – if you can believe it. There are attractive gardens for summer drinks. Near National Cycle Route 1, Sandringham Estate and the west Norfolk coast. Q☺✿P⊟(3)✿🎝

Norwich

Alexandra Tavern
16 Stafford Street, NR2 3BB (on corner of Stafford St and Gladstone St, off Dereham Rd)
✿ 12-11 (midnight Thu-Sat) ☎ (01603) 627772 ⊕ alexandratavern.co.uk
Chalk Hill Tap Bitter, CHB, Gold; 2 changing beers ⑪
Popular, bustling and friendly, this pub is a real gem found just outside the city centre. The interior is brightly decorated, with the walls featuring

pictures and articles of a nautical nature. The bar regularly serves three Chalk Hill Brewery beers as well as guest ales. Food is served daily until 7pm with a good variety available, including a soup menu. There is a dartboard and lots of board games to choose from, with children welcome until 7pm. Q☺✿🕪♣🖭✿🎝

Angel Gardens 🅛
96 Angel Road, NR3 3HT
✿ 11-midnight (1am Sat); 12-11 Sun ☎ (01603) 427490
Elgood's Black Dog; Fuller's London Pride; Oakham JHB; Sharp's Doom Bar; 5 changing beers ⑪
Friendly locals' pub with a good selection of four permanent and five changing local and national real ales. Up to six real ciders are available on gravity, depending on the season. The pub offers live entertainment on Saturday evening, a pool table, and runs darts and crib teams. It has a covered, heated drinking area at the front and a garden with play equipment at the rear. There is a small function room with bar. ✿🕪♣P✿🎝

Beehive 🅛
30 Leopold Road, NR4 7PJ
✿ 12 (4 Mon)-11; 12-midnight Fri & Sat ☎ (01603) 451628 ⊕ beehivepubnorwich.co.uk
Fuller's London Pride; Green Jack Golden Best; Oakham Bishops Farewell; 4 changing beers ⑪
A traditional friendly local with knowledgeable staff, with two bar areas and a comfortable lounge bar with sofas. A function room is upstairs with a pool table, and the pub hosts hockey, korfball, golf, darts and pool teams, a regular quiz, folk music nights and wine tasting evenings. A popular beer garden is used all year round and is great when summer barbecues are held. A beer festival with around 25 ales and ciders is held in June. The pub was Norfolk CAMRA Pub of the Year in 2015. Q✿🕪♣P⊟✿🎝

Cellar House 🅛
2 Eaton Street, Eaton, NR4 7AB
✿ 10-11; 9am-midnight Fri; 9.30am-midnight Sat ☎ (01603) 454511 ⊕ thecellarhouse.co.uk
Adnams Southwold Bitter; Woodforde's Wherry; 3 changing beers ⑪
This is an imposing Grade II-listed three-storey building. The pub was extensively refurbished in 2014, giving it a modern airy feel, while still retaining its old-world charm, with exposed brickwork, ceiling beams and an inglenook with a real fire. Up to six real ales are on the bar, some from local microbreweries. Food is served lunchtimes and evenings, plus breakfast at weekends and bank holiday Mondays. The licensing hours reflect the fact that it hosts Eaton post office. ✿🕪P⊟✿🎝

Coach & Horses
82 Thorpe Road, NR1 1BA
✿ 11-11 (1am Fri & Sat) ☎ (01603) 477077 ⊕ thecoachthorperoad.co.uk
Chalk Hill Tap Bitter, CHB, Gold; 3 changing beers ⑪
Close to the station, this coaching inn, with its iconic balcony, is the home of the on-site Chalk Hill Brewery, and serves its full range of beers. A tour of the brewery is available by appointment. Excellent-value food is served along with Burnard's cider. Sport, especially rugby, is shown on big screens, and the large fire is welcome in winter. Not far from the football ground, it gets busy before matches. ✿🕪♣🖭●P⊟✿🎝

Coach & Horses
51 Bethel Street, NR2 1NR
☼ 12–midnight; closed Sun ☎ (01603) 618522
⊕ thecoachandhorsesbethelstreet.co.uk
6 changing beers Ⓗ
Historic city-centre local near the Theatre Royal, the Forum and city hall. It is a bright, welcoming bar with several separate seating areas including cosy alcove-style seats, and it stocks a great range of ales from local breweries including Norfolk Brewhouse, Humpty Dumpty, Golden Triangle and Jo C's. A wholesome food menu is driven by the best of local produce. Ideal for a beer before or after the theatre, or any time of day. Try some celeb spotting too. Q⑤❀◑♠🚌👹 ᚋ

Cottage
9 Silver Road, NR3 4TB
☼ closed Mon; 4–11 (midnight Fri); 12–midnight Sat; 12–10.30 Sun ☎ (01603) 665535
5 changing beers Ⓗ
A large single-room pub with a lovely enclosed patio garden at the rear. Refurbished in 2015 by Grain Brewery to a high standard, it has solid oak flooring, wood panelling, exposed brickwork and a copper bar top. Six handpumps operate, with beers usually all from Grain but including the occasional special guest. A selection of quality spirits is also available. Sunday roast is offered plus burgers and wings in the evenings. There is a quiz on Wednesday and occasional live music and DJs.
❀◑♿🚌👹 ᚋ

Duke of Wellington Ⓛ
91-93 Waterloo Road, NR3 1EG
☼ 12–11 (midnight Fri & Sat); 12–10.30 Sun
☎ (01603) 441182 ⊕ dukeofwellingtonnorwich.co.uk
Fuller's London Pride Ⓗ; **Oakham JHB, Bishops Farewell; Wolf In Sheep's Clothing** Ⓖ, **Golden Jackal** Ⓗ; **15 changing beers** Ⓖ
Friendly pub with a varied range of guest ales to complement the permanent beers, the majority of which are served on gravity. The attractive enclosed rear garden/patio area accommodates a beer festival in late August plus regular barbecues at weekends in summer. Customers can bring their own food, and plates and cutlery will be provided, or they can sample the filling and inexpensive pies and sausage rolls. Events include monthly quiz evenings and folk music every Tuesday evening.
❀♿♠♥P🚌(9A,16)👹 ᚋ

Earlham Arms Ⓛ
41 Earlham Road, NR2 3AD
☼ 11–11 (11.30 Thu; midnight Fri & Sat); 9am–10.30 Sun
☎ (01603) 622993 ⊕ theearlhamarms.co.uk
11 changing beers Ⓗ
A lively pub with great food – one of Norwich's best gastro-pubs, with a good range of local real ales, either on handpump or gravity from the cellar. The large bar and dining area work well, with diners and drinkers merging seamlessly. Excellent and good-value bar snacks and tapas are served, and in the summer you can make best use of the weather in the large enclosed garden.
Q⑤❀◑♿♠P🚌👹 ᚋ

Fat Cat Ⓛ
49 West End Street, NR2 4NA
☼ 11–11 (midnight Thu–Sat) ☎ (01603) 624364
⊕ fatcatpub.co.uk

Adnams Southwold Bitter; Crouch Vale Yakima Gold; Fat Cat Bitter Ⓗ, Marmalade Cat; Fuller's ESB; Timothy Taylor Landlord; 20 changing beers Ⓖ
An outstanding example of what a real ale pub should be, with excellent, friendly service. Ales from the Fat Cat range, plus about 10 regular and 20 guest beers from all over the UK and real ciders are on offer. The Cat has been voted CAMRA National Pub of the Year twice. An amazing range of brewery memorabilia is displayed around the walls and alcoves of this traditional-style pub. Food is limited to good-value rolls and pies. A beer lover's paradise that no visitor to Norwich should miss out on. Q❀♥🚌👹 ᚋ

Fat Cat & Canary Ⓛ
101 Thorpe Road, NR1 1TR
☼ 12–11 (midnight Sat) ☎ (01603) 432393
Fat Cat Bitter, Hell Cat, Honey Ale, Marmalade Cat, Wild Cat; 7 changing beers Ⓗ
The third member of the Norwich-based Fat Cat mini chain, about 1½ miles from the centre of the city. It serves most of the Fat Cat brewery's ales, and various guests from around the UK, together with continental beers and real ciders. There is a small TV to the rear of the main bar, a large car park and terraces to the front and rear, the latter being heated. Home-made rolls are available. Busy on Norwich City match days. ❀♿♥P👹 ᚋ

Fat Cat Brewery Tap Ⓛ
98-100 Lawson Road, NR3 4LF
☼ 12–11 (midnight Fri); 11–midnight Sat; 11–10.30 Sun
☎ (01603) 413153 ⊕ fatcattap.co.uk
Adnams Southwold Bitter; Fat Cat Bitter Ⓖ, Honey Ale, Marmalade Cat Ⓗ; Oakham Bishops Farewell; 16 changing beers Ⓖ
This is the home of the Fat Cat Brewery, offering a wide-ranging choice of quality ales. Extensive breweriana adorn the walls and ceilings, with closing time indicated by a set of traffic lights. Live music on Friday and Sunday complements a variety of events including tap takeovers, themed beer evenings, a monthly cycling club, fortnightly quiz and a ladies' beer club, to name but a few. Food is specialist chipped potatoes (times vary), and cheeseboards can be provided (with 24hrs notice). Norfolk CAMRA Pub of the Year in 2016.
Q❀♿♠♥P🚌(11,11A)👹 ᚋ

Jubilee Ⓛ ✅
26 St Leonards Road, NR1 4BL
☼ 12–11 (midnight Fri & Sat) ☎ (01603) 618734
Greene King IPA; Woodforde's Wherry, Sundew, Nelson's Revenge; 2 changing beers Ⓗ
An attractive Victorian corner pub with a warm welcome. There is a choice of two bars, plus a comfortable conservatory and an enclosed patio garden. Many of the well-kept ales are local and this is also reflected in the range of lagers. This popular pub at the heart of the community caters for all tastes, from sports fans to those who enjoy local history talks, and has a village feel within easy reach of the city centre. Occasional pop-up street food fairs are held. ⑤❀◑🍴♠🚌👹 ᚋ

King's Arms
22 Hall Road, NR1 3HQ
☼ 11–11 (11.30 Fri & Sat); 12–11 Sun ☎ (01603) 477888
⊕ kingsarmsnorwich.co.uk
Batemans Gold; 10 changing beers Ⓗ
A friendly, and recently gently refurbished, Batemans house to the south of the city, which

serves an extensive and varied range of guest ales to complement the Batemans beers, usually including a stout or porter and a mild. Between three (in winter) and six (in summer) real ciders are also stocked. Customers can bring their own food from various nearby takeaways (plates and condiments provided). Monthly quiz nights, poker evenings and live music take place. Very busy on match days. Q⊛⊛◖&♣♥🍴🛜

King's Head 🍷 🄻

42 Magdalen Street, NR3 1JE (2 mins from Anglia Square)
🌐 12-midnight; 12-11 Sun ☎ (01603) 620468
⊕ kingsheadnorwich.com
11 changing beers 🄷

Friendly and welcoming traditional-style two-bar pub which offers up to a dozen quality real ales and one cider, but no keg beer. The beers are mainly from East Anglian-based microbreweries, but some from favoured breweries around the country often put in an appearance. The house beer, KHB, is brewed by Winter's. Local produce, such as fresh eggs and honey, is often sold, but there is no food except pork pies and pickled eggs. Bar billiards is well supported, with two teams in the local league. Local CAMRA Pub of the Year 2017. Q♣♥🛗🖥🛜

Leopard 🄻

98-100 Bull Close Road, NR3 1NQ
🌐 12-11 (midnight Fri & Sat) ☎ (01603) 631111
5 changing beers 🄷

A friendly and welcoming traditional single-bar corner local with a variety of changing ales from the smaller breweries, usually including at least one from Lacons. The house beer, Leopard Ale, is brewed specially by Tombstone. The pub has a clean and bright bar area which gives a spacious feel, plus a pleasant and quiet enclosed patio at the rear. Open mic events are held on the first Wednesday of the month, and food can be brought in. Q⊛&♣♥🍴🛜

Murderers 🄻

2-8 Timber Hill, NR1 3LB
🌐 10-11.30; 12-10.30 Sun ☎ (01603) 621447
⊕ themurderers.co.uk
Adnams Ghost Ship; Sharp's Doom Bar; Woodforde's Wherry; 7 changing beers 🄷

City-centre free house packed with character, beams and wood panelling. On several levels, with lots of little alcoves, the pub has been family owned for 30 years. Up to 10 real ales are available from local micros and around the country, including the house ale brewed by Coors. It is popular with shoppers, office workers and the evening going-out scene alike. Its real name is the Gardener's Arms, but nobody knows it as that since a 19th-century landlord convicted of murdering his wife gave the pub its alternative name. A regular blues night features every Thursday. ☕⊛◖♥🖥🛜

Plasterers Arms 🄻

43 Cowgate, NR3 1SZ
🌐 12-midnight (1am Fri & Sat) ☎ (01603) 387525
⊕ theplasterersarms.co.uk
Oakham JHB; 10 changing beers 🄷

This is a friendly corner local offering a wide range of microbrewery beers from around the country, specialising in new and exciting breweries. A range of bottled beers is also stocked. Regular tap takeovers and Meet the Brewer events are held. There is also sport (with a big screen for more

important events), live music from local bands on most Tuesdays and Sundays, cracking pizza all day and breakfast until 4pm at weekends, and the annual Fem.ale Festival. Q◖◗♣♥🖥⊛🛜

Plough

58 St Benedict Street, NR2 4AR
🌐 12-11 (midnight Fri & Sat) ☎ (01603) 661384
5 changing beers 🄷

Popular pub in one of the city's oldest areas near the Norwich Arts Centre. One of three Grain Brewery taps, the six ales available are usually all from the brewery. The two-bar interior is fairly small, with wooden chairs and tables, and a roaring log fire in winter. The large Mediterranean-style courtyard garden is a fine place to spend a summer's evening. A Grain-produced lager is available, along with Vic's special sausage pie, and barbecues in the summer. ⊛♣♥⊛🛜

Ribs of Beef 🄻 ✅

24 Wensum Street, NR3 1HY
🌐 11-11.30 (midnight Fri & Sat); 11-10.30 Sun
☎ (01603) 619517 ⊕ ribsofbeef.co.uk
Oakham JHB; 9 changing beers (sourced locally) 🄷

Traditional and well-decorated pub overlooking the River Wensum. A welcoming row of nine handpumps dispenses a large selection of local ales, with foreign beers and real cider also sold. The pub is popular with visitors and the kitchen offers a great selection of meals made with locally sourced ingredients. The atmosphere is relaxed and friendly, with a room downstairs as well as a big screen that regularly shows major sporting events. Just the place to watch the boats go by. ⊛◖&♣♥🖥🛜

Rosebery 🄻

94 Rosebery Road, NR3 3AB
🌐 12-midnight; 12-11 Sun & Mon ☎ (01603) 414284
⊕ theroseberynorwich.co.uk
6 changing beers 🄷

Large corner pub with high ceilings, refurbished in 2015 by Redwell Brewery, with six cask ales on handpump, usually including at least one from Bullards and another from Golden Triangle breweries. The remainder are a changing range of local and national ales. There are also four real ciders, with two each on handpump and on gravity. Live music features on a Sunday evening, food is served Thursday to Sunday, and there are four B&B rooms. ⊛🛏◖&♣♥🅿🖥(10)⊛🛜

Trafford Arms 🄻 ✅

61 Grove Road, NR1 3RL (at jct of Trafford Rd and Grove Rd)
🌐 11-11 ☎ (01603) 628466 ⊕ traffordarms.co.uk
Adnams Southwold Bitter, Ghost Ship; Woodforde's Wherry; 7 changing beers 🄷

This pub is near the city centre and continues to be a flagship for real ale in Norwich. The cask beer offering includes both regular and guest beers. High-standard pub food is served and there are special, themed food evenings. The Valentine's beer festival continues to be a major attraction, as are the regular pub quizzes on the last Sunday of the month. ⊛◖🅿🖥(9,17)🛜

Vine 🄻

7 Dove Street, NR2 1DE
🌐 11-11; closed Sun ☎ (01603) 627362 ⊕ vinethai.co.uk
4 changing beers 🄷

Just off the marketplace, serving up to four quality ales plus traditional Thai cuisine in an award-winning combination, this is Norwich's smallest pub. Beer festivals held in January and City of Ale week are highlights. The restaurant is upstairs, although customers often dine downstairs in the bar area; functions can be catered for outside normal opening hours on demand. Extra tables and chairs are set outside in the pedestrianised street. Q❀⏱❶♣🖵

Whalebone ✪

144 Magdalen Road, NR3 4BA

✿ 12-11 (midnight Fri & Sat) ☎ (01603) 425482
⊕ whalebonefreehouse.co.uk

Adnams Southwold Bitter, Broadside; Humpty Dumpty Little Sharpie; Oakham JHB; Woodforde's Wherry, Nelson's Revenge; 4 changing beers Ⓗ

A community local with eight real ales, conveniently situated just to the south of Sewell Park. The pub has three separate areas: the original front and rear bars, plus a newly refurbished area leading to a covered and heated terraced patio which is popular and used for summer barbecues. The pub holds an annual beer festival in July and supports three cricket teams as well as a golf society. Bar snacks including locally sourced pork pies, Scotch eggs and sausage rolls are available daily, plus freshly made coffee, hot chocolate and tea. ➣❀♣🖵(10,18)🐾🛜

White Lion

73 Oak Street, NR3 3AQ

✿ 12-11 (11.30 Fri & Sat); 12-10.30 Sun ☎ (01603) 632333

Milton Dionysus, Justinian, Marcus Aurelius, Nero, Pegasus, Sparta; 3 changing beers Ⓗ

Friendly award-winning pub, a short walk from the city centre, offering a range of beers from the Milton Brewery and two or three guests from non-local microbreweries. It is a former East Anglian CAMRA Cider Pub of the Year, serving over 20 types of cider and perry from near and far. Food is varied and of excellent value, using traditional local produce – check the daily specials menu. An annual beer festival is held in the autumn, and bar billiards and darts are played. Q❀❶♣🍴🐾🛜

Wig & Pen Ⓛ

6 St Martin at Palace Plain, NR3 1RN

✿ 11.30-11 (midnight Fri & Sat); 11.30-6.30 Sun
☎ (01603) 625891 ⊕ thewigandpen.com

Adnams Southwold Bitter; Humpty Dumpty Little Sharpie; Woodforde's Bure Gold; 3 changing beers Ⓗ

Pretty beamed 17th-century free house with a spacious patio immediately opposite the Bishop's Palace, and with an impressive view of Norwich Cathedral spire. Three permanent ales and three guests are always on, usually including two local beers. The small back room can be used for meetings. Good-quality food is served lunchtimes and evenings. The pub is a short walk from Tombland, where there are bus stands for several bus routes, and is an ideal starting or stopping place for a walk along the river. Q❀🛏❶🖵🛜

Old Buckenham

Ox & Plough

The Green, NR17 1RN (in centre of village overlooking green)

✿ 11-midnight; 12-midnight Sun ☎ 07887 691722

Adnams Southwold Bitter; Sharp's Doom Bar; 3 changing beers (often Hop Back, Oakham) Ⓗ

Family-friendly pub on one of the largest village greens in England, a community venue at the centre of village life. It has two open-plan drinking areas, one being quiet, without TV or electronic game machines. The garden at the front overlooks the village green. Real ale is dispensed from three to five handpumps; it is a member of the Oakham Academy and serves various changing Oakham ales. Bar snacks are available. ➣❀♿♣P🐾🛜

Old Hunstanton

Ancient Mariner ✪

6 Golf Course Road, PE36 6JJ (within Le Strange Arms Hotel complex)

✿ 11-11 ☎ (01485) 534411

Adnams Southwold Bitter, Broadside; 3 changing beers Ⓗ

A popular pub consisting of old barns and stables and including a family room and restaurants. At least four ales are on tap and live music nights are held occasionally. A large beer garden offers direct access to the beach and, as Old Hunstanton is on the east coast facing west, there are superb views of spectacular sunsets over the sea from the decking at the rear. Q➣❀🛏❶♿P🖵🐾🛜

Oxborough

Bedingfeld Arms

Stoke Ferry Road, PE33 9PS

✿ 11-11 (midnight Fri & Sat) ☎ (01366) 328300
⊕ bedingfeldarms.co.uk

Adnams Broadside; Woodforde's Wherry; 1 changing beer Ⓗ

A coaching house dating from 1723 opposite the historic Oxborough Hall. Refurbished throughout in 2012 to a high standard, this comfortable free house provides consistent high-quality meals, service, accommodation and beers from Charles Wells. It has two separate dining rooms in smart country relaxed style, and a central room with a bar and relaxed seating for lunches and coffee. Q❀🛏❶♿♣P🐾🛜

Reepham

King's Arms Ⓛ

Market Place, NR10 4JJ

✿ 11.30-3, 5.30-11; 11.30-11 Sat; 12-10.30 Sun
☎ (01603) 870345 ⊕ kingsarmsreepham.com

Adnams Southwold Bitter; Ghost Ship; Greene King Abbot; Panther Golden Panther; Woodforde's Wherry; 1 changing beer Ⓗ

A former coaching inn, dating back to 1667, in the picturesque square of this small market town, with original beams, Norfolk brickwork and open fires. There are several comfortable drinking and dining areas, tables in front with views across the square, and five permanent real ales on sale, including at least one from the local Panther Brewery, plus a guest. The comprehensive food menu is mostly sourced from nearby suppliers. Jazz bands play in the rear courtyard on summer Sundays. Dogs are welcome. Q➣❀❶🖵🐾

Roydon

Union Jack

30 Station Road, PE32 1AW (off A148)

✿ 4 (2 Mon; 1.30 Fri)-midnight; 12-midnight Sat & Sun ☎ 07771 660439

4 changing beers Ⓗ
Popular with locals, this traditional village inn has twice been local CAMRA Pub of the Year. Four handpumps dispense a variety of ales, and beer festivals held over the Easter and August bank holidays usually feature local breweries. There are occasional food nights, live music each month, regular bingo and quizzes and weekly support for darts, crib and dominoes. Dogs are welcome.
❀🛏♣💷P🖵(48)🐾

Saham Toney

Old Bell ✅
1 Bell Lane, IP25 7HD
🕐 11-11; 11-10.30 Sun ☎ (01953) 884934
Greene King IPA; Adnams Southwold Bitter; 4 changing beers Ⓗ
In appropriately named Bell Lane in Saham and in sight of the mere and beautiful medieval church, the Bell has four guest beers of good quality. It is a lovely old building with a long bar room and a restaurant. There is always a friendly atmosphere. Fundraising events are staged regularly and the Bell supports good causes both locally and nationally. Food is served daily from noon, featuring inventive fusion dishes plus themed food nights. ◑&♠♣P

St Olaves

Bell Inn ✅
Beccles Road, NR31 9HE
🕐 9am-11 ☎ (01493) 488249 ⊕ bellinn-stolaves.co.uk
Adnams Southwold Bitter, Ghost Ship; 2 changing beers Ⓗ
This brick-built building with black oak beams is reputedly Broadland's oldest recorded pub, and parts date from 1520. Adjacent to the River Waveney, it is named after the bell with which travellers used to summon the monk ferryman, before the bridge was built. It offers four real ales, pleasant gardens with their own moorings, a restaurant serving home-style food, and is popular with Broads cruisers. It may close earlier in winter, but there are two real fires for extra warmth. Food is served all day from 9am.
🛥❀◑P🖵(81,580)🐾🛜

Shouldham

King's Arms 🏆
The Green, PE33 0BY
🕐 4.30-10.30 Mon; 12-3, 4.30-11 Tue-Thu; 12-11.30 Fri; 11.30-11.30 Sat; 12-10.30 Sun ☎ (01366) 347410
⊕ kingsarmsshouldham.co.uk
2 changing beers Ⓖ
Local CAMRA Pub of the Year for 2016, this is a community-owned pub which serves two or three beers straight from the cask and uses oversized lined glasses. There is a volunteer-operated café open from 9.30am each day and, as might be expected, this hostelry is the focus of the village, with lots of events ranging from quizzes to poetry-and-a-pint nights. Locally brewed beer is usually available and cider is often for sale.
🛥❀◑♣P🖵🐾🛜

Snettisham

Rose & Crown
Old Church Road, PE31 7LX (off B1440)

🕐 11-11; 11-10.30 Sun ☎ (01485) 541382
⊕ roseandcrownsnettisham.co.uk
Adnams Broadside; Banks's Amber Ale; Marston's Pedigree; Woodforde's Wherry; 2 changing beers Ⓗ
A popular traditional village inn with cosy bars, exposed beams, a real fire and a dining room. Head through the narrow passage to find a larger bar and dining areas with a contemporary feel. Well known for quality traditional and exciting local seasonal fare, the bars also remain popular with local drinkers. The garden and play area make it appealing to families. Accommodation is available for those who wish to remain longer in this beautiful area. Q🛏❀🛏◑&♣P🖵🐾🛜

South Walsham

Ship Ⓛ
18 The Street, NR13 6DQ
🕐 12-midnight summer; 4-10 Mon & Tue; 12-11 (midnight Fri & Sat); 12-10 Sun winter ☎ (01603) 270049
⊕ lucasinns.co.uk
3 changing beers Ⓗ
The Ship is an ancient listed building, first licensed in 1789, with a bar and separate dining room offering excellent food. There is a large sun terrace to the rear, plus some seating at the front. Three beers on rotation are from the more interesting local and regional breweries such as Green Jack, Crouch Vale and Norfolk Brewhouse. Snacks are available all day. The pub is a pleasant 20-30 minute walk from the local Broads.
Q❀◑♣P🖵🖵(51)🐾🛜

Southrepps

Vernon Arms ✅
2 Church Street, NR11 8NP (NE of Thorpe Market off A149 Cromer-North Walsham road)
🕐 12-11 ☎ (01263) 833355 ⊕ vernonarms.com
Adnams Southwold Bitter; Greene King Abbot; Woodforde's Wherry; 1 changing beer Ⓗ
A thriving village-centre local, with traditional brick and flint exterior, whose welcoming atmosphere is enhanced in winter by a log fire. Regular ales are augmented by a variety of guest beers. It has an excellent reputation for fine food (prepared with locally sourced ingredients where possible), candlelit tables and good service in a recently extended dining area. Takeaway fish and chips are available Tuesday to Saturday 6-8pm. The front terrace has a heated, covered smoking area and there is a garden at the rear.
🛥❀◑&🅰♣P🖵(33,33A)🐾🛜

Sporle

Peddars Inn Ⓛ
70 The Street, PE32 2DR
🕐 closed Mon; 11-3 (not Tue), 6-10.30; 11-3, 6-11 Fri; 2-11 Sat; 12-6 Sun ☎ (01760) 788101 ⊕ thepeddarsinn.com
Adnams Southwold Bitter; 2 changing beers Ⓗ
A traditional dog-friendly village local hosting many events such as music and quiz nights. It is close to the Peddars Way long distance path, so attracts walkers. Food is served in the bar, conservatory and private dining room (no food Tue). As a member of the LocAle scheme there is always something interesting on the bar. There is a log fire for winter, and free Wi-Fi. 🛥❀◑♣P🐾🛜

Swanton Morley

Darbys
1 Elsing Road, NR20 4NY
⚙ 11.30-11; 12-6 Sun ☎ (01362) 637647
⊕ darbysfreehouse.com
**Adnams Southwold Bitter, Broadside; Lacons Legacy;
3 changing beers** G
This pub was originally two farm cottages which
became a public house in 1988, and the rooms are
decorated with a range of farming artefacts. There
is one long bar plus a split-level dining area and a
cosy function room upstairs. A varied food menu is
served both lunchtimes and evenings, and
customers may now order their meals via email
before visiting. There is a large garden and car
park, and the 12-mile Wensum Way passes the
door. Q ☯ ❀ ◑ ᵫ ♿ ᴬ P ☕ ❀ 🗣

Thetford

Albion ✅
93-95 Castle Street, IP24 2DN (opp Castle Park and Hill)
⚙ 12-11.30 (1.30am Fri & Sat) ☎ (01842) 338208
**Greene King IPA; Woodforde's Wherry; 1 changing
beer** H
Under a new management team, this classic town
pub has had a new lease of life. Its Greene King-
refurbished interior has mellowed in colour, and is
a comfortable space to drink in. The three
handpumps offer a range of standards, soon to be
expanded to six choices. There is seating outside
and you can see the 1,000-year-old castle mound
and its surrounding Iceni hill fort. Although food is
not served you are welcome to order in from one
of the food outlets in the town. ❀♿♣P

Thompson

Chequers Inn
Griston Road, IP24 1PX
⚙ 12-3, 6.30-11; 11.30-11 Sun ☎ (01953) 483360
⊕ thompsonchequers.co.uk
**Greene King IPA; Woodforde's Wherry; 1 changing
beer** H
With a steeply thatched roof and timber-framed
interior, you enter the bar ducking a beam set at
16th-century height levels. The interior is divided
into a small bar flanked by two different dining
areas in which to enjoy the excellent food, planned
and prepared by the landlord/chef and sourced
from local suppliers. A pint outside, if you are not
eating, is a great way to see how the roof nearly
touches the ground. Separate accommodation is
available. ☯ ❀ ᵫ ◑ ♿ P

Thornham

Lifeboat Inn
Ship Lane, PE36 6LT (signed from A149 coast road)
⚙ 11-11; 12-10.30 Sun ☎ (01485) 512236
⊕ lifeboatinnthornham.com
5 changing beers H
Busy pub just off the North Norfolk Coastal Path on
the edge of the salt marshes, with a wide range of
drinking areas, from the dark and cosy bar to the
light and airy conservatory. There is an enclosed
garden at the rear. It has been tastefully renovated
while retaining the atmosphere of the smugglers'
inn it undoubtedly was. Food is served in all areas
as well as in the large separate restaurant.
Accommodation comprises 12 rooms. Whatever

the season and whatever the weather, this is a
comforting place to enjoy a pint.
Q ☯ ❀ ᵫ ◑ P ☕ ❀ 🗣

Thorpe Market

Gunton Arms ⌶ ✅
Cromer Road, NR11 8TZ (on W of A149 Cromer-North
Walsham road SE of Thorpe Market; look for hanging sign,
lit at night)
⚙ 12-11; 12-10.30 Sun ☎ (01263) 832010
⊕ theguntonarms.co.uk
**Adnams Southwold Bitter, Broadside; Woodforde's
Wherry; 1 changing beer** H
National award-winning inn overlooking the
beautifully restored Gunton Park and its deer herd.
It has tasteful decor, with comfortable furnishings
and a log fire in the winter. East Anglian ales
predominate, with regular guests. First-class
cuisine is served in two restaurant areas; several
dishes are cooked on an open range in the vaulted
main room, and there is a beer garden for alfresco
dining. Interesting art and artefacts abound for the
connoisseur. Accommodation is in 16 luxurious
rooms and suites, some with parkland vistas, to
suit all tastes. Q ❀ ᵫ ◑ ♿ ♣ P 🖰 (4) ❀ 🗣

Thurlton

Queen's Head ⌶
Beccles Road, NR14 6RJ
⚙ 6 (5 Thu)-11; 5-midnight Fri; 12-midnight Sat; 12-10 Sun
☎ (01508) 548667 ⊕ queensheadthurlton.co.uk
3 changing beers (often People's) H
Community-owned pub run by locals Claire and
Mark. Three real ales are stocked, including beers
exclusively brewed by the nearby People's
Brewery. Grain and Lacons beers are regularly on
the bar, plus a selection from other breweries. The
pub is family and dog friendly, children are allowed
in the bar, and the village play area is to the rear of
the building. Regular live music features on
Saturdays. It has a new sunny beer garden, there is
a cosy log fire in winter, and an Easter beer festival.
☯ ❀ ◑ ♿ ♣ P 🖰 (577) ❀

Upton

White Horse ⌶
17 Chapel Road, NR13 6BT (10-minute walk from Upton
Dyke Staithe and moorings)
⚙ 12-midnight ☎ (01493) 750696 ⊕ whitehorseupton.com
Woodforde's Wherry; 3 changing beers H
Traditional Broadland pub dating from 1798 which
was renovated in 2012, and is owned by the local
community, with residents purchasing shares. A
community shop has recently been added in a
converted stables. Four beers are served, mostly
from local breweries. As well as the famous fish 'n'
chip Fridays (including takeaways), there are
Sunday roasts. Live music is on every first and third
Saturday and on bank holidays.
☯ ❀ ◑ ♿ ᴬ ♣ ♣ P ❀ 🗣

Watton

Willow House ⌶ ✅
2 High Street, IP25 6AE
⚙ 10.30-11.30 (midnight Sat); 12-3 Sun ☎ (01953) 881181
⊕ thewillowhouse.co.uk
3 changing beers H

The Willow House is just about the only timber-framed thatched building in Watton as it is the sole survivor of the Watton fire of 1679. It boasts annual historically themed events and beer-tasting nights from local breweries. Four handpumps offer a changing range of cask ale, and the dining areas are varied between snug and spacious. An inventive food menu is on offer as well as en-suite accommodation. ✿⭡🌜🍺♿P🐾🛜

Wells-next-the-Sea

Albatros
The Quay, NR23 1AT
🕒 12-11 ☎ 07979 087228 ⊕ albatroswells.co.uk
Woodforde's Wherry, Nelson's Revenge; 1 changing beer Ⓖ
Possibly one of the Guide's most unusual entries, the Albatros is a Dutch North Sea clipper, more or less permanently moored on the quayside of Wells harbour. The bar is in the hold of the ship and is adorned with nautical memorabilia, including many shipping maps. It sells up to four Woodforde's beers on gravity. Dutch pancakes are a speciality, and live bands perform each Friday and Saturday night, as well as Sunday afternoons in high season. As a 19th-century vessel, it is not disabled-friendly. Q⭡🌜🍺🚌🐾

Lifeboat
Station Road, NR23 1EA
🕒 closed Mon; 12-3, 6-11; 11-11 Sat & Sun
☎ (01328) 711735
Adnams Southwold Bitter, Ghost Ship, Broadside; 1 changing beer Ⓗ
Comfortable two-bar locals' town pub, a Danish/English B&B and restaurant, which reopened in 2015 under Carsten Lund, and stocks three or four ales, mostly from Adnams, and varieties of Danish schnapps. As well as home-cooked Sunday roasts, there are Danish open sandwiches filled with meatballs or marinated herring. The pub, which has portraits of the different lifeboats that have served the town on its tables, began life as the Railway Inn in the 1840s. Live music is a feature every two weeks. ✿⭡🌜🍺🐾

West Acre

Stag Ⓛ
Low Road, PE32 1TR
🕒 closed Mon; 12-3, 6.30 (5 Fri)-11 ☎ (01760) 755395
⊕ westacrestag.co.uk
3 changing beers Ⓗ
This cosy pub is well worth finding, at the east end of picturesque West Acre, and attracts locals, walkers, cyclists and riders. It is a strong supporter of local ales, maintaining a high standard of three varying beers and hosting excellent beer festivals. There is a popular monthly quiz on Sunday night. The restaurant serves a variety of great-value freshly prepared meals using locally sourced ingredients. Q✿🌜♿🅰♣P🗄

West Runton

Village Inn
Water Lane, NR27 9QP
🕒 11-11; 12-11 Sun ☎ (01263) 838000
⊕ villageinnwestrunton.co.uk
Adnams Ghost Ship; Grain Oak; 2 changing beers Ⓗ

A large pub a short distance from the station and the beach, set in pleasant gardens in the centre of this quiet coastal village. Up to six well-kept and mostly local ales are served on rotation. Excellent home-cooked meals can be enjoyed in the dining areas or outside, where the gardens can seat up to 200. In the 1970s major rock bands such as Deep Purple played secret gigs at the Pavilion which was at the rear of the pub (sadly now demolished). Q🌜✿🌜🍺♿➡🖥🐾

Weybourne

Ship Inn
The Street, NR25 7SZ
🕒 12-3, 6-11; 11-midnight Fri & Sat; 11-11 Sun
☎ (01263) 588721 ⊕ theshipinnweybourne.com
Woodforde's Wherry; 3 changing beers Ⓗ
In the heart of this attractive north Norfolk coastal village, the Ship has up to six cask ales from local brewers including Woodforde's, Humpty Dumpty, Beeston, Brewhouse, Wolf, Grain and Panther, plus a range of bottled beers. Home-cooked food is on offer lunchtimes and evenings. There is a monthly quiz night. The pub is close to the Muckleburgh collection of military vehicles (muckleburgh.co.uk). The enclosed garden is pleasant in summer and the Coasthopper bus stops outside. 🌜✿🌜🍺🅰♣P🖥

Wiveton

Wiveton Bell Ⓛ
Blakeney Road, NR25 7TL (on B1156, about 1 mile inland from Cley)
🕒 12-11 ☎ (01263) 740101 ⊕ wivetonbell.co.uk
Norfolk Brewhouse Moon Gazer Golden Ale; Woodforde's Wherry; Yetman's Red; 1 changing beer Ⓗ
The Bell has an L-shaped bar, a large conservatory which is mainly set for dining, and a stylish and spacious enclosed garden, with views to the church. Although food-led, there are always seats reserved for drinkers. A good selection of ales from local breweries is permanently on tap. A pleasant walk can be had from the pub, via the Three Swallows (or vice versa!) to Cley, around what was in medieval times the harbour. 🌜✿🌜🍺🅰P🐾🛜

Woodbastwick

Fur & Feather Inn
Slad Lane, NR13 6HQ
🕒 11-10; 10-11 Sat; 10-9 Sun ☎ (01603) 720003
⊕ thefurandfeatherinn.co.uk
8 changing beers Ⓖ
Converted from a row of three cottages, this large open-plan pub is largely food-oriented while offering customers the full range of beers from the adjoining Woodforde's Brewery. A tour of the brewery can be arranged in advance and combined with a meal. In summer the large garden provides an excellent area for a drink. The rare Norfolk Nip is occasionally available, usually as a bottle-conditioned strong ale, which is much prized locally. 🌜✿🌜♿P🐾🛜

Wortwell

Bell ⊘
52 Low Road, IP20 0HH
🕒 12 (5 Tue)-11; 12-10.30 Sun ☎ (01986) 788025
⊕ wortwellbell.pub

Adnams Southwold Bitter; house beer (by Woodforde's); 3 changing beers Ⓗ
A 17th-century coaching inn with two bars and an open fire, and a fishing lake and caravan park nearby. Enthusiastic hosts, whose family were historically linked to the licensed trade, reopened the pub in September 2015. They have rejuvenated this local to its former glory, with regular village events, and have now added to the community feel with a small village shop and a small library based at the pub and open during pub hours. A regular beer festival is staged.
🛏️⊛◑⅃★♣☂P🚌(80,81)🐾🐾🛜

Wymondham

Green Dragon Ⓛ ✔
6 Church Street, NR18 0PH (between Market St and abbey)

☼ 12-11 (midnight Fri & Sat); 12-10.30 Sun
☎ (01953) 607907 ⊕ greendragonnorfolk.co.uk
4 changing beers Ⓗ
One of the oldest pubs in the country, the Green Dragon dates back to the 14th century. This haunted, half-timbered inn with an attractive beer garden, was once connected to Wymondham Abbey via a tunnel. Formerly a merchant's shop built in the 1100s, it was converted in 1371 to the current inn. The interior features beamed timbers and carved stone, and evidence of medieval construction methods. One bar serves the downstairs bar, a snug and restaurant area. Excellent home-made food uses locally sourced ingredients where possible. The rotating real ales are mostly from local or East Anglian breweries including Humpty Dumpty, Wolf and Grain. Beer festivals take place in May and August, with live music. Q🛏️⊛◑⅃★♣🚌(14,15)🐾🐾🛜

Queen's Head, Earsham (Photo: William Wordsworth)

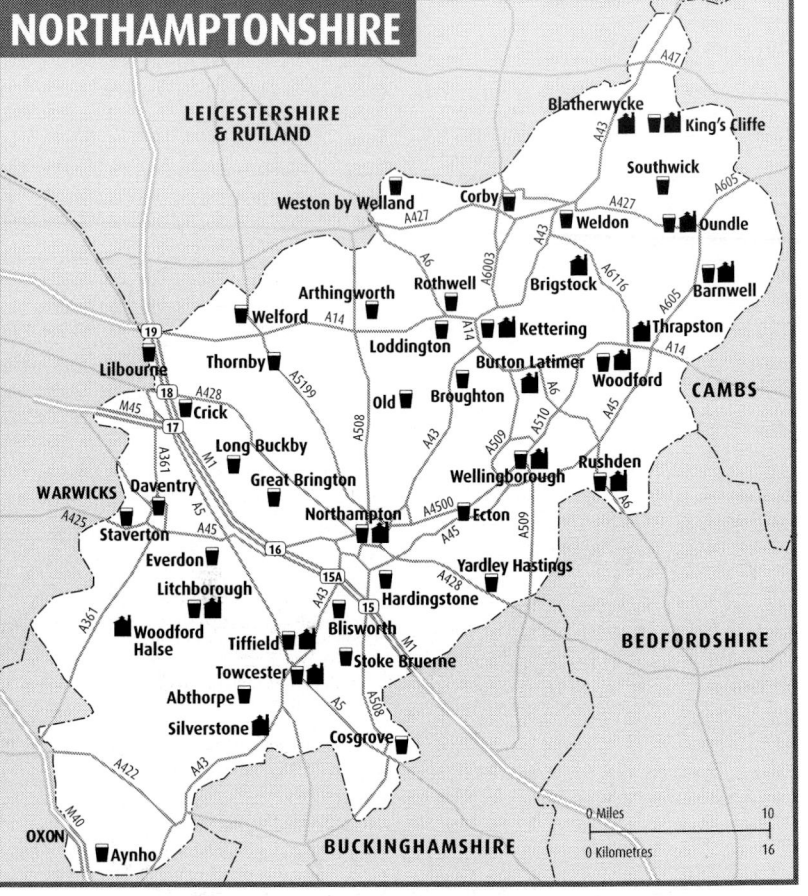

Abthorpe

New Inn L ⊘
Silver Street, NN12 8QR (off Main St, left at church)
🕙 12-2.30 (not Mon), 6-11.30; 12-11 Sun ☎ (01327) 857306
⊕ newinnabthorpe.co.uk
Hook Norton Hooky, Old Hooky; 2 changing beers (sourced locally) Ⓗ
This tranquil country hostelry is tucked away in a back street off the corner of the village green close to the church. It is a quintessentially English village pub built of local mellow sandstone complete with an inglenook fireplace with seating and low ceilings. Welcoming to visitors and locals alike, it serves good food plus ales that are still brewed in the traditional way by the Victorian Hook Norton brewery – the seasonal beers feature as guests. Traditional pub games including darts and Northamptonshire skittles are played.
Q ⛱ ❀ ◑ ♣ P 🖵 😺 🛜

Arthingworth

Bull's Head L
Kelmarsh Road, LE16 8JZ (A14 jct 2, off A508)
🕙 12-2.30, 6-11; 12-11 Sat & Sun ☎ (01858) 525637
⊕ thebullsheadonline.co.uk
Adnams Southwold Bitter; Everards Old Original; 1 changing beer (sourced locally; often Grainstore) Ⓗ
A former red-brick farmhouse dating from the 19th century featuring an opened-up bar with several cosy drinking areas and a restaurant to the front serving home-cooked fresh food from local producers. Ideal for ramblers and cyclists, this is a perfect place to finish a walk in the local area, or stay over in one of the annexe rooms. A beer festival is held over the Whitsun bank holiday on the suntrap patio. Sparklers can be removed on request. Q ⛱ ❀ ⛺ ◑ ♿ ♣ 🖕 P 🖵 😺 🛜

Aynho

Great Western Arms L ⊘
Station Road, OX17 3BP (on B4031)
🕙 11-11 ☎ (01869) 338288 ⊕ great-westernarms.co.uk
Hook Norton Hooky, Lion, Old Hooky; 1 changing beer (sourced regionally) Ⓗ
Situated on the Northants and Oxfordshire borders and between the former Great Western Railway and Oxford Canal, this is an inviting country pub with a difference. The ivy-clad traditional inn is full of Great Western Railway memorabilia. A main bar and side restaurant have photos of both the railway and the canal adorning the walls. Outdoor seating alongside the canal is pleasant in the summer. The pub is renowned for its food, and offers accommodation in four individually decorated rooms. ⛱ ❀ ⛺ ◑ ♿ 🖕 P 🖵 😺

Barnwell

Montagu Arms 🅛 ✅
PE8 5PH
⊕ 12-3 (not Mon), 6-11; 12-11 Sat & Sun ☎ (01832) 273726
Adnams Southwold Bitter; 3 changing beers ⊞
Overlooking the local river and stone bridge, this 16th-century stone-built inn has a public bar at the front and a large restaurant to the rear. The car park is behind the inn and accessed via the village hall entrance. Also at the rear is a large play and camping area. There is disabled access from the rear to the restaurant only. The traditionally decorated bar area has large original exposed beams on the ceiling and walls, and a fireplace in the middle of the room. Q🍽🚲🛏🍴👶👩‍🦽♣🅿🚌🐾

Blisworth

Walnut Tree Inn 🅛
21 Station Road, NN7 3DS (nr Bridge 49 on Grand Union Canal)
⊕ 10-11 (1am Fri & Sat) ☎ (01604) 859551
⊕ walnut-tree.co.uk
Great Oakley Tiffield Thunderbolt; Phipps NBC India Pale Ale; Towcester Mill Mill Race; 1 changing beer (sourced nationally) ⊞
An award-winning family-run hotel and bar situated just outside this historic village. The bar features leather chairs, sofas and an open fireplace, and there is a separate quieter lounge. The beer garden has tables in sunlight and others in a shaded area with heaters for chilly winter nights. An entertainment programme includes comedy, jazz, folk, blue-grass, rock and acoustic nights, as well as regular quiz nights. 🚲🛏🍴👩‍🦽🅿🚌🛜

Broughton

Red Lion 🅛 ✅
7 High Street, NN14 1NF (off A43)
⊕ 12-2 (not Mon), 5-11; 12-midnight Fri & Sat; 12-11 Sun
☎ (01536) 790239 ⊕ redlionbroughton.co.uk
Black Sheep Riggwelter; 6 changing beers (sourced nationally) ⊞
Large community-focused 18th-century ironstone inn with three main rooms. The landlady is a dark ale fan and ensures that a mild, porter, or stout is on the bar to accompany the good-value home-cooked food. The pub hosts many unusual social events along with two beer festivals. Q🍽🚲🛏🍴👩‍🦽♣🅿🚌(X43)🐾

Corby

Saxon Crown 🅛 ✅
Elizabeth Street, NN17 1PF
⊕ 8am-midnight (1am Fri & Sat) ☎ (01536) 203672
Adnams Broadside; Greene King Abbot; Sharp's Doom Bar; 6 changing beers (sourced nationally; often Hoggleys, Oakham, Phipps NBC) ⊞
This Wetherlodge is a refurbished 1960s landmark building which was formally a Co-op store and now incorporates a hotel with luxuriously fitted bathrooms. The open-plan bar has high-backed leather seating in booths, with a tiled and wooden floor leading to the rear patio. Q🍽🚲🛏🍴👩‍🦽🚲🅿🚌🛜

Cosgrove

Barley Mow ✅
7 The Stocks, MK19 7JD
⊕ 12-11 (10.30 Sun) ☎ (01908) 562957
⊕ thebarleymowcosgrove.co.uk
Everards Sunchaser, Tiger, Old Original; 1 changing beer (sourced nationally; often Titanic) ⊞
A beautiful countryside pub backing onto the Grand Union Canal by Bridge 65. The main bar and adjoining areas of this 17th-century building are full of charm – especially when the log fire is ablaze. Outside is a lovely garden and patio with a large car park. The home-cooked food menu covers all dietary requirements. Events are staged throughout the year, including murder mystery evenings and a regular quiz. Q🍽🚲🛏🍴👩‍🦽🅿🚌🐾🛜

Crick

Wheatsheaf 🅛
15 Main Road, NN6 7TU
⊕ 12-11 (midnight Fri & Sat); 12-10.30 Sun
☎ (01788) 823824 ⊕ wheatsheafcrick.com
5 changing beers (sourced locally; often Church End, Phipps NBC, Potbelly) ⊞
Village free house built from local ironstone. The comfortable front bar has exposed beams and a variety of seating areas. To the rear a large restaurant area can cater for up to 60 diners. Food, much of it sourced locally, ranges from pub favourites to restaurant specials, with a variety of vegetarian options. Themed nights with menus to match feature regularly. A pub quiz is held every Tuesday evening. Q🍽🚲🛏🍴👩‍🦽♣🅿🚌(96)🐾

Daventry

Early Doors 🅛
3 Prince William Walk, NN11 4AB
⊕ 12-9; closed Sun & Mon ☎ 07707 299959
⊕ earlydoorsdaventry.co.uk
Phipps NBC India Pale Ale ⊞; 5 changing beers (sourced locally; often Gun Dog Ales, Towcester Mill) Ⓖ
Opened in 2015, this was the first micropub in the county, situated in a former mobility shop. Warm and welcoming, the bar is simply decorated, using

---

REAL ALE BREWERIES

Boot Town Burton Latimer (NEW)
Brigstock Brigstock
Cotton End 🍴 Northampton
Digfield Barnwell
Frog Island Northampton
Great Oakley Tiffield
Gun Dog Woodford Halse
Hart Family Wellingborough
J Church 🍴 Northampton
King's Cliffe King's Cliffe
Maule Northampton
Merrimen Litchborough
Nene Valley Oundle
Nobby's Thrapston
Phipps NBC Northampton
Potbelly Kettering
Rockingham Blatherwycke
Silverstone Silverstone
Three Hills Woodford (NEW)
Towcester Mill Towcester
Weldon Rushden

reclaimed doors and weathered scaffolding planks. Beers are all on gravity and locally produced cider is made within one mile of Welton. Hand-made local pork pies are available, and pubgoers are welcome to bring their own food which will be plated up for a small donation to charity. Local CAMRA branch Cider Pub of the Year 2017. Q&♿♥P🚌

Ecton

Three Horseshoes 🅛

23 High Street, NN6 0QA (off A4500)
🕙 7 (5.30 Fri)-midnight; 12-midnight Sat & Sun
☎ (01604) 407446

St Austell Trelawny, Proper Job; 2 changing beers (sourced nationally) 🅗
A whitewashed stone building said to date from 1757 but extended over the years. The name is taken from the forge that was originally on the site – Benjamin Franklin's Uncle Thomas was the last of the family to work the family forge. The traditional multi-room layout has been retained, with a separate bar and games area with Northants skittles and darts. Q🏴🐕♣♠P🚌🐾🛜

Everdon

Plough Inn 🅛

High Street, NN11 3BL (opp church)
🕙 12-11 ☎ (01327) 361606 🌐 theploughinneverdon.com
Greene King IPA; Gun Dog Ales Jack's Spaniels; Sharp's Doom Bar; 1 changing beer (sourced regionally) 🅗
Attractive early 18th-century Northamptonshire ironstone-built village pub with a small bar and flagstone floors. From the entrance lobby on two levels there is a small lounge, formerly two small rooms, with plaster-over-stone walls, a more modern counter and a working Rayburn woodburner. More interconnected rooms to the left include a snug with leather settees. This is a quaint and unusual pub – check out the garden and the Furrow outbuildings in the summer. Q🐕🏴🐾⚓♣P🚌🐾🛜

Great Brington

Althorp Coaching Inn (Fox & Hounds) 🅛

Main Street, NN7 4JA
🕙 11-midnight; 12-11 Sun ☎ (01604) 770651
🌐 althorp-coaching-inn.co.uk
Greene King IPA, Abbot; Phipps NBC India Pale Ale; St Austell Tribute; Sharp's Doom Bar; 2 changing beers (sourced locally) 🅗
Close to Althorp House, this lovely thatched country pub dates from 1765. Oak beams and flagstone floors feature throughout, and the lounge area has a large inglenook fireplace. Outside is a courtyard, barn and enclosed garden. Excellent food is served in the bar and separate restaurant. The pub is often busy, especially on Monday quiz night. Happy hour is 5-7pm every day, with 50p off a pint. Q🏴🐕♿⚓P🐾🛜

Hardingstone

Sun Inn 🅛 ✔

7 High Street, NN4 7BT
🕙 11-11 (midnight Fri & Sat); 12-10.30 Sun
☎ (01604) 700007 🌐 thesuninnhardingstone.co.uk

Courage Directors; 5 changing beers (sourced regionally; often Gun Dog Ales, Phipps NBC) 🅗
Friendly, attractive, old white-walled pub in the older part of the village. The traditional interior is welcoming and cosy with soft lighting, a beamed ceiling, two character fireplaces and half-panelling separating numerous alcoves for drinkers and diners, which are all served by a side bar. Outside there is a courtyard with seating, a children's play area and a barn bar used as a function room. Northamptonshire Food & Drink Award Rural Community Pub of the Year winner 2016/17. 🐕🏴🌓♥🚌(7)🐾🛜

Kettering

Piper 🅛 ✔

Windmill Avenue, NN15 6PS (near Wicksteed Park)
🕙 11-3, 5-11; 11-4, 6-11 Sat; 12-10.30 Sun
☎ (01536) 513870 🌐 thepiper.net
Castle Rock Harvest Pale; Woodforde's Wherry; 3 changing beers (sourced nationally; often Cottage) 🅗
Popular 1950s two-roomed pub which has been run by an enthusiastic CAMRA member for 27 years. There is a quiet lounge to the left, while to the right is a more lively bar/games room where a quiz is held on Sunday night. A beer festival takes place on the third weekend in August. An outdoor seating area is across the road from the pub. Q🏴🌓♿⚓▲♣♥P🚌🐾🛜

Three Cocks 🅛

48 Lower Street, NN16 8DJ (opp Morrisons)
🕙 12-11.30 (11 Sun) ☎ 07909 698798
Grainstore Ten Fifty; Mighty Oak Maldon Gold; 5 changing beers (sourced regionally; often Mighty Oak, Oakham) 🅗
A popular town-centre pub with an L-shaped servery at the centre serving the two main bar areas, furnished with comfortable armchairs and high-backed stools. On an upper level is a games area featuring Northants skittles and darts. A variety of CAMRA branch magazines is available to read while sampling the well-kept ales and quality filled cobs. Four beer festivals are held in the rear function room over the solstice and equinox weekends. Q🐕🌓♿♣♥🚌🐾

King's Cliffe

Cross Keys 🅛

2 West Street, PE8 6XA
🕙 6-10 Mon; 11-3, 6-11 ☎ (01780) 470276
🌐 crosskeyskingscliffe.uk
Greene King IPA; house beer (by King's Cliffe); 1 changing beer 🅗
Stone-built pub with three main rooms – a snug, bar area and restaurant. Two of the rooms have stone inglenooks, one with its original salt cellar, and all have wood-beamed ceilings. A plaque on the wall commemorates the pub as being the last venue Glenn Miller played before he disappeared. Northamptonshire skittles is played on the first Tuesday of the month. Traditional food is served, with fish and chips night on a Friday. Q🏴🌓♣P🚌🛜

Lilbourne

Head of Steam 🅛

10 Station Road, CV23 0SX (just off Rugby Rd)

☼ 5-11.30; 12-3, 5-midnight Fri; 12-midnight Sat; 12-11 Sun
☎ (01788) 860166 ⊕ headofsteampub.co.uk
Phipps NBC India Pale Ale; 3 changing beers (sourced nationally; often Church End, Dow Bridge, St Austell) Ⓗ

Converted from a house in 2013, this thriving community free house has a wide selection of ales, many from local breweries, including nearby Dow Bridge. With a welcoming, comfortable ambience, this is a pub for friendly conversation. Locally sourced cheese boards and pies are available. Occasional folk nights and beer festivals are held. The large garden makes this a great summer venue. Q☽⊛👍⚓♣🍴P🅿️？

Litchborough

Old Red Lion ⓛ

4 Banbury Road, NN12 8JF (opp church)
☼ 12-11 (10.30 Sun) ☎ (01327) 830064
⊕ oldredlionlitchborough.co.uk
Great Oakley Wagtail; house beer (by Grainstore); 1 changing beer (sourced regionally) Ⓗ

A four-roomed stone-built village pub well worth seeking out, popular with walkers and cyclists on the Knightly Way. The bar area has flagstone flooring and seats inside the large inglenook. The snug to the rear of the bar is a comfy casual room with double doors leading to a courtyard. The extension houses a restaurant and shop with local farm produce. A wide range of locally brewed bottled beers is stocked, often from Merrimen Brewery in the village. Q☽⊛◑👍P🍴🐾？

Loddington

Hare at Loddington

5 Main Street, NN14 1LA (on village loop)
☼ 12-3, 5.30-11; 12-midnight Sat & Sun ☎ (01536) 710337
⊕ thehareatloddington.com
Greene King Abbot; Sharp's Doom Bar; Wells Bombardier; 1 changing beer (sourced regionally) Ⓗ

Set in a conservation area, the Hare is a listed building in this picturesque village built from local ironstone. The pub stands in the middle of Main Street surrounded by listed houses. Now more open, it comprises four areas – two spread around the central bar and two for dining, where home-cooked food can be enjoyed. The guest beer is often from an established or county microbrewery. Q☽⊛◑👍🍴P🅿️(35)🐾

Long Buckby

Old King's Head ⓛ

2 Harbidges Lane, NN6 7QL (off B5385)
☼ closed Mon; 12-2.30 (11 Fri & Sat); 12-10.30 Sun
☎ (01327) 842680 ⊕ oldkingsheadlongbuckby.co.uk
Everards Beacon Hill, Sunchaser, Tiger; 3 changing beers (sourced regionally; often Everards, Phipps NBC, Titanic) Ⓗ

Firmly established at the heart of village social life, this charming 17th-century thatched pub now thrives under the efficient tutelage of tenants Matt and Katie. Two quite different cosy bars, a small skittles and darts area, and a separate restaurant make it an interesting place to explore. Up to three guest ales are available along with three regulars from the Everards stable. Paintings by a local artist decorate the walls. It has a growing reputation for high-quality food. Local CAMRA branch Rural Pub of the Year 2017. Q☽⊛◑♣🍴P🅿️(11,96)🐾？

Northampton

Albion Brewery Bar ⓛ

54 Kingswell Street, NN1 1PR (bottom of Bridge St hill)
☼ closed Mon; 12-3, 5-11; 12-midnight Fri & Sat; 12-3 Sun
☎ (01604) 946606 ⊕ phipps-nbc.co.uk
Hoggleys Northamptonshire Bitter, Reservoir Hogs; Phipps NBC Red Star, India Pale Ale, Ratliffe's Celebrated Stout; house beer (by Phipps NBC); 2 changing beers (sourced locally) Ⓗ

Phipps NBC returned to its roots in a Victorian brewery in the heart of Northampton in 2014, 40 years after Phipps' Bridge Street brewery closed. This brewery bar subsequently opened, with an oak and glass partition between the bar and brewery enabling the brewing process to be viewed. Almost all the bar's fittings are reclaimed, with many coming from former Phipps pubs. There is much memorabilia to read and view. Eight handpumps serve six ales from the brewery including Hoggleys plus a rotating guest, with one pump reserved for a Northamptonshire cider. Q☽◑👍⚓♣🍴🐾？

Bold Dragoon ⓛ

48 High Street, Weston Favell, NN3 3JW (off A4500 on traffic lights)
☼ 12-11.30 (midnight Fri & Sat); 12-11 Sun
☎ (01604) 401221
Fuller's London Pride, ESB; Greene King IPA, Abbot; 3 changing beers (sourced regionally; often Phipps NBC, St Austell, Timothy Taylor) Ⓗ

A popular and well-kept pub built in the 1930s on the site of a 19th-century inn that was demolished to enable road widening. The Bold is in the centre of the village, now absorbed into Northampton borough. The spacious pub has a lively bar, carpeted lounge, games room and superb conservatory restaurant serving a full menu. Seven beers are stocked, four permanent and three changing, usually from local and regional breweries. It has the welcoming atmosphere of a country pub in the town. ☽⊛◑👍♣🍴P🅿️(1,X46)🐾？

Cordwainer ⓛ ✅

The Ridings, NN1 2AQ (near jct with Fish St)
☼ 8am-11 ☎ (01604) 609000
Greene King IPA, Abbot; Sharp's Doom Bar; 5 changing beers Ⓗ

Large, popular Wetherspoon town-centre pub on two levels boasting three sets of five handpulls. There is usually a choice of eight real ales, including LocAles, and two real ciders. The TVs are always on silent unless sporting events are shown. Curry and quiz night is every Thursday, along with the extensive Wetherspoon pub food menu. Two annual beer festivals are held. One wall is dedicated to local CAMRA activities. ☽⊛◑👍🍴🐾？

Lamplighter ⓛ

66 Overstone Road, The Mounts, NN1 3JS
☼ 12-midnight (1am Fri & Sat); 12-11 Sun
☎ (01604) 631125 ⊕ thelamplighter.co.uk
8 changing beers (sourced regionally; often Nene Valley, Oakham, Phipps NBC) Ⓗ

A popular traditional street-corner inn just off the town centre attracting young and old alike. There is a roaring fire in the bar, a lovely snug and a heated courtyard. Four local beers and four guests are from established micros, along with a selection of bottled beers. Up to six beer festivals a year add to the range. Home-cooked food is served until 9pm (7pm weekends), with children welcome during mealtimes. The pub hosts open mic, discos, live music and quiz nights each week. ⭐🌣🅾️◗🖤♣🖤🖳🐾🛜

Malt Shovel Tavern 🅛
121 Bridge Street, NN1 1QF
🕐 11.30-11; 12-10.30 Sun ☎ (01604) 234212
🌐 maltshoveltavern.com
Frog Island Natterjack; Fuller's London Pride; Oakham Bishops Farewell; 10 changing beers (sourced locally) 🅗

Close to the town centre and opposite the Carlsberg brewery, this popular pub has won many awards over the past 20 or more years, including local CAMRA Pub of the Year on numerous occasions. Breweriana features everywhere, with real cider, LocAle, Belgian draught and bottled beers available. Two beer festivals are held each year on bank holidays with live bands. Blues bands play on Wednesday nights. The pub has a strong rugby following. Home-made lunches are served 12-2pm Monday to Saturday. 🌣🅾️◗🖤≠♣🖤🖳

Olde England 🅛
199 Kettering Road, NN1 4BP (near racecourse)
🕐 5-midnight (11 Mon); 3.30-midnight Fri; 12-midnight Sat; 12-11 Sun ☎ 07981 043285 🌐 theoldeengland.com
J Church Gold Testament; Vale Gravitas 🅖; changing beers (often Great Oakley, Phipps NBC, Potbelly) 🅗/🅖

Converted end-of-terrace Victorian building on three floors with bars on two floors. The ground and first floors have a medieval theme with solid fuel burners. The cellar bar has a contemporary style and is more intimate. Over 15 beers from local micros and regional breweries are served by gravity and handpump as well as 15 ciders. Various board games, cards and dominoes are provided. Quiz night is Wednesday, live folk music is Thursday. This award-winning pub is one of only four outlets in the county for J Church and Olde England Ales beers. Q⭐🌣🅾️♣🖤🖳🐾🛜

Pomfret Arms 🅛
10 Cotton End, Far Cotton, NN4 8BS
🕐 4.30-11; 12.30-midnight Thu-Sat; 12.30-11 Sun
☎ (01604) 555119 🌐 pomfretarms.co.uk
4 changing beers (sourced locally; often Cotton End, Great Oakley, Hart) 🅗

With its own microbrewery, this town pub is situated on the south-west side of the River Nene in Cotton End. Its small central bar has six handpumps serving the front opened-out room and rear bar. The brewery and a function room are in a separate building in the lovely beer garden. Two of the beers are usually from the brewery itself or Hart Family sister brewery. ⭐🌣🅾️♣🖤🖳🛜

Queen Adelaide 🅛
50 Manor Road, Kingsthorpe, NN2 6QJ (off A5199)
🕐 11-11.30; 12-10.30 Sun ☎ (01604) 714524
🌐 queenadelaide.com
Adnams Southwold Bitter, Broadside; Nobby's Guilsborough Gold; 4 changing beers (sourced regionally) 🅗

A friendly, established pub in Kingsthorpe village, this 18th-century listed stone-built local has a main bar with low beams and an uneven floor, a small snug complete with leather sofas, and a further lounge bar to the rear. It is very popular on rugby

match days. The guest beers are often from local microbreweries. The Sunday roasts are exceptional (booking advised). An annual beer festival is held in early September. ⭐🌣🅾️◗🖤♣🖤🖳🐾🛜

Road to Morocco
Bridgwater Drive, Abington Vale, NN3 3AG
🕐 12-11 (midnight Fri & Sat); 12-10.30 Sun
☎ (01604) 632899
Greene King IPA, Abbot; Theakston Old Peculier; 4 changing beers (sourced regionally) 🅗

Run by an enthusiastic CAMRA member, this popular 1960s brick-built estate pub has a Moorish theme in some of the decor, reflecting its name. There are two connected but distinctly different rooms. The bar area, where darts and pool are played, is quite lively, particularly if there is a sporting event on TV. The homely lounge is generally the quieter part of the pub. Quiz night is Tuesday. ⭐🌣🅾️♣🖤🖳(5,9b)🐾🛜

Wig & Pen 🅛 ✅
19 St Giles Street, NN1 1JA
🕐 10-midnight (1.30am Fri & Sat) ☎ (01604) 622178
🌐 thewigandpennorthampton.com
Adnams Ghost Ship; Black Sheep Best Bitter; Fuller's London Pride; Greene King IPA; St Austell Tribute; 6 changing beers (sourced regionally; often Elgood's) 🅗

A popular 300-year-old pub close to the town hall, reputedly haunted by a young girl. A long L-shaped bar counter serves up to six guest ales, cider and a wide range of bottled beers. A retractable cover provides shelter in the garden, where jazz bands play on Tuesday nights and live bands on Sunday afternoons. Good home-cooked food features locally sourced ingredients. ⭐🌣🅾️◗🖤🖳🛜

Old

White Horse 🅛
Walgrave Road, NN6 9QX
🕐 closed Mon; 12-3, 5-11; 12-11 Fri & Sat; 12-7 Sun
☎ (01604) 781297 🌐 whitehorseold.co.uk
3 changing beers (sourced locally; often Phipps NBC) 🅗

A contemporary country pub comprising two opened-out rooms with polished wooden floors and a real fire, and a small snug towards the rear. Upstairs is the Millstone room which leads to the garden patio. A relatively small food menu offers interesting, quality home-cooked seasonal lunches and evening meals, from pub classics to specials. Monthly live music and quiz nights, and a weekly Tuesday pie night, make this local always worth a visit. Q⭐🌣🅾️◗🖤♣🖳🐾🛜

Oundle

Tap & Kitchen
Oundle Wharf, Station Road, PE8 4DE
🕐 10-11; 12-6 Sun ☎ (01832) 275069 🌐 tapandkitchen.com
6 changing beers (sourced locally) 🅗

The main outlet for the Nene Valley Brewery, this pub has spacious eating and drinking areas. Built in a revamped wharfside warehouse, the industrial theme has been retained, with chrome and wood, cogs and rails. An extensive menu of home-cooked and locally sourced food is served. Outside, there is a new seating area. Live music is hosted on occasion. At least six real ales from Nene Valley are available plus a selection of ciders. ⭐🅾️◗🖤🖳🐾🛜

Rothwell

Woolpack 🅛 ✅
Market Hill, NN14 6BW
☼ 2-10 (midnight Thu; 1am Fri); 12-midnight Sat & Sun
☎ (01536) 710284 🌐 thewoolpackrothwell.com
Phipps NBC India Pale Ale; Wells Bombardier;
Wychwood Hobgoblin; 3 changing beers (sourced
locally; often Gun Dog Ales, Grainstore) 🅷
A community-focused 17th-century ironstone inn
with three low-beamed open-plan rooms, an L-
shaped bar and a lounge area to the rear. The pub
is believed to be on the site where wool was sold
on the medieval market since the granting of the
1204 Charter. The landlady has turned this pub
around, increasing the number of changing guest
beers to three. Q🌲🏵♣🐾P🚪(19,X10)🐕 ☎

Rushden

Rushden Historical Transport
Society 🅛
Station Approach, NN10 0AW (on ring road)
☼ 7.30 (6 Wed & Thu)-11; 4.30-11 Fri; 12-11 Sat & Sun
☎ (01933) 318988 🌐 rhts.co.uk
Dark Star Hophead; Phipps NBC India Pale Ale; 5
changing beers (sourced regionally) 🅷
An award-winning club in the former Midland
Railway Station. The ladies' waiting room is now
the bar, with gas lighting and walls adorned with
enamel advertising panels, railway photos and
CAMRA awards. On the platform, carriages provide
a meeting room, Northants skittles, and a buffet for
numerous open days held during the year with
steam and diesel train rides. A beer festival is held
in September. Day membership is £1 except on
open days. Q🌲🏵♣🐾🚪🐕

Southwick

Shuckburgh Arms 🅛
Main Street, PE8 5BL
☼ 12 (6 Mon & Tue)-11 (10 Mon); 12-10 Sun
☎ (01832) 272044 🌐 shuckburghpub.co.uk
Brewster's Hophead; Nene Valley Bitter 🅷; house
beer (by Grainstore) 🅷/🅖; 2 changing beers (sourced
nationally) 🅷
Stone-built thatched inn next to the village hall in
the centre of Southwick, serving five real ales. The
bar area doubles as a restaurant for diners. To the
rear is a covered outdoor area, car park, large
garden and the village cricket pitch. Red kites can
often be seen flying. The pub is run by the local
community with shareholders and a small
committee. It hosts the annual World Conker
Championship in October and jousting in May.
Popular well-priced food is available including
weekend breakfasts from 10am by arrangement.
Q🏵♠♣P🚪🐕 ☎

Staverton

Countryman 🅛
Daventry Road, NN11 6JH (on A425)
☼ 12-3, 6-11; 12-10 Sun ☎ (01327) 311815
🌐 thecountrymanstaverton.co.uk
Hook Norton Old Hooky; Wells Bombardier; 1
changing beer (sourced locally) 🅷
The Countryman is the last of three pubs remaining
in this lovely village close to Daventry. The L-
shaped bar, with wood beams throughout, serves
four areas, some set aside for diners, and an open-

hearth fire between the spaces provides some
seclusion. The enthusiastic landlord offers a wide
choice of reasonably priced food, sourced locally
whenever possible. Three changing guest beers are
available, always including a locally brewed beer.
Q🏵🐾P🚪(66) ☎

Stoke Bruerne

Boat Inn ✅
Shutlanger Road, NN12 7SB (alongside Grand Union
Canal)
☼ 9am-11 ☎ (01604) 862428 🌐 boatinn.co.uk
Banks's Amber Ale; Jennings Cumberland Ale;
Marston's EPA, Old Empire; Wychwood Hobgoblin; 2
changing beers (sourced nationally) 🅷
Opposite the National Canal Museum, the Boat Inn
has been owned by the same family since 1877.
The stone-built, thatched pub is long and narrow,
with a wonderful tap bar with interconnecting
rooms with canal views, open fires, original stone
floors and window seats. An adjoining room has
Northants skittles. A canal boat is available to hire.
The cider is Thatchers Heritage. Breakfast is served
until 11am. Q🌲🏵♣🐾P🚪(86)🐕 ☎

Thornby

Red Lion 🅛 ✅
Welford Road, NN6 8SJ (on A5199)
☼ 12-11; 12-10.30 Sun ☎ (01604) 740238
🌐 redlionthornby.co.uk
6 changing beers (sourced regionally; often Adnams,
Grainstore, Wadworth) 🅷
An impressive whitewashed village pub dating
back more than 400 years situated on the old A50.
The compact bar has two drinking areas with a
wood-burning open fire in the lounge. A motley
collection of beer tankards, steins and framed
photos is displayed throughout. To the rear is the
restaurant, which occupies two linked rooms, one
heavily beamed. Accommodation has been added
in a converted barn. A beer festival is held in late
July. A local CAMRA award winner in 2016.
Q🌲🏵🛏◑P🚪(60)🐕 ☎

Tiffield

George at Tiffield 🅛 ✅
21 High Street North, NN12 8AD (centre of village)
☼ 12-3, 6-11; 7-11 Tue; 12-midnight Fri; 12-11 Sat; 12-7 Sun
☎ (01327) 350587 🌐 thegeorgeattiffield.co.uk
Great Oakley Tiffield Thunderbolt; Vale Best IPA, Pale
Ale; 2 changing beers (sourced regionally) 🅷
A true community inn central to many village
activities – the building dates from the 16th
century, with Victorian additions when it became a
public house. It has a cosy bar, games room with
Northants skittles and back room restaurant which
can be booked for small functions. It is the tap for
Great Oakley Brewery, just outside the village. Two
beer festivals are held at Easter and in October.
Q🌲🏵◑♣♠P🚩🐕

Towcester

Towcester Mill Brewery Tap 🍺 🅛
Chantry Lane, NN12 6AD
☼ 5-10.30 (8 Mon); 3-11 Fri; 12-11 Sat; 12-8 Sun
☎ (01327) 437060 🌐 towcestermillbrewery.co.uk

Towcester Mill Mill Race, Bell Ringer, Black Fire; 5 changing beers (sourced locally; often Towcester Mill) Ⓗ
Popular and welcoming brewery tap in a historic Grade II-listed mill dating from 1794, straddling the old mill race and adjacent to Bury Munt on which the town's fort once stood. The bar retains many original features including beams, stonework and a wooden floor, with a second room to cope with demand. A large garden runs alongside the mill, home to beer festivals in April, June and September. Four rotating guest ales are sourced from other local breweries and eight ciders are available. Local CAMRA Pub of the Year 2017. Q🕿🕭🏵🅑♿🍴🅿🚪🐾🛇

Weldon

Shoulder of Mutton 🗽
12 Chapel Road, NN17 3HP
🕒 3-10; 12-midnight Fri-Sun ☎ (01536) 601016
⊕ shoulderofmuttonweldon.co.uk
Weldon Cupola, Dragline, Galvy Stout, Oresome, Roman Mosaics; 1 changing beer (sourced locally; often Weldon) Ⓗ
Large, two-roomed pub with a locals' bar at the front and a function room to the rear. The front bar was originally three rooms which have been opened out into one, with a fire at one end. In 2016 the pub's microbrewery moved off site to Rushden and was renamed the Weldon Brewery. The food menu includes home-made Serbian dishes alongside traditional pub meals. Brewery tours can be arranged a week in advance, including transport and food back at the pub for up to eight people. 🏵🍴♣🅿🚪(X4)🐾🛇

Welford

Wharf Inn 🗽 ✅
NN6 6JQ (on A5199 by canal basin)
🕒 12-11 ☎ (01858) 575075 ⊕ wharfinn.co.uk
Grainstore Ten Fifty; Marston's Pedigree; Oakham Bishops Farewell; 3 changing beers (sourced locally) Ⓗ
This original ironstone building dates from 1814 and is situated at the end of the Welford cut on the Grand Union Canal, a few yards from the border with Leicestershire. Inside, the main room is segregated by an open fireplace between the two areas. A smaller snug/back bar is occasionally used. Several walks can be started from here – ask for the handy leaflet behind the bar. Guest beers are always sourced locally or regionally. B&B is available. Q🕿🏵🕭🅑♿🍴🅿🚪(60)🐾🛇

Wellingborough

Coach & Horses 🗽 ✅
17 Oxford Street, NN8 4HY (800yds from Market Square)
🕒 12-11 (9 Mon); 12-6 Sun ☎ (01933) 441848
⊕ coachandhorseswellingborough.co.uk
12 changing beers (sourced nationally; often Abbeydale, Great Oakley, Phipps NBC) Ⓗ
Popular town-centre local with an enthusiastic landlord who keeps a constantly changing choice of 12 beers and 12 ciders, including two or more

local ales. The central servery looks after three drinking areas adorned with breweriana. Traditional home-cooked food is served including 40 different pies (no food Sun eve, Mon and Tue). A pub quiz is hosted on alternate Wednesdays. CAMRA East Midlands Leicestershire & Northamptonshire Pub of the Year in 2016. 🏵🕭♿🍴🅿🚪🛇

Weston by Welland

Wheel & Compass 🗽
Valley Road, LE16 8HZ (off B664)
🕒 12-11 (10.30 Sun) ☎ (01858) 565864
⊕ thewheelandcompass.co.uk
Black Sheep Best Bitter; Fuller's London Pride; Greene King Abbot; Oakham JHB; Sharp's Doom Bar; 1 changing beer (sourced nationally; often Everards) Ⓗ
A rural pub in the picturesque Welland Valley with a cosy bar/lounge and a large extended dining room. An outside drinking area offers good views across the valley and is an ideal playground for children. The pub is a popular stop-off for walkers on the Jurassic Way which runs close by. Good-value food is available including lunchtime specials. Q🕿🏵🕭♿🍴🅿🚪🐾🛇

Woodford

Dukes 🗽
83 High Street, NN14 4HE (off A510)
🕒 12-11 ☎ (01832) 732224
Digfield Fools Nook; Greene King 1799; Oakham JHB; 4 changing beers (sourced nationally) Ⓗ
Originally a 17th-century manor, the Dukes was renamed in honour of the Duke of Wellington who was a frequent visitor to the village. Overlooking the green, it has a divided main bar, lounge restaurant, rear games room with 3D TV and an upstairs games room. Very much a community-focused pub, it holds a Whitsun bank holiday beer festival and August bank holiday music festival, plus regular open mic, quiz, karaoke and acoustic sessions. Traditional pub food is available, plus a pizza and chilli barn outside. Q🕿🏵🕭♿♣🅿🚪(16)🐾🛇

Yardley Hastings

Rose & Crown 🗽
4 Northampton Road, NN7 1EX
🕒 5-10 Mon; 12-11; 12-10 Sun ☎ (01604) 696276
⊕ roseandcrownbistro.co.uk
Greene King IPA, Abbot; house beer (by Hart Family Brewers); 3 changing beers (sourced nationally; often Adnams, Black Sheep) Ⓗ
An award-winning ironstone pub now extensively refurbished, with a single large room. It retains stone-flagged floors and beamed ceilings throughout, and has a small drinking area in the bay window. The emphasis is on traditional home cooking with a daily changing menu and light meals throughout the day. The house beer is from Hart Family. Board games are available and monthly music events are held. The landscaped gardens are wonderful in summer. Winner of a Northamptonshire Food & Drink Award in 2016/17. Q🏵🕭♿♣🅿🚪(41)🐾

Keep your Good Beer Guide up to date by visiting the CAMRA website camra.org.uk/gbg-updates

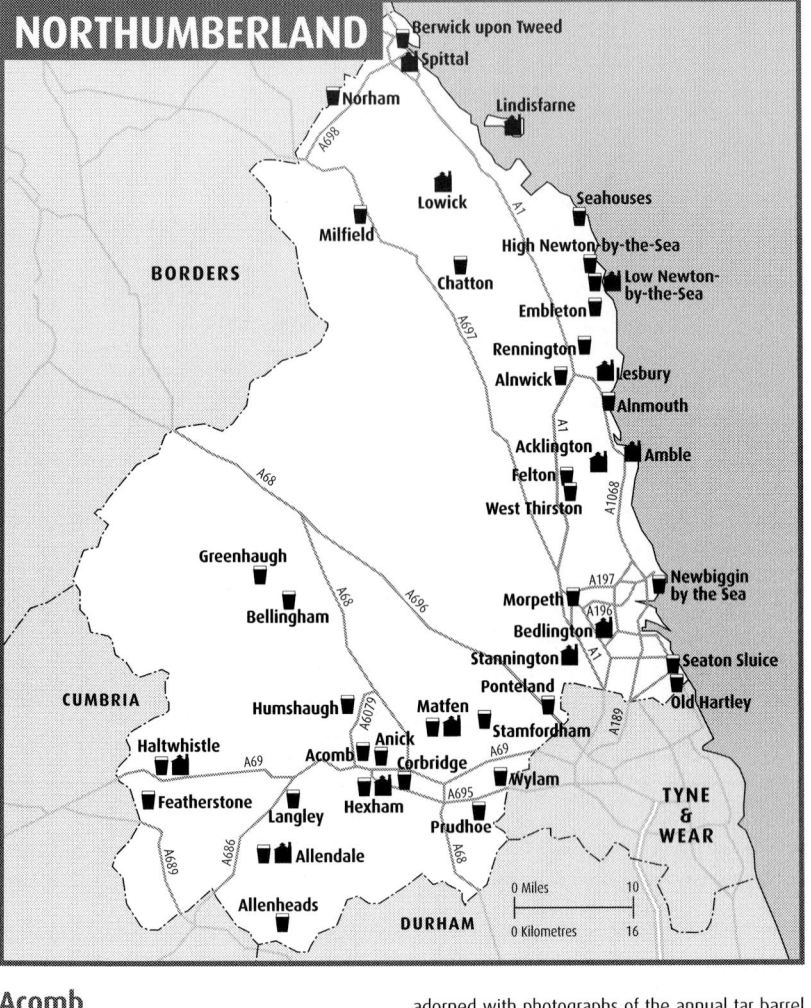

NORTHUMBERLAND

Berwick upon Tweed
Spittal
Norham
Lindisfarne
Lowick
Milfield
Seahouses
High Newton-by-the-Sea
Chatton
Low Newton-by-the-Sea
Embleton
Rennington
Alnwick
Lesbury
Alnmouth
Acklington
Amble
Felton
West Thirston
Greenhaugh
Bellingham
Morpeth
Newbiggin by the Sea
Bedlington
Stannington
Seaton Sluice
Ponteland
Old Hartley
Humshaugh
Matfen
Stamfordham
Anick
Haltwhistle
Acomb
Corbridge
Wylam
Featherstone
Hexham
Langley
Prudhoe
Allendale
Allenheads

BORDERS

CUMBRIA

TYNE & WEAR

DURHAM

0 Miles 10
0 Kilometres 16

Acomb

Miners Arms

Main Street, NE46 4PW

⏰ 5-11.30; 12-midnight Sat & Sun ☎ (01434) 603909

🌐 theminersacomb.com

Wylam Gold Tankard; Yates Bitter; 1 changing beer Ⓗ
Superb traditional 1746 inn with an emphasis on
real ale, served in oversized lined glasses. The
family-run pub hosts regular music and folk nights.
The bar has a genuine, cosy feel and is divided by a
central staircase – energetic dogs often greet
visitors here. The miners have long gone but this
pub is a superb legacy that lives on in this popular
hamlet. ➤✿❀◑&♣🖥️🚌 (680,682)♿

Allendale

Golden Lion Hotel Ⓛ

Market Place, NE47 9BD

⏰ 12-1.30am (1am Wed); 12-2.30am Fri-Sun

☎ (01434) 683225 🌐 goldenlionhotel.net

**Timothy Taylor Landlord; Wylam Gold Tankard; 3
changing beers** Ⓗ
Friendly and hospitable pub in the centre of town,
patronised by locals and tourists. The walls are

adorned with photographs of the annual tar barrel
procession, an experience in itself, and local
landscapes. Allendale's local choir practise here on
Tuesday evening, and live Irish music plays on the
last Wednesday of the month. With two regular
beers and three guests, there is always plenty of
choice of local ales. Home-cooked food is served.
The pub has a late licence at weekends.
✿🍴◑🚌 (688)♿

REAL ALE BREWERIES

Allendale Allendale
Anarchy Stannington
Beacon Brauhaus Lindisfarne (NEW)
Bear Claw Spittal
Credence Amble
Hetton Law Lowick
Hexhamshire Hexham
High House Farm Matfen
Muckle Haltwhistle (NEW)
Northumberland Bedlington
Rigg & Furrow Acklington (NEW)
Ship Inn 🍴 Low Newton-by-the-Sea
VIP Lesbury

Allenheads

Allenheads Inn 🅛

NE47 9HJ

🕑 4-11; 12-11 Sat; 12-10.30 Sun ☎ (01434) 685200
🌐 allenheadsinn.co.uk

Mordue Northumbrian Blonde; house beer (by Anarchy); 3 changing beers 🄷

Superb 18th-century, multi-roomed inn with a public bar with a log fire, games room and dining room. On the Coast-to-Coast cycle route, it is popular with cyclists, ramblers and tourists. Good bar meals are available at a decent price. Originally the home of Sir Thomas Wentworth, the premises are bedecked with memorabilia and knick-knacks from a bygone age. The pub will open early on request for coach parties and other groups.
🏠🏵️🛏️🍴◑♣️P🚌(688)🐾

Alnmouth

Red Lion Inn ✅

22 Northumberland Street, NE66 2RJ

🕑 11-midnight ☎ (01665) 830584 🌐 redlionalnmouth.com

4 changing beers 🄷

Charming family-run, 18th-century coaching inn with a cosy lounge bar with attractive woodwork and panoramic views across the Aln Estuary from the decked area at the bottom of the garden. Occasional live music plays – in the open air in summer. Guest beers usually include one local and two interesting brews from further afield. An annual beer festival is held in October. Open for breakfast from 9am, excellent en-suite B&B accommodation is available. Popular with tourists and locals. Q🏠🏵️🛏️◑♣️P🚌(x18)🐾🛜

Alnwick

John Bull Inn 🅛

12 Howick Street, NE66 1UY

🕑 12-3 (not Mon-Fri), 7-11 Sat; 12-3, 7-10.30 Sun
☎ (01665) 602055 🌐 john-bull-inn.co.uk

5 changing beers 🄷

Many-time local CAMRA Pub of the Year and a former Regional Pub of the Year, this 180-year-old inn thrives on its reputation as a back-street local. The passionate landlord offers a wide range of cask-conditioned ales at varying ABVs, real cider, the widest range of bottled Belgian beers in the county and over 120 single malt whiskies. The darts team competes in the local league and the pub upholds the North-East tradition of an annual leek show. There is a cheese club on Saturday night. Q🏵️♣️🚌(X15,X18)🐾

Tanners Arms 🅛

2-4 Hotspur Place, NE66 1QF

🕑 5-11 (midnight Fri); 12-midnight Sat; 12-10.30 Sun
☎ (01665) 602553 🌐 tannersarms.com

6 changing beers 🄷

Ivy-covered stone-built pub just off Bondgate Without and a short distance from Alnwick Garden. The rustic single room has a flagstone floor and tree beer shelf. A large fireplace provides added warmth in winter. Acoustic music nights feature regularly with open mic on the last Friday of the month. The ever-changing real ales frequently come from North-East and Scottish Borders microbreweries. 🏠&♣️🚌(X15,X18)🐾🛜

Anick

Rat Inn

NE46 4LN (follow signpost at Hexham A69 roundabout)

🕑 12-11.30; 12-10.30 Sun ☎ (01434) 602814
🌐 theratinn.com

4 changing beers 🄷

Superb 1750 country inn with spectacular views across the Tyne Valley. The pub has a welcoming and friendly ambience, with an open log fire and chamber pots hanging from the ceiling. It has an excellent local reputation for good food prepared with locally sourced ingredients and appears in several food guides. Half portions are available for children. Bottled beers are stocked to complement the handpumped ales. The first Thursday of the month is singers/poetry night. Well worth the short taxi ride from Hexham rail station.
Q🏠🏵️🛏️◑♣️👜P🚌

Bellingham

Cheviot Hotel ✅

Main Street, NE48 2AU

🕑 10-midnight (1am Fri & Sat) ☎ (01434) 220696
🌐 thecheviothotel.co.uk

4 changing beers 🄷

Friendly hotel on Main Street, now refurbished, updated and renovated, opposite the bus stop. A log-burning stove warms the bar area. Cask beer is available all year round including one ale supplied by High House Farm Brewery. There is plenty of outside seating at the front. Regular theme nights are hosted. Stay up to date with the monthly newsletter, The Sheep Dip.
🏠🏵️🛏️◑&🅰️♣️P🚌(680,880)🐾🛜

Berwick upon Tweed

Barrels Ale House

59-61 Bridge Street, TD15 1ES

🕑 12-midnight; 12-11.30 Sun ☎ (01289) 308013

5 changing beers 🄷

There is an Old Curiosity Shop ambience to this pub, located in the old part of Berwick next to the original road bridge over the Tweed. The excellent real ale no doubt helps customers brave the 'dentist's chair' at the side of the bar. A downstairs bar is used by DJs and bands at weekends. Outside is a unique open drinking area surrounded by high walls. A former winner of CAMRA Pub of the Year. 🏵️🐾

Curfew 🅛

46A Bridge Street, TD15 1AQ

🕑 12-9 (10 Fri-Sun) ☎ 07842 912268

4 changing beers 🄷

Berwick's first micropub is located up a small lane which opens out into a large courtyard off Bridge Street. It has a small bar area with a bottle fridge to one side. The courtyard makes a pleasant outdoor drinking area in summer. The cellar is in the shed at the top of the yard. Regional CAMRA Pub of the Year 2016 winner. Q🏵️🚉👜

Pilot 🅛

31 Low Greens, TD15 1LZ

🕑 12 (11 Sat)-midnight; 12-11 Sun ☎ (01289) 304214

Caledonian Deuchars IPA; 2 changing beers 🄷

This popular pub with friendly bar staff is well patronised by locals and sought out by train trippers who have heard about this gem. The stone-built end-of-terrace hostelry dates from the

19th century and has a regionally important historic interior. It retains the original small room layout and boasts several nautical artefacts over 100 years old. It is home to a darts team and hosts music nights. 🚫🏠🛏️🍴⛔♿💷♣️☀️

Chatton

Percy Arms Hotel 🄻
Main Road, NE66 5PS
🕛 11-11 ☎ (01668) 215244 ⊕ percyarmschatton.co.uk
6 changing beers Ⓗ
Once the Duke of Northumberland's 19th-century hunting lodge, the Percy Arms was licensed for alcohol sales in 1879. The pub is frequented by walkers, cyclists and holidaymakers due to the proximity of Chillingham Castle. A recent high-quality refurbishment has modernised the look and feel of the pub and its oak-panelled restaurant – however, as many original features as possible were retained during the renovation. 🚫🏠🛏️🍴🚶

Corbridge

Angel of Corbridge 🄻
Main Street, NE45 5LA
🕛 11-11; 12-11 Sun ☎ (01434) 632119
⊕ theangelofcorbridge.com
Cumberland Corby Blonde; Hadrian Border Tyneside Blonde; Wylam Angel; 3 changing beers Ⓗ
Superb former coaching inn dating from 1726 located on the main road with good transport links. Seven handpulls adorn the bar and a wonderful selection of malt whiskies is also kept. Family-friendly and with a reputation for good food, the pub is popular with tourists, ramblers and locals. A separate lounge area has comfy leather seating and outside is a relaxed seating area. The town has strong links with the Romans and Hadrian's Wall is nearby. Q🚫🏠🛏️🍴🚶🅿️🚌

Embleton

Greys Inn 🄻 ✅
Stanley Terrace, NE66 3UZ
🕛 12-11; 12-10.30 Sun ☎ (01665) 576983
5 changing beers Ⓗ
Pleasant, traditional pub in a lovely seaside hamlet, just a short walk to a wonderful beach. It has three open fires and a framed 1904 grocery list hangs on the wall. The pub is an excellent venue to enjoy a bite to eat washed down with a locally sourced real ale, sitting outside on the superb patio in good weather. It is home to a ladies' darts team, clay pigeon club and golf club.
🚫🏠🍴♣️🚌(418,X18)☀️

Featherstone

Wallace Arms 🄻
Rowfoot, NE49 0JF
🕛 5-10.30 (11.30 Wed & Thu); 3-11.30 Fri; 12-11.30 Sat; 12-10.30 Sun ☎ (01434) 298921
4 changing beers Ⓗ
Cosy, traditional country pub warmed by real fires, with no jukebox or fruit machines to disturb the peace. Split over two levels and three rooms, it has a traditional bar area and two restaurant spaces. The welcoming landlady is always prepared to open early for groups of walkers, preferably if arranged in advance. Opening hours are reduced in winter – check ahead. Q🏠🅿️☀️🛜

Felton

Fox's Den 🄻
Cellar 2, 4 Riverside, NE65 9EA
🕛 5-10.30 ☎ 07707 703182
Acton Ales Golden Cocker, Seahouses Pale; 2 changing beers Ⓗ
This recently opened micropub is a welcome addition to the mid-Northumberland pub scene. Situated in the basement below the Running Fox bakery, it has its own door on the main street. It is the sister pub to the Office in Morpeth and also run by local microbrewery Acton Ales. Four handpumps serve changing, mostly local, ales. Q🚫🅿️🚌(X15)☀️

Greenhaugh

Holly Bush Inn 🄻
NE48 1PW
🕛 4-11 ☎ (01434) 240391 ⊕ hollybushinn.net
High House Farm Nel's Best; 1 changing beer Ⓗ
Independently owned pub, over 300 years old and set in the heart of the Northumberland National Park and the Dark Sky Park, making it ideal for those with an interest in real ale and real stars. No TV and no mobile reception make for a peaceful drinking experience. The pub hosts informal jam sessions – bring your instrument if you like. Q🚫🏠🛏️🍴♿🅿️☀️🛜

Haltwhistle

Black Bull
Black Bull Lane, Market Square, NE49 0BL
🕛 3.30 (12 Wed)-11; 12-11 Sat; 12-10.30 Sun
☎ (01434) 320463
6 changing beers (sourced nationally) Ⓗ
Warm, friendly, two-roomed inn close to Hadrian's Wall and popular with locals and ramblers. An open fire warms the low wood-beamed interior, with a wooden bar and horse brasses enhancing the traditional ambience. The pub is down a cobbled lane just off the marketplace in the centre of the town. Beers are available on six handpulls. Regular theme nights are hosted. Ring to check winter hours, and meal times can vary too.
Q🚫🍴🚌(685,85)☀️

Milecastle Inn 🄻
North Road, NE49 9NN
🕛 12-11 ☎ (01434) 321372 ⊕ milecastle-inn.co.uk
Big Lamp Bitter, Prince Bishop Ale; 1 changing beer Ⓗ
This 1600s pub adjacent to Hadrian's Wall sells ale mainly from Newburn-based Big Lamp Brewery. Located a mile-and-a-half north of Haltwhistle, the rural hostelry has a homely feel, popular with ramblers and tourists. Food is locally sourced and attracts customers from as far as Newcastle and Carlisle. There are also two comfy holiday cottages. The Hadrian's Wall bus stops outside April to September. Check ahead for winter opening hours. Q🚫🏠🛏️🍴🅿️🚌🛜

Hexham

Dipton Mill Inn 🄻
Dipton Mill Road, NE46 1YA
🕛 12-2.30, 6-11; 12-3 Sun ☎ (01434) 606577
⊕ diptonmill.co.uk
Hexhamshire Blackhall English Stout, Devil's Elbow, Devil's Water, Old Humbug, Shire Bitter, Whapweasel Ⓗ

The tap for Hexhamshire Brewery, now relocated to the beer garden, this small inn is run by enthusiasts who brew their own excellent beers. Blackhall English Stout has proved so popular with drinkers that it has ousted Guinness. To complement the ales there is great home-cooked food – Saturday is curry night. A cosy atmosphere and warm welcome make this pub well worth seeking out. The large garden has a stream running through it and there is plenty of countryside to explore. Q❀❀◑➍P

Heart of Northumberland 🅛
5 Market Street, NE46 3NS
✪ 12.30-11 ☎ (01434) 608013
Timothy Taylor Landlord; 4 changing beers 🅗
Five handpumps, four selling local ales, adorn the bar in this recently refurbished and reopened, food-led pub. The single large room is divided almost in two near the end of the bar, with wooden floors throughout. A large open fire warms things nicely in the back room and another smaller fire keeps the front room cosy, too. Excellent food is served. ◑➲♣🚍❀

Tannery 🅛
22 Gilesgate, NE46 3QD
✪ 12-midnight ☎ (01434) 605537
6 changing beers 🅗
This local hostelry has been taken over by an established landlord from Newcastle with a vision to serve the best beers, ciders, whiskies and gins alongside a menu of meats, cheeses and snacks sourced from small producers in the region. The pub is split into two distinct bars, with the public bar serving six real ales including one LocAle. The lounge offers up to 12 real ciders, six on handpull and six on gravity. ➳❀◑♿➲♣◉🚍❀

High Newton-by-the-Sea

Joiners Arms ✪
Town Square, NE66 3EA
✪ 11-11; 11-10.30 Sun ☎ (01665) 576112
⊕ joiners-arms.com
Anarchy Blonde Star; Mordue Workie Ticket; 2 changing beers (often Hadrian Border) 🅗
Eighteenth-century former manor house, tastefully restored and refurbished following closure for two years. The house ale, St Mary's, reflects the name of the local church and for every pint sold a donation is made towards the church upkeep. Set in a pleasant hamlet on the B1340, the pub portrays a typical Northumbrian scene with outdoor seating overlooking the small picturesque green. Five en-suite bedrooms are fitted out to a high standard. ➳❀⛱◑♿P🚍(418)❀

Humshaugh

Crown Inn 🅛
NE46 4AG
✪ 12-11 ☎ (01434) 681231
5 changing beers 🅗
A traditional village pub located in the centre of the beautiful village of Humshaugh, five miles north of the market town of Hexham. The Crown has a homely charm, with a wood-burning stove, cask ales and traditional home-cooked food. Simple guest accommodation is offered in comfortable rooms, ideal for those wishing to explore Hadrian's Wall. ⛱◑❀

Langley

Carts Bog Inn 🅛
NE47 5NW
✪ closed Mon; 12-2.30, 5-11; 12-11 Sat; 12-10.30 Sun
☎ (01434) 684338 ⊕ cartsbog.co.uk
3 changing beers 🅗
Excellent rural pub serving the local community and tourists in Langley. The building dates from 1730 and was built on the site of an ancient brewery (circa 1521). Carts really did get bogged down here. A large open fire divides the two rooms and the walls proudly display pictures of bygone days. Good food including meat from a local farm is served (booking essential for Sunday lunch). Three real ales from local breweries are usually available, and a beer festival is held in August. Home to three quoits teams. Winter opening times vary. Q➳❀◑♿♣P🚍(688)❀ ❀

Low Newton-by-the-Sea

Ship Inn 🅛
Newton Square, NE66 3EL
✪ 11-11; 12-11 Sun ☎ (01665) 576262
⊕ shipinnnewton.co.uk
Ship Inn Sea Coal, Sea Wheat; 4 changing beers 🅗
Nestling in the corner of a three-sided square of former fishermen's cottages only a few yards from the beach, this small pub is often busy with beer drinkers seeking ales from the in-house microbrewery, walkers and diners. The excellent food menu uses fresh local ingredients. The pub is a short walk from the public car park at the top of the hill. Opening times may vary in winter so phone ahead if travelling any distance. Q➳❀◑❀

Matfen

Black Bull 🅛
NE20 0RP
✪ 4-11; 12-11 Sat & Sun ☎ (01661) 855395
⊕ theblackbullmatfen.co.uk
5 changing beers (often High House Farm, Wylam) 🅗
Recently refurbished, this pub is now the heart of the village, and home to pool and darts teams. The small, cosy bar is warmed by two real fires. Four handpumps serve beers from Wylam, High House Farm and other local breweries. Cards, dominoes, Trivial Pursuit, Scrabble and more games are available to while away those winter weekend afternoons. Dogs are warmly welcomed, with snacks and a water bowl for four-legged friends. ◑P❀

Milfield

Red Lion Inn 🅛
Main Road, NE71 6JD
✪ 11-2, 5-11; 11-11 Sat & Sun ☎ (01668) 216224
⊕ redlionmilfield.co.uk
Black Sheep Best Bitter; 2 changing beers 🅗
A true local pub at the heart of the village, just eight miles inside the border, dating back to the mid-1700s. Rescued by the current licensee from the tight grip of Scottish & Newcastle, the Red Lion is a proper free house, with many varied guest beers served through the third handpump. Freshly prepared food is available, with blackboards proudly displaying where the local produce is sourced. Home to the local leek-growing club. Q➳❀⛱◑♿♣P🚍(267)❀

Morpeth

Office 🍷 ⅃
The Toll House, Castle Square, NE61 1YL
🌣 5-11; 12-11 Sat & Sun ☎ 07707 703182
5 changing beers 🅷
The Office is the brewery tap for Acton Ales. It is a micropub with no music or games machines. It features five handpulls, all of local origin, and three real ciders served on gravity from the glass-fronted fridge opposite the bar. No food is available. Local CAMRA Pub of the Year 2016 and 2017. Q❦🖵🏃

Newbiggin by the Sea

Queen's Head ⊘
7 High Street, NE64 6AT
🌣 10-midnight ☎ (01670) 817293
2 changing beers 🅷
Single-room building, rebuilt in 1909, with the bar, lounge and snug all together. Some Edwardian features have been retained including the curved bar counter. The pub sells competitively priced real ales at advantageous opening times and displays an impressive ever-growing collection of guest beer pumpclips on the walls. One beer is usually available, two on Fridays, varying weekly. This no-nonsense pub is popular with locals and visitors alike. ➰♣🖯

Norham

Masons Arms
17 West Street, TD15 2LB
🌣 12-11 ☎ (01289) 382326 🌐 themasonsarmsnorham.co.uk
4 changing beers (often Allendale) 🅷
The cosy wood-panelled public bar, with a real fire at its heart, is the hub of this pub. Photos of bygone Norham adorn the walls, along with collections of fishing gear and joinery tools, and an old Younger's brewery mirror. The area is popular with tourists – nearby are a ruined castle and the railway station museum. Close to the Tweed Cycle Way and 67 bus stop. ❄🛏♣🖵(67)

Old Hartley

Delaval Arms ⅃
NE26 4RL (jct A193/B1325 S of Seaton Sluice)
🌣 12-11; winter 12-2.30, 4.30-10.30; 12-11 Fri-Sun
☎ (0191) 237 0489 🌐 thedelavalarms.wordpress.com
4 changing beers 🅷
Multi-roomed Grade II-listed building dating from 1748, with a listed WWI water storage tower (part of Roberts Battery) behind the beer garden. It is the first pub in Northumberland for those following the coastal route. Good-quality, affordable meals complement the beer, with guest ales coming from local micros. To the left as you enter there is a room served through a hatch from the bar and to the right a room where children are welcome. Q➰❄🕔P🖵(308,309)🐾

Ponteland

Blackbird ⅃ ⊘
North Road, NE20 9UH
🌣 12-11 (midnight Fri & Sat) ☎ (01661) 822684
🌐 theblackbirdponteland.co.uk
4 changing beers 🅷
This pub dates back over 500 years – parts of the building are the remains of Ponteland Castle. A

blend of old and new, the Blackbird is central to village life, with a good mixed clientele. The annual New Year's Day wheelbarrow race starts and finishes at the pub. Two local beers are always available as well as two nationally sourced guest ales. ➰❄🕔🚲♣P🖵(X77,X78)🛜

Prudhoe

Wor Local ⅃
Front Street, NE42 5HJ
🌣 4-9; 3-10.30 Thu & Fri; 2-10.30 Sat & Sun
☎ (01661) 598150
4 changing beers 🅷
Located on Prudhoe's Front Street, Wor Local (or Our Local if you're not a Geordie) is a micropub with room for around 40 customers. The layout of the bar, with its comfy seating, encourages conversation. There are lots of traditional pub and board games available. Four local beers in a variety of styles are offered, one always at a lower price. Real ciders are also available. Pork pies and cheese are on sale along with crisps and nuts. A welcome addition to the area. ♣🐾

Rennington

Horseshoes Inn ⅃
6 Rennington Village, NE66 3RS
🌣 closed Mon; 12-3, 6.45-11 ☎ (01665) 577665
🌐 thehorseshoesrennington.co.uk
Hadrian Border Farne Island Pale Ale; 1 changing beer 🅷
Superb traditional family-run village pub dating from 1841, with its history detailed on the chimney breast. The bar is warm and friendly without TV or jukebox and with a log fire plus dry hops hanging over the serving area. The restaurant seats 50 and has an excellent reputation for good home-cooked food. A pleasant beer garden is at the front. The pub hosts a scarecrow competition every August bank holiday Saturday and is home to two darts teams. Q➰❄🕔♣P🖯

Seahouses

Olde Ship Inn ⅃
7-9 Main Street, NE68 7RD
🌣 11-11; 12-11 Sun ☎ (01665) 720200 🌐 seahouses.co.uk
Black Sheep Best Bitter; Courage Directors; Hadrian Border Farne Island Pale Ale; Ruddles County; Morland Old Speckled Hen; Theakston Best Bitter; 2 changing beers 🅷
This 1745 farmhouse was converted to the licensed trade in 1812 and has a regionally important historic pub interior. Family-owned since 1910, the pub has three quality bars adorned with a veritable treasure trove of 19th and 20th century maritime memorabilia. Fully residential, it offers an interesting menu of fish, fresh crab meals and snacks. Q➰❄🛏🕔♿♣P🖵(418,X18)

Seaton Sluice

Melton Constable
Beresford Road, NE26 4QL
🌣 12-11; 12-10.30 Sun ☎ (0191) 237 7741
🌐 themeltonconstable.co.uk
Caledonian Deuchars IPA; Wells Bombardier; Wychwood Hobgoblin; 3 changing beers 🅷
Large roadside pub a few minutes' walk from the beach and local history sights. It is named after the

southern seat of Lord Hastings, a member of the Delaval family – Delaval Hall is close by. Tuesday is steak night, Wednesday is quiz night, Sunday evening features live music. A late-night fishing club meets here and the BSA owners' club meets on the first and third Thursdays of the month. ≿⊛⊄▷⊾P➟(308,309,X7)❀ ╗

Stamfordham

Swinburne Arms ⅃

31 North Side, NE18 0QG
✪ 12-2, 5.30-11 ☎ (01661) 886707
2 changing beers ⊞
This welcoming Grade II-listed country inn is very popular with cyclists – the yard at the back is always full of bikes. It has a relaxed, friendly atmosphere, ideal for a drink winter or summer. Children are welcome until 9pm. There is now a village shop in one of the outbuildings to the rear and the beer garden has been extensively remodelled. ≿

West Thirston

Northumberland Arms ⅃ ✔

The Peth, NE65 9EE
✪ 11.30-11; 11.30-10.30 Sun ☎ (01670) 787370
⊕ northumberlandarms-felton.co.uk

3 changing beers (often Allendale) ⊞
This fine stone-built pub was built in the 1820s by Hugh Percy, 3rd Duke of Northumberland, as a coaching inn. The building has been lovingly restored in an eclectic style while remaining warm, comfortable and welcoming. Bare stone walls and real fires add to the ambience. A large function room caters for groups of up to 30. The beer range is predominantly from local breweries.
≿⊛⇔⊄▷P➟(X15)

Wylam

Boathouse Inn ⅃

Station Road, NE41 8HR
✪ 11-11; 11-midnight Sat; 12-10.30 Sun ☎ (01661) 853431
⊕ theboathousewylam.com
12 changing beers ⊞
Superb two-roomed pub with 15 handpulls, three dedicated to cider, with more ciders served from the cellar. Beers are sourced locally and nationwide, and on bank holidays themed beer festivals are held. Toasties and sandwiches are available during the day. The pub is a popular stopping-off point for Whistle Stops II travellers. Fifteen CAMRA awards cover one wall including North East Regional Pub of the Year 2009 and 2011. Alternate Tuesdays are buskers' nights.
Q≿⊛⇔≒♣♦P❀╗

Miners Arms, Acomb

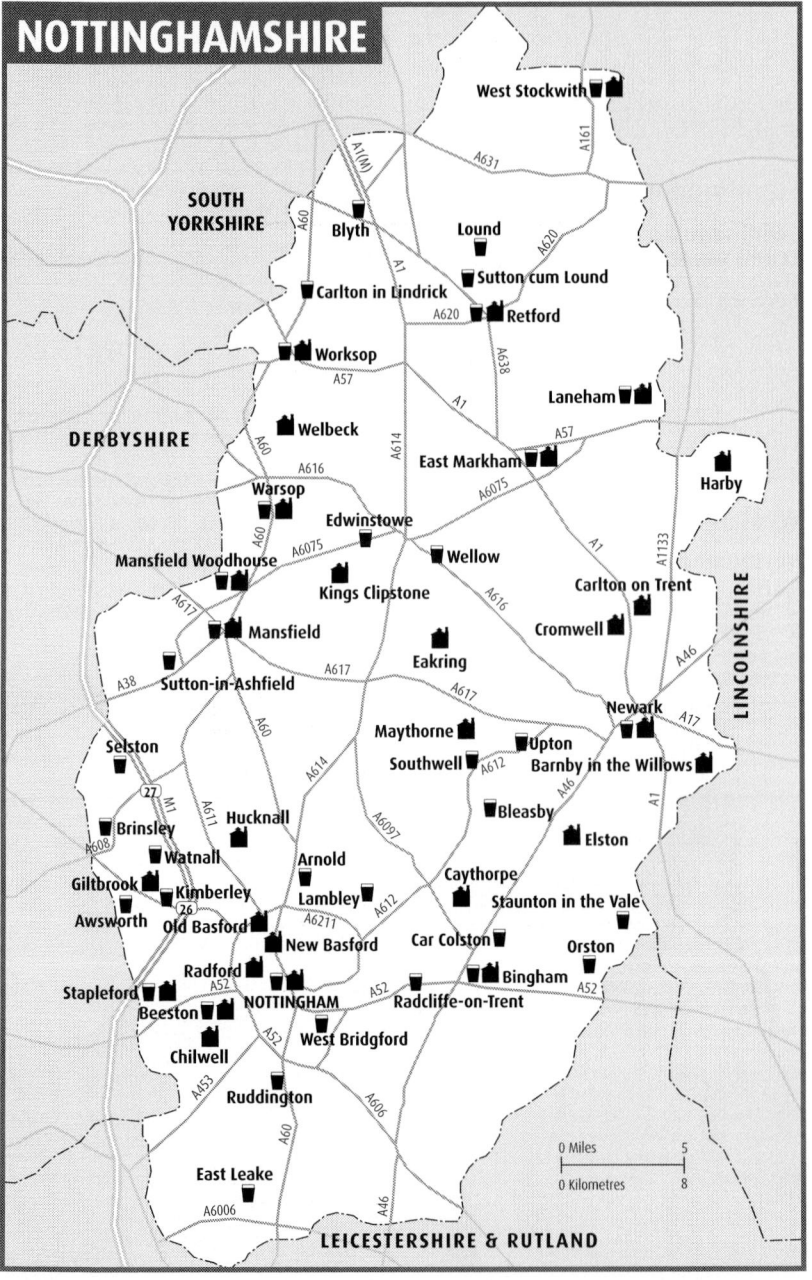

NOTTINGHAMSHIRE

West Stockwith

SOUTH YORKSHIRE

Blyth

Lound

Sutton cum Lound

Carlton in Lindrick

Retford

Worksop

Laneham

DERBYSHIRE

Welbeck

East Markham

Harby

Warsop

Edwinstowe

Wellow

Mansfield Woodhouse

Kings Clipstone

Carlton on Trent

Mansfield

Eakring

Cromwell

Sutton-in-Ashfield

Newark

Selston

Maythorne

Upton

Southwell

Barnby in the Willows

Brinsley

Hucknall

Bleasby

Watnall

Arnold

Elston

Giltbrook

Kimberley

Lambley

Caythorpe

Awsworth

Old Basford

Staunton in the Vale

New Basford

Car Colston

Orston

Radford

Stapleford

Bingham

Beeston

NOTTINGHAM

Radcliffe-on-Trent

Chilwell

West Bridgford

Ruddington

East Leake

LINCOLNSHIRE

0 Miles 5

0 Kilometres 8

LEICESTERSHIRE & RUTLAND

Arnold

Abdication ⒧

89 Mansfield Road, Daybrook, NG5 6BH (opp gates of former Home Brewery)

✪ closed Mon & Tue; 4-9.30; 2-6 Sun ⊕ theabdication.co.uk

4 changing beers Ⓗ

Built in 1936/37, this modern micropub is part of the Home Brewery Coronation Buildings opposite the former brewery, and for many years was a shop. The four changing beers and two ciders are from microbreweries, small producers or the on-

site nanobrewery, and come in a mix of styles. An archway divides the single room, giving an appearance of a much larger area. Participants in the monthly quiz are grouped into teams by a raffle. Q&♣♠🐕🌳

Robin Hood & Little John ⒧

1 Church Street, NG5 8FD (on corner of Cross St)

✪ 12-11.30 (midnight Fri & Sat); 12-10.30 Sun

☎ (0115) 920 1054 ⊕ therobinhoodandlittlejohn.co.uk

Everards Tiger; Lincoln Green Marion, Archer, Hood, Tuck; 5 changing beers Ⓗ

Two-room Project William refurbishment between Lincoln Green and Everards breweries. The bar features Home Ales memorabilia, while the lounge has details of the pub's history and the local area. The rear courtyard has outdoor seating and leads to a covered skittles alley. Along with 10 real ale pumps offering microbrewery beers, the real cider wall has eight taps dispensing ciders from small local producers and further afield. National CAMRA Cider Pub of the Year in 2015. ♿️🏡🍴♣️🚲🅿️🚭🐾📶

Awsworth

Gate Inn L ✔
Main Street, NG16 2RN
🕐 12-midnight ☎ (0115) 932 9821
7 changing beers Ⓗ
Deemed to be unviable and sold by the pub's former owners, the Gate reopened in 2010 as a free house and quickly established itself as a quality real ale outlet, going on to win a Nottingham CAMRA Award of Excellence and LocAle Pub of the Year. A truly welcoming and friendly venue, this late-19th-century inn has a bar, lounge and rooftop sun terrace. Gradually being renovated throughout, the bar area has been refurbished. ♿️♣️🚲🅿️🚭

Beeston

Crown Inn ★ L
Church Street, NG9 1FY
🕐 12-11.30; 12-11 Sun ☎ (0115) 967 8623
🌐 brownales.co.uk/crown-inn
Draught Bass; Everards Sunchaser; Nottingham Rock Ale Mild Beer; house beer (by Ashover); 6 changing beers Ⓗ
Nineteenth-century Grade II-listed alehouse, acquired and sympathetically refurbished by Everards. Up to 14 ales and several real ciders and perries are served at this former East Midlands CAMRA Pub of the Year. Five distinct drinking areas include a snug and three-seat 'confessional', once used as a hideaway by the parish vicar. Although busy, the pub retains a community feel, with a cosy atmosphere throughout. The beer garden regularly hosts events. Substantial snacks are available. Q♿️🏡🚲♣️🚲🅿️🚭🐾📶

Star Inn L
22 Middle Street, NG9 1FX
🕐 12-11 (midnight Thu-Sat) ☎ (0115) 854 5320
🌐 starbeeston.co.uk
House beer (by Nottingham); 10 changing beers Ⓗ
Former Shipstone's pub still with branded windows, restored beyond its former glory. The decor is tasteful and minimal with three separate rooms, complemented by a permanent marquee, sports/games room, spacious garden and patio outside. Visitors may recognise the bar, which featured in Boon and Auf Wiedersehen, Pet. Ten cask ales are on offer alongside a wide selection of whiskies and wines. Meals are served as well as a popular and extensive range of bar snacks. Families are welcome during the day.
♿️🏡🍴🚲♣️🚲🅿️🚭📶

Victoria Hotel L
85 Dovecote Lane, NG9 1JG
🕐 10.30-11 (midnight Fri & Sat); 12-11 Sun
☎ (0115) 925 4049 🌐 victoriabeeston.co.uk

Castle Rock Harvest Pale; Everards Tiger; Fuller's London Pride; 13 changing beers Ⓗ
Located alongside the platform of Beeston railway station, this restored Victorian masterpiece has mass appeal. Sixteen real ales are joined by real ciders and perries, an extensive whisky and wine list, and a renowned food menu. Taster trays of three third-pints are offered. Two distinct bars are complemented by a dining room and a covered, smoke-free seating area outside. VicFest is hosted in July in addition to beer festivals throughout the year. CAMRA and NUS discounts are available Sunday to Thursday. Q♿️🏡🍴♣️🚲🅿️🚭🐾📶

Bingham

Butter Cross L ✔
Market Place, NG13 8AP
🕐 8am-midnight ☎ (01949) 863100
Greene King Abbot; Ruddles Best Bitter; Sharp's Doom Bar; house beer (by Nottingham); changing beers Ⓗ
Formerly the Crown Inn, the building has been fully refurbished and features historic pictures of the town and surrounding area. The bar has 10 handpumps with between six and eight cask ales available, including the house beer, Buttercross Brew from Nottingham Brewery. The pub holds regular mini beer festivals and features in local CAMRA Mild Trails. ♿️🏡🍴♣️🚲🅿️📶

REAL ALE BREWERIES

Angel 🍴 Nottingham (NEW)
Beeston Hop Beeston
Black Iris Nottingham: New Basford
Black Market 🍴 Warsop
Blue Monkey Giltbrook
Brewhouse & Kitchen 🍴 Nottingham (NEW)
Castle Rock Nottingham
Caythorpe 🍴 Caythorpe
Double Top Worksop
Dukeries Worksop
Full Mash Stapleford
Funfair 🍴 Elston
Good Stuff 🍴 Nottingham (NEW)
Grafton Worksop
Handley's 🍴 Barnby in the Willows
Harby 🍴 Harby
Idle West Stockwith
Idle Valley Retford
Kings Clipstone Kings Clipstone
Langwith Mansfield
Lenton Lane Nottingham
Lincoln Green Hucknall
Linear Bingham (NEW)
Magpie Nottingham
Mallard Maythorne
Maypole Eakring
Milestone Cromwell
Navigation 🍴 Nottingham
Newark Newark
Nottingham 🍴 Nottingham: Radford
Pheasantry East Markham
Prior's Well Mansfield Woodhouse
Reality Nottingham: Chilwell
Robin Hood Nottingham: New Basford
Scribbler's Stapleford
Shipstone's 🍴 Nottingham: Old Basford
Springhead Laneham
Tom Herrick's Carlton on Trent
Totally Brewed Nottingham
Welbeck Abbey Welbeck

Horse & Plough 🍺 ⓛ
Long Acre, NG13 8AF
🕐 11-11 (midnight Fri & Sat) ☎ (01949) 839313
Brains Rev James; Castle Rock Harvest Pale; Wells
Bombardier; 7 changing beers Ⓗ
Situated in the heart of a busy market town, this
small pub is a former Methodist chapel with a
cottage-style interior and flagstone floor. Food is
served in the bar and upstairs restaurant, which
offers a varied seasonal menu. Up to nine cask ales
and three ciders are available. Local CAMRA Pub of
the Year in 2017, for the fourth time, and a former
Cider Pub of the Year, the range and quality of
beers makes the pub a serious draw for lovers of
cask ale. 🚼⓪&⇄🍴🚃♣🎵♿

Bleasby

Waggon & Horses ⓛ
Gipsy Lane, NG14 7GG
🕐 5 (12 Thu)-11; 12-midnight Fri & Sat; 12-11 Sun
☎ (01636) 830283 ⊕ thewaggonbleasby.co.uk
Blue Monkey BG Sips, Infinity; Sharp's Doom Bar; 5
changing beers (sourced locally) Ⓗ
Thriving free house set in a lovely Trent Valley
village, one of the prettiest in Nottinghamshire,
overlooking the village green. An open real fire
adds warmth in winter. It offers up to eight real
ales, mainly from Blue Monkey brewery. This is a
traditional pub with no gimmicks or electronic
games, just good conversation. Close to Southwell
Minster and Racecourse, this is a must-visit –
walkers with muddy boots and dogs with muddy
paws welcome. Q❀⓪Å⇄♣🍴P🚃(300)♿🎵

Blyth

Red Hart ⓛ
Bawtry Road, S81 8HG (opp church)
🕐 2.30-11.30 Mon; 11.30-midnight ☎ (01909) 591221
⊕ redhart.co.uk
3 changing beers Ⓗ
An attractive 17th-century former coaching inn in
the centre of Blyth with a lounge, taproom,
separate dining room and outside seating area. The
bar has a pool table and TV for sport. A traditional
menu offers high-quality food made from fresh
ingredients sourced from the surrounding area.
Three changing guest beers are available. The pub
runs an annual beer festival in May from a bar in an
outbuilding. Q🚼❀🚪⓪&♣🍴P🚃(25,29)♿🎵

Brinsley

Lion at Brinsley
Hall Lane, NG16 5AH
🕐 12-11; 12-9 Sun ☎ (01773) 714328
⊕ thewhitelion-brinsley.co.uk
Blue Monkey Infinity; Sharp's Doom Bar; 2 changing
beers Ⓗ
Formerly the White Lion, this is an open-plan pub
with a large car park to the rear, beer garden and
family play area. Up to four ales are available, one
a rotating guest from Blue Monkey. The modern
interior offers both comfortable sofa seating for
drinkers and large tables for family dining. TVs
show sport or music channels. 🚼❀⓪P🚃♿🎵

Car Colston

Royal Oak ✓
The Green, NG13 8JE
🕐 11.30-11 ☎ (01949) 20247 ⊕ royaloakcarcolston.co.uk
Marston's 61 Deep; Ringwood Boondoggle; 2
changing beers Ⓗ
Country inn situated on one of England's largest
village greens. The pub has a cosy bar with
comfortable seating, a real fire, plus a separate
restaurant. The bar's vaulted brickwork ceiling is a
legacy from the building's life as a hosiery factory.
Well-kept beers are complemented by excellent
food, served lunchtimes and evenings. There is a
skittle alley to the rear, beer garden and camping
facilities. The landlord maintains his 100 per cent
record for entries in the Guide.
🚼❀⓪&Å♣P♿🎵

Carlton in Lindrick

Grey Horses Inn ⓛ
The Cross, S81 9EW (centre of old village)
🕐 12-11; 11-11 Sun ☎ (01909) 730252
⊕ greyhorsesinn.com
5 changing beers (often Welbeck Abbey) Ⓗ
The brewery tap for Welbeck Brewery and within a
conservation area. It has a front bar, the Tap Room,
accessible from the street, where locals gather to
chat, play cards and dominoes, and a spacious
lounge bar area where excellent food is served.
There is also a large beer garden. You can be sure
of a warm welcome here.
Q🚼❀⓪&♣🍴P🚃(21,22)♿🎵

East Leake

Round RobINN
54 Main Street, LE12 6PG
🕐 closed Mon; 5 (4 Fri)-11; 12-11 Sat & Sun
☎ (0115) 778 8168
6 changing beers (sourced locally) Ⓖ
Micropub opened in 2015 serving six local beers on
gravity. A choice of ciders and continental bottled
beers is also available. The single room
accommodates up to 45 patrons – seating is a mix
of chairs, cushioned benches and high stools. A
small outdoor area to the front offers alfresco
drinking. Food is restricted to light bar snacks.
Q🚼&♣🍴🚃(1)♿

East Markham

Queen's Hotel
High Street, NG22 0RE
🕐 12 (2 Mon)-11 ☎ (01777) 870288
Adnams Southwold Bitter; Everards Beacon Hill,
Sunchaser, Tiger; 1 changing beer (sourced
nationally) Ⓗ
This cosy, recently refurbished pub has a friendly
atmosphere enhanced by an open fire in winter. A
single bar with five beers serves the lounge and
dining areas. Food ranges from hot and cold snacks
to full home-cooked meals. There is a large garden
area at the rear of the car park.
Q🚼❀⓪&🍴P🚃(36,37)♿

Edwinstowe

Black Swan
High Street, NG21 9QR
🕐 12-11 (12.30am Fri & Sat) ☎ (01623) 822598

Sharp's Doom Bar; 2 changing beers Ⓗ
A traditional cask ale pub in a picturesque village. Old pictures of the village decorate the walls. Up to three real ales are usually available along with real cider. Local breweries feature regularly including Castle Rock, Nottingham, Blue Monkey, Welbeck Abbey and the nearby Kings Clipstone. Three letting rooms are available above the pub.
Q ☆ ⚅ ⊯ & ● P ⊟ ✿ ☂

Forest Lodge ✔

2-4 Church Street, NG21 9QA
☼ 11.30-3, 5.30 (5 Fri)-11; 12-3, 6-10.30 Sun
☎ (01623) 824443 ⊕ forestlodgehotel.co.uk
Wells Bombardier; house beer (by Welbeck Abbey); 3 changing beers Ⓗ
Based in the heart of Sherwood Forest, this 18th-century coaching inn is a free house offering a range of guest beers including a top-quality mild and a house beer supplied by Welbeck Abbey. The high-class restaurant serves a wide choice of daily specials, and is proud to use local produce wherever possible. Private functions can be catered for. Accommodation is 4-star AA rated.
Q ☆ ⚅ ⊯ ⊙ P ⊟ ☂

Kimberley

Stag Inn 🄻 ✔

67 Nottingham Road, NG16 2NE
☼ 5 (1.30 Sat)-11; 12-10.30 Sun ☎ (0115) 938 3151
⊕ stagkimberley.co.uk
Adnams Southwold Bitter; Timothy Taylor Landlord; 3 changing beers Ⓗ
This wattle and daub Tudor-style house dates from 1737 and is near the town centre. Inside, two rooms are linked by a central bar, with an eclectic mix of seating including wooden settles. Table skittles and dominoes are played, but at most times conversation reigns. The spacious rear garden includes a children's play area and ample seating. A beer festival is held in early summer. The guest beers always include a local brew.
Q ☆ ⚅ & ♣ P ⊟ ✿

White Lion 🄻

74 Swingate, NG16 2PQ
☼ 4 (2 Fri)-11.30; 12-11.30 Sat; 12-10.30 Sun
☎ (0115) 938 3193 ⊕ whitelionswingate.co.uk
Black Iris Snake Eyes; Castle Rock Harvest Pale; Oakham Bishops Farewell; Sharp's Doom Bar Ⓗ**; 3 changing beers** Ⓗ/Ⓖ
A genuine community free house which has recently been modernised throughout while retaining its traditional two-roomed status. Seven cask beers, mainly from local microbreweries, are served on handpump from the central bar. A further selection may be available on occasion from a stillage bar adjoining the large rear garden, which is accessed by a central corridor or directly from the car park. Sandwiches can be provided on request. Q ☆ ⚅ & ♣ P ⊟ ✿ ☂

Lambley

Woodlark Inn 🄻

Church Street, NG4 4QB
☼ 12-midnight ☎ (0115) 931 2535
Castle Rock Harvest Pale; Samuel Smith Old Brewery Bitter; Timothy Taylor Landlord; 1 changing beer Ⓗ
This traditional pub dates back to the 19th century and is located in the quaint-sounding Dumbles area

of the village. It is popular with both locals and visitors, and offers a friendly welcome to all. A music-free environment enables customers and staff to engage in conversation. It has two rooms – a bare red-brick bar with exposed beams and a lounge where excellent home-cooked food is served. Q ☆ ⚅ ⊙ ♣ ● P ⊞ ✿

Laneham

Bees Knees 🄻

Springhead Brewery, Robin Hood Site, Main Street, DN22 0NA (centre of village)
☼ 4-11; 12-midnight Sat; 12-11 Sun ☎ 07884 65577
⊕ springhead.co.uk
Oakham Citra; 5 changing beers (often Springhead) Ⓗ
A country pub with three small rooms converted from a former shop on the Springhead Brewery site and well supported by locals. The interior has recently been refurbished. It offers four Springhead beers along with Oakham Citra and a rotating guest beer. Over 100 gins are also available. Excellent food is served. There is an adequate outside seating area. Q ☆ ⊙ & ⏚ ● P ⊟ ✿ ☂

Lound

Blue Bell Inn

Town Street, DN22 8RN (on main road through village)
☼ 5-11; 12-11 Sat; 12-10.30 Sun ☎ (01777) 818457
⊕ bluebellinnretford.co.uk
Black Sheep Best Bitter; 2 changing beers (sourced regionally; often Welbeck Abbey) Ⓗ
This traditional two-room village pub is gaining a growing reputation for high-quality food and beer. Black Sheep is always available alongside a Welbeck Abbey beer, usually Harley, plus a changing guest beer, often a local ale. There is a large car park and a fenced outside seating area. Boules is played in the summer on Wednesday and Sunday. Wednesday is quiz night.
Q ☆ ⚅ ⊯ ⊙ & ♣ P ⊟ ✿ ☂

Mansfield

Bold Forester

Botany Avenue, NG18 5NF
☼ 11-11.30 (12.30am Fri & Sat); 12-11.30 Sun
☎ (01623) 623970
Greene King IPA, Abbot; Hardys & Hansons Olde Trip; Morland Old Speckled Hen; 8 changing beers Ⓗ
Hungry Horse-branded pub and restaurant. Up to 12 real ales are available, usually including six from Greene King and up to six guests. Food is served daily until 9pm. The spacious open-plan interior has large-screen TVs showing all major live sport. There is a covered smoking area outside with a TV. The enclosed beer garden is popular with families in the summer months. Situated on the main road into Mansfield, it is well serviced by public transport and has a large car park.
☆ ⚅ ⊙ & ⏤ ♣ P ⊟ ☂

Brown Cow ▼

31 Ratcliffe Gate, NG18 2JA
☼ 12-11 (midnight Fri & Sat) ☎ (01623) 645854
⊕ rawbrew.com/pubs
Everards Tiger; 9 changing beers (often Raw) Ⓗ
Operated by Raw Brewery under the award-winning Project William scheme with Everards of Leicester. It has two separate bar areas and a function room upstairs. A range of up to 12 real

ales and ciders is offered alongside a selection of world bottled beers. Regular beer festivals are hosted. Folk music features on a Tuesday night and a quiz on Wednesday. The pub is located a short walk from Mansfield town centre bus and railway stations and has ample car parking. Local CAMRA branch Pub of the Year 2017. Q৬৯✿≠●P🅿🚲◔🐾🛜

Court House ✓

Market Place, NG18 1HX (next to town hall)
🕙 8am-11 (midnight Fri & Sat) ☎ (01623) 412720
5 changing beers 🅷
Family-friendly pub overlooking the marketplace. As the name suggests, this Grade II-listed historic building was previously a court house built in 1867. It has five handpulls serving regularly changing beers and one real cider. Food is served daily until 10pm. Children are welcome until 9pm. Monday is pie club, Tuesday is steak club and Wednesday is chicken club. Thursday is chip shop night and curry is the speciality on Friday. Under five minutes' walk from the bus and railway stations.
৬🕙&≠●🅿🛜

Railway Inn

9 Station Street, NG18 1EF
🕙 11-11 ☎ (01623) 623086
4 changing beers 🅷
A stone's throw from the railway and bus stations, this community pub is dog-friendly, serves home-cooked foods and has two separate rooms for diners or those desiring a little privacy. Four real ales are available, at least one a local offering, and one or more real cider. A music night is held once a month. Outside there is a walled garden and smoking area. CAMRA branch Pub of the Year in 2015 and 2016. Q৬৯✿🕙≠●🅿🐾🛜

Mansfield Woodhouse

Greyhound Inn ✓

82 High Street, NG19 8BD
🕙 12-11 (midnight Fri & Sat); 12-10.30 Sun
☎ (01623) 464403
Adnams Broadside; Caledonian Deuchars IPA; 3 changing beers 🅷
There are few pubs that have been in the Guide for 24 years, run by the same landlady for 33 years, like the Greyhound. This success has been achieved by serving quality ales in a traditional two-room pub environment. No food, just bar snacks and lively conversation. Weekly activities include open the box, play your cards right, quiz night and card bingo. Pool, darts and dominoes are played in the public bar. Dogs are welcome in the taproom.
✿♣●🅿🐾

Well

Farmway, NG19 9BG
🕙 2.30-7.30 Thu & Fri; closed Sat-Wed ☎ (01623) 632393
🌐 priorswellbrewery.co.uk
Prior's Well Priory Gold, Prior's Pale, Resurrected; 2 changing beers 🅷
The Well is the brewery tap at Prior's Well Brewery. The Victorian bar is on a mezzanine level with four handpulls dispensing beers from the Prior's Well range alongside one lager and a cider. The bar is open only Thursday and Friday afternoons, and the occasional Sunday, but will remain open later if busy. Children and dogs are welcome but this is a working brewery so supervision is advised.
৬●🅿(11,12)🐾🛜

Newark

Fox & Crown 🄻

4-6 Appleton Gate, NG24 1JY (opp parish church)
🕙 10.30-11 (midnight Fri & Sat); 10-11 Sun
☎ (01636) 605820
Castle Rock Sheriff's Tipple, Harvest Pale, Preservation Fine Ale, Elsie Mo; Everards Ascalon; 3 changing beers 🅷
Popular, friendly, town-centre local, busy with shoppers during the day. It has an open-plan layout with a central bar and three side rooms. The decor includes brewery pictures, posters, mirrors and old photos of Newark. Six real ales are available alongside more than 100 bottled beers to drink in or take away. Live music features on a Friday night. Q৬✿🕙&≠(Castle)♣●🅿(1,2)🐾🛜

Just Beer Micropub 🏆 🄻

32A Castle Gate, NG24 1BG (in Swan & Salmon Yard, off Castle Gate)
🕙 1-11; 12-midnight Fri & Sat; 12-10 Sun ☎ (01636) 312047
🌐 justbeermicropub.biz
4 changing beers 🅷
Micropub concentrating on cask ales, cider and perries. In February 2016 the milestone of 3,000 different beers from 1,000 different breweries was reached. World and unusual UK ales are available from the well-stocked fridge. Food includes locally sourced pork pies, cheeseboards and pork scratchings. Traditional pub games are played, including an annual cribbage tournament. Three beer festivals are held each year. Local CAMRA Pub of the Year for five years. Q&🅰≠♣●🅿🍽🐾

Oscar's Inn

105 Balderton Gate, NG24 1RY
🕙 12-11 (midnight Fri & Sat) ☎ (01636) 918130
House beer (by Marston's); 5 changing beers 🅷
Refurbished two-room pub situated close to the town centre, named after the owner's dog. The Oscar Wilde room is open at all times, displaying quotes from the great man, the Oscar Peterson room opens at busier times and hosts live music at the weekend. A lunchtime menu is available and the kitchen specialises in 16-inch pizzas. The house beer, Oscar's Ale, is from the Marston's group.
৬🕙🅿(2,3)🐾🛜

Prince Rupert 🄻

46 Stodman Street, NG24 1AW
🕙 11-11 (midnight Wed & Thu; 1am Fri & Sat); 12-11 Sun
☎ (01636) 918121
Brains Rev James; Oakham JHB; 4 changing beers 🅷
Reopened in 2010, this historic pub dates back to 1452. Multi-roomed on two separate levels, exposed beams are evident and various interesting artefacts and brewery memorabilia decorate the walls and ceilings. The Nelson room has an open fire. An extensive lunchtime and evening food menu is available, with pizzas a speciality. The pub has featured in the Guide for seven consecutive years. Q✿🕙≠●🅿🐾🛜

Vaults Cider & Ale House

14 North Gate, NG24 1EZ (adjacent to Newark Locksmiths)
🕙 12-3, 5-11 (midnight Thu); 12-midnight Fri & Sat; 12-10 Sun ☎ (01636) 678953 🌐 thevaultsnewark.co.uk
4 changing beers 🅷
In one of the city's historic cellars, the Vaults boasts eight handpumps offering cask ales, ciders and perries, with further cider and perry available direct

from the box. A wide selection of well-regarded lunchtime and evening food features locally sourced ingredients. Local CAMRA Cider Pub of the Year in 2016 and 2017. ◑⬤≢⬤🏠🖰😺🛜

Nottingham: Central

Canalhouse 🗓
48-52 Canal Street, NG1 7EH
🕐 11-11 (midnight Thu); 11-1am Fri & Sat; 11-10.30 Sun
☎ (0115) 955 5060 ⊕ thecanalhouse.co.uk
Castle Rock Harvest Pale; 5 changing beers 🅷
A modern Waterways warehouse conversion. The canal to the rear runs inside the building, where up to two narrowboats are moored. A good selection of real ales, real ciders and perries is complemented by quality world beers both on tap and in bottles. The pub hosts the Champion Beer of Nottinghamshire competition in the first-floor function room in February. Outside is a spacious glass-covered patio overlooking the canal, which is popular on sunny summer days. ⊛◑🚹≢�'(Nottingham Station)⬤P🖰😺🛜

Crafty Crow 🗓
102 Friar Lane, NG1 6EB
🕐 12-11; 11-midnight Fri & Sat ☎ (0115) 837 1992
⊕ craftycrownotts.co.uk
8 changing beers (often Magpie) 🅷
Magpie Brewery's first pub, with eight handpulls serving microbrewery beers and a further four offering a good variety of real ciders. Maintaining a 'green and local' ethos throughout, the majority of fittings are recycled or home-made – the sinks are made from beer casks with ex-keg fonts as taps. Snacks and light meals are served until 9pm, made from locally sourced produce. Situated on two levels, a side entrance leads directly to all facilities. Corvid birds feature strongly. 🛏◑🚹≢🚁⬤🖰😺🛜

Hand & Heart 🗓
65 Derby Road, NG1 5BA
🕐 12-11 (midnight Fri & Sat); 12-10.30 Sun
☎ (0115) 958 2456 ⊕ thehandandheart.co.uk
Maypole Little Weed; house beer (by Dancing Duck); 7 changing beers (sourced locally) 🅷
The modern frontage and bar area hide the age of this pub – there are sandstone caves to the rear used as a dining space. A high-quality menu of both food and beer is offered, with eight mostly local beers on handpump, together with three real ciders or perries. The upstairs room has a separate bar for private functions, and there is a partially covered first-floor terrace overlooking the busy street below. Live music features on Sundays and Thursdays. 🛏◑⬤🖰😺🛜

King William IV 🗓
6 Eyre Street, Sneinton, NG2 4PB
🕐 12 (2 Mon)-11; 12-11.30 Thu; 11-midnight Fri & Sat
☎ (0115) 958 9864
Oakham Citra, Bishops Farewell; house beer (by Black Iris); 5 changing beers 🅷
Nicknamed the King Billy, this cosy Victorian gem nestling on the edge of town is just a stone's throw from the Arena. A family-run free house that oozes charm and character, it is a haven for real ale drinkers, with a choice of up to eight microbrewery ales from near and far as well as real cider. Occasional live music and televised sport feature. A selection of rolls is available. The pub sign won a national award in 2015. Q⊛⬤🖰😺🛜

Lincolnshire Poacher 🗓
161-163 Mansfield Road, NG1 3FR
🕐 11-11 (midnight Thu & Fri); 10.30-midnight Sat; 12-11 Sun
☎ (0115) 941 1584
Castle Rock Harvest Pale, Elsie Mo, Screech Owl; Everards Tiger; Fuller's London Pride; 8 changing beers 🅷
Thirteen handpumps offer a wide selection of guest ales, mainly from microbreweries. A mild, stout or porter is always available alongside real ciders and perries, continental bottled beers and a good selection of whiskies. The food menu features locally sourced ingredients. Walls display artwork celebrating the pub's twinning with In de Wildeman bar in Amsterdam, and various memorabilia of local and international interest. Live music plays on Sundays and Wednesdays. Q⊛◑🚹⬤♣⬤🖰😺🛜

Newshouse 🗓
123 Canal Street, NG1 7HB
🕐 12-11 (midnight Fri & Sat) ☎ (0115) 952 3061
Castle Rock Harvest Pale; 4 changing beers (sourced locally; often Totally Brewed) 🅷
In times past, newspapers would be read out here to inform the illiterate of elections at home and military victories overseas, hence the name. The walls are covered with framed front pages of local newspapers showing headlines stretching back over many years. The public bar has a large TV screen, dartboard, bar billiards and table skittles. The lounge has more comfortable seating. Light lunches are served and snacks at all times. Beers from the local Totally Brewed Brewery are almost always available. 🛏⊛◑🚹≢🚁(Nottingham Station)♣⬤🖰😺🛜

Olde Trip to Jerusalem ★ 🗓 ✅
Brewhouse Yard, NG1 6AD (off Castle Rd)
🕐 11-11 (midnight Fri & Sat) ☎ (0115) 947 3171
⊕ triptojerusalem.com
Greene King IPA; Hardys & Hansons Olde Trip; Nottingham Extra Pale Ale; 6 changing beers 🅷
Famous pub at the bottom of Castle Road, built into the rock beneath Nottingham Castle. Several rooms on the ground and first floor are open to the public. The Cursed Galleon in the upstairs rock lounge is reputed to have claimed the lives of those who tried to clean it. Play ring the bull at quieter times in the front bar. Beer festivals are held in the enclosed courtyard. A cobblestone area outside is popular on warmer days. Q⊛◑≢♣⬤😺🛜

Organ Grinder 🗓
21 Alfreton Road, Canning Circus, NG7 3JE
🕐 12-11 (11.30 Thu; midnight Fri & Sat) ☎ (0115) 970 0630
Blue Monkey BG Sips, Infinity, Guerrilla; Sharp's Doom Bar; 3 changing beers 🅷
Previously the Red Lion, this inn was bought and refurbished by Blue Monkey Brewery. The single-room, multi-level pub boasts a wood-burning fire. To the rear is a small courtyard leading to a raised decked area and first-floor function room (where a TV is occasionally in use). The full Blue Monkey range of beers is offered, as well as a guest and three real ciders or perries. No meals, but bar snacks such as Scotch eggs and pork pies are sold. 🛏⊛♣⬤😺🛜

Room with a Brew 🗓
78 Derby Road, NG1 5FD
🕐 closed Mon; 5 (12 Wed & Thu)-10; 12-11 Fri & Sat; 2-9 Sun ☎ 07780 662244 ⊕ aroomwithabrew.pub

7 changing beers (often Scribbler's) ⓗ
This micropub was opened in February 2016 by local brewery Scribbler's Ales. Situated on the main road that links Canning Circus to the city centre, the long, narrow pub has a bar to the rear sporting seven handpumps. Seating is on either side, between the door and the bar. As with the Scribbler's beers, there is a literary theme throughout, with many books to peruse. Q&♣●🖥

Vat & Fiddle ⓛ
Queens Bridge Road, NG2 1NB
🕐 11-11 (midnight Fri & Sat) ☎ (0115) 985 0611
Castle Rock Sheriff's Tipple, Harvest Pale, Elsie Mo, Screech Owl; 7 changing beers ⓗ
Close to the railway station and HMRC offices, this 1937 Art Deco gem is the brewery tap for the adjacent Castle Rock Brewery. Twelve handpumps serve at least five from the Castle Rock stable, and a recently expanded range of ciders. Tasting trays of six third-pints are available. Hot food is served all week, with roasts on Sundays. The outside seating area features floral displays in summer. Brewery tours operate Monday to Saturday and can be booked in advance.
Q🏃🐕🍽&⇄🚉(Nottingham Station)♣●🖥😺🛜

Nottingham: East

Bread & Bitter ⓛ
153-155 Woodthorpe Drive, Mapperley, NG3 5JL
🕐 10-midnight (11.30 Mon; 11 Tue & Wed); 11-11 Sun
☎ (0115) 960 7541
Castle Rock Harvest Pale, Preservation Fine Ale, Elsie Mo, Screech Owl; Fuller's London Pride; 6 changing beers ⓗ
Castle Rock pub converted in 2007 from the premises of an old bakery on Mapperley Top. The original baker's oven fronts are still embedded in an inside wall, giving the place a warm and welcoming feel. The pub started a revival of real ale outlets in Mapperley. Twelve beers including a mild and rotating guests are available, along with a cider and an extensive foreign bottled beer list. Food is all home-cooked and changes frequently – look for the specials board. Q🏃🐕🍽&●🖥😺🛜

Old Volunteer ⓛ ✅
35 Burton Road, Carlton, NG4 3DQ
🕐 12-11 (midnight Fri & Sat) ☎ (0115) 987 2299
🌐 oldvolunteer.com
Flipside Sterling Pale, Flipping Best, Russian Rouble; 6 changing beers ⓗ
Refurbished by Flipside Brewery several years ago, the pub showcases five of its beers alongside several guests and real cider. The interior is separated into distinct areas by unusual wooden beams, with a raised corner and varied flooring. Outside is a decked patio area with parasols, leading to the main entrance. Food choices include speciality burgers with wedges. Snacks are on offer at all times. Beer festivals are held in a car park marquee. 🐕🍽&⇄●🖥😺🛜

Willowbrook ⓛ
13 Main Road, Gedling, NG4 3HQ
🕐 10-11 (midnight Fri); 9am-midnight Sat; 9am-11 Sun
☎ (0115) 987 8596
Castle Rock Harvest Pale, Preservation Fine Ale, Elsie Mo; Everards Tiger; 7 changing beers ⓗ
Formerly a club, the building was refurbished in late 2013 and again in 2015 due to a fire. The 14 handpumps always offer a stout or porter as well

as a selection of three real ciders or perries. A small side room and entrance lounge lead to the bar which opens to a rear room. Patio doors open onto a secluded paved outdoor area. Diners can enjoy a good food menu complemented by daily specials. 🏃🐕🍽&●🖥😺🛜

Nottingham: North

Doctor's Orders ⓛ
351 Mansfield Road, Carrington, NG5 2DA
🕐 12-10.30 ☎ (0115) 960 7985
🌐 doctorsordersmicropub.co.uk
5 changing beers (sourced locally) ⓗ
Small beer emporium with two distinct areas, refurbished in 2015. A square, compact lounge leads to a corridor flanked on one side by a narrow raised seating area with benches, with a small bar-cum-serving area at the rear where you will find the handpumps. Beer and cider are brought to your table. While now owned by Magpie Brewery, the pub continues its original ethos of providing a range of microbrewery beers in an intimate atmosphere. Q🐕&♣●🖥😺🛜

Nottingham: South

Embankment ⓛ
282-284 Arkwright Street, The Meadows, NG2 2GR
🕐 10-11 (midnight Fri & Sat) ☎ (0115) 986 4502
Castle Rock Harvest Pale, Preservation Fine Ale, Elsie Mo, Screech Owl; Fuller's London Pride; 10 changing beers ⓗ
Originally one of the largest shops belonging to Boots the Chemist, this former Boots Members' Social Club is now a pub. Jesse Boot's office remains upstairs in the black and white mock-Tudor building, which has been restored, retaining the oak-panelled walls and stained-glass leaded windows. It has multiple function rooms of varying sizes. Situated just off Trent Bridge, the three sports grounds are close by. Now operated by Castle Rock, it sells a large range of real ales and ciders. 🏃🐕🍽&●P🖥😺🛜

Nottingham: West

Johnson Arms ⓛ ✅
59 Abbey Street, Lenton, NG7 2NZ
🕐 12 (4 Mon)-11; 4-11 Sat ☎ (0115) 978 6355
🌐 johnsonarms.co.uk
Sharp's Doom Bar; 5 changing beers ⓗ
Popular pub close to the University of Nottingham and QMC hospital. This former Shipstone's house has a green-tiled frontage and retains the original etched windows. Beers from local breweries complement the more well-known brands. Traditional home-cooked food includes JA burgers. Events include beer festivals, Johnsonbury and various sporting events on TV, and the pub supports local real ale trails. The beer garden, with a pétanque court, is not to be missed. Q🐕🍽🚉(Gregory St)♣●🖥🛜

Plough Inn ⓛ ✅
17 St Peter's Street, Radford, NG7 3EN
🕐 12-11 (midnight Wed & Thu); 12-10.30 Sun
☎ (0115) 970 2615 🌐 nottinghambrewerytaphouse.co.uk
Nottingham Rock Ale Bitter Beer, Rock Ale Mild Beer, Legend, Extra Pale Ale; 4 changing beers ⓗ
Linked with the old Nottingham Brewery since 1887, the Plough is now the brewery tap for the

company. The four regular beers come from the brewery as well as two of the four rotating guests. The present building, a 1932 two-room house with a central servery, is largely unchanged. Attracting regulars from a wide area, this 'village pub in the city' has retained its local feel in a period of rapid change, offering real fires, a skittles alley and a popular quiz night. Q🏠🕿🍴🌆♣♠P🚆☺🐾🛜

Orston

Durham Ox
Church Street, NG13 9NS
🕒 12-3, 6-11; 12-11 Fri & Sat; 12-10.30 Sun
🕿 (01949) 850059 ⊕ thedurhamoxorston.co.uk
Castle Rock Harvest Pale; Theakston Best Bitter, Lightfoot; 2 changing beers ⊞
A traditional country pub in the picturesque Vale of Belvoir, serving a range of real ales. The bar is home to five handpumps, complemented by wines and quality home-cooked food served in the bar and separate restaurant. There is an extremely pretty beer garden to the rear, plus a function room. This lovely village pub is popular with both locals and visitors to the area. 🏠🕿🍴🌆♠P🚆☺🐾🛜

Radcliffe on Trent

Chestnut Ⓛ ✅
Main Road, NG12 2BE
🕒 12-11 (11.30 Fri); 10.30-11.30 Sat; 10.30-11 Sun
🕿 (0115) 933 1994 ⊕ thechestnutradcliffe.co.uk
Fuller's London Pride; Oakham JHB; St Austell Tribute; 4 changing beers ⊞
Well-regarded, cask beer-led village pub with a smart 1920s-style decor. Originally the Cliffe Inn, following a major refurbishment in 2006 it became the Horse Chestnut and in 2015 simply the Chestnut. Seven reasonably priced real ales are served including ever-changing guests, always including a local brew. Quality home-made food, ranging from stone-baked pizzas to classic British dishes, is served in a relaxed, casual atmosphere. 🏠🕿🌆♠Pロ=♠P🚆☺🐾🛜

Retford

BeerHeadZ
3 Town Hall Yard, DN22 6DU (off Market Square to rear of 10 Green Bottles)
🕒 1 (11 Thu)-11; 11-midnight Fri & Sat; 12-10 Sun
🕿 (01777) 949631 ⊕ beerheadz.biz
5 changing beers (sourced regionally) ⊞
A small, friendly pub serving five rotating guest beers, three ciders and a range of bottled beers. The ale is always in excellent condition and served in oversized glasses so you can be sure of a full pint – a discount scheme is available to regular customers. BeerHeadZ has won several CAMRA awards including North Notts Pub of the Season and Nottinghamshire Pub of the Year 2016. Q🕿♣🚆☺🐾🛜

Galway Arms
Bridgegate, DN22 7UZ (nr Market Square)
🕒 4 (11 Sat & Sun)-midnight 🕿 (01777) 702446
Black Sheep Ale; 3 changing beers (sourced regionally) ⊞
The interior here is open plan with four separate areas and two bars, and there are TVs for sport. The lounge area is screen-free for a more peaceful drink. There is also a quaint snug area with seating

for up to 12 people. The Black Sheep is complemented by three rotating guests. Live music plays on Fridays and Saturdays. The pub is famed for its breakfasts at the weekend. 🏠🕿🌆♠Pロ☺🐾🛜

Idle Valley Tap Ⓛ
Carolgate, DN22 6AS
🕒 12-11.30 (12.30am Thu-Sat) 🕿 (01777) 948586
Idle Valley Vacant Gesture; 7 changing beers (sourced regionally; often Idle Valley) ⊞
A great addition for real ale drinkers in Retford, with five Idle Valley and three rotating guest beers on the bar providing customers with a wider choice of beers. The brewery tap, opened in late 2015, is a one-room pub with a pool table and dartboard. The outside space has been put to good use, with bench seating attracting large numbers in fine weather. A winner of local CAMRA awards. 🏠⇄♠♣Pロ🚆🛜

Ruddington

Frame Breakers Ⓛ
High Street, NG11 6DT
🕒 11-11 (midnight Fri & Sat); 12-10.30 Sun
🕿 (0115) 859 0060 ⊕ theframebreakers.co.uk
Nottingham Rock Ale Bitter Beer, Rock Ale Mild Beer, Extra Pale Ale; 2 changing beers (sourced locally) ⊞
A large three-storey white-painted corner building. Inside, the open-plan layout features low wood beams and a decor with plenty of wood including a solid bar, plus settles and chunky furniture. Live music is confined to the rear. Run by Nottingham Brewery since October 2015, a number of its beers are featured, including a dark brew. Q🌆♠♣Pロ(3,10)☺🛜

Selston

Horse & Jockey
Church Lane, NG16 6FB
🕒 12-3.30, 5-midnight; 12-4, 7-1am Sun 🕿 (01773) 781012
Greene King Abbot; Timothy Taylor Landlord ⊞**; 4 changing beers** ⊞/Ⓖ
A drinkers' gem dating from 1664 with wooden bench seating, large open fires and flagstone floors. Up to six real ales are available, two served under gravity from casks on stone trestles. A real cider or perry is always available. A quiz is held on Sunday evening and a folk night every Wednesday. Look out for the Selstock Beer and Music Festival in July. A winner of many CAMRA awards. Q🏠🕿🌆♠♣PロŪ☺

Southwell

Final Whistle
Station Road, NG25 0ET
🕒 12-midnight 🕿 (01636) 814953
Draught Bass; 6 changing beers ⊞
Adjacent to the Southwell Trail, formerly an old railway line popular with walkers, this comfortable pub has a railway theme and features plenty of memorabilia. The rear garden is a mock station with a section of track. The bar has 10 handpumps serving two regular beers, six changing ales and two house beers brewed by Ashover Ales. Quiz nights are Tuesday and Sunday. Limited bar snacks are available. Local CAMRA Pub of the Year 2015 and 2017. 🏠🕿🌆♠♣PロŪ(28,100)🐾

Stapleford

Horse & Jockey 🅻
20 Nottingham Road, NG9 8AA
✪ 12-11 (midnight Fri & Sat) ☎ (0115) 875 9655
🌐 horseandjockeystapleford.co.uk
Full Mash Horse & Jockey; 12 changing beers ⊞
Known locally as the Jockey, it was refurbished in 2012 and has become a real ale destination pub. A choice of 13 cask ales, including five LocAles, is offered, accompanied by local ciders and a range of whiskies. There are two rooms on split levels, each with a different ambience. Pictures of local landmarks decorate the pub. There is no music, TV (other than for major sporting events) or games machines. A former CAMRA National Pub of the Year finalist. Q🖢🛋️♿🚶🍴P🚃🐾

Staunton in the Vale

Staunton Arms 🅻 ✅
NG13 9PE
✪ 12-11 (midnight Fri & Sat); 12-10 Sun ☎ (01400) 281218
🌐 stauntonarms.co.uk
Castle Rock Harvest Pale; Draught Bass; 1 changing beer ⊞
Two-hundred-year-old listed inn in the far north of the Vale of Belvoir, carefully restored to retain its original character. The large bar offers comfortable seating for drinkers and diners, with a further separate raised restaurant area. The pub serves freshly prepared meals lunchtimes and evenings and has built a reputation for good food. Three cask beers, one always a LocAle, are on the bar, and mini beer festivals are held regularly. Q🖢🏴🍴♿♠️P🐾🛜

Sutton cum Lound

Gate Inn
40 Town Street, DN22 8PT (on main road in centre of village)
✪ 12-3, 5-10; 12-11.30 Fri & Sat; 12-10 Sun
☎ (01777) 709408 🌐 the-gate-inn.co.uk
6 changing beers ⊞
Recently reopened following a massive refurbishment of the building and interior that has completely transformed this friendly village pub. The beers are well kept and usually include a brew from Welbeck Abbey. Hearty seasonal food is also excellent. Situated in the countryside, the pub is an ideal starting or finishing place for walks around the stunning local scenery. 🖢🍴♿♠️P🚃🐾🛜

Sutton-in-Ashfield

Masons Arms
Unwin Road, NG17 4NB
✪ 12-11 ☎ (01623) 610421
2 changing beers ⊞
Community pub with a lounge and public bar separated by a central bar area. Two ever-changing, usually local, real ales are available and a real cider. Darts and dominoes are popular in the bar. A large conservatory at the rear leads to the enclosed garden where mini beer festivals are held twice a year. Q🖢♿♣️🚶P🚃🐾

Scruffy Dog
Station Road, NG17 5HF
✪ closed Mon & Tue; 4-11 (11.30 Thu & Fri); 12-11.30 Sat;
12-10.30 Sun ☎ (01623) 550826 🌐 thescruffydog.co.uk
5 changing beers ⊞
A drinkers' gem, comfy sofas and a real fire on colder days welcome visitors to this dog-friendly pub. Six beers are usually available, from the likes of Abbeydale and Thornbridge alongside one or two nationals. Purchased from a large pub company, this community pub has been refurbished, with a small L-shaped bar and a large open-plan bar area. Closed on Mondays and Tuesdays except bank holidays. Q🖢❄️♿🚶P🚃🐾

Speed the Plough
Mansfield Road, NG17 4HG
✪ 12-11 (midnight Wed & Fri); 12-1am Sat; 12-midnight Sun ☎ 07821 331173
Greene King Abbot; 3 changing beers (often Blue Monkey, St Austell) ⊞
Three handpulled beers – two nationals and one local brew – are usually available at this community pub. Dogs and children are welcome except on Saturday evening when a popular, busy karaoke night is hosted. A range of home-made food including beef and onion pie, quarter-pounder burgers and steaks is available daily except Sunday. There is an enclosed beer garden to the rear. The pub is a big supporter of armed forces' charities. 🖢❄️◑♣️P🚃🐾🛜

Upton

Cross Keys
43 Main Street, NG23 5SY
✪ closed Mon; 12-3, 5-11.30 (12.30am Fri & Sat); 12-11 Sun
☎ (01636) 813269 🌐 crosskeysatupton.co.uk
Mallard Duck 'n' Dive; 3 changing beers ⊞
Situated on the main route from Newark to Southwell, this 16th-century pub has been at the centre of village life for more than 300 years. It features excellent meals, including home-made lunches and themed food evenings and events. Fish prepared by the French-born chef is a speciality and Sunday lunch is not to be missed. The Mallard Brewery tap, three of their ales are always on handpump and in excellent condition. Locals enjoy the book club and dominoes. Q🖢❄️◑P🚃🐾

Warsop

Black Market Venue
43 High Street, NG20 0AB
✪ 10-midnight ☎ (01623) 842105 🌐 blackmarketlive.co.uk
Black Market Illicit; 2 changing beers ⊞
The building that houses the Black Market Venue has been selling ales continuously for almost 100 years. In 2015 the Black Market Brewery opened, with its first beer, Illicit, appearing soon after. The 2½-barrel plant in the basement produces other seasonal beers and one guest is usually offered. The venue has a large hall where live music is hosted most weekends. All rooms are on one wheelchair-accessible level but there are no disabled toilets. The bar area is dog-friendly. ♣️🚃(11,12)🐾

Watnall

Queen's Head 🅻
40 Main Road, NG16 1HT
✪ 12-11; 11.30-midnight Thu-Sat; 11.30-11 Sun
☎ (0115) 938 6774 🌐 queensheadwatnall.co.uk

Adnams Broadside; Everards Tiger; 4 changing beers (often Lincoln Green) Ⓗ
A 17th-century rural gem, reputedly haunted, with a lounge/dining space, a small snug hidden behind the bar and an unusual area with a grandfather clock. The internal fittings around the bar are original, and photographs of locals adorn the walls. The extensive garden has children's play equipment and a marquee, making the pub particularly popular in summer. Home-cooked English food is served all day. Occasional beer festivals and live music feature.
Q ☆ ☺ ◑ & P ⊟ ❀ ☜

Wellow

Olde Red Lion ⒧
Eakring Road, NG22 0EG (opp maypole on village green)
✿ 12-11 ☎ (01623) 861000
Wells Bombardier; 2 changing beers Ⓗ
This 400-year-old pub participates in a large event on May Day. The traditional wood-beamed interior includes a restaurant, lounge and bar areas, with photographs and maps depicting the history of the village. Three real ales are available – Wells Bombardier and two rotating guest beers, usually LocAles. The food is good value and recommended. An annual beer festival is hosted. Close to Sherwood Forest and Clumber Park.
Q ☆ ☺ ◑ ♣ P ⊟

West Bridgford

Poppy & Pint ⛻ ⒧
Pierrepont Road, NG2 5DX
✿ 9.30am-11; 10-11 Sun ☎ (0115) 981 9995
Castle Rock Sheriff's Tipple, Harvest Pale, Preservation Fine Ale, Screech Owl; 8 changing beers Ⓗ
Former British Legion Club converted in 2011 to become a Castle Rock pub and café. It has a large main bar with a raised area and a family area with a café bar (children welcome until 9pm). A large upstairs function room features a folk club and the beer garden overlooks a bowling green. Twelve handpumps dispense Castle Rock beers plus guests, often from new breweries. There are usually two real ciders and excellent food is served.
☆ ☺ ◑ & ● P ⊟ ❀ ☜

Stratford Haven ⒧
2 Stratford Road, NG2 6BA
✿ 11-11 (midnight Thu & Fri); 10-midnight Sat; 10-11 Sun ☎ (0115) 982 5981
Adnams Broadside; Batemans XB; Castle Rock Harvest Pale, Elsie Mo, Screech Owl; 5 changing beers Ⓗ
A former pet shop, the pub has a single narrow bar with a larger seating area at the back and a secluded snug to one side. Up to 12 cask ales plus a cider are available at any one time, including LocAles from owner Castle Rock's portfolio. A wide food selection includes curry night on Monday and

pie night on Tuesday. Sunday is silent quiz night and new brew day is the first Thursday of the month. Q ☆ ☺ ◑ & ♣ ● P ⊟ ❀ ☜

West Stockwith

White Hart ⒧
Main Street, DN10 4EY (opp church)
✿ 11-11 ☎ (01427) 892672
4 changing beers (sourced locally; often Idle)
Small country pub close to the River Trent, Chesterfield Canal and West Stockwith Marina. One bar serves the open-plan bar, lounge and dining area. The Idle Brewery is situated in outbuildings at the side of the pub and four or five real ales are available, usually from Idle. The area is especially busy during the summer, due to the canal and river traffic. ☆ ☺ ◑ ▲ ♣ ● P ⊟ (97) ❀

Worksop

Mallard ⛻ ⒧
Station Approach, S81 7AG (just off railway platform)
✿ 12 (5 Mon; 4.15 Tue & Thu)-11; 11-11 Fri & Sat; 12-10.30 Sun ☎ 07973 521824
4 changing beers (often Double Top) Ⓗ
Formerly the Worksop station buffet, access is from the car park. The small, cosy pub offers a warm welcome. Four real ales are available – usually including a dark beer and one from the Double Top Brewery – plus two ciders, a selection of foreign bottled beers and country fruit wines. There is a room downstairs used for special occasions including four beer festivals each year. Current local CAMRA Pub of the Year. Q ☆ ⇌ ♣ ● P ⊟ ❀

Station Hotel ⒧
Carlton Road, S80 1PS (opp railway station)
✿ 11-11; 12-11 Sun ☎ (01909) 474108
⊕ thestationhotelworksop.co.uk
4 changing beers Ⓗ
On the edge of the town centre, the long bar serves a lounge drinking area with a separate dining room attached, and there is a further small room suitable for meetings. A spacious and well-maintained garden with seating is to the rear. Four regularly changing real ales are available, with a discount scheme for regulars. Food is served lunchtimes and evenings and accommodation is offered. Q ☆ ⇦ ◑ ⇌ ♣ ● P ⊟ ⊟ (5) ❀ ☜

Unicorn ⒧
37 Bridge Street, S80 1DA (opp Queen's Head)
✿ 10-11.30 (1am Sat); 12-11.30 Sun ☎ (01909) 478769
3 changing beers (sourced regionally) Ⓗ
An impressive building in the pedestrian area of the town centre, refurbished several years ago in a traditional style. The pub has three handpulled beers, often from local breweries, and one real cider. A large number of TV screens show all the major sports. A wide range of drinks is available, offering good value for money, served by efficient and friendly staff. & ♣ ● ⊟ ❀ ☜

Epitaph

She drank good ale, good punch and wine,
And lived to the age of ninety-nine.

Epitaph to Rebecca Freeland (1741) at Edwalton, Notts.

OXFORDSHIRE

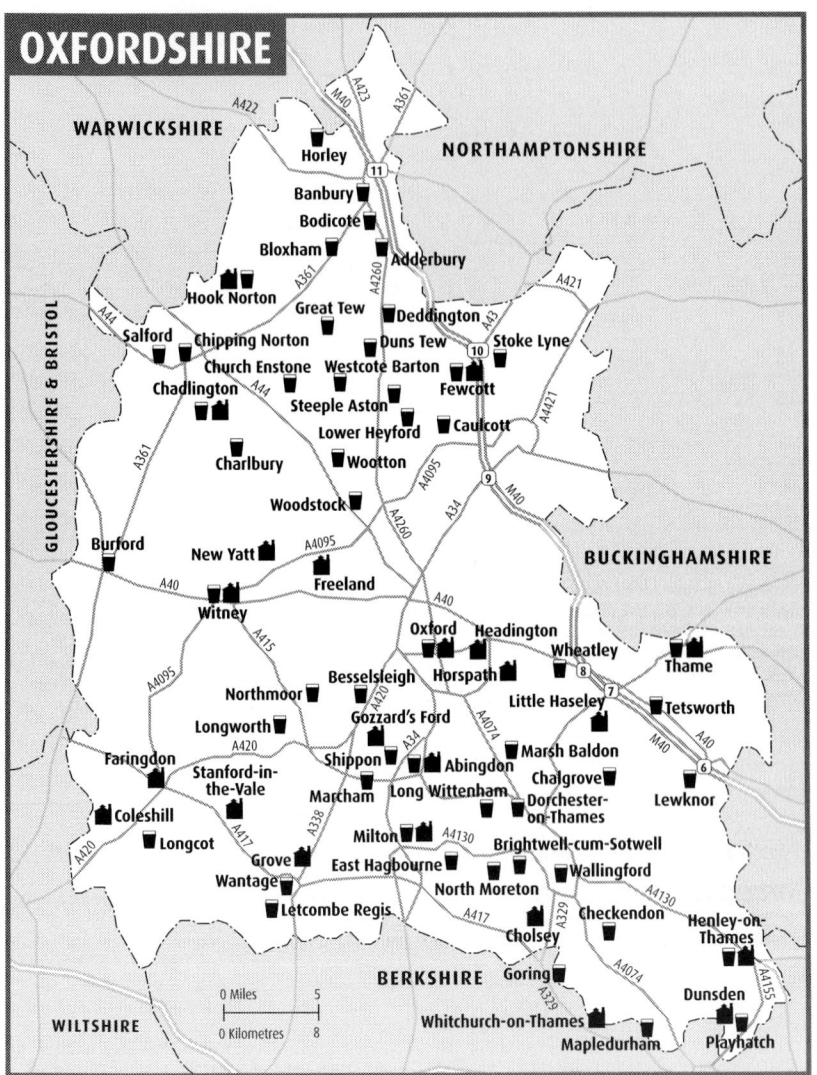

WARWICKSHIRE

NORTHAMPTONSHIRE

Horley

Banbury

Bodicote

Bloxham

Adderbury

Hook Norton

Great Tew

Deddington

Salford

Chipping Norton

Duns Tew

Stoke Lyne

Church Enstone

Westcote Barton

Fewcott

Chadlington

Steeple Aston

Lower Heyford

Caulcott

Charlbury

Wootton

Woodstock

Burford

New Yatt

Freeland

Witney

Oxford

Headington

Wheatley

Thame

Besselsleigh

Horspath

Northmoor

Little Haseley

Tetsworth

Longworth

Gozzard's Ford

Faringdon

Shippon

Abingdon

Marsh Baldon

Stanford-in-the-Vale

Marcham

Long Wittenham

Chalgrove

Dorchester-on-Thames

Lewknor

Coleshill

Milton

Brightwell-cum-Sotwell

Longcot

Grove

East Hagbourne

Wallingford

Wantage

North Moreton

Checkendon

Henley-on-Thames

Letcombe Regis

Cholsey

Goring

Dunsden

BERKSHIRE

Whitchurch-on-Thames

Playhatch

WILTSHIRE

Mapledurham

GLOUCESTERSHIRE & BRISTOL

BUCKINGHAMSHIRE

0 Miles 5

0 Kilometres 8

Abingdon

Brewery Tap ⓛ

40-42 Ock Street, OX14 5BZ

🕐 11-11.30 (1am Fri & Sat); 12-11 Sun ☎ (01235) 521655
🌐 thebrewerytap.net

Morland Original Bitter; 5 changing beers (sourced nationally; often Loose Cannon) Ⓗ

Morland created a tap for its brewery in 1993 from three Grade II-listed town houses. The brewery is no more but the award-winning pub, run by the same family since it opened, has thrived. It has always offered a diverse beer range and this is set to stay, with one or more Loose Cannon Brewery beers among the range. Three beer festivals are hosted each year. The pub has three rooms, two of them away from the bar, and a courtyard outside. It is the headquarters for the Abingdon Traditional Morris Men. Accommodation is available in three en-suite rooms. Q🌞🐾🛏️🕘👌♣👜🅿️�🌞📶

Nag's Head on the Thames ⓛ ✔

The Bridge, OX14 3HX

🕐 12-10; 11-11 Sat & Sun ☎ (01235) 524516
🌐 thenagsheadonthethames.co.uk

Loddon Ferryman's Gold; White Horse Oxford Dark Blue; house beer (by Caledonian); 5 changing beers (sourced regionally; often Plain, Shotover, XT) Ⓗ

Set on an island right on Abingdon Bridge, this Grade II-listed pub is split over two levels with a large garden area next to the River Thames and lovely views of the countryside and the town's historic buildings. A free house, it offers eight regularly changing beers, mostly local, including the house beer Nag's Island Pale Ale (4.3% ABV). Bar meals and an à la carte menu are available. Live music plays at weekends and some weekdays. Salter's Steamer cruises from Oxford pass by in the summer. A three-times local CAMRA branch Town and Village Pub of the Year. 🌞🐾🕘👜🅿️🚐🌞📶

Narrows 🄻 ✅
25 High Street, OX14 5AA
⊕ 8am-midnight (1am Fri & Sat) ☎ (01235) 467680
Greene King Abbot; Ruddles Best Bitter; 8 changing beers (sourced nationally) 🄷
Wetherspoon converted the former post office in 2013. The pub is named after this part of the High Street which during the 19th century was called the Narrow. The area at the front of the pub has a long bar with 10 handpumps offering an impressive range of real ales, some from local breweries. To the rear, the former sorting office and telephone exchange provides more space for drinkers and diners. Abingdon's was the last manual telephone exchange in England when it closed in 1975. ❀◖◗🦽🖵🛜

Adderbury

Bell Inn 🄻
High Street, OX17 3LS (off A4260 in centre of village)
⊕ 12-3, 6-11; 12-midnight Fri & Sat; 12-10.30 Sun
☎ (01295) 810338 ⊕ thebelladderbury.co.uk
Hook Norton Hooky Mild, Hooky, Hooky Gold, Old Hooky; 2 changing beers (sourced locally; often Hook Norton) 🄷
Established village pub at the heart of the community and the flagship of the Hook Norton estate. The landlord's cellar skills ensure that six handpumps dispense the full Hooky range superbly. Home-cooked food and two bedrooms make the Bell a good base for exploration of this attractive ironstone village and its environs as well as the quirky local traditions of Aunt Sally and morris dancing. Muddy boots, dogs, even folk singers, are all welcome.
Q❀🛏◖◗🦽🅰🌳🖵(S4)🐾🛜

Banbury

White Horse 🄻
50-52 North Bar Street, OX16 0TH
⊕ 2-10.30 Mon; 12-11 Tue-Thu; 12-midnight Fri & Sat; 12-10.30 Sun ☎ (01295) 277484
⊕ thewhitehorsebanbury.co.uk
Everards Ascalon; Turpin Golden Citrus; 8 changing beers (sourced nationally; often Charnwood, Cornish Crown, Derby) 🄷
A warm and welcoming ale house in an imposing building in the heart of Banbury. The White Horse keeps an extensive range of up to 10 ales and a couple of ciders on its large L-shaped bar. Home-made dishes based on locally sourced ingredients are freshly cooked to order. There is a courtyard area to the rear for alfresco drinking and dining. Regular events such as live music and a weekly pub quiz are organised. Q🛏❀◖◗🦽🛜🌳🖵🐾🛜

Besselsleigh

Greyhound 🄻
OX13 5PX
⊕ 11.30-11; 11.30-10.30 Sun ☎ (01865) 862110
⊕ greyhound-besselsleigh.co.uk
Loose Cannon Gunners Gold; North Cotswold Windrush Ale; Timothy Taylor Landlord; 3 changing beers (sourced regionally; often Three Castles) 🄷
The pub is about 400 years old and was formerly a coaching inn on one of the major turnpike roads from Oxford to the West Country. At one time a blacksmith's forge was attached to the building. Six real ales are on handpump including three

regularly changing guests, and an extensive food menu is offered. This popular pub-restaurant is now run by the Brunning & Price pub company.
Q🛏❀◖◗🦽🖵🖵(66)🐾🛜

Bloxham

Red Lion
High Street, OX15 4LX
⊕ closed Mon; 11-11; 11-5 Sun ☎ (01295) 722067
⊕ redlionbloxham.com
House beer (by Marston's); 1 changing beer (sourced nationally; often Jennings, Ringwood, Thwaites) 🄷
Rescued in 2016 from a pubco trying to sell the building for development, this externally unremarkable brick pub in a village of mainly ironstone cottages has had a full internal makeover, turning it into a contemporary, welcoming space. The operation is unashamedly food-led, but drinkers are not forgotten, with comfy bar stools to perch on and two handpumps dispensing well-kept ales from the Marston's stable. Families and dogs are welcome and there is a deck and large garden to the rear with a children's play area.
Q🛏❀◖◗🦽♣🖵🖵(488,489)🐾🛜

Bodicote

Plough Inn ✅
9 High Street, OX15 4BZ
⊕ 12-11.30 (midnight Fri & Sat) ☎ (01295) 258909
Wadworth IPA, 6X; 2 changing beers (sourced nationally; often Wadworth) 🄷
The Plough is returning to its rightful place in village life. A prominent corner building on the main street, the front entrance lobby has a traditional, but disused, jug and bottle off-sales hatch, with a comfortable bar to the right and the dining area to the left. Outside is an award-winning beer garden. On the bar two regular ales can be found alongside a seasonal from Wadworth, and guest ales make an occasional appearance.
🛏❀◖◗♣🖵(B2)🐾🛜

REAL ALE BREWERIES

Amwell Spring Cholsey (NEW)
Barn Owl Gozzards Ford
Bell Street 🍺 Henley-on-Thames
Bellinger's Grove
Brakspear Witney
Chadlington Chadlington
Church Hanbrewery New Yatt
Faringdon 🍺 Faringdon (brewing suspended)
Hen House Whitchurch-on-Thames
Hook Norton Hook Norton
Little Ox Freeland (NEW)
Loddon Dunsden
Loose Cannon Abingdon
LoveBeer Milton
Old Bog 🍺 Headington
Old Forge 🍺 Coleshill
Philsters Little Haseley
Pirate 🍺 Fewcott (NEW)
Shotover Horspath
Tap Social Movement Oxford (NEW)
Thame 🍺 Thame
Turpin Hook Norton
White Horse Stanford-in-the-Vale
Wychwood Witney

Brightwell-cum-Sotwell

Red Lion 🅻

Brightwell Street, OX10 0RT (off A4130)

🕔 12-3, 6-11; 12-9 Sun ☎ (01491) 837373 ⊕ redlion.biz

Loddon Hoppit; West Berkshire Good Old Boy; 2 changing beers (sourced nationally) Ⓗ

A popular traditional thatched inn dating from the 16th century in a quiet village. It has a comfortable bar featuring exposed beams and brick, with a restaurant area to one side. The rear courtyard garden is a summer suntrap. The beers and ciders are usually from local breweries, and good-quality reasonably priced pub food is served (no food Mon and Sun eve). Jazz evenings and charity quiz nights are held monthly. Local CAMRA Cider Pub of the Year 2016. ॐ😋🕒🌓🕁🌑🕒₽🖵(X2)🌸🛜

Burford

Golden Pheasant

91 High Street, OX18 4QA

🕔 10-11 ☎ (01993) 823223 ⊕ goldenpheasantburford.com

4 changing beers (sourced nationally) Ⓗ

Hotel on Burford High Street with an impressive Georgian-style frontage built on a 16th-century frame. Through the front door to the right is a well-lit bar dispensing at least four real ales and a cider. To the other side is the dining area serving an interesting selection of food to satisfy all tastes. At the rear is a garden for alfresco dining and drinking. Major sporting events are shown on large-screen TV. Q ॐ😋🕒🖾🕒🕁🌑🕒₽(233,853)🌸🛜

Caulcott

Horse & Groom

Lower Heyford Road, OX25 4ND

🕔 closed Mon; 12-3, 6-11; 12-3, 7-10.30 Sun

☎ (01869) 343257 ⊕ horseandgroomcaulcott.co.uk

Black Sheep Best Bitter; 3 changing beers (sourced nationally; often Tring, Vale) Ⓗ

Charming 16th-century coaching house, warm and cosy with a welcoming open fire in winter. Black Sheep Best Bitter is on handpump plus three changing guests, often from Tring, Vale or a Cornish brewer. The French landlord and chef serves excellent food based on local fresh seasonal produce, with highlights including Thursday steak night, Sunday lunch and themed French evenings (booking recommended). A Bastille Day beer festival weekend is hosted annually. The garden is popular in summer. No dogs permitted inside. Q ॐ😋🕒🌓₽🛜

Chadlington

Tite Inn

Mill End, OX7 3NY

🕔 11.30-11; 11.30-10.30 Sun ☎ (01608) 676910 ⊕ thetiteinn.co.uk

Sharp's Doom Bar; 2 changing beers (sourced nationally; often Chadlington, Cotswold Lion, Sharp's) Ⓗ

Cosy, welcoming country pub in the picturesque Evenlode Valley with one regular and two ever-changing guest ales along with a Westons cider on handpump. Tite is old local dialect for spring – water runs under the pub and down the hill to where the famous Great Brook Run takes place in December. Good-quality, reasonably priced meals are served in the comfortable bar and restaurant.

Outside, the beautiful hillside garden is an idyllic place for an alfresco pint. Q ॐ😋🕒🌓🅰🌑₽🖵(S3,X9)🌸🛜

Chalgrove

Red Lion 🅻

115 High Street, OX44 7SS

🕔 11-3, 6-midnight (1.30am Fri & Sat); 12-11 Sun

☎ (01865) 890625 ⊕ redlionchalgrove.com

Butcombe Original; Fuller's London Pride; 2 changing beers (sourced nationally; often Adnams, Rebellion, West Berkshire) Ⓗ

Church-owned village local, run by a friendly husband and wife team, both trained chefs. Good food is a speciality at this picturesque 16th-century inn. The interior is divided into several distinct areas and the pub is used by a wide cross-section of the community. The two guest beers are usually from small breweries. You can drink outside in both front and rear gardens, while a real fire awaits inside in the winter months. Real Hitchcox cider in bottles is usually available during the summer. Q ॐ😋🕒🌓🕁🌑₽🖵(T1)🌸🛜

Charlbury

Rose & Crown ⊘

Market Street, OX7 3PL

🕔 12-11 (1am Fri); 11-1am Sat ☎ (01608) 810103 ⊕ roseandcrown.charlbury.com

Ramsbury Bitter; 7 changing beers (sourced nationally; often Dark Star, Kelham Island, Salopian) Ⓗ

This popular, traditional, wet-sales-only alehouse has featured in the Guide for 31 years and continues to offer one of the best selections in the area. Eight handpumps serve Ramsbury Bitter and seven ever-changing ales along with six traditional ciders and perries. Vale, Oakham, XT, Turpin and Wye Valley breweries are regularly showcased as well as new and established breweries across the UK. Free live music is hosted fortnightly and an annual beer festival each January. Real ale is £2.50 a pint on Monday. ॐ😋🅰🌣🌑₽🖵(S3,X9)🌸🛜

Checkendon

Highwayman 🅻

Exlade Street, RG8 0UA

🕔 closed Mon; 12-3, 6-11; 12-3 Sun ☎ (01491) 682020 ⊕ thehighwaymaninn-checkendon.co.uk

Fuller's London Pride; Loddon Hoppit; West Berkshire Good Old Boy Ⓗ

The original building dates from 1625 but the pub now has a contemporary feel, with most of the internal rooms dedicated to dining. However, the landlord is keen that the Highwayman is regarded as a pub with dining rooms attached, and a bar and drinking area with woodburner, beams and exposed brickwork has been retained. There are three ales on handpump, two selected from local microbreweries, one always from Loddon – usually Hoppit - and the other two may occasionally be seasonal beers. Q ॐ😋🕒🌓🕁🌑₽🌸🛜

Chipping Norton

Crown & Cushion

23 High Street, OX7 5AD

🕔 11-11 ☎ (01608) 642533 ⊕ crown-cushion.co.uk

Draught Bass; Hook Norton Hooky Ⓗ

Formerly a coaching inn dating from the 15th century, the Crown & Cushion is now a 40-bedroom hotel, once owned by Keith Moon, legendary drummer of The Who. The bar room has tables for dining and there is a separate restaurant where you can enjoy a popular Sunday carvery. The small courtyard garden leads to the car park and heated indoor swimming pool, gym and squash court (enquire at reception). The TV is for major sporting events only. Q ☆ ⊛ ✍ ◑ P ☐ ✿ ✈

Church Enstone

Crown Inn 🄻

Mill Lane, OX7 4NN (off A44, on B4030)
🕐 12-3, 6-11; 12-4 Sun ☎ (01608) 677262
⊕ crowninnenstone.co.uk
Hook Norton Hooky; 2 changing beers (sourced nationally) Ⓗ
Seventeenth-century Cotswold stone pub set back off the road, featuring an inglenook fireplace and wooden beams. Popular with locals and visitors alike, it is ideal for a drink after a walk. Two guest ales change regularly, with one on the stronger side. Food is locally sourced and popular, with booking recommended for busier days. A pub for conversation, there is no jukebox, gaming machines or TV. Families and well-behaved dogs are welcome in this Cotswold gem.
Q ☆ ⊛ ◑ P ☐ (S3) ✿

Deddington

Deddington Arms

Horse Fair, OX15 0SH
🕐 12-11 ☎ (01869) 338364 ⊕ deddington-arms-hotel.co.uk
Adnams Southwold Bitter; Butcombe Adam Henson's Rare Breed; Hook Norton Hooky; 1 changing beer (sourced nationally) Ⓗ
Just off the A4260, this privately owned fully refurbished 16th-century hotel faces a charming village marketplace. Four handpumps dispense three regular and a monthly changing guest ale in a cosy bar area with a real fire in winter. With full hotel facilities including 27 en-suite bedrooms and an award-winning restaurant, this is an ideal base to explore the tourist attractions of north Oxfordshire. Alternatively, just watch the world go by from the outside seating area in summer.
☆ ⊛ ✍ ◑ & P ☐ (S4) ✈

Dorchester-on-Thames

George Hotel

25 High Street, OX10 7HH (opp Dorchester Abbey church lychgate)
🕐 11-midnight ☎ (01865) 340404
⊕ georgehoteloxfordshire.co.uk
Brakspear Bitter; Sharp's Doom Bar; Wadworth 6X; 1 changing beer (sourced locally; often Loose Cannon, West Berkshire) Ⓗ
Built in 1495, this coaching inn is one of the oldest in the country. The friendly locals' front bar, lounge and restaurant are complete with oak beams and inglenook fireplaces throughout. The landlord is passionate about serving real ale in perfect condition. Three regular and one guest ale are always available and are discounted by 65p per pint 5-7pm every day. Q ☆ ⊛ ✍ ◑ P ☐ ✈

Duns Tew

White Horse Inn

Daisy Hill, OX25 6JS
🕐 10-11; 10-10.30 Sun ☎ (01869) 340272
⊕ dunstewwhitehorse.co.uk
3 changing beers (sourced nationally) Ⓗ
A traditional 17th-century Hornton stone inn at the heart of the village. The landlord, a keen supporter of real ale, makes imaginative use of the Greene King guest beer list, with three ever-changing beers, usually under 4.5% ABV. Food is served daily with breakfast bookable in advance, and a village night is hosted once a month. A pleasant outdoor drinking area is well used in good weather. There is wheelchair access from the car park to the rear of the building. Eleven en-suite letting rooms are available. ⊛ ✍ ◑ & P ☐ ✿ ✈

East Hagbourne

Fleur de Lys ⛾

30 Main Road, OX11 9LN
🕐 11.30-2.30, 6-11 (10 Mon); 11.30-11 Fri & Sat; 12-10 Sun
☎ (01235) 813247 ⊕ thefleurdelyspub.co.uk
Morland Original Bitter; 3 changing beers (sourced nationally; often Morland) Ⓗ
The Fleur de Lys is a family- and dog-friendly 17th-century inn in the rural village of East Hagbourne. The Greene King tied pub offers two regular beers from Morland and two nationally sourced guests. The large bar and dining area are comfortable and cosy, warmed by a large open fire. Live music evenings feature regularly. Outside is an extensive decked area with a separate beer garden where Aunt Sally is played. No food on Monday or Sunday evenings. Local CAMRA Pub of the Year 2017.
☆ ⊛ ◑ & ♣ ♦ P ☐ (94,94A) ✿ ✈

Fewcott

White Lion 🄻

Fritwell Road, OX27 7NZ
🕐 11-2 (not Mon-Wed), 4-11; 11-2, 4-midnight Fri; 12-midnight Sat; 12-9 Sun ☎ (01869) 346676
⊕ ardleywithfewcottvillagehall.com/
the-white-lion-fewcott.html
3 changing beers (sourced nationally; often Black Sheep, Wadworth) Ⓗ
A true free house, family-friendly and the hub of the community, with its own microbrewery, the Pirate Brewery. It serves three constantly changing ales plus four changing real ciders, and also features up to two dozen gins. Sport is shown on two TVs. The large garden with a play pirate ship is popular in summer, and Aunt Sally is played here. A cider and pirate festival is held over the August bank holiday weekend. Local CAMRA Cider Pub of the Year 2016. ☆ ⊛ & ♣ ♦ P ☐ (81) ✿ ✈

Goring

Miller of Mansfield 🄻 ✓

High Street, RG8 9AW (on B4009)
🕐 12-11; 12-10.30 Sun ☎ (01491) 872829
⊕ millerofmansfield.com
West Berkshire Good Old Boy; 1 changing beer (sourced nationally) Ⓗ
Immensely improved since it was taken over by new owners in 2014, the Miller, a former 18th-century coaching inn, continues to impress with the quality of its beer and its friendly ambience. The

The attractive bar, overlooking the village memorial gardens, has a mixture of seating including comfy fireside armchairs. Top-quality food is served both in the bar and the award-winning restaurant. There is a courtyard area for outside drinking. Thirteen luxury rooms are available. Q ♿ ✿ ⚐ ◑ ➧ ⟌ (133,134,135)✿ 🐾 🛜

Great Tew

Falkland Arms ✅
19-21 The Green, OX7 4DB
✿ 8am-11; 9am-10.30 Sun ☎ (01608) 683653
⊕ falklandarms.co.uk
Wadworth IPA, Horizon, 6X, Bishop's Tipple, Swordfish; 2 changing beers (sourced nationally) Ⓗ
A quintessential 16th-century English country pub with flagstone and bare-board floors, simple wooden furniture and an array of jugs hanging from the ancient beams. Breweriana adorn the walls and a large inglenook fireplace warms you in winter. There are eight handpumps with five regular ales, two guests and a cider. Accommodation and food are available, including breakfast for non-residents. Outside is the beer garden overlooking the picturesque thatched Great Tew estate. Q ♿ ✿ ⚐ ◑ 🍴 P ⟌ (5)✿ 🛜

Henley-on-Thames

Bird in Hand
61 Greys Road, RG9 1SB
✿ 12-2, 5-11; 12-11 Sat; 12-10.30 Sun ☎ (01491) 575775
⊕ henleybirdinhand.co.uk
Brakspear Bitter; Fuller's London Pride; Hook Norton Hooky Mild; 2 changing beers (sourced locally; often Loddon, Rebellion, West Berkshire) Ⓗ
A Guide regular for over 20 years, the Bird has flourished under the stewardship of the same family throughout. Two ever-changing guest beers complement three regulars. The pub is home to darts and cribbage teams, and hosts regular quiz nights. The family room leads to a delightful garden featuring a pond and aviary. TVs show sporting events, hot and cold snacks are available all day, and dogs on leads are welcome. A frequent winner of local CAMRA Pub of the Year. Q ♿ ✿ A ➧ 🍴 ⟌ ✿ 🛜

Hook Norton

Pear Tree Inn ⓛ ✅
Scotland End, OX15 5NU
✿ 11-11 (midnight Fri & Sat); 12-11 Sun ☎ (01608) 737482
⊕ thepeartreehooky.com
Hook Norton Hooky Mild, Hooky, Hooky Gold, Old Hooky; 2 changing beers (sourced locally; often Hook Norton) Ⓗ
A warm welcome awaits at this beamed bar, the brewery tap for Hook Norton's nearby Grade II-listed Victorian tower brewery. There are always six Hook Norton ales available, delivered by horse and dray. A large child-friendly beer garden is ideal for summer drinking, with Aunt Sally played here in the summer (and featured on Penelope Keith's Hidden Villages). Three en-suite letting rooms make it the ideal base for exploring the area. Closed weekday afternoons January to Easter. Q ♿ ✿ ⚐ ◑ & A 🍴 🚲 P ⟌ (488)✿ 🛜

Horley

Red Lion ♈ ⓛ
Hornton Lane, OX15 6BQ
✿ closed Mon; 6-11; 12-6 Sun ☎ (01295) 730427
Hook Norton Hooky; Purity Pure UBU; Sharp's Doom Bar Ⓗ
This traditional village wet-sales-only pub is the focal point of the community, offering a friendly welcome to visitors including walkers and dogs. The garden provides a tranquil area for a summer evening's tipple. Three handpumped ales are served – four on special occasions. The annual beer festival for St George's Day has become a must, attracting locals and visitors alike. Darts and dominoes are played, with a TV showing live sporting events. Local CAMRA Pub of the Year 2017. ✿ 🚲 🍴 ✿ 🛜

Letcombe Regis

Greyhound Inn ⓛ
Main Street, OX12 9JL
✿ 11-11; 11.30-10.30 Sun ☎ (01235) 771969
⊕ thegreyhoundletcombe.co.uk
4 changing beers (sourced regionally; often Butts, Loose Cannon, Ringwood) Ⓗ
Large, welcoming pub in the centre of the village, recently refurbished to a high standard. Inside is a single bar with dining areas and a formerly hidden inglenook fireplace. The garden has been re-landscaped for outdoor dining during the summer months. Locally sourced home-cooked food and four constantly changing handpumped beers are served. Parking is available at the side of the pub, also provision for tethering horses. Eight boutique en-suite bedrooms are now open. Within a couple of miles of the Ridgeway, it provides a place of refreshment and rest for wayfarers. Q ♿ ✿ ⚐ ◑ & A 🍴 P ✿ 🛜

Lewknor

Leathern Bottle ✅
1 High Street, OX49 5TW (off B4009 near M40 jct 6)
✿ 11-2.30 (3 Sat), 5.30-11; 12-3, 7-10.30 Sun
☎ (01844) 351482 ⊕ theleathernbottle.co.uk
Brakspear Bitter; Marston's Pedigree; 1 changing beer (sourced nationally) Ⓗ
Classic 17th-century inn which has featured in all but one edition of the Guide. The place has a reputation for good home-cooked pub food including locally sourced meats, and also offers woodburners, a warm welcome and a family-friendly garden. The guest beer comes from the Brakspear pubco approved list. Popular with walkers from the nearby Ridgeway, it is a short walk from the Oxford Tube and the airline coach stop. Q ♿ ✿ ⚐ & 🍴 P ⟌ ✿ 🛜

Long Wittenham

Plough ⓛ
24 High Street, OX14 4QH
✿ 12-11 ☎ (01865) 407738 ⊕ theploughinnlw.co.uk
Butcombe Original; 2 changing beers (sourced regionally; often Loose Cannon, West Berkshire) Ⓗ
The Plough is Grade II-listed and dates back to the 17th century – you may need to duck when you enter the bar to avoid the wooden beams overhead. There are two cosy bars and a restaurant. Beyond the children's play area, the

long garden stretches down to the River Thames – a delightful place in summer. Changing guest ales are sourced from breweries and microbreweries in the South-east. On weekdays 5-7pm there is 30p off a pint. ⮑✿🍴◐🅰♣🅿🐾🛜

Longcot

King & Queen 🅛
Shrivenham Road, SN7 7TL
✿ 12-2 (not Mon), 5-11; 12-2.30, 5-11 Sat; 12-2.30, 5-10.30 Sun ☎ (01793) 784348 ⊕ longcotkingandqueen.com
Loose Cannon Gunners Gold; 2 changing beers (sourced nationally; often Oakham, Ramsbury, XT) 🅗
This pub enjoys one of the best views of White Horse Hill and its famous 3,000-year-old Uffington horse figure cut into the chalk. The interior comprises an extensive, open-plan drinking area and to one side a restaurant serving organic meat and local produce. The bar offers a good selection of beers from local breweries and two ciders on handpump. Q⮑✿🍴◐🅰♣🅿🚃(66)🐾🛜

Longworth

Blue Boar 🅛
Tucks Lane, OX13 5ET
✿ 12-11 ☎ (01865) 820494 ⊕ blueboarlongworth.co.uk
Brakspear Bitter; Otter Ale 🅗
Pretty wisteria-covered thatched village pub with the original tiled floor and wooden beams, and three real fires. An unusual collection of historic skis decorates the ceiling, and there are hop flowers in abundance, plus cricket, boxing and rugby memorabilia. Furniture includes large wooden tables and church pews. An excellent choice of home-cooked food is served and there is an extensive wine list. Vibrant and busy at times, the pub can also be a place for a quiet pint and a good meal. ⮑✿◐🅿🚃(T01)🐾🛜

Lower Heyford

Bell Inn
21 Market Square, OX25 5NY
✿ 12-3, 5-11; 12-11 Fri-Sun ☎ (01869) 347176
Salopian Shropshire Gold; 1 changing beer (sourced nationally) 🅗
Large multi-roomed pub in the centre of the village close to the railway and Oxford Canal. Salopian beers are regulars here, with Darwin's Origin often on the bar. There is always a choice of two ales as well as two real ciders or perries. A beer festival is held at the end of the summer. Regular live music nights showcase local bands. The large garden, where Aunt Sally is played, has a covered smoking area and is popular in summer. ✿◐🚭♣🅿🚃(25A)🐾🛜

Mapledurham

Packhorse 🅛
Woodcote Road, RG4 7UG (on A4074)
✿ 11.30-11; 11.30-10.30 Sun ☎ (0118) 972 2140
Loddon Hoppit; 4 changing beers (sourced nationally; often West Berkshire) 🅗
Originally a farm on the Mapledurham House estate dating from the 1600s, this Brunning & Price establishment is now a cosy pub and restaurant. The low-beamed bar has ample seating for drinkers and usually features local microbrewery beers. The larger restaurant area is furnished with

bookcases and numerous prints and has a wide-ranging good-value menu. A large secluded garden at the rear has a shaded seating area overlooking fields. There is 60p off a pint 5-7pm weekdays. Meet the Brewer evenings are proving popular. Q⮑✿◐&♣🅿🚃(X39,X40)🐾🛜

Marcham

Crown
1 Packhorse Lane, OX13 6NT
✿ 12 (5 Mon)-11; 12-midnight Fri & Sat; 12-10.30 Sun ☎ (01865) 391735 ⊕ thecrownmarcham.co.uk
Loose Cannon Abingdon Bridge; Sharp's Doom Bar; Wells Bombardier; 3 changing beers (sourced nationally) 🅗
Traditional friendly village local with a lively public bar and a cosy dining room with its own bar, owned by Admiral Taverns and recently refurbished. Additional handpumps have been fitted and now three regular beers and three changing guests are usually available. The pub was designated a Grade II-listed building in 1987. Marcham is home to Denman College, headquarters of the WI. ⮑✿◐♣🅿🚃(31,15)🐾🛜

Marsh Baldon

Seven Stars on the Green 🍺 🅛
The Green, OX44 9LP
✿ 12-11 (midnight Fri & Sat); 12-10 Sun ☎ (01865) 343337 ⊕ sevenstarsonthegreen.co.uk
Fuller's London Pride; 3 changing beers (sourced locally; often Loddon, Shotover, White Horse) 🅗
This 400-year-old coaching inn reopened as a community owned pub in 2013 with a refurbished main bar and a new function room/restaurant. It sits next to a village green that claims to be the largest in Europe and has a big garden for the summer. Three local ales are always available and food is served all day including extensive gluten-free options. Dogs, wellies and muddy boots all welcome. Local CAMRA Pub of the Year 2017. Q⮑✿◐&🅿🐾🛜

Milton

Plum Pudding 🅛
44 High Street, OX14 4EJ
✿ 11.30-2.30, 5-11; 11.30-11.30 Fri & Sat; 12-10 Sun ☎ (01235) 834443 ⊕ theplumpuddingmilton.co.uk
Loose Cannon Abingdon Bridge; house beer (by Ringwood); 2 changing beers (sourced nationally) 🅗
Plum Pudding refers to the Oxford Sandy and Black pig, one of the older and rarer British breeds, which features on the menu. Sitting in the pleasant walled garden, you wouldn't know it, but it is only a couple of minutes from the busy A34 and close to the thriving Milton Business Park. Regular live music is hosted, and two beer festivals each year. Local CAMRA Pub of the Year 2015. ⮑✿◐♣🅿🚃🐾🛜

North Moreton

Bear at Home 🅛
High Street, OX11 9AT (off A4130)
✿ 12-3, 6-11; 12-11 Sat; 12-10 (4 winter) Sun ☎ (01235) 811311 ⊕ bear-at-home.co.uk
Timothy Taylor Landlord; house beer (by West Berkshire); 2 changing beers (sourced locally) 🅗

Friendly village local dating back to the 15th century with an open fire and plenty of tables for diners to enjoy the excellent pub food. Two regular beers – Landlord and Bear Beer (4% ABV), brewed exclusively for the pub by West Berkshire – are complemented by two changing guests. The Bear adjoins the village cricket ground and a popular four-day beer and cricket festival is held at the end of July. ⚞🐕😄🌙⚟ ▲♣︎P🖵(94A)🐾🔊 ☕

Northmoor

Red Lion 🅛 ✅
Standlake Road, OX29 5SX
🍺 closed Mon; 12-3, 5.30-11; 11-11 Sat; 12-4 Sun
☎ (01865) 300301 🌐 theredlionnorthmoor.com
Brakspear Bitter; Wychwood Hobgoblin; 2 changing beers (sourced locally; often Hook Norton, Loose Cannon, Vale) 🖻
Traditional village inn with whitewashed stone walls, heavy oak beams, real fires and a large garden. Purchased by the local community from Greene King in 2014, the pub has gone from strength to strength ever since. The focus is on local produce, with a changing menu of home-cooked food, some of which is grown in the pub's kitchen garden. A selection of four local beers is available in the small bar, alongside locally made soft drinks from Samuelsons of Witney.
Q⚞🐕😄🌙⚟♣︎P🖵(18)🐾 ☕

Oxford

Chequers 🅛 ✅
130A High Street, OX1 4DH (down a narrow medieval passageway off High St)
🍺 11-11 (11.30 Fri & Sat); 11-10.30 Sun ☎ (01865) 727463
Brakspear Bitter; Hook Norton Hooky; St Austell Admiral's Ale; Sharp's Doom Bar; 6 changing beers (sourced nationally) 🖻
Grade II-listed, much of this pub dates back to the early 16th century when it was converted from a moneylender's tenement to a tavern, hence the name. Note the fine carvings, windows and the ceiling in the lower bar. Tasting notes are provided for all real ales including the many frequently changing guest beers, and interesting food is available. A cobbled courtyard provides alfresco drinking, dining and smoking spaces.
Q⚞🐕😄🌙⚿️⚞🔊🖵🐾 ☕

Chester 🅛
19 Chester Street, OX4 1SN
🍺 12 (5 Mon)-11; 10-11 Fri & Sat; 12-10 Sun
☎ (01865) 790438 🌐 thechesteroxford.co.uk
5 changing beers (sourced regionally; often XT, Loose Cannon) 🖻
A trendy back-street pub off the Iffley Road, now opened out with boarded floors and powder blue painted walls. The stud copperwork bar front is of interest, as are the brass light fittings, but the star of the show is some original Halls stained and leaded glasswork on the entrance surrounds. There is a large patio garden to the rear. The real ales always include at least two from Loose Cannon. Opens early for breakfast on Friday and Saturday.
⚞🐕😄🌙⚿️♣︎P🖵🐾 ☕

Gardeners Arms 🅛
39 Plantation Road, OX2 6JE
🍺 12-2.30 (not Mon & Tue), 5-midnight; 12-11 Sun
☎ (01865) 559814 🌐 thegarden-oxford.co.uk

4 changing beers (sourced nationally; often Box Steam, Ringwood, XT) 🖻
Cosy pub down a narrow street off Woodstock Road. The small bar opens up to a spacious dining area, once two rooms, serving some of the finest vegetarian food in the city (with some vegan food available). At the rear is a large and pleasant garden, as well as the outside toilets. A popular and relaxing place to eat and drink. Weekly quiz night is Sunday. Q⚞🐕😄🌙⚟♣︎🔊🖵🐾

Lamb & Flag 🅛
12 St Giles, OX1 3JS
🍺 12-11; 12-10.30 Sun ☎ (01865) 515787
Palmers Best Bitter; Skinner's Betty Stogs; Theakston Old Peculier; house beer (by Palmers); 3 changing beers (sourced nationally; often Big Hand, Tring, XT) 🖻
Grade II-listed building owned by the adjacent St John's College. Some of the profits from the pub support student scholarships. This is a classic city pub with no music, Wi-Fi or other distractions from friendly conversation. Beers from the South-west feature – the house beer Lamb & Flag Gold (4.5% ABV) is brewed by Palmers of Bridport. It is believed to be the setting for the inn in Thomas Hardy's novel Jude the Obscure and has other literary links. Local CAMRA Pub of the Year 2016 and Cider Pub of the Year 2017. Q⚞🐕🌙⚟🔊🖵

Masons Arms 🅛 ✅
2 Quarry School Place, Headington Quarry, OX3 8LH
🍺 5 (7 Mon)-11; 12-11 Sat; 12-4, 7-10.30 Sun
☎ (01865) 764579 🌐 themasonsarmshq.co.uk
Dark Star Hophead; Rebellion Mutiny; Timothy Taylor Boltmaker; 2 changing beers (sourced nationally; often Loddon, Oakham, Old Bog) 🖻
Family-run community pub hosting many pub games' leagues, including bar billiards and Aunt Sally. The guest ales are varied and regularly come from the Old Bog Brewery (named after the original purpose of the building behind the pub where it was founded). A wide range of bottled beers is stocked. The pub is home to the Headington beer festival in September. A heated decking area and garden lead to the function room. Local CAMRA City Pub of the Year 2016.
⚞😄🌙♣︎🔊P🖵(H2)🐾 ☕

Old Bookbinders ✅
17-18 Victor Street, Jericho, OX2 6BT
🍺 closed Mon; 12-midnight; 12-11 Sun ☎ (01865) 553549
🌐 oldbookbinders.co.uk
Greene King IPA; Morland Original Bitter; house beer (by Greene King); 3 changing beers (sourced nationally; often Bath Ales, Brains, Timothy Taylor) 🖻
Back-street local near the Oxford Canal, rejuvenated by new licensees. This family-run pub offers three guest beers and home-cooked food made by the French landlord. Two rooms served by a single bar are furnished in alehouse style with an eclectic mix of furniture and bric-a-brac. Free monkey nuts are available from the barrel by the entrance. Take a shortcut along the canal to get here from the city centre or railway station.
Q⚞🐕🌙⚿️⚞♣︎🖵(17)🐾 ☕

Rose & Crown 🅛
14 North Parade Avenue, OX2 6LX (½ mile N of city centre, off Banbury Rd)
🍺 11-midnight (1am Fri & Sat) ☎ (01865) 510551
🌐 roseandcrownoxford.com

Adnams Southwold Bitter; Hook Norton Old Hooky; Shotover Scholar; 1 changing beer (sourced nationally) Ⓗ
Now a free house, this popular Victorian local on a vibrant north Oxford street is a time capsule with two small rooms and many original features. A friendly community pub, it has been run by the same landlords for over 30 years. No intrusive music or mobile phones are permitted. Its fame has even spread to Everest – see the photo on the wall. To the rear is a heated, covered patio. Children are welcome until 5pm. Q➤🕭🕭❶♣🖳🛜

Royal Blenheim Ⓛ
13 St Ebbes Street, OX1 1PT
🕭 11.30-11 (11.30 Wed & Thu; midnight Fri & Sat); 12-11 Sun
☎ (01865) 242355 ⊕ royalblenheim.co.uk
White Horse Bitter; Village Idiot, Wayland Smithy; 6 changing beers (sourced nationally; often Everards, Long Man, Titanic) Ⓗ
Street-corner, single-room, Victorian pub with a bright, airy interior, next to the Museum of Modern Art. Built in 1889 on the site of two earlier pubs, the original Royal Blenheim was a stagecoach. The pub is owned by Everards but leased to the White Horse Brewery. Ten handpumps dispense a range of White Horse beers, plus guests (including one from Everards) and a real cider. Good food and bar snacks, including vegetarian and gluten-free options, are served. ❶♿⇌♣🖳🛜

St Aldate's Tavern Ⓛ ✔
108 St Aldate's, OX1 1BU
🕭 11.30-11 (midnight Thu & Fri); 11-midnight Sat; 11-11 Sun
☎ (01865) 241185 ⊕ staldatestavernoxford.co.uk
6 changing beers (sourced nationally; often Redemption, Shotover, XT) Ⓗ
Refurbished for its reopening in 2012, this friendly pub in the centre of Oxford features up to six well-kept real ales with at least two from local breweries such as XT and Shotover. Good-quality, freshly cooked food is served all day using locally sourced ingredients where possible. There is an attractive function room upstairs, available to hire, with its own bar and toilets. Q❶⇌🖳🛜

Turf Tavern ✔
4 Bath Place, OX1 3SU (in alley off Holywell St, next to Bath Hotel)
🕭 11-11 ☎ (01865) 243235 ⊕ turftavern-oxford.co.uk
Greene King IPA, Abbot; house beer (by Greene King); 8 changing beers (sourced nationally) Ⓗ
The Turf is an Oxford institution dating from the late-18th century and popular with students. It is hard to find, tucked away in a sheltered position. Outside there are three flagstoned courtyards, one retaining parts of the original city wall standing three storeys high, all with heating and umbrellas. Up to 11 real ales are available plus Westons Old Rosie cider. The pub alleges that this is where former US President Bill Clinton famously 'did not inhale'. Q➤🕭❶🖳🛜

White Hart
12 St Andrew's Road, Headington, OX3 9DL (opp church in Old Headington village)
🕭 12-11 (midnight Fri & Sat) ☎ (01865) 761737
Everards Sunchaser, Tiger; 3 changing beers (sourced nationally; often Bath Ales, Brunswick, Oakham) Ⓗ
Terraced stone-built pub with a good selection of Everards ales. The interior is divided into three with two small bars, and it has a large garden. Note the framed extract from a play The Tragi-comedy of

Joan of Hedington by Dr William King of Christ Church, written in 1712 about the proprietor of a dishonourable alehouse – thankfully the pub now has a much better reputation. The food is traditional and home made, with pies a speciality. ➤🕭❶●P🖳🛜

White Rabbit Ⓛ
21 Friars Entry, OX1 2BY (alley between Magdalen St and Gloucester Green)
🕭 12-midnight ☎ (01865) 241177
Shotover Scholar; 3 changing beers (sourced regionally; often Loose Cannon) Ⓗ
This pub reopened in 2012 as the White Rabbit following the closure of Oxford's premier rock pub, the Gloucester Arms. It is brighter and more spacious than before, with a central bar surrounded by three areas. Four real ales are on offer, three changing and often local. Bar snacks and panini are available and a wide range of hand-made pizzas, made with organic gluten-free bases on request. ❶⇌♣🖳🛜

Playhatch

Flowing Spring ✔
Henley Road, RG4 9RB (on A4155)
🕭 closed Mon; 12-3, 5.30-11; 12-11 Sat & Sun
☎ (0118) 969 9878 ⊕ theflowingspringpub.co.uk
Fuller's London Pride, ESB; Gale's Seafarers Ale; 1 changing beer (sourced nationally) Ⓗ
Sociable 18th-century country pub on the edge of the Chilterns featuring Fuller's ales, plus a changing guest from the Fuller's list. It serves home-made food with gluten-free, dairy-free, vegetarian and vegan options. Events include monthly unplugged nights, live jazz nights, classic car and bike meets, story-telling, murder mysteries, an annual ferret show and beer and cider festivals in the summer and autumn. The pleasant covered balcony and large riverside garden are ideal for summer. ➤🕭❶♣●P🖳(800)🐾🛜

Salford

Salford Inn
Lower End, OX7 5YW
🕭 closed Mon; 12-2.30, 5.30-10 (11 Fri & Sat); 12-4 Sun
☎ (01608) 642631 ⊕ thesalford.co.uk
Ruddles Best Bitter; 1 changing beer (sourced nationally; often Butcombe) Ⓗ
One-room stone-built pub just off the A44 less than two miles from Chipping Norton, tastefully renovated and reopened in early 2016 under its new name and with a father and son team at the helm. Quality food, freshly prepared and locally sourced where possible, is served alongside the two ales. There is a patio area for drinking and eating in warmer weather. Accommodation is available in a newly refurbished double letting room with kitchenette and en-suite facilities. Q➤🕭🛏❶♿♣P🖳🐾🛜

Shippon

Prince of Wales Ⓛ
60 Barrow Road, OX13 6JQ (off A415, NW of Abingdon)
🕭 5-11 Mon; 11-11.30; 12-11 Sun ☎ (01235) 538546
⊕ princeofwalesshippon.co.uk
Black Sheep Best Bitter; Loose Cannon Abingdon Bridge; Shotover Prospect; Timothy Taylor Landlord; 1

changing beer (sourced nationally; often Loose Cannon) Ⓗ
At the centre of the village, this traditional country pub is rumoured to be haunted. It has two large rooms, both with log fires – one dominating the lounge – and a separate function room. An ever-changing menu of English food is available alongside a large selection of malt whiskies and ciders. The pub hosts regular beer and cider festivals and traditional jazz and folk music evenings. All visitors are welcome including walkers, cyclists and dogs.
Q🛏️❀⏾🍺♣️🚲️P🚆(4)🐾🛜

Steeple Aston

Red Lion Ⓛ ✅
South Side, OX25 4RY
✪ 12-3, 5.30-11; 12-11 Sat; 12-5 Sun ☎ (01869) 340225
⊕ redlionsteepleaston.co.uk
Hook Norton Hooky, Hooky Gold; 1 changing beer (sourced locally; often Hook Norton) Ⓗ
Signposted from the A4260, this pleasant village pub boasts displays of hanging baskets on the front patio in summer. A Hook Norton establishment, the changing beer comes from its seasonal range. Good food is served including the popular Sunday roasts. A TV is wheeled out for major sporting events. Approximately one mile from Heyford station and the Oxford Canal, the car park is before the pub if coming from the main road.
❀⏾♿️P🚆(S4)🐾

Stoke Lyne

Peyton Arms
OX27 8SD
✪ closed Mon; 12-2 (not Wed-Fri), 5-11; 12-7 Sat & Sun ☎ 07546 066160
Hook Norton Hooky, Lion, Old Hooky Ⓖ
Just two miles from the motorway, enter here and step back in time. Up to three Hooky ales are served through a hatch direct from the casks. Regular users of the pub include members of the local farming community looking to enjoy quality ales with great conversation. The bar area is for adults only – children are welcome in the garden but dogs are not permitted. Simple filled rolls are usually available. Weekday hours can vary – call ahead to check. Q❀P🚆(81)

Tetsworth

Old Red Lion Ⓛ
40 High Street, OX9 7AS
✪ 8am-10 (midnight Fri); 8.30am-10 Sat; 9am-5 Sun
☎ (01844) 281274 ⊕ theoldredliontetsworth.co.uk
3 changing beers (sourced locally; often Loose Cannon, Vale, XT) Ⓗ
The pub has a warm and friendly atmosphere with a cosy log fire in the winter. Up to three well-kept real ales come from local breweries – CAMRA members receive a 10 per cent discount on beers. Traditional pub food is served all day. The pub is a member of Brit Stop and allows motorhomes free overnight parking. It also serves as the village shop and offers B&B accommodation. Truly an asset of community value.
Q🛏️❀🚌⏾♿️♣️🚲️P🚆(124,275)🐾🛜

Thame

Cross Keys 🍺 Ⓛ ✅
East Street, OX9 3JS
✪ 12-2, 5-11; 12-11 Sat; 12-10.30 Sun ☎ (01844) 218202
⊕ crosskeysthame.co.uk
XT Four; 7 changing beers Ⓗ
Once almost lost forever, this pub was saved by the current tenants, who have transformed it into a drinkers' local and offer a warm welcome to all. Serving an ever-changing range of ales and ciders, local brews feature alongside beers from around the country. At busy times, it is not uncommon for beers to change during the evening. Check Twitter for unusual ales, but be warned, they will go quickly. A former local CAMRA branch Pub of the Year and Cider Pub of the Year.
Q❀♣️🚌🚲️🚆(280)🐾🛜

James Figg Ⓛ ✅
21 Cornmarket, OX9 2BL
✪ 11-11; 12-10.30 Sun ☎ (01844) 260166
⊕ thejamesfiggthame.co.uk
Purity Mad Goose; Sharp's Doom Bar; Vale Best IPA; 1 changing beer (sourced locally) Ⓗ
Former 17th-century coaching inn with an early-Georgian frontage. There is a choice of bars to the left or right as you enter. Dried hops hang down from the ceiling and sporting prints adorn the walls. The bar area opens out into a larger room complete with sofas, and a beer garden beyond. Nibbles are usually available on the bar to enjoy with your drink. Previously the Abingdon Arms, it is now renamed after Thame's very own 18th-century undefeated bare-knuckle boxing champion of England. Q❀⏾♣️P🚆(280)🐾

Wallingford

George Hotel
25 High Street, OX10 0BS
✪ 11-11; 12-10.30 Sun ☎ (01491) 836665
Rebellion IPA; 2 changing beers (sourced locally; often Rebellion) Ⓗ
A Peel Hotels pub close to the town centre, this former coaching inn dates from the 16th century. The cask ales are available in the Tavern Bar, which has several separate areas in addition to the spacious hotel courtyard, ideal for alfresco eating and drinking. Three handpumps dispense beers from Marlow's Rebellion Brewery. Food ranges from bar snacks to an à la carte menu in the Bistro George. The hotel hosts various functions and is licensed for civil wedding ceremonies.
🛏️❀🚌⏾♿️🔺️♣️P🚆🛜

Wantage

Royal Oak 🍺 Ⓛ
Newbury Street, OX12 8DF (S of Market Square)
✪ 5.30-11; 12-2.30, 7-11 Sat; 12-2, 7-10.30 Sun
☎ (01235) 763129 ⊕ royaloakwantage.co.uk
Wadworth 6X; West Berkshire Maggs' Magnificent Mild, Dr Hexter's Healer; 8 changing beers (sourced nationally; often Flying Monk) Ⓖ
This multi award-winning street-corner pub is a mecca for the discerning drinker and a meeting place for many local clubs. Photographs of ships bearing the pub's name are displayed. The lounge features wrought-iron trelliswork covered in pumpclips. The pub is the primary outlet for West Berkshire ales in the area – two beers carry landlord Paul Hexter's name – together with 30-

plus ciders and perries. All beers are dispensed by gravity. A former national CAMRA Cider and Perry Pub of the Year and local branch Pub and Cider Pub of the Year 2017. Q�⚲♣♿⌂🚲🐾🛜

Shoulder of Mutton
38 Wallingford Street, OX12 8AX (E of Market Square)
🕐 12-11 (midnight Fri & Sat); 12-10.30 Sun
10 changing beers (sourced nationally) 🅷
Victorian corner pub close to the town centre with 10 constantly changing beers on handpump to suit all tastes. The sympathetically renovated interior comprises public and lounge bars, a cosy snug and a 'lay-by' leading to a small courtyard and function room. Awards include local and regional CAMRA Pub of the Year. Q😺♿🚲

Westcote Barton

Fox Inn
27 Enstone Road, OX7 7BL
🕐 12 (5 Mon)-11; 12-midnight Fri & Sat ☎ (01869) 340338
🌐 foxinnmiddlebarton.co.uk
Exmoor Fox; Hook Norton Hooky; 2 changing beers (sourced nationally) 🅷
Seventeenth-century roadside pub with a warm welcome. Four handpumps dispense two regular ales and two guest beers from micros and regionals – often taken from the SIBA list. Quiz and poker nights, regular live music and an old jukebox provide the entertainment. Home-cooked food is available in the restaurant Tuesday to Sunday lunchtime, with Sunday roasts proving popular. The spacious garden has distractions for the kids as well as an Aunt Sally pitch. 🛏😺🕪♣♿🅿🚲

Wheatley

Cricketers Arms 🄻
38 Littleworth, OX33 1TR (walk W along Littleworth Rd from Wheatley)
🕐 6 (5 Fri)-11; 12-3, 6-11 Sat; 12-4, 7-10.30 Sun
☎ (01865) 872738 🌐 cricketers-arms.co.uk
Hook Norton Hooky; 2 changing beers (sourced locally) 🅷
A friendly, traditional free house offering three cask ales from local breweries, often including darker ales. A range of local bottled beers is also available and real cider. Good-value home-cooked food is served, and there are themed nights. Beer and sausage festivals are held in February and September. A popular stop-off for walkers, and dogs and children are welcome. There is a frequent bus service to the centre of Wheatley, and the pub is on National Cycle Route 57. Q🛏😺🕪♣♿🅿🐾🛜

Witney

Angel Inn 🄻 ✅
42 Market Square, OX28 6AL
🕐 10-11 (midnight Fri & Sat); 11-11 Sun ☎ (01993) 703238
Brakspear Oxford Gold; Wychwood Hobgoblin Gold, Hobgoblin; house beer (by Marston's) 🅷
A Grade II-listed free house at one time owned by brewer Joseph Early of the blanket manufacturing dynasty. It has a fine front bar with low beams and a bay window, with plenty of space for drinkers and diners beyond. Outside is a small paved and walled courtyard. The beer range is mostly from Marston's – its Wychwood Brewery is just around the corner. One of the regular beers may be replaced by a guest on occasion. 😺🕪♣🚲(S1,S2)

Eagle Tavern 🄻 ✅
22 Corn Street, OX28 6BL
🕐 11-3, 5-midnight (2am Fri); 11-2am Sat; 12-midnight Sun
☎ (01993) 700121
Hook Norton Hooky, Hooky Gold, Old Hooky; Wychwood Hobgoblin; 1 changing beer (sourced locally; often Hook Norton) 🅷
The landlord has been running pubs in Corn Street for 25 years, this one for 10, and has won Hook Norton Pub of the Year and Best Kept Beer and Cellar on several occasions. This Grade II-listed pub has wood panelling and stone floors, and you can see the cellar through the window next to the bar. Friendly locals, welcoming staff and quality beer all add up to a must-visit pub. Wychwood Brewery is just across the road. Q😺🕪♿♣♿🚲(S1,S2)🛜

New Inn 🄻
111 Corn Street, OX28 6AU
🕐 5-midnight; 12-2.30, 5-1am Sat; 12-2.30, 5-midnight Sun
☎ (01993) 703807
Black Sheep Best Bitter; Sharp's Doom Bar; St Austell Proper Job; Tring Side Pocket for a Toad; 2 changing beers (sourced locally) 🅷
Mid-Victorian pub at the lower end of Corn Street, with an enthusiastic landlord who serves an excellent choice of real ales. There are seven handpumps, one dispensing a real cider and the other six real ales, including two guests from microbreweries. Can be noisy when major rugby tournaments are being televised. There is live music on some Fridays. Q😺♿♣♿🅿🚲(S1,S2)🐾

Woodstock

Black Prince ✅
2 Manor Road, OX20 1XJ
🕐 12-11 ☎ (01993) 811530
🌐 theblackprincewoodstock.com
Loddon Hullabaloo; St Austell Tribute; 2 changing beers (sourced nationally; often Dark Star, Vale) 🅷
Historic 16th-century pub with an attractive riverside setting by the River Glyme, opposite Blenheim Palace. The open-plan interior boasts two ancient fireplaces and a French suit of armour. The garden and terrace offer a tranquil setting to enjoy a well-kept pint. You can choose from two regular ales and two changing guests, often from local breweries. Fresh well-cooked snacks and meals are available daily at reasonable prices. Aunt Sally is played and families, walkers and well-behaved dogs are welcome. 🛏😺🕪♿♣🅿🚲🐾🛜

Wootton

Killingworth Castle
Glympton Road, OX20 1EJ
🕐 9am-11 ☎ (01993) 811401 🌐 thekillingworthcastle.com
5 changing beers (sourced locally; often Little Ox, North Cotswold, Vale) 🅷
Welcoming coaching inn, dating from 1637, on the ancient Worcester to London road. At the front is a small dining area and the bar, warmed by a wood-burning stove. To the rear in a later extension is the larger restaurant area serving award-winning food. Five handpumps usually serve two ales from sister brewery Yubberton and three guests from regionals and micros. Beers can be sampled in a tasting paddle of three third-pint glasses. Eight recently refurbished letting rooms are available. Q🛏😺🖂🕪♣🅿🐾🛜

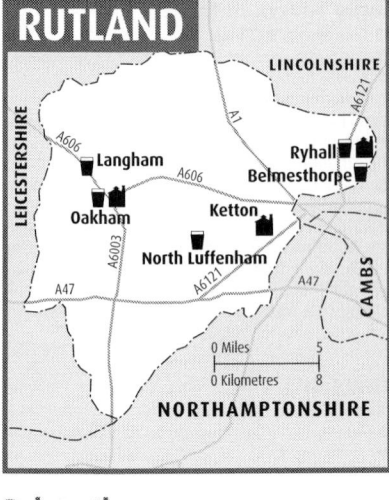

RUTLAND

LINCOLNSHIRE

LEICESTERSHIRE

Langham

Ryhall
Belmesthorpe

Oakham

Ketton

North Luffenham

CAMBS

A47

A47

0 Miles   5
0 Kilometres   8

NORTHAMPTONSHIRE

Belmesthorpe

Blue Bell ⏸
Shepherds Walk, PE9 4JG
🕐 12-2.30 (not Mon), 6-11; 12-2.30, 5-11 Fri; 12-11 Sat & Sun
☎ (01780) 753081
Draught Bass; Grainstore Ten Fifty; Greene King IPA; Oakham Bishops Farewell; 1 changing beer (often Abbeydale) ⊞
The Blue Bell is a historic village pub. Six handpulls offer a wide range of well-kept guest beers, including at least one LocAle and real cider. Dogs on leads are welcome in the bar area. Good honest home-made pub food is available Tuesday to Sunday lunchtimes (booking advisable). A former Rutland CAMRA Pub of the Year.
Q🛏️🕙🌓🕐♿♣🌳P🐕

Langham

Wheatsheaf
2 Burley Road, LE15 7HU (N of Oakham on A606)
🕐 12 (5 Mon & Tue)-11; 12-midnight Fri & Sat
☎ (01572) 869105 ⊕ thewheatsheaf-langham.co.uk
Fuller's London Pride; Greene King Abbot; 2 changing beers (often Robinsons, Woodforde's) ⊞
A former Mann's pub, it is now free of tie and serving beers from many breweries, micro and otherwise. It has an excellent reputation for its food and can be extremely busy, particularly in the summer months. A children's menu is available.
Q🛏️🌓🕐♿P🚌🐕

North Luffenham

Fox 🍺
1 Pinfold Lane, LE15 8LE
🕐 12-2.30 (not Mon), 5.30-11; 12-11.30 Sat; 11.30-10.30 Sun
☎ (01572) 720991 ⊕ thefoxrutland.co.uk
Greene King IPA; Oakham JHB; 2 changing beers (often Hopshackle, Langton) ⊞
Stone-built pub, now completely refurbished and opened out into one room. Despite the clean and modern decor it still retains the rural feel of a country pub. Happy hour is 5-7pm Monday to Thursday, with 30p off a pint or glass of wine. Rutland CAMRA Pub of the Year 2016 and 2017.
Q🛏️🌓🕐♿♣P🚌🐕📶

Oakham

Captain Noel Newton ✅
55 High Street, LE15 6AJ
🕐 8am-midnight (1am Fri & Sat) ☎ (01572) 725490
Greene King IPA, Abbot; Sharp's Doom Bar; changing beers ⊞
Acquired in the late 1940s from Captain Noel Newton, who served as a captain then major in the army during World War I and was awarded the Military Cross. He was later a member of Rutland County Council. The premises are built on to a surviving part of The Limes, a grand house named after the tall trees in its walled garden.
🛏️🌓🕐♿🚌🚇📶

Grainstore Brewery Tap
Station Approach, LE15 6EA
🕐 11-11 (midnight Fri); 9am-midnight Sat; 9am-11 Sun
☎ (01572) 770065 ⊕ grainstorebrewery.com
Grainstore Rutland Bitter, Rutland Panther, Cooking, Triple B, Daniel Lambert, Ten Fifty; 3 changing beers (often Grainstore) ⊞
A pub and brewery in a small, cleverly converted warehouse over four floors, retaining some original features (brewery tours can be booked in advance). Ten handpumps offer a wide beer range, always including a mild, alongside a range of bottle-conditioned Belgian beers. Home-made food is served at lunchtimes. Live bands feature regularly. Dogs and walkers are welcome. It has had 20 consecutive years in the Guide.
Q🛏️🕙🌓♿♣🌳💷P🚌🐕📶

Three Crowns
42 Northgate, LE15 6QS
🕐 12 (3 Mon & Tue)-11; 12-midnight Fri & Sat
☎ (01572) 757441 ⊕ steamin-billy.co.uk
Steamin' Billy Tipsy Fisherman, Bitter; 3 changing beers (often Belvoir, Brewsters, North Cotswold) ⊞
Purchased by Steamin' Billy and extensively refurbished prior to reopening in 2013, this pub appeared in the first edition of the Guide in 1972. Many events are held here, from live music to quiz nights and karaoke. The pub participates in the Oakham Ale Trail in conjunction with the annual CAMRA beer festival in June. No food is served but snacks are available. Q🛏️🌓🕙♿🚇♣🌳💷🚌🐕📶

Ryhall

Green Dragon
The Square, PE9 4HH
🕐 12-2.30 (not Mon), 5-11; 12-11 Sat & Sun
☎ (01780) 751999 ⊕ thegreendragonryhall.co.uk
Greene King IPA; 3 changing beers (often Gun Dog Ales, Oakham, Springhead) ⊞
Former Melbourn's stone-built inn in the heart of the village, Grade II-listed and dating back to the 17th century, with low ceilings and nooks and crannies adding to the cosy feel. Superb home-cooked meals are served including the pub's speciality pizzas cooked in the pizza oven. A former Rutland CAMRA Pub of the Year.
Q🛏️🌓🕙♣🚌(202)🐕📶

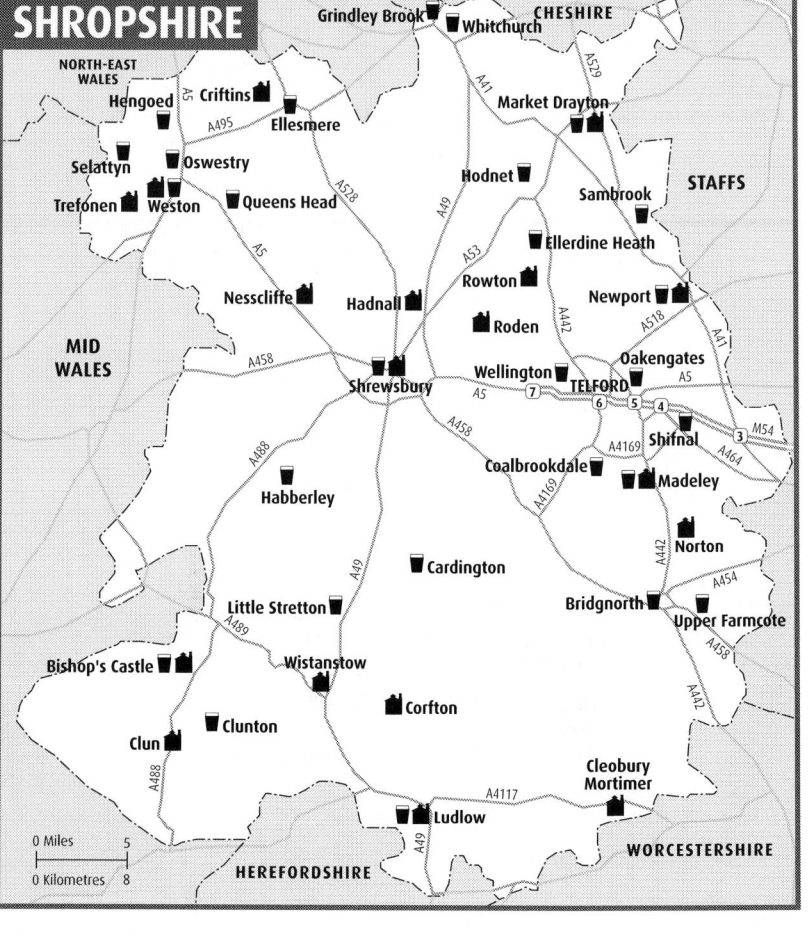

Bishop's Castle

Three Tuns Inn 🅛
Salop Street, SY9 5BW
☼ 12-11; 12-10.30 Sun ☎ (01588) 638797
🌐 thethreetunsinn.co.uk
**Three Tuns Rantipole, XXX, Stout, Cleric's Cure; 1
changing beer (often Three Tuns)** 🅗
A truly historic pub, this is one of the Famous Four
who were still brewing in the early 1970s. The
brewery is now separately owned. Refurbished and
enlarged, the pub has been extended into four
rooms – on one side is the lounge, on the other,
the ever-popular front bar leading to the central
snug and the extended oak-framed glass-sided
dining room. A function room is available for hire.
Q ☻ 😺 �(🌔 🛱 ♣ 🛱 (553) 🐾 📶

Bridgnorth

Black Boy 🅛
58 Cartway, WV16 4BG
☼ 12-11; 12-10.30 Sun ☎ (01746) 766497
**House beer (by Gorgeous); 5 changing beers (sourced
regionally; often Greene King, Salopian, Three
Tuns)** 🅗
Award-winning Grade II-listed 17th-century ale
house. First licensed in 1790, the pub stands on

historic Cartway linking High Town with the
quayside. Knowledgable staff can advise on the
range of ales from Greene King, complemented by
a choice from other breweries and the house beer
by Gorgeous. A real cider and traditional bar snacks

REAL ALE BREWERIES

Battlefield Shrewsbury
Chapel Criftins
Clun 🍺 Clun
Corvedale 🍺 Corfton
Gorgeous Madeley (NEW)
Hobsons Cleobury Mortimer
Hop & Stagger Norton
Joule's Market Drayton
Ludlow Ludlow
Ness 🍺 Nesscliffe
Offa's Dyke 🍺 Trefonen
Plan B Newport (NEW)
Rowton Rowton
Salopian Hadnall
Six Bells 🍺 Bishop's Castle
Stonehouse Weston
Target Roden
Three Tuns 🍺 Bishop's Castle
Wood Wistanstow

are also available. Local CAMRA Pub of the Year 2015 and Bridgnorth Pub of the Year 2016.
ⓑ☸❀⇒(SVR)♣●☺📶

Black Horse 🅛
4 Bridge Street, Low Town, WV15 6AF
⊕ 12-1am ☎ (01746) 762415
⊕ theblackhorsebridgnorth.co.uk
Bathams Best Bitter; Hobsons Town Crier; Three Tuns XXX; Wye Valley HPA; 3 changing beers (often Enville, Ludlow, Salopian) Ⓗ
This popular Low Town free house has two bars serving four regular and three changing guest beers. Extended into the adjacent property in late 2016, the front bar has a rustic feel with a modern touch. The wood-panelled lounge leads to a conservatory, both with widescreen TVs for sporting events. Filled rolls are often available but no meals. The smoking area leads to a long courtyard. Car parking is accessed from Severn Street. The accommodation is en-suite B&B.
☸🚌🛏⇒(SVR)♣P📶●❀📶

King's Head 🅛
3 Whitburn Street, High Town, WV16 4QN
⊕ 11-11 (midnight Fri & Sat); 12-10.30 Sun
☎ (01746) 762141 ⊕ thekingsheadbridgnorth.co.uk
Hobsons Twisted Spire, Town Crier; Wye Valley HPA; 2 changing beers (sourced nationally; often Kelham Island, Thornbridge, Three Tuns) Ⓗ
A popular Grade II-listed 16th-century coaching inn sympathetically restored with exposed timber beams, flagstone floor, leaded windows and roaring log fires in winter. There are three regular local and two changing guest beers, a carefully selected wine list, and a range of fine spirits and liqueurs. Excellent food is offered from a quintessentially English menu alongside a selection of daily specials, prepared using fresh local ingredients. The bar is dog-friendly – ask for the dog biscuits. ⓑ☸❀🚌&⇒(SVR)●📶●📶

Old Castle 🅛 ✅
10/11 West Castle Street, WV16 4AB (between SVR and town centre)
⊕ 11.30-11; 11.30-10.30 Sun ☎ (01746) 711420
⊕ oldcastlebridgnorth.co.uk
Hobsons Town Crier; Sharp's Doom Bar; Wye Valley HPA; 1 changing beer (sourced nationally; often Thwaites, Wye Valley) Ⓗ
A popular 17th-century pub, where the dining area at the front is separated from the bar by a real log fire. To the rear is a conservatory/games room with darts, pool and table football leading to a well-kept garden with excellent views. A well-balanced menu, including vegetarian and gluten-free options and a popular Sunday carvery, is offered. Meals can be served in the garden. There is a small function room.
ⓑ☸❀🚌&⇒(SVR)♣📶(436)●📶

Railwayman's Arms 🍺 🅛
Severn Valley Railway Station, Hollybush Road, WV16 5DT (Platform 1 SVR)
⊕ 11-11; 11.30-10.30 Sun ☎ (01746) 760920 ⊕ svr.co.uk
Bathams Best Bitter; Hobsons Mild, Best, Town Crier; 4 changing beers (sourced nationally) Ⓗ
A popular pub attracting locals and visitors, run by the SVR and licensed since 1861. Located on Platform 1 of the heritage railway, the bars feature railway memorabilia and the platform drinking area is an ideal place to soak up the atmosphere of a steam railway. Ten handpumps serve a selection

of local and national ales and, in summer, a cider and a perry. There are plans to turn an adjacent store room into a snug.
Q ⓑ☸❀⇒(SVR)●P📶(436,101)●📶

White Lion 🅛
3 West Castle Street, WV16 4AB (between town centre and SVR)
⊕ 12 (11 Sat)-11; 12-10.30 Sun ☎ (01746) 763962
⊕ whitelionbridgnorth.co.uk
Hop & Stagger Golden Wander; house beer (by Hop & Stagger); 3 changing beers (sourced regionally) Ⓗ
An 18th-century inn with two bars, offering a warm welcome to regulars and visitors. Murals by a local artist adorn the walls, inside and out. Eight handpumps offer a selection of the pub's own Hop & Stagger beers plus LocAles, national beers and Thatchers cider. Good snacks are served including the pub's famous home-made Scotch eggs. Outside is a terraced, lawned garden and children's play area. A regular venue for a story-telling group, folk club and quiz teams.
Q ⓑ☸❀🚌◑⇒(SVR)♣●📶(436,890)●📶

Cardington

Royal Oak
SY6 7JZ
⊕ closed Mon; 12-2.30, 6-11; 12-11 Sat; 12-4 Sun
☎ (01694) 771266 ⊕ at-the-oak.com
Ludlow Ludlow Best; Sharp's Doom Bar; 2 changing beers Ⓗ
The Royal Oak, dating back to the 15th century, is reputedly Shropshire's oldest continually licensed pub, and is the archetypal country inn. The single room is multi-functional with a bar, lounge and dining area, and has a relaxed ambience. It is low-beamed and dominated by a large inglenook fireplace which provides a home for various interesting artefacts. A good choice of beers includes a mix of local and regional brews.
Q☸❀◑🅰♣●P📶(540)●📶

Clunton

Crown Inn 🅛
SY7 0HU
⊕ 5 (4 Wed & Thu)-11; 12-midnight Fri & Sat; 12-11 Sun
☎ (01588) 660265 ⊕ crowninnclunton.co.uk
Hobsons Best; Ludlow Gold; Stonehouse Station Bitter; 1 changing beer Ⓗ
Set in the Clun Valley, a designated Area of Outstanding Natural Beauty, this genuine, community-owned inn, run by a local family, has three rooms including a smart restaurant. It hosts a popular fish and chips night every Wednesday and an acoustic folk night on the fourth Monday of the month. Ludlow Gold is available in winter, replaced by a changing guest in summer. The Crown takes part in the annual Clun Valley Beer Festival.
Q☸◑♣●P📶

Ellerdine Heath

Royal Oak 🅛 ✅
Hazles Road, TF6 6RL (midway between A442 and A53)
SJ603226
⊕ 12-11 ☎ (01939) 250300
Hobsons Best; Tring Side Pocket for a Toad; Wye Valley HPA; 3 changing beers (sourced nationally; often Rowton, Salopian, Stonehouse) Ⓗ

This long-standing Guide entry, also known as the Tiddly, is a popular pub used by young farmers, shooting parties and folk groups, and hosts various rallies. Features include a pool table, dartboard, real fires in both rooms, a dining room, smoking shed and a marquee used from Easter to October. Food is served Wednesday to Sunday.
Q🕑✿◑🚴♿♣♠P❀☕🌐

Ellesmere

White Hart 🅛
Birch Road, SY12 0ET
🕑 3-midnight; 1-1am Sat & Sun ☎ (01691) 624653
Salopian Shropshire Gold; 3 changing beers 🅗
A Grade II-listed building of the early Jacobean period with a wealth of exposed timber. The interior comprises a public bar and a lounge. Outside, the drinking area to the rear has a tented gazebo. The three guest beers include offerings from local breweries. Convenient for boating folk on the Llangollen Canal as the marina is close by.
✿P🚃❀🌐

Grindley Brook

Horse & Jockey 🅛
SY13 4QJ
🕑 12-11 ☎ (01948) 662723
8 changing beers (often Greene King, Salopian, Weetwood) 🅗
The 19th-century core of the pub is quite small, but over time it has been extended considerably. There are various nooks and crannies serving different purposes, all tastefully done, with extensive use of reclaimed timber and quality furnishings. While the emphasis is on dining, there is ample provision for drinkers. Outside, there is a lawned area with children's play equipment. Strategically placed close to the Shropshire Union Canal and Cheshire's Sandstone Trail. 🕑✿◑♿♣♠P🚃(41)❀🌐

Habberley

Mytton Arms 🅛
SY5 0TP
🕑 4 (12 Fri-Sun)-11 ☎ (01743) 792490
Hobsons Best; Three Tuns XXX; 2 changing beers (often Hobsons, Joule's) 🅗
Somewhat off the beaten track, this popular pub is worth seeking out. A well-known local character and pub regular features on the inn sign. There are four low-beamed rooms and a friendly rustic atmosphere – beer and conversation predominate. Outside are seats to the front, and a paved area with a vine-covered pergola to the side. The South Shropshire Hills shuttle bus provides transport in summer. Q✿♣♠P🚃❀

Hengoed

Last Inn
Brookside, SY10 7EU
🕑 4-midnight; 12-midnight Sat & Sun ☎ (01691) 659747
Oakham Bishops Farewell; Sharp's Doom Bar; 3 changing beers 🅗
Large pub in a small village at a rural crossroads. A former cobbler's workshop, the Last has a games room, public bar and dining room as well as a separate, extensively refurbished function room which hosts music and other entertainment. A member of the Oakademy of Excellence, there are

usually five cask ales on offer from regional, local and micro breweries. A source of pride is that the pub runs on a woodchip biomass boiler.
🕑✿◑♠♣♠P🚃(2A)❀🌐

Hodnet

Bear 🅛
Drayton Road, TF9 3NH
🕑 12-11; 12-10 Sun ☎ (01630) 685214
🌐 bearathodnet.co.uk
4 changing beers (sourced nationally; often Black Sheep, Rowton, Three Tuns) 🅗
A welcoming 17th-century village pub situated opposite a historic church famed for its Holy Grail connections. There are four main public areas, with cosy log-burning fires catering for both diners and drinkers. The original bear pit can be viewed through a glass panel in the floor of Wilfred's Retreat. Dogs are welcome in the snug. Four regularly changing real ales are sourced from both local and national breweries. Closes at 7pm on winter Sundays. Q🕑✿◑◑♠♣P🚃❀🌐

Little Stretton

Green Dragon
Ludlow Road, SY6 6RE
🕑 11.30-11.30 ☎ (01694) 722925
🌐 greendragonlittlestretton.co.uk
Draught Bass; Ludlow Gold; Wye Valley Butty Bach; 2 changing beers (often Hobsons, Wye Valley) 🅗
The pub is set in a picturesque location in the Shropshire Hills Area of Outstanding Natural Beauty, with an abundance of walks in the district. The L-shaped bar has a comfortable and welcoming feel and the pleasant separate dining room is well used. The beer is mostly from local breweries, as is the cider (at the appropriate time of year).
🕑✿◑♣♠P🚃(435)❀🌐

Ludlow

Queen's 🅛
113 Lower Galdeford, SY8 1RU (just off town centre, opp Co-op)
🕑 12-11 (midnight Fri & Sat); 12-10.30 Sun
☎ (01584) 879177 🌐 thequeensludlow.com
Hobsons Best; Wye Valley Butty Bach; 1 changing beer (sourced locally; often Hobsons, Ludlow) 🅗
Named after Queen Victoria, this is a popular pub and café bar with a good range of local ales. Look out for the guest beer offered at a competitive price. The light and airy L-shaped bar has three distinct areas, with dining down a short flight of steps. Bar meals are available with local produce a proud boast. The large enclosed patio garden has views toward Ludford. The monthly quiz is always well attended. ✿🏠◑♿♣⇄🚃❀🌐

Railway Shed 🅛
Station Drive, SY8 2PQ
🕑 10-5 (6 Fri); 11-4 Sun ☎ (01584) 873291
🌐 theludlowbrewingcompany.co.uk
Ludlow Best, Blonde, Gold, Black Knight, Boiling Well, Stairway 🅗
The brewery tap and visitor centre for the Ludlow Brewing Company, and as the name suggests, the building was once a transit depot for railway goods. An imaginative conversion on two levels, on the ground floor there are hand-crafted timber

tables and benches, together with a shop. On the upper level are two huge brewing vessels and more comfortable seating and tables. Brewery visits are welcome and the centre is available for hire. Q❀ಸ⏚⇌♠Pᄆ❀令

Market Drayton

Hippodrome Ⓛ ✅
Queen Street, TF9 1PS
❀ 8am-midnight (11 Sun) ☎ (01630) 650820
Greene King Abbot; Ruddles Best Bitter; 3 changing beers (sourced locally; often Lymestone, Slater's, Titanic) Ⓗ
The Hippodrome was Market Drayton's first cinema, closing in 1966. The pub was opened by Wetherspoon in 2007, retaining some unique features of the original building. The usual food fare is served, but what makes this pub different is that it actively supports local breweries, regularly showcasing them on the bar. ಸ❀①⏚♠ᄆ令

Red Lion ▽ Ⓛ
Great Hales Street, TF9 1JP
❀ 11-11 (midnight Fri & Sat) ☎ (01630) 652602
Joule's Blonde, Pale Ale, Slumbering Monk; 5 changing beers (sourced locally; often Joule's) Ⓗ
A previous winner of the CAMRA/Historic England Conservation Award, this Joule's brewery tap was formerly a coaching inn, built in 1623. Its unique features include an illuminated well in the main bar and the Mouse Room – a Robert Thompson-inspired function room featuring carved mice. Log fires and oak beams create a comfortable atmosphere where locally sourced food can be enjoyed from an extensive menu. The Joule's range of beers is produced in the adjacent brewery. Q ಸ❀①⏚ಸ♠Pᄆ❀令

Sandbrook Vaults Ⓛ
4 Shropshire Street, TF9 3BY
❀ 5-11; 12-midnight Fri & Sat; 11-11 Sun ☎ (01630) 478405
Joule's Blonde, Pale Ale, Slumbering Monk; 1 changing beer (often Joule's) Ⓗ
You are guaranteed a warm welcome at this Joule's pub, originally built in 1653. It has the familiar easy-on-the-eye Joule's interior and well-kept beers from the brewery 150 yards away. Free hot food is offered to customers at weekends (with an optional donation to charity). The pub holds regular high-quality live acoustic music nights on Thursdays and Sundays, featuring good regional bands. Q❀①⏚♠ᄆ令

Newport

New Inn Ⓛ
2 Stafford Street, TF10 7LX
❀ 12-11 (midnight Fri & Sat) ☎ (01952) 812295
⊕ thenewinnnewport.co.uk
Joule's Blonde, Pale Ale, Slumbering Monk; 2 changing beers (sourced locally; often Joule's) Ⓗ
Originally an old coaching inn dating from 1792, the building has been completely refurbished by Joule's but retains some of the old features such as the latch doors. There is a Yorkist fireplace in the snug area plus a central woodburner for winter comfort and an extensive garden for the summer. A friendly pub catering for all ages, it serves good food including vegetarian options. Live music often plays on Sunday evenings. Q ಸ❀①⏚ಸ♠ᄆ❀令

Oswestry

Bailey Head Ⓛ
SY11 1PZ (in Market Square opp Guildhall)
❀ 12 (3 Mon)-11.30; 12-12.30am Sat; 12-10.30 Sun
⊕ baileyhead.co.uk
5 changing beers (sourced nationally; often Oakham) Ⓗ
Near the old castle, this free house opened in 2016. It offers five constantly changing real ales plus draught cider. Beers are sourced locally, regionally and nationally, usually from microbreweries. Locally produced traditional food is served until 10pm. Events include Meet the Brewer and quiz nights. The Market car park is close by. ಸ⏚♣♠ᄆᄆ❀令

Black Lion Ⓛ
Salop Road, SY11 2RJ (S of town centre on B4579)
❀ 6-11; 4.30-midnight Fri; 12-midnight Sat; 12-11 Sun
☎ (01691) 652745 ⊕ theblacklionoswestry.co.uk
Salopian Oracle; 4 changing beers (sourced locally; often Hobsons, Salopian, Wood) Ⓗ
Just inside the town's conservation area, this family-run establishment is a true community pub and has a warm and friendly atmosphere. It is home to sports teams and social groups, with plenty of TVs for sports fans and tasting boards for beer lovers. The central bar divides the pub into a comfortable lounge at the front and public bar at the rear. Well-kept ales from various local and regional brewers can be enjoyed. Q ಸ❀❀♣♠Pᄆ❀令

Queens Head

Queen's Head
West Felton, SY11 4EB (E of Oswestry)
❀ 12-11 ☎ (01691) 610255
⊕ the-queens-head-oswestry.co.uk
Church End Fallen Angel; Stonehouse Station Bitter, Off the Rails Ⓗ
Located next to the Montgomery Canal, the pub is primarily a dining venue with a pleasant bar area. All beers are locally sourced, and local Sweeney Mountain real cider is also available. Dining areas include an attractive conservatory, with meals served until 9pm. One of only two Shropshire pubs on this canal, the front patio has views overlooking the water. Q ಸ❀①⏚♠Pᄆ(70)令

Sambrook

Three Horseshoes Ⓛ
TF10 8AP (½ mile E of A41, on main road through Sambrook)
❀ 6-11 Mon; 12-2, 5-11; 12-11 Sat & Sun ☎ (01952) 551133
⊕ threehorseshoessambrook.co.uk
Salopian Shropshire Gold; 2 changing beers (sourced regionally; often Hobsons, Three Tuns, Wood) Ⓗ
A traditional country pub for over 100 years, with three rooms including a main bar with a woodburner and a separate restaurant. This welcoming community venue hosts occasional quiz nights, music on alternate Fridays, darts and dominoes. A varied menu of home-cooked food is served weekday evenings (not Mon) and weekends to suit all tastes and budgets. Families and dogs are welcome throughout the pub, patio and garden, which has a children's play area. Real cider is available in the summer. ಸ❀①♣♠P❀令

Selattyn

Cross Keys ★ L
SY10 7DN

✪ closed Mon & Tue; 6-midnight Wed-Fri; 12-2.30, 6-midnight Sat; 12-midnight Sun ☎ (01691) 653347
Stonehouse Station Bitter; Three Tuns XXX; 1 changing beer (sourced locally) Ⓗ

A gem – this 17th-century building has been a pub since 1840 and has a nationally important historic interior. It is situated in a village close to the Welsh border and Offa's Dyke. The cosy small bar with its quarry-tiled floor and real fire is probably the soul of the pub, although original features in other rooms are being carefully restored by the new owners. Q✿🐕♣🚶P🐾🐾🛜

Shifnal

Plough Inn L
26 Broadway, TF11 8AZ

✪ 12 (4.30 Mon)-11; 12-10.30 Sun ☎ (01952) 463118
🌐 theploughinnshifnal.co.uk
Hobsons Mild, Best; 6 changing beers (sourced regionally; often Bathams, Sarah Hughes, Wood) Ⓗ

Traditional homely 17th-century free house with exposed oak beams and tiled floors. Eight handpulled ales including at least one strong and one dark beer together with two traditional ciders are on offer, as well as an array of Belgian bottles. Heartily portioned home-cooked food is served (no food Mon). A secluded yet extensive suntrap beer garden lies at the rear, and there is a function room. Work from local artists adorns the walls. A free book exchange is offered. 🚶✿🐕🍴♣🚶🐾🛜

White Hart 🍷 L ✔
High Street, TF11 8BH

✪ 12-11 ☎ (01952) 461161
Greene King Abbot; Holden's Black Country Mild; Salopian Shropshire Gold; Wye Valley HPA, Butty Bach; 4 changing beers (sourced regionally) Ⓗ

Grade II, 17th-century, two-roomed free house, with 23 years in the Guide. It now has nine handpumps, and real cider kept in the cellar. It is noted for the lunchtime food menu (no food Sun). Family-run and community-oriented, it supports darts and dominoes teams. There are no noisy games machines. Outside, there is a sunny walled patio area off the lounge, a beer garden and a large car park. Q🚶✿🐕🍴♣🚶P🚶🐾

Shrewsbury

Abbey L ✔
83 Monkmoor Road, Monkmoor, SY2 5AZ

✪ 11.30-11 (midnight Fri); 11-midnight Sat; 11-11 Sun ☎ (01743) 236788 🌐 theabbeyshrewsbury.co.uk
Morland Old Speckled Hen; Slater's Haka; Wells Bombardier; house beer (by Greene King); 3 changing beers (often Three Tuns, Titanic) Ⓗ

A large, recently refurbished pub with several alcoves and multiple fireplaces. The Abbey's publican is an ale enthusiast, running frequent Meet the Brewer sessions and several beer festivals a year. In between, he has expanded the range of guest ales and real ciders. Food is served until 10pm every evening. There are regular community events including quizzes, sometimes with live music rounds. 🚶✿🐕🍴♣🚶P🚶(1)🛜

Admiral Benbow L
24 Swan Hill, SY1 1NF (just off Main Square)

✪ 5 (12 Sat)-11; 7-10.30 Sun ☎ (01743) 244423
Battlefield 1066; Ludlow Gold; The Shropshire Brewer Spire Dancer; 3 changing beers (sourced locally; often Six Bells) Ⓗ

Spacious free house serving a range of Shropshire and Herefordshire beers plus a selection of ciders from Rosie's including Black Bart and Wicked Wasp. A good choice of Belgian, American and other foreign beers is also offered. A small room off the bar can be used for private functions, and there is a seating and smoking area outside at the rear. Children are not permitted. The Admiral was a notorious 17th-century naval officer born in Shrewsbury. Q✿🐾🚶♣🚶🛜

Coach & Horses L ✔
23 Swan Hill, SY1 1NF

✪ 11.30-midnight (12.30am Fri & Sat); 12-11.30 Sun ☎ (01743) 365661
Salopian Shropshire Gold, Oracle; Stonehouse Station Bitter; 3 changing beers Ⓗ

Set in a quiet street off the main shopping area, the pub is a peaceful haven, with magnificent floral displays in summer. Victorian in style, it has a wood-panelled bar, a small side snug area and a large lounge where meals are served lunchtimes and evenings. Bar snacks are also available at lunchtimes. Cheddar Valley or Sweeney Mountain cider is dispensed on handpull. Q🐕🍴♣🚶🐾🛜

Cross Foxes
27 Longden Coleham, SY3 7DE (close to River Severn)

✪ 11-midnight; 11-11 Sun ☎ (01743) 355050
Draught Bass; Salopian Shropshire Gold; Three Tuns XXX; Worthington's Bitter Ⓗ

A friendly locals' pub noted for its sales of the popular Draught Bass. A free house since its purchase from Mitchells & Butlers in the late 1980s, it has been run by the same family since 1985. The large L-shaped room has the main area with the bar, major drinking area and an efficient woodburner on one side, with a smaller drinking area and dartboard leading off. Q♣🚶🛜

Montgomery's Tower L ✔
Lower Claremont Bank, SY1 1RT

✪ 8am-midnight (1am Wed & Thu; 2am Fri & Sat) ☎ (01743) 239080
Greene King IPA; Salopian Shropshire Gold; Wood Shropshire Lad; 4 changing beers (often Sadler's, Sharp's, Slater's) Ⓗ

Close to the Quarry Park and handy for Theatre Severn, this Lloyds No.1 offers a choice of two bars. To the left is a large open area rich in natural light, with a smoking area to the rear. The bar to the right provides quieter surroundings and subdued lighting, except on Fridays and Saturdays when there is a DJ. The walls display prints illustrating local history and famous Salopians. 🚶✿🐕🍴♣🚶🛜

Nag's Head L
22 Wyle Cop, SY1 1XB

✪ 11.30-midnight; 10.30-1am Fri; 12-midnight Sun ☎ (01743) 362455
Hobsons Best; Sharp's Doom Bar; Timothy Taylor Landlord; Wye Valley HPA; 1 changing beer (often Titanic) Ⓗ

The main features of this Grade II-listed, timber-framed building are best appreciated externally – in particular the upper-storey jettying and, to the rear, the timber remnants of a 14th-century hall house including a screened passage which provided protection from draughts (and now offers shelter for smokers). The old-style interior has remained unaltered for many years. The pub is said to be haunted and features on the Shrewsbury Ghost Trail. ❀≠♣🚲🏵

Prince of Wales ♥ 🅛
30 Bynner Street, Belle Vue, SY3 7NZ
✪ 5 (12 Fri-Sun)-midnight ☎ (01743) 343301
🌐 theprince.pub
Greene King IPA; Hobsons Twisted Spire; Marston's Wainwright; St Austell Tribute; Salopian Golden Thread; Three Tuns Mild; 1 changing beer (sourced locally; often Rowton, Wood) ℍ
Welcoming two-roomed community pub with a heated smoking shelter and a large suntrap deck adjoining a bowling green. The green is overlooked by a 19th-century maltings. Darts, dominoes and bowls teams abound. Beer festivals take place each year in February and May. Shrewsbury Town FC memorabilia adorn the building both inside and out, with some of the seating from the old Gay Meadow ground skirting the bowling green. Westons Rosie's Pig is on handpull.
Q🛏🚲❀&♣🅟🖰🏵

Salopian Bar 🅛 ✅
Smithfield Road, SY1 1PW
✪ 11-midnight (11 Tue); 11-11 Sun ☎ (01743) 351505
Hobsons Best; Oakham Citra; Salopian Oracle; 5 changing beers (often Oakham, Salopian) ℍ
A single-room pub popular with all age groups. The bar's management strives to increase, and vary, the beer, cider and perry range to satisfy public demand. Regular cider and perry are provided by Westons and Thatchers, and a good range of Belgian and American bottled beer is also available. Large-screen TVs show coverage of major sporting events. Filled rolls and pork pies are usually available. &≠🍴🖰🏵🛜

Three Fishes 🅛
4 Fish Street, SY1 1UR
✪ 11.30-3, 5-11; 11.30-11.30 Fri & Sat; 12-10.30 Sun
☎ (01743) 344793 🌐 realaleshrewsbury.co.uk
Stonehouse Station Bitter; Three Tuns Stout; Timothy Taylor Landlord; 2 changing beers (often Oakham, Salopian) ℍ
Fifteenth-century building standing in the shadow of two churches, St Alkmund's and St Julian's, within the maze of streets and passageways in the town's medieval quarter. Freshly prepared food is available lunchtimes and early evenings Monday to Saturday. The pub offers a range of up to six local and national ales, usually including some dark beers, and a choice of real ciders and perries. A former local CAMRA Pub of the Year.
Q🍽≠♣🍴🖰🏵🛜

Woodman 🅛
32 Coton Hill, SY1 2DZ
✪ 4-midnight; 12-midnight Sat & Sun ☎ (01743) 351007
Salopian Shropshire Gold; Wye Valley Butty Bach; 3 changing beers (sourced regionally; often Abbeydale, Mallinson's, Ossett) ℍ
Half-brick and half-timbered black and white corner pub, originally built in the 1800s. The wonderful oak-panelled lounge has two real log fires and traditional settles, and the separate bar has the original stone-tiled flooring, wooden

seating, fire and listed leaded windows. The courtyard has a heated smoking area and seating. Q🛏❀≠♣🍴🖰🏵🛜

Telford: Coalbrookdale

Coalbrookdale Inn 🅛
12 Wellington Road, TF8 7DX (opp Enginuity Museum)
✪ 4-11; 12-11 Sat & Sun ☎ (01952) 432166
Hobsons Town Crier; Sarah Hughes Dark Ruby Mild; 6 changing beers (sourced regionally; often Hobsons, Salopian, Wye Valley) ℍ
Opened in 1834 and granted inn status in 1851, this historic three-room village pub sits at the heart of the local community, nestled a stone's throw from the museums within the Ironbridge Gorge World Heritage site. Simple bar food is available throughout opening hours. The pub emphasises a strong local ale focus and at least two milds are on at all times. Quiz and ukulele nights alternate on Tuesdays. Notably dog-friendly and welcoming of locals and visitors alike. 🛏❀🛋▲♣🍴🖰🅟(9)🏵♥

Telford: Madeley

All Nations 🅛
20 Coalport Road, TF7 5DP (signed off Legges Way, opp Blists Hill Museum)
✪ 12-midnight (1am Sat & Sun) ☎ (01952) 585747
Hobsons Twisted Spire; house beer (by Broughs); 2 changing beers (sourced locally; often Hobsons, Wye Valley) ℍ
Cosy, bustling 1832 brewhouse with a warm, inviting fire. The walls are decorated with old photographs, and original Jackfield tiles adorn the fireplace. Located in the Ironbridge Gorge World Heritage Site, this pub offers a homely, family- and dog-friendly atmosphere loved by locals and visitors alike. Brews are fortnightly and a selection of bar snacks is available at all times. Quiz night is Monday, live bands feature May to July.
Q🛏❀🛋▲♣🅟🏵

Telford: Oakengates

Crown Inn 🅛 ✅
Market Street, TF2 6EA (by bus station)
✪ 12-11 ☎ (01952) 610888 🌐 crown.oakengates.net
Hobsons Twisted Spire, Best; Purity Bunny Hop; 10 changing beers (sourced nationally; often Burton Bridge, Joule's, Rudgate) ℍ
Traditional town pub, warmed by real fires in the winter, with three separate drinking areas. Cask Marque-accredited, the number of handpulls rises to 34 during beer festivals held the first weekend of May and October. The pub is home to Telford Comedy Club and Telford Acoustic Club, and features live music and quiz nights. Food includes tasty pies and pasties, plus takeaways from the neighbouring Indian restaurant. At the rear is a suntrap courtyard. Q🛏❀&≠♣🍴🖰🏵🛜

Old Fighting Cocks 🅛
48 Market Street, TF2 6DU
✪ 12-11 ☎ (01952) 615607
Everards Tiger; Hop & Stagger Golden Wander, Pure Amber; 3 changing beers (sourced nationally) ℍ
Friendly old coaching inn on the former Watling Street, with woodburners in each bar. The original windows remain in the front bar. There are 10 handpulls. The pub offers a range of hot and cold snacks including home-made Scotch eggs, or you

can bring your own – plates and cutlery provided. An upstairs function room with room for up to 40 people is available to hire. Five minutes' walk from both the bus and train stations. Q☎☆&≉♣●🍴☺🎵

Station Hotel 🅛
42 Market Street, TF2 6DU
🕐 11-11 (9 Mon); 12-11 Sun ☎ (01952) 612949
Bathams Best Bitter; 8 changing beers (sourced nationally; often North Riding, Oakham, Salopian) 🅗
A basic town pub that has featured in the Guide for many years. The landlord specialises in beers from Yorkshire, but also sources locally and nationally. There is a real fire in the front room where drinkers can enjoy home-made bar snacks, pizzas and a Wednesday night curry. Beer festivals with up to 12 pumps are held in May and November – do not miss the Belgian event. Cider is available in summer. Q☆≉♣●🍴☺

Telford: Wellington

Cock Hotel 🅛
148 Holyhead Road, TF1 2DL
🕐 4 (12 Thu)-11.30; 12-11.45 Fri & Sat; 12-11 Sun
☎ (01952) 244954 ⊕ cockhotel.co.uk
Hobsons Mild, Best; 5 changing beers (sourced regionally) 🅗
This multi award-winning 18th-century coaching inn has eight handpulls dispensing mostly regional ales, always including a dark beer and a real cider. Continental beers are also kept on draught and in bottles. The two-roomed pub has a main bar decorated with hops and warmed by a fire in winter. Award-winning pork pies are served from the bar at all times. B&B accommodation and a meeting room are available.
Q☆🛏♣●P🖫(4)☺🎵

Pheasant Inn 🅛
54 Market Street, TF1 1DT
🕐 11-11 (midnight Fri & Sat); 12-10.30 Sun
☎ (01952) 260683
Everards Tiger; Wrekin Ironbridge Gold; 4 changing beers (sourced regionally; often Rowton) 🅗
Home of the Wrekin Brewing Company, based in an adjacent outbuilding – the beers are now brewed under licence by the local Rowton Brewery. The bar has nine handpulls, one often offering a dark beer and two for cider. Seasonal Wrekin and Rowton brews are also available. You can enjoy home-made food Monday to Saturday until 4pm and local pork pies at any time.
Q☆◖&≉●P🖫☺🎵

William Withering 🅛 ✔
43-45 New Street, TF1 1LU
🕐 8am-midnight (1am Fri & Sat) ☎ (01952) 642800
Ruddles Best Bitter; Salopian Shropshire Gold; Sharp's Doom Bar; Slater's Haka; 3 changing beers (sourced nationally) 🅗
Named after a local physician who is best remembered for discovering and developing the medical properties of digitalis. The large single open-plan room is styled as an 18th-century study. Four regular beers are complemented by three changing ales – local, national and sometimes even international. Ciders come from Westons and Cheddar Valley. Good-value food is served 8am-11pm. Can be very busy on a Saturday lunchtime with shoppers. ☎☆◖&≉●🍴☺🎵

Wrekin Inn 🅛
26 Wrekin Road, TF1 1RH
🕐 3-11; 12-midnight Fri-Sun ☎ (01952) 256756
Three Tuns XXX; 6 changing beers (sourced nationally; often Hobsons, Salopian, Three Tuns) 🅗
A short walk from the civic and leisure centres, this is a friendly and popular live music venue with an L-shaped bar and separate drinking area. The beer range varies, with a good selection of local and national beers. The cider selection also varies. Live music usually plays Friday to Sunday nights, with open mic nights Tuesdays. There is a decked seating area outside. Beer and cider festivals are held throughout the year. There is a 10p a pint discount for CAMRA members.
☎☆≉♣●P🖫☺🎵

Upper Farmcote

Lion o' Morfe 🅛
WV15 5PS (½ mile from A458 signpost Claverley)
SO770919
🕐 12-11.30 ☎ (01746) 389935
Enville Ale; Hobsons Mild, Town Crier; Wye Valley HPA; 2 changing beers 🅗
This former Georgian farmhouse in the heart of the countryside became a pub in the early 1850s. A bustling local, it is also popular with walkers and cyclists. The main bar has an open fire and cosy wooden bench seating. To the rear is a snug with an old-fashioned range, and to the left is a traditionally decorated lounge leading to the conservatory. Outside is a large car park and garden area with a boules piste. Q☎☆☆A♣●P☺🎵

Weston

Stonehouse Brewery 🅛
Stonehouse, Weston Road, SY10 9ES (just off A483 Oswestry bypass)
🕐 10-5; closed Sun ☎ (01691) 676457
⊕ stonehousebrewery.co.uk
Stonehouse Sunlander, Station Bitter, Zaffir, Cambrian Gold, Off the Rails; 1 changing beer (often Stonehouse) 🅗
The family-run Stonehouse Brewery Visitor Centre Bar is in part of the brewery next to the preserved Cambrian Railway and is pleasantly rustic in style. At least four Stonehouse beers are available on draught – or to buy in bottles, polypins and takeaway jugs – plus Sweeney Mountain Cider. If the weather is nice, you can enjoy your pint in the beer garden. Brewery tours are by appointment.
Q☎☆&♣●P🖫☺🎵

Whitchurch

Black Bear 🅛
High Street, SY13 1AZ (opp St Alkmund's church)
🕐 12-3, 6-11; 12-11; 12-11 Sun; 12-10.30 Sun ☎ (01948) 663800
⊕ blackbearpub.co.uk
6 changing beers (often Hobsons, Lancaster) 🅗
Tastefully renovated black and white pub dating back to 1662. The ornate bar has six handpulls serving a range of guest beers both from local and lesser-known national microbreweries, with pumpclips adorning the walls, ceiling and bar area. Cider is served on gravity. There are two separate dining areas and an upstairs meeting room.
Q☆◖●P🖫☺

SOMERSET

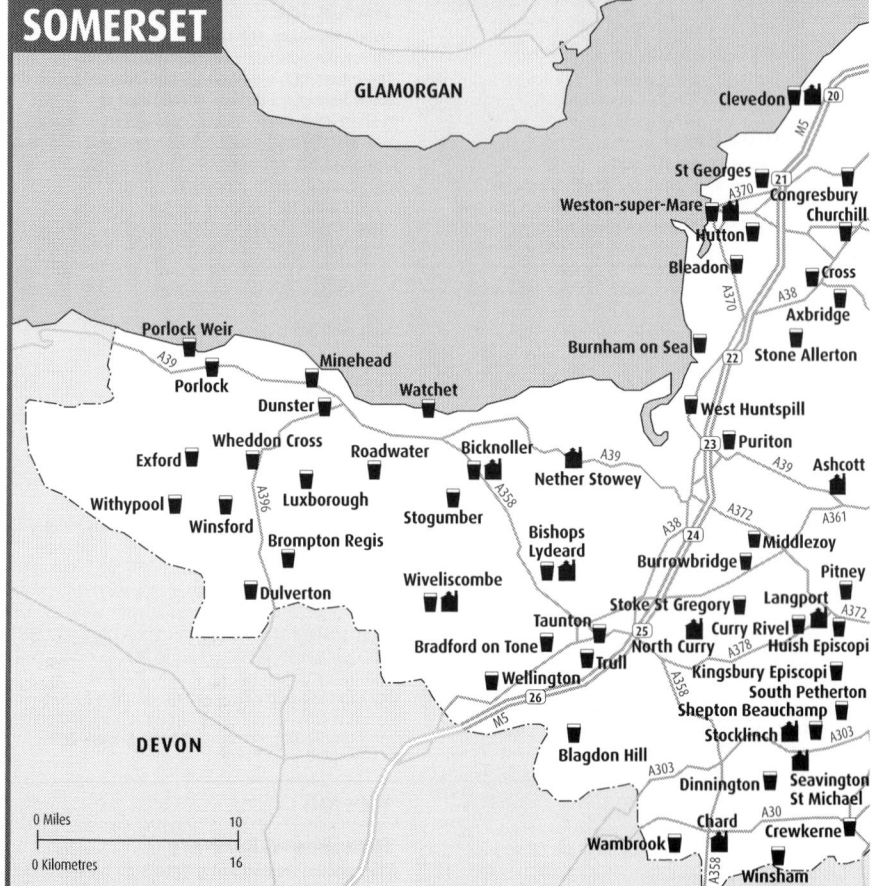

GLAMORGAN

Clevedon 20

St Georges 21
Weston-super-Mare Congresbury
Churchill
Hutton
Bleadon
Cross
Axbridge
Burnham on Sea 22 Stone Allerton
Porlock Weir West Huntspill
Minehead Puriton
Porlock Watchet 23 Ashcott
Dunster
Wheddon Cross Bicknoller A39
Exford Roadwater Nether Stowey
Withypool Luxborough Stogumber
Winsford Bishops Middlezoy
Brompton Regis Lydeard Pitney
Wiveliscombe Burrowbridge
Dulverton 24
Stoke St Gregory Langport
Taunton Curry Rivel
Bradford on Tone North Curry Huish Episcopi
Trull Kingsbury Episcopi
Wellington South Petherton
26 Shepton Beauchamp
DEVON Stocklinch
Blagdon Hill Seavington
Dinnington St Michael
Chard Crewkerne
0 Miles 10 Wambrook
0 Kilometres 16 Winsham

Ash

Bell Inn

3 Main Street, TA12 6NS
🕐 12-11; 12-10 Sun ☎ (01935) 822727
🌐 thebellinnash.co.uk
Sharp's Doom Bar; 3 changing beers (sourced regionally; often Exmoor, Plain, Teignworthy) Ⓗ
The Bell continues to be a warm, welcoming traditional pub with four ale handpumps and a real cider. Locally sourced home-cooked meals are served with a wide menu choice, blackboard specials and a Sunday roast. Regular live music nights and a quiz night take place. Skittles is popular here and the alley doubles up as a function room. Many unusual old church belfry items adorn the bar walls. It is possible to camp at the pub by prior arrangement. Q�garden🕏🐕🍴◑&♿♣🅿🚌(N9A)🌼

Axbridge

Crown Inn

St Mary's Street, BS26 2BN
🕐 5.30-midnight (2am Fri); 12-2am Sat; 12-midnight Sun
☎ (01934) 732518 🌐 crowninnaxbridge.co.uk
St Austell Tribute; Sharp's Doom Bar; 2 changing beers (sourced regionally) Ⓗ
In the heart of Axbridge, this village pub has a healthy local trade, as well as being welcoming to

visitors. There is a popular food menu including pizzas and Sunday roasts. Three en-suite bedrooms were opened in 2016 and cyclists are welcome, with bike storage available. This is a regular haunt for locals, particularly for TV sport and for its late opening hours. Q☆garden🕏🐕🍴◑&♿♣🅿🚌(126)🌼🛜

Lamb

The Square, BS26 2AP
🕐 11.30-11 (midnight Fri & Sat); 12-11 Sun
☎ (01934) 732253
Butcombe Original; 2 changing beers (often Butcombe) Ⓗ
Butcombe-owned Grade II-listed coaching house in the village square. The National Trust's medieval King John's Hunting Lodge lies directly opposite. There is a large low-beamed bar area and several smaller, quieter areas leading off it. Outside drinking spaces are to the front and rear via the courtyard. Butcombe seasonal ales are served together with a guest beer and several real ciders. Q🕏◑♣♿🚌(26,126)🌼🛜

Batcombe

Three Horseshoes Inn

BA4 6HE (off Back Lane) ST69023908
🕐 11-3, 6-11; 11-11 Sat; 12-10.30 Sun ☎ (01749) 850359
🌐 thethreehorseshoesinn.co.uk

Bell

103 Walcot Street, BA1 5BW

⊕ 11.30-11; 12-10.30 Sun ☎ (01225) 460426
⊕ thebellinnbath.co.uk

Abbey Bellringer; Bath Ales Gem; Butcombe Adam Henson's Rare Breed; Hop Back Summer Lightning; Otter Ale; RCH Pitchfork; 3 changing beers (sourced regionally; often Cotswold Lion, Stonehenge, Three Daggers) Ⓗ

Owned by 536 of its regulars, fans and staff following a community buy-out in 2013, the Bell has six regular ales plus three changing guests from micros near and far. Live music is a mainstay, with bands playing Monday and Wednesday evenings and Sunday lunchtimes and, in the separate Love Lounge to the rear, open mic nights take place on Thursday evenings. Features include bar billiards, board games and even a tiny launderette. At the rear is a walled garden with covered seating. ⊛Ⓓ♣🚌🍴♿🐾🛜

King of Wessex ✓

James Street West, BA1 2BX

⊕ 7am-11.30; 8am-11 Sun ☎ (01225) 303380

Greene King Abbot; changing beers Ⓗ

A large new-build Wetherspoon pub at the entrance to a cinema complex, refurbished in January 2016, and now with a spanking new carpet. There are up to six, mostly changing real ales, plus the usual 'Spoons regulars. Popular with the younger crowd, it can get busy in the evenings. Both the food and the beers are good value for the city centre. 🐾Ⓓ♿🚌🍴🛜

Old Green Tree ★

12 Green Street, BA1 2JZ

⊕ 11-11; 12-6 Sun ☎ (01225) 448259

Butcombe Adam Henson's Rare Breed; RCH Pitchfork; house beer (by Blindmans); 2 changing beers (sourced locally) Ⓗ

Butcombe Bitter; 3 changing beers Ⓗ
A 400-year-old country pub which has a spacious bar with an inglenook fireplace and beamed ceiling, a stunning dining room with a vaulted ceiling and a lawned garden overlooked by the church tower. Food is sourced from local suppliers. Open to all, it welcomes drinkers, foodies, walkers, children (with colouring books and games, to keep them entertained) and dogs. Local cider is from Rich's. Q🐾⊛♿Ⓓ🐾P

Bath

Bath Brew House ✓

14 James Street West, BA1 2BX

⊕ 12-midnight (1am Fri & Sat); 12-11 Sun
☎ (01225) 805609 ⊕ thebathbrewhouse.com

James Street Gladiator, Emperor; 5 changing beers (sourced regionally; often Castle Combe, James Street, Yeovil) Ⓗ

Refurbishment in 2013 saw the Midland Hotel transformed into a City Pub Company brewpub. The on-site James Street Brewery produces two regular beers, and rotating seasonal beers. Four guests are also available, usually from nearby micros. A large L-shaped bar leads to a dining area and a good-sized beer garden. The upstairs room hosts sports TV, quizzes, comedy and more. ⊛Ⓓ♿🚲🍴🚌♿🛜

Churchill

Crown Inn
The Batch, Skinners Lane, BS25 5PP (off A38)
✪ 11-11; 11-10.30 Sun ☎ (01934) 852995
Bath Ales Gem; Butcombe Original; St Austell Tribute;
4 changing beers Ⓖ
Long-time Guide regular and winner of many
CAMRA awards, it is tucked away down a small
lane yet close to the village centre. Several cosy
rooms with stone-flagged floors are warmed by
two log fires, and offer an assortment of seating.
Excellent food is provided at lunchtimes featuring
local ingredients. Up to eight beers, usually local,
are served on gravity. Outside drinking areas are to
the front and rear. Families are welcome away
from the bar itself. A classic unchanged old pub;
cash only, no cards. Q☎⊛◖Ⓐ♣P🚂(A2)🐾

Clevedon

Royal Oak ✔
35 Copse Road, BS21 7QN (behind ice cream parlour)
✪ 12-11 (midnight Fri & Sat) ☎ (01275) 563879
Butcombe Original; Fuller's London Pride; Sharp's
Doom Bar; 1 changing beer Ⓗ
Lively, friendly, mid-terrace pub close to the
seafront and connected via an alley. It has a large
front window and an unexpectedly large interior
with many rooms. This community hub is home to
cribbage and cricket teams. The winner of various
awards, it hosts many events, including cooking
competitions and dancing, ranging from morris
men through belly dance to Zulus. There is a quiz
on Monday and folk music on Wednesday.
Thatchers cider is sold. Q☎♣♠🚂🐾🛜

Combe Down

Cross Keys ✔
Midford Road, BA2 5RZ
✪ 12-3, 5-11; 12-midnight Fri & Sat; 12-11 Sun
☎ (01225) 832002 ⊕ crosskeysbath.co.uk
Butcombe Adam Henson's Rare Breed; Sharp's Doom
Bar; Wickwar BOB; 1 changing beer Ⓗ
An ivy-clad 18th-century coaching inn, right on the
outskirts of the city and close to the beautiful
Midford valley, popular with walkers. There are
usually up to four ales on, and much-
recommended gastro-standard food is served.
Inside there are two main bars with many original
features. Outside there is a large garden with
children's play area. ☎⊛◖P🚂(10)🐾🛜

Congresbury

Plough
High Street, BS49 5JA (off A370 at B3133 jct)
✪ 11.30-2.30, 4.30-11; 12-2.30, 7-10.30 Sun
☎ (01934) 877402 ⊕ the-plough-inn.net
Butcombe Original; St Austell Tribute Ⓗ/Ⓖ; Twisted
Oak Fallen Tree Ⓖ; 5 changing beers (sourced
locally) Ⓗ/Ⓖ
Characterful village pub with flagstone floors and
many original features, decorated with interesting
local artefacts. Five guest beers are delivered from
a row of old cask heads behind the bar, sourced
mainly from local breweries. Up to 16 ciders are
also stocked. Sunday is quiz night. The pub has real
fires and a large garden. Mendip morris men meet
here. Local CAMRA Pub of the Year 2015.
Q⊛◖♣♠P🚂(X1,353)🐾

Crewkerne

King William Inn
Barn Street, TA18 8BP (fringe of town)
✪ 5 (12 Sat)-midnight; 12-4 Sun ☎ (01460) 279615
Butcombe Bitter; 2 changing beers (sourced
regionally; often Arbor, Oakham, Tapstone) Ⓗ
A short walk from the town centre towards Chard
takes you to this traditional pub. There are two
changing guest ales, mainly from regional
breweries, but sometimes from further afield. A
beer festival is held on the August bank holiday.
Happy hours feature on Monday and Wednesday,
and for music lovers there is an acoustic night on
the last Wednesday of the month. The TV has
terrestrial and BT sport.
Q☎⊛◖♣♠P🚂(40/96A)🐾

White Hart
East Street, TA18 7LW
✪ closed Mon & Tue; 12-11 ☎ (01460) 73774
⊕ whitehartcrewkerne.co.uk
2 changing beers (often Butcombe, Oakham,
Thornbridge) Ⓗ
Regarded as the oldest surviving pub in Crewkerne,
dating back to circa 1500. Seating is arranged
around a U-shaped bar, with a magnificent
fireplace and a wood-burning stove, and a second
fireplace and stove in a snug area near the
entrance. There is an upstairs skittle alley that can
double up as a function room. A rotating choice of
two interesting real ales makes this pub well worth
a visit. ☎⊛◖♣🚂(40/96A)🐾🛜

Croscombe

George Inn
Long Street, BA5 3QH (on A371)
✪ 7.30am-3, 6-11; 7.30am-3, 5-midnight Fri;
7.30am-midnight Sat; 7.30am-11 Sun ☎ (01749) 342306
⊕ thegeorgeinn.co.uk
House beer (by Blindmans) Ⓗ; changing beers (often
Arbor, Cheddar Ales, Three Daggers) Ⓗ/Ⓖ
Attractive 17th-century inn refurbished by the
owner, serving at least four guest ales from West
Country independents and hosting two beer
festivals a year. Blindmans King George and
George & Dragon are exclusively brewed for the
pub. Four real ciders are available, with Hecks
Kingston Black, Thatchers Cheddar Valley and
Orchard Pig the regulars. It has a large main bar, a
snug with fireplace, a family room and a separate
dining room. Food is home-cooked using locally
sourced ingredients. The large garden has a
covered terrace. Q☎⊛◖◖♦♣♠P🚂🐾🛜

Cross

New Inn ✔
Old Coach Road, BS26 2EE (on A38/A361 jct)
✪ 12-11 (midnight Fri & Sat) ☎ (01934) 732455
⊕ newinncross.co.uk
Otter Ale; Sharp's Cornish Coaster; 3 changing
beers Ⓗ
Roadside inn on the A38, close to the historic
medieval town of Axbridge. Popular for its
extensive food menu served all day until 9pm
(8pm Sun), it usually has three guest beers, often
adventurous and rare for the area. Beer festivals
are held over the Easter and August bank holidays.
There is a function room on the first floor. Families
are welcome – dogs too. The large hillside garden
with children's play facilities offers a fine view of

the Mendip Hills, out to Glastonbury Tory, and Somerset Levels. There is a small car park opposite. ✿🌓♣P🚆(126)☺🛜

Curry Rivel

Firehouse ✓
Church Street, TA10 0HE
✿ 12-11; 11-10 Sun ☎ (01458) 887447
⊕ thefirehousesomerset.co.uk
Butcombe Adam Henson's Rare Breed, Bitter; 2 changing beers (often Oakham, Thornbridge) ℍ
This enticing village hostelry has been beautifully restored with a modern twist and yet is also packed with traditional charm. On the left when entering is the house bar where you will find four real ales with two changing choices. In addition there is real cider from local producers. Leading from the bar are five further sitting/dining areas arranged over three floors with wood-burning stoves in abundance. Well worth a visit in this delightful village. ➚✿🌓&P🚆(54)🛜

Dinnington

Dinnington Docks Inn ✓
TA17 8SX (approx 3 miles E of Ilminster off B3168)
✿ 10.30-3.30, 5.30-11; 11.30-11 Fri & Sat; 12-10.30 Sun
☎ (01460) 52397
Butcombe Bitter; Teignworthy Gun Dog; 1 changing beer (sourced regionally; often Sharp's, Teignworthy, Yeovil) ℍ
This is very much a traditional country pub where the conversation will not be interrupted by fruit machines or music. Three cask ales are served in excellent condition and meals are prepared to order from a blackboard menu above the fireplace. A garden with trestle tables can be found at the rear. There is an abundance of railway memorabilia including a spoof illustration of an old rail crossing outside. Q➚✿🌓&♣P☺

Draycott

Cider Barn
Latches Lane Crossroads, Draycott Road, BS27 3YB
✿ 12-10 (11 Thu-Sat) ☎ (01934) 741837
3 changing beers ℍ/🄶
Quirky, relaxing bar/cafe/takeaway cider and ale barn on the main A371 near Cheddar where you can also buy coffee, tea and cakes, simple locally sourced home-cooked meals and great little snacks (Somerset tapas!). Up to 13 real ciders and three usually local real ales are served, two on gravity. There is live music every Saturday evening and every other Sunday afternoon. The bar sometimes stays open until 11pm. Caravan electric hook-up and camping are available. ✿🌓&🅰♣P🚆(126)☺🛜

Dulverton

Bridge Inn 🄻
20 Bridge Street, TA22 9HJ
✿ 12-11 (3 Mon) ☎ (01398) 324130
⊕ thebridgeinndulverton.com
Exmoor Ale; 3 changing beers (sourced regionally; often Burning Sky, Butcombe, Dark Star) ℍ
A warm, welcoming pub dating from 1845. As the name implies, it is close to a bridge crossing the River Barle upstream from its confluence with the River Exe. Situated in a delightful small town, the

pub has a cosy single-room bar with a wood-burning stove and an extended restaurant area. There is always an interesting selection of national cask ales, and bottled beers include a Belgian selection. Opening hours are restricted in winter. Q➚✿🌓🅰♣P🚆☺🛜

Dunster

Luttrell Arms Hotel
36 High Street, TA24 6SG
✿ 10-11.30 ☎ (01643) 821555 ⊕ luttrellarms.co.uk
Exmoor Ale; Otter Amber; 2 changing beers (sourced locally) ℍ
The hotel, with its 28 unique bedrooms, is on the site of three ancient houses dating back to 1443. The back bar with an open log fire features some of the oldest glass windows in Somerset and there is fine plasterwork on the lounge ceiling. You can dine in the à la carte restaurant or, if you prefer, order a bar snack. The view of Dunster Castle from the back garden is wonderful. Mini beer festivals are held. Q➚✿🚪🌓🅰♣🚆(28,198)☺🛜

Emborough

Old Down Inn
BA3 4SA (close to A37/B3139 crossroads)
✿ 12-3, 6-midnight; 12-5 Sun ☎ (01761) 232398
Draught Bass; Glastonbury Lady of the Lake; Sharp's Doom Bar 🄶; 2 changing beers (sourced regionally; often Three Daggers) ℍ/🄶
An old coaching inn first licensed in 1640. The spirit of the past lives on in the main bar, where beer is served straight from the cask. Two guests from local breweries are generally available. The bar snacks are excellent value, and likewise the main meals. This friendly and popular hostelry is a classic example of a traditional Somerset inn and is the centre of many local community activities. Watch out for the parrot. Q➚✿🌓&🅰♣P🚆(173)☺

Exford

Exmoor White Horse Inn ✓
TA24 7PY (on B3224 W of Wheddon Cross)
✿ 11-11 ☎ (01643) 831229 ⊕ exmoor-whitehorse.co.uk
Cotleigh Tawny Owl; Exmoor Ale, Gold; 3 changing beers (sourced locally) ℍ
Set in a pretty village, within Exmoor National Park, this is an ideal base for walking, fishing and various country pursuits. The long bar features fine ales and a choice of 200 malt whiskies in the separate whisky bar. There are 28 en-suite rooms and a honeymoon suite. The outside tables are set on the bank of the River Exe. Enjoy fine dining or a bar snack, featuring locally sourced produce. Q➚✿🌓&♣P🚆(198)☺🛜

Faulkland

Tucker's Grave ★
BA3 5XF
✿ 12-3 (not Mon), 6-11; 12-3, 7-10.30 Sun
☎ (01373) 834230
Butcombe Adam Henson's Rare Breed, Original; 1 changing beer (sourced locally) 🄶
A gem from a bygone age with a nationally important historic pub interior, this inn was built in the mid-17th century and has changed little since. It was named after Tucker, who hanged himself and was buried at the crossroads outside, and

Built in 1906 between the harbour and the lifeboat station, the pub has 12 letting rooms with fantastic views over the Bristol Channel. Exmoor National Park is only a 20-minute drive away, and it is within walking distance of the town centre and the West Somerset Railway. Themed food nights are held throughout the week, and a carvery on Sunday. Beer festivals are staged and there is live music at the weekend. ⌂⊛�◑🕭Ġ👌▲♣🖚P🚻(28,198)🐾🛜

Mudford

Half Moon Inn
Main Street, BA21 5TF (on A359)
✪ 11-11; 11-10.30 Sun ☎ (01935) 850289
⊕ thehalfmooninn.co.uk
St Austell Proper Job, HSD Ġ
Popular 17th-century roadside inn with a strong regular trade. Real ales and cider are served from a stillage behind the bar. The courtyard, in which dogs are allowed (guide dogs only in the pub) is pleasant on warm days. The extensive menu, which includes light lunches and daily specials, is displayed on a blackboard. The pub has letting rooms in the main building, former skittle alley and log store. Q⊛🚮◑Ġ🖚P🚻(1)🐾🛜

Norton St Philip

Fleur de Lys ✪
High Street, BA2 7LG
✪ 11-3 (not Mon-Thu), 5-11; 11-11 Sat & Sun
☎ (01373) 834333 ⊕ fleurdelysnsp.co.uk
Wadworth 6X, Bishops Tipple; 1 changing beer (sourced regionally; often Dukeries)
An inn since 1584, the Fleur is a warm, welcoming pub. Its three main drinking/dining areas are served by a single bar. Old beams, stone walls and a log fire impart a cosy feeling, and on the walls old hand-painted Wadworth brewery signs can be seen. At the rear of the pub is a much-used skittle alley where a number of local teams regularly play. The food is mainly pizzas, but other dishes are available. Q◑♣🖚P🚻🛜

Pitney

Halfway House 🅛
Pitney Hill, TA10 9AB (on B3153)
✪ 11.30-3, 4-11; 11.30-11.30 Sat; 11.30-11 Sun
☎ (01458) 252513 ⊕ thehalfwayhouse.co.uk
Hop Back Summer Lightning; Otter Bright; Teignworthy Neap Tide, Reel Ale; 5 changing beers (often Cheddar Ales, Plain, Quantock) Ġ
An outstanding pub offering eight to nine regional ales on gravity alongside many bottled beers and real ciders. The inside is traditional, with flagstone flooring, old wooden tables and benches, and three real fires. This busy pub deserves its many accolades and has featured in the Guide for 25 consecutive years. It serves superb home-cooked food including roast lunch on Sunday. Q⊛◑♣🖚P🚻(54)🐾🛜

Porlock

Ship Inn 🅛 ✪
High Street, TA24 8QD
✪ 11-midnight; 12-midnight Sun ☎ (01643) 862507
⊕ shipinnporlock.co.uk

Exmoor Beast; Otter Bitter; 6 changing beers (sourced regionally)
Known locally as the Top Ship, the bar is a gem with its flagstone floor and open fire. It has changed little since featuring in RD Blackmore's novel Lorna Doone. The pub dates from the 13th century and sits at the bottom of the notorious Porlock Hill that takes you up to Exmoor. Eight ales and local cider are sold and good food can be enjoyed in its restaurant or delightful three-tiered garden in summer. Q⌂⊛🚮◑Ġ👌▲♣🖚P🚻(10)🐾

Porlock Weir

Ship Inn 🅛
TA24 8PB (take B3225 from Porlock)
✪ 11-11; 12-10.30 Sun ☎ (01643) 863288
⊕ shipinnporlockweir.co.uk
Exmoor Ale; St Austell Tribute, Proper Job; 2 changing beers
The pub, on the South-West Coast Path, boasts fantastic views of the Bristol Channel and the coastline of South Wales. It is set next to the small harbour where oyster beds have been recently installed. The 400-year-old inn, in Exmoor National Park, is a favourite with walkers. A beer festival is held in June featuring up to 50 ales. It gets busy in the summer – there is a Pay & Display car park opposite. Q⊛◑Ġ▲♣🖚P🚻(10)🐾

Portishead

Windmill Inn
58 Nore Road, BS20 6JZ (next to municipal golf course)
✪ 11-11; 11-10.30 Sun ☎ (01275) 818483
Butcombe Original; Fuller's London Pride; 3 changing beers
Large split-level pub with a spacious patio to the rear, plus an extension enjoying panoramic views. It is above the coastal path on the edge of town, and the Severn Estuary and both Severn bridges can be seen on clear days. A varied menu is served all day with table bookings available. The pub was acquired by Fuller's in 2014 but the three guest ales come from a variety of breweries, and Thatchers cider is also served. Monday is quiz night. Q⌂⊛◑Ġ🖚P🚻(X3,X4)🐾🛜

Priddy

Hunters Lodge
Hillgrove Road, BA5 3AR (on isolated crossroads 1 mile from A39 close to TV mast) ST549500
✪ 11.30-2.30, 6.30-11; 12-2, 7-11 Sun ☎ (01749) 672275
Butcombe Original; Cheddar Ales Potholer; 1 changing beer (often Blindmans) Ġ
The landlord of this timeless roadside inn has been in charge for 47 years. At a crossroads near Priddy, the highest village in Somerset, it is popular with cavers and walkers. Three rooms include one with a flagged floor, and all beer is served direct from casks behind the bar. Local cider is stocked and the home-cooked food is excellent and exceptional value. A folk musicians' drop-in session is held on Tuesday evening. The garden is pleasant and secluded. Mobile phones are not welcome but dogs are. Q⌂⊛◑♣🖚🐾

Queen Victoria Inn ✪
Pelting Drove, BA5 3BA
✪ 12-11; 12-10.30 Sun ☎ (01749) 676385
⊕ thequeenvicpriddy.co.uk

Butcombe Original; 2 changing beers (often Fuller's, Butcombe) Ⓗ
Creeper-clad inn, a pub since 1851, with four rooms that feature low ceilings, flagged floors and log fires. A wonderfully warm and relaxing haven on cold winter nights, it is popular during the Priddy Folk Festival in July and the annual fair in August. Reasonably priced, home-cooked food is a speciality. Children are welcome and there is a play area by the car park. Cheddar Valley and Ashton Still ciders are sold. May close briefly on some afternoons. Q✿🛏️🕙▲♣️🍴P🐾🎶📶

Puriton

37 Club 🅛
1 West Approach Road, Woolavington Road, TA7 8AD
✿ 4-11; 2-midnight Fri; 12-midnight Sat & Sun
☎ (01278) 685190 🌐 37club.co.uk
Otter Amber, Ale; St Austell Tribute, Proper Job; 3 changing beers (often Exmoor) Ⓗ
On the site of the former Royal Ordnance Factory which was allocated the number 37, this is a large club offering a great many facilities to members and visitors. It has two bars and its multi-roomed layout incorporates a concert room, two skittle alleys, dining room, snooker room with five tables and, outside, a beer garden, fishing lake and football pitch. CAMRA members are welcome with a membership card. The food menu includes a Sunday carvery (booking advisable). 🛏️🕙▲♣️🍴P🚉(75)

Radstock

Fromeway
Frome Road, BA3 3LG
✿ closed Mon; 12-3, 6-11; 12-11 Sun ☎ (01761) 432116
🌐 fromeway.co.uk
Butcombe Adam Henson's Rare Breed Ⓗ; 2 changing beers (sourced nationally; often Timothy Taylor, Wadworth, Yeovil) Ⓗ/Ⓐ
This friendly free house is now in its sixth generation of the same family. Emily and Andrew welcome you with a great selection of weekly changing ales. In the first year of their takeover they have provided over 100 different beers from all over the country. The food features traditional classics as well as more contemporary dishes. The pub has an award-winning garden. Regular charity events, quiz nights and walks take place from month to month. 🛏️🕙&🍴P🚉(768,178)🐾📶

Roadwater

Valiant Soldier 🅛 ✅
TA23 0QZ (off A39 at Washford)
✿ 11.30-2.30, 6-11; 12-3, 6-11 Sun ☎ (01984) 640223
🌐 thevaliantsoldier.co.uk
Exmoor Ale; Sharp's Doom Bar; 1 changing beer (sourced regionally) Ⓗ
The inn dates back to 1720 and is ideal as a base for country walks and exploring nearby Exmoor and the old Mineral Line. This vibrant local's pub has quiz, pool, darts and nine skittles teams to see it through the winter months. It is by a small river where you can relax and watch the ducks and, if you are lucky, kingfishers. It offers good-quality locally sourced food, and has been run by the same landlord for over 30 years. 🛏️🕙▲♣️🍴P📶

Rode

Cross Keys ✅
20 High Street, BA11 6NZ (on main street)
✿ 12-2.30, 5.30-11.30; 12-11.30 Sat; 12-10.30 Sun
☎ (01373) 830900 🌐 crosskeysrode.co.uk
Butcombe Adam Henson's Rare Breed; 2 changing beers (sourced nationally; often Bristol Beer Factory, Oakham, Three Daggers) Ⓗ
Reopened in 2004 after 10 years of closure, this was originally the brewery tap for the long-closed Fussell's Brewery, and more recently, a Bass depot. Sympathetically restored, it has succeeded in bringing back a strong village trade. A passageway featuring a deep well links two bars, and there is a large restaurant. Up to two guest beers can come from almost anywhere, and may be major names like London Pride but are more often from breweries rare for the area. Look out for the fascinating clock mechanism in the restaurant. Q✿🛏️🕙▲♣️🍴P🚉🐾📶

Rowberrow

Swan Inn ✅
Rowberrow Lane, BS25 1QL
✿ 12-11; 12-10.30 Sun ☎ (01934) 852371
Butcombe Original; 3 changing beers (often Butcombe) Ⓗ
Believed to date from around the late 17th century, this country pub, made up of three knocked-through miners' cottages, enjoys an attractive setting, nestling beneath the Dolebury Iron Age hill fort. A convenient stop for walkers on the Mendip Hills, the emphasis is on quality home-cooked food, but customers who just want a drink are welcome. At least one guest beer is on handpump, often from a brewery unusual to this area. The large, attractive beer garden and car park are opposite. Q✿🛏️🕙&🍴P🐾

St Georges

Woolpack
Shepherds Way, BS22 7XE (close to M5 jct 21)
✿ 11-11; 12-10.30 Sun ☎ (01934) 521670
Butcombe Original, Gold; Fuller's London Pride; 1 changing beer Ⓗ
This 17th-century coaching house was once a packing station that baled wool for local farmers. Owned by Butcombe Brewery since 2006, it has two bar areas, a conservatory and a patio. The pub is in the much-expanded St Georges area, and within walking distance of Worle station. Food is served every day from an extensive menu with daily specials, and there is a separate carvery (no table reservations on Sunday). 🛏️🕙&⇄P🚉📶

Saltford

Bird in Hand ✅
58 High Street, BS31 3EJ
✿ 11-11 ☎ (01225) 873335 🌐 birdinhandsaltford.co.uk
Butcombe Original; Sharp's Doom Bar; 2 changing beers Ⓗ
A traditional country inn dating from 1869 set among stone dwellings at the bottom of the village high street, 400 yards from the A4 and close to the Bristol to Bath cycle path and River Avon. There is a long L-shaped bar and a pleasant conservatory with fine views across the garden to the hills beyond. Old photographs feature and there is a small family

area. Food is served lunchtimes and evenings (all day at weekends), including gluten-free. It has a pétanque piste. ⌂🕮⌖🍴🛆♣♠P🖵🐾🛜

Shepton Beauchamp

Duke of York 🄻
North Street, TA19 0LW
✪ 5-midnight Mon; 3.30 (12 Thu & Fri)-11; 12-midnight Sat; 12-10.30 Sun ☎ (01460) 240314 ⊕ thesheptonduke.co.uk
Sharp's Doom Bar; Teignworthy Gun Dog; 1 changing beer (sourced regionally; often Otter, St Austell) Ⓗ
A typical south Somerset village, with the inn, school, shop and church in the centre. The pub has a split-level interior which makes it somewhat unusual. Externally, a high pavement with benches gives a village overview and to the rear is a pleasant beer garden and letting rooms. This family establishment welcomes both dogs on leads and children. On Saturday breakfast is served 9-11am. ⌂🕮⌖🍴♣P🐾🛜

South Cadbury

Camelot 🄻
Chapel Road, BA22 7EX (just off A303)
✪ 12-3, 6.30-9.30; 11-11 Fri & Sat; 12-10.30 Sun
☎ (01963) 441685 ⊕ camelotpub.co.uk
Sharp's Doom Bar; Yeovil Summerset; 2 changing beers (sourced regionally; often Cotleigh, Exmoor, Otter) Ⓗ
Legend has it that Cadbury Castle is the castle of King Arthur, and at the foot of the northern slopes, the village pub can be found. Inside the pub an informative display catalogues what is known of the local history but unfortunately no picture or selfie of King Arthur! Close to the A303 and well signposted, it makes an ideal stop-off for those travelling to or from the West Country. Dogs and children are welcome. Q⌂🕮⌖🍴♣♠P🖵(1)🐾🛜

South Petherton

Brewers Arms 🄻 ✅
18-20 St James Street, TA13 5BW (½ mile off A303)
✪ 11.30-2.30, 6-11; 11.30-midnight Fri & Sat; 12-11 Sun
☎ (01460) 241887 ⊕ the-brewersarms.com
Butcombe Bitter; Otter Bitter; 3 changing beers (sourced nationally; often Hop Back, Otter) Ⓗ
Awarded the county CAMRA Pub of the Year in 2016, the pub has been in the Guide for 22 consecutive years and in the current landlord's capable hands for 23. During this time 2,600 different ales have been presented. This establishment is the centre of village life, with its extensive support for local events and charities. Beer festivals are held twice a year and there are numerous other events such as live music and quiz nights. ⌂🕮⌖🍴🛆♣♠🖵(81)🐾🛜

Stogumber

White Horse Inn
High Street, TA4 3TA (turn left off A358 at Crowcombe)
✪ 12-2.30, 4.30-11; 6-11 Tue; 12-11 Sat & Sun
☎ (01984) 656277 ⊕ whitehorsestogumber.co.uk
Otter Bitter; St Austell Proper Job; 2 changing beers (sourced regionally; often Otter, Quantock) Ⓗ
In a picturesque village near the Brendon Hills and close to the WSR steam railway, this traditional free house is a Grade II-listed building. The bar has a friendly atmosphere with a cosy log fire, and its

ales are from local and regional breweries. There is a courtyard garden. The separate restaurant, originally the Market Hall, serves Somerset-produced food. The skittle alley doubles as a function room and hosts a music festival in September. Accommodation is reached via an outside stairwell. ⌂🕮⌖🍴♣P🐾🛜

Stoke St Gregory

Royal Oak Inn
The Square, TA3 6EH (opp church)
✪ closed Mon; 12-3, 6.30-11.30; 12-5, 6.30-12.30am Sat; 12-4.30, 7-11.30 Sun ☎ (01823) 490602
⊕ theroyaloaktaunton.co.uk
2 changing beers (often Butcombe, Quantock, St Austell) Ⓗ
In the centre of the village, this friendly, family-run pub offers a warm welcome to all. There is a varied and well-priced menu to suit all tastes, including home-made stone-baked pizzas. There are facilities for darts, pool and skittles, and the pub has a cricket team. It is ideally located for taking a break when walking the Somerset Levels or the long-distance Parrett Trail. Overnight parking is available for camper vans. ⌂🕮⌖🍴🛆♣♠P🖵(51)🐾🛜

Stone Allerton

Wheatsheaf Inn
Notting Hill Way, BS26 2NH
✪ closed Mon; 6-11; 12-2 Sun ☎ (01934) 444333
2 changing beers Ⓖ
One of the only pubs in a wide area, it was reopened in 2014 after a long closure. The modern-yet-boutique decor, including old bookshelves, makes it a comfortable and warm place to eat and drink. Local products are sold, including an unusual lager selection; the cask ales are served by gravity and often come from Cheddar Ales and Twisted Oak breweries. The restaurant is popular and all food is produced in the on-site smokery. There are no electronic gaming machines, only quiet background music. Q⌂🕮⌖🍴♣P🐾

Stratton-on-the-Fosse

King's Arms
6 South Street, BA3 4RA
✪ 12-2 (not Mon & Tue), 6-11; 12-11 Sun ☎ (01761) 233544
⊕ kingsarms-strattonotf.co.uk
4 changing beers (sourced locally; often Box Steam, Twisted, Yeovil) Ⓗ
A smart and handsome pub usually serving up to five weekly changing ales, mainly from local and other West Country breweries, plus a local cider. Lunchtime and evening meals are on offer, and there are B&B rooms available. The village is set in beautiful countryside, while the pub is directly opposite Downside Abbey. ⌂🍴⌖🛆♣♠P🖵🐾🛜

Taunton

Bank
Middle Street, TA1 1SJ
✪ 11-11 (midnight Sat); closed Sun ☎ (01823) 257788
⊕ thebanktaunton.co.uk
2 changing beers (sourced nationally; often Arbor, Moor Beer, Oakham) Ⓗ
Close to Somerset cricket ground, the Bank features two changing cask ales from small breweries. On the ground floor is a cosy bar offering a wide range

of drinks; upstairs is reserved for diners, with doors that open on to a terrace. Quality food is on offer which can be described as modern British with an international influence. Bar meals reflect the quality of the main menu. ⊛🌣⅃ᚹ≷🖵🐾🐾♿

Racehorse Inn ✓
East Reach, TA1 3HT
🕕 12-4, 6-11; 12-12.30am Fri & Sat; 12-11 Sun
☎ (01823) 327513
St Austell Trelawny, Tribute, Proper Job; 1 changing beer Ⓗ
Popular St Austell pub close to the town centre at the top of East Reach, multi-roomed with front and rear bars and a small lounge with comfortable armchairs. Skittles and darts are played regularly and there is live music every week. A large walled garden at the rear is ideal for a relaxing drink on warm summer days. No food is served.
⊛🌣♣🖵🐾🐾♿

Ring of Bells Ⓛ
16-17 St James Street, TA1 1JS
🕕 11-11; 11-8 Sun ☎ (01823) 259480
⊕ theringofbellstaunton.co.uk
5 changing beers (sourced nationally; often Oakham, Quantock) Ⓗ
Town-centre pub close to the theatre and Somerset cricket ground and therefore a favourite haunt of cricket fans. Wooden floored, there are two bar areas (one with an open fire), a downstairs dining area, an upstairs restaurant and a large courtyard. The five cask beers are from local, regional and national breweries. Excellent locally produced food is served (booking recommended). Sporting events are shown on TV in the bar area.
Q🌣⊛🌣⅃≷🖵🐾🐾♿

Wyvern Social Club Ⓛ
Mountfields Road, TA1 3BJ (off South Rd)
🕕 6 (2 Sat)-11; 12-3, 7-10.30 Sun ☎ (01823) 284591
⊕ wyvernclub.co.uk
Exmoor Ale; 2 changing beers (sourced regionally; often Exmoor, Quantock, St Austell) Ⓗ
For over 30 years this club has been a great venue to drink real ale and now real cider. It is members-only but has a visitors' licence – show a CAMRA membership card to be signed in as a guest. It is the hub for the rugby, cricket and squash clubs who use the attached playing fields. Joint Somerset CAMRA branch Club of the Year 2017, it hosts an annual beer festival in October. Bus routes are Saturday daytime only. 🌣⊛⅃🌣♣🖵P🖵(6,99)♿

Trull

Winchester Arms
8 Church Road, TA3 7LG
🕕 12-3, 6.30-11; 12-3.30, 6.30-10.30 Sun ☎ (01823) 284723
⊕ winchesterarmstrull.co.uk
4 changing beers (sourced regionally; often Exmoor, Otter, St Austell) Ⓗ
Thriving family-run community pub on the outskirts of Taunton near the Blackdown Hills. The comfortable bar area is separated from the long dining area by a fireplace. The locally sourced home-cooked food is excellent (booking is advised at popular times). The streamside gardens, perfect for families and dogs, becomes the venue for entertainment and barbecues. The pub offers good-value accommodation. A popular quiz takes place on Sunday night. Q⊛🚲⅃🌣♣P🖵(97)🐾♿

Twerton

Royal Oak
Lower Bristol Road, BA2 3BW (on A36)
🕕 2-midnight; 12-1am Fri & Sat; 12-midnight Sun
☎ (01225) 481409 ⊕ theroyaloakbath.co.uk
Butts Jester, Barbus Barbus; Downton IPA; 5 changing beers Ⓗ
Two regular beers from Butts Brewery, one from Downton and up to five guests from microbreweries near and far are served here alongside an interesting range of ciders, perries and bottled British and Belgian beers. There are folk music sessions (Irish and English) on Wednesday evening and live music most weekends. Tuesday is quiz night. Outside is a secluded garden and a small car park. CAMRA members receive a discount of 30p per pint. Beer festivals feature occasionally. ⊛≷🍴P🖵🐾♿

Wambrook

Cotley Inn
TA20 3EN (from A30 W out of Chard, by toll house, take left fork and almost immediately left again; continue for just over 1 mile on narrow lane)
🕕 closed Mon; 12-3, 6-11; 12-3 Sun ☎ (01460) 62348
⊕ cotleyinnwambrook.co.uk
Otter Bitter; 2 changing beers (often Exeter, Exmoor, Otter) Ⓖ
A traditional country pub that is well worth finding. Inside the main entrance is a bar area with a welcoming wood-burning stove to greet you in the winter months. To the right of the bar is a skittle alley and to the left you will find dining areas where you can sample the excellent food. Ales are served from gravity racking behind the bar. The pub is in a rural setting where sitting outside is a delight. Q🌣⊛⅃♣🍴P🐾

Watchet

Esplanade Club Ⓛ ✓
5 The Esplanade, TA23 0AJ (opp marina)
🕕 7 (12 Sat)-midnight; 12-3, 7-midnight Sun
☎ (01984) 634518
4 changing beers (sourced regionally; often Exmoor, Quantock) Ⓗ
Built in the 1860s as a sailmaking factory and now home to the boat owners' club, it has a fine display of old photographs and memorabilia. There are great views over the marina and Bristol Channel and it is close to the West Somerset Railway. The club has a reputation as a music venue with live acts every weekend and folk nights and open mic during the week. Joint Somerset CAMRA Club of the Year 2017. 🌣⊛🌣🏔≷♣🍴🖵(28)🐾

Pebbles Tavern Ⓛ
24 Market Street, TA23 0AN (near museum)
🕕 10.30 (5 Wed)-11; 12-10.30 Sun ☎ (01984) 634737
⊕ pebblestavern.co.uk
3 changing beers (often Moles, Otter, Stowey) Ⓖ
This small, unique tavern in the heart of the village has won numerous CAMRA branch and regional awards for Cider Pub of the Year, and in 2015 it was the national runner-up. There can be up to 30 ciders, three changing ales direct from the cask and 37 gins. You are allowed to bring in your fish and chips from the shop next door or order food from the local deli. Music nights featuring folk, sea shanty, acoustic and jazz are held regularly. 🌣≷♣🍴🖵(28)🐾♿

Star Inn Ⓛ
Mill Lane, TA23 0BZ
✪ 12-3.30, 6.30-11; 12-4, 6.30-11 Sun ☎ (01984) 631367
🌐 starinnwatchet.co.uk
4 changing beers (often Butcombe, Exmoor, Otter) Ⓗ
This 16th-century pub has been in the Guide for over 15 years. With friendly staff and a congenial atmosphere, it is well known for its good-value locally sourced food which is cooked to order. It has darts, quiz and boules teams, and hosts music nights in the summer. It also does port and cheese nights and is home to the Sunday night Bad Boys Club. Mick's beer tours have run over 80 trips from the pub. 🛏️🏵️🍴🍽️♿🚶🎏♣🚗🅿️🚃(28)🐾🎵📶

Wellington

Dolphin Ⓛ
37 Waterloo Road, TA21 8JQ
✪ 12 (4 Mon & Tue)-11; 12-10 Sun ☎ (01823) 665889
🌐 thedolphinwellington.co.uk
Otter Amber; 2 changing beers (often Exeter, Exmoor, Quantock) Ⓗ
Traditional town-centre pub offering up to four local ales at the weekend. Home-cooked food is served daily plus pizza to eat in or take away (including vegan and gluten-free varieties). Live music features twice a month, normally on Thursday or Saturday, and there are monthly themed food or charity nights. The colourful pub frontage features an unusual mural with handpumps depicting local breweries and wine bottles. Q🛏️🏵️🍴🍽️♿♣🚗🅿️(22a)🐾📶

Wellow

Fox & Badger
Railway Lane, BA2 8QG
✪ 11.30-3, 6-11; 11.30-11 Fri & Sat; 12-4 Sun
☎ (01225) 832293 🌐 thefoxandbadger.com
Butcombe Adam Henson's Rare Breed; 2 changing beers (sourced regionally; often Electric Bear, Otter, Palmers) Ⓗ
An unspoilt, popular village local, with a single central bar decorated with hops. Up to three ales will be on, including two changing guests. Rustic furniture rests on stone-flagged and wood-boarded floors, while there is a fine stone fireplace with a wood-burning stove. It is popular in the evenings for its food, so book up if you wish to eat. A great destination for walkers and cyclists (close to National Cycle Route 244). Car parking can be a problem. 🍴🍽️♣🚗🅿️(757)🐾📶

Wells

Just Ales
38 Market Street, BA5 2DS
✪ 12-9 (11 Fri & Sat) ☎ (01749) 678480 🌐 justales.com
7 changing beers (sourced nationally) Ⓖ
Wells' first micropub, opened in March 2016 by two beer enthusiasts in what was an old tea shop, just a few yards from the High Street. As well as up to seven ales on gravity, there are as many real ciders. The ales can come from any part of the country. This is a quiet, comfortable place for a pint and a natter with friends or strangers – tea and coffee, sandwiches, jackets and toast are also available. Q🛏️♣🚗🅿️🐾📶

West Huntspill

Crossways Inn 🍷 Ⓛ
Withy Road, TA9 3RA (on A38)
✪ 12-midnight (1am Fri & Sat); 12-11 Sun
☎ (01278) 783756 🌐 crosswaysinn.com
Exmoor Gold; 5 changing beers (sourced nationally; often Arbor, Marston's, Otter) Ⓗ
This 17th-century inn is a well-deserved winner of Somerset CAMRA Pub of the Year 2017. It has several bar areas, two log fires in winter and an outside fireplace for smokers. The skittle alley can also be used as a function room. Live music sessions feature regularly evenings and Sunday afternoon. A beer festival is held on August bank holiday. A separate B&B business is attached to the pub. 🛏️🏵️🛌🍴🍽️♿🚶🎏♣🚗🅿️🚃(21)🐾📶

Weston-super-Mare

Bear
66 Walliscote Road, BS23 1ED
✪ 1-11.30; 12-midnight Fri & Sat; 12-11 Sun
☎ (01934) 641722 🌐 thebearinnweston.co.uk
4 changing beers (sourced regionally) Ⓗ
Spacious and comfortable pub a few minutes' walk from the seafront. It was formerly called the Balmoral, and reopened in 2012 with a new name after a period of closure. Beers can be unusual for the area, and come in a variety of styles. Live music is popular every Saturday evening. There is a skittle alley, a refurbished function room at the back with a stage, and 23 en-suite rooms. Sport is occasionally shown on TV. 🛏️🏵️🛌🍴♿🎏♣🚗🅿️(5,7)🐾📶

Brit Bar ✔️
118 High Street, BS23 1HP
✪ 12-1am ☎ (01934) 632629
3 changing beers (often RPM) Ⓗ
Town-centre pub that has been given a bright, modern makeover while retaining the important traditional elements. Mondays to Wednesdays are gaming nights, with live music at weekends. Two or three changing beers are offered and it is not unusual for all to be dark beers, including stouts and porters. In September 2015 brewing commenced on site, under the RPM brewery label, and there is usually one RPM beer on the bar. Families are welcome in the covered, heated courtyard. 🛏️🏵️🎏🚗🅿️🐾📶

Imperial
14 South Parade, BS23 1JN
✪ 12-11.30 (10 Mon & Tue) ☎ (01934) 643333
🌐 theimperialpub.co.uk
3 changing beers (sourced locally) Ⓗ
Comfortable town-centre pub and one of the oldest in Weston, reopened after refurbishment in 2015 following a period of closure. It serves three regularly changing real ales in a variety of styles, often from local breweries, real cider and a selection of bottled beers from around the world. Lunchtime and evening meals feature locally sourced produce, with daily specials including vegetarian, vegan and gluten-free options. Tuesday is quiz night and there is occasional live music. Q🛏️🍴♿♣🚗

Regency
22-24 Lower Church Road, BS23 2AG
✪ 10-11.30 (midnight Fri & Sat); 10.45-11.30 Sun
☎ (01934) 633406 🌐 theregencyinn.co.uk

Butcombe Original; Courage Best Bitter; Draught Bass; Wells Bombardier; 1 changing beer Ⓗ
Comfortable, friendly, town-centre local, attracting a mixed clientele including students at lunchtime. The pub has pool, skittles and crib teams, but also offers a quiet refuge for conversation. The pool room with TV and jukebox is separate from the main bar area, and children are welcome here. Keenly priced home-cooked food is served lunchtimes, and there are Wednesday curry and Thursday grill evenings. Patios are to the front and rear. Pub outings feature, plus occasional live bands. ⑤🏠🕮🕙👌♣🖵

Wheddon Cross

Rest & Be Thankful Inn Ⓛ
TA24 7DR (on A396 SW of Dunster at jct with B3224)
🕓 11.30-2, 6-midnight ☎ (01643) 841222
⊕ restandbethankful.co.uk
Exmoor Ale; St Austell Tribute; 2 changing beers (sourced locally) Ⓗ
Cyclists and walkers will find this hostelry welcoming after a long climb to what is the highest pub for many miles, being nearly 1,000ft above sea level. This 19th-century coaching inn, at the heart of Exmoor National Park, has its own skittle alley, pool table, dartboard and private function room. Dunkery Beacon and Snowdrop Valley are both close by. Good locally sourced food is available at reasonable prices and there is a carvery on Wednesday and Sunday.
Q⑤🏠🕮🕙👌Å♣👤P🖵(198)🐾🛜

Wincanton

Nog Inn
South Street, BA9 9DL
🕓 10.30-11 (midnight Fri & Sat); 12-11 Sun
☎ (01963) 32998 ⊕ thenoginn.com
Otter Bitter; Sharp's Original; 2 changing beers Ⓗ
Attractive listed pub with a striking Georgian façade fronting a long, narrow building with parts dating back to the 16th century. A secluded sunny garden with covered seating can be found at the far end of the property. The guest ales are often seasonal and an extensive range of continental draught beers is always available, as are real ciders. Home-cooked pub classics are on the menu. Regular events on Thursday evenings include comedy, open mic and a quiz.
⑤🏠🕙♣👤P🖵(58)🐾🛜

Winsford

Royal Oak Inn Ⓛ
Halse Lane, TA24 7JE (left off A396 at Coppleham Cross)
🕓 11-3, 6-11 ☎ (01643) 851455 ⊕ royaloakexmoor.co.uk
Exmoor Ale, Gold; Otter Amber Ⓗ
An attractive thatched inn in the heart of a picturesque village and within Exmoor National Park. The village is noted as the birthplace of politician Ernest Bevin. The Winn Brook runs past the pub and over the ford that leads up to Exmoor and Tarr Steps. The inn has won a number of awards for its food, much of it sourced locally. Weekend hours are extended in summer.
Q⑤🏠🕮🕙👌♣P🐾🛜

Winsham

Bell Inn Ⓛ
Church Street, TA20 4HU
🕓 12-2.30 (not Mon), 7-11; 12-3, 7-11 Sat & Sun
☎ (01460) 30677 ⊕ thebellwinsham.co.uk
Branscombe Vale Branoc; 3 changing beers (sourced regionally; often Bays, Cotleigh, Exmoor) Ⓗ
Popular free house in the centre of the village. The licensees have been running this pub for over 17 years. It has two bars – one caters for darts, skittles and pool. There is a strong commitment to real ale, with up to three rotating guest ales from the West Country. Funds are raised for village and local charities through a weekly lottery and other events. Good-value food is served, including a popular Sunday roast. Q⑤🏠🕮👌♣P🖵(96)🐾

Witham Friary

Seymour Arms ★
BA11 5HF
🕓 11-3 (4 Sat), 6-11; 12-11 Sun ☎ (01749) 850742
Cheddar Ales Potholer; 1 changing beer (sourced locally) Ⓖ
A hidden rural gem, this pub has probably changed very little over the last 50 or so years. Built in the 1860s as a hotel to serve the nearby Mid-Somerset GWR branch railway station, it was part of the Duke of Somerset's estate. Sadly, in the 1960s Dr Beeching closed the station, and the hotel became a quiet country pub. The beer and cider are served from a glass-panelled hatch in the central hallway.
Q⑤🏠♣👤P🐾

Withypool

Royal Oak Inn Ⓛ
TA24 7QP (W of B3223 at Comers Cross) SS847356
🕓 12-3, 6-11 (not Mon eve) ☎ (01643) 831506
⊕ royaloakwithypool.co.uk
Exmoor Ale, Gold; 2 changing beers (sourced locally; often Exmoor) Ⓗ
Set in this remote village, the pub has been providing great ale and food for over 300 years. Larger than it first appears, it has two bars and a dining room decorated with an interesting array of historical country pursuits memorabilia, as well as eight en-suite rooms. Shooting, riding and fishing are available locally. Although remote, there is easy access to beauty spots such as Tarr Steps four miles away. Q⑤🏠🏠🕮Å♣👤🐾🛜

Wiveliscombe

Bear Inn Ⓛ
8-10 North Street, TA4 2JY
🕓 10.30-11 ☎ (01984) 623537
⊕ thebearwiveliscombe.co.uk
Black Bear Wivey Best, Black Bear; 4 changing beers (sourced locally; often Black Bear, Exmoor, Otter) Ⓗ
Welcoming family-run pub with a large garden, patio and skittle alley. This former 17th-century coaching inn can be found in the centre of the town and a warm welcome is assured. An extensive menu offers good-value meals using local produce where possible. There is an on-site microbrewery and you will find one or more of the Black Bear ales on the bar. Real cider features strongly. A beer festival is held mid-September.
⑤🏠🏠🕮👌♣👤P🖵(25)🐾🛜

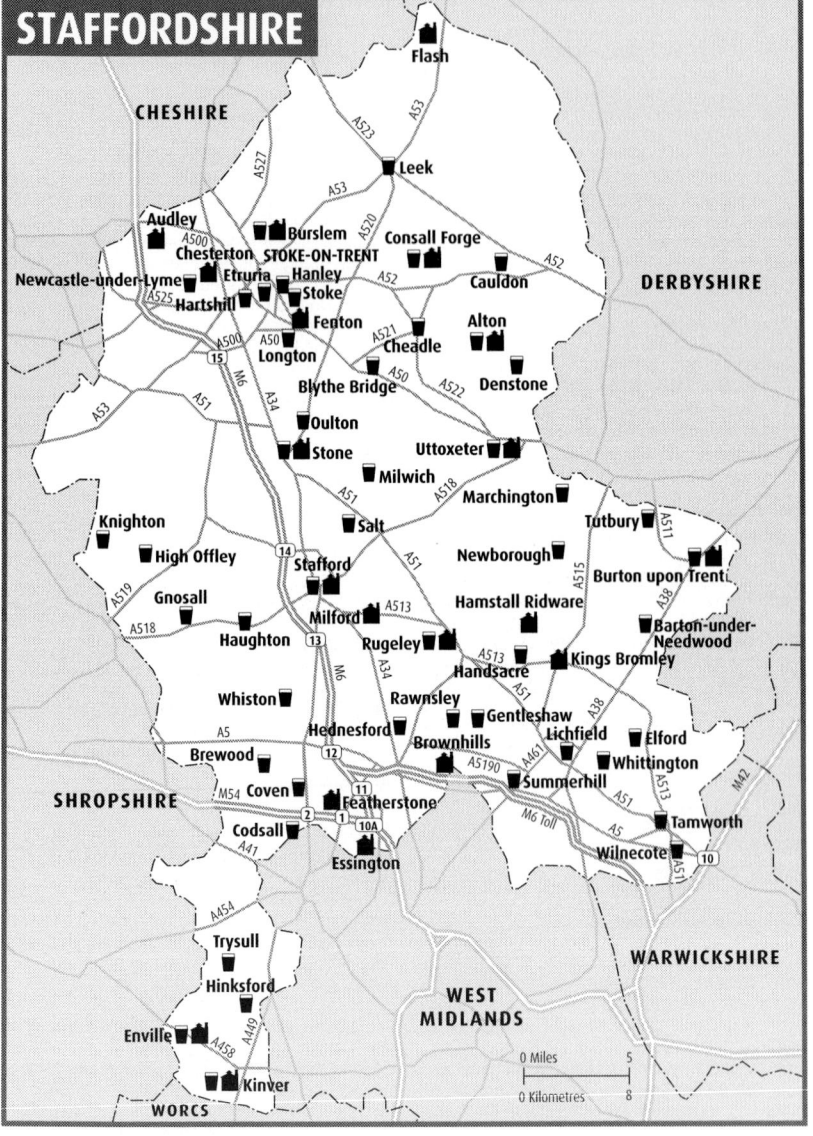

STAFFORDSHIRE

Flash

CHESHIRE

Leek

Audley

Burslem

Chesterton STOKE-ON-TRENT

Consall Forge

Newcastle-under-Lyme Etruria Hanley

Cauldon

DERBYSHIRE

Hartshill Stoke

Fenton

Alton

Cheadle

Longton

Blythe Bridge

Denstone

Oulton

Stone

Uttoxeter

Milwich

Marchington

Knighton

Salt

High Offley

Stafford

Newborough

Tutbury

Burton upon Trent

Gnosall

Milford

Hamstall Ridware

Barton-under-Needwood

Haughton

Rugeley

Handsacre

Kings Bromley

Whiston

Rawnsley

Gentleshaw

Brewood

Hednesford

Brownhills

Lichfield

Elford

Whittington

Coven

Featherstone

Summerhill

Tamworth

SHROPSHIRE

Codsall

Essington

Wilnecote

Trysull

WARWICKSHIRE

Hinksford

WEST MIDLANDS

Enville

Kinver

WORCS

0 Miles 5

0 Kilometres 8

Alton

Alton Bridge Hotel ⓛ
Station Road, ST10 4BX
☼ 12-midnight ☎ (01538) 703088 ⌖ altonbridgehotel.co.uk
Sharp's Doom Bar; 3 changing beers (often Burton Bridge, Peakstones Rock, Wincle) Ⓗ
Newly refurbished country pub, restaurant and riverside beer garden set in the heart of Alton in the Staffordshire Moorlands with views over the Churnet Valley. There is an attractive, extensive beer garden running down to the River Churnet, with glorious views of the Alton Bridge itself. Accommodation is available and delicious home-cooked food is served at lunchtimes and evenings. The changing guest beers will often hail from local breweries. ⛵🏠🅿️◑🍴🚲

Barton-under-Needwood

Barton Turns
3 Barton Turn, DE13 8EA (off B5016, ½ mile E of village)
☼ 12-11; 11-11 Sat & Sun ☎ (01283) 480682
Marston's Wainwright, Pedigree; 1 changing beer (sourced nationally) Ⓗ
Friendly traditional Victorian pub with an open-plan single room, close to the Trent & Mersey Canal, still known by locals as The Vine, its former name. The beer garden at the rear has a sheltered decking area and lawn, but outdoor drinking (with picnic tables) is also possible at the front of the pub and across the road by the side of the canal. Bar meals are served every day to 8.30pm. Boaters, cyclists and walkers are welcome. Popular with TV sport fans. ⛵🏠◑🅿️🚌(811,812)🐕🀫

Royal Oak ✿

74 The Green, DE13 8JD (½ mile from B5016 via Wales Lane)

✪ 12-11.30 (12.30am Fri & Sat); 12-11 Sun

☎ (01283) 713852

Marston's Pedigree; 2 changing beers (sourced nationally) H/G

Bustling community local on the southern edge of the village, home to many traditional pub games teams. While parts of the building date back to the 16th century, it has only been an inn since the mid-1800s. Public bar and lounge customers are served from a central sunken bar below the level of the rest of the ground floor. A separate conservatory offers access to the garden. Beers are on handpump or gravity, direct from the cask, on request. Q❀☎♣♠P➱(811,812)❀☂

Blythe Bridge

Crossways Micropub L

246 Uttoxeter Road, ST11 9LY

✪ closed Mon-Wed; 5-10 Thu; 12-10 Fri & Sat; 12-6 Sun ☎ 07527 669965 ⊕ peakstonesrock.co.uk/micropub.htm

3 changing beers (sourced regionally; often Burton Bridge, Leatherbritches, Peakstones Rock) H

At the heart of Blythe Bridge, opposite the library, this venue is just a short five-minute walk from the nearby railway station, turning right along Uttoxeter Road. It is a no-nonsense, no-frills drinking establishment, selling two house beers derived from the full range of real ales brewed by Peakstones Rock Brewery in Alton. One guest ale is also usually available. The pub is a chilled-out place where chatting to the friendly locals is compulsory. Q≈♠➱(6B,31)

Brewood

Swan Hotel L ✿

15 Market Place, ST19 9BS

✪ 11.45-midnight ☎ (01902) 850330

Courage Directors; Wye Valley HPA; 4 changing beers (sourced locally; often Salopian, Three Tuns, Weetwood) H

Characterful old coaching inn with low-beamed ceilings and seasonal log fires. Its village-centre location makes it convenient for the Shropshire Union Canal and the Staffordshire Way. Cosy snugs displaying early prints of the district flank the central bar which, unusually for the area, stocks nearly 80 malt whiskies and 20 gins from around the world. There is a traditional skittle alley upstairs, which doubles as a function room and hosts a fun quiz on Sunday evenings. Major Freeview sporting events are shown. Q❀☎❀♣P➱❀☂

Burton upon Trent

Burton Bridge Inn

24 Bridge Street, DE14 1SY (on A511, at town end of Trent Bridge)

✪ 12-2 (not Mon), 5-11; 12-2.30, 5-11 Thu; 11.30-11.30 Fri & Sat; 12-3, 7-11 Sun ☎ (01283) 536596

⊕ burtonbridgeinn.co.uk

Burton Bridge Golden Delicious, Sovereign Gold, Bitter, Porter, Stairway to Heaven, Festival Ale; 1 changing beer (sourced locally) H

This 17th-century pub is the flagship of the Burton Bridge Brewery estate and fronts the brewery

itself. It incorporates two rooms served from a central bar: a smaller front room with wooden pews and displaying many awards, brewery memorabilia, and framed old maps of Burton, and a back room featuring oak beams and panels. A dining/function room and a skittle alley are upstairs. No lunches Sunday to Wednesday. Steak nights and fish nights are held on Tuesdays monthly. Q❀☎◑♣➱❀☂

Derby Inn

17 Derby Road, DE14 1RU (on A5121, 350yds N of jct with A511)

✪ 5 (12 Thu)-11; 12-midnight Fri & Sat; 12-11 Sun

☎ (01283) 500729

Timothy Taylor Golden Best, Boltmaker; 2 changing beers (sourced nationally) H

Friendly Victorian two-roomed local, situated towards the northern edge of the town. Very much a community pub, it offers a step back in time to a more relaxed pace of life. Popular with football supporters on match days, the pub is en route between the railway station and Burton Albion's Pirelli Stadium. Evening meals, with limited choice, are available only on Wednesdays (type varies) and Saturdays (usually curries). Cheesy Quiz Night is on Tuesday, and live music is played on the second and fourth Friday of the month.

☎❀◑♣♠P➱❀☂

Dog Inn ▼

5 Lichfield Street, DE14 3QZ (opp Burton College, nr jct with High St/New St)

✪ 12-11 (11.30 Fri & Sat) ☎ (01283) 517060

Black Country Bradley's Finest Golden, Pig on the Wall, Fireside; Draught Bass; 7 changing beers (sourced regionally) H

Attractive half-timbered terrace pub near the town centre, dating back to the early 19th century. Recently purchased and refurbished by Black Country Ales, this radically revitalised pub offers an impressive selection of cask ales and ciders. Internally, a large square single room surrounds a

REAL ALE BREWERIES

Beowulf Brownhills
Black Hole Burton upon Trent
Blythe Hamstall Ridware
Burton Bridge Burton upon Trent
Burton Old Cottage Burton upon Trent
Burton Town Burton upon Trent
Consall Forge Consall Forge
Enville Enville
Flash Flash
Gates Burton Burton upon Trent
Grey Friars Featherstone (brewing suspended)
Heritage Burton upon Trent
Kinver Kinver
Lymestone Stone
Marston's Burton upon Trent
Morton Essington
Peakstones Rock Alton
Quartz Kings Bromley
RAN Stoke-on-Trent: Fenton
Shugborough Milford
Slater's Stafford
Titanic Stoke-on-Trent: Burslem
Tower Burton upon Trent
Townhouse Audley
Uttoxeter Uttoxeter (NEW)
Vine Inn ⬛ Rugeley (NEW)
Weal Chesterton

central bar and features a wood-framed ceiling and wood panelling on the walls, plus three real fires and numerous framed old photographs of Burton. Available beers are listed on two boards on opposite sides of the room. ♿♣🍴🍽🐾🐾📶

Fuggle & Nugget

81 High Street, DE14 1LD (on W side of N end of High St)
🕐 6 (5 Thu)-10; 5-10.30 Fri; 1-10.30 Sat; closed Sun & Mon ☎ 07805 526322
4 changing beers (sourced regionally) ⑥
Cosy single-room micropub on the ground floor of a Grade II-listed end-terrace building, featuring plain bench seating and high tables around the periphery, with a small raised area under the shop-style windows. The plain wood floor gives way to original red quarry tiles towards the rear, adjacent to the separate cask stillage room, visible through a window. Current and impending beers, plus ciders and perries, are listed on blackboards. There is no bar, so customers are cheerfully served at their tables. Note the unusual Gents' keg urinal!
Q🐾🍴🍽🐾

Last Heretic

95 Station Street, DE14 1BT (in terrace between Grant's Yard and Mosley St)
🕐 5-10 Mon; 4-10.30 (11 Fri); 12-11 Sat; 1-10 Sun ☎ 07715 097797 🌐 thelastheretic.co.uk
4 changing beers (sourced regionally) ⑥
Smart micropub in a terrace of commercial properties close to the station, named after Edward Wightman, a resident of Burton, who was the last person in England to be executed for heresy. The comfortable single room features a small bar counter towards the rear, with the stillage visible through a glass door and window. Available beers (occasionally up to six) and up to five ciders and perries are listed on boards near the bar. Outdoor drinking is in a narrow yard at the rear. Opening hours are reduced in January and February.
Q🐾🐾🍴🍽🐾

Roebuck Inn ✔

101 Station Street, DE14 1BT (on corner of jct with Mosley St)
🕐 12-11 ☎ (01283) 511213 🌐 roe-buck-inn.co.uk
Draught Bass; Greene King Abbot; Marston's Pedigree; Theakston Old Peculier; 2 changing beers (sourced regionally) Ⓗ
Friendly Victorian corner-terrace pub near the railway station, once the Ind Coope Brewery tap, opposite the former brewery. The original classic Draught Burton Ale was launched here in 1976. Inside, there is a long, narrow, single room with dark-wood panelling and the bar counter down one side. A small patio at the rear is available for outdoor drinking, plus a few tables and chairs outside at the front in summer. Live music is played early Sunday evenings. 🐾🍴🍽🐾🐾

Waterloo Inn ✔

50 Ashby Road, DE15 0LQ (on A511, about ½ mile E from Trent Bridge)
🕐 4-11.30; 12-midnight Fri & Sat; 12-11 Sun ☎ (01283) 354637
Draught Bass; Marston's Pedigree; 1 changing beer (sourced locally) Ⓗ
Traditional two-roomed local, probably Victorian, in the suburb of Winshill, east of the River Trent; there may have been a pub on the site since the 1700s. It was reputedly a halfway point for changing

horses on brewery drays delivering to south Derbyshire. Outdoor drinking can be enjoyed on a decking area at the front, accessed via patio doors, creating an alfresco atmosphere in warm weather. Pies, pasties and artisan cheeses are frequently sold, but customers may bring takeaways. Quiz night is Sunday. 🐾🐾♣🍽(29,29A)🐾📶

Cauldon

Yew Tree Inn Ⓛ

ST10 3EJ (turn left at Cross pub, Cauldon Lowe; approx 1 mile from jct)
🕐 12-3, 6-midnight; 12-midnight Sat & Sun
☎ (01538) 309876 🌐 yewtreeinncauldon.co.uk
Burton Bridge Bitter; Rudgate Ruby Mild; 1 changing beer (sourced nationally; often Blue Monkey, Cottage, Dancing Duck) Ⓗ
A 17th-century inn in a small village; if you want uniqueness, a visit to the Yew Tree is a must as its 'museum' has many interesting objects and curios. A warm welcome is assured on entry into this quiet hostelry with well-kept, excellent beers and one draught cider. Pork pies are always available. There is a pleasant outdoor seating area which also has objects of interest. The pub has been run by the same family since 1961.
Q🐾🐾🍴🐾♿♣🍽(108)🐾📶

Cheadle

Huntsman Ⓛ

The Green, ST10 1XS
🕐 12-midnight ☎ (01538) 750502
🌐 thehuntsmancheadle.com
Joule's Blonde; Marston's Pedigree; Sharp's Doom Bar; 3 changing beers (sourced nationally; often Newby Wyke, Peakstones Rock, Sarah Hughes) Ⓗ
Now a regular entry in this Guide, you can expect two log fires and friendly bar staff. A good range of beers is on offer for the discerning real ale drinker. Quality traditional pub food is on the menu, with excellent service. There are annual beer and cider festivals and there is a (sometimes) sunny beer garden to the rear. This is a great pub for families as well as those who enjoy a quiet pint.
🐾🐾🍴🐾♿♣🍽🐾📶

Codsall

Crown Joule's 🍽 Ⓛ

1 Wood Road, WV8 1DB
🕐 12-11 (midnight Fri & Sat) ☎ (01902) 844876
🌐 thecrownjoules.pub
Joule's Blonde, Pale Ale, Slumbering Monk; 5 changing beers (sourced regionally; often Joule's) Ⓗ
The oldest pub in Codsall was bought by Joule's and reopened in 2016 after a major refurbishment, which transformed it into a slightly grand Edwardian-style pub with a modern twist, featuring open fires, stained-glass windows, old beams and reclaimed furniture. The former function room, which in the '60s and '70s hosted a famous jazz club, has been fitted out in the style of a library. Meals are served all day and a canine cuisine meal with optional gravy is also available for dogs. Q🐾🐾🍴🐾♿♣🍽(5,10B)🐾📶

Firs Club Ⓛ

16 Wood Road, WV8 1BX (entrance from shared Co-op car park off Station Rd)

7.30-11 (midnight Fri); 12-midnight Sat; 12-11 Sun
☎ (01902) 844674 thefirscodsall.com
3 changing beers (sourced locally; often Hobsons, Ludlow, Wye Valley) Ⓗ
The club contains a bar area, quiet lounge and sports lounge with pool table, dartboard and card table. Snooker tables are upstairs. Up to three guest ales, mainly local, are stocked, and a beer festival is held in November. The large function room is available to hire. Show this Guide or a current CAMRA membership card to be signed in. A pedestrian entrance in Wood Road is handy for the bus stop. Q❀♿≠♣P🚌(5,10B)

Consall Forge

Black Lion

Wetley Rocks, ST9 0AJ (off A522 follow signs to Consall Gardens, then nature reserve on hairpin bend; go straight on, ignoring No Vehicular Access sign; at bottom of hill, go left along track to car park)
12-11; 12-10.30 Sun ☎ (01782) 550294
Peakstones Rock Black Hole; 6 changing beers (sourced nationally; often Consall Forge, Joule's, Kelham Island) Ⓗ
A rural gem set next to the Caldon Canal and the Churnet Valley Heritage Railway, and surrounded by woods. Home-cooked food is served and the portions are large, so be hungry! The beer range varies and is mainly from smaller independent breweries. A range of ciders is also available – the pub is a local CAMRA Cider Pub of the Year. Several beer festivals are held annually. Not the easiest of places to find, but that is part of the adventure.
❀◑Ⲁ≠♣●P🐾

Coven

Harrows Inn

School Lane, WV9 5AW (by traffic lights on A449, main Wolverhampton to Stafford road)
12-11 (midnight Thu-Sun) ☎ (01902) 790055
theharrowsinn.co.uk
Ludlow Gold; Three Tuns XXX; Titanic Plum Porter; 3 changing beers (sourced regionally; often Abbeydale, Broughs, Salopian) Ⓗ
This attractive privately owned pub has been a free house since 2012. A central counter serves two rooms furnished in contemporary style; one is a lounge and the other is a public bar with piano, dartboard and pool table. Six real ales are sold, always including a gluten-free beer. Usually, up to 20 real ciders and perries are stocked. Cheese and ham cobs are always available. There is a large beer garden and children's play area.
Q❀♿Ⲁ♣●P🚌🐾

Denstone

Tavern

College Road, ST14 5HR
6-11 Mon; 12-2, 5.30-11; 12-midnight Fri-Sun
☎ (01889) 590847 thetaverndenstone.co.uk
Marston's Pedigree; house beer (by Ringwood); 2 changing beers (sourced nationally; often Marston's) Ⓗ
A 17th-century village inn offering fine food and good beers in comfortable surroundings. There is a bar area with darts, a comfortable lounge area and a conservatory for dining. Quiz night is on Monday, when there is no food. Fresh, wood-fired, stone-baked pizzas are served Friday and Saturday evenings, to eat in or take away. Booking tables in advance is advisable. Guest beers come from the Marston's range. Q❀◑Ⲁ♣P🚌(32A)🐾

Elford

Crown Inn

The Square, B79 9DB (600yds E of A513) SK189106
6-11; 12-midnight Fri-Sun ☎ (01827) 383602
Burton Bridge Sovereign Gold; Draught Bass; 2 changing beers Ⓗ
Welcoming multi-room village pub, where beamed ceilings feature throughout, with real fires creating a cosy glow. A separate room to the side is dedicated to pool and darts. In the 18th century the upstairs rooms were used as a courthouse, and today's dining room once served as the cells. Burton Bridge ales often feature among the two guests. Food is served until 9pm Wednesday to Saturday, until 3.30pm on Sunday. Bar snacks are available at all times. No evening bus service.
◑♣P🚌🐾

Enville

Cat Inn 🏆

Bridgnorth Road, DY7 5HA (on A458)
12-2.30 (not Mon), 5-11; 12-11 Fri & Sat; 12-6 Sun
☎ (01384) 872209 thecatinn.com
Enville Ale, Ginger Beer; 5 changing beers Ⓗ
Parts of this traditional country pub date back to the 16th century, and the three oak-beamed rooms all have real fires. The main lounge and toilets have been refurbished and there is a function room upstairs. Hanging baskets adorn the beer garden and courtyard during the summer months. Regular Enville beers are on handpump plus guest ales, usually from local breweries. Home-made dishes and daily specials, using local produce whenever possible, are served. Local CAMRA Pub of the Year 2017. Q❀◑●P🐾

Gentleshaw

Olde Windmill

Windmill Lane, WS15 4NF SK051118
12-midnight ☎ (01543) 682468 yeoldewindmill.co.uk
Draught Bass; 3 changing beers (sourced regionally; often Burton Bridge, Castle Rock, Springhead) Ⓗ
Welcoming 400-year-old country pub, with smartly attired staff and equally sharp food and drink offerings. Free of tie, the three guest ales are usually interesting microbrews. The cosy bar is dog-friendly, while the wood-panelled lounge offers freshly cooked meals including interesting specials. Both rooms feature old beams (some cleverly fake) and open fires. A number of teams use the crown bowling green. The pub is 100 yards from the stump of an old disused windmill.
Q❀◑♿●P🚌🐾

Gnosall

George & the Dragon 🏆

46 High Street, ST20 0EX
4-10.30; 12-10.30 Sat & Sun ☎ 07779 327551
Holden's Golden Glow; Wood Shropshire Lad; 3 changing beers (sourced locally) Ⓗ
This lovely little pub opened in July 2015 and has already received acclaim, winning the local CAMRA Cider Pub of the Year 2016 and Rural Pub of the Year 2017. The building dates from 1736, with a

Tastefully restored Grade II-listed pub with a split-level bar featuring aged beams and a large, comfortable lounge to the rear. Both have real fires. Lunches are served 12-3pm Tuesday to Saturday, and pork pies are available during all sessions. A Joule's seasonal beer is usually one of the changing ales. A comprehensive malt whisky and country wine selection is also stocked. Dogs are welcome except in the lounge. An annual beer festival is held in April. Q✿⌀🌙≈♣🏠P🖵☼🏃🛜

Horse & Jockey 🍷 🅛
8-10 Sandford Street, WS13 6QA
✿ 11.30-11 ☎ (01543) 410033
Holden's Golden Glow; Marston's Pedigree; Timothy Taylor Landlord; Wye Valley HPA; 4 changing beers 🅗
Deservedly busy, this free house is a must on the Lichfield real ale circuit. The regular ales are complemented by four guests, mainly from microbreweries. There is a cosy snug and a separate games room at the back of the large open-plan bar. Hot food is served Wednesday to Saturday lunchtimes, and a pork pie/cheeseboard selection is always on offer. Sport is shown on muted TV screens. There is an over-21 entry policy, with the exception of canines. ✿⌀≈♣P🖵☼🏃🛜

Whippet Inn 🅛
21 Tamworth Street, WS13 6JP
✿ closed Mon & Tue; 12-2.30, 4.30-10; 12-10 Fri & Sat; 12-5 Sun ☎ 07858 753653
4 changing beers 🅗
A cracking little bar, holding true to micropub principles – just real ale, real cider, wines and soft drinks. With a maximum capacity of around 40, be prepared to make friends! The four ales are always interesting, and generally include one of the Hippy Killer range of beers, brewed by pub gaffer Paul. Two changing ciders are offered. Dogs are welcome and usually pampered by co-gaffer Debbie. Food is simple snacks like pork pies and cobs. Q🌙≈🚶🏃☼

Marchington

Dog & Partridge 🍷
Church Lane, ST14 8LJ (250yds along Church Lane from High St)
✿ 12-3, 6-11 (5-midnight Fri); 12-midnight Sat; 12-11 Sun ☎ (01283) 820394 🌐 dogandpartridgemarchington.co.uk
Draught Bass; 3 changing beers (sourced locally; often Abbeydale, Gates Burton, Uttoxeter) 🅗
A gem of a village pub permanently serving Draught Bass; several handpumps provide constantly changing local guest ales. Formerly a restaurant, the pub is split into four main indoor areas with open fires. Food is served lunchtimes and evenings. A pleasant beer garden to the rear is popular in the summer months. It is renowned locally for its weekly live music sessions and the hosting of regular beer festivals. Parking is to the side of the building. Children are welcome. Q🌙✿⌀🛂AP🖵(402)🛜

Milwich

Green Man
Sandon Lane, ST18 0EG (on B5027 in centre of village)
✿ 5 (12 Thu-Sat)-11; 12-10.30 Sun ☎ (01889) 505310
🌐 greenmanmilwich.com
Draught Bass; 5 changing beers (sourced nationally) 🅗

An independent pub at the heart of a vibrant village community, and a more or less permanent fixture in the Guide. It celebrated its 200th anniversary in 2015, with the licensee 25 years in situ. To top it off, it was also CAMRA branch Pub of the Year. The pub has two rooms, one of which is set aside for diners. There is a large, verdant garden area where the annual free music festival is not to be missed. A true and lively village inn. Q🌙✿⌀🛂♣🏠P☼🛜

Newborough

Red Lion ✓
Duffield Lane, DE13 8SH (on B5234, at corner of jct with Yoxall Rd)
✿ 12-11 (midnight Fri & Sat); 12-10 Sun ☎ (01283) 576182
🌐 redlionnewborough.co.uk
Draught Bass; Marston's 61 Deep, Pedigree; 1 changing beer (sourced regionally) 🅗
Popular village local, built in the 17th century as a farmhouse and converted into a pub in the early 1800s. It is now the only pub in the village and a privately owned free house. There is a comfortable, long public bar, plus a smart two-section 46-seater restaurant which incorporates the former snug and features a number of framed old local photographs. There are separate, regularly changing lunch, evening, Sunday and bar snack menus, and occasional themed food evenings (eg tapas). 🌙✿⌀P🖵(402A,403)🏃🛜

Newcastle-under-Lyme

Bridge Street Ale House 🅛 ✓
31 Bridge Street, ST5 2RY
✿ 1-11; 12-9 Sun ☎ (01782) 499394
🌐 bridgestreetalehouse.co.uk
4 changing beers (sourced nationally; often Coach House, Happy Valley, Rat) 🅗
The first micropub in the area, the Bridge is a special place for regulars and newcomers alike. From Grum, the charismatic owner, and his hospitable staff, to the quirky decor, the pub oozes charm and appeal. There are four changing guest beers on handpull from various breweries, with four alternatives always ready to replace them when required. An array of ciders also features, with several exceptional rums adding to the individuality of this fantastic pub. Q♣🚶🏃🛜

Freebird 🅛
96 Liverpool Road, ST5 2AX
✿ 5-midnight (1am Fri); 2-1am Sat; 2-11.30 Sun
12 changing beers (sourced nationally; often Falstaff, Ilkley, Salopian) 🅗
A vibrant, biker-friendly free house, five minutes' walk from the town centre, sporting up to 12 rotating ales of excellent quality and variety from across the whole of the UK, as well as at least one real cider. The pub hosts regular live bands on weekend nights, with a rock DJ on Fridays. Named after a Lynyrd Skynyrd song from the 1970s, The Freebird is well worth a visit and is always buzzing with atmosphere. 🛂♣🚶P🖵(4,4A)🏃

Hopinn
102 Albert Street, ST5 1JR
✿ 4 (12 Sat)-midnight; 12-11 Sun ☎ (01782) 711121
Black Sheep Best Bitter; Draught Bass; Oakham Citra; 5 changing beers (sourced nationally; often Mallinson's, Northern Monk, Oakham) 🅗

Comfortable and friendly family-owned free house on the edge of the town centre, comprising a front bar, lounge and snug, all with well-preserved Art Deco features, including wood panelling and a rare stained-glass skylight. Up to five guest beers come from a wide variety of breweries and, as the pub name suggests, many are hoppy, but a dark ale is usually on the bar. Real cider is also on offer. 👟♣🌭🚪🛜

Hopwater Cellar ⓛ

2 Bridge Street, ST5 2RY
🕐 12-8 (9 Fri & Sat); 12-4 Sun ☎ (01782) 713311
3 changing beers (sourced nationally; often Front Row, Twisted Barrel, Weal Ales) Ⓗ

This cellar bar is in the town centre close to other good pubs. There are two seated drinking areas and in the centre is a range of over 500 bottles from around the world. Three beers are on draught, and all will vary by brewery and style. A CAMRA discount is offered on the cask ale. Dogs are welcome and have their own beer! As the landlord says, this is more than just a bottle shop.
Q🌅👟♣🌭🚪🐈🛜

Lymestone Vaults ⓛ

Pepper Street, ST5 1PR
🕐 11-11 (midnight Fri & Sat); 12-10.30 Sun
☎ (01782) 615801
Lymestone Stone Cutter, Stone Faced, Foundation Stone, Ein Stein, Stone the Crows; 4 changing beers (sourced regionally; often Derventio, Lymestone, Springhead) Ⓗ

This well-run, multiple award-winning pub is the first of the Lymestone Brewery tap houses, which showcase its award-winning beers. In the town centre, off the High Street, it offers a relaxed and comfortable environment to sample a wide variety of beverages sourced locally, nationally and internationally. You will find yourself in traditional yet modern surroundings with a log-burning stove, comfortable seating, traditional pub games and hearty home-cooked food at lunchtime. Knowledgeable staff offer a warm welcome to every man and particularly his dog.
🌅🍺👟♣🌭🚪🐈🛜

Oulton

Brushmaker's Arms

8 Kibblestone Road, ST15 8UW (500yds W of A520, 1 mile NE of Stone)
🕐 12-midnight (1am Fri & Sat) ☎ (01785) 812062
Marston's Lancaster Bomber; Thwaites Original; 1 changing beer (sourced nationally) Ⓗ

The Brush is an exceptionally well-supported community pub which has been in the hands of the current licensee for over 25 years and has won many CAMRA awards. About the only thing that has changed in that time is the swish new pub sign. A two-room pub, it has a small, immaculate lounge to the left as you enter, and a larger bar ahead. There is a small TV in the bar but otherwise conversation rules here. Q🌅🌤🅰♣P🚪(4)🐈🛜

Rawnsley

Rag ✅

Ironstone Road, WS12 0QD
🕐 12-11; 12-10.30 Sun ☎ (01543) 277491
🌐 theragatrawnsley.co.uk

Castle Rock Harvest Pale; Fuller's London Pride; 3 changing beers (sourced nationally) Ⓗ

A free house with five ales on the bar and now a fledgling brewery on-site, supplying the bar to the front. With an award-winning 100-seat restaurant and seven en-suite rooms, this is an ideal base for visiting local attractions such as Lichfield Cathedral, Trentham Village, Monkey Forest and Chasewater Light Railway. There is a bowling green at the rear of the building, along with six recently installed camping pods. Regular summer barbecues are held. Q🌤🛏🕐👟🅰P🚪

Rugeley

Plaza ⓛ ✅

Horsefair, WS15 2EJ
🕐 9am-11.30 (12.30am Fri & Sat) ☎ (01889) 586831
Greene King Abbot; Ruddles Best Bitter; Sharp's Doom Bar; 7 changing beers (sourced locally; often Beowulf, Blythe, Salopian) Ⓗ

Previously a cinema dating from the 1930s, this spacious Wetherspoon pub retains much of the cinematic atmosphere and Art Deco flourishes of the period. The light and airy interior allows for three widely separated levels, accentuated by a large window area where the cinema screen once was; this leads to an outside drinking area, with balcony, terrace and lawned beer garden. Around seven guest ales are offered, with brews from micros such as Salopian proving popular. The small car park is Pay & Display. Q🌅🌤🕐👟🚲🚌🌭P🚪🛜

Salt

Holly Bush Inn ✅

ST18 0BX (turn W off A518 opp Weston Hall) SJ959277
🕐 12-11 ☎ (01889) 508234
Adnams Southwold Bitter; Marston's Pedigree; 1 changing beer (sourced nationally) Ⓗ

The pub claims to have originated as far back as 1190 and to have been the second oldest to be granted a licence. The oldest part of the existing building retains a thatched roof and probably dates from the early 17th century. With extensions and alterations over the centuries, there are now three distinct areas – a bar area, dining room and snug. Many awards have been won for the superb-quality meals. Q🌅🌤🕐P🚪🛜

Stafford

Floodgate Ale House

147 Newport Road, ST16 2EZ
🕐 closed Mon; 5-10; 1-11 Fri & Sat; 1-10 Sun ☎ 07917 885821
5 changing beers (sourced nationally) Ⓗ

A one-room micropub with space for up to 45 people. There are plenty of tables and it is a good pub for conversation. Up to five ciders are sold and a good selection of whiskies. Normally closed on Mondays, it is open once a month for an event. The walls are adorned with pumpclips which show the incredible range of beers that have been sold. It now has a sister pub, No.7 Market Square, in the centre of town. Q🚌🌭🚪🐈

Greyhound ⓛ

12 County Road, ST16 2PU (off A34, opp jail)
🕐 4 (12 Sat)-midnight; 12-11 Sun ☎ (01785) 222432
🌐 greyhoundfreehousestafford.co.uk

Bradfield Farmers Blonde; Wells Bombardier; 6 changing beers (sourced nationally) ⊞
A short walk from the centre of Stafford, this two-room free house is well worth a visit. The pub dates from 1831 and a newspaper article from the day it opened can be seen above the bar. Today, the bar offers a range of eight different beers, often from Yorkshire breweries, and a choice of bottled ciders. The Greyhound has won several CAMRA branch awards including Pub of the Year. Q❀☆♣🖪❀

King's Arms
11-12 Peel Terrace, ST16 3HD (off B5066, Sandon Rd)
🕒 12-11 (midnight Thu-Sat); 12-11.30 Sun
☎ (01785) 246562 ⊕ kings-arms-staffordshire.co.uk
Draught Bass; 4 changing beers (sourced nationally) ⊞
Converted a long time ago from two terraced houses, the interior has been further opened up in more recent years but retains separate bar and snug areas and a surprisingly large garden. With two dartboards, it supports a number of darts teams, with darts nights on Tuesday, Wednesday and Thursday, and a crib team on Thursday. A wide selection of guest ales is stocked. Only a 10-minute walk from the town centre. ☆❀♣●🖪(4,5)❀🌬

Market Vaults 🅛
4 St Martin's Place, ST16 2LA (in corner of Market Sq)
🕒 12 (3 Mon)-midnight; 12-1am Sat; 3-midnight Sun
☎ (01785) 256126 ⊕ themarketvaults.com
Banks's Sunbeam; Slater's Top Totty; 3 changing beers ⊞
A welcoming pub with a series of rooms and distinct areas that ramble around a central bar. It offers a selection of well-kept beers alongside a range of gourmet burgers. Regular live music is played, which includes country, blues and cover versions. ◑🅓♿🖪❀🌬

Olde Rose & Crown 🅛
10 Market Street, ST16 2JZ
🕒 12-11 (midnight Fri & Sat); 12-10.30 Sun
☎ (01785) 251343
Joule's Blonde, Pale Ale, Slumbering Monk; 1 changing beer (sourced locally; often Joule's) ⊞
This comfortable Joule's house is right in the heart of Stafford and much larger than it looks from the outside. Four handpumps serve Joule's ales. Lunches are served Monday to Saturday and bar snacks, using locally sourced ingredients, are available all day. Situated next to the Gatehouse Theatre, the pub is a favourite of theatregoers and is frequented by cast members enjoying an after-show pint. An acoustic night is held every Wednesday. Q❀◑🅓❀🖪❀🌬

Picture House ⊘
14 Bridge Street, ST16 2HL
🕒 8am-midnight (1am Fri & Sat) ☎ (01785) 222941
Greene King Abbot; Ruddles Best Bitter; 4 changing beers (sourced nationally) ⊞
A Wetherspoon conversion of a small 1914 provincial cinema. It retains a lot of original and ornate features, including the entrance foyer and projection room. Posters from the golden age of films adorn the walls. On Wednesday at 9pm films are once again shown – it is a cinemagoer's delight! A wide selection of real ales is served to a mixed clientele and the pub is often busy in the evening. There is an outdoor drinking area overlooking the River Sow. Q❀☆❀◑🅓♿🖪🌬

Spittal Brook 🅛 ⊘
106 Lichfield Road, ST17 4LP (1 mile SE of centre off A34 at Queensville Bridge)
🕒 12-3, 5-11; 12-11 Fri & Sat; 12-10.30 Sun
☎ (01785) 302246
St Austell Tribute; Sharp's Doom Bar; 2 changing beers (sourced nationally) ⊞
A two-room pub with a small front room for sports and a larger room at the back which includes the restaurant. There are five en-suite bedrooms. Entertainment includes a folk night on Tuesday, a quiz on Wednesday and a cheese night on the last Sunday of the month; bring your own cheeses to share with others. The pub holds an annual beer festival in July. Q❀☆❀🛏◑♣P🖪❀🌬

Sun 🅛
7 Lichfield Road, ST17 4JX
🕒 12-11 (midnight Fri & Sat) ☎ (01785) 248361
⊕ thesunstafford.co.uk
Everards Tiger; Titanic Steerage, Iceberg, White Star, Captain Smith's Strong Ale; 6 changing beers (sourced nationally) ⊞
One of Titanic Brewery's fleet, it has been clear sailing for this popular pub since its refurbishment by Titanic. A previous CAMRA branch Pub of the Year, it has 12 handpumps offering a constant choice from Titanic and a changing range of beers and ciders from across the country. Food is served throughout the day, using ingredients sourced as locally as possible to the pub. Keep an eye out for the original pub sign hanging inside the pub. Q❀☆◑🅓≈♣●P🖪❀🌬

Stoke-on-Trent: Burslem

Bull's Head 🅛
14 St John's Square, ST6 3AJ
🕒 3-11 (11.30 Wed & Thu); 12-midnight Fri & Sat; 12-11 Sun
☎ (01782) 834153
Titanic Steerage, Iceberg, White Star, Plum Porter; 6 changing beers (sourced nationally; often Ashover, Dancing Duck, Holden's) ⊞
Titanic's brewery tap in Burslem, 10 minutes' walk from Port Vale's ground, is open at 11am on Vale home Saturdays, welcoming to all supporters, home and away. This is a two-roomed pub with an island bar with up to 10 real ales on tap and seven or more real ciders and perries available straight from the cellar, alongside draught and bottled Belgian beers. Bar billiards, table skittles and a jukebox are in the bar. Local CAMRA Cider Pub of the Year 2016. Q❀☆❀♣●🖪❀🌬

Duke William 🅛
2 St Johns Square, ST6 3AJ
🕒 12-11 (midnight Fri & Sat) ☎ (01782) 814809
⊕ dukewilliamburslem.com
Draught Bass; Joule's Slumbering Monk; Oakham Citra; Sarah Hughes Dark Ruby Mild; 4 changing beers (sourced nationally; often Abbeydale, Acorn, Salopian) ⊞
An imposing mock-Tudor building in the heart of the Potteries mother town, with a friendly and relaxed atmosphere. This family-run free house is a popular haunt both for drinkers and diners since reopening in 2010 after a sympathetic refurbishment. Original features, such as the horseshoe-shaped bar and heated foot rail, have been preserved. The ground floor has a lounge and a snug, plus a large public bar. The splendid restaurant is on the first floor. ◑🅓♿●❀

Post Office Vaults

3 Market Place, ST6 3AA

✪ 11-11 (1am Fri & Sat); 12-11 Sun ☎ (01782) 811027

Greene King Abbot; Oakham Bishops Farewell; Wye Valley Butty Bach; 1 changing beer (sourced regionally) Ⓗ

This establishment is on the main road and on a good bus route. There are eye-catching hanging baskets and the windows have classical engraving. Once you step through the main door, the pub is tiny and has a single bar, but you are made to feel at home; the covered smoking area at the rear of the pub is a gem and the toilets may be cramped, but they have character. ♿♣🚌(3,98)☀

Stoke-on-Trent: Etruria

Holy Inadequate 🍺 Ⓛ

67 Etruria Old Road, ST1 5PE

✪ 12-midnight ☎ 07771 358238

Joule's Pale Ale; 5 changing beers (sourced nationally; often Beartown, Burton Bridge, Hawkshead) Ⓗ

Having achieved yet another CAMRA Pub of the Year award, this superb venue has now moved on to the next, and highly anticipated, level, with the opening of the on-site Inadequate Brewery. The ever-popular Joule's Pale remains among the six handpulled beers, complemented by Inadequate ales served alongside rotating guests, plus real draught cider. The pork pies and Scotch eggs are always in demand. Beer festivals are held every bank holiday. Q❄♣🚌☀🛜

Stoke-on-Trent: Hanley

Coachmakers Arms ★ Ⓛ

65 Lichfield Street, ST1 3EA (off A5008 Potteries Way ring road)

✪ 4-11 (midnight Fri); 12-11 Sat & Sun

Draught Bass; 3 changing beers (sourced regionally; often Lymestone, Titanic, Weal Ales) Ⓗ

The Coach is a regular and well-deserved entry in this Guide. Now saved from the threat of demolition, this gem of the Potteries continues to trade and thrive. A Victorian drinking passage pub with four small rooms on CAMRA's National Inventory of Historic Pub Interiors, this is a must-visit place when arriving in the city centre. In winter, a roaring fire welcomes, while in summer there is nothing finer than to sit outside on a bench with a pint and people-watch in the sunshine. A true classic. Q🚲♣P🚌☀

Victoria Lounge Bar Ⓛ

5 Adventure Place, ST1 3AF (next to Hanley bus station)

✪ 9.30am-11 ☎ (01782) 273530 🌐 thereardon.com

Draught Bass; Greene King Abbot; 4 changing beers (sourced nationally; often Blue Monkey, Brains, Cottage) Ⓗ

Now a regular entry, the elegant Victoria Lounge Bar is often mistakenly called Reardon's as it is connected to the Reardon Snooker Club. This hostelry is conveniently located right behind the new bus station. Two permanent beers are complemented by a changing and adventurous list of guests in this true free house. It can get busy at lunchtime as good-value food is served every day, with evening meals available on request. It is popular with the nearby evening theatre clientele. A self-contained upstairs function room is available for hire. Q🚲🕑♿P🚌🛜

Stoke-on-Trent: Hartshill

Greyhound Ⓛ

67 George Street, ST5 1JT

✪ 12-11 (11.30 Wed & Thu; midnight Fri); 11-midnight Sat; 11-11 Sun ☎ (01782) 635814

Everards Tiger; Titanic Steerage, Iceberg, White Star, Plum Porter; 4 changing beers (sourced nationally; often Nethergate, RCH, Rooster's) Ⓗ

A warm welcome awaits at this dog-friendly pub on the outskirts of Newcastle. The second pub in the Titanic fleet, the Greyhound boasts nine handpumps showcasing Titanic ales as well as a fantastic and varied range of ales from across the UK. A great selection of bottled beers as well as country wines and real cider make this a pub for everyone. Tasty bar snacks are served. There is occasional live music from local groups and a Sunday pub quiz. Q♣🐕🚌☀🛜

Stoke-on-Trent: Longton

Congress Inn Ⓛ

14 Sutherland Road, ST3 1HJ (¼ mile from Longton bus and rail stations and opp police station)

✪ 2-11; 12-midnight Fri-Sun ☎ (01782) 763667

🌐 congressinnlongton.co.uk

Adnams Broadside; Castle Rock Sheriff's Tipple, Elsie Mo; Townhouse Styrian Pale, Gladstone Strong Ale; 4 changing beers (sourced nationally; often Acorn, Wadworth, Welbeck Abbey) Ⓗ

Award-winning two-room free house, in the same ownership for over a decade. A wide range of real ales and real ciders awaits the thirsty customer, plus bottled UK and Belgian beers. Inside, breweriana deck the walls, while outside, recently revealed Joule's Ales lettering has been authentically restored to its former glory. A beer festival is staged over three bars every May. If you feel peckish, consider a delicious pork pie and imbibe again! ≥♣🐕🚌

Stoke-on-Trent: Stoke

Glebe Ⓛ

35 Glebe Street, ST4 1HG

✪ 12-11 (midnight Thu-Sat); 12-10.30 Sun

☎ (01782) 860670

Joule's Blonde, Pale Ale, Slumbering Monk; 1 changing beer (sourced nationally; often Bank Top, Joule's, Kelham Island) Ⓗ

A short walk from Stoke railway station, this superb Joule's establishment has justifiably become one of the must-visit pubs in the city. Magnificent features including beautifully restored stained-glass windows, along with candlelit tables, all add to the welcoming atmosphere. Three mainstay Joule's ales are complemented by one guest beer. Home-made meals are served at lunchtimes and early evenings and are of a high standard; there is also an extensive cheeseboard to choose from all day. 🕑🍴≥♣🚌☀

London Road Ale House Ⓛ

241 London Road, ST4 5AA

✪ 3 (12 Fri & Sat)-10; 12-10 Sun

6 changing beers (sourced nationally; often Coach House, Great Orme, Pig & Porter) Ⓗ

A free house and micropub just a short walk from Stoke town centre serving up to six real ales and six real ciders from across the UK, plus a bottled beer selection. Opened in 2015, this has quickly become a firm favourite on the Stoke pub scene and has won accolades from the local CAMRA branch. Knowledgable, friendly staff and a varied and exciting drinks choice have made this a pub to visit. Q≈♣♠🍴(21,21A)❀

Olde Bull & Bush 🅛
9 Hartshill Road, ST4 7QT
☼ 12-11 (midnight Sat) ☎ (01782) 920209
Draught Bass; 5 changing beers (sourced nationally; often Greene King, Lymestone, RAN Ales) 🄷
A welcome new addition to the Guide, this pub is a delightfully refurbished free house in Stoke town centre. Among its most outstanding features are the mural depicting local history, the Minton floor tiling and its magnificent beer garden. The split-level bar has six handpull beers, with Lymestone Drunken Bull and a RAN Ale usually available, plus six handpulled ciders. CAMRA members receive a 10 per cent discount at all times. ⛵❀◖◗≈♠🍴

Wheatsheaf 🅛
84-92 Church Street, ST4 1BU
☼ 8am-midnight (1am Fri & Sat) ☎ (01782) 747462
Greene King Abbot; Ruddles Best Bitter; Sharp's Doom Bar; 5 changing beers (sourced nationally; often Lymestone, Summerskills, Titanic) 🄷
Unlike a lot of the JD Wetherspoon chain, the Wheatsheaf has always been a pub, originally an 18th-century coaching inn. Proud of its community links, it is often customer-led in its choice of beers via a suggestion box located in the CAMRA Corner. It has deservedly been awarded Wetherspoon Regional Real Ale Pub of the Year for the past four years. Popular on match days due to its proximity to the shuttle bus link to the Britannia Stadium. Q⛵◖◗&≈♣♠🍴🛜

Stone

Borehole 🅛
Mount Road Industrial Estate, ST15 8LL
☼ 12-10 (11 Fri & Sat) ☎ (01785) 817796
⊕ theborehole.com
Lymestone Stone Cutter, Stone Faced, Foundation Stone, Ein Stein, Stone the Crows; 2 changing beers (sourced locally) 🄷
A traditional pub that has proved a hit with beer and cider fans since its opening in 2015. Small and friendly, there are eight handpumps. A nice variety of home-baked cakes and pickled egg of the month are available for the peckish. A good selection of single malts and Belgian beers adds to the craic. Children are welcome until 8pm and dogs are well provided for. A small meeting room caters for local groups. Q⛵❀◖◗≈♣♠P🍴(10)❀

Royal Exchange 🅛
26 Radford Street, ST15 8DA (on corner of Northesk St and Radford St)
☼ 12-11 (midnight Fri & Sat) ☎ (01785) 812685
Everards Tiger; Titanic Steerage, Iceberg, White Star, Plum Porter, Captain Smith's Strong Ale; 4 changing beers (sourced nationally) 🄷
A one-roomed corner pub with four distinct drinking areas and real fires at both ends. Ten real ales are stocked together with a real cider. The four changing beers are mainly from microbreweries. There are no TVs but acoustic music and quiz nights are hosted, together with a number of clubs including knitting, reading, gaming and photography. Light snacks, as well as Friday and Saturday lunches using local ingredients, are served. Q⛵❀◖◗≈♣♠🍴❀🛜

Swan Inn 🅛
18 Stafford Street, ST15 8QW (on A520 near Trent & Mersey Canal)
☼ 12-1am (11 Mon; midnight Tue & Wed); 12-11 Sun
☎ (01785) 815570 ⊕ swaninnstone.co.uk
House beer (by Coach House); 9 changing beers (sourced nationally) 🄷
A carefully renovated Grade II-listed building, this thriving free house has served beers from well over 700 breweries. Regular beers come from Blythe, Holden's, Joule's and Lymestone, supported by breweries from across the country. There is also a good range of real ciders. The pub hosts quiz nights and live music, and also holds a popular beer festival in early July. Strictly over-18s only. ❀♣♠🍴❀🛜

Summerhill

Boat
Walsall Road, WS14 0BU
☼ 12-3, 6-11; 12-11 Sun ☎ (01543) 361692
⊕ oddfellowsintheboat.com
3 changing beers (often Cottage) 🄷
Primarily a popular dining venue, this free house does have a bar area where drinkers are welcome. Diners can peruse the extensive chalkboard menu in the reception area while watching the cooking. A Cottage beer is generally featured, plus two different ales which are usually interesting and often local. There is an enclosed garden area adjacent to the large car park. If approaching by car from the north, a U-turn is required after passing the pub on the right. Q❀◖◗&P🍴❀🛜

Tamworth

King's Ditch 🅛
51 Lower Gungate, B79 7AS
☼ closed Mon; 5-9 (10.30 Thu); 4-10.30 Fri; 12-10.30 Sat & Sun ☎ 07989 805828 ⊕ kingsditch.co.uk
🄶
This is Tamworth's first micropub, formerly a cycle shop. There is a single ground-floor room with a simple decor of bare brick and wood, plus a small drinking area upstairs. Between three and six gravity-served ales are complemented by a range of 20 real ciders – the pub was a finalist in CAMRA's national Cider Pub of the Year competition in 2016. There are occasional mini beer festivals showcasing a particular brewery. Children are welcome until 7pm. Q⛵≈♠🍴❀🛜

Market Vaults ✅
7 Market Street, B79 7LU
☼ 12-11 ☎ (01827) 66552
Joule's Pale Ale; 7 changing beers 🄷
Traditional and historic town-centre pub, close to the attractive town hall and Norman castle. A Joule's seasonal ale often features among the changing guest beers. A wide range of real ciders is available, from a chilled cabinet. In winter, the pub is cheered by solid fuel stoves, while a peaceful walled beer garden at the rear provides sanctuary to drinkers on fine days. Hot food is served daily except Mondays. ❀◖◗≈♠🍴❀🛜

Sir Robert Peel 🅛
13-15 Lower Gungate, B79 7BA
☼ 2 (4 Tue)-11; 12-11 Sat & Sun ☎ (01827) 300910
5 changing beers (often Oakham) 🄷

Popular free house celebrating its 13th consecutive year in the Guide. Named after the town's historic statesman, it is twinned with a pub in Tamworth's German twin town of Bad Laasphe and attracts regular exchange visits. Attentive staff dispense up to five changing ales including a Church End house beer, plus four real ciders and a large selection of foreign bottled beers. It has a small beer terrace on the pedestrianised street front. The up-to-date jukebox ensures a lively atmosphere at the weekend. ≈●🖥♣🛜

Trysull

Bell Inn 🅛
Bell Road, WV5 7JB
☼ 11.30-3, 5-11 (midnight Fri); 11.30-midnight Sat; 12-11 Sun ☎ (01902) 892871 ⊕ holdensbellinntrysull.co.uk
Bathams Best Bitter; Holden's Black Country Bitter, Golden Glow, Special; 2 changing beers (often Burton Bridge, Enville) 🅗
A fine 18th-century building next to the village church. It has a small yet cosy bar, a pleasant lounge and a large dining room; the lounge and restaurant serve an extensive food menu. There is a large patio area at the front of the pub which overlooks several picturesque residential properties. Popular with walkers, the Staffordshire & Worcestershire Canal is a 15-minute walk away. Q🕮🌂⏺🄿♣

Tutbury

Cask & Pottle
2 High Street, DE13 9LP (close to mini roundabout at centre of village)
☼ 5-9 Mon; 12-2, 5-9 (10 Fri); 1-10 Sat; 1-4 Sun ☎ 07595 423614 ⊕ caskandpottle.co.uk
4 changing beers (sourced regionally) 🄶
East Staffordshire's first micropub, opened in 2013 in a former sweet shop. The small, bright single room on the ground floor of a Victorian terrace features pine benches (with cushions) and tables, but no bar counter. One wall is decorated with an aphorism, a mural, and a table of ale measures (a pottle is an archaic name for a half-gallon measure). A window at the rear offers a view of the stillage. Three ciders and a perry are usually available, from varying sources. Q🕮🖥●♣

Cross Keys ✔
39 Burton Street, DE13 9NR (E side of village, 300yds from A511)
☼ closed Mon; 11-3, 5-11; 12-9 Sun ☎ (01283) 813677
Burton Bridge Draught Burton Ale; 2 changing beers (sourced regionally) 🅗
Privately owned 19th-century free house, overlooking the Dove Valley and providing a fine view of Tutbury Castle. The split-level public bar and lounge have a homely feel and are served from a similarly split-level bar. There is a separate large dining room to the rear (no meals Sun eve). This is the only pub in the area which has offered Draught Burton Ale since its launch by Ind Coope in 1976 through to its 2015 reincarnation from Burton Bridge. 🌂⏺♣🄿♣🛜

Uttoxeter

Old Swan 🅛 ✔
Market Place, ST14 8HN
☼ 8am-midnight (1am Fri & Sat) ☎ (01889) 598650

Greene King Abbot; Ruddles Best Bitter; Sharp's Doom Bar; 4 changing beers (sourced locally; often Backyard, Lymestone, Slater's) 🅗
Centrally located close to the town's marketplace, this Wetherspoon pub attracts a varied clientele throughout the day. Up to six handpumps are in use at any one time, with a varied choice of changing local and national ales. A large open-plan seating area downstairs is supplemented with a quieter upper level to the rear. A small rear outdoor patio and separate smoking area are also provided. Food is served all day. Very busy on race days. Q🕮🌂⏺●♣Å≈●🖥🛜

Whiston

Swan Inn 🅛
ST19 5QH (in Penkridge turn W off A449 at roundabout by Hodsons on to Bungham Lane, cross Cuttlestone Bridge and follow signs to Whiston) SJ895144
☼ 6-8.30 Mon; 12-3, 5-11; 12-11 Sat; 12-10.30 Sun
☎ (01785) 716200 ⊕ swanwhiston.co.uk
Holden's Black Country Bitter; 4 changing beers (sourced nationally) 🅗
Although remote, the Swan's high-quality, well-kept ales and superb food make this a thriving pub. Built in 1593, burnt down and rebuilt in 1711, the oldest part today is the small bar housing an inglenook fireplace. The lounge features an intriguing double-sided log fire. Six acres of grounds include a children's obstacle course, aviary and rabbits. Open all day on bank holidays noon-11pm (except Christmas Day). Q🕮🌂⏺●♣🄿🖥(878,76)♣🛜

Whittington

Bell Inn ✔
27 Main Street, WS14 9JR
☼ 11-11 (midnight Fri & Sat); 12-10.30 Sun
☎ (01543) 432377 ⊕ bellwhittington.co.uk
Draught Bass; Greene King Abbot; Marston's Pedigree; 1 changing beer 🅗
Old-fashioned and cosy local at the centre of the village, within walking distance of the canal. Dating from 1834, the pub features a wealth of wooden beams, plus lovely open fires in winter. The central island bar serves a small room to the front and a larger area to the rear, with a large spillover room to one side. The small beer terrace at the front offers outdoor drinking. The guest ale is usually from one of the bigger players. 🌂♣🄿🖥(785,786)♣🛜

Wilnecote

Globe Inn
91 Watling Street, B77 5BA
☼ 3-11; 12-midnight Fri & Sat; 12-11 Sun ☎ (01827) 254554
Marston's Pedigree; 2 changing beers 🅗
Friendly community pub, renowned for the quality of its Pedigree, which has a rapid turnover. The guest ales, of which there are at least two, are free of tie and often local. Bar staff are happy to provide guidance to the uncertain. The single L-shaped room is complemented by an enclosed beer terrace to the rear, surrounded by leafy trees in summer. The pub is just over half a mile from Wilnecote rail station. 🌂♣🖥♣🛜

Britain's Best Real Heritage Pubs

Geoff Brandwood

This definitive listing is the result of 25 years' research by CAMRA to discover pubs that are either unaltered in 70 years or have features of truly national historic importance. Fully revised, this 2nd edition boasts updated information and a new set of evocative illustrations. Among the 260 pubs, there are unspoilt country locals, Victorian drinking palaces and mighty roadhouses. The book has features describing how the pub developed, what's distinctive about pubs in different parts of the country, how people a century ago could expect to be served drinks at their table, and how they used the pub for take-out sales in the pre-supermarket era.

RRP £9.99 ISBN: 978-1-85249-334-9 **320 pages**

For this and other books on beer and pubs visit CAMRA's online bookshop at **www.camra.org.uk/books** or call **01727 867201**. Discounts are available for CAMRA members.

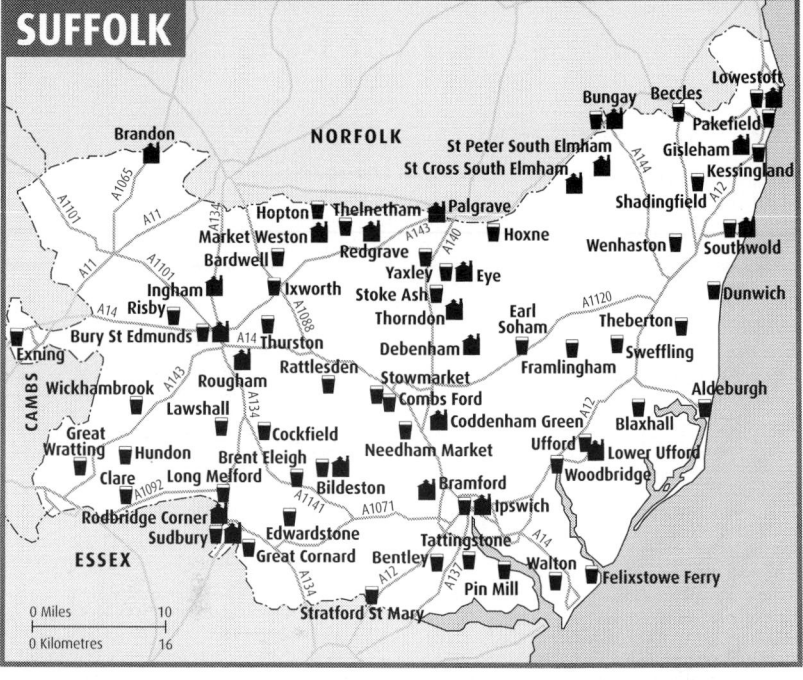

Aldeburgh

White Hart 🄻

222 High Street, IP15 5AJ (next to fish & chip shop)
🕐 11.30-11; 12-10.30 Sun ☎ (01728) 453205
🌐 whitehartaldeburgh.co.uk
Adnams Southwold Bitter, Ghost Ship, Broadside; 3 changing beers (often Adnams) 🄷
Friendly single bar where drinkers can buy fish and chips from next door and eat them in the garden in fine weather together with a drink from the bar. This local was formerly used as a public reading room. Occasional live music features. Families are welcome outside in summer, where there is covered seating, barbecues and a wood-fired pizza oven Easter until mid-Sept. 🌺🏠♣🚍🐾🛜

Bardwell

Dun Cow 🅥

Up Street, IP31 1AA (approx 1 mile off A143 at Stanton)
🕐 11.30-2.30, 5-midnight; 12-midnight Sat; 12-10.30 Sun
☎ (01359) 250806
Greene King IPA; 3 changing beers 🄷
A traditional pub in a pleasant village set in the Suffolk countryside. The pub has two bars and offers speciality food nights. Six real ales are available at weekends. Outside is a covered smoking area and large family space in the garden. Party bookings and coaches are welcome if booked in advance. The picturesque restored village windmill is worth a visit and has occasional threshing open days. 🌺🏠🍷♣🅿🚍🐾

Beccles

Butchers Arms 🄻

51 London Road, NR34 9YT
🕐 4-midnight; 12-12.30am Fri & Sat; 12-midnight Sun
☎ (01502) 712243 🌐 mypub.org.uk

Woodforde's Nelson's Revenge; 5 changing beers (sourced locally; often Barrell & Sellers, Greene King, Woodforde's) 🄷
Situated on the outskirts of town opposite Beccles Cemetery, this popular locals' pub serves up to six ales mainly from East Anglian breweries. Jazz nights and other live music are hosted along with regular monthly quiz nights, open mic nights and charity events. The original lounge and public bars are now open plan, with the bar and a real fire in the old part of the building and pool tables in the extended area. Customers are welcome to bring their own food to eat on the premises. 🏠♣♥🅿🚍(60H,60S)🐾🛜

Caxton Club 🄻

Gaol Lane, NR34 9SJ
🕐 12-1.30 (not Tue), 7-11; 12-2, 6.30-11 Fri; 12-11 Sat; 12-10.30 Sun ☎ (01502) 712829
4 changing beers (sourced nationally; often Green Jack, Greene King, Woodforde's) 🄷
Spacious club conveniently situated a short walk from bus and train stations and the town centre, serving four ever-changing beers and a large choice of real cider. All members and guests are warmly welcomed (a small charge is made to cover entertainment on Saturday evenings). It has a central bar, TV and darts room and a separate snooker room. There is also a large function room where music events are held. CAMRA Suffolk Cider Pub of the Year 2016. Guide dogs only are allowed. 🌺🏠♿🚲♣🚍🛜

Bentley

Case is Altered 🅥

Capel Road, IP9 2DW
🕐 closed Mon & Tue; 12-2.30 (3 Sat), 6-11.30; 12-4, 7-10.30 Sun ☎ (01473) 805575 🌐 thecasepubbentley.co.uk

Adnams Southwold Bitter; 3 changing beers (sourced locally) Ⓗ

Local community-owned and run pub with a single bar serving two drinking areas, a restaurant area with a wood-burning stove, and a pretty beer garden with plenty of seating. Various music evenings and themed food nights are hosted but there is no TV. Traditional pub games are available including darts, cards and dominoes. A quiz is held on the last Saturday of the month. Local artists' work is on display. Some of the produce used in the kitchen is now grown by the local community. As this is a community-run pub please check opening hours before travelling. ⛵🏮🅓&♣️🅿️🚍🐾🐱📶

Bildeston

King's Head Ⓛ ✅

132 High Street, IP7 7ED

❂ closed Mon & Tue; 6-11.30 Wed; 4-11.30 Thu & Fri; 12-11.30 Sat; 12-10.30 Sun ☎ (01449) 741434

🌐 bildestonkingshead.co.uk

King's Head Bildeston Best, Brettvale Gold; 4 changing beers (sourced locally) Ⓗ

Home of the King's Head Brewery since 1996, the building's carved timbers indicate its history as part of a larger complex dating from around 1530. Now a single bar with a large, cosy inglenook fireplace, a friendly alehouse atmosphere has evolved, with food available at weekends only. There is a fully enclosed rear garden with a covered patio area, lawns and play equipment for children. The late May bank holiday beer festival is long established and popular. ⛵🏮🅓&♣️🚍🐾🐱📶

Blaxhall

Ship Ⓛ ✅

School Road, IP12 2DY

❂ 12 (11 Mon)-11.30 ☎ (01728) 688316

🌐 blaxhallshipinn.co.uk

Adnams Southwold Bitter; Greene King IPA; Woodforde's Wherry; 2 changing beers Ⓗ

A cosy two-roomed 16th-century pub on the edge of the 'Suffolk Sandlings' with a long reputation for traditional singing in the bar. The menu offers a wide choice of home-made dishes and daily specials using locally sourced ingredients (book for breakfast from 10.30am in the summer months). Live entertainment includes folk music, bands and story-telling every week, and the pub hosts a Folk East stage during the festival weekend. Letting chalets are available beside the pub and camping at the nearby village hall is by arrangement. ⛵🏮🅓&♣️🅿️🚍🐾🐱📶

Brent Eleigh

Cock ★

Lavenham Road, CO10 9PB

❂ 12-4, 6-11; 12-11 Fri & Sat; 12-10.30 Sun

☎ (01787) 247371

Adnams Southwold Bitter; 3 changing beers (sourced locally) Ⓗ

The Cock remains a real gem and has been identified by CAMRA as having a nationally important historic interior. It has two bars, the smaller one ideal for families. The landlady provides good food throughout opening times, including popular Sunday lunches, keeping visiting walkers and cyclists more than happy. Real cider comes from local suppliers. Seating outside is ideal for watching the world go by. The pub has cats but well-behaved dogs are always welcome. Q🏮🅗🅓♣️🅿️🚍(111)🐾📶

Bungay

Chequers Ⓛ

23 Bridge Street, NR35 1HD

❂ 11-midnight; 12-midnight Sun ☎ (01986) 893579

Green Jack Golden Best; 3 changing beers (sourced locally; often Adnams, Grain, Woodforde's) Ⓗ

Situated close to the town centre, this inn dates from the 17th century and has retained the original timber frame, wood panelling and doors. It comprises two rooms separated by an archway with TV screens in both for sporting events. Ample parking is available adjacent to a partially covered area leading to a large paved beer garden. An ever-changing range of ales is usually sourced locally, often including a dark beer in the winter months. 🏮🅓&♣️🅿️🚍🐾📶

Green Dragon Ⓛ

29 Broad Street, NR35 1EE

❂ 11 (12 Sat)-midnight; 12-5 Sun ☎ (01986) 892681

🌐 greendragonbungay.co.uk

Green Dragon Chaucer Ale, Gold, Bridge Street Bitter Ⓗ**, Strong Mild; 1 changing beer (sourced locally; often Green Dragon)** Ⓖ

On the northern edge of town, this is Bungay's only brewpub and the home of the Green Dragon brewery. Ales are brewed in outbuildings adjacent to the car park at the rear (brewery tours by appointment). Bottle-conditioned and seasonal brews are often available. The pub has a public bar and a spacious lounge with a side room where families are welcome, leading to a small enclosed garden. Curry night is Wednesday. ⛵🏮♣️🅿️🚍🐾📶

REAL ALE BREWERIES

Adnams Southwold
Barrell & Sellers St Cross South Elmham
Bartrams Rougham
Brandon Brandon
Brewshed Ingham
Briarbank 🍺 Ipswich
Calvors Coddenham Green
Cliff Quay Debenham
Dove Street Ipswich
Earl Soham Debenham
Green Dragon 🍺 Bungay
Green Jack Lowestoft
Greene King Bury St Edmunds
Hellhound Bramford
Hoxne Palgrave
Kings Head 🍺 Bildeston
Mauldons Sudbury
Nethergate Rodbridge Corner
Old Cannon 🍺 Bury St Edmunds
Old Chimneys Market Weston
Shortts Thorndon
St Judes 🍺 Ipswich
St Peter's St Peter South Elmham
Star Wing Redgrave (NEW)
Station 119 Eye
Trinity Gisleham
Uffa 🍺 Lower Ufford

Bury St Edmunds

Beerhouse ⓛ
1 Tayfen Road, IP32 6BH
🕒 5 (12 Sat)-11; 12-10 Sun ☎ (01284) 766415
🌐 burybeerhouse.co.uk
Brewshed Best; 7 changing beers (sourced nationally) Ⓗ
Traditional beer house in an unusual semi-circular Victorian building (previously called the Ipswich Arms), handy for the railway station, and refurbished with a modern feel. Seven beer engines provide an ever-changing selection of well-kept real ales. It also serves its own beers from the Brewshed Brewery, which is now located out of town and supplies the brewery's three other local pubs. Three real ciders are also available. Regular beer festivals and an annual cider festival are hosted. Major sporting events are shown on a big screen. ᐅ🏵🌳🍴P🎫🐾🎶

Dove � ⓛ
68 Hospital Road, IP33 3JU (5 mins walk from town centre)
🕒 5-11; 12-3, 6-11 Sat; 12-3, 6-10.30 Sun ☎ (01284) 702787
🌐 thedovepub.co.uk
Woodforde's Wherry Ⓗ**; changing beers** Ⓗ/Ⓖ
No lager, TVs, pool or gaming machines here – the Dove is how pubs used to be. This back-street community venue has a traditional, basic main bar and a parlour area. It offers ever-changing beers on six handpumps and a good selection of real ciders, and the staff are knowledgable about the ales. Locally made pies and snacks are available. A former East Anglian CAMRA Regional Pub of the Year and local Cider Pub of the Year. Q🏵🍴🍴P🎫🐾

Oakes Barn
St Andrews Street South, IP33 3PH (opp Waitrose car park)
🕒 11-11.30; 12-5 Sun ☎ (01284) 761592 🌐 oakesbarn.co.uk
Oakham JHB; Woodforde's Wherry; 4 changing beers (sourced nationally) Ⓗ
A real ale free house and social hub near the town centre with some period features and historic links to the medieval town. Six real ales are always available including one dark beer alongside real cider. Home-made food comprises lunchtime specials and snacks served all day. There is a covered smoking area outside and an open courtyard with seating. Regular events are held in the bar and upstairs function room which is available for hire. Local CAMRA Pub of the Year 2016. ᐅ🏵🍴🍴P🎫🐾🎶

Rose & Crown ✅
48 Whiting Street, IP33 1NP (on corner of Whiting St and Westgate)
🕒 11.30-11.30; 11.30-3, 7-11.30 Sat; 12-2.30, 8-11.30 Sun ☎ (01284) 755934
Greene King XX Mild, IPA, Abbot; 3 changing beers (sourced nationally) Ⓗ
In sight of Greene King's Westgate Brewery, this is a traditional inn with two bars and a separate off-sales hatch. The present tenants have run the pub for over 30 years and it has been in the same family for over 40 years. Good-value wholesome food is served lunchtimes Monday to Saturday. Children are not allowed in the bars but are welcome in the garden. The pub is a listed building within the conservation area of Bury St Edmunds, and is on CAMRA's Regional Inventory of Historic Pub Interiors. Q🏵🍴🍴🎫🐾

Clare

Globe
10 Callis Street, CO10 8PX
🕒 5 (4 Fri)-11.30; 11-11.30 Sat; 12-7 Sun ☎ (01787) 278122
Young's Bitter; 3 changing beers (sourced nationally) Ⓗ
A phoenix risen from the ashes, the Globe reopened in 2013 after a two-year closure. Serving one well-kept regular beer and up to three changing guests, it is now a thriving local where beer and conversation dominate. Live music plays every other Saturday night and afternoon sessions every other Sunday. It has a separate pool room at the rear and a newly refurbished garden for summer drinking. No food is served. Q ᐅ🏵🍴P🎫🐾🎶

Cockfield

Horseshoes Inn ✅
Stow's Hill, IP30 0JB
🕒 closed Mon; 12-3, 6-11 (11.30 Fri); 11.30-11 Sat; 12-6.30 Sun ☎ (01284) 828177 🌐 thehorseshoes-inn.co.uk
Adnams Southwold Bitter, Broadside; Black Sheep Best Bitter; 1 changing beer (sourced nationally) Ⓗ
A sympathetically refurbished thatched 14th-century building on the A1141 road to Lavenham. The large long bar room is divided by a chimney breast into two areas, and there is a separate spacious conservatory dining area. The bar area features an exposed crown post and many original beams dating from 1350. Good-value meals are available, with speciality food nights. The hilltop beer garden enjoys fabulous views. Q ᐅ🏵🍴P🎫🐾🎶

Combs Ford

Gladstone Arms
2 Combs Road, IP14 2AP
🕒 12-midnight; 12-11 Sun ☎ (01449) 771608
🌐 gladstonearms.co.uk
Adnams Southwold Bitter, Broadside; Crouch Vale Brewers Gold; Fuller's London Pride; Sharp's Doom Bar; Woodforde's Wherry Ⓗ**; 4 changing beers** Ⓗ/Ⓖ
The owners of this pub also run the Dove Street Inn in Ipswich. The two pubs share a similar beer range, with between 12 and 14 ales, including house beers brewed in Ipswich. Four or five ciders and a wide range of imported foreign beers and whiskies are also available. Good-value food is served with vegetarian options. Sky Sports and BT Sport are screened, monthly live music is hosted and board games are available. A beer festival features over the Easter weekend. The garden at the rear leads to the river. Q ᐅ🏵🍴🍴P🎫🐾🎶

Dunwich

Ship
St James Street, IP17 3DT
🕒 11-11 ☎ (01728) 648219 🌐 shipatdunwich.co.uk
Adnams Southwold Bitter; 3 changing beers Ⓗ
Once a haunt of smugglers, this is now a great place to eat, drink, relax and get away from it all. The small public bar is simply furnished with wooden furniture and a woodburner. Comfortable, traditionally furnished rooms have views across the sea or nearby marshes. Beers come from local brewers and bottled local cider is available. There is an extensive food menu. The enormous garden is

dotted with fruit trees including a 300-year-old fig. The beach is just a couple of minutes' walk away. Beer festivals are held in March and September. ⚑☆🅱🅿🐾📶

Earl Soham

Victoria 🅛
The Street, IP13 7RL
☼ 11.30-3, 5.30-11; 11-3, 7-10.30 Sun ☎ (01728) 685758
Earl Soham Victoria Bitter; 2 changing beers (often Cliff Quay, Earl Soham) 🅷
Although recently refurbished, this popular, traditional pub has changed little over the years, with two small bars and a prominent fireplace (now fitted with a woodburner). It still has an outside toilet. An ever-changing food menu with daily specials is offered lunchtimes and evenings, all home-cooked. The pub gets very busy at weekends, especially on sunny days when even a seat in the garden can be hard to find. Dogs and children are welcome. The Earl Soham Brewery was originally behind the pub. Q⚑☆🅱♣🅿🐾📶

Edwardstone

White Horse Inn 🅛
Mill Green, CO10 5PX
☼ 12-midnight ☎ (01787) 211211
⊕ edwardstonewhitehorse.co.uk
Timothy Taylor Landlord; Woodforde's Wherry 🅷; 6 changing beers (sourced nationally) 🅷/🅶
Off the beaten track in rural countryside, this is a traditional Suffolk free house, hard to find but well worth seeking out. Eight beers are usually available, four on handpump and the remainder on stillage, plus up to 14 ciders. Two small holiday cottages and a campsite are within the grounds. Reasonably priced home-prepared food uses mainly locally sourced and home-grown ingredients, with Sunday roasts ever popular. Beer festivals and the annual Eddyfest in August are highlights in the events calendar. Q⚑☆🅱🅐♣🖤🅿🐾📶

Exning

White Horse
23 Church Street, CB8 7EH
☼ 12-midnight ☎ (01638) 577323
⊕ whitehorseexning.co.uk
Changing beers 🅷
Mentioned in the Domesday Book, this fine free house has been run by the same family since 1923. It comprises a public bar, cosy lounge and separate restaurant offering a good choice of home-cooked food. Beers vary from week to week but often include Bass, Doom Bar and Directors. Happy hour is 5.30-6.30pm, extended to 7pm on Friday. A private room can be hired. Q☆🅱♣🅿🐾

Eye

Queen's Head ✅
7 Cross Street, IP23 7AB
☼ 11-11; 11-9 Sun ☎ (01379) 870153
⊕ queensheadeye.co.uk
Adnams Southwold Bitter, Broadside; 3 changing beers (often Batemans, Nethergate) 🅖
Dating from 1590, this is now the only pub remaining in this delightful north Suffolk town with

many buildings of character and historic significance. The main bar has a wood-burning stove, Cross Street bar is a former butcher's shop, and there is also a snug bar. Beers are dispensed direct from casks (with water-cooling jackets) in the main bar. Traditional pub food and daily specials are served, including breakfast 8.30-10.30am. Families are welcome. ⚑☆🅱🅐♣🅿🐾📶

Felixstowe Ferry

Ferry Boat Inn ✅
Ferry Road, IP11 9RZ
☼ 11-3, 5.30-11; 11-11 Sat; 12-10.30 Sun ☎ (01394) 284203
⊕ ferryboatinn.org.uk
Adnams Southwold Bitter; Woodforde's Wherry; 2 changing beers 🅷
Popular coastal pub set in a small hamlet one mile north of the main town. The split-level bar has old stone-flagged flooring and traditional seating around a large fireplace with a woodburner. Food is mostly locally sourced and freshly prepared on the premises, including fish from nearby fishermen's huts. Daily specials, gluten-free dishes and vegetarian options are available lunchtimes and evenings. A room to the rear can cater for private functions, while the large garden to the front is busy in summer months. ⚑☆🅱🅐♣🅿🐾

Framlingham

Station Hotel 🅛
Station Road, IP13 9EE
☼ 12-2.30, 5-11; 12-11 Sat; 11-2.30, 7-10.30 Sun
☎ (01728) 723455 ⊕ thestationhotel.net
Earl Soham Gannet Mild, Victoria Bitter, Brandeston Gold; 2 changing beers (often Earl Soham) 🅷
Cosy two-bar pub set in a former station buffet (the branch line closed in 1963). It enjoys a good reputation for food, made with locally sourced ingredients and prepared on the premises. An ever-changing menu is displayed on chalkboards. Beers and a guest cider are dispensed from a set of Edwardian German silver handpumps. On Sundays, brunch and beers are available from 11am. The garden bar has a wood-fired pizza oven. A beer festival is held over the third weekend in July. Children and dogs welcome. Q⚑☆🅱🖤🅿🐾📶

Great Cornard

Five Bells
63 Bures Road, CO10 0HU
☼ 12-midnight ☎ (01787) 379016
Adnams Southwold Bitter; Greene King XX Mild, IPA; 2 changing beers (sourced nationally) 🅷
A friendly community free house situated near the church (home of the five bells) on the main Sudbury to Bures road. The main bar has a library and a piano. A separate small bar is home to a Tunisian restaurant. Outside is a large beer garden. Pub games include bar billiards. An open mic session is hosted every third Thursday and karaoke every second Friday of the month. The home-made pies are legendary. A rare outlet for Greene King XX Mild. Q⚑☆🅱🅐♣🅿🐾📶

Great Wratting

Red Lion
School Road, CB9 7HA

⏲ 11-2.30, 5-11; 11-1.30am Sat; 12-3, 7-10 Sun
☎ (01440) 783237
Adnams Southwold Bitter, Broadside; 1 changing beer Ⓗ
A whale's jawbones frame the doorway to this village local dating from the 17th or 18th century, making an unusual and amusing entrance. Now a free house, this ex-Adnams pub offers good beer, quality food and conversation as its mainstay. Locals love this hostelry and are passionate supporters of the activities overseen by an enthusiastic landlord of long experience. Quiz nights and a darts league thrive here.
Q♘❀◐⛺♣●P🚌🐾

Hopton

Vine
High Street, IP22 2QX
⏲ 3-11; 12-midnight Sat; 12-10.30 Sun ☎ (01953) 688581
Adnams Southwold Bitter, Broadside; Greene King IPA, IPA Reserve; 5 changing beers (sourced locally; often Colchester, Lacons, Wolf) Ⓗ
On the main road near the church, this village local has been revitalised by an enthusiastic landlord and friendly staff since it was taken over in 2013. Nine ales including a selection of local and regional guests are currently offered at reasonable prices, with Adnams Southwold, Broadside and Greene King IPA the regulars. The pub has a pool table in one of its three separate areas. Outside is a large play area for children. Popular with locals and visitors. ♘❀♿♣●P🚌(100)🐾📶

Hoxne

Swan ✔
Low Street, IP21 5AS
⏲ 12-11; 11-midnight Fri & Sat ☎ (01379) 668275
🌐 swaninnhoxne.co.uk
Adnams Southwold Bitter, Broadside; Timothy Taylor Landlord; Woodforde's Wherry Ⓖ
The Swan reopened in 2016 after temporary closure and is once again a thriving village local. The 15th-century building has a colourful history – it claims to be both the former home of the Bishop of Norwich and later a brothel. There is a large open fire in the main bar and a woodburner in the adjacent bar. The restaurant serves excellent home-cooked food, with an emphasis on local produce. To the rear is a large garden. An annual beer festival features in August. Buskers' night is Thursday. ♘❀◐♿♣P🚌🐾📶

Hundon

Rose & Crown
20 North Street, CO10 8ED
⏲ 6-9 Mon & Tue; 12-2, 6-11 Wed & Thu; 12-midnight Fri & Sat; 12-9 Sun ☎ (01440) 786261 🌐 hundon-village.co.uk/roseandcrown.html
Sharp's Doom Bar; 3 changing beers (sourced nationally; often Fuller's, St Austell, Timothy Taylor) Ⓗ
Since it became a free house, this refurbished two-roomed pub has developed a reputation for good ale. The three changing beers are dictated by customer demand. A true village atmosphere prevails and the welcome is warm and friendly. Home-cooked food is served Wednesday evening to Sunday lunchtime. A folk evening is held on the third Wednesday of the month and an autumn family festival over the August bank holiday. Weddings can be catered for in a marquee in the extensive garden. Q♘❀◐♿♣P🚌🐾

Ipswich

Arcade Street Tavern
Arcade Street, IP1 1EX (behind Corn Exchange)
⏲ closed Mon; 10.30-3 Tue (11 Wed & Thu; midnight Fri; 1am Sat); closed Sun ☎ (01473) 805454 🌐 arcadetavern.co.uk
2 changing beers Ⓗ
A stylish and multi-roomed café bar with a traditional wooden interior. Two handpumps dispense a varied range of ales alongside a selection of around 130 imported bottles. Street-food Fridays are hosted in conjunction with various other local traders. There are some heated seating areas outside and two function rooms; one upstairs, and one to the rear often used for product launches. Artisan coffee is available.
Q❀🚌📶

Cricketers 𝕃 ✔
51 Crown Street, IP1 3JA
⏲ 8am-midnight (12.30am Fri & Sat) ☎ (01473) 225910
Adnams Ghost Ship; Greene King IPA, Abbot; Sharp's Doom Bar; 6 changing beers Ⓗ
Situated opposite the Tower Ramparts bus station, this large 1930s town centre pub was once a 'Tolly Folly'. Now run by Wetherspoon, it has various seating areas set around a central bar and kitchen. Popular at most times of day, it offers a choice of 12 ever-changing beers on handpump. Regular beer festivals add to the range. The patio area to the side includes a heated smoking area.
Q♘❀◐♿♣●P🚌📶

Dove Street Inn 𝕃 ✔
76 St Helen's Street, IP4 2LA
⏲ 12-midnight; 12-10.30 Sun ☎ (01473) 211270
🌐 dovestreetinn.co.uk
Adnams Broadside; Crouch Vale Brewers Gold; Fuller's London Pride; Greene King Abbot Ⓗ**; changing beers (often Dove Street)** Ⓗ/Ⓖ
Popular multi-roomed inn with a large selection of real ales including milds, plus ciders and continental beers. Some ales are from its own brewery adjacent, and there is a brew shop next door. Home-cooked food and bar snacks are served at all times. Sports TV is shown in the conservatory. The green room, a covered and heated seating area outside, hosts various events. Well-behaved dogs and children are welcome. Three beer festivals are held annually. Last admission is 10.45pm. ♘❀🛏◐♿♣●🚌(66)🐾📶

Fat Cat
288 Spring Road, IP4 5NL
⏲ 12-11 (midnight Fri & Sat) ☎ (01473) 726524
🌐 fatcatipswich.co.uk
Adnams Southwold Bitter Ⓗ**; Fuller's London Pride; Woodforde's Wherry; changing beers** Ⓖ
Ever popular, this small, multi-roomed drinking bar is free from background music and games machines. Bar snacks include Scotch eggs and pasties cooked on the premises. Up to 18 gravity beers are dispensed from the taproom and up to five ciders. An airy conservatory behind the main bar leads out to the pretty garden – the patio and garden provide extra space on sunny afternoons, with the occasional barbecue. Often voted the best pub in town by local CAMRA branch members. No children under 16. Q❀◐●🚌🐾📶

Greyhound

9 Henley Road, IP1 3SE

⏰ 11.30-2.30, 5-11; 11.30-midnight Fri; 11.30-11.30 Sat; 10-10.30 Sun ☎ (01473) 252862

🌐 thegreyhoundipswich.co.uk

Adnams Southwold Bitter, Ghost Ship, Broadside; 3 changing beers (often Adnams) Ⓗ

The Greyhound has a traditional, small public bar at the front and a larger, more modern drinking and dining room to the side and rear. The outside drinking space can be busy during the summer months and hosts occasional barbecues. A menu of freshly prepared food is complemented by daily specials, with vegetarian options, and breakfasts 10-11.30am Sunday only. Quiz nights are held twice a month on Sunday evenings. The TVs are only used for sporting events.

Q🕎🏠🕀🍴👌♣P🚃(116)🛜

Spread Eagle

1-3 Fore Street, IP4 1JW

⏰ closed Mon; 12-midnight; 12-10.30 Sun
☎ (01473) 256093

Grain Oak, Best Bitter, Redwood, Slate, Lignum Vitae; 1 changing beer (often Grain) Ⓗ

This distinctive Grade II-listed building is the sole survivor of four pubs that once stood at this junction. Recent refurbishment has restored the building to a high standard and the split-level bar room has been sympathetically furnished throughout. Six real ales are on handpump, all from Grain, plus a selection of specialist beers and imported bottles. Some daytime food options and bar snacks are available, and quality, locally roasted coffee. There is seating outside.

Q🏠🚃🐕🛜

Steamboat Tavern ✓

78 New Cut West, IP2 8HW

⏰ 12-11 (midnight Sat); 12-8 Sun ☎ (01473) 601902

🌐 thesteamboat.co.uk

4 changing beers Ⓗ

Popular L-shaped bar in a historic riverside location, featuring live music and good food prepared on the premises. It has various drinking areas and a recently refurbished beer garden. Live music includes jazz on alternate Sundays and folk music on the third Thursday of the month. Occasional blues and punk music nights are held, and an annual folk music weekend – see the website for details. Suffolk song writers play here monthly.

🕎🏠🕀♣🐕🛜

Thomas Wolsey

9-13 St Peters Street, IP1 1XF (300yds from bus station)

⏰ 4.30-11.30 (1am Fri & Sat); closed Sun ☎ (01473) 210055

Adnams Ghost Ship; Crouch Vale Brewers Gold; Woodforde's Wherry; 1 changing beer Ⓗ

Large single-room lounge bar set in a historic Grade II-listed building. It has a patio area to the side and two nicely furnished function rooms upstairs, used for a wide variety of events including story-telling nights, charity quizzes and meetings. A range of ales is available on draught plus over 25 bottled beers and 40 quality wines. Games are available including darts. Home supporters only on football match days.

🏠🚃♣🚃🛜

Ixworth

Greyhound ✓

49 High Street, IP31 2HJ

⏰ 11.30-2.30, 6 (5 Fri & Sat)-11; 12-3, 7-11 Sun
☎ (01359) 230887

Greene King XX Mild, IPA, Abbot; 2 changing beers (sourced nationally) Ⓗ

Situated on the village's attractive high street, this welcoming traditional inn has three bars, one a lovely central snug. The heart of the building dates back to Tudor times. The pub is a rare outlet for Greene King XX Mild. Good-value lunches and early evening meals are served in the restaurant including a daily special. Dominoes, crib, darts and pool are played in leagues and for charity fundraising. Dogs and children are welcome.

Q🕎🏠🕀⚲♣P🚃🐕

Kessingland

Sailors Home Ⓛ ✓

302 Church Road, NR33 7SB

⏰ 12-11 ☎ (01502) 740245 🌐 sailorshome.co.uk

Adnams Southwold Bitter Ⓗ; **6 changing beers (sourced locally; often Green Jack, Humpty Dumpty, Wolf)** Ⓗ/🅶

Situated on the seafront with coastal views, the Sailors is popular in summer with holidaymakers from nearby caravan parks and guest houses. The interior has a mock-Tudor design with four adjoining rooms – one for diners, a games room, a side room and a large central bar area with a TV screen. Four handpulled beers are available, with up to three served on gravity, plus a regularly changing real cider. Beer festivals are held in June and August. 🕎🏠🕀⚲♣P🚃(61)🐕🛜

Lawshall

Swan

The Street, IP29 4QA

⏰ 12-2.45 (not Mon), 6-11; closed Tue; 12-2.45, 5-11 Fri; 12-11 Sat & Sun ☎ (01284) 828477 🌐 swaninnlawshall.com

4 changing beers (sourced nationally; often Adnams, Black Sheep) Ⓗ

Set in the heart of rural Suffolk in the village of Lawshall, the Swan is everything a country pub should be. The beautiful 18th-century thatched building was lovingly restored in 2013 and is crammed full of period features. On the menu you will find all the traditional pub classics and a few extra culinary delights. The large garden encourages children to play. A real ale festival is held in May. Q🕎🏠🕀♣P🐕🛜

Long Melford

Crown Inn

Hall Street, CO10 9JL

⏰ 11-11; 12-10.30 Sun ☎ (01787) 377666

🌐 thecrownhotelmelford.co.uk

Adnams Southwold Bitter, Ghost Ship; 2 changing beers (sourced nationally) Ⓗ

A busy family-run free house and cosy hotel set in the popular antiques centre of Long Melford. Two regular ales and two changing guests, together with real cider, are on handpump. A high-quality home-cooked menu is served in the spacious bar and separate restaurant. There is a large attractive patio garden for summer dining and drinking. Eleven comfortable bedrooms are available for those wishing to stay and explore this picturesque area. Q🕎☎🏠⚲🕀👌🐕P🚃🐕🛜

Lowestoft

Norman Warrior L ✔
Fir Lane, NR32 2RB
🕐 11-11.30 (12.30am Fri & Sat); 12-11.30 Sun
☎ (01502) 561982 ⊕ thenormanwarrior.co.uk
Greene King IPA; 4 changing beers (sourced nationally; often Greene King, Lacons, Sharp's) Ⓗ
Large estate pub with ample parking, situated between the town centre and Oulton Broad North. It comprises a public bar where pool and darts are played and a comfortable lounge leading to a spacious restaurant serving reasonably priced home-cooked food daily. Booking is advisable at weekends. Outside is a large garden and terrace where a beer and cider festival with live music is held annually over the August bank holiday weekend. A popular quiz takes place weekly.
🕭❀◑&♣➡️P🖵(102)🐾☀️📶

Stanford Arms � L
Stanford Street, NR32 2DD
🕐 4-10 (midnight Tue & Wed); closed Thu; 3-1am Fri;
12-midnight Sat; 12-10 Sun ☎ (01502) 587444
12 changing beers (sourced locally; often Golden Triangle, Grain, Shortts Farm) Ⓗ
This quality free house is a short walk from Lowestoft train and bus stations. Nicely refurbished, the open-plan, L-shaped bar has a large array of handpumps serving mainly local ales, with a fine collection of beer trays adorning the walls. To the rear is a courtyard garden with an aviary and a wood-fired pizza oven (Friday is pizza night). Wednesday is usually speciality food night (booking required) and there is live music on Sunday afternoon. CAMRA National Pub of the Year finalist 2016. 🕭❀♣➡️🖵🐾☀️📶

Triangle Tavern L
29 St Peters Street, NR32 1QA
🕐 11-11 (midnight Thu; 1am Fri & Sat); 12-10.30 Sun
☎ (01502) 582711 ⊕ green-jack.com
Green Jack Golden Best, Trawlerboys Best Bitter, Orange Wheat Beer, Lurcher Stout, Gone Fishing ESB, Ripper Tripel Ⓗ**; 2 changing beers (sourced locally; often Crouch Vale, Oakham)** Ⓖ
This lively town-centre tavern is the brewery tap for Green Jack Brewery. The characterful front bar is decorated with many brewery and pub awards and hosts live music every Friday evening. The back bar is more popular with a younger clientele and has a central pool table. Alongside the full Green Jack range are guest ales, real ciders and occasional continental beers. Quarterly beer festivals are held. Customers are welcome to bring in their own food.
❀≈♣➡️🖵🐾

Needham Market

Rampant Horse L
Coddenham Road, IP6 8AU
🕐 12-3, 5-11 (10 Mon); 12-11 Fri & Sat; 12-10 Sun
☎ (01449) 722044 ⊕ therampanthorse.co.uk
Calvors Lodestar Festival Ale, Smooth Hoperator; 1 changing beer Ⓗ
Calvors Brewery of Coddenham Green purchased and reopened this pub in 2012. It now sells a wide range of locally sourced food and drink including its own high-quality lagers and real ales. Beer festivals and live music feature occasionally. There is a garden and car park to the rear. The pub is close to the railway station which was built in an area previously known as 'camping land' – the local

pitch for an ancient ball game, a precursor to football, dating back to at least the 17th century.
❀◑≈♣P🖵🐾☀️📶

Pakefield

Oddfellows L
6 Nightingale Road, NR33 7AU
🕐 11-11; 12-10.30 Sun ☎ (01502) 538415
Adnams Southwold Bitter; 3 changing beers (sourced locally; often Green Jack, Lacons, Woodforde's) Ⓗ
Small, cosy pub close to the clifftop, popular with locals, holidaymakers and those walking the coastal heritage path. The pub comprises three open-plan areas including one for diners, with wooden flooring and panelling throughout. The walls are festooned with pictures of old Pakefield, and sporting events are shown on TV screens. Up to four ales are available, usually including one or two from Green Jack Brewery. Beer festivals are held in summer and winter, the former on the green opposite the pub. 🕭❀◑🖵🐾📶

Pin Mill

Butt & Oyster ★ ✔
Pin Mill Road, IP9 1JW
🕐 10 (9am Sat & Sun)-11 ☎ (01473) 780764
⊕ debeninns.co.uk/buttandoyster
Adnams Southwold Bitter, Ghost Ship, Broadside; 1 changing beer (often Adnams) Ⓖ
Traditional 17th-century pub on the bank of the River Orwell with three separate rooms and a connecting corridor with flagstone floors. Famous for its fabulous setting overlooking the water, there is plenty of outdoor seating for drinkers and diners at the front. Inside, there are some high-backed settles and a large open fire in the main bar area, making it cosy on cold winter days. Breakfast is available until 11.45am, weekends only.
Q🕭❀◑&♣P🖵🐾📶

Rattlesden

Five Bells
High Street, IP30 0RA
🕐 12-midnight; 12-11 Sun ☎ (01449) 737373
3 changing beers (sourced locally; often Earl Soham, Woodforde's) Ⓗ
Set on the high road through a picturesque village, this is a good old Suffolk drinking house – few of its kind still survive. Three well-chosen ales on the bar are usually sourced direct from the breweries. The cosy single-room interior has a games area on a lower level and there is occasional live music. Pub games include shut-the-box and shove-ha'penny plus pétanque in the garden in summer. A motorcycle show is hosted in May. Q❀♣🖵🐾

Risby

Crown & Castle
South Street, IP28 6QU
🕐 12-3, 5 (6.30 Sat)-11; 12-3, 7-10.30 Sun
☎ (01284) 810393 ⊕ crownandcastle.com
Adnams Southwold Bitter; 2 changing beers (sourced nationally) Ⓗ
This attractive flint-faced building opened as a pub and shop in the late 1800s and was sold by Greene King in 2014. A 120ft unrecorded well was discovered during alterations in recent times and is now a feature beneath a grille in the entrance

lobby. The pub has classic back and front bars, with food served in both. The back bar is the public, dominated by games and conversation – well-behaved dogs are also allowed in here.
Q🕏🏵◖♣🅿🖰🌣

Shadingfield

Fox 🖳

London Road, NR34 8DD

🟢 12-11.30; 12-10.30 Sun ☎ (01502) 575100

🌐 shadingfieldfox.co.uk

Young's London Gold; 7 changing beers (sourced locally; often Green Jack, Lacons, Wolf) 🗓

A charming and cosy rural inn on the road between Beccles and Southwold. The original inn dates from the 16th century, comprising a central bar with comfortable seating leading to a conservatory on one side and a restaurant on the other. Outside is a small garden and a heated sun terrace. Two beer festivals are held annually, one over Father's Day weekend and the other close to Guy Fawkes Night. Curry night is Thursday and there is live music on Friday evenings. Q🕏🏵◖♿♣🅿🖰(60S)🌣🌣

Southwold

Lord Nelson 🖳 🗸

42 East Street, IP18 6EJ

🟢 10.30-11; 12-10.30 Sun ☎ (01502) 722079

🌐 thelordnelsonsouthwold.co.uk

Adnams Lighthouse, Southwold Bitter, Ghost Ship, Broadside; 2 changing beers (sourced locally; often Adnams) 🗓

Always busy and lively, the pub is popular with locals and visitors alike, with the nearby clifftop enjoying fine coastal views. It is situated next to the Sailors' Reading Room museum and close to the town centre. The interior has a flagstone floor with an open fire in winter months and is decorated throughout with naval and seafaring memorabilia. The large central bar offers a good range of Adnams beers. Children are welcome in the side room and patio garden to the rear.
🕏🏵◖▲🖰🌣🌣

Stoke Ash

White Horse

Ipswich Road, IP23 7ET

🟢 7.30am-11pm ☎ (01379) 678222

🌐 whitehorse-suffolk.co.uk

Adnams Southwold; Greene King Abbot; Morland Old Speckled Hen; Woodfordes Wherry 🗓

This former coaching inn sits at a crossroads on the A140 halfway between Ipswich and Norwich. Dating from the 1700s it has been sympathetically extended to create several seating areas. Motel-style accomodation is available. Local legend tells of a tunnel running from here to the Four Horseshoes Inn at nearby Thornham Magna. Breakfast is served 7.30am-noon Mon-Fri, 8am-noon Saturday and Sunday. Full menu 12-9.30 daily. Q🕏🏵🖰◖♿🅿🖰🌣

Stowmarket

King's Arms 🗸

Station Road, IP14 1RQ

🟢 11-11; 10.30-11 Sun ☎ 07852 497412

Woodforde's Wherry; 2 changing beers (often Adnams) 🗓

Multi-roomed hostelry, just a short walk from the historic railway station and town centre. Pub games are popular, and occasional live music and barbecues are hosted. Food includes snacks, stews, hotpots, chilli and omelettes. The patio to the rear leads to a smoking room and various other spaces used for live music and private parties. There is a children's play area and dogs are welcome when the pub is not busy. Two or three beer festivals are held each year. The cider is usually Old Rosie.
🏵◖🍴♣🖰🅿🖰🌣🌣🌣

Royal William 🖳

53 Union Street East, IP14 1HP

🟢 11-11 (midnight Fri & Sat); 12-10.30 Sun

☎ (01449) 674553

Greene King IPA; 10 changing beers 🅶

Tucked away down a narrow side street, just a short walk from the town centre and railway station. An end-of-terrace back-street bar, it is well supported by locals and visitors alike. Ales are served by gravity dispense from the cellar behind the bar, with up to 10 guest beers and five ciders. There is a games room, home to regular dominoes, darts and crib matches, and a smoking area in the enclosed garden to the rear. Sport is shown on TV. Home-made bar snacks are available. A winner of many local CAMRA awards.
🕏🏵◖♿♣🍴🖰🌣🌣

Stratford St Mary

Swan 🗸

Lower Street, CO7 6JR

🟢 closed Mon & Tue; 11-11; 11-10.30 Sun

☎ (01206) 321244 🌐 stratfordswan.com

3 changing beers 🗓

The building is part of a historic former coaching inn dating from about 1520. It has a small, friendly bar retaining many historic features, several other wood-panelled rooms mainly used for dining, and a large garden to the rear. The pub has its own house brewery – brewing started in summer 2015 – with some beers now available on draught. A wide range of bottled beers is also available and an annual beer festival is held in summer.
🕏🏵◖♣🍴🅿🌣

Sudbury

Bay Horse

61-65 Melford Road, CO10 1JS

🟢 12 (6 Mon)-midnight ☎ (01787) 377450

🌐 bayhorsesudbury.co.uk

4 changing beers 🗓

A traditional family-run local pub run as a free house by the owners since 2003. On the outskirts of the town centre, the pub has a single bar and a large beer garden backing on to the River Stour and water meadows. At the front is a comfortable covered, heated patio area. A range of pub games is available and TVs show sports events. Five letting rooms are at the rear of the building.
🕏🏵🖰◖♿♣🅿🖰

Brewery Tap 🖳

21 to 23 East Street, CO10 2TP (200yds from market place)

🟢 11-11 (midnight Fri & Sat); 12-10.30 Sun

☎ (01787) 370876 🌐 blackaddertap.co.uk

Mauldons Moletrap Bitter, Suffolk Pride, Black Adder 🗓; 5 changing beers (sourced nationally) 🗓/🅶

A mecca for real ale drinkers, the Mauldons Brewery tap is a comfortable, friendly pub in the old traditional style. Soup, rolls, filled baps, occasional chillies, stews and locally made pies are available and takeaways can be ordered in. Events include a Sunday breakfast club, quiz nights, live music and beer festivals in April and October. The pub is home to golf, darts, crib and bar billiards clubs. A must for beer and pub lovers. Q❀◑&≋♣●🛢️🚃❀

Waggon & Horses ✅
Church Walk, Acton Square, CO10 1HJ
❀ 11-11 (midnight Fri & Sat) ☎ (01787) 312147
🌐 thesudburywaggon.co.uk
Nethergate Augustinian Ale Ⓗ; **3 changing beers (sourced nationally)** Ⓗ/Ⓖ
Originally refurbished by Growler (now Nethergate) Brewery, the pub is these days run by independent owners. One regular and three changing guest beers complement the home-cooked high-quality food. The interior comprises a long main bar room with real fire, a small dining area and a snug with a glass floor looking into the cellar. Regular quiz nights are held and live music plays on the last Sunday of the month. Two beer festivals are held each year. Q🐾❀◑&≋♣🚃❀

Sweffling

White Horse ♥ 🅛
Low Road, IP17 2BB
❀ 7-11 Mon, Fri & Sat; closed Tue-Thu; 12-3, 7-11 Sun
☎ (01728) 664178 🌐 swefflingwhitehorse.co.uk
3 changing beers Ⓖ
A cosy, traditional two-room pub, warmed by a woodburner and wood-fired range. The owners have refurbished the building in an environmentally-friendly manner. Gravity dispensed beers from local brewers are served through a taproom door. Fair-trade, organic and locally produced bottled beers are also available, and cider too. Hot and cold bar snacks are sold. Pub games include bar billiards, darts, crib and board games, and live music features twice a month. Horse and trap rides are available in summer. CAMRA East Anglian Pub of the Year in 2015. Q🐾❀🚪▲♣●P❀🛜

Tattingstone

Wheatsheaf 🅛
Church Road, IP9 2LY
❀ closed Mon; 12-3, 6-11; 12-midnight Fri & Sat; 12-9 Sun
☎ (01473) 805470 🌐 wheatsheaftattingstone.com
2 changing beers (sourced locally) Ⓖ
Comfortable open-plan single bar pub, fully refurbished over the past three years by the owners. It is located on the outskirts of a small village divided by the nearby Alton Water Park reservoir. Beers are usually from local brewers. Themed food nights and Sunday roasts are popular. Live music and quiz nights feature occasionally. The pub hosts local cribbage league matches and caters for social events and weddings. There is a large garden to the side. 🐾❀◑▲♣P🚃❀🛜

Theberton

Lion
The Street, IP16 4RU
❀ 12-3, 6-11 ☎ (01728) 830185

Woodforde's Wherry; **2 changing beers (sourced locally)** Ⓗ
Large and lively Grade II-listed village bar dating from the early 19th century with various seating areas, a central fireplace, many local pictures on the walls and horse brasses on the beams. Patio seating areas to the front of the pub have been recently reinstated and a former shop has been converted into a games room. The outdoor toilets remain. Real local cider is available in bottles. Accommodation is in two en-suite log cabins. Winter opening hours vary. 🐾❀🚪◑&♣●P❀🛜

Thelnetham

White Horse 🅛
Hopton Road, IP22 1JN
❀ closed Mon; 12-3, 5-10.30; 12-10.30 Sat; 12-8 Sun
☎ (01379) 898779 🌐 whitehorsethelnetham.co.uk
Adnams Southwold Bitter; Woodforde's Wherry; 1 changing beer (often Buffy's, Shortts Farm) Ⓗ
Friendly 1800s-built pub in a remote location near the windmill, well worth seeking out. Closed for a couple of years, it reopened at the end of 2012. Dog-, family- and wellie-friendly, it is popular with walkers and cyclists, and welcomes drinkers and diners alike. It has two bar areas and a restaurant offering a monthly changing menu, featuring old favourites and some unusual dishes, using locally sourced ingredients. Wine comes from Thelnetham Vineyard and ciders from local cider makers. Live music plays on Tuesday evening. Q🐾❀◑&●P❀🛜

Thurston

Fox & Hounds
Barton Road, IP31 3QT
❀ 11.30-11 ☎ (01359) 232228
🌐 thurstonfoxandhounds.co.uk
Adnams Broadside; Greene King IPA; 4 changing beers (sourced nationally; often Cliff Quay, Green Jack, Tring) Ⓗ
A listed building, this popular local sits in the middle of the village a short walk from the railway station. The restaurant, serving good home-cooked food, is within the public bar area, separated by uplights from an original wall. There is a separate bar for pool and darts. Regular quiz nights and bingo feature, and on bank holidays and special occasions live music is hosted. A conker competition is held in the autumn. Accommodation is available in a single-bedroom apartment at the rear of the pub. 🐾❀🚪◑▲≋P🚃❀🛜

Ufford

White Lion 🅛
Lower Street, IP13 6DW (1 mile from village between church and river)
❀ closed Mon; 11-3.30, 6-11; 11-4 Sun ☎ (01394) 460770
🌐 uffordwhitelion.co.uk
Adnams Southwold Bitter; 3 changing beers (often Uffa) Ⓖ
Cosy, small, single-bar pub with a quarry-tiled floor, offering various beers including home-brewed ales on gravity stillage. Food is all locally sourced and freshly prepared on the premises. The large garden leads to the River Deben and includes a substantial marquee used for various events on summer days including car rallies, an annual beer festival (over the August bank holiday), quiz nights,

hog roasts and private events. A pizza oven and rotisserie are available for summer events.
Q🛇🏮🌗⓪P🐾

Walton

Half Moon 🅛
303 High Street, IP11 9QL
🕑 12-3 (not Mon), 5-11 ; 12-3, 5-midnight Fri; 12-11 Sat; 12-3, 7-11 Sun ☎ (01394) 285586
Adnams Lighthouse, Southwold Bitter, Broadside; 3 changing beers (often Adnams) 🅷
An excellent, traditional, two-bar local community pub with wood panelling and an open fire in the public bar in winter. A meeting place for local groups of all kinds, it has quiz nights, darts matches, cribbage and a selection of books to read. There are no gaming machines or music. The secure garden has a children's play area which has proved popular with families in the summer. Food is available lunchtimes only. Monthly folk nights are hosted as well as other live music on occasion.
🛇🏮🌗🌙♿🐾P🖪🐾📶

Wenhaston

Star Inn 🅛
Hall Road, IP19 9HF
🕑 12-3, 6-11; 12-11 Sun ☎ (01502) 478240
🌐 wenhastonstar.co.uk
Adnams Southwold Bitter; 5 changing beers (sourced locally; often Colchester, Green Jack, Wolf) 🅷
Free house situated on the outskirts of the village, with fine views of the Blyth Valley from the lawned garden. It has three small public rooms – the front bar is full of character with old enamel advertising signs and an open fire in winter. Good food is all home-cooked and sourced locally. Beer festivals are held over the late May and August bank holiday weekends. Camping is available by prior arrangement. Q🛇🏮🌗⓪🅰♿🐾P🖪(88A)🐾📶

Wickhambrook

Greyhound
Meeting Green, CB8 8XS
🕑 12-2 (not Mon & Wed), 4-11; 12-midnight Fri & Sat; 12-11 Sun ☎ (01440) 821017 🌐 greyhoundwickhambrook.co.uk
2 changing beers (sourced nationally) 🅷
The Greyhound opened its doors under its current owners in 2011 after being purchased from Greene King. It has since undergone a thorough refurbishment including the addition of a new building housing a kitchen and restaurant Twenty One. Regular events include an annual beer festival in the large garden. The pub is committed to supporting the local community and was local CAMRA branch Community Pub of the Year in 2015.
🛇🏮🌙⓪🌙♿P

Woodbridge

Angel
2 Theatre Street, IP12 4NE
🕑 2-11 (midnight Fri & Sat); 12-10.30 Sun
☎ (01394) 383808 🌐 theangelwoodbridge.co.uk
Adnams Southwold Bitter; 5 changing beers 🅷

Traditional two-bar drinking pub with beams and tiled floors, on this site since 1153 and in its current building since 1678. A regularly changing range of real ales is available alongside a selection of over 270 gins. There is seating outside, a garden with a wood-fired pizza oven and former stables at the rear. Live music features regularly, with open mic on the second and fourth Wednesday of the month, and a DJ every Saturday evening.
🛇🏮🌗≈♣P🖪🐾📶

Cherry Tree 🅛
73 Cumberland Street, IP12 4AG
🕑 7.30am-11; 9am-11 Sat & Sun ☎ (01394) 384627
🌐 thecherrytreepub.co.uk
Adnams Southwold Bitter, Ghost Ship, Broadside; Elgood's Black Dog; 5 changing beers (often Adnams) 🅷
Spacious lounge bar/diner with a large central counter and several distinct seating areas. Nine beers are usually on offer and an annual summer beer festival is hosted. Food is locally sourced and home-cooked, including some gluten-free options, with breakfast until 11am. Board games and cards are available to play and a quiz is held on Thursday. The large garden has children's play equipment. Accommodation is offered in a converted barn. Wheelchair-, child- and dog-friendly.
🛇🏮🌗⓪🌛≈♣P🐾📶

Olde Bell & Steelyard ✅
103 New Street, IP12 1DZ
🕑 12-3, 5-11.30; 11-12.30am Fri & Sat; 12-11 Sun
☎ (01394) 382933 🌐 yeoldebellandsteelyard.co.uk
Greene King IPA, Abbot; 2 changing beers (often Greene King) 🅷
Large multi-roomed pub with oak beams in two bars and a separate function room. The steelyard – a former cart weighbridge that dates from 1650 and still works – was on show at the Great Exhibition in 1851. Traditional games include bar billiards, chess and bar skittles. Live rugby is shown on TVs in the side-bar area. Good home-cooked food is served. To the rear of the building is a large heated and covered patio area and disabled access.
🛇🏮⓪🌛≈♣🖪🐾📶

Yaxley

Cherry Tree 🅛
Old Norwich Road, IP23 8BH
🕑 closed Mon; 12-2.30, 5-11 (midnight Fri & Sat); 12-3, 6-10 Sun ☎ (01379) 788050
Grain Oak, Best Bitter; Greene King IPA; 1 changing beer (often St Peter's) 🅷
Reopened in 2015, this traditional and comfortable pub is situated in a quiet village just off the A140. It has two bar areas, a separate bar/games room with darts and a pool table, and a large enclosed garden to the rear. Regular community events include quiz nights and live music by local musicians. Four handpumps usually feature ales from Grain and Greene King plus a local guest.
🛇🏮🌛♣P🖪(456)🐾

Good ale is the true and proper drink of Englishmen. He is not deserving of the name of Englishman who speaketh against ale, that is good ale. **George Borrow, Lavengro**

SURREY

(Map of Surrey showing locations including Staines-upon-Thames, Egham, Englefield Green, Walton on Thames, Shepperton, Lyne, Chertsey, Thames Ditton, Chobham, Weybridge, Hersham, Esher, Camberley, Horsell, Claygate, Woodmansterne, Knaphill, Oxshott, Epsom, Banstead, Whyteleafe, Pirbright, Woking, Leatherhead, Mugswell, Caterham, Worplesdon, Mickleham, Redhill, Oxted, Upper Hale, Weybourne, Guildford, Westcott, Dorking, Godstone, Limpsfield Chart, Farnham, Tongham, Shere, Reigate, Tilford, Bramley, Friday Street, Boundstone, Godalming, Albury Heath, Coldharbour, Lingfield, Frensham, Dockenfield, Hambledon, Newdigate, Churt, Cranleigh, Chiddingfold, Dunsfold. Bordered by BERKSHIRE, GREATER LONDON, HANTS, WEST SUSSEX)

0 Miles 5
0 Kilometres 8

Albury Heath

William IV 𝕃

Little London, GU5 9DG TQ06554673
🕐 11-3, 5.30-11; 11-11 Sat; 12-11 Sun ☎ (01483) 202685
🌐 williamivalbury.com

Surrey Hills Ranmore, Shere Drop; Young's Bitter; 1 changing beer Ⓗ

This wonderfully old-fashioned 16th-century country pub is deservedly a Guide regular. It is situated on a quiet lane adjoining extensive woodland and is popular with walkers. The pub features beams, flagstones and a magnificent fireplace where a welcoming wood fire burns in winter. There are two traditional bars – shove-ha'penny is played in the rear room. Up a couple of steps from the main bar is a dining room where excellent home-made meals are served (not Sun eve). Q❀🌙♣P❀

Banstead

Woolpack

186 High Street, SM7 2NZ
🕐 11-11; 12-10.30 Sun ☎ (01737) 354560
🌐 thewoolpackbanstead.co.uk

Shepherd Neame Master Brew, Spitfire, Bishops Finger; 2 changing beers Ⓗ

Smartly furnished brick and tile Shepherd Neame pub at the top end of the High Street, just a short walk from the town centre. The regular ales are complemented by two frequently changing guest beers. A separate restaurant serves a range of good food (no food Sun eve). Live jazz features on the first Tuesday afternoon of each month and a beer festival is held on the late-August bank holiday. ❀🌙♿P🖳❀🎵

Boundstone

Bat & Ball 𝕃

15 Bat & Ball Lane, GU10 4SA (off Sandrock Hill Rd via Upper Bourne Lane) SU833444
🕐 11-11; 12-10.30 Sun ☎ (01252) 792108
🌐 thebatandball.co.uk

Dark Star Hophead; Hogs Back TEA; 4 changing beers (sourced locally; often Bowman) Ⓗ

Popular family-owned free house offering six interesting beers, mainly from adjoining counties, alongside excellent reasonably priced food. A family-friendly front room complements the beamed, panelled and log-fired bar – a cosy inner sanctum for adults. The garden, with a children's playground, hosts an annual charity beer festival. Quiz night is every Tuesday and the last Thursday of the month is open mic night.
Q🚲❀🌙♿P🖳(16,17)❀🎵

Bramley

Jolly Farmer 𝕃

High Street, GU5 0HB
🕐 11-11; 12-11 Sun ☎ (01483) 893355 🌐 jollyfarmer.co.uk

Greene King IPA; 7 changing beers (often Crafty Brewing, Hammerpot, Long Man) Ⓗ

Privately owned traditional free house in the village centre. The decor is full of character and oak beams add to a cosy, welcoming atmosphere. Good-quality food is served (booking is essential for the Sunday lunchtime carvery). The changing beers are from a rota of small breweries, several from Hampshire and Sussex, and usually include a dark beer in winter. Real cider is added during the summer months. Dogs are welcome in the bar. Easily accessible by bus at all times.
🚲❀🍴🌙♣🍺P🖳❀🎵

Camberley

Claude du Vall L ✓

77-81 High Street, GU15 3RB

☼ 8am-midnight (1am Fri & Sat) ☎ (01276) 672910

Fuller's London Pride; Greene King Abbot; Ruddles Best Bitter; Sharp's Doom Bar; 5 changing beers (often Dark Star, Surrey Hills, Windsor & Eton) ⊞

Located on the High Street close to the shopping area, station and bus stops, this large Wetherspoon pub attracts a variety of customers throughout the day. The long bar offers five guest ales at one end and four regular ales and a real cider at the other end. The seating area is imaginatively divided into various large and small areas, some with lounge furniture. ⬚❀◑♿♺♣♿⬚🞄

Caterham

King & Queen L

34 High Street, CR3 5UA (on B2030)

☼ 11-11 (midnight Fri & Sat); 12-11 Sun ☎ (01883) 345438

⊕ kingandqueencaterham.co.uk

Fuller's London Pride, ESB; Gale's Seafarers Ale; 1 changing beer ⊞

A friendly welcome awaits you at this popular community pub. Once three cottages, this 400-year-old building became an inn in the 1840s. It features a traditional public bar together with a beamed room with an inglenook fireplace. A side room has a dartboard and there is an outside patio at the rear. Portraits of King William and Queen Mary, after whom the pub is named, adorn the walls. ⬚❀◑♣P⬚♿🞄

Chertsey

Olde Swan

27 Windsor Street, KT16 8AY

☼ 12-11 (midnight Fri & Sat) ☎ (01932) 562129

⊕ theoldeswanhotel.co.uk

Marston's Wainwright; Sharp's Doom Bar; Tring Side Pocket for a Toad; 1 changing beer (sourced nationally; often Fuller's) ⊞

The Olde Swan had a comprehensive refurbishment when acquired by McLean Inns, without spoiling its charm. The shabby chic decor is intended to give drinkers and diners a mellow experience. Four ales are usually on offer. The food menu features stone-baked pizzas, home-made burgers and sizzling steaks – Friday is Mexican night. Chertsey is handy for the M3 junction 11 and Thorpe Park. ⬚❀🏠◑♺P⬚🞄

Thyme at the Tavern ♟ L

20 London Street, KT16 8AA (jct of London St and Heriot Rd)

☼ 12-11 (1am Fri & Sat) ☎ (01932) 429667

⊕ thymeatthetavern.co.uk

Courage Best Bitter; 5 changing beers (sourced locally; often Thames Side, Thurstons, Windsor & Eton) ⊞

Family-run, dog-friendly free house, and current local CAMRA Pub of the Year. Alongside the regular cask beers are up to five guests, mostly sourced locally. Regular beer festivals are held, usually on a LocAle or regional theme. An extensive food menu is available (no food Sun, Mon and Fri eves). Friday is live music night. There is a comfortable marquee for smokers. The pub is heavily involved in fundraising for local good causes. ⬚❀🏠◑♿♺♣⬚🞄

Chiddingfold

Winterton Arms L

Petworth Road, GU8 4UU

☼ 12-11 (11.30 Fri & Sat); 12-6 Sun ☎ (01428) 776151

⊕ thewinterton.pub

Little Beer Corporation Little Haka; 5 changing beers (sourced regionally; often Crafty Brewing, Firebird, Little Beer Corporation) ⊞

Set back from the the A283 north of Chiddingfold, the pub was once the northern gateway to the estate of Lord Winterton. It has timbered gables, bay windows and ivy-covered walls together with a large tree-filled garden. Inside the decor is modern with dark grey walls and heavy wooden tables. Up to six real ales are available, with a strong focus on local breweries. Food is available all day, except Sunday evening.

Q⬚❀◑P⬚⬚(71)🞄🞄

Chobham

White Hart L

58 High Street, GU24 8AA (on High St near Bagshot roundabout)

☼ 11-11; 9am-11 Sat; 9am-10.30 Sun ☎ (01276) 857580

Brunning & Price Original; 4 changing beers (sourced locally) ⊞

The White Hart is a lovely rambling building with interesting nooks and crannies, situated a few miles north of Woking. Five local ales are on offer in a range of strengths and styles. Brunning & Price Original is always available – the others can come from any of the many local breweries, with the distance from the pub prominently displayed. There are two restaurant areas and a less formal area for drinkers as you enter the pub.

Q⬚❀◑♿P⬚(73)🞄🞄

Churt

Crossways Inn L

Churt Road, GU10 2JS

☼ 11-3, 5-11; 11-11 Fri & Sat; 12-4, 7-10.30 Sun ☎ (01428) 714323 ⊕ weydonian.net/crossways

Arundel Sussex IPA; Courage Best Bitter; Hop Back Crop Circle ⊞; 4 changing beers ⑤

Friendly two-bar pub with a homely ambience. At the centre of village life, it is popular with local groups as well as visitors from further afield including ramblers and cyclists. Guest beers are fetched from casks in the cellar, usually including local ales and a stout or porter. Good-value food is served at lunchtimes, plus fish and chips night on a Wednesday (no food Sun). ✿❍♣♠P🚌(19)🐾

Claygate

Platform 3 🗓

Claygate Station, The Parade, KT10 0PB
✿ closed Mon-Wed; 3-9.30 (10.30 Fri); 12-8 Sun; Jan-Apr 3-8.30 Thu & Fri; closed Sat-Wed ☎ 07802 316389
🌐 brightwaterbrewery.co.uk
3 changing beers (sourced locally; often Brightwater) Ⓗ
One of the smallest pubs in the UK, but Platform 3 has established itself as a focal point for the local community. Housed in a former coal office at Claygate Station, it is the outlet for locally brewed Brightwater beers. A guest ale from another brewer is sometimes available. All seating is outside on the station forecourt under a gazebo, heated in winter. Call before travelling to visit as opening is weather-dependent. Bonus opening times are advertised on social media.
Q🕭🐕✿🐾🎸♣🚌(K3)🐾📶

Coldharbour

Plough Inn 🗓

Coldharbour Lane, RH5 6HD
✿ 11.30-11; 12-9 Sun ☎ (01306) 711793 🌐 ploughinn.com
Hogs Back TEA; Leith Hill Crooked Furrow, Smiler's Happiness, Surrey Puma; Tillingbourne Falls Gold Ⓗ
The 17th-century inn is to be found down narrow lanes amid lovely countryside close to Leith Hill, the highest point in south-east England. The pub has its own Leith Hill microbrewery and its beers complement the excellent home-made food, featuring seasonal dishes and daily specials. Understandably popular with walkers and cyclists, it also has a shop providing hot drinks and snacks alongside local produce (open 8am-6pm). Six en-suite letting rooms are available.
Q🕭✿🛏❍♿P🚌(50,433)📶

Cranleigh

Three Horseshoes

4 High Street, GU6 8AE (on B2128)
✿ 12-11 ☎ (01483) 276978
🌐 threehorseshoescranleigh.co.uk
Bowman Swift One; Sharp's Doom Bar; Triple fff Moondance Ⓗ; **2 changing beers** Ⓖ
This 17th-century pub features an inglenook fireplace with a roaring wood fire in winter. The long-gone Brufords Brewery used to stand behind the pub and some photos in the lounge bar show the building. Good home-made food is available daily (not Sun eve). The rear garden contains children's play equipment. Two constantly changing guest beers are available, often served straight from the cask. 🕭✿❍♿♣P🚌🐾📶

Dockenfield

Bluebell 🗓

Batts Corner, GU10 4EX (½ mile N of village) SU820410
✿ 12-3, 5.30-11; 12-11 Fri & Sat; 12-7 Sun
☎ (01252) 792801 🌐 bluebell-dockenfield.com
4 changing beers (sourced locally; often Frensham, Langham, Triple fff) Ⓗ
This rural pub, with a cosy fireplace and four real ales, is a perfect place to visit after a walk around Alice Holt forest. The breweries are regulars and their beers rotate. Dogs and children are welcome. Outside, there is plenty of parking and seating, and a large children's play area. No food on Sunday evening. Q🕭✿❍◑♿🛏♣P🐾📶

Dorking

Cobbett's 🗓

23 West Street, RH4 1BY (on A25 one-way system eastbound)
✿ 12 (10 Fri & Sat)-8; 12-6 Sun ☎ (01306) 879877
🌐 cobbettsrealales.com
3 changing beers Ⓖ
This excellent off-licence and micropub is a must-visit when in the area. The bar, open daily from noon (earlier Friday and Saturday opening is off-sales only), is situated in a tiny back room, complete with garden. The number of cask beers varies from three early in the week to six at weekends and usually includes hop-monsters. Draught ciders (plus perry in summer) provide more choice. Over 200 interesting bottled beers and ciders are also on sale. Q🕭✿❧✿❍🐾📶

Cricketers 🗓 ✅

81 South Street, RH4 2JU (on A25 one-way system westbound)
✿ 12-11 (midnight Thu & Sat; 12.30am Fri)
☎ (01306) 889938 🌐 cricketersdorking.co.uk
Fuller's Oliver's Island, London Pride, ESB; 2 changing beers Ⓗ
Small and well-run pub with an excellent mix of customers. The single bare-bricked L-shaped room is covered with old photographs and adverts. Rugby is popular – when England play it is standing room only. The multi-level walled Georgian garden is the scene of the pub's May bank holiday and autumn beer festivals. Basic lunches are available weekdays and tasty home-made snacks are sold Wednesday to Saturday evenings. On alternate Monday evenings a classic film is shown.
🕭✿❍◑🚌📶

Red Bar & Lounge 🗓

45 Dene Street, RH4 2DW (off A25 opp post office)
✿ 12-11 (midnight Fri & Sat); 12-10.30 Sun
☎ (01306) 882222 🌐 redbar-dorking.com
Dark Star Hophead; Surrey Hills Shere Drop; 2 changing beers Ⓗ
A welcoming modern lounge bar in a 1920s building set back from the road. It is brightly lit and features an eclectic mix of contemporary and traditional decor with a variety of pub tables, comfy sofas and benches. Food is popular and locally sourced ingredients play a big part in the menu. There is live music two or three Saturdays a month. The guest beers are from local brewers such as Tillingbourne. Outside is a patio garden.
🕭✿◑♣P🚌🐾📶

Dunsfold

Sun Inn 🗓 ✅

The Common, GU8 4LE
✿ 11-midnight (1am Fri & Sat); 12-11.30 Sun
☎ (01483) 200242 🌐 suninndunsfold.co.uk
5 changing beers (sourced locally; often Crafty Brewing, Firebird, Triple fff) Ⓗ
Grade II-listed 18th-century pub, part of which is a converted coach house about 400 years old. The interior is cosy and the older part has subdued

lighting. Exposed wooden beams and an open log fire add to the character. Darts is played. The pub offers a seasonal food menu. There is plenty of outdoor seating at the front overlooking the common. Q ☺ ♿ 🐕 ◗ ♣ ◖ P 🚌 (42) 🐾 🌐 📶

Egham

Egham United Services Club 🅛

111 Spring Rise, TW20 9PE (close to A30 Egham Hill)
☼ 12-11 (midnight Fri & Sat) ☎ (01784) 435120
🌐 eusc.co.uk
Sixpenny 6d Best Bitter; Surrey Hills Ranmore; 3 changing beers (sourced nationally; often Burning Sky, Red Cat, Thames Side) 🅗
Once again local CAMRA Club of the Year and featuring in the Guide for the 10th consecutive year. The bar offers an ever-changing range of guest ales including something dark, plus a wide choice of ciders from the cellar. Three beer festivals a year feature an eclectic list of ales, mostly from the newest micros around. Satellite TV is screened and live music hosted on most Saturday evenings. Show a copy of this Guide or CAMRA membership card for entry. ☺ ♿ & ♿ ⇌ ♣ ◖ P 🚌 📶

Englefield Green

Bailiwick 🅛

Wick Road, TW20 0HN
☼ 10-11; 9am-11 Sat & Sun ☎ (01784) 477877
Bruning & Price Original; Windsor & Eton Guardsman; 2 changing beers (sourced locally; often Thames Side, Tillingbourne) 🅗
A new entry to the Guide. After several incarnations, this is now a proper pub serving local ales, with a front bar leading through to a large dining area with an extensive food menu. A small front patio overlooks the adjacent Windsor Great Park, where the landlord organises occasional rambles, and Meet the Brewer evenings are proving popular. Dogs are welcome in the bar. Tea and coffee are always available.
Q ☺ ♿ ◗ & ◖ P 🐾 📶

Happy Man 🅛

12 Harvest Road, TW20 0QS (off A30)
☼ 12-11.30 (midnight Fri & Sat); 12-10.30 Sun
☎ (01784) 433265 🌐 thehappyman1.weebly.com/ index.html
Hop Back Summer Lightning; 3 changing beers (sourced nationally; often Crouch Vale, Purity, Reunion) 🅗
Formerly two houses, in Victorian times they were converted to a pub serving workers building Royal Holloway College. Refurbished but virtually unchanged, this is a popular haunt for both students and locals. Four handpumps dispense Hop Back Summer Lightning plus changing guest ales, both local and national. Beer festivals are held on the rear patio, where there is a heated smokers' refuge. Darts and quiz nights are hosted. Food is available all day. Local CAMRA Pub of the Year 2015. ♿ ◗ ♣ ◖ 🚌 🐾

Epsom

Cricketers ✅

1 Stamford Green Road, KT18 7SR (off B280)
☼ 10-11 (midnight Fri & Sat) ☎ (01372) 729384
🌐 thecricketersinnepsom.co.uk

4 changing beers (often Dorking, Surrey Hills, Wimbledon) 🅗
Weatherboarded pub with a brick extension in an idyllic setting next to a pond with its waterfowl and opposite the cricket green. The building is 250 years old and parts were once police stables before it became a pub in 1836. Inside it has been modernised and is comfortably furnished. There is one bar with a lounge area on several levels. Breakfast is served until midday. Lilley's cider is sold. ☺ ♿ ◗ & ◖ 🚌 (E9) 🐾 📶

Jolly Coopers 🅛 ✅

84 Wheelers Lane, KT18 7SD (off B280 via Stamford Green Rd)
☼ 12-11; 12-8 Sun ☎ (01372) 723222 🌐 jollycoopers.co.uk
Fuller's London Pride; 4 changing beers (sourced locally; often Dark Star, Surrey Hills, Triple fff) 🅗
On the edge of Epsom Common and the nearest to the wells that once made Epsom a spa town, this pub is more than 200 years old. The decor is modern, with a carpeted bar area to the left and another larger area with polished parquet flooring to the right used mainly for dining. There is a large paved garden at the rear. A varying cider is sold in summer. Q ☺ ♿ ◗ ◖ P 🚌 (E9) 🐾 📶

Rifleman 🅛

5 East Street, KT17 1BB (on A24)
☼ 12-11 (midnight Fri & Sat); 12-10.30 Sun
☎ (01372) 721244 🌐 therifleman.co.uk
Greene King London Glory; house beer (by Hardys & Hansons); 3 changing beers (sourced locally; often Hogs Back, Windsor & Eton) 🅗
Small corner pub in the shadow of a bridge carrying the railway to and from London. It is decorated in a traditional style with wood panelling and two fireplaces, but also has some modern features such as bare brickwork and high tables at the front. There is a pleasant garden to the rear, an oasis of calm close to central Epsom. The name may derive from the formation of the Surrey Volunteers to meet the threat of a French invasion. Children are welcome until 6pm. ☺ ♿ ◗ ⇌ ◖ 🚌 🐾 📶

Esher

Wheatsheaf 🏆 🅛

40 The Green, KT10 8AG
☼ 11-11 (11.30 Fri & Sat); 11-10.30 Sun ☎ (01372) 464014
🌐 wheatsheafesher.co.uk
Sharp's Doom Bar; Surrey Hills Shere Drop; 2 changing beers 🅗
Imposing inn about 200 years old opposite Esher Green. A smart community pub where diners and drinkers alike are looked after with the same friendly service. Comfortably furnished throughout in a modern style, the original oak flooring in the main part has been retained and replicated in the extended areas. The bar area has an open fire, and there is a private dining room. A bicycle rack is provided at the rear. Changing guest beers may be local. Local CAMRA joint Pub of the Year 2017. ☺ ♿ & P 🚌 🐾 📶

Farnham

Hop Blossom ✅

50 Long Garden Walk, GU9 7HX (between Waitrose and Castle St) SU838469
☼ 12-11.30 (12.30am Fri & Sat); 12-11 Sun
☎ (01252) 710770 🌐 hopblossom.co.uk

Fuller's London Pride, ESB; Gale's Seafarers Ale; 1 changing beer (often Fuller's) Ⓗ
A traditional quintessentially English pub used and loved by some colourful local characters. The staff are always friendly and helpful. Bare floorboards and hops above the bar create a pleasant ambience and in winter the real log fire is warming and welcoming. The paved conservatory area is charming. The pub can be busy during local events such as the food festival and carnival.
Q🌲🕭≠♣🖵(4)🏵🛜

Jolly Sailor 🏆 Ⓛ ✅
64 West Street, GU9 7EH
🕑 12-11 (12.30am Fri & Sat); 12-10.30 Sun
☎ (01252) 719139 🌐 jollysailorfarnham.com
Greene King Abbot; Morland Old Speckled Hen; 6 changing beers (sourced locally; often Thurstons, Tillingbourne, Triple fff) Ⓗ
Ten minutes' walk from the town centre is sufficient to escape the hurly-burly at this warm, friendly, good-value local. Traditional wooden flooring and an occasional log fire add to the pleaant ambiance. A great choice of beers – usually four from nearby microbreweries and four from the Greene King portfolio – is served by knowledgable bar staff. The thriving darts club meets on alternate Thursdays and there are weekly quizzes. A decked patio captures the evening sun, great for relaxing in the summer. Local CAMRA Pub of the Year 2017.
🌲🏵🕭🕪P🖵(65)🏵🛜

Friday Street

Stephan Langton Inn Ⓛ
RH5 6JR TQ12804559
🕑 closed Mon; 11-11; 11-7 Sun ☎ (01306) 730775
🌐 stephanlangton.pub
Tillingbourne The Source, AONB, Hop Troll; 1 changing beer Ⓗ
Named after a local man who became Archbishop of Canterbury and was involved in the writing of Magna Carta. The pub is in a beautiful position, hidden away down narrow country lanes and surrounded by National Trust land. The bar is warmed by a real fire and is popular with walkers and cyclists. Excellent food including local game and fish is served in the bar and restaurant. There is a large and attractive garden to the rear. The guest beer is usually from Tillingbourne.
Q🌲🏵🕭🕪&♣P🏵🛜

Godalming

Jack Phillips Ⓛ ✅
48-56 High Street, GU7 1DY
🕑 9am-11 (midnight Thu; 1am Fri & Sat) ☎ (01483) 521750
Greene King IPA, Abbot; Sharp's Doom Bar; 7 changing beers (often Tillingbourne, Triple fff, Westerham) Ⓗ
Wetherspoon pub, converted from a shop, with a light, airy interior styled to look like an Art Deco ocean liner passenger saloon. It is named after local hero Jack Phillips who was the radio operator on the Titanic. There is a patio area to the front, overlooking the pavement. Up to seven guest beers supplement the regulars, usually including at least one from a local brewery. Two or more real ciders are usually available. Opens at 8am for breakfast. Q🌲🏵🕭🕪&≠🍺🛜

Star Inn ✅
17 Church Street, GU7 1EL
🕑 11.30 (12 Mon)-11; 11.30-12.30am Fri & Sat; 12-11 Sun
☎ (01483) 417717
Hardys & Hansons Olde Trip Ⓗ; 9 changing beers (sourced nationally; often Greene King) Ⓗ/Ⓖ
Dating from the 1830s or earlier, the Star has a small public bar at the front and the main rooms to the side, leading to a separate lounge where dogs are welcome and a patio with a smoking area. Between the dark oak beams of the ceiling hang hundreds of pump clips. Up to 10 real ales are stocked, some from the Greene King range, with beer festivals at Easter and Halloween. The pub regularly wins local and regional CAMRA cider awards, with many ciders and perries on the bar.
🏵🕭≠♣🖂🏵🛜

Guildford

King's Head Ⓛ
27 King's Road, GU1 4JW (on A320 Stoke Rd)
🕑 11-11 (midnight Fri & Sat); 12-10.30 Sun
☎ (01483) 568957 🌐 kingsheadguildford.co.uk
Fuller's Oliver's Island, London Pride, ESB; 2 changing beers (sourced locally; often Fuller's, Surrey Hills, Tillingbourne) Ⓗ
Originally built in 1860 as two cottages that soon became a beer house, the pub is noted for its attractive hanging baskets. It is deceptively spacious inside after much enlargement and features service from both sides of a central bar. There is plenty of seating including a covered, heated courtyard used mainly by smokers and benches along the outside of the building. The circular floor hatch at the rear covers a well. There is live music on three nights, a quiz on Wednesday and sport on TV in most areas.
🌲🏵🕭&≠(London Rd)♣P🖵🏵🛜

Row Barge Ⓛ
7 Riverside, GU1 1LW
🕑 12-11 (midnight Fri & Sat) ☎ (01483) 570242
🌐 therowbargeguildford.com
Dartmoor Jail Ale; St Austell Tribute; 4 changing beers (often Ascot Ales, Hogs Back, Surrey Hills) Ⓗ
Built in 1856 and extended for the post-war Bellfields Estate, this two-bar pub with pool room is a mile and a half along the River Wey towpath from the town centre, close to the A320 Woking Road. Day and night moorings are available for customers and a cycle rack is provided. Poker night is Thursday, live music features on Friday and Saturday. Food is served until 7pm (5pm Sun).
🌲🏵🕭♣P🖵🏵🛜

Hambledon

Merry Harriers Ⓛ
Hambledon Road, GU8 4DR SU967391
🕑 5.30-10.30 Mon; 11-2.30, 5.30-10.30 (11 Fri); 11-11 Sat; 12-6 Sun ☎ (01428) 682883 🌐 merryharriers.com
Dark Star Hophead; Surrey Hills Shere Drop; 2 changing beers (sourced locally; often Firebird, Pilgrim) Ⓗ
Traditional country pub set in the Surrey Hills. The main bar has an inglenook fireplace, to the left is a small quiet side room and to the right a restaurant/function room. All food (except fish) is sourced from within a 15-mile radius. Accommodation is offered in the converted barn and there is a field for camping. Llamas can be

admired from the garden or even walked. Live music features monthly on a Saturday. Opening times are reduced in winter – check ahead.
🖕❀⛱🍽️♿ΔP♣🐾🛜

Hersham

Royal George
130 Hersham Road, KT12 5QJ (off A244)
🕐 11-11 (midnight Fri & Sat); 12-11 Sun ☎ (01932) 220910
🌐 theroyalgeorge-hersham.co.uk
Young's Bitter, Special; 1 changing beer (often Young's) Ⓗ
The pub was built in 1964 – the name refers to a 100-gun ship from the Napoleonic Wars. It has one L-shaped bar with tartan carpet and upholstered banquette seating. A real fire adds to the comfortable atmosphere. It holds a quiz night every Tuesday and offers a menu featuring excellent Thai food alongside more traditional British fare. There are paved outdoor seating areas to the front and rear for the warmer months.
Q🖕❀⛱🍽️♿♿P🚌(555)🐾🛜

Horsell

Crown Ⓛ
104 High Street, GU21 4ST
🕐 12-11 (midnight Fri); 11-midnight Sat ☎ (01483) 771719
5 changing beers (sourced nationally; often Thurstons) Ⓗ
Welcoming two-bar community local offering five real ales. One handpump is reserved for a beer either from Thurstons Brewery, which started brewing in the Crown and is now located next door, or from another local microbrewery. To the rear is a sturdy smokers' shelter and well beyond that a large garden with two pétanque pistes. The pub hosts a weekly quiz on Wednesday evening and an annual beer festival in late May.
🖕❀♣P🚌(48)🐾🛜

Knaphill

Garibaldi ✅
134 High Street, GU21 2QH
🕐 12-11 (midnight Fri & Sat); 12-10.30 Sun
☎ (01483) 473374 🌐 thegaribaldi-knaphill.co.uk
West Berkshire Mr Chubb's Lunchtime Bitter; 2 changing beers (sourced nationally) Ⓗ
Enterprising pub on the edge of Knaphill serving a mixed clientele. It has a compact interior with exposed beams and wooden floors. It features three beers, two of which are constantly changing, chosen from the Punch or SIBA lists. Real ale club on Monday night offers beers at reduced prices. There is a quiz on Sunday evening, a Tuesday curry night and a Thursday steak night. A beer festival is held in April with live music. ❀🍽️P🚌(34,91)🛜

Royal Oak Ⓛ
Anchor Hill, GU21 2JH
🕐 12-11 (midnight Fri & Sat); 12-10.30 Sun
☎ (01483) 473330 🌐 royaloakknaphill.co.uk
5 changing beers (often Exmoor, Ringwood, Wye Valley) Ⓗ
An attractive 17th-century building situated at the bottom of the hill and set back from the road. Five beers are available including one of premium strength, with local breweries including Thurstons, Andwell and Surrey Hills well represented. Seven ciders are also kept. It has one central bar with a

slightly elevated dining area and a superb garden with a barbecue and children's play equipment. An annual cider and beer festival is hosted and live bands play. The pub raises funds for a Woking hospice. 🖕❀⛱🍽️♣🐾P🚌(48,91)🐾🛜

Leatherhead

Running Horse Ⓛ ✅
38 Bridge Street, KT22 8BZ (off B2122)
🕐 11.30-11; 12-10.30 Sun ☎ (01372) 372081
🌐 running-horse.co.uk
Shepherd Neame Master Brew, Spitfire; Surrey Hills Ranmore; 1 changing beer (sourced regionally; often Shepherd Neame) Ⓗ
Overlooking the River Mole, this Grade II*-listed two-room pub, dating from 1403, features a real log fire, home-made food, an outside courtyard seating area plus a large back garden. The public bar has TV, pool table and dartboard, and the cosy lounge bar has low ceilings and exposed beams. Traditional pub games include bar skittles and shove-ha'penny, with a quiz night on Tuesday. Live jazz plays on Sunday lunchtime and live bands monthly, with a charity music event on May Day. Children are allowed until 9pm.
Q🖕❀⛱🍽️🚲♣P🚌🐾🛜

Limpsfield Chart

Carpenters Arms Ⓛ
12 Tally Road, RH8 0TG (off B269)
🕐 12-11 Mon-Wed; 11-midnight Thu-Sat; 12-10.30 Sun
☎ (01883) 722209 🌐 carpenterslimpsfield.co.uk
Westerham Finchcocks Original, British Bulldog, 1965 Special Bitter Ale; 2 changing beers Ⓗ
A Westerham Brewery tied house, located adjacent to the National Trust's Limpsfield Common attracting both walkers and horse riders. The L-shaped bar has parquet flooring and a copper-topped bar. One side caters for diners enjoying the good home-made food on offer. The other retains a dartboard and a rare snakes and ladders table. There is a quiz on the first Sunday of the month.
🖕❀🍽️♣P🚌(594)🐾🛜

Lingfield

Star Inn Ⓛ
Church Road, RH7 6AH
🕐 10-11.30 (midnight Fri); 10-1am Sat; 12-10.30 Sun
☎ (01342) 832364 🌐 thestar-lingfield.co.uk
Harvey's Sussex Best Bitter; Sharp's Doom Bar; 3 changing beers Ⓗ
Brick-built pub dating from 1938 situated on the edge of the village with a path leading to the railway station. The L-shaped bar has wood panelling but gradual refurbishment is exposing the original brickwork. Good food is served noon-9pm daily. The guest beers vary, with Long Man and Otter always popular. A selection of games is available including dominoes and giant Jenga. Accommodation comprises 12 en-suite rooms.
🖕❀⛱🍽️🚲♣P🚌🐾🛜

Lyne

Royal Marine
Lyne Lane, KT16 0AN (off B386 in village centre)
🕐 12-2.30, 5.30-11; closed Sat; 12-3 Sun ☎ (01932) 873900
🌐 royalmarinelyne.co.uk

Ruddles Best Bitter; 2 changing beers (sourced nationally; often Cotleigh, Goff's) Ⓗ
The name of this one-time beer house in a rural setting commemorates Queen Victoria's review of her troops in 1853 on nearby Chobham Common. Royal Marines memorabilia, a large collection of drinking jugs and other bric-a-brac are on display. Guest beers come mainly from microbreweries and occasional beer festivals are held. Generous portions of home-cooked food are served (no food Sun eve). Friday is bingo quiz night. Note that the pub is closed Saturdays. Q☆☺⚫❶P❀🎜🛜

Mickleham

King William IV Ⓛ
4 Byttom Hill, RH5 6EL (behind Frascati restaurant)
🕑 11-11 (11.30 Fri & Sat); 11-10.30 Sun ☎ (01372) 372590
🌐 thekingwilliamiv.com

Hogs Back TEA; Surrey Hills Shere Drop; 2 changing beers (sourced regionally; often Dorking) Ⓗ
A welcoming, quaint country pub, nestled on a hillside. The main bar is homely with a log fire and there is a smaller bar to the front. An attractive outside terrace, with some tables under cover, gives stunning views over the Mole Valley. Good home-made food is served – book ahead for lunch, especially on summer weekends. Steep steps can make access difficult. A shared car park is on the A24 southbound. Q☆☺⚫❶P🚌(465)❀🛜

Mugswell

Well House Inn Ⓛ ✅
Chipstead Lane, CR5 3SQ (off A217) TQ25845526
🕑 12-11 ☎ (01737) 830640
🌐 wellhouseinn.timewellspent.co.uk

Fuller's London Pride; Surrey Hills Shere Drop; 2 changing beers Ⓗ
Part of the local Time Well Spent group, the Well House originated as three cottages in the 1560s and became a pub in the 1950s. It is a rural gem with a secluded feel and has retained many original features. Its three small bars all have log fires and there is a conservatory to the rear. Food is served all day. Tuesday is quiz night. The garden contains St Margaret's Well which is mentioned in the Domesday Book. ☆☺⚫❶♣P❀🛜

Newdigate

Surrey Oaks Ⓛ
Parkgate Road, Parkgate, RH5 5DZ (between Newdigate and Leigh) TQ20524363
🕑 11.30-2.30, 5.30-11; 9am-11 Fri & Sat; 9am-9 Sun
☎ (01306) 631200 🌐 surreyoaks.co.uk

Surrey Hills Ranmore, Shere Drop; 3 changing beers Ⓗ
This attractive 16th-century inn is renowned for its commitment to good-quality real ale. The guest beers always include one dark ale, alongside a number of ciders and perries. The main bar features low beams, flagstones and an inglenook fireplace with a log-burning stove. Excellent food is available including home-made pizzas and daily specials. Outside is a large garden where the extremely popular late-spring and August bank holiday beer festivals are held.
☆☺⚫❶♣👍P🚌(21,50)❀

Oxshott

Victoria ✅
High Street, KT22 0JR (on A244)
🕑 11-11; 12-10 Sun ☎ (01372) 841900
🌐 victoriaoxshott.com

Sharp's Doom Bar, Atlantic; Timothy Taylor Landlord; 1 changing beer (often Surrey Hills) Ⓗ
A recently modernised pub and brasserie at the centre of the village. The interior has a mix of painted wood, bare brick and some pictures, producing a light and airy bar area with a real fire. There is a large restaurant area but an extensive bar snack menu is available too. Quiz nights and occasional live music evenings are laid on. Outdoor seating is available at the front and rear.
☆☺⚫❶♿🚆🚌❀🛜

Oxted

Crown Inn Ⓛ
53 High Street, Old Oxted, RH8 9LN (just off A25)
🕑 12-3 (not Mon), 5.30-11; 12-3, 5.30-midnight Fri & Sat; 12-10.30 Sun ☎ (01883) 717853

Fuller's London Pride; 3 changing beers (often Godstone, Oxted, Westerham) Ⓗ
Dating from the 17th century, this pub is reputedly haunted. It has two contrasting bars, each operating different hours (so check the other if one seems closed). There are a number of interesting features including Victorian wood panelling and irregularly shaped windows. A selection of board games is available and live music is hosted on occasion. Home-cooked food is served Tuesday to Sunday. The guest ales come from Godstone, Oxted and Westerham breweries. ☆☺⚫❶♣🚌(410)❀🛜

Oxted Inn Ⓛ ✅
Units 1-4 Hoskins Walk, Station Road West, RH8 9HR
🕑 8am-11 ☎ (01883) 723440
Greene King IPA, Abbot; Sharp's Doom Bar; 3 changing beers Ⓗ
Small purpose-built Wetherspoon pub opened in 1997 and right next to the station. The walls display many photographs of former pubs and other buildings of local historic interest. Oxted is on the Greenwich Meridian and the interior is decorated with more than 20 working clocks showing the time in various parts of the world. Guest beers change frequently and are often from local microbreweries. Food is served all day. Q☆☺⚫❶♿🚆🚌🛜

Pirbright

Cricketers Inn Ⓛ ✅
The Green, GU24 0JT
🕑 5-10 Mon; 12-2.30, 5-11; 12-11 Sat; 12-10.30 Sun
☎ (01483) 473198
Fuller's London Pride; 2 changing beers Ⓗ
The Cricketers is set opposite Pirbright's large village green with its duck pond and cricket pitch. Formerly an Ind Coope house, the pub still sports a large Burton Ale sign on an external wall. Inside, the area to the left of the bar has sofas and high tables for groups, while a more intimate space in front of the bar is set with small tables and has a real fire. No food Sunday evening or Monday.
☆☺⚫❶P🚌(28,91)❀🛜

Redhill

Garland ♥

5 Brighton Road, RH1 6PP (on A23 S of town)
✪ 12-11 (12.30am Fri & Sat) ☎ (01737) 764612
Harvey's Sussex XX Mild Ale, IPA, Sussex Best Bitter, Armada Ale; 2 changing beers ⊞

Harvey's only tied house in Surrey, the Garland is a classic Victorian street-corner local less than five minutes' walk from the town centre. Alongside the ales listed there are usually another two or three seasonal beers. Darts is popular here, with two boards, and there is a bar billiards table. Good-value food is served weekday lunchtimes and Friday evenings. Live music plays on some Saturday evenings and a function room is available.
광⊛◑⇥♣●P☺❄🐾🛜

Sun ⓛ ✓

17-21 London Road, RH1 1LY (on A25 in town centre)
✪ 8am-midnight (1am Fri & Sat) ☎ (01737) 766886
Adnams Ghost Ship; Greene King Abbot; Ruddles Best Bitter; Sharp's Doom Bar; 5 changing beers ⊞

A large, modern town-centre Wetherspoon pub a short walk from the railway and bus stations. It has one large room with a long bar, a raised dining area, a few sofas and a corner allocated to children (families welcome until 6pm). An extensive menu of reasonably priced food is available all day. TVs show major sporting events but with the sound turned off. There is no garden, but there is a smoking area outside at the front.
Q광⊛◑&⇥●🛜

Reigate

Bell Inn ⓛ ✓

21 Bell Street, RH2 7AD (on A217)
✪ 11-11 (midnight Thu-Sat); 12-10 Sun ☎ (01737) 244438
⊕ thebellreigate.co.uk
Greene King IPA, Abbot; 4 changing beers ⊞

A long, narrow pub with low ceilings, wooden floors and tables, and a comfortable and welcoming feel. The guest beers change frequently and are often from local microbreweries. Food is served daily lunchtimes and evenings – the menu includes over a dozen varieties of burger sourced from local butchers. There is a selection of board games available. Note the large old Ordnance Survey map on the ceiling. 광⊛◑⇥🐾🛜

Shepperton

Barley Mow ⓛ

67 Watersplash Road, TW17 0EE (off B376 in Shepperton Green)
✪ 12-11; 12-10.30 Sun ☎ (01932) 225326 ⊕ themow.co.uk
Hop Back Summer Lightning; 4 changing beers (sourced locally; often Thames Side, Twickenham, Windsor & Eton) ⊞

Friendly community local in Shepperton Green to the west of the main village centre. Five handpumps serve Hop Back Summer Lightning plus up to four usually local guest ales. Many pumpclips adorn the bar and beams. Entertainment includes jazz on Wednesday, a quiz night on Thursday, live rock or blues bands on Friday or Saturday night and a traditional charity meat raffle on Sunday afternoon. Outside is a covered, heated patio area for smokers. Local CAMRA Pub of the Year 2016.
⊛♣●P☺❄🛜

Staines-upon-Thames

Beehive

35 Edgell Road, TW18 2EP
✪ 12-11 (midnight Fri & Sat) ☎ (01784) 452663
Courage Best Bitter; 1 changing beer (often Thames Side) ⊞

Unspoilt 19th-century two-bar community local. The saloon bar is wood-panelled and the public bar has a pool table and dartboard. In keeping with the historic theme, the toilets are on an outside passage, but modern and warm. A regularly rotating guest beer is drawn mainly from regional brewers, though more recently local microbeers have featured. There is no food but pickled eggs are available. ⇥♣🚍(458,570)

Bells

124 Church Street, TW18 4ZB (off B376)
✪ 12-4, 5-11; 12-midnight Fri & Sat; 12-11 Sun
☎ (01784) 454240 ⊕ thebellspub.co.uk
Young's Bitter, Special; 2 changing beers (often Sharp's, St Austell) ⊞

Friendly, comfortable, 18th-century pub opposite historic St Mary's Church. It is close to the Thames Path and within easy walking distance of the town centre. Regular beers and seasonals from Wells and Young's are available plus two guests. The pub is noted locally for the quality of its food (no food Sun eve). The pleasant rear patio garden, with a large heated smokers' canopy, is especially popular in summer, attracting local workers and shoppers.
Q⊛◑&🚍

George ✓

2-8 High Street, TW18 4EE (on A308, opp town hall)
✪ 8am-midnight (1am Fri & Sat) ☎ (01784) 462181
Courage Best Bitter; Greene King Abbot; Ruddles Best Bitter; Sharp's Doom Bar; 6 changing beers (sourced nationally; often Adnams, Hogs Back, Thames Side) ⊞

Ever-popular, two-storey, town-centre Wetherspoon pub built in the 1990s. The spacious downstairs bar with its mixture of tables and booths is always busy but there is a quieter bar upstairs. Up to six guest ales are dispensed from one bank of handpumps, with the national brands and two real ciders from Westons on the rear bank. A varied selection of foreign bottled beers and ciders is also stocked. Value-for-money pub food is served all day. Q광⊛◑&⇥●🚍🛜

Wheatsheaf & Pigeon ⓛ ✓

Penton Road, TW18 2LL (corner of Wheatsheaf Lane and Penton Rd)
✪ 12-11 ☎ (01784) 452922
⊕ thewheatsheafandpigeon.co.uk
Fuller's London Pride; Otter Ale; Sharp's Doom Bar; 2 changing beers (sourced regionally; often Reunion, Windsor & Eton) ⊞

Welcoming and friendly community local between Staines and Laleham, a short walk signposted from the Thames Path. Staines Town FC, home to Chelsea Ladies FC, is nearby. Ales often include local micro or West Country guests. Good-value food is served every day (no food Mon and Sun eves). There is outside seating front and back plus a covered smoking area. Quiz night is Sunday. Beer festivals are held occasionally. The local bus stops in Laleham Road. 광⊛◑&♣P☺(458,570)❄🛜

Thames Ditton

Red Lion
85 High Street, KT7 0SF
🕒 11-11 (midnight Fri); 10-midnight Sat; 10-10.30 Sun
☎ (020) 8398 8662
2 changing beers (sourced locally) Ⓗ
Situated near the church, this eclectically styled pub has an island bar surrounded by quirky decor including odd bits of wooden door panels fronting the bar. There is a wooden floor, two open fireplaces and seating in a wide variety of styles. The original mottled leaded windows have mostly been retained. The restaurant is in the conservatory, where vinyl LPs are used as place mats. Food is served all day.
🏠🕌🍺🅿🚪(515)♣🛜

Tilford

Donkey
Charles Hill, GU10 2AU
🕒 12-3, 5-11; 12-11 Sat; 12-10.30 Sun ☎ (01252) 702124
🌐 donkeytilford.co.uk
3 changing beers (sourced regionally; often Hogs Back, Triple fff) Ⓗ
A cosy, friendly, food-led country pub, converted from two small cottages in 1850. The bar is small with up to three ales available depending on the season. There is a restaurant and conservatory to the rear where good food is served, and plenty of outside seating to admire the donkeys, Pip and Dusty. 🏠🕌🍺🅿🚪(46)♣🛜

Tongham

White Hart 𝕃
76 The Street, GU10 1DH
🕒 12-11 (10.30 Mon); 12-midnight Fri & Sat; 12-10.30 Sun
☎ (01252) 782419 🌐 thewhitehearttongham.co.uk
Hogs Back TEA; 5 changing beers (sourced nationally; often Surrey Hills, Triple fff) Ⓗ
At the heart of the village, the White Hart is used by a cross-section of the community. A three-roomed pub, the rear games room is the liveliest; the listed older room has old village photos on the walls. The pub serves up to seven real ales and a real cider, with one pump dedicated to a rotating dark beer. Live music plays at the weekend. The pub is conveniently sited for visitors to the Hogs Back Brewery. No food on Monday.
Q🏠🕌🍺♣🍺🅿🚪(3)♣🛜

Upper Hale

Alfred Free House
9 Bishops Road, GU9 0JA
🕒 5.30-11 (11.30 Fri & Sat); 12-11.30 Sun ☎ (01252) 820385
🌐 thealfredfreehouse.co.uk
Bowman Wallops Wood Ⓗ**; 3 changing beers (sourced nationally; often Red Cat, B&T, Triple fff)** Ⓗ/Ⓖ
This friendly local pub, tucked away in a residential area, has a bar area and a restaurant/function room. Up to three guest ales include one from B&T Brewery. Fresh home-made food, using locally sourced ingredients, is served Thursday to Saturday evenings and Sunday lunchtime. Two beer festivals are held a year in May and October, and there is live music every month. Q🏠♣🍺🅿🚪(5)♣🛜

Walton on Thames

Regent 𝕃 ✓
19 Church Street, KT12 2QP (on A3050)
🕒 8am-midnight (1am Fri & Sat) ☎ (01932) 506379
🌐 theregent-waltononthames.co.uk
Greene King Abbot; Sharp's Doom Bar; 8 changing beers (often Sambrook's, Twickenham) Ⓗ
A pleasant pub in what was the old Regent cinema. At the far end, steps lead to a small seating area for customers seeking a more secluded spot. The walls are hung with lots of photos of old Walton plus relics of local connections with the film industry. Live sport is screened. Westons cider is supplemented by guests. Alcohol is served from 9am. Local CAMRA joint Pub of the Year 2016.
🏠🕌🍺♣🍺(459,461)🛜

Weir
Riverside, KT12 2JB (off Waterside Way)
🕒 10.30-11.30; winter 11.30-11; 11-midnight Fri (11 Sat); 11.30-11 Sun ☎ (01932) 784530 🌐 weirhotel.co.uk
Greene King Abbot; Sharp's Doom Bar; 2 changing beers Ⓗ
In a superb location by the river's edge, attracting walkers, cyclists, boaters and families, with extensive outside seating including an adults-only area. The Victorian-style bar area is mainly carpeted, with comfortable upholstered benches around the walls. There are more intimate areas to the rear and along the front. The decor includes copper pans, plates, ornaments and old pictures. Roasts are a highlight on Sunday lunchtime. Poker night is Monday. Real ale and cider festivals are held over the May and August bank holidays. There are six en-suite letting rooms. 🏠🕌🛏🍺🅿♣🛜

Weybourne

Running Stream ✓
66 Weybourne Road, GU9 9HE
🕒 11-3, 4.30 (4 Thu)-11; 11-11 Fri & Sat; 11-3, 7-11 Sun
☎ (01252) 323750
Greene King IPA, Abbot; 1 changing beer (often Morland, Ruddles) Ⓗ
Friendly, quiet locals' pub with a horseshoe-shaped room surrounding a central bar. Basic tables are dotted around the outside of the room, with stools at the bar. The walls are decorated with historic pictures of the pub. Greene King beers are invariably in excellent condition. Good-value home-cooked food, including a daily special Monday to Friday, is served at lunchtimes.
🕌🍺🚪(17,18,19)

Weybridge

Old Crown
83 Thames Street, KT13 8LP (off A317)
🕒 10-11; 12-10.30 Sun ☎ (01932) 842844
🌐 theoldcrownweybridge.co.uk
Courage Best Bitter, Directors; Young's Bitter; 1 changing beer (sourced regionally) Ⓗ
A Grade II-listed pub with a weatherboarded façade that dates back to at least 1729. There are several areas to meet the needs of drinkers and diners. The two gardens are popular in summer, and mooring for small boats is provided at the waterside, which is at the confluence of the River Wey with the Thames. The changing beer varies in source and can be from a microbrewery. Food is served every lunchtime, and in the evenings Wednesday to Saturday. Q🏠🕌🍺♣🍺🅿🚪♣🛜

Whyteleafe

Radius Arms

205 Godstone Road, CR3 0EL (on A22)

✪ closed Mon; 4-9.30 Tue-Thu; 12-10.30 Fri & Sat; 12-5 Sun ☎ 07514 916172

4 changing beers Ⓖ

Friendly micropub which opened in former commercial premises in 2015. The walls are decorated with dried hops, bottles and pumpclips, and the wooden benches were recycled from the Olympic Park in London. An ever-changing selection of beers from around Britain is served from the cask, although on rare occasions handpumps are used. 13 ciders and perries are also available. Dominoes is played.
Q⇌(Whyteleafe/Upper Warlingham)♣♠🚍🐾

Woking

Herbert Wells Ⓛ ✅

51-57 Chertsey Road, GU21 5AJ

✪ 8am-midnight (1am Fri & Sat) ☎ (01483) 722818

Courage Best Bitter; Fuller's London Pride; Greene King Abbot; Hogs Back TEA; Sharp's Doom Bar; 7 changing beers (sourced nationally) Ⓗ

An ever-changing range of up to seven guest beers, plus eight ciders and perries are available in this popular town-centre Wetherspoon, which is close to both bus and railway stations. A varied clientele makes up this busy pub – shoppers and office workers by day and drinkers young and old in the evening. Note the novel nod to HG Wells dotted around the walls and ceiling.
Q🕐&⇌♠🚍🐾

Woking Railway Athletic Club

Goldsworth Road, GU21 6JT (behind offices at E end of Goldsworth Rd) TQ003585

✪ 10.30-11 (11.30 Fri & Sat); 12-10.30 Sun
☎ (01483) 598499

2 changing beers Ⓗ

Friendly and lively social club tucked away near Victoria Arch, serving between two and four beers. One side of the bar is sports-oriented, with darts, pool and Sky Sports, while the other side is quieter. Children are welcome at all times. Filled rolls are available on Saturday afternoon. For entry show a CAMRA membership card or a copy of this Guide. Local CAMRA Club of the Year 2017. 🖼☘♣🚍🐾

Woodmansterne

Woodman ✅

Woodmansterne Street, SM7 3NL (on B278)

✪ 12-11 (midnight Fri & Sat); 12-10.30 Sun
☎ (01737) 371841 ⊕ thewoodmanbanstead.co.uk

Sharp's Doom Bar; 3 changing beers Ⓗ

This attractive brick, flint and tile building has some late-Gothic flourishes on show. Food is served all day with breakfast available at the weekend. Guest beers change frequently, often including ales from local microbreweries as well as from national brewers. There are hand-pulled ciders in the summer. Cricket can be viewed from the large beer garden, and there is a sandpit for children to play in. A beer festival is held on the last weekend in May. 🖼🕐♣♠P🚍(166)🐾🛈

Worplesdon

Fox Inn Ⓛ

Fox Corner, GU3 3PP

✪ 12 (4 Mon)-11; 12-midnight Fri & Sat ☎ (01483) 234024
⊕ foxinn.org

3 changing beers (sourced nationally; often Brains, Thurstons, Tillingbourne) Ⓗ

Convivial and welcoming free house recently rescued from closure by a local resident. The two separate bars have subdued lighting and low beams, and contain an eclectic collection of artwork that makes the rooms interesting without being cluttered. To the side of the pub is a patio, and beyond that a substantial garden. Lunch is served daily except Monday, dinner Thursday to Saturday. The menu changes daily.
Q🖼🕐🍴P🚍(28,91)🐾🛈

The language of beer

Nose: the aroma. Gently swirl the beer to release the aroma. You will detect malt: grainy and biscuity, often likened to crackers or Ovaltine. When darker malts are used, the nose will have powerful hints of chocolate, coffee, nuts, vanilla, liquorice, molasses and such dried fruits as raisins and sultanas. Hops add superb aromas of resins, herbs, spices, fresh-mown grass and tart citrus fruit – lemon and orange are typical, with intense grapefruit notes from some American varieties. Sulphur may also be present when waters are 'Burtonised': i.e. gypsum and magnesium salts have been added to replicate the famous spring waters of Burton-on-Trent.

Palate: the appeal in the mouth. The tongue can detect sweetness, bitterness and saltiness as the beer passes over it. The rich flavours of malt will come to the fore but hop bitterness will also make a substantial impact. The tongue will also pick out the natural saltiness from the brewing water and fruit from darker malts, yeast and hops. Citrus notes often have a major impact on the palate.

Finish: the aftertaste, as the beer goes over the tongue and down the throat. The finish is often radically different to the nose. The aroma may be dominated by malt whereas hop flavours and bitterness can govern the finish. Darker malts will make their presence felt with roast, chocolate or coffee notes; fruit character may linger. Strong beers may end on a sweet or biscuity note but in mainstream bitters, bitterness and dryness come to the fore.

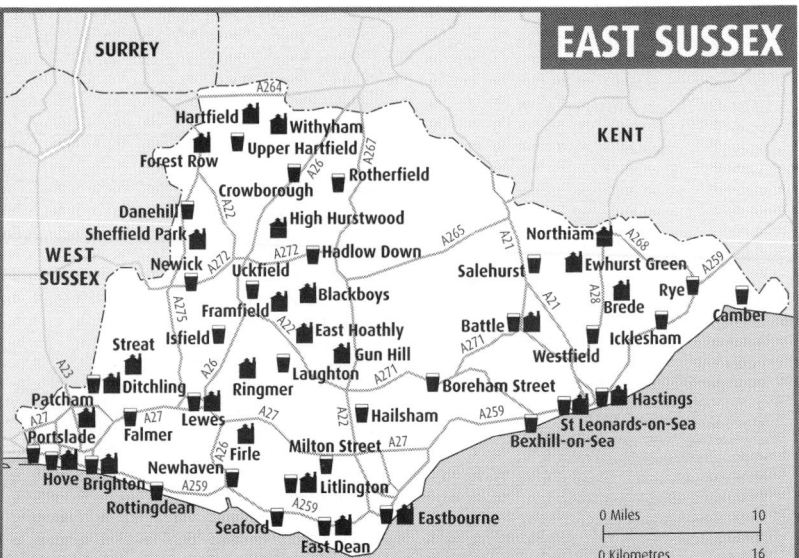

EAST SUSSEX

SUSSEX (EAST)

Battle

Squirrel 🅛
North Trade Road, TN33 9LJ
🕐 11-11; 12-10.30 Sun ☎ (01424) 772717
🌐 thesquirrelinn-battle.co.uk
Harvey's Sussex Best Bitter; 3 changing beers (sourced locally) Ⓗ
Traditional village pub, built in the 18th century, just to the west of the town. It serves home-cooked food, mostly locally sourced, and there are two bars and four handpumps, with one regular and three changing local ales. It has plenty of seating inside, a restaurant and function room and a large garden to the side of the pub, with plenty of tables and a play area for children.
🌥️🏵️🕮👌🅰️🅿️🖵(95)🎖️🛜

Bexhill on Sea

Albatross Club (RAFA) 🅛
15 Marina Arcade, TN40 1JS (on seafront 200yds E of De La Warr Pavilion)
🕐 11-2.30, 7 (5 Thu)-11; 12-2.30 Sun ☎ (01424) 212916
🌐 bexhillrafa.co.uk
4 changing beers (sourced nationally) Ⓗ
A most welcoming and friendly RAFA club, awarded National CAMRA Club of the Year in 2016 and a consistent winner of CAMRA local and regional awards. At least one local beer is always available, often from Franklins, Gun or Rother Valley; other beers are nationally sourced. Regular, popular beer festivals are held, open to the public. Additionally there are folk, jazz and quiz nights. CAMRA members are always welcome. No food Monday. Q🌥️🕮🌮🖵(98,99)🎖️🛜

Boreham Street

Bull's Head 🅛
Boreham Hill, BN27 4SG

🕐 12-11; 12-8 Sun ☎ (01323) 831981
🌐 bullsheadborehamstreet.com
Harvey's Sussex Best Bitter; house beer (by Harvey's); 2 changing beers (often Harvey's) Ⓗ
A popular pub with locals and visitors alike for a meal or just a drink. Tied to Harvey's Brewery, its regular beers include the house beer, Bull's Head Bitter, while two handpumps dispense Harvey's seasonal ales and another cider, usually Westons. It is a rustic, rural pub, dating from the 18th century, with wooden flooring and furniture and panelled walls. Outdoor seating is behind the building, next to the spacious car park. The campsite at the rear belongs to the pub and offers toilet and shower facilities. Q🌥️🏵️🕮🌮🅰️🌮🅿️🖵(98)🎖️🛜

Brighton

Admiral 🅛
2-6 Elm Grove, BN2 3DD
🕐 12-11 (midnight Thu; 1am Fri & Sat) ☎ (01273) 691028
🌐 theadmiralbrighton.com
Downlands Bramber; 4 changing beers (sourced locally; often Downlands, Gun, Hurst) Ⓗ
This pub, originally the Admiral Napier, was named after Sir John Napier, also known as Black or Dirty Charlie, who died in 1860. The 1860s building was extended and rebuilt by the Kemp Town Brewery. It remains a fine example of neo-Georgian architecture. The former three bars have long since been converted into one, but an area of comparative privacy still remains.
🏵️🕮👌🚞(London Road)🍴🖵🎖️🛜

Basketmakers Arms ✪
12 Gloucester Road, BN1 4AD
🕐 11-11 (midnight Fri & Sat); 12-11 Sun ☎ (01273) 689006
Fuller's Oliver's Island, London Pride, Bengal Lancer, ESB; Gale's Seafarers Ale, HSB; 1 changing beer (sourced nationally; often Butcombe) Ⓗ
A Guide regular for many years, the pub is a two-roomed gem in the heart of the North Laine area of the city and within half a mile of the Royal Pavilion. Popular with all ages, the Fuller's beers are complemented by locally sourced fish and meats,

with vegetarian options. Plans are in place to relocate the kitchen in order to form an additional seating area. ◐🕭♿🍴🚪🐾🛜📶

Brighton Beer Dispensary ♟
38 Dean Street, BN1 3EG
🕭 12-11 (midnight Fri & Sat) ☎ (01273) 710624
6 changing beers (sourced nationally; often Brighton Bier) Ⓗ/Ⓖ
Formerly the Prince Arthur, these terraced premises are on a steep hill off the Western Road shopping area. Reopened in 2014, the bar has six changing beers and three ciders. A blackboard shows beers available with prices. At the rear is a conservatory seating area, and at the front a decked area with seating for smokers. A varied food menu is available. Local CAMRA City Pub of the Year 2015 and Pub of the Year 2017.
🛏◐🍴♣🍴🐾🛜📶

Craft Beer Co
22-23 Upper North Street, BN1 3FG (short walk from Churchill Square shopping centre)
🕭 4-11 (1am Fri); 12-1am Sat; 12-10.30 Sun
☎ (01273) 723736
House beer (by Kent); 4 changing beers (sourced regionally; often Dark Star, Kent) Ⓗ
A simple, wood-floored pub, part of the Craft Beer Co group, selling cask ales and Lilley's cider. A large selection of national and international bottled beers is also available. There is additional seating upstairs, including a slightly secluded smaller area with space for up to 10 people. A range of burgers is served from 5.30pm during the week and from noon at weekends, plus roasts on Sunday.
🛏◐🍴♣🍴🐾🛜📶

Evening Star 🅛
55-56 Surrey Street, BN1 3PB (200yds S of station)
🕭 12-11; 11.30-midnight Fri & Sat ☎ (01273) 328931
Dark Star Hophead, American Pale Ale; 6 changing beers (sourced regionally; often Dark Star) Ⓗ
What can be said about this pub that has not already been said? It has been Brighton's real ale mecca for many years, was the birthplace of the Dark Star Brewing Co, and is conveniently placed for Brighton station. Though fairly basic, it is dearly loved by many Brightonians. Three or four Dark Star beers will always be found, together with three guests. There are continental beers on tap and a large range of bottled beers from around the world. Popular at weekends. 🐾♿🍴♣🍴🐾🛜📶

Hanover 🅛
242 Queens Park Road, Hanover, BN2 9ZB
🕭 3-11 (midnight Thu); 12-midnight Fri & Sat; 12-11 Sun
☎ (01273) 679902 🌐 hanoverbrighton.co.uk
4 changing beers (sourced locally) Ⓗ
An estate pub from circa 1927, since opened out but retaining its well-used function/meeting room. Although the venue is quite large there are discrete areas with a variety of seating and tables. Part of the Indigo chain, it serves a variety of Sussex ales plus a local cider on handpump. Food is served 12.30-10pm, a feature of the bar area being the pizza oven. Sunday roasts are available midday-9pm. It hosts a quiz night on Tuesday and occasional live music. 🛏🐾◐♣🍴(21,23)🐾📶

Mitre Tavern 🅛 ✔
13 Baker Street, BN1 4JN
🕭 10.30-midnight; 12-10.30 Sun ☎ (01273) 683173
🌐 mitretavern.co.uk

Harvey's Sussex XX Mild Ale, Sussex Best Bitter, Armada Ale; 2 changing beers (sourced locally; often Harvey's) Ⓗ
There is a 1950s feel to this cosy two-bar corner house with its full range of Harvey's beers and back-street location, just off London Road. Free Wi-Fi is available but otherwise it is light on technology, and has chintzy wallpaper. A smaller snug bar is on the right of the front entrance and there is a small smoking yard to the rear. A change of landlord in 2016 has altered it little. Westons Old Rosie cider is sold. 🐾♣🍴🐾🛜📶

Prince Albert 🅛
48 Trafalgar Street, BN1 4ED
🕭 12-midnight (12.30am Fri & Sat) ☎ (01273) 730499
5 changing beers (sourced locally) Ⓗ
A former Victorian hotel on the railway station's doorstep, this welcoming free house offers five changing, mainly local, ales plus a cider on handpump. There are several drinking areas off the main bar, with a large seating area on the pavement at the front and a smaller one to the rear. Portuguese food is served during the week, with a traditional roast on Sunday. There is live music most days. 🛏🐾◐🍴♣🍴🐾🛜📶

Victory Inn 🅛
6 Duke Street, BN1 1AH
🕭 12-midnight (2am Fri & Sat) ☎ (01273) 326555
4 changing beers (sourced locally; often Dark Star, Laine) Ⓗ
Built in 1765, this is one of the oldest pubs in the city, well situated in the city centre and in the historic Brighton Lanes. There are several rooms including a large upstairs area, plus an enclosed smoking yard and outside seating on the

REAL ALE BREWERIES

1648 🍶 East Hoathly
360° Sheffield Park
Ashdown Withyham
Bartleby's Brighton
Battle Battle (NEW)
Beachy Head East Dean
Beer Me 🍶 Eastbourne
Beercraft 🍶 Hove
Brewing Brothers 🍶 Hastings (NEW)
Brick House Patcham (brewing suspended)
Brighton Bier Brighton
Burning Sky Firle
Cellar Head Framfield (NEW)
Engineer High Hurstwood (NEW)
Ewhurst Ewhurst Green (NEW)
FILO Hastings
Franklins Ringmer
Goldstone Ditchling
Gun Gun Hill
Hand 🍶 Brighton
Harvey's Lewes
Hastings St Leonards-on-Sea (brewing suspended)
High Weald Hartfield
Holler Boys Blackboys (NEW)
Hop Yard Forest Row
Laine 🍶 Brighton
Long Man Litlington
Old Tree Brighton
Pells Lewes
Rectory Streat
Rother Valley Northiam
Three Legs Brede
Unbarred Hove

pavement. Original Tamplin's Brewery tiles and etched window panes remain. Orchard Pig cider is on handpump. Evening meals are served 5-8pm. 🕮🕮🕮🕮🕮🕮🕮🕮🕮

Camber

Owl ℒ
11 Old Lydd Road, TN31 7RE
🕮 12-midnight (2am Fri & Sat) ☎ (01797) 225284
🌐 theowlcamber.co.uk
Long Man Best Bitter; 3 changing beers (sourced locally; often Romney Marsh) Ⓗ
A traditional English pub built in the 1920s, set behind the iconic dunes of Camber Sands beach. An all-year-round, friendly establishment for locals, visitors and holidaymakers, it is traditionally furnished inside with a wraparound bar selling regular Romney Marsh and guest ales. Locally sourced home-cooked food is served at set times and letting rooms are available. During quiet times in winter only one changing beer may be available. No food Monday. 🕮🕮🕮🕮🕮🕮🕮(100)🕮🕮

Crowborough

Coopers Arms ℒ
Coopers Lane, St John's, TN6 1SN
🕮 12-2.30 (not Mon), 5-11; 12-11 Sat & Sun
☎ (01892) 654796
Long Man Best Bitter; 3 changing beers (sourced nationally) Ⓗ
A Guide regular, this friendly Victorian local is well worth seeking out. One permanent real ale and at least three changing beers, often local, are usually on tap. Bottled beers are also offered. Beer festivals are held throughout the year with all 11 handpumps put to use. Food is available Wednesday to Sunday lunchtimes. There are real fires in winter. Other features include a small function room and a secluded garden with superb views over Ashdown Forest.
Q🕮🕮🕮P🕮(29,29B)🕮🕮

Wheatsheaf ℒ ✔
Mount Pleasant, Jarvis Brook, TN6 2NF
🕮 12-11; 12-10.30 Sun ☎ (01892) 663756
🌐 wheatsheafcrowborough.co.uk
Harvey's Sussex XX Mild Ale, IPA, Sussex Best Bitter; 1 changing beer (often Harvey's) Ⓗ
A white weatherboarded building that first became a pub in 1853. Three distinct drinking areas surround a central bar, which had been a separate servery until the mid-1960s. There are real fires in the lower and middle bars, creating a cosy feel in the winter months. Two beer festivals are held a year, at Whitsun and in October. In addition to Harvey's seasonal beers, the rare Dark Mild is on offer. Evening food is available Tuesday to Thursday only. Q🕮🕮🕮🕮🕮🕮P🕮(228,229)🕮🕮

Danehill

Coach & Horses ℒ
School Lane, RH17 7JF
🕮 12-3, 5.30-11; 12-11 Sat; 12-10.30 Sun ☎ (01825) 740369
🌐 coachandhorses.co
Harvey's Sussex Best Bitter; 1 changing beer (sourced locally; often Franklins, Isfield, Long Man) Ⓗ
A traditional country pub built in 1847 and retaining many original features. The former adjoining stables have been converted to a

restaurant serving high-quality locally sourced food. There are separate public and saloon bars with real fires and simple farmhouse-style furniture. It has a large garden to the front with a children's play area and a rear patio with extensive farmland views. Q🕮🕮🕮🕮🕮P🕮(270)🕮

Ditchling

White Horse
16 West Street, BN6 8TS
🕮 11-11; 12-11 Sun ☎ (01273) 842006
🌐 whitehorseditchling.com
Dark Star Hophead; Harvey's Sussex Best Bitter; 2 changing beers (sourced regionally) Ⓗ
This 12th-century inn lies below the parish church in a picturesque and historic village. Its cellar leads to a network of tunnels under the village, thought to have been used for smuggling in times past. The accommodation at the White Horse can cater for weddings, birthday parties or as a stopover while walking the South Downs Way. Log fires in winter, excellent food and ever-changing quality guest beers are certain to fortify the traveller.
Q🕮🕮🕮🕮P🕮(167,168)🕮🕮

East Dean

Tiger Inn ℒ ✔
The Green, BN20 0DA
🕮 10-10.30 (11 Fri & Sat); 10-10 Sun ☎ (01323) 423209
🌐 beachyhead.org.uk/the_tiger_inn
Beachy Head Legless Rambler; Harvey's Sussex Best Bitter; Long Man Long Blonde; 4 changing beers (sourced locally) Ⓗ
With a history streching back several centuries, this idyllic country pub sits on the edge of East Dean village green. Ducking into the main entrance brings you to the cosy central bar area, warmed by a real log fire. There are dining rooms to the left and right, with the latter accessible by wheelchair from the side entrance. The pub is traditionally decorated, and has stone floors and beamed ceilings adding to the atmosphere. Good-quality, locally sourced food is available.
Q🕮🕮🕮🕮🕮🕮P🕮🕮🕮

Eastbourne

Crown ℒ ✔
22 Crown Street, Old Town, BN21 1PB
🕮 11-11 (midnight Fri & Sat); 12-11 Sun ☎ (01323) 724654
Dark Star Hophead; Harvey's Sussex Best Bitter; Shepherd Neame Spitfire; Wadworth 6X Ⓗ**; Young's Special** Ⓗ**/**Ⓖ**; 1 changing beer (sourced locally)** Ⓖ
Local CAMRA branch LocAle Pub of the Year 2015 and Community Pub of the Year 2016, this is a friendly, homely pub. It has two bars with log fires, and a separate pool room. The large enclosed garden has children's play equipment, and hosts regular barbecues during the summer months. Three beer festivals are held every year. Home-made bar snacks and beer discounts are offered on Sunday lunchtime. Monthly quiz nights include a complimentary hot buffet and there is occasional live music. 🕮🕮🕮🕮🕮🕮🕮

Dew Drop Inn
37-39 South Street, BN21 4UP
🕮 12-midnight (1am Fri & Sat) ☎ (01323) 723313
Greene King Abbot; Hardys & Hansons Olde Trip; 2 changing beers Ⓗ

Situated in the Little Chelsea area of Eastbourne near the town hall, this two-bar local offers a comfortable oasis a little away from the main town centre. Leather chairs and low coffee tables abound, dark-wood panels and interesting knick-knacks hang on the walls. The younger clientele gather here mainly in the evenings; there are occasional music evenings at weekends, but daytime visitors will find it much quieter. The Greene King Local Heroes scheme provides a range of guest beers. ➰🍴🍺❤✳🖳(3,3A)✿🎵📶

Eagle 🅛

57 South Street, BN21 4UT
🕐 11-11 (12.30am Fri & Sat) ☎ (01323) 417799
Harvey's Sussex Best Bitter; 4 changing beers (sourced regionally) 🅗
This well-kept corner hostelry is located in the Little Chelsea area of town, a short walk from the town centre. A variety of ales, both local and national, are on offer, also Westons Old Rosie or Orchard Pig ciders. Good-value food is served daily, lunchtimes and evenings. It has a pool table and dartboard, and TVs for sporting events. An unusual feature is the semi-arch stained-glass window behind the bar. ➰🍴🍺❤♣🍴🖳✿🎵📶

Hurst Arms 🅛

76 Willingdon Road, BN21 1TW
🕐 12-2 (not Mon), 5-11.30; 12-midnight Fri & Sat; 12-11.30 Sun ☎ (01323) 419440 ⊕ thehurstarms.pub
Harvey's Sussex Best Bitter, Armada Ale; 3 changing beers (sourced locally; often Harvey's) 🅗
There is always a warm welcome at this Victorian-built Harvey's tied house. One bar has pool, darts and a jukebox, while the saloon offers a complete contrast. Three regular Harvey's beers are stocked, often including one or two seasonals. The Sunday meat raffle and evening quiz are popular. Various events are held during the year. 🍴♿♣🖳✿🎵📶

Lamb Inn 🅛 ✅

36 High Street, Old Town, BN21 1HH
🕐 11-11 (midnight Fri & Sat) ☎ (01323) 720545
⊕ thelambeastbourne.co.uk
Harvey's Sussex Best Bitter, Armada Ale; 1 changing beer (often Harvey's) 🅗
A Harvey's tied pub that is one of the oldest houses of entertainment in the country, dating from 1240, and the cellars from 1180. Cellar tours can be arranged to view the crypt. The interior has great character and is rich in timber beams, with the unusual feature of two traditional bars and a sunken area all having access to a U-shaped bar. Good-quality food is served lunchtimes and evenings. A function room with its own bar is available for hire. Q➰🍴🍺♿♣P🖳✿📶

London & County 🅛 ✅

46 Terminus Road, BN21 3LX
🕐 8am-midnight (1am Fri & Sat) ☎ (01323) 746310
Greene King Abbot; Ruddles Best Bitter; Sharp's Doom Bar; 4 changing beers (sourced nationally) 🅗
A Wetherspoon Lloyds No.1 Bar in the town centre, close to the railway station and bus stops. The large ground-floor bar has dining areas and muted news screens; a smaller upstairs bar is also used for functions, and there is outside seating. Seven handpumps feature regular, guest and local ales, and three ciders are offered. Good-value food is served all day. Music is played each evening, with a DJ at weekends when a smart casual dress code applies. ➰🍺♿🍴🖳📶

Falmer

Swan Inn 🅛 ✅

Middle Street, BN1 9PD (just off A27 N of village)
🕐 closed Mon; 12-11; 12-10.30 Sun ☎ (01273) 681842
⊕ swanfalmer.co.uk
Palmers Best Bitter, Tally Ho!; 4 changing beers (sourced locally; often Downlands, Franklins, Long Man) 🅗
This is a traditional family-run free house in a village near the universities. It has three bar areas and a barn available for functions. Good-value food is served at lunchtimes plus Thursday and Friday evenings. It gets busy when Brighton & Hove Albion play at home. The pub opens at 11am on Saturday match days and will also open in the event of Monday evening games. A small courtyard area sits to the rear of the pub.
Q➰🍴🍺♿🍴❤♣P🖳(28,29)✿📶

Hadlow Down

New Inn ★ 🅛

Main Road, TN22 4HJ
🕐 6-11; 12-11 Sat & Sun ☎ (01825) 830939
Harvey's IPA, Sussex Best Bitter; 1 changing beer (often Harvey's) 🅗
That rare gem, a village pub that does not sell food. The building is Grade II listed, was rebuilt in 1885, and it is likely the interior has changed little since then, hence its inclusion on CAMRA's National Inventory of Historic Pub Interiors. Simple surroundings and a warm welcome mean that locals, hikers and dog walkers can be comfortable, enjoying the beer and occasional music nights, at which everyone is encouraged to sing along.
Q➰🍴♣P✿

Hailsham

George Hotel 🅛 ✅

3 George Street, BN27 1AD
🕐 8am-11 (midnight Fri & Sat) ☎ (01323) 445120
Greene King Abbot; Ruddles Best Bitter; Sharp's Doom Bar; 2 changing beers (sourced nationally) 🅗
A spacious town-centre Wetherspoon, with an enclosed beer garden to the rear and additional outside seating areas. Opposite is the Hailsham Pavilion, a classic Edwardian auditorium. The George offers a range of reasonably priced ales, with at least one LocAle, and customers are encouraged to suggest ales from the Wetherspoon seasonal guest list. At least four real ciders are stocked, served from a dedicated cool room for optimum temperature. Q➰🍴🍺♿♣🖳📶

Hastings

Crown 🅛

64-66 All Saints Street, Old Town, TN34 3BN
🕐 11-11; 11-10.30 Sun ☎ (01424) 465100
⊕ thecrownhastings.co.uk
4 changing beers (sourced locally) 🅗
A good selection of real ales and continental draught and bottled beers is sold in this traditional pub, with a board floor and wooden tables and chairs. It is popular with diners, especially at weekends and holidays. At the front is a small outdoor seating area. Please note that on Sunday the premises open at 11am but alcohol is not served until midday. ➰🍺♣🍴🖳✿📶

Dolphin ✅

11-12 Rock-A-Nore Road, Old Town, TN34 3DW
🕓 11-11 (midnight Fri & Sat) ☎ (01424) 431197
Dark Star Hophead; Harvey's Sussex Best Bitter; Young's Special; 3 changing beers (sourced nationally) Ⓗ
Atmospheric pub in the heart of the Old Town, offering a friendly welcome to locals and tourists alike. It has a wood-burning stove and is adorned with memorablia and old photographs of the fishing community. Six cask beers are served from a newly refurbished cellar including three varied guest ales. Fish and chips are served on Monday evening, live music plays on Tuesday, Friday and Saturday, real cider is summer only, and there are no Sunday lunches in January and February.
Q ⑤ ⑧ ◑ ♣ ◘ ⏰ ⚐ 🐾 🛜

First In Last Out Ⓛ

14-15 High Street, Old Town, TN34 3EY (near Stables Theatre)
🕓 12-11; 11-midnight Fri & Sat ☎ (01424) 425079
🌐 thefilo.co.uk
FILO Brewery Crofters, Churches Pale Ale, Old Town Tom, Gold; 2 changing beers Ⓗ
A popular pub, in the heart of Hastings Old Town, serving six cask beers, mainly from its own brewery located nearby and, usually, two guest beers. The large single bar is warmed by a central open fire in winter. Good food is served in the restaurant area at the back (Monday is tapas night and Thursday thali). Live music features on Tuesdays and Thursdays, and Jazz Sunday is once a month. Q ⑤ ◑ ♣ ⏰ ⚐ 🐾 🛜

White Rock Hotel Ⓛ

White Rock, TN34 1JU (opp pier)
🕓 10-11; 12-11 Sun ☎ (01424) 422240
🌐 thewhiterockhotel.com
4 changing beers Ⓗ
Adjacent to the White Rock Theatre, this friendly hotel has a spacious contemporary bar with ample seating. The adjoining terrace overlooks the seafront and the newly refurbished pier. Non-residents are welcome. Four beers are offered from various Sussex breweries, one of which is usually dark. Freshly prepared food is served until 10pm. The guest rooms are en-suite, many with fantastic sea views. The best are on the first floor, with Juliet balconies. Q ⑤ 🛏 ◑ ⇌ ♣ ◘ ⏰ 🐾 🛜

Hove

Neptune Inn Ⓛ

10 Victoria Terrace, BN3 2WB (E of King Alfred leisure complex)
🕓 12-1am (2am Fri & Sat); 12-midnight Sun
☎ (01273) 736390 🌐 theneptunelivemusicbar.co.uk
Dark Star Hophead; Greene King Abbot; Harvey's Sussex Best Bitter; 2 changing beers (sourced locally) Ⓗ
Five handpumps serve regular favourites plus changing guest ales, always in good condition. This traditional single-bar pub is frequented by a regular local clientele. Live music is strongly supported with blues and rock every Friday and jazz on Sunday, together with monthly open mic and vinyl nights on the second and fourth Mondays. This pub is on the Brighton to Shoreham coast road near central Hove. The interior features music-related pictures, posters and other memorabilia.
⚐ (700) 🐾 🛜

Sussex Cricketer ✅

Eaton Road, BN3 3AF
🕓 11-11 (midnight Fri & Sat) ☎ (01273) 771645
Harvey's Sussex Best Bitter; house beer (by Black Sheep); 6 changing beers (sourced regionally) Ⓗ
A stylish single-bar Ember Inn sitting right next to the Sussex county cricket ground at Hove, with up to eight real ales on offer including beers from Sussex and other national and regional brewers. There is try-before-you-buy on all ales. Cask club is all day Monday, with all real ales at £2.49. Quizzes are held on Tuesday and Sunday. A good selection of food includes various meal deals on different days of the week. ⑤ ⑧ ◑ ⅙ ◘ ⏰ ⚐ 🛜

Watchmaker's Arms

84 Goldstone Villas, BN3 3RU
🕓 closed Mon; 12-2, 5-9 (11 Fri); 12-11 Sat; 12-3 Sun
☎ (01273) 776307 🌐 thewatchmakersarms.co.uk
5 changing beers (sourced regionally) Ⓖ
The city's only micropub is an excellent conversion of a former shop. All the beers are dispensed by gravity from a cool room behind the bar. An on-site brewery, Beercraft, is at the rear of the premises. A good selection of local ciders is also available. As the name suggests, clocks and watches are displayed on the walls. Locally made sausage rolls are on sale. Q ⇌ ◘ ⚐ (7,21) 🐾

Westbourne

90 Portland Road, BN3 5DN
🕓 12-11 (midnight Fri & Sat) ☎ (01273) 823633
🌐 thewestbournehove.co.uk
4 changing beers (sourced locally; often Dark Star, Downlands, Franklins) Ⓗ
A large two-bar Victorian pub in a busy shopping area and popular with all ages. Four changing beers come mainly from Sussex micros and up to six ciders are available in the Cider Shack. Good-quality food includes vegan and vegetarian dishes. Several bus routes stop just outside. Family and dog friendly, it has a large covered outside drinking area and a rear patio garden. One bar is available for hire. ⑤ ⑧ ◑ ⇌ ◘ ⚐ 🐾 🛜

Icklesham

Queen's Head Ⓛ

Parsonage Lane, TN36 4BL (opp village hall)
🕓 11-11; 12-10.30 Sun ☎ (01424) 814552
🌐 queenshead.com
Greene King IPA, Abbot; Harvey's Sussex Best Bitter; 3 changing beers (sourced locally) Ⓗ
Wonderful 17th-century inn just off the A259 which has been in the Guide for more than 30 years. Three changing ales are often from local breweries and at least one real cider is available. There are open fires in each bar and outside the garden has fantastic views. Excellent, good-value home-made food is served every day. There is live music on Sunday afternoons, a quiz night on Wednesdays (ring for dates), and occasional mini beer festivals on bank holiday weekends.
⑤ ⑧ ◑ ♣ ◘ P ⏰ ⚐ (100) 🐾 🛜

Robin Hood

Main Road, TN36 4BD (on A259 at W end of village)
🕓 11-3, 6-11; 11-11 Fri & Sat; 12-10.30 Sun
☎ (01424) 814277 🌐 robinhoodicklesham.co.uk
Greene King IPA; 5 changing beers (sourced nationally) Ⓗ

This warm, friendly locals' pub has a striking ceiling display of hops, coppers and brasses built up over 20 years. There is a magnificent open fire, and a large dining area to the rear offers locally sourced, home-cooked food. Six ales and at least two ciders are served. The pub hosts pool and pétanque teams and is the home of the local Bonfire Society. The large garden has a children's play area.
Q ⏱ ❀ ⦿ ◑ ⅗ ♣ ♠ P ⏰ (100) ❀ 🛜

Isfield

Laughing Fish 🅛 ✅
Station Road, TN22 5XB (off A26 between Lewes and Uckfield)
⏱ 11.30 (10 Thu)-10; 11.30-11 Fri & Sat ☎ (01825) 750349
⊕ laughingfishonline.co.uk
Greene King IPA; Hardys & Hansons Olde Trip; Morland Old Golden Hen; 3 changing beers (sourced locally; often Burning Sky, Gun) Ⓗ
Formerly the Half Moon, then the Station Hotel, this 1860s pub is next to the preserved Lavender Line. WWII brought the custom of Canadian troops, not without incident. In the 1950s it was the HQ of the District Angling Club, the probable origin of the present name. It combines the Greene King portfolio and guest beers from other Sussex breweries. Good pub food and a range of games including bar billiards is on offer.
⏱ ❀ ◑ ⅗ Å ♣ ♠ P ⏰ (29,29B) ❀ 🛜

Laughton

Roebuck Inn 🅛 ✅
Lewes Road, BN8 6BG
⏱ 12-11 ☎ (01323) 811244
Burning Sky Plateau; Harvey's Sussex Best Bitter; 3 changing beers (sourced locally) Ⓗ
An attractive 17th-century former coaching inn in the centre of this quiet village, it is largely open plan and was once owned by Tamplins Brewery. The main bar has an attractive fireplace with a tiled surround, there is a small snug at the rear for a quiet drink, and a large refurbished function room. Home-made food is locally sourced and always includes a vegetarian option. Toad in the hole can be played here. Q ⏱ ❀ 🛏 ◑ ⅗ ♣ ♠ P ⏰ ❀ 🛜

Lewes

Black Horse ✅
55 Western Road, BN7 1RS
⏱ 11-11; 12-10.30 Sun ☎ (01273) 473653
⊕ theblackhorselewes.co.uk
Burning Sky Plateau; Greene King Abbot; Morland Old Speckled Hen; house beer (by Greene King); 3 changing beers (sourced regionally) Ⓗ
A traditional pub with large bay windows, towards the western end of town. The main bar has plenty of seating and a real fire plus pub games. There are two TVs showing most sporting events. The smaller, quieter back bar has further seating. The terrace at the rear of the pub is popular in the summer. Home-made food is served lunchtimes and evenings. Friendly poker is played every Wednesday and a quiz is held alternate Sundays.
⏱ ❀ 🛏 ◑ ⅗ ♣ ♠ ⏰ (28,29) ❀ 🛜

Brewers Arms 🅛
91 High Street, BN7 1XN (near Lewes Castle)
⏱ 10-11; 12-10.30 Sun ☎ (01273) 475524
⊕ brewersarmslewes.co.uk

Harvey's Sussex Best Bitter; 4 changing beers (sourced regionally) Ⓗ
Close to Lewes Castle, this genuine second generation family-run free house has two contrasting bars – a quiet, comfortable front bar and a back bar with a jukebox, pool table, darts and the old Sussex game of toads. It is popular on match days with Lewes FC, Brighton & Hove Albion and away fans alike. Traditional, good-value pub food is served daily until 8pm. Dogs are welcome. The exterior proclaims former owners Page and Overton, Brewers of Croydon.
Q ❀ ◑ ⅗ ⤙ ♣ ♠ ⏰ (28,29) ❀ 🛜

Elephant & Castle 🅛
White Hill, BN7 2DJ (off Fisher St, near old police station)
⏱ 11.30-11 (midnight Fri & Sat); 12-11 Sun
☎ (01273) 473797 ⊕ elephantandcastlelewes.com
Harvey's Sussex Best Bitter; 3 changing beers (sourced locally) Ⓗ
A spacious pub with three rooms around a central bar. It has several large screens for sport, making it popular with Lewes, Brighton FC and away fans alike on match days. Good-value food is served lunchtime and evening including the famous Elly burger. It has a large selection of bottled beers, which on Crafty Thursday are available to drink in at take-away prices. It is also home to a number of clubs. ❀ ◑ ⅗ ⤙ ♣ ♠ ⏰ (127,132) 🛜

Gardener's Arms 🅛
46 Cliffe High Street, BN7 2AN
⏱ 11-11; 12-10.30 Sun ☎ (01273) 474808
Harvey's Sussex Best Bitter; 5 changing beers (sourced regionally; often Harvey's) Ⓗ
A traditional, genuine free house near Harvey's Brewery. It is a one-roomed pub with a wooden floor and central bar. Five changing guest ales are dispensed, generally from small breweries across the country. Food consists of locally made pies and pasties. A real cider is always sold and an Old and Dark beer festival is held in February. No children are allowed but dogs are especially welcome, and it is popular with Lewes and Brighton FC fans on match days. ⤙ ♣ ♠ ⏰ (28,29) ❀ 🛜

John Harvey Tavern 🅛 ✅
Bear Yard, BN7 2AS (opp Harvey's Brewery)
⏱ 11-11; 12-10.30 Sun ☎ (01273) 479880
⊕ johnharveytavern.co.uk
Harvey's IPA, Sussex Wild Hop Ⓗ, Sussex Best Bitter Ⓗ/Ⓖ, Armada Ale Ⓗ; 2 changing beers (sourced locally; often Harvey's) Ⓗ/Ⓖ
Housed in a former stable block of the Bear Inn, opposite Harvey's Brewery and next to the River Ouse, the bar here boasts wooden beams, a slate floor, logburner and two large wine vats, providing cosy seating areas. There is a large function/dining room upstairs. The outside tables are a suntrap in summer and therefore very popular. There is folk on Tuesday and other live music on Sunday. Children are allowed in the restaurant only, until 9pm. Q ❀ ◑ ⅗ ⤙ ⏰ (28,29) ❀

Lewes Arms ✅
1 Mount Place, BN7 1YH
⏱ 11-11; 10-midnight Fri & Sat; 12-11 Sun
☎ (01273) 473152
Fuller's London Pride; Gale's Seafarers Ale, HSB; Harvey's Sussex Best Bitter; 2 changing beers (sourced regionally; often Fuller's) Ⓗ
An historic pub in the heart of the county town, made up of three small rooms. You will find a real

fire in winter, with a raised terrace and courtyard garden for the summer. Home-made food is served every day from noon. It is home to the world pea throwing championship, dwyle flunking matches, spaniel racing and other unusual events. A pantomime is held every March in the upstairs function room in aid of local charities. Dogs are welcome. Q✿☻❀◑➡♣⛽(28,29)❀🐾🗢

Rights of Man 🄻 ✅
179 High Street, BN7 1YE
✿ 12-11; 12-10.30 Sun ☎ (01273) 486894
⊕ rightsofmanlewes.com
Harvey's IPA, Sussex Best Bitter; 4 changing beers (sourced locally; often Harvey's) Ⓗ
A small two-bar pub near the law courts. The front bar sports dark oak-panelled walls and etched-glass screens to form booths. It has two tall tables near the front windows, wonderful for having a pint and watching the world go by. The small Martyr's Bar has pictures of each local bonfire society on the wall and more seating. Good-quality food is served, lunchtime and evening. The Astroturf-covered roof terrace is a real suntrap in the summer. ❀◑➡⛽(28,29)❀🐾🗢

Snowdrop Inn 🄻 ✅
119 South Street, BN7 2BU
✿ 12-midnight; 12-11 Sun ☎ (01273) 471018
⊕ thesnowdropinn.com
Burning Sky Plateau; Harvey's Sussex Best Bitter; 4 changing beers (sourced locally; often Burning Sky) Ⓗ
On the outer edge of the Cliffe area of this historic town, the Snowdrop is a popular and welcoming free house serving six cask ales, one cider and four other, often unusual, beers. The pub has a central bar, with additional seating upstairs and two outside drinking areas. It is family friendly and serves good home-cooked food all day. It hosts a jazz night every Monday and music most Saturdays. A beer festival is held in October. ✿❀◑➡♣⛽(28,29)❀🗢

Litlington

Plough & Harrow 🄻 ✅
The Street, BN26 5RE
✿ 11.30-11; 12-10.30 Sun ☎ (01323) 870632
⊕ ploughandharrowlitlington.co.uk
Long Man Best Bitter; 4 changing beers (sourced locally; often Long Man) Ⓗ
Quintessentially English local in a picturesque setting within the South Downs National Park. The oldest parts date from the 16th century while an inglenook fireplace features in the unusual snug. A pleasant and sizeable garden can be enjoyed during the summer months. At least four real ales from the nearby Long Man brewery, just along the road, are dispensed together with carefully chosen guests, mainly from other Sussex microbreweries. Quality food is served every day. ✿❀◑●P⛽❀🗢

Milton Street

Sussex Ox 🄻
BN26 5RL
✿ 11.30-3, 5.30-11; 11.30-11 Sat; 12-10.30 Sun
☎ (01323) 870840 ⊕ thesussexox.co.uk
Harvey's Sussex Best Bitter; 2 changing beers (sourced locally) Ⓗ

This traditionally decorated popular pub nestling above the Cuckmere Valley has stunning views over the South Downs from its large rear garden. The separate bar and spacious restaurant cater for all. Three ales are served, two of them LocAles, plus a local real cider on handpump. It was grand finalist for the Sussex Food and Drink Awards 2016 and 2017, ensuring gastronomes are suitably catered for, with many ingredients from its own farm nearby. Q✿❀◑♣●P❀🗢

Newhaven

Hope Inn ✅
West Pier, BN9 9DN
✿ 11-10.30 (midnight Wed); 11-midnight Fri & Sat
☎ (01273) 515389 ⊕ hopeinnnewhaven.co.uk
Harvey's Sussex Best Bitter; 2 changing beers (sourced regionally) Ⓗ
Spacious pub at the far end of Newhaven with a covered balcony overlooking the harbour entrance and close to Newhaven Fort. The interior has a timber-panelled beamed ceiling, timber-panelled bar walls and polished timber floors. Look out for the stained-glass panels, the multitude of nautical-themed pictures and the flag signals on the ceiling beams. Heed the sign warning you against feeding the pub dog. Quiz night is Wednesday. Home-cooked food is served every day. There is a raised patio smoking area out front. ◑♣●P🐾❀🗢

Newick

Crown Inn 🄻 ✅
22 Church Road, BN8 4JX
✿ 12-11; 12-10.30 Sun ☎ (01825) 723293
⊕ thecrownatnewick.co.uk
Harvey's Sussex Best Bitter; 2 changing beers (sourced regionally) Ⓗ
This family-run free house is at the southern end of the village near the post office. The 121 bus stops just round the corner. There is a central bar with two smaller rooms off to either side and a pleasant garden to the rear. Good-value meals are served using local produce. With two other pubs on the village green, Newick is well worth a whole afternoon's stay, but do not miss the last bus! ✿❀◑♣●P⛽(31,121)❀🗢

Portslade

Stag's Head
35 High Street, Old Portslade, BN41 2LH
✿ 12-3, 4.30-11; 12-11.30 Fri & Sat; 12-10.30 Sun
☎ (01273) 416058
Harvey's Sussex Best Bitter; Long Man American Pale Ale; 3 changing beers (sourced nationally; often Brains, Goddards) Ⓗ
This pub, originally the Bull, dates from the 16th century. It stands in the shadow of John Dudney's magnificent 1881 brewery to which it was allegedly linked by a tunnel fitted with rails to allow the rolling of barrels. The brewery was closed in 1930. The pub was enlarged in 1959, with the adjacent cottage becoming the saloon bar. The interior shows little sign of the pub's age but some evidence of Watneyisation remains. Q✿❀♣⛽(1,1A)❀🗢

Stanley Arms
47 Wolseley Road, BN41 1SS (on corner of Wolseley Rd and Stanley Rd)

✪ 3 (4 Mon & Tue)-11; 12-11 Sat; 12-10.30 Sun
☎ (01273) 430234 ⊕ thestanley.com
5 changing beers (sourced regionally; often Downlands, Long Man, Sharp's) Ⓗ
Family-run free house named after Henry Morton Stanley of 'Doctor Livingston, I presume' fame. Beer festivals are held in spring, summer and autumn, and reduced price cellar nights with free nibbles take place on the first Monday every month 7-9pm. A varied range of UK beers is served from seven handpumps, plus UK and imported bottled and real ciders on draught. It has a football team, sport is shown on TV, there are weekly quiz and crib evenings, occasional live music features and it has talks by sports personalities. There is a stained-glass tiled canopy over the bar.
Q ☺ ❀ ⧖ ♣ ● ⊟ ⊟ (2,46) ♣ ☎

Rotherfield

King's Arms Ⓛ
High Street, TN6 3LJ
✪ 12-midnight; 12-10.30 Sun ☎ (01892) 853441
Harvey's Sussex Best Bitter; 2 changing beers (sourced locally) Ⓗ
A 17th-century tile-hung building, with exposed timber beams and three large open fireplaces in separate rooms. It is a friendly local, with a good reputation for food, served in a separate restaurant area. Regular events are held, including a summer beer and music festival. There are panoramic views from the outside terrace and a large garden where the tenants keep pigs and chickens. There is ample parking. Disabled access is to the front bar and toilets only. ☺ ❀ ⧖ ♣ P ⊟ (252) ♣ ☎

Rottingdean

Queen Victoria Ⓛ ✔
54 High Street, BN2 7HF
✪ 12-11 (midnight Fri & Sat); 12-10.30 Sun
☎ (01273) 302121 ⊕ thequeenvic.co.uk
Harvey's Sussex Best Bitter; Long Man Long Blonde; 4 changing beers (sourced locally; often 360 Degree, Goldstone, Long Man) Ⓗ
A real, local, one-bar pub at the bottom of the High Street with a mock-Tudor frontage, constructed in the 1930s to replace an original pub which stood opposite, now the site of the public car park. Former licensees were local folk singers, the Copper family. Worth noting are the chandelier and the 19th-century harmonium. Food is home cooked using locally sourced ingredients. Live jazz and brunch take place every Saturday afternoon. A large range of gins is stocked. ☺ ❀ ⧖ ♣ ● ⊟ ♣ ☎

Rye

Globe Inn Marsh
10 Military Road, TN31 7NX
✪ 8am-11 ☎ (01797) 225220 ⊕ globeinnmarshrye.com
Harvey's Sussex Best Bitter; house beer (by Tonbridge); 2 changing beers (sourced locally) Ⓗ
A unique open-plan bar serving five mainly local beers and a selection of five real ciders from Duddas is the centrepiece of this creatively designed and furnished, food-oriented pub, built about 1834. Decorated with lobster pots and fishing nets, and warmed by open fires, it was recently voted third cosiest pub in Britain by readers of a national newspaper. There is a covered outdoor area. Good-quality locally sourced meals

are served, including breakfast from 8am, and pizza cooked in a wood-fired oven.
☺ ❀ ⧖ ⧖ ♣ ● ⊟ (100,344) ♣ ☎

Standard Inn Ⓛ
The Mint, TN31 7EN
✪ 12-11 (midnight Fri & Sat); 12-10 Sun ☎ (01797) 225231
⊕ thestandardinnrye.co.uk
House beer (by Old Dairy); 3 changing beers (sourced locally; often Three Legs) Ⓗ
Dating from the 15th century, this well-established inn with five en-suite bedrooms has a front bar partitioned by a rustic wooden screen and separate back room, both with exposed beams and brickwork, the former with a quarry-tiled floor, the latter with a wooden one. A rear courtyard is a suntrap in summer months. The menu includes pub standards with some interesting additions, locally sourced where possible. The house beer is by Old Dairy, and Three Legs beers feature prominently. No evening meals Sunday.
Q ☺ ❀ ⧖ ⧖ ⧖ ♣ ⊟ (100,101) ♣ ☎

Ypres Castle Inn Ⓛ ✔
Gun Gardens, TN31 7HH
✪ 12-11 (midnight Fri); 12-10.30 Sun ☎ (01797) 223248
⊕ yprescastleinn.co.uk
Harvey's Sussex Best Bitter; 4 changing beers (sourced locally) Ⓗ
An attractive weatherboarded pub built in 1640, with fantastic views across Romney Marsh; the outside drinking areas include part of the top of the town ramparts. The Wipers has one large bar with an open fire, and an adjoining room which can be used for functions. The cider is Biddenham Bushells, while the menu usually includes locally sourced seafood. Music is on Friday evenings and Sunday afternoons, and the large garden accommodates musical Wipers Weekends in August. The pub is closed winter Mondays.
☺ ❀ ⧖ ⧖ ♣ ⊟ (100,344) ♣ ☎

St Leonards on Sea

Tower ♈
251 London Road, TN37 6NB
✪ 11-11.30 (12.30am Fri & Sat); 11-11 Sun
☎ (01424) 721773
Dark Star Hophead, American Pale Ale; 4 changing beers (sourced locally) Ⓗ
A self-proclaimed proper boozer that truly lives up to its name. A friendly welcome and an excellent selection of reasonably priced ales and ciders are guaranteed, with a wood-burning stove adding to the convivial atmosphere. The main football and rugby matches are shown on HDTV screens, with the week's fixtures chalked on a board. It has been local CAMRA Pub of the Year for the last two years and Sussex Pub of the Year in 2015.
⧖ ♣ ● ⊟ ⊟ ♣ ☎

Salehurst

Salehurst Halt Ⓛ
Church Lane, TN32 5PH (by church)
✪ closed Mon; 12-11 ☎ (01580) 880620
⊕ salehursthalt.co.uk
Harvey's Sussex Best Bitter; 2 changing beers Ⓗ
A popular, dog-friendly pub in the heart of the village, with excellent views from the beautiful garden over the hop fields of the Rother Valley. You can usually find a beer from a local

microbrewery as well as good locally sourced food and, on summer Wednesday evenings, freshly baked pizza from the outside oven. In 2016 it received the Community Pub of the Year and Consistency of Excellence awards from the local CAMRA branch. Q✿♿⏰&●☀❀🖢

Seaford

Old Boot Inn
16 South Street, BN25 1PE
✪ 10-11; 10.30-9.30 Sun ☎ (01323) 895454
Harvey's Sussex Best Bitter; 3 changing beers (sourced regionally; often Dark Star, Harvey's, Thornbridge) Ⓗ
Deceptively large pub with three entrances, one in South Street and two in High Street. The South Street entrance has a large outside seating area; the one in High Street has wheelchair access. The pub is now under the same ownership as the Gardener's Arms in Lewes. Food is available; there are plenty of tables and a wide choice of roasts on a Sunday. There are five handpumps with three changing guest beers, and a real cider is stocked. 🖢✿⏰&≈●🖵❀🖢

Wellington Hotel Ⓛ ✔
33 Steyne Road, BN25 1HT
✪ 12-11 (midnight Fri & Sat); 12-10 Sun ☎ (01323) 899517
⊕ thewellington-hotel.com
Dark Star Hophead, American Pale Ale; Long Man Best Bitter; 7 changing beers (sourced nationally; often Moorhouse's, Springhead, Timothy Taylor) Ⓗ
Greene King supplies the beers but the pub boasts ten handpumps serving local and national brews, imaginative food deals and accommodation. It is on the former quayside in the old part of the town, close to the beach and town centre, handy for buses to Brighton and Eastbourne. There are three rooms: a small sports TV bar, a comfortable main bar, and a third room across the corridor. Dogs are welcome in the TV bar.
Q🖢🛏⏰≈●🖵(12,12A)❀🖢

Uckfield

Alma Arms Ⓛ ✔
65 Framfield Road, TN22 5AJ (on B2102)
✪ 11-11 (11.30 Fri & Sat); 12-10.30 Sun ☎ (01825) 762232
⊕ alma-arms.co.uk
Harvey's Sussex XX Mild Ale, Sussex Best Bitter; 2 changing beers (often Harvey's) Ⓗ
This Harvey's pub is about five minutes' walk from the town centre, station and buses. The large main bar has smaller seating areas and there are independent meeting/function rooms. A separate area houses a number of traditional games including toad in the hole. Harvey's XX Mild is served all year round and the cider is Thatcher's Heritage. There is a fair-sized garden seating area across the car park. Q✿⏰&≈♣●🖵(31)❀

Upper Hartfield

Gallipot Inn Ⓛ
Gallipot Street, TN7 4AJ
✪ 11-11 ☎ (01892) 770008 ⊕ the-gallipot-inn.co.uk
Harvey's Sussex Best Bitter; Larkins Traditional Ale; 1 changing beer (sourced locally) Ⓗ
Dating from 1597 and originally built as three almshouses, this traditional pub can be found in Winnie the Pooh country. There is a welcoming log

fire in winter and an attractive garden in summer. Local cask ales are always stocked, together with locally sourced freshly cooked food. The pub's name comes from the fact that gallipots (a type of ointment jar) were made in one part of the building, with clogs produced in another.
Q✿⏰▲♣P🖵(291)❀🖢

Westfield

New Inn Ⓛ
Main Road, TN35 4QE
✪ 12-11 (11.30 Sat); 12-8 Sun ☎ (01424) 752800
⊕ newinnwestfield.com
5 changing beers (sourced locally) Ⓗ
This village pub reopened in 2015, following a complete renovation. It serves up to six ales, normally including Harvey's, Rother Valley, Three Legs and Old Dairy, and others from regional and national breweries. It has gained a reputation for good home-cooked locally sourced food at reasonable prices (booking is advisable to avoid disappointment) and was voted More Radio Best Eatery in 2016. A warm, friendly, family-run place which is popular with locals and visitors alike.
Q🖢✿⏰&P🖵(2,342)❀🖢

SUSSEX (WEST)

Amberley

Bridge Inn Ⓛ ✔
Houghton Bridge, BN18 9LR (on B2139 just W of railway bridge at Amberley station)
✪ 11-11; 12-9 Sun ☎ (01798) 831619
⊕ bridgeinnamberley.com
Harvey's Sussex Best Bitter; Long Man Long Blonde; 1 changing beer (sourced nationally; often Timothy Taylor) Ⓗ
Close to Amberley Museum and Heritage Centre, the South Downs Way, and Amberley railway station, this Grade II-listed inn serves three real ales. Inside is a single cosy bar, open log fires and a large dining area to the side, serving mainly locally sourced home-cooked produce. There is a patio at the front and an attractive gated garden to the side. Q🖢✿⏰≈●P🖵(73)❀🖢

Billingshurst

King's Head ✔
40 High Street, RH14 9NY
✪ 11-11 (midnight Fri & Sat); 12-11 Sun ☎ (01403) 782012
Hogs Back TEA; 7 changing beers (sourced regionally) Ⓗ
A former Enterprise pub and now a free house, the King's Head is enjoying a resurgence after many years out of the Guide, boasting a wide range of real ales from the eight handpumps. It is a large town-centre pub dating from the 18th century, with plenty of space for drinkers and diners. A great pub for watching sport. 🖢✿⏰●P🖵🖢❀🖢

Bognor Regis

Hatters Ⓛ ✔
2-10 Queensway, PO21 1QT (at W end of High St opp Iceland)
✪ 8am-midnight (1am Fri & Sat) ☎ (01243) 840206
Greene King Abbot; Sharp's Doom Bar; changing beers (sourced locally; often Ballard's, Dark Star, Irving) Ⓗ

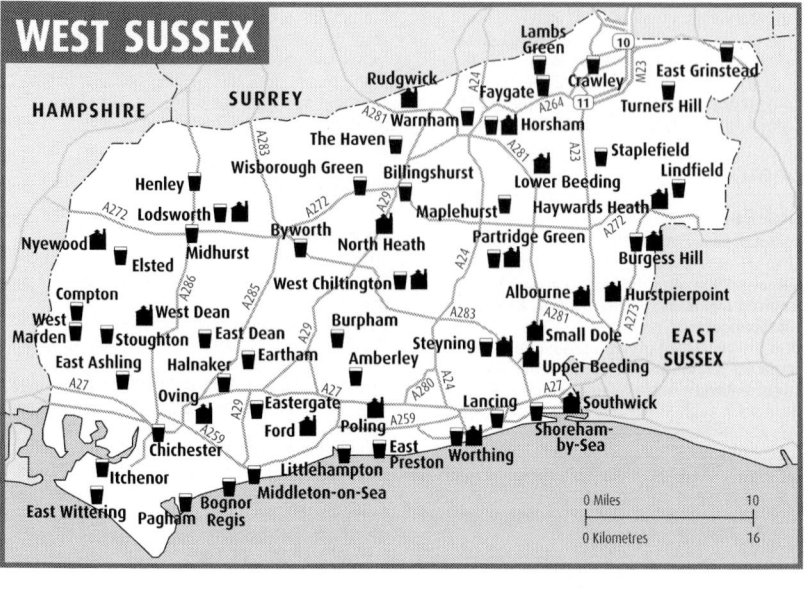

WEST SUSSEX

Large town-centre Wetherspoon pub that was once a Sainsbury's store, part of a concrete '60s retail development at one end of the main shopping street. The usual JDW beer range of regulars plus changing guests (with an emphasis on local micros) can be found, plus good-value food all day. There is a small patio garden for outside drinking and smoking. Public parking is available in Queensway car park or the adjacent multi-storey. ✿❀◗◐⛵◆⬛�

Burgess Hill

Quench Bar & Kitchen Ⓛ

2-4 Church Road, RH15 9AE

✪ 9am-11 (12.30am Fri; 1am Sat); 10-10.30 Sun
☎ (01444) 253332 ⊕ quenchbar.co.uk

Harvey's Sussex Best Bitter; 2 changing beers (sourced locally; often Downlands, Franklins, Kissingate) Ⓗ

Within sight of the railway station, this venue is at the top end of the town's original shopping street. It comprises a bar area together with a comfortable lounge. Quality local beers prevail, together with a range of bottled beers, spirits, teas and espresso coffees. Occasional live music events and beer festivals are held. A limited number of tables and chairs are provided outside. ◗⬛�

Burpham

George at Burpham Ⓛ

Main Street, BN18 9RR (turn N off A27 near Arundel station and follow country lane through Wepham to Burpham)

✪ 10.30-3, 6-11; 10.30-11 Sat; 10.30-10 Sun
☎ (01903) 883131 ⊕ georgeatburpham.co.uk

Hammerpot Red Hunter; house beer (by Arundel); 2 changing beers (sourced locally)

This attractive village inn was saved from possible closure by local residents and, following tasteful renovation, reopened in 2013. A small single bar, with four handpumps, offers local ales. The restaurant features an innovative menu. The car park behind the pub, shared with the recreation

ground, affords great views across the Arun Valley and is the starting point for a network of local walks. Walkers are welcome. The pub closes earlier in winter. Q✿❀◗◆🅿🅰◗❀

Byworth

Black Horse Inn Ⓛ

The Street, GU28 0HL (head E from Petworth on A283 for about 1 mile, then left into The Street) SU987211

✪ 12-11; 12-8 Sun ☎ (01798) 342424
⊕ theblackhorseatbyworth.com

Flowerpots Bitter; Fuller's London Pride; 2 changing beers (sourced locally) Ⓗ

Friendly unspoilt village pub dating from 1791, still with some original timbers. There is a large fire in the front bar, and several dining areas at the back. A spiral staircase leads to the function room. Flowerpots Bitter has been the main beer for a while – a rarity in Sussex. The spectacular terraced garden, with a stream at the bottom, gives splendid views over the local countryside. A previous local CAMRA Country Pub of the Year. Q✿❀◗◐◆⬛🅿◗(1)❀

Chichester

Belle Isle

32 Chapel Street, PO19 1AB (off West St, behind post office)

✪ 11-11 (midnight Fri); 10-midnight Sat; 11-10 Sun
☎ (01243) 781085 ⊕ thebelleisle.co.uk

House beer (by Franklins); 3 changing beers (sourced nationally; often Sharp's, Tiny Rebel, Titanic) Ⓗ

Spacious American-style bar, café and restaurant close to the cathedral. The atmosphere is relaxed and retro yet modern, attracting families by day and a younger crowd in the evening. Food from the bar and table service area includes international fare such as Mexican and Jamaican. The ale range includes one from Sharp's, one from a Sussex, Kent or Hants brewery, plus others from further afield micros such as First Chop, Magic Rock or Tiny Rebel. A large selection of bottled beers is available. ✿❀◗◐⛵�

Chichester Inn 🄻

38 West Street, PO19 1RP (at Westgate roundabout)
🕔 12-11.30 (midnight Fri & Sat); 12-10.30 Sun
☎ (01243) 783185 ⊕ chichesterinn.co.uk
Harvey's Sussex Best Bitter; 3 changing beers (sourced locally; often Dark Star, Downlands, Vibrant Forest) 🄷

Pleasant two-bar pub with a real fire in the front lounge surrounded by comfortable chairs, with a mix of seating and table types elsewhere. The larger public bar to the rear features regular live music on Wednesday, Friday and Saturday evenings. Outside is an attractive walled garden with a heated and covered smoking area. Food includes Sunday lunches. There is a strong emphasis on LocAles. Four B&B rooms are available. Closes 6pm Sunday January to March.
🏨🛏🕪🍴🚲🚪P🚽🐾🛜

Eastgate ✅

4 The Hornet, PO19 7JG (500yds E of Market Cross)
🕔 12 (11 Wed)-11; 10-12.30am Sat; 12-11.30 Sun
☎ (01243) 774877
Fuller's London Pride; Gale's Seafarers Ale, HSB; 2 changing beers (sourced nationally; often Adnams, Castle Rock, Fuller's) 🄷

Welcoming town pub with an open-plan bar and tables for diners. Good-quality traditional pub meals are served daily. There is a heated patio garden to the rear, which is the venue for a beer festival in July. The pub attracts locals, holidaymakers and shoppers from the nearby market, with a warm welcome and traditional pub games such as darts, cribbage and pool. Music is turned up on Friday and Saturday late evenings, while live bands perform once a month.
🏨🕪🍴🚪(51,700)🐾🛜

Rainbow 🄻

56 St Paul's Road, PO19 3BW (on B2188 150yds NW of Northgate)
🕔 11-10.30 (11 Wed & Thu; 11.30 Fri & Sat); 12-10.30 Sun
☎ (01243) 783122 ⊕ rainbowchichester.co.uk
3 changing beers (sourced locally; often Bowman, Dark Star, Downlands) 🄷

A popular Georgian suburban local with a part wood-panelled L-shaped bar and plenty of seating. The ambience is cosy in winter and airy in summer. There is a coal fire at one end and a restaurant area in a conservatory at the other. On Wednesday to Saturday the full menu of home-made bar snacks and meals is available lunchtimes and evenings after 6pm. Sunday lunches are also served. The restaurant area can be used for private functions. Quiz night is Wednesday. Q🏨🕪P🚪🐾🛜

Compton

Coach & Horses 🄻

The Square, PO18 9HA (on B2146)
🕔 closed Mon; 12-3, 6-11; 12-3, 7-10 Sun
☎ (023) 9263 1228 ⊕ coachandhorsescompton.com
Red Cat Prowler Pale; house beer (by Ballard's); 3 changing beers (sourced locally; often Ballard's, Burning Sky, Dark Star) 🄷

A 16th-century pub in a quiet, pleasant downland village, popular both with walkers and cyclists. The front bar, with internal wooden shutters and wooden floors, has a wood-burning stove at one end and an open fire at the other. The oldest part of the building is the rear, which is now the restaurant where an adventurous menu of high-

quality food is served daily. The well-loved owners, David and Christiane, have been here for over 30 years. Q🏨🕪▲🍴🚲🚪🚽(54)🐾

Crawley

Brewery Shades 🄻

85 High Street, RH10 1BA
🕔 11-11.30 (1am Fri & Sat); 11-10.30 Sun ☎ (01293) 514105
Greene King Abbot; Morland Old Speckled Hen; 8 changing beers 🄷

Arguably the oldest building in Crawley High Street, dating back to the 1400s and complete with two active ghosts. The pub is wet-sales led. The licensee has a true passion for the trade, demonstrated by the inspired range of guest ales and cider which are always in excellent condition. The haunted upstairs room is now available for meetings. Good food is served during the day and evening – check the specials board.
🏨🕪🍴🚪🛜

Eartham

George 🄻 ✅

PO18 0LT (turn N off A27 at Crockerhill or W of Fontwell and proceed 2 miles to centre of this tiny village)
🕔 closed Mon; 11.30-11; 12-6 Sun ☎ (01243) 814340
⊕ thegeorgeeartham.com
House beer (by Otter); 3 changing beers (often Downlands, Gun, Langham) 🄷

A tastefully refurbished old village pub whose landlord's passion for the best of English, and especially Sussex, extends to the entire drinks and food menu. All changing beers are LocAle and always include one from Langham. Usually one is a hoppy golden ale while another is a porter, old ale or mild. The food menu features locally sourced ingredients. Popular with walkers and cyclists, the pub holds a beer festival in its garden each April featuring LocAles and live music.
Q🏨🕪♿P🚪(99)🐾🛜

REAL ALE BREWERIES

81 Artisan West Dean (NEW)
Adur Steyning
Arundel Ford
Ballard's Nyewood
Bedlam Albourne
Dark Star Partridge Green
Downlands Small Dole
Firebird Rudgwick
Goldmark Poling
Greyhound West Chiltington
Gribble 🍴 Oving
Hammerpot Poling
Heathen Haywards Heath
Hepworth North Heath
Hurst Hurstpierpoint
Kiln Burgess Hill
Kissingate Lower Beeding
Langham Lodsworth
Lister's Ford
Pin-Up Southwick
Polarity Worthing (NEW)
Ridgeway North Heath
Riverside Upper Beeding
Top-Notch Haywards Heath
Two Tribes Horsham
Weltons Horsham

East Ashling

Horse & Groom 🅛
PO18 9AX (on B2178 in village) SU820077
☼ 12-11; 12-6 Sun ☎ (01243) 575339
🌐 thehorseandgroomchichester.co.uk
Dark Star Hophead; Hop Back Summer Lightning; Long Man Best Bitter; Young's Bitter; 1 changing beer (sourced regionally; often Wadworth) Ⓗ
Between the South Downs and the sea, and an inn for over 200 years, this fine country free house has a compact bar featuring flagstones, settles, half-panelled walls and a fine old range. Sympathetically extended, it remains unspoilt. The beers are meticulously presented and are sold at consistently good-value prices. A blackboard reveals the diverse, high-quality menu of hearty home-made dishes, all sourced locally (no food Sun eve). En-suite accommodation is dog friendly, some in a converted 17th-century oak-beamed flint barn. Q✿🏠◁①🕭👶♣P☐🚌(54)🐾🌣 ≈

East Dean

Star & Garter
PO18 0JG (overlooking pond in village centre)
☼ 12-3, 6-11; 11-11 Sat; 12-11 Sun ☎ (01243) 811318
Arundel Black Stallion, Castle; 2 changing beers (sourced regionally; often Arundel, Ballard's) Ⓖ
An 18th-century free house nestled opposite the duckpond in this charming downland village. The large bar has an area for dining and it is renowned for good food, using local seasonal produce, with fresh fish a speciality (Sunday lunchtime booking is essential). Local Arundel beer is poured straight from the cask from a cold room behind the bar. A guest beer may be available in the summer which can be enjoyed in the large walled garden to the rear. Q🏠✿🏠◁①🕭♣●🐾🌣 ≈

East Grinstead

Old Dunnings Mill
Dunnings Road, RH19 4AT
☼ 11-11 ☎ (01342) 821080 🌐 olddunningsmill.co.uk
Harvey's Sussex Best Bitter, Armada Ale; 2 changing beers (often Harvey's) Ⓗ
This large but basically quiet pub on the edge of town is based on an old water mill. Separate bar and restaurant areas are on various levels but the main parts are disabled-friendly. A heated, covered area to the rear has a working waterwheel. Two beer festivals a year are planned. Music is played on appropriate occasions. Q🏠✿①🕭P☐(84)🐾

East Preston

Clockhouse Bar 🅛 ✅
103-105 Sea Road, BN16 1NX (near sea and beach)
☼ 12-11 (midnight Fri & Sat); 12-10.30 Sun
☎ (01903) 788367 🌐 theclockhousebaranddeli.co.uk
St Austell Tribute; 2 changing beers (sourced locally; often Hammerpot) Ⓗ
This ex-bank building, built in 1929, has plenty of character, complete with its own deli next door. There are cork-style tables and a raised area with comfy seating. A working clock above the pub serves as a war memorial, and in the pub itself there are many different clocks on the walls. The emphasis is on local ales, with Hammerpot beer a regular on one of three handpumps in use. Q🏠◁🕭☐(700)🐾🌣 ≈

East Wittering

Shore 🅛
Shore Road, PO20 8DZ (50yds from sea)
☼ 11-11; 11-10.30 Sun ☎ (01243) 674454
🌐 theshorepub.co.uk
Dark Star Hophead, American Pale Ale; Palmers Copper Ale, Dorset Gold; Sharp's Doom Bar, Atlantic; 1 changing beer (sourced regionally; often Hop Back) Ⓗ
Friendly beachside pub popular with the locals (particularly dog owners) and the many summer visitors. There are two main bars, a children's area, and a fair-sized decked area for outside drinking as well as smoking. The good-quality lunchtime menu can be enjoyed either in the bar or restaurant. Evening meals are served on the last Friday of the month, when extremely inviting food is on offer at fair prices. Occasional live music features. Q🏠✿①🕭👶♣P☐🚌(52,53)🐾 ≈

Eastergate

Wilkes' Head 🅛 ✅
Church Lane, PO20 3UT (off A29 in old village, 350yds S of B2233 roundabout, 1¼ miles W of Barnham station) SU943053
☼ 12-11 ☎ (01243) 543380
Adnams Southwold Bitter; 5 changing beers (sourced nationally; often Langham, Long Man) Ⓗ
Small Grade II-listed red-brick pub, built in 1803 and named after the 18th-century radical John Wilkes. There is a cosy lounge left of the central bar, and to the right a larger room with inglenook fireplace, flagstones and low beams, plus a separate restaurant. At the rear is a permanent marquee with seating plus a heated smokers' shelter and a large garden. There are five well-chosen changing beers, and regular beer festivals are held. Q🏠✿①🕭♣●P☐🐾 ≈

Elsted

Three Horseshoes
GU29 0JY (at E end of village)
☼ 11-2.30, 6-11; 12-3, 7-10.30 Sun ☎ (01730) 825746
Bowman Wallops Wood; Flowerpots Bitter; Young's Bitter; 2 changing beers (sourced locally; often Ballard's, Langham) Ⓖ
Old and cosy rural inn divided into small rooms, including one reserved for dining and one with a blazing log fire in winter. Outside, the large, pleasant garden enjoys superb views of the South Downs. In summer there are five beers (mainly from local micros) and in winter three, all served by gravity from a stillage alongside the bar. Meals are substantial and of high quality. This is a popular and homely pub which you will be reluctant to leave. Q✿①🕭♣P🌣

Faygate

Frog & Nightgown 🅛
Wimland Road, RH12 4SS
☼ 10.30-3, 5.30-10.30 (10 Mon; 11 Fri); 12-10 Sat; 12-6 Sun ☎ (01293) 852764
Dark Star Hophead Ⓗ; Fuller's London Pride Ⓗ/Ⓖ; 2 changing beers (often Harvey's) Ⓗ
Coral and Ritchie bought the pub in 2015 and spent several months refurbishing it; it is now run by son Lewis and girlfriend Joely – and pub dog Otto. They sell three regular ales and one changing ale from a

local brewery. They also plan to hold quiz nights, open mic nights, a classic car show, live music, wine tasting, morris dancing, and more. The tearoom is the only part of the pub open weekday lunchtimes – although ales are available.
🛇🕮🅙🏃P❀

Halnaker

Anglesey Arms 🅛 ✅
Stane Street, PO18 0NQ (on A285)
🕐 11-3, 5.30-11; 11-11 Fri & Sat; 12-7 Sun
☎ (01243) 773474 🌐 angleseyarms.com
Harvey's Sussex Best Bitter; Young's Bitter; 2 changing beers (sourced locally; often Bowman, Langham) 🅗
Close to the Goodwood estate, which owns the freehold, this family-run, listed Georgian pub and dining room features a wood and flagstone-floored public bar with a log fire, plus a comfortable restaurant renowned for good food made with local produce (booking for meals essential). Two local SIBA guest beers are usually on the bar. The 2½-acre rear garden with pétanque court is popular for wedding receptions and classic car meetings, as well as regular boules matches in summer. Dogs are welcome.
Q🛇🕮🅙🏃P🚌(55,99)❀🛜

Henley

Duke of Cumberland 🅛
GU27 3HQ (off A286, 3 miles N of Midhurst) SU894258
🕐 11-11; 12-10.30 Sun ☎ (01428) 652280
🌐 dukeofcumberland.com
Harvey's Sussex Best Bitter; Langham Hip Hop, Best; 1 changing beer (sourced locally; often Langham) 🅖
Stunning 15th-century inn nestling against the hillside in over three acres of terraced gardens with extensive views. The rustic front bar has scrubbed-top tables and benches, plus log fires at both ends, while to the rear is a dining extension that blends in perfectly with the original pub and offers much-needed additional space. Outside is a smokers' shelter with its own woodburner. A former local CAMRA Pub of the Year, this is a rural gem. May close Sunday evening in winter.
Q🕮🅙🏃P🚌(70)❀

Horsham

Anchor Hotel 🅛 ✅
3 Market Square, RH12 1EU
🕐 11-11 (midnight Fri & Sat); 12-10.30 Sun
☎ (01403) 250640
Greene King IPA; Harvey's Sussex Best Bitter; 5 changing beers (often Andwells) 🅗
This Taylor Walker pub is an impressive Victorian building in the heart of town, and comprises a large ground-floor room and balcony room, plus a heated courtyard to the rear. Freshly prepared great British pub food is served daily. There is an emphasis on local ales, complemented by the occasional festival featuring beers from around the country. CAMRA members receive a 10 per cent discount on ales. The Anchor hosts a variety of entertainment including live music, comedy, DJs and quizzes. 🛇🕮🅙🅗♿🌲🅙🚌🛜

Anchor Tap ♟ 🅛
16 East Street, RH12 1HL
🕐 closed Mon; 12-10.30 (11 Fri & Sat)

Dark Star Partridge Best Bitter, American Pale Ale, Festival; 2 changing beers (sourced regionally) 🅗
Having been closed for 30 years, this pub was reopened in February 2016 by Dark Star Brewery. A much-welcome addition to the town's drinking establishments, it is popular with customers both local and from afar. Refurbished in an early-20th century style, there are six handpumps offering Dark Star beers together with other ales from across the country, and real cider. Bar snacks are served lunchtimes. 🛇♿🌲🅙🚌🛜

Beer Essentials 🅛
30a East Street, RH12 1HL
🕐 10-6 (7 Fri & Sat); closed Sun & Mon ☎ (01403) 218890
🌐 thebeeressentials.co.uk
Arundel Sussex Gold; 7 changing beers (sourced locally) 🅖
A mecca for the connoisseur, this shop opened in Horsham following the demise of King & Barnes in 2000. Up to seven cask ales are served on gravity to take away in 2, 4 and 8 pint containers, along with JB medium cider and occasionally perry. The shop also stocks over 150 bottled beers from all over. A popular beer festival is organised each September in the nearby Drill Hall. Every town should have a shop like this! 🛇♿🌲🅙🚌❀

Black Jug
31 North Street, RH12 1RJ
🕐 11.30-11; 12-10.30 Sun ☎ (01403) 253526
🌐 blackjug-horsham.co.uk
Long Man Best Bitter; 6 changing beers (sourced locally; often Brains, Marston's, Robinsons) 🅗
A large, bustling town-centre pub, the Jug is something of a Horsham institution. It has a welcoming interior with bookshelves, pictures, a fire and friendly, efficient staff. Two regular ales are available plus rotating guests and a cider, as well as an extensive range of malt whiskies and gins. The pub is popular with diners for excellent food served all day, and as a venue to meet and chat with no intrusive music. It is close to the railway station and arts complex.
Q🛇🕮🅙♿🌲🅙🚌🛜

Malt Shovel 🅛
15 Springfield Road, RH12 2PG
🕐 11-midnight (1am Fri & Sat); 12-midnight Sun
☎ (01403) 252302
Long Man Best Bitter; Robinsons Trooper; Timothy Taylor Landlord; 4 changing beers (often Pilgrim, Surrey Hills) 🅗
Located close to the town centre, the pub serves seven real ales and two ciders/perries at all times. There is live music every Saturday night, as well as regular open mic and jam events. The landlord takes great pride in his real ale and his friendly staff are equally proud. Good parking for a town-centre pub. 🕮🅙♿🌲🅙P🚌❀🛜

Piries Bar 🅛
Piries Place, RH12 1NY
🕐 11-midnight (1am Fri-Sun) ☎ (01403) 267846
🌐 piriesbar.co.uk
Dark Star Hophead; 2 changing beers (sourced locally; often Long Man) 🅗
In a building dating from the 15th century, with exposed original timber beams, the pub is tucked away down a narrow alley adjoining Horsham's Carfax. It comprises a small downstairs room, an upstairs lounge bar, and a small modern extension in character with the building. Regular charity

events are organised. Evenings here can be lively, with karaoke on Sunday, a quiz on Tuesday night and occasional live music. Two cask ales are always stocked. This bar is well worth a visit. 🛏🍴♿🚂🚌🐾☕🛜

Itchenor

Ship

The Street, PO20 7AH (on main street, 100yds from waterfront)
🕚 11-11; 11-10.30 Sun ☎ (01243) 512284
🌐 theshipinnitchenor.co.uk
Arundel Castle; Ballard's Best Bitter; Langham Hip Hop; 1 changing beer (sourced locally; often Hammerpot) Ⓗ
Popular pub in an attractive village on the shore of picturesque Chichester harbour. A cosy bar decorated with yachting memorabilia adds to the pub's character, complemented by the pleasant patio, a suntrap in summer. A separate restaurant area offers a wide range of traditional meals, including locally landed fish. Accommodation includes a self-contained three-bed cottage, together with separate B&B rooms. Buses 52 and 53 stop on the B2179 over a mile away, but the infrequent 150 stops opposite the pub.
Q🛏🏠🍴◐♣P🐾☕🛜

Lambs Green

Lamb Inn Ⓛ

RH12 4RG (2 miles N of A264)
🕚 11.30-3, 5.30-11; 11.30-11 Fri & Sat; 12-10.30 Sun
☎ (01293) 871336 🌐 thelambinn.org
Dark Star Hophead; Gale's HSB; 3 changing beers Ⓗ
Lovely old pub with a mixture of flagstones and wood floors interspersed with wrought-iron work, low-beamed ceilings and exposed brick walls. Furnishings include high-backed settles and soft sofas, and a real fire adds warmth in winter. This welcoming pub with a friendly landlord and staff is committed to LocAle – all beers come from within 25 miles and customers elect the guest beer. Home-made lunchtime and evening meals are served daily, featuring quality locally sourced ingredients. Q🛏🏠◐♿♣👜P🚆🐾☕🛜

Lancing

Stanley Ale House Ⓛ

5 Queensway, BN15 9AY (200yds N of Lancing railway station)
🕚 12 (2 Mon)-10; 12-8 Sun ☎ (01903) 366820
🌐 thestanleyalehouse.com
3 changing beers (sourced regionally; often Downlands, Langham) Ⓗ/Ⓖ
This former launderette opened as a welcoming, family-oriented ale house in 2014. Near the station and local shops, it offers up to four changing ales, plus ciders. There is ample seating, both inside and out. Bar snacks are sold, and you can bring in takeaways. There is a weekly quiz, regular music nights, and a variety of board games.
Q🛏♿🚂♣👜🚌☕🛜

Lindfield

Red Lion ✅

60 High Street, RH16 2HL
🕚 11-11 (midnight Thu-Sat); 12-11 Sun ☎ (01444) 484305
Brakspear Bitter; Harvey's Sussex Best Bitter; 4 changing beers (sourced nationally) Ⓗ

Situated in the historic High Street, the pub has a wealth of interesting features including mathematical tiles on the bay windows, an unusual raised bench facing the bar, panelled rooms and a reconstructed horse gin house in the large garden. The pub started life as a coaching inn in 1720; the original Red Lion stands next door. There is try-before-you-buy on all ales. Cask Club is all day on Monday. Most buses serving Lindfield stop nearby. Q🛏🏠◐♿♣P🚌🛜

Littlehampton

New Inn ✅

5 Norfolk Road, BN17 5PL (N from Sea Road)
🕚 12-11 (midnight Fri & Sat); 12-10.30 Sun
☎ (01903) 713112 🌐 newinnla.co.uk
3 changing beers (sourced nationally) Ⓗ
A friendly community pub offering three ales. It is just a short walk from the beach. This traditional inn has two bar areas: the front bar has ample seating, a real fire and hosts weekly pub quizzes and poker nights; the rear bar has a pool table and dartboard, as well as showing live sport. A free jukebox is a feature of Monday nights. There is a heated courtyard at the back. 🛏🏠♣🚌☕🛜

Lodsworth

Hollist Arms

The Street, GU28 9BZ (1 mile N of A272)
🕚 11-midnight; 12-11 Sun ☎ (01798) 861310
🌐 thehollistarms.com
Dark Star Hophead; Timothy Taylor Landlord; 3 changing beers (often Langham) Ⓗ
The pub is in the village centre overlooking the green, complete with a chestnut tree planted in 1897 to mark Queen Victoria's diamond jubilee. The building was formed from two cottages in 1825. A small bar leads to a larger restaurant area and a small snug with an ancient inglenook fireplace. At the rear, the raised beer garden has a barbecue area, and in front there are seats on the green. The rear car park houses the village's community shop. Home-cooked food is served all week. Q🏠◐♣☕🛜

Maplehurst

White Horse Ⓛ

Park Lane, RH13 6LL
🕚 12-2.30 (not Mon), 6-11 (11.30 Fri & Sat); 12-3, 7-11 Sun
☎ (01403) 891208 🌐 whitehorsemaplehurst.co.uk
Weltons Pride 'n' Joy; 4 changing beers Ⓗ
Under the same ownership for 35 years, this splendid and welcoming country pub has featured in the Guide 33 times. Popular with locals, cyclists and walkers, the cosy interior, with an unusually large wooden bar, boasts real fires and many interesting artefacts and bric-a-bac. While good honest pub fare is provided, the emphasis is on beer and conversation. Many local beers feature including a good selection of dark ales, and local JB cider is stocked. Q🛏🏠◐♣👜P🐾☕🛜

Middleton-On-Sea

Cabin

167-169 Elmer Road, Elmer, PO22 6JA
🕚 12-11.30 (midnight Fri & Sat) ☎ (01243) 585643
Sharp's Doom Bar; 3 changing beers (sourced nationally; often Castle Rock, Exmoor, Orkney) Ⓗ

A friendly locals' pub, a stone's throw from the beach. The large patio garden area at the front is popular in summer. Inside is a spacious single bar, and there is an area for sitting and watching the sports TV. Another is set aside for high-quality meals – with an emphasis on seafood – which are served Tuesday to Sunday. There is a pool table and dartboard. Live music nights are popular. Three changing guest beers are available.
🏠🕮⟨⟩P🖭(600)🐾📶

Midhurst

Greyhound
Cocking Causeway, Cocking, GU29 9QH (on A286 between Cocking and Midhurst)
🕐 11-11; 12-10.30 Sun ☎ (01730) 814425
🌐 thegreyhoundpub.com
4 changing beers (sourced regionally; often Greyhound, Hop Back, Long Man) Ⓗ
Traditional free house close to the South Downs. The front bar is largely unspoilt and relaxing both for drinkers and diners. To the rear is a large modern conservatory that serves as a restaurant offering locally sourced seasonal food. With extensive gardens to the front and rear, the rear garden has a large children's play area and a patio for alfresco dining. The four beers usually come from a mix of traditional regional brewers alongside more local micros from Sussex and Hampshire. Q🏠🕮⟨⟩♣🖭(60)🐾📶

Swan Ⓛ ✅
Red Lion Street, GU29 9PB (opp church in old town area)
🕐 10.30-midnight; 12-10.30 Sun ☎ (01730) 812853
🌐 theswaninn.pub
Harvey's Sussex Best Bitter; 2 changing beers (often Harvey's) Ⓗ
Now a single-bar pub as the upstairs area has been given over exclusively to dining. There is a dartboard along with a TV and quiz machines that emit no noise. During the week it may only be the Sussex Best on the bar, but the other handpumps are always operating at weekends. During the spring and summer all three handpumps will be dispensing Harvey's tasty beers. Accommodation is in six en-suite rooms. Limited public parking is available nearby. Q🏠🕮⟨⟩♣🖭(1,60)🐾📶

Pagham

Inglenook 🍷
255 Pagham Road, PO21 3QB
🕐 11-11 (midnight Fri & Sat) ☎ (01243) 262495
🌐 the-inglenook.com
Fuller's London Pride; Young's Special; 3 changing beers (sourced nationally; often Brighton Bier, Dark Star, Staggeringly Good) Ⓗ
A 16th-century Grade II-listed hotel, restaurant and free house, owned and run by the Honour family for over 40 years. There is always a selection of excellent well-hopped real ales available from highly regarded microbreweries alongside local real ciders. The cosy bar areas have real fires and there is a large garden to the rear and a patio area at the front. Local CAMRA Pub of the Year 2015-2017. 🏠🕮⟨⟩P🖭(600)🐾📶

Partridge Green

Partridge Ⓛ
Church Road, RH13 8GW (on B2135 at jct of High St & Church Rd)
🕐 12-11; 12-10.30 Sun ☎ (01403) 710391
Dark Star Hophead, Partridge Best Bitter; 4 changing beers (sourced nationally; often Dark Star) Ⓗ
This former railway hotel is a spacious village pub and the Dark Star Brewery tap, offering up to six ales. It is near the brewery and adjacent to the popular Downs Link trail that follows the track bed of the disused Shoreham-by-Sea to Guildford railway line. The large, wood-panelled lounge has a huge fireplace. There is a pleasant patio, garden and play area. The front bar has a display of local photographs, and pool and darts can be played here. Q🏠🕮⟨⟩♿♣🖭(17)🐾📶

Shoreham-by-Sea

Duke of Wellington Ⓛ
368 Brighton Road, BN43 6RE (on A259)
🕐 12-11 (12.30am Fri & Sat) ☎ (01273) 441297
🌐 dukeofwellingtonbrewhouse.co.uk/home
Burning Sky Aurora; Dark Star American Pale Ale; 5 changing beers (sourced regionally) Ⓗ
A pub of contrasts – on some nights it is a quiet drinking emporium and on others packed to the gills with a ukulele band, the Wellington Wailers, or a local group. What is consistent is the beer quality and range. Its pedigree is Dark Star and the original brewer has a small shrine of certificates together with back issues of this Guide in a display case. There are original Kemp Town Brewery windows. 🏠🕮🚲♣🖭(2,700)🐾📶

Old Star Ale & Cider House
Church Street, BN43 5DQ
🕐 12-9 ☎ 07982 842057
6 changing beers (sourced locally; often Burning Sky, Franklins) Ⓗ
This well-run micropub is just off the High Street. At least six beers are sold, mainly from Sussex microbreweries, served direct from the casks on stillage behind the bar. Up to 12 ciders may also be on sale. A cider festival is held over the autumn bank holiday. A complimentary cheese board is on offer every Saturday after 6pm.
Q🚲♣🖭(2,700)🐾📶

Staplefield

Jolly Tanners Ⓛ ✅
Handcross Road, RH17 6EF
🕐 11-3, 5.30-11; 11-11 Fri & Sat; 12-10.30 Sun
☎ (01444) 400335 🌐 jollytanners.com
Fuller's London Pride; Harvey's Sussex Best Bitter; changing beers Ⓗ
Independently run free house on the north corner of the cricket green. The pub takes great pride in providing a wide selection of real ale and cider, and tasty food made using local ingredients where possible. This is a very friendly establishment and well worth a visit. A roaring fire welcomes you in winter. Open mic evenings feature on Tuesdays and beer festivals are held regularly during the year, with an excellent range of ales to be enjoyed. Q🏠🕮⟨⟩♿🅰♣🖭(271)🐾📶

Steyning

Chequer Inn L ✓
41 High Street, BN44 3RE (in centre of village)
☼ 10-11 (midnight Fri & Sat) ☎ (01903) 814437
⊕ chequerinnsteyning.co.uk
Shepherd Neame Spitfire, Bishops Finger; 3 changing beers (sourced nationally; often Shepherd Neame, Timothy Taylor) Ⓗ
A 15th-century coaching inn with many original design features. It has several drinking areas, including a covered courtyard garden and a cosy saloon bar with an open log fire. Live sport is shown in the public bar. There is a 100-year-old three-quarter-size snooker table. Five handpumps offer ales from national brewers. Home-cooked food using locally sourced ingredients is served, with the breakfast recommended. Live music takes place, usually Thursday or Saturday. Handy for those walking the South Downs Way or Downs Link. Q ⌂ 🕏 🏠 ⑩ ♣ ● ☀ 📶

Stoughton

Hare & Hounds L
PO18 9JQ (off B2146, through Walderton) SU803115
☼ 11-11; 12-10.30 Sun ☎ (023) 9263 1433
⊕ hareandhoundspub.co.uk
Dark Star Hophead; Flack Manor Double Drop; Harvey's Sussex Best Bitter; Otter Amber; 1 changing beer (sourced locally) Ⓗ
Traditional country pub in a beautiful setting that makes it an ideal base for walking. The large dining room serves fresh local produce in comfortable surroundings, with an open fire in winter. A separate public bar has pictures of vintage racing cars and its own open fire, which attracts locals. The fires, stone-flagged floors and simple furniture create a wonderful atmosphere. Outside, the paved patio area complements a rear garden for alfresco dining and drinking. Two ciders are sold. Q 🕏 ⑩ Å ♣ ● P 📶

The Haven

Blue Ship ★
RH14 9BS (opp Okehurst Rd North)
☼ closed Mon; 11.30 (11 Fri & Sat); 12-4 Sun
☎ (01403) 822709 ⊕ theblueship.co.uk
Badger Autumn Red; 1 changing beer (often Badger) Ⓖ
The Blue Ship dates from the 15th/16th centuries. It has four separate rooms retaining many original features, with log fires and a coal-burning stove. Beer is served from two hatches and is on stillage. Excellent pub food is available, with Sunday lunches particularly popular. The pub hosts a gun club and in July the Newfoundland Dog Show. Included in CAMRA's National Inventory of Historic Pub Interiors. Q ⌂ 🕏 🏠 ⑩ & Å ♣ ● P ☀

Turners Hill

Red Lion L ✓
Lion Lane, RH10 4NU
☼ 11-3, 5-11; 11.30-11 Sat; 12-10.30 Sun ☎ (01342) 715416
⊕ redlionturnershill.com
Harvey's Sussex XX Mild Ale, IPA, Sussex Best Bitter, Armada Ale; 2 changing beers (often Harvey's) Ⓗ
Still very much a village local, this inn offers a warm welcome to all who enter. It has a split-level interior with a large inglenook fireplace and has

recently had a tasteful extension to the dining area. Good-value and high-quality lunchtime food is served. Children and dogs are welcome and there is a fortnightly quiz. North Sussex CAMRA held its first meeting here in 1974.
Q ⌂ 🕏 🏠 ⑩ & ♣ ● P 🖺 (84,272) ☀ 📶

Warnham

Sussex Oak L ✓
2 Church Street, RH12 3QW
☼ 11-11; 11-10.30 Sun ☎ (01403) 265028
⊕ thesussexoak.co.uk
Dark Star Hophead; Long Man American Pale Ale; 3 changing beers (sourced locally) Ⓗ
Popular village pub with a separate dining area. Six handpumps deliver three regular beers and up to three guests, with LocAle actively supported. Two handpumps dispense real cider and perry in the summer months. An extensive menu of high-quality, reasonably priced food is available. There is a large garden and dogs are welcome. Quiz nights are held fortnightly, jazz night on the last Thursday of the month, and beer festivals on bank holidays. Q ⌂ 🕏 🏠 ⑩ & ♣ ● P 🖺 ☀ 📶

West Chiltington

Five Bells L
Smock Alley, RH20 2QX (approx 1 mile S of old village centre) TQ092171
☼ 12-3, 6-11; 12-4, 7-10.30 Sun ☎ (01798) 812143
⊕ thefivebellsinn.com
5 changing beers (sourced nationally; often Jennings, Palmers) Ⓗ
This friendly village free house is a Guide regular. Dating from 1935, the former King & Barnes pub has been run by the same couple since 1983. Five handpumps are on what is probably Sussex's longest copper-top counter. One of the ales is usually a dark brew. There is a large copper-hooded open fire. Locally sourced home-cooked food is served in the bar and large conservatory (no food Sun eve). CAMRA branch Country Pub of the Year in 2016. Q 🕏 🏠 ⑩ ● P 🖺 (1,74) ☀ 📶

Queens Head L
The Hollow, RH20 2JN (on main crossroads between East St and Church St) TQ091185
☼ 12-2.30, 6-9 (9.30 Fri & Sat); 12-4 Sun ☎ (01798) 812244
⊕ queensheadwestchilt.com
Harvey's Sussex Best; Sharp's Doom Bar; 2 changing beers (often Long Man) Ⓗ
This welcoming 17th-century low-beamed pub is situated in the centre of the charming old village, some distance from the newer housing to the south. It has been tastefully refurbished and is now a thriving part of the community, with a popular weekly quiz and other events. Drinkers can enjoy four well-kept ales in the cosy main bar, with its open fire. There are separate areas for dining and a pleasant patio garden. 🕏 🏠 ⑩ ♣ ● P 🖺 (1,74) ☀ 📶

West Marden

Victoria L
PO18 9EN (just W of B2146 in village)
☼ closed Mon; 12-2.30, 6-10.30 (11 Fri); 12-11 Sat; 12-10 Sun
☎ (023) 9263 1330 ⊕ victoriainnwestmarden.co.uk
3 changing beers (sourced locally; often Bowman, Dark Star, Langham) Ⓗ

Comfortable old rural inn at the heart of its tiny downland community. Cricket and bar billiards teams plus a golf society help maintain its local involvement, and all kinds of country pursuits, including walking, riding and shooting are supported. Inside there are several intimate spaces in which to drink and dine, with a log-burning stove for cold evenings. The front garden has splendid views of the surrounding hills. Changing beers usually come from local breweries and occasional beer festivals celebrate local beers.
Q❀❀◑♣P🖵(54)❀❀

Wisborough Green

Three Crowns 🅛 ✅
Billingshurst Road, RH14 0DX
🕑 11-11; 12-10.30 Sun ☎ (01403) 700239
🌐 thethreecrownsinn.com
Harvey's Sussex Best Bitter; Shepherd Neame Spitfire Gold; 4 changing beers (often Dark Star, Downlands, Long Man) 🅗
A warm welcome awaits at this cosy village pub adjacent to the cricket green. A fireplace with a woodburner creates an inviting atmosphere. The pub serves a selection of hand-picked local ales including Three Crowns Crowning Glory Ale by Downland, and home-cooked food from local produce within a 20-mile radius. Live music features on a Tuesday night, and a seven-course food and beer matching evening was introduced in 2013. Well worth a visit. Q❀❀❀◑&♣P🖵❀❀

Worthing

Anchored in Worthing ♥ 🅛
27 West Buildings, BN11 3BS (close to seafront)
🕑 closed Mon; 12-9.30; 12-5.30 Sun ☎ (01903) 529100
🌐 anchoredinworthing.co.uk
3 changing beers (sourced locally; often Gun, Isfield, Long Man) 🅖
Look for the Anchor hanging outside Sussex's first micropub. High wooden tables are arranged so customers face each other and conversation quickly flows. On offer are three ales, ciders, perry and wine, all from local producers. The ceiling is adorned with pumpclips of the many ales sold since opening. The walls have maps showing breweries and micropubs, plus CAMRA and local event information. An ale home delivery service can be accessed via the website. Q♣❀🖵❀❀

Brooksteed Alehouse 🅛
38 South Farm Road, BN14 7AE (N of Worthing Central railway crossing) TQ143034
🕑 closed Mon; 12-9.30; 12-5.30 Sun ☎ 07786 084020
🌐 brooksteedalehouse.co.uk
5 changing beers (often Goldmark, Holler Boys, Lister's) 🅖
Named after the former name for South Farm Road, Worthing's second micropub opened in 2014. Up to five ever-changing ales are on offer from local and national brewers, served from a purpose-built cool room, plus cider and perry, and a good selection of bottled beers from around the world. The pub recently changed hands, but the new owners have maintained the atmosphere and beer quality. The decor is stylish and quirky with comfortable areas and outdoor seating in the forecourt. Local, county and regional CAMRA Pub of the Year in 2016. Q❀❀❀❀

Corner House 🅛 ✅
80 High Street, BN11 1DJ (opp Waitrose) TQ151029
🕑 12-11 (midnight Sat); 12-10.30 Sun ☎ (01903) 215464
🌐 cornerhouseworthing.co.uk
4 changing beers (often Goldmark, Harvey's, Long Man) 🅗
Originally the Anchor, this pub dates back to 1805 and is one of Worthing's oldest. It was rebuilt in 1895 and has an interesting history. The new owners, who have a sister establishment, the Beach House Bar, on the seafront, have greatly improved the pub. Reopened in 2015, with a gold and black exterior, the Corner House occupies a prominent position at the town centre's eastern edge. A family-friendly place to eat and drink, the decor is bright and cheerful with a log-burning stove. The large beer garden features cosy pods with heaters. Monday is quiz night. ❀❀❀◑≈🖵

Egremont 🅛
32 Brighton Road, BN11 3ED (short walk from seafront and town centre)
🕑 12-11.30 (midnight Thu; 12.30am Fri & Sat); 12-11 Sun ☎ (01903) 600064
Harvey's Sussex Best Bitter; house beer (by Goldmark); 3 changing beers (sourced regionally; often Burning Sky, Dark Star) 🅗
Previously, when Worthing was its HQ, the English Bowls Association nicknamed this pub the Bowlers' Arms. Now, thoroughly refurbished before reopening in May 2015, it feels much lighter, brighter and more spacious, while retaining the lovely old doors and stained-glass Kemp Town Brewery windows, whose adjoining Tower Brewery closed in 1926. Several different seating areas still allow space for regular mini beer festivals, quizzes and weekend live music. Two house beers are on tap, plus up to four other ales. ❀◑♣🖵❀❀

Green Man Ale & Cider House 🅛
17 South Street, Tarring, BN14 7LG (NW of West Worthing railway crossing) TQ133034
🕑 12-9 (4 Sun) ☎ 07984 793877
🌐 green-man-ale-and-cider-house.co.uk
5 changing beers (often Goldmark, Gun, Wantsum) 🅖
This former café opened in 2016 as a micropub and quickly gained a reputation for offering an interesting and varied range of up to five ales and up to seven ciders, all kept in fine condition and served from a cool room visible from the drinking area. There are large windows on two sides of the room giving much natural light. Steps inside take you to the rear toilets. Q≈(West)❀🖵❀

Hare & Hounds ✅
79-81 Portland Road, BN11 1QG
🕑 11-11 (11.30 Tue & Thu; midnight Fri & Sat); 12-11 Sun ☎ (01903) 230085 🌐 hareandhoundsworthing.co.uk
Fuller's London Pride; Gale's HSB; Sharp's Doom Bar; 2 changing beers (sourced nationally; often Harvey's) 🅗
In the heart of Worthing, this 18th-century flint building became a pub in 1814, extending into the adjoining property in the 1990s. The large, wood-panelled, U-shaped bar leads to a rear conservatory and a heated and covered patio. Old prints focusing on hunting hang from the walls. There are five handpumps, serving national ales. Tuesday evening features live jazz, Wednesday is quiz night, Saturday evening live bands play, and Sunday is music quiz night. Q❀❀❀◑≈🖵❀

Parsonage Bar & Restaurant L ✓

6-10 High Street, BN14 7NN (at S end of Tarring High St)
◷ 11-11 (midnight Fri & Sat); 12-9 Sun & Mon
☎ (01903) 820140 ⊕ theparsonage.co.uk
Burning Sky Plateau; Harvey's Sussex Best Bitter ⒣; **3 changing beers (sourced nationally; often Downlands, Harvey's, St Austell)** ⒣/Ⓖ

This interesting Grade II-listed 15th-century building was originally three cottages. Once the Museum of Sussex Folklore, it has been a quality restaurant since 1987 which, several years ago, added a handpump in the bar area serving a popular local bitter. There are now four pumps offering a selection of beer styles. Guest ales usually include a dark brew, typically Old Ale during winter. The secluded courtyard garden is great for the warmer weather. Local CAMRA branch Pub of the Year in 2015. Q❀◑➤●⊓🖳(6,16)🛜

Selden Arms

41 Lyndhurst Road, BN11 2DB (about 5 mins from centre of town and 2 mins from Worthing Hospital on Lyndhurst Rd, opp gasometer)
◷ 11-11; 12-10.30 Sun ☎ (01903) 523361
⊕ seldenarms.co.uk
6 changing beers (sourced nationally; often Downlands, Kissingate) ⒣

This welcoming 19th-century free house is a Guide regular. There are six handpumps serving varying national ales, one of which is a dark brew. A blackboard displays upcoming beers. The single bar has a copper-plated top. Pumpclips are stuck on the ceiling and nostalgic photos adorn the walls. The choice of Belgian bottled beer is extensive. Lunch is available Monday to Saturday, and curry night every Friday. It has an annual winterfest in January and a monthly quiz night. ◑➤♣●🖳😺🛜

Tiger Inn, East Dean, East Sussex

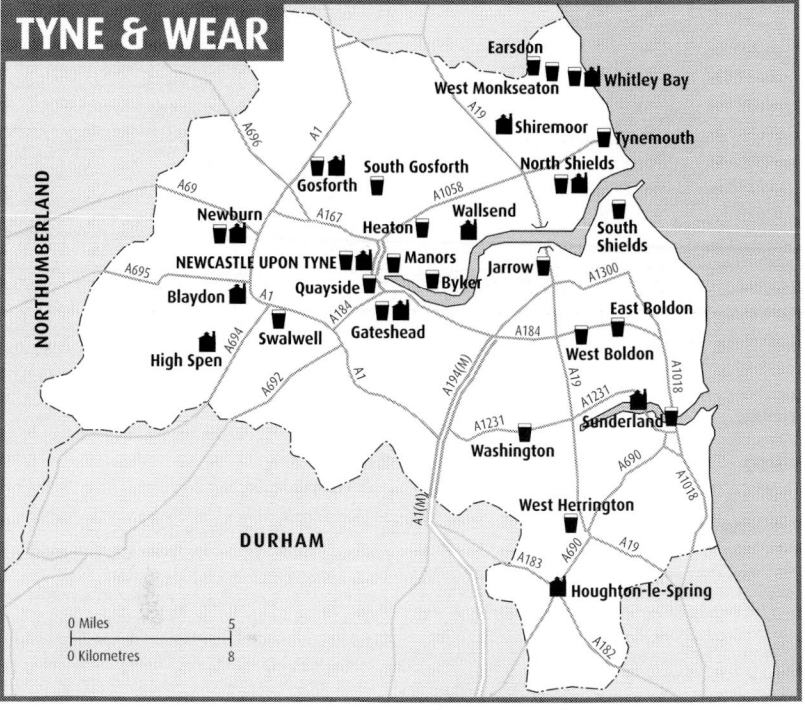

Earsdon

Beehive 🅛
Hartley Lane, NE25 0SZ
🕐 11-11; 12-9 Sun ☎ (0191) 252 9352
🌐 beehiveearsdon.co.uk
Mordue Workie Ticket; 2 changing beers Ⓗ
This 18th-century Grade II-listed building has been an inn since 1896. The superb three-room country pub is now back to its best, with the owners taking great pride in the quality of their ale. A choice of blonde, pale and dark beers is usually available. Excellent food is served, made with ingredients sourced from local suppliers. The car park has been extended and there is a mini goat area, children's secret garden, a picnic site and extra seating.
🛇😊🍴🛆♣●P🐾

East Boldon

Grey Horse ✪
Front Street, NE36 0SJ
🕐 11-11 (midnight Fri & Sat); 12-11 Sun ☎ (0191) 519 1796
🌐 greyhorseeastboldon.co.uk
6 changing beers Ⓗ
Large and distinctive mock-Tudor building with separate lounge and bar areas, situated next to the Boldon Auction Rooms. There are large-screen TVs in the bar for football and other sport, and an upstairs function room. Six changing ales come from a mixture of local and national breweries. Meals are served daily with themed nights during the week. A folk club meets on the first Thursday of the month and the Boldon History Society on the last Tuesday. Q🛇😊🍴🛆🖶P➋(9,30)🛜

Gateshead

Wheat Sheaf 🅛
26 Carlisle Street, Felling, NE10 0HQ
🕐 5 (3 Thu; 12 Fri & Sat)-11; 12-10.30 Sun
☎ (0191) 597 2981
Big Lamp Bitter, Prince Bishop Ale, Sunny Daze; 1 changing beer Ⓗ
Welcoming street-corner pub owned by Big Lamp Brewery and patronised by a loyal band of regulars who often travel quite a distance to drink here. The pub features some original details, mismatched furniture and, when needed, real coal fires. The outdoor toilets have original Victorian urinals. There is a fortnightly Monday night quiz, traditional folk music featuring local musicians on Tuesday night and dominoes on Wednesday night. An original CAMRA clock keeps time behind the bar. Snacks are available. 🛇🚆🛆♣●🖶🐾🛜

Jarrow

McConnell's Gin & Ale House 🅛
Walter Street, NE32 3PQ (behind town hall)
🕐 12-11.30 (12.30am Fri-Sun) ☎ (0191) 483 6792
4 changing beers Ⓗ
A well-appointed conversion of the old Crusader, with an emphasis on wooden panelling, carpets, vintage photographs and pub memorabilia. The pub serves up to four ales, with at least one from Arbier, and also promotes over a dozen gins. An ale of the day is offered at a discount. A quiz is held every Sunday night and a buskers' night on Thursday. Note the ornate tiling on the outside of the building. 🐾🖶🖶

Newburn

Keelman 🄻

Grange Road, NE15 8NL
🕓 11-11; 12-10.30 Sun ☎ (0191) 267 1689
🌐 keelmanslodge.co.uk
Big Lamp Bitter, Prince Bishop Ale, Summerhill Stout, Sunny Daze; 1 changing beer 🄷

This tastefully converted Grade II-listed former pumping station is now home to the Big Lamp Brewery and the Keelman is the brewery tap. A conservatory restaurant serves excellent food, and quality accommodation is provided in the adjacent Keelman's Lodge and Salmon Cottage. Attractively situated by Tyne Riverside Country Park, the Coast-to-Coast cycleway and Hadrian's Wall National Trail. 🛏️🏵️🍴◑🅿️🚪(22)🛜

Newcastle upon Tyne: Byker

Cluny 🄻

36 Lime Street, NE1 2PQ
🕓 12-11; 12-10.30 Sun ☎ (0191) 230 4474
7 changing beers 🄷

Large, former industrial building converted into a pub, art gallery and live music venue. The pub runs frequent themed beer festivals and always has a good selection of British and foreign draught and bottled products available. The art gallery shows work of all kinds ranging from final degree shows to local independent established artists in all media, with the displays changing monthly. Live music sessions are held most evenings and feature a wide range of British, European and American musicians. Q◑&🅡🏵️🚪🛜

Cumberland Arms 🄻

James Place Street, NE6 1LD (off Byker Bank)
🕓 3-11 (midnight Fri); 12-midnight Sat; 12-11 Sun
☎ (0191) 265 1725 🌐 thecumberlandarms.co.uk
6 changing beers 🄷

Three-storey venue rebuilt over 100 years ago and relatively little changed since. It stands in a prominent position overlooking the lower Ouseburn Valley. The pub is home to dance and music groups and its house beer, Rapper from Wylam Brewery, is named after the traditional rapper sword dance. A multiple winner of CAMRA regional Cider Pub of the Year awards, it generally offers up to 12 ciders and perries. Winter and summer beer festivals are held each year. Closing time may vary. Q🛏️🏵️🍴🅡🏵️🏵️🅿️🏵️🛜

Free Trade Inn 🏆 🄻

St Lawrence Road, NE6 1AP
🕓 11-11 (midnight Fri & Sat); 12-10.30 Sun
☎ (0191) 265 5764
7 changing beers 🄷

Unique former S&N pub with wonderful views of the Tyne bridges and the Newcastle and Gateshead quaysides. Up to nine beers and two ciders are available on the bar, with cellar runs willingly offered. Interesting ales come from far and wide including an extensive range of foreign bottled beers. Service is with a smile, friendly and knowledgable. Tasty sandwiches are supplied by a local delicatessen. The jukebox is classic and free. The beer garden is excellent. Local CAMRA Pub of the Year and Cider Pub of the Year 2017. Q🛏️🏵️🅡🏵️🏵️🚪(Q3)🏵️🛜

Newcastle upon Tyne: City Centre

Bacchus 🄻

42-48 High Bridge, NE1 6BX
🕓 11.30-midnight; 12-11 Sun ☎ (0191) 261 1008
🌐 thebacchusnewcastle.co.uk
6 changing beers 🄷

Former local CAMRA Pub of the Year four years running, this smart city-centre pub boasts nine handpumps offering a range of changing guest beers, with one pump dedicated to cider. A seasonal house beer is brewed by Yorkshire Dales, and a large range of draught and bottled foreign beers is available. Photographs and posters show the industries in which this region used to lead the world. 🛏️◑&🅡(Monument)🏵️🛜

Bodega 🄻

125 Westgate Road, NE1 4AG
🕓 12-11 (midnight Fri); 11-midnight Sat; 12-10.30 Sun
☎ (0191) 221 1552 🌐 thebodeganewcastle.co.uk
Big Lamp Prince Bishop Ale; Fyne Ales Jarl; Oakham Citra; 5 changing beers (often Almasty) 🄷

Two fine stained-glass domes are the architectural highlights of the pub, which is popular with football and music fans. TVs show sporting events and the pub can be busy on match days. The interior offers a number of standing and seating areas with separate booths for more intimate drinking. A number of old brewery mirrors adorn the walls. Eight handpumps include beers from Oakham and Fyne Ales, alongside a good selection of foreign bottled beers. 🚆🅡(Central Station)🏵️🏵️🏵️🛜

Bridge Hotel Ⓛ
Castle Square, NE1 1RQ
☼ 11.30-11 (midnight Fri & Sat); 12-10.30 Sun
☎ (0191) 232 6400 ∰ bridgehotelnewcastle.co.uk
Anarchy Blonde Star; Sharp's Doom Bar; Three Kings Castle Keep; 7 changing beers Ⓗ
Large Fitzgerald pub situated next to Stephenson's spectacular High Level Bridge – the rear windows and patio have views of the city walls, River Tyne and Gateshead Quays. The main bar area, with many stained-glass windows, is divided into a number of seating areas with a raised section at the rear. Guest beers come from far and wide. What claims to be the oldest folk club in the country is among live music events hosted in the upstairs function room. ❀◐≉ℚ(Central Station)●

Fitzgeralds Ⓛ
60 Grey Street, NE1 6AF
☼ 11-midnight; 12-11 Sun ☎ (0191) 230 1350
∰ fitzgeraldsnewcastle.co.uk
House beer (by Brinkburn Street); 5 changing beers (sourced nationally) Ⓗ
Large, open-plan, friendly Sir John Fitzgerald pub, recently refurbished with six handpulls serving local and national beers. The pub is much bigger inside than it appears from the outside owing to its depth, with the bar situated towards the back. There is plenty of seating in various areas as well as a large standing area in front of the bar. The experienced landlady likes to offer an ale selection not found elsewhere locally, including an extensive range of bottled beers.
◐≉ℚ(Monument)🚌(Q1,Q2)

Five Swans ✅
14 St Mary's Place, NE1 7PG
☼ 8am-midnight (1am Fri & Sat) ☎ (0191) 232 3893
Adnams Broadside; Fuller's London Pride; Greene King Abbot; Ruddles Best Bitter; Sharp's Doom Bar; 6 changing beers Ⓗ
Multi-roomed Wetherspoon pub, very busy at times, opposite Newcastle Civic Centre and close to the main shopping areas. The beer range includes guests from all the local brewers and from further afield. Food is served all day. There is a drinking area outside to the front and a 'secret' courtyard through the maze of rooms. Children are welcome until 9pm. The pub area can be booked for private functions. Q≤❀◐&≉ℚ♣🚌

Head of Steam
1 Neville Street, NE1 5EN
☼ 12-2am (3am Fri & Sat) ☎ (0191) 230 4236
6 changing beers (often Camerons) Ⓗ
Facing the central railway station, this is an unusual pub in that there is nothing on the ground floor. Upstairs is the main bar with six cask beers, three real ciders and a good selection of continental draught beers. Downstairs is one of the most popular music venues in the city centre (no draught beers here although there is an extensive range of cans and bottles). ≉ℚ(Central Station)●

Lady Greys Ⓛ ✅
20 Shakespeare Street, NE1 6AQ
☼ 11-11pm ☎ (0191) 232 3606 ∰ ladygreys.co.uk
Mordue Northumbrian Blonde; 7 changing beers Ⓗ
Close to the historic Theatre Royal and busy shopping areas, this pub, formerly the Adelphi, is a welcome addition to the city-centre real ale scene. Beers are mainly from local brewers Mordue, Hadrian Border, Allendale and Wylam, with guests

from all over the country. A refurbishment has added two more handpumps for beer and two for real cider. Food is served all day.
◐≉ℚ(Monument)●

Old George Ⓛ ✅
Old George Yard, NE1 1EZ
☼ 11-11 (1am Thu; 2am Fri & Sat); 12-midnight Sun
☎ (0191) 260 3035 ∰ oldgeorgeinnnewcastle.co.uk
Draught Bass; 6 changing beers Ⓗ
Built in 1582, this historic pub is alleged to have been frequented by King Charles I and is a welcoming watering hole for customers who like a piece of old England. The corridors and stairs creak and the ambience is mostly original. A cabinet of five handpulls complements the traditional bar area, and a smaller bar has an additional three handpulls. Buskers' nights are Thursday and Sunday. In summer bands play regularly in the yard. ⌂◐&≉ℚ(Monument)

Pleased To Meet You Ⓛ
High Bridge, NE1 1EW
☼ 11-1am (2am Fri & Sat) ☎ (0191) 340 5137
∰ ptmy-newcastle.co.uk
Mordue Five Bridges; 6 changing beers Ⓗ
Refurbished to a high standard and serving a multitude of drinks, this gin and real ale eatery has a busy mixed clientele. Situated on Newcastle's premier real ale street, it offers six handpulls serving a variety of brews, both local and national, with a trend towards the out of the ordinary. The front of the building features full-height windows which fold away in summer. To the rear are outdoor cabins. ◐≉ℚ(Monument)

Split Chimp Ⓛ
Arch 7, Westgate Road, NE1 1SA
☼ 3-8; 11-11 Fri & Sat ∰ splitchimp.pub/home
House beer (by Errant); 4 changing beers (sourced nationally) Ⓗ
Newcastle's first micropub opened in 2015 in a recently refurbished railway arch behind Central Station opposite the site of the former Federation Brewery. It relocated to a larger arch on Westgate Road in 2016. More spacious than some micropubs and split over two levels, six handpumps serve an ever-changing selection of real ales, with one dedicated to the house beer, Clever Chimp, from nearby Errant Brewery. Foreign bottled beers are also available. The popular skittles alley upstairs can be noisy. ❀≉ℚ(Central Station)♣●

Strawberry Ⓛ
7 Strawberry Place, NE1 4SF
☼ 9am-2.30am; 12-10.30 Sun ☎ (0191) 232 6865
∰ thestrawberrypub.co.uk
Caledonian Deuchars IPA; Mordue Northumbrian Blonde; 3 changing beers Ⓗ
A single-room pub situated directly opposite St James' Park, the Strawberry can be busy on match days. The walls are covered in Newcastle United memorabilia, and silent TV screens show sporting events. A new roof terrace with canopies and heaters overlooks the city centre. Two guest beers are available, and above-average food at below-average prices is served all day – check out the giant filled Yorkshire puddings.
⌂◐&≉ℚ(St James)♣P

Trent House Ⓛ
1-2 Leazes Lane, NE1 4QT
☼ 12-11 ☎ (0191) 261 2154

6 changing beers Ⓗ
Friendly and laid back, the Trent is popular with students. It is home to the best jukebox in town, featuring an eclectic mix of classic rock, jazz and electronica. There is an upstairs room with a pool table, and board games are available at the bar. The pub has a nightly happy hour 8-9pm, with cask ales priced at £2 per pint, and on the first Sunday of the month ales are just £1 between 5-10pm.
🅰(Haymarket)♣🚌(32,32A)🛜

Tyneside Cinema Bar Café Ⓛ
Pilgrim Street, NE1 6QG
⊕ 8am-11 (midnight Fri & Sat); 10-11 Sun ☎ 0845 217 9909
⊕ tynesidecinema.co.uk/food-drink/tyneside-bar-cafe
House beer (by Wylam); 3 changing beers Ⓗ
Part of Tyneside Cinema, the Bar Café is a large open-plan bar with its own curtained-off cinema screen. The bar has three handpumps serving a range of locally brewed cask ales including the house beer, 35mm from Wylam Brewery. Beer can be taken into cinema screenings. A tasty selection of cakes and pastries is also available. The cellar is in the vault of a former bank.
◑♿🚊🅰(Monument)●🛜

Victoria Comet
38 Neville Street, NE1 5DF
⊕ 10-11.30 (12.30am Fri & Sat) ☎ (0191) 261 7921
Durham White Gold; St Austell Nicholson's Pale Ale; Sharp's Doom Bar; 5 changing beers Ⓗ
Formerly O'Neills, following a stylish refurbishment this became Nicholson's most northerly English pub in 2014. The welcome addition of several more handpulls has provided a choice of eight cask beers. Note the chandeliers and the butcher's block high tables. The pub is opposite the portico of Newcastle Central railway station and handy for other public transport links.
🛏◑♿🚊🅰(Central Station)🚌🛜

Newcastle Upon Tyne: Gosforth

County Ⓛ ✅
High Street, NE3 1HB
⊕ 11-11; 12-10.30 Sun ☎ (0191) 285 6919
Caledonian Deuchars IPA; Greene King London Glory, IPA; Ruddles County; Wells Bombardier; 6 changing beers Ⓗ
This large L-shaped bar, with pleasant stained-glass windows on the main road frontage, attracts a variety of visitors, from office workers to students, and can get busy, especially at weekends. A separate quiet room at the back offers respite from the hustle and bustle of the main bar, and also doubles as a small meeting or function room. Several guest beers are available. ✿●P🚌✿🛜

Gosforth Hotel Ⓛ ✅
High Street, NE3 1HQ
⊕ 11-11 (midnight Fri & Sat) ☎ (0191) 285 6617
⊕ gosforthhotelnewcastle.co.uk
Allendale Pennine Pale; Mordue Workie Ticket; 4 changing beers Ⓗ
On the corner of a busy junction at the top of the High Street, this is a stalwart of the Gosforth pub scene. Popular with a wide clientele, from nearby office workers to locals and students, the pub often gets busy. Three ales are regularly available along with the occasional guest beer. A quieter adjoining bar opens at busier times and also serves as a function room. Another function room is available upstairs. ◑♿🚌🛜

Job Bulman Ⓛ
St Nicholas Avenue, NE3 1AA
⊕ 8am-11 ☎ (0191) 223 6230
Greene King Abbot; Ruddles Best Bitter; 6 changing beers Ⓗ
Wetherspoon pub located just off the High Street, which strives to serve a wide range of real ales. Aside from the two core beers, up to six guests may be available, often from local established breweries or local micros. There is a raised area to the right set aside for families and diners.
🛏✿◑♿🅰(Regent Centre or S Gosforth)●🚌🛜

Newcastle upon Tyne: Heaton

Chillingham Ⓛ
Chillingham Road, NE6 5XN
⊕ 11-11 (midnight Fri & Sat); 12-11 Sun ☎ (0191) 265 3992
⊕ thechillinghamnewcastle.co.uk
Anarchy Blonde Star; Sharp's Atlantic; 8 changing beers Ⓗ
Close to Chillingham Road Metro station, this large two-roomed pub was extensively renovated, refurbished and reopened in 2016. It has a comfortable bar and lounge, with sport shown on TVs, appealing to the widest possible clientele. The food menu is popular with locals and visitors alike. An excellent choice of local microbrewery beers is offered – and look out for the bottled beer, whisky and wine of the month. A function room upstairs hosts regular quiz nights. ◑🅰♣●P🚌(62,63)🛜

Newcastle upon Tyne: Manors

New Bridge Ⓛ
2-4 Argyle Street, NE1 6PF
⊕ 11-11 (11.30 Thu & Fri); 12-10.30 Sun ☎ (0191) 232 1020
⊕ thenewbridgenewcastle.co.uk
Anarchy Blonde Star; 4 changing beers Ⓗ
Just east of Newcastle city centre, and well served by buses and the Metro, this pub has no regular beers but offers an ever-changing choice from independent brewers. It is very much a locals' venue, but all are made welcome. The building is next to a business park and facing a large extension to Northumbria University, so attracts a mixed lunchtime and early evening crowd enjoying the beer and home-made food. ◑🚊●🚌🛜

Newcastle upon Tyne: Quayside

Bridge Tavern Ⓛ
7 Akenside Hill, NE1 3UF
⊕ 12-midnight (1am Fri & Sat); 12-11 Sun
☎ (0191) 261 9966 ⊕ thebridgetavern.com
7 changing beers Ⓗ
A popular pub with its own microbrewery – the Bridge Tavern's one-barrel plant brews a range of beers under the Tavernale name. Food ranging from bar snacks to buffets and full meals is prepared and cooked by a professional chef. There has been an alehouse on this site for over 200 years – the original building was demolished in 1925 and a new premises built following the construction of the town's most famous landmark, the Tyne Bridge. Children welcome until 7pm.
🛏✿◑♿🚊🅰(Central Station)●🚌✿🛜

Broad Chare Ⓛ
25 Broad Chare, NE1 3DQ
⊕ 11-11 (10 Mon) ☎ (0191) 211 2144
⊕ thebroadchare.co.uk

Wylam Writer's Block; 3 changing beers Ⓗ

A warm welcome awaits at this cosy pub just off Newcastle's historic, bustling Quayside. Stripped floors, exposed brickwork and comfy leather banquettes make the bar an attractive, quiet place to relax in and enjoy a pint. Bar food is served all day and there is a restaurant upstairs if you wish to dine in style. The house beer is The Writer's Block from Wylam. ◖▶≠Ө●呂(Q3)🛜

Crown Posada Ⓛ

31 Side, NE1 3JE

✿ 12 (11 Thu)-11; 11-midnight Fri; 12-midnight Sat; 12-10.30 Sun ☎ (0191) 232 1269 ∰ crownposadanewcastle.co.uk

Allendale Pennine Pale; Hadrian Border Tyneside Blonde; 4 changing beers (often Hadrian Border) Ⓗ

An architecturally fine pub, on CAMRA's Regional Inventory of Historic Pub Interiors. Behind the narrow street frontage with its two impressive stained-glass windows lie a small snug, bar counter and a longer seating area. There is an interesting coffered ceiling, as well as local photographs and cartoons of long-gone customers and staff on the walls. Small brewers are enthusiastically supported. Q≠Ө(Central Station)呂 🛜

Hop & Cleaver Ⓛ

40 Sandhill, NE1 3JF

✿ 12-1am ☎ (0191) 261 1037

6 changing beers Ⓗ

Interestingly renovated pub now stripped back to the brickwork throughout. One room is home to a microbrewery, and leads through to the Red House next door. The food majors on smoked American-style meats and burgers, while the Red House features specialist pies, peas and mash. A good range of real ales is served from a bar with an open front. ◖▶ᕫ≠Ө(Central Station)呂

Newcastle upon Tyne: South Gosforth

Brandling Villa Ⓛ ✅

Haddricks Mill Road, NE3 1QL

✿ 12-11 (midnight Fri & Sat) ☎ (0191) 284 0490 ∰ brandlingvilla.co.uk

7 changing beers Ⓗ

Large double-fronted establishment with enthusiastic staff. It offers a constantly changing selection of 10 beers – also available in third-pint tasting glasses – plus two ciders on handpump. The manager organises various well-attended beer-related events, including brewery takeovers, local sausage and pie festivals, music, cinema and beer festivals. The house beer, Frank & Bird, is from Hadrian Border and is a special brew, not a rebadge. ⛷❀◖▶ᕫӨ♣●P呂(55)❀🛜

Millstone Ⓛ

Haddricks Mill Road, NE3 1QL

✿ 12-11 (midnight Fri & Sat) ☎ (0191) 285 3429

Anarchy Blonde Star; Draught Bass; Sharp's Doom Bar; 5 changing beers Ⓗ

A modern, stylish, two-roomed pub with the lounge to the front and a small public bar to the rear serving beers from local microbreweries as well as national favourites. Bass has been the regulars' choice for many years. The function room upstairs is available to hire and hosts CAMRA events. Complimentary nibbles are on the bar every Sunday from noon. ⛷❀◖▶ӨP呂(55)🛜

North Shields

Exchange Ⓛ

Howard Street, NE30 1SE

✿ 10-11 ☎ (0191) 258 4111

5 changing beers (sourced locally; often Flash House, Hadrian Border, Three Kings)

Bar, café and performance venue within the Exchange Building, an arts and culture centre at the end of Howard Street. The bar, which opened at the end of 2015, is accessed through the archway and courtyard. Beers from local breweries including Hadrian Border, Cullercoats and Three Kings are available, alongside traditional cider. Open mic nights are hosted. ᕫӨ●呂

South Shields

Alum Ale House ✅

Ferry Street, NE33 1JR (next to Ferry Landing)

✿ 11-11 (midnight Fri & Sat); 12-11 Sun ☎ (0191) 427 7245

Jennings Cumberland Ale, Cocker Hoop; Wychwood Hobgoblin; 14 changing beers Ⓗ

Small, traditional pub adjacent to the Market Square, River Tyne and ferry landing. It is popular with local ale drinkers as a haven of good beer. Fourteen handpumps dispense beers from the Marston's range and a real cider. The pub has three rooms including a cellar bar, with low ceilings throughout. There is a lively Irish folk session on the first Sunday of each month. Outside seating offers fine river views. ❀Ө♣●

Marine Ⓛ

230 Ocean Road, NE33 2JQ

✿ 11-11 (midnight Fri & Sat); 12-10.30 Sun ☎ (0191) 455 0280

3 changing beers Ⓗ

Large 1840s pub opposite Marine Park, close to the seafront. This free house offers three changing real ales and a real cider. To the left of the bar are two raised seating areas, and to the right is a games area. There is a function room upstairs. Unobtrusive background music is played. Pub food is served daily, including a traditional Sunday lunch. ◖▶Ө♣●P呂(E1,516)❀

Steamboat 🍷 Ⓛ ✅

Mill Dam, NE33 1EQ (follow signs for Customs House)

✿ 12-11 (midnight Thu-Sat); 12-11.30 Sun ☎ (0191) 454 0134

9 changing beers Ⓗ

Under the same management for the past 25 years, the Steamboat has one of the largest selections of cask ales in South Shields. Nine handpumps dispense a range of beers from small and family brewers across the country, and Meet the Brewer events and beer festivals take place throughout the year. The split-level bar has a nautical theme. The pub is a short walk from bus stops, the Shields Ferry and Customs House Theatre. QӨ●❀🛜

Wouldhave ✅

16 Mile End Road, NE33 1TA

✿ 8am-midnight ☎ (0191) 427 6014

Greene King Abbot; Ruddles Best Bitter; 3 changing beers Ⓗ

Wetherspoon pub opposite South Shields Metro station rear entrance and close to the main bus stops. The bar is on the ground floor with plenty of seats and tables, and there is more seating upstairs where children are welcome until 7pm. Six handpumps serve two regular beers and four guest beers or ciders. Wetherspoon's popular beer and cider festivals are regular events. Reasonably priced food is available all day from breakfast until late. Q ⊛ ⛲ ◑ ⓵ & ♠ ◉ P 🛜

Sunderland

Avenue
Zetland Street, Roker, SR6 0EQ (just off Roker Avenue)
🕐 12-11.30 (12.30am Fri); 11-12.30am Sat; 11-11.30 Sun
☎ (0191) 567 7412 ⊕ theavenuepub.net
8 changing beers Ⓗ
Fifteen minutes' walk from the Stadium of Light, this local pub hosts various themed nights throughout the week including music, bingo, football and a popular Thursday night quiz, often followed by a live band. The bar has six handpulls for ale and cider. There is a pool table and an upstairs games room with a snooker table and two dartboards. A function room with two handpulls provides extra space during busier periods and is available to hire. 🛡♠🚌🚃(E1,E6)🐾🛜

Chaplins
Stockton Road, SR1 3NR
🕐 10-11; 12-10.30 Sun ☎ (0191) 567 3562
Thwaites Original; 5 changing beers Ⓗ
A city-centre pub with eight handpulls including a house ale brewed by Thwaites and a real cider. Good-value food is served daily including fish on Friday. A quiz is held on Thursday evening and live music on Saturday. There is plenty of seating either side of the main entrance. Some table tops depict scenes of Sunderland's heritage. Handy for public transport with Park Lane Interchange two minutes away. ⊛◑≒🛡♠🚌🛜

Chesters Ⓛ ✅
Chester Road, SR4 7DR
🕐 10-11 (midnight Fri & Sat); 12-10.30 Sun
☎ (0191) 565 9952
6 changing beers Ⓗ
This popular pub just outside the city centre has a smart yet comfortable interior, with a large main bar and a more intimate area at the back. With six handpulls, there is always one beer from a local brewery as well as guest ales from other brewers. Outside is car parking and a large beer garden. A function room with private bar is also available. ⛲⊛◑&🛡P🛜

Dun Cow ★ Ⓛ
High Street West, SR1 3HA
🕐 12-midnight ☎ (0191) 567 2262 ⊕ theheadofsteam.co.uk
Anarchy Blonde Star; Camerons Strongarm; 5 changing beers Ⓗ
Dating back to 1900, the pub was purchased and reopened by Sunderland MAC Trust in 2014 following a major restoration, revealing many original features, and was awarded both the CAMRA/Historic England Conservation and Refurbishment awards in 2015. It offers seven cask beers complemented by an extensive range of bottled beers, real cider and craft gins. The pub is next to the Empire Theatre and close to Sunderland Minster and city-centre restaurants. Q◑≒🛡♠🛜

Fitzgeralds Ⓛ
12-14 Green Terrace, SR1 3PZ
🕐 11.30-11 (11.30 Fri & Sat); 12-11 Sun ☎ (0191) 567 0852
Fyne Ales Jarl; Titanic Plum Porter; 8 changing beers Ⓗ

Part of the real ale-friendly Sir John Fitzgerald chain, this city-centre pub serves two regular beers complemented by up to eight guests. There are two separate rooms offering a choice of seating areas, with the smaller nautically themed Chart Room quieter than the main bar. Meals are served all day from an extensive menu. Live music features on Tuesday and Saturday, a buskers' night on Monday evening. Q⛲⊛◑≒🛡♠🛜

Harbour View
Harbour View, Roker, SR6 0NU
🕐 10.30-11.30 (midnight Fri & Sat) ☎ (0191) 567 3878
6 changing beers Ⓗ
A modern local pub with six handpulls offering regularly changing beers chosen by local CAMRA members. A blackboard proudly displays the brewer, name of ale and ABV, along with a tally of beers to date from 1 January. The aim is to offer in excess of 600 ales a year. If real ale is for you, then you have found home. ⊛🛡🚃(E1,18)🐾🛜

Ivy House
7A Worcester Terrace, Ashbrooke, SR2 7AW
🕐 12-11 (midnight Fri & Sat) ☎ (0191) 567 3399
5 changing beers Ⓗ
Tucked away but close to the bus and metro interchange, the Ivy House is well worth seeking out. Five different guest ales are on offer as well as a guest cider. An extensive range of bottled international beers is also kept. Home-made pizzas and burgers are freshly prepared in an open kitchen next to the bar. Quiz night is Wednesday, live music plays on the last Sunday of the month and happy hour is weekdays from 5pm. ⊛◑&≒🛡♠P🛜

Museum Vaults Ⓛ
33 Silksworth Row, SR1 3QJ
🕐 5-11; 3-midnight Fri; 12-midnight Sat; 12-10.30 Sun
☎ (0191) 565 9443
3 changing beers Ⓗ
This small former beer house on the edge of the city centre has been run by the same family for over 40 years. The single room is divided in two, both sides with open fires. The pub offers three cask beers from local breweries and is a regular outlet for student brews from Brewlab in Sunderland. The real ale is complemented by a real cider and a small range of bottled beers. ⊛≒🛡♠P🚃🐾🛜

Poetic License Ⓛ
Roker Terrace, Roker, SR6 9ND
🕐 11-11 (1am Fri & Sat) ☎ (0191) 567 1786
⊕ poeticlicensebar.co.uk
Sonnet 43 Abolition, Seraphim, The Aurora, The Raven; 1 changing beer Ⓗ
Poetic License has fine views of the mouth of the River Wear and seashore. Up to four Sonnet 43 beers are on offer plus a guest. The decor is a blend of modern and traditional, with separate dining areas featuring wood-panelled ceilings and comfortable seating. Meal deals are available Monday to Friday. It is also home to a gin distillery, visible from the bar. Disabled access is to the left of the hotel reception. ⛲🏠◑&P🚃(18,E1)

Ship Isis Ⓛ
26 Silksworth Row, SR1 3QJ
🕐 12-midnight; 12-11.30 Sun ☎ (0191) 514 7684
Camerons Strongarm; 8 changing beers Ⓗ

Restored to its original Victorian splendour by Jarrow Brewery and acquired by Camerons, the Isis is now part of the Head of Steam group. Twelve handpumps offer nine cask beers and three real ciders, complemented by an extensive selection of bottled beers and a range of craft gins, served by knowledgable staff. Monday is quiz night, Wednesday is buskers' night and there is live music on Sunday. Just a short walk from the city centre, the Ship Isis has something for everyone. ◑⑤&⇌요➡︎🖥🛜

William Jameson ✅
30-32 Fawcett Street, SR1 1RH
✪ 8am-11 ☎ (0191) 514 5016
Greene King Abbot; Ruddles Best Bitter; 6 changing beers Ⓗ

Sunderland's first Wetherspoon is in a former department store opposite the Winter Gardens. All the usual features associated with the chain can be found is this busy corner pub at the heart of the city centre, including good-value meals served all day. Twelve handpumps offer up to six guest beers and a cider to complement the regular range. The pub is a keen supporter of local brewers and holds twice-yearly beer festivals. Q🌣◑⇌요➡︎🛜

Swalwell

Sun Inn ✅
Market Lane, NE16 3AL (just off roundabout at end of Front St)
✪ 11-11; 12-11 Sun
Marston's Pedigree; 2 changing beers Ⓗ

Situated in the heart of the historic village that spawned many internationally renowned engineers and industrialists, and of course the famous Swalwell cabbage. This truly no-nonsense community pub provides good company for locals and strangers alike. Sword dancers, darts, dominoes handicaps, a monthly pie competition and Saturday buskers' night all feature. Bar food and snacks are available, free on Sundays. There is a regular bus service from Newcastle. 🌣❀♣●요👕

Tynemouth

Tynemouth Lodge Hotel Ⓛ
Tynemouth Road, NE30 4AA
✪ 11-11; 12-10.30 Sun ☎ (0191) 257 7565
⊕ tynemouthlodgehotel.co.uk
Caledonian Deuchars IPA; Draught Bass; Mordue Northumbrian Blonde; 1 changing beer Ⓗ

This attractive externally tiled 1799 free house, next to a former house of correction, has featured in every issue of the Guide since 1983. The comfortable pub has a U-shaped lounge with the bar on one side and a serving hatch on the other, and is noted in the area for the quality of its Draught Bass. A popular stopping-off point for those completing the Coast-to-Coast cycle route. Q❀요➡︎(1,1A)🛜

Washington

Courtyard Ⓛ
Biddick Lane, NE38 8AB
✪ 11-11 (midnight Fri & Sat); 12-11 Sun ☎ (0191) 417 0445
⊕ artscentrewashington.co.uk/courtyard.aspx
Timothy Taylor Landlord; 7 changing beers Ⓗ

Located within the lively arts centre, this light and airy café/bar offers a warm welcome to drinkers and food lovers alike. Eight handpumped beers, two real ciders, a perry and a range of bottled Belgian beers are available. Food is served lunchtime and early evening. Quiz nights are Sunday and Thursday and buskers' night is Monday. Outdoor seating is within the spacious courtyard. Two beer festivals are held annually, on the Easter and August bank holidays. Q🌣❀◑⑤&●🖥❀🛜

Sir William de Wessyngton ✅
2-3 Victoria Road, Concord, NE37 2SY
✪ 7am-11 (midnight Fri & Sat); 8am-11 Sun
☎ (0191) 418 0100
Greene King Abbot; Ruddles Best Bitter; 6 changing beers Ⓗ

Large open-plan Wetherspoon pub housed in a former snooker hall and ice cream parlour. It is named after a Norman knight and lord of the manor whose descendants later emigrated to the United States. The pub offers value-for-money beer and the usual well-priced Wetherspoon menu. The regular ales are complemented by up to four guests and at least two real ciders. Twice-yearly beer festivals are held. A large selection of local and international bottled beers is available. Q🌣❀◑⑤&●🖥🛜

Steps
47 Spout Lane, NE38 7HP
✪ 3.30-11; 12-11 Sat; 12-10.30 Sun ☎ (0191) 415 0733
5 changing beers Ⓗ

Opened in 1894 as the Spout Lane Inn, the pub was renamed the Steps in 1976. The small, comfortable and friendly single-room lounge bar is divided into two drinking areas and the walls are decorated with pictures of old Washington. Five ever-changing beers are on offer, frequently from local microbreweries. Quiz night is Tuesday. Opening hours vary. Q❀♣🖥(82,86)

West Boldon

Black Horse
Rectory Bank, NE36 0QQ (off A184)
✪ 11-11; 11-11.30 Sun ☎ (0191) 536 1814
Jennings Cumberland Ale; 1 changing beer Ⓗ

An old-fashioned pub with one small L-shaped bar and unusual bric-a-brac adorning the walls. Prints of the photographs on display are available to buy. Two handpulls offer Cumberland Ale and a guest beer. With a popular restaurant serving high-quality food, the pub can get busy in the evenings and at weekends. Live music features on Sunday night. Q◑🖥요

West Herrington

Stables
DH4 4ND (off B1286)
✪ 12-11 (midnight Fri & Sat) ☎ (0191) 584 9226
⊕ thestablespub.co.uk
Black Sheep Best Bitter; Timothy Taylor Landlord; 2 changing beers Ⓗ

This conversion from a former riding school is well worth a visit and you can be sure of a friendly welcome. The bar has a small snug behind it, and the main restaurant features original beams and stonework. Four handpulls offer two permanent and two guest ales. An extensive food menu is available daily, with tapas on Friday and Saturday evenings (the food is popular so it is wise to book ahead). There is a pleasant outdoor seating area. ⌂⊛◖⅙P🖫❀

West Monkseaton

Beacon Hotel ✅
Earsdon Road, NE25 9PT
✪ 11-midnight ☎ (0191) 253 6911
Brakspear Bitter; house beer (by Durham); 5 changing beers (often Black Sheep) 🅷
Superb modern pub serving excellent food, popular with locals, set back from the main road. The manager sources a wide range of ales and there is a rapid turnover. The cellar has dedicated lines so beers are served at the correct temperature. Ales can be ordered in wooden paddles of three third-pints, allowing a wider range to be sampled. There are themed food nights Monday to Thursday and chef's specials Friday and Saturday. Quiz nights are Sunday and Wednesday. Q⊛◖⅙♿P🖫

Whitley Bay

Dog & Rabbit 🅛
36 Park View, NE26 2TH
✪ 12-10; 3-10 Sun ☎ 07944 552716
4 changing beers 🅷
This new micropub, converted from a women's clothing shop, is a welcome addition to the pub scene in Whitley Bay. It features a corner bar with four handpumps serving mostly local beers. There are plans to move the owner's microbrewery from its current location into the building. No music, no Wi-Fi and no sports TV encourages conversation among pubgoers.
Q⌂🚲(Monkseaton or Whitley Bay)●🖫❀

King George
56 North Parade, NE26 1PB
✪ 12-11 (midnight Fri & Sat) ☎ 07538 880371
2 changing beers 🅷
This small pub is home to the Whitley Bay microbrewery and serves beer from its range including A Dog Called Mouse and Ghost Ships, as well as guest beers from other local microbreweries. Regular buskers' nights are hosted along with the adjoining 42nd Street bar. The brewery is located in a small room at the back of the pub. ◖🚲♣❀

Bridge Hotel, Newcastle upon Tyne (Photo: Cat Button)

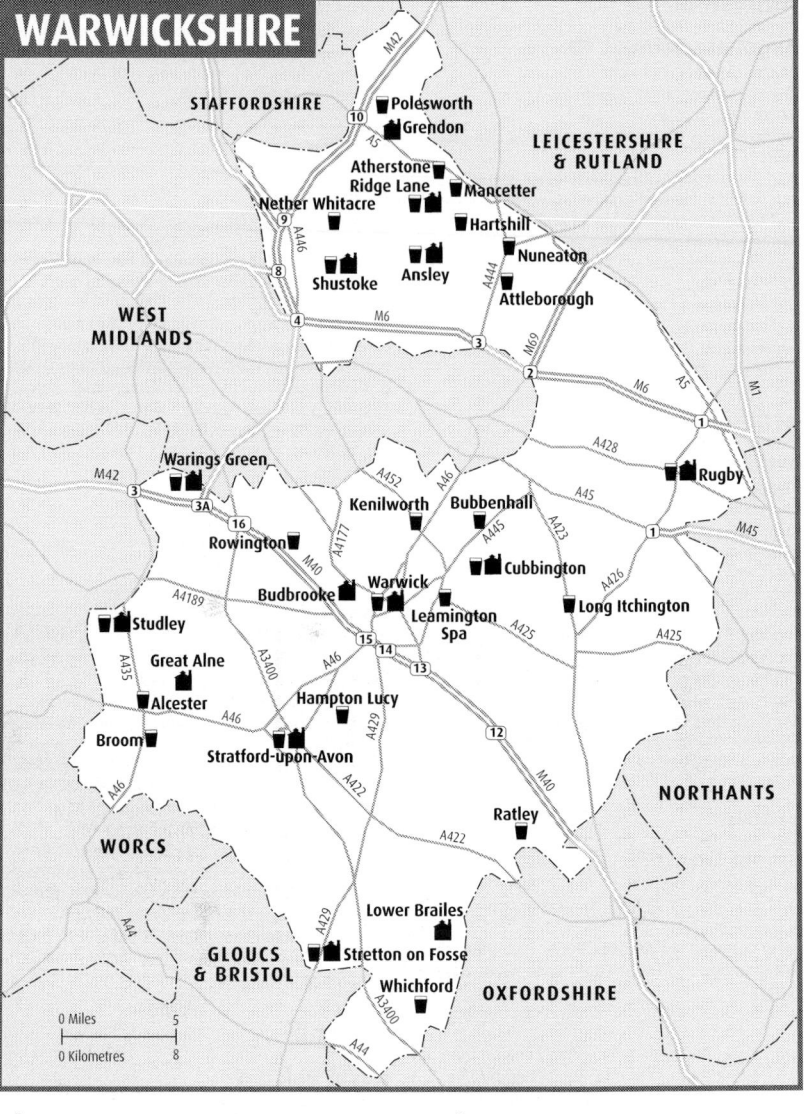

Alcester

Turk's Head
4 High Street, B49 5AD
⏰ 12 (10 Sat)-11; 12-10.30 Sun ☎ (01789) 765948
🌐 theturkshead.net
Wye Valley HPA; 3 changing beers (often Brains, Otter, Skinner's) Ⓗ
A central location helps make this a popular place. The publican is a real ale enthusiast, staging beer festivals during the summer months, either from the garden bar or from the mobile bar outside the pub during Alcester's popular food festivals. Beers are sourced from Cornwall, South Wales, Shropshire and Yorkshire to give an ever-changing range of styles and flavours. A busy dining pub, it sources the best quality ingredients to deliver classic and modern pub dishes (booking advisable).
🐾◑🚻♿🖥🛜

Ansley

Lord Nelson Inn Ⓛ ✔
Birmingham Road, CV10 9PQ
⏰ 12-11; 12-10.30 Sun ☎ (024) 7639 2305
🌐 thelordnelsoninnansley.co.uk
Sperrin Ansley Mild, Head Hunter, Band of Brothers, Third Party, Thick as Thieves; 3 changing beers Ⓗ
This nautically themed pub, thought to date back to the late 16th century, has been run by the Sperrin family since 1974 and has featured in the Guide for more than 20 consecutive years. Nine handpulls dispense Sperrin brews, ales from other breweries local and not so local, plus a real cider. There is an extensive food menu with meal nights and tribute nights hosted. The suntrap courtyard and garden are a venue for beer festivals and barbecues.
🚲🐾◑🍴🅿🖥♿

Atherstone

Angel Ale House 🄻 ✅
24 Church Street, CV9 1RN
🄾 4-11 (midnight Fri); 12-midnight Sat; 12-10.30
Sun ☎ 07525 183056
Blythe Palmers Poison; Oakham Citra; 4 changing beers 🄷
Real ale flagship with a pretty black and white exterior. The bar looks out on the market square and there is a comfortable lounge to the rear where children are allowed. Music in the bar is via customer select-and-play from the large vinyl LP collection. Six real ales are offered, often local and usually including two dark beers. A good range of real ciders is also available. Wednesday is gourmet burger night. There is a large free council car park to the rear. ⛵❀❀≈●🄡 (48,65)❀

Attleborough

Attleborough Arms
Highfield Road, CV11 4PL
🄾 11-11 (midnight Fri & Sat); 12-11 Sun ☎ (024) 7638 3231
⊕ attleborougharmspub.co.uk
Banks's Amber Ale; Marston's Pedigree; 4 changing beers 🄷
Large open-plan pub selling a good and often interesting range of various beers from the Marston's stable. Many value-for-money meal deals are on offer and the place is popular with lunchtime diners. It can get busy at times, particularly when Nuneaton Town are playing at home. Buffets can be catered for on special occasions. There is seating outside for warmer weather. ❀🄤👥P🄡❀🛜

Broom

Broom Tavern 🄻
32 High Street, B50 4HL
🄾 12-3, 5-11; 12-11 Sat & Sun ☎ (01789) 778199
⊕ broomtavern.co.uk
North Cotswold Shagweaver; Purity Pure UBU; 2 changing beers (often Stratford Upon Avon, Wye Valley) 🄷
A lovely brick and timber multi-room building which retains a great amount of character. It has been tastefully made over, while keeping the cosy snug and log fire in winter. Reopened by two experienced chefs with a good pedigree in the kitchen, it serves great food lunchtimes and evenings, made with local ingredients. Local beers are frequently found here alongside the Cornish contingents and at least one real cider. There is a choice of beer gardens. A former CAMRA branch award winner and current local CAMRA Cider Pub of the Year. ❀🄤👥👄

Bubbenhall

Malt Shovel 🄻
Lower End, CV8 3BW
🄾 12-11 ☎ (024) 7630 1141
Church End Fallen Angel; Greene King Abbot; 2 changing beers (sourced regionally; often Goff's, Purity) 🄷
An old traditional village pub at the heart of the community, offering excellent real ale and friendly service to a mixed clientele. There is a large L-shaped lounge bar and patio area at the front, and a small public bar to the rear. Good quality home-cooked food is available lunchtimes and evenings except Sundays. Behind the spacious car park lies the pleasant large walled garden. Handy for the nearby Ryton Pools Country Park and Ryton Organic Gardens. ❀🄤👥P🄡 (539)❀

Cubbington

King's Head
2 Church Hill, CV32 7JY (E end of village next to church)
🄾 12-11.30 (midnight Fri & Sat) ☎ (01926) 887142
Greene King Abbot; Sharp's Doom Bar; Wells Bombardier; Wye Valley HPA; 2 changing beers 🄷
Attractive village pub dating back to the 1890s in the shadow of the church. It comprises two cottages with varying roof lines, now knocked together and painted white. Inside, a number of distinct drinking areas reflect the original rooms. The pub is popular with ramblers and has several sports teams who raise funds for charitable causes. The large games area was once a garage. There are a few pub tables outside. A mixed clientele gives a nice feel to this hostelry. ⛵❀🄤👥👥♣P🄡 (68/67)❀🛜

Hampton Lucy

Boar's Head 🄻 ✅
Church Street, CV35 8BE
🄾 12-11 (midnight Fri & Sat); 12-8 Sun ☎ (01789) 840533
⊕ theboarsheadhamptonlucy.com
Ringwood Razorback; 4 changing beers (sourced locally; often Church End, Slaughterhouse, Stratford Upon Avon) 🄷
A friendly, popular village pub dating back to the 17th century. Originally built as a cider house, the present kitchen was once a mortuary. On a Sustrans route and close to the River Avon, it is frequented by cyclists, walkers and visitors to nearby Charlecote Park. Five real ales are served including at least two LocAles. The menu offers fresh, locally sourced home-made food. The sheltered, walled rear garden is popular in good weather. An annual themed beer festival is held in summer. ❀🄤👥P🛜

Hartshill

Royal Oak 🄻 ✅
Oldbury Road, CV10 0TD
🄾 4-11; 12-midnight Fri-Sun ☎ (024) 7639 6442
⊕ theroyaloakhartshill.co.uk
Draught Bass; 2 changing beers 🄷

REAL ALE BREWERIES
Atomic 🍺 Rugby
Blue Bell 🍺 Warings Green (brewing suspended)
Church End Ridge Lane
Church Farm Budbrooke
Clouded Minds Lower Brailes
Freestyle Shustoke
Merry Miner Grendon
North Cotswold Stretton-on-Fosse
Old Pie Factory Warwick
Purity Great Alne
Slaughterhouse Warwick
Sperrin 🍺 Ansley
Stratford Upon Avon Stratford-upon-Avon
Warwickshire Cubbington
Weatheroak Studley

A former Charles Wells pub and now a free house, the Royal Oak has been refurbished to give a good old-fashioned community feeling, with many pictures of old Hartshill on display. It offers a constantly changing range of beers from breweries near and far, alongside a cider always on handpull. A good-sized garden at the rear accommodates live music and beer festivals during the summer months. ✿❀♣♠🖤🐾✿🛜

Kenilworth

Green Man 🅛 ✅
Warwick Road, CV8 1HS
✿ 11-11 (midnight Fri); 10-midnight Sat; 10-11 Sun
☎ (01296) 863061
Brakspear Bitter; Purity Pure UBU; 8 changing beers (sourced nationally; often Black Sheep) Ⓗ
Popular and efficiently run Ember Inn within walking distance of Kenilworth town centre. The central bar has two banks of five handpumps dispensing a range of permanent and changing beers. Good-quality food is available all day until 10pm, plus brunch from 10am on Saturday and Sunday. There is an assortment of distinct seating areas and a pleasant patio. Ample parking is available and dogs are welcome throughout. Public transport passes the door.
✿❀🌙♿️P🖤(11,X17)✿🛜

Old Bakery 🏆 🅛
12 High Street, CV8 1LZ (near A429/A452 jct)
✿ 5.30-11.30; 5-11 Sun ☎ (01926) 864111
🌐 theoldbakery.eu
Wye Valley HPA; house beer (by Byatt's); 2 changing beers (sourced regionally) Ⓗ
Located in the old part of Kenilworth near St Nicholas Church and Abbey Fields, this two-roomed bar has been fashioned out of an oak-beamed 400-year-old building. There are no TV screens, music or noisy games machines, just convivial conversation and good beer. Discerning drinkers can enjoy four ales served with friendly efficiency. Home-made Monday night food is always popular. Disabled access is to the rear of the building. En-suite accommodation is available. Q✿❀🚐♿️P🖤(11)🛜

Virgins & Castle
7 High Street, CV8 1LY (A429/A452 jct)
✿ 11-11 (midnight Fri & Sat); 11-10.30 Sun
☎ (01926) 853737 🌐 virginsandcastle.co.uk
Everards Beacon Hill, Sunchaser, Tiger, Old Original; 1 changing beer (sourced nationally) Ⓗ
Established in the 16th century, this historic, multi-roomed, split-level pub lies near Abbey Fields in Kenilworth's old town. It was here that the original Coventry & Warwickshire branch of CAMRA was formed in 1974. Diners enjoy English and Filipino cuisine (no food Sun eve). A folk night is held on the second Thursday of the month. Popular beer and cider festivals feature in May and October. Dogs are welcome except in the restaurant area. Street parking is limited but there is a nearby public car park. Q✿❀🌙♿️🖤🖤(11)✿🛜

Leamington Spa

New Inn
197 Leam Terrace, CV31 1DW
✿ 12 (4 Mon)-11 ☎ (01926) 422861
Greene King Abbot; Sharp's Doom Bar, Atlantic; Wells Eagle IPA; 2 changing beers Ⓗ

A traditional and popular town pub located in a wide Victorian terrace on the outskirts of Leamington Spa. The original Victorian pub has been extended into the next-door property. A central door opens directly on to the bar, with a seating area to left and a games area to the right leading to an extension at the rear. Outside is a good-sized walled garden. Good home-cooked food is available. A quiz is hosted fortnightly on a Wednesday. ✿❀🌙♿️🖤(63/64)✿🛜

Woodland Tavern 🅛 ✅
3 Regent Street, CV32 5HW
✿ 12-midnight (1am Fri & Sat); 12-11.30 Sun
☎ (01926) 425868
Slaughterhouse Saddleback Best Bitter; Wychwood Hobgoblin; 4 changing beers Ⓗ
Characterful Victorian street-corner pub situated close to the centre of Leamington Spa and enjoyed by locals and visitors alike. It has a public bar and a separate lounge, also used as a function room. The unique partially covered courtyard features murals depicting local references and jokes. On the side of the building is a large colourful mural showing a dray and horses delivering ale to the pub. Real ciders are from Westons and Thatchers. ❀♿️♣♠🖤🐾✿🛜

Long Itchington

Green Man ✅
Church Road, CV47 9PW
✿ 5-11.30 (midnight Fri); 12-midnight Sat; 12-10.30 Sun
☎ (01926) 812208 🌐 greenmanlongitchington.co.uk
Black Sheep Best Bitter; Fuller's London Pride; Purity Mad Goose; St Austell Tribute; 1 changing beer Ⓗ
An old-fashioned village community pub, originally a farmhouse dating back to 1690 and retaining some of the original beams and low ceilings. The building has a small central bar with a number of linked drinking areas, and to the rear is a large function room. It is home to several pub teams. There are benches in the front courtyard and a good-sized garden at the back. Beyond that is a camping and caravan site. Q✿🌙🚐♿️🅰♣♠🖤P🖤(64)✿🛜

Harvester 🅛
6 Church Road, CV47 9PE
✿ 12-2.30, 6-11; 12-3, 7-10.30 Sun ☎ (01926) 812698
🌐 theharvesterinn.co.uk
Hook Norton Hooky; 2 changing beers Ⓗ
This white-fronted pub is 100 yards from the village pond, on the corner of the square. Inside is a main bar, a small drinking area and a restaurant specialising in good-value steaks. Real cider and a Belgian fruit beer are available. The pub hosts a beer festival each May bank holiday. A large walled courtyard garden to the rear has a wood-fired pizza oven. Gruntfuttocks Speciality Pickles can be purchased. ✿❀🌙♿️🅰🖤(64)✿🛜

Mancetter

Blue Boar 🅛 ✅
Watling Street, CV9 1NE
✿ 12-11 ☎ (01827) 716166 🌐 blueboarmancetter.co.uk
Marston's Pedigree; Sperrin Band of Brothers; 1 changing beer Ⓗ
Spacious multi-roomed 1940s rebuild of an earlier Blue Boar on the same site. Choose between the boisterous bar, comfy lounge, function room or

spacious conservatory restaurant. Well-regarded food is served throughout the pub, and good-value en-suite B&B is available. The Sperrin ales, nicely priced, come from the brewery located at nearby sister pub, the Lord Nelson in Ansley. The guest ale is generally a Sperrin beer. Cask ales are sold at bargain prices on Wednesday evening. ♨☆🏠◑♿P🖂

Nether Whitacre

Dog Inn ✅
Dog Lane, B46 2DU SP232930
✪ 12-3, 6-11; 12-11 Sat & Sun ☎ (01675) 481318
5 changing beers Ⓗ
Well-hidden black-and-white rural classic, with a peaceful beer garden which includes a pets' corner. Inside, brass knick-knacks abound, and in winter two hefty log fires add warmth. Easily missed is the marvellously elaborate carved frontage to the bar, including two pairs of stuffed jays. There are two cosy, intimate dining rooms to the side. The four or five guest ales are generally well-known names and change slowly – try-before-you-buy is offered. Complimentary bar nibbles are available on Sunday lunchtimes. ♨☆◑P🌸

Nuneaton

Crown
10 Bond Street, CV11 4BX (between rail and bus stations)
✪ 12-11 (midnight Fri & Sat) ☎ (024) 7637 3343
5 changing beers Ⓗ
Close to the railway and bus stations, this regular Guide entry boasts 10 handpulls dispensing five real ales and five ciders/perries, plus a large selection of malt whiskies and a choice of foreign bottled beers. Live music plays on Saturday nights. There is a large garden to the rear and a function room available for hire. Beer festivals are held in June and December. Sunday lunch is served until 4pm. The pub hosts the Nuneaton Folk Club on the first Wednesday of the month. 🌸≠●P🖂🕏

Felix Holt Ⓛ
3 Stratford Street, CV11 5BS
✪ 8-midnight (1am Wed & Thu; 2am Fri & Sat; 11 Sun)
☎ (024) 7634 7785
Byatt's Regal Blond; Greene King Abbot; Ruddles Best Bitter; Sharp's Doom Bar; changing beers Ⓗ
Large Wetherspoon outlet in the town centre. The pub takes its name from one of novelist George Eliot's works and the literary theme is reflected in the décor of books and pictures of local history. A good range of guest beers includes local ales, with Byatt's and Oakham often represented. Food is served 8am-10pm. There is a heated area for smokers. Q♨◑♿≠●🖂🕏

Horseshoes Ⓛ
2 Heath End Road, CV10 7JQ
✪ 11-11 (midnight Fri & Sat); 12-11 Sun ☎ (024) 7767 5066
Everards Sunchaser, Tiger, Old Original; 3 changing beers (sourced nationally) Ⓗ
An Everards pub selling a large range of the brewery's own beers alongside a choice of guests plus cider and perries. The pub is close to the George Eliot Hospital and Coventry Canal and has been refurbished to provide more room. The family-friendly venue is popular with diners and features various themed food nights throughout

the week. Quiz night is Wednesday. There is an outside drinking area at the side of the building. Q♨☆◑♿●P🖂🕏🕏🌸

Lord Hop ☕ Ⓛ
38 Queens Road, CV11 5JX
✪ 12-10 ☎ (024) 7798 1869
4 changing beers Ⓗ
Town-centre micropub on two levels, run by two local CAMRA members. Four or more real ales are served on handpull or straight from the cask from both local and far away breweries, plus two ciders or perries on handpull and up to six more in the chiller. Wine and soft drinks are also stocked. CAMRA magazines from various branches are available to read. No under-18s, and guide dogs only. Current local CAMRA Pub of the Year and Cider Pub of the Year. Q≠●🖂🕏

Polesworth

Bull's Head
Tamworth Road, B78 1JH (by canal bridge on B5000)
✪ 11-midnight; 11-11.30 Sun
John Smith's Bitter; Sharp's Doom Bar; Titanic Plum Porter; 1 changing beer 🌸
Pleasantly down-to-earth local next to the canal. The community feel is reflected in a wide range of activities including darts and bowls clubs, quizzes, raffles and sports screenings. There is an L-shaped bar which is generally busy plus a small lounge through the archway which tends to be quieter. The guest handpump usually features something novel. No food, but the independent Indian restaurant upstairs is happy to fetch ale for you from downstairs. ♣P🖂🕏

Ratley

Rose & Crown
OX15 6DS
✪ 12-3 (not Mon), 5-11; 12-midnight Fri & Sat; 12-11 Sun
☎ (01295) 678148 ⊕ roseandcrown-ratley.co.uk
Otter Bitter; St Austell Tribute; Wells Bombardier; 2 changing beers (sourced locally; often Derby, North Cotswold) Ⓗ
Superb rural inn on the northern extremity of the Cotswolds escarpment close to the National Trust's Upton House. Dating back to the 11th century, this gold-stone pub has a wealth of detail, exposed beams and a flagstone floor. It is cosy in winter with log stoves, and in the summer the garden proves a suntrap. High-quality food is served. Walkers and their dogs are welcome. This friendly local is reputedly haunted by the ghost of a Roundhead soldier. Q♨☆◑♣♿Å🖂🕏🌸

Ridge Lane

Church End Brewery Tap Ⓛ
CV10 0RD (2 miles SW of Atherstone)
✪ closed Mon-Wed; 6-11 Thu; 12-11 Fri & Sat; 12-10.30 Sun
☎ (01827) 713080 ⊕ churchendbrewery.co.uk
Church End Poachers Pocket, Gravediggers Ale, What the Fox's Hat, Fallen Angel; 4 changing beers Ⓗ
This brewery tap is hidden from the road, with access signposted by a board positioned at the entrance. The brewery can be viewed from the bar area. Eight handpulls serve the bar and vestry. Beers change regularly but always include a mild. The ever-changing ciders are dispensed direct from the barrel. Children are not allowed inside but

there is a large meadow garden with ample seating. The pub opens on the third Wednesday of the month for live entertainment.
Q🕭🕭&🛆🍴P🖵🐾🛜

Rowington

Rowington Club 🅛

Rowington Green, CV35 7DB (just off B4439 between Rowington and Lapworth; follow signs for Rowington Village Hall) SP1988070150
🕭 2 (12 Sat)-midnight; 12-11 Sun ☎ (01564) 782087
Sharp's Doom Bar; Wye Valley HPA; 2 changing beers (sourced nationally) Ⓗ
Busy and thriving community club, popular with locals and also open to visitors. Four real ales are on offer at all times plus a varying choice of traditional ciders. Darts matches are held on Thursday evenings. Bar snacks are available. The large beer garden overlooks the village cricket ground, and the club is handy for local walking and cycling. Always friendly, it is well worth seeking out. Q🚌🕭🕭&♣🍴P🐾🛜

Rugby

Alexandra Arms 🅛

72-73 James Street, CV21 2SL (next to John Barford car park)
🕭 11.30-11.30 (midnight Fri & Sat); 12-11.30 Sun
☎ (01788) 578660 🌐 alexandraarms.co.uk
Abbeydale Deception; Atomic Strike, Half life; Fuller's London Pride; 5 changing beers (sourced nationally) Ⓗ
This town-centre hostelry has a comfortable refurbished lounge bar where good-value pub food is served at lunchtimes. The large back bar accommodates a pool table and an excellent jukebox. There is a large rear garden which hosts a summer beer festival. The Atomic Brewery is at the back and its beers are available in the pub. Seven times local CAMRA Pub of the Year.
🚌🕭🕭&🍴≒♣🐾🐾🛜

London Calling!

11-13 Castle Street, CV21 2TP
🕭 closed Mon; 5-11 Tue-Thu; 10-1am Fri & Sun; 10-2 Sun
☎ (01788) 575430
Sharp's Doom Bar; 2 changing beers (often Church End) Ⓗ
A contemporary bar in the town centre with a music-themed decor. Up to three real ales are on offer, regularly from Church End Brewery, including its seasonal specials. Live music may be enjoyed on Saturday night, with rock, mod and ska bands often featuring in keeping with the venue's theme. Traditional English breakfasts are served on Saturday and Sunday mornings, and gourmet burger nights are held on Tuesday and Wednesday.
🚌🛜

Merchants Inn 🅛

5-6 Little Church Street, CV21 3AW
🕭 12-midnight (1am Fri & Sat); 12-11 Sun
☎ (01788) 571119 🌐 merchantsinn.co.uk
Nethergate Suffolk County Best Bitter; Oakham Bishops Farewell; Purity Mad Goose; 6 changing beers (sourced nationally) Ⓗ
Up to nine real ales are available in this flagstoned gem of a pub. Comfortable seating and an open fire make this a welcoming place to enjoy real ales, ciders, perries and foreign beers. Excellent home-

cooked food is served at lunchtime. The walls are covered in an impressive range of pub and brewery memorabilia. Rugby and cricket feature on the big screen. There are regular beer festivals, theme nights and quizzes. Situated a mile from the railway station. 🚌🕭🕭&🍴🍴♣🍴🖵🐾🛜

Raglan Arms

50 Dunchurch Road, CV22 6AD (on A426 near gyratory and town centre)
🕭 4-midnight (1am Fri); 12-1am Sat; 12-midnight Sun
☎ (01788) 544441
Abbeydale Moonshine; Fuller's London Pride; Greene King Abbot; Morland Old Golden Hen; 4 changing beers (sourced nationally; often Newby Wyke, North Cotswold) Ⓗ
Up to eight handpumps serving a fine selection of real ales await you at the friendly Raglan Arms. Full of character and a winner of many CAMRA awards, the pub hosts monthly quiz nights and screens major rugby and football sports fixtures in two bars. It offers tasty locally sourced bar snacks and can cater for corporate and special events. Outside is a heated, covered area. Pop in and you will not be disappointed at this little gem.
🚌🕭♣🍴P🖵🐾🛜

Rugby Tap 🍺 🅛

3 St Matthews Street, CV21 3BY (close to town centre adjacent to A426 gyratory)
🕭 10-6 (10 Fri & Sat); 12-3 Sun ☎ (01788) 576767
🌐 rugbytap.co.uk
6 changing beers (sourced locally; often Byatt's, Church End, Purity) Ⓖ
The Rugby Tap off-licence and adjacent Tap Room micropub stock a large selection of draught and bottled ales and ciders, and a good range of imported beers. The Tap Room offers an environment that shuns electronic entertainment, promoting conversation in an intimate setting. Acoustic music is a regular feature on Thursday evenings. The Rugby Tap serves up to six LocAles and ciders and has a range of traditional pub snacks. Q🍴🖵🐾🛜

Seven Stars

40 Albert Street, CV21 2SH
🕭 4-11 Mon; 12-11 (midnight Fri & Sat); 12-10 Sun
☎ (01788) 535478 🌐 sevenstarsrugby.co.uk
Everards Tiger; Grainstore Ten Fifty; Gun Dog Ales Booze Hound; Oakham JHB; 8 changing beers (sourced nationally) Ⓗ
Quintessential back-street local with plenty of charm and character, offering a warm and friendly welcome. The interior features plenty of Rugby Union memorabilia, and quiet background music makes conversation a delight. The bar boasts 14 handpumps, with mild and two ciders permanently on offer, and guest beers available alongside the Everards, Oakham and Grainstore regulars. A winner of many CAMRA awards in recent years.
Q🚌🕭≒🍴🖵🐾🛜

Squirrel Inn 🅛

33 Church Street, CV21 3PU
🕭 2-11; 4-11 Sun ☎ (01788) 578527
Marston's Pedigree; 4 changing beers (sourced regionally; often Cottage, Dow Bridge, Merry Miner) Ⓗ
A small, historic pub with a big welcome. A real fire in winter creates a cosy atmosphere and adds to the Squirrel's genuine charm. Live music is a big part of the pub's culture, with open mic on

Wednesday evenings and bands of various genres playing most Saturday evenings. Ales from local and independent brewers feature alongside brands from the Marston's stable. ♣♠🚲🐾

Victoria Inn 🅛
1 Lower Hillmorton Road, CV21 3ST
🕐 12 (4 Mon-Wed)-midnight ☎ (01788) 544374
🌐 downthevic.com
Atomic Strike, Half Life; Hook Norton Hooky; 7 changing beers (sourced nationally; often Abbeydale, Hop Studio, RCH) Ⓗ
A traditional Victorian real ale pub owned by the Atomic Brewery with 10 handpumps offering rapidly changing ales. Real cider is also on handpull and a selection of foreign beers is available. There is a bustling period lounge and a traditional bar with darts and pool. TV sport is regularly screened and quiz nights are held on Sunday and Wednesday evenings. Themed beer festivals feature twice a year. The railway station is less than a mile away. ♿🌟🍴♣♠🐾🛜

Shustoke

Griffin Inn 🅛
Church Road, B46 2LB (on B4116 on sharp bend)
🕐 12-2.30, 7-11; 12-11 Fri; 12-10.30 Sun ☎ (01675) 481205
Marston's Pedigree; RCH Pitchfork; Theakston Old Peculier; 7 changing beers (often Oakham) Ⓗ
Popular Guide regular which draws an audience from miles around. The interior, free from music and TV, features beams and inglenook fireplaces with solid fuel stoves. Seven guest ales always include a mild and beers from the recently upgraded Griffin Inn on-site brewery. There is always one real cider, up to four in summertime. A large, busy beer festival is the highlight of the summer. Children are welcome in the conservatory, beer terrace and meadow-style garden. No food is served on Sunday.
Q♿🌟🍴Å♣P🐾🛜

Plough ✓
The Green, B46 2AN
🕐 12-3, 5.30-11; 12-11 Fri & Sat; 12-10.30 Sun
☎ (01675) 481557 🌐 theploughinnshustoke.co.uk
Draught Bass; 4 changing beers Ⓗ
Attractive 200-year-old village green pub, popular with both locals and visitors. The bar area with a real fire is compact and cosy, with games in a separate room. There are more rooms for diners. Four guest ales are usually available, with effort invested to provide the most interesting from the Punch range. Children enjoy the feathered-and-furry pets area to the rear, while the front has a tidy beer terrace with greenery. A quiz night is held monthly. ♿🌟🍴🐶♣P🐾🛜

Stratford-upon-Avon

Bear (Swans Nest) 🅛 ✓
Swans Nest Hotel, CV37 7LT
🕐 12-midnight; 12-11 Sun ☎ (01789) 265540
🌐 thebearfreehouse.co.uk
Hook Norton Old Hooky; North Cotswold Windrush Ale; Purity Pure Gold; Stratford Upon Avon Stratford Gold; Wye Valley Butty Bach; 3 changing beers (often Brakspear, Greene King, Sadler's) Ⓗ
Historic pub in a waterside location, five minutes' walk from the town centre, serving eight real ales. The focus tends to be on local and regional brewers

such as Wye Valley, Hook Norton, Stratford Upon Avon and Purity, with seasonal beers available. The interior is decked out with wood panelling and has a pewter bar; outside, there are picnic tables for riverside drinking. Excellent home-made meals are served in a warm, friendly, welcoming atmosphere. Board games and newspapers are available. ♿🌟🛏🍴🐶♿P🖥🐾🛜

Stratford Alehouse 🅛
12B Greenhill Street, CV37 6LF
🕐 1-10.30; 2-9 Sun ☎ 07746 807966
🌐 thestratfordalehouse.com
4 changing beers (often North Cotswold, Prescott, Stratford Upon Avon) Ⓗ
A family-run, one-bar micropub serving the finest real ales, ciders and wines. There is no loud music (except on live music nights), noisy children or gaming machines to distract you here – just a friendly welcome in a relaxing environment for drinking, chatting, making new friends or reading the newspapers. Snacks are served. Since opening in 2013, more than 600 different beers have made an appearance. Home to Stratford Folk Club on a Wednesday and live bands on a Sunday. Local CAMRA branch Pub of the Year in 2016.
Q♿🚲🐶🐾

Stretton-on-Fosse

Plough Inn 🅛
Moreton-in-Marsh, GL56 9QX
🕐 11-11 ☎ (01608) 661053 🌐 strettonplough.com
North Cotswold Shagweaver; Sharp's Doom Bar; 2 changing beers (sourced regionally; often Marston's, Prescott) Ⓗ
Visitors including walkers enjoy a warm welcome at this smallish, stone-built, 17th-century Cotswold pub with oak beams, open fires and a strong focus on local produce. Ale is always on offer from North Cotswold Brewery two miles away, while Pearson's draught cider and perry have travelled less than seven miles. The food has a well-deserved reputation – booking is advisable at busy times. Spit-roasted meat is served on Sunday lunchtime (vegetarian options available). Transport to nearby accommodation is willingly arranged if needed. Q♿🌟🍴♣🐶P🛜

Studley

Weatheroak Tap House 🅛
21A High Street, B80 7HN
🕐 4-9 Mon; 12.30-10.30 Tue-Thu; 12.30-11 Fri; 12-11 Sat; 12-9 Sun ☎ (01527) 854433 🌐 weatheroakbrewery.co.uk
Weatheroak Bees Knees, Ale, Victoria Works, Redwood, Keystone Hops; 1 changing beer (sourced locally) Ⓗ
This micropub with two small, cosy rooms opened in 2016 and is the outlet for the nearby Weatheroak Brewery. Basic snacks are available and there is a chip shop next door – you are welcome to bring food into the pub. Off-sales from the nearby brewery are also available.
Q♿🐶🖥🐾🛜

Warings Green

Blue Bell Cider House
Warings Green Road, Hockley Heath, B94 6BP (S of Cheswick Green, off Ilshaw Heath Rd) SP1286074275

🕒 11.30-11 (11.30 Fri & Sat); 12-10.30 Sun
☎ (01564) 702328 ⊕ bluebellciderhouse.org
Sharp's Doom Bar; Wye Valley HPA; 3 changing beers Ⓗ
Friendly canalside free house offering five real ales and three draught ciders. Two or three beers usually come from the on-site brewhouse. The pub is popular with boaters and walkers – muddy boots and dogs welcome in the bar. The spacious lounge and cosy bar have real fires in winter, and families are welcome in the large conservatory and canalside garden. Reasonably priced food includes a Sunday carvery. Quiz night is Wednesday, poker night Thursday and live music plays on occasion.
Q🛏️🏡🍽️🍴♿♣P🐾🌾🎵

Warwick

Cape of Good Hope Ⓛ
66 Lower Cape, CV34 5DP (off Cape Rd)
🕒 11-11; 10-midnight Fri-Sun ☎ (01926) 498138
⊕ thecapeofgoodhopepub.com
Church Farm Harry's Heifer; Hook Norton Hooky; Wye Valley Butty Bach; 3 changing beers Ⓗ
This historic 1820s alehouse on the Grand Union Canal welcomes canal users and locals alike. The original building on the waterside is now the front bar, with a modern extension to the rear. Internal decorations include canal memorabilia. Three permanent real ales along with three locally sourced guest beers are offered. The staff are knowledgable and proud to serve local ales and foods. There is outside seating alongside the canal next to a sometimes busy double lock.
🛏️🏡🍴♿🅰️♣P🚆(G1)🐾🌾🎵

Old Post Office Ⓛ
12 West Street, CV32 6AN
🕒 closed Mon; 12-9; 12-5 Sun ☎ 07765 896155
Slaughterhouse Saddleback Best Bitter; Young's Special Ⓗ**; 4 changing beers** Ⓗ/Ⓖ
Warwick's first alehouse offers a relaxed atmosphere and traditional beers served on handpump and straight from the cask. Popular with local residents, the small bar is housed in a former shop below the West Gate and within walking distance of Warwick Castle. It is decorated with a collection of pub memorabilia and Batman hangs from the ceiling drinking a pint. No food is served but you are welcome to bring your own.
🛏️🅰️♥🚆🐾

Punch Bowl
1 The Butts, CV34 4SS
🕒 12 (5 Mon)-11; 12-11.30 Thu; 12-10 Sun
☎ (01926) 403846 ⊕ punchbowlwarwick.co.uk
5 changing beers Ⓗ
The building is an old coaching inn and hostelry dating back to the early-19th century. It has a large, open bar area on different levels – a raised area acts as a stage for popular music evenings held every Thursday and on special occasions. International sports events are shown on a large

screen. Five changing guest beers are available at all times. A blackboard behind the bar keeps a tally of different beers sold under the current ownership. 🛏️🏡🏨🅰️🚆♣♥P🚆(X17)🐾🌾

Tilted Wig ✅
11 Market Place, CV34 4SA
🕒 11-11 (midnight Fri & Sat) ☎ (01926) 400110
⊕ tiltedwigwarwick.co.uk
Morland Old Golden Hen; Purity Mad Goose; Sharp's Doom Bar; 1 changing beer Ⓗ
The pub is set in a Grade II-listed, 17th-century Georgian building, once part of a market hall. The frontage is made up of a series of arches. Located in the market square, it has one light airy bar, but the layout and decor divide into three distinct spaces. Seating outside in the square on fine days has a relaxed continental feel, and there is also a small courtyard to the rear. Real cider is available.
Q🛏️🏨🏡🍴♿🚆♥🚆🐾🌾

Wild Boar 🍺 Ⓛ
27 Lakin Road, CV34 5BU
🕒 12-11.30 (12.30am Fri & Sat); 12-10.30 Sun
☎ (01926) 499968 ⊕ thewildboarwarwick.co.uk
Slaughterhouse Saddleback Best Bitter; 9 changing beers (often Everards, Slaughterhouse) Ⓗ
Award-winning Project William community pub, close to the railway station. An end-of-terrace Victorian building, it has a bar, snug and separate beer hall which was formerly a skittle alley. The taphouse for Slaughterhouse Brewery, the on-site microbrewery can be viewed from within the pub. Ten handpumps deliver Slaughterhouse, Everards and guest ales alongside two real ciders. Outside there is a hop garden – the hops are used for Slaughterhouse's annual brew, the Green Hopper.
Q🛏️🏡🏨♣♥P🚆(X17)🐾🌾

Whichford

Norman Knight 🍺 Ⓛ
CV36 5PE
🕒 12-3 (not Mon), 6-11; 12-11 Fri & Sat; 12-6 Sun
☎ (01608) 684621 ⊕ thenormanknight.co.uk
Hook Norton Hooky; Stratford Upon Avon Stratford Gold, Mosaic, Malty Pig Bitter, Immortal; 1 changing beer (sourced locally) Ⓗ
Stratford Upon Avon Brewery taphouse, with six handpumps showcasing an eclectic range alongside local beers and organic cider. The pub has a well-earned reputation as a drinking destination and also offers wonderful food served fresh to order made with local ingredients. It has two flagstone-floored rooms, a restaurant and a beer garden overlooking the green. Live music plays most weeks and a quiz night is held once a month. Classic cars gather on the third Thursday of the month throughout the summer. Glamping pods and a holiday apartment are available. Local CAMRA Pub of the Year 2017. 🏡🏨🍴♥P

Join CAMRA

The Campaign for Real Ale has been fighting for over 45 years to save Britain's proud heritage of cask-conditioned ales, independent breweries, and pubs that offer a good choice of beer. You can help that fight by joining the campaign: use the form at the back of the guide or see **www.camra.org.uk**

WEST MIDLANDS

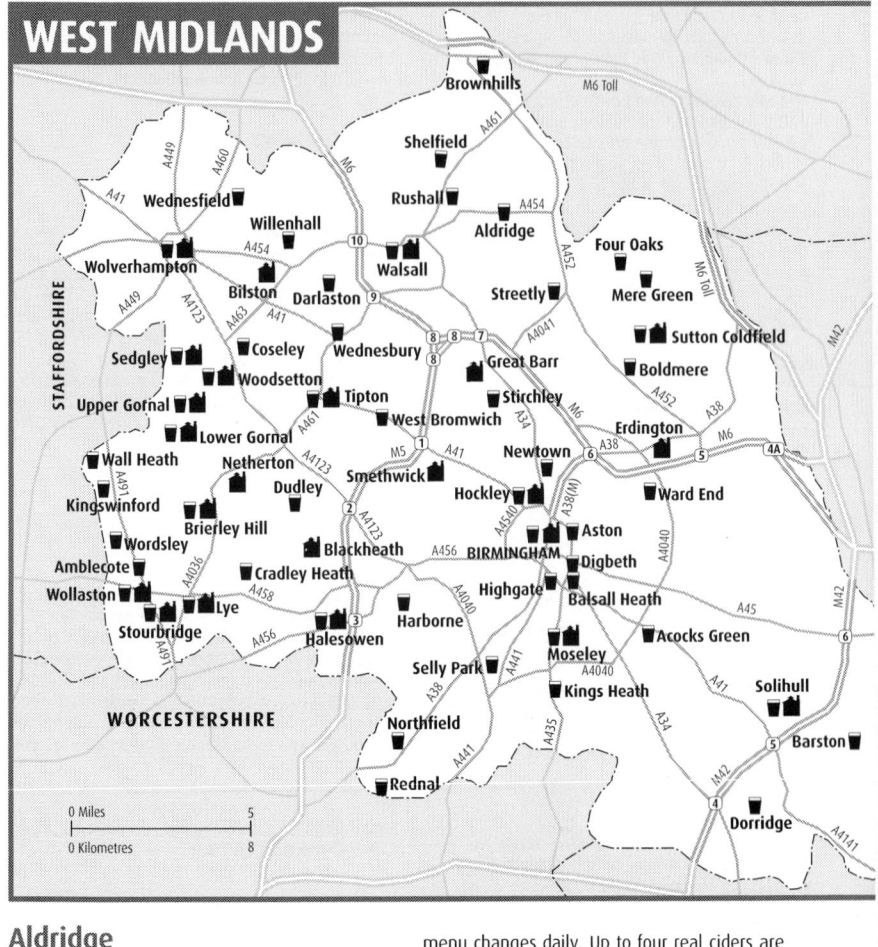

Aldridge

Lazy Hill Tavern 🅛
196 Walsall Wood Road, WS9 8HB
☼ 6-11; 12-2.30, 7-10.30 Sun ☎ (01922) 457244
Blythe Staffie; Greene King Abbot; Holden's Black Country Mild, Golden Glow; Morland Old Speckled Hen; Wye Valley Butty Bach; 1 changing beer (sourced nationally) Ⓗ
Large and welcoming family-run free house with the same licensee for nearly 40 years. The building was originally a farmhouse which was converted into a country club, then finally a pub in 1986. Four separate areas are all similarly and comfortably furnished, with a logburner in two. The large 160-seater function room is used midweek by local sports/community organisations. A car park is at the rear of the pub, but plenty of off-road parking is nearby. P🖳🛜

Turtle's Head 🅛
14 Croft Parade, WS9 8LY
☼ 12 (5 Mon)-10; 12-10.30 Fri & Sat; 12-9 Sun
☎ (01922) 325635
4 changing beers (sourced locally; often Backyard, Church End, Fixed Wheel) Ⓗ
Micropub with a warm welcome, opened in November 2015 in the centre of town. Four handpulls serve a range of ales from throughout the UK. No regular beers are sold and the beer

menu changes daily. Up to four real ciders are available, increasing to eight in summer months. Food consists of filled rolls and bar snacks, with a selection of complimentary cheeses and pates provided on Sunday. Dogs are welcome.
🛏🛆🍴🖳🐾🛜

Amblecote

Robin Hood 🅛
196 Collis Street, DY8 4EQ (on A4102 one-way street off Brettell Lane, A461)
☼ 12 (4 Mon & Tue)-11; 12-midnight Fri & Sat ☎ 07436 793462
Bathams Best Bitter; Enville Ginger Beer; Holden's Golden Glow; St Austell Proper Job; Sarah Hughes Dark Ruby Mild; Wye Valley Bitter; 4 changing beers (often Titanic) Ⓗ
Good ales, quality food and a warm welcome – this is a fine traditional Black Country local. In 2015 the Robin Hood celebrated 160 years as a licensed house and was CAMRA branch Pub of the Year. The front rooms house a wonderful beer bottle collection, including international and historic brews. The pub hosts occasional themed culinary nights, and is set to resume its beer festivals. The LocAle scheme is emphasised, with more local beers available. The real cider is Thatchers Heritage. Q🛏🐕🍴🚲🛆🅿🖳🛜

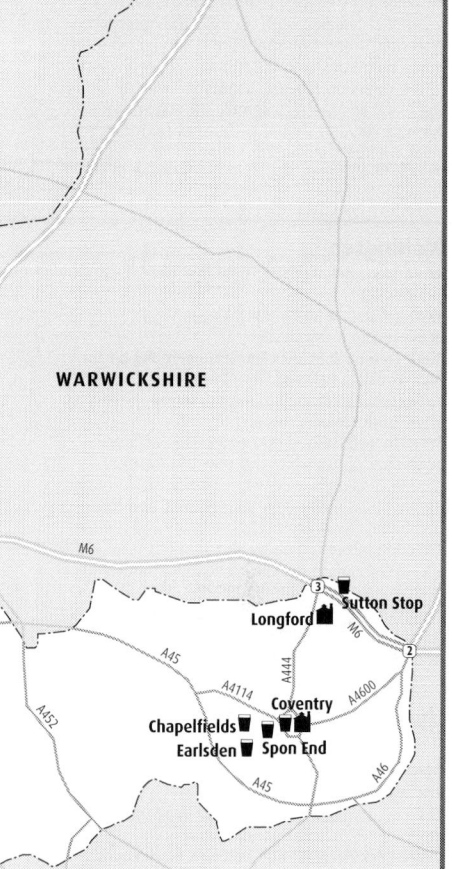

WARWICKSHIRE

M6

3 Sutton Stop
Longford
M6
A45
A444
2
A4114
Coventry A4600
A452
Chapelfields
Earlsden Spon End
A45
A46

Swan

10 Brettell Lane, DY8 4BN (on A461, ½ mile after A491)
🕐 7 (12 Sat)-11; 12-3, 7-10.30 Sun ☎ (01384) 76932
3 changing beers Ⓗ
This free house separates into a basic, lively public bar and a more sedate, cosy lounge, with a well-kept garden to the rear. Three changing beers are permanently offered. If you want a beer you have never seen before, let alone tasted, this is the place to go. Cobs are sold at lunchtime and there is a varied selection of whiskies to choose from.
🏮🕩🖩(246)🛜

Barston

Bull's Head 🅛 ✓

Barston Lane, B92 0JU (on main street in village, opp church) SP2073378090
🕐 11-2.30, 5-11; 11-11 Fri & Sat; 12-11 Sun
☎ (01675) 442830 ⊕ thebullsheadbarston.co.uk
Adnams Southwold Bitter; Purity Mad Goose; 2 changing beers (sourced nationally) Ⓗ
A true country village local, formerly a 15th-century coaching inn, with two comfortable bars with real fires and an intimate restaurant. A friendly welcome from locals and staff is assured. The pub is Cask Marque accredited, with two regular ales and two guests always of reliable quality. It has been local CAMRA Pub of the Year

seven times and has featured in this Guide almost continuously since 1993. A good-value food menu is complemented by seasonal home-cooked food. The pub hosts the annual village fête on the August bank holiday. Q🏮🐾🕩P🐾🛜

Birmingham: Acocks Green

Inn on the Green 🍺 🅛

2 Westley Road, B27 7UH
🕐 11-11 (midnight Fri); 10-midnight Sat & Sun
☎ (0121) 708 0108 ⊕ innonthegreen.pub
6 changing beers (sourced nationally; often Wye Valley) Ⓗ
Run by a keen and passionate landlord who is an active CAMRA member, with friendly and knowledgable staff. The pub hosts regular entertainment and shows live sport, with live music at the weekend. Excellent beer festivals are held four times a year. Four handpulls are in use during the week and six at weekends. The same beer is rarely on twice, making this a great place to discover ales from new breweries. Local CAMRA branch Pub of the Year for 2015. 🏮♿≉🖤P🖩🛜

Birmingham: Aston

Eagle & Ball

Gopsal Street, B4 7RJ
🕐 11-11 (2am Fri); 12-11.30 Sat; 4-11 Sun
☎ (0121) 331 7777 ⊕ eagleandball.co.uk
Greene King IPA; Sadler's Peaky Blinder Ⓗ
The Eagle & Ball was built in the 1840s and opened as a back-street public house some time in the 1850s. Originally one of the first Ansells pubs in

REAL ALE BREWERIES

AJ's Walsall
Angel Ales Halesowen
Backyard Walsall
Banks's Wolverhampton
Bathams Brierley Hill
Birmingham Birmingham (NEW)
Black Country 🍴 Lower Gornal
Blue Bear Smethwick
Brewhouse & Kitchen 🍴 Sutton Coldfield
Broughs Wolverhampton
Burning Soul Birmingham: Hockley (NEW)
Byatt's Coventry
Craddock's 🍴 Stourbridge
Dhillon's Longford
Edmunds 🍴 Birmingham
Fixed Wheel Blackheath
Fownes Upper Gornal
Froth Blowers Erdington
Green Duck Stourbridge
Holden's Woodsetton
Indian Great Barr
Moseley Moseley (NEW)
Newbridge Bilston
Olde Swan Netherton
Pig Iron Brierley Hill
Rock & Roll Birmingham: Hockley
Sadler's Lye
Sarah Hughes 🍴 Sedgley
Silhill Solihull
Thousand Trades Birmingham (NEW)
Toll End 🍴 Tipton
Twisted Barrel Coventry
Two Towers Birmingham
Websters 🍴 Wollaston

GOOD BEER GUIDE 2018

Birmingham, it promised the local residents good ale, good times and an array of musical entertainment. Now a Grade II-listed building, it has been lovingly restored and incorporated into the new Birmingham City University building. 🐕🍽️♿

Birmingham: Balsall Heath

Old Moseley Arms 🄻
53 Tindal Street, B12 9QU (400yds off Moseley Rd)
🕐 12-11 (midnight Fri & Sat) ☎ (0121) 440 1954
🌐 oldmoseleyarms.co.uk
Church End Cuthberts; Enville Ale; Wye Valley HPA, Butty Bach; 1 changing beer (sourced nationally) Ⓗ
This is a traditional 19th-century pub; nowadays, the left bar has an 80-inch screen for sport, the right bar has the jukebox. There is an upstairs room for functions, pool table and Sunday evening music, and there are comfy sofas in the covered garden/smoking area. A superb tandoori menu is served Monday to Saturday evenings, and from 1pm on Sunday. Regular beer festivals feature 16 ales, cider and perry. Live music showcasing local talent is on upstairs every Sunday evening.
🐕🐾🍽️♣🚃(50)📶

Birmingham: City Centre

Gunmakers Arms 🄻
93 Bath Street, B4 6HG
🕐 12-midnight ☎ (0121) 439 7253 🌐 gunmakersarms.com
Two Towers Hockley Gold, Complete Muppetry, Chamberlain Pale Ale; 2 changing beers (often Two Towers) Ⓗ
This is the Two Towers Brewery tap, with the brewery next to the beer garden. The Grade II-listed pub is a small traditional venue opposite the Children's Hospital, just a few minutes' walk from Snow Hill station and St Chad's metro. Six handpulls serve a range of Two Towers ales and occasional guest beers. There are also locally sourced ciders. The pub hosts a range of events from book readings to beer festivals. Traditional pub food, often incorporating Two Towers beers, is available.
🐾🍽️≠🍴♣👆

Post Office Vaults 🄻
84 New Street, B2 4BA (entrances on both New St and Pinfold St)
🕐 11-11 (midnight Fri & Sat); 12-11 Sun ☎ (0121) 643 7354
🌐 postofficevaults.co.uk
Hobsons Mild; house beer (by Kinver); 6 changing beers (sourced nationally) Ⓗ
Only a two-minute walk from the Stephenson Street entrance to New Street station and close to Victoria Square, this subterranean pub offers a range of eight traditional beers in excellent condition. At least 350 different bottled beers are also available from all over the world, one of the largest ranges in the country, as well as 14 ciders and perries. The extremely knowledgable staff will make your visit a pleasure. Q≠🍴♣👆🚃🐾📶

Pure Craft Bar & Kitchen 🄻
30 Waterloo Street, B2 5TJ (5 mins from New St and Snow Hill stations)
🕐 11-11 (midnight Fri & Sat); 12-10 Sun ☎ (0121) 237 5666
Purity Bunny Hop, Pure Gold, Mad Goose; 4 changing beers (sourced nationally; often Kirkstall, Rooster's, Tiny Rebel) Ⓗ

Birmingham's newest real ale outlet, set in a traditional building with an industrial interior on Waterloo Street. Gourmet food is served, all food is made with beer, and the menu has been matched to the beers on the bar. Landlord James describes the place as a perfect democratic environment where everyone should be able to find their ideal beer. A large chalkboard behind the bar provides details of all beers available. 🐕🍽️≠🍴♣🚃📶

Wellington 🄻
37 Bennetts Hill, B2 5SN (5 mins from New St and Snow Hill stations)
🕐 10-midnight ☎ (0121) 200 3115
🌐 thewellingtonrealale.co.uk
Black Country Bradley's Finest Golden, Pig on the Wall, Fireside; Oakham Citra; Purity Mad Goose; Wye Valley HPA; 10 changing beers (sourced nationally; often Froth Blowers, Titanic) Ⓗ
Recently refurbished and extended, with an additional upstairs bar and roof terrace beer garden, this multiple award-winner is a veritable beer festival every day. Sixteen ales and three traditional ciders are on handpump, and a wide selection of bottled beers and whiskies is served to a varied clientele by knowledgable staff. Regular quizzes, cheese nights and darts competitions are held. No food is served, but you are welcome to bring your own – plates, cutlery and condiments provided. Q🐾≠🍴♣🚃📶

Birmingham: Digbeth

Spotted Dog 🄻
104 Warwick Street, B12 0NH
🕐 5-11; 3-1am Fri; 12-1am Sat; 12-midnight Sun
☎ (0121) 772 3822 🌐 spotteddog.co.uk
Castle Rock Harvest Pale; Holden's Black Country Mild; 2 changing beers (sourced nationally) Ⓗ
This is a traditional multi-roomed pub with an Irish feel, off the beaten track but well worth a trip. Excellent Holden's Mild is sold at a competitive price. It has a large covered garden/smoking area with heaters and a barbecue area. Live traditional Irish music plays on Monday, jazz night is Tuesday, blues night Thursday. There is a mixture of sports on the large screen, but especially rugby. Excellent Scotch eggs, including vegetarian and gluten-free, are sold. The pub can be busy when Birmingham City are at home. 🐕🐾🍽️≠🍴♣📶

Woodman ★ 🄻
New Canal Street, B5 5LG (opp old Curzon St by Millennium Point)
🕐 12-11 (midnight Fri) ☎ (0121) 643 4960
Castle Rock Black Gold, Harvest Pale; 6 changing beers (sourced nationally) Ⓗ
This environmentally friendly and recently refurbished pub is Grade II-listed and on CAMRA's National Inventory of Historic Pub Interiors. It has a red-bricked tile and terracotta exterior, with an L-shaped bar tiled above a wooden dado. A tiled lobby on Albert Street leads to a small, attractive drinking area, with a hatch to the servery, as well as a real fire. The third plain room on the left now makes for a pleasant dividing area. Good food is served daily. It has a quiz night every Wednesday and an outside seating/dining area.
Q🐾🍽️♿≠🍴♣🚃📶

Birmingham: Harborne

White Horse ✓
2 York Street, B17 0HG

🕓 11 (12 Mon)-11.30; 11-12.30am Fri & Sat; 12-11.30 Sun
☎ (0121) 427 8004 ⊕ whitehorseharborne.com

Greene King Abbot; 9 changing beers (sourced nationally; often Bathams, Holden's, Three Tuns) Ⓗ
A much-improved and extended free house just off the busy High Street. There is an island bar with a front snug and a rear heated area. With a strong emphasis on real ale, it has an electronic beer board linked to its website. Regular live music nights are held on Friday and Saturday, and an open mic night on the last Wednesday of the month. Quiz night is every Tuesday. The food menu is basic. The artwork on the walls is by local artists, including the landlord. Ostlers Ales is brewed on the premises. 🏠&♿🍴🚃🅿🐾🛜

Birmingham: Highgate

Lamp Tavern Ⓛ
157 Barford Street, B5 6AH (500yds from A441
Pershore Rd near bottom of Hurst St)

🕓 12.30-11 ☎ (0121) 688 1220

Everards Ascalon; Hobsons Mild; Rock & Roll Brew Springsteen; Stanway Stanney Bitter; 2 changing beers (sourced nationally; often Abbeydale, Malvern Hills, Rock & Roll) Ⓗ
A warm welcome awaits from Eddie, a landlord of more than 20 years standing, at this characterful, single-roomed, street-corner local. The Lamp was the original home to Rock & Roll Brewery and regularly sells one of its beers. It is also the only Birmingham pub to supply Stanway Stanney Bitter. A Guide regular, it hosts a weekly folk club on Friday evening. Q&♿♣🚃

Birmingham: Hockley

1000 Trades
16 Frederick Street, B1 3HE

🕓 4-11 (midnight Thu & Fri); 12-midnight Sat; 12-10 Sun
☎ (0121) 233 6291 ⊕ 1000trades.org.uk

4 changing beers (sourced nationally; often Titanic) Ⓗ
This delightful addition to the Jewellery Quarter has distinctive bare boards and brickwork, and full-width doors opening on to the pavement, helping to give it its distinctive atmosphere. An independent beer bar, it has four handpumps, usually with at least one beer from a local micro. The cask offering is supported by an interesting range of bottled beers. It runs kitchen residencies, often street food and characterised by ever-changing variety. Also a music venue, it showcases independent labels. ♦&♿🚃🅿

Black Eagle Ⓛ
16 Factory Road, B18 5JU (turn right out of Soho Benson Road metro station, cross road and walk 200yds)

🕓 11.30-3, 5.30-11; 11.30-11 Fri; 12-11 Sat; 12-3 Sun
☎ (0121) 523 4008 ⊕ theblackeaglepub.co.uk

Marston's Pedigree; Sadler's Peaky Blinder; Timothy Taylor Landlord; 3 changing beers (often Dark Star, Holden's, Salopian) Ⓗ
Traditional award-winning multi-room pub that also features a restaurant to the rear. While slightly off the beaten track, this real ale oasis is well worth seeking out for its excellent range of beers and good-value food. Three guest ales are always stocked and an annual beer festival is staged in the summer. Occasional barbecues are held. Real cider and perry usually come from Westons and Gwynt y Ddraig. 🏠&♿🍴🚃🐾🛜

Red Lion Ⓛ
95 Warstone Lane, B18 6NG

🕓 10-midnight (2am Fri & Sat) ☎ (0121) 233 9144
⊕ theredlionbirmingham.com

Wye Valley Butty Bach; 3 changing beers (sourced nationally; often Bathams) Ⓗ
Traditional two-roomed pub, rich in local heritage and modern art. It has a lively front bar, a cosy back lounge and a good-sized club room upstairs. There is a sheltered patio and smoking area to the rear. An excellent and extensive food menu is served all day, with a Cow Club on Monday. There are three changing guest beers and two changing ciders. Regular quiz nights are held and large screens show sporting events. 🏠🌰♦🍴🚃🐾🛜

Rock & Roll Tap House Ⓛ
Unit 2, 60 Regent Place, B3 1UG

🕓 5-9 Fri; 12-9 Sat; closed Sun-Thu

Rock & Roll Brew Springsteen, Thirst Aid Kit; 1 changing beer (often Rock & Roll) Ⓗ
A small, quirky brewery taproom bedecked with music memorabilia. There are usually three vegan-friendly ales available, always including a dark ale. 🚃🅿

Rose Villa Tavern ★ ✓
172 Warstone Lane, B18 6JW

🕓 12-midnight (1am Fri); 11-1am Sat & Sun
☎ (0121) 236 7910 ⊕ therosevillatavern.co.uk

Sharp's Doom Bar; 4 changing beers Ⓗ
A former red-brick corner pub now owned by the Bitters 'n' Twisted chain that also runs the Victoria (John Bright Street) and New Inn (Harborne). The Grade II-listed building is on CAMRA's National Inventory of Historic Pub Interiors. The interior has beautiful tiling and stained-glass windows. There are five handpumps offering a changing range of ales, over 100 vodkas and an interesting cocktail menu. Various forms of entertainment feature throughout the week. It serves an American diner-style food menu. 🏠♦&♿🚃🅿🛜

Birmingham: Kings Heath

Kings Heath Cricket & Sports Club ✓
Charlton House, 247 Alcester Road South, B14 6DT

🕓 12-midnight ☎ (0121) 444 1913
⊕ kingsheathsportsclub.com

Wye Valley HPA, Butty Bach; 2 changing beers (sourced nationally; often Greene King) Ⓗ
Welcoming sports club where CAMRA members are permitted entry on production of a membership card (maximum 10 visits per year). The club has two rooms – a comfortable lounge for relaxed drinking and a large room for watching sporting events on large screens, also housing two full-size snooker tables. The beer range always includes two rotating guest ales. Varying social events are held throughout the year, including live music. Q🏠🌰♦&♣🐾🅿🛜

Pear Tree Ⓛ ✓
25-27 Alcester Road South, B14 7JQ

🕓 9am-11.30 (midnight Thu; 1am Fri & Sat)
☎ (0121) 441 6710

Greene King Abbot; Ruddles County; 6 changing beers Ⓗ

An excellent Wetherspoon outlet run by an enthusiastic manager who is a keen CAMRA member. The guest beers are highly driven by the LocAle policy, and many local beers feature. Between four and six guest ales are available, plus a selection of real ciders and perries. The building is a former bank and easily accessible by public transport. In winter months a large gas fire in the middle of the room gives the impression of an open fire. Food is the standard Wetherspoon fare. ⛄🍽️♿♣🚅🚌🚃🛜

Birmingham: Moseley

Prince of Wales 🄻 ✅
118 Alcester Road, B13 8EE
🕐 12-11.30 (1am Fri & Sat) ☎ (0121) 449 4198
🌐 theprincemoseley.co.uk
Oakham Citra; Purity Mad Goose; Timothy Taylor Landlord; 3 changing beers (often Castle Rock, Holden's) Ⓗ
Serving cask ales since 1861, this pub is a real community local – the front bar boasts an authentic Victorian bar back and there are two further rooms to the rear leading to a beer garden and cigar smoke room boasting the largest selection of Cuban cigars in the country. Two ciders are on sale, alongside a good selection of whiskies and interesting cocktails. There is a TV for sport, a real fire and a quiz night every Tuesday. 🕷🍽️🚌🛜🛜

Birmingham: Newtown

Bartons Arms ★ ✅
144 High Street, B6 4UP
🕐 12-11; 12-10.30 Sun ☎ (0121) 333 5988
🌐 thebartonsarms.com
Oakham JHB, Inferno, Citra, Bishops Farewell; 2 changing beers (sourced nationally; often Oakham) Ⓗ
A stunning red-bricked pub run by Oakham Brewery from Peterborough. The 1901 interior is Grade II listed and mentioned in CAMRA's National Inventory of Historic Pub Interiors. It has ornate Minton tiles throughout, including a central tiled staircase, original stained-glass windows and snob screens on the bar. Superb Thai food is served in the lounge. A range of Oakham Ales is available, plus usually one guest beer and a cider. Quiz night is Monday and regular music and beer festivals are held. ⛄🍽️🍴🅿🚌🛜

Birmingham: Northfield

Black Horse ★ 🄻 ✅
Bristol Road South, B31 2QT (opp Sainsbury's)
🕐 8am-11 (1am Fri & Sat); 8am-midnight Sun
☎ (0121) 477 1800
Greene King Abbot; Ruddles Best Bitter; Sharp's Doom Bar; 7 changing beers (sourced nationally; often Adnams, Fuller's, Purity) Ⓗ
Large inter-war mock-Tudor roadhouse offering the only extensive real ale choice in this part of the city, transformed from being an undesirable local to a popular pub serving consistently good-quality beer. Unusually for Wetherspoon's, this pub has a multi-room layout and bars on two levels. It still retains the original baronial hall entrance but the bar has been tastefully refurbished with an etched-glass entrance door. There is a bowling green with original outbuildings to the rear.
Q⛄🕷🍽️♿🍴🅿🚌🛜

Birmingham: Rednal

Old Hare & Hounds ✅
426 Lickey Road, B45 8UU
🕐 11.30-11 (12.30am Fri); 10-12.30am Sat; 11-10.30 Sun
☎ (0121) 457 9743
Black Sheep Best Bitter; Brakspear Bitter; house beer (by Black Sheep); 3 changing beers Ⓗ
A large, one-roomed Ember Inns pub at the foot of the Lickey Hills, near to buses from the city centre, Halesowen, Bromsgrove and Redditch. There is a discount on the price of real ales on Monday. Good-quality food is served daily. The pub has open fires in the winter, a beer garden and a covered smoking area. ⛄🕷🍽️♿🅿🚌(47,98)🛜

Birmingham: Selly Park

Selly Park Tavern 🄻 ✅
592 Pershore Road, B29 7HQ
🕐 11.30-11 (midnight Fri & Sat); 12-11 Sun
☎ (0121) 472 4392
House beer (by Black Sheep); 6 changing beers (sourced nationally) Ⓗ
An Ember Inns red-bricked pub dating to 1901, with a varied clientele, run by the same manager for over 10 years. The large one-roomed pub has smaller areas providing some privacy. The regular and guest ales are served by friendly staff. There is an active bowling club and a skittle alley at the rear. Less than one mile from Edgbaston Cricket Ground, it is handy for visiting fans.
🕷🚐🍽️♿🚑♣🚅🚌(45,47)

Birmingham: Stirchley

Wildcat Tap
1466 Pershore Road, B30 2NT
🕐 closed Mon & Tue; 5-11 Wed-Fri; 12-11 Sat; 12-6 Sun
🌐 stirchleywildcat.co.uk
3 changing beers (sourced nationally) Ⓖ
A small, independent pub offering three cask beers served via gravity dispense, complemented by a selection of bottled beers, gins, whiskies and soft drinks. If you are planning to travel far to come and have a drink here, please check it is open beforehand by dropping an email to liam@stirchleywildcat.co.uk. ✍

Birmingham: Ward End

Hornet ✅
991 Alum Rock Road, B8 2LY
🕐 8am-11 ☎ (0121) 789 5920
Greene King IPA, Abbot; Sharp's Doom Bar; 2 changing beers Ⓗ
Herbert Austin's famous motor works stood near this establishment, which bears the name of his famous Hornet model, produced from 1930 until the mid-1970s. The usual selection of house beers and lagers is found and the food is the standard Wetherspoon fare. It is somewhat smaller than the average Wetherspoon house. ⛄🍽️♿🚅🚌🛜

Boldmere

Bishop Vesey 🄻 ✅
63 Boldmere Road, B73 5UY
🕐 8am-11 (midnight Fri & Sat) ☎ (0121) 355 5077
Backyard Blonde; Greene King Abbot; Oakham Citra; Ruddles Best Bitter; Sharp's Doom Bar; 7 changing beers Ⓗ

This busy Wetherspoon pub is named after Sutton Coldfield's Tudor benefactor; his ghost is not thought to use the wooden pulpit at the pub entrance. The open-plan interior includes upstairs seating, and there is a pleasantly green rear patio. With 17 consecutive years in the Guide, it is a frequent Pub of the Year for the local CAMRA branch. The loyal local clientele includes a thriving darts team. Up to seven interesting guest beers, many from local micros, are served, and one changing real cider. ☺🕭🌑🕩🕭🚆🌲🍴🛒🛜

Brierley Hill

Rose & Crown 🅛
161 Bank Street, DY5 3DD (on B4179)
🕮 12-11 (midnight Fri & Sat) ☎ (01384) 936166
Holden's Black Country Mild, Black Country Bitter, Golden Glow, Special; house beer (by Holden's); 1 changing beer (often Holden's) 🅗
A traditional pub that was originally two terraced properties. One end of the bar is dominated by a dartboard. A conservatory provides extra space and is used as a separate dining area, opening on to a small garden with tables and benches. A selection of good-value food is served. There is a bus stop outside the pub, or a five-minute walk takes you to Brierley Hill High Street which is served by several bus routes. Q☺🕭🕩🌲🅿🚆(222,255)🐾🛜

Vine
10 Delph Road, DY5 2TN
🕮 12-11; 12-10.30 Sun ☎ (01384) 78293
Bathams Mild Ale, Best Bitter 🅗
Unspoilt brewery tap with an ornately decorated façade proclaiming the Shakespearian quotation: 'Blessing of your heart, you brew good ale.' In this elongated pub with a labyrinthine feel the front bar is staunchly traditional, while the larger rear room has its own servery, leather seating and a dartboard. The homely lounge was partly converted from former brewery offices. Black Country lunches, such as faggots and pie, are served weekdays, and generously filled rolls at other times. CAMRA branch Pub of the Year 2016. Q☺🕭🕩🌲🅿🚆(X96)🐾🛜

Brownhills

Swan 🅛
Pelsall Road, WS8 7DL
🕮 4 (2 Fri)-midnight; 12-midnight Sat & Sun
☎ (01543) 820628
Holden's Golden Glow; 2 changing beers 🅗
A cracking local pub with two rooms served by a central bar. The main drinking area is to the right of the front entrance, with a lounge to the left. Beyond the lounge, a separate space houses the pool table. There is room for outside drinking at the front and a covered smoking area to the rear. A comfortable and welcoming venue both for locals and visitors, it was recent local CAMRA Pub of the Year. ☺🕭🌲🅿🐾🛜

Coseley

Old Chainyard 🅛
63 Castle Street, WV14 9DW
🕮 12-11 (11.30 Fri & Sat)
2 changing beers (often Fixed Wheel, Oakham, Salopian) 🅗

Single-roomed community pub full of local character in the heart of Roseville village. The A4123 Wolverhampton-Birmingham road is close by and the public transport is excellent. Two real ales from local breweries are available. The manageress, Amanda, takes great pride in her cellar management and welcomes suggestions for future guest beers. It is a brief walk from Coseley train station, which has regular services between Wolverhampton and Birmingham. ☺🕭🚆🌲🅿🚆🐾🛜

Coventry: Chapelfields

Nursery Tavern
38-39 Lord Street, CV5 8DA (1 mile W of city centre, off Allesley Old Rd)
🕮 12-11.30 (midnight Fri & Sat); 12-11 Sun
☎ (024) 7667 4530
Courage Best Bitter; Fuller's London Pride; 4 changing beers (sourced nationally) 🅗
Very much a community pub, in a Victorian terraced street in the old watchmaking quarter. Comprising three rooms, the front two are served by a central bar where conversation dominates. The rear room hosts local societies and clubs, charity events, quizzes and music nights promoting local talent. It also serves as a restaurant providing excellent-value traditional roast meals on Sunday lunchtime. Beer festivals are held in the rear garden every June and December. Dogs are welcome. Q☺🕭🕩🌲🍴🛒🚆🐾🛜

Coventry: City Centre

Drapers 🅛
Earl Street, CV1 5RU
🕮 10-10 (11 Wed & Thu; midnight Fri & Sat); closed Sun
☎ (024) 7622 1100
Purity Mad Goose; 2 changing beers (sourced nationally; often Purity, Siren, Thornbridge) 🅗
A retro-style, two-floor café bar conveniently located next to the Herbert Art Gallery and the city's famous cathedrals. Popular with students, university staff and city-centre workers, it features a roof terrace and street-level sliding doors that are opened in fine weather. The bar stocks a wide range of bottled beers, and hosts a variety of popular events such as film screenings, board games and themed evenings. The bar can sometimes close early on weeknights if quiet. ☺🕭🕩🚆🚆(8,9)🐾🛜

Earl of Mercia
18 High Street, CV1 5RE
🕮 8am-midnight (1am Fri & Sat) ☎ (024) 7643 3990
Greene King Abbot; Ruddles Best Bitter; Sharp's Doom Bar; 5 changing beers (sourced nationally; often Sadler's) 🅗
This well-established Wetherspoon pub is a conversion of a former bank building. Located opposite the Council House and near the cathedral quarter, the pub is popular with city-centre workers, shoppers and families during the day and early evening. There is a good range of international bottled beers. Seating is available in the ground-floor bar area, mezzanine and pavement patio. It gets busy on Friday and Saturday nights, with a mixed crowd. ☺🕭🕩🚆🚆🚆(8,9)🛜

A traditional taproom, within the brewery and right next to the brewery kit, with a vibrant community atmosphere, where all people are friends of the brewery; if you are not, you will soon be welcomed into the community. In addition to two cask beers there are up to four rotating guest ciders on offer, together with bottle-conditioned beers brewed on-site. Q ☜ ♣ P ⏍ ➌ (241,140) ☙

Waggon & Horses ▼ ⏸

21 Stourbridge Road, B63 3TU (on main A458, ½ mile from bus station)
☼ 12-11 (11.30 Fri & Sat); 12-10.30 Sun ☎ (0121) 585 9699
Black Country Bradley's Finest Golden, Pig on the Wall, Fireside; 8 changing beers (sourced nationally) Ⓗ
Following a major refurbishment by Black Country Ales, this thoroughly welcoming pub has an enviable reputation for its wide selection of expertly kept beers. Fifteen handpulls serve three regular ales and 12 guests, and real ciders are also available. The traditional interior with a long bar and a famous sloping floor now extends into an old adjoining shop. Dogs are welcome but not in the carpeted area. Cobs and snacks are served.
Q ♿ ♣ ➌ (9) ☙ 🛜

Kingswinford

Cottage ✔

534 High Street, DY6 8AW
☼ 12-11 (midnight Fri & Sat); 12-10.30 Sun
☎ (01384) 287133
Enville Ale; St Austell Tribute; 2 changing beers Ⓗ
Interesting former Scottish & Newcastle pub with a cosy feel. Good-value food dominates in the early evening but drinkers will not struggle to find a comfortable spot. The spacious L-shaped venue is organised into separate areas. Four real ales including two guests selected from the Punch list are served. A carvery is available every day and there is a separate restaurant.
Q ☜ ⓓ P ➌ (205,255) 🛜

Park Tavern ⏸

182 Cot Lane, DY6 9QG (corner of Cot Lane and Broad St)
☼ 11-11 (midnight Thu-Sat) ☎ (01384) 287178
Bathams Best Bitter; Enville Ale, Ginger Beer; Holden's Golden Glow; 2 changing beers Ⓗ
Lively pub in the back streets of Kingswinford, currently serving six real ales. Opened as the Brickmakers Arms in 1855, it changed its name to the Park Tavern in 1859. The bar and lounge each have their own feel, but TV dominates when sporting events are on. The pub recently introduced a basic food menu with a drink included with some meals, otherwise there is a selection of cobs. A patio attached to the rear is for smokers. Card-carrying CAMRA members are offered a discount.
⊛ⓓ ♣ P ➌ (226) ☙ 🛜

Lower Gornal

Black Bear

86 Deepdale Lane, DY3 2AE
☼ 5 (12 Fri & Sat)-11; 12-10.30 Sun ☎ (01384) 253333
House beer (by Kinver); 5 changing beers (often Abbeydale, Oakham) Ⓗ
Once a farmhouse, this building has been a pub for over 180 years. Subsidence has taken its toll and there is a distinct slope to the split-level interior, and large buttresses support the downhill exterior

walls. The views from the garden are stunning. Up to six ales include the house beer from Kinver. There are bus stops are close by, or you can take an uphill walk from the Gornal Wood bus station or go downhill from the main number 1 bus route.
⊛ ♣ ➌ (27,257) ☙

Fountain

8 Temple Street, DY3 2PE (on B4157 5 mins from Gornal Wood bus station)
☼ 12-11; 12-10.30 Sun ☎ (01384) 242777
🌐 fountaininnrealale.co.uk
Hobsons Best; RCH Pitchfork; 7 changing beers (sourced nationally; often Wood) Ⓗ
Longstanding Guide entry and twice winner of the CAMRA branch Pub of the Year. This excellent free house serves nine real ales accompanied by draught Belgian beers, a real cider and 12 fruit wines. The busy, vibrant bar is complemented by an elevated dining area serving excellent food (12-9pm Mon-Sat), and Sunday lunches until 5pm. A wide selection of cobs and baguettes is available at lunchtime. During the summer months the rear garden is a suntrap.
☜ ⊛ⓓ ♿ ♣ ♣ P ➌ (27,257) ☙ 🛜

Old Bull's Head

1 Redhall Road, DY3 2NU (at jct with Temple St, B4175)
☼ 12-11 (midnight Fri & Sat) ☎ (01384) 231616
Black Country Bradley's Finest Golden, Pig on the Wall, Fireside; 5 changing beers Ⓗ
This imposing late-Victorian pub has two separate rooms, both recently refurbished and now including three real fires. The Black Country Ales Brewery is at the rear. Guest beers are usually from small independent brewers. Beers can be purchased in third-pint measures. Large crusty cobs are available daily. It is a five-minute uphill walk from Gornal Wood bus station where the numbers 27 and 257 call. The 27 also stops outside going downhill towards the bus station.
⊛ ♣ ♣ P ➌ (27,257) ☙ 🛜

Red Cow ⏸

84 Grosvenor Road, DY3 2PR
☼ 4-midnight; 12-midnight Sat & Sun ☎ 07943 189351
9 changing beers (sourced nationally; often Abbeydale, Holden's, Wye Valley) Ⓗ
An early 19th-century hostelry in a cul-de-sac, which is part of Grosvenor Road. This community local supports numerous pub games teams. To the left is a large bar. The cosy lounge to the right is divided into two by a large chimney breast, which has openings either side to afford passage between them. A large garden is at the rear. It is a five-minute walk to the bus stop in Corncrake Road. ☜ ⊛ ♣ P ➌ (257) ☙ 🛜

Lye

Shovel ⏸

81 Pedmore Road, DY9 7DZ (on A4036, just S of Lye Cross)
☼ 5.30-11 (midnight Fri); 1-midnight Sat; 12-midnight Sun
☎ (01384) 423998
Enville Ale, Ginger Beer; Holden's Golden Glow; Morland Old Speckled Hen; Salopian Oracle; 7 changing beers (sourced nationally) Ⓗ
Extensive refurbishment has given this pub a smart feel. The central bar serves three separate spaces – a bar with sports TV, a plush lounge and a rear seating area. The Mediterranean area outside is covered, with a real-fire heated smokers' space;

the Real Ale Wall features over 1,000 pumpclips. Good evening food includes Mexican and balti nights, and traditional lunch is served on Sunday. Fresh filled rolls are the only food on Friday and Saturday. Opens some lunchtimes during the football season. ❀◑よ☒(9,276)

Mere Green

Mare Pool 🄻 ✓
297 Lichfield Road, B74 2UG (behind shops on E side of Lichfield Rd)
❀8am-midnight (1am Fri & Sat) ☎ (0121) 323 1070
Greene King Abbot; Ruddles Best Bitter; Sharp's Doom Bar; 6 changing beers ⊞
Suburban Wetherspoon pub with the usual food offerings and child-friendly policy. The name refers to one of the many pools which used to surround Sutton, and the watery theme includes hundreds of hanging glass droplets. Café-style seating around the frontage is complemented by a beer terrace to the side, accessed from inside the pub. There are occasional showings of big-screen sport. Guest ales often come from breweries in the region such as Purity or Slaters. Q❀❀◑よ❧P☒�

Rushall

Manor Arms ★ 🄻 ✓
Park Road, WS4 1LG (off Daw End Lane) SK032004
❀12-11 (midnight Thu-Sat) ☎ (01922) 642333
Banks's Mild, Amber Ale, Sunbeam; 1 changing beer (sourced locally) ⊞
A canalside pub built around 1105, thought to have held a licence for ale since 1248, and one of the oldest pubs in the country. It retains exposed beams and open fires in both bars. Unusually, beer comes from handpumps situated on the bar back – the pub is known locally as 'the pub with no bar'. Situated next to a country park and nature reserve, it is a little off the beaten track, but well worth a visit. Q❀❀☒❀�

Sedgley

Beacon Hotel ▼ ★ 🄻
129 Bilston Street, DY3 1JE (a463)
❀12-2.30 (3 Fri), 5.30-11; 12-3, 6-11 Sat; 12-3, 7-10.30 Sun
☎ (01902) 883380 ⊕ sarahhughesbrewery.co.uk
Sarah Hughes Pale Amber, Sedgley Surprise, Dark Ruby Mild; 3 changing beers (often Kinver, Sarah Hughes, Shiny) ⊞
In the shadow of the ancient Sedgley Beacon, this old hotel has remained virtually unchanged for decades. It is a Grade II-listed building and has a nationally important historic pub interior. At its heart is a small central servery with hatches serving four rooms, including a family room. The Sarah Hughes Brewery lives in a tower out the back and supplies the pub. The Beacon lives up to its name – it shines. Local CAMRA Pub of the Year 2017. Q❀❀P☒(229,224)

Bull's Head
27 Bilston Street, DY3 1JA (on A463)
❀10-11 (midnight Fri & Sat) ☎ (01902) 671499
Holden's Black Country Bitter, Golden Glow, Special; 1 changing beer (often Holden's) ⊞
Not far from the centre of Sedgley sits this listed building. The bar area extends across the front of the pub and into the two bay windows. More drinking space is available further back in a raised

area to the side. Beyond that is a busy Thai restaurant which also serves takeaways. A warm welcome awaits regulars and visitors alike. Live entertainment is a feature on Sunday evening. ❀❀◑☒❀�

Mount Pleasant
144 High Street, DY3 1RH (on A459)
❀6.30 (7 Mon & Tue)-11; 12-3, 7-10.30 Sun ☎ 07950 195652
Oakham Bishops Farewell; 8 changing beers (sourced nationally; often Holden's, RCH, Salopian) ⊞
Known locally as the Stump, this friendly, popular free house serves a selection of eight beers. It possesses a mock-Tudor frontage and a Tardis-like interior. The front bar has a convivial atmosphere. The lounge has an intimate feel with two rooms on different levels housing various nooks and crannies to hide away in and two real coal stoves. Dog-friendly, it is on the Dudley to Wolverhampton bus route, or five minutes' walk from Sedgley centre. Q❀❀P☒(1)❀

Shelfield

Four Crosses 🄻
1 Green Lane, WS4 1RN (off A461)
❀12-midnight
3 changing beers (sourced nationally; often AJ's Ales, Backyard, Stonehenge) ⊞
Traditional friendly three-roomed pub with two bars. Sky Sports TV is shown in all areas. Music is supplied via a jukebox, plus live music every Saturday. This is a community pub with a warm atmosphere. It was closed for an extended period of time, but reopened at the end of 2015 and is now back to its former glory, popular with locals and visitors alike. ❀❀❀❀P☒�

Solihull

Fieldhouse ✓
10 Knightcote Drive, Monkspath, B91 3JU
❀11.30-11.30 Mon; 11.30-11.30 Tue & Wed; 11.30-midnight Thu & Fri; 10-midnight Sat & Sun ☎ (0121) 703 9209
Black Sheep Ember Pale Ale; Brakspear Bitter; Hook Norton Old Hooky; 4 changing beers (sourced nationally) ⊞
Part of the Ember Inns chain, this large, modern pub is tastefully decorated and comfortably furnished following a recent makeover. It features three large fires (one real, two coal-effect) and pleasant patio areas. It normally serves seven ales, with three guest ales from across the country, often unusual ones, changing frequently. Often busy, it attracts a wide age range. Quiz nights are Sunday and Tuesday, on Monday cask ales are discounted. The pub holds monthly tribute acts and occasional Meet the Brewer events. ❀❀◑よP☒(S15,5)�

Pup & Duckling ▼
1 Hatchford Brook Road, Olton, B92 9AG
❀closed Mon & Tue; 5-10; 12-3 Sun ☎ (0121) 247 8358
⊕ pupandduckling.co.uk
6 changing beers (sourced nationally; often Byatt's, Fixed Wheel, Twisted Barrel) ⊞
Solihull's first micropub, opened in 2016 in a vacant shop. Family-run, it has added a garden area to the initial two-room layout. Six rapidly changing real ales are on handpull, along with six ciders. The latest ales are listed on Facebook, but

can sell out in an evening. Bar snacks are served and customers are welcome to bring in their own food from the nearby Chinese, Indian and fish and chip shop takeaways. Q☺♿🚌(73,957)🐾 🛜

Stourbridge

Badelynge Bar 🇱

Rufford Road, DY9 7ND (entrance is a green door next to Base Studios on Rufford Rd)
☻ 4-11 Fri; 1-7 Sat; closed Sun-Thu ☎ (01384) 377666
5 changing beers (sourced locally; often Green Duck) Ⓗ
Brewery tap for the Green Duck Brewery located in a large converted industrial unit, which is light and airy with a unique atmosphere among Stourbridge pubs. The working brewery is visible through a glass partition. Seating is plentiful. Cask ale can be bought using a token system, with four pints for £10, or by the pint. The bar is available to hire for functions and regular beer festivals are held featuring many guest beers. 🚲🚆♿🚌(287)🐾

Barbridge

Victoria Passage, DY8 1DP (at end of Victoria Passage on Talbot St)
☻ 10.30-11 (1.30am Fri & Sat) ☎ (01384) 379898
4 changing beers (sourced nationally; often Fixed Wheel) Ⓗ/Ⓖ
Opened in 2015 in an old retail unit behind the Rye Market, this is a busy, bustling venue appealing to all age ranges. Four ales are stocked, usually one from Fixed Wheel, served from a chiller unit to the rear through handpulls at the end of the bar. Eight real ciders are also available. Cobs are also sold. ♿🚆♿🚌🐾🛜

Red House Boutique 🇱

21-26 Foster Place, DY8 1EL
☻ 11-11 (midnight Fri & Sat); 12-8 Sun ☎ (01384) 936430
Enville Ale; Holden's Golden Glow; Wye Valley HPA; 5 changing beers (sourced nationally; often Fixed Wheel, Three Tuns) Ⓗ
Large, single-bar free house near to Stourbridge Interchange. Originally part of the Hogshead chain, this refurbished pub has returned to being an alehouse. Beers from Enville, Fixed Wheel and Three Tuns will usually be available but may change from those listed. Tasty snacks are sold at all times including gourmet Scotch eggs and flavoured scratchings. Fridges behind the bar are stocked with 50 bottles from around the world. ☺♿🚆🚌🛜

Royal Exchange 🇱

75 Enville Street, DY8 1XW (on A458 just off ring road)
☻ 1-11; 12-11 Sat; 12-10.30 Sun ☎ (01384) 396726
Bathams Mild Ale, Best Bitter Ⓗ
The busy traditional bar is to the front and a small cosy lounge to the rear, accessed through a side passage. The bar is decorated with whisky bottles and boxes, pewter tankards and foreign bank notes. The beer is served in handled glasses on request. A heated smoking area exists within the large beer garden to the rear, and a function room is upstairs and may be booked for free. Bathams XXX is available winter only. A public car park is directly opposite. Q☺♣P🚌

Waggon & Horses 🇱

31 Worcester Street, DY8 1AT
☻ 12-11 (midnight Thu-Sat) ☎ (01384) 395398

Enville Ale, Ginger Beer; Holden's Golden Glow; 3 changing beers Ⓗ
Recent refurbishment has created a comfortable, welcoming alehouse. There is a small cask ale bar to the front with a narrow passageway leading to a larger rear bar. To the side is a cider bar with a small serving hatchway. Two or more real ciders are usually stocked. Parking can be difficult in the narrow surrounding streets. ☺♿🚆♿🚌🐾🛜

Streetly

Queslett ✅

Queslett Road East, B74 2EY
☻ 11.30-11 (midnight Thu-Sat) ☎ (0121) 580 8123
Marston's Pedigree; Purity Pure UBU; house beer (by Black Sheep); 4 changing beers Ⓗ
Busy community Ember Inn with a large front patio. The open-plan interior is split into a variety of cosily furnished areas, enhanced by flaming gas fires. Well-presented food is served daily until 10pm. Three to four guest beers from the Ember seasonal range are offered, and Cask Ale Monday sees all real ales offered at a special price. Live music and sports screenings feature occasionally, and there is a weekly quiz. 🚲☺🕙♿♣P🚌

Sutton Coldfield

Duke Inn ✅

12 Duke Street, B72 1RJ
☻ 12-11 (midnight Fri & Sat); 12-10.30 Sun
☎ (0121) 355 1767 ⊕ dukeinnsutton.co.uk
Butcombe Original; Caledonian Deuchars IPA; Greene King Abbot; Young's Bitter; 1 changing beer Ⓗ
Tucked away from the centre of Sutton, this side-street pub is a welcome break from chain pubs. Regulars play darts in the main bar, which features a pale-wood gantry complete with mirrors and clock. A delightful small lounge to the rear is more cosy. The corridor abutting the bar features elaborate floor tiles, decorated mirrors, and even a short panel of snob screens. Children are welcome in the beer garden. The guest ale tends to be from a larger brewer. ☺🚆♣P🚌🛜

Three Tuns

19 High Street, B72 1XS
☻ 11.30-midnight (11 Mon; 11.30 Tue; 1am Fri & Sat); 12-11 Sun ☎ (0121) 355 2996 ⊕ threetuns.net
Marston's Wainwright, Lancaster Bomber; Thwaites Original; 1 changing beer Ⓗ
A 16th-century coaching inn with some old timbers still visible, and the central coach track still evident. The bar area leads off to three rooms, all different in style. There is live music on Saturday and a quiz on Thursday. Televised sports are often shown. The guest ale is frequently a special from Thwaites. Food is served noon-9pm (8pm Sun) and children are welcome during food hours (no food Mon). Pay & Display parking is nearby. Q🚲🕙♿🚆♣🚌🐾🛜

Tipton

Rising Sun 🇱

116 Horseley Road, DY4 7NH (off B4517)
☻ 12-midnight ☎ (0121) 557 1940
Black Country Bradley's Finest Golden, Pig on the Wall, Fireside; 7 changing beers Ⓗ
A former CAMRA National Pub of the Year, reopened in March 2013 following a superb refurbishment by Black Country Ales. It is an

imposing Victorian hostelry with two distinct rooms warmed by open fires. For the summer, there is a tidy yard at the back. There are seven changing guest beers and two traditional ciders, usually including Black Rat. Cobs are available. It is 10 minutes' walk from Great Bridge, which has frequent services to Dudley, West Bromwich and Birmingham. ✿♣●🖵(22)🐾🎅

Tamebridge

45 Tame Road, DY4 7JA (off A461)
✪ 12-11 ☎ (0121) 557 2496
Wye Valley HPA; 3 changing beers ⓗ
Situated alongside the Oldbury arm of the River Tame. The bar, which has a large coal fire, leads to a small, cosy snug area. There is also a family room. A large-screen TV is mounted above the coal fire. Outside is a covered, heated smoking area and garden. The pub has a separate toilet for wheelchair users. A 'coming soon' board is regularly updated to keep customers informed about future offerings. ♿✿≠P🖵(74)🐾🎅

Upper Gornal

Jolly Crispin

25 Clarence Street, DY3 1UL (on A459)
✪ 4 (12 Fri & Sat)-11; 12-10.30 Sun ☎ (01902) 672220
⊕ thejollycrispin.co.uk
Fownes Crispin's Ommer; 8 changing beers (sourced nationally; often Abbeydale, Oakham, Salopian) ⓗ
A shoemaker's house in the 18th century, then a pub for more than 180 years. It sits on the top of the Black Country ridge, with distant views from the rear. Inside, the locals are friendly, the fires glow and dogs are welcome. The pub's house beer, Crispin's Ommer, comes from the on-site Fownes brewery. Real ale is complemented by changing real ciders, and a cider festival is held in the garden (usually in May) in aid of charity.
✿♣●P🖵(1)🐾🎅

Wall Heath

Wall Heath Tavern ⓛ

14 High Street, DY6 0HA (on A449)
✪ 12-11 (midnight Fri & Sat); 12-10.30 Sun
☎ (01384) 287319 ⊕ thewallheathtavern.co.uk
Bathams Best Bitter; Enville Ale, Ginger Beer; Holden's Golden Glow; 4 changing beers (often Three Tuns, Wye Valley) ⓗ
A bustling pub on the A449 approaching Wall Heath village centre, serving up to 10 real ales, with a major emphasis on Enville Ales. With a sports TV in the bar, it can get busy, particularly at weekends. The lounge is predominantly food-driven, especially in the evening when tables can be reserved. The menu features good-value cooking. There is a large patio area at the rear, which is busy in the summer months. Card-carrying CAMRA members receive a discount.
♿✿◑●P🖵🐾🎅

Walsall

Black Country Arms ⓛ

High Street, WS1 1QW (in market, opp Asda)
✪ 11-11 (midnight Fri); 12-midnight Sat; 12-11 Sun
☎ (01922) 640588 ⊕ blackcountryarms.co.uk
Black Country Bradley's Finest Golden, Pig on the Wall, Fireside; 11 changing beers (sourced nationally) ⓗ

A large, imposing multi award-winning pub on three levels, part of which was originally the Green Dragon Inn that dated back to the 18th century. The place lay empty for 70 years until extensive refurbishment saw it reopen in 1987. The impressive bar boasts 16 handpumps serving up to 11 guest ales, mainly from microbreweries, with two real ciders always on. Live music features frequently. Booking is recommended for Sunday lunches. ♿✿◑≠♣●P🖵🎅

Fountain Inn ♥ ⓛ

49 Lower Forster Street, WS1 1XB (off A4148 ring road)
✪ 12-2, 5-11; 12-midnight Fri & Sat; 12-11 Sun
☎ (01922) 633307
Backyard Blonde, The Hoard; 6 changing beers (sourced nationally; often Holden's, St Austell) ⓗ
A family-run pub, this is the brewery tap for Backyard Brewhouse, with up to eight real ales to choose from. It has a friendly atmosphere and welcoming staff. Bar snacks include cobs and pork pies. Regular music nights are held including vinyl, indie, classic rock, reggae, funk and soul. There are also monthly Monday film nights, and drawing classes. Both rooms feature log fires.
Q♿◑≠♣🖵

Longhorn ⓛ ✅

255 Sutton Road, WS5 3AR
✪ 11-11 (midnight Wed-Fri); 10-midnight Sat; 10-11 Sun
☎ (01922) 625065
Brakspear Bitter; Marston's Wainwright; Purity Pure UBU; house beer (by Black Sheep); 4 changing beers (sourced nationally) ⓗ
Large 1930s roadside inn with a real community feel. The rear of the pub is given over to diners while drinkers tend to occupy the front section. Many charity events are hosted throughout the year, with quiz nights on Sunday and Wednesday. Regular food and drinks deals are on offer, with all ales reduced in price on Monday. There is a function area available free of charge. Breakfast is served from 10am at weekends. ♿✿◑&P🎅

Pretty Bricks ⓛ

5 John Street, WS2 8AF (near magistrates court, off B4210)
✪ 12-11 ☎ (01922) 612553
Black Country Bradley's Finest Golden, Pig on the Wall, Fireside; 7 changing beers (sourced nationally; often Mallinson's, Salopian, Swannay) ⓗ
Small, friendly, comfortable pub, dating from 1845. It has a front bar with wood fire, a lounge, an upstairs function room and a small blue brick courtyard with a couple of benches. Originally the New Inn, its was renamed due to its attractive part-glazed frontage. Great cobs and pork pies provide sustenance alongside the great range of ales. A folk night is held every second Thursday of the month. Q✿≠♣●🖵(301)🐾

Walsall Cricket Club

Gorway Road, WS1 3BE (off A34, by university campus)
✪ 8-10.30; 6-11 Fri; 12-11 Sat; 12-8 Sun; closed Mon
☎ (01922) 622094
Sharp's Doom Bar; Wye Valley HPA; 1 changing beer (sourced nationally) ⓗ
On a fine summer evening, the click of bat on ball welcomes you to a green oasis in the heart of town. The club room has had a major renovation and now provides luxurious comfort with a panoramic view of the field. The club contains much local cricket memorabilia and two large

sporting screens. There is occasional entertainment and the venue is popular for function hire. Show a CAMRA membership card for entry. In winter, weekend hours are 5-11pm Saturday and 12-8.30pm Sunday. ⌂❀&♣P🖳(51)🛜

White Lion 🅛

150 Sandwell Street, WS1 3EQ (at jct of Sandwell St and Little London)
✪ 12-11 (midnight Fri & Sat) ☎ 07746 219452
Adnams Southwold Bitter; Holden's Golden Glow; Wye Valley HPA, Butty Bach; 2 changing beers (sourced nationally) 🅗
Imposing late-Victorian back-street corner local. The pub's classic sloping bar, with its deep and shallow ends, is certainly one of the best in town. There is a plush lounge for the drinker who wants to languish. This venue is a great community melting pot. Regular open mic and quiz nights are hosted. Outside there is a small, walled garden. ⌂❀&♣●🖳(4)🐾🛜

Wednesbury

Cottage Spring 🅛

106 Franchise Street, WS10 9RG
✪ 3 (1 Thu)-11.30; 12-midnight Fri & Sat; 12-11.30 Sun
☎ (0121) 531 7191
Holden's Black Country Mild, Black Country Bitter, Golden Glow; 1 changing beer (sourced locally; often Holden's) 🅗
The front bar has photos of the pub and owners from yesteryear. Darts is played at one end. The lounge also has old-world prints and old-fashioned manufacturing devices, and there is a stage area in one corner. The bar features a classic red phone box. Friday is quiz night, live music features on Saturday night and Sunday afternoon, and Sunday lunches are served. Q❀●♣P🖳

Queen's Head ✅

100 Brunswick Park Road, WS10 9QR
✪ 12 (5 Mon)-11; 12-midnight Fri & Sat ☎ 07713 756570
⊕ queensheadwednesbury.com
Salopian Shropshire Gold; Wye Valley HPA; 2 changing beers 🅗
Enthusiastically run, this brick-built, twin-gabled pub offers a warm welcome to all. There are two rooms – the front bar has tables and booths and is popular with diners, the side bar has a TV and dartboard. Home-made food, good beer and entertainment (frequent live bands and DJs) ensure that the Queen's Head is well supported by the local community. Tennis, football and water polo teams all meet here. Summer barbecues and the occasional beer festival also feature. Q⌂❀◑&♣●P🖳🐾🛜

Wednesfield

Vine ★ 🅛

35 Lichfield Road, WV11 1TN
✪ 12-11 (midnight Fri & Sat) ☎ (01902) 733529
Black Country Bradley's Finest Golden, Pig on the Wall, Fireside; 6 changing beers (sourced nationally) 🅗
Built in 1938, this Grade II-listed community local is a rare intact example of a simple inter-war working-class pub. It has been identified by CAMRA as having a nationally important historic pub interior for retaining its original bar, lounge and snug. Darts and dominoes are played and there are

TVs showing live sport and horse racing. A covered smokers' shelter and a beer garden provide outdoor drinking areas. Cobs and pork pies are available at all times. ❀♣●P🖳(59,89)🐾🛜

West Bromwich

Crown & Cushion ✅

2 Lloyd Street, B71 4AT
✪ 12-11 ☎ (0121) 553 4493
Harviestoun Bitter & Twisted; St Austell Tribute; 1 changing beer (sourced nationally; often Castle Rock) 🅗
Family-friendly hostelry comprising a single L-shaped room, run by a welcoming landlady. The pub is popular in summer with visitors to nearby Dartmouth Park. It is within easy walking distance of West Bromwich Albion's football ground and can therefore get busy on match days; however, away supporters are made welcome. A popular quiz night is held on Thursday. ⌂❀◑♣P🖳

Old Hop Pole

474 High Street, B70 9LD
✪ 12-3 (not Wed), 5-11; 12-midnight Fri; 12-1am Sat; 12-11 Sun ☎ 07946 579957
Wye Valley HPA; 2 changing beers 🅗
Popular community hostelry a short distance from West Bromwich town centre. The central bar is surrounded by a bustling, traditional front bar, with two conversely quieter and homelier drinking areas. The pub gets busy at weekends when there is a West Bromwich Albion home fixture (opens at 11am), as it is a mecca for fans, as testified by the club memorabilia decorating the walls. Entertainment on Saturday evenings alternates between live music and a disco. ⌂❀♙♣🖳(74,79)

Royal Oak 🅛

14 Newton Street, B71 3RQ (down side road off Hollyhedge Rd)
✪ 2-11; 12-midnight Fri & Sat; 12-11 Sun ☎ (0121) 588 5857
Marston's Wainwright; St Austell Proper Job; Sharp's Doom Bar; Wye Valley HPA; 2 changing beers (sourced nationally) 🅗
Traditional back-street local with two small rooms. There is a sports TV in both rooms, but the sound is normally reduced. The bar on the left is adorned with West Bromwich Albion football club pictures and on the right is the quieter lounge. There is a terrace in the rear yard for smokers and two benches outside the front to bask on in the summer. Parking is difficult, but available on the neighbouring streets. ⌂❀♣🖳

Sow & Pigs 🅛 ✅

26 Hill Top, B70 0PS
✪ 12-11 ☎ (0121) 553 1191
6 changing beers (sourced locally) 🅗
Traditional pub recently brought back to life by the Two Crafty Brewers and Sadler's breweries. It has recently been refurbished throughout while keeping the majority of the original features in place. Families are welcome in the pub; a pleasant garden area is at the rear. A number of Two Crafty Brewers ales feature alongside a range of guest ales. Believed to be the oldest public house in West Bromwich. ❀◑♙♣🖳🐾🛜

Vine

152 Roebuck Street, B70 6RD
✪ 11.30-2, 5-11; 11.30-11 Fri & Sat; 12-10.30 Sun
☎ (0121) 553 2866 ⊕ thevine.co.uk

2 changing beers ⓗ
From the street this appears a traditional corner pub, but be prepared for a surprise! The traditional part consists of three small rooms off the corridor. Continue further in and the building opens up into a large dining area, where an extensive range of Indian meals is available together with British and vegetarian options, which are all excellent value. Two guest ales are regularly on tap. This popular establishment gets busy, especially when West Bromwich Albion are at home.
🛇❀◐♿⚞♫🖥🖵(74,79)

Willenhall

Falcon
77 Gomer Street West, WV13 2NR (off B4464, behind flats)
🕓 12-11; 12-10.30 Sun ☎ (01902) 633378
Moorhouse's Blond Witch; Salopian Oracle; 3 changing beers (sourced nationally) ⓗ
A two-roomed pub with a lively public bar and quieter lounge at the rear, just a short walk from the town centre. Dating back to 1936, the Falcon has been in the same family for over 30 years. Old pub memorabilia adorn both rooms, where keenly priced beers are served. There is a beer garden at the rear. On-street parking is plentiful.
Q🛇❀♣◐🖥🖵(529)❀

Jolly Collier
112 Lucknow Road, WV12 4QG
🕓 2-11; 12-midnight Fri & Sat; 12-11 Sun ☎ (01902) 413083
Enville Ale; Wye Valley HPA; 2 changing beers ⓗ
A welcoming two-roomed, family-run pub. It has recently been refurbished and is popular with locals and visitors alike. The lounge area has a real fire. Live entertainment is usually provided once a month on a Saturday, and quiz night is Tuesday. Bar snacks include cobs, with fresh pork sandwiches on Friday night. Sunday lunches are served in an adjacent room. A large beer garden and play area can be found at the rear.
🛇❀♣P🖵(41)☎

Robin Hood ⓛ
54 The Crescent, WV13 2QR (200yds from A462/B4464 jct)
🕓 12-11 (midnight Fri & Sat) ☎ (01902) 635070
Black Country Bradley's Finest Golden, Pig on the Wall ⓗ**, Fireside** ⓗ/ⓖ**; 6 changing beers (sourced nationally)** ⓗ
Black Country Ales-owned pub with an old-fashioned feel and welcoming, friendly staff. One central bar serves both drinking areas – a large bar and quieter lounge. The three permanent beers are supplemented by six changing guest beers from throughout the UK. Two real ciders are also stocked. Bar snacks including cobs and pork pies are available all day. A heated and covered smoking area is to the rear. A beer festival is held every July in the beer garden, and barbecues throughout the year. ❀♣◐P🖵(529)

Wollaston

Unicorn ⓛ
145 Bridgnorth Road, DY8 3NX (on A458 towards Bridgnorth)
🕓 12-11; 12-4, 7-10.30 Sun ☎ (01384) 394823
Bathams Mild Ale, Best Bitter ⓗ

A former brewhouse purchased by Bathams, which has barely altered in appearance since the Billingham family sold up in the early 1990s. The brewhouse is still there but not used anymore. This is a traditional two-bar drinking house, with a small back room where children are welcome, and it is popular with all age groups – conversation is the order of the day. Fresh cobs can be provided on request; hot pork cobs with stuffing are available on Saturday lunchtime. Bathams XXX is sold in winter only. Q🛇❀♣P🖵❀☎

Wolverhampton

Chindit ⓛ ✅
113 Merridale Road, WV3 9SE
🕓 4-11 (midnight Fri); 12-midnight Sat; 2-11 Sun ☎ 07986 773487 🌐 thechindit.co.uk
Castle Rock Harvest Pale; Hop Back Summer Lightning; Wye Valley HPA; 2 changing beers (sourced locally; often Burton Bridge, Salopian, Three Tuns) ⓗ
Originally built in the 1950s as an off-licence and since extended, the first landlord served in the Chindit Regiment in Burma in WWII and named the pub after his comrades. It is thought this is the only pub in the country honouring Major General Orde Wingate's special forces; their history is displayed on the wall in the lounge. It has two rooms – a small lounge and a large bar where music events are regularly held. 🛇❀♣P🖵(3,4)☎

Combermere Arms
90 Chapel Ash, WV3 0TY (on A41 Tettenhall Rd)
🕓 12-3 (not Mon winter), 5-11; 12-midnight Fri & Sat; 12-10.30 Sun ☎ (01902) 421880
5 changing beers (sourced nationally; often Greene King) ⓗ
Grade II-listed building with original sash windows. A short walk or bus ride from the city centre, the pub comprises three charming rooms with cosy fireplaces, classic adverts and a comical Guinness cartoon series. A pub-favourites menu is available weekday lunchtimes except Monday. Cheese, pie and sausage-tasting festivals are held annually and there is occasional live entertainment. Character features include the tree in the Gents. Beers are from the Greene King portfolio. Q🛇❀◐●P🖵

Dog & Doublet ⓛ
9 North Street, WV1 1RE
🕓 12-10 Mon; 12-11 Tue & Wed; 12-2am Thu & Fri; 12-3am Sat; 2.30-10.30 Sun ☎ (01902) 423805
🌐 thedoganddoubletinn.co.uk
Ludlow Gold; Oakham Bishops Farewell; 4 changing beers (sourced nationally) ⓗ
City-centre pub, near the Civic and Wulfrun Halls, a mix of modern and traditional, with real fires and chesterfield furniture. The outside drinking area includes a cocktail bar. Music features heavily here, with open mic on Thursday, live bands on Friday and a DJ on Saturday (admission charges apply after 10pm Sat). No food is served but you are welcome to bring your own – plates and cutlery are provided. Harry's Cider is always available.
🛇❀⚞♣●🖵☎

Dog & Gun ⓛ ✅
1 Wrottesley Road, Tettenhall, WV6 8SB (off A41 Wergs Road)
🕓 11.30-11 (midnight Fri & Sat) ☎ (01902) 747943
Brakspear Bitter; Marston's Wainwright; house beer (by Black Sheep); 3 changing beers (sourced nationally) ⓗ

Comfortable Ember Inns pub arranged around a large U-shaped bar with a family dining area and a bar/lounge space. It is well attended, particularly on weekend evenings, with a friendly atmosphere. An imaginative choice of guest ales greets a broad range of customers including a local writers' group and a rambling club. Fortnightly open mic nights on Wednesdays and a weekly Sunday quiz provide entertainment. A patio allows outside drinking. Monday is Cask Ale Club, offering all ale at reduced prices. ⛲🕭🍴ᵭ🅿🖵(1,891)🛜

Great Western 🅛

Sun Street, WV10 0DJ (pedestrian access from city centre via subway at station)
🕐 11-11; 11-10.30 Sun ☎ (01902) 351090
Bathams Best Bitter; Holden's Black Country Mild, Black Country Bitter, Golden Glow, Special; 3 changing beers (sourced regionally) 🅗
A previous CAMRA National Pub of the Year, close to the former low-level railway station. It attracts a varied clientele, including rock climbers and motorbike and railway groups, who meet here regularly. Plenty of railway and Wolverhampton Wanderers memorabilia is on display and cosy real fires blaze in the winter. Meals are served at lunchtimes and snacks are available until 10pm, except Sunday. A beer festival is held over November's Remembrance weekend.
Q⛲🕭🍴➡🅿🖵🐾🛜

Hail to the Ale 🅛

2 Pendeford Avenue, Claregate, WV6 9EF (on Claregate island)
🕐 closed Mon-Wed; 5-10 Thu & Fri; 12-10 Sat; 12-5 Sun ☎ 07846 562910 🌐 hailtothealemicropub.co.uk
4 changing beers (sourced locally; often Beowulf, Lymestone, Morton) 🅗
Welcoming one-room beer-focused pub converted from a shop. This was West Midlands' first micropub, opened in 2013 by Morton Brewery, and follows a simple formula of good ale and conversation. Four handpulls serve at least one Morton beer and different guests, usually from local microbreweries. Also available on handpull and from the cellar are four ciders or perries. Locally sourced pies, cheese, sausage rolls and Scotch eggs are served along with 10 fruit wines. Regional CAMRA Pub of the Year 2015.
Q⛲🕭ᵭ🍃🖵🅿🖵(5,6)🐾

Hogshead 🅛 ✅

186 Stafford Street, WV1 1NA
🕐 10-midnight (1am Fri); 10-2am Sat ☎ (01902) 717955
🌐 hogsheadwolverhampton.co.uk
10 changing beers (sourced nationally) 🅗
Large 19th-century traditional city-centre pub with an attractive brick terracotta exterior. A stained-glass window above the entrance still displays the original name, the Vine. The large single room interior is divided into separate areas, with large-screen TVs showing sport and music videos throughout. It serves a wide range of 10 guest ales, often from local microbreweries, up to three changing ciders, and is popular with all age groups. It holds a quiz on Wednesday evening.
⛲🕭🍴ᵭ➡🍃🖵🛜

Lych Gate Tavern 🅛

44 Queen Square, WV1 1TX (off Queen Sq between Nationwide and Barclays bank by St Peter's Church)
🕐 11-11 (midnight Fri & Sat) ☎ (01902) 399516
🌐 lychgatetavern.co.uk

Black Country Bradley's Finest Golden, Pig on the Wall, Fireside; 6 changing beers (sourced nationally) 🅗
Friendly, traditional city-centre pub housed in one of the oldest timber-framed buildings in Wolverhampton; the Georgian frontage dates from 1726, the timber-framed rear from about 1500. The bar area is reached by a short flight of stairs down from street level and there is a function room available for hire upstairs. Cobs are sold, or you may bring your own food (plates and cutlery provided). All floors are accessible via a lift. A previous CAMRA branch Pub of the Year.
Q🕭➡🍃🖵🛜

Newhampton 🅛 ✅

17 Riches Street, Whitmore Reans, WV6 0DW
🕐 11-11 (midnight Fri & Sat) ☎ (01902) 680766
Courage Best Bitter, Directors; Enville Ale; Three Tuns XXX; Timothy Taylor Landlord; Wye Valley HPA; 1 changing beer (sourced nationally) 🅗
A Victorian street-corner local catering for a cosmopolitan customer base. Hatches service the (former) smoke room and pool room, which has a jukebox. The bar has an additional handpump for Thatcher's Heritage cider. Regular music events, including folk and jazz, are held in the bar and in an upstairs function room (the Blind Wolf, no wheelchair access). The large garden includes a popular seating area, children's small adventure playground, a crown green bowls lawn, an occasional pavilion bar and a smoking shelter.
⛲🕭🍴ᵭ🍃🖵(1,6)🐾🛜

Posada 🅛

48 Lichfield Street, WV1 1DG
🕐 12-11 (1am Fri); 11.30-1am Sat; 12-6 Sun
Hobsons Town Crier; Sharp's Doom Bar; 3 changing beers (often AJ's Ales, Salopian, Wye Valley) 🅗
Victorian Grade II-listed city-centre pub with tiled walls and original bar fittings, including rare snob screens, and little altered since 1900. It attracts a varied clientele and is quiet during the day but busy in the evenings and weekends, especially when Wolverhampton Wanderers are at home. There is a courtyard to the rear with a smoking area. Cobs are sold and Westons Old Rosie is served on handpump. ⛲➡🍃🖵🛜

Royal Oak 🅛 ✅

70 Compton Road, WV3 9PH
🕐 11.30-11 (midnight Fri & Sat); 12-11 Sun
☎ (01902) 422845 🌐 royaloakwolverhampton.co.uk
Banks's Mild, Amber Ale, Sunbeam; Wychwood Hobgoblin Gold; 3 changing beers (sourced nationally; often Jennings, Ringwood, Wychwood) 🅗
Friendly local, a short walk or bus ride from the city centre, serving a wide range of changing real ales from Marston's. The bustling pub has good sports coverage and hosts an open mic night on Wednesday, and live bands on Friday and Saturday (also Sunday afternoon in summer). Part of the community, the pub raises money for local and national charities, features a book swap library and is the headquarters of Old Wulfrunians Hockey Club. Fresh cobs are available at the bar.
⛲🕭ᵭ🍃🅿🖵(10,890)🐾🛜

Slater's 🅛

41 Queen Square, WV1 1TX
🕐 11-11 (midnight Fri & Sat); closed Sun ☎ (01902) 426475
10 changing beers (sourced nationally; often Slater's) 🅗

Developed by Slater's Brewery, this former Costa coffee bar was opened in 2016 in a contemporary style with a brushed stainless-steel bar counter and handpulls. An upstairs room offers great opportunities for viewing passers-by in Queen Square and the 'mon on 'is 'oss'. The pub serves 10 real ales, five from Slater's Brewery, two ciders, a draught sparkling wine, and an excellent range of bottled worldwide beers. Q✿🍴🕔🕭♿⚒♨🅿🚪🛏🐾📶

Stile Inn ⓛ ✔

3 Harrow Street, Whitmore Reans, WV1 4PB (off Newhampton Rd East/Fawdry St)
✿ 11.30-11 (midnight Fri; 1am Sat) ☎ (01902) 425336
Banks's Mild, Amber Ale, Sunbeam; 1 changing beer (sourced nationally) Ⓗ
A typical late-Victorian street-corner pub, built in 1900, featuring a public bar, smoke room and snug. It is a true community local with an emphasis on sport – darts and dominoes feature inside, crown green bowls on the unusual L-shaped green outside, and it gets busy with Wolverhampton Wanderers fans on match days. Excellent-value food, including Polish dishes, is served all day. Friday is open mic night and Saturday is karaoke. Sky Sports is shown in all rooms.
🚲✿🍴♣♨🚪(5,6)🐾📶

Swan ⓛ

Bridgnorth Road, Compton, WV6 8AE (at Compton Island, on A454)
✿ 12-11 (11.30 Thu; midnight Fri & Sat) ☎ (01902) 754736
🌐 swanpubwolverhampton.co.uk
Banks's Mild, Amber Ale, Sunbeam; Marston's Wainwright, Old Empire; 3 changing beers (sourced nationally; often Brakspear, Jennings, Wychwood) Ⓗ
Built around 1780, this Grade II-listed former coaching inn is popular with locals, boaters, ramblers and cyclists – it is close to the Staffordshire & Worcestershire Canal and Smestow Valley Nature Reserve. It comprises a lively bar full of local banter, a games room and a more sedate snug. It hosts charity dog shows, three beer festivals featuring ales from outside the Marston's range, and the weekly local pigeon-flyers club. A well-considered and sympathetic refurbishment was carried out mid-2016.
Q🚲✿♣♨🚪(10,890)🐾📶

Woodsetton

Park Inn ⓛ

George Street, DY1 4LW (on A457, 200yds from A4123)
✿ 12-11; 12-10.30 Sun ☎ (01902) 661279
Holden's Black Country Mild, Black Country Bitter, Golden Glow, Special; 3 changing beers Ⓗ

Vibrant suburban brewery tap, owned by the Holden family since 1915. Radiating out from the bar are a small games room, a raised dining area and a separate conservatory. Functions are catered for and reasonably priced food is served 12-8pm. The pub adjoins the recently refurbished and extended brewery (the new brewery centre is on the right of the car park). Sporting events on BT are shown on a large-screen TV in the bar. Card-carrying CAMRA members receive a small discount.
🚲✿🍴♣🅿🚪🐾

Wordsley

Bird in Hand

57 John Street, DY8 4AZ
✿ 12 (3 Mon-Wed)-11
Enville Ale; Hobsons Town Crier; Holden's Golden Glow; 1 changing beer Ⓗ
Quiet back-street pub, not far from the Red House Cone and old glassworks. There is a separate bar and a lounge which has a warm, homely feel, plus a covered beer garden and smoking area at the rear. It changed ownership in 2013, but the manager remains the same. The pub serves three regular beers and a changing guest, normally from a local brewery. There is light and inoffensive background music. Q🚲✿♣🚪(256,257)🐾📶

New Inn ⓛ

117 High Street, DY8 5QR (on A491)
✿ 12-11; 12-10.30 Sun ☎ (01384) 295614
Bathams Mild Ale, Best Bitter Ⓗ
The building has an imposing three-storey Victorian façade. Definitely a locals' pub, it has become extremely popular and is usually busy. An L-shaped bar serves a single room with a small annexe at one end, plus a patio area and newly refurbished garden outside. Children are not allowed in the pub. A variety of cobs is available.
🚲✿♣🅿🚪(256,257)🐾📶

Queen's Head ⓛ

129 High Street, DY8 5QS (on A491)
✿ 12-11 (midnight Fri & Sat) ☎ (01384) 402967
Black Country Bradley's Finest Golden, Pig on the Wall, Fireside; 6 changing beers Ⓗ
Comfortable roadside pub on the main Stourbridge to Wolverhampton road. The layout echoes its multi-roomed past, although most of the walls have gone. The decor is cosy Victorian or Edwardian in style. It offers up to nine real ales, with three from the parent brewery, and a traditional cider. To the right is a bar-type area which has a large-screen TV and dartboard. The pub now sells food (book ahead for Sunday lunch).
🚲✿🍴♣♨🅿🚪(256,257)🐾📶

The soul of beer

Brewers call barley malt the 'soul of beer'. While a great deal of attention has been rightly paid to hops in recent years, the role of malt in brewing must not be ignored. Malt contains starch that is converted to a special form of sugar known as maltose during the brewing process. It is maltose that is attacked by yeast during fermentation and turned into alcohol and carbon dioxide. Other grains can be used in brewing, notably wheat. But barley malt is the preferred grain as it gives a delightful biscuit / cracker / Ovaltine note to beer. Unlike wheat, barley has a husk that works as a natural filter during the first stage of brewing, known as the mash. Cereals such as rice and corn / maize are widely used by global producers of mass-market lagers, but craft brewers avoid them.

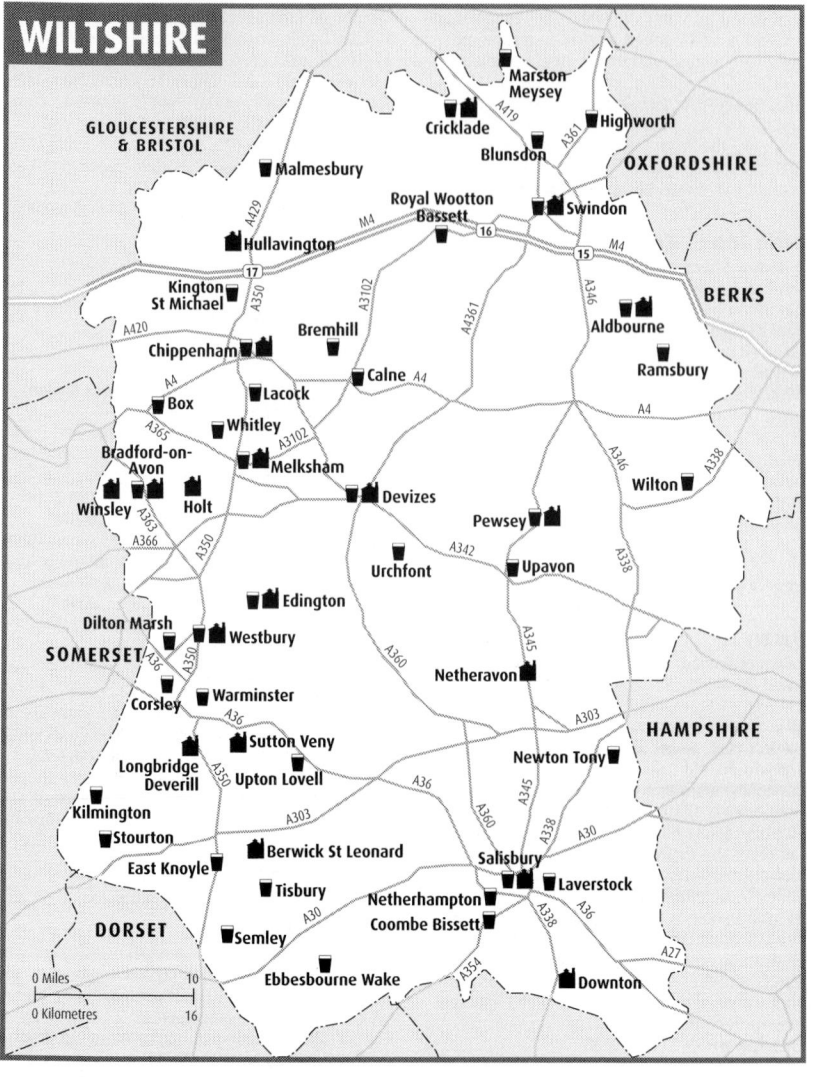

WILTSHIRE

GLOUCESTERSHIRE
& BRISTOL

Malmesbury

Marston
Meysey

Cricklade

Blunsdon

Highworth

OXFORDSHIRE

Royal Wootton
Bassett

Swindon

Hullavington

Kington
St Michael

Aldbourne

BERKS

Bremhill

Chippenham

Calne

Ramsbury

Box

Lacock

Whitley

Bradford-on-
Avon

Melksham

Winsley Holt

Devizes

Wilton

Pewsey

Urchfont

Upavon

Edington

Dilton Marsh

Westbury

SOMERSET

Netheravon

Corsley

Warminster

HAMPSHIRE

Sutton Veny

Newton Tony

Longbridge
Deverill

Upton Lovell

Kilmington

Stourton

East Knoyle

Berwick St Leonard

Salisbury

Laverstock

DORSET

Tisbury

Netherhampton

Semley

Coombe Bissett

Ebbesbourne Wake

Downton

0 Miles   10

0 Kilometres   16

Aldbourne

Crown Hotel ✓
The Square, SN8 2DU
🕐 12-midnight; 12-10.30 Sun ☎ (01672) 540214
🌐 thecrownaldbourne.co.uk
Sharp's Doom Bar; Shepherd Neame Spitfire; 2
changing beers (sourced nationally; often Castle
Combe, Timothy Taylor) Ⓗ
The Crown is set in the middle of the village
opposite the duck pond. A Dalek stands guard
outside. Much improved in recent years, it has a
relaxed and pleasant atmosphere, with two bars.
The main bar is stylishly refurbished and has a
welcoming fire during the colder seasons. The
smaller bar shows films on a Monday night. Quiz
nights, live music and other entertainments also
feature regularly. The restaurant serves freshly
prepared food with daily specials until 9.30pm. On
Sundays there is a carvery until it runs out, then the
usual menu. Accommodation comprises of four en-
suite bedrooms. ❀🚗🍴◑▲♣🚲(46,48)♥🐾📶

Blunsdon

Heart in Hand
43 High Street, SN26 7AG
🕐 11-3, 5.30-11; 11.30-midnight Fri & Sat; 12-10.30 Sun
☎ (01793) 721314 🌐 heartinhand.co.uk
3 changing beers (sourced regionally; often
Ramsbury) Ⓗ
Family friendly village local with darts and crib
teams and a quiz night on Thursday. Two guest
beers are on offer during the week, three at
weekends. The high-quality home-cooked food is
good value. A beer festival is held on the first
Sunday of September. There are four en-suite
rooms and a large garden. 🚗❀🚗◑♣🅿🚲(12)♥

Box

Quarryman's Arms 🄻
Box Hill, SN13 8HN (off A4, follow signs)
🕐 8am-11 (midnight Fri & Sat) ☎ (01225) 743569
🌐 quarrymans-arms.co.uk

Butcombe Bitter; Moles Best Bitter; Wadworth 6X; 2 changing beers (sourced nationally; often Flying Monk, Kennet & Avon) ⓗ

A 300-year-old former miner's cottage – some of the stone for Georgian Bath was mined below Box Hill. It has a separate snug bar with a linked main bar and dining area with a fabulous view towards Bath and across the valley to Colerne. The walls are decorated with stone-mining paraphernalia and pump labels from the many guest beers served. Food is locally sourced, the cider is Black Rat and there are four B&B rooms.

Q ⭑ ✿ ⏀ ⓓ ♿ ▲ ✦ ● P 🛏 (X31) 🛜

Bradford-on-Avon

Castle Inn ⓣ

Mount Pleasant, BA15 1SJ

🕐 9am-11; 10-10.30 Sun ☎ (01225) 865657

🌐 flatcappers.co.uk/the-castle-inn

Three Castles Barbury Castle, Vale Ale; 3 changing beers (often Electric Bear) ⓗ

A popular, comfortable pub commanding splendid views across the town towards Salisbury Plain. The refurbishment by Flatcappers earned a CAMRA Pub Design award. A wide range of handpulled real ales is complemented by excellent food, served all day until 10pm. The guest beers are usually sourced from micros in Wiltshire and east Somerset. There is a good-sized garden at the front and children are welcome. Local CAMRA Pub of the Year 2017. ⭑ ✿ ✦ ⏀ ⓓ ♿ ▲ ⇌ ● P 🛏 (265) 🐾 🛜

Timbrell's Yard

49 St Margaret's Street, BA15 1DE

🕐 9am-11 (10.30 Sun) ☎ (01225) 869492

🌐 timbrellsyard.com

Kettlesmith Faultline; 3 changing beers (sourced regionally; often Bristol Beer Factory, Cotleigh, Otter) ⓗ

Newly reopened in 2015, Timbrell's Yard has been beautifully restored and transformed into an upmarket pub with rooms. Originally the home of wealthy local mill owner Mr Timbrell, the building has been returned to its former glory. The beers – two regulars and two guests – are usually locally brewed, while ciders are on tap too. The food is excellent and highly recommended, including substantial all-day bar snacks and restaurant meals.

Q ⭑ ✿ ✦ ⏀ ⓓ ♿ ⇌ ● P 🛏 (265) 🐾 🛜

Bremhill

Dumb Post Inn ⓛ

Dumb Post Hill, SN11 9JZ (1 mile N of A4, just W of Calne)

🕐 12-3, 6-11; 12-midnight Fri & Sat; 12-10.30 Sun

☎ (01249) 813192 🌐 the-dumb-post-inn.co.uk

Butcombe Adam Henson's Rare Breed; St Austell Cornish Best Bitter; 2 changing beers (sourced regionally; often Bristol Beer Factory, Castle Combe) ⓗ

Thought to be the only Dumb Post Inn in the country, this stone-built pub with real fires dates from the 18th century, although the building is older. The management are enthusiastic innkeepers, with plans to add a fifth beer and a real cider on handpump. Good-quality home-cooked food is available, with Wiltshire faggots a speciality. The huge garden offers views over the Bowood Estate. Say hello to Oscar, the parrot who has been in residence for over 35 years.

Q ⭑ ✿ ⏀ P 🐾 🛜

Calne

White Hart Hotel ⓛ

London Road, SN11 0AB (on A4 jct with Silver St)

🕐 12-11 (1am Fri & Sat) ☎ (01249) 812413

🌐 whitehartcalne.com

Bath Ales Gem; Box Steam Piston Broke; 3 changing beers (sourced locally; often Castle Combe, Cottage, Goff's) ⓗ

An old coaching inn built in 1659, popular with locals and welcoming to visitors. The bar and restaurant feature an eclectic decor, and there is a medieval-style banqueting hall decorated with armour and swords. The area behind the fire has a homely feel with sofas and plenty of books to read. Local and regional charities are supported with fundraising events. ⭑ ⏀ ⓓ ♿ ✦ ● P 🛏 (33) 🛜

Chippenham

Bridge House ⓛ ✅

Borough Parade, SN15 3WL (next to river just off town bridge)

🕐 8am-11 (1am Fri & Sat) ☎ (01249) 450980

Greene King Abbot; Ruddles Best Bitter; Sharp's Doom Bar; 4 changing beers (sourced nationally; often Box Steam) ⓗ

Recent changes in management have seen major improvements in beer quality at this busy Wetherspoon pub, with meticulous attention to delivering the highest quality ale and cider. Good food, friendly yet informal service and great value have made it a focal point for many in the local community. With views over the River Avon and an outside decking area, the large pub attracts a diverse range of highly satisfied and loyal customers. ⭑ ✿ ⏀ ♿ ⇌ ● P 🛏 🛜

Old Road Tavern

Old Rd, SN15 1JA (over bridge from railway station)

🕐 11-11.30 (12.30am Fri & Sat); 12-11.30 Sun

☎ (01249) 652094

Bath Ales Gem; Hop Back Summer Lightning; Otter Bitter; Wye Valley HPA; 2 changing beers (sourced nationally; often Adnams, Moorhouse's) ⓗ

REAL ALE BREWERIES

Arkell's Swindon
Box Steam Holt
Chippenham Chippenham (brewing suspended)
Dark Revolution Salisbury (NEW)
Downton Downton
Flying Monk Hullavington
Hop Back Downton
Hop Kettle 🍴 Cricklade/Swindon
Kennet & Avon Melksham
Kettlesmith Bradford-on-Avon (NEW)
Keystone Berwick St Leonard
Moles Melksham
Plain Sutton Veny
Ramsbury Aldbourne
Shed Pewsey
Stonehenge Netheravon
Three Castles Pewsey
Three Daggers Edington
Twisted Westbury
Wadworth Devizes
Weighbridge 🍴 Swindon
Wessex Longbridge Deverill
Willy Good Ale Winsley
World's End 🍴 Pewsey

A traditional community local occupying a 140-year-old listed building. The diverse mix of regulars ensures lively and friendly conversation. Four regular beers and two guests are available alongside simple bar food served Thursday to Saturday lunchtimes. A live music and comedy night venue, it is always extremely busy during the Chippenham Folk Festival over the late May bank holiday weekend. The large garden with plenty of seating is popular in summer. ⊛◑&≠♣♠🐾🐱🛜

Three Crowns 🍷 ⃞Ⓛ

18 The Causeway, SN15 3DB (S of town opp Kwik Fit)
🕓 5-11; 12-midnight Fri & Sat; 12-11 Sun ☎ (01249) 449029
⊕ threecrownschippenham.co.uk
7 changing beers (sourced nationally; often Arbor, Slater's, XT) Ⓗ
Originally an 18th-century wagon inn on the London to Bath road, this is now a community free house offering seven cask beers from local microbreweries and from further afield. The range always includes two dark beers and one strong brew. A multiple CAMRA award winner, it sells three ciders, mainly sourced from Wiltshire producers, and a perry, and hosts four beer festivals each year. A popular venue for quiz, music and various other ad hoc theme nights.
Q≠♣♠P🚲🖵(55)🐱🛜

Coombe Bissett

Fox & Goose ⃞Ⓛ

Blandford Road, SP5 4LE
🕓 11-11; 12-10.30 Sun ☎ (01722) 718437
⊕ foxandgoose-coombebissett.co.uk
Sharp's Doom Bar; 2 changing beers (sourced locally) Ⓗ
Eighteenth-century coaching inn on the A354 three miles south of Salisbury. A popular community pub, it has a loyal village clientele and a welcoming atmosphere. It is divided into a bar and restaurant, offering an extensive food menu with ever-changing specials. There is a loyalty card scheme for regular diners. Two regularly changing ales are sourced mostly from local microbreweries. Outside there is a covered smoking area and gardens to the rear. Q🛏⊛◑P🖵(X12,29)🐱🛜

Corsley

Cross Keys Inn

Lye's Green, BA12 7PB
🕓 12-3, 6-11; 12-11 Sun ☎ (01373) 832406
⊕ crosskeyscorsley.co.uk
Three Daggers Daggers Ale; 3 changing beers (sourced locally; often Moles, Twisted) Ⓗ
This rural gem in the shadow of Cley Hill (famed for its UFO sightings) was taken over by a village consortium in 2016. It has a large open fire and a warm, welcoming atmosphere. A good selection of guest ales is available, mainly sourced from local breweries, along with excellent bar food and restaurant meals. The pub is set in an excellent walking area, close to the Somerset border, with Longleat House and Safari Park nearby.
🛏⊛◑♣♠P🐱🛜

Cricklade

Red Lion 🍷 ⃞Ⓛ

74 High Street, SN6 6DD

🕓 12-11 (10.30 Sun) ☎ (01793) 750776
⊕ theredlioncricklade.co.uk
Butcombe Bitter; Hop Kettle seasonal beers; Wadworth 6X; 4 changing beers Ⓗ
Friendly, popular and comfortable inn, parts of which are quite ancient – the old Saxon town wall passes through the building. It is home to the Hop Kettle Brewing Co, which started brewing in 2012. Ten real ales – two regular, four from Hop Kettle and four guests – are on handpump, plus real cider. Food is served lunchtimes and evenings Monday-Saturday, lunchtime only on Sunday. There is a large garden at the back, and accommodation in five rooms. A winter beer festival is held in February, a summer festival in June.
Q⊛🛏◑&♠🖵(51,53)🐱🛜

Devizes

British Lion ✅

9 Estcourt Street, SN10 1LQ (on A361 London road opp Kwik Fit)
🕓 11-11 (midnight Fri & Sat); 12-11 Sun ☎ (01380) 720665
⊕ britishliondevizes.co.uk
4 changing beers (sourced nationally; often Bath Ales, Palmers, Stonehenge) Ⓗ
A Guide regular now for well over 20 years. With friendly locals, excellent staff and a landlord who knows the industry inside out, the Lion is an essential port of call in Devizes. Four handpumps dispense ever-changing ales mainly from West Country breweries, and a large selection of chilled bottles and real cider is always available. Inside, there are wooden floors, comfy settles and plenty of tables and chairs. Outside there is a huge beer garden and a covered smoking area.
⊛♠P🖵(49)🛜

Southgate Inn

Potterne Road, SN10 5BY
🕓 4-11; 12-midnight Fri & Sat; 12-11 Sun ☎ (01380) 722872
3 changing beers (often Downton, Hop Back) Ⓗ
The five-minute stroll from the town centre to find the Southgate is well worth it – this popular pub attracts regulars and visitors alike. Warm, cosy and friendly, it has a three-sided bar, lots of nooks and crannies, and is carpeted throughout. A Hop Back house, it offers two beers from Hop Back or Downton and a guest ale on the third pump. Live music is hosted several times a month plus an annual beer festival. Outside is a smart courtyard with benches and parasols. Dogs are welcome.
🛏♣♠P🖵(2,49)🐱🛜

Vaults

28A St John's Street, SN10 1BN (opp town hall)
🕓 12-9 (6 Sun) ☎ (01380) 721443 ⊕ thevaultsdevizes.com
6 changing beers (sourced nationally; often Kennet & Avon) Ⓗ
The Vaults maintains its high standards, with six handpumps usually offering two from Kennet & Avon plus three or four ever-changing beers from breweries including Tiny Rebel and Old Dairy. A vast selection of bottles and tins from around the world is also stocked. Paddles are available – three third-pint glasses allow you to sample several ales at a time. It has a long, galley-style bar and a huge cellar used for events. Conversation rules here – there is no music or fruit machines but a great atmosphere. ♠P🐱🛜

Dilton Marsh

Prince of Wales

94 High Street, BA13 4DZ (on main road through village)
🕐 5-11; 12-11 Fri-Sun ☎ (01373) 865487
⊕ powdiltonmarsh.co.uk
Otter Ale; St Austell Cornish Best Bitter, Trelawny; 1 changing beer (sourced regionally; often Bath Ales, Otter, St Austell) Ⓗ
A smart, friendly local, refurbished in 2013, with a bar, separate dining area and skittle alley/function room. Outside is a paved area to one side and the beer garden. The menu offers traditional pub food including a popular Sunday lunch. The guest beer can be from St Austell – HSD or Proper Job – but quite often comes from elsewhere and has included London Pride, Bass and beers from local micros such as Box Steam and Twisted.
🏮🕪👌♣♠P🖵🐾📶

East Knoyle

Fox & Hounds

Wise Lane, The Green, SP3 6BN ST87113135
🕐 11.30-3, 5.30-11 ☎ (01747) 830573
⊕ foxandhounds-eastknoyle.co.uk
3 changing beers Ⓗ
Attractive old thatched black-and-white pub situated high on a hillside with extensive panoramic rural views. Comfortable and cosy inside, the warm welcome is enhanced in winter by a blazing log fire in a huge inglenook fireplace. Three ales are always available encompassing a wide range of strengths and varying continuously, with local beers given prominence. The real cider is Thatchers Cheddar Valley. Food is served at all sessions. An adjacent skittle alley doubles as a function room. Q🐕🏮🕪♠P🐾

Ebbesbourne Wake

Horseshoe

The Cross, SP5 5JF
🕐 closed Mon; 12-3, 6.30-11; 12-4 Sun ☎ (01722) 780474
Bowman Swift One; Otter Bitter; Palmers Copper Ale; 2 changing beers (sourced nationally; often Flack Manor) Ⓖ
Unspoilt 18th-century pub in a remote rural setting at the foot of an old ox drove. This friendly pub has two small bars that display an impressive collection of old farm implements, tools and lamps, plus a restaurant, conservatory and pleasant garden. Good local food is available Tuesday to Sunday and the four beers are served direct from casks stillaged behind the bar. The original serving hatch just inside the front door is still in use. Real cider is usually available, often from Thatchers or Wessex.
Q🐕🏮🕪Å♠P🖵(29)🐾

Edington

Three Daggers

Westbury Road, BA13 4PG
🕐 8am-11; 9am-10.30 Sun ☎ (01380) 830940
⊕ threedaggers.co.uk
Three Daggers Daggers Blonde, Daggers Ale, Daggers Edge, seasonal beer; 1 changing beer Ⓗ
This refurbished village pub is now the brewery tap for the eponymous brewery situated in an adjacent farm shop. The pub has a main bar with three distinct drinking areas, leading to a seating area and a dining room. Two mirrors hide TV screens that are occasionally used for sporting events. Regular seasonal beers are brewed, and carryouts and bottles are available from the farm shop.
Q🐕🏮🕪🛏◑👌P🖵🐾📶

Highworth

Rose & Crown Ⓛ

19 The Green, SN6 7DB
🕐 9am-11 (midnight Fri); 11-midnight Sat; 12-11 Sun
☎ (01793) 764699 ⊕ roseandcrownhighworth.co.uk
Brains Rev James; Sharp's Doom Bar; Timothy Taylor Landlord; 2 changing beers (sourced regionally; often Halfpenny, Old Forge) Ⓗ
This is one of the oldest pubs in Highworth. It opened as a free house in 2014 after a major facelift, and has a pleasant ambience. Cheerful and friendly staff serve a changing range of ales on five handpumps. The lunchtime menu is good quality and great value. There is a boules pitch in the garden. Open mic and folk sessions are hosted once a month. Q🐕🏮🕪◑♠P🖵(6)🐾📶

Kilmington

Red Lion Inn Ⓛ ✅

BA12 6RP (on B3092 between Mere and Frome)
🕐 11-3, 6.30-10 (9 Mon & Tue); 12-3, 7-10 Sun
☎ (01985) 844263 ⊕ theredlionkilmington.co.uk
Butcombe Bitter; Wessex Stourton Pale Ale; 1 changing beer Ⓗ
A warm and friendly traditional free house with a low-beamed, flagstoned front bar with cushioned walls and window seats, curved high-backed settle seats and woodburners. The larger back bar has tables for diners to enjoy the home-cooked food sourced from high-quality local food producers (some from the village itself). Thatchers Heritage cider completes the excellent drinks range. Dogs are welcome to join their owners in the front bar or in the large attractive garden which has fine views of White Sheet Hill. Q🐕🏮🕪◑♣♠P🐾📶

Kington St Michael

Jolly Huntsman Ⓛ

SN14 6JB
🕐 11.30-2.30, 6-11 (midnight Fri & Sat); 12-3, 7-10.30 Sun
☎ (01249) 750305 ⊕ jollyhuntsman.com
Moles Gold; Wadworth 6X; 2 changing beers (sourced locally; often Flying Monk, Ramsbury) Ⓗ
A former brewery situated on the village high street, this free house offers a warm and friendly welcome, with a large open fire in the winter. It serves a selection of locally brewed real ales and often regional ciders. An excellent food menu is available lunchtimes and evenings, featuring a range of traditional fare and chef's specials. Themed evenings are held on occasion. Accommodation is en suite. Q🐕🛏🕪◑👌♠P🖵(99)

Lacock

Bell Inn Ⓛ

The Wharf, SN15 2PJ (½ mile out of Lacock towards Bowden Hill)
🕐 11-2.30, 5-11; 11.30-11 Sat; 12-10.30 Sun
☎ (01249) 730308 ⊕ thebellatlacock.co.uk
House beer (by Bath Ales); 3 changing beers (sourced regionally; often Cottage, Great Western, Plain) Ⓗ

Renowned for its friendly welcome, this popular free house is on the edge of the National Trust village of Lacock and one of only two pubs sitting on the Wilts & Berks Canal. Local CAMRA Pub of the Year on numerous occasions, it has an excellent reputation for the quality of its ale and food. Four ales and a real cider are usually available, and two beer festivals are held each year. The house beer, Red Wharf, is brewed to the pub's own recipe by Bath Ales. Q🕭🏠🍴🕐🅰♣🐕P🖪🐾🌣📶

George Inn 🅛 ✅
4 West Street, SN15 2LH

🕐 11-3, 6-11; 11-11 Sat; 11-10.30 Sun ☎ (01249) 730263

🌐 georgeinnlacock.co.uk

Wadworth IPA, Horizon, 6X; 1 changing beer (sourced nationally; often Oakham) Ⓗ

Timber and stone pub near the centre of this beautiful National Trust village, dating from the mid-14th century. Look for the original fireplace and dog-driven spit in the oak-beamed interior. A changing range of cider is available and good-quality locally sourced meals are served. A beer festival is held in August and the Boxing Day barbecue is popular. Photographs and cuttings on display reflect the popularity of the village with film and TV programme makers. A Wadworth seasonal beer is always on the bar.
Q🕭🏠🍴🕐🅰🕐P🖪(X34)🐾📶

Laverstock

Duck 🅛
Duck Lane, SP1 1PU

🕐 12-midnight; 12.30-midnight Sun ☎ (01722) 327678

🌐 theduckatlaverstock.co.uk

Hop Back GFB, Crop Circle, Summer Lightning; 2 changing beers (sourced nationally) Ⓗ

A busy community village pub serving popular home-cooked lunches, including traditional roasts on Sunday, in a large, well-furnished, open-plan bar. A variety of entertainment includes open-mic nights, quizzes, live music at weekends and themed barbecues. There is full disabled access and dogs and children are welcome. Ideally located for walkers on the Clarendon Way. Local CAMRA Country Pub of the Year 2017.
🏠🕐🕓P🖪(66,R6)🐾📶

Malmesbury

Whole Hog 🅛
8 Market Cross, SN16 9AS

🕐 11-11; 12-midnight Fri & Sat; 12-11 Sun

☎ (01666) 825845

Stonehenge Pigswill; Wadworth 6X; Young's Bitter; 1 changing beer (sourced locally) Ⓗ

Located between the 15th-century market cross and the abbey in the oldest borough in England, this is a popular town-centre pub, serving well-kept ales and freshly prepared food. There is a diverse range of seating areas, from a former shop window overlooking the Market Square to cosy nooks and crannies. A pub central to the community with many regulars and equally welcoming to visitors looking for respite from sightseeing. Q🕐♣🕐🖪📶

Marston Meysey

Old Spotted Cow
SN6 6LQ

🕐 11-11 (6.30 Sun) ☎ (01285) 810264

🌐 theoldspottedcow.co.uk

Butcombe Gold; Otter Bitter; 1 changing beer (sourced nationally) Ⓗ

With large gardens and a cosy interior featuring beamed ceilings, log fires and three real ale handpumps, this pub is popular with locals and visitors alike. There is a strong emphasis on good food sourced from local producers and suppliers. The Thames Path is nearby and the pub is attractive to hikers. A classic car show features in late May.
Q🕭🏠🕐🕓♣P🐾📶

Melksham

Bear 🅛 ✅
3 Bath Road, SN12 6LL

🕐 8am-midnight ☎ (01225) 792690

Greene King Abbot; Ruddles Best Bitter; Sharp's Doom Bar; 3 changing beers (sourced nationally; often Exmoor, Shepherd Neame, Titanic) Ⓗ

A spacious Wetherspoon pub with interesting local history storyboards adorning the walls, and a real fire in winter. Friendly and helpful staff serve a range of three regular ales and three guests, often including LocAle, as well as three varying ciders. A full range of food is always available, including the popular weekly steak, curry and fish nights. The large paved garden area includes a smoking area. Frequent buses stop directly outside the pub.
Q🕭🏠🕐🕓🕭P🖪(272)📶

Netherhampton

Victoria & Albert
SP2 8PU

🕐 11-3, 5.30 (5 Sat)-11; 12-3, 7-10.30 Sun

☎ (01722) 743174 🌐 victoriaandalbert.org

4 changing beers (sourced nationally) Ⓗ

Classic thatched inn dating from 1540 in a village setting three miles from Salisbury and close to the racecourse. A log fire provides a winter welcome and for summer there is a large garden and covered patio area. Four varying beers are usually sourced from small breweries, alongside real cider. An established family business, the pub provides quality food ranging from hearty snacks to full meals. A former local CAMRA and Wessex regional and country Pub of the Year. Q🕭🏠🕐♣🕐P🐾📶

Newton Tony

Malet Arms 🅛
SP4 0HF

🕐 11-3, 6-11; 12-3 Sun ☎ (01980) 629279

4 changing beers (sourced locally; often Itchen Valley, Ramsbury, Stonehenge) Ⓗ

Charming and historic pub, with a restaurant extension, in the conservation area of the village and with the river Bourne flowing past in winter. The window in the larger bar is reputed to come from a galleon. The long-standing landlord is as enthusiastic and proud of his high-quality food as he is of his ales. Four beers change weekly and include local ones and occasionally others from further afield. The pub welcomes walkers and dogs. Q🕭🏠🕐🕐P🖪(67)🐾

Pewsey

Crown Inn 🅛
60 Wilcot Road, SN9 5EL

🌠 4 (12 Wed & Thu)-11; 12-11.30 Fri; 12-midnight Sat; 12-10.30 Sun ☎ (01672) 562653
🌐 thecrowninnpewsey.com

Wadworth 6X; 3 changing beers (sourced locally; often Stonehenge, Three Castles, World's End) 🅷
This traditional local is the brewery tap for World's End and always features at least two of its own beers among the five on offer. The small bar has an attractive stone and brick fireplace in the centre. Chess and poetry nights are hosted as well as live music twice a month. There are beer festivals to mark the summer and winter solstices. Food is served Friday evening, Sunday lunchtime and theme nights only, unless by prior arrangement. Q 🕭 🕭 🕭 ⛄ 🕭 (X5) 🕭 🕭

Shed Alehouse

20 North Street, SN9 5EX
🌠 closed Mon & Tue; 5-9.30 Wed & Thu; 4-10 Fri; 2-10 Sat; 1-5 Sun ☎ 07769 812643 🌐 theshedalehouse.com

5 changing beers (sourced regionally) 🅷
A former shop converted to a cosy micropub, the interior reflecting its name with a basic wood-panelled decor complete with tools. This is a free house with five handpumps serving a changing range of beers from local and regional brewers, often including Shed Ales from Pewsey, alongside four real ciders. There is not much space inside, so you soon get to know your fellow drinkers. No dogs allowed. Q ⛄ 🕭 🕭 (X5)

Ramsbury

Crown & Anchor 🅻

1 Crowood Lane, SN8 2PT
🌠 12-11 (10.30 Sun) ☎ (01672) 520335
🌐 crownandanchorramsbury.co.uk

Wickwar BOB; house beer (by Wickwar); 2 changing beers (sourced nationally; often Fuller's, West Berkshire) 🅷
A welcoming 19th-century country pub on several levels, with a cosy feel enhanced by fireplaces and low ceiling beams. Interesting bric-a-brac including 200-year-old blacksmith's fixings and a Victorian beer engine add to the ambience. There are four ales on offer including the house beer from Wickwar. Food, including breakfast, is served daily except Sunday evening. The garden area to the rear has a barbecue for the summer. Two en-suite B&B rooms are available. Q 🕭 🕭 🕭 🕭 🕭 P 🕭 🕭 🕭

Royal Wootton Bassett

Five Bells 🅻 🕭

Wood Street, SN4 7BD
🌠 12-3, 5-midnight; 12-1am Fri & Sat; 12-midnight Sun
☎ (01793) 849422

Black Sheep Best Bitter; Fuller's London Pride; 4 changing beers (sourced nationally; often Sharp's, Timothy Taylor) 🅷
Dating from before 1841, this is a busy and cosy traditional thatched local with a beamed ceiling and open fires. The bar, which has recently been extended, has seven handpumps for two regular beers, four guests and a cider. Food is served lunchtimes and Wednesday and Thursday evenings (booking recommended). The pub has darts and crib teams. Special events are held throughout the year including a festival in the summer. Q 🕭 🕭 🕭 🕭 P 🕭 (55) 🕭 🕭

Salisbury

Duke of York 🅻

34 York Road, SP2 7AS
🌠 6 (4 Sat)-midnight; 2-midnight Sun ☎ (01722) 503872

Hop Back GFB; 4 changing beers (sourced nationally) 🅷
Dating back to 1901 and formerly owned by Ushers, the pub has a strong community focus with an emphasis on conversation. Quiz night is every Sunday and a presentation by the resident Fisherton History Society is on the second Wednesday of the month. Other occasional events include beer festivals. The range of often local beers may be reduced midweek – up to two real ciders are also usually available.
🕭 ⛄ 🕭 🕭 (R1) 🕭 🕭

Haunch of Venison ★

1 Minster Street, SP1 1TB
🌠 11-11 (midnight Fri & Sat); 11-10 Sun ☎ (01722) 411313
🌐 haunchpub.co.uk

Courage Best Bitter; Hop Back GFB, Summer Lightning; 1 changing beer (sourced nationally) 🅷
One of the oldest and most haunted hostelries in the city, the pub was first recorded in 1320, housing craftsmen building the Cathedral. Identified by CAMRA as having a nationally important historic interior, there are three areas: the Horsebox, a tiny bar with a pewter bar-top and original spirit taps; the Commons, wood-panelled with a large fireplace, bench seats and a floor laid with tiles from the Cathedral; and the Lords, another wood-panelled room with an inglenook fireplace. In an alcove is the mummified hand of a card cheat still holding his last cards. 🕭 ⛄ 🕭 🕭 🕭

King's Head 🕭

Bridge Street, SP1 2ND
🌠 7am-midnight (1am Thu-Sat) ☎ (01722) 342050

Greene King Abbot; Sharp's Doom Bar; 6 changing beers (sourced nationally) 🅷
Formerly the County Hotel, this fine stone building sitting alongside the River Avon is now a Wetherspoon. A pub or brewery has occupied this site since 1470. The spacious interior is spread over two levels. The riverside beer garden has recently had new furniture and grass added, making it a popular spot for alfresco drinking and dining. Q 🕭 🕭 🕭 🕭 🕭 🕭 ⛄ 🕭 🕭

Rai d'Or 🅻

69 Brown Street, SP1 2AS
🌠 5-10 (11 Thu-Sat); closed Sun ☎ (01722) 327137
🌐 raidor.co.uk

2 changing beers (sourced locally) 🅷
Characterful 13th-century free house with a fascinating history. An inglenook fireplace and low ceilings make for an appealing ambience. Excellent, reasonably priced Thai food is complemented by two ever-changing, usually local beers. It can be busy at mealtimes, but drinkers are always welcome. There is a discount on food before 6.30pm. A former local CAMRA Pub of the Year with 13 years in the Guide. 🕭 🕭 🕭 🕭 🕭 🕭

Railway Inn/Dust Hole 🅻

59 Tollgate Road, SP1 2JG
🌠 12-2 (not Mon-Wed), 7-11; 12-3, 6-11 Sun
☎ (01722) 324537 🌐 thedusthole.vpweb.co.uk

Downton Honey Blonde; 1 changing beer (sourced locally) 🅷

Friendly local pub close to Salisbury College, a short walk from the city centre. This is the only public house in the country to be licensed under two official names – look at the sign hanging outside. The Railway refers to its proximity to the now closed goods railway station and the Dust Hole to the coal dust that used to be blown into the bar. Bought by a local in 2013, it is now a free house. ⛺🕮🕽🌙♣🚌(X7)📶

Rugby Club 🅛
Castle Road, SP1 3SA
🕓 closed Mon; 7-11; 12-midnight Sat; 8-11 Sun
☎ (01722) 325317 ⊕ salisburyrfc.org
Hop Back GFB, Crop Circle, Summer Lightning; 1 changing beer (often Hop Back) 🅗
Occupying a corner of the large club house, this cosy, recently refurbished lounge bar is open to the public. Retaining its sporting roots, the bar features rugby memorabilia. Two TVs generally show rugby or other sport. The function room bar is open at busy times such as match days. The changing beer is occasionally from Downton. Quiz night is Wednesday. A beer festival is held in May. There are camping facilities close by. ⛺🕮♣AP🚌🐾📶

Village Freehouse 🅛
33 Wilton Road, SP2 7EF
🕓 5-midnight; 12-midnight Fri-Sun ☎ (01722) 329707
Downton Quadhop; 4 changing beers (sourced nationally) 🅗
Friendly, lively pub close to the railway station with a decor featuring railway memorabilia and books. Microbrewery beers from near and far are core to the spirit of this pub, with requests welcomed. Unique in the area, there is always a dark beer – either mild, porter or stout. Major sporting events are screened on terrestrial TV. Filled rolls are available or you are welcome to bring your own food. Local CAMRA Pub of the Year three times in the past decade. 🚃🖥(R8, PR3)🐾📶

Wyndham Arms 🍷 🅛
27 Estcourt Road, SP1 3AS
🕓 4.30 (12 Thu)-11.30; 12-midnight Fri & Sat; 12-11.30 Sun
☎ (01722) 331026
Hop Back GFB, Citra, Crop Circle, Summer Lightning 🅗
The birthplace of Hop Back Brewery, now celebrating 31 consecutive years in the Guide. A traditional ale house, it has a single bar with six handpumps serving a selection of Hop Back ales including its seasonal offering. There is also a fine selection of bottled beers and wines. This is a pub for conversation, good-natured banter and fine ales. Local CAMRA Pub of the Year 2017. ⛺♣🖥(R2,R6)🐾

Semley

Benett Arms
Village Green, SP7 9AS (1 mile E of A350) ST891270
🕓 12-3, 5-11 ☎ (01747) 830221 ⊕ benettarms.co.uk
House beer (by Ringwood); 2 changing beers 🅗
A genuine free house sitting by the green and pond in a quiet village, with a single small bar and separate dining areas. The beer choice varies but there are usually three to choose from, either on handpump or direct from the cellar. The cider is from Bridge Farm. Excellent home-cooked food is available at all sessions. A warm welcome is extended to all, including families and dogs, in an area popular with walkers. Local CAMRA branch Pub of the Year 2016. Q🕮🕽♿♣P🖥(84,247)🐾

Stourton

Spread Eagle
Church Lawn, BA12 6QE
🕓 10-11; 12-10.30 Sun ☎ (01747) 840587
⊕ spreadeagleinn.com
Butcombe Bitter; Wessex Kilmington Best; 1 changing beer 🅗
Mellow brick and slate pub owned by the National Trust within the Stourhead Estate and adjacent to the famous Stourhead House and garden. Spacious and comfortable, the inn offers a selection of local ales and bottled ciders. Excellent English cooking features dishes made with locally sourced ingredients. Breakfast is served 8-9am and afternoon refreshments are also available. It can be busy during the peak tourist season. Q🕮🛌🕽♿P

Swindon

Beehive ✅
55 Prospect Hill, SN1 3JS
🕓 12-midnight (1am Thu-Sat) ☎ (01793) 523187
⊕ bee-hive.co.uk
Hardys & Hansons Olde Trip; house beer (by Hardys & Hansons); 4 changing beers (sourced regionally; often Greene King) 🅗
Multi-levelled, four-room pub with a quirky charm. The beer range has a local focus including Meet the Brewer evenings as part of Greene King's Local Hero initiative. A popular live music venue, it hosts performances on most Thursday and Friday evenings and some Mondays. The walls feature pictures and other artwork, often for sale. Locally sourced pies are available lunchtime until early evening, with complimentary crisps and snacks from late afternoon. Poker night is Monday. 🕽♣🖥🐾📶

Blunsdon Arms ✅
Lady Lane, SN25 2NA
🕓 11-midnight; 10-12.30am Fri & Sat ☎ (01793) 729801
Brakspear Oxford Gold; house beer (by Black Sheep); 6 changing beers (sourced nationally; often Bath Ales, Butcombe) 🅗
This Ember Inns pub opened in 2006 and has a large open-plan interior with lots of comfortable seating. The six guest beers rotate from a selection of 12 ales changing quarterly. There are also three real ciders. CAMRA members receive a discount. Food is served every day until 10pm. Quiz nights are Wednesday and Sunday, poker night every Monday. Live music features on the last Saturday of the month. A friendly welcome is assured from the pleasant staff. ⛺🕮🕽♿♣🍽P🖥(11,15,15A)📶

Glue Pot
5 Emlyn Square, SN1 5BP
🕓 12 (4.30 Mon)-11; 11.30-11 Fri & Sat; 12-10.30 Sun
☎ (01793) 497420
Downton New Forest Ale; Hop Back Citra, Crop Circle, Entire Stout, Summer Lightning; 2 changing beers (sourced regionally; often Downton, Hop Back) 🅗
The Glue Pot is part of the historic Swindon Railway Village built in the 1840s. One window still shows the Allsopp's logo. The inside is basic with wooden bench seats. There are seven Hop Back or Downton ales, one guest, and 10 real ciders. A range of sandwiches, wraps and subs is always available. There is a pub quiz on Thursday night and a beer festival over the Easter weekend. Local CAMRA Cider Pub of the Year in 2016. Q🕮🚃🍽🖥(8,14)🐾

Hop Inn ⓛ

7 Devizes Road, SN1 4BJ

☼ 12-11 (midnight Fri & Sat); 12-10.30 Sun
☎ (01793) 976833 ⊕ hopinnswindon.co.uk
House beer (by Ramsbury); 4 changing beers (sourced regionally) Ⓗ

A genuine free house, this former shop has become a popular destination for real ale lovers. The small bar has five handpumps, four with an ever-changing variety of guest ales sourced from smaller breweries. There are also two real ciders in boxes. The interior is furnished in an eclectic style with bright plastic chairs and tables made from reclaimed wood. A former local CAMRA Pub of the Year. Q❤️🌑👌🍴🖵(12,15)❀🛜

Savoy ⓛ ✅

38-40 Regent Street, SN1 1JL

☼ 8am-midnight (1am Fri & Sat) ☎ (01793) 533970
Greene King Abbot; Ruddles Best Bitter; Sharp's Doom Bar; Wychwood Hobgoblin; changing beers (sourced nationally) Ⓗ

This lively town-centre pub is the oldest Wetherspoon in Swindon, converted from the foyer and ground floors of a 1930s cinema. Cinema photos and information from the era decorate the walls. It has a spacious interior on different levels, divided into separate areas. There is a TV screen in one corner, mainly silent. A large selection of well-kept beers is available and food is served all day until 11pm. Handy for the theatre, cinema, restaurants and shopping. Q❤️🌑🌑👌🍴🖵(1,1A)🛜

Wheatsheaf ⓛ

32 Newport Street, SN1 3DP

☼ 12-3, 5-11; 12-midnight Fri & Sat; 12-8 Sun
☎ (01793) 266754
Wadworth IPA, Horizon, 6X, Swordfish; 1 changing beer Ⓗ

The focus here is on real ale, with six handpumps and six wooden casks behind the bar. However, these casks do not store beer, it is pumped from steel casks in the cellar. The guest ale comes from the Wadworth list. The front bar is cosy while the back bar opens up into a larger area. Live music plays occasionally, usually on the third Sunday of the month. Q❤️🌑♣️🍴🖵❀🛜

Tisbury

Benett Arms ⓛ

High Street, SP3 6HD

☼ 12-midnight (1am Thu-Sat) ☎ (01747) 870428
⊕ benetttisbury.co.uk
Keystone Bedrock, Large One; 1 changing beer (sourced regionally) Ⓗ

A warm welcome awaits you at this Keystone Brewery pub. Two Keystone beers – Large One is badged as Gordon Benett – are accompanied by another from Wiltshire, Dorset or Somerset, and a real cider. The front bar is furnished with a range of tables while the rear bar has a pool table. In fine weather you can sit on the front patio and watch the world go by. Lunchtime paninis are served, and traditional roasts on Sunday. The popular curry night is the first Monday of the month.
❤️🌑🌑🍴♣️🍴🖵(25,26)❀🛜

Boot Inn ⓛ

High Street, SP3 6PS

☼ 12-2.30 (not Mon & Tue), 7-11; 12-3 Sun
☎ (01747) 870363
3 changing beers (sourced regionally) Ⓖ

Fine village pub built of Chilmark stone, licensed since 1768, with a relaxed, friendly atmosphere appealing to locals and visitors alike. Run by the same landlord since 1976, it became a free house in 2009 and has three or four ales behind the bar. Excellent food is served and there is a spacious garden. A pub for conversation and a former local CAMRA Pub of the Year. Q🌑🌑♣️🍴(25,26)

Upavon

Ship ⓛ

10 High Street, SN9 6EA

☼ 11.30-11.30 (1am Fri & Sat); 12-11 Sun ☎ (01980) 630313
⊕ theshipinnupavon.co.uk
Wadworth 6X; 4 changing beers (sourced locally; often Cottage, Plain, Stonehenge) Ⓗ

Parts of this thatched pub date from the 15th century. Inside it combines traditional wooden beams with a light, airy appearance. The decor, including a huge model of the Cutty Sark, is of nautical and local interest. A wood-burning pizza oven in the garden is fired up Thursday to Saturday evenings from 5.30pm. The three guest ales are locally sourced and there are four real ciders and 40 malt whiskies. Tuesday is fish and chips night. 🌑🌑👌♣️🍴🖵(X5)❀🛜

Upton Lovell

Prince Leopold Inn

54 Upton Lovell, BA12 0JP

☼ 12-3 (not Mon), 6-11; 12-4 Sun ☎ (01985) 850460
⊕ princeleopold.co.uk
Butcombe Adam Henson's Rare Breed; 2 changing beers (sourced regionally) Ⓗ

Hidden away in the beautiful Wylye Valley, the pub is now back to being a proper local as well as catering for visitors. The main bar is reserved for those wishing to enjoy a drink, and there is a small snug with an open fire, books, newspapers and board games. There are several areas dedicated to excellent food, including the large restaurant overlooking the River Wylye. It has a lovely garden which runs right down to the riverbank. Q❤️🌑🖾🌑P❀🛜

Urchfont

Lamb Inn ✅

The Green, SN10 4QU

☼ 12-3 (not Mon), 6-11; 12-11 Sun ☎ (01380) 848848
⊕ lambinnurchfont.co.uk
Wadworth IPA, 6X; 1 changing beer (often Wadworth) Ⓗ

The quintessential village pub – this lovely thatched inn in the heart of the village has a wooden bar, panelled walls and beamed ceilings. A Wadworth house, 6X and IPA are always on handpump, with a third pump dispensing a seasonal ale from the brewery. Cosy, warm and inviting, there are plenty of tables and chairs, a large beer garden and a covered smoking area. It offers a varied dining menu, as well as a skittle alley, darts and a large function room. 🌑🌑♣️P🖵(271)❀

Warminster

Fox & Hounds
6 Deverill Road, BA12 9QP
☼ 11-11 ☎ (01985) 216711
Wessex Warminster Warrior; house beer (by Wessex); 2 changing beers (sourced regionally; often Flack Manor, Otter, Palmers) Ⓗ
This friendly two-bar inn is a local CAMRA multiple award-winning pub. The main bar has a pool table and TV for sport at the back; a quiet snug bar is to the right of the entrance. There is also a large skittle alley and function room. Regular ciders are from Thatchers and Rich's, with up to five guests. Guest real ales are usually from local and regional breweries. Closing time may be later than 11pm.
Q❀&♣■P❀�

Organ Inn ✔
49 High Street, BA12 9AQ
☼ 4 (12 Sat)-midnight; 4-11 Sun ☎ (01985) 211777
⊕ theorganinn.co.uk
3 changing beers (sourced regionally; often Cottage, Plain, Stonehenge) Ⓗ
An inn until 1913, the Organ reopened as a pub in 2006. The welcoming interior comprises several rooms with a traditional feel, with a snug games room and a skittle alley. The beer range constantly changes but always includes Organ Bitter (the brewer is a secret). The cider is mainly Westons or a guest. Bar snacks are interesting. There is an art gallery upstairs. A beer festival is held in September. A former local CAMRA Rural Pub of the Year. Q❀&≈♣●■❀�

Westbury

Hollies
55A Westbury Leigh, BA13 3SF
☼ 12-11 (midnight Fri & Sat); 12-10.30 Sun
☎ (01373) 864493 ⊕ theholliesinn.com
Twisted Gaucho; 2 changing beers (sourced locally; often Plain, Twisted) Ⓗ
A handsome old red-brick village pub in the Westbury Leigh area of town. Inside there is plenty of comfortable seating in multiple areas including a separate dining room. An outlet for the local Twisted Brewery, at least two of its extensive range are on offer, and usually a guest from elsewhere. The food is highly rated and there is good-quality accommodation in three rooms.
➳❀⇦◑≈P■(58)❀�

Horse & Groom
18 Alfred Street, BA13 3DY

☼ 12-10 (11 Fri & Sat); 12-9 Sun ☎ (01373) 859433
⊕ horseandgroomwestbury.co.uk
Sharp's Doom Bar; 2 changing beers (sourced regionally; often Twisted) Ⓗ
A large pub on the north-eastern edge of the town centre, fully refurbished several years ago. There are two separate bars, one of which is essentially a restaurant. At the front is an attractive patio-style drinking area which can be a suntrap in the summer, and there is a large garden with plenty of seating and a good-sized car park. Opposite the pub is a skittle alley which can be used as a function room. ❀⇦◑&♣P■(58,87)❀�

Whitley

Pear Tree Inn
Top Lane, SN12 8QX (¾ of a mile off B3353 on Purlpit/Atworth Rd)
☼ 10-11; 11-11.30 Fri & Sat ☎ (01225) 704966
⊕ peartreewhitley.co.uk
Bath Ales Gem; 2 changing beers (often Box Steam, Kennet and Avon) Ⓗ
Recently sympathetically refurbished pub-restaurant with accommodation. This 18th-century former working farm has a small rustic and cosy bar area with a large open fire, stone walls and flagstone floors. Three local ales and a real cider are stocked. Large areas at the rear of the pub form the restaurant where a wide range of fine food is served. The pub has an extensive garden with trimmed lawns and fragrant plants to the front and rear, with a decent-sized car park.
Q➳❀⇦◑&●P■❀�

Wilton

Swan Ⓛ
SN8 3SS
☼ 12-3, 6-11; 12-11 Sat; 12-10.30 Sun ☎ (01672) 870274
⊕ theswanwilton.co.uk
5 changing beers (sourced regionally; often Flying Monk, Plain, Stonehenge) Ⓗ/Ⓖ
This popular village pub near the Kennet & Avon Canal has an open and attractive interior. Real ale dispense is a mixture of handpump and gravity – a beer board displaying the distance from the brewery underlines the pub's commitment to local produce. Good-quality food also features local ingredients. Themed food nights include steak night on Tuesday. No evening meals on Sunday.
❀◑P■(21,22)❀�

Pepys on the road

Thence (from Salisbury) about 6 o'clock, and with a guide went over the smooth plain indeed till night; and then by a happy mistake, and that looked like an adventure, we were carried out of our way to a town where we would lie, since we could not go as far as we would. And there with great difficulty came about 10 at night to a little inn, where we were fain to go into a room where a pedlar was in bed, and made him rise; and there wife and I lay, and in a truckle-bed, Betty Turner and Willet. But good beds, and the master of the house a sober, understanding man, and I had a pleasant discourse with him about country matters. Up, finding our beds good, but we lousy; which made us merry. We set out, the reckoning and servants coming to 9s. 6d.

Samuel Pepys (1633-1703), diary for Thursday and Friday, 11 and 12 June 1668

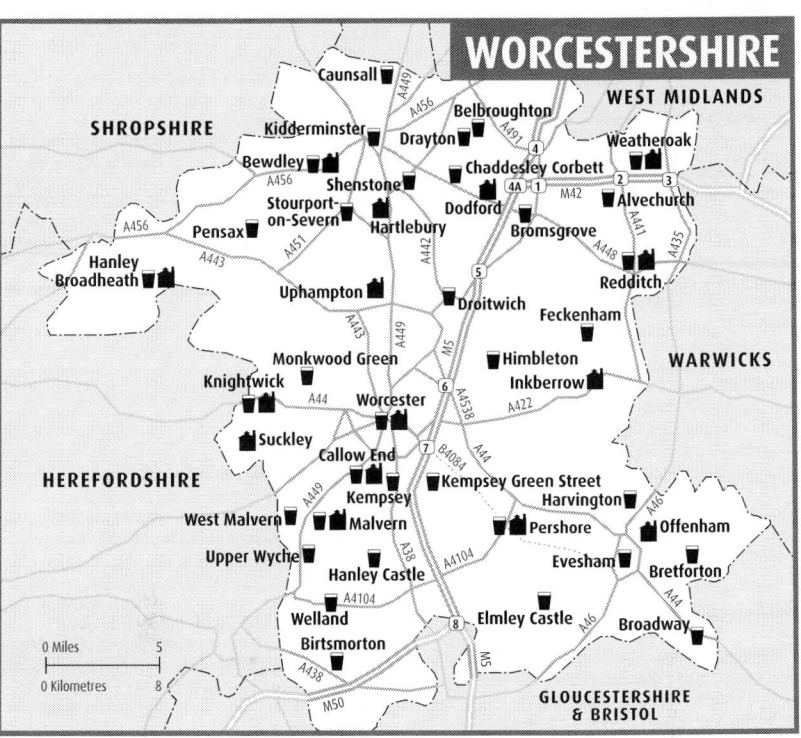

Alvechurch

Weighbridge L

Scarfield Wharf, Scarfield Hill, B48 7SQ (follow signs to marina from village) SP022721

☼ 12-3, 7-11; 12-3, 7-10.30 Sun ☎ (0121) 445 5111

⊕ the-weighbridge.co.uk

House beer (by Weatheroak); 4 changing beers (often Wye Valley) Ⓗ

This cosy canalside pub is a regular local CAMRA Pub of the Year. It has two small lounges, a public bar and a pleasant garden. Good-value home-cooked food is served lunchtimes and evenings (no food Tue and Wed) and excellent Sunday lunches. A covered area outside can be used for functions. Its quality beer is served by enthusiastic and knowledgable staff. House beers are Weatheroak Tillerman's Tipple and Kinver Bargees Bitter. Changing guest beers include a mild, and real cider or perry is available. Spring and autumn beer festivals are held. Q❄☎☸◐➤♿P☐(146)📶

Belbroughton

Holly Bush Inn

Stourbridge Road, DY9 9UG (on A491 Stourbridge Rd)

☼ 11.30-11; 11.30-3, 6-11 Sat; 12-3, 7-10.30 Sun

☎ (01562) 730207

Hobsons Mild, Twisted Spire, Town Crier; 1 changing beer (sourced regionally; often Hobsons) Ⓗ

A pub since 1845, this low-level white building was originally a row of terraced cottages. It is set back from the A491 dual carriageway between Hagley and the M5 motorway. Full of character, with low ceilings, it has a single bar serving three separate areas including a dining room. Excellent-value traditional home-made meals are available – the fish options are particularly good. Thatchers

cider is on handpump. It is near to the National Trust Clent Hills. Local CAMRA Pub of the Year 2015. Q❄☎◐♿P☐❀

Bewdley

Great Western L

Kidderminster Road, DY12 1BY (near SVR station – walk past signal box and under viaduct)

☼ 11.30-11 ☎ (01299) 488828

Bewdley Worcestershire Way; Morland Old Golden Hen; house beer (by Bewdley); 2 changing beers (sourced nationally; often Belhaven, Greene King) Ⓗ

Conveniently located within a short walk of the Severn Valley Railway station, the pub has a simple railway theme reminiscent of an earlier age. Overlooking the bar is an upper level from which to admire the fine glazed decorative wall tiles. Pub snacks such as pork pies and cobs go with the concept of a traditional pub, and on the bar there are five real ales including regulars from Greene King and Bewdley, and two Westons ciders. Q❄☸♿⇌(SVR)♣♿P☐📶

Mug House L ✓

12 Severnside North, DY12 2EE (150yds along Severnside North from river bridge)

☼ 12-11 (11.30 Fri & Sat) ☎ (01299) 402543

⊕ mughousebewdley.co.uk

Bewdley Worcestershire Way; Purity Mad Goose; Timothy Taylor Landlord; Wye Valley HPA; 1 changing beer (sourced locally; often Bewdley, Holden's, Wye Valley) Ⓗ

Located on the side of the Severn, the Mug House is not to be missed. A friendly pub that welcomes locals and visitors alike, it serves five beers from Bewdley, Purity, Wye Valley and Timothy Taylor, plus a guest. There are cosy settles and a log fire in the lounge bar, and to the rear is a sun terrace with a glass-covered patio with grapevines and wisteria. The restaurant serves an a la carte menu as well as bar meals at lunchtime. Q♣☺⌂◑♿≒(SVR)●🅿☕🌡🛜

Old Waggon & Horses 🅛

91 Kidderminster Road, DY12 1DG (on Bewdley to Kidderminster road, Catchems End)
☼ 12-11; 11.30-1am Fri & Sat ☎ (01299) 403170
🌐 waggonbewdley.co.uk
Banks's Mild, Amber Ale; Bathams Best Bitter; 2 changing beers (sourced locally; often Hobsons, Ludlow) 🅷
Popular locals' and visitors' pub with a central bar serving three distinct areas. The small wooden-floored snug has a dartboard and the larger room a woodburner. There is a roll-down screen for major sporting events, but at most times conversation prevails. An old kitchen range in the dining area adds to the cottagey feel. Food includes a curry night on Friday, monthly pie night on Wednesday and a carvery on Sunday. The terraced flower garden is on many levels. Guest ales come from local independents. Q☺◑♿≒(SVR)♣●🅿🛒🌡🛜

Birtsmorton

Farmers Arms

Birts Street, WR13 6AP (off B4208) SO790363
☼ 11-4, 6-midnight; 12-4, 6-midnight Sun
☎ (01684) 833308 🌐 farmersarmsbirtsmorton.co.uk
Hook Norton Hooky, Old Hooky; 2 changing beers (sourced locally) 🅷
Grade II-listed black-and-white village pub dating from 1480, down a quiet country lane. The large bar area features an inglenook fireplace while the cosy lounge has old settles and low beams. Good-value, home-made food is on offer daily (lunch until 2pm, eve meals until 9.30pm weekdays, 9pm Sun). A beer from a local brewer is often available. The pub holds a beer festival in August. The spacious garden, with swings, provides fine views of the Malvern Hills. A caravan site is nearby. Q♣☺◑♿♣🅿(577)🌡🛜

Bretforton

Fleece Inn ★ 🅛

The Cross, WR11 7JE
☼ 11-11 ☎ (01386) 831173 🌐 thefleeceinn.co.uk
Uley Pig's Ear Strong Beer; Wye Valley Bitter; 3 changing beers (often Cotswold Lion, Hook Norton, Purity) 🅷
Fifteenth-century timber-framed village pub owned by the National Trust on the edge of the Cotswolds. Sensitively restored in 2005 after a fire, it is recognised by CAMRA as having a nationally important historic pub interior, and houses a world-famous 17th-century pewter collection. Morris dancers and music feature all year round, with entertainment evenings in the medieval barn. Local breweries are represented among the three changing beers, and one of the three or four ciders is made at the Fleece itself. A pub not to be missed. Q♣☺⌂◑●🌡🛜

Broadway

Crown & Trumpet Inn 🅛 ✅

14 Church Street, WR12 7AE

☼ 11-10.30 (11.45 Fri & Sat) ☎ (01386) 853202
🌐 crownandtrumpet.co.uk
Bath Ales Gem; Prescott Chequered Flag; Stroud Tom Long; 2 changing beers (sourced locally; often North Cotswold, Stanway) 🅷
Picturesque 17th-century Cotswold-stone inn just off the village green. The landlord is a real ale enthusiast and has 32 years' experience as a Guide licensee. This hostelry has welcoming and friendly staff and an abundance of character, with oak beams, log fire and Flowers Brewery memorabilia. Good, honest, well-cooked pub favourites are offered at reasonable prices alongside a range of regular ales and guests plus ciders and perries. Current local CAMRA Cider Pub of the Year. Entertainment includes live jazz and blues nights. Q☺⌂◑♣●🅿🛜

Bromsgrove

Golden Cross Hotel 🅛 ✅

20 High Street, B61 8HH (S end of High St)
☼ 8am-midnight (1am Fri & Sat) ☎ (01527) 870005
Greene King Abbot; Ruddles Best Bitter; Sharp's Doom Bar; 9 changing beers 🅷
This stylish split-level Wetherspoon pub in the town centre was previously a coach house. It has 12 individual booths with interesting glass throughout. Nine guest beers are available, many sourced locally, and regular themed beer festivals are held. There is a Pay & Display car park at the rear which is free after 7pm. Q♣☺⌂◑♿♣●🅿🛒🛜

Ladybird 🅛

2 Finstall Road, B60 2DZ (on B4184, on roundabout) SO969695
☼ 11-11; 12-10.30 Sun ☎ (01527) 878014
🌐 ladybirdinn.co.uk
Bathams Best Bitter; Sharp's Doom Bar; Wye Valley HPA, Butty Bach; 2 changing beers (often Malvern Hills) 🅷
This popular local is adjacent to the town's railway station. The light, airy lounge, with polished wooden floor, is decorated with historic railway photographs. A function/meeting room is available on the first floor. Food is served every day, and

REAL ALE BREWERIES

Ambridge Inkberrow
Bewdley Bewdley
Black Tap Redditch
Boat Lane Offenham (NEW)
Cannon Royall Uphampton
Crafted Bewdley (NEW)
Firefly Worcester
Friday Beer Malvern
Joseph Herbert Smith Hanley Broadheath
Lakehouse Malvern (NEW)
Malvern Hills Malvern
Pershore Pershore (NEW)
Pope's Worcester
Sociable Worcester (NEW)
St George's Callow End
Teme Valley Knightwick
Three Shires Worcester
Unity Brew House Suckley (NEW)
Weatheroak Hill Weatheroak
Winning Post Worcester
Woodcote Manor Dodford
Worcester Worcester
Worcestershire Hartlebury

Rosado's, a privately run Italian restaurant, is on the same site. A token is needed to exit the car park. ✿✿✿✪◑ᕦᕤ♣P☷♬☺🞉

Little Ale House

21 Worcester Road, B61 7DL (on corner of Station St)
✿ 12 (3 Mon-Wed)-10 ☎ 07791 698641
Malvern Hills Black Pear; 7 changing beers (often Ambridge, Bewdley, Prescott) 🅖
Bromsgrove's first micropub has a friendly and cosy atmosphere. It offers one permanent beer and a range of seven constantly rotating ales from three permanent and four changing breweries, all served straight from the cask. A selection of real cider and perries is also available, as are take-out containers. A council car park is nearby and the bus station is parallel with the High Street. Q&♣●☷🞉☺🞉

Park Gate

Kidderminster Road, Park Gate, B61 9AJ
✿ 12-11 (midnight Fri & Sat) ☎ (01527) 870158
🌐 parkgateinn.co.uk
Hobsons Mild; house beer (by Ambridge); 5 changing beers 🅗
This functional but welcoming roadside inn is a popular stop-off for weekend walkers and displays a selection of marked walks on the noticeboard in the car park. There are excellent views from the large, attractive gardens. A range of snacks, including cobs with various fillings, pies and pickled eggs is available, alongside a choice of up to 10 different ales. The bus stop is near the pub. ✿✿✪▲♣●P☷(42)☺🞉

Callow End

Old Bush

Upton Road, WR2 4TE (small lane off B4424) SO835497
✿ 12-3, 5-11.30; 12-midnight Fri & Sat; 12-11.30 Sun
☎ (01905) 830792 🌐 old-bush.com
Butcombe Adam Henson's Rare Breed, Original; Hobsons Twisted Spire; 1 changing beer (sourced locally; often Malvern Hills) 🅗
Village local with a pretty black and white exterior down a quiet lane off the main road. It was recently rescued from closure by a strong local campaign and bought in 2017 by the landlord. The interior is cosy with a logburner – good home-made food is served in the bar and a separate dining area. The large and attractively laid-out garden has country views and a play area for children. Events include regular live music and an annual blues festival. A guest cider is available in the summer. ✿✿✪◑▲♣●P☷☺🞉

Caunsall

Anchor Inn 🅛

DY11 5YL (off A449 Kidderminster/Wolverhampton road)
✿ 11-4, 7-11; 11-3, 7-10.30 Sun ☎ (01562) 850254
🌐 theanchorinncaunsall.co.uk
Hobsons Best, Town Crier; Three Tuns XXX; Wye Valley HPA, Butty Bach 🅗
Popular and friendly village inn renowned for its five real ales, traditional ciders and especially its well-filled cobs. A central doorway leads into the bar with its original 1920s furniture and horse-racing memorabilia. Outside, the garden is a sun-trap in summer. The friendly staff welcome an impressive mix of customers and the pub gets especially busy at lunchtimes. Easily reached from

the nearby canal, this gem is well worth visiting. Local CAMRA Pub of the Year finalist in 2016 and 2017. Q✿✿✪◑ᕦ♣●P☷☺🞉

Chaddesley Corbett

Swan 🍷 🅛

High Street, DY10 4SD (along High St from A448) SO892737
✿ 11-11 (midnight Fri); 12-11 Sun ☎ (01562) 777302
🌐 theswanchaddesleycorbett.co.uk
Bathams Mild Ale, Best Bitter 🅗
Characterful village pub dating from 1606 with an impressive lounge with a raised stage area for entertainment, a cosy side room with a real fire, and a traditional public bar. Live jazz is hosted on Thursday evening and open mic on the first Friday of the month. There is a large garden at the rear overlooking the beautiful local countryside. Guest still cider is available on handpull. The pub is popular with walkers and cyclists and close to historic Harvington Hall. Q✿✿✪◑ᕦ▲♣●P☷☺🞉

Drayton

Robin Hood

Drayton Road, DY9 0BW (on Chaddesley Corbett to Belbroughton road) SO905758
✿ 12-11 ☎ (01562) 730526 🌐 robinhoodinn-drayton.co.uk
Enville Ale, Ginger Beer; Holden's Golden Glow; Sharp's Doom Bar; Wye Valley HPA, Butty Bach 🅗
A traditional pub, refurbished but retaining the ambience of a rural retreat. The original bar has been extended into the old store room and a small passageway leads to the comfortable lounge. Six real ales plus real cider are available and snacks and cooked meals are served. Outside is a paved patio and garden with a covered smoking area. Barbecues are held regularly in the summer with drinks served from an outside bar. CAMRA branch Pub of the Year in 2016. ✿✿✪◑ᕦ●P🞉

Droitwich

Hop Pole 🅛

40 Friar Street, WR9 8ED
✿ 12-11; 12-10.30 Sun ☎ (01905) 770155
Malvern Hills Black Pear; Wye Valley HPA, Butty Bach; 2 changing beers 🅗
Popular and unchanging 18th-century pub located at a dead end in the old part of Droitwich between the Norbury Theatre and the fire station. There is a separate pool room adjoining the bar and a heated patio area at the rear to accommodate smokers. Three locally sourced beers are usually available with an occasional guest. Good-value food is served at lunchtimes, and pub games and live music on some weekends ensure a convivial atmosphere. ✿✿✪◑⇌♣☷☺

Elmley Castle

Queen Elizabeth

Main Street, WR10 3HS
✿ 11 (5 Mon)-11; 11-8 Sun ☎ (01386) 710215
🌐 elmleycastle.com
4 changing beers (sourced locally; often Goff's, North Cotswold, Purity) 🅗
An old pub with a fresh, modern feel inside, named after Elizabeth I's visit to the village in August 1575. This is a community pub, owned by local residents who rescued it from closure. The bar has

a flagstone floor, timber beams and a roaring fire. There is a comfortable lounge and a separate dining room. Themed food evenings are held weekly and beer festivals twice a year. The café opens 10-4pm Tuesday to Friday and 9am on Saturday for breakfast. Q ➤ ✿ ◑ P 🚐 🐾 🛜

Evesham

Red Lion 🅛
6 Market Place, WR11 4RE
✿ 11-11; 12-9 Sun ☎ (01386) 761688
Cannon Royall Fruiterers Mild, King's Shilling, Arrowhead Bitter, Blond Bombshell; 2 changing beers (sourced locally; often North Cotswold) 🅗
Closed for over 100 years, this basic town-centre pub has been sympathetically refurbished. It has seating areas to the front and side, and to the rear a separate area incorporating the recently discovered inglenook fireplace. It is tucked away in a corner of the marketplace and, with no TV or music, it is a great place for people-watching and conversation. Up to six real ales are served from a central bar including five well-priced Cannon Royall beers, and two ciders. Q ⇄ 🐾 🛜

Feckenham

Rose & Crown ✅
High Street, B96 6HS
✿ 11-3, 6-11; 12-11 Sat & Sun ☎ (01527) 892188
⊕ roseandcrownfeckenham.co.uk
Banks's Amber Ale; Brakspear Oxford Gold; 2 changing beers (often Marston's, Wye Valley) 🅗
A welcoming family-run, 19th-century, Grade II-listed village pub standing in what was once the historic Forest of Feckenham. Up to four real ales and at least one real cider are available. An annual beer festival is held over the August bank holiday. There is a large beer garden. Parking is limited, but there is a free car park 200 yards away. The Monarch's Way footpath lies one-and-a-half miles to the east of the village. Q ➤ ✿ ◑ ♣ 🐾 🛜

Hanley Broadheath

Fox Inn 🅛
WR15 8QS (on B4204 E of Tenbury Wells) SO671652
✿ 5-11; 3-12.30am Fri; 12-12.30am Sat; 12-10 Sun
☎ (01886) 853189
Bathams Best Bitter; Joseph Herbert Smith Foxy Lady; 2 changing beers (often Hogarths) 🅗
The main bar of this 16th-century black-and-white timbered free house is decorated with hops and has a large fireplace with a wood-burning stove. The panelled dining area is separated from the bar by wood beams. The games room has a pool table, TV and darts. Home-made food, including Sunday lunch, is available, with bar snacks at any time. One guest beer is usually from Hogarths Brewery in Bolton. Q ➤ ✿ ◑ Å ♣ 🐾 🛜

Tally Ho! 🅛
WR15 8QX (on B4204 road E of Tenbury Wells) SO662655
✿ 12-midnight ☎ (01886) 853241 ⊕ tallyhorestaurant.co.uk
Ludlow Gold; Wye Valley HPA; 2 changing beers (sourced nationally) 🅗
An inviting, cosy, 14th-century inn with an abundance of beams and stonework, featuring local beers on the bar. Pool and darts are popular. The separate restaurant in the conservatory has grand views of the countryside. The garden enjoys

more panoramic views of Titterstone Clee Hill and the Teme Valley, and has a children's playground. Food is served lunchtimes and evenings every day, with a carvery on Sunday.
➤ ✿ 🍴 ◑ & Å ♣ 🐾 P 🐾 🛜

Hanley Castle

Three Kings ★ 🅛
Church End, WR8 0BL (signed off B4211) SO838420
✿ 12-3, 7-11; 12-3, 7-10.30 Sun ☎ (01684) 592686
Butcombe Original; Hobsons Best; 3 changing beers (often Beowulf, Malvern Hills, Slater's) 🅗
On CAMRA's National Inventory of Historic Pub Interiors, this unspoilt 15th-century country pub on the village green near the church has been run by the Roberts family since 1911. The three-room interior comprises a small snug with large inglenook, serving hatch and settle wall, a small side room, and Nell's Lounge with another inglenook, beams and its own entrance. Westons Old Rosie draught cider is served. Live music sessions feature regularly and a popular beer festival is held in November.
Q ➤ ✿ ◑ ♣ 🐾 P 🚐 (363) 🐾

Harvington

Coach & Horses 🍷 ✅
Station Road, WR11 8NJ
✿ 5 (12 Sat)-midnight; 12-11.30 Sun ☎ (01386) 870249
⊕ coachandhorsesharvington.com
Greene King IPA; 4 changing beers (sourced nationally) 🅗
Traditional village pub having a separate bar, a real fire and a lounge with a logburner in the inglenook. Photos of old Harvington adorn the walls. The pub's real ale drinkers select the guest beers from Finest Cask and SIBA lists. Good-value food is served. A local ukulele group plays on Tuesday and a fun quiz is hosted on Sunday. The skittle alley doubles as a function/training room. An annual beer festival is held in September. Worcestershire CAMRA Pub of the Year and local CAMRA Pub of the Year 2014-17.
➤ ✿ ◑ Å ♣ 🐾 P 🚐 🐾 🛜

Himbleton

Galton Arms 🅛
Harrow Lane, WR9 7LQ
✿ 12-2 (not Mon), 4.30-11; 11-11 Sun ☎ (01905) 391672
Banks's Amber Ale; Bathams Best Bitter; Wye Valley HPA; 1 changing beer (sourced locally) 🅗
Splendid rural pub, situated on the edge of the village, with a friendly welcome and popular with locals and visitors alike. The unspoilt interior, warmed by open fires, retains the original beams that divide up the space. The guest beer is often from a local brewery. TV sport is shown in the bar area and two separate dining areas serve good-value food. Q ➤ ✿ ◑ & P 🐾

Kempsey

Walter de Cantelupe 🅛
34 Main Road, WR5 3NA (on A38 next to post office)
✿ closed Mon; 12-2, 6-11; 12-9 Sun ☎ (01905) 820572
⊕ walterdecantelupe.co.uk
Timothy Taylor Landlord; Wye Valley Bitter; 2 changing beers 🅗

A comfortable pub named after a 13th-century Bishop of Worcester. Divided into three cosy drinking areas, it has a large settle from the 1700s one end and an imposing inglenook fireplace at the other. It serves traditional but inventive food made with local ingredients where possible. Lighter meals are often available outside restaurant hours. Events include a paella party in the attractive walled garden in June. Opening hours may vary. 🏠🞉🚭◖◗&♣♠P🏨🐾☕🎵

Kempsey Green Street

Huntsman Inn 🅛

Green Street, WR5 3QB (from A38 at Kempsey via Post Office Lane) SO868490

🞉 5-11; 12-11 Sat & Sun ☎ (01905) 820336

Bathams Best Bitter; Greene King IPA; Morland Original Bitter Ⓗ

A 300-year-old ex-farmhouse with exposed beams, this cosy and friendly multi-roomed local has a small main bar with a real fire to the front and a larger bar down some steps. The separate restaurant serves reasonably priced home-cooked food. There is also a skittle alley with its own bar, an attractive garden and a large car park. Dogs are welcome in the bar and lounge. 🏠🞉◖◗♣P🐾

Kidderminster

Beer Emporium & Cider House

Oxford Street, DY10 1AR

🞉 closed Mon & Tue; 4-10 Wed; 12-11 Thu-Sat; 12-8 Sun ☎ 07803 357362

4 changing beers (sourced nationally) Ⓖ

Micropub situated between the station and the town centre. The single room, furnished with a mixture of barrel furniture and low and high tables, is lively with the buzz of conversation. Table service is the norm. A chalkboard shows up to six real ales sourced locally and from around the country. Four ciders and two perries, an interesting selection of bottled foreign beers, wines and soft drinks ensure there is something for everyone. Q🏠&♿♠P🏨🐾☕

King & Castle 🅛

Comberton Hill, DY10 1QX (next to mainline station and part of SVR terminus)

🞉 8-11; 10-11.30 Sat; 11-11 Sun ☎ (01562) 747505

Bathams Best Bitter; Bewdley Worcestershire Way; Hobsons Mild, Town Crier; 4 changing beers (sourced nationally; often Cotleigh, Cottage, Exmoor) Ⓗ

Atmospheric recreation of a GWR terminus station bar and gateway to the Severn Valley Railway. Eight handpumps dispense beers from Hobsons, Bewdley and Bathams, with changing beers from regional and national breweries. Three still ciders are also available. Breakfast is served until 11am, then pub meals, cobs and snacks until 9pm. Bottled beers from Bewdley Brewery are served on trains, and pubs along the line are an attraction for locals and visitors using the railway. Q🏠🞉◖◗&♿♠🐾P🏨🐾☕

Olde Seven Stars 🅛 ✅

13-14 Coventry Street, DY10 2BG (facing Swan Centre)

🞉 11-11 (11.30 Fri & Sat); 12-11 Sun ☎ (01562) 755777

6 changing beers Ⓗ

With six ever-changing real ales and one draught cider, this town-centre family-friendly pub is well worth visiting. The front and rear bars display many

old features from previous ages. It serves cobs and pork pies, and customers can bring their own food (there are plenty of takeaways nearby), with tableware and condiments provided. Live music plays on Friday evenings. It has a quiet rear garden which is popular in summer. A former local CAMRA Gold Pub of the Year. 🏠🞉&♣🍴🐾☕🎵

Station Inn 🅛 ✅

7 Farfield, DY10 1UG

🞉 12-11 ☎ (01562) 569621 🌐 stationkidderminster.co.uk

Enville Ale; Holden's Golden Glow; Wye Valley HPA, Butty Bach; 1 changing beer (sourced locally; often Bewdley, Enville, Hobsons) Ⓗ

A friendly pub just a short walk from the railway station. Two rooms are served from a central bar and there is a large beer garden to the rear. Five handpulled ales always include some from Enville, Holden's and Wye Valley. Home-cooked food is available during the day, with traditional roast dinners on Sundays. The warm welcome, community atmosphere and excellent ales won it local CAMRA Community Pub of the Year 2015 and Pub of the Year finalist in 2016 and 2017. Q🏠🞉&🞉≒♣P🏨🐾☕

Swan 🅛 ✅

Vicar Street, DY10 1DE (opp town hall)

🞉 10-7 (10 Thu); 10-1am Fri & Sat; 12-6 Sun ☎ (01562) 823008 🌐 swankidderminster.co.uk

Bewdley Worcestershire Way; Sir Keith Park, Worcestershire Sway; 3 changing beers (sourced nationally; often Purity, Sharp's, Wye Valley) Ⓗ

A one-room pub opposite the town hall dating from 1865, serving six well-kept real ales and real ciders. The long, single room has quiet tables for meals towards the rear, while the front bar gets lively on rugby match days. Breakfast is available from 10am, followed by fresh bar meals Monday to Saturday. A beer festival is held over the August bank holiday. A former local CAMRA Pub of the Year. 🏠◖&🍴🐾☕

Weavers at Park Lane 🅛

40 Park Lane, DY11 6TG (opp Tesco)

🞉 4 (12 Wed & Thu)-10; 12-11 Fri & Sat; 12-6 Sun ☎ (01562) 742717

Three Tuns XXX; Wye Valley HPA; 4 changing beers (sourced regionally; often Bewdley, Fixed Wheel) Ⓗ

Canalside pub in a listed Georgian building dating from 1804. The beer garden overlooks the canal and moorings are on the towpath side, a short walk over the nearby bridge. It offers cobs, pork pies and an impressive range of well-kept beers and ciders. There are six real ales and eight ciders and perries, some from local breweries, and also unusual beers from further afield. Summer hours are usually 12-11pm but opening times can vary. Q🏠🞉≒♣P🐾☕

Weavers Real Ale House 🍺 🅛

98 Comberton Hill, DY10 1QH (300yds down hill from railway station)

🞉 2 (12 Thu-Sat)-11; 12-10.30 Sun ☎ (01562) 229413

Pig Iron Unbeweavable; Three Tuns XXX; 12 changing beers (sourced nationally; often Bewdley, Fixed Wheel, Fownes Brewing) Ⓗ

This micropub is deceptively spacious inside, with bench seating along the sides, plenty of tables and a conversational atmosphere. Light and airy, the walls display pictures of old Kidderminster and beer memorabilia. It serves eight beers, four ciders and a perry on handpump. Cobs are always available. Just a short walk from the railway station, this is a convenient stop-off for a pint and a chat on the way into town. Public parking is a short distance away. Q&♿🚲🍴🅿️🚃🐕🛜

Knightwick

Talbot 🅻
WR6 5PH (on B4197, 400yds from A44 jct)
🕒 8am-11 ☎ (01886) 821235 ⊕ the-talbot.co.uk
Teme Valley T'Other, This, That 🅷; **changing beers (often Teme Valley)** 🅶
A 14th-century coaching inn with a large lounge bar divided in two by a large fireplace, a separate tap room and a fine conservatory. The small wood-panelled restaurant serves an imaginative menu using local ingredients (6-9pm). The bar usually offers three or four beers from the Teme Valley Brewery behind the pub. There is a farmers' market outside on the second Sunday of the month. Beer festivals are held in April, June and early October (for green hop beers). Dogs and walkers are welcome.
Q🐕🏡🍴◑♿🅰♣🅿️(420)🐾🛜

Malvern

Great Malvern Hotel 🅻
Graham Road, WR14 2HN (by crossroads with Church St)
🕒 10-11; 11-10.30 Sun ☎ (01684) 563411
⊕ great-malvern-hotel.co.uk
Malvern Hills Black Pear; Wye Valley HPA, Butty Bach; 2 changing beers (often Friday Beer Co) 🅷
Popular hotel with a public bar, a short walk from the Malvern Theatres complex, ideal for pre- and post-performance refreshment. The beer range usually includes something from Malvern's two breweries. Meals are served in the bar and the adjoining brasserie, including Sunday lunches. There is also a comfortable lounge with lots of sofas, fresh coffee and newspapers. Live music sessions are hosted weekly. The Great Shakes cellar bar has sport on TV and is available for hire. On-site parking is limited but there is plenty of public parking nearby. 🐕🏡🍴◑🚃🅿️🐾🛜

Morgan 🅻 ✅
52 Clarence Road, WR14 3EQ
🕒 12-3, 5-11; 12-11 Fri & Sat; 12-10.30 Sun
☎ (01684) 578575
Wye Valley Bitter, HPA, Butty Bach; 2 changing beers (sourced locally) 🅷
Named after the town's Morgan car factory, this Wye Valley Brewery-owned premises has an open-plan interior divided into a games area for darts, a drinking space and a slightly raised seating area with comfy settees. The landscaped patio has ample seating, a fish pond and 'Them Organ' gates. Activities include a monthly book club and weekly quizzes. The pub is muzak-free and the TV is only turned on for major sporting events. Up to two guest beers come from the Wye Valley range. 🐕🏡🚃♣🅿️🐾🛜

Nag's Head ✅
19-21 Bank Street, WR14 2JG (off Graham Rd at Link Top common)
🕒 11-11.15 (11.30 Fri & Sat); 12-11.15 Sun
☎ (01684) 574373 ⊕ nagsheadmalvern.co.uk
Banks's Amber Ale; Bathams Best Bitter; St George's Friar Tuck, Charger, Dragons Blood; Wood Shropshire Lad; 2 changing beers (often Otter, Ringwood) 🅷

A free house serving beers from the owner's brewery, St George's in nearby Callow End, alongside others from all over the county, plus two draught ciders. Mismatched furniture, nooks and crannies, newspapers and foliage create a homely environment. Quality food is served in the bar and separate restaurant (open until 9pm Fri and Sat). Outside is a large covered and heated area to the front and a garden to the rear. The car park is small but there is ample on-street parking. Dogs are welcome and numerous. 🏡◑♣🅿️🅿️(44)🐾🛜

Monkwood Green

Fox
WR2 6NX (S edge of Monkwood Nature Reserve)
SO803601
🕒 5 (12 Sat)-11; 12-10.30 Sun ☎ (01886) 889123
Malvern Hills Feelgood; Wye Valley HPA, Butty Bach 🅷
Single-bar village local set on the common near the nature reserve renowned for butterflies and moths. There is seating around the fireplace and hearth at one end, games at the other. Many events feature here including skittles, indoor air rifle shooting, and a music night on the last Friday of the month. There is no food on general sale but meals can be provided for groups and parties by arrangement. The pub is a rare outlet for Barker's cider and perry. There is a limited bus service.
Q🐕🏡🅰♣🅿️(308)🐾

Pensax

Bell 🅻
WR6 6AE (on B4202 Clows Top to Great Witley road S of Pensax)
🕒 12-2.30 (not Mon), 5-11; 12-10.30 Sun ☎ (01299) 896677
Bewdley Worcestershire Way; Exmoor Gold; Hobsons Best; Wye Valley Bitter; 3 changing beers (sourced regionally; often Three Tuns) 🅷
This friendly country and community pub is well worth making a detour to visit. Seven real ales plus local cider and perry feature on the bar. There is a separate dining room and a snug where families are welcome. Home-cooked meals are made using local seasonal ingredients. Wooden floors, hanging hops, open fires and some pew seating give a true country feel. Local CAMRA Pub of the Year and runner-up West Midlands Pub of the Year in 2015.
Q🐕🏡◑♿🅿️🐾

Pershore

Pickled Plum
135 High Street, WR10 1EQ
🕒 12-11 (midnight Fri & Sat) ☎ (01386) 556645
⊕ pickledplum.co.uk
Banks's Sunbeam; Brakspear Bitter; Dark Star Hophead; Wychwood Hobgoblin; 2 changing beers (often Malvern Hills, Pope's, Three Shires) 🅷
A large, smart pub with a modern, airy interior, divided into several areas, with exposed beams and real fires adding old-world charm. The bar serves up to six ales including Dark Star, always features brews from local breweries, and has six real ciders. A three third-pint tasting option is offered. Food is available lunchtimes and evenings. The pub hosts a regular Sunday night quiz and acoustic jam on the first Monday of the month. 🏡◑♿🅿️

Redditch

Black Tap Brew Pub ⬧

Church Green East, B98 8BP (near top of Church Green East opp fountain)

☼ 4 (12 Thu-Sat)-11; 12-5 Sun ☎ (01527) 549997

⊕ blacktap.co.uk

4 changing beers ⬧

A recently converted office building with two rooms and an outside drinking area. Conveniently located near the town centre, the pub has a small brewing plant on site which produces most of the Black Tap beers available here, although guest ales are also usually kept. A good range of snacks is offered. Live music plays every Saturday evening. ⬧♣⬧(57,58)⬧

Rising Sun ⬧ ✅

4 Alcester Street, B98 8AE (opp town hall)

☼ 8am-midnight (1am Fri & Sat) ☎ (01527) 62452

Greene King IPA, Abbot; Morland Old Speckled Hen; Sharp's Doom Bar; 9 changing beers ⬧

Large open-plan town-centre pub in the Wetherspoon style with a raised seating area and booths. Local histories of Redditch's manufacturing industries adorn the walls, and a large metal horse and rider stands in the centre. Two screens at each end of the pub show news and sport. The bar gets busy at lunchtimes and weekends. Outside, a glass canopy and café-style seating are ideal for people-watching. ⬧⬧⬧⬧⬧P⬧⬧

Rocklands Social Club

59 Birchfield Road, Headless Cross, B97 4LB (opp green on Birchfield Rd)

☼ 12 (3 Tue-Thu)-11 ☎ (01527) 544356

⊕ therocklands.co.uk

3 changing beers ⬧

This family club has won multiple CAMRA awards and is a former West Midlands Regional Club of the Year. Three real ales are available from independent brewers, including a mild or stout, and up to two real ciders. The club runs a beer festival and an ale tasting society (RATS). Ales can also be bought to take away. The large function room hosts live entertainment, and outside there is landscaped decking and a sheltered smoking area. Show this Guide or a CAMRA membership card for entry. ⬧⬧⬧♣⬧P⬧(26,47)⬧⬧

Shenstone

Plough ⬧

DY10 4DL (off A450/A448) SO865735

☼ 12.30-3.30, 6-11; 12-11 Fri-Sun ☎ (01562) 777340

Bathams Mild Ale, Best Bitter ⬧

A traditional rural community pub which has been at the heart of the village since 1840. The long single bar serves both the lounge and public areas, with a real fire in the lounge. A large enclosed courtyard serves as an overflow area in which children are permitted. There is a small patio with seating to the front. Cobs and pork pies are available. Bathams XXX is kept in winter. The Elizabethan Harvington Hall is nearby. Q⬧⬧⬧P⬧⬧

Stourport-on-Severn

Black Star ⬧ ✅

Mitton Street, DY13 8YP (just off top end of High St next to canal)

☼ 12-11 (midnight Fri & Sat) ☎ (01299) 488838

Wye Valley Bitter, HPA, Dorothy Goodbody's Golden Ale, Butty Bach, Dorothy Goodbody's Wholesome Stout; 1 changing beer (sourced nationally; often Exmoor) ⬧

Next to the canal, the pub has a historic feel. The main bar has a real fire, low ceilings and cosy corners. At the back overlooking the water is an attractive beer garden with shelter, tables and raised flowerbeds. Moorings are just through the bridge towards the basins. The varied food menu includes everything from doorstep sandwiches and baguettes to rib-eye steaks and everything in between. Food requests are encouraged. The beers are from Wye Valley plus a guest. ⬧⬧⬧⬧⬧⬧⬧⬧

Rock Tavern ⬧

80 Wilden Lane, DY13 9LR (on back road between Stourport and Kidderminster at Wilden)

☼ 12-11.30 (midnight Sat); 12-10.30 Sun ☎ (01299) 822962

⊕ therocktavern.com

St Austell Tribute; Three Tuns XXX; Wye Valley HPA; 1 changing beer (sourced locally; often Bewdley, Wye Valley) ⬧

An old pub in a comfortable modern style with a lounge bar and restaurant serving home-cooked, locally sourced and free-range food daytimes and most evenings. Four beers are on offer including some from local breweries. A traditional music session features on the fourth Tuesday of the month. The smoking area outside is next to a cave cut into the rock which can be explored, and the pub is handy for an adjacent walk along the old railway line. ⬧⬧⬧⬧P⬧⬧

Upper Wyche

Wyche Inn ⬧

Wyche Road, WR14 4EQ (on B4218, follow signs from Malvern to Colwall)

☼ 12-11; 11-11 Sat & Sun ☎ (01684) 575396

⊕ thewycheinn.co.uk

Wye Valley HPA; 3 changing beers (sourced regionally) ⬧

The highest pub in Worcestershire, this free house has panoramic views towards the Cotswolds. Ideally situated for hill walkers, it offers two bars – one with pool and darts, the other dedicated to drinking and dining. The range of real ales always features some from local breweries. Home-cooked food is served lunchtimes and evenings, with a different theme every day including steak nights on Tuesday and Saturday. B&B accommodation and a holiday cottage are AA 4-star. Q⬧⬧⬧♣P⬧(675)⬧⬧

Weatheroak

Coach & Horses ⬧

Weatheroak Hill, B48 7EA (Alvechurch to Wythall road) SP057740

☼ 11.30-11; 12-10.30 Sun ☎ (01564) 823386

⊕ coachandhorsesinn.co.uk

Holden's 101; Hook Norton Old Hooky; Weatheroak Hill Hill Top Bitter, Gold, Icknield Pale Ale, Cofton Common; 10 changing beers (sourced nationally; often Hobsons, St Austell, Wood) ⬧

Award-winning free house with a traditional bar with a real fire and quarry-tiled floor, a modern lounge bar and a restaurant. Formerly a coach house, it has been in the same family for 50 years. Eleven real ales are served from breweries across the West Midlands, including five from the on-site

Weatheroak Hill, and two constantly changing guests. Beers can also be bought in takeaway containers. Fresh rolls are always available. Outside, the garden is popular in summer. The pub is adjacent to Icknield Street Roman road. Q🕏🌞🕪❶🛪♣P🐾🐾🛜

Welland

Marlbank Inn 🅛
Marlbank Road, WR13 6NA (on A4104 W of Welland) SO786404
✪ 12-midnight ☎ (01684) 310603 ⊕ themarlbankinn.co.uk
Greene King Abbot; Wye Valley HPA 🅖; 3 changing beers (sourced nationally) 🅗
A sizeable pub in the countryside at the foot of the Malvern Hills. It has an interesting interior with two main rooms around a central bar. Live music nights and themed dinners feature regularly throughout the year, and the pub hosts party nights on St Patrick's Day, Halloween and New Year's Eve. The real cider is Westons Old Rosie. B&B is available and a camping and caravan site is adjacent with a children's play area. 🕏🌞🛏🕪❶🛪♣❶P🐾🐾🛜

West Malvern

Brewers Arms 🅛
Lower Dingle, WR14 4BQ (S end of village, down track off B4232)
✪ 12-midnight ☎ (01684) 561989
Malvern Hills Black Pear; Wye Valley Butty Bach; 4 changing beers 🅗
An ideal refreshment stop for visitors to the Malvern Hills, this welcoming traditional pub is the centre of the village community. Home-cooked food is served lunchtimes and evenings. The garden offers splendid views across to the Black Mountains. The single bar can get busy, but extra space is available in the function room across the yard. Live music features on Fridays. Q🕏🌞🕪❶🛪(675)🐾🛜

Worcester

Bull Baiters Inn
22 St Johns, WR2 5AH
✪ 12-2 (not Mon), 5.30-9.30; 12-9.30 Fri & Sat; 12-2 Sun
☎ (01905) 421579 ⊕ bullbaiters.com
7 changing beers (sourced locally) 🅗
Worcester's first micropub in the St Johns area of the city, a short walk across the river from the city centre. A small single room housed in a former patisserie, it has wood-panelled walls and bench seating and stools covered in replica hop pocket sacks. Up to seven ever-changing beers are available, mostly from local brewers, with eight ciders and perries, also locally sourced. Interesting pub games, including ringing the bull, can be played. Q♣❶🛪

Dragon Inn
51 The Tything, WR1 1JT (on A449, 300yds N of Foregate St Station)
✪ 4 (12 Fri & Sat)-11; 12-10.30 Sun ☎ (01905) 25845
⊕ thedragoninnworcester.co.uk
Church End Goats Milk, What the Fox's Hat, Fallen Angel; 5 changing beers (often Church End) 🅗
A Georgian building on the edge of the city centre run by Church End Brewery. The bar is towards the back while the front area offers the opportunity to watch the world go by. Behind the pub is a large

quiet patio area with a covered space in the old side passage. A changing variety of Church End beers is on the bar plus two guest ales from other small breweries. Pork pies and sausage rolls are always available. Q🌞🛪♣❶🛪🐾🛜

Firefly 🅛
54 Lowesmoor, WR1 2SE
✪ 12-midnight (1am Thu & Fri); 12-2am Sat; 12-11 Sun
☎ (01905) 616996
5 changing beers (often Dark Star, Oakham, Tiny Rebel) 🅗
Once the old vinegar works' manager's Georgian residence, this is now a comfortable, stylish bar with its own on-site microbrewery (brewing October to March). It has five handpulls for beers and two for ciders – one usually from Snails Bank. The interior has soft furnishings, subtle lighting and an open fire. Downstairs is a cosy snug with bench sofas, upstairs is a bar that hosts live music. There is a paved, partially covered beer garden. 🌞🕪🛪❶🛪🐾🛜

King Charles II
29 New Street, WR1 2DP
✪ 11.30-11 (11.30 Fri & Sat) ☎ (01905) 726100
⊕ thekingcharleshouse.com
Craddock's Saxon Gold, Crazy Sheep, Goat Herder Stout, Troll; 3 changing beers (sourced locally) 🅗
A black-and-white listed building in the heart of the historic city. Be sure to check out the skeleton in the oubliette and the rollercoaster ride that is the first floor, where there is a piano for passing musicians. The bar features a range of beers from Craddock's, Two Thirsty Brewers and Bridgnorth. Barbourne Cider on the pumps is occasionally joined by its perry. Quiz night is Tuesday, board games night Wednesday. Speciality pies feature large on the menu. Q🕏🕪🛪♣❶🛪🐾🛜

Plough 🍺 🅛
23 Fish Street, WR1 2HN (on Deansway)
✪ 12-11 (11.30 Fri & Sat); 12-10.30 Sun ☎ (01905) 21381
Hobsons Best; Malvern Hills Black Pear; 4 changing beers (sourced regionally; often Froth Blowers, Mighty Oak, Salopian) 🅗
Grade II-listed pub near the cathedral with a tiny bar. The beers usually come from breweries in Worcestershire and the surrounding counties, but occasionally from further afield. Draught cider and perry are from Barbourne in the city. There is also an ever-changing range of whiskies for the connoisseur. Outside is a small patio area. Rolls are available at weekends and when the cricket is on. Hot meals are served Friday and Saturday lunchtimes, roasts on Sundays. 🕏🌞🛪♣❶🛪🐾

Postal Order ✅
18 Foregate Street, WR1 1DN ☎ (01905) 22373
✪ 8am-midnight (1am Fri & Sat) 🅗
Greene King Abbot; Ruddles Best Bitter; 10 changing beers (sourced nationally; often Pope's) 🅗
A classic Wetherspoon pub, formerly the old Worcester telephone exchange. The Postal Order has one of the largest real ale sales in the chain's West Midlands region and a wide range of beers is served, with regular beer festivals adding even more variety. A cider from local producer Barbourne and Old Rosie from Westons are always available plus two others. Good-value food is served daily 8am-11pm (alcohol from 9am). The volume on the TV may be turned up for important games. Q🕏🕪❶🛪🛪❶🛪🛜

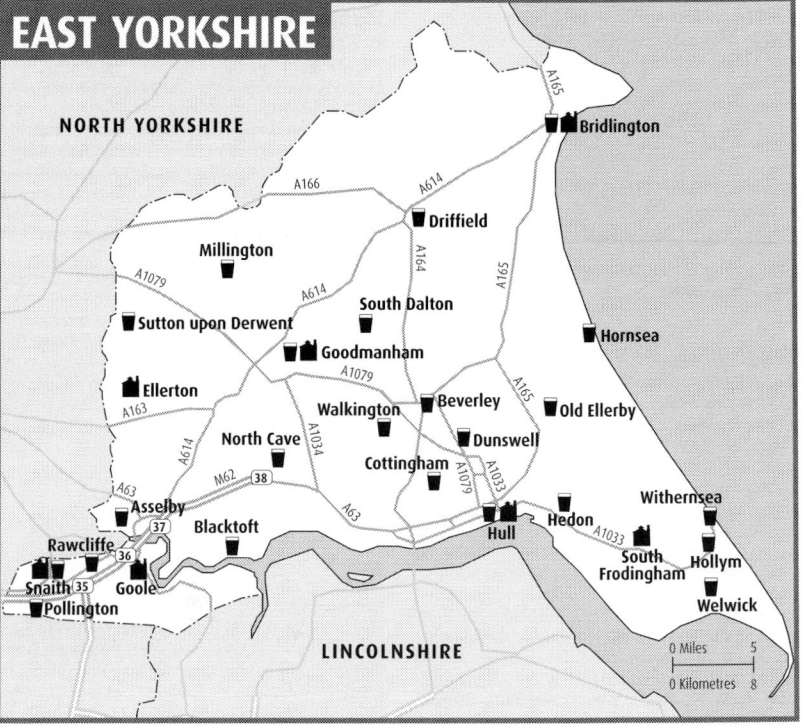

YORKSHIRE (EAST)

Asselby

Black Swan 🄻
Main Street, DN14 7HE
🕐 5-11; 12-11 Sat & Sun ☎ (01757) 630409
John Smith's Bitter; 5 changing beers (sourced locally; often Bird Brain, Half Moon, Sunbeam) Ⓗ
A traditional and family-friendly village pub with an interesting array of regional beers permanently available. Four rotating guest beers frequently include collaborations with local breweries, and there is always a handpulled cider on the bar. A refurbished garden room can be used for such functions as the annual beer festival. The pub is on the Transpennine Cycle Trail - which is a good way to visit it as local transport is scarce.
🐕🏠🍽🍴●P🐾🍲📶

Beverley

Chequers Micropub 🄻
15 Swaby's Yard, Dyer Lane, HU17 9BZ (off Saturday Market)
🕐 12-10 (11 Thu-Sat) ☎ 07964 227906
5 changing beers (sourced regionally; often Atom, Brass Castle, North Riding) Ⓗ
Yorkshire's first micropub in a former baker's shop, near the bus station. Local breweries are well represented on the bar plus micros from throughout the UK. Eight ciders/perries are also on offer. Typically for a micropub, no lager, keg beer or spirits are sold. There is no TV or loud music, making it a place for real conversation, like pubs used to be. A selection of board games is available. The cellar is above the bar. Q🏠🍲♣●🍴🍲🐾

Cornerhouse
2 Norwood, HU17 9ET
🕐 closed Mon; 5-midnight (1am Fri); 10-1am Sat; 10-11 Sun
☎ (01482) 882652
Abbeydale Deception; Black Sheep Best Bitter; Greene King IPA; Timothy Taylor Landlord; 8 changing beers (sourced nationally) Ⓗ
The Cornerhouse looks like a gastro-pub, but the customers are mainly here for the real ale on 12 handpumps and the real cider on two. Beers from local and regional micros are featured, including mild. A coal fire warms the far end of the bar and there is unusual gallery seating off the bar. Curry night is Tuesday and quiz night Wednesday. Breakfast, served 10am-1pm at the weekend, is popular, as is Sunday lunch, served until 8pm.
🐕🏠🍽🍴🚲●P🍲📶

Dog & Duck
33 Ladygate, HU17 8BH (off Saturday Market adjacent to Brown's store)
🕐 11-4, 7-midnight; 11-midnight Fri & Sat; 11.30-3, 7-11 Sun
☎ (01482) 862419 🌐 bedandbreakfastbeverley.com

REAL ALE BREWERIES
Aire Heads Goole (NEW)
All Hallows 🍺 Goodmanham
Atom Hull
Bricknell Hull
Bridlington 🍺 Bridlington
Gene Pool Hull (NEW)
Great Newsome South Frodingham
Half Moon Ellerton
Old Mill Snaith
Yorkshire Hull

Black Sheep Best Bitter; Copper Dragon Golden Pippin; John Smith's Bitter; York Guzzler; 2 changing beers (sourced nationally; often Adnams, Timothy Taylor) Ⓗ
On a side street, the pub was built in the 1930s and has been run by the same family for 45 years. It comprises three areas: a bar with a period brick fireplace and bentwood seating, a front lounge with an open fire, and a rear snug. The home-cooked lunches are good value and popular. Guest accommodation is in six purpose-built self-contained rooms to the rear. It is dog-friendly after food service. Close to Beverley bus station. 🛏◖◀♣♠🛢🖵🐾🛜

Green Dragon ✪
51 Saturday Market, HU17 8AA
☼ 9am-11 (midnight Fri & Sat) ☎ (01482) 889801
⊕ thegreendragonbeverley.co.uk
Greene King IPA; Marston's Wainwright; Sharp's Doom Bar; Timothy Taylor Landlord; 4 changing beers (sourced nationally; often Adnams, Purity, Rudgate) Ⓗ
Historic black and white-fronted inn renamed the Green Dragon in 1765. The entrance is down a side passageway; the front bar retains some wood panelling where a long bar counter originates. Breakfast is served from 9am (alcohol from 10am) and the extensive menu is available until late, including drinks and meal offers. Families are welcome. Tuesday and Thursday are quiz nights, with open mic on Wednesday and live music on the last Friday of the month. There are TV screens for sports fans. 🛏🌣◖◀♠♠🛢🖵🛜

Monks Walk Ⓛ
19 Highgate, HU17 0DN
☼ 12-11; 12-10.30 Sun ☎ (01482) 864972
⊕ monkswalkinn.co.uk
5 changing beers (sourced locally; often Atom, Brass Castle, Yorkshire) Ⓗ/Ⓖ
Dating back to the 13th century and built as a merchants' warehouse, records show there was a brewery attached in the 19th century. There are two bars, the Minster and Monks Bar, divided by an open passageway, plus a dining room which features exposed roof beams and an open fire. Conversation is encouraged at this genuine free house. Known as the George & Dragon until the 1980s, the sheltered beer garden has splendid views of the minster. Access to the car park is off Eastgate. Q🌣◖◀&♣♠P🖵🐾🛜

Sun Inn
1 Flemingate, HU17 0NP (adjacent to Beverley Minster)
☼ 4-11 (12.30am Fri); 12-12.30am Sat; 12-10.30 Sun ☎ 07541 456215 ⊕ suninnbeverley.co.uk
Black Sheep Best Bitter; Morland Old Speckled Hen; Timothy Taylor Landlord; York Guzzler; 1 changing beer (sourced nationally; often Robinsons) Ⓗ
The Sun Inn's medieval timber-framed building is set opposite the eastern front of Beverley's famous minster, so the view from the courtyard beer garden should not be missed. Formerly a Tap & Spile, the pub's stripped-back interior featuring bare brick walls reflects that style. It is a live music venue, with blues and rock bands on a weekend and folk sessions on Saturday teatime; among other events, there is a popular quiz on Thursday. Sunday lunches are served 12-3pm. 🌣◖🛏≈♣♠🛢🖵

Woolpack
37 Westwood Road, HU17 8EN (W of Saturday Market via Newbegin)
☼ 4.30-10 Mon; 12-3, 4.30-11; 12-11 Sat; 12-10 Sun
☎ (01482) 867095
Banks's Sunbeam; Jennings Bitter, Cocker Hoop, Sneck Lifter; Marston's EPA; Wychwood Hobgoblin; 1 changing beer (sourced nationally) Ⓗ
In a Victorian residential street, the Woolpack started life as pair of cottages and became a public house around 1831, later developing its own brewhouse and stables, and is now owned by Marston's. It retains a quarry-tiled snug that is dog-friendly, an open fire in the winter, and has a more recent extension to the rear. Meals are served lunchtimes and evenings, 12-7pm on Sunday. Quiz night is Thursday. Q🌣◖◀♠♠

Blacktoft

Hope & Anchor Ⓛ
Blacktoft Lane, DN14 7YW (3½ miles S of Gilberdyke rail station; follow signs to Blacktoft) SE842242
☼ 12 (5 Mon & Tue)-11; 12-10.30 Sun ☎ (01430) 440441
⊕ hopeandanchorblacktoft.co.uk
Marston's Pedigree; 3 changing beers (sourced regionally; often Copper Dragon, Great Newsome, Half Moon) Ⓗ
Thriving village local in a superb location on the bank of the River Ouse; the RSPB's Blacktoft Sands bird sanctuary is visible on the far bank. Laurel and Hardy memorabilia is prominent, as is a collection of jugs suspended from wooden beams. The conservatory offers fine river views. Popular home-cooked meals are served lunchtimes and evenings during the week (no food Mon and Tue) and all day at the weekend (booking for Sunday recommended). A mild is often on tap. 🛏🌣◖◀▲♣P🛜

Bridlington

Marine Bar Ⓛ
North Marine Drive, YO15 2LS (1 mile NE of centre)
☼ 12-11 (11.30 Sat) ☎ (01262) 675347 ⊕ marinebar.net
John Smith's Bitter; Timothy Taylor Landlord; Wold Top Bitter; 2 changing beers (sourced regionally; often Daleside, Rooster's) Ⓗ
Large open-plan bar, part of the Expanse Hotel. Spectacular sea views are the perfect accompaniment to enjoying the home-cooked food served here daily. Attracting a good mix of regulars, a warm welcome awaits the influx of summer visitors. Twice-weekly quizzes and live music nights are popular. Two regional guest beers complement the three regular ales, with real cider also available. There is ample parking along the promenade, where a land train operates during the summer. 🛏🌣🛏◖◀&▲♣♠P🖵 (512,513)

Cottingham

King William IV
152 Hallgate, HU16 4DB
☼ 11-11 (midnight Fri & Sat); 12-11 Sun ☎ (01482) 875996
⊕ kingwilliamcottingham.co.uk
Banks's Sunbeam; Jennings Cumberland Ale; Marston's Wainwright, Pedigree; Wychwood Hobgoblin; 2 changing beers (sourced nationally; often Brakspear, Ringwood, Wychwood) Ⓗ
Village-centre pub with a traditional bar and quiet lounge. The pub hosts weekly quiz nights and is a

venue during the village's annual music festival. At the rear a former brewery has been converted into a function room offering live music and special events. The beer garden and side courtyard have covered smoking areas. Excellent-value meals are served in large and small portions. Thatchers cider is on handpump. Local CAMRA Village Pub of the Year runner-up for the past two years.
Q✿◑⊱♣●♟☕🅴

Driffield

Butcher's Dog ♈ 🅻
24 Middle Street South, YO25 6PS
☯ closed Mon; 12-11 (10 Tue & Wed); 12-10 Sun
☎ (01377) 254032 ⊕ thebutchersdog.co.uk
5 changing beers (sourced locally; often Wold Top, Yorkshire, Yorkshire Heart) 🅗
One-room micropub but returning to traditional pub values with modern twists. Five real ales from local and regional breweries are served in oversized glasses (tasting paddles available) alongside a wide selection of real ciders, but no spirits. Customers are encouraged to rely on good conversation in the Wi-Fi and music-free environment. It does simple bar snacks, including a cheese board on Sunday afternoon, but customers may bring their own food. Local CAMRA Town Pub of the Year for the past two years.
Q♿⊱♣●🖥🚆(121)☕

Mariners Arms
47 Eastgate South, YO25 6LR (on back street parallel with Middle St)
☯ 3-midnight; 12-midnight Sat & Sun ☎ (01377) 253708
Banks's Sunbeam; Jennings Bitter; Ringwood Razor Back; 1 changing beer (often Ringwood) 🅗
A street-corner local well worth seeking out. The beer range is from the Marston's portfolio, as an alternative to the other breweries more commonly available in the town. Formerly part of the Hull Brewery estate, its four small rooms have now become two: a public bar and a more comfortable lounge. Live terrestrial broadcast sport is shown and the pub fields various sports teams. The long-standing licensees enjoy a loyal following among locals and offer a friendly welcome to all visitors.
✿⊱♣P🚆(121)

Dunswell

Ship Inn 🅻
Beverley Road, HU6 0AJ
☯ 11.30-11 (11.30 Thu; midnight Fri & Sat); 12-11.30 Sun
☎ (01482) 859160 ⊕ shipsquarters.co.uk
Great Newsome Frothingham Best; Hardys & Hansons Bitter; 2 changing beers (sourced regionally; often Great Newsome, Partners, Pennine) 🅗
Fronting the old Hull-Beverley road, this inn once served traffic on the nearby River Hull, and is decorated with nautical memorabilia including the bell from the shipwrecked Caroline. Log fires warm the convivial interior, which is partly divided to create a separate dining area with church pew seating. Former outbuildings have been developed to create en-suite accommodation in the Ship's Quarters. The large garden has an outside bar and barbecue area for summer events. The pub maintains good links with the local primary school and church. ➤✿⛺◑♿♣●P🚆☕🅴

Goodmanham

Goodmanham Arms ♈ 🅻
Main Street, YO43 3JA
☯ 11-midnight; 11-11 Sun ☎ (01430) 873849
⊕ goodmanhamarms.co.uk
All Hallows Peg Fyfe Dark Mild, Ragged Robyn, No Notion Porter, Goodmanham Best; Black Dog Whitby Abbey Ale; Hambleton Stallion Premium Bitter; 3 changing beers (sourced regionally; often Great Newsome, Leeds, Yorkshire) 🅗
Situated close to the Wolds Way footpath, this brewery pub makes an ideal resting place for walkers. With gardens front and back, you can sample nine ales including four from the on-site brewery, and seven ciders. A central corridor leading to the bar serves two separate atmospherically lit rooms, both with open fires, one complete with an old cooking range. Reclaimed farm tools give the ambience of a farmhouse kitchen. Local CAMRA Village Pub of the Year winner 2015 and 2016. Q➤✿◑●P☕

Hedon

Hed'On Inn 🅻
7 Watmaughs Arcade, St Augustine Gate, HU12 8EZ
☯ 1-11 (11.30 Fri & Sat) ☎ 07768 723333
Black Sheep Best Bitter; Titanic Plum Porter; 5 changing beers (sourced regionally; often Atom, Great Newsome, Wold Top) 🅗
Micropub adjacent to a car park at the end of a shopping arcade in the centre of this old market town, it was converted from a disused carpet shop office. The premises are tastefully decorated with recycled fittings. There are two regular and five changing beers covering the full spectrum of styles, together with seven real ciders, bottled beers and a range of spirits and wines. Acoustic music sessions take place on Tuesday night and Sunday afternoon, with a quiz and games night on Wednesday. Q♣●P🚆

Shakespeare Inn 🅻 ✅
9 Baxtergate, HU12 8JN
☯ 12-11 (11.30 Fri & Sat); 12-10.30 Sun ☎ (01482) 891892
Tetley Bitter; Timothy Taylor Landlord; 3 changing beers (sourced nationally; often Great Newsome, Hardys & Hansons, Jennings) 🅗
A 300-year-old pub in the centre of historic Hedon, largely unaltered for the past 50 years, featuring original Darley's wall sconces. Frequented by customers of all ages, it puts on live music fortnightly on Saturdays during summer. Rugby League memorabilia, reflecting the landlord's previous career, adorn the walls, and a friendly atmosphere encourages the art of conversation. The menu has freshly cooked local produce with popular changing specials. Of the three guest beers, one is usually from a local brewery.
➤✿◑♣P🚆☕

Hollym

Plough Inn 🅻
Northside Road, HU19 2RS
☯ closed Mon; 5 (3 Fri)-midnight; 12-midnight Sat & Sun
☎ (01964) 612049 ⊕ theploughinnhollym.co.uk
Greene King IPA; 4 changing beers (sourced nationally; often Great Newsome, Rudgate, Yorkshire Heart) 🅗
Family-run free house, parts of which date from the 17th century – see the wattle and daub front

wall in the public bar. Offering five real ales, both bars have coal fires bringing warmth and cheer during the winter. Primarily a locals' pub, it is a base for Withernsea Rugby Club, Withernsea Harriers and Withernsea Pigeon Flyers. A haven for holidaymakers in summer, the pub opens on bank holiday Mondays. A former local CAMRA Village Pub of the Year. Q ☎ 🕏🏠🌰🕭▶️🅰🔌P🖵🖵😺🐾🛜

Hornsea

Stackhouse Bar 🅛
8a Newbegin, HU18 1AG
✪ 4 (2 Fri)-11; 12-midnight Sat & Sun ☎ (01964) 534407
4 changing beers (sourced regionally; often Brass Castle, Great Newsome, Yorkshire) Ⓗ
Former shop converted to a micropub in October 2014 with an interesting choice of regional ales and a large range of real ciders. Attracting a mixed clientele, customers are encouraged to engage in conversation. Regular quiz nights and board game evenings are held, together with folk nights. There is a separate function room. An autumn beer festival is held in the nearby Hornsea Museum gardens. Although no food is provided, customers are allowed to bring their own. Vaping-friendly. 🛏🅰🌰🔌🖵(240,246)😺🛜

Hull

Furley & Co 🅛
18-20 Princes Dock Street, HU1 2LP (opp dockside entrance to Princes Quay shopping centre)
✪ 11-10 (midnight Thu-Sat); 11-8 Sun ☎ (01482) 229649
Atom Blonde Ale; 4 changing beers (sourced nationally; often Atom, Half Moon, North Riding) Ⓗ
Popular family-friendly bar, offering local and regional beers, overlooking the waterfront of the former Princes Dock. Historically, it was warehousing and offices for a local shipping company and the first bottled gas merchant in Hull; the decor is now neo-industrial, portraying music and film iconography on the walls. Varied events include occasional live music and monthly visits from the chess society. There is an upstairs function room. Local CAMRA Pub of the Year runner-up in 2016 after only two years of operation. 🛏🌰▶️🕭&🐟♣🌰😺

George Hotel
Land of Green Ginger, HU1 2EA
✪ 12-midnight ☎ (01482) 226373
Abbeydale Moonshine; Bradfield Farmers Blonde; Theakston Old Peculier; 4 changing beers (sourced regionally) Ⓗ
In the heart of the old town on Hull's most famous street, this one-roomed pub is of historic interest. The Georgian interior, with beamed ceilings, wood-panelled walls and pictures of old Hull, remains virtually unaltered. The fine glazed leaded windows have been retained and of note is the reputedly the smallest pub window in England, dating from its former coaching days. Meals are served daily except Monday. Two Westons ciders are stocked, with four guest beers sourced mainly from Yorkshire. ▶️🌰♣🌰🖵

Larkin's 🅛
48-52 Newland Avenue, HU5 3AE (near jct of De Grey Street)
✪ 12-11 (11.30 Fri & Sat) ☎ (01482) 440991
🌐 larkinsbar.co.uk

Wold Top Wold Gold; 3 changing beers (sourced regionally; often Abbeydale, Gene Pool, Great Newsome) Ⓗ
One-roomed café-bar named after poet Philip Larkin; it was once two shops and can still be partitioned for small private functions. A good selection of home-cooked food is served every day. There is a paved area to the front and a newly extended family-oriented beer garden to the side and rear. Beer festivals with live music from local acts are usually held over bank holiday weekends during spring and summer. 🛏🌰▶️&🖵🛜

Lord Nelson
163 Endike Lane, HU6 7UA (3 miles N of city centre)
✪ 1-11; 12-midnight Fri & Sat; 12-11 Sun ☎ (01482) 801844
3 changing beers (sourced nationally; often Adnams, Backyard, Wadworth) Ⓗ
Comfortable, friendly estate pub with traditional appeal, easily accessible by bus and a short walk from the main Hull-Beverley road. The main bar has an open fire with traditional-style blue and white tiling, walls of half-brick/half-wood cladding and a display of rugby shirts on the ceiling. The pub supports various sports clubs from the local estate. The back bar/function room, featuring a dance floor and stage, is used for karaoke/discos at weekends. It has an unusual side-of-bar pool room with wood-clad walls. 🛏🌰♣P🖵(115,5)😺🛜

Minerva Hotel
Nelson Street, HU1 1XE
✪ 11.30-11.30 (midnight Fri & Sat) ☎ (01482) 210025
🌐 minerva-hull.co.uk
Tetley Bitter; 5 changing beers (sourced regionally; often Atom, Revolutions, Yorkshire) Ⓗ
Overlooking the Humber estuary and Victoria Pier, this famous pub, built in 1829, is a great place from which to watch the ships go by. Photos and memorabilia are a reminder of the area's maritime past. The central bar serves various rooms including a tiny three-seat snug. The former brewhouse was converted to provide an additional drinking area and is available for functions. It is connected to The Deep visitor attraction by a footbridge at the mouth of the River Hull. 🌰▶️🖵(16)🛜

New Adelphi Club 🅛
89 De Grey Street, HU5 2RU
✪ 8-11 ☎ (01482) 348216 🌐 theadelphi.com
Great Newsome Frothingham Best; 3 changing beers (sourced regionally; often Atom, Brass Castle, Great Newsome) Ⓗ
Hull's justifiably famous music venue has been the launchpad to many an illustrious career and has hosted a veritable Who's Who of popular music since opening in 1984. The main music room is supplemented by a small front bar that accommodates a pool table and features a cut-off bus front as the bar counter. Access to the small bar is free at all times and no membership restrictions apply. Benefit from a £1 reduction on ale when no musicians are booked. A genuinely idiosyncratic venue. ♣🌰P🖵😺🛜

Olde Black Boy ★
150 High Street, HU1 1PS
✪ 5-11 Mon & Tue; 11.30-11.30
🌐 yeoldeblackboy.weebly.com/index.html
6 changing beers (sourced nationally) Ⓗ
Historic pub, licensed since 1729, with a beamed ceiling and panelled walls, previously a wine merchant's and tobacco dealer. It has a front snug

bar with an open fire, a main back bar and a heated rooftop smoking terrace. Historic black and white photos of old town pubs are displayed. Folk music features monthly on the first Monday. Several museums and Hull Minster are within five minutes' walk. Guest beers, mainly from Yorkshire breweries, and Weston's Old Rosie cider, are served, together with bar snacks. It sells 35-40 single malt whiskies. Q♣●🖥🐈🛏📶

Olde White Harte ★

25 Silver Street, HU1 1JG (in alley between Silver St and Bowlalley Lane)
✿ 11-midnight ☎ (01482) 326363 ⊕ yeoldewhiteharte.com
Caledonian Deuchars IPA; Theakston Best Bitter, Old Peculier; house beer (by Caledonian); 3 changing beers (sourced nationally) 🅷

Historic pub in a 17th-century merchant's house, with strong connections to the English Civil War, hidden down an alley near Hull's Old Town. The existing ground floor interior dates back to a major refurbishment in 1881, which was an idealised re-creation of an old English inn, complete with massive inglenook fireplaces and stained-glass windows. The first floor features the Plotting Parlour, which is available for meetings and functions. There is also a heated courtyard providing an all-weather outdoor drinking area. 🐈♣🛏

Pave 🅻 ✅

16-20 Princes Avenue, HU5 3QA
✿ 11-11 (11.30 Fri & Sat) ☎ (01482) 333181
⊕ pavebar.co.uk
Tetley Gold; Theakston Best Bitter; 3 changing beers (sourced regionally; often Great Yorkshire, Saltaire, Scarborough) 🅷

The original pavement café in this popular area of the city, a continental-style bar that attracts a diverse range of customers. As well as the regular ales, there are three guests, usually sourced regionally, and a varied range of European draught and bottled beers. Home-cooked food including vegetarian and gluten-free options is served daily. Live music is provided on Tuesday evenings and Sunday afternoons. A changing Westons cider is sold. 🛏🐈🕽🛏📶

St John's Hotel ✅

10 Queens Road, HU5 2PY
✿ 12-11.30 (midnight Tue & Thu; 12.30am Fri & Sat)
☎ (01482) 341013 ⊕ stjohnshull.com
Marston's EPA, Old Empire; 3 changing beers (sourced nationally; often Brakspear, Ringwood) 🅷

Grade II-listed classic street-corner local that boasts one of the least altered interiors in the city. The welcoming front-corner public bar complements a quiet back room, with original bench seating. A more basic larger room accommodates the pool table and is home to the beer festival bar three times a year. A community local, it has two darts teams, a football team and the Oddfellows cricket league which hosts quiz nights in the winter. Open mic night is Tuesday. Q🛏🐈♣P🖥🐈📶

Three John Scotts 🅻 ✅

Lowgate, HU1 1AA
✿ 8am-midnight (1am Fri & Sat) ☎ (01482) 381910
Greene King Abbot; Ruddles Best Bitter; Sharp's Doom Bar; 7 changing beers (sourced regionally; often Great Heck, Great Newsome, Wold Top) 🅷

Originally an Edwardian post office, this open-plan Wetherspoon features modern decor and works of art. The name derives from three successive 19th-century vicars of St Mary's Church opposite. The pub has established a broad customer base appealing to all types of clientele. Up to 10 real ales and two real ciders are on the bar. Children are welcome up to 9pm. There is a large rear courtyard seating area which is a great suntrap in the summer. 🛏🐈🕽🛏♣●🛏📶

Whalebone 🏆 🅻

165 Wincolmlee, HU2 0PA
✿ 12-midnight (11 Tue & Wed) ☎ 07506 868461
Great Newsome Frothingham Best; Rudgate Viking; 5 changing beers (sourced regionally; often Abbeydale, Rat, Sonnet 43) 🅷

Local CAMRA City Pub of the Year for the last three years and 2016 Cider Pub of the Year, this is a rare gem sited within the old Greenland whaling trading area. Continuously licensed since 1791, the current building dates from 1890 though much altered internally. A genuine free house since 2002, seven real ales, six ciders/perry plus continental draught and bottled beers are served in a comfortable saloon bar. Photos celebrating the city's sporting heritage and bygone Hull pubs adorn the walls. An old illuminated M&R brewery sign hangs outside. 🛏🐈♣🐈

Millington

Gait

Main Street, YO42 1TX
✿ closed Mon; 12-3 (not Mon), 6.30-11; 12-4, 6-11 Sat; 12-3, 6-11 Sun ☎ (01759) 302045 ⊕ gait-inn-millington.co.uk
Black Sheep Best Bitter; Tetley Bitter; Theakston Best Bitter; 2 changing beers (sourced locally; often Half Moon, Wold Top) 🅷

Delightful Yorkshire Wolds pub that provides a warm welcome (seasonally by means of a wood-burning stove) both to locals and the many walkers enjoying the attractions of Millington woods and pastures. The idiosyncratic bar is filled with a range of ornaments and local pictures. Sit at kitchen-style tables to enjoy hearty, home-made food served from an extensive menu. It has an annual beer festival with up to 35 ales. Three regular beers are stocked and at least one guest, when surveyed, all from Yorkshire. 🛏🐈🕽♣P🐈

North Cave

White Hart 🅻

20 Westgate, HU15 2NJ
✿ 4-11 (midnight Fri & Sat) ☎ (01430) 470940
⊕ whitehartnorthcave.co.uk
House beer (by Great Newsome); 2 changing beers (sourced regionally; often Great Newsome, Theakston, Wold Top) 🅷

This welcoming, traditional village pub is a credit to the community it serves. There is a long bar to the side and rear while the quieter front bar has comfortable seating and is where the three real ales are on offer. The house beer, 1776, provides an insight to the history of the pub. Open fires are lit during the winter months, providing further home comforts. Walkers and dogs are welcome. Third-pint taster trays are now available. A popular stopping-off point for Beverley racegoers. Q🛏🐈♣P🖥(155)🐈

Old Ellerby

Blue Bell 🛈

Crabtree Lane, HU11 5AJ
☼ 7-11.30 Tue & Wed; 7-midnight Fri & Sat; 12-6, 8-11.30 Sun; closed Mon & Thu ☎ (01964) 562364
Great Newsome Sleck Dust; Tetley Bitter; 2 changing beers (sourced regionally; often Great Newsome, Tom Wood's) Ⓗ
A 16th-century inn with an L-shaped bar and a single room divided into distinct areas, including a snug to the right and a rear pool area where children are welcome until 8.30pm. The pub has a strong community focus and is home to several darts and dominoes teams. Two guest beers in winter increase to three in summer. Outside there is a fishing pond and bowling green together with a sun terrace. Popular with walkers (wipe your boots, please). Q❄🚲🐕&🅰♣P🐾

Pollington

King's Head 🛈 ✅

Main Street, DN14 0DW
☼ 5-11 (midnight Fri); 10-midnight Sat; 12-11 Sun
☎ (01405) 861507
Isaac Poad 1863 Best Bitter; Old Mill Blonde Bombshell; Tetley Bitter; 2 changing beers (sourced locally; often Black Sheep, Theakston, Timothy Taylor) Ⓗ
Traditional pub with real ales, proper pub grub and a warm, friendly atmosphere, run by a local family. It upholds village traditions, with vintage weekends to coincide with the local RAF base reunions. The full-time chef prides himself on his home-made pies, puddings and specials menu. All produce is locally sourced. There is a quiz and rock 'n' roll bingo on Friday nights, with monthly theme nights on Saturdays. Q❄🚲🍴🍺&🅰♣P🐾🛜

Rawcliffe

Jemmy Hirst at the Rose & Crown 🛈

26 Riverside, DN14 8RN (from village green turn N on Chapel Lane)
☼ 6 (5 Fri)-midnight; 12-midnight Sat & Sun
☎ (01405) 831038 ⊕ jemmyhirst.freeservers.com
Timothy Taylor Landlord; 4 changing beers (sourced locally; often Abbeydale, Ossett, Wold Top) Ⓗ
An outstanding free house that locals say is the heart of the village, well known regionally and winner of numerous CAMRA branch awards including Pub of the Year eight times. There is always a warm, friendly welcome from the owners, locals and Bruno the dog. Book-lined walls and an open fire provide a haven on a cold winter's day. You can sample five real ales and a traditional cider here. The patio or river bank beckon in warmer weather. Q❄🚲♣🍺P🚌(88,401)🐾

Snaith

Brewers Arms Hotel 🛈

10 Pontefract Road, DN14 9JS (on main road)
☼ 12 (5.30 Mon)-11 ☎ (01405) 862404
⊕ thebrewersarms.co.uk
Old Mill Traditional Bitter, Blonde Bombshell; 1 changing beer (sourced locally; often Old Mill) Ⓗ
Fine example of a large village pub, with many worn oak beams in evidence, as well as three fireplaces. It is split into a large main room and bar, with four individual side rooms leading off. One

side room has an angling theme, with fishing rods and stuffed wildlife. It always has three real ales on handpull, with an additional one in the summer. Q❄🚲🍴🍺&🚼♣P🚌🛜

South Dalton

Pipe & Glass 🛈 ✅

West End, HU17 7PN (at end of West End lane)
☼ closed Mon; 12-11; 12-10.30 Sun ☎ (01430) 810246
⊕ pipeandglass.co.uk
Black Sheep Best Bitter; house beer (by Great Yorkshire); 3 changing beers (sourced regionally; often John Smith's, Wold Top, York) Ⓗ
Delightful hostelry that stands at the site of the original gatehouse to Dalton Hall, featuring exposed beams and custom-made furniture. The owner and chef holds a Michelin star for the eighth consecutive year. Three guest ales come from around Yorkshire, as does the real Moorlands Farm cider. Five boutique rooms, with views of Dalton Hall, are available to let. Closed for the first two weeks of January, but open on bank holiday Mondays. Q❄🚲🍴🍺&🚼P🚌(142)

Sutton upon Derwent

St Vincent Arms 🛈

Main Street, YO41 4BN
☼ 11.30-3, 6-11; 12-3, 6.30-10.30 Sun ☎ (01904) 608349
⊕ stvincentarms.co.uk
Fuller's London Pride, ESB; Greene King IPA; Theakston Old Peculier; Timothy Taylor Landlord; York Guzzler; 1 changing beer (sourced nationally) Ⓗ
A winner of many local CAMRA awards, this pretty white-painted village free house on a bend in the road has been family owned and well run for many years. A long-time supporter of Fuller's beers, it has a consistent and large beer range. The bar, featuring a large Fuller, Smith & Turner mirror, is popular with locals. Another small bar with a serving hatch leads to the dining rooms. It serves excellent food, catering for a variety of tastes. Q❄🚲🍺P

Walkington

Barrel Inn

35 East End, HU17 8RX
☼ 4.30-midnight (1am Fri); 12-1am Sat; 12-midnight Sun ☎ 07550 078833 ⊕ barrelwalkington.co.uk
Marston's Wainwright, Lancaster Bomber; 1 changing beer (sourced regionally) Ⓗ
Friendly drinkers' local in a quiet three-pub village, and one of only two Thwaites pubs in East Yorkshire. The front bar has a log fire and beamed ceiling; a step leads to a connecting lounge, also with a log fire. To the rear is a secluded cottage-style garden. Families and dogs are welcome throughout. Although essentially a quiet pub, major Premier League football matches and some other sporting events are shown. Thursday is quiz night. 🚲🍺♣🚌🐾

Welwick

Coach & Horses 🛈

Main Street, HU12 0RY
☼ 12-midnight ☎ (01964) 630788
Great Newsome Frothingham Best; 2 changing beers (sourced regionally; often Black Sheep, Theakston, Timothy Taylor) Ⓗ

A family-run free house with a friendly atmosphere, focused on village life and activities, with local charity auctions and fundraising events. It has a decent-sized bar area for those wanting to sample the three real ales on offer. A designated dining area offers a menu featuring local produce, served all day. Regular heritage weekends are held, with a beer festival in the marquee set up across the road from the pub.
Q ⚓ ❀ ⇌ ◑ ♿ Ⓐ ♣ P 🚌 (71) 🐾 📶

Withernsea

Old Boat Shed 🄻

2 Seaside Road, HU19 2DL
closed Mon; 12-midnight summer; closed Mon & Tue; 5-9.30 (10.30 Thu; 11 Fri); 1-11.30 Sat; 1-10 Sun winter ☎ 07975 539534
4 changing beers (sourced regionally; often Great Newsome, Isaac Poad, Wold Top) 🄷
Originally built in 1881 to house the Withernsea lifeboat station before it was decommissioned in 1913, the building was virtually derelict when the current owners took over. Following 11 months of hard work, the micropub opened in April 2016. Four cask ales and six real ciders are served in this community-focused bar where conversation is actively encouraged in preference to loud music or TV. A selection of unusual board games such as shove-ha'penny and bar skittles is available.
Q ⚓ ❀ ♿ Ⓐ ♣ 🍎 🅱 🚌 (76,129) 🐾 📶

YORKSHIRE (NORTH)

Acaster Malbis

Ship ✔

Moor End, YO23 2UH
12-11 (4 Mon & Tue); 12-10.30 Sun ☎ (01904) 703888
shipinnacastermalbis.co.uk
Black Sheep Best Bitter; Camerons Strongarm; Timothy Taylor Golden Best; 3 changing beers (sourced regionally; often Ossett, Theakston) 🄷
Located by the river (and attractively refurbished after the December 2015 floods), this friendly country pub serves a good range of real ales and quality food in a pleasant and relaxing location. A welcoming real fire inside and the riverfront garden offer choices depending on the weather. Popular in spring and summer, it has four nearby camping/caravan sites and boats, but is quieter the rest of the year. The York waterbus in the summer makes an interesting trip.
Q ⚓ ❀ ⇌ ◑ Ⓐ P 🚌 (21) 🐾 📶

Aldbrough St John

Stanwick 🄻 ✔

High Green, DL11 7SZ (1 mile from B6275)
closed Mon & Tue; 12-3, 5.30 (6 Sat)-11; 12-9 Sun
☎ (01325) 374258 thestanwick.co.uk
Daleside Bitter; house beer (by Great North Eastern); 2 changing beers 🄷
In a picturesque North Yorkshire village on one of the country's largest village greens, this multi award-winning and welcoming 19th-century inn has two bars – one for drinkers and one for the two excellent restaurants where locally sourced food is served. It is the brewery tap for the village's Mithril Ales, and one of its beers is always featured. Cricket, quoits and darts are supported. It does takeaway fish and chips 5.30-8pm Wednesday, roast baguettes 2-5pm Sunday, and has a food theme night on the last Friday of the month. Local CAMRA Country Pub of the Year 2017.
Q ⚓ ❀ ◑ ♿ ♣ P 🚌 (29) 🐾 📶

Appleton-le-Moors

Moors Inn 🄻

YO62 6TF
11-11 ☎ (01751) 417435 moorsinn.co.uk
Bradfield Farmers Brown Cow; 2 changing beers (sourced locally; often Bradfield, Helmsley, Pennine) 🄷
Grade II-listed 17th-century pub in a pretty village. It is a welcoming place with a coal fire in a cast-iron range in winter. The single bar has three handpulls, two with changing guest ales from local breweries. Two separate dining rooms serve quality locally sourced food. It has outside seating at the front, a patio and a delightful beer garden to the rear. Q ⚓ ❀ ⇌ ◑ P 🐾

Appletreewick

Craven Arms 🄻

BD23 6DA
12-11; 12-10.30 Sun ☎ (01756) 720270
craven-cruckbarn.co.uk
Dark Horse Craven Bitter, Hetton Pale Ale, Night Jar; Theakston Best Bitter, Old Peculier; Wharfedale Blonde; 3 changing beers (sourced regionally; often Greene King, Saltaire) 🄷
Dating from 1548, this multi-roomed free house has stone-flagged floors, oak beams and gas lighting. The bar features an original Yorkshire range while the cosy taproom has an open fire and ring the bull. A snug behind the bar leads to the cruck barn, added in 2006 using traditional techniques, with its minstrels' gallery and large open fireplace. This can be hired for functions. Seven regular beers are supplemented by two guests in summer. Accommodation is in three shepherd's huts. Q ⚓ ❀ ⇌ ◑ Ⓐ ♣ 🍎 P 🚌 (74A) 🐾 📶

Arncliffe

Falcon Inn 🄻

BD23 5QE
12-3, 7-11 (not Tue & Thu eve winter); 12-11 Fri & Sat; 12-10.30 Sun ☎ (01756) 770205
thefalconinnskipton.co.uk
Timothy Taylor Boltmaker 🄷/🄶**; 1 changing beer (sourced locally)** 🄷
Unspoilt traditional Dales pub-cum-hotel nestled next to the village green; it was the original Woolpack in Emmerdale Farm. Eschewing modern gimmickry, the last significant changes to the pub interior occurred in the 1950s. Timothy Taylor Boltmaker is served from the jug or via a recently installed handpump. A second handpump offers a changing guest beer from a local brewery. Loved by visitors from near and far, the pub is also well supported by Dales folk. Q ⚓ ❀ ⇌ ◑ 🐾 📶

Askrigg

King's Arms 🄻

Main Street, DL8 3HQ
11-11.30 (midnight Fri & Sat) ☎ (01969) 650113
kingsarmsaskrigg.co.uk
Black Sheep Best Bitter; Theakston Best Bitter; house beer (by Yorkshire Dales) 🄷

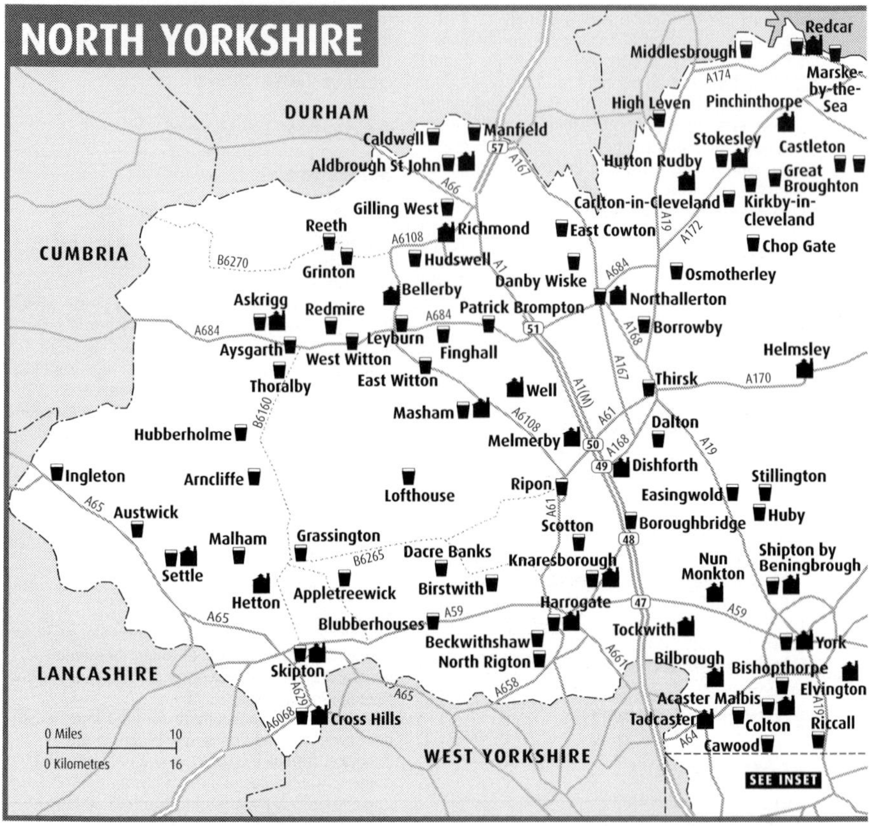
NORTH YORKSHIRE
DURHAM
CUMBRIA
LANCASHIRE
WEST YORKSHIRE
Middlesbrough
Redcar
Marske-by-the-Sea
High Leven
Pinchinthorpe
Stokesley
Castleton
Hutton Rudby
Great Broughton
Carlton-in-Cleveland
Kirkby-in-Cleveland
Chop Gate
Caldwell
Manfield
Aldbrough St John
Gilling West
Reeth
Richmond
East Cowton
Hudswell
Grinton
Danby Wiske
Osmotherley
Askrigg
Redmire
Bellerby
Patrick Brompton
Northallerton
Leyburn
Borrowby
Aysgarth
West Witton
Finghall
Helmsley
Thoralby
East Witton
Well
Thirsk
Masham
Dalton
Hubberholme
Melmerby
Dishforth
Ingleton
Arncliffe
Lofthouse
Ripon
Stillington
Easingwold
Austwick
Scotton
Huby
Boroughbridge
Malham
Grassington
Dacre Banks
Knaresborough
Nun Monkton
Shipton by Beningbrough
Settle
Hetton
Appletreewick
Birstwith
Harrogate
Blubberhouses
Tockwith
York
Beckwithshaw
Bilbrough
North Rigton
Bishopthorpe
Skipton
Elvington
Acaster Malbis
Cross Hills
Tadcaster
Colton
Riccall
Cawood
0 Miles 10
0 Kilometres 16

This historic multi-roomed Dales free house of great character starred as the Drover's Arms in TV's All Creatures Great and Small. A huge open fireplace and painting of the local friendly society add character to the stone-flagged bar. There are separate dining rooms plus a vaulted games room to the rear, and a small outdoor courtyard. Three house beers are from the Yorkshire Dales Brewery, a few hundred yards away.

Austwick

Game Cock

LA2 8BB (on Horton road)
closed Mon; 11.30-1am ☎ (015242) 51226
gamecockinn.co.uk
Marston's Wainwright; Thwaites Nutty Black, Original; 1 changing beer Ⓗ
Most of the licensed area is a restaurant but there is a lovely little old-fashioned bar at the end of the building. It has three drinking rooms – two small rooms were added to the drinking area in 2010 without spoiling it. It has three weekly specials nights for food and gluten-free dishes are available on request. Austwick is a quiet and non-touristy village compared to neighbouring Clapham, but there are usually a few hikers alongside the locals in the bar. Q P (581)

Aysgarth

Aysgarth Falls Hotel

DL8 3SR
11.30-11 ☎ (01969) 663775 aysgarthfallshotel.com
Black Sheep Best Bitter; 3 changing beers (sourced regionally) Ⓗ
The torrents of Aysgarth Falls provide a world-famous spectacle just a few hundred yards below this imposing hotel, which has its own fishing stretch on the River Ure. On the main A684, the building has been comfortably refurbished and its public bar serves up to five real ales from local and regional brewers. The hotel has its own campsite in a field to the rear, within sight and sound of the falls. Q P

George & Dragon

DL8 3AD (on main A684 between Hawes and Leyburn)
11-midnight ☎ (01969) 663358
georgeanddragonaysgarth.co.uk
Black Sheep Best Bitter; Theakston Best Bitter; house beer (by Yorkshire Dales); 1 changing beer Ⓗ
The famous Aysgarth Falls lie less than a mile away from this attractive 17th-century coaching inn. Drinkers are welcome in its cosy, wood-panelled bar which serves up to five locally brewed real ales, while for diners there is a separate restaurant. En-suite accommodation is also offered. An outside drinking area has thatched umbrellas and great views of the stunning surrounding Dales countryside. Q P

Beck Hole

Birch Hall Inn ★

YO22 5LE (approx 1 mile N of Goathland)

Birstwith

Station Hotel
Station Road, HG3 3AG
⌂ 10.30-11 (midnight Fri); 12-10 Sun ☎ (01423) 770254
⊕ station-hotel.net
Black Sheep Golden Sheep; Copper Dragon Best Bitter; 2 changing beers Ⓗ
This former station hotel has undergone a high-quality refurbishment and is now a popular drinking and dining pub. It has three open-plan bar spaces and a separate dining area at the rear. Outside is a large beer garden. The pub is noted for its locally sourced food, served all day. The guest beers are usually from local Yorkshire breweries. Five letting rooms are available, one adapted for disabled customers. ⏚❀✿◑&P🚲(24)🐾🛜

Bishopthorpe

Ebor
46 Main Street, YO23 2RB
⌂ 11-midnight; 12-11.30 Sun ☎ (01904) 706190
Samuel Smith Old Brewery Bitter Ⓗ
Officially haunted and with 16th-century origins, this two-bar pub is uniquely the only tenanted Samuel Smith's property. Landlord of 36 years Gordon Watkins provides a welcoming ambience, well kept Old Brewery Bitter, and an extensive, home-cooked menu (Whitby fish a speciality and vegetarian options) lunchtimes and evenings (no food Sun). The Ebor is at the heart of the local community, with a family atmosphere and a large beer garden – children and dogs welcome. ⏚❀◑&▲♣P🚲(11)🐾🛜

Marcia Ⓛ ✅
29 Main Street, YO23 2RA
⌂ 11-midnight; 12-11 Sun ☎ (01904) 706185
⊕ themarciayork.co.uk
Leeds Pale; Rooster's Yankee; Timothy Taylor Landlord; 3 changing beers (sourced locally; often Half Moon, Treboom, York) Ⓗ
Welcoming and popular village local with a landlord passionate about real ale. Six handpumps offer three permanent and three rotating real ales (mainly LocAle). An annual summer beer and cider festival is staged in the large rear garden, which has a children's play area. A good range of food is served every day in the bar and in the large restaurant/conservatory. The pub has a relaxed and friendly atmosphere, with games and occasional live music. There is a quiz on Wednesday night. Q⏚❀✿◑&▲♣P🚲(11)🐾🛜

Blubberhouses

Hopper Lane Hotel
Skipton Road, LS21 2NZ
⌂ closed Mon; 12-11; 12-10.30 Sun ☎ (01943) 880010
⊕ hopperlanehotel.co.uk
3 changing beers Ⓗ
A family-owned establishment on the main A59 Harrogate to Skipton road above Fewston Reservoir. Double fronted and stone built, the three original front rooms are pleasantly decorated and furnished; beyond are dining areas set out with tables and chairs. The front rooms have open fires and the original stone flags remain by the front door. An old glass-covered well is an unusual feature in the lounge, which is furnished with leather settees and chairs. ⏚❀✿◑&♣P🐾

⌂ 11-11 ☎ (01947) 896245 ⊕ beckhole.info
Black Sheep Best Bitter; North Yorkshire Beckwatter; 1 changing beer Ⓗ
Unspoilt, family-run rural gem, resting among a hamlet of cottages, run by the same licensee, an accomplished fine artist, for 37 years. A winner of multiple CAMRA awards, only beers from Yorkshire are served. It comprises the Big Bar and the Small Bar, which sandwich a sweet shop. Pleasant outdoor drinking facilities overlook the Murk Esk. The house beer, Beckwatter, is brewed organically by North Yorkshire. Sandwiches, pies, beer cake and traditional sweets are always available. Hours change during winter. Q⏚❀&♣🐾🌸

Beckwithshaw

Smith's Arms Ⓛ ✅
Church Row, HG3 1QW
⌂ 11-11 (midnight Sat); 12-10.30 Sun ☎ (01423) 504871
Black Sheep Best Bitter; Greene King IPA; 3 changing beers Ⓗ
A Chef & Brewer food-led pub in an 18th-century inn that, as the name suggests, was formerly a blacksmith's forge. In a quiet hamlet to the south-west of Harrogate, the pub comprises an L-shaped bar area and a separate restaurant. An excellent menu with many seasonal dishes is available throughout the day in both the restaurant and bar. The five handpumps serve two permanent beers and three widely sourced guest ales. ⏚❀◑&P🐾🛜

Boroughbridge

Black Bull Inn
6 St James Square, YO51 9AR
☼ 11-midnight; 12-11 Sun ☎ (01423) 322413
⊕ blackbullboroughbridge.co.uk
John Smith's Bitter; Timothy Taylor Boltmaker; 1 changing beer ⊞
Nestling in a corner of the market square, this 13th-century inn is immaculately kept, comfortably furnished and popular with locals and tourists alike. A Grade II-listed gem, it has a resident ghost. Three drinking and dining areas include a small, cosy snug and a larger bar with open fires and good-value beers. A wide range of bar meals is served and there is a separate restaurant. A local CAMRA Pub of the Year. Q❤️◑▶▲♣P🖵🐾🛜

Borrowby

Wheatsheaf Inn 🄻
YO7 4QP (800yds from A19)
☼ 5.30-11; 12-10.30 Sun ☎ (01845) 537274
Daleside Bitter; 2 changing beers (sourced locally) ⊞
A well-kept and welcoming free house in a rambling, attractive village a short hop from the busy A19 trunk route. The cosy public bar features a low-beamed ceiling and a splendid canopied fireplace, showing its 17th-century origins and giving a traditional feel, particularly in winter. There is a small dining room (no food Sun eve) and a further drinking area to the rear. Guest beers are usually from Yorkshire microbreweries.
Q🍴🐕♣P🐾🛜

Brompton by Sawdon

Old Post Office Tavern
High Street, YO13 9DP (on A170)
☼ closed Mon; 5-10; 12-10 Sat & Sun summer; closed Mon; 5 (3 Sun)-10 winter ☎ 07957 214161
⊕ oldpostofficetavern.co.uk
4 changing beers (sourced regionally) ⊞
The latest addition to the local CAMRA branch rural pub scene is on the Scarborough to Pickering road. This former village post office has been recently converted into a cosy single-roomed pub which encourages good old-fashioned conversation. Four varying guest beers are offered, predominantly from Yorkshire microbreweries, together with many real ciders. Q🍴♿♣P🖵(128)🐾

Burn

Wheatsheaf 🄻
Main Road, YO8 8LJ
☼ 12-11 (midnight Fri & Sat) ☎ (01757) 270614
⊕ wheatsheafburn.co.uk
6 changing beers (often Brown Cow, Great Heck, Ossett) ⊞
Traditional country pub serving a varied range of guest beers mainly from Yorkshire breweries. A narrow entrance leads to the bar, a small room to the left, and a spacious lounge with a huge open fire to the right. There is a collection of artefacts from bygone days and memorabilia of 578 and 431 Squadrons stationed at Burn in WWII. Food is served every lunchtime and Wednesday to Saturday evenings. Regular beer festivals, a popular Sunday quiz night and occasional live entertainment take place.
Q🍴🐕◑♣P🖵(476,405)🐾🛜

Caldwell

Brownlow Arms
DL11 7QH
☼ 5.30-11; 12-11 Sat & Sun ☎ (01325) 718471
⊕ brownlowarms.co.uk
Timothy Taylor Landlord; 2 changing beers ⊞
The Brownlow Arms, in this quiet village, could be described as the perfect country inn. It boasts a fine dining restaurant as well as two cosy bars accompanied by open log fires, where you are guaranteed to find some welcoming locals. Serving three cask ales (up to six in summer), always including Timothy Taylor Landlord, requests are welcome. Whether you are coming for a quick pint or a romantic dinner for two, a huge choice of home-cooked food is on offer alongside the ales. Q🐕🍴◑♿P🐾🛜

Carlton-in-Cleveland

Blackwell Ox Inn
TS9 7DJ (800yds E of A172)
☼ 11.30-11 ☎ (01642) 712287 ⊕ blackwellox.co.uk

REAL ALE BREWERIES

Ainsty Acaster Malbis (NEW)
BAD Dishforth
Bad Seed Malton
Bilbrough Top Bilbrough (NEW)
Black Sheep Masham
Brass Castle Malton
Brew York York (NEW)
Brown Cow Barlow
Captain Cook Stokesley
Daleside Harrogate
Dark Horse Hetton
Great British Breworks 🍴 Pickering (NEW)
Great Heck Great Heck
Great Yorkshire 🍴 Cropton
GreyHawk Skipton
Hambleton Melmerby
Harrogate Harrogate
Helmsley Helmsley
Hop Studio Elvington
Jolly Sailor 🍴 Selby
Little Black Dog Carlton (NEW)
Mithril Aldbrough St John
Naylor's Cross Hills
North Riding (Brewery) Scarborough
North Riding (Brewpub) 🍴 Scarborough
North Yorkshire Pinchinthorpe
Northallerton Northallerton (NEW)
Pennine Well
Redscar 🍴 Redcar
Richmond Richmond
Rooster's Knaresborough
Rudgate Tockwith
Ryedale Cross Hills (brewing suspended)
Samuel Smith Tadcaster
Scarborough Scarborough
Settle Settle
Theakston Masham
Three Peaks Settle
Treboom Shipton-by-Beningbrough
Wainstones Hutton Rudby
Wensleydale Bellerby
Whitby Whitby
Wold Top Wold Newton
York York
Yorkshire Dales Askrigg
Yorkshire Heart Nun Monkton

Marston's Wainwright; Ringwood Boondoggle; 2 changing beers Ⓗ
Set in a beautiful area on the northern edge of the North York Moors, with the same licensee for 29 years, this popular, multi-roomed village inn is as renowned for its fine beers as it is for its Thai food and more traditional menus. Look out for the lunchtime and early doors food offers. But you do not have to eat – four handpumps provide an eclectic range of beers in various styles. The garden has an extensive, well-designed children's play area. Q❤🕙🅿🚃(89)

Castleton

Downe Arms Ⓛ ⦿
3 High Street, YO21 2EE (500yds S of Castleton Moor railway station)
🕙 12-midnight; 12-11 Sun ☎ (01287) 660223
🌐 thedownearms.co.uk
Black Sheep Best Bitter; Camerons Strongarm; 2 changing beers Ⓗ
Overlooking the Esk Valley, this recent CAMRA branch Pub of the Year is a family-run country inn under the stewardship of enthusiastic members who serve two regular and two guest beers. Lunchtime and early doors midweek Beat the Clock specials are available from the menu. The pub hosts a wide range of events and also supports charitable causes. Pleasant days are enhanced by the superb views over the North York Moors. There are four letting bedrooms. Check winter opening hours. ❤🕙🛏🅿🚃♿🐾🚲🅿🚃🐾📶

Cawood

Ferry Ⓛ
2 King Street, YO8 3TL
🕙 4-8 Mon; 4-10 Tue & Wed; 12-11 Thu; 12-1am Fri & Sat; 12-10 Sun ☎ (01757) 268515 🌐 ferryinncawood.com
Leeds Pale; Timothy Taylor Landlord; 3 changing beers (sourced regionally; often Bradfield, Theakston, Wold Top) Ⓗ
Wooden-beamed 16th-century inn on the river in this historic village. Cosy, with open fires and numerous rooms, there is a real air of history to the pub. Outside, a pleasant terrace and beer garden are home to Ferry Fest in August where local crafts, food and beer are celebrated. Five handpumps on the bar provide mainly regional brews, and real cider is available. Good food is served Thursday to Sunday. ❤🕙🅿♿🅿🚃(42)🐾📶

Chop Gate

Buck Inn Ⓛ
Chop Gate, TS9 7JL (on B1257, between Stokesley and Helmsley)
🕙 12 (5 Mon-Wed)-9 ☎ (01642) 778334
🌐 the-buck-inn.co.uk
3 changing beers Ⓗ
Set amid a walkers' paradise, in the centre of the North York Moors, this picturesque family-run village pub offers a truly Yorkshire/Teutonic twist. Three locally sourced beers and seven draught German lagers, brewed under the 502-year-old purity laws, are served, together with real home-made food, again half-Yorkshire, half-German. Live music features monthly. There are six en-suite bedrooms, some designated dog-friendly, while free camping is offered to campers who choose to dine here. Q❤🕙🛏🅿🅿🐾📶

Church Fenton

Fenton Flyer Ⓛ ⦿
Main Street, LS24 9RF
🕙 5-11; 4-midnight Thu & Fri; 12-midnight Sat; 12-10.30 Sun ☎ (01937) 558137 🌐 thefentonflyer.com
John Smith's Bitter; 4 changing beers (sourced regionally; often Ilkley, Leeds, Ossett) Ⓗ
Friendly village pub with pictures of the nearby WWII airbase that is now a commercial airport. The beers, chosen from the SIBA list and often LocAle, are always in good condition. It has live music on the first Friday of each month, a monthly Saturday disco with karaoke, and a quiz night on Wednesday raising money for local charities. Sky and BT sports TV are in the main bar and an adjacent games room has a pool table and darts. ❤🅿🅿🚃(492)📶

Cliffe

New Inn Ⓛ
York Road, YO8 6NN
🕙 2-11; 12-midnight Fri & Sat; 12-10.30 Sun
☎ (01757) 633888
John Smith's Bitter; 5 changing beers (sourced regionally; often Half Moon, Small World, Sunbeam) Ⓗ
Now established as a superb example of how a village local can be a real ale emporium, this award-winning pub is a delight to visit. Comfortable and two-roomed, it serves five guest beers – almost always local and certainly from Yorkshire. Blazing log fires for cosy winter drinking are complemented by a shady beer garden for summer. The annual beer festival is held every August, ramping up the number of ales served alongside live local music and a traditional barbecue. ❤🅿♿🅿🚃🐾📶

Colton

Old Sun Inn Ⓛ ⦿
Main Street, LS24 8EP
🕙 closed Mon; 12-3 (not Tue), 6-11; 12-11 Sun
☎ (01904) 744261 🌐 yeoldsuninn.co.uk
Timothy Taylor Landlord; 4 changing beers (sourced locally; often Black Sheep, Revolutions) Ⓗ
A 17th-century village pub with an award-winning restaurant featuring locally sourced produce. There are four cosy dining areas together with a drinkers-only bar with five handpumps; it also has an extensive wine list. The interior has traditional low-beamed ceilings and in the winter there are two fires. For the summer there is a patio and a large picnic area, and functions are catered for. A studio barn can sleep up to six on a B&B or self-catering basis. Q❤🕙🛏🅿♿🅿🚃(21)🐾📶

Cropton

New Inn Ⓛ
Cropton Lane, YO18 8HH (leave A170 at Wrelton and follow signs for Cropton)
🕙 11-11 (midnight Fri & Sat) ☎ (01751) 417330
🌐 newinncropton.co.uk
Great Yorkshire Pale, Classic, Golden; 3 changing beers (sourced locally; often Great Yorkshire) Ⓗ
A family-run pub on the edge of the North Yorkshire Moors National Park, the tap for the Great Yorkshire Brewery (formerly Cropton Brewery). It is a perfect base for walking and cycling, serving good food in the bars, conservatory or restaurant,

and offering both B&B accommodation and camping. Many real ales are on offer, and there is a legendary beer festival every November. Other festivals and music events are put on during the year. A positive and chatty pub, it is dog and rambler friendly. Q❀😊🍴🍽◐🍺♦♣P🚪🚃🐾🏮

Cross Hills

Beer Belly Bar & Kitchen 🅛

Midland Mills Station Road, BD20 7DT (in industrial estate on right over railway bridge from Cross Hills)
🕐 closed Mon & Tue; 3 (12 Sat & Sun)-11 ☎ 07743 795199
🌐 beerbellykitchen.co.uk
Naylor's Bitter, Pinnacle Blonde; 3 changing beers (sourced locally) 🅷
This is part of Naylor's Brewery and has a downstairs bar and an upstairs eatery. The emphasis in the bar is on good company, friendly chatter and the appreciation of good beer. In fine weather customers spill out into the yard outside. Five reasonably priced ales are available, with at least four supplied by Naylor's, one of which is usually dark. Brewery merchandise and bottled beers can also be purchased. Occasional music evenings and events take place.
Q❀&P🚃(66)🐾🏮

Gallagher's Ale House 🅛

1-3 East Keltus, BD20 8TD
🕐 closed Mon & Tue; 3-10 Wed & Thu; 1-11 Fri; 12-11 Sat;
12-10 Sun ☎ 07834 456134
5 changing beers (sourced nationally) 🅷
Popular micropub in what used to be Gallagher's bookmaker's shop. The five changing beers usually include a dark ale, a pale bitter and a strong or speciality brew. No electronic music or TV disturb the conversation. Parking is available adjacent to the Co-op store round the corner. The phone number given is shared with the Beer Engine in Skipton. Q🍺🚃(M4,66)🐾🏮

Dacre Banks

Royal Oak Inn

Oak Lane, HG3 4EN
🕐 11.30-11 (11.30 Fri & Sat); 12-10.30 Sun
☎ (01423) 780200 🌐 the-royaloak-dacre.co.uk
6 changing beers 🅷
A family-run Grade II-listed pub, dating from 1752, in the heart of Nidderdale. From the rear snug are views of the dale while the rest of the interior is broken up into smaller spaces by panelled walls and glazed partitions. A large restaurant is at the rear and pool is available in one of the front rooms. Outside is an attractive garden and boules is played beside the car park. Up to six real ales from the Marston's group are on tap. Food majors on local produce and themed food nights are regularly held.
Q❀😊🍴🍽◐♣P🚃(24)🏮

Dalton

Jolly Farmers Inn

Brookside, YO7 3HY
🕐 4-11; 12-midnight Sat & Sun ☎ (01845) 595004
John Smith's Bitter; 1 changing beer 🅷
A large village local in the heart of a working village. The three rooms offer drinking, dining and pub games, with sports TV in the bar and the games room. Various pub games league teams are supported by the regulars. Accommodation is

available across the courtyard from the main building in what were formerly outbuildings. The village is conveniently close to the A1M and the A19 near the foot of the North York Moors escarpment. 😊🍴🍽◐♣P🏮

Danby

Duke of Wellington 🅛

West Lane, YO21 2LY (300yds N of railway station)
🕐 12-2.30 (not Mon), 7-11; 12-11 Fri & Sat; 12-2.30, 7-10.30
Sun ☎ (01287) 660351 🌐 dukeofwellingtondanby.co.uk
Copper Dragon Scotts 1816; Daleside Bitter; 1 changing beer 🅷
This 18th-century inn, and previous CAMRA branch Pub of the Year, is set in idyllic countryside, close to the popular visitor centre and equally popular traditional local bakery. The inn was used as a recruiting post during the Napoleonic Wars, with a cast-iron plaque of the first Duke, unearthed during restorations, hanging above the fireplace. All beers are from Yorkshire, while the kitchen offers traditional British home-cooked meals at their best, using local produce. Cider and perry are served Easter-October. Q😊🍴🍽◐🍻♣🍺🚃🏮

Danby Wiske

White Swan 🅛

DL7 0NQ (approx 3 miles N of Northallerton off A167)
🕐 12-11 ☎ (01609) 775131
🌐 thewhiteswandanbywiske.co.uk
4 changing beers (sourced locally) 🅷
This haven for Coast-to-Coast walkers offers welcome accommodation and camping, and champions local beers, notably from Northallerton Brewery. A real village local, its attractive single-room bar has wood-burning stoves and is home to the local sword dancers plus a monthly folk club on the third Tuesday. Lunchtime snacks and evening meals are available April-October (booking advised), using locally sourced produce. Opening hours vary in winter – check ahead.
Q😊❀🍴🍽♦♣🍺🐾🏮

Easingwold

George Hotel 🅛 ✅

Market Place, YO61 3AD
🕐 11-11 ☎ (01347) 821698 🌐 the-george-hotel.co.uk
Black Sheep Best Bitter; Timothy Taylor Landlord; 1 changing beer (sourced regionally) 🅷
If it were a theme pub, the theme would be 'no change'. The George is a fine example of a smart, confident, country town hotel pub, with an excellent range of beer and food to match. Just step off the bus in the market square and straight into a calm, welcoming home-from-home which even has the style to pull off a tartan carpet without appearing loud. Q😊❀🍴🍽◐&P🚃

East Cowton

Beeswing ✅

Main Street, DL7 0BD
🕐 5-11; 11.30-11 Sat & Sun ☎ (01325) 378349
🌐 thebeeswing.weebly.com
4 changing beers 🅷
Traditional country village pub with two bars, a pool room and a highly rated restaurant. Named after a locally bred champion racehorse, there are numerous racing references. It has up to four

different beers from breweries countrywide and one real cider. Real fires create a relaxing atmosphere, and the staff are welcoming. The pub supports the local community with regular music and quizzes. Q🏠🛏️🍴🍺♣🐕P🚲

East Witton

Cover Bridge Inn 🅛
DL8 4SQ (½ mile N of village on A6108)
☼ 11-midnight; 12-11.30 Sun ☎ (01969) 623250
🌐 thecoverbridgeinn.co.uk
Black Sheep Best Bitter; John Smith's Bitter; Theakston Old Peculier; Timothy Taylor Landlord; 3 changing beers (sourced locally) Ⓗ
A splendidly traditional Dales inn where numerous CAMRA awards tell their tale. The River Cover runs along the foot of the attractive garden and play area, near its confluence with the River Ure. Fathom out the door latch and enjoy a warm welcome in the unspoilt public bar, with its giant hearth, in the tiny lounge or pleasant beer garden. Eight handpumps dispense locally brewed beers and guests from further afield; there are two real ciders and perry.
Q🏠🛏️🍴🍺♣🐕P🚉🚲(159)🐕🛜

Egton

Wheatsheaf Inn 🅛
YO21 1TZ
☼ closed Mon; 11.30-2.45, 5.30-11; 11.30-11 Sat & Sun
☎ (01947) 895271 🌐 wheatsheafegton.com
Black Sheep Best Bitter; Timothy Taylor Landlord; 2 changing beers Ⓗ
Winner of many CAMRA awards, this Grade II-listed 19th-century pub serves four Yorkshire beers. It is now in its 18th year in the Guide, and remains under the stewardship of a licensee with over 30 years of continuous Guide recognition. Church pews, country collectables and a roaring range add to the ambience. The grassy area to the front and boules to the rear are ideal for summer drinking. The renowned first-class restaurant always features local meat, fish and game.
Q🛏️🍴🍺♣P🚉🚲(99)🐕

Egton Bridge

Horseshoe Hotel
YO21 1XE
☼ 11.30-3, 6-11; 12-11 Sun ☎ (01947) 895245
🌐 egtonbridgehotel.co.uk
Theakston Best Bitter; 3 changing beers Ⓗ
Secluded 18th-century gem in a horseshoe-shaped hollow and accessed either by road, from the railway station, or by walking over the stepping stones across the River Esk. Old-fashioned settles, a large fire and angling memorabilia adorn the bar, while picnic tables, on a large raised grassy bank, make outdoor drinking a pleasure. Four handpumps (three in winter) feature some interesting beers. The menu and specials board are locally sourced and represent good value. Accommodation is in six letting bedrooms.
Q🏠🛏️🍴🚉♣P🚲(99)🐕

Filey

Bonhommes' Bar
Royal Crescent Court, The Crescent, YO14 9JH

☼ 11-midnight (1am Fri & Sat) ☎ (01723) 515325
🌐 bonhommesbar.co.uk
5 changing beers (sourced nationally) Ⓗ
Just off the fine Victorian Royal Crescent Hotel complex, the bar's name celebrates John Paul Jones, father of the American Navy. His ship, the Bonhomme Richard, was involved in a battle off nearby Flamborough Head during the War of Independence. Five handpumps serve rotating guest beers. Food is served daily (except Mon). A quiz is held on Thursday evening and Saturday afternoon each week. Local CAMRA Rural Pub of the Year runner-up 2015.
🛏️🍴Å🚉♣🐕🍺(121)🐕🛜

Cobbler's Arms
2 Union Street, YO14 9DZ
☼ closed Mon; 4-10; 12-11 Sat; 3-10 Sun ☎ (01723) 512511
5 changing beers (sourced nationally; often Scarborough, Wold Top) Ⓗ
Recently opened in the centre of Filey, the bar started out as a private residence before becoming the cobbler's shop from which it takes its name. It offers five changing guest ales and four real ciders. A discount is available to card-carrying CAMRA members. The bar is dog and family friendly. There is a regular quiz on a Tuesday night and live music once a month. The rear snug can be used for meetings free of charge. 🛏️♿🚉🐕🍺🛜

Star Inn ✓
23 Mitford Street, YO14 9DX
☼ 12-midnight (1am Fri & Sat) ☎ (01723) 512031
🌐 thestarfiley.co.uk
York Guzzler; Black Sheep Ale; Theakston Best Bitter; 3 changing beers (sourced nationally) Ⓗ
The Star Inn is just off the Filey town centre and has a large main room and separate restaurant/ function room. Three regular beers and three rotating guests are offered. Freshly cooked meals are served lunchtimes and evenings (except Mon). Live entertainment features at weekends, and pub teams participate in a local pool league. Smokers are catered for at both the front and rear of the building, while parking is provided behind the pub. Runner-up local CAMRA Rural Pub of the Year 2016.
🛏️🍴🍺♿🚉♣P🚲(121)🛜

Finghall

Queen's Head 🅛
DL8 5ND
☼ 12-3, 6-11 ☎ (01677) 450259 🌐 queensfinghall.co.uk
4 changing beers Ⓗ
Comfortably appointed 18th-century free house in an isolated village, overlooking the Wild Wood said to have inspired the author Kenneth Grahame's Wind in the Willows. Bar meals or restaurant dining are the main focus here, but it remains a community pub, with oak beams, nooks and crannies and a real fire. The beer garden has pleasant views over Wensleydale, and the Wensleydale Railway's Finghall Lane station is a few minutes' walk away.
🛏️🍴🍺♿Å🚉P🚲(155)🛜

Gilling West

White Swan 🅛
51 High Street, DL10 5JG (1 mile W of Scotch Corner, off A66)
☼ 12 (9am Sat)-11 ☎ (01748) 825122 🌐 thewhiteswan.co

House beer (by Mithril); 2 changing beers ⊞
A historic coaching inn, recently modernised, with bar, restaurant and rooms. An open fire, courtyard garden and traditional beams continue the tradition, while the granite bar, tin tables and modern rooms bring this charming village pub into the present. Real ales are sourced locally, always including one from local microbrewery Mithril, who brew the house beer, The Swan. There is also an extensive wine and gin menu. The kitchen specialises in steaks, seafood and Yorkshire tapas, and sources its famous steaks from a local Yorkshire farm. Quiz nights are fortnightly, there is regular live music, and it has a modern pool room. Q ⌂ ❀ ⚲ ◖ ▲ ♣ P ⊟ (29) ❀ ☞

Grassington

Foresters Arms ⅃ ⦿
20 Main Street, BD23 5AA
❁ 11-midnight (1am Fri & Sat) ☎ (01756) 752349
⊕ forestersarmsgrassington.co.uk
Black Sheep Best Bitter, Riggwelter; Tetley Mild, Bitter; Timothy Taylor Landlord; 2 changing beers (sourced locally; often Timothy Taylor, Wharfedale) ⊞
Just off the cobbled town square, the Foresters is a lively inn and popular with locals and visitors alike. The main bar and pool/TV area are to the left and further seating leads to a separate dining room. Accommodation is in seven en-suite rooms, and fishing permits for the local River Wharfe can be bought at the pub. There is a quiz on Monday. Secure cycle storage is available for overnight guests. ❀ ⚲ ◖ ♣ ⊟ (72,74) ❀ ☞

Great Broughton

Bay Horse ⅃
88 High Street, TS9 7HA (at S end of village)
❁ 11.30-3, 5.30-11; 11.30-11 Sat; 12-11 Sun
☎ (01642) 712319 ⊕ thebayhorse-greatbroughton.co.uk
Camerons Strongarm; Jennings Sneck Lifter; 2 changing beers ⊞
Visitors and locals alike enjoy the welcoming hospitality offered by friendly bar staff at this spacious village country inn, situated at one of the northern entrances to the North York Moors. While the emphasis is on good-value, freshly prepared, home-cooked meals, drinkers are also especially well catered for. As well as the regulars, Strongarm and Sneck Lifter, for which the pub has been renowned for serving for many years, two changing beers from the Marston's stable are also now on the bar. Q ⌂ ❀ ◖ P ⊟ (89,X89)

Grinton

Bridge Inn
DL11 6HH (on B6270, 1 mile E of Reeth)
❁ 12-midnight; 12-11 Sun ☎ (01748) 884224
⊕ bridgeinn-grinton.co.uk
Jennings Cumberland Ale; Marston's Wainwright; 3 changing beers (sourced nationally; often Marston's) ⊞
Set beneath the towering hills of Fremington Edge and Harkerside, this friendly, well-run inn lies close to the River Swale. Its comfortable lounge, wood-panelled bar and two restaurant rooms offering home-made food are a haven for walkers and cyclists on the Coast-to-Coast and Inn Way walks and Dales Cycle Way; a youth hostel is half a mile up the hill. Guest beers are from the Marston's

range. May close early at quiet times. Accommodation is offered in five en-suite rooms. Q ⌂ ❀ ⚲ ◖ ◖ ♣ P ⊟ ❀ ☞

Grosmont

Crossing Club ⅃
Co-operative Building, Front Street, YO22 5QE (opp NYMR car park – ring front door bell)
❁ 8-11 ☎ 07766 197744
5 changing beers ⊞
Set amid beautiful scenery in the Esk Valley, this CAMRA branch Club of the Year is opposite the NYMR/Esk Valley railway stations in what was the local Co-op's upstairs delivery bay. Converted by dedicated villagers into a railway-themed private members' club 19 years ago, a warm welcome always awaits CAMRA members. The five handpumps have now served over 1,100 different beers. For railway enthusiasts, both steam and diesel memorabilia adorn the walls. Opening hours are extended during NYMR galas. Q ⇌ ♣ ⑊ ❀

Harrogate

10 Devonshire Place
10 Devonshire Place, HG1 4AA
❁ 3-midnight; 12-midnight Fri-Sun ☎ (01423) 202356
⊕ 10devonshireplace.com
Timothy Taylor Boltmaker; 8 changing beers ⊞
Restored and renovated in 2014, the original semicircular counter with its stained-glass canopy has been refurbished and is complemented by a newly installed reclaimed floor. Ten handpumps serve local cask ales and a cider. Flights of thirds are offered and a changing style of street food is available afternoons and evenings. To one side at the front is the bottle shop, with a stock of interesting bottled beers and wines which can be drunk on or off the premises. ⌂ ◖ ⇌ ♣ ❀ ☞

Blues Café Bar
4 Montpellier Parade, HG1 2TJ
❁ 12-1am; 12-11 Sun ☎ (01423) 566881 ⊕ bluesbar.co.uk
4 changing beers (often Daleside, Ossett, Rooster's) ⊞
A small single-room live music bar modelled on an Amsterdam café bar. There is live music seven evenings a week with two sessions on a Sunday. Popular with music lovers, it can get busy. Four rotating guest beers are offered, sourced from far and wide. Food is served from 10am until early evening (2pm Sun). Children are permitted until 7pm. ◗ ⇌

Coach & Horses
16 West Park, HG1 1BJ
❁ 11-11; 12-10.30 Sun ☎ (01423) 561802
⊕ thecoachandhorses.net
Daleside Bitter; Tetley Bitter; Timothy Taylor Landlord; 5 changing beers ⊞
A busy, traditional pub popular with locals and visitors, by Harrogate's famous Stray. The counter is surrounded by snugs and alcoves creating a cosy atmosphere inside. Tables and chairs are provided outside for customers in summer while window boxes create a spectacular display and add year-round colour. The pub offers a guest beer range and serves excellent meals at lunchtime. It also holds themed evenings and a popular Sunday night quiz, which help to raise a considerable amount of money for a local children's hospice. Q ◖ ⇌ ⊟ ☞

Harrogate Tap

Station Parade, HG1 1TE
⏰ 11-11 (midnight Fri); 10-midnight Sat ☎ (01423) 501644
🌐 harrogatetap.co.uk
11 changing beers (often Harrogate, Rooster's) Ⓗ
Just off platform 1 of Harrogate station is this impressive transformation of a neglected railway building into a fine pub of similar style to the Tapped Brew Company's other bars at York and Sheffield. Comprising a long bar room and a separate snug, the decor features dark-wood panelling, a tiled floor and tasteful Victorian-style fittings. A diverse range of cask ales is available on 12 handpumps, with one devoted to cider. These are complemented by bottled world beers. Bar snacks are also available. Q🕏ᕙ⇌🍽🚃🕏

Little Ale House 🏆

7 Cheltenham Crescent, HG1 1DH
⏰ closed Mon; 2-9 (10 Thu & Fri); 12-10 Sat; 1-7 Sun
☎ (01423) 391996
5 changing beers Ⓗ
Harrogate's first micropub, comprising one room with the counter at the back, and a pleasant drinking yard to the rear. As in many other micropubs, the beers are kept cool in a glass cabinet to one side. Four handpumps dispense cask beers, plus a fifth at the weekend. There are also ciders in boxes, a selection of German bottled beers, and a range of wines and gins. Q🕏⇌🍽🕏🕏

Major Tom's Social

The Ginnel, HG1 2RB
⏰ 12-11.30 (1am Fri & Sat) ☎ (01423) 566984
🌐 majortomssocial.co.uk
House beer (by Rooster's); 3 changing beers Ⓗ
An unusual café bar housed upstairs in a former antiques emporium. It provides real ale, pizza, music and art in one fun package, and is simply furnished and decorated in a mix of styles to suit the eclectic customers. The artwork on display is for sale. The four handpumps dispense a changing variety of ales, usually including some from Rooster's, and from a variety of smaller breweries. There are also interesting bottles from the UK, US and Europe. ◑⇌🕏🕏

Montpellier

14 Montpellier Parade, HG1 2TG
⏰ 11-11 ☎ (01423) 817248
Theakston Old Peculier; Timothy Taylor Landlord; 1 changing beer (often Theakston) Ⓗ
A narrow but long pub in Harrogate's Montpellier quarter of small exclusive shops, bars and restaurants. Very much a food-led pub, it offers three local beers. The front part is laid out for dining while the rear is furnished in a more traditional public house style. Tables and chairs are provided on the pavement outside in the pleasant setting of Montpellier Hill with its trees and manicured lawns. 🕏◑⇌

Winter Gardens ⦿

4 Royal Baths, HG1 2RR
⏰ 8am-midnight (1am Thu; 2am Fri & Sat)
☎ (01423) 877010
Black Sheep Best Bitter; Daleside Bitter; Greene King Abbot; Ruddles Best Bitter; Sharp's Doom Bar; 6 changing beers Ⓗ
Converted from part of the Royal Baths complex in 2002, this magnificent building has a large, spacious interior reached from the Parliament

Street entrance by a sweeping double stone staircase. Wheelchair access is from the entrance in The Ginnel. In addition to the usual Wetherspoon core range, a number of locally sourced guests is always available across three sets of handpumps. The pub can get busy due to its location near Harrogate's conference and exhibition centre. 🕏🕏◑🕏⇌🕏🕏

Hensall

Railway Tavern Hotel

Station Road, DN14 0QJ (off A645 between Eggborough and Great Heck)
⏰ closed Mon; 5 (4 Sat)-9; 12-11 Sun ☎ 07546 900203
1 changing beer (sourced nationally; often Brains, Revolutions, St Austell) Ⓗ
Friendly community free house featuring a changing guest beer, sourced nationally, and often from a small independent brewery. Recently refurbished to a high standard, the pub comprises a lounge bar and separate dining areas. Food is available on Sunday lunchtime only, served throughout the pub, and advance booking is advisable due to its popularity. Regular charity events are hosted and, on Macmillan day, the charity has full use of the pub. Sunday is quiz night. Q🕏🕏🏠▲⇌♣P🚃 (150)

High Leven

Fox Covert Ⓛ

Low Lane, TS15 9JW (on A1044, 2 miles E of Yarm)
⏰ 11.30-11 (11.30 Fri & Sat); 12-11 Sun ☎ (01642) 760033
🌐 thefoxcovert.com
Black Sheep Best Bitter; Sharp's Doom Bar; Theakston Old Peculier; Timothy Taylor Landlord Ⓗ
A warm welcome is guaranteed at this popular, long-established and uniquely named pub, which has been in the same family for more than 36 years. Originally a farmstead, it was built in the traditional longhouse style, with whitewashed walls and a pantiled roof. Inside it is warm and cosy, with two open fires, and four handpumps serving superbly kept beers. The pub is also noted for its good-value food, served all day every day. Conference facilities are available. Q🕏🕏◑🕏P🚃 (17)

Hubberholme

George Inn Ⓛ

Kirk Gill, BD23 5JE (opp church, 1 mile NW of Buckden)
⏰ 12 (4 Mon)-10.30; closed Tue summer; 12-3 (not Mon), 6-10.30; 12-10.30 Sat; 12-5 Sun; closed Tue winter
☎ (01756) 760223 🌐 thegeorge-inn.co.uk
Black Sheep Best Bitter; 3 changing beers (sourced locally; often Dark Horse, Wensleydale, Yorkshire Dales) Ⓗ
A favourite haunt of JB Priestley, this Grade II-listed whitewashed building dates from the 1600s and boasts mullioned windows, heavy oak beams and flagstone floors. A lighted candle on the bar denotes that it is open and is associated with the Hubberholme Parliament, an annual auction for letting church land. George of the George (the owners' Jack Russell) eagerly greets visitors. The inn stays open later on winter Sundays if busy, and closes for a short annual holiday around the end of January. Q🕏🏠◑◑P🕏

Huby

Mended Drum ⃝

Tollerton Road, YO61 1HT

☼ 5 (4 Fri)-11; 12-midnight Sat; 12-11 Sun
☎ (01347) 810264 ⊕ themendeddrumhuby.blogspot.co.uk
Black Sheep Best Bitter; 5 changing beers (sourced locally; often Bad, Brass Castle) ⊞
You need to make an effort to get to Huby, but once inside this pub it is well rewarded. Bright, lively and dedicated to real ale is a fitting description both of the pub and its staff. With a better beer range than many big city pubs (plus an excellent bottle range to take home if constrained by driving), there is never a dull moment – a destination pub, but what a destination!
➰ ☻ ⓓ ♿ ♠ ♣ ⌂ 🚲 (x30) ♥ 🎜

Hudswell

George & Dragon 🍷 ⃝

DL11 6BL

☼ 11-3, 5-11; 11-11 Sat & Sun ☎ (01748) 518373
⊕ georgeanddragonhudswell.com
Wensleydale Falconer Session Bitter; 4 changing beers (sourced locally) ⊞
CAMRA named this homely, two-roomed village inn its current National Pub of the Year. Rescued and refurbished in 2010 after a successful community buy-out, it now features its own library, shop, allotments and other local facilities as well as great food and Yorkshire-brewed beers. Either Northallerton Dark or Rudgate Ruby Mild is always on. A large beer terrace to the rear offers stunning panoramic views over the Swale Valley. Open all day bank holidays. Q ➰ ☻ ⓓ ♿ ♠ ♣ ⌂ 🚲 (32) ♥ 🎜

Hunmanby

PieBald Inn

65 Sands Lane, YO14 0LT

☼ 12-11 (10.30 Sun) ☎ (01723) 447577
⊕ thepiebaldinn.co.uk
House beer (by Greene King); 3 changing beers ⊞
The Piebald Inn is located on the outskirts of Hunmanby village adjacent to the Sands Lane level-crossing. It's a large multi-roomed pub, which is predominantly food oriented. PiePub Co Bitter is the house beer with three to five guest ales offered depending on the time of year. Food is served all day every day. A particular feature of the menu is the extensive range of fifty different pies on offer. At the side is a terraced area and large garden. ➰ ☻ ⓓ ♿ ♠ ⇄ P

Ingleton

Masons

New Road, LA6 3HL

☼ 11.30-11; 12-10.30 Sun ☎ (015242) 42040
⊕ masonsismoran.co.uk
Black Sheep Best Bitter; Sharp's Doom Bar; 3 changing beers ⊞
Early-Victorian building on the busy main road away from the centre of this popular tourist village. Extensively refurbished in 2016, it is now a true family-run free house. A small bar counter serves a long drinking space of linked areas with a light and airy decor. Live music features but not yet regularly. ☻ ⇄ ⓓ ♠ P 🚲 (80) ♥ 🎜

Kirk Smeaton

Shoulder of Mutton

Main Street, WF8 3JY (follow signs from A1)

☼ 12-midnight; 11.30-midnight Sun ☎ (01977) 620348
Black Sheep Best Bitter; 1 changing beer (sourced regionally; often Theakston, Wharfe Bank) ⊞
Convenient for the Went Valley and Brockadale Nature Reserve, this rural gem is popular with walkers and the local community. The friendly clientele assures a warm welcome and the beer is always in superb condition. An award-winning free house, the pub comprises a large lounge with open fires and a cosy, dark-panelled snug. The spacious beer garden has a covered and heated shelter for smokers and there is ample parking. Quiz night is Tuesday. ➰ ☻ ♣ ⌂ 🚲 (409) ♥ 🎜

Kirkby-in-Cleveland

Black Swan ⃝

Busby Lane, TS9 7AW (800yds W of B1257) NZ539060

☼ 12-midnight ☎ (01642) 712512
Black Sheep Best Bitter; Bradfield Farmers Blonde; Timothy Taylor Landlord; Wainstones Amber; 1 changing beer ⊞
Nestling at the foot of the North York Moors, at the crossroads of an ancient village, this warm and cosy free house, comprising a bar, a lounge/restaurant and a conservatory, affords a friendly and genuine welcome. Four regular beers, with the house beer, Kirkby Blonde, brewed by Wainstones, together with a guest beer, are served in a convivial atmosphere, where making conversation with locals seems a must. Bar snacks and a full menu, including daily specials, represent good value. ➰ ☻ ⓓ ♿ ♣ P ⌂ 🚲 (89) ♥ 🎜

Knaresborough

Blind Jack's ⃝

19 Market Place, HG5 8AL

☼ 4 (5 Mon; 3 Fri; 12 Sat)-11; 12-10.30 Sun
☎ (01423) 869148
Bad Comfortably Numb; Black Sheep Best Bitter; 7 changing beers ⊞
A multi-roomed pub with bare brick walls, wooden floorboards and panelling, and in this Guide for over 25 years. An award-winning ale house, it provides a focal point both for locals and the many visitors who appreciate the excellent selection of ales, the cosy ambience and lively banter. The beer range usually includes several from Bad Company Brewery, as the head brewer of Bad Co is the co-owner of Blind Jacks. Q ⇄ 🚲 (1) ♥

Cross Keys ✔

17 Cheapside, HG5 8AX

☼ 4-11; 12-midnight Fri & Sat; 12-11 Sun ☎ (01423) 863562
Jennings Bitter; Ossett Yorkshire Blonde, Big Red Bitter, Silver King; Rat White Rat; 3 changing beers (sourced regionally; often Rat) ⊞
A former Tetley's house, it was refurbished by Ossett Brewery in its trademark style of stone-flagged floors, bare brick walls and stained glass. This traditional pub serves four regular beers and two guests, one of which is usually a dark beer or stout from either a microbrewery or from one of the other breweries within the Ossett company. Thursday is quiz night and a live band plays on most Saturday nights. Lunches are served on Sunday. ⓓ ♿ ⇄ 🚲 (1) ♥ 🎜

Half Moon 🅛

1 Abbey Road, HG5 8HY
☼ 5 (4 Fri)-11; 12-11 Sat & Sun ☎ (01423) 313461
4 changing beers 🅗
A popular watering hole down from the town at
river level, this recently restored independent free
house, with bare brick walls, real fire and wood-
burning stove, provides a welcoming atmosphere.
Four handpumps dispense a varying range of
beers, one of which is usually from local Rooster's
Brewery. The pub hosts a popular quiz every
Tuesday at 8pm, and a grazing menu of boards and
light snacks is available every evening until 10pm.
Dogs are welcome in the outdoor area.
🌡😼◑⇌🖫(22)🛜

Mitre Hotel ✅

4 Station Road, HG5 9AA (opp railway station)
☼ 12-11 ☎ (01423) 868948
**Black Sheep Ale; Okells Manx Pale Ale; Timothy Taylor
Boltmaker; 4 changing beers** 🅗
The Mitre offers a modern split-level bar, a side
function room and another in the basement, along
with a beer garden with views of the local church.
As with other Market Town Taverns pubs, there are
eight handpumps dispensing beers mainly from
Yorkshire, including the town's own Rooster's
Brewery, and cider. Look out for the speciality
bottled beer menu; some foreign beers are also
available on draught. There is accommodation in
four en-suite rooms and food is served every day.
Dogs are welcome. 🌡😼🛏◑ఉⴰ⇌❀🖫(1)😼🛜

Lastingham

Blacksmiths Arms

Anserdale Lane, YO62 6TN
☼ 11.30-11.30 ☎ (01751) 417247
🌐 blacksmithslastingham.co.uk
**Theakston Best Bitter; 3 changing beers (sourced
regionally)** 🅗
Pretty stone inn in a conservation village, opposite
St Mary's Church, famous for its 11th-century crypt.
The interior comprises a cosy bar with a York range
lit in winter, a snug, and two dining rooms.
Excellent-quality food including local game dishes
is served alongside interesting guest beers. A
secluded beer garden is to the rear. This remote
pub is popular with locals, walkers and shooting
parties. Sorry, no dogs. Q🌡😼🛏◑

Lealholm

Board Inn 🅛

Village Geen, YO21 2AJ
☼ 9am-midnight (2am Fri & Sat) ☎ (01947) 897279
🌐 theboardinn.com
3 changing beers 🅗
Overlooking the Esk, this family-run 17th-century
pub is at the heart of village life. Three beers, four
ciders and 60 whiskies are served. It comprises a
locals' bar, a lounge/restaurant, and a riverside
patio, where an Easter beer festival is held. The
food is virtually all traceable to within a mile of the
pub. The licensees air-cure their own hams, keep
hens, ducks and livestock, and have salmon fishing
rights. A recent winner of local CAMRA branch
Community Pub and Cider Pub awards.
Q🌡😼🛏◑ఉⴰ❀🖫🖫(99)😼

Leavening

Jolly Farmers 🅛

Main Street, YO17 9SA
☼ 5.30-midnight (1am Fri); 12-1am Sat; 12-midnight Sun
☎ (01653) 658276 🌐 thejollys.co.uk
**Timothy Taylor Landlord; York Guzzler; 3 changing
beers (sourced locally; often Brass Castle, Half Moon,
Wold Top)** 🅗
Seventeenth-century pub on the edge of the
Yorkshire Wolds between York and Malton. The
multi-room interior retains old-world cosiness in
two small bars, a games/family room and a
separate dining room. It is community focused,
with meetings, charity events, darts and quiz
leagues, occasional live music and beer festivals.
Varied guest beers come from independent
breweries. It has an extensive menu of quality food
including locally caught game dishes in season (no
food Mon or Tue eves). Q🌡😼◑ఉ♣P🖫😼

Leyburn

Golden Lion 🅛

Market Place, DL8 5AS
☼ 11-11 (midnight Fri & Sat) ☎ (01969) 622161
🌐 goldenlionleyburn.co.uk
**John Smith's Bitter; Wensleydale Semerwater
Summer Ale, Coverdale Gamekeeper; 1 changing
beer (sourced locally)** 🅗
A traditional market town pub facing the main
square of this busy and attractive Dales centre, a
short walk from the revived Wensleydale Railway,
with steam trains in summer. The comfortable
main bar area is opened out and largely wood
panelled, with a real fire at both ends. There is a
separate dining room to the rear, particularly
popular for the Sunday carvery.
🌡😼🛏◑🅰⇌♣🖫🛜

Lofthouse

Crown Hotel

Thorpe Lane, HG3 5RZ
☼ 12-3, 7-11; 12-3, 7-10.30 Sun ☎ (01423) 755206
**Black Sheep Best Bitter; Theakston Best Bitter; 1
changing beer (sourced locally)** 🅗
A traditional Dales pub and hotel in the Nidderdale
Area of Outstanding Natural Beauty, a short way
uphill from the main part of the village on a road
with spectacular views. There is an unusual
panelled entrance corridor leading to a traditionally
furnished, comfortable bar decorated with local
pictures, maps and brassware; a more formal
dining room is reached through the bar. Local ales
from Masham predominate and a guest is usually
available in summer. There is no cellphone
coverage inside the pub and payment by card is
not accepted. 🛏◑😼

Loftus

Station Hotel 🅛

Station Road, TS13 4QB (100yds S of A174)
☼ 3-11; 12-11.30 Sat & Sun ☎ (01287) 640373
2 changing beers 🅗
This once-bustling railway hotel is now a free
house. The last passenger train left in 1953 – the
overgrown platform is still in situ. The licensee, a
keen musician and local independent councillor,
has served best/premium bitters for 26 years, and
anything under 4% ABV generally meets with the

locals' disapproval. The pub comprises a cosy bar, a lounge and a function room where live music plays Thursday/Saturday. Fans of particularly eccentric railway memorabilia are well catered for. ❀&🖵🖵(X4,5)❀

Malham

Lister Arms 🅛 ✅
Gordale Scar Road, BD23 4DB
❀ 8am-11 ☎ (01729) 830330 ⊕ listerarms.co.uk
Marston's Wainwright, Lancaster Bomber; Thwaites Nutty Black; 3 changing beers (sourced locally; often Dark Horse, Naylor's, Settle) Ⓗ
A 17th-century coaching inn overlooking the village green. The tiled entrance hall opens to the stone-flagged main bar, with separate areas to the left and right and a dining room/restaurant beyond. The large secluded garden at the rear has ample comfortable seating. Food is served all day, with breakfast/brunch on offer before midday and the main menu thereafter. Home-made cakes, cream teas and luxury hot chocolate are also to be had. It does low season accommodation deals. 🛏❀🚲🌐Å♥P🖵❀🛜

Malton

Blue Ball 🅛
14 Newbiggin, YO17 7JF
❀ 12-midnight ☎ (01653) 690692
Tetley Bitter; Timothy Taylor Landlord; 1 changing beer (sourced locally; often Great Yorkshire) Ⓗ
This Grade II-listed Yorkshire Heritage pub dates from the 16th century and was named the Blue Ball in 1823. The low frontage hides a maze-like interior with the frontward cosy bar, compact servery and linking corridor retaining most of the pub's historic flavour. A smoking area is at the rear of the pub. Home-cooked food is available daily (except Wed). The Blue Ball Folk Club meets on the second Tuesday of each month. Q🛏🐕🌐➥♥P🖵🖵(843)❀🛜

Manfield

Crown Inn 🅛
Vicars Lane, DL2 2RF (500yds from B6275)
❀ 4 (10.30 Fri)-11.30; 12-11.30 Sat & Sun ☎ (01325) 374243
Village White Boar; 7 changing beers Ⓗ
Local CAMRA Country Pub of the Year 14 times and previously Yorkshire Pub of the Year, this 18th-century inn is in a quiet village. It has two bars and a games room where a mix of locals and visitors creates a friendly atmosphere. Up to seven guest beers from microbreweries plus occasional ciders or perry are available, and two seasonal beer festivals are held. A real log fire is in the main bar. Q🛏🐕🌐♥P🖵🖵(29)❀🛜

Marske-by-the-Sea

Clarendon 🅛
88-90 High Street, TS11 7BA
❀ 11-11; 11-11.30 Fri-Sun ☎ (01642) 490005
Black Sheep Best Bitter; Camerons Strongarm; Copper Dragon Golden Pippin; Theakston Old Peculier, Best Bitter; 1 changing beer Ⓗ
Recent CAMRA branch award winner, the Middle House is a family-run, one-room locals' pub, where the walls are adorned with photographs of yesteryear. Six beers are served from a mahogany

island bar – a rarity on Teesside. There is no TV/ jukebox, no pool table, no children/teenagers – just locals indulging in convivial conversation. There is no catering either, but tea and coffee are available, together with excellent home-made scones at lunchtimes, while a free buffet is provided on Tuesday evening. Q❀➥P🖵(X3,X4)

Masham

White Bear ✅
Wellgarth, HG4 4EN
❀ 11-midnight ☎ (01765) 689319
⊕ thewhitebearhotel.co.uk
Caledonian Deuchars IPA; Theakston Best Bitter, Black Bull Bitter, XB, Old Peculier; 1 changing beer Ⓗ
The de facto brewery tap for Theakston, the White Bear offers food, drink, accommodation and conference facilities. There is a large dining area to one side and a small cosy taproom to the other serving almost the full range of Theakston beers. The pub hosts a popular three-day beer festival in late June with over 30 beers on offer. During the war the building was a victim of bombing and was left derelict for many years before being renovated to a high standard. ❀🚲🌐&♣P🖵(159,144)❀🛜

Middlesbrough

Dr Phil's Real Ale House 🅛
10 Pilkington Buildings, Roman Road, Linthorpe, TS5 6DY (100yds N of Roman Rd and The Crescent jct)
❀ 1-10 (11 Fri); 12.30-11 Sat; 12.30-8 Sun ☎ 07883 072389
⊕ drphilsrealalehouse.co.uk
4 changing beers Ⓗ
The first micropub in the area, set among a terrace of shops in the leafy suburbs of Linthorpe, a mile south of the town. It was opened in 2013 by an enthusiastic CAMRA member and soon became a local branch award winner. The five-yards-square space accommodates an eclectic mix of drinkers, who have a choice of four changing beers, together with cider and perry. Over 700 different beers have been served and, often, a cask does not even last the day. Q&♣●🖵(11,17)🛜

Infant Hercules 🍺 🅛
84 Grange Road, TS1 2LS (just S of Cleveland centre)
❀ 1-10 (11 Fri & Sat) ☎ 07539 169704
3 changing beers Ⓗ
One of several micropubs in the town's original solicitors' quarter, all within a stone's throw of each other and all located in a series of parallel streets of Victorian terraced houses, close to the university. It is named after Gladstone's description of the town in 1862, after he had witnessed the expansion of the steel and shipbuilding industries. Three interesting beers are served on a try-before-you-buy basis. Third-pint tasting bats are available. Local CAMRA Pub of the Year 2017. Q➥●🖵

North Rigton

Square & Compass ✅
Hall Green Hill, LS17 0DJ
❀ 10-11 (midnight Thu-Sat); 10-10 Sun ☎ (01423) 733031
⊕ thesquareandcompass.com
Leeds Pale; Theakston Best Bitter; York Guzzler; 3 changing beers Ⓗ
An elegant dining pub with multiple areas, although the main bar at the front of this large establishment is pleasant for drinking. The bar is

furnished with tables and leather armchairs while the dining spaces are more formal. Six handpumps dispense ales from local small breweries, usually including a guest from nearby Ilkley, and there are well-stocked fridges with a selection of interesting bottled beers. ⑤❀❶◗&P🖵❀🛜

Northallerton

Little Tanner 🄻
227A High Street, DL7 8LU
❂ closed Mon; 4.30 (2 Sat)-11; 12-9 Sun ☎ (01609) 778801
3 changing beers (sourced locally) Ⓗ
Accessed down a narrow passageway beside the White Horse chippy on the High Street, this small bar – virtually a micropub – has a strong focus on Yorkshire-brewed real ale. Other than an impressive display of beer bottles, a comfy sofa and a few bar stools, there is little room for anything more in the tiny bar, while upstairs a larger room is furnished with former cinema seats and hosts monthly music nights. ⑤❀&🖵❀🛜

Oddfellows Arms 🄻
251 High Street, DL7 8DJ (off main part of High St behind parish church)
❂ 4-11 Mon; closed Tue; 12-midnight; 12-11 Sun
☎ (01609) 259107 ⊕ theoddies.uk
3 changing beers (sourced locally; often Copper Dragon) Ⓗ
Hidden behind the parish church by the cemetery gates, the Oddies does not appear to be on the High Street, despite its address. A thriving back-street community pub, it handles a mainly local trade and is popular with darts players, TV football fans and church bell ringers. Refurbished in a simple but traditional style with an open-plan interior, its regular beers are usually from Northallerton, Pennine or Black Sheep breweries. Q⑤❀❶♣🖵❀🛜

Tithe ⬤
2A Friarage Street, DL6 1DP (off High St near hospital)
❂ 12-11 (midnight Fri & Sat) ☎ (01609) 778482
Okells Manx Pale Ale; Timothy Taylor Boltmaker; 5 changing beers (sourced regionally) Ⓗ
Part of the small, real-ale-friendly Market Town Taverns chain, this is a pleasant town-centre bar. There is a strong commitment to cask beer and numerous continental and speciality beers are also available, plus a good range of gins. The decor is simple, with wooden floors throughout, and often the only sound is the buzz of conversation. Upstairs, a brasserie is open most evenings. Children are welcome during the daytime. ⑤◗&♣🖵❀🛜

Osgodby

Wadkin Arms 🄻 ⬤
Cliffe Road, YO8 5HU
❂ 12-11 (midnight Fri & Sat) ☎ (01757) 702391
⊕ wadkinarms.co.uk
Brown Cow White Dragon; John Smith's Bitter; Sharp's Doom Bar; house beer (by Tetley); 1 changing beer (sourced locally; often Treboom) Ⓗ
A true community pub at the heart of the village, with five handpumps dispensing ales largely sourced from Yorkshire breweries. The Wadkin has a homely feel, with open fires and a friendly welcome, and is popular with locals and visitors alike. The nearby Transpennine Cycle Trail sees

cyclists and walkers visiting in the summer months, and a local bus service passes too. You will see much evidence of CAMRA sympathies on display. Bar meals are served daily except Monday and Tuesday. ⑤❀❶♣P🖵(4)❀🛜

Osmotherley

Golden Lion 🄻
6 West End, DL6 3AA (in village centre, 1 mile E of A19)
❂ 12-3 (not Mon & Tue), 5-11; 12-midnight Sat; 12-11 Sun
☎ (01609) 883526 ⊕ goldenlionosmotherley.co.uk
Timothy Taylor Landlord; 3 changing beers (sourced locally) Ⓗ
This village on the edge of the North York Moors National Park is the start/finish of the long-distance Lyke Wake Walk, and hikers and others can enjoy a well-earned rest at this pub. With an emphasis on local sources, the food has a fine reputation and there is also a warm welcome for drinkers. Regularly changing beers are from Northallerton and other local Yorkshire breweries, with a beer festival each November. There are drinking tables outside and dogs are welcome. Q❀❶◗A🖵(80,89)❀🛜

Patrick Brompton

Green Tree Inn 🄻
DL8 1JW
❂ closed Mon & Tue; 7-11; 12-3, 7-10.30 Sun
☎ (01677) 450262
3 changing beers (sourced locally) Ⓗ
Grade II-listed family-run village pub by the parish church, overlooking the main A684 Wensleydale road. The small, cosy bar has a real fire and brick-built chimney breast, with the restaurant in a larger room but still with a country pub atmosphere. Home-cooked meals include vegetarian options and a children's menu, with takeaway fish and chips available on Wednesday night. Note the limited opening hours, and narrow car park entrance. Q⑤❀❶♣🖵❀

Pickering

Sun Inn 🍺 🄻
136 Westgate, YO18 8BB (on A170 400yds W of traffic lights in town centre)
❂ 4-11; 12-midnight Fri & Sat; 12-11 Sun ☎ (01751) 473661
⊕ thesuninn-pickering.co.uk
Helmsley Yorkshire Legend; Tetley Bitter; 4 changing beers (sourced regionally) Ⓗ
Friendly local CAMRA Rural Pub of the Year, close to the town and steam railway. Four guest ales are offered (three from Yorkshire micros) as well as several traditional ciders. A cosy bar with real fire leads to a separate room, ideal for families and special events, opening on to a large beer garden. Children, walkers and dogs (on leads) are welcome. Regular events include bi-weekly acoustic music sessions and charity quizzes, together with monthly vinyl nights. The pub opens from noon every day during bank holidays and through Easter, summer and Christmas school holidays. ⑤❀&≠♣●🖵🖵❀

Redcar

Turner's Mill ⬤
Greenstones Road, TS10 2RA (off B1269, 800yds S of town)

✪ 11.30–midnight; 10–midnight Sat & Sun ☎ (01642) 496021
10 changing beers Ⓗ
This increasingly popular Ember Inn and recent
CAMRA branch award winner is close to the town's
racecourse. A cosy, relaxing and welcoming
ambience prevails. The ever-enthusiastic bar staff
serve 10 changing beers on a try-before-you-buy
basis. Reasonably priced food is available all day
every day. An email-based newsletter details the
pub's latest offers, including seasonal specials. Cask
ale club is on Monday, while quiz nights are
Wednesday and Sunday. Children are allowed up to
8pm. ❧❀◍♿≉🅿️🚆(22,64)📶

Redmire

Bolton Arms Inn Ⓛ ⊘
DL8 4EA
✪ 11–midnight; 12–midnight Sun ☎ (01969) 624336
∰ boltonarmsredmire.co.uk
**Black Sheep Best Bitter; 3 changing beers (sourced
locally)** Ⓗ
This attractive village lies at the western terminus
of the revived Wensleydale Railway and less than a
mile from the historic Bolton Castle. The stone-built
pub is a 10-minute walk from the station, and
trains provide a good way to travel as parking can
be limited. Inside, lunchtime and evening meals
are served in the large dining area with snacks
available all day, as well as four real ales, usually
locally brewed. ❧❀🛏◍♿🅰≉🅿️🐾📶

Reeth

Buck Hotel Ⓛ
DL11 6SW
✪ 11–midnight ☎ (01748) 884210 ∰ buckhotel.co.uk/index
**Black Sheep Best Bitter, Golden Sheep; Ossett Silver
King; Wensleydale Semerwater Summer Ale,
Coverdale Gamekeeper** Ⓗ
At the top of the green in the centre of this
attractive Swaledale village, this 18th-century
former coaching inn, known as the top house,
retains its beamed ceilings, open fire and even an
ice house. Home-cooked food is offered along with
five cask ales and six real ciders. Quoits is popular
in the summer, with three teams based here along
with two darts teams. During winter, beer choice
and opening hours may be reduced.
❧❀🛏◍♿🅰♣🚆🐾📶

Riccall

Greyhound Ⓛ ⊘
82 Main Street, YO19 6TE
✪ 12–midnight; 12–11.30 Sun summer; 3 (12 Sat)–midnight;
12–11.30 Sun winter ☎ (01757) 249101
∰ thegreyhoundriccall.co.uk
**Tetley Mild, Bitter; Theakston Best Bitter; 4 changing
beers (sourced regionally; often Acorn, Ossett,
Rudgate)** Ⓗ
Four miles north of Selby, you will find this pub in
the heart of a historic village. It is a friendly family-
run inn dating back to the late-1800s. It is popular
with locals and visitors alike, many of who enjoy
the attractions of River Ouse walks and the
Transpennine Cycle Trail. The large beer garden can
get busy on warmer days. Home-made food is
served daily. Winter opening hours may vary.
❧❀🛏◍♣🅿️🐾📶

Ripon

One Eyed Rat ⊘
51 Allhallowgate, HG4 1LQ
✪ 5 (12 Fri & Sat)–11; 12–10.30 Sun ☎ (01765) 607704
∰ oneeyedrat.com
7 changing beers Ⓗ
A family-run hostelry that is well known and highly
regarded for the quality of its ales; it has been in
this Guide for over 25 years. Set within a terrace of
200-year-old houses, its narrow frontage belies a
long interior with traditional seating and an open
fire. Seven changing real ales and a real cider are
on offer, invariably including a dark ale and a
stronger beer. Sarah Hughes Dark Ruby from the
Black Country is sometimes available. The pub
hosts regular live music and holds two beer
festivals a year. Q❀●🚆(36)🐾📶

Royal Oak ⊘
36 Kirkgate, HG4 1PB
✪ 11–11 (midnight Fri & Sat) ☎ (01765) 602284
∰ royaloakripon.co.uk
**Timothy Taylor Dark Mild, Golden Best, Boltmaker,
Landlord; 2 changing beers (often Saltaire)** Ⓗ
An 18th-century coaching inn, beautifully
renovated in a modern idiom, in the centre of
historic Ripon between the Cathedral and the
Market Square. As Timothy Taylor's most northerly
tied house, the Royal Oak serves a top-quality
range of its beers alongside a regular guest from
another Yorkshire brewery, often Saltaire. The pub
is separated into relaxed dining areas with log-
burning stoves and comfortable seating, and has a
first-class locally sourced menu. Accommodation is
in six stylish and comfortable bedrooms and
includes a hearty English breakfast.
❧❀🛏◍●🅿️🚆(36)🐾📶

Saltburn-by-the-Sea

Saltburn Cricket, Bowls & Tennis
Club
Marske Mill Lane, TS12 1HJ (next to leisure centre)
✪ 8–midnight (1am Fri & Sat); 11.30–3, 8–midnight Sun
☎ (01287) 622761 ∰ saltburn.play-cricket.com
2 changing beers Ⓗ
Visitors are made most welcome at this local
CAMRA branch multi award-winner, now
celebrating 22 years of continuous Guide
recognition. A private sports club, it is run by an
enthusiastic steward and is well supported by the
local community. It is also the watering hole for the
local diving club. The balcony, ideal for those lazy
summer afternoons, overlooks the cricket field. On
match day Saturdays the club opens at 2pm. Two
changing beers are served, often not even lasting
the evening. ♿≉♣🅿️🚾🚆(X3,X4)🐾

Ship Inn Ⓛ ⊘
Saltburn Road, TS12 1HF
✪ 11.30–11; 12–11 Sun ☎ (01287) 622361
**Black Sheep Best Bitter; Timothy Taylor Landlord; 1
changing beer** Ⓗ
Dating from the 1500s and once at the centre of
the smuggling trade, this is the last remaining of
several ancient pubs in Old Saltburn, close to
Skelton Beck. Much refurbished over the years, it
still retains its original timbers and keeps that old-
world, traditional feel. Warm and welcoming
throughout, four beers – including the house beer,
Shipwrecked – are served by friendly staff, and it is
praised for its good-value food. The beach-side

seating area provides pleasant views of the sea, the cliffs and the award-winning Victorian pier. ☺❀◑◐⇒P🚲(X4)

Scagglethorpe

Ham & Cheese Inn 🄻
Bull Piece Lane, YO17 8DY
🌣 11-11 ☎ (01944) 758249 ∰ hamandcheese.pub
3 changing beers (sourced regionally) Ⓗ
This village pub is 50 yards off the A64, some three miles east of Malton. There is a spacious single-roomed bar divided into two main areas, together with a separate restaurant which doubles as a function room. Three rotating guest ales from Yorkshire microbreweries are offered, and home-cooked meals are served throughout the day. To the rear is a drinking/smoking area and large car park. Local CAMRA runner-up Rural Pub of the Year 2015. En-suite accommodation is available.
☺❀🛏◑◐🕭♣P🚲(843)♥🛜

Scarborough

Angel ⊘
46 North Street, YO11 1DF
🌣 11-midnight; 12-midnight Sun ☎ (01723) 365504
Copper Dragon Golden Pippin; Tetley Bitter; Timothy Taylor Landlord; 3 changing beers (sourced nationally) Ⓗ
Friendly and popular town-centre local close to the main shopping area, recently refurbished with a single-room horseshoe bar. Three regular beers are offered together with three guests. An interest in sport and games is reflected in the impressive array of trophies won by various pub teams and the large-screen TVs for viewing sporting events. It has a surprisingly spacious and well-appointed patio garden at the rear. ❀⇒♣🚲🛜

Hole in the Wall 🄻
26-32 Vernon Road, YO11 2PS
🌣 12-11 (midnight Fri & Sat) ☎ 07544 775051
4 changing beers (sourced nationally) Ⓗ
Built in the 1840s, the pub has a split-level interior with three seating areas. This friendly, conversational venue is handy for the town centre and spa complex. The former Marston's pub is now privately owned and matches its former status as a real ale mecca. Up to seven guest beers are offered at weekends. Sky and BT satellite TV may be enjoyed. There is an outside covered and heated smoking area to the side. Runner-up local CAMRA Town Pub of the Year 2016. ❀🕭⇒♣🚲♥

North Riding Brewpub 🄻
161-163 North Marine Road, YO12 7HU
🌣 12-midnight (1am Fri & Sat) ☎ (01723) 370004
∰ northridingbrewpub.com
6 changing beers (sourced nationally; often North Riding Brewpub, North Riding Brewery) Ⓗ
Scarborough's only brewpub, serving at least six continually changing beers from local and microbreweries around the UK; available are always one or more North Riding beers together with beers brewed at the pub. These are complemented by an extensive range of bottled beers. The pub has a public bar and a quiet lounge, both with real fires. Quiz night is Thursday. Local CAMRA Town Pub of the Year 2008-2014.
Q☺🛏♣●🚲(3)♥🛜

Scholars Bar 🄻
6 Somerset Terrace, YO11 2PA
🌣 4.30-midnight; 12-midnight Fri-Sun ☎ (01723) 372826
7 changing beers (sourced regionally; often North Riding Brewery, Ossett) Ⓗ
A warm, friendly atmosphere prevails at this town-centre pub at the rear of the main shopping centre, voted as CAMRA runner-up Town Pub of the Year 2015. It has a large front bar and a games room. Seven rotating guest beers, usually from Yorkshire microbreweries, are offered, plus numerous ciders and perries. TV screens show major sporting events. Twenty-eight pints are the prize at the Thursday quiz. ⇒♣●🚲

Stumble Inn 🍷 🄻
59 Westborough, YO11 1TS (approx 200yds SW of railway station)
🌣 12-11; 12-10.30 Sun ☎ 07837 716774
∰ stumbleinnmicropub.weebly.com/home.html
6 changing beers (sourced nationally) Ⓗ
This first micropub in Scarborough is a welcome addition to the local real ale scene, a short walk from the railway station and formerly a solicitors' office. This single-roomed pub offers six rotating guest ales, with local breweries always represented. Up to 26 real ciders and perries are also served. It is a quiet establishment, ideal for a cosy chat and chill out. Local CAMRA Town Pub of the Year 2016. Q🕭⇒●🚲♥

Tap & Spile ⊘
94 Falsgrave Road, YO12 5AZ
🌣 4 (12 Sat)-midnight; 12-11 Sun ☎ (01723) 507666
Black Sheep Best Bitter; Camerons Strongarm; Theakston Old Peculier; Timothy Taylor Landlord; 1 changing beer (sourced nationally) Ⓗ
Sympathetically restored Grade II-listed public house, not far from the town centre, serving five cask ales. There are two main rooms plus a small snug – local memorabilia is displayed. This thriving local has a friendly atmosphere and is a venue for live music, with Sunday afternoons particularly popular. TV sport is shown in one bar, and a beer garden is at the rear. Dogs are welcome in the taproom. ☺❀◑🕭⇒♣P🚲♥🛜

Valley Bar
51 Valley Road, YO11 2LX
🌣 12-midnight (1am Thu-Sat) ☎ (01723) 372593
∰ valleybar.co.uk
Dark Star Hophead; 5 changing beers (sourced nationally; often Scarborough, Theakston) Ⓗ
A cellar bar with six handpumps offering mainly microbrewery beers, usually including one or more from Scarborough Brewery. Up to eight real ciders and perries are also available, Broadoak perry being a regular, together with over 100 bottles of Belgian beers including Cantillon. Further rooms offer additional seating upstairs, which can be used for meetings. There is also a pool table upstairs.
☺🛏♣●🕭🚲(4)♥🛜

Scotton

Guy Fawkes Arms
Main Street, HG5 9HU
🌣 12 (4 Mon)-11 ☎ (01423) 868400
∰ guyfawkesarms.co.uk
Black Sheep Best Bitter; 3 changing beers Ⓗ
Popular village pub which was rescued from closure in 2013 by two local families. The L-shaped

interior features a cosy lounge area, part flagged, part carpeted, with a mix of traditional and modern furniture and a real fire in winter. A separate dining room occupies one end, and a raised seating area is at the other with its own mini library. Guy Fawkes lived in the village and there are several related items displayed. Complementing the regular Black Sheep Bitter are three changing guests from Yorkshire breweries. ◑PⓅ(22)✿ 🗢

Selby

Giant Bellflower 🅛 ✅
47a Gowthorpe, YO8 4HF
✪ 8am-midnight (1am Fri & Sat) ☎ (01757) 293020
Greene King Abbot; Ruddles Best Bitter; 6 changing beers (sourced nationally; often Adnams, Rudgate, Sharp's) Ⓗ
Named after a flower closely associated with a local 17th-century botanist, and converted from a furniture showroom, this modern and spacious pub is completely different from all the others in Selby. Artefacts and pictures from Selby's past complement the light and airy interior and the pub is deceptively large from its small frontage, with an enormous stainless steel bar taking pride of place. Offering a typical Wetherspoon's range of keenly priced beers, real ciders and LocAles, it is an important addition to the town's pub scene.
🗢✿◑&≒🚋✿🗢

Settle

Talbot Arms 🅛 ✅
High Street, BD24 9EX
✪ 12-11 ☎ (01729) 823924 ⊕ talbotsettle.co.uk
Theakston Best Bitter; 5 changing beers (sourced regionally; often Settle, Three Peaks) Ⓗ
Just off the square, this family-run free house offers a welcoming and friendly atmosphere. A stove glows in the large stone feature fireplace to the left of the main entrance, with a pool table, dartboard and dominoes tables beyond providing a base for teams in local leagues. A pleasant terraced beer garden is at the rear. The three to five guest beers and cider are usually from Cumbria, Lancashire or Yorkshire. Good-value food is served 12-8pm all week. 🗢✿◑≒♣✿PⓅ✿🗢

Shipton by Beningbrough

Dawnay Arms 🅛 ✅
Main Street, YO30 1AB
✪ closed Mon; 5.30-10.30 Tue & Thu; 12-2, 5.30-midnight Wed & Fri; 12-2, 6-11 Sat; 12-11 Sun ☎ (01904) 470334
⊕ thedawnayarms.co.uk
Tetley Bitter; 2 changing beers (sourced nationally; often Caledonian, Robinsons, Treboom) Ⓗ
A traditional country inn dating from 1730 in the village centre. There are three interconnecting rooms, with old pictures and items of local history on display. One of the handpumps always serves a LocAle. The wide-ranging pub food includes gluten-free/vegetarian options. It has a weekly steak night (Tue), a quiz night (Wed), fish lunch (Fri), a monthly music quiz (Sun), and a weekly supper club (Thu). Occasional live music features. The car park and decked sitting area is to the rear. It is served by daytime buses between York and Easingwold. 🗢✿◑PⓅ🗢

Skipton

Beer Engine 🅛
1 Albert Street, BD23 1JD
✪ 12-8 Mon; closed Tue; 12-10 Wed & Thu; 12-11 Fri & Sat; 12-10.30 Sun ☎ 07834 456134 ⊕ thebeerengine.co
5 changing beers (sourced nationally) Ⓗ
Micropub in a tiny street between the town centre and the canal. Five handpumps dispense a variety of beers; there is always one blonde/pale ale and one dark beer, plus a character beer. A still cider and a fruit cider are also on tap alongside a selection of bottled beers and wines. The beers are stored in refrigerated cabinets behind the bar. The ambience is friendly and welcoming, and closing time can be flexible. Well-behaved dogs are welcome. Q≒♣🚋✿🗢

Boat House 🅛
19 Coach Street, BD23 1LH
✪ 12-10 ☎ (01756) 701660
5 changing beers
Accessed through an arch from Coach Street, this recent addition to Skipton's pub scene opened in March 2016. The bar is light and airy with windows looking out onto the canal basin, and the decor is canal themed. A pleasant cobbled outdoor drinking area offers the opportunity to enjoy a beer while watching the boats go by in summer and an old-style stove keeps it warm in winter. One dark beer is usually available. 🗢✿◑&≒♣🚋✿🗢

Early Doors 🅛
14 Newmarket Street, BD23 2HX
✪ closed Mon; 12-8; 2-6 Sun ☎ 07550 079925
⊕ earlydoorspub.co.uk
Moorhouse's Blond Witch; 5 changing beers (sourced locally) Ⓗ
A recently opened micropub with no frills, no music, no Wi-Fi and no food, just good beer and conversation. The bar in the long narrow room has six handpumps and is without keg fonts or other clutter. Beers, including a dark brew, are usually from Yorkshire or Lancashire and are priced the same no matter what the strength. A small range of foreign bottled beers is also available. There is a small covered smoking area in the rear yard. Q≒🚋✿

Narrow Boat 🅛 ✅
38 Victoria Street, BD23 1JE (alleyway off Coach St near canal bridge)
✪ 12-11 ☎ (01756) 797922
Ilkley Mary Jane; Okells Bitter; Timothy Taylor Landlord; 5 changing beers (often Black Sheep) Ⓗ
Spread over two rooms with an upstairs gallery, the pub has recently been refurbished with heavy wood-style furniture. Note the somewhat unusual interpretation of the Leeds & Liverpool Canal in a mural. There is usually a dark beer and a good range of continental bottled and draught beers, plus up to three ciders or perries. A folk club is on Monday evening and a quiz night on Wednesday. Well-behaved dogs are welcome. 🗢✿◑&≒♣🚋🗢

Woolly Sheep 🅛 ✅
38 Sheep Street, BD23 1HY
✪ 10-11 (midnight Thu; 1am Fri & Sat); 12-11 Sun
☎ (01756) 700966 ⊕ woollysheepinn.co.uk
Timothy Taylor Dark Mild, Golden Best, Boltmaker, Knowle Spring Blonde, Landlord, Ram Tam; 1 changing beer Ⓗ

An 18th-century pub at the bottom of the High Street and handy for the bus station and town-centre shops. The cosy front lounge has a roaring fire in winter and the area around the main bar has stone flags; the traditional cobbled courtyard has decking with comfortable seating, a canopy and heaters. The split-level restaurant serves food throughout the day. Accommodation is in 12 en-suite rooms upstairs. ✿⊯◑▶⇌🚌🛜

Staithes

Cod & Lobster Inn

High Street, TS13 5BH (at end of High St)
✪ 10-11 ☎ (01947) 840330 ⊕ codandlobster.co.uk
4 changing beers Ⓗ
Superbly positioned at the seawater's edge in this sleepy, picturesque fishing village. During high tides and easterly winds you are advised to use the roadside door or risk getting wet. It comprises a large single open-plan room, where three changing beers are dispensed alongside the house beer, Old Jack's Tipple, and named after a locally filmed children's TV character. Good-value traditional meals are served. On sunny days, a pleasant patio, directly overlooking the chilly sea, becomes popular. ⍧◑

Stillington

White Bear Ⓛ

Main Street, YO61 1JU
✪ 12-2.30 (not Mon), 5.30-11; 12-midnight Sat; 12-11 Sun
☎ (01347) 810338 ⊕ thewhitebearinn-york.co.uk
Leeds Pale; 4 changing beers (sourced regionally) Ⓗ
If you want to try regularly changing beers from small and medium-size Yorkshire breweries then this is an excellent choice. The multi award-winning pub is the beating heart of the village and is becoming accustomed to visitors from far and wide. Turn right for a traditional taproom bar and left for an unpretentious restaurant bar, but turn up or miss out. ⍧⊯◑♣P🚌(40)

Stokesley

White Swan ✅

1 West End, TS9 5BL (150yds beyond shops)
✪ 11-midnight (1am Fri & Sat); 11-11.30 Sun
☎ (01642) 710263 ⊕ thewhiteswanstokesley.co.uk
Captain Cook Black Porter, Botany Bay, Endeavour, IPA, Slipway, Sunset; 2 changing beers Ⓗ
Home of the Captain Cook Brewery, this 18th-century pub, winner of many local CAMRA branch awards, is at the west end of this pretty market town. At least six Captain Cook beers, two guest beers and two ciders are served from 12 handpulls. Beer festivals are held Easter and October. An award-winning, good-value, home-baked pie menu is served Monday-Saturday lunchtimes. Quiz night is Wednesday, music night Thursday. The sheltered outdoor drinking area overlooks the brewery. Over-18s only, and dogs welcome. ✿◑&♣🍴🚌(81,89)🐾🛜

Thirsk

Little 3 Ⓛ

13-15 Finkle Street, YO7 1DA
✪ 12-10 (11 Thu; midnight Fri & Sat) ☎ (01845) 523782
⊕ littlethree.co.uk

Theakston Best Bitter; 5 changing beers (sourced nationally) Ⓗ
Low-beamed pub just off Market Place claiming a history from 1214. It is a warren of nooks and crannies, all decorated in mock half-timbering, with an impressive fireplace in the main bar. Originally the Old Three Tuns, it was renamed to avoid confusion with the nearby Three Tuns. Regularly changing guest beers are from local and national brewers. Food is served in the upstairs bistro and there is live music every Thursday. ⍧✿◑🚌🐾🛜

Thixendale

Cross Keys

YO17 9TG
✪ 6-11; 12-3, 6-11 Fri & Sat; 12-3, 7-10.30 Sun
☎ (01377) 288272
Tetley Bitter; 2 changing beers (sourced locally; often Great Newsome, Half Moon, Wold Top) Ⓗ
This single-room hostelry appears on a map dated 1851. At the heart of five dry valleys, it is popular with walkers, including those on the Wolds Way and, though remote, is well worth seeking out. It has had the same landlord for over 30 years. The two guest beers come from independent breweries and are usually not more than 4% ABV. Children are welcome in the beer garden. Good-value, traditional home-cooked food is served. Accommodation is in the adjoining converted stable. It will open weekday lunchtimes on request for six or more people. Q✿⊯◑♣

Thoralby

George Inn Ⓛ

DL8 3SU (on small lane off village centre)
✪ 12-2, 6.30-11 Sat & Sun ☎ (01969) 663256
⊕ thegeorgeinnthoralby.com
3 changing beers (sourced locally) Ⓗ
Dating from 1732, this small, off-the-beaten-track inn lies tucked away in a little village just off the B6160 Bishopsdale road. The interior has been opened up into a single room but retains two distinct halves and is cosy and comfortable, with a particularly impressive stone fireplace with a stove at one end. Separate apartments offer accommodation. Beers are usually from local Yorkshire brewers and home-cooked food is offered. Opens 7pm in the winter. Q⍧⊯◑▲♣🚌🐾🛜

West Witton

Fox & Hounds Ⓛ

DL8 4LP (on A684)
✪ 12-3, 6-midnight; 12-midnight Sat & Sun
☎ (01969) 623650 ⊕ foxwitton.com
Black Sheep Baa Baa; Theakston Best Bitter; 3 changing beers (sourced regionally; often Salamander, Yorkshire Dales) Ⓗ
Once a rest house for 15th-century Jervaulx Abbey monks, this welcoming, Grade II-listed family-run free house is full of character. A real community local, it has a down-to-earth bar and games room popular with locals and visitors alike. Good-value meals are served all week with a roast on Sunday, and the dining room boasts an inglenook fireplace with quaint stone oven. It has a pleasant patio at the rear; beware the tight entry to the car park. Q⍧✿◑♣🍴P🚌🐾🛜

Whitby

Black Horse Ⓛ ✪

91 Church Street, YO22 4BH (on E side of swing bridge on way to abbey steps, close to marketplace)
🕒 11-11; 12-10.30 Sun ☎ (01947) 602906
🌐 the-black-horse.com
5 changing beers Ⓗ
Former CAMRA branch award winner, this little multi-roomed gem, dating from the 1600s, offers a warm welcome. The frontage, with its frosted glass, together with one of Europe's oldest public serving bars, was built in the 1880s and remains largely unchanged. Beer is served from five handpumps. Snuff, tapas, olives, Yorkshire cheeses and hot drinks are always available, while hot lunches are served during the winter months. The cider is Westons Rosie's Pig. Accommodation is in four bedrooms. Q ⏰ 🛏 🍴 ◑ & ≽ ♣ ● 🚌 (X93,840) ● 🐾 🛜

Board Inn Ⓛ

125 Church Street, YO22 4DE (at N end of Church St, by abbey steps)
🕒 11.30-11; 11-11 Sun ☎ (01947) 602884
🌐 theboardinnwhitby.co.uk
Caledonian Deuchars IPA; Theakston XB, Old Peculier Ⓗ
The last remaining Board of several that existed during the 1800s on Church Street – traditional family-run shops that sold ale, among other produce, displaying the brews available on that day on chalkboards. Nowadays, three beers are served. From the front snug, drinkers can admire the 199 steps up to the abbey. To the rear, where the lounge/restaurant serves reasonably priced meals, there are fine harbour views. The famous Fortune's kipper smokehouse can be found nearby. ⏰ 🛏 ◑ ≽ 🚌 (X93,840)

Dolphin Hotel Ⓛ ✪

Bridge Street, YO22 4BG (on E side of swing bridge)
🕒 8.30am-midnight ☎ (01947) 821455
🌐 thedolphinwhitby.co.uk
6 changing beers Ⓗ
Originally known as the Custom House Coffee House, this large, prominent building was developed into a public house in 1823 and then rebuilt in 1912 to its present form. The pub provides the complete package of six local and national beers on a try-before-you-buy basis, real cider, good-value food, a patio with harbour views, six bedrooms fitted with king-size beds, live music Tuesday and weekends, and even a friendly welcome for your dog. ⏰ 🎔 🛏 ◑ ≽ ● 🚌 (X93,840) ● 🛜

Endeavour ✪

66 Church Street, YO22 4AS (on W side of swing bridge, close to award-winning fish and chip shop)
🕒 12-11 ☎ (01947) 603557 🌐 endeavourpub.com
4 changing beers Ⓗ
A welcome return to the Guide for this cosy one-room 1935 pub named after the ship in which James Cook made his voyages to the Antipodes. The warming fire and pleasant conversation add to the welcome from an enthusiastic licensee, who serves 140 different beers annually. Four handpumps, Yorkshire tapas bar snacks, and permission to bring your own fish and chips into the pub all make for a relaxing visit. Folk/Irish music both on Friday evenings and Sundays are well supported. Manic during Goth weekends. Q ⏰ 🛏 ≽ ♣ 🚌 (X93,840) ● 🛜

Little Angel Inn ✪

18 Flowergate, YO21 3BA (200yds W of swing bridge, 200yds N of railway/bus stations)
🕒 12-midnight (1am Fri & Sat) ☎ (01947) 820475
6 changing beers Ⓗ
Just off the main tourist route and up a slight incline, locals and visitors alike are afforded a genuine friendly welcome at this extremely popular pub where, it is rumoured, the remains of the castle form part of the structure. Pub food, large-screen TVs, live music, outside drinking and even a horse mount – for those requiring this facility - complement the six beers served to three separate rooms from a central bar. CAMRA branch Best Whitby Pub for three years running. ⏰ ≽ ♣ ● 🚌 (X93,840) 🐾

Station Inn Ⓛ ✪

New Quay Road, YO21 1DH (opp bus and railway stations)
🕒 10-midnight; 10-11.30 Sun ☎ (01947) 603937
🌐 stationinnwhitby.co.uk
Black Dog Whitby Abbey Ale; Camerons Strongarm; Copper Dragon Scotts 1816; Whitby Platform 3; 4 changing beers Ⓗ
Next to the harbour and marina, this multi-roomed pub and recent CAMRA branch Pub of the Year offers a warm welcome. The enthusiastic licensees ensure that the eight beers, including the house beer, Whitby Platform 3, always encompass a superb range of varying styles, while cider and fruit wines mean there is something for everybody. Opposite the bus station and NYMR/Esk Valley railway station, the pub has become the discerning travellers' waiting room. Live music features three evenings a week. 🛏 ≽ ● 🚌 (X93,840) 🐾

Waiting Room

2 Whitby Station, Langborne Road, YO21 1YN (by main entrance to station)
🕒 closed Mon & Tue; 4.30-9 Wed & Thu; 4-9 Fri; 12-9 Sat; 12-5 Sun ☎ 07584 311886
5 changing beers Ⓗ
On the station platform that NYMR steam trains use, the friendly owners of Whitby's first micropub strive to adhere to the original micropub values – no craft beer/lager, no spirits, no jukebox and no TV. Five handpumps and nine ciders help promote a pleasant atmosphere together with lots of convivial conversation. The six-yards-square pub gets busy at times, so please do not be disappointed if you cannot even get in. Local CAMRA branch 2017 Cider Pub of the Year. & ≽ 🚌 (X93,840) 🐾 🛜

York

Blue Bell ★ Ⓛ ✪

53 Fossgate, YO1 9TF
🕒 11-11 (midnight Fri & Sat); 12-10.30 Sun
☎ (01904) 654904
Bradfield Farmers Blonde; Kelham Island Best Bitter; Rudgate Ruby Mild; Timothy Taylor Landlord; 3 changing beers (sourced locally; often Half Moon, Ilkley, Rooster's) Ⓗ
This small Edwardian Grade II*-listed pub has a nationally important historic interior comprising a central bar supplying two small rooms and, through a hatch, the side corridor. It can get full so it has a strict no-groups policy and entry may be restricted at busy times. Permanent beers are complemented by a great range of rotating guests.

Bar snacks and pork pies are available. It has a new landlord, together with a friendly and welcoming atmosphere. Q♣♠🖪❀🛜

Brew York Tap Room ⎣

Unit 6, Enterprise Complex, Walmgate, YO1 9TT

◷ 5-11 Thu; 12-11 Fri & Sat; closed Sun-Wed
☎ (01904) 848448 ⊕ brewyork.co.uk
7 changing beers (sourced locally; often Brew York) ⓗ

Venture down a courtyard off Walmgate to be rewarded with a brewery showcase that neighbours a day nursery, cycle shop and boxing club. Sit inside by brew tanks, on benches, or at high tables, or outside in the yard with rare views of the River Foss. The clean, functional lines give the bar a contemporary feel, with plenty of room for all. Additional opening days/hours are a future possibility. ❀♿🖪

Brigantes ⎣ ✅

114 Micklegate, YO1 6JX

◷ 12-11 ☎ (01904) 675355
Okells Manx Pale Ale; 9 changing beers (sourced nationally; often Brass Castle, Great Heck, Leeds) ⓗ

Popular, welcoming Market Town Taverns pub in a smart Georgian building just inside the city walls on Micklegate. It offers 10 ales, at least one dark, featuring good Yorkshire breweries and interesting guests from across the UK, plus a good range of bottled beers. At least one real cider is on tap and there is a Wall of Cider festival in October with 25+ ciders and perries. A high-quality food menu is served every day. A function room upstairs can be used for social group meetings/dining/special events. Dog-friendly and wheelchair-accessible throughout. Q🌥🕪♿⇌🍴🖪❀🛜

Falcon Tap ⎣

94 Micklegate, YO1 6JX

◷ 3-11; 1-1am Fri; 12-1am Sat; 1-10.30 Sun
☎ (01904) 622225 ⊕ thefalcontap.co.uk
6 changing beers (sourced locally; often Bad, Bad Seed, Brass Castle) ⓗ

Originally the Falcon, dating from 1770, it had a period when it was called Rumours, and was then refurbished and renamed the Falcon Tap. A small carpeted front bar overlooks busy Micklegate. A large back bar has six handpumps and real cider, and it has a large outdoor area to the rear, partly covered and with comfy seating. The enthusiastic landlord is keen to offer a wide range of styles and strengths of beers, mostly from local breweries, as well as a growing selection of bottled beers. It occasionally has a DJ playing vinyl records. ❀⇌🍴❀

Maltings ⎣

Tanners Moat, YO1 6HU

◷ 11-11; 12-10.30 Sun ☎ (01904) 655387 ⊕ maltings.co.uk
Black Sheep Best Bitter; Treboom Yorkshire Sparkle; York Guzzler; 4 changing beers (sourced nationally; often Hop Studio, Pig & Porter, Sunbeam) ⓗ

A popular pub close to the station. The cask ales from microbreweries, both local and from further afield, change regularly. At any one time customers can choose from seven real ales and four traditional ciders, with three permanent beers. The four changing ales always include a beer from Rooster's. An extension has provided more seating and a small outside area, while maintaining the original character. ❀🕪⇌🍴🖪❀

Phoenix

75 George Street, YO1 9PT

◷ 12-11 (11.30 Fri & Sat); 12-10.30 Sun ☎ (01904) 656401
⊕ york-pm.co.uk/the-phoenix-inn
Copper Dragon Golden Pippin; Timothy Taylor Landlord; Wold Top Bitter; 2 changing beers (sourced regionally; often Brampton, Hop Studio) ⓗ

An independently run CAMRA heritage pub, where a friendly welcome always awaits. Relax in the traditional pub atmosphere without the noise of gaming machines, TVs or jukebox. Enjoy your pint while reading a selection of newspapers or playing a game of bar billiards. In the winter months you can warm to a real log fire in the front room, while the beer garden overlooking the ancient city walls is a delight in summer. The pub hosts regular jazz nights and quizzes. Q❀♣♠🖪❀🛜

Pivni

6 Patrick Pool, YO1 8BB

◷ 11.30 (12 Mon)-11.30; 12-11.30 Sun ☎ (01904) 635464
5 changing beers (sourced nationally; often Tapped Sheffield) ⓗ

Founding bar of the Pivovar UK group, it's five cask ales are sourced nationally from highly regarded breweries. Two real ciders and an extensive selection of bottled beers are also available. The beautiful three-storeyed timber-framed building dates back to 1190. There is a Monday night quiz, a jukebox and occasional live music. Bar snacks include local pork pies. ♠❀

Rook & Gaskill ⎣

12 Lawrence Street, YO10 3WP

◷ 4-11.30 (12.30am Thu); 2-12.30am Fri & Sat
☎ (01904) 533105 ⊕ rookandgaskillyork.co.uk
Castle Rock Harvest Pale; 7 changing beers (sourced nationally; often Blue Bee, Great Heck, Rooster's) ⓗ

Just outside Walmgate Bar, this pub focuses on good-quality beer and cider at competitive prices, and is popular with locals, beer enthusiasts and the university community. A large range of carefully chosen cask ales, and up to three real ciders, are on offer on handpump. Home-made burgers and wood-fired pizzas are available. There is a quiz on Thursdays. Local CAMRA Pub and Cider Pub of the Year 2016. ❀♦♣♠🖪❀🛜

Slip Inn ⎣

Clementhorpe, YO23 1AN

◷ 5-11.30; 4-midnight Fri; 12-midnight Sat; 12-11 Sun
☎ (01904) 621793 ⊕ theslipinnyork.co.uk
Leeds Pale; Rudgate Ruby Mild; Timothy Taylor Boltmaker; 2 changing beers (sourced regionally; often Great Heck, Revolutions, Ridgeside) ⓗ

Just outside the walls and close to river, this independent free house is a thriving local community venue with two bars, a snug and a sheltered courtyard and beer garden to the rear. The pub runs regular Battle of the Brewery events, and several beer festivals each year, including one run jointly with the Swan just up the road. It supports traditional pub games, such as darts, dominoes and cribbage. 🌥❀♣🖪(11)❀🛜

Swan ★ ⎣ ✅

16 Bishopgate Street, YO23 1JH

◷ 4-11 (11.30 Thu; midnight Fri); 12-midnight Sat; 12-10.30 Sun ☎ (01904) 634968 ⊕ theswanyork.co.uk
Tetley Bitter; Timothy Taylor Landlord; house beer (by Treboom); 3 changing beers (sourced regionally) ⓗ

Just outside the city walls, this is a thriving traditional street-corner pub with a typical West

Riding-style drinking lobby, two bars and a snug. It is cosy, comfortable and unspoilt. Grade II listed, it has a nationally important historic interior (a Tetley Heritage Inn), and a beer garden to the rear which is covered and heated. It hosts an annual beer festival jointly with the Slip Inn nearby.
❀♣●▭(11)🐾

Waggon & Horses 🏆

19 Lawrence Street, YO10 3BP
3-11.30; 12-midnight Fri & Sat; 12-11 Sun
☎ (01904) 637478 🌐 waggonandhorsesyork.com
Batemans XB, XXXB; Oakham Citra; 4 changing beers (sourced nationally; often Ossett, Rooster's, Titanic) H
Batemans-owned multi-roomed family-run pub. The bar area and front room have TVs showing BT Sport. The two rooms at the back of the pub are quieter and used by various local groups to hold meetings. There is a free bar billiards table and a selection of board games. Good-value accommodation (CAMRA members get a 10 per cent discount) and food are also on offer.
❀♣●▭🐾

York Tap

Railway Station, Station Road, YO24 1AB
11-11 (11.45 Fri); 10-11.45 Sat ☎ (01904) 659009
🌐 yorktap.com
18 changing beers (sourced nationally; often Anarchy, Tapped Sheffield, Thornbridge) H
On York railway station, this stunning Grade A-listed Edwardian building has a circular wooden bar selling 18 cask beers plus two ciders or perries. The ornate ceiling, Art Deco stained-glass windows and ceiling domes create an award-winning backdrop. Regularly changing beers – all styles and strengths are represented – are chosen from a wide selection of Britain's finest breweries, usually including some from its own Tapped Brewery. ❀♿⇌●▭🐾

YORKSHIRE (SOUTH)

Arksey

Plough Inn L

2 High Street, DN5 0SF (behind church)
7 (6.30 Thu)-11; 12-2, 6.30-11 Fri; 12-3.30, 6.30-11 Sat; 12-3.30, 7-11 Sun ☎ (01302) 872472 🌐 arkseyplough.co.uk
Old Mill Blonde Bombshell; house beer (by Hilltop); 1 changing beer (sourced locally; often Abbeydale, Hilltop, White Rose) H
A friendly, multi-roomed village free house featuring beers from small independent breweries. The lounge, which is heated by a log-burning stove, has horse harnesses and brasses on display along with photographs of the village, some depicting floods of long ago. Reasonably priced bar meals are available on Thursday, Friday and Saturday evenings, and also on Saturday lunchtime. The excellent Sunday lunch is popular. Quiz night is Sunday. Q❀♣▭(64,64A)

Armthorpe

Wheatsheaf L

Church Street, DN3 3AE
12 (5 Mon)-11 ☎ (01302) 835868
Purity Pure UBU; Sharp's Doom Bar; 4 changing beers (sourced nationally; often Black Sheep, Sharp's, Theakston) H
Large roadside hostelry in the centre of Armthorpe which serves four rotating guest beers. Typical guests include one from Jennings, Woodforde and Skinner's as well as customer favourites like Sharp's Doom Bar and Purity UBU. It has a separate dining area, two bars, a public bar, lounge and an outside area with tables. The landlord is keen to promote real ales and offers a discount to card-carrying members of CAMRA.
Q❀♿♣●P▭(81,82)🐾

Auckley

Eagle & Child

24 Main Street, DN9 3HS
11.30-11 (11.30 Fri & Sat); 12-10.30 Sun
☎ (01302) 770406 🌐 eagleandchildauckley.co.uk
Black Sheep Best Bitter; John Smith's Bitter; Timothy Taylor Landlord; 2 changing beers (sourced regionally; often Bradfield, Ossett, Springhead) H
A much-loved pub on the main road in the village and winner of numerous CAMRA awards. Dating from the early 19th century, it has real character. There are two bars, one with a TV, the other quieter with tables for bar meals. The separate restaurant is decorated with photographs of local historic interest, and the home-cooked meals have a deserved reputation. Recently voted Doncaster's Best Pub by TRAX FM listeners. It is only one mile from Robin Hood Airport. Q❀♣P▭(57)

Barnsley

Arcade Alehouse 🏆 L

31 The Arcade, S70 2QP
closed Mon-Wed; 12-10 Thu-Sat; 12-8 Sun ☎ 07843 930974
6 changing beers (sourced regionally) H
Barnsley's first ever micropub, this is a tiny one-up, one-down bar serving up to six real ales and up to three real ciders. Most beers and ciders are sourced locally or regionally. The owners recently ran their own brewery, Two Roses. This excellent refurbishment of a former cake shop maximises what space is available and there is a cosy feel in both rooms. The welcoming staff are happy to offer a try-before-you-buy taster. Q⇌●▭🐾

Commercial L

74 Summer Lane, S70 2NN
4.30-11; 12-11 Sat & Sun
Tetley Bitter; 2 changing beers (sourced locally) H
Busy pub on the edge of the town centre which is still family owned. One large room contains the bar area, sports section and TV lounge. All three real ales are served in oversized lined glasses. To the rear is a large shelter and paved garden. Popular with darts and pool players and epitomising what a local community pub should be, there is a vibrant atmosphere here. Well worth the 10-minute walk from the interchange. ❀⇌♣▭(43,44)

Joseph Bramah L ✔

Market Hill, S70 2PX
8am-midnight (1am Fri & Sat) ☎ (01226) 320890
Greene King Abbot; Sharp's Doom Bar; 4 changing beers (sourced nationally) H
This Lloyds No.1 bar offers the standard Wetherspoon range of real ales with up to four changing guest beers, often from microbreweries. The hardworking staff are keen to promote the real ale experience with occasional Meet the Brewer

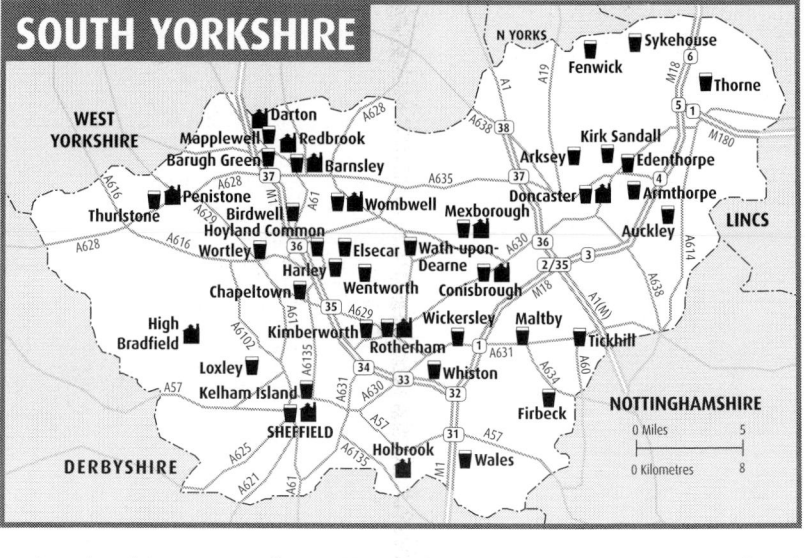

SOUTH YORKSHIRE

evenings. The pub is set over two floors and has quieter areas upstairs, with a sheltered courtyard to the rear downstairs. The unusual pub name celebrates Barnsley's most famous inventor of unpickable locks and beer engines. ❀◑♿⬛🚲🚌📶

Old No.7 🄻

7 Market Hill, S70 2PX
❀ 11-11 (midnight Wed-Sat) ☎ (01226) 244735
🌐 oldno7barnsley.co.uk
Acorn Barnsley Bitter, Blonde; 6 changing beers Ⓗ
The Acorn Brewery tap opened in August 2011. Two bars offer a range of up to eight real ales from Acorn and other microbreweries, plus real ciders and perries, and a wide choice of bottled beers and lagers. The upper bar is open each day, the cellar bar (available for functions and meetings) Friday and Saturday. Two beer festivals are held each year. Winner of local CAMRA Pub of the Year 2015, other regional awards and cider awards.
≈♣●🛢🚌🐾📶

Silkstone Inn 🄻 ⊘

64 Market Street, S70 1SN
❀ 8am-midnight ☎ (01226) 320860
Greene King Abbot; Ruddles Best Bitter; Sharp's Doom Bar; 4 changing beers (sourced locally) Ⓗ
This JD Wetherspoon outlet prides itself on offering a high turnover of excellent real ales and gives a friendly welcome. The outside seating forecourt can be a suntrap in good weather as you watch passing shoppers. Inside, the dark-themed decor emphasises the coal seam on which Barnsley sits. The large one-roomed bar has plenty of snugs dotted around its central fireplace, creating a cosy feel. Q❀◑●≈🚌📶

Barugh Green

Crown & Anchor 🄻

Barugh Lane, S75 1LL (on B6428)
❀ 11.30-11.30 (midnight Thu; 1am Fri; 12.30am Sat)
☎ (01226) 387200 🌐 thecrownandanchor.com
6 changing beers Ⓗ
This pub, part of the True North Brewery, serves its own and changing guest beers from local and regional breweries. Also known to locals as the

White House, it has three distinct areas inside, with a wood-burning stove in winter months, and a vast beer garden. It offers excellent-value food freshly prepared on site, and has won a best pie award. It also hosts various food clubs and events such as gin school. ❀◑♿⬛🐾P🚌📶

Birdwell

Cock Inn 🄻 ⊘

Pilley Hill, off The Walk, S70 5UD
❀ 12 (4 Mon)-11; 12-11.30 Fri & Sat; 12-10.30 Sun
☎ (01226) 744227
Tetley Bitter; 4 changing beers Ⓗ
This lovely, small stone-built village pub always offers a warm welcome. The main bar area has a slate floor and an inviting large open fire, leading into a large lounge area with carpeting and plush seating. The smaller room is ideal for small parties or meetings. Well known for good food, it gets busy for lunches and evening meals (booking for Sunday lunch is advised). Five cask ales are on offer and one real cider. Q❀◑Å♣●P🚌(7A,67A)

Conisbrough

Hilltop Hotel 🄻

Sheffield Road, DN12 2AY (on main road)
❀ closed Mon; 5-11; 4-midnight Fri; 12-midnight Sat & Sun
☎ (01709) 868811 🌐 thehilltophotel.co.uk
Hilltop Classic Bitter, Blonde, Stout, Porter Ⓗ
A traditional free house on the outskirts of Conisbrough, offering a relaxed and friendly atmosphere and serving four real ales from its own on-site brewery. It is split into a public bar and lounge area, the latter serving an excellent Sunday lunch. Quiz night is on a Wednesday and includes supper. Panel games are hosted on Thursday evening. Q❀❀◑♣P🚌(X78)🐾📶

Doncaster

Corner Pin 🍷 🄻

145 St Sepulchre Gate West, DN1 3AH (5 mins' walk from railway station)
❀ 12-11; 12-midnight Sun ☎ (01302) 340670

Leeds Pale; 4 changing beers (sourced locally; often Dukeries, Geeves, Stancill) H
Multi award-winning traditional pub close to the railway and bus stations and town centre. Beers, in a variety of styles, are mainly from local independent breweries. Mini beer festivals are held twice a year. Food is served weekday afternoons and there is a popular Sunday lunch until 2pm (later if pre-booked). Inside are both lounge and public bars and outside to the rear is a decked area. Local CAMRA Pub of the Year 2017.
🛆🏠🕽🗢♣🖫🖫(71,73A)🛜

Doncaster Brewery Tap 🍷 🄻

7 Young Street, DN1 3EL
🕒 closed Mon; 5 (12 Fri & Sat)-11; 12-5 Sun
☎ (01302) 376436 🌐 doncasterbrewery.co.uk
Doncaster Sand House, Cheswold; 4 changing beers (sourced locally; often Doncaster) H
Conveniently situated in the town centre, Doncaster Brewery Tap was opened in 2014. The brewery, originally launched in 2012, was relocated to the rear and provides up to six beers, all served from handpumps into lined glasses. This welcoming pub also offers a range of six real ciders and perries. There is always something different going on at the Tap, from quiz night on Tuesday, spoken word night on Thursday, to ukulele singalongs on some Saturday afternoons.
Q🗢♣🛒🖫🗮🐾🛜

Leopard ✅

2 West Street, DN1 3AA (less than 5 mins' walk from railway station)
🕒 10-10 (11 Mon & Fri; 11.30 Sat); 12-9 Sun
☎ (01302) 739460 🌐 leopard-doncaster.co.uk
5 changing beers (sourced nationally; often Ossett, York) H
This street-corner local close to the town centre has been a regular award winner over the years. It has a superb tiled frontage recalling its days as a Warwick and Richardson house. There are two distinct rooms downstairs, one often used for functions and meetings. Upstairs is a room that regularly hosts rock and pop gigs. The pub serves a good range of afternoon food to go with the five real ales usually on offer.
Q🛆🏠🕽🕭🗢♣🗮P🖫(71,72)🐾🛜

Plough ★ 🄻

8 West Laith Gate, DN1 1SF (close to Frenchgate shopping centre)
🕒 11-11 (midnight Fri & Sat); 11-4, 7-11.30 Sun
☎ (01302) 738310
Acorn Barnsley Bitter; 2 changing beers (sourced regionally; often Bradfield, Moorhouse's, Mordue) H
Known as the Little Plough, this is a friendly haven to anyone wishing to escape the town-centre bustle. CAMRA-friendly, three real ales are served and there are mini beer festivals. The interior dates from 1934 and is mentioned in CAMRA's National Inventory of Historic Pub Interiors. There is a public bar at the front and a lounge to the rear. The pub is adorned with pictures of old agricultural scenes, and it has won many local CAMRA awards.
Q🏠🗢♣🖫🐾🛜

Queen (Crafthouse & Kitchen)

1 Sunny Bar, DN1 1LY (on corner of Sunny Bar and Market Place)
🕒 closed Mon; 5-11; 11-midnight Fri & Sat; 12-10 Sun
☎ (01302) 562908

5 changing beers (sourced nationally; often Hopjacker, Siren, Steel City) H
Town-centre pub with five rotating casks and real cider. The Queen is a former Tetley's pub which has gone from strength to strength since being taken over and completely refurbished by the current owners, Kath and Rachel. There is a large public bar and a small snug on the side. It is a live music venue at weekends. Q🛆🗢●🖫(76)🐾🛜

White Swan 🄻

34 French Gate, DN1 1QQ (adjacent to Church Way and Frenchgate shopping centre)
🕒 10-11 (10 Mon); 11.30 Fri & Sat); 11-10 Sun
☎ (01302) 344757
Black Sheep Best Bitter; 3 changing beers (sourced locally; often Doncaster) H
Town-centre pub with a narrow frontage disguising a roomy interior, serving food daily including breakfast. There is a cosy drinking area at the front and a long narrow room beyond the bar, where diners can eat in a comfortable setting. Up to three guest beers are usually on tap, including some from local breweries. Live jazz is played on the first Saturday of the month, and there are also occasional bands on weekend evenings.
🏠🕽🛆🗢🖫🛜

Edenthorpe

Eden Arms ✅

Eden Field Road, DN3 2QR (adjacent to Tesco)
🕒 11.30-11 (midnight Wed, Fri & Sat) ☎ (01302) 888682
Abbeydale Moonshine; Brakspear Oxford Gold; 3 changing beers (sourced nationally; often Black Sheep, Marston's, Thornbridge) H
A fine, modern and busy estate pub built in the late 1980s. Attractive and comfortable, it is one of the area's most CAMRA-friendly pubs. On Monday all cask ales are generously discounted all day. Five

REAL ALE BREWERIES		
Abbeydale	Sheffield	
Acorn	Wombwell	
Blue Bee	Sheffield	
Bradfield	High Bradfield	
Chantry	Rotherham	
Concertina 🍺	Mexborough	
Doncaster	Doncaster	
Emmanuales	Sheffield (NEW)	
Exit 33	Sheffield	
Fuggle Bunny	Holbrook	
Geeves	Barnsley	
Hilltop 🍺	Conisbrough	
Imperial 🍺	Mexborough	
Jolly Boys	Redbrook (NEW)	
Kelham Island	Sheffield	
Little Critters	Sheffield (NEW)	
Lost Industry	Sheffield	
Mitchell's Hop House	Sheffield (NEW)	
Neepsend	Sheffield	
On the Edge	Sheffield	
Penistone 🍺	Penistone (NEW)	
Regather	Sheffield	
Sentinel 🍺	Sheffield (NEW)	
Sheffield	Sheffield	
Stancill	Sheffield	
Tapped 🍺	Sheffield	
Toolmakers	Sheffield	
True North	Sheffield (NEW)	
Two Roses	Darton	

real ales are usually on offer, with a display at the entrance informing customers about present and future cask beers. It has a large outside drinking area, and pleasant gas flame fires indoors. Meet the Brewer evenings are popular, and it is notable for good-quality meals. Q⌂✿◑ⓓ♿P🖾(87,8)🛜

Elsecar

Crown Inn ⑂
22 Hill Street, S74 8EL
✿ 12 (4 Mon)-midnight ☎ (01226) 743823
Acorn Yorkshire Pride, Blonde; 1 changing beer (often Ossett) Ⓗ
Stone-built roadside pub in a picturesque village, a family business run by well-known local licensees who have previously managed two other pubs in the area. Two rooms to the left give that community feel, while the lounge to the rear leads to a large new conservatory overlooking gardens and a play area. The guest beers are from local breweries; one of the changing guest beers is always from Ossett. CAMRA branch Pub of the Year 2016. ⌂✿◑ⓓ♿≈♣P🖾✿🛜

Market Hotel ⑂
2-4 Wentworth Road, S74 8EP
✿ 12-11.30 (12.30am Fri & Sat) ☎ (01226) 742240
Acorn Barnsley Gold; 4 changing beers Ⓗ
Multi-roomed pub with a popular drinking corridor. Look for the 'horse and gig for hire' sign chiselled into the stonework. Constantly changing beers from local microbreweries are all sold at the same price regardless of strength. To the rear is a beer garden with a large brick-built barbecue. It is a popular meeting place for various groups and for walkers, with plenty of open scenic countryside. Next to Elsecar Heritage Centre. Q✿⌂≈♣🖾✿

Fenwick

Baxter Arms 🏆
Fenwick Lane, DN6 0HA (between Askern and Moss)
✿ 11.30 (5.30 Mon)-11 ☎ (01302) 702671
Theakston Best Bitter; 2 changing beers (sourced regionally; often Bradfield, Ossett, York) Ⓗ
This award-winning multi-room free house, run by the same family for over 25 years, is a rural gem well worth seeking out. Popular with locals and visitors alike, a warm welcome is extended to all. Fresh food, sourced locally, is served all day and beers are from small independent breweries. A smaller room includes a snooker table and, outside, there is ample parking and seating. Wednesday is quiz night. Local CAMRA Pub of the Year 2017. Q⌂✿◑Å♣P✿🛜

Firbeck

Black Lion ⑂
9 New Road, S81 8JY (opp village hall)
✿ 12-3, 5.30-11 (11.30 Sat); 12-5 Sun ☎ (01709) 812575
John Smith's Bitter; 4 changing beers (often Bradfield, Chantry, Kelham Island) Ⓗ
Traditional village pub, now a free house, which has returned to its former glory under new ownership. It attracts diners, walkers and the local farming community. Four guest beers are offered, usually from local microbrewers such as Chantry. The food is home cooked to order and highly recommended. Pictures of old Firbeck adorn the walls of the snug area. Handy for visiting the ruins

of Roche Abbey. A winner of numerous local CAMRA branch awards and a regular in the Guide. Q✿⌂◑ⓓ♿♣P🖾(20)✿

Harley

Horseshoe ⑂
9 Harley Road, S62 7UD (off A6135 on B6090, 1 mile from Wentworth)
✿ 4-11 (10 Mon); 2-11 Sun; 12-10.30 Sun ☎ (01226) 742204
⊕ thehorseshoeharley.co.uk
Bradfield Farmers Blonde; 3 changing beers Ⓗ
Popular village street-corner local, which has been in the same family for many years. It hosts regular events and is home to football and pool teams. Guest beers change regularly, ensuring their quality, with ales often coming from local breweries. A carvery is held 12-3pm Sunday; book to avoid disappointment. The Horseshoe has been the hub of the local community for well over a century and is handy if walking around the Wentworth estate and for the Needles Eye and Elsecar Heritage Centre. Can be busy when the pool team has a home fixture. ✿◑♣🖾(44)✿

Hoyland Common

Keys ⑂
Sheffield Road, S74 0PY
✿ 12-11 (11.30 Fri & Sat); 12-10.30 Sun ☎ (01226) 824437
⊕ thekeyshoyland.co.uk
3 changing beers Ⓗ
This large, modern pub is set back from the roadside, offering open-plan seating for diners, with room for drinkers. It opened in December 2014 following a £500,000 refurbishment. The real ales are from all over the UK with at least one LocAle. The pub is part of the CAMRA discount scheme (ask at the bar for details). Two popular beer festivals are held in the outdoor areas, with live entertainment. ✿◑P🖾

Kimberworth

Manor Barn ⑂ ✅
109 Church Street, S61 1EP
✿ 4-11 (midnight Fri); 11.30-midnight Sat & Sun
☎ (01709) 551089 ⊕ manorbarnrotherham.co.uk
3 changing beers (often Bradfield, Castle Rock, Moorhouse's) Ⓗ
Tasteful conversion of a barn in the grounds of the former listed Kimberworth Manor, which can be viewed to the rear of the car park. New tenants took over in January 2016 following a problematic time for the pub. Real ale was reinstated, with three handpumps dispensing changing beers from national breweries and micros. This has proved popular, as have the open mic and quiz nights. The food is home-cooked from a varied menu. The large upstairs function room can accommodate 120 people. ⌂✿◑P🖾

Kirk Sandall

Glasshouse
1 Doncaster Road, DN3 1HP
✿ 12-11 (midnight Fri & Sat) ☎ (01302) 884268
⊕ glassh.co.uk
4 changing beers (sourced regionally; often Bosun's, Courage, Old Mill) Ⓗ
This venue has a long historic connection with the glass industry, being close to the site of the

Pilkington Glass works. There has been a pub here since 1934, originally known as the Kirk Sandall Hotel, and then the Glassmaker. The open-plan single-room bar has many large-screen TVs showing sport. Four changing real ales on handpull are served, and good-quality meals are available all day. 😋🏠🍴🚆👥♿🅿️🚃📶

Maltby

Queen's Hotel ✅
Tickhill Road, S66 7NQ
🕐 8am-midnight (1am Thu-Sat) ☎ (01709) 812494
Greene King Abbot; Ruddles Best Bitter; 4 changing beers Ⓗ
Former residential hotel completely refurbished by Wetherspoon after a lengthy period of closure. It won the local CAMRA best pub refurbishment award in 2013, and led to a much-needed raising of the profile of real ale in this small town. Now firmly established, this spacious pub has an attractive family dining area offering typical Wetherspoon value-for-money food and drink. Handy for Coronation Park next door, and the shops. 😋🏠🍴♿🅿️🚃(X1,10)📶

Mapplewell

Talbot Inn Ⓛ ✅
Towngate, S75 6AS
🕐 12-11 (11.30 Wed); 11.30-midnight Fri & Sat; 11.30-11 Sun
☎ (01226) 385629 🌐 thetalbotmapplewell.co.uk
5 changing beers (sourced locally; often Acorn, Thornbridge) Ⓗ
This 17th-century coaching house is popular with diners. The 1776 Restaurant is upstairs, with an extensive beer and wine list to complement the food offerings. Meals are also served in the bar. It offers four varying beers from breweries both local and slightly further afield, such as Acorn and Magic Rock, and has a buy-local policy.
Q😋🏠🍴♣🅿️🚃(1,97)🐾📶

Mexborough

Concertina Band Club Ⓛ
9a Dolcliffe Road, S64 9AZ (off Bank St, halfway up hill, on left-hand side)
🕐 2-4 (5 Sat), 7.45-11; 2-11 Fri; 12-3, 7.45-10.30 Sun
☎ (01709) 580841
Concertina Club Bitter, Old Dark Attic, Bengal Tiger; John Smith's Bitter Ⓗ
Long-established club and brewery with an interesting history, and a regular in the Guide. The Tina, as it is known locally, was originally home to a concertina band formed in 1887. Pictures and memorabilia, as well as many CAMRA awards, decorate the main room, and it also has a small TV and pool room. The cellar brewery provides three regular ales including the award-winning Bengal Tiger. CAMRA members are welcome – just show the Guide or your membership card.
Q🏠🚆👥🅿️🚃(220,221)🐾

Imperial Brewery Tap Ⓛ
Arcadia Hall, Cliff Street, S64 9HU (opp bus station)
🕐 closed Mon & Tue; 4.30-12.30am Wed-Fri; 12-12.30am Sat; 12-10 Sun ☎ (01709) 584000
Imperial Bitter, Blonde, Darkness, Bees Knees, Hop Bomb, Stout; 2 changing beers (sourced nationally; often Great Heck, Ossett, Revolutions) Ⓗ

This friendly brewery tap has a large main bar with a cosy lounge area, plus a separate games/function room. Eight handpumps dispense excellent-quality Imperial ales, which may include seasonal specials and one-off brews, as well as guest beers – all served in lined glasses. A real cider is sometimes available. There is entertainment most nights with live bands on Friday, Saturday and Sunday evenings, featuring music for a wide range of tastes. Thursday is acoustic open mic night. 😋🏠🍴♿🚆👥🅿️🚃(220,221)🐾📶

Rotherham

Bluecoat Ⓛ ✅
The Crofts, S60 2DJ (behind town hall, off Moorgate Road, A618)
🕐 8am-midnight (1am Fri & Sat) ☎ (01709) 539500
Greene King Abbot, IPA; Kelham Island Pale Rider; 7 changing beers (sourced locally) Ⓗ
Originally a charity school, opened in 1776, it became a Wetherspoon pub in 2001. A Guide regular, the selection of up to 10 beers is listed on a screen at the end of the bar. At least two real ciders or perries are served from bags behind the bar. The pub commissions a specially brewed beer four times a year from a local brewery and holds regular Meet the Brewer nights. Local breweries feature strongly in the guest beer selection. Winner of local CAMRA Pub of the Year five times.
😋🏠🍴♿🚆♣🅿️🚃📶

Cutler's Arms Ⓛ
29 Westgate, S60 1BQ
🕐 12-11 (1am Fri & Sat) ☎ (01709) 382581
🌐 cutlersarms.co.uk
Chantry New York Pale, Iron & Steel Bitter, Diamond Black Stout; house beer (by Chantry); 2 changing beers (sourced locally; often Chantry) Ⓗ
Originally dated 1825, and rebuilt for Stones Brewery in 1907, the pub was restored to its Edwardian splendour by Chantry Brewery, reopening in February 2014. It retains some Art Nouveau windows, tiling and the original curved bar counter with elegant dividing screen. It is Grade II and ACV listed, and offers a full range of Chantry beers among the eight pumps, plus two real ciders or perries. Live music plays every Saturday evening, Sunday afternoon and most Friday evenings. Snacks are offered. It gets busy on Rotherham United home match days. On CAMRA's Regional Inventory of Historic Pub Interiors.
Q🏠🍴🚆👥🚃🐾📶

New York Tavern Ⓛ
84 Westgate, S60 1BD
🕐 12-midnight ☎ (01709) 375596 🌐 newyorktavern.co.uk
Chantry New York Pale, Iron & Steel Bitter, Diamond Black Stout; house beer (by Chantry); 2 changing beers (sourced locally; often Chantry) Ⓗ
A pub since 1856, reopened by a team from Chantry Brewery in September 2013, and refurbished as a real ale-led pub. At least six Chantry beers are on tap, plus two real ciders or perries, all at competitive prices. A large selection of foreign bottled beers, pickled eggs and snuff is available. Formerly the Prince of Wales Feathers, it was renamed after a pub that was demolished when the nearby ring road was built and is near New York football stadium. Rotherham United memorabilia adorn the walls. The jukebox has an eclectic selection of music. Local CAMRA Town Pub of the Year 2014-2017. 🍴🚆👥🚃🐾

Rhinoceros L ✅

35-37 Bridgegate, S60 1PL

🕑 8am-11 (midnight Fri & Sat) ☎ (01709) 361422

Greene King Abbot; Marston's 61 Deep; 5 changing beers Ⓗ

Busy town-centre pub popular with shoppers and bigger than it looks from the outside. A single long room on one level features booths down one side and many local pictures – look for one explaining the name. The usual good-value fare is on offer at this Wetherspoon outlet. Beer quality and range have improved recently. The pub can be busy in the afternoon and early evening, and on Rotherham United home match days. Several real ciders and perries are available. ◑&≈●🚍🎵

Stag L ✅

111 Wickersley Road, Broom, S60 4JN (on A6021)

🕑 11-midnight (11 Mon & Tue); 10-midnight Sat & Sun
☎ (01709) 838929

4 changing beers (often Bradfield, Exmoor) Ⓗ

Vastly improved popular suburban roadhouse on a busy roundabout. Keenly priced real ales often come from local microbreweries, and the food is good value too. A conservatory leads to an extensive garden with a covered, raised area. Sport is popular at the pub. It was originally a coaching house that stood on its own on a main route between Rotherham and Bawtry, and acted as the centre of operations for the local Home Guard in WWII. The pub was refurbished in March 2017. ⊛◑♣P🚍(X1,19)🎵

Sheffield: Central

Bath Hotel ★

66-68 Victoria Street, S3 7QL

🕑 12-11 (midnight Fri & Sat); closed Sun ☎ (0114) 249 5151
🌐 beerinthebath.co.uk

Thornbridge Wild Swan; 6 changing beers (sourced regionally; often Thornbridge) Ⓗ

A careful restoration of the 1930s interior gave this two-roomed pub a conservation award and identified by CAMRA as having a nationally important historic pub interior. The bar lies between the tiled lounge, a small corridor drinking area and the cosy well-upholstered snug. Three Thornbridge beers and three guests are usually on the bar. There is regular live music and a weekly quiz on Thursday. Light snacks are available. Q🚍♣●🚍❀

Devonshire Cat ✅

49 Wellington Street, S1 4HG

🕑 12-2am ☎ (0114) 279 6700 🌐 devonshirecat.co.uk

Abbeydale Deception, Moonshine, Absolution; 7 changing beers (often Abbeydale) Ⓗ

With 12 handpumps adorning the bar and over 100 beers from around the world, the Dev Cat is a great place for the discerning drinker. Now operated by Abbeydale Brewery, there are usually up to six of its beers as well as a number of interesting guests. A recent refurbishment has created a central island bar with various seating areas around. The menu ranges from light snacks through to full meals served all day until 9pm (6pm Sun). 🚍◑&🚇(West St)●🚍🎵

Red Deer L ✅

18 Pitt Street, S1 4DD

🕑 12-midnight (1am Fri & Sat); 12-11 Sun
☎ (0114) 272 2890 🌐 red-deer-sheffield.co.uk

Blue Bee Reet Pale; Kelham Island Easy Rider; Moorhouse's Pride of Pendle; Welbeck Abbey Portland Black; 4 changing beers (sourced regionally) Ⓗ

A genuine, traditional local in the heart of the city. The small frontage of the original three-roomed pub hides an open-plan interior extended to the rear with a gallery seating area. As well as the impressive range of eight cask beers, including four guest ales, there is also a selection of continental bottled beers. Meals are served lunchtimes and evenings daily. The popular quiz is held Tuesday night, and an upstairs function room is available for bookings. Q⊛◑🚇(West St)●🚍❀🎵

Rutland Arms L

86 Brown Street, S1 2BS

🕑 12-11 (midnight Fri & Sat) ☎ (0114) 272 9003
🌐 therutlandarmssheffield.co.uk

Blue Bee Hillfoot Best Bitter, Reet Pale; 6 changing beers (sourced regionally) Ⓗ

Occupying a corner site in the Cultural Industries Quarter and near Sheffield's main railway station, the pub has operated as a free house since 2009. The comfortable interior provides ample seating either side of the central entrance, and the wall displays include photos of old Sheffield pubs. Most of the guest beers come from local and regional microbreweries together with specials from Blue Bee. Food is served throughout the day to 9pm (6pm Sunday). ⊛◑≈🚇●🚍❀🎵

Sheffield Tap ★ L

Platform 1b, Sheffield Station, Sheaf Street, S1 2BP

🕑 11-11; 10-midnight Fri & Sat ☎ (0114) 273 7558
🌐 sheffieldtap.com

Tapped Mojo, Rodeo; Thornbridge Jaipur IPA; 7 changing beers (sourced nationally) Ⓗ

Opened in 2009, this was originally the First Class refreshment room for Sheffield Midland Station, built in 1904. After years of neglect, the main bar area has been the subject of an award-winning restoration, retaining many original features. Further seating has been provided in the entrance corridor and to the right of the bar. Usually three beers are from the on-site Tapped Brewery, opened in 2013 in the impressive former dining room. The brewery can be viewed behind a glass screen. Q🚍⊛&≈🚇●🚍❀🎵

Sheffield: Chapeltown

Commercial L

107 Station Road, S35 2XF

🕑 12-11 (midnight Fri & Sat) ☎ (0114) 246 9066
🌐 thecommie.co.uk

Abbeydale Moonshine; Neepsend Blonde; 6 changing beers (sourced nationally; often Durham, Toolmakers, White Rose) Ⓗ

In addition to six guest beers, including a stout or porter, this friendly, well-established free house serves at least one real cider. Built in 1890, an island bar serves the lounge, games room and snug. Beer festivals are held in May and November. There is an outdoor area to the rear, and an upstairs function room which hosts regular live folk sessions. Monthly tutored whisky tastings take advantage of the extensive range. Children are welcome. No meals Sunday evening. 🚍⊛◑≈(Chapeltown)♣●P🚍(265,31A)❀🎵

Sheffield: Kelham Island

Fat Cat ⓛ

23 Alma Street, S3 8SA

🌐 12-11 (midnight Fri & Sat) ☎ (0114) 249 4801

🌐 thefatcat.co.uk

Kelham Island Best Bitter, Pale Rider; Timothy Taylor Landlord; 8 changing beers (sourced nationally; often Kelham Island) Ⓗ

Opened in 1981, this is the pub that started the real ale revolution in the area. Beers from around the country are available alongside those from the adjacent Kelham Island Brewery. Vegetarian and gluten-free dishes feature on the menu. The walls are covered with many awards presented to the pub and brewery. Beer festivals are held every August and at various other times. Monday is curry and quiz night. Q☕️❄️◑🕹️♿️Ⓡ(Shalesmoor)♣️P🚃🚌

Harlequin ⓛ

108 Nursery Street, S3 8GG

🌐 12-11 (11.30 Thu & Fri; midnight Sat) ☎ (0114) 249 4181

🌐 theharlequinpub.wordpress.com

Exit 33 Blonde, New England Best; 8 changing beers (often Exit 33) Ⓗ

Operated by Exit 33 Brewing, the Harlequin takes its name from another former Ward's pub just round the corner, now demolished. The large open-plan interior features a central bar with seating on two levels. There are two regular and usually four other beers from Exit 33, as well as guests from far and wide, with the emphasis on microbreweries. A large range of real ciders is also available. Wednesday is quiz night and there is live music at weekends. ❄️◑Ⓡ(Castle Sq)♣️🍴🚃🚌🐕

Kelham Island Tavern 🍴 ⓛ ✅

62 Russell Street, S3 8RW

🌐 12-midnight ☎ (0114) 272 2482 🌐 kelhamtavern.co.uk

Abbeydale Deception; Acorn Barnsley Bitter; Bradfield Farmers Blonde; Pictish Brewers Gold; 8 changing beers (sourced nationally; often Brass Castle, North Riding Brewery) Ⓗ

Former CAMRA National Pub of the Year and regular regional and local winner, this small gem was rescued from dereliction in 2002. Twelve handpumps dispense an impressive range of beers, always including a mild, a porter and a stout. In the warmer months you can relax in the pub's multi award-winning beer garden. Regular folk music features on Sunday evening and quiz night is Monday. No meals Sunday. Q☕️❄️◑Ⓡ(Shalesmoor)♣️🍴🚃🚌🐕

Shakespeare's Ale & Cider House ⓛ

146-148 Gibraltar Street, S3 8UB

🌐 12-midnight (1am Fri & Sat) ☎ (0114) 275 5959

🌐 shakespeares-sheffield.co.uk

Abbeydale Deception; Stancill Barnsley Bitter; 8 changing beers (sourced nationally; often Brass Castle, North Riding Brewery) Ⓗ

Originally built in 1821, it reopened as a free house in 2011 following a refurbishment including incorporation into the pub of the archway to the rear yard. The central bar serves three rooms including the extension, and there is a further room across the corridor. The eight handpumps have featured more than 4,000 different beers over the last five years, and over 100 whiskies are also stocked. There is regular live music, a quiz is held on Thursday, and beer festivals feature annually. Q❄️Ⓡ(Shalesmoor)♣️🍴🚃🚌🐕📶

Ship Inn ⓛ ✅

312 Shalesmoor, S3 8UL

🌐 11-11 (midnight Fri & Sat) ☎ (0114) 275 6231

Black Sheep Bitter; Timothy Taylor Landlord; 6 changing beers (sourced regionally; often Revolutions) Ⓗ

Edwardian street-corner pub with a stunning tiled Tomlinson's Brewery exterior; refurbished in 2015 and subsequently commended in the 2016 National CAMRA/English Heritage pub design awards. As well as two regular beers the eight handpumps usually dispense up to four rotating beers from the Revolutions Brewing Co, together with two local guest ales. There are varied seating areas around the central bar and the walls are decorated with locally themed pictures. ☕️❄️Ⓡ(Shalesmoor)♣️🚃🚌📶

Wellington ⓛ

1 Henry Street, S3 7EQ

🌐 3-11; 12-midnight Fri & Sat; 12-11 Sun ☎ (0114) 249 2295

Neepsend Blonde; 4 changing beers Ⓗ

This traditional two-roomed local opened as a free house in 1993. Now part of the small Sheaf Inns group of pubs, it is the brewery tap for the nearby Neepsend Brewery. Sympathetically refurbished following the recent takeover, the rooms are comfortably furnished and welcoming. The seven handpumps feature at least three Neepsend beers and up to three changing guests, mainly from micros, together with a real cider. An extensive range of malt whiskies is also on offer. Q❄️Ⓡ(Shalesmoor)♣️🍴🚃🚌🐕📶

Sheffield: Loxley

Nag's Head Inn ⓛ

Stacey Bank, S6 6SJ

🌐 11.30-11.30; 10-11.30 Sat & Sun ☎ (0114) 285 1202

Bradfield Farmers Bitter, Farmers Blonde, Farmers Brown Cow, Farmers Pale Ale; 2 changing beers (sourced locally; often Bradfield) Ⓗ

The tap for the nearby Bradfield Brewery, this friendly two-roomed country pub is on the main road towards High Bradfield. Six beers are sold, including both seasonal and special one-offs, all at competitive prices. Good home-cooked food is served (no food Sun eve, Mon and Tue). Excellent views of the Loxley Valley can be enjoyed from the outdoor drinking area. The games room includes a three-quarter-size snooker table. Opens 10am at weekends to cater for anglers and walkers. Q☕️❄️◑♣️P🚌(61,62)🐕

Sheffield: North

Blake Hotel

53 Blake Street, Walkley, S6 3JQ

🌐 12-11.30 (midnight Fri & Sat) ☎ (0114) 233 9336

Acorn Blonde; 5 changing beers Ⓗ

The five guest beers usually include a stout or porter, the majority from small independent breweries. The pub also provides probably the largest selection of whisky in Sheffield, with over 200 to choose from. At the top of a steep hill (pedestrian handholds provided), this community pub reopened as a free house in 2010 after seven years of closure. Extensively restored, it has retained many Victorian features, with original etched windows and mirrors. At the rear is a large decked garden. No electronic games, TV or jukebox. Q❄️♣️🍴🚃🚌🐕

Gardeners Rest

105 Neepsend Lane, Neepsend, S3 8AT

🕑 3-11; 12-midnight Fri & Sat; 12-11 Sun ☎ (0114) 272 4978

Sheffield Crucible Best, Five Rivers, Blanco Blonde, Porter; 8 changing beers (sourced nationally) Ⓗ

This friendly well-run free house is the tap for the nearby Sheffield Brewery. There are up to eight guest beers sourced nationwide from small independent breweries and at least two real ciders. The main bar, with its clean, bright interior, houses art exhibitions. To the rear is a conservatory leading to a beer garden overlooking the River Don. The cosy Dram Shop includes a restored bar billiards table. There is live music at weekends. It reopened in 2009 after refurbishment following extensive flood damage in June 2007.

Q🏵️&♿(Infirmary Rd)♣🍴🚻🚃🐾

Hillsborough Hotel Ⓛ

54-58 Langsett Road, Hillfoot, S6 2UB

🕑 2-10 Mon; 12-11 (midnight Fri & Sat) ☎ (0114) 232 2100

Acorn Barnsley Bitter; Tapped Mojo; 5 changing beers (sourced nationally) Ⓗ

Privately owned 4-star hotel with six en-suite rooms, providing beer from a wide range of independent breweries. There are regular themed events, with a quiz on Tuesday, live bands at weekends, and folk music sessions on the second and fourth Sundays in the month. The conservatory at the rear offers extensive views over the Don Valley, and a function room is available.

Q🛏️🏵️🛌◑&♿(Langsett)♣🍴🐾🤶

Walkley Beer Company

362 South Road, Walkley, S6 3TF

🕑 closed Mon & Tue; 4-10 Wed-Thu; 2-10 Fri & Sat; 12-8 Sun

🌐 walkleybeer.co.uk

3 changing beers (sourced regionally; often Siren, Wild Beer) Ⓖ

A small specialist beer shop and micropub, open Tuesday to Sunday. It has a tasting bar offering the choice of beers to drink inside. Three gravity-served cask beers are on tap, with a frequently changing range. Two-pint takeouts can be purchased and occasional events are held in this friendly converted shop unit.

Q🛏️&♿(Hillsborough)🚃🐾🤶

Sheffield: South

Broadfield

452 Abbeydale Road, Nether Edge, S7 1FR

🕑 11.30-midnight (1am Fri & Sat); 11.30-11 Sun

☎ (0114) 255 0200 🌐 thebroadfield.co.uk

Abbeydale Moonshine; 7 changing beers (sourced regionally; often Abbeydale) Ⓗ

Dating from 1896, the Broadfield became part of what is now the True North Brew Co in 2011. Nine cask ales, always including beers from True North, are complemented by a large range of bottled beers and whiskies. The pub has established a deserved reputation for quality food, with an extensive menu including hearty pies and home-made sausages. Situated within the city's antiques quarter, the Broadfield is now a leading player in the Abbeydale social scene. 🛏️🏵️◑&🍴🚃🐾🤶

Brothers Arms ✪

106 Well Road, Heeley, S8 9TZ

🕑 12-11 (midnight Fri & Sat) ☎ (0114) 258 3544

Bradfield Farmers Blonde; house beer (by Abbeydale); 6 changing beers (sourced locally; often Blue Bee) Ⓗ

A classic, traditional local – although the interior is open plan, it is designed so the various seating areas and games area all feel individual and cosy. The pub's name reflects its association with locally renowned parody ukulele band The Everly Pregnant Brothers, and live music is hosted every Monday evening, supplemented by folk sessions on the third Sunday. The bar features eight real ales with two regular beers and six changing guests, together with a real cider.

🛏️🏵️♣🍴🚃🐾🤶

Mount Pleasant

293 Derbyshire Lane, Norton Woodseats, S8 8SG

🕑 11-midnight (1am Thu-Sat) ☎ (0114) 255 4997

Abbeydale Moonshine; Adnams Ghost Ship; Bradfield Farmers Blonde; Greene King Abbot; 1 changing beer (sourced locally) Ⓗ

Small, welcoming two-roomed pub housed in a former quarryman's cottage built in 1820, and largely unspoilt by progress. The two rooms comprise a public bar to the right of the entrance and a comfortable quieter lounge where the Whisky Club meets. There are two quiz nights weekly, a darts team and a fishing club. Occasional beer festivals also feature. The current licensee is only the 11th since 1841. Q🛏️🏵️♣P🚃(18)🐾🤶

Sheaf View

25 Gleadless Road, Heeley, S2 3AA

🕑 11.30-11.30 (12.30am Fri & Sat) ☎ (0114) 249 6455

Kelham Island Easy Rider; Neepsend Blonde; 6 changing beers (sourced regionally; often Neepsend, Pictish, Saltaire) Ⓗ

A 19th-century pub near Heeley City Farm, the Sheaf experienced a chequered history before becoming a real ale oasis since reopening as a free house in 2000. The walls and shelves are adorned with assorted breweriana and provide an ideal background for good drinking and conversation. A wide range of international beers, together with malt whiskies and a real cider, complement the eight reasonably priced real ales. It is a busy pub, especially on Wednesday quiz nights and Sheffield United match days. Q🏵️&♣🍴P🚃🐾🤶

White Lion Ⓛ

615 London Road, Heeley, S2 4HT

🕑 4-midnight (1am Fri); 12-1am Sat; 2-midnight Sun

☎ (0114) 255 1500 🌐 whitelionsheffield.co.uk

Abbeydale Moonshine; Tetley Bitter; Wychwood Hobgoblin; house beer (by Kelham Island); 8 changing beers (sourced regionally) Ⓗ

This Grade II-listed pub has been respectfully refurbished over the years. A tiled central corridor links a number of delightful small rooms and leads to a larger rear concert room. There are four regular beers and up to eight changing guests, always including one gluten-free and one vegan option, and a good selection of malts. The pub hosts many community events along with live music every night except Wednesday which is quiz night. 🛏️🏵️♣🍴🚃🐾🤶

Sheffield: West

Beer Engine Ⓛ

17 Cemetery Road, Highfield, S11 8FJ

🕑 12-11 (midnight Fri & Sat) ☎ (0114) 272 1356

🌐 beerenginesheffield.com

Neepsend Blonde; 5 changing beers (sourced regionally) Ⓗ
A traditional-style multi-roomed pub reopened in 2015 as a free house following a sympathetic refurbishment. The changing beer range is mainly sourced from local and regional microbreweries, and there is a quality spirits offering. Food is served lunchtimes and evenings (except Sun eve) – mainly tapas-style dishes, supplemented by a roast on Sunday lunchtime. The large beer garden has a heated, covered area. ⊛◑●🅿🗕🐾🛜

Beer House Ⓛ
623 Ecclesall Road, Sharrow, S11 8PT
✪ 12-11
6 changing beers (sourced nationally; often Blue Bee, Exit 33) Ⓗ
Sheffield's first micropub opened in a small former shop unit in late 2014. The front room of the two has level access from the street and contains the bar, with its bank of six handpumps displaying a varied range of beers mainly from microbreweries, with local breweries well represented. The rear room has seating focused around the fireplace, and there is a quiz on Wednesday evening.
Q⍩⊛♣🗕🐾

Closed Shop Ⓛ ✅
52-54 Commonside, S10 1GG
✪ 4-11 (midnight Fri); 12-midnight Sat; 12-11 Sun
☎ (0114) 266 0330 ⊕ theclosedshopsheffield.co.uk
Blue Bee Reet Pale; 7 changing beers (sourced regionally; often Blue Bee, Little Critters) Ⓗ
Following a significant refurbishment in 2013, there are now eight handpumps, dispensing beers from Blue Bee, other local breweries, and guests, alongside three real ciders and a perry. There are two large bay windows at the front which provide comfortable seating. The smaller space at the end of the bar has photos of the local surroundings, and there is a display of limited edition prints by a local artist for sale. A pool table is in the raised part at the rear. ⍩⊛◑♣🅿🗕(95)🐾🛜

Hallamshire House
49 Commonside, S10 1GF
✪ 4-11.30; 2-12.30am Fri; 12-12.30am Sat; 12-11.30 Sun
☎ (0114) 266 4466 ⊕ myhallamshire.co.uk
Thornbridge Wild Swan; house beer (by Thornbridge); 5 changing beers (sourced locally; often Thornbridge) Ⓗ
Operated by Thornbridge Brewery, and known locally as the Tardis, the pub has two small comfy rooms at the front, and leading through the bar area are a large lounge and a snooker room. There is a courtyard drinking area downstairs with ample seating, and comfortable furniture under a covered space. Quiz night is Monday and live music or a DJ play on some Saturdays. ⍩⊛&♣🗕(95)🐾

Portland House
286 Ecclesall Road, Sharrow, S11 8PE
✪ closed Mon; 12 (5 Tue)-11 ☎ (0114) 266 9511
⊕ theportlandhouse.co.uk
Welbeck Abbey Henrietta; 4 changing beers (often Welbeck Abbey) Ⓗ
Welbeck Abbey's first micropub, and its only tied outlet in Sheffield, opened in late 2015 in a former sandwich shop close to the Sheffield Hallam University collegiate campus. The limited space is well utilised to maximise the seating available, and there is also bench seating outside. Six handpumps usually feature three or four Welbeck beers, a

guest beer and a real cider. The food offering is limited to pork pies, cheese platters and the usual bar snacks. Q⊛♣🗕🐾🛜

Rising Sun ✅
471 Fulwood Road, Nether Green, S10 3QA
✪ 12-11 (11.30 Fri & Sat) ☎ (0114) 230 3855
⊕ risingsunsheffield.co.uk
Abbeydale Daily Bread, Deception, Moonshine; 8 changing beers (sourced nationally; often Abbeydale, Ulverston) Ⓗ
This pub is a large suburban roadhouse operated by local brewer Abbeydale. There are two comfortably furnished rooms with a log-burning fire between the main bar and the glass-roofed extension, which also has glass panels in the end wall. A range of Abbeydale beers is always served, with up to six guests mainly from micros, dispensed from the impressive bank of 13 handpumps. Quizzes are on Sunday and Wednesday evenings. The Sunfest beer festival is in July.
Q⍩⊛◑&●🅿🗕(120,83a)🐾🛜

University Arms Ⓛ
197 Brook Hill, Broomhall, S3 7HG
✪ 12-11 (midnight Fri & Sat); closed Sun ☎ (0114) 222 8969
Kelham Island Pale Rider Ⓗ; Welbeck Abbey Red Feather Ⓗ/Ⓖ; house beer (by Acorn); 5 changing beers (sourced regionally) Ⓗ
Owned by the University of Sheffield, this former staff club has an open-plan lounge with a bar at one end adjacent to a small alcove seating area, and a conservatory leading to the large garden. There is additional seating upstairs with separate rooms for snooker and darts. The guest beers are mostly local and there are regular beer festivals. Entertainment includes a quiz on Tuesday and live blues or jazz some weekends.
⍩⊛◑&🗕♣●🗕(51,52)🐾🛜

York Ⓛ
243-247 Fulwood Road, Broomhill, S10 3BA
✪ 11.30-midnight (1am Fri & Sat) ☎ (0114) 266 4624
⊕ theyorksheffield.co.uk
6 changing beers (sourced regionally; often Abbeydale) Ⓗ
Occupying a prominent site in the centre of Broomhill, the York was built in the 1830s and was originally a blacksmith's and alehouse called the Travellers Inn. Extensively refurbished in 2010, with parquet flooring and wood-panelled walls, it now offers high-quality dining. There are two regular beers from the group's own True North Brewery together with a range of six local and regional guest ales, two real ciders, and over 60 gins. Beer and food events feature regularly throughout the year. ⍩⊛◑&●🐾🛜

Sykehouse

Old George Inn
Broad Lane, DN14 9AU (in centre of village)
✪ 12-midnight; 11.30-midnight Sun ☎ (01405) 785635
Tetley Bitter; 2 changing beers (sourced nationally; often Black Sheep, Ossett, Thwaites) Ⓗ
Friendly village pub in a building over 200 years old. It has several rooms including a lounge with an open fire, a restaurant and a games room. Excellent food is served throughout, with a Sunday carvery which is particularly popular. The guest beer range in this free house is sourced nationally and often includes ales seldom seen locally. Outside is a camping field, a patio area and garden

where barbecues are held in summer, and a large playground with a bathing pool and helter-skelter. ☺❀◑⟨♣Å♣⚫P📶

Thorne

Windmill ✓
19 Queen Street, DN8 5AA
☼ 2-11 (midnight Fri); 12-midnight Sat; 12-11 Sun
☎ (01405) 812866
Kelham Island Easy Rider; Sharp's Doom Bar 🅷
Two well-kept real ales are on offer in this friendly community pub. There is a smart lounge linked by an archway to another room with a pool table, plus a conservatory at the side. Outside there is a large beer garden with play equipment. Close to the town centre, but located in a quiet back street, it is convenient for public transport. The Windmill Golf Club meets here. Q☺❀≉♣P🚃(87,86)🐾📶

Thurlstone

Huntsman 🄻
136 Manchester Road, S36 9QW (on main A628 through village)
☼ 5-11; 3-midnight Fri; 12-midnight Sat; 12-11 Sun
☎ (01226) 764892 ⊕ thehuntsmanthurlstone.co.uk
Black Sheep Best Bitter; Tetley Bitter; Timothy Taylor Landlord; 3 changing beers (sourced locally) 🅷
A popular award-winning pub and regular entry in the Guide. It has a fantastic ambience created by a chatty and appreciative clientele, and is a hub for many local activity groups. Regular music sessions are hosted. Food is served on Tuesday evening and Sunday lunchtime only. Dogs are especially welcome. Oh, and the six cask ales are superb! Q☺❀◑♣⚫🚃🐾

Tickhill

Scarbrough Arms 🄻
Sunderland Street, DN11 9QJ (on A631 near Buttercross)
☼ 12-11; 12-10.30 Sun ☎ (01302) 742977
Greene King Abbot; John Smith's Bitter; Timothy Taylor Landlord; 2 changing beers (sourced locally; often Abbeydale, Kelham Island, Welbeck Abbey) 🅷
A deserving Guide entry since 1990, this three-roomed stone-built pub has won several CAMRA awards over the years. Originally a farmhouse, the building dates back to the 16th century although it has undergone structural changes since then. The snug is a delight with its barrel-shaped furniture and real fire; there is also a rejuvenated front lounge with logburner and a traditional rear bar. An outbuilding doubles as a covered smoking area and an extension for beer festivals. Q☺❀📮♣⚫P🚃(22,205)🐾📶

Wales

Duke of Leeds
16 Church Street, S26 5LQ (off A618 into School Rd, opp parish church)
☼ 12-11 ☎ (01909) 515490 ⊕ thedukeofleeds.co.uk
Theakston Old Peculier; Timothy Taylor Landlord; 2 changing beers (sourced regionally; often Abbeydale) 🅷
Reopened in October 2015 following substantial refurbishment after a period of closure. There are four real ales on including one from Abbeydale Brewery. Once the coaching inn of the Duke of

Leeds, it is more than 300 years old. The bar opens into three other areas where drinks and meals can be taken. Outdoor drinking spaces afford views of the village. Ample parking is provided behind the pub, while buses travel along the main Wales road, a few minutes' walk away. It is also a popular area for walkers. The food menu is extensive and freshly cooked to order. ❀◑P🚃

Wath-upon-Dearne

Wath Tap 🄻
49 High Street, S63 7QB
☼ 12-11 ☎ (01709) 872150
6 changing beers (sourced locally; often Geeves) 🅷
Rotherham district's first micropub, opened in a former butcher's shop in March 2016. Six real ales are on tap at any one time, mostly from local breweries, plus five real ciders. The beers and ciders are listed on chalkboards, at reasonable prices. Food may be brought in from the surrounding takeaways. Welcoming, it can get busy at the weekend. It also offers a range of wines, gins, malt whiskies and soft drinks. The former walk-in cold store is now the cellar. Q♿⚫🚃🐾📶

Wentworth

George & Dragon 🄻
85 Main Street, S62 7TN (stands back from road on B6090)
☼ 11-11 (11.30 Thu; midnight Fri & Sat) ☎ (01226) 742440
Theakston Old Peculier; 7 changing beers (often Bradfield, Chantry) 🅷
In a picturesque and popular village, this free house offers up to eight ales from local, regional and national brewers. The pub has a car park, patio and a grassed area at the rear with a children's adventure playground and craft shop. There is also a marquee in the garden. Home-cooked food is popular here. This local, licensed since 1804, is handy for walking to historic Wentworth Woodhouse and Hoober Stand. It can also be accessed through the rear garden from the parish church. Q☺❀◑P🚃(44,227)🐾📶

Rockingham Arms 🄻 ✓
8 Main Street, S62 7TL
☼ 11-11 (midnight Fri & Sat); 11-10.30 Sun
☎ (01226) 742075
Black Sheep Best Bitter; Theakston Old Peculier; 5 changing beers (sourced regionally) 🅷
Country pub dating from 1814 in this picturesque village, close to historic Wentworth Woodhouse and the Fitzwilliam Follies. An ideal stop-off point for walkers, the pub offers accommodation across the road in converted cottages. An extensive range of home-cooked meals is served. A crown green bowling green is attached, with a patio and gardens for summer drinking. Welcoming and warmed by real fires in winter, there are three rooms plus a large function/dining room and, in addition, a barn for events. It stocks up to seven real ales, and guest ales may be local or from further afield. Q☺❀📮◑♣⚫P🚃(44,227)🐾📶

Whiston

Hind 🄻 ✓
285 East Bawtry Road, S60 4ET (on A631 link road between M1 and M18)
☼ 11.30-midnight; 10-midnight Sat & Sun ☎ (01709) 532490

Abbeydale Moonshine; Tetley Bitter; house beer (by Black Sheep); 3 changing beers (sourced nationally) ⊞
Large roadhouse built for Mappins Brewery of Rotherham in 1936. Originally named the King Edward VIII, it was renamed when the king abdicated. Following refurbishment the interior has been opened out, creating good disabled access. There are extensive gardens and a patio to the rear, with a snooker table upstairs (membership required to play). Daytime, evening and, now, takeaway food is popular. Guest beers are from the Ember Inns portfolio, and are cheaper on Monday. There is also a cask club. Q➤❀◑▶&P🖳❂

Wickersley

Three Horseshoes ✿
133 Bawtry Road, S66 2BW (on A631)
❀ 11-11 (midnight Fri & Sat) ☎ (01709) 704310
⊕ greatukpubs.co.uk/threehorseshoeswickersley
Black Sheep Best Bitter; Fuller's London Pride; 6 changing beers (sourced locally; often Dukeries, Partners) ⊞
Much-improved pub in the centre of the village, which reopened in February 2016 following refurbishment. Standing back from the busy M1/M18 link road, this mock Tudor-style pub now boasts eight real ales. The six guest beers may be sourced locally or from further afield and usually cover a range of styles including a stout or porter – the manager is keen to promote real ale. A large upstairs function room is used for a variety of events and live acts. Regular beer festivals feature ales on the bar and in an outside marquee. The food menu includes breakfast, lunch and dinner. ➤❀◑▶♣P🖳(X1)

Wickersley Old Village Cricket Club ℹ
Northfield Lane, S66 2HL (opp Wickersley Northfield Primary School, down driveway beside pitch)
❀ 5-10 (11 Wed, Fri & Sat); 12-10 Sun ☎ (01709) 700536
Sharp's Doom Bar; 3 changing beers (often Bradfield, Moorhouse's, Chantry) ⊞
Popular cricket club, comfortably appointed and friendly, open to the public and now boasting four handpulled beers. The large lounge offers a more peaceful location for a quality beer than the local pubs. CAMRA members are more than welcome for a good-value well-kept pint, and of course you can always watch the cricket. Opening hours are likely to be extended when home matches are staged and it can get busy. Local CAMRA branch Club of the Year 2014-17. ❀▶♣P🖳(10)

Wombwell

Anglers Rest ℹ
66 Park Street, S73 0HS
❀ 5-midnight (11 Mon & Tue; 8 Wed); 12-8 Sun
☎ (01226) 345747
Geeves Clear Cut; 5 changing beers (sourced locally) ⊞
This small gem of a pub on the edge of Wombwell town centre is the Geeves Brewery tap – the landlord being the founding father of the brewery. It is very much a locals' pub while still welcoming all visitors. The emphasis is on friendly chit-chat and banter over an excellent pint of Geeves or a guest beer from a range of small breweries. Opening hours vary on the second Wednesday of

the month for the ever-popular music night. A selection of traditional pub games are on offer and a free pool night is hosted on Thursdays. Q❀♣P🖳❂🛆

Horseshoe ℹ ✿
30 High Street, S73 0AA
❀ 8am-midnight (1am Fri & Sat) ☎ (01226) 273820
Greene King Abbot; Ruddles Best Bitter; 3 changing beers (sourced regionally) ⊞
Built in the 1930s to replace a terraced pub of the same name, this impressive red-brick building stands in the heart of the main town shopping area. It is a JD Wetherspoon outlet that offers a standard range of cask ales alongside a selection of guest beers often from local breweries. The pub hosts occasional Meet the Brewer evenings. The interior is a large open space divided into convenient comfortable areas which allow for the provision of several different pub experiences. Q❀◑▶P🖳❂

Wortley

Wortley Men's Club ℹ ✿
Reading Room Lane, S35 7DB (in centre of village at back of Wortley Arms public house)
❀ 2-11; 12-11 Sat & Sun ☎ (0114) 288 2066
Timothy Taylor Landlord; 2 changing beers (sourced regionally) ⊞
CAMRA national, regional and branch Club of the Year award winner in this pretty rural village near to Wortley Hall and gardens. The opulent building features exposed timber frames, ornate ceilings, wooden panelling and a real fire. Guest ales are from local and national breweries, and a guest cider is always stocked. The club runs an annual beer festival in July. Show your CAMRA membership card or a copy of this Guide on entry. Q❀&▶P🖳(29)

YORKSHIRE (WEST)

Ackworth

Masons Arms ℹ
Bell Lane, WF7 7JD (turning off A628 by defunct railway bridge)
❀ 4-midnight; 1.30-1am Fri; 12-1am Sat; 12-midnight Sun ☎ 07966 501827
Bradfield Farmers Blonde, Farmers Brown Cow; 2 changing beers (sourced regionally) ⊞
One of seven real ale establishments in the village, this Grade II-listed former coaching house dates from 1682 and is built of locally quarried stone. It has a central bar serving the main room, pool room and smaller lounge. Log-burning fireplaces in both the main rooms were discovered 15 years ago during a sensitive refurbishment. Live music plays Saturday evening and late afternoon Sunday, games night is Tuesday and quiz night Thursday – all well attended by locals and visitors alike. ➤❀♣P🖳❂

Altofts

Robin Hood ℹ
10 Church Road, WF6 2NJ (from Normanton town centre take road over railway into Altofts, continue through Lee Brigg, then High Green Rd & left on to Church Rd)
❀ 4-11; 3-midnight Fri; 12-midnight Sat; 12-11 Sun
☎ (01924) 892911

Acorn Barnsley Bitter; 5 changing beers (sourced locally; often Tarn 51) Ⓗ
Locally owned free house/brewpub at the top end of the village. Local CAMRA Pub of the Year 2015, it has a new large patio area seating 70 people. Tarn 51 microbrewery is on-site next to the patio. The pub is within easy reach of the Pennine Trail and Aire and Calder Navigation, and only a mile from Stanley Ferry marina. Q✿⬤♣⬤P☐❄☂

Alverthorpe

Alverthorpe WMC Ⓛ

111 Flanshaw Lane, WF2 9JG (on road from Alverthorpe to Flanshaw; from Wakefield turn left at traffic lights in middle of Alverthorpe)
✿ 2-11; 11.30-11 Fri & Sat; 12-11 Sun ☎ (01924) 374179
Timothy Taylor Landlord; 3 changing beers (sourced locally) Ⓗ
Multi-roomed CIU-affiliated club with a cosy interior with unusual stained-glass features. A wide selection of guest ales is featured, mainly from local micros. The club is a regular winner of local CAMRA awards, and puts on live entertainment Saturdays and Sundays. Snooker and darts are among the traditional games, with wide-screen TV for the armchair enthusiasts. It has sporting teams and also a floodlit bowling green. Local CAMRA Club of the Year 2015. ✿✿♣P☐

Baildon

Bull's Head Inn Ⓛ ✅

6 Westgate, BD17 5ES
✿ 12-11.30 Mon; 11-11 ☎ (01274) 976416
Goose Eye Chinook Blonde; Saltaire Blonde; Sharp's Doom Bar; Tetley Bitter; 2 changing beers (sourced nationally) Ⓗ
A popular village local where visitors and well-behaved dogs are always welcome. Log fires in both rooms give a homely atmosphere, and local photos of Baildon adorn the walls. Two independent guest beers are offered alongside the four regular real ales. Sunday and Tuesday evenings are busy quiz nights and live bands play occasionally. There is often piped background music. The separate taproom houses darts and dominoes. ✿♣P☐❄☂

Junction Ⓛ

1 Baildon Road, BD17 6AB (on A6038)
✿ 12-midnight (1am Fri & Sat) ☎ (01274) 582009
Fuller's ESB; Junction Blonde; Oakham JHB; Tetley Bitter; 3 changing beers (sourced nationally) Ⓗ
A popular three-roomed local comprising a lounge, public bar and games area. The four regular ales include at least one from the in-house Junction brewery and are complemented by two guest ales. Real cider and foreign bottled beers are also sold. Food is available weekday lunchtimes and other times by arrangement. A quiz night is held on

REAL ALE BREWERIES

Baildon Baildon
Beer Ink Huddersfield
BEEspoke ⬤ Shipley
Bingley Wilsden
Blue Square Leeds: Morley (NEW)
Boothtown Halifax (NEW)
Bosun's Horbury Bridge
Bradford ⬤ Bradford
Bridestones Hebden Bridge
Bridge ⬤ Holmbridge
Bridgehouse Keighley
Briggs Huddersfield
Briscoe's Otley
Burley Street ⬤ Leeds
Cap House Batley
Chin Chin South Elmsall (NEW)
Clark's Wakefield
Cobbydale ⬤ Silsden (NEW)
Eagles Crag Todmorden (NEW)
Elland Elland
Empire Slaithwaite
Fernandes ⬤ Wakefield
Five Towns Wakefield
Ghost Baildon
Golcar Golcar
Goose Eye Keighley
Halifax Steam ⬤ Hipperholme
Hamelsworde Hemsworth
Haworth Steam ⬤ Cleckheaton
Hedge Row Bradford
Here Be Monsters Holmbridge
Hogs Head ⬤ Sowerby Bridge (NEW)
Horbury Ossett (NEW)
Hungry Bear Leeds
Ilkley Ilkley
James & Kirkman ⬤ Pontefract
Junction ⬤ Baildon
Kirkstall Leeds: Kirkstall
Landlord's Friend ⬤ Luddendenfoot

Leeds Leeds: Holbeck
Linfit ⬤ Linthwaite
Little Valley Hebden Bridge
Lord's Golcar
Magic Rock Huddersfield
Mallinson's Huddersfield
Mill Valley Cleckheaton
Milltown Milnsbridge
Morton Collins Ryhill (NEW)
New Inn ⬤ Liversedge
Nook ⬤ Holmfirth
North Leeds
Northern Monk Holbeck
Old Spot Cullingworth
Ossett Ossett
Partners Hightown
Quirky Garforth
Rat ⬤ Huddersfield
Revolutions Whitwood
Ridgeside Leeds: Meanwood
Riverhead ⬤ Marsden
Salamander Bradford
Saltaire Shipley
Slightly Foxed Mytholmroyd
Small World Shelley
Steampunk Castleford (NEW)
Stod Fold Halifax
Summer Wine Honley
Sunbeam Leeds
Tapped ⬤ Leeds
Three Fiends Meltham
Tigertops Wakefield
Timothy Taylor Keighley
Trinity Wakefield
Vocation Hebden Bridge
Wharfe Bank Pool-in-Wharfedale (brewing suspended)
Wharfedale ⬤ Ilkley
Wilde Child Leeds (NEW)
Wishbone Keighley

WEST YORKSHIRE

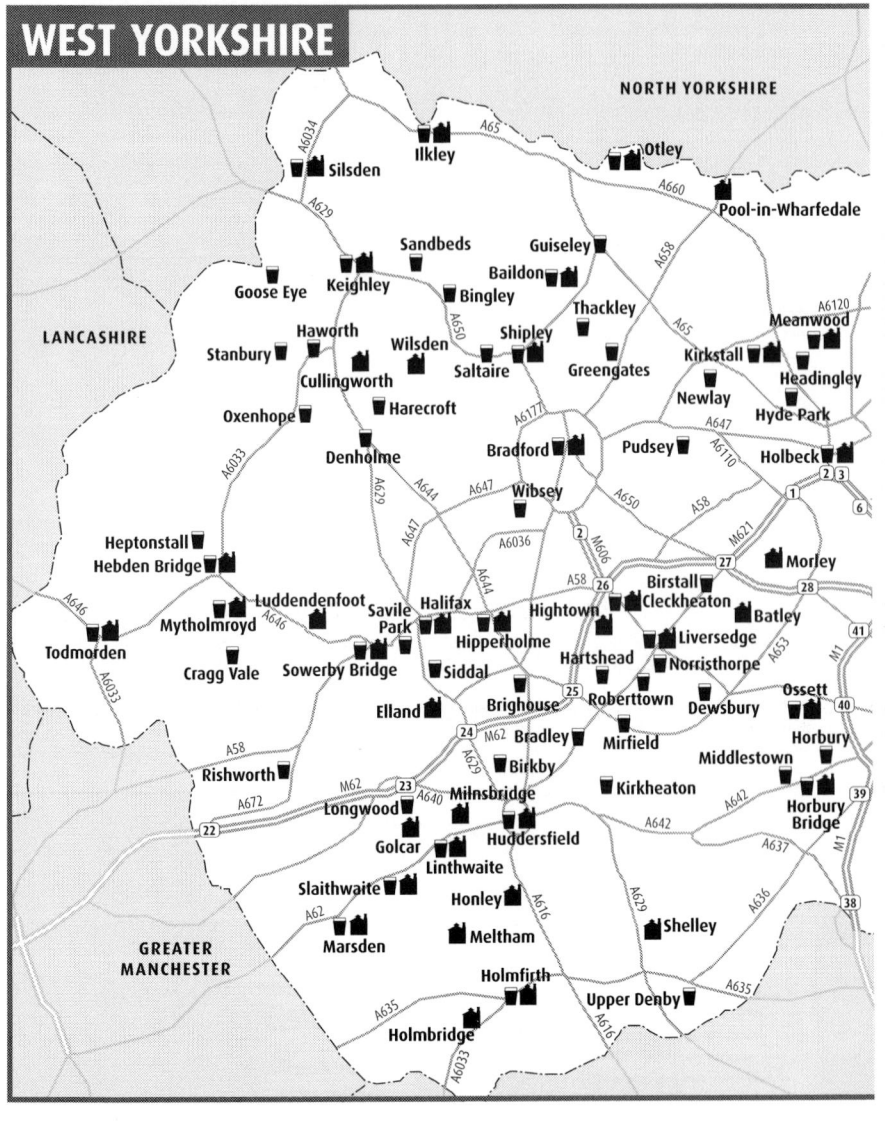

Thursday, an acoustic session on Sunday night and varying pub games during other evenings. An annual beer festival is staged at the end of July. 🏠🍴♣🍺🚃🐾

Bingley

Chip N Ern
73 Main Street, BD16 2JA
☼ 4 (12 Sat)-midnight; 12-11 Sun
6 changing beers (sourced locally; often Bingley, Bridgehouse, Wishbone) 🅷

Centrally located on Bingley's Main Street near the railway station, this friendly micropub opened in 2015 and features a wood-panelled ground-floor bar and a well-furnished room upstairs. It has quickly established itself as a popular addition to the emerging local beer scene. The six cask ales come chiefly from local microbreweries such as Bingley, Bridgehouse and Wishbone. Handy for

exploring the famous Five Rise Locks on the adjacent Leeds-Liverpool canal.
🛏👶🚌🚃🚽(662)🎵🐾🛜

Foundry Hill
Wellington Street, BD16 2NB (opp railway station)
☼ closed Mon & Tue; 12-midnight; 12-9 Sun
☎ (01274) 566144 ⊕ foundryhillbar.co.uk
House beer (by Slightly Foxed); 4 changing beers (sourced nationally; often Bingley, Slightly Foxed, Wishbone) 🅷

Opposite the railway station, this modern basement pub comprises a small bar area and an adjacent larger room for drinking and dining. A changing range of real ales is sold, sourced both locally and nationally. A real cider is usually on. The pub can get quite busy, especially at weekends. Meals are home made and popular on Sunday lunchtime, when bookings are advised. Events are occasionally held. Q🛏◐🚃🚌🚽🛜

Birstall

Horse & Jockey ⏚ ✅

97 Low Lane, WF17 9HB (on A643 W of village centre)

🕐 12 (4 Wed)-midnight; 12-1am Fri & Sat ☎ (01924) 472559

Jennings Cumberland Ale; John Smith's Bitter; Ossett Yorkshire Blonde, Silver King; Sharp's Doom Bar; 2 changing beers (sourced nationally; often Durham, Naylor's, Rudgate) Ⓗ

A country-style pub licensed from the 1750s. The open-plan bar is divided into four areas, with half-panelled walls and beamed ceilings. Darts, dominoes and pool are played, on Thursdays there is a music and knowledge quiz, and on Saturdays karaoke. Guest beers come mainly from independent breweries. Outside, the patio with a beautiful flower display has won the Birstall in Bloom award for the past three years. Pub policy says no hats, no tracksuit bottoms, and last admission 11pm. ✲♣☗P🚌🛜

Bradford

Castle Hotel ⏚

20 Grattan Road, BD1 2LU

🕐 12-11; 1-9 Sun ☎ (01274) 393166

Jennings Cumberland Ale; 3 changing beers (often Cross Bay, Empire) Ⓗ

Traditional city-centre pub kept alive by an enthusiastic Indian landlord. The imposing stone building, dating from 1898, comprises a large open-plan room with a wraparound bar to one side. Formerly a Webster's house, it now sells a variety of beers in a relaxed atmosphere. Guest ales include at least one from a local brewery. A dartboard and TV are located to one end. Live folk music is popular on Friday evening and a DJ plays on Saturday night. Within easy reach of the city centre transport network. 🚅♿🚆♣🚌☗

Corn Dolly ⏚

110 Bolton Road, BD1 4DE

🕐 11.30-11; 12-10.30 Sun ☎ (01274) 720219

🌐 corndolly.pub

Everards Ascalon; Moorhouse's Pride of Pendle; Timothy Taylor Boltmaker; 5 changing beers (sourced nationally) Ⓗ

Award-winning free house run by the same family for over 25 years, a short distance from the city centre and Forster Square railway station. Previously called the Wharf due to its location near the former Bradford Canal, it first opened its doors in 1834. An open-plan layout incorporates a games area to one end. Good-value food is served weekday lunchtimes. It has a friendly atmosphere and is popular before Bradford City matches. A collection of pumpclips adorns the beams. ◖🚆♣P🚌

Fighting Cock ⏚

21-23 Preston Street, BD7 1JE (close to Grattans, off Thornton Rd)

🕐 11.30-11; 12-10.30 Sun ☎ (01274) 726907

Ilkley Mary Jane; Theakston Old Peculier; Timothy Taylor Golden Best, Boltmaker, Landlord; 7 changing beers (often Phoenix, Pictish, Stancill) Ⓗ

Drinkers' paradise in an industrial area, this multi award-winning pub is 20 minutes' walk from the city centre and close to bus routes along Thornton Road and Legrams Lane. A large beer garden on the opposite side of the street was added in 2015 and summer beer festivals now take place. Twelve real ales are usually on sale, including at least one

Birkby

Magic Rock Brewery Tap

Willow Park Business Centre, Willow Lane, HD1 5EB

🕐 closed Mon; 4-10 Tue-Thu; 1-11 Fri; 12-11 Sat; 12-9 Sun

🌐 magicrockbrewing.com

Magic Rock Ringmaster; 4 changing beers (sourced locally; often Magic Rock) Ⓗ

The Tap opened in 2015 following a relocation from Quarmby, and has been a growing success among beer drinkers ever since. It sells five cask beers from the brewery. Less than 10 minutes' walk from the town centre, the Tap itself is housed in a 1,700 square foot area to the far end of the brewery, with a view directly into it so that you can watch during production. Street food outlets and other unusual caterers are laid on every weekend to feed the masses. Regular events include brewery tours, a Tap social (every second Sunday), exhibitions and festivals. Well worth a visit. 🚅♿P🚌☗🛜

Map labels: A661, 45, A61, A58, A1(M), A64, 44, A58, A64, 47, 48/43, Garforth, LEEDS, 46, A642, A63, A639, 45, M1, Ledsham, 42, 7, 44, A656, A639, A1(M), 43, M62, 29/42, 30, Whitwood, Castleford, 41, Stanley, A642, 31, 32, 33, M62, Alverthorpe, Altofts, Pontefract, 40, Wakefield, A645, Heath, A628, A638, Ryhill, Ackworth, Hemsworth, A628, A638, A61, South Elmsall, SOUTH YORKSHIRE, 0 Miles 5, 0 Kilometres 8

dark beer. A choice of real ciders and foreign bottled beers is also offered. Good-value lunches are served Monday to Saturday. ❀🍴♿🚶🚌♫🐾🛜

Jacobs Beer House 🅛

14 Kent Street, BD1 5RL (by Jacobs Well roundabout at end of Hall Ings)
❀ 4-11 (10 Mon); 12-11 Sat; closed Sun ☎ (01274) 394479
Half Moon Dark Masquerade; 8 changing beers (sourced nationally; often Salamander, Stancill, Sunbeam) Ⓗ
Refurbished and reopened in 2013, this pub was formerly known as Jacobs Well, dating from about 1830. The layout is open plan but with a snug to the side of the bar. Nine handpulls offer a changing range of beers from local and regional independents, always featuring some darker ales. Five ciders are also available, together with a good range of foreign bottled beers. Sit outside and watch the city's bustle while supping good ale. ❀🚅🚶🚌🛜

Monkey 🅛

931 Great Horton Road, BD7 4AQ
❀ 3-11; 12-11 Fri-Sun
Junction Blonde; 2 changing beers (sourced locally) Ⓗ
Located between Bradford and Queensbury, this welcoming free house was originally two 17th-century cottages and comprises a games room and lounge with a real fire. The real ales are from Junction Brewery plus other locals such as Salamander and Abbeydale. One of the outdoor areas has a barbecue and a covered, seated smoking area. The other is elevated and offers magnificent views over and beyond Bradford. The pool table, jukebox and Wi-Fi are all free. 🐕❀♿🚶🌳🐾🛜

Record Café 🍸

45-47 North Parade, BD1 3JH
❀ 11-11 (midnight Fri & Sat); 12-11 Sun ☎ (01274) 723143
🌐 therecordcafe.co.uk
4 changing beers (sourced regionally; often Magic Rock, Northern Monk, Vocation) Ⓗ
Located in the city's independent quarter, this café-style bar sells ale, vinyl and ham. Four real ales are on handpull, all regional and in a variety of styles. A dark beer is usually on the bar, and there is an extensive selection of imported bottled beers. Food is offered in a charcuterie style, particularly hams and cheeses from Spain. In the upstairs mezzanine area it is possible to browse and purchase vinyl records. Occasional live acoustic music features on Sunday evening. 🐕❀🍴♿🚅🚶🚌(662,680)🐾🛜

Sparrow Bier Café 🅛

32 North Parade, BD1 3HZ
❀ 11-11 (midnight Thu-Sat); 12-11 Sun ☎ (01274) 270772
4 changing beers (sourced regionally; often Kirkstall, Squawk, Wishbone) Ⓗ
Located in Bradford's popular independent quarter, this busy café-bar is simply furnished in a minimalist style. A large main bar is complemented by the basement area with additional seating. Four cask ales are offered plus at least two real ciders and a varied selection of international draught and bottled beers. Deli-style sandwiches and platters are available and free snacks are served on Bradford City FC match days. ❀🚅🚶🚌(680)🐾🛜

Bradley

White Cross ✓

2 Bradley Road, HD2 1XD (on A62, 3 miles from Huddersfield centre, at Leeds Rd/Bradley Rd crossroads)
❀ 11.45-11 (midnight Fri & Sat); 12-10.30 Sun
☎ (01484) 425728
Marston's Wainwright; St Austell Admiral's Ale; 3 changing beers Ⓗ
This friendly Bradley pub has been in the Guide for 15 years. It has been serving the community since about 1806 and still retains the Bentley Yorkshire Breweries green-tiled entrance and windows. The dining area and lounge sit either side of the central bar, where two regular beers are supported by up to three varied guests. You will always get a warm welcome in this popular and cosy pub. No food Saturday. ❀🍴♿P🚌🛜

Brighouse

Market Tavern

2 Ship Street, HD6 1JX
❀ closed Mon & Tue; 2 (12 Fri & Sat)-10 ☎ 07908 698360
6 changing beers (often Abbeydale, Salopian, Vocation)
A single-storey former butcher's shop has been transformed into a micropub, next to the canalside open-air market. Seating is available in the bar, in a small snug by the entrance, and in an outside drinking area. At least one dark beer is sold at all times. Real ciders include Thirsty Cross and one other which varies. Appropriately, pork pies are among the snacks offered. Q🐕❀🚅🚶🐾🛜

Red Rooster

123 Elland Road, HD6 2QR (on A6025 towards Elland)
❀ 4-11; 12-midnight Fri & Sat; 12-10.30 Sun
☎ (01484) 721291
Abbeydale Moonshine; Saltaire Blonde; Timothy Taylor Boltmaker; 6 changing beers (often Oakham, Salopian) Ⓗ
Half a mile from Brighouse town centre, it is well worth the walk to this excellent free house. Formerly known as the Wharf, the alehouse was purpose built around 1900 for the adjacent coal wharf, which served much of western Yorkshire. Three wharfmen's cottages still stand alongside the pub by the Red Beck. Locally sourced pie and peas are available at all times, as is fresh ground coffee. Dark beers are always on tap. Q🐕❀♿P🚶🚌🐾🛜

Castleford

Junction 🅛

Carlton Street, WF10 1EE (enter Castleford on A655; pub is on corner with Carlton St at top of town centre)
❀ 2-8.30 Mon & Tue; 2-11 Wed & Thu; 12-11.30 Fri-Sun
☎ (01977) 277750 🌐 thejunctionpubcastleford.com
6 changing beers Ⓗ
Rejuvenated pub handy for bus and train stations, specialising in beers in the landlord's own wooden casks. Up to six guest beers are sold in the wood from enterprising local brewers. An annual Easter Woodfest Beer Festival is staged. The large horseshoe-shaped bar is kept warm with open fires, and there is a stove-heated snug available for functions. Folk night is on the last Sunday of each month and a live band plays on Friday evenings. Quiz night is Wednesday. Q🐕❀🚶♿🚶🚌🐾🛜

Cleckheaton

Rose & Crown ⅃

6 Westgate, BD19 5ET (on A643, W off A638)
🕓 12-11; 12-10.30 Sun ☎ (01274) 861530
🌐 rosebrewpub.co.uk
6 changing beers (sourced locally; often Empire,
Ossett, Salamander) Ⓗ

A cosy town-centre pub with a five-barrel
microbrewery on-site beyond the sheltered patio,
producing beers under the Whitechapel and
Haworth Steam brands. It is newly refurbished to a
high specification with lots of woodwork in the
three rooms, plus comfortable seating and
attractive features. Great-quality food is served
lunchtimes and evenings. A good choice of mainly
local beers is available, including one or two
brewed here – dark beers being especially popular.
The bus station is a three-minute walk.
ᗜ❀⊛◗●🖵😺🕏

Cragg Vale

Robin Hood ⅃

Cragg Road, HX7 5SQ (on B6138 1½ miles S of
Mytholmroyd)
🕓 3-11; 12-11 Fri-Sun ☎ (01422) 885899
Timothy Taylor Boltmaker, Landlord; 4 changing
beers (sourced regionally; often Mallinsons, Small
World, Vocation) Ⓗ

Compact and welcoming two-roomed split-level
local, set in the scenic wooded Cragg Valley. Ideal
for investigating the history of the infamous Cragg
Vale Coiners. There is a cosy real fire in the winter,
and food is served Friday to Sunday (telephone to
check times). The pub is customer-led and guest
ales are usually from West Yorkshire breweries.
Real cider is sometimes available.
Q ᗜ❀🖵 (900,901) 😺🕏

Denholme

New Inn ✓

Keighley Road, BD13 4JT (on A629)
🕓 4-11; 12-11 Sat & Sun ☎ 07887 510354
Tetley Bitter; 3 changing beers (sourced regionally;
often Empire, Phoenix, Saltaire) Ⓗ

A warm welcome is assured in this cosy free house
on the Keighley-Halifax road in the village of
Denholme. The premises has an open-plan layout
but still retains a multi-room feel. Real fires add
warmth and a conservatory extension houses a
pool table. Three rotating guest ales regularly come
from local breweries. The pub sits high on the
hillside with stunning views over the Aire Valley.
For the energetic, the Great Northern walking/
cycling trail is nearby. ᗜ❀♣●P🖵 (502,696)😺

Dewsbury

Leggers ⅃

Calder Valley Marina, Mill Street East, WF12 9BD (off
B6409, follow brown signs to canal basin)
🕓 11-11 (midnight Fri & Sat); 11-10.30 Sun
☎ (01924) 502846 🌐 leggersinn.co.uk
Sharp's Atlantic; house beer (by Tapped Sheffield); 5
changing beers (sourced nationally; often Dark Star,
Leeds, Oakham) Ⓗ

A hidden gem in a former stable hayloft
overlooking the canal basin. Outside, a large
decked area welcomes cyclists and walkers, while
inside, the interesting bar has a unique decor. A

raging fire warms while you study the beer
blackboard, but watch out for the low beams. The
large function room hosts live music and annual
beer festivals. Good, simple pub food features local
pie and peas as a speciality. Guest beers always
include a dark beer. ᗜ❀⊛◗♣●P🖵😺🕏

West Riding Refreshment Rooms ▼ ⅃ ✓

Dewsbury Railway Station, Wellington Road,
WF13 1HF
🕓 11 (12 Mon)-11; 11-midnight Fri; 10-midnight Sat
☎ (01924) 459193
Black Sheep Best Bitter; Timothy Taylor Landlord; 7
changing beers (sourced nationally; often Brass
Castle, Magic Rock, Rooster's) Ⓗ

Multi award-winning pub in a Grade II-listed station
building. The excellent range of nine real ales
always includes a dark beer. Real cider is sold, as
well as a selection of speciality bottled beers. Live
music plays outside in summer and occasional beer
festivals are held. Good food is served daily. The
pub is a mainstay of the Transpennine Rail Ale Trail
and consequently tends to be busy on Saturday.
There are monthly Meet the Brewer sessions.
⊛◗&⇌●P🖵😺🕏

Goose Eye

Turkey Inn ⅃

BD22 0PD SE028406
🕓 12-11 (midnight Fri & Sat) ☎ (01535) 681339
🌐 theturkeyinn.com
Goose Eye Bitter, Chinook Blonde; Timothy Taylor
Golden Best, Landlord; house beer (by Settle); 3
changing beers Ⓗ

Friendly, historic pub in a tiny hamlet approached
by steep roads or a riverside footpath. Three snugs
all have real fires to keep out the winter chill. It has
a pool table, holds a quiz night on Wednesday, and
hosts occasional live music and special theme
nights. Food is served every day until 8pm (9pm Fri
and Sat). Three to six guest beers are usually
available. A good base for exploring the
surrounding countryside. ᗜ❀⊛◗♣P🖵😺🕏

Greengates

Albion

25 New Line, BD10 9AS
🕓 12-11 ☎ 07973 641104
Acorn Barnsley Bitter Ⓗ; Tetley Bitter Ⓗ/Ⓐ; 2
changing beers (sourced regionally; often Old Spot,
Salamander) Ⓗ

Comfortable, traditional community venue with an
L-shaped lounge and separate public bar where
pub games can be played. Previously pubco-
owned, this hostelry became a free house in
February 2014, probably saving it from the usual
fate of closure and conversion. A thriving social
club is testament to the local appeal of this warm
and welcoming place. Two rotating guest ales
come from local Bradford-based breweries such as
Old Spot and Salamander. The 760 bus passes the
front door. ⊛♣●P🖵 (760)😺

Guiseley

Coopers ⅃ ✓

4-6 Otley Road, LS20 8AH
🕓 12-11 (midnight Fri & Sat) ☎ (01943) 878835

Okells Bitter; Rooster's Yorkshire Pale Ale; Timothy Taylor Landlord; 5 changing beers (sourced regionally; often Hawkshead, Okells, Thornbridge) Ⓗ
A light, modern, airy bar/diner converted from a former Co-operative store, the interior includes a separate dining area and upstairs function room. Eight ales are served, generally from Yorkshire or northern micros, with a dedicated dark-beer pump and a large selection of continental beers in bottle and on tap. A diverse range of meals is available until 9pm. The large function room has regular music events and a monthly comedy club, and this area also serves as extra dining space.
Q❀⊕◑&⇌●🛏❤️🎵🛜

Guiseley Factory Workers Club Ⓛ

6 Town Street, LS20 9DT
🕐 1-11 (midnight Fri); 11.30-midnight Sat; 11-11 Sun
☎ (01943) 874793 ⊕ guiseleyfactoryworkersclub.co.uk
Tetley Bitter; 3 changing beers (sourced locally; often Acorn, Pennine, Salamander) Ⓗ
Three-roomed club founded over 100 years ago by the Yeadon and Guiseley Factory Workers Union. The bar serves both the lounge and the concert room and has changing guest ales from micros and independents. There is also a snooker room and a small outdoor drinking area. Varied musical acts perform on Friday and Saturday nights, and the venue hosts many local clubs and organisations. An annual beer festival is held in April. CAMRA members are welcome with this Guide or a membership card. ❀⇌♣P🛏❤️🛜

Halifax: Savile Park

Big Six

10 Horsfall Street, HX1 3HG (off A646 Skircoat Moor Rd at King Cross)
🕐 4 (3.30 Fri)-11; 12-midnight Sat & Sun ☎ (01422) 350169
Old Mill Traditional Bitter; 4 changing beers (sourced regionally) Ⓗ
Close to the Free School Lane recreation ground and Crossley Heath School, this is a characterful hidden gem in a row of terraces, comprising two houses knocked together. The emphasis in this friendly pub is on good beer and conversation. It has a regionally important historic interior with a through corridor separating the bar, cosy snug and games room from the two lounges. Four rotating guest beers from regional or microbreweries are sold alongside an extensive range of gins and malt whiskies. Q❀♣●🛏(577)❤️

Halifax: Siddal

Cross Keys 🍸

3 Whitegate, HX3 9AE
🕐 3-11; 12-11 Fri-Sun ☎ (01422) 300348
8 changing beers Ⓗ
This 17th-century pub has a real traditional feel. The front of bar area is split into a snug and two rooms divided by an original inglenook fireplace. There is also a separate taproom. The large beer garden (heated and covered during the winter) has a children's play area and displays the pub's old signs. Walkers and cyclists are welcome and two letting rooms are available.
Q❀🛏♣●🛏(542,555)❤️🛜

Halifax: Town Centre

Barum Top Ⓛ ✅

17 Rawson Street, HX1 1NX
🕐 8am-midnight (1am Fri & Sat) ☎ (01422) 300488
Greene King Abbot; Ruddles Best Bitter; 8 changing beers Ⓗ
This popular Wetherspoon pub occupies the site of a former garage in an area once known as Barum Top. The name derives from the old Yorkshire word bourum, meaning a natural watercourse. The interior has an open-plan layout with a long bar. There are steps leading up to a family dining area, and further seating on the balcony round the sides. Food is served daily until 11pm, with breakfast 8am-noon. 🛏⊕◑&⇌●🛏🛜

Grayston Unity

1-3 Wesley Court, HX1 1UH
🕐 closed Mon; 4-10 Tue & Wed; 4-11 Thu; 12-11 Fri & Sat; 1-10 Sun ☎ 07807 136520
Goose Eye Chinook Blonde; 2 changing beers Ⓗ
This micropub is opposite Halifax's town hall, in a Grade II-listed building. There is a café-style seating area in front of the bar, a side room with comfy chairs and, to the side of the bar, a vestibule leading to an outside seating area. It hosts music nights and has an ale of the day offer. You can bring your own food, with cutlery provided. There is a selection of board games to choose from.
Q⇌🛏❤️🛜

Gundog

Crown Street, HX1 1JB
🕐 3-11 (10 Mon); 1-1am Fri & Sat; 1-11 Sun
☎ (01422) 380135
Bootleg Lawless; Stod Fold Gold; 4 changing beers (sourced regionally) Ⓗ
This Grade II-listed building dates from the 18th century, though the elaborate façade is Edwardian. Note the fine tiles in the entrance, the original terrazzo floor tiles, and the staircase. The open-plan room to the left has comfy seats and a bar billiards table. To the right is an enclosed room with fine original Edwardian panelling and leaded windows. The original tap room at the back has been opened out to provide additional space.
Q⇌♣🛏🛜

Pump Room Micropub Ⓛ

33 Northgate, HX1 1UR
🕐 2-9 Mon & Tue; 12-11 Wed-Sat; 11-10 Sun
6 changing beers (often Bingley, Mallinsons, Vocation) Ⓗ
Quirky, atmospheric, one-room micropub situated in an old Army recruiting office on Northgate, just across from the bus station. It takes its name from an old recently demolished pub on New Road – some of the artefacts, including a door from the old pub, have been incorporated into the new place. Behind the bar are glass panels with four shelves, the lower three hosting casks of real ale while the top shelf has real cider. Q🛏⇌●🛏❤️🛜

Three Pigeons ★ ✅

1 Sun Fold, HX1 2LX
🕐 4-11; 12-11 Fri-Sun ☎ (01422) 347001
Ossett Pale Gold, Big Red Bitter, Silver King; 5 changing beers (sourced nationally; often Fernandes, Jennings, Rat) Ⓗ
A Grade II-listed building rebuilt by Webster's Brewery in 1932 in an Art Deco style. The main feature is the octagonal stand-up drinking area by

the bar, from which three rooms radiate. A further two rooms can be found at the rear. The pub attracts a variety of local groups and societies, and welcomes football and Rugby League visitors to the nearby Shay ground. Q✿≈♣●🖫

Victorian Craft Beer Café

18-22 Powell Street, HX1 1LN
✪ 11-11; 12-10 Sun ⊕ victorian.beer
8 changing beers ⊞
This bar is behind the Halifax Victoria Theatre and can be easily missed due to lack of signage. On entering you find the main seating and drinking area, with a tiled bar and wooden floors. To the left is a more secluded area and steps to an upper level which offers several seating spaces. The handpumps are in two sets of five – the nearest to the door in each set dispenses the ciders. Q≈●🖫 ?

Harecroft

Station Hotel ℓ

122 Harecroft, BD15 0BP (on B6144)
✪ 4-midnight; 12-midnight Sun ☎ (01535) 272430
Timothy Taylor Landlord; 2 changing beers (often Cottage, Salamander) ⊞
In the heart of a small village between Bradford and Haworth, this homely community pub is named after a station on the long-gone Great Northern Railway. It comprises two linked rooms with real fires and a games room. A jazz/swing band plays on Monday night, as does the local pool team. The local bus runs Monday to Saturday until early evening. ♿✿♣P🖫(727)●

Hartshead

Hartshead ℓ

86 Prospect Road, WF15 8AY
✪ 5-11; 12-midnight Sat & Sun ☎ (01274) 873365
⊕ thehartshead.co.uk
Copper Dragon Scotts 1816; 3 changing beers (sourced regionally; often Abbeydale, Moorhouse's, Saltaire) ⊞
Attractive club in a rural location, founded 1895. The layout is open plan, featuring a large horseshoe bar, comfortable seating, full-size snooker table and a small stage regularly used for live music and open mic sessions on Fridays plus quiz night on Wednesdays. The friendly community club, popular with walkers and ramblers, also serves non-members and has carefully chosen guest beers. There are good views from the small beer garden. ♿✿♣P🖫(229,259)● ?

Haworth

Fleece Inn ℓ ✔

67 Main Street, BD22 8DA
✪ 11-11 (11.30 Fri & Sat); 11-10.30 Sun ☎ (01535) 642172
⊕ fleeceinnhaworth.co.uk
Timothy Taylor Golden Best, Boltmaker, Knowle Spring Blonde, Landlord, Ram Tam; 1 changing beer ⊞
Stone-built coaching inn on Haworth's famous cobbled Main Street with spectacular views over the Worth Valley and close to the KWVR historic heritage railway. A cosy room to the right and a dining area offer quiet alternatives to the busy bar. Accommodation and locally sourced food are available. Cyclists are welcome; there is safe bicycle storage for guests. The beer garden is three

storeys up from the bar, on the roof. The Fleece is popular with tourists and locals alike. ♿✿🖨🌶🍴👟≈♣🖫●?

Heath

King's Arms ★ ℓ ✔

Heath Common, WF1 5SL (at edge of Heath Village, off A655 Wakefield-Normanton road)
✪ 12-11 (midnight Fri & Sat) ☎ (01924) 377527
⊕ thekingsarmsheath.co.uk
Ossett Yorkshire Blonde, Silver King; Rat White Rat; house beer (by Ossett); 4 changing beers ⊞
The King's Arms, acquired by Clark's Brewery in 1989, is now leased to Ossett Brewery. Built in the early 1700s and converted into a public house in 1841, it comprises three oak-panelled rooms with gas lighting plus a conservatory and gardens to the rear. In the summer months you can sit outside and relax peacefully amid the acres of common grassland surrounding the area. There is a quiz on Tuesday. Time may be called early on quieter evenings. Q♿✿🖨🌶🍴♣P🖫(188)●?

Hebden Bridge

Calan's Micropub

3 The Courtyard, Bridge Gate, HX7 8EX (from A646 turn into Bridge Gate; at start of pedestrian section turn into yard on right)
✪ 12-8 (9 Wed & Thu; 10 Fri & Sat); closed Tue ☎ 07739 563983
5 changing beers (often Great Heck, Mallinsons, Vocation) ⊞
Calderdale's first micropub, set in a suntrap courtyard just off the main pedestrianised shopping street, is an intimate, friendly and welcoming experience. Five rotating ales, mainly from Northern microbreweries, are complemented by cider. No piped music or other distractions disturb the conversation, but there are books, cards and dominoes to while away the time. Dogs are welcome. Q✿≈♣●🖫●

Fox & Goose ℓ ✔

7 Heptonstall Road, HX7 6AZ (on A646 at bottom of Heptonstall Rd; on foot, walk through Hebden Bridge W along A646 towards Todmorden; pub is on your right)
✪ 12-midnight (2am Fri & Sat) ☎ (01422) 648052
⊕ foxandgoose.org
6 changing beers (sourced nationally; often Vocation) ⊞
West Yorkshire's first community co-operative pub has a small bar serving three flagstone-floored rooms. The main bar has a roaring fire in winter. The left-hand room is frequently used for live music events, while there is a dartboard in the room to the right. A welcoming, inclusive atmosphere and eclectic clientele ensure that customers who enter as strangers leave as friends. Beer festivals are held in May and November. Quiz night is Monday. Q✿♣●🖨🖫(590,592)●?

Old Gate Bar & Restaurant

1-5 Old Gate, HX7 8JP
✪ 10-midnight; 10-11 Sun ☎ (01422) 843993
⊕ oldgatehebden.co.uk
7 changing beers (sourced nationally; often Abbeydale, Marble, Vocation) ⊞
Smart, modern inn and restaurant on two floors with an impressive long copper-topped bar, whose 10 handpumps dispense the biggest selection of

real ales in the town, plus one rotating cider. Quality food is served all day. An eclectic mix of furniture and the large picture windows make it an ideal spot for relaxing with a pint and observing the comings and goings of Hebden's diverse and colourful population. At least one dark beer is always on the bar. Q ► ► ○ ○ ❅ ♣ ● ☾ ❀ ⓦ

Hemsworth

Hamelsworde Brewery Tap L
41B Kirkby Road, WF9 4BA (on road out of town past marketplace in direction of South Kirkby)
✪ closed Mon & Tue; 3-9; 5-11 Fri; 1-11 Sat; 1-6 Sun
☎ (01977) 619528 ⊕ hamelsworde.co.uk
6 changing beers (sourced locally; often Hamelsworde) ⓗ
A friendly, quirky, family-run pub with a great community spirit. All Hamelsworde beers are produced on site in a 2½-barrel plant. Locally sourced produce is part of the ethos. Six handpulls provide three Hamelsworde beers and three changing guest ales from local microbreweries. Bottled German beers are also stocked. A local food menu is offered on selected dates. Entertainment includes quiz night on the last Thursday of the month, occasional Meet the Brewer nights, brewery tours and mini-festivals. Private bookings are available. ► ❅ ○ ○ ● ☾ ⓦ

Heptonstall

White Lion
58 Towngate, HX7 7NB
✪ 12-midnight ☎ (01422) 842027
Goose Eye Chinook Blonde; Marston's Wainwright; 3 changing beers (sourced nationally; often Abbeydale, Leeds, Saltaire) ⓗ
Friendly local in the cobbled main street of a historic conservation village. The single bar serves two distinct drinking areas – to the left with a real fire in winter, and to the right, a piano and food service. A recently uncovered historic inglenook fireplace is in the corridor leading to the beer garden. The pub is developing a range of gins – currently there are 107 varieties. Irish music plays on Tuesday evening and quiz night is Thursday.
Q ❅ ○ ♣ ● ☾

Hipperholme

Travellers Inn L ✓
53 Tanhouse Hill, HX3 8HN (off A58)
✪ 12-11.30; 11-midnight Thu-Sat; 11-11 Sun
☎ (01422) 202434
Ossett Pale Gold, Yorkshire Blonde, Silver King, Excelsior; 4 changing beers (sourced locally; often Fernandes, Rat, Saltaire) ⓗ
Opposite the site of the former railway station, this 18th-century local has taken in adjoining cottages to create a series of distinct spaces. Well-behaved children and dogs on leads are welcome until 7pm. Thursday is quiz night. A covered and heated yard is provided for smokers. A dark beer is always among the guest ales from Ossett group breweries and other microbreweries. ► ❅ ♣ ● ☾ ⓦ

Holmfirth

Nook (Rose & Crown) L ✓
7 Victoria Square, HD9 2DN (down alley behind Barclays Bank)

✪ 11.30-midnight ☎ (01484) 682373
⊕ thenookbrewhouse.co.uk
Nook Yorks, Baby Blond, Rescue Red, Best, Blond, Oat Stout; 2 changing beers ⓗ
The Nook (properly, the Rose & Crown) is a well-known pub in the village dating from 1754, and has been dispensing beers from its own brewhouse since 2009. Guest beers and Pure North ciders are also available. Home-cooked food is served until 8pm. It has a popular folk evening every Sunday and real ale festivals on the weekend before Easter and August bank holiday. The log fire is particularly warming. The Tap House next door is under the same management.
► ❅ ○ ○ ♣ ● ☾ ⓦ

Horbury

Cricketers Arms L ✓
22 Cluntergate, WF4 5AG (in a right fork off the High St)
✪ 4-11; 12-midnight Fri & Sat; 12-11 Sun ☎ (01924) 267032
⊕ thecricketershorbury.co.uk
Bosun's Horbury Blond; Timothy Taylor Landlord; 6 changing beers ⓗ
On the edge of the town centre, this former Tetley's house is now a genuine free house. There is a frequent bus service to Wakefield, Ossett and Dewsbury. Poker night is Monday, quiz night Wednesday and open mic night the second Sunday of each month. Beer festivals take place in late May (Yankee Fest) and mid October (Oktoberfest). ❅ ♣ ● P ☾ ⓦ

Horbury Bridge

Bingley Arms L ✓
221 Bridge Road, WF4 5NL (on A642 by bridge over River Calder, facing viaduct)
✪ 4-11; 12-midnight Fri & Sat; 12-10.30 Sun
☎ (01924) 272838 ⊕ bingleyarms.co.uk
Ossett Silver King; 5 changing beers (sourced regionally) ⓗ
This pub, built in 1822, is bordered by the River Calder and the Aire & Calder Navigation Canal, and has its own moorings. It is named after the Earl of Bingley, who funded the building of the canal. It comprises two rooms, both with open fires, and is reputed to be haunted. Outside is a good-sized beer garden, home to the resident donkey, Nellie. There is folk music on Thursday evening. Functions can be catered for. ► ❅ ○ ♣ ● P ☾

Huddersfield

Corner
5 Market Walk, HD1 2QA
✪ 11-11 (midnight Fri & Sat); 12-11 Sun
House beer (by Mallinsons); 6 changing beers (sourced nationally; often Mallinsons, Outstanding, Vocation) ⓗ
With the brewing pedigree of Tara and Elaine at Mallinsons and the award-winning front of house persona of Sam Smith, something special was expected when this Mallinsons tap opened in September 2016. Those expectations have been fully realised. Seven cask ales are on offer, three Mallinsons and four rotating guests, always including a dark beer. A membership scheme gives a 10 per cent discount Sunday to Thursday. Food is available. A light, modern bar is on the first floor of the premises, with a function room on the second floor. ► ○ ❅ ● ☾ ⓦ

Grove 🅛

2 Spring Grove Street, HD1 4BP
🕒 2-11 (midnight Thu); 12-midnight Fri & Sat; 12-11 Sun
☎ (01484) 430113 ⊕ thegrove.pub
Marble Pint; Oakham Citra; Thornbridge Jaipur IPA; Timothy Taylor Landlord; changing beers (often Durham, Hawkshead, Northern Monk) 🅗
The Grove Inn has a phenomenal list of 19 cask ales. It has four permanent beers, five rotating brewery pumps and 10 beers representing breweries from across the UK. New breweries feature regularly, along with stouts and strong ales. In addition there is a superb list of 200-plus bottled beers. This is a friendly pub with quirky, surreal artwork. No food is served, but a unique range of bar snacks is on offer. Real cider is also sold here.
Q🌑🎈🚲🍴🖥️🐾🛜

King's Head 🅨

St George's Square, HD1 1JF (in station buildings, on left when exiting station)
🕒 11.30-11; 12-11 Sun ☎ (01484) 511058
Bradfield Farmers Blonde; Magic Rock Ringmaster; Timothy Taylor Golden Best, Landlord; 6 changing beers (sourced regionally; often Abbeydale, Oakham, Pictish) 🅗
Recent restoration work has revealed the superb high ceilings to complement the wonderful tiled floors. It is decorated to a high standard, and a new bar has been installed. Conveniently situated in the listed railway station, it has a warm and friendly atmosphere. Ten beers are available (four regular, six guest), sold at competitive prices. There are always two dark ales, and real cider is also stocked. Live music plays on Saturday afternoons. It can get busy at weekends. 🚲🍴🖥️🐾

Rat & Ratchet 🅛 ✅

40 Chapel Hill, HD1 3EB (on A616, just off ring road)
🕒 3-midnight (11 Mon); 12-midnight Fri & Sat; 12-11 Sun
☎ (01484) 542400
Ossett Yorkshire Blonde, Silver King; Rat White Rat, King Rat; 8 changing beers (sourced regionally; often Acorn, Fernandes, Riverhead) 🅗
Multi award-winning pub, now dwarfed by Kirklees College. It is owned by Ossett, but has its own on-site Rat microbrewery. The 12 handpumps offer beers from both of these, and other breweries. A good range of ciders and perries is also available. The large open-plan main area still retains the feel of separate rooms. A further room at the back leads to the outside drinking area. A popular quiz is on Wednesday. 🌑🍴♣🍴P🖥️🐾🛜

Sportsman ★ 🅛 ✅

1 St John's Road, HD1 5AY
🕒 12-11; 11-midnight Fri & Sat; 11.30-11 Sun
☎ (01484) 421929
Timothy Taylor Boltmaker; 7 changing beers (sourced regionally; often Mallinsons, North Riding Brewery) 🅗
This 1930s pub, with a 1950s refit by Hammonds (note the windows), has won a CAMRA English Heritage Conservation Pub Design award. The superb curved bar has eight handpumps, including a dedicated Mallinsons beer pump. Guest beers often include some from North Riding. A stout/porter is usually available, along with two ciders, one from Pure North. The central bar has a parquet floor and an interesting wooden entrance, and the two rooms off are regularly used for meetings. 🌑🍴🚲🍴🖥️🐾🛜

Star 🅛

7 Albert Street, Folly Hall, HD1 3PJ (off A616)
🕒 closed Mon; 5 (12 Sat)-11; 11.30-10.30 Sun
☎ (01484) 545443 ⊕ thestarinn.info
Pictish Brewers Gold; Timothy Taylor Landlord; 9 changing beers (often Briggs Signature Ales, Mallinsons, Timothy Taylor) 🅗
Multi award-winning local which has featured in this Guide for many years. It is a showcase for new breweries, with changing ales sourced countrywide, plus dedicated pumps for Taylor, Mallinsons and a dark beer. It has no jukebox, pool table or games machine, but there is lively conversation around the bar and a real fire in winter. The ambience is summed up by a sign that reads 'Be nice or leave'. Three beer festivals are held annually. Q🍴🌑🖥️🐾🛜

Ilkley

Crescent Inn

Brook Street, LS29 8DG (within Crescent Hotel)
🕒 12-11 (midnight Fri & Sat) ☎ (01943) 811250
⊕ thecrescentinn.co.uk
Goose Eye Bitter; Ilkley Crossroads IPA; Leeds Funfair; Saltaire Blonde; 4 changing beers (sourced regionally; often Brass Castle, Phoenix) 🅗
Busy town-centre bar occupying the ground floor of a 19th-century hotel. Furnishings are smart, while original internal finishes are retained. Eight real ales are always on the bar and the guests are usually from local and regional breweries such as Brass Castle and Phoenix. Bar meals are served until 9.30pm, with meal deals during the week. There is also an adjacent bistro restaurant. It has full disabled facilities but the rear door provides best access. 🌑🍴🛏️🐾♿🚲🖥️🐾🛜

Flying Duck 🅛 ✅

16 Church Street, LS29 9DS (on A65)
🕒 12-11; 11-12.30am Fri & Sat ☎ (01943) 609587
Wharfedale Black, Blonde, Best; 6 changing beers (sourced regionally; often Dark Horse) 🅗
Originally constructed as a farmhouse in 1709, this is reputed to be Ilkley's oldest pub building. Substantially refurbished and reopened in late 2013, this Grade II-listed building retains many original features such as the York stone, oak flooring, beamed ceilings, internal stonework and mullioned windows. Up to nine real ales and two real ciders are sold. Wharfedale Brewery is to the rear and tours can be arranged. The first-floor function room includes a bar. 🌑🍴🛏️🚲🍴🖥️🐾🛜

Keighley

Brown Cow 🅛

5 Cross Street, BD21 2LQ
🕒 4-11; 12-10.30 Sun ⊕ browncowkeighley.co.uk
Timothy Taylor Golden Best, Landlord; 5 changing beers 🅗
Family-run community local where a no-bad-language policy is in force. The ethos of this award-winning free house is quality, beer choice and customer comfort. The pub is adorned with local breweriana, including the original sign from the entrance to Bradford's now-defunct Trough Brewery. The back room can be booked for meetings. Five guest beers, often from local micros, usually include a dark beer and one beer at a higher strength. Discounted beer on Super Saver Sunday is popular. 🌑🍴♣🍴P🖥️🐾🛜

Livery Rooms ●

89-97 North Street, BD21 3AA

✪ 8am-midnight ☎ (01535) 682950

Greene King Abbot; Ruddles Best Bitter; Sharp's Doom Bar; 5 changing beers Ⓗ

Substantial, open-plan Wetherspoon with several partially enclosed raised areas. In times past the building has been a stables, home to the Temperance Movement, a bingo hall and a row of shops. This varied history is illustrated using artworks throughout the pub. Handy for the bus station, services to Burnley, Ilkley and Skipton stop outside the door. Alcohol is served from 9am.
Ⓨ☼◑ᕼ☂♿🐾🍴🚍🛜

Lord Rodney Bar & Kitchen Ⓛ ●

Church Street, BD21 5HT

✪ 11.30-11 (2am Fri & Sat); 12-10 Sun ☎ (01535) 603053

⊕ lordrodney.co.uk

Timothy Taylor Golden Best, Boltmaker, Knowle Spring Blonde, Landlord Ⓗ

On the site of Keighley's oldest pub, the Olde Red Lion, the Lord Rodney is next to the parish church and offers a splendid view along North Street. A Timothy Taylor-managed house, it is a bright and modern town-centre pub. A variety of furniture from tall stools to armchairs surrounds the bar in the long single room, warmed by a real fire. A separate eating area leads to a heated beer garden at the rear. Ⓨ☼◑ᕼ☂🚍🐾🛜

Kirkheaton

Yeaton Cask

4 Town Road, HD5 0HW

✪ 4-9 Mon; 4-11 Tue & Wed; 12-11 Thu; 12-11.30 Fri & Sat; 12-10.30 Sun ☎ 07796 641003

Marston's Wainwright; 5 changing beers Ⓗ

Formerly the Junction, the pub was bought as a true free house by the current owner in 2010. Beautiful furniture and flooring with the backdrop of striking exposed stonework give a traditional yet contemporary feel. Two permanent ales are served including the house beer from a secret West Yorkshire microbrewery. Five changing guests are sourced countrywide, always including a dark beer. Food is not available but there is complimentary bar food daily. A highly rated beer festival is held in October. Q❄Ⓨ♣🚍(262)🐾🛜

Ledsham

Chequers Inn Ⓛ

Claypit Lane, LS25 5LP

✪ 11-11; 12-6 Sun ☎ (01977) 683135

⊕ thechequersinn.com

Leeds Best; Theakston Best Bitter; Timothy Taylor Landlord; house beer (by Brown Cow); 1 changing beer (sourced locally; often Brown Cow) Ⓗ

Close to the oldest church in Yorkshire and handy for Fairburn Ings RSPB reserve, this delightful 16th-century country pub is popular for its good food and Yorkshire beers. The entrance, past the stepped garden area is through a stone-flagged yard. A passageway inside opens up at the bar and divides into rooms at either side with low beams and open fires. These in turn each lead to another cosy room complete with local photographs and other memorabilia.
Q☼◑P🚍(175,405)🛜

Leeds: City Centre

Duck & Drake Ⓛ ●

43 Kirkgate, LS2 7DR

✪ 10-11 (midnight Fri & Sat); 11-11 Sun ☎ (0113) 245 5432

⊕ duckndrake.co.uk

Brains Bitter; Rooster's Yankee; Saltaire Blonde; Theakston Old Peculier; Timothy Taylor Landlord; York Centurion's Ghost Ale; 9 changing beers (sourced locally; often Abbeydale, Elland, Salamander) Ⓗ

Victorian corner pub whose marble door jambs are a fine example of the era. There are a number of original light fittings and some of the floorboards have survived 200 years of trade. The central bar, with 15 handpumps, sits in between and serves both rooms. As a pub noted for the quality of its live music, it is appropriate that the front room has a mural on the back wall depicting many blues and rock legends. 🅿🚆🍴🚍🐾🛜

Foleys Tap House Ⓛ

159 The Headrow, LS1 5RG

✪ 12-11; 11-1am Fri & Sat; 12-10 Sun ☎ (0113) 242 9674

⊕ mrfoleysleeds.co.uk

York Guzzler, Centurion's Ghost Ale; 8 changing beers (sourced locally; often Brass Castle, Hardknott, York) Ⓗ

Four beers from York Brewery's range plus eight guest beers are usually on offer at this city-centre pub. Also available is a wide range of real ciders, along with bottled beers from around the world. The building is an impressive edifice built of Portland stone and previously owned by the Pearl Assurance Company. The company was founded by Patrick James Foley, hence the name of the pub. The interior is on several levels. ☂🚆🍴🚍🐾

Head of Steam Ⓛ

13 Mill Hill, LS1 5DQ

✪ 11-midnight (1am Fri & Sat); 12-11 Sun

☎ (0113) 243 6618 ⊕ theheadofsteam.co.uk

9 changing beers (sourced locally; often Camerons, Northern Monk, Timothy Taylor) Ⓗ

A large single-room pub with a central island bar loaded with nine handpumps serving a variety of brews from Yorkshire and the North-east. If none of these tickle your fancy then there are a further 20 or more international beers on draught as well as a selection of bottles and cans in the fridges. Comfortable seating and proximity to the railway station makes this a busy pub enjoyed by people from all walks of life. 🚆🍴🚍🐾🛜

Hop Ⓛ ●

Granary Wharf, Dark Neville Street, LS1 4BR

✪ 12-midnight ☎ (0113) 243 9854 ⊕ thehop-leeds.co.uk

Ossett Yorkshire Blonde, Big Red Bitter, Silver King, Excelsior; 6 changing beers (sourced locally; often Ilkley, Rat, Thornbridge) Ⓗ

Beneath the arches of Leeds station's platform 17, the Hop serves 10 real ales from the Ossett family of brewers, together with several guests and real cider. The bar is surrounded by comfortable seating with bare-brick walls decorated with murals and pictures depicting rock bands. The stairs on either side of the bar lead to another seating area which hosts live music. A good-value pie and pint deal is available. ☼◑🚆🍴🚍🛜

Lamb & Flag Ⓛ

1 Church Row, LS2 7HD

✪ 11-11 (midnight Thu-Sat); 11-10.30 Sun

☎ (0113) 243 1255 ⊕ lambandflagleeds.co.uk

Leeds Pale, Yorkshire Gold, Best, Midnight Bell; 4 changing beers (sourced regionally; often Camerons, RedWillow, Rooster's) Ⓗ

A stone's throw from Leeds minster, this 19th-century building has been tastefully restored to its former usage – as a pub – with no expense spared. A suntrap rear courtyard is overlooked by an upstairs balcony. The upstairs bar has two handpulls while the downstairs bar has eight. Plenty of exposed brickwork is in evidence, as are high ceilings, big open windows and oak beams, and there are a number of distinct drinking areas. ᗷ✦ⓓ🏛ⓓ❧🚃🐾🛜

North Bar Ⓛ

24 New Briggate, LS1 6NU

🕙 11-2am (1am Mon & Tue); 12-midnight Sun
☎ (0113) 242 4540

North Prototype; 4 changing beers (sourced locally; often Magic Rock, Ridgeside, Thornbridge) Ⓗ

Opened in 1997, this was the first of the continuing wave of new bars opening in the city centre. The bar along one wall has five handpumps and a large range of beers from around the world both on draught and in bottles. Behind the bar are tankards belonging to staff and regulars. The wooden-floored drinking area has wooden chairs and tables, and pictures from local artists on the wall. Bar food such as pork pies and cheese platters are on offer. ⓓ❧🚃👕🚃

Reliance

76-78 North Street, LS2 7PN

🕙 12-11 (midnight Fri & Sat); 11-10.30 Sun
☎ (0113) 295 6060 🌐 the-reliance.co.uk

House beer (by Acorn); 3 changing beers (sourced locally; often Rooster's) Ⓗ

On the northern fringes of town, this light and laid-back pub can be identified by its tall windows and the inevitable bicycle parked outside. The bar offerings and food menu are always interesting, and includes the pub's popular charcuterie, cured in the kitchen. Eat in the bare-boarded bar area or the dining room behind the bar. Handpulled cider, board games and Sunday quizzes make this a great city local. One handpump is dedicated to Rooster's Brewery beers. 🏛ⓓ👕🚃

Scarbrough Hotel Ⓛ ✅

Bishopgate Street, LS1 5DY

🕙 10-midnight (1am Fri & Sat); 8am-10 Sun
☎ (0113) 243 4590

St Austell Nicholson's Pale Ale; Tetley Bitter; 5 changing beers (sourced regionally; often Adnams, Great Heck, Vocation) Ⓗ

Being close to Leeds railway station, the Scarbrough is great for a swift one before your train, as well as for longer stays relaxing in the comfortable seating at either end of the long bar, which is opposite the entrance. The selection of ales includes guests both from local breweries and those further afield. The building dates from 1765 and became a pub in 1826. It is named after Henry Scarbrough, the first owner of the pub. 🏛ⓓ👕🚃🛜

Stick or Twist Ⓛ ✅

Podium Buildings, Merrion Way, LS2 8PD

🕙 8am-midnight (1am Fri & Sat) ☎ (0113) 234 9748

Greene King IPA, Abbot; Sharp's Doom Bar; 9 changing beers (sourced locally; often Elland, Kelham Island, Ossett) Ⓗ

The oldest Wetherspoon pub in Leeds, the Stick remains a local in the city, despite its close proximity to the newer Arena —it can get busy at showtimes. Very wide, with an outdoor patio to match, it has more handpulls than you can shake a stick at —12 in total —and the usual all-day menu, good bottle selection and vibrant atmosphere you associate with the chain. A former casino, it is now a well-established CAMRA award-winning pub. Q🏛🍴ⓓ👕🚃🛜

Tapped Leeds

51 Boar Lane, LS1 5EL

🕙 11-11 (midnight Thu; 1am Fri & Sat) ☎ (0113) 244 1953

13 changing beers (sourced regionally; often Tapped Sheffield) Ⓗ

This modern bar consists of one room with a bar to the right of the entrance and brewing equipment to the left. Tapped Brewing Company real ales are usually brewed at Tapped's sister pub on Sheffield station. Clipboards above the bar give details of the 13 cask beers available; the house beers are shown in yellow. There are no handpumps but the lower set of taps on the back wall dispense the real ale. Food includes the popular Big Dan's pizzas. ⓓ👕🚃🛜

Templar Ⓛ ✅

2 Templar Street, LS2 7NU

🕙 11-11; 12-10.30 Sun ☎ (0113) 243 0318

Tetley Bitter; 7 changing beers (sourced locally; often Abbeydale, Acorn, Ilkley) Ⓗ

The Templar has eight handpulls serving ales both from local breweries and those further afield, which can be enjoyed in great surroundings. The interior features wooden panels, still with their service bells in place, while the outside is adorned with green and cream glazed Burmantoft tiles. The bowing courtier logo can be seen in the leaded window panes from when it was a Melbourne Brewery pub. There are large-screen TVs throughout the pub showing a range of sporting events. 🚃♣🚃

Veritas Ale & Wine Bar Ⓛ

43 Great George Street, LS1 3BB

🕙 11-11 (midnight Fri & Sat); 12-7 Sun ☎ (0113) 242 8094

Ilkley Mary Jane; Okells Manx Pale Ale; Timothy Taylor Boltmaker; 5 changing beers (sourced locally; often Kirkstall, Ridgeside, Rooster's) Ⓗ

Part of the Market Town Taverns local chain. The pub has an L-shaped continental café-style open-plan layout but with separate areas and levels. The large shop front-type windows afford a fine view of Gilbert Scott's classic Leeds General Infirmary building which is opposite. The five guest beers are mainly from local breweries. Other beers from around the world are also sold both in bottle and on draught. Qⓓ👕🚃🚃👕🏛

Victoria Family & Commercial Hotel Ⓛ

28 Great George Street, LS1 3DL

🕙 11-11.30 (midnight Fri & Sat); 12-10 Sun
☎ (0113) 245 1386

St Austell Nicholson's Pale Ale; Tetley Bitter; 4 changing beers (sourced locally; often Kirkstall, Leeds, Rooster's) Ⓗ

Hidden away behind Leeds town hall and built by the Victoria Hotel Company in 1865 as a 28-room hotel to accommodate visitors to the Assizes Court, the building has an impressive Victorian exterior and an ornate interior with high ceilings. There is a long main bar area and two separate rooms, all of which feature an array of polished wood and shiny brass. The guest beers are a selection both of local ales and beers from around the country. ⑪➡≒🖴🐾🛜

Wapentake 🅛

92 Kirkgate, LS2 7DJ

⚙ 7.30am-11 (9 Mon); 10-11 Sat; 10-9 Sun

☎ (0113) 243 6248

Sharp's Atlantic; 3 changing beers (sourced locally; often Kirkstall, Northern Monk, Ridgeside) Ⓗ

Referring to a parcel of land in northern England, as far as dedication to local produce and community goes, the pub name could not be more apt. This little bar and bakery has many strings to its bow. It makes its own bread and cakes, serves meals using locally sourced ingredients, and of course has a good range of real ales and bottles, predominantly from Leeds and Yorkshire. Wapentake is welcoming and woody, with a locally customised piano, sports TV upstairs and friendly bartenders. 🐾⑪➡≒🖴🐾🛜

Whitelock's Ale House ★ 🅛 ✅

Turk's Head Yard, LS1 6HB (off Briggate)

⚙ 11-midnight (1am Fri & Sat); 11-11 Sun

☎ (0113) 245 3950 🌐 whitelocksleeds.com

Ilkley Mary Jane; Kirkstall Pale Ale; Theakston Best Bitter, Old Peculier; Timothy Taylor Landlord; 6 changing beers (sourced locally; often Acorn, Great Heck, Saltaire) Ⓗ

Described by John Betjeman as the very heart of Leeds, Whitelock's dates from 1715 and occupies a long narrow yard. The interior is unchanged from 1895 and has been identified by CAMRA as having a nationally important historic pub interior. The pub is a feast of mirrors, woodwork, stained glass and has a fine faience bar, making this a must-visit hostelry. A new modern bar, The Turk's Head, with two real ales, is further up the yard. 🐾⑪➡🍴🖴🐾🛜

Leeds: Headingley

Arcadia Ale House 🅛 ✅

34 Arndale Centre, Otley Road, LS6 2UE (corner of Alma Road)

⚙ 12-11 ☎ (0113) 274 5599

Okells Manx Pale Ale; Timothy Taylor Boltmaker; 6 changing beers (sourced locally; often Elland, Ilkley, Rooster's) Ⓗ

This cleverly converted bank is now a well-established and multi award-winning pub. There are two ground-floor rooms plus an upstairs mezzanine level. The unusual modern decor includes a chandelier formed of foreign beer crates. Eight real ales are offered along with a range of foreign bottled and draught beers plus a cider. There is also a wide selection of gins, some locally produced. Children, large groups (over eight people) and fancy dress are not permitted. Q♿🍴🖴🐾🛜

Woodies Craft Ale House 🅛 ✅

104 Otley Road, LS16 5JG

⚙ 11-11 (11.30 Thu; midnight Fri & Sat) ☎ (0113) 278 4393

🌐 woodies-leeds.co.uk

Greene King IPA; Ilkley Pale; Leeds Pale; Saltaire Blonde; 8 changing beers (sourced locally; often Kirkstall, Naylor's, Rooster's) Ⓗ

Roadside pub which over time has been opened out into a single space with a bar along one wall and drinking areas on three sides. Twelve real ales

are usually dispensed. The eclectic decor includes a range of differently upholstered furniture. Two satellite TV boxes enable different events to be shown at the same time. This is the starting point of the well known Otley Run pub crawl, so can be busy in the early evening. Quiz nights are Thursday and Sunday. 🐾⑪♿🖴🐾🛜

Leeds: Holbeck

Cross Keys 🅛

107 Water Lane, LS11 5WD

⚙ 12-11 (midnight Fri & Sat); 12-10.30 Sun

☎ (0113) 243 3711

North Prototype; 3 changing beers (sourced locally; often Kirkstall, North, Rooster's) Ⓗ

The Cross Keys is owned by the North Bar pub group and has plenty to offer both drinkers and diners. The ground floor has a small food area to the left, and a larger traditional pub area to the right with four handpumps. Upstairs is a function room which is available to hire and has two handpumps. To the rear is a courtyard drinking area. There is a selection of mainly British bottled beers and some Trappist-style bottles. 🐾⑪♿➡🖴🐾🛜

Grove Inn 🅛

Back Row, LS11 5PL

⚙ 11-midnight ☎ (0113) 244 2085

🌐 thegroveinnleeds.co.uk

Daleside Blonde; 7 changing beers (sourced regionally; often Acorn, Moorhouse's, Stancill) Ⓗ

A traditional Yorkshire pub nestled among modern offices. Eight real ales from local and regional breweries are served from the bar, with service both to the public bar and corridor. There are two small side rooms and the Concert Room to the rear which houses an eclectic range of music including, every Friday since 1962, reputedly the oldest folk club in the world. Live music features six nights a week, with a live band playing every Thursday, Saturday and Sunday night. 🐾⑪➡🍴🖴🐾🛜

Midnight Bell 🅛

101 Water Lane, LS11 5QN

⚙ 12-11 (midnight Fri & Sat) ☎ (0113) 244 5044

🌐 midnightbell.co.uk

Leeds Pale, Yorkshire Gold, Best, Midnight Bell; 2 changing beers (sourced locally; often Rooster's, Sonnet 43) Ⓗ

In the regenerated area to the south of the River Aire known as the Holbeck Urban Village, this award-winning pub caters for office workers, diners and discerning drinkers who can enjoy the Leeds Brewery range of beers in a relaxed atmosphere. To the rear of the building is a pleasant courtyard area, which in the warmer weather is served from the bar via a hatch. The upstairs area is more food-oriented. Real cider is available in the summer months. 🐾⑪♿➡🖴🐾🛜

Leeds: Hyde Park

Brudenell Social Club 🅛

33 Queen's Road, LS6 1NY

⚙ 11-1am ☎ (0113) 275 2411 🌐 brudenellsocialclub.co.uk

Kirkstall Pale Ale, Three Swords; 3 changing beers (sourced locally; often Northern Monk, Saltaire, Summer Wine) Ⓗ

A three-roomed premises with two music rooms and a games room with six sports TVs. Bar service is from the larger music room and the games room. Live music plays most days of the week, with artists of international status regularly booked. Voted LiveUK Best Small Music Venue 2015/16 and Yorkshire Gig Guide's Venue of the Year 2015 and 2016. An annual beer festival is held in January with around 40 beers and up to 18 ciders and perries. ✪◑&≈♣♠P🍴(56)👟🐾🛜

Leeds: Kirkstall

Kirkstall Bridge Inn ▼ ⓛ

12 Bridge Road, LS5 3BW
✪ 12-11.30 (12.30am Fri & Sat) ☎ (0113) 278 4044
⊕ kirkstallbridge.co.uk

Kirkstall Pale Ale, Three Swords, Dissolution IPA, Black Band Porter; 4 changing beers (sourced regionally; often Butcombe, Okells, Thornbridge) Ⓗ
Located on the bank of the River Aire, with a stunning garden/outdoor drinking area. Entering the pub from the car park via the downstairs bar, a staircase leads up to the centre of the main bar. The walls of the premises are hung with memorabilia from long-gone breweries. A regular award winner, it was local CAMRA Pub of the Year 2014-2016. Booking is advised if planning to dine here on a Saturday or Sunday. ✪◑♣P🍴👟🛜

Leeds: Meanwood

East of Arcadia ⓛ ✅

607 Meanwood Road, LS6 4HQ
✪ 11-11 (midnight Fri & Sat); 12-11 Sun ☎ (0113) 275 5488

Leeds Pale; Okells Manx Pale Ale; Timothy Taylor Boltmaker; 5 changing beers (sourced locally; often Ilkley, Ridgeside) Ⓗ
This modern bar occupies a prominent corner position in the heart of Meanwood. Open plan and on one level, there is a carpeted area which follows the sweep of tall windows curving around the pub. Closer to the bar there is a bare-boarded area with large casks which have been converted to small tables complete with foot rails. The light-coloured walls display international breweriana. Beers from Ridgeside and Ilkley breweries are normally available. Quiz night is on Wednesday. ⛵◑&🍴👟🛜

Leeds: Newlay

Abbey Inn ⓛ

99 Pollard Lane, LS13 1EQ (vehicle access from B6157 only)
✪ 12-11 ☎ (0113) 258 1248 ⊕ abbeyinn.org

8 changing beers (sourced locally; often Kirkstall, Leeds, Ossett) Ⓗ
Solid stone-built former farmhouse, dating from 1714, between the River Aire and the Leeds-Liverpool canal. Tuesday is a traditional folk night, Wednesday is pool league and games night, on Thursday there is a music quiz. Saturday has free live music and a general knowledge quiz takes place on Sunday. There is plenty of outside seating. A popular beer and music festival is held in July each year. One of the handpumps is dedicated to dark beers. ⛵✪◑&♣♠P👟

Linthwaite

Sair ⓛ ✅

139 Lane Top, HD7 5SG (top of Hoyle Ing, off A62)
✪ 5 (12 Sat)-11; 12-10.30 Sun ☎ (01484) 842370

Linfit Bitter, Gold Medal, Special, Swift, Autumn Gold, Old Eli Ⓗ
High on the edge of the Colne Valley, the Sair has been home to Linfit Brewery since 1982. It is a traditional multi-roomed stone building with a central bar and real fires. The beer range is the ultimate in LocAle, with up to 10 ales unique to the pub, including three dark brews, and real cider from Pure North. It is a popular community venue providing a welcome for all – locals, visitors, walkers and their dogs alike. A former CAMRA National Pub of the Year. Q✪♣♠🐾🛜

Liversedge

Black Bull ⓛ ✅

37 Halifax Road, WF15 6JR (on A649, close to A62)
✪ 12-midnight (1am Fri & Sat) ☎ (01924) 403779

Ossett Pale Gold, Yorkshire Blonde, Big Red Bitter, Silver King, Excelsior; 4 changing beers (sourced nationally) Ⓗ
Ossett Brewery's first pub. The five rooms each have a unique, skilfully honed style, including one dubbed the Chapel with a high ceiling and a mix of tasteful artefacts. A new, covered area by the stream outside adds to the choices. Nine handpumps always offer a mild or dark ale, plus good guest beers from the group and from independents. A regular Guide entry, the Black Bull is a popular, sociable community local with a warm welcome. Quiz night is Tuesday. ⛵✪&♣P👟🛜

Longwood

Dusty Miller Inn ⓛ ✅

2 Gilead Road, HD3 4XH
✪ 5-11; 4-midnight Fri; 12-midnight Sat; 12-11 Sun ☎ 07946 589645 ⊕ dustymillerlongwood.com

Milltown Platinum Blonde, Black Jack Porter, Weaver's Bitter; Timothy Taylor Landlord; 3 changing beers (often Phoenix, Pictish, Rooster's) Ⓗ
A Punch house, but operated by local brewery Milltown as its brewery tap. Local historic photographs adorn the walls, and stone floors dominate in this multi-roomed, cosy pub. From the outside benches there are great views of the Colne Valley. It is dog friendly and a haven for walkers. Seven real ales are served – three permanent beers from Milltown, Taylor Landlord and three rotating guests. A dark beer is always on offer. You can also get a locally made pie with chutney. Q⛵♣♠(356)👟🛜

Marsden

Riverhead Brewery Tap ⓛ ✅

Peel Street, HD7 6BR
✪ 12-midnight ☎ (01484) 844324
⊕ theriverheadmarsden.co.uk

Ossett Yorkshire Blonde, Silver King; Riverhead Butterley Bitter, March Haigh, Redbrook Premium; 5 changing beers Ⓗ
A brewpub since 1995, now owned by Ossett Brewery, and welcoming to all. The brewery is visible from the bar – beers do not get more LocAle than this. Ten ales are available – four from the on-site brewery, two from Ossett, plus guests. A dark beer is usually on the bar and occasionally real cider. A popular stop on the Real Ale Rail Trail, Saturdays are extremely busy. Great food is served in the restaurant and there is a riverside terrace for alfresco drinking. ⛵✪◑&≈♠P🍴(185)👟🛜

Middlestown

Little Bull 🄻

72 New Road, WF4 4NR (on A642 at crossroads in centre of village)
✪ 12-11.30 (12.30am Thu-Sat) ☎ (01924) 726142
⊕ thelittlebull.co.uk
Abbeydale Deception; Rat White Rat; 3 changing beers (sourced locally) Ⓗ
This pub has been established since 1814 and is free of tie. Beers come from local and regional breweries, alongside a range of world bottled beers. All food is locally sourced and home cooked. A single bar services a number of smaller rooms, and there is an open fire in colder weather. The National Coal Mining Museum is nearby. Meals are served 12-3pm (4pm Sun) daily and 5-9pm Wednesday and Thursday, plus steak night on the first Friday of the month. A beer festival is on the last weekend in July. Q 🛇 🏵 ◑ Ⓟ 🚍 (232,128) 🐾 📶

Mirfield

Flowerpot 🄻 ✅

65 Calder Road, WF14 8NN (over river, 400yds S of railway station)
✪ 12-12.30am (1.30am Fri & Sat); 12-midnight Sun
☎ (01924) 496939
Ossett Yorkshire Blonde, Big Red Bitter, Silver King, Excelsior; 4 changing beers (often Acorn, Marston's, Riverhead) Ⓗ
An 1807 pub, sensitively and tastefully restored by Ossett Brewery, comprising three rooms, all with real fires, off the central bar, which features an impressive tiled flowerpot. The riverside terrace is popular in good weather. There are eight ales on offer from Ossett, Rat, Riverhead, Fernandes and independents, including a mild or stout, plus a rotating cider. Local farm shop Haigh's supplies five different pies with peas, served until 4pm Monday to Saturday. There is a quiz on Tuesday.
Q 🛇 🏵 ◑ 🕭 ♿ ⇄ ♣ ♠ Ⓟ 🚍 (262) 🐾 📶

Navigation Tavern

6 Station Road, WF14 8NL (next to railway station)
✪ 11.30-11; 12-11 Sun ☎ (01924) 492476
Caledonian Deuchars IPA; John Smith's Bitter; Theakston Black Bull Bitter, Lightfoot, XB, Old Peculier; 3 changing beers (sourced nationally) Ⓗ
A canalside free house serving eight regular beers including five from Theakston, plus up to four guests at weekends, all at keen prices. The pub features on the Transpennine Rail Ale Trail and holds renowned beer festivals twice a year. It hosts Saturday night entertainment and active sports and pool teams. A large function room and en-suite B&B with stairlift are available, and winter heating is aided by a large wood-burning fire.
🛇 🏵 🕭 🔥 ♿ ⇄ ♣ Ⓟ 🚍 📶

Old Colonial

Dunbottle Lane, WF14 9JJ (off A644 up Church Lane, 1 mile NE of station)
✪ 5-11; 12-midnight Fri & Sat; 12-10 Sun ☎ (01924) 496920
⊕ theoldcolonial.webplus.net/index.html
Copper Dragon Best Bitter; 3 changing beers Ⓗ
Former club with fascinating colonial memorabilia offering a cosy retreat with sofas around the fire. There is a Royal British Legion memorial in the prize-winning garden and local charities are well supported. The spacious conservatory is popular for functions and meetings. Three to five guests, including a dark ale, from the likes of Thwaites,

Lees and Marston's, and small brewers, are dispensed. Evening meals are served Thursday to Saturday and the excellent-value Sunday lunch is recommended. 🛇 🏵 ◑ Ⓟ 🚍 (202,205) 📶

Mytholmroyd

Dusty Miller 🄻 ✅

Burnley Road, HX7 5LH
✪ 12-11 ☎ (01422) 885959 ⊕ dustymillerinn.co.uk
Elland Nettlethrasher; 2 changing beers (sourced locally; often Trinity, Vocation) Ⓗ
Built in 1760, this former coaching inn has a rich history, mainly associated with the Cragg Vale Coiners who reputedly held regular meetings here. This Grade II-listed building, originally a farmhouse and an adjoining barn, is open as a drinking venue seven days a week. The pub entrance, from the main Burnley Road, leads to the bar area to the left which has a natural tiled floor. There are regular bus services stopping right outside the pub.
Q 🛇 🏵 🛏 ⇄ ≠ Ⓟ 🚍 🐾 📶

Norristhorpe

Rising Sun 🄻

254 Norristhorpe Lane, WF15 7AN (turn off A62 by Yew Tree pub, then ½ mile on right)
✪ 12-11.30 (12.30am Fri & Sat) ☎ (01924) 400190
Acorn Barnsley Bitter; Saltaire Blonde; 5 changing beers (sourced locally; often Bradfield, Partners, Timothy Taylor) Ⓗ
Now under family ownership, this village local has been tastefully refurbished inside and out, featuring cosy lounge areas with exposed brickwork and several real fires, plus an open, light and spacious bar area. The seven beers on offer are mainly from Yorkshire. There are fine views across the valley from the attractive beer garden, and a smoking area with seating. Outdoor music and barbecues are held in summer. 🛇 🏵 ♣ Ⓟ 🚍 🐾 📶

Ossett

Bier Huis 🄻

17 Towngate, WF5 9BL (in shopping precinct opp town hall)
✪ 9.30am-6.30 (8 Fri & Sat); 11-3 Sun ☎ (01924) 565121
⊕ bierhuis.co.uk
3 changing beers (sourced locally; often Whippet) Ⓗ
A beer shop selling bottled beers from many Yorkshire breweries and also an extensive selection of foreign bottled beers. Two draught beers come mainly from Bradfield and Saltaire breweries and can be drunk on the premises. Meet the Brewer evenings are held at regular intervals and brewery visits are popular. It also holds Thirsty Friday events when more beers are on draught.
Q 🛇 ♿ ♠ Ⓟ 🚇 🚍 📶

Brewers Pride 🄻

Low Mill Road, Healey, WF5 8ND (bottom of Healey Rd, 1½ miles from town centre)
✪ 12-11; 12-10.30 Sun ☎ (01924) 273865
⊕ brewers-pride.co.uk
Rudgate Ruby Mild; 8 changing beers (often Horbury Ales) Ⓗ
An independent free house on the outskirts of Ossett, in what is now largely the Healey Mills industrial area close to the Calder & Hebble canal. Two regular beers plus eight guest ales are stocked. Bar meals are served lunchtimes and

Miller's Restaurant is open Friday and Saturday evenings and Sunday midday onwards. Themed evenings are Monday pies, Tuesday tapas, Wednesday and Thursday specials. Monday is also quiz night. Live music features on the first Saturday of the month and a beer festival on the August bank holiday, with charity events throughout the year. Q ⊃ ⊛ ◑ ♣ ● ☰ (102) ✿

Old Vic 🄻 ✅

47 Manor Road, South Ossett, WF5 0AU (Manor Rd is a left turn from B6128 at S end of Ossett, or a right turn from The Green near Ossett School)
✪ 4-11; 12-midnight Fri & Sat; 12-11 Sun ☎ (01924) 273516
Fuller's London Pride; Ossett Pale Gold, Yorkshire Blonde, Silver King, Excelsior; 2 changing beers (often Abbeydale) Ⓗ
Friendly local pub, previously known as the Victoria, a 10-minute walk from Ossett town centre. Fresh home-cooked food is served. Two varying guest beers and an alternating stout or porter complement the regular well-kept beers. Taken over by Ossett Brewery a couple of years ago, this pub has undergone a renaissance. It holds a beer festival in November featuring beers from every brewery in the local CAMRA branch area.
⊃ ⊛ ◑ ♿ ♣ ● P ☰ ✿ ☞

Otley

Junction Inn 🄻

44 Bondgate, LS21 1AD
✪ 11-11 (11.30 Thu; midnight Fri & Sat); 12-11 Sun
☎ (01943) 463233
Robinsons Dizzy Blonde; St Austell Proper Job; Theakston Best Bitter, Old Peculier; Timothy Taylor Boltmaker, Landlord; 5 changing beers (sourced regionally; often Acorn, Adnams, Hambleton) Ⓗ
A solid-looking stone-built pub on a prominent street-corner site on the approach from Leeds. To the front, roadside tables allow for outdoor drinking. Eleven real ales are on the bar, along with a real cider and a wide range of malt whiskies. There is a central fireplace, and comfortable fixed seating runs around the walls. A collection of farming implements hangs from the ceiling, and on the walls are pictures of old Otley. Several brewery enamel signs complete the decor. ⊛ ♣ ● 🐾 ☞

Old Cock 🄻

11-13 Crossgate, LS21 1AA
✪ 11-11 ☎ (01943) 464424 ⊕ theoldcockotley.co.uk
Ilkley Mary Jane; Theakston Best Bitter; 7 changing beers (sourced locally; often Bradfield, Briscoe's, Mallinsons) Ⓗ
Although it only opened in 2010, this genuine free house has already won multiple local CAMRA awards. It was painstakingly converted from a former café to create a pub that feels like it has been in situ for many years. There are two rooms downstairs with low ceilings and stone-flagged floors, and a further room upstairs. The guest ales are mostly from local breweries. At least two real ciders are also sold plus a range of foreign beers. No admittance to under-18s. Q ♿ ● ☰ ✿ ☞

Oxenhope

Bay Horse 🄻 ✅

20 Uppertown, BD22 9LN (on A6033)
✪ 3.30-11; 12-midnight Sat; 12-10.30 Sun
☎ (01535) 642921

Timothy Taylor Landlord; 4 changing beers Ⓗ
Family and dog friendly village local, with a pleasant single-bar setup, with a pool room to the rear and a separate dining area up a flight of steps. The four changing guest beers come from local breweries such as Goose Eye and Little Valley. The changing traditional cider is served from the cellar, so please ask. Home-made food is available Tuesday to Sunday except in winter. Evening meals can be booked in advance. ⊃ ⊛ ◑ ≈ ♣ ● P ☰ ✿ ☞

Pontefract

Robin Hood 🄻

4 Wakefield Road, WF8 4HN (on A645/A639 jct on S side of town)
✪ 5-midnight; 12-1am Fri & Sat; 12-midnight Sun
☎ (01977) 702231
House beer (by James & Kirkman); 5 changing beers Ⓗ
Busy locals' pub with a public bar and three other drinking areas. It holds quizzes twice weekly and has darts and dominoes teams in the local charity league. It has an open mic night once a month and holds a beer festival over the August bank holiday weekend. The James & Kirkman Brewery is behind the pub. A winner of several local CAMRA awards.
Q ⊃ ⊛ ♿ ≈ (Tanshelf/Monkhill/Baghill) ♣ ● ☰ ✿

Pudsey

Fleece 🄻 ✅

100 Fartown, LS28 8LU
✪ 12-11 ☎ (0113) 236 2748 ⊕ fleecepudsey.co.uk
Tetley Bitter; Timothy Taylor Golden Best, Landlord; 2 changing beers (sourced locally; often Elland, Ossett, Pennine) Ⓗ
A traditional, warm and friendly community pub. The lounge room has a theme of Laurel and Hardy and other film stars of the golden age of Hollywood. The games room, where you can play dominoes or watch sports TV, has an open fire. To the back of the pub is an attractive garden. This award-winning venue holds regular quizzes, charity events and a summer beer festival in August with all proceeds going to Yorkshire Air Ambulance. ⊛ ♣ P ☰ ☞

Rishworth

Booth Wood Inn

Oldham Road, HX6 4QU (on A672 towards jct 22 of M62) SE034170
✪ 12-10 (11 Fri & Sat) ☎ (01422) 825600
⊕ boothwoodinn.co.uk
Holt Bitter; 4 changing beers (sourced locally; often Bradfield, Pennine, Salopian) Ⓗ
A traditional family country pub and restaurant close to the scenic Yorkshire Moors, on the A672. It is open plan with a large central bar and two restaurant areas featuring beams and stone-flagged floors. All food is freshly prepared each day. Daily specials are available in addition to the main menu. There is always a good selection of carefully sourced real ales. ⊃ ⊛ ◑ ♿ P ☞

Roberttown

New Inn 🄻 ✅

Roberttown Lane, WF15 7NP

🍺 3-10.30 Mon; 3-11 Tue; 3-11.45 Wed & Thu; 12-11.45 Fri & Sat; 12-10.30 Sun ☎ (01924) 402069
🌐 thenewinnroberttown.com

Abbeydale Moonshine; Leeds Best; house beer (by Mallinson's); 3 changing beers (sourced nationally) ⊞
A traditional village local, popular with all ages. It is the brewery tap for the New Inn Brewery, with one of the family's beers always on. There is a snug with comfy chairs, and a function room. The Wednesday quiz is popular, along with the occasional Sunday race day. An annual beer festival is now well established, featuring rare beers. Guest ales are from local and national sources.
🛏️🕮♣️P🚃(229,253)🐾🐱🛜

Saltaire

Cap & Collar ⓛ
4 Queens Road, BD18 4SJ
🍺 closed Mon; 5-10; 4-11 Fri & Sat; 1-6 Sun
4 changing beers (sourced regionally; often Northern Monk, Saltaire, Wishbone) ⊞
Popular micropub with an open-plan café-style layout accommodating up to 35 customers. A beer garden and smoking area is at the rear. Four handpulls serve a varied range of beers, many sourced regionally. Real cider is delivered on draught and there is a good selection of bottle-conditioned ales. Meet the Brewer and tap takeover events are held regularly and a homebrew club meets here. Live music plays on Sunday afternoon and occasional evenings.
🛏️🕮≈🍴🚃(760)🐱🛜

Fanny's Ale & Cider House ⓛ ⊘
63 Saltaire Road, BD18 3JN (on A657, opp fire station)
🍺 12 (4 Mon)-11; 12-midnight Fri & Sat ☎ (01274) 591419
Timothy Taylor Golden Best, Landlord; 6 changing beers (sourced regionally; often Bingley, Bridgehouse, Naylor's) ⊞
Located near the UNESCO World Heritage Site of Saltaire village and the historic Salts Mill, this cosy pub is popular with residents and visitors alike. An extension has increased seating capacity downstairs and added disabled access. Upstairs there is a room with comfortable seating. It is now a free house serving two regular ales, up to six guests and real ciders. The gas-lit lounge is adorned with breweriana and real fires add nicely to the welcome. ♿≈🍴🚃(760)🐱🛜

Hop ⓛ ⊘
199 Bingley Road, BD18 4DH
🍺 12-midnight ☎ (01274) 582111 🌐 thehopsaltaire.co.uk
Black Sheep Best Bitter; Ossett Yorkshire Blonde; Big Red Bitter; Silver King, Excelsior; Rat White Rat; 2 changing beers (sourced regionally; often Ilkley, Wishbone) ⊞
Adjacent to the main A650 road and built within an old tram depot originally constructed in 1904. It features a large open-plan main room with horseshoe bar and an upper mezzanine floor primarily used for dining. A large outdoor seating area is popular in good weather. Excellent food is served, from snacks to full restaurant meals. Wood-fired pizzas can be seen being prepared from the main bar area. Regular live music events take place. Local CAMRA Pub of the Year 2016.
🛏️🕮◐♿≈🍴🚃🛜

Sandbeds

Airedale Heifer ⓛ
Bradford Road, BD20 5LY
🍺 11.30-11 ☎ (01274) 515870 🌐 theairedaleheifer.co.uk
Bridgehouse Blonde, Aired Ale, Porter, Holy Cow; 2 changing beers (sourced locally; often Bridgehouse) ⊞
An extensive roadside venue with a substantial food presence, where many dishes feature the brewery's beers. It is the tap for Bridgehouse Brewery situated in the car park behind. The pub is named after the famous Airedale heifer of the early 1800s, the heaviest cow in the UK (see the statue at the front). The open-plan layout has a single L-shaped bar and a sizeable, south-facing garden with patio heaters. Children are welcome until 8pm, later if dining. Brewery tours can be booked. 🛏️🕮◐♿P🚃(662)🐱🛜

Shipley

Fox ⓛ
41 Briggate, BD17 7BP
🍺 10.30-11 (midnight Fri & Sat); 12-10.30 Sun ☎ (01274) 594826 🌐 thefoxshipley.co.uk
BEEspoke Plan Bee; 5 changing beers (sourced regionally; often Great Heck, Mallinsons) ⊞
An independent, single-roomed café-style bar, simply but smartly furnished featuring recycled church pews. Friendly and welcoming, it has six handpulled ales including one from the in-house BEEspoke microbrewery in the cellar. Real ciders are sold, as is a wide range of international bottled beers. It is handy for a quick refreshment when waiting for trains at Shipley station as the train times appear on a TV monitor. Live acoustic music plays Tuesday and Wednesday evenings. You can get good home-made food at lunchtimes.
🛏️🕮◐♿≈🚃🐱🛜

Ring o' Bells ⓛ
3 Bradford Road, BD18 3PR (on A650)
🍺 11-midnight; 12-11 Sun ☎ (01274) 584386
Greene King IPA; Leeds Pale; Tetley Bitter; 3 changing beers (often Moorhouse's, Naylor's, Saltaire) ⊞
Situated close to the UNESCO World Heritage village of Saltaire, this traditional roadhouse-type pub has an impressive frontage. Sensitively refurbished in 2014, it retains a comfortable, homely feel. Up to three guest ales are mainly sourced regionally. Sport is shown on several TV screens and there is occasional live music. A small Edwardian smoke room merits a place in CAMRA's book, Yorkshire's Real Heritage Pubs, and is used by local community groups, including writers and anglers.
🕮◐♿♣️P🐱🛜

Silsden

King's Arms ♟️ ⓛ ⊘
Bolton Road, BD20 0JY
🍺 12-midnight (11 Mon) ☎ (01535) 653216
Black Sheep Best Bitter; Saltaire Blonde; 4 changing beers (sourced nationally; often Rudgate, Wishbone) ⊞
Award-winning, bustling community pub, run by the same couple since 2003, with music nights on Tuesday and Thursday, quiz night on Wednesday, a pool table and beer festivals all combining to make it a great place to visit. Partitions divide the main bar into three distinct areas, each with its own feel. Westons cider and four to six guest beers from near

and far, including a darker beer, provide something for all tastes. Regular buses between Keighley and Ilkley stop close by. ✿♣●P🚌(762,903)😺🏳

Slaithwaite

Swan Inn 🅛 ✅
Carr Lane, Crimble, HD7 5BQ
✿4-midnight (10 Tue); 12-midnight Sat & Sun
☎ (01484) 841115
Bradfield Farmers Blonde; 5 changing beers (often Bingley, Empire, Thornbridge)
Huddersfield's long-closed Palace Theatre and 40-year-old CAMRA posters, plus interesting old books, are displayed in the taproom. Saturday's disco is in the larger, more vibrant lounge, with an impressive bar with ornate etched glass. A blackboard lists current and forthcoming beers, six normally being on tap. A good selection of bottled beers and bar snacks is served. A quiz is held on Wednesday, and occasional live music. The Swan plays a part in the Slawit Moonraker Festival and the famous ale trail. Q🌛✿🍽♣●P🚌😺🏳

Sowerby Bridge

Firehouse 🅛
1 Town Hall Street, HX6 2QD
✿closed Mon; 4 (12 Sat)-11.30; 12-10.30 Sun
☎ (01422) 832586 ⊕ firehousesowerbybridge.co.uk
Moorhouse's Pride of Pendle; Vocation Heart & Soul; 3 changing beers (sourced regionally; often Dark Star, Hawkshead, Saltaire)
Close to the bridge crossing the River Calder in the centre of Sowerby Bridge, this prominent building, dating from 1874, is a popular venue for those who like to eat out with the option of a traditional pint. The family-run outlet has built a reputation for food and real ale, in particular pizza cooked in an open oven, and its tapas menu. Three guest beers are served, with at least one from a local or regional brewer. ◗🅑♿🍽●🚌(560,579)🏳

Hog's Head Brew House & Bar 🅛
1 Stanley Street, HX6 2AH
✿3-11; 12-midnight Fri & Sat; 12-11 Sun ☎ (01422) 836585
⊕ hogsheadbrewhouse.co.uk
Hogs Head Olde Maltings, 6 to 8 Weeks, White Hog, Hoppy Valley, Old Schnozzler; 3 changing beers (often Phoenix, Salopian, Vocation)
Close to the centre of Sowerby Bridge, this establishment is in a former 18th-century malthouse which has been extensively renovated. The brewery is at the back of the building and can be viewed from the bar area. Five core Hogs Head beers are served as well as guest ales. There is plenty of seating in the huge, sprawling bar area where snacks are also served. Q♿🍽🚌😺🏳

Jubilee Refreshment Rooms 🅛
Station Road, HX6 3AB (on railway station)
✿9.30am (9am Sat)-10; 12-9 Sun ☎ (01422) 648285
⊕ jubileerefreshmentrooms.co.uk
3 changing beers (often Bingley, Goose Eye, Mallinsons)
Located in the only surviving part of the 1876 station building, the bar serves three changing local beers and offers a pleasant place to while away the time or stop off for refreshments. Alcohol is served from noon onwards, and hot food noon-1.30pm. The walls are adorned with interesting railway and brewery related memorabilia, and

events and talks take place frequently. Trains depart regularly for Leeds and Manchester. Q✿♿🍽P😺🏳

Shepherd's Rest ✅
125 Bolton Brow, HX6 2BD (on A58 towards Halifax)
✿3-11; 12-11.30 Fri & Sat; 12-11 Sun ☎ (01422) 831937
Ossett Pale Gold, Yorkshire Blonde, Silver King; Rat White Rat; 4 changing beers (often Phoenix)
Built in 1877 and halfway up Bolton Brow out of Sowerby Bridge, this friendly local was purchased by Ossett Brewery in 2005. From the door, a triangular area leads to the bar, which faces a cosy lounge with a large brick-arched fireplace. To the left is a comfortable seating area with flagged floor, going through to an enclosed outside area. A selection of pork pies is always available. Monday is dominoes league night while Tuesday is quiz night, with free supper for entrants. Q✿🍽♣🚌😺🏳

Stanbury

Wuthering Heights Inn 🅛 ✅
Main Street, BD22 0HB
✿12-midnight ☎ (01535) 643332
⊕ thewutheringheights.co.uk
Marston's Wainwright; Theakston Best Bitter; 2 changing beers (sourced nationally)
A popular, friendly local dating from 1763. Warmed by logburners, the traditional main bar has photographs showing the history of the village and an internet terminal for customers' use. The cosy dining room has a Bronte theme. A third room hosts regular folk music gatherings and can be booked for parties and meetings. The rear garden has spectacular views down the Worth Valley, and a separate camping area (no caravans). Well-behaved dogs and children are welcome. Quiz night is Thursday. 🌛✿🍽◗▲♣P😺🏳

Stanley

Graziers Inn
116 Aberford Road, WF3 4NN (on A642 at bottom of hill after hospitals, near jct with road to Stanley Ferry)
✿12-midnight; 12-11 Sun ☎ (01924) 200283
Abbeydale Moonshine; John Smith's Bitter; 2 changing beers (sourced regionally; often Black Sheep, Theakston)
The pub dates from 1890 and is a deserved addition to the Guide. It has served consistently good-quality beers for a number of years. Traditional and welcoming, this pub boasts numerous rooms separated from a central bar. In addition, copper-topped tables and a real fire in winter add to the atmosphere. Pictures of old Stanley adorn the walls. 🌛✿♿♣P🚌😺🏳

Thackley

Commercial Inn
61 Park Road, BD10 0RR (3 mins' walk along Thackley Rd from Thackley Corner)
✿2.30-11.30; 12-12.30am Fri & Sat; 12-11.30 Sun
☎ (01274) 962295
Tetley Bitter; 3 changing beers (often Goose Eye, Naylor's, Stancill)
A true local community pub providing a warm family welcome to all, in a quiet residential street off the beaten track in a semi-country setting near Thackley football and cricket ground. Once a BYB

(Bentley's Yorkshire Brewery) house, this building has a multi-roomed layout with a free-to-hire function room to the rear and a beer garden/ smoking area at the back. There is a popular quiz night on Wednesday and occasional live music is featured. Children are welcome until 9pm.
🛏☺♣P🚌(612,760)☺

Todmorden

Staff of Life ⓛ

550 Burnley Road, OL14 8JF (on A646 between Todmorden and Cornholme)
🕑 12-3, 5.30-11; 12-11 Fri-Sun ☎ (01706) 819033
🌐 staffoflifeinn.org.uk
Timothy Taylor Golden Best, Landlord; 3 changing beers (often Goose Eye, Moorhouse's, Rooster's) Ⓗ
Set in a dramatic valley landscape beneath Eagles Crag, this welcoming free house was built in 1838. The layout is semi-open with seating around the cosy bar area. There are two further rooms, one with a vaulted stone chamber, originally used as the cellar. Good-quality, home-cooked food with regular changing specials is on the menu, and there are regular quiz nights. Accommodation is also available. Parking for the pub is on Knotts Road, 70 yards to the east.
🛏☺🛌◀◗P🚌(589,592)☺🛜

Upper Denby

George Inn ⓛ ✅

114 Denby Lane, HD8 8UE
🕑 5-10.30; 12-11.30 Fri & Sat; 11.30-10.30 Sun
☎ (01484) 861347 🌐 thegeorgeinn-upperdenby.co.uk
Tetley Bitter; Timothy Taylor Landlord; 1 changing beer (often Great Heck, Ossett, Small World) Ⓗ
This family-run village local is going from strength to strength since becoming a free house in late 2012, and is a former winner of the local CAMRA branch Rural Pub of the Year. The pub hosts regular 'pie and pea walks', with a reward of home-made food at the end. Other entertainment includes monthly jazz on a Thursday and folk on the first and third Mondays, as well as occasional traditional sing arounds. Walkers and dogs are welcome, families until 8.30pm. Q🛏☺🛌◗🅰♣P🚌☺🛜

Wakefield

Black Rock ♟ ✅

19 Cross Square, WF1 1PQ (between Bull Ring and top of Westgate)
🕑 11-11 (midnight Sat); 12-10.30 Sun ☎ (01924) 375550
Kelham Island Easy Rider; Tetley Bitter; 4 changing beers (sourced regionally) Ⓗ
An arched, tiled façade leads into this compact city-centre local with a warm welcome and a comfy and surprisingly large interior, which includes photographs of old Wakefield. The Rock stands as one of the few proper pubs left in the middle of the clubs and bars of Westgate, and is popular with drinkers of all ages looking for a real pint. Customers are encouraged to suggest beers to try, with four regularly changing guest ales on offer. There is a free function room for private use.
Q➡🚌

Fernandes Brewery Tap & Bier Keller ⓛ ✅

5 Avison Yard, Kirkgate, WF1 1UA (turn right approx 100 yards S of the George St/Kirkgate jct near Scartop Pine)
🕑 4-11 (11.30 Thu); 12-12.30am Fri & Sat; 12-11 Sun
☎ (01924) 386348
10 changing beers (sourced regionally; often Fernandes, Ossett) Ⓗ
Owned by Ossett Brewery, the Fernandes Brewery operates in the cellar. It has 11 handpulls, with two dedicated to dark beers. There are four Fernandes beers, two Ossett, plus a choice of guests, plus draught cider. The Bier Keller, which opens 6-midnight Friday and Saturday, has premier foreign beers on draught plus an Ossett beer and a cider on handpump. There is a quiz on Wednesday evening, folk music on the first third Sunday of the month and open mic on the third. Q➡(Kirkgate)🚌☺🛜

Harry's Bar ⓛ ✅

107B Westgate, WF1 1EL (turn right from Westgate Station, cross road at traffic lights and pub is at back of car park on right)
🕑 5 (4 Sat)-1am ☎ (01924) 373773
House beer (by Five Towns); 7 changing beers (often North Riding Brewery) Ⓗ
This small, one-roomed pub is set in an alleyway just off Westgate. A real fire and a bare-brick and wood interior plus vintage sporting pictures enhance this cosy hostelry. There is also a fantastic view of Wakefield's 99-arch viaduct – if only steam trains were a regular feature. A selection of bottled Belgian beers adds to the temptation.
Q☺🛜➡(Westgate/Kirkgate)🍴🚌☺🛜

Hop ⓛ ✅

19 Bank Street, WF1 1EH (in a cobbled street off Westgate almost opp Theatre Royal)
🕑 4-11 (midnight Thu); 12-2.30am Fri & Sat; 12-10.30 Sun
☎ (01924) 367111 🌐 thehopwakefield.co.uk
Ossett Yorkshire Blonde, Big Red Bitter, Silver King, Excelsior; Rat White Rat; 4 changing beers Ⓗ
Converted into a venue for music and conversation, this Georgian building retains bare-brick walls, fireplaces and other original features along with an extension that includes an open fire. The main bar has nine handpumps, one reserved for a dark beer, and a selection of bottled Belgian and American beers. Open mic night is Monday, quiz night is Tuesday and live music plays on Thursday, Friday and Saturday. Kebabs are served on Friday and Saturday nights. Rooms are available for hire (midweek only). ☺🛜➡(Westgate/Kirkgate)🍴🚌

Old Printworks ⓛ

WF1 1EL (down an alley off Westgate next door to Harry's Bar)
🕑 4-midnight; 12-12.30am Thu; 12-1.30am Fri & Sat; 12-12.30am Sun ☎ 07771 861129
Abbeydale Moonshine; Leeds Pale; Rat White Rat; 2 changing beers (sourced regionally) Ⓗ
Formerly an Indian restaurant, this pub is a welcome addition to the real ale quarter of Wakefield. Just off Westgate, it has an outdoor drinking area that is particularly popular during the summer months. The bar was rescued from the closed Union pub in Wakefield. The beers come from a range of Yorkshire breweries. It hosts regular darts and dominoes nights as well as showing live sporting events.
☺🛜➡(Westgate)♣P🚌☺🛜

Wakefield Beer Exchange L

14 Bull Ring, WF1 1HA (at top of Westgate; bar is almost on jct with Wood St)

☼ 11-11 (midnight Fri & Sat) ☎ (01924) 339913

6 changing beers (sourced locally; often Revolutions) H

Barely a year after opening by Revolutions Brewery, the pub has become one of the most popular in Wakefield. It has bare boards and minimalist furnishings, with paintings from local artists adorning the walls. A friendly welcome awaits all, with cask beer drinkers getting a choice of straight or dimple glasses. The pub hosts frequent Meet the Brewer nights, Hang the DJ on the last Wednesday of the month, and a monthly quiz. Pie and peas with a pint of Revolutions beer is available at all times.

ᗰ◑₺≉(Westgate/Kirkgate)♣●🖵🛜

Wakefield Labour Club L

18 Vicarage Street, WF1 1QX (at top of Kirkgate, round corner from Wakey Tavern)

☼ 7-11 (midnight Fri); 11-midnight Sat; 7-midnight Sun

☎ (01924) 215626 ⊕ theredshed.org.uk

5 changing beers (sourced regionally) H

The Red Shed is a secondhand army hut which has been extensively refurbished, and is home to many union, community and charity groups. Quiz night is Wednesday, there is occasional live music on the second Saturday, and open mic folk music night on the last Saturday of each month. There are three rooms, two of which can be hired for functions. An extensive collection of union plates and badges is displayed over the bar and numerous CAMRA awards adorn the walls.

Q🖰₺≉(Kirkgate/Westgate)♣P🖵❀

Wibsey

Hooper Micropub L

209 High Street, BD6 1JU

☼ closed Mon; 4.30-10.30 (11.30 Fri); 2-11.30 Sat; 2-9 Sun

⊕ thehoopermicropub.co.uk

5 changing beers (sourced regionally; often Moorhouse's, Saltaire, Wharfedale) H

Opened on Christmas Eve 2015, this cosy, split-level bar in the micropub style has quickly established itself with local people in the urban village of Wibsey. The bar is on the upper level and there is comfortable seating in the lower part. Photographs of old Wibsey provide a simple relief from the otherwise minimalist decor. The bar attracts a loyal and discerning clientele for the five rotating guest beers that come mainly from regional independent brewers. Q🖵

Blue Bell, York, North Yorkshire (Photo: Melissa Reed & Allan Conner)

Historic Coaching Inns of the Great North Road

Roger Protz

The Great North Road is part of British folklore, the Route 66 of Britain, except instead of gas stations and diners we have magnificent coaching inns, part of the living history of our islands. Taking in the history of these buildings as well as the literature that has celebrated them – from Charles Dickens through to J B Priestley – Roger Protz describes these coaching houses with an expert and discerning eye, producing not only a great pub guide but a gazetteer of the history and culture that are draped along this iconic road.

RRP £12.99 **ISBN** 978-1-85249-339-4 **224 pages**

For this and other books on beer and pubs visit CAMRA's online bookshop at **www.camra.org.uk/books** or call **01727 867201**. Discounts are available for CAMRA members.

NORTHERN
ISLES

SHETLAND

HIGHLANDS
&
WESTERN ISLES

ABERDEEN
& GRAMPIAN

TAYSIDE

LOCH LOMOND,
STIRLING
& THE
TROSSACHS

FIFE

ARGYLL &
THE ISLES

EDINBURGH & LOTHIANS

GREATER
GLASGOW &
CLYDE

BORDERS

AYRSHIRE
& ARRAN

NORTHERN
IRELAND

DUMFRIES &
GALLOWAY

NORTHUMBERLAND

TYNE &
WEAR

CUMBRIA

DURHAM

ISLE OF
MAN

NORTH
YORKSHIRE

LANCASHIRE

WEST
YORKS

EAST
YORKS

MERSEYSIDE

GREATER
MANCHESTER

SOUTH
YORKS

CHESHIRE

DERBYSHIRE

NOTTINGHAM-
SHIRE

LINCOLNSHIRE

NW
WALES

NE
WALES

SHROPSHIRE

STAFFORD-
SHIRE

LEICESTERSHIRE

NORFOLK

CAMBRIDGE-
SHIRE

MID
WALES

WORCESTER-
SHIRE

WEST
MIDLANDS

WARWICK-
SHIRE

NORTHAMPTON-
SHIRE

SUFFOLK

WEST
WALES

HEREFORD-
SHIRE

BEDFORD-
SHIRE

HERTFORD-
SHIRE

ESSEX

GWENT

GLOUCS &
BRISTOL

OXFORD-
SHIRE

BUCKINGHAMSHIRE

GREATER
LONDON

GLAMORGAN

WILTSHIRE

BERKSHIRE

SURREY

KENT

SOMERSET

HAMPSHIRE

WEST
SUSSEX

EAST
SUSSEX

CHANNEL
ISLANDS

DEVON

DORSET

CORNWALL

ISLE OF
WIGHT

Wales

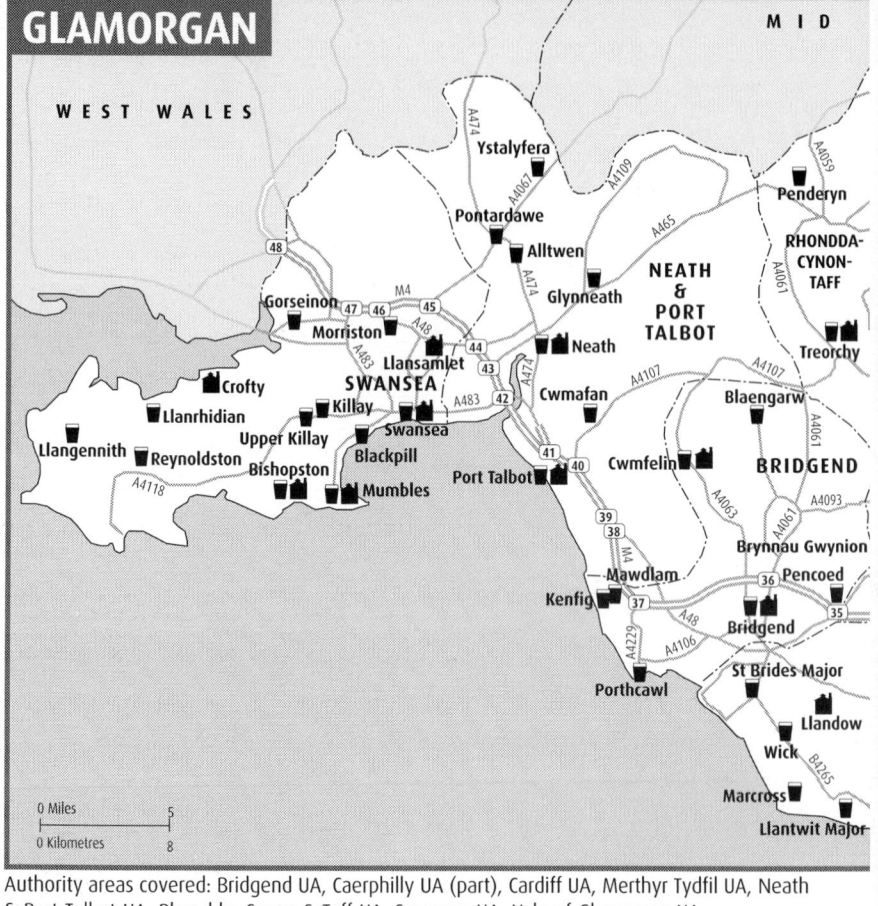

GLAMORGAN

WEST WALES

MID

Ystalyfera

Penderyn

Pontardawe

RHONDDA-
CYNON-
TAFF

48

Alltwen

NEATH
&
PORT
TALBOT

Gorseinon 47 46

M4

45

Glynneath

Morriston

A463

44

Neath

Treorchy

A4107

A4107

Crofty

Llansamlet

43

Cwmafan

Blaengarw

SWANSEA

Killay

42

A483

Llanrhidian

Upper Killay

Swansea

Cwmfelin

BRIDGEND

Llangennith

Reynoldston

Bishopston

Blackpill

41

A4063

A4061

A4118

Mumbles

Port Talbot

40

39
38

Brynnau Gwynion

M4

Mawdlam

36

Pencoed

Kenfig

37

Bridgend

35

A4229

A48

A4106

St Brides Major

Porthcawl

Llandow

Wick

0 Miles   5
0 Kilometres   8

Marcross

Llantwit Major

Authority areas covered: Bridgend UA, Caerphilly UA (part), Cardiff UA, Merthyr Tydfil UA, Neath & Port Talbot UA, Rhondda, Cynon & Taff UA, Swansea UA, Vale of Glamorgan UA

Aberdare

Ieuan ap Iago
High Street, CF44 7AA
🕐 8am-midnight (1am Fri & Sat) ☎ (01685) 880080
Greene King Abbot; Ruddles Best Bitter; Sharp's Doom Bar; 5 changing beers (sourced nationally; often Boss, Glamorgan) Ⓗ
Located on the edge of the town centre and within walking distance of Dare Valley Country Park, this former post office celebrates the poet who wrote the lyrics to the Welsh national anthem, Ieuan ap Iago (the bardic name of Evan James). His son James James composed the music and a memorial stands opposite. Many old photographs recall local history. ⏰❀◑ও♿♣🚆🅿️🎵

Rhoswenallt Inn
Abernant Road, CF44 0YS (top end of village, approx 1 mile from Aberdare)
🕐 12-midnight (9 Mon); 12-11 Sun ☎ (01685) 886428
Grey Trees Diggers Gold; Morland Old Speckled Hen; 1 changing beer (sourced locally; often Grey Trees) Ⓗ
Out of town, friendly pub/restaurant with a beer garden. Located on the Cynon Valley edge of Merthyr Mountain, the pub is attractive to walkers – Merthyr Tydfil is an approximate four-mile walk over the top of the mountain. Historic photographs

of the locality decorate the walls. Good food is served all day including vegetarian dishes. The pub gets busy when major sporting events are on, with three TVs in the bar. Singers perform frequently on Sunday evenings. ⏰❀◑🅿️(1)🎵

Whitcombe Inn
Whitcombe Street, CF44 7DA
🕐 12-12.30am; 11.30-12.30am Sat & Sun ☎ (01685) 875106
Wye Valley Butty Bach; 3 changing beers (sourced nationally; often Bragdy Twt Lol, Bullmastiff, Moles) Ⓗ
Welcoming and friendly street-corner traditional local, near the town centre. Owned by the licensee for over 12 years, it has a proud real ale tradition. The large front bar backs on to a pool room at the rear. Interesting photographs of long-gone local pubs hang in the bar. Sport sometimes plays on TV, with projector screens for major sporting events, though it is rarely intrusive. Live music is hosted occasionally. Approximately a mile from the picturesque Dare Valley Country Park.
♿🅰️🚶♣🚆🐾🎵

Aberthin

Hare & Hounds
Aberthin Road, CF71 7LG

Swansea Valley, there is plenty of scope for walkers and cyclists (National Cycle Route 43 is nearby). Q❄♣🚌(122)

Barry

Barry West End Club L

54 St Nicholas Road, CF62 6QY
🕐 1-11.30; 12-midnight Sat & Sun ☎ (01446) 735739
🌐 barrywestendclub.webs.com
Brains Dark; Wychwood Hobgoblin; Wye Valley HPA; 2 changing beers ⓗ
Visitors are welcome to sample the keenly priced ales at this multiple winner of the local CAMRA Club of the Year title. Housed in a building overlooking Barry Old Harbour, it features a bar, lounge, function room and snooker room. The club holds a number of beer festivals during the year and has been home to a cricket club for over 30 years. It fields skittles, adult and junior football and snooker teams, and even has chess, fishing and scuba diving clubs. Q❄🐕🍴◑👶♣🚌🅿🛏🪑

Sir Samuel Romilly L ✅

Romilly Buildings, Broad Street, CF62 7AU
🕐 8am-midnight (1am Fri & Sat) ☎ (01446) 724900
Greene King Abbot; Ruddles Best Bitter; Sharp's Doom Bar; 3 changing beers ⓗ
This spacious Wetherspoon pub is named after an 1800s landowner and legal reformer. It opened in 2009 in a building that was previously a market hall, theatre and bank – the vault remains and is used as a seating area. A large mural above the side entrance depicts life in old Barry, with many more pictures of the town inside. A typical range of guest ales comes from local breweries including Vale of Glamorgan. Q❄🐕◑👶♿🚌🛏🪑

🕐 12 (3 Mon & Tue)-midnight; 12-1am Fri & Sat
☎ (01446) 774892 🌐 hareandhoundsaberthin.com
Hancocks HB; Wye Valley HPA; 2 changing beers (sourced regionally; often Evan Evans, Glamorgan) ⓗ
A characterful village pub whose cosy public bar with its traditional stone walls, wooden beams and log fire is the focal point where the locals gather. Outside, the beer garden has its own bar and, occasionally, live music. High-quality fare is served from a seasonal menu, with most ingredients freshly bought on the day or grown by the chef. A more limited menu is available in the bar. The guest ales are mainly sourced locally, as are the ciders. There is limited parking.
Q❄🐕◑👶♿♣🛏🅿(321)🐾🪑

Alltwen

Gwyn Arms

Gwyn's Place, SA8 3AJ
🕐 4-midnight; 12-midnight Sat & Sun ☎ 07749 360555
Wye Valley Butty Bach; 2 changing beers (sourced regionally) ⓗ
Cosy, traditional village pub where the landlord and locals provide a convivial atmosphere, ensuring a warm welcome. Guest ales are often based on the recommendations of regular visitors, to complement the pub's permanent beer. Gradual refurbishment is ongoing. Live music is a regular feature at weekends. Situated in the picturesque

Bishopston

Joiners Arms ⓛ
50 Bishopston Road, SA3 3EJ
☼ 3-10.30; 11.30-11 Wed-Sat; 12-8.30 Sun
☎ (01792) 232658 ⊕ thejoiners.info
Marston's Pedigree; Swansea Bishopswood Bitter,
Three Cliffs Gold, Original Wood; Theakston Best
Bitter; 2 changing beers (sourced nationally) Ⓗ
Situated in the heart of the village, this 1860s free
house remains popular with locals and visitors.
Home of the Swansea Brewing Company, the pub
has two bars and holds beer festivals and
occasional music events, usually around public
holidays. Good-value food is served lunchtimes and
evenings (except Mon and Sun eve). The pub has
won several local CAMRA awards. There is a small
car park. ⏤🕮🌣🕭♣P🖳(14)🐾🛜

Valley
41 Bishopston Road, SA3 3EJ
☼ 11.30-11 ☎ (01792) 234820
⊕ valleyhotelbishopston.co.uk
Brains Rev James; Courage Best Bitter; 2 changing
beers (sourced nationally) Ⓗ
Traditional family-run country pub set in the heart
of this Gower village. A large porch area (which
doubles as a convenient bus shelter) leads to a
split-level bar and dining area, with exposed
beams, a large open fire and hearth. A wide variety
of home-cooked meals using local ingredients is
served daily and a Sunday lunch takeaway service
is available. Live music plays on occasion.
🌣🕭👌♣●P🖳(14)🐾🛜

Blackpill

Woodman ✅
120 Mumbles Road, SA3 5AS (near turn off for B4436)
☼ 11.30-11; 11.30-10.30 Sun ☎ (01792) 402700
Greene King IPA; 3 changing beers (sourced
nationally; often Mumbles) Ⓗ
This historic pub and restaurant has recently been
attractively refurbished. The deceptively spacious
establishment, with its various nooks and alcoves,
is situated on the main seafront road and the
entrance to the beautiful Clyne Gardens. Popular
with both families and diners, the pub also
welcomes those only seeking liquid refreshment. A
constantly changing range of guest ales is offered.
There are three seating areas outside including a
small beer garden. ⏤🌣🕭👌♣P🖳🛜

Blaengarw

Blaengarw Hotel
The Strand, CF32 8AA
☼ 11.30-11 (midnight Fri & Sat); 11-10.30 Sun
☎ (01656) 870287
1 changing beer (often Evan Evans, Glamorgan,
Rhymney) Ⓗ
Recently refurbished, large street-corner local at
the heart of the community. Just one carefully
chosen changing cask beer is on sale along with up
to four ciders. The public bar is popular for sports TV
and hosts pool and darts league teams, and there
is a fine jukebox. Meals are available in the
lounge/dining room until 8pm Tuesday and
Thursday; Sunday lunches (until 3pm) are also
popular. The famous Welsh hymn Calon Lan was
written upstairs. ⏤🌣🕭👌👌♣●🖳🛜

Bridgend

Coach Inn
37 Cowbridge Road, CF31 3DH
☼ 11.30-11; 12-10.30 Sun
Wye Valley Butty Bach Ⓗ; 6 changing beers (often
Grey Trees, Otley, VOG) Ⓗ/Ⓖ
Basically furnished free house with a passion for
real ale and cider from Wales and beyond, with
three guest beers on handpump and two served
straight from the cask. A popular weekend venue,
customers enjoy open mic nights, themed
evenings, brewery trips, an Easter beer festival, a
stout and porter festival in November, Meet the
Brewer and tap takeover events. Continental beers
are also available including takeaway bottles.
⏤🌣🕭⇋♣●🖳(303,X2)🐾🛜

King's Head ✅
44-44A Nolton Street, CF31 3BN
☼ 11-11.30; 8am-1am Fri & Sat; 12-11 Sun
☎ (01656) 648729 ⊕ thekingsheadbridgend.co.uk
Brains Rev James; 2 changing beers (often Brecon,
Felinfoel, Gower) Ⓗ
A new entry in this Guide, the King's Head has
reverted to its original name and to the cask ale
fold after many years as an Irish theme pub. Within
a year, it has gone from serving no real ale to
offering three beers and a cider, attracting drinkers
of all ages. A good range of pub food is also
available. The Tuesday night quiz is popular. Voted
local CAMRA branch Most Improved Pub of the Year
for 2017. ⏤🌣🕭👌⇋●🖳🛜

Brynnau Gwynion

Mountain Hare
Brynna Road, CF35 6PG
☼ 4 (5 Mon)-11; 3-midnight Fri; 12-midnight Sat; 12-10.30
Sun ☎ (01656) 860453 ⊕ mountainhare.co.uk
Mountain Hare Gold; Wickwar BOB; 2 changing
beers (sourced nationally; often Glamorgan, Mountain
Hare, St Austell) Ⓗ
This is a typical Welsh village pub and has featured
regularly in the Guide for more than 10 years. The
licensee and self-taught brewer began brewing on
site in 2014 and one of his two beers is always
available, plus cider in summer. The pub has been
in the same family for over 40 years and boasts a
traditional public bar, games room and a lovely old
stone-walled lounge. Sport is often on TV in this
rugby lovers' pub. Q⏤🌣🕭♣●P🖳(64,404)🐾🛜

Caerphilly

Green Lady
Pontygwindy Road, CF83 3HF
☼ 10-11 (midnight Fri); 9am-midnight Sat; 9am-11 Sun
☎ (029) 2085 1510
3 changing beers (sourced nationally; often
Marston's, Ringwood, Wychwood) Ⓗ
Open-plan Marston's pub alongside the old main
road, north of the town centre. Comfortable and
spacious, it has a separate dining/function room.
Three handpumps dispense a widely varying
selection of ales from the wider Marston's group,
including seasonals. Good-value meals are
available (no food Sun eves). Live music features
most Saturday evenings and there is a quiz night
every Sunday.
⏤🌣🕭👌⇋(Energlyn & Churchill Park)P🖳(26,50)

Malcolm Uphill ✓

89-91 Cardiff Road, CF83 1FQ

⊙ 8am-midnight (1am Fri & Sat) ☎ (029) 2076 0720

Greene King Abbot; Ruddles Best Bitter; Sharp's Doom Bar; 3 changing beers (sourced nationally; often Moles, Tring) H

Busy Wetherspoon pub, handy for the rail and bus interchange. Up to five guest beers are usually on sale, plus one or two guest ciders. The usual JDW deals and promotions are offered. This pub can be crowded at weekends and hosts a popular quiz on Sunday. The back room is the quieter area. A separate accessible entrance is available if required. Q ⛱ ⛲ ◑ ♿ ♻ ● ♻ 훟

Caerphilly Mountain

Black Cock Inn L

Waunwaelod Way, CF83 1BD (off A469, along Ffordd Waenwaelod)

⊙ 12-11; 12-10.30 Sun ☎ (029) 2088 0534

Wye Valley Butty Bach; 3 changing beers (sourced regionally; often Grey Trees, St Austell) H

Slightly off the beaten track yet easily accessible, with a large car park. The pub has two bars with a rustic atmosphere – the corner bar has a wood-burning stove set into a brick fireplace. There are separate dining areas. The staff are welcoming and informative, offering a good range of well-kept ales. Lunches and evening meals are popular (booking for the evening is recommended). Quiz nights feature regularly. Dogs are welcome in one bar. Q ⛲ ◑ ● P ♣ 훟

Cardiff

Andrew Buchan

29 Albany Road, Roath, CF24 3LH

⊙ 11-11

Rhymney Hobby Horse, Dark, Bitter, Export; 1 changing beer H

This pub, a converted shop, offers a range of Rhymney beers and a variety of real ciders from local producers. It is named after the founder of the original, now defunct, Rhymney Brewery and features an open fireplace with the brewery moose head hanging above. The walls are decorated with a collection of modern art. On an outside wall is an allegoric mural featuring the brewery's hobby horse logo. The pub has a good reputation for live music. ⛲ ♿ ♻ (Cathays) ● ♻ ♣ 훟

Cambrian Tap ✓

51 St Mary Street, CF10 1AD

⊙ 11-11 (midnight Fri & Sat); 12-10.30 Sun

☎ (029) 2064 4952 ⊕ thecambriantap.com

6 changing beers (often Brains) H

Brains' refurbishment of a historic street-corner city centre pub has created the company's newest beer bar. It sports eight handpumps, two or three showcasing the cask products of the Brains Craft Brewery. A mural depicts the various real ales, which have often been brewed in collaboration with others. Guest beers are sourced from UK-wide microbreweries, often rare for the area. Pork pies are a speciality here. ◑ ● ♻ (Central) ♻ 훟

Chapter Arts Centre

Market Road, Canton, CF5 1QE (off Cowbridge Rd E behind Iceland store)

⊙ 10-11; 12-12.30am Fri; 12-midnight Sat; 10-10.30 Sun

☎ (029) 2030 4400 ⊕ chapter.org

Ringwood Razorback; 5 changing beers (sourced nationally) H

Arts centre and cinema complex situated in a converted Victorian school. The open-plan bar/diner has plenty of seating, and there is additional space in a covered area outside. The five guest beers are sourced from across the UK, usually from small independent or local breweries. A number of fridges contain an impressive range of bottled beers from continental producers, with the accent on German beers. ⛱ ⛲ ◑ ♿ ⚘ ♻ (17,18) 훟

City Arms L ✓

10-12 Quay Street, CF10 1EA

⊙ 12-midnight (2am Fri & Sat); 12-10 Sun

☎ (029) 2064 1913

Brains Bitter, SA, Rev James H**; 7 changing beers** H/G

A traditional pub in the heart of Cardiff's real ale and music district, with the feel of an Amsterdam brown bar about it. Just off Westgate Street, it is a mere penalty kick away from the Principality Stadium, meaning it gets busy on match days. The central three-sided bar separates two drinking areas. Nine traditional ciders and perries are served from a stillage in the centre of the bar area, with another on handpump. ⛲ ♿ ⚘ ♻ (Central) ♣ ● ♻ ♣ 훟

Discovery L

Celyn Avenue, Lakeside, CF23 6EH

⊙ 12-11.30 (12.30am Fri & Sat); 12-11 Sun

☎ (029) 2075 2720

Sharp's Doom Bar; 5 changing beers (often Otley, VOG) H

A spacious contemporary pub, situated uphill in a residential area, close to the north end of Roath Park Lake. The public bar has a large-screen TV, dartboard and access to a covered outdoor area. The larger and quieter lounge/dining room serves a variety of changing dishes showcasing the head chef's skills. A large, impressive function room is available for private hire. There are usually five ever-changing guest beers, including at least one from a local brewery. ⛲ ◑ ♿ ♻ (Heath) ♣ P ♻ (54) ♣ 훟

Four Elms

1 Elm Street, CF24 3QR (off Newport Rd)

⊙ 10-11 (midnight Fri); 11-midnight Sat; 12-11 Sun

☎ (029) 2046 2120

Felinfoel Double Dragon; 3 changing beers H

Lively community pub, recently refurbished and extended, with a large beer garden. The three changing beers can come from anywhere in the UK, with the accent on smaller brewers. Three real bag-in-box ciders are also offered. A good menu of reasonably priced pub food is served all day. The pub is divided between a lively bar with a pool table at the front and a quieter lounge area (which has replaced the skittle alley) at the rear. ⛲ ◑ ♣ ● ♻ 훟

Gatekeeper ✓

9 Westgate Street, CF10 1DD

⊙ 8am-midnight (2am Fri & Sat) ☎ (029) 2064 6020

Greene King Abbot; Ruddles Best Bitter; 5 changing beers H

Three-level, two-bar Wetherspoon pub, near the Principality Stadium. It gets busy when something is on at the stadium and when sporting events are shown on the many TV screens. Up to five handpumps dispense real ciders, frequently from

WALES

the Gwynt y Ddraig range. Bars are on the lower and upper floors, but the lower bar offers the greater choice, with five handpumps serving a range of countrywide real ales, invariably including a locally brewed ale. ♿🛋️🕐🍺👶🅿️🚶🗙🚉(Central)🍴🍺🚃🛜

Hopbunker 🏆
Kingsway, CF10 5AF
🕐 12-11; 11-midnight Fri & Sat; 11-11 Sun
☎ (029) 2039 8889
14 changing beers (sourced regionally; often Pixie Spring/Hopcraft) Ⓗ
Modern basement bar and brewery tap for Hopcraft Brewery. Fifteen handpumps dispense a variety of cask ales, sourced mainly from small brewers and invariably including ales from Hopcraft. A row of taps behind the serving area dispenses up to 20 other beers. The bag-in-box real cider range has recently increased, with up to 20 examples. Prices are reasonable for a city centre pub. Not surprisingly, this is Cardiff CAMRA Cider Pub of the Year as well as local CAMRA Pub of the Year 2017.
🚉(Queen St/Central)🍴🍺🛜

Lansdowne
71 Beda Road, Canton, CF5 1LX
🕐 12-11 (11.30 Fri & Sat); 12-10.30 Sun ☎ (029) 2022 1312
4 changing beers (often Grey Trees, Tiny Rebel) Ⓗ
A landmark former hotel with a strong community focus, hosting a community beer festival in June. The upper storeys have been converted to flats and the ground floor has been refurbished into three distinct areas. The decor is fairly basic but bright and attractive with plenty of woodwork. Beers are sourced from microbreweries including a few local examples. A multiple winner of Cardiff CAMRA branch Pub of the Year.
♿🛋️🕐🚉(Ninian Park)🐾🍴🍺🐕🛜

Mochyn Du
Sophia Close, Pontcanna, CF11 9HW
🕐 12-11 (midnight Fri & Sat); 12-10.30 Sun
☎ (029) 2037 1599 🌐 ymochyndu.com
House beer (by VOG); 3 changing beers (sourced nationally) Ⓗ
Located near Glamorgan County Cricket Club ground, the pub is a short walk from the city centre. A spacious, attractive free house, formerly a lodge, it offers a choice of up to five real ales. The house beers from VOG (Vale of Glamorgan) Brewery are rebadges of its usual range. This is a popular meeting place for Welsh speakers. The conservatory provides a smart and comfortable environment in which to enjoy home-cooked food. Large decked areas outside offer pleasant surroundings in fine weather. Q🛋️🕐🅿️🍴

Pen & Wig 🅻 ✅
1 Park Grove, CF10 3BJ
🕐 11.30-midnight; 11-1am Fri & Sat; 11.30-11.30 Sun
☎ (029) 2037 1217 🌐 penandwigcardiff.co.uk
8 changing beers (sourced nationally; often Brecon) Ⓗ
Victorian-built terraced pub, just off the city centre and near the university. The clientele is a mix of students, young professionals and office workers. A varied beer range is offered, sourced from local, regional and national breweries, plus two ciders. The large garden includes a covered section and a smokers' area. The pub can become crowded at peak periods and weekends. 🛋️🕐🚉(Queen St)🍴🍺

Queens Vaults ✅
29 Westgate Street, CF10 1EH
🕐 10-11 (midnight Fri & Sat); 11-11 Sun ☎ (029) 2022 7966
Felinfoel Double Dragon; Sharp's Doom Bar; 5 changing beers Ⓗ
Large sports-oriented pub on one floor opposite the Principality Stadium. There is a raised lounge/dining area at the front and a games area with three pool tables and two dartboards to the rear. The competitively priced guest beers can be sourced from any size of brewery, near or far, but are often from microbreweries. A former Cardiff CAMRA Cider Pub of the Year, up to six ciders or perries are also available. Reasonably priced meals are served. 🛋️🕐🍺👶🗙🚉(Central)🐾🍴🚃🛜

Rummer Tavern ✅
14 Duke Street, CF10 1AY
🕐 11.30-midnight; 12-11 Sun ☎ (029) 2023 5091
🌐 therummertaverncardiff.co.uk
Wye Valley HPA; 5 changing beers (often Grey Trees, Purity) Ⓗ
Opposite Cardiff Castle, this is Cardiff's oldest licensed premises, with a distinctive half-timbered frontage and leaded windows, and a history spanning more than three centuries. The interior is narrow but long, comprising a series of simply furnished areas, with dark-wood panelling throughout. There is also an upstairs room available for hire. The regularly changing guest beers can come from anywhere in the UK. Real cider complements the beer range, and food is served until early evening.
🍺👶🗙🚉(Queen St/Central)🍴🚃🛜

Tiny Rebel
26 Westgate Street, CF10 1DD
🕐 12-2am ☎ (029) 2039 9557 🌐 urbantaphouse.co.uk
8 changing beers (often Tiny Rebel) Ⓗ
This popular city-centre pub is opposite the Principality Stadium. There are several rooms, upstairs and downstairs, decorated in Tiny Rebel brewery's unique style, with some available for private hire. The pub hosts regular quiz, bring your own vinyl, Americana and board game nights, and occasional brewery tap takeovers. Eight handpumps offer four Tiny Rebel beers and a range of independent brewery beers from across the UK. There are four further handpumps for ciders and perries. A former Cardiff CAMRA Pub of the Year winner. 🛋️🕐🍺👶🗙🚉(Central)🐾🍴🚃🐕🛜

Cowbridge

Edmondes Arms
Cardiff Road, CF71 7EP
🕐 4 (1 Sat)-11; 4-10.30 Sun ☎ (01446) 773192
Hancocks HB; Wye Valley HPA; 1 changing beer (sourced nationally; often Glamorgan, Sharp's) Ⓗ
Situate in a prominent position at busy crossroads on the eastern edge of Cowbridge and dating from 1899, this three-roomed pub has a strong local following. The building is of brick and local limestone with a traditional unspoilt interior featuring stained-glass panels in the windows, wood panelling and other original features. The main bar and games room have wooden floors and open fires. There is a separate cosy lounge to the rear with a piano and a door leading to a small patio area outside. Live bands play most Saturday evenings. Q🛋️🐾🚌(X2,321)🛜

Vale of Glamorgan Inn

51 High Street, CF71 7AE

🌑 12-11 (midnight Fri & Sat) ☎ (01446) 772252

Draught Bass; Hancocks HB; Sharp's Atlantic; Wye Valley HPA, Butty Bach; 1 changing beer (sourced nationally; often Borough Arms, Grey Trees, VOG) Ⓗ

Popular single-room pub in the centre of town. The wooden-floored bar area has a warming range fire, and recent work has added a flagstone floor to the rear area plus more seating around another stove. Outside is an attractive enclosed beer garden with a separate covered and heated smoking area. An annual beer festival coincides with the town's food and drink festival in May. Good-value home-made food is served lunchtimes (no food Sun). A former local CAMRA Pub of the Year.

Q ☺ ❀ ◐ ● 🖾 (X2,321) ❀ 🛜

Cross Inn

Cross Inn Hotel

Main Road, CF72 8AZ

🌑 12-11 ☎ (01443) 223431

Hancocks HB; Sharp's Doom Bar; Wye Valley HPA; 1 changing beer (sourced nationally) Ⓗ

Traditional terrace pub with a convivial atmosphere, enjoyed by a regular clientele as well as visitors to the area. Immaculately clean, the ground floor is divided into a bar with a flagstone floor and a comfortable lounge area. A good range of well-kept beers is offered. Sunday lunches are popular (booking recommended) and regularly curry nights are held. Q ❀ ◐ ♿ ♣ P 🖾 🛜

Cwmafan

Brit Pub Ⓛ

London Row, SA12 9AH

🌑 6-10 Mon; 11.30-11 (midnight Fri & Sat); 11.30-10.30 Sun
☎ (01639) 680247 🌐 thebrit.wales

Morland Old Speckled Hen; 4 changing beers (sourced locally; often Borough Arms, Grey Trees, Mumbles) Ⓗ

Dating back to 1845, this pub offers a warm welcome to drinkers, diners, backpackers, locals and tourists. A selection of up to five real ales and cider (mostly sourced locally) is available. It has a bunkhouse and award-winning food, not to mention a picturesque riverside beer garden. Music jam sessions feature regularly. A gem found nestled in the beautiful Afan Valley, quirkiness mixes with tradition in this establishment.
Q ☺ ❀ 🛏 ◐ ♿ ♣ ● P 🖾 (1,23) ❀ 🛜

Cwmfelin

Cross Inn

Masteg Road, CF34 9LB

🌑 11.45-midnight (1am Fri & Sat); 11-midnight Sun
☎ (01656) 732476

Cerddin Solar, Cascade; 3 changing beers (often Cerddin) Ⓗ

Winner of numerous local CAMRA awards and home to the on-site Cerddin Brewery, this is a must-visit pub. Five cask beers are on offer alongside the bottle-conditioned range, as well as eight real ciders. This is a traditional two-roomed valleys' pub with strong community links. The Tuesday night quiz raises money for the local food bank and 'locals' come from as far away as Australia. Local CAMRA County Pub of the Year for 2017. Q ❀ 🛒 (Garth) ● 🖥 🖾 (71) ❀ 🛜

Dinas Powys

Cross Keys Inn ✔

Elm Grove Road, CF64 4AA

🌑 12-midnight ☎ (029) 2051 3910
🌐 thecrosskeysinndinaspowys.co.uk

Brains Rev James; Hancock's HB; 1 changing beer (often Brecon) Ⓗ

An active local pub, one of three situated in the centre of the village, with a pool table, darts team and sport on TV. It has a cosy and snug atmosphere inside, with comfortable seating and music kept comfortably low for conversation. Beers are chosen in a good range of strengths, and often come from local breweries such as Vale of Glamorgan. There is limited parking outside, but spaces can usually be found within easy walking distance.
Q ❀ ❀ ◐ ♿ 🛒 ♣ P 🖾 ❀ 🛜

Gilfach Fargoed

Real Ale Farm (RAF) Ⓛ

Gilfach Fargoed Fawr Farm, Cardiff Road, CF81 8NY

🌑 7-11 Mon (midnight Tue & Thu); closed Wed;
6.30-midnight Fri & Sat; 12-8 Sun ☎ 07837 006276

Felinfoel Cambrian Best Bitter, Double Dragon; 4 changing beers (sourced nationally; often Grey Trees, Salopian, VOG) Ⓗ

CAMRA award-winning club, offering the best range and quality of beer for miles, with up to four guest ales and two ciders or perries, selected for flavour and interest and sourced from breweries both near and far. The building pre-dates the industrial age and has a complex history. Numerous charity events feature and also the occasional beer festival. Visitors are welcome but must be signed in. The short walk from Gilfach Fargoed station presents a modest but energetic climb. Q ☺ ❀ 🛒 ♣ ● P 🖾 (50) ❀

Glan-y-Llyn

Fagins Ale & Chop House Ⓛ

9 Cardiff Road, CF15 7QD

🌑 3-11 Mon; 12-11.30; 12-10.30 Sun ☎ (029) 2081 1800

Dark Star Hophead Ⓗ**; 2 changing beers (sourced nationally; often Bragdy Twt Lol, Salopian)** Ⓖ

Welcoming free house just north of Taffs Well. It is a rare outlet for Dark Star, and also offers up to two more hoppy guest beers on gravity. A unique house beer from Grey Trees is also sometimes available. One handpump serves a cider, alongside a bottled range from Gwynt y Ddraig. Good-value pub food is available (no food Mon). Live music plays on occasion. The pub is well served by bus and an easy 15-minute walk from Taffs Well station. Q ☺ ❀ ◐ ● 🖾 (26,132) ❀ 🛜

Glynneath

Dinas Rock Hotel Ⓛ

High Street, SA11 5AP

🌑 closed Mon; 5-11 Tue-Thu; 4-midnight Fri; 1-midnight Sat;
12-midnight Sun ☎ (01639) 720105

2 changing beers (sourced locally; often Glamorgan, Gower, Grey Trees) Ⓗ

Recently refurbished, this traditional local is a reliable outlet for real ale in an area where it can be hard to find. Two wood-burning stoves make for a cosy atmosphere in winter. Six Nations and Ospreys rugby fixtures feature prominently on TV at weekends. The beers are predominantly local, often from Gower and Grey Trees, and the real cider, when available, is also sourced locally from the village. The pub is close to the famous waterfall walks. Q🌳🏵️🐾♿🍺🚍(8,X55)🐾

Gorseinon

Mardy Inn ✅
117 High Street, SA4 4BR
🕐 8am-midnight (1am Fri & Sat) ☎ (01792) 890600
Greene King Abbot; Ruddles Best Bitter; Sharp's Doom Bar; 4 changing beers Ⓗ
This modern Wetherspoon establishment opened in April 2013 following a major refurbishment of a former traditional high-street pub. It has a large single bar with several TVs for news and sport, and an adjoining airy extension overlooking the furnished patio area. Some interesting pictures of old Gorseinon adorn the walls. A good selection of local and national beers can be enjoyed in the beer garden. 🌳🏵️🕐♿🐾♿🍺🚍🛜

Groeswen

White Cross Inn
CF15 7UT (overlooking Groeswen Chapel)
🕐 4-midnight; 12-midnight Fri-Sun ☎ (029) 2085 1332
5 changing beers (sourced nationally) Ⓗ
Just outside Caerphilly, this cosy stone pub is well worth finding. Six handpumps dispense five changing beers and a cider. The beers are good value and carefully chosen to suit modern and traditional tastes, usually including a dark ale. Small and emerging breweries regularly feature, many making their debut in the area. The large back room often hosts meetings, including the popular monthly Beer Bellies gathering, with visiting brewers and beer industry speakers. Occasional beer festivals are hosted. Road access is narrow. 🌳🏵️🐾🍺🐾🛜

Gwaelod y Garth

Gwaelod y Garth Inn
Main Road, CF15 9HH
🕐 10-11; 12-10.30 Sun ☎ (029) 2081 0408
🌐 gwaelodinn.co.uk
Dark Star American Pale Ale; Violet Cottage Shine On; Wye Valley Bitter; 4 changing beers (often Dark Star, Thornbridge) Ⓗ
A stone-built, multi award-winning village local. Located on the extreme outskirts of Cardiff and situated on the slope of Garth Mountain, in the centre of Gwaelod village, it is frequented by locals as well as cyclists and walkers. Expect to find at least one beer from the on-site Violet Cottage Brewery, complementing a varying range of real ales which can originate from anywhere across the UK. There is a separate games room and upstairs restaurant. Q🌳🏵️🛏️🕐♿🍺🚍(26B)

Hendreforgan

Griffin Inn Ⓛ
CF39 8YL (turn down lane off A4093 after Gilfach Goch village sign)
🕐 7 (6 Fri)-11; 12-11 Sat & Sun ☎ (01443) 670379
Brains SA; 1 changing beer (sourced locally; often Glamorgan) Ⓗ
Recognised by CAMRA as one of the Real Heritage Pubs of Wales, the Griffin has been in the same family for over 50 years. It can be difficult to find,

but persistence pays off and it is well worth the effort. The Brains SA is always superb quality. The decor is worth a look in itself, featuring oak furniture, gleaming brasses and a splendid Victorian counter with an 1870 till. A heartfelt welcome is assured. Q🌳🏵️Å♿🍺🚍(150,172)🐾

Kenfig

Prince of Wales
CF33 4PR
🕐 4-8 Mon; 12-11 ☎ (01656) 740356 🌐 princekenfig.co.uk
Draught Bass; Sharp's Doom Bar; Worthington's Bitter Ⓖ
With the current landlord only the 11th since 1816, this heritage award-winning inn dates from around the 15th century and is steeped in local history. Visitors can expect three or four quality ales on gravity, good locally sourced food, and a warm welcome. Family- and dog-friendly, the interior is comfortable and cosy, and outside there is a stunning view over Kenfig Nature Reserve. The Draught Bass outsells all the pub's lagers combined. Regular local guest beers and cider are also sold. Q🌳🏵️🕐♿🍺🚍(63B)🐾🛜

Killay

Village Inn
5-6 Swan Court, The Precinct, SA2 7BA
🕐 10.15-11 (11.30 Fri & Sat); 12-11 Sun ☎ (01792) 203311
Fuller's London Pride; Timothy Taylor Landlord; 2 changing beers Ⓗ
Cosy pub with an L-shaped bar and wood panelling, situated in a small shopping precinct in Killay, a gateway to Gower. The pub has a strong community focus, with Sunday and Tuesday quiz nights, traditional and electronic community noticeboards, and occasional music and themed food evenings (or challenge the bar manager to a game of chess). Home-made food, including speciality pizzas, is served from a daily-changing menu. This former local CAMRA Pub of the Year holds an annual beer festival at Easter. 🕐♿🐾🍺🚍🐾🛜

Llangennith

King's Head Ⓛ
SA3 1HX
🕐 11-11; 12-10.30 Sun ☎ (01792) 386212
🌐 kingsheadgower.co.uk
Gower Brew 1, Gower Gold; 3 changing beers (often Gower) Ⓗ
A row of three 17th-century stone-built cottages, the pub offers quality 4-star accommodation, with some rooms pet-friendly. It is situated at the Western end of the Gower Peninsula, a short distance from the sandy stretches of Llangennith Beach. Ales from nearby Gower Brewery are available (up to six in summer) plus a cask cider. An impressive variety of home-made food is served, with dishes inspired by fresh local produce. An annual beer festival is held in October and a themed fancy dress event over the August bank holiday. 🌳🏵️🛏️🕐Å♿🍺🚍(116)🐾🛜

Llanharry

Fox & Hounds
Llanharan Road, CF72 9LL

✪ 12-11 (midnight Fri & Sat) ☎ (01443) 222124
⊕ fox-and-hounds-inn-llanhari.co.uk
4 changing beers (sourced regionally; often Boss, Glamorgan) Ⓗ
Traditional construction materials combined with modern furnishings result in a pub well worth a visit. The stone-built inn is family owned and offers a good selection of varying beers, usually about four in number. It has a growing reputation for high-quality food. Bottled ciders are usually available. There is a large car park beside the pub.
Q✿⛱⏺◑♿♣🅿🚍(64,404)🐾🤝

Llanrhidian

Dolphin Inn

Mill Lane, SA3 1EH (just off B4295 N Gower Road)
✪ 1 (12 Sun)-11 summer; 4.30 (6 Tue)-11; 1-11 Fri & Sat;
12-10.30 Sun winter ☎ (01792) 391069
Exmoor Gold; Fuller's London Pride; 1 changing beer Ⓗ
Cosy village pub dating from the 18th century on the north side of Gower next to a 13th-century church, with stunning views of the estuary from the lovely beer gardens. The characterful single room is warmed by a solid fuel stove. A limited range of hot and cold meals is available, plus tea and coffee. There is a children's play area at the rear with an enclosure for rabbits and poultry to roam. Quiz night is Sunday. Check ahead for afternoon opening times.
Q✿⛱⏺◑♣🅿🚍(116,115)🐾

Greyhound Inn Ⓛ

Oldwalls, SA3 1HA (1 mile W of Llanrhidian on B4295)
✪ 11-11 ☎ (01792) 391027 ⊕ greyhoundgower.com
Draught Bass; Gower Gold, Power; 2 changing beers Ⓗ
Traditional 19th-century inn with a welcoming atmosphere, and spiritual home to the Gower Brewery, with a wide range of its ales on offer at the bar. An extensive home-cooked bar menu is served every day, with Sunday lunches particularly popular. Outside at the rear is a large beer garden with a children's play area and wonderful views over the Gower countryside.
⛱✿⏺◑♿♣🅿🚍🐾🤝

Llantrisant

Wheatsheaf Hotel

High Street, CF72 8BQ
✪ closed Mon & Tue; 4-11 Wed-Fri; 12-11 Sat; 12-8 Sun
St Austell Tribute; 3 changing beers (sourced nationally) Ⓟ
This street-front pub in Llantrisant's historic old town reopened in 2016, with a completely independent outlook. It has been extensively modernised in a rustic-chic style. Up to six cask ales are available, all dispensed from free-flow taps on the back wall. Buses stop close by, and free car parks are a short walk away.
Q⛱♣🅿🚍(100,404)🐾🤝

Llantwit Major

King's Head

East Street, CF61 1XY
✪ 11.30-11.30 (midnight Fri & Sat); 11.30-10.30 Sun
☎ (01446) 792697
Brains Bitter; 1 changing beer (often Belhaven, Brains) Ⓗ

A family-run town-centre pub, in the Guide for the 19th consecutive year. The traditional two-bar inn has a strong local following and the stone-floored public bar is popular for darts and pool. The comfortable lounge features wood panelling and an eclectic mix of furnishings, and leads to the patio beer garden. Large-screen TVs for sport are in both bars. Guest beers come from both local and national brewers. Karaoke features in the bar on Thursday. Q⛱✿⏺≈♣🅿🚍🐾🤝

Old Swan Inn

Church Street, CF61 1SB
✪ 12-11; 12-10.30 Sun ☎ (01446) 792230
5 changing beers (sourced nationally; often Grey Trees, Springhead, VOG) Ⓗ
The town's oldest inn, overlooking the historic St Illtyd's Church and the town hall. It boasts an ever-changing range of four or five ales, often sourced from local brewers. There is a popular front bar and a new restaurant at the back, with excellent food served in both. Beer festivals are held in spring and summer featuring local bands. The town car park is nearby. Cider is occasionally available, more so in summer. Q⛱✿⏺◑≈♣🅿🚍🐾🤝

Llanwonno

Brynffynon Hotel

CF37 3PH (opp church) ST030955
✪ closed Mon; 12-11; 12-10.30 Sun ☎ (01443) 790272
⊕ brynffynonhotel.com
3 changing beers (sourced nationally; often Draught Bass) Ⓗ
Set on top of the ridge between the urban Cynon and Rhondda Fach valleys, this tranquil country inn is well worth the effort to seek out. The lounge has a timeless atmosphere with its relaxing leather couches and log-burning fire. The dining room serves food of an excellent standard (booking advised), including cream teas. Three guest beers are available, and beer festivals are held throughout the year. A patio offers views of the forest and ancient churchyard. Q⛱✿⏺◑Ⓐ🅿🐾

Marcross

Horseshoe Inn

CF61 1ZG
✪ 12-2.30 (not Mon), 6-11; 12-11 Sat; 12-10.30 Sun
☎ (01656) 890568 ⊕ theshoesmarcross.co.uk
Sharp's Atlantic; Wye Valley Butty Bach; 2 changing beers (often Gower, VOG) Ⓗ
The Shoes is a beautiful 19th-century pub in the hamlet of Marcross. It offers a varied menu of good food and three excellent ales, usually including one from a Welsh brewery. When sunny the beer garden is delightful and in winter the compact interior is cosy with a large logburner in the bar. The location is convenient for Nash Point lighthouse – from here you can walk along the coastal path and enjoy spectacular views across the Bristol Channel. Q⛱✿⏺◑🅿🚍(303)

Mawdlam

Angel Inn ✪

Marlas Road, CF33 4PG
✪ 12-11; 12-10.30 Sun ☎ (01656) 743995
⊕ theangelinnmaudlam.co.uk
Gower Gold Ⓗ; **Sharp's Doom Bar; 2 changing beers (often Grey Trees, Mumbles, VOG)** Ⓖ

Close to the M4 motorway and the Kenfig Nature Reserve, most of the pub's trade is in high-quality food, but there is a comfortable bar for drinkers with a TV for sport. Four ales are kept at a perfect temperature served straight from the cask. The pub has greatly improved under the current licensee and occasional food theme nights are hosted, as well as a successful summer beer festival. Dogs are welcome in the bottom bar. Accommodation comprises three double rooms, one dog-friendly. Q ☜ ❀ ⛺ ◑ ♣ P ⋤ (63B) ❁ 📶

Morriston

Red Lion Hotel ✅
Sway Road, SA6 6JA
🕐 8am-midnight (1am Fri & Sat) ☎ (01792) 761870
Greene King Abbot; Ruddles Best Bitter; 4 changing beers Ⓗ
The Red Lion, part of the Wetherspoon chain, has a large dining area with an open log fire at the front and high bar stools at the back. On the walls are a number of pictures depicting former local industry, and a community board advertises trips to breweries and other events. Outside is a large patio area with tables and chairs and a smoking area. There are good parking facilities and disabled access. ☜ ❀ ◑ ⛭ ♣ P ⋤ (4) 📶

Mumbles

Mumbles Ale House
2 Dunns Lane, SA3 4AA
🕐 4-9 Mon-Wed; 12-11 ☎ 07971 194838
Butcombe Gold Ⓗ; 6 changing beers (sourced nationally; often Butcombe, Glamorgan, Oakham) Ⓗ/Ⓖ
Wales' first micropub, this intimate bar is on the ground floor of a terraced house about 50 yards from the main road, and has become popular as a pub for conversation. It offers a regularly changing real ale range – no keg beers here – along with real cider, wine, limited spirits and soft drinks, all listed on a large blackboard alongside the bar. Traditional bar snacks are available. Local CAMRA Pub of the Year in 2016. Q ❀ ● ⋤ ❁

Park Inn Ⓛ
23 Park Street, SA3 4DA
🕐 4-11; 2-11 Fri-Sun ☎ (01792) 366738
5 changing beers (sourced regionally; often Evan Evans, Mumbles, Tiny Rebel) Ⓗ
The convivial atmosphere in this small establishment in a village side street attracts discerning drinkers of all ages. Five handpumps dispense an ever-changing range of beers, with particular emphasis on independent breweries from Wales and the west of England. Alongside a fine display of pumpclips are pictures of old Mumbles and its pioneering railway. A popular quiz is held on Thursday, with occasional music at weekends. Q ☜ ❀ ♣ ● ⋤ (2,3) ❁ 📶

Pilot Inn Ⓛ
726 Mumbles Road, SA3 4EL
🕐 12-11 (midnight Fri & Sat) ☎ 07897 895511
⊕ thepilotofmumbles.co.uk
Draught Bass; 6 changing beers (sourced nationally) Ⓗ
Welcoming and friendly local on the seafront at Mumbles and home to the Pilot Brewery. Seven ales are always available, usually including up to

three rotating beers brewed on site. A wide range of bottled ciders is also kept and hot drinks are served. This historic pub, built in 1849, is next to the coastal path and popular with lifeboatmen, locals, real ale fans, walkers and cyclists. A former Welsh CAMRA Pub of the Year. Q ☜ ● ⋤ (2B) ❁ 📶

Neath

Borough Arms Ⓛ
2 New Henry Street, SA11 1PH (off Briton Ferry road, near Stockhams Corner roundabout)
🕐 4.30-9 Mon (11 Tue & Wed); 4-11 Thu & Fri; 12-11 Sat; 12-4 Sun ☎ (01639) 644902 ⊕ boroughbreweryneath.com
Draught Bass; house beer (by Borough Arms); 4 changing beers (sourced locally; often Borough Arms, Butcombe, Evan Evans) Ⓗ
This pub is the home of the Borough Brewery and is cosy, welcoming and well worth a visit. The Borough beer names generally have a steelworks theme, paying homage to the area and the landlord's ties to the Port Talbot steelworks. Favourites include Full Blast, Puddlers Peril and Nut Red Coke. This is probably the best back-street pub in Wales, much to the delight of the locals. Q ☜ ❀ ⛭ ♣ ⋤ ❁ 📶

David Protheroe ✅
7 Windsor Road, SA11 1LS
🕐 8am-midnight (1am Fri & Sat) ☎ (01639) 622130
Greene King Abbot; Ruddles Best Bitter; Sharp's Doom Bar; 5 changing beers (sourced nationally) Ⓗ
Situated opposite Neath railway station and a short walk from the bus terminus, this popular town centre venue is a typical Wetherspoon pub. The building is the former Neath Police Station and is named after the town's first policeman. It has an open-plan interior with a family area at the rear. A Welsh food menu is available. It gets busy on rugby international days. ☜ ❀ ◑ ⛭ ⋤ 📶

Penarth

Golden Lion 🏆 Ⓛ
69 Glebe Street, CF64 1EF
🕐 10-11; 11-midnight Fri & Sat; 12-10.30 Sun
☎ (029) 2070 1574
4 changing beers (often Grey Trees, Otley, VOG) Ⓗ
Situated a short walk from the town centre, three or four excellent ales from Welsh breweries are usually available along with good-value food. Sports TV is shown throughout, even in the small beer garden, which includes a popular table tennis table. Inside, the jukebox has a huge catalogue and is well used – the pub can be lively! Regulars include local sports teams, including football and darts sides. Local CAMRA Pub of the Year in 2016 and 2017. ☜ ❀ ◑ ⛭ ♣ ⋤ 📶

Pilot
67 Queen's Road, CF64 1DJ
🕐 12-11 (midnight Fri & Sat) ☎ (029) 2071 0615
4 changing beers (often Dukeries, Milton, VOG) Ⓗ
The Pilot has gained a reputation for high-quality food, wine and beer. Ales are chosen from all over the country, and some of the best Welsh breweries often feature, including Vale of Glamorgan. Five handpumps offer up to four quality cask beers and a real cider. There is seating outside at the front for warm weather, and the rear restaurant area with its log-fired stove is comfortable in winter. Q ☜ ◑ ♣ ● ⋤ ❁ 📶

Pencoed

Little Penybont Arms

11 Penybont Road, CF35 5PY

🕒 3-11; closed Tue; 12-11 Fri & Sat ☎ 07734 767937

4 changing beers (often Grey Trees, Mumbles, VOG) Ⓖ

A cosy micropub converted from a café, offering up to four changing beers on gravity, 20 plus ciders and 15 plus single malt whiskies. The Steak & Stamp restaurant two doors down is under the same ownership and offers the same range of drinks. In the pub, excellent bar snacks include pork pies, pickles, nuts and home-made pork scratchings. Families are admitted until 9pm. A gem which can get busy quickly. Q🏠◑≉♣●🚍🐾🛜

Penderyn

Red Lion

Church Road, CF44 9JR

🕒 closed Mon; 12-3, 6-11; 12-11 Sat; 12-10.30 Sun
☎ (01685) 811914 🌐 redlionpenderyn.com

Brains Rev James; Draught Bass; Fuller's ESB; Gower Gold; Tomos Watkin Old Style Bitter; 1 changing beer (sourced nationally; often Rhymney, Wadworth, Wychwood) Ⓖ

Quaint old pub on the edge of the Brecon Beacons National Park with two log fires to keep it cosy in the colder months. Between six and 10 local and national beers are on gravity, with Fuller's ESB a favourite over the years. Up to five real ciders and perries are also available, with some from local producer Bragdy Brodyr. High-quality traditional home-cooked pub food is served (booking essential). Q🏵◑ঌ●P🛜

Pontardawe

Pontardawe Inn 🍽 Ⓛ ✅

123 Herbert Street, SA8 4ED

🕒 12-midnight ☎ (01792) 447562 🌐 pontardaweinn.co.uk

Marston's Pedigree; Ringwood Fortyniner; 4 changing beers (sourced nationally; often Jennings, Mumbles, Thwaites) Ⓗ

Originally a drovers' pub on the route to Neath mart, the Gwachel, as it is known locally, is worth the short walk from the town centre, under the flyover. Live music is prominent on Friday and Saturday evenings, with Welsh language bands playing on the third Friday of the month. Beer festivals are held in May, August and November. The landscaped garden is popular in fine weather. A popular stop-off for cyclists on Route 43 of the National Cycle Network. Local CAMRA Pub of the Year 2014-2017. 🏠🏵◑ঌ♣P🚍🐾🛜

Pontsarn

Aberglais Hotel

CF48 2TS (near Vaynor, between Trefechan and Pontsticill) SO043098

🕒 10.30-11 ☎ (01685) 377344

Wye Valley Bitter; 2 changing beers (sourced locally; often Grey Trees, Wye Valley) Ⓗ

Rescued from near oblivion, the Aberglais makes an ideal stop for visitors exploring the picturesque Pontsticill Reservoir and Morlais Castle. This wonderful country inn offers good food and great beers. The landlord has a long local association, having moved from a nearby pub. Holidaymakers and locals are all welcome, and there is a children's play area. Set midway along Sustrans Taff Trail Route 8 between Cefn Coed and Pontsticill, the pub also attracts cyclists. The car park is over the road. 🏠🏵◑ঌ●P🐾🛜

Pontsticill

Red Cow

CF48 2UN

🕒 11-11 (8.30 Mon; 9.30 Tue); 11-10 Sun ☎ (01685) 387775

Wye Valley Bitter; 2 changing beers (sourced locally; often Bragdy Twt Lol, Grey Trees, Tiny Rebel) Ⓗ

Impressive traditional pub with flagstone floors and a warm fire in winter. Within the Brecon Beacons National Park, and not far from the Brecon Mountain Railway, it is popular with walkers and cyclists, not to mention real ale lovers. The beer range focuses predominantly on locally produced brews. Food is served 12-4pm Tuesday to Sunday. Pontsticill Reservoir is close by. 🏠🏵◑♣●P🚍🐾

Pontypridd

Bunch of Grapes Ⓛ ✅

Ynysangharad Road, CF37 4DA (off A4054)

🕒 11-1am; 11-midnight Sun ☎ (01443) 402934
🌐 bunchofgrapes.org.uk

Otley O2 Croeso; 9 changing beers (often Dark Star, Otley, Salopian) Ⓗ

A short stroll from the town centre, this popular multiple award-winning pub has distinct areas around a central bar. Six guest beers accompany four from Otley Brewery, plus two ciders and perries. Guest ales are varied and wide ranging. A separate and acclaimed restaurant serves locally sourced food with themed nights a regular feature (booking suggested, especially at weekends). Events include beer, cider and cheese festivals and much more. Q🏠🏵◑≉●P🚍🐾

Llanover Arms Ⓛ

Bridge Street, CF37 4PE (opp N entrance to Ynysangharad Park, off A470)

🕒 11-midnight; 11-11 Sun ☎ (01443) 403215

3 changing beers (sourced nationally; often Brains, Salopian) Ⓗ

Built around 1794 to serve thirsty boatmen working the newly opened Glamorganshire Canal, this historic free house has been in the same family for over a century. Three rooms are linked by a central passageway, each room with its own regulars. The canal is long gone, though Ynysangharad Park and the famous town bridge and museum are close by, as is the Taff Trail path. Q🏵≉♣P🚍🐾

Patriot Bar Ⓛ

25B Taff Street, CF37 4UA

🕒 12-midnight ☎ (01443) 407915

Rhymney Best, Hobby Horse, Dark, Bitter; 1 changing beer (often Rhymney) Ⓗ

A Rhymney Brewery tied house, this is a popular no-frills bar offering a range of well-kept beers. Prices are reasonable, helping to ensure a constant turnover of beers. The central location on Taff Street makes it easy to find. Converted from a shop unit and known fondly as the Wonky Bar, it is an easy walk from both the rail and bus stations. Wheelchair access is possible, but requires some assistance. ≉●🚍🐾🛜

Port Talbot

Lord Caradoc L ⊘
69-73 Station Road, SA13 1NW (5 mins' walk from Parkway station)
✪ 8am-midnight (1am Fri & Sat) ☎ (01639) 896007
Greene King Abbot; Ruddles Best Bitter; Sharp's Doom Bar; 7 changing beers (sourced regionally; often Brains, Neath Ales, Tomos Watkin) ⊞
A comfortable Wetherspoon pub with a relaxed atmosphere, in the centre of town and easily accessible from Parkway station and bus terminus. The choice of beers is open to suggestion from regular customers, with a wide range of Welsh beers always available from both regional and microbreweries. The pub has a spacious layout plus an outdoor area for drinkers and diners at the rear. It is family-friendly throughout and has a strong local following. Q🏠🛏️🍴◐♿�‹P🚃🛜

Porth

Rheola
Rheola Road, CF39 0LF
✪ 2-midnight; 1-1am Fri; 12-1am Sat; 12-midnight Sun
☎ (01443) 682633
Rhymney Best, Dark, Bitter ⊞
Acquired by Rhymney Brewery in 2015, this friendly local sells a range of good-value Rhymney beers. A large, detached building it is situated at the confluence of the two Rhondda rivers, and is well served by both rail and bus. The bar features a jukebox, pool table and dartboard, and is often quite lively, whereas the comfortable lounge will provide a quiet haven and only tends to get busy at weekends. Activities include a quiz night and whist night. 🌟🚋♣P🚃(132)🛜

Porthcawl

Lorelei Hotel
36-38 Esplanade Avenue, CF36 3YU
✪ 5-11 Mon; 12-1.30, 5-11 Tue; 12-11 Wed-Sat; 12-10.30 Sun
☎ (01656) 788342 ⊕ loreleihotel.co.uk
Draught Bass G; Rhymney Export; 3 changing beers (often Boss, Grey Trees, VOG) ⊞
Near the seafront and the Grand Pavilion, the Lorelei is a multiple award winner, with good-quality and good-value food served evenings (not Mon) and Sunday lunchtime. Four draught beers are available plus cider in summer. Beer festivals are held twice a year on Grand National and Halloween weekends. Built around the end of the 19th century, during World War I it was two separate buildings – one used as a hospice for injured soldiers. Q🏠🛏️◐♣🍴🚃🛜

Reynoldston

King Arthur Hotel
Higher Green, SA3 1AD (on village green)
✪ 10-11 ☎ (01792) 390775 ⊕ kingarthurhotel.co.uk
Felinfoel Double Dragon; Sharp's Doom Bar; 3 changing beers (often Gower, Tiny Rebel) ⊞
Traditional family-owned hotel and acclaimed wedding venue, situated at the foot of Cefn Bryn in beautiful Gower, overlooking the village green. There is covered outdoor seating by the pub entrance and a large seating area on the green itself. The cosy, atmospheric main bar is welcoming to drinkers and diners, serving home-cooked food made with local produce. Main meals and bar snacks are available all day, breakfasts for non-residents 9-11am.
🛏️🌟🍴◐♿♣🍴P🚃(118,116)🛜

St Brides Major

Fox & Hounds
Ewenny Road, CF32 0SA
✪ 4-11; 12-11 Fri-Sun ☎ (01656) 880285
⊕ thefoxandhoundstbrides.co.uk
Draught Bass; Hancocks HB; 2 changing beers ⊞
An Enterprise Inns tenant, the landlord has done excellent work over the years and the Fox & Hounds is a welcome addition to this Guide. The village inn attracts regulars from nearby towns as well as local residents, and is popular with ramblers as several walking routes start from the car park. The pub has pool, darts and air rifle teams, and raises funds for charity. Local CAMRA Community Pub of the Year 2017.
Q🌟◐♣P🚃(303)🐾🛜

Swansea

Bank Statement ⊘
57/58 Wind Street, SA1 1EP
✪ 8am-midnight (1am Wed & Fri); 8am-2am Sat
☎ (01792) 455477
Sharp's Doom Bar; 5 changing beers (sourced nationally; often Boss, Exmoor, Fuller's) ⊞
A former bank, sympathetically transformed by Wetherspoon, while retaining its original ornate interior. Trading as a Lloyds No.1, the pub is at the heart of the city's bar quarter and has a large ground floor with plenty of seating. Popular with all ages, it is busy throughout the week as well as at the weekend. Sports fixtures are shown on its many screens. It offers a wide selection of bottled beers, some of which are RAIB (Real Ale in a Bottle). 🛏️◐♿🚋♣🚃🛜

Hogarths
2-3 St Mary's Street, SA1 3LH
✪ 11-midnight (1am Wed); 11-1am Fri & Sat
☎ (01792) 465169
6 changing beers (sourced nationally; often Hogarths, Marston's, Wychwood) ⊞
Hogarths is styled as a Victorian gin palace. The venue attracts large crowds for sporting and live music events. One long bar and seating area is accompanied by several snugs and a partially covered outdoor area. The bar aims to offer between five and six real ales, constantly changing depending on demand. A large beer garden is to the rear. 🌟🚋♣🚃🛜

No Sign Bar
56 Wind Street, SA1 1EG
✪ 11-11 (midnight Wed & Thu; 1am Fri & Sat); 12-11 Sun
☎ (01792) 465300 ⊕ nosignwinebar.com
Gower Gold; 3 changing beers (sourced nationally; often Bristol Beer Factory, Monty's, Mumbles) ⊞
Historic narrow bar established in 1690, reputedly a regular haunt of Dylan Thomas. Architectural signs from various periods of the pub's past remain, some dividing the interior into separate areas. Quality food and wine are available, and up to five real ciders. Live music features in the bar on Fridays, Saturdays and often Sundays. Bands also play in the Vault basement later in the evening. Swansea CAMRA Pub of the Year 2015.
🛏️🌟◐🚋♣🚃🛜

Potters Wheel ✓

85-86 The Kingsway, SA1 5JE

☼ 8am-midnight (1am Thu-Sat) ☎ (01792) 465113

Adnams Broadside; Fuller's London Pride; Ruddles Best Bitter; Sharp's Doom Bar; 6 changing beers (sourced nationally) ℍ

A city-centre Wetherspoon outlet with a long sprawling bar area offering various seating arrangements, attracting customers of all ages and backgrounds. An interesting selection of guest beers is kept, with a commitment to local breweries. Cask cider is always available. Photographs on the walls feature local dignitaries associated with the area's industrial past, particularly the ceramics and pottery industries. Look for the CAMRA board and beer suggestion box. ⏃◑&♥⊟➚

Queen's Hotel ▼

Gloucester Place, SA1 1TY (near Waterfront Museum)

☼ 11-11 (11.30 Sat); 12-11 Sun ☎ (01792) 521531

Theakston Best Bitter, Old Peculier; 2 changing beers (sourced nationally; often Bristol Beer Factory, Fuller's, Glamorgan) ℍ

This vibrant free house is near the Dylan Thomas Theatre, City Museum, National Waterfront Museum and marina. The walls display photographs depicting Swansea's rich maritime heritage. The pub enjoys strong local support and home-cooked lunches are popular. Evening entertainment includes live music on Saturday, a Sunday quiz and bingo on Wednesday. This is a rare local outlet for Theakston Old Peculier in addition to two seasonal guest beers sometimes from a local microbrewery. Local CAMRA Pub of the Year 2017. ◑⊟➚

Uplands Tavern ✓

42 Uplands Crescent, Uplands, SA2 0PG

☼ 11-11 (midnight Fri & Sat) ☎ (01792) 458242

Greene King IPA, Abbot; 2 changing beers (sourced nationally) ℍ

In the heart of Swansea's student quarter, the Tav is a large single-room Greene King pub attracting regulars from all walks of life. It is another former haunt of Dylan Thomas, commemorated in a separate snug area. The pub has a deserved reputation for the quality and variety of its live music at weekends, and hosts an open mic night on Monday. Tuesday is quiz night. There is a large heated outdoor drinking area at the front. ❀&♣⊟(20,21)➚

Vivian Arms ✓

104 Gower Road, Sketty, SA2 9BZ (Sketty Cross, jct of A4118 and A4216)

☼ 11.30-11 (midnight Fri & Sat); 12-11 Sun

☎ (01792) 516194

Brains Bitter, Rev James Gold, SA, Rev James; 1 changing beer ℍ

Situated on the main crossroads in Sketty, the Vivs is a spacious pub that attracts a wide range of customers young and old. It has a mixture of seating areas, and plenty of TV screens throughout that show live sport. There is a small meeting room (seating about 18 people), and the pub is suitable for family dining, with a popular carvery on Sundays. Live music plays on Fridays and occasional Saturdays, a general knowledge quiz is held on Sundays and a music quiz on Wednesdays. ⏃❀◑&⊟(20,21)➚

Westbourne

1 Brynymor Road, SA1 4JQ

☼ 11-11.30 (11 Mon); 11-12.30am Fri & Sat; 11-11 Sun

☎ (01792) 476637 ⊕ westbourneswansea.com

Greene King Abbot; Sharp's Doom Bar; 4 changing beers ℍ

Located on the western fringe of the city centre, this street-corner pub has a single split-level bar with various drinking areas including a heated terrace outside. Home to the first self-service beer wall in Wales and iPad tabletop ordering, it is now the place to go for young and old alike. Four to six ales are always available – customers are able to request a particular beer on the pub's website. A quiz is held on Tuesday evening. ❀◑&⊟(2,3)➚

Trefforest

Otley Arms ⌶

Forest Road, CF37 1SY (on gyratory system)

☼ 12-midnight (1am Sat) ☎ (01443) 402033

⊕ theotley.co.uk

Otley O1; 5 changing beers (sourced regionally; often Otley) ℍ

The Otley's diverse clientele, including university students, locals and visitors, have several comfortable rooms to explore. Guest beers include one or two Otley ales plus a well-chosen selection that can come from anywhere. The mostly traditional food is of a high standard. Live music plays on the last Friday of the month, and also features at the popular spring cider festival and Oct-O-Bar beer festival. Handy for buses and trains. ⏃◑&≥♣⊟(90,100)🐾

Treorchy

Pencelli Hotel ▼ ✓

Pencae Terrace, CF42 6HL

☼ 2-11 (midnight Thu & Fri); closed Wed; 12-midnight Sat; 12-10.30 Sun ☎ (01443) 775181

6 changing beers (sourced nationally; often Bragdy Twt Lol, Cwm Rhondda Ales, Glamorgan) ℍ

Proudly independent and welcoming, the Pencelli Hotel is an excellent community pub with a central bar serving two large rooms. Local CAMRA Pub of the Year, and also Cider Pub of the Year 2017, the superb range of beers and ciders contrasts with other venues nearby. Weekly events include a quiz on Monday, pool night on Tuesday and live music Thursday to Saturday, where you might spot the landlord among the band members. Easily reached by bus and train, with ample parking opposite. ⏃❀◑≥♣⊟

Tyla Garw

Boar's Head

Coedcae Lane, CF72 9EZ (600yds from A473 over level crossing)

☼ 4-10 Mon; 12-11; 12-10 Sun ☎ (01443) 225400

9 changing beers (often Oakham, Salopian, Skinner's) ℍ

The pub has five rooms – bar, lounge, dining room, coffee bar/lounge and central bar. Up to eight changing beers are available, staff and locals are always happy to advise on choices. Regular beer festivals are held, often with beers direct from the cask. Booking is advised for the popular Sunday lunch. The direct walking route from Pontyclun station cuts through a small industrial area. Q⏃❀◑&≥♥P

Upper Church Village

Farmers Arms ✅
St Illtyd Road, CF38 1EB
❀ 3-11 Mon-Wed; 12-midnight Thu-Sat; 12-10.30 Sun
☎ (01443) 205766
Brains Rev James; 1 changing beer (sourced nationally; often Greene King, Wells) ⊞
Comfortable village local with one large bar, and a pleasant split-level beer garden and patio outside. The changing beers tend to be national brands, though often less common for the area. A popular quiz night is hosted on Tuesday, but beer and conversation are the main attractions. Traditional pub food and a logburner add to the appeal.
❀◑Pᗺ(90)❀

Upper Killay

Railway Inn ⓛ
553 Gower Road, SA2 7DS
❀ 12-11; 12-10.30 Sun ☎ (01792) 203946
Swansea Deep Slade Dark, Bishopswood Bitter, Three Cliffs Gold, Original Wood; 1 changing beer ⊞
A classic locals' pub set in woodlands at the top end of Clyne Valley. The adjacent former railway line now forms part of Route 4 of the National Cycle Network. In winter the real fire in the lounge provides welcome warmth and cheer. Traditional cider and at least one guest beer are kept alongside the Swansea Brewing Company beers. A large area outside hosts occasional barbecues, music events and boules tournaments in summer.
Q❀♣●Pᗺ

Wick

Star Inn
Ewenny Road, CF71 7QA
❀ 12 (5 Mon)-11.30; 12-10.30 Sun ☎ (01656) 890080
⊕ thestarinnwick.co.uk
Wye Valley Bitter; 1 changing beer (often Brecon, Evan Evans, St Austell) ⊞

Originally three farm cottages, the interior has a traditional bar and a lounge/diner with flagstone floors and efficient fires in both rooms for when the temperature drops. An upstairs pool room also serves as a function room. The lounge bar was refurbished in 2016 and the public bar in spring 2017. The locals and staff make this a friendly and comfortable pub to spend time in and, with excellent food on offer, the Star is well worth a visit. Q❀❀◑♣●Pᗺ(303)❀☎

Ystalyfera

Corner House
70 Commercial Street, SA9 2HS
❀ 4-midnight; 3-1am Fri; 12-1am Sat; 12-10.30 Sun
☎ (01639) 849420
2 changing beers (sourced regionally) ⊞
Traditional village local, run by the same family for two generations. As the name suggests, it is situated on a corner site on the main (top) road in Ystalyfera. The main bar is to the left as you enter, with a separate lounge across the corridor. Live music and karaoke often feature on weekend evenings. A welcome addition in an area where real ale is hard to find. ᗺ♣●ᗺ(X50)❀☎

Wern Fawr ⓛ
47 Wern Road, SA9 2LX
❀ 2-5, 7 (6.30 Fri)-11; 12-3, 7-11 Sat; 12-midnight Sun
☎ (01639) 843625
Bryncelyn Holly Hop, Buddy Marvellous, Oh Boy; 1 changing beer (sourced locally; often Bryncelyn) ⊞
Recently celebrating over two decades of continuous entry in the Guide, this rare, unspoiled locals' pub is the tap for the Bryncelyn Brewery – the beers all adopting Buddy Holly-themed names. The pub has a central bar serving both the bar and lounge and hosts an interesting display of old mining, industrial and domestic artefacts. With a warm welcome for all, this is a must-visit for real ale and historic pub enthusiasts.
Q❀♣●ᗺ(X50)❀☎

Mountain Hare, Brynnau Gwynion

GWENT

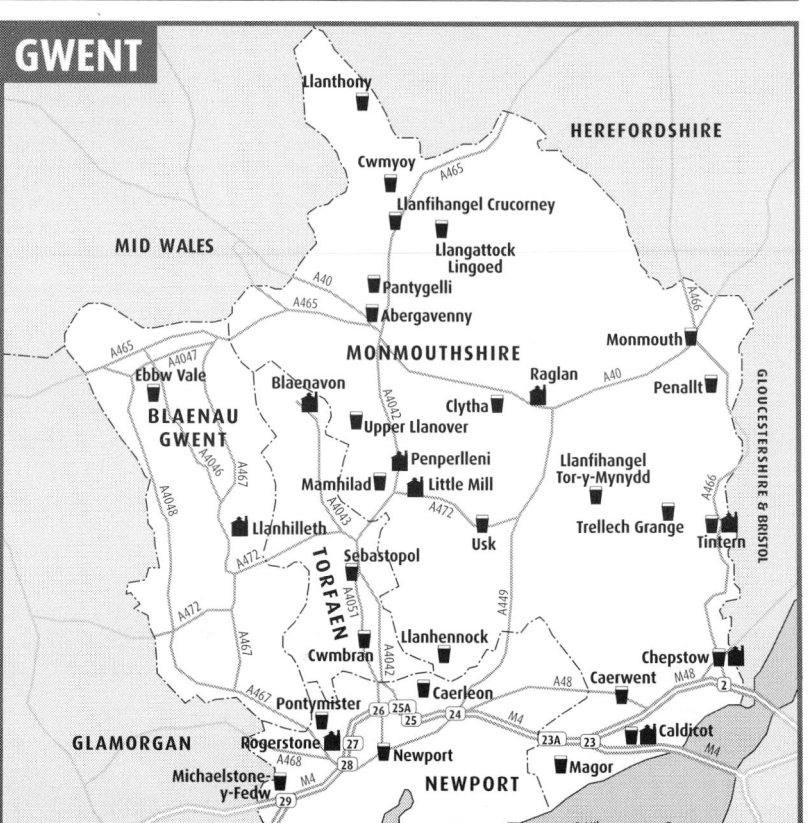

WALES

Authority areas covered: Blaenau Gwent UA, Caerphilly UA (part), Monmouthshire UA, Newport UA, Torfaen UA

Abergavenny

Grofield ⛚

Baker Street, NP7 5BT

☼ 5-11 Mon; 11-11.30 ☎ (01873) 858939 ⊕ grofield.com
Rhymney Bitter; Sharp's Doom Bar; 1 changing beer (sourced nationally; often St Austell, Wadworth, Wye Valley) ⒣

Just off the main street, opposite the cinema, this family owned and run free house has a U-shaped lounge around a central bar. The experienced licensee is committed to real ale and hosts an annual beer festival in the summer. On warm days the pleasant garden provides an oasis of green in the town centre. The pub is a popular lunch venue – evening food is also available Thursday to Saturday. Quiz night is Sunday. Q⛚🕸◑♣🖥🐾

Station Hotel

37 Brecon Road, NP7 5UH

☼ 5 (2 Wed & Thu)-11; 1-11.30 Fri; 12-11.30 Sat; 11.30-11 Sun ☎ (01873) 854759
Draught Bass; Rhymney Bitter; Wye Valley HPA; 1 changing beer (sourced nationally) ⒣

A pub like they used to be, with a separate bar and lounge, no piped music and no meals – and with close-to-legendary status in the locality. A CAMRA Real Heritage Pub of Wales, this no-frills hostelry

went slightly upmarket when the gents' toilet was moved inside! Apart from that little changes and the beer remains as good as ever. Even though the railway that gave the place its name has gone, the pub goes on, as strong as ever. ♣P🖥🐾

Caerleon

Priory Hotel ⛚

High Street, NP18 1AG

☼ 12-3, 6.30-11 ☎ (01633) 421241
⊕ thepriorycaerleon.co.uk
Felinfoel Double Dragon; Wye Valley Butty Bach; 2 changing beers (sourced regionally) ⒣

REAL ALE BREWERIES

Baa Chepstow
Castles Caldicot
Kingstone Tintern
Mad Dog Penperlleni
Melin Tap 🍺 Little Mill (NEW)
Rhymney Blaenavon
Tiny Rebel Rogerstone
Tudor Llanhilleth
Untapped Raglan

This historic gem of a building was once an old priory and is now a thriving hotel and restaurant. A long well-appointed bar offers an extensive range of drinks, including up to four real ales (two in winter) at upmarket prices. The decor around the bar is dark and the lighting subdued – easy listening background music adds to the relaxing ambience. Note the wood carvings near the rear entrance. A spacious patio looks towards manicured lawns and gardens. ♿🏵🍴🛏◑🅿️🚗🛜

Red Lion 🅛 ⏣

Backhall Street, NP18 1AR
⏣ 12-11 (12.30am Fri & Sat); 12-10.30 Sun
☎ (01633) 420284 ⊕ theredlioncaerleon.co.uk
St Austell Proper Job; Sharp's Doom Bar; 1 changing beer (sourced locally; often Tiny Rebel) Ⓗ
Popular back-street pub attracting a loyal following from local customers as well as those from further afield. The open-plan interior links what were once a separate public bar and lounge. At the rear is a spacious garden that has an ancient Roman wall as part of its perimeter. Food is a big attraction (booking is advised). The guest beer is nearly always sourced from Tiny Rebel Brewery.
♿🏵◑♣🅿️🛜

Caerwent

Coach & Horses

Green Lane, NP26 5AX
⏣ 12-11 ☎ (01291) 420352
⊕ caerwent-coachandhorses.co.uk
Brains Rev James; Wye Valley HPA, Butty Bach; 1 changing beer (sourced regionally; often Baa, Evan Evans, Glamorgan) Ⓗ
Central village inn near extensive Roman walls – this famous Roman site has a CADW (Welsh Government historic environment service) visitor centre. The pub has a traditional public bar with tiled floor, comfortable seating, darts and pool. There is also a cosy lounge, restaurant and tea rooms. Food is sourced primarily from local suppliers. The large garden has a patio and play area alongside the Roman walls.
♿🏵🍴◑♣🅿️ (73)🐾🛜

Caldicot

Castle Inn

64 Church Road, NP26 4HW
⏣ closed Mon; 12-11 (midnight Fri & Sat) ☎ (01291) 420509
⊕ thecastleinncaldicot.com
2 changing beers (sourced nationally; often Greene King) Ⓗ
In keeping with its location near Caldicot Castle & Country Park, there are miniature cannons near the entrance to this pub and an impressive play fort for children in the garden. The pleasant low-beamed interior has a spacious lounge/dining area and a cosy bar with a large fireplace as its focal point. Two or three guest ales are sourced from national, regional and family brewers. Food is popular, with a good choice from an extensive menu.
♿🏵◑♿🅿️ (74)

Chepstow

Beaufort Hotel ⏣

Beaufort Square, St Mary's Street, NP16 5EP
⏣ 12-11 (1am Sat); 12-10.30 Sun ☎ (01291) 622497
⊕ beauforthotelchepstow.com

Sharp's Doom Bar; 1 changing beer (sourced regionally; often Butcombe) Ⓗ
Popular with locals and the business community, this relaxed town-centre hotel sports a single recently refurbished L-shaped bar, with a large side room for busy times. There is an air of reassuring continuity here, with 'Beaufort Hotel Circa 1650' on panels above the bar giving a clue to the hotel's longevity. Local scenes are framed within wall panels and a glass cabinet displays racing colours either side of a picture of champion jockey Lester Piggott. Q♿🏵🛏◑⟿🅿️🐾🛜

Chepstow Athletic Club 🅛

Mathern Road, Bulwark, NP16 5JJ (off Bulwark Rd)
⏣ 7-11 (11.30 Fri); 12.30-11.30 (midnight summer) Sat; 7-11 Sun ☎ (01291) 622126
Brains SA; Greene King IPA; 2 changing beers (sourced regionally) Ⓗ
This long-standing Guide entry caters for a broad range of local people and community groups, including sports players and enthusiasts of all ages. The consistent quality and high turnover of the two regular ales and two guests, often from smaller independent breweries, reflect the dedication of the bar management team – who also ensure CAMRA members receive a warm welcome. Real ale is also available in an upstairs function room, while a pleasant patio suits sunny weekend afternoons. ♿🏵♿♣🅿️🛜

Five Alls

Hocker Hill Street, NP16 5ER
⏣ 12-midnight (11 Mon-Wed) ☎ (01291) 622528
2 changing beers (sourced nationally; often Butcombe, Robinsons) Ⓗ
An old pub built in 1849 on a cobbled street with a superb sign above the entrance depicting the Five Alls. A pub of character, the interior retains most of the original layout with some touches of modernity. The emphasis here is on rock music with a digital jukebox and live music. It has a pinball machine and pool is free to play on Sunday and Monday. 🏵⟿♣🅿️🐾🛜

Queen's Head 🍺 🅛

Moor Street, NP16 5DD
⏣ closed Mon; 5-11; 12-2.30, 5-11 Sat; 12-4 Sun ☎ 07793 889613
8 changing beers (sourced regionally; often Castles, Gower, Untapped) Ⓖ
This welcoming micropub has achieved local CAMRA recognition as it ticks so many boxes. An eclectic range of furniture provides comfort while you sup your drink and take in the atmosphere. Chatter and laughter dominate – there is no obtrusive noise from TVs or electronic games here – and you cannot help but be drawn into friendly conversation. The ale and cider range is mainly from Wales although occasional themed weeks are held featuring beers from other regions. Q⟿♥🅿️

Clytha

Clytha Arms 🅛

Groesonen Road, NP7 9BW (on B4598 old road between Abergavenny and Raglan)
⏣ 12-3.30 (not Mon), 6-midnight; 12-midnight Fri & Sat; 12-11 Sun ☎ (01873) 840206 ⊕ clytha-arms.com
Brecon Three Beacons; Untapped Sundown; Wye Valley Bitter; 3 changing beers (sourced regionally) Ⓗ
This acclaimed multi award-winning classic country free house strikes a happy balance between being

both a pub and a restaurant. Six ales, usually from Wales, complement up to four mostly local ciders. Several festivals each year including an Oktoberfest celebrate ale, cider and other tasty delights such as cheese and dumplings, while the pub's high-quality home-cooked meals have gained a fine reputation far beyond Wales. Top-rate accommodation, including a room with a four-poster bed, is popular year-round.
Q☕🍴🕭🍽🛊♿♣🚗P🚃(83)♨

Cwmbran

John Fielding ⓛ ✔
1 Caradoc Road, NP44 1PP
☕ 8am-midnight; 7am-1am Fri & Sat ☎ (01633) 833760
Greene King Abbot; Ruddles Best Bitter; Sharp's Doom Bar; 2 changing beers Ⓗ
The only pub serving Cwmbran's shopping and entertainment centre keeps its clientele happy with the Wetherspoon package of competitively priced food and drinks. The regular real ales are supplemented by two guest ales often sourced from Welsh breweries. The large-open plan room offers a choice of drinking and dining areas. John Fielding, masquerading as John Williams, is a local hero who won the VC at the Battle of Rorke's Drift (1879) in the Zulu Wars. Q☕🕭🍽♿🚃♣🚗P🚃

Mount Pleasant
Wesley Street, Old Cwmbran, NP44 3LX
☕ 4-9 Mon; 12-11; 12-midnight Fri & Sat ☎ (01633) 712176
2 changing beers (sourced regionally; often Evan Evans, Kingstone) Ⓗ
A cosy and welcoming community hub in the heart of old Cwmbran village. The L-shaped layout is partly split-level, comfortable and tastefully decorated. While very much a locals' pub, there is always a welcome for a visitor. Two handpumps are kept busy dispensing constantly changing ales primarily from Welsh breweries, which the pub is keen to support, especially those from Kingstone. The food is popular. Well-behaved dogs are welcome outside prime dining times.
☕🕭🍽♣🚗P(6)♨

Cwmyoy

Queen's Head 🏆
NP7 7NE (leave A465 at Llanfihangel Crucorney and in centre of village near Skirrid Inn, take lane signposted to Llanthony; pub is about a mile on right) SO311221
☕ 10.30-2 (not Tue & Fri), 6-11; closed Wed; 11-3, 6-11 Sat; 12-4 Sun ☎ (01873) 890241
Kingstone Classic Ⓗ
Situated in beautiful countryside just a couple of miles from the main road, the pub is often known as Billy's in honour of its licensee of nearly 40 years standing. The antiquity of the building is reflected in its solid wooden beams and heavy flagstone floors. With good walking country all around you can leave your car in the car park (for a small charge), stretch your legs and return later for a beer. The regular Kingstone beer might at times be joined by another from the brewery. Q🕭🕭P

Ebbw Vale

Picture House ✔
Market Street, NP23 6HP
☕ 8am-11 (midnight Fri & Sat) ☎ (01495) 352382

Greene King Abbot; Ruddles Best Bitter; Sharp's Doom Bar; 3 changing beers (sourced nationally) Ⓗ
This popular Wetherspoon pub derives its name from a former cinema that once stood on part of the site, although the present building is a converted supermarket. The spacious interior offers several levels for drinking and dining including a cosy upstairs area with a fireplace and small pictures of film scenes. Elsewhere the decor includes a remarkable 3D-effect picture of the town alongside local scenes and colourful artwork. Interesting guest ales complement the standard favourites. Q☕🕭🕭♿≠(Town)🚃🚃?

Llanfihangel Crucorney

Skirrid Inn
Hereford Road, NP7 8DH
☕ 11.30-2.30 (not Mon), 5.30-11; 11.30-11 Sat; 12-5 Sun
☎ (01873) 890258 ⊕ skirridmountaininn.co.uk
2 changing beers (sourced nationally; often Wye Valley) Ⓗ
The Skirrid claims to be the oldest pub in Wales. Owain Glyndwr is reputed to have rallied his troops here and the building once doubled as a court house, with many men sentenced to hang from a beam in the corridor behind the bar. Stone floors, heavy beams and a huge fireplace emphasise the scale of the building, part of the estate of the Marquis of Abergavenny until 1900. Beers come from national breweries, usually including one from Wye Valley. Q🕭🍴🕭 ♠P🚃(X3)♨

Llanfihangel Tor-y-Mynydd

Star Inn ✔
NP15 1DT (near Llansoy)
☕ 4-8 Mon; 5-9 Tue; 5-11 Wed-Fri; 12-11 Sat; 12-5 Sun
☎ (01291) 650256 ⊕ thestarllansoy.co.uk
2 changing beers (sourced regionally; often St Austell) Ⓗ
The public bar has a separate entrance from the restaurant and is comfortably furnished with sofas and a large wood-burning stove. The restaurant serves home-cooked food made to order, and extends into a large conservatory, with three more fireplaces. Disabled access is at the back through the conservatory. The pub produces its own cider and occasionally perry, which are sold seasonally. Well worth seeking out. ☕🕭🕭♿♠♣🚗P♨

Llangattock Lingoed

Hunter's Moon Inn
NP7 8RR SO363201
☕ 12-11 ☎ (01873) 821499 ⊕ hunters-moon-inn.co.uk
Wye Valley HPA Ⓗ/Ⓖ, Butty Bach Ⓗ; 1 changing beer (sourced regionally) Ⓗ/Ⓖ
A haven for walkers on Offa's Dyke, providing accommodation as well as excellent beer. Run by three generations of the same family, the pub has undoubtedly become the hub of social activity in the village. Whatever time of day you arrive, you are assured of a warm welcome, sustenance and conversation. The traditional flagstone-floored bar has an owl gazing down from beneath a bright hunter's moon. Adjacent to the pub is a most interesting 14th-century church.
Q☕🕭🍴🕭♣♨?

Llanhennock

Wheatsheaf

NP18 1LT (turn right 1 mile along Usk road heading N from Caerleon; bear left at fork) ST353927
☼ 11 (2 Sat)-11; 12-4, 8-11 Sun ☎ (01633) 420468
Fuller's London Pride; 2 changing beers (sourced regionally) Ⓗ
This traditional inn has over three decades in this Guide under its belt, a run which looks likely to continue. The country pub has two bars adorned with old photographs and memorabilia, fine views of the hills on both sides, and a secluded outside drinking area with swings. Boules is played in one section of the car park. One of the two ever-changing guest ales is usually locally produced.
⌂✿◐▲♣P🐾

Llanthony

Half Moon

NP7 7NN SO286279
☼ 12-11; closed Wed; 12-10.30 Sun ☎ (01873) 890611
⊕ halfmoon-llanthony.co.uk
Wye Valley Butty Bach; 1 changing beer (sourced regionally; often Wye Valley) Ⓗ
Set in a remote spot in the Black Mountains, the pub is situated a couple of hundred yards beyond the romantic ruins of Llanthony Abbey. Spectacular walking and trekking country, it said to be one of the most beautiful areas in Wales and is a remarkable place to enjoy a beer. Formed out of two workman's cottages dating back to the 1700s the pub features stone-flagged floors and a warm fire on cold days, which emphasises the simplistic style, with the focus on rest and relaxation. Closed weekday lunchtimes in winter.
Q⌂✿✿╬◐▲♣P🐾🛜

Magor

Wheatsheaf Ⓛ

The Square, NP26 3HN
☼ 10-11 (midnight Fri & Sat); 12-11 Sun ☎ (01633) 880608
4 changing beers (sourced regionally; often Castles, Rhymney, Sharp's) Ⓗ
Just off the village square, this old whitewashed pub is welcoming with its charming multi-roomed interior. The Tap Room public bar is lively with games while the lounge is cosy with a warming fire on colder days – it is here where the handpumps dispense an interesting mix of local and national ales from breweries large and small. Off the lounge is a small snug and restaurant. The decor exudes character with plenty of exposed stone and low wooden beams.
⌂✿◐♿♣P🚌(62,74)🐾🛜

Mamhilad

Horseshoe Inn ✔

Old Abergavenny Road, NP4 8QZ
☼ 12-3, 5-11; 11.30-midnight Fri-Sun ☎ (01873) 880542
⊕ horseshoeinn.org
Mad Dog Y Ffoledd/Holy Well; 2 changing beers (sourced nationally) Ⓗ
This welcoming 200-year-old pub has an outside drinking area with fine views of the surrounding hills, where you can sup to the sound of bleating sheep. The bar with its slate floor retains the cosy feel of a country pub and attracts walkers seeking refreshment. An appetising menu of fresh food has

a fine reputation. The guest ales, which sit alongside the locally brewed house ale, are usually interesting for the area, while real cider is also served. Q⌂✿◐▲♣P🐾🛜

Michaelstone-y-Fedw

Cefn Mably Arms ✔

CF3 6XS
☼ 12-11; 12-10.30 Sun ☎ (01633) 680347
⊕ cefnmablyarms.com
Brains Bitter; Butcombe Gold; Wye Valley HPA, Butty Bach Ⓗ
Pleasant local pub slightly off the beaten track a couple of miles from the A48 at Castleton. The interior is divided into three distinct areas, mainly laid out for diners, with a good selection of well-kept ales available. A recently opened 'cwtch' next to the bar provides an additional dining space without encroaching on the drinking area.
Q⌂✿◐▮P🐾🛜

Monmouth

Old Nag's Head

Granville Street, NP25 3DR
☼ 2 (12 Sat)-midnight; 12-11 Sun ☎ (01600) 712220
Brains Bitter, Rev James; 1 changing beer (sourced locally; often Brains) Ⓗ
This venerable pub is one of the oldest in Wales. While the main building is believed to date from at least 1765, it embraces the Gate Room which forms part of the 13th-century Dixton Gate. The multi-roomed interior recalls a pub of yesteryear with low beams and wood panelling. Music is popular and draws in folk from all around. A collection of old bank notes and rugby tickets is displayed on beams in the front snug.
⌂✿▲♣🚌🐾🛜

Newport

McCann's Rock 'n' Ale Bar Ⓛ

10 High Street, NP20 1FQ
☼ 12-11 (3am Fri & Sat) ☎ 07953 238194
Robinsons Trooper; 1 changing beer (sourced regionally; often Untapped) Ⓗ
Risen from the ashes of the much missed Hornblower at the other end of town (now scheduled for demolition) in April 2016, McCann's is owned by its former manager. Much of the Blowers memorabilia has been transferred here. The long bar has a raised stage area on the left for live bands on Saturday nights. If you like your music loud 'n' heavy, this is the place for you. The ales are sometimes accompanied by a traditional cider. ✿⇌♣🚌🐾🛜

Olde Murenger House

52-53 High Street, NP20 1GA
☼ 12-11; 12-3, 7.30-10.30 Sun ☎ (01633) 263977
Samuel Smith Old Brewery Bitter Ⓗ
A Tudor building that served many purposes in the past before becoming a pub in 1903. The hostelry is a local institution – behind its leaded windows is a characterful interior of dark wood, high-back settles, and a gallery of brewery scenes and images of Newport, including sporting greats. It has a friendly ambience with no obtrusive noise, just chatter and laughter, and has been well run by the same management team for over 25 years – visit, relax, enjoy. ◐⇌🚌🐾

Pen & Wig 🅛

22-24 Stow Hill, NP20 1JD

🕐 10-11 (midnight Fri); 11-midnight Sat; 12-10.30 Sun
☎ (01633) 666818

Brains SA; Draught Bass; Felinfoel Celtic Pride; 3 changing beers (sourced regionally; often Brains, Gloucester) Ⓗ

Former business premises transformed into a pub for all ages. It has plenty of seating spread over several areas, all within sight of a TV to watch the sport. The kitchen serves up an appetising range of food that can be washed down by the regular ales or those from Welsh and West Country brewers, or the ciders stacked behind the bar. Upstairs is a large function area, while the deck patio at the rear also has its own TV. ❀◑≠♣●P🖶

Ruperra Arms ✔

73 Caerphilly Road, Bassaleg, NP10 8LJ

🕐 12-midnight ☎ (01633) 894255 🌐 theruperraarms.co.uk

Brains Bitter; Fuller's London Pride; 2 changing beers (sourced locally) Ⓗ

Small but busy local with an emphasis on quality locally sourced food. Four ales are always available, with at least one from the nearby Tiny Rebel Brewery. While much of the pub is set up for dining, drinkers are welcome in the cosy bar area. Outside is a small drinking/smoking area next to the modest car park. The regular menu is complemented by an ever-changing selection of chef's specials. Q❀◑●P🖶(37,50)🛜

St Julian Inn ✔

Caerleon Road, NP18 1QA

🕐 11.30-11.30 (midnight Fri & Sat); 12-11 Sun
☎ (01633) 243548 🌐 stjulian.co.uk

Wells Bombardier; Young's Bitter; 2 changing beers (sourced regionally; often Bath Ales, Ludlow, Wye Valley) Ⓗ

This wonderful edge-of-town inn has now featured in 26 consecutive issues of the Guide. Set in a beautiful riverside location alongside the River Usk, the balcony, garden and bar areas all offer superb scenic views. Handily placed for the Roman village and tourist attractions of Caerleon, the pub has a loyal following from all age groups. Cask ale is the central feature and although tied to a pubco, the guest ales are unusual for the area.
❀◑♣P🖶🐾🛜

Tiny Rebel

22-23 High Street, NP20 1FX

🕐 12-11 (1am Fri & Sat); closed Sun ☎ (01633) 252538

Tiny Rebel Fubar, Dirty Stopout; 4 changing beers (sourced nationally; often Tiny Rebel) Ⓗ

Tiny Rebel's spiritual home is Newport and this refreshingly airy and spacious outlet is where the brewery showcases its regular ales as well as new additions to the portfolio. Collaborative swaps with other innovative breweries add to an already exciting range of beers, to be savoured along with a tasty burger or pizza from a creative food menu. Downstairs, the Cwtch lounge is cosy, while a view into the cellar gives an insight into the pub's operation. ❀◑&≠🖶🐾🛜

Pantygelli

Crown Inn 🅛

Old Hereford Road, NP7 7HR

🕐 12-2.30 (not Mon), 6-11; 12-3, 6-11 Sat; 12-3, 6-10.30 Sun
☎ (01873) 853314 🌐 thecrownatpantygelli.com

Draught Bass; Rhymney Best; Wye Valley HPA; 1 changing beer (sourced regionally; often Grey Trees, Kingstone, Monty's) Ⓗ

This family-owned gastro-pub has a reputation for the quality of its food and beers that goes far beyond the hamlet in which it is found. Situated beneath the National Trust owned Sugar Loaf and with long views across to the Skirrid Mountain, this is walking country and ramblers are made welcome. On warm days the patio is a lovely place for alfresco dining and drinking, while in the cold of winter a log-burning stove helps create a cosy atmosphere. ❀◑●♣P

Penallt

Boat Inn

Lone Lane, NP25 4AJ

🕐 12-11 ☎ (01600) 712615 🌐 theboatpenallt.co.uk

Wye Valley Butty Bach; 2 changing beers (sourced regionally; often Butcombe, Goff's, Wickwar) Ⓖ

Perched on the banks of the River Wye, a wooded embankment behind it and cascading streams beside it, this pub is in an idyllic spot. Two simply furnished rooms cater for local and passing trade. Ales served from their casks and a choice of ciders accompany tasty wholesome food. Park in England then cross the river alongside a disused railway bridge to sup in Wales. Closed on Tuesday in winter. ❀◑♣●P🖶(69)🐾

Pontymister

Commercial Inn 🅛 ✔

Commercial Street, NP11 6BA

🕐 11 (10 Sat)-11.30; 12-11.30 Sun ☎ (01633) 612608
🌐 thecommercialpontymister.com

4 changing beers (sourced nationally; often Tiny Rebel) Ⓗ

On the main street, this popular open-plan pub caters for sports lovers, with up to five TVs always on, showing different sporting events at the same time, but muted except for major events. One of the four ales is usually from Tiny Rebel Brewery – sometimes two. Other ales tend to include one well-known national traditional bitter, while the rest are from microbreweries and often tend to be light and hoppy. Good-value food is available.
❀◑&≠♣🖶🛜

Sebastopol

Sebastopol Social Club 🅛

Wern Road, NP4 5DU (on corner of Wern Rd with Austin Rd)

🕐 12-11 (midnight Fri & Sat); 12-10.30 Sun
☎ (01495) 763808 🌐 sebastopolsocial.org.uk

Wye Valley HPA; 3 changing beers (sourced regionally; often Grey Trees, RCH) Ⓗ

A smart building with an equally tidy and comfortably furnished interior, providing a warm welcome for club members and CAMRA members (subject to entry rules). The club has been a regular award winner over many years and maintains its commitment to real ale and cider. The beer range usually includes a returning favourite or two, and sometimes surprises with a new ale from one of the many local regional breweries. The venue caters for indoor sports, functions and live entertainment. ❀&♣●P🖶🐾🛜

WALES

Tintern

Anchor Inn
NP16 6TE (off A466 at Tintern Abbey)
☼ 9am-11; 12-10.30 Sun ☎ (01291) 689582
⊕ theanchortintern.com
3 changing beers (sourced regionally; often Otter, Wye Valley, Kingstone) Ⓗ
A stone's toss from the surging River Wye, the Anchor oozes with the rich history of this beautiful valley, at one time pounding with industry and at another solemnly and silently monastic – the local Cistercian monks made their cider here and their massive press is still the centrepiece of the bar. The large pub has gained a strong reputation for its food and ales – Kingstone, Wye Valley and Otter beers are usually available and enjoy a high turnover. Muddy boots and pets are welcome. ☎☼❀◑➦PⒺ(69)☞

Wye Valley Hotel
Monmouth Road, NP16 6SQ
☼ 11-3, 6-11; 12-3, 6.30-10.30 Sun ☎ (01291) 689441
⊕ thewyevalleyhotel.co.uk
Wye Valley HPA, Butty Bach; 1 changing beer (sourced locally; often Kingstone) Ⓗ
A Tintern landmark since the 1930s, this distinctive and welcoming roadside pub at the north end of the village is a fine base from which to explore the magnificent scenery and history of the lower Wye Valley. It is a long-standing outlet for Wye Valley ales and also often offers a guest ale from the nearby Kingstone Brewery. Good home-cooked food is available in the bar and adjoining traditional restaurant. With accommodation too, the pub is popular with locals and visitors all year round. ☎☼❀◑➦⑤APⒺ(69)❀☞

Trellech Grange

Fountain Inn
NP16 6QW SO503101
☼ closed Mon; 4-10 (11 Fri); 12-10 Sat & Sun
☎ (01291) 689303 ⊕ fountaininntrellech.co.uk
Kingstone Gold; Untapped Border Bitter; 1 changing beer (sourced locally) Ⓗ

Welcoming 17th-century pub with a stream flowing beneath it, helping to keep the ales cool. The pleasant open-plan bar has a real fire in winter. It offers an appetising range of food and caters for parties and functions. Midweek activities include cribbage on Tuesday, a quiz on Wednesday and darts on Thursday. The landlord takes great pride in serving well-kept ales from local breweries. In summer, opening time is midday on Thursday and Friday. ☎☼❀◑➦Å➦PⒺ

Upper Llanover

Goose & Cuckoo Ⓛ
NP7 9ER SO292073
☼ closed Mon; 11.30-3, 7-11 Tue-Thu; 11.30-11 Fri & Sat; 12-10.30 Sun ☎ (01873) 880277
Rhymney Bitter; Tudor Skirrid; Untapped Border Bitter; 1 changing beer (sourced regionally) Ⓗ
It is definitely worth making the effort to seek out this refreshingly unchanged traditional pub. The interior is particularly interesting, with a pictorial history of the area on the walls and comfortable settles. It serves three beers from local breweries as well as an excellent range of whiskies. Popular with walkers and cyclists alike, on a fine summer's day there are marvellous panoramic views from the garden towards the Skirrid Mountain and England. Q☎☼❀◑➦♣P❀

Usk

Nag's Head Ⓛ
Twyn Square, NP15 1BH
☼ 9.30am-2.30, 5-11 (10.30 Fri-Sun) ☎ (01291) 672820
⊕ nagsheadusk.co.uk
Brains Rev James; Sharp's Doom Bar Ⓗ
A fascinating pub dating from 1641, well known for a good range of tasty locally sourced food. There is an almost bewildering array of artefacts on display, including a gallery of old black-and-white and sepia pictures, agricultural implements, a fine collection of plaques from former businesses and the unusual brass taps on the front panel of the bar. During summer the front is a blaze of colour with hanging baskets and potted plants. Q☎☼◑⑤Ⓔ(60,63)

Of Ale
Ale is made of malte and water, and they the which do put any other thynge to ale than is rehersed, except yest, barme or godisgood (other forms of yeast) do sofysticat (adulterate) theyr ale. Ale for an englysshe man is a natural drynke. Ale must have these propertyes, it must be freshe and cleare, it must not be ropy (cloudy) or smoky, nor it must have no welt nor tayle (sediment or dregs). Ale should not be dronke under V days olde. Newe ale is unholsome for all men. And soure ale and deade ale the which doth stande a tylt is good for no man. Barley malte maketh better ale then oten malte or any other corne doth, it doth engender grosse humoures, but yette it maketh a man stronge.

Of Bere
Bere is made of malte, of hoppes, and water, it is a natural drinke for a dutche man. And nowe of late dayes it is moche used in Englande to the detryment of many englysshe men, specyally it kylleth them the which be troubled with the colycke and the stone & strangulion (quinsy), for the drynke is a colde drynke: yet it doth make a man fat and doth inflate the bely, as it doth appere by the dutche mens faces & belyes. If the beer be well served and be fyned & not newe, it doth qualify ye heat of the lyver.
Andrew Boorde (c.1490-1549),
A 'Compendyous Regyment' or 'a Dyetary of Helth', 1542

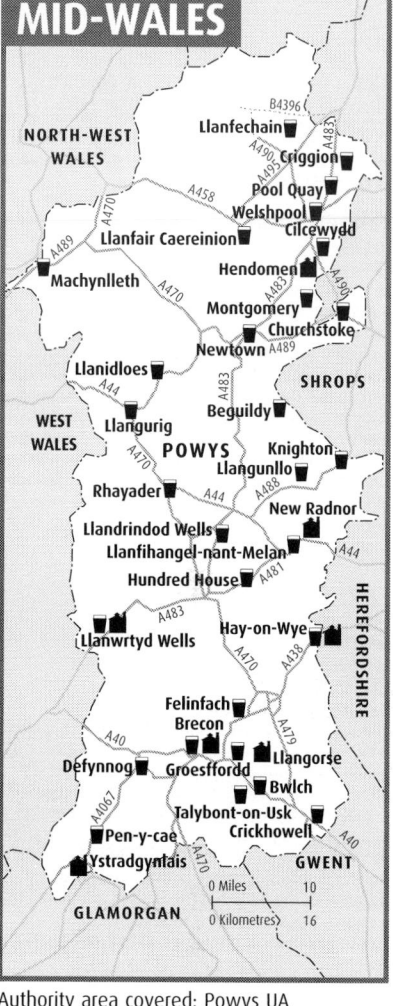

MID-WALES

Authority area covered: Powys UA

Beguildy

Radnorshire Arms
LD7 1YE

🌣 closed Mon; 12-2, 6-11 (midnight Fri & Sat); 12-3.30, 7-11 Sun ☎ (01547) 510634

2 changing beers (sourced regionally; often Ludlow, Stonehouse) Ⓗ

The Radnorshire Arms dates back to the 16th century and was probably a drovers' pub at one time. There is a cosy bar with an inglenook, an intimate dining area and a pleasant garden to the side. The beers are from Ludlow and Stonehouse breweries. The pub is popular with diners and offers separate menus for lunchtimes, evenings and Sunday lunches as well as daily specials.
🏠◑P🖾

Brecon

Brecon Rugby Club
63 The Watton, LD3 7EL

🌣 5-11; 11-11 Sat & Sun ☎ (01874) 624848

🌐 breconrfc.co.uk

3 changing beers Ⓗ

A founder member of the Welsh RFU, this friendly and welcoming club is open to all. A main bar with separate lounge is towards the front, and there is a large function room with a big screen beyond the bar. Outside is a spacious patio garden and the Brecon Pétanque Club. Beers from local brewers are frequently available plus bottled ciders from Gwynt y Ddraig. The pub is often busy during the rugby season, particularly when Wales are playing.
🚫🏠◑♣P🖾😊♿🛜

Brecon Tap
6 Bulwark, LD3 7LB

🌣 11-11 (midnight Fri & Sat); 12-11 Sun ☎ (01874) 623888

🌐 breconinns.co.uk

Brecon Three Beacons, Copper Beacons, Gold Beacons; 3 changing beers (sourced regionally) Ⓗ

Owned by Brecon Brewing, the Tap is in a prime central location. Contemporary in style, it has a light and airy feel, with comfortable seating throughout and walls lined with bottle-filled shelves. Three Brecon ales are usually on tap plus three guests, often from Welsh breweries, sometimes from further afield. There is also an interesting range of international ales, plus simple food – good-value pies, sandwiches and the like. Bottled beers, wines, craft spirits and local artisan produce are available to take away.
Q🏠◑♿🍴🖾😊🛜

Clarence
25 The Watton, LD3 7ED

🌣 12-midnight (2am Fri & Sat) ☎ (01874) 622810

🌐 clarenceinn.co.uk

Wye Valley Bitter, Butty Bach; 1 changing beer (often Brecon) Ⓗ

Two-roomed town-centre community pub with a contemporary, welcoming and relaxed atmosphere. The newly extended front bar tends to be frequented by locals, while the larger back bar is popular with diners. A large TV screen draws a crowd for big sporting events. Outside, the spacious garden is an attraction, especially during the renowned Brecon Jazz Festival. Guest beers are usually sourced from local breweries.
🏠😊🍴◑♣●🖾😊

Bwlch

New Inn 🍺
Brecon Road, LD3 7RQ (on A40 between Brecon and Crickhowell)

🌣 5 (12 Sat)-11; 12-8 Sun ☎ (01874) 730215

🌐 beaconsbackpackers.co.uk

Felinfoel Double Dragon; Wye Valley Butty Bach; 2 changing beers (sourced regionally; often Dark Star, Salopian, Tiny Rebel) Ⓗ

Lively and cosy village pub popular both with locals and visitors. A comfortable dining area sits to the side of the stone-flagged public bar, with armchairs

REAL ALE BREWERIES

9 Lives Ystradgynlais (NEW)
Brecon Brecon
Heart of Wales 🍺 Llanwrtyd Wells
Lithic Llangorse (NEW)
Lucky 7 Hay on Wye (NEW) (brewing suspended)
Monty's Hendomen
Radnorshire New Radnor
Tydwals Llangorse

and settles arranged around a huge fireplace. Two always interesting guest ales supplement the two regulars, and good-value home-cooked food is served evenings, and lunchtimes at weekends. The pub is an excellent base for exploring the surrounding Brecon Beacons and Black Mountains, with bunkhouse accommodation available. Local CAMRA Pub of the Year 2017.
Q ⑤ ❀ 🍴 ◑ ♣ ➌ P 🚃 (X43) ❀ 🛜

Churchstoke

Horse & Jockey
SY15 6AE
🕐 12 (4.30 Mon & Tue)-11 ☎ (01588) 620060
2 changing beers (sourced regionally) H
A prominent stone-built pub on the edge of the village, offering an ever-changing range of guest ales, and up to nine real ciders and perries during the summer. The public bar is wooden beamed with a pool table, darts and a bar billiards table. The lounge is carpeted, with comfortable armchairs and wall seating. There is a stone fireplace with a wood-burning stove. A large well-appointed restaurant is off the lounge.
⑤ ❀ ◑ ⅙ ♣ ➌ P 🚃 (81) 🛜

Cilcewydd

Square & Compass
SY21 8RU
🕐 4.30 (1 Sat)-11; 12-11 Sun ☎ (01938) 580360
Sharp's Doom Bar; 1 changing beer (sourced regionally) H
A popular community pub with two rooms – a long main room divided in two by comfortable bench seating, and a second room with seating around the sides. Old agricultural photos decorate the walls. This welcoming rural local mainly survives on wet sales, with bar snacks available. It has a large rear beer garden, and gents have the choice of inside or outside toilets. Situated just off the road, it can easily be missed. Q ❀ ◑ ♣ P 🚃 (71,81) ❀ 🛜

Crickhowell

Bear Hotel
High Street, NP8 1BW
🕐 10-11; 11-10.30 Sun ☎ (01873) 810408
🌐 bearhotel.co.uk
Brains Rev James; Sharp's Doom Bar; 2 changing beers (sourced regionally) H
Originally a 15th-century coaching inn, this is now an award-winning hotel. The multi-roomed bar enjoys grand surroundings with exposed beams, wood panelling, fine settles and an eclectic selection of furnishings and decorations. The two bar rooms have exposed fireplaces, as does one of the side rooms. Food is excellent, with a varied menu featuring much local produce. The hotel is an excellent base for exploring the surrounding Black Mountains and Brecon Beacons National Park.
Q ⑤ ❀ 🍴 ◑ ⅙ A P 🚃 (43/X43) ❀

Criggion

Admiral Rodney Inn
SY5 9AU
🕐 12-11; 12-10 Sun ☎ (01938) 570313
Salopian Oracle; Wye Valley Butty Bach H
This unspoilt rural inn dates back to the mid-1700s and is named after an admiral who harvested local

oak to build his ships – he is honoured with a pillar on the adjacent hill. The pub is a base for walkers exploring the area. The single-room interior has a fireplace at both ends and a restaurant area to the right as you enter. Posters of Terry Pratchett's Discworld novels decorate the dining space.
Q ⑤ ❀ 🍴 ◑ ♣ ⅙ P ❀

Defynnog

Tanners Arms
LD3 8SF (on A4067)
🕐 5-midnight; 12-midnight Fri-Sun ☎ (01874) 638032
🌐 tannersarmspub.com
5 changing beers H/G
Family-run country pub known for its warm welcome to both locals and tourists, set in a delightful village in the Brecon Beacons National Park. It has traded continuously since 1870 but the original buildings, cottages for workers at the nearby tannery, date from circa 1806. A selection of real ciders is usually on offer alongside home-cooked food. A number of beer and cider festivals are held throughout the year. A multiple local CAMRA award winner.
⑤ ❀ 🍴 ◑ A ♣ ➌ P 🚃 (T6) ❀ 🛜

Felinfach

Griffin L
LD3 0UB (just off A470 3 miles NE of Brecon)
🕐 12-11.30 ☎ (01874) 620111
4 changing beers (sourced locally) H
The pub's ethos – the simple things in life done well – says it all. A welcoming country pub, restaurant and rooms, the emphasis here is on good beer and excellent food. The multi-roomed layout allows for discrete areas for drinking and dining. The huge fireplace between the bar and the main dining area dominates in winter, while an Aga lurks in a side room, providing warmth throughout the building. The garden affords superb views of the surrounding mountains. Beers are sourced from local breweries. Q ⑤ ❀ 🍴 ◑ ⅙ P 🚃

Groesffordd

Three Horseshoes ✔
LD3 7SN (just off B4558 in centre of village)
🕐 12-3 (not Mon), 5-11; 12-11 Fri-Sun ☎ (01874) 665672
🌐 threehorseshoesgroesffordd.co.uk
St Austell Tribute; 2 changing beers (sourced regionally) H
Busy village-centre inn in the heart of the Brecon Beacons, boasting superb views from both the front and rear outdoor seating areas. The pub is only a 10-minute walk from the Brynich Lock on the Monmouthshire & Brecon Canal and is a popular stop for boaters and other visitors. The emphasis here is very much on food, but the beers are always varied and interesting. Brynich Caravan Site and the Brecon YHA are nearby.
⑤ ❀ ◑ ⅙ A ♣ ❀ 🛜

Hay-on-Wye

Blue Boar
Oxford Road, HR3 5DF
🕐 9am-11 ☎ (01497) 820884
Brains Rev James; Timothy Taylor Landlord; 2 changing beers (sourced regionally) H

Comfortable and friendly pub in the centre of the town famed for its literary festival, owned and run by the same family for many years. A large central bar dominates, with two separate seating areas around it, each with a log fire. Two regular beers are usually supplemented by one or two guests. Food is available all day in the bar and the separate dining area. Q✿ᔑ◑ᕵ⬇️🚌(39)❤🛜

Hundred House

Hundred House
LD1 5RY (on A481, near Builth Wells)
✪ 12-2, 5.30-11; 11-11 Sat & Sun ☎ (01982) 570231
Greene King Abbot; Wye Valley Butty Bach; 1 changing beer (sourced nationally) Ⓗ
Located among rolling Welsh hills, the Hundred House Inn takes its name from the Saxon hundred, which was an administrative area. At one time a drovers' inn, this is now a traditional pub, well patronised by the local farming community. There is a lounge, locals' bar, pool room with TV (for rugby), restaurant area and beer garden. The pub is welcoming and friendly – afternoon closing times are flexible depending on custom.
Q✿ᔑ✿᯽◑ᕵᘁ👣ᐊᕵP

Knighton

Red Lion Ⓛ
West Street, LD7 1EN
✪ closed Mon & Tue; 5.30-11; 12-4 Sun ☎ (01547) 428080
⊕ redlionknighton.co.uk
2 changing beers (sourced locally; often Hobsons, Six Bells, Wye Valley) Ⓗ
This 150-year-old pub is in the centre of town opposite the clock tower. Rotating beers are from local breweries Hobsons, Joule's, Wye Valley, Six Bells and Clun. The pub lies on the Offa's Dyke Path and the Offa's Dyke Information Centre is close by. Food and drink are sourced from within 30 miles where possible. Live music plays on the last Sunday of the month. Lunches are served Sunday only in winter. There are four letting rooms.
Q✿ᔑ◑⬇️🚌❤🛜

Llandrindod Wells

Arvon Ale House 🍷 Ⓛ
Temple Street, LD1 5DP
✪ closed Mon & Tue; 4-10 (11 Fri & Sat) ☎ 07477 627267
5 changing beers (sourced regionally) Ⓗ
The first micropub in this part of Wales, offering sensibly priced ales from Wales, the Borders and the Midlands, plus eight real ciders. Formerly shop premises, this is a proper alehouse for the quiet enjoyment of beer with no distractions. Snacks are available. Monthly all-comers folk music sessions are held on the second, third and fourth Sundays. Welsh CAMRA Pub of the Year and Cider Pub of the Year in 2016. Q⬇️🔴🚌❤

Conservative Club
South Crescent, LD1 5DH (opp bandstand)
✪ 11-2, 5.30-11 Mon-Wed; 11-11 Thu; 11-11.30 Fri & Sat; 11.30-10.30 Sun ☎ (01597) 822126
Marston's Pedigree; 1 changing beer (sourced nationally) Ⓗ
Located in the centre of this historic spa town, the Con Club is a regular Guide entry. It has a large lounge, TV room, games bar, snooker and pool tables and a small front patio/smoking area. Until

the early 1970s the building was the Lansdown Hotel. Good-value lunches are served Wednesday to Friday and Sunday. CAMRA members are welcome but visitors must be signed in.
Q✿◑🔴⬇️🚌❤🚌🛜

Llanfair Caereinion

Goat Hotel
High Street, SY21 0QS (off A485)
✪ 11-11 (midnight Fri & Sat) ☎ (01938) 810428
⊕ thegoathotel.co.uk
3 changing beers (sourced locally; often Stonehouse, Wood) Ⓗ
Excellent 300-year-old beamed coaching inn with a welcoming atmosphere which attracts both locals and tourists. The plush lounge, dominated by a large inglenook and open fire, has comfortable leather armchairs and sofas. There is a dining room serving home-cooked food and a games room to the rear. The choice of real ale always includes one from Wood Brewery. Beware the low-beamed entrance to the gents!
Q✿ᔑ✿◑🔴⬅️(Welshpool & Llanfair Light Railway)
ᐊPᕵ(87)❤🛜

Llanfechain

Plas-yn-Dinas Inn
SY22 6UJ (off B4393)
✪ closed Mon; 12-2.30, 5-11 Wed-Fri; 12-11 Sat; 12-10.30 Sun ☎ (01691) 829055 ⊕ plasyndinas.co.uk
3 changing beers (sourced locally; often Monty's, Purple Moose, Stonehouse) Ⓗ
Early 18th-century, Grade II-listed public house which started life as a courthouse. Following a lengthy closure and a complete makeover, the Plas reopened in 2015. The interior features wooden beams and supports and has a number of handsome drinking areas with tiled floors, the rear restaurant/lounge is carpeted. Outside is a patio with benches and a garden. Note the bottle collection from old Shropshire breweries.
Q✿ᔑ✿◑ᐊPᕵ(72,74)❤🛜

Llanfihangel-nant-Melan

Fforest Inn
LD8 2TN (jct A44 and A481)
✪ 12-11; closed Mon winter ☎ (01544) 350526
⊕ thefforest.co.uk
3 changing beers (sourced nationally) Ⓗ
Built in the 16th century as a drovers inn, the pub is steeped in history and following renovation retains many original features, with a comfortable and welcoming ambience. Three regularly changing real ales are served in the summer (two in winter). The food menu features fresh local produce and delicious home-made puddings all day Tuesday to Sunday. Well-behaved dogs are welcome in the bar and, subject to prior arrangement, in the guest rooms. Open seven days a week July and August.
ᔑ✿◑🔴ᐊᘁPᕵ(461)❤

Llangunllo

Greyhound Ⓛ
LD7 1SP (on B4356, off A488)
✪ closed Mon & Tue; 4.30-11 (2am Fri); 2-2am Sat; 2-11 Sun ☎ (01547) 550400
3 changing beers (sourced regionally; often Broughs, Six Bells, Wrekin) Ⓗ

This unique 16th-century inn, set in picturesque countryside, is the first stop on the Glyndwr's Way long-distance trail. The beers are usually from Broughs and Six Bells breweries, and the cider is Westons Family Reserve. Beer festivals are held on the May and August bank holidays and regular music sessions are hosted. You are welcome to bring your own food. Opening times are approximate – ring the doorbell any time after midday and with luck you will be served.
🏠♣🛷🚲🐾

Llangurig

Black Lion Hotel
SY18 6SG
🕐 closed Mon; 6-11 Tue-Thu; 12-3, 6-11 Fri-Sun
☎ (01686) 440223 🌐 llangurig.org.uk
2 changing beers (sourced nationally; often Greene King, Hardys & Hansons) Ⓗ
Built originally as a shooting lodge, the Black Lion was first licensed in 1633, and rebuilt as a hotel in the late-19th century. The interior is divided into two bars and a conservatory, with wood beams and low ceilings. The first bar serves as the games area, with a pool table, dartboard and seating around the bar. The lounge/dining area has wall seating, a stone fireplace and settles. There is a side room with comfortable armchairs.
Q🕐🏠🛷🕐♿♣P🖵(X75,525)🐾🛜

Llanidloes

Old Mill
40-44 High Street, SY18 6BZ
🕐 closed Mon & Tue; 12-3, 5-midnight Wed-Fri; 11-midnight Sat; 12-3, 6-midnight Sun ☎ (01686) 412008
🌐 oldmillbar.co.uk
3 changing beers (sourced regionally) Ⓗ
Opened in the former premises of the United Services Club, the decor features an eclectic mix of furniture including a baby grand piano and other curios. The main bar has subdued lighting and wall seating, creating a relaxed atmosphere. A second room to the left has a pool table and walls decorated with pages from encyclopedias. Three rotating ales are served, one usually from Hopcraft, and a stout or porter is often available. Regular live music is hosted. 🕐🏠🕐♿♣🖵(X75,525)🐾🛜

Llanwrtyd Wells

Neuadd Arms Hotel Ⓛ
The Square, LD5 4RB
🕐 11-midnight (2am Fri & Sat) ☎ (01591) 610236
🌐 neuaddarmshotel.co.uk
Felinfoel Double Dragon; Heart of Wales Irfon Valley Bitter, Aur Cymru, Welsh Black, Noble Eden Ale; 4 changing beers (sourced locally) Ⓗ
Large Victorian hotel serving as the tap for the Heart of Wales Brewery. The Bells Bar features a large fireplace and an eclectic mix of furniture. The bells formerly used to summon servants remain on one wall, along with the winners' boards from some of the town's unusual competitions. The

lounge bar is a little more formal. The hotel takes part in the town's annual events including a major beer festival over two weekends in November. A good range of real ciders is kept.
Q🏠🚲🕐🕐🚲♣🛷P🐾

Machynlleth

Dyfi Forester
4 Heol y Doll, SY20 8BQ
🕐 11.45-1am; 11-1am Sat & Sun ☎ (01654) 703239
1 changing beer (sourced regionally; often Evan Evans, Wood, Wye Valley) Ⓗ
Halfway between the railway station and the bustling centre of Machynlleth, this friendly, down-to-earth free house has a welcoming central bar with jukebox, pool and dartboards. Pub games are played with enthusiasm here. Original stained glass features in the quirky exterior. Outside, there is a patio to the rear with tables. A variety of events is hosted including comedy and classical music festivals. 🕐🏠🚲🚲♣P🖵🐾🛜

White Horse
42 Heol Maengwyn, SY20 8DT
🕐 closed Mon; 6 (7 Tue)-11; 4-midnight Sat; 12-11 Sun
☎ (01654) 702247
Purple Moose Cwrw Glaslyn/Glaslyn Ale; 2 changing beers (sourced regionally; often Ludlow, Purple Moose, Three Tuns) Ⓗ
Traditional town pub opposite Owain Glyndwr's Parliament House with two separate bars. One has darts and a jukebox, the other a pool table and log fire in winter. The building was destroyed by fire and rebuilt in 1911 with the present magnificent frontage – look above the fireplace in the right-hand bar for before and after pictures. Bar meals are served including Sunday lunches, but times vary so it is best to phone ahead. Real cider is sometimes available in the summer.
🕐🏠🕐♿🚲♣P🖵🐾

Montgomery

Dragon Hotel
Market Square, SY15 6PA
🕐 11-11; 11-10.30 Sun ☎ (01686) 668359
🌐 dragonhotel.com
4 changing beers (sourced regionally; often Monty's) Ⓗ
Dating from the mid-1600s, this former coaching inn has a distinctive Tudor black-and-white, half-timbered frontage. The bar has recently been relocated to the rear of the hotel, giving more space to its clientele. There are patio areas outside to the front and rear for alfresco drinking. The hotel boasts an indoor swimming pool and a large function room. Q🕐🏠🚲🕐🕐♿🛷P🖵(71,81)🛜

Newtown

Railway Tavern
Old Kerry Road, SY16 1BH (off A483)
🕐 11-2, 7 (5 Mon)-midnight; 11-1am Fri & Sat; 11-midnight Tue & Sun ☎ (01686) 626156
3 changing beers (sourced regionally; often Clun, Stonehouse, Three Tuns) Ⓗ
This is the 23rd consecutive year in the Guide for Dave and Eileen, the longest serving publicans in town. Two guest beers from regional or small breweries are always on offer. The Railway hosts darts and dominoes, and can get crowded on

match nights. A TV shows sporting events and the jukebox is well patronised. The interior is essentially divided in two – a lower bar area and a rear area with wall benches and tables. Note the poster listing over 50 pubs that once operated in Newtown. Q✿≈♣🖳

Sportsman 🅛

17 Severn Street, SY16 2AQ (off A483)
✪ closed Mon; 12-10 (11 Wed & Thu); 12-11.30 Fri & Sat
☎ (01686) 623978
Monty's Old Jailhouse, MPA, Sunshine, Masquerade, Mischief; 3 changing beers (sourced nationally; often Brains, Robinsons, Wychwood) Ⓗ
Monty's tap house, with up to five of the brewery's beers available alongside up to three guest ales and a varying number of ciders. The pub is divided into three areas – a snug with comfortable wall seating, a main bar area with a wood-burning stove and a rear tiled games area with pool table, TV and darts. There is a patio at the rear for summer drinking. A former local CAMRA Pub of the Year and Welsh Cider Pub of the Year.
Q✿&≈♣🍺🖳🛜

Pen-y-cae

Ancient Briton

Brecon Road, SA9 1YY (on A4067 between Ystradgynlais and Dan-yr-Ogof caves)
✪ 12-midnight ☎ (01639) 730273 ⊕ ancientbriton.co.uk
Wye Valley Butty Bach; 10 changing beers (sourced nationally; often Rooster's, Salopian, Thornbridge) Ⓗ
Situated in the Brecon Beacons National Park and Forest Fawr Geopark, the Ancient Briton is a winner of numerous CAMRA Pub of the Year awards. Visitors are greeted by the welcome sight of 15 handpumps dispensing a fascinating selection of between five and 11 ales and a perry. On cold days, a real log fire provides a warm welcome. The pub has its own camping and caravan site with full facilities. A gem not to be missed when in the area.
⛵✿🚪🌙Å🍺P🖳(T6)😺🛜

Pool Quay

Powis Arms

SY21 9JS
✪ 12-11 (midnight Fri & Sat) ☎ (01938) 590255
⊕ powisarmshotel.co.uk
3 changing beers (sourced regionally) Ⓗ
This 18th-century coaching inn is located in what was once a major port on the River Severn before the demise of water transport. Locally known as the Quay, it was saved from closure in 2007 when Powis Estates tried to convert it to housing. It has a main bar with beams and a stone-tiled floor, a

snug with armchairs, and a restaurant to the far right. The large beer garden at the front enjoys some fine views. Q⛵✿🚪🌙&♣P😺🛜

Rhayader

Cornhill Inn

West Street, LD6 5AB (400yds W of clock tower on main A470)
✪ 4-midnight; 12-midnight Sat & Sun ☎ (01597) 810029
3 changing beers (sourced nationally) Ⓗ
Sixteenth-century inn providing a pub experience sometimes lost in this modern world. There are two separate rooms and a cosy log fire in winter, and a lively, friendly atmosphere is assured. The beer range can include national, regional and local ales. Outside are a beer garden and a covered smoking area. For many years there was a blacksmith's forge at the rear, now converted into a holiday cottage. Q⛵✿🚪&🖳🛜

Talybont-on-Usk

Star Inn 🅛

LD3 7YX (on B4558 between Brecon and Crickhowell)
✪ 5-11; 12-11 Sat & Sun ☎ (01874) 676635
4 changing beers (sourced regionally; often Brecon, Dark Star, Grey Trees) Ⓗ
Traditional village pub tucked in alongside the Monmouth & Brecon Canal, popular with both locals and visitors. Two separate rooms with stone floors and log fires link to a small central bar, which usually offers up to four ales from local and regional breweries. The pub is an ideal stop-off for boaters on the canal, walkers and cyclists taking advantage of the forest trails accessible from the village. ⛵✿🚪🌙&Å♣🍺🖳(43/X43)😺🛜

Welshpool

Pheasant Inn

43 High Street, SY21 7JQ
✪ 1-11; 12-11 Fri-Sun ☎ (01938) 553104
2 changing beers (often Salopian, Three Tuns) Ⓗ
The Pheasant is a Grade II-listed building in a terrace of what were formerly 18th-century town houses. Much modified internally, it has one long room with a wooden floor, comfortable seating at the far end and a pool table and dartboard. To the rear is a door leading to an outside drinking and smoking area. A third guest beer is often available at weekends; all beers are usually from small or regional breweries. ✿≈♣🖳🛜

Choosing pubs

CAMRA members and branches choose the pubs listed in the Good Beer Guide. There is no payment for entry, and pubs are inspected on a regular basis by personal visits; publicans are not sent a questionnaire once a year, as is the case with some pub guides. CAMRA branches monitor all the pubs in their areas, and the choice of pubs for the guide is often the result of democratic vote at branch meetings. However, recommendations from readers are welcomed and will be passed on to the relevant branch: write to Good Beer Guide, CAMRA, 230 Hatfield Road, St Albans, Hertfordshire, AL1 4LW; or send an email to: **gbgeditor@camra.org.uk**

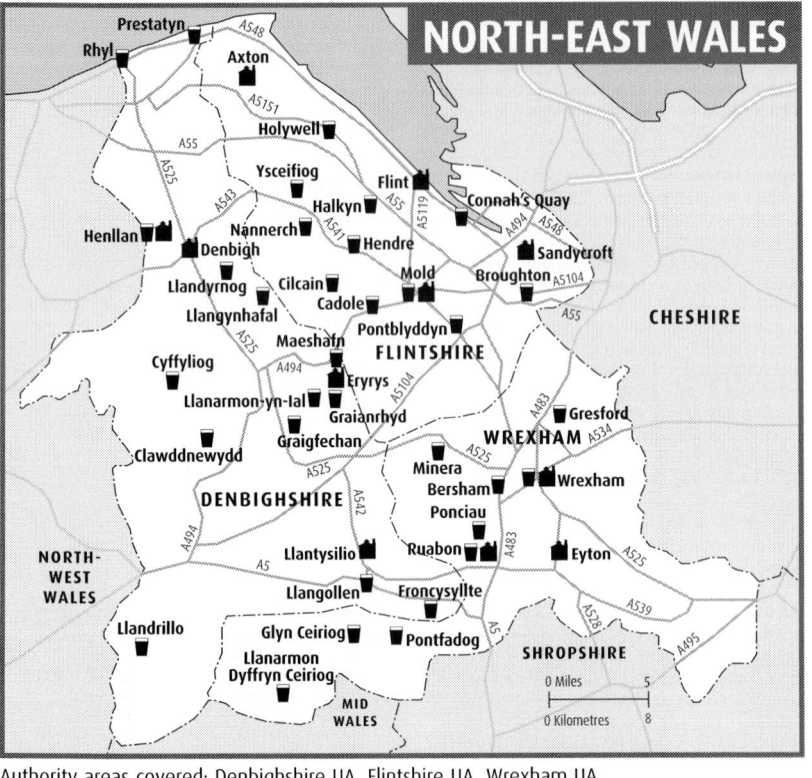

NORTH-EAST WALES

Authority areas covered: Denbighshire UA, Flintshire UA, Wrexham UA

Bersham

Black Lion ✅
Y Ddol, LL14 4HN (off B5099 near Bersham Heritage Centre)
🕐 11.30-12.30am ☎ (01978) 290193
🌐 blacklioninnbersham.com
Hydes 1863, Hydes Original; 1 changing beer (sourced regionally; often Hydes) Ⓗ
Known locally as the Hole in the Wall, this friendly hostelry sits adjacent to the Clywedog Industrial Trail overlooking the beautiful Clywedog River. The pub provides a welcome stop-off for walkers and visitors. The wood-panelled bar serves two rooms, warmed by real fires in winter. Bar food is available lunchtimes and early evenings. A popular beer festival is held over the August bank holiday weekend. The pub may close early if quiet.
🛏🕮🌐💷🅿(6)🐾🛜

Broughton

Offa's Dyke ✅
Broughton Hall Road, CH4 0QN
🕐 12-11 (midnight Thu; 1am Fri & Sat) ☎ (01244) 520133
🌐 offasdyke-hotel.co.uk
Greene King IPA; 5 changing beers (sourced nationally; often Brains, St Austell) Ⓗ
This popular estate pub has served the needs of the Broughton community for 40 years and is now part of the Golden Oak pub brand. Two or three beers are available during the week and up to five at weekends from breweries such as St Austell, Brains and Bass. Meals are served in the large family-friendly lounge. In the livelier public bar you will

find TV sport, pool tables and poker nights. There is a spacious beer garden at the rear.
🛏🕮🌐💷🅑🅰🅿🚭🛜

Cadole

Colomendy Arms
Village Road, CH7 5LL (off A494 Mold-Ruthin road)
🕐 7-11 (11 Thu); 4-11 Fri; 2-11 Sat & Sun ☎ (01352) 810217
5 changing beers Ⓗ
A wonderful pub in the middle of the village, run by the same family for over 25 years and featuring in the Guide for most of that time. It has two cosy rooms warmed by real fires and festooned with local history and photographs. Conversation is king here. Five ever-changing beers come from far and

REAL ALE BREWERIES

Axiom Wrexham
Axton Axton
Big Hand Wrexham
Black Brook Mold (NEW)
Buzzard Denbigh
Denbigh Denbigh
Deva Craft Sandycroft
Dovecote Denbigh (NEW)
Facer's Flint
Hafod Mold
Heavy Industry Henllan
Iâl Eryrys
Llangollen 🍺 Llantysilio
McGivern 🍺 Ruabon
New Plassey Eyton
Sandstone Wrexham

wide. Be aware that the Black Sheep clock keeps dubious time. The Loggerheads Country Park is close by. Q✿♣P🎵♿

Cilcain

White Horse

Ffordd Y Llan, CH7 5NN (signed from A451 Mold-Denbigh road)

🕿 12-3, 6-11; 12-11 Sat; 12-10.30 Sun ☎ (01352) 740142

2 changing beers (sourced nationally) H

A picturesque and cosy village pub with a separate quarry-tiled public bar with a set of antique beer engines. The original building dates from the early-19th century and now has an added lounge and dining area. Beers generally rotate but some may serve longer stints. Close to the Clwydian mountain range, the pub attracts many walkers. Q🌳✿🍴♣P🚽(14C)♿

Clawddnewydd

Glan Llŷn Inn L

Ruthin Road, LL15 2NA (on B5105)

🕿 5-11; 12-midnight Fri & Sat; 12-9 Sun ☎ (01824) 750754

2 changing beers (sourced locally) H

This pub is now owned and run by the community, and a warm welcome awaits when you enter the lounge bar. Dating in parts back to the 16th century, it has been refurbished to include a lounge area with real fire and stove, a dining room and a separate public bar. Another extension provides an additional dining area and space for the community shop. The Sunday carvery is popular. Two changing beers are always from Welsh brewers. Q🌳✿🍴♿🅰♣P♿🎵🛜

Connah's Quay

Ship Inn

275 High Street, CH5 4DJ (on B5129)

🕿 3-midnight; 12.30-12.30am Sat & Sun ☎ (01244) 818916

1 changing beer (sourced locally; often Big Hand, Deva Craft, Heavy Industry) H

A simple no-frills pub, it has a comfortable open-plan main lounge with side rooms for darts and pool. A small area by the bar has banquette seating, an upright piano and reading material. Karaoke and open mic sessions are held most weekends and live sport is shown on large-screen TVs. One real ale is usually served which may be a local or a national beer. Dee Cider is often available. 🌳✿♣🍴🚽♿

Cyffyliog

Red Lion Hotel L

LL15 2DN (off B5105 at Llanfwrog)

🕿 closed Mon; 5-10.30 (midnight Fri); 12-midnight Sat; 12-3 Sun ☎ (01824) 710351 ⊕ redlionhotel.biz

Marston's 61 Deep, Pedigree; 1 changing beer (sourced locally) H

Family-run village inn with parts dating back to the 17th century. The focal point is the welcoming lounge with a bar and open fire. There is a cosy adjacent dining area and a further dining/function room. The public bar includes a pool table, TV and a gents' toilet bedecked in numerous wall tiles from a bombed Liverpool factory. Wednesday quiz nights and Thursday curry nights are popular. The pub also serves as the village shop. Q🌳🍴🅰♣♿🛜

Froncysyllte

Aqueduct Inn L ✔

Holyhead Road, LL20 7PY (on A5)

🕿 12-11 ☎ (01691) 777118

4 changing beers (sourced locally; often Hafod, Peerless, Stonehouse) H

The pub continues to thrive under new owners who took over in 2016 and are making further improvements to the interior. It is a simple three-roomed affair with a central bar, small games room and comfortable lounge with woodburner. The rear verandah offers panoramic views, not least of the Llangollen Canal as it approaches the world-famous Pontcysyllte Aqueduct. The menu features an extensive selection of good-value home-cooked food. There is additional parking down the lane. 🌳✿🍴♣P🚽(64)♿🛜

Glyn Ceiriog

Oak

High Street, LL20 7EH

🕿 6-midnight; closed Sun & Mon ☎ (01691) 718810 ⊕ y-dderwen.co.uk

Stonehouse Station Bitter; 1 changing beer (sourced nationally; often Stonehouse) H

Friendly free house, back in the hands of the owner after a period of community ownership. The small bar serves a simple lounge area with a side room and a function room to the rear. Outside, there is decking and a verandah. High-quality food is freshly prepared by a local chef. Both real ales are usually from Stonehouse Brewery but can vary. 🌳✿🍴P🚽♿🛜

Graianrhyd

Rose & Crown

Llanarmon Road, CH7 4QW (on B5430 off A5104)

🕿 4 (12 Sat)-11; 12-10.30 Sun ☎ (01824) 780727 ⊕ theroseandcrownpub.co.uk

Black Sheep Best Bitter; 2 changing beers H

A traditional early 19th-century pub with a strong local following. The long bar serves two rooms – the main room has an open fire, copper-topped tables and a vast array of pumpclips. Guest beers are usually from local breweries. Popular with tourists, walkers and fell runners keen to fuel up on post-race chip baps following the local Dash in the Park. Q🌳✿🍴🅰♣●P🚽(2)♿

Graigfechan

Three Pigeons Inn

LL15 2EU (on B5429 about 3 miles from Ruthin)

🕿 closed Mon; 5 (12 Sat)-11; 12-10 Sun ☎ (01824) 703178 ⊕ threepigeonsinn.co.uk

Sharp's Doom Bar; 3 changing beers H

Fine old drovers' inn with parts originating from the 12th century. The interior is tastefully decorated throughout, retaining the original features and open log fires. An extensive lounge area has a sports room to one side and a large dining area to the other. Cellars are ideal for keeping the cask ale that is still, on occasion, served in jugs. An outdoor area to the rear has great views over the Vale of Clwyd. Regular live music and other special events are hosted. A campsite is adjacent. 🌳✿🛏🍴🅰♣●P🚽(76)♿🛜

Gresford

Griffin Inn
Church Green, LL12 8RG
☼ 4 (5 Tue; 7.30 Wed)-11.30; 4-11 Sun ☎ (01978) 855280
Adnams Southwold Bitter; Courage Best Bitter; 1 changing beer (sourced nationally; often Moorhouse's, Weetwood) Ⓗ
Friendly community inn where the landlady has presided since 1973. Included in CAMRA's Real Heritage Pubs of Wales, it has changed little since 1947. The irregular open-plan layout has a comfortable lounge and distinct bar area, the walls adorned with interesting pictures and objects. The garden to one side has views of the 15th-century All Saints Church whose bells are one of the Seven Wonders of Wales. Children are welcome in some areas until 8pm. The guest ale comes from the Punch list. Q☾❀♣P🖵(1)🥂

Pant-yr-Ochain Ⓛ
Old Wrexham Road, LL12 8TY (off A5156, E from A483, follow signs to The Flash)
☼ 11-11; 11-10.30 Sun ☎ (01978) 853525
⊕ pantyrochain-gresford.co.uk
Purple Moose Cwrw Eryri/Snowdonia Ale; Stonehouse Off the Rails; Timothy Taylor Landlord; Weetwood Eastgate; house beer (by Phoenix); 3 changing beers (sourced locally) Ⓗ
Impressive 16th-century dower house which retains many historic features and sits beside a small lake within extensive gardens. The central room, dominated by a large double-fronted bar, leads to a variety of seating areas including a garden room, a small snug behind the period inglenook fireplace, and the patio and lawn outside. Hugely popular with diners, food is served all day. Five regular beers are supplemented by three guests, often local, and draught cider, plus perry in summer. Q☾❀◑&♣♠P❀🥂

Halkyn

Blue Bell Inn Ⓛ
Rhosesmor Road, CH8 8DL (on B5123)
☼ closed Tue; 3 (5 Wed)-11; 5-midnight Fri; 12-midnight Sat; 12-11 Sun ☎ (01352) 780309 ⊕ bluebell.uk.eu.org
House beer (by Facer's); 2 changing beers (sourced locally) Ⓗ
Situated on Halkyn Mountain, the Blue Bell is an excellent community pub with weekly events including free guided walks, conversational Welsh classes and trad jazz on Sunday afternoon. It is also a much-needed post office for the village. There are usually four beers – two house ales from local brewery Facer's (Blue Bell Bitter and Dark Blue Porter) plus two from other local producers. Ciders feature strongly, with three or four regularly available. A frequent winner of many local CAMRA awards. Q☾❀Å♣♠P🖵(126)❀🥂

Hendre

Y Dderwen (The Oak) Ⓛ
Denbigh Road, CH7 5QE (on A541)
☼ 7-11; 7-midnight Sat & Sun ☎ (01352) 741466
2 changing beers Ⓗ
A roadside pub with a central bar serving two rooms, both with ceilings adorned with impressive collections of pottery. Up to four cask ales are available from a variety of north Wales microbreweries. This 300-year-old pub has a strong community focus, hosting a range of social activities including folk nights and Welsh singing. It is popular with walkers and visitors to the nearby Clwydian hills. Q☾❀&Å♣P🖵❀

Henllan

Llindir Inn Ⓛ
Llindir Street, LL16 5BH
☼ 5 (12 Thu)-11; 12-midnight Fri & Sat; 12-11 Sun ☎ (01745) 812188
Heavy Industry Electric Mountain; 4 changing beers (sourced locally; often Heavy Industry) Ⓗ
Rambling 13th-century Grade II-listed thatched inn. On entry you are welcomed by a long bar room with an inglenook fireplace and a comfortable TV lounge. Three steps take you up to another bar and a further three steps to a pleasant restaurant. The interior retains its character with old beams, tiled floors, copper and brassware. This is also the home of Heavy Industry Brewing situated close by and serves up to five cask beers. Q☾❀◑♣P🖵(6)❀🥂

Holywell

Market Cross ✓
9-11 High Street, CH8 7LA (on main walkway)
☼ 8am-midnight (1am Fri & Sat) ☎ (01352) 717800
Ruddles Best Bitter; Sharp's Doom Bar; 3 changing beers (often Big Bog, Purple Moose) Ⓗ
Converted in 2011 from a large retail outlet, this small Wetherspoon pub is named after the obelisk of the same name that stood outside. There are many pictures of local interest on the walls remembering Holywell and the Greenfield Valley in times gone by. The standard Wetherspoon beer range is complemented by three guest ales, usually including a brew from Purple Moose or Big Bog, plus a real cider in summer. Q☾◑&🖵(X11,11)🥂

Llanarmon Dyffryn Ceiriog

Hand at Llanarmon
LL20 7LD (end of B4500 from Chirk)
☼ 11-11 (12.30am Fri & Sat); 12-11 Sun ☎ (01691) 600666
⊕ thehandhotel.co.uk
2 changing beers (sourced regionally; often Stonehouse, Weetwood) Ⓗ
Welcoming free house standing at the head of the wonderful Ceiriog Valley. The pub is easily identified by the giant hand sculpture outside the entrance. The cosy bar offers seating by a large fire, with a games room and restaurant to the rear. Two real ales are usually available, one each from Weetwood and Stonehouse breweries. High-quality food is popular and booking is advisable before travelling. A favourite destination for cyclists, walkers and tourists, there is accommodation and a spa on site. Q☾❀🛏◑&♣♠P🖵❀🥂

Llanarmon-yn-Ial

Raven Inn Ⓛ
Ffordd-Rhew-Ial, CH7 4QE (signed 500yds W of B5430)
☼ closed Mon; 5-10.30 (11 Fri); 12-11 Sat; 12-9 Sun
☎ (01824) 780833 ⊕ raveninn.co.uk
3 changing beers (sourced locally) Ⓗ
Community-run by volunteers since 2009, this delightful old pub goes from strength to strength, with profits used to benefit the community.

Refurbished in 2013, there is a friendly and inviting ambience from the moment you enter. The three guest beers are from local breweries, usually including one from sister enterprise, Cwrw Ial Brewery. Excellent locally sourced home-cooked food is served Thursday to Sunday. Three self-catering bedrooms are available.
Q ☺ ⚫ ⌂ ◐ ♿ ♣ ✪ P ⊒ (2) ☕ 🛜

Llandrillo

Dudley Arms Hotel
High Street, LL21 0TL
☺ 6-11; closed Tue; 12-midnight Sat; 12-10.30 Sun
☎ (01490) 440223 ⊕ dudleyarms.wales
Stonehouse Station Bitter; 1 changing beer (sourced locally) Ⓗ
Traditional early 18th-century Welsh village inn nestling within the Berwyn mountains. New owners took over in 2015 and have carried out extensive refurbishment to create a pub full of charm with many period features and exposed oak beams. There are several discrete areas including a lounge, dining area and pool room with stone walls, tiled floors and cosy fires. The guest beer is always from a local brewery. B&B accommodation is available upstairs and in an adjacent refurbished cottage. Q ☺ ⚫ ⌂ ◐ ▲ ♣ P ⊒ (T3) ☕ 🛜

Llandyrnog

Kinmel Arms Ⓛ
Waen, LL16 4HN
☺ 12-3, 5-9.30 (11 Wed-Fri); 12-11 Sat; 12-5 Sun
☎ (01824) 790291 ⊕ kinmelarms.com
Marston's Lancaster Bomber; Thwaites Original; 2 changing beers Ⓗ
A friendly pub on the edge of the Clwydian Range and close to Offa's Dyke path and Moel Arthur hill fort. The front bar area features a large woodburner. There is a separate dining space, children's play area and games room. Guest beers are usually from Buzzard or Heavy Industry breweries. Food is served daily although times may vary. Q ☺ ⚫ ◐ ♿ ▲ ♣ P ⊒ (76) ☕ 🛜

Llangollen

Chainbridge Hotel Ⓛ
Berwyn, LL20 8BS (off B5103)
☺ 11-11 ☎ (01978) 860215 ⊕ chainbridgehotel.com
Stonehouse Station Bitter; 1 changing beer (sourced locally; often Purple Moose, Stonehouse) Ⓗ
Situated in a picturesque spot between the Llangollen Canal and River Dee, the hotel enjoys excellent views. It can be reached by bus or steam train to Berwyn and then across the restored pedestrian chainbridge. It is also a pleasant, half-hour stroll along the canal towpath from the centre of Llangollen. Ales are typically from Stonehouse and other local breweries.
Q ☺ ⚫ ⌂ ◐ ♿ ▲ ≈ P ⊒ (T3) ☕ 🛜

Ponsonby Arms Ⓛ
Mill Street, LL20 8RY (near steam railway)
☺ 12-midnight Fri-Sun & summer; closed Mon; 5-midnight Tue-Thu winter ☎ (01978) 447985 ⊕ ponsonbyarms.com
Bollington Long Hop; Elland 1872 Porter; Ulverston Flying Elephants; 7 changing beers (sourced nationally; often Elland, Salopian, Saltaire) Ⓗ
Just north-east of Llangollen Bridge, this welcoming independent free house is run by the same owners as the nearby Sun Inn. An extensive beer garden overlooks the river. Up to 10 beers and two ciders are available, with Ulverston and Bollington regularly represented. There is a cask ale promotion every Friday 6-7pm and a folk evening every other Sunday. A free ticket for the adjacent council car park can be obtained at the bar.
Q ☺ ⚫ ▲ ≈ ♣ ✪ P ⊒ (5,T3) ☕ 🛜

Sun Inn Ⓛ
49 Regent Street, LL20 8HN (400yds E of town centre on A5)
☺ 5-2am (3am Fri); 12-3am Sat; 12-2am Sun summer; closed Mon; 7-2am (3am Fri & Sat) winter ☎ (01978) 860079
5 changing beers (often Bollington, Ulverston) Ⓗ
A lively free house across the River Dee from its sister pub, the Ponsonby Arms. The stone-flagged bar room has two open fires and a games area with pool and table football. A quieter back room can be reached via a seating area outside. Wednesday to Saturday evenings feature live music. Five changing ales, often including Bollington and Ulverston, plus a changing cider, are available. Cask ale promotions are offered at various times during the week.
⚫ ▲ ≈ ♣ ✪ ⊒ (5,T3) ☕ 🛜

Llangynhafal

Golden Lion Inn
LL16 4LN (at village crossroads)
☺ closed Mon; 6 (4 Fri & Sat)-11; 12-10.30 Sun
☎ (01824) 790451 ⊕ thegoldenlioninn.com
Thwaites Original; 2 changing beers (sourced locally) Ⓗ
Traditional and welcoming 18th-century village inn at the foothills of the Clwydian hills. The bar serves two distinct areas – the bar room with a pool table, and the lounge, which leads down to a dining area. The landlord has been at the helm for over 13 years and takes particular pride in his beers and whiskies. The guest beer is often from the local Buzzard Brewery. There is a campsite to the rear. A regular in the Bus Route 76 Real Ale Festival.
Q ☺ ⌂ ◐ ▲ ♣ ✪ P ⊒ (76) ☕ 🛜

Maeshafn

Miners Arms
Village Road, CH7 5LR (off A494 in village centre)
☺ closed Mon & Tue; 6-11.30; 12-11.30 Sat & Sun
☎ (01352) 810464 ⊕ miners-arms-maeshafn.co.uk
Greene King IPA; 2 changing beers (sourced locally) Ⓗ
Built in the 1820s as part of the development of lead mining in the area, the pub is now popular with hikers visiting local nature reserves. The central bar area has a large wood-burning stove and there is a side room which can accommodate groups. A pleasant area outside at the front of the pub is used for occasional beer and music festivals. The food menu includes daily specials and 'miners mess tin' meals for simpler tastes.
☺ ⚫ ◐ ♣ P ⊒ (2) ☕ 🛜

Minera

Tyn-y-Capel Ⓛ
Church Road, LL11 3DA
☺ 12-11 (midnight Fri & Sat); 12-10.30 Sun
☎ (01978) 269347 ⊕ tyn-y-capel.com

House beer (by Facer's); 3 changing beers (sourced locally; often Cwrw Llyn, Heavy Industry) ⊞
Former coaching inn rescued and now run by the local community, largely staffed by volunteers. Part of the original bar survives and a large, modern extension caters for both drinking and dining. The split-level interior is a focal point for many local activities. Outside, the impressive terrace affords panoramic views of Esclusham Mountain and the surrounding area. The house beer is by Facer's and guests ales are usually from local microbreweries. Food is available every day. Q ⮔ ⌂ ⊛ ◑ & ♣ P ❒ ❀ �

Mold

Glasfryn 🅛
Raikes Lane, CH7 6LR (off A5119 ½ mile N of Mold)
🕒 11-11; 11-10.30 Sun ☎ (01352) 750500
⊕ glasfryn-mold.co.uk
Brunning & Price Original; Hobsons Best; Purple Moose Cwrw Eryri/Snowdonia Ale; house beer (by Brunning & Price); 6 changing beers (often Black Brook) ⊞
Near Theatre Clwyd and set in its own grounds, this is a large upmarket pub and restaurant. Food predominates and is served all day in three dining areas. Nine handpumps supply national and local beers, guest beers often come from the local Black Brook Brewery. The walls are covered with many interesting and unusual pictures. There are extensive views over the surrounding countryside from the large beer garden.
Q ⮔ ⌂ ⊛ ◑ & P ❒ (28) ❀ ☍

Mold Alehouse ❦ 🅛
Unit 2, Earl Chambers, Earl Road, CH7 1AL
✪ closed Mon & Tue; 4 (2 Wed & Sat)-10; 4-9 Sun
☎ (01352) 218188 ⊕ moldalehouse.co.uk
4 changing beers (sourced locally) ⊞
Established in 2016 and one of the first of its type in North Wales, this micropub sets the standards for others to follow. It is centrally situated in a Grade II-listed building opposite Daniel Owen Square – named after the renowned Welsh novelist and home to Mold museum and library. An arched entrance leads to a single room with a central column. No food, spirits or music, just real ale and cider. Q ● ❒ (6) ❀ ☍

Nannerch

Cross Foxes 🅛
Village Road, CH7 5RD (close to church)
✪ closed Mon; 6-11; 12-10.30 Sun ☎ (01352) 741464
⊕ nannerch.com
3 changing beers (sourced locally; often Big Hand, Buzzard, Cwrw Ial) ⊞
This delightful village pub was built in 1780 and originally also served as a pub and butcher's – the meat hooks still remain over the bar. The entrance leads to a main bar with a large fireplace. Off this is another small bar, a lounge and a function room. Three pumps serve changing beers, usually sourced locally from breweries including Big Hand, Buzzard and Cwrw Ial. Beer festivals are held in March and October. ⮔ ◑ ▲ ♣ P ❒ ☍

Ponciau

Colliers Arms
Chapel Street, LL14 1SE (off B5426)
✪ 7 (5 Wed & Thu; 4 Fri; 2 Sat)-11; 1-10.30 Sun

Facer's Flintshire Bitter; 3 changing beers (sourced regionally; often Deva Craft, Rat, Salopian) ⊞
This splendid cream-rendered free house on a narrow terraced street is a rare cask ale outlet for the area. The front room has a slate floor, comfortable bench seating, stools and small cast-iron tables. There is also a tiny snug area and a rear room with a pool table and jukebox. To the rear is a pleasant decked area and lawn. Public parking is located nearby. Guest ales are often from local micros. CAMRA branch Pub of the Year in 2016.
⮔ ⊛ & ♣ ● ❒ (3,3E) ❀ ☍

Pontblyddyn

Bridge Inn
Wrexham Road, CH7 4HN (on A541 3 miles S of Mold)
🕒 12-11 ☎ (01352) 770087
2 changing beers ⊞
Fine old building situated at a crossroads, with the River Alyn to the rear. The unspoilt interior has a warm and cosy front bar with a real fire, separate restaurant and private back room. There is also a courtyard area to the front and an extensive riverside beer garden and children's play area. Good-value food includes separate lunchtime and children's menus and regular themed evenings. The two guest beers are usually from independent breweries. Q ⮔ ⌂ ⊛ ◑ & P ❒ (26,27) ❀ ☍

Pontfadog

Swan Inn
Llanarmon Road, LL20 7AR (on B4500 next to post office)
🕒 4.30-11; 12-3, 6-11 Sat; 12-3, 7.30-10.30 Sun
☎ (01691) 718273 ⊕ theswaninnpontfadog.co.uk
1 changing beer (sourced nationally; often Conwy, Felinfoel) ⊞
Welcoming village free house in the scenic Ceiriog Valley. The red-tiled bar room features a central fireplace which separates the TV and darts area from the bar. The dining room, Elle's Kitchen, is to the side and leads to an outside decking area. One real ale is available which may be local or national, a second is often added during the summer months. Opening times may vary so please check before travelling. ⮔ ⊛ ⊛ ◑ & ♣ P ❒ (64,65) ❀ ☍

Prestatyn

Archies 🅛
151 High Street, LL19 9AS
✪ 5-11 Mon; 12-midnight; 12-11 Sun ☎ (01745) 855657
⊕ archiesbar.co.uk
Facer's Flintshire Bitter; 2 changing beers (often Axton) ⊞
This modern, family-run pub, situated at the southern end of the High Street, has one room with wall-to-wall TV and a large pull-down screen for sports fans. The regular beer is from Facer's Brewery and other beers are often local – one may be from Axton Brewery in which the landlord has an interest. A wide range of traditional British food is available. At the entrance is a decking area suitable for outside drinking. The northern end of Offa's Dyke is nearby. ⮔ ◑ & ▲ ⇌ ❒ ☍

Bar 236 🅛
236 High Street, LL19 9BP
✪ 10.30 (5 Mon & Tue)-11; 10.30-12.30am Fri & Sat
☎ (01745) 850084 ⊕ bar236.co.uk

3 changing beers (sourced locally; often Heavy Industry) Ⓗ
This café bar was fully refurbished in December 2014. The L-shaped room has a minimalist but pleasant feel with a wooden floor and blue-tiled bar front. Glass-fronted on two sides, it has open views to and from the outside world. Sport is well catered for. Three guest beers are usually sourced from local breweries. ⏰&⇌🚋🚲🛜

Halcyon Quest Hotel Ⓛ
17 Gronant Road, LL19 9DT (on A547 just E of town centre)
✪ 3-11 (midnight Fri); 12-midnight Sat; 12-11 Sun
☎ (01745) 852442 ⊕ halcyonquest-hotel.com
Facer's Flintshire Bitter; 3 changing beers (sourced nationally) Ⓗ
The HQ, as it is known, is located on the southern edge of the town, just off the High Street. It has just one room, packed with sporting memorabilia, including a rowing boat suspended from the ceiling. The garden at the rear, for sunny days, has a covered area. The beer is from local brewery Facer's, backed up by three changing ales. Accommodation is available in nine rooms. ⏰🏵🛏🅰⇌🚲🅿🚲(35,36)

Rhyl

Cob & Pen
143 High Street, LL18 1UF
✪ 11-11 (midnight Fri & Sat); 12-11 Sun ☎ (01745) 350446
Banks's Mild; Marston's 61 Deep, Pedigree; 2 changing beers Ⓗ
Respected and welcoming pub serving drinks and lunchtime meals from a central bar. It has a number of themed seating areas, all decorated imaginatively in recognition of the local heritage. Televised sports events are shown on several large screens. A weekly acoustic night is a popular attraction, as are darts, pool and dominoes. This is one of the few local pubs serving cask-conditioned mild. Located close to the bus and railway stations. ⏰🏵🍺⇌♣🚲🛜🛜

Ruabon

Bridge End Inn 🏆 Ⓛ
5 Bridge Street, LL14 6DA
✪ 5 (4 Fri)-11; 12-11 Sat & Sun ☎ (01978) 810881
⊕ mcgivernales.co.uk
8 changing beers (sourced nationally; often Ossett, Rat, Salopian) Ⓗ
Welcoming former coaching inn close to the station. The pub has won numerous awards since it was revitalised by the McGivern family in 2009, including the ultimate accolade of CAMRA National Pub of the Year in 2011. At least one beer from the on-site McGivern Brewery features among the ever-changing range of eight ales. Real cider is also available. Families and well-behaved dogs are welcome in the lounge. A hugely popular beer festival is held over the August bank holiday weekend. Q⏰🏵🅰⇌♣🚲🅿🚌🐕🛜

Wrexham

Acton Park ✅
Chester Road, LL11 2SN (on A5152, ¾ mile N of town centre)
✪ 10-midnight (11 Mon & Tue); 10-11 Sun
☎ (01978) 314336
Brains Bitter; Marston's Wainwright; Sharp's Doom Bar; 5 changing beers (sourced nationally; often Purity, Timothy Taylor) Ⓗ
Large open-plan estate pub, well furnished and with a cosy family dining area with comfortable seating towards the rear. A U-shaped bar serves all areas and there are a couple of real fires to keep you warm on winter evenings. Three permanent beers are served alongside up to five guests. Real cider is available in summer. On Monday all beers are reduced in price. Toilets are on the first floor but there is an accessible WC on the ground floor. ⏰🏵🕦&🌶🅿🚲(1)🛜

Elihu Yale ✅
44-46 Regent Street, LL11 1RR
✪ 8am-midnight (1am Fri & Sat) ☎ (01978) 366646
Greene King Abbot; Ruddles Best Bitter; Sharp's Doom Bar; 6 changing beers (sourced nationally) Ⓗ
Formally the Majestic Cinema and then a supermarket, this popular Wetherspoon town centre pub is handily placed for both the railway and bus stations. It serves three regular beers plus six guests, often from local breweries, and at least two real ciders. The standard Wetherspoon food menu is offered with the addition of Welsh dishes. Quiz night is Wednesday, poker night Sunday. Q⏰🕦&⇌(Central/General)🌶🚲🛜

North & South Wales Bank ✅
14 High Street, LL13 8HP
✪ 8am-12.30am ☎ (01978) 367940
Greene King Abbot; Ruddles Best Bitter; Sharp's Doom Bar; 2 changing beers Ⓗ
As the name suggests, this Wetherspoon Lloyds No.1 is a conversion of a former bank. Situated close to St Giles' Church, it celebrated 15 years as a pub in late 2016. The fine listed building has a magnificent stained-glass window in the high ceiling, adding to the character of the large open-plan interior. The bar can become lively and noisy especially on weekend evenings or when sport is shown on the large screen. ⏰🕦&⇌🌶🚲🛜

Ysceifiog

Fox ★ Ⓛ
Village Road, CH8 8NJ (signed from B5121)
✪ 4-11; 1-11 Sat & Sun ☎ (01352) 720241
⊕ foxinnysceifiog.co.uk
Brimstage Trappers Hat Bitter; Tetley Bitter; Weetwood Ambush; 2 changing beers (often Big Bog, Big Hand, Hafod) Ⓗ
Built around 1730, the Fox is well worth seeking out and a warm welcome awaits. The interior comprises four small rooms, two for dining. Beer was originally brewed here in a room with a stone floor. The bar has a sliding door to the public bar that takes you back to the 1930s. A choice of four beers is offered. Identified by CAMRA as having a nationally important historic pub interior, this is a rare classic. Q⏰🏵🕦&🅰♣🅿🐕🛜

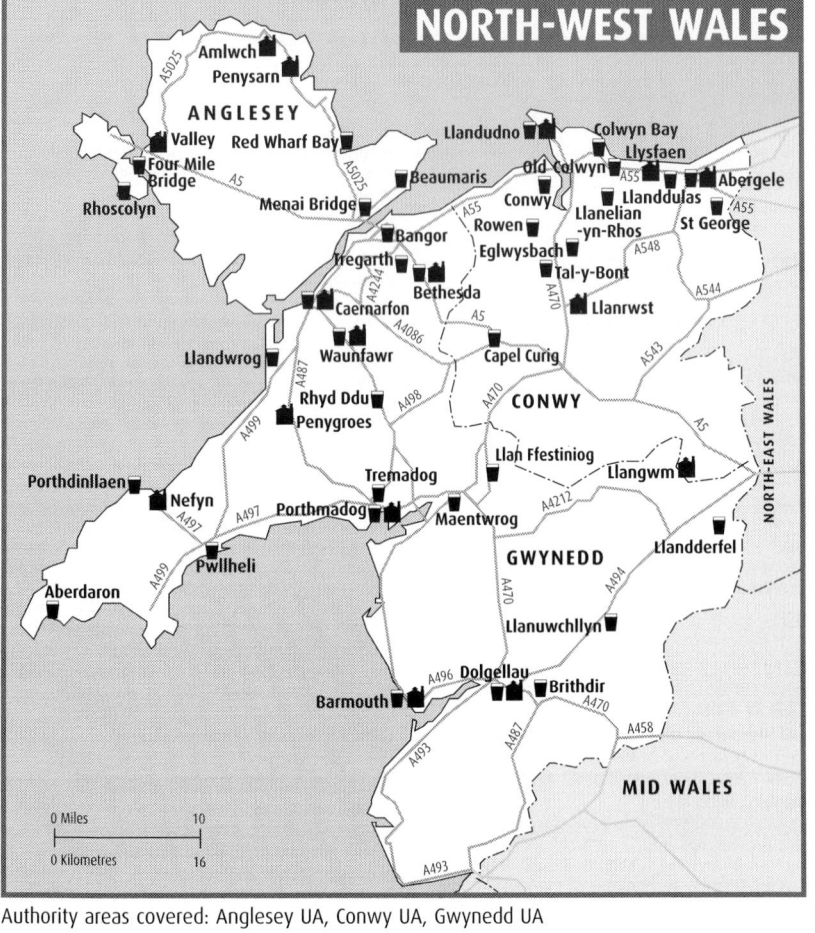

NORTH-WEST WALES

Authority areas covered: Anglesey UA, Conwy UA, Gwynedd UA

Aberdaron

Ty Newydd
LL53 8BE
🕛 11-midnight; 11-10.30 Sun ☎ (01758) 760207
🌐 gwesty-tynewydd.co.uk
Purple Moose Calon Lan; 2 changing beers (sourced locally) Ⓗ
The hotel is situated at the centre of a picturesque and historic village at the end of the Llŷn Peninsula. Beers are from two local breweries. Freshly caught Bardsey lobster and crab are on the menu, as well as afternoon teas. The Wales coastal footpath passes through the village. Eleven en-suite bedrooms offer stunning sea views. Bus services run from Pwllheli. Q🌞🏠🍴◀🚶▲🚲🚭🛜

Abergele

Castle ✓
67 Water Street, LL22 7SN
🕛 12-midnight ☎ (01745) 823322
Lees Bitter, John Willie's; 1 changing beer (often Lees) Ⓗ
Large multi-room former Bass pub just off the town centre, built in the 1850s, serving the north-east of the town and acquired by Lees in 2007. It reopened in 2015 following a short closure for an extensive internal refurbishment. The licensees pride themselves on promoting and serving quality real ale. Photographs of old Abergele adorn the walls in the snug/bar area, with two dartboards and a pool table in the games room. Q🌞♣🚲(12)🛜

Bangor

Patricks
59 Holyhead Road, LL57 2HE
🕛 11-2am (2.30am Wed & Thu; 3am Fri & Sat)
☎ (01248) 353062 🌐 patricksbar.com
3 changing beers (sourced regionally) Ⓗ
Situated in upper Bangor, this lively Irish-themed bar is popular with both the locals and students of Bangor University. Numerous TVs display sporting events. There are usually two locally sourced ales and one regional beer on the bar. Note the late opening hours for sport and late-night drinking. On the bus route towards the Menai Straits and near the railway station. 🚆🚲

Barmouth

Royal Hotel
LL42 1AB
🕛 12-11 (midnight Sat) ☎ (01341) 280455

4 changing beers Ⓗ
Located beneath the main hotel with access from the main road, the hotel has had a major structural refurbishment including the kitchens. The pub is on two levels, with the main bar next to the entrance, and the lower level primarily for playing pool. There is a beer garden to the rear. Beers are usually from Welsh breweries but occasionally come from just over the border. Local CAMRA Pub of the Year runner-up. 🏠🕙Å≠♣🐾🐕🏨📶

Beaumaris

Castle Court Hotel
Castle Square, LL58 8DA
✪ 12-11 ☎ (01248) 810078 🌐 castlecourtbeaumaris.co.uk
Facer's This Splendid Ale; 1 changing beer (sourced regionally) Ⓗ
Situated in the centre of this historic town and opposite the castle, the guest house was originally called the White Lion Hotel. The present owners have renovated the reception and dining areas. It has a small beer garden to the rear, but in spring and summer the courtyard outside the main door is used as an alfresco seating area. Alongside the permanent ale is one guest beer from a small independent brewery. Lunchtime meals are served 12-3pm during school holidays only. 🏠🕙🛏Å🅿📶

Olde Bull's Head Inn ✪
Castle Street, LL58 8AA
✪ 11-11 ☎ (01248) 810329 🌐 bullsheadinn.co.uk
Draught Bass; Hancocks HB; 4 changing beers (sourced nationally) Ⓗ
This Grade II-listed building was the original posting house for the borough. In 1645 General Mytton, a Parliamentarian, commandeered the inn while his forces laid siege to the nearby castle. The Royalists surrendered on 25 June 1646. Dr Johnson and Charles Dickens were famous guests and each bedroom is named after a Dickens character. The beamed bar has a large open fire. Parking is limited. Q🏠🕙🛏Å🅿🏨📶

Bethesda

Sior
35-37 Carneddi Road, LL57 3SE
✪ 7-midnight; 5-1am Fri; 1-1am Sat; 1-midnight Sun
☎ (01248) 600072
4 changing beers (sourced locally) Ⓗ
A friendly locals' pub in the village of Carneddi just outside Bethesda. A few minutes' drive from the A5, there is plenty of parking nearby. Free of tie, the pub offers a variety of ales from the Marston's range as well as locally brewed beers. There are views across the valley to the local slate quarry, which has the longest zip wire in Britain. Q🏨🐕

Brithdir

Cross Foxes
LL40 2SG (jct of A470 and A487)
✪ 11-midnight ☎ (01341) 421001
Cwrw Cader Gold; 2 changing beers Ⓖ
A refurbished Grade II-listed building situated near the foot of Cader Idris mountain and four miles from the historic town of Dolgellau. Beers are usually from Cader Ales and other local microbreweries. Breakfast is served from 8am and meals are available all day until 9pm. Dogs are welcome in the bar area. The hotel has Welsh

Tourist Board 5-star grading. Bus service T2 passes by, but please check times.
Q🏠🕙🛏🍽Å🅿🏨(T2)🐕📶

Caernarfon

Black Boy Inn ✪
Northgate Street, LL55 1RW (near marina)
✪ 11-11 (11.30 Fri & Sat); 12-10.30 Sun ☎ (01286) 673604
Draught Bass; 4 changing beers (sourced locally) Ⓗ
The pub is set within the town walls between the marina and castle. This historic town, a World Heritage Site, is well worth a visit, ending with a welcome pint at the Black Boy. The public bar and small lounge are warmed by roaring fires. Good-value food is served and the guest beer usually comes from Purple Moose. There is a drinking area outside on the traffic-free street. A previous local CAMRA award winner. Q🛏🍽🕙♿≠(WHR)♣🐕🏨📶

Tafarn Y Porth ✪
5-9 Eastgate Street, LL55 1AG (just off Bangor Rd near Barclays Bank)
✪ 9am-midnight ☎ (01268) 662920
Big Bog Bog Standard Bitter; Greene King Abbot; Ruddles Best Bitter; 2 changing beers Ⓗ
Friendly, welcoming Wetherspoon pub opposite the town walls and close to the castle. It has a large open-plan interior and a spacious, partly covered courtyard outside with plenty of seating. The real ale range often includes a beer from a local brewery. The pub's location is handy for the Welsh Highland Railway, which takes you to the heart of Snowdonia. Q🏠🕙Å≠(WHR)♣🐕🏨

Capel Curig

Tyn-y-Coed Inn
Holyhead Road, LL24 0EE
✪ 3 (12 Fri & Sat)-11; 12-10.30 Sun ☎ (01690) 720331
🌐 tyn-y-coed.co.uk
Black Sheep Best Bitter; Purple Moose Cwrw Eryri/Snowdonia Ale; 2 changing beers (sourced regionally) Ⓗ
A spacious old multi-roomed pub with a hotel extension. To mark its historic past on the coaching route, the Tyn-y-Coed has a majestic stagecoach opposite the entrance on the A5. It is popular with outdoor enthusiasts owing to its location in the Snowdonia National Park. Log fires provide a warm welcome in winter. Locally sourced ales and a good selection of whiskies are available. Dogs are admitted on leads. 🏠🛏🕙♣🅿📶

REAL ALE BREWERIES

Anglesey Valley
Cader Dolgellau
Conwy Llysfaen
Coppertown Amlwch
Druid Penysarn (NEW)
Geipel Llangwm
Great Orme Llandudno
Llŷn Nefyn
Lleu Penygroes
Myrddins 🍴 Barmouth
Nant Llanrwst
North Wales Abergele
Ogwen Bethesda (NEW)
Old Market 🍴 Caernarfon
Purple Moose Porthmadog
Snowdonia 🍴 Waunfawr

Colwyn Bay

Bay Hop 🏆 ⓛ
17 Penrhyn Road, LL29 8LG
🕒 closed Mon; 4-9 Tue & Wed; 2-10 Thu-Sat; 2-8 Sun
🌐 thebayhop.co.uk
5 changing beers (sourced regionally) Ⓗ
This micropub and bottle shop opened in 2016, making a welcome addition to the Colwyn Bay drinking experience. Two large barrel tables are available for vertical drinkers and attractive high-backed wooden settles for those who prefer to sit down. Five ales are on at weekends, complemented by pies sourced from local butchers. Beer is sold in two-pint cartons to take away. Q🌥�🚗❀

Pen-y-Bryn ⓛ
Pen-y-Bryn Road, LL29 6DD
🕒 11-11; 12-10.30 Sun ☎ (01492) 533360
🌐 penybryn-colwynbay.co.uk
Purple Moose Cwrw Eryri/Snowdonia Ale; house beer (by Phoenix); 4 changing beers (sourced regionally) Ⓗ
Spacious, open-plan pub with large bookcases, antique furniture and real fires during the winter. The walls are decorated with old photographs and memorabilia from the local area. Panoramic views of the Bay of Colwyn and the Great Orme can be admired from the terrace and garden. Food is served throughout the day – the menu is updated daily on the website. A boardroom-style function room, for get-togethers and meetings, has been created in the cellar, opening on to the garden. Q🌥🏵️🌓🚻♿🅿️🚗(23)❀🛜

Station
Abergele Road, LL29 8BP
🕒 11-11; 12-11 Sun ☎ (01492) 532818
🌐 thestationcolwynbay.co.uk
4 changing beers (sourced regionally) Ⓗ
Large town-centre pub originally built around 1870 and reopened in 2015 by the management team from the successful Albert in Llandudno, following an extensive modern refurbishment and change of name. Food is served throughout the day. Beers are displayed on blackboards near the bar, with third-pint glasses available. With many tables overlooking the street, it is handy for a quick drink while waiting to travel home from the adjacent bus stop. 🌥🌓♿🌥foot🚗🛜

Conwy

Albion Ale House ★ ⓛ
Uppergate Street, LL32 8RF
🕒 12-11 (midnight Fri & Sat) ☎ (01492) 582484
🌐 albionalehouse.weebly.com
8 changing beers (sourced regionally; often Conwy, Great Orme, Nant) Ⓗ
Multi-room heritage pub superbly refurbished by the current owners. Each room retains original 1920s features and several have wonderful fireplaces. There is no music or TV, just pleasant conversation. The pub is managed by four local brewers – Conwy, Great Orme, Nant and Purple Moose – and showcases their beers as well as guests. There are two guest Welsh ciders and a good selection of wines and malt whiskies. CAMRA awards include branch and Welsh Pub of the Year. Q🏵️🌥🌓🚗(5,19)❀🛜

Bank of Conwy ⓛ
1 Lancaster Square, LL32 8HT
🕒 12-11 (midnight Fri & Sat) ☎ (01492) 573741
🌐 bankofconwy.com
4 changing beers (sourced locally) Ⓗ
The Bank of Conwy is a modern continental-style beer and wine bar which opened in 2015 in a Grade II-listed former bank. It uses many fittings from the original building – the bar used to be the counter and the manager's officer is now a snug with a fire. The basement, which was formerly the vault, is available for private hire. There are four real ales. 🌥🌓🌥🚗❀🛜

Bridge Inn/Y Bont ⓛ
Rosehill Street, LL32 8LD
🕒 12-11 (midnight Fri & Sat) ☎ (01492) 572974
🌐 bridgeinnconwy.co.uk
5 changing beers (sourced regionally; often Conwy, Great Orme, Nant) Ⓗ
Busy, traditional corner inn within sight of historic Conwy Castle and inside the town walls. It has an open-plan lounge with a central bar area. Local ales come from Bragdy'r Nant, Great Orme, Purple Moose and Conwy breweries, usually including a dark beer. Real Welsh cider is also on handpump. Good-quality food is available lunchtimes and evenings. Thursday is quiz night. Excellent accommodation includes a Welsh breakfast. The sister pub to the Albion Ale House. 🛏️🌓🌥♣🚗(5,19)❀🛜

Liverpool Arms
Lower Gate Street, LL32 8BE
🕒 12-11 (11.30 Fri & Sat); 12-10 Sun ☎ (01492) 573393
🌐 liverpoolarmsconwy.net
Draught Bass; 2 changing beers (sourced regionally) Ⓗ
This small one-roomed historic pub reopened in 2015 after a major refurbishment. A popular family-friendly pub attracting locals and visitors alike, it is set in a unique location next to the town walls with a fantastic seating area outside overlooking the historic Conwy Quays. Beer is served in plastic glasses for those wishing to enjoy this facility. Locally sourced real ales are always available. 🌥🏵️🌥♣🚗(5,19)❀🛜

Dolgellau

Torrent Walk Hotel 🏆 ⓛ
Smithfield Street, LL40 1AA
🕒 11-midnight ☎ (01341) 422858
Purple Moose Cwrw Eryri/Snowdonia Ale; Wychwood Hobgoblin; 3 changing beers (sourced nationally) Ⓗ
An 18th-century hotel in the narrow streets of the town centre, retaining most of its multi-roomed interior and old fireplaces, although the bar fittings date from circa 1970. Note the 'Coffee Room' etched panel in the door from the lobby to the room on the right. A real cider is always served and up to five ales, mostly from local breweries. Dolgellau is an ideal base for walking in the Cader Idris area. Local CAMRA Pub of the Year. 🛏️🌓♣🌥🚗🛜

Eglwysbach

Bee Inn ⓛ
LL28 5UD
🕒 closed Mon & Tue; 12-11; 12-6 Sun ☎ (01492) 650291

House beer (by Marston's); 2 changing beers (sourced locally) H
This newly refurbished country pub is located in the heart of the Conwy Valley and offers a menu of superb locally sourced home-cooked food. Themed food nights featuring pies or pizzas are also held occasionally and good-value Sunday lunches. The one-roomed bar has a mixture of stone and wood flooring and the walls are adorned with Welsh artwork, Welsh rugby pictures and a selection of musical instruments. Friday is singalong night and open mic nights are sometimes hosted.
⛵✿◖P🚌(25)🛜

Four Mile Bridge

Anchorage Hotel
LL65 2EZ (on B4545, just past bridge to Holy Island)
✿ 11-11; 12-11 Sun ☎ (01407) 740168
⊕ the-anchorage-hotel.com
Draught Bass; Theakston XB; Timothy Taylor Landlord; 2 changing beers H
Family-run hotel on Holy Island close to Treaddur Bay. It has a comfortable, spacious lounge bar and a large dining area serving a wide selection of meals. The hotel is near some fine sandy beaches and coastal walks. Its proximity to the A55 makes it a useful stopping-off point for Holyhead Port. Hourly bus services from Bangor pass by the hotel entrance. Q⛵🚪◖🅿🚌

Llan Ffestiniog

Y Pengwern ✓
Church Square, LL41 4PB
✿ 7-11.30; 5-midnight Fri; 12-midnight Sat & Sun
☎ (01766) 762200 ⊕ pengwern.org.uk
Purple Moose Cwrw Eryri/Snowdonia Ale; 1 changing beer H
This community-run hostelry was formerly an old drovers' inn. It has one regular beer from Purple Moose and guests from other local breweries such as Big Bog, Cwrw Llŷn and Heavy Industry. The pub holds a beer festival over the August bank holiday with around 20 beers. An ideal stop-off for walkers in the local area, and there is a bus stop right outside. Q✿🚪◖🅿🚌✿🛜

Llandderfel

Bryntirion Inn L
B4401, LL23 7RA (on B4401 4 miles E of Bala)
✿ 11-11; 12-11 Sun ☎ (01678) 530205
⊕ bryntirioninn.co.uk
Purple Moose Cwrw Eryri/Snowdonia Ale; 1 changing beer (sourced locally) H
Dating back to 1695, this former hunting lodge and coaching inn overlooks the Dee Valley. The cosy and comfortable bar area with a log fire is open all day. There are a number of other rooms to accommodate diners and families including a large function room for special events. There is also a small covered and heated courtyard at the rear. The guest beer varies and may be from a local or national brewer. Two ensuite guest rooms are available upstairs. Q⛵✿🚪◖🅿🚌(T3)✿🛜

Llanddulas

Valentine ✓
9 Mill Street, LL22 8ES

✿ 3-11; 12-midnight Fri & Sat; 12-11 Sun ☎ (01492) 515898
⊕ valentine-inn.co.uk
Marston's Pedigree; 1 changing beer (sourced regionally) H
At the centre of a semi-rural seaside village, this traditional village inn, dating from the 18th century, is built on the site of an old clay cottage. To the left is a well-furnished, comfortable lounge and straight ahead is a separate public bar with TV, both with an open fire in winter. Brewery memorabilia and many old framed photographs relating to the Valentine decorate the walls. An attractive drinking area and walled garden are at the rear. Q⛵✿Å🚪🚌(12,13)✿🛜

Llandudno

Cottage Loaf L ✓
Market Street, LL30 2SR
✿ 11-11 ☎ (01492) 870762 ⊕ the-cottageloaf.co.uk
Conwy Welsh Pride; Courage Directors; Marston's Wainwright; 2 changing beers (sourced regionally) H
The building was previously a bakery, hence the name. The interior features stone-flagged floors, an impressive fireplace and a raised timber-floored area – much of the wood came from the Flying Foam, a schooner shipwrecked at Llandudno's West Shore. The Loaf is a popular meeting place for people of all ages, with excellent home-cooked food served all day every day. A major refurbishment and extension a few years ago added a conservatory restaurant area with an enclosed outdoor terrace. ⛵✿◖🚪🚌(5,12)🛜

King's Head ✓
Old Road, LL30 2NB
✿ 12-11 (midnight Fri & Sat) ☎ (01492) 877993
⊕ kingsheadllandudno.co.uk
Greene King IPA, Abbot; 2 changing beers (sourced regionally) H
The 300-year-old King's Head is the oldest inn in Llandudno. It has a traditional split-level bar dominated by a large open fire and a grill restaurant at the rear serving good-quality food. The pub makes an ideal stop after walking on the Great Orme or riding on Britain's only cable-hauled tramway. Quiz night is Wednesday and folk night the first Sunday of the month.
⛵✿◖Å🚌(Great Orme Tramway)🅿🚌

Snowdon
11 Tudno Street, LL30 2HB
✿ 12-11 (11.30 Fri & Sat) ☎ (01492) 872166
⊕ the-snowdonhotel.co.uk
Draught Bass; 4 changing beers (sourced regionally) H
This attractively refurbished pub just off the town centre and near the tram station is one of the oldest in Llandudno, with excellent multilingual bar staff. The interior comprises a large main drinking area and a small side snug – look for the Snowdon mirror above the fireplace. Four real ales are usually available, with three thirds on offer for the price of a pint. The garden, with fine views of the Great Orme, won Llandudno in Bloom for its floral display.
✿🚌(Great Orme Tramway)♣🚌(5,12)✿🛜

Llandwrog

Harp Inn/Ty'n Llan
LL54 5SY

✪ 12-11; 12-10.30 Sun ☎ (01286) 831071

Bragdy Lleu Blodeuwedd; Bragdy Llŷn Brenin Enlli; Nant Cwrw Coryn; 3 changing beers (sourced locally) Ⓗ

Hidden on a back road to Dinas Dinlle and Caernarfon airport, this beautiful old stone inn boasts many cosy rooms and a resident parrot called Dylan. The ever-changing beers come from smaller breweries, with one pump in use in winter and two in summer. Legend says there was a tunnel from the cellar to the church – look out for the pirate's grave in the churchyard. ◖▶

Llanelian-yn-Rhos

White Lion Inn
LL29 8YA

✪ closed Mon; 11.30-3, 6-11; 11.30-4, 5-11.30 Sat; 12-10.30 Sun ☎ (01492) 515807 ∰ whitelioninn.co.uk

Marston's 61 Deep; 2 changing beers (sourced regionally) Ⓗ

A regular in the Guide for more than 20 years, this 16th-century inn situated in the hills above Old Colwyn, next to St Elian's Church, offers a warm welcome. Gracing the entrance are two white stone lions, leading into the bar area with slate-flagged flooring and large comfortable chairs around the log fires. Decorative stained glass is mounted above the bar in the tiny snug. The restaurant serves delicious home-cooked food. Jazz night is Tuesday, quiz night Thursday.
Q🕏🏵◖▶Å♣P🐾🐾奈

Llanuwchllyn

Eagles Inn (Tafarn Yr Eryrod) Ⓛ
Llanuwchllyn, LL23 7UB

✪ 11-11 (midnight Thu-Sat); closed Sun ☎ (01678) 540278 ∰ yr-eagles.co.uk

3 changing beers (sourced locally; often Cwrw Cader, Purple Moose) Ⓗ

A friendly welcome awaits visitors to this little gem – an old stone-built village local opposite the church. The bar also serves as a shop and is open most of the day. It retains plenty of historic features including a wonderful stone floor. The adjacent restaurant serves highly rated locally produced food. The patio garden has good mountain views. It is a 10-minute walk to Llanuwchllyn station on the Bala Lake Railway. Opening hours are reduced in winter.
🕏🏵◖▶Å➤(Bala Lake)♣P🖵(T3)🐾奈

Maentwrog

Grapes Hotel Ⓛ
LL41 4HN (on A496 near A487 jct)

✪ 12-midnight ☎ (01766) 590365 ∰ grapeshotelsnowdonia.co.uk

Purple Moose Cwrw Eryri/Snowdonia Ale; Sharp's Doom Bar; 1 changing beer (sourced locally) Ⓗ

A former coaching inn, this hotel dates back to the 17th century and overlooks the Vale of Ffestiniog. The interior comprises a lounge, public bar, verandah and large dining room, and outside there is a sheltered beer garden. Most of the beers are sourced locally. The railway station nearby at Rhyd is on the Ffestiniog line. The village is an ideal spot for visiting this beautiful area.
Q🕏🏵🖂◖▶🕭Å♣🖷P🖵

Menai Bridge

Liverpool Arms ⊘
St George's Pier, LL59 5EY

✪ 12-2, 5-11.30; 12-11.30 Fri-Sun ☎ (01248) 712453

Facer's Flintshire Bitter; Purple Moose Cwrw Eryri/Snowdonia Ale Ⓗ/Ⓖ**, Ochr Tywyll y Mws/Dark Side of the Moose; 1 changing beer** Ⓗ

Refurbished to a high standard, the Livvy has four cask ales on offer and serves good-quality home-cooked food. This nautically themed pub is frequented by locals, students in term time and the local sailing fraternity. A short walk takes you beneath the famous suspension bridge and it is close to the quay for local tourist boats. The Anglesey and Welsh Coast footpaths are nearby.
🕏◖▶🕭🖵奈

Old Colwyn

Red Lion
385 Abergele Road, LL29 9PL

✪ 5-11; 4-midnight Fri; 12-midnight Sat; 12-11 Sun ☎ (01492) 515042

House beer (by Marston's); changing beers (sourced nationally) Ⓗ

This free house serves up to five guest ales from independent and local brewers. It has an L-shaped lounge featuring a real coal fire, antique brewery mirrors and other memorabilia, and a traditional public bar with a pool table, darts and TVs. To the rear is a Victorian-style covered and heated smoking conservatory. The real ale club every Thursday offers nine beers at reduced prices. The traditional pub sign is worth a look.
Q🏵♣🖷🖵🐾奈

Porthdinllaen

Ty Coch Inn
LL53 6DB (access by foot only)

✪ closed Mon-Thu; 12-6 Fri & Sat; 12-4 Sun ☎ (01758) 720498 ∰ tycoch.co.uk

Bragdy Llŷn Brenin Enlli; Purple Moose Cwrw Ysgawen/Elderflower; 1 changing beer (sourced regionally) Ⓗ

The building, in an iconic position on the beach at beautiful Porthdinllaen, opened as a pub in 1842 to serve the local fishermen. It can only be reached on foot either along the beach or across the golf course, and is rated to be one of the top 10 beach bars in the world. Parking is available at the NT car park or the golf clubhouse. Check for out-of-season opening times. 🕏◖▶🐾

Porthmadog

Spooner's Bar
Harbour Station, LL49 9NF

✪ 9am-11; 12-10.30 Sun ☎ (01766) 516032 ∰ festrail.co.uk

Purple Moose Cwrw Eryri/Snowdonia Ale; 5 changing beers (sourced nationally) Ⓗ

Spooner's beer range varies, but there are always at least two ales from the local Purple Moose Brewery. Situated in the terminus of the world-famous Ffestiniog and Welsh Highland Railway, steam trains are outside the door most of the year. Food is served every lunchtime, evening meals Tuesday to Saturday, but check first out of season. A former local CAMRA Pub of the Year award winner. Q🕏◖▶Å➤(Ffestiniog & WHR)🖷🖵奈

Station Inn

LL49 9HT (on mainline station platform)
☼ 11-11 (midnight Thu-Sat); 12-11 Sun ☎ (01766) 512629
Brains Bitter; Purple Moose Cwrw Eryri/Snowdonia Ale; 1 changing beer ⒣
Situated on the Cambrian Coast railway platform, this pub is popular with locals and visitors alike. It has a large lounge and a smaller public bar, and can get busy at weekends and on nights when live football is shown on TV. A range of pies and sandwiches is available all day. There is a pleasant beer garden at the back. Local buses stop outside the station. �&▲≒♣♠🖵🐾

Pwllheli

Pen Cob ✓

Station Square, LL53 5HG
☼ 7am-11 ☎ (01758) 704970
Greene King Abbot; Ruddles Best Bitter; 4 changing beers ⒣
Wetherspoon pub opened in 2013 opposite the train station at the start of the scenic Cambrian Line. Formerly a shop, it has been tastefully refurbished and is now a light and airy venue popular with people of all ages. It gets especially busy with locals and tourists at weekends and during the holiday season. The area is popular for sailing. ⏰⏸&≒🖵🖃

Red Wharf Bay

Ship Inn ✓

LL75 8RJ (off A5025 between Pentraeth and Benllech)
☼ 11-11; 11-10.30 Sun ☎ (01248) 852568
⊕ shipinnredwharfbay.co.uk
Adnams Broadside; Brains SA; 2 changing beers ⒣
Red Wharf Bay was once a busy port exporting coal and fertilisers in the 18th and 19th centuries. Previously known as the Quay, the Ship enjoys an excellent reputation for its bar and restaurant, with meals served lunchtimes and evenings. It gets busy with locals and visitors in the summer. The garden has panoramic views across the bay to south-east Anglesey. The resort town of Benllech is two miles away and the coastal path passes the front door. Q⏰⏸⏸&P

Rhoscolyn

White Eagle

LL65 2NJ (off B4545 signed Traeth Beach)
☼ 12-3, 6-11; 12-11 Sat; 12-10.30 Sun ☎ (01407) 860267
⊕ white-eagle.co.uk
Marston's 61 Deep, Pedigree; Weetwood Ambush; 2 changing beers ⒣
Saved from closure by new owners, this pub has been renovated and rebuilt with an airy, brasserie-style ambience. It has a fine patio enjoying superb views over Caernarfon Bay and the Llŷn Peninsula to Bardsey Island. The nearby beach offers safe swimming with a warden on duty in the summer months. The pub is also close to the coastal footpath. Excellent food is available lunchtimes and evenings – all day during the school holidays. Q⏰⏸&▲♣P

Rhyd Ddu

Cwellyn Arms

LL54 6TL

☼ 11-11 ☎ (01766) 890321 ⊕ snowdoninn.co.uk
Conwy Welsh Pride; Cottage Golden Arrow; 5 changing beers (sourced regionally) ⒣
A traditional Welsh country inn, in a fabulous situation in the village of Rhyd Ddu at the foot of Snowdon. The pub's boast that it has nine real ales nine days a week is only slightly exaggerated. There are usually four handpulls in use, dispensing ales from local breweries. The lovely log fire makes the pub cosy and welcoming after a walk on Snowdon, or after a ride on the nearby Welsh Highland Railway. ※🛏⏸&▲≒(WHR)P🖵🐾

Rowen

Ty Gwyn

High Street, LL32 8YU
☼ 4-10 Tue; 12 (4 Mon)-midnight; 12-10 Sun
☎ (01492) 650232
Lees Bitter; 2 changing beers (often Lees) ⒣
Community village inn in an idyllic setting with a warm welcome for locals and visitors alike. The comfortable lounge has horse brasses and old pictures on the walls, and there is a cosy restaurant serving good food made with locally sourced ingredients. Traditional Welsh singing features on Fridays, live entertainment most Saturdays and charity quiz nights on occasion. The pub has two walled gardens, one with a river running by. ⏰※🛏⏸▲♣P🖵(19A)🐾🎵

St George

Kinmel Arms

LL22 9BP
☼ closed Mon; 11-11 (11.30 Fri & Sat); closed Sun
☎ (01745) 832207 ⊕ thekinmelarms.co.uk
Thwaites Original; 1 changing beer (sourced regionally) ⒣
Seventeenth-century former coaching inn on the hillside overlooking the sea. A central bar serves a large combined drinking and dining area with a real log fire in one corner and a spacious conservatory dining area at the rear. Two guest beers come from local breweries, plus a cider from Gwynt y Ddraig. The pub has a reputation for good food, and luxury accommodation is available in four comfortable suites. The owner's art gallery and shop is on site. Q※🛏⏸&♠P🐾🎵

Tal-y-Bont

Y Bedol ⓛ

Conway Road, LL32 8QF
☼ closed Mon; 5-11 (midnight Fri); 12-12.30am Sat; 12-11 Sun ☎ (01492) 660164
Conwy Clogwyn Gold; Purple Moose Cwrw Ysgawen/Elderflower; 2 changing beers (sourced locally) ⒣
A traditional country pub on the main route down the west side of the Conwy Valley. It reopened in 2016 following a lengthy closure and refurbishment by the new owners. Food and real ales are sourced with the emphasis on local suppliers. Popular with walkers, outdoor enthusiasts and families, it has a large attractive beer garden to the side and rear. ⏰※⏸P🖵(19)🐾

Tregarth

Pant Yr Ardd

LL57 4PL

4 (2 Mon)-midnight; 4-1am Fri; 12-1am Sat; 12-midnight Sun ☎ (01248) 605546

Conwy Surfin' IPA; Hafod Hopper; 1 changing beer (sourced regionally) Ⓗ

This pub divides into two rooms either side of the bar. The walls are adorned with pictures of the village from the past. A free house, the ale is sourced mostly from local breweries, but sometimes national beers are available. The beer garden is adjacent to the car park over the road. The inn has been an integral part of the village community for generations and you will always receive a warm welcome here. ➳⊛P🅿🐾🌸

Tremadog

Union Inn ✅

7 Market Square, LL49 9RB

12-2, 5.30-12.30am; 12-2, 5.30-11 Sun ☎ (01766) 512748

⊕ union-inn.com

Big Bog Bog Standard Bitter; Great Orme Atlantis; Purple Moose Cwrw Eryri/Snowdonia Ale Ⓗ

Friendly village local situated in the village square, with two separate cosy bars and a restaurant at the rear. The pub has a policy of using locally sourced produce, and the ale range mainly features local

beers. Children are welcome and there are board games. Excellent food is served in the bar and restaurant. Tremadog was the birthplace of Thomas Edward Lawrence (Lawrence of Arabia) in 1888. Frequent bus services pass the building.

Q➳⊛◑&Å🚲🌸🚌🚋(1A,T2)

Waunfawr

Snowdonia Park

Beddgelert Road, LL55 4AQ

11-11; 11-10.30 Sun ☎ (01286) 650409

⊕ snowdonia-park.co.uk

Snowdonia Trithro, Snowdonia Gold, Carmen Sutra, Cais, Dark and Delicious, Welsh Highland Bitter Ⓗ

Home of the Snowdonia brewery, this is a popular pub for walkers, climbers and families, with children's play areas inside and out. Meals are served all day. The pub adjoins Waunfawr station on the Welsh Highland Railway – stop off here before continuing on one of the most scenic sections of narrow-gauge railway in Britain. There is a large campsite adjacent on the riverside. A former local CAMRA Pub of the Year.

Q➳⊛◑&Å🚲(WHR)♣🌸P🅿🐾🌸📶

Kinmel Arms, St George

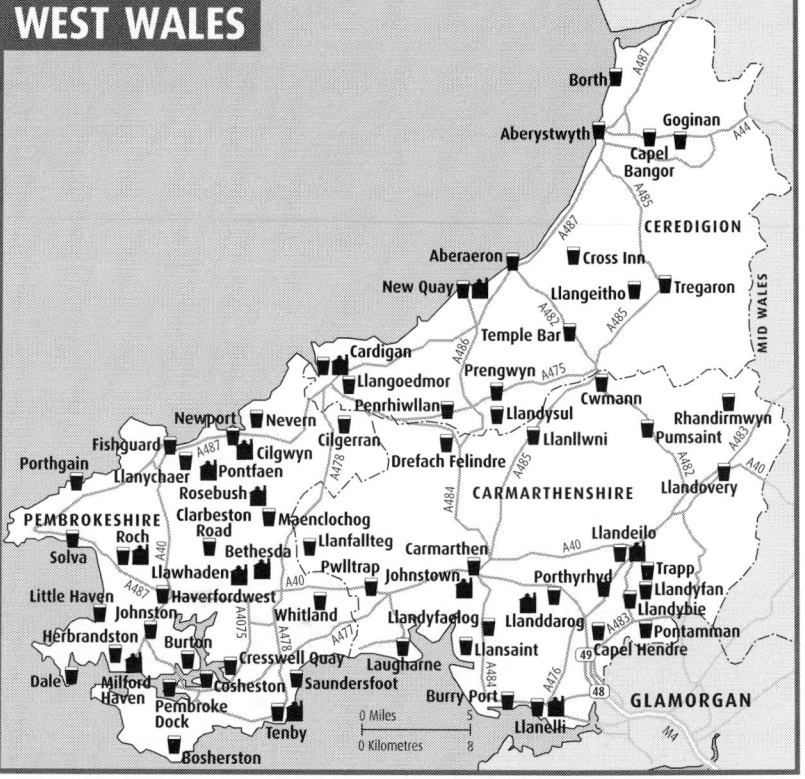

WEST WALES

WALES

MID WALES

Borth
Goginan
Aberystwyth
Capel Bangor
CEREDIGION
Aberaeron
Cross Inn
New Quay
Llangeitho
Tregaron
Temple Bar
Cardigan
Prengwyn
Llangoedmor
A475
Cwmann
Penrhiwllan
Llandysul
Newport
Nevern
Cilgerran
Llanllwni
Rhandirmwyn
Pumsaint
Fishguard
Cilgwyn
Drefach Felindre
Porthgain
Llanychaer
Pontfaen
Llandovery
Rosebush
CARMARTHENSHIRE
Clarbeston
PEMBROKESHIRE
Road
Maenclochog
Roch
Llanfallteg
Llandeilo
Solva
Bethesda
Carmarthen
Llawhaden
Pwlltrap
Johnstown
Porthyrhyd
Trapp
Little Haven
Haverfordwest
Llandyfan
Johnston
Whitland
Llandyfaelog
Llanddarog
Llandybie
Herbrandston
Burton
Llansaint
Pontamman
Cresswell Quay
Laugharne
Capel Hendre
Dale
Milford
Cosheston
Saundersfoot
Burry Port
GLAMORGAN
Haven
Pembroke
Llanelli
Dock
Tenby
0 Miles
5
Bosherston
0 Kilometres
8

Authority areas covered: Carmarthenshire UA, Ceredigion UA, Pembrokeshire UA

Aberaeron

Cadwgan Inn

10 Market Street, SA46 0AU (off A487, overlooking harbour)

☼ 12 (5 Mon)-11; 12-midnight Fri & Sat; 12-5 Sun
☎ (01545) 570149
Hancock's HB; 2 changing beers (sourced nationally; often Bluestone, Cottage, Evan Evans) Ⓗ
Named after the last ship to be built in this attractive Regency planned town, this old-fashioned single-bar pub offers a friendly welcome and lively conversation. It is popular for its sports coverage, mainly rugby and racing. The guest beers are chosen from a wide range of micro and regional breweries. A small pavement drinking area at the front of the building is a suntrap. The free public car park opposite fills up quickly, especially in summer. ❀🅰️🚌(T1,T5)🐱🛜

Aberystwyth

Glengower Hotel ✅

3 Victoria Terrace, SY23 2DH (on seafront at N end of promenade)

☼ 12-11 ☎ (01970) 626191 ⊕ glengower.co.uk
Mantle Rock Steady; Wye Valley Butty Bach; 3 changing beers (sourced regionally; often Cwrw Cader, Purple Moose, Three Tuns) Ⓗ
Excellent coastal views of Cardigan Bay can be enjoyed from the suntrap front terrace at this newly refurbished seafront hotel. The central front bar is the main drinking area, with a logburner for the winter months. There is also a quieter dining

area and a large rear games room. An annual beer festival and raft race is held over the May bank holiday weekend. Food is locally sourced wherever possible. Up to five ciders come from Gwynt y Ddraig, plus regional guests.
Q🐱🚲🛏️🍴🅰️♣️🚌(03)🐱🛜

Ship & Castle

1 High Street, SY23 1JG

☼ 2-midnight (1am Fri & Sat) ☎ 07773 778785
Wye Valley HPA, Butty Bach; 3 changing beers (sourced nationally; often Grey Trees, Magic Rock, Oakham) Ⓗ
The town's real ale flagship offering microbrewery guests from the UK and Ireland. Small amounts of excellent beer in other formats are also on offer, plus real cider and perry from Gwynt y Ddraig. A five-pump platter of third-pint measures is available. Midweek beer festivals in spring and autumn offer extended choice. The well-considered décor reflects the pub's name and history. The venue can be busy on rugby days, but is welcoming at all times. 🅰️⇌♣️🚌P🚌🐱🛜

Borth

Victoria Inn

High Street, SY24 5HZ

☼ 11-2am ☎ (01970) 871417
Mantle MOHO; Sharp's Doom Bar, Atlantic; Wye Valley HPA; 1 changing beer (sourced nationally) Ⓗ
Family-friendly beach-side pub with two bars downstairs and outside decking. Upstairs is another

613

bar and restaurant leading to a terrace with stunning sea views of Cardigan Bay. Logburners provide warmth all year round. The food menu offers speciality fish dishes and many other home-made options, plus an outside grill Easter to October. The ale range is complemented by cider from Gwynt y Ddraig. Live music features most weekends. Trains run until late seven days a week, the bus service is limited in the evening.
♿🕭🌢🌙🕭🚲♣🍴🚌(512)🐾🛜

Bosherston

St Govan's Country Inn
SA71 5DN
🕭 12-2.30, 6-9; 12-9 Sat & Sun ☎ (01646) 661311
🌐 stgovanscountryinn.webeden.co.uk
Evan Evans Cwrw; 3 changing beers (sourced nationally; often Adnams, Elgood's, Navigation) Ⓗ
Bosherston village (estimated population 300) lies a short walk from the stunning south Pembrokeshire coast and the Bosherston lily ponds which are renowned for their beauty and their varied wildlife. Up to four ales are available in the summer from regional and national brewers. The pub has a comfortable interior, with exposed beams, horse brasses and a large stone fireplace with a logburner giving a cosy feel. It can get busy in the summer months. Q🕭🌢🌙🕭🌢♣🍴🚌P🚌🐾🛜

Burry Port

Cornish Arms
1 Gors Road, SA16 0EL
🕭 12-11; 12-10.30 Sun ☎ (01554) 833224
5 changing beers (sourced regionally; often Boss, St Austell) Ⓗ
Centrally located in this coastal town and conveniently within 100 yards of the train and bus stations. The friendly pub and restaurant is popular with locals and visitors to the area. The bar offers a choice of four real ales, while the restaurant is well known for its good-quality food, specialising in fish dishes. Outside, there is a beer garden and smoking area. Q🕭🌢🌙🕭🚲🚌🛜

Burton

Jolly Sailor ✔
SA73 1NX
🕭 11.30-3, 5-11.30 summer; 11.30-3, 6-11 winter ☎ (01646) 600378 🌐 jollysailorburton.co.uk
Brains Rev James; Draught Bass; Morland Old Speckled Hen Ⓗ
Overlooking the expanse of the River Cleddau and in the shadow of the toll bridge that traverses it, there has been a public house here for over 150 years. It was from this point that travellers would come to Burton to cross by rowing boat ferry to Pembroke Dock. They would leave their supply donkeys outside the Jolly Sailor until their return. The large family- and food-oriented pub has a huge garden with a children's play area and aviary.
🕭🌢🌙P

Capel Bangor

Tynllidiart Arms
SY23 3LR
🕭 closed Mon; 11.30-3, 5-11; 11.30-11 Fri & Sat; 12-4 Sun ☎ (01970) 880248 🌐 tynllidiartarms.co.uk

Wye Valley Butty Bach; 2 changing beers (sourced regionally; often Purple Moose) Ⓗ
Situated in the charming village of Capel Bangor on the main A44 leading to Aberystwyth, the Tynllidiart Arms offers a warm welcome to tourists and locals alike. The bar area downstairs is perfect for a cosy pint. The restaurant upstairs serves fine British cuisine, locally sourced wherever possible, including a tasty and flexible children's menu. Dogs are welcome downstairs and on the front terrace outside. The bus service finishes early evening.
Q🕭🌢🌙P🚌(525,X47)🐾🛜

Capel Hendre

King's Head Hotel Ⓛ
Waterloo Road, SA18 3SF
🕭 4-midnight; 12-midnight Sun ☎ (01269) 842377
Glamorgan Cwrw Gorslas/Bluestone Bitter, Jemimas Pitchfork; 2 changing beers (sourced regionally) Ⓗ
Local village pub tucked away just a couple of miles from the former mining town of Ammanford. The main bar has pool and darts, with a sliding door leading to a separate snug. Usually two - sometimes three - real ales are mainly from Wales, often from Glamorgan and Neath breweries, plus Doom Bar from Sharp's. There is a large car park.
🕭🌢🌙🚲♣🍴P🚌(128,129)🐾🛜

Cardigan

Grosvenor
Bridge Street, SA43 1HY SN177459
🕭 11-11 ☎ (01239) 613792
Greene King Abbot; Sharp's Doom Bar; 1 changing beer (sourced nationally) Ⓗ
Situated on the edge of the town centre next to Cardigan Castle and the River Teifi, this large pub offers a good choice of ales, including a selection of bottled beers. The large open-plan bar/lounge provides various areas to relax, eat and drink, and there is an extra room upstairs for dining and functions. Good-value food is served lunchtimes and evenings every day. An outdoor patio area overlooks the river and the revamped quay area.
🕭🌢🌙🕭🚲♣🚌🛜

Carmarthen

Friends Arms 🍷
Old St Clears Road, SA31 3HH
🕭 11-midnight ☎ (01267) 234073

REAL ALE BREWERIES
4Four Bethesda (NEW)
Bluestone Cilgwyn
Caffle Llawhaden
Castlegate Johnstown
Coles Family 🍴 Llanddarog
Evan Evans Llandeilo
Felinfoel Llanelli
Friends Arms 🍴 Johnstown
Gwaun Valley Pontfaen
Harbwr Tenby Tenby
Little Dragon Milford Haven
Mantle Cardigan
Penlon Cottage New Quay
Seal Bay Cardigan (NEW)
Seren Rosebush
Tenby Tenby
Victoria Inn 🍴 Roch (NEW)

Mantle MOHO; Thornbridge Jaipur IPA; 3 changing beers (sourced locally; often Castlegate, Mantle, Thornbridge) Ⓗ

Excellent local hostelry half a mile from Carmarthen town centre, with a cosy and friendly atmosphere and a warm welcome, enhanced by two open fires. Popular with sports fans, it has BT and Sky sport on TV, and darts is played. Three real ales are usually offered, sometimes including a beer from its own microbrewery. An outbuilding on two floors has function rooms for meetings and parties. Current local CAMRA Pub of the Year. ➳❀♿🚲🍴🎵🛜

Queen's Hotel

10 Queen Street, SA31 1JR

✪ 10-11 (midnight Thu-Sat); 11-8 Sun ☎ (01267) 231800

4 changing beers (sourced regionally; often Evan Evans) Ⓗ

Town-centre pub near Carmarthenshire County Hall with a bar, lounge and small function room. The public bar is where you will find the locals and it has a TV for sporting events. The patio nestles beneath the castle walls and is a suntrap during the summer months. Upstairs function rooms are available, and the local CAMRA branch meets here. Locally sourced ales are usually among the beer range. ➳❀◑≉🚲🍴🛜

Stag & Pheasant

34 Spilman Street, SA31 1LQ

✪ 12-11 (midnight Sat) ☎ (01267) 232040

Marston's Pedigree; 3 changing beers (sourced nationally) Ⓗ

A busy locals' pub with a warm and friendly atmosphere on the main thoroughfare in Carmarthen, making it a popular venue for tourists and locals. The pub boasts an excellent beer garden with outdoor heaters at the rear. There is always a choice of two real ales – either Fortyniner, Boondoggle or Hobgoblin Gold – alongside another guest from Marston's. This is a popular venue for watching sporting events, with two large TV screens. ❀♿≉♣🍴🛜

Yr Hen Dderwen ✓

47-48 King Street, SA31 1BH

✪ 8am-midnight (1am Sat) ☎ (01267) 242050

Greene King Abbot; Ruddles Best Bitter; 3 changing beers (sourced nationally) Ⓗ

This Wetherspoon pub is named after the Carmarthen legend of Merlin and the Old Oak which is depicted throughout the premises. Local Welsh ales are always available alongside a good selection of beers from around the world. Two international beer festivals are held in the spring and autumn – a chance to try something new. A cider festival also features in summer. Food is served all day. Q◑P🏚🚲

Cilgerran

Masons Arms

Cwnce, SA43 2SR

✪ 4-11 Mon; 1-11; 12-11 Fri & Sat; 11-11 Sun ☎ 07989 990461

Hancock's HB; 1 changing beer (often Mantle) Ⓗ

The Mason's Arms, also known as the Rampin, was thought to have opened in 1836. It is a small, cosy and friendly village pub with an open fire (an old kitchen range). Many local characters can be found here and a great atmosphere awaits your visit. One real ale changes regularly, usually from a local

brewery. Various charity events are held during the year along with an occasional musical evening. ➳❀🅰♣P❀

Clarbeston Road

Cross Inn

SA63 4UL (N of railway station)

✪ 12-midnight (1am Fri & Sat) ☎ (01437) 731506

Courage Directors; Greene King Abbot; 1 changing beer (sourced nationally; often Caledonian) Ⓗ

Multi-roomed village inn, well worth seeking out, with stone and wood floors and original oak beams in abundance. The beer range is regional and national. The large bar area housing pool, TV for sport and jukebox is complemented by two small snugs and a dining room where reasonably priced home-cooked food from a largely grill-based menu is served Thursday to Saturday evenings and Sunday lunchtime. Outside there are more spacious drinking areas. A beer festival is held in summer. Q➳❀◑♿≉♣P🏚❀🛜

Cosheston

Brewery Inn

SA72 4UD

✪ closed Mon; 12-3, 6-11 (midnight Sat); 12-4, 6-11 Sun ☎ (01646) 686678 ⊕ thebreweryinn.com

Coles Family Cwrw Blasus; 1 changing beer (often Llangollen) Ⓗ

Set between Cosheston Pill and the Carew Estuary just north east of Pembroke, this light and airy stone-built inn boasts a traditional slate floor and bar, roof beams and comfortable seating with old tables. Paintings and drawings by local artists adorn the walls. The outdoor smoking area is heated in winter. Despite the name, there has been no brewery here since 1889. Q➳❀◑🅰🏚

Cresswell Quay

Cresselly Arms 🅛

SA68 0TE

✪ 12-3, 5-11; 12-11 Sat; 12-3, 5-10.30 Sun ☎ (01646) 651210

Sharp's Doom Bar Ⓗ**; Worthington's Bitter** Ⓖ**; house beer (by Caffle); 2 changing beers (sourced locally; often Bluestone, Mantle)** Ⓗ

Situated on the Cresswell River, this 250-year-old ivy-covered hostelry is a throwback to the Victorian age. The homely farm kitchen interior, where a roaring fire burns in the hearth, is a haven for locals and visitors alike. Accessible by boat from the Milford Haven estuary at high tide, the pub also lies on a series of interesting walking routes. The house beer from Caffle is complemented by Worthington's Bitter dispensed from the cask by jug. Q➳❀🅰♣🌑P🏚(361)

Cross Inn

Rhos yr Hafod Inn

SY23 5NB (at B4337/B4577 crossroads, about 3 miles from Llanon)

✪ 5-11; closed Sun ☎ (01974) 272644

2 changing beers (sourced regionally; often Evan Evans, Glamorgan, Mantle) Ⓗ

Although a bit off the beaten track, this friendly and traditional pub is well worth a visit. Cosy drinking areas cluster around the small central bar and a larger back room decorated with old

WALES

photographs of local scenes provides additional seating. Sunny days can be enjoyed either at the front of the pub in the roadside drinking area or in the large rear garden. A traditional turntable and vinyl collection are available for customers to peruse. A regular quiz night is hosted. There is ample parking. ⏰❄♣P🛜

Cwmann

Cwmann Tavern
SA48 8DR SN582473
✪ closed Mon; 4-11; 12-11 Sun ☎ (01570) 423861
🌐 cwmannetavern.co.uk
2 changing beers (sourced nationally; often Cottage) Ⓗ
A former coaching inn dating from the 1600s, within easy walking distance of the town of Lampeter. The stone floors and low beams help create a cosy atmosphere. The varied menu (available evenings only in the week) includes pub favourites, interesting specials and vegetarian options. There is a folk night every Thursday and a 'not so high stake' poker night every Friday. ⏰❄◗&♣●P🖳

Dale

Griffin Inn
SA62 3RB
✪ 12-11; 12.30-2.30, 5.30-10.30 Sun summer; 12-2, 5.30-11; 12.30-2.30, 5.30-10.30 Sun winter ☎ (01646) 636227
Brains Rev James; Evan Evans Cwrw; 1 changing beer (often Evan Evans) Ⓗ
In an enviable location at the water's edge close to the slipway on the Milford Haven waterway, the Griffin is popular with locals and visitors, including those exploring the Pembrokeshire Coast Path. Some of the outside seats are right alongside the water. Inside you can have some fun playing table skittles. The village is the centre for a thriving sailing club. A National Tourism for Wales award-winner. Q❄◗&♣🖳

Drefach Felindre

John Y Gwas
SA44 5XG SN354383
✪ 5-11; 4-midnight Fri; 12-midnight Sat; 12-11 Sun ☎ (01559) 370469
2 changing beers (sourced regionally; often Bluestone, Brains, Shepherd Neame) Ⓗ
Early 19th-century village tavern with a striking yellow and black livery, attracting locals and tourists alike with snugs, a wood-burning stove, quality beer and cider, and a warm welcome, especially for dogs. Two ales are generally offered, and a wide variety of bottled beers and ciders. A beer festival, showcasing more than 10 different ales, is held over the August bank holiday weekend. Basket meals are available most evenings, bar meals on Friday and Saturday evenings. ⏰❄◗♣●P🖳(460)❄🛜

Red Lion
SA44 5UH (centre of village 1 mile off A484 Llandysul to Newcastle Emlyn road) SN354388
✪ 4-11 (midnight Fri & Sat); 12-10 Sun ☎ (01559) 371677
Mantle Cwrw Teifi Ⓗ
Located in the small village of Drefach Felindre near the National Wool Museum, a warm welcome is assured at this 19th-century pub, which has been

renovated in recent years. It is now mostly open plan but with a separate dining room and a large outside drinking area. Community-focused, it hosts regular fundraising events for charity. The car park is small but on-street parking is available. The original tiled entrance porch is worthy of note. Q⏰❄◗&♣🖳(460)🛜

Fishguard

Pendre Inn
High Street, SA65 9AT (S of town towards Haverfordwest)
✪ 11 (4 Mon)-midnight; 11-1am Fri & Sat; 12-11.30 Sun
☎ (01348) 874128 🌐 thependreinn.co.uk
Hancock's HB; 2 changing beers (sourced nationally; often Greene King, Ruddles, St Austell) Ⓗ
Built around 1790, close to the tollgate on the turnpike road to Haverfordwest on the main road south out of town, this friendly, traditional pub has a good local following and an established reputation for its beer. Two guest beers change regularly and may come from anywhere in the UK. Pool and darts are played in the large back bar, while the front bar boasts an inglenook fireplace. Meals, available all day in summer, lunchtimes and evenings in winter (not Mon), include home-made specials. Q⏰❄◗▲♣P🖳(T5)❄🛜

Goginan

Druid Inn 🍷
SY23 3NT (on A44 6 miles E of Aberystwyth)
✪ 12-midnight (1am Fri & Sat) ☎ (01970) 880650
Wye Valley Bitter; 3 changing beers (sourced nationally; often Mantle, Purple Moose, Wood) Ⓗ
A family-run community pub celebrating its 43rd year in the Guide. The dining room and pool room flank the L-shaped main bar where dogs are welcome. Two guest beers are available summer and weekends plus a range of bottled real ales and ciders. Occasional music nights (sometimes with acts of more than local renown) and beer festivals are hosted. Food is popular and high quality. Buses run until early evening Monday to Saturday. A pub-owned B&B can be found next door. ⏰❄◗♣●P🖳(525,X47)❄

Haverfordwest

Pembroke Yeoman
11 Hill Street, SA61 1QQ
✪ 11-11 ☎ (01437) 762500
Draught Bass; Hancock's HB; 2 changing beers (sourced nationally) Ⓗ
A little off the beaten track, conversation rules at this local pub, though there is a well-stocked jukebox should it flag. Two guest ales come from small breweries and change often. Food is served in generous portions. Known as the Upper Three Crowns until the 1960s, the pub's name was changed in recognition of the local yeomanry headquarters nearby. Q⏰◗⇌●🖳(301)❄

William Owen Ⓛ ✔
6 Quay Street, SA61 1BG
✪ 9am-midnight (1am Fri & Sat) ☎ (01437) 771900
Greene King IPA, Abbot; Sharp's Doom Bar; 5 changing beers Ⓗ
Pembrokeshire's first and so far only Wetherspoon pub occupies a handsome 19th-century building, formerly a shop, hotel and restaurant, now with a

spacious extension to the rear. It was reputedly built in 1856 for Joseph Thomas, a corn and manure merchant, by local architect William Owen. It has also been a saddler's and more recently the Wilton House Hotel. Beer from one of the county's four breweries is regularly available. The pub offers the chain's standard menu and promotional deals, and opens from 7am for breakfast. Local CAMRA Cider Pub of the Year. Q☎🕮👪◑👭♿⇋P🖵🚃♿

Herbrandston

Taberna Inn 🅛
SA73 3TD (3 miles W of Milford Haven)
☀ 12-11 ☎ (01646) 693498 ⊕ taberna.org.uk
Caffle Drop Squint; Purple Moose Ochr Tywyll y Mws/ Dark Side of the Moose; 1 changing beer (sourced nationally) 🅗
Designed and built in 1963 by a local carpenter and builder with an eye to the area's then rapidly developing oil and petrochemical industry. A bus (service 300) is available from Milford Haven and the marina for visitors and crews looking for a choice of real ales. Local, regional and national beers are available alongside Westons and Moles Black Rat ciders. The pub maintains a list of all the guest beers sold throughout the year. A former Pembrokeshire CAMRA Pub of the Year.
Q☎🚌◑♿🅰♣P🖵(300,315)

Johnston

Vine Inn
Vine Road, SA62 3NY
☀ 11-2, 6-11; 12-11 Sat & Sun ☎ (01437) 890611
Sharp's Doom Bar; Wye Valley Bitter; 2 changing beers (sourced regionally; often Mantle, Purple Moose) 🅗
First licensed in 1810 to Thomas Evans, the pub has been trading ever since, except for a brief closure a few years ago. A smart black-and-white roadside establishment, it has a good local and countywide following. Local and regional guest ales are available. Inside is a long bar area with exposed beams where many pumpclips tell of past and present beer delights. A former Pembrokeshire CAMRA Pub of the Year. ☎🕮◑⇋●P🖵(302,349)

Laugharne

New Three Mariners Inn 🅛
Victoria Street, SA33 4SE
☀ 3-11 (midnight Fri); 12-1am Sat; 6-11 Sun
☎ (01994) 427426
Brains Rev James; 2 changing beers 🅗
The building is located in the centre of the historic township of Laugharne and only yards from its early 11th-century castle. Dylan Thomas lived in the town for a number of years and he and his wife Caitlin are laid to rest in the graveyard of St Martin's Church. The pub moved to its current site when the original ale house opposite was converted to a carpentry shop. Popular with locals, it hosts a weekly quiz night. ☎🕮🚌◑♿🅰♣P🖵🐾🚃

Little Haven

Saint Bride's Inn 🅛
St Brides Road, SA62 3UN
☀ 11-midnight ☎ (01437) 781266 ⊕ saintbridesinn.co.uk

Brains Rev James; Caffle Catchypole; Hancock's HB; 2 changing beers (sourced regionally; often Bluestone, Brecon) 🅗
Little Haven is a quaint old fishing village in a conservation area of the Pembrokeshire Coast National Park. This family-run pub in the centre of the village is open all year round, selling a range of Welsh, often Pembrokeshire, ales. It is noted for the ancient well in the cellar. The attractive interior includes a separate dining area, and there are heaters on the patio in the pretty suntrap garden for outdoor drinking. Q☎🕮◑🅰P🖵🚃(311,400)🚃

Llandeilo

Cottage Inn
Pentrefelin, SA19 6SD (on A40, 3 miles W of Llandeilo)
☀ 10.30-11 ☎ (01558) 824645 ⊕ cottageinnbandb.co.uk
Gower Gold; 2 changing beers (sourced locally) 🅗
A popular family-run local community pub on the A40. Dating back to the 1850s, it was formerly a coaching inn and a drovers' hostelry. Sky TV is available and the pub gets busy when major sporting events are screened. It has a separate restaurant/function room. At the rear is a spacious covered smoking area and outside is a garden and a large car park with caravanning and camping space. Two or three guest real ales are offered. B&B accommodation is available.
Q☎🕮◑♿🅰P🖵🐾🚃

Salutation Inn
33 New Road, SA19 6DF
☀ 12-11; 12-10.30 Sun ☎ (01558) 824256
Gower Gold; Grey Trees Afghan Pale; Timothy Taylor Landlord; 2 changing beers (sourced nationally) 🅗
The landlord at this locals' pub is a cask beer enthusiast and friendly staff dispense five rapidly changing ales. The interior is divided into two areas, with a pool table on one side and a wood fire on the other. Live music often features at weekends. There is a garden and function area to the rear. The pub hosts a beer festival in the summer. 🕮♿♣🖵🐾🚃

White Horse
Rhosmaen Street, SA19 6EN
☀ 11-11; 12-10.30 Sun ☎ (01558) 822424
Evan Evans BB/Best Bitter, Cwrw, Warrior; 2 changing beers 🅗
Grade II-listed coaching inn dating from the 16th century, tucked away just off the high street. The tap for the local Evan Evans Brewery, this multi-roomed hostelry is popular with all ages. There is a small outdoor drinking area to the front and a large council car park to the rear with access to the pub down a short flight of steps. A covered area is available for smokers with its own TV showing sport. A former Carmarthenshire CAMRA Pub of the Year winner. ◑⇋●🖵🐾(103,X13)🐾

Llandovery

King's Head 🅛
1 Market Square, SA20 0AB
☀ 10-11 ☎ (01550) 720393 ⊕ kingsheadcoachinginn.co.uk
Evan Evans Cwrw; 2 changing beers 🅗
Set in the main square of this historic town on the edge of the Brecon Beacons National Park, this former coaching inn dates from the 1700s. It is a popular base for many organisations including the Rotary Club and cattle breeders. Good food ranges

from bar meals to à la carte. Guest beers are usually from Welsh breweries and often local.
Q❄️✎🕭🍴🅰️⇌♣️🚌🐾

Llandybie

Ivy Bush

18 Church Street, SA18 3HZ (100yds from church)
⏰ 12-midnight (11 Mon); 11-midnight Sat & Sun
☎ (01269) 850272
Timothy Taylor Landlord; 1 changing beer (sourced regionally) Ⓗ
The oldest pub in the village, this friendly local dates back nearly 300 years. The single-bar room has two comfortable seating areas. Pub games and quizzes are held weekly and a large-screen TV shows sport. Timothy Taylor Landlord is usually joined by at least one regularly changing guest beer. The local bird-watching group holds its meetings here. The railway station nearby is on the scenic Heart of Wales line.
🛏️❄️⇌♣️🖐️P🚪(103,X13)🛜

Red Lion Hotel

6 Llandeilo Road, SA18 3JA
⏰ 12-3, 6-11; 12-11 Sat; 12-9 Sun ☎ (01269) 851202
Evan Evans Warrior; Gower Gower Gold Ⓗ
A family-run pub that serves food and quality beers in a convivial atmosphere. It is handy for the local railway station on the popular Heart of Wales line. The drinking area is in an enclosed comfortable sitting area. Food is served in a separate dining area. There are benches in the garden at the rear of the pub. 🛏️❄️🕭♿️⇌🖐️P🚪🛜

Llandyfaelog

Red Lion

SA17 5PP (300yds off A484)
⏰ 11-midnight ☎ (01267) 267530
🌐 redlionllandyfaelog.co.uk
Evan Evans Cwrw; Glamorgan Cwrw Gorslas/Bluestone Bitter; Wye Valley Bitter; 3 changing beers (often Butcombe) Ⓗ
This family-run village hostelry can truly be described as at the heart of the community. The pub has a separate annexe hosting concerts and functions including the local choir practice. The large public bar, with darts and a pool table, is complemented by a restaurant and a separate family room. Food is served throughout the bar and restaurant. Q❄️✎🕭♿️🅰️♣️🖐️🚪(198,X12)🛜

Llandyfan

Square & Compass

SA18 2UD (between Ammanford and Trapp)
⏰ 4.30 (12 Sat)-11; 12-10.30 Sun ☎ (01269) 850402
Tomos Watkin Old Style Bitter; 2 changing beers (sourced locally) Ⓗ
Originally the village blacksmith's, this 18th-century building was converted to a pub in the 1960s. Nestling on the western edge of the Brecon Beacons National Park, it enjoys magnificent local views and plenty of walking opportunities. A traditional family hostelry, it has a wonderful rustic charm and offers a warm, friendly welcome. Usually two, occasionally three, guest beers are available, at least one from a local brewery. Opening hours vary in winter – ring ahead to check.
Q🛏️❄️🕭♿️🅰️♣️🖐️P🚪

Llandysul

Porth Hotel

Church Street, SA44 4QS SN418407
⏰ 12-11; 12-5.30 Sun ☎ (01559) 362202 🌐 porthhotel.co.uk
2 changing beers (sourced locally; often Brecon, Glamorgan) Ⓗ
Set on the banks of the River Teifi, this 17th-century coaching inn is now a family-run village hotel with a bar, restaurant and function room. The public rooms still retain the original oak beams and panels. Beers from the local Castlegate Brewery are regularly featured alongside ales from other Welsh breweries such as Brecon, Glamorgan, Coles and Gower. An ideal location for walks and fishing.
🛏️❄️🕭🍴P🚪🛜

Llanelli

York Palace

51 Stepney Street, SA15 3YA (opp Town Hall Square Gardens)
⏰ 8am-midnight (1am Fri & Sat) ☎ (01554) 758609
Greene King Abbot; Ruddles Best Bitter; Sharp's Doom Bar; 5 changing beers Ⓗ
This former cinema in the town centre is a typical Wetherspoon conversion spread over two levels. The walls are adorned with photographs of local industrial history including Llanelli's famous tin plate industry. Guest beers are often sourced locally, and discounted on Monday. There is easy access to the bus station, and the railway station is a 10-minute walk. Q🍴♿️⇌🖐️🚪🛜

Llanfallteg

Plash

SA34 0UN (off A40 at Llanddewi Velfrey)
⏰ 12 (4 Mon & Tue)-11; 12-9 Sun ☎ (01437) 563472
🌐 theplashinn.co.uk
Wye Valley Butty Bach; 2 changing beers Ⓗ
At the centre of village life, this terrace-style cottage pub and garden has been an inn for more than 180 years and visitors are made welcome. It holds a quiz night on Tuesday, a regular folk night and a number of other special events. The guest beers are usually from small, independent breweries. Home-made food, using locally sourced ingredients, includes specials on Wednesday, Friday and Saturday. The disabled entrance is to the rear. A former local CAMRA Pub of the Year.
Q🛏️❄️🕭🍴♿️🅰️♣️🖐️P🐾🛜

Llangeitho

Three Horse Shoe

SY25 6TW
⏰ 5.30-11; 12-2 Sun ☎ (01974) 821244
2 changing beers (sourced regionally; often Evan Evans, Ludlow) Ⓗ
Friendly pub situated in a pretty village with historic connections to the Methodist revival in the 1700s. It has a main bar, games room and separate dining area also used for functions and events. An attractive outside seating area overlooks the village square and is a lovely place to enjoy a beer in the evening sun. Excellent-value, home-cooked meals are served, with a popular special offer menu on Wednesday. Pool and darts are played and there is a jukebox, plus a big screen for major sporting events. 🛏️❄️🕭🍴♣️P🚪🐾🛜

Llangoedmor

Penllwyndu

SA43 2LY (on B4570 4½ miles from Cardigan) SN240458
☼ 12 (3 Mon)-11; 11-11 Sat & Sun ☎ (01239) 682533
Hancock's HB; 2 changing beers (sourced regionally; often Brains) Ⓗ
Old-fashioned ale house standing at an isolated crossroads where Cardigan's evil-doers were once hanged – the pub sign is worthy of close inspection. The cheerful and welcoming public bar retains its quaintness, with a slate floor and inglenook with wood-burning stove. Good home-cooked food including traditional favourites is available all day in the bar and the separate restaurant. Live music plays on the third Thursday evening of the month. ▧❀◑♣Pॐ

Llanllwni

Talardd Arms

SA39 9DX SN487392
☼ 12-3, 6-11 ☎ (01559) 395633 ⊕ talardd.com
1 changing beer (sourced regionally; often Evan Evans) Ⓗ
There are records of this old inn dating back to 1626, when drovers would stop for refreshments for man and beast before driving their livestock over Llanllwni Mountain on their way to markets over the border. Sympathetically modernised, Tafarn y Talardd continues to offer a traditional warm and friendly welcome. Live music, quizzes and film nights are organised most Mondays. ▧◑♣P◨ॐ☞

Llansaint

King's Arms

13 Maes yr Eglwys, SA17 5JE
☼ closed Mon-Fri; 6-11 Sat; 12-11 Sun ☎ (01267) 267487
Glamorgan Cwrw Gorslas/Bluestone Bitter, Jemimas Pitchfork; Young's Special Ⓗ
A former local CAMRA Pub of the Year, this friendly village hostelry has been a pub for more than 200 years. Situated near an 11th-century church, it is reputedly built from stone recovered from the lost village of St Ishmaels. Music and poetry nights often feature on the third Friday of the month. Two guest beers from smaller breweries are usually offered. Good-value home-cooked food is served. Carmarthen Bay Holiday Park is a few miles away. ▧⛺◑&♣P◨(198)☞

Llanychaer

Bridge End Inn ⛾ Ⓛ

SA65 9TB (on B4313, 2 miles SW of Fishguard)
☼ 12-11 ☎ (01348) 872545
Mantle Rock Steady, Dark Heart Ⓗ**; 1 changing beer (sourced locally; often Bluestone, Mantle)** Ⓗ/Ⓖ
Known locally as the Bont, this friendly country pub, over 150 years old, nestles in the beautiful Gwaun Valley at a bridging point across the river. The cosy bars with log fires serve mainly local real ales. The dining room is housed in the smithy, once run as a complementary business to the inn, and features an external water wheel. Home-made food is served daily, with the Sunday lunch particularly popular. Check ahead for winter hours and food service. Q▧❀◑&Å♣●P◨(345)ॐ☞

Maenclochog

Globe Inn

SA66 7LE
☼ 4 (12 Sat)-11; 7-10 Sun ☎ (01437) 532269
Wadworth 6X; 1 changing beer (sourced regionally; often Box Steam) Ⓗ
In the 19th century Maenclochog was an important trading centre for slate from nearby quarries, and held a monthly livestock market – because of this trade there were once 19 public houses in the village. Now the Globe, run by the same family for over 150 years, is the only survivor, and has become the social centre for villages in the area. ▧♣P

Nevern

Trewern Arms

SA42 0NB (off A487, 2 miles N of Newport)
☼ 11-11 ☎ (01239) 820395
Bluestone Rocketeer; 2 changing beers (sourced nationally; often 4Four, Gwaun Valley) Ⓗ
A picturesque 16th-century pub, situated within a secluded valley astride the banks of the River Nevern. The village of Nevern is less than a mile from the beautiful fishing town of Newport. This multi-roomed pub can cater for all, from those who just want a drink, to large events such as wedding receptions. An ideal place to stay as a base for some of the best walks in West Wales. Food times vary in winter. Q▧❀⛺◑&Å♣P◨(T5)ॐ☞

New Quay

Black Lion

Glanmor Terrace, SA45 9PT
☼ 11-11 ☎ (01545) 560122 ⊕ blacklionnewquay.co.uk
Sharp's Doom Bar; 1 changing beer (sourced locally; often Bluestone, Mantle) Ⓗ
Refurbished in 2013, this pub has genuine connections to Dylan Thomas. There are stunning sea views from the garden. It has a main bar with seating, a tiny and cosy side area with one table and a separate dining room. A large TV screen dominates when a big game is on. A guest beer is available at busy times of year. The food is good value and high quality. Nine en-suite bedrooms are available for visitors. ▧❀⛺◑☞

Newport

Golden Lion Ⓛ

East Street, SA42 0SY (on A487)
☼ 12-midnight; 12-11 Sun ☎ (01239) 820321
⊕ goldenlionpembrokeshire.co.uk
Bluestone Bedrock Blonde; Sharp's Doom Bar; Worthington's White Shield; 1 changing beer (sourced nationally; often Thwaites) Ⓗ
Situated in an area of outstanding natural beauty close to the Pembrokeshire Coast Path, the Golden Lion is another of Newport's sociable locals and is reputed to have its own resident ghost. A number of internal walls have been removed to create a spacious open-plan bar area, with distinct sections helping to retain a cosy atmosphere. Locally caught fish and Welsh Black beef are specialities, served in the bar and restaurant. The pub offers a rare sighting of White Shield on draught: see also entry for Pembroke Dock. Car parking space is available on the opposite side of the road. Q▧❀⛺◑Å♣P◨◨(T5)ॐ☞

WALES

Llwyngwair Arms

East Street, SA42 0SY (town centre, Newport Square)
🕐 2-11 (12.30am Fri); 12-12.30am Sat; 12-11 Sun
☎ (01239) 821554
Bluestone Bedrock Blonde; Brains Rev James; 2 changing beers (often Gower) 🅷
A centrally situated stone-built traditional pub within easy reach of the coastal path with good beers and a great atmosphere. The Grade II-listed coaching inn was built around the early- to mid-19th century, with stabling opposite. The Court Leet, an ancient institution, meets here, and the annual mayoral ceremony is held here each November. Q ☞ 🏵 ♿ ▲ P 🖵 🐾 🛜

Pembroke Dock

First & Last

London Road, SA72 6TX (on A477)
🕐 10-1am (1.30am Thu-Sat) ☎ (01646) 682687
Brains Rev James; Worthington's White Shield; 1 changing beer (sourced nationally; often Skinner's) 🅷
Formerly the Commercial, the pub acquired its more distinctive name in 1991 to reflect its edge-of-town location. The friendly single-bar local has been run by the same family for 50 years. The walls display an eclectic mix of photos and prints. The guest beer can be from anywhere, local or national, and the food is good pub fare. There is a popular quirky Sunday evening quiz. It is handy for the Cleddau Bridge, giving easy access to Haverfordwest, and close to the historic naval dockyard and Irish ferry. Q ☞ 🏵 🌗 ⇌ P 🖵 🛜

Penrhiwllan

Daffodil

SA44 5NG SN370419
🕐 12-11 ☎ (01559) 370343 🌐 daffodilinn.co.uk
Greene King Abbot; 2 changing beers 🅷
Formerly the Penrhiwllan Inn, the Daffodil is a gastro-pub dating from 1750 in the beautiful countryside village of Penrhiwllan near the market town of Newcastle Emlyn. It has been modernised in an elegant style and provides separate, intimate dining sections and cosy drinking areas catering for all, with excellent disabled facilities. Two handpumps, three in summer, dispense beers mostly from national breweries, with guest beers from Welsh breweries. ☞ 🏵 🌗 ♿ P 🐾

Pontamman

Red Kite Inn

89 Pontamman Road, SA18 2JD (a little over 1 mile N of Ammanford on A474 towards Neath)
🕐 closed Mon & Tue; 12-3, 5-11; 12-11 Sat & Sun
☎ (01269) 597177 🌐 theredkiteinn.co.uk
2 changing beers (sourced regionally) 🅷
Previously known as the Perrivale, the pub reopened as the Red Kite Inn (or Y Barcud Coch in Welsh). Two or three real ales are usually available, mostly sourced from Welsh breweries. Live music and quiz nights feature at the weekend. There are a number of quiet corners and a separate restaurant. Meals are served lunchtimes and evenings Wednesday to Saturday, and Sunday lunchtimes. ☞ 🏵 ⇌ 🌗 ♿ P 🖵 🛜

Porthgain

Sloop Inn

SA62 5BN
🕐 9.30am-11 (midnight Sat) ☎ (01348) 831449
🌐 sloop.co.uk
Brains Rev James; Hancock's HB; 1 changing beer (sourced nationally; often Gower, Sharp's) 🅷
Situated in the beautiful fishing harbour of Porthgain, this sympathetically renovated and extended old inn has served both the locally based fishing industry and the nearby now-defunct quarry and brickworks on the opposite side of the valley. Interesting quarrying, brick-making and shipping artefacts are on display. The Sloop is a popular refreshment stop for walkers on the scenic Pembrokeshire Coast National Park footpath, with stunning beaches and dramatic cliff views nearby. Seasonal fresh fish and local lobster are often on the menu. Q ☞ 🏵 🌗 ▲ ♣ ♠ P 🖵 🛜

Porthyrhyd

Mansel Arms

Banc y Mansel, SA32 8BS (on B4310 between Porthyrhyd and Drefach)
🕐 4.30-11; 3-midnight Sat; 12-6 Sun ☎ (01267) 275305
Courage Directors; Wye Valley Butty Bach; 2 changing beers (sourced regionally) 🅷
Friendly 18th-century former coaching inn with wood fires in each room. The original limestone flags have been broken up and used in the fireplace, and low beams have been added to create atmosphere, with numerous jugs hanging from them in the bar. Pool and darts are played in a room to the rear, which was originally used for slaughtering pigs. Beers are varied, with the Young's range always popular as well as local ales. Q ☞ 🌗 ♠ P 🖵 (129)

Prengwyn

Gwarcefel Arms

SA44 4LU (on crossroads of A475 and B4476) SN424442
🕐 4-11; 12-11 Sat & Sun ☎ (01559) 363126
Sharp's Doom Bar; 1 changing beer (sourced nationally) 🅷
A traditional country inn with a friendly atmosphere where everyone is welcome, including families and dogs. Situated at the junction of five roads, three miles north of Llandysul, the pub has a main bar with a wood-burning stove, cosy seating, pool table and dartboard. A separate restaurant area, which caters for functions and parties, offers evening meals Thursdays to Saturdays, and Sunday lunches. The beer garden and car park are to the rear. ☞ 🏵 🌗 ♣ P 🐾

Pumsaint

Dolaucothi Arms

SA19 8UW (on A482 midway between Llanwrda and Lampeter)
🕐 closed Mon; 12 (5 Tue)-11; 12-8 Sun ☎ (01558) 650237
2 changing beers (sourced regionally) 🅷
A substantial stone-built coaching inn with a friendly welcome, owned by the National Trust and tastefully restored in traditional style. There is an excellent food menu and two real ales, usually sourced from Welsh breweries, alongside real cider. A large beer garden offers views over the valley and the rivers Cothi and Twrch. The pub is

located close to the National Trust's Dolaucothi Gold Mines. Opening hours may vary so it is advisable to check before travelling. 🌡️🛏️🍴🕽️👌🐾♣️🖤P🚃🐾🛜

Pwlltrap

White Lion

SA33 4AT

🕐 12-11; 11-10.30 Sun ☎ (01994) 230370

Courage Directors; Greene King Abbot; Shepherd Neame Bishops Finger; Young's Bitter; 1 changing beer (sourced nationally) 🖫

This roadside pub, just outside St Clears on the road to Whitland, is warm and welcoming with a real fire in winter. It has an old-world charm with oak beams and panelled walls, and boasts a large restaurant serving good food. Pool and darts are played and a large TV screen shows regular sporting fixtures. The pub organises events throughout the year. Two cask beers are available in winter, four in summer.

Q🕽️👌♣️🚃(224,322)🐾🛜

Rhandirmwyn

Royal Oak 🖳

SA20 0NY

🕐 closed Mon; 12-2, 6-11; 12-2 Sun ☎ (01550) 760201 🌐 theroyaloakinn.co.uk

3 changing beers 🖫

Remote, stone-flagged inn with excellent views of the Towy Valley and close to an RSPB bird sanctuary. Originally built as a hunting lodge, it is now a focal point for community activities and popular with fans of outdoor pursuits. The village shop is alongside. Two or three guest beers are offered and the good wholesome food is recommended. There are panoramic views from the beer garden at the side of the pub. Five times local CAMRA Pub of the Year.

Q🌡️🛏️🕽️🍴♣️🖤P🐾🛜

Roch

Victoria Inn

SA62 6AW (on A487)

🕐 closed Mon; 12-2.30, 5-11; 12-11 Sat & Sun ☎ (01437) 710426 🌐 thevictoriainnroch.com

2 changing beers (sourced nationally) 🖫

Now a brewpub, just a mile from the vast expanse of Newgale Beach, which can be seen from the pub, this little gem is worth seeking out. Dating back to at least 1851, it was reputedly at one time a stop-off for drovers on their way home from Haverfordwest market. With low doorways and beamed ceilings, and a log fire in winter, it has a warm atmosphere. A popular quiz night is held on Wednesday, curry-and-a-pint on Friday. In addition to the changing beers it serves its own brews; the house bitter is called Fine & Dandy.

Q🌡️🛏️🍴🕽️🍴♣️🖤P🚃(411)🛜

Saundersfoot

Royal Oak Inn ✅

Wogan Terrace, SA69 9HA

🕐 10-11 ☎ (01834) 812546 🌐 theroyaloaksaundersfoot.co.uk

Courage Best Bitter; Sharp's Doom Bar; 4 changing beers (sourced nationally; often Courage, Mantle) 🖫

An old pub and restaurant in the centre of town offering a wide selection of real ales. To the right is a cosy drinkers' bar where locals and visitors are made welcome. To the left is another bar and a further dedicated restaurant with an extensive menu. Food is available throughout the day during the summer months. At the front is a heated terrace with sea and harbour views.

Q🌡️🌡️🕽️🍴AP🚃(381)🐾

Solva

Cambrian Inn 🖳

SA62 6UU (on A487 by bridge)

🕐 12-3, 5.30-midnight summer; 12.30-3, 5.30-9.30 winter ☎ (01437) 721210 🌐 thecambrianinn.co.uk

Gwaun Valley Blodwen; 2 changing beers (sourced locally; often Coles Family, Mantle) 🖫

Set in the harbour village of Solva, you cannot miss this trendy modernised pub as you come down the hill from the south. The large bar offers comfortable seating for drinkers and diners. There are paintings by local artists on the walls. The beers come mainly from local and regional brewers – two in winter and four in summer. The food is all sourced as locally as possible throughout the year.

Q🛏️🕽️AP🚃(411)🐾🛜

Temple Bar

Fronfelen Arms

SA48 8BQ (on A482 at B4337 jct)

🕐 4-11 ☎ 07837 358130

2 changing beers (sourced regionally; often Ludlow, Mantle, Wye Valley) 🖫/🖪

A warm welcome is assured at this easy-to-find one-room pub, which reopened a couple of years ago and is undergoing a gradual refurbishment. The beer choice changes regularly, often complemented by a guest cider on handpump and four bag-in-a-box ciders. A '70s jukebox plays 7-inch records but otherwise this is a quiet pub.

🌡️A♣️🖤P🚃(T1)🐾🛜

Tenby

Buccaneer Inn 🖳

St Julian Street, SA70 7AS

🕐 11-12.30am; 11-11 Sun ☎ (01834) 842273

Harbwr Tenby MV Enterprise, North Star, RFA Sir Galahad; 1 changing beer (sourced regionally; often Glamorgan) 🖫

The Buccaneer is in a quaint street which links the town square to the harbour and beaches. The bar area is large but has a cosy feel with beams, stove and Tenby memorabilia adorning the walls. A sunny walled beer garden is to the rear. The pub is the brewery tap for the adjacent Tenby Harbour Brewery, offering its full range of beers. Food is served all day with locally sourced fresh fish on the menu. 🌡️🌡️🕽️🚃🚃🐾

Hope & Anchor 🖳

St Julian Street, SA70 7AS

🕐 11-midnight; 11-10.30 Sun ☎ (01834) 842131

Felinfoel Double Dragon; Harbwr Tenby MV Enterprise 🖫, North Star 🖪, Caldey Lollipop; Sharp's Atlantic; 2 changing beers (sourced nationally; often Bluestone, Mantle) 🖫

Welcoming pub set in the old town on the way down to the harbour. Food is important here and specials supplement the standard menu. The convivial atmosphere and interesting local décor make it an excellent place to relax over a beer. Up to four guest beers are sourced mainly from Welsh breweries including Evan Evans, Mantle and Purple Moose, while Wye Valley sometimes sneaks over the border. Ciders include Somerset Tree Shaker West Country Cider. ⏰☺⌂◑▲≷●P☐🚐🛜

Trapp

Cennen Arms
SA19 6TP
☺ 12-3 (not Mon), 5.30-midnight; 12-10.30 Sun
☎ (01558) 822330 ⊕ cennenlodge.co.uk
Joule's Slumbering Monk; 1 changing beer (sourced regionally) Ⓗ

The pub has two main bars, one sharing a historic glass bar screen with the cosy snug, and three separate dining areas. There are also tables outside. The landlord has consistently delivered quality food and real ale for more than 17 years. The regular beer is Joule's Slumbering Monk, and another ale is often available. A good selection of food is served lunchtimes and evenings. The pub is the starting point for some pleasant walking routes. Q⏰☺⌂◑▲♣●P☺🛜

Tregaron

Talbot
The Square, SY25 6JL

☺ 11-11; 11-10.30 Sun ☎ (01974) 298208 ⊕ ytalbot.com
4 changing beers (sourced regionally; often Evan Evans, Mantle, Purple Moose) Ⓗ

Former drovers' inn of immense character offering a public bar at the rear with TV, a small front lounge with an open fire, and a delightful beamed and flagstoned snug with inglenook fireplace. Four real ales are available, always including one from the Mantle Brewery, and a varying selection of cider and perry from Gwynt y Ddraig. Excellent locally sourced food includes good vegetarian options. The terrace drinking area has fine views and a memorial to a circus elephant reputedly buried here. Q⏰☺⌂◑▲&♣●P☐(585,588)☺🛜

Whitland

Station House Hotel
St Johns Street, SA34 0AP
☺ 9am-1am (2am Fri & Sat) ☎ (01994) 240556
⊕ stationhousewhitland.co.uk
Courage Directors; 2 changing beers Ⓗ

A smile and a warm welcome are always on tap at this friendly hostelry. Very much a locals' pub for all ages, there is something for everyone here, with pool and darts teams and bingo on Sunday evenings. A small separate room is available for people looking for a quiet corner. The outside drinking area is partly under cover. Car parking is to the rear and the railway station is close by.
☺◑≷♣●P☐☺🛜

John Y Gwas, Drefach Felindre

NORTHERN
ISLES

SHETLAND

HIGHLANDS
&
WESTERN ISLES

ABERDEEN
& GRAMPIAN

TAYSIDE

FIFE

ARGYLL &
THE ISLES

LOCH LOMOND
STIRLING
& THE
TROSSACHS

EDINBURGH & LOTHIANS

GREATER
GLASGOW &
CLYDE

BORDERS

AYRSHIRE
& ARRAN

DUMFRIES &
GALLOWAY

NORTHERN
IRELAND

NORTHUMBERLAND

TYNE &
WEAR

CUMBRIA

DURHAM

ISLE OF
MAN

NORTH
YORKSHIRE

LANCASHIRE

WEST
YORKS

EAST
YORKS

MERSEYSIDE

GREATER
MANCHESTER

SOUTH
YORKS

CHESHIRE

DERBYSHIRE

NOTTINGHAM-
SHIRE

LINCOLNSHIRE

NW
WALES

NE
WALES

STAFFORD-
SHIRE

NORFOLK

SHROPSHIRE

LEICESTERSHIRE

CAMBRIDGE-
SHIRE

WEST
MIDLANDS

WORCESTER-
SHIRE

NORTHAMPTON-
SHIRE

SUFFOLK

MID
WALES

HEREFORD-
SHIRE

WARWICK-
SHIRE

BEDFORD-
SHIRE

WEST
WALES

GWENT

GLOUCS &
BRISTOL

OXFORD-
SHIRE

HERTFORD-
SHIRE

ESSEX

GLAMORGAN

GREATER
LONDON

WILTSHIRE

BERKSHIRE

SURREY

KENT

CHANNEL
ISLANDS

SOMERSET

HAMPSHIRE

WEST
SUSSEX

EAST
SUSSEX

DEVON

DORSET

CORNWALL

ISLE OF
WIGHT

Scotland

ABERDEEN & GRAMPIAN

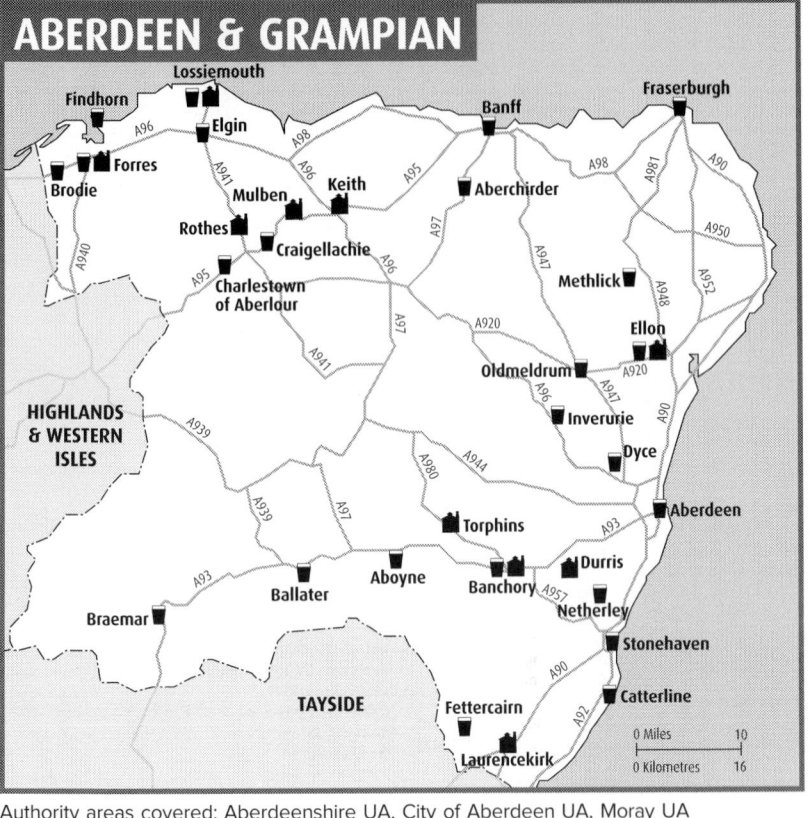

Authority areas covered: Aberdeenshire UA, City of Aberdeen UA, Moray UA

Aberchirder

New Inn

79 Main Street, AB54 7TB
🕑 12 (5 Mon)-12.30am; 12-11 Sun ☎ (01466) 780633
🌐 newinnaberchirder.co.uk
**Windswept Wolf Ⓖ; 4 changing beers (sourced
nationally; often Caledonian, Orkney)** Ⓗ
Traditional, welcoming inn with wood-burning
stoves, candlelit areas and a vintage atmosphere,
offering a changing selection of five quality ales
from local and national breweries. A separate
dining area provides home-made food featuring
locally sourced produce cooked by the owner/chef
– the pork pies are highly recommended. Families
with children are welcome in the dining room until
9pm (booking for food is advised). No food
Monday and no lunches Tuesday. A beer festival
may be held in September.
Q✿🏠🍴🚗♿🚪(301)🐕🐾🛜

Aberdeen

Aitchies Ale House

10 Trinity Street, AB11 5LY (opp Union Square shopping
centre)
🕑 8am-10 (11 Fri & Sat); closed Sun ☎ (01224) 581549
Greene King IPA; Orkney Dark Island Ⓗ
This small corner bar is the closest real ale outlet to
the city rail/bus stations and the Union Square
shopping complex. Family-owned, it retains the
flavour of an old-fashioned Scottish pub with
service second to none and bar staff wearing

traditional white aprons. Food is best described as
basic Scottish pub grub, including roast beef
stovies. A good selection of whiskies includes Bell's
special editions. Q♿≡🚗🛜

Archibald Simpson

5 Castle Street, AB11 5BQ (E end of Union St)
🕑 8am-midnight (1am Fri & Sat); 9am-midnight Sun
☎ (01224) 621365
**Greene King Abbot; Sharp's Doom Bar; 10 changing
beers (sourced nationally; often Lerwick, Orkney,
Windswept)** Ⓗ
The former local headquarters of Clydesdale Bank,
this Wetherspoon is in one of many monumental
granite buildings in central Aberdeen designed by
local architect Archibald Simpson. It has a pillared
entrance and retains many original architectural
features – the main room is a central hall with a

REAL ALE BREWERIES

22 Bake & Brew ≡ Torphins (NEW)
7 Durris (NEW)
BrewDog Ellon
Burnside Laurencekirk
Deeside Banchory
Keith Keith
Quiet ≡ Banchory
Rothes Rothes
six north Laurencekirk
Spey Valley Mulben
Speyside Craft Forres
Windswept Lossiemouth

high ceiling and additional seating areas to the sides. The long bar has up to 12 handpumps offering a variety of beers, frequently from Scottish breweries. There is a narrow outside drinking area on the pavement on Union Street corner.

Carriages

101 Crown Street, AB11 6HH (below Brentwood Hotel)
🕑 11-2.30, 4.30-midnight; 11-midnight Fri & Sat; 5.30-11 Sun
☎ (01224) 595440 ⊕ brentwood-hotel.co.uk
8 changing beers (sourced nationally; often Orkney, Swannay, Windswept) Ⓗ
A mirrored downstairs bar in the basement of the Brentwood Hotel with lots of comfortable couches and seating areas. A winner of several local CAMRA awards, it has eight changing ales, usually a mix of national brands and Scottish microbrews, with tasters offered if undecided. Beer prices are reduced at weekends. Lunchtime meals are available in the bar and the adjoining restaurant serves good food in the evening. Railway and bus stations are close and easily reached by descending the stairs from nearby Crown Terrace to Bridge Street.

Grill ★

213 Union Street, AB11 6BA
🕑 10-midnight (1am Fri & Sat); 12.30-midnight Sun
☎ (01224) 573530 ⊕ thegrillaberdeen.co.uk
Harviestoun Bitter & Twisted; 3 changing beers (sourced regionally; often Fyne, Orkney, Windswept) Ⓗ
With an exquisite interior redesigned in 1926 and remaining largely unchanged since, this is the only pub listed on CAMRA's National Inventory of Historic Pub Interiors in the area. For men only until 1975, a ladies' toilet was eventually provided in 1998. Situated across from the soon-to-be-reopened Music Hall, musicians often visit during concert breaks. Guest ales are frequently from a variety of Scottish micros and the large selection of malts has won the pub several awards. Bar snacks are available. CAMRA Branch Pub of the Year 2016.

Justice Mill ✓

423 Union Street, AB11 6DA
🕑 8am-midnight (1am Fri & Sat); 9am-midnight Sun
☎ (01224) 252410
Caledonian Deuchars IPA; Greene King Abbot; Sharp's Doom Bar; 3 changing beers (sourced nationally) Ⓗ
Long, narrow, dark Wetherspoon outlet with some raised seating near the bar and booths at both the main entrance and at the rear entrance on Justice Mill Lane, hence the name of the pub. The quieter family-friendly atmosphere changes to a loud maelstrom favoured by many of its younger clientele in the evenings, with DJs at weekends. The pub has two statement art pieces – a statue of an upside-down man and a fire behind glass. Alcohol is served from 11am (12.30pm Sunday).

Krakatoa

2 Trinity Quay, AB11 5AA (facing quayside at bottom of Market St)
🕑 1-midnight; 2-3am Fri & Sat; 2-midnight Sun
☎ (01224) 587602 ⊕ krakatoa.bar
Windswept Weizen; changing beers (sourced regionally; often Cromarty, Spey Valley, Swannay) Ⓟ
Historic harbourside bar with a unique interior, refurbished in recent years, frequented by a

friendly crowd of regulars. A wide selection of Scottish beers is served on up to 12 American-style fonts on the far left of the bar, complemented by two similar banks dispensing various other beers. Live music features on Friday and Saturday nights, often local band competitions, and there may be a cover charge. A multiple local CAMRA City Pub of the Year winner and branch winner in 2015.

Prince of Wales ✓

7 St Nicholas Lane, AB10 1HF (lane opp Marks & Spencer and parallel to Union St)
🕑 10-midnight (1am Fri & Sat); 11-midnight Sun
☎ (01224) 640597 ⊕ princeofwales-aberdeen.co.uk
9 changing beers (sourced nationally; often Cromarty, Swannay, Windswept) Ⓗ
Refurbished in late 2016, the Prince is one of the oldest bars in town and features in Scotland's True Heritage Pubs, with possibly the longest bar counter in the city. It has a friendly atmosphere and a large following of regulars. Owned by Belhaven, it serves a varied selection of mainly Scottish ales with some of the usual Greene King varieties. Sunday is folk music night and the pub quiz is on Monday. Food is served daily until 9pm. CAMRA City Pub of the Year 2017.

Queen Vic

126 Rosemount Place, AB25 2YU
🕑 12-midnight (1am Fri & Sat); 12.30-midnight Sun
☎ (01224) 638500
Caledonian Deuchars IPA; Timothy Taylor Landlord; 2 changing beers (sourced nationally; often Deeside, Windswept) Ⓗ
A cosy one-room locals' lounge bar in a converted former opticians/bakers in the highly populated area of Rosemount. As well as two interesting changing beers often chosen by customers from various guest lists, an extensive range of bottled beers is stocked from many Scottish breweries. A popular quiz is held on Monday, culminating in a Play Your Cards Right jackpot session. Occasional Meet the Brewer nights are hosted, with matching cheeses from a local cheese shop. Food is mostly restricted to sandwiches and wraps, plus free stovies on Friday nights. When sporting events are shown the pub may be extremely busy and noisy.

St Machar Bar

97 High Street, Old Aberdeen, AB24 3EN
🕑 11-11 (midnight Fri); 12.30-11 Sun ☎ (01224) 483079
Caledonian Deuchars IPA; 2 changing beers (sourced regionally; often Caledonian, Drygate) Ⓗ
Located in the photogenic and historic Old Aberdeen conservation area amid the university buildings and close to King's College, this friendly and historic pub is frequented by academia and locals alike. A splendid mirror from the long-gone Thomson Marshall Aulton Brewery is near the entrance and one from the original Devanha Brewery beside the toilets. Up to three guest beers are served alongside a comprehensive selection of whiskies. The bar is home to a darts team, university football team and rugby team. Now serving Tex-Mex food.

Under the Hammer

11 North Silver Street, AB10 1RJ (off Golden Square)
🕑 5-11 (midnight Wed & Thu); 4-1am Fri & Sat; closed Sun
☎ (01224) 640253

Fyne Jarl; 2 changing beers (often Cromarty, Timothy Taylor) ℍ
A warm, welcoming long-established basement pub near Golden Square just minutes off Union Street. The pub takes its name from the auction rooms next door. Unobtrusive background music plays, allowing for conversation, with no TV to disturb. Convenient for the Music Hall and His Majesty's Theatre, many use it for a pre- or post-theatre drink. Frequently changing works by local artists decorate the walls and are for sale. An open mic session is hosted on the first Sunday of the month. Q�⇌❀❄

Aboyne

Boat Inn
Charleston Road, AB34 5EL (N bank of River Dee next to Aboyne Bridge)
✪ 11-11 (midnight Fri & Sat) ☎ (01339) 886137
⊕ theboatinnaboyne.co.uk
Deeside 80/-, Macbeth; 3 changing beers (sourced locally) ℍ
Popular riverside inn with a food-oriented lounge. Junior diners (and adults) may request to see the model train, complete with sound effects, traverse the entire pub at picture-rail height upon completion of their meal. The local Rotary Club regularly meets here. The public bar has been extended, with a recess at the back for musicians – live music features twice-monthly on a Thursday or Friday evening. Accommodation includes seven en-suite twin rooms plus a family room.
Q➢✿⛺◐&♣❀❄

Ballater

Alexandra Hotel
12 Bridge Square, AB35 5QJ
✪ 11-2.30, 5-midnight; 11-midnight Fri; 11-midnight Sun
☎ (01339) 755376 ⊕ alexandrahotelballater.co.uk
Cairngorm Trade Winds; 2 changing beers (sourced regionally; often Cairngorm, Inveralmond) ℍ
Originally built as a private home in 1800 and becoming the Alexandra Hotel in 1915, this smart and recently refurbished lounge bar is popular with locals for bar suppers and regular bar drinkers too. It is easily spotted when entering Ballater from the east side. Handy for a stop off on your way to Braemar for the Highland Games or for a visit with the royals at Balmoral. ➢⛺◐&♣P🚗❀❄

Glenaden Hotel
6 Church Square, AB35 5NE
✪ 11-1am (midnight Mon-Wed) ☎ (01339) 755488
3 changing beers (sourced regionally; often Burnside, Deeside, Loch Lomond) ℍ
Situated on the far side of the picturesque town square, this small hotel displays a prominent external sign for its Barrel Lounge. It now serves three beers in busy periods, usually Scottish, mostly from Burnside and Deeside. Darker ales are apparently favoured by the locals. A large function suite is at the rear of the hotel.
Q➢✿⛺◐&♣P🚗❀❄

Banchory

Burnett Arms Hotel
25 High Street, AB31 5TD
✪ 11-2.30, 5-11.30 (1am Fri); 11-1am Sat; 11-midnight Sun
☎ (01330) 824944 ⊕ burnettarms.co.uk

2 changing beers (sourced regionally; often Deeside) ℍ
Centrally located, whitewashed hotel, part of the Best Western chain. The public bar is now a separate American diner; the lounge has a separate dining area and an adjacent family area. A large function room to the rear has its own bar, and local Rotary and Round Table clubs use the meeting rooms. The lounge is popular for bar suppers and an all-day carvery on Sunday. Two ales are served in the lounge only; one is the house special, Burnett Gold, brewed by local Deeside Brewery.
➢⛺◐&♣P🚗❀❄

Ravenswood Club (Royal British Legion)
25 Ramsay Road, AB31 5TS (up Mount St from High St, then second right)
✪ 11-11 (midnight Fri & Sat) ☎ (01330) 822347
⊕ banchorylegion.co.uk
2 changing beers (sourced nationally) ℍ
Large British Legion club with a comfortable lounge adjoining the pool and TV room and a spacious function room well used by local clubs and societies as well as members. Darts and snooker are popular and played most evenings. The two handpumps offer excellent value and the beer choice is constantly changing, with ales consistently the best quality in the village. An elevated terrace has fine views of the Deeside hills. Show a copy of this Guide or your CAMRA membership card for entry. ➢✿⛺◐&♣P❄

Banff

Market Arms
5 High Shore, AB45 1DB
✪ 11-midnight (1am Fri & Sat) ☎ (01261) 812261
2 changing beers (sourced locally) ℍ
This fine building is one of the oldest in historic Banff, dating back to 1585. It is worth stepping out the back to take a look at the courtyard, which retains many original features. The long public bar has several fine examples of historic brewery and distillery mirrors. The two handpumps serve an ever-changing range of beers, usually from local Scottish microbreweries. ➢♣🚗❀❄

Braemar

Moorfield House Hotel
19 Chapel Brae, AB35 5YT (well signposted from village centre)
✪ 4-11 (10 Tue & Wed); 1-7 Sun ☎ (01339) 741244
⊕ moorfieldhousehotel.com
Cairngorm Trade Winds; 3 changing beers (sourced regionally; often Cairngorm, Loch Lomond) ℍ
Small family-run hotel – the current owners took over in January 2016 – overlooking the Highland Games ground at the edge of this historic village, with one of only two bars in Braemar open to the public for some time to come. Hours can vary depending on season and weather, particularly in the ski season. Check the website or phone in advance. If required, meals can often be arranged outwith official times by prior arrangement. Four varying ales are served – even in winter.
Q➢✿⛺◐&♣P🚗❀❄

Brodie

Old Mill Inn

IV36 2TD (on main A96 between Forres and Nairn)
☼ 11.30-11; 11.45-11 Sun ☎ (01309) 641605
⊕ oldmillinnbrodie.com
5 changing beers (sourced regionally; often Speyside Craft, Swannay, Windswept) Ⓗ
This gem is a spacious, family-friendly pub-restaurant with a cosy fireside area, smart restaurant, function room and a charming conservatory with views of the old watermill and garden. An excellent range of meals is offered, including a full restaurant menu with steak on Monday, fish on Friday and roasts on Sunday, plus traditional Scottish high teas. Live Scottish/Irish instrumental music plays on Sunday evening. Brodie Castle is nearby and the popular Brodie Countryfare is opposite. A beer festival is usually held in June. Q☼👪✦Ⓓ&⚓P🚃(10,11)🗢

Catterline

Creel Inn

AB39 2UL (on coast off A92, 5 miles S of Stonehaven)
☼ 12-2, 6-midnight (1am Fri); 12-1am Sat; 12-midnight Sun
☎ (01569) 750254 ⊕ thecreelinn.co.uk
4 changing beers (sourced regionally; often Cromarty, Fyne, Swannay) Ⓗ
Set in a scenic clifftop location, the view from the rear garden of this small village inn is not to be missed. Catterline is known as an artists' village, the most famous being Joan Eardley – one of her paintings is on display in the pub along with other artists' work. The Creel is primarily a food venue but the bar area serves as the village local with up to four beers, usually from Scottish micros. Todhead Lighthouse, Crawton Bird Sanctuary and Kinneff old church are nearby. ☼✿Ⓓ&♣P🖵👹

Charlestown of Aberlour

Mash Tun

8 Broomfield Square, AB38 9QP (signposted from village square)
☼ 12-12.30am (1am Fri & Sat); 12.30-12.30am Sun
☎ (01340) 881771 ⊕ mashtun-aberlour.com
2 changing beers (sourced locally; often Cairngorm, Spey Valley) Ⓗ
A busy traditional bar promoted as a whisky bar. It has the only full collection of Glenfarclas whisky in the world and more than 100 other malts. The Speyside Way is just outside the door, as is Alice Little Park and the River Spey itself, making it popular with fishermen. Built in 1896 as the Station Bar, a pledge in the title deeds allowed a name change if the railway closed – but it must revert to the Station Bar if a train ever pulls up again outside. ☼✿✦Ⓓ⚓P🚃(36)👹🗢

Craigellachie

Copper Dog

Victoria Street, AB38 9SR (part of Craigellachie Hotel)
☼ 12-11 (1am Fri & Sat) ☎ (01340) 881204
⊕ craigellachiehotel.co.uk/copper-dog
3 changing beers (sourced locally; often Spey Valley, Windswept) Ⓗ
In a beautiful village, the impressive Victorian building boasts picturesque views across the forests and mountains, and is next to the Fiddich and Spey rivers. The hotel has a traditional bar, and

all rooms have en-suite facilities, a TV and seating area. There are over 800 whiskies in the Quaich Bar, with tasting sessions available. It can be busy, especially during whisky festivals. If you wish to eat there, booking is recommended. ☼✿✦Ⓓ&⚓P🚃(36)👹🗢

Highlander Inn

10 Victoria Street, AB38 9SR (on A95, opp post office)
☼ 12-11 (12.30am Fri & Sat) ☎ (01340) 881446
⊕ whiskyinn.com
3 changing beers (often Rothes, Spey Valley, Windswept) Ⓗ
Picturesque whisky and cask ale bar on Speyside's Whisky Trail, close to the Speyside Way which runs along the car park. It is twinned with the Highlander Whisky Bar in Tokyo and offers a fine selection of malt whiskies, including many from Japan, as well as a selection of ales from local breweries. CRAC (Craigellachie Real Ale Club) meets regularly and its members help to choose the pub's guest ales. An outside decked area with tables and chairs is a delight on a sunny afternoon. Q☼✿✦Ⓓ⚓♣P🚃(36)🗢

Dyce

Granite City ✓

Main Terminal, Aberdeen Airprt, AB21 7DU
☼ 6am (8am Sat)-10; 8am-9 Sun ☎ (01224) 725711
Sharp's Doom Bar; 4 changing beers (sourced nationally; often Windswept, Wooha) Ⓗ
In the main terminal of Aberdeen Airport, close to the entrance, this Wetherspoon bar is popular with airport staff, travellers and offshore workers. Alcohol is served throughout opening times. The walls display informative framed photographs of local personalities including 'The Scottish Samurai' Thomas Blake Glover – one of the prime movers of Japan's industrialisation in the late-19th century. An extensive outdoor area features the Baby Boar, a sculpture carved from a one-ton boulder of local Kemnay granite. ☼✿Ⓓ&🚃(727,16)🗢

Elgin

Drouthy Cobbler ✓

Shepherd's Close, 48A High Street, IV30 1BU
☼ 8am-12.30am (1.30am Fri & Sat) ☎ (01343) 596000
⊕ thedrouthycobbler.co.uk
Harviestoun Bitter & Twisted; Inveralmond Ossian, Lia Fail; 1 changing beer (sourced regionally) Ⓗ
A long, elegant pub named after John Shanks, who was a shoemaker and an important figure in the conservation of Elgin Cathedral. Excellent coffee and cakes are available, plus an imaginative breakfast, lunch and dinner menu, and brunch on Sunday. A growing whisky collection stands at around 100, alongside a large gin and cocktail selection. There are benches outside in the lane and a small garden area. Alcohol is served from 11am. Q☼✿Ⓓ&⇌🚃🗢

Muckle Cross ✓

34 High Street, IV30 1BU
☼ 8am-midnight (1am Fri & Sat); 9am-11.45 Sun
☎ (01343) 559030
Caledonian Deuchars IPA; Greene King Abbot; Sharp's Doom Bar; 4 changing beers (sourced nationally; often Windswept) Ⓗ
Typical small Wetherspoon pub converted from what was once a bicycle repair shop, then a

Halfords branch. The pleasant long room has ample seating, a family area and a long bar. Deservedly popular, it can be busy, particularly at weekends. Eight handpumps offer a wide range of beers from national and Scottish microbreweries, and ciders are available during the annual cider fest. The pub also stocks a wide range of malt whiskies from more than 20 local distilleries. Alcohol is served from 11am. Q☆🕭🚲🎐⇌🖤🚪🛇

Ellon

Tolbooth
21-23 Station Road, AB41 9AE
🟢 12-11 (midnight Thu; 12.30am Fri & Sat); 12.30-11.30 Sun
☎ (01358) 721308
Greene King Abbot; 2 changing beers (sourced regionally) 🅗
A large pub, popular with all ages, close to the centre of the town and just a short walk from the bus stops to Aberdeen/Peterhead/Fraserburgh on Market Street. There are separate seating areas on split levels as well as an airy conservatory with barrel tables. One Scottish and one English guest ale are usually available. No food is served. Several National Trust Scotland properties are nearby.
🏵♿🚪(61,62)🐾🛇

Fettercairn

Ramsay Arms
Burnside Road, AB30 1XX
🟢 12-3, 5.30-11; 12-11.30 Fri & Sat; 12.30-11 Sun
☎ (01561) 340334 🌐 ramsayarmshotel.co.uk
Inveralmond Ossian, Thrappledouser 🅗
In the shadow of the Victoria Commemorative Arch, erected in recognition of the Queen's first trip to the north-east of Scotland when she spent the night in the hotel, its Victorian heritage lends itself to the cuisine in the open, modern lounge. It is close to Fasque Estate, residence of Sir William Gladstone, and near the visitor centre at the Fettercairn distillery. May close at 10pm in winter if there are few customers. ☆🏵🕭♿P🛇

Findhorn

Kimberley Inn
94 Findhorn, IV36 3YG
🟢 12-midnight ☎ (01309) 690492 🌐 kimberleyinn.com
2 changing beers (sourced regionally; often Cairngorm, Deeside, Orkney) 🅗
'Moray's seafood pub' is situated on the shore of Findhorn Bay in a charming seaside village with a fine stretch of beach. The wood-panelled interior divides into three areas – the bar with an excellent open log fire, a family room, and a snug with splendid views of the hills across the Moray Firth. Two ales (one in winter) are mainly from Scottish micros. The extensive menu features home-cooked food, especially local seafood, and even local ice cream. Q☆🕭♿🎐♣P🚪(31)🐾

Forres

Mosset Tavern
Gordon Street, IV36 1DL
🟢 11-12.30am (1.30am Fri & Sat); 12-midnight Sun
☎ (01309) 672981 🌐 mossettavern.com
5 changing beers (sourced regionally; often Speyside Craft, Swannay, Windswept) 🅗

Described as 'the country pub in the heart of Forres', this smart, extremely popular Scottish lounge bar/restaurant is situated next to the Mosset burn and pond, with swans and ducks. Friendly, efficient staff serve ale from a single handpump in the lounge and five in the spacious, comfortable public bar, where there are pool tables and large screens showing sport. A large function room is also available. Live music plays on Friday evenings, and there is a pub quiz every Tuesday.
☆🏵🖂🕭♿⇌♣P🚪(10,11)🛇

Fraserburgh

Elizabethan Bar & Lounge
36 Union Grove, AB43 9PH
🟢 10-1am; 9am-1am Sat & Sun
3 changing beers (sourced regionally; often Cairngorm, Fyne, Kelburn) 🅗
Set in the middle of a housing estate, with a mock-Tudor exterior, the large bar and lounge have three distinct sections, with sport on TV in two of them. Darts and pool are played. The bar has a formidable reputation for offering a wide range of quality ales sourced from throughout the country, and also features well over 200 malts – the largest collection in the area. ☆🅰♣P🚪🐾🛇

Saltoun Inn ⊘
Saltoun Square, AB43 9DA
🟢 7am-midnight (1am Fri & Sat) ☎ (01346) 519548
Greene King Abbot; Sharp's Doom Bar; 5 changing beers (sourced nationally) 🅗
A Wetherspoon renovation of the historic, long-derelict Saltoun Arms Hotel, built in 1801. It comprises several interconnecting rooms with low ceilings, and includes a lounge area to the left of the entrance. A garden area has been created to the rear (smoking not permitted). Accommodation is available in 11 rooms. The Scottish Lighthouse Museum is close by, as is the main fishing harbour.
Q☆🏵🖂🕭♿🅰🚪(67,68)🛇

Inverurie

Black Bull ⊘
50 North Street, AB51 4RS (on B9001 heading N)
🟢 2-11 (midnight Tue); 12-1am Fri; 11-1am Sat; 11-11 Sun
☎ (01467) 621242
2 changing beers (sourced regionally; often Orkney, Strathaven, Strathbraan) 🅗
An old staging inn, now a family-run small hotel and locals' pub with a separate pool room. The pub is home to three pool teams and five darts teams – hence the later hours on Tuesday darts night. Live music features on Saturday evening. One Strathbraan beer is usually served with up to two guests often from Scottish micros but sometimes from further afield. Bar snacks made on the premises include toasties and interesting pies, such as chicken and haggis.
🏵🖂♿⇌♣P🚪(41,493)🐾🛇

Gordon Highlander ⊘
West High Street, AB51 3QQ
🟢 9am-11.30 (1am Fri & Sat) ☎ (01462) 626780
Sharp's Doom Bar; 4 changing beers (sourced nationally; often Inveralmond, Strathaven, Windswept) 🅗
A fine Wetherspoon conversion of a splendid Art Deco building which used to be the Victoria Cinema. The name refers to the famous local

regiment, and also to a preserved steam engine named after the regiment, which was based at the now defunct Inverurie Locomotive Works nearby. Both historic references are documented in various displays. The books on the shelves are free to read and take home, with donations welcome. There are at least three guest ales and the usual Wetherspoon beer festivals feature. Alcohol is served from 11am. ♿❶❺⬅🚍(10,37)🛜

Lossiemouth

Skerry Brae Hotel
Stotfield Road, IV31 6QS
🟢 12-11 (midnight Fri & Sat) ☎ (01343) 812040
🌐 skerrybrae.co.uk
Windswept Blonde, APA Ⓗ
Modern lounge bar with commanding views across the championship golf course, West Beach and the Moray Firth – spacious outside decking and a large conservatory enhance the viewing experience. The 19-bed hotel serves hearty food all day. One or more beers from the local Windswept Brewery are available. The bar also stocks a decent selection of malt whiskies. The bar may close afternoons Monday to Thursday in winter.
Q♿🏨❶❺▲P🚍(33C)🐕🛜

Methlick

Ythanview Hotel
Main Street, AB41 7DT
🟢 11-2.30, 5-11; 11-2.30, 4.30-1am Fri; 11-12.30am Sat; 12-11 Sun ☎ (01651) 806235 🌐 ythanviewhotel.co.uk
2 changing beers (sourced regionally; often Fyne, Swannay, Windswept) Ⓗ
Traditional inn in the village centre, home to the MCC (Methlick Cricket Club) at Lairds nearby. Log fires warm both the lounge and the friendly sports-themed public bar at the rear. The pub is renowned for the owner Jay's special chicken curry, and Thursday's steak night is popular. Meals are served all day at weekends. Live music and quiz nights take place on most Saturdays. Beers are exclusively from Scottish micros. Haddo House, Tolquhon Castle and Pitmedden Garden are nearby.
♿🏨❶♣P🚍(290,291)🐕🛜

Netherley

Lairhillock Inn
AB39 3QS (off B979 signposted, 3 miles S of B9077)
🟢 11-11 (midnight Fri & Sat) ☎ (01569) 730001
🌐 lairhillock.co.uk
Timothy Taylor Landlord; 1 changing beer (sourced regionally; often Burnside, Deeside, Strathbraan) Ⓗ
The INN sign on the roof of this rambling building in attractive open countryside makes it easy to spot from the road. It has a traditional wood-panelled bar warmed by a large log fire in winter, a lounge with an open fireplace and a large conservatory area, popular for dining. A separate function room, the Crynoch, is also available. The guest beer is usually sourced from a Scottish brewery. Convenient for the attractions of Stonehaven and Royal Deeside. Q♿🏨❶❺♣P🐕

Oldmeldrum

Redgarth 🍷
Kirk Brae, AB51 0DJ (outskirts of village, signed off A947)
🟢 11-3, 5-11 (11.45 Fri & Sat); 12-11 Sun ☎ (01651) 872353
🌐 redgarth.com
3 changing beers (sourced locally; often Cromarty, Fyne, Swannay) Ⓗ/Ⓖ
This renowned local inn has imposing views over the eastern Grampian mountains. A winner of many local CAMRA awards and CAMRA branch Pub of the Year 2017, it has a strong reputation for its imaginative choice of beers, sourced from Swannay Brewery and many other Scottish micros. During occasional Brewers in Residence evenings, the three handpumped ales may be supplemented by many more on gravity. A successful blend of popular family restaurant and marvellous real ale pub, it is appreciated by a dedicated core of regulars. ♿🏨❶▲♣P🚍(35)🛜

Stonehaven

Marine Hotel
9-10 Shorehead, AB39 2JY (overlooking harbour)
🟢 11-midnight (1am Fri & Sat) ☎ (01569) 762155
🌐 marinehotelstonehaven.co.uk
Timothy Taylor Landlord; house beer (by six°north); 4 changing beers (sourced regionally; often Burnside, Cairngorm, Windswept) Ⓗ
Small harbourside hotel featuring simple wood panelling in the bar, a rustic lounge with an open fireplace and an upstairs restaurant. Seating outside offers a splendid view of the harbour. Two to three beers from the hotel-owned six°north brewery are served alongside several Belgian beers on draught and a massive choice of bottles. Dunnottar Castle is one mile south. local CAMRA Country Pub of the Year 2016 and a winner of many more awards. ♿🏨❶▲🍴🚍🐕🛜

Ship Inn
5 Shorehead, AB39 2JY (on harbour front)
🟢 11-midnight (1am Fri & Sat) ☎ (01569) 762617
🌐 shipinnstonehaven.com
2 changing beers (sourced regionally; often Strathbraan) Ⓗ
Built in 1771, this harbour-front hotel has a maritime-themed, wood-panelled bar featuring a mirror from the defunct Devanha brewery, and a seating area outside overlooking the water. Two beers are offered, at least one from a Scottish microbrewery, and an extensive range of malt whiskies is stocked. A modern restaurant with panoramic harbour views is adjacent to the bar – food is served all day at the weekend. Accommodation is available in 11 guest rooms.
♿🏨❶❺▲🍴🐕🛜

SCOTLAND

ARGYLL & THE ISLES

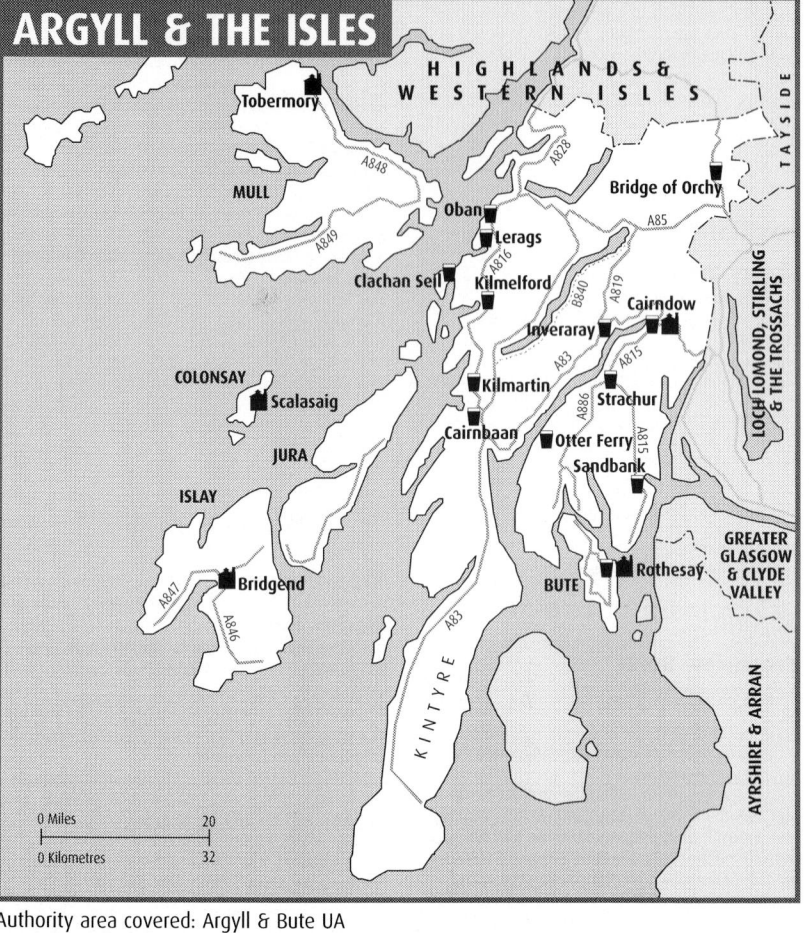

Authority area covered: Argyll & Bute UA

Bridge of Orchy

Bridge of Orchy Hotel

PA36 4AD

🕔 7am-10; 8am-9 winter ☎ (01838) 400208
🌐 bridgeoforchy.co.uk

**Harviestoun Bitter & Twisted; 1 changing beer
(sourced regionally; often Harviestoun)** Ⓗ

Large, attractive hotel situated in the middle of
remote, stunning scenery, but at the same time
remarkably accessible. The proximity of Munros
and other mountains, the West Highland Way and
River Orchy makes it popular with walkers and
canoeists. The views can be enjoyed from the
comfortable public bar to the left of the hotel, and
the restaurant behind. Closing time may vary
depending on custom. Alcohol is served from
11am. 🏠🕮🖾📶➡🅿️🚃(915)🐾 🛜

Cairnbaan

Cairnbaan Hotel

PA31 8SQ

🕔 11-11; 12.30-11 Sun ☎ (01546) 603668 🌐 cairnbaan.com

3 changing beers (sourced regionally) Ⓗ

The hotel was built in 1801 at the same time as the
Crinan Canal, at its midpoint beside lock five, and
has been accommodating travellers using the canal

or visiting mid-Argyll ever since. The dark-painted
bar and restaurant are housed in a more recent
addition to one side. The bar opens on to a
conservatory furnished with comfortable sofas and
a small outdoor seating area looking across to the
canal. There are usually only two beers available in
winter. Q🏠🕮🖾📶◖🅿️🚃🐾 🛜

Cairndow

Fyne Ales Brewery Tap Ⓛ

Achadunan, PA26 8BJ (up side road at head of Loch
Fyne)

🕔 10-6 ☎ (01499) 600120 🌐 fyneales.com/brewery-tap

**Fyne Jarl; 4 changing beers (sourced locally; often
Fyne)** Ⓗ

The brewery tap was opened a few years ago in an
old farm barn next to the original brewery. The bar
front is made from local granite etched and

polished by the owner's son and displays the names of the founders and the beers and ingredients used. In good weather there is seating outside in the courtyard to enjoy views of the hills above and red deer roaming the slopes. Hot pies made from beef produced on the farm provide sustenance. Q⏁♿🅿🐾🐾🛜

Stagecoach Inn 🅛

PA26 8BN (on slip road off A83)
🕐 11-11 (1am Fri & Sat); 11-midnight Sun
☎ (01499) 600286 ⊕ cairndowinn.com
2 changing beers (sourced regionally; often Fyne, Loch Lomond) Ⓗ

Nestling in tall trees at the foot of Glen Kinglas, the inn has provided a welcome resting place before the long climb over the Rest And Be Thankful since the 1790s, and is well placed to enjoy the mountain, woodland and lochside scenery. The old stables have been converted into a restaurant with a comfortable lounge and function room to one side. Through an archway to the other side is a small, cosy public bar with a pool table in an alcove. ⏁♿🚲🍴♿🅰♣🅿🚃 (926,976)🐾🛜

Clachan Seil

Tigh an Truish Inn 🅛

PA34 4QZ
🕐 11 (12 Sun)-11 summer; 11-2.30, 5-11; 11-11 Fri & Sat; 12-11 Sun winter ☎ (01852) 300242 ⊕ tigh-an-truish.co.uk
2 changing beers (sourced nationally; often Fyne, Orkney) Ⓗ

Scenic, whitewashed pub established in the 18th century, so called because it was reputedly the place where islanders stopped to swap their kilts for trousers before crossing to the mainland. The wood-panelled bar features a gantry designed like a ship's galley, and is warmed by an old stove. The cosy lounge is decorated with pictures of the historic Atlantic Bridge which stands outside. Good weather can be enjoyed in the garden and patio to one side. No meals are available in the winter. Q⏁♿🚲🍴🅰🅿🚃 (418)🐾🛜

Inveraray

George Hotel

Main Street East, PA32 8TT
🕐 11-midnight; 12-midnight Sun ☎ (01499) 302111
⊕ thegeorgehotel.co.uk
2 changing beers (sourced locally; often Fyne) Ⓗ

Originally built as two private homes in 1770, these were combined to form the hotel 90 years later by the Clark family, who still own and manage it. Much of the old ambience and original features remain, including the flagstone floors and peat and log fires throughout. The meals have an emphasis on local produce. Beer is available in both the main lounge and the lively public bar to one side. Live blues, folk and rock play on Friday and Saturday evenings. Q⏁♿🚲🍴♿🅰🅿🚃 (926,976)🐾🛜

Kilmartin

Kilmartin Hotel 🅛

PA31 8RQ (on A816 10 miles N of Lochgilphead)
🕐 12-11 (1am Fri) summer; 5-11; 11-1am Fri winter; 11-midnight Sat; 12-11 Sun ☎ (01546) 510250
⊕ kilmartin-hotel.com
3 changing beers (sourced regionally; often Caledonian, Loch Lomond, Orkney) Ⓗ

Prominent whitewashed hotel overlooking Kilmartin Glen with its many sites of religious and historic significance dating back 5,000 years. The small, intimate bar has a cosy fireside nook and leads to a pool room at the rear. Good home-made food is served in the restaurant in the evenings and some lunchtimes (check ahead). A small shed for smokers is available at the back next to a pleasant beer garden. There are usually only two beers in winter. ⏁♿🚲🍴♿🅰🅿🚃 (423)🐾🛜

Kilmelford

Cuilfail ★

PA34 4XA
🕐 11-11; 12.30-11 Sun ☎ (01852) 200274 ⊕ cuilfail.co.uk
2 changing beers (sourced nationally; often Loch Lomond) Ⓗ

Victorian country hotel, first built as a coaching inn around 1840 next to a drovers' inn – what is now the main part of the building was added some 30 years later. The bar is located in the old inn, renovated in 1957 with a rugged stonework feel – the original bricks remain around the fireplace. The clean and cosy snug behind the bar was built as part of the hotel and is accessed off the corridor leading to it. ⏁♿🚲🍴♿🅿🚃 (423)🐾🛜

Lerags

Barn 🅛

Kilbride, PA34 4SE
🕐 12-11 (1am Fri & Sat) summer; closed Mon-Thu; 4 (12 Sat & Sun)-11 winter ☎ (01631) 564618 ⊕ cologin.co.uk/country-inn
2 changing beers (sourced locally; often Fyne) Ⓗ

Cologin farmhouse forms the centre of a range of holiday chalets and lodges in a secluded glen a couple of miles south of Oban. The Barn was originally the cattle byre and some of the slate stalls have been retained to provide the backrest for seating, helping to contribute to the cosy ambience. An enclosed verandah at the front provides extra seating, overlooking the play area and duck pond. Q⏁♿🚲🍴🅰🅿🐾🛜

Oban

Corryvreckan ✅

The Waterfront Centre, Railway Pier, PA34 4LW
🕐 7am-midnight (1am Fri & Sat) ☎ (01631) 568910
Caledonian Deuchars IPA; Greene King Abbot; Sharp's Doom Bar; 6 changing beers (sourced nationally) Ⓗ

A well-placed Wetherspoon pub on the seafront with views across the bay to the islands beyond. It is part of a modern complex sandwiched between the station and the ferry terminal, making it ideal for a drink before continuing your journey. Named after a famous whirlpool off the Argyll coast, the pub's light and airy interior has many nautical references and is presided over by a sea eagle. Alcohol is served from 11am. ⏁♿🍴♿🚃🚃🛜

Otter Ferry

Oystercatcher 🅛

PA21 2DH (on B8000 E coast of Loch Fyne)
🕐 11-11; closed Tue & Wed ☎ (01700) 821229
⊕ theoystercatcher.co.uk
2 changing beers (sourced locally; often Fyne) Ⓗ

Attractive pub on Argyll's Secret Coast accessed by a scenic trip down the single track B8000. The comfortable bar and lounge are warmed by real fires and offer views across the loch to Kintyre. In summer visitors can sit out in the beer garden or lochside lawn and wander down to the beach and pontoon. Quality meals feature local seafood. Winter opening varies – phone ahead at quiet times of the year. ⌂✿◑♿ẢP✿❀

Rothesay

Black Bull Inn
West Princes Street, PA20 9AF (opp harbour)
✪ 11-11 (midnight Fri & Sat); 12.30-11 Sun
☎ (01700) 502366
3 changing beers (sourced regionally; often Bute Brew Co) Ⓗ
An ever-popular pub in the centre of town close to the harbour, approached via the splendid Wemyss Bay rail station and the ferry. A fine example of Victorian toilets is close by. This two-bar pub, always popular with yachtsmen, is ideally situated as a meeting point for food and ale before trips to all corners of the island. One of the three real ales comes from the Bute Beer Co nearby, others from Scottish micros. ◑🖥️❀✿

Sandbank

Holy Loch Inn Ⓛ
Springfield Place, PA23 8PJ (on A815 at jct with Shore Rd)
✪ 12-11 ☎ (01389) 706903
2 changing beers (sourced locally; often Fyne) Ⓗ
Attractive whitewashed building across from a small marina on a quiet loch where US submarines were once serviced. Recently refurbished, the two-room interior has a welcoming light and airy feel. The lively public bar features two handpumps and is presided over by a stag's head; the lounge is set for dining – good food is made from local produce where possible. Breakfast is served on Sunday morning and there is a beer festival in October. Q◑P🖥️✿❀

Strachur

Creggans Inn Ⓛ
PA27 8BX (on A815 at N end of village)
✪ 11-11; 12-11 Sun ☎ (01369) 860279
⊕ creggans-inn.co.uk
2 changing beers (sourced locally; often Fyne) Ⓗ
Historic coaching inn with connections to Mary Queen of Scots, situated on the shores of Loch Fyne where a ferry once left for Inveraray. The old public bar, MacPhunn's Bar, has a modern extension with a pool table, and welcomes the local shinty team as well as locals and travellers. Other rooms lead off, including a separate dining room open in the evening. The meals concentrate on local produce and there are warming real fires throughout. Q⌂✿⇌◑P🖥️(484,486)✿❀

Stagecoach Inn, Cairndow (Photo: Tom Ord)

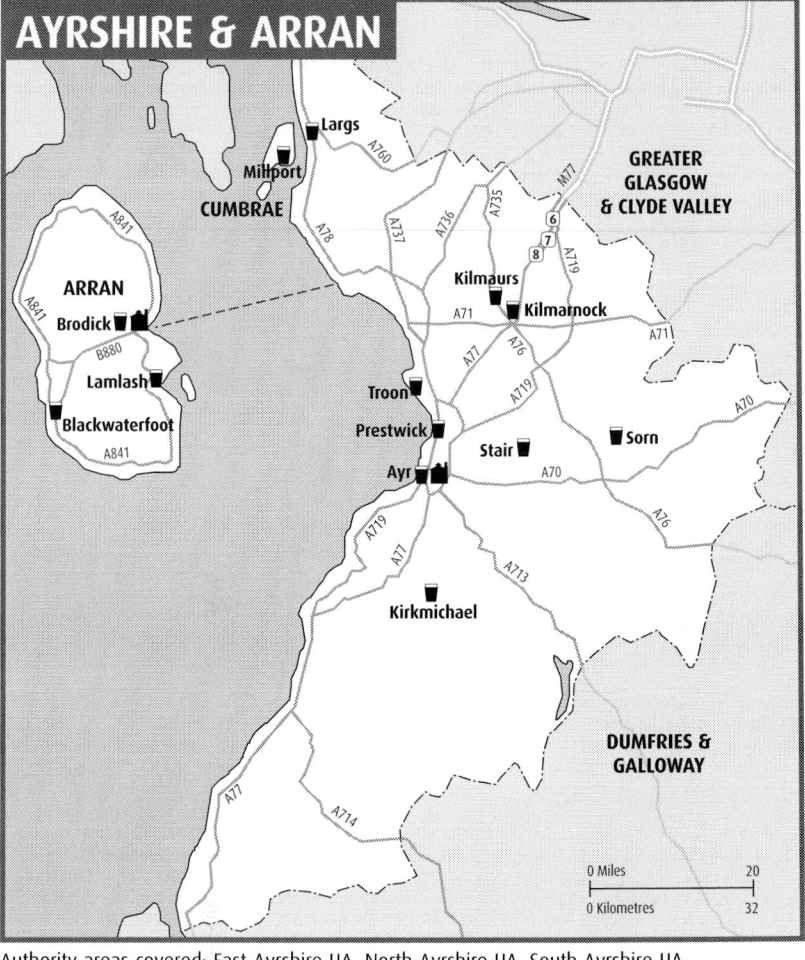

AYRSHIRE & ARRAN

SCOTLAND

Authority areas covered: East Ayrshire UA, North Ayrshire UA, South Ayrshire UA

Ayr

Abbotsford Hotel

14 Corsehill Road, KA7 2ST (1 mile S of town centre)
☼ 10-12.30am; 10-midnight Sun ☎ (01292) 261506
⊕ abbotsfordhotel.co.uk
3 changing beers (often Fyne, Hop Back, Thwaites) Ⓗ
A fine Scottish baronial building, under the same ownership since 1966. The real ale is to be found in the delightful and aptly named Copper Bar. There is also a pleasant dining room and games room with TV showing sport. Good Scottish-style meals feature local meats, vegetables and seafood.
🏨🏴🛏️🌙❺♣️P🚌(57,361)🐾🛜

Chestnuts Hotel

52 Racecourse Road, KA7 2UZ (on A719, 1 mile S of centre)
☼ 10-11 (12.30am Fri & Sat) ☎ (01292) 264393
⊕ chestnutshotel.com
3 changing beers Ⓗ
Ales from a range of breweries are offered in The 19th Hole, a delightful oak-beamed hall with an interesting history. The family-run hotel welcomes both locals and visitors. Excellent food is available in the bar and separate restaurant. Open log fires add to the comfortable atmosphere in winter and a pleasant beer garden is popular when the weather allows. 🏨🌙🏴🌙❺♣️AP🚌(9)🛜

Geordie's Byre

103 Main Street, KA8 8BU (in Newton, N of centre, over river towards Prestwick)
☼ 11-11 (midnight Thu-Sat); 12.30-11 Sun
☎ (01292) 264925
4 changing beers (often Fyne, Kelburn) Ⓐ
Under the same ownership for over 40 years, this CAMRA award-winning 18th-century pub serves up to four guest ales. It is one of the few Scottish pubs using traditional Scottish tall founts. A wide selection of malt whiskies and rums is also available. Q🚌🐾🛜

Glen Park Hotel Ⓛ

5 Racecourse Road, KA7 2DG
☼ 10-midnight; 12-midnight Sun ☎ (01292) 263891
⊕ glenparkhotel.co.uk

633

Ayr Leezie Lundie, Jolly Beggars; 2 changing beers (often Ayr) Ⓗ
This comfortable lounge bar, in an attractive 1860s B-listed Victorian building, is the brewery tap for Ayr Brewing Co in the rear of the building. Bar and restaurant meals are available daily except Monday. ⮑⚘🍴◑🍽️♿⚑P🚆🚲(9)🐾🛜

Smoking Goat
2A Academy Street, KA7 1HS (opp town hall)
☼ closed Mon; 12-12.30am (1am Fri & Sat)
☎ (01292) 857137 ⊕ thesmokinggoat.com
2 changing beers (often Ayr, Fyne Ales) Ⓗ
Basement bar with two handpumps. The full food menu is available Tuesday to Saturday, roasts are served on Sunday. The pub hosts a quiz night on Tuesday and DJ nights Thursday to Saturday. ⚘◑🚆🛜

Wellingtons Bar ▼
17 Wellington Square, KA7 1EZ
☼ 11-12.30am; 12-midnight Sun ☎ (01292) 262794
⊕ welliesbar.weebly.com
3 changing beers (often Fyne, Kelburn) Ⓗ
Close to the seafront, bus station and local government offices, it attracts tourists and office workers alike. The Wednesday evening quiz is popular and weekend music includes live music or a DJ on Saturday and an acoustic session on Sunday evening. The three changing ales constantly vary between brewers. ◑🍽️🚆🐾🛜

Blackwaterfoot: Isle of Arran

Kinloch Hotel
KA27 8ET
☼ 12-midnight ☎ (01770) 860444 ⊕ bw-kinlochhotel.co.uk
Ayr Uisge Dubh; 1 changing beer (often Ayr, Caledonian) Ⓗ
A hidden gem on the west coast of Arran. The family hotel has 37 bedrooms, a restaurant and three refurbished bars, and facilities including a heated indoor swimming pool. It serves fabulous local produce including fish and seafood. A summer beer festival is held. ⮑⚘🍴◑♿🅰♣🐾P🚆🐾🛜

Brodick: Isle of Arran

Ormidale Hotel
Knowe Road, KA27 8BY (off A841 at W end of village)
☼ 12.30-14.30 (not winter), 4-midnight; 12-12.30am Sat; 12-midnight Sun ☎ (01770) 302293 ⊕ ormidale-hotel.co.uk
House beer (by Caledonian); 1 changing beer (often Arran, Ayr) Ⓐ
Beers are served from traditional Scottish tall founts on the boat-shaped bar, with Arran Blonde often available in summer. Home-cooked meals are recommended. Discos and folk nights are held, and the attractive beer garden has views across Brodick Bay. Accommodation is available all year round. ⮑⚘🍴◑♣P🚆(322,324)🐾🛜

> Give my people plenty of beer, good beer and cheap beer, and you will have no revolution among them.
> **Queen Victoria**

Kilmarnock

Braehead Bar
8 Langlands Street, KA1 2AH (top of Gas Brae, up from John Finnie St)
☼ 11-11 (1am Thu-Sat) ☎ (01563) 258846
2 changing beers Ⓗ
Traditional pub close to the town centre which has had many names in recent years but which is probably still best known as the Jolly Farmer, from the days when the town's cattle market was opposite. The welcoming local serves the cheapest quality ale in the area. It has a new free-to-use pool table and a free jukebox on some days. Food is available on special event days. It hosts monthly party nights and barbecue events in summer in the garden. ⚘♿≉♣🚆🐾🛜

Brass & Granite
53 Grange Street, KA1 2DD
☼ 11-midnight (1am Thu-Sat); 12.30-midnight Sun
☎ (01563) 523431
3 changing beers (often Kelburn, Strathaven) Ⓗ
Open-plan pub near Kilmarnock town centre, close to Rugby Park football ground. Guest beers are usually from local or Cumbrian brewers and a wide range of draught and bottled Belgian beers is also on sale. Families are welcome and food is available all day. Several TVs show live sport. Quizzes are held every Sunday, Monday and Wednesday. ⮑◑♿≉♣🚆🛜

Wheatsheaf Inn
70 Portland Street, KA1 1JG
☼ 8am-midnight (1am Fri & Sat) ☎ (01563) 572483
Greene King Abbot; Sharp's Doom Bar; 7 changing beers Ⓗ
Sizeable town-centre Lloyds No.1 bar, originally the historic Wheatsheaf Hotel, famous for its links to Robert Burns, who was first published in Kilmarnock. The bar is divided into various seating areas, with booths, sofas and a raised dining space. DJs entertain on a Friday and Saturday, and karaoke features early Friday evening, but otherwise conversation holds sway. Food is the standard Wetherspoon fare and nine handpumps dispense a range of ales plus real cider. Licensed from 11am. ⮑⚘◑♿≉🍴🚆🛜

Kilmaurs

Weston Tavern
27 Main Street, KA3 2RQ
☼ 11-midnight (1am Fri & Sat); 12.30-midnight Sun
☎ (01563) 538805 ⊕ westontavern.co.uk
1 changing beer Ⓗ
Housed in the former manse of reformist minister David Smeaton, a contemporary of Robert Burns, this classic country pub and restaurant has a tiled floor, stone walls and a wood-burning fire. It sits beside the Jougs, a former jailhouse and tollbooth. A single pump dispenses ale from a rotating list of local breweries. The pub holds regular live music and quiz nights. The restaurant and bar areas were refurbished in 2016. ⚘◑♿≉P🚆🐾🛜

Kirkmichael

Kirkmichael Arms
3-5 Straiton Road, KA19 7PH
☼ 12-midnight (12.30am Fri & Sat) ☎ (01655) 750200
⊕ kirkmichaelarms.co.uk
2 changing beers (often Ayr) Ⓗ

A friendly country pub with a lounge bar and separate dining room. Two handpumps dispense an Ayr Brewing Co beer plus a guest. This is a pub at the heart of the community, serving excellent food made with locally sourced produce where possible. Small functions can be catered for. Well placed for Galloway Forest Park to the south, walkers and dogs are welcome. Q ♿ 🏠 🕸 🍴 ♿ ♣ ♠ ➡ 🚗 (358,361) 🐾 🛜

Lamlash: Isle of Arran

Pierhead Tavern
Shore Road, KA27 8JN
☼ 11-midnight (1am Fri & Sat) summer; 12-midnight (1am Fri & Sat) winter ☎ (01770) 600418 ⊕ thepht.co.uk
3 changing beers (often Ayr, Cairngorm, Kelburn) Ⓗ
Saved by new owners from being converted into flats, this famous village local has reopened following extensive refurbishment. Three handpumps serve a variety of rotating ales from breweries such as Ayr, Inveralmond, Cairngorm and Orkney, in addition to local Arran ales in the summer season. The pub grub is all home made and chef's specials change weekly. There is a pool table at one end of the bar. Karaoke is hosted every second Friday. ♿ 🕸 🍴 ♣ ♠ ➡ (323) 🐾 🛜

Largs

JG Sharps Bar ✓
34-36 Nelson Street, KA30 8LW (off seafront at Nardini's)
☼ 11-midnight (1am Fri & Sat); 12.30-midnight Sun
☎ (01475) 675515 ⊕ jgsharps.co.uk
Sharp's Doom Bar; 1 changing beer Ⓗ
On the corner of Nelson Street and Boyd Street, this is a large traditional pub with several drinking areas and an open fire in the bar area. Good-quality pub meals are served lunchtimes and Friday to Sunday evenings. Pub games are played and sport screened on TV, and there is occasional live music. The beer garden outside has space for smokers. Q ♿ 🕸 🍴 ♣ ♠ 🐾 🛜

Millport: Isle of Cumbrae

Fraser's Bar Ⓛ
7 Cardiff Street, KA28 0AS
☼ 11-midnight (1am Thu-Sat) ☎ (01475) 530518
2 changing beers (often Kelburn) Ⓗ
Well maintained and tidy, this pub caters for visitors to the island as well as locals. Buses meet every ferry from Largs and terminate just across the road. Two handpumps serve mostly light-coloured ales, usually including one from a local brewery. Good-value pub food is available lunchtimes and early evenings. Children are welcome in the rear lounge until 8pm. There is an open fire in the main bar. Q ♿ 🕸 🍴 ♣ ♠ ➡ (320) 🐾 🛜

Prestwick

Prestwick Pioneer ✓
87 Main Street, KA9 1JS
☼ 8am-midnight (12.30am Fri & Sat) ☎ (01292) 473210
Greene King Abbot; Sharp's Doom Bar; 8 changing beers (often Ayr, Loch Lomond) Ⓗ
Modern Wetherspoon outlet in a former Woolworths store, named after the first Scottish Aviation Pioneer built in 1947 at the nearby international airport. It has an airy feel with a light wood decor, and features photos of early Open Golf Championships at Prestwick and of Elvis at the nearby airport, the only place in the UK that he stepped foot on. Ten handpumps serve local and national ales and food is available all day. Licensed from 10am. ♿🕸🍴➡♦🚗☎

Sorn

Sorn Inn
35 Main Street, KA5 6HU
☼ closed Mon; 12-2.30, 6-10 (midnight Fri); 12-midnight Sat; 12-10 Sun ☎ (01290) 551305 ⊕ sorninn.com
1 changing beer (often Orkney) Ⓗ
The inn is the major community hub for the residents of the conservation village of Sorn. It has an award-winning restaurant with a menu that offers a mix of fine dining and brasserie-style food, featuring locally sourced produce. The cosy bar has one handpump and a selection of bottled ales. It offers accommodation in four rooms with en-suite facilities. ♿ 🕸 🏠 🍴 ♦ 🚗 (X50,X76) 🐾 🛜

Stair

Stair Inn
KA5 5HW (on B730 7 miles E of Ayr)
☼ 12-11 (1am Fri & Sat) ☎ (01292) 591650 ⊕ stairinn.co.uk
1 changing beer (often Kelburn, Orkney, Strathaven) Ⓗ
This family-run hotel on the banks of the River Ayr is not accessible by public transport but is well worth seeking out. The comfortable bar and adjacent restaurant feature hand-made furniture and the bedrooms are furnished in a similar style. The food menu relies heavily on local produce and fish from the inn's own smokehouse is a speciality (booking recommended at weekends). Freshly cooked pizzas are available to eat in or take away. Q ♿ 🕸 🏠 🍴 ♦ P 🛜

Troon

Bruce's Well ✓
91 Portland Street, KA10 6QN (nr town centre and station)
☼ 12-midnight; 11-1am Fri & Sat ☎ (01292) 311429
Caledonian Deuchars IPA; 2 changing beers (often Caledonian, Greene King, Inveralmond) Ⓗ
A friendly, spacious and comfortable lounge bar. A number of quiet TVs show sport. The guest ales come from the Belhaven list and change regularly. Unusually, the cellar is in a temperature-controlled room off the main bar area. ➡🚗🛜

McKay's
69 Portland Street, KA10 6QU
☼ 10-12.30am; 10-midnight Sun ☎ (01292) 737372
3 changing beers (often Cairngorm, Fyne, Inveralmond) Ⓗ
Popular town-centre bar with a large well-furnished beer garden which is busy in summer. The ale range varies but beers are usually from Scottish breweries including Harviestoun and Inveralmond. Food is served lunchtimes Monday to Thursday and until 8pm Friday to Sunday. The bar hosts various food-themed evenings including a steak night every Wednesday (booking required). It also holds local dominoes competitions. ♿🕸🍴➡🚗🐾🛜

BORDERS

EDINBURGH &
THE LOTHIANS

Auchencrow
Burnmouth

Duns

West Linton

A1107

A1

A6105

A697

Leitholm

A6112

B6461

Peebles

Clovenfords Galashiels

Earlston

A6105

Coldstream

A68

Broughton

Innerleithen

Tweedbank

Melrose

Kelso

GREATER GLASGOW & CLYDE VALLEY

A72

A701

A703

A701

A702

A72

A708

B7009

Hawick

Jedburgh

Town Yetholm

A699

A6089

A6091

A698

B6436

A698

A698

A6088

A68

A7

DUMFRIES
&
GALLOWAY

B6357

NORTHUMBERLAND

CUMBRIA

| 0 Miles | | 10 |
| 0 Kilometres | | 16 |

Authority area covered: Scottish Borders UA

Auchencrow

Craw Inn

TD14 5LS (signed from A1)

🕐 12-2, 6-11 (midnight Fri); 12-midnight Sat; 12.30-11 Sun
☎ (01890) 761253 ⊕ thecrawinn.co.uk

**2 changing beers (sourced nationally; often Hadrian
Border, High House Farm, Swannay)** Ⓗ

A friendly 18th-century listed country inn where
banter with the locals is guaranteed. The bar has a
wood-burning stove and tables for dining and
drinking. The real ales (three in summer) are
usually from smaller breweries, as can be seen
from the many pumpclips that festoon the roof
beams. Excellent home-cooked food is served in
both the bar and the well-appointed restaurant.
Beer festivals are held in August and November.
Accommodation includes a self-catering annexe.
Q ➤ 🏠 🛏 ◀◑ ♣ ● P 🚗 (34) 🛜

Burnmouth

First & Last

Upper Burnmouth, TD14 5SL

🕐 12-11 (1am Sat); 12.30-midnight Sun ☎ (01890) 781306
⊕ thefirstandlastpub.co.uk

2 changing beers (often Born in the Borders) Ⓗ

This comfortable and welcoming pub is frequented
by locals and travellers on the adjacent A1.
Following refurbishment in 2016 it is carpeted
throughout, and has a small dance floor in the
dining/function area. The bar area, with a real fire
and sports TV, is decorated with old photographs

and nautical artefacts. Meals are served all day,
except Monday in winter. Handy for a walk down
the steep hill to the charming little harbour at
Lower Burnmouth. It offers B&B accommodation in
four en-suite bedrooms. ➤ 🏠 🛏 ◀◑ & ♣ P 🚗 🛜

Clovenfords

Clovenfords Hotel

1 Vine Street, TD1 3LU

🕐 11-11 (1am Fri & Sat); 12-11 Sun ☎ (01896) 850203

**2 changing beers (sourced nationally; often
Sharp's)** Ⓗ

Set in the heart of the old vineyard village and hard
to miss with a striking white statue of Sir Walter
Scott outside, this family-run hotel was refurbished
in 2016. Old photos adorn the walls, giving
testimony to the hotel's literary history. Families
are welcome in the lounge and adjacent
conservatory restaurant, with games and a
children's menu provided. The hotel has plenty to
offer visitors, including walkers, cyclists and
tourists. Q ➤ 🏠 🛏 ◀◑ & ♣ P 🚗 (62) 🛜

REAL ALE BREWERIES

Born in the Borders Jedburgh
Broughton Broughton
Freewheelin' Peebles
Old Worthy Broughton
Tempest Tweedbank
Traquair House Innerleithen

Coldstream

Besom ✔

75-77 High Street, TD12 4AE
⚙ 11-midnight (1am Fri & Sat); 12.30-midnight Sun
☎ (01890) 882391 ⊕ besom-inn.co.uk
House beer (by Tetley); 1 changing beer (sourced nationally; often Black Sheep, Firebrick) Ⓗ
Another of the first and last pubs in Scotland, this three-roomed gem has remained relatively unchanged since it was built in the 1890s and revamped circa 1910. The cosy bar retains its original counter and gantry, while the diverse range of memorabilia, bookshelves and sofa seating gives the feel more of a living room than a pub. The lounge (where families are welcome) leads to a room dedicated to the history of the Coldstream Guards. Q ☎ ❀ ◑ ♣ ➡ (67,904) 🐾 🌢 ☞

Castle Hotel

11 High Street, TD12 4AP
⚙ 11-midnight (1am Fri & Sat) ☎ (01890) 882830
1 changing beer (sourced nationally; often Belhaven, Harviestoun, Inveralmond) Ⓗ
A small hotel towards the western edge of the town, convenient for the Hirsel Estate and Country Park. As you enter, the bar forms part of an open-plan area with a pool table at one end and sports TV for entertainment. The pub is known for its friendly and relaxed atmosphere. Meals are served in the bar including a children's menu, as well as simple bar snacks. There is a separate restaurant for those who prefer quieter dining.
☎ ❀ ⊠ ◑ ♣ ➡ (67) 🐾 🌢 ☞

Duns

Black Bull Hotel

15 Black Bull Street, TD11 3AR (between town square and A6109)
⚙ 11-midnight (1am Fri & Sat); 12-midnight Sun
☎ (01361) 883379 ⊕ blackbullhotelduns.co.uk
3 changing beers (sourced regionally; often Born in the Borders, Firebrick, Tempest) Ⓗ
This family-run 200-year-old hotel has a cosy wood-panelled bar popular with the locals and a lounge more suited to families. The restaurant specialises in fresh local produce, with an intimate, relaxed, candlelit atmosphere (no food Mon and winter Sun). The secluded beer garden is lovely in good weather, with a gazebo and play area. A beer festival is usually held in the summer.
☎ ❀ ⊠ ◑ ♿ ♣ P ➡ (60,260) 🐾 ☞

Earlston

Red Lion ✔

The Square, TD4 6DB
⚙ 11-11 (midnight Fri); 9am-11 Sat & Sun
☎ (01896) 848994 ⊕ redlionearlston.co.uk
2 changing beers (sourced regionally; often Born in the Borders, Freewheelin', Orkney) Ⓗ
Dating from the 1800s, this former coaching inn stands well back from the main street in this small

> How easy can the barley-bree
> Cement the quarrel.
> It's aye the cheapest lawyer's fee
> To taste the barrel.
> **Robert Burns**

town. Upgraded over the past few years, the pub boasts a spacious bar with a huge fireplace and open fire, and a pool table in the far corner. Food is served all day in the bar and attractive dining room, including breakfast on Saturday and Sunday. A children's menu and games are provided. Alcohol is sold from 11am. ☎ ❀ ⊠ ◑ ♣ P ➡ 🐾 ☞

Galashiels

Ladhope Inn ✔

33 High Buckholmside, TD1 2HR (on A7, ⅓ mile N of centre)
⚙ 4-11 (midnight Thu; 1am Fri); 11-1am Sat; 12-11 Sun
☎ (01896) 752446
1 changing beer (sourced regionally; often Born in the Borders, Caledonian) Ⓗ
Very much a community hub, this is a comfortable, friendly local with a vibrant Borders atmosphere. Originating circa 1792, it has been altered considerably over the years, with more refurbishment in 2016. Now a single room, it is decorated with a large inked map of the Galashiels area, and has a wee alcove with a golfing theme. Three TVs ensure the pub is busy during sporting events. Excellent home-made soup is served on Sunday. Children are not allowed. ❀ Ⓐ ❦ ♣ ➡ 🐾 ☞

Hawick

Exchange Bar (Dalton's)

1 Silver Street, TD9 0AD (off SW end of High St)
⚙ 11-11 (1am Fri & Sat); 12.30-11 Sun ☎ (01450) 376067
2 changing beers (sourced regionally; often Born in the Borders) Ⓗ
Tucked away between St Mary's Kirk and the Heart of Hawick Heritage Centre, and now without its iconic No Entry sign, the pub used to overlook the Corn Exchange, hence the name – however, a previous owner was called Dalton and that name has stuck. It is a Victorian gem with original dark-wood panelling and ornate cornice work. The bar is popular with locals and there is a comfy lounge used for parties, Friday karaoke and Sunday folk sessions. Children are not admitted. Ⓐ ♣ ➡ 🐾 ☞

Jedburgh

Canon (Exchange Inn)

8 Exchange Street, TD8 6BH
⚙ 3-midnight (1am Fri); 12-1am Sat; 12.30-midnight Sun
☎ (01835) 863243
2 changing beers (sourced regionally; often Caledonian, Thwaites) Ⓗ
Compact town-centre pub with a traditional atmosphere, featuring a welcoming real fire, original stone wall and dark-wood beams. The long bar has a small alcove-like area at the end. Real ales are usually from Scotland or northern England. The walls are adorned with rugby memorabilia and local history material. Phased renovations are in sympathy with the pub's original layout. Children are not admitted. Closed on Tuesdays in January and February. ♿ Ⓐ ♣ ➡ 🐾 ☞

Kelso

Cobbles Freehouse & Dining

7 Bowmont Street, TD5 7JH (off NE side of town square)
⚙ 11.30-11; 11-midnight Fri & Sat; 12-11 Sun
☎ (01573) 223548 ⊕ thecobbleskelso.co.uk
2 changing beers (sourced locally; often Tempest) Ⓗ

Diners and drinkers are well catered for at this long-established gastro-pub. The bright and airy interior includes a cosy bar on the right and a dining area to the left, with food served throughout. There is a menu to suit all tastes including children's, available lunchtimes and evenings during the week, all day at the weekend. The three handpumps are dedicated solely to Tempest beers, but at most times only two are on. Please ask before bringing in your dog.
🛏🏵🌗🖑🍴🚭💷🐾🛜

Rutherfords
38 The Square, TD5 7HL
🕒 3 (4 Mon)-9; 12-10 Fri & Sat; 12-9 Sun ☎ 07803 208460
🌐 rutherfordsmicropub.co.uk
4 changing beers (sourced nationally; often Allendale, Firebrick, Stewart) Ⓖ
This tiny shop conversion is the first micropub in Scotland; with no TV or music to distract, it is the ideal place for a friendly chat or to play board games. Real ales are served directly from the cask, and third-pint paddles are available. A selection of locally produced charcuterie, pies and cheeses is served all day. Opening times are extended in summer. CAMRA Borders Pub of the Year 2017 runner-up. Q🛏🏵♣🖑🐾

Leitholm
Plough Inn
Main Street, TD12 4JN
🕒 closed Mon; 12-10 (11 Fri & Sat) ☎ (01890) 840408
🌐 theploughinnleitholm.co.uk
2 changing beers (sourced nationally; often Born in the Borders, Hetton Law) Ⓗ
Set in the main street of a quiet village, this former ailing pub has been transformed into a charming family-run inn. The wood-floored bar and dining room are decorated and furnished to create a bright, modern and welcoming ambience. A massive clock dominates the fireplace in the bar. Full meals are served evenings and Sunday lunchtime, with a café style menu at other times.
🛏🏵🍴🌗♣🐾🛜

Melrose
King's Arms Hotel ✅
High Street, TD6 9PB
🕒 11-11 (1am Fri & Sat); 12-11 Sun ☎ (01896) 800335
🌐 kingsarms-melrose.co.uk
3 changing beers (sourced nationally; often Timothy Taylor) Ⓗ
Old coaching inn dating from 1793. The bar has a wooden floor, church pew seating and a large-screen TV for sporting events. It is decorated with rugby memorabilia and old local photographs. The quieter lounge, where families are welcome, is comfortably furnished and has a lovely old carved door set in the ceiling. There are additional dining rooms upstairs. Food is served all day on Saturday and Sunday. National Cycle Route 1 passes the door. Q🛏🏵🍴🌗🅰♣P🖑🐾🛜

Peebles
Bridge Inn (Trust) 🏆
Portbrae, EH45 8AW
🕒 11-midnight (1am Thu-Sat); 12-midnight Sun
☎ (01721) 720589

Fyne Jarl; 3 changing beers (sourced nationally; often Born in the Borders, Stewart, Tempest) Ⓗ
Cheerful, welcoming, single-roomed town-centre local, also known as the Trust. The mosaic entrance floor shows it was once the Tweedside Inn. The bright, comfortable bar is decorated with jugs, bottles, memorabilia of outdoor pursuits and photos of old Peebles. An outdoor heated patio area overlooks the river. The Gents is superb, with well-maintained original Twyford Adamant urinals. There is TV sport and live music on Sunday evening. Children are not admitted. Local CAMRA Pub of the Year 2017. 🏵🅰♣🖑(X62)🐾🛜

Cross Keys ✅
Northgate, EH45 8RS
🕒 7am-midnight (1am Fri & Sat) ☎ (01721) 723467
Greene King Abbot; Sharp's Doom Bar; 2 changing beers (sourced nationally; often Acorn, Wells, Wychwood) Ⓗ
Old coaching inn, now a Wetherspoon pub and hotel. The large, pleasant main bar, with a low ceiling, is on the ground floor. A smaller, attractive bar is situated one floor up, with easy access to an excellent beer garden. Food is served all day from the extensive Wetherspoon menu. Somerset Tree Shaker and Westons Old Rosie ciders are often available. Alcohol is served from 11am (noon Sun).
🛏🏵🛌🌗🖑🅰🏠🖑(X62)🐾🛜

Town Yetholm
Plough Hotel
High Street, TD5 8RF
🕒 11-midnight (1am Fri & Sat) ☎ (01573) 420215
🌐 theploughhotelyetholm.co.uk
2 changing beers (sourced regionally; often Belhaven, Born in the Borders, Broughton) Ⓗ
A friendly inn dating from 1710 at the heart of a rural village, which is a haven for walkers with the Pennine Way, St Cuthbert's Way and the Scottish National Trail all nearby. A large wood-burning stove dominates the bar, where the locals are happy to chat with visitors. There is also a separate lounge and an attractive little dining room. Lunchtime meals are not always available in winter. Enjoy the beer garden in summer.
🛏🏵🛌🌗🅰♣P🖑(81)🐾🛜

West Linton
Gordon Arms Hotel
Dolphinton Road, EH46 7DR (on A702)
🕒 11-midnight (1am Fri & Sat); 12-11 Sun
☎ (01968) 660208 🌐 thegordon.co.uk
Black Sheep Best Bitter; Stewart Pentland IPA; 2 changing beers (sourced nationally; often Cross Borders, Speyside Craft) Ⓗ
Situated in a picturesque village on the road from Edinburgh to Biggar. The large L-shaped, airy bar has stone walls and cornicing more reminiscent of an Edinburgh pub than a village local. There is a roaring log fire in winter and you can relax in comfortable seating. Meals including a children's menu are served in the bar, restaurant and covered outdoor area, and are available all day on Sunday.
🛏🏵🛌🌗🅰♣P🖑🐾🛜

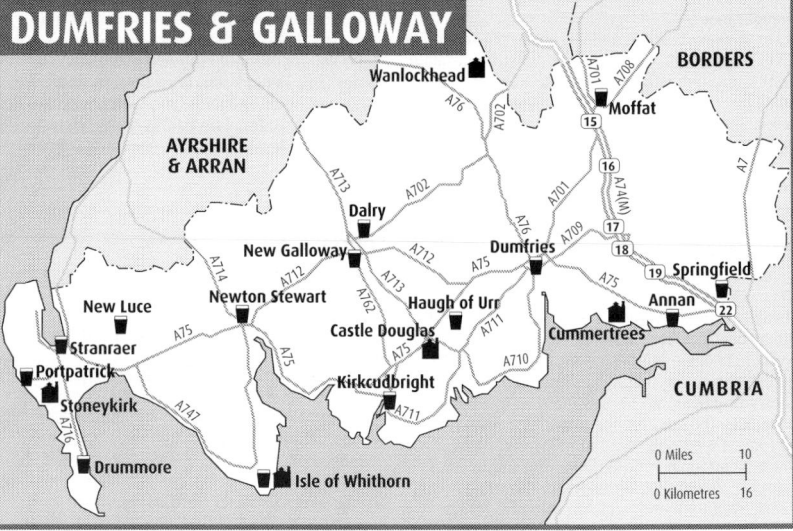

DUMFRIES & GALLOWAY

BORDERS
Wanlockhead
Moffat
15
AYRSHIRE & ARRAN
16
Dalry
17
New Galloway
Dumfries
18
19 Springfield
New Luce
Newton Stewart
Haugh of Urr
Annan
22
Stranraer
Castle Douglas
Cummertrees
Portpatrick
Kirkcudbright
CUMBRIA
Stoneykirk
Drummore
Isle of Whithorn

0 Miles 10
0 Kilometres 16

SCOTLAND

Authority area covered: Dumfries & Galloway UA

Annan

Blue Bell Inn
10 High Street, DG12 6AG
11-11 (midnight Thu-Sat); 12.30-11 Sun
☎ (01461) 202385
Caledonian Deuchars IPA; 3 changing beers (sourced nationally; often Andrews Ales, Kelburn, Strathaven) Ⓗ
Former coaching inn dating from 1770 where Hans Christian Andersen is said to have stayed. The Blue Bell was part of the Gretna State Management Scheme from 1917 to 1972 when it was owned by the government. The pub is home to many community activities along with annual beer and cider festivals. The red sandstone building houses some traditional features, notably the panelled interior and rear stables. The Gents has a panelled ante-room, tiled inner room and original Shanks urinals. ☺☺♿★➴♣●P🚪(79,383)♣🚭

Dalry

Clachan Inn
8-10 Main Street, DG7 3UW
12-midnight ☎ (01644) 430241 ⊕ theclachaninn.co.uk
2 changing beers (sourced regionally; often Ayr, Fallen, Fyne) Ⓗ
The Clachan has a reputation for excellent food, cosy, well-equipped bedrooms and a welcoming atmosphere. The menu is varied with excellent daily specials, and the kitchen makes use of local produce including organic lamb and venison. The pub has an attractive traditional main bar, a relaxing lounge bar and a separate restaurant – both bars have wonderfully warming open log fires in winter. A handy stop for walkers on the Southern Upland Way. Q☺☺♿◐♿♣●P🚪(520,521)♣🚭

Drummore

Clashwhannon
Stair Street, DG9 9QE (on A716 S from Stranraer)
12-midnight summer; 4 (12 Fri-Sun)-11 winter
☎ (01776) 840632 ⊕ clashwhannon.co.uk

2 changing beers (often Hadrian Border, Portpatrick, Timothy Taylor) Ⓗ
A friendly and relaxing place, this bar serves the adjacent caravan park and is open all year round. Demand from visitors and locals alike has seen the emergence of real ale in this remote location, close to the Mull of Galloway. There is a bar area plus large family room and restaurant where local produce is served at reasonable prices. Three handpumps are used in summer, one in winter. Music and variety events feature during the high season. ☺☺♿◐♿★♣P🚪(407)♣🚭

Dumfries

Cavens Arms 🏆
20 Buccleuch Street, DG1 2AH
11-midnight (11 Mon & Tue); 12-11 Sun
☎ (01387) 252896
Fyne Jarl; Marston's Wainwright; Morland Old Speckled Hen; Thornbridge Jaipur IPA; 4 changing beers (sourced nationally) Ⓗ
Busy food-oriented pub, popular with diners for its range of good-value meals. A separate restaurant space has been created to cope with demand at peak times. Drinkers are welcome in the bar area but seating can be limited during food service times. Guest ales are from a wide range of breweries including some rarely seen in this locality. There are regular charity quizzes and other theme nights. Local CAMRA Pub of the Year 2017. ◐♿➴P🚪🚭

Coach & Horses
66 Whitesands, DG1 2RS
closed Mon; 11-11 (midnight Sat); 12.30-11 Sun ☎ 07746 675349

REAL ALE BREWERIES
Andrews Cummertrees
Five Kingdoms █ Isle of Whithorn
Lola Rose █ Wanlockhead
Portpatrick Stoneykirk
Sulwath Castle Douglas

Draught Bass Ⓗ
A small, lively former coaching inn overlooking the River Nith. Situated next to the Tourist Information Centre, the pub is handy for local attractions. The small bar can feel cramped but service is always quick. The bar features a flagstone floor with a warming open fire during the colder months. There is a great atmosphere in this gem of a pub, enhanced on regular live music nights. Winter opening times may vary. ⏰≠♣P🖵♨

New Bazaar
39 Whitesands, DG1 2RS
☼ 11-11; 12-8 Sun ☎ (01387) 268776
Theakston XB; 3 changing beers (sourced nationally; often Fuller's, Greene King, Timothy Taylor) Ⓗ
Former coaching inn beside the River Nith with an attractive airy bar featuring a splendid Victorian gantry displaying an impressive malt whisky collection. The cosy lounge provides a quiet retreat and has a warming coal fire in winter. A small room is available for meetings. The pub is a favourite with football supporters attending nearby Palmerston Park and is ideally situated for car parking, local buses and tourist attractions. Winter opening times may vary. ⏰≠♣P🖵♨🛜

Riverside Bar
Dock Park, DG1 2RY
☼ 12-11 (midnight Thu; 1am Fri & Sat); 12.30-11 Sun
☎ (01387) 254477
Morland Old Speckled Hen; 3 changing beers (sourced nationally; often Cairngorm, Fallen, Orkney) Ⓗ
The Riverside Bar is now an established venue on the Dumfries real ale scene. Comfortable and friendly, it has seating on two levels and a large conservatory. Two outside seating areas include a terrace with open views over the Dock Park and down to the River Nith. The pub is accessible from the St Michaels area near Robert Burns Mausoleum or from Dock Park. Guest beers can be sourced from local brewers as well as from further afield. ⏰⏰P🖵♨🛜

Robert the Bruce ✅
81 Buccleuch Street, DG1 2AB
☼ 8am-midnight (1am Fri & Sat) ☎ (01387) 270320
Caledonian Deuchars IPA; Greene King Abbot; Sharp's Doom Bar; Thornbridge Jaipur IPA; 2 changing beers (sourced nationally) Ⓗ
This former Methodist church, sensitively converted by Wetherspoon in 2001, has a relaxed atmosphere and is a popular meeting place in the town centre. There is a pleasant outside seating area to the rear. The pub stands near the site where Robert the Bruce killed John Comyn in 1306 in an incident linked to Scotland's fight for independence. The food menu offers a range of good-value meals all day, every day. Alcohol is served from 11am. ⏰⏰⏰♿≠♣P🖵🛜

Tam o' Shanter
113-117 Queensberry Street, DG1 1BH
☼ 11-11 (midnight Fri & Sat); 12-10 Sun ☎ (01387) 267880
Broughton Clipper IPA, 6.2 IPA; 4 changing beers (sourced nationally; often Andrews Ales, Broughton, Sulwath) Ⓗ
Established in 1630, this 17th-century coaching inn with a connection to Robert Burns has been a

> Bread is the staff of life, but beer is life itself. **Traditional**

mainstay of the Dumfries beer scene for many years. It is a small traditional pub with a main bar and a couple of quiet cosy rooms including a games area behind. An upstairs room hosts live music and other functions. It is well positioned just off the High Street. Two of the guest beers are usually from local breweries. ⏰≠♣P🖵♨🛜

Haugh of Urr

Laurie Arms Hotel
11-13 Main Street, DG7 3YA
☼ 12-2, 5-11 (9 Mon & Tue); 12-11 Sat & Sun
☎ (01556) 660246 ⊕ haugh-of-urr.co.uk
4 changing beers (sourced nationally; often Caledonian, Fyne, Strathaven) Ⓗ
Welcoming family-run pub and restaurant in a charming, quiet village, popular for its range of beers and freshly cooked food featuring local produce. It has a good village-pub atmosphere, enhanced on winter nights by a warming log fire in the bar. Up to four beers are available depending on the season, mainly from independent breweries. National Cycle Route 7 passes nearby. A former local CAMRA award winner. Winter opening times may vary. ⏰⏰⏰♣P🖵(501)♨🛜

Isle of Whithorn

Steam Packet Inn ✅
Harbour Row, DG8 8LL (on B7004 from Whithorn)
☼ 11-11 (12.30am Fri & Sat) summer; 11-11 (midnight Fri & Sat); 12-11 Sun winter ☎ (01988) 500334
⊕ thesteampacketinn.biz
Morland Old Speckled Hen; 8 changing beers (often Five Kingdoms, Fyne, Kelburn) Ⓗ
Traditional and historic family-run hotel overlooking the harbour, welcoming to all including families and pets. The public bar has stone walls and a multi-fuel stove, and there are pictures of the village and maritime events throughout. Four guest ales from a wide variety of breweries and up to four ales from the in-house brewery, Five Kingdoms, are available in both bars. The extensive food menu features local produce – the Sunday hot buffet is a speciality and there are various themed food nights.
Q⏰⏰⏰⏰♣♨P🖵(415)♨🛜

Kirkcudbright

Masonic Arms
19 Castle Street, DG6 4JA
☼ 12-midnight; 12.30-midnight Sun ☎ (01557) 330517
2 changing beers (sourced nationally; often Black Sheep, Caledonian, Thwaites) Ⓗ
This friendly pub in the town has been a firm favourite with real ale enthusiasts for many years. The tables and bar fronts are made from old malt whisky casks from Islay's Bowmore Distillery. There is a smaller back bar and a garden with a smoking area. A wide selection of more than 50 malt whiskies and over 60 gins is available, as well as a good range of world beers.
Q⏰⏰A P🖵(431,502)♨🛜

Selkirk Arms Hotel ✅
High Street, DG6 4JG
☼ 11-11 ☎ (01557) 330402 ⊕ selkirkarmshotel.co.uk
3 changing beers (sourced nationally; often Fyne, Sulwath, Timothy Taylor) Ⓗ

Refurbished 18th-century hotel with a restaurant, bistro and lounge bar, renowned for locally sourced food, highlighted by the menus and photos of suppliers on the walls. The large garden area with tables is popular in summer. Robert Burns wrote his famous Selkirk Grace at the hotel in 1794. Kirkcudbright is notable for its artistic heritage and houses a number of interesting galleries and museums. One or two real ales are available in winter, three in summer.
Q ⍟ ⚲ ⏢ ◑ ⅃ & ▲ P ⊟ (431,502) ⚘ 🛜

Moffat

Stag Hotel ✅
21-22 High Street, DG10 9HL
🕓 11-11 (midnight Thu-Sat) ☎ (01683) 220343
🌐 staghotelmoffat.com
Caledonian Deuchars IPA; 1 changing beer (sourced nationally; often Greene King) Ⓗ
A family-run hotel situated at the north end of the High Street, offering a warm welcome and home-cooked food. The bar features a range of malt whiskies. There is a separate games room with sofas, and an enclosed courtyard and garden at the rear of the building. This multi-roomed pub offers accommodation and is a good base for exploring the local countryside. ⍟ ⚲ ⏢ ◑ ▲ ♣ P ⊟ ⚘ 🛜

New Galloway

Ken Bridge Hotel
Galloway Forest Park, DG7 3PR (at jct of A713 and A712, 14 miles N of Castle Douglas)
🕓 11-11; 12-11 Sun ☎ (01644) 420211
🌐 kenbridgehotel.co.uk
2 changing beers (sourced regionally; often Born in the Borders, Harviestoun, Stewart) Ⓗ
Eighteenth-century former coaching inn, now a family-run hotel with local connections reaching back several generations. Situated on the banks of the lovely River Ken with its good fishing and picturesque views, it provides an ideal base for exploring the Galloway Forest Park and some of the darkest skies in Europe. Wooden benches, original stone walls and a natural slate floor create a relaxed atmosphere in the bar. Winter opening times may vary.
Q ⍟ ⚲ ⏢ ◑ & ▲ ♣ P ⊟ (520,521) 🛜

New Luce

Kenmuir Arms Hotel
31 Main Street, DG8 0AJ (8 miles N of Glenluce along old military road)
🕓 closed Mon; 5-11 ☎ (01581) 600218 🌐 kenmuirarms.com
1 changing beer (often Goose Eye, Orkney) Ⓗ
Situated in a beautiful village on the banks of the River Luce, this picturesque hotel has well-kept gardens by the river. The public bar offers one real ale all year round, two in summer, sourced from all over the UK. Home-cooked, freshly prepared food is served in the evenings. This is a popular stopping-off point for walkers on the Southern Upland Way and the hotel offers a luggage transfer service. Opening hours vary. Q ⚲ ⏢ ◑ & ▲ ♣ P 🛜

Newton Stewart

Creebridge House Hotel
Minnigaff, DG8 6NP (on B7079, E of river)

🕓 12-2.30, 6-midnight ☎ (01671) 402121
🌐 creebridge.co.uk
2 changing beers (often Belhaven, Greene King, Harviestoun) Ⓗ
This traditional country house hotel close to the town centre is set in three acres of gardens and woodland next to the River Cree. It offers two Greene King ales, and occasional guest ales from the Greene King list. A choice of excellent food is available featuring locally sourced meat, game and fish, served in the top-class restaurant and adjacent informal brasserie. The bar and lounge areas have real fires. Occasional dominoes league games, quiz nights and charity events are held.
⚲ ⏢ ◑ & ▲ P ⊟ (X75,430) ⚘ 🛜

Portpatrick

Crown Hotel
9 North Crescent, DG9 8SX (facing harbour)
🕓 11-midnight (1am Fri & Sat); 12-midnight Sun
☎ (01776) 810261 🌐 crownhotelportpatrick.com
2 changing beers (often Hadrian Border, Portpatrick, Wells) Ⓗ
Hotel overlooking the picturesque and historic Portpatrick harbour with views on a clear day across to Ireland. The large comfortable bar area at the front is adorned with fine pictures and ornaments and warmed by an open fire. Two regularly changing ales are available from across the UK, including the local Portpatrick Brewery. Live music plays on Friday and Saturday nights, featuring both local and visiting musicians and groups. ⚲ ⏢ ◑ & ▲ ♣ ⊟ (367) ⚘ 🛜

Springfield

Queen's Head
Main Street, DG16 5EH
🕓 5-11 (midnight Thu & Fri); 12-midnight Sat; 12.30-11 Sun
☎ (01461) 337173
1 changing beer (sourced regionally; often Andrews Ales, Caledonian, Strathaven) Ⓗ
A small single-roomed village pub dating from 1760. This friendly, unpretentious local is slightly off the beaten track, although it is close to Gretna, wedding capital of the country. In the 18th and early-19th centuries marriages were conducted in the Queen's Head and wedding parties still celebrate here. One beer is on handpump all year with a second on rare occasions. No food is available. ⚲ ⇌ ♣ P ⊟ (382) ⚘ 🛜

Stranraer

Grapes
4-6 Bridge Street, DG9 7HY
🕓 11-11.30 (midnight Thu-Sat); 12.30-11.30 Sun
☎ (01776) 703386 🌐 thegrapes1862.co.uk
2 changing beers (often Portpatrick) Ⓗ
Popular historic public bar, with an impressive mirror and gantry, which has altered little in over 50 years. It has a separate refurbished snug bar downstairs, an upstairs Art Deco lounge/function room, and a courtyard with seating. Local musicians play in the public bar most Friday evenings, and touring American-style bands often perform upstairs. There is a strong commitment to real ales sourced both locally and from all over the UK. Mini beer festivals are held twice yearly.
⚲ ⏢ ⇌ ♣ ⊟ 🛜

EDINBURGH & THE LOTHIANS

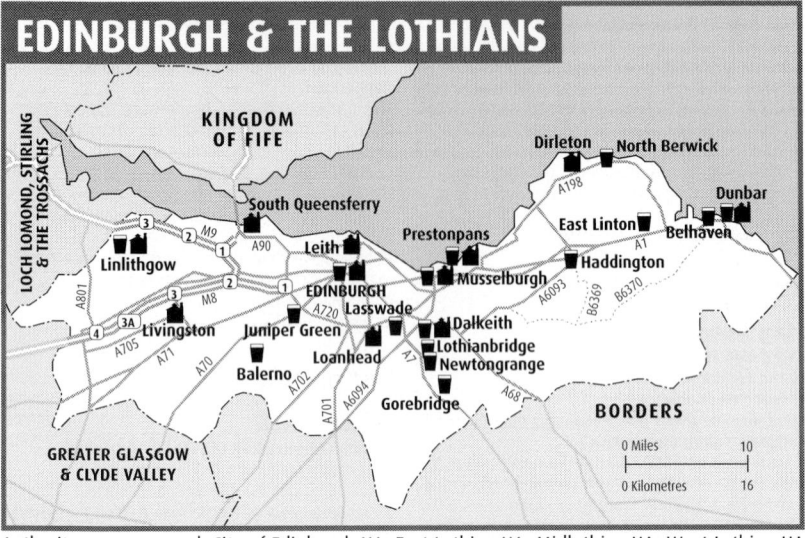

Authority areas covered: City of Edinburgh UA, East Lothian UA, Midlothian UA, West Lothian UA

Balerno

Grey Horse
20 Main Street, EH14 7EH (off A70, in pedestrian area)
☼ 10-11 (midnight Fri & Sat); 12.30-11 Sun
☎ (0131) 449 2888 ⊕ greyhorsebalerno.com
Fyne Jarl; 4 changing beers (sourced regionally; often Alechemy, Orkney, Stewart) Ⓗ
Traditional stone-built village pub, dating from the 18th century. The lounge, refurbished in 2016, is furnished with tables and chairs and features a gastro-pub style menu as well as Chinese street food options. There is one folk and one jazz evening each month, often on a Sunday. Alcohol is served from 11am (12.30pm Sun). Local CAMRA Pub of the Year runner-up 2017.
Q☜◑&♣☐♨?

Belhaven

Masons Arms
8 High Street, EH42 1NP (1 mile W of Dunbar)
☼ 12-2.30, 6-11; 12-midnight Fri & Sat; 12.30-11 Sun
☎ (01368) 864566
1 changing beer (sourced locally; often Belhaven, Knops, Stewart Brewing) Ⓗ
Just a few minutes' walk from Belhaven Brewery, this friendly pub has a bright, comfortable bar overlooking the superb beer garden with views to the distant Lammermuir Hills. It has a plain wooden floor, bench seating around the walls and is warmed by a real fire in winter. A further small room is used for functions. ☜♨A♣♨?

Dalkeith

Blacksmith's Forge ✓
5 Newmills Road, EH22 1DU
☼ 8am-midnight (1am Fri & Sat) ☎ (0131) 561 5100
Greene King Abbot; Sharp's Doom Bar; 6 changing beers (sourced regionally; often Cairngorm, Harviestoun, Stewart) Ⓗ
Large open-plan Wetherspoon pub divided into several distinct areas with a mix of tables and chairs, high tables and booths with bench seating.

Changing real ales are often from Scottish breweries. Families are welcome until 10pm for meals, which are available all day. Alcohol is served from 11am (12.30pm Sun).
Q☜♨◑&♣☐?

Dunbar

Volunteer Arms
17 Victoria Street, EH42 1HP (near swimming pool)
☼ 12-11; 11-midnight Thu; 11-1am Fri & Sat; 12.30-midnight Sun ☎ (01368) 862278 ⊕ volunteerarmsdunbar.co.uk
2 changing beers (sourced nationally; often Harviestoun, Orkney, Tryst) Ⓗ
Close to Dunbar harbour, this is a friendly, traditional locals' pub. The cosy panelled bar is decorated with lots of fishing and lifeboat-oriented memorabilia. The two real ales are often from smaller breweries. Upstairs is a restaurant serving an excellent, good-value range of food including a children's menu, with an emphasis on seafood. Meals are available all day. Dogs must be on a lead. ☜♨◑A≈♣☐♨?

East Linton

Linton Hotel & Steakhouse
3 Bridge End, EH40 3AF
☼ 12-11 (1am Fri & Sat) ☎ (01620) 860202
⊕ thelintonhotel.co.uk
3 changing beers (sourced regionally) Ⓗ
Small, welcoming hotel by the historic brig over the Tyne in a pretty conservation village. There is a comfortably furnished public bar with at least one real ale from a Scottish microbrewery. To the rear is a pleasant coffee/dining lounge while upstairs is a large restaurant. Food is served all day and the emphasis is on local produce, especially quality steaks – the owner was previously a butcher.
Q☜♨☐◑&♣☐(107,120)♨?

Edinburgh: Central

Abbotsford Bar & Restaurant ★
3-5 Rose Street, EH2 2PR

✪ 11-11 (midnight Fri & Sat) ☎ (0131) 225 5276
⊕ theabbotsford.com
6 changing beers (sourced regionally) Ⓗ/Ⓐ
A traditional Scottish bar listed on CAMRA's National Inventory of Historic Pub Interiors. The magnificent island bar and gantry in dark mahogany have been a fixture since 1902. Six real ales are served, usually from Scottish microbreweries. There is an extensive food menu, available all day in the bar. Diners in the restaurant upstairs can order real ale from downstairs.
Q ☎ ✿ ⓓ ≅ (Waverley) 🚌🚌 ✿ 🛜

Blue Blazer

2 Spittal Street, EH3 9DX (SW of centre)
✪ 11-1am; 12.30-1am Sun ☎ (0131) 229 5030
⊕ theblueblazer.co.uk
Fallen Oddysey; Stewart Pentland IPA Ⓐ; **5 changing beers (sourced regionally; often Edinbrew, Kelburn, Knops)** Ⓗ
Two-roomed pub with wooden floors, high ceilings and old brewery window panels, and candles in the evening adding to the traditional feel. The pub specialises in real ales from smaller Scottish breweries. Toasties are available all day. Close to theatres and cinemas, closing time is later in August and December. Children are not admitted.
🚌 ✿ 🛜

Bow Bar

80 West Bow, EH1 2HH (Old Town, off Grassmarket)
✪ 12-midnight; 12.30-11.30 Sun ☎ (0131) 226 7667
⊕ thebowbar.co.uk
Fallen Oddysey; Stewart 80/-; Tempest Cascadian; 5 changing beers (sourced nationally; often Arbor, Cromarty, Swannay) Ⓐ
A re-creation of a classic Scottish one-roomed ale house, dedicated to traditional Scottish air pressure dispense and upright drinking. Regular beer festivals are held in January and June. The walls are festooned with original brewery mirrors and the superb gantry does justice to an award-winning selection of over 300 single malt whiskies and international bottled beers. Pies and bridies are available at lunchtime. Children are not admitted.
Q ≅ (Waverley) 🚌🚌 ✿ 🛜

Cafe Royal ★ ✅

19 West Register Street, EH2 2AA (off E end of Princes St)
✪ 11-11 (midnight Thu; 1am Fri & Sat); 12.30-11 Sun
☎ (0131) 556 1884 ⊕ caferoyaledinburgh.co.uk
6 changing beers (sourced regionally; often Broughton, Kelburn, Stewart) Ⓗ
One of the finest Victorian pub interiors in Scotland, dominated by an impressive oval island bar with ornate brass light fittings and magnificent ceramic tiled murals of innovators made by Doulton from pictures by John Eyre. The sporting windows of the adjacent Oyster Bar/Restaurant were made by the same firm that supplied windows for the House of Lords. The real ales are mainly from Scottish breweries. Meals are served all day. Children are only allowed in the restaurant.
Q ☎ ⓓ ≅ (Waverley) 🚌🚌 🛜

Guildford Arms

1 West Register Street, EH2 2AA (off E end of Princes St)
✪ 11-11 (midnight Thu & Fri); 10-midnight Sat; 10-11 Sun
☎ (0131) 556 4312 ⊕ guildfordarms.com
Fyne Jarl; Orkney Dark Island; Stewart Pentland IPA; Swannay Orkney IPA; 5 changing beers (sourced nationally; often Alechemy, Fallen, Wells) Ⓗ

A large establishment built in the golden age of Victorian pub design. The high ceiling, cornices and friezes are spectacular, as are the window arches and screens. There is a large standing space around the canopied bar plus extensive seating areas. The diverse range of 10 real ales includes many from Scottish micros, and real cider is occasionally on handpump. Bar snacks are available 3-9pm. Children permitted in the restaurant only. Alcohol is served from 11am. ☎ ⓓ ≅ (Waverley) 🚌🚍🚌 ✿ 🛜

Halfway House

24 Fleshmarket Close, EH1 1BX (up steps opp Waverley Station's Market St entrance)
✪ 11-11.30 (midnight Thu; 1am Fri & Sat)
☎ (0131) 225 7101
4 changing beers (sourced nationally; often Alechemy, Broughton, Stewart) Ⓗ
Cosy, characterful bar hidden halfway down an Old Town close. Railway memorabilia decorates the interior of this small, often busy, bar. At the front are tables with window seats and stools. The rear area has more comfortable semicircular booth seating. Meals and bar snacks are served all day. The bar may stay open until 1am during busy times of year. ✿ ⓓ ≅ (Waverley) 🚌🚌 ✿ 🛜

Haymarket ✅

11-14 West Maitland Street, EH12 5DS (W of centre)
✪ 11-midnight (1am Fri & Sat) ☎ (0131) 228 2537
Caledonian Deuchars IPA; St Austell Nicholson's Pale Ale; Stewart Jack Back; 7 changing beers (sourced nationally; often Acorn, Harviestoun, Kelburn) Ⓗ
On the busy corner of the Haymarket, the pub has a comfortable interior decorated with historic prints of the pub and locality. An island bar overlooks a large central area with a raised mezzanine floor to one side and arches leading through to a restaurant. Twelve real ale handpumps dispense a varied and interesting range. Food is served all day from the Nicholson's menu. Children are welcome if dining. ☎ ✿ ⓓ ♿ ≅ (Haymarket) 🚌🚍🚌 ✿ 🛜

Jolly Judge

7A Lawnmarket, EH1 2PB (Old Town, in James Court)
✪ 12-midnight (11 Tue & Wed); 12-11 Sun
☎ (0131) 225 2669 ⊕ jollyjudge.co.uk
3 changing beers (sourced regionally; often Cromarty, Kelburn, Windswept) Ⓗ
Comfortable bar with an attractive painted ceiling hidden down an Old Town close just off the Royal Mile. This is a welcome spot for refreshment after

REAL ALE BREWERIES

Alechemy Livingston
Barney's Edinburgh
Belhaven Dunbar
Black Metal Edinburgh
Caledonian Edinburgh
Campervan Edinburgh
Cross Borders Dalkeith (NEW)
Edinbrew Livingston
Ferry South Queensferry (NEW)
Hanging Bat 🍺 Edinburgh
Hurly Burly Musselburgh (NEW)
Kentwood 🍺 Prestonpans
Knops Dirleton
Krafty Brew 🍺 Linlithgow
Pilot Leith
Stewart Loanhead
Top Out Loanhead
Valve Edinburgh (NEW)

visiting the castle. There are steps down to the entrance, as was common in the past. The real ales are often from smaller Scottish breweries. This is one of Edinburgh's top pubs for cider, selling a varying selection of three APPLE-certified ciders. Dogs are permitted after 3pm, but no children inside. Q✿🕙◀≉(Waverley)🛏♣🚐🐾🍴🎅

Monty's
185 Morrison Street, EH3 8DZ (W of centre)
🕙 4-11 Mon; 12-midnight (11 Tue); 12-1am Fri; 12.30-11 Sun
☎ (0131) 629 1104
6 changing beers (sourced nationally; often Fyne, Timothy Taylor) Ⓗ
Busy street-corner bar favoured by a younger clientele which reopened in late 2016 under new management with a positive attitude towards real ale (unusually the pub has a dedicated cask ale cellar). The wood-panelled interior has large windows and a range of comfortable seating. There is also an upstairs area with cosy seating. Children are not allowed. ✿≉(Haymarket)🛏🚐🍴🎅

Oxford Bar ★
8 Young Street, EH2 4JB (New Town, off Charlotte Sq)
🕙 11-midnight (1am Fri & Sat); 12.30-11 Sun
☎ (0131) 539 7119 ⊕ oxfordbar.co.uk
Caledonian Deuchars IPA; 3 changing beers (sourced regionally; often Belhaven, Cairngorm, Inveralmond) Ⓗ
A real taste of New Town past, this small, basic, vibrant drinking shop has remained largely unaltered since the late-19th century. The bar counter nearly fills the small front room but there is more space in the side room. It is renowned as one of the favourite pubs of Rebus and his creator Ian Rankin, and a haunt of many other famous and infamous characters over the years. Children are not admitted. Q🛏🚐🍴🎅

Thomson's Bar ✅
182-184 Morrison Street, EH3 8EB (W of centre)
🕙 12-11.30 (midnight Thu & Sat; 1am Fri); 4-11.30 Sun
☎ (0131) 228 5700 ⊕ thomsonsbaredinburgh.co.uk
Caledonian Deuchars IPA; Fyne Jarl Ⓗ; **4 changing beers (sourced nationally; often Alechemy, Oakham, Swannay)** Ⓗ/Ⓐ
Superb single-roomed bar modelled on the style of Glasgow architect Alexander 'Greek' Thomson. The walls are decorated with rare mirrors, adverts and point of sale material from long-forgotten breweries. The bar is a member of Oakham Ales' Oakademy, and up to six, often hoppy, real ales are served from a variety of breweries. No food is served on Sunday and pies only on Saturday. Children are not admitted.
Q✿🕙≉(Haymarket)🛏♣🚐🍴🎅

Edinburgh: East

Regent
2 Montrose Terrace, EH7 5DL (1 mile E of centre)
🕙 12-1am; 12.30-1am Sun ☎ (0131) 661 8198
⊕ theregentbar.co.uk
Caledonian Deuchars IPA; 2 changing beers (sourced nationally) Ⓗ
Large tenement bar with two rooms, popular with LGBT real ale drinkers. The comfortable seating includes banquettes, leather sofas and armchairs. Real ales are served without sparklers on request. The cider is Westons Old Rosie. Bar snacks and simple meals, including good vegetarian and vegan options, are available all day. A novel slant

on pub games is the gymnastic pommel horse. Children over 5 are permitted until 8pm.
🎅🕙♣🚐🍴🐾🎅🎶

Edinburgh: North

Cask & Barrel
115 Broughton Street, EH1 3RZ (E of New Town)
🕙 11-12.30am (1am Thu-Sat); 12.30-12.30am Sun
☎ (0131) 556 3132
Caledonian Deuchars IPA; Edinburgh Castle 80/-; Draught Bass; Swannay Orkney Best; house beer (by Hadrian Border); 5 changing beers (sourced nationally) Ⓗ
Spacious and busy alehouse drawing a varied clientele of all ages, ranging from business people to football fans. The interior features an imposing horseshoe bar, bare floorboards, a splendid cornice and a collection of brewery mirrors. Old barrels serve as tables. The guest beers, often from smaller Scottish breweries, come in a range of strengths and styles. Sparklers can be removed on request. Children are not permitted.
✿🕙&≉(Waverley)🛏(York Place)🚐🎅

Kay's Bar ✅
39 Jamaica Street West, EH3 6HF (New Town, off India Street)
🕙 11-midnight (1am Fri & Sat); 12.30-11 Sun
☎ (0131) 225 1858 ⊕ kaysbar.co.uk
Caledonian Deuchars IPA; Fyne Jarl; Theakston Best Bitter; 4 changing beers (sourced nationally; often Cross Borders, Fyne, Timothy Taylor) Ⓗ
A cosy and convivial pub, hidden away in the new town, that retains many features from its days as a Victorian wine merchant and that is decorated with whisky barrels. Considering its size it offers an impressive range of real ales. It also specialises in malt whisky, with a large selection behind the bar. If the front bar is busy, try the small room at the back. Lunches consist mainly of traditional Scottish fare. Children are not admitted. Dogs are not permitted 12-2.30pm. Q🕙♣🚐🐾🎅

Malt & Hops
45 The Shore, Leith, EH6 6QU (1½ miles N of centre)
🕙 12-11 (midnight Wed & Thu; 1am Fri & Sat); 12.30-11 Sun
☎ (0131) 555 0083 ⊕ barcalisa.com
8 changing beers (sourced nationally; often Fallen, Hadrian Border, Swannay) Ⓗ
Single-roomed, old-fashioned bar by the Water of Leith dating from 1747. The walls are bedecked with mirrors, prints and beer-related artefacts. A large collection of pumpclips, many from long-lost breweries and distilleries, hangs from the ceiling along with hop bines that are renewed every harvest. The wide variety of real ales has an emphasis on smaller breweries. Bar snacks including toasties are always available. Children are welcome until 6pm. 🎅🎶♣🚐🐾🎅🎶

Stockbridge Tap
2-4 Raeburn Place, Stockbridge, EH4 1HN (N of centre)
🕙 12-midnight (1am Fri & Sat); 12.30-midnight Sun
☎ (0131) 343 3000
Swannay Island Hopping; 6 changing beers (sourced nationally; often Alechemy, Cromarty, Oakham) Ⓗ
Very much a specialist real ale house, the pub offers interesting ales from all over the UK and holds occasional beer festivals. The L-shaped room, with a bright bar area, boasts mirrors from lost breweries including Murray's and Campbell's. There is plenty of seating and ample space for vertical

drinking. No food is served on Monday or Tuesday. Children are not admitted. Closing time may be a little earlier if quiet. CAMRA Edinburgh Pub of the Year 2017. ◑♿♣🚪😺🛜

Teuchters Landing

1c Dock Place, Leith, EH6 6LU (2 miles N of centre)
🕑 10.30-1am ☎ (0131) 554 7427 ⊕ aroomin.co.uk/teuchters-landing-bar-edinburgh
Caledonian Deuchars IPA; Fyne Jarl; Inveralmond Ossian; Timothy Taylor Landlord; 2 changing beers (sourced regionally; often Fallen, Knops, Stewart) Ⓗ
Formerly the waiting room for the Leith to Aberdeen ferry, the attractive bar has a wood-panelled ceiling edged with tiles featuring random Scottish place names from Teuchterland. There are also some smaller rooms and a large conservatory extension that opens out onto a pontoon floating on the Water of Leith. The food menu, available all day, includes meals served in small or large mugs. An excellent selection of malt whiskies is available. Alcohol is served from 11am. ▷☺◑♿♣🚪😺🛜

Edinburgh: South

Bennets Bar ★

8 Leven Street, EH3 9LG (SW of centre)
🕑 12-1am ☎ (0131) 229 5143
⊕ bennetsbaredinburgh.co.uk
Caledonian Deuchars IPA; Harviestoun Bitter & Twisted Ⓗ**, Schiehallion** Ⓟ**; Orkney Dark Island** Ⓗ**; 3 changing beers** Ⓟ
One of the city's top pub interiors and housed in a Grade B listed building, this is the zenith of late Victorian Edinburgh pub architecture, from the Jeffrey's Brewery etched door panels and window screens to the snug and magnificent gantry, which houses a top class range of malts and spirit barrels. Daytime food is typically pub grub but in the evening a restaurant-style menu is available.
Q▷◑🚪😺🛜

Cask & Barrel (Southside)

24-26 West Preston Street, EH8 9PZ (1 mile S of centre)
🕑 12-midnight (1am Fri); 11-1am Sat; 12.30-midnight Sun
☎ (0131) 667 0856
Caledonian Deuchars IPA; Swannay Orkney Best; Tryst Drovers 80/-; 5 changing beers (sourced nationally; often Ayr, Hardknott, Loch Lomond) Ⓗ
Modern re-creation of a Scottish city or tenement bar. The single room, with windows front and back, is divided by a horseshoe bar with a dark-wood gantry adorned with decorative wooden casks. The walls feature a fine range of old photos, framed advertisements and historic brewery and distillery mirrors. A good place to try real ales from interesting breweries UK-wide. Children are not admitted. CAMRA Edinburgh Pub of the Year runner-up in 2016. 🚉(York Pl)🚪🛜

Cloisters Bar

26 Brougham Street, EH3 9JH (SW of centre)
🕑 12-midnight (1am Fri & Sat); 12.30-midnight Sun
☎ (0131) 221 9997 ⊕ cloistersbar.com
Stewart Pentland IPA; Holy Grale; 7 changing beers (sourced nationally; often Alechemy, Swannay, Thornbridge) Ⓗ
Established in 1995 in the former All Saints Parsonage, many traditional features have been maintained in this warm and friendly bar. The wide range of single malt whiskies, gins and rums does justice to the outstanding gantry. The real ales are generally from interesting breweries UK-wide.

Frequent beer festivals and Meet the Brewer events are held. Meals are freshly prepared (no food Mon or Sun eve). Under-16s are not admitted. Q◑♣🚪😺🛜

Dagda Bar

93-95 Buccleuch Street, EH8 9NG (S of centre)
🕑 12.30-1am; 1-1am Sun ☎ (0131) 667 9773
4 changing beers (sourced regionally; often Oakham, Orkney, Tryst) Ⓗ
Small ground-floor bar in an 18th-century tenement terrace, in the heart of a university area. A stone-flagged floor surrounds the large rectangular counter which takes up at least a third of the room. The colourful, mirrored gantry blends with the cornice – the joins blurred by a collection of pumpclips. Children are not admitted. ♣🚪😺🛜

John Leslie (Leslie's Bar) ★

45-47 Ratcliffe Terrace, EH9 1SU (1½ miles S of centre)
🕑 11-midnight (1am Fri & Sat) ☎ (0131) 667 7205
⊕ realalepubedinburgh.co.uk
Caledonian Deuchars IPA; Timothy Taylor Landlord; house beer (by Allendale); 3 changing beers Ⓗ
In the basement of a four-storey tenement, a fine mahogany counter, mirrored snob screen and clock divide this bar in two. The bar has an alcove with banquettes while the lounge has three areas – a small snug by the door, an area around the fire and a quieter corner with more banquettes. The late-19th-century decorative plasterwork, including a Lincrusta frieze, and the snob screen suggest the bar once catered for a genteel Victorian clientele. Food is served all day. ▷◑♣🚪😺🛜

Edinburgh: West

Athletic Arms (Diggers) ✔

1-3 Angle Park Terrace, EH11 2JX (1 mile SW of centre)
🕑 11-1am ☎ (0131) 337 3822 ⊕ athleticarms.com
Caledonian Deuchars IPA; Stewart 80/- Ⓐ**; 4 changing beers (sourced nationally; often Alechemy, Caledonian)** Ⓗ
Situated between two graveyards, the name Diggers became synonymous with this Edinburgh pub legend which opened in 1897. Banquette seating lines the walls and a compass features on the floor. A smaller back room has a dartboard and further seating – children are welcome here if dining. Quieter now than in its heyday, it gets packed when Hearts are at home. The pies are outstanding. ▷♣🚪😺🛜

Golden Rule ✔

30 Yeaman Place, EH11 1BT (1 mile W of centre)
🕑 12-midnight (1am Fri & Sat); 12.30-midnight Sun
☎ (0131) 229 3413 ⊕ goldenruleedinburgh.co.uk
Stewart Jack Back; 4 changing beers (sourced nationally; often Drygate, Magic Rock, Stewart) Ⓗ
A split-level Victorian tenement bar close to the Union Canal and the Fountain Park entertainment complex. The pub is a real ale showcase, with a great selection from breweries UK-wide. The upstairs bar is pleasantly furnished. The downstairs bar comes into its own at weekends, but real ale has to be carried down the steps. There is live music on Saturday evening and a quiz on Tuesday evening. Children are not admitted. 😺♣🚪😺🛜

Roseburn Bar

1 Roseburn Terrace, EH12 5NG (1½ miles W of centre)
🕑 9am-11 (midnight Thu-Sat); 11-11 Sun
☎ (0131) 337 1067 ⊕ roseburnbar.co.uk

Caledonian Deuchars IPA; Fyne Jarl; 2 changing beers (sourced nationally) ⊞

A traditional pub that is popular with locals. It boasts high ceilings and a largely wooden interior. There are numerous comfortable booths along the walls and two separate lounge areas. Three TVs show sporting events, though the volume is typically kept low. Live music plays on Friday and Saturday evenings. Close to Murrayfield for rugby and also handy for Tynecastle for football. Children are not admitted. ⊛₺옷묘☜令

Gorebridge

Stobsmill Inn (Bruntons)
25 Powdermill Brae, EH23 4HX (S of town)
🕑 12-11 (11.30 Mon & Thu; midnight Fri & Sat); 12.30-11 Sun
☎ (01875) 820202
1 changing beer (sourced nationally; often Kelburn, Stewart, Tryst) ⊞

Built in 1866 as a public house, the single-room wood-floored bar has one area containing a long L-shaped counter lined with stools and another with bench seating, tables and chairs. Wooden panels engraved with sporting scenes hide an intriguingly tiny jug bar. The single real ale is often from a smaller Scottish brewery. Simple bar snacks are available at all times. Over-21s only.
⊛⇌♣P묘(29,33)☜令

Haddington

Golf Tavern
5 Bridge Street, EH41 4AU
🕑 11-11 (midnight Thu; 1am Fri & Sat) ☎ (01620) 822327
⊕ golftavernhaddington.co.uk
1 changing beer (sourced regionally; often Broughton, Knops, Tryst) ⊞

A traditional locals' bar nestling behind the Waterside Bistro on the eastern side of the River Tyne. The public bar has a pool table and dartboard. The one handpump is likely to feature a Scottish real ale. The spacious lounge acts mainly as a popular restaurant and function room. Food, renowned for its generous portions, is available all day Saturday and until 7pm on Sunday.
👈🛏◑₺♣묘令

Juniper Green

Juniper Green Inn
542 Lanark Road, EH14 5EL
🕑 11-midnight (11 Mon & Tue); 12.30-11 Sun
☎ (0131) 458 5395
Caledonian Deuchars IPA; Timothy Taylor Landlord; 2 changing beers (sourced nationally; often Black Isle, Fuller's, Hadrian Border) ⊞

Well-appointed, single-room lounge bar in a late-1800s building, with a strong community spirit. The decor is clean and attractive throughout. The mahogany bar counter has a more modern gantry to match. A secluded patio and garden are popular in summer. The varied menu includes meal deals. Children over 12 are permitted if dining.
Q👈⊛◑묘令

> 'I think now would be a good time for a beer' – **Franklin Delano Roosevelt, 15 December 1933, on the day Prohibition ended**

Lasswade

Laird & Dog Inn ✓
5 High Street, EH18 1NA (on A768 near river)
🕑 11-11 (midnight Thu; 1am Fri & Sat); 11-12.30am Sun
☎ (0131) 663 9219 ⊕ lairdanddoginn.co.uk
3 changing beers (sourced regionally; often Clockwork Beer Co, Stewart) ⊞

Comfortable village local, just five miles from central Edinburgh. It caters for all tastes, with different areas for a quiet drink, a meal, or a game of pool accompanied by music. There is also a conservatory restaurant with an unusual bottle-shaped well by the entrance. The three guest ales are usually from smaller breweries.
👈⊛🛏◑₺♣P묘☜令

Linlithgow

Four Marys ✓
65-67 High Street, EH49 7ED
🕑 11-11 (11.30 Wed & Thu; 1am Fri & Sat); 12.30-11 Sun
☎ (01506) 842147 ⊕ thefourmarys.co.uk
Belhaven St Andrew's Ale; Caledonian Deuchars IPA; 6 changing beers (sourced regionally) ⊞

A stone's throw from Linlithgow Palace, birthplace of Mary Queen of Scots, the building dates back to around 1500. The pub is named after the Queen's ladies-in-waiting. Initially a dwelling house, the building has had several changes of use over the years – at one time it was a chemist's run by the Waldie family whose most famous member, David, helped establish the anaesthetic properties of chloroform in 1847. Q⊛◑⇌묘令

Linlithgow Tap
111 High Street, EH49 7AB
🕑 11-11 (midnight Wed & Thu; 1am Fri & Sat)
☎ (01506) 843590
Fyne Jarl; Orkney Dark Island; 4 changing beers (sourced regionally; often Belhaven, Inveralmond, Kinneil) ⊞

Situated a short distance west of Lithgae Cross and formerly known as the Footballers & Cricketers Arms, the pub underwent a makeover in 2015 and introduced six real ale taps. The stained-glass panels of footballer and cricketer have been replaced by clear glass windows, with a window depicting a footballer to the side. The pub has an island bar and there is a map of old Linlithgow on the ceiling. Snacks are available, and music plays on Friday and Saturday nights. ⇌묘☜令

Platform 3 🄻 ✓
1A High Street, EH49 7AB
🕑 10.30-midnight (1am Fri & Sat); 12.30-midnight Sun
☎ (01506) 847405 ⊕ platform3.co.uk
Caledonian Deuchars IPA; 2 changing beers (sourced regionally; often Cairngorm, Harviestoun, Stewart) ⊞

Small, friendly hostelry on the railway station approach, originally the public bar of the hotel next door and renovated in 1998 as a pub in its own right. Look for the goods train that journeys from the station above the bar. Two Scottish beers are served in addition to the regular ale. Dogs are welcome, with biscuits 'on tap'. A live train departures board keeps travellers informed. Alcohol is served from 11am (12.30pm Sun).
⇌묘☜令

Lothianbridge

Sun Inn

EH22 4TR (on A7 near Newtongrange)
🕒 8am-11 (midnight Fri & Sat) ☎ (0131) 663 2456
🌐 thesuninnedinburgh.co.uk
2 changing beers (sourced regionally; often Alechemy, Kelburn, Stewart) Ⓗ
A well-appointed award-winning gastro-pub overlooked by the impressive 23-span Waverley Line viaduct. The tasteful interior has a mixture of exposed stone, papered walls, wooden floors and carpets. A new bar area for drinkers and a function room/coffee shop overlooking the river opened in 2017. Meals are served all day on Sunday until 7pm and breakfast and afternoon tea are available during the week. The bar may close earlier if quiet. Alcohol is available from 11am.
🕭😷🖂�𝄞🖐ㅅ☇P🖵(29,39)🌞🛜

Musselburgh

David MacBeth Moir ✅

Bridge Street, EH21 6AG (opp The Brunton)
🕒 8am-11 (midnight Thu; 1am Fri & Sat) ☎ (0131) 653 1060
Caledonian Deuchars IPA; 4 changing beers (sourced nationally) Ⓗ
Wetherspoon pub named after a local physician and writer, set in a former cinema dating back to 1935. Many original features have been beautifully restored, and the vast single-room bar is filled with Art Deco cinema-themed artefacts. Food is available all day. Last entry may be restricted on Friday and Saturday. Alcohol is served from 11am (12.30pm Sun). Q🕭😷🖂𝄞ㅅ🖐🖵🛜

Levenhall Arms

10 Ravensheugh Road, EH21 7PP (on B1348, 1 mile E of centre)
🕒 12-11 (midnight Thu; 1am Fri & Sat); 12.30-midnight Sun
☎ (0131) 665 3220
Inveralmond Ossian Ⓐ**; 2 changing beers (sourced regionally; often Knops, Sonnet 43, Strathaven)** Ⓗ/Ⓐ
A three-roomed hostelry dating from 1830 and close to the racecourse. The lively, cheerfully decorated public bar is half timber-panelled and carpeted. Dominoes is popular here and there is a TV for sporting events. A smaller area leads off, with a dartboard and pictures of old local industries. The pleasant lounge has a hardwood floor and comfortable seating. Expect to find some interesting beers from smaller, mainly Scottish breweries. A quiz is held on the penultimate Sunday of the month. Q🕭😷🌞ㅅ♣P🖵🌞🛜

Volunteer Arms (Staggs) 🍺

81 North High Street, EH21 6JE (behind The Brunton)
🕒 12-11 (11.30 Thu; midnight Fri); 11-midnight Sat; 12.30-11 Sun ☎ (0131) 665 9654 🌐 staggsbar.com
Oakham JHB, Bishops Farewell; 4 changing beers (sourced nationally) Ⓗ
Superb pub run by the same family since 1858. The bar and snug are traditional, with wooden floors, wood panelling and mirrors from defunct local breweries. The attractive gantry is topped with old casks. The more modern lounge opens at the weekend. The real ales, mostly pale and hoppy but one often darker, change regularly. Local CAMRA Pub of the Year 2017 and a winner of many previous awards – see the bar wall. Children are permitted until 7pm. 🕭😷♣🖐🖵🌞🛜

Newtongrange

Dean Tavern

80 Main Street, EH22 4NA
🕒 11-11 Mon; 9am-11 (midnight Fri & Sat); 10-11 Sun
☎ (0131) 663 2419 🌐 deantavern.co.uk
1 changing beer (sourced regionally; often Born in the Borders, Inveralmond, Stewart) Ⓗ
Superb pub run by trustees using the Gothenburg public house system, with the profits returned to the local community. The large, light and airy bar area was designed to help miners recover from their day in darkness, with roof lights in a high ceiling supported by arched iron beams. There is also the Lamp Room restaurant, and a function room with a large mural depicting the town's mining past. Children are permitted until 8pm if dining. Alcohol is served from 11am (12.30pm Sun). 🕭😷𝄞ㅅㅈ♣🖵🌞🛜

North Berwick

Nether Abbey Hotel

20 Dirleton Avenue, EH39 4BQ (on A198, W of centre)
🕒 9am-11 (midnight Thu; 1am Fri & Sat) ☎ (01620) 892802
🌐 netherabbey.co.uk
Knops East Coast Pale; 3 changing beers (sourced nationally; often Stewart, Timothy Taylor, Williams Bros) Ⓗ
Busy, family-run hotel in a stone-built villa, offering a bright, contemporary, open-plan interior. The Fly Half Bar is in a split-level glass extension, with large folding doors opening out onto the patio. Real ales are often from Scottish breweries – sparklers can be removed on request. The upper central area is an award-winning restaurant. The Nethers is famous for its good, freshly cooked and locally sourced food, available all day Friday to Sunday. Alcohol is served from 11am.
🕭😷🖂𝄞ㅅㅈP🖵(124,X24)🌞🛜

Ship Inn ✅

7-9 Quality Street, EH39 4HJ (at E end of town)
🕒 11-11 (1am Thu-Sat) ☎ (01620) 890699 🌐 50mls.co.uk/ship-inn
Harviestoun Schiehallion; 3 changing beers (sourced nationally; often Greene King, Stewart, Theakston) Ⓗ
Spacious, open-plan bar with a wide variety of seating and tables. The bar area has pine floorboards, a mahogany counter and a dark-stained wooden gantry. To the side and rear is a quieter carpeted area. The pub is popular for food, with good vegetarian options, served all day until 8pm (earlier in winter). Sparklers are happily removed on request. 🕭😷𝄞🖵🌞🛜

Prestonpans

Prestoungrange Gothenburg ★

227 High Street, EH32 9BE (W edge of town)
🕒 closed Mon; 12-2.30 Tue; 12-2.30, 5-11 Wed; 11-11 Thu, Fri & Sun; 11-midnight Sat ☎ (01875) 819922
3 changing beers (sourced locally; often Kentwood) Ⓗ
Superb Gothenburg pub listed on CAMRA's National Inventory of Historic Pub Interiors with a magnificent painted ceiling in the bar. The on-site microbrewery, which can be viewed from the bar, is now used by Kentwood brewing to produce the in-house real ales. There is an upstairs lounge and function room with superb views over the Forth. Meals include gluten-free options.
🕭😷𝄞ㅅP🖵🌞🛜

GREATER GLASGOW & CLYDE VALLEY

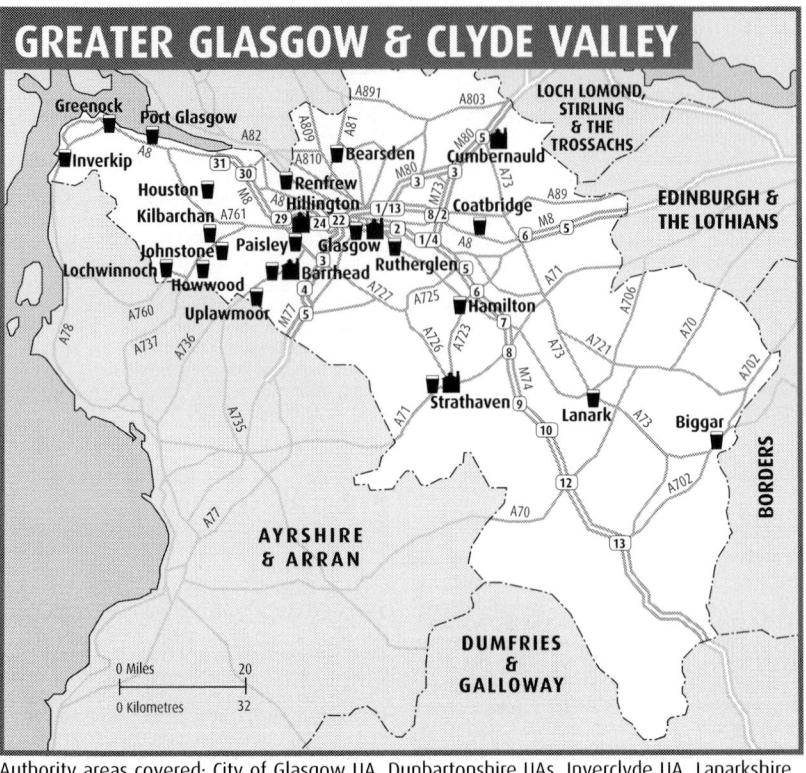

Authority areas covered: City of Glasgow UA, Dunbartonshire UAs, Inverclyde UA, Lanarkshire UAs, Renfrewshire UAs

Barrhead

Cross Stobs Inn ⓛ

2-6 Grahamston Road, G78 1NS (jct of B771/B774)
☼ 11-11 (midnight Thu & Sat; 1am Fri); 12.30-11 Sun
☎ (0141) 881 1581 ⊕ crossstobsinn.co.uk
2 changing beers (often Kelburn) Ⓗ
Eighteenth-century coaching inn on the road to Paisley. The public bar has a real coal fire and retains much of its original charm with antique furniture and service bells. The spacious lounge is mostly used for dining and leads to an enclosed garden to the rear. There is also an outside drinking area at the front. A pool room and function suite are situated off the public bar.
৬🏠🕪৬⇌P🚲(54,101)🛜

Bearsden

Burnbrae ✅

281 Milngavie Road, G61 3EA
☼ 7am-11 (midnight Fri); 8am-11 Sat & Sun
☎ (0141) 942 5951
6 changing beers (sourced nationally; often Greene King) Ⓗ
Relatively recently built but old world-style pub-restaurant with real fires and oak beams, situated in front of a Premier Inn. The interior is open plan with several distinct areas mostly for dining but there is space around the bar for drinkers. The licensee is enthusiastic about real ale and runs a mini festival every Easter with a stillage set up in the bar. Alcohol is served from 11am (12.30pm Sun). ৬🏠🛏🍴৬৬P🚲(60A)🐾🛜

Biggar

Crown Inn 🏆 ✅

109-111 High Street, ML12 6DL
☼ 9am-1am ☎ (01899) 220116 ⊕ thecrownbiggar.co.uk
6 changing beers (sourced nationally) Ⓗ
Attractive, long-established 17th century coaching inn in the centre of a small, historic market town situated in rolling hills just north of the Southern Uplands. Recently modernised and refurbished, the central bar now serves a wide, almost Q-shaped seating area. The beer range has also widened significantly, with six handpumps offering ales from the Borders, around Glasgow, and further afield. There is live music every second Friday and a beer festival twice a year. Current local CAMRA Pub of the Year. ৬🏠🕪🍴🚲(191)🐾🛜

Elphinstone Hotel ✅

145 High Street, ML12 6DL
☼ 11-1am ☎ (01899) 220044 ⊕ elphinstonehotel.co.uk
3 changing beers (sourced regionally; often Broughton, Fyne, Strathaven) Ⓗ
A coaching inn with a history going back over 400 years in the centre of this small market town. Three handpumps are to be found in the public bar, the Elph, which is an L-shaped room offering comfortable seating and an impressive logburner at the front and pool and other games towards the back. The ales can also be carried through to the lounge and, weather permitting, to the terrace at the back. 🏠🛏🕪🍴🚲(191)🐾🛜

Coatbridge

Vulcan ✓
181 Main Street, ML5 3HH (jct with Dunbeth Rd)
🕐 8am-midnight (1am Thu-Sat) ☎ (01236) 437972
Greene King Abbot; 5 changing beers (sourced nationally) Ⓗ
Fairly modern Wetherspoon establishment in the town centre at the end of the main street, named after the first iron-built boat that used to travel on the Monkland Canal. It is modest in size compared to many in the chain – the building was previously a pub and it retains an intimate atmosphere. A good selection and variety of beers are offered.
🏃😋🌙◐♿🚲(Sunnyside)🅿🍴🛏�widefi

Glasgow

Babbity Bowster
16-18 Blackfriars Street, Merchant City, G1 1PE
🕐 11-midnight; 12.30-midnight Sun ☎ (0141) 552 5055
🌐 babbitybowster.com
3 changing beers (sourced regionally; often Fyne) Ⓗ
This Adams-designed merchant's house dating from 1790 was saved from demolition and restored as a bar, restaurant and hotel in the early 1980s. It is named after an 18th-century Scottish dance, reflecting the building's vintage. The bright, airy bar offers three cask beers from Scottish breweries and serves good-quality food all day. There is traditional music on Wednesday and Saturday afternoons, and jazz on alternate Sundays. The pleasant beer garden has a boules alley.
Q😋🛏🍴◐🚲(High St)🚆🚌🛏

Blackfriars Ⓛ
36 Bell Street, Merchant City, G1 1LG
🕐 11-midnight; 12.30-midnight Sun ☎ (0141) 552 5924
🌐 blackfriarsglasgow.com
5 changing beers (sourced nationally; often Kelburn) Ⓗ
Vibrant pub in the centre of the Merchant City area. The bar has three main areas – the central bar, a brighter café-style corner overlooking the streets, and a quieter rear area suited to dining. Five handpumps serve beers from all over the UK, with an emphasis on Scottish brewers, generally including one beer from the Kelburn brewery. There is a good selection of American and European bottled beers. Live music features on Tuesday and Sunday nights.
◐♿🚲(High St)🚌🍴🛏widefi

Bon Accord Ⓛ
153 North Street, Charing Cross, G3 7DA
🕐 11-midnight; 12.30-midnight Sun ☎ (0141) 248 4427
🌐 bonaccordpub.com
Caledonian Deuchars IPA; 8 changing beers (sourced nationally; often Lawman) Ⓗ
The first stop for many beer enthusiasts when visiting Glasgow, the Bon Accord has long been renowned for its commitment to real ale, and now sells more than 1,000 different ales annually. Complementing the ale is an impressive range of 400 malts which has led to its recognition as one of the top whisky bars in Britain. A recent addition is the online whisky shop. Food is served all day, quiz night is Wednesday and bands play on Saturday night. 🏃😋◐♿🚲(Charing Cross)🚌🍴🛏widefi

Clockwork Beer Co Ⓛ ✓
Cathcart Road, Mount Florida, G42 9HB
🕐 11-midnight ☎ (0141) 649 0184
Clockwork Beer Co Original Amber, Cartside Red, Craft Lager, Oregon IPA, Hampden Roar; house beer (by Clockwork Beer Company); 4 changing beers (sourced regionally; often Clockwork Beer Co) Ⓐ
Brewpub close to Hampden Park with a bar, a raised area mainly for meals and a balcony upstairs with a large screen for sporting events. Families are welcome. A glass roof keeps the pub light and airy. Parts of the brewery are visible and tours are available on request. There is open mic on Monday, quiz night on Thursday and live music on the last Friday of the month.
🏃😋◐♿🚲(Mount Florida)🅿🚌widefi

Drum & Monkey ✓
91-93 St Vincent Street, G2 5TF
🕐 11-11 (midnight Fri & Sat) ☎ (0141) 221 6636
St Austell Nicholson's Pale Ale; 4 changing beers (sourced nationally) Ⓗ
Upmarket Nicholson's pub handy both for Central and Queen Street stations; this former bank dating from 1924 has an opulent marble and wood-panelled interior and an ornate ceiling. The large U-shaped central bar featuring five handpumps is often busy, particularly with the after-work crowd in the early evening. There are two raised seating areas and an extra dining room at the rear. Toilets are down a spiral staircase. Food is served all day until 10pm. ◐♿🚲(Central)🚌🛏widefi

Drygate Ⓛ
85 Drygate, Dennistoun, G4 0UT (off John Knox St)
🕐 11-midnight ☎ (0141) 212 8815 🌐 drygate.com
Drygate Pale Duke, Seven Peaks; 2 changing beers (sourced nationally; often Drygate) Ⓗ
Large brewpub just east of the Merchant City offering Drygate beers and guests. The majority of space is for diners – the food is excellent – but the bar area, from where you can view the brewery, is popular with drinkers. An upstairs beer hall is used for various events including live music, and there is a roof terrace for outdoor drinking. The bottle shop has a fine selection of beers to take away.
🏃😋◐♿🚲(High St)🅿🚌🛏widefi

Hengler's Circus ✓
351-363 Sauchiehall Street, Charing Cross, G2 3HU
🕐 8am-midnight ☎ (0141) 331 9810
Greene King Abbot; Sharp's Doom Bar; 12 changing beers (sourced nationally) Ⓗ
Situated in Sauchiehall Street to the west of the city centre, this Wetherspoon pub is thriving in a competitive area. The L-shaped bar is usually fairly busy with diners at lunchtimes, and in the evenings, especially at the weekend, the clientele is a mix of older folk and young people enjoying a drink before going on to nearby clubs. Staff are keen to supply what the customers request so the regular beers are supplemented by an eclectic mix of guests. Q🏃😋◐♿🚲(Charing Cross)🚌🛏widefi

REAL ALE BREWERIES	
Clockwork 🍺	Glasgow
Drygate 🍺	Glasgow
Jaw	Hillington
Kelburn	Barrhead
Lawman	Cumbernauld
Shilling 🍺	Glasgow (NEW)
Strathaven	Strathaven
WEST 🍺	Glasgow

Hippo Taproom

323 Sauchiehall Street, G2 3HW (opp bus stop at Dental Hospital)

🌐 12-midnight; 12.30-midnight Sun ☎ (0141) 353 3400

🌐 hippotaproom.co.uk

3 changing beers (sourced nationally) Ⓗ

Friendly, unpretentious basement bar with booths and tables, opened in 2016 and aimed squarely at serious beer aficionados. Knowledgable staff are happy to recommend beers and offer tasters, and regular beer events are held with the newest start-up breweries. Pork pies, cheese platters and other snacks are available. ≈(Charing Cross)🏠🚌♣🛜

Inn Deep

445 Great Western Road, Hillhead, G12 8HH

🌐 12-midnight; 12-11 Sun ☎ (0141) 357 1075

🌐 inndeep.com

3 changing beers (sourced nationally; often Williams Bros) Ⓟ

Situated below the Great Western Road and occupying railway arches beside the River Kelvin, Inn Deep is a modern pub. The three cask ales, served from the tall founts near the riverside entrance, are usually from small breweries around the country, with Williams beers regularly available. Although a bit on the pricey side, the pub makes an ideal place for cyclists and walkers to take a break. 🐕❄️◑🚲🌳🚌(20,6)♣🛜

Laurieston Bar ★ Ⓛ

58 Bridge Street, Tradeston, G5 9HU

🌐 11-11; 12.30-11 Sun ☎ (0141) 429 4528

Fyne Jarl; 2 changing beers (sourced locally; often Fyne, Jaw) Ⓗ

Friendly and unpretentious, this is a welcome oasis in an area of Glasgow otherwise devoid of pubs, let alone real ale. It is owned by brothers whose family have been in the pub trade for generations. The horseshoe bar is surrounded by formica-top tables and walls covered in vintage photographs, mirrors, memorabilia and the occasional painting. Dogs are welcome. Listed in CAMRA's National Inventory of Historic Pub Interiors and Scotland's True Heritage Pubs. ≈(Central)🏠🚌♣🛜

Mulberry St

778 Pollokshaws Road, Strathbungo, G41 2AE

🌐 11-11 (midnight Fri & Sat); 12.30-11 Sun

☎ (0141) 424 0858 🌐 mulberry.st

Harviestoun Bitter & Twisted; 2 changing beers (sourced locally; often Fyne) Ⓗ

This community pub in the conservation area of Strathbungo is conveniently placed near to Queens Park. It has a snug comfortable bar and an excellent bistro, with a varied menu available throughout. In good weather the alfresco drinking area on the pavement surrounding the pub proves popular. The third guest beer is usually only available in summer. A quiz is hosted every Monday. 🐕◑≈(Queens Park)🚌♣🛜

Pot Still Ⓛ

154 Hope Street, G2 2TH

🌐 11-midnight ☎ (0141) 333 0980 🌐 thepotstill.co.uk

4 changing beers (sourced regionally) Ⓗ

A gem of a pub going back 150 years. Locally known as the Whisky Pub, connoisseurs come from all over the world to sample rare malts from the hundreds covering various shelves, accessed by bar staff via a ladder. Four varying ales are available, normally from Scottish breweries. Good-value pies, with peas or beans, are served, along with soup

and sandwiches, with a more limited selection after 5pm. Dogs are welcome, except when the pub is busy. ◑≈(Central)🏠🚌♣🛜

Raven

81-85 Renfield Street, G2 1LP

🌐 12-11 (midnight Thu-Sat) ☎ (0141) 332 6151

🌐 theravenglasgow.co.uk

3 changing beers (sourced nationally) Ⓗ

Modern pub, opened in 2014, situated close to the main shopping areas. It offers a light and airy split-level bar and separate restaurant with both bench and table seating. A mezzanine level provides extra dining space and a function room and bar. The beers are predominately Scottish from smaller breweries and often local. Meet the Brewer nights are held regularly. Barbecue food is served throughout the day cooked in the smokehouse. 🐕◑🦽≈(Queen St)🏠🚌🛜

Sir John Moore

260-292 Argyle Street, G2 8QW

🌐 7am-midnight; 8am-midnight Sat & Sun

☎ (0141) 222 1780

8 changing beers (sourced nationally) Ⓗ

Close to Central Station's Hope Street and Argyle Street exits, this Wetherspoon pub is an ideal place to wait for a train from either the high- or low-level platforms. Converted from several shops, it has a number of distinct areas on different levels and a covered outdoor area overlooking the busy street. It is named after a Glasgow-born soldier whose likeness was cast from brass cannons and whose statue was the first to be unveiled in George Square in 1819. ❄️◑🦽≈(Central)🚲🚌🛜

Sir John Stirling Maxwell ⊘

136-140 Kilmarnock Road, Shawlands, G41 3NN

🌐 8am-midnight ☎ (0141) 636 9024

Caledonian Deuchars IPA; Greene King Abbot; Sharp's Doom Bar; 7 changing beers (sourced nationally; often Kelburn) Ⓗ

Wetherspoon supermarket conversion in an elevated position overlooking the main shopping street in Shawlands. The wide-ranging choice of beers usually includes dark and/or strong ales. The pub is split level with a raised area to the rear popular with families during the day and primarily used for dining, although food is served throughout. The lower level is favoured by a more mixed clientele and has a good community feel. A constantly busy pub that never feels too crowded. Alcohol is served from 11am. 🐕◑🦽≈(Pollokshaws East)🍴🚌🛜

State Bar

148 Holland Street, Charing Cross, G2 4NG (just off Sauchiehall Street, opp The Hengler's Circus)

🌐 12-midnight ☎ (0141) 332 2159

House beer (by Stewart Brewing); 6 changing beers (sourced nationally; often Oakham) Ⓗ

CAMRA branch Pub of the Year for the past three years, this popular town-centre bar gets busy at lunchtimes and at the weekend. It has a traditional island bar, offering a changing range of beers often unusual for Glasgow, usually including at least one from Oakham. The pub's proximity to the King's Theatre is reflected in old pictures and show bills displayed around the walls. There is a weekly blues session on Tuesday in the main bar and a comedy club in the small bar downstairs on Friday. ◑🦽≈(Charing Cross)🏠🚌🛜

Tennents

191 Byres Road, Hillhead, G12 8TN
🕓 10-11 (midnight Thu-Sat) ☎ (0141) 339 7203
🌐 thetennentsbarglasgow.co.uk
Belhaven 80/- Ale; Caledonian Deuchars IPA; Draught Bass; Harviestoun Bitter & Twisted; St Austell Tribute; Timothy Taylor Landlord; 3 changing beers (sourced nationally) Ⓗ
Large traditional pub situated at a busy junction in the centre of the West End in the shadow of Glasgow University. It was established in the 1880s by a member of the Tennent family but not originally associated with the brewery. The open-plan room is dominated by the rectangular bar which prominently features 12 handpumps. TV screens show mostly sporting events. A small lounge to one side provides extra seating at busy times. Alcohol is served from 11am. ⓓ&🖨🕏🌞🛜

Three Judges Ⓛ ✅

141 Dumbarton Road, Partick, G11 6PR
🕓 11-midnight ☎ (0141) 337 3055 🌐 threejudges.co.uk
Caledonian Deuchars IPA; 8 changing beers (sourced nationally) Ⓗ
A traditional corner tenement pub at a busy junction which has showcased real ale for over 25 years. A raised area at the front overlooks Partick Cross and provides a stage for Sunday afternoon jazz bands, while there is a quieter area at the rear. Regular beer festivals are held including one dedicated to dark beers, as well as a cider and perry festival. Pork pies are often available and other food can be brought in from nearby takeaways. Q⇌(Partick)🖨🕏🖨🌞🛜

Greenock

James Watt ✅

80-92 Cathcart Street, PA15 1DD
🕓 8am-midnight (1am Fri & Sat); 9am-midnight Sun
☎ (01475) 722640
Greene King Abbot; Sharp's Doom Bar; 4 changing beers Ⓗ
Situated across the road from Greenock Central Station and 200 yards from the bus station, this large open-plan Wetherspoon, in a former post office, is named after one of Greenock's famous sons who improved steam engine technology and has the SI unit of power named after him. The chain's standard value-for-money food is available all day and beer festivals are held at various times throughout the year. This pub is an oasis in a beer desert. ⓓ&⇌🛜

Hamilton

George Bar

18 Campbell Street, ML3 6AS
🕓 12-midnight (1am Fri); 12.30-midnight Sun
☎ (01698) 424225
3 changing beers (sourced nationally; often Strathaven) Ⓗ
This traditional, family-run pub is situated in a pedestrianised area just off the inner ring road in the town. The single-bar room is quite small but full of character. It can be cramped at busy times but there are high tables for those who are standing to rest their drinks. Tasty home-cooked meals are available until 6pm. In warmer weather café-style seating provides extra space outside. ⓓ&⇌(Central)🖨🌞

Houston

Fox & Hounds Ⓛ

South Street, PA6 7EN
🕓 11-midnight (1am Fri & Sat); 12-midnight Sun
☎ (01505) 808604 🌐 foxandhoundshouston.co.uk
5 changing beers (often Kelburn) Ⓗ
Established in 1779, this iconic village pub reopened in December 2015 under new ownership and has been refurbished while retaining many traditional features. Downstairs is the quiet Vixens Bar Lounge and Stables Restaurant, with the Hunters Bar, a sports bar with TV and games, upstairs. Five handpumps downstairs offer beers from across the UK and two handpumps upstairs serve a smaller selection. The old Houston Brewery area is now an open kitchen. Q🕏ⓓ&P🖨🌞

Houston Inn

North Street, PA6 7HF
🕓 11-midnight (1am Fri & Sat) ☎ (01505) 614315
🌐 houston-inn.com
Kelburn Goldihops; 1 changing beer Ⓗ
Friendly village country inn with an L-shaped bar area warmed by a log fire and a separate restaurant. Three handpumps offer a variety of Scottish and occasionally English beers. There is a quiz night each Wednesday and live music on Saturday featuring performers from the local area. Only a short drive from Glasgow, the large restaurant offers flavoursome traditional food made with locally sourced ingredients. 🕏🌞🚙ⓓ&P🖨🌞🛜

Howwood

Boarding House

Main Street, PA9 1BQ
🕓 11-midnight (1am Fri & Sat) ☎ (01505) 703119
🌐 theboardinghouse.co.uk
Kelburn Jaguar; 2 changing beers Ⓗ
A recent renovation has transformed this old coaching inn into an upmarket gastro-pub, building on its reputation for excellent food and considerably expanding its cask ale offering. The comfortable village inn offers meals in the bar as well as the restaurant, which caters for customers looking for something extra special. With friendly staff too, it is both a destination outlet and a hub for the community and surrounding villages. 🌞ⓓ⇌P

Inverkip

Inverkip Hotel

Main Street, PA16 0AS
🕓 11-11 (11.30 Thu-Sat); 12.30-11 Sun ☎ (01475) 521478
🌐 inverkip.co.uk
Fyne Jarl; 1 changing beer Ⓗ
Small, family-run hotel just a short walk from the large Inverkip Marina, making it an ideal staging post for those just messing about on the river or passing through on the way to Largs and the Ayrshire coast. This is the only outlet in the area that regularly sells beer from the Isle of Arran Brewery – the second beer is from another local brewery. 🌞🚙ⓓ⇌P🖨(578,580)🛜

Johnstone

Callum's 🍷 Ⓛ

26 High Street, PA5 8AH

✪ 11-11.30 (1am Fri & Sat); 12.30-midnight Sun
☎ (01505) 322925 ⊕ callums-bar.com
Kelburn Jaguar; Orkney Dark Island; Sharp's Doom Bar; 4 changing beers Ⓗ
An oasis in another real-ale desert, this is a popular town-centre pub offering a friendly welcome and a comfortable atmosphere. A large TV screen shows sporting events. The lounge is set for dining, with themed nights including curry on Thursday. There is a small function room available for private parties and occasional live music at weekends. Two regular beers are offered alongside five changing guests. ★🍴🕭☕🚃🚌(36,38)🛜

Kilbarchan

Trust Inn
8 Low Barholm, PA10 2ET
✪ 12-midnight; 12-1am Fri & Sat ☎ (01505) 702401
⊕ thetrustinn.com
3 changing beers Ⓗ
Small, single-room, local pub in the centre of a conservation village, with old village photographs adorning the walls. A superior bar menu and special promotions mean it can be busy at mealtimes. Live music plays fortnightly on Friday evening, featuring local bands. Children are welcome in the evening until 9pm if dining.
★🍴🕭🚌(38)🛜

Lanark

Clydesdale Inn ✓
15 Bloomgate, ML11 9ET
✪ 9am-midnight (1am Fri & Sat) ☎ (01555) 678740
Caledonian Deuchars IPA; Greene King Abbot; 2 changing beers (sourced nationally) Ⓗ
Old coaching inn built in the late-18th century by local worthies in the centre of the historic old county town. The bar area is quite small but there are several rooms nearby. A former Wetherspoon conversion, it has been bought by a new chain who have retained many of its previous features including the commitment to cask ale. The guest beers are usually Scottish real ales. Meals are available all day until 10pm. Q★🍴🕭⚓🚃🅿🚌🛜

Lochwinnoch

Brown Bull
32 Main Street, PA12 4AH
✪ 12-11 (midnight Fri & Sun); 12.30-11 Sun
☎ (01505) 843250
Harviestoun Bitter & Twisted; 3 changing beers (sourced regionally) Ⓗ
This village pub is a family-run free house more than 200 years old and popular with locals and visitors alike. Quiz night is Tuesday and live music features every second Sunday. An ever-changing choice of four ales is offered, mainly from Scottish breweries. At the rear is a quirky outdoor seating area and garden. The popular upstairs restaurant uses local produce and bar meals are also available. Located close to Lochwinnoch RSPB nature reserve and Castle Semple visitor centre.
Q★🌳🍴🕭☕🚌☕🛜

Paisley

Bull Inn ★ Ⓛ ✓
7 New Street, PA1 1XU
✪ 11-11 (1am Fri & Sat) ☎ (0141) 849 0472

4 changing beers (sourced regionally; often Kelburn, Lerwick, Loch Lomond) Ⓗ
Established in 1901 and identified by CAMRA as having a nationally important historic interior, this is the oldest inn in Paisley. The pub retains many original features including stained-glass windows, three small snugs and a spirit cask gantry, and boasts the only original set of spirit cocks left in Scotland. Four changing guest ales are from the likes of Fyne, Inveralmond, Kelburn, Loch Lomond, Orkney, Skye, Stewart, Strathaven and Lerwick breweries. 🕭🚃🚌☕🛜

Harvies Bar Ⓛ
86 Glasgow Road, PA1 3NU
✪ 11-11 (1am Fri; midnight Sat); 12.30-midnight Sun
☎ (0141) 889 0911 ⊕ harviesbar.co.uk
Caledonian Deuchars IPA; Kelburn Goldihops; 1 changing beer Ⓗ
Popular tenement-style local situated on the main Paisley to Glasgow road. The spacious open-plan bar, with raised seating, has three large TV screens showing sport and music videos with the volume turned down low. The pub can get busy during major football matches. Sunday features a quiz night and Wednesday is poker night. Live music or a DJ play occasionally. 🕭🕭🚃🚌🛜

Last Post Ⓛ ✓
2 County Square, PA1 1BN
✪ 8am-midnight ☎ (0141) 849 6911
Caledonian Deuchars IPA; Greene King Abbot; Sharp's Doom Bar; 6 changing beers Ⓗ
Large Wetherspoon pub converted from the town's main post office. Open plan in design on two levels, there is plenty of seating and good wheelchair access. The standard Wetherspoon food menu is served and six guest ales are usually available. Next to Gilmour Street railway station and close to the bus station, it is handy for a pint between trains or buses. 🕭🕭🚃🚌(9,36)🛜

Sandpiper ✓
Glasgow Airport, PA3 2SW
✪ 4-10 ☎ (0141) 842 7858
Caledonian Deuchars IPA; Greene King Abbot; Sharp's Doom Bar; 3 changing beers Ⓗ
Positioned on the ground floor, in the public area of the airport, this Wetherspoon outlet is ideal if you are looking for an ale before heading through security, waiting for family or friends arriving on an incoming flight or, if you are a plane spotter, in need of refreshment. With eight handpumps you are spoilt for choice and can relax watching one of the many TV screens showing 24-hour news and sporting events. Q★🕭🕭☕🚌🅿🛜

Port Glasgow

Waterwheel
Russel Way, Greenock Road, PA14 5DX
✪ 11-11 ☎ (01475) 742167
Marston's Pedigree; Wychwood Hobgoblin Ⓗ
This is a modern family-friendly food-led Marston's pub/restaurant, situated on the A8 on the site of the old Lithgow's Kingston Yard ship-building site, with great views of the River Clyde. While the focus is on carvery meals which are served all day, up to three handpumps offer a choice of cask ales from the Marston's family of breweries. ★🕭🚃🅿

Renfrew

Lord of the Isles ✓
Unit 21 Xscape, Kings Inch Road, PA4 8XQ
☼ 8am-midnight (1am Fri); 7am-1am Sat; 7.30am-midnight
Sun ☎ (0141) 886 8930
Greene King Abbot; 3 changing beers ⊞
Large, purpose-built Wetherspoon establishment
attached to the Soar leisure complex at the
Braehead shopping centre. The walls display
photographs depicting the history of industry on
the River Clyde. The outside seating area is south-
facing and a suntrap on summer days. Food is
available all day and three ever-changing guest
ales are on handpump. A short stroll allows you to
view the ships docked at Yarrow Shipyard. Alcohol
is served from 11am. ⊛◐&P⊟🖥

Steam Wheeler
1 Row Avenue, G51 4SY
☼ 11-11; 11-10.30 Sun ☎ (0141) 886 3995
Marston's Pedigree; Wychwood Hobgoblin ⊞
Modern, family-friendly Marston's pub/restaurant,
in close proximity to Braehead shopping centre and
the King George V Dock, with good access to the
M8 motorway. While the focus is on carvery meals,
served all day, there is also a selection of up to
three different ales – usually English and from the
Marston's range. ☎⊛◐&P⊟🖥

Rutherglen

An Ruadh Ghleann ✓
40-44 Main Street, G73 2HY
☼ 8am-midnight (1am Fri & Sat) ☎ (0141) 613 2370
**Caledonian Deuchars IPA; Greene King Abbot; 7
changing beers (sourced nationally)** ⊞
Popular Wetherspoon bar at the west end of the
main street. The bright interior is rather more
contemporary than usual with a long, fairly narrow
bar and large windows letting in plenty of light.
The beer garden at the back is on two levels, the
upper one with a wooden canopy handy for

smokers. Varied guest beers tend towards the
more popular light side. Alcohol is served from
11am. Q☎⊛◐&⇌⊟🖥

Strathaven

Weavers Ⓛ ✓
1-3 Green Street, ML10 6LT
☼ 11-midnight Mon; 4.30-midnight (1am Thu); 11-1am Fri &
Sat; 2-1am Sun ☎ 07749 332914
**4 changing beers (sourced nationally; often
Strathaven)** ⊞
A good family-run country pub which takes its
name from the traditional trade of the town. It acts
as a local community hub and is home to local
clubs and groups, and supports the nearby
Strathaven Ales. The modernised single-room bar,
with a cosy space around the fire, is decorated with
black and white photographs of film and pop stars,
and attracts a clientele who enjoy conversation. A
frequent winner of local CAMRA Pub of the Year.
&⊟(254,256)🖥

Uplawmoor

Uplawmoor Hotel Ⓛ
66 Neilston Road, G78 4AF (off A736)
☼ 11-11 (10 Mon & Tue; midnight Fri); 11-10 Sun
☎ (01505) 850565 ⊕ uplawmoor.co.uk
2 changing beers (sourced locally; often Kelburn) ⊞
In a tranquil village setting just over 10 miles from
Glasgow, the building dates back to the 18th
century. It was originally a coaching inn used by
travellers and customs officers chasing smugglers
en-route between Glasgow and the south-west
coast of Scotland. Today the hotel continues to
offer travellers the opportunity to relax and
explore. The interior is rustic and cosy, with a public
bar, pool room and lounge bar. The beer is from
the local Kelburn Brewing Company.
☎⊛⇌◐&P⊟⊟(395,X44B)🐾🖥

Bon Accord, Glasgow

HIGHLANDS & WESTERN ISLES

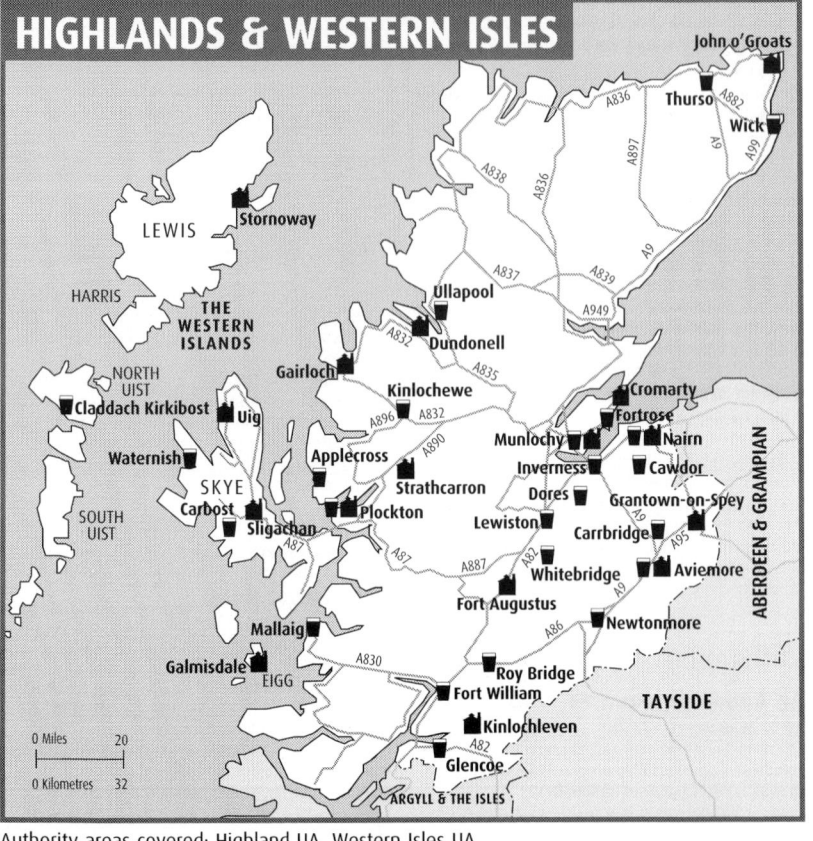

Authority areas covered: Highland UA, Western Isles UA

Applecross

Applecross Inn
Shore Street, IV54 8LR NG70974444
🕓 11-midnight (1am Fri); 12.30-11.30 Sun
☎ (01520) 744262 🌐 applecross.uk.com/inn
2 changing beers (sourced locally; often An Teallach, Applecross, Isle of Skye) Ⓗ
This remote multi award-winning iconic inn is reached by a hair-raising drive on one of the steepest roads in Britain or by a longer scenic coastal route and is well worth the journey. Isle of Skye and An Teallach beers are served in rotation, joined by ales from the new local micro, Applecross. Renowned for its local seafood and venison, with a massive chalkboard menu, the pub is a must for foodies. ら🏠🛏🌐🕭♿🅰🅿🚌🐾🖤

Aviemore

Cairngorm Hotel Ⓛ
77 Grampian Road, PH22 1PE (on B9152 opp railway station)
🕓 11-11; 12-10.30 Sun ☎ (01479) 810233 🌐 cairngorm.com
Cairngorm Stag, Gold Ⓗ
Just over the road from the train station and bus stop, this is often the first watering hole for many after a long journey. The privately owned Cairngorm Hotel has a warm and familiar feel about it, with comfy seats in the lobby to the bar and seating under cover outside. Although not tied, Cairngorm beers feature on the two handpumps.

Large-screen TVs show popular sporting events and there is Scottish entertainment for the many visitors most evenings. Food is available throughout the day. ら🏠🛏🌐🕭♿🅰🅿🚌🖤

Mackenzies Highland Inn ❷
125 Grampian Road, PH22 1RL (N end of village)
🕓 11-1am ☎ (01479) 810672
Cairngorm Trade Winds; Orkney Dark Island; house beer (by Greene King); 3 changing beers Ⓗ
The licensee is enthusiastic about Scottish real ales, with five handpumps offering two regular beers, a choice of guests, and a house beer, Mackenzies Lodge Inn. There is also a cider on handpump. Good honest pub food including excellent-value meal deals is available all day until 9pm. Entertainment features every evening. Open for breakfast from 8am. ら🏠🛏🌐🕭♿🅰🍴🅿🖤🖤

Old Bridge Inn Ⓛ
23 Dalfaber Road, PH22 1PU
🕓 12-11 (1am Fri & Sat) ☎ (01479) 811137
🌐 oldbridgeinn.co.uk
Cairngorm Stag, Trade Winds; Caledonian Flying Scotsman, Deuchars IPA Ⓗ
Close to the gently flowing River Spey, this gem of a pub is worth seeking out and is an ideal place to relax after a busy day on the hills, or even just touring in the area. Four handpumps offer a mix of Caledonian and Cairngorm beers. Booking is recommended for the restaurant with a quality menu featuring produce with low food miles. Local

654

entertainment is hosted most nights, and there is a selection of games and books to pass away the time over a pint. Handy for the Strathspey Steam Railway. ♿🍽🛏🍴🅿️♿🅰️🚶🅿️🅿️🌶☕️📶

Winking Owl 🄻 ✅

123 Grampian Road, PH22 1RH (N end of village)
🕐 12-11; 11-11am Fri & Sat; 12.30-11 Sun ☎ (01479) 812368
🌐 thewinkingowl.co
Cairngorm Stag, Trade Winds, Wildcat; 3 changing beers (sourced locally; often Cairngorm, Caledonian) Ⓗ
The Winky, said to be the oldest hostelry in Aviemore, has been the brewery tap for the Cairngorm Brewery, half a mile away, since 2014. An innovative partial brewery tie means that Caledonian beers are also available. The menu has something for everyone, including children. Access to the bar on the first floor is via steps, but staff are more than happy to help if assistance is required. There are benches outside for hardy folk.
♿🍽🍴🅰️🚶🅿️🅿️📶

Carbost: Isle of Skye

Old Inn

IV47 8SR (follow directions for distillery, B8009)
NG379318
🕐 11-1am (12.30am Sat); 12.30-11.30 Sun
☎ (01478) 640205 🌐 theoldinnskye.co.uk
3 changing beers (often Cuillin, Isle of Skye) Ⓗ
On the shores of Loch Harport, the Old Inn nestles on the tideline. Outside, trestle tables take advantage of the views that Skye is famous for – there can be no better place to enjoy a pint. Three handpumps offer beers from both of the island's breweries. The pub is busy all year round with an eclectic mix of outdoor folk, and those touring Skye or visiting the Talisker Distillery close by. Seafood is top of the menu, most of it coming from the loch.
Q♿🍽🍴🅿️🚶

Carrbridge

Cairn Hotel 🄻

Main Road, PH23 3AS (on B9153 N of Carrbridge)
🕐 12-midnight (1am Fri & Sat); 12.30-midnight Sun
☎ (01479) 841212 🌐 cairnhotel.co.uk
3 changing beers (sourced regionally; often Cairngorm, Cromarty, Orkney) Ⓗ
The licensee is passionate about the beer he selects for his three handpumps and the Cairn is popular with loyal locals and the many visitors to the area. The excellent pub grub is a draw, as is the open fire on cooler days. A Cairngorm beer is regularly available alongside a Cromarty brew, with Two Thirsty Men making an occasional appearance. The Cairn is the community hub of the village and can be busy when porridge-making or chainsaw-carving events are on.
♿🍽🍴🅿️🚶📶

Cawdor

Cawdor Tavern ✅

The Lane, IV12 5XP (B9090 to Cawdor village)
NH845500
🕐 11-11 (midnight Sat); 12.30-11 Sun summer; 11-3, 5-11; 11-midnight Sat; 12.30-11 Sun winter ☎ (01667) 404777
🌐 cawdortavern.co.uk
Orkney Northern Light, Red MacGregor, Dark Island; 1 changing beer (sourced regionally; often Orkney) Ⓗ

The Cawdor Tavern has been in the same hands since 1994 – the family also owns the Orkney/Atlas brewery at Quoyloo. Accordingly, up to five handpumps feature its beers. Oak panelling covers the walls of the public areas including the spacious cosy bar room with its water taps for whisky on the bar. The lounge is mainly for dining, alongside a separate baronial dining hall. The tempting menus cater for all tastes and ages – leave room for pudding! Q♿🍽🍴🅿️🅿️(252)📶

Claddach Kirkibost

Westford Inn

HS6 5EP (2½ miles NW of Clachan on A865)
NF7751066195
🕐 12-11 (midnight Fri); 12-1am Sat; 12.30-11 Sun
☎ (01876) 580653
Isle of Skye Skye Red; 2 changing beers (sourced regionally; often Fyne, Isle of Skye) Ⓗ
The owners took on the Westford Inn in 2015 and have turned around its fortunes. Now very much the hub of the community, it hosts live music and an annual beer festival. Skye Red is available all year and a second Skye beer in winter, with three ales in summer, as well as a range of bottled beers. Good-quality pub food is served. Although probably one of the most remote pubs in the Guide, it is well worth making the effort to visit.
Q♿🍽🍴🅰️🚶🅿️🌶📶

Dores

Dores Inn 🄻

IV2 6TR (on B862) NH59753476
🕐 11-11 (midnight Fri & Sat); closed Mon winter
☎ (01463) 751203 🌐 thedoresinn.co.uk
4 changing beers (sourced regionally; often Cairngorm, Cromarty, Inveralmond) Ⓗ
Set on the shores of the north-east end of Loch Ness, the location offers excellent Nessie-spotting opportunities, and is popular all year round – a must stop, just for the views. The cosy wood-finished bar has up to four handpumps offering ales from a selection of local and regional independents and occasionally an English ale. During the summer, a second OutDores Inn bar opens in the beer garden. Great food is available all day. Tea and coffee are served from 10am. A free minibus service is provided to/from Inverness.
Q♿🍽🍴🅰️🅿️🌶☕️📶

REAL ALE BREWERIES

An Teallach Dundonell
Black Isle Munlochy
Cairngorm Aviemore
Cromarty Cromarty
Cuillin 🍴 Sligachan: Isle of Skye
Hebridean Stornoway: Isle of Lewis
Isle of Skye Uig: Isle of Skye
John o'Groats John o'Groats
Laig Bay Galmisdale: Isle of Eigg (NEW)
Nessie Fort Augustus (NEW)
Old Inn 🍴 Gairloch
Plockton Plockton
River Leven Kinlochleven
Strathcarron Strathcarron (NEW)
Two Thirsty Men Grantown-on-Spey (NEW)
Wooha Nairn

Fort William

Ben Nevis Inn L ✔

Achintee Road, Claggan, PH33 6TE (signed from A82)
NN12477293
☼ 12-11 summer ☎ (01397) 701227 ⊕ ben-nevis-inn.co.uk
3 changing beers (sourced locally; often Cairngorm, Isle of Skye) ⊞

Traditional stone-built barn at the start of the Ben Nevis mountain path, popular with outdoor enthusiasts. The small bar counter has three handpumps offering beers from local breweries. The interior, with long beer hall-style tables and a beckoning stove, is a warm, informal and friendly setting, an ideal venue for the regular live music. The hearty menu changes daily and is available until 9pm. Bunkhouse accommodation sleeps 24 people. Check ahead for opening hours in winter.
Q❀🛏🍽🕭♿♠P

Great Glen ✔

104 High Street, PH33 6AD (in pedestrianised area)
☼ 7am-midnight (1am Fri & Sat) ☎ (01397) 709910
Adnams Broadside; Caledonian Deuchars IPA; 8 changing beers (sourced nationally) ⊞

Purpose built in 2013, with a spacious and modern interior, the pub is named after the 78-mile Great Glen (An Gleann Mor), the geological feature that runs up to Inverness. Up to 10 handpumps offer mostly local and regional beers. An outside seating area is reached by an internal staircase, above a separate Travelodge handy for accommodation. Alcohol is served from 11am (noon Sunday).
♿❀🍽🕭♿⇌P🚅🛜

Grog & Gruel L ✔

66 High Street, PH33 6AE (in pedestrianised area)
☼ 12-11.30 (12.30am Thu-Sat); 12.30 (5 winter)-11.30 Sun
☎ (01397) 705078 ⊕ grogandgruel.co.uk
6 changing beers (sourced locally; often An Teallach, Isle of Skye) ⊞

The Grog is busy throughout the year and has justifiably featured in the Guide since 1997. A real draw for real ale enthusiasts, it offers a combination of up to six ales from local breweries, including River Leven, and ales from further afield, plus a great food menu. The upstairs restaurant opens in the evening to provide more tables. There is no better place to end the 96-mile walk along the West Highland Way. Entertainment is hosted most evenings and there's an annual beer festival.
♿🕭⇌🚅🚶♣🛜

Fortrose

Anderson

Union Street, IV10 8TD
☼ 4-11.30; closed Sun-Tue winter ☎ (01381) 620236
⊕ theanderson.co.uk
3 changing beers (sourced nationally; often Cromarty, Inveralmond) ⊞

Not only is owner Jim Anderson a beer writer, but he fanatically keeps his real ale in tip-top condition in the natural cellar. Three handpumps offer mostly Scottish ales and a fourth dispenses real cider. More than 100 Belgian and 30 Mikkeller bottled beers are also kept as well as approaching 300 malts. The multi award-winning kitchen has a well-deserved reputation for foodie excellence. Quiz, music, film and knitting nights are weekly regulars, complemented by mini beer festivals and special food nights. Closed November to early December.
Q♿❀🛏♿♠🚶♣♠P🚅🛜

Glencoe

Clachaig Inn L ✔

PH49 4HX (3 miles SE of Glencoe village, off A82)
NN12705668
☼ 11-11 (11.30 Fri; midnight Sat); 12.30-11 Sun
☎ (01855) 811252 ⊕ clachaig.com
10 changing beers (sourced locally; often Cairngorm, Orkney, River Leven) ⊞

Isolated amid breathtaking scenery, the Clachaig has been a regular in the Guide since 1984. This real ale stronghold has a forest of handpumps in its three open-plan bars offering mainly Scottish beers to suit all tastes. Although quieter during the day, it is busy in the evening when walkers and climbers descend to slake thirsts and fill hungry stomachs with hearty fare after a day out on the hills. Superlatives abound, as do the wood-burning stoves that keep the place warm and cosy.
♿❀🛏🕭♿♣P🛜

Inverness

Black Isle Bar L

68 Church Street, IV1 1EN
☼ 11-1am ☎ (01463) 229920 ⊕ blackislebar.com
Black Isle Yellowhammer, Red Kite; 4 changing beers (sourced locally; often Black Isle) ℗

Opened in 2016, the bar has grown in popularity, offering up to six real ales. Two big screens show the beer menu, with prices for pints, halves and thirds. The open-plan bar area offers a mix of seating including comfy sofas. Upstairs is a secret garden, with upcycled cable drums, pallet tables and stools under a cover of reclaimed corrugated iron. Other than pizza, prepared in an oven at the rear, sides, salads and soups are available, as is accommodation. Q🛏🕭♿⇌P🚅🛜

Castle Tavern L

1 View Place, IV2 4SA (top of Castle St)
☼ 11-1am (12.30am Sat); 12-midnight Sun
☎ (01463) 718178 ⊕ castletavern.net
6 changing beers (sourced regionally; often Cromarty, Isle of Skye, Windswept) ⊞

A five-minute walk from town will take you to the Castle Tavern, which is popular with tourists visiting the castle opposite – and locals who know their beer. The impressive covered canopy area is always busy, even in winter, with fine views along the River Ness. Inside, six handpumps offer a changing selection of beers and styles from Scottish independents, and a few LocAles. Bar meals are available all day and there is a restaurant upstairs for evening meals. ♿❀🕭🚶⇌🚅🛜

Clachnaharry Inn

17-19 High Street, Clachnaharry, IV3 8RB (on A862 Beauly road)
☼ 11-11 (midnight Thu; 1am Fri & Sat); 12-11 Sun
☎ (01463) 239806 ⊕ clachnaharryinn.co.uk
Fyne Jarl; Harviestoun Bitter & Twisted; Inveralmond Ossian; 1 changing beer (sourced nationally; often Cairngorm, Greene King, Timothy Taylor) ⊞

The Clach has featured in the Guide for more than 30 years and is the place where many have discovered the joys of real ale. The 17th-century coaching inn is a must-visit pub, with a warm welcome for all. The bar oozes heritage, with an open fire on cooler days. Food is available in the bar area and the quieter dining area. On warmer days, the view from the terrace over the Caledonian Canal sea locks and Beauly Firth with

Ben Wyvis beyond never fails to satisfy. Wednesday is quiz night, with a Scottish music jam on Thursday. Q🌠🐕🏮🍴🛏️♣P🖪(28,28A)😺📶

Corriegarth 🅛

5-7 Heathmount Road, IV2 3JU (in Crown area of Inverness)
🕐 8am-midnight (1am Fri & Sat) ☎ (01463) 242730
🌐 corriegarth.com
Caledonian Deuchars IPA; Cromarty Happy Chappy; 2 changing beers (sourced nationally) Ⓗ
The Corrie is located in the quiet Crown area of Inverness, just five minutes from the town centre. The imposing red sandstone building was once a hotel and also did a stint as a club for Navy and RAF officers. In addition to the regular beers, two others from the Punch list are usually available in this popular local. In summer, the large area outside is busy. Six boutique en-suite rooms make it a great place to stay. Q🌠🐕🏮🍴🛏️🍴♣P🖪📶

Hootananny

67 Church Street, IV1 1ES
🕐 12-3am; 6.30-midnight Sun ☎ (01463) 233651
🌐 hootananyinverness.co.uk
Black Isle Yellowhammer, Red Kite Ⓗ
There is a great craic every night at Hoots – this lively award-winning pub celebrates Scottish folk music and all things Scottish. The well-trodden wooden floorboards are a testimony to the popularity of this real ale pub. Although not tied, the two handpumps offer beers from Black Isle Brewery. Food with a Scottish theme is available until 8.30pm when the usually free entertainment starts. 🐕🏮🍴♣🖪

Kings Highway ✓

72-74 Church Street, IV1 1EN
🕐 7am-1am ☎ (01463) 251830
Adnams Broadside; Caledonian Deuchars IPA; Fuller's London Pride; Greene King Abbot; Sharp's Doom Bar; 5 changing beers (sourced regionally; often An Teallach) Ⓗ
Conveniently situated just a few minutes from the main shopping area, bus and train stations, Kings Highway is an ideal place to meet up. It is busy throughout the day with a wide spectrum of customers taking advantage of its breakfast, tea and coffee. Like many Wetherspoon pubs, it offers good-value fare and is popular with families. Up to 10 real ales are available, generally Scottish, with many local to the Highland area. Alcohol is served from 11am. 🐕🏮🍴♣P🖪📶

Phoenix Ale House 🅛

106-110 Academy Street, IV1 1LX
🕐 11-midnight (1am Fri & Sat); 12-midnight Sun
☎ (01463) 240300 🌐 phoenixalehouse.co.uk
10 changing beers (sourced nationally; often Cairngorm, Loch Ness, Windswept) Ⓗ
The Phoenix rose from the ashes in 2014 after returning to the safe hands of a previous owner. A choice selection of Scottish real ales beckons from up to 10 handpumps. Listed in CAMRA's Scottish Inventory of Historic Pub Interiors, the island bar is surrounded by a spittoon and there is even talk of sawdust returning! Mostly standing only, but the restaurant next door has plenty of seating for hearty meals all day. Popular with tourists and those who know their ales. Q🏮🍴♣P🖪

Kinlochewe

Kinlochewe Hotel (Beinn Eighe Bar)
🍷 🅛
IV22 2PA (on A832 Gairloch Road) NH028619
🕐 11-11; 12.30-11 Sun summer; 4-10; 12-midnight Fri & Sat; 12-10 Sun winter ☎ (01445) 760253
🌐 kinlochewehotel.co.uk
6 changing beers (sourced regionally; often Cromarty, Orkney, Windswept) Ⓗ
Set amid the magnificent Torridon Hills, the approach from Achnasheen offers one of the best views in the Highlands, and the area is popular with many visitors. There are six handpumps in this former 18th-century coaching inn, offering a tempting selection of local and regional beers plus a real cider. Great pride is taken in the tasty and simply prepared locally sourced fish, meat and game. A favourite stop on the North Coast 500 route. Local CAMRA Pub of the Year for 2017. Q🏮🍴🛏️🍴♣P🖪😺📶

Lewiston

Loch Ness Inn (Brewery Bar)
IV63 6UW (just off A82)
🕐 11.30-11 ☎ (01456) 450991 🌐 staylochness.co.uk
3 changing beers (sourced locally; often Applecross) Ⓗ
An ideal central location to stay on Loch Ness or a watering hole after visiting Urquhart Castle or the local Nessie tourist haunts. Up to three handpumps offer a great selection of mainly local ales, with some from the new Applecross Brewery. The Loch Ness Inn has been heaped with awards for its food and takes great pride in the provenance of its ingredients. It is popular with walkers and cyclists covering the Great Glen route. A free pick-up/drop-off minibus is available within five miles. 🐕🏮🍴🛏️🍴♣P🖪📶

Mallaig

Chlachain Inn ✓
Davies Brae, PH41 4QY (past ferry terminal and up brae)
🕐 11-midnight (1am Thu-Sat); 12-11.45 Sun
☎ (01687) 460289 🌐 westscotlandinn.co.uk
House beer (by Caledonian); 2 changing beers (often Isle of Skye, Orkney) Ⓗ
Mallaig is the landing port for arguably the best seafood in Scotland, and the ferry port for Skye and the small isles. Arrive there by the scenic Road to the Isles, train or steam train from Fort William. The Chlachain Inn provides an excellent destination in its own right with an open-plan bar and dining area, and a roaring log fire as its focal point on cooler days. Up to three handpumps offer Scottish beers. Of course, excellent seafood is on the menu. Children, backpackers, dogs and muddy boots are welcome. Q🌠🐕🏮🍴🍴♣P🖪(500,501)😺📶

Munlochy

Allangrange Arms 🅛
58 Millbank Road, IV8 8NL (on B9161)
🕐 11-11 (1am Fri & Sat) summer; 11 (4.45 Mon)-11; 11-1am Fri & Sat; 12.30-11 Sun winter ☎ (01463) 819862
🌐 allangrangearms.com
Cromarty Happy Chappy; Orkney Red MacGregor Ⓗ
Busy, family-friendly pub with a deserved reputation for innovative and generous food at a keen price. Two handpumps serve the two regular

ales, which are proven favourites, with just one or the other available during the quieter months. The bar offers a mix of comfy sofa, booth and open-plan seating, with a separate restaurant area, and outside there is bench seating front and back. Check ahead for winter opening times. Q ☺ ❀ ⇦ ⓘ ⅃ ♣ P ⊟ ❀ ☞

Nairn

Braeval Hotel ⃝ ✓
Crescent Road, IV12 4NB (E end of town, near beach)
☼ 12-11 (12.30am Fri; 1am Sat) summer; 4-10; 12-midnight Fri & Sat; 12-10 Sun winter ☎ (01667) 452341
⊕ braevalhotel.co.uk
9 changing beers (sourced regionally; often Cairngorm, Cromarty, Orkney) ⅃
The family-run hotel's Bandstand Bar has up to nine handpumps offering an excellent selection of local and regional Scottish ales, with the occasional English brew. It is also a haven for whisky lovers with around 120 Scottish single malts available. Live music plays every weekend. The biggest independent beer festival in the Highlands is held here after Easter with around 150 ales and 10 ciders, alongside excellent live music. The Seaview Restaurant offers fine food and great views. Winner of CAMRA Highland Pub of the Year three times. Q ☺ ❀ ⇦ ⓘ ⅃ ♣ ⚭ ⊟ ☞

Newtonmore

Glen Hotel ⃝
Main Street, PH20 1DD (S of village)
☼ 11-midnight; 12.30-midnight Sun ☎ (01540) 673203
⊕ theglenhotel.co.uk
4 changing beers (often Cairngorm, Caledonian) ⅃
This is the first of what now totals 200 real ale pubs as you enter the CAMRA branch area travelling north up the A9. The Glen was a trailblazer in what was a real ale desert. It offers up to four handpumps featuring Cairngorm, Caledonian and guest beers, plus real cider in the summer. Good honest pub grub is served in the comfy bar, restaurant and outside on trestle tables. Quiz nights and a games room make this a popular evening retreat for locals and visitors alike.
☺ ⇦ ⓘ ⅃ ♣ P ⊟ ☞

Plockton

Plockton Hotel ✓
41 Harbour Street, IV52 8TN NG80293343
☼ 11-midnight; 12.30-11 Sun ☎ (01599) 544274
⊕ plocktonhotel.co.uk
5 changing beers (often Cromarty, Swannay) ⅃
Plockton was the setting for TV's Hamish Macbeth, which is a major draw for visitors to this pretty village, many of whom arrive by train on the picturesque Kyle Line. The hotel owner and chef proudly offers four handpumps dispensing both local and regional beers and also prepares the tempting food menu featuring locally sourced seafood, beef and venison. Take your beer on to

> A glass of bitter beer or pale ale, taken with the principal meal of the day, does more good and less harm than any medicine the physician can prescribe.
> **Dr Carpenter, 1750**

the terrace and from the shade of the palm trees watch the tide. A real ale and gin festival is held in May. Closed for the first two weeks of January.
Q ☺ ❀ ⇦ ⓘ ⅃ ♣ P ⊟ ☞

Roy Bridge

Stronlossit Inn ⃝ ✓
Main Street, PH31 4AG (on A86) NN27228117
☼ 11-11.45 (1am Thu-Sat); 12.30-11.45 Sun
☎ (01397) 712253 ⊕ stronlossit.co.uk
4 changing beers (sourced locally; often Cairngorm, Isle of Skye, Orkney) ⅃
The location of the Stronlossitt makes it attractive to those keen on the outdoors, and with the railway station just over the road, you can abandon the car and arrive by train from Fort William or London. The train can also take you for a day trip to Corrour to walk around Loch Ossian. Four handpumps spoil real ale fans, with beers from varying Scottish breweries. Great food is available all day as well as rooms for all budgets.
Q ☺ ❀ ⇦ ⓘ ⅃ ⚭ ⚭ P ⊟ ☞

Thurso

Weigh Inn (Ashes Bar)
Burnside, KW14 7UG (on A9 at jct for Scrabster)
☼ 12-2.30, 4.30-midnight; 12-midnight Fri-Sun
☎ (01847) 893722 ⊕ weighinn.co.uk
John o' Groats Swelkie; Orkney Corncrake ⅃
Overlooking the Pentland Firth with panoramic views of the Orkney Isles, the hotel is close to the Orkney ferry. The Ashes is the main bar, with screens for sport and occasional live entertainment, and there are two more bars used for functions. Two handpumps dispense Orkney and John o' Groats ales. Bar meals are served lunchtime and evening. Outside there is an enclosed children's play area and a patio with tables and seating. Q ☺ ❀ ⇦ ⓘ ⅃ ♣ P ⊟ ☞

Ullapool

Morefield Motel ⃝
North Road, IV26 2TQ (signed from A835)
☼ 12-11 ☎ (01854) 612000 ⊕ morefieldmotel.co.uk
3 changing beers (sourced locally; often An Teallach, Cairngorm) ⅃
The family-friendly Morefield Motel is a popular place to stay for those exploring the spectacular west coast, or overnighting to catch the ferry to the Western Isles. Ullapool is a pretty fishing village and you can be assured that fresh seafood takes centre stage. The bar is open to all, with three handpumps featuring Scottish beers including at least one from An Teallach. A beer festival is held in October. Q ❀ ⇦ ⓘ ⅃ ♣ P ⊟ ❀ ☞

Waternish: Isle of Skye

Stein Inn ⃝ ✓
MacLeod's Terrace, IV55 8GA (N of Dunvegan, on B886)
NG26255643
☼ 11-midnight (1am Fri); 11-12.30am Sat; 11.30-11 summer; winter hours vary ☎ (01470) 592362 ⊕ steininn.co.uk
3 changing beers (often Caledonian, Isle of Skye) ⅃
Probably the oldest pub on Skye, the Stein is set at the end of a whitewashed terrace on the shores of Loch Bay, proudly run by the same owners for more than 20 years. Two beers are usually available plus a third guest in the summer. The

seafood is landed from the slipway 100 yards away. A large double-fronted stove radiates warmth throughout the low-beamed bar on cooler days; there is ample seating outside to soak up the view in the summer. Q ⛄ ⛄ 🛏 🍴 & ♣ P 🐾

Whitebridge

Whitebridge Hotel 🅛

IV2 6UN (on B862) NH487152
☼ 11 (12 Sun)-11 summer; winter hours vary
☎ (01456) 486226 🌐 whitebridgehotel.co.uk
3 changing beers (often Cairngorm, Cromarty, Orkney)

Built in 1899 and located on the quiet east side of Loch Ness, this hotel has fishing rights on three local lochs. Inside, the attractive pitch pine-panelled bar has a welcoming wood-burning stove. An adjacent room has a pool table and also a separate area for dining. Three ales are usually available, one or two in winter. The traditional pub food is all home cooked. The hotel has a green tourism policy. Q ⛄ 🛏 🍴 & ♣ 🚌 🐾 📶

Wick

Mackays Hotel 🅛

1 Ebenezer Place, KW1 5ED (close to bridge)
☼ 11-11 ☎ (01955) 602323 🌐 mackayshotel.co.uk
John o' Groats Duncansby, Swelkie 🅗

Mackays Hotel is in the Guinness Book of Records as being on the shortest street in the world – the front door of the bistro is the only building. In the bar it has just one handpump, supplied with a beer from the relatively new John o' Groats Brewery 16 miles away. Wick is a pretty town and a convenient stopping-off point on the way to John o' Groats, or a base to explore the landscape and features of Caithness's sometimes wild but stunning coast and hinterland. Q 🛏 🍴 & 🅰 ⇌ P 🚌

Grog & Gruel, Fort William (Photo: Daniel Neilson)

SCOTLAND

KINGDOM OF FIFE

Authority area covered: Fife UA

Anstruther

Ship Tavern
49 Shore Street, KY10 3AQ
☼ 11-midnight (1am Fri & Sat); 12.30-midnight Sun
☎ (01333) 310347
2 changing beers (sourced nationally; often Eden Mill) Ⓗ
Next door to the famous Anstruther Fish Bar, this traditional pub on the harbour front is a popular meeting place for fishermen, locals and visitors to the museum. The bar has all the character you would expect from a historic fishing village inn. Two ever-changing ales come from breweries all over the UK, including the local Eden Mill. Take in the views of the harbour or relax in the comfort of the back room. ◑▷▲♣☐(X60,95)

Crail

Golf Hotel ⊘
4 High Street, KY10 3TD
☼ 11-midnight (1am Thu-Sat); 12.30-midnight Sun
☎ (01333) 450206 ⊕ thegolfhotelcrail.com
3 changing beers (sourced nationally) Ⓗ
The Golf Hotel is a listed 16th-century coaching inn in a picturesque village in the East Neuk of Fife. The historic bar dates back to 1721, making it one of the oldest in Scotland. The room retains the original low-beamed ceiling, wooden floor and a 16th-century fireplace with a marriage lintel over it bearing the initials of the original owners. Relax with a beer in the garden or enjoy a meal in the restaurant after walking the coastal path.
⊛⇔◑☐(95)♣ ⎙

Cupar

Boudingait
43 Bonnygate, KY15 4BU
☼ 11-11 (10 Mon); 11-1am Fri & Sat ☎ (01334) 654681
⊕ theboudingaitcupar.co.uk
2 changing beers (sourced regionally; often Eden Mill) Ⓗ

This wee gem hidden off Main Street in Cupar is a bustling family-friendly outlet, traditionally decorated with a rustic feel. Two handpulls feature a variety of regional and local ales from Eden Mill and Orkney breweries. Meals are served daily and a loyalty card is available. A quiz night features weekly, live music fortnightly, and bingo every Sunday evening. ⏻◑♿⇌☐ ⎙

Dunfermline

Commercial Inn
13 Douglas Street, KY12 7EB
☼ 10-11 (midnight Fri & Sat) ☎ (01383) 733876
7 changing beers (sourced nationally; often Alechemy, Eden Mill) Ⓗ
This cosy town-centre establishment, just off the High Street adjacent to the main post office, is a renowned ale house situated in a historic building dating back to the 1820s. Seven real ales and a cider are always on offer. Good food and friendly service attract an eclectic clientele. A former Kingdom of Fife CAMRA Pub of the Year and Scottish finalist. ◑⇌(Town)♣☐

East Port Bar ⊘
7 East Port, KY12 7JG
☼ 11.30-11 (midnight Fri & Sat); 12-11 Sun
☎ (01383) 736678
2 changing beers (sourced nationally) Ⓗ
The East Port Bar is a terrific pub to visit during a day out in Dunfermline. This busy town-centre establishment has cosy sofas and booths in which

REAL ALE BREWERIES
Beath Cowdenbeath
Brew Shed Limekilns (NEW)
Craft Originale Markinch (NEW)
de bRus ⊟ Dunfermline
Eden St Andrews Guardbridge
Inner Bay Inverkeithing (NEW)
Kingdom Rosyth (NEW)
Luckie Leven
St Andrews St Andrews

to enjoy a drink or two. The interior features wood panelling and a wood bar and gantry. Value-for-money bar food is served at lunchtime. Sport from football to golf are shown on the plasma screens, with soft background music usually playing. ❀◑&≑(Town)🖳🛜

Elie

Ship Inn
The Toft, KY9 1DT
✪ 10.30-11 (midnight Fri & Sat) ☎ (01333) 330246
🌐 shipinn.scot
4 changing beers (sourced nationally; often Eden Mill) Ⓗ
A cracking pub/restaurant with a fabulous beach view, worth the 10-minute walk from the High Street. In winter, relax in the comfort of open fires and wood-burning stoves. During the summer when the tide is out, beach cricket can be viewed from the beach bar. Four handpulls offer a wide range of local, regional and national ales. Food is served throughout, featuring the ever-popular Ship Inn's famous fish and chips, as well as local shellfish and Scottish seafood. ❀🍴◑🖳(95)❀

Freuchie

Albert Tavern
2 High Street, KY15 7EX
✪ 5-midnight; 12-1am Fri & Sat; 12.30-midnight Sun ☎ 07876 178863 🌐 alberttavern.wixsite.com/albert
5 changing beers (sourced nationally; often Elland, Mallinson's, Phoenix) Ⓗ
A cosy local with a low-beamed ceiling reminiscent of an English village pub. The small bar has five handpumps with a choice of ales from microbreweries from Devon to Orkney. The lounge hosts various events such as a malt whisky club and is popular during rugby internationals. The village is renowned for its cricket team, once national village champions. A multi award-winning Local CAMRA Pub of the Year and twice the Scottish winner, this gem of a pub is not to be missed. Q❀🖴🖳(64,36)❀

Glenrothes

Bankhead Gate
Beaufort Drive, KY7 4UJ
✪ 6.30am-11; 7am-11 Sat & Sun ☎ (01592) 773473
Caledonian Deuchars IPA; Sharp's Doom Bar Ⓗ
This Brewers Fayre pub sells alcohol from 11am (noon Sunday) but opens earlier for breakfast and coffee. Here you will find pub food as it should be, with a great value everyday menu and buffet nights. The family-friendly premises has children's play areas inside and out. The two core ales may change from time to time. ⏰❀🍴&P🖳(32)🛜

Golden Acorn ⊘
1 North Street, KY7 5NA
✪ 7am-midnight (1am Fri) ☎ (01592) 751175

> Where village statesmen talked with looks profound,
> And news much older than the ale went round.
> **Alfred, Lord Tennyson**

Caledonian Deuchars IPA; Greene King Abbot; Sharp's Doom Bar; 4 changing beers (sourced nationally) Ⓗ
Near the town centre and only two minutes' walk from the bus station, this Wetherspoon establishment comprises a large open-plan bar and hotel. Real ale is available on seven handpumps and a regular cider, as well as the usual Wetherspoon special deals and beer festivals. Large TV screens show some sporting events and rolling news. A dartboard can be found tucked away in a corner. ⏰❀🍴◑&♣🖴P🖳🛜

Hillend

Hillend Tavern 🍷
37 Main Street, KY11 9ND
✪ 4 (3 Fri)-midnight; 1-midnight Sat & Sun
☎ (01383) 415391 🌐 hillendtavern.co.uk
Greene King IPA; 2 changing beers (sourced nationally) Ⓗ
A small, traditional pub, welcoming with two real fires. A hidden gem not far from Dalgety Bay, it has a spacious room at the back and a large covered area outside. The Hillend offers a wide variety of traditional events, live music, TV sport such as football and rugby, quizzes and karaoke. Three handpulls dispense a wide range of regional and national ales. Local CAMRA Pub of the Year 2017. ❀≑🖳(7,87)❀

Kinghorn

Crown Tavern ⊘
55-57 High Street, KY3 9UW
✪ 11-11.45; 12.30-11.45 Sun ☎ (01592) 890340
2 changing beers (sourced nationally; often Tryst) Ⓗ
A bustling two-roomed local, also called the Middle Bar, situated to the west of the High Street. Attractive stained-glass panels adorn the windows, and the high ceilings feature ornate plaster work. Mainly a sports bar, two TVs screen a wide range of sporting events. A pool table can be found to the side. Two guest ales from microbreweries throughout the UK are available here. Kingdom of Fife CAMRA Cider Pub of the Year in 2015 and 2016. ≑♣🖴🖳(7)🛜

Kirkcaldy

Betty Nicols
297 High Street, KY1 1JL
✪ 12-8.30 (midnight Thu & Fri); 11-midnight Sat; 1-8.30 Sun
☎ (01592) 642083 🌐 bettynicolsbarandbistro.co.uk
2 changing beers (sourced regionally; often Broughton, Fyne, Orkney) Ⓗ
Betty Nicols has long been one of Kirkcaldy's most popular places for a high-quality drink in a relaxed and comfortable atmosphere. Its traditional decor and unrushed pace attract people of all ages looking for good conversation and company. A wide range of real ales is another attraction that ensures this high-street pub remains a unique and well-loved fixture in the town. Live music plays every Thursday, and a quiz is held on the first Tuesday of the month. ◑&≑🖳❀🛜

Harbour Bar
471-475 High Street, KY1 2SN
✪ 11-3 (not Mon & Tue), 5-midnight; 11-midnight Thu-Sat; 12.30-midnight Sun ☎ (01592) 264270
6 changing beers (sourced nationally) Ⓗ

The building dates from around 1870 and was a ship chandler's before it became a pub in 1924. It is one of just a few pubs to still have the historic jug bar. The lounge is light and airy with ornate cornices. Six handpumps sell up to 20 different beers a week from micros all over Britain. Kingdom of Fife CAMRA Pub of the Year on numerous occasions, and a previous Scottish Pub of the Year winner. Q♣☺️Ⓗ❀

Robert Nairn ✅
2-6 Kirk Wynd, KY1 1EH
☼ 8am-midnight (1am Fri & Sat); 8am-11 Sun
☎ (01592) 205249
Caledonian Deuchars IPA; Greene King Abbot; 4 changing beers (sourced nationally) Ⓗ
A Wetherspoon pub just off the main pedestrianised area of the town with a split-level lounge and pictures of old Kirkcaldy on the walls. Six handpulls dispense a variety of beers and regular Meet the Brewer evenings are hosted. With its central location, this lively pub attracts a mixed clientele, young and old, who all enjoy the real ales. ☺️Ⓓ♿️♣️Ⓗ♠

Leslie

Burns Tavern
184 High Street, KY6 3DB
☼ 11-midnight (1am Fri & Sat); 12.30-midnight Sun
☎ (01592) 741345
Timothy Taylor Landlord; 1 changing beer (sourced nationally; often Kelburn, Stewart) Ⓗ
A friendly two-roomed local in a small former paper-making town, north of Glenrothes. The public bar is split level with the bar on the lower level and a pool table on the upper. The spacious lounge hosts karaoke on Saturday, folk music on Sunday and a quiz on Thursday. Unusually for the area, Timothy Taylor Landlord is always on tap. Q🏮♣️P🚌(39A)❀

Limekilns

Ship Inn Ⓛ
Halketts Hall, KY11 3HJ
☼ 11-11 (11.30 Thu; midnight Fri & Sat) ☎ (01383) 872247
3 changing beers (sourced nationally; often Brew Shed) Ⓗ
The first pub in Fife to be accredited on the LocAle 2017 scheme for stocking Brew Shed Ales, brewed in Limekilns itself. Set on the waterside in a small rural village, this establishment has excellent views across the River Forth. Three guest ales are available, mostly from microbreweries throughout the UK. The bar has a cosy alcove to the left, and a maritime theme features throughout the building. Meals are served lunchtimes with fish and seafood the speciality (booking is essential). Q❀ⓄP🚌(6)

Lower Largo

Railway Inn
1 Station Wynd, KY8 6BU
☼ 11-midnight (1am Thu-Sat) ☎ (01333) 320239
🌐 railwayinnlargo.co.uk
5 changing beers (sourced nationally; often Born in the Borders, Eden Mill, Hawk Hill) Ⓗ
This friendly and traditional village pub has been established in Lower Largo since 1749. Situated near the Fife coastal path, close to the picturesque harbour of Largo, it is a welcome place to take a

break for ramblers, dog walkers and locals. The small two-roomed interior has a cosy real fire. Bar snacks are available. Five handpumps serve beers from all over the UK. Q☺️❀🚌(95)❀

Pitlessie

Village Inn
Cupar Road, KY15 7SU
☼ 12-2.30, 5-11 (midnight Thu); 12-midnight Fri; 12-11.30 Sat; 12-11 Sun ☎ (01337) 830595 🌐 pitlessievillageinn.com
2 changing beers (sourced nationally) Ⓗ
A family-run business with a warm, local atmosphere serving great-value freshly produced meals and using the best seasonal produce from around Scotland. The former coaching inn is decorated with pictures of the maltings that were once opposite. A lovely real fire adds warmth to the wood-panelled, stone and plaster-walled bar. The room has a corner bar with bar stools and a separate seating area for bar meals or drinks. Two varying ales are offered. 🏮Ⓓ♣️P🚌

St Andrews

Central Bar ✅
77 Market Street, KY16 9NU
☼ 11-11.45 (midnight Fri & Sat); 12.30-11.45 Sun
☎ (01334) 478296
8 changing beers (sourced nationally) Ⓗ
This bar is, as its name suggests, centrally located in the town of St Andrews. A Greene King outlet, it has a Victorian-style island bar, large windows and ornate mirrors creating a late 19th-century feel. A good mix of students, tourists and locals adds to the character of the pub. A wide selection of ales is dispensed from eight handpulls. ❀Ⓓ🚌♠

Criterion ✅
99 South Street, KY16 9QW
☼ 10-midnight (1am Fri & Sat) ☎ (01334) 474543
Caledonian Flying Scotsman, Deuchars IPA; changing beers (sourced nationally; often Eden Mill, St Andrews) Ⓗ
A cracking hostelry at the far end of South Street – relax with a few drinks and watch life go by in this bustling university town. Oak-panelled walls are adorned with photographs of St Andrews in days gone by. The pub is renowned for its home-made meals and the legendary Cri-pie. Background music plays and a TV shows sport. Open music night on Monday is popular with local artists, and a regular quiz night is hosted during the week. ❀Ⓓ♣️Ⓗ❀

Strathkinness

Tavern
4 High Road, KY16 9RS
☼ 5-11; 12-1am Fri & Sat; 12-midnight Sun
☎ (01334) 850085 🌐 strathkinnesstavern.co.uk
2 changing beers (sourced nationally; often Cromarty, Stewart) Ⓗ
The Tavern, owned and run by the same family since 2008, is at the heart of the village and well known for its welcoming hosts, great food and cracking ales – two handpulls offer a choice of changing guests. Lunches and evening meals are served in the bar and restaurant. Quiz nights and folk evenings are regular events. There is seating at the front of the building with lovely views over the river estuary. Q❀Ⓓ♿️♣️P🚌(64,64A)❀

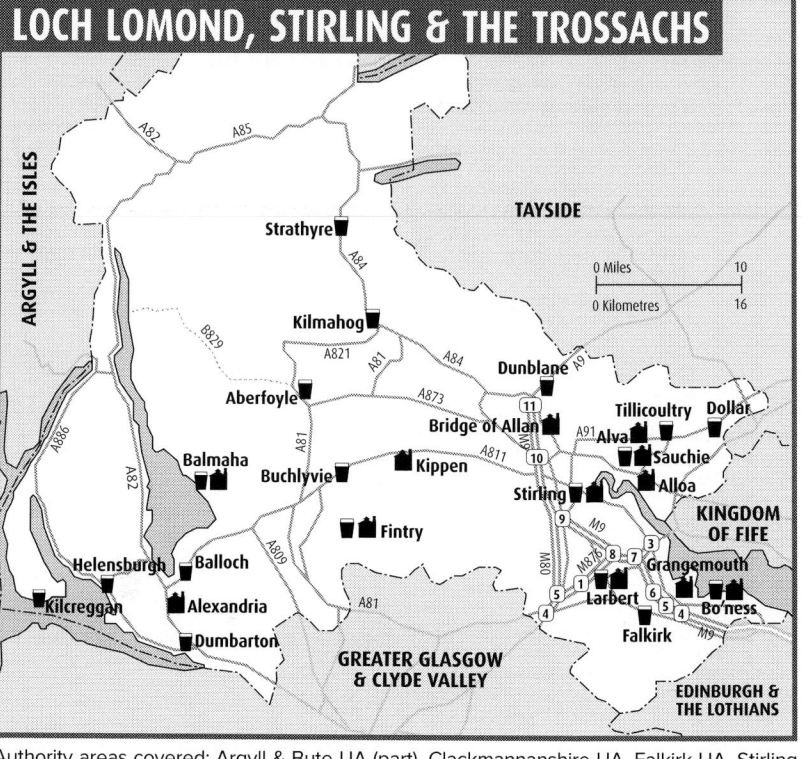

LOCH LOMOND, STIRLING & THE TROSSACHS

Authority areas covered: Argyll & Bute UA (part), Clackmannanshire UA, Falkirk UA, Stirling UA, West Dumbartonshire UA

Aberfoyle

Forth Inn ✓
Main Street, FK8 3UQ
🕐 9am-midnight (1am Fri & Sat) ☎ (01877) 382372
🌐 forthinn.com
Harviestoun Schiehallion; 4 changing beers (sourced regionally; often Belhaven, Cairngorm, Fallen) 🅗
This 100-year-old inn is situated by the River Forth within the Trossachs National Park. The cosy wood-panelled bar is decorated with old photographs of the area and is a magnet for tourists and locals alike. The innovative landlord is proud to serve only Scottish ales from up to eight handpumps, with third-pint taster glasses available, and wholesome food featuring locally sourced produce. There is a separate dining room and a 'baronial' dining hall.
Q ★ ⊛ 🛏️ ◑ ♿ 🅰 ✦ P 🚆 (C11)

Balloch

Balloch House Hotel ✓
Balloch Road, G83 8LQ
🕐 12-11; 12.30-10.30 Sun ☎ (01389) 752579
Sharp's Doom Bar; 4 changing beers 🅗
A prime location on the River Leven by Loch Lomond affords sylvan views from the garden. The well-appointed building offers a choice of seating and dining areas with many exposed beams. Friendly staff serve ales from the Vintage Inns list through five handpumps. A great spot from which to explore the National Park or just to spend some time on the Bonnie Banks.
★ ⊛ 🛏️ ◑ ♿ 🅰 ≈ P 🚆 🐾 ✦ 🛜

Balmaha

Oak Tree Inn
Main Street, G63 0JQ
🕐 9.30am-midnight (1am Fri & Sat) ☎ (01360) 870357
🌐 theoaktreeinn.co.uk
4 changing beers (often Fallen, Jaw, Loch Lomond) 🅗
Balmaha is a picturesque village situated on the quieter eastern shore of Loch Lomond, on the route of the West Highland Way and close to the statue of climber and broadcaster Tom Weir. Meals are served all day in this award-winning pub-restaurant, with four handpumps on the bar dispensing local microbrewery ales. There is a large outdoor drinking area under the eponymous tree. Alcohol is served from 11am (12.30pm Sun). Local CAMRA Rural Stirlingshire Pub of the Year 2016.
★ ⊛ 🛏️ ◑ ♿ P 🚆 (309) 🛜

REAL ALE BREWERIES

Balmaha 🍺 Balmaha
Black Wolf Stirling
Devon 🍺 Sauchie
Fallen Kippen
Fintry Fintry
Harviestoun Alva
Hybrid Grangemouth (NEW)
Kinneil Bo'ness
Loch Lomond Alexandria
Tinpot Bridge of Allan
Tryst Larbert
Williams Bros Alloa

Bo'ness

Corbie Inn ♈
84 Corbiehall, EH51 0AS

✪ 12-11; 12.30-11 Sun ☎ (01506) 825307 ⊕ corbieinn.co.uk
Changing beers (sourced nationally; often Kinneil) Ⓗ
This pub opened in 2011 and has been hand-crafted by the owners. Six ales are usually on handpump, including one from the Kinneil Brew Hoose at the back of the premises. An ideal refreshment stop after a visit to the Bo'ness & Kinneil Railway or the Bo'ness Motor Museum, the pub is also handy for the Hippodrome, Scotland's oldest purpose-built picture house. It is a community venue and involved in local charity projects. Local CAMRA Pub of the Year 2017.
Q ॐ ⊛ ◑ P ☞

Buchlyvie

Buchlyvie Inn ✅
Main Street, FK8 3LX

✪ 12-midnight (1am Fri & Sat); 12.30-midnight Sun
☎ (01360) 850058
2 changing beers (sourced nationally) Ⓗ
A central hub for the community, hosting entertainment at weekends. The small, friendly bar has stone flooring and comfortable seating. The large dining room is furnished in a contemporary rustic style. The rear garden with a children's play area, barbecue, pétanque and splendid views across Flanders Moss to the Trossachs is popular in summer. Two handpumps serve ale from national and local brewers. ॐ ⊛ ≝ ◑ ♣ ▯ ☞ (B12)

Dollar

King's Seat ♈
23 Bridge Street, FK14 7DE

✪ 4-midnight; 12-1am Fri & Sat; 12-midnight Sun
☎ (01259) 742515 ⊕ kingsseat.com
Fyne Jarl; Harviestoun Bitter & Twisted; 4 changing beers (sourced nationally; often Fuller's, Harviestoun) Ⓗ
Cosy, welcoming bar and separate American restaurant situated in a quaint old village. Up to six ales and real cider are on offer during the summer, along with bar snacks and good-value food. Dogs and children are welcome and there are tables and chairs outside for warmer weather. Occasional barbecues and live folk music are hosted. There are many great walks and attractions nearby. Local CAMRA Pub of the Year 2017. Q ⊛ ≝ ◑ ♿ ▲ ☎ ☞ ☀

Dumbarton

Captain James Lang ⓛ ✅
97-99 High Street, G82 1PH

✪ 8am-midnight (1am Fri & Sat) ☎ (01389) 742112
Greene King Abbot; Kelburn Jaguar; 4 changing beers (sourced nationally; often Loch Lomond) Ⓗ
Attractive conversion of a former Woolworths store in an Art Deco-style building on the High Street. One long room stretches from the main entrance through to the beer garden at the rear overlooking the River Leven. The pub is named after a local paddle steamer captain and is decorated with local ephemera reflecting the shipbuilding heritage of the town. The regular beers are supported by guests both from local micros and national breweries. Alcohol is served from 11am.
ॐ ⊛ ◑ ♿ ≝ (Central) ☞ ☀

Dunblane

Riverside
Stirling Road, FK15 9EP

✪ 8am-midnight (1am Fri & Sat); 9am-midnight Sun
☎ (01786) 823318 ⊕ theriversidedunblane.co.uk
Caledonian Deuchars IPA; 2 changing beers (sourced regionally; often Loch Ness, Orkney, Strathaven) Ⓗ
If in the Dunblane area, visit the Riverside for a healthy or hearty breakfast, a coffee and a home-bake beside the wood-burning stove, fantastic food with the family in the restaurant, or a glass of wine or a local beer with friends in the bar or on the terrace. There is a play area for children. The pub is close to Dunblane Cathedral and overlooks the Allan Water. Licensed from 11am.
ॐ ◑ ♿ ≝ ▯ ☀

Tappit Hen
Kirk Street, FK15 0AL

✪ 11-midnight (1am Fri & Sat) ☎ (01786) 825226
⊕ thetappithen-dunblane.co.uk
Belhaven IPA; 4 changing beers Ⓗ
A traditional single-room pub with the interior split into different areas by wooden dividers. It is a cosy meeting point for local people as well as a delightful discovery for visitors. It hosts a weekly folk music night on a Tuesday and a real ale festival once or twice a year. Fundraising events in support of local charities are held regularly at this hospitable and generous community venue.
≝ ▯ ☀ ☎

Falkirk

Behind the Wall ✅
14 Melville Street, FK1 1HZ

✪ 11-midnight (3am Fri & Sat); 12-midnight Sun
☎ (01324) 633338 ⊕ behindthewall.co.uk
Changing beers (often Fyne, Tryst) Ⓗ
This spacious venue for drinking, dining and entertainment was once a bra factory. Upstairs was previously the Eglesbrech Brewery but is now a real ale and whisky bar, with two rooms, timber furnishings and a wood-burning stove. When the brewery closed, Eglesbrech became popular for watching sport events, music and comedy, and hosting bands and comedians from all over the UK. If the upstairs bar is closed, ale can be ordered downstairs and staff will get it for you.
ॐ ⊛ ◑ ≝ ▯ ☎

Wheatsheaf Inn
16 Baxters Wynd, FK1 1PF

✪ 11-midnight (1am Fri & Sat); 12.30-midnight Sun
☎ (01324) 638282 ⊕ thewheatsheaffalkirk.co.uk
Caledonian Deuchars IPA; 3 changing beers (sourced nationally; often Hadrian Border, Ilkley, Knops) Ⓗ
Dating from the late-18th century and retaining much of its original character, this public house is to be found off the High Street via one of the vennels. The wood-panelled bar is furnished in traditional style with plenty of interesting features from the past. Guest ales come from microbreweries in Scotland and England, with two on offer mid-week and three at the weekend. Tea, coffee and snacks are served daily. A must-visit venue when in the area. ⊛ ≝ ▯

Fintry

Fintry Inn
23 Main Street, G63 0XA

✪ 12-midnight; 12.30-midnight Sun ☎ (01360) 860224
⊕ thefintryinn.co.uk
2 changing beers (sourced locally; often Fintry) Ⓗ
The Fintry Inn was established in 1750 and has a long tradition as a country pub. Since 2012, it has been owned and managed by the Fintry Inn Collective whose aim is to ensure that the traditional values of the village pub are maintained for the whole community. A full restaurant service is available along with ales from the Fintry Brewing Co based at the rear of the pub. ☎◑ৈ♣P✿❀

Helensburgh

Ashton Ⓛ
74 West Princes Street, G84 8UG
✪ 11-midnight (1am Fri & Sat) ☎ (01436) 675900
Belhaven IPA; 2 changing beers (sourced nationally; often Loch Lomond) Ⓗ
A warm welcome awaits at this genuine local where the bar has been tastefully modernised and decorated with a nautical theme while retaining its original charm. During the work a set of tiles depicting scenes from Sir Walter Scott's Waverley novels was revealed. There is a small room for playing darts. An ever-changing selection of ales from Scottish microbreweries is supported by quality English beers. Live music is a regular Saturday night feature.
⪪(Central)♣🚍(1B,316)❀🛈

Henry Bell ✪
19-29 James Street, G84 8AS
✪ 8am-midnight (1am Fri & Sat) ☎ (01436) 863060
Greene King Abbot; Sharp's Doom Bar; changing beers (sourced nationally; often Loch Lomond) Ⓗ
Close to the recently revamped town centre and esplanade, this sympathetic Wetherspoon conversion of an old furniture showroom has now established itself as an important real ale outlet in the area. The interior is in the style of Charles Rennie Mackintosh, whose Hill House draws celebrities and visitors to the town, and the walls are adorned with TVs in homage to Helensburgh-born John Logie Baird. A busy and popular venue at the heart of the town. Alcohol is served from 11am. Q☎✿◑ৈ⪪(Central)🚍(1B,316)🛈

Kilcreggan

Kilcreggan Hotel Ⓛ
Argyll Road, G84 0JP (turn off Shore Road at Donaldson's Brae)
✪ 4-midnight; 11.30-1am Fri & Sat; 12.30-midnight Sun
☎ (01436) 842243 ⊕ kilcregganhotel.com
2 changing beers (sourced nationally; often Strathaven) Ⓗ
Perched on an elevated position above the Clyde, the views are stunning. The interior is decorated with a nautical theme and the lounge and patio overlook well-established gardens. An ever-changing choice of two ales is sourced mostly from Scottish breweries, particularly Orkney, Strathaven and Fyne. The pub can be approached via the ferry from Gourock or the bus from Helensburgh. Opening hours vary in winter.
☎✿⇆◑P🚍(316)❀🛈

Kilmahog

Lade Inn Ⓛ
FK17 8HD

✪ 12-11 (1am Fri & Sat); 12.30-10.30 Sun ☎ (01877) 330152
⊕ theladeinn.com
House beer (by Tryst) Ⓗ
A pleasant, friendly pub in a handy spot on the Trossachs Trail to Loch Katrine, next to the multi-use path from Callander to Ben Ledi and beyond. Locally sourced fresh food is an attraction. The three house beers are brewed by Tryst Brewery. The Scottish Real Ale Shop, with its tremendous range of bottled ales, is next door. Scottish folk music features at weekends. Phone ahead to check opening hours in January and February.
Q☎✿◑ৈP🚍(C60)❀

Larbert

Station Hotel ✪
2 Foundry Loan, FK5 4AW
✪ 12-11 (midnight Thu; 1am Fri & Sat); 12.30-11 Sun
☎ (01324) 557186 ⊕ thestationhotellarbert.co.uk
5 changing beers (sourced nationally; often Cairngorm, Greene King, Strathaven) Ⓗ
A popular local, situated next to the railway station and on a regular bus route, this hotel prides itself on the support it gives to a number of community groups. Three to five cask ales are usually on offer and efforts are made to provide a variety of local, regional and national ales. Large-screen TVs show sporting events. The Station is a sponsor of CAMRA's Larbert Real Ale Festival in the nearby Dobbie Hall. ✿⇆⪪P🚍(6,7)

Sauchie

Mansfield Arms ✪
7 Main Street, FK10 3JR
✪ 11-midnight ☎ (01259) 722020 ⊕ devonales.com
Devon Original 70/-, Black, IPA, Pride Ⓗ
The oldest operating microbrewery in the county, this traditional two-bar pub brews four Devon ales dispensed via T-bar founts. Situated within an ex-mining community and family-owned and run, the bar is popular with locals, who enjoy lively banter, and families who come to enjoy a meal in the comfortable lounge. Beer and food are both excellent value for money. The pub is on the Stirling via Alloa circular bus route. ☎◑ৈP🚍❀

Stirling

No.2 Baker Street ✪
2 Baker Street, FK8 1BJ
✪ 11-midnight (1am Fri & Sat) ☎ (01786) 448722
⊕ no2bakerstreet-stirling.co.uk
Belhaven 80/- Ale; Greene King Abbot; 2 changing beers Ⓗ
City-centre pub popular with locals, students and tourists. The single room has plenty of seating and tables, all on street level, and more seating outside for when the weather is good. Music, poker or quiz nights are held most evenings and it can get busy. A Belhaven-managed house, it has eight handpumps, with four or five usually serving Belhaven, Greene King and Scottish micro ales.
◑ৈ⪪🚍🛈

Portcullis Hotel
Castle Wynd, FK8 1EG (adjacent to castle esplanade)
✪ 11-11 Mon & Tue; 11.30-midnight; 11.30-11 Sun
☎ (01786) 472290 ⊕ theportcullishotel.com
2 changing beers (sourced regionally; often Isle of Skye, Orkney) Ⓗ

Popular pub at the top of town, originally the old grammar school building. Exposed stone walls and an open fireplace with ornate surround create a warm welcome in the heart of old Stirling. Frequented by tourists and supported by locals, the pub is renowned for its food and regularly changing selection of Scottish ales from the far north and west. Always busy, diners are advised to reserve a table. Q☰☆⊛≠◑◐↻⇌P⊛

Settle Inn
90 St Marys Wynd, FK8 1BU
☼3-midnight (1am Fri & Sat) ☎ (01786) 474609
3 changing beers (sourced nationally) Ⓗ
Warm, friendly and atmospheric inn popular with a mixed clientele of locals, students and tourists. Situated on a route descending from Stirling Castle, the Settle Inn was built in 1733 and is the oldest pub in Stirling. The pub lives up to its name – settle down in front of the cosy fire and you may not want to leave, ghosts or no ghosts. There is music on Monday, Wednesday, Friday and Saturday, and a quiz on Sunday. ≠⊛🐾📶

Strathyre

Inn & Bistro
Main Street, FK18 8NA
☼12-midnight (1am Fri & Sat); 12.30-midnight Sun
☎ (01877) 384224
3 changing beers (sourced locally; often Inveralmond, Tryst) Ⓗ

Cosy, popular pub, serving meals in the bar or bistro, with an emphasis on local produce. The beers are mainly Scottish. The raised beer garden enjoys panoramic views. Accommodation is available and dogs and children are permitted in the bar. Hill walking, fishing, golf and watersports are all close at hand, and Stirling, Callander and the Trossachs are within easy travelling distance. Opening hours vary in winter. Local CAMRA Rural Stirlingshire Pub of the Year 2017.
Q☰☆⊛≠◑◐♣P⇌(C60)⊛📶

Tillicoultry

Woolpack Inn
1-3 Glassford Square, FK13 6AU
☼2 (11 Mon)-midnight; 11-1am Fri & Sat; 11-midnight Sun
☎ (01259) 750109
House beer (by Greene King); 3 changing beers (sourced nationally; often Belhaven, Greene King, Inveralmond) Ⓗ
Originally a drovers' inn on the southern foothills of the Ochil Hills, this pub is well-used by friendly locals and hill walkers, and has a comfortable feel, log stove and low ceilings. Lively banter dominates rather than TV, muzak or machines. Occasional live music, tasting evenings and quiz nights are hosted. Up to four ales from the Belhaven list change regularly and a good selection of malt whiskies is also available. A former CAMRA Scotland & Northern Ireland Pub of the Year. Q☰♣⊛📶

Lade Inn, Kilmahog

NORTHERN ISLES

Haroldswick

UNST

YELL

SHETLAND

MAINLAND

Wormadale Lerwick

Scalloway

ORKNEY

Swannay

Quoyloo

Kirkwall

Stromness

MAINLAND

HOY

0 Miles   20

0 Kilometres   32

Authority area covered: Highland UA

Kirkwall: Orkney

Auld Motor Hoose

26 Junction Road, KW15 1AB
🌣 11-midnight (1am Fri & Sat) ☎ (01856) 871422
Swannay Scapa Special Ⓗ
A friendly pub with a single-room bar scattered throughout with motoring memorabilia, car parts and illuminated petrol pump tops. The jukebox tends to blast out rock classics. There is regular live music, mainly at weekends, and the pub is one of the venues for the Orkney Rock Festival. Outside, the patio has a smoking area. It is the sister bar to the Torvhaug on Bridge Street. Convenient for the bus station nearby and close to St Magnus Cathedral. CAMRA Northern Isles Pub of the Year 2016. 🌣🍴&🅰🚻🐾🛜

Bothy Bar (Albert Hotel)

Mounthoolie Lane, KW15 1HW (lane between Junction Lane and Bridge St)
🌣 11-midnight (1am Sat); 12-midnight
Sun ☎ 0800 050 9037 ⊕ hotelorkney.co.uk
Swannay Scapa Special; 2 changing beers (sourced locally; often Orkney, Swannay) Ⓗ
After reconstruction using much of the original materials following a fire a few years ago, this popular bar in the town centre has more space than previously, with intimate alcoves offering some privacy. Handy for buses, North Isles ferries and the shops, it is frequented by locals and after-work drinkers, and features on the weekend circuit. A roaring fire adds warmth in winter. Historic St Magnus Cathedral is close by. In the winter months there may be only one beer. A premium is paid for half pints. 🛏🍴&🅰🚻🐾🛜

Helgi's Bar

14 Harbour Street, KW15 1LE (by harbour)
🌣 12.30-midnight ☎ (01856) 879293 ⊕ helgis.co.uk
Swannay Scapa Special; 2 changing beers (sourced locally; often Swannay) Ⓗ
Converted from a former shipping office, this small, smart bar has the look of a modern café with a local stone floor and wood panelling. Set on the harbour front where seafood is landed daily, it is a handy place to fill in time before island hopping on the many ferries to outlying parts. Special food nights where food is matched with ales are hosted, as well as regular music sessions and Thursday quiz nights. One dark beer is always available. A former CAMRA Northern Isles Pub of the Year. Over-18s only. 🍴&🅰🚻🛜

St Ola Hotel

Harbour Street, KW15 1LE
🌣 11-11.30 (midnight Thu; 1am Fri); 10-1am Sat;
10-midnight Sun ☎ (01856) 875090 ⊕ stolahotel.co.uk
Swannay Orkney Best, Scapa Special; 1 changing beer (sourced locally; often Orkney, Swannay) Ⓗ
The Ola is on Kirkwall's waterfront with a traditional public bar facing the harbour and a larger more contemporary lounge to the rear, both serving two beers and an extensive range of whiskies. The busy, friendly pub is close to the ferry for the northern isles of Orkney and all major attractions of Kirkwall are a short walk away. Breakfast is served at the weekend 10am-3pm. 🐾🛏🍴&🅰♣🚻🛜

Scalloway: Shetland

Scalloway Hotel

Main Street, ZE1 0TR
🌣 11-11 ☎ (01595) 880444 ⊕ scallowayhotel.com
1 changing beer (often Lerwick) Ⓗ
Harbourside hotel in the centre of the village with tremendous views. Recently refurbished, it has a small lounge bar where sport is sometimes shown and an award-winning restaurant, where locally caught fish is a speciality. An extensive range of gins and malt whiskies is also available. The neighbouring Scalloway Castle is a listed ancient

REAL ALE BREWERIES

Lerwick Lerwick: Shetland
Orkney Quoyloo: Orkney
Swannay Swannay: Orkney
Valhalla Haroldswick: Unst

SCOTLAND

monument and the Scalloway Museum is close by, providing an interesting insight into life in the village through the ages. Both loch and sea fishing can be arranged, and there are golf courses within three miles. ❄️🛏️🕪️🅿️🚆🛜

Stromness: Orkney

Ferry Inn
10 John Street, KW16 3AD (opp ferry terminal)
☼ 9am-midnight summer; 4-11 (11.30 Fri); 9am-11.30 Sat; 9.30am-11 Sun winter ☎ (01856) 850280 ⊕ ferryinn.com
Swannay Scapa Special; 3 changing beers (sourced locally; often Orkney, Swannay) ℍ
An easy walk from the harbour front, the Ferry Inn is handy for buses to Kirkwall and the ferry from Scrabster. It is popular with locals and visitors, including divers who come to Orkney to explore the sunken German fleet at Scapa Flow. Various attractions nearby include the Ring of Brodgar and Scara Brae village. Annual folk and blues festivals are held, with a marquee erected outside complete

with an ale pump. During the winter months there may be fewer beers available.
❄️🛏️🕪️🅰️🕪️🅿️🚆🐾🛜

Wormadale: Shetland

Westings Inn
ZE2 9LJ (8 miles N of Lerwick on A971)
☼ 7.30-10.30 Thu-Sat; closed Sun-Wed ☎ (01595) 840242
⊕ westings.shetland.co.uk
2 changing beers (sourced nationally; often Fuller's, Timothy Taylor) ℍ
Isolated white-painted inn in a stunning location near the summit of Wormadale Hill. There are marvellous sea views from the comfortable lounge, and adjacent games area, of Whiteness Voe, western Shetland and the outlying islands. Caravans are welcome and camping is available in the pub grounds. Two ales are usually served in summer and one in winter, typically from Fuller's or Timothy Taylor. Phone ahead to check opening hours. 🛏️❄️🛏️🕭️🅰️🕪️🅿️🛜

Ferry Inn, Stromness: Orkney (Photo: George Howie)

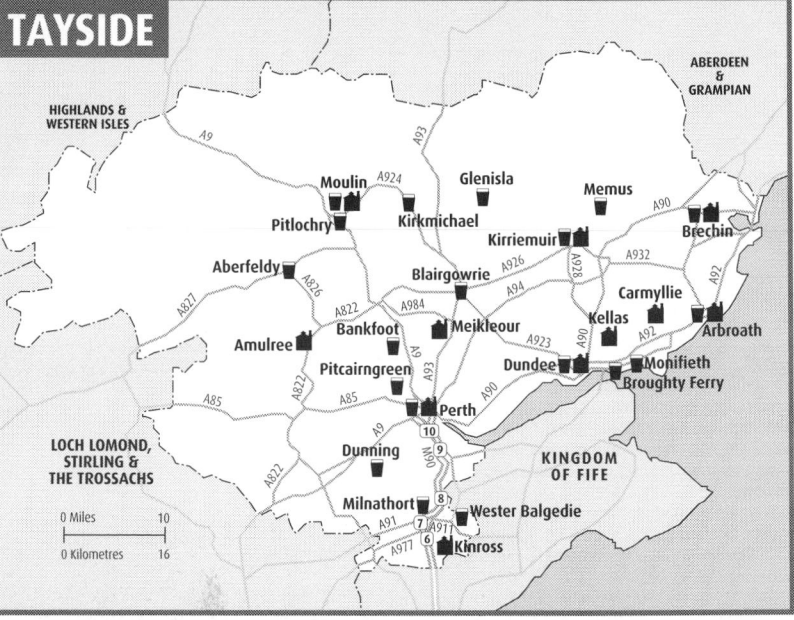

Authority areas covered: Angus UA, City of Dundee UA, Perth & Kinross UA

Aberfeldy

Ben Lawers Hotel

Loch Tay, PH15 2PA

⏱ 11-11 ☎ (01567) 820436 ⊕ benlawershotel.co.uk

1 changing beer (sourced locally; often Inveralmond)

In the heart of one of Scotland's most beautiful and accessible unspoilt areas, this small hotel offers fabulous views over Loch Tay. One handpull always serves a different Inveralmond ale, with a taster happily provided. Staff are welcoming and good food and accommodation are available. The hotel is a popular stop-off for walkers. ⌂◖

Arbroath

Corn Exchange ✅

14 Olympic Centre, Market Place, DD11 1HR

⏱ 8am-midnight (1am Fri & Sat) ☎ (01241) 432430

Caledonian Deuchars IPA; Greene King Abbot; Sharp's Doom Bar; 3 changing beers Ⓗ

Located just off the High Street, this Wetherspoon pub occupies a 19th-century former corn exchange. Although it is largely open plan there are a number of booths providing some privacy. A varied selection of real ales is always available. Boat trips offering fishing or a visit to the 200-year-old Bell Rock lighthouse are available from the nearby harbour. ◖≈⊟🖥

Bankfoot

Bankfoot Inn

Main Street, PH1 4AB

⏱ 12-2 (not Mon & Tue), 6-11; 12-2, 5-12.30am Fri; 12-12.30am Sat; 12-midnight Sun ☎ (01738) 787243 ⊕ bankfootinn.co.uk

3 changing beers (sourced locally) Ⓗ

The hotel has a public bar and a small lounge bar with an adjoining restaurant, warmed by two real fires in winter. The owners are real ale enthusiasts and strongly committed to local breweries. Two ale fests are held each year. Good food is available lunchtimes and evenings Wednesday to Sunday. Quality live folk music features every Wednesday evening. There is outdoor seating at the front and rear of the building. A former Tayside CAMRA Pub of the Year. ⌂🅿⌂◖♣🖥🐾🛜

Blairgowrie

Ericht Alehouse

13 Wellmeadow, PH10 6ND

⏱ 1.30-11 ☎ (01250) 872469

6 changing beers Ⓗ

Classic town-centre pub with a friendly atmosphere. There are two seating areas separated by a well-stocked bar offering a wide range of changing ales and ciders catering for all tastes, alongside a dozen gins. No food is served but customers are welcome to bring their own. A winner of Tayside CAMRA Pub of the Year several times over the past decade. 🅿♣🖥🐾🛜

Fair o' Blair ✅

25-29 Allan Street, PH10 6ND

⏱ 8am-11 ☎ (01250) 871890

SCOTLAND

Greene King Abbot; Sharp's Doom Bar; 3 changing beers ⊞
A Wetherspoon pub since 2013, in the centre of town, with a clean, bright and appealing interior. It offers the chain's typical wide range of good-value food, expertly prepared and well presented, alongside a great choice of well-priced ales.
⊕💷&🐾🛜

Brechin

Caledonian
43 Southesk Street, DD9 6DZ
🕓 closed Mon & Tue; 5-10 Wed & Thu; 4.30-11.30 Fri; 3-11.30 Sat; 3-11 Sun ☎ (01356) 624345
3 changing beers (sourced regionally; often Inveralmond, Park Brew) ⊞
Named after the privately run railway whose terminus is opposite, the Caledonian features a large bar and dining area. The extensive use of wood creates a warm and inviting interior. Park Brew and Inveralmond provide the regular ales, alongside guest beers sourced by the landlord on trips to Hampshire. A wide range of continental bottled beers is also offered. Live folk music on the last Friday of the month is popular. Opening hours are extended in summer. ▶️🚌

Broughty Ferry

Fisherman's Tavern ✅
10-16 Fort Street, DD5 2AD
🕓 11-midnight (1am Thu-Sat) ☎ (01382) 775941
🌐 fishermanstavern-broughtyferry.co.uk
5 changing beers (sourced nationally) ⊞
Licensed since 1857, this famous hostelry was originally three fishermen's cottages, later converted into a small hotel. The bar is to the right of the entrance, and a snug to the left, leading to the dining room/lounge, warmed by a real fire. The lounge to the rear has disabled access from Bell's Lane. An annual beer festival is held in late May. A Belhaven/Greene King managed house, the ales come from Scottish and English breweries.
🏵️🛏️⊕💷🚌🐾🛜

Jolly's Hotel ✅
43A Gray Street, DD5 2BJ
🕓 7am-midnight (1am Fri & Sat) ☎ (01382) 734910
Caledonian Deuchars IPA; Greene King Abbot; 2 changing beers ⊞
Closed for several years, this 25-room hotel was bought by Wetherspoon and reopened in early 2014 after a major refit. There are two large areas, one for drinking and dining, the other principally for dining. Many handpulls serve a wide selection of ales, popular with a mixed clientele of all ages. The outdoor patio area has a number of tables.
🛏️⊕💷🚌🐾🚍🛜

Royal Arch ✅
285 Brook Street, DD5 2DS
🕓 11-midnight (1am Fri & Sat); 12.30-midnight Sun
☎ (01382) 779741
Caledonian Deuchars IPA; 2 changing beers (sourced nationally) ⊞
A popular locally owned pub in the centre of the Ferry. There are three TVs in the public bar for the many sports fans, and good-quality meals are served in the Art Deco lounge. Three handpulls dispense ales from local brewers as well as from all over Britain. The gantry in the public bar was

rescued long ago from the demolished Craigour Bar in Dens Road, and the exterior was refurbished in 2014. 🏵️⊕💷🚌🐾🚍🛜

Ship Inn
121 Fisher Street, DD5 2BR
🕓 11-11; 12.30-11 Sun ☎ (01382) 214235
🌐 theshipinn-broughtyferry.co.uk
Timothy Taylor Landlord; 2 changing beers (sourced regionally) ⊞
The Ship Inn is a traditional free house on the waterfront at Broughty Ferry, with views over the Tay towards Fife. Dating back to 1847, this cosy retreat is interesting and atmospheric, with some nautical features. Three well-kept real ales are usually available. A range of tasty bar meals is on offer and there is a restaurant upstairs. Pavement seating just outside is pleasant in good weather.
⊕💷🚌🐾🛜

Dundee

Bank Bar ✅
7-9 Union Street, DD1 4BN
🕓 11-midnight (10 Mon & Tue); 12.30-7 Sun
☎ (01382) 205037
3 changing beers ⊞
A former bank with bare-board floors, wooden furnishings and a series of alcoves with tables, in the tradition of older Scottish city pubs. A collection of themed pictures decorates the walls. Two or three ales are usually available and food is served until 7pm every day. Quality live music features on most Friday and Saturday nights. ⊕💷🚌🐾🐾

Counting House ✅
67-71 Reform Street, DD1 1SP
🕓 8am-midnight ☎ (01382) 225251
Caledonian Deuchars IPA; Greene King Abbot; 2 changing beers ⊞
Now a Wetherspoon pub, this impressive building first opened as a bank in 1856 and was once a branch of the Royal Bank of Scotland. It was originally designed by George Angus, then modified by William Scott and reconstructed by Robert Gibson in the 1930s. Customers entered his new-look bank via a revolving door, crossed a terrazzo marble floor and were served at handsome mahogany counters topped with shiny bronze grilles. A great city-centre location to enjoy a few ales. ⊕💷&🚍🛜

Market Bar
7-9 Seagate, DD1 2EG
🕓 8am-11 ☎ (01382) 205950
Greene King Abbot; 4 changing beers (often Greene King) ⊞
Formerly the Capitol cinema, built in 1945, but converted into a Lloyd's in 2003 and then sold to become the Market Bar. A staircase rises to the large upper seating area which is primarily used as a family area. Popular with shoppers during the day and lively with revellers on Friday and Saturday evenings. Live music is a regular feature.
🛏️⊕💷🚍(73)🛜

Phoenix
103 Nethergate, DD1 4DH
🕓 11-midnight ☎ (01382) 200014
Caledonian Deuchars IPA; Timothy Taylor Landlord; 3 changing beers ⊞
One of Dundee's oldest pubs, this traditional inn has a great atmosphere. Subdued lighting, sturdy

wooden tables and chairs, and green leather benches give the place character, and there is a rare Ballingall Brewery mirror. Five ales are on offer, and excellent pub food at conservative prices. The location is handy for the Rep Theatre, Dundee Contemporary Arts and Bonar Hall. Warm and cosy, like pubs used to be. ◑🚲≠🖫(73)

Speedwell Bar (Mennie's) ♟ ★ ⊘
165-167 Perth Road, DD2 1AS
🌣 11-11; 12.30-11 Sun ☎ (01382) 667783
🌐 speedwell-bar.co.uk
3 changing beers Ⓗ
Built in 1903 for James Speed, the bar is known as Mennie's after the family who ran it for more than 50 years. The L-shaped interior is divided by a part-glazed screen and has a magnificent mahogany gantry and counter, dado-panelled walls and an anaglypta Jacobean ceiling. It has two sitting rooms, separated by a glass screen. There are usually three ales to choose from, alongside a selection of Belgian bottled beers and around 150 malt whiskies. You can take in your own food. Local CAMRA Pub of the Year 2017. 🖫(73)🏵🎇

Dunning

Kirkstyle Inn ⊘
Kirkstyle Square, PH2 0RR
🌣 5-11 Mon & Tue; 11-2.30, 5-11 (midnight Fri); 11-midnight Sat; 12.30-11 Sun ☎ (01764) 684248
🌐 kirkstyle-dunning.co.uk
2 changing beers Ⓗ
Traditional village inn dating from 1760 overshadowed by the impressive Norman steeple of St Serf's Church, home to the ancient Dupplin Cross and other Pictish relics. One or two ales in the cosy public bar come from a variety of Scottish independents, as well as English and Welsh regional breweries. There is a separate restaurant. Around a mile west of the village stands a 20-foot high stone cross, a memorial to Maggie Wall who was burned here as a witch in 1657. ◑

Glenisla

Kirkton of Glenisla Hotel
PH11 8PH
🌣 12-midnight (1am Fri-Sun) ☎ (01575) 582223
2 changing beers Ⓗ
A welcoming hostelry in a magnificent Angus glen. This 17th-century former coaching inn has been refurbished to a high standard but retains a traditional feel. An excellent selection of real ales from local breweries is served in the cosy, oak-beamed bar, which features an open log fire. Good-value traditional food is available. ◑

Kirkmichael

Strathardle Inn
PH10 7NS (on A924)
🌣 11-11 ☎ (01250) 881224 🌐 strathardleinn.co.uk
3 changing beers Ⓗ
Small, friendly hotel with a bar room with a coal fire and horse brasses around the mantelpiece. Up to three ales are available from Scottish micros, and good lunches and evening meals are served. The historic coaching inn, dating back to the late 1700s, has a 700-yard fishing beat on the River Ardle which flows in front of the building. The

Cateran Trail is also nearby and the Southern Highlands, Glenshee ski slopes, Deeside and Angus Glens are all within reach. 🐕🏵🖢🛏◑P🐾🎇

Kirriemuir

Airlie Arms
St Malcolm's Wynd, DD8 4HB
🌣 11-midnight (1am Fri & Sat); 12.30-1am Sun
☎ (01575) 218080 🌐 airliearms.net
2 changing beers Ⓗ
After many years left closed and in poor condition, this large, B-listed, 18th-century establishment was substantially renovated and reopened in 2015 by the local Ewart family. Real ale has made a welcome appearance, with two handpulls on the bar dispensing a good selection of beers. Food is served daily in the bar and also in the restaurant at weekends. 🛏◑

Glen Clova Hotel
Glen Clova, DD8 4QS
🌣 11-11 (1am Fri & Sat); 12-11 Sun ☎ (01575) 550350
🌐 clova.com
2 changing beers Ⓗ
Situated near the head of one of Scotland's most beautiful glens and popular with walkers after a day on the hills, the hotel's bar has a log-fired stove and plenty of character. Two handpumps supply the ale, usually from Scottish breweries. Local food including lamb and venison is served in the bar and adjoining restaurant. The hotel has a range of accommodation from bunkhouse to en-suite rooms to self-catering luxury lodges. A summer beer festival is held in the field opposite. 🛏◑P

Memus

Drovers Inn
DD8 3TY
🌣 11-11 (midnight Fri & Sat); 12.30-10 Sun
☎ (01307) 860322 🌐 the-drovers.com
2 changing beers (sourced regionally) Ⓗ
In a rural setting just north of Forfar and handily placed for the Angus Glens, the Drovers is a traditional Scottish inn with a contemporary look. An old range fire in the bar adds to the atmosphere, especially on a chilly day. Two real ales are usually served, and excellent food using locally sourced seasonal produce is available daily. There is a large outdoor dining area under the trees with an adjoining play area for children. Q🐕🏵◑

Milnathort

Village Inn
36 Wester Loan, KY13 9YH
🌣 2-11 (midnight Fri); 12-midnight Sat; 12.30-11 Sun
☎ (01577) 863293
3 changing beers (sourced locally) Ⓗ
Friendly local with a semi open-plan interior featuring classic brewery mirrors and local historic photographs. The comfortable lounge area has low ceilings, exposed joists and stone walls, and the bar area is warmed by a log fire. At the rear is a games room with a pool table. This pub has been family owned since 1985 and usually serves three - often local - beers. Milnathort links some great cycling routes through the Ochils, via Burleigh Castle, to the more leisurely Loch Leven Heritage Trail. 🏵🚲♣🖫(23)

Monifieth

Milton Inn ✓
Grange Road, DD5 4LU

✪ closed Mon; 12-2.30, 5-11; 12-midnight Fri & Sat; 12-11 Sun ☎ (01382) 532620 ⊕ themiltoninn.co.uk

3 changing beers (sourced nationally) Ⓗ

The only premises in Monifieth serving real ale, which this traditional inn does with a passion. There are usually three beers to choose from, alongside good home-made food at fair prices. The pub is set back from the road, with large gardens and a sunny decked area to the rear providing a nice sheltered spot for a pint in the fresh air, or to enjoy a barbecue. Entertainment features regularly.
✿⇰◑⇌P⊟ 🛜

Moulin

Moulin Inn
11-13 Kirkmichael Road, PH16 5EH

✪ 11-11 ☎ (01796) 472196 ⊕ moulininn.co.uk

Moulin Light, Braveheart, Ale of Atholl, Old Remedial Ⓗ

First opened in 1695, the inn is the oldest part of the Moulin Hotel, situated within the village square of an ancient crossroads, just east of Pitlochry. Full of character and charm, it is traditionally furnished and has two log fires. A good choice of home-prepared local fare is available, along with four Moulin beers, brewed in the old coach house behind the hotel. There is an area outside for dining and drinking in good weather. An ideal base for outdoor pursuits, with several marked walks nearby. Q⌂ప✿⇰◑♣P

Perth

Cherrybank Inn
210 Glasgow Road, PH2 0NA

✪ 11-11 (12.30am Thu-Sat); 12-midnight Sun
☎ (01738) 624349 ⊕ cherrybankinn.co.uk

Inveralmond Ossian; 5 changing beers (sourced regionally; often Inveralmond) Ⓗ

This 250-year-old former drovers' inn is a popular watering hole and stopover for travellers. Ales from Inveralmond and other Scottish independents are dispensed from six handpulls in the multi-roomed public bar or the larger L-shaped lounge, with views up to a woodland walk. Good bar lunches and evening meals are served. The inn has seven well-appointed en-suite rooms, and golf can be arranged for residents. ప✿⇰◑♣P⊟(7)♣🛜

Green Room Ⓛ
97 Canal Street, PH2 8HX

✪ 12-11 (12.30am Thu; 1.30am Fri & Sat); 12-midnight Sun
☎ (01738) 248121 ⊕ thegreenroomperth.com

Inveralmond Rascal London Porter; 6 changing beers Ⓗ

Following a major makeover, this establishment now has three bars, one with six handpulls, plus a large selection of bottled beers from around the world. Live entertainment plays seven nights a week, which pulls in plenty of customers. A must-visit venue in Perth for ale enthusiasts, in a convenient city-centre location near to the railway station. ⇌

Greyfriars Ⓛ
15 South Street, PH2 8PG

✪ 11-11 (11.45 Fri & Sat); 3-11 Sun ☎ (01738) 633036
⊕ perth-bars.co.uk/greyfriars.php

Inveralmond Lia Fail; 3 changing beers (sourced regionally; often Inveralmond) Ⓗ

Small city-centre lounge bar selling up to four ales, often including an Inveralmond beer. Good-value lunches are served in the bar and a small seating area upstairs. The pub takes its name from the former Greyfriars monastery. Nearby attractions include a Victorian theatre, art gallery, museum and concert hall. This may well be the smallest lounge bar in the Fair City but it has an enviable reputation among locals and visitors as one of the friendliest. ◑⇌

Pitcairngreen

Pitcairngreen Inn
PH1 3LP

✪ 10.30-11 (midnight Fri & Sat) ☎ (01738) 583022
⊕ pitcairngreeninn.co.uk

3 changing beers (sourced locally) Ⓗ

A fairly large establishment with several different areas including a snug warmed by an open log fire. The inn has a real enthusiasm for good beer, served on three handpulls. This is the finest place in Tayside to enjoy real ciders and perries, presented professionally and with passion. Good-value, home-cooked meals are also available. The car park is just across the road. Tayside CAMRA Cider Pub of the Year in 2016.
Q✿◑♣P⊟(14,15)♣

Pitlochry

Old Mill Inn
Mill Lane, PH16 5BH

✪ 11-11; 11-midnight Sat & Sun ☎ (01796) 474020
⊕ theoldmillpitlochry.co.uk

Strathbraan Due South, Head East; 2 changing beers Ⓗ

A family-owned, well-run establishment in the town centre, built in the 19th century as a mill, with the mill wheel still driven by the stream. Customers can sit beside it in fine weather. The large bar serves a varied selection of three or four guest ales alongside beers from local Scottish microbrewery Strathbraan. ప✿⇰◑&⇌♣P⊟🛜

Wester Balgedie

Balgedie Toll Tavern
KY13 9HE (2 miles E of M90 at jct of A911 and B919)

✪ 11-11 (11.30 Thu; 12.30am Fri & Sat); 12.30-11.30 Sun
☎ (01592) 840212

Harviestoun Bitter & Twisted; 1 changing beer Ⓗ

Welcoming and comfortable rural tavern dating from 1534 where travellers had to break their journey to pay tolls. Now much extended, the oldest part of the building, the toll house, is at the southern end. It has three seating areas plus a small bar with low ceilings, oak beams, horse brasses, wooden settles and works of art by a local painter. A good selection of meals and bar snacks is available. Guest beers are rotated, mainly from Scottish independent breweries. ✿◑P⊟

NORTHERN ISLES

SHETLAND

HIGHLANDS
&
WESTERN ISLES

ABERDEEN
& GRAMPIAN

TAYSIDE

ARGYLL &
THE ISLES

LOCH LOMOND
STIRLING
& THE
TROSSACHS

FIFE

EDINBURGH & LOTHIANS

GREATER
GLASGOW &
CLYDE

BORDERS

AYRSHIRE
& ARRAN

NORTHERN
IRELAND

DUMFRIES &
GALLOWAY

NORTHUMBERLAND

TYNE &
WEAR

CUMBRIA

DURHAM

NORTH
YORKSHIRE

ISLE OF
MAN

LANCASHIRE

EAST
YORKS

WEST
YORKS

MERSEYSIDE

GREATER
MANCHESTER

SOUTH
YORKS

NW
WALES

NE
WALES

CHESHIRE

DERBYSHIRE

NOTTINGHAM-
SHIRE

LINCOLNSHIRE

STAFFORD-
SHIRE

NORFOLK

SHROPSHIRE

LEICESTERSHIRE

RUTLAND

CAMBRIDGE-
SHIRE

SUFFOLK

WEST
MIDLANDS

NORTHAMPTON-
SHIRE

MID
WALES

HEREFORD-
SHIRE

WORCESTER-
SHIRE

WARWICK-
SHIRE

BEDFORD-
SHIRE

WEST
WALES

GWENT

GLOUCS &
BRISTOL

OXFORD-
SHIRE

BUCKINGHAM-
SHIRE

HERTFORD-
SHIRE

ESSEX

GLAMORGAN

GREATER
LONDON

BERKSHIRE

WILTSHIRE

SURREY

KENT

SOMERSET

HAMPSHIRE

WEST
SUSSEX

EAST
SUSSEX

CHANNEL
ISLANDS

DEVON

DORSET

ISLE OF
WIGHT

CORNWALL

Northern Ireland
Channel Islands
Isle of Man

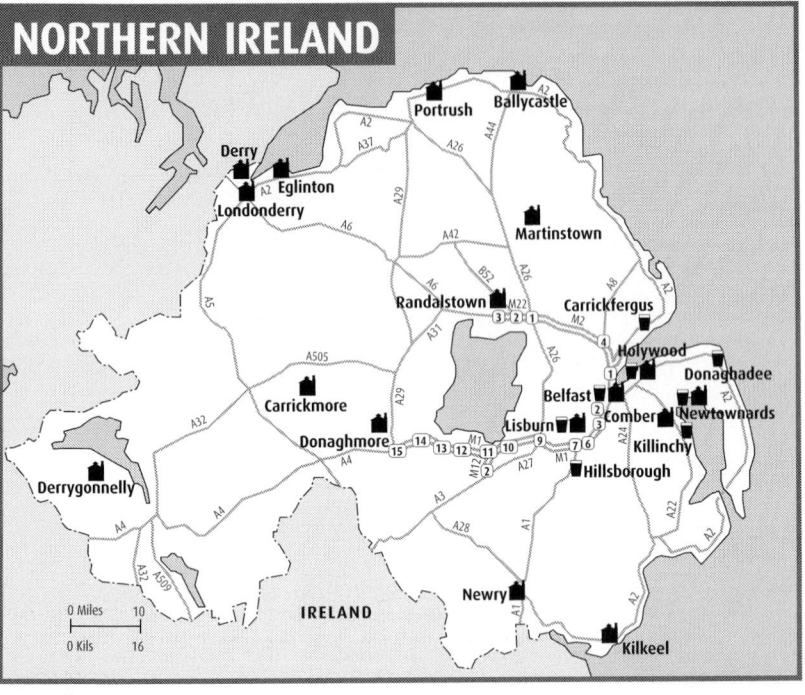

NORTHERN IRELAND

Belfast

Bridge House ✓
37-43 Bedford Street, BT2 7EJ
🕑 8am-midnight (1am Fri & Sat); 12-midnight Sun
☎ (028) 9072 7890
Greene King Abbot; Sharp's Doom Bar; changing beers (sourced nationally) ⊞
The Bridge House is reputed to be one of the Wetherspoon's busiest bars and sells a lot of real ale from eight handpumps. In the downstairs bar, seating ranges from comfy booths to large craft bar-style tables. Upstairs is more of a restaurant experience, and there are plans to add a beer garden. A two-times winner of local CAMRA Pub of the Year. Alcohol is served from 11.30am (12.30pm Sun). Q🕭🕼❍🕇🖳🏠🛜

Crown 🏆 ★ ✓
46 Great Victoria Street, BT2 7BA (opp Europa Hotel and Great Victoria St station)
🕑 11.30-11; 12.30-10 Sun ☎ (028) 9024 3187
St Austell Nicholson's Pale Ale; Whitewater Belfast Ale; 3 changing beers (sourced nationally) ⊞
The Crown is known for its outstanding interior and exterior, and looks even better now following a facelift. It is also a top spot for real ale, with five handpumps serving Nicholson's Pale Ale and local ales mainly from Whitewater Brewery. Three guests vary, especially during the regular beer festivals. Good food is available upstairs in the Crown Dining Rooms and downstairs in the main bar. Current local CAMRA Pub of the Year.
Q❍🕇🖳🏠

Errigle Inn
312-320 Ormeau Road, BT7 2GE
🕑 11.30-1am; 10-midnight Sun ☎ (028) 9064 1410
🌐 errigle.com

Hilden Scullion's Irish; Shepherd Neame Whitstable Bay Pale Ale; Whitewater Belfast Ale; 1 changing beer (often Farmageddon Brewing Co-op) ⊞
On the Ormeau Road in the south side of the city, this pub has been trading since 1935. The Errigle, in particular the Oak Lounge, has become something of a haven for ale enthusiasts. It has five handpumps, with an emphasis on local beer from Hilden, Whitewater and Farmageddon. Shepherd Neame ales are also available. The Lounge is a quiet back bar where beer and food can be enjoyed in peace. Q❍🕇🖳🏠🛜

Garrick Bar
29 Chichester Street, BT1 4JB
🕑 11.30-1am; 12.30-midnight Sun ☎ (028) 9032 1984
🌐 thegarrickbar.com
Sharp's Atlantic ⊞
The Garrick Bar is a long-established public house close to the city centre. It has a pleasingly traditional-style front bar and a more modern lounge at the back featuring a collection of barometers. The food is good and available in both bars. The handpump is in the front bar and dispenses ales from Sharp's. Sports TV is a major feature along with live entertainment – bands or DJs – throughout the week. 🕼🖳

John Hewitt
51 Donegal Street, BT1 2FH (100yds from St Anne's Cathedral)
🕑 11.30 (12 Sat)-1am; 7-midnight Sun ☎ (028) 9023 3768
🌐 thejohnhewitt.com
Shepherd Neame Master Brew ⊞
Named after the poet John Hewitt, this is a busy single-room bar with a large snug. It is different from most bars in that it is run by the Belfast Unemployed Resource Centre, and profits fund the centre's work. It is also a venue for live music, charity evenings, art exhibitions and other events.

High-quality food is served at lunchtime with specials on the blackboard. A single handpump dispenses Shepherd Neame beers and occasional guests. Q⊃◖&⚏

Kitchen Bar

1 Victoria Square, BT1 4QB (adjacent to Victoria Shopping Centre, Victoria St side)
⚙ 11.30-11.30 (midnight Mon); 11.30-1am Fri & Sat; 12-11 Sun ☎ (028) 9024 5268 ⊕ thekitchenbar.com
Whitewater Maggie's Leap IPA Ⓗ
The Kitchen is very much a shopping-centre bar and as part of the Victoria Square development it is extraordinarily busy. The bar is in the middle, with a restaurant/music area on one side and a sports TV on the other. Whitewater's Maggie's Leap is the sole real ale. Food served all day and music up to four nights a week are the other attractions.
◖&⇌⚏

McHugh's

29-31 Queens Square, BT1 3FG (near Albert Clock)
⚙ 12-1am; 12-midnight Sun ☎ (028) 9050 9999
⊕ mchughsbar.com
Whitewater Maggie's Leap IPA Ⓗ
Long-established, traditional hostelry which has been sympathetically upgraded and extended to incorporate the adjacent premises, formerly a renowned brothel. The interior comprises a basement function room, a ground-floor bar with new and old areas, and a galleried restaurant on the first floor. There is one handpump dispensing Whitewater's Maggie's Leap. The patrons include regulars, tourists and visitors to nearby music venues. A variety of live music from folk to jazz features throughout the week.
Q◖&⇌(Central)⚏🔊

Sunflower

65 Union Street, BT1 2JG
⚙ 11.30-midnight (1am Thu-Sat); 5-11 Sun
☎ (028) 9023 2474 ⊕ sunflowerbelfast.com
Hilden Twisted Hop Ⓗ
A renovated corner pub with a lively atmosphere and a colourful beer garden. It is slightly out of the way, just north of the city centre, behind Belfast Central Library. The bar downstairs is cosy and has one handpump offering a changing Hilden ale. Upstairs hosts musical events, though bands play downstairs too and the pub has become a renowned live music venue. Pizza is available Thursday to Saturday evenings. Q⚙◖⚏

Carrickfergus

Central Bar ⊘

13-15 High Street, BT38 7AN (opp castle)
⚙ 8am-midnight (1am Fri & Sat); 8am-midnight Sun
☎ (028) 9335 7840
Greene King Abbot; Sharp's Doom Bar; 3 changing beers (sourced nationally) Ⓗ
Busy town-centre Wetherspoon with a lively downstairs bar and a quieter family dining area upstairs. The dining area and the beer garden enjoy a fantastic view which takes in Belfast Lough and Carrickfergus Castle. Up to 10 handpumps dispense the two regular beers plus three or more changing guests. Not far from bus and rail stations. Alcohol is served from 11.30am (12.30pm Sun).
Q⊃⚙◖&⇌⚏(563)

Donaghadee

Moat Inn

102 Moat Street, BT21 0ED
⚙ 11.30-11.30; 12.30-10 Sun ☎ (028) 9188 3297
⊕ moatinn.co.uk
Whitewater Belfast Ale; 1 changing beer (sourced locally; often Whitewater) Ⓗ
On the main road into Donaghadee, the Moat Inn has a public bar, lounge, upstairs restaurant and garden area for summer days. There are two handpumps in the public bar supplying beers mainly from Whitewater Brewery, often Belfast Ale and Copperhead, and occasional guests. The seaside town is well known for the lighthouse and the picturesque harbour just a few hundred yards away. The pub and locality are well worth a visit.
Q⊃⚙◖&⚏(7)

Hillsborough

Hillside

21 Main Street, BT26 6AE
⚙ 12-11.30 (12.30am Fri & Sat); 12-11 Sun
☎ (028) 9268 9233 ⊕ hillsidehillsborough.co.uk
Hilden Nut Brown, Twisted Hop; 1 changing beer (sourced nationally) Ⓗ
The Hillside is a bar and restaurant dating from 1752. It is located halfway up the hill in Hillsborough, which is about 12 miles from Belfast. Inside there are a number of drinking and dining areas. Three handpumps dispense beers from Hilden Brewery and occasional national guests. The annual beer festival is popular, and the bar takes part in Oyster Festival events. It is home to local groups such as Hillsborough's bell ringers, and hosts a variety of musical acts.
Q⊃⚙◖&⚏(38,238)❀

Holywood

Dirty Duck Ale House

3 Kinnegar Road, BT18 9JN
⚙ 12-11 (1am Thu-Sat); 12.30-11 Sun ☎ (028) 9059 6666
⊕ thedirtyduckalehouse.co.uk
3 changing beers (sourced nationally; often Barney's Beer, Inveralmond, Shepherd Neame) Ⓗ
The Dirty Duck is a two-times winner of CAMRA Northern Ireland Pub of the Year. The single room bar has a restaurant upstairs but good food is

REAL ALE BREWERIES

Ards Newtownards
Barrahooley Craft Martinstown (NEW)
Boundary Belfast
Bullhouse Newtownards (NEW)
Dopey Dick Derry (NEW)
Farmageddon Comber
Glens of Antrim Ballycastle (NEW)
Hercules Holywood
Hilden Lisburn
Hillstown Randalstown
Inishmacsaint Derrygonnelly
Knockout Belfast
Lacada Portrush
Northbound Eglinton
Pokertree Carrickmore
Red Hand 🍴 Donaghmore
Station Works Newry
Walled City 🍴 Londonderry
Whitewater Kilkeel

served throughout. Three regularly changing real ales are available plus the house beer, Dirty Duck Ale, brewed by Hilden. There is much to admire here – a great view over Belfast Lough, a roomy beer garden, a collection of pumpclips and a corner in honour of golfer Rory McIlroy. Q☺️🛏🍴◑♿⇌

Killinchy

Daft Eddy's ⌊

Sketrick Island, BT23 6QH (2 miles N of Killinchey at Whiterock Bay)

🕐 11.30-11.30 (1am Fri); 12-10.30 Sun ☎ (028) 9754 1615
🌐 dafteddys.co.uk

1 changing beer (sourced locally; often Farmageddon Brewing Co-op)

Northern Ireland's most remote, yet pleasantly situated real ale bar. It is on an island in Strangford Lough about two miles from the nearest town. The main bar has one handpump dispensing beers from Farmageddon. The pub is well known for the quality of the restaurant, where seafood is a speciality. Meals are also served in the adjacent coffee bar. A covered verandah has been added. With its impressive view this is one of the country's treasures. Q☺️🛏◑♿P

Lisburn

Tap Room

BT27 4TY (5 mins' walk from Hilden railway halt)

🕐 closed Mon; 12-2.30, 5.30-9; 12-3 Sun ☎ (028) 9266 3863
🌐 taproomhilden.com

Hilden Irish Stout; 1 changing beer (sourced locally; often Hilden) ⒣

The Tap Room is set in Hilden Brewery's courtyard. It is next to the brewhouse in the grounds of a magnificent Georgian mansion. There are usually two ales from the brewery, complementing the locally sourced cuisine. As a licensed restaurant, alcohol is only available with a meal. The venue also hosts functions including an annual beer festival. Tours can be arranged around the brewery, which recently celebrated its 35th year. Q☺️◑♿⇌🚌 (325H)

Tuesday Bell ✓

4 Lisburn Square, BT28 1TS

🕐 8am-11 (midnight Fri & Sat) ☎ (028) 9262 7390

Greene King Abbot; Sharp's Doom Bar ⒣

The Tuesday Bell is a large two-floor pub in the middle of Lisburn, close to the bus station. Established now for 15 years, it continues to be a popular location for dining and drinking. There are five handpumps downstairs and three upstairs offering a changing range of beers to complement the two regulars. Local ale from Hilden and real cider are often available. Alcohol is served from 11.30am (12.30pm Sun). Q☺️◑♿⇌♣🍴P🚭🛜

Newtownards

Spirit Merchant ✓

54-56 Regent Street, BT23 4LP (next to bus station)

🕐 8am-midnight ☎ (028) 9182 4270

Greene King Abbot; Sharp's Doom Bar; 2 changing beers (sourced nationally) ⒣

This large single-bar Wetherspoon pub on the main street retains the ambience of the local pub that it once was. In addition to the regular beers, up to two changing guests are offered on the pub's five handpumps. A popular feature is the large heated courtyard to the side. The usual good-value Wetherspoon's menu is served, with breakfast from 8am. Alcohol is available from 11.30am (12.30pm Sun). Q☺️🛏◑♿🚭 (7)

Bridge House, Belfast (Photo: Jim Taylor)

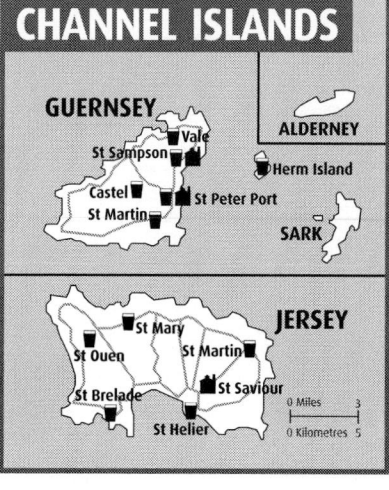

GUERNSEY
Castel

Fleur du Jardin 🅥
Kings Mills, GY5 7JT
🕐 10.30-11.45 ☎ (01481) 257996 ⊕ fleurdujardin.com
2 changing beers Ⓗ
A building of unique charm with two bars – one traditional, small and cosy, attached to the restaurant, the other renovated in a more contemporary style to create a comfortable, relaxing area to enjoy a beer. A door from here leads to a large covered patio and out to the garden. Menus in both the bar and restaurant feature fresh local produce. The car park can be busy during the summer months.
Q🏠🕏🏨🕪🛏️P🖵🕏

La Grand Mare Hotel & Golf Club
Vazon Bay, GY5 7LL (on Vazon coast road)
🕐 10-11.45; 12-11.45 Sun ☎ (01481) 256576
⊕ lagrandemare.com
Shepherd Neame Spitfire; 2 changing beers Ⓗ
The hotel is open all year for guests and locals alike. It is situated opposite the beach at Vazon, one of the popular west coast bays. The Club bar is open every day, with a large-screen TV showing sports and a fire in the winter months. There is also a separate bar with comfy seats attached to the large restaurant. Children are welcome.
🏠🏨🕪🛏️&P🖵🕏

Rockmount Hotel
Cobo, GY5 7HB
🕐 10.30-midnight (12.45am Fri & Sat) ☎ (01481) 252778
⊕ therocky.gg
5 changing beers
The pub, overlooking Cobo beach, has a taproom with sport on TV and a large lounge bar. The lounge has an emphasis on food, serving a good range of dishes featuring locally sourced produce, but there are comfy chairs near the fire for drinkers. Five handpumps offer a changing range of beers and you can also try a tasting paddle of different ales.
Q🕪&🖵🕏

Herm Island

Mermaid Tavern 🏆 🅥
GY1 3HR (travel Trident ferry from St Peter Port to Herm, then follow signs)
🕐 11-10.30; 12-10.30 Sun ☎ (01481) 750050 ⊕ herm.com/mermaid
House beer (by Liberation); 2 changing beers Ⓗ
A short trip by ferry from Guernsey takes you to Herm. A large courtyard acts as a suntrap in the summer while in winter an open fire creates a cosy atmosphere. Real ale and cider festivals are held twice a year. The house beer is Herm Island Gold. A trip to Herm to discover the island's tranquillity and outstanding natural beauty is a must for any visitor to Guernsey. Guernsey CAMRA Pub of the Year 2016. 🏠🕏🏨🕪Å♣♥🐾🕏

St Martin

Captain's Hotel 🅥
La Fosse, GY4 6EF
🕐 11-11 (midnight Fri & Sat); 12-4 Sun ☎ (01481) 238990
⊕ thecaptainshotel.co.uk
Butcombe Original; Sharp's Doom Bar Ⓗ
In a secluded location down a country lane, this is a popular locals' pub with a lively, friendly atmosphere. It has a small, raised area in front of the bar furnished with a sofa to make a comfy zone. Good-quality meals can be eaten in the bar or bistro area, or you can take away a pizza. A meat draw is held on Friday. The car park to the rear fills up quickly. Accommodation is offered in nine en-suite bedrooms. 🏨🕪P🖵

Les Douvres Hotel 🅥
La Fosse, GY4 6ER
🕐 10.30-12.30am ☎ (01481) 238731
⊕ lesdouvreshotel.co.uk
Black Sheep Best Bitter; Timothy Taylor Landlord; 2 changing beers Ⓗ
Former 18th-century manor house, set in private gardens in St Martin near the south coast, two-and-a-half miles from St Peter Port, with cliff walks and a tiny fishing harbour. A well-maintained, changing range of beers is offered on two handpumps, and seasonal real cider. Excellent meals are served in the bar and separate restaurant. Live music features on Friday nights and occasional Wednesdays. The venue is popular with locals and visitors. 🕏🏨🕪🐾P🖵

St Peter Port

Cock & Bull
Lower Hauteville, GY1 1LL
🕐 11-12.45am; closed Sun ☎ (01481) 722660
⊕ cockandbullguernsey.com
5 changing beers Ⓗ
Just up the hill from the town church, the pub has five handpumps providing a changing range of beers, and real cider in summer. Seating is on three levels, with a pool table in the lower level. Live music features throughout the week, with open mic on Tuesday, Irish on Thursday, baroque once a month on Monday, and on Saturday a silent set –

REAL ALE BREWERIES

Liberation St Saviour: Jersey
Randalls St Peter Port: Guernsey
White Rock St Sampsons: Guernsey

ISLANDS

gentle music that won't hinder conversation. A meat draw is held on Friday. The pub only opens on Sunday when rugby is on. ♿🍺🚐🛜

Cornerstone 🅛

2 La Tour Beauregard, GY1 1LQ
✪ 11-12.30am; 12-11 Sun ☎ (01481) 713832
⊕ thecornerstone.gg
White Rock Wonky Donkey; 4 changing beers (often White Rock) Ⓗ
The Cornerstone has a small bar area to the front and further seating to the rear, with a large screen for sporting events. White Rock beer is always on handpump together with a varying range of other ales – visit the website to see the current brews. Gluten-free beer is kept in bottles and gluten-free meals are available with advance notice. There is a meat draw on a Sunday. ⏻🍺🚐🛜

Golden Lion

7 Market Street, GY1 1HF
✪ 10-12.30am; 12-11 Sun ☎ (01481) 726634
⊕ thegoldenlion.gg
White Rock Wonky Donkey; 7 changing beers (often White Rock) Ⓗ
Town-centre pub opposite the former Market. This is the second White Rock Brewery pub in Guernsey. One room with a long bar offers up to 10 real ales, usually including three from White Rock. The pub has the modern feel of a craft beer bar. Live music plays on occasion in the downstairs bar. The first floor has been renovated and is now the Lions Den, open in the evenings and available for private hire. Gluten-free beer is available in bottles. 🚐🛜

Red Lion

Les Banques, GY1 2RX (on seafront to N of St Peter Port)
✪ 11-11 (midnight Fri & Sat) ☎ (01481) 724042
3 changing beers Ⓗ
On the outskirts of St Peter Port, the Red Lion has two bar areas – a seafront lounge overlooking Belle Greve Bay to the front and a public area at the rear. Large-screen TVs show sport in both bars – just ask if there is something you would like to view. Meat draws are held on Friday and Saturday evenings. A changing variety of beers is offered on handpump and gluten-free beer in bottles. Real cider is added in the summer months. The pub is on several bus routes and on the cycle route between St Peter Port and St Sampson. 🐕🏠⏻🍺🚐🐾🛜

St Sampson

Pony Inn ✅

Les Capelles, GY2 4GX (on main road between Guernsey Candles and Oatlands Centre)
✪ closed Mon; 11 (10 Sat)-11; 12-6.30 Sun
☎ (01481) 244374
Butcombe Original; 1 changing beer Ⓗ
Well-maintained beer and good food in generous portions is served in the main bar, conservatory area and separate family dining room (booking is advisable for food, particularly at weekends). The public bar at the side shows sports events on TV and has a pool table. The staff are friendly and families are welcome. There is disabled access for wheelchair users. 🐕🏠⏻♿♣P🚐

> Beer is proof that God loves us and wants us to be happy. **Benjamin Franklin**

Vale

Houmet Tavern ✅

Rousse, GY6 8AR (between church and Rousse Tower)
✪ 10-12.45am (6 Sun) ☎ (01481) 242214
Butcombe Gold; 2 changing beers Ⓗ
A popular pub, the Houmet has two bars – the Anchor Bar, which is the public bar at the rear with pool and darts, and the Front Bar, which has more of an emphasis on food, and enjoys picturesque views of the north of the island. Only the public bar is open in the afternoon during the week. The same choice of beer is available in both bars. ⏻P🚐🛜

JERSEY
St Brelade

Old Smugglers Inn

Le Mont du Ouaisne, JE3 8AW
✪ 11-11 ☎ (01534) 741510 ⊕ oldsmugglersinn.com
Draught Bass Ⓗ**; Greene King Abbot** Ⓖ**; 1 changing beer** Ⓗ
Perched on the edge of Ouaisne Bay, the Smugglers has been the crown jewel of the Jersey real ale scene for many years. Steeped in history, dating back to when pirates came to enjoy an ale or two here, it is set within granite-built fishermen's cottages with foundations reputedly from the 13th century. Up to four ales are available including one from Skinner's, and mini beer festivals are regularly held. The pub is known for its good food including fresh daily specials. Q🐕🏠⏻🍺P🚐(12,15)🐾

St Helier

Forum 🅛 ✅

13 Grenville Street, JE2 4UF
✪ 11-11 ☎ (01534) 768105
Box Steam Tunnel Vision, Piston Broke; 1 changing beer (often Liberation) Ⓗ
On the outskirts of town, the pub is named after the cinema that once stood opposite. It has a modern interior but with a classic feel and includes a number of brass plaques taken from the old Royal Court building. Three real ales are always available, and a large range of real ciders. Upstairs is a sports bar with darts, pool and football tables, and sports TV. A former local CAMRA Pub of the Year. ⏻♿♣🚐(3)🐾🛜

Lamplighter 🍷 🅛 ✅

9 Mulcaster Street, JE2 3NJ
✪ 11-11 ☎ (01534) 723119 ⊕ randallsjersey.com
Ringwood Fortyniner; Wells Eagle IPA, Bombardier; 5 changing beers Ⓖ
A traditional pub with a modern feel. The gas lamps that gave the pub its name remain, as does the original antique pewter bar top. An excellent range of up to eight real ales is available – the largest selection on the island – including one from Skinner's. All real ales are served direct from the cellar. A real cider is sometimes also on offer. Winner of local CAMRA Pub of the Year in 2016 and many times previously. ⏻🍺🚐🛜

Peirson 🅛 ✅

17 Royal Square, JE2 4WA
✪ 10-11; 11-11 Sun ☎ (01534) 722726
Draught Bass; Liberation Ale Ⓗ**; 1 changing beer** Ⓖ

Nestled in the corner of the Royal Square in the centre of St Helier. Named after Major Francis Peirson, it displays historical reminders of the Battle of Jersey in 1781. Two ales are always on handpump plus an occasional guest ale on gravity. Excellent food is served at lunchtime throughout the year, with evening meals also on offer in summer. The pub has a good reputation with locals and visitors alike. Outside seating is extremely popular in the summer months. Q ⌂ ◐ & ⊟ ❀

Post Horn ⎣ ✅
Hue Street, JE2 3RE
✿ 10-11; 11-11 Sun ☎ (01534) 872853
Liberation Ale; 2 changing beers (often Liberation) ⊞
Busy, friendly pub adjacent to the precinct and five minutes' walk from the Royal Square. Popular at lunchtimes with its own nucleus of regulars, it offers up to four draught ales. The large L-shaped public bar extends into the lounge area where there is an open fire and TV showing sport. A good selection of freshly cooked food is served. There is a large function room on the first floor, a drinking area outside and a public car park nearby. ⊛ ◐ & ⊟ ❀ 🛜

St Martin
Royal
La Grande Route de Faldouet, JE3 6UG
✿ 10-11; 11-11 Sun ☎ (01534) 856289
Draught Bass; Ringwood Fortyniner ⊞; **1 changing beer** ⒢
Originally a coaching inn, this large country-style hostelry is located at the centre of St Martin with sizeable public and lounge bars, a restaurant area and a spacious alfresco area. The interior features traditional furnishings, cosy corners, and a real fire in colder months. Owned by Randalls Brewery, it serves guest ales from the Marston's, Sharp's and Skinner's stables. Quality food is popular with locals and visitors alike, with a good menu available lunchtimes and evenings until 8.30pm (no food Sun eve). ⌂ ⊛ ◐ & A P ⊟ (3) ❀

Rozel Bar & Restaurant ⎣ ✅
La Valle de Rozel, JE3 6AJ
✿ 10-11; 11-11 Sun ☎ (01534) 863438
⊕ rozelpubanddining.co.uk
Draught Bass; Liberation Ale; 1 changing beer ⊞
A charming hostelry tucked away in the north-east corner of the island in the picturesque fishing village of Rozel, with a delightful beer garden. Bar meals are served in the public bar and snug, where there is a wood-burning stove in the winter. The excellent restaurant upstairs is available for private

functions. A Liberation Group partner pub, guest ales are often from Skinner's and Ringwood. Locals are friendly, if sometimes a little boisterous. ⌂ ⊛ ◐ & ⊟ ❀

St Mary
St Mary's Country Inn ⎣ ✅
La Rue des Buttes, JE3 3DS
✿ 11-11 ☎ (01534) 482897
Liberation Ale; 3 changing beers ⊞
An archetypal country inn from the outside, this 17th-century farmhouse is opposite the 13th-century parish church. The interior is contemporary with a main bar and an extensive dining area. The four handpumps serve Liberation and three guest beers. Reasonably priced, good food is available daily. The inn has a comfortable and relaxed atmosphere, with seating outside at the front and rear for when the sun shines. The north coast is a half-hour walk away, including the Devil's Hole blow hole. ⌂ ⊛ ◐ & P ⊟ ❀ 🛜

St Ouen
Farmers Inn ✅
La Grande Route de St Ouen, JE3 2HY
✿ 10-11; 11-11 Sun ☎ (01534) 485311
Draught Bass; Liberation Ale; 1 changing beer ⊞
Situated in the hub of St Ouen, near the war memorial and parish hall, the rustic Farmers Inn is a typical country pub offering up to three ales as well as a locally made cider when available (usually April to July). Traditional pub food is served in generous portions. Best described as a friendly community local, there is a good chance of hearing Jersey French (Jerriais) spoken at the bar. There is outside seating at the front of the pub. ▶ ♣ P ⊟

Moulin de Lecq ✅
Le Mont de Ste Marie, JE3 2DT
✿ 11-11 ☎ (01534) 482818 ⊕ moulindelecq.com
House beer (by Liberation) ⊞; **2 changing beers (often Greene King)** ⒢
A free house on the island offering a range of real ales, the Moulin is a converted 12th-century watermill situated in the valley above the beach at Greve de Lecq. The waterwheel is still in place and the turning mechanism can be seen behind the bar. A large restaurant adjoins the mill and can be hired for functions. The children's play space and a barbecue area are used extensively in the summer. There is a pool table in the second floor games room. Q ⌂ ⊛ ◐ & ♣ ● P ⊟ (9) ❀ 🛜

Beer not brandy

Before brandy, which has now become common and sold in every little alehouse, came to England in such quantities as it now doth, we drank good strong beer and ale, and all laborious people (which are the greater part of the kingdom), their bodies requiring after hard labour some strong drink to refresh them, did therefore every morning and evening used to drink a pot of ale or a flagon of strong beer, which greatly helped the promotion of our grains and did them no great prejudice; it hindereth not their work, neither did it take away their senses nor cost them much money, whereas the prohibition of brandy would prevent the destruction of his majesty's subjects, many of whom have been killed by drinking thereof, it not agreeing with their constitution.
Petition to the House of Commons, 1673

CAMRA's Home-Brewing Problem Solver

Erik Lars Myers

Real ale and other craft beers have become increasingly popular over the past few years, and as a result more people have been compelled to try making their own homebrew. However, while the concept behind making beer is simple, the execution can at times seem complex and confusing. The key to bridging the gap between brewing in theory and practise is being able to spot the signs of trouble and know how to respond. CAMRA's *Home-Brewing Problem Solver* provides the information you need to nip problems in the bud – and, better still, to avoid them in the first place.

RRP £12.99 **ISBN** 978-1-85249-347-9 **224 pages**

For this and other books on beer and pubs visit CAMRA's online bookshop at **www.camra.org.uk/books** or call **01727 867201**. Discounts are available for CAMRA members.

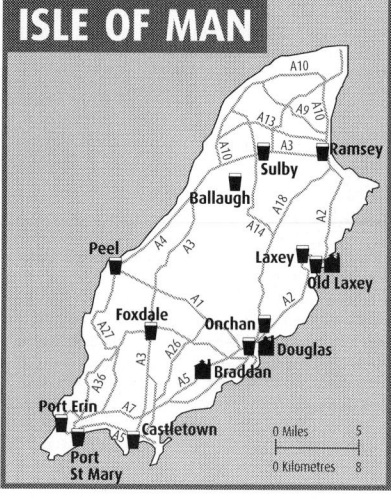

ISLE OF MAN

Ballaugh

Raven ✔

The Main Road, IM7 5EG
❂ 12-11 (midnight Fri & Sat) ☎ (01624) 896128
Okell's Bitter; house beer (by Okell's); 2 changing beers (sourced nationally) Ⓗ
Village-centre pub situated on the world-famous TT motorbike circuit adjacent to Ballaugh Bridge. A family-friendly local, following some sympathetic refurbishments, the Raven retains a comfortable main bar, an intimate dining area and a separate games room for pool and darts. There are seating areas outside for the summer months and for watching the races. Rarely for the island, a house brew, Ravens Claw, is permanently available.
Q ➤ ⌖ ◑ 点 ♣ P 🖵 (5,6) ☙ 🛜

Castletown

Castle Arms ✔

The Quay, IM9 1LD
❂ 12-11.30 (12.30am Fri & Sat) ☎ (01624) 824673
Okell's Bitter; 3 changing beers (often Okell's) Ⓗ
An attractive and historic pub, the Castle Arms is also known as the Glue Pot. It is next to Castletown harbour beneath the walls of Castle Rushen and handy for other heritage attractions. Two small ground-floor rooms have nautical and Manx motor racing themes. The patio is ideal for watching quayside vessels and waterfront wildlife. This is the only pub in the British Isles to feature on a banknote (to the left of Castle Rushen on the Manx £5 note). Q ⌖ ▲ ⇌ ♣ 🖵 (1,2) ☙ 🛜

Sidings

Victoria Road, IM9 1EF (next to railway station)
❂ 11.30-11 (midnight Fri & Sat) ☎ (01624) 823282
Bushy's Castletown Bitter, Ruby (1874) Mild, Bitter; Okell's Bitter; 8 changing beers (sourced nationally) Ⓗ
The Sidings (a former railway ticket office) comprises three distinct lounges, a bar area, a light and airy lounge mainly for dining and live music, and a refurbished games and TV room. Outside, it has an extensive beer garden and smoking area. A long line of handpumps sitting on the bar is an impressive sight, with four for local ales. Ales are

sourced from all over the UK, usually including a wide choice of bitters. The pub is ideally placed to wait for a bus or a train. Q ⌖ ◑ ⇌ ♣ P 🖵 ☙ 🛜

Douglas

Albert Hotel ✔

3 Chapel Row, IM1 2BJ (next to bus station, near indoor market)
❂ 10-11 (11.45 Fri & Sat); 12-11 Sun ☎ (01624) 673632
Bushy's Bitter; Okell's Bitter; 2 changing beers (sourced locally) Ⓗ
The nearest real ale pub to the sea terminal, the Albert is an unspoilt local with many regulars, plus darts and pool teams. It has a traditionally laid-out central bar and dark-wood panelling, with a pool table in one room and interesting historic pictures of Steampacket boats in the other. Sport is often on TV but never loud enough to spoil conversation. The drinks are competitively priced – the resident beers include those from local breweries Okell's and Bushy's. Q ⇌ ♣ 🖵 ☙ 🛜

Hooded Ram at Clinch's

North Quay, IM1 4LH
❂ 11-midnight (1am Fri & Sat) ☎ (01624) 612464
🌐 hoodedram.com
Hooded Ram Amber Ram, Black Pearl Oyster Stout; 6 changing beers (sourced nationally; often Hooded Ram) Ⓗ
Following substantial and stylish refurbishment to the former Clinch's Bar and Grill, which many years ago housed the historic Clinch's brewery, this place now offers a range of innovative ales. Up to six real ales come from the Hooded Ram brewery as well as a real cider. It has comfortable seating and TVs for the sporting crowd, plus a back room for diners. A particularly fine shuffleboard takes centre stage in the main lounge area. ➤ ◑ ⇌ ♣ ● 🖵 🛜

Horse & Plough ✔

Isle of Man Business Park, Bradden, IM2 2QZ
❂ 12-11 (midnight Fri & Sat) ☎ (01624) 626060
Okell's Manx Pale Ale, Bitter; 2 changing beers Ⓗ
A large, modern Heron & Brearley pub, serving the Isle of Man Business Park and nearby housing estate. The spacious interior comprises a large conservatory, a smaller dining area off a comfortable lounge with TVs, and a quieter raised area. The pub is a popular venue for functions and offers in-house catering. An interesting food menu accompanies up to four real ales.
➤ ⌖ ◑ 点 ♣ P 🖵 ☙ 🛜

Old Market Inn

Chapel Row, IM1 2BJ
❂ 9am-11
2 changing beers (often Bushy's)
Under the same ownership for many years, the Old Market Inn has the smallest bar on the island, serving two separate rooms. What it lacks in size is more than made up for in character, and few pubs like this remain in the British Isles. Two ales, often from Bushy's, are served in this friendly hostelry, where the visitor is almost bound to end up in

ISLANDS

conversation with other drinkers. In close proximity to the bus station and ferry terminal, the pub makes a great waiting room. Q❧☷🖵

Prospect Hotel ✪
Prospect Hill, IM1 1ET
✪ 12-11 (midnight Fri & Sat); closed Sun ☎ (01624) 616773
Okell's Manx Pale Ale, Bitter; 9 changing beers (often Okell's) Ⓗ
Opened in 1857, the pub is in the finance sector of the island's capital. The law courts are in close proximity, and the walls feature many pictures of luminaries of the law profession from the UK and the Isle of Man. Up to 14 handpumps, the largest number in one venue on the island, dispense a range of local, national and smaller brewery ales. Real cider and perry are also usually available.
◧☷♣♠🖵😺♟

Queen's Hotel ✪
Queens Promenade, IM2 4NL
✪ 12-midnight (1am Fri & Sat) ☎ (01624) 674438
Okell's Bitter; 3 changing beers Ⓗ
One of just a few remaining pubs situated on Douglas promenade, the refurbished Queen's is popular with visitors and locals alike. There is a great view of Douglas Bay, ferries and trams from the terrace, which has plenty of seating under heated awnings. Inside there are three distinct areas, one with a pool table, two with low-volume TVs featuring sport. Pub grub is served seven days a week and there is live music at the weekend.
Q❧☷🌟◧♿☷♣🖵😺♟

Rovers Return
11 Church Street, IM1 2AG
✪ 12-11 (midnight Fri & Sat) ☎ (01624) 676459
Bushy's Ruby (1874) Mild, Bitter; 5 changing beers Ⓗ
The Rovers is a fascinating pub, with handpumps fashioned from fire hoses, a traditional coal fire, and a shrine to Blackburn Rovers in a back room. The interior comprises an almost warren-like series of rooms, frequented by a truly eclectic and loyal clientele. Famously large food portions are available at lunchtimes, and rare and unusual guest ales complement the Bushy's regular and seasonal ales. Real cider is also always available. The pub is tucked away down a narrow street directly behind Douglas town hall. 🌟◧☷♣♠🖵😺♟

Samuel Webbs
Marina Road, IM1 2HG
✪ 12-midnight (1am Fri & Sat) ☎ (01624) 675595 ⊕ None
Okell's Manx Pale Ale, Bitter; 1 changing beer Ⓗ
Sam Webbs is a busy and vibrant town-centre bar. It an ideal location both for pre- and post-theatre drinks, situated just a few yards from the Gaiety Theatre. It can be quite a lively venue, with an eclectic mix of customers, regular live entertainment and nearly always a sporting event on TV. This is a popular sports bar as well as a favourite venue for starting or finishing a tour of Douglas bars. ♣😺♟

Terminus Tavern ✪
Strathallan Crescent, IM2 4NR
✪ 12-11 (midnight Fri & Sat) ☎ (01624) 624312
Okell's Bitter; 3 changing beers (often Okell's) Ⓗ
Located next to the starting point for the seasonal Manx Electric Railway and horse trams, the Terminus has a comfortable, spacious front bar with alcoves around its large front windows. There is also a side bar for pool and darts, and a large

outside seating area with views across Douglas Bay. This award-winning pub is popular for dining throughout the year, but nevertheless retains a local focus. Q❧☷🌟◧♿☷(MER)♣P🖵♟

Woodbourne Hotel
Alexander Drive, IM2 3QF
✪ 12-midnight ☎ (01624) 676754
Okell's Bitter; 8 changing beers Ⓗ
Large three-bar Victorian local in a residential area within walking distance of Douglas centre. What was once the gents-only bar is now used to promote cask ale, offering a range of Okell's beers alongside four or five guests. The Woody is a popular, friendly pub with a varied clientele and boasts a genuine community spirit, with a proud record of charity fundraising. A regular pub quiz is held on Sunday evening, and there is a separate pool room, also used for meetings and live music. Local CAMRA Pub of the Year in 2015. Q😺♣♠🖵♟

Foxdale

Baltic Inn
1 Glentramman Terrace, IM4 3EE
✪ 4 (2 Fri & Sat)-midnight ☎ (01624) 801305
Okell's Manx Pale Ale, Bitter; 1 changing beer (sourced locally) Ⓗ
Quiet, cosy local, with one main room divided into separate seating areas. A roaring real fire in winter adds to the atmosphere. Real ales on handpump supplement bottled Okell's IPA, Maclir and Hooded Ram beers. There are some fascinating historic photos on the walls of Foxdale during the mining boom. This friendly village pub continues to thrive following new ownership and a sympathetic refurbishment, and is well worth a visit.
Q🛏♣😺♟

Laxey

Bridge Inn
6 New Road, IM4 7BE
✪ 12-11 (midnight Fri & Sat) ☎ (01624) 862414
⊕ bridgeinn.im
Bushy's Bitter; 2 changing beers (sourced locally) Ⓗ
Popular and lively local pub in the centre of the village. The Bridge has been refurbished but retains its friendly atmosphere and continues to serve an excellent pint. It offers occasional live music, wide-screen TV and a pool table. In 1897, after the Snaefell mining disaster in which 20 men perished, the cellar area was used as a temporary morgue. There are rumours of a resident ghost.
🌟🛏◧Å☷♣♠🖵😺♟

Mines Tavern ✪
Captains Hill, IM4 7AY
✪ 12-11 (midnight Fri & Sat) ☎ (01624) 861484
Okell's Bitter; 2 changing beers (often Okell's) Ⓗ
The Mines Tavern is a little Manx gem nestled in the picturesque setting of the Laxey Tram Station. It has a tram-shaped bar and is dotted about with traditional Manx memorabilia. The recently refurbished outdoor seating and smoking area is a great place to watch the trams in summer. The food is good solid traditional pub fare and the real ales are mainly from Okell's. 🌟◧Å☷(MER)♣🖵

Old Laxey

Shore Hotel

Old Laxey Hill, IM4 7DA (follow signs to Old Laxey from Laxey main road)

☺ 12-midnight ☎ (01624) 861509

Old Laxey Bosun Bitter Ⓗ

A popular community pub all year round, the Shore attracts many additional visitors in the summer due to its proximity to the beach and promenade. A comfy hostelry with a nautical theme, and featuring memorabilia of international cycling star and local hero Mark Cavendish, it is well worth the detour from the main road through Laxey. The island's only brewpub, you might even meet the brewer in the bar. ❀❹ὒ🛆🎋P🖵

Onchan

Manx Arms ✅

Main Road, IM3 1BE

☺ 12-11 (midnight Fri-Sun) ☎ (01624) 675484

Okell's Manx Pale Ale, Bitter; 1 changing beer (sourced nationally) Ⓗ

Traditional village pub on the main road with two separate bar areas with pub games including pool, darts and dominoes, and large-screen TVs for sport. Live music features most Saturday evenings as well as an occasional karaoke night. There are attractive heated patios at the front and rear for smokers and a substantial car park. The regular real ale is from Okell's with another seasonal or guest beer usually available, as well as a real cider.
Q❀ὒ🎋●P🖵(3,23)❀🛜

Peel

Creek Inn ✅

Station Place, IM5 1AT

☺ 10-midnight (12.30am Fri & Sat) ☎ (01624) 842216

⊕ thecreekinn.co.uk

Okell's Bitter; Sharp's Doom Bar; changing beers (often Hooded Ram) Ⓗ

Traditional harbourside pub popular with locals and tourists, with ample outdoor seating on the edge of the picturesque harbour. The lounge bar has a nautical theme with etched-glass screens featuring sailing ships separating the cosy seating areas, and there is also some interesting beer memorabilia on display. A large selection of local, national and small brewery real ales is on offer, plus real cider. The comprehensive food menu includes locally caught Manx queenies (queen scallops) and locally cured kippers. Live music features at the weekends. 🐾❀❹🛆●🖵(5,6)❀🛜

Marine Hotel

Shore Road, IM5 1AH

☺ 10-midnight ☎ (01624) 842337 ⊕ marinehotelpeel.co.uk

Okell's Bitter; 3 changing beers (sourced locally) Ⓗ

The Marine Hotel overlooks the beach and historic Peel Castle. It has two bar areas, one a traditional drinking corridor, and a lounge area. There is also a large restaurant accessed via a separate entrance, serving excellent, value-for-money meals seven days a week. The landlord is a staunch supporter of local breweries and cider makers, though guest ales from all over the UK are often available.
❹🎋●🖵(5,6)❀🛜

White House Hotel ☖ ✅

2 Tynwald Road, IM5 1LA (150yds from bus station)

☺ 11-midnight ☎ (01624) 842252

Bushy's Ruby (1874) Mild, Bitter; Moorhouse's Pride of Pendle; Okell's Manx Pale Ale, Bitter; 2 changing beers (sourced nationally) Ⓗ

The White House, run by the same family for many years, features a public bar area, a separate pool room and a larger room for TV sport and live music at the weekend. There is also a cosy snug with nautical memorabilia, accessed internally via a sliding door. Local CAMRA Pub of the Year 2017, the venue has long supported the now-growing cider market on the island.
Q❀🛆🎋●P🖵(5,6)❀🛜

Port Erin

Falcon's Nest Hotel

Station Road, IM9 6AF

☺ 11-midnight (12.30am Fri & Sat) ☎ (01624) 834077

⊕ falconsnesthotel.co.uk

Bushy's Bitter; 4 changing beers (sourced nationally; often Okell's) Ⓗ

The Falcon's Nest Hotel is on the south-west coast in a spectacular location overlooking the beautiful crescent-shaped bay of Port Erin. A free house with two bars, the residents' lounge, also open to the public, is in the true tradition of the public house, where visitors can enjoy an ever-changing choice of guests and local beers relaxing in front of an open fire. One bar has pub games and TVs showing sport. The Victorian-style Gladstone restaurant offers an extensive à la carte menu and an ever-popular Sunday lunch carvery.
Q🛏❹🍽🎋P🖵❀🛜

Port St Mary

Albert Hotel

Athol Street, IM9 5DS

☺ 11-midnight (1am Fri & Sat); 12-midnight Sun ☎ (01624) 832118

Bushy's Bitter; Okell's Bitter; 2 changing beers (sourced nationally) Ⓗ

A hidden gem in the heart of this coastal village, the Albert boasts impressive views over the harbour. It has a public bar with games area, a cosy lounge bar complete with newly installed wood-burning stove, and an overflow area of tables and seating. Immaculately decorated and furnished, the walls are adorned with many paintings by local artists who frequent the pub. Isle of Man CAMRA Pub of the Year 2016. Q❀🛏🎋P🖵(1,2)🛜

Railway Station Hotel

Station Road, IM9 5LF

☺ 11-11 (midnight Fri & Sat) ☎ (01624) 832494

⊕ therailwaystationhotel.com

Bushy's Bitter, Old Bushy Tail; Okell's Bitter; 1 changing beer (often Okell's) Ⓗ

A welcoming venue for drinkers and diners, situated on the steam railway station platform and convenient for rail and bus travellers. The beer garden is now complete along with a secure and safe children's playground. The pub has a restaurant for finer dining as well as serving pub lunches and snacks in the lounge area. There are band nights in the Sports Bar most weekends. Four guest bedrooms are available. Q❀🛏❹🍽🎋🖵

Shore Hotel

Shore Road, Gansey, IM9 5LZ

☺ 12-11 (midnight Fri & Sat) ☎ (01624) 832269

⊕ theshore.im

Bushy's Old Bushy Tail; Okell's Bitter; 1 changing beer (sourced nationally) Ⓗ
Large, sturdy building with stunning views over Carrick Bay, also known as Gansey. There is a separate bar with a mixture of seating and tables, and a lounge-style area. The wooden bar area is fashioned partly from former door panelling and ships' handrails and features old sepia pictures of the hotel. The outdoor seating area is sheltered from what can be biting winds. Food is served throughout the day in both the bar and a separate dining room. This is one of only a few outlets to regularly sell Bushy's Old Bushy Tail. Check out the interesting fittings in the gents. ✪🏠◑♨P🖵🐾🛜

Ramsey

Mitre
16 Parliament Street, IM8 1AP
✪ 10-11 (1am Fri & Sat); 10-midnight Sun ☎ (01624) 813257
Bushy's Bitter; Okell's Bitter; house beer (by Okells); 1 changing beer (sourced locally) Ⓗ
A large building with views of the quayside and entrances on both sides. The interior has been much refurbished in recent years but retains its comfortable seating and friendly atmosphere. The pub is on three levels – the basement Schooner bar is popular with young revellers at the weekend, while live music is hosted in the upstairs bar, where food is served, including Sunday lunches, and the real ales are to be found. The Mitre is a staunch supporter of island breweries, with the house beer Jough Bitter supplied via Okell's.
◑≈♣🐾🛜

Trafalgar Hotel ✓
West Quay, IM8 1DW
✪ 11-11 (12.15am Fri & Sat); 11.30-11 Sun
☎ (01624) 814601
Moorhouse's Black Cat; Okell's Bitter; 2 changing beers (sourced nationally) Ⓗ
Traditional twin-room pub situated on the harbour behind the main shopping street. The real ale range includes guests sourced from all over the UK. Friendly, welcoming and always busy, it is particularly popular during TT week. It is just around the corner from spectacular views of the races and not far from the electric tram stop. A CAMRA Isle of Man branch Pub of the Year finalist on several occasions. Q≈♣♨🖵🐾🛜

Sulby

Ginger Hall
Ballamanagh Road, IM7 2HB
✪ 12-midnight; 12-11 Sun ☎ (01624) 897231
Bushy's Castletown Bitter; Okell's Bitter; 1 changing beer (sourced nationally) Ⓗ
The Ginger Hall has been repainted white. Inside there is the same welcome in the bar, with a real fire and an impressive beer engine which dispenses two local real ales and guests that change every Thursday. The pub is situated on the TT course and the windows feature black and white pictures of TT riders. Be careful not to spill your beer while admiring the huge TT map on the ceiling! A large mirror behind the bar is also worthy of note. The restaurant serves good-value food in generous portions with takeaways available.
🛏✪🏠♿Å♣P🖵

Ginger Hall, Sulby (Photo: Tom Stainer)

The Breweries

Breweries overview

Global beer giants are on the march, buying small breweries in UK and US

The *Good Beer Guide* proves that choice for beer drinkers has never been better. New small breweries continue to open and add to the diversity of beers on offer. But there are storm clouds gathering as global brewers attempt to stifle choice.

America's independent brewers have a neat description for global brewers: they call them Big Beer. The craft sector in the US, with its trade group the Brewers' Association, is so concerned by the manner in which Big Beer is muscling in on the independent sector that in 2017, they launched a Seal of Approval scheme. The seal will appear on labels and the aim is to enable consumers to differentiate between craft beer and the products made by the global brewers who use the names of smaller companies they have taken over.

In Britain, SIBA – the Society of Independent Brewers – has launched a similar accreditation scheme. The American and British organisations have worked closely together, with SIBA's chief executive Mike Benner visiting the US to discuss the need to combat the rise of Big Beer with members of the Brewers' Association.

The concern over the erosion of drinkers' choice is not exaggerated. In 2016, the world's biggest brewing group, AB InBev, bought SABMiller, its major rival, for £71 billion. It was the third biggest takeover in corporate history and gave AB InBev control of 30 per cent of global beer production and sales.

The group is the result of earlier mergers between Anheuser Busch of the US, AmBev of Brazil and InBev of Belgium. It owns such mass market beers as Budweiser, Brahma, Beck's and Stella Artois. The takeover of SABMiller has given the group an important foothold in southern Africa where SAB stands for South African Breweries.

But AB InBev has been busy in both the US and UK markets. In 2016, it bought the Camden Brewery in North London for £80 million and built a much-enlarged site for the brewery in Enfield a year later. Before the takeover, SABMiller had bought the leading craft brewery Meantime in Greenwich for the staggering amount of £120 million. When regulators in the US and the EU told AB InBev it had to drop some of its brands to satisfy competition rules it sold off Grolsch, Peroni,

Pilsner Urquell and Meantime. The Greenwich brewery is now owned by Asahi of Japan.

The stage was set for the takeover of independent brewers by Big Beer in 2011, when Molson Coors bought Sharp's of Cornwall. Molson Coors is a Canadian-American company that occupies the former Bass breweries in Burton-on-Trent. It has invested £7.5 million in Sharp's, boosted production from 60,000 barrels a year to 200,000 and turned Doom Bar into the biggest-selling cask and bottled beer in the UK.

Heineken, another global giant, owns the Caledonian Brewery in Edinburgh where Deuchars IPA is a leading brand in cask and package. In the summer of 2017, Carlsberg, another world giant, bought the London Fields Brewery in Hackney.

The reason for this activity by Big Beer is caused by declining sales of their mass market lager brands in traditional markets. In the US, AB InBev has bought a raft of craft breweries, including 10 Barrel, Blue Point, Breckenridge, Devils Backbone, Elysian, Four Peaks, Golden Road, Goose Island and Shock Top. It has substantial stakes in a number of other breweries. Miller Coors, now wholly owned by Coors, has taken Blue Moon, Leinenkugel's and Saint Archer under its wings while Heineken has turned a 50 per cent stake in Lagunitas into complete ownership.

British consumers will have noticed that Goose Island and Lagunitas beers are now widely available here in major supermarkets and at remarkably cheap prices of around £1.70 a bottle. They can sell their brands at low prices as a result of being able to dramatically reduce the costs of production. As a result of their sheer size, the global brewers can buy malt and hops in vast bulk and can drive down the prices they pay. It's estimated that Big Beer has 40 per cent lower costs than even big and medium sized brewers. When AB InBev bought Modelo in Mexico, it stripped 20 per cent of costs out of the company. With Beck's in Germany it reduced costs by 15 per cent. It's estimated that in the long term buying SABMiller will generate cost savings of $1.4 billion.

Low production costs enable the global brewers to advertise on TV, posters and social media at prices smaller brewers cannot afford. While British

SIBA's Assured scheme identifies breweries that are truly independent

Now a brand of AB InBev, Goose is far removed from its origins as Goose Island

national and regional brewers have to match supermarket prices with those of the globals, smaller independents can't afford such low prices if they are to stay in business. As a result they have to confine their sales to specialist beer shops.

Consumers will also have spotted that Goose Island has been re-branded Goose by AB InBev. What has happened to the brewery is an object lesson in the behaviour of global brewers when they buy smaller ones. Goose Island started out as a brewpub in Chicago in 1988 and later moved to a bigger brewery at Wrigley Field. In 2011, it was bought by Anheuser Busch, the American arm of AB InBev. The main beers – IPA, Honkers Ale and 312 Urban Wheat – are now brewed in a giant AB factory in Fort Collins, Colorado, and at two Labatts plants in Canada, also owned by the group, which has built what it calls a new 'facility' for the beers on the East Coast of the US.

The recipe for Goose IPA has changed. AB no longer imports Saaz hops from the Czech Republic as a result of the long-running trademark dispute between the American and Czech version of Budweiser. A different yeast culture is used as the original yeast wasn't suitable for big batch brewing in conical vessels: yeast makes a vital contribution to beer flavour.

AB InBev has moved into others areas of the beer world. In June 2017 it was announced that ZX Ventures, a wholly-owned subsidiary of the global giant, had taken a substantial minority stake in RateBeer. This is an online scoring and rating system for beers that drinkers find useful and illuminating. The involvement by AB InBev caused such outrage that several leading craft breweries said they would no longer allow their beers to be tested by RateBeer. The breweries include Dogfish Head, Harpoon, Black Project Ales and Prison City in the US and the renowned brewer of Belgian lambic beers, Cantillon. The arrogance of the giant brewers can be seen from the response given by RateBeer when Black Project asked for its beers to be taken down: 'Nope'.

In the UK in 2017, the online beer retailer Beer Hawk partnered with AB InBev. In a statement, Beer Hawk said it had 'hooked up' with the global group, which would bring a 'new dimension to the scope' of its work by bringing a new set of beers from 'some of the best and toughest to source breweries on the planet'. It will be interesting to see how Beer Hawks' portfolio develops but expect to find some Brazilian beers on offer.

Big Beer not only seeks to dominate what we can drink but is also attempting to control the ingredients used to make beer. In June 2017, the German campaign group No Patents on Beer! (**www.no-patents-on-beer.org**) revealed that Carlsberg and Heineken have had patents granted to cover two strains of barley, along with a third patent that will allow the two strains to be used together: the aim is to develop strains of barley with low levels of the type of enzymes that create a cardboard flavour in beer, a problem usually associated with lager brewing.

No Patents on Beer! raised a petition to implore the European Patents Office in Munich to cease granting patents on beer ingredients on the grounds that beer and brewing have been in the public domain for thousands of years and should remain so.

First Big Beer buys up a swathe of independent breweries. Now it's attempting to control the natural ingredients used to make beer. The power of the global behemoths is frightening and has to be vigorously resisted.

A German campaign is fighting patents on barley after moves by Carlsberg and Heineken

How to use the Breweries section

This section lists breweries operating in the United Kingdom, the Isle of Man and the Channel Islands. Breweries are listed in alphabetical order. They include independent companies (regional, family, micro-brewers and brewpubs), national brewers and global groups. If a brewery owns more than one site, these are cross-referenced. Within each brewery entry, regular beers are listed in increasing order of strength. Websites should be consulted when breweries produce occasional or seasonal beers that are available for less than six months of the year. We mention when breweries produce bottle-conditioned beers but do not list or evaluate them: for further information, see CAMRA's *Good Bottled Beer Guide*.

KEY TO BREWERY ENTRIES

BREWERY SYMBOLS

Brewpub: a pub that brews beer on the premises.

Cyclops: the brewery is affiliated with the Cyclops system for describing beers to consumers.

CAMRA tasting notes, supplied by a trained CAMRA tasting panel. Beer descriptions that do not carry this symbol are based on more limited tastings or have been obtained from other sources.

A CAMRA Beer of the Year in 2016.

One of CAMRA's Beers of the Year 2017: a finalist in the Champion Beer of Britain competition held during the Great British Beer Festival in London in August 2017, or in the Champion Winter Beer of Britain competition held earlier in the year.

Serve with tight sparkler: the brewery's beers can be acceptably served through a 'tight sparkler' attached to the nozzle of the beer pump, designed to give a thick collar of foam on the beer.

Do not serve with tight sparkler: the brewery's beers should NOT be served through a tight sparkler. CAMRA is opposed to the growing tendency to serve southern-brewed beers with the aid of sparklers, which aerate the beer and tend to drive hop aroma and flavour into the head, altering the balance of the beer achieved in the brewery. When neither symbol is used it means the brewery in question has not stated a preference.

Brewery tours available: check with individual breweries for details.

Brewery shop: beer available to take away. Check opening hours in advance.

RAIB **Real Ale in a Bottle:** the brewery produces bottle-conditioned beer (known by CAMRA as Real Ale in a Bottle).

Seasonal beers: the brewery produces seasonal beers in addition to its regular range.

V **Vegan:** the brewery produces vegan beers (check with brewery for further details. Not all beers produced may be vegan).

GF **Gluten free:** the brewery produces gluten-free beers (check with brewery for further details. Not all beers produced may be gluten free).

ABBREVIATIONS

OG Stands for Original Gravity, the measure taken before fermentation of the level of 'fermentable material' (malt sugars and added sugars) in the brew. It is only a rough indication of strength and is no longer used for duty purposes.

ABV Stands for Alcohol by Volume, which is a more reliable measure of the percentage of alcohol in finished beer. Many breweries now only disclose ABVs but the Guide lists OGs where available. Often the OG and the ABV of a beer are identical, i.e. 1035 and 3.5 per cent. If the ABV is higher than the OG, i.e. OG

1035, ABV 3.8, this indicates that the beer has been 'well attenuated' with most of the malt sugars turned into alcohol. If the ABV is lower than the OG, this means residual sugars have been left in the beer for fullness of body and flavour: this is rare but can apply to some milds or strong old ales, barley wines and winter beers.

SIBA Indicates a member of the Society of Independent Brewers.

IFBB Indicates a member of the Independent Family Brewers of Britain.

NOTE: The Breweries section was correct at the time of going to press and every effort has been made to ensure that all regularly-available cask-conditioned beers are included.

The Breweries

The breweries listed in this section include micro, small, family, regional, national and global companies. Please use the Beer index (p987) to help locate beers.

1648 SIBA

Old Stables Brewery, Mill Lane, East Hoathly, East Sussex, BN8 6QB
☎ (01825) 840830 ⊕ 1648brewing.co.uk

The 1648 brewery, set up in the old stable block at the King's Head pub in 2003, derives its name from the year of the deposition of King Charles I. One pub is owned and more than 40 outlets are supplied.

Hop Pocket (OG 1039, ABV 3.7%)

Triple Champion (OG 1041, ABV 4%)
A chestnut-coloured, full-bodied, traditional English ale.

Signature (OG 1044, ABV 4.4%)
Pale, light and crisply refreshing ale with a bitter aftertaste.

Laughing Frog (OG 1052, ABV 5.2%)
Dark golden in colour, full-bodied beer, lightly-hopped with a full, malty flavour.

22 Bake & Brew (NEW)

Platform 22, 22a Station Road, Torphins, AB31 4JF
☎ (01339) 882807 ⊕ platform22.co.uk

Platform 22 is a café-bar in rural Aberdeenshire. Brewing began in 2015 as a spin-off from its bakery. Producing a range of traditional beers to suit the soft water, it still produces, from time to time, tasty beer bread and chocolate stout cake.

3 Brewers of St Albans SIBA ◉

The Potato Shed, Symonds Hyde Farm, Symonds Hyde Lane, Hatfield, Hertfordshire, AL10 9BB
☎ (01707) 271636 ☎ 07941 854615
⊕ 3brewers.co.uk

⊠ Launched in 2013 by three brewers from St Albans who turned a potato shed into an eight-barrel plant brewery. Spent malt becomes compost for the farm. Its range of six beers is supplied to pubs and beer festivals around the St Albans district. ‼🍺

Dark Mild (OG 1036, ABV 3.6%)
Dark ruby in colour this smooth, well-balanced and creamy mild combines a malty sweetness with a touch of liquorice bitterness.

Golden English Ale (OG 1038, ABV 3.8%)
A refreshing beer with a subtle citrus flavour and a hint of sweetness.

Classic English Ale (OG 1040, ABV 4%)
Deep amber in colour with a light, hoppy aroma and a rich, rounded malty taste balanced by subtle hoppiness to give a clean, smooth and refreshing ale.

Ruby English Ale (OG 1043, ABV 4.3%)
A ruby-coloured ale, rich and malty with a hint of spiciness.

IPA (OG 1046, ABV 4.6%)
Golden-coloured IPA with a clean, dry finish.

Special English Ale (OG 1048, ABV 4.8%) 🍺

A copper-coloured, robust and full-bodied premium ale. Well-balanced and smooth with a hint of berries.

3 Potts

8 Russell Avenue, Southport, Merseyside, PR9 7RD
☎ 07926 178707 ⊠ simon@3potts.co.uk

3 Potts is a nanobrewery creating small batch beers. RAIB

Sparkplug (ABV 4.6%)

Gasket (ABV 5.8%)

Short Circuit (ABV 6%)

Wingnut (ABV 6%)

360° SIBA ◉

Unit 24b, Bluebell Business Estate, Sheffield Park, East Sussex, TN22 3HQ
☎ (01825) 722375 ⊕ 360degreebrewing.com

⊠ Brewing began in 2013 using a six-barrel plant. Beers are available across Sussex, the South East, and London. ‼🍺♦

Pale (ABV 3.9%)
A light-bodied but full-flavoured zesty golden ale.

Best (ABV 4.2%)
A traditional copper-coloured best bitter. Aromatic with a clean bitterness

American Pale Ale (ABV 5%)
A contemporary pale ale with intense tropical fruit flavours and a long bitter finish.

40FT

Bootyard, Abbot Street, Dalston, London, E8 3DP

Office: The Printhouse, 18-20 Ashwin Street, Dalston, London, E8 3DL ⊕ 40ftbrewery.com

40FT began brewing in 2015. It is a six-barrel microbrewery, located in a 40-ft shipping container in a disused car park close to Ridley Road Market. Beers are produced for its brewery tap room as well as pubs, bars, restaurants and off licences.

#alesnotdead (OG 1045, ABV 4.5%)
An amber-coloured hoppy ale.

4Four (NEW)

Sarngwm, Bethesda, SA67 8HG
☎ (01834) 474440 ☎ 07789 186503 ⊕ 4four.beer

4four began brewing in 2016 using a 2.5-barrel plant. Steve and Christie have had a passion for real ale for more than 12 years in their CAMRA award-winning pub and wanted to turn their hand at producing it themselves. Beers are music themed. ♦RAIB

Session (OG 1036, ABV 3.6%)
A refreshing traditional amber-coloured session bitter.

Allegro (OG 1039, ABV 3.9%)

A light and fresh pale ale.

BPM (OG 1044, ABV 4.4%)
Premium golden ale, refreshing with a bitter finish.

Overture (OG 1047, ABV 4.7%)
An easy-drinking ale with hidden strength. Malt and chocolate flavours, not sweet.

4Ts

Unit 20, Manor Industrial Estate, Lower Wash Lane, Latchford, Warrington, Cheshire, WA4 1PL
☎ (01925) 747463 ☎ 07917 730184
⊕ 4tsbrewery.co.uk

Brewing returned to Warrington in 2015. Beers are usually available in the Tavern, Warrington. ‼♦

Pale Ale (OG 1037, ABV 3.7%)
A refreshing session ale with spicy hop notes.

APA (OG 1040, ABV 4%)
Spicy and citrus hints throughout with a hint of bitterness at the end, leaving a citrus burst of flavour.

WSB (Warrington Special Bitter) (ABV 4.2%)
A bitter with a malty base and lots of hops. A crisp, refreshing bitterness with aromas of blackcurrant and citrus.

IPA (OG 1046, ABV 4.6%)
Hints of citrus and passion fruit with a bitter punch.

Pilsner (ABV 4.8%)
Earthy and fresh bread aromas with hints of honeysuckle followed by malty sweetness with pleasing bitterness.

Stout (OG 1050, ABV 5%)
An English stout with biscuit, chocolate and burnt notes at the start. Hoppy notes break through giving a burst of flowery tones.

Big Daddy IPA (ABV 7.2%)
A double IPA, clean and crisp with intense amounts of resinous, citrus and grapefruit aromas.

7 (NEW)

16 Woodlands Park, Durris, AB31 6BF ☎ 07890 814636 ⊕ 7reasonstobrew.co.uk

Brewing began in 2016 using a four-barrel plant. RAIB

8 Sail SIBA

Heckington Windmill, Hale Road, Heckington, Lincolnshire, NG34 9JW
☎ (01529) 469308 ☎ 07866 183479
⊕ 8sailbrewery.co.uk

8 Sail Brewery was established in 2010 and operates on a six-barrel brew plant. The brewery nestles in the shadow of Heckington Windmill, Britain's only eight-sailed windmill, from where the brewery takes its name. The mill is now working and helping to mill malted grain for the brewery. The brewery shop stocks bottle-conditioned beers alongside local ciders. The front of the brewery has been converted into a Victorian-style bar. 🍺♦RAIB

8 Sail Ale (OG 1040, ABV 3.8%)
A refreshing, traditional English pale ale.

Windmill Bitter (OG 1040, ABV 3.8%)

Blonde (OG 1042, ABV 4%)

Millwright (OG 1042, ABV 4%)
A mild with rich, dark flavours, lightly balanced with hops. The aroma is chocolate with a dry roast and liquorice flavour.

Merry Miller (OG 1043, ABV 4.1%)
A traditional bitter. Mid brown in colour with a nutty, malty flavour.

Rolling Stone (OG 1044, ABV 4.3%)
A pale ale using locally grown barley milled at the adjacent Heckington Windmill.

King John's Jewels (OG 1045, ABV 4.5%)

Little Willie (OG 1045, ABV 4.5%)

Millstone (OG 1046, ABV 4.5%)
A modern premium bitter with a good balance of malt and hops.

After the Gold Rush (OG 1047, ABV 4.6%)
An ale/lager hybrid. Mildly fruity with an assertive hop bitterness.

Kibbled (OG 1047, ABV 4.6%)
A red-coloured ale, well-rounded and balanced with a pleasant malt character.

Windy Miller (OG 1047, ABV 4.6%)
A rich, dark, smooth-flavoured stout brewed with a generous amount of oat malt.

Damson Porter (OG 1053, ABV 5%)
Damsons have been added to give a full-bodied fruitiness to the rich, complex flavours. The aroma is bitter with caramel tones. Flavour is malty, slightly fruity with a bitter finish.

Victorian Porter (OG 1053, ABV 5%) 🍷
An aroma of berries and roasted malts and deep, intense chocolaty flavours give this beer a rich and full-bodied flavour.

Old Colony (OG 1052, ABV 5.3%)

Black Widow (OG 1054, ABV 5.5%)
A strong dark ruby mild. Dark malt and liquorice flavours dominate.

John Barleycorn IPA (OG 1053, ABV 5.5%)
Brewed to recreate the taste of an original English IPA.

81 Artisan

The Courtyard, Crowshall Farm, Chilgrove Road, West Dean, West Sussex, PO18 9HP
☎ (01243) 527444 ☎ 07990 035736
⊕ 81artisan.com

Brewing began in 2017 using a 10-barrel plant. RAIB

9 Lives (NEW)

Unit 303, Ystradgynlais Workshops, Trawsffordd Road, Ystradgynlais, SA9 1BS ☎ 07743 559736
⊕ 9livesbrewing.co.uk

☺9 Lives was established in 2017 by Robert Scott, formerly the brewer at the now defunct Bryncelyn Brewery, using the same six-barrel plant. ‼♦RAIB

A-B InBev UK

Porter Tun House, 500 Capability Green, Luton, Bedfordshire, LU1 3LS
☎ (01582) 391166 ⊕ inbev.com

No real ale.

Abbey SIBA

Abbey Brewery, Camden Row, Bath, BA1 5LB
☎ (01225) 444437 ⊕ abbeyales.co.uk

Founded in 1997, Abbey Ales was the first brewery in Bath for over 50 years. It supplies more than 80 regular outlets within a 20-mile radius. It operates four pubs in Bath. ‼◆

Somerset Ale (OG 1038, ABV 3.8%)
Amber-coloured, full-bodied, malty ale with hints of caramel, balanced with a hoppy and floral finish.

Bath Best (OG 1040, ABV 4%)
A good balance of malt and hops. Sweet to the nose with a bitter finish.

Bellringer (OG 1042, ABV 4.2%) ◆
A notably hoppy ale, light to medium-bodied, clean-tasting, refreshingly dry, with a balancing sweetness. Citrus, pale malt aroma and dry, bitter finish.

Abbey Grange

See Llangollen

Abbeydale SIBA ◉

Unit 8, Aizlewood Road, Sheffield, South Yorkshire, S8 0YX
☎ (0114) 281 2712 ⊕ abbeydalebrewery.co.uk

☺Since starting in 1996, Abbeydale Brewery has grown steadily; it now produces upwards of 130 barrels a week. ◆

Deception (OG 1043, ABV 4.1%)
A pale beer with aromas of elderflower and grapes. Strong citrus flavours, especially grapefruit. Long lasting bitter finish.

Moonshine (OG 1041.2, ABV 4.3%) 🍴
A well-balanced pale ale with a full hop aroma. Pleasant grapefruit traces may be detected.

Absolution (OG 1050, ABV 5.3%)
A fruity pale ale, deceptively drinkable for its strength. Sweetish but not cloying.

Black Mass (OG 1065, ABV 6.7%)
A strong black stout with complex roast flavours and a lasting bitter finish.

Abernyte (NEW)

South Latch Farm, Abernyte, Perthshire, PH14 9SU
☎ 07827 715915 ⊕ abernytebrewery.com

Brewing began in 2016. No real ale.

Abington (NEW)

Buckingham Garden Centre, Tingewick Road, Buckingham, MK18 4AE ⊕ abingtonales.com

Started by Peter Brown as a home brewery, commercial production began in 2016 in 50-litre batches at the family garden centre in Buckingham. Beer is sold in bottles at the garden centre and two other Northampton outlets. RAIB

Abstract Jungle

Unit 14, Bailey Brook Industrial Estate, Amber Drive, Langley Mill, NG16 4BE ☎ 07481 849332

Office: 2 Manor Farm Mews, Brinsley, Nottinghamshire, NG16 5AG
✉ simon@abstractjunglebrewery.co.uk

Abstract Jungle was established in 2016 by a husband and wife team, using a custom-built six-barrel plant. A range of five core beers is brewed along with occasional beers that stretch the boundaries of modern day brewing. ‼🍺

Pride (OG 1040, ABV 3.9%)
Crisp and clean pale ale, low mellow bitterness with a tropical aroma.

Jackal (OG 1043, ABV 4.2%)
Traditional-style porter with four different malts and a subtle, spicy aroma.

Restless (OG 1045, ABV 4.5%)
A hoppy session beer. Resinous and fruity.

Casual (OG 1048, ABV 4.6%)
A bold, complex stout using unrefined chocolate and a hint of blueberries.

Sturdy (OG 1054, ABV 5.6%)
A classic IPA with pine notes and citrus fruits.

Acorn SIBA ◉

Unit 3, Aldham Industrial Estate, Mitchell Road, Wombwell, Barnsley, South Yorkshire, S73 8HA
☎ (01226) 270734 ⊕ acorn-brewery.co.uk

☺Acorn was set up in 2003 with a 10-barrel expanding to a 20-barrel plant when the brewery moved to larger premises and currently has a 160-barrel a week capacity. All beers are produced using the Barnsley Bitter yeast strain, dating back to the 1850s. ‼🍺◆RAIB

Yorkshire Pride (OG 1037, ABV 3.7%) ◆
This session beer is golden in colour with pleasing fruit notes. A mouthwatering blend of malt and hops create a fruity taste which leads to a clean bitter finish.

Barnsley Bitter (OG 1038, ABV 3.8%) 🍴🍺◆
This brown bitter has a smooth malty bitterness throughout with notes of chocolate and caramel. Fruity bitter finish.

Blonde (OG 1040.5, ABV 4%) ◆
A clean-tasting, golden-coloured hoppy beer with a refreshing bitter and fruity aftertaste.

Barnsley Gold (OG 1041.5, ABV 4.3%) ◆
This golden ale has fruit on the aroma with a hoppy and fruity flavour throughout. A well-hopped, clean, dry finish.

Old Moor Porter (OG 1045, ABV 4.4%) 🍴◆
A rich-tasting, porter, smooth throughout with a hint of chocolate and liquorice.

Gorlovka Imperial Stout (OG 1058, ABV 6%) ◆
This black stout is rich and smooth and full of chocolate and liquorice flavours with a fruity, creamy finish.

Ad Hop (NEW)

Unit B3, Prospect Street, Liverpool, L6 1AU ☎ 07957 165501

Ad Hop started life in 2014 in a tiny room off the kitchen of the Clove Hitch pub and has moved twice since with plans for further relocation and expansion. Currently using a 5.5 and a 2.5-barrel plant, the brewery specialises in innovative beers.

Low ABV beers are occasionally produced for local festivals.

Adnams SIBA 👁

Sole Bay Brewery, East Green, Southwold, Suffolk, IP18 6JW
☎ (01502) 727200 ☎ 07787 151311
⊕ adnams.co.uk

⊠ The company was founded by George and Ernest Adnams in 1872. About 50 pubs are owned around East Anglia plus an outpost in London and there is national distribution. Beers are from a 300-barrel plant within the confines of the present site. ‼ 🍺 ♦

Lighthouse (OG 1037, ABV 3.4%) 🍺
A quaffable beer with bitterness predominating.

Southwold Bitter (OG 1037, ABV 3.7%) 🍺 🍺
Aromas of toffee apple, caramel and sulphur. Taste is a complex mix of malt, toffee and roast bitterness with hops. Malty bitter and apple flavours linger into the aftertaste.

Mosaic (OG 1041, ABV 4.1%) 🍺
Tropical fruit nose, intensely fruity flavour with complex hop characteristics, which linger in the aftertaste.

Old Ale (OG 1044, ABV 4.1%) 🍺 🍺

Ghost Ship (OG 1046, ABV 4.5%) 🍺
A pale ale with an assertive pithy bitterness, biscuit flavours and fresh citrus aroma.

Broadside (OG 1049, ABV 4.7%) 🍺
Rich, malty aroma with blackberries and dried fruit. Rich and full flavours of malt and fruit, with roast and caramel notes and subtle hops. Well-balanced, long-lasting aftertaste.

Adur

Brick Barn, Charlton Court, Mouse Lane, Steyning, West Sussex, BN44 3DG
☎ (01903) 867614

Office: 2 Sullington Way, Shoreham-by-Sea, BN43 6PJ
⊕ adurvalleycoop.com

⊠ Adur Brewery, nestled in the heart of the South Downs, was launched in 2008 on a 5.5-barrel plant, marking the return of brewing to the Adur Valley after an interval of nearly 100 years. The brewery was sold to the Adur Valley Co-Operative Ltd in 2012, including the Adur Brewery name and recipes. A large part of the output is sold as bottle-conditioned beer. ‼ ♦ RAIB

Ropetackle Golden Ale (OG 1036, ABV 3.4%)
A light, golden ale with an initial sweetness and delicate aroma, balanced by a dry finish.

Hop Token: Amarillo (OG 1040, ABV 4%)
An amber-coloured bitter with notes of peach and grapefruit in both aroma and taste, a good bitterness and a long, dry finish.

Hop Token: Summit (OG 1040, ABV 4%)

Velocity (OG 1044, ABV 4.4%)
Traditional best bitter with a hoppy aroma and a hint of marmalade in the taste.

Black William (OG 1055, ABV 5%)
A rich, black stout with dark chocolate aromas and roasted flavours.

Robbie's Red (OG 1050, ABV 5.2%)

Slight initial sweetness leads to flavours including orange peel and a satisfying bitterness which persists into the long finish.

Affinity (NEW)

39a Markfield Road, South Tottenham, London, N15 4QA ☎ 07904 391807 ⊕ affinitybrewco.com

Established in 2016, Affinity is located in two shipping containers, one of which contains the 2.5-barrel plant. Beers are mainly available in KeyKeg but there are plans to produce cask-conditioned beers. No real ale. ♦

Ainsty (NEW) SIBA 👁

Manor Farm, Intake Lane, Acaster Malbis, North Yorkshire, YO23 3UJ
☎ (01904) 703233 ☎ 07983 604989
⊕ ainstyales.co.uk

☺ Launched by a former policeman in 2014, initially Ainsty cuckoo brewed, opening its own brewery in 2016 in the ancient York and Ainsty Wappentake, a few miles south-west of York. Beers are available in around 20 outlets in the York area. Home-grown hops are planned. ‼ 🍺 ♦

Angel (ABV 3.7%)
An easy-drinking session pale ale with a refreshing, clean and smooth finish.

Flummoxed Farmer (ABV 4%)
A light blonde ale with a grapefruit and tropical nose, giving a refreshing and slightly hoppy, dry finish.

Wankled Waggoner (ABV 4.5%)
A golden ale with a sweet nose, giving a good balance of malt and hop character, delivering a slightly bitter finish.

Crafty Chocolatier (ABV 4.8%)
A smooth porter crafted with chocolate from York based 'Choc-Affair'.

Kolkata Karma (ABV 5%)
A classic IPA using only English hops.

Aire Heads (NEW)

Unit 4d, Rawcliffe Road Industrial Estate, Lidice Road, Goole, East Yorkshire, DN14 6XL ☎ 07842 141584
✉ aireheadsbrewery@gmail.com

Aire Heads began brewing in 2017. It was founded by former journalist Ben Pindar and ex-music producer Craig Sanderson.

AJ's

Unit 12, Ashmore Industrial Estate, Longacre Street, Walsall, West Midlands, WS2 8QG ☎ 07860 585911
✉ ajs-ales@hotmail.com

⊠ AJ's was established in 2015 and use a four-barrel plant with three fermenting vessels and a cool room. Local Black Country pubs, local wholesalers and Wetherspoon pubs are supplied. ♦

Stuck on Blondes (ABV 3.9%)
A straw-coloured session ale.

Best Bitter (ABV 4%)
A fruity golden bitter.

SPA (ABV 4.2%)
A smooth, straw-coloured, easy-drinking pale ale.

Stuck in the Mud (ABV 4.3%)
A smooth, dark stout.

Ruby (ABV 4.4%)
A full-bodied ruby ale.

Stuck in the Doghouse (ABV 4.7%)
A bittersweet golden ale.

Albion (NEW)

5 Milton Avenue, Bear Flat, Bath, BA2 4QZ
☎ (01225) 480465 ⊕ albionbrewing.co.uk

Picobrewery established in 2016. All output is
bottle conditioned. ♦ RAIB

Alcazar

See Shipstone's

Alchemist

See Golden Duck

Alechemy SIBA

**Unit B, 1 Gregory Road, Kirkton Campus, Livingston,
EH54 7DR**
☎ (01506) 413634 ☎ 07748 156973
⊕ alechemy.beer

Dr James Davies, a keen traditional brewer and
chemist, started brewing in 2012. A 12-barrel plant
is used. New beers are being produced regularly:
see website for details. Beers can be found in pubs
across the UK. ♦ RAIB

Starhopper (OG 1036, ABV 3.5%)

Rhapsody (OG 1038, ABV 3.8%)

Ritual (OG 1042, ABV 4.1%) ◕
A golden ale with a strong hop character, balanced
by malt and fruit with a long, dry finish.

Five Sisters (OG 1045, ABV 4.3%) ◕
Flavoursome tawny beer with good balance of
malt, hops and fruit plus hints of roast and caramel.
Lingering distinctive finish.

Photon (OG 1043, ABV 4.3%)

10 Storey Malt Bomb (OG 1049, ABV 4.5%)

Bad Day at the Office (OG 1047, ABV 4.5%)

Secret Citra (ABV 5%) 🍾

Damona (OG 1056, ABV 5.3%)

EH54 (OG 1056, ABV 5.7%)
Pale ale bursting with grapefruit and tangerine
aromas with a pleasant bitter aftertaste.

Brake Neck (OG 1076, ABV 7.5%)

AleCraft

Office: 17 Springhill, Nuneaton, CV10 0NP ☎ 07939
634677 ⊕ alecraftmanagement.co.uk

AleCraft began brewing in 2012 as a cuckoo
brewery utilising the equipment at the Verulam
brewery in St Albans, which has since closed. Beers
are delivered direct to Yorkshire, the Midlands and
the South East. Brewing is currently suspended. RAIB

Ales of Scilly SIBA

**2b Porthmellon Industrial Estate, St Mary's, Isles of
Scilly, TR21 0JY**
☎ (01720) 423233 ⊕ alesofscilly.co.uk

⊗ Opened in 2001, Ales of Scilly is the most south-
westerly brewery in Britain. Several island pubs are
supplied, with occasional exports to mainland beer
festivals. ‼🍺♦

Challenger (OG 1039, ABV 4.2%)

Alfred's SIBA

**Unit 5B, Scylla Industrial Estate, Winnall Valley Road,
Winchester, Hampshire, SO23 0LD**
☎ (01962) 859999 ⊕ alfredsbrewery.co.uk

Alfred's is a 3.5-barrel brewhouse opened by Steve
and Isabelle Haigh in 2012. Steve previously
brewed for three other renowned Hampshire
breweries. Deliveries are made to pubs within 15
miles of Winchester. ‼🍺♦

Saxon Bronze (OG 1038, ABV 3.8%)
Crisp, straw-coloured session ale with light, hoppy
citrus notes.

All Day

**Salle Brewery Barns 14, 15, 16 Salle Moor Farm,
Wood Dalling Road, Salle, Norfolk, NR10 4SB**
☎ (01603) 951173 ☎ 07825 604887
⊕ alldaybrewing.co.uk

⊗ Located in former farm buildings, the brewery
has established its own hop yard, to be self-
sufficient in traditional varieties of hop. Hops are
frozen and used to produce a range of green hop
beers throughout the year. A tap room and shop
are open at weekends and other ad hoc hours.
Organic cider is also produced. A changing range of
beers is available. ♦ V

All Hallows

**⊜ Main Street, Goodmanham, East Yorkshire,
YO43 3JA**
☎ (01430) 873849 ⊕ goodmanhamarms.co.uk

Abbie Logozzi, landlady of the Goodmanham Arms,
started brewing in 2012 in outbuildings behind the
pub. The ex-Goodmanham Brewery Buildings were
purchased and a five-barrel plant installed. The
brewery name comes from the adjacent 12th-
century All Hallows Church. Local legendary
characters are used in the naming of some of the
beers. Brews are supplied to the pub, beer festivals
when requested, and mainly to local free trade.

Peg Fyfe Dark Mild (OG 1040, ABV 3.6%)

Ragged Robyn (OG 1058, ABV 4.8%)
A traditional ruby-coloured heritage ale.

No Notion Porter (OG 1060, ABV 5.6%)

Allendale SIBA 👁

Allen Mill, Allendale, Northumberland, NE47 9EA
☎ (01434) 618686 ⊕ allendalebrewery.com

☺Established in 2006, the brewery is a state-of-
the-art 20-barrel plant in a historic lead smelting
mill, which formed the centre of the mining
industry of the area during the industrial

revolution. Many of the beer names reflect this and the local area. ‼️🍴♦️

Wagtail Best Bitter (OG 1037, ABV 3.8%) ◆
Amber-coloured bitter with spicy aromas and a long, bitter finish.

Golden Plover (OG 1039, ABV 4%) ◆
Light, refreshing, easy-drinking blonde beer with a clean finish.

Pennine Pale (OG 1040, ABV 4%)
Pale ale brewed with American hops for a full fruity aroma and flavour and a refreshing citrus finish.

Mosaic (OG 1045, ABV 4.4%)
Single hop pale ale. Fruity and soft bitter taste.

APA (OG 1056, ABV 5.5%)
A full-bodied beer with citrus and tropical aromas.

Wolf (OG 1053, ABV 5.5%) ◆
Full-bodied red ale with bitterness in the taste giving way to a fruity finish.

Red Rye (OG 1060, ABV 6%)

AllGates

The Old Brewery, Brewery Yard, off Wallgate, Wigan, WN1 1JU
☎ (01942) 234976

☺AllGates commenced brewing in 2006 in a fully restored Grade II-listed tower brewery at the rear of Wigan's General Post Office. A modern five-barrel plant is used. Beers are principally delivered to its own nine-pub estate. Brewing is currently suspended. ‼️♦️

Allsaints

c/o Coastal Brewery, Unit 10B, Cardrew Industrial Estate, Redruth, Cornwall, TR15 1SS ☎ 07790 274112

⊗ Formerly known as Doghouse Brewery, which closed in 2007, Allsaints recommenced production in 2008 using spare capacity at Keltek Brewery. In 2009 the brewery began using spare capacity at Coastal Brewery in Redruth. Brewing is currently suspended. ♦️

Almasty

Unit 11, Algernon Industrial Estate, New York Road, Shiremoor, NE27 0NB
☎ (0191) 253 1639 ⊕ almasty.co.uk

⊗ Opened in 2014, this two-man operated 10-barrel plant produces an ever-changing range of unfined, unfiltered beers. A barrel ageing programme is also in place. Twice yearly open days are held (in spring and summer). Pumpclips are made from screen-printed, hand-sawn logs. The brewery tap is the Free Trade Inn, Byker, while the beers are supplied nationwide. ‼️♦️

Alnwick

See Cumberland and Daleside

Alphabet SIBA

99 Northern Western Street, Ardwick, Manchester, M12 6JL
☎ (0161) 272 6532 ☎ 07540 534350
⊕ alphabetbrewing.co.uk

Alphabet began brewing in 2014 and is situated in Manchester city centre under railway arches. It has an 80-barrel capacity with a 10-barrel kit and focuses mainly on keg beers, which are unfiltered and unpasteurised. The brewery also cans its own beers on site. Cask-conditioned beers are sometimes available. Regular brewery tap events are held.

Alphabeta

🍴 Pittcue, 1 The Avenue, Devonshire Square, London, EC2M 4YP
☎ (020) 7324 7770

Alphabeta is a small in-house brewery contiguous with the Pittcue restaurant.

Altarnun SIBA

Inner Trenarrett, Altarnun, Launceston, Cornwall, PL15 7SY
☎ (01566) 86069

⊗ Formerly known as Penpont, Altarnan began brewing in 2008 and has steadily increased the range and production since then. The award-winning brewery currently uses a 25-barrel plant with an eight-barrel plant for special brews. Beers are available in pubs across Cornwall. Beer is also brewed under the Firebrand Brewing Co label. ‼️🍴♦️RAIB

St Nonna's (OG 1037, ABV 3.7%) ◆
Tawny-coloured session bitter with floral nose and balanced malt and hop bitterness throughout with roast and sweet notes. Bitter finish.

Cornish Arvor (OG 1040, ABV 4%) ◆
Well-balanced, tawny-coloured best bitter. Principally bitter with fruity sweetness and some malt. Bitter hop-fruit finish.

Creation Pale Ale (OG 1039.2, ABV 4.2%) 🍴 ◆
Gold-coloured bitter with a hop aroma. Quite hoppy taste with sweet peach, citrus zing and roast malt. Bitter, slightly dry finish.

Shipwreck Coast (OG 1044, ABV 4.4%) ◆
Golden ale with citrus aroma. Powerful lemon citrus hop dominates the taste and finish with bitterness and fruits. Faint dryness.

Roughtor (OG 1047, ABV 4.7%) ◆
Copper-coloured strong bitter with malt and citrus hop aroma. Hop bitterness balanced by malt, plum and marmalade. Bitter, dry finish.

Beast of Bodmin (OG 1046.5, ABV 5%) ◆
Brown-coloured strong bitter with malt aroma. Smooth roast malt, chestnuts and complex fruits in the mouth. Refreshing malty, bitter finish.

Stormer IPA (OG 1046.7, ABV 5.2%)

Brewed under the Firebrand Brewery name:

Big Hop, Little Beer (OG 1035, ABV 3.6%)
A golden-coloured, malty ale with a fruity aroma and taste.

Cross Pacific Pale Ale (ABV 4%)
A pale ale with a malty taste, which gives way to a burst of hop flavour.

Graffiti IPA (ABV 5%)
A smooth, malty, full-bodied ale with a fruity finish.

Amazing

▤ Ship Inn, 65 High Street, Sandgate, Kent, CT20 3AH
☎ (01303) 248525

Amazing was set up in 2016 using a four-barrel plant and is situated at the Ship Inn, Sandgate. The pub, beer festivals and selected free trade outlets are supplied.

Amber SIBA

Unit 7 Outram Business Centre, Whiteley Road, Ripley, Derbyshire, DE5 3QL
☎ (01773) 512864 ⊕ amberales.co.uk

⊗ Amber Ales began production in 2006 on a five-barrel plant from the Firkin brewpub chain. Around 100 outlets are supplied in the Derby/Nottingham/Chesterfield area, further afield via distributors. ‼ ♦ RAIB V

Sunrise (ABV 3.8%)

Chocolate Orange Stout (OG 1040, ABV 4%)
A stout with additional chocolate malt and Curacao orange peel. Vanilla pods are added during fermentation.

Original Black Stout (OG 1040, ABV 4%)
Traditional stout, full-flavoured, smooth and easy drinking with a subtle hop aroma.

Barnes Wallis (OG 1040, ABV 4.1%)
An easy-drinking IPA-style bitter, copper-coloured with a full malt flavour.

Revolution (OG 1047, ABV 4.5%)
Spicy golden ale with a touch of rye and a citrus-packed flavour explosion.

Dambuster (OG 1051, ABV 5.5%)
Well-hopped golden ale.

Imperial IPA (OG 1058, ABV 6.5%)
Traditional IPA with a substantial malty base and a big hop profile.

Ambridge

Unit 2a, Priory Piece Business Park, Priory Farm Lane, Inkberrow, Worcestershire, WR7 4HT
☎ (01386) 792191 ☎ 07500 046391
⊕ ambridgebrewery.co.uk

☺Ambridge commenced brewing in 2013, initially for the family pub, the Bulls Head in Inkberrow, the model for the Bull in the Archers. Later that year they acquired the Wyre Piddle Brewery and relocated it to the outskirts of the village. The beers from both breweries continue to be brewed. On-demand brews supplement the core range, and some small-run bottling is carried out. ‼ ♦ RAIB

Sticky Dog (OG 1040, ABV 4%)
Smooth and easy drinking beer with a citrus hop aroma and refreshing finish.

Honey Bunny (OG 1043, ABV 4.2%)
Full-flavoured, light ale. Smooth with hints of honey.

**Worcestershire Pale Ale (WPA)
(OG 1043, ABV 4.2%)**
A premium pale ale with a good balance of hops and malt. Hops carry on from the taste to a bittersweet finish.

Citra (OG 1044, ABV 4.4%)
Light and refreshing single hop ale with a zesty lemon and lime bitter finish.

Mosaic (OG 1044, ABV 4.4%)

Jester (OG 1048, ABV 4.8%)
Pale gold-coloured beer with a punchy aroma of grapefruit and tropical fruits and a delicate bitter finish.

Ampersand (NEW)

Camphill Farm, Middle Road, Earsham, Norfolk, NR35 2AH ☎ 07791 086689 ⊕ ampersandbrew.co

A small batch brewery established in 2017 and based on a family farm in South Norfolk. ♦ RAIB

Ampthill SIBA ◉

Unit D, The Sidings, Station Road, Ampthill, Bedfordshire, MK45 2QY
☎ (01525) 620015 ⊕ ampthillbrewhouse.co.uk

A six-barrel microbrewery established in 2015.
🍺 ♦ RAIB

Session Ale (ABV 3.4%)
A light beer with a subtle spice and honey aroma ending with a citrus kick.

Best Bitter (ABV 3.9%)

Hoppy Birthday (ABV 3.9%)

Golden Ale (ABV 4.1%)

India Pale Ale (ABV 4.5%)

Amwell Spring (NEW)

Westfield Farm House, Cholsey, Oxfordshire, OX10 9LS
☎ 07812 396619 ✉ gibbo_seven@hotmail.com

Brewing began in 2017 on a 70-litre plant using water from a spring in the farm house grounds. Unfined bottle-conditioned beers are produced, available in local free houses. RAIB V

An Teallach SIBA

Camusnagaul, Dundonnell, Garve, IV23 2QT
☎ (01854) 633306 ✉ ataleco1@yahoo.co.uk

An Teallach was formed in 2001 by husband-and-wife team David and Wilma Orr, on the family croft on the shores of Little Loch Broom, Wester Ross. More than 60 pubs are supplied. ‼ ♦

Beallach Na Ba (ABV 3.8%) 🍺
Golden-amber citrus hoppy brew with some background malts.

Beinn Dearg Ale (OG 1044, ABV 3.8%) 🍺
A well-balanced malty, hoppy, sweetish beer with a long, malty bitter aftertaste.

Ale (OG 1042, ABV 4.2%) 🍺
A classic pint in the Scottish 80/- tradition. Plenty of malt in the balanced bittersweet taste.

Crofters Pale Ale (OG 1042, ABV 4.2%) 🍺
Refreshing mix of citrus hops and malts.

Suilven (OG 1043, ABV 4.3%) 🍺
A refreshing yellow brew with plenty of citrus fruits and hops throughout.

Kildonan (OG 1044, ABV 4.4%) 🍺
Plenty of fruit and a good smack of bitterness in this golden ale.

Anarchy SIBA

Unit 5, Whitehouse Farm Centre, Stannington, Northumberland, NE61 6AW
☎ (01670) 789755 ☎ 07702 810111
⊕ anarchybrewco.com

☺⊙A 10-barrel brewery ran by an enthusiastic team producing a range of hand-crafted beers and lagers with big, bold flavours. ‼ ⌑ RAIB

Smoke Bomb (OG 1043, ABV 3.9%)
A bitter with a light, smoky nose and Bavarian smoked ham and citrus flavours matched with dark, smooth toffee malts.

Blonde Star (OG 1041, ABV 4.1%)
Lemon, grapefruit and passion fruit hop flavours combine with pale malts to give a crisp and fresh session blonde.

Citra Star (OG 1041, ABV 4.1%)
Grapefruit, lemon, lime and passion fruit flavours come from the hops to give a clean, crisp blonde ale.

Urban Assault (OG 1050, ABV 5%)
Red-coloured pale ale with heavy notes of lemon, orange and passion fruit in the flavour, followed by a bitter finish.

Crime Scene (OG 1056, ABV 5.5%)
Fruit-flavoured, amber-coloured beer made using caramel malts that melts into a long-lasting bitter aftertaste.

Quiet Riot (OG 1063, ABV 6.6%)
Kiwi fruit, lime and orange zest flavours combine to give a big bitterness that is balanced with sweet malts.

Sublime Chaos (OG 1075, ABV 7%)
Liquorice, chocolate and caramel flavoured breakfast stout infused with Ethiopian Guji natural coffee beans.

Andrews

1 Railway Cottages, Cummertrees, Annan, DG12 5QG
☎ (01461) 700387 ☎ 07785 613321
⊕ andrews-ales.co.uk

Andrews Ales began brewing in 2011 and is situated at the family home in Cummertrees. Brewing capacity is three barrels. Cask and bottle-conditioned beers are supplied direct by the brewery to pubs and independent shops. ♦ RAIB

Supus Lupus (OG 1036, ABV 3.6%)
A straw-coloured session ale with a light, zesty finish.

Cummertrees Pale Ale (OG 1040, ABV 4%)
Full-bodied, IPA-style beer, refreshingly clean and crisp.

Into The Darkness (OG 1046, ABV 4.3%)

Andwells SIBA ◉

Andwell Lane, Andwell, Hampshire, RG27 9PA
☎ (01256) 761044 ⊕ andwells.com

⊠ Brewing commenced in 2008 on a 10-barrel plant. The brewery relocated and expanded in 2011 to an idyllic riverside location with a new bespoke 20-barrel plant. Beer is distributed within a 40-mile radius and to the Isle of Wight. ‼ ⌑ ♦ RAIB

Resolute Bitter (OG 1038, ABV 3.8%) ◕

An easy-drinking session bitter. A malty aroma leads into an initially malty flavour with some bitterness and a sweetish finish.

Gold Muddler (OG 1039, ABV 3.9%) ◕
Light golden-coloured standard bitter. Aroma of hops and malt, characteristics carried into the flavour with solid bitterness and dry, biscuity finish.

Red Mist (ABV 4.1%) ◕
Pale brown best bitter brewed for Red Mist Leisure. Predominantly bitter with a malty backbone and a dry bitter finish.

King John (OG 1042, ABV 4.2%) ◕
Malty best bitter, low in hops with short initial bitterness and underlying sweetness, leading to some dryness in the finish.

Ruddy Darter (OG 1047, ABV 4.6%)
A ruby chestnut-coloured ale with a hoppy, spicy aroma. Full-bodied and fruity to taste with a dry finish.

Angel (NEW)

🯈 **Angel, 7 Stoney Street, Nottingham, NG1 1LG**
☎ (0115) 948 3343 ⊕ angelmicrobrewery.com

Situated inside one of Nottingham's oldest pubs, the Angel Microbrewery is a 2.5-barrel plant nestled in the tap room. Beers are only available in the pub.

Angel Ales SIBA

62a Furlong Lane, Halesowen, West Midlands, B63 2TA ☎ 07986 382919 ⊕ angelales.co.uk

Angel Ales began commercial brewing in 2011 and is expanding outlets. The brewery building has been a Chapel of Rest, a coffin makers' workshop and a pattern makers before becoming a brewhouse. Beers are produced using organic materials where possible, and all stouts are vegan-friendly. ♦ RAIB V

Angel Ale (OG 1042, ABV 4.1%)
Ultra pale and intensely hopped bitter with a citrus nose and a lingering bitter finish.

Ginger Stout (OG 1048, ABV 4.8%)
A stout produced using fresh ginger root.

Angels & Demons (NEW) SIBA

Great Cauldham Farm, Cauldham Lane, Capel-le-Ferne, Kent, CT18 7HQ
☎ (01303) 255666 ⊕ fantasticbeer.co.uk

Brewing began in 2016 using a 20-barrel plant. The brewery produces two ranges of beers, the McCanns range of more traditional ales and the Angels & Demons range of more experimental brews. ♦ RAIB V

Bombay Social (ABV 3.8%)

Racing Tiger (ABV 4.2%)
A cask-conditioned lager.

Panama Jazz (ABV 4.8%)

A.D.H-Me (ABV 5.2%)

Brewed under the McCanns brand name:

Harry Hop (ABV 3.7%)

Graham's (ABV 4.2%)

Hockley Soul (ABV 4.2%)

Angles (NEW)

Unit 54, Culley Court, Peterborough, Cambridgeshire, PE2 6WA ☎ 07500 362007 ⊕ angles-ales.uk

A highly qualified microbiologist and an Exciseman with a passion for real ales and lagers got together to found Angles Ales.

Anglesey

Cheawn Ddu, Valley, LL71 7DE
☎ (01248) 717734
⊕ angleseybrewingcompany.co.uk

Brewing began in 2014 in Llanbadrig as Bragdy'r Bwthyn, producing bottle-conditioned beers. In 2017 the brewery relocated to Valley under the Anglesey Brewing Co name and cask production began. RAIB

APA (OG 1040, ABV 4%)

Golden Ale (ABV 4.4%)

Amlwch Old Porter (OG 1056, ABV 5.6%)

Animal

See XT

Anspach & Hobday

118 Druid Street, Bermondsey, London, SE1 2HH
☎ (020) 8617 9510 ⊕ anspachandhobday.com

⊠ Anspach & Hobday began brewing in 2014 using a one-barrel plant, upgrading to 2.5 barrels later that year. In 2016 the brewery was upgraded again to a seven-barrel plant. It is based in a railway arch in Bermondsey. A taproom is open at weekends. ⌷RAIB V

The Smoked Brown (OG 1061, ABV 6%)

The Porter (OG 1062, ABV 6.7%) ◢
Black/brown beer with roasted notes throughout with caramel, fruit and hops in the flavour and finish, which is slightly dry

The Stout Porter (OG 1080, ABV 8.5%)

Anstey

40 Dalby Road, Anstey, Leicestershire, LE7 7DJ
☎ 07960 776843 ✉ stuartslessor@me.com

Anstey is a small two-barrel brewery, which commenced brewing in 2015.

Father's Favourite (OG 1036, ABV 3.7%)
Light, easy-drinking pale session ale with a slight sweetness.

Packhorse Bridge (OG 1043, ABV 4%)
Dark-coloured bitter with a caramel flavour and aroma.

Darkroom (OG 1040, ABV 4.7%)
A well-rounded, triple-hopped stout.

Paleface (OG 1050, ABV 5%)
An English IPA with a fresh flavour.

Antoine's

The Garden Shed at 25 Ashley Road, Westcott, Surrey, RH4 3QJ ☎ 07545 828589 ✉ antoine@1beer.co.uk

Tiny brewery which produces occasional KeyCasks in a variety of styles.

Appleby

The Brewery at the Stables, Morland House, Morland, Cumbria, CA10 3AZ
☎ (01931) 714348 ⊕ applebybrewery.co.uk

Established by Fred Mills in 2015, the brewery outgrew its original premises in Appleby within a year and moved to a former horse stable in an Eden Valley village in 2016. The beers are available at selected pubs across Cumbria, but mainly in the Eden Valley area. ‼◆RAIB

Senior Moment (OG 1039, ABV 3.9%)
An old-fashioned bitter.

Vanya Yam (ABV 4%)
Amber-coloured IPA with a malty taste and a hoppy, citrus finish.

Midlife Crisis (OG 1042, ABV 4.2%)

Middle-Aged Spread (OG 1052, ABV 5.2%)
A rich stout; dark, nutty and chocolaty.

Applecross (NEW)

c/o Applecross Inn, Shore Street, Applecross, IV54 8LR

A microbrewery co-funded by 14 stakeholders. The head brewer, John Johnston, was cuckoo brewing in 2016 until the new brewery was ready in 2017.

Sanctuary (ABV 3.8%)

Red Rock (ABV 4%)

Inner Sound (ABV 4.7%)

Arbor SIBA ⊙

181 Easton Road, Easton, Bristol, BS5 0HQ
☎ (0117) 329 2711 ⊕ arborales.com

⊠ Arbor Ales began brewing in 2007 and has relocated and expanded several times, most recently in 2015. A wide range of beers is brewed, with particular pride taken in darker ales. ◆RAIB

Pocket Rocket (OG 1038, ABV 3.9%)

Shangri La (OG 1040, ABV 4.2%)

Oz Bomb (OG 1045, ABV 4.7%) ◢
Strong, bitter, hoppy flavour. Citrus fruit flavours balanced with pale malt. Quite an astringent finish.

The Devil Made Me Brew It
(OG 1056, ABV 5.5%) ◢
A velvety speciality beer. Floral and citrus hops in the aroma, coffee and slightly burnt toffee flavours – sweet but with a bitter finish.

Why Kick a Moo Cow (OG 1052, ABV 5.5%)

Yakima Valley (OG 1067, ABV 7%) ◢
A strong, full-bodied IPA. Hoppy and fruity. Sweetness is well balanced with bitterness, lasting into a soft bitter aftertaste.

Arcane Bridge

Arch 5, King Edward Bridge, Newcastle upon Tyne, NE1 3TQ ☎ 07932 774745 ✉ arcanebridge@aol.com

Brewing began in 2016 using a 5.5-barrel plant, supplying local outlets within a 20-mile radius. A tasting bar is located on the premises (please ring for opening hours). Brewing is currently suspended.

Archerfield

See Knops

Archers

See Evan Evans

Ards

34b Carrowdore Road, Newtownards, Co Down, BT22 2LX ☎ 07515 558406
✉ ardsbrewing@blackwood34.plus.com

Ards began brewing in 2011 using a 100-litre plant. A five-barrel plant is now in operation, allowing cask production in addition to the increasing range of bottle-conditioned beers. RAIB

Rockin' Goose (OG 1044, ABV 4.4%)

BallyBlack (OG 1046, ABV 4.6%)

Hip Hop (OG 1050, ABV 5%)

Cardy Man (OG 1051, ABV 5.1%)

Pig Island (OG 1052, ABV 5.2%)

Argyll SIBA

Unit 8a, Baliscate Industrial Estate, Tobermory, Isle of Mull, PA75 6QA
☎ (01688) 302821
✉ isleofmullbrewing@btinternet.com

Argyll Breweries was formed in 2010 following the merger of Oban Bay and Isle of Mull breweries, continuing to trade under those names. A small brewing plant now supports the Isle of Mull beers in Tobermory, primarily producing bottles but some cask-conditioned ale is still available. !!

Kilt Lifter (OG 1039, ABV 3.9%)

Skinny Blonde (OG 1041, ABV 4.1%)

Ginger Jakey (OG 1042, ABV 4.2%)

Skelpt Lug (OG 1042, ABV 4.2%)

Fair Puggled (OG 1045, ABV 4.5%)

Arkell's SIBAIFBB 👁

Kingsdown, Swindon, Wiltshire, SN2 7RU
☎ (01793) 823026 ⊕ arkells.com

Arkell's Brewery was established in 1843 by John Arkell and the Arkell family still brew beer in the original Victorian brewhouse every day. The brewery owns 96 pubs in Berkshire, Gloucestershire, Oxfordshire and Wiltshire. !!➡◆

Wiltshire Gold (OG 1038, ABV 3.7%)
A gold-coloured ale with a mellow floral hop aroma and distinctive hoppy taste.

3B (OG 1040, ABV 4%) ◆
A medium brown beer with a strong, sweetish malt/caramel flavour. The hops come through strongly in the aftertaste, which is lingering and dry.

HOPeration IPA (OG 1041, ABV 4.2%)
A powerfully hoppy beer with a smooth, rounded finish.

Bee's Organic (OG 1045, ABV 4.5%)
Organically produced honey gives this golden ale a light, fresh taste.

Moonlight (OG 1046, ABV 4.5%)
Auburn-coloured beer with a warm, toasty aroma and distinctive citrus hoppy flavour.

Arkwright's

See Darkwave

Arran SIBA

Cladach, Brodick, Isle of Arran, KA27 8DE
☎ (01770) 302353

Office: 100 Wellington Street, Glasgow, G2 6DH
⊕ arranbrewery.com

The brewery opened in Brodick in 2000 using a 20-barrel plant. Around 300 outlets around the UK are supplied direct. Beers are also produced under the Devil's Dyke Brewery name in Cambridgeshire, which trials new recipes. !!➡◆RAIB

Guid Ale (OG 1038, ABV 3.8%)
A refreshing session ale with a delicate balance of malt and fruit.

Dark (OG 1042, ABV 4.3%) 🍺 ◆
A well-balanced malty beer with plenty of roast and hop in the taste and a dry, bitter finish.

Sunset (OG 1042, ABV 4.4%)
An amber-coloured ale with a lightly perfumed aroma, a good balance of malt, fruit and hops and a pleasant dry finish.

Clyde Puffer (OG 1045, ABV 4.5%)
A stout with a deep, dark colour. Sweet and mellow.

Blonde (OG 1048, ABV 5%) ◆
A hoppy beer with substantial fruit balance. The taste is balanced and the finish increasingly bitter. An aromatic strong bitter that drinks below its weight.

Brewery Dug (OG 1055, ABV 5.5%)
An American-style IPA with a refreshing citrus body and a dry lemon zest bitter finish.

ID (ABV 6%)
A dark, hoppy beer in the style of a dark IPA.

Arrow

c/o Wine Vaults, 37 High Street, Kington, Herefordshire, HR5 3BJ
☎ (01544) 230685 ✉ deanewright@yahoo.co.uk

Brewer Deane Wright built this five-barrel brewery at the rear of the Wine Vaults and started brewing in 2005. The Wine Vaults is the only pub outlet for Arrow Bitter.

Bitter (OG 1042, ABV 4%)

Art Brew SIBA

Brightwater Farm, Sutcombe, Devon, EX22 7QE
☎ 07881 783626 ✉ artbrewdorset@googlemail.com

⊠ Brewing started in 2008 on a five-barrel plant near the Jurassic Coast. In 2016 the brewery relocated to a new site in Devon with a brewery tap using a 2.5-barrel plant. In addition to its core

ales a rolling programme of beers is also produced.
🚚 ♦ RAIB V

Baby Anarchist (OG 1034, ABV 3.2%)

Pale (OG 1034, ABV 3.2%)

Outsider Ale (OG 1042, ABV 4.4%)

Milk Stout (OG 1045, ABV 4.5%)

Ginger & Chilli IPA (OG 1055, ABV 6%)

Love Or Nothing (OG 1055, ABV 6%)

Orange IPA (OG 1055, ABV 6%)

Anarchist Party Bitter (OG 1068, ABV 7.2%)

Artisan

See Evan Evans

Artisan Brew Company (NEW)

🏠 3 Mile Inn, Great North Road, Newcastle upon Tyne, NE3 2DS
☎ (0191) 255 2100 ⊕ threemileinn.co.uk/the-artisan-brew-co

Nanobrewery based at the Three Mile Inn in Gosforth. Beers are not always available on the bar so it advisable to ring first to check.

Artisan Brewing

See Pipes

Arundel SIBA 👁

Unit C7, Ford Airfield Industrial Estate, Ford, Arundel, West Sussex, BN18 0HY
☎ (01903) 733111 ⊕ arundelbrewery.co.uk

⊗ Founded in 1992, Arundel Brewery is the historic town's first brewery in 70 years. A brewery shop opened in 2014 by the quayside with a good selection of beers, both its own and from other breweries. The brewery also brews for the Bison Crafthouse in Brighton. ‼🚚♦

Black Stallion (OG 1037, ABV 3.7%) 🍺
A dark mild with well defined chocolate and roast character. The aftertaste is not powerful but the initial flavours remain in the clean finish.

Castle (OG 1038, ABV 3.8%) 🍺
A pale tawny-coloured beer with fruit and malt noticeable in the aroma. The flavour has a good balance of malt, fruit and hops, with a dry, hoppy finish.

Maltravers Session IPA (ABV 4.2%)
An easy-drinking session IPA with a powerful hop character.

Sussex Gold (OG 1042, ABV 4.2%) 🍺
A golden-coloured best bitter with a strong floral hop aroma. The ale is clean-tasting and bitter for its strength, with a tangy citrus flavour. The initial hop and fruit die to a dry and bitter finish.

Sussex IPA (OG 1045, ABV 4.5%)
Formerly known as Heritage IPA. A special bitter with a complex roast malt flavour leading to a fruity, hoppy, bittersweet finish.

Hirondelle Coffee Milk Stout (ABV 5%)
A rich, smooth coffee milk stout, brewed using Edgcumbes coffee beans.

Wild Heaven (OG 1052, ABV 5.2%)
An American-style pale ale, full-flavoured with strong grapefruit, orange and lime notes resulting in a lingering, dry bitter finish.

Smokehouse (ABV 6%)
A rich, smooth beer with subtle smoky overtones.

Ascot SIBA 👁

Unit 5, Compton Place Business Centre, Surrey Avenue, Camberley, Surrey, GU15 3DX
☎ (01276) 686696 ⊕ ascot-ales.co.uk

⊗ Ascot Ales started production in 2007 on a four-barrel plant in a small industrial unit. The brewery has successfully expanded over the years.
‼🚚♦RAIB

Alley Cat Ale (OG 1038, ABV 3.8%) 🍺
A pale brown session bitter with malt flavours present throughout. Dry with a lasting sharp and bitter finish.

On the Rails (OG 1039, ABV 3.8%) 🍺
Chocolaty mild with a notable hop character throughout, bittersweet in the taste and aftertaste, with a dry finish.

Aureole Ale (OG 1039, ABV 4%) 🍺
A lemony aroma leads to a dry, bitter taste, with more citrus flavours. Hoppy finish with a hint of sweetness.

Posh Pooch (OG 1042, ABV 4.2%) 🍺
A best bitter with balancing biscuity malt sweetness. Some citrus fruitiness and a clean, hoppy aftertaste.

Penguin Porter (OG 1045, ABV 4.5%)
A chestnut-coloured ale with an initial subtle hoppiness giving way to coffee malt flavour with rich chocolate in the finish.

Alligator Ale (OG 1047, ABV 4.6%) 🍺
Some grapefruit in the aroma, with hop and bitterness in the taste and plenty of balancing biscuit in the aroma and aftertaste.

Single Hop (OG 1045, ABV 4.6%)
Copper-coloured IPA brewed each month showcasing a different single hop variety.

Anastasia's Exile Stout (OG 1049, ABV 5%) 🍺
Burnt coffee aromas lead to a roast malt flavour in this black beer. Notably fruity throughout, with a bittersweet aftertaste.

Rhino Rye (OG 1049, ABV 5%)
A rye IPA with a slightly spicy note and a good hoppy bitterness.

Red IPA (OG 1054, ABV 5.5%)
An intensely-hopped red IPA with a citrus, grapefruit taste.

Anastasia's Imperial Stout (OG 1078, ABV 8%) 🍾
A deep black beer with intense aromas of roasted coffee and chocolate.

Ash Valley

🏠 Prince of Wales, Green Tye, nr Much Hadham, Hertfordshire, SG10 6JP
☎ (01279) 842139 ☎ 07966 474730
⊕ thepow.co.uk/the-brewery

The brewery is part of the Prince of Wales pub in Green Tye, run by the landlord. Most of the beer is sold at the pub and occasional CAMRA beer festivals, and a small amount is swapped with other brewers. A micro pilot brewery is used to produce one-off experimental beers all year round.

Ashdown 👁

Buckhurst Park, Withyham, East Sussex, TN7 4BN
☎ (01892) 770532 ☎ 07530 604064
🌐 ashdownales.co.uk

Brewing began in 2016.

Ashley Down

15 Wathen Road, St Andrews, Bristol, BS6 5BY
☎ (0117) 983 6567 ☎ 07563 751200
✉ ashleydownbrewery@gmail.com

⊗ Ashley Down began brewing in 2011 using a 5.5-barrel plant in the owner's garage. There are plans for expansion and to relocate to new premises. ♦ RAIB

Sideways (OG 1037, ABV 3.7%) ◥
Strong citrus aroma. Lemony hops with a light sweetness, leaving a faint astringency.

Remedy (OG 1037.5, ABV 4%) ◥
Characteristics of a dark mild and a red. A pronounced aroma of crystal malt precedes a malty astringent taste with hints of toffee and dark fruit.

Landlords Best (OG 1039.5, ABV 4.2%) ◥
Malty best bitter with balancing hops and astringency in the aftertaste.

Pale Ale (OG 1040.5, ABV 4.3%) ◥
Sweet best bitter balanced with hoppy bitterness which continues to the aftertaste.

Ashleyhay SIBA

🏠 **Royal Oak, North End, Wirksworth, Derbyshire, DE4 4FG**
☎ (01629) 823000 ☎ 07708 050019
✉ jim@ashleyhaybrewery.co.uk

Brewing began in 2014. The 2.5-barrel plant was relocated to the Royal Oak in Wirksworth in 2017. Brewing is currently suspended.

Ashover SIBA

Unit 1, Derby Road, Clay Cross, Derbyshire, S45 9AG
☎ 07803 708526 🌐 ashoverbrewery.com

⊗ Brewing began in 2007 on a 3.5-barrel plant in the garage of the cottage next to the Old Poets' Corner, Ashover. Since its acquisition of a 10-barrel brewery in the neighbouring village of Clay Cross in 2015, Ashover now brews at both sites. The brewery serves local freehouses across Derbyshire and further afield as well as the Poets' Corner and Brown Ales pub groups. ‼ RAIB

Font (OG 1037, ABV 3.8%)
A golden-coloured session beer.

Poets Tipple (OG 1040, ABV 4%) ◥
Complex, tawny-coloured beer that drinks above its strength. Predominantly malty in flavour, with increasing bitterness towards the end.

Littlemoor Citra (OG 1041, ABV 4.1%)
Clean, pale, crisp and refreshing.

The Fabrick (OG 1042, ABV 4.4%)
Golden ale with a soft, fruity flavour, full mouthfeel and a crisp, clean finish.

Red Lion (OG 1044, ABV 4.6%)

A full-bodied red ale with malt complementing the hop fruitiness.

Coffin Lane Stout (OG 1050, ABV 5%) ◥
A chocolate and coffee flavour, balanced by a little sweetness. Finish is long and quite dry.

Liquorice (OG 1050, ABV 5%)
Rich, full-bodied stout with added liquorice.

Butts Pale Ale (OG 1051.3, ABV 5.5%) ◥
Pale and strong yet easy-drinking golden bitter. Combination of bitter and sweet flavours mingle with an alcoholic kick, leading to a warming yet bitter finish and aftertaste.

Milk Stout (OG 1060, ABV 6%)
Smooth and rich stout with chocolate roasted essences and hints of coffee and caramel.

Atlantic

Treisaac Farm, Treisaac, Cornwall, TR8 4DX
☎ (01637) 880326 🌐 atlanticbrewery.com

⊗ Specialist microbrewery producing organic and vegan ales. All ales are unfiltered and finings-free. There are nine core brews including four food-matched Dining Ales developed with Michelin chef Nathan Outlaw. Casks are supplied locally and to London, with bottle-conditioned beers available nationally. ♦ RAIB V

Ale (OG 1038, ABV 4%) ◥
A pale amber ale, with good body, sweet malt and hints of vanilla. Well-hopped yet balanced.

Azores (OG 1042, ABV 4.2%) ◥
Pale brown golden ale. Citrus and resinous hops dominate the aroma and taste with tropical fruits. Refreshing bitter and dry finish.

Earl Grey PA (OG 1045, ABV 4.5%) ◥
Cloudy amber-coloured organic speciality ale. Hop aroma leads to powerful citrus fruit flavours becoming intense. Fairly bitter and dry.

Madarina Cornovia (OG 1045, ABV 4.5%) ◥
Gold-coloured beer with added orange peel. Citrus hop aroma with strong bitter lemon and orange flavours and a rising dryness.

Masala Chai PA (OG 1045, ABV 4.5%)
Classic Indian roadhouse spices and black tea tannins in this pale session ale.

Smoked Green Tea PA (OG 1045, ABV 4.5%)
A fresh pale ale with gentle hint of smoked green tea.

Gold (OG 1043, ABV 4.6%) ◥
Refreshing, crisp golden ale lightly spiced with zingy ginger. Dry finish with the lingering light marmalade of First Gold hops.

Bee Keeper (OG 1046, ABV 4.8%)
A smooth, balanced golden-coloured honey beer.

Blue (OG 1045, ABV 4.8%) ◥
Rich black porter with heavy roast malt aroma and taste. Smoky liquorice, bitter coffee and chocolate flavours with sweet fruit.

Red (OG 1047, ABV 5%) ◥
Malty, smooth red ale with nutty flavours and natural cloudiness. Dryness of the hop finish is balanced by sweet malt.

Fistral (OG 1048, ABV 5.2%) ◥
Full-flavoured copper wheat beer. Sweet, stone-fruit flavours blend with biscuit malt and citrus hops. Malty finish with hops and dryness.

Discovery – Easterly (OG 1050, ABV 5.5%) ◈
A golden pale ale with crisp distinct flavours of lime, chilli and ginger. Sweet malt balancing the citrus aroma tones.

Discovery – Northerly (OG 1050, ABV 5.5%) ◈
Rich Cornish porter with blackcurrant and molasses. Full-bodied dark roasted malts, hints of chocolate, ripe blackcurrants and black cherries.

Discovery – Southerly (OG 1050, ABV 5.5%) ◈
Smooth blonde ale with elderflower and lemon. Gentle hops, sweet malt with a floral and citrus zest finish.

Discovery – Westerly (OG 1050, ABV 5.5%) ◈
Red Celtic ale with cinnamon and orange. Full-bodied bitter with gentle citrus marmalade and mild nutty spice flavours.

Atlas

See Orkney

Atom SIBA

Unit 4 Food & Tech Park, Malmo Road, Sutton Fields Industrial Estate, Hull, East Yorkshire, HU7 0FY ⊕ atombeers.com

⊠ Atom is a collaboration between Allan Rice and Sarah Thackray, set up in 2013 in a modern industrial unit north-west of Hull city centre. The 10-barrel brewing equipment, which came from Oban Ales, is supplemented by a fermentation capacity of 180 barrels and a conditioning capacity of 180 barrels. ‼◆

Schrodingers Cat (OG 1035, ABV 3.5%)
A full-bodied hop bomb.

Blonde Ale (OG 1040, ABV 4%)
A fresh, smooth pale beer with citrus notes.

Camomile (OG 1042, ABV 4.2%)
An easy-drinking ale with a fragrant floral aroma.

Pale Ale (OG 1045, ABV 4.5%)

Dark Alchemy (OG 1049, ABV 4.9%)
A rich, complex porter with bitterness and aroma from cardamom and coriander but no hops.

India Pale Ale (OG 1056, ABV 5.6%)

Atomic

⬚ c/o Alexandra Arms, 72-73 St James Street, Rugby, Warwickshire, CV21 2SL
☎ (01788) 576194 ☎ 07986 983984

Office: 1 Lower Hillmorton Road, Rugby, Warwickshire, CV21 3ST ⊕ atomicbrewery.com

Originally set up in 2006, the brewery stands in the garden of the Alexandra Arms in Rugby.

Aurora (NEW)

Unit 6, Gallows Industrial Park, off Furnace Road, Ilkeston, Derbyshire, DE7 5EP ☎ 07740 783631

The former North Star brewery, which was taken over by new owners and renamed in 2016.

Austendyke

The Beeches, Austendyke Road, Weston Hills, Spalding, Lincolnshire, PE12 6BZ ☎ 07866 045778

Austendyke Ales began brewing in 2012 using a seven-barrel plant. The brewery is operated on a part-time basis by brewer Charlie Rawlings and business partner Nathan Marshall, who handles sales. The brewery owns and runs its micropub, the Prior's Oven, Spalding.

Long Lane (OG 1039, ABV 4%)

Sheep Market (OG 1040, ABV 4%)

Bakestraw Bitter (OG 1041, ABV 4.1%)

Holbeach High Street (OG 1045, ABV 4.5%)

Hogsgate (OG 1050, ABV 5%)

Axholme SIBA

7 Lakes Country Park, Wharf Road, Crowle, Lincolnshire, DN17 4JS
☎ (01724) 781804 ☎ 07551 910040

Office: 2 Garthorpe Road, Luddington, Lincolnshire, DN17 4QT ⊕ axholmebrewing.co.uk

Former Abbeydale and Thorne brewer Mike Richards commissioned Scunthorpe's first microbrewery in 2012 using a 2.5-barrel plant. In 2013 the brewery relocated to a brand new four-barrel plant in Crowle. Bespoke beers are also available. Beers are distributed nationwide. ◆RAIB

Best Bitter (OG 1038, ABV 3.8%)
Malty fruitcake flavours dominate with a peppery hop finish.

Cleethorpes Pale Ale (OG 1041, ABV 4.2%)

Clearwater Pale Ale (OG 1041, ABV 4.3%)
A fresh and spicy take on the pale ale style, with grassy and herbal flavours dominating with a rounded bitter finish.

Special Reserve (OG 1066, ABV 7.2%)
Powerful old ale with flavours of brandy and dried fruits.

Axiom

Unit 4a, Wrexham Enterprise Park, Ash Road, North Wrexham Industrial Estate, Wrexham, LL13 9JT
☎ 07544 280353 ⊕ axiombrewing.co.uk

Brewing commenced in 2014 on a self-built four-barrel plant. A core range of beers is available, as well as occasional experimental beers and collaboration brews.

Reversion (ABV 4.1%)

Conclusion (OG 1049, ABV 4.6%)
Rich and dark with notes of figs, raisins and dark chocolate.

Axton

Pentre Lane, Axton, CH8 9DH
☎ (01745) 855657 ☎ 07756 636415

Correspondence: Archies Bar, 151 High Street, Prestatyn, LL19 9AS ⊠ jamesmcgeown@live.co.uk

☺Axton commenced brewing in 2015 on a 1.5-barrel plant, mainly supplying Archies Bar in Prestatyn. ◆

Nicky Nacky Noo (OG 1043, ABV 4.3%)
Hoppy with a caramel butterscotch aftertaste.

Aylesbury

🍺 **83 Bicester Road, Aylesbury, Buckinghamshire, HP19 9AZ**
☎ **(01844) 239237** ⊕ **aylesburybrewhouse.co.uk**

Established in 2011 at the Hop Pole as a sister brewery to Vale (qv). One-off beers are brewed on a weekly basis using a 12-barrel kit.

Ayr

5 Racecourse Road, Ayr, KA7 2DG
☎ **(01292) 263891**
✉ **info@ayrbrewingcompany.com**

Ayr began brewing in 2009 on a five-barrel plant and is located at the Glenpark Hotel. As well as the hotel around 50 other outlets are supplied throughout Scotland and England. ➤♦ RAIB

Leezie Lundie (OG 1037.5, ABV 3.8%) ◈
A pale golden session ale with hints of grapefruit and a dry, lingering finish.

Jolly Beggars (OG 1041, ABV 4.2%) ◈
A complex best bitter with plenty of character and lingering malty aftertaste.

Rabbie's Porter (OG 1042.5, ABV 4.3%) 🍺 ◈
A robust, full-bodied porter with well-balanced toffee, fruity malt and a slightly smoky finish.

Burning Gull (OG 1048, ABV 5%)
A strong bitter with toffee, caramelised oranges and grapefruit on the palate leading to a creamy, rich, bitter finish.

Betty and the Gardens (OG 1049.5, ABV 5.2%)
A blonde ale with hints of pineapple, passion fruit and strawberries leading to a smooth, fruity finish.

B&T SIBA

The Brewery, Shefford, Bedfordshire, SG17 5DZ
☎ **(01462) 815080** ⊕ **banksandtaylor.com**

⊠ Banks & Taylor – now just B&T – was founded in 1982. It produces 13 regular beers, plus monthly specials and occasional beers, in an industrial unit close to the town centre. There are five tied houses. ‼♦

Two Brewers Bitter (OG 1036, ABV 3.6%) ◈
Bronze-coloured bitter with citrus hop aroma and taste and a dry finish.

Plum Mild (OG 1038, ABV 3.8%)
A rich, dark mild with a strong malty aroma, hints of plum flavour on the tongue and a fruity plum finish.

Shefford Bitter (OG 1038, ABV 3.8%) ◈
A pale brown beer with a light hop aroma and a hoppy taste leading to a bitter finish.

Shefford Dark Mild (OG 1038, ABV 3.8%) ◈
A dark beer with a well-balanced taste. Sweetish, roast malt aftertaste.

Golden Fox (OG 1041, ABV 4.1%)
A golden, hoppy ale, dry tasting with a fruity aroma and citrus finish.

Black Dragon Mild (OG 1043, ABV 4.3%) ◈
Black in colour with a toffee and roast malt flavour and a smoky finish.

Dunstable Giant (OG 1044, ABV 4.4%)
Dark tawny bitter with a subtle blend of malt and hops.

Dragon Slayer (OG 1045, ABV 4.5%) 🍺 ◈
A golden beer with a malt and hop flavour and a bitter finish. More malty and less hoppy than is usual for a beer of this style.

**Edwin Taylor's Extra Stout
(OG 1045, ABV 4.5%)** ◈
A complex black beer with a bitter coffee and roast malt flavour and a dry bitter finish.

Fruit Bat (OG 1045, ABV 4.5%) ◈
A warming straw-coloured beer with a taste of apricots and a bitter finish.

Shefford Pale Ale (SPA) (OG 1045, ABV 4.5%) ◈
A well-balanced beer with hop, fruit and malt flavours. Dry, bitter aftertaste.

SOD (OG 1050, ABV 5%)
SOS with caramel added for colour.

SOS (OG 1050, ABV 5%) ◈
A rich mixture of fruit, hops and malt is present in the taste and aftertaste of this beer. Predominantly hoppy aroma.

Baa SIBA

Unit 4, Station Road Industrial Estate, Chepstow, NP16 5PF ⊕ **baabrewing.com**

Established in 2015 using an eight-barrel plant with five fermenters and a bright beer tank. ‼➤♦

BQ Blonde (ABV 3.7%)

Best Bitter (ABV 4%)

Hopping (ABV 4.2%)

Two Bridges (ABV 4.5%)
Smooth and full-bodied with a gentle citrus hoppy aftertaste.

IPA (ABV 5%)

Bacchus

🍺 **Bacchus Hotel, 17 High Street, Sutton-on-Sea, Lincolnshire, LN12 2EY**
☎ **(01507) 441204** ⊕ **bacchushotel.co.uk**

Bacchus began brewing in 2010 and now has a two-barrel plant supplying the Bacchus Hotel.

Backyard SIBA ◉

Unit 8a, Gatehouse Trading Estate, Lichfield Road, Brownhills, Walsall, West Midlands, WS8 6JZ
☎ **(01543) 360145** ⊕ **tbb.uk.com**

Backyard began brewing in 2008 and expanded in 2012 to a 12-barrel plant brewing up to 50 barrels a week. Two pubs are owned: the Fountain, Walsall and the Saddlers Arms, Solihull. A half-barrel experimental plant is also in operation and a tap house is open every Friday (1-8pm). ‼➤♦ RAIB

Bitter (OG 1038, ABV 3.8%)
A blonde beer, slightly sweet with hints of tangerine and fruit salad.

The Hoard (OG 1040, ABV 3.9%)
A golden bitter, refreshing and dry with a light malt flavour with a hint of lemon the palate.

Blonde (OG 1041, ABV 4.1%)
A blonde bitter with a citrus and pine aroma and a dry, crisp, hoppy taste.

Americana (ABV 4.3%)

A light, fruity pale ale with powerful orange and lemon aromas and malty biscuit, fruity hops and vanilla flavours.

Gold (OG 1045, ABV 4.5%)
A golden bitter with a hoppy tropical fruit taste.

Coaltown Coffee Stout (OG 1052, ABV 5%)
A stout with a roast malt and coffee aroma and a fruity coffee taste.

IPA (OG 1049, ABV 5%)
An IPA with an intense floral and herbal aroma and strong, rich and fruity bitterness.

Antipodean (OG 1052, ABV 5.6%)
Complex flavours of exotic fruits, apricot and pine with an undercurrent of spicy cedar and oak.

BAD 👁

Unit 3, North Hill Road, Dishforth, North Yorkshire, YO7 3DH
☎ (01423) 324005 ⊕ wearebad.co

Brewing commenced in 2014, originally using a 13-barrel plant, since upgraded to cope with demand. Monthly specials often incorporate seasonal ingredients and the brewery also produces more experimental and radical brews pushing the boundaries of conventional brewing. ‼◆

Comfortably Numb (ABV 3.8%)
Fruity and slightly bitter. Hoppy with notes of tangerine, mango, grapefruit and pineapple.

Love Over Gold (ABV 4.1%)
A blonde ale, light and hoppy. Well-balanced with grapefruit and grassy notes.

Wild Gravity (ABV 5.2%)
An IPA with a malty backbone and tropical hop flavours.

Dazed & Confused (ABV 5.5%)
Dark rich milk stout with hints of cherry, chocolate, coffee and almond.

Bad Bunny (NEW)

4 Wallace Street, Derby, DE22 3FB ☎ 07519 605362
⊕ badbunnybrewery.co.uk

Small 300-litre brewery that started production in 2016. Most output is naturally conditioned KeyKegs and bottle-conditioned beers but cask-conditioned beers are available for festivals. RAIB

Bad Seed SIBA

Unit 6, 7 Rye Close, York Way Industrial Estate, Malton, North Yorkshire, YO17 6YD
☎ (01653) 695783 ⊕ badseedbrewery.co.uk

☺Started in 2013 by James Broad and Chris Waplington, the four-barrel brewery was increased to a 12-barrel plant in 2016. ◆

NZ Pale Ale (ABV 3.8%)

Session IPA (ABV 4%)

Single Hop Pale Ale (ABV 4.5%)

Cascade: American Pale (ABV 5.4%)

Badger

See Hall & Woodhouse

Baildon SIBA

Unit D, Tong Park Business Centre, Otley Road, Baildon, West Yorkshire, BD17 7QD
⊕ baildonbrewing.co.uk

Brewing began in 2014 using a six-barrel plant. The brewery is run by Leigh Terry, head brewster. ◆RAIB

Blonde (ABV 3.6%)
A refreshing and zesty summer ale.

Brunette (ABV 3.9%)
A well-rounded ruby-coloured ale.

Auburn Flame (ABV 4.2%)
A crisp ale with spicy hop and soft fruit flavours.

Bakers Dozen

Unit 5, Ketton Business Estate, Pit Lane, Ketton, PE9 3SZ
☎ (01780) 238180 ⊕ bakersdozenbrewing.co.uk

Brewing takes place on a five-barrel plant installed in 2015 by the owners of the Jolly Brewer, Stamford, where the beers are regularly available. ◆

Jentacular (OG 1034, ABV 3.5%)

Magic Potion (OG 1036, ABV 3.8%)

Stamford Pale (OG 1038, ABV 4%)

System of a Brown (OG 1038, ABV 4.1%)

Bearded Archway (OG 1043, ABV 4.6%)
A refreshing, unfined lemon and lime saison-style beer.

Electric Landlady (OG 1045, ABV 5%)

Bale (NEW)

Janie Craig Cottage, Liddaton, Devon, EX20 4AD
☎ 07540 283014 ⊕ baleale.com

Bale Ale is a nanobrewery established in 2016 situated near Dartmoor National Park in Devon. Only bottle-conditioned beers are produced at present. RAIB

Ballard's SIBA 👁

The Old Sawmill, Nyewood, Petersfield, West Sussex, GU31 5HA
☎ (01730) 821362 ⊕ ballards-brewery.co.uk

Launched in 1980 by Mike and Carola Brown at Cumbers Farm, Trotton, Ballard's has been trading at Nyewood since 1988 and now supplies 70-80 outlets. ‼🍺◆RAIB

Midhurst Mild (OG 1034, ABV 3.4%)
Traditional dark mild, well-balanced and refreshing with a biscuity flavour.

Golden Bine (OG 1038, ABV 3.8%) 🔖
Amber-coloured, clean-tasting bitter. A roast malt aroma leads to a fruity, slightly sweet taste and a dry finish.

Best Bitter (OG 1042, ABV 4.2%) 🔖
A copper-coloured beer with a malty aroma. A good balance of fruit and malt in the flavour gives way to a dry, hoppy aftertaste.

Wild (OG 1047, ABV 4.7%)
A blend of Midhurst Mild and Wassail.

Nyewood Gold (OG 1050, ABV 5%)

Wassail (OG 1060, ABV 6%) 🔖

A strong, full-bodied, tawny-red, fruity beer with a predominance of malt throughout, but also an underlying hoppiness.

Balmaha

▤ Oak Tree Inn, Balmaha, Loch Lomond, G63 0JQ
☎ (01360) 870357 ⊕ oak-tree-inn.co.uk

Balmaha began brewing in 2012 using a one-barrel plant.

Bang-On (NEW) SIBA

Unit 3, George Street, Bridgend Industrial Estate, Bridgend, CF31 3TS
☎ (01656) 760790

Office: 51 Angel Way, North Cornelly, Bridgend, CF33 4PB ⊕ bangonbrewery.beer

Launched in 2016 using a five-barrel plant. The brewery has a tap room on site and offers tours and brew day experiences. The beer range is expanding as new recipes are developed. ‼️ 🏭

Doris (OG 1031, ABV 3.4%)
A session IPA, fruity and fragrant.

Steven (OG 1041, ABV 4%)
A light stout, warming with deep notes of coffee and hints of fruit.

Arthur (OG 1039, ABV 4.4%)
A lightly-hopped amber-coloured ale with floral and berries on the nose.

Craig (OG 1052, ABV 5.6%)
A fruity beer with a spicy edge and subtle liquorice hints.

Bank Top SIBA ◉

The Pavilion, Ashworth Lane, Bolton, BL1 8RA
☎ (01204) 595800 ⊕ banktopbrewery.com

☺Bank Top was established in 1995. Since 2002 the brewery has occupied a Grade II listed tennis pavilion housing an 11-barrel plant. Bank Top Brewery Estates was formed in 2010 and now owns two pubs, Bank Top Brewery Tap and Bank Top Ale House. ‼️♦

Barley to Beer (OG 1036, ABV 3.6%)
A pale bitter with a citrus lemon and herbal finish.

Sweeneys (OG 1038, ABV 3.8%)
An amber-coloured bitter with a bold, crisp flavour and a delicate, slightly spicy aroma.

Bad to the Bone (OG 1040, ABV 4%)
A tan-coloured beer with floral qualities and delicate citrus notes.

Dark Mild (OG 1040, ABV 4%) ◄
Dark brown beer with a malt and roast aroma. Smooth mouthfeel, with malt, roast malt and hops prominent throughout.

Flat Cap (OG 1040, ABV 4%) 🏆 ◄
Amber-coloured ale with a modest fruit aroma leading to a beer with citrus fruit, malt and hops. Good finish of fruit, malt and bitterness.

Gold Digger (OG 1040, ABV 4%) ◄
Golden-coloured, with a citrus aroma, grapefruit and a touch of spiciness on the palate; a fresh, hoppy citrus finish.

Old Slapper (OG 1042, ABV 4.2%)

A golden-amber beer with citrus, floral and peach notes on the nose. Lightly hopped with a soft fruity taste.

Pavilion Pale Ale (OG 1045, ABV 4.5%) ◄
A yellow beer with a citrus and hop aroma. Big fruity flavour with a peppery hoppiness; dry, bitter yet fruity finish.

Blonde (OG 1050, ABV 5%)
A pale ale with a pleasant woody flavour and distinct berry aroma.

Port O Call (OG 1050, ABV 5%) ◄
Dark brown beer with a malty, fruity aroma. Malt, roast and dark fruits in the bittersweet taste and finish.

Banks's

Park Brewery, Wolverhampton, West Midlands, WV1 4NY
☎ (01902) 711811 ⊕ bankssbeer.co.uk

Banks's was founded as a firm of maltsters in 1840, commencing brewing in 1874 and moved to the current Park Brewery the following year. It became the principal brewery of the Wolverhampton & Dudley Breweries, founded in 1890 by an amalgamation with two other local companies. Several other breweries were later acquired, notably Hanson's of Dudley in 1943, which continued brewing until 1991. Following the takeover of Marston's of Burton-on-Trent in 1999, W&DB subsequently adopted this name for the PLC in 2007. While continuing to produce the original Banks's Mild and Bitter beers for which they gained fame throughout the Midlands, many new beers have been developed notably Sunbeam, which was introduced in 2011 to coincide with the 10th anniversary of Wolverhampton's city status, and the Single Hop and Revisionist ranges. In recent years, Marston's PLC has taken on contract brewing of several well-known national ales, many produced at the Banks's site. These include Tetley Bitter for Carlsberg and Original Bitter for Thwaites. Wainwright and Lancaster Bomber (formerly Thwaites) were brewed under licence from 2014 and purchased outright by Marston's the following year. Part of Marston's PLC. ‼️ 🏭

Mild (OG 1036, ABV 3.5%) ◄
An amber-coloured, well-balanced, refreshing session beer.

Amber Ale (OG 1038, ABV 3.8%) ◄
A pale brown bitter with a pleasant balance of hops and malt. Hops continue from the taste through to a bittersweet aftertaste.

Sunbeam (OG 1042, ABV 4.2%)
Zesty golden blonde beer, with refreshing gooseberry and grapefruit citrus hops prominent. A vibrant hop aroma leads to a long clean finish

Brewed under the Mansfield brand name:

Cask Ale (OG 1038, ABV 3.9%)
A copper-coloured bitter with fruity notes from the Mansfield yeast, subtle hop aromas, and a restrained bitterness.

Brewed under the Thwaites brand name:

Original (OG 1036, ABV 3.6%)
A classic copper-coloured, traditional session bitter, with balance between malt flavour and hop bitterness.

Contract brewed for Carlsberg:

Tetley Mild (OG 1034, ABV 3.3%)

Tetley Bitter (OG 1035, ABV 3.7%)
A classic session bitter. A distinct hop character prevails with subtle clove-like notes.

Tetley Gold (OG 1041, ABV 4.1%)
A straw-coloured golden ale. A dry, refreshing citrus/herbal hop character predominates

Contract brewed for Marston's:

EPA (OG 1036, ABV 3.6%)

Wainwright (OG 1042, ABV 4.1%)
Refreshing golden ale with gentle bitterness and a sweet lemon hop finish.

Lancaster Bomber (OG 1044, ABV 4.4%)
Full-bodied deep amber-coloured beer, with a raisin-like sweetness and a noticeable dry hop character.

Barlow

Units 5 & 6, Shippen Rural Business Centre, Church Farm, Barlow, Derbyshire, S18 7TR
☎ (0114) 360 3676 ☎ 07976 884703
⊕ barlowbrewery.co.uk

Brewing started in 2009 on a self-built 2.5-barrel plant located in farm outbuildings. Expansion to five-barrel capacity was completed in 2014. Beers are supplied to the Hare & Hounds in Barlow and other local outlets. The brewery aquired its first pub, the Tap House, Brampton in 2014. ➤◆RAIB

Heath Robinson (OG 1039, ABV 3.8%)
A traditional dark bitter with a malty background and a balanced, bitter finish.

Betty's Blonde (OG 1042, ABV 4%)
Light golden in colour with subtle citrus and passion fruit flavours and a clean, crisp finish.

Beyond the Pale (OG 1042, ABV 4%)
A well-balanced, straw-coloured pale ale. A floral aroma with light citrus grapefruit taste and a hint of lemon; light bitter finish.

Carnival Ale (OG 1042, ABV 4%)
A light, golden pale ale with a citrus finish.

Dark Horse (OG 1043, ABV 4.2%)
A dark bitter with a coffee aroma.

Black (OG 1051, ABV 5%)
A dark ale with strong roast and malty flavours and a well-balanced, bitter finish.

Three Valleys IPA (OG 1052, ABV 5%)
An American-style IPA bursting with tropical fruit and citrus flavours; clean bitter finish.

Jolly Roger (OG 1053, ABV 5.2%)
A robust porter, smooth, dark and satisfying. Coffee and chocolate flavours with a warming finish.

Full Monty (OG 1067, ABV 6.5%)
A strong, full-flavoured IPA. Golden in colour with complex passion fruit, citrus and mandarin orange flavours with a warming finish.

Anastasia (OG 1076, ABV 7.5%)
Strong, dark and smooth with complex malt flavours, chocolate, coffee and a hint of fruit.

Barn Owl

Buildings Farm, Faringdon Road, Gozzards Ford, Oxfordshire, OX13 6QH ☎ 07724 551086

⊠ Located in a spacious barn on a farm just outside Abingdon, brewing began in 2016 using a four-barrel plant. Beers are often to be found in the Black Horse in Gozzard's Ford and other local free trade outlets.

Golden Gozzard (OG 1040, ABV 4%)
A light, refreshing golden ale with a soft bitterness and long finish.

Gozzard's Guzzler (OG 1044, ABV 4.4%)
A dark best bitter with a sweetish nose and fruity tones.

Barnaby's (NEW) SIBA

The Old Stable, Hole Farm, Staverton, Devon, TQ11 0LA
☎ (01803) 762730 ⊕ barnabysbrewhouse.com

New Soil Association-certified organic brewery established in 2016. No real ale.

Barnet

🍺 **Black Horse, Wood Street, High Barnet, Hertfordshire, EN5 4BW**
☎ (020) 8449 2230 ⊕ blackhorsebarnet.co.uk

The brewery opened in 2013 using a 2.5-barrel plant located behind the Black Horse pub. Brewing takes place three times a week using traditional recipes from long since closed breweries. The beers are supplied mainly to the Black Horse, but small quantities may be found in other local pubs.

Barney's SIBA

Summerhall Brewery, 1 Summerhall, Edinburgh, EH9 1PL ☎ 07512 253660 ⊕ barneysbeer.com

The only microbrewery in Edinburgh's city centre, Barney's Beer was founded in 2010 and now brews on the site of the original 1800s Summerhall brewery. Summerhall is Edinburgh's centre for the arts and science. ‼RAIB

Vital Juices (ABV 3.8%)

Extra Pale (OG 1040, ABV 4%)
Light and refreshing blonde ale.

Red Rye (OG 1044, ABV 4.5%)
Copper-coloured ale with a clean, crisp, dry and fruity taste.

Volcano IPA (OG 1049, ABV 5%)
A hoppy, light-coloured American-style pale ale.

Barngates SIBA ⊚

Barngates, Cumbria, LA22 0NG
☎ (01539) 436575 ⊕ barngatesbrewery.co.uk

⊚Barngates was established in 1997 to supply only the Drunken Duck Inn. It became a limited company in 1999. Expansion over the years plus a new purpose-built 10-barrel plant in 2008 means it now supplies more than 150 outlets throughout Cumbria, Lancashire, Yorkshire and Northumberland. ‼◆

Pale (OG 1036, ABV 3.3%) 🍂
A well-balanced, fruity, hoppy bitter with plenty of flavour for its strength.

Cat Nap (OG 1037, ABV 3.6%) 🍂
Pale beer, unapologetically bitter, with a dry, astringent finish.

Cracker (OG 1038, ABV 3.9%) 🍷 ◆
A full-bodied, hoppy beer with some balancing sweetness and fruit. There is plenty of taste in this brown beer.

Brathay Gold (OG 1042, ABV 4%) ◆
A sweet and rich aroma is followed by plenty of fruit and hops then a long bitter finish.

Goodhew's Dry Stout (OG 1045, ABV 4.3%) 🍷 ◆
The inviting roast aroma leads to an easy-drinking, full-bodied and well-balanced roasty stout.

Tag Lag (OG 1044, ABV 4.4%) 🍷 ◆
This traditional bitter is full on: fruit, noble hops, malt balance and a good body with a crisp, clean finish.

Red Bull Terrier (OG 1048, ABV 4.8%) 🍷 ◆
An assertive roasty red beer with full mouthfeel. Initial sweetness and luscious fruit, give way to a lingering bitter finish.

Barrahooley Craft (NEW)

122 Glenravel Road, Martinstown, BT43 6QL
⊕ barrahooleybrewery.com

Located in the heart of the Glens of Antrim, Barrahooley started brewing in 2014. RAIB

Barrell & Sellers SIBA

Spring Farm, St Cross South Elmham, Suffolk, IP20 0NZ
☎ (01986) 783902 ☎ 07788 561455
⊕ barrellandsellers.co.uk

⊠ Brewing began in 2014, producing easy-drinking classic beers using only English-grown hops and malt. The cask beers are supplied to a small number of local pubs and its bottled-conditioned beers are available direct from the brewery, via the website shop or through selected retail outlets. ‼ ◆ RAIB

Barrowden

See Co Pilot

Bartleby's

Coachwerks, 19 Hollingdean Terrace, Brighton, East Sussex, BN1 7HB
☎ (01273) 275012 ☎ 07518 485342
⊕ bartlebysbrewery.com

Bartleby's began trading in 2014 in Brighton. Since opening it has expanded its distribution to local pubs and has established an on-site shop with home deliveries by veloelectric tricycle. An on-site venue is used for music, community events and art shows. ‼ ◆

Bartrams

Rougham Estate, Ipswich Road (A14), Rougham, Suffolk, IP30 9ND ☎ 07768 062581
⊕ bartramsbrewery.co.uk

⊠ Established in 1999, the brewery was moved to Rougham Airfield in 2005 to a building formerly used to pack parachutes during WW2. Its small capacity enables the brewery to produce a great diversity and number of specialist beers including its legendary dark brews. Beers are supplied to a

select number of local pubs with the majority of sales being via music festivals and local events. ‼ 🍷 ◆ RAIB V

Marld (OG 1033, ABV 3.4%)
Spicy hops and malt with a hint of chocolate, slightly smoky with a light, roasted finish.

Washing Machine Bitter (OG 1036, ABV 3.6%)

Adams Ale (OG 1036, ABV 3.7%)
A traditional full-bodied bitter with English hops.

Premier Bitter (OG 1038, ABV 3.7%)
A traditional quaffing ale, full-flavoured but light, dry and hoppy.

Cambridge Rock (OG 1038, ABV 3.8%)

Rougham Ready (OG 1038, ABV 3.8%)
A light, crisp bitter, surprisingly full bodied for its strength.

Milkmaid Bitter (OG 1040, ABV 4%)

Thy Last Drop (OG 1040, ABV 4%)

Bee's Knees (OG 1042, ABV 4.2%)
An amber-coloured beer with a floral aroma; honey softness on the palate leads to a crisp, bitter finish.

Captain Bill Bartram's Best Bitter (OG 1048, ABV 4.8%)
Modified from a 100-year old recipe, using full malt and traditional Kentish hops.

Captain's Stout (OG 1049, ABV 4.8%)
Biscuity dark malt leads to a lightly smoked aroma, plenty of roasted malt character, coffee notes and a whiff of smoke.

Cherry Stout (OG 1048, ABV 4.8%)
Sensuous hints of chocolate lead to a subtle suggestion of cherries.

Darkside (OG 1050, ABV 5%)

Suffolk 'n' Strong (OG 1050, ABV 5%)
A light, smooth but strong bitter, well-balanced malt and hops with an easy finish.

Flirtatious Ungulate (OG 1056, ABV 5.6%)

Red Rye Ding Hood (OG 1066, ABV 6.6%)

Comrade Bill Bartram's Egalitarian Anti Imperialist Soviet Stout (OG 1070, ABV 6.9%)
A Russian stout by any other name, a luscious easy-drinking example of the style.

For the John Peel Centre, Stowmarket:

John Peel Centre (OG 1037, ABV 3.7%)

Barum SIBA

🏠 c/o Reform Inn, Pilton High Street, Pilton, Barnstaple, Devon, EX31 1PD
☎ (01271) 329994 ⊕ barumbrewery.co.uk

Barum was established in 1996 by Tim Webster, and is housed in a conversion attached to the Reform Inn that acts as the brewery tap and main outlet. Distribution is exclusively within Devon.

Original (OG 1044, ABV 4.4%) ◆
A smooth, tawny-coloured best bitter. A malt and fruit aroma leads to fruity, hoppy tastes into a short-lived bitter finish.

EPA (OG 1046, ABV 4.6%)
Pale golden ale with citrus grapefruit notes throughout. Clean, dry finish.

Breakfast (OG 1048, ABV 5%)

Copper-coloured malty premium bitter with a floral nose and bittersweet finish.

Batemans SIBAIFBB 👁

Salem Bridge Brewery, Mill Lane, Wainfleet, Lincolnshire, PE24 4JE
☎ (01754) 880317 🌐 bateman.co.uk

⊚Bateman's Brewery is one of Britain's few remaining independent family-owned and managed brewers. Established in 1874, it has been brewing award-winning beers for four generations. All 62 tied and managed houses serve cask-conditioned beer. ‼️🍺◆

XB (OG 1037, ABV 3.7%) 🍺 🔸
A well-rounded, smooth malty beer with a blackcurrant fruity background. Hops flourish initially before giving way to a bittersweet dryness that enhances the mellow malty ending.

Gold (OG 1039, ABV 3.9%)
A golden-coloured, refreshing beer with a citrus flavour and aroma. Quite dry.

XXXB (OG 1045, ABV 4.5%) 🔸
A blend of malt, hops and fruit on the nose with a bitter bite over the top of a faintly banana maltiness that stays the course. A russet-tan brown classic.

Salem Porter (OG 1048, ABV 4.7%) 🍺 🔸
A black and complex mix of chocolate, liquorice and cough elixir.

Bath 👁

Hare House, Southway Drive, Warmley, Bristol, BS30 5LW
☎ (0117) 947 4797 🌐 bathales.com

⊗ Established in 1995, Bath Ales was taken over by St Austell Brewery in 2016. The Bath Ales and subsidiary Beerd brands are still being brewed as before, on the same sites. More than 400 regional outlets are supplied. 10 pubs and sites are operated across the South-west. ‼️🍺◆RAIB

Special Pale Ale (OG 1039, ABV 3.7%) 🔸
Hoppy, pale golden session bitter. Light citrus aroma with bittersweet flavours and a bitter aftertaste.

Prophecy (OG 1040, ABV 3.9%)
Fruity pine-like aroma, light colour and crisp bitter finish.

Gem (OG 1042, ABV 4.1%) 🍺 🔸
Pale brown best bitter with sweet fruit and malt flavours and a hint of caramel. Little aroma but a balanced taste with a short bitter finish.

Barnsey (OG 1045, ABV 4.5%) 🔸
A dark brown old ale with a grainy mouthfeel. Malt, dark fruits and toffee flavours combine to provide sweetness before a lingering bitter finish.

Platform 3 (OG 1044, ABV 4.5%)
A refreshing IPA with tropical fruit aromas, hints of citrus honey flavours, and a long bitter finish.

Brewed under the Beerd brand name:

Monterey (OG 1040, ABV 3.9%)
A West Coast-style pale ale brewed with American-sourced hops. Pine and tropical fruits on the nose, more pine on the tongue followed by a quick, sharp, bitter finish.

Silver Tip (OG 1046, ABV 4.7%)

A refreshing pale ale with a fruity aroma and a flavour that has hints of white wine with a fresh, quick bitter finish.

Bathams IFBB

Delph Brewery, Delph Road, Brierley Hill, West Midlands, DY5 2TN
☎ (01384) 77229 🌐 bathams.com

⊚A classic Black Country small brewery established in 1877. Tim and Matthew Batham represent the fifth generation to run the company. The Vine, one of the Black Country's most famous pubs, is also the site of the brewery. The company has 10 tied houses and supplies around 30 other outlets. Batham's Bitter is delivered in 54-gallon hogsheads to meet demand. ◆

Mild Ale (OG 1036.5, ABV 3.5%) 🍺 🔸
A fruity, dark brown mild with malty sweetness and a roast malt finish.

Best Bitter (OG 1043.5, ABV 4.3%) 🍺 🔸
A pale yellow, fruity, sweetish bitter, with a dry, hoppy finish. A good, light, refreshing beer.

Battle (NEW)

Netherfield Hill Farm, Netherfield Hill, Battle, East Sussex, TN33 0LH
☎ (01424) 864235 🌐 battlebrewery.co.uk

Located on a working farm close to the iconic abbey in the heart of 1066 Country, Battle Brewery commenced brewing in 2016. ‼️🍺RAIB

Conquest (OG 1043, ABV 4.1%)

Abbey Pale (OG 1050, ABV 5%)

Battledown SIBA 👁

Dowdeswell Park, London Road, Cheltenham, Gloucestershire, GL52 6UT
☎ (01242) 693409 ☎ 07734 834104
🌐 battledownbrewery.com

⊗ Battledown was established by Roland and Stephanie Elliot-Berry in 2005, joined by Ben Jennison-Phillips the following year. The brewery relocated to new premises in 2016 and supplies around 250 outlets. ‼️🍺RAIB

Pale Ale (OG 1037, ABV 3.8%)
Pale with a refreshing aroma and sharp but smooth taste, leaving a dry, hoppy aftertaste which lingers on the palate.

Amber Ale (OG 1041, ABV 4.2%)
A deep golden beer, the malt is evident but gives way to a spicy hop and slightly citrus finish.

Original (OG 1046, ABV 4.6%)
A rich amber-coloured ale. A malty aroma and taste with a deep, full-bodied fruit and malt texture leaving a well-rounded, mellow aftertaste.

Four Kings (OG 1066, ABV 7.2%)
A strong ale with a heady aroma.

Battlefield (Shrewsbury) SIBA

Harlescott Lane, Shrewsbury, SY1 3AH
☎ (01743) 465000 🌐 battlefieldbrewery.co.uk

Battlefield Brewery began brewing in 2015 using a 25-hectolitre European system. It is located in the famous Battlefield area of Shrewsbury. ‼️◆

THE BREWERIES

Saxon Gold (OG 1038, ABV 3.8%)
A golden ale with a subtle orange marmalade aroma on the nose and crisp maltiness with touches of soft hops.

1403 (OG 1043, ABV 4.3%)
A light, dry and crisp ale. Slight malt backbone with a subtle citrus/apricot note. The dry hop finish leaves a grapefruit and floral flavour.

1066 (OG 1045, ABV 4.5%)
An easy-drinking dark ale with rich malt and striking hop aromas.

Archers (OG 1049, ABV 4.9%)
A strong pale ale full of clean malt flavours with a hoppy finish.

Sabut Jung (ABV 5.8%)

Battlefield

See Tunnel

Bays SIBA 👁

Aspen Way, Paignton, Devon, TQ4 7QR
☎ (01803) 555004 ⊕ baysbrewery.co.uk

Bays Brewery opened in 2007 in an old steel fabrication unit in Paignton using a 20-barrel plant. The brewery delivers to many pubs, hotels and restaurants in the south-west and further afield. ‼️🍺♦

Topsail (OG 1040, ABV 4%) 🍺
A traditional session bitter. Fruity-malt aroma, bittersweet hoppy taste with a little malt. Malt and fruit aftertaste.

Gold (OG 1042, ABV 4.3%)
An easy-drinking, light golden ale. The unique blend of hops create lemon citrus overtones.

Devon Dumpling (OG 1048, ABV 5.1%)
A strong golden-coloured beer with a fresh hop character. Smooth with a balanced sweetness throughout.

Beachy Head SIBA

Seven Sisters Sheep Centre, Birling Manor Farm, Gilberts Drive, East Dean, East Sussex, BN20 0AA
☎ (01323) 423313 ☎ -

Offfice: Estates Office, The Green, East Dean, BN20 0BS ⊕ beachyhead.org.uk

⊠ The 2.5-barrel brew plant was installed in 2006 at the rear of the sheep centre. Around 25 outlets are supplied regularly, including three local pubs. The full range of ales (including seasonals) can be sampled at the Tiger Inn, East Dean village, which is the brewery tap. ‼️♦RAIB

Beachy Original (OG 1045, ABV 4.5%)

Legless Rambler (OG 1050, ABV 5%)

Beacon Brauhaus (NEW)

Pilgrims Coffee, Falkland House, Marygate, Lindisfarne, TD15 2SJ
☎ (01289) 389109 ⊕ pilgrimscoffee.com

Nanobrewery situated on Holy Island, the first brewery to be based there in around 500 years. Local outlets are supplied. RAIB

Bear Claw

Unit 3, Meantime Workshops, Spittal, Northumberland, TD15 1RG ☎ 07919 276715
⊕ bearclawbrewery.weebly.com

Bear Claw began brewing in 2012 using a two-barrel plant, producing an ever-changing range of mainly highly-hopped cask-conditioned ales and many bottle-conditioned beers, including continental styles. Expansion is planned as demand is high. RAIB

Beardface & Bines (NEW)

c/o Crafty Devil Brewing, Cardiff ☎ 07850 119481

Office: Full Moon Club, Womanby Street, Cardiff

⊠ Cuckoo brewery set up by two local pub managers. It operates from the brewery premises of Crafty Devil although it is looking at brewing at other sites. No real ale at present.

Beardy Monkey

22 Thorpe Road, Melton Mowbray, Leicestershire, LE13 1SG ☎ 07866 477504
✉ tobychaplin71@gmail.com

Beardy Monkey commenced brewing in 2016 using a half-barrel plant which ex-science teacher turned brewer Toby Chaplin operates from the rear of his own house. There are usually eight brews a month. A small number of local outlets and beer festivals are supplied direct. Beers can be designed and brewed to order.

Pale Ale (OG 1040, ABV 3.9%)
A well-balanced malty brew with a floral hop and soft citrus aftertaste.

Beartown

Bromley House, Spindle Street, Congleton, Cheshire, CW12 1QN
☎ (01260) 299964 ⊕ beartownbrewery.co.uk

☺ Beartown began brewing in 1994 and uses a 25-barrel plant. It supplies more than 250 outlets. It recently joined forces with Manning Brewers (qv), also of Congleton. ‼️🍺♦

Best Bitter (OG 1037, ABV 3.7%)
A copper-coloured session beer with a full palate of malt and crisp hops.

Bear Ass (OG 1040, ABV 4%)
Dark ruby-red, malty bitter with good hop nose and fruity flavour with dry, bitter, astringent aftertaste.

Ginger Bear (OG 1040, ABV 4%)
The flavours from the malt and hops blend with the added bite from the root ginger to produce a quenching blonde ale.

Kodiak Gold (OG 1040, ABV 4%) 🍺
Hops and fruit dominate the taste of this crisp yellow bitter and these follow through to the dryish aftertaste. Biscuity malt also comes through on the aroma and taste.

Bearskinful (OG 1042, ABV 4.2%) 🍺
Biscuity malt dominates the flavour of this amber-coloured best bitter. There are hops and a hint of sulphur on the aroma. A balance of malt and bitterness follows through to the aftertaste.

Bearly Literate (OG 1045, ABV 4.5%)

Golden pale ale. Floral scented and packed with the flavours of summer fruits and lemon, ending with a smooth dryness.

Polar Eclipse (OG 1048, ABV 4.8%) 🏳️ 🍺
Classic black-coloured, dry and bitter stout, with roast flavours to the fore. Good hop on the nose follows through the taste into a long, dry finish.

Blackbear (OG 1050, ABV 5%)
Dark ruby-coloured strong mild ale. Subtle roast and malt flavours fill the taste, complemented by a mellow sweetness.

Bruins Ruin (OG 1050, ABV 5%)
Deep copper-coloured premium ale. Full of malty character and a palate of sweet, smooth, fruity flavours.

Beat Ales SIBA 👁

Old Coach House, Church Road, North Curry, Somerset, TA3 6LH
☎ (07821) 132297 ☎ 07821 132297
Office: 11 Sydenham Hill, Bristol, BS6 5SL
⊕ beatales.com

⊠ Established on the same site as the now closed North Curry Brewery in the Somerset village of the same name. Beer names reflect the owners musical inspiration, taking in different genres. Music can be played from the pumpclips. ♦ RAIB

Raver (OG 1034, ABV 3.8%)

Mod (OG 1038, ABV 4.3%)

Metal Head (OG 1042, ABV 4.8%)

Rockabilly (OG 1044, ABV 5.3%)

Beath SIBA

54 Foulford Road, Cowdenbeath, KY4 9AS ☎ 07792 369678 ⊕ beathbrewing.com

Beath began brewing in 2016, originally with a 20-litre capacity upgraded to 100-litre within a few months. RAIB

Beatnikz Republic (NEW) SIBA

Unit 15, Redbank Court, Green Quarter, Manchester, M4 4HF ☎ 07825 077832 ⊕ beatnikzrepublic.com

Brewing began in 2017 using an eight-barrel plant. An on-site tap room serves the beers. No real ale. ‼️ 🍻

Beavertown SIBA

Units 17 & 18, Lockwood Industrial Park, Mill Mead Road, Tottenham Hale, London, N17 9QP
☎ (020) 8525 9884 ☎ 07976 984173
⊕ beavertownbrewery.co.uk

⊠ Beavertown began brewing in 2014. No real ale. 🍻♦

Beckstones

Upper Beckstones Mill, The Green, Millom, Cumbria, LA18 5HL ☎ 07761 605782
⊕ beckstonesbrewery.co.uk

⊠ On the site of an 18th-century mill, with its own water supply, this five-barrel operation continues to win awards. Beer names have connections to

the long-closed Millom Iron Works or local characters; the brewer designs the distinctive pumpclips. ♦

Leat (OG 1036, ABV 3.6%) 🍺
A refreshing golden bitter with tangy fruit and a rising hop finish.

Barley Blonde (ABV 3.7%) 🍺
Full-flavoured, well-balanced, emphatically fruity, hoppy beer.

Black Dog Freddy Mild (OG 1038, ABV 3.8%) 🍺
A full-bodied, well-balanced ruby dark mild, replete with fruit and roast malt.

Border Steeans (OG 1040, ABV 4.1%) 🍺
An old-fashioned, tawny-coloured bitter with a sweet start, some bitter notes and plenty of aftertaste.

Iron Town (ABV 4.1%) 🍺
Creamy sweet brown ale full of well-balanced fruit and hop.

Rev Rob (OG 1044, ABV 4.6%) 🍺
A golden beer with a pronounced grapefruit aroma and taste. The hoppy bitterness lasts through to the aftertaste.

Bedlam SIBA

Albourne Farm, Shaves Wood Lane, Albourne, West Sussex, BN6 9DX
☎ (01273) 978015 ☎ 07801 822645
⊕ bedlambrewery.co.uk

The brewery, named after Bedlam Street, the Roman road that once ran through the adjacent countryside, has been brewing in the shadow of the South Downs since 2012. The Bull in Ditchling serves as the taphouse. ‼️RAIB

Benchmark (OG 1040, ABV 4%)
A classic English amber-coloured best bitter, full of old-style roasted barley malts and bittering hops.

Golden (OG 1042, ABV 4.2%)
An alternative to the contemporary American-style golden ales, with a full bitterness and mouthfeel.

IPA (OG 1048, ABV 4.8%)
A rich, full-flavoured IPA.

Beer Bores

Pixtons Green, Ashwicke, Gloucestershire, SN14 8AL
☎ (01225) 8599959 ☎ 07790 715464
⊕ thebeerbores.co.uk

Mark Hempleman-Adams, Paul Clarke-Dabson and Marshall Ewart established Box Steam Brewery in 2004, before selling the business in 2007. However, Mark and Paul missed brewing so much that they set up a three-barrel microbrewery in 2015. Plans are in place to increase capacity with a new six-barrel plant and to distil their own West Country gin. ♦

American Beauty (OG 1035, ABV 3.5%)
A blonde American-style pale ale using a single grain malt, producing a malty beer with hints of hazelnut and honey.

Toad Stabber (OG 1043, ABV 4.3%)
A traditional, full-flavoured beer, with a crisp, dry aftertaste.

Blindhouse (OG 1046, ABV 4.6%)
A dark, malty, full-bodied beer, with added molasses, giving hints of red wine and cinnamon.

Wiltshire Wheat (OG 1047, ABV 4.7%)
A naturally hazy wheat beer in the style of a traditional German Weissbier, giving notes of banana and clove with subtle hints of citrus and spice flavours.

Beer Brothers

335 Ranglet Road, Walton Summit Centre, Bamber Bridge, Lancashire, PR5 8AR ☎ 07921 519129 ⊕ beerbrothers.co.uk

Brewing started in 2015. The brewery moved in 2017 and expanded to a 10-barrel brew plant due to demand. ‼

Best Bitter (OG 1044, ABV 3.8%)
A ruby-coloured, smooth, full-bodied malty session ale made with only British hops.

Blonde (OG 1040, ABV 3.8%)
Refreshing session beer with a crisp taste.

IPA (OG 1035, ABV 3.8%)
A full-bodied, full-flavoured IPA.

Milk Stout (OG 1058, ABV 4%)
An initial creamy sweet hit on the palate is followed by a gentle roasted barley bitterness.

Chocolate Porter (OG 1058, ABV 4.3%)
Full-bodied, well-balanced with heavy bitter with notes of full roast coffee and dark chocolate. Made with real cocoa.

Altbier (OG 1058, ABV 5%)
A dark copper-coloured ale with a crisp, fruity finish.

Cloudy Wheat Beer (OG 1052, ABV 5.5%)
A German-style crisp, golden wheat beer.

Dark Wheat Beer (OG 1067, ABV 6.5%)
A dark, lightly carbonated, full-bodied wheat beer with hints of liquorice and tart berries to round off a long-lasting, fruity finish.

Black Widow (OG 1100, ABV 9.9%)
Rich, dark, full and intense, brewed with liquid molasses.

Beer Engine SIBA

Newton St Cyres, Devon, EX5 5AX
☎ (01392) 851282 ⊕ thebeerengine.co.uk

The Beer Engine was established in 1983 and is the oldest working microbrewery in Devon. The brewery is visible downstairs in the pub through multiple viewing windows. Several outlets are supplied, as well as local beer festivals. Off sales are available.

Beer Ink

Plover Road Garage, Plover Road, Lindley, Huddersfield, West Yorkshire, HD3 3PJ
☎ (01484) 655262 ☎ 07739 754816

The Beer Ink Brewery Company is based in Lindlay and occupies the premises previously used by the Hand Drawn Monkey Brewery. Ryan Stoppard, owner and brewer, took possession of the brewery and eight-barrel plant in late 2015. ◆

Beer Me

⊟ Belgian Café, 11-23 Grand Parade, Eastbourne, East Sussex, BN21 3YN

☎ (01323) 729967 ⊕ thebelgiancafe.co.uk

Beer Me was launched in 2014 by the owners of the Belgian Café in Eastbourne, building on 10 years in the catering industry. It uses a 2.5-barrel plant and produces continental-style beers which are served direct from the brewery.

Beer Nouveau

75 Temperance Street, Ardwick, Manchester, M12 6HU ⊕ beernouveau.co.uk

Beer Nouveau started brewing in 2014 in Prestwich, on a 42-litre kit that owner Steve built in his garage. In 2015 the brewery relocated, taking over the six-barrel brewing plant in the railway arch previously occupied by Privateer Beers and now specialising in recreating historical recipes. In 2016 the adjoining arch was acquired for a brewery tap located on North Western Street. The original kit has been retained for experimental and one-off brews. RAIB

Peterloo (OG 1042, ABV 4%)
A rich, roasted porter, full of flavour on the nose and body, leading to a long, dry, roasted finish.

Rum Porter (OG 1042, ABV 4%)
A smooth, velvety porter with gentle coffee and rum aromas leading to a long, creamy finish.

Challenger (OG 1042, ABV 4.2%)
A light, hoppy, easy-drinking beer with an underlying dryness.

Ginger (OG 1042, ABV 4.2%)
A light, refreshing ginger beer with a slight spiciness enhancing the malt base.

Body Snatcher (OG 1040, ABV 4.4%)
A rich, copper-coloured session beer. A slightly sweet malt base sits underneath a fresh, spicy hop aroma. Dry, crisp and clean hop flavours linger to produce a balanced, bitter aftertaste.

Beer Refinery

Chapel Court Enterprise Centre, Wervin Road, Wervin, Chester, CH2 4BP ☎ 07939 875308
✉ enquiries@thebeerrefinery.co.uk

⊠ The Beer Refinery is a partnership of 10 engineers, some home brewers, and some just beer lovers. They are not reliant on the brewery for an income so are able to brew the beers they want to drink rather than the ones they think will sell the best. ‼◆

Beerblefish (NEW) SIBA

Unit 6, Georgiou Business Park, Second Avenue, Upper Edmonton, London, N18 2PG ☎ 07946 634555 ⊕ beerblefish.co.uk

Beerblefish began brewing in 2015. It brews a wide variety of styles and experiments with new hops and malts. ‼◆

Holy Smoke (OG 1034, ABV 3.1%)
An amber-coloured ale with a light smoky flavour.

ESB (OG 1048, ABV 4.8%)
A darker ale with a rich malt finish.

Black Beerblefish (OG 1053, ABV 5.2%)
A mellow stout using chocolate malts.

Bloodletter (OG 1050, ABV 5.2%)
A red IPA with a hint of citrus.

1892 (OG 1065, ABV 7.2%)
An IPA based on an 1890s recipe with a hint of modern aroma hops.

Beercraft

🍴 Watchmaker's Arms, 84 Goldstone Villas, Hove, East Sussex, BN3 3RU ⊕ beercraftbrighton.co.uk

Beercraft Brighton is a 100-litre pilot kit based out of the Watchmaker's Arms micropub in Hove. Brewing started in 2016 with different beers being produced each time. There are plans for expansion to a full-size plant.

Beerd

See Bath

BEEspoke

🍴 Fox, 41 Briggate, Shipley, West Yorkshire, BD17 7BP
☎ (01274) 594826 ⊕ thefoxshipley.co.uk

Brewing began in 2015 in the cellar of the Fox pub using a one-barrel plant. Four regular beers are produced along with monthly specials. Beers are available in the pub and at local festivals.

Beeston SIBA

Fransham Road Farm, Beeston, Norfolk, PE32 2LZ
☎ (01328) 700844 ☎ 07768 742763
⊕ beestonbrewery.co.uk

⊠ The brewery was established in 2006 in an old farm building using a five-barrel plant. Brewing water comes from a dedicated borehole and raw ingredients are sourced locally whenever possible.
‼ RAIB

The Squirrels Nuts (OG 1035, ABV 3.5%) ◆
Cherry, chocolate and vanilla aroma. A malt and cherry sweetness comes to the fore but quickly fades. Short finish.

Worth the Wait (OG 1041, ABV 4.2%) ◆
Hoppy throughout with a growing dryness. Complex and grainy with fruit notes, malt and understated bitterness.

Stirling (OG 1045, ABV 4.5%)
Rich, malty red-coloured bitter with toffee notes.

The Dry Road (OG 1048, ABV 4.8%)

Village Life (OG 1047, ABV 4.8%) ◆
Copper-coloured with a nutty character. Malty throughout, a bittersweet background gives depth. Strong toffee apple finish.

On the Huh (OG 1048, ABV 5%) ◆
A fruity raisin aroma. A bittersweet maltiness jousts with caramel and roast. A dry hoppiness adds to a strong finale.

Old Stoatwobbler (OG 1065, ABV 6%)

Contract brewed for Brancaster Brewery:

Best (ABV 3.8%)
A refreshing session ale with a touch of citrus on the finish.

Malthouse Bitter (ABV 4.2%)
An amber-coloured ale with malty character and distinct bitterness on the finish.

Beeston Hop

Gwenbrook Avenue, Beeston, Nottingham, NG9 4BA
⊕ beestonhop.co.uk

A nano-brewery launched in 2015 producing mainly bottle-conditioned beers. Cask beers are occasionally produced for festivals using capacity at other breweries. The beers are unfined, unfiltered and unpasteurised. RAIB V

Belhaven

Brewery Lane, Dunbar, EH42 1PE
☎ (01368) 862734

Office: Spott Road, Dunbar, EH42 1RS
⊕ belhaven.co.uk

☺Belhaven brewery is one of the oldest brewing sites in Scotland. Established in Dunbar in 1719, it brews beers made with water from its own well and local Scottish barley. Part of Greene King PLC.
‼🍺

60/- Ale (OG 1030, ABV 2.9%) ◆
A fine example of a Scottish light. This bittersweet, reddish-brown beer is dominated by fruit and malt with a hint of roast and caramel, and increasing bitterness in the aftertaste.

IPA (OG 1038, ABV 3.8%)
A golden ale with refreshing floral and citrus tones produced by a well-balanced fusion of malt and hops giving a clean, crisp flavour.

80/- Ale (OG 1040, ABV 4.2%) ◆
One of the last remaining original Scottish 80 Shillings. Malt is the predominant flavour characteristic, though it is balanced by fruit and a little hop.

Black (OG 1041, ABV 4.2%)
A smooth, balanced stout with malty body and roast notes of dark chocolate and coffee.

St Andrew's Ale (OG 1046, ABV 4.9%)
A bittersweet beer with lots of body. The malt, fruit and roast mingle throughout with hints of hop and caramel.

Bell Street

🍴 57-59 Bell Street, Henley-on-Thames, Oxfordshire, RG9 2BA
☎ (01491) 570200 ⊕ bellstreetbrewery.co.uk

Bell Street Brewery opened in 2013 at the rear of Brakspear pub company's refurbished Bull on Bell Street. A four-barrel plant is used. The beers are sold at the pub and through the Brakspear estate.

Brakspear Special (OG 1043, ABV 4.3%)
Tawny-coloured, full-bodied beer with a well-balanced aroma and a hint of sweetness. The initial sweetness gives way to a dry hop bitterness.

Belleville SIBA

36 Jaggard Way, Wandsworth Common, London, SW12 8SG ☎ 07712 298273
⊕ bellevillebrewing.co.uk

Belleville began brewing in 2012. It was formed by a group of parents who met in the playground of a local primary school and specialises in American-style beers. ‼♦

Northcote Blonde (OG 1042, ABV 4.2%) ◆

Smooth, dark golden ale with biscuity character and a trace of hoppy bitterness. Fruit is pineapple, orange and mixed citrus.

Picnic Session IPA (ABV 4.4%)

Commonside Pale Ale (OG 1050, ABV 5%) ◣
Full-flavoured amber beer with hops and fruit throughout. Initial palate is sweet but bitterness develops, particularly in the finish.

Thames Surf IPA (OG 1057, ABV 5.7%) ◣
Strong, amber-coloured IPA with citrus, hops, honey, caramel and spicy notes. There is a long-lasting, faintly hoppy, bitter finish.

Bellfield (NEW)

46 Stanley Place, Edinburgh, EH7 5TB ☎ 07713 987005

Office: 6 Logie Mill, Beaverbank Business Park, Edinburgh, EH7 4HG ⊕ bellfieldbrewery.com

Founded by two coeliacs, Bellfield Brewery is the UK's first dedicated gluten-free microbrewery, with the first beers launched in 2016. Accredited by Coeliac UK. No real ale. ◆ GF V

Bellinger's SIBA

**Station Road, Grove, Oxfordshire, OX12 0DH
☎ (01235) 772255 ⊕ bellingersbrewery.co.uk**

⊠ The late Mike Bellinger established the brewery as a family partnership in 2011. Now run by his nephew and son-in-law, it is currently a five-barrel plant producing mainly bottled beers with the occasional cask ale being supplied to local festivals and a few pubs. All beers, when available, are sold in the garage forecourt shop. !! ☕ ◆ RAIB

Original Bitter (OG 1040, ABV 4.1%)
A light and refreshing, easy-drinking beer with a delicate malt flavour.

Cavalry (OG 1045, ABV 4.6%)
A malty, robust bitter.

IPA (OG 1050, ABV 5%)
Gently hoppy with a lingering bitter taste.

Gallipoli Stout (OG 1053, ABV 5.3%)
A stout with a big chocolate taste.

Belvoir SIBA ◉

**Crown Park, Station Road, Old Dalby, Leicestershire, LE14 3NQ
☎ (01664) 823455 ⊕ belvoirbrewery.co.uk**

Belvoir (pronounced 'beaver') Brewery was set up in 1995 by former Shipstone's and Theakston's brewer Colin Brown. Long-term expansion has seen the introduction of a 20-barrel plant that can produce 50 barrels a week. There is also a visitor centre incorporating brewery memorabilia, a bar, restaurant and shop (open seven days a week). Around 150 outlets are supplied direct. !! ◆ RAIB

Dark Horse (OG 1034, ABV 3.4%)

Whippling (OG 1037, ABV 3.6%)

Star Bitter (OG 1039, ABV 3.9%) ◣
Reminiscent of the long-extinct Shipstone's Bitter, this mid-brown bitter lives up to its name as it is bitter in taste but not unpleasantly so.

Gordon Bennett (OG 1041, ABV 4.1%)

Light chestnut-coloured beer with a biscuity character and a pleasant hop finish.

Beaver Bitter (OG 1043, ABV 4.3%) ◣
A light brown bitter that starts malty in both aroma and taste, but soon develops a hoppy bitterness. Appreciably fruity.

Old Dalby (OG 1050, ABV 5.1%)
A rich, smooth ruby red strong ale with pleasant hop character.

Contract brewed for Hoskins Brothers:

Hob Bitter (OG 1040, ABV 4%)

IPA (OG 1040, ABV 4%)

Contract brewed for Steamin' Billy:

Tipsy Fisherman (OG 1036, ABV 3.6%)
Traditional light amber-coloured bitter with a mellow, crisp flavour and hoppy aftertaste.

Bitter (OG 1043, ABV 4.3%)
A light golden-coloured English bitter with a pronounced floral flavour and aroma, followed by a lingering hoppy aftertaste.

1485 (OG 1050, ABV 5%)

Skydiver (OG 1050, ABV 5%)
Mahogany-coloured beer with a fine balance of malty sweetness and hop bitterness.

Beowulf SIBA ◉

**Forest of Mercia, Chasewater Country Park, Pool Lane, Brownhills, Staffordshire, WS8 7NL
☎ (01543) 454067 ☎ 07714 291226
⊕ beowulfbrewery.com**

Beowulf Brewing Company is based at the Chasewater County Park. Its beers appear as guest ales predominantly in the central region, but also across the country. !! ◆ RAIB

Beorma (OG 1038, ABV 3.9%) ◣
A well-balanced session ale with a malty hint of fruit giving way to a lingering bitterness. Background spice excites the palate.

Chasewater Bitter (OG 1043, ABV 4.4%) ◣
Golden bitter, hoppy throughout with citrus and hints of malt. Long mouth-watering, bitter finish.

Chase Buster (OG 1045, ABV 4.5%)
A pale golden bitter.

Dark Raven (OG 1048, ABV 4.5%) ▱ ◣
Dark in colour with apple and bonfire in the aroma. Sweet and smooth like liquid toffee apples with a sudden bitter finish.

Swordsman (OG 1045, ABV 4.5%) ◣
Pale gold in colour with a light fruity aroma and tangy hoppy flavour. Faintly hoppy finish.

Folded Cross (OG 1045, ABV 4.6%) ◣
Malt and caramel aromas and tastes with hints of fruity biscuits are nudged aside by the robust hops, which give lingering bitter edges.

Hurricane (OG 1041, ABV 4.6%)

Dragon Smoke Stout (OG 1048, ABV 4.7%) ▤ ◣
Black with a light brown creamy head. Tobacco, chocolate, liquorice and mixed fruity hints on the aroma. Bitterness fights through the sweet and roast flavours and eventually dominates. Hints of a good port emerge.

Finn's Hall Porter (OG 1049, ABV 4.7%) ◣

Dark chocolate aroma, after dinner mints, coffee and fresh tobacco. Good bitterness with woodland hints of autumn. Long late bitterness.

Heroes Bitter (OG 1046, ABV 4.7%) ◆
Gold in colour, malt aroma, hoppy taste but sweetish finish.

Mercian Shine (OG 1048, ABV 5%) ◆
Amber to pale gold with a good bitter and hoppy start. Plenty of caramel and hops with background malt leading to a good bitter finish with caramel and hops lingering in the aftertaste.

Beowulf IPA (OG 1067, ABV 7.2%)

Killer Stout (OG 1080, ABV 7.3%)
A dark, smooth stout with dark chocolate and coffee hints in the aftertaste.

Bere (NEW)

**Homefield, Bere Alston, Devon, PL20 7JA
☎ (01822) 840382 ⊕ berebrewery.co.uk**

Established in 2016 by growers Jerry and Buffy on their smallholding on the Bere Peninsula in the Tamar Valley. The brewery produces bottle-conditioned beers using hops grown on the holding, with a 1.3-barrel plant and a 50-litre small batch kit. Building on its horticultural background, the brewery is working towards being self-sufficient in hops from 2019. In addition to four regular beers, occasional, seasonal and one-off brews are available, with sales at Tavistock Farmers' Market, by arrangement from the brewery, and at the Olde Plough Inn, Bere Ferrers.
◆ RAIB

Bespoke SIBA

**Unit 5, The Mews, Mitcheldean, Gloucestershire, GL17 0SL
☎ (01594) 546426 ⊕ bespokebrewery.co.uk**

⊠ Brewing commenced in 2012 on a 5.5-barrel plant on the site of the former Wintles Brewery, which closed in the early 1900s. In 2014 capacity was increased to 12 barrels. Speciality-labelled bottles are offered for celebratory occasions. An on-site brewery tap opens Fri-Sun. !! ☰ ◆

Saved by the Bell (OG 1037, ABV 3.8%)
A light, refreshing session bitter with a spicy hop bite and a light floral aroma from the late hop addition.

Golden Rule (OG 1041, ABV 4%)
A light golden session ale with a subtly refreshing and fruity finish.

Running the Gauntlet (OG 1046, ABV 4.4%)
Full malty flavoured bitter with rich roasted undertones balanced with good hop bitterness with spicy blackcurrant aromas.

Going Off Half-Cocked (OG 1043, ABV 4.6%)
A spicy-hopped golden ale.

Money for Old Rope (OG 1050, ABV 4.8%)
Classic stout with rich, dry flavours of malt and grain with deep hop bitterness.

Over a Barrel (OG 1052, ABV 5%)
A fruity strong ale with generous peppery finish.

Betteridge's

**Coopers Barn, The Dene, Hurstbourne Tarrant, Hampshire, SP11 0AG ☎ 07771 966058
⊕ betteridgesbrewery.co.uk**

Microbrewery trading since 2014 using a 2.5-barrel plant. The founder and brewer, Mark Betteridge, brews four core beers using principally English hops and traditional floor-malted barley. Beers are supplied to beer festivals, private events and to a growing number of pubs in the Test Valley area and occasionally further afield. RAIB

Old Chap (ABV 3.8%)
An easy-drinking session bitter. Amber in colour with good malt flavour, lightly hopped.

Jenny Wren (ABV 4.2%) ◆
A dark golden-coloured single hop beer. Initial fruit in the aroma and taste leads to a bitter finish.

Private Sector (ABV 4.2%)
A full-flavoured amber-coloured ale.

Serious Black (ABV 4.2%)
A complex stout with coffee, chocolate notes and roast flavours but with some underlying sweetness from added lactose.

Bewdley SIBA

**Unit 7, Bewdley Craft Centre, Lax Lane, Bewdley, Worcestershire, DY12 2DZ
☎ (01299) 405148 ⊕ bewdleybrewery.co.uk**

⊠ Bewdley began brewing in 2008 on a six-barrel plant in an old school. This was upgraded to a 10-barrel plant in 2014. Beers are brewed with a railway theme for the nearby Severn Valley Railway. A brewery tap is open 12-6pm Fri, Sat and bank holidays. !! ☰ ◆ RAIB

Worcestershire Way (OG 1036, ABV 3.6%) ◆
Refreshing golden ale with a citrus, faintly orange peel aroma, leads to a balanced hop, malt and grapefruit taste and a lingering hoppy finish.

Old School (OG 1038, ABV 3.8%)
A traditional English ale with a hoppy finish.

Jubilee (OG 1043, ABV 4.3%) ◆
Pale in colour, fruit and citrus aroma, sweet malt with underlying citrus taste.

Sir Keith Park (OG 1045, ABV 4.5%) ◆
Pale amber in colour, full, fruity and balanced flavour followed by a long, hoppy finish.

Worcestershire Sway/2857 (OG 1050, ABV 5%) ◆
Complex amber-coloured bitter, sometimes badged as 2857. Fragrant malty aroma, well-balanced slightly sweet malt and hops with hints of toffee and marmalade, malt with citrus and meadow grass finish.

William Mucklows Dark Mild (OG 1060, ABV 6%) ◆
Dark in colour, malty, sweetish fruity flavour with slight liquorice finish.

Bexar County

**8 Belgic Square, Padholme Road, Peterborough, Cambridgeshire, PE1 5XF ☎ 07934 722584
⊕ bexarcountybrewery.com**

Bexar was established in 2013, brewing American-style beers. ◆

Poquito Pequeno (OG 1040, ABV 3.5%)

Prospect (OG 1048, ABV 4.5%)

Phantasmagorical (OG 1075, ABV 7.4%)

Bexley SIBA 👁

18 Manford Industrial Estate, Erith, Kent, DA8 2AJ
☎ (01322) 337368 ⊕ bexleybrewery.co.uk

Opened in 2014, brewers Cliff and Jane Murphy produce regular, seasonal and experimental brews as well as selling own-brand beer mustard. The premises also houses a chilli jam producer. ‼🍴♦

Session Golden Ale (OG 1042, ABV 3.6%)

Session Ruby Ale (OG 1042, ABV 3.7%)

Session Pale Ale (OG 1044, ABV 3.8%)

Golden Acre (OG 1042, ABV 4%) ◀
Smooth golden ale with a citrus aroma. Flavour is of grapefruit, hops and a strong bitterness, continuing in the dry-fruity finish.

Bexley's Own Beer (OG 1044, ABV 4.2%) ◀
Pale brown beer with a balance of fudge, floral hop, stone fruit and some bitterness growing in the dry finish.

Redhouse Premium (OG 1042, ABV 4.2%) ◀
Copper-coloured best bitter with roast and sweet orange marmalade. Dry finish with a touch of chocolate in finish and aroma.

Bianca Road (NEW)

Unit 1, 95 Haymerle Road, Bianca Road, Peckham, London, SE15 6SJ
☎ (020) 7732 2587 ☎ 07557 646610
⊕ biancaroad.com

Brewing began in 2016. No real ale.

Big Bog SIBA

74 Venture Point West, Evans Road, Speke, Merseyside, L24 9PB
☎ (0151) 558 0290

Office: 164 Walkden Road, Worsley, M28 7DP
⊕ bigbog.co.uk

Big Bog was established in 2011. The brewery, which used to share its site with the Snowdonia Parc brewpub, underwent rapid expansion in 2013. In 2016 it moved to its present location in Speke, using a custom-built plant with a 10-barrel brew length. ♦

Bog Standard Bitter (OG 1036, ABV 3.6%)
A light-coloured session beer with medium bitterness and a distinctive hoppy finish.

Blonde Bach (ABV 3.9%)
A pale-coloured ale with citrus/grapefruit notes.

Hinkypunk (OG 1041, ABV 4.1%)
A pale ale, hoppy with intense citrus notes.

Welsh Pale Ale (OG 1042, ABV 4.2%)
Tawny-coloured classic British ale with a medium bitterness and dry finish.

Swampy (OG 1044, ABV 4.7%)
Ruby red in colour with a robust bitterness that is offset by a slightly sweet finish.

Will O the Wisp (OG 1047, ABV 4.7%)
Premium golden-coloured ale with a distinctive hoppy aroma, good bitterness and loads of floral/ citrus character.

Bog Trotter (OG 1051, ABV 5.3%)
Rich chestnut in colour with a hint of roasted flavours offset by classic spicy hop notes.

Quagmire (OG 1058, ABV 6%)
A strong but deceptively easy-drinking beer. Mid-brown in colour with a medium to high bitterness.

Bog Super IPA (OG 1068, ABV 7%)
A proper IPA with a tawny colour and robust bitterness.

Big Clock SIBA 👁

🏠 Grants, 1 Manchester Road, Accrington, Lancashire, BB5 2BQ
☎ (01254) 393938 ⊕ thebigclockbrewery.co.uk

Brewing commenced in 2014. A 6.5-barrel plant is used.

Big Drop (NEW)

c/o 5a Frascati Way, Maidenhead, Berkshire, SL6 4UY
⊕ bigdropbrew.com

Established in 2016 this company brews low-alcohol bottled beers on the rental facilities at U-Brew, Bermondsey, London.

Big Hand SIBA

Unit A1, Abbey Close, Redwither Business Park, Wrexham, LL13 9XG
☎ (01978) 660709 ☎ 07946 514238
⊕ bighandbrewing.co.uk

☺Big Hand is a family owned and run brewery that began brewing in 2013 using a 10-barrel plant. It opens on the first Friday of each month for its Weekend Wind Down event where you can enjoy beer served from a bar in the brewery itself. The brewery sponsors the Focus Wales music festival in Wrexham. ‼🍴♦

Solaris (OG 1035.9, ABV 3.7%)

King's Bane (OG 1038, ABV 3.9%) ◀
A clean-tasting malty bitter with a fruity aroma and peppery hops evident in the full, smooth mouthfeel.

Seren (OG 1038, ABV 3.9%)
American pale ale, light and malty. The citrus hop is balanced and mellowed by classic hops.

Melyn (OG 1039, ABV 4%) ◀
A malty, hoppy beer with a faint fruit aroma and bittersweet taste. The initial sweet malt flavours combine with hoppy bitterness in the aftertaste.

Bastion (OG 1041, ABV 4.2%) ◀
A dry, malty best bitter, mahogany in colour with a full mouthfeel. Biscuity flavours and faint roast notes feature throughout.

Domino (OG 1046, ABV 4.4%) ◀
A smooth and fruity stout, quite hoppy and roasty with hints of berries in the initial sweetness leading to a satisfying hoppy finish.

Havok (OG 1049, ABV 5%)
Intense American pale ale with a signature brash grapefruit explosion.

Bad Gorilla (OG 1060, ABV 6%)
A strong dark mild that is paradoxically sweet yet dry.

Brewed for the Tyn-y-Capel, Minera:

Tyn-y-Capel Ale (OG 1041, ABV 4.2%)

Big Lamp

Grange Road, Newburn, Newcastle upon Tyne,
NE15 8NL
☎ (0191) 267 1689 ⊕ biglampbrewers.co.uk

☺Big Lamp started in 1982 and relocated in 1997
to a 55-barrel plant in a former water pumping
station. It is the oldest microbrewery in the North-
east of England. Around 160 outlets are supplied
and two pubs are owned, one of which (the
Keelman) is attached to the brewery. ‼♦RAIB

Sunny Daze (OG 1036, ABV 3.6%) ◖
Golden, hoppy session bitter with a clean taste and
finish.

Bitter (OG 1039, ABV 3.9%) ◖
A clean-tasting bitter, full of hops and malt. A hint
of fruit with a good, hoppy finish.

Lamplight Bitter (OG 1042, ABV 4.2%)
Crisp, light, refreshing ale with a dry aftertaste.

Summerhill Stout (OG 1044, ABV 4.4%) ◖
A rich, tasty stout, dark in colour with a lasting rich
roast character. Malty mouthfeel with a lingering
finish.

Prince Bishop Ale (OG 1048, ABV 4.8%) ◖
A refreshing, easy-drinking bitter. Golden in colour,
full of fruit and hops. Strong bitterness with a spicy,
dry finish.

Premium (OG 1052, ABV 5.2%) ◖
Hoppy ale with a good bitter finish.

Keelman Brown (OG 1057, ABV 5.7%)
A full-bodied ale with a hint of toffee.

Big Smoke SIBA

▤ Antelope, 87 Maple Road, Surbiton, Surrey,
KT6 4AW
☎ (020) 8339 9721 ☎ 07859 884190
⊕ bigsmokebrew.co.uk

Big Smoke is a purpose-built brewery established
in 2014 in courtyard buildings behind the Antelope
pub, Surbiton. The five-barrel brew kit is used twice
weekly. Beers can be found in the Antelope and
the Sussex Arms in Twickenham, the Lyric in Soho,
the Express in Brentford and occasionally in other
local pubs and at beer festivals.

Biggar

Queens Arms Courtyard, Biggar Village, Cumbria,
LA14 3YG
☎ (01229) 474335 ⊕ biggarbrewing.co.uk

This 2.5-barrel brewery, an independent co-
operative of several shareholders, opened in late
2015 in the courtyard of the Queens Arms in Biggar
Village on Walney Island. The beer names are
themed on Barrow's shipbuilding heritage, and the
brewery logo features a representation of Barrow's
dockside cranes, a strong visual motif of the town's
history.

Mikasa (OG 1035, ABV 3.6%)

Vanguard (OG 1041, ABV 3.8%)

Oriana (OG 1039, ABV 4%)

Biggleswade (NEW)

▤ c/o New Inn Ale House & Kitchen, Market Square,
Biggleswade, Bedfordshire, SG18 8AS
☎ (01767) 222938
⊕ thenewinnalehouseandkitchen.co.uk

Brewing began in 2016 at the rear of the New Inn,
using a 2.5-barrel plant. Brewing is weekly unless
demand requires more.

Bilbrough Top (NEW)

St James House, Main Street, Bilbrough, North
Yorkshire, YO23 3PH

Brewing began in 2016 using a six-barrel plant.

Top Beer (ABV 3.9%)

Billericay SIBA

▤ Essex Beer Shop, 54c Chapel Street, Billericay,
Essex, CM12 9LS
☎ (01277) 500121 ☎ 07788 373129
⊕ billericaybrewing.co.uk

Billericay Brewing opened at its present site in
2014, using a 4.5-barrel plant. A micropub and
beershop are next door.

Binghams SIBA

Unit 10, Tavistock Industrial Estate, Ruscombe,
Berkshire, RG10 9NJ
☎ (0118) 934 4376 ⊕ binghams.co.uk

⊗ Binghams began brewing in 2010, producing 40
firkins in each batch. The brewery is situated in an
industrial unit on the site of a former brickworks –
hence the name of one of the beers. Head brewer
Chris Bingham is a member of the local branch of
CAMRA and had extensive experience in
homebrewing and a local brewery prior to starting
up. ‼⌷RAIB

Twyford Tipple (OG 1040, ABV 3.7%)
Tawny-coloured bitter with a good balance of malt
and hops in the flavour and a citrus hop finish.

Brickworks Bitter (OG 1047, ABV 4.2%)
Chestnut-coloured best bitter with a sweetish,
malty nose. Hops balance the maltiness to give a
well-rounded flavour with a slightly nutty hint and
a sweet, earthy aftertaste.

Coffee Stout (OG 1056, ABV 5%)
A mellow beer with dark malts that complement
the coffee flavour.

Doodle Stout (OG 1056, ABV 5%)
A blend of dark malts provide a complex character.

Ginger Doodle Stout (OG 1056, ABV 5%)
A dark stout with a subtle hint of ginger, which
rounds off the bitterness.

Hot Dog Chilli Stout (OG 1056, ABV 5%)
Doodle Stout with a hint of chilli to provide a warm
glow on the aftertaste.

Space Hoppy IPA (OG 1052, ABV 5%)
Pale golden in colour and packed with hops to
create a complex flavour and a long, citrus finish.

Vanilla Stout (OG 1052, ABV 5%) ⌷
Infused with vanilla pods that complement the
dark malts to create a smooth-drinking, dark stout.

Bingley SIBA

Unit 2, Old Mill Yard, Shay Lane, Wilsden, West
Yorkshire, BD15 0DR
☎ (01535) 274285 ⊕ bingleybrewery.co.uk

Bingley is a small, family-run brewery that opened
in 2014 using a six-barrel plant. It is located in a
rural setting in the village of Wilsden, part of
Bingley Rural Ward. Beers are distributed coast to
coast and as far south as Derby. ‼

Goldy Locks Blonde (ABV 4%)
A blonde ale with a hoppy and citrus aroma and a
delicate toffee aftertaste.

Session IPA (ABV 4.2%)

Steady State (ABV 4.2%)

Centennial (ABV 4.4%)

Tri State (ABV 4.5%)

1848 Stout (ABV 4.8%)
Creamy stout with hints of chocolate and liquorice
with a pleasant bitter finish.

Birchover

⊟ Red Lion, Main Street, Birchover, Derbyshire,
DE4 2BN
☎ (01629) 650363 ⊕ red-lion-birchover.co.uk

Brewing commenced in 2016, mainly to supply the
owner's own pub, the Red Lion Inn plus other free
trade outlets. The four core beers are often
complemented by occasional beers.

Birmingham Brewing (NEW)

Unit 15, Stirchley Trading Estate, Hazelwell Road,
Birmingham, B30 2PF ☎ 07717 704929
⊕ birminghambrewingcompany.co.uk

Birmingham Brewing Co was established in 2016
and supplies the local area. Further beers are
planned.

Pale Brummie (ABV 4%)

Bitter Brummie (ABV 4.1%)

Bishop Nick SIBA ◉

33 East Street, Braintree, Essex, CM7 3JJ
☎ (01376) 349605 ⊕ bishopnick.com

⊠ Bishop Nick was launched in 2011 by Nelion
Ridley, a member of the family that started
Ridley's brewery near Chelmsford in 1842. In 2013
a new brewery was established in Braintree using
a 20-barrel plant. A limited edition range of beers
is also available. ➤ ◆ RAIB

Ridley's Rite (OG 1036, ABV 3.6%) ⬗
A classic bitter with a floral aroma and subtle but
long-lasting bitter aftertaste.

Heresy (OG 1041, ABV 4%)
Refreshing golden ale with a spicy bitterness
before the hops deliver citrus and floral notes.

1555 (OG 1043, ABV 4.3%)
Full-bodied, rich, tawny-coloured ale. A sweet,
nutty taste underlined by ginger and fruit.

Bishop's Crook SIBA

51 Woodcroft Close, Penwortham, Lancashire,
PR1 9BX ☎ 07516 478003
⊕ bishopscrookbrewery.com

A small brewery based at the home of one of the
owners, it started brewing commercially in 2013
and currently has just a handful of regular outlets.

Galaxy (OG 1037, ABV 3.7%)
A light pale ale with citrus and distinct passion fruit
flavours.

Winding Staircase (OG 1038, ABV 3.8%)
A golden ale with a slight malty taste and
tangerine overtones.

Initiate (OG 1040, ABV 4%)
A golden ale with strong citrus and tropical fruit
flavours.

Lancashire's Invaders (OG 1042, ABV 4.2%)
A refreshing amber-coloured ale, well-hopped and
providing a burst of grapefruit, lemon and pine.

Bishop's Stortford

c/o Prince of Wales, Green Tye, Much Hadham,
Hertfordshire, SG10 6JP
☎ (01279) 503224

Office: 24 Trinity Street, Bishop's Stortford,
Hertfordshire, CM23 3TJ
✉ bishopsstortfordbrewery@hotmail.co.uk

⊠ Established in 2012, the brewery has produced
beer on various other brewer's equipment. Since
the start of 2014 the brewery has used spare
capacity at Ash Valley Brewery (qv) in Green Tye,
Hertfordshire. ◆

Stortford Pale Ale (OG 1039, ABV 3.8%)

Stortford Sunrise (OG 1041, ABV 3.8%)

Stortford Sunset (OG 1042, ABV 3.8%)
A complex beer with a golden hue and a long, firm
finish.

Stortford Citra (OG 1039, ABV 3.9%)
A light golden ale with good balance of malts and
citrus hops.

Bitter (OG 1040, ABV 4.1%)
Classic copper-coloured bitter with a complex
balance of malts.

Bitter End

See Tirril

Black Bear

⊟ c/o Bear Inn, 8-10 North Street, Wiveliscombe,
Somerset, TA4 2JY
☎ (01984) 623537 ✉ liquidbrighton@hotmail.com

Originally established in 2014 at the Northbrook
Arms, East Stratton, Hampshire, before relocating
to the Bear Inn, Wiveliscombe, Somerset in 2015.
Five beers are currently regularly brewed for the
pub and a steady stream of other local outlets.

Wivey Best (ABV 3.8%)

Baby Bear (ABV 4%)

Black Bear (ABV 4%)

Goldie Hops (ABV 4%)

Strong One (ABV 5.1%)

Black Brook (NEW)

Holland Farm, Blackbrook, Mold, CH7 6LU ☎ 07455 005932 ⊕ blackbrookbeer.com

Brewing commenced in 2016 using a six-barrel plant. Initially producing cask-conditioned beers, the brewery has since moved to KeyKeg with limited edition cask beers still available for festivals.

Pale Ale (OG 1040, ABV 4%)

Breakfast (OG 1045, ABV 4.5%)
Easy-drinking stout brewed with lactose.

Golden State (OG 1046, ABV 4.6%)
West Coast-style American pale ale.

Black Country ◉

⚏ Rear of Old Bulls Head, 1 Redhall Road, Lower Gornal, West Midlands, DY3 2NU ☎ (01384) 401820

Office & unit for beer delivery: 69 Third Avenue, Pensnett Trading Estate, Kingswinford, DY6 7FD ⊕ blackcountryales.co.uk

Brewery located at the rear of the Old Bulls Head since 2004. Its sister company, Black Country Inns/Taverns, own 35 pubs across the West Midlands. Beers are also brewed under the Thomas Guest Brewing Company name.

Bradley's Finest Golden (OG 1040, ABV 4.2%)
A straw-coloured quaffing beer with a bold citrus hop aroma, fruity balanced sweetness and a lingering, refreshing aftertaste.

Pig on the Wall (OG 1042, ABV 4.3%)
A refreshing chestnut brown beer with a complex flavour of light hops giving way to a bittersweet blend of roasted malt. Suggestions of chocolate and coffee undertones.

Fireside (OG 1047, ABV 5%)
A well-rounded premium bitter, amber in colour, clean in taste, leading to a pleasant, dry finish.

Black Dog

See Hambleton

Black Falls

See Neath

Black Flag

Unit 4D, Bridge Road Industrial Estate, Goonhavern, Cornwall, TR4 9QL ☎ (01872) 858004 ⊕ blackflagbrewery.com

⊠ Black Flag began brewing in 2013 using an eight-barrel plant. Much use is made of New Zealand and American hops. ♦ RAIB

Chameleon (OG 1038, ABV 3.8%) ◈
Golden ale. Grassy and floral hops throughout. Punchy lemon citrus flavour with apricot and peaches. Bitter, dry and crisp finish.

Fang (OG 1040, ABV 4%) ◈
Golden bitter with powerful citrus hop aroma. Refreshing ale with lemon, orange, mango and grapefruit throughout. Long, bitter, hoppy finish.

Naughty Pilchard (OG 1040, ABV 4%) ◈
Tawny bitter with malt aroma. Dominant biscuit malt flavour with a sharp bite of crisp hops. Short malty, bitter finish.

Crab Claw (OG 1050, ABV 5%) ◈
Red-coloured strong bitter with intense hop fruit nose. Powerful citrus hop flavour, lightly bittersweet. Dry hop and sweet finish.

Galaxy & Amarillo Pale Ale (OG 1055, ABV 5.5%)
Malty golden ale with mango and orange hops throughout.

Mosaic IPA (OG 1055, ABV 5.7%) ◈
Smooth, easy-drinking golden ale with heady citrus hop nose. Powerful grassy and citrus hop flavours throughout, with mango fruit and bitterness.

White Cross IPA (OG 1057, ABV 5.7%) ◈
Amber-coloured strong bitter with hop nose. Robust hop bitterness balanced by sweetness and malt. Fruit flavours emerge. Long, bitter finish.

Black IPA (OG 1060, ABV 6%)
Smooth coffee and chocolate maltiness with Black Flag's trademark punchy, hoppy finish.

Captain Haddock (OG 1056, ABV 6.5%)
Smooth Belgian-style ale, with vibrant mango and banana tones, with a prolonged rich finish.

Black Hole SIBA

Unit 63GF, IMEX Business Park, Shobnall Road, Burton upon Trent, Staffordshire, DE14 2AU ☎ (01283) 619943 ☎ 07812 812953 ⊕ blackholebrewery.co.uk

⊠ Black Hole was established in 2007 with a purpose-built 10-barrel plant in the former Ind Coope bottling stores. Fermenting capacity was increased in 2012 to enable the production of up to four brews per week. Around 600 outlets, mainly in the Midlands, are supplied direct, and many more via wholesalers. The brewery was bought by the owners of Mr Grundy's Brewery (qv) in 2014. ‼♦

Golden Ale (OG 1040, ABV 3.8%)
An amber-coloured session beer, malty with a spicy hop aroma, a clean, crisp finish, hoppy dryness and a touch of astringency. Occasionally available as Black Hole Bitter.

Cosmic (OG 1044, ABV 4.2%) ◈
Almost golden with an initial malt aroma. The complex balance of malt and English hops give lingering tastes of nuts, fruit and dry hoppy bitterness.

Supernova (OG 1048, ABV 4.8%) ◈
Pure gold. Like marmalade made from Seville oranges and grapefruit, the aroma mimics the sweet start but gives in to the hops, which deliver a dry, lingering bitter finish.

Milky Way (OG 1059, ABV 6%) ◈
Honey and banana nose. Sweet, dry spicy finish from this wheat beer.

Brewed for Small Beer:

Lincoln Imperial Ale (OG 1036, ABV 3.8%)

Black Horse SIBA

26 Nottingham Court, Nottingham Road, Louth, Lincolnshire, LN11 0WB ☎ (01507) 354330 ☎ 07557 789060 ⊕ blackhorsebrewing.co.uk

⊕Black Horse is a five-barrel microbrewery situated in the Lincolnshire Wolds. It boasts its own small, fully licensed brewery tap, always serving at least two cask ales. Retail outlets are supplied throughout Lincolnshire, Yorkshire and Nottinghamshire. ‼☰♦

**Lincolnshire Traditional Bitter
(OG 1038, ABV 3.8%)**
A traditional English session bitter with a smooth hop finish.

Wheres My Fiorucci (OG 1038, ABV 3.8%)
Amber-coloured session beer with delicate malt flavours and a slightly spicy aroma.

Aisey Dubitz (OG 1042, ABV 3.9%)

Farming County (OG 1040, ABV 4%)

Saturdays Blonde (OG 1042, ABV 4%)
Delicate pale ale with a subtle, yet refreshing aftertaste.

Wet Pocket (OG 1041, ABV 4.1%)
An amber-coloured rye beer.

Best Bitter (OG 1046, ABV 4.2%)

Pleasant Blonde (OG 1042, ABV 4.2%)
Refreshing blonde ale with a clean citrus hop flavour and flowery grapefruit aroma.

Executioners Assistant (OG 1044, ABV 4.3%)

Obliging Blonde (OG 1044, ABV 4.3%)

Black Frog (OG 1044, ABV 4.4%)
A dark-coloured ale with complex malt flavours. Bitter with a slight smoky aroma.

Queens (OG 1040, ABV 4.4%)

**Willy Wickams Posthumous Ale
(OG 1044, ABV 4.4%)**

Englands Finest Hour (OG 1046, ABV 4.5%)

Fat Cat Fuller (OG 1052, ABV 5%)

Nicholas De Luda (OG 1050, ABV 5.4%)
A rich, dark, old-style English stout, full-bodied and packed with flavour.

Seek Medical Help (OG 1057, ABV 5.5%)
A zesty IPA full of American hops.

Thanks PA (OG 1057, ABV 6%)
Traditional IPA with a floral bouquet and citrus finish.

Black Iris SIBA

Unit 1, Shipstone Street, New Basford, Nottingham, NG7 6GJ
☎ (0115) 979 1936 ✉ blackirisbrewery@gmail.com

Black Iris began brewing in 2011 using a six-barrel plant behind the Flowerpot pub in Derby. It expanded to a brand new 10-barrel plant in 2014 and relocated to premises in Nottingham. ‼♦

Snake Eyes (OG 1038, ABV 3.8%) ◥
Golden-coloured ale with an intense hoppy aroma and taste, and a lingering bitter finish.

Bleeding Heart (OG 1044, ABV 4.5%) ◥
Red rye malty ale balanced with roast and hops and a bitter finish.

Endless Summer (OG 1041.9, ABV 4.5%) ◥
Golden in colour with a tropical citrus fruit presence throughout, from aroma to aftertaste, with a gentle bitter finish.

Better The Devil You Know (OG 1053, ABV 5.5%)

Pale, citrus Australian-style IPA with big fruity aromas and a lingering bitterness.

Black Isle

Old Allengrange, Munlochy, IV8 8NZ
☎ (01463) 811871 ⊕ blackislebrewery.com

⊕Black Isle Brewery was set up in 1998 in the heart of the Scottish Highlands. It expanded substantially in 2011 with a new brewhouse and bottling line. All beers are organic with Soil Association certification. ‼☰♦V

Yellowhammer (ABV 4%)

Red Kite (OG 1042, ABV 4.2%) ◥
Tawny ale with light malt on the nose and some fruit on the palate. Slight sweetness in the taste.

Blonde (ABV 4.5%)

Heather Honey (OG 1045, ABV 4.6%) ◥
A sweet, honey-flavoured brew.

Porter (OG 1046, ABV 4.6%) ◥
A hint of liquorice and burnt chocolate on the nose and a creamy mix of malt and fruit in the taste.

Black Lodge (NEW)

4 Kitchen Street, Baltic Triangle, Liverpool, L1 0AN
☎ 07565 299879 ⊕ blacklodgebrewing.co.uk

Small-batch and one-off brewery producing beers in keg, bottle and can formats that can be drunk in its own Tap Room. No real ale.

Black Market

☰ The Workman's, 43 High Street, Warsop, Nottinghamshire, NG20 0AE ☎ 07824 363373

Beers first appeared from Black Market in 2016. The 2.5-barrel plant is situated in the basement of the brewery tap, the Workman's. Further beers are planned.

Black Metal

Unit 4, 6b Dryden Road, Loanhead, EH20 9LZ
☎ (0131) 623 3411 ☎ 07711 295385
⊕ blackmetalbrewery.com

Black Metal Brewery was established in 2012 by two old friends – metalheads and inspired brewers. Equipment was shared with Top Out (qv) brewery but it has now moved next door to its own site.
♦RAIB

Blood Revenge (ABV 6.6%)

Will-o'-the-Wisp (ABV 6.6%)

Yggdrasil (ABV 6.6%)

Louhi (ABV 7%)

Battering Ram (ABV 7.1%)

Gates of Valhalla (ABV 7.9%)

Jotunblod (ABV 8.1%)

Black Paw

Unit 4, Westgate Road, Bishop Auckland, County Durham, DL14 7AX
☎ (01388) 602144 ☎ 07557 020664
⊕ blackpawbrewery.co.uk

Black Paw began brewing in 2011 using a 12-barrel plant and now supplies pubs across the North-east of England. Occasional open days are held. ♦ RAIB

Bishop's Best (OG 1038, ABV 3.8%)
Session bitter with a slight hint of chocolate.

Paw's Gold (OG 1040, ABV 4%)
A rich golden bitter with the malt and hop taste coming through.

Archbishop's Ale (OG 1041, ABV 4.1%)
Full-flavoured and smooth.

Polar Paw (OG 1044, ABV 4.4%)
Bittersweet dark ale with a pleasant hoppy aroma and aftertaste.

Dark Seam (OG 1050, ABV 5%)
A dark and full-flavoured beer with definite chocolate taste and a hint of coffee.

IPA (OG 1050, ABV 5%)
Amber-coloured beer brewed to an American recipe with a strong complex aroma and refreshing bitter finish.

Black Rock SIBA

Unit 6c, Empire Way, Tregoniggie Industrial Estate, Falmouth, Cornwall, TR11 4SN
☎ (01326) 379477 ⊕ blackrockbrewing.com

⊗ Black Rock began brewing in 2013, producing just one beer. It now has a core range of four beers, which are available in Five Degrees West, Falmouth, and a number of other local outlets. Relocation to larger premises within Falmouth is planned. ♦ RAIB

Endless IPA (ABV 3.8%) ◈
Gold-coloured bitter with assertive fruity hop aroma and taste. Refreshing bitter citrus flavour followed by hints of caramel. Dry finish.

Pale Ale (OG 1042, ABV 4.2%) ◈
Golden best bitter. Balance of earthy malt and bitter hop flavours. Apricot and limes in the mouth. Long bitter finish.

Deep (OG 1048, ABV 5%) ◈
Faintly sulphurous malt and light hop aroma. Strong malt and grassy hop bitterness with sweet tropical fruit. Bitter, dry finish.

Black IPA (OG 1058, ABV 6%) ◈
Black porter with pronounced roast malt from aroma to the long finish. Light bitterness with smoky stone fruit and toffee.

Black Sheep SIBA ◉

Wellgarth, Masham, North Yorkshire, HG4 4EN
☎ (01765) 689227 ⊕ blacksheepbrewery.co.uk

☺Established in 1992 by Paul Theakston, a member of Masham's famous brewing family, in the former Wellgarth Maltings, using the traditional Yorkshire Square fermenting system, the company now supplies around 600 free trade outlets, with national exposure through pubcos and wholesale channels, but owns no pubs. Production is 75% cask with the remainder bottled. Paul has now handed over operations to his sons. ‼️🎬♦

Best Bitter (OG 1038, ABV 3.8%) ◈
A hoppy and fruity beer with strong bitter overtones, leading to a long, dry, bitter finish.

Golden Sheep (OG 1039, ABV 3.9%)

A balanced blonde beer with a dry and refreshing bitterness. Light golden in colour with fresh citrus fruit flavours and a clean, crisp finish.

Baa Baa (ABV 4%)
A juicy pale ale with a generous hoppy tone and subtle zesty twang but low in bitterness.

Holy Grail (ABV 4%)
A fresh zesty golden ale with a long, crisp finish. Clean and refreshing.

Ale (OG 1044, ABV 4.4%)
A premium bitter with robust fruit, malt and hops.

Riggwelter (OG 1059, ABV 5.9%) 🍶 ◈
A fruity bitter, with complex underlying tastes and hints of liquorice and pear drops leading to a long, dry, bitter finish.

Black Tap

🏠 Beech House, Church Green East, Redditch, Worcestershire, B98 8BP
☎ (01527) 549997 ⊕ blacktap.co.uk

Originally based in Staffordshire, Black Tap relocated to Redditch in 2015, now operating as a brewpub with a focus on serving high-quality cask ales, designed and brewed on site.

Black Tor SIBA

Unit 5, Gidley's Industrial Estate, Christow, Exeter, Devon, EX6 7QB
☎ (01647) 252120 ⊕ blacktorbrewery.com

⊗ Brewing began on this site in 1998 under the Scattor Rock name using a five-barrel plant. The brewery changed hands in 2009, trading under the Gidley's name, before another change of hands in 2013 when it became Black Tor. It changed hands again in 2015. The brewery is located in the Teign Valley in the beautiful East Dartmoor National Park. Outlets are supplied in Devon and on the Cornish border. ♦

Pride of Dartmoor (OG 1040, ABV 4%)
This mid-brown session bitter has a gentle floral aroma and pleasant taste.

Raven (OG 1042, ABV 4.2%)

Devonshire Pale Ale (OG 1044, ABV 4.5%)

Black Wolf

Unit 7c, Bandeath Industrial Estate, Throsk, Stirling, FK7 7NP
☎ (01786) 817000 ⊕ blackwolfbrewery.com

☺Established in 2005, and now owned by VC2 Brands, the brewery is located in a former torpedo factory on the shores of the River Forth. In 2014 the brewery changed its name from Traditional Scottish Ales to Black Wolf Brewery and rebranded its range of beers. ♦

Nevis (OG 1040, ABV 4%)

RoK (OG 1040, ABV 4%)

Florida Black (OG 1045, ABV 4.5%)

Glencoe (OG 1045, ABV 4.5%)

William Wallace (OG 1045, ABV 4.5%)

Lomond Gold (OG 1050, ABV 5%)

Valente's Double Espresso (OG 1060, ABV 6%)

Blackbeck SIBA

⊟ Blackbeck Inn, Blackbeck, Cumbria, CA22 2NY
☎ (01946) 841661 ⊕ blackbeckbrewery.co.uk

A five-barrel brewery, established in 2009 and owned by a father-and-daughter team, producing handcrafted ales using English malts and hops. Beers have fairground themed names.

Blackedge SIBA

Moreton Mill, Hampson Street, Horwich, BL6 7JH
☎ (01204) 692976 ☎ 07795 654895
⊕ blackedgebrewery.co.uk

⊠ Blackedge Brewery, established in 2011, has expanded from a five to a 10-barrel plant, visible through a viewing window on the ground floor beneath the brewery bar. !! 🍽 ♦RAIB

Session (OG 1038, ABV 3.5%)
A full-bodied golden session bitter with a grapefruit flavour and aroma.

HoP (OG 1039, ABV 3.8%)
A clean, dry and refreshing session beer with hoppy citrus and floral flavours.

Black (OG 1047, ABV 4%)
A velvety stout with intense roasted barley flavours and rich undertones of chocolate and coffee with a liquorice finish.

Pike (OG 1042, ABV 4%) 🍺
A pale ale with plenty of sweet citrus hop flavour.

American Pale Ale (OG 1043, ABV 4.2%)
Light hoppy beer with intense citrus aromas.

Platinum (OG 1046, ABV 4.4%)
Blonde ale, light in colour, lightly hopped to give a clean, citrus flavour and aroma.

BLONDe (OG 1046, ABV 4.5%)
Full-flavoured, full-bodied blonde ale, well-hopped to give a clean, crisp fruity flavour and aroma.

Dark Rum (OG 1045, ABV 4.6%)
Dark, rich porter with roasted coffee and chocolate flavours, hints of liquorice and finished with sweetness from dark rum.

IPA (OG 1047, ABV 4.7%)
Full-bodied, full-flavoured and well-balanced hoppy and intensely citrus beer with a grapefruit aroma.

Black Port (OG 1045, ABV 4.9%) 🍺 ◆
Black-coloured beer with malty, fruity aroma. Rich, with chocolate and dark fruits to taste with a slightly dry finish.

Blackened Sun (NEW)

3 Heathfield, Stacey Bushes, Milton Keynes, Buckinghamshire, MK12 6HP
⊕ blackenedsunbrewing.co.uk

Blackened Sun began brewing unpasteurised, unfiltered beers in 2017, available in KeyCasks and bottles. ◆

Hedone Saison (ABV 3.6%)
A Saison with a spicy, fruity yeast character and notes of citrus and berries from the hops.

Crossover Pale Ale (ABV 4.2%)
Between a fruity pale ale and a Belgian-style single beer. Citrus/tropical hop flavours with a spicy yeast character.

Collision ESB (Extra Special Belgian) (ABV 4.7%)
A malty, spicy, fruity beer.

Blackhill SIBA

Unit 1a, Pontop Business Park, Harelaw Industrial Estate, Stanley, County Durham, DH9 8HN
☎ (01207) 230632 ☎ 07905 788286
⊕ blackhillbrewery.com

Blackhill began brewing in 2012 using spare capacity at Geltsdale Brewery. In 2013 it moved to its own premises using a 10-barrel plant. Beers are named after Durham coal mining seams and are available on rotation. ◆

Blackjack SIBA

36 Gould Street, Manchester, M4 4RN
☎ (0161) 819 2767 ⊕ blackjack-beers.com

⊛Blackjack was established in 2012 and brews a large range of regular beers in many different styles, often using Belgian farmhouse yeasts. Beers are widely available across the North-west and specialist beer outlets nationally. The brewery also owns Glassworks Drinks, a distribution business specialising in craft breweries. ◆RAIB V

Pokies (OG 1036, ABV 3.6%)
A pale, hoppy session bitter.

Shuffled Deck (OG 1039, ABV 3.9%)
Aromas are marmalade with pine and grapefruit. Flavours are woody with sweet citrus and bitter grapefruit and a dry finish.

Bramling Cross (OG 1040, ABV 4%) 🏷
Amber-coloured beer with hops and tart fruit in aroma and taste. Good bitterness throughout.

You Bet (ABV 4%)

New Deck (OG 1042, ABV 4.2%)
A crisp, hoppy ale with a satisfying finish.

Solitaire (OG 1042, ABV 4.3%)
A session pale ale.

First Deal (OG 1044, ABV 4.4%)
A ruby-coloured ale with a dried fruit aroma with flavour of berries, earthy malts and a spicy, bitter finish.

Rabbit Hunt (ABV 4.5%)
A hoppy pale ale.

Small Saison (OG 1042, ABV 4.5%)
A spicy, dry beer.

Double Bluff (OG 1048, ABV 4.8%)
An amber-coloured ale with full aroma and bitter notes.

The River (OG 1049, ABV 4.8%)
Brown ale with farmhouse yeast.

Beginners Luck (OG 1050, ABV 5%)
A pale ale with a punchy, fruity aroma with a golden IPA bitterness.

Schafkopf (OG 1050, ABV 5%)
German lemongrass and ginger Witbier.

Stout (OG 1050, ABV 5%)
Aroma is roasted malts and chocolate syrup. The palate has a hint of maple syrup and light bitter hops. Finish is slightly fruity.

Aces High (OG 1055, ABV 5.5%)

Aroma has some ripe citrus notes of melon and orange. Flavour is sweet, with mild grass and pine, along with more ripe tangerine and melon.

Black Maria (OG 1057, ABV 5.8%)
A dark ale with hoppy aroma and light body.

Dragon's Tears (OG 1054, ABV 5.8%)
Jasmine tea infused golden Saison.

Four Of A Kind (OG 1060, ABV 6.2%)
An American-style IPA.

Brewed for Jack in the Box, Altrincham:

House Ale (ABV 4%)

Brewed for the Crescent, Salford:

Crescent Ale (ABV 4%)

Brewed for the Moorbrook, Preston

Moorbrook Pale Ale (ABV 3.9%)

Blackmore

🏠 Trooper Inn, Golden Hill, Stourton Caundle, Dorset, DT10 2JW
☎ (01963) 362405 ✉ kevinstaunton@aol.com

This small 0.5-barrel brewpub began brewing in 2011, in the adjacent garage. Beers are brewed only for the pub.

Blackpit (NEW)

Blackpit Farm, Silverstone Road, Stowe, Buckinghamshire, MK18 5LJ ⊕ blackpitbrewery.co.uk

Brewing began in 2017 in a converted stable yard on Blackpit farm, four miles south of Silverstone. ♦

Goshawk (ABV 3.9%)
A golden-coloured session ale with a grapefruit and herbal nose.

Woodlands (ABV 4.2%)

Blindmans SIBA

Talbot Farm, Leighton, Somerset, BA11 4PN
☎ (01749) 880038 ⊕ blindmansbrewery.co.uk

Established in 2002 in a converted milking parlour and purchased by its current owners in 2004, this five-barrel brewery has its own water spring. The range of ales is regularly on tap at the Cornerhouse, Frome. !! ♦

Buff (OG 1036, ABV 3.6%)
Amber-coloured, smooth session beer.

Golden Spring (OG 1040, ABV 4%)
Fresh and aromatic straw-coloured beer.

Mine Beer (OG 1042, ABV 4.2%)
Full-bodied, copper-coloured blended malt ale.

Icarus (OG 1045, ABV 4.5%)
Fruity, rich, ruby-coloured ale.

Bloomfield (NEW)

🏠 Bloomfield Brewhouse, 47 Ansdell Road, Blackpool, FY1 6PW
☎ (01253) 693219 ⊕ bloomfield-brewhouse.co.uk

Brewing began in 2015. The beers are finished on site using wort from a third-party brewery.

Blue Anchor SIBA

🏠 50 Coinagehall Street, Helston, Cornwall, TR13 8EL
☎ (01326) 562821 ⊕ spingoales.com

15th-century thatched brewpub, the oldest continuously brewing plant in the country. Home of the famous Spingo ales, which are produced from the well water beneath the pub.

Blue Bear SIBA

Unit 5, Empire House, 11 New Street, Smethwick, West Midlands, B66 2AJ
☎ (0121) 565 5622 ✉ info@bluebearbrewery.com

☺Blue Bear brewery, formerly in Worcestershire, relocated to an industrial unit in Smethwick on the outskirts of Birmingham. The nine-barrel plant produces a selection of beers, most of it under contract for the now defunct Highgate & Davenports brewery of Walsall. Much of the beer is keg but cask-conditioned beers are now being promoted. ♦

Contract brewed under the Highgate & Davenports brand name:

Dark Mild (OG 1036.8, ABV 3.4%)

Pale Ale (OG 1038, ABV 3.8%)

Original Bitter (OG 1041.8, ABV 4%)

Red Baron (OG 1046, ABV 4.8%)

Imperial IPA (OG 1048, ABV 5.2%)

Blue Bee SIBA

Unit 29-30, Hoyland Road Industrial Estate, Sheffield, South Yorkshire, S3 8AB ☎ 07375 659349
⊕ bluebeebrewery.co.uk

Blue Bee was established in 2010. The 10-barrel brewery supplies beer to the free trade throughout Yorkshire and the East Midlands. The core range of beers is complemented by an ever-changing range of specials often including a single hopped IPA. ♦V

Hillfoot Best Bitter (OG 1040, ABV 4%)
Traditional dark chestnut-coloured fruity best bitter.

Reet Pale (OG 1040, ABV 4%)
A pale ale with floral and citrus flavours leading to a dry bitter finish.

American 5 Hop (OG 1043, ABV 4.3%)
Pale ale hopped with five different varieties of American hops.

Ginger Beer (OG 1048, ABV 4.8%)
A pale ale with the addition of fiery ginger.

Tempest Stout (OG 1048, ABV 4.8%)
Rich, well-balanced stout with hints of coffee and chocolate, leading to a bitter finish.

Blue Bell

🏠 Cranesgate South, Whaplode St Catherine, Lincolnshire, PE12 6SN
☎ (01406) 504300 ☎ 07788 136663
⊕ thebluebell.net

Founded in 1998 behind the Blue Bell pub, the brewery is now back under the ownership of the pub after several years as a separate business. Beers are only available at the pub and to private customers.

Blue Bell Brewhouse

▤ Warings Green Rd, Warings Green, B94 6BP
☎ 07922 554181 ✉ rnrbrewhouse@outlook.com

A two-barrel plant set up in 2013 by Mark Shepherd to resurrect on-site brewing at the Blue Bell Cider House (brewing ceased in 1968). Brewster Lynn Crossland, who joined in 2014, continues the tradition of female brewers in the original brewhouse, producing solely for the Blue Bell and local festivals. The brewery likes to experiment with unusual flavours, and using ingredients foraged from local hedgerows. Brewing is currently suspended.

Blue Monkey SIBA

10 Pentrich Road, Giltbrook Industrial Park, Giltbrook, Nottinghamshire, NG16 2UZ
☎ (0115) 938 5899 ⊕ bluemonkeybrewery.com

☺Blue Monkey was established in 2008 as a 10-barrel plant but moved in 2010 to a bigger site to meet increasing demand. It now brews around 15,000 pints a week to supply more than 200 local outlets and selected national distributors. The name stems from a nickname for the blue flames that used to rise from the chimneys of Stanton Ironworks, which was a prominent local foundry. ‼▰

Marmoset (OG 1038, ABV 3.6%)
Highly-hopped citrus-flavoured golden beer with a dry, bitter finish.

BG Sips (OG 1041, ABV 4%) ◆
Pale golden hoppy beer. Very fruity and bitter.

Funky Gibbon (OG 1041.8, ABV 4.1%)
Copper-coloured malty beer.

99 Red Baboons (OG 1042, ABV 4.2%) ▰ ◆
Red in colour with a malty fruitiness. Not overly hoppy.

Centennial (ABV 4.3%)
A fresh floral aroma and flavour with a deep bitter finish.

Infinity (OG 1045.7, ABV 4.6%) ▱ ▰ ◆
Golden ale packed with hops.

Guerrilla (OG 1052, ABV 4.9%) ◆
A creamy stout, full of roast malt flavour and a slightly sweet finish.

Ape Ale (OG 1052, ABV 5.4%) ▰ ◆
Intensely hopped strong golden ale with dry bitter finish.

Blue Square (NEW) SIBA

c/o MSS City Mills, Peel Street, Morley, Leeds, West Yorkshire, LS27 8QL
☎ (0113) 238 0382 ⊕ bluesquarebrewery.com

☺Blue Square was established in 2016 . ▰

Morley Rocket (OG 1038, ABV 3.8%)

Moonlight (OG 1039, ABV 4%)

Supernova (OG 1042, ABV 4.3%)

Abyss (OG 1045, ABV 4.8%)

Polaris (OG 1047, ABV 5.1%)

Bluestone (Lancashire) SIBA

Unit 6, Daniel Street Industrial Estate, Whitworth, Lancashire, OL12 8BX
☎ (01706) 853009 ☎ 07802 792536
⊕ bluestonebrewery.co.uk

Bluestone is a small 3.5-barrel brewery using traditional methods including 'double dropping' fermentation.

Quarrymans Stout (OG 1041, ABV 4%)

EPA (English Pale Ale) (OG 1042, ABV 4.2%)
A traditional dry pale ale with strong malt and hop flavours.

Night Hops Stout (OG 1043, ABV 4.2%)
Dark, dry stout with a good hop flavour through roasted malt, liquorice and spice.

AKA (Amber Kitchen Ale) (OG 1043, ABV 4.4%)
A mild, brown-coloured ale with a caramel and liquorice malty flavour.

Spodden Pilsner (OG 1048, ABV 4.4%)
A full-bodied, Bohemian-style Pilsner. Hoppy, golden and full of flavour.

Bluestone (Pembrokeshire) SIBA

Tyriet, Cilgwyn, Newport, Pembrokeshire, SA42 0QW
☎ (01239) 820833 ⊕ bluestonebrewing.co.uk

A family-run business established in 2013 on a working hill farm in the Preseli Hills within the Pembrokeshire Coast National Park. The 10-barrel brewery has been installed in a renovated 200-year-old stone barn, which also doubles as a visitor facility and office, with the surrounding yard becoming an events venue throughout the summer months. The brewery uses water from a private supply, which filters down through the Preseli Hill. Numerous local outlets are supplied as well as wholesalers around the UK. ‼▰◆RAIB

Rockhopper (OG 1039, ABV 3.9%)
Classic amber-coloured bitter, with a light malt base and a spicy fruitiness from the hops.

Bedrock Blonde (OG 1040, ABV 4%)
A straw-coloured blonde ale with creamy soft malt flavours.

Elderflower Blonde (OG 1040, ABV 4%)
Straw-coloured, delicately-hopped ale finished with a hint of elderflower.

Crystal Ruby (OG 1042, ABV 4.2%)
A balanced combination of rich malty flavours with a touch of caramelised grain on top.

Hammerstone IPA (OG 1044, ABV 4.5%)
A modern IPA, fruity and refreshing.

Moonstone (OG 1046, ABV 4.6%)
A full-bodied porter. Spicy bitterness complements its chocolate and nut flavours.

Rocketeer (OG 1046, ABV 4.6%)
A traditional full-bodied bitter with a rich malty base.

Blythe SIBA

Blythe House Farm, Lichfield Road, Hamstall Ridware, Staffordshire, WS15 3QQ
☎ (01889) 504661 ☎ 07483 248723
⊕ blythebrewery.co.uk

⊠ Blythe began brewing in 2003 using a 2.5-barrel plant in a converted barn. 15 outlets are supplied direct. **‼♦RAIB**

Bagot's Bitter (OG 1040, ABV 3.8%)
Amber in colour with a fruity start and sweetness which develops to a smooth, bitter finish.

Ridware Pale (OG 1042, ABV 4.3%) ◥
Bright and golden with a bitter floral hop aroma and citrus taste. Good and hop-sharp, bitter and refreshing. Long, lingering bite with ripples of citrus across the tongue.

Staffie (OG 1044, ABV 4.4%) ◥
Hoppy and grassy aroma with hints of sweetness from this amber beer. A touch of malt at the start is soon overwhelmed by hops. A full hoppy, mouthwatering finish.

Palmers Poison (OG 1045, ABV 4.5%) ◥
Refreshing dark-coloured beer. Coffee truffle aroma, pleasingly sweet to start but with a good hop mouthfeel.

Johnsons (OG 1056, ABV 5.2%) ◥
Black with a thick head. Refreshingly hoppy and full bodied with lingering bitterness of chocolate, dates, coal smoke and liquorice.

Boat Lane (NEW)

Unit 3, Streamside Business Park, Boat Lane, Offenham, Worcestershire, WR11 8RS
☎ (01386) 48212 ⊕ boatlanebrewery.co.uk

Brewing began in 2016 using a 200-litre brew kit. **RAIB V**

Satsumo Stout (ABV 4.2%)

Offenham Orange (ABV 4.5%)

Phantom Falls (ABV 5.1%)

Valentine Moon (ABV 5.5%)

Bohem

227 Whittington Road, Bowes Park, London, N22 8YW
☎ 07999 014294 ⊕ bohembrewery.com

No real ale.

Bollington SIBA

⊟ **Adlington Road, Bollington, Cheshire, SK10 5JT**
☎ (01625) 575380 ⊕ bollingtonbrewing.co.uk

Bollington began brewing in 2008 with the Vale Inn, Bollington, as the brewery tap. The Park Tavern, Macclesfield, and the Cask Tavern, Poynton, are also owned. Around 40 outlets are supplied direct.

Chinook & Grapefruit (OG 1036, ABV 3.6%)
Fresh grapefruit zest and juice paired with punchy hops.

Ginger Brew (OG 1041, ABV 3.6%)
A classic ginger beer with a hoppy, bitter flavour and a smooth taste with fresh root ginger added at the end.

White Nancy (OG 1038, ABV 3.6%)
Extremely pale bitter with a good hoppiness and light body.

Long Hop (OG 1039, ABV 3.9%)
Pale lager-style bitter with fruity, refreshing hops.

Best (OG 1041, ABV 4.2%)
A hoppy bitter. Clean and crisp, light golden in colour with a refreshing bitter aftertaste.

Dinner Ale (OG 1042, ABV 4.3%)
Deep copper-coloured beer with a fresh, slightly fruity nose. A traditional-style bitter with a dry, hoppy finish.

Oat Mill Stout (OG 1049, ABV 5%)
An oatmeal stout with a twist. A hoppy bitter taste keeps the sweetness in check.

Eastern Nights (OG 1056, ABV 5.6%)
A pale gold-coloured IPA with a modest hop content.

Bolthole

2a Shipley Road, Westbury on Trym, Bristol, BS9 3HS
☎ 07771 902393 ⊕ bolthole.beer

The brewery was set up in 2015, running from the owner's premises in North Bristol. A range of five beers is regularly produced, with occasional specials. Most of the production is bottle-conditioned and sold at local farmers' markets.
☛♦RAIB

Bond Brews

Units 3 & 4, South Barns, Gardeners Green Farm, Heathlands Road, Wokingham Without, Berkshire, RG40 3AS
☎ (01344) 775450 ⊕ bondbrews.co.uk

⊠ Bond Brews was established in 2015 on the outskirts of Wokingham, using a six-barrel plant. Beers are delivered to free trade outlets within a 30-mile radius and there are plans to open a brewery shop. **‼♦RAIB**

Goldi-hops (OG 1039, ABV 3.9%)
A refreshing amber-coloured pale ale with a malty and delicately citrus nose, followed by a bitter flavour and a long, dry, bitter finish.

Best of British (OG 1040, ABV 4%)
A tawny best bitter with malt and fruit on the nose, dry fruity flavours balancing the bitterness, followed by a touch of blackcurrant in the aftertaste.

Railway Porter (OG 1045, ABV 4.5%)
An easy-drinking dark brown porter with a reddish tint. It has a subtle toasty maltiness with a gently lingering fruity finish.

Boot

⊟ **12 Boot Hill, Repton, Derbyshire, DE65 6FT**
☎ (01283) 346047 ⊕ thebootbeer.co.uk

An eight-barrel brewery installed at the rear of the Boot Inn, Repton, home of the eponymous public school, during 2015. The brewery supplies the three pubs within the group and a small number of free trade outlets.

Boot Town (NEW)

Copper Kettle Brewing, Bosworths Garden Centre, 110 Finedon Road, Burton Latimer, Northamptonshire, NN15 5QA
⊕ boottownbrewery.co.uk

Brewing began in 2017.

St Georges Ale (ABV 4.3%)

Boothtown (NEW)

4 Ladyship Business Park, Mill Lane, Halifax, West Yorkshire, HX3 6TA ☎ 07957 068009 ✉ david-bamforth@hotmail.com

⊛Boothtown was established in 2011, producing traditional Yorkshire ales. The full range of beers is available at the brewery tap, which is attached to the brewery.

Blonde (OG 1038, ABV 3.8%) ◣
Refreshing golden ale with a delicate citrus aroma and flavour. Hoppy bitterness lingers in the aftertaste.

Copper (OG 1040, ABV 4%) ◣
A traditional copper-coloured bitter with a fruity nose and a dominate malt flavour. It ends with a long, hoppy, bitter aftertaste.

Liquid Gold (OG 1041, ABV 4.1%) ◣
This light-drinking amber beer has caramel initially in the palate with malt and hops that linger into a dry and bitter finish.

Proud Miner (OG 1040, ABV 4.1%) ◣
A smooth, fruity, pale brown-coloured ale, deceptively easy drinking with a clean hop finish.

Old Cockerel (OG 1042, ABV 4.3%) ◣
A rich, creamy, malty and well-balanced amber-coloured best bitter. Good dry finish with lingering malt notes.

Hoppy Valley IPA (OG 1046, ABV 4.5%) ◣
A robust golden IPA with a hoppy aroma and a malty, bitter taste.

Bootleg IFBB

▤ Horse & Jockey, 9 The Green, Chorlton-cum-Hardy, M21 9HS ☎ 07774 937910 ⊕ bootleg-brewingco.com

A microbrewery, established in 2010, nestled in a space where the original brewery would have been in a 200 year old pub. Some beers may be brewed at Joseph Holt (qv) when a larger volume is required.

Bootlegger

▤ The Bootlegger, 3 Amersham Hill, High Wycombe, Buckinghamshire, HP13 6NQ
☎ (01494) 525457 ⊕ thebootleggerpub.co.uk/brewco

A small-scale brewery operating out of the Bootlegger pub in High Wycombe. It currently produces five bottle-conditioned beers. Cask-conditioned beer may be available in the future.

Born in the Borders

Lanton Mill, Jedburgh, TD8 6ST
☎ (01835) 830495 ☎ 07802 416494
⊕ bornintheborders.com

Born in the Borders Brewery is Scotland's original plough-to-pint brewery, and started brewing as Scottish Borders Brewery in 2011 using barley from its own farm. Beyond its core range of ales, recent projects include the brewery's 'Wild Harvest' initiative, which sources locally foraged ingredients for its ales. The brewery has recently launched a visitor centre, offering brewery tours, a café/

restaurant and retail units featuring Borders beer, produce and food. ‼🍽♦

Foxy Blonde (OG 1037.5, ABV 3.8%)
A golden ale bursting with citrus and floral flavours.

Game Bird (OG 1039.5, ABV 4%) 🏵 🍺
An amber-coloured ale with a balance of malty sweetness and late summer fruit with a long and easy finish.

Holy Cow (OG 1041, ABV 4.2%)
Hints of dark malt combine with a long floral finish.

Gold Dust (OG 1041.5, ABV 4.3%)
A light IPA with a big burst of hops.

Dark Horse (OG 1044, ABV 4.5%)
A classic dark ale that has overtones of coffee and chocolate with a spicy finish that lingers on the tongue.

Borough (Crewe)

▤ 33 Earle Street, Crewe, Cheshire, CW1 2BG
☎ (01270) 254999
✉ info@borougharmscrewe.co.uk

A two-barrel brewery opened in 2005 to supply the pub but with beers occasionally available at festivals. Brewing is currently suspended.

Borough (Lancaster) SIBA 👁

Brook Street, Lancaster, LA1 1SL ☎ 07912 679761
⊕ theboroughbrewery.co.uk

⊛Borough Brewery moved from the cellar of the Borough, a free house in the centre of Lancaster, in 2016. A eight-gallon plant is used to create four regular beers, which are available in the Borough and the recently purchased Britannia, Lancaster. ♦V

Pale (OG 1038, ABV 3.7%) ◣
Dry, refreshing up front hoppy bitter beer.

Bitter (OG 1040, ABV 4%) ◣
Sweet malty bitter with caramel flavours and light hop balance.

Summertime Dark (OG 1040, ABV 4%) ◣
A rich, dark, sweet mild with gentle roast.

Wintertime Dark (OG 1050, ABV 5%) ◣
Well-balanced, roasty dry stout with a full body and lingering finish.

Borough Arms SIBA

Unit 5, Tonmawr Business Park, Neath, SA10 9UU
☎ (01639) 644902 ☎ 07577 461915

Correspondence: Borough Arms, 2 New Henry Street, Neath, SA11 2PH ✉ boroughbrewery@gmail.com

⊛Opened in 2014, the brewery was built by the landlord Kevin Davies in a converted outbuilding at the rear of the Borough Arms, Neath. By 2016 the brewery had expanded to 10 barrels and relocated to a nearby industrial estate. The original kit remains at the pub but is used for experimental brews only. Beers are named primarily after the local coal and steel industry. ‼RAIB

Welsh Gold (OG 1038, ABV 3.8%)
A stout with hints of chocolate, a nutty taste and a slightly bitter finish.

Bit 'o' Sweet (OG 1042, ABV 4.2%)

A light brown-coloured malty beer with a biscuit taste and a subtle aroma, backed with the taste of British hops.

Iron Runner (OG 1042, ABV 4.3%)
A best bitter with a roasted nutty aftertaste.

Triple Bleeder (OG 1046, ABV 4.3%)
Amber-coloured bitter ale with a dry, hoppy taste.

IPA (OG 1044, ABV 4.4%)
Strong-tasting with a crisp, clean mouthfeel.

Full Blast (OG 1050, ABV 4.7%)
Golden, fruity and zesty ale.

Puddlers Peril (OG 1048, ABV 4.8%)
A strong, copper-coloured ale with a malt aroma and distinct hoppy aftertaste.

Nut Red Coke (OG 1051, ABV 4.9%)
Chestnut-coloured ale with malt overtones.

Pit Head Porter (OG 1058, ABV 5.4%)
Full-bodied porter with nutty overtones and a hint of chocolate aftertaste.

Boss SIBA 👁

14 Worcester Court, Mannesmann Close, Llansamlet, SA7 9FD
☎ (01792) 790726 ☎ 07825 525735
⊕ bossbrewing.co.uk

⊠ Established in 2015 by Roy Alkin and Sarah John, using a 10-barrel plant. Subsequent expansion has provided bottling and casking facilities. 250 outlets are supplied with bottles available via national retailers. Exports to France and Germany commenced in 2017. A brewery tap named Copper is now open in Swansea city centre. ♦RAIB

Blonde (OG 1040, ABV 4%)
Aromas of pine forest, spice and grapefruit peel, followed by taste of grapefruit, resinous pine. Clean bitterness to finish.

Brawn (OG 1043, ABV 4.4%)
A hoppy beer, matured to bring out lychee and sherbet flavours. A sweet, hoppy start leads to bitter fruit flavours and finishes with a dry, hoppy palate.

Blaze (OG 1045, ABV 4.5%)
Floral, herbal aroma gives way to a zingy citrus, spicy flavour.

Bix (ABV 4.6%)
A Belgian-style Witbier. Orange and coriander seeds present, with a fuller body and rounder mouthfeel than expected for a wheat beer.

Bare (OG 1050, ABV 5%)
Lager-style beer, lemon zest with malty biscuit undertone. Hints of caramel leading to a clean, spicy finish.

Black (OG 1050, ABV 5%) 🍺
Aroma of roasted coffee and warm chocolate, with flavour of fire roasted nuts, toffee and chocolate.

Brave (OG 1055, ABV 5.5%)
Initial tropical fruit cocktail, elderflower and rose, with a grapefruit, citrus, pine kick to finish.

Bosun's SIBA 👁

Unit 20, Wakefield Commercial Park, 97 Bridge Road, Horbury Bridge, West Yorkshire, WF4 5NW ☎ 07703 535735 ⊕ bosunsbrewery.co.uk

The first brew was produced in 2013 by a father-and-son team who have both served in the armed forces. The regular beers are produced on a 10-barrel plant with some given military themed names. ‼♦

Horbury Blond (OG 1039, ABV 3.9%)
A straw-coloured bitter.

Maiden Voyage (OG 1039, ABV 3.9%)
A chestnut-coloured traditional English ale.

Bermuda Triangle (OG 1041, ABV 4.1%)
Fruity golden blonde ale with soft citrus aroma and flavour.

Botley SIBA

Botley Mills, Mill Hill, Botley, Hampshire, SO30 2GB
☎ (01489) 784867 ☎ 07909 337212
⊕ botleybrewery.com

⊠ Botley Brewery was established in 2010 and uses a five-barrel plant. ♦RAIB

Hampshire Bitter (OG 1038, ABV 3.8%)
Yorkshire-style amber-coloured session bitter.

Mill (OG 1038, ABV 3.8%)
A light session bitter, copper in colour, with a fresh aftertaste.

Cobbett's (OG 1045, ABV 4.5%)
A light, fruity golden ale with a clean bitter finish.

Bottle Brook

Church Street, Kilburn, Belper, Derbyshire, DE56 0LU
☎ (01332) 880051 ☎ 07971 189915

⊠ A sister brewery to Leadmill (qv), Bottle Brook was established in 2005 using a 2.5-barrel plant on a tower gravity system. New World hops are predominantly used. The core range of beers is supplemented by one-off brews.

Columbus (OG 1040, ABV 4%)

Heanor Pale Ale (OG 1041, ABV 4.2%)

Roadrunner (OG 1047, ABV 4.8%)

Mellow Yellow (OG 1054, ABV 5.7%)

Rapture (OG 1058, ABV 5.9%)

Sand in the Wind (OG 1060, ABV 6.1%)

Boudicca

The Old Store, Walsingham Road, West Barsham, NR21 9NP ☎ 07864 321732
⊕ boudiccabrewing.co.uk

⊠ An indepedent Norfolk brewery, set up in 2015 exclusively producing vegan beers. ♦RAIB V

Queen of Hops (OG 1036.5, ABV 3.7%)
A refreshing pale ale with a grassy, fruity aroma with hints of marmalade. On the palate it has a tangy and fruity hit of hops with some underpinning of malt and bitterness.

Three Tails (OG 1036.5, ABV 3.9%)
Amber-coloured classic English bitter with a touch of peppery spiciness in the hop character.

Golden Torc (OG 1039.5, ABV 4.3%)
Subtle on the nose, hops start to come through in the mouth and grow in the lasting finish.

Spiral Stout (OG 1045, ABV 4.6%)

Stout with undertones of coffee and dark chocolate and aromas of dark autumn berries. A gentle, lingering dry roast finish with a hint of smoke.

Prasto's Porter (OG 1053.5, ABV 5.2%)
Dark fruit and hops on the nose, with hints of roast malt and smoke. Full-bodied in the mouth. A dry, subtle smoky finish with fruit and hop notes.

Boundary

Unit A5, 310 Portview Trade Centre, Newtownards Road, Belfast, BT4 1HE ⊕ boundarybrewing.coop

Boundary is a cooperative brewery based in Belfast, established in 2014. A taproom is open to the public, see website for details. ♦RAIB

APA (OG 1035, ABV 3.5%)

Export Stout (OG 1070, ABV 7%)

IPA (OG 1070, ABV 7%)

Bournemouth

Unit 6, 4-6 Abingdon Road, Nuffield Industrial Estate, Poole, Dorset, BH17 0UG
☎ (01202) 280405 ⊕ bournemouthbrewery.co.uk

⊗ Brewing began in 2013 using a one-barrel plant but has since increased capacity to seven barrels. Most of the beer is sold directly from the brewery bar or from the brewery's two pubs. A small proportion goes to local pubs and beer festivals. ‼️☰♦

Sandbanks (OG 1038, ABV 3.9%)
A session bitter with a slighty malty taste.

Wessex Wobble (OG 1041, ABV 4.3%)
Best bitter with a mildly hoppy taste.

Golden Grains (OG 1044, ABV 4.6%)
This pale golden beer has a mild sweetness and a strong hop flavour.

Sandbanks Export (OG 1052, ABV 5.7%)
Sweeter, maltier and hoppier version of Sandbanks Bitter.

Battleaxe (OG 1058, ABV 6.3%)
Lots of dark malts rounded off with powerful hops.

Sandbanks Extra Reserve (OG 1059, ABV 6.6%)
Strong and well-aged beer emphasising the hops.

Sandbanks Tempestatum (OG 1068, ABV 7%)
A rich, dark, velvety black IPA.

Boutilliers (NEW)

The Hop Shed, Macknade Fine Foods, Selling Road, Faversham, Kent, ME13 8XF ☎ 07743 372434 ⊕ boutilliers.com

Boutilliers began brewing in 2016 in the heart of Kent. Further beers are planned. Around 20 outlets are supplied direct. ♦RAIB V

Rye Pale Ale (OG 1041, ABV 4.3%)

Smoked Oatmeal Stout (OG 1045, ABV 4.4%)

90 Minute Saison (OG 1039, ABV 4.9%)

Anniversary Porter (OG 1050, ABV 5%)

Bowland SIBA 👁

Holmes Mill, Greenacre Street, Clitheroe, Lancashire, BB7 1EB

☎ (01200) 443592 ⊕ bowlandbrewery.com

☺Founded in 2003, this family-run business uses a 30-barrel plant together with a nanobrewery for experimental brews. The site features a beer shop and beer hall with 42 handpumps featuring beers from Lancashire and beyond. ‼️☰♦RAIB

Pheasant Plucker (OG 1038, ABV 3.7%)
A copper-coloured bitter with rounded blackcurrant flavours and a malty aftertaste.

Gold (OG 1039, ABV 3.8%)
A hoppy, golden bitter with intense grapefruit flavours and aromas.

AONB (Ale of Outstanding Natural Beauty) (OG 1040, ABV 4%)
A straw-coloured refreshing ale with a delicate gooseberry flavour and aroma.

Hen Harrier (OG 1040, ABV 4%) ◀
The malty start belies what comes next: fruity, sweet, hoppy bitter with a long-lasting finish comprising of all the previous elements.

Buster IPA (OG 1046, ABV 4.5%)
Well-balanced, medium-bodied and rounded. Generous hops provide long, tropical undertones.

Bowman SIBA 👁

Wallops Wood, Sheardley Lane, Droxford, Hampshire, SO32 3QY
☎ (01489) 878110 ⊕ bowman-ales.com

⊗ Brewing started in 2006 in converted farm buildings. The brewery supplies more than 100 outlets. A new 40-barrel plant came on stream in 2013, which is now working alongside the original 20-barrel plant. ‼️♦RAIB

Swift One (OG 1038, ABV 3.8%) ◀
Easy-drinking bitter, well-balanced with sweet maltiness leading to a bittersweet finish and slightly dry, hoppy aftertaste.

Meon Valley Bitter (OG 1040, ABV 3.9%) ◀
Well-balanced, copper-coloured bitter; sweet with an initial maltiness in taste and aroma leading to a more bitter finish.

Lapwing (OG 1040, ABV 4%)
A hoppy, golden bitter.

Wallops Wood (OG 1040, ABV 4%) ◀
Malt flavours throughout balanced by toffee notes, sweetness and slightly dry finish.

Contract brewed for Suthwyk Ales:

Old Dick (OG 1038, ABV 3.8%) ◀
Pleasant, clean-tasting pale brown bitter. Easy-drinking and well-balanced.

Liberation (OG 1042, ABV 4.2%)
Light-coloured with a soft, berry fruit flavour.

Skew Sunshine Ale (OG 1046, ABV 4.6%) ◀
An amber-coloured beer. Initial hoppiness leads to a fruity taste and finish.

Palmerston's Folly (OG 1050, ABV 5%)
A clear wheat and barley beer. Slightly dry with a hint of honey in the aftertaste.

Bowness Bay

Unit 10, Castle Mills, Aynam Road, Kendal, Cumbria, LA9 7DE ☎ 07885 171210
⊕ bownessbaybrewing.co.uk

Bowness Bay Brewery moved to Kendal in 2015, increasing capacity from five to 15 barrels. The original five-barrel plant is used for small experimental brews. The brewery now has its own tap house, the Factory Tap. ◆

Amazon Amber (OG 1038, ABV 3.8%)
A light ale with a distinctive partnering of oranges and spiced berries.

Swift Best (OG 1044, ABV 3.8%) ◀
A tawny bitter where caramel sweetness dominates, leading to a gentle bitter finish.

Swallow Gold (OG 1039, ABV 3.9%)
A golden ale with smooth, floral hints of apricot, lime and peach.

Swan Blonde (OG 1039, ABV 4%) ◀
A sweet malty start with a finish dominated by hop bitterness.

Swan Black (OG 1046, ABV 4.6%) ◀
Stout-like beer with a fruity raisiny middle, grainy mouthfeel and roast bitter finish.

Term IPA (OG 1043, ABV 5%)
A crisp, golden ale brewed from an 80 year old recipe from the old Whitwell Mark Brewery of Kendal. Full-flavoured, with a balanced hoppiness and caramel sweetness giving a deep, smooth finish.

Box Social SIBA

Units 1-3, Winnings Courtyard, Newburn, Newcastle upon Tyne, NE15 9RU ☎ 07803 791761 ⊕ boxsocial.pub

Launched in 2015, this family-run brewery has a licence and is open to the public most days (12-9pm). ‼️🍺◆

Convive Blond (ABV 3.9%)

Kaffir (ABV 4.2%)

India Brown Ale (ABV 5.6%)

Box Steam SIBA ◉

15, The Midlands, Holt, Wiltshire, BA14 6RU ☎ (01225) 782700 ⊕ boxsteambrewery.com

⊠ The brewery was founded in 2004 and boasts a Fulton steam-fired copper, hence the name. New ownership since 2006 meant expansion and increased capacity with the brewery moving to larger premises in Holt in 2011. Two pubs are owned and more than 100 outlets supplied. ‼️🍺◆

Golden Bolt (OG 1037.5, ABV 3.8%)
A straw-coloured bitter with a slightly dry, hoppy aftertaste.

Tunnel Vision (OG 1040.5, ABV 4.2%)
A well-rounded light amber bitter. Clean tasting, with a slight bitterness on the finish.

Piston Broke (OG 1045, ABV 4.5%)
A full-bodied deep golden ale with a refreshing hoppy, citrus palate and a subtle fruit-hop aroma.

Brack'N'Brew

🏠 Brackenrigg Inn, Watermillock, Cumbria, CA11 0LP ☎ (01768) 486206 ⊕ brackenrigginn.co.uk

Brewing started in 2015 in a converted 16th-century stable overlooking Ullswater. Brewing takes place three times a week on a four-barrel plant. A 70-litre plant is used for experimental brews and one-offs.

Bradfield SIBA ◉

Watt House Farm, High Bradfield, South Yorkshire, S6 6LG
☎ (0114) 285 1118 ⊕ bradfieldbrewery.com

☺Established in 2005, Bradfield is a family-run business, based on a working farm in the Peak District using pure Milstone Grit springwater. In 2009 the brewery bought its first brewery tap, the Nags Head, Loxley. 🍺◆RAIB

Farmers Bitter (OG 1039, ABV 3.9%)
A traditional copper-coloured malt ale with a floral aroma.

Farmers Blonde (OG 1041, ABV 4%)
Pale, blonde beer with citrus and summer fruit aromas.

Yorkshire Farmer (OG 1041, ABV 4%)
A gold-coloured beer with a smooth bitter finish.

Farmers Brown Cow (OG 1042.5, ABV 4.2%)
A smooth, chestnut-coloured ale with a citrus aftertaste.

Farmers Stout (OG 1045, ABV 4.5%)
A dark stout with roasted malts and flaked oats and a subtle, bitter hop character.

Farmers Pale Ale (OG 1049, ABV 5%)
A fruity, full-bodied pale ale with a dry aftertaste.

Bradford

🏠 22 Rawson Road, Westgate, Bradford, West Yorkshire, BD1 3SQ
☎ (01274) 379054 ⊕ bradfordbrewery.com

The brewery was established in 2015, seeing the return of brewing to Bradford city centre for the first time in 60 years. It is based in converted former factory buildings and uses a 10-barrel plant. The beers are available at the on-site Brewfactory pub, where a feature glass wall allows visitors to view the brewery in operation.

Brains IFBB ◉

Crawshay Street, Cardiff, CF10 1SP
☎ (029) 2040 2060 ⊕ sabrain.com

☺Brains was established in 1882 at the Old Brewery, moving to the former Hancock's brewery site in 1999. The company has remained in family ownership and runs more than 270 pubs throughout Wales, the Midlands and the West Country and is heavily involved in sponsoring Welsh sport. A new microbrewery within the existing site produces an ever-increasing range of new beers, which have proved popular within the Brain's estate. ◆

Dark (OG 1035.5, ABV 3.5%) ◀
A classic dark brown mild, a mix of malt, roast, caramel with a background of hops. Bittersweet, mellow and with a lasting finish of malt and roast.

Bitter (OG 1036, ABV 3.7%) ◀
Amber-coloured with a gentle aroma of malt and hops. Malt, hops and bitterness combine in an easy-drinking beer with a bitter finish.

Rev James Gold (OG 1041, ABV 4.1%)

SA (OG 1042, ABV 4.2%) ◀

Dark brown mild with a hint of maple syrup.

Legacy (ABV 4%)
Easy-drinking pale ale with citrus notes.

Best (OG 1042, ABV 4.2%) ▤
A traditional, light-coloured best bitter with a well-rounded flavour and aroma.

Gold (OG 1043, ABV 4.3%)
A heavily-hopped golden beer with a fruity taste and bitter finish.

Hope & Glory (ABV 4.5%)
A premium, full-bodied, red-coloured bitter. Well-balanced with full malt flavours and light hops, with a lingering bitter finish.

Lumberjack (ABV 5.2%)
A strong, slightly sweet, full-bodied bitter with a round, hoppy finish.

Chockwork Orange (OG 1067, ABV 6.5%)
A deep chocolate malty beer brewed with oranges.

Brewed under the Elephant School brand name:

Cheru Kol (ABV 4.5%)
A fig and rosemary Belgian-style beer.

Sombrero (ABV 4.5%)
A chia and passion fruit Saison.

Porter in A Storm (ABV 4.9%)
A chocolate and cranberry porter.

Brew Buddies

Unit 14, Highlands Farm Business Park, Highlands Hill, Swanley Village, Kent, BR8 7NA ☎ 07962 369717
⊕ brew-buddies.co.uk

⊠ Established by two friends in 2015, Brew Buddies operates on a six-barrel plant set up in a post-war farm building. The brewery supplies free trade outlets in Kent and local beer festivals, while a wholesaler distributes beers more widely. ‼▭

Brew By Numbers

79 Enid Street, Bermondsey, London, SE16 3RA
☎ (020) 7237 9794 ☎ 07528 684105
⊕ brewbynumbers.com

Brew By Numbers is a small brewery established in 2012, specialising in Saisons and hop-forward pale beers, all bottled on site. Most beers undergo secondary fermentation and conditioning in bottle and keg, but hop-forward styles are conditioned and carbonated in tank. All beers are named by a four digit number, the first two digits denoting style and the second denoting recipe. The latest releases are served in its taproom. ▭RAIB

Brew Foundation SIBA ⊙

c/o Wincle Brewery, Toll Barn, Wincle, Cheshire, SK11 0QE
☎ (0114) 282 3098 ☎ 07545 618894

Office: 18 Jarrow Road, Sheffield, South Yorkshire, S11 8YB ⊕ thebrewfoundation.co.uk

A father-and-son brewery, currently using spare capacity at Wincle Brewery (qv). Beer is distributed both east and west of the Pennines.

Pop (ABV 3.6%)
A session pale ale with a tropical hop flavour.

Little Bitter That (ABV 3.8%)

Hops & Dreams (ABV 4%)
A session IPA with a citrus, floral and tropical hop flavour and aroma.

Laughing Water (ABV 4.3%)
A tropical fruit pale ale with a subtle citrus base.

First Light (ABV 4.6%)
A pale session beer.

Janet's Treat Porter (ABV 4.8%)
The flavour of cherries is balanced by chocolate malt bitterness and provides a subtle dark cherry aroma. Brewed in collaboration with Wincle Brewery.

Hop & Glory (ABV 4.9%)

Bitter That (ABV 5%)

Brew Shack

Unit 3, Old Manor Farm Buildings, 187 Leigh Road, Wimborne Minster, Dorset, BH21 2BT ☎ 07580 120258 ⊕ thebrewshack.co.uk

⊠ Brewing began in 2015 on a 1.5-barrel plant in purpose-built premises and has now increased to a 4.5-barrel plant.

Pale Ale (OG 1045, ABV 4.5%)
Smooth, well-hopped, refreshing pale-coloured bitter.

Eight Grain Porter (OG 1050, ABV 5%)
A sweetish brown-coloured porter using eight different malts.

Sump Oil Stout (OG 1060, ABV 6%)
Rich, full-bodied beer with big roast flavours and a bitter finish.

Brew Shed (NEW)

Wellheads House, Sandilands, Limekilns, KY11 3JD
☎ 07484 727672 ⊕ brewshedbeers.wordpress.com

Brewing began in 2016 in a tiny brewery behind the owner's house, the first brewery in Limekilns since 1849. Brew Shed Beers revives a tradition of local breweries serving the neighbourhood. RAIB

Ramsay Lane (ABV 4.4%)

Sandilands (ABV 4.4%)

Cocket Hat (ABV 4.5%)

Brew York (NEW) SIBA

Unit 6, Enterprise Complex, Walmgate, York, YO1 9TT
☎ (01904) 848448 ⊕ brewyork.co.uk

⊙Brew York is a brewery and tap room within York's historic city walls, launched in 2016. The tap room overlooks the brew house. More than 180 outlets are supplied. ‼▭♦V

JARSA (Juicy & Refreshing Session Ale) (OG 1035, ABV 3.7%)

Maris the Otter (OG 1037, ABV 3.9%)

X-Panda (OG 1043, ABV 4.5%)

Brew York (OG 1045, ABV 4.9%)

Viking DNA (OG 1052, ABV 5%)

Big Eagle (OG 1060, ABV 6.5%)

BrewDog

Balmacassie Industrial Estate, Ellon, AB41 8BX

☎ (01358) 724924 ⊕ brewdog.com

Established in 2007 by James Watt and Martin Dickie. 31 UK bars and 17 overseas bars are open as of early 2017. Most of the production goes into bottles and keg. In 2016 a KeyCask initiative began, described as 'real ale for modernists', which has now been expanded to include more beers. ‼️🍺

Dead Pony (OG 1040, ABV 3.8%)

5am Saint (OG 1048, ABV 5%)

Brewheadz (NEW)

Unit 16a, Rosebery Industrial Park, Rosebery Avenue, Tottenham Hale, London, N17 9SR ⊕ brewheadz.com

Established in 2016, Brewheadz is the newest independent microbrewery in Tottenham Hale, producing unpasteurised and unfiltered beers. The range is currently available in KeyCasks and bottle-conditioned from some speciality pubs, beer shops and online retailers. A tap room is open on Saturdays. RAIB

Brewhouse & Kitchen SIBA

🍴 **Bedford: 115 High Street, Bedford, MK40 1NU** ☎ (01234) 342931

Bournemouth (NEW): 154 Commercial Road, Bournemouth, Dorset, BH2 5LU ☎ (01202) 055221

Bristol: 31-35 Cotham Hill, Bristol, BS6 6JY ☎ (0117) 973 3793

Cheltenham: Unit 7, The Brewery, St Margaret's Road, Cheltenham, GL50 4EQ ☎ (01242) 509946

Chester (NEW): Forest House, Love Street, Chester, CH1 1QY ☎ (01244) 365361

Dorchester: 17 Weymouth Avenue, Dorchester, Dorset, DT1 1QY ☎ (01305) 265551

Gloucester Quay: Unit R1, St Anne Walk, Gloucester Quay, Gloucester, GL1 5SH ☎ (01452) 222965

Highbury: 2a Corsica Street, Highbury, London, N5 1JJ ☎ (020) 7226 1026

Islington: 5 Torrens Street, Angel, London, EC1V 1NQ ☎ (020) 7064 9943

Nottingham (NEW): Trent Bridge, Nottingham, NG2 2GS ☎ (0115) 986 7960

Poole: 3 Dear Hay Lane, Poole, Dorset, BH15 1NZ ☎ (01202) 771246

Portsmouth: 26 Guildhall Walk, Portsmouth, Hampshire, PO1 2DD ☎ (023) 9389 1340

Southampton: 47 Highfield Lane, Southampton, Hampshire, SO17 1QD ☎ (023) 8055 5566

Southbourne: 147 Parkwood Road, Southbourne, Dorset, BH5 2BN ☎ (01202) 055209

Sutton Coldfield: 8 Birmingham Road, Sutton Coldfield, West Midlands, B72 1QD ☎ (0121) 796 6838

Wilmslow: 6-12 Swan Street, Wilmslow, Cheshire, SK9 1HE ☎ (01625) 441850 ⊕ brewhouseandkitchen.com

Brewing started in 2013 in Portsmouth, the first in the growing Brewhouse & Kitchen chain. There are now 15 brewpubs, with more planned, each producing its own particular range of beers and with its brewery on open display in the bar area. Local freehouses and beer festivals can be

supplied. Carry outs and brewery experience days are available at all venues.

Brewing Brothers (NEW)

🍴 **The Imperial, 119 Queens Road, Hastings, East Sussex, TN34 1RL** ⊕ brewingbrothers.org

Brewing began in 2016 behind the bar of the Imperial, Hastings, using a 2.5-barrel plant. There are plans for expansion.

Brewshed SIBA

Place Farm, Ingham, Suffolk, IP31 1NQ ☎ (01284) 848066 ⊕ brewshedbrewery.co.uk

⊠ Brewshed began brewing in 2011 using a five-barrel plant in buildings located behind the Beerhouse, one of its pub outlets. It's now located in the nearby village of Ingham, using a 12-barrel plant, which has resulted in greater capacity and a wider beer range. ♦

Pale (OG 1040, ABV 3.9%)

Best (OG 1044, ABV 4.3%)

American Blonde (OG 1055, ABV 5.5%)

Brewshine

4 Littledale, Kendal, Cumbria, LA9 7SG ☎ 07817 873997 ⊕ brewshine.co.uk

Brewing began in 2014 using a nine-gallon plant situated in a garage in Kendal. There are plans for expansion.

Silly Billy (OG 1038, ABV 3.8%)
A smooth, copper-coloured bitter with balanced flavours and a caramel finish.

Billonde (OG 1040, ABV 4%)
A refreshing beer with a light, citrus fruit flavour.

Billy Goat Ale (OG 1040, ABV 4%)
Dark amber in colour. with a rich malty taste. Well-balanced with hops to leave a dry, caramel-chocolate finish.

Billyonaires Gold (OG 1040, ABV 4%)
A light, refreshing beer with a citrus fruit flavour.

Oatmeal Stout (ABV 4%)
A smooth, easy-drinking stout with a rich, creamy head leading to a long chocolate finish.

Little Billy Wheat (ABV 4.6%)
A refreshing lower ABV version of Big Billy Wheat.

Big Billy Wheat (ABV 6.6%)
Wheat beer with a spicy nose, laced with coriander and full of sweet orange flavour.

Brewsmith SIBA

Unit 11, Cuba Industrial Estate, Ramsbottom, BL0 ONE ☎ (01706) 829390 ⊕ brewsmithbeer.co.uk

Brewsmith is a 10-barrel microbrewery established in 2014 by the Smith family – James, Jennifer and Ted. It produces a range of cask and bottle-conditioned ales in traditional British beer styles. ‼️♦ RAIB

Mosaic (ABV 3.5%)
A session strength light ale with tropical fruit flavours.

Amarillo (ABV 3.8%)

Golden-coloured beer with floral, citrus and orange tones.

Bitter (OG 1039, ABV 3.9%)
A pale session bitter. Moderate bitterness, pronounced floral/citrus hop aromas.

Gold (ABV 4.2%)
Golden ale made with English hops. Moderate bitterness with a hint of marmalade.

New Zealand Pale (ABV 4.2%)
A pronounced floral and pine aroma beer with moderate bitterness.

Pale (OG 1042, ABV 4.2%)
A refreshingly bitter and hoppy pale ale.

Anvil Ale (OG 1045, ABV 4.5%)
Full-bodied dark bitter with pine and fruit aromas.

APA (ABV 5%)
Pale ale with resinous pine, grapefruit and floral aromas.

Oatmeal Stout (OG 1052, ABV 5.2%)
A full-bodied, richly-textured stout.

IPA (OG 1060, ABV 6%)
Rich mouthfeel, big hop aromas, long dry finish.

Brewster's SIBA ◉

Unit 5, Burnside, Turnpike Close, Grantham, Lincolnshire, NG31 7XU
☎ (01476) 566000 ⊕ brewsters.co.uk

⊗ Brewster is the old English term for a female brewer and Sara Barton is a modern example. Originally established in the Vale of Belvoir in 1998, moving to Grantham in 2006, Brewster's produces a range of traditional and innovative beers with two regularly-changing ranges; Women of Wonder (4.8% ABV) and WhimsicAles (4.0% ABV). ‼ 🍴 ♦

Hophead (OG 1036, ABV 3.6%) 🍺
An amber-coloured beer with a floral hop character. Hops predominate throughout before yielding to grapefruit in the lasting dry finish.

Marquis (OG 1038, ABV 3.8%) ◆
A well-balanced and refreshing session bitter with maltiness and a dry, hoppy finish.

Aromantica (OG 1042, ABV 4.2%)
A light amber-coloured brew with a slightly sweet, nutty flavour. Tropical hop notes and aromas of lime and passion fruit with a refreshingly long, aromatic finish.

Hop A Doodle Doo (OG 1043, ABV 4.3%)
A copper-coloured ale, rich and full-bodied with a fruity hop character.

Decadence (OG 1044, ABV 4.4%)
A golden ale with a hint of malt sweetness with passion fruit and grapefruit aromas on the nose. A complex zesty hop palate leads to a fresh, herby finish.

Aromatic Porter (OG 1045, ABV 4.5%)
A rich, roasty, dark porter. Generous amounts of aromatic hops give citrus and tropical fruit flavours.

Stilton Porter (OG 1049, ABV 4.9%)
A rich, roast-flavoured porter brewed with four types of malt and balanced with spicy, rich hop flavours.

Briarbank SIBA

⬍ 70 Fore Street, Ipswich, IP4 1LB
☎ (01473) 284000 ⊕ briarbank.org

The Briarbank Brewing Company was established in 2013, and is situated on the site of the old Lloyds Bank on Fore Street. The brewery is a small two-barrel plant. The bar above offers the range of beers.

Brick SIBA

Arch 209, Blenheim Grove, Peckham, London, SE15 4QL ☎ 07747 787636 ⊕ brickbrewery.co.uk

Brick began brewing in 2013. A tap room is open on Saturdays from 12-6pm. The beers brewed vary from week to week. Local pubs, bars and restaurants are also supplied. 🍴 ♦

Sir Thomas Gardyner (OG 1038, ABV 3.8%) ◆
Unfined golden ale. Grapefruit and orange peel dominate, overlaid with hops lingering in the dry finish; increasing bitterness on drinking.

Kinsale (ABV 4%) ◆
Fruity, tawny-coloured best bitter with a little nutty roast character and hops throughout. Sweetish with a little honey on the palate.

Blenheim Black (OG 1053, ABV 5.3%) ◆
Roasted notes throughout with black cherry and blackcurrant and a trace of hops. Finish is bitter and dry with some malt.

Brick House

Patcham, East Sussex, BN1 8HQ ☎ 07708 384604
✉ brickhousebrewingco@gmail.com

⊚ Brick House has grown organically from humble homebrewing beginnings and plans to continue in this vein. Current output is a single firkin and 24 bottles a week. Brewing is currently suspended.
RAIB

Bricknell

67 Bricknell Avenue, Hull, East Yorkshire, HU5 4ET
☎ (01482) 446563 ☎ 07729 722953
⊕ bricknellbrewery.co.uk

Commercial brewing began in 2015. Brew size is currently 150 litres, once or twice a week. A large proportion of each brew is bottle-conditioned, with some going into 36 pint pins. 🍴 RAIB V

Bridestones SIBA

Smithy Farm, Long Causeway, Blackshaw Head, Hebden Bridge, West Yorkshire, HX7 7JB
☎ (01422) 847104 ⊕ bridestonesbrewery.co.uk

⊚ Bridestones, situated close to a rock outcrop from which it takes its name, started brewing in 2006 and currently supplies more than 60 outlets. Its brewery tap is the New Delight Inn, Blackshaw.
♦ RAIB

Indians Head (OG 1037, ABV 3.7%)
Light amber-coloured session bitter with a citrus hop finish.

Bridge

🏠 The Bridge, Woodhead Road, Holmbridge, West Yorkshire, HD9 2NQ
☎ (01484) 687652 ☎ 07970 779762

Brewing began in 2014 using a 2.5-barrel plant, in premises at the Bridge pub, Holmbridge. The brewery produces beers for the pub and also for its companion pub, Brambles, Holmfirth.

Bridgehouse SIBA

Airedale Heifer, Bradford Road, Sandbeds, Keighley, West Yorkshire, BD20 9LY
☎ (01535) 601222

Office: Unit 1, Aireworth Mills, Aireworth Road, Keighley, BD21 4DH ⊕ bridgehousebrewery.co.uk

☺Bridgehouse began brewing in 2010 using a 10-barrel plant. The brewery purchased the recipes and branding of Old Bear Brewery in 2014 and moved into its premises in Keighley. In 2015 the brewery relocated again to its present address behind the Airedale Heifer pub in Sandbeds, which it also operates. A bespoke 15-barrel brewery is used and the site includes a visitor centre. ‼◆

Tequila Blonde (OG 1038, ABV 3.8%)

Blonde (OG 1040, ABV 4%) ◄
A strong, fruity aroma with a sharp burst of grapefruit on the tongue and a touch of sweetness in the background. Bitter finish.

Aired Ale (OG 1042, ABV 4.1%) ◄
Brown beer with a malty aroma. Malt, hops and fruit in equal balance with lingering fruitiness in a long bitter finish.

Porter (OG 1045, ABV 4.5%) ◄
Dark brown beer with red hints. Aromas of malt and liquorice lead to coffee and wine fruit flavours, which carry through to a dry finish.

Holy Cow (OG 1057, ABV 5.6%) ◄
Light brown strong ale with juicy malt and full hop flavour, citrus overtones. Light hop aroma and a bitter, slightly astringent finish.

Brewed under the Old Bear brand name:

Yorkshire Ale (OG 1043, ABV 4.2%) ◄
A malty, robust best bitter with slight fruit aroma. Sweet fruitiness follows through into the bitter aftertaste.

Bridgetown

🏠 Albert Inn, Bridgetown Close, Totnes, Devon, TQ9 5AD
☎ (01803) 863214 ⊕ albertinntotnes.com/bridgetown-brewery

Bridgetown started brewing in 2008 on a two-barrel plant in the outbuildings of the Albert Inn, Totnes.

Bridlington

🏠 Pack Horse, 7 Market Place, Bridlington, East Yorkshire, YO16 4QJ
☎ (01262) 603502

The brewery, founded in 2014 in the grounds of the Telegraph Inn, Bridlington, is now based in the beer garden of the Pack Horse, Bridlington.

Briggs

c/o Unit 1, Waterhouse Mill, 65-71 Lockwood Road, Huddersfield, West Yorkshire, HD1 3QU ☎ 07427 668004 ⊕ briggssignatureales.weebly.com

Nick Briggs, former head brewer at Elland, has branched out on his own, producing his first brew on the Mallinson's plant. Now producing various regular, rotating, modern, hop-forward beers. 🍺

Northern Soul (OG 1038, ABV 3.8%)
Pale bitter with a citrus and zesty hop aroma.

Brighton Bier SIBA

Unit 10, Bell Tower Industrial Estate, Roedean Road, Brighton, East Sussex, BN2 5RU ☎ 07967 681203 ⊕ brightonbier.com

Brighton Bier was established in 2012. Originally based at the Hand in Hand pub in Brighton, it moved into new premises in 2014 with the opening of a new 15-barrel brewery. Beers are available throughout the South-east, and increasingly across the country. The brewery also part-owns the Brighton Beer Dispensary pub in Brighton with Late Knights Brewery.

Thirty Three (OG 1035, ABV 3.3%)

Brighton Bier (ABV 4%)

West Pier (OG 1042, ABV 4%)

Underdog (ABV 4.2%)

IPA (OG 1062, ABV 5%)

No Name Stout (ABV 5%)

Grand Porter (ABV 5.2%)

Brightside SIBA

Unit 10, Dale Industrial Estate, Radcliffe, M26 1AD
☎ (0161) 725 9644 ☎ 07870 207442
⊕ brightsidebrewing.co.uk

Brightside is an 18-barrel plant established in 2009 which began commercial production in 2011. It moved from the back room of the family bakery into dedicated industrial premises in 2014 and continues to expand. In 2017 the brewery introduced the Wildside Beers range, usually one-off beers brewed in small batches. ◆

Odin (OG 1038, ABV 3.8%)
A fresh, light-bodied blonde ale with a fruity, citrus flavour and moderately bitter finish.

Our Town (OG 1040, ABV 4%)
A copper-coloured beer with tropical fruit flavoured hops and a maltiness and depth of flavour.

B-Side (OG 1042, ABV 4.2%)
Light and refreshing with fruity notes and a gentle malty, lightly bitter finish.

Best Bitter (OG 1044, ABV 4.3%)
A dark amber-coloured traditional English best bitter.

Underworld (OG 1049, ABV 4.4%)
A dry, medium-bodied porter. A little more bitter than you might expect from a traditional porter. Aromas of coffee and dried fruit.

Academy Ale (OG 1044, ABV 4.5%)

Darkside Stout (OG 1052, ABV 4.6%)
A jet black stout with flavours reminiscent of espresso coffee and dark chocolate, with more

than a touch of smoke on the finish. More hops than are usual for a stout enhance the roast malt bitterness.

Manchester Skyline (OG 1044, ABV 4.6%)
A deep golden-coloured beer with a complex flavour.

Maverick IPA (OG 1047, ABV 4.8%)
An amber-coloured IPA with a rich, malty base and punchy citrus hop character. Refreshingly bitter but not overpowering.

Amarillo (OG 1048, ABV 5%) ◆
Enticing fruity and hoppy aromatic start, gives way to a sweet, full mouth, developing a good balance with a long-lasting bitter finish.

Brightwater SIBA

9 Beaconsfield Road, Claygate, Surrey, KT10 0PN
☎ (01372) 462334 ☎ 07802 316389
⊕ brightbrew.co.uk

⊠ Established in 2013 at Claygate in Surrey, Brightwater is a five-barrel brewery producing traditional beers. The range is available at its brewery tap, Platform 3, outside Claygate Station, and other Surrey and South London pubs.

Little Nipper (OG 1033, ABV 3.3%) ◆
A rather thin hoppy bitter with a hint of a citrus taste and a bitter, slightly dry finish.

Top Notch (OG 1035, ABV 3.5%) ◆
Citrus notes dominate the aroma of this mid brown bitter. It has a reasonably well-balanced taste with some bitterness in the finish.

Daisy Gold (OG 1040, ABV 4%) ◆
Golden-coloured ale with a moderate tropical fruit hoppy character and some balancing malt leading to a bittersweet finish.

Wild Orchid (OG 1040, ABV 4%)
Dark oatmeal porter enhanced with a vanilla pod in each cask giving the beer fragrant vanilla undertones.

All Citra (OG 1043, ABV 4.3%)
Bitter with a hoppy bite and distinctly citrus flavour.

Brigstock

7 Park Walk, Brigstock, Northamptonshire, NN14 3HH
☎ (01536) 373428 ⊕ brigstockbrewhouse.co.uk

Philip Wilks began brewing in 2012 on a small 52-litre plant using local spring water. **RAIB**

Brimstage SIBA

Home Farm, Brimstage, Merseyside, CH63 6HY
☎ (0151) 342 1181 ☎ 07870 968323
⊕ brimstagebrewery.com

Brewing started in 2006 on a 10-barrel plant in a redundant farm dairy in the heart of the Wirral countryside. This is Wirral's first brewery since the closure of the Birkenhead Brewery in the late 1960s. More than 100 outlets are supplied across the Wirral, Merseyside, Cheshire and North Wales. ◆

Sandpiper Light Ale (OG 1036.5, ABV 3.6%)
A session beer, well-balanced, light and refreshing with tropical fruit flavours.

Trapper's Hat Bitter (OG 1037.5, ABV 3.8%)

Gold-coloured with a complex bouquet. It provides a mouthful of fruit zest, with hints of orange and grapefruit. A refreshingly hoppy session brew.

Rhode Island Red Rye (OG 1039, ABV 4%) ◆
Red-coloured, smooth and well-balanced malty beer with a good dry aftertaste. Some fruitiness in the taste.

Elderflower Wheat (ABV 4.1%)
A light, refreshing wheat beer brewed with dried elderflower. It has a delicate vanilla and honey-like aroma.

Scarecrow Bitter (OG 1041, ABV 4.2%)
Orange marmalade in colour, this well-balanced session brew has a distinct citrus fruit bouquet and a bitter finish.

Oyster Catcher Oatmeal Stout (ABV 4.4%)
Chocolate and vanilla flavours, with a rich smoothness due to added oatmeal.

IPA (OG 1055.5, ABV 6%)
A modern IPA with a floral aroma and dry bitter finish.

Brinkburn Street SIBA

Unit 1, Maling Court, Hoults Yard, Walker Road, Newcastle upon Tyne, NE6 2HL
☎ (0191) 260 0688 ⊕ brinkburnbrewery.co.uk

Brewing began in 2015, much influenced by West Coast US beer styles. Citrus flavours and highly-hopped bitterness is a feature of many of its beers.

Fools Gold Session (ABV 3.8%)

The Pursuit of Hoppiness Session (ABV 3.9%)

Byker Brown (ABV 4.8%)

Tino (ABV 4.8%)

Briscoe's

16 Ash Grove, Otley, West Yorkshire, LS21 3EL
☎ (01943) 466515 ✉ briscoe.brewery@talktalk.net

☺The brewery was launched in 1998 by microbiologist/chemist Dr Paul Briscoe in the cellar of his house with a one-barrel brew length. Dr Briscoe is currently producing one brew per week on his original plant, while several beers are produced on an irregular basis.

Otley Gold (OG 1040, ABV 3.9%)

Bristol Beer Factory SIBA

Unit A, The Old Brewery, Durnford Street, Ashton, Bristol, BS3 2AW
☎ (0117) 902 6317

Office: Tobacco Factory, Raleigh Road, Southville, Bristol, BS3 1TF ⊕ bristolbeerfactory.co.uk

⊠ A 30-barrel microbrewery in a part of the former Ashton Gate Brewing Co, which closed in 1933. A visitor centre opened in 2016. ‼ ▬ ◆ **RAIB**

Nova (OG 1040, ABV 3.8%) ◆
Citrus hop aroma to this straw-coloured, light-bodied and bitter session ale. Hop-led taste with lemon fruit and pale malt following into a bitter hop aftertaste.

Seven (OG 1043, ABV 4.2%) ◆
Mid-brown best bitter with a fruity aroma. Balanced malt and hops with hints of fruit and

caramel flavours. Malt and bitterness remain on the aftertaste.

Enigma (ABV 4.4%)

Milk Stout (OG 1049, ABV 4.5%) ◆
Sweet, full-bodied black stout with lactose creaminess. Finishes with smoky roast bitterness.

Independence (OG 1046, ABV 4.6%) ▣ ◆
Strong, hoppy aroma and initial flavour. Sweet fruitiness follows, leading to a bitter hoppy finish. Well-balanced with impressive flavour for its strength.

Britman

The Stables, Atelier Suite, Burton Manor, Burton, Cheshire, CH64 5SJ ☎ 07925 875836
✉ britmanbreweryburtonmanor@gmail.com

Britman is a small, quirky independent brewery established in 2013. It brews to the Reinheitsgebot German purity law, and produces vegetarian-friendly beers. The brewery has been recognised by the Sustainable Restaurants Association as a sustainable product; all spent grain is sent to happy pigs locally. ◆

Best Bitter (OG 1044, ABV 4.5%)
Smooth, light and pleasantly bitter.

London Porter (OG 1043, ABV 4.5%)
Dark, hoppy and slightly bitter with a treacle and coffee aftertaste.

Golden Ale (OG 1044, ABV 4.6%)
A true golden ale, hoppy and slightly bitter with a mild, sweet aftertaste.

Brixton SIBA

Arch 547, Brixton Station Road, Brixton, London, SW9 8PF
☎ (020) 3609 8880 ☎ 07761 436757
⊕ brixtonbrewery.com

Located in a railway arch in central Brixton, the brewery opened in 2013. The bulk of the production is currently bottled, but cask-conditioned ales feature as occasional guests in several pubs in the Brixton area. Beers are generally named after places in Brixton. ╦◆RAIB

Reliance Pale Ale (OG 1042, ABV 4.2%) ◆
Tropical notes and a little malt are noticeable in this refreshing amber-coloured beer. A gentle bitterness grows on drinking.

Effra Ale (OG 1045, ABV 4.5%) ◆
Dry, copper-coloured best bitter with peppery hops and fruit in flavour and bitter finish. A little caramel malt provides balance.

Atlantic APA (OG 1054, ABV 5.4%) ◆
A strong aroma of flowery hops, melon and citrus. Biscuit, grapefruit and melon flavours, with a little bitterness. Dry, complex finish.

Electric IPA (OG 1065, ABV 6.5%) ◆
Sweet biscuit balances the bitterness in this golden ale. Strong citrus, passion fruit and melon with spicy hop flavours. Dry, hoppy aftertaste.

Brockley SIBA

31 Harcourt Road, Brockley, London, SE4 2AJ
☎ 07814 584338 ⊕ brockleybrewery.co.uk

Established in 2013 by a group of local beer enthusiasts who installed a five-barrel plant in a converted builder's workshop. The brewery concentrates on supplying outlets within a four-mile radius. A bar is open on Friday and Saturday. ╦◆

Golden Ale (OG 1038, ABV 3.8%) ◆
A hoppy golden ale with some citrus throughout and a bitter finish. Trace of caramelised malt.

Pale Ale (OG 1041, ABV 4.1%) ◆
Well-balanced, dry, hoppy best bitter with some apricot fruit overlain with some biscuit malt.

Porter (OG 1043, ABV 4.3%) ◆
Roast malt with a hint of blackcurrant becoming more hoppy and bitter late in the taste and aftertaste.

Red Ale (OG 1048, ABV 4.8%)
A deep red-coloured ale; the malty backbone is complemented by a distinctive hoppy aroma.

IPA (OG 1052, ABV 5.2%)
Medium-bodied, amber-coloured beer. Citrus notes and hints of tropical fruit are followed by a bitter finish.

Brodie's

⬛ **816a High Road, Leyton, London, E10 6AE ☎ 07828 498733**

Office: Unit 40, 4 Lammas Road, Fairways Business Park, London, E10 7QT ⊕ brodiesbeers.com

Established in 2008 by James Brodie, beers are currently brewed using spare capacity at Rhymney Brewery (qv). A new 30-barrel plant is planned to accommodate international demand.

Citra (OG 1031, ABV 3.1%) ◆
Citrus and tropical fruit in aroma and flavour, which is dry and bitter and faintly sweet. Bitterness grows on drinking.

Mild (OG 1038, ABV 3.6%) ◆
Roast notes on the nose of this well-balanced black fruity mild. Some bitter character from the dark malt on the palate, which lingers into a dry finish.

Shoreditch Sunshine (OG 1038, ABV 3.9%)
A pale beer with lots of tropical aroma and character. Hops linger into the soft bitter aftertaste.

Bethnal Green Bitter (OG 1040, ABV 4%) ◆
A brown-coloured, refreshing but full-bodied bitter with a malty sweetness. Finish is dry with an increasing bitterness.

London Field Pale Ale (OG 1040, ABV 4%)
A refreshing golden-coloured beer with a strong hop character balanced by a biscuity sweetness. Long, dry aftertaste.

Piccadilly Pale Ale (OG 1042, ABV 4.2%)

Whitechapel Weissen (OG 1043, ABV 4.5%)
Prominent hops and banana yeast flavours complemented by an intensely hoppy long and dry finish.

Old Street Pale Ale (OG 1048, ABV 5%) ◆
Hops and citrus fruit are balanced in this golden beer by the bitterness, a biscuity sweetness and a creamy mouthfeel.

California (OG 1053, ABV 5.3%) ◆
Smooth yellow-coloured beer with a citrus fruit aroma. Sweet citrus fruit is balanced with bitterness on the palate and aftertaste.

Jamaican Stout (OG 1050, ABV 5.4%)
Complex roasted malt flavours with lots of hop flavours and aromas.

Saison Citron (OG 1058, ABV 6%)
Complex prominent spicy yeast flavours complemented by intense fresh citrus flavours. A long and dry finish.

Hackney Red IPA (OG 1058, ABV 6.2%)
A red-coloured American IPA full of citrus and tropical fruit flavours complemented by a malty roasted body, balanced by bitterness.

Hoxton Special IPA (OG 1064, ABV 6.6%)
Intense tropical and citrus aroma and flavours backed up with a strong biscuity malt body and balanced bitterness. A long, dry finish.

Dalston Black IPA (OG 1071, ABV 7%)
Huge tropical fruit flavour and aroma, balanced bitterness.

Kiwi IPA (OG 1062, ABV 7.1%) 🌱
A smooth-drinking yellow-coloured beer. Flavour is malty sweet overlaid by green fruit, a little hops and a bitter character.

Mocha Milk Stout (OG 1085, ABV 9%)
Complex dark roasted malt flavours with coffee, chocolate and sweet lactose shining through.

Romanov Empress Stout (OG 1110, ABV 12.1%)

Broken Bridge (NEW) SIBA

Unit 5, Lycroft Farm, Upper Swanmore, Hampshire, SO32 2QQ ☎ 07720 212895

Office: 2 Frys Cottage, Frys Lane, Meonstoke, Hampshire, SO32 3NL
✉ jim@brokenbridgebrewing.co.uk

⊠ Brewing began in 2016 in a small farm industrial unit previously housing Stumpy's Brewery. A 2.5-barrel plant is used with two fermenters, giving an annual capacity of 250 barrels. Many one-off brews complement the core range. ♦RAIB

Henchman (ABV 3.8%)

Broken Biscuit (ABV 4%)

No Chaff (ABV 4%)

Wayfarer (ABV 4%)

Hygge (ABV 4.2%)

It's 5 O'Clock Somewhere (ABV 5%)

Broughs

Unit 26, Steel Drive, Fordhouse Road Industrial Estate, Bushbury, Wolverhampton, West Midlands, WV10 9XD ☎ 07814 158292

Office: 192 Staveley Road, Wolverhampton, WV1 4RL
✉ broughsltd@yahoo.co.uk

⊚Broughs is a family-run brewery which began trading in 2008 using spare capacity at several breweries around the West Midlands region. In 2011 it moved into rented premises at the former Butlers Springfield brewery (1873-1991). Redevelopment of the site in 2015 forced Broughs to relocate to more modern premises. It continues to brew three times a week on its five-barrel plant. More than 30 outlets in the West Midlands, Staffordshire and Shropshire are supplied direct. ‼♦RAIB

Springfield (OG 1040, ABV 4%)

A light golden session ale with a subtle clean taste.

Light Pale Ale (OG 1042, ABV 4.2%)
Light, smooth and creamy ale with a subtle bitter finish.

Blonde (OG 1045, ABV 4.5%)
A hoppy and fruity pale yellow-coloured ale.

India Pale Ale (OG 1050, ABV 5%)
Traditional strong IPA bursting with a sweet, fruity, hoppy flavour. Followed by pleasant spices and bitterness to finish.

Sledgehammer (OG 1056, ABV 5.6%)
Traditional strong English IPA, dark golden colour and full of flavour with a subtle hop finish.

Superior (OG 1060, ABV 6%)
A strong, dark mild with a sweet, malty finish.

Broughton SIBA

Broughton, ML12 6HQ
☎ (01899) 830345 ⊕ broughtonales.co.uk

⊚Founded in 1979, Broughton Ales was then one of the first microbreweries. Broughton has developed since then and though more than 60% of production goes into bottle for sale in Britain and abroad, it retains a sizeable range of cask ales. All beers are suitable for vegetarians. ‼🏳♦

Hopopotamus (OG 1038, ABV 3.8%)

Greenmantle (OG 1038, ABV 3.9%)
A dark, bittersweet ale with a pleasant hop aftertaste.

Brewer's Gold (OG 1060, ABV 4%)

Clipper IPA (OG 1042, ABV 4.2%)
A light-coloured, crisp, hoppy beer with a clean aftertaste.

Merlin's Ale (OG 1042, ABV 4.2%) 🌱
A well-hopped, fruity flavour is balanced by malt in the taste. The finish is bittersweet, light but dry.

Dark 'n' Cloudy (OG 1046, ABV 4.4%)

Exciseman's 80/- (OG 1046, ABV 4.6%)
A traditional 80/- cask ale. A dark, malty brew with a good hop aftertaste.

Jeddart Justice (OG 1046, ABV 4.7%)

Dark Dunter (OG 1050, ABV 4.8%)
Bursting with oatmeal and chocolate aromas complemented by dark roasted malts and a rich aftertaste.

Proper IPA (OG 1050, ABV 5%)

6.2 IPA (OG 1060, ABV 6%)
With quadruple the hops of a typical IPA, this dark chestnut brown-coloured beer has a bold citrus aroma and a biscuit and bitter aftertaste.

Old Jock (OG 1070, ABV 6.7%) 🍺
Strong, sweet and fruity in the finish.

Brown Cow

Brown Cow Road, Barlow, North Yorkshire, YO8 8EH
☎ (01757) 618947 ⊕ browncowbrewery.co.uk

⊚Brewing since 1997, Brown Cow has won awards at many festivals. Keith and Sue Simpson operate a six-barrel plant at its maximum capacity of 17 barrels per week. Handcrafted cask beers brewed using traditional methods are delivered direct from the brewery. ♦RAIB V

Sessions (OG 1033, ABV 3.6%)
A pale, hoppy session beer with a refreshing finish and citrus notes in the aftertaste.

White Dragon (OG 1039, ABV 4%)
A pale, aromatic beer with a good level of bitterness, citrus undertones and a clean finish.

Over the Moon Gold (OG 1041, ABV 4.2%)
Well-balanced golden traditional English ale, round and full-flavoured with a smooth finish.

Captain Oates Mild (OG 1044, ABV 4.5%)
A dark mild with a complex mix of malts and oats. Well-balanced with undertones of coffee and chocolate.

Mrs Simpsons Thriller in Vanilla (OG 1049, ABV 5.1%)
A rich porter brewed with fresh vanilla pods complementing the dark malts.

Broxbourne

See Fallen Angel

Brumaison (NEW) SIBA

Unit 7, Crest Industrial Estate, Pattenden Lane, Marden, Kent, TN12 9QJ ☎ 07831 704089 ⊕ brumaison.beer

⊠ The name Brumaison came about from ideas to set up in a small village in France. However, Peter and Caroline decided to keep their 'Brewing Maison' in England after another brewery got there first. Trading since 2017, beers are available in the local area.

BB (OG 1036, ABV 3.6%)

GB (OG 1042, ABV 4.4%)

Brunning & Price

See Phoenix

Brunswick SIBA ◉

⌗ 1 Railway Terrace, Derby, DE1 2RU ☎ (01332) 410055 ☎ 07534 401352 ⊕ brunswickbrewingcompany.co.uk

Derby's oldest brewery, it is a 10-barrel tower plant built as an extension to the Brunswick Inn in 1991. Bought by Everards in 2002, the brewery is now run separately yet in conjunction with the pub. It supplies the Brunswick Inn, Everards, wholesalers and the free trade within 100 miles. Brunswick also swaps with other breweries.

White Feather (OG 1038, ABV 3.6%)
Pale yet full-bodied session beer, easy-drinking with a citrus twist.

Triple Hop (OG 1040, ABV 4%)
Straw-coloured ale with a bitter astringency.

The Usual (OG 1042, ABV 4.2%)
A traditional English malty best bitter, smooth with hints of toffee.

Railway Porter (OG 1045, ABV 4.3%)
A classic dark porter with chocolate and coffee notes, lightly hopped.

Rocket (OG 1047, ABV 4.7%)
A New World IPA with citrus, apricot and mango flavours.

Black Sabbath (OG 1058, ABV 6%)
A strong dark ale with finely balanced flavours of liquorice, coffee and chocolate.

Buccaneer (NEW)

Sycamore House, Sutton Quays Business Park, Sutton Weaver, Cheshire, WA7 3EH

Buccaneer began brewing in 2016. Beers are usually named with a pirate theme.

Bucks Star

23 Twizel Close, Stonebridge, Milton Keynes, Buckinghamshire, MK13 0DX ☎ (01908) 590054 ⊕ bucksstar.beer

⊠ Possibly the first microbrewery to be solar-powered from panels on the brewery roof, Bucks Star opened in 2015 using a 10-barrel, purpose-built plant. Only organic malt is used and no sugars or syrups are added. The beers are distributed to local pubs, restaurants and garden centres. ‼ ☞RAIB

No. 1 (OG 1040, ABV 4%)
A deep golden-coloured beer with a good balance between malt and hops. It has a light, dry and refreshing character with a lingering bitter finish.

Waltone (OG 1041, ABV 4%)
A refreshing wheat beer with a strong, distinctive taste.

Magiovinum (OG 1045, ABV 4.5%)
A dark, sweet stout.

Mideltone Pils (OG 1051, ABV 5%)
A dark lager wit a balanced hop aroma and flavour.

Bude

Unit 14c, Kings Hill Industrial Estate, Bude, Cornwall, EX23 8QN ☎ (01288) 359937 ⊕ budebrewery.co.uk

⊠ Originally established in 2011 near Launceston as Fry's Brewery, and now relocated to Bude, it started beer production under the Bude Brewery name in 2014.

Neet (OG 1037, ABV 3.7%)
An easy-drinking light bitter with hints of elderflower and citrus.

Porthbud (OG 1040, ABV 4%)
A session pale ale with a tropical, citrus taste.

Haven (OG 1042, ABV 4.2%) ◣
Amber-coloured best bitter with light hop aroma. Balanced hop and malt character in the mouth with fruit notes. Bitter finish.

Summerleaze (OG 1047, ABV 4.7%) ◣
Refreshing pale brown strong bitter. Sweet malt with stone fruit flavours balanced by hops, becoming bitter.

Black Rock (OG 1051, ABV 5.1%) ◣
Red porter with malt aroma. Sweet roast malt and stone fruit flavours with bitterness. Malt, hops and dry bitter finish.

Buffy's SIBA

Church Lane, Wicklewood, Norfolk, NR18 9QH ☎ (01953) 606962 ⊕ buffys.co.uk

⊠ Established in 1993, Buffy's brewing capacity is 20 barrels. The brewery owns two pubs, the

Wicklewood Cherry Tree, close to where the brewery has recently relocated, and the Foulden White Hart. Barley for all brewing is grown in Norfolk. Around 100 outlets are supplied. ◆ RAIB

Norfolk Terrier (OG 1038, ABV 3.8%) ◕
A strong plummy aroma leads into a sweet malty beginning. Caramel notes add depth to a long fruity finish.

Beagle (OG 1040, ABV 4%)

Mild (OG 1042, ABV 4.2%) ◕
Complex with a smooth but grainy feel. Caramel and blackcurrant initially bolster the heavy malt influence. Short malty finish.

Polly's Folly (OG 1043, ABV 4.3%) ◕
Well-balanced with a definitive malty spine. Elderberry notes and a long, dry, bittersweet finale.

Hopleaf (OG 1044.5, ABV 4.5%) ◕
A gentle hop nose. Strawberries mingle with the hops as the malt gently subsides to leave a bittersweet, dry finish.

Mucky Duck (OG 1044, ABV 4.5%) ◕
Roasted malt throughout with a sweet fruitiness giving depth without becoming dominant. Chewy mouthfeel and lingering finish.

India (OG 1046, ABV 4.6%)

Norwegian Blue (OG 1049, ABV 4.9%) ◕
Nutty caramel aroma. A well-balanced mix of malt and bitterness with caramel, hops, and sweetness. Strong, increasingly bitter finish.

Ale (OG 1055, ABV 5.5%)

Bull Lane

See Stables

Bullards ◉

7 The Arches, Bracondale, Trowse Newton, Norwich, NR1 2EF
☎ (01603) 624072 ⊕ bullardsbeers.co.uk

Beers were originally produced by Redwell brewery. Bullards is now a separate company sharing premises and brewer but not brewing kit. ◆

No. 4: Session IPA (OG 1041.8, ABV 3.8%)
A golden, juicy session beer packed full of American hops.

No. 5: Best Red Bitter (OG 1040, ABV 4%)
A deep red-coloured malty bitter.

No. 1: East Coast Pale Ale (OG 1042, ABV 4.2%) ◕
Grapefruit and lemon join the hoppy signature to create a distinctive, easy drinking brew. Well-balanced, complex strong finish.

No. 6: Rye Pale Ale (OG 1045, ABV 4.4%)
A brown rye ale brewed with spicy hops.

No. 3: Amber Ale (OG 1047, ABV 4.7%)
A malty amber-coloured ale with hints of caramel as well as peppery and fruity hops.

No. 2: India Pale Ale (OG 1058, ABV 6%)
A deep copper-coloured IPA full of rich caramel and burnt brown sugar flavours, with a bitter orange aroma.

Bullfinch

Arches 886 & 887, Rosendale Road, Herne Hill, London, SE24 9EH ☎ 07899 795823
⊕ thebullfinchbrewery.co.uk

Bullfinch began brewing in 2014 using a 2.5-barrel plant. Production is mainly keg but cask and bottle-conditioned beers are available. ‼ ⬝ RAIB

RosendAle (OG 1039, ABV 3.8%)
A traditional bitter with earthy hop notes.

South Eastern Bloc Stout (OG 1060, ABV 5.2%) ◕
Roasty nose and flavour with chocolate, earthy, plum notes. The finish is dry with some dark roast bitterness.

Bullhouse (NEW)

10 Greengraves Road, Newtownards, BT23 5AG
☎ 07562 702825

Brewing began in 2016 on a farm in Co Down where the old bull's house has been refurbished into a 2.5-barrel brewhouse producing a range of bottle-conditioned beers. RAIB

Bullmastiff SIBA

14 Bessemer Close, Leckwith, Cardiff, CF11 8DL
☎ (029) 2066 5292

Office: Units 7-8, Curran Rd Industrial Estate, Cardiff, CF10 5DF ✉ bob.bullmastiff@live.co.uk

The brewery has recently been purchased following the retirement of the founders Bob and Paul Jenkins. The new brewster, Ramphai, is believed to be the only Thai brewster currently brewing in the UK. The beers are still brewed using the founders' recipes and are available in Southeast Wales, with the JD Wetherspoon Bears Head in Penarth serving as the informal brewery tap. ◆

Slobberchops (OG 1046, ABV 4.6%)

Welsh Red (OG 1048, ABV 4.8%)

Olde Snarler (OG 1053, ABV 5.1%)

Son of a Bitch (OG 1062, ABV 6%) ◕
A complex, warming amber ale with a tasty blend of hops, malt and fruit flavours, with increasing bitterness.

Special Reserve (OG 1068, ABV 6.5%)

Buntingford

Greys Brewhouse, Therfield Road, Royston, Hertfordshire, SG8 9NW
☎ (01763) 250749 ☎ 07879 698541
⊕ buntingford-brewery.co.uk

⊠ Brewing commenced on the current site in 2005 and has expanded to a capacity of around 60 barrels per week. Two regular beers are brewed year round alongside seasonal/occasional brews and various themed specials. The beers are brewed using water from an on-site well and all liquid waste is treated in a reed bed. The brewery is located on a conservation farm and there is a wide variety of bird life visible from the doors of the brewhouse, often including rare and endangered species. ‼◆

Highwayman (OG 1036, ABV 3.6%)

Twitchell (OG 1038, ABV 3.8%) 🗂

Polar Star (OG 1045, ABV 4.4%)

Burley Street

■ Fox & Newt, 7-9 Burley Street, Leeds, LS3 1LD
☎ (0113) 245 4527 ⊕ burleystreetbrewhouse.co.uk

Burley Street Brewhouse is in the cellar of the Fox & Newt pub where the first brewery was installed by Whitbread in the 1980s. The freehold was purchased by the current owners and brewing recommenced in 2010 and then again, after a two-year break, in 2015 by the team from the Whippet Brewing Company. The Pack Horse at Woodhouse is the only other outlet supplied.

Burning Sky SIBA

Place Barn, The Street, Firle, East Sussex, BN8 6LP
☎ (01273) 858080 ⊕ burningskybeer.com

⊗ Burning Sky started brewing in 2013 using a 15-barrel plant, based on the Firle Estate in the South Downs. It is owned and run by Mark Tranter (ex-Dark Star head brewer). The brewery has its own yeast strains suited to the beer styles. It specialises in pale ales and Belgian-inspired farmhouse beers and has an extensive barrel-aging programme. RAIB

Plateau (OG 1035, ABV 3.5%)
Pale gold in colour, with a crisp malt edge and sharp bitterness.

Aurora (OG 1056, ABV 5.6%)
A premium pale ale, with a juicy malt backbone. Big citrus and tropical fruit flavours are prominent.

Devil's Rest IPA (OG 1070, ABV 7%)
A full-flavoured, hoppy IPA.

Burning Soul (NEW)

Unit 1, 51 Mott Street, Hockley, Birmingham, B19 3HE
☎ (0121) 439 1490 ☎ 07793 026624
⊕ burningsoulbrewing.com

Established in 2016 by Chris Small and Richard Murphy, who chose the name Burning Soul to reflect their passion for beer and brewing, it's a five-barrel full mash brewery with an on-site brewery tap. ‼️🍴♦

Mount Olympus (ABV 5.2%)
Yellow in colour with a crisp hop aroma. Aromatic hops in the taste with resinous flavours. A long bitter finish.

OCT IPA (ABV 6.7%)
Pale gold in colour with a fruity hop aroma and long, bitter aftertaste.

Coconut Porter (ABV 6.9%)
Dark brown in colour with coconut in the aroma. A good balance of malt and hops in the taste leading to a fruity aftertaste.

Burnside SIBA

Laurencekirk Business Park, Laurencekirk, Aberdeenshire, AB30 1EY
☎ (01561) 377316 ⊕ burnsidebrewery.co.uk

Burnside began brewing in 2010 using a 2.5-barrel plant and by 2012 had expanded to a 10-barrel plant. Since then the focus has been to establish the brand and range of cask-conditioned ales locally and to develop a range of bottle-conditioned beers. ‼️🍴RAIB

Black Katz (OG 1036, ABV 3.6%)

No 1 Pale Ale (OG 1036, ABV 3.6%)

3-BULLZ (OG 1038, ABV 3.8%)

Mad Dogz (OG 1038, ABV 3.8%) ◄
Slight mix of roasted malt and citrus hop session brew.

Golden X (OG 1042, ABV 4.1%)

Wild Rhino (OG 1045, ABV 4.5%)

Chieftains Export (OG 1048, ABV 4.6%)

India Pale Ale (OG 1049, ABV 4.8%) ◄
Full on citrus hop aroma declining through the taste.

After Dark (OG 1050.5, ABV 5%)
A double chocolate oatmeal stout.

M-PIRE (OG 1052, ABV 5.2%) ◄
Sweetish, peachy, hoppy brew. Very warming.

Stealth (OG 1058, ABV 6%)
A full-bodied, rich, dark ale.

Burscough

See Hop Vine

Burton Bridge SIBA 👁

24 Bridge Street, Burton upon Trent, Staffordshire, DE14 1SY
☎ (01283) 510573 ⊕ burtonbridgebrewery.co.uk

☺The brewery was established in 1982 by Bruce Wilkinson and Geoff Mumford and owns five pubs in the local area, including its CAMRA award-winning brewery tap. More than 300 outlets are supplied direct. ‼️🍴♦RAIB

Golden Delicious (OG 1037, ABV 3.8%) ◄
A Burton classic with sulphurous aroma and well-balanced hops and fruit. An apple fruitiness, sharp and refreshing start leads to a lingering mouth-watering bitter finish with a hint of astringency. Light, crisp and refreshing.

Sovereign Gold (OG 1040, ABV 4%) ◄
Sweet caramel aroma with a grassy hop start with malt overtones. Fresh and fruity with a bitterness that emerges and continues to develop.

XL Bitter (OG 1039, ABV 4%) ◄
Another Burton classic with sulphurous aroma. Golden with fruit and hops and a characteristic lingering aftertaste hinting of toffee apple sweetness.

XL Mild (OG 1040, ABV 4%)

Bridge Bitter (OG 1041, ABV 4.2%) ◄
Gentle aroma of malt and fruit. Good balanced start finishing with a robust hop mouthfeel.

Burton Porter (OG 1044, ABV 4.5%) ◄
Chocolate aromas and sweet, smooth taste of smoky roasted grain and coffee.

Damson Porter (OG 1044, ABV 4.5%)

Draught Burton Ale (OG 1048, ABV 4.8%) ◄
Fruity orange aroma leads to hoppy start, hop and fruit body then fruity aftertaste. Dry finish with fruity hints

Stairway to Heaven (OG 1049, ABV 5%) ◄
Golden bitter. A perfectly balanced beer. The fruity and hoppy start leads to a hoppy body with a mouthwatering finish.

**Top Dog Stout/Bramble Stout
(OG 1049, ABV 5%)** ◈
Black and rich with a roast and malty start. Fruity
and abundant hops give a fruity, bitter finish with a
mouthwatering edge. Also available as Bramble
Stout.

Festival Ale (OG 1054, ABV 5.5%) ◈
Caramel aroma with plenty of hop taste balanced
by a full-bodied malty sweetness.

Thomas Sykes (OG 1095, ABV 10%) ◈
Kid in a sweetshop aroma. Rich fruity spirited tastes
– warming and dangerously drinkable.

Burton Old Cottage IFBB

**Unit 10, Eccleshall Business Park, Unit 10, Eccleshall
Business Park, Burton upon Trent, Staffordshire,
DE14 1PT ☎ 07909 931250 ⊕ oldcottagebeer.co.uk**

☺The brewery was originally installed in the old
Heritage Brewery. When the site was taken over, it
moved to a modern industrial unit. The brewery
was sold in 2005, the following year saw heavy
investment in new production and storage facilities
by the new owners. ‼◆

Oak Ale (OG 1044, ABV 4%) ◈
Tawny, full-bodied bitter. A sweet start with
balanced fruit gives way to a slight roast taste with
some caramel for interest. A dry, hoppy finish
satisfies the palate.

Chestnut (OG 1042, ABV 4.2%)
A dark session ale with a touch of bitterness and a
pleasant, full aftertaste.

Stout (OG 1047, ABV 4.7%) ◈
Roast aroma with background fruit, roast tastes
with gentle sweetness. Bitterness develops
surprisingly from the sweet start to leave a sharp
edged mouthfeel. Roast throughout with a malt
background.

Pastiche (OG 1050, ABV 5.2%)
A smooth, balanced ale with a complex taste and
aroma.

Halcyon Daze (OG 1050, ABV 5.3%) ◈
Tawny and creamy with touches of hop, fruit and
malt aroma. Fruity taste and finish.

Burton Road (NEW)

✉ contact@burtonroadbrewing.co.uk

Burton Road is a Manchester brewery currently
focusing on bottle production. It is cuckoo brewing
in the Piccadilly area.

Burton Town SIBA

**Unit 8, Falcon Close, Burton upon Trent, Staffordshire,
DE14 1SG**
☎ (01283) 510839 ☎ 07595 333889 ⊕ burton.town

⊗ Brewing since 2015, Burton Town is run by head
brewer Helen Gallimore from converted premises
off Hawkins Lane. Currently using a six-barrel plant,
there are plans for expansion via crowdfunding. An
on-site tap is open to the public on Friday and
Saturdays and before Burton Albion home games.
‼ ☰ ◆ RAIB

Swan/Albion (OG 1040, ABV 3.9%)
Layers of toasted malt and a balanced hop finish in
this pale ale.

Scorned Woman (OG 1040, ABV 4%)

Dark Burton Ale (OG 1047, ABV 4.7%)
Caramel and malt notes with a vanilla and chestnut
finish.

Modwena (OG 1052, ABV 4.8%)
A thick, velvety oatmeal stout with chocolate
notes.

Thomcat (OG 1051, ABV 5.1%)
An unfined amber-coloured ale with a strong citrus
hop aroma and taste and a hint of biscuity
maltiness. A high, lingering bitterness with a dry
finish.

Burton IPA (OG 1054, ABV 5.6%)
A traditional strong IPA. Full-flavoured, with a hint
of toffee and a long-lasting bittersweet finish.

Burtonwood

**Bold Lane, Burtonwood, Warrington, Cheshire,
WA5 4TH**
☎ (01925) 220022 ⊕ thomashardybrewery.co.uk

Thomas Hardy's only brewery was acquired by
Molson Coors in 2015. Currently producing no real
ale, and operating solely as a contract brewer.

Bushy's SIBA

**Mount Murray Brewery, Mount Murray, Braddan, Isle
of Man, IM4 1JE**
☎ (01624) 661244 ⊕ bushys.com

☺Launched in 1986 as a brewpub, Bushys
relocated in 1990 when demand outgrew capacity.
Bushys goes one step further than the Manx Pure
Beer Law preferring the German Reinheitsgebot
(Pure Beer Law). ‼◆

Castletown Bitter (OG 1035, ABV 3.5%)
A light, golden beer full of floral and citrus hints. A
refreshing session beer.

Ruby (1874) Mild (OG 1035, ABV 3.5%) ◈
Classic full-bodied malty ruby mild with sweet
caramel flavours throughout, and well-balanced
hops.

Bitter (OG 1038, ABV 3.8%) ◈
A traditional malty and hoppy beer with good
balnace. The fruit lasts through to the bitter finish.

Old Bushy Tail (OG 1045, ABV 4.5%)
A reddish-brown beer with a pronounced hop and
malt aroma, the malt tending towards treacle.
Slightly sweet and malty on the palate with distinct
orangey tones. The full finish is malty and hoppy
with a hint of toffee.

Butchers Arms (NEW)

▤ Butchers Arms, Woolhope, Herefordshire, HR1 4RF
☎ (01432) 860281 ⊕ butchersarmswoolhope.com

Founded in 2016 in a building adjacent to the 17th
century Butchers Arms.

Butcombe SIBA ◉

Cox's Green, Wrington, Somerset, BS40 5PA
☎ (01934) 863963 ⊕ butcombe.com

⊗ Originally established in 1978, Butcombe was
bought by the Channel Islands-based Liberation
Group for a reported £15m in 2015. It moved to a
new purpose-built brewery with a 150-barrel plant

in 2005. Around 500 outlets are supplied direct and similar numbers via wholesalers and pub companies. The brewery has an estate of 13 managed and 12 tenanted pubs. ‼️🍽️♦

Adam Henson's Rare Breed (OG 1038, ABV 3.8%) 🍺
Sulphurous aroma with undertones of unripe fruit combine in this thin-bodied ale. Bitterness and astringency dominate and continue into the finish.

Original (OG 1039, ABV 4%) 🍺 🍺
A brown-coloured bitter with little aroma. Sweet and malty taste with faint fruit notes. The hop gradually asserts itself, leaving a slightly bitter finish.

Gold (OG 1045, ABV 4.4%) 🍺
Golden ale with light aroma of fruit and hops, leading to well-balanced flavours of malt, pale fruit and hops. Bitter aftertaste.

Bute

15-17 Columshill Street, Rothesay, Isle of Bute, PA20 0DN
☎ (01700) 504260 ☎ 07980 259511
🌐 butebrewco.co.uk

Situated in the centre of Rothesay on the Isle of Bute, brewing began in 2015. Beers are supplied to several local outlets, and further afield. Beer festivals are also supplied. ‼️

Scalpsie Blonde (OG 1038, ABV 3.8%)

Red (OG 1042, ABV 4.2%)

The Maids (OG 1043, ABV 4.3%)

Butts

Northfield Farm, Wantage Road, Great Shefford, Berkshire, RG17 7BY
☎ (01488) 648133 🌐 buttsbrewery.com

⊠ The brewery was set up in a converted barn in 1994. In 2002 the owners took the decision to become dedicated to organic production; all the beers brewed use organic malted barley and organic hops and are certified by the Soil Association. 🍽️♦RAIB

Jester (OG 1036, ABV 3.5%) 🍺
A pale brown session bitter with a hoppy aroma and a hint of fruit. The taste balances malt, hops, fruit and bitterness with a hoppy aftertaste.

Traditional (OG 1040, ABV 4%) 🍺
A pale brown bitter that is quite soft on the tongue with hoppy citrus flavours accompanying a gentle bittersweetness. A long, dry aftertaste is dominated by fruity hops.

Barbus Barbus (OG 1046, ABV 4.6%) 🍺
Golden ale with a fruity hoppy aroma and a hint of malt. Hops dominate taste and aftertaste, accompanied by fruitiness and bitterness, with a hint of balancing sweetness.

Buxton SIBA

Units 4, Staden Business Park, Staden Lane, Buxton, Derbyshire, SK17 9RZ
☎ (01298) 244200 ☎ 07754 015743
🌐 buxtonbrewery.co.uk

Buxton Brewery was set up in 2009 as a five-barrel brewery and now currently operates on a 24-barrel plant. Water is drawn from its own borehole. Its brewery tap is in Buxton and it exports to 25 countries. ♦RAIB

Moor Top (OG 1038, ABV 3.6%)
A pale ale with a refreshing grapefruit bitterness.

Rednik Stout (OG 1045, ABV 4.1%)
Classic stout with big roast malt character.

SPA (Special Pale Ale) (OG 1041, ABV 4.1%)

Axe Edge (OG 1065, ABV 6.8%)
IPA with big tropical and zesty fruit nose and palate.

Buzzard

Unit 3, Vale Park, Colomendy Industrial Estate, Denbigh, LL16 5TA ☎ 07972 202880
🌐 buzzardbrewery.co.uk

Brewing commenced in 2013 on a 2.5-barrel plant in a former farm building. The brewery has now relocated to Denbigh to larger premises. 30-50 pubs are supplied within a 30-mile radius. ♦

Buzzard Session Ale (BSA) (OG 1037, ABV 3.6%)

Hoppin Buzzard (OG 1038, ABV 3.9%)
A hoppy pale ale.

Village Bitter (OG 1039, ABV 3.9%) 🍺
A malty session bitter with a dry taste and subtle hop characteristics leading to a bitter finish.

Bwncath (OG 1042, ABV 4.2%)
A hoppy best bitter.

Pale of Clwyd (OG 1042, ABV 4.2%) 🍺
A light and fruity best bitter with a sweetish initial taste and a hoppy, dry finish.

Vale Ale (OG 1045, ABV 4.5%) 🍺
A dark-brown best bitter, smooth and malty with a dry, hoppy finish.

Golden Buzzard (OG 1045, ABV 4.7%)

Bwthyn

See Anglesey

By The Horns SIBA

Unit 25, Summerstown, London, SW17 0BQ
☎ (020) 3417 7338 🌐 bythehorns.co.uk

⊠ By the Horns began brewing in 2012 using a 5.5-barrel plant, since upgraded to a 12-barrel. It is located in an industrial unit near Wimbledon Stadium. The brewery tap is open six days a week (Tue-Sun) and hosts regular events. 🍽️

Stiff Upper Lip (OG 1038, ABV 3.8%) 🍺
A classic amber-coloured bitter, well-balanced with hops to the fore and a hint of citrus. Dry bitter finish.

Mayor of Garratt (OG 1042, ABV 4.3%) 🍺
Amber-coloured best bitter with sweet biscuit and orange fruit flavour. Long dry finish with some bitterness and peppery hop.

Diamond Geezer (OG 1049, ABV 4.9%) 🍺
Malty, hoppy red ale with blackcurrant, citrus and faint roast notes. Bitterness develops and builds in the aftertaste.

Lambeth Walk (OG 1051, ABV 5.1%) 🍺 🍺

Well-balanced black porter with hops and a little fruit throughout. The roasted bitterness is complemented by the malt notes.

By The Mile (NEW)

22 Detling Avenue, Broadstairs, Kent, CT10 1SL
☎ 07900 954680 ✉ jon@bythemilebrewery.co.uk

⊠ By the Mile began brewing in 2016 in domestic premises. RAIB

Snowdown Mild (OG 1036, ABV 3.7%)

Ramblers' Gold (OG 1039, ABV 4%)

Waypoint Bitter (OG 1040, ABV 4.2%)

Sea Breeze Ale (OG 1048, ABV 4.9%)

Gobbolino (OG 1051, ABV 5.1%)

Byatt's SIBA

Unit 7-8, Lythalls Lane Industrial Estate, Lythalls Lane, Coventry, CV6 6FL
☎ (024) 7663 7996 ⊕ byattsbrewery.co.uk

☺Byatt's was established in 2011. In 2016 it expanded to a 12-barrel plant, still located on the north side of Coventry, just two doors down from the old brewery. A brewhouse bar is open on Saturdays and some Sundays. Beers are supplied across the region. ‼🍺♦RAIB

XK Dark (OG 1038, ABV 3.5%) ◆
Liquorice aroma, soft smoky tastes. Sweet but giving hoppy sides. One to savour.

Coventry Bitter (OG 1039, ABV 3.8%)

Platinum Blonde (OG 1039, ABV 3.9%)

Big Cat (OG 1042, ABV 4%)

Phoenix Gold (OG 1043, ABV 4.2%)

Urban Red (OG 1047, ABV 4.5%)

Regal Blond (OG 1053, ABV 5.2%)

Cader SIBA

Unit 4, Marian Mawr Enterprise Park, Dolgellau, LL40 1UU ☎ 07931 734655 ⊕ caderales.com

Cader Ales was founded in 2012 by a husband-and-wife team. It was expanded in 2013 to its present five-barrel capacity. It is situated close to the centre of the picturesque market town of Dolgellau, which is also home to its brewery tap, the Unicorn. ‼

Cwrw Cregennan (ABV 3.8%)
A golden ale with citrus notes and soft malt flavour enhanced by a little local honey.

Gold (OG 1038, ABV 3.8%)
A light, hoppy golden ale with a subtle aroma of honey, lemon and tarragon.

Machlyd Mawddach (ABV 3.9%)
A light and refreshing ale with a fruity citrus aroma using kaffir lime leaves.

Idris Bitter (OG 1041, ABV 4.1%)
Traditional bitter with caramel and spicy notes.

Tallyllyn Pale Ale (OG 1044, ABV 4.4%)
Refreshingly bitter with citrus floral notes.

Red Bandit (OG 1050, ABV 5%)
A warm ruby-coloured ale based on a traditional recipe with spicy berry aromas.

Caffle

The Old School, Llawhaden, SA67 8DS
☎ (01437) 541502 ⊕ cafflebrewery.co.uk

⊠ Caffle began brewing in 2013 using a four-barrel plant producing ale in small batches, mainly for the local market. Each year a green hop ale is produced using Pembrokeshire grown hops via Caffle's hop co-op. ‼🍺RAIB

Skirp Gold (OG 1039, ABV 3.8%)
Golden ale with fruity, spicy aromas. Bitter grapefruit flavour.

Quay Ale (OG 1044, ABV 4%)
A amber-coloured ale, caramel with light hoppy citrus flavour. Balanced slightly to the malty side.

Sholly Amber (OG 1044, ABV 4%)
Light chestnut in colour with a good malt/hop balance.

Sprilly Maid (OG 1044, ABV 4%)
Light chestnut in colour and infused with rosemary to give a slight ginger finish.

Kift Blonde (OG 1044, ABV 4.3%)
Straw-coloured ale with citrus and floral notes, flavoured with nettle tips.

In The Grip (OG 1052, ABV 4.7%)
Ruby-red in colour, malty caramel, slightly sweet and warming.

Skaddly Puck (OG 1048, ABV 4.8%)
An IPA using a blend of hops to give a distinctive hoppy citrus flavour.

Drop Squint (OG 1052, ABV 5.2%)
Light golden in colour, smooth and clean-tasting with honey, malt and biscuit flavours.

Cairngorm SIBA ◉

Unit 12, Dalfaber Industrial Estate, Aviemore, PH22 1ST
☎ (01479) 812222 ⊕ cairngormbrewery.com

☺Cairngorm brews using a 20-barrel plant. Now with its own bottling line, it supplies the free trade as far south as the central belt and nationally via wholesalers. In 2016, in partnership with the Cobbs Group, it bought the brands of the Loch Ness Brewing Co and now brews selected beers under the Loch Ness brand name. ‼🍺♦

Nessies Monster Mash (OG 1040, ABV 4.1%) ◆
A good traditional English-type bitter with plenty of bitterness and strong malt flavour and a fruity background. Lingering bitterness in the aftertaste with diminishing sweetness.

Stag (OG 1040, ABV 4.1%) ◆
A fine best bitter with plenty of roast and hop throughout. This tawny brew also has plenty of malt in the lingering bittersweet aftertaste.

Trade Winds (OG 1043, ABV 4.3%) ◆
Citrus fruit, hop and elderflower nose leads to hints of grapefruit in the mouth. The bittersweetness in the taste lasts through the long, lingering aftertaste.

Black Gold (OG 1044, ABV 4.4%) 🍺 ◆
Roast malt dominates throughout, slight smokiness in aroma leading to a liquorice and blackcurrant background taste giving it a background sweetness. Very long, dry bitter finish.

Cairngorm Gold / Sheepshaggers Gold (OG 1044, ABV 4.5%) ◆

Fruit and hops to the fore with a hint of caramel in this sweetish brew.

Highland IPA (OG 1049, ABV 5%) ◆
Refreshing, light-coloured, citrus-hopped IPA.

Wildcat (OG 1049.5, ABV 5.1%) ◆
A full-bodied warming strong bitter. Malt predominates but there is an underlying hop character through to the well-balanced aftertaste. Drinks dangerously less than its strength.

Brewed under the Loch Ness Brewery brand name:

LightNESS (OG 1039, ABV 3.9%)

WilderNESS (OG 1039, ABV 3.9%)

CaithNESS (OG 1044, ABV 4%)

RedNESS (OG 1042, ABV 4.2%)

DarkNESS (OG 1052, ABV 4.5%)

SaaziNESS (OG 1045, ABV 4.5%)

HoppyNESS (OG 1050, ABV 5%)

LochNESS (OG 1049, ABV 5.1%)

Caledonian 👁

42 Slateford Road, Edinburgh, EH11 1PH
☎ (0131) 337 1286 ⊕ caledonianbeer.com

☺ The brewery was founded by Lorimer and Clark in 1869 and was sold to Vaux of Sunderland in 1919. In 1987 the brewery was saved from closure by a management buy-out and became independent. The brewery was purchased by S&N in 2004 and became part of Heineken in 2008. Guest beers, sometimes of an unusual style, are produced for occasions throughout the year, and there is a rolling programme of special beers covering each of the seasons. A pilot brewery 'Wee George' named after the founding father George Lorimer, was opened in 2015 to allow small scale brews of new recipes. ‼◆

Deuchars IPA (OG 1039.5, ABV 3.8%) ◆
Golden session ale with hop aroma and dry bitter finish. Malt adds body and there is a balancing fruity sweetness.

Edinburgh Castle 80/- (OG 1042.4, ABV 4.1%) ◆
A predominantly malty, brown beer with soft roast and caramel throughout. Fruit gives sweetness, typical of a Scottish 80/-.

Golden XPA (OG 1044, ABV 4.3%) ◆
Well-balanced golden ale with malt and fruit throughout, Hops come to the fore in the increasingly dry, bitter aftertaste.

Brewed for Heineken:

John Smith's Bitter (ABV 3.8%)

Calverley's SIBA

🍺 23a Hooper Street, Cambridge, CB1 2NZ
☎ (01223) 312370 ☎ 07769 537342
⊕ calverleys.com

This small central Cambridge brewery was started in 2013 by Sam Calverley and his brother Tom. The one-barrel plant is located in an old industrial unit close to the city centre. The major part of production is sold on the premises, but beer festivals and local pubs are supplied on demand.

Calvors SIBA 👁

Home Farm, Coddenham Green, Suffolk, IP6 9UN
☎ (01449) 711055 ⊕ calvorsbrewery.com

Calvors Brewery was established in 2008 and brews three craft lagers, as well as cask-conditioned beers.

Lodestar Festival Ale (OG 1038, ABV 3.8%)
A rich, straw-coloured ale with a gentle sweetness and a honey aroma.

Smooth Hoperator (OG 1040, ABV 4%)
A pale ale combining four different malts to give a copper colour and a background sweetness.

Session IPA (ABV 4.2%)
A crisp, light and hoppy IPA.

American Red (ABV 4.5%)
A red-coloured ale, malty but well balanced.

Cambridge

🍺 Cambridge Brew House, 1 King Street, Cambridge, CB1 1LH
☎ (01223) 858155 ⊕ thecambridgebrewhouse.com

Brewing began in 2013 on an on-site microbrewery in the Cambridge Brew House.

Cambrinus

See Liverpool Organic

Camden Town

55-59 Wilkin Street Mews, Kentish Town, London, NW5 3NN
☎ (020) 7485 1671 ⊕ camdentownbrewery.com

✗ No real ale. Bought by A-B InBev in 2016. A modern, automated brewhouse situated in five railway arches underneath Kentish Town West railway station with an on-site brewery tap. A second, new brewery in Ponders End opened in 2017. ‼

Camerons 👁

Lion Brewery, Stranton, Hartlepool, County Durham, TS24 7QS
☎ (01429) 852000 ⊕ cameronsbrewery.com

☺Founded in 1865, Camerons was bought in 2002 by Castle Eden. The brewery has an estate of more than 70, including the Head of Steam pubs. ‼☰◆

Best Bitter (OG 1036, ABV 3.6%) ◆
A light bitter, but well-balanced, with hops and malt.

IPA (OG 1038, ABV 3.8%)
A straw-coloured, light IPA.

Strongarm (OG 1041, ABV 4%) ◆
A well-rounded, ruby-red ale with a distinctive, tight creamy head; initially fruity, but with a good balance of malt, hops and moderate bitterness.

Trophy Special (OG 1040, ABV 4%)
An amber-coloured ale, slightly sweet and malty, fruity and hoppy.

A-Hop-Alypse Now (ABV 4.3%)
A golden-coloured ale with a citrus aroma and full hop flavour.

Gold Bullion (OG 1043, ABV 4.3%)

Gold-coloured, full-bodied ale with a good hop flavour.

Campervan SIBA

PO Box 28626, Comely Bank, Edinburgh, EH4 9DQ
☎ 07786 566000 ⊕ campervanbrewery.com

Campervan began brewing in 2016 in a private garage but also in a 1973 VW campervan, hence the name. The van is used as a mobile sales outlet at beer festivals and other outdoor events. It expanded to a new 10-barrel facility in Edinburgh in 2017.

Blonde Voyage (OG 1038, ABV 3.8%)

All Shook Up (OG 1040, ABV 4%)

Mutiny on the Bounty (OG 1042, ABV 4.2%)

Cannon Royall IFBB

⬢ Fruiterer's Arms, Uphampton Lane, Uphampton, Worcestershire, WR9 0JW
☎ (01905) 621161 ⊕ cannonroyall.co.uk

Cannon Royall's first brew was in 1993 in a converted cider house behind the Fruiterer's Arms. The brewery supplies a number of mainly local outlets.

Fruiterers Mild (OG 1037, ABV 3.7%) ◤
Fruity aroma with a hint of damsons, slightly sweet fruity taste balanced with roasted malt. Fruity finish with smoky malt undertones.

Hunny Bear (OG 1038, ABV 3.8%)

King's Shilling (OG 1038, ABV 3.8%)

Arrowhead Bitter (OG 1039, ABV 3.9%) ◤
Well-balanced, fruity aroma with hints of banana, fruit and hop taste with mango and peach, followed by a long, sweet, hoppy finish.

Arrowhead Extra (OG 1043, ABV 4.3%)
A hop punch leads to a smooth palate and pleasant finish with a good malt balance.

Best Bitter (OG 1043, ABV 4.3%) ◤
Hops with a slight hint of gooseberry aroma followed by a slightly sweet hop and grapefruit taste then a dry finish.

Blond Bombshell (OG 1043, ABV 4.3%)

Grapeshot (OG 1043, ABV 4.3%)
Gold in colour with a citrus bite.

Hood (OG 1043, ABV 4.3%)

Teddy Bear (OG 1043, ABV 4.3%)
A pale, easy-drinking bitter.

Canopy SIBA

Arch 1127, Bath Factory Estate, 41 Norwood Road, Herne Hill, London, SE24 9AJ
☎ (020) 8671 9496 ⊕ canopybeer.com

⊠ Canopy started brewing in 2014 and opened a tap room in 2015. ‼ ◆ RAIB

Sunray Pale Ale (ABV 4.2%)
A light-coloured pale ale, refreshing and hoppy.

Champion Kölsch (ABV 4.5%)
Crisp, fresh and light, this is a Kölsch-style beer based on the Cologne original.

Full Moon Porter (ABV 5%)

Rich flavours of chocolate, caramel and coffee with light hop notes on the finish.

Brockwell IPA (ABV 5.6%)
Smooth and rounded with a tropical fruit hop flavour. A hoppy, easy-drinking IPA.

Troy Town Saison (ABV 6.1%)

Canterbury Ales SIBA

Unit 7, Stour Valley Business Park, Ashford Road, Chartham, Kent, CT4 7HF
☎ (01227) 732541 ☎ 07944 657978
⊕ canterbury-ales.co.uk

⊠ Brewing commenced in 2010. In addition to the six regular beers, two new specials are brewed each month. These specials include single hop varieties, regional and international styles showcasing a particular country's hops. ‼ ◆

The Pardoner's Ale (OG 1037, ABV 3.8%)
A light session pale ale with honey notes, citrus hops and a gentle spiciness.

The Wife of Bath's Ale (OG 1038, ABV 3.9%) ◤
A golden beer with strong bitterness and grapefruit hop character, leading to a long, dry finish.

The Merchant's Ale (OG 1043, ABV 4%)
A mild stout with a hint of hops in the smooth, fruity, roasted base giving a clean finish.

The Reeve's Ale (OG 1040, ABV 4.1%)
Copper-coloured bitter with berry fruit hops and a clean, hoppy finish.

The Miller's Ale (OG 1044, ABV 4.2%)
A red-coloured best bitter with toffee malts and rich, fruity hops with a hint of citrus.

The Knight's Ale (OG 1047, ABV 4.6%)
A dark red-coloured malty old ale with earthy hops and a smooth, long malty finish.

Canterbury Brewers ◉

⬢ Foundry Brew Pub, White Horse Lane, Canterbury, Kent, CT1 2RU
☎ (01227) 455899 ⊕ thefoundrycanterbury.co.uk

Canterbury Brewers started brewing in the Foundry Brewpub (formerly a Victorian foundry) in the heart of Canterbury in 2011. The six-barrel plant is purpose-built. Gluten-free bottled beer is planned. Beer is also supplied to events and beer festivals.

Cap House

444-446 Bradford Road, Batley, West Yorkshire, WF17 5LW
☎ (01924) 479909 ☎ 07981 858270
⊕ caphousebrewery.co.uk

☺Cap House began in 2011 using a 2.5-barrel plant as a joint venture between Peter Lister, who has a plastics business at the location, and Gary Wardman of the Reindeer Inn in Overton, which is the brewery tap. ◆

Miners A Pint (OG 1038, ABV 3.8%)
A tangy session bitter with a smooth mouthfeel balanced by a toffee undertone and a deep, dry finish with lingering fruit notes.

Hey Blondie (OG 1044, ABV 4.2%)
A light, golden ale.

Hoppylicious (OG 1040, ABV 4.2%)

A light hoppy beer with a well-balanced fruity taste. Refreshing citrus and grapefruit flavours for a bittersweet finish.

Temptress (OG 1054, ABV 5.6%)
A rich, ruby red ale with a smooth finish with fruity nut/toffee aroma and a tangy palate.

Captain Cook 👁

White Swan, 1 West End, Stokesley, North Yorkshire, TS9 5BL
☎ (01642) 710263 ⊕ captaincookbrewery.com

☺The Captain Cook Brewery is located behind the 18th-century White Swan pub. The brewery, which started in 1999, uses a four-barrel plant. Under new ownership from July 2017. ‼◆

Botany Bay (OG 1040, ABV 4%)
A light ale with a hint of grapefruit and spruce.

Sunset (OG 1040, ABV 4%)
A smooth, light ale with hint of citrus.

Slipway (OG 1042, ABV 4.2%)
A light-coloured, full-flavoured, hoppy ale with a smooth malt aftertaste.

Endeavour (OG 1043, ABV 4.3%)
Brown-coloured ale with a bitter finish.

Black Porter (OG 1044, ABV 4.4%)
Chocolate notes and dominant roast flavours lead to a dry, bitter finish.

IPA (OG 1051, ABV 5.1%)

Carbon Smith SIBA

80 North Western Street, Manchester, M12 6DY
☎ 07518 106487 ⊕ carbonsmith.co.uk

✖ Carbon Smith started brewing in a fourth-floor tenement flat bedroom in Edinburgh before moving to a small unit in Newington with a self-built and designed two-barrel plant. It moved to a archway near Piccadilly station in Manchester in 2016. ◆

Carlisle SIBA 👁

Unit 2, 12a Kingstown Broadway, Kingstown Industrial Estate, Carlisle, Cumbria, CA3 0HA
☎ (01228) 594959

Office: Spinners Arms, Cummersdale, Carlisle, Cumbria, CA2 6BD ⊕ thespinnersarms.org.uk

☺Carlisle Brewing Company is a family-run brewery established in 2013. Initially using a 2.5-barrel plant in a shed behind the owner's freehouse, by 2015 it had expanded to a 10-barrel plant in an industrial unit. Beer is available in the Spinners Arms and other local outlets. ‼◆GF

Bell (ABV 3.8%)
A pale ale with light citrus and tropical fruit flavours. Gluten-free.

Spun Gold (OG 1043, ABV 4.2%)
A gold-coloured ale with a sweet taste followed by hops to complement the balanced finish.

Flaxen (OG 1042, ABV 4.5%)
A blonde ale, well-balanced with a hoppy bouquet.

Magic Number (OG 1045, ABV 4.5%)
A premium bitter with caramel and toffee flavours, lightly bittered to give a refreshing, malty beer.

Oatmeal Stout (OG 1048, ABV 4.5%)
A well-balanced stout with a soft mouthfeel and coffee, chocolate and dark smoke aromas.

Nut Brown (OG 1048, ABV 4.7%) 🔹
Sweet, mild and characterful amber ale with predominately nutty and roast flavours to make a long, quaffable strong ale.

The Carlisle Experiment (ABV 5.6%)
An international pale ale with a fresh, citrus taste.

Carlsberg-Tetley

Jacobson House, 140 Bridge Street, Northampton, NN1 1PZ
☎ (01604) 668866 ⊕ carlsberg.co.uk

International lager brewery, which, while brewing no real ale, is a major distributor of cask beer. The Tetley-owned real ales are brewed under contract by Marston's.

Castle SIBA

Unit 9a-7, Restormel Industrial Estate, Liddicoat Road, Lostwithiel, Cornwall, PL22 0HD ☎ 07880 349032 ⊕ castlebrewery.co.uk

The brewery was established in 2007 using a one-barrel plant. It was re-equipped in 2016 with a new 200-litre plant. All brews are unfined, and are suitable for vegans. The brewery carries out its own bottling, and some for other breweries. ◆RAIB V

Golden Gauntlet (OG 1040, ABV 4%) 🔹
Light, golden bitter with gentle fruity nose. Heavy malt and bitter taste dominate the fruity hop, persisting into the finish.

Cornish Best Bitter (OG 1042, ABV 4.2%)

Once a Knight (OG 1050, ABV 5%)

Castle Combe

See Flying Monk

Castle Eden (NEW)

8 East Cliff Road, Spectrum Business Park, Seaham, SR7 7PS
☎ (0191) 581 5711 ☎ 07768 044484 ⊕ castleedenbrewery.com

Small independent brewery that has its own range of ales as well as undertaking contract brewing. ◆

Castle Rock SIBA 👁

Queensbridge Road, Nottingham, NG2 1NB
☎ (0115) 985 1615 ⊕ castlerockbrewery.co.uk

☺Castle Rock was established in 1998. From small beginnings, the brewery now has a capacity of 360 barrels per week, distributed through its estate of 22 pubs and further afield via wholesalers. Regular beers produced include a core range of four, three rotating beers combining traditional and modern styles, a variety of yearly seasonals and specials, which include four Nottinghamian Celebration Ales a year, plus an offshoot range of experimental, unfined, vegan-friendly beers called The Traffic Street Specials. ‼◆RAIB V

Sheriff's Tipple (OG 1034, ABV 3.4%) 🔹
Tawny-coloured malty beer with Goldings hops.

Black Gold (OG 1037, ABV 3.8%) ◥
A dark ruby mild. Full-bodied and fairly bitter.

Harvest Pale (OG 1037, ABV 3.8%) ◥
Pale yellow-coloured beer, full of hop aroma and flavour. Refreshing with a mellow aftertaste.

Red Riding Hood (OG 1042.5, ABV 4.3%) ◥
Reddish brown-coloured fruity bitter with initial malt, caramel and hops leading to a lasting, malty, bitter finish.

Preservation Fine Ale (OG 1044, ABV 4.4%) ◥
A traditional copper-coloured English best bitter with malt predominant. Fairly bitter with a residual sweetness.

Sherwood Reserve (OG 1045, ABV 4.5%) ◼ ◥
An earthy yet smooth tasting dark stout with a smoked roastness through to a roast bitter finish.

Elsie Mo (OG 1045, ABV 4.7%) ⬚ ◼ ◥
A strong golden ale with floral hops evident in the aroma. Citrus hops are mellowed by a slight sweetness.

Midnight Owl (OG 1055, ABV 5.5%) ⬚ ◥
Black IPA with roast malts, fruity hops and a slightly sweet finish.

Screech Owl (OG 1055, ABV 5.5%) ⬚ ◥
A classic golden IPA with an intensely hoppy aroma and bitter taste with a little balancing sweetness.

Castlegate SIBA

Unit 13, Cillefwr Industrial Estate, Johnstown, SA31 3RB
☎ (01267) 468150
✉ castlegatebrewery@outlook.com

Castlegate began brewing in 2015 as a one-man operation. RAIB

Best Bitter (OG 1044, ABV 4.4%)

Towy Gold (OG 1044, ABV 4.4%)

Merlins Own (OG 1052, ABV 5.2%)

Castles SIBA 👁

Symondscliffe Way, Caldicot, NP26 5PW
☎ (01291) 422032 ☎ 07825 992604
⊕ castlesbrewery.co.uk

Brewing began in 2014. Capacity increased in 2015 to seven barrels and a brewery shop was opened. ⌂ ◆ RAIB

Court Jester (OG 1038, ABV 3.8%)
A session pale ale with vibrant tropical aromas and a fruity taste.

White Knight (OG 1041, ABV 4.1%)
American-style pale ale with a peach aroma.

Portcullis (OG 1042, ABV 4.2%)
A russet-coloured ale with a vibrant tropical fruit aroma. Full-bodied with a malty yet rounded taste.

Kings Reserve (OG 1043, ABV 4.3%)
Amber-coloured ale brewed with a blend of malts. An orange, dry taste.

Ironclad (OG 1052, ABV 5%)
An American-style IPA. Dry and fruity on the palate with hints of pithy orange and mango backed up with sweet malt.

Castor SIBA

30 Peterborough Road, Castor, Cambridgeshire, PE5 7AX
☎ (01733) 380337 ⊕ castorales.co.uk

This three-barrel brewery, established in 2009, is located in a specially converted outhouse in the garden of the founder brewer. Several local outlets feature the beers as well as many national beer festivals. ‼ ◆

Roman Gold (OG 1037, ABV 3.7%)
A golden-coloured session bitter with refreshing citrus and fruit notes.

Hopping Toad (OG 1040, ABV 4.1%)
A light golden bitter with a refreshing citrus, flowery finish and a fruity aftertaste.

Salters Tree (OG 1043, ABV 4.3%)
Biscuit malt gives a sweetness balanced by a bitter hoppy finish.

Old Scarlet (OG 1045, ABV 4.6%)
A ruby-coloured malty beer balanced by subtle hops with a fine aroma and citrus finish.

Caveman

The Cave (below The George & Dragon), 1 London Road, Swanscombe, Kent, DA10 0LQ ☎ 07900 234644 ⊕ cavemanbrewery.co.uk

Caveman began brewing in 2012 and moved to its current site beneath the George & Dragon pub in 2013 using a four-barrel plant. It is named for the local discovery in the 1930s of skull fragments from a Palaeolithic human, then the oldest remains found in the UK. Beers can be found nationwide through various wholesalers with direct supply to London, Kent and parts of Sussex. ◆ RAIB

Palaeolithic (OG 1038, ABV 3.8%)
A pale ale, hoppy with some slight malt sweetness.

Neolithic (OG 1041, ABV 4.1%)
A hoppy pale ale with a straightforward malt character that lets the citrus, grapefruit and pine hop flavours shine through.

Neanderthal (OG 1044, ABV 4.4%)
An ale full of roast and caramel malt flavours and traditional Kent hops.

Cavedweller (OG 1059, ABV 5.8%)
A rich porter with a full body and balanced hop bitterness. Chocolate and coffee notes come through in the malt and dark berry flavours from the hops.

Caythorpe SIBA

⬚ c/o Black Horse, 29 Main Street, Caythorpe, Nottinghamshire, NG14 7ED
☎ (0115) 966 4933 ☎ 07807 583724

Office: Trentham Cottage, Boat Lane, Hoveringham, Nottinghamshire, NG14 7JP
⊕ caythorpebrewery.co.uk

Established in 1996 using a 2.5-barrel plant in a building at the rear of the Black Horse pub, the brewery upgraded to a six-barrel plant in 2010.

Cellar Head (NEW) SIBA

Unit 16, New Place Farm, Pump Lane, Framfield, East Sussex, TN22 5EQ
☎ (01825) 890078 ⊕ cellarheadbrewing.com

Cellar Head is a microbrewery in the heart of the Weald countryside.

Session Bitter (ABV 3.5%)

Golden Ale (ABV 4.3%)

Single Hop Ale (ABV 4.6%)

India Pale Ale (ABV 5%)

Celt Experience

See Evan Evans

Cerddin SIBA

■ c/o Cross Inn, Maesteg Road, Cwmfelin, CF34 9LB
☎ (01656) 732476 ☎ 07949 652237
⊕ cerddinbrewery.co.uk

Established in 2010 using a 2.5-barrel plant with conditioning and malting rooms in a converted garage adjacent to the owner's pub, now enlarged to a four-barrel plant. Beer is usually only available in the pub.

Cerne Abbas SIBA

Black Hill Barn, Sherborne Road, Cerne Abbas, Dorset, DT2 7SJ ☎ 07506 303407

Office: The Mill House, Mill Lane, Cerne Abbas, Dorset, DT2 7LB ⊕ cerneabbasbrewery.com

⊠ Established in 2014 using a five-barrel plant, the beers are made as naturally as possible using local, chalk-filtered water. Many seasonal beers are produced, occasionally using locally-sourced barley and interesting non-conventional ingredients. ♦

Responsibly (OG 1035, ABV 3.2%)
A well-balanced English pale ale.

Ale (OG 1040, ABV 3.8%)
A well-balanced tawny-coloured ale with a full mouthfeel and refreshing finish.

Blonde (OG 1042, ABV 4.2%)
Single-hopped blonde ale.

Watercress Warrior (OG 1042, ABV 4.5%)
A pale ale made using local watercress; crisp with distinct spicy and mineral tones.

Gurt Stout (OG 1058, ABV 6.2%)
Silky smooth, full-bodied and rich stout.

Chadlington

Chapel Road, Chadlington, Oxfordshire, OX7 3LZ
☎ 07931 482807 ⊕ chadlingtonbrewery.com

Chadlington began brewing in 2015 on an occasional basis using local spring water, supplying the local area. A new 12-barrel plant is planned. ♦

Golden Ale (OG 1040, ABV 4%)
Light, fruity and refreshing golden ale.

Oxford Blonde (OG 1040, ABV 4%)
A well-balanced, light and refreshing golden ale.

Chadwick's

Unit 16, Castle Mills, Aynam Road, Kendal, Cumbria, LA9 7DE ☎ 07983 543724 ⊕ chadwicksbrewery.co.uk

⊚Chadwick's Brewery is based in the historic town of Kendal. Established in 2014 it is situated on the old Goodacre Carpets site.

Castle Mills Mild (OG 1036, ABV 3.6%) ◣
A well-balanced traditional, fruity dark mild.

Kirkland Blonde (OG 1036, ABV 3.6%) ◣
A pale ale with a slight bitter finish.

Miller Bridge Bitter (OG 1040, ABV 4%) ◣
A refreshing, malty brown ale with a sweetish middle. The long finish is gently hoppy and roasty.

Castle Pale (OG 1042, ABV 4.2%) ◣
A well-balanced, sweet and fruity beer with a full palate and a long-lasting bitter finish.

Chalk Hill

■ Rosary Road, Norwich, NR1 4DA
☎ (01603) 477078 ⊕ thecoachthorperoad.co.uk

Chalk Hill began production in 1993 on a 15-barrel plant. It supplies local pubs and festivals.

Tap Bitter (OG 1036, ABV 3.6%) ◣
Well-balanced with a light, hoppy character in both aroma and taste. Malt provides contrast. Short dry and bitter finish.

CHB (OG 1042, ABV 4.2%) ◣
Yeasty aroma with malt and hop. Light biscuity airs flow over malt and floral hoppiness. Good balance, gentle finish.

Gold (OG 1043, ABV 4.3%) ◣
A light, hoppy nose. Grapefruit, banana and hops mingle in a well-balanced beginning. The finish develops a growing bitterness.

Dreadnought (OG 1049, ABV 4.9%) ◣
Red brown beer with a malty, sulphurous nose. Malty with fruit and nut notes. Full-bodied with a long finish.

Chantry SIBA

Units 1 & 2, Callum Court, Gateway Industrial Estate, Parkgate, Rotherham, South Yorkshire, S62 6NR
☎ (01709) 711866 ☎ 07766 384606
⊕ chantrybrewery.co.uk

☺Brewing returned to Rotherham with the opening of Chantry in 2012 using the latest brewing technology in a 20-barrel state of the art plant built by Sheffield-based Moeschle UK. ‼♦

New York Pale (OG 1039, ABV 3.9%)
A refreshing pale ale with a hint of citrus flavours and a crisp, dry finish.

Iron & Steel Bitter (OG 1040, ABV 4%)
Chestnut-coloured bitter, full-flavoured with subtle hints of dark fruits.

Steelos (ABV 4.1%)
Easy-drinking, well-balanced ale with light, subtle citrus aromas of sweet orange, apricot and blackcurrant.

Diamond Black Stout (OG 1045, ABV 4.5%)
A full-bodied stout with liquorice tones and subtle hints of chocolate and coffee.

Kaldo (ABV 5.5%)
An English pale ale, well-balanced with a subtle citrus taste and hints of orange and grapefruit.

Special Reserve (ABV 6.3%)
Rich and full-bodied with undertones of liquorice and toffee.

Chapel

Dinesfield, Chapel Lane, Criftins, Shropshire, SY12 9LZ
☎ (01691) 690412 ☎ 07928 682174
⊕ chapelbrewery.co.uk

☺Chapel began brewing in 2013 using a one-barrel plant behind the owner's bungalow. In 2016 the brewery moved to larger premises across the road. Occasional specials are brewed for festivals.

Angels Share (OG 1040, ABV 4%)

Miracle (OG 1044, ABV 4.4%)

Babylon (OG 1048, ABV 5%)

Chapel-en-le-Frith (NEW)

5 Market Place., Chapel-en-le-Frith, Derbyshire, SK23 0EW ☎ 07951 524003
✉ timboothman@aol.com

Opened in 2016, this is a small operation located at the rear of Chapel-en-le-Frith Post Office. The brewing kit consists of a single 200-litre capacity integrated system supplemented by a 60-litre trial kit. Beers are available in bottles and five-litre minicasks from Chapel-en-le-Frith and Whaley Bridge Post Offices. Casks are available from a limited number of local outlets. RAIB

Siena (OG 1041, ABV 4.1%)
A crisp, light ale hopped to give a unique balance of flavour and aroma.

Leningrad (OG 1052, ABV 5%)
A strong ruby red-coloured ale full of malt character.

Elysium Amber Ale (OG 1056, ABV 5.4%)
A full-bodied, rich, sweet and malty amber-coloured ale with a clean, crisp bitter finish.

Acadian (OG 1057, ABV 5.6%)
A New England-style IPA with a delicate malt character and a crescendo of tropical citrus fruit hop flavours.

Hoppy as Funk (OG 1055, ABV 5.8%)
A light ale with a strong malt backbone, finished with a blend of citrus flavour hops.

Sinamarian (OG 1060, ABV 6%)
A smooth, dry black IPA with rich roast flavours and hints of chocolate, finished with tropical fruit flavour hops.

Chapel Street

🍴 Thatched House, Ball Street, Poulton-le-Fylde, Lancashire, FY6 7BG ☎ 07963 860080
⊕ thatchedhousepoulton.co.uk

This four-barrel plant is situated in the coach house of the award-winning Thatched House pub in Poulton-le-Fylde and has been brewing almost to capacity since opening in 2014. High local demand means that the whole of production is sold in the pub, at a few local outlets plus selected beer festivals.

Chapter (NEW)

Unit 2a, Sutton Quays Business Park, Clifton Road, Sutton Weaver, Cheshire, WA7 3EH ☎ 07791 516948
✉ chapterbrewing@gmail.com

Chapter Brewing was established in 2016 using a 10-barrel brew plant. RAIB V

Bread and Circuses Pale (ABV 3.9%)
A session pale ale.

Dead Man's Fist Smoked Porter (ABV 5.5%)
A smoked porter with freshly crushed black pepper.

As Lazarus IPA (ABV 6.2%)
An IPA with a different aroma hop used for each brew.

Charnwood SIBA ⊙

22 Jubilee Drive, Loughborough, Leicestershire, LE11 5XS
☎ (01509) 218666 ☎ 07872 651561
⊕ charnwoodbrewery.co.uk

☺Charnwood is a family-run 10-barrel brewery established in 2014 in a former mozzarella factory. Beers are available in many local pubs. The front of the building has been fitted out as a shop, bar and reception area, with large glass windows giving a good view into the brewery. ‼🍴♦

Salvation (OG 1038, ABV 3.8%)
A light, refreshing golden-coloured ale with tropical fruit, citrus and floral flavours. A citrus aroma, and crisp, clean bitterness on the finish.

Vixen (OG 1040, ABV 4%)
A well-balanced, copper-coloured best bitter with subtle hints of honey, spice and hedgerow fruits. A fruity hop nose and finish.

Checkstone

🍴 First & Last Inn, 10 Church Street, Exmouth, Devon, EX8 1PE
☎ (01395) 263275

Checkstone Brewery, named after the Checkstone reef outside the Exe Estuary, is a one-barrel plant inside the First & Last pub, Exmouth, established in 2016. Like the brewery, the beers are named after various sea features around Exmouth.

Cheddar SIBA ⊙

Winchester Farm, Draycott Road, Cheddar, Somerset, BS27 3RP
☎ (01934) 744193 ⊕ cheddarales.co.uk

⊗ Established in 2006 in the heart of the Mendips, Cheddar Ales has expanded capacity to enable it to brew up to 100 barrels a week. Production is split approximately 75% cask-conditioned ale with the remainder bottle conditioned. Its bottling plant produces around 120,000 bottles annually. Around 450 outlets are supplied including pubs, clubs and off trade. ‼🍴♦RAIB

Bitter Bully (OG 1038.5, ABV 3.8%) 🍺
Light session bitter with flowery hops on the nose and a dry, bitter finish.

Gorge Best (OG 1040, ABV 4%) 🍺
Malty bitter with caramel and fruit notes followed by a short bittersweet aftertaste.

Potholer (OG 1043.5, ABV 4.3%) 🍺
A well-balanced golden ale with fruit and sweetness throughout and some bitterness to finish.

Totty Pot (OG 1044.5, ABV 4.5%) 🍺
Roasted malts dominate this smooth, well-flavoured porter. Hints of coffee and rich fruits follow with a well-balanced bitterness.

Crown & Glory (OG 1045, ABV 4.6%)

Goat's Leap (OG 1054.5, ABV 5.5%)

Cheeky Imp

The Old Dairy, Monson Farm, Jerusalem Road, Skellingthorpe, Lincolnshire, LN6 4RP ☎ 07884 022236 ⊕ cheekyimp.com

☺Brewing began in 2015 in Waddington using a 0.5-barrel plant. The brewery relocated and upgraded to a 2.5-barrel unit in Skellingthorpe in 2017. RAIB

Cheshire Brew Brothers SIBA

Unit 6, Stanney Mill Industrial Estate, Dutton Green, Ellesmere Port, Cheshire, CH2 4SA ☎ 07890 567582 ⊕ cheshirebrewbrothers.co.uk

Brewing began in 2013. The brewery is run by two friends who call themselves the 'Brew Bros' after being inspired by a beer trip to Belgium. They supply the free and tied trade across Merseyside, Cheshire, North Wales and beyond.

Chester Gold (ABV 3.6%) ◆
A fruity, hoppy bitter with a pleasant sweet finish.

Earl's Eye Amber (ABV 3.8%)
Dry, hoppy, fruity amber-coloured ale with a spicy, malty aroma.

Roodee Dark (ABV 4%)
Deep red-coloured porter with a hoppy, dry, coffee taste and roasted, malty aroma.

Cheshire Best Bitter (ABV 4.5%)
A traditional bitter, malty, lightly spicy and dry with a sweet aftertaste.

Cheshire Brewhouse SIBA

Units 5 & 6, Daneside Business Park, Riverdane Road, Congleton, Cheshire, CW12 1UN
☎ (01260) 274788 ⊕ cheshirebrewhouse.co.uk

☺ Cheshire Brewhouse was established in 2012 using a five-barrel plant, expanding in 2014 to a 10-barrel one. The business has taken over adjacent premises and the brewery is now capable of producing 160 firkins a week. Bottling is carried out on site. An on-site brewery tap opened in 2016. !!◆V

Cheshire Gap (ABV 3.8%)
A light English pale ale.

Cheshire Set (ABV 4%)
A pale and refreshing ale.

Engine Vein (ABV 4.2%)
A traditional copper-coloured best bitter.

Lindow (ABV 4.5%)
A lighter take on stout, malty and easy-drinking with a hint of espresso and dark chocolate balanced with vine fruits.

DBA (ABV 4.6%)
A Burton-style bitter. Strong and malty with a peppery finish.

Dane'ish (ABV 5%)
A German Pilsner-style kellerbier lager.

Conger Tun Ale (ABV 6.3%)
A wee heavy-style ale.

Chew Valley

Sunningdale, Hillcrest, Pensford, Somerset, BS39 4AS
⊕ chewvalleybrewery.co.uk

⊗ The brewery opened in 2014 using a one-barrel plant supplying the Chew Valley and surrounding areas. Production has been suspended at the brewery premises; bottled beer and occasional casks are contract-brewed elsewhere while new premises are sought.

Chiltern SIBA ⊚

Nash Lee Road, Terrick, Buckinghamshire, HP17 0TQ
☎ (01296) 613647 ⊕ chilternbrewery.co.uk

⊗ Founded in 1980, Chiltern was one of the first microbreweries in the country and is the oldest independent brewery in Buckinghamshire and the Chiltern Hills, growing from a capacity of five to its present 15-barrel plant. Now run by the second generation of the Jenkinson family, George and Tom, it supplies around 100 outlets including its own brewery tap, the Farmers' Bar, at the historic King's Head in Aylesbury. !!➤◆RAIB GF

Pale Ale (OG 1037, ABV 3.7%) ◆
An amber-coloured, refreshing beer with a slight fruit aroma, leading to a good malt/bitter balance in the mouth. The aftertaste is bitter and dry.

Black (OG 1040, ABV 3.9%)
Dark treacle tones, hints of roast barley and well hopped. Rich, smooth flavours abound leading to a light finish.

Beechwood Bitter (OG 1043, ABV 4.3%) ◆
This pale brown beer has a balanced butterscotch/toffee aroma, with a slight hop note. The taste balances bitterness and sweetness, leading to a long bitter finish.

Chin Chin (NEW)

35 Caddon Avenue, South Elmsall, West Yorkshire, WF9 2WJ ☎ 07896 253650
✉ david@chinchinbrewing.co.uk

☺Chin Chin was established in 2016 by brothers David and Andrew Currie. Brewing began on a one-barrel plant based in a domestic garage. Seasonal and experimental cask-conditioned beers are produced with a view to developing a regular range. Beers are supplied to local outlets and festivals nationwide. ◆

Chippenham

Unit 109, The Citadel, Bath Road, Chippenham, Wiltshire, SN15 2AB ⊕ chippenhambrewery.co.uk

Small scale brewery established in Chippenham in 2016. It may relocate during the currency of this Guide. Brewing is currently suspended. ◆RAIB

Chorlton

69 North Western Street, Ardwick, Manchester, M12 6DX ⊕ chorltonbrewingcompany.com

Founded in 2014 by Londoner Mike Marcus, lack of available space means that, despite the name, the brewery is in fact based in Ardwick. Mike is passionate about sour beers and yeast experiments inspired by classic European beer styles. The vegan-friendly beers are neither filtered nor pasteurised and generally available in can, KeyCask and occasionally bottles. RAIB

J Church

⊟ Black Prince, 15 Abington Square, Northampton, NN1 4AE ☎ 07956 050183

Julian Church started brewing in 2009 at the Alexandra Arms in Kettering. In 2014 the brewery moved to bigger premises in an old dairy at Cransley near Kettering. It was relocated to the Black Prince, Northampton in 2016. Beers are also brewed under the house brand 'Olde England Ales'.

Church End SIBA ⬤

Ridge Lane, Warwickshire, CV10 0RD
☎ (01827) 713080 ⊕ churchendbrewery.co.uk

⊠ The brewery started in 1994 in an old coffin shop in Shustoke. It moved to the present site and upgraded to a 10-barrel plant in 2001 with further expansion to a 20-barrel plant in 2008. Many one-off specials and old recipe beers are produced. Beers are available at the Brewery Tap, Ridge Lane, and its sister pubs, the George & Dragon, Stoke Golding and the Dragon Inn, Worcester. ‼ ☞ ♦ RAIB

Poachers Pocket (OG 1036, ABV 3.5%)

Cuthberts (OG 1038, ABV 3.8%) ◕
A refreshing, hoppy beer, with hints of malt, fruit and caramel taste. Lingering bitter aftertaste.

Goats Milk (OG 1038, ABV 3.8%) ◕

Gravediggers Ale (OG 1038, ABV 3.8%) ⬚

What the Fox's Hat (OG 1044, ABV 4.2%) ◕
A beer with a malty aroma, and a hoppy and malty taste with some caramel flavour.

Vicar's Ruin (OG 1044, ABV 4.4%) ◕
A straw-coloured best bitter with an initially hoppy, bitter flavour, softening to a delicate malt finish.

Stout Coffin (OG 1046, ABV 4.6%)

Fallen Angel (OG 1050, ABV 5%)

Church Farm SIBA ⬤

Church Farm, Budbrooke, Warwickshire, CV35 8QL
☎ (01926) 411084 ☎ 07939 607027
⊕ churchfarmbrewery.co.uk

Brewing began in 2012 using a plant converted from the farm's old milk processing equipment. A new 20-barrel gas fired plant was commissioned in 2016 to meet growing demand. Beers are brewed from local ingredients and the water comes from the farm's own well. Main trading area is a 30-mile radius from Warwick; look out for portable bars at local festivals. ♦ RAIB

Pale Ale (OG 1041, ABV 3.8%)
Lightly-hopped, easy-drinking golden bitter with a tangy finish.

Ren's Pride (OG 1044, ABV 4%)
An amber-coloured best bitter with a slightly sweet taste.

Brown's Porter (OG 1042, ABV 4.2%)
A porter with a smooth coffee taste and a long-lasting, creamy aftertaste.

Harry's Heifer (OG 1044, ABV 4.2%)
A light amber-coloured best bitter with slight floral notes.

IPA (OG 1052, ABV 5%)
Light amber-coloured, hoppy IPA. Slight citrus fruit and toffee notes.

Church Hanbrewery

Unit F2, New Yatt Business Centre, New Yatt, Oxfordshire, OX29 6TJ
☎ (01993) 774986 ☎ 07907 272617

Office: Tithe Barn South, Church Hanborough, OX29 8AB ⊕ churchhanbrewery.com

Brewing commenced in early 2016 on a small scale until later that year when a 2.5-barrel plant came on stream. ☞ RAIB

Ale X IPA (ABV 4.5%)
A powerful and complex IPA with citrus, pine, spice and herbal notes.

RAUK (ABV 5%)
Inspired by Rauchbier (smoked lager) from Bamberg.

Red Beetter (ABV 5%)
Brown-red in colour from a small amount of organic beetroot juice. Malty and smooth with low hop aroma and a balanced hop bitterness.

Bluenette (ABV 5.5%)
A porter with a smoothness that comes from the addition of Scottish rolled oats, a delicate sweetness from organic honey and rich, roasted chocolate flavours.

Mat Black (ABV 5.5%)
A black IPA with a strong lemon and herbal hop aroma and the smoothness of a stout.

Ciren

⊟ Twelve Bells, 12 Lewis Lane, Cirencester, Gloucestershire, GL7 1EA
☎ (01285) 652230 ☎ 07702 489589

Ciren Ales is a small microbrewery at the rear of the Twelve Bells pub in Cirencester, established in 2012. The brewer is the owner, Steve. Brewing is currently suspended.

City of Cambridge

See Wolf

Clanconnel

Unit 5 , 2 New Line, Gibson's Hill, Lurgan, Co Armagh, BT66 8TA ☎ 07711 626770

Correspondence: PO Box 316, Craigavon, BT65 9AZ
⊕ clanconnelbrewing.com

Beers are contract brewed by the Rye River Brewery in Co Kildare in the Republic of Ireland under the McGraths Craft Beer brand. No real ale.

Clark's SIBA ⬤

Westgate Brewery, Wakefield, West Yorkshire, WF2 9SW
☎ (01924) 373328 ☎ 07801 922473 ⊕ hbclark.co.uk

☺Founded in 1906, Clark's ceased brewing during the 1960s/70s but resumed cask ale production in 1982 and now delivers to around 220 outlets throughout the Midlands and the north of England using its own wholesale network of depots. Its two pubs serve cask ale. A new range of ales was introduced in 2014 called Merrie City Craft Beers. Recently taken over by Kitwave, a drinks wholesaler in the North-east. ◆

Classic Blonde (OG 1039, ABV 3.9%)
Pale straw-coloured beer with a fruity aroma and light spicy taste.

Brewed under the Merrie City Craft Beers brand name:

Atlantic Hop (OG 1040, ABV 4%)

Cascadian (OG 1040, ABV 4%)

Crystal Gold (OG 1042, ABV 4.2%)

Clarkshaws SIBA

Arch 497, Ridgway Road, Loughborough Junction, London, SW9 7EX ☎ 07989 402687
⊕ clarkshaws.co.uk

Clarkshaws is a small brewery established in 2013 focusing on using ingredients sourced in the UK and on reducing beer miles. The beers are suitable for vegetarians and are accredited by the Vegetarian Society. All beers are unfined and may be hazy. An on-site tap room is open Thursday-Sunday.

Gorgon's Alive (OG 1040, ABV 4%) ◣
Unfined golden-coloured beer with spicy hops throughout. The flavour has hints of orange and peach with a dry bitterness.

Phoenix Rising (OG 1040, ABV 4%) ◣
Tawny-coloured beer with a creamy toffee nose. Bananas, pineapple, hops and caramel flavours. Dryish, short, fruity biscuit finish.

Strange Brew No. 1 (OG 1040, ABV 4%) ◣
Easy-drinking, yellow-coloured ale. Flavour is of peppery hops, tropical fruits and biscuit sweetness with a trace of bitterness.

Coldharbour Hell Yeah Lager (ABV 5.3%) ◣
Hops and mango notes that are also present on the flavour with some butterscotch. Dryish palate.

Hellhound IPA (OG 1056, ABV 5.5%) ◣
Spiced and citrus notes in this unfined amber-coloured beer with a bitterness in the flavour and finish, which is dry.

Clearsky

See Hilden

Clearwater SIBA

Unit 1, Little Court, Manteo Way, Gammaton Road, Bideford, Devon, EX39 4FG
☎ (01237) 420492 ⊕ clearwaterbrewery.co.uk

⊠ Established in 1999, Clearwater is a 10-barrel brewery regularly supplying more than 250 outlets across the South-west and nationally with its 'Devon's Own' labelled beers. Beers are also available at the brewery tap, the Champ, Appledore. !! ◆ RAIB

Best Bitter (OG 1037.3, ABV 3.5%)
A traditional brown ale with hints of blackcurrant. Well-balanced and hoppy with a bitter finish.

Real Smiler (OG 1037, ABV 3.7%)
Golden-coloured, crisp and hoppy.

Devon Dympsy (OG 1039, ABV 4%) ◣

Fruity aroma leads to crisp and fruity yet bitter taste. The aftertaste continues a balanced sweet/fruit/bitterness, which is slightly dry.

Proper Ansome (OG 1041, ABV 4.2%)
Full-flavoured dark beer, full of malty goodness.

Submariner (OG 1042.9, ABV 4.2%)
Golden-coloured, clean, crisp and hoppy with a fresh grapefruit zestiness and lingering hint of bitterness.

Devon Darter (OG 1043, ABV 4.5%)
A fruity, copper-coloured ale with a grape aroma, nutty taste and a light bitterness to finish.

Artists Rifles (OG 1048.4, ABV 5%)
A refreshing, hoppy and crisp pale ale with spicy notes.

Cliff Quay

Unit 1, Meadow Works, Kenton Road, Debenham, Suffolk, IP14 6RT
☎ (01728) 861213 ⊕ cliffquay.co.uk

⊠ Cliff Quay was established in 2008 by former Wychwood brewer Jeremy Moss and John Bjornson (owner of the Earl Soham Brewery) in part of the historic Tolly Cobbold brewery in Ipswich. In 2012 the brewery relocated to Debenham, a small, picturesque market town, due to redevelopment of the former brewery site. Now re-established alongside Earl Soham brewery, with shared shop and offices. !! ☞ ◆

Bitter (OG 1034, ABV 3.4%) ◣
Pleasantly drinkable, well-balanced, malty, sweet bitter with a hint of caramel, followed by a sweet/malty aftertaste. A good flavour for such a low gravity beer.

Anchor Bitter (OG 1040, ABV 4%)

Black Jack Porter (OG 1042, ABV 4.2%) ◣
Unusual dark porter with a strong aniseed aroma and rich liquorice and aniseed flavours, reminiscent of old-fashioned sweets. The aftertaste is long and increasingly sweet.

Tolly Roger (OG 1042, ABV 4.2%) ◣
Well-balanced, highly drinkable, mid-gold summer beer with a bittersweet hoppiness, some biscuity flavours and hints of summer fruit.

Tumblehome (OG 1047, ABV 4.7%) ◣
Aroma of marzipan and dried fruit. Flavour reminiscent of Amaretto, leading to a short, bitter, slightly spicy aftertaste.

Sea Dog (OG 1053, ABV 5.5%)
Bursting with the flavours of lemon and grapefruit with a full maltiness in contrast.

Dreadnought (OG 1065, ABV 6.5%)

Clockwork

🗲 1153-1155 Cathcart Road, Glasgow, G42 9HB
☎ (0141) 649 0184 ⊕ clockworkbeercompany.co.uk

Established in 1997, Clockwork is owned by Thistle Pub Company III. The beers are stored in cellar tanks where fermentation gases from the conditioning vessel blanket the beers (but not under pressure). A wide range of ales, lagers and specials is produced. Most beers are naturally gassed while the Craft Lager is pressurised. The establishment has parted ways with its previous managing company, Maclays, and in 2014 the pub underwent a full refurbishment.

Clouded Minds SIBA 👁

Unit 5B, Brailes Industrial Estate, Winderton Road, Lower Brailes, Warwickshire, OX15 5JW ☎ 07530 998149 ⊕ cloudedminds.co.uk

Brewing began in 2013 using spare capacity at various breweries around London and Derbyshire. In 2015 the brewery moved to its own site near Banbury using a 15-barrel plant. The London area is mainly supplied but also some outlets in Birmingham, Nottinghamshire, Warwickshire and Oxfordshire. Wholesalers also distribute the beers more widely. RAIB

N29 (OG 1036, ABV 3.7%)
Citrus pale ale brewed with a small amount of rye malt.

N253 (OG 1037, ABV 3.9%)
An oatmeal American pale ale. Fruity and resiny.

99 Steps (ABV 4%)
Refreshing pale ale brewed with citrus and pine English hops.

N18 (OG 1038, ABV 4%)
A pale ale. Mild citrus, pine and resin.

Luppol (OG 1040, ABV 4.2%)
Refreshing with a good bitter finish.

Clout Stout (OG 1048, ABV 4.5%)
Velvet mouthfeel with an aroma of roasted malts, cocoa, dried fruits and figs. Mildly sweet and sour with a smoky and bitter finish.

Hazelnutter (OG 1048, ABV 5%)
Well-balanced, smooth, American-style brown ale brewed with organic Italian hazelnuts.

Elisir (OG 1052, ABV 5.3%)
Caramel and biscuit taste from the malts balanced by a generous amount of American hops. Very fruity.

Black Pike (OG 1057, ABV 6.1%)
Medium-bodied Black IPA.

Dolce Vita (OG 1058, ABV 6.2%)
West Coast American-style IPA. Fruity and mildly spicy with a dry finish.

Double Clout Stout (OG 1064, ABV 6.6%)
A complex fusion of coffee, cocoa, liquorice, dark fruit and burnt sugar.

Cloudwater

**Units 7-8 Piccadilly Trading Estate, Manchester, M1 2NP
☎ (0161) 661 5943 ⊕ cloudwaterbrew.co**

Cloudwater commenced brewing in 2015, specialising in creating and brewing modern, seasonal and special one-off brews, along with collaborations in conjunction with other micro and regional brewers. Regular cask ale production ceased in 2017. ♦

Clun SIBA 👁

**⊟ White Horse Inn, The Square, Clun, Shropshire, SY7 8JA
☎ (01588) 640305 ⊕ whi-clun.co.uk**

Formerly a tiny brewery, capacity was increased to 2.5 barrels in 2010. Established behind the White Horse in Clun, beers are produced for the pub and, increasingly, the local trade.

Loophole (OG 1035, ABV 3.5%)
A dry, hoppy, light-coloured beer.

Clun Pale (OG 1040, ABV 4.1%)
Pale, clean-tasting bitter beer.

Solar (OG 1043, ABV 4.3%)

Citadel (OG 1065, ABV 5.9%)
Golden in colour the rich and fruity malt flavours are met head on by intense hop bitterness and aroma which gives rise to a long-lasting, dry finish.

Co Pilot

Unit 4, Sam Brown Industrial Units, Dog and Gun Lane, Whetstone, Leicestershire, LE8 6LJ ☎ 07342 040567 ✉ martinjallsopp@gmail.com

⊠ Blencow Brewery was established in 1998 at the Exeter Arms in Barrowden, Rutland. In 2005 Martin Allsopp bought the pub and brewery and renamed the latter as Barrowden. In 2016 Martin sold the pub and relocated the brewery to an industrial unit on the outskirts of Leicester, adopting the name Co Pilot. ♦

Pilot (OG 1028, ABV 2.6%)

Beech (OG 1040, ABV 3.8%)

Own Gear (OG 1040, ABV 4%)

Hop Gear (OG 1046, ABV 4.4%)

Coach House SIBA 👁

**Wharf Street, Howley, Warrington, Cheshire, WA1 2DQ
☎ (01925) 232800 ⊕ coachhousebrewery.co.uk**

☺Established in 1991 by three former employees of Greenall Whitley Brewery, the brewery was bought by Martin Bailey in 2015. The 40-barrel plant produces up to 240 barrels per week. A wide range of seasonal and special occasion beers is produced. ♦

Coachman's Best Bitter (OG 1037, ABV 3.7%) ⬟
A well-hopped, malty bitter, moderately fruity with a hint of sweetness and a peppery nose.

Gunpowder Mild (OG 1037, ABV 3.8%) ⬟
Biscuity dark mild with a blackcurrant sweetness. Bitterness and fruit dominate with some hints of caramel and a slightly stronger roast flavour.

Honeypot Bitter (OG 1037, ABV 3.8%)
A medium-bodied, golden-coloured bitter, lightly hopped. Brewed with Cheshire honey which adds a silkiness to the beer.

Farrier's Best Bitter (OG 1038, ABV 3.9%)
A smooth, tawny-coloured beer, slightly sweet but with rich hop flavours developed in the mouth.

Cromwells Best Bitter (OG 1040, ABV 4%)
Amber-coloured, well-balanced beer with a smooth, clean hop finish.

Blonde (OG 1041, ABV 4.1%)
A thirst-quenching ale with hints of citrus and grapefruit.

Cheshire Gold (OG 1042, ABV 4.1%)
A pale golden-coloured beer with a pine and lemon crispness.

Dick Turpin (OG 1042, ABV 4.2%) ◀
Malty, hoppy pale brown beer with some initial sweetish flavours leading to a short, bitter aftertaste. Sold under other names as a pub house beer.

ClIPAty Hop (OG 1043, ABV 4.3%)
A light-coloured IPA with a hoppy aroma and flavour but a well-balanced malty finish.

Flintlock Pale Ale (OG 1044, ABV 4.4%)
A pale golden beer, light on the palate with a touch of sweetness in the finish.

**Innkeeper's Special Reserve
(OG 1045, ABV 4.5%)** ◀
A dark, full-flavoured bitter. Quite fruity, with a strong, bitter aftertaste.

Postlethwaite (OG 1045, ABV 4.6%)
A distinctive dry and fruity pale ale. Traditionally dry hopped to give a fine hop aroma.

Posthorn Premium (OG 1050, ABV 5%)
A rich, straw-coloured, smooth premium ale. The beer has a robust malty palate and well-balanced bitterness with a complexity of flavours.

Coastal SIBA

Unit 20, Cardrew Trade Park South, Cardrew Way, Redruth, Cornwall, TR15 1SW
☎ (01209) 212613 ☎ 07875 405407
⊕ coastalbrewery.co.uk

⊠ Launched in 2006 by Alan Hinde, Coastal operates a six-barrel plant and supplies pubs all around England. It has a brewery tap on site, with Coastal beers on draught, plus a bottle shop offering a range of speciality beers, including its own. 🍽 ◆ RAIB

Cornish Bronze (OG 1037, ABV 3.7%)
A traditional session bitter.

Hop Monster (OG 1038, ABV 3.7%) ◀
Powerfully hoppy golden ale with grassy grapefruit and marmalade flavours. Quite sweet, somewhat dry. Rising dryness and bitterness in the finish.

Handliner (OG 1040, ABV 4%) ◀
Red-coloured bitter with faintly roasted malt aroma. Smoky malt taste balanced by hop bitterness and gentle dryness, finishing bitter.

Merry Maidens Mild (OG 1040, ABV 4%) ◀
A black mild. Smooth and creamy with roasted malt, charcoal and liquorice sweetness fading slowly to a refreshing, dry finish.

Angelina (OG 1042, ABV 4.1%) ◀
Golden ale with delicate floral aroma. Grassy, citrus hops with sweet grapefruit, marmalade and apricot throughout. Crisp, dry, fruity finish.

Golden Hinde (OG 1044, ABV 4.3%) ◀
Golden ale with orange marmalade aroma. Apricot and citrus fruit flavours with dominant bitter and grassy hop. Refreshing long finish.

Pier Porter (OG 1043, ABV 4.3%)
A full-bodied porter. Heavy malt flavour gives way to a malt character.

Poseidon Extra (OG 1046, ABV 4.5%) ◀
Yellow-coloured ale. Oranges and lemons aroma. Strong bitterness and grassy hops with grapefruit notes. Long bitter and dry finish.

Cornish Cascade (OG 1050, ABV 5%) ◀

Golden ale with hoppy aroma. Strong citrus hop taste, bitter and fruity with sweet malt. Long bitter and dry finish.

Cornish Porter (OG 1050, ABV 5%) ◀
Black porter with strong roast malt and hop nose. Intense bitter roast malt flavour with a hop balance. Finish becoming dry.

St Pirans Porter (OG 1060, ABV 6%)
A traditional, full-bodied porter using seven different malts. Roasty, toasty malt notes mix with abundant hops.

Erosion (OG 1077, ABV 7.5%) ◀
After an aroma promising roast caramel this powerful, warming, dark old ale bursts with molasses and roast malt. Liquorice adds to the finish.

Kernow Imperial Stout (OG 1090, ABV 9%)
This full-flavoured, warming dark stout bursts with molasses and roast malts. Roast caramel adds to the dry stout finish.

Cobbydale (NEW)

🛏 Red Lion, 47 Kirkgate, Silsden, West Yorkshire, BD20 0AQ

Brewing began in 2017 at the Red Lion in Silsden.

Cocksure (NEW)

Unit 3, Great Leaze Farm, Oldbury Lane, Oldbury on Severn, BS35 1RF ☎ 07787 453222

Office: 1a Quaker Lane, Thornbury, BS35 2AD
⊕ cocksurebrewing.com

10-barrel brewery near Thornbury, established in 2017. Further beers are planned.

Red (OG 1040, ABV 4.1%)
An American-style red-coloured ale with citrus and mango aromas accompanied with a gentle spice and peppery finish from the rye.

P'Ale (OG 1045, ABV 4.5%)
A complex, fruity ale.

Session IPA (OG 1046, ABV 4.8%)
Highly-hopped IPA with aromas of watermelon, pear and blueberries.

Colchester SIBA

Viaduct Brewhouse, Unit 16, Wakes Hall Business Centre, Wakes Colne, Essex, CO6 2DY
☎ (01787) 829422 ⊕ colchesterbrewery.com

⊠ Set up in 2012 by three friends, Tom Knox, Roger Clark and Andy Bone, using the double drop process. Popular during the early 20th century this process requires additional brewing vessels in a two-tier system resulting in clean beer with pronounced flavours. ‼ 🍽 ◆ RAIB

AKA Pale (OG 1039, ABV 3.7%)
A mildly-hopped pale ale. Fresh and fruity.

Metropolis (OG 1040.5, ABV 3.9%)
A golden-coloured, hoppy beer with enormous depth of flavour and a long, spicy finish.

Jack Spitty's Smuggler's Ale (OG 1041.5, ABV 4%)

No. 1 (OG 1042.5, ABV 4.1%) 🍴
A classic English best bitter, copper in colour.

Red Diesel (OG 1043.5, ABV 4.2%)

Red-coloured best bitter, well-balanced with a long, rich finish.

Brazilian Coffee & Vanilla Porter (OG 1048, ABV 4.6%)

Cats Whiskers (OG 1050, ABV 4.8%)
Smooth-drinking, full-bodied cream stout with a slight sweetness.

Old King Coel London Porter (OG 1052, ABV 5%)
A rich, dark porter brewed the original way with brown malt.

Cold Black

See Brecon, Rhymney and Untapped

Coles Family

🍺 White Hart Thatched Inn & Brewery, Llanddarog, SA32 8NT
☎ (01267) 275395 ⊕ thebestpubinwales.co.uk

The brewery is based at the ancient White Hart Inn, built in 1371, which historically had a brewery on site. Brewing started again in 1999 on a nine-gallon plant. A one-barrel plant was fitted in 2000 and in 2012 the brewery was opened to the public. Cider is also produced.

Colonsay SIBA

The Brewery, Scalasaig, Isle of Colonsay, PA61 7YT
☎ (01951) 200190 ⊕ colonsaybrewery.co.uk

Colonsay began brewing in 2007 on a five-barrel plant. Beer is mainly bottled or brewery conditioned for the local trade. RAIB

Concertina SIBA

🍺 9a Dolcliffe Road, Mexborough, South Yorkshire, S64 9AZ
☎ (01709) 580841 ✉ concertina@btconnect.com

Concertina started in 1992 in the cellar of a club once famous as the home of a long-gone concertina band. The plant produces up to eight barrels a week for the club and other occasional direct outlets and the wider trade, via beer wholesalers.

Club Bitter (OG 1038, ABV 3.9%) ◈
A fruity session bitter with a good bitter flavour.

Bengal Tiger (OG 1043, ABV 4.6%) ◈
Light amber-coloured ale with an aromatic hoppy nose followed by a combination of fruit and bitterness.

Concrete Cow

59 Alston Drive, Bradwell Abbey, Milton Keynes, Buckinghamshire, MK13 9HB
☎ (01908) 316794 ☎ 07889 665745
⊕ concretecowbrewery.co.uk

⊠ Concrete Cow opened in 2007 on a 5.5-barrel plant. The beers are named after aspects of local history. The brewery supplies pubs, farmers' markets, local shops and restaurants. English single malt whisky is also available. ‼ 🍺 ◆ RAIB

Pail Ale (OG 1036, ABV 3.7%)
A light-coloured ale brewed using lager malt.

Fenny Popper (OG 1039, ABV 4%)

A light-coloured, zesty ale.

Cock 'n' Bull Story (OG 1041, ABV 4.1%)
A dark amber-coloured, malty beer.

Coniston SIBA ⊙

Coppermines Road, Coniston, Cumbria, LA21 8HL
☎ (01539) 441133 ⊕ conistonbrewery.com

⊙A 10-barrel plant started in 1995 behind the Black Bull Inn in Coniston, it now brews 40 barrels a week and supplies numerous outlets locally and nationally. Some bottle-conditioned Coniston beers are brewed using Hepworth's Horsham plant.
‼ 🍺 RAIB

Oliver's Light Ale (OG 1035, ABV 3.4%) ◈
A fruity, hoppy, straw-coloured bitter with plenty of flavour for its strength.

Bluebird Bitter (OG 1036, ABV 3.6%) ◈
A yellow-gold, predominantly hoppy and fruity beer, well-balanced with some sweetness and a rising bitter finish.

Asrai (OG 1039, ABV 4%) ◈
Crisp on the palate, a gently-hopped beer with a full-bodied finish.

Bluebird Premium XB (OG 1040.5, ABV 4.2%) ◈
Well-balanced, hoppy and fruity golden bitter. Bittersweet in the mouth with dryness building.

Old Man Ale (OG 1040.5, ABV 4.2%) ◈
Delicious fruity, winey beer with a complex, well-balanced richness.

Special Oatmeal Stout (OG 1045, ABV 4.5%) ◈
A well-balanced, easy-drinking stout, fruity with a balanced ratio of malt to hop bitterness. A good starting point for novice stout drinkers.

K7 (OG 1045, ABV 4.7%) ◈
Balanced, fruity, hoppy bitter, plenty of body and a long, hoppy, bitter finish.

Thurstein Pilsner (OG 1044.5, ABV 4.8%) ◈
True to style; mild but unusually sweet, with a hoppy fruitiness.

Blacksmiths Ale (OG 1047.5, ABV 5%) ◈
A tawny-coloured ale which holds both roastiness and fruitiness in a pleasing balance.

Infinity IPA (OG 1055, ABV 6%) ◈
High impact strong bitter. Fruity aromas persist in the powerful but well-balanced hoppiness and sweetness with nothing being lost in the finish.

No. 9 Barley Wine (OG 1087.5, ABV 8.5%) ◈
Hops and alcohol dominate with appropriate sweetness and fruit on the tongue. A full-bodied and beautifully balanced beer.

Connoisseur

(Rear of) Wolverhampton House, 121-125 Church Street, St Helens, Merseyside, WA10 1AJ ☎ 07921 838831 ⊕ connoisseurales.com

Launched in 2014 by Mark Gillian and Kevin Yates using a five-barrel plant. Brewery open days with free tours are a regular occurrence. Beers tend to stay within 30 mile of the brewery with occasional appearances further afield.

The Usual (ABV 3.8%)
A traditional ale making use of all English ingredients with characteristic hop bitterness.

Black Smoker (ABV 4.1%)

Ruby Ruby Ruby Ruby (ABV 4.1%)
A well-balanced ale with a malty character.

Lucem Light Ale (ABV 4.3%)
A hoppy ale with a distinctive nose and floral citrus taste.

Toff in a Shed (ABV 4.3%)

Sparkling WIT (ABV 4.6%)
Complex malt flavours and a hint of chocolate combined with a hoppy aroma.

Bete Noir Dry Stout (ABV 5%)
Full-flavoured dry stout with coffee, chocolate and a hint of smoke. Delicate molasses and spice on the nose.

Ex Terra Lupus IPA (ABV 5.6%)
A strong, clean and crisp beer with a well-balanced hop profile.

Consall Forge

3 Railway Cottages, Consall Forge, Staffordshire, ST9 0AJ

A one-barrel brewery set in the heart of the Staffordshire Moorlands adjacent to the Churnet Valley Railway. The Black Lion at Consall Forge is a regular outlet.

Dark Ruby Mild (OG 1050, ABV 5.2%)

Equilibrium (OG 1054, ABV 6%)
Traditional stout with flavours of coffee and molasses.

Consett Ale Works SIBA 👁

🏠 **Grey Horse Inn, 115 Sherburn Terrace, Consett, County Durham, DH8 6NE**
☎ **(01207) 591540** 🌐 **thegreyhorse.co.uk**

The brewery opened in 2006 in the stables of a former coaching inn at the rear of the Grey Horse, Consett's oldest pub. The name commemorates the historic Consett Steel Works that closed in 1980. The brewery expanded in 2007 to cope with demand. More than 100 outlets are supplied direct.

Steel Town Bitter (OG 1039, ABV 3.8%)

White Hot (OG 1040, ABV 4%)

Cast Iron (OG 1040, ABV 4.1%)

Consett Stout (OG 1045, ABV 4.3%)

Men of Steel (OG 1045, ABV 4.3%)

Red Dust (OG 1045, ABV 4.5%)

Conwy SIBA

Unit 2, Ty Mawr Enterprise Park, Tan y Graig Road, Llysfaen, LL29 8UE
☎ **(01492) 514305** 🌐 **conwybrewery.co.uk**

☺Conwy started brewing in 2003 and was the first brewery in Conwy for at least 100 years. In 2013 it increased capacity and moved to bigger premises in Llysfaen. Monthly seasonals are available as well as the West Coast range showcasing American-style beers. Around 100 outlets are supplied.
‼ 🍺 ♦ RAIB

Clogwyn Gold (OG 1037, ABV 3.6%) ◣
A full-flavoured golden ale featuring strong citrus fruit flavours throughout. Hoppy bitterness dominates the full mouthfeel and lasting finish.

Welsh Pride (OG 1040, ABV 4%)

A clean-tasting malty bitter. Fruit in aroma and taste with a crisp, grainy mouthfeel and a lingering, hoppy, bitter aftertaste.

Beachcomber Blonde (OG 1042, ABV 4.2%)
Crisp, dry refreshing ale with a delicate grapefruit flavour.

Honey Fayre (OG 1044, ABV 4.5%)
Golden-coloured best bitter with a hint of honey sweetness, balanced by an increasingly hoppy, bitter finish, slightly watery mouthfeel for a beer of this strength.

Rampart (OG 1045, ABV 4.5%) ◣
A dark, fruity beer with a sweetish initial taste. Fruit flavours accompanied by the underlying hoppiness continue into the bittersweet aftertaste.

Coppertown

Unit D, Site 7, Business Park, Amlwch, LL68 9BX
☎ **(01407) 832564**

Brewing began in 2015. Beers are produced for the island county of Anglesey.

Anglesey Bitter (OG 1038, ABV 3.8%)

Anglesey Gold (OG 1040, ABV 4%)

Anglesey Best (OG 1045, ABV 4.5%)

Corinium

Unit 1a, The Old Kennels, Cirencester Park, Cirencester, Gloucestershire, GL7 1UR ☎ **07716 826467** 🌐 **coriniumales.co.uk**

⊗ Corinium Ales was established in 2012. The one-barrel plant relocated to newly refurbished ex-dog kennels in Cirencester. The award-winning beers are mainly available bottle-conditioned and make up the brewer's 'Roman Collection' but cask-conditioned production of the beers is increasing.
‼ 🍺 ♦ RAIB

Gold (OG 1043, ABV 4.2%)
An easy-drinking fruity ale with a mellow blend of malt and hops and a soft bitter finish.

Bodicacia (OG 1045, ABV 4.7%)
A full-bodied golden ale with a long-lasting citrus finish.

Centurion (OG 1051, ABV 4.7%)
A rich, malty stout with toasty chocolate undertones. Lightly-hopped leaving a well-rounded aftertaste.

Ale Caesar (OG 1050, ABV 5%)
A well-hopped IPA with a tropical fruit aroma balanced with a pleasing bitterness.

Cornish Chough SIBA

Trethvas Farm, Lizard, Cornwall, TR12 7AR
☎ **(01326) 290908**

⊗ Cornish Chough, the most southerly brewery on the UK mainland, commenced brewing in 2011 at its present location on Trethvas Farm, Lizard village. The brewery has its own borehole and draws water from between two seams of serpentine rock. ‼ RAIB

Kynance Blonde (OG 1039, ABV 4.2%) ◣
Refreshing golden ale with crisp, hop taste and light bitterness. Lemon, peach and honey flavours and a hoppy finish.

Cadgwith Crabber (OG 1043, ABV 4.3%) ◣

THE BREWERIES

Smooth, copper-coloured best bitter. Biscuit malt balanced with citrus hop character, apples, toffee and vanilla. Gentle fruity and astringent finish.

Fire Raven (OG 1047, ABV 4.7%) ◈
Black porter with a hop aroma. Velvety roasted barley with bitter chocolate and liquorice. Faint sweet malt and hops. Short finish.

Lizard Storm (OG 1048, ABV 4.8%) ◈
Smooth, red-coloured strong bitter with malty fruitiness in the taste. Apples and hops balance the malt. Lingering sweet, fruity finish.

Kilcobben IPA (ABV 5%) ◈
Smooth, amber-coloured strong bitter. Crisp citrus hop bitterness balanced by biscuit malt with dried and tropical fruits. Bitter hoppy finish.

Cornish Crown SIBA

End Unit, Badger's Cross Farm, Badger's Cross, Penzance, Cornwall, TR20 8XE
☎ (01736) 449029 ☎ 07870 998986
⊕ cornishcrown.co.uk

⊗ Cornish Crown began brewing in 2012 on a six-barrel plant and is based on a farm high above Mounts Bay. It was established by the brewer and landlord of the Crown Inn in Penzance, which acts as the brewery tap. Beer is available in local outlets and can be found as far away as the Southampton Arms in London. **RAIB**

Mousehole (OG 1039, ABV 3.9%) ◈
Refreshing copper-coloured bitter with a hop aroma. Biscuit malt and bitter hops in the mouth, becoming drier in the finish.

St Michaels (OG 1040, ABV 4%) ◈
Copper-coloured best bitter with a dry bitter aftertaste. Flavours of apple and tropical fruits with moderate hop bitterness and malt.

Causeway (OG 1041, ABV 4.1%) ◈
Copper-coloured best bitter with a light fragrant nose. Biscuit malt and hops with damson and rum butter flavours. Bitter, dry finish.

One Hop One Grain (OG 1041, ABV 4.1%) ◈
Amber-coloured best bitter with hops dominant from aroma to finish. Taste balanced by malt, marmalade and caramel. Refreshing dry, bitter finish.

Honeyfuggle (OG 1043, ABV 4.5%) ◈
Yellow-coloured hoppy beer with sweet honey and malt in the mouth. Hop aroma and a bitter finish with some dryness.

SPA (OG 1048, ABV 4.8%) ◈
Heavily-hopped, refreshing golden strong bitter with biscuit malt and stone fruits in the mouth. Finish is bitter, hoppy and dry.

Porter (OG 1053, ABV 5.2%) ◈
Black vanilla porter with roast malt aroma. Smooth chocolate, liquorice, deep plum and black cherry, laced with cream. Burnt coffee aftertaste.

IPA (OG 1055, ABV 5.5%) ◈
Amber-coloured strong bitter with a hop nose. Powerful hop bitter taste, persistent malt. Orange marmalade, lemon and peach. Bitter, dry finish.

Red IPA (OG 1057, ABV 5.9%) ◈
Strong, brown-coloured beer with hops, vine fruit and honey aroma. Rich, sweet malt and fruit cake. Long bitter, dry finish.

Corvedale SIBA ◉

⊟ **Sun Inn, Corfton, Shropshire, SY7 9DF**
☎ (01584) 861239 ⊕ corvedalebrewery.co.uk

Brewing started in 1999 behind the pub. Landlord Norman Pearce is also the brewer and uses only British malt and hops, with water from a local borehole. Ten regular beers are brewed for the pub and wider distribution.

Cotleigh SIBA

Ford Road, Wiveliscombe, Somerset, TA4 2RE
☎ (01984) 624086 ⊕ cotleighbrewery.com

Established in 1979, Cotleigh is based in the historic town of Wiveliscombe. It supplies direct to 750 pubs, 200 retailers and selected wholesalers and is now contracted to supply Co-op and Lidl, predominantly with IPA. A visitor centre is now established and available for functions. Monthly events include Folk, Jazz, Open Mike and curry nights. ‼ ☕ ◆ RAIB

Harrier (OG 1035, ABV 3.5%)
A light and golden-coloured beer with a delicate floral and fruity aroma for a refreshing sweet and slightly hoppy finish.

Tawny Owl (OG 1038, ABV 3.8%) ◈
Well-balanced, tawny-coloured bitter with malt and fruity aroma, major malt taste followed by hop fruit, developing to a satisfying bitter finish.

IPA (OG 1039, ABV 3.9%)
A well-hopped and zesty IPA.

25 (OG 1040, ABV 4%)
A pale golden-coloured beer with a fresh aroma and fruit-filled finish.

Commando Hoofing (OG 1040, ABV 4%)
A pale golden beer, refreshing and slightly sparkling.

Golden Seahawk (OG 1042, ABV 4.2%) ◈
Gold-coloured, well-hopped ale with flowery hop aroma and fruity hop flavour, clean mouthfeel, leading to a dry, hoppy finish.

Barn Owl (OG 1045, ABV 4.5%) ◈
Mid-brown beer with well-balanced malt and hop aroma; a smooth, full-bodied taste where hops dominate, balanced by malt.

Honey Buzzard (OG 1045, ABV 4.5%)
Uses pure honey giving a smooth, creamy and chocolate palate and a subtle bittersweet finish.

Old Buzzard (OG 1048, ABV 4.8%)
A traditional dark ale, deep copper red in colour with the roasted chocolate malt giving a dry nutty flavour with hints of amarone biscuit. The finish in the mouth is dry, smoky and smooth.

Cotswold SIBA

College Farm, Stow Road, Bourton-on-the-Water, Gloucestershire, GL54 2HN
☎ (01451) 824488 ☎ 07760 889100
⊕ cotswoldbrewco.uk

An independent producer of craft lager and speciality beers. The brewery was established in 2005 and expanded in 2010. More than 150 outlets are supplied, mainly in the Cotswolds and London. ‼ ◆ RAIB

Cask (OG 1040, ABV 4%)

Copper-coloured, well-hopped, easy-drinking ale.

Cotswold Lion SIBA

Grain Store 5, Dowmans Farm, Coberley, Gloucestershire, GL53 9QY
☎ (01242) 870164 ⊕ cotswoldlionbrewery.co.uk

⊠ Brewing began in 2012 using a 10-barrel plant located in a grain store on a farm in the Cotswolds. Established by John Kemp, former head brewer at Nailsworth Brewery, and Andy Forbes, formerly of Festival Brewery. ‼ ☛ RAIB

Shepherd's Delight (OG 1036, ABV 3.6%)
A session ale, light, crisp and full of citrus flavours.

Hogget (OG 1039, ABV 3.8%)
A copper-coloured best bitter. Fruity, light on the citrus with a hint of spice.

Best in Show (OG 1042, ABV 4.2%)
A well-balanced best bitter with plenty of blackberry fruit and a hint of honey.

Golden Fleece (OG 1044, ABV 4.4%)
A non-traditional IPA, filled with Jamaican fruit.

Drover's Return (OG 1050, ABV 5%)
A strong, ruby-coloured bitter.

Cottage ◉

The Old Cheese Dairy, Hornblotton Road, Lovington, Somerset, BA7 7PS
☎ (01963) 240551 ⊕ cottagebrewing.co.uk

⊠ The brewery was established in 1993 in West Lydford and moved to larger premises in 1996, doubling brewing capacity at the same time. In 2001 a 30-barrel plant was installed. Around 1,500 outlets are supplied. Brewing is currently suspended. ‼ ♦

Cotton End

Pomfret Arms, 10 Cotton End, Northampton, NN4 8BS
☎ (01604) 765544

Brewing began in 2014 on a small brew plant located in an outhouse behind the Pomfret Arms, focusing on experimental and specialist beer styles for sale in the pub and at local beer festivals. Customers are invited to suggest beers for brewing. Expansion is planned.

Country Life SIBA

The Big Sheep, Abbotsham, Devon, EX39 5AP
☎ (01237) 420808 ☎ 07971 267790
⊕ countrylifebrewery.co.uk

⊠ Country Life is based at the Big Sheep tourist attraction. The brewery offers a beer show and free samples in the shop during the peak season (Apr-Oct). A 15.5-barrel plant was installed in 2005, making Country Life the biggest brewery in north Devon. Around 100 outlets are supplied. ‼ ☛ ♦ RAIB

Old Appledore (OG 1037, ABV 3.7%)

Reef Break (OG 1039, ABV 4%)

Shore Break (OG 1042, ABV 4.4%)

Black Boar/Board Break (OG 1044, ABV 4.5%) ◣
Complex, well-balanced aromas. Unusual dry bitter hop taste leading to a softer aftertaste with unexpected roasted malt and caramel.

Golden Pig (OG 1046, ABV 4.7%)

Country Bumpkin (OG 1058, ABV 6%)
A malty, full-flavoured, smooth taste.

CrackleRock SIBA

The Old Cooperage, High Street, Botley, Hampshire, SO30 2EA ☎ 07733 232806 ⊕ cracklerock.co.uk

⊠ CrackleRock began brewing in 2014 at the Old Cooperage in the centre of Botley with experienced head brewer Andy Ingram. In 2015 the Taproom bar opened (Thu-Sun) with seating for 28 people. ‼☛♦

Crackerjack (OG 1039, ABV 3.8%)
A clean, crisp, light-coloured ale with a slight citrus aftertaste.

Fire Cracker (OG 1043, ABV 4.2%)
A well-balanced traditional English best bitter.

Gold Rush (OG 1046, ABV 4.5%)
A premium golden ale with a subtle sweetness, but not too overpowering. Leaves a clean, crisp taste in the mouth.

Dark Destroyer (OG 1049, ABV 4.9%)
A rich, strong, dark, smooth, porter-style ale. A little caramel but not too burnt, well balanced with chocolate malt.

Crafty Shag (OG 1050, ABV 5%)
A smooth, strong, full-bodied, well-balanced ale. Big malt tastes but still clean on the palate with a hoppy, fresh aftertaste.

Craddock's

Duke William, 25 Coventry Street, Stourbridge, West Midlands, DY8 1EP
☎ (01384) 440202 ⊕ craddocksbrewery.com

Craddock's began brewing at the rear of the Duke William pub in Stourbridge, though the brewing is now also carried out in the courtyard of the Stable Bar, Bridgnorth. It is a four-barrel plant selling exclusively to its four pubs; the Duke William and the Plough & Harrow, Stourbridge, the King Charles, Worcester, and the Talbot, Droitwich.

River Steam (ABV 3.8%)

Saxon Gold (OG 1041, ABV 4%)

King's Escape (ABV 4.2%)

Crazy Sheep (OG 1045, ABV 4.5%)

Hop & Glory (OG 1045, ABV 4.5%)

Monarch's Way (ABV 4.5%)

Troll (OG 1052, ABV 5.4%)
A deceptively strong, sophisticated golden ale, with a bittersweet taste and dry hop finish.

Craft, The

29a Part Street, Southport, Merseyside, PR8 1HY
☎ 07870 160934 ⊕ thecraftbrewery.com

The Craft is a small-batch, independently owned microbrewery producing vegan-friendly, unfined, hand-crafted ales using traditional techniques. ♦ RAIB V

Crafty Gold (OG 1045, ABV 4%)
A smooth single malt beer with slight fruit flavours and a refreshing finish.

Crafty Ale (OG 1055, ABV 4.5%)

A rich, dark ale with chocolate undertones and a malty finish.

Crafty IPA (OG 1055, ABV 4.5%)
A full-flavoured IPA, slightly bitter with citrus notes, good mouthfeel and a clean, dry finish.

Crafty Devil (OG 1062, ABV 5%)
A dark, rich, traditional porter with a hint of cherry.

Crafty Smoke (OG 1064, ABV 5%)
A pale ale with a pleasant smoky aftertaste.

Craft Originale (NEW)

1 Tofthill, Markinch, KY7 6HN ☎ 07790 172708

Small scale brewing began in 2017.

Crafted (NEW) SIBA ⊙

Unit 3c, Bewdley Business Park, Long Bank, Bewdley, Worcestershire, DY12 2TZ
☎ (01299) 269382 ☎ 07851 862254
⊕ craftedbrewing.co.uk

Set up in 2016, the brewery uses a five-barrel plant from Woodbury Brewery in Worcestershire. Beers are currently only available in the local area.

White Goose (OG 1036, ABV 3.8%)
Toffee aromas, fruity, smooth bitterness with a sweet, dry finish.

The Revolution (OG 1039, ABV 4%)
Honey and pine aromas with light toffee and caramel flavours.

Wyre (OG 1048, ABV 5%)
Amber-coloured strong bitter, apricot and light citrus aromas with a smooth and light, fruity taste.

Crafty Beers

The Stables, Hall Farm, Stetchworth, Cambridgeshire, CB8 0TY
☎ (01223) 813938 ⊕ craftybeers.co.uk

⊗ Crafty Beers are brewed by Robert Beardsmore in an old stable building situated between Cambridge and Newmarket. Beer is available at a number of pubs in and around Cambridge. RAIB V

Mild Mannered (OG 1040, ABV 3.5%)
Dark mild with a pleasant balance of sweet malt and tempered bitterness.

Carpenter's Cask (OG 1038, ABV 3.8%) ◥
A well-balanced amber brew with biscuit malt character giving way to hops on the palate and a long finish.

Sixteen Strides (OG 1037, ABV 3.8%)
Generously hopped pale ale with plenty of citrus aroma.

Wilbraham (OG 1042, ABV 4.1%)
Amber-coloured ale with rich malt flavours and good balancing bitterness. Subtle hop aroma with the characteristic earthy notes of Fuggles.

Sauvignon Blonde (OG 1043, ABV 4.4%)
An aromatic golden ale.

Crafty Brewing SIBA ⊙

Thatched House Farm, Loxhill, Dunsfold, Surrey, GU8 4BW
☎ (01483) 276300 ☎ 07702 305595
⊕ craftybrewing.co.uk

⊗ Opened in 2014 and situated on Luke Herman's family farm behind Dunsfold aerodrome, Crafty's base has a historic connection with the Canadian troop presence during WWII. The five-barrel plant supplies more than 100 pubs across the region plus local events and markets. RAIB

Loxhill Biscuit (OG 1038, ABV 3.8%)
Well-balanced session golden ale with floral notes.

Dunsfold Best (OG 1040, ABV 4%)
An English ale made with classic English hops, grain and yeast.

Crafty One (OG 1042, ABV 4.2%)
A pale, straw-coloured beer, smooth and complex, yet refreshing.

Hop Tipple (OG 1042, ABV 4.2%)

Crafty Devil

Ninian Park Road, Cardiff
☎ (029) 2021 8099 ☎ 07766 014550
⊕ craftydevilbrewing.co.uk

⊗ Crafty Devil began brewing in 2014. It currently only produces bottled, canned and keg beers but cask-conditioned beer can be arranged by special request, particularly for local events. ‼ ☛

Crafty Pint

≣ c/o Half Moon, 130 Northgate, Darlington, County Durham, DL1 1QS
☎ (01325) 469965 ☎ 07804 305175
⊕ thecraftypint.co.uk

The Crafty Pint Brewery was established in 2013 in the cellar of the Half Moon in Darlington. Originally a 10-gallon brew length, it was upgraded to a one-barrel plant in 2015. One-off beers are produced solely for the pub with a few other outlets being occasionally supplied.

Crankshaft (NEW)

17e Boxer Place, Leyland, Lancashire, PR26 7QL
☎ 07827 289200 ⊕ crankshaftbrewery.co.uk

☺Crankshaft was launched in 2016, brewing from home on a 0.5-barrel plant. It moved to new premises in 2017 using a 2.5-barrel plant due to demand. The beers have been available at several local micropubs and beer festivals and in bottled form at specialist shops and markets.

Propshaft (ABV 3.8%)
A classic session beer, pale golden in colour. English hops give a refreshing, grassy, earthy taste.

Crankcase (ABV 5%)

Ribble Red (ABV 5%)

Dryveshaft (ABV 5.2%)

Sumners Steam (ABV 6.6%)

Crate SIBA

Unit 7, White Building, Queens Yard, Hackney Wick, London, E9 5EN ☎ 07834 275687
⊕ cratebrewery.com

Crate is a brewery and pizzeria opened in 2012 and situated in a canalside former print factory. RAIB

Best Bitter (OG 1045, ABV 4.3%) ◥

Copper-coloured beer with roast and berry fruitiness. Sweetness and biscuit character is offset by bitterness that lingers with roast notes.

Stout (OG 1057, ABV 5.7%) ◣
Slightly smoky nose with blackcurrant fruit. Caramelised toffee and liquorice flavour that lingers. A little black roast notes throughout.

Credence SIBA

Unit 16b, Coquet Enterprise Park, Amble, Northumberland, NE65 0PE
☎ (01665) 714855 ⊕ credencebrewing.co.uk

Credence began brewing in 2015. ◆

Blonde (ABV 3.8%)

Carnelian Pale (ABV 4.2%)

Clearwater Pale (ABV 4.2%)

White Session IPA (ABV 4.8%)

Elemental IPA (ABV 5.5%)

Cromarty

Davidston, Cromarty, IV11 8XD
☎ (01381) 600440 ⊕ cromartybrewing.co.uk

Cromarty began brewing in 2011 in a purpose-built brewhouse. Additional fermenters were installed in 2014 and again in 2015 to meet demand. ‼ ⛟ ◆

Atlantic Drift (OG 1035, ABV 3.5%) ◣
Good golden amber-coloured beer with a grapefruit hop flavour throughout.Tasty for its strength.

Hit the Lip (OG 1037, ABV 3.8%) ◣
A good mouth-puckering grapefruit hoppy brew with a dry finish.

Whiteout (ABV 3.8%)
A session IPA.

Happy Chappy (OG 1040, ABV 4.1%) ◣
A golden ale with plenty of hop character. Floral citus hop aroma with a good bitter taste, which increases in the aftertaste.

Kowabunga (OG 1046, ABV 4.6%) ◣
Refreshing, golden-coloured, peachy, hoppy brew.

Brewed Awakening (ABV 4.7%)
A coffee-infused stout.

Red Rocker (OG 1048.5, ABV 5%) ▣ ◣
Red-coloured rye speciality hop monster with a malty background leading to a bitter finish.

Rogue Wave (OG 1052, ABV 5.7%) ▣ ◣
Easy-drinking, strong, peachy, hoppy bitter.

Ghost Town (OG 1058, ABV 5.8%) ◣
Dark roasted malty brew with a blackcurrant and liquorice background.

AKA IPA (OG 1067, ABV 6.7%) ◣
Strong IPA with a smooth, citrus, hoppy taste.

Man Overboard (ABV 8.8%)

Cronx SIBA

Unit 6, Vulcan Business Centre, Vulcan Way, New Addington, CR0 9UG
☎ (01689) 809093 ☎ 07793 974395
⊕ thecronx.com

⊠ Cronx began brewing in 2012 and is the first commercial brewery in the area since 1954. ‼ ⛟ ◆

Standard (ABV 3.8%) ◣
Easy-drinking brown-coloured bitter with sweetish fudge and spicy hoppy notes throughout. A malty bitter finish with a dryness that remains.

Kotchin (ABV 3.9%) ◣
Grapefruit beer with pleasant hoppy notes. A little sweetness is balanced by a crisp, bitter finish that grows on drinking.

Nektar (ABV 4.5%) ◣
Full-bodied, dark gold-coloured best bitter. Peach with citrus, sweet biscuit and floral hops gently fade in the lingering bitter finish.

Entire (ABV 5.2%) ◣
Dark brown-coloured porter with chocolate roast notes in the aroma, flavour and finish. The fruit character is of caramelised raisins.

Cropton

See Great Yorkshire

Cross Bay ◉

White Lund Industrial Estate, Morecambe, Lancashire, LA3 3PT
☎ (01524) 39481 ⊕ crossbaybrewery.co.uk

◉Cross Bay commenced brewing in 2011 on a 28-barrel brew plant and has a brewing capacity of 168 barrels a week. ‼ ⛟ ◆

Halo (OG 1037, ABV 3.6%) ◣
A crisp and hoppy pale bitter.

Nightfall Pale Bitter (OG 1038, ABV 3.8%) ◣
A sweet, malty, gently-hopped bitter with some fruit.

Sunshine (OG 1041, ABV 4%) ◣
Smooth blonde beer with a strong, fruity flavour. Forest fruits on the nose.

Sunset Blonde (OG 1043, ABV 4.2%) ◣
Sweet and fruity best bitter with a rising bitter finish.

Dusk Ruby Ale (OG 1045, ABV 4.5%)
A ruby-coloured ale, roasted bitter body with hints of cocoa, following through with a red berry aroma.

Zenith (OG 1049.5, ABV 5%) ◣
Gentle bitterness and fruity sweetness with some astringency in the finish.

Cross Borders (NEW) SIBA

28-1, Hardengreen Industrial Estate, Dalkeith, EH22 3NX
☎ (0131) 629 3990 ⊕ crossborders.beer

Established in 2016 by two friends, Jonathan Wilson and Gary Munckton.

Pale (OG 1038, ABV 3.8%)
Notes of mint and lemon on the nose with a balanced citrus bitter finish.

Heavy (OG 1054, ABV 4.1%)
A modern take on a traditional Scottish style. Rich and well-balanced with a slight bite to the finish.

IPA (OG 1044, ABV 4.5%)
Aromas of pear and pineapple, followed by a resinous, bitter finish.

Porter (OG 1045, ABV 4.5%)

Porter with a roasted, smooth mouthfeel. Flavours of coffee, chocolate and subtle spice come through in the finish.

Braw (OG 1055, ABV 5.2%)
A juicy, refreshing pale ale with citrus and tropical notes.

Crossed Anchors SIBA

▤ c/o Grapevine, 2 Victoria Road, Exmouth, Devon, EX8 1DL
☎ (01395) 222208 ☎ 07980 806582
⊕ crossedanchors.co.uk

Crossed Anchors was established in 2015, with the beer initially produced using spare capacity at another brewery. In 2016 a six-barrel plant became operational in the old stables of the Grapevine in Exmouth town centre. Beers are available across Devon and the South-west, as well as in the Grapevine.

CSH (OG 1038, ABV 3.8%)
A single-hopped pale ale.

Three Cs Gold (OG 1040, ABV 4.3%)
A triple-hopped, golden-coloured ale.

Black IPA (OG 1042, ABV 4.5%)

American Pale Ale (OG 1045, ABV 4.6%)
A golden-coloured pale ale, with citrus and stone fruit aromas.

Red Right Hand (OG 1045, ABV 4.6%)
An American-style, red-coloured ale with stone fruit and citrus flavours.

Weisse Guy (OG 1047, ABV 5%)
A German-style wheat beer, naturally hazy.

Crouch Vale SIBA

23 Haltwhistle Road, South Woodham Ferrers, Essex, CM3 5ZA
☎ (01245) 322744 ⊕ crouchvale.co.uk

⊠ Founded in 1981 by two CAMRA enthusiasts, Crouch Vale is now well established as a major player in Essex brewing, having moved to larger premises in 2006. The company is also a major wholesaler of cask ale from other independent breweries, which it supplies to more than 100 outlets, as well as beer festivals throughout the region. A tap room opened on the brewery site in 2016. One tied house, the Queen's Head in Chelmsford, is owned. ‼ ⇌ ◆ RAIB

Blackwater Mild (OG 1037, ABV 3.7%) ◆
A dark bitter rather than a true mild. Roasty and very bitter towards the end.

Essex Boys Best Bitter (OG 1038, ABV 3.8%)
Full-bodied, traditional-style best bitter.

Brewers Gold (OG 1040, ABV 4%) ◆
Pale golden ale with a striking citrus nose. Sweet fruit and bitter hops are well matched throughout.

Yakima Gold (OG 1042, ABV 4.2%)
Golden ale with earthy, aromatic hops.

Amarillo (OG 1050, ABV 5%)
A premium golden ale with hop aromas and a lasting spicy and orange flavour.

Cryptic SIBA ⊙

3 Carrington Field, Heaviley, Stockport, SK1 3JN

☎ (0161) 222 8840 ☎ 07590 438360
⊕ crypticales.co.uk

⊠ Cryptic Ales was founded in 2014 using a 10-barrel plant after discussion between four quiz team members. Four core beers and up to six occasional beers are brewed with dark beers proving popular. Further ales are planned with a one-barrel experimental plant used for speciality and unusual ales. ◆ RAIB

Anagram (OG 1033, ABV 3.5%)
A golden session ale with a hoppy and fruity aroma. A refreshing and light, dry finish.

The Ghost (OG 1036, ABV 3.7%)
A dark and fruity mild with a hint of chocolate, enriched with a hazelnut flavour.

Tip of the Tongue (OG 1041, ABV 4.2%)
A copper-coloured premium bitter with a toffee and chocolate aroma, delivering a malty, gentle bitterness.

1049 Dead (OG 1047, ABV 4.9%)
A dark, fruity, vibrant mild with a chocolate taste.

1049 Grey (OG 1047, ABV 4.9%)
A dark, fruity, vibrant mild with a chocolate taste. The addition of Earl Grey tea in the brew provides a subtle hint of bergamot.

Enigma (OG 1046, ABV 5%)
A spicy and citrus aroma is followed by a full-bodied, well-hopped, honeyed taste.

Acrostic (OG 1047, ABV 5.1%)
A dark porter with a fruity aroma. Made with just one hop variety it has a liquorice and creamy coffee taste.

Cuillin

▤ Sligachan Hotel, Sligachan, Isle of Skye, IV47 8SW
☎ (01478) 650204 ☎ 07795 250808
⊕ sligachan.co.uk

The five-barrel brewery opened in 2004 and is situated in central Skye at the foot of the Cuillin mountains. The water from the Cuillins provides a distinctive colour and taste to the ales. The brewery is closed in winter.

Eagle (ABV 3.8%)
Slightly hoppy, smooth session ale with a light caramel taste.

Old Bridge (ABV 4.1%) ◆
Some malts and a background citrus hop in this bittersweet brew.

Black Face (ABV 4.3%) ◆
A good balance of blackcurrants and malts highlight this dark ruby red-coloured strong mild. Liquorice and roast also evident in the creamy mouthfeel.

Pinnacle (ABV 4.7%) ◆
The hoppy and fruity nose leads to more hop and plenty of pale malt flavour in this drinkable golden amber-coloured bitter.

Cullercoats SIBA ⊙

Westfield Court, 19 Maurice Road Industrial Estate, Wallsend, Tyne & Wear, NE28 6BY
☎ (0191) 252 8765 ☎ 07895 692881

Office: 17 St Oswins Avenue, Cullercoats, NE30 4PH
⊕ cullercoatsbrewery.co.uk

☺Ex-solicitor Bill Scantlebury established Cullercoats in 2011 and brews twice a week. ♦RAIB V

Shuggy Boat Blonde (OG 1039, ABV 3.8%)
A refreshing blonde beer, smooth and fresh.

Lovely Nelly (OG 1039, ABV 3.9%)
A full-bodied bronze-coloured session beer with a biscuit malt flavour balanced with a smooth hop bitterness.

Jack the Devil (OG 1045, ABV 4.5%)
A rich, dark chestnut-coloured ale with well-balanced malty nuttiness and a fresh, hoppy aroma.

Shuggy Boat Blonde Special (OG 1050, ABV 5%)

Rocket Brigade (OG 1054, ABV 5.5%)
An English pale ale, strong and bitter yet easy drinking.

Cumberland SIBA 👁

The Forge, Great Corby, Cumbria, CA4 8LR
☎ (01228) 560899 ⊕ cumberlandbreweries.co.uk

☺Cumberland was established in 2009 with a bespoke 10-barrel plant and is situated in a building at the heart of the village, previously the farriers shop from 1833. The brewery was purchased by American brewer Alltech in 2015 and expansion is planned. ‼

Corby Ale (OG 1038, ABV 3.8%) ◄
A fruity session beer with sweetness leading to gentle bitterness in the aftertaste.

Corby APA (ABV 4%)
A light-bodied, amber-coloured American-style pale ale, strong on grapefruit and stone fruit flavours with a hint of vanilla in the aroma.

Corby Blonde (OG 1039, ABV 4%) ◄
Melon fruity hoppiness gives a light, refreshing drink.

Corby Red (OG 1041, ABV 4.2%)
A deep red-coloured, sweet ale, rich in caramel and toffee flavours.

Corby Stout (OG 1044, ABV 4.5%) ◄
Fruity aroma, sweet roast middle and dry finish.

Corby Fox (OG 1048, ABV 4.6%) ◄
A pleasing brown ale with a slight bitter finish.

Cumbrian Legendary SIBA 👁

Old Hall Brewery, Hawkshead, Cumbria, LA22 0QF
☎ (01539) 436436 ⊕ cumbrianlegendaryales.com

☺First established in 2003, the brewery is located in an idyllic position in a renovated barn on the shores of Esthwaite Water. The success of Loweswater Gold has meant the brewery is thriving. ‼♦

Esthwaite Bitter (OG 1038.5, ABV 3.8%) ◄
Robust, refreshing bitter with plenty of hops, lasting well into the finish.

Langdale (OG 1040, ABV 4%) ◄
Fresh grapefruit aromas with hoppy fruity flavours and crisp, long hop finish, make for a well-balanced beer.

Grasmoor Dark Ale (OG 1043, ABV 4.3%) ◄
Dark fruity beer with complex character and roast nutty tones leading to a short, refreshing finish.

Loweswater Gold (OG 1041, ABV 4.3%) ◄

A dominant fruity body develops into a light bitter finish. A beer that belies its strength.

Vanilla Oatmeal Stout (ABV 4.8%)
A creamy stout brewed with vanilla pods.

American Invasion (OG 1047, ABV 5%) ◄
Well-balanced gold-coloured beer with big hop impact and long, fruity finish.

Cwm Rhondda

Fforch Farm, Cemetery Road, Treorchy, CF42 6TF
☎ (01443) 777491 ⊕ cwmrhonddaales.co.uk

Cwm Rhondda is a family-run brewery situated on a farm in the Rhondda Valley. Brewing commenced in 2015 on a 2.5-barrel plant using the brewery's own spring water, which gives a unique taste to the ales. Pubs in South Wales are supplied. Expansion to the brewery and an online shop are planned.

Shwmae But (OG 1039, ABV 3.8%)

Pit Head (OG 1045, ABV 4%)

Boyo (OG 1044, ABV 4.5%)

Tommy Box (OG 1044, ABV 4.5%)

Afon Aur (OG 1046, ABV 4.6%)

Daleside SIBA 👁

Camwal Road, Starbeck, Harrogate, North Yorkshire, HG1 4PT
☎ (01423) 880022 ⊕ dalesidebrewery.com

☺Opened in 1991 in Harrogate with a 20-barrel plant, the brewery delivers direct to a range of outlets including pubs, restaurants and farm shops from Newcastle to Chesterfield as well as nationally via wholesalers. �♦

Bitter (OG 1039, ABV 3.7%) ◄
Pale brown in colour, this well-balanced, hoppy beer is complemented by fruity bitterness and a hint of sweetness, leading to a long, bitter finish.

Blonde (OG 1040, ABV 3.9%) ◄
A pale golden beer with a predominantly hoppy aroma and taste, leading to a refreshing hoppy, bitter but short finish.

Old Leg Over (OG 1043, ABV 4.1%)
Well-balanced, mid brown-coloured refreshing beer that leads to an equally well-balanced fruity, bitter aftertaste.

Square Rigger IPA (ABV 4.5%)
Light amber-coloured IPA with a floral aroma.

Monkey Wrench (OG 1055, ABV 5.3%) ▣
Premium deep chestnut-coloured ale with a spicy fruit aroma and warming spicy flavour.

Dalrannoch (NEW)

Unit 16, The Old Dairy, Meikleour, PH2 6FB
⊕ dalrannochbrewing.co.uk

Brewing began in 2016 using a five-barrel plant.

Manky Blonde (ABV 4.4%)

Red Skelp (ABV 5.4%)

Blind Growler (ABV 5.7%)

Stoatin' Stoat (ABV 6.5%)

Dan's (NEW)

98 North Western Street, Manchester, M12 6HR
☎ (0161) 661 3676 ✉ danwdeb@gmail.com

Dan's Brewery was set up in 2016 in a railway arch under Piccadilly Station, mainly to supply house beers to the Knott Bar, Manchester city centre, the Macc, Macclesfield, and Chorlton Tap, Chorlton.

Pale Ale (ABV 3.9%)

Porter (ABV 5.2%)
Deep mahogany-coloured porter with a smooth texture and sweet notes of hazelnut balanced with roasted malts to give a dry and toasty finish.

Dancing Cows

Sadlers Farm Workshops, Lower Pennington Lane, Lymington, Hampshire, SO41 8AL
☎ (01590) 676071 ☎ 07952 639465
⊕ dancingcows.co.uk

⊠ Dancing Cows is a small-batch brewery and distillery close to the Lymington-Keyhaven Nature Reserve, sourcing local grains, hops, herbs and spices. Operated by the former owner of Bowland Brewery in Lancashire and inspired by a trip to Lake Michigan to bring a fresh outlook on brewing. New recipes are being developed constantly. ⅋ ⊟ ♦ RAIB

Lighthouse (OG 1038, ABV 3.8%)
A golden ale with grapefruit hop flavours and aromas.

Pony (OG 1040, ABV 4%)
A traditional amber-coloured ale with rounded fruit flavours and good malt characteristics.

Admiral (OG 1045, ABV 4.5%)
A traditional best bitter with subtle orange hop notes.

Dancing Duck SIBA ◉

1 John Cooper Buildings, Payne Street, Derby, DE22 3AZ
☎ (01332) 205582 ☎ 07581 122122
⊕ dancingduckbrewery.com

Dancing Duck was established in 2010 by Rachel Mathews using a 10-barrel brew plant. Its name comes from the local greeting 'ay up me duck'. The brewery operates two local pubs, the Exeter Arms and the Duck House at the Derby Rowing Club. ♦

Ay Up (OG 1040.5, ABV 3.9%) ▮
A pale session bitter. Subtle malt and floral notes are matched with citrus hop, rounded off with a slightly dry finish.

Waitangi (OG 1041.3, ABV 4%)
An easy-drinking, crisp, clean pale ale. Subtle malt character is balanced with zesty lemon and lime hops.

Ginger Ninja (OG 1042, ABV 4.1%)
Refreshing ale, well-balanced with citrus notes from the hops and a subtle ginger flavour.

Nice Weather (OG 1042, ABV 4.1%)
Copper-coloured fruity ale. Blackberry, strawberry and floral rose notes are in perfect balance with just the right amount of malt character. A refreshing summer thirst quencher, it's fruit salad in a glass

Back, Sack & Quack (ABV 4.2%)

A traditional mild, full-bodied with malty flavours. Black cherry, cola and toffee with a caramel finish and berry aroma.

22 (OG 1044.1, ABV 4.3%)
A well-balanced best bitter with good malty flavour and dark fruit notes offset by a strong hop with a clean finish.

DCUK (OG 1042, ABV 4.3%)
A pale ale with a fruity aroma. A juicy citrus flavour with hints of orange, mango, lemon and pine.

Dark Drake (OG 1051, ABV 4.5%)
Malty caramel liquorice flavours combine in a smooth-drinking velvety oatmeal stout with a freshly roasted coffee and tea finish.

Waddle It Be? (OG 1045.2, ABV 4.5%)
Pale ale with a complex mouthfeel and intense fruity flavours of oranges, peaches and blackcurrants with a spicy black pepper kick.

Gold (OG 1046.5, ABV 4.7%)
A modern IPA with powerful hoppy bitterness and aroma balanced with strong malt notes. English First Gold hops give peppery, plum-like and orange zesty flavours.

Amberillo (OG 1047.2, ABV 4.8%)
An easy-drinking amber-coloured ale. Earthy aromatic hops are balanced with biscuit malt flavours leading to a spicy, peppery finish.

Indian Porter (OG 1051.8, ABV 5%)
Smoky bonfire flavours with a spicy hop and pleasant warming afterglow.

Seduction (OG 1051.3, ABV 5.2%)
A malt-led ruby-coloured beer, dark fruity flavours are followed by a lingering powerful hop.

Abduction (OG 1053, ABV 5.5%)
A myriad of tropical flavours in balance with an enjoyable level of hoppy bitterness, a good malt character and clean finish. This is a dangerously drinkable 5.5 IPA

Dancing Man

Wool House, Town Quay, Southampton, Hampshire, SO14 2AR
☎ (023) 8083 6666 ⊕ dancingmanbrewery.co.uk

⊠ Dancing Man began brewing in 2011 in the Platform Tavern. In 2015 the brewery moved to the historic Wool House in order to expand and include an on-site bar and restaurant. One-off and rare brews are available throughout the year. ♦ RAIB

Pilgrim's Pale Ale (OG 1039, ABV 3.9%)
A pale golden ale with tropical fruit aromas, a smooth bitter flavour and a clean, crisp finish.

Congo Driftwood (OG 1042, ABV 4.2%)
A modern pale ale with the addition of fresh mango and papaya, which delivers unique tropical flavours.

Jack O'Diamonds (OG 1045, ABV 4.5%)
Complex malty red-coloured ale. Lots of hops play off the malt body to give a fruity, rich beer.

Fiddler's Jig (OG 1047, ABV 4.8%)
A rich malt body, with fruity hop flavours.

Last Waltz (OG 1052, ABV 5.3%)
A black IPA with an intense hoppy nose with tropical fruit notes, a smoky roasted malt flavour and a dry bitter finish.

Big Casino (OG 1056, ABV 5.7%)

Pine and citrus fruit aroma with a warming malt body and a smooth bitterness with juicy hop flavours.

Dancing Men

🏠 Hill House Inn, The Hill, Happisburgh, Norfolk, NR12 0PW
☎ (01692) 650004 ☎ 07818 038768
🌐 hillhouseinn.co.uk

Brewing began in 2014 at the 16th-century Hill House Inn on Happisburgh's fast-eroding clifftop. The microbrewery is named in honour of a famous Sherlock Holmes story written by Sir Arthur Conan Doyle after he visited the pub in 1903. The five-barrel plant was acquired from Bees Brewery after its partial destruction during the tidal surge events in Walcott in 2013.

Dark Horse SIBA

Coonlands Laithe, Hetton, North Yorkshire, BD23 6LY
☎ (01756) 730555 🌐 darkhorsebrewery.co.uk

☺Dark Horse began brewing in 2008. The brewery is based in an old hay barn within the Yorkshire Dales National Park. Around 50 outlets are supplied direct.

Craven Bitter (OG 1038, ABV 3.8%) ◀
Well-balanced bitter with biscuity malt and fruit on the nose continuing into the taste. Bitterness increases in the finish.

Blonde Beauty (OG 1040, ABV 3.9%)

Hetton Pale Ale (OG 1041, ABV 4.2%) ◀
Golden, well-balanced, full-bodied, with hoppy bitterness on the palate overlaying a malty base and a spicy citrus character.

Night Jar (OG 1042, ABV 4.2%)
A dark premium ale.

Dark Revolution (NEW) SIBA

Unit 9, Lancaster Road, Salisbury, Wiltshire, SP4 6FB
☎ (01722) 411179 🌐 darkrevolution.co.uk

Dark Revolution started commercial brewing in 2015; the owner had been home-brewing for the previous decade. 🚚◆RAIB

So.LA (ABV 4.5%)

Velveteen (ABV 4.8%)

Deviant (ABV 5.6%)

ViPA (ABV 6%)

Dark Star SIBA ◉

22 Star Road, Partridge Green, West Sussex, RH13 8RA
☎ (01403) 713085 🌐 darkstarbrewing.co.uk

⊗ The Dark Star Brewing Co was established in the cellar of the Evening Star in Brighton back in 1994, moving to their current home in Partridge Green in 2010. The 45-barrel plant produces a wide range of beers. ‼🚚◆RAIB

Hophead (OG 1040, ABV 3.8%) 🍺 ◀
A golden-coloured session bitter with a fruity/hoppy aroma and a citrus bitter taste and aftertaste. Flavours remain strong to the end.

Partridge Best Bitter (OG 1042, ABV 4%)

Traditional Sussex-style best bitter.

Espresso (OG 1048, ABV 4.2%)
Freshly ground Arabica coffee beans are added to the copper for a few minutes after the boil of this rich black beer.

American Pale Ale (OG 1048, ABV 4.7%)
American-style pale ale, dry with a crisp taste and full hop aroma.

Festival (OG 1052, ABV 5%)
A bronze-coloured bitter with a smooth mouthfeel and freshness.

Original (OG 1052, ABV 5%)
A dark, strong and bitter beer with a complex malt flavour.

Revelation (OG 1057, ABV 5.7%) 🗒
A big, hoppy American pale ale.

Dark Tribe

🏠 Dog & Gun, High Street, East Butterwick, Lincolnshire, DN17 3AJ
☎ (01724) 782324 🌐 darktribe.co.uk

Situated on the banks of the River Trent in the Dog & Gun pub, this 2.5-barrel brewing plant produces beers for the pub and local outlets. The award-winning brewery has been established since 1996. A range of one-off beers is produced throughout the year.

Darkwave

52-54 Aqueduct Street, Preston, Lancashire, PR1 7RE
☎ 07970 110459 ✉ darkwave-ale@outlook.com

Previously known as Arkwright's, brewing began at the rear of the Real Ale Shop on Lovat Road in 2010 using a 2.5-barrel plant. In 2014 the plant was upgraded to a 10-barrel plant and moved to the current premises. Darkwave are now producing a range of modern artisan beers, always unfined and vegan. ◆V

Dartmoor SIBA ◉

The Brewery, Station Road, Princetown, Devon, PL20 6QX
☎ (01822) 890789 🌐 dartmoorbrewery.co.uk

⊗ Formerly named Princetown, Dartmoor Brewery was established in 1994 and is the highest brewery in England at 1,465 feet above sea level. In 2006 the brewery moved to a purpose-built building and in 2012 capacity was increased to 360 barrels a week by the addition of another 60-barrel fermenter with a further increase in 2013. All beer is brewed using Dartmoor and Devon-grown barley. ‼◆RAIB

Best (OG 1037, ABV 3.7%)
An amber-coloured ale with a dry hop citrus fruit character.

IPA (OG 1039.5, ABV 4%) ◀
There is a flowery hop aroma and taste with a bitter aftertaste to this full-bodied, amber-coloured beer.

Dragon's Breath (OG 1044, ABV 4.4%)
Deep ruby brown in colour, rich and full bodied with an aftertaste of cherries.

Legend (OG 1043.5, ABV 4.4%) ◀

Malt and caramel dominate, balanced in an aftertaste of bitter hops. Well-rounded and complex.

Jail Ale (OG 1047.5, ABV 4.8%) ◆
Well-balanced yet complex. Lingering malty, caramel aroma with hints of hops and fruit continues into full aftertaste.

Darwin SIBA

1 West Quay Court, Sunderland Enterprise Park, Sunderland, SR5 2TE
☎ (0191) 549 9450 ⊕ darwinbrewery.com

☺Established in 1994, Darwin Brewery is based in purpose-built premises in Sunderland with a 3.5-barrel brew plant. The brewery supports students on Brewlab brewing courses at the university, who produce many unique specialist and international beers, often available locally. A range of established Darwin beers is also produced, some based on analysis of historic recipes or student initiatives. ‼◆RAIB

Dawkins SIBA

Unit 2, Lawnwood Industrial Units, Lawnwood Road, Easton, Bristol, BS5 0EF
☎ (0117) 955 9503 ⊕ dawkinsales.com

⊠ The established Dawkins Taverns group of independent Bristol pubs bought the Somerset-based Matthews Brewery in 2009. New premises in Easton, Bristol, opened in 2015 with a 20-barrel plant. The brewery distributes to its own five pubs and directly to another 80 outlets in the area. A sister company was set up in Edinburgh in 2017, reviving the long-defunct 'Steel Coulson' brewing name for a bar in Leith with an on-site microbrewery planned. ‼ 🍺◆RAIB

Bristol Blonde (OG 1036, ABV 3.8%) ◆
Pale yellow-coloured golden ale. Citrus aroma. Refreshing lemon taste with grassiness, which fades to astringent bitterness.

Bristol Best (OG 1040, ABV 4%) ◆
Copper-coloured bitter with malty aroma and taste. Hints of apple. Astringent aftertaste.

Tremendous Delicious (OG 1042, ABV 4.2%)
Amber-coloured beer with a biscuity malt aroma and flavour, and a bitter finish.

Bristol Gold (OG 1043, ABV 4.4%)
Golden ale with a slightly spicy fruit aroma and flavour.

Easton IPA (OG 1041, ABV 4.4%)
Hazy gold-coloured unfined ale. Fruity and citrus.

Resolution IPA (OG 1046, ABV 5%)
A hazy amber gold-coloured IPA with mango and grapefruit flavours.

de Brus

▤ The Bruery, 25 Canmore Street, Dunfermline, KY12 7NU
☎ (01383) 747757 ⊕ debrusbrewery.com

Located near Dunfermline's city centre and just along the road from the renowned Alhambra Theatre, the brewery opened in 2013. The Bruery is unique to Dunfermline as it is the only bar in town to brew its own beer.

Deeply Vale

Unit 25, Peel Industrial Estate, Chamberhall Street, Bury, BL9 0LU
☎ (0161) 761 7334 ☎ 07736 936973
⊕ deeplyvalebrewery.com

☺Deeply Vale is a family-run business established in 2012 using a 2.5-barrel plant. The brewery's name immortalises the Deeply Vale area near Bury, famed for legendary 1970s music festivals.

Equilibrium (OG 1036, ABV 3.8%)

Citra Storm (ABV 4%)
A session ale, bursting with the flavours and aromas of lemon and grapefruit.

Deeply Red (ABV 4.2%)
Fruity and smooth beer with a gentle red fruit and light spice aroma. A slightly spicy taste and astringency.

Golden Vale (OG 1041, ABV 4.2%)
A complex but well-balanced bitterness with a slight caramel finish and fairly fruity aroma. The flavour is refreshing, robust and satisfyingly malty.

Deeply Blonde (ABV 4.5%)
An easy-drinking beer with a citrus and tropical fruit explosion.

DV8 (OG 1050, ABV 4.8%)
A smooth, easy-drinking breakfast stout.

Deeside 👁

The Steading, Lochton of Leys, Banchory, AB31 5QB
☎ (01330) 825598 ⊕ deesidebrewery.co.uk

First established in 2005, a change of ownership and location in 2012 led to substantial growth in the Scottish retail sector as well as export markets in Europe, USA, the Middle East and Asia, while maintaining its independent status. RAIB

APA (OG 1038, ABV 3.8%) ◆
Light, citrus, hoppy session ale.

Blonde (OG 1038, ABV 3.8%)

Macbeth (OG 1042, ABV 4.1%) ◆
Roasted malt and hops come through in the taste.

80/- (OG 1048, ABV 4.5%)

IPA (OG 1054, ABV 5.2%) ◆
Slightly sweet with a mix of malt and hops and a slight raspberry background.

Denbigh

Crown Workshop, Crown Lane, Denbigh, LL16 3SY
☎ (01745) 817021 ⊕ bragdybinbych.co.uk

Brewing commenced in 2012 at the rear of the Hope & Anchor pub. The brewery relocated in 2015 to a dedicated brewhouse in the town. A micropub next to the brewery, Y-Goron-Fach, is owned. ◆RAIB

Earls Folly (OG 1042, ABV 3.6%)

John the Thumb (OG 1038, ABV 3.6%)

Goblin Tower (OG 1038, ABV 3.8%)

Cadlas Ceiliogod (Cock Pit) (OG 1045, ABV 4.5%)
A tawny-coloured bitter. Well-hopped, with caramel and malt highlights.

**Cwrw Du'nbych (Denbigh Black)
(OG 1050, ABV 5%)**
A traditional Celtic black porter with a rich, roasted flavour and hints of muscovado.

I Presume Ale (IPA) (OG 1050, ABV 5.5%)

Dent SIBA

Hollins, Cowgill, Dent, Cumbria, LA10 5TQ
☎ (01539) 625326 ⊕ dentbrewery.co.uk

☺Dent was set up in 1990 in a converted barn next to a former farmhouse in the Yorkshire Dales National Park. In 2005 the brewery was completely refurbished and capacity expanded. One pub is owned. More than 150 outlets are supplied direct.
‼🍺

Golden Fleece (OG 1035, ABV 3.7%) ◆
Light, hoppy and fruity, with a bitter aftertaste.

Station Porter (OG 1042, ABV 3.8%) ◆
A veritable malt feast for the beer's strength. A complex porter ending with roast highlights.

Aviator (OG 1039, ABV 4%) ◆
This amber-coloured ale is characterised by citrus, caramel and hop flavours that evolve into a bitter finish.

Rambrau (OG 1042, ABV 4.5%)
A cask-conditioned lager, clean, crisp and refreshing.

Ramsbottom Strong Ale (OG 1042, ABV 4.5%) ◆
A well-balanced, malty best bitter.

Kamikaze (OG 1047, ABV 5%) ◆
Hops and fruit dominate this full-bodied, golden-coloured, strong bitter, with a dry bitterness growing in the aftertaste.

T'owd Tup (OG 1056, ABV 6%) ◆
A rich, full-flavoured, strong stout with a coffee aroma. The dominant roast character is balanced by a warming sweetness and a raisiny, fruitcake taste that lingers on into the finish.

Derby SIBA ◉

Masons Place Business Park, Nottingham Road, Derby, DE21 6AQ
☎ (01332) 365366 ⊕ derbybrewing.co.uk

A family-run microbrewery, established in 2004 in the old Masons Paintworks Varnish Shed by head brewer Trevor Harris, founder and former brewer at the Brunswick Inn, Derby (qv). The business has grown over the years and four pubs are now owned around Derby. More than 400 outlets are supplied including major retailers. In addition to the core range there are at least four new beers each month which includes the new monthly Craft Collection range. ‼🍺◆

Hop Till You Drop (OG 1039, ABV 3.9%)
A blonde ale with fruity overtones and a dry finish.

Triple Hop (OG 1041, ABV 4.1%)
A well-balanced, classic pale ale.

Business As Usual (OG 1044, ABV 4.4%)
An easy-drinking, copper-coloured beer, well-balanced, smooth and malty with a satisfying finish.

Double Mash (OG 1046, ABV 4.6%)
A balanced ruby brew.

Penny's Porter (OG 1046, ABV 4.6%)
A rich, dark, robust brew, with a fine hop balance.

Dashingly Dark (OG 1048, ABV 4.8%)
A smooth, dark brew with complex flavours and a chocolate roasted finish.

Mercia IPA (OG 1050, ABV 5%)
A well-balanced IPA with a modern twist.

Old Intentional (OG 1050, ABV 5%)
A full-bodied, malty premium beer, rich chestnut in colour and well balanced with a delicate sweet aroma and smooth finish.

Quintessential (OG 1058, ABV 5.8%)
Complex and well-rounded with fruit and citrus flavours.

Derventio SIBA

The Brew Shed, Darley Abbey Mills, Darley Abbey, Derbyshire, DE22 1DZ
☎ (01332) 380199 ☎ 07975 944242
⊕ derventiobrewery.co.uk

⊠ A six-barrel microbrewery that first brewed in 2006. In 2011 it moved to the Grade I-listed Mill Complex, which is part of the Derwent Valley Mills World Heritage Site. Derventio is one of the founder members of the Derbyshire Brewers Collective. Spent grain goes to a local farmer. A popular 'Day with the Brewer' is available, by prior arrangement. ‼🍺◆

Minerva (OG 1036.8, ABV 3.8%)

Gold (OG 1040.7, ABV 4.2%)
A pale bitter with subtle character, lemon and pine notes and a hoppy finish.

Hoplite (ABV 4.2%)
Pale and hoppy best bitter.

Et tu Brutus (OG 1043.6, ABV 4.5%)
A dark-coloured ale, smooth but with a long, bitter finish.

Civitas (ABV 4.8%)
A hoppy, traditional IPA.

Cleopatra (OG 1048.4, ABV 5%) 🍴
A complex beer with a hint of apricot.

Spartan (ABV 5.3%)
A crisp, refreshing IPA.

Barbarian (OG 1053.3, ABV 5.5%)
A dark beer, smooth with a lingering subtle hop finish.

Lucretius (ABV 5.5%)
A cherry flavoured stout.

Derwent SIBA

Units 2a-2c, Station Road Industrial Estate, Silloth, Cumbria, CA7 4AG
☎ (01697) 331522 ⊕ derwentbrewery.co.uk

☺Derwent was set up in 1996 in Cockermouth and moved to Silloth in 1998. Owners Mark and Allie bought the brewery in 2013. ◆RAIB

Cote Light (OG 1034, ABV 3.6%)

Carlisle State Bitter (OG 1036, ABV 3.7%) ◆
Malty, biscuity, hoppy beer with a gold colour.

W&M Mild (OG 1036, ABV 3.7%)

Parsons Pledge (OG 1039, ABV 4%) ◆
Amber-coloured ale with a biscuity tang and a slightly fruity finish.

Blonde (OG 1039, ABV 4.2%)

Hudson Bay (OG 1043, ABV 4.2%)

Reaper (OG 1042, ABV 4.3%)

Mutineer (OG 1043, ABV 4.4%)

W&M Pale Ale (OG 1042, ABV 4.4%) ◣
A sweet, fruity, hoppy beer with a bitter finish.

Marshall Port Stout (OG 1054, ABV 5.2%)

Deva Craft

Unit 14, Engineer Park, Babbage Road, Sandycroft, CH5 2QD
☎ (01244) 630670 ☎ 07841 384143
⊕ devacraftbeer.co.uk

☺Deva Craft was set up in 2014 by father-and-son team Ade and Nick Gilbody. Brewing started in 2015 on a five-barrel plant. Beers are available in many outlets throughout North Wales and Cheshire. ‼

Eureka (OG 1038, ABV 3.8%)

568 (OG 1040, ABV 4%)

Oatimus Prime (OG 1042, ABV 4.2%)

Deverell's

Unit 16, Globe Industrial Estate, Grays, Essex, RM17 6ST ☎ 07843 627791

Established in 2012 using a 2.5-barrel plant, Deverell's was the first commercial brewer in Thurrock since Charringtons acquired and closed Seabrooks Brewery more than 80 years ago. The brewery operates its own pub, the Traitors Gate, Grays. It also contract brews for a Chelmsford-based company selling beers under its own brand names. A move is planned to new premises, which have been obtained and are being renovated, which will increase capacity to six barrels. ♦RAIB

Rock n Rolla (OG 1040, ABV 4%)

Redemption (ABV 4.5%)
Full-flavoured, amber-coloured ale with a well-balanced hop profile.

Devil's Dyke

See Arran

Devon

🍺 Mansfield Arms, 7 Main Street, Sauchie, FK10 3JR
☎ (01259) 722020 ⊕ devonales.com

Established in 1992 to produce cask ales for the Mansfield Arms, Sauchie, Devon is the oldest operating brewery in the county. A second pub, the Inn at Muckhart, was purchased in 1994 and the only beers sold there are from the Devon Ales brewery. The brewery also sells beer to the open market.

Original (70/-) (OG 1038, ABV 3.8%)
A full-bodied session ale with a prominent malty flavour and a distinct hoppiness.

Black (OG 1042, ABV 4.2%)

IPA (OG 1042, ABV 4.2%)

Pride (OG 1046, ABV 4.8%)

Devon Earth SIBA

Buckfastleigh, Devon ☎ 07927 397871

Office: 7 Fernham Terrace, Torquay Road, Paignton, Devon, TQ3 2AQ ✉ info@devonearthbrewery.co.uk

⊠ Devon Earth was launched in 2008 on a 2.5-barrel plant located on the banks of the River Dart on the edge of Dartmoor and is run on a part-time basis. It supplies beer festivals, pubs and clubs in the Torbay area and supports local charity events. ♦

Devon Earth (OG 1042, ABV 4.2%)
A light, refreshing ale with a satisfying bitter finish.

Grounded (OG 1047, ABV 4.7%)
A well-rounded, traditional session ale.

Lost in the Woods (OG 1052, ABV 5.2%)
A dark, full-flavoured porter with roasted malt flavours and a touch of liquorice.

Devon's Own

See Clearwater

DEYA (NEW)

33-34 Lansdown Industrial Estate, Gloucester Road, Cheltenham, Gloucestershire, GL51 8PL
☎ (01242) 269189 ☎ 07887 537356
⊕ deyabrewing.com

DEYA Brewing Company was established in 2016. No real ale. ⌦

Dhillon's SIBA

14a Hales Industrial Estate, Rowleys Green Lane, Longford, West Midlands, CV6 6AL
☎ (024) 7666 7413 ⊕ dhillonsbrewery.com

Originally named Lion Heart, the brewery was established in 2014. It relaunched as Dhillon's in 2016 with a new range of beers. Located on an industrial unit near the Ricoh Arena, a five-barrel plant is used. The main focus is on bottled beer but cask-conditioned ales are also brewed. ♦

Golden Pale Ale (ABV 3.8%)

Amber (OG 1048, ABV 4.5%)

Mild (ABV 4.5%)

Stout (ABV 4.5%)

Dark Ruby (ABV 5.1%)

Red IPA (ABV 6.2%)

Dickens

🍺 Great Expectations, 33 London Street, Reading, Berkshire, RG1 4PS
☎ (0118) 950 3925
✉ greatexpectations@relaxinnz.co.uk

A 2.5-barrel microbrewery situated in the Great Expectations pub, Reading, it went into full production in 2015. Its beers are named after Dickens' characters and are only available at the pub.

Dicks

c/o Crafty Little, Building 40, Humber Enterprise Park, Saltgrounds Road, Brough, East Yorkshire, HU15 1EQ
☎ (01482) 667329 ☎ 07792 417564
✉ farmersboilerdick@gmail.com

☺Brewing began in 2016. Spare capacity is used at Crafty Little Brewery.

Big Head Bitter (ABV 4.5%)

Turpins (ABV 4.5%)
A well-hopped pale ale with honey notes.

Digfield SIBA

Lilford Ldge Farm, Barnwell, Northamptonshire, PE8 5SA
☎ (01832) 273954 ⊕ digfield-ales.co.uk

✕ Digfield Ales started brewing in 2005 on a five-barrel plant, which was later expanded to seven barrels. Increased demand led to a move to larger premises in 2012, still in the Barnwell area. A reed bed effluent system has been installed and brewing capacity increased to 15 barrels with new equipment. More than 40 free houses are supplied.
♦

Fools Nook (OG 1037, ABV 3.8%) ◣
The floral aroma, dominated by lavender and honey, belies the hoppy bitterness that comes through in the taste of this golden ale. A fruity balance lasts.

Chiffchaff (OG 1038, ABV 3.9%) ◣
An amber-coloured pale ale with a distinct hoppy aroma.

Barnwell Bitter (OG 1039, ABV 4%) ◣
A fruity aroma introduces a beer in which sharp bitterness is balanced by dry, biscuity malt.

Tipple (ABV 4.2%) ◣
A strong-flavoured pale ale with a hoppy aroma and a dry, lingering finish.

Old Crow Porter (OG 1042, ABV 4.3%) ◣
A rich, full-bodied porter with a balanced roasted malt finish.

Shacklebush (OG 1044, ABV 4.5%) ◣
This amber-coloured brew begins with a balance of malt and hop on the nose which develops on the palate, complemented by a mounting bitterness. Good dry finish with lingering malt notes.

Mad Monk (OG 1047, ABV 4.8%) ◣
Fruity beer with bitter, earthy hops in evidence.

Dog & Rabbit

▤ Dog & Rabbit Micro Brew Pub, 36 Park View, Whitley Bay, Tyne & Wear, NE26 2TH ☎ 07944 552716 ⊕ dogandrabbitbrewery.co.uk

The Dog & Rabbit Brewery was established in 2015 and relocated to new premises as a micro brewpub in 2016.

Doghouse (NEW)

Unit 6, Watery Lane Industrial Estate, Watery Lane, Darwen, Lancashire, BB3 2EB
☎ (01254) 366338 ☎ 07860 913679
⊕ doghousebrewery.co.uk

First brewed in 2016 having purchased the equipment from the brewery of the same name based in the Isle of Man.

UPA (ABV 4%)

Bitter (ABV 4.2%)
Classic English bitter packed with British hops.

Pale Ale (ABV 4.6%)

Columbus Brown (ABV 5%)
Modern brown-coloured ale with a strong resin aroma and bitter kick.

IPA (ABV 5.5%)

Dominion SIBA

Unit Z, New House Farm, Little Laver Road, Moreton, Essex, CM5 0JE
☎ (01277) 890580 ☎ 07931 120806
⊕ dominionbrewerycompany.com

✕ Dominion was established in 2012 by Andy Skene, renting the premises and Pitfield brand names from the founder of Pitfield, Martin Kemp. All Pitfield beers are certified organic by the Soil Association and vegan by the Vegan Society. The Pitfield Brewery range of beers is more traditional and include historic recipe beers, while Dominion Brewery beers are more experimental.
‼RAIB

The Few (ABV 3.5%)
A pale beer brewed to a 1949 Cobbold Brewery of Ipswich recipe using hops from the original hop fields.

Theodore Pinchbeck's Spurious Stout (ABV 4.2%)
A medium-bodied chocolaty, dark stout.

Woodbine Racer (OG 1042, ABV 4.2%)
A golden-coloured beer using only American hops.

Canada (ABV 4.9%)
A dark red-coloured beer, robust and hoppy with a long-lasting bitter finish.

Amber Porter (ABV 5.5%)
A dark beer with biscuity, coffee flavours.

Mad Trappiste (OG 1095, ABV 10%)
A Belgian Trappist-style red-coloured ale, aged in cognac casks and deliberately soured to result in a beer with a complex flavour.

Brewed under the Pitfield Brewery brand name:

Light Ale (OG 1036, ABV 3.6%)

Bitter (OG 1036, ABV 3.7%)

Lager (OG 1037, ABV 3.7%)

Chococino Dark Beer (OG 1038, ABV 4%)

Shoreditch Stout (OG 1040, ABV 4%)

Eco Warrior (OG 1043, ABV 4.5%) ◣
Golden ale with a vivid, citrus hop aroma. The hop character is balanced with a delicate sweetness in the taste, followed by an increasingly bitter finish.

Red Ale (OG 1046, ABV 4.8%) ◣
Complex beer with a full, malty body and strong hop character.

1850 London Porter (OG 1048, ABV 5%) ◣
Big-tasting dark ale dominated by coffee and forest fruits. The finish is dry but not acrid.

Ginger Beer (ABV 5%)
Sweet, malty beer with a good hit of ginger.

N1 Wheat Beer (OG 1048, ABV 5%)

1837 India Pale Ale (OG 1065, ABV 7%)
A light copper-coloured IPA with a floral aroma.

Imperial Chocolate Stout (OG 1070, ABV 7.3%)
A traditional stout with overtones of chocolate.

1890 Stock Ale (OG 1070, ABV 10%)
Sweet malty flavours with hints of sherry and whisky.

Doncaster

7 Young Street, Doncaster, South Yorkshire, DN1 3EL

☎ (01302) 376436 ☎ 07770 958394
⊕ doncasterbrewery.co.uk

Established in 2012 and initially based at an industrial unit in Kirk Sandall, Doncaster, the brewery moved to new premises in the centre of Doncaster in 2014 and opened a micropub tap room. ◆

Sand House (OG 1038, ABV 3.8%)

Cheswold (OG 1042, ABV 4.2%)

Donnington

Upper Swell, Stow-on-the-Wold, Gloucestershire, GL54 1EP
☎ (01451) 830603 ⊕ donnington-brewery.com

Thomas Arkell bought a 13th-century watermill in 1827 and began brewing on the site in 1865; the waterwheel is still in use. Thomas's descendant Claude owned and ran the brewery until his death in 2007, supplying 20 outlets direct. It has now passed to Claude's cousin, James Arkell, also of Arkells Brewery, Swindon (qv). 🚂 RAIB

BB (OG 1035, ABV 3.6%) ◆
A pleasant amber-coloured bitter with a slight hop aroma, a good balance of malt and hops in the mouth and a bitter aftertaste.

Gold (OG 1041, ABV 4%)
A golden ale with a citrus flavour followed by a rounded malt finish.

SBA (OG 1045, ABV 4.4%) ◆
Malt dominates over bitterness in the subtle flavour of this premium bitter, which has a hint of fruit and a dry, malty finish.

Dopey Dick (NEW)

Skeoge Industrial Estate, Derry, BT48 8SE
☎ (028) 7141 8920 ✉ dopeydickderry@gmail.com

A microbrewery founded by the proprietors of the Grand Central Bar in Londonderry.

Dorking SIBA

Engine Shed, Dorking West Station Yard, Station Road, Dorking, Surrey, RH4 1HF
☎ (01306) 877988 ⊕ dorkingbrewery.com

⊗ Dorking started brewing in 2008 and supplies an increasing number of local pubs and clubs. New fermenters were purchased in 2013 and brewing takes place at least twice a week. New owners took over in 2016 and plans are in place to move to Capel, just south of Dorking. ‼🚂◆

Pacific Gold (OG 1042, ABV 3.8%)

Pilcrow Pale (OG 1043, ABV 4%)

Smokestack Lightnin' (OG 1043, ABV 4%)

DB One (OG 1043, ABV 4.2%) ◆
Hoppy best bitter with underlying orange fruit notes. Some balancing malt sweetness in the taste leads to a dry bitter finish.

Black Noise (OG 1045, ABV 4.5%)

Lunar White (OG 1045, ABV 4.6%)

Red India (OG 1052, ABV 5%)

Buffalo Buffalo (OG 1050, ABV 5.1%)

Dorset SIBA ◉

Unit 7, Hybris Business Park, Warmwell Road, Crossways, Dorset, DT2 8BF
☎ (01305) 777515 ⊕ dbcales.com

⊗ Founded in 1996, Dorset Brewing Company relocated from Hope Square, Weymouth, once the old Devenish and Groves breweries site, to new purpose-built premises in 2010. In 2008 it took over the running of Dorchester's brewpub, Tom Brown's (Goldfinch Brewery). Beers are available in local pubs and selected outlets throughout the south west. ‼◆

Dorset Knob (OG 1039, ABV 3.9%) ◆
Complex bitter ale with strong malt and fruit flavours despite its light gravity.

Tom Brown's (OG 1039, ABV 4%)
A pale bitter with a fruity nose. The taste is bittersweet with malt, fruit and some hop. Complex aftertaste.

Jurassic (OG 1040, ABV 4.2%) ◆
Clean-tasting, easy-drinking bitter. Well-balanced with lingering bitterness after moderate sweetness.

Yachtsman (OG 1048, ABV 4.7%)
A pale golden-coloured, bitter-tasting beer with hints of vanilla and honey in the aroma and aftertaste.

Durdle Door (OG 1046, ABV 5%) ◆
A tawny hue and fruity aroma with a hint of pear drops and good malty undertone, joined by hops and a little roast malt in the taste. Lingering bittersweet finish.

Brewed under the Goldfinch Brewery name:

Flashman's Clout (OG 1045, ABV 4.5%)

Double Top

Unit 4, Kilton Terrace, Worksop, Nottinghamshire, S80 2DQ ☎ 07973 521824

Office: Mallard, Station Approach, Carlton Road, Worksop, Nottinghamshire, S81 7AG
⊕ doubletopbrewery.co.uk

☺ Double Top procured a 2.5-barrel plant in 2012, with fermenting capacity for 7.5 barrels a week. This was expanded to a five-barrel plant in 2015 with a fermenting capacity of 20 barrels. It caters for its brewery tap, the Mallard on Platform 1 of Worksop railway station, and for regional beer festivals and free houses. ‼◆

Nelson Mild (OG 1037, ABV 3.5%)
A traditional dark mild with a delicate balance of malts.

Golden Arrow (OG 1038, ABV 3.9%)
A golden ale with citrus notes.

Shanghai (OG 1041, ABV 4.2%)
A light and hoppy session ale.

Adonis (OG 1042, ABV 4.3%)
A pale bitter with a dry, biscuity finish.

Treble 20 (OG 1043, ABV 4.5%)
Straw-coloured, hoppy and bitter.

Bad Boy (OG 1047, ABV 4.6%)
Chestnut-coloured bitter, sweet in taste.

Citra Tip (OG 1050, ABV 5.2%)
An American-hopped pale ale.

Madhouse (OG 1053, ABV 5.2%)
A modern-style porter.

IPA (OG 1055, ABV 5.5%)
A deep golden-coloured, strong, traditional IPA.

Old Stoneface (OG 1058, ABV 6%)
A black treacle stout.

Dove Street SIBA

82 St Helens Street, Ipswich, Suffolk, IP4 2LB
☎ (01473) 211270 ☎ 07880 707077
⊕ dovestreetbrewery.co.uk

⊠ Dove Street began brewing in 2011 using a 2.5-barrel plant in a garage opposite the Dove Street Inn. The Dove Street Inn, its sister pub and beer festivals are supplied. ‼ ↥

Underwood Mild (OG 1033, ABV 3.2%)
Dark, traditional mild packed with aroma and flavour, with freshness and spice.

Gladstone Guzzler (OG 1037, ABV 3.6%)
Easy-drinking, light-coloured bitter with a hoppy flavour.

Bitter (OG 1038, ABV 3.7%)
A traditional bitter with a dryish finish.

CITRA (OG 1039, ABV 3.9%)
Light beer with a dry, citrus flavour.

**Incredible Taste Fantastic Clarity
(OG 1041, ABV 4%)**
Golden-coloured, hoppy session beer. Clean, clear and crisp.

Dove Elder (OG 1042, ABV 4.1%)
Traditionally brewed speciality beer.

Thirsty Walker (OG 1047, ABV 4.6%)
A strong, well-balanced ale.

Old Ipswich Liquor (OG 1055, ABV 5.5%) ◆
Malty and slightly winey nose, carried through in the taste, along with hints of liquorice and chocolate.

Dovecote (NEW)

Unit 2, Denbigh Enterprise Centre, Colomendy Industrial Estate, Denbigh, LL16 5TA
✉ dovecote.brewery@gmail.com

Also known as Bragdy Colomendy, named after the industrial estate where it is located. Owner and head brewer Richard Green commenced brewing in 2017 on a five-barrel plant previously used at the former Frodsham brewery. A brewery bar is planned. RAIB

Dove Ale (ABV 4%)

Dow Bridge SIBA ⊙

2-3 Rugby Road, Catthorpe, Leicestershire, LE17 6DA
☎ (01788) 869121 ⊕ dowbridgebrewery.co.uk

Dow Bridge commenced brewing in 2001 and takes its name from a local bridge where Watling Street spans the River Avon. The brewery uses English whole hops and malt with no adjuncts or additives. More than 50 outlets are supplied direct.
‼ ◆ RAIB

Bonum Mild (OG 1035, ABV 3.5%) ◆
Complex dark brown-coloured, full-flavoured mild, with strong malt and roast flavours to the fore and

continuing into the aftertaste, leading to a long, satisfying finish.

Acris (OG 1037, ABV 3.8%)
Classic session bitter, packed with flavour.

Centurion (OG 1039, ABV 4%)
Copper-coloured, well-rounded best bitter. Good balance of malt and hops in the flavour.

Legion (OG 1041, ABV 4.1%)
Golden-coloured hoppy ale. A good balance of malt and fruity hop on the nose and palate.

Ratae'd (OG 1041, ABV 4.3%) ◆
Tawny-coloured, full-bodied beer with bitter hop flavours against a grainy background, leading to a long, bitter and dry aftertaste.

Dark (OG 1042, ABV 4.4%)
A strong, dark, full-bodied ale with roast malt giving hints of chocolate.

Gladiator (OG 1046, ABV 4.5%)
Ruby chestnut-coloured, well-balanced beer. Smooth and malty, but with a bitter, dry finish. Some fruit aroma and slight toffee sweetness.

Fosse Ale (OG 1046, ABV 4.8%)
Well-balanced, premium beer with caramel and burnt toffee flavours leading to a hoppy, dry finish.

Praetorian Porter (OG 1048, ABV 5%)
Dark, rich, full-bodied porter. Slightly sweet with hoppy undertones.

Onslaught (OG 1049, ABV 5.2%)
A deep ruby-coloured strong ale. A good balance of fruit and hops with rich flavours and aroma.

Downlands SIBA ⊙

Unit Z (2a), Mackley Industrial Estate, Small Dole, West Sussex, BN5 9XE
☎ (01273) 495596 ⊕ downlandsbrewery.com

⊠ A 10-barrel brewery set up in 2012 distributing beers across the South-east of England. ‼ ◆

Root Thirteen (OG 1033, ABV 3.6%)
Crisp, light golden-coloured ale that layers floral zesty aromas over a grapefruit and citrus flavour.

Best (OG 1042, ABV 4.1%)
A traditional malty, fruity, best bitter.

Bramber (OG 1047, ABV 4.5%)
Powerfully-hopped, American-style, amber-coloured ale.

Devils Dyke Porter (OG 1052, ABV 5%)
Toffee, chocolate and smoky flavours are complemented by a subtle hint of marmalade.

Devils Dyke Salted Caramel (OG 1052, ABV 5%)
The sweetness of caramel enriches the already present chocolate and coffee flavours with a surprising hint of salt in the finish.

Black Seven Four (OG 1074, ABV 7.1%) 🍷

Downton SIBA

Unit 11, Batten Road, Downton Industrial Estate, Downton, Wiltshire, SP5 3HU
☎ (01725) 513313 ⊕ downtonbrewery.com

⊠ Downton was set up in 2003. The brewery has a 20-barrel brew length and produces around 1,500 barrels a year. Around 100 outlets are supplied direct. Eight regular beers are produced together with speciality and experimental beers. The brewery has no pub estate but offers an off-site mobile bar service and an online shop. A bar and sales are available on site. ☛RAIB

New Forest Ale (OG 1037, ABV 3.8%) ◆
An amber-coloured bitter with subtle aromas leading to good hopping on the palate. Some fruit and predominate hoppiness in the aftertaste.

Quadhop (OG 1038, ABV 3.9%) ◆
Pale golden-coloured session beer, initially hoppy on the palate with some fruit and a strong hoppiness in the aftertaste.

Elderquad (OG 1039, ABV 4%) ◆
Golden yellow-coloured bitter with a floral, fruity aroma leading to a good well-hopped taste with hints of elderflower. Dryish finish with a good fruit and hop balance.

Honey Blonde (OG 1041, ABV 4.3%) ◆
Straw-coloured golden ale, easy drinking with initial bitterness giving way to slight sweetness and a lingering, balanced aftertaste.

Nelson's Delight (OG 1044, ABV 4.5%)
An amber-coloured bitter full of hoppy character and a rich resinous aroma. Underlying sweetness and strength are provided by the addition of navy rum.

Dark Delight (OG 1053, ABV 5.5%) ◆
A strong, dark brown-coloured best bitter with malt and roast in the aroma and on the palate, giving way to a balanced, lingering aftertaste with noticeable hoppiness.

Chocolate Orange Delight (OG 1052, ABV 5.8%)
A speciality old ale with pronounced chocolate flavours. A pleasant orange addition combines perfectly in this delightfully different offering.

IPA (OG 1063, ABV 6.8%) ◆
Golden yellow-coloured strong bitter with good balance of hops and fruit, slight sweetness and some malt notes, all through to the aftertaste.

Dowr Kammel (NEW)

Deaconstowe, Lower Lank, Cornwall, PL30 4PW
☎ 07774 427635
Office: 9 Tregarne Terrace, St Austell, PL25 4DD
✉ camelbrewingcompany@btinternet.com

Brewing began in 2016. A small number of local free houses are supplied.

Amber Rambler (ABV 4%)

Devil's Jump (ABV 4.6%)

Delank Dynamite (ABV 5.1%)

Brewards Droop IPA (ABV 6%)

Big Cat (ABV 7.7%)

Brewed for the Blisland Inn, Blisland:

Blisland Dark (ABV 3.5%)

Blsiland Gold (ABV 3.6%)

Dragonfly

⧉ George & Dragon, 183 High Street, Acton, London, W3 9DJ
☎ (020) 8992 3712 ☎ 07788 859450
✉ dragonflybrewery@gmail.com

Brewing began in 2014 with a Chinese-built brewing kit installed in the back bar of the George

& Dragon. The pub is supplied along with other outlets in the same pub group.

2 O'Clock Ordinary (OG 1043, ABV 4%) ◆
Pale brown-coloured best bitter with hops and fruit aroma and flavour, with a bitterness that is present in the finish.

Early Doors (OG 1042, ABV 4.3%) ◆
Dark golden-coloured best bitter with grapefruit and hops building and lingering in the dry, bitter finish, balanced by some malty sweetness.

Draycott (Cambridgeshire)

Low Farm, 30 Mill Road, Buckden, Cambridgeshire, PE19 5SS
☎ (01480) 812404 ☎ 07740 374710
⊕ draycottbrewery.co.uk

The brewery is located in an old farm complex and was set up by Jon and Jane Draycott in 2009. Only bottle-conditioned beers are produced. RAIB

Draycott (Derbyshire) SIBA

Ladywood Lodge Farm, Spondon Road, Dale Abbey, Derbyshire, DE7 4PS ☎ 07834 728540
✉ draycottbrewingcompany@yahoo.co.uk

⊠ Small microbrewery established in 2014, supplying local pubs and beer festivals. Relocation to new premises in 2015 saw beer range and capacity increased.

Top of the Hops (OG 1042, ABV 3.8%)
A single hop pale ale with a good malt/hop balance.

Heisenberg's Principle (OG 042, ABV 4.2%)
A traditional dark ale with a toasted flavour and good hop balance.

Piano Man Blues (OG 1042, ABV 4.2%)
An American-style ruby-coloured ale with good malt tones and a clean taste and finish.

Butcher's Bitter (OG 1042, ABV 4.5%)
Traditional bitter. Caramel notes with a hint of nut.

California Steam (OG 1042, ABV 4.5%)
American-style red-coloured beer. Dry and refreshing, with a hint of citrus.

Kentucky Common American Ale (OG 1042, ABV 4.5%)
American-style, amber-coloured bitter with big flavours.

Tap House Tipple (OG 1042, ABV 4.5%)
A traditional English pale ale with all English hops.

Minnesota North Star (OG 1042, ABV 4.7%)
Complex American-style, red-coloured bitter with American malt and hops.

Christmas in July (OG 1042, ABV 5%)
A traditional porter with chocolate and coconut notes in the background.

Irish Red Ale (OG 1042, ABV 5%)
A traditional red-coloured fruity ale.

Driftwood SIBA

⧉ Driftwood Spars Hotel, Trevaunance Cove, St Agnes, Cornwall, TR5 0RY
☎ (01872) 552591 ⊕ driftwoodsparsbrewery.co.uk

Brewing since 2000 on a custom-built five-barrel plant, the brewery has since expanded to incorporate additional fermentation and conditioning capacity plus a brewery shop and visitor centre with annual production now standing at 1,300 barrels. Monthly specials are produced for selected circulation only. Besides the pub, other outlets and beer festivals are supplied.

Bawden Rocks (OG 1037, ABV 3.8%) ◀
Refreshing bitter with a floral hop aroma. Balanced biscuit malt and hop bitterness with orange, apple and plum notes. Bitter finish.

Blackheads Mild (OG 1037, ABV 3.8%) ◀
Dark mild with coffee aroma. Silky, smoky roast malt, raisins and liquorice flavours persist to the finish with dry bitterness.

Blue Hills Bitter (OG 1039, ABV 4%) ◀
Medium-bodied refreshing bitter with a hoppy aroma. Flowery, grassy hops dominate the flavour to the end with gentle biscuit malt.

Booskor (OG 1042, ABV 4.2%) ◀
Smooth red-brown mild with light roast malt throughout. Sweetness, toffee apples, roast nuts and stone fruits. Light malty, sweet finish.

Forest Blond (OG 1044, ABV 4.3%) ◀
Yellow-coloured ale with apple and woody aroma. Bitter lemon, apricot, melon and elderflower with grassy hop bitterness, sweetness and perfumed esters.

Sundrift (OG 1046, ABV 4.5%) ◀
Copper-coloured best bitter packed full of fruit and hop flavours with malt and spices. Bitter finish with persistent sweet malt.

Bolster's Blood (OG 1049, ABV 4.8%) ◀
Full-bodied, dark brown porter. Coal-smoke and peaty malt flavour with dark chocolate and dried fruits. Bitterness and burnt malt persist.

Red River Rye (OG 1048, ABV 4.8%)

Lou's Brew (OG 1049, ABV 5%) ◀
Golden-coloured beer with strong lemon and grapefruit flavours, bitterness and dryness throughout. Long, tangy finish with hop bitterness fading at the end.

JSB (OG 1050, ABV 5.2%)

Alfie's Revenge (OG 1060, ABV 6.5%) ▯ ◀
Brown-coloured old ale with malt, sweet fruit aroma and flavours, balanced by spicy hop bitterness. Malt and fruit finish.

Drone Valley

Unstone Industrial Complex, Main Road, Unstone, Derbyshire, S18 4AB ☎ 07794 277091 ⊕ dronevalleybrewery.com

☺Community-owned five-barrel brewery that began brewing commercially in 2016. The brewery is entirely volunteer operated and welcomes new members and investors. Brewery open days are planned at approximately bi-monthly intervals. ♦ RAIB

Dronny Bottom Bitter (ABV 3.7%)
A traditional English Bitter.

Gosforth Gold (ABV 4%)
A pale straw-coloured beer with a full body for its strength. Well-balanced with a citrus hop finish.

Dronfield Best (ABV 4.3%)
Bright copper-coloured best bitter, full of flavour and depth.

Coal Aston Porter (ABV 4.5%)
Traditional, smooth and fruity porter.

Fanshaw Blonde (ABV 4.8%)
An American-hopped IPA.

Stubley Stout (ABV 5%)
A rich, smooth stout

IPA (ABV 5.2%)
Classic English IPA; deep amber in colour with a rich malt base and generously hopped giving a full mouthfeel and a dry, bitter finish.

Drop The Anchor (NEW)

Avon Works, Bridge Street, Christchurch, Dorset, BH23 1DY ⊕ droptheanchorbrewery.co.uk

Brewing began in 2017.

Druid (NEW)

4 Dinorben Terrace, Penysarn, LL69 9YR ✉ alan@druidbrewery.co.uk

A new microbrewery in the north of the Island County of Anglesey. The brewery is fitted into an 18th-century cottage that was built to house miners working in the historic copper mines of the nearby Parys Mountain. It is also the home of the brewery owners. The beers and ciders are made in a purpose-built brew room. Further beers are planned. RAIB

Golden Venture (ABV 6.5%)
An IPA-style brew with satisfying bitterness and a hint of orange marmalade at the finish.

Reality Shift (ABV 6.8%)
Big, bold IPA with a grapefruit finish.

Drygate SIBA

▤ 85 Drygate, Glasgow, G4 0UT ☎ (0141) 212 8810 ⊕ drygate.com

Restaurant, bar and microbrewery, Drygate is a joint venture of Tennent's and Williams Bros, though operationally independent. The on-site brewery began production in 2014.

Dukeries SIBA

Carlton Forest Distribution Centre, Unit 6, Blyth Road, Worksop, Nottinghamshire, S81 0TP ☎ (01909) 731171 ☎ 07584 305027 ⊕ dukeriesbrewery.co.uk

☺Founded in 2012 and located in the heart of the Dukeries in Nottinghamshire using a five-barrel plant. The brewery tap is located at 18 Newcastle Avenue, Worksop, serving five rotating ales. ♦

Elsi Pale (OG 1036, ABV 3.6%)
Traditional chestnut-coloured bitter with a slight nutty flavour mixed with hints of fruit leading to a dry bitter finish.

Blonde (OG 1038, ABV 3.8%)
Blonde ale with citrus notes and low level bitterness ensuring a clean, crisp feel throughout.

A Ray of Sunshine (OG 1041, ABV 4.2%)
A fruity beer with tropical fruits throughout and a clean, fresh feel on the palate.

Castle Hill (OG 1041, ABV 4.2%)

Well-hopped bitter balanced throughout offering soft malt flavours with a smooth, mellow bitter finish.

De Lovetot (OG 1041, ABV 4.2%)
Golden-coloured pale ale. Well-balanced with a citrus fruit aroma and feel, leading to a bitter finish.

Lime Tree Porter (OG 1043, ABV 4.4%)
Porter with a gentle smoke taste, some liquorice and a malt sweetness. The nose has peat and liquorice with a hint of sweetness. Gentle bitterness with hints of citrus.

Mining Stout (OG 1044, ABV 4.5%)
A dark-coloured ale bursting with robust, rich flavours leading to a well-balanced, dry finish.

Farmers Branch (OG 1047, ABV 5%)
A pale, strong ale, zesty with fresh, clean citrus notes.

Chapmans Map (OG 1051, ABV 5.2%)
Chestnut in colour. Medium-bodied with a creamy head. Nose is cinnamon and cloves, caramel, biscuit and a slight hint of coffee. Taste is strong biscuit, lots of malt sweetness. Gentle bitterness in the finish.

Wersheshope Gold (OG 1051, ABV 5.2%)
Golden-coloured ale with a light body. Nose has orange marmalade and limes. Taste is bitter orange marmalade, lime and slightly grassy hop. Sharp bitterness mid tongue into the finish.

Gunsmoke (OG 1050, ABV 5.5%)
Russet brown-coloured beer with hints of chocolate and liquorice, with a soft, dry finish.

Bess of Hardwick (OG 1052, ABV 5.7%)
An American pale ale with floral and citrus flavours in abundance with herbal characteristics.

Dunham Massey

100 Oldfield Lane, Dunham Massey, WA14 4PE
☎ (0161) 929 0663 ⊕ dunhammasseybrewing.co.uk

⊛Opened in 2007, Dunham Massey brews traditional North-western ales using only English ingredients. Around 30 outlets are supplied direct, along with the brewery tap, Costello's Bar, Altrincham. A sister brewery, Lymm (qv), opened in 2013 with Costello's Bar in Stockton Heath tied to both breweries. ⌂◆RAIB

Little Bollington Bitter (OG 1037, ABV 3.7%) ◀
Straw-coloured light ale with malt and citrus fruit taste and a dry, bitter finish.

Chocolate Cherry Mild (OG 1040, ABV 3.8%)
A speciality beer, it has the all dark chocolate, coffee and liquorice flavours of a dark mild blended with a dry, bittersweet cherry flavour.

Dunham Dark (OG 1040, ABV 3.8%) ◀
Dark brown-coloured beer with a malty aroma. Fairly sweet, with malt, some roast, hop and fruit in the taste and finish.

Big Tree Bitter (OG 1041, ABV 3.9%)
A session bitter, golden in colour, full bodied, with a good balance of hops and malt.

Obelisk (OG 1040, ABV 3.9%)
Light and hoppy but not too bitter, with hints of citrus and grapefruit.

Dunham Milk Stout (OG 1051, ABV 4%)
A classic, full bodied, sweet stout with a creamy, roast malt character.

Landlady (OG 1040, ABV 4%)
A light, refreshing, biscuit, dry ale, with a spicy hop finish.

Dunham Stout (OG 1046, ABV 4.2%)
A creamy, full-bodied, dry stout, with a classic bitter, burnt, dark roast flavour.

Stamford Bitter (OG 1045, ABV 4.2%)
A golden-coloured, full-bodied bitter, with a complex blend of hops giving a slightly dry finish.

Deer Beer (OG 1047, ABV 4.5%)
A clean, full-bodied, malty English ale, with a hint of toffee, and a distinct hop finish.

Cheshire IPA (OG 1047, ABV 4.7%)
A fairly strong, pale, hoppy and bitter IPA.

Dunham Porter (OG 1056, ABV 5.2%) 🗄 🍺
A classic old-style English porter, creamy, full bodied and packed with flavour.

East India Pale Ale (OG 1062, ABV 6%)
A strong but light and hoppy IPA.

Dunham Gold (OG 1070, ABV 7.2%)
A Belgian-style English ale. Strong, light and fruity, with a hoppy finish.

Dunscar SIBA

Unit 13a, Dunscar Bridge Business Park, Blackburn Road, Bolton, BL7 9PQ
☎ (01204) 563516 ⊕ dunscarbridge.co.uk

⊛Brewing began in 2009. In 2012 a 25-barrel plant was installed in a new brewery within the business park at Dunscar Bridge, Bolton. The brewery supplies several of the groups own pubs plus Wetherspoon outlets in the North-west. ‼

Dunscar Blonde (ABV 3.8%)

Dunscar Gold (ABV 4%)

Lancashire Stout (ABV 4%)
A full-bodied flavour with biscuity aromas and a dry bitter roasted taste.

Dunscar Best Bitter (ABV 4.1%)
A smooth beer, lightly caramelised and distinctly hoppy with a slightly dry finish. Aromas from wood and pine to soft fruits and roasted coffee.

Dunscar Amber Ale (ABV 4.5%)

Durham SIBA

Unit 6a, Bowburn North Industrial Estate, Bowburn, County Durham, DH6 5PF
☎ (0191) 377 1991 ⊕ durhambrewery.co.uk

⊛Established in 1994, County Durham's oldest brewery has a portfolio of around 40 beers, some permanent, some on rotation and with new beers appearing regularly. Beers are available throughout the North-east. ‼⌂RAIB V

Magus (OG 1036, ABV 3.8%) ◀
Pale malt gives this brew its straw colour but the hops define its character, with a fruity aroma, a clean bitter mouthfeel, and a lingering dry, citrus-like finish.

Citra Nova (OG 1039, ABV 3.9%)
Massive hop bouquet with a lively, fresh grape bitterness.

Pale Ice (OG 1039, ABV 3.9%)
A refreshing pale beer with a clean bitterness and floral aroma.

Apollo (OG 1040, ABV 4%)
Pale, aromatic and hoppy American-style IPA. Full-bodied, grapefruity and refreshing.

Black Velvet (OG 1040, ABV 4%)
Dark malts and English hops give rich coffee and roast flavors.

White Gold (OG 1040, ABV 4%)
A satisfying floral hop aroma and grapefruit body.

White Amarillo (OG 1041, ABV 4.1%)
Easy-drinking, clean and satisfying beer.

Columbus IPA (OG 1042, ABV 4.2%)
Full-bodied, hoppy, American-style IPA. Peachy aroma with a full grapefruit body.

White Velvet (OG 1042, ABV 4.2%)
Smooth and clean, with American hops.

Evensong (OG 1050, ABV 5%)

White Stout (OG 1072, ABV 7.2%)
A pale stout, full-bodied and strong with a massive floral and resinous character.

Dynamite Valley

Unit 5, Viaduct Works, Frog Hill, Ponsanooth, Cornwall, TR3 7JW
☎ (01872) 864532 ☎ 07775 570235
⊕ dynamitevalley.com

⊗ Dynamite Valley was set up in 2015 following a successful Crowdfunder campaign. The brewery is located near a historic gunpowder site near Falmouth. Investment in equipment has allowed for an increase in production. Regular events are held at the brewery's own Beer Café. Collaboration brews are welcomed. ☞

Gold Rush (OG 1040, ABV 4%) ◆
Pale brown-coloured bitter with a light malt nose. Malt dominates throughout with bitterness, honey, lemon and apricot flavours. Long, malty, bitter finish.

TNT IPA (OG 1048, ABV 4.8%) ◆
Robust, straw-coloured strong bitter with fruity hop aroma. Heavy hop bitter taste with sweet caramel, peaches and good malt balance.

Black Charge (OG 1051, ABV 5.1%) ◆
Creamy, black oatmeal-style stout with strong roast aroma. Roast coffee and molasses burst, then sweet malt, figs and peaty flavours.

Prospector (OG 1052, ABV 5.2%)
A Bavarian-style wheat beer.

Big Bang (ABV 5.3%)
A dark-coloured Belgian-style IPA.

Eagles Crag (NEW)

Unit 21, Robinwood Mill, Todmorden, West Yorkshire, OL14 8JA
☎ (01706) 810394 ⊕ eaglescragbrewery.com

Brewing began in 2016 using an eight-barrel plant. It consists of a two-man team with 30 years of home brewing experience between them. The building was designed by Sir Christopher Wren. ◆ RAIB V

Pale Eagle (ABV 4%)

Earl Soham SIBA

Meadow Works, Cross Green, Debenham, Suffolk, IP14 6RP
☎ (01728) 861213 ⊕ earlsohambrewery.co.uk

⊗ Earl Soham was set up behind the Victoria pub in 1984 and continued there until 2001 when the brewery relocated, moving again in 2013 to Debenham. The Victoria and the Station in Framlingham both sell the beers on a regular basis, as does the Brewery Tap in Ipswich. When there is spare stock, beer is supplied to local free houses and as many beer festivals as possible. 30 outlets are supplied and two pubs are owned. ‼ ☞ ◆ RAIB

Gannet Mild (OG 1034, ABV 3.3%) ◆
A beautifully balanced mild, sweet and fruity flavour with a lingering, coffee aftertaste.

Victoria Bitter (OG 1037, ABV 3.6%) ◆
A light, fruity, amber-coloured session beer with a clean taste and a long, lingering hoppy aftertaste.

Elizabeth Ale (OG 1040, ABV 4.2%)
A clean, bitter premium beer.

Sir Roger's Porter (OG 1042, ABV 4.2%) ◆
Roast/coffee aroma and berry fruit introduce a full-bodied porter with roast/coffee flavours. Dry roast finish.

Albert Ale (OG 1045, ABV 4.4%)
Hops dominate every aspect of this beer, but especially the finish. A fruity, astringent beer.

Brandeston Gold (OG 1045, ABV 4.5%) ◆
Popular beer brewed with local ingredients. Sharp clean flavour, malty/hoppy and heavily laden with citrus fruit. Malty finish.

East London SIBA

Unit 45, Fairways Business Centre, Lammas Road, Leyton, London, E10 7QB
☎ (020) 8539 0805 ⊕ eastlondonbrewing.com

⊗ The East London Brewing Company is an award-winning 10-barrel brewery established in 2011 by a husband-and-wife team. ◆ RAIB

Orchid (OG 1040, ABV 3.6%) ◆
Delicate vanilla on nose and flavour. Fruity overtones coupled with cocoa dark roast character that is present in the finish.

Pale Ale (OG 1042, ABV 4%) ◆
Amber-coloured best bitter with spicy hops, bitter lemon, tropical fruits and biscuit continue into the dry aftertaste.

Foundation Bitter (OG 1044, ABV 4.2%) ◆
Well-balanced, brown-coloured best bitter with fresh green fruity hop in aroma and flavour with caramelised pineapple. Short bitter marmalade finish.

Nightwatchman (OG 1046, ABV 4.5%) ◆
Dark ruby-brown best bitter. Peach, caramelised fruit and toffee balanced by bitter, nutty and roasted malt flavours. Dry aftertaste.

**Cowcatcher American Pale Ale
(OG 1045, ABV 4.8%)** ◆
Fruity, hoppy, rich golden ale with honey sweetness, mango and hints of passion fruit, lingering in the dry bitter finish.

Jamboree (OG 1048, ABV 4.8%) ◆

THE BREWERIES

Golden-coloured strong bitter with grassy and woody hop aroma. Flavour has spice with kiwi and sweet biscuit. Dry bitter finish.

Quadrant Oatmeal Stout (OG 1063, ABV 5.8%) ◆
Smooth, rich oatmeal stout with liquorice, mocha and caramelised fruit. Roasted coffee aroma. A dry, slightly roast bitter finish lingers.

Eccleshall

See Slater's

Eden SIBA

Hawksdale House, Hartness Road, Penrith, Cumbria, CA11 9DB
☎ (01768) 210565 ☎ 07729 677692
⊕ edenbrewery.com

Set up in 2011, Eden Brewery is run by Jason Hill, assisted by Linda and Chris. The five-barrel brewery was located at historic Brougham Hall but moved in 2017 to premises on a Penrith industrial estate.
‼◆RAIB

Best (OG 1039, ABV 3.8%) ◆
A traditional bitter, with a hoppy beginning; a malty, bittersweet middle, and a gentle finish.

Fuggle (OG 1039, ABV 3.8%) ◆
Initially sweet, a gently-hopped pale beer with a more bitter finish.

Blonde Knight (OG 1040, ABV 4%)
Brewed with rye for a crisp, clean and refreshing taste.

Atomic Blonde (OG 1041, ABV 4.1%) ◆
The initially inviting aroma of hops is followed by an intense hop flavour with some fruitiness.

Gold (OG 1042, ABV 4.2%) ◆
Gentle fruity and honey aromas to start leading to a well-balanced sweet beer with a lasting hoppy finish.

First Emperor (OG 1046, ABV 4.6%) ◆
Fruity beer with balanced malt and hops and a hint of butterscotch combining to a rich bitter finish.

Eden St Andrews

Main Street, Guardbridge, KY16 0UU ☎ 07786 060013 ⊕ edenbrewerystandrews.com

⊚The brewery was established in 2012 using a five-barrel plant in part of the former Guardbridge paper mills. In 2014 a new 20-barrel plant and distillery was installed. ‼ 🍺 RAIB

St Andrews Blonde (OG 1040, ABV 3.8%)

19th (OG 1041, ABV 3.9%)

Clock Brew (OG 1045, ABV 4.3%)

1882 Lager (OG 1048, ABV 4.5%)

Seggie Porter (OG 1053, ABV 5.5%) 🍾

Shipwreck IPA (ABV 6%)
Refreshing, tropical fruit aroma with a mellow floral hop character, which leads to a dense hoppy body. A good bitterness develops alongside ripe, fruity notes, mellowing into a gentle, sweet finish.

Edenfield

🍺 Rostron Arms, 1 Market Place, Edenfield, Lancashire, BL0 0JZ
☎ (01706) 821756

Edenfield commenced brewing in 2014. Brewing is currently suspended.

Edinbrew SIBA ⊚

Unit 5, Knightsridge East Industrial Estate, Livingston, West Lothian, EH54 8RA ☎ 07736 680755
⊕ edinbrew.beer/index

⊚ Edinbrew opened in 2015 within a small industrial estate in the Knightsridge area of Livingston. The brewery, operated by Ross Hamilton, who trained at the Milestone Brewery, uses a 5.5-barrel plant. ‼◆

Little Monster (OG 1040, ABV 3.7%)

70/- (OG 1039, ABV 3.8%)

The Good Stuff (OG 1039, ABV 3.9%)

Black Current (OG 1043, ABV 4.2%)

CommRed (OG 1043, ABV 4.2%)

Luxury IPA (OG 1041, ABV 4.2%)

Friendly Fire (OG 1045, ABV 4.3%)

85 Shilling (OG 1043, ABV 4.6%)

Super Stout (ABV 4.6%)

Industrial (OG 1054, ABV 5%)
Traditional IPA with soft fruit and gentle malt taste.

Monster (OG 1065, ABV 5.7%)

Edmunds

🍺 Edmunds Brewhouse, 106-110 Edmund Street, Birmingham, B3 2ES
☎ (0121) 200 2423 ⊕ edmundsbrewhouse.co.uk

Brewing began in 2015 at Edmunds Brewhouse in the heart of Birmingham's financial district. Beers are only available in the pub.

Eight Arch

Unit 3a, Stone Lane Industrial Estate, Wimborne, Dorset, BH21 1HB
☎ (01202) 889254 ☎ 07554 445647
⊕ 8archbrewing.co.uk

Brewing commenced in 2015 on a five-barrel plant situated in a unit on a small industrial estate on the outskirts of Wimborne. Local pubs and clubs are supplied. A brewery bar opens on Fridays 4-8pm.
🍺◆RAIB

Session Ale (ABV 3.8%)
A light-coloured session IPA with a crisp finish.

Parabolic Pale Ale (ABV 4.5%)
Pale ale with floral and grapefruit aromas.

Corbel (ABV 5.5%)
An IPA packed full of hops, backed up with a firm bitterness.

Electric Bear SIBA ⊚

Unit 12, Maltings Trading Estate, Locksbrook Road, Bath, BA1 3JL
☎ (01225) 424088 ⊕ electricbearbrewing.com

Electric Bear began brewing in 2015 using a purpose-built 15-barrel plant, expanding capacity in 2016. It brews classic beer styles with a modern twist. Its brewery tap showcases a selection of the range, including exclusive one-offs. ‼◆RAIB

Laid Back (ABV 3.3%)
Low in bitterness with a soft body and citrus hop taste. A blend of grapefruit, subtle peach and apricot aromas.

Red Bear (OG 1041, ABV 4%)
A deep brown-coloured beer with a red hue. Roast malt character, balanced bitterness and toffee, biscuit and red apple aromas

Werrrd! (ABV 4.2%)
A well-balanced, session-strength American-style pale ale.

Drop (ABV 4.3%)
A red-coloured ale with a jam/marmalade malt base and a strong orange aroma backed up with pine and grapefruit.

NZ Pale (OG 1046, ABV 4.5%)
Citrus, easy-drinking session ale.

Inspector Remorse (ABV 4.7%)

Spilt Milk (OG 1054, ABV 5%)
A classic, creamy milk stout with a touch of sweetness along with coffee flavours and a big hit of chocolate.

Livewire (OG 1051, ABV 5.4%)
An American-style IPA with citrus and floral herb notes and a well-balanced bitterness.

Above the Clouds (ABV 6.2%)
An IPA with a strong hoppy aroma, balanced bitterness and a smooth malt backbone.

Surface Area (ABV 8.2%)
A double IPA with aromas of over ripe mango, sweet orange and a medley of peach and apricot.

Elephant School

See Brentwood

Elgood's SIBAIFBB 👁

North Brink Brewery, Wisbech, Cambridgeshire, PE13 1LW
☎ (01945) 583160 ⊕ elgoods-brewery.co.uk

⊠ The North Brink brewery was established in 1795. Owned by the Elgood family since 1878, the fifth generation are now involved in running the business. Elgood's has approximately 30 tied pubs within a 50-mile radius of the brewery and a substantial free trade. Lambic style beers have been produced recently using the brewery's old open cooling trays as fermenting vessels. Off sales are available all year round from the shop in the brewery office when the visitor centre is closed. ‼🖳◆

Black Dog (OG 1036.8, ABV 3.6%) ◣
Black-red mild with liquorice and chocolate. Dry roasty finish.

Cambridge Bitter (OG 1037.8, ABV 3.8%) ◣
Fruit and malt on the nose with increasing hops and balancing malt on the palate. Dry finish.

Golden Newt (OG 1041.5, ABV 4.1%) ◣
Golden ale with floral hops and sulphur aroma. Floral hops and a fruity presence on a bittersweet

background lead to a short, muted hoppy and fruity finish.

Elixir

Office: 2.1 Merchiston Place, Edinburgh, EH10 4NR
☎ 07760 330122 ✉ elixir.brew.co@gmail.com

Elixir Brew Company is an award-winning experimental brewery that produces beers using New World hops, unusual ingredients and novel techniques. Established in 2012, Elixir beers are produced at a variety of breweries throughout the UK, including frequent collaborations with the host brewers.

Elland SIBA 👁

Units 3-5, Heathfield Industrial Estate, Heathfield Street, Elland, West Yorkshire, HX5 9AE
☎ (01422) 377677 ⊕ ellandbrewery.co.uk

☺Orginally formed in 2002 as Eastwood & Sanders by the amalgamation of the Barge & Barrel and West Yorkshire Breweries, the company was renamed Elland in 2006 to reinforce its links with the town. The brewery has a capacity of 50 barrels (200 firkins) a week with further expansion planned. ‼◆RAIB

White Prussian (OG 1039, ABV 3.9%) ◣
A straw-coloured, lightly-flavoured, easy-drinking and refreshing lager-style speciality beer.

Blonde (OG 1041, ABV 4%) ◣
Creamy yellow-coloured, hoppy ale with hints of citrus fruits. Pleasantly strong bitter aftertaste.

Beyond the Pale (OG 1042, ABV 4.2%) ◣
Gold-coloured, robust, creamy beer with ripe aromas of hops and fruit. Bitterness predominates in the mouth and leads to a dry, fruity and hoppy aftertaste.

Nettlethrasher (OG 1044, ABV 4.4%) ◣
Smooth, amber-coloured beer. A rounded nose with some fragrant hop notes followed by a mellow nutty and fruity taste and a dry finish.

1872 Porter (OG 1065, ABV 6.5%) 🖺🖻◣
Creamy, full-flavoured porter. Rich liquorice flavours with a hint of chocolate from roast malt. A soft but satisfying aftertaste of bittersweet roast and malt.

Elliswood 👁

Unit 3, Southways Industrial Estate, Coventry Road, Hinckley, Leicestershire, LE10 0NJ
☎ (01455) 635239 ☎ 07795 954392

Office: 24 Leicester Road, Hinckley, Leicestershire, LE10 1LS ⊕ elliswoodbrewery.co.uk

☺Founded in 2013 by Tracy Ellis and Phil Woodward and taken over in 2016 by Darren and Louise Lavender, who continue to brew using the David Porter 5.5-barrel system with a capacity to brew twice weekly. Beers are available across the Midlands.

Hansom Ale (OG 1036, ABV 3.9%)
Traditional, easy-drinking session ale.

Barrel of Laughs (OG 1042, ABV 4.2%)
Copper-coloured ale, well-balanced with spicy vanilla undertones. Slight bitterness all the way through with a sweet, pleasant aftertaste.

Just One More (OG 1042, ABV 4.2%)
A citrus beer with blackberry and grapefruit undertones.

Black Rose (OG 1045, ABV 4.5%)
A mild porter with a subtle chocolate aftertaste.

Nelson's Right Arm (OG 1044, ABV 4.5%)
A deep mahogany-coloured, spicy beer with heavy hints of autumn fruits.

Royal Standard 1485 (OG 1047, ABV 4.8%)
A deep red-coloured bitter, sweet toffee taste with caramel undertones.

Legless (OG 1048, ABV 4.9%)
Gold in colour and easy on the palate. Full-bodied with undertones of blackberry and spice.

Elmtree SIBA

Snetterton Brewery, Unit 10, Oakwood Industrial Estate, Harling Road, Snetterton, Norfolk, NR16 2JU
☎ (01953) 887065 ☎ 07939 549241
⊕ elmtreebeers.co.uk

⊗ Established in 2007, Elmtree brews on a six-barrel plant. More than 120 free trade outlets are supplied direct. Bespoke beers for individual pubs are also brewed. !! ☞ ♦ RAIB V

Burston's Cuckoo (OG 1038, ABV 3.8%) ◣
Gentle malt airs. Biscuity sweet beginning with delicate lime hints. Full-bodied, short, sweet finish.

Bitter (OG 1041, ABV 4.2%)
A well-balanced, copper-coloured crisp beer, the early malt notes give way to a distinctively complex hop finish.

Norfolk's 80 Shilling Ale (OG 1044, ABV 4.5%) ◣
Roast malt and caramel provide balance to an inherent hoppy bitterness. A mix of well-balanced flavours. Finish becomes chewy.

Snetterton Scary Tree (OG 1044, ABV 4.5%)
A tan-coloured beer with a complex bitterness combined with generous hop aromas.

Dark Horse Stout (OG 1050, ABV 5%) ◣
Solid coffee and malt aroma. A cornucopia of vanilla, dark chocolate, and roast with a sweet foundation. Long, strong finale.

Golden Pale Ale (OG 1048, ABV 5%) ◣
Full bodied, with a swirling malty aroma. Lime fruit adds depth to the sweet malty character. Short sweetening finish.

Nightlight Mild (OG 1057, ABV 5.7%) ◣
A heavy mix of liquorice, roast and malt infuses aroma and first taste. A sweet spiciness slowly develops.

Elusive

Unit 5, Marino Way, Hogwood Lane Industrial Estate, Finchampstead, Berkshire, RG40 4RF ☎ 07917 541718 ⊕ elusivebrewing.com

Established in 2016, Elusive is a five-barrel brewery located on the Hampshire/Berkshire border.

Cherrywood Road (ABV 3.8%)
Lightly smoked ruby mild.

Starship Fleet (ABV 4.2%)
An English pale ale.

EMAL

See Powderkeg

Emmanuales (NEW)

Unit 111, JC Albyn Complex, Burton Road, Sheffield, South Yorkshire, S3 8BT
☎ (0114) 272 7256 ⊕ emmanuales.co.uk

Emmanuales began brewing in 2014. Beer names and the brewery ethos draw inspiration from the Christian faith in a quirky, joyful way. Based at the Sheffield Brewery Company. ♦

As the Deer Pants for Porter (OG 1054, ABV 5%)
A dark brown-coloured porter with a subtle smoky twist.

Jonah and the Pale (OG 1046, ABV 5%)
A Transatlantic pale ale.

Ryejoice (OG 1052, ABV 5.4%)
A spicy, red-coloured rye beer.

Oh Hoppy Day (OG 1056, ABV 6.1%)
An IPA bursting with hops.

Empire SIBA

The Old Boiler House, Unit 33, Upper Mills, Slaithwaite, West Yorkshire, HD7 5HA
☎ (01484) 847343 ☎ 07966 592276
⊕ empirebrewing.com

☺Empire Brewing was set up 2006 in a mill on the bank of the scenic Huddersfield Narrow Canal, close to the centre of Slaithwaite. In 2011 the brewery upgraded from a five-barrel to a 10-barrel plant. Beers are supplied to local free houses and through independent specialist beer agencies and wholesalers. !! ♦ RAIB

Golden Warrior (OG 1039.5, ABV 3.8%)
Pale bitter, quite fruity with a sherbet aftertaste, moderate bitterness.

Strikes Back (OG 1041, ABV 4%)
Pale golden-coloured session bitter with a hoppy aroma and good hop and malt balance with a citrus flavour, light on the palate.

Valour (OG 1042.5, ABV 4.2%)

Longbow (OG 1043, ABV 4.3%)

Imperium (OG 1050, ABV 5.1%)

Emsworth Brewery

Rear of 16 West Street, Emsworth, Hampshire, PO10 7DY ☎ 07717 510294
⊕ theemsworthbrewery.co.uk

⊗ Michael and Hilary Bolt began their family-run brewery in 2011 on a 2.5-barrel plant, obtained from Oban Ales, in a shed behind an antiques shop in Emsworth. ♦ RAIB

Slipper (OG 1040, ABV 3.9%)

Wayfarer (OG 1042, ABV 4.1%)

Fairfield (OG 1042, ABV 4.2%)

Emsworth Brewhouse

44 Hollybank Lane, Emsworth, Hampshire, PO10 7UE
☎ 07852 000865 ⊕ theemsworthbrewhouse.co.uk

Launched in 2015, the Emsworth Brewhouse originally used a half-barrel plant but upgraded in 2016. A small number of pubs are supplied direct. The brewery has a strong sustainability ethic, using rooftop solar electric and thermal energy to brew the beer, which is then delivered using zero-emission electric vehicles.

Mainsail (OG 1038, ABV 3.8%)
A floral aroma with hints of citrus peel and tangerine with a refreshing, crisp taste.

Flotilla (OG 1044, ABV 4.4%)
A dark amber-coloured ale with fruity flavours. Hints of sultana in the final finish.

Wodehouse (OG 1048, ABV 4.8%)
A rich, chestnut-coloured ale delivering a smooth, full-bodied taste. A slight hint of Christmas cake.

Enfield (NEW) SIBA

Unit 17a, Eley Road, Upper Edmonton, London, N18 3BB
☎ (0208) 8807 1533 ⊕ enefeld.com

☺Brewing began in 2015. It is believed that it is the only brewery that uses mineral water from deep beneath London to brew its beers. More than 125 outlets are supplied direct. GF

London Pale Ale (OG 1038, ABV 4%)
A London pale ale with a cedar-like bitterness and medium body, finishing with a refreshing mango and citrus burst.

London Porter (OG 1053, ABV 5.5%)
A traditional London porter with chocolate, caramel, coffee, liquorice, dark fruits and berry flavours.

London IPA (OG 1043, ABV 6%)
An IPA with powerful citrus and spice aromas leading to a balanced malt body and sustained hop character.

Engineer (NEW)

Russetts, Burnt Oak Road, High Hurstwood, East Sussex, TN22 4AE ☎ 07841 669096
⊕ theengineerbrewery.co.uk

A picobrewery supplying a small number of local outlets. It also offers bespoke beers to the public for events and anniversaries. V

Ennerdale SIBA

Chapel Row, Rowrah, Cumbria, CA26 3XS
☎ (01946) 862977 ☎ 07918 626652
⊕ ennerdalebrewery.co.uk

☺Ennerdale started brewing in 2010 as a 10-barrel brewery in a converted barn. In 2016 the brewery moved to larger premises with plans for expansion. Beers are distributed throughout the north of England and south Scotland. ‼◆

Blonde (OG 1039, ABV 3.8%) ◣
A sweet, fruity, light-coloured beer with gentle bitterness.

Darkest (OG 1044, ABV 4.2%) ◣
Sweet, roasty, black mild with a fruity, hoppy flavour.

Wild Ennerdale (OG 1043, ABV 4.2%)

Amber in colour with a fruity base and spicy finish yielding a good hop aroma and well-rounded bitterness.

Enville SIBA

Coxgreen, Hollies Lane, Enville, DY7 5LG
☎ (01384) 873728 ⊕ envilleales.com

⊗ Enville Brewery is sited on a picturesque Victorian, Grade II-listed farm complex, using natural well water, traditional steam brewing and a reed and willow effluent plant. Enville Ale is infused with honey and is from a 19th-century recipe for beekeeper's ale passed down from the former proprietor's great-great aunt. ‼☞◆

LPA (Light Pale Ale) (OG 1039, ABV 4%)
Traditional session bitter; dry and golden with a mellow, hoppy flavour.

Nailmaker Mild (OG 1041, ABV 4%)
A well-defined hop aroma and underlying sweetness give way to a dry finish.

Simpkiss (OG 1039, ABV 4%)

Cherry Blonde (OG 1042, ABV 4.2%)
A light blonde bitter, delicately infused with essence of cherry to produce a Belgian-style fruit beer, with a bitter finish.

Saaz (OG 1042, ABV 4.2%) ◣
Golden lager-style beer. Lager bite but with more taste and lasting bitterness. The malty aroma is late arriving but the bitter finish, balanced by fruit and hops, compensates.

White (OG 1041, ABV 4.2%) ◣
Yellow-coloured with a malt, hops and fruit aroma. Hoppy but sweet finish.

Ale (OG 1044, ABV 4.5%) ◣
Sweet malty aroma and taste, honey becomes apparent before bitterness finally dominates.

Old Porter (OG 1044, ABV 4.5%) ◣
Black with a creamy head and sulphurous aroma. Sweet and fruity start with touches of spice. Good balance between sweet and bitter, but hops dominate the finish.

Ginger Beer (OG 1045, ABV 4.6%) ◣
Golden bright with gently gingered tangs. A drinkable beer with no acute flavours but a satisfying aftertaste of sweet hoppiness.

Epicurus SIBA

1-1c Grey Street, Denton, Manchester, M34 3RU
☎ (0161) 320 5627 ☎ 07903 712805

Formerly known as Hornbeam Brewery, it was taken over in 2016 by new owners, James Thompson and Nick Taylor, and completely rebranded as Epicurus in 2017 with a range of seven core beers, some using popular Hornbeam recipes. ◆RAIB

Lemon Blossom (OG 1040, ABV 3.7%)
A light straw-coloured ale, crisp, citrus and slightly floral. An aroma of citrus lemon and well-balanced sweetness with a delicate bitterness to finish.

Lime Blossom (ABV 3.7%)
A light straw-coloured, refreshing and smooth session beer with sweet lime citrus tastes.

Orange Blossom (OG 1038, ABV 3.8%)
Crisp citrus tangerine notes with a balanced sweetness and orange peel in the finish.

THE BREWERIES

Apollo (ABV 3.9%)
A light citrus, spicy ale with a grapefruit, spicy character.

Poseidon (ABV 4.2%)
A full-bodied ale with malt appeal and ample bitterness. Crisp citrus with hints of honey and a grassy finish.

IPA Lite (ABV 4.3%)
Well-balanced light IPA with lime in the finish.

Hades (ABV 4.5%)
Dark and full-bodied stout with a creamy head, subtle bitterness and coffee aftertaste. Malt, coffee, liquorice and spice.

Errant ⊙

Arch 8, King Edward Bridge, off Pottery Lane, Newcastle upon Tyne, NE1 3TQ ☎ 07736 333303
⊕ errantbrewery.com

⊠ Brewing began in 2015 in an old Victorian railway arch in central Newcastle upon Tyne. The brewery taproom is a work in progress. A range of speciality beers is available seasonally or on request. ♦

Knight (ABV 3.8%)
An amber-coloured session ale, well-balanced with a caramel and malty taste.

Clever Girl (ABV 4.1%)
A pale gold-coloured session IPA. Hoppy with citrus and grapefruit notes.

Comanche (ABV 4.5%)
A black porter with chocolate, roasted and treacle notes.

Tusk (ABV 5.2%)
An amber-coloured IPA, hoppy, bitter and citrus with a resinous hop aroma.

Essex Street

🍺 **46 Essex Street, Temple, London, WC2R 3JF**
☎ (020) 7936 2536 ⊕ templebrewhouse.com

Opened in 2014 within the Temple Brew House pub. Beers are neither filtered nor pasteurised. The pub company also operates sister brewpubs in London, Bath, Bristol, Cambridge and Norwich.

Evan Evans SIBA

The New Brewery, 1 Rhosmaen Street, Llandeilo, Carmarthenshire, SA19 6LU
☎ (01558) 824455 ⊕ evanevansbrewery.com

☺Evan Evans opened in 2004. The range of brands produced includes the regional Welsh brand Evan-Evans, J Buckley Brewer focusses on hop flavour. Artisan is a US-style craft beer brand and Fire-Island specialises in organic beer. In 2016 the iconic Celt Experience brand was acquired and its production moved to Llandeilo. Beers may also appear under the name of Archers and Porter Street. ‼🍺♦

BB (Best Bitter) (OG 1036, ABV 3.6%)
A light, malty character with a dry hop palate.

WPA (Welsh Pale Ale) (OG 1040, ABV 4%)
A golden ale, with hints of tropical fruits, malty finish.

Cwrw (OG 1043, ABV 4.2%)
Rich, malty flavour, and a distinct fruity palate.

Britannia Celebration Ale (ABV 4.6%)
Dark amber-coloured beer with a rich malt fruity hedgerow berry finish.

Warrior (OG 1046, ABV 4.6%)
Full-bodied and malty, with a fruity flavour and dry hop finish.

Brewed under the Celt Experience brand name:

Castro Mosaic (ABV 3.9%)
An American-style pale ale infused with lemon peel to create a tropical fruit palate and citrus aroma.

Chieftain (ABV 4.3%)
A complex malt flavour balanced with citrus aromas.

Silures (ABV 4.6%)
A powerfully-hopped brew with tropical fruit flavours.

Brewed under the J Buckley Brewer brand name:

Original Best (ABV 4.4%)
A rich, malty bitter with a fruit aroma.

Everards SIBA ⊙

Devana Avenue, Optimus Point, Glenfield, Leicestershire, LE3 8JS
☎ (0116) 201 4100 ⊕ everards.co.uk

Everards was established in 1849 by William Everard and remains an independent family-owned company. It has a pub estate of more than 170 tenanted houses throughout the Midlands. It plans to move its brewing operation to a new site, Everards Meadows, but this cannot go ahead until the sale of the Castle Acres site is complete. The company closed the old brewery in the summer of 2017 and for the duration of this edition of the Guide its beers will be produced by what it calls Brewing Partners. Robinson's of Stockport will brew Tiger and Beacon Hill, while Joules of Market Drayton will produce Old Original, Sunchaser and limited edition beers. The new brewery will have a capacity of 15,000 barrels a year.

Ewhurst (NEW)

The Barn, Ewhurst Green, East Sussex, TN32 5TD
☎ (01580) 830049 ⊕ ewhurstales.com

Brewing began in 2016 in a barn situated on a hill overlooking Bodiam Castle. The White Dog pub next door serves as the brewery tap. A micropub, Bakes & Ales in Wadhurst, is owned.

Exe Valley SIBA ⊙

Land Farm, Silverton, Devon, EX5 4HF
☎ (01392) 860406 ⊕ exevalleybrewery.co.uk

⊠ Exe Valley was established as Barron's Brewery in 1984. The brewery is located in a converted barn overlooking the Exe Valley and Dartmoor hills. Locally sourced malt and English hops are used, along with the brewery's own spring water. Around 100 outlets are supplied within a 45-mile radius of the brewery. Beers are also available nationally via wholesalers. ♦RAIB

Bitter (OG 1036, ABV 3.7%) 🍺
Mid-brown bitter, pleasantly fruity with underlying malt through the aroma, taste and finish.

Darkest Devon (OG 1039, ABV 3.9%) 🍺

Barron's Hopsit (OG 1040, ABV 4.1%) ◈
Straw-coloured beer with strong hop aroma, hop and fruit flavour and a bitter hop finish.

Dob's Best Bitter (OG 1040, ABV 4.1%) ◈
Delicate aroma, well-balanced taste with malt, hops and sweet fruit continuing into a bitter, hoppy aftertaste.

Devon Glory (OG 1046, ABV 4.7%)
Mid-brown, fruity-tasting pint with a sweet, fruity finish.

Mr Sheppard's Crook (OG 1046, ABV 4.7%) ◈
Smooth, full-bodied, mid-brown beer with a malty-fruit nose and a sweetish palate leading to a bitter, dry finish.

Exeter Old Bitter (OG 1046, ABV 4.8%) ◈
Mid-brown old ale with a rich fruity taste and slightly earthy aroma and bitter finish.

It's Phil's Ale (OG 1046, ABV 4.8%) ▌
Deep golden-coloured, hoppy beer.

Exeter SIBA ◉

Unit 1, Cowley Bridge Road, Exeter, Devon, EX4 4NX
☎ (01392) 259059 ⊕ exeterbrewery.co.uk

⊗ Exeter Brewery, formerly Topsham & Exminster, began brewing in 2003 and is the largest brewery in the city, supplying more than 600 outlets throughout the country. It moved to its present site in 2012, having outgrown its previous location. ‼ ═ ◆ RAIB

Lighterman (OG 1036, ABV 3.5%)
A light copper-coloured ale, fruity malt flavour with a traditional bitter finish.

Avocet (OG 1038.5, ABV 3.9%) ▌ ◈
Gold-coloured bitter that is smooth, fruity and hoppy with a sweet aftertaste. Crisp, light and refreshing.

'fraid Not (OG 1040, ABV 4%)
A golden-coloured, hoppy beer. A distinct clean, citrus bitterness and lasting dry finish.

Ferryman (OG 1041, ABV 4.2%)
Classic copper-coloured session ale. Well-balanced, sweet, warm malt flavour. Crisp bitter finish.

County Best (OG 1045, ABV 4.6%)
Premium strength best bitter. Rich malt fruity flavour. Smooth, bittersweet finish.

Darkness (OG 1050, ABV 5.1%) ◈
Full-bodied stout. Roasted malt dominates the aroma. Complex taste with roast chocolate. Hints of liquorice in a bitter finish.

Exit 33

Unit 7, 106 Fitzwalter Road, Sheffield, South Yorkshire, S2 2SP
☎ (0114) 270 9991 ⊕ exit33.beer

☺ This eight-barrel brewery was founded in Sheffield in 2008 as Brew Company but rebranded in 2014. The brewer is also a joint partner at the Harlequin pub. Regular house beers are brewed for local pubs and also deliver nationally. ◆

Blonde (OG 1038.8, ABV 4%)
A light and fruity, easy-drinking blonde session ale.

Thirst Aid (OG 1038.8, ABV 4%)
A light, clean-drinking session ale with a juicy hop-forward flavour.

Mosaic (OG 1039.7, ABV 4.1%)
A single-hop pale ale.

New England Best (OG 1040.7, ABV 4.2%)
A dark-coloured premium bitter with a smooth, well-balanced malty base and rich flavour.

Hop Monster (OG 1043.6, ABV 4.5%)
Hoppy golden ale with resinous pink grapefruit, biting citrus and a soft floral character and a long bitter finish.

Stout (OG 1048.4, ABV 5%)
A dark roasted traditional stout. The initial flavour hints of cocoa followed by delicate coffee and molasses with a silky, thick mouthfeel.

Exmoor SIBA ◉

Golden Hill Brewery, Old Brewery Road, Wiveliscombe, Somerset, TA4 2PW
☎ (01984) 623798 ⊕ exmoorales.co.uk

Somerset's largest independent brewery was founded in 1980 in the old Hancock's brewery, which closed in 1959. In 2015 Exmoor moved to new and larger premises within 100 yards of the original site, thus doubling brewing capacity. Around 250 outlets in the South-west are supplied and others nationwide via wholesalers and pub chains. ‼ ◆

Ale (OG 1039, ABV 3.8%) ◈
Mid-brown, medium-bodied session bitter. Mixture of malt and hops in the aroma and taste lead to a hoppy, bitter aftertaste.

Fox (OG 1043, ABV 4.2%)
The slight maltiness on the tongue is followed by a burst of hops with a lingering, bittersweet aftertaste.

Gold (OG 1045, ABV 4.5%) ▌ ◈
Golden best bitter with balance of malt and fruity hop on the nose and palate with sweetness following. Bitter finish.

Stag (OG 1050, ABV 5.2%) ◈
A pale brown beer, with a malty taste and aroma, and a bitter finish.

Beast (OG 1066, ABV 6.6%)
A dark-coloured beer with the characteristics of a strong porter. A good blend of malt and hops with a complex, long aftertaste.

Eyeball (NEW)

Office: Unit 2, Cockenzie Business Centre, Edinburgh Road, Cockenzie, EH32 0XL ⊕ eyeballbrewing.co.uk

Eyeball Brewing was established in 2016 by James Dempsey, producing three lagers in cask, keg and bottle.

Black (ABV 4.9%)

Yellow (ABV 4.9%)

Orange (ABV 6.5%)

Eyes (NEW) SIBA

Manor Farm, Intake Lake, Acaster Mablis, York, North Yorkshire, YO23 3UJ ☎ 07837 898749

Office: 54 Eden Crescent, Leeds, West Yorkshire, LS24 2TW ⊕ eyesbrewing.com

THE BREWERIES

⊕Brewing began in 2016 using spare capacity at Ainsty Ales in York. Eyes is the first wheat-focused brewery in the UK.

Facer's

A8-9, Ashmount Enterprise Park, Aber Road, Flint, CH5 5YL ☎ 07713 566370 ⊕ facers.co.uk

Facer's is the oldest brewery in Flintshire. Sales average some 30 barrels per week to around 100 outlets in North Wales and North-west England. Established in 2003 by ex-Boddingtons head brewer Dave Facer, the brewery now has three employees. ‼◆

Mountain Mild (OG 1035, ABV 3.3%) 🍺 ◆
A fruity dark mild, not too sweet, with underlying roast malt flavours and a full mouthfeel for its low ABV.

Clwyd Gold (OG 1034, ABV 3.5%) ◆
Clean-tasting session bitter, mid-brown in colour with a full mouthfeel. The malty flavours are accompanied by increasing hoppiness in the bitter finish.

Flintshire Bitter (OG 1035, ABV 3.7%) ◆
Well-balanced session bitter with a full mouthfeel. Some fruitiness in aroma and taste with increasing hoppy bitterness in the dry finish.

Abbey Original (OG 1038, ABV 4%) ◆
A sweetish golden-coloured beer with a good hop and fruit aroma, juicy taste and a dry hoppy finish.

Abbey Red (OG 1038, ABV 4%) ◆
A darker version of Abbey Original, copper-coloured with a sweet, malty taste and a bittersweet aftertaste.

North Star Porter (OG 1042, ABV 4%) 🍺 ◆
Dark, smooth, porter-style beer with good roast notes and hints of coffee and chocolate. Some initial sweetness and caramel flavours followed by a hoppy bitter aftertaste.

Summer Ale (OG 1037, ABV 4%)

Sunny Bitter (OG 1040, ABV 4.2%) ◆
An amber-coloured beer with a dry taste. The hop aroma continues into the taste where some faint fruit notes are also present. Lasting dry finish.

DHB (Dave's Hoppy Beer) (OG 1041, ABV 4.3%) ◆
A dry-hopped version of This Splendid Ale with some sweet flavours also coming through in the mainly hoppy, bitter taste.

This Splendid Ale (OG 1041, ABV 4.3%) ◆
Refreshing, tangy best bitter, yellow in colour with a sharp hoppy, bitter taste. Good citrus fruit undertones with hints of grapefruit throughout.

Landslide (OG 1047, ABV 4.9%) ◆
Full-flavoured, complex premium bitter with tangy orange marmalade fruitiness in aroma and taste. Long-lasting hoppy flavours throughout.

Fallen Acorn (NEW) SIBA 👁

Unit 7, Clarence Wharf Industrial Estate, Mumby Road, Gosport, Hampshire, PO12 1AJ ☎ (023) 9307 9927 ⊕ fallenacornbrewing.co

⊠ Investment firm Just Develop It in Hampshire bought Oakleaf Brewery in 2016. The brewery was renamed Fallen Acorn and went into full production later that year. Ed Anderson remains head brewer. ‼◆RAIB

Twisted Oak (OG 1040, ABV 4%)
A traditional mid-brown bitter with an initial malty flavour leading to a long, hoppy finish.

Pot Kettle (OG 1046, ABV 4.6%)

Hole Hearted (OG 1048, ABV 4.7%) ◆
Amber-coloured with a strong floral hop aroma. Continuing into the flavour, with some malt, leading to a long, bittersweet finish.

Expedition IPA (OG 1053, ABV 5.5%)
This beer is initially dry and bitter. Full-flavoured and complex marmalade/aniseed notes to follow, which leaves a lingering bitterness on the palate.

Fallen Angel SIBA

Unit 12c, Reeds Farm Estate Office, Roxwell Road, Writtle, Essex, CM1 3ST ⊕ fallenangelbrew.co.uk

Formerly known as the Broxbourne Brewery, a name change to Fallen Angel occurred in 2017. Brewing began in 2013 using a 12-barrel plant. A 15-barrel plant has been in operation since the brewery's move from Hertfordshire to Essex in 2015. RAIB

Cowgirl (OG 1045, ABV 4.2%)
A full-flavoured, hoppy, copper-coloured ale with a smooth taste and finish.

Mr & Mrs Smith's Smooth Alcoholic Ginger Beer (OG 1030, ABV 4.2%)
A traditionally-made smooth ginger beer.

Angry Ox Bitter (OG 1048, ABV 4.8%)
A traditional English bitter full of malt and hop taste.

Fire in the Hole (OG 1045, ABV 4.9%)
A golden ale flavoured with fresh green chillies. This beer has the aromatic taste of fresh chilli with moderate heat.

Black Death Chilli Stout (OG 1053, ABV 5.3%)
An oatmeal stout with the extreme heat of Naga chilli, but also smooth and slightly sweet to taste.

Fallen

Station House, Kippen, FK8 3JA ☎ 07507 862167 ⊕ fallenbrewing.co.uk

Fallen began brewing in 2014 using a 10-barrel plant. ◆RAIB

Odyssey (OG 1040, ABV 4.1%)

Dragonfly (OG 1046, ABV 4.6%)

Blackhouse (OG 1052, ABV 5%)

Grapevine (OG 1054, ABV 5.4%)

Falstaff SIBA 👁

🏠 **24 Society Place, Normanton, Derby, DE23 6UH ☎ (01332) 342902 ☎ 07947 242710 ⊕ falstaffbrewery.co.uk**

Attached to the Falstaff freehouse, the brewery dates from 1999 but was refurbished and re-opened in 2003 under new management. Themed special beers are produced all year round, including exclusive specials for the Babington Arms in Derby.

Famous Railway Tavern

🏠 **58 Station Road, Brightlingsea, Essex, CO7 0DT**

The brewery started life as a kitchen-sink affair in 1998. In 2012 the brewery was completely refurbished; a two-barrel plant is used to create a selection of dark beers suitable for vegetarians.

Faringdon

🏠 1 Park Road, Faringdon, Oxfordshire, SN7 7BP
☎ (01367) 241480

Faringdon opened in 2010 using a one-barrel plant; brewing on a larger-scale began in 2011. All beers are supplied to the brewery tap, the Swan, when available. Production is currently suspended.

Farm Yard (NEW)

Gulf Lane, Cockerham, Lancashire, LA2 0ER ☎ 07717 081170 ⊕ farmyardales.co.uk

Situated on a family-run farm in the fertile North Fylde, brewing began in 2017.

Farmageddon

25 Ballykeigle Road, Comber, BT23 5SD
⊕ farmageddonbrewery.com

Brewing began in 2014. All beers are unfiltered with no preservatives and are suitable for vegans. RAIB V

California Common (ABV 4%)

Gold Pale Ale (ABV 4.2%)

Porter (ABV 5.2%)

IPA (ABV 5.5%)

Farmer's

See Maldon

Farr Brew SIBA ◉

Unit 7, The Courtyard, Samuels Farm, Coleman Green Lane, Wheathampstead, Hertfordshire, AL4 8ER
☎ 07734 857881 ⊕ farrbrew.com

⊗ Farr Brew began brewing in 2014. The beers proved popular necessitating a move to a brand new 10-barrel brewery in 2016. Ecological and environmental concerns are at the forefront of everything Farr Brew creates. ‼♦

Chief Jester (OG 1036, ABV 3.6%)
A thirst-quenching light amber-coloured ale.

Our Greatest Golden (OG 1041, ABV 4.1%)
A dark golden-coloured ale with a well-rounded but not overpowering hoppiness.

Our Most Perfect Pale (OG 1042, ABV 4.2%)
A pale, refreshing golden ale full of tropical and citrus flavours with a fine, crisp bitter finish.

The Best Bitter (OG 1042, ABV 4.2%)
A dark-coloured traditional bitter with a hint of caramel.

Black Listed IBA (OG 1045, ABV 4.5%)
Smoky, powerfully-hopped India black ale with a well-rounded, punchy flavour.

Our Most Potent Porter (OG 1050, ABV 5%)
Some honey and treacle notes combine to create a complex porter with a deep chocolate nose and a rich, fruity, hoppy flavour. Made with honey from local hives.

Farriers Arms

🏠 The Forstal, Mersham, Kent, TN25 6NU
☎ (01233) 720444 ⊕ thefarriersarms.comcontact

Brewing commenced in 2010 in this brewpub owned by a consortium of villagers.

Fat Belly (NEW)

🏠 c/o Cottage Inn, Lynton, Devon, EX34 6NR
☎ (01598) 753496 ⊕ thecottageinnlynton.co.uk

Established in 2016 using a 3.5-barrel plant at the rear of the Cottage Inn. Beers are available in the pub plus a few other local free houses, hotels and restaurants. Further beers are planned.

Fat Cat

🏠 Fat Cat Brewery Tap, 98-100 Lawson Road, Norwich, NR3 4LF
☎ (01603) 788508 ☎ 07795 633368
⊕ fatcatbrewery.co.uk

Fat Cat Brewery was founded by the owner of the Fat Cat free house in Norwich. Brewing started in 2005 at the Fat Cat's sister pub, the Fat Cat Brewery Tap, under the supervision of former Woodforde's owner Ray Ashworth.

Fat Pig SIBA

🏠 2 John Street, Exeter, Devon, EX1 1BL
☎ (01392) 437217 ⊕ fatpig-exeter.co.uk

Brewing commenced in 2013 using a 2.5-barrel plant to supply the Fat Pig and its sister pub Tabac, also in Exeter. It is run as an experimental brewery, constantly playing with combinations of malts, hops and temperatures to improve the range of beers and push the boundaries. Grain liquor is also produced for its in-house distillery.

Faversham Steam

See Shepherd Neame

Felinfoel SIBA

Farmers Row, Felinfoel, Llanelli, SA14 8LB
☎ (01554) 773357 ⊕ felinfoel-brewery.com

Founded in the 1830s, the company is still family-owned and is now the oldest brewery in Wales. The present buildings are Grade II*-listed and were built in the 1870s. It supplies cask ale to half its 84 houses, though some use top pressure dispense, and to approximately 350 free trade outlets. ‼🍴♦

IPA (OG 1036, ABV 3.6%)

Celtic Pride (OG 1045, ABV 3.9%)
A light, golden-coloured premium ale with a bright, clean flavour and citrus overtones.

Double Dragon (OG 1042, ABV 4.2%) 🍂
This pale brown beer has a malty, fruity aroma. The taste is also malt and fruit with a background hop presence throughout. A malty and fruity finish.

Stout (OG 1048, ABV 5%)
A Welsh stout created with a subtle blend of chocolate malt giving a predominantly roast barley flavour and a rich, creamy head.

Fell

Unit 27, Moor Lane Business Park, Flookburgh,
Cumbria, LA11 7NG
☎ (01539) 558980 ☎ 07967 503689
⊕ fellbrewery.co.uk

⊠ Fell Brewery was founded in 2012 by
homebrewer Tim Bloomer and friend Andrew
Carter, brewing beers inspired by their travels in
the US and Belgium.

YOLO (OG 1035, ABV 3.7%) ◀
A yellow-coloured, highly drinkable hoppy session
bitter with a long, drying, bitter finish.

Nectar (OG 1038, ABV 4.2%)
Intensely hoppy West Coast American-style pale
ale.

Robust Porter (OG 1051, ABV 4.8%) ◀
Roast dominates throughout; fruit comes through
on drinking, with a dry and bitter finish.

Tinderbox IPA (OG 1059, ABV 6.3%)
A strongly-hopped IPA with an initial sweetness
leading to a lingering bitter aftertaste.

Fellows

2 Leopold Walk, Cottenham, Cambridgeshire,
CB24 8XS
☎ (01954) 250262 ⊕ fellowsbrewery.co.uk

⊠ Fellows began production in 2010 though
brewer Mark Burton had been developing recipes
for a year or so before. Five regular beers are
available with plans for a series of special ales.
Beers are increasingly visible in the local free trade.

Cambridge Fellow (OG 1038, ABV 3.8%)
A golden-coloured session ale, light and clean-
tasting.

Gulping Fellow (OG 1042, ABV 4.2%)
A dry bitter finish complements the spicy hop
character of this well-balanced best bitter.

Burton Snatch (OG 1048, ABV 4.8%)
Blonde ale with a citrus aroma and refreshing
mouthfeel. A hint of wet leather completes the
finish.

Jolly Fellows (OG 1050, ABV 5%)
Full-bodied, clean-tasting premium bitter.

Clever Fellow (OG 1052, ABV 5.2%)
Malt loaf and toffee flavours combine with back of
the tongue bitterness to achieve a balanced
richness.

Felstar

Felsted Vineyards, Crix Green, Felsted, Essex, CM6 3JT
☎ (01245) 361504 ☎ 07546 096374
⊕ felstarbrewery.co.uk

⊠ Felstar Brewery opened in 2001 with a five-
barrel plant based in the old bonded warehouse of
the Felsted Vineyard. A small number of outlets are
supplied. ‼ 🍺 ◆ RAIB

Felstar (OG 1036, ABV 3.6%)
Amber-coloured session bitter with an aroma of
traditional English hops and a long bitter finish.

Summer Light (OG 1038, ABV 3.8%)

Old Essex (OG 1039, ABV 3.9%)

Crix Forest (OG 1040, ABV 4%)

A toasty dark mild with hints of berries, a hoppy
nose and a bitter finish.

Lightburst (OG 1040, ABV 4%)

Witchcraft (OG 1044, ABV 4.4%)

Good Knight (OG 1050, ABV 5%)
A dark porter with gentle smoky and spicy flavours
balancing the bitter hoppiness.

Hoppy Hen (OG 1050, ABV 5%)
An old ale with rich malty and spicy flavours and
strong, hoppy nose and bitter finish.

Pecking Order (OG 1050, ABV 5%)

Fernandes

🏠 5 Avison Yard, Kirkgate, Wakefield, West Yorkshire,
WF1 1UA
☎ (01924) 291709 ⊕ ossett-brewery.co.uk

Opened in 1997 and housed in a 19th-century
malthouse, Ossett Brewing Company purchased
the brewery and tap in 2007 but independent
brewing continues. Around 90 different beers are
brewed each year. The tap sells Fernandes and
Ossett beers as well as guest ales; the former are
more widely available through Ossett's supply
chain.

Malt Shovel Mild (OG 1038, ABV 3.8%)
A dark, full-bodied, malty mild with roast malt and
chocolate flavours, leading to a lingering, dry,
malty finish.

Ale to the Tsar (OG 1042, ABV 4.1%)
A pale, smooth, well-balanced beer with some
sweetness leading to a nutty, malty and satisfying
aftertaste.

Centaur (OG 1045, ABV 4.5%)
A dry, pale ale with balanced notes of orange zest,
coriander and pine.

Black Voodoo (OG 1050, ABV 5.1%)
Smooth, full-bodied black stout with chocolate,
orange and vanilla flavours coming through.

Double Six (OG 1062, ABV 6%)
A powerful, dark and rich strong beer with an array
of malt, roast malt and chocolate flavours and a
strong, lasting malty finish, with some hoppiness.

Ferry Ales (NEW) SIBA

Ferry Hill Farm, Ferry Road, Fiskerton, Lincolnshire,
LN3 4HU ☎ 07790 241999 ⊕ ferryalesbrewery.co.uk

Ferry Ales Brewery (FAB) began brewing in 2016
using a five-barrel brew plant. The two brewers/
directors are currently brewing once or twice a
week. ◆

Just Jane (ABV 3.8%)
Amber-coloured session ale with a fruity finish.

Witham Shield (ABV 4.5%)

49 SQN (ABV 4.9%)
A well-balanced beer of malt, fruit and citrus hop
flavour.

Smokey Joe (ABV 4.9%)
A classic porter with a hint of smokiness in the
finish.

Ferry Brewery (NEW)

Bankhead Farm Steading, Bankhead Road, South
Queensferry, EH30 9TF

☎ (0131) 331 1851 ⊕ ferrybrewery.co.uk

The first brewery in South Queensferry since 1851, Ferry Brewery was established in 2016 by husband-and-wife team Mark and Jan Moran. Its beers combine traditional and historic beer recipes with a contemporary twist. Tours and tasting sessions are planned. ⌭♦

Ferry Fair (OG 1038.8, ABV 4%)
Refreshing, golden-coloured, dry pale ale with a moderate bitterness.

40/- Fine (OG 1040.7, ABV 4.2%)
Traditional 80/- style Scottish ale. Easy-drinking with aromas of malt, light hops and fruit to complement its smooth and creamy texture.

Ferry Crossing (OG 1043.6, ABV 4.5%)
A light, hoppy, crisp, fruity blonde ale.

Ferry Witches Brew (OG 1043.6, ABV 4.5%)
A reddish copper-coloured, well-balanced ale with a hoppy flavour.

Ferry Stout (OG 1055, ABV 4.9%)
Black and rich with a roasted malty flavour and balanced bitter finish.

Thomas Miller 1785 (OG 1054.2, ABV 5.5%)
A smooth, smoky, bitter-coffee porter with a sweet liquorice finish and aromas of smoke and coffee.

Fierce

Unit 46, Howe Moss Avenue, Dyce, AB21 0GP
☎ (01224) 729131 ⊕ fiercebeer.com

Initially started by an enthusuastic home brewer, the brewery re-located to a factory unit in 2016. No real ale.

FILO

The Old Town Brewery, Torfield Cottage, 8 Old London Road, Hastings, East Sussex, TN34 3HA
☎ (01424) 420212 ⊕ filobrewing.co.uk

⊠ The brewery at the First In Last Out public house was established in 1985, with the current owners taking over in 1988. In 2011 the brewery relocated two minutes' walk away, remaining in the Old Town. The First In Last Out (FILO) is still supplied direct together with pubs throughout Sussex and Kent. ‼⌭♦

Crofters (OG 1037, ABV 3.8%)

Bourne Blonde (ABV 4%)

Churches Pale Ale (OG 1042, ABV 4.2%)

Old Town Tom (OG 1044, ABV 4.5%)

Cardinal (ABV 4.8%)

Gold (OG 1050, ABV 4.8%)

Our Auld Ale (ABV 5.8%)

Fine Tuned (NEW)

24 Moor Park, Langport, Somerset, TA10 9PX
☎ 07872 139945 ⊕ finetunedbrewery.com

Brewing began in 2016. A core range of three beers are brewed. ♦RAIB

Langport Bitter (OG 1040, ABV 4%)
A traditional English bitter, amber in colour.

Rack & Roll (OG 1041, ABV 4%)
Hoppy, amber-coloured ale.

Sunshine Reggae (OG 1043, ABV 4.2%)
An American-style pale ale, refreshing and hoppy.

Fintry SIBA

23 Main Street, Fintry, G63 0XA
☎ (01360) 860224 ☎ 07833 662820
✉ bill@fintrymusos.co.uk

⊠ Fintry Brewing was established in 2013 in premises at the Fintry Inn. After expansion in 2015, it now uses an eight-barrel plant with a capacity of 2,600 litres a week. The beers are named after local hills and streams. ‼♦

Clachertyfarlie (OG 1039, ABV 3.9%)

Knockbuckle (OG 1041, ABV 4.1%)

Meikle Bin (OG 1041, ABV 4.1%)

Firebird SIBA 👁

Old Rudgwick Brickworks, Lynwick Street, Rudgwick, West Sussex, RH12 3UW
☎ (01403) 823180 ⊕ firebirdbrewing.co.uk

⊠ Firebird began brewing in 2013 and has grown rapidly with new beers, new vessels, an extended warehouse and an expanded team of seven people. ‼⌭♦RAIB

Heritage XX (OG 1041, ABV 4%)
A fresh, hoppy, full-bodied ale.

No. 79 (OG 1043, ABV 4.3%)
A full and fruity golden ale.

Old Ale XXXX (OG 1045, ABV 4.5%)
A smooth, bittersweet, dark-coloured ale with hints of roasted chocolate.

Paleface APA (OG 1053, ABV 5.2%)
A zesty and aromatic American-style pale ale.

Firebrand

See Altarnun

Firebrick SIBA 👁

Units 10 & 11, Blaydon Business Centre, Cowen Road, Blaydon, Tyne & Wear, NE21 5TW
☎ (0191) 447 6543 ⊕ firebrickbrewery.com

Firebrick began brewing on a 2.5-barrel plant in 2013, expanding to a 12-barrel plant in 2014. Regular beers are brewed on the 12-barrel plant while the 2.5-barrel plant is used to brew specials. Beers are found in pubs within the Tyne & Wear area. ♦

Blaydon Brick (OG 1038, ABV 3.8%)

Coalface (OG 1039, ABV 3.9%)

Elder Statesman (OG 1043, ABV 3.9%)

Tyne 9 (OG 1039, ABV 3.9%)

Pagan Queen (OG 1040, ABV 4%)

Trade Star (OG 1041, ABV 4.2%)

Stella Spark (OG 1043, ABV 4.4%)

Toon Broon (OG 1046, ABV 4.6%)

Wey-Aye P.A. (OG 1058, ABV 5.8%)

Firefly

🍺 Firefly, 54 Lowesmoor, Worcester, WR1 2SE
☎ (01905) 616996 ☎ 07525 445988
✉ thefirefly@hotmail.co.uk

A pub microbrewery, Firefly started brewing in 2012 using a 0.5-barrel plant. Brewing takes place from October to March. Each beer is unique as different recipes are used each time.

Firehouse

13 Thames Street, Louth, Lincolnshire, LN11 7AD
☎ (01507) 608202 ☎ 07961 772905
⊕ firehouse-brewery.co.uk

☺Firehouse was founded by Jason Allen in 2014 in the village of Manby using a 2.5-barrel plant. In 2016, along with Louise Darbon, the Fulstow Brewery in Louth was purchased and the brewery was relocated there. Beers from the Fulstow range are also produced. Beers are available in the free trade and from the bar located at the brewery, the Gas Lamp Lounge. ♦

Mainwarings Mild (ABV 3.6%)
A dark malty mild based on a wartime recipe.

Marsh Mild (ABV 3.8%)
Traditional ruby red-coloured mild ale with a rich roast, full-bodied flavour.

FGB (ABV 3.9%)
An amber-coloured English session ale.

Northway IPA (OG 1042.5, ABV 4.2%)
A pale-coloured IPA with a clean citrus flavour and dry finish.

Woodman Pale Ale (ABV 4.4%)
Pale yellow-coloured, fruity, sweetish session bitter with a dry, hoppy finish.

Pride of Fulstow (OG 1044, ABV 4.5%)
Premium English pale ale with a full-bodied flavour and rich mouthfeel.

Wobbly Weasel (ABV 4.9%)
Complex ale, rich and fruity in the mouth with an intense bittersweet finish.

Lincolnshire Country Bitter (ABV 5.1%)
A smooth, full-bodied dark ale with fruity flavours. Intense bitter aftertaste that lingers.

Firestorm

See Wharfe Bank

First Chop SIBA ⊙

B2, Barton Hall Business Park, Hardy Street, Eccles, M30 7NB ☎ 07970 241398
⊕ firstchopbrewingarm.com

Brewing began at Outstanding Brewery (qv) in Bury in 2012 before transferring to Salford in 2013. The brewery relocated again to Eccles in 2017 with increased capacity. It specialises in producing gluten-free beers. GF

AVA (OG 1034, ABV 3.5%)
A hoppy, blonde session ale.

SYL (OG 1064, ABV 6.2%)

Fish Key

Unit 4, Granite Quay, Looe, Cornwall, PL13 1DX
☎ (01726) 870007 ☎ 07814 019250
⊕ fishkeybrewingcompany.com

Fish Key started production in 2016. Five local outlets are supplied at present.

Hop2It (OG 1039, ABV 4%) ◆
Yellow-coloured bitter with citrus hop aroma. Overpowering grassy citrus hop flavour with grapefruit, pith and robust bitterness. Finish becomes dry.

Brew.T (OG 1043, ABV 4.4%)
Fresh hop and fruit aroma with strong hop bitterness.

Hip Hop (OG 1044, ABV 4.5%)

Red IPA (OG 1049, ABV 4.9%)

Fisher's

Unit 8, Central Park Business Centre, Bellfield Road, High Wycombe, Buckinghamshire, HP13 5HG
☎ 07789 007876 ⊕ fishersbrew.co.uk

Established in 2013 and orginally operating out of his garage at home, owner and brewer Mike Fisher moved the brewery to larger premises in 2017. Beers are supplied to two pubs in High Wycombe, the Bootlegger and Sausage Tree. RAIB

Golden Hour (ABV 3.5%)

Sundown (ABV 4.1%)

Five Kingdoms

🍺 Steam Packet Inn, Harbour Row, Isle of Whithorn, DG8 8LL
☎ (01988) 500334 ⊕ thesteampacketinn.biz

Five Kingdoms was established in 2015 by Alastair Scoular, owner of the Steam Packet Inn, using a 2.5-barrel plant. The pub, selected beer festivals and a few local outlets are supplied.

Five Oh

83 Agecroft Road West, Prestwich, M25 9RF ☎ 07772 243089 ✉ fiveohbrewco@sky.com

Five Oh began brewing in 2014 on a small scale focusing on bottled beers, which are based on international styles or have some unusual ingredients. Beers are available from selected specialists in Manchester's Northern Quarter and Prestwich. RAIB V

Five Points SIBA ⊙

3 Institute Place, Hackney Downs, London, E8 1JE
☎ (020) 8533 7746 ⊕ fivepointsbrewing.co.uk

Five Points commenced brewing in 2013 on a 10-barrel plant in the heart of Hackney. Based in a railway arch under Hackney Downs Railway Station, the brewery takes its name from the five-way junction where Dalston Lane, Amhurst Road and Pembury Road meet, the Five Points. Beers are available unfiltered in bottles. ‼RAIB V

Pale (OG 1044, ABV 4.4%) ◆
Strong, fruity, bitter, golden-coloured ale with citrus and tropical fruit fading in the aftertaste where the bitterness lingers.

Railway Porter (ABV 4.8%) ◆
Roasted black malt throughout creating a dry roasted finish softened by a treacle sweetness. Some caramelised fruit and peppery hops.

Brick Field Brown (OG 1054, ABV 5.4%)

Hook Island Red (ABV 6%) ◆
Treacle notes on nose and flavour linger in the dry bitterness, which builds on drinking. The mouthfeel is creamy.

Five Towns

651 Leeds Road, Outwood, Wakefield, West Yorkshire, WF1 2LU
☎ (01924) 781887
✉ malcolmbastow@googlemail.com

☺Five Towns began production on a 2.5-barrel plant in 2008 and mostly supplies outlets in Yorkshire. ◆RAIB

Mi Usual (ABV 3.7%)

Middle Un (ABV 4.6%)

Owt L Do (ABV 4.6%)
An easy-drinking dark mile with added rum.

Nowt Stout (ABV 6.7%)
A full-bodied stout with an intense roasted malt and coffee flavour.

One At T'end (ABV 6.7%)
An American-style IPA with tropical, citrus and grapefruit flavours.

Summat Else (ABV 7.2%)
An IPA with a strong tropical fruit nose, biscuit malt with gooseberry flavour and a hoppy, maple syrup aftertaste.

Fixed Wheel SIBA ◉

Unit 9, Long Lane Trading Estate, Long Lane, Blackheath, West Midlands, B62 9LD ☎ 07766 162794 ⊕ fixedwheelbrewery.co.uk

⊠ Set up in 2014 by cycling and brewing enthusiasts Scott Povey and Sharon Bryant, this full mash brewery is situated on a trading estate on the Blackheath/Halesowen border. It brews three times a week using an eight-barrel plant. ‼ 🍴 ◆RAIB

Through & Off (OG 1038, ABV 3.8%)
A session IPA concentrating on big, fruity hops.

Chain Reaction Pale Ale (OG 1042, ABV 4.2%)
An American-style pale ale with orange and citrus flavours.

Century Gold (OG 1048, ABV 4.8%)
A bright golden-coloured ale with a big hop presence, firm lemon bitterness and a big orange aroma.

Blackheath Stout (OG 1050, ABV 5%)
Full-bodied, fruity stout with an oaky bitterness and a big, smooth, creamy dark fruit finish.

Mild Concussion (OG 1055, ABV 5.5%) ◆
Ruby in colour with a creamy head. Aroma is red fruit with a rich, balanced taste and satisfying finish.

No Brakes IPA (OG 1059, ABV 5.9%)
An American-style IPA delivering upfront fruity, citrus flavours with a touch of sweetness.

Flack Manor SIBA ◉

8 Romsey Industrial Estate, Greatbridge Road, Romsey, Hampshire, SO51 0HR
☎ (01794) 518520 ⊕ flackmanor.co.uk

⊠ Flack Manor commenced brewing in 2010 using a 20-barrel plant purchased from Canada. The brewery employs the 'double drop' method of fermentation. Beers are supplied to local outlets within approximately 30 miles of Romsey, and may also be found in Wetherspoon pubs. ‼ 🍴 ◆RAIB

Flack's Double Drop (OG 1037, ABV 3.7%) ◆
Brown-coloured session bitter. Hops and some bitterness in the taste with more hoppiness and some malt in a long finish.

Flack Catcher (OG 1045, ABV 4.4%) ◆
Well-balanced best bitter with malty nose and citrus hints. Hoppy taste balanced with fruity sweetness and a lingering finish.

Hedge Hop (OG 1050, ABV 4.9%)
Deep, biscuity maltiness balanced with exotic fruit and spicy flavours.

Flash

Moss Top Farm, Moss Top Lane, Flash, Staffordshire, SK17 0TA ✉ flashbrewery@hotmail.com

The brewery that is located high in the Peak District was founded by two friends who brew on a part-time basis. All natural ingredients are used including spring water and seaweed finings which make the beer suitable for vegans. Due to the altitude, a brick boiler was found and is used in the brewing process rather than electrical equipment. Three bottle-conditioned beers are produced and are sold at Leek Market, which is the only sales outlet. RAIB

Flash House (NEW)

5 Northumberland Terrace, North Shields, NE30 4BA
☎ 07481 901875 ⊕ flashhousebrewing.co.uk

Flash House was set up by Jack O'Keefe in 2016 using a five-barrel plant. Nestled on a hill overlooking the River Tyne, not far from the revitalised Fish Quay, it is surrounded by workshops and fishmongers. Small batch world beers are brewed.

Session IPA (OG 1043, ABV 4.4%)
A West Coast US-style IPA with a good hit of citrus and hops on the nose.

Original Porter (OG 1044, ABV 4.5%)
A traditional, full-bodied dark porter with a smoky, sweet aroma and smooth mouthfeel.

American Pale Ale (ABV 5.2%)
A well-balanced American pale ale with a pine, floral, citrus aroma.

Flipside SIBA ◉

c/o Black Horse, 29 Main Street, Caythorpe, Nottinghamshire, NG14 7D
☎ (0115) 987 7500 ☎ 07958 752334

Office: Old Volunteer, 35 Burton Road, Carlton, NG4 3DQ ⊕ flipsidebrewery.co.uk

⊠ Andrew and Maggie Dunkin established their six-barrel brewery in an industrial unit in Colwick in 2010, expanding to 12 barrels in 2013. The brewery opened its own tap, the Old Volunteer, in nearby Carlton in 2014. In 2016 brewing was moved to share the plant at Caythorpe Brewery (qv) and the offices relocated to the Old Volunteer. ◆ RAIB

Sterling Pale (OG 1039, ABV 3.9%) ◆
Golden ale with a citrus aroma and hoppy taste, leading to a bitter and peppery finish.

Dark Denomination (OG 1041, ABV 4%)
Well-rounded, mildly-hopped beer. Chocolate and caramel malt flavours combine delicately with blackcurrant hop flavours.

Bitcoin (OG 1041, ABV 4.1%)

Copper Penny (OG 1043, ABV 4.2%)
An easy-drinking session bitter. Light brown in colour, moderately bitter but with good hop flavours, ending with a hint of tangerine.

Golden Sovereign (OG 1043, ABV 4.2%)
A golden-coloured session ale. Refreshingly bitter with dry biscuit flavours. American hops are added to produce a pleasant citrus and grapefruit flavour in the finish.

Franc in Stein (OG 1043, ABV 4.3%) ◆
Golden ale with a floral hop aroma, leading to a hoppy and bitter finish.

Random Toss (OG 1044, ABV 4.4%)
A refreshing pale ale with lemon and lime tropical fruit flavours.

Kopek Stout (OG 1046, ABV 4.5%) ◆
Full-bodied, dark stout with a coffee aroma and assertive roast flavours throughout and a balanced bitterness.

Flipping Best (OG 1046, ABV 4.6%) ◆
Brown-coloured, malty, strong bitter with lasting malt, bitterness and subtle hop flavours.

Dusty Penny (OG 1052, ABV 5%)
A full-bodied porter bursting with chocolate and caramel malt flavours, rounded off with hop bitterness.

Clippings IPA (OG 1062, ABV 6.5%)
A traditional IPA, golden in colour with crushed gooseberry and bitter white wine hop flavours.

Russian Rouble (OG 1072, ABV 7.3%) ◆
Strong, dark stout with balanced malt, roast and fruit flavours.

Flowerpots SIBA

🏠 Brandy Mount, Cheriton, Hampshire, SO24 0QQ
☎ (01962) 771534 ⊕ flowerpotscheriton.co.uk

Flowerpots began production in 2006. The brewery is in a pretty Hampshire village, and stands across the car park from the pub of the same name. Its beers are supplied direct to the Flowerpots, its two sibling pubs, and many other local outlets.

Perridge Pale (OG 1035.5, ABV 3.6%) ◆
Pale, easy-drinking golden ale. Honey-scented with high hops, grapefruit and bitterness throughout. Crisp with some citrus notes.

Bitter (OG 1038, ABV 3.8%) ◆
Dry, earthy hop flavours balanced by malt. Good bitterness with some hop in aroma and sharp, bitter finish. Refreshing bitter.

Goodens Gold (OG 1046, ABV 4.8%) 🍴 ◆

Complex, full-bodied golden ale, bursting with hops and citrus fruit and a snatch of sweetness, leading to long, dry finish.

Flying Monk SIBA 👁

Unit 1, Bradfield Farm, Hullavington, Wiltshire, SN14 6EU
☎ (01666) 838415 ☎ 07917 804517
⊕ flyingmonk.beer

⊠ Established in 2014, Flying Monk uses a 20-barrel plant and supplies more than 200 outlets regionally and utilises national wholesalers. It uses only the best local ingredients and is developing its portfolio to incorporate more adventurous seasonal beers. Castle Combe Brewery merged with Flying Monk in 2017. 🛒 ◆

Elmers (OG 1040, ABV 3.8%) ◆
A refreshing session beer with floral and citrus aromas, followed by an encouraging bitter finish.

Habit (OG 1045, ABV 4.2%) ◆
An amber-coloured traditional English best bitter with a contrast of sweet and bitter flavours.

Jackdaw (OG 1045, ABV 4.3%)

Birdman (OG 1049, ABV 4.6%) ◆
A refreshing, pale golden-coloured premium bitter, well-hopped to give a full-bodied flavour.

Brewed under the Castle Combe Brewery name:

Bybrook Bitter (OG 1034, ABV 3.5%) ◆
Pale single malt/single hop easy-drinking beer with a citrus taste.

Pendulum Pale Ale (OG 1037, ABV 3.8%) ◆
Well-hopped, full-bodied, golden-coloured bitter.

Doing Little Bitter (OG 1040, ABV 4.1%) ◆
Light copper-coloured ale with a gentle bitter taste from the English hops.

Circuit Bitter (OG 1043, ABV 4.4%) ◆
Chestnut-coloured, well-balanced premium bitter.

Dark Lane Porter (OG 1055, ABV 5.5%) ◆
Full-flavoured but easy-drinking for its strength.

Fool Hardy SIBA

🏠 Hope Inn, 118 Wellington Road North, Heaton Norris, SK4 2LL
☎ (0161) 637 6191 ⊕ foolhardyales.co.uk

Martin and Samantha Wood bought the Hope Inn in 2012 and installed the brewery in the cellar. The beers first went on sale in 2013. In 2014 the brew kit was upgraded, almost doubling capacity to 4.5 barrels. A sister pub, Spring Gardens in Marple Bridge, opened in 2016. Local festivals are also supplied.

Foragers (NEW)

🏠 Verulam Arms, 41 Lower Dagnall Street, St Albans, Hertfordshire, AL3 4QE
☎ (01727) 836004 ⊕ the-foragers.com

Brewing began in 2015. Four base beers are brewed with different wild ingredients added throughout the year.

Force

Unit 2, Global Business Park, Wilkinson Road, Cirencester, Gloucestershire, GL7 1YZ ☎ 07532 097050 ⊕ forcebrewery.com

Force Brewery was established in 2014 using a four-barrel gravity-fed brew plant. Carry-out ales are available direct from the brewery, which hosts regular tours and is a licensed venue for events. Licensed for tap room drinking on Fridays and Saturdays. ‼ ☛ ◆ RAIB V

Chasing Leather (OG 1040, ABV 4%)
An aromatic pale ale with grapefruit hop notes.

Yankee Zulu (OG 1040, ABV 4%)
A golden-coloured bitter. Subtle, spicy bitterness and mellow, floral aromas.

Thunderball (OG 1051, ABV 5%)
A robust stout. Deep, roasty flavours are met with a gentle smoothness and hop aroma.

Withershins (OG 1044, ABV 5%)
A Bohemian-style Pilsner.

Forge SIBA 👁

Wilderland, Woolley, Cornwall, EX23 9PW ☎ (01288) 331669 ☎ 07837 487800 ⊕ forge-brewery.co.uk

⊠ This multi-award-winning brewery was set up near Bideford in Devon by Dave Lang, who commenced brewing in 2008 using a five-barrel plant. The brewery relocated to Cornwall in 2017. ◆ RAIB

Discovery (OG 1039, ABV 3.8%) ◗
Gold-coloured bitter bursting with hops from start to finish. Some subtle hints of fruit to the discerning palate too.

Devon Maid (OG 1040, ABV 4%)

Hartland Blonde (OG 1040, ABV 4%)
A light, hoppy beer with citrus notes.

Litehouse (OG 1042, ABV 4.3%)
Golden in colour. Hints of elderflower with a citrus bite.

IPA (OG 1044, ABV 4.5%)
A light, hoppy beer with grapefruit and citrus notes.

Ascension (OG 1046, ABV 4.6%)
An amber-coloured beer with complex hop notes.

Rev Hawker (OG 1046, ABV 4.6%)

Dreckly (OG 1046, ABV 4.8%)
A warm, ruby-coloured strong premium ale fortified with gorse and heather, rich in malt with a spicy aroma and a malty aftertaste.

Handsome (OG 1048, ABV 5.1%)
A light brown-coloured, well-balanced and hoppy beer.

Four Candles SIBA

🛢 1 Sowell Street, St Peters, Kent, CT10 2AT ☎ 07947 062063 ⊕ thefourcandles.co.uk

Based in the cellar of the micropub of the same name, Four Candles uses a 2.5-barrel plant and produces up to 10 nine-gallon casks with each brew. Never brewing the same ale twice, the brewery supplies the micropub, which is named after the well known Two Ronnies sketch.

Four Kings (NEW)

Unit 15G, Newton Moor Industrial Estate, Lodge Street, Hyde, SK14 4LD ☎ 07951 699428 ⊕ fourkingsbrewery.com

☺Four Kings is a six-barrel brewery established by five friends with a mutual love of beer. Brewing began in 2016 using only British ingredients. Regular events are held at the brewery, which boasts an in-house bar. Beers can be found in the Hyde and Denton areas. ‼ ☛ RAIB

Gold (ABV 4%)
A golden-coloured beer with a tart hop bitterness and a long finish.

IPA (ABV 4%)
A pale-coloured beer with a fresh, hoppy aroma and malty flavour. Well-balanced, it has an intense bitterness leading to a long, dry finish.

Bitter (ABV 4.5%)
A bitter tasting beer with a slight sweetness. A moderate bitter finish with toffee in the aftertaste.

Porter (ABV 5.2%)
A rich, smooth, chocolaty porter with roasted coffee in the aftertaste.

Fourpure SIBA

22 Bermondsey Trading Estate, Rotherhithe New Road, Bermondsey, London, SE16 3LL ☎ (020) 3744 2141 ⊕ fourpure.com

Fourpure began brewing in 2013. No real ale. ☛ RAIB

Fowey (NEW)

Unit 9D, Restormel Industrial Estate, Liddicoat Road, Lostwithiel, Cornwall, PL22 0HD ☎ (01208) 871385 ☎ 07443 504644

Office: Pawton Mill, St Breock, PL27 7LH ⊕ foweybrewery.co.uk

Fowey began brewing in 2016. Only bottle-conditioned ales are available at present. ◆ RAIB

Fownes

25 Clarence Street, Upper Gornal, West Midlands, DY3 1UL ☎ 07790 766844

Office: 42 The Ridgeway, Sedgley, DY3 3UR ⊕ fownesbrewing.co.uk

☺The brewery was established in 2012 by James and Tom Fownes in premises to the rear of the Jolly Crispin in Upper Gornal. It expanded to a three-barrel plant in 2014. Beers are available in the Jolly Crispin and a number of free houses in the Midlands. ‼ ◆ RAIB

Gunhild (OG 1041, ABV 4%) ◗
Bright with creamy, lingering head. Smooth mouthfeel. Pleasant earthy aroma with hints of blackcurrants and honey. Peardrops and caramel with some malt and blackcurrant flavour. Dry, malty aftertaste

Crispin's Ommer (OG 1038, ABV 4.1%)
Jolly Crispin house beer.

Frost Hammer (OG 1047, ABV 4.6%) ◗
Blonde and bright with a clingy head. Pine resin, nutmeg, malt, lemon and floral aroma. Dry

mouthfeel with coffee, sweet malt and grapefruit flavours. Grapefruit and hoppy aftertaste.

Firebeard's Old Favourite No. 5 Ruby Ale (OG 1051, ABV 5%) ◆
Creamy head, rich red in colour. Malty, fresh earth, rhubarb and some coffee in the aroma. Smooth mouthfeel, dark chocolate and plum dominate the flavour with hints of malt and coffee. A pleasant dryness in the aftertaste, with hints of coffee, plum and cocoa.

King Korvak's Saga (OG 1058, ABV 5.4%) ⬚ ◆
Pear drop and cocoa aroma with hints of coffee. Coffee, toasted malt, blackcurrant and slight cocoa taste, with rich malty tones in the aftertaste.

Fox

🏠 22 Station Road, Heacham, Norfolk, PE31 7EX
☎ (01485) 570345 ⊕ foxbrewery.co.uk

Based in an old cottage adjacent to the Fox & Hounds pub, Fox Brewery was established in 2002 and now supplies around 30 outlets as well as the pub. All the Branthill beers are brewed from barley grown on Branthill Farm and malted at Crisps in Great Ryburgh. A hop garden next to the brewery, trialled during 2009, has been enlarged.

Foxfield SIBA

🏠 Prince of Wales, Foxfield, Cumbria, LA20 6BX
☎ (01229) 716238 ⊕ princeofwalesfoxfield.co.uk

Foxfield is a 4.5-barrel plant in old stables attached to the Prince of Wales. Several other outlets are supplied. Tiger Tops in Wakefield is also owned. The beer range constantly changes.

Dark Mild (OG 1040, ABV 3.7%) 🍺 ◆
Traditional dark mild, low hop bitterness is compensated for with sweetness and roast malts.

Framework (NEW)

The Old City Depot, 7-74 Friday Street, Leicester, LE1 3BW
☎ (0116) 262 4037 ⊕ frameworkbrewery.com

⊠ Established in 2016 using a six-barrel brew plant, Framework is a vegan-friendly modern brewery producing a constantly evolving range of beers. ‼ RAIB V

US PA (ABV 3.8%)
An American-style IPA with a deep taste of malt and citrus fruit and a pleasing floral, grapefruit and lemon bitter finish.

Stout (ABV 4%)
A dark, smooth and rich stout with caramel maltiness offset against passion fruit and berry characteristics.

Red Rye (ABV 4.2%)

Porter (ABV 4.3%)
A rich, dark porter, well-balanced with caramel and dark chocolate malty flavours.

Franklins SIBA

Highfields Farm, The Broyle, Ringmer, East Sussex, BN8 5AR ☎ 07900 218584 ⊕ franklinsbrewery.co.uk

⊠ Owned by Steve Medniuk, Franklins have recently moved to a new site in Ringmer in order to aid expansion. A 10-barrel brew plant is curently used with building work underway to add a new chilling system and 15-barrel conditioning tanks. Beers are also brewed under the Hastings Brewery name. Beers are available throughout the South East, London and beyond. ‼

English Garden (OG 1042, ABV 3.8%)
A hoppy, golden ale perfect for session drinking.

Mama Knows Best (OG 1043, ABV 4.1%)
A refreshing traditional English best bitter, rich in mango, lemon and earthy pine.

Resurrection Stout (ABV 5.3%)

Citra IPA (OG 1056, ABV 5.5%)
Single-hopped IPA bursting in citrus and lychee flavours and aroma.

North Shore IPA (ABV 5.5%)

Smoked Porter (OG 1052, ABV 5.5%)
A rich, intense porter made with oatmeal. Added chipotle chillies accentuate the smokiness and provide a touch of heat.

Free Radical

Manchester ☎ 07575 538385
✉ freeradicalbrewco@gmail.com

Production began in 2016 using spare capacity at breweries around Manchester.

Freedom SIBA 👁

1 Park Lodge House, Bagots Park, Abbots Bromley, Staffordshire, WS15 3ES
☎ (01283) 840721 ⊕ freedomlager.com

No real ale. Freedom specialises in producing hand-crafted English lagers, all brewed in accordance with the German Reinheitsgebot purity law. ‼ ⚑

Freestyle

Church Road, Shustoke, Warwickshire, B46 2LB
☎ (01675) 481205 ⊕ griffininnshustoke.co.uk

Brewing started in 2008 in the old coffin shop premises adjacent to the Griffin Inn. The 2.5-barrel brewery is a venture between Griffin licensee Mick Pugh and his son Oliver. Beers are available for the free trade but most output goes to the pub. Occasional experimental brews are produced. ‼ ◆

Yeti (OG 1047, ABV 4.7%)
A light-coloured pale ale with a grapefruit aftertaste.

Freewheelin'

Peebles Hydro, Innerleithen Road, Peebles, EH45 8LX
☎ 07802 175826 ⊕ freewheelinbrewery.co.uk

Freewheelin' began brewing in 2013. ◆

Blonde (OG 1040, ABV 3.8%)

XX Bitter (OG 1044, ABV 4.2%)

XX IPA (OG 1044, ABV 4.2%)

Dizzy Blonde (OG 1045, ABV 4.3%)

Ruby (OG 1046, ABV 4.4%)

Frensham SIBA

The Old Dairy, Pierrepont Home Farm, The Reeds, Frensham, Surrey, GU10 3BS
☎ (01252) 793956 ☎ 07505 798380
⊕ frenshambrewery.co.uk

⊠ Set in the Surrey countryside, Frensham is a microbrewery situated in a 17th-century restored barn on a working dairy farm. A tap room opened in 2017. ⌾♦

Soul (OG 1038, ABV 3.8%)
A light, floral session beer with biscuit orange notes.

Rambler (OG 1039, ABV 3.9%)
A golden-coloured, refreshing session ale, fruity hops with an oak edge give rise to a satisfying bitterness.

Silent Flight (ABV 4.2%)

Forager (OG 1045, ABV 4.5%)
Rich copper-coloured ale. A complex floral aroma with subtle vanilla notes, offset with a caramel/ spicy hop balance. Lingering bitter finish.

Friday Beer

Unit 4, Link Business Centre, Malvern, Worcestershire, WR14 1UQ
☎ (01684) 572648 ⊕ thefridaybeer.com

Founded in 2011, the Friday Beer Co primarily produces bottle-conditioned ales, selling across the Three Counties. Available cask-conditioned in a small number of local pubs. ‼⌾RAIB

Friends Arms

▤ Old St Clears Road, Johnstown, SA31 3HH
☎ (01267) 234073 ⊕ thefriendsarms.co.uk

Friends Arms Brewery opened in 2011 on the premises of the Friends Arms, a traditional local community pub, which acts as the brewery tap.

Frisky Bear (NEW)

The Brewery, 21 Weavers Close, Morley, Leeds, West Yorkshire, LS27 9FF ⊕ friskybear.com

Established in 2016 using a one-barrel plant. No real ale.

Frog Island

The Maltings, Westbridge, St James Road, Northampton, NN5 5HS
☎ (01604) 587772 ⊕ frogislandbrewery.co.uk

Established in 1994, Frog Island specialises in beers with personalised bottle labels, available by mail order. The brewery changed hands in 2013 and again in 2017. It is now run by Graeme Swanson. ‼♦RAIB

Best Bitter (OG 1038, ABV 3.8%) ◣
Blackcurrant and gooseberry enhance the full malty aroma with pineapple and papaya joining on the tongue. Bitterness develops in the fairly long hop finish.

Lock, Stock & Barrel (OG 1040, ABV 4%)
A rounded bittersweet malt taste leads to a refreshing, bitter finish.

Shoemaker (OG 1043, ABV 4.2%) ◣

An orange aroma of fruity hops is balanced by malt. Citrus and hoppy bitterness last into a long, dry finish. Amber colour.

TOC (That Old Chestnut) (OG 1044, ABV 4.4%)
A smooth, easy-drinking porter-style beer with subtle roasted notes.

Natterjack (OG 1048, ABV 4.8%) ◣
Deceptively robust, golden and smooth. Fruit and hop aromas fight for dominance before the grainy astringency and floral palate give way to a long, dry aftertaste.

Fire Bellied Toad (OG 1048, ABV 5%) ◣
Amber-gold brew with an extraordinary long bitter, fruity finish. Huge malt and hop flavours have a hint of apples.

Croak & Stagger (OG 1054, ABV 5.6%) ◣
The initial honey/fruit aroma is quickly overpowered by roast malt then bitter chocolate and pale malt sweetness on the tongue. Gentle, bittersweet finish.

Front Row SIBA

Unit 1, Hopkins Close, Greenfield Farm Industrial Estate, Congleton, Cheshire, CW12 4TR
☎ (01260) 289055 ☎ 07861 718673
⊕ frontrowbrewing.co.uk

After starting operations on a 2.5-barrel plant in 2012, Front Row expanded to an eight-barrel plant in 2014 to meet demand. Beers are available nationally through brewery swaps and wholesalers. ‼♦

Crouch (OG 1039, ABV 3.8%)

LOHAG (Land of Hops and Glory) (OG 1036, ABV 3.8%)

Sin Bin (OG 1042, ABV 4.2%)

Pause (OG 1049, ABV 4.5%)

Pride (ABV 4.6%)

Collapsed (OG 1051, ABV 5.6%)

Froth Blowers SIBA

Unit P35, Hastingwood Industrial Park, Wood Lane, Erdington, West Midlands, B24 9QR ☎ 07908 056009
⊕ frothblower.co.uk

⊠ Froth Blowers began brewing in 2013. The brewery now has the capacity to brew 20 barrels at a new site only metres away from its original, with the new site used for the core beers and the original six-barrel plant used for special beers. ♦

Piffle Snonker (OG 1038, ABV 3.8%) ◣
Straw-coloured. Aroma is almost jammy with a little malt and hop. Taste is well-balanced with a slightly hoppier aftertaste.

Bar-King Mad (OG 1042, ABV 4.2%)

Wellingtonian (OG 1043, ABV 4.3%)

John Bull's Best (OG 1044, ABV 4.4%)
A golden-coloured, balanced bitter, using traditional British malts and hops.

Gollop With Zest (OG 1045, ABV 4.5%)
A blonde beer with a floral start and a citrus finish.

Hornswoggle (OG 1050, ABV 5%)
A full-bodied blonde beer, floral nose and sweetish start, soon replaced by a dry and satisfying bitterness.

Fuddy Duck (NEW)

Unit 12, Kirton Business Park, Willington Road, Kirton, Lincolnshire, PE20 1NN ☎ 07881 818875
⊕ thefuddyduckbrewery.co.uk

Small brewery based in Kirton near Boston, where brewing commenced in 2016.

Pale Ale (ABV 4%)
A golden ale with a grapefruit citrus flavour.

American Red Ale (ABV 4.5%)

Blonde Ale (ABV 4.5%)
A blonde ale with flavours and aromas of banana and clove.

Dark Porter (ABV 4.5%)
A porter with flavours of chocolate and liquorice.

German Ale Altbier (ABV 4.5%)

Biere De Garde (ABV 6.5%)

Fuggle Bunny SIBA

Unit 1, Meadowbrook Park Industrial Estate, Station Road, Holbrook, South Yorkshire, S20 3PJ
☎ (0114) 248 4541 ☎ 07813 763347
⊕ fugglebunny.co.uk

⊗ A husband-and-wife team commenced brewing in 2014. The plant, originally obtained from Flipside Brewery, has recently been expanded and can now brew 24 barrels per week. Beers are delivered direct within a 40-mile radius of the brewery and available nationally through wholesalers. ‼ ▆

Chapter 5 Oh Crumbs (OG 1038, ABV 3.8%)
Amber-coloured with hints of spice, cedar and pine. Sweet caramel and biscuit flavours gives this a distinctive finish.

Chapter 2 Cotton Tail (OG 1040, ABV 4%)
Uplifting, fruity aromas of lychees and citrus with a dry, hoppy finish.

Chapter 6 Hazy Summer Daze (OG 1042, ABV 4.2%)
Totally tropical with mango, lime, apricot, melon, lychees and grapefruit with fresh, floral aromas.

Chapter 8 Jammy Dodger (OG 1045, ABV 4.5%)
A ruby red-coloured ale with hints of blackcurrant, liquorice and caramel and a malty undertone.

Chapter 1 New Beginnings (OG 1049, ABV 4.9%)
Amber-coloured, classic bitter with a sweet edge of honey and spice leading to a dry, hoppy aftertaste.

Chapter 3 Orchard Gold (OG 1050, ABV 5%)
Golden ale with hints of spice and honey and an earthy undertone.

Chapter 7 Russian Rare-Bit (OG 1050, ABV 5%)
Malty and complex with a twist of chocolate, coffee and liquorice aromas. British hops lend bittering qualities.

Chapter 4 24 Carrot (OG 1060, ABV 6%)
Smooth aromas of citrus and blackberry with a spicy blanket of malt-flavoured hoppiness.

Full Mash SIBA

17 Lower Park Street, Stapleford, Nottinghamshire, NG9 8EW
☎ (0115) 949 9262 ⊕ fullmash.net

⊛Brewing commenced in 2003 and has grown steadily since, with a gradual expansion in outlets and capacity. ◆

Horse & Jockey (OG 1039, ABV 3.8%) ◣
Easy-drinking golden ale with moderate hoppy aroma and finish.

Seance (OG 1041, ABV 4%) ◣
Predominantly hoppy golden beer, with a refreshing bitter finish.

Illuminati (OG 1043, ABV 4.2%) ◣
Gently-hopped golden ale with initial hops and bitterness giving way to a short bitter finish.

Wheat Ear (OG 1043, ABV 4.2%)
Pale, clear wheat beer, fruity and aromatic.

Warlord (OG 1045, ABV 4.4%) ◣
Amber-coloured beer with an initial malt taste leading to a dry bitter finish.

Apparition (OG 1046, ABV 4.5%) ◣
A pale, hoppy bitter brewed with Brewers Gold hops.

Nevermore (OG 1047, ABV 4.6%)
Well-rounded stout with soft roast chocolate flavours.

Manhaton Pale?? (OG 1053, ABV 5.2%)
Refreshing American-style IPA with a complex citrus aroma and big hop finish.

Bhisti (OG 1063, ABV 6.2%)
Strong IPA with a warning kick of bitterness.

Fuller's ◉

Griffin Brewery, Chiswick Lane South, Chiswick, London, W4 2QB
☎ (020) 8996 2000 ⊕ fullers.co.uk

⊗ Fuller, Smith and Turner's Griffin Brewery has stood on the same site in Chiswick for more than 350 years. The partnership from which the company now takes its name was formed in 1845 and members of the founding families are still involved in running the company today. At the end of 2005 Fuller's announced an agreed acquisition of Hampshire brewer George Gale. The company now operates 362 pubs and hotels. Fuller's stopped brewing at the Gale's Horndean site in 2006 and all the brands, including some seasonals, are now brewed at Chiswick. ‼ ▆ ◆ RAIB

Oliver's Island (OG 1038, ABV 3.8%)
Gold-coloured ale with distinctive biscuity, malty base notes balanced with a subtle bitterness. Delicate floral, tropical and citrus aromas. Added orange peel brings refreshing, zesty qualities before the crisp finish.

London Pride (OG 1040.5, ABV 4.1%) ◣
Well-balanced, smooth best bitter with orange citrus fruit, malt and hops in aroma and flavour, which linger into a slightly bitter aftertaste. Honey and toffee develop as the beer matures.

Bengal Lancer (OG 1049.5, ABV 5%) ◣
Rich, creamy and well-balanced pale brown-coloured IPA with a gold hue. Hops with a dryish bitterness harmonise with the fruit and malty sweetness that linger into the aftertaste.

ESB (OG 1054, ABV 5.5%) ◣
Bitter orange marmalade with hops, creamy toffee and some raisins are all present in this multi-faceted strong brown bitter. A satisfying long, bitter, dry finish balanced by a malty sweetness.

Brewed under the Gale's brand name:

Seafarers Ale (OG 1036.8, ABV 3.6%) ◣

A pale brown bitter, predominantly malty, with a refreshing balance of fruit and hops that lingers into the aftertaste, where a dry bitterness unfolds.

HSB (OG 1050, ABV 4.8%) ◆
Dates and dried fruit with some spicy hops in the nose add to the caramelised orange and treacle in the flavour of this smooth brown-coloured beer. Malty throughout with a bittersweet finish.

Fulstow

See Firehouse

Funfair

▣ Chequers Inn, Toad Lane, Elston, Nottinghamshire, NG23 5NS
☎ (01636) 525257 ☎ 07971 540186
⊕ funfairbrewingcompany.co.uk

Funfair was launched in 2004 in Holbrook, relocated to Ilkeston, Derbyshire and then relocated again in 2012 to the Chequers Inn in Elston, where a new 10-barrel plant is used. The Chequers also serves as the brewery tap. More than 40 outlets are supplied.

Gallopers (OG 1037, ABV 3.8%)
Well-hopped, pale session bitter.

Teacups (OG 1040, ABV 4%)
A traditional ginger beer.

Waltzer (OG 1044, ABV 4.5%)
Copper-coloured, easy-drinking bitter.

Brandy Snap (OG 1046, ABV 4.7%)
Golden ale containing root ginger.

Dive Bomber (OG 1047, ABV 4.7%)
Refreshing, straw-coloured premium ale.

Dodgem (OG 1047, ABV 4.7%)
Golden-coloured premium pale ale with a unique blend of hops.

Fuzzy Duck SIBA

18 Wood Street, Poulton Industrial Estate, Poulton-le-Fylde, Lancashire, FY6 8JY ☎ 07904 343729
⊕ fuzzyduckbrewery.co.uk

Fuzzy Duck was established in 2006. It relocated to Poulton-le-Fylde later that year, expanding capacity to an eight-barrel plant. The brewery delivers over a wide area of North-west England and Yorkshire. !! ◆ RAIB

Golden Cascade (OG 1038, ABV 3.8%)
Golden-coloured ale with a citrus flavour and floral aroma.

Mucky Duck (OG 1042, ABV 4%)
Dark stout, slightly sweet with chocolate and coffee notes from the roasted malt.

Pheasant Plucker (OG 1042, ABV 4.2%)
Amber-coloured beer with a slightly spicy taste and citrus finish.

Cunning Stunt (OG 1044, ABV 4.3%)
Amber-coloured beer with a blackcurrant and herbal aroma.

Ruby Duck (OG 1053, ABV 5.3%)
Dark ruby-coloured beer with a rich, full body and complex fruit flavours.

Fyne SIBA

Achadunan, Cairndow, PA26 8BJ
☎ (01499) 600120 ⊕ fyneales.com

⊛Fyne Ales has been brewing since 2001 and is situated at the head of Loch Fyne. In 2012 an on-site brewery tap was added. Expansion has allowed for the production of experimental brews. FyneFest runs annually, celebrating local fare and showcasing other breweries. !! ☰ ◆ RAIB

Jarl (OG 1038, ABV 3.8%) 🜚 🍺
A light golden-coloured ale with strong citrus notes.

Maverick (OG 1040.5, ABV 4.2%) ◆
Full-bodied, roasty, tawny-coloured best bitter. It is balanced, fruity and well hopped.

Hurricane Jack (OG 1042.5, ABV 4.4%)
Smooth golden ale, deep citrus flavours which mellow to a lingering citrus bitter finish.

Vital Spark (OG 1042.5, ABV 4.4%)
A rich, dark beer that shows glints of red. The taste is clean and slightly sharp with a hint of blackcurrant.

Avalanche (OG 1043.5, ABV 4.5%) ◆
This true golden ale starts with citrus hops on the nose. Well-balanced with good body and fruit balancing a refreshing hoppy taste, it finishes with a long, bittersweet aftertaste.

Highlander (OG 1046, ABV 4.8%) ◆
Full-bodied, bittersweet ale with a good dry hop finish. In the style of a Heavy although the malt is less pronounced and the sweetness ebbs away to leave a bitter, hoppy finish.

Sublime Stout (OG 1067, ABV 6.8%)
Stout with a hint of liquorice on the aftertaste.

Superior IPA (OG 1070, ABV 7.1%)
A full-bodied beer with an oily mouthfeel. The aroma of apricot and pine resin is present. A dry, fruity and hoppy aftertaste.

G2 SIBA 👁

Unit 5, Ashford Works, Brunswick Road, Cobbs Wood, Ashford, Kent, TN23 1EH
☎ (01233) 630277 ⊕ g2brewing.com

Brewing began in 2015. Outlets are supplied across the South-east and in London.

Orion (OG 1038, ABV 3.8%)
Chestnut-coloured ale, well-balanced with blasts of mint, rustic, malty, earthy tones and floral and lavender aromas.

Sail (OG 1038, ABV 4.2%)
A blonde ale with citrus lemon flavours, loganberry notes and a spicy aroma.

Plough (OG 1040, ABV 4.4%)
A deep gold-coloured beer with pine, orange and toffee notes.

Southern Cross (OG 1044, ABV 4.8%)
Gold-coloured beer with passion fruit, spicy lemon and grapefruit aromas.

Gadds

See Ramsgate

Gale's

See Fuller's

Gaol SIBA

The Old Lock Up, 46 North End, Wirksworth, Derbyshire, DE4 4FG ☎ 07981 220734
✉ sales@gaolales.co.uk

A small brewery established in 2015. Currently producing up to two barrels a week. RAIB

Jailbird (ABV 4%)

Black Maria (ABV 4.1%)
Traditional-style porter with complex dark malt tastes and hints of woodsmoke and chocolate. An initial bitterness followed by a smooth but complex taste.

Jailbreak (ABV 4.5%)
Traditional copper-coloured English bitter with a dry, balanced taste and caramel notes.

Strong Arm of the Law (ABV 5.1%)
A dark, strong ale with a roasted malt and hints of dark fruits, liquorice and chocolate.

No Prisoners (ABV 5.7%)
Strong IPA-style ale. A pleasant hoppy taste with a hint of spice and citrus flavours.

Garden City

⬛ 22 The Wynd, Letchworth, Hertfordshire, SG6 3EN
☎ 07932 739558 ⊕ gardencitybrewery.co.uk

A brewbar established in 2016 using a 2.5-barrel plant, serving a selection of its own ales plus guests on gravity.

Gas Dog

⬛ Noel's Arms, 31 Burton Street, Melton Mowbray, Leicestershire, LE13 1AE ☎ 07921 260063

Office: 9 Westview, Somerby, Leicestershire, LE14 2QH ⊕ gasdogbrewery.co.uk

Gas Dog began brewing in 2013 at the same premises as Parish Brewery, but using a separate 0.5-barrel plant. In 2014 it relocated to an outbuilding at the rear of the Noel's Arms in Melton Mowbray and in 2016 upgraded to a 2.5-barrel plant.

Gasworks (NEW)

⬛ First Street, Manchester, M15 4FN

Gasworks is a six-barrel brewpub from the team behind Dockyard, opened in 2016. It supplies Gasworks Tap, Dockyard, Salford Quays and Dockyard, Spinningfields.

Gates Burton

Reservoir Road, Burton upon Trent, Staffordshire, DE14 2BP
☎ (01283) 532567
✉ gatesburtonbrewery@talktalk.net

☺The Gates Burton Brewery was established in 2011 using a one-barrel plant. This has now expanded to a three-barrel plant. ‼◆

Reservoir (OG 1048, ABV 4.6%) 🍷

Pale brown in colour with a malty aroma and roast hint. Caramel and malt lead to a sweet hop balanced taste. Hops arrive late on the palate to urge another mouthful.

Gates Burton Ale (GBA) (OG 1050, ABV 4.8%)
A robust, amber-coloured ale with a floral aroma and sweet finish. Based on the original recipe for Ind Coope Draught Burton Ale.

Damn (OG 1050, ABV 5%)
Smooth-drinking ruby ale with chocolate malt tones. Delicately hopped with a subtle, sweet finish.

Reservoir Gold (OG 1075, ABV 7.5%)
Full-bodied, amber-coloured beer balanced with roast barley and subtly-hopped. Smooth with a sweet finish.

Geeves SIBA

Unit 12, Grange Lane Industrial Estate, Carrwood Road, Stairfoot, Barnsley, South Yorkshire, S71 5AS
☎ 07859 039259 ⊕ geevesbrewery.co.uk

Geeves began brewing in 2011 using a 5.5-barrel plant with recipes developed when the owners lived on a narrow boat. ‼◆RAIB

Rococo (OG 1037, ABV 3.6%)
A smooth, dark mild with a hint of chocolate. Aromas are cocoa, dark fruits and berries with a subtle but lingering bitter finish.

Topaz Session Pale (OG 1040, ABV 3.8%)
A light pale ale with a soft citrus palate.

Renaissance (OG 1040, ABV 4.1%)
A deep red-coloured ale packed with sweet malts giving flavours of dark fruits and molasses while the hops bring a diverse array of spicy earthiness, lemon citrus and hints of floral apricot and peach.

Aurelian (OG 1043, ABV 4.2%)
English hops dominate this golden ale with flavours of sweet, tangy orange citrus. A refreshingly crisp and bitter finish.

Captain Gingerbread (OG 1043, ABV 4.3%)
A naturally hazy wheat beer infused with ginger. Spicy and refreshing with a hint of citrus.

Clear Cut (OG 1044, ABV 4.4%)
An extra pale ale with bags of American hops for a real citrus kick.

Oaty McOatface (ABV 4.5%)
A rich and full stout packed with malted oats to create a smooth and silky mouthfeel balanced by a lightly spicy hop character.

Smokey Joe Stout (OG 1050, ABV 5%)
A rich, bold stout with flavours of black coffee, dark chocolate and a lingering smokiness. A combination of hops give a spicy, oaky finish.

Fully Laden (OG 1060, ABV 6%)
A strong IPA with a juicy, citrus, sweet floral taste and aroma and a satisfying bitterness.

Geipel SIBA

Pant Glas, Llangwm, LL21 0RN
☎ (01490) 420838 ☎ 07549 526287 ⊕ geipel.co.uk

Geipel commenced brewing in 2013 producing classic German-style, unpasteurised and unfiltered beers in keg, KeyKeg and bottle form only, mainly supplying bars and off-licences across Wales and Greater Manchester. RAIB

Aloha from Bala (OG 1047, ABV 4.4%)

Pilsner (OG 1046, ABV 4.6%)

Dunkelweizen (OG 1057, ABV 5.4%)

Zoigl (OG 1053, ABV 5.4%)

Hefeweizen (OG 1054, ABV 5.6%)

Zoiglator Bock (OG 1067, ABV 6.7%)

Gene Pool (NEW)

Unit 6, 23 Arthur Street, Hull, East Yorkshire, HU3 6BH
☎ 07760 669157 ⊕ genepoolbrewing.com

☺Father and son enterprise, hence the brewery's name, established in 2016 using a two-barrel brew plant currently brewing twice a week.

Primordial Ooze (OG 1044, ABV 4.3%)

D.N.Ale (OG 1044, ABV 4.5%)

Helix (OG 1050, ABV 5%)

Genetic Code (OG 1060, ABV 5.8%)

George Samuel

Spennymoor, County Durham ☎ 07840 892751
⊕ georgesamuelbrewingcompany.co.uk

A small, two-barrel brewery originally set up at the Duke of Wellington pub in the small village of Welbury near Northallerton, and named after the brewer's two sons. It has now moved to a private address in Spennymoor and supplies a small number of outlets around County Durham and the North-east.

By George She's Got It (OG 1036, ABV 3.6%)
Blonde session ale with a good hoppy punch.

Brew It Again Sam (OG 1042, ABV 4.2%)

Golden Wellingtons (OG 1050, ABV 5%)
Golden premium ale with a bittersweet character.

George Wright

See under Wright

George's SIBA

Common Road, Great Wakering, Essex, SS3 0AG
☎ (01702) 826755 ☎ 07771 871255
⊕ georgesbrewery.com

⊠ George's Brewery and Hop Monster Brewing Company (qv) are owned by the same brewer, using the same plant. George's concentrates on traditional styles and Hop Monster on the more unusual. A taproom/micropub called Mawson's has now opened in Southend. ‼️ 🍴 ◆ RAIB V

Wallasea Wench (OG 1037.5, ABV 3.6%)
Pale copper-coloured, easy-drinking ale with a smooth mouthfeel.

Wakering Gold (OG 1039.5, ABV 3.8%)
Bursting with fresh hop aroma; a refreshing blend of hops.

Best (OG 1041, ABV 4%)
Copper-coloured session bitter.

Cockleboats (OG 1039, ABV 4%)

Empire (OG 1040, ABV 4%)

Broadsword (OG 1046, ABV 4.7%)

Ruby/copper-coloured with a malty, smooth start and a well-balanced dry finish.

Ghost

Unit D, Tong Business Centre, Otley Road, Baildon, West Yorkshire, BD17 7QD
☎ (0113) 418 2002 ☎ 01896 097882
⊕ ghostbrew.co.uk

Ghost Brewing Co is the creation of Steve Crump and James Thompson.

Wraith (ABV 3.8%)

Spectre (ABV 4.4%)

Phantom (ABV 5.3%)

Gipsy Hill SIBA

Unit 11 Hamilton Road Industrial Estate, 160 Hamilton Road, West Norwood, London, SE27 9SF
☎ (020) 8761 9061 ⊕ gipsyhillbrewing.com

Founded in 2014, Gipsy Hill is a small, independent microbrewery producing mainly for the local market in London. A tap room is open to the public at weekends. ◆ RAIB

Anorak (ABV 4.4%)
A classic mild with a fruity twist. A biscuity base with British hops for a stone fruit bittering. The addition of plums balances the malt and hops for a sweet and tart finish.

Aviator (ABV 5.5%)
An easy-drinking wheat beer.

Glamorgan SIBA

Unit J, Llantrisant Business Park, Llantrisant, CF72 8LF
☎ (01443) 406080 ⊕ glamorganbrewingco.com

☺This family-run brewery moved to its present site in 2013. Expansion in 2017 included increased production capacity, a brewery tap and a brewery shop. Direct deliveries are made throughout Wales and distributed further afield by selected wholesalers and breweries. 🍴◆

Cwrw Gorslas/Bluestone Bitter (OG 1040, ABV 4%)
A well-rounded bitter delivering softly roasted undertones to a malty body, complemented by a smooth and robust hoppiness from nose to finish.

Welsh Pale Ale (OG 1042, ABV 4.1%)
A crisp pale ale, light gold in colour, and full of bright citrus aromas and flavours. Finishes dry, fruity and hoppy.

Jemimas Pitchfork (OG 1044, ABV 4.4%)

Thunderbird (OG 1045, ABV 4.5%)

Glastonbury SIBA

Unit 11, Wessex Park, Somerton Business Park, Somerton, Somerset, TA11 6SB
☎ (01458) 272244 ⊕ glastonburyales.com

Glastonbury Ales was established in 2002 on a five-barrel plant. In 2006 the brewery changed ownership and moved to Somerton, enlarging capacity to a 20-barrel plant. Cider is also produced. ‼️🍴◆

Mystery Tor (OG 1040, ABV 3.8%) 🍂

Golden-coloured bitter with floral hop and fruit on the nose and palate, sweetness giving way to a bitter hop finish. Full-bodied.

Lady of the Lake (OG 1042, ABV 4.2%) ◥
Full-bodied amber-coloured best bitter with hops balanced by fruity malt flavour and a hint of vanilla. Clean, bitter hop aftertaste.

Love Monkey (OG 1042, ABV 4.2%)
Golden ale loaded with zesty, fruity hops and a variety of malts.

Black As Yer 'At (OG 1043, ABV 4.3%)

Hedge Monkey (OG 1048, ABV 4.6%)
A well-rounded deep amber-coloured bitter. Malty, rich and hoppy.

Golden Chalice (OG 1048, ABV 4.8%)
A golden-coloured ale with a good balance of malt and fragrant hops, a robust bitterness and lingering bittersweet finish.

Thriller Cappuccino Porter (OG 1050, ABV 5%)

Glen Affric (NEW)

Unit 3, Lightbox, Knox Street, Birkenhead, Merseyside, CH41 5JG

Office: 53 Wood Street, Ashton-under-Lyne, OL6 7NB
⊕ glenaffricbrewery.com

Established in 2016, a small batch brewery producing only keg beers.

Glens of Antrim

10 Murlough Road, Ballycastle, BT64 6RG
☎ (028) 2076 9696

Small, family-run brewery founded in 2014 producing bottle-conditioned beers. RAIB

Globe

⬛ 144 High Street West, Glossop, Derbyshire, SK13 8HJ
☎ (01457) 852417 ⊕ globepub.co.uk

Globe was established in 2006 by Ron Brookes on a 2.5-barrel plant in an old stable behind the Globe pub. Grandson Toby now has a major role in the brewery under the watchful eye of Ron. The beers are mainly for the pub but special one-off brews are produced for beer festivals.

Gloucester SIBA

Fox's Kiln, West Quay, The Docks, Gloucester, GL1 2LG
☎ (01452) 668043 ☎ 07503 152749
⊕ gloucesterbrewery.co.uk

⊗ Situated in the historic Gloucester Docks, brewing began in 2011. The brewery expanded into larger premises in the docks area to cope with increased demand while retaining and sympathetically restoring its original converted stables site for experimental brews and a bar named Tank. The full range of beers is regularly available in pubs throughout Gloucestershire and further afield. ‼ ♦ RAIB V

Session Pale (OG 1037, ABV 3.7%)
A refreshing, hoppy ale with citrus and tropical notes.

Gold (OG 1040, ABV 3.9%)
A crisp, hoppy golden ale.

Cascade (OG 1042, ABV 4.2%)
Big malty backbone with bold hops.

Session IPA (OG 1045, ABV 4.5%)

Six Malt Porter (OG 1045, ABV 4.5%)
A full-bodied and smooth porter with aromas of roasted malt and dark fruits.

West Coast Red (OG 1048, ABV 4.8%)

Goacher's

Unit 8, Tovil Green Business Park, Burial Ground Lane, Tovil, Kent, ME15 6TA
☎ (01622) 682112 ⊕ goachers.com

A traditional brewery that uses only malt and Kentish hops for all its beers. Phil and Debbie Goacher have concentrated on brewing good wholesome beers without gimmicks. Two tied houses and around 30 free trade outlets in the mid-Kent area are supplied. Special is brewed for sale under house names. ‼ ♦

Real Mild Ale (OG 1033, ABV 3.4%) ◥
A rich, flavourful mild with moderate roast barley and a generous helping of chocolate malt.

Fine Light Ale (OG 1036, ABV 3.7%) ◥
A pale, golden brown-coloured bitter with a strong, floral, hoppy aroma and aftertaste. A hoppy and moderately malty session beer.

Special/House Ale (OG 1037, ABV 3.8%)

Best Dark Ale (OG 1040, ABV 4.1%) ◥
Dark in colour but light and quaffable in body, this ale features hints of caramel and chocolate malt throughout.

Crown Imperial Stout (OG 1044, ABV 4.5%) ◥
A well-balanced roasty stout, dark and bitter with just a hint of caramel and a lingering creamy head.

Gold Star Strong Ale (OG 1050, ABV 5.1%) ◥
A strong pale ale.

Goddards SIBA ◉

Barnsley Farm, Bullen Road, Ryde, Isle of Wight, PO33 1QF
☎ (01983) 611011 ⊕ goddardsbrewery.com

⊠ Anthony Goddard established what is now the oldest active brewery on the Isle of Wight in 1993. Originally occupying an 18th-century barn, a new brewery was built in 2008, quadrupling its capacity, which has since been further increased. Goddard's remain a locally-focused business distributing ales on the Isle of Wight and the easily accessible counties of southern England. ♦

Ale of Wight (OG 1037, ABV 3.7%)
An aromatic, fresh and zesty pale beer.

Scrumdiggity (OG 1039, ABV 4%) ◥
Well-balanced session beer that maintains its flavour and bite with compelling drinkability.

Wight Squirrel (OG 1042.5, ABV 4.3%)
A russet-coloured best bitter with an initial dry taste.

Fuggle-Dee-Dum (OG 1047, ABV 4.8%) ◥
Brown-coloured strong ale with plenty of malt and hops.

Godstone

Flower Farm, Oxted Road, Godstone, Surrey, RH9 8BP
☎ 07791 570731

Office: 3 Willow Way, Godstone, Surrey, RH9 8NQ
⊕ thegodstonebrewers.com

The Godstone Brewers was established in 2015 with a one-barrel plant and has moved to larger premises on a farm in Godstone using a five-barrel plant. Beers are named with local themes. The brewery supplies the nearby Fox & Hounds, Tilburstow Hill, and appears in micropubs in Surrey and Kent. ♦ RAIB V

Not So Black & White (ABV 3.7%)
An amber-coloured ale based on a milk stout recipe.

Trenchman's Hop (OG 1041, ABV 3.8%)
A pale bitter with a good balance of malt and hops.

Pondtail Pale (OG 1044, ABV 4.1%)
Citrus and exotic fruit flavours predominate from the American hops used.

Rusty's Ale (ABV 4.4%)

Bitter Entropy (ABV 5.3%)

Polly Paine's Porter (OG 1070, ABV 6.5%)
Full-bodied and complex porter with caramel, coffee and chocolate notes.

Goff's SIBA

9 Isbourne Way, Winchcombe, Gloucestershire, GL54 5NS
☎ (01242) 603383 ⊕ goffsbrewery.com

Goff's is a family concern that has been brewing cask-conditioned ales since 1994. The ales are available regionally in more than 200 outlets and nationally through wholesalers. ♦

Jouster (OG 1040, ABV 4%) ⬣
A drinkable, tawny-coloured ale, with a light hoppiness in the aroma. It has a good balance of malt and bitterness in the mouth, underscored by fruitiness, with a clean, hoppy aftertaste.

Tournament (OG 1038, ABV 4%) ⬣
Dark golden in colour, with a pleasant hop aroma. A clean, light and refreshing session bitter with a pleasant hop aftertaste.

White Knight (OG 1046, ABV 4.7%) ⬣
A well-hopped bitter with a light colour and full-bodied taste. Bitterness predominates in the mouth and leads to a dry, hoppy aftertaste.

Golcar

60a Swallow Lane, Golcar, West Yorkshire, HD7 4NB
☎ (01484) 644241 ☎ 07970 267555
⊕ golcarbrewery.co.uk

Golcar started brewing in 2001 and production has increased from 2.5 barrels to five barrels a week. The brewery owns one pub, the Rose & Crown at Golcar, and occasionally supplies other outlets in the local area. ‼

Dark Mild (OG 1034, ABV 3.4%) ⬣
Dark mild with a light roasted malt and liquorice taste. Smooth and satisfying.

Town End Bitter (OG 1039, ABV 3.9%) ⬣
Amber-coloured bitter with a hoppy, citrus taste, with fruity overtones and a bitter finish.

Pennine Gold (OG 1038, ABV 4%)
A hoppy and fruity session beer.

Guthlac's Porter (OG 1047, ABV 5%)
A robust all grain and malty working man's porter.

Golden Duck SIBA

Unit 2, Redhill Farm, Top Street, Appleby Magna, Leicestershire, DE12 7AH ☎ 07846 295179
⊕ goldenduckbrewery.com

Golden Duck began brewing in 2012 using a five-barrel plant. It is run by the father-and-son team of Andrew and Harry Lunn. Beers have a cricket-related theme and are always available in Mushroom Hall, Albert Village. Beers are also contract brewed for Alchemist Brewery. ♦ RAIB

LFB (Lunns First Brew) (OG 1043, ABV 4.3%)
Traditional golden-coloured, hoppy session ale with citrus overtones.

Wristy Fitzy (OG 1046, ABV 4.6%)
Deceptively smooth and rich chestnut-coloured ale, hoppy but with slight malty overtones.

Lunnys No. 8 (OG 1048, ABV 4.8%)
Hoppy bitter with a fruity and lasting aroma.

Golden Owl (NEW)

28 Alder Hill Grove, Leeds, West Yorkshire, LS7 2PT
☎ 07534 958250

A cuckoo brewery using spare capacity at breweries in the Leeds area. No real ale.

Golden Triangle SIBA

Unit 9, Watton Road Industrial Estate, Norwich, NR9 4BG
☎ (01603) 757763 ☎ 07976 281132
⊕ goldentriangle.co.uk

Golden Triangle, named after an area of Norwich, has been brewing modern, hop-forward ales on a 10-barrel plant since 2011. The brewery moved to its current address in 2012, and continues to add new beers to its range. Beers are mainly found in pubs across Norwich. ♦

City Gold (OG 1038, ABV 3.8%) ⬣
A lemony hop aroma introduces a mix of citrus, hop, and bitterness. Finish develops a dry astringency.

Mosaic City (OG 1038, ABV 3.8%) ⬚
Light golden ale made exclusively with Mosaic hops. A distinctive flavour with plenty of body.

Citropolis (OG 1039, ABV 3.9%)
Light, refreshing and zesty with citrus hop notes and fruity aroma.

Bonny's Gold (OG 1040, ABV 4%)
Golden ale with a definite American citrus hop profile and a good malt backbone.

Black Hops IBA (OG 1047, ABV 4.6%) ⬣
Intense hop and cherry aroma. Complex mix of malt, cherry and bitterness dominated by hops. Challenging, increasingly bitter ending.

Red Square (OG 1046, ABV 4.6%)
A red-coloured beer with balanced complex flavours developing into a strong, hoppy finish.

Shenanigans (ABV 5.2%)

Hop Lobster (OG 1053, ABV 5.5%)

A strong golden ale with plenty of citrus hop character.

Golden Valley

Abbeydore, Herefordshire ☎ 07828 935675

Correspondence: Unit 7, Three Elms Trading Estate, Hereford, HR4 9PU

Occasional brewing began in 2015 in Abbeydore, Herefordshire. Brewing is currently suspended.

Goldmark SIBA ◉

Unit 23 The Vinery, Arundel Road, Poling, West Sussex, BN18 9PY
☎ (01903) 297838 ☎ 07900 555415
⊕ goldmarks.co.uk

⊠ Ex-biochemist and home brewer Mark Lehmann began commercial brewing in 2013 using an 11-barrel plant. ‼RAIB

Ebony Mild (OG 1035, ABV 3.5%)
Black spicy mild with hints of chocolate, coffee and toffee.

Liquid Gold (OG 1040, ABV 4%)
A refreshing, full-bodied, golden-coloured beer with bursts of fruit and citrus.

Phoenix (OG 1041, ABV 4.1%)
A brown-coloured ale with hints of toffee, caramel and a smooth hop finish.

Red IPA (OG 1043, ABV 4.3%)

American Hop Idol (OG 1040, ABV 4.4%)
A pale ale using six American hop varieties balanced with roasted malt.

Warrior (OG 1046, ABV 4.6%)
A brown-coloured ale with hints of honey and caramel, ending with a smooth hop note.

Black Lion Porter (OG 1048, ABV 4.8%)
A rich, smooth and satisfying black porter with chocolate hints and a coffee end note.

Goldstone

The Forge, Ditchling Common Industrial Estate, Streat Lane, Ditchling, East Sussex, BN6 8SG
☎ (01444) 257053

Office: 257 Dyke Road, Hove, BN3 6PA
⊕ goldstonebrewery.co.uk

⊠ Located in an old forge in the South Downs, Goldstone is the brainchild of Mark Francis, who, while running a bar in Brussels, fell in love with the vast selection of Belgian beers. The brewery is named after a 20-ton rock found in Sussex, believed to have been used by druids for worship.

Old Charmer (OG 1041, ABV 4.1%)
A light ale with an assertive bitterness and a tropical fruit and spicy aroma.

Ruddy Duck (OG 1041, ABV 4.1%)
Medium-bodied, dark-coloured ale with notes of caramel, chocolate and coffee. A dry finish.

Beacon Best Bitter (OG 1042, ABV 4.2%)
Well-balanced amber-coloured ale with maltiness on the palate and a pleasant, dry bitter finish.

Cascade (OG 1044, ABV 4.4%)
An American-style ale with strong aromas of citrus fruit.

East Slope Ale (OG 1044, ABV 4.4%)
Golden ale with a smooth, light, hoppy flavour.

Amarillo (OG 1045, ABV 4.5%)
Golden-coloured, American-style ale with strong aromas of grapefruit and gooseberry with a dry bitter finish.

Good Chemistry

Unit 2, William Street, St Philips, Bristol, BS2 0RG
☎ (0117) 903 9930 ⊕ goodchemistrybrewing.co.uk

⊠ Good Chemistry was established in 2015 in a warehouse in Brewmuda Triangle, St Philips, Bristol by Bob Cary and Kelly Sidgwick, using a 10-barrel plant. As the name suggests, all brewery and beer logos have a scientific theme. Frequent brewery open days are held. ♦RAIB

Big Bang (OG 1044, ABV 4.4%) ◥
Unfined brown speciality beer, hoppy aroma with hint of apple. Complex fruit taste with perfumy background. Lingering bitter aftertaste.

Redstart Rye (OG 1048, ABV 5.3%)

Good Stuff (NEW)

🝗 Abdication, 89 Mansfield Road, Daybrook, Nottingham, NG5 6BH ⊕ theabdication.co.uk

A nanobrewery located inside the Abdication micropub. Capacity is 0.5 barrels so occasional beers can only be found at the pub.

Goodall's

🝗 The Lodge, 88 Crewe Road, Alsager, ST7 2JA
☎ (01270) 873669
✉ goodalls.brewery@hotmail.co.uk

Goodall's began brewing in 2010 at the Lodge in Alsager using a 2.5-barrel plant. Mainly seasonal ales are brewed.

Goody SIBA

Bleangate Brewery, Braggs Lane, Herne, Kent, CT6 7NP
☎ (01227) 361555 ⊕ goodyales.co.uk

Goody Ales began brewing in 2012 using a 10-barrel plant. A wood-burning boiler is used to heat the water for the brews using wood from its copse, thereby minimising the use of non-renewable fuel. An on-site bar, the Cathedral, is now open (limited hours). ‼ 🍽 ♦RAIB GF V

Good Evening (OG 1034, ABV 3.4%)
A smooth, dark mild with a tinge of chocolate.

Genesis (OG 1035, ABV 3.5%)
A dark ruby-coloured ale with a full flavour and lasting bitter finish.

Good Health (OG 1038, ABV 3.6%)
A honey-coloured golden ale with a fresh, hoppy finish and undertones of zesty orange.

Good Life (OG 1040, ABV 3.9%)
Fresh-tasting pale ale, bursting with citrus flavours and a host of golden hops.

Good Heavens (OG 1042, ABV 4.1%)
Amber-coloured, hoppy ale.

Good Sheppard (OG 1045, ABV 4.5%)
Deep amber-coloured ale with a warm vanilla twist on the palate and a soft feel on the tongue.

796

Goodness Gracious Me (OG 1047, ABV 4.8%)
Robust, citrus-flavoured, highly-hopped IPA.

Goose Eye SIBA

Ingrow Bridge, South Street, Keighley, West Yorkshire, BD21 5AX
☎ (01535) 605807 ⊕ goose-eye-brewery.co.uk

☺Goose Eye is a family-run brewery supplying 60-70 regular outlets, mainly in North and West Yorkshire and Lancashire. The beers are available through national wholesalers and pub chains. The brewery is looking for new premises. ♦

Springwell (OG 1036, ABV 3.6%)

Barm Pot Bitter (OG 1038, ABV 3.8%) 🍺
Bitter, hop and fruit flavours dominate this golden session bitter, over a malty base. Increasingly dry and bitter finish.

Bitter (OG 1038, ABV 3.9%) 🍺
Traditional Yorkshire brown-coloured session bitter, well-balanced malt and hops with a pleasingly bitter finish.

Blackmoor (OG 1040, ABV 4%)
A dark-coloured session beer.

Chinook Blonde (OG 1042, ABV 4.2%) 🍺 🍺
An increasingly tart bitter finish follows assertive grapefruit hoppiness in the aroma and tropical flavours in this satisfying brew.

Golden Goose (OG 1045, ABV 4.5%)
A straw-coloured beer, light on the palate with a smooth and refreshing hoppy finish.

Over & Stout (OG 1052, ABV 5.2%) 🍺
A full-bodied stout with roast and malt flavours mingling with hops, dark fruit and liquorice on the palate. Look also for tart fruit on the nose and a growing bitter finish.

Pommies Revenge (OG 1052, ABV 5.2%) 🍺
Golden-coloured, strong bitter combining grassy hops, a cocktail of fruit flavours, a peppery hint and a hoppy, bitter finish.

Goosnargh SIBA

🍺 Horns Inn, Horns Lane, Goosnargh, Lancashire, PR3 2FJ
☎ (01772) 864382 ⊕ yehornsinn.co.uk

Brewing began in 2013 using a five-barrel plant in a tiny outbuilding at Horns Inn. Most of the equipment came from the Grindleton Brewery, which closed in 2010. The beer is served at the pub and in local free houses.

Gorgeous Beer (NEW) SIBA 👁

Unit 16, Tweedale Court, Madeley, Shropshire, TF7 4JZ
☎ (01952) 583656 ⊕ gorgeousbeer.co.uk

☺Brewing was established in 2016 by a small group of real ale enthusiasts. A 10-barrel plant is used, supplying three core beers plus seasonals to the free trade. A one-barrel plant is used for trial brews. ♦

Golden Bitter (OG 1034.5, ABV 3.8%)

Blonde Ale (OG 1046.5, ABV 4.8%)
Smooth-tasting with a slightly citrus bitterness.

Porter (OG 1051, ABV 5.5%)
Sweet, malty and dark.

Gorgeous Brewery (NEW)

🍺 Bull, 13 North Hill, Highgate, London, N6 4AB
☎ (020) 8341 0510 ⊕ thebullhighgate.co.uk

Brewing began in 2016 using a six-barrel plant.

Gower SIBA 👁

Unit 25, Crofty Industrial Estate, Crofty, SA4 3RS
☎ (01792) 850681 ⊕ gowerbrewery.com

⊠ Established in 2011 on a five-barrel brew plant at the Greyhound Inn in Llanrhidian, Gower moved to a new 20-barrel brewery in Crofty in 2015. 🚚♦

Brew 1 (OG 1039, ABV 3.8%)
Honey-coloured ale with a pronounced floral aroma.

Best Bitter (OG 1045, ABV 4.5%)
A traditional honey-coloured ale with a full-bodied, balanced malty flavour and crisp, lingering hop bite.

Gold (OG 1045, ABV 4.5%)
Thirst-quenching golden ale with refreshing citrus flavours and a hop aroma.

Rumour (OG 1050, ABV 5%)
Strong ruby red-coloured ale with complex tastes and aromas.

Power (OG 1052, ABV 5.5%)

Grafton SIBA 👁

Walters Yard, Unit 4, Claylands Industrial Estate, Worksop, Nottinghamshire, S81 7DW
☎ (01909) 476121 ☎ 07436 282779

Office: 8 Oak Close, Crabtree Park Estate, Worksop, S80 1BH ⊕ graftonbrewing.co.uk

☺Grafton is a 12-barrel brewery established in 2007. The brewery tap is the Grafton Hotel, Worksop. In 2017 the brewery took over the operation of the former Hale's Brewery, which was based in an adjacent unit, but utilised the Grafton plant, and now produces Hale's beers as a sub-brand within its portfolio. ‼♦

Framboise (OG 1038, ABV 4%) 🍺
Golden ale with a raspberry aroma and taste, leading to a sweet and slightly bitter finish.

Silhouette (OG 1038, ABV 4%)
A pale beer, the addition of vanilla pods gives a unique vanilla flavour.

Lady Julia (OG 1041, ABV 4.3%)
A golden ale. Wheat and barley produce a crisp beer with a floral hop aroma.

Bananalicious (OG 1043, ABV 4.5%)
Mid brown-coloured ale with a banana and toffee aftertaste.

Lady Catherine (OG 1043, ABV 4.5%)
Well-balanced with a malty, slightly sweet biscuit flavour. A golden-coloured beer, easy-drinking with a gentle bitterness.

Lady Ruby (OG 1043, ABV 4.5%)
A dark ruby-coloured ale made with the addition of cherries. Hint of cherries on the nose, on the palate a bitter start which then finishes with a cherry bomb on the back of the tongue.

Apricot Jungle (OG 1046, ABV 4.8%)

THE BREWERIES

A fruity, golden beer with honey, apricot and almond notes. The sweetness is balanced by hop bitterness.

Blondie (OG 1046, ABV 4.8%)
A strong, golden-coloured beer whose aroma is dominated by citrus notes. Hops and fruit on the palate are balanced by malt, leading to a hoppy finish with soft fruit flavours.

Mint Chocolate Stout (OG 1046, ABV 4.8%)
Dark ale brewed with chocolate malt and mint which gives a mint chocolate flavour.

Caramel Stout (OG 1048, ABV 5%)
A black-coloured ale, made with chocolate malt, caramel and dark roast.

Coco Loco (OG 1048, ABV 5%) ◆
Dark-coloured, smooth-drinking ale with a gentle bitterness, infused with coconut.

Charioteer (OG 1063, ABV 6.5%)
A deceptively easy-drinking strong beer. Subtle, with citrus flavours, giving a fruity berry aroma and fruity flavour, with a hint of malty sweetness, leading to a smooth, long finish.

Brewed under the Hale's Brewery brand name:

Sacred Heart (OG 1034, ABV 3.6%)
Golden-coloured session ale, low in strength but with bags of flavour.

Grey Heart (OG 1038, ABV 4%)
Hazy beer infused with Earl Grey, which has bergamot and jasmine overtones, followed by a refreshing, gentle citrus flavour.

Black Heart (OG 1048, ABV 5%)
A black IPA packed with intense flavours, followed by a smooth roast background.

Grain SIBA

South Farm, Tunbeck Road, Alburgh, Norfolk, IP20 0BS
☎ (01986) 788884 ⊕ grainbrewery.co.uk

⊠ Grain Brewery was launched in 2006 by Geoff Wright and Phil Halls in a converted dairy in the Waveney Valley. It upgraded to a 15-barrel plant in 2012. Four pubs are owned, the Plough and the Cottage, both in Norwich, the Spread Eagle, Ipswich, and the Corn Hall Bar, Diss. ‼🍺◆RAIB

Oak (OG 1038, ABV 3.8%) ◆
A balanced mix of malt and hops with marmalade overtones. A hint of molasses in the short, sharp ending.

ThreeOneSix (OG 1039, ABV 3.9%) 🍴 ◆
Strong citrus notes throughout. Tangerine, lemon and lime mix with a solid hoppy base. A well-balanced, bitter finish.

Best Bitter (OG 1042, ABV 4.2%) ◆
A well-balanced, complex bitter. A blend of flavours with malt and hops ably supported by caramel and bitterness.

Redwood (OG 1043, ABV 4.3%) ◆
Heavy blackcurrant airs give way to a rich fruity bitterness with malt overtones. Copper-coloured, crisp and satisfying.

Slate (OG 1060, ABV 6%) ◆
Coffee, caramel and plum on the nose. Dried fruit and sweet maltiness dominate a creamy roast background. Long, strong finish.

Lignum Vitae (OG 1065, ABV 6.5%) ◆

Powerful, complex and rich throughout. Malt and hops vie with tropical fruit and bitterness for dominance.

Grainstore SIBA ◉

Station Approach, Oakham, Rutland, LE15 6RE
☎ (01572) 770065 ⊕ grainstorebrewery.com

☺ Grainstore, the smallest county's largest brewery, has been in production since 1995, founded by Tony Davis and Mike Davies. After 30 years in the industry Tony decided to set up his own business after finding a derelict Victorian railway grainstore building. Now retired, he has handed the reins to his son, William. More than 200 outlets are supplied. ‼◆

Rutland Bitter (OG 1032, ABV 3.4%)
Well-balanced, light session beer.

Rutland Panther (OG 1034, ABV 3.4%) ◆
This reddish-black mild punches above its weight with malt and roast flavours combining to deliver a brew that can match the average stout for intensity of flavour.

Cooking (OG 1036, ABV 3.6%) ◆
Tawny-coloured beer with malt and hops on the nose and a pleasant grainy mouthfeel. Hops and fruit flavours combine to give a bitterness that continues into a long finish.

Red Kite (OG 1038, ABV 3.8%)
A malty, sweet beer with a good body.

Steelback IPA (OG 1042, ABV 4.2%)
A full-bodied, golden IPA with a classic blend of English hops.

Triple B (OG 1042, ABV 4.2%) ◆
Initially hops dominate over malt in both the aroma and taste, but fruit is there too. All three linger in varying degrees in the sweetish aftertaste of this brown brew.

GB Best (OG 1043, ABV 4.3%)
A light beer with a pronounced floral aroma and flavour.

Ten Fifty (OG 1050, ABV 5%) ◆
Pungent banana and malt notes on the nose. On the palate, rich malt and fruit is joined by subtle hop on a bittersweet base. Dry malt aftertaste with some fruit.

Rutland Beast (OG 1053, ABV 5.3%) 🍴
A strong mild ale with complex flavours of chocolate/coffee and those of raisins and autumn fruits.

Nip (OG 1073, ABV 7.3%) 🍴
A well-balanced barley wine, smooth and warming with raisins and winter fruit dominant.

Grampus

🍴 **Grampus Inn, Lee Bay, Devon, EX34 8LR**
☎ (01271) 862906 ⊕ thegrampus-inn.co.uk

Grampus was opened in 2014 at the back of the Grampus Inn by Bill Harvey, the owner. It is a small plant using traditional brewing methods, but combining some unique and unusual ingredients. At present, all production is sold though the pub.

Granite Rock

Unit 19, Kernick Road Industrial Estate, Penryn, Cornwall, TR10 9EP
☎ (01326) 379251 ☎ 07436 817974
⊕ graniterockbrewery.co.uk

⊗ Granite Rock was established in 2013 as a brewery and home brew shop. Located on an industrial estate in Penryn, the two-barrel plant currently supplies the free trade in west Cornwall. ‼ ➤ ◆ RAIB

Penryn Company Pale Ale (OG 1040, ABV 4%) ◆
Tawny-coloured bitter with fruity hop and malt nose. Assertive bitterness, lightly sulphurous roast malt with stone fruit traces and dry finish.

Summer Solstice (OG 1040, ABV 4%) ◆
Golden ale with a floral grapefruit aroma. Refreshing essences of oranges, lemons and grapefruit. Assertive bitterness throughout with some dryness.

Penryn Pride (OG 1042, ABV 4.5%)
A red/brown-coloured ale with full malt, coffee and chocolate notes; strong hopping ensures the malt does not overwhelm.

Bronescombe's Vision (OG 1048, ABV 5.2%) ◆
Well-balanced, red-coloured, strong bitter with malt and hop aroma. Strong malt flavour, hop bitterness, some sweetness. Refreshing bitter, dry finish.

Glasney College Porter (OG 1050, ABV 5.4%) ◆
Black porter with roast malt aroma. Full-bodied taste of creamy coffee and dark chocolate, liquorice and pear drops. Light finish.

Grasshopper (NEW)

Unit F2, Langley Bridge Industrial Estate, Linkmel Road, Langley Mill, Derbyshire, NG16 3RZ ☎ 07900 806277 ⊕ grasshopperbrewery.co.uk

Grasshopper commenced brewing in 2017 using a 10-barrel plant.

Nymph (ABV 4.8%)

Great British Breworks (NEW)

⊟ The Brew House, Black Swan, 18 Birdgate, Pickering, North Yorkshire, YO18 7AL
⊕ blackswan-pickering.co.uk/breworks

Brewing started on a permanent basis in the rear yard of the Black Swan in 2016, using a 2.5-barrel plant.

Great Heck SIBA

Harwinn House, Main Street, Great Heck, North Yorkshire, DN14 0BQ
☎ (01977) 661430 ☎ 07723 381002
⊕ greatheckbrewery.co.uk

☺ Great Heck began production in 2008 in a converted slaughterhouse. The brewery moved across the road to a converted cottage in 2012 and now produces its regular beers on a 15-barrel plant with capacity for 45 barrels per week. ‼ ◆

Amish Mash (OG 1045
A cloudy wheat beer with notes of banana and clove and fruity hop flavours.

Chopper (OG 1037, ABV 3.8%)
A dry-hopped pale session beer.

Dave (OG 1038, ABV 3.9%)
A dark-coloured session bitter with a satisfying roasty taste.

Mercy (OG 1039, ABV 3.9%)

Navigator (OG 1039, ABV 3.9%)
Traditional mahogany-coloured session bitter with subtle yet exotic hop aromas.

Blonde (OG 1043, ABV 4.3%)
A rich, well-balanced blonde beer with a zesty finish.

Voodoo Mild (OG 1043, ABV 4.3%)
Rich, black mild bursting with flavour from the roasted malts.

Christopher (OG 1043, ABV 4.5%)
A clean, dry and moderately bitter pale ale with loads of American aroma hops.

Mount Hood (OG 1043, ABV 4.5%)

Treasure IPA (OG 1045, ABV 4.8%)
Smooth, golden IPA with moderate bitterness and distinctive tropical fruit notes.

Shankar IPA (OG 1055, ABV 5.9%)
A pale, hoppy, fruity beer with a clean, zesty finish.

Black Jesus (OG 1060, ABV 6.5%)

Yakima IPA (OG 1070, ABV 7.4%)
Deep golden in colour, very low in bitterness, the alcohol balances the fruity hop flavours and aromas perfectly.

Great Newsome SIBA ◉

Great Newsome Farm, South Frodingham, East Yorkshire, HU12 0NR
☎ (01964) 612201 ⊕ greatnewsomebrewery.co.uk

☺ Nestled in the Holderness countryside, Great Newsome began brewing in 2007 in renovated farm buildings. A range of beers is now brewed using barley from the farm and brewing can be seen from a newly-built viewing area. Beer is distributed throughout the UK and overseas. ‼ ➤ ◆

Sleck Dust (OG 1037, ABV 3.8%)
Straw-coloured, refreshingly bitter session beer with floral aroma and subtle dry finish.

Ploughman's Pride (OG 1042, ABV 4.2%)
Easy-drinking, moderately bittered ale, deep chestnut in colour. Malty with liquorice tones.

Pricky Back Otchan (OG 1042, ABV 4.2%)
Golden-coloured bitter with nutty, toffee aroma. Complex with mild citrus notes.

Frothingham Best (OG 1042, ABV 4.3%)
Dark amber-coloured best bitter. Fruit and nut aroma with hop resin and peach notes leading to a sweetish finish.

Holderness Dark (OG 1042, ABV 4.3%)
Dark, strong mild. Chocolate malt and hazelnut notes with a hint of sweetness in a long satisfying finish.

Jem's Stout (OG 1044, ABV 4.3%)
Dark, smooth beer with smoky, roasted malt flavours and aroma.

Liquorice Lads Stout (OG 1044, ABV 4.3%)
Black stout flavoured by real liquorice.

Great North Eastern (NEW) SIBA 👁

Contact House, Wellington Road, Dunston, Gateshead, NE11 9HS
☎ (0191) 447 4462 ☎ 07514 787483
⊕ greatnortheasternbrewingco.com

The Great North Eastern Brewing Company began brewing in 2016 on a 10-barrel plant. In 2017 the brewery expanded into the adjacent premises and a brewery shop has now opened. There are plans to open a brewery tap and instal a bottling plant in the near future. Beers are available throughout the North-east.

Claspers Citra Blonde (OG 1038, ABV 3.8%)
A pale ale with strong citrus notes.

Jarrow Bitter (OG 1038, ABV 3.8%)

Gold (OG 1039, ABV 4%)
Single-hopped golden ale with strong hop flavours.

Rivet Catcher (OG 1040, ABV 4%)
A light, smooth, golden-coloured ale with a subtle fruity hop taste.

Joblings Swinging Gibbet (OG 1041, ABV 4.1%)
A copper-coloured, well-balanced beer with a good hop aroma and fruity finish.

Caulker (OG 1042, ABV 4.2%)

Shipwright Blonde (OG 1042, ABV 4.2%)

Red Ellen (OG 1044, ABV 4.4%)
A rich, ruby-coloured, full-bodied ale with a citrus hop aroma.

McConnells Irish Stout (OG 1046, ABV 4.6%)

Minnikins Stout (OG 1045, ABV 4.6%)
A rich, creamy stout with a long, lingering liquorice and chocolate finish.

Westoe IPA (OG 1044.5, ABV 4.6%)
A pale golden-coloured ale with a soft malt character and complex hop aroma.

Great Oakley SIBA 👁

Ark Farm, High Street South, Tiffield, Northamptonshire, NN12 8AB
☎ (01327) 351759 ☎ 07850 327658
⊕ greatoakleybrewery.co.uk

The brewery commenced production in 2005 in Great Oakley and relocated to Tiffield in 2012. It is run by husband-and-wife team Phil and Hazel Greenway. More than 60 outlets are supplied, including the George, Tiffield, which is the brewery tap. ‼ ◆ RAIB

Welland Valley Mild (OG 1037, ABV 3.6%)
A dark, traditional mild. Full of flavour.

Egret (OG 1038, ABV 3.8%)

Wagtail (OG 1040, ABV 3.9%)
Light-coloured with a unique bitterness derived from New Zealand hops.

Wot's Occurring (OG 1040, ABV 3.9%)
A mid-golden session bitter with a subtle hop finish.

Walter Tull (OG 1040, ABV 4%)

Tiffield Thunderbolt (OG 1043, ABV 4.2%)

Harpers (OG 1044, ABV 4.3%)
Traditional mid-brown bitter with a malty taste and slight hints of chocolate and citrus in the finish.

Gobble (OG 1045, ABV 4.5%)
Straw-coloured beer with a pleasant hop aftertaste.

Delapre Dark (OG 1047, ABV 4.6%)
A dark, full-bodied ale made from five different malts.

Abbey Stout (OG 1051, ABV 5%)
A dark, rich stout brewed with generous amounts of roast barley and German hops.

Tailshaker (OG 1051, ABV 5%)
A complex golden ale with a great depth of flavour.

Great Orme SIBA

Builder Street, Llandudno, LL30 1DR
☎ (01492) 330680 ⊕ greatormebrewery.co.uk

☺Great Orme began brewing in 2005 on a five-barrel plant, situated in the Conwy Valley. It moved to larger premises in the Victorian seaside town of Llandudno, within sight of the Great Orme, from which the brewery takes its name. It now brews on an 18-barrel plant. Around 100 outlets are supplied. ‼ ◆

Welsh Gold (OG 1036, ABV 3.6%) ◣
A pale brown malty session bitter with a dry taste. Some hoppy flavours develop in the bitter aftertaste.

Welsh Black (OG 1042, ABV 4%) ◣
Smooth-tasting dark beer with roast coffee notes in aroma and taste. Sweetish in flavour and having some characteristics of a mild ale with hoppiness also present in the aftertaste.

Orme (OG 1042, ABV 4.2%) ◣
Malty best bitter with a dry finish. Faint hop and fruit notes in aroma and taste, but malt dominates throughout.

Celtica (OG 1045, ABV 4.5%) ◣
Yellow in colour with a zesty taste full of citrus fruit flavours. Some initial sweetness followed by peppery hops and a bitter finish.

Red Dragon (OG 1045, ABV 4.5%) ◣
A light-brown best bitter with a sweet, malty taste accompanied by faint fruit notes and peppery hops in the finish.

Ynys Mon (OG 1045, ABV 4.5%) ◣
A copper-coloured, malty best bitter with a smooth, sweetish taste and a satisfying finish.

Great Western SIBA 👁

Stream Bakery, Bristol Road, Hambrook, Bristol, BS16 1RF
☎ (0117) 957 2842 ⊕ gwbrewery.co.uk

⊗ Great Western is a 12-barrel brewery set up in 2008 by Kevin Stone in a former bakery. The property has been renovated resulting in a bespoke showpiece brewery retaining many of the building's original features. The brewery owns a single pub – the Rising Sun, Frampton Cotterell – and 500 outlets are supplied. ‼ 🛒 ◆

HPA (OG 1040, ABV 4%) ◣
Hoppy, yellow-coloured bitter with clean citrus flavours leading to a lingering, astringent finish.

Maiden Voyage (OG 1040, ABV 4%) ◣
An amber-coloured bitter with a light aroma of malt and fruit which continues to the palate before leading to a strong bitter finish.

Bees Knees (OG 1041, ABV 4.2%) ◣

Golden-coloured beer, bitter with malt nose and flavour and some honey. Lasting astringent bitter aftertaste.

Exhibitionist (OG 1044, ABV 4.5%)
Deep copper-coloured beer, full-bodied with a fruity taste.

Classic Gold (OG 1044, ABV 4.6%) ◀
Golden ale with subtle aromas of pale malt and fruits. Citrus fruits with balanced hop and malt character with a lingering bitter finish.

Old Higby (OG 1045, ABV 4.8%) ◀
Full-bodied, malty bitter with roast notes on the nose. Hints of fruit flavour give way to a bitter hop finish with some astringency throughout.

Moose River (OG 1047, ABV 5%) ◀
Light citrus aroma, delicate hop taste with long-lasting bitter finish.

Great Yorkshire

Cropton, North Yorkshire, YO18 8HH
☎ (01751) 417330
⊕ thegreatyorkshirebrewery.co.uk

Great Yorkshire took over the Cropton Brewery in 2012 concentrating on the production of keg beers. Check the website for limited edition and other cask ales.

Green Dragon

▤ Green Dragon, 29 Broad Street, Bungay, Suffolk, NR35 1EF
☎ (01986) 892681

The Green Dragon pub was purchased in 1991 and the rear converted to a brewery. In 1994 the plant was expanded and moved to a converted barn. The doubling of capacity allowed the production of a larger range of ales.

Chaucer Ale (OG 1037, ABV 3.8%)

Gold (OG 1045, ABV 4.4%)

Bridge Street Bitter (OG 1045, ABV 4.5%)

Magnum IPA (ABV 5%)

Strong Mild (OG 1054, ABV 5.5%)
A dark, ruby-coloured ale. Plum and dark chocolate on the nose with a rich and smooth taste full of dark malt notes. It is mildly hopped to allow the malt character to prevail.

Green Duck SIBA

Unit 13, Gainsborough Trading Estate, Rufford Road, Stourbridge, West Midlands, DY9 7ND
☎ (01384) 377666 ⊕ greenduckbrewery.co.uk

☺ Green Duck began brewing in 2012 and relocated to its present site in Stourbridge in 2013. Experimental beers are brewed alongside a core range. The brewery has an onsite brewery tap, the Badelynge Bar, where the brewing equipment is visible through a glass partition. Private parties and quarterly beer festivals are hosted. ‼◆

Duck & Cover (OG 1041, ABV 4%) ◀
Pale gold with a tropical aroma. Refreshing with a dry pine and resin aftertaste.

Duck Blonde (OG 1042, ABV 4.2%) ◀

Gold with a sharp fruity aroma. Lots of passionfruit in the taste. Aftertaste is balanced with fruit sweetness and hops.

Duck Under (OG 1045, ABV 4.5%)
A strong malt backbone with an intense hop flavour delivers a well-balanced drink with a bitter citrus finish.

Duck Dastardly (OG 1050, ABV 5%) ◀
This creamy stout is dark brown to black. Aroma contains chocolate and coffee. Pronounced roast flavours in the taste and aftertaste.

Duck & Dive (OG 1056, ABV 5.9%) ◀
Amber-coloured with a fruity aroma. Citrus hop and spicy orange peel sweetness in the taste with a long bitter finish.

Green Jack SIBA ◉

Argyle Place, Love Road, Lowestoft, Suffolk, NR32 2NZ
☎ (01502) 562863 ☎ 07902 219459
⊕ green-jack.com

⊠ After 10 years at Oulton Broad, Green Jack moved to the Triangle Tavern, Lowestoft in 2003 and then to a nearby 35-barrel plant in 2009. One pub is owned and more than 150 outlets supplied. ‼◆RAIB

Golden Best (OG 1037, ABV 3.8%)

Orange Wheat Beer (OG 1041, ABV 4.2%) ◀
Marmalade aroma with a hint of hops, leading to a well-balanced blend of sweetness, hops and citrus with a malt background. Mixed fruit flavours in the aftertaste.

Trawlerboys Best Bitter (OG 1045, ABV 4.6%) ◀
Tawny-coloured beer with aroma of apple, sultana and malt plus hints of caramel and hops. Rich fig and plum base with malt and roast overtones. Strong finish with a sticky mouthfeel.

Lurcher Stout (OG 1046, ABV 4.8%) ◀
Pleasant malt, roast and fruit aromas. Blackberry, raisin and port flavours. Long, dry, bitter roast finish.

Rising Sun (OG 1047, ABV 4.8%)

Red Herring (OG 1048, ABV 5%)

Gone Fishing ESB (OG 1052, ABV 5.5%)

Mahseer IPA (OG 1056, ABV 5.8%)

Ripper Tripel (OG 1074, ABV 8.5%) ▮

Baltic Trader Export Stout (OG 1092, ABV 10.5%)

Green Mill SIBA

▤ Harewood Arms, 2 Market Street, Broadbottom, SK14 6AX ☎ 07967 656887 ⊕ greenmillbrewery.com

Green Mill started brewing in 2007 on a 2.5-barrel plant and moved in 2010 to the Cask & Feather in Rochdale. The brewery relocated again in 2013 to the Harewood Arms in Broadbottom. A number of occasional beers are brewed. Around 40 outlets are supplied.

Gold (OG 1035, ABV 3.6%)

Chief (OG 1041, ABV 4.2%)
A smooth, pale bitter with American hop varieties.

Citrus Snap (OG 1040, ABV 4.2%)
A copper-coloured bitter with citrus notes.

Old Git (OG 1040, ABV 4.2%)
A refreshing golden ale with a fusion of hops.

Talisman (OG 1040, ABV 4.2%)
A straw-coloured golden ale with tropical fruit notes.

Flavia (OG 1042, ABV 4.5%)
A blonde beer with a fresh hop aroma, leading to a clean, dry finish.

Northern Lights (OG 1045, ABV 4.5%)
A pale, well-hopped premium bitter.

Big Chief (OG 1052, ABV 5.5%)

Greene King ⊚

Westgate Brewery, Westgate Street, Bury St Edmunds, Suffolk, IP33 1QT
☎ (01284) 763222 ⊕ greeneking.co.uk

⊗ Greene King has been brewing in the market town of Bury St Edmunds since 1799. It brews its beers using water drawn from artesian chalk wells below its brewhouse as well as local East Anglia malt. ‼ ➥ ♦ RAIB

XX Mild (OG 1035, ABV 3%)
A dark mild with a sweet and roast flavour.

IPA (OG 1036, ABV 3.6%) ◥
Hop-infused fruit cake aromas. Complex flavours of malt, caramel and hop with both sweetness and bitterness. A lingering mellow aftertaste with blackberries.

London Glory (OG 1041.1, ABV 4%)
Rich, fruity and full of flavour.

IPA Gold (OG 1041, ABV 4.1%)
A deep golden ale brewed with a blend of tropical fruit flavours, mango and spicy notes.

Abbot (OG 1049, ABV 5%) ◥
Strong malt, toffee and caramel aromas. Rich, malty caramel flavours with vine fruit and a little hop bite. Heavy, sweet finish with a subtle hint of bitterness in the aftertaste.

IPA Reserve (OG 1055.5, ABV 5.4%)
A full-bodied, amber-coloured ale. Grapefruit and orange citrus tones combine with the floral and herbal hop notes and lead to a dry bitter finish.

Brewed for the Taylor Walker pub chain:

1730 (ABV 4%)

Brewed under the Hardys & Hansons brand name:

Bitter (OG 1038, ABV 3.9%)
A balance of sweetness and bitterness that combines with a subtle hop character. A distinctive beer with a full finish.

Olde Trip (OG 1043, ABV 4.3%)
A rich toffee-flavoured beer with a fruity character and clean, bitter finish.

Brewed under the Morland brand name:

Original Bitter (OG 1039, ABV 4%)
A subtle malt and fruit character and a pronounced bitter finish.

Old Golden Hen (OG 1038.6, ABV 4.1%)
Light golden-coloured beer with tropical fruit notes.

Old Speckled Hen (OG 1045, ABV 4.5%) ◥
Smooth, malty and fruity with a short finish.

Brewed under the Ruddles brand name:

Best Bitter (OG 1037, ABV 3.7%) ◥

An amber/brown-coloured beer, strong on bitterness but with some initial sweetness, fruit and subtle, distinctive Bramling Cross hop. Dryness lingers in the aftertaste.

County (OG 1043, ABV 4.3%) ◥
Sweet, malty and bitter, with a dry and bitter aftertaste.

Brewed under the Tolly Cobbold brand name:

English Ale (OG 1033.6, ABV 2.8%)
Amber-coloured ale with balanced bitterness and strong tropical notes.

Greenfield SIBA ⊚

Unit 8, Waterside Mills, Greenfield, OL3 7NH
☎ (01457) 879789 ⊕ greenfieldbrewery.co.uk

⊚ Greenfield was launched in 2002 and is situated in an old spinning mill next to the River Chew on the edge of the Peak District National Park. Spring water from the National Park is used for brewing. It is open to the public and supplies beer to them and to more than 100 outlets. ‼ ➥ ♦

Greenfield (OG 1039, ABV 3.8%)

Silver Owl (OG 1042, ABV 4%)
A golden-amber beer with aromas of citrus fruits and hints of vanilla – oranges, dryness and lightly hopped taste.

Thirst Born (OG 1041, ABV 4.1%)
Floral citrus aroma with malt and hops. Taste of citrus, peach, floral malt.

Dobcross Bitter (OG 1041, ABV 4.2%)
An amber-coloured beer with lemon flavours and a dry finish.

Copper Caskade (OG 1042, ABV 4.3%)
Full-bodied, single hop, copper-coloured beer with a hoppy finish. Citrus and fruit tones to finish.

Vanilla Stout (OG 1048, ABV 5.2%)
A black stout with initial flavours of both chocolate and coffee before the roasted malts give way to a natural vanilla finish, created by the use of real vanilla pods.

Greenodd

⬛ Ship Inn, Main Street, Greenodd, Cumbria, LA12 7QZ ☎ 07782 655294
✉ greenoddbrewery@yahoo.co.uk

Established in 2010 at the Ship Inn on a two-barrel plant. Majority of production goes to the Ship with remainder going to local free trade.

Greg's

⬛ Dambusters Inn, 23 High Street, Scampton, Lincolnshire, LN1 2SD
☎ (01522) 730123

Greg's is a microbrewery launched in 2013 on the premises of the Dambusters Inn.

Grey Friars SIBA

Featherstone Hall Farm, New Road, Featherstone, Staffordshire, WV10 7NW ☎ 07966 361443
⊕ greyfriarsbrewery.co.uk

Established in 2014 and using equipment originally from Upham Brewery in Hampshire, the three-barrel plant is installed in a barn, formerly used as a snooker room and which still contains the original wood panelling. Brewing is currently suspended.

Grey Trees SIBA 👁

Unit 5-6, Gasworks Road, Aberaman, CF44 6RS
☎ (01685) 267077 ⊕ greytreesbrewing.com

Grey Trees began brewing at the Red Cow Inn in 2011 on the outskirts of Aberdare and relocated to its present location in 2013, upgrading to a 10-barrel plant. It supplies an increasing number of local outlets, as well as those in other parts of South Wales. There are a number of open nights throughout the year (see website for details). ‼ RAIB

Caradogs (OG 1038, ABV 3.9%)
Copper in colour, with a crisp flavour and dry finish.

Black Road Stout (OG 1040, ABV 4%)
A dark, smooth stout with delicate roasted flavours and a bittersweet aftertaste.

Diggers Gold (OG 1040, ABV 4%) 🍷 🍴
A golden ale with fresh citrus aromas, which leave a subtle bitterness.

Drummer Boy (OG 1042, ABV 4.2%)

Jagar Weizen (OG 1046, ABV 4.5%)
A Bavarian-style wheat beer with banana and clove notes.

Valley Porter (OG 1046, ABV 4.6%)
Warming and rich, with notes of dark fruits, coffee, chocolate and hazelnuts.

JPR Pale (OG 1046, ABV 4.7%)

Afghan Pale (OG 1054, ABV 5.4%) 🍴
A full-flavoured, crisp beer brewed in the the style of an American pale ale.

GreyHawk SIBA

Units 3 & 4, Enterprise Way, Airedale Business Park, Skipton, North Yorkshire, BD23 2TZ
☎ (01756) 701289 ⊕ greyhawkbrewery.com

☺GreyHawk Brewery has taken on the mantle of brewing quality real ales in Skipton at its modern brewery on the southern edge of town. Brewing takes place on a Bavarian specified 30-barrel plant using water from the brewery's own bore hole. 12 annual limited edition beers are sold under the Crafty Dog brand name. ‼ 🍴 ♦

Best Bitter (OG 1036, ABV 3.8%) 🍴
A traditional Yorkshire bitter with a malty aroma, a hoppy bitter taste with hints of fruit and a bitter finish.

Pippin (OG 1037, ABV 3.9%) 🍴
This golden-coloured ale has a citrus aroma and flavour. The dry, bitter astringency increases in the aftertaste.

Yorkshire Myst (OG 1040, ABV 4%)
A cask Pilsner; crisp, smooth and refreshing.

Greyhound SIBA 👁

Watershed, Smock Alley, West Chiltington, RH20 2QX
☎ 07973 625510 ⊕ greyhoundbrewery.co.uk

⊗ Established in 2015 in West Sussex by husband-and-wife team Nick and Sarah Allen, Greyhound is a 7.5-barrel brewery. There are plans to open a brewery tap and to expand the brewery on a new site. ‼ ♦ RAIB

Good Ordinary Bitter (OG 1038, ABV 3.8%)
A classic English-style session bitter with a nutty flavour and subtle bitterness.

Blonde Bird (OG 1039, ABV 3.9%)
A refreshing pale ale with a well-rounded, dry finish and a subtle fresh lemon aroma.

Amber Eyes (OG 1040, ABV 4.2%)
A rich and well-balanced golden amber-coloured ale with complex floral aromas, rounded light biscuit malt flavours and a bitter finish.

B-46 (OG 1044, ABV 4.6%)
A rich, dark amber-coloured ale. A good balance of warm biscuity malt flavours move towards toast and blackberry, which linger on the palate assisting a clean, hoppy finish.

Gribble

🍺 Gribble Inn, Oving, West Sussex, PO20 2BP
☎ (01243) 786893 ⊕ gribbleinn.co.uk

Established in 1980 using a five-barrel plant, the Gribble Brewery is the longest-serving brewpub in the Sussex area, independently owned and run by the licensees. A number of local outlets are supplied.

Sussex Quadhopper (OG 1043, ABV 4%)

Ale (OG 1041, ABV 4.1%)

Fuzzy Duck (OG 1045, ABV 4.3%)

Reg's Tipple (OG 1050, ABV 4.5%)
A smooth nutty flavour with a pleasant afterbite.

Plucking Pheasant (OG 1052, ABV 5.2%)

Pig's Ear (OG 1058, ABV 6%)

Wobbler (OG 1058, ABV 7.2%)

Griffin

See Freestyle

Grill & Grain (NEW)

🍺 Grill & Grain at the Boatyard, 2 Bolton Road, Hoghton, Lancashire, PR5 0SP
☎ (01254) 209841 ⊕ grillandgrainboatyard.co.uk

Thwaites installed a one-barrel plant in 2016 in this canal side pub/restaurant. Brewing is currently suspended.

GT

Unit 5, The Old Aerodrome, Chivenor Business Park, Braunton, Devon, EX31 4AY
☎ (01271) 267420 ☎ 07909 515170 ⊕ gtales.co.uk

⊗ GT Ales was established in Barnstaple in 2013, producing only bottle-conditioned beers, before relocating to larger premises in Braunton in 2015. All five regular award-winning ales are now available in cask. ‼ ♦ RAIB

Thirst of Many (OG 1043, ABV 4.2%)
An amber-coloured best bitter. A fruity taste with slight caramel.

North Coast IPA (OG 1045, ABV 4.3%)
American-style IPA with a strong fruity aroma, sweet taste and hints of tropical fruits. A complex, lingering hop finish.

Blonde Ambition (OG 1044, ABV 4.5%)

Golden ale with good hop and citrus/gooseberry notes. Refreshing with a floral aroma.

Dark Horse Milk Stout (OG 1048, ABV 4.5%)
Smooth, slightly sweet mouthfeel. Fruity taste with hints of blackcurrant and a slight coffee bitterness in the finish.

Crimson Rye'd (OG 1048, ABV 4.8%)
A specialty beer with a distinct red colour. A strong fruity malted taste and good fruity residual hop finish.

Gun SIBA 👁

Hawthbush Farm, Gun Hill, East Sussex, TN21 0JY
☎ (01323) 700200 ☎ 07900 683355
⊕ gunbrewery.co.uk

Gun Brewery is located on a beautiful 140-acre organic mixed farm in the Sussex Weald. It generates much of its own power from a 15-kW solar array and heating comes from a wood-powered boiler. Spent grains keep the local livestock happy and all the water used for brewing comes from the brewery's own spring. More than 30 outlets are supplied. RAIB V

Scaramanga Extra Pale (OG 1038, ABV 3.9%)

Parabellum Milk Stout (OG 1057, ABV 4.1%)

Project Babylon Pale Ale (OG 1044, ABV 4.6%)

Base Ejection Smoked Rye (OG 1046, ABV 4.7%)

Velo Dog (OG 1051, ABV 5.5%)

Zamzama IPA (OG 1060, ABV 6.5%)

Gun Dog SIBA

Unit 5b, Great Central Way, Woodford Halse, Northamptonshire, NN11 3PZ
☎ (01327) 264005 ☎ 07834 374751
⊕ gundogales.co.uk

Gun Dog is a family-run brewery established in 2012. A six-barrel plant is used to brew modern crafted ales with a nod to brewing traditions of the past. Beers are available in a number of pubs and shops locally. ‼ 🍺 ♦ RAIB

Jack's Spaniels (OG 1038, ABV 3.8%)
A careful blend of malt and hops create this floral, refreshing blonde.

Scrum Dog (OG 1040, ABV 4%)
An amber-coloured beer with a taste of fruit and hops.

Booze Hound (OG 1042, ABV 4.2%)
A copper-coloured IPA with a slightly sweet taste but a bitter twist.

Lord Barker (OG 1042, ABV 4.2%)
Rich, dark and smooth stout with a chocolate nose, round taste in the mouth and a clean finish.

Bad to the Bone (OG 1045, ABV 4.5%) 🌢
A light brown-coloured bitter with a fruity nose, biscuit malt flavour and a bitter finish.

Yankee Poodle (OG 1047, ABV 4.7%) 🌢
A golden-coloured beer with a citrus hop aroma, citrus bitter flavour and bitter finish.

Gwaun Valley

Kilkiffeth Farm, Pontfaen, SA65 9TP
☎ (01348) 881304 ⊕ gwaunvalleybrewery.co.uk

Gwaun Valley began brewing in 2009 on a four-barrel plant in a converted granary. The brewery offers views of the Preseli Hills and has a camp site, a holiday cottage and pitches for five caravans. Folk music sessions are held every Saturday evening. Each year a Bluegrass Festival is held at the brewery over a July weekend. ‼ 🍺

Farmhouse Ale (OG 1040, ABV 4%)
A malty ale with a smooth, balanced character, made from only English hops.

Golden Bitter Ale (OG 1040, ABV 4%)
A smooth, bitter ale with a strong, hoppy flavour and crisp finish.

Light Ale (OG 1040, ABV 4%)
Refreshing and easy-drinking, with citrus undertones and a clean finish.

St Davids Special (OG 1040, ABV 4%)
A light, fruity beer with a refreshingly citrus flavour.

Valley Brew (OG 1040, ABV 4.1%)
Double-hopped bitter ale with a mellow taste and balanced sweetness.

Blodwen (OG 1043, ABV 4.3%)
Creamy, full-bodied bitter, ruby red in colour with a hint of caramel.

Cascade (OG 1043, ABV 4.3%)
Refreshing, clear, hoppy pale ale.

Calon Lan (OG 1044, ABV 4.5%)
Rich and malty beer with a bittersweet aftertaste.

King of the Road (OG 1045, ABV 4.5%)
A full-bodied, smooth, classic light chestnut-coloured ale with a well-balanced finish.

Pembrokeshire Best Bitter (OG 1045, ABV 4.5%)
A full-flavoured, malty bitter ale with a hoppy finish.

Gyle 59 SIBA

The Brewery, Sadborow Estate Yard, Thorncombe, Dorset, TA20 4PW
☎ (01297) 678990 ☎ 07508 691178 ⊕ gyle59.co.uk

Gyle 59 is a 10-barrel brewery that began commercial production in 2014. Bottling takes place on site with bottles being available by mail order. ‼ 🍺 ♦ RAIB V

Take It Easy (OG 1029, ABV 2.5%)

Freedom Hiker (OG 1038, ABV 3.7%)

Tropical Thunder (OG 1033.7, ABV 3.7%)

Toujours (OG 1042, ABV 4%)

Vienna Session Lager (OG 1040, ABV 4.2%)

Caribbean Cocktail (OG 1043, ABV 4.5%)

Halcyon Daze (OG 1046.5, ABV 5%)

Pale & Bitter (OG 1046, ABV 5%)

IPA (OG 1050, ABV 5.3%)

Dorset Gipa (OG 1050, ABV 5.4%)
A ginger-infused IPA.

Dark & Bitter (OG 1054, ABV 5.8%)

Starstruck (OG 1060, ABV 6.6%)
A fruity porter enhanced by the addition of star anise.

The Favourite (OG 1060, ABV 6.6%)

Double IPA (OG 1063, ABV 7.3%)

Hackney SIBA

Arch 358, Laburnum Street, Haggerston, London, E2 8BB
☎ (020) 3489 9595 ⊕ hackneybrewery.co.uk

⊠ Founded in 2011, Hackney Brewery is the oldest brewery in the area. Weekly cask-conditioned specials are available locally. RAIB

Golden Ale (OG 1041, ABV 4%) ◣
Perfumed hops, honey and fruit balanced by a dry pleasant bitterness that builds as the fruit and hops diminish.

Best Bitter (OG 1044, ABV 4.4%) ◣
Pale brown beer with a sweet citrus aroma and full, smooth mouthfeel. Citrus and floral hops on the palate.

American Pale Ale (OG 1045, ABV 4.5%)

Hadham SIBA

Unit 6C, Hadham Industrial Estate, Church End, Little Hadham, Hertfordshire, SG11 2DY
☎ (01279) 771916 ☎ 07770 766376
⊕ hadhambrewery.co.uk

⊠ Hadham began brewing in 2015 with a 10-barrel plant, using its own spring water found on site. Outlets are supplied within a 25-mile radius of the brewery.

18ct Golden Ale (OG 1038, ABV 3.7%)
Golden ale with a light citrus and fresh hop character; crisp and lightly bitter with some sweetness developing.

First Brewed (OG 1042, ABV 4%)
Reddish brown-coloured best bitter with a fruity, bitter body, caramel notes and a full finish.

Hadrian Border SIBA

Unit 5, The Preserving Works, Newburn Industrial Estate, Shelley Road, Newburn, NE15 9RT
☎ (0191) 264 9000 ⊕ hadrian-border-brewery.co.uk

Based in Newburn near Newcastle-upon-Tyne using a 40-barrel plant, the brewery can produce up to 200 barrels per week. Beer is delivered directly to the area between Edinburgh, North Yorkshire, Carlisle and the East Coast. Beers are also available nationally through wholesalers. A three-barrel plant is used for experimental craft brews. ‼◆RAIB GF

Tyneside Blonde (OG 1039, ABV 3.9%) ◣
Refreshing blonde ale with zesty notes and a clean, fruity finish.

Farne Island Pale Ale (OG 1040, ABV 4%) ◣
A copper-coloured bitter with a refreshing malt/hop balance.

Secret Kingdom (OG 1042, ABV 4.3%)
Dark, rich and full-bodied, slightly roasted with a malty palate ending with a pleasant bitterness.

Coast to Coast (OG 1043, ABV 4.4%)
Light amber-coloured and hoppy beer with a good malt balance.

Reiver's IPA (OG 1043, ABV 4.4%)
Golden bitter with a clean citrus palate and aroma with subtle malt flavours breaking through at the end.

Northumbrian Gold (OG 1044, ABV 4.5%)

Light golden-coloured ale with a biscuit malt flavour countered with floral and aromatic hops.

Grainger Ale (OG 1045, ABV 4.6%)
Gluten free. A pale-coloured ale, well-balanced with a refreshing bitter finish.

Ouseburn Porter (OG 1052, ABV 5.2%) ◣
Traditional robust porter, made with chocolate and black malt. Distinct bitter coffee finish.

Hafod

Old Gas Works, Gas Lane, Mold, CH7 1UR
☎ (01352) 750765 ☎ 07901 386638
⊕ welshbeer.com

☺Hafod began brewing in 2011 on a small scale and moved to new premises in 2014, retaining the original kit for low volume brewing. A number of speciality beers using ingredients from the local upland areas and heathlands are also produced on a limited basis. ‼◆RAIB

Sunrise (OG 1037, ABV 3.8%) ◣
A pale and refreshing golden ale with citrus fruit bitterness evident throughout and a mouthwatering astringent finish.

Moel Famau Ale (OG 1039, ABV 4.1%) ◣
A speciality dark ale brewed using local heather giving a dry, roasty taste with underlying sweet malt flavours.

H:E (OG 1040.5, ABV 4.3%) ◣
A clean-tasting best bitter, pale and hoppy with hints of vanilla in the dry taste.

Hopper (OG 1040.5, ABV 4.3%) ◣
A full-flavoured session bitter with a mouthwatering taste of peppery hops and a lasting dry finish.

Moel Fenlli (OG 1045, ABV 4.4%)
A speciality golden ale made with heather honey.

Landmark (OG 1046, ABV 4.6%)
Copper-coloured ale with juicy malt flavours.

Big Red (OG 1055, ABV 5.5%)

Empyre (OG 1061, ABV 6.1%)

Hammer (OG 1059, ABV 6.6%) ◣
A sweet, strong bitter full of tropical fruits in aroma and taste, balanced by a powerful, hoppy finish.

Dark Times (OG 1069, ABV 6.9%)

Dubbel (OG 1069, ABV 7.2%)
Dark-coloured Belgian trappist-style beer.

Hairy Brewers

Venture Garage, Belper Road, Holbrook, Derbyshire, DE56 0SX ☎ 07415 209489
✉ info@hairybrewersales.co.uk.

Hairy Brewers Ales was established in 2015, with the first brew being released in 2016. The eight-barrel plant was born from two bearded friends and their love for fine ale, with six years of experience already in the brewing trade. Beers are available in the Derbyshire area with an increasing demand further afield.

Hair of the Dog (ABV 3.8%)
Traditional, well-balanced English bitter. Full-bodied and rich on the palate, the malt gives a gentle caramel aroma with a spiced, aromatic, bitter finish.

Blonde Bombshell (ABV 4.3%)
Well-balanced, pale straw-coloured ale with a floral aroma, leading to a citrus taste and a bitter finish.

Fear the Beard (ABV 5%)
A rich copper-coloured ale with a gentle floral aroma and a soft, smooth sweetness. Leading to a bittersweet finish.

Devils Whiskers (ABV 5.2%)

Dead Beard IPA (ABV 5.5%)
Rich, golden-coloured ale with a big grapefruit and mango aroma and a soft, smooth sweetness, leading to a crisp, dry, hoppy and bitter grapefruit finish.

Hale's

See Grafton

Half Moon SIBA 👁

Forge House, Main Street, Ellerton, East Yorkshire, YO42 4PB
☎ (01757) 288977 ☎ 07741 400508
⊕ halfmoonbrewery.co.uk

Established in 2013 by Tony and Jackie Rogers, the brewery is based in the original blacksmith's forge next to their house. A five-barrel plant is used. The brewery welcomes visitors and hosts a bottle shop alongside its taproom. ‼ ☕ ◆

Dark Masquerade (OG 1038, ABV 3.6%)
A rich ruby/brown-coloured ale packed with dark chocolate and liquorice flavours.

Old Forge Bitter (OG 1040, ABV 3.8%)
A bright amber-coloured ale with a soft spiced lemon and honeyed flavour. The hop character is well-balanced with a mellow bitter finish.

F'Hops Sake (OG 1039, ABV 3.9%)
A bright golden ale with a refreshing hit of grapefruit and a good hoppy finish.

Blonde (OG 1038, ABV 4.2%)
A bright blonde ale with a spicy blackcurrant and loganberry aroma and a rounded, fruity bitterness.

Robustus Lunam (OG 1045, ABV 5%)
A dark stout, full bodied with a rich aroma of espresso and treacle. Initial sweetness develops into a dark honeycomb flavour and a smoky bitter finish with a lingering touch of liquorice.

Lunar (OG 1047, ABV 5.5%)
A refreshing golden bitter with an intense hop aroma and fine malt flavour. Hints of caramel followed by a floral hop aftertaste.

Halfpenny

🍺 **Crown Inn, High Street, Lechlade, Gloucestershire, GL7 3AE**
☎ (01367) 252198 ⊕ halfpennybrewery.co.uk

Halfpenny was established in 2008 on a four-barrel plant at the Crown at Lechlade, visible in a glazed outbuilding. Beers are mainly brewed for the pub but some appear in the local free trade. Brewing is currently suspended.

Halifax Steam

🍺 **The Conclave, v, Hipperholme, West Yorkshire, HX3 8EF** ☎ 07506 022504 ⊕ halifax-steam.co.uk

Brewing since 1999, the five-barrel plant supplies only the brewery tap, the Cock o' the North. A range of permanent beers and around 200 different rotating beers are brewed, including the only rice beers in the country. 10-12 Halifax Steam beers are available in the pub at any one time, plus occasional guests on a fair trade basis.

Hall & Woodhouse (Badger) IFBB 👁

Bournemouth Road, Blandford St Mary, Blandford Forum, Dorset, DT11 9LS
☎ (01258) 452141 ⊕ hall-woodhouse.co.uk

⊠ Hall & Woodhouse has been brewing in the heart of the Dorset countryside since 1777. As one of the leading independent brewers in the UK, Hall & Woodhouse is well known for its range of award-winning ales brewed under the Badger brand and its estate of around 190 pubs across the south of England. The brewery, owned and run by the seventh generation of the Woodhouse family, brews with Dorset spring water filtered through the Cretaceous chalk downs and drawn-up 120 feet from its own wells. Badger cask ales are available exclusively in Hall & Woodhouse public houses. Bi-monthly seasonal ales are also available. ‼ ☕ ◆

Best Bitter (ABV 3.7%)
Refreshing auburn-coloured beer with a subtle, yet defined, floral hop character.

Fursty Ferret (ABV 4.1%)
A sweet, nutty palate, hoppy aroma and a hint of Seville oranges give this tawny amber-coloured ale its distinctive personality.

Tanglefoot (ABV 4.9%) 🥄
Relatively sweet-tasting and deceptive, given its strength. Pale malt provides caramel overtones and a bittersweet finish.

Hambleton SIBA 👁

Melmerby Green Road, Melmerby, North Yorkshire, HG4 5NB
☎ (01765) 640108 ⊕ hambletonales.co.uk

⊚ Established in 1991 on the banks of the River Swale in the Vale of York, after several moves Hambleton now occupies purpose-built premises. Capacity is 100 barrels a week with a monthly special supplementing the core range. Village Brewer and Black Dog beers are contract brewed and a bottling line handles brands for other brewers. ‼ ◆ GF

Session Pale (OG 1036, ABV 3.6%)
A golden-coloured bitter with a good balance of malty and refreshing citrus notes leading to a mellow, tangy finish.

Stallion Amber (OG 1041, ABV 4.2%) 🥄
A premium bitter, moderately hoppy throughout and richly balanced in malt and fruit, developing a sound and robust bitterness, with earthy hops drying the aftertaste.

Stud Blonde (OG 1042.5, ABV 4.3%) 🥄
A strongly bitter beer, with rich hop and fruit. It ends dry and spicy.

Nightmare Porter (OG 1050, ABV 5%) 🥄

This impressively flavoured beer satisfies all parts of the palate. Strong roast malts dominate, but hoppiness rears out of this complex blend.

Contract brewed for Black Dog Brewery, Whitby:

Whitby Abbey Ale (OG 1037.5, ABV 3.8%)

Schooner (OG 1041.5, ABV 4.2%)

Rhatas (OG 1045, ABV 4.6%)

Contract brewed for Village Brewer:

White Boar (OG 1037.5, ABV 3.8%)

Bull (OG 1039, ABV 4%)

Hamelsworde

41b Kirkby Road, Hemsworth, West Yorkshire, WF9 4BA ☎ 07530 669332 ⊕ hamelsworde.co.uk

☺The brainchild of enthusiastic home brewer Dan Jones, his beers were originally brewed using a 50-litre boiler in a converted garage. A one-barrel plant was installed in 2013, which has now been moved into a converted shop with a tap house at the front. ‼♦RAIB

Spanish Stout (OG 1045, ABV 4.2%)
A traditional stout with strong roasted flavours and a sweet liquorice taste complemented by aniseed.

Haley's Comet (OG 1047, ABV 4.5%)
A fresh, light ale with a citrus aroma and taste.

Jumping Pirate (OG 1051, ABV 4.9%)
A light golden-coloured ale in a Bavarian style with floral, pine and citrus notes. Complex but smooth on the finish.

Colin Brown Ale (OG 1054, ABV 5.2%)
A deep amber/red-coloured beer. A fruity hop aroma leads onto a malty, nutty, bittersweet flavour with a long, dry aftertaste, while the late hop addition creates a citrus burst.

Scalded Shoulder (OG 1054, ABV 5.2%)
A single-hop golden wheat beer finished with coriander and orange.

Cherokee America IPA (OG 1063, ABV 6%)
A copper-coloured IPA with a strong, fruity hop aroma.

Hammerpot SIBA

Unit 30, The Vinery, Arundel Road, Poling, West Sussex, BN18 9PY
☎ (01903) 883338 ⊕ hammerpot-brewery.co.uk

⊠ Hammerpot started brewing in 2005 using a five-barrel plant, which was upgraded to 10 barrels in 2011. The brewery supplies as far as London and Southampton. ♦RAIB

Shooting Star (OG 1038, ABV 3.8%)

HPA (OG 1044, ABV 4.1%)
A light, golden-coloured, tangy pale ale with a full, fresh hop flavour.

Red Hunter (OG 1046, ABV 4.3%)
A ruby red-coloured bitter with a full-bodied, rich character.

Woodcote (OG 1047, ABV 4.5%)
A tangy, amber-coloured bitter with a pleasant, dry finish.

Brighton Belle (ABV 4.6%)
Pale amber-coloured bitter. Fresh floral hop notes, spicy orange, crisp grapefruit and a hint of caramel.

Bottle Wreck Porter (OG 1047, ABV 4.7%)
A traditional pitch black porter with coffee, chocolate and rich roast malt flavours.

Madgwick Gold (OG 1050, ABV 5%)
A golden ale with a fresh citrus spice hop aroma.

Hammerton SIBA ☺

Unit 8 & 9, Roman Way Industrial Estate, 149 Roman Way, Barnsbury, London, N7 8XH
☎ (020) 3302 5880 ⊕ hammertonbrewery.co.uk

Hammerton began brewing in London in 1868. It ceased to brew in the late 1950s and the brewery was later demolished. In 2014, a member of the Hammerton family decided to resurrect the family name in brewing. A 15-barrel plant is used. RAIB

N1 (OG 1044, ABV 4.1%) ◗
Refreshing, smooth pale ale. Honey, some citrus and pineapple flavours, fading in the finish where a spicy, hoppy bitterness builds.

Life on Mars (OG 1045, ABV 4.6%) ◗
Ruby-coloured ale with roast, toffee and fruit aroma. Peppery hops, nutty roasty flavour with dark bitter marmalade. Dry, lingering finish.

N7 (OG 1052, ABV 5.2%) ◗
Cocoa throughout with a pleasant sweetness, balanced by a lingering dark-roast dryness and a raisin fruitiness. A trace of liquorice.

Pentonville Oyster Stout (OG 1057, ABV 5.3%) ◗
Liquorice and fruit on the palate. Dry finish with a little dark roast character and a touch of caramelised fruit.

Hand SIBA

▤ 33 Upper St James's Street, Kemptown, Brighton, East Sussex, BN2 1JN
☎ (01273) 699595 ☎ 07508 814541
⊕ handbrewpub.com/brew

Founded in 1989, the brewery is the smallest commercially operating tower brewery in the world. Originally operating under the Kemptown Brewery name before being used as a gypsy brewery by Brighton Bier for four years. Now operating as the Hand Brew Co since 2016. Around 10 other outlets are supplied.

Pale Ale (ABV 4%)

Irish Red (ABV 4.4%)

Tomahawk Chop (ABV 5%)

Quicker Than The Eye (ABV 5.4%)

Handley's

▤ Willow Tree, Front Street, Barnby in the Willows, Nottinghamshire, NG24 2SA
⊕ willowtreebarnby.co.uk

Handley's began brewing in 2011 on a 0.5-barrel plant installed behind the Willow Tree pub. Beer is mostly sold in the pub, with at least two being on pump at all times, and can occasionally be found at local beer festivals.

Handsome (NEW)

Bowston Bridge Garage, Bowston, Cumbria, LA8 9HD
☎ 0344 848 0888 ⊕ handsomebrew.co.uk

Originally Houston Brewery in Renfrewshire, it was re-established as Handsome in 2016 in the Lake District. It is situated on the River Kent in an old MOT garage, formerly the blacksmith's for James Cropper's paper mills.

Top Knot (ABV 3.7%)

Peter's Well (ABV 4.2%)

Stranger (ABV 4.2%)

Bar Steward (ABV 4.4%)

Blacksmith (ABV 4.6%)

FKR (ABV 4.8%)

Hanging Bat

c/o 133 Lothian Road, Edinburgh, EH3 9AB
☎ (0131) 229 0759
⊕ hangingbatbrewco.tumblr.com

Brewing began in 2012 from within the Hanging Bat bar using a 50-litre brew kit from the United States. No regular range available.

Hanlons SIBA 👁

Hill Farm, Half Moon Village, Newton St Cyres, Half Moon Village, EX5 5AE
☎ (01392) 851160 ⊕ hanlonsbrewery.com

⊠ Formerly known as O'Hanlons, the brewery moved to Half Moon, near Exeter, in 2013. The building comprises a shop, bar and restaurant. !! ⇌ ♦

Firefly (OG 1038, ABV 3.7%) ◗
Malty and fruity light bitter. Hints of orange in the taste.

Dry Stout (OG 1043, ABV 4.2%) ◗
A dark malty, well-balanced stout with a dry, bitter finish and plenty of roast and fruit flavours up front.

Yellowhammer (OG 1041, ABV 4.2%) ◗
Golden ale dominated by hops and fruit throughout. Sweetness develops through to a lingering aftertaste.

Port Stout (OG 1048, ABV 4.8%) ◗
Complex black beer. Malt and fruit dominate throughout. Fruit and caramel develop. Rich and smooth.

Stormstay (OG 1050, ABV 5%) ◗
Tawny-coloured and full-bodied. Caramel with hints of malt on the nose. Triumvirate of malt, caramel and hops develop into lingering bitterness.

Happy Valley SIBA

8 Hazelhurst Drive, Bollington, Cheshire, SK10 5QT
☎ 07758 512080 ⊕ happyvalleybrewery.co.uk

⊠ Happy Valley was established in 2010 by David and Nicola Hughes using a 2.5-barrel plant. Pubs are supplied in Cheshire, Derbyshire, Greater Manchester and Staffordshire. !! ♦

Little Mill Town (OG 1036, ABV 3.6%)

Small & Mighty (OG 1036, ABV 3.6%)
A clean, crisp and refreshing ale with a lasting, floral, citrus aroma and a hint of lemon.

Sworn Secret (OG 1038, ABV 3.8%)
Pale straw-coloured ale with a strong hop character. A pleasant hoppy nose with a citrus aftertaste.

Little Rascal (OG 1039, ABV 3.9%)
A light golden-coloured session ale. Well-balanced with a lingering citrus and grapefruit aftertaste.

Five Rings (OG 1040, ABV 4%)
Crisp, clean-tasting ale brewed with three aroma hops.

Lazy Daze (OG 1042, ABV 4.2%)
Golden-coloured ale made with a hoppy finish.

Black Out XO Rum Porter (OG 1044, ABV 4.4%)
A full-bodied porter with a deep malty flavour. Dark roasted and chocolate malts with a lingering aroma of Barbadian oak-aged rum.

Black Magic (OG 1046, ABV 4.6%)

Tie the Knot (OG 1050, ABV 5%)
A straw-coloured strong bitter with malt tastes and a big hop character.

Dangerously Dark (OG 1056, ABV 5.6%)

Bollywood IPA (OG 1058, ABV 5.9%)
A full-bodied, straw-coloured strong bitter with rounded malt flavours blended with bitterness and a big hop character. A deep and intensely rich taste.

Harbour SIBA

Trekillick Farm, Kirland, Bodmin, Cornwall, PL30 5BB
☎ (01208) 832131 ☎ 07870 305063
⊕ harbourbrewing.com

⊠ Harbour is an innovative brewery founded on the outskirts of Bodmin in 2011. Brewed using local spring water, the regular beers are established in an increasing number of outlets. A new 30-barrel plant was installed in 2016. ♦

Light (OG 1037, ABV 3.7%) ◗
Light, golden ale with hop aroma. Hops dominate the taste with some pineapple, citrus and pear drops. Hoppy, dry finish.

Daymer Extra Pale (ABV 3.8%)

Amber (OG 1037.5, ABV 4%) ◗
Pale brown-coloured bitter with a floral hop aroma. Peach and citrus flavours with biscuit malt. Quite sweet taste and finish.

Cornish Bitter (ABV 4%)

New Zealand Gold (ABV 4.2%) ◗
Golden ale with light hop nose. Strong pine needle hop flavour. Bitter, sweet and dry throughout.

Ellensberg (ABV 4.3%)

Session IPA (OG 1043, ABV 4.3%)

India Brown Ale (OG 1049, ABV 4.9%) ◗
Smooth, copper-coloured strong bitter. Heavy body and balanced sweet malt and bitter hop flavour, with plums, prunes and some butterscotch.

IPA (OG 1048.5, ABV 5%) ◗
Amber-coloured strong bitter-cum-golden ale with heady citrus hop aroma. Hoppy bitter taste and finish with citrus fruits but subdued malt.

Cascadia (ABV 5.2%)

Light no2 (ABV 5.2%)

Antipodean IPA (ABV 5.5%)

Little Rock IPA (ABV 5.5%)

Porter (OG 1055, ABV 5.5%) ◗

Smooth, creamy, black porter with roast malt aroma. Malty, smoky and sweet followed by a bitter tang. Sweet finish.

Pale (OG 1059, ABV 6%) ◣
Amber-coloured ale with a powerful citrus hop aroma. Intense citrus hop flavour with marmalade, orange and bitterness. Hoppy, dry finish.

Harbwr Tenby

Sargeants Lane, St Julian Street, Tenby, SA70 7BU
☎ (01834) 845797 ⊕ harbwr.wales

Brewing commenced in 2015 on a five-barrel plant in an outbuilding of the Buccaneer Inn, Tenby. Beers are available in the pub, at the nearby Hope & Anchor and further afield. A mezzanine bar area is available for tastings, tapas and tours. ‼◆

MV Enterprise (OG 1040, ABV 4%)
A citrus pale ale with spicy, herbal bitterness finished with a floral and zesty aroma.

North Star (OG 1042, ABV 4.2%)
Smooth, malty, amber-coloured ale blending herbal bitterness with a spicy blackcurrant and lemon aroma.

Caldey Lollipop (OG 1044, ABV 4.5%)
Hoppy, golden-coloured IPA with hints of pine and grapefruit blended with New World hop aroma.

RFA Sir Galahad (OG 1046, ABV 4.6%)
A rich, ruby-coloured beer with a deep, complex malt character. Four different hop varieties provide cedar, grapefruit and floral aromas.

Harby

🍾 Bottle & Glass, 5 High Street, Harby, Nottinghamshire, NG23 7EB
☎ (01522) 703438
✉ email@bottleandglassharby.com

Harby Brewstore is a four-barrel malt extract brewery established in 2015 and located at the Bottle & Glass in Harby. Most output goes to the three pubs in the small Wig & Mitre pub group; the Wig & Mitre, Lincoln, Caunton Beck, Caunton and the Bottle & Glass itself.

Hardknott SIBA

Unit 10, Devonshire Road Industrial Estate, Millom, Cumbria, LA18 4JS
☎ (01229) 779309 ⊕ hardknott.com

Hardknott began brewing in 2005 at the Woolpack Inn in Boot. The brewery relocated to Millom and expanded in 2010. It supplies beers both nationally and internationally, in a variety of formats. The 16-hectolitre brewhouse is complemented with modern multi-purpose fermentation tanks and a bottling line. ‼◆RAIB

Light Cascade (OG 1030, ABV 3.4%)

Katalyst (OG 1034, ABV 3.8%) ◣
An assertively hoppy, bitter beer, with a sweet, fruity taste which diminishes in the finish.

Lux Borealis (OG 1034, ABV 3.8%) ◣
Fruity, hoppy aromas lead to a well-balanced middle with hops increasing in the finish.

Continuum (OG 1036, ABV 4%) ◣

An amber-coloured beer with pronounced hops and bitterness through to the aftertaste. Some maltiness in the aroma and taste.

Cool Fusion (OG 1043, ABV 4.4%)
A pale straw-coloured beer with a hint of ginger and a mild finish.

Brownian Motion (OG 1042, ABV 4.5%)

Nuclear Sunset (OG 1039, ABV 4.7%)
A wheat beer made with orange peel, orange juice, coriander and nutmeg.

Long Drop (ABV 4.8%)

Dark Energy (OG 1046, ABV 4.9%) ◣
A hoppy aroma leads to a dry hoppy beer with plenty of roast.

Intergalactic Space Hopper (OG 1045, ABV 5.2%)

Code Black (OG 1052, ABV 5.6%) ◣
High impact hops and roast malt leave a lasting impression.

Azimuth (OG 1051, ABV 5.8%) ◣
Floral and fruity esters and lots of interesting hops with complex bitterness.

Infra Red (OG 1058, ABV 6.2%)
Hints of toffee and popcorn. Citrus fruits dominate.

Hardys & Hansons

See Greene King

Haresfoot SIBA

Global Infusion Court, Nashleigh Hill, Chesham, Buckinghamshire, HP5 3FE
☎ (01494) 790783 ⊕ haresfoot.com

⊠ Established in Berkhamsted in 2014, the move to the current site in 2017 brought brewing back to the town of Chesham after an absence of 60 years. As well as the regular beers, a range of short run, limited edition beers under the Crafty Hare brand are brewed using a dual-channel 12- and 2.5-barrel plant. Beers can be found across the Chiltern area and London. ◆

Wild Boy (OG 1037.5, ABV 3.7%)
A modern pale ale hopped to give floral and citrus aromas. Smooth malt and vanilla in the mouth give way to long, bittersweet notes.

Sundial Golden Ale (OG 1038, ABV 3.8%)
A refreshing light golden ale with an undercurrent of exotic fruits.

Lock Keeper's Launch Ale (OG 1039, ABV 3.9%)
A complex blend of malts with a hoppy edge and delicate fruit notes, leading to a long, bittersweet aftertaste.

Stardust (OG 1042.5, ABV 4.2%)
A red-coloured beer with fruit and floral aromas and a nutty sweetness rounded off with a crisp finish.

Conqueror's Premium Bitter (OG 1043, ABV 4.4%)
A full-bodied bitter with roasted barley creating a chestnut-coloured ale with a lingering malty taste and rounded bitter finish.

Totem American IPA (OG 1042, ABV 4.5%)
American-style IPA with citrus flavours and hop aromas balanced by subtle malt character.

Old Tiney (OG 1049, ABV 4.8%)

A deep, dark porter with a well-rounded richness. An undertone of natural plum is balanced by the hops.

Harrogate SIBA

41 Claro Court Business Centre, Harrogate, North Yorkshire, HG1 4BA ☎ 07774 891664 ⊕ harrogatebrewery.co.uk

Started in 2013, the brewery also uses the names Spa Town Ales and It's Quicker By Ale on its logo and pumpclips. The brewery has a capacity of four barrels and brews several times each week.

Pale (OG 1040, ABV 4.2%)
A single hopped session ale.

Cold Bath Gold (OG 1042, ABV 4.4%)

Pinewoods Pale Ale (OG 1044, ABV 4.4%)
Pale beer with citrus flavours.

Vanilla Porter (OG 1048, ABV 4.8%)
Rich porter with added vanilla pods.

No. 5 Porter (OG 1053, ABV 5.3%)
A rich, fruity dark beer, ruby brown in colour with roasted malt, fruit and spice.

Kursaal Porter (OG 1054, ABV 5.4%)
A rich, bittersweet porter tasting of espresso, liquorice and chocolate.

Hart Family

The 1833 Brewery, 21 Nene Court, The Embankment, Wellingborough, Northamptonshire, NN8 1LD ☎ (01933) 228324 ☎ 07891 212476 ⊕ hartfamilybrewers.com

⊠ Hart Family Brewers was established in 2012 using an eight-barrel plant. It is owned and operated by Rob and Sarah Hart, who are indulging their passion after a combined 25 years in the drinks industry. Recent expansion, including a third fermenter, gives weekly production of up to 38 barrels. ‼ ☞ ◆ RAIB

House Beer (OG 1036, ABV 3.6%)
A classic country bitter with straightforward flavours of British malt and English hops.

Harts No. 1 (OG 1043, ABV 4.1%)
A tawny-coloured premium bitter with fruity, malty aromas and grassy citrus notes. Fresh and fruity on the palate with spicy bitterness and citrus, hay-like aromas on the finish.

Harts No. 9 (OG 1044, ABV 4.3%)
A golden-coloured beer with spicy grapefruit aromas. Fresh and light on the palate with pithy grapefruit flavours supported by biscuity malt.

Harts No. 3 (OG 1047, ABV 4.7%)
A fruity, ruby-coloured beer with full malty, spicy aromas. Full and forward on the palate with rounded, rich malty flavours supported by gentle spicy hoppiness.

Harts No. 8 (OG 1052, ABV 5%)
A dark-coloured beer with toasted fruit aromas and hints of espresso. Full and warming roasted fruit and molasses flavours balanced by bitter coffee, chocolate and spice aromas over a long finish.

Pale (OG 1052, ABV 5%)
Strong bitter beer. Biscuity malt complemented by a marked orange-scented bitterness.

1833 India Pale Ale (ABV 6.6%) ◆

Hart SIBA

Unit 5, Oxhey Trading Estate, Greenbank Street, Preston, Lancashire, PR1 7PH ☎ (01282) 616192

Office: Unit 1, Riverside Works, Brunswick Street, Nelson, BB9 0HZ ⊕ lancashirebeer.co.uk

Formerly known as Hart, brewing began in 1995 in Little Eccleston and moved to Preston in 2010. Brewing ceased in 2016 and in 2017 it was sold to the Lancashire Beer Company, a pub supplies wholesaler in Nelson, Lancs. Hart's ex-owner John Smith has been retained to brew most of the previous range of beers.

Citra (OG 1038, ABV 3.8%)

Spring Gold (OG 1038, ABV 3.8%)

Lancashire Best Bitter (OG 1039, ABV 3.9%)

Ice Maiden (OG 1040, ABV 4%) ◆
Hoppy, crisp, straw-coloured bitter with floral notes and a dry finish.

Lord of the Glen (OG 1042, ABV 4.2%)

Hart of Stebbing

🍺 **White Hart, High Street, Stebbing, Essex, CM6 3SQ** ☎ (01371) 856383 ✉ nickeldred@hotmail.com

The brewery was established in 2007 by Nick Eldred, who is also the owner of the White Hart pub where the brewery is based. At present only the White Hart and local beer festivals are supplied.

Hartshorns

Unit 4, Tomlinsons Industrial Estate, Alfreton Road, Derby, DE21 4ED ☎ 07830 367125 ⊕ hartshornsbrewery.com

⊠ Hartshorns began brewing in 2012 using a six-barrel plant installed by brothers Darren and Lindsey Hartshorn. In 2015 the brewery acquired its first pub, the Little Chester Ale House, Derby. ☞

Ignite (OG 1039, ABV 3.9%)

Highgate (OG 1044, ABV 4.3%)
Smooth, easy-drinking, pale copper-coloured ale. Perfectly balanced malt sweetness with fruity hop flavour and a well-rounded bitterness.

Porter (OG 1045, ABV 4.5%)

Brooklyn Nights (OG 1052, ABV 5.4%)
A punchy American brown ale with a complex malt base, assertive bitterness and a clean, dry finish.

Shakademus (OG 1052, ABV 5.4%)
Full-bodied with a citrus hop bite, a satisfying premium golden ale.

Apocalypse (OG 1055, ABV 6.2%)
Surprisingly easy-drinking golden ale with a clean bitter finish. Refreshingly crisp and packed with hop character.

Harvey's IFBB ◉

Bridge Wharf Brewery, 6 Cliffe High Street, Lewes, East Sussex, BN7 2AH ☎ (01273) 480209 ⊕ harveys.org.uk

A golden amber-coloured beer with a honey malt and orange marmalade hop aroma, a strong malt, marmalade and spice taste, with a dry bitter finish.

⊗ Established in 1790, this independent family brewery operates from the banks of the River Ouse in Lewes. A major development in 1985 doubled the brewhouse capacity and subsequent additional fermenting capacity has seen production rise to more than 38,000 barrels a year. There is also a microbrewery on site used to brew special beers including replicating old Lewes Brewery recipes using the County Town Beers name. Harveys supplies real ale to all its 48 pubs and 550 free trade outlets in the south-east. ‼ ⬛ ♦ RAIB

R (ABV 2.8%)

Sussex XX Mild Ale (OG 1030, ABV 3%) ◄
A dark copper-brown colour. Roast malt dominates the aroma and palate leading to a sweet, caramel finish.

IPA (OG 1033, ABV 3.5%)

Sussex Wild Hop (OG 1037, ABV 3.7%)

Sussex Best Bitter (OG 1040, ABV 4%) ◄
Full-bodied brown bitter. A hoppy aroma leads to a good malt and hop balance, and a dry aftertaste.

Old Ale (OG 1043, ABV 4.3%)

Olympia (OG 1042, ABV 4.3%)

Armada Ale (OG 1045, ABV 4.5%) ◄
Hoppy, amber-coloured best bitter. Well-balanced fruit and hops dominate throughout with a fruity palate.

Harviestoun SIBA ◉

Alva Industrial Estate, Alva, FK12 5DQ
☎ (01259) 769100 ⊕ harviestoun.com

Harviestoun has grown from one-man brewing in a bucket in the back of a shed in 1983 to a 60-barrel, multi-award-winning brewery today. With a reputation for experimentation, the brewery adds around eight to ten short-run seasonals to its core range of two ales. ‼ ⬛ ♦ RAIB

Bitter & Twisted (OG 1039, ABV 3.8%) ◄
Refreshingly hoppy beer with fruit throughout. A bittersweet taste with a long bitter finish. A golden session beer.

Schiehallion (OG 1048, ABV 4.8%) 🗂 ◄
A Scottish cask lager, brewed using a lager yeast and Hersbrucker hops. A hoppy aroma, with fruit and malt, leads to a malty, bitter taste with floral hoppiness and a bitter finish.

Harwich Town

Station Approach, Harwich, Essex, CO12 3NA
☎ (01255) 551155 ⊕ harwichtown.co.uk

Brewing started in 2007 on a five-barrel plant next to Harwich Town railway station. The brewer is a CAMRA member and former customs officer. Beers are named after local landmarks, characters or events. 50 outlets are supplied. The brewery holds a beer festival in July and a festival special is brewed for the Harwich & Dovercourt Bay Winter Ale Festival in December. ‼ ⬛ ♦ RAIB

Bay Bitter (OG 1036, ABV 3.6%)

Ha'Penny Mild (OG 1036, ABV 3.6%)

EPA 100 (OG 1038, ABV 3.8%)

Leading Lights (OG 1038, ABV 3.8%)

Ganges (OG 1040, ABV 4%)

Misleading Lights (OG 1040, ABV 4%)

Bathside Battery Bitter (OG 1042, ABV 4.2%)

Redoubt Stout (OG 1042, ABV 4.2%)

Parkeston Porter (OG 1045, ABV 4.5%)

Lighthouse Bitter (OG 1048, ABV 4.8%)

Phoenix APA (OG 1052, ABV 5%)

Hastings

Unit 12, Conqueror Industrial Estate, Moorhurst Road, St Leonards-on-Sea, East Sussex, TN38 9NB
☎ (01424) 572050 ⊕ hastingsbrewery.co.uk

⊗ Hastings is a small five-barrel brewery established in 2010, exclusively producing unfined beers suitable for vegetarians and vegans. Brewing is currently suspended. RAIB

Hattie Brown's

Unit 1, The Sidings, Victoria Avenue Industrial Estate, Swanage, Dorset, BH19 1AU
☎ (01929) 439229

⊗ Hattie Brown's began brewing in 2014 at Wessex brewery. In 2015 it moved to its present location. Beers are produced for the Square & Compass in Worth Matravers, and occasionally for local beer festivals. ♦

HBA (OG 1039, ABV 3.8%)
A well-balanced, copper-coloured, lightly malted beer.

Moonlite (OG 039, ABV 3.8%)
A hoppy pale ale with strong citrus notes and a big finish.

Hawk Hill (NEW)

5 Sugarhouse Wynd, Dundee, DD1 2SH

Brewing began in 2016.

Red Falcon (OG 1046, ABV 4.5%)

Scuttlebutt IPA (OG 1060, ABV 6%)

Hawkshead SIBA ◉

Mill Yard, Staveley, Cumbria, LA8 9LR
☎ (01539) 822644 ⊕ hawksheadbrewery.co.uk

◉ The brewery takes its name from the village in which it was founded in 2002. It outgrew its original barn and moved to Staveley in 2006 to a purpose-built 20-barrel brewery. Capacity has been increased several times since, a new micro packaging plant added and the Beer Hall, brewery tap, developed as a showcase for real ale. In 2017 Hawkshead signed a deal with Halewood International that will triple capacity. Packaged beers will be sold globally but founder Alex Brodie and his team remain in control of draught beer production. ‼ ⬛ ♦ RAIB

Iti (OG 1036, ABV 3.5%) ◄
A beer packed with grapefruit aroma and taste. Beautifully balanced with a long-lasting, hoppy, bitter finish.

Windermere Pale (OG 1036, ABV 3.5%) 🍺 ◄
Crisp and fruity yellow-coloured beer with hints of melon and grapefruit and a strong bitter aftertaste.

Bitter (OG 1037, ABV 3.7%) 🗂 ◄

THE BREWERIES

Well-balanced, thirst-quenching beer with fruit and hops aroma, leading to a lasting bitter finish.

Red (OG 1042, ABV 4.2%) ◄
An impressive colour for this richly-flavoured beer; lots of fruitiness and good hop flavour with a lingering aftertaste.

Lakeland Gold (OG 1043, ABV 4.4%) ◄
Fresh, well-balanced fruity, hoppy beer with a clean bitter aftertaste.

Dry Stone Stout (OG 1044, ABV 4.5%) ◄
Black, dry, bitter stout with an astringent, roast finish.

Great White (OG 1048, ABV 4.8%)
A spiced wheat beer brewed with coriander seeds and Seville orange peel. Served cloudy.

Brodie's Prime (OG 1048, ABV 4.9%) ◄
Complex, dark brown-coloured beer with plenty of malt, fruit and roast taste. Satisfying full body with clean finish.

Cumbrian Five Hop (OG 1050, ABV 5%) ◄
A robust, hoppy bitter with citrus hops and fruity middle.

Lakeland Lager (OG 1045, ABV 5%)

NZPA (OG 1056, ABV 6%) ◄
A hoppy bitter with a sweet, fruity taste and a resounding dry bitter finish.

IPA (OG 1065, ABV 7%)
A modern IPA, amber in colour, with huge hop flavours.

Haworth Steam

Rose & Crown, 2 Westgate, Cleckheaton, West Yorkshire, BD19 5ET
☎ (01535) 646059 ☎ 07974 483310
⊕ haworthsteambrewery.co.uk

Established in 2011, beer is brewed at the Rose & Crown in Cleckheaton.

Hay Rake

Blackstone Edge Old Road, Littleborough, OL15 0JX
☎ (01706) 379689 ☎ 07775 792684
⊕ hayrakebrewery.info

Mark Wickham, the landlord of the Rake Tapas Restaurant, resurrected the Hay Rake microbrewery in 2013. The Rake brewed its own beer during the reign of Queen Victoria but stopped in 1901. Beers are available in the restaurant, occasionally the nearby White House and at local beer festivals.

Dawn's Hopping Mad (OG 1038, ABV 3.8%)
A blend of five hops with a hint of chilli and ginger.

Dawn's Called Thyme (OG 1040, ABV 4%)
Citrus with a blend of thyme and fresh peaches.

Early Dawn (OG 1041, ABV 4.1%)
An IPA with a hint of honey and lemongrass.

Dawn's Dark Side (OG 1044, ABV 4.4%)
A blend of four hops with molasses and coriander.

Dawn's Autumn Gold (OG 1045, ABV 4.5%)
A blend of four hops with a hint of liquorice and golden syrup.

Haywood Bad Ram SIBA

Callow Top Holiday Park, Buxton Road, Sandybrook, Ashbourne, Derbyshire, DE6 2AQ
☎ (01335) 344020 ☎ 07974 948427
⊕ callowtop.co.uk/ccallow-top-brewery

⊠ Established in 2003, the brewery was based in a converted barn but a new brewery and bottling plant became operational in 2012. One pub is owned (on site) and several other outlets are supplied. ‼ ⋿ RAIB

Thoroughbred Bad Ram (OG 1038, ABV 3.8%)
A refreshing, straw-coloured ale with a crisp bite and spice and flowery notes.

Dr Samuel Johnson (OG 1044, ABV 4.5%)
A slightly fruity and refined spicy flavour.

Callow Top Imperial IPA (OG 1050, ABV 5.2%)
A full-bodied, rich ale with a fruity and slightly citrus aftertaste.

Healey's

Wellington Inn, Main Street, Loppergarth, Cumbria, LA12 0JL
☎ (01229) 582388

Healey's began brewing in the Wellington in 2012 using a custom-made 2.5-barrel stainless steel plant, which can be viewed through full-length windows in the pub. A range of different beer styles is brewed, available in more than 15 pubs.

Heaney Farmhouse (NEW)

c/o Boundary Brewing, Portview Trade Centre, Newtownards Road, Belfast, BT4 1HE
⊕ heaneyfarmhousebrewing.com

Founded in 2014. Bottled beers are currently brewed at Boundary (qv) in Belfast while its brewhouse project is underway at a farm in Bellaghy, Co Londonderry. No real ale.

Heart of Wales

Stables Yard, Zion Street, Llanwrtyd Wells, LD5 4RD
☎ (01591) 610236 ⊕ heartofwalesbrewery.co.uk

The brewery was set up with a six-barrel plant in 2006 in old stables at the rear of the Neuadd Arms Hotel. Beers are brewed using water from the brewery's own borehole. Cambrian Heart Ale was commissioned by and is brewed for the Cambrian Mountains Initiative, inspired by the Prince of Wales, which aims to promote and support rural producers and communities in the region.

Heathen

Grape & Grain, 51 The Broadway, Haywards Heath, West Sussex, RH16 3AS
☎ (01444) 456217 ☎ 07825 429428
⊕ heathenbrewers.co.uk

Located in the basement of the Grape & Grain off-licence and delicatessen, brewing began in 2014 using a full mash, two-barrel plant. Local outlets and beer festivals are supplied. ‼ ♦ RAIB

ISA (OG 1040, ABV 3.9%)

ipaD (OG 1055, ABV 4.5%)

Farmhouse (OG 1048, ABV 4.7%)
A Belgian-style hazy IPA.

Porter (OG 1055, ABV 5%)

Pale (OG 1050, ABV 5.3%)

West Coast (OG 1049, ABV 5.4%)

Iceni Genie (OG 1057, ABV 5.5%)

Hopler Effect (OG 1058, ABV 5.8%)
A full-hopped, full-bodied pale ale.

Honey (OG 1060, ABV 6%)
An IPA with copious amounts of Greek honey.

Heathton

c/o Old Gate, Heathton, Shropshire, WV5 7EB

This brewery is planned to be resurrected at the Old Gate pub, but its three beers are produced at present in three different breweries, and served only in the Old Gate. Brewing is currently suspended.

Heavy Industry SIBA

The Old Slaughterhouse, Denbigh Street, Henllan, LL16 5AR
☎ (01745) 814655 ☎ 07813 024161
⊕ heavyindustrybrewing.com

Established in 2012, Heavy Industry is an award-winning brewery using a 10-barrel plant situated in an old slaughterhouse in the village of Henllan. ♦

Diawl Bach (OG 1036.5, ABV 3.8%) ◈
Citrus fruit flavours feature strongly in this uncompromising, hoppy bitter. The acerbic, tart taste continues long into the aftertaste.

Electric Mountain (OG 1036.5, ABV 3.8%) ▪ ◈
A full-bodied session bitter, dry and well-balanced with a satisfying hoppy finish.

Nelsons Eye (OG 1041, ABV 4.4%) ▪ ◈
Heavily-hopped with a strong, sharp bitter taste. Citrus fruit notes, mainly grapefruit, in the aroma and palate continue into the hoppy, bitter aftertaste.

Freak Chick (OG 1042, ABV 4.5%) ◈
A well-balanced dark best bitter, initially sweet with caramel undertones complemented by hoppy bitterness in the aftertaste.

77 (OG 1046, ABV 4.9%) ▯ ◈
A strong bitter with a powerful smack of fruit and hops. Tangy fruit flavours and hoppy bitterness feature strongly in the aroma, taste and finish.

Collaborator (OG 1046, ABV 5%) ▪ ◈
A smooth and satisfying dark, hoppy beer. The juicy malty taste is quite roasty and leads to a dry, hoppy aftertaste.

Pigeon Toed Orange Peel (OG 1048.5, ABV 5.2%) ◈
A naturally hazy half wheat beer with a strong orange fruit aroma and taste and a tangy, hoppy, bitter finish.

Nos Smoked Porter (OG 1055.5, ABV 5.5%)
A dark porter, wreaths of smoke mingle with coffee and roast notes.

Hebridean

10 Shell St, Stornoway, Isle of Lewis, HS1 2BS
☎ (01851) 700123 ⊕ hebridean-brewery.co.uk

☺Hebridean relocated its 14-barrel brew plant just around the corner to new premises in 2016 and now includes and on-site bar and shop. ☛

Celtic Black Ale (OG 1036, ABV 3.9%)
A dark ale full of flavour, balancing an aromatic hop combined with a subtle bite and a pleasantly smooth caramel aftertaste.

Clansman Ale (OG 1036, ABV 3.9%)
A light beer, brewed with Scottish malts and lightly hopped to give a subtle bittering.

Seaforth Ale (OG 1042, ABV 4.2%) ◈
A light, quaffable beer with a delicate nose. A complex mixture of biscuity malt and fruit in the taste leads to a lasting, bittersweet finish.

Islander Strong Premium Ale (OG 1044, ABV 4.8%) ◈
A malty, fruity strong bitter drinking dangerously below its ABV.

Berserker Export Pale Ale (OG 1068, ABV 7.5%) ◈
This malty, fruity winter warmer is packed full of flavour, with toffee apple and caramel notes right through to the long, satisfying aftertaste.

Hedge Row

115 Lynfield Drive, Haworth Road, Bradford, West Yorkshire, BD9 6EP ☎ 07714 435599
✉ hedgerowbrewingco@gmail.com

Hedge Row was established in 2015 by young, enthusiastic brewer Michael Coffey after gaining experience in local breweries. It is located in a back garden shed with a brew length of a half barrel.

Bradford's Wrath (OG 1041, ABV 3.9%)

Daisy Hill Blonde (OG 1043, ABV 4%)
Zesty blonde ale with a biscuity dry finish.

Pale Ale (OG 1048, ABV 4.8%)
Well-balanced pale ale with a pronounced floral hop character.

Sweet Michael (OG 1060, ABV 5.6%)
Distinctive malty stout.

Heidrun

Inn House Brewery, 449 Great Western Road, Glasgow, G12 8HH ✉ hello@valhallasgoat.com

A small batch brewery with beers contract brewed by Drygate Brewery (qv). RAIB

Heineken Royal Trafford

Royal Brewery, 201 Denmark Road, Manchester, M15 6LD

Brews Kronenbourg (for owner Carlsberg) and Fosters brands among others. No real ale.

Hellhound

Sycamore Farm, Somersham Road, Bramford, Suffolk, IP8 4NN
☎ (01473) 831200 ☎ 07850 076202
⊕ hellhoundbrewery.co.uk

Hellhound was established in 2009, initially producing bottled beers. In 2014 the brewery relocated to its current site, a farm in Bramford with its own private water supply. Around 100 outlets are supplied across East Anglia. ♦

Dirty Blond (OG 1039, ABV 3.9%)
A blonde ale with a citrus finish.

Helm Bar

Ellerholme, Appleby-in-Westmorland, Cumbria, CA16 6JG ☎ 07736 364478 ⊕ helmbarbrews.com

Inspired by a passion for strong, distinctive beers from the US Pacific North West and Belgium, Helm Bar currently brews small batch beers using the highest quality grain and hops. RAIB

Jabberwock (ABV 5.2%)

Ghost Tractor (ABV 5.3%)
Robust porter with a hint of vanilla.

Jub Jub (ABV 5.5%)

Bandersnatch (ABV 6%)
An American-style IPA, mid-brown in colour, bitter and dry-hopped.

Vorpel Blade (ABV 6.4%)

Helmsley 👁

18 Bridge Street, Helmsley, North Yorkshire, YO62 5DX
☎ (01439) 771014 ☎ 07525 434268

☺Located within the North York Moors National Park, brewing began in 2014. The brewery has a viewing gallery, tasting room and brewery tap. Local pubs are supplied. RAIB

Yorkshire Legend (ABV 3.8%)

Striding the Riding (ABV 4%)

Howardian Gold (ABV 4.2%)

Honey (ABV 4.5%)

H!PA (ABV 5.5%)

Hen House

The Old Dairy, Walliscote Farm, High Street, Whitchurch-on-Thames, Oxfordshire, RG8 7EP
⊕ henhousebrewery.co.uk

Hen House began brewing in 2012 on a 30-litre plant. Only bottle-conditioned beers are produced, available from the brewery shop and the Wallingford Local Producers' Market every Saturday. ☞♦RAIB

Hepworth SIBA 👁

The New Brewery, Stane Street, North Heath, West Sussex, RH20 1DJ
☎ (01403) 269696 ⊕ hepworthbrewery.co.uk

⊠ Hepworth's was established in 2001 with draught beer brewing beginning in 2003 using Sussex malt and hops. 274 outlets are supplied. Originally situated in Horsham, a new brewery site in North Heath opened in 2016. ‼☞♦RAIB

Traditional Sussex Bitter (OG 1035, ABV 3.5%) ◆
A fine, clean-tasting amber-coloured session beer. A bitter beer with a pleasant fruity and hoppy aroma that leads to a crisp, tangy taste. A long, dry finish.

Dark Horse (OG 1038, ABV 3.8%)
Nutty and roasted malt characters with a complementary bitterness.

Summer Ale (OG 1038, ABV 3.8%)

Pullman First Class Ale (OG 1041, ABV 4.2%) ◆
A sweet, nutty maltiness and fruitiness are balanced by hops and bitterness in this easy-drinking, pale brown best bitter. A subtle bitter aftertaste.

Prospect Organic (OG 1045, ABV 4.5%)
A well-balanced and traditional brew.

Classic Old Ale (OG 1046, ABV 4.8%)
A traditional winter brew, rich with a variety of roasted malts balanced with sweetness and hop bitterness.

Iron Horse (OG 1048, ABV 4.8%) ◆
There's a fruity, toffee aroma to this light brown, full-bodied bitter. A citrus flavour balanced by caramel and malt leads to a clean, dry finish.

Hercules

Unit 5b, Harbour Court, Heron Road, Sydenham, Holywood, BT3 9HB
☎ (028) 9036 4516 ✉ niall@herculesbrewery.com

The original Hercules Brewing Company, founded in the 19th century, was one of 13 breweries in Belfast at the time. The company has been re-established to produce small batch brews using old brewing traditions. Its output is all under the Yardsman brand name.

Yardsman IPA (OG 1043, ABV 4.3%)

Yardsman Lager (OG 1048, ABV 4.8%)

Yardsman Belfast Pale Ale (OG 1056, ABV 5.6%)

Here Be Monsters

Unit 1, Holmbridge Mill, Holmbridge, West Yorkshire, HD9 2NE ☎ 07792 174863
⊕ herebemonstersbrewery.co.uk

A small brewery producing cask and bottle-conditioned beers using a six-barrel plant. RAIB

Hereford SIBA

▤ 88 St Owen Street, Hereford, HR1 2QD
☎ (01432) 342125 ✉ jfkenyon@aol.com

Hereford began life as the Spinning Dog Brewery in 2000, changing its name in 2010. It is now primarily a brew pub but supplies outlets on request, usually by social media.

Heritage

National Brewery Centre, Horninglow Street, Burton upon Trent, Staffordshire, DE14 1NG
☎ (01283) 777006
⊕ heritagebrewingcompany.co.uk

☺Heritage Brewing Company (formerly William Worthington's Brewery) was established in 2015 by Planning Solutions Limited, operators of the National Brewery Centre (NBC). They purchased the 25-barrel brewery and nearby bottling plant from the previous owners, Molson Coors. The team, led by master brewer Steve Wellington, has set out to utilise the resources, history and knowledge available at the NBC to breath new life into heritage beers, including those produced 10-15 years ago by the former Museum Brewing Co. ‼☞♦RAIB

Victoria Ale (OG 1034, ABV 3.8%)
Light but full flavoured, rich amber in colour.

Charrington Oatmeal Stout (OG 1041, ABV 4%)
Mellow and drinkable yet full bodied stout.

Offilers' Best Bitter (OG 1038, ABV 4%)
Amber-coloured with a light hop finish.

St. Modwen Golden Ale (OG 1040, ABV 4.2%)
Refreshing, but not too bitter, with a subtle malted wheat biscuit taste.

Charrington IPA (OG 1046, ABV 4.5%)
Deep amber in colour with a creamy foam and has a pleasant hoppy bite leading to a smooth, malty flavour and a balanced, lingering bitterness.

Masterpiece IPA (OG 1055, ABV 5.6%)
Aromatic hops, toasted cereal notes and hints of smoke and spice enhanced by fragrant fruity character and a top note of fresh bread. A full mouthfeel combines with a subtle peppery character.

Hermitage

Heathwaite, Slanting Hill, Hermitage, Berkshire, RG18 9QG
☎ (01635) 200907 ☎ 07980 019484
⊕ hermitagebrewery.co.uk

⊠ Brewing began in 2013 in the village of Hermitage, West Berkshire, using a 0.5-barrel plant. The owner, Richard Marshall, taught food science at degree level and has been brewing his own beers for more than 40 years. Bottle-conditioned beers are sold in local shops and post offices. Casks are supplied to some independent pubs as well as local beer festivals. New beers are frequently introduced. RAIB

Tom Herrick's

The Stable House, Main Street, Carlton on Trent, Nottinghamshire, NG23 6NW ☎ 07877 542331
✉ tomherricksbrewery@hotmail.com

Tom Herrick installed his bespoke 2.5-barrel stainless steel brewery at the front of his premises during 2014 and began small scale commercial brewing in 2015. The brewery is only operated on a part-time basis with output going to festivals and local pubs.

Black Lace (OG 1046, ABV 4.2%)
Roasted coffee and dark chocolate notes with a bittersweet aftertaste and smooth, well-rounded mouthfeel.

Bomber Command (OG 1045, ABV 4.2%)
A pale copper-coloured ale, full-bodied and malty with a delicate, well-balanced hop profile.

East India IPA (OG 1057, ABV 5.4%)
Pale golden in colour with a low malt profile complemented with generous amounts of citrus hops.

Hesket Newmarket SIBA

Old Crown Barn, Back Green, Hesket Newmarket, Cumbria, CA7 8JG
☎ (01697) 478066 ⊕ hesketbrewery.co.uk

☺Founded in 1988, and bought by a co-operative in 1999 to preserve a community amenity. All the beers are named after local fells, except for Doris' 90th Birthday Ale. ‼◆

Haystacks (OG 1037, ABV 3.7%) ◣

Light, easy-drinking, thirst-quenching blonde beer; pleasant for its strength.

Skiddaw Special Bitter (OG 1037, ABV 3.7%)
An amber-coloured session beer, malty throughout, well-balanced with a dryish finish.

Red Pike (OG 1038, ABV 3.8%)
A dark red-coloured ale with a complex malty backbone but plenty of hop flavour, balanced with a big hit of hops. The hop blend gives notes of resin and pine as well as some citrus and fruit.

Black Sail (OG 1042.1, ABV 4%) ◣
A sweet stout with roast flavours.

Helvellyn Gold (OG 1039, ABV 4%) ◣
Complex, hoppy and fruity beer with malt presence and refreshing finish.

High Pike (OG 1042, ABV 4.2%) ◣
A traditional-style bitter; fruity with a dry finish.

Doris' 90th Birthday Ale (OG 1045, ABV 4.3%)
A fruity premium beer.

Scafell Blonde (OG 1043, ABV 4.4%) ◣
A hoppy, sweet, fruity, pale-coloured bitter.

Brim Fell (OG 1047, ABV 4.5%)
A light copper-coloured IPA. Enough body to back up the hop bitterness, and a little residual sweetness from the malt balances the beer well. A light malt gives way to floral and citrus hops.

Catbells Pale Ale (OG 1050, ABV 5%) ◣
Golden ale with a good balance of fruity sweetness and bitterness, almost syrupy but with an unexpectedly dry finish.

Old Carrock Strong Ale (OG 1060, ABV 6%) ◣
Reddy brown-coloured strong ale, vine fruit in flavour with a slightly astringent finish.

Hetton Law

Hetton Law Farm, Lowick, Northumberland, TD15 2UL
☎ (01289) 388558 ☎ 07889 457140
⊕ hettonlawbrewery.co.uk

Brewing began in 2015 using a 2.5-barrel plant. Run by retired dentists Judith and Nicholas Grasse, it uses local spring water and locally grown malt, which gives the beers a distinctive character. ◆

Hetton Harvest (ABV 3.9%)

Hetton Howler (ABV 4.2%)
A traditional bitter with a rich, malty taste and hoppy overtones.

Hetton Harlot (ABV 4.8%)

Hetton Hare-raiser (ABV 5.2%)
A light, golden-coloured, hoppy beer.

Hewitt's

c/o Brentwood Brewery, Calcott Hall Farm, Ongar Road, Brentwood, Essex, CM15 9HS ☎ 07949 565424

Office: 40 Marconi Road, Chelmsford, Essex, CM1 1QD
⊕ hewittsbrewery.co.uk

Hewitt's was founded in 2010, using spare capacity at Brentwood Brewery (qv). Brewing is currently suspended.

Hexagon

PO Box 174, Marple, SK6 9BR ☎ 07903 264243
⊕ hexagonbrew.co.uk

Hexagon was founded in 2015 and is run by a husband-and-wife team. The brewery produces small batch bottle-conditioned beers supplying bars and bottle shops locally and in Manchester. There are plans for expansion. RAIB

Hexhamshire SIBA 👁

Dipton Mill Road, Hexham, Northumberland, NE46 1YA
☎ (01434) 606577 ⊕ hexhamshire.co.uk

Hexhamshire is Northumberland's oldest brewery and is run by the same family since it was founded in 1993. The Brooker family also run the brewery tap, the Dipton Mill. Outlets are supplied direct and via the SIBA Beerflex scheme.

Devil's Elbow (OG 1036, ABV 3.6%) ◆
Amber-coloured brew full of hops and fruit, leading to a bitter finish.

Shire Bitter (OG 1037, ABV 3.8%) ◆
A good balance of hops with fruity overtones, this amber-coloured beer makes an easy-drinking session bitter.

Blackhall English Stout (OG 1040, ABV 4%)
A pleasant bitter beer with a strong roast malt flavour.

Devil's Water (OG 1041, ABV 4.1%) ◆
Copper-coloured best bitter, well-balanced with a slightly fruity, hoppy finish.

County IPA (ABV 4.5%)
A sessionable English IPA.

Whapweasel (OG 1048, ABV 4.8%) ◆
An interesting smooth, hoppy beer with a fruity flavour. Amber in colour, the bitter finish brings out the fruit and hops.

Old Humbug (OG 1055, ABV 5.5%)

High House Farm SIBA

Matfen, NE20 0RG
☎ (01661) 886192 ⊕ highhousefarmbrewery.co.uk

The brewery was founded in 2003 by a Brewlab graduate on a working farm, with visitor centre, brewery shop and function room. This has now expanded to include a restaurant and wedding venue. More than 350 regional outlets are supplied with beers made using many ingredients from the farm. ♩▤◆

Sundancer (OG 1036, ABV 3.6%)

Pullet Please (OG 1037, ABV 3.7%)
A pale golden-coloured refreshing ale with a delicate grapefruit nose and a crisp, dry finish.

Auld Hemp (OG 1038, ABV 3.8%) ◆
Tawny-coloured ale with hop, malt and fruit flavours and a good bitter finish.

Nel's Best (OG 1041, ABV 4.2%) ◆
Golden hoppy ale full of flavour with a clean, bitter finish.

Matfen Magic (OG 1046.5, ABV 4.8%) ◆
Well-hopped brown ale with a fruity aroma. Malt and chocolate overtones with a rich, bitter finish.

High Peak

41a Market Street, Chapel-en-le-Frith, Derbyshire, SK23 0HP ☎ 07936 174364 ⊕ highpeakbrewco.com

High Peak is a microbrewery based in Chapel-en-le-Frith on the edge of the Peak District that specialises in hand crafted, small batch, unfined, unfiltered and unpasteurised beers in batches of 600 litres. There is no core range of beers as set recipes are not followed.

High Weald SIBA 👁

Unit 24, Bassetts Manor, Butcherfield Lane, Hartfield, West Sussex, TN7 4LA ☎ 07836 291430

Office: 23 Hermitage Road, East Grinstead, RH19 2BP
⊕ highwealdbrewery.co.uk

⊠ Established in 2013, High Weald Brewery has grown from its home brew origins to a four-barrel plant size, which moved to Hartfield in 2017. The brewery supplies local (and not so local) free houses, shops and festivals and is increasing direct sales at farmers' and community markets. Further expansion of both the beer range and capacity is planned.

Chronicle (OG 1038, ABV 3.8%)

Greenstede (OG 1040, ABV 4%)

Charcoal Burner (OG 1043, ABV 4.3%)

Off the Chart (OG 1049, ABV 5%)

First Gold IPA (OG 1052, ABV 5.4%)
Punchy and zesty, this IPA has a bitter orange flavour, a resinous aroma and a long, smooth finish.

Hilden SIBA

Hilden House, Hilden, Lisburn, Co Antrim, BT27 4TY
☎ (028) 9266 0800 ⊕ hildenbrewery.co.uk

☺Established 1981, Hilden is Ireland's oldest independent brewery. Now in the second generation of family ownership, the beers are widely distributed across the UK. The beers are regularly available in Wetherspoon outlets in Northern Ireland. ♩▤◆

Nut Brown (OG 1038, ABV 3.8%)

Ale (OG 1038, ABV 4%) ◆
An amber-coloured beer with an aroma of malt, hops and fruit. The balanced taste is slightly slanted towards hops, and hops are also prominent in the full, malty finish.

Barney's Brew (OG 1043, ABV 4.2%)
Belfast bap wheat beer, spiced with cardamon, coriander and black pepper.

Irish Stout (OG 1043, ABV 4.3%)

Scullion Irish Ale (OG 1046, ABV 4.6%)

Scullion's Irish (OG 1045, ABV 4.6%)
A bright amber-coloured ale, initially smooth with a slight taste of honey that is balanced by a long, dry aftertaste that lingers on the palate.

Twisted Hop (OG 1047, ABV 4.7%)

Halt (OG 1058, ABV 6.1%)
A premium traditional Irish red ale with a malty, mild hop flavour.

Contract brewed for Clearsky Brewing:

Fulcrum (ABV 4.5%)

Prism Red (ABV 4.5%)

Rowlock (ABV 4.5%)

Tidefall (ABV 4.5%)

Hill Island

Unit 7, Fowlers Yard, Back Silver Street, Durham,
DH1 3RA ☎ 07740 932584
✉ mike@hillisland.freeserve.co.uk

☺Established in 2002, the brewery name is a literal translation of Dunholme from which Durham is derived. It is situated in the Fowlers Yard complex by the banks of the Wear in the heart of Durham City. Beers can be crafted exclusively for individual pubs. Beer festivals take place at the brewery each month. ‼ 🍴◆

Peninsula Pint (OG 1036.5, ABV 3.7%)
Blonde and hoppy with a zesty aroma.

Bitter (OG 1039, ABV 3.9%)
A red gold-coloured bitter with pronounced caramel flavour and zesty bitterness.

Stout for the Count (OG 1040, ABV 4%)
A traditional, full-bodied stout. Almost black in colour with roast coffee flavors and a clean hop bitterness.

Neptune's Gold (OG 1042, ABV 4.2%)
Subtle bitterness balanced with hop flavours and a hint of tropical fruit.

Cathedral Ale (OG 1042, ABV 4.3%)
Ruby red in colour with hints of roast malts and a crisp bitterness.

ThaIPA (OG 1043, ABV 4.3%)

Griffin's Irish Stout (OG 1045, ABV 4.5%)
Black and bitter. Traditional Irish-style stout.

Hillfire SIBA

23 Edison Road, Aylesbury, Buckinghamshire,
HP19 8TE
☎ (01296) 338521 ⊕ hillfirebrewing.com

☒ Hillfire commenced brewing in 2016 using a 2.5-barrel plant. Sole owner and CAMRA member Neil Coxhead brews once a week. Further beers and direct sales are planned.

California Gold (OG 1043, ABV 4.3%)

Nighthawk (OG 1050, ABV 5%)

Hillside SIBA 👁

Holly Bush Farm, Ross Road, Longhope,
Gloucestershire, GL17 0NG
☎ (01452) 830222 ⊕ hillsidebrewery.com

☒ A six-barrel plant in a reconstructed farm dairy that started in 2011. A 200-foot bore hole produces pure water rich in minerals ideally suited to brewing. The regular beers are supplemented by limited run specials that explore different styles and flavours. ‼ 🍴◆RAIB

Over the Hill (OG 1042, ABV 3.5%)
Full-bodied, single-hopped dark mild, the hops complement the cocoa and roast malt character.

Pinnacle (OG 1038, ABV 3.8%)
A good session beer with a fresh and fruity finish.

Legless Cow (OG 1044, ABV 4.2%)
A well-balanced and full-flavoured best bitter. Rich caramel flavour with a smooth and citrus hop finish.

HCL (OG 1038, ABV 4.3%)
A clean and crisp lager with a subtle honey flavour and a refreshing peach and zesty finish.

Legend of Hillside (OG 1047, ABV 4.7%)
A traditional English IPA with a subtle honey flavour and a strong hop finish.

Summit Ruby Ale (OG 1049, ABV 4.9%)
Packed with rich, malty flavours, deep caramel notes and hints of chocolate and toffee to finish.

Hillstown

128 Glebe Road, Randalstown, BT41 3DT
⊕ hillstownbrewery.com

Brewing began in 2014 in a converted barn on a farm in Randalstown producing bottle-conditioned beers. ◆RAIB

Hilltop

🏠 Sheffield Road, Conisbrough, South Yorkshire,
DN12 2AY
☎ (01709) 868811 ☎ 07947 146746
⊕ thehilltophotel.co.uk

Established in 2016, Hilltop Brewery is a 3.5-barrel plant in the recently refurbished outbuildings of the Hilltop Hotel in Conisbrough. Beers are available in the hotel and other local outlets.

Hippy Killer (NEW)

c/o Whippet Inn, 21 Tamworth Street, Lichfield,
WS13 6JP ☎ 07858 753653

Paul Hudson, owner of the Whippet micropub in Lichfield, began commercial brewing in 2016. He currently uses spare capacity at Merry Miner Brewery (qv) in Warwickshire. Beer is mainly available at the micropub but can occasionally be found in the free trade.

Lowrider (OG 1040, ABV 4%)
Pale ale with citrus notes and a dry bitter finish.

Filthy Juicebox (OG 1042, ABV 4.2%)
New Zealand-hopped golden ale with rounded tropical fruit notes.

Sleeping With Trash (OG 1050, ABV 5%)

Hobsons SIBA 👁

Newhouse Farm, Tenbury Road, Cleobury Mortimer,
Shropshire, DY14 8RD
☎ (01299) 270837 ⊕ hobsons-brewery.co.uk

Established in 1993 in a former sawmill, Hobsons relocated to a farm site with more space in 1995. A second brewery, bottling plant and a warehouse have been added along with significant expansion to the first brewery. Beers are supplied within a 50-mile radius. The brewery has an onsite wind turbine and utilises environmental sustainable technologies where possible. ‼ 🍴RAIB

Mild (OG 1034, ABV 3.2%) 🍺
A classic mild. Complex layers of taste come from roasted malts that predominate and give lots of flavour.

Twisted Spire (OG 1036, ABV 3.6%)
Vibrant blonde beer with a light fizz and sweet floral aroma bringing bursts of refreshing flavour and crisp, dry finish.

Best (OG 1038.5, ABV 3.8%) 🍽 🍺
A pale brown to amber-coloured, medium-bodied beer with strong hop character throughout. It is

THE BREWERIES

consequently bitter, but with malt discernible in the taste.

Old Prickly (OG 1042, ABV 4.2%)
Pale ale with complex hop flavours with floral and citrus notes and a lingering but subtle bitterness.

Town Crier (OG 1044, ABV 4.5%)
A full-flavoured, crisp golden ale. A hint of sweetness complemented by subtle hop flavours leads to a dry finish.

Hogarths SIBA

🍺 Hogarths, 37-41 Churchgate, Bolton, BL1 1HU
☎ (01204) 386964

Microbrewery located in the old kitchen of a Bolton pub of the same name. Beers are available in the pub, other Amber Taverns up and down the country and at festivals.

Beer Street (ABV 3.8%)

Liberty (ABV 3.8%)

The Bruiser (ABV 4%)

Enraged Musician (ABV 4.2%)

Hoggleys

See Phipps

Hogs Back SIBA 👁

Manor Farm, The Street, Tongham, Surrey, GU10 1DE
☎ (01252) 783000 ∰ hogsback.co.uk

⊠ This traditionally-styled brewery, established in 1992, boasts an extensive range of award-winning ales. The shop sells all the brewery's beers and related merchandise plus over 400 beers and ciders from around the world. In 2014 the brewery planted hops on neighbouring farmland, restoring the ancient Farnham White Bine variety. ‼ 🍺 ◆ RAIB

HBB (OG 1039, ABV 3.7%) 🍺
Biscuity aroma with some hops and lemon notes. Well-balanced, plenty of hop in the mouth with a long-lasting dry bitter aftertaste.

TEA (OG 1044, ABV 4.2%) 🍺
A tawny-coloured best bitter with toffee and malt present in the nose. A well-rounded flavour with malt and a fruity sweetness.

Hop Garden Gold (OG 1048, ABV 4.4%) 🍺
Full-bodied with an aroma of malt, hops and fruit. Hoppy bitterness grows in an increasingly dry aftertaste with a hint of sweetness.

A over T (OG 1094, ABV 9%) 🍺
Full-bodied, tawny-coloured barley wine. The malty aroma with hints of vanilla lead to a well-balanced taste where the hops cut through the underlying sweetness and dominate in the finish.

Hogs Head (NEW)

🍺 1 Stanley Street, Sowerby Bridge, West Yorkshire, HX6 2AH
☎ (01422) 836585
✉ hogsheadbrewpub@outlook.com

The Hogs Head Brewery opened in a huge 18th-century former malthouse at the end of 2015. The eight-barrel brewhouse is situated at the back of the accompanying bar with the copper and stainless steel brewing vats on display at the back of the building.

Holden's SIBAIFBB 👁

George Street, Woodsetton, West Midlands, DY1 4LW
☎ (01902) 880051 ∰ holdensbrewery.co.uk

⊛A family brewery spanning four generations, Holden's began life as a brewpub in 1915. Continued recent expansion enables 20 tied pubs, a new brewhouse and a shop. ‼ 🍺 ◆

Black Country Mild (OG 1037, ABV 3.7%) 🍺
A good, red/brown mild; a refreshing, light blend of roast malt, hops and fruit, dominated by malt throughout.

Black Country Bitter (OG 1039, ABV 3.9%) 🍺
A medium-bodied, golden ale; a light, well-balanced bitter with a subtle, dry, hoppy finish.

Golden Glow (OG 1045, ABV 4.4%)
A pale golden-coloured beer with a subtle hop aroma plus gentle sweetness and light hoppiness.

Special (OG 1052, ABV 5.1%) 🍺
A sweet, malty, full-bodied, amber-coloured ale with hops to balance in the taste and in the good, bittersweet finish.

Holler Boys (NEW)

Little Goldsmiths Farm, Beechy Road, Blackboys, East Sussex, TN22 5JG
☎ (01825) 890856 ∰ hollerboysbrewery.co.uk

⊠ Steve worked with Fullers and Late Knights Brewery in London before moving down to Sussex with his partner Bethany to open Holler Boys Brewery in 2017. 40 outlets are supplied direct. ‼ ◆ RAIB

Cheat Mode (OG 1040, ABV 3.8%)
A fresh-tasting, American-hopped pale ale.

Brass Hand (OG 1042, ABV 4%)
A traditional golden ale with a fruity bitterness and fresh honey aroma.

Heavy Lifting (OG 1044, ABV 4.2%)
An easy-drinking stout with complex chocolate and coffee malt notes and sweet, tropical hop flavours.

Fog Cutter (OG 1046, ABV 4.5%)
A session IPA with citrus and piny aromas. Hoppy but not too bitter, balanced with sweetness and biscuity malt notes.

The Rouser (OG 1062, ABV 5.9%)
A full-bodied IPA with a citrus and spicy character.

Holsworthy

Unit 5, Circuit Business Park, Clawton, Clawton, EX22 6RR
☎ (01566) 783678 ☎ 07879 401073
∰ holsworthyales.co.uk

⊠ Holsworthy Ales began brewing in 2011 using a six-barrel plant, serving the local rural community. ‼ 🍺 ◆ RAIB V

Mine's a Mild (OG 1035, ABV 3.5%)
A traditional English mild with a rich, malty taste.

Paler Shade of Ale (ABV 3.6%)
A vibrant, hoppy pale ale.

Original (ABV 3.8%)

A rounded session ale with a good bitterness and some fruity, hoppy notes.

Sunshine (OG 1040, ABV 4%) ◣
Smooth golden ale. Hops overwhelm all else. Hints of fruit. Fresh and bitter hoppy aftertaste.

Boom! (ABV 4.2%)
A beer loaded with hops, with a spicy finish.

Green Hop (ABV 4.3%)

Muck 'n' Straw (OG 1044, ABV 4.4%) ◣
Hops dominate with hints of malt in aroma and taste. Well balanced with slight dryness in aftertaste

Okey Smokey (ABV 4.5%)
A rich, full-flavoured ruby-coloured ale with a warming smokiness on the nose.

Make Me Hoppy (OG 1046, ABV 4.7%)
Classic modern IPA, triple hopped for a big flavour.

Tamar Black (OG 1048, ABV 4.8%) ◣
Dark stout with hints of liquorice and coffee. A complex mix full of malt, roast, fruit, hops and caramel.

Dark Bomb (OG 1050, ABV 5%)
A dark, rich, smooth, lightly smoked porter.

Hop on the Run (ABV 5%)
An American-style IPA, packed full of vibrant hops, with a good body and lasting flavour.

Proper Lager (ABV 5%)

Old Market Monk (OG 1059, ABV 6.1%)
A Belgian-style ale with a deep, rich tone with hints of coriander.

Holt SIBAIFBB ◉

The Brewery, Empire Street, Cheetham, Manchester, M3 1JD
☎ (0161) 834 3285 ⊕ joseph-holt.com

☺ The brewery, established in 1849 by Joseph and Catherine Holt, is still a family-run business and is now in the hands of the great, great-grandson of the founder. In 2017 the great, great, great granddaughter, Jane Kershaw, a qualified brewster, joined the business. It supplies approximately 350 free trade outlets as well as its own estate of 130 tied pubs. ➤

Mild (OG 1033, ABV 3.2%) ◣
A dark brown/red-coloured beer with a fruity, malty nose. Roast, malt, fruit and hops in the taste, with strong bitterness for a mild, and a dry malt and hops finish.

IPA (OG 1038, ABV 3.8%) ◣
Golden bitter with biscuity malt, hops and restrained lemony notes. Dry, bitter finish.

Bitter (OG 1040, ABV 4%) ◣
Copper-coloured beer with malt and hops in the aroma. Malt, hops and fruit in the taste with a bitter and hoppy finish.

Two Hoots (OG 1043.8, ABV 4.2%)
It is a light, crisp and refreshing ale with a hint of citrus.

Holy Well

4 Barnfield Close, Egerton, Bolton, BL7 9UP ☎ 07949 179338 ⊕ holywellbrewing.com

Holy Well is a nanobrewery with a 1.5-barrel brew length split between producing firkins for a few local outlets and bottles for direct sale at local farmers' markets and online. The owners have strong links with Halliwell, an ancient township of Bolton whose name derives from the original Holy Well. **RAIB V**

Home Ales

See Oldershaw

Hooded Ram SIBA

Hills Meadow, Douglas, Isle of Man, IM3 1LE
☎ (01624) 612464 ⊕ hoodedram.com

☺ Brewing began in 2013 on a 2.5-barrel plant. Expansion in 2014 saw an increase to a 10-barrel plant with a 100-litre pilot plant added in 2016. A tied pub has recently opened in the old Clinch's Brewery building on the North Quay in Douglas with the Hooded Ram Beer & Spirits store adjacent to this, from which all beers and merchandise are available. ◆**RAIB**

Coco le Ram (ABV 3.5%)

Rams Head Bitter (OG 1037, ABV 3.7%)

Sovereign Ram Single Hop (OG 1037, ABV 4.1%)

Amber Ram (OG 1038, ABV 4.3%)

Jack The Ram Stout (OG 1044, ABV 4.7%) ◣
Roast dominates the aroma and taste, with bitterness coming through in the finish. Plenty of body from the sweetness and fruit make this an easy drinking stout.

Mosaic Single Hop Pale Ale (OG 1044, ABV 5%) ◣
A notably hoppy aroma gives a clear indication of what is to come. The hop-led taste is complemented with plenty of fruitiness, underlying sweetness, bitterness and a touch of malt, all of which are well matched.

Hook Norton SIBAIFBB ◉

Brewery Lane, Scotland End, Hook Norton, Oxfordshire, OX15 5NY
☎ (01608) 737210 ⊕ hooky.co.uk

⊗ One of the finest examples of a Victorian tower brewery and the oldest independent brewery in Oxfordshire, Hook Norton has been brewing since 1849. The current premises were built in 1900 and still house much of the original machinery, including a 25hp steam engine, which operates occasionally. Shire horses are used to make deliveries to local pubs in Hook Norton and the surrounding area. Remaining family-owned, it combines its brewing heritage with a modern approach. The boardroom and Cellar Bar are available for hire. Customers can spend a day brewing their own beer. ‼➤◆RAIB

Hooky Mild (OG 1033, ABV 2.8%) ◣
A chestnut brown-coloured, easy-drinking mild. A complex malt and hop aroma give way to a well-balanced taste, leading to a long, hoppy finish that is unusual for a mild.

Hooky (OG 1036, ABV 3.5%) ◣
A classic golden session bitter. Hoppy and fruity aroma followed by a malt and hops taste and a continuing hoppy finish.

Hooky Gold (ABV 4.1%)
A pale, crisp beer with a hoppy character, a fruity aroma and a pleasant, light taste.

Old Hooky (OG 1048, ABV 4.6%) ◆
A strong bitter, tawny in colour. A well-rounded fruity taste with a balanced bitter finish.

Hop & Cleaver

▤ 44 Sandhill, Newcastle upon Tyne, NE1 3JF
☎ (0191) 261 1037 ⊕ hopandcleaver.com

Established in 2014 the brewery is situated in the Hop & Cleaver pub, where the brewing equipment is on view. Its constantly changing beer range is supplied solely to the pub.

Hop & Stagger SIBA

Unit 1, The Old Cow Shed, Astol Farm, Norton, Shropshire, TF11 9EW
☎ (01952) 730737 ☎ 07487 898151
⊕ hopandstaggerbrewery.co.uk

Hop & Stagger began brewing in 2012 having set up a 2.5-barrel plant at the White Lion Inn in Bridgnorth. Initially brewing a range of bitters and occasional seasonal ales exclusively for the White Lion, it has now moved to a larger premises in rural Shropshire using a six-barrel plant. ◆

Shropshire Pale Ale (OG 1038, ABV 3.8%)
A pale straw-coloured session ale with a good balance of fruit and hops.

Golden Wander (OG 1042, ABV 4.1%)
Mid gold in colour, slight citrus notes and a well-balanced, fruity bitterness.

Bridgnorth Porter (OG 1055, ABV 5%)
A traditional porter with hints of chocolate and some dark fruit notes coming through alongside the suggestion of caramel.

Triple Hop IPA (OG 1052, ABV 5%)
Subtle citrus flavours with back notes of cedar and pine.

Hop Back SIBA ◉

Units 22-24, Batten Road Industrial Estate, Downton, Wiltshire, SP5 3HU
☎ (01725) 510986 ⊕ hopback.co.uk

⊗ Founded in 1987, Hop Back owns 10 pubs and distributes nationally. The flagship beer, Summer Lightning, has won numerous CAMRA awards.
‼ ⌇ ◆ RAIB GF V

GFB (OG 1035, ABV 3.5%) ◆
A light gold-coloured refreshing session bitter. The hoppy aroma leads to bitterness initially, lasting through to the finish with some fruit.

Citra (OG 1040, ABV 4%) ◆
Pale yellow, almost straw coloured with lemon and grapefruit on the aroma and taste, rapidly developing a balanced, hoppy aftertaste.

Crop Circle (OG 1041, ABV 4.2%) ◆
A pale yellow-coloured best bitter with a fragrant hop aroma, complex hop, fruit and citrus flavours with a balanced hoppy, bittersweet aftertaste.

Taiphoon (OG 1041, ABV 4.2%) ◆
A clean-tasting, light, fruity beer with hops and fruit on the aroma, complex hop character and lemongrass notes in the taste, slight sweetness balanced with some astringency in the aftertaste.

Entire Stout (OG 1044, ABV 4.5%) ◆
A smooth, rich, ruby-black stout with strong roast and malt aromas and flavours, with a long bitter, sweet and malty aftertaste.

Summer Lightning (OG 1048, ABV 5%) ◆
Golden-coloured strong bitter with a hoppy aroma and slightly astringent bitterness in the taste, balanced with some fruit sweetness in the dry aftertaste.

Hop Fuzz SIBA

Unit 8, Riverside Industrial Estate, West Hythe, Kent, CT21 4NB ☎ 07730 768881 ⊕ hopfuzz.co.uk

Hop Fuzz was started by two friends in 2011 and situated on an industrial estate next to the Royal Military Canal at West Hythe. In 2016, the brewery tap, Unit Number One, opened at the entrance to the estate. ◆

Fallout (OG 1036, ABV 3.6%)
A delicate and hoppy IPA.

Yellow Zinger (OG 1038, ABV 3.7%)

Martello (OG 1038, ABV 3.8%)

English (OG 1044, ABV 4%)

Northern Star (OG 1044, ABV 4.4%)

Galleon (OG 1046, ABV 4.6%)
A hardy and rich coffee best bitter.

Tomahawk (OG 1048, ABV 4.8%)

Bullion Bomb (OG 1050, ABV 5%)

Hop Kettle SIBA

▤ Red Lion, 74 High Street, Cricklade, Wiltshire, SN6 6DD
☎ (01793) 750776

Unit 4, Hawksworth Industrial Estate, Newcombe Drive, Swindon, Wiltshire, SN2 1DZ
⊕ theredlioncricklade.co.uk

Brewing began in 2012 using a four-barrel plant. The brewery is situated in a stone barn behind the Red Lion Inn, Cricklade. A second 10-barrel brew plant came on stream in 2016 in an old Royal Mail warehouse in Swindon. This supplements the original, smaller plant at the Red Lion. It is anticipated that this plant will be used to supply beer to the free trade in the local area, and the original plant will be used for experimental brews.

Cricklade Ordinary Bitter (ABV 3.8%)

Chameleon (ABV 4%)

North Wall (OG 1043, ABV 4.3%)
Traditional English best bitter, with a mildly bitter finish.

Hop Monster

See George's

Hop Studio SIBA ◉

3 Handley Park, Elvington Industrial Estate, York Road, Elvington, North Yorkshire, YO41 4AR
☎ (01904) 608029 ⊕ thehopstudio.co.uk

Founded in 2012 the Hop Studio brews on a 10-barrel plant in an industrial unit just outside York. Some barrel-aged specials are produced. Outlets in Yorkshire are supplied direct and the rest of the UK via wholesalers. A tap room is open on Fridays. ♦RAIB

Blonde (OG 1039, ABV 3.5%)
A refreshing blonde ale with a gooseberry, grapefruit and citrus aroma and flavour.

Pale (OG 1037, ABV 4%)
A pale, hoppy session ale. Grapefruit, lemons and tropical fruits linger into a dry finish.

Porter (OG 1050, ABV 4.3%)
A dark-coloured vanilla ale with intense chocolate malt and berry flavours.

Gold (OG 1048, ABV 4.5%)
A juicy, easy-drinking golden ale with a soft, rounded bitterness and citrus, peach and tropical fruit flavours.

India (OG 1046, ABV 5%)
A modern IPA with refreshing grapefruit and tropical fruit flavours.

XS (OG 1061, ABV 5.5%)
A strong, complex, chestnut-coloured ale. Spicy dark fruit flavours. Malty and bitter with hints of floral and citrus aromas.

Avenoir (OG 1072, ABV 6%)
A rich, velvety oatmeal stout. Coffee, chocolate and oat notes with subtle blackcurrant and cherry flavours.

Hop Stuff SIBA

Unit 7, Gunnery Terrace, Cornwallis Road, Woolwich, London, SE18 6SW
☎ (020) 8854 9509 ☎ 07850 086461
⊕ hopstuffbrewery.com

Hop Stuff began brewing in 2013. ♦

Fusilier (OG 1041, ABV 4.3%)
Biscuity, malty best bitter with spicy hop notes. Finish is sweetish, slightly dry with a faint bitterness. Rich, smooth mouthfeel.

Pale (OG 1045, ABV 4.5%)
Slightly dry amber-coloured bitter with a complex hop character throughout. Citrus notes in the flavour and finish, which is bitter.

Renegade IPA (OG 1056, ABV 5.6%)
Smooth, dark-gold IPA with grapefruit and spiced hops aroma and flavour. Warm, lingering finish that is bitter and dry.

Hop Vine

▤ c/o Hop Vine, Liverpool Road North, Burscough, Lancashire, L40 4BY
☎ (01704) 893799 ☎ 07920 002783

Hop Vine began brewing in 2017 using the four-barrel plant of the defunct Burscough Brewery. It is situated in old stable buildings in the courtyard to the rear of the Hop Vine. Beer is usually only supplied to the pub and the Legh Arms, Mere Brow.

Hop Yard

The Yard, Lewes Road, Forest Row, East Sussex, RH18 5AA
☎ (01342) 824272 ⊕ hopyardbrewing.co.uk

Hop Yard began brewing in 2014 using a 100-litre brew plant. Cask-conditioned Golden Ale is now brewed using spare capacity at Westerham Brewery (qv). The original plant is used for test brews. Beers are available at its on-site brewery bar. 🛢

Hopburst (NEW)

80 Grange Road, Darlington, DL1 5NP
☎ (01325) 787912 ⊕ hopburstbrewing.com

Focussing on small batch ales, commercial brewing began in 2016. A micropub is planned. Around five outlets are supplied direct. ‼RAIB

Blonde (OG 1040, ABV 3.6%)

Pale (OG 1050, ABV 5%)

IPA (OG 1053, ABV 5.6%)

Hopcraft

See Pixie Spring

Hopdaemon SIBA

Unit 1, Parsonage Farm, Seed Road, Newnham, Kent, ME9 0NA
☎ (01795) 892078 ⊕ hopdaemon.com

Tonie Prins originally started brewing in Tyler Hill near Canterbury in 2000 and moved to a new site in Newnham in 2005. The brewery currently supplies more than 100 outlets and is working at full capacity. ‼♦RAIB

Golden Braid (OG 1039, ABV 3.7%)
A refreshing golden session bitter with a good blend of bittering and aroma hops underpinned by pale malt.

Incubus (OG 1041, ABV 4%)
A well-balanced, copper-hued best bitter. Pale malt and a hint of crystal malt are blended with bitter and slightly floral hops to give a lingering, hoppy finish.

Skrimshander IPA (OG 1045, ABV 4.5%)
An aromatic copper-coloured pale ale with a refreshing taste and fruity finish.

Green Daemon (OG 1048, ABV 5%)
A golden-coloured beer with tropical fruit aromas and a crisp, clean finish.

Leviathan (OG 1057, ABV 6%)
A strong ruby-coloured ale with spicy hop aromas and a rich, malty finish.

Hope

Unit 15, Towers Road, Globe Industrial Estate, Grays, Essex, RM17 6ST ☎ 07903 793223

Office: 76 Corringham Road, Stanford le Hope, SS17 0AE ⊕ hopebrewery.co.uk

Hope was founded in 2013 using a 0.25-barrel plant, expanding to 2.5-barrels in 2014. The brewery relocated and expanded to a five-barrel plant in 2016. ♦RAIB

SX Pale (OG 1039, ABV 3.9%)

SX Dark (OG 1041, ABV 4.2%)

SX Gold (OG 1041, ABV 4.2%)

Hope Springs (NEW)

Courtfield, Bacombe Lane, Wendover,
Buckinghamshire, HP22 6EQ ☎ 07793 132829
⊕ hopespring.net

Commercial brewing began in 2016. Bottle-
conditioned beers are produced in small batches on
a 25-litre kit. RAIB

Hophurst SIBA

Unit 8, Hindley Business Centre, Platt Lane, Hindley,
WN2 3PA
☎ (01942) 522333 ⊕ hophurstbrewery.co.uk

☺Hophurst Brewery was started in 2014 by Stuart
Hurst, whose passion for producing craft ales
combined with 20 years of supporting businesses
and re-skilling unemployed people created a
unique social enterprise brewery that employs
people over the age of 50 and guides them
through their training programme in the Wigan
area. ◆

Flaxen (OG 1038, ABV 3.7%)
A pale golden ale with a fresh, earthy, hoppy
aroma with hints of honey and a long, refreshing
finish.

Mellors (OG 1039, ABV 3.8%)
A citrus blonde ale with hop flavours of lemon and
blackcurrant.

Campfire (OG 1042, ABV 3.9%)
A dark mild with a smoky, malty taste and aromas
of roasted coffee and chocolate.

Joust (OG 1040, ABV 4%)
A refreshing citrus pale ale, well-rounded with
flavours of spice, citrus and zesty orange.

Twisted Vine (OG 1041, ABV 4.1%)
A golden bitter with citrus hoppy aromas of
grapefruit and passion fruit.

Cosmati (OG 1042, ABV 4.2%)
A hoppy, citrus golden ale with flavours of
blueberry, citrus and tropical fruit.

50 Gyle (OG 1044, ABV 4.4%)
An IPA with hop flavours of berries, tropical fruit
and citrus.

Debonair (OG 1052, ABV 4.9%)
A robust stout with flavours of roasted coffee and
liquorice and a pleasant bitter aftertaste.

Hopjacker

Dronfield Arms, 91 Chesterfield Road, Dronfield,
Derbyshire, S18 2XE ☎ 07841 487247
⊕ hopjacker.co.uk

☺Established in 2015 in the old restaurant space
beneath the Dronfield Arms. Hopjacker specialises
in unfined, vegan-friendly, hop-forward beers. ‼

The Long Con (OG 1037, ABV 3.8%)
Light copper in colour with floral and pine hop
notes to complement the subtle malt backdrop.

Pyrites (OG 1038, ABV 4.1%)
Easy-drinking golden ale with berry notes and a
balanced yet lingering bitterness.

Beer House Pale (OG 1039, ABV 4.2%)
Tropical hop flavours and a citrus finish.

The Grifter (OG 1043, ABV 4.6%)

Rich, smooth and chocolaty oatmeal stout with a
full body and complex malt character.

Hopshackle SIBA

Unit F, Bentley Business Park, Blenheim Way,
Northfields Industrial Estate, Market Deeping,
Lincolnshire, PE6 8LD
☎ (01778) 348542 ⊕ hopshacklebrewery.co.uk

☺Hopshackle was established in 2006 using a five-
barrel plant. A 10-barrel plant was installed in
2015. More than 40 outlets are supplied direct.
‼ ◆ RAIB

Simarillo (OG 1037, ABV 3.8%)
Burnished gold in colour with an aroma of citrus
and soft fruits. The taste is tangy fruit with
blackberry, plum and pineapple.

Zen (OG 1037, ABV 3.8%)
Brown-coloured, traditional, full-flavoured bitter;
malty and fruity with a bittersweet finish.

American Pale Ale (OG 1042, ABV 4.3%)
An amber-coloured ale with a fruity, zesty aroma.
The taste is citrus hop with background gooseberry
and lychees and a dry bitter finish.

Hopnosis (OG 1050, ABV 5.2%)
Golden-coloured beer with a strong aroma of
sweet malt and fruit. The taste is of strong citrus
and tropical fruits with a dry finish.

Hopstar SIBA

Unit 9, Rinus Business Park, Grimshaw Street,
Darwen, Grimshaw Street, BB3 2QX ☎ 07933 590159
⊕ hopstarbrewery.co.uk

☺Hopstar first brewed in 2004 on a 2.5-barrel
plant and expanded in 2010 to a new unit with a
six-barrel plant. More than 100 outlets are supplied
around Lancashire and the Greater Manchester
area. The brewery tap is Number 39 in Darwen.
‼ ◆ RAIB

Chilli (OG 1039, ABV 3.8%)

Dark Knight (ABV 3.9%)

Off t' Mill (OG 1039, ABV 3.9%)

Smokey Joe's Black Beer (ABV 3.9%)

Lancashire Gold (OG 1041, ABV 4%)

Lush (OG 1041, ABV 4%)

Saaz Blonde (OG 1038, ABV 4%)
A light and refreshing beer brewed with extra pale
malt and continental hops.

JC (ABV 4.1%)

Horbury (NEW)

Low Mill Road, Ossett, West Yorkshire, WF4 6LT
☎ 07970 299292

Following the closure of Bob's Brewing Co, Horbury
Ales took over the plant in 2016.

Gold (ABV 3.9%)

5 Hop (ABV 4.1%)

First Light (ABV 4.1%)

Tiramisu (ABV 4.3%)

Sundown (ABV 5.2%)

Hornbeam

See Epicurus

Horncastle

⚏ Old Nicks Tavern, 8 North Street, Horncastle, Lincolnshire, LN9 5DX
☎ (01507) 526862 ⊕ horncastleales.co.uk

Brewing began in 2014 using a 3.75-barrel plant. The brewery is situated in Old Nicks Tavern with beer available in the pub plus other Lincolnshire outlets. It has its own bottling plant and a beer in box scheme is also available for pre-ordering.

Midnight Tempter (OG 1036.5, ABV 3.6%)
Smooth roasted flavours with a hoppy edge.

Damned Deceiver (OG 1038, ABV 3.8%)
Smooth, rich, chestnut-coloured beer with a full body.

Wicked Blonde (OG 1039, ABV 3.9%)
A blonde beer with a distinctive flavour.

Angel of Light (OG 1039.5, ABV 4%)
Light and malty beer with a nutty finish.

Lilith's Lust (OG 1040.5, ABV 4.1%)
Traditional red-coloured bitter, malty and full bodied.

Satan's Fury (OG 1040.5, ABV 4.1%)
Full-bodied, fruity IPA with a dark golden colour.

Dragon's Flame (ABV 4.3%)
Light chestnut-coloured, smooth bitter, with hints of vanilla and spice.

Dragon's Flame (OG 1042, ABV 4.3%)
A smooth bitter with hints of vanilla and spice.

Sacrificed Soul (OG 1042, ABV 4.3%)
Chestnut-coloured, full-bodied bitter with caramel flavours and a slight, sweet edge.

Lucifer's Desire (OG 1046, ABV 4.8%)
Deep golden-coloured beer with citrus flavours and hoppy finish.

Hornes SIBA

19b Station Road, Bow Brickhill, Buckinghamshire, MK17 9JU
☎ (01908) 647724 ⊕ hornesbrewery.co.uk

A purpose-built six-barrel brewery established in 2015 and producing a range of beers called Triple Goat after the three goats kept in a paddock at the brewery. There is no shop, but beers can be purchased at the brewery. RAIB

Featherstone Amber Ale (OG 1037, ABV 3.6%)
A robust traditional bitter with a soft, fruity finish.

Dark Fox (OG 1039, ABV 3.8%)
A rich, malty, brown-coloured brew with burnt notes and a lasting, dry bitter finish.

Triple Goat Pale Ale (OG 1039, ABV 3.9%)
Easy-drinking, golden-coloured beer, bitter with hints of grapefruit.

Triple Goat Porter (OG 1047, ABV 4.6%)
Dark brown-coloured, sweet and fruity giving way to a lasting bitterness with hints of liquorice.

Triple Goat IPA (OG 1049, ABV 5%)
Deep golden-coloured beer, well-balanced with notes of orange and a touch of spice.

Hoskins Brothers

See Belvoir

Howard Town SIBA

Hawkshead Mill, Hope Street, Glossop, Derbyshire, SK13 7SS
☎ (01457) 869800 ⊕ howardtownbrewery.co.uk

Established in 2005, this eight-barrel, award-winning brewery moved to its current location in 2007. An on-site bar caters for members' evenings and open days. !! ᛒ ♦ RAIB V

Mill Town Mild (OG 1038, ABV 3.5%)
Dark and lightly hopped with hints of toffee and coffee.

Longdendale Lights (OG 1039, ABV 3.9%)
A light-bodied, blonde, refreshing ale.

Monk's Gold (OG 1040, ABV 4%)
A golden-coloured session ale with subtle orange notes.

Wren's Nest (OG 1041, ABV 4.2%)
Citrus, floral hops dominate this uncompromising bitter.

Super Fortress (OG 1044, ABV 4.4%)
Well-balanced, premium chestnut-coloured bitter with malty caramel notes and fruity hops.

Glott's Hop (OG 1050, ABV 5%)
A strong and assertively bitter, straw-coloured ale with citrus notes.

Dark Peak (OG 1064, ABV 6%)
Strong and dark with a hint of liquorice and a warming rum kick.

Howling Hops

⚏ Unit 9a, Queen's Yard, White Post Lane, Hackney Wick, London, E9 5EN
☎ (020) 3583 8262 ⊕ howlinghops.co.uk

Brewing began in 2012. Originally brewing at the Cock Tavern in Hackney, a new plant opened in 2015 in Hackney Wick. The original brewery at the Cock is still in place as a boutique bewery, brewing one-off speciality beers. Beers are available at the on-site tap room, the Tank Bar, the Cock and occasionally in local free houses and at beer festivals.

Hoxne

Unit 12, Forge Business Centre, Palgrave, IP22 1AP
☎ 07515 003503 ⊕ hoxnebrewery.co.uk

Hoxne Brewery is a small village producer handcrafting real ales in small batches. The beers can be found in numerous pubs around East Anglia. ♦ RAIB

Old Forge Amber (ABV 4%)

Suffolk Punch Bitter (ABV 4.5%)

Churchyard Oatmeal Stout (ABV 5%)

Defender Oatmeal IPA (ABV 5%)

Hubsters (NEW) SIBA

Kenyons Farm, Gough Lane, Clayton Brook, Lancashire, PR5 6AR

THE BREWERIES

☎ (01772) 837655 ☎ 07050 685795
⊕ hubstersbrewery.co.uk

☺Hubsters started brewing commercially in 2017 using a five-barrel plant. A brewery tap is planned.
◆ RAIB

Hop & Glory (ABV 3.8%)

Hop on the Good Foot (ABV 4%)

Hopscotch (ABV 5%)

Hop Mama (ABV 6%)

Sarah Hughes

▤ Beacon Hotel, 129 Bilston Street, Sedgley, West Midlands, DY3 1JE
☎ (01902) 883381 ⊕ sarahhughesbrewery.co.uk

Traditional Black Country Victorian tower brewery, taken over by Sarah Hughes in 1921. Brewing ceased in the 1950s and recommenced in 1987. The original grist case and rare open-topped copper give a unique character to the brews. The Beacon Hotel is the brewery tap.

Pale Amber (OG 1038, ABV 4%)
A well-balanced beer, initially slightly sweet but with hops close behind.

Sedgley Surprise (OG 1048, ABV 5%) ◄
A bittersweet, medium-bodied, hoppy ale with some malt.

Dark Ruby Mild (OG 1058, ABV 6%) ▉ ◄
A dark ruby strong ale with a good balance of fruit and hops, leading to a pleasant, lingering hops and malt finish.

Humpty Dumpty SIBA

Church Road, Reedham, Norfolk, NR13 3TZ
☎ (01493) 701818 ☎ 07843 248865
⊕ humptydumptybrewery.co.uk

⊗ Established in 1998, this 11-barrel, award-winning brewery continues to grow and expand its range of beers. The on-site shop sells bottled beer from the brewery and local cider. !! ☰ ◆ RAIB

Little Sharpie (OG 1039, ABV 3.8%) ◄
Swirling toffee apple bouquet. Biscuity beginning with bittersweet lemon nuances giving contrast. Full-bodied with a growing bitterness.

Lemon & Ginger (OG 1041, ABV 4%)
An amber-coloured, crisp ale with a ginger and lemon tang.

Swallowtail (OG 1041, ABV 4%) ◄
Malt and fruit on the nose. Well-balanced with hops adding to the fruity sweetness. Some malt in a rounded finish.

Ale (OG 1042, ABV 4.1%) ◄
A hoppy vanilla fudge edge in both nose and taste. Malt provides balance as a gentle bitterness quickly recedes. Lengthy finish.

Broadland Sunrise (OG 1043, ABV 4.2%) ◄
Rolling malt bouquet with tangerine notes. Well-balanced mix of malt, tangerine, gentle bittersweet hoppiness and caramel. Refreshing bitter finish.

Red Mill (OG 1045, ABV 4.3%) ◄
A peppery redcurrant nose and grainy mouthfeel. Bittersweet base with vine fruit adding depth and gravity. Long, sherry-like finish.

Reedcutter (OG 1045, ABV 4.4%) ◄
A sweet, malty beer; golden-hued with a gentle malt background. Smooth and full-bodied with a quick, gentle finish.

Cheltenham Flyer (OG 1047, ABV 4.6%) ◄
A full-flavoured, golden-coloured, earthy bitter with a long, grainy finish. A strong hop bitterness dominates throughout. Little evidence of malt.

EAPA (East Anglian Pale Ale) (OG 1047, ABV 4.6%) ◄
Amber gold in colour with an orange marmalade nose. A bittersweet caramel beginning slowly dries out as malty nuances fade away.

Hungry Bear

10-14 Stonegate Road, Leeds, West Yorkshire, LS6 4HY
☎ (0113) 274 0241 ⊕ thehungrybear.co.uk

Hungry Bear began brewing in 2013 in the upstairs rooms of the Hungry Bear restaurant. A wide range of ales is produced in batches of about 70 litres, which are bottled and conditioned on site and supplied to the restaurant and also on sale from the off licence facility on the premises. !! RAIB

Hunters SIBA ◍

Bulleigh Barton Farm, Ipplepen, Devon, TQ12 5UA
☎ (01803) 873509 ☎ 07540 657115
⊕ huntersbrewery.com

⊗ Hunters began brewing in 2008. The award-winning brewery has a 60-barrel brew length and 4,000 gallon fermenting capacity. A bottling, labelling and packing plant means it can produce bottled beers for other breweries. !! ☰ ◆ RAIB

Old Charlie (OG 1038, ABV 3.8%)
Good malt feel in the mouth, dry, tangy bitter finish.

Crispy Pig (OG 1042, ABV 4%)
Speciality beer with a hint of apples, refreshingly sharp and hoppy.

Half Bore (OG 1040, ABV 4%) ◄
Light colour and body. Malt dominates from start to finish. Lots of flavour and slightly flowery.

Devon Dreamer (OG 1042, ABV 4.1%) ◄
Amber-coloured best bitter with hop aroma and undertones of caramel. Hops in the taste and slight bitterness develop later.

Pheasant Plucker (OG 1044, ABV 4.3%)
Full-flavoured ale with a bittersweet finish.

Premium (OG 1040, ABV 4.8%)
A light amber-coloured premium bitter with malty flavours and a fruity aroma.

Royal Hunt (OG 1055, ABV 5.5%)

Black Jack (OG 1062, ABV 6%)
Premium triple-hopped stout made with Devon honey.

Full Bore (OG 1070, ABV 6.8%)
Malt flavours, made with Devon honey.

Hurly Burly (NEW)

15 Wedderburn Terrace, Musselburgh, EH21 7TJ
☎ (0131) 665 8135

Office: 15 Glenorchy Road, North Berwick, EH39 4PH
⊕ hurlyburlybrewery.co.uk

Small, family-run brewery producing bottle-conditioned ales in the brewer's back kitchen. RAIB

Hurns

See Tomos Watkin (under W)

Hurst SIBA

Western Road, Hurstpierpoint, West Sussex, BN6 9SP
☎ 07866 438953 ⊕ hurstbrewery.co.uk

Hurst is a four-barrel microbrewery, founded in 2012 but reviving a name dating back to 1862. More than 100 outlets are supplied between south London and Brighton. !!♦

Oldland Sussex Pale Ale (ABV 3.7%)
A copper-coloured session ale with a nutty and biscuity depth and an earthy, spicy hop aroma.

Founders Best Bitter (ABV 4.2%)
Nutty brown in colour with a rounded malty taste, suffused with subtle caramel.

Keepers Gold (ABV 4.4%)
Smooth, amber-coloured ale with a floral aroma. Citrus notes are finely balanced with a subtle infusion of South Downs honey and a refreshing, hoppy finish.

1862 Premium Bitter (ABV 4.8%)
A full-flavoured, smooth, dark ale with spicy, nutty and resinous characteristics and hints of dark fruits.

Watchtower (ABV 5.5%)
A strong, dark porter with a distinctive bitterness and a rich, creamy head.

Husk

Unit 58a, Railway Arches, North Woolwich Road, West Silvertown, London, E16 2AA
☎ (020) 7474 3827 ☎ 07803 271160
⊕ huskbrewing.com

Commercial brewing began in 2016 after the husband-and-wife team outgrew their kitchen. Expansion is planned. RAIB

Pale Ale (OG 1050, ABV 5.1%)
A pale ale with citrus and stone fruit flavours and aromas and a decent malty body.

Hybrid (NEW)

Unit 14c, Abbotsinch Road Industrial Estate, Grangemouth, FK3 9UX ⊕ hybridbrewing.com

Hybrid began brewing in 2016 using a 10.5-barrel dual train brewplant, allowing for two different beers to be brewed at a time. 40 outlets are supplied direct.

Ctrl Alt Del (ABV 3.8%)

Apex (ABV 4.1%)

Hindsight (ABV 4.4%)

Hippy Chick (ABV 4.6%)

Magic Porridge (ABV 4.7%)

Street Legal (ABV 4.7%)

Jar Nektar (ABV 5.7%)

Hydes ◉

The Beer Studio, 30 Kansas Avenue, Salford, M50 2GL
☎ (0161) 226 1317 ⊕ hydesbrewery.com

◉Hydes Brewery has been in the Manchester area since 1863 and currently focuses entirely on cask beer production. Based in the Media City area, it brews around 40 different beers throughout the year. Beer is supplied to its own estate, as well as the free trade and wholesale market. ♦

1863 (OG 1033.5, ABV 3.5%) ⬥
Lightly hopped, pale brown-coloured session beer with some hops, malt and fruit in the taste and a short, dry finish.

Old Indie (OG 1033.5, ABV 3.5%) ⬥
Dark brown/red in colour, with a fruit and malt nose. Taste includes biscuity malt and green fruits, with a satisfying aftertaste.

Original (OG 1036.5, ABV 3.8%) ⬥
Pale brown-coloured beer with a malty nose, malt and an earthy hoppiness in the taste, and a good bitterness through to the finish.

Lowry (ABV 4.7%)

Iâl SIBA ◉

Pant Du Road, Eryrys, CH7 4DD ☎ 07956 440402
⊕ cwrwial.com

Cwrw Iâl Community Brewery is run as a social enterprise assisted by EU funding with all profits used for local community projects. The 10-barrel plant brews a core range as well as regular specials. It supplies outlets along the North Wales coast and in the North-west. ♦

The Volunteer (OG 1037, ABV 3.8%)
Light copper-coloured session ale.

Pocket Rocket (OG 1040, ABV 4%)
A pale session IPA.

Kia Kaha! (OG 1043, ABV 4.3%) ⬥
A dry, bitter beer, gold in colour with a fruity aroma leading to a good hoppy taste and finish.

Limestone Cowboy (OG 1045, ABV 4.5%) ⬥
A copper-coloured best bitter, malty with faint roast notes and fruit flavours. Hops dominate in the dry bitter finish.

Pothole Porter (OG 1054, ABV 5.1%)
Black and roasted with the addition of British-grown hops.

Iceni SIBA

Foulden Road, Ickburgh, Norfolk, IP26 5HB
☎ (01842) 878922 ☎ 07949 488113
⊕ icenibrewery.co.uk

Iceni was launched in 1995 by Brendan Moore. The brewery is also the headquarters of the East Anglian Brewers Co-op (EAB). !!♦RAIB

Fine Soft Day (OG 1038, ABV 4%) ⬥
Golden hued with toffee notes throughout. A creamy, lightly-hopped backdrop softly sinks into a pleasant sweetness.

Idle

White Hart Inn, Main Street, West Stockwith, Nottinghamshire, DN10 4EY

☎ (01427) 892672 ☎ 07949 137174
⏺ theidlebrewery.co.uk

☺The brewery began production in 2007 and is situated in a converted stable at the back of the White Hart Inn, which Brian Cooper, the brewer, now owns, alongside the River Idle. ‼♦

Golden Crown (OG 1038, ABV 3.8%)

Dog (OG 1041, ABV 4.2%)
A copper-coloured ale, moderately hoppy with a good balance of malt and hops leading to a bitter finish.

Sod (OG 1041, ABV 4.2%)
Light golden-coloured ale with a deep, fruity aroma and a well-balanced bittering.

Tongue (OG 1041, ABV 4.2%)

Black & Tan (OG 1042, ABV 4.3%)

Black Abbot (OG 1044, ABV 4.6%)
Strong, black-coloured ale with deep roasted notes.

Idle Landlord (OG 1044, ABV 4.6%)
A dark brown-coloured ale with plenty of body, a malty flavour and a caramel/coffee finish.

Idle Valley SIBA 👁

Barham House, Aurillac Way, Hallcroft Industrial Estate, Retford, Nottinghamshire, DN22 7PX
☎ (01777) 860327 ☎ 07850 228383
⏺ idlevalleybrewing.com

Idle Valley began brewing in 2014 using a 1.46-barrel plant. High demand plus the opening of the Idle Valley Tap in Retford led to the brewery upgrading to a 12-barrel plant in 2016. RAIB

Mild Revolution (OG 1036, ABV 3.6%)

Summer Breeze (OG 1036, ABV 3.8%)

Vacant Gesture (OG 1036, ABV 3.8%)
A light, fresh, hoppy, blonde beer.

Jaded Pioneer (OG 1040, ABV 4.1%)
A medium-bodied pale ale, well-balanced with a fist full of hops on the nose and a crisp, dry, citrus taste.

Torpid Expression (OG 1039, ABV 4.1%)
A deep copper/amber-coloured traditional bitter with a fruity and toffee aroma and and a malty, toffee taste.

Coconut Shy PA (OG 1041, ABV 4.2%)
A coconut pale ale brewed in collaboration with Pinfold Brewery, Chesterfield.

Indolent Philosopher (OG 1052, ABV 5.3%)
A dark stout with a relatively light body. Roast notes include chocolate and coffee.

Unpretentious Declarant (OG 1053, ABV 5.6%)
Almost copper in colour with a tropical and hoppy aroma. The beer is crisp, bitter and hoppy with a citrus flavour.

Ilkley SIBA 👁

The New Brewery, Ashlands Road, Ilkley, West Yorkshire, LS29 8JT
☎ (01943) 604604 ⏺ ilkleybrewery.co.uk

☺Ilkley brewery was founded in 2009 and now produces up to 160 barrels per week. The brewery consistently wins awards and last year produced over 40 different beers. It continues to expand,

having acquired a new units on the same site in 2016 and 2017. ‼♦RAIB

Mary Jane (OG 1036, ABV 3.5%)
A crisp, pale ale with citrus aromas.

Pale (ABV 4.2%)

Rombald (ABV 4.6%)
American amber-coloured ale with crisp and fruity hop flavours.

Hanging Stone (ABV 5%)
Rich and creamy, with a bitter finish of forest fruits and coffee.

Crossroads IPA (ABV 5.4%)
Aromas of orange rind and citrus peel with dry, spicy finish.

Imperial

⬛ **Arcadia Hall, Cliff Street, Mexborough, South Yorkshire, S64 9HU**
☎ (01709) 584000 ☎ 07428 422703
✉ imperialclub@hotmail.co.uk

Brewing began in 2010 using a six-barrel tower brewery system located in the basement of the Imperial Club, Mexborough. Beer is available in the club as well as local outlets.

Incredible SIBA

214-224 Broomhill Road, Brislington, Bristol, BS4 5RG
☎ 07780 977073 ⏺ incrediblebrewingcompany.com

⊠ This microbrewery specialises in producing small batches of beer using a 2.5-barrel plant. It was established in 2014 by head brewer Stephen Hall with the aim of promoting experimental beers and traditional recipes. ‼♦RAIB V

Milk Stout (OG 1044, ABV 4.4%)

Pale Ale (OG 1043, ABV 4.4%)

Amber Ale (OG 1052, ABV 5.2%)

Black IPA (OG 1056, ABV 5.6%)

Grapefruit IPA (OG 1054, ABV 5.6%)

Indian Pale Ale (OG 1063, ABV 6.6%)

Independent Lakeland

See Strands

Indian

119b Baltimore Trading Estate, Baltimore Road, Great Barr, B42 1DD
☎ (0121) 296 9000 ⏺ indianbrewery.com

This six-barrel brewery, established in 2005 as the Tunnel Brewery at the Lord Nelson Inn, relocated to the picturesque stable block at Red House Farm in 2011. In 2015 the owners of Tunnel Brewery went their separate ways, with Mike Walsh retaining the brewery and renaming it the Indian Brewery. Later that year the Indian Brewery was sold to new owners and relocated to the outskirts of Birmingham. ‼

Summer (ABV 4%)
A full-flavoured, well-balanced beer with a distinct citrus hop flavour.

IPA (ABV 4.9%)

A traditional IPA with a citrus punch, tropical fruit flavours and a well-rounded body.

Bombay Honey (ABV 5%)
A blonde beer, brewed with real honey.

Peacock (ABV 5%)
Vibrant amber-coloured ale with sweet mellow and spiced berry tastes.

Indigenous

Peacock Cottage, Main Street, Chaddleworth, Berkshire, RG20 7EH
☎ (01488) 505060 ⊕ indigenousbrewery.co.uk

⊠ An occasional and informal microbrewer for many years, Kevin Brady established Indigenous in 2014, increasing production using a 2.5-barrel plant. Availability is restricted to local pubs, shops and an increasing number of regional beer festivals. !! ⊨ ♦ RAIB

Baldrick (ABV 3.4%)
A smooth mild ale that delivers plenty of malty flavours.

Forager's Gold (OG 1040, ABV 4%)
A crisp golden ale with a slight amber touch. Smooth and refreshing with caramel notes.

Summer Solstice (OG 1042, ABV 4.1%)
A straw-coloured pale ale with a fresh, hoppy aroma coupled with a subtle bitterness and a long, dry finish.

Frisky Mare (ABV 4.2%)
A generously-hopped, golden-coloured ale, with notes of gooseberry, grape and floral accents, leading to a long, dry finish.

Monocle (OG 1049, ABV 4.5%)
A smooth stout with a malty aroma and a slightly dry finish.

Nutcracker (ABV 4.5%)
A brown-coloured ale that delivers a good mix of roasted malts and fruity hops.

Old Cadger (OG 1046, ABV 4.5%)
Rich malts and fruity hops combine to produce a balanced, full-flavoured beer.

Moonstruck (OG 1051, ABV 4.8%)
Plenty of chocolate and coffee notes, complemented by a subtle bitterness and smooth finish.

Nosey Parker (OG 1058, ABV 5.5%)
A strong ruby-red mild with a sweet malty base and a hint of hops.

AMMO Belle (OG 1055, ABV 5.6%)
A well-hopped American-style pale ale that delivers lots of fruity notes, a floral aroma and a moderately dry finish.

Double Warp (ABV 5.8%)
A rich, dark, full-flavoured brown stout with plenty of deep chocolate notes and a hint of spice.

Inishmacsaint

7 Drumadown Road, Drumskimly, Derrygonnelly, Co Fermanagh, BT93 6DN
☎ (028) 6864 1031 ⊠ gordyfallis@hotmail.com

⊠ Inishmacsaint is a small-scale brewery that has been in production since 2009. A larger brew plant is now in use producing a range of bottle-conditioned beers. RAIB

Inkspot (NEW)

The Rookery Barn, Streatham Common South, London, SW16 3BZ ☎ 07787 832292
⊕ theinkspotbrewery.com

Inkspot began cuckoo brewing in 2012. A 10-barrel plant at the address listed is due to come on stream during the currency of this guide.

Geronimo20 (ABV 4.1%)
An American-style pale ale, well-hopped with citrus notes of grapefruit and orange against sweet malts.

5.56 (ABV 5.56%)
A copper-coloured IPA with resinous, hoppy qualities and floral hints, balanced well with malted sweetness.

Inner Bay (NEW) SIBA

Seacliffe Villa, Hill Street, Inverkeithing, KY11 1AB
☎ 07871 172939 ⊕ innerbay.co.uk

Brewing began in 2016. Inner Bay is a family-run brewery using traditional ingredients and methods producing bottle-conditioned beers in small batches. RAIB

INNformal

⊟ **Five Bells, Baydon Road, Wickham, RG20 8HH**
☎ (01488) 657300 ⊕ fivebellswickham.co.uk

INNformal was established in 2015 in a purpose-built building behind the Five Bells pub in Wickham. A bore hole in the pub garden supplies water for the 2.5-barrel plant. A secondary 0.5-barrel kit is used for experimental brews. Beers are supplied mainly to the Five Bells and the John O'Gaunt, Hungerford.

Innis & Gunn

See Inveralmond

Instant Karma

⊟ **4 John Street, Clay Cross, Derbyshire, S45 9NQ**
☎ (0124) 250366 ⊕ instantkarmabrewery.co.uk

nstant Karma began brewing in 2012 using a five-barrel plant with a brew length of 15 barrels per week. The brewery is part of the Rykneld Turnpyke brewpub.

Interbrew UK

Porter Tun House, Capability Green, Luton, Bedfordshire, LU1 3LS
☎ (01582) 391166

Interbrew (Magor): Magor Brewery, Magor, NP26 3DA

Interbrew (Samlesbury): Cuerdale Lane, Samlesbury, PR5 0XD

UK subsidiary of A-B InBev. No real ale.

Inveralmond SIBA ◉

22 Inveralmond Place, Perth, PH1 3TS
☎ (01738) 449448 ⊕ inveralmond-brewery.co.uk

◉Established in 1997, Inveralmond was the first brewery in Perth for more than 30 years. Around

250 outlets are supplied. In 2016, Innis & Gunn, the Edinburgh company that specialises in oak-aged beers, bought Inveralmond following a successful crowdfunding scheme that raised £3 million. I&G had planned to build a new brewing operation but decided instead to buy the Perth brewery, where the current 30-barrel plant will be expanded, with a new maturation plant for the I&G beers. I&G makes no real ale but the Inveralmond range will continue. ‼ 🍴 ♦

EPA (ABV 3.8%)
A vibrant, hoppy ale.

Ossian (OG 1042, ABV 4.1%) 🍴
Well-balanced best bitter with a dry finish. This full-bodied amber-coloured ale is dominated by fruit and hop with a bittersweet character although excessive caramel can distract from this.

Lia Fail (OG 1048, ABV 4.7%) 🍴
The Gaelic name means Stone of Destiny. A dark, robust, full-bodied beer with a deep malty taste. Smooth texture and balanced finish.

Daracha (ABV 5.2%)
An oak matured, ruby-coloured Scotch ale.

Irving SIBA ◉

Unit G1, Railway Triangle, Walton Road, Portsmouth, Hampshire, PO6 1TQ
☎ (023) 9238 9988 ⊕ irvingbrewers.co.uk

⊗ Established in 2007 by former Gale's brewer Malcolm Irving using a 15-barrel plant. Around 120 outlets are supplied in Hampshire, Sussex and Surrey with beers available further afield through beer swaps with other breweries. Speciality beers may be ordered for festivals. ‼ 🍴 ♦

Frigate (OG 1039, ABV 3.8%) 🍴
Satisfying session bitter. Hoppy, with a floral aroma and initial sweetness, leading to bitterness and a smooth, slightly dry finish.

Type 42 (OG 1042, ABV 4.2%)
A robust best bitter with a deep ruby red hue balancing sweet hedgerow berry notes with a long, roasted malt finish and a deep bitterness.

Admiral Stout (OG 1042.5, ABV 4.3%) 🍴
Well-balanced stout, with plenty of fruit and roast, together with pleasant hint of coffee and short bitter finish.

Invincible (OG 1048, ABV 4.6%) 🍴
Tawny-coloured strong bitter. Sweet and fruity with underlying maltiness throughout and gradually increasing dryness, contrasting with the sweet finish.

Iron Duke (OG 1053, ABV 5.3%)
A refreshing, well-balanced strong IPA. Hoppy – but not overly so.

Irwell Works SIBA

Irwell Street, Ramsbottom, BL0 9YQ
☎ (01706) 825019 ⊕ irwellworksbrewery.co.uk

⊕ Irwell Works started brewing in 2010 in a building dating from 1888 that once housed the Irwell Works steam, tin, copper and iron works. It now houses a six-barrel plant. The brewery tap is on the first floor and hosts regular live music events. ‼

Lightweights & Gentlemen (OG 1031, ABV 3.2%) 🍴
Light, refreshing pale ale with some fruitiness and a hoppy, bitter finish.

Tin Plate (OG 1033, ABV 3.6%)
Brewed as a traditional dark mild, low in strength and a rich creamy flavour but with a slight bitterness to contrast.

Copper Plate (OG 1036, ABV 3.8%) 🍴
Traditional northern bitter. Copper-coloured with a satisfying blend of malt and hops and good bitterness.

Richard Mason 1888 (OG 1039, ABV 4%)
A mid-strength, single-hopped beer with a mild bitterness and pleasant, mildly-hopped aftertaste.

Costa Del Salford (OG 1039, ABV 4.1%)
A hoppy summer ale, this beer is light in colour with bags of flavour.

Steam Plate (OG 1042, ABV 4.3%)
A golden-coloured best bitter balanced with a slight sweetness. A slightly nutty flavour and a pleasant hop aroma.

Iron Plate (OG 1043, ABV 4.4%) 🍴
Roast malt in the aroma is joined by hop and a toasty bitterness in the taste and finish.

Mad Dogs & Englishmen (OG 1052, ABV 5.5%)
Export-style pale ale. Little sweetness for its strength and a strong hop character make this a smooth, easy-drinking beer.

Isaac Poad (NEW)

Office: Axholme Croft, Chapel Street, Cattal, York, North Yorkshire, YO26 8DY
☎ (01423) 358114 ⊕ isaacpoad.co.uk

⊕ Established in 2016, this is a subsidiary of a long established grain merchant known for supplying malting barley to many local maltsters. Currently using spare capacity at another local brewery pending the construction of its own plant, the emphasis is on using local Yorkshire malt and only British hops.

No. 86 Golden Ale (ABV 3.6%)

1863 Best Bitter (ABV 3.8%)

No. 84 India Pale Ale (ABV 4.5%)

Isca SIBA

Court Farm, Holcombe, Devon, EX7 0JT ☎ 07773 444501 ⊕ iscaales.co.uk

⊗ Isca Ales has developed a niche market by bottling much of its production and supplying beer festivals outside its region. RAIB V

Citra (OG 1038, ABV 3.8%)
Light, refreshing beer with a grapefruit aroma leading to a dry bitter finish.

Dawlish Summer (OG 1038, ABV 3.8%)

Golden Ale (OG 1038, ABV 3.8%)

Dawlish Bitter (OG 1042, ABV 4.2%)

Glorious Devon (OG 1044, ABV 4.4%)
A grassy hop aroma with hoppy aftertaste.

Gold (OG 1045, ABV 4.5%)
Golden-coloured beer, hoppy with a dry bitter finish.

Holcombe White (OG 1045, ABV 4.5%)
Cloudy wheat beer with hints of banana, oranges and spice.

Dawlish Pale (OG 1050, ABV 5%)
Grassy hop aroma with intense hoppy aftertaste.

Black IPA (OG 1060, ABV 6%)

Devon Pale (OG 1068, ABV 6.8%)

Isla Vale

17 Westbrook Gardens, Margate, Kent, CT9 5DJ
☎ (01843) 292451 ☎ 07980 174616
⊕ islavalealesmiths.co.uk

⊠ Established in 2014 from a residential address in Westbrook (Margate) supplying local micropubs. There are plans to expand the brewery and increase the range and styles of ales to supply establishments further south and west. ♦

Golding Delicious (OG 1038, ABV 3.8%)
A light, copper-coloured session ale with a slight malty sweetness.

Hopping Mad (OG 1042, ABV 4%)
A traditional session bitter with a variety of hops, complex aromas and malty flavours.

Two Halves (OG 1040, ABV 4%)
Session bitter made with English hops.

Ninkasi Pale Ale (OG 1045, ABV 4.5%)
A hoppy pale ale with added elderflower.

Big Red Beer (OG 1046, ABV 4.6%)
A session beer, fruity with plenty of locally-grown hops and a hint of honey.

Cock-A-Snook (OG 1045, ABV 4.6%)
A dark golden-coloured session ale with good hop aroma and hints of fruit.

Natural Blonde (OG 1046, ABV 4.7%)
A refreshing blonde ale, initial floral notes with a lasting hoppy bitterness throughout.

Befuggled (OG 1052, ABV 5.2%)
A rich malty ESB-style ale, with plenty of hops.

IPA (OG 1058, ABV 5.5%)
A modern take on a traditional IPA using a variety of New World hops. A hint of fruit with an intense hoppy aroma and flavour.

Island SIBA

Dinglers Farm, Yarmouth Road, Newport, Isle of Wight, PO30 4LZ
☎ (01983) 821731 ⊕ islandbrewery.co.uk

⊠ Island Brewery is the realisation of Tom Minshull's ambition to brew real ales to complement the existing family-owned drinks distribution business. Brewing commenced in 2010 using a 12-barrel brewery. More than 100 outlets are supplied direct. ‼♦

Nipper Bitter (OG 1038, ABV 3.8%)
Straw-coloured, light and refreshing with a distinguishable balance of malt and hops and a satisfying afterbite.

Wight Gold (OG 1040, ABV 4%)
Golden in colour with rounded malt and hops throughout and a pleasing bitter finish.

Yachtsmans Ale (OG 1042, ABV 4.2%)

Chestnut-coloured ale with a rich, malty mouthfeel, counterbalanced with sufficient hops to give a subtle complexity of flavours and texture.

Wight Knight (OG 1045, ABV 4.5%)
Strong, full-bodied, amber-coloured ale with malty caramel flavours.

Vectis Venom (OG 1048, ABV 4.8%)
Malty, easy-drinking, ruby red-coloured ale.

Earls RDA (OG 1052, ABV 5%)
Rich, dark ale with flavours of chocolate and coffee leading to a classic espresso finish.

Islay SIBA

The Brewery, Islay House Square, Bridgend, Isle of Islay, PA44 7NZ
☎ (01496) 810014 ⊕ islayales.com

☺Brewing started on a four-barrel plant in a converted tractor shed in 2004. The brewery shop is next door. The island is more famous for its whisky, but the brewery has established itself as a must-see place for those visiting the eight working distilleries. ‼ ☞♦RAIB

Isle of Avalon SIBA

Little Whitley, Stagman Lane, Ashcott, Somerset, TA7 9BJ
☎ (01458) 210050 ☎ 07809 056855
⊕ avalonwholesaleandbrewing.co.uk

⊠ Brewing began in 2008. Isle of Avalon is a five-barrel plant brewing for the parent company Avalon Wholesale and occasionally for one-off events and local supply.

Isle Ale (OG 1039, ABV 3.8%)

Sunrise (OG 1042, ABV 4.3%)

Pomparles Porter (OG 1045, ABV 4.5%)

Sunset (OG 1051, ABV 5%)

Arthurs Ale (OG 1066, ABV 6.5%)

Isle of Mull

See Argyll

Isle of Purbeck SIBA

⊟ Manor Road, Studland, Dorset, BH19 3AU
☎ (01929) 450227 ⊕ isleofpurbeckbrewery.com

Founded in 2003, the brewery is situated in the grounds of the Bankes Arms Hotel, overlooking Studland Bay on the Jurassic Coast. A 10-barrel plant is used. The core beers are available nationwide via exchange swaps with other small breweries.

Purbeck Best Bitter (OG 1036, ABV 3.6%) ◆
A classic malty best bitter with rich malt aroma and taste and smooth, malty, bitter finish.

Force Four (OG 1040, ABV 4%)
A balanced, smooth-drinking beer packed with roasted malt flavours with a subtle whisper of spicy hops.

Fossil Fuel (OG 1040, ABV 4.1%) ◆
Amber-coloured bitter with complex aroma with a hint of pepper; rich malt dominates the taste, leading to a smooth, dry finish.

Solar Power (OG 1043, ABV 4.3%) ◆
Tawny-coloured, mid-range ale brewed using Continental hops. Well-balanced flavours combine to provide a strong bitter taste but short, dry finish.

Studland Bay Wrecked (OG 1044, ABV 4.5%) ◆
Deep red-coloured ale with slightly sweet aroma reflecting a mixture of caramel, malt and hops that lead to a dry, malty finish.

Purbeck IPA (OG 1047, ABV 4.8%) ◆
Mid-brown beer with hop/malt balance in the flavour and a long, dry aftertaste

Isle of Skye SIBA

The Pier, Uig, Isle of Skye, IV51 9XP
☎ (01470) 542477 ⊕ skyeale.com

☺The Isle of Skye Brewery was established in 1995. Originally a 10-barrel plant, it was upgraded to 20 barrels in 2004. Further expansion is planned. ☗◆

Skye Light (OG 1038, ABV 3.8%) ◆
A slightly hoppy nose leads to a powerful hop and fruit taste and a sharp finish.

Tarasgeir (OG 1040, ABV 4%) ◆
The peat roasted barley dominates giving a mellow, peaty whisky taste.

Young Pretender (OG 1039, ABV 4%) ▣ ◆
A refreshing, amber-coloured, hoppy grapefruit-tasting bitter. Some sweetness in the taste but continuing into a lingering bitter finish.

Skye Red (OG 1041, ABV 4.2%) ◆
A light, fruity nose with a hint of caramel lead to a hoppy, malty, fruity flavour and a dry, bittersweet finish.

Skye Gold (OG 1041.5, ABV 4.3%) ◆
Porridge oats are used to produce this speciality beer. Nicely balanced, it has a refreshingly soft lemon, bitter flavour with an oat background.

Skye Black (OG 1044, ABV 4.5%) ▣ ◆
A complex Scottish old ale. Full-bodied with a malty richness. Malt holds sway but there are plenty of hops and fruit to be discovered in its varied character.

Skye IPA (OG 1046, ABV 4.5%) ◆
Well-balanced with a good malty background and complemented with Sorachi hops.

Skye Blaven (OG 1047, ABV 5%) ◆
A well-balanced, strong, amber-coloured bitter with kiwi fruit and caramel in the nose and a lingering sharp bitterness.

Skye Blonde (ABV 5.5%) ◆
Citrus hoppy brew with some caramel sweetness.

Cuillin Beast (OG 1066, ABV 7%) ◆
A winter warmer; sweet and fruity, and much more drinkable than the strength would suggest. Plenty of caramel throughout with a variety of fruit on the nose.

Itchen Valley SIBA

Unit D, Prospect Commercial Park, Prospect Road, Alresford, Hampshire, SO24 9QF
☎ (01962) 735111 ⊕ itchenvalley.com

▧ Established in 1997, Itchen Valley moved to new premises in 2006 with a 20-barrel plant. More than 350 pubs are supplied, with wholesalers used for further distribution. ‼☗◆RAIB

QED (OG 1041, ABV 4.1%) ◆
Copper-coloured best bitter with a hint of crystal malt and a pleasant bitter aftertaste.

Hampshire Rose (OG 1042, ABV 4.2%)
A golden amber-coloured ale. Fruit and hops dominate the taste throughout, with a good mouthfeel.

Pure Gold (OG 1046, ABV 4.8%) ◆
Aromatic, hoppy, strong bitter. Golden-coloured with initial maltiness and grapefruit counter-balanced with some sweetness, leading to a dry finish.

James & Kirkman

▤ 4 Wakefield Road, Pontefract, West Yorkshire, WF8 4HN
☎ (01977) 702231
✉ jamesandkirkmanbrewery@gmail.com

Brewing began in 2013 behind the Robin Hood pub using a 2.5-barrel plant. Two pubs are owned, the Robin Hood in Pontefract and the Rising Sun, Wakefield.

James Street

▤ City Pub Company, 14 James Street West, Bath, BA1 2BX
☎ (01225) 805609

Office: City Pub Company (West) Plc, Essel House, 2nd Floor, 29 Foley Street, London, W1W 7TH
⊕ thebathbrewhouse.com

The James Street Brewery opened in 2013 and is owned by the City Pub Company (West), which owns several other pubs around the country. The compact brewery is on the ground floor of the Bath Brewhouse, with the fermenting vessels and conditioning tanks on the first floor. The company's other pub, the Cork, Bath, is also supplied.

Jaw SIBA ◉

Unit 9, The Centre Point, 67b Montrose Avenue, Hillington Industrial Estate, Hillington, G52 4LA
☎ (0141) 237 5840 ⊕ jawbrew.co.uk

Brewing began in 2014. RAIB

Drop (OG 1042, ABV 4.2%)

Surf (OG 1043, ABV 4.3%)

Drift (OG 1047, ABV 4.6%)

Wave (OG 1048, ABV 4.7%)

Jennings ◉

Castle Brewery, Cockermouth, Cumbria, CA13 9NE
☎ (01900) 820362 ⊕ jenningsbrewery.co.uk

☺Jennings Brewery was established as a family concern in 1828 in the village of Lorton. The company moved to its present location in 1874. Pure Lakeland water is still used for brewing, drawn from the brewery's own well. Part of Marston's PLC. ‼☗◆

Bitter (OG 1035, ABV 3.5%) ◆
A malty beer with a good mouthfeel that combines with roast flavour and a hoppy finish.

Cumberland Ale (OG 1038, ABV 4%) ▣ ◆
A tawny-coloured, hoppy beer with a dry aftertaste.

Cocker Hoop (OG 1044, ABV 4.6%) ◆
Full-bodied, complex, bitter beer with plenty of hops and a rising bitter finish.

Sneck Lifter (OG 1051, ABV 5.1%) ◆
A strong, dark brown-coloured ale with a complex balance of fruit, malt, sweet and roast flavours through to the finish.

John o'Groats

County Road, John o'Groats, KW1 4YR ☎ 07825 729680 ✉ johnogroatsbrewery@gmail.com

⊛Brewing began in 2015 using a four-barrel plant.

Swelkie (OG 1041, ABV 4%) ◆
Slight honey taste in this citrus, hoppy brew.

Duncansby (OG 1044, ABV 4.5%)
A fruity, amber-coloured ale.

Jolly Boys (NEW) SIBA

Unit 16a, Redbrook Business Park, off Wilthorpe Road, Redbrook, South Yorkshire, S75 1JN ☎ 07808 085214 ⊕ jollyboysbrewery.co.uk

⊛Jolly Boys started brewing using spare capacity at another brewery in early 2016. Brewing began on its own plant later the same year.

Jolly Collier Stout (OG 1035, ABV 3.5%)

Blonde (OG 1041, ABV 4%)

Golden Best (OG 1042, ABV 4.5%)

Jolly Collier Porter (OG 1052, ABV 5%)

Jolly Sailor SIBA

🍺 Olympia Hotel, 77 Barlby Road, Selby, North Yorkshire, YO8 5AB
☎ (01757) 268918 ☎ 07923 635755
⊕ jolly-sailor-brewery.webplus.net

Jolly Sailor began brewing in 2012 at Ricall Business Park, a former mine site near York. Production was moved to the Olympia Hotel, Selby, in 2013, where the regular beers are always available and increasingly in other local pubs.

Jollyboat SIBA

Coach House, Buttgarden Street, Bideford, Devon, EX39 2AU
☎ (01237) 424343

⊠ Established in 1995, the brewery is named after a sailor's leave vessel and all the beers have a nautical theme. Most outlets supplied are in Devon. ‼◆

Mainbrace (OG 1042, ABV 4.2%) ◆
Pale brown-coloured brew with a rich, fruity aroma and a bitter taste and aftertaste.

Plunder (OG 1049, ABV 4.8%)
Red/brown-coloured beer with an aromatic nose, a good balance of malt, hops and fruit present throughout, leading to a bitter finish.

Joule's SIBA ◉

The Brewery, Great Hales Street, Market Drayton, Shropshire, TF9 1JP
☎ (01630) 654400 ⊕ joulesbrewery.co.uk

Re-established in 2010, following a break of 40 years, Joule's is situated in Market Drayton and uses its own mineral water. It runs a collection of 40 pubs across the region. ‼◆

Blonde (OG 1038, ABV 3.8%)
Light, refreshing and aromatic, this well-balanced blonde ale delivers a crisp, clean palate coupled with a pleasing aroma of citrus fruit.

Pale Ale (OG 1042, ABV 4.1%)
Brewed using the original Joule's recipe dating back to 1779. Full-bodied and well-balanced with a pleasant bitter finish.

Slumbering Monk (OG 1045, ABV 4.5%)
Full-bodied with complex malt and nut character, this bright copper ale has hints of caramel which give a round, soft smoothness to the palate.

Contract brewed for Everards Brewery:

Sunchaser (OG 1038, ABV 4%)
A golden brew with a slightly sweet, lightly-hopped character. Some citrus notes to the fore in a quick finish that becomes increasingly bitter.

Old Original (OG 1050, ABV 5.2%)
Full-bodied, mid-brown strong bitter with a pleasant rich, grainy mouthfeel. Well-balanced flavours, with malty slightly to the fore, merging into a long, satisfying finish.

Junction

🍺 1 Baildon Road, Baildon, West Yorkshire, BD17 6AB
☎ 07539 923744 ✉ andydoug48@gmail.com

Junction is a microbrewery established in 2012 in the cellar of the Junction pub in Baildon, brewing around 300 gallons a week. Beer is sold in the pub and other local outlets.

Keep

🍺 Village Inn, The Cross, Nailsworth, Gloucestershire, GL6 0HH ☎ 07963 200768 ✉ paul@dropinpubs.com

After a break of 96 years, brewing returned to Nailsworth in 2004 at the Village Inn. The pub and brewery were sold in 2016 to Paul Sugden and Adam Pavey, who changed the brewery name from Nailsworth to Keep Brewing.

Keith SIBA

Unit R, Isla Bank Mills, Keith, AB55 5DD
☎ (01542) 488006 ⊕ keithbrewery.co.uk

Formerly known as Brewmeister and established in 2012, the brewery was renamed Keith Brewery in 2015. Beer is mainly available in bottles in selected specialist off-licenses but cask-conditioned beer is available to a few outlets and beer festivals. The Brewmeister brand name is kept for export-only orders. ◆RAIB

Herr Keith (OG 1044, ABV 4.5%) ◆
Cloudy white/yellow-coloured wheat beer with hints of coriander.

Larger Keith (OG 1048, ABV 4.5%)

Pale Keith (OG 1048, ABV 5%) ◆
Grapefruit hoppy bitter.

Stout Keith (OG 1048, ABV 5%)
Coffee stout made with chocolate and coffee beans.

THE BREWERIES

Sir Keith (OG 1096, ABV 10.1%)
Slightly sweet but hoppy with a fruity aroma and complex malty character.

Kelburn SIBA 👁

10 Muriel Lane, Barrhead, G78 1QB
☎ (0141) 881 2138 ⊕ kelburnbrewery.com

⊠ Kelburn is an award-winning family business established in 2002. ‼◆

Sunriser (OG 1034, ABV 3.4%)
A well-balanced, hoppy, refreshing beer with a touch of rye and a blend of six hops leaving a long-lasting biscuit and grapefruit finish.

Goldihops (OG 1038, ABV 3.8%) ◥
Well-hopped session ale with a fruity taste and a bitter finish.

Pivo Estivo (OG 1038, ABV 3.9%)

Misty Law (OG 1040, ABV 4%) ▣
A dry, hoppy amber-coloured ale with a long-lasting bitter finish.

Red Smiddy (OG 1040, ABV 4.1%) ◥
This bittersweet ale predominantly features an intense citrus hop character that assaults the nose and continues into the flavour, balanced perfectly with fruity malt.

Regnitz (OG 1042, ABV 4.4%)

Dark Moor (OG 1044, ABV 4.5%) ▣
A dark, fruity ale with undertones of liquorice and blackcurrant.

Jaguar (OG 1043, ABV 4.5%)
A golden-coloured, full-bodied ale with undertones of grapefruit and a long-lasting citrus, hoppy aftertaste.

Cart Noir (OG 1046, ABV 4.8%)

Cart Blanche (OG 1048, ABV 5%) ◥
A golden-coloured, full-bodied ale. The assault of fruit and hop camouflages the strength of this easy-drinking ale.

Kelham Island SIBA

23 Alma Street, Sheffield, South Yorkshire, S3 8SA
☎ (0114) 249 4804

Office: Prospect House, 17 Alma Street, Sheffield, S3 8RY ⊕ kelhambrewery.co.uk

☺Opened in 1990 behind the Fat Cat pub, the brewery moved to new purpose-built premises in 1999. The old building is used as a visitor centre. A brewery shop is housed with new offices in nearby Prospect House. ‼ ⊨ ◆RAIB

Best Bitter (OG 1038, ABV 3.8%)
Classic amber-coloured Yorkshire bitter with spicy, earthy aromas and a sweet, refreshing, malty finish.

Pride of Sheffield (OG 1040.5, ABV 4%)
A full-flavoured, amber-coloured bitter.

Easy Rider (OG 1041.8, ABV 4.3%) ◥
A pale, straw-coloured beer with a sweetish flavour and delicate hints of citrus fruits. A beer with hints of flavour rather than full-bodied.

Riders on the Storm (OG 1045, ABV 4.5%)
A robust golden-coloured pale ale with berry notes and slight roasted notes.

Pale Rider (OG 1050, ABV 5.2%) ▣ ◥

A full-bodied, straw-coloured pale ale, with a good fruity aroma and a strong fruit and hop taste. Its well-balanced sweetness and bitterness continue in the finish.

Kelpaul

Wellington, HR4 8DZ ☎ 07941 027134

Office: 1 Churchway Cottage, Holmer, Hereford, HR1 1LL ✉ kelpaulbrewco@gmail.com

⊠ Established in 2015, Kelpaul originally used spare capacity at Hereford Brewery (qv). In 2017 it moved to the former Mulberry Duck premises in Wellington. Around 10 outlets across Herefordshire and beyond are supplied. ◆RAIB

Madagascar Mild (OG 1036, ABV 3.8%)
A lightly-hopped, full-flavoured mild. A complex, rich roast malt flavour with a hint of berries and chocolate overlaid with Madagascan vanilla.

Seville (ABV 3.8%)

Sunshine Session (OG 1036, ABV 3.8%)
A refreshing pale ale with a hint of spicy lemon marmalade on the aroma, a hit of grapefruit bitterness on the first taste, leading to grassy, nutty notes and a floral aftertaste.

Tribal Elder (ABV 3.8%)

Bonneville (OG 1041, ABV 4.4%)
A well-rounded, easy-drinking bitter. A malty aroma with green tea notes, giving way to a flavour comprising hop earthiness and hints of blackcurrant and grapefruit.

Lambretta (OG 1044, ABV 4.9%)
A smooth, well-hopped pale ale. Initial sweet bitterness giving way to a smooth finish.

Keltek SIBA 👁

Candela House, Cardrew Way, Redruth, Cornwall, TR15 1SS
☎ (01209) 313620

Office: Unit 5, Kernick Business Park, Annear Road, Penryn, Cornwall, TR10 9EW ⊕ keltekbrewery.co.uk

⊠ Keltek, meaning 'Celtic' in Cornish, was founded in 1997 by Stuart Heath. It started life as a 2.5-barrel plant in Stuart's disused stable block on the Roseland Peninsula but several moves and expansions means it is now based in Redruth and has the capacity to brew more than 250 barrels a week. In 2013 Keltek acquired four pubs in south-west Cornwall, becoming only the second brewery in Cornwall to own its own estate of public houses. In 2016 Keltek acquired a further two (closed) pubs, saving them from permanent closure. These two pubs reopened in 2017, bringing the estate to six pubs. ⊨ ◆RAIB

Even Keel (OG 1034, ABV 3.4%) ◥
Pale brown-coloured session bitter. Light malt and hop taste with apple, plum and pear drops. Gentle dry and bitter finish.

Golden Lance (OG 1038, ABV 4%) ◥
Gold-coloured bitter with slight fruity aroma. Grassy citrus hops, apples, gentle malt, hints of elderflower and butterscotch. Long bitter finish.

Magik (OG 1040, ABV 4%) ◥
Copper-coloured best bitter. Sweet honey-like flavour with toffee butterscotch. Quite malty with

balancing English hop bitterness. Bitter citrus hop finish.

King (OG 1049, ABV 5.1%) ◆
Pale brown-coloured strong bitter. Vine fruits and malt aroma. Sweet summer fruits, esters and biscuit malt balanced by hop bitterness.

Beheaded (OG 1068, ABV 7.5%) ◆
Smooth, brown-coloured, strong old ale. Christmas pudding with port wine. Smoked peat, figs and plums. Sweet, fruity finish, lightly dry.

Kemptown

See Hand

Kendal

☰ Tanners Yard, Kendal, Cumbria, LA9 4DH
☎ (01539) 733803 ⊕ burgundyswinebar.co.uk

Kendal Brewing Company was established in 2011. Brewing take place twice a week.

Kendricks

c/o Pig In Muck, Manor Road, Claybrooke Magna, Leicestershire, LE17 5AY ☎ 07947 812147
⊕ kendricksbrewing.co.uk

☺Linden and Jane Kendricks took over the operation of the Wood Farm Brewery in Willey near Rugby in 2015 and renamed it Kendricks. At the start of 2017 they moved out of Wood Farm and began sharing the brewing plant at the Pig Pub Brewery in Claybrooke Magna to produce their full range of beers. ◆RAIB

1823 Mild (OG 1035, ABV 3.5%)
Full-bodied dark mild with hints of caramel, finishing with a smooth, malty palate.

Barbarella (OG 1038, ABV 3.8%)
Pale session bitter that is hoppy and fruity throughout, with a distinctive dryness to the palate to finish.

Scrum (OG 1040, ABV 4%)
Deep russet red-coloured, full-bodied beer with a malty, nutty flavour. A long, dry finish with a hint of wild berries.

Boudicea (OG 1042, ABV 4.2%)
Crisp ale, golden in colour with a hoppy nose and a slight hint of bitterness on the palate to finish.

Victoria (OG 1042, ABV 4.2%)
Dark amber in colour with a distinctive malty aroma. Slightly bitter on the palate but with a mellow aftertaste.

Harlot (OG 1050, ABV 5%)
Strong, heavyweight, full-bodied ale, amber in colour with a full hoppy aroma leading to a malty finish.

Kennet & Avon SIBA

34 Old Broughton Road, Melksham, Wiltshire, SN12 8BX
☎ (01225) 707111 ☎ 07917 272482
⊕ kennetandavonbrewery.co.uk

Kennet & Avon began brewing in 2014, with the beers originally brewed by Wessex Brewery (qv) while the plant was under construction. The brewery relocated to its present site in 2015. The

beers are available at the owner's micropub, the Vaults in Devizes, the Bowbridge Lock, Stroud, and in outlets throughout the West Country. A specialist beer shop has been built, selling beers from all over the world, with a beer garden planned. A tap room is open Fridays and Saturdays. ☲◆RAIB V

Bedwyn (OG 1037, ABV 3.7%)
A malty session ale.

Foxhangers (OG 1040, ABV 3.8%)

Pillbox (OG 1039, ABV 4%) ◆
A light, refreshing ale with a hoppy bite.

Dundas (OG 1041, ABV 4.2%) ◆
A copper-coloured best bitter with a pleasant bitterness and citrus hoppy aroma.

Rusty Lane (OG 1044, ABV 4.4%) ◆
A rusty-coloured Irish-style red ale with rounded toffee malt flavour and floral hop finish.

Wilcot Wide (OG 1047, ABV 4.6%)

Bruce (OG 1048, ABV 4.8%) ◆
A rich and liquorice-tasting dark porter with an underlying roasted chocolate maltiness and slight coffee aroma.

Caen Hill Hop (OG 1050, ABV 5%) ◆
A strong golden ale with a powerful floral hop flavour.

Savernake (OG 1053, ABV 5.3%) ◆
Full-bodied black-coloured beer with aromas of liquorice, roast coffee and chocolate, with a delicate pleasant aftertaste. This barley and oat brewed beer is certified gluten-free.

Crofton IPA (OG 1054, ABV 5.4%) ◆
A traditional strong IPA-style beer balanced with the latest New World hops giving a full on flavour of exotic fruits with a light bitter finish.

Kent SIBA 👁

The Long Barn, Birling Place Farm, Stangate Road, Birling, Kent, ME19 5JN
☎ (01634) 780037 ⊕ kentbrewery.com

Kent Brewery was founded in 2010 by Toby Simmonds (ex-brewer from Dark Star) and Paul Herbert. Originally brewed at Larkins, a 10-barrel plant has been in operation at the Birling site since 2011. More than 200 outlets are supplied direct, mainly throughout Kent, Sussex and London. ◆RAIB

Session Pale (OG 1037, ABV 3.7%)
A light and hoppy session beer with hints of citrus and elderflower.

Black Gold (OG 1040, ABV 4%)
Dark-coloured beer with the easy-drinking qualities of a golden ale.

Pale (OG 1040, ABV 4%)
A full-flavoured and aromatic pale ale.

Cobnut (OG 1041, ABV 4.1%)
Generously-hopped, dark and nutty.

KGB (Kent Golding Bitter) (OG 1041, ABV 4.1%)

Summit (ABV 4.5%)
A strong citrus flavour and aroma.

Prohibition (ABV 4.8%)
A citrus pale ale, highly-hopped.

Brewers Reserve (OG 1050, ABV 5%)
A strong hop flavour of citrus and resin.

THE BREWERIES

Kentwood

⚏ **Prestoungrange Gothenburg, 227-229 High Street, Prestonpans, EH32 9BE**
⊕ kentwoodbrewery.wordpress.com

A microbrewery was installed at the award-winning pub, the Prestoungrange Gothenburg, in 2004. In 2015 the Kentwood Brewery took ownership of the five-barrel plant. Visitors to the pub are able to see the brewing process through windows separating the brewery and the main bar. Ales from the traditional Fowler's Ales range are also produced under the 'Kentwood at the Goth' label.

Kernel SIBA

Arch 11, Dockley Road Industrial Estate, Dockley Road, Bermondsey, London, SE16 4QT
☎ (020) 7231 4516

Office: 01 Spa Terminus, Spa Road, London, SE16 4QT
⊕ thekernelbrewery.com

Kernel was established in 2010 by Evin O'Riordain and moved to larger premises in 2012 to keep up with demand. The brewery produces bottle-conditioned and keg beers, and has won many awards for its wide, ever-changing range. Bottles are available from the brewery on a Saturday as well as a selection of pubs around the country.
🍺 RAIB

Keswick SIBA 👁

The Old Brewery, Brewery Lane, Keswick, Cumbria, CA12 5BY
☎ (01768) 780700 ⊕ keswickbrewery.co.uk

Keswick, owned by Sue Jefferson, began brewing in 2006 using a 10-barrel plant on the site of a brewery that closed in 1897. Outlets include Middle Ruddings Hotel in Braithwaite, the Dog & Gun, Keswick, and many other Lakeland pubs. ‼🍺◆

Gold (OG 1035, ABV 3.6%)

Bitter (OG 1036, ABV 3.7%)

Icknield (OG 1036, ABV 3.7%)

Park Your Thirst (OG 1038, ABV 3.9%)

Thirst Run (OG 1041, ABV 4.2%) 🍺
A well-balanced golden-coloured beer that maintains its fruitiness from start to finish.

Thirst Quencher (OG 1042, ABV 4.3%)

Special (OG 1047, ABV 4.8%)
Full malt flavour with notes of chocolate and roast barley.

Thirst Celebration (OG 1065, ABV 7%)

Kettlesmith (NEW) SIBA

Unit 16, Treenwood Industrial Estate, Bradford-on-Avon, Wiltshire, BA15 2AU
☎ (01225) 864839 ⊕ kettlesmithbrewing.com

⊠ Kettlesmith is a small, independent microbrewery established in 2016. It brews modern interpretations of a wide variety of beer styles, drawing inspiration from its background in America and England, as well as a love of Belgian beer. ‼◆

Outline (OG 1040, ABV 3.8%)

An amber-coloured session ale with hints of chocolate and molasses, balanced with floral and pine hops.

Faultline (OG 1043, ABV 4.1%)
A hoppy pale ale with resinous floral citrus notes of grapefruit.

Plotline (OG 1047, ABV 4.4%)
Flavours of dark chocolate, rich coffee and roast barley, with fruity hops.

Fogline (OG 1046, ABV 4.7%)
A Belgian-style ale, with hints of clove and honey and a subtle tart finish.

Ridgeline (OG 1051, ABV 5%)
A rich and powerful American rye ale. The peppery, nutty rye malt is balanced by juicy resinous hops.

Timeline (OG 1055, ABV 5.4%)
Hop-driven IPA, with malty undertones. The American and English hops combine for herbal, berry and citrus flavours.

Skyline (OG 1051, ABV 5.6%)
A Belgian Saison-style beer, spicy and earthy with hints of orange and lemon with a refreshing tart finish.

Kew

477 Upper Richmond Road West, East Sheen, London, SW14 7PU
☎ (020) 8878 9415 ⊕ kewbrewery.co.uk

⊠ Established in 2015, Kew is a family-run, independent brewery situated less than a mile from, and inspired by, the world-famous Royal Botanic Gardens at Kew. ‼🍺◆RAIB

Botanic (OG 1038, ABV 3.8%) 🍺
Refreshing, amber-coloured beer with hints of spicy hops and citrus. There is a little sweetness and a dry, lingering bitterness.

Kew Green (& Black) (OG 1040, ABV 3.9%) 🍺
Strong chocolate note to the aroma which continues into a dry, bitter taste and dry finish. A hint of sweetness.

Nightshade (OG 1045, ABV 4.2%)

Petersham Porter (OG 1045, ABV 4.3%) 🍺
Dark chocolate character in the aroma and flavour, which is malty with toffee, treacle and blackberry notes. Dry bitter finish.

Richmond Rye (OG 1045, ABV 4.3%) 🍺
Dry amber-coloured beer with hints of tangerine and spice. Bitter hops throughout with a touch of caramel in the aroma.

Sandycombe Gold (OG 1040, ABV 4.4%)
Pale golden-coloured ale, hopped and dry-hopped with fruity varieties.

Pagoda Pale (OG 1052, ABV 4.5%) 🍺
Unfined dark gold-coloured beer with biscuit sweetness balancing the citrus fruit and dryness that builds in a long bitter finish.

Keystone SIBA

Old Carpenters Workshop, Berwick St Leonard, Wiltshire, SP3 5SN
☎ (01747) 820426 ⊕ keystonebrewery.co.uk

⊠ Set up in 2006 with a 10-barrel plant, the brewer aims to be as sustainable and efficient as possible, brewing traditional southern English-style beers using local ingredients whenever possible. The beers are available in the brewery-run Benett Arms, Tisbury. Around 150 other outlets are also supplied. ‼️🍴♦️

Bedrock (OG 1035, ABV 3.6%) 🍺
Copper-coloured bitter, hops and malt in the aroma, followed by fruit and bitterness in the taste. Long, lingering aftertaste.

Gold Hill (OG 1039, ABV 4%) 🍺
Amber-coloured bitter with floral/citrus aroma, clean-tasting with a balanced bittersweet taste right through to the aftertaste, which has a slightly hoppy astringency.

Large One (OG 1041, ABV 4.2%) 🍺
Copper-coloured malty best bitter, fruit and bitterness to the fore initially, long fruit and bitter hop flavours to the finish.

Kiln SIBA

4 Alexandra Road, Burgess Hill, West Sussex, RH15 0EW ☎ 07800 556729

Office: 1st Floor, 30 Church Road, Burgess Hill, RH15 9AE ⊕ thekilnbrewery.co.uk

Kiln brewery was set up by two friends in 2014. The beers are available locally. ♦️

Mischief Maker (ABV 3.8%)
A fresh-tasting version of a classic bitter with hints of fig and black pepper and a slightly fruity aroma.

Session IPA (OG 1040, ABV 4.4%)
An IPA with a tropical juicy fruit aroma and smooth, light body. Low in bitterness with a crisp finish.

Boardwalk (OG 1046, ABV 4.5%)
A refreshing pale ale with a citrus aroma, light malt and spicy taste and a pleasing green fruit finish.

Southern Pale (OG 1046, ABV 5.2%)
A full-bodied pale ale with a citrus herbal aroma, a spicy oak dryness and a crisp finish.

Bricks & Porter (OG 1056, ABV 5.6%)
A combination of malts with hints of chocolate, coffee and a subtle smokiness balanced by a single hop. Full-bodied with a crisp finish.

King Alfred

11 Mill Rise, Bourton, Dorset, SP8 5DH ☎ (01747) 840967 ✉ kingalfredales@aol.com

❌ King Alfred is a 0.5-barrel garage brewery that started production in 2012. It currently brews about once a month. A few local pubs and beer festivals are supplied.

871 (OG 1043, ABV 4.3%)
Mid brown-coloured malty bitter with balanced hop flavours.

Saxon Gold (OG 1048, ABV 4.8%)
Mid gold-coloured bitter with prominent hop flavours and aroma.

King Street

⧉ Riverside House, Welsh Back, Bristol, BS1 4RR ☎ (0117) 405 8948

Office: The City Pub Company (West) Plc, Essel House, 2nd Floor, 29 Foley Street, London, W1W 7TH ⊕ kingstreetbrewhouse.co.uk

The King Street Brew House is owned by the the City Pub Company (West) which owns several pubs around the country. The compact brewery is on the ground floor, with the fermenting vessels and conditioning tanks in the basement. It also supplies the company's other pub in Bristol, the Prince Street Social.

King's Cliffe

Unit 10, Kingsmead, Station Road, King's Cliffe, Northamptonshire, PE8 6YH ☎ 07843 288088 ⊕ kcbales.co.uk

❌ In 2014, exactly 100 years after the last brewery in King's Cliffe ceased brewing, village resident Jeremy O'Neill set up this new venture. It currently produces five barrels a week. ‼️♦️

5C (OG 1038, ABV 3.8%) 🍺
A light bitter with a balanced taste of malt and hops and a refreshing bitter finish.

No. 10 (OG 1040, ABV 4%) 🍺
Amber-coloured beer with a clean, malty taste and a long bitter finish.

66 Degrees (OG 1046, ABV 4.6%) 🍺
Amber-coloured beer with a floral aroma, a balanced taste of malt and hops, and a long bitter finish.

Kingdom (NEW)

12 Jutland Street, Rosyth, KY11 2ZL ✉ joe.vettese@thekingdombrewery.com

Kingdom Brewery is run by the husband and wife team of Joe and Lois Vettese. It is situated in Joe's garage where he produces occasional small batch runs of beer.

Kings Clipstone

Keepers Bothy, Kings Clipstone, Nottinghamshire, NG21 9BT
☎ (01623) 823589 ☎ 07790 190020 ⊕ kingsclipstonebrewery.co.uk

Located in the heart of Sherwood Forest, Kings Clipstone began brewing in 2012 using a five-barrel plant. The owners, David and Daryl Maguire, brew a range of core beers plus one-off brews and seasonals. Beers are available nationwide to freehouses, festivals and wholesale markets. ‼️♦️

Palace Pale (OG 1036, ABV 3.6%)
Golden ale which is light and crisp with a refreshing taste.

Hop On (OG 1039, ABV 3.8%)
A pale and refreshing session beer with fruity hops.

Amazing Gazing (OG 1040, ABV 4%)
A red-coloured, easy-drinking bitter with a floral aroma and pleasant aftertaste.

Tabaknakas (OG 1041, ABV 4.1%)
A golden ale with overtones of spiced berries with floral characteristics.

Moonbeam (OG 1042, ABV 4.2%)
A mid strength, chestnut-coloured bitter with a full flavour and well-rounded finish.

Sire (OG 1043, ABV 4.2%)
A well-rounded beer with a clean bitter finish.

Queen Bee (OG 1051, ABV 5.1%)

A ruby red-coloured strong ale, classically rich and smooth.

Kings Head

⊟ Kings Head, 132 High Street, Bildeston, Suffolk, IP7 7ED
☎ (01449) 741434 ⊕ bildestonkingshead.co.uk

Kings Head has been brewing since 1996 in an old cart lodge at the back of the pub. Under new ownership since 2008, the 2.5-barrel plant brews fortnightly.

Kingstone SIBA

Tintern, NP16 7NX
☎ (01291) 680111 ⊕ kingstonebrewery.co.uk

Kingstone Brewery is located in the Wye Valley close to Tintern Abbey. Brewing began on a four-barrel plant in 2005. Special brews are marketed under the Hapax Brewing Co label. !! ➡ ♦ RAIB

Tewdric's Tipple (OG 1038, ABV 3.8%)
An ale with a dry, bitter character and a tangy core.

Challenger (OG 1040, ABV 4%)
A smooth, richly-hopped, well-balanced ale with a malty nose and toffee undertones.

Gold (OG 1040, ABV 4%)
A straw-coloured smooth ale with citrus notes and a balanced, hoppy finish.

Llandogo Trow (OG 1042, ABV 4.2%)
A ruby red-coloured ale with a smooth, fruity finish.

Premium Stout (OG 1044, ABV 4.4%)
A smooth, rich stout with a bitter finish.

Classic (OG 1045, ABV 4.5%)
A balanced, distinctly hoppy, dry ale with a floral nose and a smooth, well-balanced finish.

1503 (OG 1048, ABV 4.8%)
A deep chestnut red in colour, lightly-hopped and bursting with complex, rich flavours.

Abbey Ale (OG 1051, ABV 5.1%)
An amber-coloured, full-flavoured ale. The hoppy edge is balanced by a smooth, malty richness.

Humpty (OG 1058, ABV 5.8%)
An IPA with a slightly sweet, floral nose, a balanced level of malt supporting the hops and finally a subtle but slightly citrus finish.

Kinneil

84 Corbiehall, Bo'ness, EH51 0AS ☎ 07789 204008
⊕ kinneilbrew.co.uk

⊛Kinneil began brewing in 2011 using a 2.5-barrel plant. The brewery is adjacent to the Corbie Inn but separately owned.

Wonderfu' Jake (OG 1037, ABV 3.6%)

Katie Wearie's (OG 1039, ABV 3.8%)

Wayfinder (OG 1038, ABV 3.8%)

Pennvael Amber (OG 1042, ABV 4%)

Kincardine Sunset (OG 1042, ABV 4.1%)

Caer Edin Dark (OG 1044, ABV 4.2%)

Kinver SIBA ◉

Unit 1, Britch Farm, Rocky Wall, Kinver, Staffordshire, DY7 5NW ☎ 07715 842676 ⊕ kinverbrewery.co.uk

⊛Established in 2004, Kinver produces a wide range of different beer styles including one-off specials. The brewery relocated in 2012 to a new 10-barrel plant on the edge of Kinver due to increased demand. Around 30 outlets are supplied direct including several in Kinver. !! ♦ RAIB

Light Railway (OG 1038, ABV 3.8%) ◆
Straw-coloured session beer. A fruity and malty start quickly gives way to well-hopped bitterness and a lingering hoppy aftertaste.

Cavegirl Bitter (OG 1040, ABV 4%)
Pale straw-coloured, well-balanced bitter.

Edge (OG 1041, ABV 4.2%) ◆
Amber in colour with a malty aroma. Sweet fruity start with a hint of citrus marmalade in the spicy edged malt; lasting hoppy finish that is satisfyingly bitter.

Noble (OG 1043, ABV 4.5%) ▣ ◆
Fruity hop aroma. Fruity start then the grassy hops give a sharp bitter finish with malt support.

Maybug (OG 1045, ABV 4.8%)

Half Centurion (OG 1047, ABV 5%) ▢ ◆
A golden-coloured best bitter; malty before the hop takes command to give a balanced, hoppy finish.

Black Ram Stout (OG 1048, ABV 5.2%)
Full-bodied, roasty dark stout.

Khyber (OG 1054, ABV 5.8%) ◆
Golden-coloured strong bitter with a hop bite that overwhelms the fleeting malty sweetness and drives through to the long, dry finish.

Over the Edge (OG 1068, ABV 7.5%) ▢ ▣

Kirkby Lonsdale SIBA

Unit 2F, Old Station Yard, Kirkby Lonsdale, Cumbria, LA6 2HP
☎ (01524) 272221 ☎ 07793 149999
⊕ kirkbylonsdalebrewery.com

⊛Kirkby Lonsdale is a family-run business established in 2009 on a six-barrel plant. In 2016 a further six-barrel plant was installed in its new brewery tap, the Royal Barn, Kirkby Lonsdale. !! ♦

Crafty Mild (OG 1036, ABV 3.6%) ◆
A typical mild with powerful malty aromas and some caramel, which follows through in the taste and finish.

Tiffin Gold (OG 1036, ABV 3.6%) ◆
A full-flavoured, grapefruit hoppy and bitter beer with a dry finish.

Stanley's Pale Ale (OG 1038, ABV 3.8%) ◆
Hops dominate this sweet and fruity, well-balanced beer.

Ruskins Bitter (OG 1039, ABV 3.9%) ◆
A tawny-coloured bitter with a distinctive aroma of fruit and malt. The clean, hoppy flavour is well-balanced with fruity sweetness leading to a sustained bittersweet finish.

Singletrack (OG 1040, ABV 4%) ◆
Crisp citrus hops predominate in a well-balanced beer with a pleasant bitter finish.

Radical Red (OG 1042, ABV 4.2%) ◆

Malty beer with a caramel sweetness that is balanced by a bitter finish.

Monumental Blonde (OG 1045, ABV 4.5%) ◆
Distinctly hoppy, a fruity, sweet, pale-coloured, full-bodied bitter.

Jubilee Stout (OG 1055, ABV 5.5%) ◆
Rich, well-balanced stout with malt. A long aftertaste retains this complexity and is surprisingly refreshing.

Westmorland Pale Ale (OG 1060, ABV 6.2%)
A pale ale with fruity, spicy hop flavours and aroma together with a delicate hint of chocolate malt.

Imperial Dragon (OG 1080, ABV 8.2%)
Dry-hopped and dangerously drinkable IPA.

Kirkstall SIBA

100 Kirkstall Road, Leeds, West Yorkshire, LS3 1HJ
☎ (0113) 898 0280 ⊕ kirkstallbrewerycompany.com

☺ The brewery was established in 2011 a few yards from the original Kirkstall Brewery beside the Leeds-Liverpool canal. Nearby Kirkstall Abbey, which had its own brewhouse, and lost local industries are the inspiration for the beer names. The range can be sampled in the Kirkstall Bridge Inn, the brewery tap. ‼◆

BYB (Best Yorkshire Bitter) (OG 1036, ABV 3.5%)

Pale Ale (OG 1040, ABV 4%)

Three Swords (OG 1045, ABV 4.5%) ◆
Pithy grapefruit flavours characterise this light-coloured golden ale, plenty of hops from the start to the lingering finish.

Dissolution IPA (OG 1050, ABV 5%) ◆
Full-flavoured ale – hops lead the charge with bitter fruit just behind.

Black Band Porter (OG 1055, ABV 5.5%) ◆
Dark, smooth and complex. Expect sumptuous fruit cake flavours, hints of malted chocolate, coffee and liquorice plus occasional smokiness.

Generous George (OG 1060, ABV 6%)

Kirrie

Bon Scott Brewery, 8 Bon Scott Place, Kirriemuir, DD8 4LD ☎ 07855 808975 ⊕ kirrie-ales.co.nf

Established in 2014, Kirrie Ales is situated in the picturesque town of Kirriemuir, birthplace of JM Barrie, creator of Peter Pan, and gateway to the Angus Glens. The brewery space measures only 8 by 9 feet. RAIB

Fruity Wee Blonde (OG 1037, ABV 3.8%)
American-style pale ale with lots of grapefruit and other citrus flavours but not overly dry and bitter.

Hoppy Daze (OG 1039, ABV 4%)
Well-balanced classic session IPA.

Red from the Shed (OG 1044, ABV 4.5%)
Scottish 80/- style beer with subtle fruity notes on the finish.

Thrums Best (OG 1044, ABV 4.5%)
Well-balanced bitter with hints of orange on the finish.

Kissingate

Pole Barn, Church Lane Farm Estate, Church Lane, Lower Beeding, West Sussex, RH13 6LU

☎ (01403) 891335 ⊕ kissingate.co.uk

⊠ Kissingate Brewery is an eight-barrel plant that began brewing commercially in 2010. It is located in a barn conversion in a quiet wooded valley near the village of Lower Beeding. The brewery is available for private hire. Brew days can be booked. ‼☭◆

Storyteller (OG 1036, ABV 3.5%)

Sussex (OG 1040, ABV 4%)

Black Cherry Mild (OG 1042, ABV 4.2%)

Gardenia Mild (OG 1045, ABV 4.5%)

Moon (OG 1045, ABV 4.5%)
A taste of lightly roasted malts, late autumn apples and a lingering hop bitterness.

Old Tale Porter (OG 1045, ABV 4.5%)

Mandarina Red (OG 1048, ABV 4.8%)
A complex, red-coloured IPA with multiple flavour layers of malt and prominent citrus fruits. A pine and citrus bitter finish.

Chennai Premium IPA (OG 1050, ABV 5%)

Micro Lot Coffee Porter (OG 1050, ABV 5%)

Toffee Cog (OG 1052, ABV 5%)

Smelter's Stout (OG 1052, ABV 5.1%)

Power Blue (OG 1058, ABV 5.5%)

Metal Cat (OG 1060, ABV 5.8%)

Stout Extreme Jamaica (OG 1060, ABV 6%)

Mary's Ruby Mild (OG 1064, ABV 6.5%)
Deep ruby in colour with gentle aromas of well-aged port. Intense and rounded malt flavours and a light and floral hop aftertaste.

Six Crows (OG 1068, ABV 6.6%)

Knockout

Unit 10, Alanbrooke Park, Alexander Road, Belfast, BT6 9HB

Founded in 2009 by Joseph McMullan, Knockout produces a range of bottle-conditioned beers. Each brew is usually in small 900-litre batches. RAIB

Knops SIBA

The Walled Garden, Archerfield Estate, Dirleton, EH39 5HQ ☎ 07949 879147 ⊕ knopsbeer.co.uk

☺Knops began brewing in 2010 under contract. In 2013 it moved to new premises on the Archerfield Estate at Dirleton on the East Lothian coastline with an 11-barrel plant. Beers are based on modern interpretations of traditional styles and are bottled in-house. Cask-conditioned beers are available in Eastern Scotland and the Glasgow area. ‼RAIB

East Coast Pale (OG 1039, ABV 3.8%)
An aromatic session beer.

Musselburgh Broke (OG 1045, ABV 4.5%)
Full malt flavour with a clean, brisk finish.

California Common (OG 1048, ABV 4.6%)
A clean hop finish and light toffee notes followed by lingering bitterness.

India Pale Ale (OG 1047, ABV 5%)
A citrus and apricot aroma, well-balanced by a smooth, honeyed malt backbone.

Black Cork (OG 1066, ABV 6.5%)

A dark beer with a prominent chocolate/coffee bitterness and hop aroma.

Contract brewed for Archerfield Fine Ales:

Golden Ale (OG 1039, ABV 3.8%)

Dark Ale (OG 1046, ABV 4.7%)

India Pale Ale (OG 1047, ABV 5%)

Krafty Brew

▤ Star & Garter, 1 High Port, Linlithgow, EH49 7AB
☎ 07763 873596 ⊕ kraftybrew.com

A small brewery with six Braumeister systems specialising in 'brew it yourself' and own label products. A range of bottle-conditioned beers is also sold under the Krafty brand name. Some cask-conditioned beer is available at the brewery's pub, Woodland Creatures, Leith.

Lacada

7a Victoria Street, Portrush, BT56 8DL
☎ (028) 7082 5684 ⊕ lacadabrewery.com

Lacada was established in 2015 and produces its Salamander series alongside three core beers. RAIB

Giant's Organ (OG 1045, ABV 4.5%)

Sorley Boy's Stash (OG 1045, ABV 4.5%)

Stranded Bunny (OG 1045, ABV 4.5%)

Lacons SIBA ⊙

Falcon Brewery, Main Cross Road, Great Yarmouth, Norfolk, NR30 3NZ
☎ (01493) 850578 ⊕ lacons.co.uk

⊠ Lacons Brewery has a rich history dating back to 1760 but was closed by Whitbread in the 1960s. It relaunched in 2013 and the Falcon Brewery is now nestled within a stunning courtyard in Great Yarmouth. Its award-winning beers are available across East Anglia and beyond. The brewery also produces a range of 'Heritage' seasonal ales based on the brewery's original recipes from the archives. Beers are brewed with the original Lacons yeast strains, which had been stored at the National Collection of Yeast Cultures since 1959. ‼ ▅ ♦ RAIB

Encore (OG 1038, ABV 3.8%) ◥
Grapefruit and hops dominate throughout. Well-balanced with soft sweetness contributing to a gently tapering finish.

Falcon Ale (OG 1042, ABV 4.2%) ◥
Complex with malt, caramel, hop and plum vying for supremacy. Both smooth and grainy with a well-rounded, bittersweet finale.

Legacy (OG 1043, ABV 4.4%) ◥
Malty nose with some biscuit. Orange maltiness. Malt, hop and citrus beginning. Increasingly bitter finish.

Affinity (OG 1046, ABV 4.8%) ◥
A bouncy citrus nose. Orange notes soar over an astringent hoppiness softened by a gentle malt background. A growing hop finish.

Audit (OG 1072, ABV 8%)
Barley wine with flavours of berry fruit, laced with pronounced spice. The finish is warming, smooth and sweet.

Laig Bay (NEW)

Galmisdale, Isle of Eigg, PH42 4RL
⊕ laigbaybrewingco.wordpress.com

Laig Bay began brewing in 2014 and brews 150 litres per week, most of which stays on Eigg.

I am the Eiggman (ABV 4%)

Cleadale 80/- (ABV 4.5%)

Five Pennies Pilsner (ABV 4.8%)

Charadail Pale Ale (ABV 5.5%)

Killdonnan (ABV 5.5%)

Independence IPA (ABV 6.2%)

Red Martyr (ABV 8.5%)

Laine

▤ Brighton: North Laine Bar & Brewhouse, 27 Gloucester Place, Brighton, East Sussex, BN1 4AA
☎ (01273) 683666

Battersea: Four Thieves, 51 Lavender Gardens, London, SW11 1DJ ☎ (020) 7223 6927

Victoria Park: People's Park Tavern, 360 Victoria Park Road, London, E9 7BT ☎ (020) 8533 0040

Laine launched its first brewery in 2012, in Brighton, using a five-barrel plant based within the North Laine pub, which is owned by the drinkinbrighton pub group. The brewing equipment and process can be viewed from the bar. In 2013 a sister brewery was opened in Acton, London (currently derelict due to fire), with the brewing equipment - three fermenters producing 60 firkins of beer a week - visible behind the left-hand bar. Since then two more Laine breweries have been established in London, in Hackney (2014) and Battersea (2015). The beer range varies in each establishment.

Lakehouse (NEW)

Lake House, Peachfield Road, Malvern, Worcestershire, WR14 3LE ☎ 07532 440634
⊕ lakehousebrewery.com

Lakehouse was established in 2016 by Dan Frost and Graeme Gordon on a 2.5-barrel plant. Situated below the Malvern Hills, within the grounds of a country house and fishing lake, from which it takes its name. Beers can be found at food & drink festivals and Farmers' Markets as well as trade outlets.

Amber Session Ale (OG 1038.5, ABV 3.9%)
Light, sweet and refreshing session ale.

Citrus Pale Ale (OG 1039.5, ABV 4%)
A light, refreshing pale ale with punchy citrus notes.

Cherry-Chocolate Porter (OG 1063, ABV 5.5%)
A soft and fruity speciality beer with a sweet chocolate influence. Infused with fresh cherries.

LAM

Unit 68, Sandford Lane Industrial Estate, Sandford Lane, Kennington, Oxfordshire, OX1 5RP ☎ 07913 061025 ⊕ lambrewing.com

LAM began brewing in 2014. No real ale. ▅

THE BREWERIES · L

Lancaster SIBA 👁

Lancaster Leisure Park, Wyresdale Road, Lancaster, LA1 3LA
☎ (01524) 848537 ⊕ lancasterbrewery.co.uk

⊕Lancaster began brewing in 2005. The brewery moved to new premises in 2010 and installed a larger 60-barrel brewing plant. As well as the regular beers, seasonal beers are brewed under the T'ales from the Brewhouse name. ‼️🍽♦V

Amber (OG 1037, ABV 3.6%) ◆
Amber malt flavours lead to an increasingly astringent bitter finish.

Blonde (OG 1041, ABV 4%) ◆
A pale, gently-hopped, easy-drinking, mild bitter with an astringent finish.

Black (OG 1045, ABV 4.5%) ◆
A satisfying and robust roast bitter beer with hints of sweet fruitiness.

Red (OG 1047, ABV 4.8%) ◆
Sweet start with lasting roast malts leads to a satisfying bitter finish.

Landlocked

🍺 Handle Bar, 54a King Street, Alfreton, Derbyshire, DE55 7DD ☎ 07845 609585
✉ brewhousemike@gmail.com

Landlocked began brewing in 2014 using a five-barrel plant in outbuildings behind the Beehive Inn in Ripley. In 2016 it moved to the Handle Bar in Alfreton, which is now the brewery tap. The beers can also be found in the Beehive, the Honeypot bar, the Five Lamps and other local free houses.

Honeypot Pale (OG 1036, ABV 4%)
Pale golden ale brewed with a touch of honey.

Island IPA (OG 1044, ABV 4.7%)
A golden-coloured IPA, powerfully hopped.

A & E (OG 1064, ABV 7.4%)
An amber-coloured IPA, strong and powerful.

Landlord's Friend

🍺 Kershaw House Inn, Luddenden Lane, Luddendenfoot, West Yorkshire, HX2 6NW
☎ (01422) 882222 ✉ landfriendbeers@aol.co.uk

Landlord's Friend began brewing in 2010 using a 2.5-barrel plant. Around 30 outlets are supplied direct.

Last Leaf (ABV 4%)
Golden-coloured, fruity ale with a hint of dryness in a grainy malt finish.

Mr Cuddle (ABV 4%)
Combines coriander with a malt base and light spicy notes.

Chestnuts Roasting (ABV 4.1%)
Chestnut-coloured beer, malty with nutty hints. Dry and malty finish.

Mr Webster's Brown Ale (ABV 4.2%)
Moderate malty aroma with molasses, caramel and toffee. Flavour is sweetish, with some nutty malts and a touch of toffee.

Mr JK's Itish (ABV 4.4%)
Rich, black body with roast. coffee and nuts flavours and a bitter, dry finish.

Not Just For Mother (ABV 4.5%)

Light-bodied with a blend of malt and hops.

Langham SIBA

Old Granary, Langham Lane, Lodsworth, GU28 9BU
☎ (01798) 860861 ⊕ langhambrewery.co.uk

⊠ Langham Brewery was established in 2006 in an 18th-century granary barn and is set in the heart of West Sussex with fine views of the rolling South Downs. It is owned by Lesley Foulkes and James Berrow who brew and run the business. The brewery is a 10-barrel steam-heated plant and more than 200 outlets are supplied. ‼️🍽

Halfway to Heaven (OG 1035, ABV 3.5%)
A chestnut-coloured beer with a balanced biscuit maltiness and citrus and fruit hop character with a hint of spice.

Saison (OG 1039, ABV 3.9%)
A zesty, unfined, Saison-style beer, light and well hopped.

Hip Hop (OG 1038, ABV 4%)
A blonde beer, clean and crisp. The nose is loaded with floral hop aroma while the pale malt flavour is overtaken by a dry and bitter finish.

Sundowner (OG 1042, ABV 4.2%)
Tropical fruit, pineapple and citrus on the nose with a smooth maltiness in the background. A balanced bitter finish with floral hop aroma.

Best (OG 1043, ABV 4.5%)
A tawny-coloured classic best bitter with well-balanced malt flavours and bitterness.

Arapaho (OG 1046, ABV 4.9%)

LSD (Langham Special Draught) (ABV 5.2%)
An auburn-coloured beer with a sweet maltiness balanced by spicy hop aromas and a dry finish.

Black Swallow (OG 1055, ABV 6%)

Langton SIBA 👁

Grange Farm, Welham Road, Thorpe Langton, Leicestershire, LE16 7TU
☎ (01858) 540116 ☎ 07840 532826
⊕ langtonbrewery.co.uk

Established in 1999 in outbuildings behind the Bell Inn, East Langton, the brewery relocated in 2005 to a converted barn at Thorpe Langton, where a four-barrel plant was installed. Further expansion in 2010 and 2016 significantly increased capacity. ‼️♦RAIB

Caudle Bitter (OG 1039, ABV 3.9%) ◆
Copper-coloured session bitter that is close to pale ale in style. Flavours are relatively well-balanced throughout with hops slightly to the fore.

Inclined Plane Bitter (OG 1042, ABV 4.2%)
A straw-coloured bitter with a citrus nose and long, hoppy finish.

Hop On (OG 1044, ABV 4.4%)
A premium bitter, deep chestnut in colour with a good balance of flavours and aroma.

Bowler Strong Ale (OG 1048, ABV 4.8%)
A strong traditional ale with a deep red colour and a hoppy nose.

Bullseye (OG 1050, ABV 4.8%)
Intensely dark stout with flavours of liquorice and chocolate.

THE BREWERIES

839

Langwith SIBA

Unit 16, Hermitage Way, Hermitage Way Industrial Estate, Mansfield, Nottinghamshire, NG18 5ES
☎ (01623) 740607 ⏚ langwithbrewing.co.uk

Purpose-built six-barrel brewhouse that opened in 2016. A 100-litre pilot plant is also utilised for small run and experimental brews.

Stumpys Bitter (ABV 3.8%)
A light golden-coloured bitter with slightly earthy overtones. Full-bodied and dry with balanced malty sweetness.

Mystic Peg (ABV 4.1%)
Unfined pale ale with a floral and fresh aroma with a hint of grapefruit. The taste is crisp and clean with a zesty bite.

Dickie MiG (ABV 4.4%)

Pocket Locket (ABV 4.7%)
Rich honey IPA with a smooth, clean taste.

Lord Humungous (ABV 4.8%)
A deep brown-coloured porter with dry oatmeal and bitter chocolate aroma. Soft and smooth with liquorice overtones.

Lucy Locket (ABV 5.1%)
A light honey-coloured IPA with subtle hop aroma. Crisp and sweet with a citrus aftertaste.

Mozza (ABV 5.9%)
A light amber-coloured ale with a deep earthy fragrance. Full-bodied, rich and smooth.

Larkins SIBA

Larkins Farm, Hampkins Hill Road, Chiddingstone, Kent, TN8 7BB
☎ (01892) 870328

⊠ Larkins brewery was founded by the Dockerty family in Rusthall in Kent in 1986, on the site of the original Royal Tunbridge Wells Brewery. In 1988 the brewery relocated to Larkins Farm in Chiddingstone. All beers include hops grown on the farm itself. The brewery delivers direct to around 40-50 pubs and restaurants within a 20-mile radius. ‼◆

Traditional Ale (OG 1035, ABV 3.4%)
Tawny in colour, a full-tasting hoppy ale with plenty of character for its strength.

Pale (ABV 4.2%)
Pleasantly hoppy pale ale with a soft, fruity rather than astringent aftertaste.

Best (OG 1045, ABV 4.4%) ◈
Full-bodied, slightly fruity and unusually bitter for its gravity.

Law (NEW)

Unit 17, Mid Wynd, Dundee, DD1 4JG ☎ 07893 538277 ⏚ lawbrewing.co

Law brewing Co was established in 2016 and is named after Dundee's most distinctive landmark; the volcano-like slopes of the Law. RAIB V

All-Nighter Gold Ale (OG 1044, ABV 4.5%)
A refreshing golden-coloured beer with tropical/citrus notes and a hint of marmalade.

Liquid Bread Ale (OG 1049, ABV 5%)
A pale ale using surplus bread and various hop combinations in collaboration with Clark's Bakery in Dundee.

Weekender Pils Style (OG 1049, ABV 5%)
A refreshing Pilsner/lager hybrid with lemon and lime notes and spicy hop flavours.

Mod IPA (OG 1052, ABV 5.5%)
A sharp, modern IPA with a clean hit of tropical fruits.

Lawman

Craigmarloch, Cumbernauld
☎ (0141) 212 9570 ☎ 07872 525762
⏚ lawmanbrew.co.uk

Lawman began brewing in 2015 using a five-barrel brew plant located in an industrial unit near Cumbernauld town centre. ◆

Pixel Bandit (OG 1040, ABV 4%)
A session ale with a citrus aroma and flavours of lemongrass and tangerine.

Steadfast Koln-ish Bier (OG 1044, ABV 4.4%)
A session lager with an elderflower twist.

Onyx (OG 1048, ABV 4.8%)
A full-bodied stout with a clean coffee bitterness and dark chocolate finish.

Horizon APA (OG 1052, ABV 5.2%)
A deep golden-coloured American pale ale, packed with tropical fruits and pine.

Weatherall IPA (OG 1064, ABV 6.4%)
A heavily-hopped IPA with an orange marmalade bitterness and full flavour.

Leadmill

Unit 3, Heanor Small Business Centre, Adams Close, Heanor, Derbyshire, DE75 7SW ☎ 07971 189915
⊠ leadmill@fsmail.net

⊠ Set up in Selston in 1999, Leadmill moved to Denby in 2001 and again in 2010 to Heanor. A sister brewery to Bottle Brook (qv), the brewery tap is at the Old Oak, Horsley Woodhouse. ◆

Langley Best (OG 1036, ABV 3.6%)

Mash Tun Bitter (OG 1036, ABV 3.6%)

Old Oak Bitter (OG 1037, ABV 3.7%)

B52 (OG 1050, ABV 5.2%)

Slumdog (OG 1058, ABV 5.9%)

Leafy Hollow

Ferkins Barn, Lower Burlone, Washaway, Cornwall, PL30 3AJ ☎ 07592 310182
⊠ leafyhollowbrewery@yahoo.com

This nanobrewery was established in 2015 and brews bottle-conditioned beers by hand crafting without machinery, using traditional methods and containing no modern chemicals. RAIB

Leatherbritches

⛁ **Brewery Yard, Tap House, Annwell, Smisby, Derbyshire, LE65 2TA** ☎ 07976 279253
⏚ leatherbritches.co.uk

The brewery, founded in 1993 in Fenny Bentley, has relocated and expanded over the years, moving to its current address in 2011 where it effectively took over the existing Tap House Brewery (established 2010) but continued to brew the latter's beers. Since 2015, however, Tap House beers have become re-badged Leatherbritches products.

Goldings (OG 1036, ABV 3.6%)
A light golden beer with a flowery hoppy aroma and a bitter finish.

Lemongrass & Ginger (OG 1036, ABV 3.8%)
Pale and hoppy ale infused with lemongrass and ginger. Crisp and refreshing.

Ashbourne Ale (OG 1040, ABV 4%)
A pale bitter with a crisp, lasting taste.

Scoundrel (OG 1040, ABV 4.1%)
Full-bodied porter with a well-rounded, sweet finish.

Dovedale (OG 1044, ABV 4.4%)
A copper-coloured bitter with a crisp finish.

Ginger Helmet (OG 1047, ABV 4.7%)
A pale bitter with a sweet finish and a hint of ginger.

Hairy Helmet (OG 1047, ABV 4.7%)
Pale bitter, well-hopped but with a sweet finish.

Ashbourne IPA (OG 1047, ABV 4.9%)
Pale ale with a flowery, hoppy aroma and a strong bitter finish, crisp and refreshing.

Bespoke (OG 1048, ABV 5%)
Full-bodied, well-rounded premium bitter.

Stouter (OG 1049, ABV 5.2%)
Stout with a coffee and vanilla taste.

Scary Hairy (OG 1057, ABV 5.9%)
Pale and hoppy, a stronger version of Hairy Helmet.

Scary Hairy Export (OG 1064, ABV 7.2%)
Strong pale bitter produced with New World hops creating a bitter, dry finish.

Leazes Lane

⊟ Trent House, 1-2 Leazes Lane, Newcastle upon Tyne, NE1 4QT
☎ (0191) 261 2154

Leazes Lane began brewing in 2013 using a one-barrel plant. Beer is only available in the pub.

Ledbury SIBA

Gazerdine House, Hereford Road, Ledbury, Herefordshire, HR8 2PZ
☎ (01531) 671184 ☎ 07957 428070
⊕ ledburyrealales.co.uk

☺Established in 2012, Ledbury Real Ales uses hops grown in Herefordshire and Worcestershire with other materials sourced locally where possible. The beers are sold mainly within a 15-mile radius of the brewery. ‼◆

Bitter (OG 1038, ABV 3.8%)
A traditional, copper-coloured ale with a noticeably bitter start and an enjoyable finish with hints of spice and citrus.

Dark (OG 1039, ABV 3.9%)
A chocolate and coffee start with a smooth, mellow finish with notes of spice, marmalade and honey.

Gold (OG 1040, ABV 4%)

A golden bitter, well-balanced with a honey and fruit finish.

Dr Rudi's Extra Pale (ABV 4.1%)
A light beer with a slight bitter finish.

Phoenixx (ABV 4.5%)
A dark beer brewed with a complex mix of malts and hops that impart a taste of chocolate, spice and molasses.

Leeds SIBA ⊚

3 Sydenham Road, Holbeck, Leeds, West Yorkshire, LS11 9RU
☎ (0113) 244 5866 ⊕ leedsbrewery.co.uk

☺Production began in 2007 using a 20-barrel plant. The largest independent brewer in the city, it uses a unique strain of yeast originally used by a defunct West Yorkshire brewery. Beer is supplied direct as far as South Yorkshire, Lancashire, the North East and North Lincolnshire. A separate brew plant is situated in the Leeds Brewery Tap. In 2016 Camerons of Hartlepool (qv) bought the Leeds' pub estate. Beers are also brewed for Suddaby's. ◆

Pale (OG 1037.5, ABV 3.8%) ◣
Hops and fruit, sometimes citrus or lemon, last through to the bitter, dry, hoppy finish. Light gold in colour.

Yorkshire Gold (OG 1040, ABV 4%) ◣
Plenty of zesty citrus flavours, a wallop of hops and a long-lasting bitter finish make this a refreshing beer.

Best (OG 1041, ABV 4.3%) ⬚ ◣
There is a pleasing mix of malt and hops in this smooth, amber-coloured, bittersweet beer.

Midnight Bell (OG 1047.5, ABV 4.8%) ⬚ ◣
A full-bodied strong mild, deep red to dark brown in colour. Chocolate and strong malt flavours are present throughout.

Lees IFBB ⊚

Greengate Brewery, Middleton Junction, Manchester, M24 2AX
☎ (0161) 643 2487 ⊕ jwlees.co.uk

☺Family-owned since its foundation by John Lees in 1828, the brewery has a tied estate of around 150 pubs, mostly in north Manchester, Cheshire, Lancashire and North Wales. The vast majority serve cask beer. The current head brewer is a family member. ‼

Brewer's Dark (OG 1032, ABV 3.5%) ◣
Formerly GB Mild, this is a dark brown beer with a malt and caramel aroma. Creamy mouthfeel, with malt, caramel and fruit flavours and a malty finish. Becoming rare.

Supernova (OG 1035, ABV 3.5%)

Manchester Pale Ale (OG 1038, ABV 3.7%) ◣
Yellow in colour, with malt, hops and a good bitterness throughout.

The Governor (OG 1038, ABV 3.8%)
Malty auburn/amber-coloured beer with floral and citrus notes and a clean, dry finish.

Bitter (OG 1037, ABV 4%) ◣
Copper-coloured beer with malt and fruit in aroma, taste and finish.

Dragon's Fire (OG 1037, ABV 4%)

Game On (OG 1042, ABV 4.2%)

John Willie's (OG 1041, ABV 4.5%)
A well-balanced, full-bodied premium bitter.

Moonraker (OG 1073, ABV 6.5%) ◀
A reddish brown-coloured beer with a strong, malty, fruity aroma. The flavour is rich and sweet, with roast malt, and the finish is fruity yet dry.

Left Bank

☎ 07815 849523 ⊕ leftbankbrewery.co.uk

Brewing began in 2013 in Walthamstow. In 2016 the brewery began using spare capacity at other breweries while a permanent premises is sought in Wales.

Left Handed Giant SIBA

Unit 9, Wadehurst Industrial Park, St Philips Road, St Philip's, Bristol, BS2 0JE ⊕ lefthandedgiant.com

Originally launched in 2015 as a cuckoo brewery using spare capacity at other local breweries for commercial brews and its own 200-litre plant for more experimental beers, Left Handed Giant have recently installed a 12.5-barrel plant. The brewery shares premises with Big Beer Distribution, where there is a tap room (open Apr-Sep). The head brewer, Richard Poole, is a former home brewer and also has his own nanobrewery, Rocket Science (qv). **RAIB**

Pale (OG 1039, ABV 4.3%)

Lactose Tolerant (OG 1059, ABV 5.1%)

Legitimate Industries (NEW)

10 Weaver Street, Leeds, West Yorkshire, LS4 2AU ⊕ legitimateworldwide.com

Founded in 2016. No real ale.

Leighton Buzzard SIBA ◉

Unit 31, Harmill Industrial Estate, Grovebury Road, Leighton Buzzard, Bedfordshire, LU7 4FF ☎ 07538 903753 ⊕ leightonbuzzardbrewing.co.uk

The first brewery to operate in Leighton Buzzard for over 100 years. Established in 2014 by local CAMRA member and home brew enthusiast Jon d'Este-Hoare, the first beers were upscaled versions of his home brews. ‼️🛒◆

Cuckoo Ale (OG 1038, ABV 3.8%)
A traditional British bitter.

Narrow Gauge (OG 1040, ABV 3.9%)
A golden ale, light and refreshing with a dry bitter taste and crisp, citrus finish.

Restoration Ale (OG 1049, ABV 4.6%)
A mid brown-coloured best bitter, fruity and refreshing.

Rebel Yell (OG 1053, ABV 5%)
A black IPA with an initial smooth malt richness followed by sharp, dry hops.

Black Buzzard (OG 1061, ABV 5.8%)
A complex, robust porter.

Leila Cottage SIBA

🏠 Countryman, Chapel Road, Ingoldmells, Skegness, Lincolnshire, PE25 1ND
☎ (01754) 872268
✉ countryman_inn@btconnect.com

Brewing began in 2007. The brewery is situated at the Countryman pub – Leila Cottage was the original name of the building before it became a licensed club and more recently a pub. The history of the Countryman and the brewery is on display in the pub.

Leith Hill

🏠 c/o Plough Inn, Coldharbour Lane, Coldharbour, Surrey, RH5 6HD
☎ (01306) 711793 ⊕ ploughinn.com

Leith Hill was established in 1996 at the Plough Inn and was moved to converted storerooms at the rear in 2001, increasing capacity to 2.5 barrels in 2005. All beers brewed are sold only on the premises. New owners took over in 2016.

Lenton Lane

Unit 5G, The Midway, Lenton Industrial Estate, Nottingham, NG7 2TS ☎ 0333 003 5008
⊕ lentonlane.co.uk

⊠ Lenton Lane began brewing in 2014 under the name Frontier, after taking over the brewing plant at the Flower Pot pub in Derby. Lenton Lane changed its name in 2016 and relocated to a purpose-built brewery in Nottingham using a 10-barrel plant. ◆

Gold Rush (OG 1037, ABV 4%)

Pioneer (OG 1040, ABV 4.3%)
A golden, crisp, hoppy pale ale with a dry finish.

Ramification (OG 1042, ABV 4.5%)

Atlas Stout (OG 1046, ABV 5%)
A full-bodied, rich, dry stout. Coffee and chocolate notes give way to a dry finish.

Lerwick SIBA

Staneyhill, North Road, Lerwick, Shetland, ZE1 0QA
☎ (01595) 694552 ☎ 07738 948336
⊕ lerwickbrewery.co.uk

Lerwick Brewery was established in 2011 using a 12-barrel plant and sits at the very edge of the North Atlantic. Originally only brewing keg beer, a cask-conditioned range was launched in 2015.

Shetland Pale Ale (ABV 3.8%) ◀
Malt and citrus hops with a background sulphur taste.

Azure (ABV 4.3%) ◀
Refreshing, grapefruit/peach, hoppy, golden bitter.

IPA (ABV 5%) ◀
Grapefruit hoppy bitter with a slight biscuit background.

Tushkar (ABV 5.5%) ◀
Dark brown-coloured liquorice malty stout.

Leyden

🏠 Lord Raglan, Walmersley Old Road, Nangreaves, BL9 6SP

☎ (0161) 764 6680 ⊕ lordraglannangreaves.co.uk

Leyden was established in 1999 at the Lord Raglan pub. Both the pub and the free trade are supplied.

Balaclava (OG 1040, ABV 3.8%)
A copper-coloured session bitter with malty and hoppy flavours.

Black Pudding (OG 1039, ABV 3.8%)
A dark brown-coloured, creamy mild with a malty flavour, followed by a balanced finish.

Nanny Flyer (OG 1036, ABV 3.8%)
A session bitter with an initial dryness, original bitterness, followed by a strong, malty finish.

Oyster Stout (OG 1039, ABV 4%)
Dark red-coloured, smooth beer with hint of chocolate.

Light Brigade (OG 1042, ABV 4.2%) ◆
Copper in colour with a citrus aroma. The flavour is a balance of malt, hops and fruit, with a bitter finish.

Rammy Rocket (OG 1042, ABV 4.2%)
A smooth, straw-coloured ale.

Raglan Sleeve (OG 1048, ABV 4.6%) ◆
Dark red/brown-coloured beer with a hoppy aroma and a dry, roasty, hoppy taste and finish.

Crowning Glory (OG 1068, ABV 6.8%)

Liberation ◉

Tregar House, Longueville Road, St Saviour, Jersey, JE2 7WF
☎ (01534) 764089 ⊕ liberationgroup.com

⊠ The Liberation Brewery is located at Longueville, just outside St Helier using a 40-barrel and an eight-barrel plant. Its multi-award-winning flagship beer, Liberation Ale, is now regularly seen on the mainland, as well as on the other Channel Islands. 68 pubs are owned with around two-thirds of these serving cask ale. In 2016 Liberation, including Butcombe (qv), was bought by Caledonia Investments. ‼◆

Ale (OG 1039, ABV 4%)
Golden beer with a hint of citrus on the nose.

IPA (OG 1047, ABV 4.8%)
Traditional IPA with a coriander, citrus hop flavour and a crisp, balanced finish.

Lincoln Green SIBA ◉

Unit 5, Enterprise Park, Wigwam Lane, Hucknall, Nottingham, NG15 7SZ
☎ (0115) 963 4233 ☎ 07748 111457
⊕ lincolngreenbrewing.co.uk

☺ Anthony Hughes established the Lincoln Green Brewing Company in 2012 using a 10-barrel plant. The brewery takes its name from the colour of dyed woollen cloth associated with the legend of Robin Hood. ☛◆RAIB

Marion (OG 1038, ABV 3.8%) ⊡ ◆
Subtly-hopped golden ale with citrus aroma and a dry bitter finish.

Archer (OG 1040, ABV 4%)

Hood (OG 1042, ABV 4.2%) ◆
Tawny-coloured ale with balanced hops and bitterness.

Tuck (OG 1047, ABV 4.7%) ◆

Full-bodied, rich dark ale with roast and malt flavours throughout.

Lincolnshire SIBA ◉

🯅 George, 15 Main Road, Langworth, Lincolnshire, LN3 5BJ ☎ 07508 554890
⊕ lincolnshirebrewingco.co.uk

An events company that operates mobile bars, in 2014 it started brewing for its own bars and has since expanded into the free trade. An eight-barrel plant brews both cask and bottle-conditioned beers, with bottling carried out in-house. Beers can be found at local fairs, shows, markets and free houses and nationally via wholesalers.

Great Tom (OG 1037, ABV 3.7%)
A dark-coloured ale with elements of chocolate and coffee in the nose. A fruity and dark malt mouthfeel with a long, but soft bitter finish.

Spicy Sausage (OG 1041, ABV 4.1%)
An amber-coloured ale with a sharp bitterness and dry finish.

Friendly Rottweiler (OG 1045, ABV 4.5%)
A light, crisp ale with a subtle hoppy taste.

Cheeky Imp (OG 1046, ABV 4.6%)
A malty ale with caramel notes and hoppy aromas, a good mouthfeel and slightly sweet taste.

Linear (NEW)

Bingham, Nottinghamshire, NG13 8EU ⊕ linear.beer

Small-scale 50-litre brewery, which started production in 2016 and is located at the owner's house. Currently producing a pin of each brew for the Horse & Plough in Bingham with the rest of production bottle-conditioned. Limited capacity prevents the supply of cask beers to other outlets at present. RAIB

Lines (NEW)

Unit 2e, Pontygwindy Estate, Caerphilly, CF83 3HU
☎ (029) 2085 0706

Office: 23 Jim Driscoll Way, Cardiff, CF11 7JA
⊕ linesbrewco.com

Lines has been formed out of the remains of the former Celt Experience brewery after it ceased trading.

Linfit

🯅 Sair Inn, 139 Lane Top, Linthwaite, Huddersfield, West Yorkshire, HD7 5SG
☎ (01484) 842370

A 19th-century brewpub that started brewing again in 1982. The beer is only available at the Sair Inn.

Lion's Lair (NEW)

2 Lochlair Farm Cottage, Arbroath, DD11 2RF
✉ brewhouse@lionslairbrewery.co

Brewing began in 2015.

Rusty Nail (OG 1039, ABV 3.9%)

Rusty Fang (OG 1040, ABV 4%)

Sonny Blonde (OG 1042, ABV 4.2%)

Black Mamba (OG 1052, ABV 5.2%)

Lister's SIBA ◉

The Old Dairy, Ford Lane, Ford, West Sussex, BN18 0DF
☎ (01903) 739117 ☎ 07775 853412
⊕ listersbrewery.com

Brewing began in 2012 using a 0.25-barrel kit. The brewery relocated in 2014 and expanded to a five-barrel plant. Lister's donates 5p from every pint and bottle sold to the Battersea Dogs & Cats Home.

Best Bitter (ABV 3.9%)

Golden Ale (ABV 4.1%)

Limehouse Porter (ABV 4.1%)

American Pale Ale (ABV 4.2%)

IPA (ABV 4.3%)

Special Ale (ABV 4.6%)

Lithic (NEW) SIBA

TY Newydd Farm, Llangorse, LD3 7UA ☎ 07542 425408 ✉ info@lithicbrewing.com

Brewing began in 2016 at the premises of the former Redstone Brewery.

Little Beer SIBA ◉

Building 3, 14-15 Midleton Road, Guildford, GU2 8XW
☎ (01483) 497201 ☎ 07941 061241
⊕ littlebeer.co.uk

⊠ Little Beer Corporation is a Guildford-based 10-barrel brewery, the first to open there since Friary Meux closed in the 1970s. It is run by Jim Taylor, alongside around 300 local shareholders. A monthly beer club (including beer, food and music) is for paid membership only. ‼🍴RAIB

Little Haka (OG 1035, ABV 3.5%) ◆
An easy-drinking session ale. Predominantly bitter but with a good malt character and light hoppy tones.

Little Geyser (OG 1036, ABV 3.6%)
A steam beer brewed with English hops.

Little Vienna (ABV 3.8%)

Little Kahuna (ABV 3.9%)
An easy-drinking American-style pale ale.

Little Black Dog (NEW) SIBA

Carlton Towers Brewery, Carlton Towers, Carlton, North Yorkshire, DN14 9LZ ☎ 07495 026173
⊕ littleblackdogbeer.com

A small batch, family-run brewery based in the village of Carlton in North Yorkshire. RAIB

Yorkshire Bitter (ABV 3.8%)

India Pale (ABV 3.9%)

New World Pale (ABV 4%)

Yorkshire Gold (ABV 4%)

American Pale (ABV 4.1%)

Alt Bier (ABV 4.2%)

Little Bush

🏠 51 Brook Lane, Marehay, Derbyshire, DE5 8JA

☎ (01773) 570830 ⊕ hollybushmarehay.co.uk

A four-barrel plant, located in the cellar of the Hollybush pub in the village of Marehay, Little Bush commenced brewing in 2015. Beers are only available in the pub.

Little Critters (NEW) SIBA ◉

80 Parkwood Road, Sheffield, S3 8AG
☎ (0114) 276 3171

Office: Horizon House, 2 Whiting Street, Sheffield, S8 9QR ⊕ littlecrittersbrewery.com

A small batch, family-owned microbrewery, opened in 2016. It runs two pubs in Sheffield; the Fox & Duck, Broomhill, and the Doctor's Orders. Pubs are supplied throughout Yorkshire and the East Midlands.

Little Hopper (OG 1038, ABV 3.6%)
Golden-coloured session ale with a malty, refreshing finish.

Blonde Bear (OG 1040, ABV 4.2%)
Smooth blonde ale with a balanced taste and tropical notes.

Shire Horse (OG 1043, ABV 4.3%)

Sleepy Badger (OG 1043, ABV 4.5%)
An oatmeal stout brewed with locally-sourced honey.

Malty Python (OG 1046, ABV 4.8%)
A beer with a spicy taste and smooth bitter finish.

White Wolf (OG 1048, ABV 5%)
A refreshing, light beer with bitterness and a citrus finish.

Chameleon Series (OG 1052, ABV 5.5%)
A single hopped pale ale with a strong bitter finish. Different hop versions brewed simultaneously.

Hazelnut Milk Stout (OG 1059, ABV 6%)
Smooth stout with a hazelnut nose, supported by coffee and chocolate notes for a well-balanced taste.

C Monster (OG 1060, ABV 6.5%)
Citrus IPA made with American hops, lime leaves and fresh citrus peel for a bold, refreshing taste.

Imperial Coffee Stout (OG 1068, ABV 7.2%)
Smooth stout with a strong coffee taste brewed with ethically sourced espresso coffee from a local café.

Little Dragon SIBA

Unit 3, Havens Head Business Park, Milford Haven, SA73 3LD ☎ 07999 030254
⊕ littledragonbrewery.co.uk

Morgan Coe established the Little Dragon Brewery in 2015 using a five-barrel plant. It is located in an industrial unit close to the historic port of Milford Haven. The beers are unfiltered and no finings are used unless requested. 🍴◆RAIB

Cleddau Gold (OG 1044, ABV 4.2%)
A golden ale full of hop flavour.

Jack Sound (OG 1044, ABV 4.3%)
A well-rounded beer, good malt/chocolate notes with a balanced hop character.

Milford Trawler Smoked Porter (OG 1052, ABV 5.2%)

A rich porter with chocolate/espresso notes and a lightly smoked flavour.

Little London SIBA

Unit 6B, Ash Park Business Centre, Ash Lane, Little London, Hampshire, RG26 5FL
☎ (01256) 533044 ☎ 07785 225468
⊕ littlelondonbrewery.com

⊗ Brewing began in 2015 using a six-barrel plant. Three fermentation vessels ensure a production capability of 60 firkins per week, with capacity for expansion. ♦

Doreen's Dark (OG 1035, ABV 3.2%)
Treacle-coloured with hints of liquorice and coffee, but a dry finish.

Red Boy (OG 1036, ABV 3.7%)
A light, balanced session bitter with a delicate hop aroma and subtle hop flavours on the palate.

Hoppy Hilda (OG 1039, ABV 3.8%)

Pryde (OG 1040.5, ABV 4.2%)
A fruity, dark amber-coloured best bitter with caramel and toffee aromas and spicy hop notes.

Ash Park Special (OG 1048, ABV 4.9%)
A russet-coloured ale with malt and raisin on the nose. Slightly sweet with a long finish.

Little Ox (NEW) SIBA

Unit 6, Wroslyn Road Industrial Estate, Freeland, Oxfordshire, OX29 8HZ
☎ (01993) 881941 ☎ 07730 496525

Office: 25 Castle Road, Wootton, Oxfordshire, OX20 1EQ ⊕ littleoxbrewery.co.uk

Little Ox began production in 2016 using a 10-barrel plant.

Oddbod (OG 1040, ABV 4%)
A bitter with a malty backbone and a floral, bitter finish with hints of orange marmalade.

Wipeout (OG 1042, ABV 4.2%)
A zesty pale gold-coloured ale with a full-bodied, fruity flavour and citrus and tropical notes.

Filthy Rich (OG 1044, ABV 4.5%)
A porter with a rich, smooth body balanced with a generous portion of English hops. Finishes smooth and creamy with berry notes.

Little Valley SIBA ⟨◉⟩

Unit 3, Turkey Lodge Farm, New Road, Cragg Vale, Hebden Bridge, West Yorkshire, HX7 5TT
☎ (01422) 883888 ⊕ littlevalleybrewery.co.uk

☺Little Valley began brewing in 2005 on a 10-barrel plant. All beers are organic and vegan, and Ginger Pale Ale uses Fairtrade ingredients. Around 300 outlets are supplied. Several beers are contract brewed for Suma Wholefoods and in 2012 the brewery was contracted by the Benedictine Order of Ampleforth Abbey to brew and bottle their Ampleforth Abbey Beer (ABV 7%). 🍺♦RAIB

Withens Pale Ale (OG 1037, ABV 3.9%) ◣
Creamy, gold-coloured, refreshingly light ale. Floral, spicy hop aroma, lightly-flavoured with hints of lemon and grapefruit. Clean, bitter aftertaste.

Ginger Pale Ale (OG 1037, ABV 4%) ◣

Full-bodied speciality ale. Ginger predominates in the aroma and taste. It has a pleasantly powerful, fiery and spicy finish.

Cragg Vale Bitter (OG 1039, ABV 4.2%) ◣
Creamy, pale brown-coloured session bitter, light on the palate with a delicate flavour of malt and fruit and a bitter finish.

Hebden's Wheat (OG 1043, ABV 4.5%) ◣
A pale yellow-coloured, creamy wheat beer with a good balance of bitterness and fruit, a hint of sweetness but with a lasting, dry finish.

Vanilla Porter (ABV 4.5%) ◣
Dark and complex speciality beer. Fresh taste of vanilla dominates both the aroma and taste. Smooth mellow finish.

Stoodley Stout (OG 1044, ABV 4.8%) ◣
Dark brown-coloured creamy stout with a rich roast aroma and luscious fruity, chocolate, roast flavours. Well-balanced with a clean bitter finish.

Tod's Blonde (OG 1045, ABV 5%) ◣
Bright yellow-coloured, smooth, speciality beer with a citrus hop start and a dry finish. Fruity, with a hint of spice. Similar in style to a Belgian blonde beer.

Moor Ale (OG 1051, ABV 5.5%) ◣
Tawny in colour with a full-bodied taste. It has a strong malty nose and palate with hints of heather and peat-smoked malt. Well-balanced with a bitter finish.

Python IPA (OG 1055, ABV 6%) ◣
Amber-coloured, creamy beer with a complex bitter fruit palate subtly balance by a malty sweetness, leading to a strongly lingering bitter aftertaste.

Littleover SIBA

Unit 9, Robinson Industrial Estate, Shaftesbury Street, Derby, DE23 8NL
☎ (01332) 987100 ☎ 07449 586811
⊕ littleoverbrewery.co.uk

Littleover was established in 2015, using a new six-barrel plant from PBC installations. ♦

Gold Pale Ale (ABV 3.8%)
Pale, golden-coloured session ale with a subtle hoppy aroma.

Apex Amber Ale (ABV 4.1%)
An easy-drinking, amber-coloured ale with a solid backbone of malts.

The Panther Oatmeal Stout (ABV 4.2%)
A rich, smooth and warming stout with hints of coffee and Irish whiskey.

Dazzler IPA (ABV 4.5%)
A refreshing ale with the taste and aroma of tropical fruits.

Liverpool Craft SIBA

10 Love Lane, The Railway Arches, Liverpool, L3 7DD
☎ (0151) 236 9400 ⊕ liverpoolcraftbeer.com

☺ Brewing began in 2011 using a 10-barrel plant. Work is undergoing on new premises in the Baltic Triangle area of Liverpool. The brewery owns the rights to use the name of the old Higson's Brewery. ♦RAIB

Liverpool Organic SIBA

39 Brasenose Road, Liverpool, L20 8HL
☎ (0151) 933 9660 ⊕ liverpoolorganicbrewery.com

⊠ Liverpool Organic started brewing in 2009. Outlets are supplied around the extended Merseyside area. The brewery also supports many local beer festivals and also runs festivals of its own. Beers are also brewed under the name of the now defunct Cambrinus brewery. ‼◆RAIB

Cascade (OG 1038, ABV 3.8%)
An intensely-hopped light session bitter.

Joseph Williamson (OG 1039, ABV 4%)
Traditional malty bitter flavours with floral elements building to a smooth, satisfying finish.

Liverpool Pale Ale (OG 1039, ABV 4%)
Dry hoppy notes with floral complexity giving way to spicy tones and a slightly creamy malt finish.

Bier Head (OG 1040, ABV 4.1%)
Sharp, hoppy foretaste with complex spice and crisp malt tones, building to a rich, mellow aftertaste.

24 Carat Gold (OG 1041, ABV 4.2%)
Generously hopped with a bitterness that builds steadily towards a lingering finish with spicy, orange notes.

Liverpool Stout (OG 1048, ABV 4.3%)
Strong, dark and dry stout with a smooth, spicy finish.

William Roscoe (OG 1042, ABV 4.3%)
Hoppy and fruity with a hint of dryness and bitterness building to a crisp and slightly earthy malt finish.

Honey Blond (OG 1043, ABV 4.5%)
A subtle and not cloyingly sweet honey aftertaste married to a solid malt backbone and a good hoppy character.

Josephine Butler (OG 1043, ABV 4.5%)
Initial citrus hops followed by elderflower fruit and pale, biscuity malt with a refreshing, sharp finish.

Kitty Wilkinson (OG 1047, ABV 4.5%)
Vanilla, butterscotch and chocolate combine in the roasted malty taste with a fairly dry finish and a generous cocoa bitterness.

Empire Ale (OG 1056, ABV 5.3%)
A strong ruby-coloured ale with slightly sweet finish.

Shipwreck IPA (OG 1066, ABV 6.5%)
Grapefruit, aniseed and peach notes feature in the hoppy bite that builds to tropical fruit and a generous pine bitterness in the finish.

Imperial Russian Stout (OG 1078, ABV 7.4%)
Featuring a rich, strong, hoppy bitterness with a full-bodied sweetness and bitter coffee finish with a little fruity malt on the aftertaste.

Brewed under the Cambrinus Brewery name:

Deliverance (OG 1042, ABV 4.2%)
Pale gold-coloured beer with a sharp, hoppy taste.

Endurance (OG 1044, ABV 4.3%)
A beer with vanilla notes made with English malt and hops.

Lizard

The Old Nuclear Bunker, Pednavounder, Coverack, Cornwall, TR12 6SE

☎ (01326) 281135 ⊕ lizardales.co.uk

⊠ Launched in 2004, Lizard Ales is now based at former RAF Treleaver, a massive disused nuclear bunker in the countryside near Coverack on the Lizard Peninsula. Specialising in bottle-conditioned ales, it mainly supplies west Cornwall. ‼RAIB

Kernow Gold (OG 1037, ABV 3.7%)
A light, dry without being acidic, gently-hopped, golden ale.

Bitter (OG 1041, ABV 4.2%) 🍺
Pale brown-coloured beer with aroma of ripe apples. Roast malt with fruit esters balanced by bitterness. Bitter finish with dryness.

Frenchman's Creek (OG 1042, ABV 4.8%)
A fruity pale ale with a blend of hops.

An Gof (OG 1049, ABV 5.2%) 🍺
Robust and smooth tawny-coloured ale dominated by malt in the mouth with a hint of smoke. Fruity hops follow on into the bitter finish.

Horseshoe Special Reserve (OG 1062, ABV 6.2%)
A dark-coloured, rich, strong beer, matured for several months.

Llangollen SIBA

🏠 Abbey Grange Brewing Ltd, Abbey Grange Hotel, Horseshoe Pass Road, Llantysilio, LL20 8DD
☎ (01978) 861916 ⊕ llangollenbrewery.com

Brewing began in 2010 on a 2.5-barrel plant. The brewery was updated and upgraded in 2014.

Lleu

Unit A9, Penygroes Industrial Estate, Penygroes, LL54 6DB ☎ 07724 902532 ⊕ bragdylleu.cymru

Brewing began in 2014 using a 1.25-barrel plant. The beer reflects the Welsh folklore tales of the Mabinogi in both name and character. Capacity was upgraded to 5.5 barrels in 2016. ‼

Blodeuwedd (OG 1036, ABV 3.6%)

Lleu (OG 1040, ABV 4%)
Full-bodied ale with a good mouthfeel and a lasting hoppy aftertaste.

Gwydion (OG 1047, ABV 4.7%)
A dark chestnut-coloured bitter, malty with a subtle hop character and lasting aftertaste.

Llŷn

1 Parc Eithin, Ffordd Dewi Sant, Nefyn, LL53 6EG
☎ (01758) 721981 ☎ 07823 320148
⊕ cwrwllyn.cymru

☺Cwrw Llŷn began brewing in 2011. In 2016 it moved to a new purpose-built 15-barrel plant that includes a shop, tap house and a visitor's gallery for tours. ‼🍴◆

Y Brawd Houdini (OG 1040, ABV 3.5%)
A pale ale, citrus and aromatic.

Brenin Enlli (OG 1041, ABV 4%) 🍺
A fruity bitter, the initial malty taste leads to a hoppy, bitter aftertaste.

Cwrw Glyndwr (OG 1041, ABV 4%) 🍺
A full-bodied and well-balanced amber-coloured beer, quite fruity with a good hoppy finish.

Seithenyn (OG 1042, ABV 4.2%) 🍺

A fruity golden ale with a tangy citrus taste and a dry hoppy finish.

Porth Neigwl (OG 1044, ABV 4.5%)
An American-style, amber-coloured IPA.

Loch Leven (NEW)

The Muirs, Kinross, KY13 8AS

A new venture opposite the Green Hotel in Kinross, the brewery started production in 2017. Brewing plant and casks have been acquired from the former Loch Leven Brewery in Fife.

Loch Lomond SIBA

Unit 5, Block 1, Lomond Industrial Estate, Alexandria, G83 0TL
☎ (01389) 755698 ☎ 07891 920213
⊕ lochlomondbrewery.com

Established in 2011 by Fiona and Euan MacEachern, it is the only brewery around Loch Lomond. !! ➡ ◆

Southern Summit (OG 1040, ABV 4%)
The palate is fresh and fruity with hints of grapefruit and lemon, leading to a crisp, light bitter finish.

Bonnie 'n' Clyde (OG 1046, ABV 4.6%)
An amber-coloured ale with a big citrus hit on the nose that follows through to the rich, bitter finish.

Silkie Stout (OG 1050, ABV 5%) 🍺
A black-coloured stout with chocolate orange spicy notes.

Loch Ness

See Cairngorm

Loddon SIBA 👁

Dunsden Green Farm, Church Lane, Dunsden, Oxfordshire, RG4 9QD
☎ (0118) 948 1111 ⊕ loddonbrewery.com

⊠ This family-run brewery was established in 2002, in a brick-and-flint barn that was originally a grain store. The custom-built 17-barrel plant typically produces 120 barrels per week, and supplies more than 500 outlets far and wide. Popular open evenings are held quarterly. !! ➡ ◆

Hoppit (OG 1036.2, ABV 3.5%) ◆
Hops dominate the aroma of this drinkable, light-coloured session beer. Malt and hops create a balanced taste and a pleasant bitterness carries through to the aftertaste.

Reading Best (OG 1041.5, ABV 4%)
A light copper-coloured best bitter with a smooth but nutty body and a lingering bitter aftertaste.

Hullabaloo (OG 1043.8, ABV 4.2%) ◆
A hint of fruit in the initial taste develops into a balance of hops and malt in this well-rounded, medium-bodied bitter with a bitter aftertaste.

Ferryman's Gold (OG 1045.8, ABV 4.4%) ◆
Golden-coloured with a strong, hoppy character throughout, accompanied by fruit in the taste and aftertaste.

Bamboozle (OG 1049.5, ABV 4.8%) ◆
Full-bodied and well-balanced. Distinctive bittersweet flavour with hop and caramel to accompany.

Forbury Lion (OG 1056.5, ABV 5.5%)
A malty IPA with a strong, complex hop finish.

Lola Rose

🏠 Wanlockhead Inn, Wanlockhead, ML12 6UZ
☎ (01659) 74535 ☎ 07500 663405
⊕ lola-rose-brewery.co.uk

Lola Rose is based in the family-run Wanlockhead Inn, situated in the scenic Lowther Hills of the Scottish Lowlands. Local outlets only are supplied at present.

Blonde (OG 1041, ABV 4.1%)

Stout (OG 1042, ABV 4.2%)

Red Ale (OG 1043, ABV 4.3%)

London Beer Factory SIBA 👁

Unit 4, 160 Hamilton Road, West Norwood, London, SE27 9SF ☎ 07760 290489
⊕ thelondonbeerfactory.com

The London Beer Factory started brewing in 2014 using a 20-barrel plant. Local outlets are supplied. A tap room is open to the public at weekends.

Chelsea Blonde (ABV 4.3%) ◆
Grapefruit dominates the flavour and aroma with trace of spiciness and a dry bitterness balanced by a little honey sweetness.

Sayers Stout (ABV 4.5%) ◆
Copper-coloured bitter with a pleasant malty aroma, soft, well-balanced taste and a dry aftertaste that continues into the finish.

Paxton Pale Ale (ABV 5%)

London Beer Lab SIBA

Arch 41, Nursery Road, Brixton, London, SW9 8BP
⊕ londonbeerlab.com

Started as a bottle shop, brewing workshop and home brew supplies outlet, London Beer Lab began commercial brewing in 2015. Initially offering only KeyKeg and bottled beers, it now offers some cask-conditioned ales. Originally sharing facilities with Clarkshaws (qv), it now brews on its own equipment in Brixton.

London Brewing SIBA

🏠 Bohemia, 762-764 High Road, North Finchley, London, N12 9QH
☎ (020) 8446 0294 ⊕ londonbrewing.com

London Brewing Co began brewing in 2011 at the Bull in Highgate using a 2.5-barrel plant. In 2014 it acquired its second pub, the Bohemia in North Finchley, at which brewing began in 2015 in a new 6.5-barrel brewhouse. The Bull was sold in the summer of 2016 to concentrate all production at the North Finchley site. Beer is now supplied widely beyond the Bohemia itself.

High Rise (OG 1040, ABV 3.9%) ◆
A fruity, yellow-coloured ale with a bitter character balanced by a fudge sweetness and a touch of lemon/lime peel.

Beer Street (OG 1042, ABV 4%) ◆
Well-balanced, coppery brown-coloured best bitter with the hoppy bitterness underpinned by the

THE BREWERIES

caramelised malt character. Fruit is present throughout.

Oyster Stout (OG 1049, ABV 4.6%) 🍴 🍂
Sweet dark treacle and soft citrus fruit on this smooth stout. Finish is dry roast with a little bitterness.

Vista (OG 1047, ABV 4.7%) 🍂
Smooth, brown-coloured best bitter. Some nutty notes with hints of chocolate balanced by fruit. Lingering dry bitter finish.

Skyline (OG 1053, ABV 5.3%) 🍂
Pale brown-coloured beer with a honey sweetness and a some soft fruit notes. Sweetness is balanced by a bitter dryness.

Never Mind the Kent Hops
(OG 1056, ABV 5.5%) 🍂
A smooth, brown-coloured beer with spicy hops on the palate, lingering in the dry finish, which is slightly bitter. There is a sweet toffee character throughout.

London Road (NEW)

🍺 London Road Brew House, 67-75 London Road, Southampton, Hampshire, SO15 2AB
☎ (023) 8098 9401 ☎ 07399 999947
🌐 londonroadbrewhouse.com

Brewing commenced in 2017 in the London Road Brew House using a six-barrel plant. Beer is brewed for the pub, the City Pub Co estate and the trade.

Athena (OG 1040, ABV 3.8%)

Kodiak (ABV 4.2%)

Long Arm

🍺 Ealing Park Tavern, 222 South Ealing Road, South Ealing, London, W5 4RL
☎ (020) 8758 1879 ☎ 07857 257970
🌐 ealingparktavern.com

A brewpub on the Brentford/Ealing border. Beers are also available across London and at the ETM chain of bars and restaurants.

Lucky Penny (OG 1041, ABV 4%) 🍂
Smooth, dark golden-coloured ale with a sweet and lightly fruity flavour followed by a sharply dry, strong bitter finish.

Birdie Flipper (OG 1045, ABV 4.5%) 🍂
A complex bitter beer with malt and hops and a hint of blackcurrant. A bitter finish.

IPA OK (OG 1051, ABV 5.5%) 🍂
Fruity brown-coloured beer with a malty toffee sweetness and a bitter hop character that is also in the dry finish.

Shadow Wolf (OG 1054, ABV 5.5%)
Smoked stout inspired by Bamberg rauch bier.

Long Hop (NEW)

c/o 26 Nottingham Court, Nottingham Road, Louth, Lincolnshire, LN11 0WB ☎ 07730 407404
🌐 longhopbrewery.com

Cuckoo brewery utilising the Black Horse Brewery plant. Production commenced in 2016.

Plain Jane (ABV 3.8%)
Blonde ale with a citrus finish.

Phoenix Pale (ABV 4.5%)
A pale ale with grapefruit notes and a dry bitter finish.

Brewed for the Tale of Two, Cleethorpes:

Solitude (ABV 5%)

Long Man SIBA 👁

Church Farm, Litlington, East Sussex, BN26 5RA
☎ (01323) 871850 ☎ 07976 777992
🌐 longmanbrewery.com

⊠ Long Man began brewing in 2012 using a 20-barrel stainless steel plant. Hops and grain are sourced locally with a view to using home-grown barley, as well as a traditional strain of Sussex yeast. ‼

Long Blonde (OG 1039, ABV 3.8%)
A light-coloured golden ale with a distinctive hoppy aroma and crisp, clean bitterness on the finish. Smooth, light and refreshing.

Best Bitter (OG 1040, ABV 4%)
Well-balanced with a complex bittersweet malty taste, fragrant hops and a characteristic long deep finish.

Copper Hop (ABV 4.2%)

Old Man (OG 1048, ABV 4.3%)
Dark-coloured beer with soft malt notes of coffee and chocolate combined with a pleasant light hoppiness creating a rich, full-tasting old ale.

Sussex Pride (OG 1045, ABV 4.5%)
A classic strong pale ale. Bronze-coloured with a fruity nose and full round flavours.

American Pale Ale (OG 1046, ABV 4.8%)
A triple-hopped American pale ale with a pleasant citrus fruit aroma and characteristic robust bitterness.

Longdog SIBA

Unit A1, Moniton Trading Estate, West Ham Lane, Worting, Basingstoke, Hampshire, RG22 6NQ
☎ (01256) 324286 ☎ 07827 618733
🌐 longdogbrewery.co.uk

⊠ Longdog was established in 2011 using a six-barrel plant. The name is inspired by the owner's lurcher. ‼ 🍺 ◆ RAIB

Bunny Chaser (OG 1036, ABV 3.6%)
A light copper-coloured session bitter with plenty of malt in the mouth and a big hit of bitterness.

Golden Poacher (OG 1039, ABV 3.9%) 🍂
A fruity nose with plenty of hops, balanced by a malty sweetness in the flavour. The hops build to a faint astringent finish.

Red Runner (OG 1041, ABV 4.2%)
A mahogany-coloured best bitter, fruity and hoppy.

Kismet (OG 1045, ABV 4.5%)
A pale ale with assertive hop bitterness, flavour and aroma coming from a blend of fragrant American hops.

Lamplight Porter (OG 1048, ABV 5%) 🍷 🍂
A smoky, dry porter with strong roast flavours giving way to a blackberry taste and slightly vinous finish.

848

Longhill

Longhill Cottage, Whitstone, Cornwall, EX22 6UG
☎ (01288) 341466

⊠ Longhill began brewing in 2011 using a 0.5-barrel plant, upgraded in 2012 to a four-barrel plant to meet demand. The beers are named with a wind theme. Eight outlets are supplied direct.

Whistler (OG 1038, ABV 3.8%) ◄
Smooth, pale brown-coloured bitter with little aroma. Gentle balance of caramel malt, bitter hops and sweet fruit. Slowly fading bittersweet finish.

Westerly (OG 1040, ABV 4%) ◄
Copper-coloured best bitter with malt and toffee aroma. Mainly malt and caramel flavour. Light finish with malt, fruit and bitterness.

Gale Force (OG 1048, ABV 4.8%) ◄
Copper-coloured strong bitter. Malt and almonds aroma. Malty flavours with toffee and nuts. Short, malty, dry finish with stone fruit.

Hurricane (OG 1048, ABV 4.8%) ◄
Sulphurous malt nose. Assertive malt taste with some sweetness and a little roast. Distinct nutty, earthy and sulphur flavours.

Loose Cannon SIBA

Unit 6, Suffolk Way, Abingdon, Oxfordshire, OX14 5JX
☎ (01235) 531141 ⊕ lcbeers.co.uk

Brewing began in 2010 using a 15-barrel plant, reviving Abingdon's brewing history after the Morland Brewery closed in 2000. Beers can be found in an increasing number of local pubs and within 50 miles of the brewery. Popular brewery evenings take place on the first Tuesday of the month. ‼🍺♦

Gunners Gold (OG 1034.5, ABV 3.5%)
Golden-coloured, easy-drinking session ale with a subtle peach flavour.

Abingdon Bridge (OG 1041, ABV 4.1%)
Full-flavoured and smooth, with well-rounded hop bitterness and a floral aroma.

Porter (OG 1054, ABV 5%)
Moderately sweet with hints of dark chocolate and a smooth espresso finish.

India Pale Ale (OG 1053, ABV 5.4%)
Balanced floral aroma and fruity taste with a smooth bitter kick and a warming quality.

Lord Conrad's

Unit 21, Dry Drayton Industrial Estate, Scotland Road, Dry Drayton, Cambridgeshire, CB23 8AT ☎ 07736 739700 ⊕ lordconradsbrewery.co.uk

⊠ Lord Conrad's was established in 2007 and moved to Dry Drayton in 2011 using a 2.5-barrel plant. One permanent outlet is supplied, the Abbot's Elm in Abbots Ripton, along with other local free houses and beer festivals. The brewery adheres strongly to 'green' principles, using low energy systems, recycled materials and local ingredients. ‼🍺

Stoat Warbler (OG 1035, ABV 3.4%)

Zulu Dawn (OG 1037, ABV 3.5%)

Hedgerow Hop (OG 1039, ABV 3.7%)
An amber-coloured ale made with locally-picked hops and supporting the RSPB.

Lickety Split (OG 1038, ABV 3.8%)
Sweet, malty, brown-coloured ale, light but not overly hoppy.

Conkerwood (OG 1044, ABV 4%)
Dark porter with hints of liquorice.

Gubbins (OG 1040, ABV 4%)

Slap N' Tickle (OG 1042, ABV 4.3%)
A blonde ale with a big slap of bitterness and just a tickle of hops.

Zulu (OG 1047, ABV 4.5%)
A strong black-coloured bitter with an exotic nature.

Pheasant's Rise (OG 1050, ABV 5%)
Smoky, woody traditional strong ale.

Stubble Burner (OG 1050, ABV 5%)
A straw-like beer with a good earthy nose and a well-balanced fruity bitterness.

Lord's

Unit 15, Heath House Mill, Heath House Lane, Golcar, West Yorkshire, HD7 4JW ☎ 07976 974162 ⊕ lordsbrewing.com

Established in 2015, Lord's is the brain child of three brothers-in-law, Ben, John and Tim. Initially cuckoo brewing at Golcar (qv), the brewery moved to new premises in 2017 with a eight-barrel plant and a tap room, with plans for a bottle shop. ♦

Tithe House Bitter (OG 1037, ABV 3.9%)
Light copper-coloured bitter with subtle malt flavours balanced by English hops. It has a soft malt and caramel base with a mellow pine and grapefruit flavour.

Expedition Pale Ale (OG 1038, ABV 4%)
Pale and delicately hopped. Refreshing, with citrus notes.

Mount Helix West Coast Pale (OG 1047, ABV 5%)
American-style ale bursting with citrus, pine and floral overtones, which give way to a lightly toasted crisp malt base.

Havelock IPA (OG 1054, ABV 5.7%)
An IPA with an abundance of hops, a touch of coriander seed and a hint of orange peel.

Lost + Found (NEW)

12/13 Ship Street, Brighton, East Sussex, BN1 1AD ⊕ lostandfoundbrewery.com

Brewing began in 2016. No real ale.

Lost & Grounded (NEW) SIBA

🍴 Barley Mow, 91 Whitby Road, Bristol, BS4 4AR ⊕ lostandgrounded.co.uk

Brewing began in 2016 at the Barley Mow. No real ale.

Lost Industry

Nutwood Trading Estate, Sheffield, South Yorkshire, S6 1NJ
☎ (0114) 231 6393 ⊕ lostindustrybrewing.com

Lost Industry began brewing in 2015. A wide range of beer styles is brewed.

LoveBeer SIBA

95 High Street, Milton, Oxfordshire, OX14 4EJ
☎ 07889 455845 ⊕ lovebeerbrewery.com

Jim Southey has been brewing ale since 2013 and became fully licensed as a brewer in 2014. The 0.5-barrel plant supplies local pubs such as the Nags Head in Abingdon, the regular beer festival at the Plum Pudding in Milton, and local farm shops.

Doctor Roo (OG 1038, ABV 3.7%)
A balanced, light pale ale. Late flavour hops contribute a zesty, tropical flavour.

Molly's Malt (OG 1041, ABV 4%)
A well-hopped, amber-coloured ale with a caramel biscuit aroma and hints of citrus.

Bonnie Hops (OG 1048, ABV 4.6%)
A hoppy pale ale with full-flavour American hops.

Hair of the Doug (OG 1053, ABV 5.1%)
A pale ale brewed with a hint of ginger and caramel.

Widget (OG 1055, ABV 5.3%)
A well-hopped black IPA.

Purdy Peculiar (OG 1056, ABV 5.4%)
A smooth, dark and smoky stout with hints of molasses and black treacle.

Monty's Jem (OG 1058, ABV 5.6%)
A traditional ale with full body and good hop flavour with a hint of lime or mandarin.

Lovibonds

Rear of 19-21 Market Place, Henley-on-Thames, Oxfordshire, RG9 2AA
☎ (01491) 576596 ⊕ lovibonds.com

Lovibonds was founded by Jeff Rosenmeier in 2005 and is named after Joseph William Lovibond, who invented the Tintometer to measure beer colour. The beers are unfiltered and unpasteurised, but served with top pressure. Currently brewing on the kit at Old Luxters (qv), its own brewery is being built near Henley. ‼ ☕

Luckie

Unit 4, Block 5, Banbeath Industrial Estate, Leven, KY8 5HD ☎ 07979 364906 ⊕ luckie-ales.com

Luckie Ales was established in 2009 and is an artisan microbrewery specialising in handcrafted Scottish beers and historic British ales. Brewing moved to Markinch in 2012, operating on a one-barrel plant. The brewery was sold in 2016, and relocated to new premises in Leven. RAIB

Lucky 7 (NEW)

Hay on Wye, HR3 5AW ☎ 07815 853353
⊕ lucky7beer.co.uk

Established in 2014, brewing is currently suspended while larger premises are sought.

Ludlow SIBA 👁

The Railway Shed, Station Drive, Ludlow, Shropshire, SY8 2PQ
☎ (01584) 873291
⊕ theludlowbrewingcompany.co.uk

Established in 2006, the brewery occupies a converted railway sidings shed. Brews are produced using a 20-barrel plant. The premises also function as a brewery tap, visitor centre and events area. ‼ ☕

Best (OG 1037, ABV 3.7%)
An amber-coloured, well-balanced session beer with a banana, pineapple and toffee aroma and a resinous, dry finish.

Blonde (OG 1040, ABV 4%)
A pale blonde ale, aromatic and hoppy.

Gold (OG 1041, ABV 4.2%) 🍺
A golden yellow-coloured ale with a papaya, pineapple and lemon aroma and a soft, full-bodied, creamy taste.

Black Knight (OG 1045, ABV 4.5%)
A ruby black-coloured stout with a smoky, liquorice aroma and sweet, roasted, nutty flavour.

Boiling Well (OG 1045.5, ABV 4.7%)
An auburn-coloured beer with a grassy aroma of autumn fruit with a full-bodied sweet then dry taste.

Stairway (OG 1047, ABV 5%)
A honey gold-coloured beer with a grassy, citrus floral aroma and a sharp, sweet, full-bodied taste.

LWC

Beers brewed under the Gray's brand. See Marston's

Lyme Regis SIBA

Mill Lane, Lyme Regis, Dorset, DT7 3PU
☎ (01297) 444354

Office: 15a Broad Street, Lyme Regis, Dorset, DT7 3QE
⊕ lymeregisbrewery.com

⊠ Lyme Regis Brewery, formerly known as Town Mill, began brewing in 2010 using a four-barrel plant in a part of the mill that at one time housed the Lyme Regis electricity generator, although historic use of the building was as a brewer's malthouse. The outside area is licensed. The brewery offers cuckoo brewing capability for other brewers. ‼ ☕ ♦ RAIB

Cobb (OG 1041, ABV 3.9%)
An amber/brown-coloured bitter with a full flavour and traditional-tasting fruity hop finish.

Lyme Gold (OG 1042, ABV 4.2%)
A pale summer ale, easy-drinking with a refreshing citrus aroma.

Rebel (OG 1041, ABV 4.2%)
A light ruby-coloured ale with a malted biscuit aroma and a pleasant fruity flavour.

Dorset Pearl (OG 1041, ABV 4.3%)
A traditional English pale ale; crisp, floral and refreshing.

Town Mill Best (OG 1045, ABV 4.5%)
A reddish brown-coloured bitter with a fruit and nut flavour.

Black Ven (OG 1050, ABV 5%)
A dark brown-coloured porter with a pronounced depth of flavour, enhanced with the blackcurrant fruitiness of the hops.

Revenge (OG 1052, ABV 5.3%)

A traditional IPA with a well-balanced hop and spiced fruit flavour.

Lymestone SIBA ⊙

The Brewery, Mount Road, Stone, Staffordshire, ST15 8LL
☎ (01785) 817796 ☎ 07891 782652
⊕ lymestonebrewery.co.uk

☺Lymestone commenced brewing in 2008. Rapid growth has seen the beers supplied direct to 300 outlets, with beer also being available via wholesalers. Two pubs are owned. ‼️🍺♦

Stone Cutter (OG 1037, ABV 3.7%) ◥
Hoppy and grassy aroma, clean, sharp and refreshing. A hint of caramel start then intense bitterness emerges with a good bitter aftertaste and touch of mouthwatering astringency.

Stone Faced (OG 1040, ABV 4%)
Subtle citrus and toffee flavours balanced by a hoppy aroma and bitter finish.

Foundation Stone (OG 1047, ABV 4.5%) ◥
An IPA-style beer with pale and crystal malts. Faint biscuit and chewy, juicy fruits burst on to the palate then the spicy hops pepper the tastebuds to leave a dry bitter finish.

Ein Stein (OG 1052, ABV 5%)
A pale, citrus, hoppy ale.

Stone the Crows (OG 1056, ABV 5.4%) ◥
A rich, dark-coloured beer. Fruit, roasts and hops abound to leave a deep, lingering bitterness from the hop mix.

Abdominal Stoneman (OG 1072, ABV 7%)
A crisp American-style pale ale with a massive hoppy finish.

Lymm

18 Bridgewater Street, Lymm, Cheshire, WA13 0AB
☎ (0161) 929 0663 ✉ info@lymmbrewing.co.uk

☺Lymm is a small, family-run brewery, launched in 2013. Located in an old post office, the brewing equipment is downstairs in what used to be the mess rooms with a brewery tap upstairs in what was the sorting office/post office counter. A sister brewery to Dunham Massey (qv), a joint bar opened in 2013, Costello's Bar, Stockton Heath. ♦

Bitter (OG 1040, ABV 3.8%)
A light, refreshing, medium-bodied session bitter, with a good balance of malt and hops.

Bridgewater Blonde (OG 1041, ABV 4%)
Light, delicate, hoppy, subtle and refreshing.

Heritage Trail Ale (OG 1046, ABV 4.5%)
An easy-drinking, well-balanced best bitter, fruity with a light, crisp hop.

Dam Strong Ale (OG 1071, ABV 7.2%)
Belgian-style ale, strong, malty and fruity with a dry finish.

Lytham SIBA

8 Cambell's Court, Lord Street, St Annes, Lancashire, FY8 2DF
☎ (01253) 725440 ⊕ lythambrewery.co.uk

☺Lytham is a well-established, family-run brewery that began brewing in 2007. ‼️♦

Amber (OG 1037, ABV 3.6%)
A traditional malty beer using English hops.

Blonde (OG 1038, ABV 3.8%) ◥
Smooth golden ale with a dry finish.

Gold (OG 1042, ABV 4.2%)
A golden-coloured beer with a fruity aroma and lasting bitter finish.

Royal (OG 1044, ABV 4.4%)
A full-bodied English ale with a crisp, fruity aroma and a smooth, dry finish.

Stout (OG 1046, ABV 4.6%)
Dark-coloured, rich, roasty, full-bodied stout.

IPA (OG 1054, ABV 5.6%)
A pale bitter with a fresh, sweet, hoppy flavour leading to a long, dry finish.

McColl's (NEW)

Unit 4, Randolph Industrial Estate, Evenwood, DL14 9SJ
☎ (01388) 641250 ⊕ mccollsbrewery.co.uk

Brewing commenced in 2017 using a 20-barrel plant. Outlets are supplied across the North-east and further afield. ‼️♦RAIB

Golden Ale (OG 1038, ABV 4%)
Light malt and citrus hop flavours with lemon and floral aromas building to a soft bitterness and medium dry finish.

Best Bitter (OG 1045, ABV 4.4%)
Rich and resinous malts with spicy marmalade hop flavours and deep citrus aromas building to an assertive bitterness balanced by a sweet body.

Pale Ale (OG 1044, ABV 4.5%)
A smooth, full-bodied pale ale that builds from light spicy notes to citrus and soft fruit aromas.

IPA (OG 1050, ABV 5%)
Earthy hop flavours and punchy citrus and grapefruit aromas. The body is well-balanced with a firm bitterness and lingering, dry finish.

McGivern

⬛ c/o The Bridge End Inn, 5 Bridge Street, Ruabon, LL14 6DA
☎ (01978) 810881 ☎ 07891 676614
⊕ mcgivernales.co.uk

The brewery was established in 2008 and was originally based at the brewer's home in Wrexham but moved in 2011 to the award-winning Bridge End Inn in Ruabon using a 2.5-barrel plant.

McMullen SIBAIFBB ⊙

26 Old Cross, Hertford, SG14 1RD
☎ (01992) 584911 ⊕ mcmullens.co.uk

McMullen, Hertfordshire's oldest independent brewery, was founded in 1827 – its famous brew, AK, is traceable back into the 19th century. The 'Authentic Heritage' tag promotes its four core beers. Ten additional seasonal ales are produced throughout the year, sometimes produced under the Rivertown Brewery name. A new microbrewery supplements the main plant. All 125 tied pubs, spread across South-east England, serve cask beer. A number of open days are held for the public to view the brewery. ♦

AK (OG 1035, ABV 3.7%) ◥

THE BREWERIES

A pleasant mix of malt and hops leads to a distinctive, dry aftertaste that isn't always as pronounced as it used to be.

Cask Ale (OG 1039, ABV 3.8%)
A well-balanced ale with subtle biscuit malt and citrus hop flavours.

Country Bitter (OG 1042, ABV 4.3%) ◣
A full-bodied beer with a well-balanced mix of malt, hops and fruit throughout.

IPA (OG 1047, ABV 4.8%)
A strong bitter with deep, rich flavours.

Macclesfield

76 Brown Street, Macclesfield, Cheshire, SK11 6RY
⊕ maccbrew.co

A small-batch 100-litre brewery producing bottled beers using seasonal ingredients. No core range.

Mad Cat SIBA

Brogdale Farm, Brogdale Road, Faversham, Kent, ME13 8XZ
☎ (01795) 597743 ☎ 07960 263615
⊕ madcatbrewery.co.uk

Established in 2012 by Peter Meaney in a refurbished cold store using an eight-barrel plant. ‼️ 🍺 ♦

Red Ale (ABV 3.9%)
A chestnut-coloured best bitter, malty, fruity and nutty.

Crispin Ale (ABV 4%)

Crispin Pale Ale (ABV 4%)

Mild Disobedience (ABV 4%)
A black mild with fruits of the forest flavours.

Golden IPA (ABV 4.2%)
A golden ale with a peppery hop aroma.

Platinum Blonde (ABV 4.2%)
A pale beer with a citrus hop aroma.

Mad Dog

Shed 4, Unit 9, Park Farm, Plough Road, Penperlleni, NP4 0AL ☎ 07703 731197 ⊕ maddogbrew.co.uk

Brewing began in 2014 based at the brewer's home in Cwmbran. The brewery relocated in 2015 expanding to a brew length of five barrels. An upgrade to larger premises on the same site later the same year has enabled a significant increase in production capacity.

Third Eye Blind (ABV 3.8%)
A pale ale with tropical and citrus hop flavours.

Now In A Minute (ABV 4.2%)
A traditional Welsh red-coloured ale with flavours of sweet chocolate and citrus.

Stouty McStoutface (ABV 4.5%)
Full-bodied and smooth with chocolate and roast flavours.

Bohemian Hipster (ABV 4.9%)
Pale ale with flavours of lemongrass and pine needles.

It's All Propaganda (ABV 5%)
A black IPA with no roast flavour but full of lemon, coconut and grapefruit, finishing on a spicy note.

Mad Hatter

Unit 1, Palmer Hill Building, 15-37 Caryl Street, Liverpool, L8 5SQ ☎ 07474 797450
⊕ madhatterbrewing.co.uk

Mad Hatter began brewing in 2013.

Mad Scientist (NEW)

🚊 c/o The Quakerhouse, 2-3 Mechanics Yard, Darlington, DL3 7QF
☎ (01325) 245052

Brewing commenced in 2017 on a half-barrel plant situated in the cellar of the Quakerhouse.

Mad Squirrel SIBA 👁

Unit 19, Boxted Farm, Berkhamsted Road, Potten End, Hertfordshire, HP1 2SQ
☎ (01442) 256970 ⊕ madsquirrel.uk

⊗ Established in 2004 and formerly Red Squirrel, the company changed name in 2017 to coincide with the installation of a larger brew kit and opening of a new shop and taproom at the brewery with pizzeria, outdoor seating and countryside views. ‼️ 🍺 ♦

Hopfest (OG 1037.5, ABV 3.8%)
A pale golden ale with a floral/citrus aroma and elderflower notes.

De La Creme (OG 1040, ABV 4%)
A smooth milk stout, full-bodied with hints of caramel, cream and chocolate.

Mister Squirrel (OG 1040, ABV 4%)
A chestnut-coloured bitter, lightly-hopped with a creamy texture. Hints of caramel and vanilla complement the slightly hoppy and malty overtones.

Sumo (OG 1046, ABV 4.7%)
An American-style pale ale with tropical fruit notes and some bitterness.

London Porter (OG 1052, ABV 5%)
Dark brown/black-coloured porter with a good balance of chocolate and roasted barley. Full-bodied on the palate with bittersweet liquorice, rich chocolate flavours and a creamy finish.

Roadkill (OG 1060, ABV 6.5%)
An unfiltered and unfined, yellow-coloured New England-style IPA containing wheat and oats.

Madrigal

The Manor House, Manor Green, Lynmouth, Devon, EX35 6EN ☎ 07857 560677 ⊕ madrigalbrewery.co.uk

⊗ The brewery was established in 2014 in the village of Combe Martin. It relocated to larger premises in Lynmouth in 2016 to help meet increased demand. ‼️ ♦ RAIB V

Garland (OG 1036, ABV 3.5%)
A wheat beer with hints of fruits from the tropics.

Surfer Rosa (OG 1036, ABV 3.6%)
A unique ale, made with English hops and a spicy red rye malt.

Burning House (OG 1042, ABV 4%)
A dark brown-coloured speciality beer, with a smooth mouthfeel and a gradual smoke and hop finish.

Fossil (OG 1043, ABV 4%)

A well-rounded, amber-coloured ale.

Hanged Man (OG 1042, ABV 4.2%)
Well-rounded stout made with raw cacao nibs. Smooth, soft taste with slight spicy notes.

Severed Hand (OG 1043, ABV 4.3%)
A velvety porter.

Monkey's Fist (OG 1048, ABV 5%) ◣
Smooth, dark old ale with strong fruit and roast from start to lingering, slightly sour finish. Heavy, sweet but satisfying.

North Coast Voodoo (OG 1050, ABV 5%)
An aromatic IPA made with a fruity aroma and a gradual hop finish.

Wheatear (OG 1048, ABV 5.1%)
Wheat beer made with fresh ginger and coriander.

Magic Rock SIBA

Units 1-4, Willow Lane, Huddersfield, West Yorkshire, HD1 5EB
☎ (01484) 649823 ⊕ magicrockbrewing.com

Magic Rock began brewing in 2011. ♦RAIB

Ringmaster (OG 1038, ABV 3.9%)
Pale ale with a floral, grassy aroma and citrus hops.

Rapture (OG 1044.5, ABV 4.6%)
Full-bodied, red-coloured ale with grapefruit and pine aromas, pithy orange, and a rich, malty body.

High Wire (OG 1051, ABV 5.5%)
West Coast-style pale ale, with mango, lychee and grapefruit flavours.

Dark Arts (OG 1057, ABV 6%) ▨
Chocolate, liquorice, blackberry and fig flavours with a long, roasted bitter finish.

Magic Spells (NEW)

Leyton, London, E10
☎ (0203) 475 1781 ☎ 07740 428952
⊕ magicspellsbrewery.co.uk

Magic Spells is an independent brewery located in East London, owned and operated by Jas Hare. Brewing takes place on a 10-barrel plant with a half-barrel kit used for experimental brews. RAIB

Magpie SIBA ◉

Unit 4, Ashling Court, Ashling Street, Nottingham, NG2 3JA ☎ 07738 762897 ⊕ magpiebrewery.com

☺Launched in 2006 using a six-barrel plant, the brewery upgraded to 15 barrels in 2017. Only British hops and malt are used. ♦RAIB

Hoppily Ever After (OG 1035, ABV 3.8%) ◣
Golden-coloured bitter, gently hopped with biscuit malt flavours and a bitter finish.

Flyer (OG 1038.8, ABV 4.1%)
A light golden-coloured ale with a fruity and slightly spicy flavour.

Best (OG 1040.7, ABV 4.2%) ◣
A malty, traditional pale brown-coloured best bitter, with balancing hops giving a bitter finish.

Raven Stout (OG 1044, ABV 4.4%) ◣
Dark stout with roast coffee aroma and taste, leading to a dry bitter finish.

Thieving Rogue (OG 1042, ABV 4.5%) ◣

A hoppy golden ale with a long-lasting, bitter finish.

Jay IPA (OG 1048.6, ABV 5.2%)
Mature hops, citrus fruit nose with a balance of hops and malt in the mouth with a smooth, hoppy aftertaste.

Maidstone

Unit 11, The Old Brewery, Rocky Hill, London Road, Maidstone, Kent, ME16 0DZ ☎ 07736 149014
⊕ maidstonebrewing.co.uk

⊠ A four-barrel brewery situated in the former stable block of the old Style & Winch brewery in Maidstone. Test brewing commenced in 2013 and the first beer went on sale in 2015. Beers are available locally, particularly at the Flower Pot in Maidstone.

Alpha 38 (OG 1040, ABV 3.9%)

First Light (OG 1040, ABV 3.9%)
A pale ale with a slightly sweet initial taste and a dry, bitter finish.

Eight (OG 1052, ABV 4.5%)
A smooth, dark-coloured ale with gentle bitterness and a hint of chocolate.

Maldon SIBA

▤ **Stable Brewery, Silver Street, Maldon, Essex, CM9 4QE**
☎ (01621) 851000 ⊕ maldonbrewing.co.uk

Established in 2002, this family-run brewery is tucked away behind the 14th-century Blue Boar Hotel. The six-barrel plant is at full production serving more than 50 outlets including many Gray & Sons houses and the brewery's micropub on the High Street.

Farmer's IPA (OG 1036, ABV 3.6%)
A crisp IPA based on an old Ridley's recipe.

Drop of Nelson's Blood (OG 1038, ABV 3.8%)
An easy-drinking bitter. A tot of brandy is added to each cask.

Hotel Porter (OG 1041, ABV 4.1%)
A classic stout with a smoky tang.

Pucks Folly (OG 1038, ABV 4.2%)
A pale golden ale with a spicy character and pineapple in the aroma and taste.

Farmer's Golden Boar (OG 1050, ABV 5%)
An amber-coloured beer with a hoppy aroma.

Essex Strong Ale (OG 1053, ABV 5.3%)
An American-style pale ale, slightly sweet.

Dark Horse (OG 1064, ABV 6.6%)
A chestnut-coloured bitter, smooth but with spice in the finish.

Mallard SIBA

Unit A, Maythorne, Nottinghamshire, NG25 0RS
☎ 07811 193930 ⊠ stevenhussey@tiscali.co.uk

☺Mallard is a 2.25-barrel brewery run by Steve Hussey and Alison Ryan, brewing for their own pub, the Cross Keys in Upton, and local outlets in and around the county. ‼♦RAIB

Duck 'n' Dive (OG 1039, ABV 3.7%) ◣
A bitter, pale golden beer, with a dry finish.

Greet Ale (OG 1037, ABV 3.7%)

A copper-coloured, traditional, malty ale, pleasantly bitter on the palate.

Golden Duck (OG 1039, ABV 3.9%)
Golden-coloured bitter brewed with a combination of four hops.

Quacker Jack (OG 1040, ABV 4%)
Copper-coloured bitter with a well-balanced hop/malt bitterness.

Feather Light (OG 1040, ABV 4.1%) ◥
A straw-coloured lager-style beer with a hoppy taste and aroma.

Duckling (OG 1041, ABV 4.2%) ◥
A dry-hopped golden ale. Bitter; hops dominate in the aroma and aftertaste.

Specduckular (OG 1042, ABV 4.2%)
A refreshing golden ale full of fruity hops with a malty undertone.

Mallinson's

Unit 1, Waterhouse Mill, 65-71 Lockwood Road, Huddersfield, West Yorkshire, HD1 3QU
☎ (01484) 654301 ☎ 07850 446571
⊕ drinkmallinsons.co.uk

☺The brewery was originally set up in 2008 on a six-barrel plant by CAMRA members Tara Mallinson and Elaine Yendall. The company moved to new premises in 2012 with a 15-barrel plant. Its first tap house opened in Huddersfield in 2016. ☞◆RAIB V

Malt SIBA

Collings Hanger Farm, 100 Wycombe Road, Prestwood, Buckinghamshire, HP16 0HP
☎ (01494) 865063 ☎ 07815 187113
⊕ maltthebrewery.co.uk

⊗ Family-owned brewery, founded in 2012 using a 10-barrel plant. Based on a dairy farm in the heart of the Chiltern Hills, it has sustainability built-into its brewing with spent grains going to feed the pigs on the farm and spent hops being composted. In-house deliveries are made to trade and direct customers within 30 miles of the brewery. National distribution is through leading distributors and wholesalers. ‼☞◆RAIB

Missenden Pale (OG 1035, ABV 3.6%)
Easy to drink session ale, light amber in colour.

Golden Ale (OG 1038, ABV 3.9%)
Light and refreshing with a citrus finish.

Malt Dark Ale (OG 1038, ABV 3.9%)
Smooth, mild ale. Full of deep malt tones.

Starry Nights (OG 1040, ABV 4%)
A light, fruity ale with a dark side.

Anniversary Ale (OG 1043, ABV 4.4%)
Classic-style bitter with a dry finish. Made with a blend of traditional British hops.

Voyager (OG 1048, ABV 5%)
Aromatic with a bitter finish.

Malvern Hills SIBA

15 West Malvern Road, Malvern, Worcestershire, WR14 4ND
☎ (01684) 560165 ⊕ malvernhillsbrewery.co.uk

⊗ Founded in 1998 in an old quarrying dynamite store and an established presence in the Three

Counties, Birmingham and the Black Country. Seasonal and special beers are directed more by ad-hoc requests from publicans rather than a planned brewery timetable apart from green-hopped beers in September. ‼◆

Beacon Gold (OG 1036, ABV 3.7%)

Feelgood (OG 1037, ABV 3.8%)
A light bitter, with a floral spicy aroma.

Malvern Spring (OG 1040, ABV 4.2%)

Black Pear (OG 1042, ABV 4.4%) ◥
A sharp citrus hoppiness is the main constituent of this golden-coloured best bitter that has a long, dry aftertaste.

Manchester

66 North Western Street, Manchester, M12 6DX
☎ (0161) 273 6167 ⊕ manchesterbrewing.co.uk

Brewing commenced in 2016 in a railway arch on Manchester's 'beer mile' using an eight-barrel plant. Local pubs and beer festivals are supplied. ◆

Factory Pale Ale (OG 1040, ABV 4%)
Dry, straw-coloured pale ale.

King Cotton (OG 1043, ABV 4.2%)

Cuts Like a Buffalo (OG 1045, ABV 4.5%)

Pick Me Up Coffee Porter (OG 1050, ABV 4.7%)
A porter spiked with cold brew coffee after fermentation.

Mad Carew (OG 1055, ABV 5.9%)

Manning

Lower Overton Farm, Overton Road, Congleton, Cheshire, CW12 3QW ☎ 07946 278018
⊕ manningbrewers.co.uk

A family-owned and run brewery using only British hops, opened in 2015. It has recently joined forces with the established Beartown Brewery (qv), also of Congleton.

Woah Man (ABV 3.8%)
A clean-drinking, golden-coloured pale ale with a floral aroma.

Man Up! (ABV 4%)
A bronze-coloured, malty session beer.

Cave-Man (ABV 4.2%)
A well-balanced bitter. A crisp finish with some blackberry aromas, and a lasting gentle bitterness.

Mantle SIBA ◉

Unit 16, Pentood Industrial Estate, Cardigan, SA43 3AG
☎ (01239) 623898 ☎ 07552 609909
⊕ mantlebrewery.com

Mantle began brewing in 2013 using a 10-barrel plant. More than 200 outlets are supplied direct with wider distribution via selected wholesalers. ‼☞◆

Rock Steady (OG 1038, ABV 3.8%)
Golden-coloured session ale with great depth of flavour.

MOHO (OG 1041.5, ABV 4.3%) 🍶
Robust and aromatic Welsh pale ale.

Cwrw Teifi (OG 1045, ABV 4.5%)

Full-bodied, malt-driven best bitter with a well-balanced and pleasant hop finish.

Dark Heart (OG 1052, ABV 5.2%)
Rich, dark and smooth porter with a hint of spice.

Marble SIBA

41 Williamson Street, Manchester, M4 4JS
☎ (0161) 819 2694 ⊕ marblebeers.com

☺Marble began brewing in 1997 at the Marble Arch Inn in Manchester but now brews at a larger 12-barrel plant in a nearby unit, producing vegan beers. It supplies its own three pubs and more than 70 other outlets. ‼♦

Pint (OG 1038.5, ABV 3.9%) ◣
Pale yellow in colour with a citrus aroma. Hop, fruit and bitterness in the taste, with a dry finish.

Manchester Bitter (OG 1040.5, ABV 4.2%) ◣
Yellow-coloured beer with a fruity and hoppy aroma. Hops, fruit and bitterness on the palate and in the finish.

Lagonda IPA (OG 1047, ABV 5%) ⌂ ◣
Golden yellow-coloured beer with a spicy, fruity nose. Fruit, hops and malt in the mouth, with a dry fruitiness continuing into the bitter aftertaste.

Built to Fall APA (ABV 5.6%)

Earl Grey IPA (OG 1065, ABV 6.8%) ⌂
A citrus fruit aroma and smooth texture. Hop notes are complemented by bergamot and a light tannic finish.

Maregade

▤ Cock Tavern, Mare Street, Hackney, London, E8 1EJ
⊕ maregade.com

Microbrewery in the basement of the Cock Tavern in Hackney.

Market Bosworth (NEW)

Unit 10, Willow Farm Business Centre, Stoke Golding, Leicestershire, CV13 6EU
☎ (01455) 377855 ⊕ marketbosworthbrewery.co.uk

▨ The brewery was set up by Jon Skinner in 2016 as a natural progression from his homebrew retail business. Rich Brine joined in partnership in 2017 and the kit was doubled in size to two barrels to meet demand. ♦

Stout (ABV 4.2%)
A dark-coloured stout with roasted notes.

Best Bitter (ABV 4.8%)
A dark copper-coloured beer with a malty mouthfeel and lingering bitter finish.

Porter (ABV 5%)
Old-fashioned, traditional porter. Deceptively easy to drink.

Pale Ale (ABV 5.2%)
Golden-coloured ale; hoppy with citrus aromas.

Market Harborough

71 St Marys Road, Market Harborough, Leicestershire, LE16 7DS
☎ (01858) 461682 ⊕ mhbrew.co.uk

Brewing commenced in 2015 on a six-barrel plant. The brewery merged with the former Tres Bien

Brewery in 2017, with the beers being brewed as a separate brand. Beers are supplied to a limited number of pubs and shops in the area. ‼▤♦RAIB

Best (ABV 3.8%)
A complex malty backbone with traditional English hops.

Hoppy Pale (ABV 4.1%)
Crisp, refreshing, pale and bursting with citrus hop notes.

SuperHop Ahtunum (ABV 4.1%)
A smooth, dry pale ale with subtle fruitiness.

SuperHop Falconers Flight (ABV 4.1%)
A crisp, refreshing pale ale with tropical fruit aromas.

Brown (ABV 5.1%)
A modern brown-coloured ale with chocolate and caramel malt flavours.

Dry Stout (ABV 5.2%)
A well-balanced stout with a long, dry finish.

Hibiscus (ABV 5.5%)
A refreshing beer brewed with hibiscus flowers. Delicate and smooth with a wine-like finish.

IPA (ABV 6.3%)
An English IPA, smooth and deceptively strong with a long, hoppy finish.

Brewed under the Tres Bien brand name:

My Name is Earl (ABV 3.3%)
A mild with a delicate background of bergamot.

Air Mail (ABV 3.8%)
A refreshing pale ale with fruity, pine and citrus flavours and aromas.

Cottontail (ABV 3.8%)
Light and fruity session pale ale with floral and pine aromas.

Porter (ABV 5%)
Traditional porter. A little chocolaty, a little smoky.

Parakeet (ABV 5.2%)
Strong and pale with grapefruit, orange and pine notes.

Marko Paulo (NEW)

▤ Owl & The Pussycat, 106 Northfield Avenue, Northfields, London, W13 9RT ⊕ markopaulo.co.uk

A 1.25-barrel brewpub opened in 2016 in a former bookshop by two ex-teachers. It produces unfiltered, unpasteurised and unfined beers.

Marlpool

5 Breach Road, Marlpool, Derbyshire, DE75 7NJ
☎ (01773) 711285 ☎ 07963 511855
⊕ marlpoolbrewing.co.uk

Marlpool was set up by brothers Andy and Chris McAuley in 2010 using a 2.5-barrel plant situated in an old slaughterhouse. The majority of the beer is sold through its own micro pub built into the old butcher's shop attached to the brewery. The remainder is sold to local outlets. ‼♦RAIB

Blind Boris (OG 1038, ABV 3.5%)

Otters Pocket (OG 1040, ABV 4%)
Easy-drinking, smooth, amber-coloured ale.

Scratty Ratty (OG 1044, ABV 4.4%)
Pale ale, lightly hopped with a bitter, dry finish.

Frank (OG 1045, ABV 4.5%)
A dark red-coloured ale, fairly bitter.

Derbyshire Classic (OG 1048, ABV 4.8%)

Black Oss (OG 1058, ABV 5.4%)

Marston's 👁

Shobnall Road, Burton upon Trent, Staffordshire,
DE14 2BW
☎ (01283) 531131 ⊕ marstons.co.uk

☺ Marston's has been brewing cask beer in Burton since 1834 and the current site is the home of the only working Burton Union fermenters, housed in rooms known as the Cathedral of Brewing. Burton Unions were developed in the 19th century to cleanse the new style of pale ale yeast. Only Pedigree is fermented in the unions but yeast from the system is used to ferment the other Marston's branded beers. In 2016 a small 2.5-barrel nanobrewery was installed within the DE14 visitors centre. Beers from this nanobrewery are available locally. Marston's continues to take contract brewing, and brews the iconic cask beer Draught Bass on behalf of AB Inbev. ‼ 🍺 ◆ RAIB

61 Deep (OG 1038, ABV 3.8%)
A mellow, understated hop bitterness complemented by a blast of tropical fruit flavours. A light citrus tingle follows, leading to a fragrant and refreshing finish.

Saddle Tank (OG 1037, ABV 3.8%) 🍺
Overwhelming sulphurous aroma supports a scattering of hops and fruit with an easy-drinking sweetness. The taste develops from the sweet middle to a satisfyingly hoppy finish.

Pedigree (OG 1043, ABV 4.5%) 🍺
Pale brown with a sweet hoppy aroma. Malt with a dash of hop flavours give a satisfying tasty finish.

Old Empire (OG 1057, ABV 5.7%) 🍺
Sulphur dominates the gentle malt aroma. Malty and sweet to start but developing bitterness with fruit and a touch of sweetness. A balanced aftertaste of hops and fruit leads to a lingering bitterness.

For AB InBev:

Draught Bass (OG 1043, ABV 4.4%) 🍺
Hints of caramel aroma and taste, lightly hopped for a short bitter finish.

Martland Mill SIBA

Unit 5, Otterwood Square, Martland Mill, Wigan,
WN5 0LF
☎ (01942) 665656 ⊕ martlandmillbrewery.co.uk

☺ Founded in 2014 by a husband-and-wife team using a six-barrel brew plant, the brewery is located close to the town centre of Martland Mill Park. Numerous local outlets are supplied including the brewery tap, the Tap 'n' Barrel in Wigan, that opened in 2015. ‼ ◆

Chonkin Feckle (OG 1038, ABV 3.8%)
A yellow-coloured ale with a citrus hop aroma, floral notes and a pine finish.

Spinner's Gold (OG 1038, ABV 3.8%)
A golden ale with well-balanced hoppiness, a pleasant citrus taste and a hint of spiciness.

Knocker Upper (OG 1040, ABV 3.9%)

A straw-coloured ale with a floral aroma, a rich honey taste and hints of fruit.

Clogmaker (OG 1041, ABV 4%)
A rich, golden-coloured, full-bodied ale with a refreshing fruity flavour and an inkling of cedar and honey.

Lancashire Loom (OG 1043, ABV 4%)
A light golden-coloured ale bursting with a real fruit punch of grapefruit, lychees and lemon with a slight floral note.

D Day Dodger (OG 1041, ABV 4.1%)
A red-hued beer with subtle malt aromas, a refreshing rounded bitterness and a clean, crisp, fruity finish.

Bomber's Blonde (OG 1043, ABV 4.4%)
A pale blonde ale with an intense hoppy aroma and a crisp, refreshing citrus taste, leading to a slightly dry finish.

Arctic Convoy (OG 1045, ABV 4.5%)
A traditional, full-bodied stout with rich roasted malt palate, giving a pleasant hint of bitterness and smooth, chocolaty finish.

MASH SIBA 👁

Middle Barn, Burcot Farm, East Stratton, Hampshire,
SO21 3DZ
☎ (01962) 795023 ⊕ mashbrewery.com

☒ Brewing began in 2013 using a one-barrel plant. A 10-barrel plant was installed in 2014. RAIB

Pale (OG 1035, ABV 3.8%)
A pale ale with a subtle aroma and a long, bitter finish.

Copper (OG 1037, ABV 3.9%)
A copper-coloured beer with fruity, peachy aromas and a dry bitter flavour.

Gilt (OG 1038, ABV 4.1%)
Golden ale with citrus orange aroma and spice. Dry bitter finish.

Amber (OG 1042, ABV 4.3%)
A well-balanced beer with floral aromas.

Ruby (OG 1045, ABV 4.8%)
Red-coloured ale with a malty, full-bodied finish.

Chocolate Stout (OG 1047, ABV 5%)
A rich, black stout with roasted malt and burnt coffee flavours. Dark chocolate is added during the brew.

Matlock Wolds Farm SIBA

South Barn, Cavendish Road, Farm Lane, Matlock,
Derbyshire, DE4 3GZ
☎ (01629) 697989 ☎ 07852 263263
⊕ woldsfarm.co.uk

☒ Brewing began in 2014 using a 50-litre kit. The brewery expanded to a 250-litre kit in 2015 and 2017 saw further expansion to a five-barrel plant. Beers are available at many local outlets. ◆ RAIB

The Bitter End (OG 1034, ABV 3.4%)
Ruby-coloured ale with a rich, malty background. Earthy, grassy hop flavours with notes of chocolate, nuts and pine and a long, bitter finish.

Apogee (OG 1038, ABV 3.8%)
Amber-coloured ale with fruit and citrus aromas. Flavours include orange and grapefruit combined with a light bitterness.

Simcoe (OG 1038, ABV 3.8%)
Aromas of pine and apricot with earthy citrus flavours and hints of tropical fruit leading to a strong bitter finish.

Smedley's Folly (OG 1039, ABV 3.9%)
A well-balanced ale with a slightly dry, bitter taste, which finishes with a hint of toffee.

Riber Gold (OG 1043, ABV 4.3%)
Traditional golden ale with floral and apricot aromas, hints of tropical fruit and a complex finish.

100cc (OG 1049, ABV 4.9%)
Light chestnut-coloured ale with a malty aroma complemented by orange and pine. Huge citrus flavours with orange and lemon coming through a good hop bitterness.

Classic Porter (OG 1049, ABV 4.9%)
Full-bodied porter with a chocolate aroma and a hint of vanilla. Full of roasted malt and coffee with a lingering bitterness.

Mauldons SIBA ◉

Black Adder Brewery, 13 Church Field Road, Sudbury, Suffolk, CO10 2YA
☎ (01787) 311055 ⊕ mauldons.co.uk

The Mauldon family started brewing in Sudbury in 1795. The brewery with 26 pubs was bought by Greene King in the 1960s. The current business, established in 1982, was bought by Steve and Alison Sims in 2000. They relocated to a new brewery in 2005, with a 30-barrel plant that has doubled production. One pub is owned and around 150 outlets are supplied. ‼🍺♦RAIB

Micawber's Mild (OG 1035, ABV 3.5%) 🍺
Light, easy-drinking mild. Malty smoothness with a rich, roast flavour turns into a caramel liquorice aftertaste.

Moletrap Bitter (OG 1038, ABV 3.8%) 🍺
Plum and toffee on the nose. A good balance of malt, hops and fruit, leading to an increasingly bitter aftertaste.

Christies Golden Ale (OG 1040, ABV 3.9%)
A light, golden-coloured, hoppy and refreshing beer.

Silver Adder (OG 1042, ABV 4.2%) 🍺
Light fruity aroma, dry hoppiness and citrus fruit with rich honey in the taste, and a long, fruity, sweet aftertaste. Refreshing and well-balanced.

Blackberry Porter (OG 1048, ABV 4.8%)
A full-bodied, black porter with balanced hop aroma and a rich blend of chocolate and roast flavours, giving way to a subtle sweet fruit finish.

Suffolk Pride (OG 1048, ABV 4.8%) 🍺
A full-bodied, copper-coloured beer. A bubblegum nose leads to a spicy taste, with mild astringency in the aftertaste.

Black Adder (OG 1053, ABV 5.3%) 🍺
Malty, roasty aroma leads to a well-balanced, full-bodied beer, malty with roast and dark soft fruit overtones.

Maule SIBA

42 Rothersthorpe Avenue, Northampton, NN4 8JH
⊕ maulebrewing.com

Brewing began in 2014 on a self-built plant. Production is mainly unfiltered keg and bottle-conditioned beers, but cask-conditioned ales are occasionally produced for festivals. Most output is supplied to London outlets. RAIB

Maxim SIBA ◉

1 Gadwall Road, Rainton Bridge South, Houghton-le-Spring, DH4 5NL
☎ (0191) 584 8844 ⊕ maximbrewery.co.uk

◉Rising from the ashes of Sunderland brewer Vaux, Maxim was set up with a 20-barrel plant in Houghton-le-Spring in 2007. More than 100 outlets are supplied direct and two pubs are owned. ‼🍺♦

Lambtons (OG 1039, ABV 3.8%)
Smooth golden ale with citrus and hoppy flavours.

Samson (OG 1040, ABV 4%)
Traditional best bitter, chestnut brown in colour with a caramel taste and a balanced bitterness.

Ward's Best Bitter (OG 1040, ABV 4%)
A tawny-coloured best bitter with a sweet, toasted biscuit flavour. Slightly hoppy, slightly fruity.

Swedish Blonde (OG 1042, ABV 4.2%)
A smooth, light-coloured beer, refreshing and hoppy with complex grapefruit flavours on the palate.

Double Maxim (OG 1048, ABV 4.7%)
A fruity, caramel, malty and nutty taste with a hint of sweetness.

American Pride IPA (OG 1055, ABV 5.2%)

Maximus (OG 1062, ABV 6%)
Dark ruby-coloured, full-bodied premium ale. Sweet with a liquorice flavour, caramel and dark fruits.

Mayflower

🍴 Charles Dickens, 14 Upper Dicconson Street, Wigan, WN1 2AD ☎ 07984 404567
✉ info@mayflowerbeer.co.uk

Originally established in Standish in 2001 as a 2.5-barrel plant, which was acquired by the current owner in 2007. Between 2012 and 2016 brewing was undertaken using spare capacity at various other breweries but a five-barrel plant has now been established at the rear of the owner's pub.

Maypole

North Laithes Farm, Wellow Road, Eakring, Nottinghamshire, NG22 0AN ☎ 07971 277598
⊕ maypolebrewery.co.uk

◉The brewery opened in 1995 in a converted 18th-century farm building. After changing hands in 2001 it was bought by the former head brewer, Rob Neil, in 2005. ♦

Midge (OG 1035, ABV 3.5%)
Pale ale with a lasting bitter finish.

Little Weed (OG 1037, ABV 3.8%)
Deep golden in colour with a subtle hop bitterness.

Celebration (OG 1038, ABV 4%)
Amber-coloured traditional English ale, slightly nutty overtones.

Gate Hopper (OG 1040, ABV 4%)
A golden ale with a floral aroma and lingering, hoppy bitterness.

Hop Fusion (OG 1040, ABV 4.2%)

A pale golden ale, pleasantly bitter.

Major Oak (OG 1042, ABV 4.4%)
A well-balanced red/brown-coloured, full-bodied
bitter. Hints of fruit and burnt malt.

Wellow Gold (OG 1044, ABV 4.6%)
Refreshing blonde ale, citrus on the nose and in the
aftertaste.

Meantime ◉

Lawrence Trading Estate, Blackwall Lane, East
Greenwich, London, SE10 0AR
☎ (020) 8293 1111

Head Office: Norman House, 110-114 Norman Road,
London, SE10 9EH ⊕ meantimebrewing.com

⊠ Founded in 2000, Meantime brews a wide
range of continental-style beers. Two pubs are
owned. In 2010 the brewery relocated to larger
premises in Greenwich. Taken over by SABMiller in
2015 and now owned by Asahi UK. No real ale.
‼ ▤ ♦ V

Melbourn

All Saints Brewery, All Saints Street, Stamford,
Lincolnshire, PE9 2PA
☎ (01780) 752186

No real ale. A famous Stamford brewery that
opened in 1825 and closed in 1974. It re-opened in
1994 and is owned by Samuel Smith of Tadcaster
(qv). ‼

Melin Tap (NEW)

🢒 Halfway House, Little Mill, NP4 0HL

Melin Tap is a small-scale brewery. Beers are
available at the Halfway House as well as a few
other local outlets.

Melwood SIBA

7 Stanley Grange, Knowsley Park, Merseyside,
L34 4AR
☎ (0151) 214 3340 ☎ 07545 265283
⊕ melwoodbeer.co.uk

Melwood began brewing in 2013 using a five-
barrel plant in an old dairy that used to house the
Cambrinus Brewery. In 2016 the brewery moved to
bigger premises in nearby old kennels on the
Knowsley Estate. ♦

Lovelight (OG 1038, ABV 3.8%)
Light, hoppy blonde beer with a crisp, biting
flavour.

Father Ted (ABV 4.2%)
A traditional English bitter, floral in flavour.

Knowsley Blonde (OG 1043, ABV 4.3%)
Crisp, refreshing pale ale with a fresh, hoppy aroma
and a pleasant bitter taste.

Stanley Gold (ABV 4.3%)
A crisp, hoppy beer with a citrus aroma.

Merlin SIBA

3 Spring Bank Farm, Congleton Road, Arclid, Cheshire,
CW11 2UD
☎ (01477) 500893 ☎ 07812 352590
⊕ merlinbrewing.co.uk

◉Established in 2010 using an eight-barrel plant in
a farm unit just outside Sandbach. The beers are
principally supplied to outlets within a 30-mile
radius. Brewing uses renewable energy from solar
panels and wind power, and spent grain and hops
are used on the farm. ‼ ♦ RAIB

Merlin's Gold (OG 1038, ABV 3.8%)
Light golden ale with rounded floral citrus flavours.

Excalibur (OG 1039, ABV 3.9%)
A light-coloured session ale. Bitter, hoppy flavours
are accompanied by a faint sweetness.

Spellbound (OG 1040, ABV 4%)
A full-flavoured bitter, light chestnut in colour with
a dry finish.

Avalon (OG 1041, ABV 4.1%)
A pale ale with grapefruit, lemon and spicy hop
flavours.

The Wizard (OG 1042, ABV 4.2%)
A hoppy, bitter, golden-coloured ale with generous
hints of grapefruit flavour.

Dark Magic (OG 1048, ABV 4.8%)
A strong, well-bodied dark mild with a caramel
aftertaste.

Dragonslayer (OG 1056, ABV 5.6%)
A dark-coloured brew with complex flavours.

Merrie City

See Clark's

Merrimen SIBA ◉

Unit 12, Litchborough Industrial Estate, Northampton
Road, Litchborough, Northamptonshire, NN12 8JB
☎ (01327) 831308 ☎ 07763 494673
⊕ merrimen.co.uk

Merrimen commenced brewing on an eight-barrel
plant in 2013. All beers are named on a 'Merri'
theme. Outlets include JD Wetherspoon, SIBA, pubs
and off-licences in Northampton, Coventry,
Warwick and surrounding areas. ♦ RAIB

Merri One (OG 1035, ABV 3.6%)
A light amber-coloured ale with medium
bitterness, combining three spicy hops.

**MPG (Merrimen's Pure Gold)
(OG 1035, ABV 3.7%)**
A pale golden-coloured beer with a lemon citrus
floral aroma and a dry, biscuity, bitter finish.

Hail Merri (OG 1036, ABV 3.8%)
Deep amber in colour, with a fruity, floral and
malty aroma and a biscuit, bitter taste with a dry
finish.

Black Beauty (OG 1037, ABV 3.9%)
A black-coloured bitter with a light roast coffee
aroma and a smooth caramel, refreshing finish.

Merri Weather (OG 1038, ABV 4%)
Rich and refreshing golden-coloured beer.

Be Merri (OG 1042, ABV 4.5%)
Premium amber-coloured bitter with roasted
chocolate malt and a smooth, rounded taste.

Very Merri (OG 1045, ABV 5.2%)
Vibrant citrus fruits, fresh aroma. A crisp citrus and
gentle malt finish.

Merry Miner 👁

Unit 20-21, Grendon House Farm, Grendon, Warwickshire, CV9 3DT ☎ 07811 932721
⊕ merryminerbrewery.com

Brewing began in 2010, based in farm buildings on the outskirts of the village of Grendon. The brewery and beers are named after the brewer's former occupation. It also brews under the name of Morgans. ‼◆

Miners Best Bitter (OG 1035, ABV 3.7%)
A pale, smooth, traditional best bitter with a crisp, bitter aftertaste.

Warwickshire's Finest (OG 1036, ABV 3.8%)
Light, amber-coloured session bitter.

Self Rescuer (OG 1039, ABV 3.9%)
Deep golden in colour with a pleasing bitterness and a smooth, malty aftertaste.

Davy's Lamp (OG 1038, ABV 4%)
Pale, full-flavoured bitter.

Bevin Boys (OG 1039, ABV 4.1%)
An American-style IPA with a pleasant finish.

Cap Lamp (OG 1039, ABV 4.2%)
Mid gold-coloured ale with a refreshing, crisp bitterness.

Deputy Drop (OG 1040, ABV 4.3%)

Going Underground (OG 1041, ABV 4.4%)

Pit Pony (OG 1041, ABV 4.5%)
Deep golden-coloured, smooth bitter.

Methane (OG 1045, ABV 5%)
Light golden-coloured bitter with a citrus finish.

Brewed under the Morgans brand name:

Chedhams Ale (OG 1036, ABV 3.8%)
Dark golden in colour. Tangy with a bitter fruit taste and a tart, hoppy aftertaste. Finishes dry.

Mersea Island

Rewsalls Lane, East Mersea, Essex, CO5 8SX ☎ 07970 070399 ⊕ merseabrewery.co.uk

⊠ The brewery was established at Mersea Island Vineyard in 2005. It supplies several local pubs on a guest beer basis as well as most local beer festivals. It holds its own festival of Essex-produced ales over the four-day Easter weekend. 🍴RAIB

Mersea Mud (OG 1036, ABV 3.8%)
An easy-drinking mild with a refreshing, malty flavour.

Yo Boy! (OG 1038, ABV 3.8%)
A session bitter with a long-lasting bitterness on the finish.

Gold (OG 1043, ABV 4.4%)
A refreshing, golden-coloured ale.

Monkeys (OG 1044, ABV 4.4%)
Sweet, lightly smoky and lightly roasted in aroma, while having smoky, fruity and light herbal flavours.

Skippers (OG 1047, ABV 4.8%)
A dark amber-coloured best bitter with a good malty flavour and a smooth bitterness.

Oyster Stout (OG 1048, ABV 5%)
A traditional oyster stout with local Mersea Island oysters added.

Middle Earth

Rowditch Inn, 246 Uttoxeter New Road, Derby, DE22 3LL ☎ 07504 304564

Office: 53 Springfield Road, Etwall, Derbyshire, DE65 6JZ ⊕ mebrewco.com

⊠ Set up in 2011, Middle Earth uses the 3.-75-barrel plant at the Rowditch Inn, Derby (also used by the Rowditch Brewery, qv). Steve Twells (the Rowditch brewer) established Middle Earth as a separate venture to utilise spare capacity to produce different brews for free trade sale. Following the successful start of its first micropub, the brewery will concentrate on house ales and one stout, with all other products to be brewed periodically.

Rivendale (OG 1044, ABV 4.3%)
A well-balanced, golden-coloured bitter.

Honey Dragon (OG 1044, ABV 4.5%)
Well-balanced, golden-coloured bitter with subtle honey notes.

Mighty Medicine (NEW)

Unit 4, Daniel Street, Whitworth, Lancashire, OL12 8BX
☎ (01706) 558980 ⊕ mightymedicine.com

Established in 2016 this brewery is committed to using the finest ingredients to produce an eclectic range of beers. A tap room is attached to the brewery. 🍴

Stunning Blonde (ABV 3.9%)
Easy-drinking, fruity blonde ale.

Madchester Cream (ABV 4.2%)
Creamy and smooth pale ale.

Mighty Oak

14b West Station Yard, Spital Road, Maldon, Essex, CM9 6TW
☎ (01621) 843713 ⊕ mightyoakbrewing.co.uk

⊠ Mighty Oak was formed in 1996 and has expanded considerably following a move to Maldon in 2001. Current capacity is 8,000 barrels a year following the acquisition of two adjacent buildings and enlarged plant. Some 450 outlets are supplied. Twelve monthly ales are brewed to a theme, which for 2018 is aircraft. ‼🍴◆

Oscar Wilde (OG 1039.5, ABV 3.7%) 🗒 🍂
Roasty dark mild with suggestions of forest fruits and dark chocolate. A sweet taste yields to a more bitter finish.

Captain Bob (OG 1039.5, ABV 3.8%)
A traditional deep amber-coloured bitter with a fruity and hoppy aroma. A slight sweet maltiness balances an easy going bitterness, followed by hints of gooseberry, elderflower and grape in the finish.

Maldon Gold (OG 1039.5, ABV 3.8%) 🍂
Pale golden ale with a sharp citrus note moderated by honey and biscuity malt.

Endeavour (OG 1042.6, ABV 4.2%)
A rich, copper-coloured ale with subtle blackcurrant, grapefruit and spice flavours.

Kings (OG 1042.6, ABV 4.2%)

A deep golden-coloured beer bursting with hoppy fruitiness with orange, nectarine and passion fruit flavours lasting into the finish.

Mile Tree SIBA

Mile Tree Lane, Wisbech, Cambridgeshire, PE13 4TR
☎ 07858 930363
⊕ thesecretgardentouringpark.co.uk

Mile Tree began brewing in 2012 using a five-barrel plant. Local outlets and beer festivals are supplied. ♦ RAIB

Adventurer (OG 1040, ABV 4%)
Golden-coloured, full-flavoured beer with a ripe, generous fruitiness and a fresh light hop character.

Wellstream (OG 1049, ABV 4.9%)
Ruby-coloured, full-bodied, malty beer with a deep bittersweet finish.

Milestone SIBA ◉

Great North Road, Cromwell, Nottinghamshire, NG23 6JE
☎ (01636) 822255 ⊕ milestonebrewery.co.uk

☺Established in 2005, Milestone currently brews on a 12-barrel plant. More than 150 outlets are supplied. ‼ ⊨ ♦ RAIB

Best Bitter (OG 1037, ABV 3.7%)
An amber-coloured, traditional session bitter.

Liberty Ale (OG 1037, ABV 3.7%)
Straw-coloured session ale infused with American hops.

Sherwood Pale Ale (OG 1039, ABV 3.9%)

Classic Dark Mild (OG 1040, ABV 4%)

Shine On (OG 1039, ABV 4%)
Straw-coloured session ale with floral and citrus notes.

Azacca Gold (OG 1042, ABV 4.2%)
A single hop blonde beer.

Loxley Ale (OG 1042, ABV 4.2%)
Golden-coloured beer with a subtle hint of honey.

Black Pearl (OG 1043, ABV 4.3%)
A traditional Irish-style stout.

Crusader (OG 1044, ABV 4.4%)
Belgian-style blonde beer with a zesty, clean finish.

Rich Ruby (OG 1044, ABV 4.5%)
Rich, smooth and creamy Celtic red-coloured ale.

American Pale Ale (OG 1046, ABV 4.6%)
A blonde, hoppy, citrus ale.

Olde English (OG 1049, ABV 4.9%)
Full-bodied winter warmer with a pleasing nutty finish.

Raspberry Wheat Beer (OG 1055, ABV 5.6%)
Continental-style ale infused with fresh fruit.

Milk Street ◉

Frome Brewing Co, Unit L13, Marshall Way, Commerce Park, Frome, Somerset, BA11 2FB
☎ (01373) 467766

Office: The Griffin, 25 Milk Street, Frome, Somerset, BA11 3DB ⊕ milkstreetbrewery.co.uk

⊠ Milk Street was established in 1999 behind the Griffin pub in Frome. In 2016 the brewery relocated

to an industrial unit having outgrown the cramped facilities behind the pub and increased its capabilities to 60 barrels. Beer is supplied direct to its own estate of two pubs and other local outlets. ‼ ♦

Same Again (OG 1039, ABV 3.9%)

Funky Monkey (OG 1040, ABV 4%)
Copper-coloured ale with fruity flavours and aromas. A dry finish with developing bitterness and an undertone of citrus fruit.

Ra (OG 1041, ABV 4.1%)

The Usual (OG 1045, ABV 4.4%)
A well-rounded fruitiness with hints of caramel in the taste. The slight sweetness is balanced by a bitter, grainy finish with hints of raspberry.

Zig-Zag Stout (OG 1046, ABV 4.5%)
A stout with characteristic roastiness and dryness. Bitter chocolate and citrus fruit in the background.

Gulp IPA (OG 1048, ABV 4.8%)
A session beer with a lemon and citrus aroma and good hop balance. The finish has a clean bitterness with spicy blackcurrant notes.

Beer (OG 1049, ABV 5%)
A hoppy blonde beer with citrus fruit on the nose, while more fruit surges through on the palate before the bittersweet finish.

Mill Valley

Woodroyd Mills, Cleckheaton, BD19 3AF
☎ (0113) 815 1624 ☎ 07565 229560
⊕ millvalleybrewery.co.uk

☺Steve Hemingway began brewing in 2016. A six-barrel plant is used supplying more than 40 outlets and beer festivals. An on-site bar and bottle shop are planned. ‼ V

Luddite Ale (ABV 3.8%)

Panther Ale (ABV 4%)

The Dukes IPA (ABV 4%)
A pale ale with a hoppy bitter taste and citrus finish.

Mill Blonde (ABV 4.2%)

Mill Bitter (ABV 4.3%)

Luddite Dark (ABV 4.6%)

Millis (Dartford Wobbler) SIBA ◉

Dartford Wobbler Brewery, St Margaret's Farm, St Margaret's Road, South Darenth, Kent, DA4 9LB
☎ (01322) 866233 ⊕ dartfordwobbler.com

☺John and Miriam Millis started with a 0.5-barrel plant at their home in Gravesend. Demand outstripped the facility and Millis moved in 2003 to its current location – a former farm cold store – using a 10-barrel plant. It now supplies around 40 outlets within a 50-mile radius. ♦ RAIB

Curiously Dark (OG 1036, ABV 3.6%)
A dark mild with a roasted malt flavour and some background fruit notes, leading to a dry aftertaste.

Guinea Guzzler (OG 1037, ABV 3.7%)
An amber-coloured session beer with a malty and fruity taste and a dry finish.

Penny Red (OG 1039, ABV 3.9%)
A burnished red-coloured beer that has pungent hop notes, a dry finish and a malty base.

Peddlars Best (OG 1040, ABV 4%)
A copper-coloured bitter with floral fruit notes and an oaky, dry flavour to finish.

Golden Wobbler (OG 1041, ABV 4.1%)
A golden-coloured malty beer with complex citrus and lightly-spiced flavours.

Dartford Wobbler (OG 1043, ABV 4.3%)
A full-bodied, russet brown-coloured premium bitter with a dark malt profile, fruit notes and a dry finish.

Thieves & Fakirs (OG 1043, ABV 4.3%)
A dark porter with a full-bodied malt and hop base, and a long, dry aftertaste.

Country Wobbler (OG 1048, ABV 4.8%)
Bold flavours of malt and hops with a long, clean and dry finish.

Mills (NEW)

c/o Salutation Inn, Ham, Gloucestershire, GL13 9QH
☎ 07848 922558

Office: Jumpers Lane Yard, Berkeley, GL13 9BW

Mills was established in Berkeley in 2016 by Genevieve Kaye and Jonny Mills. Wort is produced at Tiley's Brewery (qv), which is then fermented in wooden vessels at their premises in Berkeley using 100% wild yeasts and bacteria from the local surroundings.

Millstone SIBA 👁

Unit 4, Vale Mill, Micklehurst Road, Mossley, Lancashire, OL5 9JL
☎ (01457) 835835 ⊕ millstonebrewery.co.uk

Established in 2003 by Nick Boughton and Jon Hunt, the brewery is located in an 18th-century textile mill. The eight-barrel plant produces a range of pale, hoppy beers and a traditional stout. More than 30 regular outlets are supplied. ♦

Vale Mill (OG 1039, ABV 3.9%)
A pale gold-coloured session bitter with a floral and spicy aroma building upon a crisp and refreshing taste.

Three Shires Bitter (OG 1040, ABV 4%) 🍺
Yellow-coloured beer with hop and fruit aroma. Fresh citrus fruit, hops and bitterness in the taste and aftertaste.

Tiger Rut (OG 1040, ABV 4%)
A pale, hoppy ale with a distinctive citrus/grapefruit aroma.

Stout (OG 1045, ABV 4.5%)
A traditional dry stout; pale chocolate malt, roasted barley, and a hint of sweetness to the aroma.

True Grit (OG 1050, ABV 5%)
A well-hopped strong ale with a mellow bitterness and a citrus/grapefruit aroma.

Milltown SIBA

The Brewery, The Old Railway Goods Yard, Scar Lane, Milnsbridge, West Yorkshire, HD3 4PE ☎ 07946 589645 ⊕ milltownbrewing.co.uk

☺Milltown began brewing in 2011 using a four-barrel plant. One pub is owned, the Dusty Miller in Longwood, Huddersfield, which acts as the brewery tap. ‼♦

Sorachi Pale (OG 1039, ABV 3.8%)

American Pale Ale (OG 1040, ABV 3.9%)

Weavers Bitter (OG 1040, ABV 3.9%)

Willett's Notion (OG 1040, ABV 3.9%)

Platinum Blonde (OG 1041, ABV 4%)

Sterling Gold (OG 1045, ABV 4.3%)

Black Jack (OG 1049, ABV 4.5%)

Milton SIBA

Pegasus House, Pembroke Avenue, Waterbeach, Cambridgeshire, CB25 9PY
☎ (01223) 862067 ⊕ miltonbrewery.co.uk

⊠ The brewery has grown steadily since it was founded in 1999. In 2012 the brewery moved to larger premises in the village of Waterbeach. It now operates pubs in Cambridge, London and Norwich through a sister company. In 2016 a separate brand, Beach Brewery, was created to market unpasteurised and unfiltered keg beers. ‼

Minotaur (OG 1035, ABV 3.3%) 🍺
A dark ruby-coloured mild with liquorice and raisin fruit throughout. Light, dry finish.

Dionysus (OG 1037, ABV 3.6%) 🍺
Yellow-coloured bitter with good balance of biscuity malt and citrus hop. Some malt and hops linger on long, dry aftertaste.

Justinian (OG 1039, ABV 3.9%) 🍺
Straw-coloured bitter with pink grapefruit hop character and light malt softness. Very dry finish.

Pegasus (OG 1043, ABV 4.1%) 🍺
Malty, amber-coloured, medium-bodied bitter with faint hops. Bittersweet aftertaste.

Sparta (OG 1043, ABV 4.3%) 🍺🍺
A yellow/gold-coloured best bitter with floral hops, kiwi fruit and balancing malt softness which fades to a long, dry finish.

Minerva (OG 1046, ABV 4.6%)
A powerful hop punch and satisfying bitterness.

Nero (OG 1050, ABV 5%) 🍺
A complex black beer comprising a blend of milk chocolate, raisins and liquorice. Roast malt and fruit complete the experience.

Cyclops (OG 1055, ABV 5.3%)
Deep copper-coloured ale with a rich hoppy aroma and full body; fruit and malt notes develop in the finish.

Marcus Aurelius (OG 1075, ABV 7.5%) 🍺🍺
A powerful black brew brimming with raisins and liquorice. Big balanced finish.

Brewed under the Beach Brewery brand name:

Waikiki (OG 1061, ABV 6%)
A refreshing beer with generous quantities of bergamot.

Mitchell's Hop House (NEW) SIBA

352-354 Meadowhead, Sheffield, South Yorkshire, S8 7UJ
☎ (0114) 274 0311 ⊕ mitchellswine.co.uk

☺Brewing began in 2016 in a converted space at the back of an award-winning off-licence. 🚚♦RAIB

Butchers (ABV 4%)

Independent (ABV 4%)

Marilyn (ABV 4.3%)

Dennis (ABV 4.5%)

Madness (ABV 5%)

Mithril

Mithril, Aldbrough St John, North Yorkshire, DL11 7TL
☎ (01325) 374817 ☎ 07889 167128
⊕ mithrilales.blogspot.co.uk

⊚Mithril started brewing in 2010 in old stables opposite the brewer's house on a 2.5-barrel plant. Owner/brewer Pete Fenwick, a well-known craft brewer, brews twice a week to supply the local area of Darlington and Richmond. A new beer is brewed every week. ♦

Dere Street (OG 1039, ABV 3.8%)
Amber-coloured bitter with a fruity, malty sweetness and a smooth. hoppy finish.

A66 (OG 1041, ABV 4%)
A crisp, refreshing, satisfying golden-coloured beer. A dry bitterness with a lingering citrus and spicy hop taste and aroma.

Flower Power (OG 1043, ABV 4.3%)
This pale ale packs massive citrus, fruity hop flavours. Hints of grapefruit and floral on the tongue from the late addition of elderflower.

Mix

3 Cemmaes Court Road, Hemel Hempstead, Hertfordshire, HP1 1ST ⊕ mixbrewery.co.uk

⊠ A small brewery established in 2013 and based in a domestic garage. Beer is produced in small batches allowing for an ever-changing range.

Mobberley SIBA

Unit 2, Barncroft Farm, Woodend Lane, Mobberley, Cheshire, WA16 7LZ
☎ (01565) 873601 ☎ 07879 771209
⊕ mobberleyfineales.co.uk

⊠ Mobberley began brewing in 2011 in an old milking parlour on a working farm in the heart of the Cheshire countryside. Expansion is planned. ♦

HedgeHopper (OG 1039, ABV 3.8%)
A golden-coloured, refreshing ale, light and aromatic.

RoadRunner (OG 1039, ABV 3.8%)
A pale yellow-coloured ale with a delicate, lightly spicy finish. Rich in flavours, sweet to the taste and smooth.

Mandalay (OG 1040, ABV 4%)

Maori (OG 1040, ABV 4%)

WhirlyBird (OG 1040, ABV 4%)
A pale ale, sweet yet full bodied with a smooth, subtle, zesty finish.

Red Vienna (ABV 4.2%)

Legacy (ABV 4.4%)
A zesty pale ale.

1924 (ABV 4.5%)
Amber-coloured, powerful and fruity.

Solstice (ABV 4.5%)

Elysium (ABV 4.7%)

Origin (ABV 4.7%)

Moles SIBA ◉

5 Merlin Way, Bowerhill, Melksham, Wiltshire, SN12 6TJ
☎ (01225) 708842 ⊕ molesbrewery.com

Moles was established in 1982 by Roger Catte, a former Ushers brewer, using his nickname for the brewery. 10 pubs are owned, all serving cask beer. More than 200 outlets are supplied direct. Moles' beer brands were acquired by Wickwar Wessex Brewing Co in mid 2017. All brewing equipment and brewing may relocate to the Wickwar Wessex site during the currency of this guide. ‼️☞♦

Gold (OG 1038, ABV 3.8%) ◀
Golden-coloured, hoppy beer with subtle citrus fruit aroma and flavour with a malty background.

Best (OG 1040, ABV 4%) ◀
An amber-coloured bitter, clean, dry and malty with some bitterness, and delicate floral hop flavour.

Elmo's (OG 1044, ABV 4.4%) ◀
Medium-bodied bitter with subtle fruit aroma and flavours, leading to a long bitter finish.

Dark (OG 1045, ABV 4.5%) ◀
A dark, strong, smooth porter with a rich, fruity palate and malty finish.

Rucking Mole (OG 1045, ABV 4.5%) ◀
A chestnut-coloured premium ale, fruity and malty with a smooth bitter finish.

Molson Coors

Molson Coors (Burton): 137 High Street, Burton upon Trent, Staffordshire, DE14 1JZ
☎ (01283) 511000

Molson Coors (Tadcaster): Tower Brewery, Wetherby Road, Tadcaster, LS24 9SD
⊕ molsoncoorsbrewers.com

Molson Coors is the result of a merger between Molson of Canada and Coors of Colorado, US. Coors established itself in Europe in 2002 by buying part of the former Bass brewing empire, when Interbrew (now A-B InBev) was instructed by the British government to divest itself of some of its interests in Bass. Coors owns several cask ale brands. It brews 110,000 barrels of cask beer a year (under licensing arrangements with other brewers) and also provides a further 50,000 barrels of cask beer from other breweries. In 2011 Molson Coors bought Sharp's brewery in Cornwall (qv) in a bid to increase its stake in the cask beer sector. No cask ale is produced in Burton or Tadcaster.

Moncada SIBA ◉

37 Humber Road, Dollis Hill, London, NW2 6EN
☎ (020) 8964 0829 ⊕ moncadabrewery.co.uk

⊠ Moncada began brewing in 2011 using a six-barrel plant. ♦RAIB

Notting Hill Bitter (ABV 3.7%) ◀
Brown-coloured bitter with a good balance of hops and sweetness and a pleasant finish.

Notting Hill Blonde (ABV 4.2%) ◀
Continental-style golden beer with a smooth mouthfeel, sweetish with a touch of honey and fruity hops. Short, crisp finish.

Notting Hill Amber (ABV 4.7%) ◀

Full-bodied, creamy, amber-coloured beer with a citrus peel aroma and flavour well-balanced by the sweet biscuit character.

Notting Hill Stout (ABV 5%) ◆
A dry, malty beer with roast, caramel and a little malty sweetness. The pleasant aftertaste is long and lingering.

Notting Hill Ruby Rye (ABV 5.2%) ◆
Sweetish ruby red-coloured beer with a full, fruity aroma, a creamy mouthfeel and a little roast throughout.

Mondo

86-92 Stewarts Road, South Lambeth, London, SW8 4UG
☎ (020) 7720 0782 ☎ 07453 312170
⊕ mondobrewingcompany.com

⊠ The brewery opened in 2015 using a 10-hectolitre brew kit. A taphouse has been added.
‼◆

Monty's SIBA

Unit 1, Castle Works, Hendomen, SY15 6HA
☎ (01686) 668933 ⊕ montysbrewery.co.uk

Monty's began brewing in 2009 and was the first brewery in Montgomeryshire since the Eagle brewery in Newtown closed in 1990. It leases one pub, the Sportsman in Newtown, through its sister company, Hophouse Inns. The Cottage Inn in Montgomery is owned and acts as the brewery's visitor centre. It also houses a 250-litre plant producing small runs of experimental beers. ◆ RAIB

Old Jailhouse (OG 1039.5, ABV 3.9%) 🍺
Copper-coloured bitter with a good blend of malt and hops.

Best Offa (OG 1040, ABV 4%)
A golden-coloured, toasty bitter.

Moonrise (OG 1040, ABV 4%)
A copper-coloured, gently malty, well-balanced traditional brew.

MPA (OG 1040.5, ABV 4%)
Pale ale with a good bitter character.

Sunshine (OG 1041, ABV 4.2%)
A golden-coloured, hoppy, floral/citrus ale with a pleasantly dry finish.

Masquerade (OG 1046, ABV 4.6%)
A gluten-free premium golden-coloured bitter with tropical fruit flavour and hop aroma.

Mischief (OG 1050, ABV 5%)
Strong golden ale with a good balance of malt and hop bitterness.

Dark Secret (OG 1056, ABV 5.6%)
Gluten free oatmeal stout with chocolate and coffee flavours.

Eastbound (OG 1073, ABV 7.3%)
An Imperial IPA with good hop bitterness and aroma.

Magnitude (OG 1075.5, ABV 7.5%) 🍺

Moody Fox (NEW)

Hilcote Country Club, Hilcote Lane, Hilcote, Derbyshire, DE55 5HR

Established in 2016, Moody Fox is a microbrewery specialising in traditional ales using the finest hops and barley from around the world.

Cub (ABV 3.8%)
A smooth session bitter with a slightly dry finish.

Pale Tale (ABV 5.4%)
An IPA-style beer, full of citrus flavour with a slightly bitter finish.

Moody Goose

🏠 King William IV, 114 London Road, Braintree, Essex, CM77 7PU
☎ (01376) 567755 ⊕ moodygoosebrewery.co.uk

A three-barrel brewery, brewing approximately 15 times a year. The beers are currently only available in the King William IV, where the brewery is located, and select beer festivals.

moogBREW

1 Copeland Cottages, Marsh Lane, Taplow, SL6 0DF
☎ 07941 241954 ⊕ moogbrew.co.uk

⊠ Situated in a converted garden shed, this 100-litre brewery was set up in 2016. The majority of the output is bottle-conditioned with inspiration for the range coming from world-wide beer hunting. Distribution is targeted to within a 10-mile radius of the brewery. ‼ 🍺 ◆ RAIB

Royal Standard Pale (ABV 3.8%)
Easy-drinking golden ale with distinctive hop flavours.

Porter (ABV 4.7%)
Traditional bittersweet, dark-coloured ale with a caramel aroma.

Bastard Bunny Strikes Back (ABV 6%)
A well-balanced, amber-coloured American-style IPA.

Moonchild

2 Church Gate, Petrockstow, Devon, EX20 3HL
☎ 07585 914120

Moonchild was established in 2016 by Fred and Sophie Caure. All beers are unfined, unfiltered and unpasteurised. Small batch brews are planned.
◆ RAIB V

Bird Of Paradise (OG 1035, ABV 3.5%)
A pale wheat beer.

Street Urchin (OG 1046, ABV 4.4%)
An American-style pale ale.

Gypsy Queen Baltic Porter (OG 1055, ABV 5.5%)
Raisins, dark fruit and chocolate, with a slight hint of roasted coffee.

Harvest Home Red Rye (OG 1055, ABV 5.5%)
Light spices and coffee with a generous amount of New World hops, adding a fruity note.

Moonshine

Hill Farm, Shelford Road, Fulbourn, Cambridgeshire, CB21 5EQ ☎ 07906 066794

Office: 28 Radegund Road, Cambridge, CB1 3RS
⊕ moonshinebrewery.co.uk

⊠ Established in 2004, the brewery produces up to 35 barrels a week. Locally-produced ingredients are used including water from the brewery's own well and barley grown on the farm where the brewery is based. CAMRA beer festivals are supplied throughout the country, with 30 local outlets supplied direct. ◆ RAIB V

Sundowner (OG 1036, ABV 3.6%)
Light amber-coloured session beer with balanced malt and a rounded hop finish.

Trumpington Tipple (OG 1036, ABV 3.6%)
Deep amber-coloured ale, medium malt flavours, fragrant hop aroma.

Cambridge Pale Ale (OG 1038, ABV 3.8%)
A well-balanced beer with a smooth malt profile complemented by a restrained hop flavour.

Shelford Crier (OG 1038, ABV 3.8%)
An amber-coloured beer with a citrus fruit bouquet and taste that continues through to a refreshing, dry finish.

Harvest Moon Mild (OG 1040, ABV 3.9%)
Well-balanced and slightly sweet with plenty of character. Smooth fruit notes combine with coffee and chocolate flavours.

Barton Bitter (OG 1040, ABV 4%) ◆
Pale brown in colour with red and amber highlights, balanced malt and hops and a fruity backdrop on both nose and palate. A bittersweet flavour dries as fruit and sweetness diminish.

Heavenly Matter (OG 1041, ABV 4.1%)
A straw-coloured beer with a hoppy citrus, tropical fruit aroma and taste, which leads to a generous bitterness in the finish.

Blueberry Ale (OG 1042, ABV 4.2%)
A red-coloured beer brewed with the addition of fresh blueberries. Light, fruity and refreshing.

Cambridge Best Bitter (OG 1041, ABV 4.2%)
The malt and hop aromas carry through to the taste. The finish is rounded with a growing hop bitterness.

Night Watch Porter (OG 1043, ABV 4.5%)
A well-rounded, sweet-starting and dry-finishing traditional porter.

Raspberry Porter (OG 1043, ABV 4.5%)
Night Watch Porter with added raspberries to give a mellow, fruity finish.

Raspberry Wheat Beer (OG 1044, ABV 4.5%)
A fruity wheat beer with a tropical fruit, citrus and berry finish.

Black Hole Stout (OG 1048, ABV 5%)
Full-bodied stout with a complex malt profile. The roasted flavours are rich, smooth and long-lasting.

Hot Numbers Coffee Stout (OG 1057, ABV 5.5%)
Rich, coffee flavoured milk stout made with two different varieties of coffee beans.

**Chocolate Orange Stout
(OG 1068, ABV 6.7%)** 🗇 🍫
Full-bodied stout loaded with chocolate and coffee flavours and a hint of orange on the nose.

Wheat Wine Ale (OG 1091, ABV 10.5%)
Barley wine made with wheat. Spicy fruit aromas combine with caramel to give a long finish.

Moonstone

🏠 Ministry of Ale, 9 Trafalgar Street, Burnley, Lancashire, BB11 1TQ
☎ (01282) 830909 ⊕ moonstonebrewery.co.uk

A small, three-barrel brewery, based in the front room of the Ministry of Ale pub. Brewing started in 2001 and beer is only available in the pub.

Moor SIBA

Days Road, Bristol, BS2 0QS
☎ (0117) 941 4460 ⊕ moorbeer.co.uk

⊠ Moor Beer was founded in 1996, originally brewing in Ashcott. Since being relaunched in 2007 in Long Sutton the brewery has gone through a steady expansion programme, resulting in the relocation to larger premises featuring a shop and brewery tap. All beers are produced without isinglass finings and are naturally hazy. Moor's cans have been the first in the UK to be recognised as real ale by CAMRA. ‼ 🍺 ◆ RAIB

Revival (OG 1038, ABV 3.8%)
An immensely hoppy and refreshing pale ale.

Nor'Hop (OG 1041, ABV 4.1%)

So'Hop (OG 1041, ABV 4.1%)

Union Hop (ABV 4.1%)
Ultra pale ale. Zingy, citrus and refreshing, with some sweet pale malt to balance.

Raw (OG 1043, ABV 4.3%) ◆
Pale brown-coloured best bitter with a powerful aroma. Bitter orange fruit with a hint of tropical lychee on the tongue. Sweetish background and a bitter finish.

Amoor (OG 1045, ABV 4.5%)
Rich porter with chocolate and nut flavours to the fore and a balancing bitterness.

Claudia (ABV 4.5%)
Hoppy wheat beer. Flavours of banana, lemon and cloves together with herbal and citrus hop character.

Dark Alliance (OG 1045, ABV 4.5%)
A hoppy coffee stout.

Illusion (OG 1045, ABV 4.5%)
Session strength version of a black IPA, powerfully hopped on the dark side.

Confidence (OG 1046, ABV 4.6%)
Hoppy, American-style red-coloured ale.

Ported Amoor (OG 1047, ABV 4.7%)
Amoor with added Reserve Port.

Radiance (OG 1048, ABV 5%)

Smokey Horyzon (OG 1050, ABV 5%) ◆
A speciality beer made using smoked rye. Hoppy, pale brown-coloured strong ale with plenty of body, balanced by sweetness of unfermented rich dry rye malt and very smoky.

Stout (OG 1050, ABV 5%) ◆
A classic black stout. Smoky roast malts and dark fruit aroma with hint of vanilla. Prunes and liquorice notes follow into the taste. Pleasant dark chocolate aftertaste.

PMA (ABV 5.3%)
Hoppy pale ale with oats.

Return of the Empire (OG 1057, ABV 5.7%)
Modern English IPA. Light caramel honey malt with honeydew melon, citrus, apricot and peach.

B-Moor (OG 1060, ABV 6%)
A rich porter, with flavours of blueberry chocolate cheesecake.

Hoppiness (OG 1065, ABV 6.5%)

All the rich malt and fruit flavours of a barley wine combined with the hoppy crispness of a pale ale.

Old Freddy Walker (OG 1073, ABV 7.3%) 🍺 🍷
Rich, dark, strong ale with a fruity complex taste, leaving a fruitcake finish.

Moorhouse's SIBA 👁

The Brewery, Moorhouse Street, Burnley, Lancashire, BB11 5EN
☎ (01282) 422864 ⊕ moorhouses.co.uk

Established in 1865 as a soft drinks manufacturer, the brewery started producing cask-conditioned ale in 1978. A new brewhouse and visitor centre opened in 2012. Three pubs are owned. ‼◆

Black Cat (OG 1036, ABV 3.4%) 🍺
A dark mild-style beer with delicate chocolate and coffee roast flavours and a crisp, bitter finish.

Premier Bitter (OG 1036, ABV 3.7%) 🍺
A clean and satisfying bitter aftertaste rounds off this well-balanced hoppy, amber-coloured session bitter.

White Witch (OG 1039, ABV 4%)
A refreshing blonde ale with a touch of citrus flowers and peppery spice on the aroma.

Pride of Pendle (OG 1040, ABV 4.1%) 🍺 🍺
Well-balanced, amber-coloured best bitter with a fresh initial hoppiness and a mellow, malt-driven body.

Blond Witch (OG 1045, ABV 4.5%) 🍺
A light ale, fruity with lasting finish.

Pendle Witches Brew (OG 1050, ABV 5.1%) 🍺
Well-balanced, full-bodied, malty beer with a long, complex finish.

Moorstone SIBA

Axna Farm, Horndon, Devon, PL19 9NF
☎ (01822) 810418 ☎ 07738 098572
✉ moorstonebrewery@btinternet.com

Paul and Joanna Barton began brewing in 2016 using a 2.5-barrel plant. The brewery is in a barn conversion on Axna Farm near Mary Tavy and uses the farm's own spring water. RAIB

Wheal Betsy (OG 1041, ABV 4.1%)
A golden-coloured best bitter with a malty finish and well-balanced, subtle lemon citrus hop aroma.

Theo's Brew (OG 1045, ABV 4.5%)
A pale golden ale with a refreshing, crisp taste.

Ruby Red (OG 1050, ABV 4.7%)
A full-bodied porter with a silky smooth mouthfeel and long-lasting finish with hints of chocolate and coffee.

MòR SIBA

Old Mill, Kellas, DD5 3PD ☎ 07884 346351
⊕ morbrewing.co.uk

Retired lifeboat coxswain Jim Hughan teamed up with family friend Ross Niven to establish the 2.5-barrel brewery in 2012. Just over a year later it expanded to a 4.5-barrel plant. In 2016 Matt Forrest joined the business as a co-director following Ross' retirement. ‼◆RAIB

MòR Tea Vicar? (OG 1038, ABV 3.8%)

A pale amber-coloured bitter with a pleasant balance of malt and hops, a malty, fruity aroma and a pronounced bitter finish.

MòR Ish! (OG 1042, ABV 4.2%)
A bright amber-coloured ale with a malty, fruity aroma and a well-balanced and controlled bitter finish.

MòR Please! (OG 1045, ABV 4.5%)
A clean-tasting, full-bodied, golden-coloured bitter bursting with malt and hops with a hint of honey in the hoppy finish.

Mordue SIBA 👁

Units D1 & D2, Narvic Way, Tyne Tunnel Estate, North Shields, Tyne & Wear, NE29 7XJ
☎ (0191) 296 1879 ⊕ morduebrewery.com

In 1995 the Fawson brothers revived the Mordue Brewery name (the original closed in 1879). High demand required moves to larger premises and replacing the original five-barrel plant with a 20-barrel one. The beers are distributed nationally and 300 outlets are supplied direct. ‼🍺◆RAIB

Five Bridges (OG 1038, ABV 3.6%) 🍺
Crisp, golden-coloured beer with a good hit of hops, the bitterness carries on in the finish.

Northumbrian Blonde (OG 1040, ABV 4%) 🍺
A blonde beer with a citrus aroma and hoppy finish.

Panda Frog Pandarillo (OG 1042, ABV 4.2%)

Workie Ticket (OG 1045, ABV 4.5%) 🍺 🍺
Complex, tasty bitter with plenty of malt and hops, long satisfying bitter finish.

Panda Frog Project Pils (OG 1047, ABV 4.7%)
Straw-coloured Czech-style Pilsner with a herbal, grassy aroma and a fruity citrus undertone.

Radgie Gadgie (OG 1048, ABV 4.8%) 🍺
Strong, easy-drinking bitter with plenty of fruit and hops.

Panda Frog Project Allelic Drift (OG 1050, ABV 5%)
A pale golden-coloured ale with floral, pine and citrus notes and a clean bitterness.

IPA (OG 1051, ABV 5.1%) 🍺
Easy-drinking golden ale with plenty of hops, the bitterness carries on in the finish.

Morgans

See Merry Miner

Morland

See Greene King

Morton Collins (NEW)

39 Brunswick, Ryhill, West Yorkshire
☎ (01226) 728746 ☎ 07812 111960

Office: 49 Willow Garth, Durkar, Wakefield, West Yorkshire, WF4 3BX

Set up in 2016 by Ged Morton and Sam Collins using a 100-litre plant in Ged's garage. The brewery produces to demand but can brew every day if required. It took over the lease of the Star, Sandal, in 2016. ◆

Wintersett Gold (OG 1041, ABV 4.1%)

Amber No. 9 (OG 1048, ABV 4.8%)

Morton

Unit 10, Essington Light Industrial Estate, Essington, Staffordshire, WV11 2BH ☎ 07988 69647

Office: 96 Brewood Road, Coven, WV9 5EF
⊕ mortonbrewery.co.uk

⊛ This family-run brewery was established in 2006 on a three-barrel, purpose-built plant. Beers are supplied locally plus various beer festivals and a selection is always available at the brewery's own micropub, Hail to the Ale. !!♦

Essington Dark Mild (OG 1036, ABV 3.6%)

Essington Bitter (OG 1037, ABV 3.8%)

Merry Mount (OG 1037, ABV 3.8%)

Essington Blonde (OG 1039, ABV 4%)

Essington Ale (OG 1041, ABV 4.2%)

Jelly Roll (OG 1041, ABV 4.2%)

Essington Gold (OG 1044, ABV 4.4%)

Essington Supreme (OG 1046, ABV 4.6%)

Scottish Maiden (OG 1045, ABV 4.6%)

Essington IPA (OG 1046, ABV 4.8%)

Moseley (NEW)

14 Cleveland Court, St Agnes Road, Moseley, B13 9PR
⊕ moseleybeercompany.co.uk

Moseley Beer Company began brewing in 2016, set up by a family of four brothers. V

Sightseer Wheat Beer (ABV 4.5%)
A bright and hoppy, light and refreshing ale with a citrus aftertaste.

Pale Ale (ABV 5%)

Marianna Porter (ABV 8%)
A dark and roasty porter with a sweet honey kick, based on a Victorian recipe.

Iron Man Stout (ABV 9%)

Moulin

🍴 2 Baledmund Road, Moulin, Pitlochry, PH16 5EL
☎ (01796) 472196

Office: Moulin Hotel, 11-13 Kirkmicheal Road, Moulin, Pitlochry, PH16 5EH ⊕ moulinhotel.co.uk

The brewery opened in 1995 to celebrate the Moulin Hotel's 300th anniversary. Two pubs are owned and four outlets are supplied.

Mountain Hare

🍴 Mountain Hare Inn, Brynna Road, Brynnau Gwynion, CF35 6PG
☎ (01656) 860453 ⊕ mountainhare.co.uk

Paul Jones, licensee of the Mountain Hare, finally realised his ambition of installing a brewery in his family-owned pub. A 1.5-barrel custom-built brewing plant was installed in 2013, supplying only the pub itself. There are plans for expansion to a six-barrel plant to meet demand.

Mourne Mountains (NEW)

Milltown East Industrial Estate, Upper Dromore Road, Warrenpoint, BT34 3PN
☎ (028) 4175 2299
⊕ mournemountainsbrewery.com

Brewing began in 2015. No real ale. ♦

Mouselow Farm

3 Mouselow Farm, Dinting, Derbyshire, SK13 7QQ
☎ 07920 048252 ✉ glossopowl@btinternet.com

Mouselow Farm began brewing in 2013 using a 2.5-barrel plant housed in a converted barn. Brewing is on a part-time basis. Local free houses, clubs and beer festivals are supplied. ♦

Golden Gosling (OG 1037, ABV 3.6%)

Cluckstar (ABV 3.7%)

Udder the Influence (OG 1041, ABV 4%)

Flying Goose (ABV 4.2%)

Mr Grundy's SIBA

🍴 Georgian House Hotel, 34 Ashbourne Road, Derby, DE22 3AD
☎ (01332) 349806 ⊕ mrgrundysbrewery.co.uk

The brewery opened in 2010 using a four-barrel plant which was made-to-measure to fit into a converted hotel bedroom. Beers are produced for the company's own tavern (Mr Grundy's) and hotels.

Mr Majolica

Units 7a & 15, Thurrock Enterprise Centre, Maidstone Road, Grays, Essex, RM17 6NF ☎ 07834 539761
⊕ mrmajolica.co.uk

⊠ A family-run microbrewery situated in Grays town centre, Mr Majolica began brewing in 2014 on a 2.5-barrel plant. Pubs and clubs are supplied around Essex, Kent and London.

Buccaneer (ABV 3.8%)

Phantom (ABV 4%)

Vanguard (ABV 4.1%)

Enterprise (ABV 4.5%)

Evolution (ABV 4.8%)

Muckle (NEW) SIBA

3 Bellister Close, Park Village, Haltwhistle, Northumberland, NE49 0HA ☎ 07711 980086
⊕ mucklebrewing.co.uk

Established in 2016, Muckle Brewing is a tiny brewery in rural Northumberland, close to Hadrian's Wall. RAIB

Tickle (OG 1039, ABV 4%)

Chuckle (OG 1040, ABV 4.2%)

Moss Stout (OG 1042, ABV 4.3%)

Buster (OG 1043, ABV 4.5%)

Muirhouse

Unit 1, Enterprise Court, Manners Avenue, Manners Industrial Estate, Ilkeston, Derbyshire, DE7 8EW
☎ 07916 590525 ⊕ muirhousebrewery.co.uk

Muirhouse was established in 2009 in a domestic garage in Long Eaton. It expanded in 2011 to the present location in Ilkeston and the plant was upgraded in 2016 to 7.5 barrels. ‼ ◆ RAIB

Summit Hoppy (OG 1041, ABV 4%)
Pale session beer packed with hops.

Magnum Mild (OG 1047, ABV 4.5%)
Dark, smooth, strong mild.

Pirate's Gold (OG 1045, ABV 4.5%)
Pale golden-coloured beer with a hint of caramel.

Hat Trick IPA (OG 1052, ABV 5.2%)
Bitter with a citrus hop taste.

Mumbles SIBA ⊚

Unit 8, Clarion Court, Clarion Close, Swansea Enterprise Park, Swansea, SA6 8RF
☎ (01792) 792612 ☎ 07757 109938
⊕ mumblesbrewery.co.uk

⊗ Mumbles was established in 2011 and began brewing in 2013. The beers are supplied to numerous pubs in South Wales and the Bristol area. In 2014 brewing took place using spare capacity at other local breweries but a permanent home was found in 2015 using a 10-barrel plant. ◆

Hop Kick (OG 1038, ABV 4%)
A light pale ale that makes a refreshing session beer.

Mile (OG 1039, ABV 4%)
A light-coloured session bitter with big hop flavours.

Gold (OG 1042, ABV 4.3%)
A light, refreshing pale ale, golden in colour. Well-hopped with lingering lemon and lime flavours.

Oystermouth Stout (OG 1043, ABV 4.4%)
A rich, creamy head and dark roasted malt flavours distinguish this classic stout.

Lifesaver Strong Bitter (OG 1048, ABV 4.9%)
A smooth, malty, bronze-coloured ale with a clean, rewarding hop finish.

India Pale Ale (OG 1052, ABV 5.3%)
A traditional IPA, light gold in colour with a distinct marmalade taste and aroma.

Musket SIBA

Unit 7, Loddington Farm, Loddington Lane, Linton, Kent, ME17 4AG
☎ (01622) 749931 ☎ 07967 127278
⊕ musketbrewery.co.uk

Musket began production in 2013 in refurbished mushroom sheds at Loddington Farm, in the heart of the Kent countryside. The family-owned brewery supplies more than 250 pubs, micropubs and clubs throughout Kent. ◆

Trigger (OG 1032, ABV 3.6%)
A hoppy, easy-drinking session ale.

Fife & Drum (OG 1034, ABV 3.8%)
A golden ale with tastes and aromas of spice, honey, marmalade and a hint of wild blackcurrant.

Matchlock (OG 1034, ABV 3.8%)

A tasty mild with a selection of four malts, roasted barley and Kentish hops.

Ball Puller (ABV 4%)

Flintlock (OG 1037, ABV 4.2%)
A best bitter with spicy orange undertones and a hint of marmalade.

Muzzleloader (OG 1039, ABV 4.5%)
Smoky and dark in colour with the faint spicy aroma of orange.

Myrddins

⊟ Church Street, Barmouth, LL42 1EH
☎ (01341) 388060 ✉ myrddins@talktalk.net

Established in 2016, Myrddins is a small brewery within a café bar in the centre of Barmouth.

Nailsworth

See Keep

Nant SIBA

Penrhwylfa, Maenan, Llanrwst, LL26 0UF ☎ 07723 036862 ⊕ bragdynant.co.uk

⊗ Nant commenced brewing in 2007 with a plant purchased from the Yorkshire Dales Brewery. Capacity is currently 10-15 nine gallon firkins a week. ◆ RAIB

Brenin (OG 1038, ABV 3.8%)
A light golden-coloured session ale with balanced hops and malt.

Cwrw Chwarel (OG 1036, ABV 3.8%)
A pale gold-coloured session ale.

Cwrw Coryn (OG 1042, ABV 4.2%)
Traditional amber-coloured beer. Slightly malty with good bitter overtones.

Chwaden Aur (OG 1043, ABV 4.3%)
Golden-coloured ale with a citrus aroma and full mouthfeel. Grapefruit and lemon citrus taste balance with biscuity malt for a long, fruity finish.

Rwster (OG 1046, ABV 4.6%)
Deep copper-coloured sweet and malty ale.

Mwnci Nel (OG 1055, ABV 5.5%)
A dark-coloured ale, not excessively sweet but dominated by burnt chocolate flavours, balanced with hops.

NauticAles (NEW)

Sowell Street, St Peters, Broadstairs, Kent, CT10 6SG
☎ 07552 600919

Office: 347 Margate Road, Ramsgate, Kent, CT12 6SG
✉ nauticales@outlook.com

Beers are only available at the brewery's micropub in Ramsgate and at local beer festivals.

Maiden Voyage (ABV 4.2%)

Navigation SIBA

⊟ Trent Navigation Inn, 17 Meadow Lane, Nottingham, NG2 3HS
☎ (0115) 986 9877 ⊕ navigationbrewery.com

Brewing began in 2012 in the old stable block of the Trent Navigation Inn. The brewery is owned by sister company Great Northern Inns and supplies cask beers to the pubs in its estate.

Britannia (OG 1038, ABV 3.8%) ◄
Tawny-coloured malty bitter.

New Dawn Pale (OG 1039, ABV 3.9%) ◄
Golden-coloured ale with initial fruit and hops and a bitter finish.

Golden Anchor (OG 1041.8, ABV 4.3%) ◄
Golden best bitter.

Apus (OG 1054, ABV 5.5%)

Naylor's SIBA 👁

Midland Mills, Station Road, Cross Hills, North Yorkshire, BD20 7DT
☎ (01535) 637451 ⊕ naylorsbrewery.com

☺The Naylor brothers started brewing in 2005 at the Old White Bear pub in Cross Hills. The brewery moved to Midland Mills in 2006 and transferred to a larger unit on the same site in 2012. 70 outlets are regularly supplied and around 1,000 on an occasional basis. The on-site bar and restaurant (the Beer Belly Bar & Kitchen) is open Tuesday to Sunday. ‼🍴♦RAIB

Bitter (OG 1037, ABV 3.8%) ◄
Predominantly malty traditional mid-brown bitter with subtle fruit and hops in the nose and taste and a growing bitter finish.

Gold (OG 1040, ABV 4%)
Golden-coloured ale, bitter to taste with a classic grapefruit hop finish.

Velvet (OG 1040, ABV 4%) ◄
Chocolate and roast aromas and flavours predominate in this dark brown-coloured mild, which has an increasingly roast bitter finish.

Pinnacle Blonde (OG 1041.5, ABV 4.3%) ◄
Hoppy, fruity aroma followed by grassy hop and tropical fruit flavours. The finish remains hoppy with a bitter, fruity edge.

Black & Tan (OG 1042, ABV 4.4%) ◄
Dark brown-coloured best bitter with a roast edge and a hop hit. Liquorice and a malty sweetness lead to a bitter finish.

Old Ale (OG 1054, ABV 5.9%)
A smooth beer with sweet maltiness, balanced by subtle bitterness. Strong but easy drinking.

Neath

Endeavour Close, Port Talbot, SA12 7PT ☎ 07772 468436 ⊕ neathales.co.uk

Neath Ales was established in 2009 and produces a range of single hop variety beers. Some beers are released under the Black Falls brand name. ♦RAIB V

Firebrick (OG 1042, ABV 4.2%)
Amber-coloured best bitter with quintessential British hop flavour and aroma.

Deliverance (OG 1045, ABV 4.5%)
A smooth, bronze-coloured beer.

Dewi Sant (OG 1048, ABV 4.8%)
A pale ale with a well-balanced hop fruit flavour.

Neatishead

▤ **White Horse Inn, The Street, Neatishead, Norfolk, NR12 8AD**

☎ (01692) 630828
⊕ thewhitehorseinnneatishead.com

Brewing began in 2015 at the White Horse Inn. The brew kit can be viewed through glass from the restaurant. Beer is only available in the pub at present. A range of semi-regular beers is brewed with at least one ever-changing ale.

Neckstamper (NEW) SIBA

Unit 3, Cromwell Industrial Estate, Staffa Road, Leyton, London, E10 7QZ ☎ 07968 150075
⊕ neckstamper.com

Neckstamper began brewing in 2016 using a 10-barrel plant. No real ale. ♦

Neepsend

Units 1-3, Lion Works, Mowbray Street, Sheffield, South Yorkshire, S3 8EN
☎ (0114) 276 3406 ☎ 07545 323427
✉ gavin@neepsendbrewco.com

☺Established in 2015 by James Birkett and Gavin Martin after taking over Little Ale Cart Brewery and moving to new premises in Sheffield's 'Valley of Beer'. A 10-barrel plant is used, supplying beers locally, including to the company's own pubs, Sheaf View, the Blake Hotel and the Wellington. ♦

Blonde (OG 1039, ABV 4%)
Mellow and easy-drinking session pale ale.

Nelson SIBA

Unit 2, Building 64, The Historic Dockyard, Chatham, Kent, ME4 4TE
☎ (01634) 832828 ⊕ nelsonbrewery.co.uk

☺Based in Chatham's Historic Dockyard and brewing on a nautical theme, the brewery supplies award-winning ales direct to more than 330 outlets. ‼🍴♦RAIB

Pieces of Eight (OG 1040, ABV 3.8%)
A light, refreshing ale with full-flavoured hops and a hint of chocolate aftertaste.

Admiral IPA (OG 1040, ABV 4%)
A traditional IPA brewed with citrus flavours on the palate.

Midshipman Dark Mild (OG 1040, ABV 4%)
A dark mild brewed with a roasted aftertaste on the palate.

Trafalgar Bitter (OG 1040, ABV 4.1%)

Powder Monkey (OG 1043, ABV 4.3%)
A golden ale with a smooth aftertaste, which leaves a sweetness on the palate.

Friggin' in the Riggin' (OG 1046, ABV 4.5%)
Premium bitter with a smooth malt flavour and bittersweet aftertaste.

Pursers Pussy Porter (OG 1051, ABV 4.8%)

Nelsons Blood (OG 1062, ABV 6%)
A strong, malty ale with mellow roast tones, slightly nutty and fruity with a warm aftertaste.

Nene Valley SIBA

Oundle Wharf, Station Road, Oundle, Northamptonshire, PE8 4DE
☎ (01832) 272776 ⊕ nenevalleybrewery.com

⊗ Established in 2011, a bespoke 15-barrel plant was installed in former Water Board premises on expansion in 2012. Further expansion in 2016 has doubled the floorspace. A brewery tap, Tap & Kitchen, opened on the same site in 2014. ‼ 🍴 ♦ RAIB GF

Unexpected Pleasures Ale
(OG 1036, ABV 3.6%) 🝮
A light, clean and refreshing beer with a pleasing citrus hop aroma and flavour.

Lone Star (OG 1037, ABV 3.7%)
Amber-coloured ale with biscuit and toffee apple flavours and a satisfying fruity hop bitterness.

Blonde Session Ale (OG 1038, ABV 3.8%)
A light golden-coloured session ale with a refreshing citrus hop finish.

Dark Horse (OG 1039, ABV 3.8%)
A dark ruby-coloured mild with roasted grains giving hints of chocolate, coffee and liquorice.

Jim's Little Brother (OG 1038, ABV 3.8%)
A light, clean and refreshing beer with a pleasing citrus hop aroma and flavour.

Bitter (OG 1040, ABV 4.1%) 🝯 🝮
Floral hop and malt aroma introduces a full, clean biscuit malt taste balanced by bitterness and some fruit, ending with a long malt and bitter finish.

Australian Pale (OG 1043, ABV 4.4%)
A rich golden ale with a floral aroma preceding citrus and tropical fruit hop flavours.

Release the Chimps (OG 1043, ABV 4.4%)
An IPA with a crisp mouthfeel and a clean, punchy bitterness.

Egyptian Cream (OG 1053, ABV 4.5%)
A milk stout with a velvety mouthfeel and a deep, full richness.

Dick's Extraordinary Bitter (OG 1045, ABV 4.6%)
Chestnut in colour with plenty of maltiness. Balanced with late-hopped spicy character.

Pulp Fiction (OG 1052, ABV 5.2%)
Fresh whole grapefruits make this an immensely refreshing Saison.

Big Bang Theory (OG 1051, ABV 5.3%) 🝮
Well-balanced pale ale with a huge hop aroma giving way to malty sweetness and a gentle bitter finish.

Jim Irving Pale (OG 1053, ABV 5.6%)
Full bodied with a big malty taste backed with zesty hop flavour.

Supersonic (OG 1055, ABV 6%)

Bible Black (OG 1068, ABV 6.5%) 🝮
An inviting aroma of malt and fruit leads to a rich-tasting beer where blackberry dominates but is balanced by malt, hops and some bitterness. The lingering finish is bittersweet with fruit assertive.

Fenland Farmhouse Saison (OG 1057, ABV 7.2%)
A complex and refreshing Saison with spicy clove notes and a fruity citrus aroma.

Mid-Week Bender (OG 1072, ABV 7.4%)
Dark amber-coloured beer with flavours of rich malt, molasses and candied orange and a big hop hit throughout.

Neon Raptor

Office: 23 Hope Street, Derby, DE1 1RZ ☎ 07821 586342 ⊕ neonraptorbrewingco.com

Established in 2016, Neon Raptor is a small independent brewery that utilises spare capacity at neighbouring breweries until able to establish a plant of its own. Beers were originally brewed at Songbird Brewery (qv) and more recently at Black Hole Brewery (qv). However, towards the end of 2017 plans were in progress to move to unit in Sneinton Market, Nottingham, with a new 10-barrel plant on order and a licence already granted to open an on-site taproom. All beers are unfiltered, unfined and unpasteurised.

Neptune

Unit 1, Sefton Lane Industrial Estate, Maghull, Merseyside, L31 8BX
☎ (0151) 222 3908 ⊕ neptunebrewery.com

☺ Neptune began brewing in 2015, upgrading from a one-barrel plant to six barrels. RAIB V

Riptide (OG 1038, ABV 3.7%)

Triton (OG 1044, ABV 4.4%)

Abyss (OG 1053, ABV 5%)

Ness

▤ c/o Old Three Pigeons, Nesscliffe, Shropshire, SY4 1DB
☎ (01743) 741279 ✉ info@3pigeons.co.uk

Brewing commenced in 2015 at the Three Pigeons pub using a two-barrel plant.

Nessie (NEW)

Westoaks, Fort William Road, Fort Augustus, PH32 4BH

Set up in 2017 this nanobrewery markets to the tourist trade around Fort Augustus.

Really Dumb Blonde (ABV 4.5%)

Nethergate SIBA

The Brewery, Rodbridge Corner, Suffolk, CO10 9HJ
⊕ nethergatebrewery.co.uk

⊗ Nethergate was formed in 1986 by Dick Burge and Ian Hornsey in Clare, Suffolk, and was one of the original UK microbreweries. It was sold in 2010, but in 2014 Dick Burge re-purchased the business and in 2017 a brand new brewery, visitor centre and shop was built at Rodbridge Corner, a couple of miles from its original home. ‼ 🍴 ♦

Priory Mild (OG 1036, ABV 3.5%) 🝮
A black bitter rather than a true mild. Strong roast and bitter tastes dominate throughout.

Umbel Ale (OG 1039, ABV 3.8%) 🝮
Pleasant, easy-drinking bitter, infused with coriander, which dominates.

Venture (OG 1039, ABV 3.8%) 🝮
Light-tasting, sweetish and fruity session beer.

Suffolk County Best Bitter (OG 1041, ABV 4%) 🝮
Dark bitter with roast grain tones off-setting biscuity malt and powerful hoppy, bitter notes.

Hopweaver (OG 1043, ABV 4.2%)
A light golden-coloured beer with citrus overtones and a fruity aroma. Refreshing on the palate with a generous hoppy finish.

Old Growler (OG 1051, ABV 5%) 🝮

Well-balanced porter in which roast grain is complemented by fruit and bubblegum.

Umbel Magna (OG 1051, ABV 5%) ◆
Old Growler flavoured with coriander. The spice is less dominant than in Umbel Ale, with some of the weight and body of the beer coming through.

New Bristol

20a Wilson Street, Bristol, BS2 9HH ☎ 07837 976871
⊕ newbristolbrewery.co.uk

⊗ Brothers Tom and Noel commenced brewing in 2013 on a five-barrel plant. Capacity has since been increased to fifteen barrels. All beers are unfined, unfiltered and unpasteurised. !! ◆ RAIB

365 (OG 1041, ABV 4%)
A session bitter with plenty of up front malt and toffee.

Oolala (OG 1040, ABV 4.2%)
An amber-coloured beer balanced by sweet, spicy notes with hints of citrus and herbs, and the zest of 60 lemons.

Beer Du Jour (OG 1046, ABV 4.6%) ◆
A bittersweet, strong bitter with citrus fruit aromas and flavours which continue in the aftertaste. Unfined so may be hazy.

New Inn

⊟ New Inn, 112 Roberttown Lane, Roberttown, Liversedge, West Yorkshire, WF15 7NP
☎ (01924) 402069 ⊕ thenewinnroberttown.com

Brewing commenced in 2012 using a half-barrel brew plant located in the cellar of the New Inn, Liversedge. The beer is produced in wood-clad vessels by Andrew Kenyon, the son of ex-brewer at the Riverhead Brewery, Joe Kenyon.

New Lion SIBA

Station Road, Totnes, Devon, TQ9 5JR
☎ (01803) 226277 ⊕ lioncraftbrewery.com

⊗ The original Lion Brewery closed in 1926 and was restarted in 2013 by four local business people. A five-barrel plant is used. Brewery supporters provide hops from a patchwork of hop gardens for annual green hop ale and a series of traditional Belgian-style beers are being re-created. Beer is distributed throughout South Devon. !! ◆ RAIB

Mane Event (OG 1039, ABV 3.8%)
A golden brown-coloured, well-balanced, modern session bitter.

TQ9 (OG 1042, ABV 4.2%)
A golden-coloured, refreshing ale with a hint of Earl Grey.

Totnes Stout (OG 1045, ABV 4.4%) ◆
Full-bodied stout with roasted malts and some smoky chocolate and liquorice. Dry bitterness finishes.

Pandit IPA (OG 1046, ABV 4.9%)
A citrus and floral nose complemented on the palate by a well-defined biscuity malt character.

**Smokestack Lightning Porter
(OG 1067, ABV 6.8%)**
A rich, dark porter with hints of smoke, chocolate, plums and liquorice.

New Plassey

Eyton, LL13 0SP ☎ 07769 155874
⊠ plassey.brewery@gmail.com

Plassey brewery was founded in 1985 on the 250-acre Plassey Estate. Following the merger of Plassey and the Gertie Sweet Brewery in 2012, the New Plassey Brewery was formed. New owners, Magic Dragon Brewing, took over the brewery in 2017.

New World Pale (OG 1039, ABV 3.9%)
A pale beer, well-balanced with a hoppy bite.

Plassey Bitter (OG 1040, ABV 4%) ◆
Smooth and malty best bitter, reddish brown in colour with a good hop and fruit balance and a dry finish.

Midnight Mild (OG 1042, ABV 4.2%)
A medium strength dark mild with a real fullness of character and flavour.

Offa's Dyke (OG 1043, ABV 4.3%)
Pale, crisp and refreshing bitter .

Dusky Maiden Stout (OG 1044, ABV 4.4%)
A dark-coloured, complex stout.

Deep Porter (OG 1045, ABV 4.5%)
A smooth, deep brown-coloured porter.

Cherry Diva (OG 1047, ABV 4.7%)
A pale beer with a subtle flavour of maraschino cherry.

Cwrw Tudno (OG 1050, ABV 5%)
A pale, strong bitter.

Dragons Breath (OG 1060, ABV 6%) ◆
Well-balanced strong bitter. Plum fruit in aroma with the initial sweetness followed by a powerful smack of hops and fruit.

New Religion (NEW)

Office: 75 Brynhyfryd, Groesyceiliog, Cwmbran, NP44 2LN

New Religion was established in 2016. Beers were contract brewed by Mad Dog Brewery (qv), Gwent, but brewing is currently suspended.

New River SIBA ⊙

Unit 47, Hoddesdon Industrial Centre, Pindar Road, Hoddesdon, Hertfordshire, EN11 0FF
☎ (01992) 446200 ⊕ newriverbrewery.co.uk

⊗ New River commenced brewing in 2015 on a brand new 10-barrel plant. !! ◆

London Tap (OG 1038, ABV 3.8%)
A refreshing, hoppy pale ale, light citrus with hints of toffee and a refreshing, dry finish.

Riverbed Red (OG 1041, ABV 4.2%)

Five Inch Drop (OG 1044, ABV 4.6%)
A triple-hopped IPA with a toffee, malty aroma. Pine resin and citrus fruit flavours.

New Wharf (NEW)

Hyde Farm, Marlow Road, Maidenhead, SL6 6PQ
☎ 07815 717251 ⊠ kevinblack2001@hotmail.com

A 20-barrel brewery set up in 2017 with an ever-changing range of beers. RAIB

Newark 👁

77 William Street, Newark, Nottinghamshire, NG24 1QU ☎ 07804 609917 ⊕ newarkbrewery.co.uk

Established in 2012 on the site of a former maltings using an eight-barrel plant. The bulk of production is supplied to local pubs. Its brewery tap is the Ram in Castle Gate, Newark.

Best (OG 1038, ABV 3.8%)
Deep copper-coloured beer with a biscuity malt nose. Sweet toffee dominates the palate with a long, fruity finish

NPA (Newark Pale Ale) (OG 1039, ABV 3.8%)
Pale gold in colour, citrus lemon on the nose, leading to a fruity finish.

BLH4 (OG 1040, ABV 4%)

Norwegian Blue (OG 1040, ABV 4%)
Deep gold in colour. Grapefruit and citrus orange on the nose. Malty lemon on the palate with a long finish.

Winter Gold (OG 1040, ABV 4%)
A dry golden ale with bittersweet lemon citrus flavours.

Pure Gold (OG 1045, ABV 4.5%)
A rich gold in colour with biscuit and burnt orange on the nose, leading to a soft biscuit finish.

Summer Gold (OG 1045, ABV 4.5%)
Deep gold in colour with a strong, sweet citrus nose. The lime character and light malt balance produce a lasting finish.

Phoenix (OG 1048, ABV 4.8%)
Russet brown in colour, slight spice and roasted malt on the nose with a fruity, treacle, full-bodied finish.

5.5 (OG 1055, ABV 5.5%)
Deep gold-coloured strong ale, honey on the nose with sweet, soft fruits on the finish.

Newbridge

Unit 3, Tudor House, Moseley Road, Bilston, West Midlands, WV14 6JD ☎ 07970 456052 ⊕ newbridgebrewery.co.uk

First established in 2014, the five-barrel plant incorporates six original Grundy cellar tanks. The brewery closes during the winter months and resumes production around March.

Little Fox (OG 1042, ABV 4.2%)

Solaris (OG 1045, ABV 4.5%)

Indian Empire (OG 1051, ABV 5.1%)

Newby Wyke SIBA

Unit 24, Limesquare Business Park, Alma Park Road, Grantham, Lincolnshire, NG31 9SN ☎ (01476) 565682 ⊕ newbywyke.co.uk

⊠ The brewery is named after a Hull trawler skippered by brewer Rob March's grandfather. It started life in 1998 as a 2.5-barrel plant in a converted garage then moved to premises behind the Willoughby Arms, Little Bytham. In 2009 it moved back to Grantham. ‼◆

Banquo (OG 1036, ABV 3.8%)
Pale blonde beer with a full, hoppy taste and a long, fruity finish.

Orsino (OG 1037, ABV 4%)

A blonde ale with a fruity citrus and mango taste, moving to a soft citrus hop finish.

Comet (OG 1039, ABV 4.1%)
Amber-coloured ale with slight malt undertones and a gooseberry citrus fruit finish.

Kingston Topaz (OG 1039, ABV 4.2%)
A single-hopped ale with floral undertones.

Black Beerd (OG 1040, ABV 4.3%)
An oat malt stout with a balanced malt palate and fruit undertones.

Bear Island (OG 1043, ABV 4.6%)
A blonde beer with a hoppy aroma and a crisp, dry finish.

White Squall (OG 1044, ABV 4.8%) ◣
Blonde beer with a hoppy aroma. Generous amounts of hop are well-supported by a solid malty undercurrent. An increasingly bittersweet tang makes itself known towards the finish.

Newcastle (NEW)

Arch 2, Stepney Bank, Ouseburn, Newcastle upon Tyne, NE1 2NP ☎ 07446 011941 ⊕ newcastlebrewingltd.co.uk

Inspired by other local brewers, father and son Mike and Leo Bell initially founded the brewery in the Quayside Development Centre in Ouseburn before moving to new premises under Byker Bridge. This also includes a café bar and beer garden. RAIB

Newtown (NEW)

25 Victoria Street, Gosport, Hampshire, PO12 4TX ☎ (023) 9250 4294 ⊕ newtownbrewery.co.uk

Brewing commenced in 2016 in this nanobrewery with just a half-barrel plant, although the brewer has had many years previous experience of home brewing. Full mash beers are produced on demand for local Gosport pubs and CAMRA Beer Festivals.

Nine Standards

See Settle

Nirvana (NEW)

Unit T6, Leyton Industrial Village, Argall Avenue, Leyton, London, E10 7QP ☎ (020) 3417 5580 ⊕ nirvanabrewery.com

Established in 2017 producing a range of non-alcoholic beers. No real ale.

No. 18 Yard

See Shepherd Neame

Nobby's SIBA

Unit 2, Cottingham Way, Thrapston, Northamptonshire, NN14 4PL ☎ (01832) 730800 ⊕ nobbysbrewery.co.uk

Paul 'Nobby' Mulliner started commercial brewing in 2004 on a 2.5-barrel plant at the rear of the Alexandra Arms, Kettering. The brewery relocated to Guilsborough in 2007 and again in 2014 to larger premises in Thrapston. ‼ ▬ ◆ RAIB

Claridges Crystal (OG 1036, ABV 3.6%)
A pale ale, crisp and fresh with a slightly citrus hop finish.

Guilsborough Guzzler (OG 1036, ABV 3.6%)
An easy-drinking, malty, auburn-coloured ale with a gentle hop finish.

Best (OG 1037, ABV 3.8%)
A fine session ale with a good hop finish.

Guilsborough Gold (OG 1041, ABV 4%)
A full-bodied golden ale with a well-balanced traditional hop finish.

Northampton Red (OG 104, ABV 4%)
Mahogany-coloured beer, full and flavoursome.

Tow'd Navigation (OG 1067, ABV 6.1%)
Dark, strong ale with rich malt and hops. Wonderfully warming.

Nomadic (NEW)

c/o 29 Skelton Terrace, Leeds, West Yorkshire, LS9 9ES ☎ 07868 345228
✉ **nomadicbeers@gmail.com**

Nomadic Beers was established in 2017 by Katie Marriott and Ross Nicholson. Beers are produced using spare capacity at the Burley Street Brewhouse (qv). **V**

Pale (OG 1035, ABV 3.8%)

Nook SIBA

🍴 **Riverside, 7b Victoria Square, Holmfirth, West Yorkshire, HD9 2DN**
☎ **(01484) 682373 ⊕ thenookbrewhouse.co.uk**

The Nook Brewhouse is built on the foundations of a previous brewhouse dating back to 1754, next to the River Ribble. Two brewery taps are supplied, one with a restaurant whose dishes are matched with the beer brewed on site.

Norfolk SIBA ⊙

Moon Gazer Barn, Harvest Lane, Hindringham, Norfolk, NR21 0PW
☎ **(01328) 878495 ⊕ norfolkbrewhouse.co.uk**

⊠ Brewing began in 2012 using a 10-barrel plant. The brewery is owned and run by Rachel and David Holliday. Chalk-filtered water is used from the brewery's own well. ‼♦

Dewhopper Cask Lager (OG 1038, ABV 3.8%)

Moon Gazer Amber Ale (OG 1040, ABV 4%)
An amber-coloured ale with a full-bodied bitterness and fruity overtones. A smooth, lasting finish.

Moon Gazer Golden Ale (OG 1040, ABV 4%)
A golden ale with a fresh, citrus aroma. Well-hopped with a fruit and hop flavour carrying through to the refreshing, crisp, dry finish.

Moon Gazer Ruby Ale (OG 1040, ABV 4%)
A ruby-coloured ale with a rich, spicy, roasted aroma and a full malty body resulting in a full-bodied mouthfeel.

Moon Gazer Dark Mild (OG 1051, ABV 4.9%)
A strong dark mild with a subtle blackcurrant aroma. Full-bodied with a rich, fruity, sweet finish.

Stubblestag Cask Lager (OG 1049, ABV 5%)

North Cotswold SIBA ⊙

Unit 3, Ditchford Farm, Stretton-on-Fosse, Warwickshire, GL56 9RD
☎ **(01608) 663947 ⊕ northcotswoldbrewery.co.uk**

⊙ North Cotswold started in 1999 as a 2.5-barrel plant, which was upgraded in 2000 to 10 barrels. 🚚 ♦ RAIB

Windrush Ale (OG 1036, ABV 3.6%)
An amber-coloured session bitter with a malty, slightly sweeter palate.

Fosseway Flanker (OG 1038, ABV 3.8%)
A refreshing, pale and hoppy session ale.

Moreton Mild (OG 1038, ABV 3.8%)
A classic dark mild with a nutty palate.

Cotswold Best (OG 1040, ABV 4%)
An easy-drinking, copper-coloured best bitter.

Shagweaver (OG 1045, ABV 4.5%)
A pale, hoppy bitter made with a trio of New Zealand hops.

**Hung, Drawn 'n' Portered
(OG 1050, ABV 5%)** 🗐 🍺
Strong, dark-coloured porter with a malty finish.

Contract brewed for Yubberton Brewing Co:

Yubbie (ABV 3.8%)
Strong caramel malty notes carry through to a fruity hop character with a pleasant bitter finish.

Goldie (ABV 4%)
A refreshing IPA-style beer with a strong hoppy character.

Yawnie (ABV 4.3%)
A well-balanced, chestnut-coloured ale with toffee malt notes persisting through a complex hop character.

North

Unit 6, Taverner's Walk Estate, Sheepscar Grove, Leeds, West Yorkshire, LS7 1AH
☎ **(0113) 345 3290 ⊕ northbrewing.com**

⊙ Brewing began in 2015, originally supplying the North Bar group of bars in Leeds. It has since grown and supplies other outlets. ‼♦V

Prototype (OG 1038, ABV 3.8%) 🔶
Light amber-coloured hoppy beer with an ever present bitterness.

Sputnik (OG 1046, ABV 5%)
A pale ale, light and crisp with citrus, pine, tropical and stone fruit aromas.

Full Fathom 5 (OG 1065, ABV 6.5%)
A full-bodied coffee and coconut porter.

Transmission (OG 1063, ABV 6.9%)
A classic American-style IPA with a light body and dry finish.

North Riding (Brewery)

Unit 9, Betton Business Park, Racecourse Road, East Ayton, Scarborough, North Yorkshire, YO13 9HD
☎ **(01723) 864845 ☎ 07930 843868**
⊕ **northridingbrewery.com**

Brewing commenced in 2015 on a 10-barrel plant with four core beers. ♦ RAIB

USA Session IPA (OG 1039, ABV 3.8%)
A pale and hoppy session IPA.

Cascade Pale Ale (OG 1042, ABV 4%)
A pale ale with unique citrus qualities.

Mosaic Pale Ale (OG 1044, ABV 4.3%)
A pale ale packed with blueberry and citrus flavours.

Citra Pale Ale (OG 1045, ABV 4.5%)
Easy-drinking premium pale ale with a grapefruit and lemon taste and aroma.

North Riding (Brewpub)

North Marine Road, Scarborough, North Yorkshire, YO12 7HU
☎ (01723) 370004 ⊕ northridingbrewpub.com

Brewing commenced in 2011 using a two-barrel plant situated in the cellar of the pub, which is now brewing to capacity with three fermenting vessels.

North Union

Matrix Business Centre, Nobel Way, Dinnington, Sheffield, South Yorkshire, S25 3QB
☎ (01909) 547033 ⊕ northunionbrewing.co.uk

Brewing began in 2016 using spare capacity at Harthill Village Brewery (qv). No real ale.

North Wales

Tan-y-Mynydd, Moelfre, Abergele, LL22 9RF ☎ 0800 083 4100 ⊕ northwalesbrewery.net

John Wood established his brewery in 2007. In 2012 a bore hole was drilled to supply water for brewing. Mead and soft drinks are also produced. RAIB

Bodelwyddan Bitter (OG 1038, ABV 3.8%)

Chilli Beer (OG 1040, ABV 4%)

Dandelion & Burdock (OG 1040, ABV 4%)

Abergele Ale (OG 1050, ABV 5%)

Welsh Stout (OG 1052, ABV 5.2%)

North Yorkshire SIBA

Pinchinthorpe Hall, Pinchinthorpe, North Yorkshire, TS14 8HG
☎ (01287) 630200

Founded in Middlesbrough in 1989 the brewery moved to Pinchinthorpe Hall, a moated, listed medieval estate near Guisborough in 1998. Its own spring water produces a distinctive flavour. More than 20 different beers are produced. ‼ ➳ ♦ RAIB

Northallerton (NEW)

2 Binks Close, Standard Way Business Park, Northallerton, North Yorkshire, DL6 2YB
☎ (01609) 258226 ⊕ northallertonbrewery.co.uk

Northallerton Brewery was established in 2016 using the old Wall's Brewery 5.5-barrel equipment and recipes. The beers can be found locally as well as in outlets across the country. ‼ ♦ RAIB

Gun Dog Bitter (OG 1039, ABV 3.8%)

Snow Storm (OG 1039, ABV 3.8%)
A beer with fruity and spicy hop characteristics.

Brewers Gold (OG 1039, ABV 4%)
A malty, golden-coloured session beer.

Dark (OG 1045, ABV 4.4%)
Dark-coloured ale with an orange finish.

Uncle Sam's Black IPA (OG 1049, ABV 4.8%)
A full-bodied American-style IPA, strongly hoppy with a hint of roast malt.

Northbound

Campsie Industrial Estate, McLean Road, Eglinton, BT47 3XX ⊕ northboundbrewery.com

Established in 2015, Northbound produce a range of bottle-conditioned beers named after their measurement of bitterness (IBUs). RAIB

Northern Alchemy

The Lab, Cumberland Arms, St James Street, Newcastle upon Tyne, NE6 1LD ☎ 07834 386333
⊕ wearenorthernalchemy.com

Brewing began in 2014. Production is mostly keg but some cask-conditioned beer is available.

Northern FC

McCracken Park, Great North Road, Gosforth, Newcastle upon Tyne, NE3 2DT
⊕ northernfootballclub.co.uk

Established in 2012 to supply the clubhouse for the Northern RUFC. The range is developing.

Northern Monk SIBA ◉

The Old Flax Store, Marshalls Mill, Holbeck, Leeds, West Yorkshire, LS11 9YJ
☎ (0113) 243 6430 ⊕ northernmonkbrewco.com

☺Based in a Grade II-listed mill building in the centre of Leeds, Northern Monk started brewing as cuckoo brewers in 2013 and set up at its present site in 2014 using a 10-barrel plant.

True North (OG 1037, ABV 3.7%)
Hops dominate this light yellow-coloured beer but there is a bitterness which builds in strength then lingers in the finish.

Monacus NZ Pale Ale (OG 1045, ABV 4.5%)

Northern Monkey (NEW)

The Link, Bow Street, Bolton, BL1 2EQ ☎ 07737 125629

Ryan Bailey and Liam Covey were homebrewers for a number of years before setting up Northern Monkey Brew Co in 2016 using a one-barrel plant. The local area and beer festivals are supplied. ♦

The Last Drop (ABV 3.6%)

Winter Hill (ABV 3.8%)
A golden ale with a caramel flavour and fruity finish.

Sheephouse (ABV 4.2%)
A pale ale with subtle peach and lime flavours followed by a hoppy finish.

Underdog (ABV 6%)
A chocolate treacle porter.

Northern Whisper (NEW)

Hill End Mill, Hill End Lane, Cloughfold, Lancashire, BB4 7RN

☎ (01706) 230082
⊕ northernwhisperbrewingco.co.uk
Brewing began in 2017.

Northumberland ⬿

North Blyth Bar & Brewery, Accessory House, Barrington Road, Bedlington, Northumberland, NE22 7AP
☎ (01670) 822112 ⊕ northumberlandbrewery.co.uk

☺Brewing began in 1996 in Ashington using a five-barrel plant. Relocation and expansion mean that the brewery now uses a 10-barrel plant and has an on-site brewery tap, Fuggles. 30-40 barrels are brewed each week of a wide range of ales. ‼◆

Pit Pony (OG 1039, ABV 3.8%)

Fog on the Tyne (OG 1040.5, ABV 4.1%)

Norton

Norton Priory, Tudor Road, Manor Park, Runcorn, Cheshire, WA7 1SX
☎ (01928) 716971 ☎ 07767 354674
⊕ nortonbrewing.com

Situated within the grounds of Norton Priory, the brewery was created as a social enterprise by Halton Borough Council to provide employment opportunities for people with learning disabilities, autism and other disabilities. It opened in 2011 with a 2.5-barrel plant.

Noss Beer Works SIBA

Unit 6, Ash Court, Pennant Way, Lee Mill, Devon, PL21 9GE ☎ 07977 479634 ⊕ nossbeerworks.co.uk

⊠ Noss Beer Works, based in Lee Mill, was formed in 2012 using a six-barrel plant. The beers are made from only the finest locally sourced hops and malts. ‼RAIB

Black Rock (ABV 4%)
A black IPA with liquorice, citrus and caramel notes. Slightly bitter aftertaste.

Church Ledge (OG 1040, ABV 4%)
A light IPA, hoppy and zesty.

Mew Stone (OG 1043, ABV 4.3%)
A copper-coloured beer, well-balanced and refreshing.

Ebb Rock (OG 1049, ABV 4.9%)
A dark copper-coloured, full-bodied beer.

Nottingham SIBA ⬿

⬢ Plough Inn, 17 St Peter's Street, Radford, Nottingham, NG7 3EN
☎ (0115) 942 2649 ☎ 07815 073447
⊕ nottinghambrewery.co.uk

The former owners of the Bramcote and Castle Rock Breweries re-established the Nottingham Brewery in 2000 in a purpose-built brewhouse behind the Plough Inn. Philip Darby and Niven Balfour set out to revive the brands of the original Nottingham Brewery, closed by Whitbread in the 1950s. Within the LocAle ethos, beers are supplied widely to the local trade including the brewery tap house, the Plough Inn, and its two other tied houses the Ned Ludd, Nottingham and the Frame Breakers, Ruddington.

Rock Ale Bitter Beer (OG 1038, ABV 3.8%) ⬿
A pale and bitter, thirst-quenching, hoppy beer with a dry finish.

Rock Ale Mild Beer (OG 1038, ABV 3.8%) ⬡ ⬿
A reddish-coloured malty mild with some refreshing bitterness in the finish.

Legend (OG 1040, ABV 4%) ⬿
A fruity and malty pale brown-coloured bitter with a touch of sweetness and bitterness.

Extra Pale Ale (OG 1042, ABV 4.2%) ⬿
A hoppy and fruity golden ale with a hint of sweetness and a long-lasting bitter finish.

Broadway Reel Ale (OG 1044, ABV 4.4%) ⬿
Hoppy golden ale with a lingering bitter finish.

Dreadnought (OG 1045, ABV 4.5%) ⬿
Well-balanced best bitter. Blend of malt and hops give a rounded fruity finish.

Bullion (OG 1047, ABV 4.7%) ⬿
A refreshing premium golden ale. Brewed with a single malt variety, it is triple-hopped and exceptionally bitter.

Supreme (OG 1052, ABV 5.2%) ⬿
A strong, amber-coloured, fruity ale. A touch of malt in the taste is followed by a sweet and slightly hoppy finish.

Brewed for the Trent Bridge Inn, West Bridgford:

Trent Bridge Inn Ale (OG 1038, ABV 3.8%)
Tawny-coloured, traditionally-hopped bitter.

Nutbrook

6 Hallam Way, West Hallam, Derbyshire, DE7 6LA
☎ 0800 458 2460 ⊕ nutbrookbrewery.com

Nutbrook was established in 2007. In addition to a regular range, special beers are brewed to order for domestic and corporate clients. The brewery's unique 'Design-a-Beer' system allows customers to design and brew their own beer. On Saturdays cask-conditioned beer is sold at Oakfield Farm, Stanley Common. ‼ 🚊RAIB

The Mild Side (OG 1036, ABV 3.6%)
A golden-coloured mild with a traditional malt taste and fruit tones.

Responsibly (OG 1041, ABV 4%)
A light bronze-coloured, crisp beer with a fruity flavour.

Banter (OG 1040.8, ABV 4.5%)
A light golden yellow-coloured beer with a traditional hoppy taste and floral notes.

Daft Apeth (OG 1050, ABV 4.5%)

More (OG 1047, ABV 4.8%)
Dark-coloured beer with a subtle red tint, burnt roasted barley taste and sweet bitterness.

Black Beauty (OG 1054, ABV 5%)
A traditional milk stout with undertones of chocolate, honey and nuts.

The Perfect Fifth (OG 1047.8, ABV 5%)
A strong pale ale with honey tones.

Moderation (OG 1057, ABV 5.5%)
A golden ale with subtle hop flavours and medium bitterness.

O'Brien

Unit 13, Enderby Road Industrial Estate, Whetstone, Leicestershire, LE8 6HZ
☎ (0116) 286 3166 ⊕ dobrienbrewery.co.uk

Brewing commenced in 2016 using a four-barrel plant. One regular beer is produced along with a rotating selection of seasonal and one-off brews. ♦

Rebel Porter (OG 1040, ABV 4%)
Roast malt infused with spicy hops.

O'Connor (NEW)

12 Lime Road, Faughanvale, Greysteel, Northern Ireland, BT47 3EH ☎ 07748 004065

Brewing began in 2013. No real ale.

Oakham SIBA ⊙

⊟ 2 Maxwell Road, Woodston, Peterborough, Cambridgeshire, PE2 7JB
☎ (01733) 370500 ⊕ oakhamales.com

The brewery started in 1993 in Oakham, Rutland, and moved to Peterborough in 1998. The brewery's main production site is a 75-barrel plant. An additional six-barrel plant is located at its city-centre brewpub, which makes special and one-off brews. Around 350 outlets are supplied and four pubs are owned.

JHB (OG 1038, ABV 3.8%) ◆
Straw-coloured golden ale dominated by citrus hop character throughout. Long, dry, slightly astringent finish.

Inferno (OG 1039, ABV 4%) ◆
The citrus hop character of this straw-coloured brew begins on the nose and builds in intensity on the palate. Clean, dry, citrus finish.

Citra (OG 1042, ABV 4.2%) ▮ ◆
Refreshing grapefruit and peach aroma and flavour characterise this golden ale. Bittersweet palate gives way to a long, dry aftertaste.

Scarlet Macaw (OG 1043, ABV 4.4%)
Tart gooseberry and soft peach on the nose and intense bitter finish.

Bishops Farewell (OG 1046, ABV 4.6%) ◆
Powerfully citrus, the hops and fruit on the aroma of this golden/yellow-coloured beer become bittersweet on the palate. Zesty citrus aftertaste.

Oakleaf

See Fallen Acorn

Oakwood

Northfield Crescent, Wells-next-the-Sea, Norfolk, NR23 1LP ☎ 07512 111211 ⊕ oakwoodbrewery.com

Oakwood was established in 2015. After producing beers on a small scale from home the brewer decided to turn his hobby into a full-time job. Barley is locally-grown by Teddy Maufe at Branthill Farm on the Holkham Estate in Norfolk. RAIB

Oast House (NEW)

Correspondence: 32 Brynystywyth, Penparcau, SY23 1SS

☎ (01970) 627907 ☎ 07943 374730
✉ beer@oasthousebrewery.co.uk

Cuckoo brewery using spare capacity at Brecon Brewery (qv). Location of brewery to change in due course to a recently purchased pub in Aberystwyth with the intention of larger brews to continue to be carried out at Brecon Brewery.

Larger Than Life (ABV 3.8%)
A light and refreshing lager-style brew.

AberDabbaDoo (ABV 4.2%)
Amber-coloured with soft, hoppy aromas and a caramel flavour, carrying an edge of gentle spice.

Oban Bay

See Argyll

Occasional

Roosters of Babylon, Babylon Lane, Silverton, Devon, EX5 4DT ☎ 07506 355318 ⊕ occasionalbrewing.co.uk

⊠ The Occasional Brewing Company was established in 2014. It concentrates on producing bottle-conditioned beers, although the occasional cask does get into the trade. Brewing is currently suspended as the brewery is in the process of relocating. RAIB

Odcombe

⊟ Masons Arms, 41 Lower Odcombe, Odcombe, Somerset, BA22 8TX
☎ (01935) 862591 ⊕ masonsarmsodcombe.co.uk

Odcombe opened in 2000, but closed a few years later. It re-opened in 2005 with assistance from Shepherd Neame (qv). Brewing takes place once a week and beers are available only in the Masons Arms.

Oddly (NEW)

Unit 12, Platt's Eyot, Hampton, TW12 2HF
☎ (020) 3741 7741 ⊕ oddlybeer.com

Brewing began in 2017. Oddly is a small batch brewery producing mostly keg beers. Cask-conditioned ale is occasionally available.

Odyssey

Brockhampton Brewery, Oast House Barn, Whitbourne, Herefordshire, WR6 5SH
☎ (01885) 483496 ☎ 07918 553152
⊕ odysseybrewco.com

⊠ This six-barrel brewery was bought in 2014 by Alison and Mitchell Evans, who also own the Beer in Hand in Hereford. The original building, a restored barn on a National Trust estate, has been retained. ☛

Syren (OG 1039, ABV 3.9%)

Mo' Citra (OG 1040, ABV 4%)

Little India Pale Ale (OG 1045, ABV 4.5%)

Latte Stout (OG 1062, ABV 5.4%)

Nirvana (OG 1052, ABV 5.4%)

31st State (OG 1049, ABV 5.8%)

Crowd Control (OG 1060, ABV 6%)

Cookie Monster (OG 1045, ABV 6.5%)

Offa's Dyke

🍴 Chapel Lane, Trefonen, Shropshire, SY10 9DX
☎ (01691) 656889 ⊕ trefonen.org/
offas-dyke-brewery.html

Established in 2007, the brewery and adjoining pub straddle the old England/Wales border, Offa's Dyke. The Olde Vaults and adjacent Ironworks in Oswestry serve as alternative brewery taps.

Offbeat SIBA

Units 4-5, Thomas Street, Crewe, Cheshire, CW1 2BD
☎ 07502 096438 ⊕ offbeatbrewery.com

☺Offbeat began brewing in 2010 and in 2016 scaled down to a two-barrel plant focusing on local sales and its own bar in the brewery. The brewery tap is open Thursday and Friday evenings. A monthly open night is held the first Friday of the month with live music. ‼ 🍺 ♦ RAIB

Outlandish Pale (OG 1037.8, ABV 3.9%)
A pale session ale with a fresh burst of lemony hoppiness.

Kooky Gold (OG 1041, ABV 4.1%)
Light, golden-coloured session ale, easy-drinking with low bitterness.

Odd Ball Red (OG 1040.4, ABV 4.2%)
A ruby-coloured ale with masses of hops giving a spicy flavour and finish.

Disfunctional Functional IPA (ABV 4.8%)

Out of Step IPA (OG 1055.3, ABV 5.8%)
An American-style IPA, hoppy with citrus flavours leading to a dry, bitter finish.

Ogwen (NEW)

5 Rhes Ogwen, Bethesda, LL57 3AY ☎ 07545 684752
⊕ cwrwogwen.cymru

The first brewery in the Ogwen Valley for over a century. Beers are named after characters from Welsh folklore.

Cwrw Caradog (OG 1039, ABV 3.9%)

Okells SIBA 👁

Kewaigue, Douglas, Isle of Man, IM2 1QG
☎ (01624) 699400 ⊕ okells.co.uk

☺Founded in 1874 by Dr Okell, this is the main brewery on the island and moved in 1994 to a new, purpose-built plant at Kewaigue. All the beers are produced under the Manx Brewers' Act. ‼ ♦

MPA (Manx Pale Ale) (OG 1036, ABV 3.6%) 🍴 ♦
A golden-coloured, fruity session bitter with background sweetness and a rising hoppy finish.

Bitter (OG 1035, ABV 3.7%) ♦
A gently bittered, sweet beer with some fruit and malt flavours.

Dr Okell's IPA (OG 1044, ABV 4.5%) ♦
A clean, fruity, sweetish bitter with an alcoholic bite.

Old Bog

🍴 Masons Arms, 2 Quarry School Place, Headington, Oxfordshire, OX3 8LH
☎ (01865) 764579 ⊠ theoldbog@hotmail.co.uk

Originally established in 2005 behind the Masons Arms, Headington, the brewer is again producing Old Bog beers at the pub after a short spell of brewing them at the Old Forge brewery. The beers, when available, are sold at the Masons Arms and occasionally at local beer festivals. A number of one-off brews appear throughout the year.

Old Cannon

🍴 86 Cannon Street, Bury St Edmunds, Suffolk, IP33 1JR
☎ (01284) 768769 ⊕ oldcannonbrewery.co.uk

The former St Edmunds Head pub re-opened in 1999 as the Old Cannon Brewery complete with a unique state-of-the-art brewery housed in the bar area. A growing number of outlets are supplied.

Best Bitter (OG 1037, ABV 3.8%) ♦
Traditional East Anglian bitter. Rich, hoppy aroma and bitterness dominate throughout with just a hint of sweetness in the aftertaste.

Elveden IPA (OG 1038, ABV 3.9%)

Gunner's Daughter (OG 1052, ABV 5.5%) ♦
A well-balanced strong ale with a complexity of hop, fruit, sweetness and bitterness in the flavour, and a lingering, hoppy, bitter aftertaste.

Old Chimneys

Hopton End Farm, Church Road, Market Weston, Suffolk, IP22 2NX
☎ (01359) 221013 ⊕ oldchimneysbrewery.com

Old Chimneys opened in 1995, moving to a converted farm building in 2001. Most of the beers are named after rare species found nearby.
‼ 🍺 ♦ RAIB

Military Mild (OG 1035, ABV 3.3%) ♦
A rich, dark mild with good body for its gravity. Sweetish toffee and light roast bitterness dominate, leading to a dry aftertaste.

Great Raft Bitter (OG 1040, ABV 4%)
Pale copper-coloured bitter bursting with fruit. Malt and hops add to the sweetish fruity flavour, which is rounded off with hoppy bitterness in the aftertaste.

Black Rat Stout (OG 1048, ABV 4.4%)
Roast malt and coffee flavours with body and sweetness from added lactose.

Golden Pheasant (OG 1044, ABV 4.5%)
Pale, dry bitter with citrus, apple and malt, balanced with robust hop bitterness.

Arrowhead (OG 1047, ABV 4.8%)
A premium ruby-coloured ale with smooth, malty tones.

Old Cross

🍴 Old Cross Tavern, 8 St Andrew Street, Hertford, SG14 1JA
☎ (01992) 583133

The microbrewery was set up in 2008 and is located within the pub. Owner Nigel Beviss brews solely for the Old Cross Tavern. A range of beers is produced during the year including beers brewed with single variety hops. One of these is usually available at the bar.

Old Dairy SIBA 👁

Tenterden Station Estate, Station Road, Tenterden, Kent, TN30 6HE
☎ (01580) 763867 ⊕ olddairybrewery.com

⊗ Old Dairy was founded in 2009. It relocated from Rolvenden in 2014 to larger premises near the Kent & East Sussex Railway in Tenterden in order to increase capacity. There is a brewery shop offering discounts to CAMRA members. ‼ 🍺 ♦ RAIB

Red Top (OG 1038, ABV 3.8%) 🍺
A sweetish, copper-coloured bitter with hints of caramel and a subtle hop character.

Uber Brew (OG 1038, ABV 3.8%)
Full-bodied, hoppy pale ale with a strong floral aroma.

Copper Top (OG 1041, ABV 4.1%)
Dark-coloured, full-flavoured best bitter.

Gold Top (OG 1043, ABV 4.3%) 🍺
A well-balanced golden ale with a good blend of malt and hops followed by a long, bittersweet finish.

Blue Top (OG 1048, ABV 4.8%) 🍺
Rich and full bodied, this pale brown ale has a long bittersweet finish and a hint of aroma hop.

Snow Top (OG 1060, ABV 6%) 🍺 🍺

Old Forge

🍺 Radnor Arms, 32 Coleshill, Coleshill, Oxfordshire, SN6 7PR
☎ (01793) 861575 ⊕ oldforgebrewery.co.uk

Old Forge began brewing in a converted outbuilding at the Radnor Arms in 2010 using a four-barrel plant.

Old Inn

🍺 Old Inn, Flowerdale Glen, Gairloch, IV21 2BD
☎ (01445) 712006 ⊕ theoldinn.net

Brewing began in 2010 using a 150-litre plant.

Old Laxey

🍺 Shore Hotel Brew Pub, Old Laxey, Isle of Man, IM4 7DA
☎ (01624) 863214 ⊕ shorehotel.im

Beer brewed on the Isle of Man is brewed to a strict Beer Purity Act. Additives are not permitted to extend shelf life, nor are chemicals allowed to assist with head retention. Old Laxey's beer is sold mostly through the adjacent Shore Hotel.

Old Luxters

Chiltern Valley Vineyard, Hambleden, Buckinghamshire, RG9 6JW
☎ (01491) 638330 ⊕ chilternvalley.co.uk

Situated in a 17th-century barn beside the Chiltern Valley Vineyard, Old Luxters is a traditional brewery established in 1990 and was awarded a Royal Warrant of Appointment in 2007. The core range is bottle-conditioned beers. ‼ 🍺 ♦ RAIB

Old Market

🍺 Old Market Hall, Palace Street, Caernarfon, LL55 1RR

Situated in a 19th-century former market hall building, close to Caernarvon Castle, the six-barrel plant can be viewed within the premises. The beer is usually only available in the Old Market Hall bar, but may sometimes be found in other local outlets.

Old Mill SIBA

Mill Street, Snaith, East Yorkshire, DN14 9HU
☎ (01405) 861813 ⊕ oldmillbrewery.co.uk

☺ Opened in 1983 in a 200-year-old former malt kiln and corn mill, the brew-length is 60 barrels. The brewery is building a tied estate, now standing at 17 houses. Beers can be found nationwide through wholesalers and around 80 free trade outlets are supplied direct. ‼ ♦

Traditional Mild (OG 1034, ABV 3.4%) 🍺
A satisfying roast malt flavour dominates this easy-drinking dark mild.

Traditional Bitter (OG 1038.5, ABV 3.9%) 🍺
A malty nose is carried through to the initial flavour. Bitterness runs throughout.

Blonde Bombshell (OG 1042, ABV 4%)
An easy-drinking, straw-coloured beer with refreshing fruity flavours.

Yorkshire Porter (OG 1044, ABV 4.4%) 🍺
A slightly sweet porter with roasted chocolate flavours and a pleasant hop aroma.

Old Curiosity (OG 1044.5, ABV 4.5%) 🍺
Slightly sweet amber-coloured brew, malty to start with. Malt flavours all the way through.

Bullion (OG 1047.5, ABV 4.7%) 🍺
The malty and hoppy aroma is followed by a neat mix of hop and fruit tastes within an enveloping maltiness. Dark amber in colour.

Old Pie Factory SIBA 👁

4 Montague Road, Warwick, CV34 5LW ☎ 07816 413026 ✉ josh@oldpiefactorybrewery.co.uk

☺ Brewing began in 2011 using a 5.5-barrel plant and is a joint venture between Underwood Wines, Stratford upon Avon, and the Case is Altered, Five Ways. Spare capacity at the brewery is leased to cuckoo brewers Urban Huntsman.

Case Bitter (OG 1036, ABV 3.9%)
Classic English session bitter with only English ingredients.

Pie In The Sky (OG 1042, ABV 4.1%)

Humble Pie (OG 1045, ABV 4.2%)

American Pie (OG 1051, ABV 5.5%)

Old Sawley SIBA

🍺 White Lion, 352a Tamworth Road, Sawley, Derbyshire, NG10 3AT
☎ (0115) 946 3061 ☎ 07722 311209
⊕ oldsawley.com

Established in 2013, initially on a 0.5-barrel plant, upgraded to a 10-barrel plant in 2016. Beers are available in the White Lion, at Midlands beer festivals and in outlets across the East Midlands.

THE BREWERIES

Jobber (OG 1040, ABV 3.9%)
Traditional amber-coloured bitter with good balance of malt and hops to give a smooth, easy-drinking session ale.

Figaro (OG 1040, ABV 4%)

Gold (OG 1043, ABV 4.3%)
A crisp, golden ale with a delicate minty, grassy taste and a slightly floral aroma.

Little Jack (OG 1044, ABV 4.3%)
Crisp, refreshing pale ale with a fruity, citrus taste from a unique blend of four American hops.

Tollbridge Porter (OG 1047, ABV 4.5%)
A dark-coloured porter with smooth, subtle flavours of chocolate, coffee and vanilla.

Old School SIBA

Holly Bank Barn, Crag Road, Warton, Lancashire, LA5 9PL
☎ (01524) 740888 ☎ 07515 376700
🌐 oldschoolbrewery.co.uk

☺A 12-barrel brewery, founded in 2012, located in a renovated 400-year-old former school outbuilding overlooking the picturesque village of Warton. Beer is mainly sold to free houses within a 40-mile radius. ‼◆

Hopscotch (OG 1037, ABV 3.7%) 🍺
Initially hoppy, astringency builds in this satisfying beer, ending with a bitter finish.

Textbook (OG 1039, ABV 3.9%)

Detention (OG 1041, ABV 4.1%) 🍺
Light, malty bitter, sweetish middle with a gentle finish.

Headmaster (OG 1045, ABV 4.5%)
A dark-coloured, strong best bitter. It mixes a complex malty flavour with a blackcurrant aroma, leaving a subtle, sweet, nutty aftertaste.

Old Spot SIBA

Manor Farm, Station Road, Cullingworth, Bradford, West Yorkshire, BD13 5HN
☎ (01535) 691144 🌐 oldspotbrewery.co.uk

☺Old Spot, named after the owner's sheepdog, started brewing in 2005. The beers are available locally with the acting brewery tap, the George Hotel in Cullingworth, being the main outlet. ‼◆

Light But Dark (OG 1043, ABV 4%)
Chestnut-coloured session bitter with a slight malty taste and pleasant bitter finish.

Spot Light (OG 1040, ABV 4.2%) 🍺
This smooth-drinking golden ale has a slightly fruity, hoppy aroma leading to a well-balanced fruity hop flavour with hints of pineapple and a long, bittersweet finish.

Inn-Spired (OG 1043, ABV 4.3%)
Light-coloured bitter with a light, hoppy taste and a slight, fruity finish.

OSB (OG 1042, ABV 4.5%)
A golden-coloured, full-bodied bitter.

Spot O'Bother (OG 1060, ABV 5.5%)
Porter with a chocolate ice cream taste and slight liquorice bitterness to finish. A complex brew.

Old Tree

Field House, Preston Barracks, Lewes Road, Brighton, East Sussex, BN2 4GL ☎ 07413 064346
🌐 oldtree.house

A co-operative based in an old barracks and supplying its own Field café and zero-waste Silo restaurant. It combines brewing and gardening and uses a production process that contributes to land regeneration. RAIB

Old Worthy

Broughton, ML12 6HQ ☎ 07955 113083
🌐 oldworthybeer.co.uk

☺Brewing takes place on a 10-barrel plant. The beers are designed to be drunk as a 'half 'n' half', a beer served with a dram of whisky on the side. The malt used is sourced from Scottish whisky distilleries. 200 outlets are supplied.

Wee XP (OG 1045, ABV 4.4%)

Wee Blonde (OG 1048, ABV 4.7%)

The Old Worthy (OG 1050, ABV 5%)

Wild Bill's Aces & Eights (OG 1050, ABV 5%)

A Midnight Caper (OG 1050, ABV 5.5%)

Mighty XP (OG 1060, ABV 6%)

Olde Potting Shed

Collingdon Buildings, Collingdon Road, High Spen, Tyne & Wear, NE39 2EQ
☎ (01207) 545577

Olde Potting Shed began brewing in 2013 using a five-barrel plant.

Cygnet (ABV 4%)

Dark Wing (ABV 4.3%)

Swan Song (ABV 4.8%)

Olde Swan

⬛ 89 Halesowen Road, Netherton, West Midlands, DY2 9PY
☎ (01384) 253075

A famous brewpub best known as Ma Pardoe's after the matriarch who ruled it for years. The pub has been licensed since 1835 and the present brewery and pub were built in 1863. Brewing continued until 1988 and restarted in 2001.

Oldershaw SIBA 👁

Heath Lane, Barkston Heath, Grantham, Lincolnshire, NG32 2DE
☎ (01476) 572135 🌐 oldershawbrewery.com

☺Oldershaw Brewery has been brewing since 1997. Owned and run by brewster Kathy Britton, it is a nine-barrel plant and brews in the region of 500,000 pints a year. The brewery produces around 20 different beers of varying styles. Beers branded as Home Ales are brewed under contract for Brands Reunited. ‼🍺◆

Heavenly Blonde (OG 1038, ABV 3.8%)
A pale blonde session beer packed with zesty, refreshing tropical fruit flavours. A crisp, dry finish.

Newton's Drop (OG 1041, ABV 4.1%) 🍺

Balanced malt and hops but with a strong bitter, lingering taste in this mid-brown beer.

Great Expectations (OG 1040, ABV 4.2%)
A pale gold-coloured, citrus beer.

Grantham Stout (OG 1043, ABV 4.3%)
Dark brown-coloured and smooth with rich roast malt notes. Warming, fruity, complex flavours.

Mosaic Blonde (OG 1041, ABV 4.3%)
Lager-style beer. Powerfully citrus, tropical.

Old Boy (OG 1047, ABV 4.8%) ◆
A full-bodied, amber-coloured ale, fruity and bitter with a hop/fruit aroma. The malt that backs the taste dies in the long finish.

Blonde Volupta (OG 1050, ABV 5%)
Straw gold-coloured, zesty premium beer packed with complexity and intense tropical fruit flavours leading to a crisp, dry finish.

Ollie's

616 Newport Road, Cardiff, CF3 4FG ☎ 07896 296259 ⊕ olliesbrewery.com

Ollie's was established in 2016 using a 100-litre brew kit, named after the owner's rescue dog. Only bottle-conditioned beers are produced at present but cask-conditioned beers are planned. A further 100-litre kit was added in 2017 and there are plans for relocation to larger premises. RAIB

On the Edge

Woodseats, Sheffield, South Yorkshire ☎ 07854 983197 ⊕ ontheedgebrew.com

On the Edge started brewing commercially in 2012 using a 0.5-barrel plant in the brewer's home. Brewing takes place once a week. Three local pubs are supplied as well as beer festivals. There is no regular beer list as new brews are constantly being tried.

One Mile End SIBA

⊟ Unit 2, Compass West Estate, West Road, Tottenham, London, N17 0XL
☎ (020) 7998 0610 ☎ 07912 411147

Correspondence: White Hart, 1-3 Mile End Road, Whitechapel, London, E1 4TP
⊕ the-white-hart.co.uk/index.php

One Mile End took over the former premises of the Redemption Brewery (qv) using a 12.5-barrel plant brewing up to four times a week. A three-barrel plant is also in operation at the White Hart in Whitechapel. Beer is also brewed using the Under the Street brand name.

Temperance Session Ale (ABV 3.5%)

Great Tom Mild (ABV 3.8%)

Dockers Delight Bitter (ABV 4.2%) ◆
Best bitter with caramelised toffee and fruit on palate and aroma. Earthy, spicy hops fade in the dry lingering finish.

Salvation Pale Ale (ABV 4.4%) ◆
Golden ale with passion fruit, biscuit and lemon flavours. Lingering, dry, bitter aftertaste. Trace of metallic lemon in the aroma.

Hospital Porter (ABV 5.2%) ◆

Dark brown-coloured porter with a smoky, roasty nose. Sweet mocha, roast and nuts on the palate. Dry, dark roast finish.

Opa Hay's

Glencot, Wood Lane, Aldeby, Norfolk, NR34 0DA
☎ (01502) 679144 ☎ 07916 282729
⊕ engelfineales.com

Opa Hay's began brewing in 2008. It is a small, family-run brewery, taking its name from the brewer's great grandfather. Only traditional brewing methods are used, with ingredients that are, where possible, sourced locally. ◆ RAIB

Engels Fruity Little Number (ABV 3.6%) ◆
Powerful citrus/grapefruit aroma with malt and hops. Smoky, sweetish flavours with fruit notes and a fruity, hoppy aftertaste.

Engel's Best Bitter (ABV 4%)
A triple-hopped, aromatic beer.

Hop Hop Hooray (ABV 4.3%)

Matilda's Revenge (ABV 4.3%)

SEMP (Samuel Engels Meister Pils) (ABV 4.8%)
A Pilsner-style beer, light in colour with a hoppy aroma.

Liquid Bread (ABV 5.2%)
Bavarian-style wheat beer, naturally cloudy with a distinct aroma of cloves and banana.

Orbit

Arches 225 & 228, Fielding Street, Walworth, London, SE17 3HD
☎ (020) 7703 9092 ⊕ orbitbeers.com

Established in 2014, Orbit is a microbrewery producing keg and bottle-conditioned beers. RAIB

Origami (NEW)

75 Temperance Street, Manchester, M12 6HU

Office: 23 Bradshaw Lane, Stretford, Manchester, M32 8WF ⊕ origamibrewingcompany.com

Brewing began in 2016 using its own brew plant on the premises of Beer Nouveau (qv) on the 'Piccadilly Beer Mile'. Brewster Erin Guy was previously head brewer at Bootleg Brewery (qv) in Chorlton.

Fortune Teller (ABV 4%)

Rabbit Ear (ABV 4.8%)

1000 Cranes (ABV 5%)

Valley Fold (ABV 5.2%)

Arctic Fox (ABV 7%)

Orkney SIBA ◉

Quoyloo, Stromness, Orkney, KW16 3LT
☎ (01667) 404555 ☎ 07721 013227

Office: Sinclair Breweries Ltd, Cawdor, IV12 5XP
⊕ orkneybrewery.co.uk

◉Orkney was established in 1988 in an old village school building. Having incorporated sister brewery Atlas (qv), it moved next door in 2010 to enable an increase in capacity and the completion of an award-winning visitor centre in 2012. ‼ ☰ ◆

Raven (OG 1038, ABV 3.8%) ⬦ ◆

A well-balanced, quaffable bitter. Malty fruitiness and bitter hops last through to the long, dry aftertaste.

Dragonhead (OG 1040, ABV 4%) ◆
A strong, dark roasted malt aroma flows into the taste. The roast malt continues to dominate the aftertaste, and blends with chocolate to develop a strong, dry finish.

Northern Light (OG 1040, ABV 4%) ◆
A well-balanced golden ale with a real smack of fruit and hops in the taste and an increasing bitter aftertaste.

Red MacGregor (OG 1040, ABV 4%) ◆
This tawny red-coloured ale has a red fruit, malt and hop mix. Generally a well balanced bitter.

Corncrake (OG 1042, ABV 4.1%) ◆
A straw-coloured beer with soft citrus fruits and a floral aroma.

Puffin Ale (OG 1045, ABV 4.5%) ◆
Bittersweet mix of some malts and plenty of hops.

Dark Island (OG 1045, ABV 4.6%) ◆
The roast malt and chocolate character varies. A sweetish roast malt taste leads to a long-lasting roasted, slightly bitter, dry finish.

Skull Splitter (OG 1080, ABV 8.5%) 🗂 ▣ ◆
An intense velvet malt nose with hints of apple, prune and plum. The hoppy taste is balanced by satiny smooth malt with sweet, fruity, spicy edges, leading to a long, dry finish with a hint of nut.

Brewed for Atlas Brewery:

Latitude (OG 1036, ABV 3.6%)
A light citrus taste with a smack of hops and grapefruit in the light bitter finish.

Wayfarer (OG 1044, ABV 4.4%) ◆
Full of citrus fruits and hops.

Golden Amber (OG 1045, ABV 4.5%) ◆
Refreshing hops, honey, marmalade and grapefruit to the fore with a dry, hoppy finish.

Blizzard (OG 1047, ABV 4.7%) ◆
Light on malts and hops with ginger and spices coming through.

Ossett SIBA 👁

Kings Yard, Low Mill Road, Ossett, West Yorkshire, WF5 8ND
☎ (01924) 261333 ⊕ ossett-brewery.co.uk

☺Ossett began brewing in 1998, moving to a new site in 2005. An extra 40-barrel fermenter was added in 2014, increasing total brewing capacity to 280 barrels a week. The brewery owns 23 pubs, five of which are 'Hop'-branded bars – larger city centre venues with real ale and live music. ‼▐◆

Pale Gold (OG 1038, ABV 3.8%)
A light, refreshing pale ale with a light, hoppy aroma.

Yorkshire Blonde (OG 1040, ABV 3.9%)
A pale, full-bodied and well-rounded ale. Slightly sweet on the palate.

Big Red Bitter (OG 1042, ABV 4%) 🗂
Deep red-coloured, malty Yorkshire bitter.

Silver King (OG 1041, ABV 4.3%)
A lager-style beer with a crisp, dry flavour and citrus fruity aroma.

Treacle Stout (OG 1050, ABV 5%) 🗂
A rich and robust stout. The addition of black treacle gives intense depth and roasted malts impart a coffee flavour. Generous amounts of hops add a dry citrus finish to this complex ale.

Excelsior (OG 1051, ABV 5.2%)
A strong pale ale with a full, mellow flavour and a fresh, hoppy aroma with citrus/floral characteristics.

Otley SIBA 👁

Unit 39, Albion Industrial Estate, Pontypridd, CF37 4NX
☎ (01443) 480555 ⊕ otleybrewing.co.uk

☺Otley Brewing was established in 2005 and since then the brewery has almost tripled in size, taking over adjacent industrial units. There is now an on-site shop. The beers are supplied to many outlets across South Wales and in the London area. The brewery was sold in 2017 but sale was conditional on the best traditions being maintained. ‼▐◆RAIB

01 (OG 1038, ABV 4%) 🗂 ◆
A pale golden-coloured beer with a hoppy aroma. The taste has hops, malt, fruit and a thirst-quenching bitterness. A satisfying finish completes this beer.

02 Croeso (OG 1040, ABV 4%)
Light golden ale full of citrus hop aromas.

04 Colombo (OG 1038, ABV 4%)

03 Boss (OG 1042, ABV 4.4%)
Chestnut-coloured bitter using American hops for bitterness and aroma.

12 Thai Bo (OG 1045, ABV 4.6%)
Clear wheat beer with lemongrass, lime leaf and galangal.

05 Hop Angeles (OG 1047, ABV 4.8%)

09 Blonde (OG 1047, ABV 4.8%)
Clear wheat beer flavoured with roasted orange peel, coriander and cloves.

07 Weissen (OG 1048, ABV 5%)
Cloudy German-style wheat beer.

10 Oxymoron (ABV 5.5%)

06 Porter (OG 1063, ABV 6.6%)

11 Motley Brew (OG 1072, ABV 7.5%)
Double IPA with big hop aromas and high bitterness.

Otter SIBA 👁

Mathayes, Luppitt, Devon, EX14 4SA
☎ (01404) 891285 ⊕ otterbrewery.com

⊠ A family-run brewery set high up in the Blackdown Hills. Environmental responsibility lies at the heart of its ethos. Otter's eco cellar has been built underground and is naturally chilled. The beers are made from the brewery's own springs and locally-sourced ingredients. ◆

Bitter (OG 1036, ABV 3.6%) ◆
Well-balanced, amber-coloured session bitter with a fruity nose, bitter taste and aftertaste.

Amber (OG 1038.5, ABV 4%) 🗂 ◆
Light, refreshing and mellow with hints of citrus hoppiness. Creamy and delicate with hops and fruit.

Bright (OG 1039, ABV 4.3%) ◆

A light and refreshing golden ale with delicate malt and fruit leading through hops to a lingering bitter aftertaste.

Ale (OG 1043, ABV 4.5%) ◈
Malt dominates from nose to throat. Sweet fruit, toffee and caramel with a dry aftertaste, full of flavour.

Head (OG 1054, ABV 5.8%) ⬚ ⬛
Fruity aroma and taste with a pleasant bitter finish. Dark brown in colour and full-bodied.

Oud Craft

c/o Dulcimer, 567 Wilbraham Road, Manchester, M21 0AE
☎ (0161) 860 6444 ✉ brewedbyoud@gmail.com

Established in 2015, Oud Craft Brewery was set up by the team behind Dulcimer Bar, Chorlton-cum-Hardy, and Saison, West Didsbury, using spare capacity at Outstanding Brewing Company (qv). Beers are currently exclusive to the two bars.

Ouseburn Valley

11 Dilston Terrace, Gosforth, Tyne & Wear, NE3 1XX
☎ 07932 677899 ⊕ ouseburnvalleybrewery.co.uk

Ouseburn Valley started in the owner's garage in 2010, and in 2011 the plant was moved to the cellar of the Brandling Villa Pub where both capacity and beer range were increased. After a flood in 2012, brewing is back in the owner's garage. ◆

Armstrong Bitter (OG 1042, ABV 4.1%)
Yellow-coloured beer with a light, spicy aroma and soft caramel overtone. A long, bitter finish.

Golden Ale (OG 1044, ABV 4.4%)
Dark gold in colour with light hop aroma, sweet malty taste and a smooth finish.

India Pale Ale (OG 1047, ABV 4.7%)
Pale gold in colour with a strong hop aroma and a long, dry finish.

Milk Stout (OG 1047, ABV 4.7%)
Traditionally dark in colour with a liquorice aroma, sweet liquorice and a coffee taste.

American Honey (OG 1049, ABV 5%)
Rich dark gold in colour with sweet honey taste and strong dry hop aroma.

Out There SIBA

Unit 4, Foundry Lane Industrial Estate, Newcastle upon Tyne, NE6 1LH ☎ 07946 579534
⊕ outtherebrewing.com

Out There was established in 2012 by Steve Pickthall. Branding and beer names are themed around the 1950s space race.

Space is the Place (OG 1034, ABV 3.5%)
An amber-coloured beer with aromas of digestive biscuits and brown bread. A sweet malt flavour with floral notes.

Laika (OG 1049, ABV 4.8%)
A straw-coloured, cloudy beer, the aroma is citrus with a hint of custard cream biscuits. Flavours of orange peel and spices liven the malt base.

Celestial Love (OG 1051, ABV 5.1%)

Red-coloured ale with aromas of caramel and a hint of malt loaf. The taste is sweet malt with floral and grapefruit hop flavours.

Outlaw

See Rooster's

Outstanding SIBA 👁

Units 1 & 2, Foundry, Ordsall Lane, Ordsall, Manchester, M5 3AN
☎ (0161) 873 8090 ⊕ outstandingbeers.com

Established in 2008, the brewery operates a dual system, brewing on a 15-barrel plant and using a 2.5-barrel plant for special and experimental brews. Originally based in Bury, it moved to Ordsall in 2017. ◆

3.9 (OG 1036, ABV 3.9%)

Ultra Pale (OG 1041, ABV 4.1%) ◈
Straw in colour, with a light citrus aroma. Lemony fruit with hop bitterness to taste and a bitter, astringent finish.

Red (OG 1045, ABV 4.4%)

Blond (OG 1044, ABV 4.5%)

IPA (OG 1058, ABV 5.5%)

Stout (OG 1061, ABV 5.5%)

Imperial IPA (OG 1065, ABV 7.4%) ⬚

Oxted

Flower Farm, Oxted Road, Godstone, Surrey, RH9 8BP
☎ 07867 541700 ⊕ theoxtedbrewery.co.uk

⊗ Oxted Brewery was established in 2015 at a farm in Godstone using a two-barrel plant. Beers are regularly available at the Crown and Wheatsheaf pubs, Old Oxted. Open events are held locally most months. ▰ ◆ RAIB

Hopfather (OG 1038, ABV 3.8%)
A hoppy pale ale.

Single Hop (OG 1037, ABV 3.8%)
Light, fresh, mildly-hopped session beer which often uses a different hop for each brew.

Amber Ale (OG 1039, ABV 3.9%)
Citrus and grapefruit with a light, malty finish.

BOB (Best Oxted Bitter) (OG 1041, ABV 4%)
Biscuity, mild chocolate with a light, hoppy finish.

Pacific Red (OG 1043, ABV 4.3%)
A smooth bitter with a hint of kiwi fruit and a long, malty finish.

The Black Perle (OG 1044, ABV 4.4%)
Roasted flavours with a clean aftertaste.

Treehouse IPA (OG 1048, ABV 4.9%)
Well-balanced IPA with citrus and grapefruit to the fore.

Padstow SIBA

The Brewery, Unit 4a, Trecerus Industrial Estate, Padstow, Cornwall, PL28 8RW
☎ (01841) 532169 ☎ 07834 924312
⊕ padstowbrewing.co.uk

⊗ The brewery started commercially in 2013 using a 0.5-barrel plant. Owners Des and Caron Archer,

Caron being the brewster, have since installed a custom-built 10-barrel plant. Beer festivals and an increasing number of local outlets are supplied. ‼ ☛ ♦ RAIB

Pale Ale (OG 1037, ABV 3.6%) ◆
Golden-coloured beer with assertive hop aroma. Citrus hops dominate the taste with bitterness and dryness. Hoppy, refreshing and crisp finish.

Kor Dorgel (OG 1040, ABV 4%) ◆
Refreshing, gold-coloured ale with fruity hop nose. Crisp citrus, apple and pineapple flavours colour the grassy hop bitterness and balancing malt.

Windjammer (OG 1042, ABV 4.3%) ◆
Copper-coloured best bitter. Biscuit malt with pear drops and delicate stone fruits. Bitterness grows and lasts well into the finish.

Lobster Tale (OG 1044, ABV 4.5%) ◆
A smooth, yellow-coloured and cloudy wheat beer with a fruity aroma. Bitter lemon hop and coriander flavours with light malt.

Pride (OG 1044, ABV 4.5%) ◆
Tawny-coloured with added honey. Malt dominates throughout with some toffee sweetness and light roast notes balanced by bitterness, plums and hops.

IPA (OG 1046, ABV 4.8%) ◆
Amber-coloured, strong bitter. Fully hopped on nose and taste with orange bitterness. Sweet finish with citrus hops and faintly dry.

The Smoke (OG 1049, ABV 4.9%) ◆
Smooth, dark red-coloured stout with gentle roast aroma. Smoky roast and earthy, peaty malt dominates the taste. Long finish.

May Day (OG 1048, ABV 5%) ◆
Yellow-coloured ale with powerful citrus hop aroma and flavour. Grapefruit and moderate bitterness. Strong grassy hop finish with dryness.

Sundowner (OG 1060, ABV 6.8%) ◆
Strong, gold-coloured ale with fruity hop aroma. Dominant apricot with citrus hops and malt flavours. Quite bitter, slightly sweet and dry.

Palmers SIBAIFBB ⊙

The Old Brewery, West Bay Road, Bridport, Dorset, DT6 4JA
☎ (01308) 422396 ⊕ palmersbrewery.com

⊠ Palmers is Britain's only thatched brewery and dates from 1794. It is situated in Bridport, the heart of the Jurassic Coast in south-west Dorset. The company continues to make substantial investment in its 54 tenanted pubs, all serving cask ale. An additional 400 outlets are supplied. ‼☛♦

Copper Ale (OG 1036, ABV 3.7%) ◆
Beautifully balanced, copper-coloured light bitter with a hoppy aroma.

IPA (OG 1040, ABV 4.2%) ◆
Hop aroma and bitterness stay in the background in this predominately malty best bitter, with some fruit on the aroma.

Dorset Gold (OG 1046, ABV 4.5%) ◆
More complex than many golden ales thanks to a pleasant banana and mango fruitiness on the aroma that carries on into the taste and aftertaste.

200 (OG 1052, ABV 5%) ◆

This is a big beer with a touch of caramel sweetness adding to a complex hoppy, fruit taste that lasts from the aroma well into the aftertaste.

Tally Ho! (OG 1057, ABV 5.5%) ⬚ ◆
A complex, dark-coloured old ale. Roast malts and treacle toffee on the palate lead in to a long, lingering finish with more than a hint of coffee.

Panther

Unit 1, Collers Way, Reepham, Norfolk, NR10 4SW
☎ 07766 558215 ⊕ pantherbrewery.co.uk

⊠ Panther began brewing in 2010 on an industrial estate near the old railway station, formerly the home of Reepham Brewery. ‼☛♦RAIB

Mild Panther (OG 1035, ABV 3.3%) ◆
A smooth, malty character with notes of chocolate, which give this beer plenty of flavour and aroma.

Ginger Panther (OG 1037, ABV 3.7%) ◆
Refreshingly clean ginger wheat beer with a distinct fiery kick.

Golden Panther (OG 1039, ABV 3.7%) ◆
Refreshing orange and malt notes flow through this well-balanced, easy-drinking bitter. Hops and a soft bitterness add depth.

Honey Panther (OG 1044, ABV 4%) ◆
A gentle, flowing brew with honey and malt throughout. Amber-coloured with a tapering bittersweet finale.

Red Panther (OG 1041, ABV 4.1%) ◆
Full-flavoured brew. Solidly malty in both aroma and taste. Hops, and a residual sweetness, provide balance.

American Pale Ale (OG 1044, ABV 4.4%)
A light malt base lets tropical flavours and aromas shine through, with a crisp dry finish.

Black Panther (OG 1050, ABV 4.5%) ◆
This dark ale is full flavoured, smooth and complex. It has a bittersweet balance that leads to a dry finish.

Beast of the East (OG 1052, ABV 5.5%)
An amber-coloured IPA, refreshing with floral and grapefruit notes.

Papworth (NEW)

7 Byfield Road, Papworth Everard, Cambridgeshire, CB23 3UQ
☎ (01480) 830248 ☎ 07835 845797
⊕ papworthbrewery.com

Brewing began in 2014.

Mad Jack (ABV 3.8%)
A well-balanced session bitter with a light copper colour and gentle citrus aroma. Caramel overtones lead to a long and hoppy finish.

Half Nelson (ABV 4.1%)
A well-balanced, ruby-coloured IPA with a fresh and zesty finish.

Red Kite (ABV 4.4%)
A sweet, ruby-coloured ale with a strong hop finish bursting with tropical fruit flavours.

Crystal Ship (ABV 4.5%)
An amber-coloured ale with a light body and a strong citrus finish.

Big Sur (ABV 5%)

A West Coast-style pale ale with a light malt body and a finish of floral and citrus flavours.

Robin Goodfellow (ABV 5.4%)
A dark-coloured and full-bodied ale with a strong hop aroma. Heavy and complex malts softened with dark fruit flavours give way to a smooth yet hoppy finish.

Paradigm SIBA

4d Green End Farm, 93a Church Lane, Sarratt, Hertfordshire, WD3 6HH
☎ (01923) 291215 ⊕ paradigmbrewery.com

⊗ Founded by two friends, Neil Hodges and Rob Atkinson, Paradigm went into production in 2015. Its five-barrel plant is located in an industrial unit on a farm. One-off beers are also brewed. The brewery and beer names are based on corporate jargon and buzzwords. ‼◆RAIB

Watercress Ale (OG 1036, ABV 3.6%)
Produced with locally grown watercress to add a peppery flavour to this bitter, amber-coloured beer.

Low Hanging Fruit (OG 1038, ABV 3.7%)
Refreshing with citrus flavours, particularly tangerine and grapefruit.

Touch Point (OG 1039, ABV 3.9%)
A light-coloured, hoppy pale ale.

Synergy (OG 1052, ABV 5.1%)
A full-bodied, fruity IPA.

Black Friday (OG 1062, ABV 6%)
A dark, strong mild. Smooth and sweetish with a hint of smoked malt.

Paradise

⬗ **Bird in Hand, Trelissick Road, Hayle, Cornwall, TR27 4HY**
☎ (01736) 753974
✉ birdinhand@paradisepark.org.uk

Brewing first started in 1981 under the name Paradise Brewery, named after its location, the Paradise Bird Park. The name was changed to Wheal Ale in 1995. Brewing ceased in 2004 but re-started in 2009 under the original Paradise name.

Parish

6 Main Street, Burrough on the Hill, Leicestershire, LE14 2JQ
☎ (01664) 454801 ☎ 07715 369410
✉ bazbrewery@gmail.com

Parish began in 1983 and now operates on a 20-barrel plant, with capacity to brew a further 12 barrels. The brewery is located in a 400-year-old building next to Grants Freehouse, which stocks the full range of beers. Other local outlets are also supplied and one-off brews are produced for beer festivals. ‼RAIB

PSB (OG 1038, ABV 3.9%)
Hoppy session beer with a malty aftertaste.

Burrough Bitter (OG 1047, ABV 4.8%)
Darker version of PSB with a good balance of malt and hops. Reddish brown in colour.

Poachers Ale (OG 1060, ABV 6%)
Deep ruby red-coloured, full bodied, malty beer.

Baz's Bonce Blower (OG 1098, ABV 12%)

Strong, dark-coloured beer with a rich, malty character. A Christmas pudding ale.

Park Brew (NEW)

The Shed, Park View, Brechin, DD9 7AT ☎ 07905 998740 ⊕ parkbrew.com

Established in 2016 by John Leatherbarrow and Andrew Donald.

Park Brewery SIBA ◉

95 Elm Road, Kingston, Surrey, KT2 6HX ☎ 07932 624395

Office: 38 St Georges Road, Kingston, Surrey, KT2 6DN
⊕ theparkbrewery.com

⊗ The Park Brewery was founded in 2014 in a former greengrocer's premises, using a one-barrel plant, increasing in 2015 to four barrels. Beers are available locally as well as across London. ‼◆RAIB

Killcat Pale (OG 1037, ABV 3.7%) ◀
Unfined golden-coloured bitter with grapefruit throughout and a strong, hoppy, bitter flavour and finish, which is dry and slightly tart.

Gallows Gold (OG 1044, ABV 4.4%) ◀
Unfined hoppy golden ale with citrus notes. Bitterness develops in the taste and finish, which has some pineapple fruitiness.

Spankers IPA (OG 1055, ABV 5.5%) ◀
An amber-coloured, hoppy, citrus, dry golden ale with a similar finish and a touch of dry bitterness.

Parker

Unit 3, Gravel Lane, Banks, Lancashire, PR9 8BY
☎ (01704) 620718 ☎ 07949 797889
⊕ theparkerbrewery.co.uk

☺Parker was established in 2014 using a 25-litre plant, and has since expanded to a five-barrel plant. ‼RAIB

Centurion Pale Ale (OG 1040, ABV 3.9%)
A light, refreshing pale ale with zesty fruit flavours with a crisp, dry and hoppy finish.

Barbarian Bitter (OG 1041, ABV 4.1%)
Amber-coloured traditional ale with notes of caramel. Smooth and well balanced.

Saxon Red Ale (OG 1046, ABV 4.5%)
Ruby red in colour, packed full of warm fruit flavours and a subtle hint of spice on the finish.

Viking Blonde (OG 1045, ABV 4.7%)
A blonde ale with subtle hints of blackcurrant and summer berry fruit flavours with a refreshing, full, crisp finish.

Dark Spartan Stout (OG 1052, ABV 5%)
Silky smooth with hints of chocolate and coffee.

Partizan SIBA

8 Almond Road, South Bermondsey, London, SE16 3LR
☎ (020) 8127 5053 ⊕ partizanbrewing.co.uk

Partizan began brewing in 2012. There is a constantly changing range based on a variety of international styles. All are vegan-friendly and bottled by hand on site. ⬚◆RAIB V

Partners SIBA 👁

The Brew House, 589 Halifax Road, Hightown, Liversedge, West Yorkshire, WF15 8HQ
☎ (01924) 457772 ⊕ partnersbrewery.co.uk

☺Partners was formed in 2011 following the purchase of the long-established Anglo Dutch Brewery by Richard Sharp. The brewery moved into newly renovated premises in 2015 and invested in a 15-barrel state-of-the-art brew plant to meet increased demand for its beers. Three pubs are owned; the Brew House in Hightown, Halfway House in Morley and the Shant in Halifax. ‼◆

Blonde (OG 1039, ABV 3.9%)
A blonde, crisp, aromatic session beer.

Black Lion (ABV 4%)
Roasted malt delivers a smooth ale with a unique character.

White Lion (ABV 4.3%)

Tabatha (OG 1054, ABV 6%) ◣
Golden-coloured, Belgian-style Tripel with a strong, fruity, hoppy and bitter character. Powerful and warming, slightly thin with a bitter, dry finish.

Patriot

Upcott Farm, Bicknoller, Somerset, TA4 3HZ

Office: Farmer's Arms, Combe Florey, Somerset, TA4 3HZ ⊕ thepatriotbrewery.co.uk

☒ Patriot began brewing in Warwickshire in 2010 using a four-barrel plant before relocating to Bickoller, Taunton, in 2015. All beers are available at the Farmer's Arms, Combe Florey, plus a few other local outlets. ‼◆

Somerset Blonde (OG 1038, ABV 3.8%)

Broomsquire (OG 1040, ABV 4%)

Black Beauty (OG 1056, ABV 5.6%)

Peak SIBA

Barn Brewery, Chatsworth, Derbyshire, DE45 1EX
☎ (01246) 583737 ⊕ peakales.co.uk

☺Peak Ales opened in 2005 in former derelict farm buildings on the Chatsworth estate aided by a DEFRA Rural Enterprise Scheme grant and support from trustees of Chatsworth Settlement. Main beer production moved to a new facility at Ashford in the Water in 2014 to increase capacity. Beers are available throughout the Peak District. ‼◆

Swift Nick (ABV 4%) ◣
Easy-drinking, copper-coloured bitter with balanced malt and hops and a gentle, hoppy, bitter finish.

Bakewell Best Bitter (ABV 4.2%) ◣
Full-bodied, tawny-coloured bitter with a hoppy bitterness against a malty background, leading to a hoppy, dry aftertaste.

Chatsworth Gold (ABV 4.6%) 🏁 ◣
Speciality beer made with honey, which gives a pleasant sweetness leading to a hop and malt finish.

IPA (ABV 6%)
A classic IPA-style ale, bold and hoppy with a modern citrus twist.

Peakstones Rock SIBA 👁

Peakstones Farm, Cheadle Road, Alton, Staffordshire, ST10 4DH ☎ 07891 350908 ⊕ peakstonesrock.co.uk

☒ Peakstones Rock was established in 2005 with a five-barrel plant located on a farm in the Peak District Park. The brewery was expanded to 10-barrel capacity in 2009. It supplies an expanding free trade market in the North Midlands and surrounding areas. The brewery is connected to Crossways Micropub in Blythe Bridge. ‼◆RAIB

Nemesis (OG 1042, ABV 3.8%) ◣
Biscuity aroma with some hop background. Sweet start, sweetish body then hops emerge to give a fruity middle. Bitterness develops slowly to a tongue tingling finish.

Pugin's Gold (OG 1043, ABV 4%)

Chained Oak (OG 1045, ABV 4.2%)
A copper-coloured beer with a bitter finish and hop aroma.

Alton Abbey (OG 1051, ABV 4.5%)

Black Hole (OG 1048, ABV 4.8%) 🏁 ◣
Grassy aroma with malt background. Hops hit the mouth and intensify. Bitterness lingers with some mouth-watering astringency.

Oblivion (OG 1055, ABV 5.5%)

Peerless SIBA 👁

The Brewery, 8 Pool Street, Birkenhead, Merseyside, CH41 3NL
☎ (0151) 647 7688 ⊕ peerlessbrewing.co.uk

Peerless began brewing in 2009 and is under the directorship of Steve Briscoe. Beers are sold through festivals, local pubs and the free trade. ‼◆

Pale (OG 1036, ABV 3.8%)
Pale session ale. Good initial bitterness and a hint of grapefruit on the finish.

Deadbeat (ABV 4%)
A toasted wheat backbone leads to a fruity finish.

Triple Blonde (OG 1040, ABV 4%)
A blonde ale with a fruity, citrus finish.

Lottie Dod (ABV 4.2%)
An amber-coloured ale with a good malt backbone and a hint of bitterness.

Langton Spin (ABV 4.4%)
A well-balanced, dry-hopped golden ale with an initial bitterness and a crisp, dry, citrus finish.

Oatmeal Stout (OG 1050, ABV 5%)
Full-bodied, black-coloured stout with toffee and caramel notes.

Red Rocks (OG 1047, ABV 5%)
Full-bodied, ruby-coloured ale. Rich malt flavours combine with the hops for fruity overtones.

Knee-Buckler IPA (ABV 5.2%)
Initial hop bitterness is matched with a hint of sweetness. A distinct fruity finish.

Full Whack (OG 1054, ABV 6%)
Strong ale, bitter with a fruity hop finish.

Tectonic (ABV 6.2%)
A deep honey-coloured ale with lots of hop aroma and flavour.

Pells

c/o Elephant & Castle, White Hill, Lewes, East Sussex, BN7 2DJ ⊕ pellsbrewingcoop.org

⊗ A brewing co-operative established in 2015. All beers are sold through the Elephant & Castle pub in Lewes.

House IPA (ABV 6.4%)

Penistone (NEW)

🯆 White Heart, 77 Gate Bridge Street, Penistone, South Yorkshire, S36 7AH ☎ 07885 251603 ⊕ thewhiteheart.co.uk/penistone_brewers

Brewing began in 2017 at the back of the White Heart pub, which dates back to 1377.

Penlon Cottage

Panteg Farm, New Quay, SA45 9TL ☎ (01545) 561492 ⊕ penlon.biz

After 10 years' operation, Penlon Cottage, strongly focussed on an ethos of sustainability, changed hands in 2014 and in 2015 moved to new premises nearby. It produces mainly bottle-conditioned beers. ‼RAIB

Pennine SIBA ◉

Well Hall Farm, Well, North Yorkshire, DL8 2PX ☎ (01677) 470111 ⊕ pennine-brewing.co.uk

☺Pennine began brewing in Batley in 2012 using an 18-barrel lager plant complete with lauter tun. In 2013 the brewery relocated to Well. ‼♦

Amber Necker (OG 1039, ABV 3.9%)
A session beer with a smooth and creamy texture and a hoppy aftertaste.

Best Bitter (OG 1040, ABV 3.9%)

Hair of the Dog (OG 1036, ABV 3.9%)
Bright blonde ale with a good aroma and smooth, refreshing aftertaste.

Real Blonde (OG 1041, ABV 4%)
Well-balanced blonde ale with a fruity aftertaste.

Natural Gold (OG 1043, ABV 4.2%)

Penpont

See Altarnun

Pentrich SIBA ◉

Unit B, Asher Lane Business Park, Asher Lane, Pentrich, Derbyshire, DE5 3RB ☎ (01773) 741700 ✉ pentrichbrewingco@gmail.com

Two former home brewers began producing beer for sale in their garage in Pentrich, before moving to share the plant of the Landlocked Brewing Co at the Beehive Inn, Ripley, in 2014. In 2016 the brewery moved into its own premises. ♦RAIB

Shoot the Servant (OG 1038, ABV 3.8%)
Dark bitter with flavours of toasted caramel and subtle chocolate. English hops add blackcurrant aromas and an understated spicy character.

Soma (OG 1044, ABV 4.3%)

A session pale ale with vibrant citrus and floral flavours.

1817 (OG 1045, ABV 4.5%)
A full-bodied, amber-coloured ale with a dry fruit aroma and a pleasing bitter finish.

Kiama (OG 1047, ABV 5%)
A hoppy pale ale with punchy citrus flavours and huge stone fruit aromas.

Death Valley (ABV 5.2%)
A subtle caramel malt character balanced with huge citrus and tropical flavours plus pine and floral notes.

Dry River (ABV 5.8%)
Huge pine, grapefruit and orange flavours with big, punchy citrus notes. A delicate caramel malt backbone complements the hops.

Three Graves (OG 1060, ABV 6%)
A strong, dark-coloured porter.

Northfield Garage (ABV 6.5%)

Black Ale (ABV 7.4%)
A black IPA with a silky texture. Pungent pine and stone fruit flavours.

Penzance

🯆 Star Inn, Crowlas, Penzance, Cornwall, TR20 8DX ☎ (01736) 740375 ⊕ penzancebrewing.wordpress.com

Owner Peter Elvin began brewing in 2008 on a self-built five-barrel plant in the old stable block of the Star Inn. The fermentation capacity has since been expanded, increasing the volume and range of beers produced. Production is now at full capacity of 1,400 barrels a year. Besides the pub, selected outlets and beer festivals are supplied.

People's

Mill House, Mill Lane, Thorpe-next-Haddiscoe, Norfolk, NR14 6PA ☎ (01508) 548706 ✉ peoplesbrewery@mail.com

⊗ A one-barrel brewery associated with the community-owned Queen's Head pub in Thurlton, which takes most of its draught output. RAIB

Northdown Bitter (OG 1038, ABV 3.8%)

Raveningham Bitter (OG 1040, ABV 3.9%)

Thurlton Gold (OG 1042, ABV 4.2%)

Cascade (OG 1043, ABV 4.5%)

Imperial Stout (OG 1072, ABV 7.3%)

Pershore (NEW) SIBA ◉

Unit 5, Lyttleton Road, Pershore, Worcestershire, WR10 2DF ☎ (01386) 561578 ☎ 07495 578397 ⊕ pershorebrewery.co.uk

☺Pershore began commercial brewing in 2016 using a six-barrel plant. Around 50 outlets are supplied direct. RAIB V

Summertime (OG 1038, ABV 3.8%)

Wobbly Angel (OG 1040, ABV 4%)

Croft (OG 1042, ABV 4.2%)

Pale Ale (OG 1045, ABV 4.5%)

Black Moon (OG 1050, ABV 5%)

Oh Betty (OG 1050, ABV 5%)

Tahkir Khing (OG 1068, ABV 6.5%)

Pheasantry SIBA 👁

High Brecks Farm, Lincoln Road, East Markham,
Nottinghamshire, NG22 0SN
☎ (01777) 872728 ☎ 07948 976749
⏾ pheasantrybrewery.co.uk

☺Pheasantry began brewing in 2012 using a new
10-barrel plant from Canada. Situated in a listed
barn on a farm, the brewery and visitor centre
incorporate a wedding and events venue, with the
brewery visible through glass partitions. It supplies
some 400 pubs and retail outlets. ‼ 🍴

Best Bitter (OG 1038, ABV 3.8%)
Smooth-tasting, copper-coloured beer with a light,
spicy aroma.

Pale Ale (OG 1040, ABV 4%)
A pale-coloured, smooth-tasting beer with floral
and citrus notes and a dry finish.

Ringneck Amber Ale (OG 1041, ABV 4.1%) ◀
Amber-coloured best bitter, initial malt and
caramel leading to a brief bitter, dry finish

Dark Ale (OG 1042, ABV 4.2%)
A smooth, soft, satisfying dark ale with malty
flavours, balanced bitterness and a velvety texture.

Lincoln Tank Ale (OG 1042, ABV 4.2%)
Amber-coloured, well-hopped beer.

Dancing Dragonfly (OG 1050, ABV 5%)
Refreshing blonde beer with exotic fruit flavours.

Philsters

Beehive Brewery, Beehive Cottage, Little Haseley,
Oxfordshire, OX44 7LH ☎ 07747 827489
⏾ philsters.co.uk

⊠ Named after the owner/brewer's nickname,
this small 200-litre brewery was established in
2015. It supplies local pubs, including the Plough,
Great Haseley and the White Rabbit, Oxford. There
are plans to increase production when funding and
premises become available. ◆

Haseley Gold (OG 1039, ABV 4.1%)
A golden-coloured, light ale with a good balance of
malt and hops, giving an initial bright, fresh
bitterness with soft woody, honey notes following.

Boosh (OG 1041, ABV 4.5%)
A light copper-coloured best bitter with an easy-
drinking, crisp, dry bitter finish to balance the rich
malts.

Glass Blower (ABV 4.6%)

Phipps SIBA 👁

The Albion Brewery, 54 Kingswell Street,
Northampton, NN1 1PR
☎ (01604) 946606 ☎ 07717 078402
⏾ phipps-nbc.co.uk

Originally founded in Towcester in 1801, Phipps
had been brewing in Northampton since 1817 until
taken over by Watney Mann, who closed the
brewery in 1974. The company name and recipes
were acquired and in 2008 the first Phipps draught
beer reappeared after 40 years, brewed to the
original recipe at Grainstore Brewery (qv) in
Oakham. The Albion Brewery site, once owned by

Phipps, was acquired and a new 15-barrel brewing
plant installed in 2014 to enable Phipps beers to be
once again brewed in the town. Hoggleys brewery,
which was established in 2002, merged with
Phipps NBC at the end of 2013 and all Hoggleys
beers are now brewed on the Phipps plant, with
the former Hoggleys plant sold to Merrimen
Brewing (qv). ‼ ◆ RAIB

Diamond Ale (OG 1037, ABV 3.7%)

Red Star (OG 1038, ABV 3.8%)

Cobbler's Ale (ABV 4%)
A chestnut-coloured session bitter with a dry finish.

India Pale Ale (OG 1043, ABV 4.3%)
A residual malt sweetness and grapefruit note from
the hops gives a fresh, crisp finish.

Ratliffe's Celebrated Stout (OG 1043, ABV 4.3%)
A creamy, well-balanced stout with just a hint of
bitterness.

Becket's Ale (ABV 4.5%)
A sweet, dark and malty brew with honey.

Bison Brown (OG 1046, ABV 4.6%)
Strong, smooth and sweet brown-coloured ale.

Cascadia (OG 1050, ABV 5%)

Gold Star (OG 1050, ABV 5.2%)

Brewed for Hoggleys Brewery:

Mill Lane Mild (OG 1040, ABV 4%)

Northamptonshire Bitter (OG 1040, ABV 4%)

Reservoir Hogs (OG 1042, ABV 4.3%)
Mid golden in colour, hoppy and refreshing.

Pump Fiction (OG 1045, ABV 4.5%)

India Pale Ale (OG 1050, ABV 5%)
A hoppy, full-bodied IPA.

Solstice Stout (OG 1050, ABV 5%)

Phoenix SIBA 👁

Green Lane, Heywood, OL10 2EP
☎ (01706) 627009 ✉ tony@phoenixbrewery.co.uk

☺ Established in Ellesmere Port in 1982, Oak
Brewery moved to the old Phoenix Brewery in
Heywood and adopted the name in 1991. It now
supplies more than 400 outlets plus wholesalers.
Restoration of the old brewery, built in 1897, is
ongoing. ◆

Hopsack (OG 1038, ABV 3.8%)
A light-drinking, hoppy session beer.

Navvy (OG 1039, ABV 3.8%) ◀
Amber-coloured beer with a citrus fruit and malt
nose. Good balance of citrus fruit, malt and hops
with bitterness coming through in the aftertaste.

Monkeytown Mild (OG 1039, ABV 3.9%)
Dark-coloured mild with fruitiness, bitterness and a
smooth, full malt finish.

Arizona (OG 1040, ABV 4.1%) ◀
Yellow in colour with a fruity and hoppy aroma. A
refreshing beer with citrus, hops and good
bitterness, and a shortish dry aftertaste.

Spotland Gold (OG 1041, ABV 4.1%)
A pale, hoppy beer with a lingering bitter finish.

Pale Moonlight (OG 1042, ABV 4.2%)
Quite bitter with lingering grassy hop finish.

Black Bee (OG 1045, ABV 4.5%)

Brewed with honey, this porter has a malty aroma with tastes of dark fruit, honey and a hint of coffee.

White Monk (OG 1045, ABV 4.5%) ◆
Yellow-coloured beer with a citrus fruit aroma, plenty of fruit, hops and bitterness in the taste, and a hoppy, bitter finish.

Thirsty Moon (OG 1046, ABV 4.6%) ◆
Tawny-coloured beer with a fresh citrus aroma. Hoppy, fruity and malty with a dry, hoppy finish.

West Coast IPA (OG 1046, ABV 4.6%) ◆
Golden in colour with a hoppy, fruity nose. Strong hoppy and fruity taste and aftertaste with good bitterness throughout.

Double Gold (OG 1050, ABV 5%)
A full-bodied premium bitter.

Wobbly Bob (OG 1060, ABV 6%) ◆
A red/brown-coloured beer with malty, fruity aroma and creamy mouthfeel. Strongly malty and fruity in flavour, with hops and a hint of herbs. Both sweetness and bitterness are evident throughout.

Brewed for Brunning & Price Pub Co:

Original (ABV 3.8%)

Pictish

Unit 9, Canalside Industrial Estate, Rochdale, OL16 5LB
☎ (01706) 522227 ⊕ pictish-brewing.co.uk

☺ The brewery was established in 2000 and supplies free trade outlets in the North-west and West Yorkshire. Famed for the consistency and clarity of its brews and the ever-changing single hop series of beers. ◆

Brewers Gold (OG 1038, ABV 3.8%) ◆
Yellow in colour with a hoppy, fruity nose. Soft maltiness and a strong hop/citrus flavour lead to a dry, bitter finish.

Talisman IPA (OG 1042, ABV 4.2%)
A golden-coloured session IPA.

Alchemists Ale (OG 1043, ABV 4.3%) ◆
Yellow-coloured beer with generous hop and fruit on the nose and palate. Good bitter hop finish.

Piddle SIBA ◉

Unit 24, Enterprise Park, Piddlehinton, Dorset, DT2 7UA
☎ (01305) 849336 ☎ 07730 436343
⊕ piddlebrewery.co.uk

⊠ Established in 2007, the brewery boasts a large range of beers crafted beside the River Piddle in Dorset, hence the name. A new bottling plant was installed in 2017. Beers are available in pubs and other outlets across Dorset and beyond. ◆GF

Dorset Rogue (OG 1038, ABV 3.9%)
A well-balanced and complex chestnut brown-coloured best bitter. Malty and fruity with a hint of caramel and toffee.

Piddle (OG 1043, ABV 4.1%)
Easy-drinking, amber-coloured session ale. Slightly sweet but malty with a fruity nose and a citrus twist.

Cocky IPA (OG 1047, ABV 4.3%)
Golden-coloured, hoppy IPA with a crisp grapefruit finish and pine/floral notes.

Bent Copper (OG 1050, ABV 4.8%)

A silky smooth, full-bodied English strong bitter with a herbal and fresh cut grass aroma.

Slasher (OG 1053, ABV 5.1%)
A strong, blonde, lager-style beer. Slightly sweet with a gentle floral aroma and refreshing dry finish.

Pied Bull

🏠 Pied Bull Hotel, 57 Northgate Street, Chester, CH1 2HQ
☎ (01244) 325829 ⊕ piedbull.co.uk

Pied Bull began brewing in 2011 using a one-barrel plant. Beer is mainly for in-house consumption but local beer festivals are supplied and occasional brewery swaps occur.

Pig & Porter

18h Chapman Way, Tunbridge Wells, Kent, TN2 3EF
☎ (01424) 893519 ⊕ pigandporter.co.uk

Originally brewing at several microbreweries in Sussex and Kent, brewing has taken place on its own plant in Tunbridge Wells since 2013 using a 10-barrel plant. ◆

Ashburnham Pale Ale (ABV 3.8%)

Red Spider Rye (ABV 5.5%)

Pig Iron SIBA

Unit 3, Venture Way, Brierley Hill, West Midlands, DY5 1RG ☎ 07816 018777 ⊕ pigironbrewingco.co.uk

☺Set up in 2015, this three-barrel plant is situated on the edge of the Merry Hill shopping centre. The brewer, from a former baking family, acquired the kit from Brewmeister in Northern Scotland. The brewery supplies free trade outlets within 15 miles of the brewery and the brewer's home. ◆

Blonde (OG 1038, ABV 3.8%)

EPA (OG 1042, ABV 4.2%)
Floral, grapefruit, pine and cedar flavours with a spicy honey aroma give this golden-coloured beer a smooth, light texture.

IPA (OG 1042, ABV 4.2%)

Unbeweavable (OG 1042, ABV 4.2%)

APA (OG 1045, ABV 4.5%)
An American-style IPA with pronounced citrus, blackcurrant and grapefruit flavours.

Pig Pub

🏠 Pig In Muck, Manor Road, Claybrooke Magna, Leicestershire, LE17 5AY
☎ (01455) 202859 ⊕ piginmuck.com/brewery

Brewing began in 2013 using a two-barrel plant, recently upgraded to a five-barrel one. Special beers are brewed for the pub by customers.

Pigeon Fishers

Unit B1, Devonshire Buildings, Works Road, Hollingwood, Chesterfield, Derbyshire, S43 2PE
☎ 07506 000989 ⊕ pigeonfishers.com

Pigeon Fishers is a small batch, award-winning brewery. It was founded in 2014 by head brewer Ade Cole using a pilot plant donated by Thornbridge Brewery (qv), recently upgraded to a

3.75-barrel plant. Ade is the landlord of the Derby Tup, where the beers can be found. ♦

House Pale (ABV 4%)
A single-hopped session pale ale. Clean and fresh.

House IPA (ABV 5%)
Fruity and strong IPA.

Pilgrim SIBA

11 West Street, Reigate, Surrey, RH2 9BL
☎ (01737) 222651 ⊕ pilgrim.co.uk

⊗ Pilgrim was the first microbrewery in Surrey, set up in 1982 in Woldingham before moving to its current premises in Reigate in 1984. The original owner, Dave Roberts, is still in charge. Beers are sold to around 40 local outlets. ‼️🍺♦

Quench (OG 1037, ABV 3.6%)
Light on the palate with a restrained hop structure and floral, lime notes.

Surrey Bitter (OG 1038, ABV 3.7%) 🍻
Pineapple, grapefruit and spicy aromas. Biscuity maltiness with a hint of vanilla balanced by a hoppy bitterness and refreshing bittersweet finish.

Progress (OG 1041.5, ABV 4%) 🍻
Well-rounded tawny-coloured bitter. Predominantly sweet and malty with an underlying fruitiness and hint of toffee, balanced with a subdued bitterness.

Quest (OG 1045, ABV 4.3%)

Pillars (NEW)

Unit 2, Ravenswood Industrial Estate, Shernhall Street, Walthamstow, London, E17 9HQ
☎ (020) 8521 5552 ⊕ pillarsbrewery.com

Brewing began in 2016 and is the only exclusively lager brewery and taproom in London. No real ale.

Pilot Beer

22 Jane Street, Leith, EH6 5HD
☎ (0131) 561 4267 ⊕ pilotbeer.co.uk

Pilot started brewing in 2013 in an industrial unit in Leith using a salvaged five-barrel plant. Graduates of the Heriot-Watt University Brewing degree course, the owners infuse a number of flavours in their hop-forward beers. Distribution is to the Edinburgh area. Beers are mostly unfiltered and unfined but much of the current output is keg.

Pilot Brewery

🏠 726 Mumbles Rd, Mumbles, Swansea, SA3 4EL
☎ 07897 895511 ⊕ thepilotbrewery.co.uk

The Pilot Brewery began production on its 2.5-barrel plant in 2013. It is located at the rear of the Pilot Inn on the Mumbles sea front. The output is mainly for the Pilot Inn but can be found at festivals and other select outlets.

Pin-Up SIBA

Unit 3, Block 3, Chalex Industrial Estate, Manor Hall Road, Southwick, Brighton, West Sussex, BN42 4NH
☎ (01273) 411127 ☎ 07888 836892
⊕ pinupbrewingco.com

⊗ Pin-Up began brewing in 2011, initially having its beers contract brewed at an Essex brewery. In 2014 it obtained its own plant and began brewing in Southwick, expanding from a five-barrel to a 10-barrel plant in 2015. Its first pub, the United Brethren, Chelmsford, opened in 2016. ♦RAIB

Session IPA (OG 1040, ABV 4.1%)

Gold Rush (OG 1043, ABV 4.2%)

Tank 3 (OG 1043, ABV 4.2%)

Milk Stout (OG 1044, ABV 4.5%)

Fernie Red (OG 1045, ABV 4.7%)

Pipes

183a Kings Road, Cardiff, CF11 9DF ☎ 07776 382244
⊕ pipesbeer.co.uk

Formery known as Artisan, the brewery was established in 2008. All beers are unfiltered, without additives or preservatives and suitable for vegans. The main output is bottled and keg beers, although cask-conditioned beers are occasionally produced. 🍺♦

Pirate (NEW)

🏠 White Lion, Fritwell Road, Fewcott, Oxfordshire, OX27 7NZ
☎ (01869) 346676 ⊕ whitelionfewcott.uk

Pirate Brewery set sail in 2017 and is located in a large log cabin behind the White Lion in Fewcott. With its two-barrel capacity, beer is mainly for in-house consumption, but local pubs and beer festivals are suppplied. The name comes from a large children's pirate play ship in the pub garden.

Pitfield

See Dominion

Pixie Spring/Hopcraft

Unit C1, Coed Cae Lane Industrial Estate, Pontyclun, CF72 9HG ☎ 07814 255943 ⊕ pixiespring.com

Pixie Spring began brewing in 2011 in the Wheatsheaf, Llantrisant. In 2012 there was a joining of forces with Gazza Prescott of Steel City Brewing and a move to the present 12-barrel plant. Output under the Pixie Spring banner is restricted to a few regular beers, whereas the Hopcraft brand is used for mostly one-off, well-hopped recipes, although many beers are now permanent. The brewery opened the Hopbunker, a cellar bar in the centre of Cardiff, in 2015.

Golden Pixie (OG 1038, ABV 3.8%)
Golden-coloured, balanced, malty beer and a restrained citrus and fruity character.

Brewed under the Hopcraft Brewing name:

Temple of Love (OG 1938, ABV 3.8%)
Hoppy and bitter session beer.

Profits of Doom (ABV 4.5%)
A sweet stout brewed with lactose.

Oceanic (OG 1048, ABV 4.8%)
Pale ale with a soft tropical fruit character.

Graveyard Eyes (OG 1053, ABV 5.3%)

Citra Plus (ABV 5.4%)

A hoppy pale ale.

Mate, Spawn & Die (OG 1054, ABV 5.4%)
Pale gold in colour with a tropical fruit punch aroma and taste.

Brewed under the Waen Brewery name:

Lemon Drizzle (OG 1037, ABV 3.7%)
Pale ale with lemon citrus flavours.

Pamplemousse (OG 1042, ABV 4.2%) 🍶
Pale ale with grapefruit flavours.

Plain SIBA

17c Deverill Trading Estate, Sutton Veny, Wiltshire, BA12 7BZ
☎ (01985) 841481 ⊕ plainales.co.uk

⊠ Plain Ales started production in 2008 on a 2.5-barrel plant in a garage, and expanded to a 10-barrel plant in 2011 to keep up with demand for its award-winning ales. ‼◆

Sheep Dip (OG 1040, ABV 3.8%)
A session ale with a zesty start leading to a dry and hoppy finish.

Innocence (OG 1042, ABV 4%)
A straw-coloured, fragrant bitter.

Innspiration (OG 1042, ABV 4%)
A traditional, copper-coloured, easy-drinking bitter.

Inntrigue (OG 1044, ABV 4.2%)
Ruby-coloured best bitter with flavours of woodland berries and a whisper of dark chocolate.

Inncognito (OG 1053, ABV 4.8%) 🍶
A stout with sweet, roasted malt, aged port and mature fruits of the vine flavours.

Inndulgence (OG 1055, ABV 5.2%)
A dark ruby-coloured porter with coffee, chocolate and a hint of smoke.

Plan B (NEW)

Audley Avenue Enterprise Park, Audley Avenue, Newport, TF10 7DW
☎ (01952) 810091

☺ Plan B was set up in 2016 using a 10-barrel brew plant. ☞

Nova Gold (ABV 3.9%)

NPA (Newport Pale Ale) (ABV 4.4%)

Woodlands Midnight Stout (ABV 4.7%)

New India IPA (ABV 6%)

Platform 5 SIBA

Railway Brewhouse, 197 Queen Street, Newton Abbot, Devon, TQ12 2BS
☎ (01626) 437140 ⊕ platform5brewing.co.uk

⊠ Established in 2013 using a six-barrel plant. The Railway Inn is supplied along with Molloys in Teignmouth and Torquay. This family-run brewery is situated in part of an enclosed alley under the disused Platform 5 of Newton Abbot station. ◆

The Coaster (OG 1040, ABV 4%)
A light and refreshing session ale.

The Antelope (OG 1043, ABV 4.3%)
A hoppy pale ale.

APA (OG 1046, ABV 4.6%)

Plockton

5 Bank Street, Plockton, IV52 8TP
☎ (01599) 544276 ☎ 07823 322043
⊕ theplocktonbrewery.com

The brewery started trading in 2007 and expanded to a 2.5-barrel plant in 2009. ‼◆RAIB V

Ciste Dhubh (OG 1040, ABV 3.9%) ◣
Excellent mix of malts and hops in this dark brew. Initial bitter turning bittersweet.

Hitched (ABV 4.1%)

Bay (OG 1047, ABV 4.6%) ◣
A well-balanced, tawny-coloured best bitter with plenty of hops and malt which give a bittersweet fruity flavour.

Fiddlers Fancy (OG 1046, ABV 4.6%) ◣
Refreshing grapefruit aroma and taste turning to a more malty finish.

Serendipity (ABV 4.6%)

Starboard! (ABV 5.1%)

Ring Tong (ABV 5.6%)

Poachers

439 Newark Road, North Hykeham, Lincolnshire, LN6 9SP
☎ (01522) 807404 ☎ 07954 131972
⊕ poachersbrewery.co.uk

☺ Brewing started in 2001 on a five-barrel plant. In 2006 it was downsized to 2.5-barrel and relocated to outbuildings at the rear of the brewer's home. 2011 saw capacity returned to five barrels. Regular outlets in Lincolnshire and surrounding counties are supplied direct. ‼◆

Trembling Rabbit Mild (OG 1034, ABV 3.4%)
Rich, dark mild with a smooth, malty flavour and a slightly bitter finish. Local honey used.

Shy Talk Bitter (OG 1037, ABV 3.7%)
A crisp-tasting session beer, pale golden in colour. Refreshing with citrus overtones.

Rock Ape (OG 1038, ABV 3.8%)
Traditional brown-coloured session bitter.

Poachers Pride (OG 1040, ABV 4%)
Amber-coloured bitter with a fine hop flavour and an aroma that lingers.

Bog Trotter (OG 1042, ABV 4.2%)
An amber-coloured, full-flavoured, malty beer with a bitter aftertaste.

Lincoln Best (OG 1042, ABV 4.2%)
A flowery hop-nosed, brown-coloured beer with a well-balanced but bitter taste that stays with the malt, becoming more apparent in the drying finish.

Billy Boy (OG 1044, ABV 4.4%)
A rich, full-flavoured, brown-coloured beer.

Imp Ale (OG 1044, ABV 4.4%)
Copper-coloured, fruity and floral with a bitter finish.

Black Crow Stout (OG 1045, ABV 4.5%)
Full-bodied stout with burnt toffee and caramel flavours.

Hykeham Gold (OG 1045, ABV 4.5%)
A cask-conditioned lager.

Monkey Hanger (OG 1045, ABV 4.5%)
A ruby-coloured bitter with a smooth, fruity flavour balanced by hop bitterness.

Jock's Trap (OG 1050, ABV 5%)
A strong, pale brown-coloured bitter with a good hop flavour and aroma. A slightly dry fruit finish.

Trout Tickler (OG 1055, ABV 5.5%)
A strong, ruby-coloured bitter with intense flavour and character, sweet undertones with a hint of chocolate. A rich, malty beer.

Pokertree

The Brewhouse, 357b Drumnakilly Road, Carrickmore, Co Tyrone, BT79 9JY
☎ (028) 8076 1923 ⊕ pokertreebrewing.co.uk

Opened in 2014, Pokertree brews small batch beers using all natural and, where possible, local ingredients. RAIB

Ghrain Golden Ale (OG 1045, ABV 4.5%)

Seven Sisters Treacle Oat Stout (OG 1052, ABV 5.2%)

Red Earl Ruby Ale (OG 1055, ABV 5.5%)

Dark Nirvana (OG 1065, ABV 6.5%)

Polarity (NEW)

5 Abbotts Close, Worthing, West Sussex, BN11 1JB
☎ 07872 105300 ⊕ polaritybrewing.co.uk

A small brewery established in 2016 by two home-brewing enthusiasts.

Rosetta's Comet (OG 1052, ABV 5.4%)
A traditional IPA with a malt-forward flavour balanced with hops to give a lasting, bitter, fruity finish.

Pope's

73a, Blackpole Trading Estate West, Worcester, WR3 8TJ
☎ (01905) 755016 ✉ popesbrew@btconnect.com

Pope's is a family-run brewery established in 2012. A 4.5-barrel brew plant is used with brewing taking place twice a week, supplying the local free trade and further afield. Beer names are influenced by the local area. ‼ ▭ ♦ RAIB

Cavalier (OG 1036, ABV 3.6%)

Hop Market (OG 1038, ABV 3.8%)

Worcester Gold (OG 1040, ABV 4%)

Hope & Glory (OG 1046, ABV 4.6%)

Pope's Yard

477-479 Whippendell Road, Watford, Hertfordshire, WD18 7PU
☎ (01923) 510850 ⊕ popesyard.co.uk

Pope's Yard began commercial brewing in 2012 using a one-barrel plant. Relocation in 2015 also meant expansion to a five-barrel plant with a one-barrel pilot plant. RAIB

Luminaire (OG 1041, ABV 3.9%)
A hoppy beer with hints of citrus, passion fruit and pineapple and a classic bitter finish.

Quartermaster (OG 1044, ABV 4.4%)

Club Hammer Stout (OG 1060, ABV 5.5%)
A stout with a chocolate sweetness and rich, roast character.

Strong Dark Mild (OG 1063, ABV 6.8%)

Galaxian IPA (OG 1066, ABV 7.4%)

Poppyland

46 West Street, Cromer, Norfolk, NR27 9DS
☎ (01263) 513992 ☎ 07887 389804
⊕ poppylandbeer.com

Established in 2012 by Martin Warren as a working retirement project, the two-barrel plant produces unfiltered and vegan-friendly beers. Many of the beers are gluten-free, most are experimental and brewed with local wild ingredients such as damson, sea purslane, wild hops and dandelions. ▭ RAIB GF V

Porter Street

See Evan Evans

Portobello SIBA

Unit 6, Mitre Bridge Industrial Estate, Mitre Way, North Kensington, London, W10 6AU
☎ (020) 8969 2269 ⊕ portobellobrewing.com

⊠ Portobello began brewing in 2012 using a 10-barrel plant. ♦

Pale (OG 1040, ABV 4%) ⬧
Golden-coloured, well-balanced best bitter with citrus and spiced hops. Biscuit sweetness fades in the clean, dry finish becoming bitter.

Star (OG 1044, ABV 4.3%) ⬧
Pale brown-coloured malty best bitter with a sweetish nose, a fruity flavour and a bitter finish. Hints of nut on the palate and some hops throughout.

APA (OG 1050, ABV 5%) ⬧
Full-bodied, straw-coloured strong ale. The honey sweetness and soft citrus fruit are balanced by bitter hops. Dry aftertaste.

Portpatrick

The Neuk, Stoneykirk, DG9 9EF ☎ 07826 542149
⊕ portpatrick-brewery.co.uk

☺The brewery opened in 2015 using a 1.5-barrel plant in converted space in outbuildings. A number of local pubs are supplied. ♦

16-21 Bitter (OG 1040, ABV 3.8%)

Beltie Blonde (OG 1042, ABV 4%)

Dorn Rock Best Bitter (OG 1043, ABV 4.3%)

Gulf Stream Golden Ale (OG 1044, ABV 4.4%)

Fog Horn IPA (OG 1048, ABV 4.8%)

Potbelly SIBA 👁

Sydney Street Entrance, Kettering, Northamptonshire, NN16 0JA
☎ (01536) 410818 ☎ 07834 867825
⊕ potbelly-brewery.co.uk

Potbelly started brewing in 2005 on a 10-barrel plant and supplies some 200 outlets. ‼ ▭ ♦ RAIB GF V

Best (OG 1037, ABV 3.8%)

Hop-trotter (OG 1040, ABV 4.1%)
Golden in colour, spicy aromas and citrus notes.

Beijing Black (OG 1044, ABV 4.4%)

Pigs Do Fly (OG 1042, ABV 4.4%)

Hedonism (OG 1043, ABV 4.5%)
A light-coloured bitter with a citrus hoppy finish.

Captain Pigwash (OG 1048, ABV 5%)
An easy-drinking dark porter.

Crazy Daze (OG 1051, ABV 5.5%)

Powderkeg SIBA

10 Hogsbrook Units, Woodbury Salterton, Devon,
EX5 1PY
☎ (01395) 488181 ⊕ powderkegbeer.co.uk

⊠ Powderkeg was established in 2015 brewing
small batches of beer. It combines International
beer styles with new ingredients sourced from
around the world.

**Speak Easy Transatlantic Pale Ale
(OG 1041.5, ABV 4.3%)**
Uniting robust malt and fruitiness with balanced
bitterness and a clean finish.

Fours & Five5 (OG 1045, ABV 4.5%)
A bittersweet best bitter with a hoppy aftertaste.

Contract brewed for EMAL Brewery:

Castra (ABV 3.5%)
A session pale ale with a light malt base, gentle
bitterness and a well-rounded, hoppy finish.

Isca Gold (ABV 4%)
An easy-drinking golden ale balancing a hint of
caramel sweetness with a gentle bitter finish, and
a fruity hop aroma.

Legio (ABV 4.5%)
A full-bodied, mahogany-coloured ale with sweet
caramel notes, balanced bitterness and a rounded
hop finish.

Poynton SIBA

⬚ Royal British Legion Club, St George's Road West,
Poynton, Cheshire, SK12 1JY ☎ 07771 722403

The Poynton Brewery was established in 2015 by
Colin Bavens and Andy King, located at the Poynton
Legion Club. Around 20 pubs, clubs and bars are
supplied in the Stockport, Altrincham, East Cheshire
and Macclesfield areas.

Hoppy Daze (ABV 3.8%)
A zesty aroma with a crisp, dry finish.

Aurora (ABV 3.9%)
A well-rounded, refreshing bitter with a good dry
finish.

Citra Pale (ABV 4%)
An intense citrus and tropical fruit flavour.

Kiwi (ABV 4%)
A light golden-coloured beer with mellow fruit
flavours.

Chinook Pale (ABV 4.2%)
A refreshing pale ale with a distinctive grapefruit
hop character.

Idaho (ABV 4.2%)
A robust, fruity, thirst-quenching pale ale.

Vulcan (ABV 4.2%)
Traditional copper-coloured bitter with a satisfying,
balanced flavour.

Dark Side (ABV 4.5%)

A smooth and balanced dark-coloured beer with a
combination of chocolate and roast barley.

Mosaic Pale (ABV 4.5%)
A soft, clean bitterness and complex fruit flavour
with hints of berry.

Black Pearl (ABV 5%)
A rich, dark-coloured, aromatic chocolate stout.

Simcoe Red (ABV 5%)
A full-bodied, amber-coloured ale with woody,
pine, earthy and citrus characteristics.

Prescott SIBA

Unit 1, The Bramery Business Park, Alstone Lane,
Cheltenham, Gloucestershire, GL51 8HE ☎ 07526
934866 ⊕ prescottales.co.uk

Established in 2008, Prescott Ales brews on a 25-
barrel plant, clad in wood, brass and copper. It
takes its name from the famous Prescott Hill Climb,
which is also the home of the UK Bugatti Owners
Club. In 2015, a number of craft ales brewed under
the Super-6 banner was introduced. ‼◆

Hill Climb (OG 1039.5, ABV 3.8%)
A straw-coloured IPA-style session beer with a
refreshing fruity finish.

Chequered Flag (OG 1042, ABV 4.1%)
A well-hopped, amber-coloured ale with a malty
finish.

Track Record (OG 1044, ABV 4.4%)
A fruity, light copper-coloured best bitter with a
slightly sweet finish.

Grand Prix (OG 1050, ABV 5.2%)
A dark amber-coloured strong ale with a rich,
smooth finish.

Pressure Drop

Lockwood Industrial Estate, Mill Mead Road,
Tottenham Hale, London, N17 9QP
☎ (020) 8533 0614 ⊕ pressuredropbrewing.co.uk

Run by three partners who were home brewers but
began commercial brewing in 2013 using a five-
barrel plant and a small pilot kit. RAIB

Street Porter (ABV 5.2%) 🥄
Roast notes and a bitter character dominate this
black porter. Long, enjoyable aftertaste.

Priest Town (NEW)

139 Ribbleton Avenue, Preston, Lancashire, PR2 6YS
⊕ priesttownbrewing.com

Brewing began in 2017 using a 2.5-barrel plant. RAIB

Prior's Well SIBA

Unit 8, Block 21, Old Mill Lane Industrial Estate,
Mansfield Woodhouse, Nottinghamshire, NG19 9BQ
☎ (01623) 632393 ☎ 07970 885204
⊕ priorswellbrewery.co.uk

Originally established in a National Trust building
on the Clumber Park Estate, but brewing ceased
there in 2014. The brewery was subsequently sold
and the five-barrel plant modernised and relocated
to a new site in Mansfield Woodhouse in 2016 with
an on-site bar. ‼

Silver Chalice (OG 1014.7, ABV 4.2%)

A straw-coloured ale with a balanced hop flavour and good bitterness. Orange peel and coriander seed give further layers of flavour.

Blade (OG 1043.1, ABV 4.7%)

Priory Gold (OG 1045.2, ABV 4.7%)
Pale gold in colour with a citrus aroma and pleasant hop flavours culminating in an intense bitter finish.

Prior's Pale (OG 1047.1, ABV 4.8%)
A pale ale full of hop flavour with a lingering bitter finish.

Resurrected (OG 1046.7, ABV 4.8%)
Dark ruby in colour, complex nutty overtones, smooth classic English ale flavours with a dry finish.

Wolfcatcher (OG 1047.1, ABV 4.8%)
American-style pale ale with intense citrus, grapefruit tones.

Dirty Habit (OG 1054.4, ABV 5.8%)
An American-style IPA with a complex hop profile and pleasant maltiness.

Problem Child

🍺 Wayfarer Inn, Alder Lane, Parbold, Lancashire, WN8 7NL
☎ (01257) 464600 ☎ 07588 736926
⊕ problemchildbrewing.co.uk

Problem Child began brewing in 2013, at the Wayfarer Inn, Parbold, owned by Johnny and Rachel Birkett. A five-barrel plant is used.

Prospect SIBA 👁

Unit 10a, Great George Street, Off Wallgate, Wigan, WN3 4DL
☎ (01257) 421329 ⊕ prospectbrewery.com

☺Prospect brewery was founded as a five-barrel plant in 2007, extending capacity on relocation in 2010 and again relocating and moving their 12-barrel plant to its present premises in 2017. The brewery features an on-site bar as well as owning a popular local bar, Wigan Central. ♦

Silver Tally (OG 1037, ABV 3.7%)
A clean, pale golden-coloured bitter with citrus aromas and a full hop flavour with a dry bitter finish.

Whatever! (OG 1040, ABV 3.8%)
Pale bitter packed with hop flavour and aroma.

Nutty Slack (OG 1039, ABV 3.9%) 🍷 🍂
Mild ale with malt and fruit in the aroma. Creamy and chocolaty on the palate, with both malt and fruit in evidence. Malty and moderately bitter finish.

Pioneer (OG 1040, ABV 4%)
A light-bodied, amber-coloured beer with aromas of dry pale malt and earthy hops.

Cascade Blonde (OG 1039, ABV 4.1%)
A yellow/gold-coloured beer with zesty citrus notes; clean and refreshing lemon taste.

Blinding Light (OG 1042, ABV 4.2%)
A pale, refreshing beer with citrus and spicy notes.

Gold Rush (OG 1045, ABV 4.5%)
A deep golden-coloured ale with hoppy and bitter flavours, light fruity notes and a grassy floral finish.

Big John (OG 1047, ABV 4.8%)

A dark-coloured stout bursting with smoky liquorice flavour with a satisfying bitter aftertaste.

Pumphouse

🍺 Green Man, Church Lane, Toppesfield, Essex, CO9 4DR ☎ 07421 994518
⊕ pumphousecommunitybrewery.com

Community-owned brewery established in 2015. Most of the output is sold in the Green Man, with the rest supplied to other local outlets. Experimental beers are added to the range if popular.

Purity SIBA 👁

The Brewery, Upper Spernal Farm, Spernal Lane, Great Alne, Warwickshire, B49 6JF
☎ (01789) 488007 ⊕ puritybrewing.com

☺Brewing began in 2005 in a purpose-designed plant housed in converted barns. The brewery incorporates an environmentally-friendly effluent treatment system. It supplies the free trade within a 70-mile radius, plus London postcodes, and delivers to more than 500 outlets. ‼🍺♦

Bunny Hop (OG 1037, ABV 3.5%)

Pure Gold (OG 1039.5, ABV 3.8%) 🍷
An easy-drinking beer with a dry and bitter finish.

Mad Goose (OG 1042.5, ABV 4.2%)
Light copper in colour with a zesty hop character and citrus overtones.

Pure UBU (OG 1044.8, ABV 4.5%)
A full-flavoured, well-balanced, premium amber-coloured beer.

Purple Moose SIBA 👁

Madoc Street, Porthmadog, LL49 9DB
☎ (01766) 515571 ⊕ purplemoose.co.uk

Purple Moose opened in 2005 using a 10-barrel plant in a former iron works in the coastal town of Porthmadog. In 2013 a new 40-barrel plant was installed, significantly increasing production. The names of the beers reflect local history and geography. ‼🍺♦

**Cwrw Eryri/Snowdonia Ale
(OG 1035.3, ABV 3.6%)** 🍂
Golden-coloured, refreshing bitter with citrus fruit hoppiness in aroma and taste. The full mouthfeel leads to a long-lasting, dry bitter finish.

**Cwrw Madog/Madog's Ale
(OG 1037, ABV 3.7%)** 🍂
Full-bodied session bitter. Malty nose and an initial nutty flavour but bitterness dominates. Well balanced and refreshing with a dry roastiness on the taste and a good dry finish.

**Cwrw Ysgawen/Elderflower
(OG 1039, ABV 4%)** 🍶 🍂
A pale and refreshing elderflower beer with a good citrus fruit aroma, bittersweet taste, and a zesty, hoppy, mouthwatering finish.

**Cwrw Glaslyn/Glaslyn Ale
(OG 1040.5, ABV 4.2%)** 🍂
Refreshing light and malty, amber-coloured ale. Plenty of hop in the aroma and taste. Good smooth mouthfeel leading to a slightly chewy finish.

Ochr Tywyll y Mws/Dark Side of the Moose (OG 1045, ABV 4.6%) 🍺 ◈
A dark, complex beer quite hoppy and bitter with roast undertones. Malt and fruit flavours also feature in the smooth taste and dry finish.

Q

16 The Ringway, Queniborough, Leicestershire, LE7 3DL ☎ 07762 300240 ⊕ qbrewery.co.uk

A microbrewery situated in a converted building behind the house of head brewer Tim Lowe. It was established in 2014 and uses a 0.5-barrel brew kit. Beers are brewed on demand.

Quantock 👁

Westridge Way, Broadgauge Business Park, Bishops Lydeard, Somerset, TA4 3RU
☎ (01823) 433812 ⊕ quantockbrewery.co.uk

Quantock is a family-run brewery that started trading in 2008 on an eight-barrel plant. The brewery supplies beers to outlets throughout the South-west and further afield via wholesalers.
🚲◈RAIB

Ale (OG 1036, ABV 3.8%)
An amber-coloured beer with a fruity, full-bodied flavour and a dry finish to the palate. The blend of English hops creates a balanced, fruity character with a delicate spicy aroma.

Ginger Cockney (OG 1037, ABV 4%)
A copper-coloured ale with a hint of fresh ginger.

Rorke's Drift (OG 1039, ABV 4.2%)
A light, refreshing, lager-style beer. A fruit-filled experience with a delicate citrus aroma.

Sunraker (OG 1039, ABV 4.2%)
A pale straw-coloured beer, light and refreshing with a delicate, clean grassy hop finish.

Wills Neck (OG 1040, ABV 4.3%)
A golden ale with a malty flavour with aromas of grapefruit and cherries and a lasting bitterness on the palate.

White Hind (OG 1042, ABV 4.5%)
A best bitter with a full-bodied, malty flavour, a dry finish and a biscuity, spicy aroma.

Stag (OG 1056, ABV 6%)
A copper-coloured beer with a malty, fruity flavour and a smoky aroma with hints of banana and toffee.

UXB (OG 1088, ABV 9%)
A strong beer, slightly sweet with a full, malty flavour.

Quartz SIBA 👁

Archers, Alrewas Road, Kings Bromley, Staffordshire, DE13 7HW
☎ (01543) 473965 ⊕ quartzbrewing.co.uk

☺Quartz was established in 2005 by Scott and Julia Barnett. Around 50 outlets are supplied direct.
‼🚲◈

Blonde (OG 1038, ABV 3.8%) ◈
Little aroma, gentle hop and background malt. Sweet with unsophisticated sweetshop tastes.

Crystal (OG 1040, ABV 4.2%) ◈

Sweet aroma with some fruit and yeasty Marmite hints. Hoppiness begins but dwindles to a bittersweet finish.

Extra Blonde (OG 1042, ABV 4.4%) ◈
Sweet malty aroma with a touch of fruit. Sweet start, smooth with a hint of hops in the sugary finish.

Heart (OG 1045, ABV 4.6%) ◈
Pale brown in colour with some aroma of fruit and malt. Gentle tastes of fruit and hops eventually appear to leave a bitter finish.

Cracker (OG 1050, ABV 5%)
Chestnut in colour with a slight roasted aroma, smooth fruit notes leaving a dry hop finish.

Queen Inn

🏠 28 Kingsgate Road, Winchester, Hampshire, SO23 9PG
☎ (01962) 853898 ⊕ thequeeninnwinchester.co.uk

Brewing began in 2014 using a 1.5-barrel brew plant. At present beers are only brewed for the pub.

Queens Head

🏠 Queen's Head, 66 Acton Street, St Pancras, London, WC1X 9NB
☎ (020) 7713 5772

Situated in the basement of the Queen's Head pub, brewing began in 2014. Beer is mainly keg and supplied direct to the pub. Brewing is currently suspended.

Quiet

🏠 Buchanan's Bistro, Banchory, AB31 5QA
☎ (01330) 826530 ⊕ buchananfood.com

Quiet Brewery is situated at Buchanan's Bistro. Beers are available bottle-conditioned only and are supplied to the bistro and local outlets.

Quirky

Units 3 & 4, Ash Lane, Garforth, Leeds, West Yorkshire, LS25 2HG
☎ (0113) 286 2072 ⊕ quirkyales.com

☺Established in 2015, Quirky Ales brews only ten or so nine-gallon firkins at a time. A tap room and bottle shop opened in 2016. ‼🚲◈RAIB V

Porter (ABV 3.5%)
A smooth, dark-coloured ale with a malty finish.

Blonde (ABV 3.8%)
A light, crisp, refreshing beer with a tropical citrus finish.

Pilsner (ABV 3.8%)

Bitter (ABV 4%)
An easy-drinking session bitter with well-balanced malt and hops.

Ruby (ABV 4%)
A classic bitter with a crisp flavour.

Gold (ABV 4.1%)
An easy-drinking, light golden-coloured ale with a citrus flavour and caramel finish.

Long Hop (ABV 4.2%)

A thirst-quenching, aromatic IPA with a classic American hop finish.

Black IPA (ABV 4.8%)

Phoenix (ABV 5.3%)
Brewed with a special malt for a distinctive smoky flavour.

Radlett

See Watling Street

Radnorshire SIBA

Timberwork, Brookside Farm, Mutton Dingle, New Radnor, LD8 2SU
☎ (01544) 350456 ☎ 07789 909748
⊕ radnorhillsholidaycottages.com

⊛Set up in 2012 in a barn on the grounds of a farm offering holiday cottage accommodation, Radnorshire uses its own spring water. Drinkers staying at the cottages are supplied as well as a few local pubs. ‼️ 🍺

Whimble Gold (OG 1038, ABV 3.8%)
Light and hoppy golden ale.

Four Stones (OG 1040, ABV 4%)
A light amber-coloured ale with a subtle maltiness.

Smatcher Tawny (OG 1042, ABV 4.2%)
Mellow, tawny-coloured best bitter.

Water-Break-Its-Neck (ABV 5.7%)
A well-hopped IPA.

Rail Ale

See Reynolds

Ralph's Ruin (NEW)

🍴 c/o Royal Oak, Lower Bristol Road, Bath, BA2 3BW
☎ (01225) 481409

Brewing commenced in 2017 using a two-barrel plant in the old kitchen of the Royal Oak. Beer is only available in the pub.

Ramsbottom Craft SIBA ⊚

1 Heapworth Avenue, Ramsbottom, BL0 9EH
☎ 07976 263344 ⊕ rammycraft.com

Established in a garage in 2011, the brewery began full time production in 2014 with cask ale distribution being around the North-west. Larger premises are being sought in order to expand from its current 2.5-barrel plant. Beers are sold under the Rammy Craft name. ◆ RAIB

Stellar IPA (OG 1040, ABV 3.7%)
Refreshing, medium-bodied ale with an intensely fruity finish.

Waterfall Pale (OG 1041, ABV 3.9%)

Bumble's Honeyed Ale (OG 1039, ABV 4%)
Elderflower and honey based EPA.

Rammy Ale (OG 1041, ABV 4%)

Flaori Maori (OG 1042, ABV 4.1%)
Balanced session ale, initial light malt gives way to increasingly red fruit finish.

Chocolate Porter (OG 1043, ABV 4.2%)

Yankie Lip Smacka (OG 1042, ABV 4.2%)

Fat Lady Stout (OG 1043, ABV 4.3%)
Dark brown, almost black-coloured stout with a hint of roast in the aroma and a smooth taste.

Crafty Ram (OG 1045, ABV 4.4%)

Oh Sunny Day (OG 1046, ABV 4.5%)
A pale yellow-coloured, mellow ale with balanced malt sweetness and fruitiness.

Mango Beach (OG 1054, ABV 5.5%)

Ramsbury SIBA ⊚

Stockclose Farm, Aldbourne, Wiltshire, SN8 2NN
☎ (01672) 541407 ☎ 07843 289527
⊕ ramsbury.com/brewery

⊗ The Ramsbury Brewing & Distilling Company started brewing in 2004 using a 10-barrel plant, situated high on the Marlborough Downs in Wiltshire. The brewery uses home-grown barley from the Ramsbury Estate. Expansion in 2014 saw an upgrade to a 30-barrel plant with a visitor centre and a well to provide the water. A distillery that uses grains grown on the estate became operational in 2015. ‼️ 🍺◆

Bitter (OG 1036, ABV 3.6%)
Amber-coloured beer with a smooth, delicate aroma and flavour.

Popham's Pride (ABV 3.6%)
An amber-coloured ale with a smooth, delicate flavour.

Same Again (ABV 3.8%)
Pale amber-coloured ale with a citrus finish.

Deerstalker (OG 1040, ABV 4%)
Amber-coloured best bitter with a smooth bitter finish.

Kennet Valley (OG 1041, ABV 4.1%)
A light amber-coloured, hoppy bitter with a long, dry finish.

Flint Knapper (OG 1042, ABV 4.2%)
Rich amber in colour with a malty taste.

Gold (OG 1045, ABV 4.5%)
A rich golden-coloured beer with a light, hoppy aroma and taste.

Chalk Stream (OG 1050, ABV 5%)
Pale, lightly-hopped premium ale.

Belapur IPA (OG 1055, ABV 5.5%)
English-style, well-hopped IPA with a fruity, citrus finish.

Ramsgate SIBA ⊚

1 Hornet Close, Pyson's Road Industrial Estate, Broadstairs, Kent, CT10 2YD
☎ (01843) 868453 ⊕ ramsgatebrewery.co.uk

Ramsgate was established in 2002 at the back of a Ramsgate pub. In 2006 the brewery moved to its current location, allowing for increased capacity and bottling. ‼️ 🍺◆ RAIB

Gadds' No. 7 Bitter Ale (OG 1037, ABV 3.8%)

Gadds' Seasider (OG 1042, ABV 4.3%)

Gadds' No. 5 Best Bitter Ale (OG 1043, ABV 4.4%)

Gadds' No. 3 Kent Pale Ale (OG 1047, ABV 5%) 🍺

Gadds' Faithful Dogbolter Porter (OG 1054, ABV 5.6%)

Gadds' Black Pearl (OG 1062, ABV 6.2%)

RAN SIBA

Unit 8, Ormonde Street, Fenton, Stoke-on-Trent, Staffordshire, ST4 3NP ☎ 07843 092620
⊕ ranales.co.uk

⊗ Brewing began in 2014 using a one-barrel kit in the garage to the rear of the owner's house. It relocated in 2015 to larger, purpose-built premises nearby, increasing capacity to 2.5 barrels. ♦

Coppa Flya (OG 1040, ABV 4%)
A copper-coloured bitter with a dry finish and a complementary caramel aftertaste.

American Pale Ale (OG 1045, ABV 4.5%)

Flya (OG 1045, ABV 4.5%)
Easy-drinking session ale. Amber in colour with a malty bitterness.

Hedge Hopper (OG 1045, ABV 4.5%)
A light golden-coloured bitter with refreshing fruity notes.

Owd Flya (OG 1050, ABV 5%) ◆
Malt and roast aromas. Liquorice flavours, sweet finish with gentle hops.

Cherry Chilli Stout (OG 1053, ABV 5.3%)

Rum 'n' Raisin Stout (OG 1053, ABV 5.3%) ◆
Chocolate aroma with cocoa. Sweet fruity start with hoppy background which develops to a mouthwatering finish.

Stout (OG 1053, ABV 5.3%)
Rich and flavoursome dark ale with hints of coffee and chocolate.

Randalls SIBA

La Piette Brewery, St Georges Esplanade, St Peter Port, Guernsey, GY1 3JG
☎ (01481) 720134 ⊕ randallsbrewery.com

Randalls has been brewing in Guernsey since 1868. The company was bought out in 2006 and moved into a modern, purpose-built brewery in 2008. 19 pubs are owned and a further 70 outlets are supplied. ‼◆

Range SIBA

Unit N4, Lympne Industrial Estate, Otterpool Lane, Lympne, Kent, CT21 4LR
☎ (01303) 230842 ☎ 07912 207775
⊕ rangealesbrewery.co.uk

⊗ Range Ales was planned and set up in 2016 by two friends over a few pints in their local. The brewery name comes from associations with the Hythe small arms ranges nearby, which provides the names of the beers. A four-barrel plant is used to supply pubs and clubs in the Hythe and Folkestone areas. ‼

Golden Shot (ABV 3.7%)
Hoppy, citrus flavour.

CQB (ABV 4%)
English pale ale with sharp, hoppy note to the nose and the tastes of lemon sorbet to follow.

One in the Chambers (ABV 4%)

Double Tap (ABV 4.1%)
A sweetish, gentle hop aftertaste.

Black Ops (ABV 4.8%)

A modern black IPA with a smooth coffee-like finish.

Rat

⊟ Rat & Ratchet, 40 Chapel Hill, Huddersfield, West Yorkshire, HD1 3EB
☎ (01484) 542400 ☎ 07906 279038
✉ ratandratchet@ossett-brewery.co.uk

The Rat & Ratchet was originally established as a brewpub in 1994. Brewing ceased and it was purchased by Ossett Brewery (qv) in 2004. Brewing re-started in 2011 with a capacity of 30 barrels per week.

Raw SIBA

Units 3 & 4, Silver House, Adelphi Way, Staveley, Derbyshire, S43 3LJ
☎ (01246) 475445 ⊕ rawbrew.com

Raw began brewing in 2010 using a five-barrel plant, upgraded in 2016 to a 15-barrel one. Specials are available including the Xtreme range, which are one-off brews that push the ingredients a little further. ‼◆ GF

Baby Ghost IPA (OG 1039, ABV 3.9%)
Powerful, citrus-hopped session IPA.

Independence American Pale (ABV 4.1%)

JR Best Bitter (OG 1042, ABV 4.2%)
Traditional brown-coloured bitter with sweet biscuit malt flavours. Smooth, balanced bitterness

Edge American Pale (OG 1045, ABV 4.3%)

Dark Peak Stout (OG 1045, ABV 4.5%)
Easy-drinking stout with plenty of malt flavours and a smooth bitter finish.

Anubis Porter (OG 1051, ABV 5.2%) ⬚
Smooth roast malt and mild coffee flavours with a lingering bitterness and gentle hop aroma.

Grey Ghost IPA (OG 1056, ABV 5.9%)
Powerful American-hopped IPA with citrus and grapefruit flavours. Smooth and deceptively easy to drink.

Reality

127 High Road, Chilwell, Nottingham, NG9 4AT
☎ 07801 539523
✉ alandenismonaghan@hotmail.com

Reality began brewing in 2009 in the unused space of an IT business, hence the pun on Real-ITy. Core beers are mainly themed around the brewery name and can be found locally and at beer festivals across the country. ♦

Virtuale Reality (OG 1039, ABV 3.8%)
A pale session brew.

No Escape (OG 1043, ABV 4.2%)

Bitter Reality (OG 1044, ABV 4.3%)

Stark Reality (OG 1046, ABV 4.5%)
Amber-coloured bitter with a hint of rum.

Reality Czech (OG 1047, ABV 4.6%)

Rebel

Century House, Kernick Industrial Estate, Penryn, Cornwall, TR10 9EP
☎ (01326) 379362 ⊕ rebelbrewing.co.uk

⊠ Rebel began brewing in 2011. It expanded to a nine-barrel plant with a shop and bar in 2012, supplying local pubs. In 2015 an 18-barrel plant was installed to meet local and national demand. **‼ ⬛ ♦ RAIB**

Surf Bum IPA (OG 1034, ABV 3.5%) ◣
Gold-coloured session bitter with a fruity hop nose. Dominant hop bitterness with a hint of apples, apricots and grassy grapefruit. Lingering hop bitterness.

Bal Maiden (OG 1041, ABV 4%) ◣
Pale brown-coloured best bitter with malt aroma. Full malt and bitter ale with apple and lemon flavours. Lingering bittersweet finish.

Sail Ale Golden Ale (OG 1041, ABV 4%) ◣
Gold-coloured best bitter. Balanced malt and bitter, grapefruit citrus hop flavour. Malt fades, with grassy hops and rising dryness at the end.

Penryn Pale Ale (OG 1043, ABV 4.3%) ◣
Amber-coloured best bitter with hop and mango nose. Bitter taste, fruit, biscuit malt and toffee. Short, fresh hop bitter finish.

Eighty Shilling (OG 1051, ABV 5%) ◣
A dark brown-coloured porter with roast malt aroma. Roast and biscuit malt balanced by sweet plum and bitterness. Long finish.

Mexi-Cocoa Choc-Vanilla Stout (ABV 7.2%)

Rebellion SIBA

Rebellion Brewery, Bencombe Farm, Marlow Bottom, Buckinghamshire, SL7 3LT
☎ (01628) 476594 ⊕ rebellionbeer.co.uk

⊠ Established in 1993, Rebellion has grown steadily with one site move and several expansion projects, including an on-site shop. It currently brews approximately 100,000 pints per week, supplying more than 400 local pubs and clubs within a 30-mile radius of Marlow. **‼ ⬛ ♦**

IPA (OG 1039, ABV 3.7%) ◣
Copper-coloured bitter, sweet and malty, with resinous and red apple flavours. Caramel and fruit decline to leave a dry, bitter and malty finish.

Smuggler (OG 1042, ABV 4.2%) ◣
A red/brown-coloured beer, well-bodied and bitter with an uncompromisingly dry, bitter finish.

Roasted Nuts (OG 1046, ABV 4.6%)
A deep ruby-coloured, complex winter warmer, packed with intense malt and hop character.

Zebedee (OG 1047, ABV 4.7%)
A clean and fresh, straw-coloured pale ale with a crisp bitterness and a tropical fruit aroma.

Recoil (NEW)

Unit 9, Lincoln Park, Salthill Industrial Estate, Clitheroe, Lancashire, BB7 1QD
☎ (01200) 613777 ⊕ recoilbrewing.com

☺Recoil began brewing in 2017. 70 outlets are supplied direct.

Back to Best (OG 1038, ABV 3.8%)
A traditional amber-coloured Yorkshire session ale.

Blonde Avenger (OG 1039, ABV 3.9%)
A blonde beer with fruity undertones and a citrus finish.

Collision Pilsner (OG 1038, ABV 4%)

Boomslang Pale (OG 1041, ABV 4.1%)
A full-bodied, well-rounded ale with a distinctive hoppy palate and aroma.

Rectory SIBA

Streat Hill Farm, Streat Hill, Streat, East Sussex, BN6 8RP
☎ (01273) 890570 ⊠ rectoryales@hotmail.com

⊠ Rectory was founded in 1995 by the Rev Godfrey Broster to generate funds for the maintenance of his three parish churches. 107 parishioners are shareholders. Production is split between Streat Hill Farm (specials/seasonal beers) and Harvey's Brewery (qv) microplant. **‼ ♦**

Rector's Light Relief (OG 1045, ABV 4.5%)
Golden ale with a fresh, floral aroma and distinctly hoppy, bitter characteristics.

The Rector's Revenge (OG 1050, ABV 5%)
Traditional-style strong bitter with a good balance of malt and hops and a long, bitter finish.

Red Cat SIBA

Unit 10, Sun Valley Business Park, Winnall Close, Winchester, Hampshire, SO23 0LB
☎ (01962) 863423 ☎ 07824 876489
⊕ redcatbrewing.co.uk

Established in 2014 by Andy Mansell and Iain McIntosh using an 11-barrel plant. It supplies Hampshire and bordering counties. A small bar sells a range of products. **⬛ ♦**

Prowler Pale (OG 1034.5, ABV 3.6%) ◣
A refreshing, light session bitter, predominantly hoppy with some malt and a dry bitter finish.

Bitter (OG 1037, ABV 3.7%) ◣
A fresh, hoppy bitter, light brown in colour with an enticing hoppy aroma and a lasting dryness throughout.

Scratch (ABV 4%)

Best (OG 1042.3, ABV 4.2%)
A traditional best bitter with a deep red/bronze colour and a rounded malty flavour.

Mr M's Porter (OG 1050, ABV 4.5%)
Aromas of chocolate, vanilla and soft coffee. Full in the mouth yet surprisingly easy to drink.

TomCat (OG 1044.4, ABV 4.7%)
A golden-coloured premium ale with a full hop flavour that is not overly bitter.

MaCavity (OG 1055.5, ABV 5.3%)

Red Fox SIBA

The Chicken Sheds, Upp Hall Farm, Salmons Lane, Coggeshall, Essex, CO6 1RY
☎ (01376) 563123 ⊕ redfoxbrewery.co.uk

Red Fox began brewing in 2008 and has continued to expand in line with increasing demand. Brewery experience days are available. Numerous local pubs stocks the beers. **‼ ♦ RAIB**

Mild (OG 1037, ABV 3.6%)
A classic dark-coloured, full-flavoured mild with hints of chocolate and a deep roast barley flavour.

IPA (OG 1038, ABV 3.7%)
An East Anglian-style copper-coloured beer with a delicate flavour.

Bitter (OG 1039, ABV 3.8%)
A traditional-style bitter which perfectly balances malt and fruit flavours.

Hunter's Gold (OG 1040, ABV 3.9%)
A golden-coloured beer with a delicate citrus aroma.

Best Bitter (OG 1040, ABV 4%)
A light brown-coloured best bitter with a full flavour and malty backbone.

Coggeshall Gold (OG 1041, ABV 4%)
An aromatic golden-coloured beer, packed full of citrus and exotic fruit flavours.

Surrex Gold (OG 1041, ABV 4.1%)
A highly-hopped, aromatic beer. Pink grapefruit and peach aromas abound leading to a slightly bitter finish.

Black Fox Porter (OG 1046, ABV 4.8%) 🍺
A rich-flavoured, black-coloured beer packed with malty flavour and undertones of chocolate.

Wily Ol' Fox (OG 1050, ABV 5.2%)
An aromatic, amber-coloured traditional IPA made from English hops and malt with a soft, fruity palate.

Ruby Red Mild (OG 1065, ABV 6.9%)
A dark ruby mild, full bodied and rounded.

Red Hand

⬛ 38 Main Street, Donaghmore, County Tyrone, BT70 3EZ ☎ 07748 637056

Established in 2013, Red Hand Brewing Company forms part of the award-winning Brewers House pub in Donaghmore, County Tyrone.

Red Kite (NEW) SIBA

Unit 1, Tweed Road Trading Estate, Clevedon, Somerset, BS21 6RR ☎ 07802 702367
✉ tuckers@redkitebrewing.co.uk

Founded in the Chilterns by Howard Tucker in 2016, the brewery relocated to Clevedon, Somerset, in 2017.

Golden Dawn (ABV 4%)

Tucker's Tipple (ABV 4.1%)

Tucker's Nuts (ABV 4.5%)

Red SIBA 👁

Unit 1, The Orchard, Garden Farm, The Town, Great Staughton, Cambridgeshire, PE19 5BE ☎ 07557 207013 ⊕ redbrewery.com

Red Brewery was established using a four-barrel plant in 2012 in a converted farm building in the village of Great Staughton. ♦RAIB

One Brown Mouse (OG 1041, ABV 4%)
Brown-coloured session ale. Caramel and toffee flavours.

Pathfinder (OG 1045, ABV 4.8%)
Amber-coloured ale with orange and grapefruit notes.

Sundial Gold (OG 1046, ABV 4.8%)
Golden ale with a balanced, deep hop character.

White Duck (OG 1045, ABV 4.8%)
Pale, highly-hopped ale with grapefruit and melon flavours.

Staughton Bitter (OG 1050, ABV 5.2%)
Copper-coloured hoppy bitter with light fruit notes.

Kangaroo (OG 1053, ABV 5.4%)
Garnet-coloured ale. Light hop, floral and slightly sweet.

Valhalla (OG 1053, ABV 5.5%)
Bronze-coloured strong beer with a rounded fruit taste.

Red Rock SIBA

Higher Humber Farm, Bishopsteignton, Devon, TQ14 9TD
☎ (01626) 879738 ⊕ redrockbrewery.co.uk

⊠ Red Rock first started brewing in 2006 with a four-barrel plant and upgraded in 2011 to a 7.5-barrel one. It is based in a converted barn on a working farm using locally-sourced malt, fresh hops and the farm's own spring water. It has a bar and can accommodate private functions. ‼🛒♦RAIB

Back Beach (OG 1038, ABV 3.8%)
A golden-coloured beer with a crisp and clean finish.

Red Rock (OG 1041, ABV 4.2%)

Red Shoot

⬛ Toms Lane, Linwood, Ringwood, Hampshire, BH24 3QT
☎ (01425) 475792 ⊕ redshoot.co.uk

The 2.5-barrel brewery was commissioned in 1998 and can be viewed from inside the pub. Most of the output is sold in the pub, but sometimes the beers are made available to Wadworth outlets.

Red Squirrel

See Mad Squirrel

Red Star SIBA 👁

54b Stephenson Way, Formby Business Park, Formby, Merseyside, L37 8EG
☎ (01704) 461120 ☎ 07899 904270
⊕ redstarbrewery.co.uk

Production started in 2015 using a 10-barrel plant. Pubs and bars are supplied in Merseyside and the wider North-west region. ♦

Formby Blonde (ABV 3.9%)
A light ale with a malty base and an orange peel finish.

Formby IPA (ABV 4%)
A session IPA with a hint of elderflower.

Lakota (ABV 4.1%)
An amber-coloured ale with a smooth, sweet edge.

Havana Moon (ABV 4.2%)
An oatmeal stout with notes of chocolate, coffee and raisins.

Samba (ABV 4.7%)
An easy-drinking, golden-coloured premium ale.

Hurricane (ABV 4.8%)
A premium copper-coloured ale with a bittersweet finish.

Weissbier (ABV 5.3%)
A naturally cloudy wheat beer with big hitting orange and coriander flavours.

Partisan (ABV 5.4%)
Dark chestnut in colour with a smooth and malty finish following a flavour combo of mocha and caramel.

Redcastle (NEW) SIBA

Drummygar Mains, Carmyllie, DD11 2RA
☎ (01241) 860516 ☎ 07967 226357
⊕ redcastlebrewery.co.uk

⊠ Established by local farmer and Clydesdale horse breeder John Anderson, Redcastle started brewing in rural Angus in 2016 in a purpose-built brewery on the family farm. The brewery takes its name from the nearby ruined 'red castle' at Lunan Bay and the beers are named accordingly with a historic theme. In addition to the 10-barrel plant, the brewery also includes a bottling line. RAIB

Crusader (OG 1043, ABV 4%)

Red Lady (OG 1044, ABV 4%)

Nobleman (OG 1042, ABV 4.2%)

Tower IPA (OG 1046, ABV 4.8%)
American-style IPA with a fruity aroma and a hint of toffee on the palate.

Redchurch

275-276 Poyser Street, Bethnal Green, London, E2 9RF
☎ (020) 3487 0255 ⊕ theredchurchbrewery.com

Redchurch was established in 2011 using an eight-barrel plant and is situated in a pair of units under the railway arches in Bethnal Green. A second brewery in Harlow is also in operation. No real ale.
🍺

Redemption Brew SIBA

Unit 16, Compass West Industrial Estate, 33 West Road, Tottenham, London, N17 0XL
☎ (020) 8885 5227 ⊕ redemptionbrewing.co.uk

⊠ Redemption began brewing in 2010 on a 12-barrel plant. In 2016 it moved into a larger unit with a 30-barrel plant and a tasting room (open to the public on Saturdays). Most of the beer is supplied in cask to pubs in north and central London and to beer festivals. ‼🍺◆RAIB

Trinity (OG 1036.6, ABV 3%)
Refreshing golden-coloured beer with strong citrus notes throughout. The strong bitterness is softened by a little sweet malt character.

Pale Ale (OG 1037.5, ABV 3.8%) 🍺
Well-balanced, amber-coloured bitter with peppery hops and citrus throughout. Sweet toffee and fruit fades in the slightly dry bitter finish.

Rock the Kazbek (ABV 4%)
A blonde, single-hopped ale with refreshing, zesty lemon, lime and grapefruit flavours and a delicate lemon aroma.

Hopspur (OG 1044.5, ABV 4.5%) 🍺
Smooth, brown-coloured best bitter. Sweet coffee roast notes, a little nuttiness with resinous hops on the flavour. Dry bitter finish.

Urban Dusk (OG 1044.5, ABV 4.6%) 🍺
Full-bodied, brown-coloured best bitter; chocolate and fudge in the aroma and flavour overlaid with citrus. Lingering, dry bitter finish.

Fellowship Porter (OG 1051.5, ABV 5.1%) 🍺
Sweetish, smooth porter. Liquorice, treacle and caramelised fruit balances the dry, dark roast coffee and chocolate notes in the flavour.

Big Chief (OG 1052.5, ABV 5.5%) 🍺
Golden ale with a smooth mouthfeel and a strong fruity aroma, flavour and finish, which is also dry and bitter.

Redscar SIBA

⊟ c/o Cleveland Hotel, 9-11 High Street West, Redcar, North Yorkshire, TS10 1SQ
☎ (01642) 513727 ☎ 07828 855146
⊕ redscar-brewery.co.uk

Redscar first brewed in 2008. In 2014 it increased its capacity to a five-barrel plant. The brewery supplies the hotel, local pubs and beer festivals.

Redwell SIBA

7 The Arches, Bracondale, Trowse Millgate, Norwich, NR1 2EF
☎ (01603) 624072 ⊕ redwellbrewing.com

⊠ Redwell began brewing in 2013 using a 10-barrel plant. Production is mostly keg or bottled but occasional cask-conditioned ales are produced for beer festivals or by special request for local outlets.
‼

RedWillow SIBA

The Lodge, Sutton Garrison, Byrons Lane, Macclesfield, Cheshire, SK11 7JW
☎ (01625) 502315 ⊕ redwillowbrewery.com

☺Established in 2010 by home brewer Toby McKenzie and his wife Caroline. In 2015 brewing moved to a larger, purpose-built unit on the same site. The award-winning beers are distributed nationwide and are available from the brewery's own RedWillow bar in Macclesfield. Experimental brews are branded under the Faithless and Clueless labels. ◆RAIB

Seamless (OG 1034, ABV 3.6%)
A light and hoppy pale ale.

Headless (OG 1037, ABV 3.9%)
Refreshingly floral pale ale with a restrained orange-led bitterness and a light, straw-hued colour.

Stateless (OG 1038, ABV 3.9%)
A classic English session ale, well-rounded with citrus, pine and grapefruit notes.

Feckless (OG 1040, ABV 4.1%)
A classic best bitter, rich toffee and malt balanced with subtle hop flavours.

Directionless (OG 1041, ABV 4.2%)
A balanced session ale, warm amber in colour with a subtle candied orange fruitiness.

Weightless (OG 1042, ABV 4.2%)
A session IPA with pithy grapefruit and mango flavours and a well-rounded body.

Wreckless (OG 1046, ABV 4.8%)
A hoppy pale ale with a big tropical fruit flavour and a clean finish.

Sleepless (OG 1052, ABV 5.4%)
Rich toffee malt flavours followed by juicy hops and a long, clean bitter finish.

Smokeless (OG 1055, ABV 5.7%)
A smooth, smoky porter infused with chipotle.

Shameless (OG 1055, ABV 5.9%)
An American-style IPA.

Reedley Hallows SIBA

Unit B3, Farrington Close, Farrington Road Industrial Estate, Burnley, Lancashire, BB11 5SH ☎ 07749 414513 ⊕ reedley-hallows-brewery.co.uk

☺Brewing started on this four-barrel plant in 2012. Having moved to larger premises the brewery now has nine fermenters to cope with demand. ‼

Old Laund Bitter (OG 1038, ABV 3.6%)
A good session beer, smooth and creamy with a distinctive hoppy aftertaste.

Filly Close Blonde (OG 1040, ABV 3.9%)
A well-balanced ale, bitter and spicy with a good fruity finish.

Pendleside (OG 1042, ABV 4%)
A light-coloured beer with hints of tropical fruits and a spicy aftertaste.

Monkholme Premium (OG 1042, ABV 4.2%)
A premium golden ale, smooth with a hoppy taste throughout.

New Laund Dark (OG 1044, ABV 4.4%)
A dark-coloured stout, sweet with a smoky, bitter finish.

Griffin IPA (OG 1045, ABV 4.5%)
Well-hopped classic IPA balanced with traditional malty sweetness.

Nook of Pendle (OG 1050, ABV 5%)
An amber-coloured, warming ale with a dried fruit and malty aroma. Tropical fruits in the taste with a bittersweet finish.

Regather

57-59 Club Garden Road, Sheffield, South Yorkshire, S11 8BU
☎ (0114) 273 1258 ⊕ regather.net/food-drink/regather-brewery

Regather Brewery is one of Sheffield's smallest microbreweries. It runs as part of the Regather Co-op. Beers are available at all Regather events and to order online. RAIB

Remedy

☰ 10-11 Market Place, Stockport, SK1 1EW
☎ (0161) 477 1842
⊕ remedybarandbrewhouse.co.uk

Opened in 2016, the 1.5-barrel plant is located in a glazed-off area in the main bar of the Remedy pub, Stockport. The brewery supplies the pub and local festivals with its ever-changing range of beers.

Reunion SIBA 👁

Unit 17, Vector Park, Forest Road, Feltham, TW13 7EJ
☎ 07818 014430 ⊕ reunionales.com

⊠ Reunion Ales was founded in 2015 by Francis Smedley using a Moeschle 10-barrel plant. Beers are available across London, from the brewery tap room and sometimes further afield. ‼♦

Opening Gambit (OG 1038, ABV 3.8%) ◣

Traditional bitter with a pleasant balance of biscuit, hop and bitter orange. Bitterness builds strongly in the lingering finish.

Beardtongue (OG 1044, ABV 4.5%) ◣
Reddish brown-coloured best bitter with chocolate and damson aroma and flavour with some honey. Lingering sweet finish with dry cocoa.

Talwar (OG 1042, ABV 4.5%) ◣
Yellow-coloured beer with sweet earthy hops overlaid with a lemony fruitiness and a touch of spice from the added coriander.

Incredible Pale Ale (OG 1047, ABV 5%) ◣
Smooth, amber-coloured beer with honey sweetness overlaid with a mix of fruits. Earthy hop character is present throughout. Bitter finish.

Single Hop Knot (ABV 5.2%) ◣
Amber-coloured, smooth, strong bitter with faint orange blossom aroma. Building dry bitterness builds with green apples, citrus and residual sweetness.

Revolutions SIBA

Unit B7, Whitwood Enterprise Park, Speedwell Road, Whitwood, West Yorkshire, WF10 5PX
☎ (01977) 552649 ☎ 07801 701089
⊕ revolutionsbrewing.co.uk

Revolutions began brewing in 2010. All beers are musically inspired. The Rewind 33 series of bi-monthly specials references music from 33 years ago. ‼♦

Candidate Session Pale (OG 1039, ABV 3.9%)
A pale, hoppy session ale.

Grip Yorkshire Ale (OG 1039, ABV 3.9%)
Chestnut-coloured session bitter.

Clash Porter (OG 1048, ABV 4.5%)
A complex, dark, malty beer rounded off with a smooth hop finish.

Switch (OG 1044, ABV 4.5%)
Light golden-coloured ale with a hop bill that switches every two months.

Treasure Ruby Ale (OG 1048, ABV 4.5%)
Deep ruby-coloured ale made with a subtle hop flavour.

Rudy English IPA (OG 1049, ABV 5%)
Deep golden-coloured IPA made with English hops.

Hex Six Hop IPA (OG 1058, ABV 6%)
Pale golden-coloured, hoppy IPA.

Manifesto Stout (OG 1059, ABV 6%)
Stout with berry fruit hop notes.

Reynolds

☰ c/o Schooner, South Shore Road, Gateshead, Tyne & Wear, NE8 3AF

Established in 2013 as Rail Ale Brewery in the cellar of the Schooner pub in Gateshead. The brewery changed its name to Reynolds Brewing in 2017. Beers are available at the Schooner and other local outlets.

Rhymney SIBA

Gilchrist Thomas Industrial Estate, Blaenavon, NP4 9RL
☎ (01495) 790456 ⊕ rhymneybreweryltd.com

⊕Established in 2005 by father and son team Steve and Marc Evans. The brewery and its visitor centre is situated in a UNESCO World Heritage Site, adjacent to the National Mining Museum at Big Pit, using a 75-hectolitre plant. The company owns nine tied houses and its beers are available across South Wales. !! ⇌ ♦ RAIB

Best (OG 1037, ABV 3.7%)

Hobby Horse (OG 1038, ABV 3.8%)

Dark (OG 1040, ABV 4%)

Bevans Bitter (OG 1042, ABV 4.2%)

General Picton (OG 1043, ABV 4.3%)

Bitter (OG 1045, ABV 4.5%)

Export (OG 1050, ABV 5%)

Contract brewed for Cold Black Label:

Glyder Fawr (ABV 4%)
Dark golden-coloured ale with a smooth, malty, rounded finish.

Guardian (ABV 4.1%)
Rich bronze-coloured bitter with a balance of hoppy and tangy citrus flavours. Refreshing.

Harlech Castle (ABV 4.4%)
Deep golden brown in colour with a strong amber glow and toffee notes.

Red Beast (ABV 4.4%)
Smooth, ruby-coloured beer with fresh citrus aroma and well-hopped character.

Chirk Castle (ABV 4.6%)
A golden sparkle and subtle citrus tones.

Crib Goch (ABV 5%)
A full-bodied beer with dark coffee and chocolate notes.

Nutty Ale (ABV 5%)
Dark ruby-coloured beer with a rich, nutty, complex finish.

Richmond SIBA

Station Brewery, Station Yard, Richmond, North Yorkshire, DL10 4LD
☎ (01748) 828266 ⊕ richmondbrewing.co.uk

⊕Richmond opened in 2008 in the Victorian station complex beside the River Swale. Beers are available in the local area in the Hildyard Arms, Colburn, and the Castle Tavern, Richmond. Ownership changed in 2013. !! ⇌ ♦ RAIB

SwAle (OG 1035, ABV 3.7%)
Dark mild brewed using chocolate malt with slightly more bitterness than a traditional mild.

Station Ale (OG 1039, ABV 4%)
Light golden-coloured bitter brewed using hedgerow hops.

Greyfriars Stout (OG 1042, ABV 4.2%)

Dale Strider (OG 1043, ABV 4.5%)

Stump Cross Ale (OG 1046, ABV 4.7%)
Dark, malty and full flavoured dark-coloured beer.

Ridgeside SIBA

Unit 24, Penraevon 2 Industrial Estate, Meanwood, Leeds, West Yorkshire, LS7 2AW ☎ 07595 380568
⊕ ridgesidebrewery.co.uk

⊕Ridgeside began brewing in 2010 using a four-barrel plant. Regular outlets are supplied around Leeds and beers can be found across West and North Yorkshire. ♦

Jailbreak (OG 1038, ABV 3.8%)

Cascadia (OG 1041, ABV 4.1%)

Stonegate (OG 1043, ABV 4.4%)
A cask Pilsner. Pale in colour, grassy, floral and refreshing.

Black Night (OG 1050, ABV 5%)
A strong, dark-coloured oatmeal stout with a complex malt character and smooth mouthfeel.

Stargazer (OG 1049, ABV 5%)
Light amber in colour, a juicy hop IPA; bitter, pithy and aromatic.

Ridgeway SIBA ⊚

Stane Street, North Heath, West Sussex, RH20 1DJ
☎ (01491) 873474

Office: Beer Counter Ltd, South Stoke, RG8 0JW
⊕ ridgewaybrewery.co.uk

Set up by ex-Brakspear head brewer Peter Scholey, Ridgeway specialises in bottle-conditioned beers, although cask beers are occasionally available at beer festivals and locally. A new brewery has been operational since 2016, co-located within Hepworth Brewery's new premises near Pulborough, sharing some facilities. RAIB

Rigg & Furrow (NEW)

Acklington Park Farm, Acklington, Northumberland, NE65 9AA ⊕ riggandfurrow.com

Brewing began in 2017 at this authentic farmhouse brewery situated in a former milking parlour. It is a family-run business incorporating its own home-grown Golden Promise malt. ♦ RAIB V

The Pale Ale (OG 1037, ABV 3.8%)
A balanced, easy-drinking pale ale with notes of peach and stone fruits. A biscuity middle and satisfyingly bitter finish.

Owl Porter (OG 1044, ABV 4%)
A robust porter with smooth, roasty, toasty flavours and notes of chocolate, coffee and toffee.

Run, Hop, Run (OG 1040, ABV 4.2%)
A session IPA with a soft bitterness and flavours of pine, citrus and tropical fruits.

Trickster (OG 1042, ABV 4.3%)
A ruby-coloured ale with a jam-like aroma and berry, biscuit and caramel flavours. A hoppy, bitter finish.

Ringwood ⊚

Christchurch Road, Ringwood, Hampshire, BH24 3AP
☎ (01425) 471177 ⊕ ringwoodbrewery.co.uk

⊗ Ringwood was bought in 2007 by Marston's for £19 million. Production has been increased to 50,000 barrels a year. Some 750 outlets are supplied. Ringwood beers are now available in Marston's pubs all over the country. Part of Marston's PLC. !! ⇌ ♦

Razorback (OG 1038, ABV 3.8%) ◗

A malty session bitter with strong toffee notes in the aroma, leading to a short, bittersweet finish. Malt tends to dominate throughout.

Boondoggle (OG 1042, ABV 4.2%)
A golden-coloured beer, full of zesty hop flavours and aromas.

Fortyniner (OG 1049, ABV 4.9%) ◆
A caramel, biscuity aroma, with hints of damson, lead to a sweet but well-balanced taste with malt, fruit and hop flavours.

Old Thumper (OG 1055, ABV 5.1%) ◆
A powerful, sweet, copper-coloured beer. A fruity aroma preludes a sweet, malty taste with fruit and caramel and a bittersweet aftertaste.

Ripple Steam SIBA

Parsonage Farm, Vale Road, Sutton, Kent, CT15 5DH
☎ 07917 037611 ⊕ ripplesteambrewery.co.uk

Ripple Steam began brewing commercially on a farm in Kent in 2012. ◆

Milk Stout (ABV 3.5%)

Best Bitter (ABV 4.1%)

Green Hopped IPA (ABV 4.5%)

IPA (ABV 4.5%)

Rising Sun

▤ Rising Sun, 235 Stockport Road, Mossley, OL5 0RQ
☎ (01457) 238236 ⊕ risingsunmossley.co.uk

Brewing began in 2016 using a two-barrel plant at the side of the Rising Sun. The beers are primarily produced for sale in the pub. In addition to the regular beer, various other brews are produced on demand.

River Leven

Lab Road, Kinlochleven, PH50 4SG
☎ (01855) 831519 ☎ 07901 873273
⊕ riverlevenales.co.uk

Established in 2011 in the former carbon bunker of the aluminium smelter factory in Kinlochleven. Only pure malt cask-conditioned ale is produced.

Blonde (OG 1040, ABV 4%)
A clean-tasting, golden-coloured beer with hints of citrus.

Dark (ABV 4%)

Traditional IPA (OG 1040, ABV 4%)

Pilsner (ABV 4.8%)

Riverhead

▤ 2 Peel Street, Marsden, Huddersfield, West Yorkshire, HD7 6BR
☎ (01484) 841270 (pub) ⊕ ossett-brewery.co.uk

Riverhead is a brewpub that opened in 1995. Ossett Brewing (qv) purchased the site in 2006 but runs it as a separate brewery. It has since opened the Dining Room on the first floor, which uses Riverhead beers in its dishes. Many different beers are produced on a rotating basis.

Riverside

Unit 6, Beeding Court Business Park, Shoreham Road, Upper Beeding, West Sussex, BN44 3TN
☎ (01903) 898030 ⊕ riversidebreweryltd.co.uk

Riverside began brewing in 2015 using a five-barrel plant. Beers are available locally. RAIB

Steyning Stinker (OG 1042, ABV 4%)
A slight fruity/spicy edge complements the earthy, smoked flavour.

Beeding Best Bitter (OG 1038, ABV 4.2%)
A pine/floral characteristic with just a hint of liquorice.

Sneaky Steamer (OG 1050, ABV 5.1%)
A pine/floral characteristic with a hint of grapefruit.

Tubbers' Tipple (OG 1051, ABV 5.6%)
A premium bitter with earthy/spicy notes and a hint of honey.

Riviera

4 Yonder Meadow, Stoke Gabriel, Devon, TQ9 6QE
☎ 07714 715044 ⊕ rivierabrewing.co.uk

⊗ Riviera started brewing commercially in 2015 using a one-barrel plant. ◆

RBC Best (ABV 3.8%)
A light-hopped session ale.

Gold (OG 1040, ABV 4.2%)
A golden ale, citrus and fruity.

Porterhead (ABV 4.3%)

Torbay Express (OG 1046, ABV 4.8%)
Copper-coloured premium ale with a fruity, spicy bitterness and a citrus aroma.

Rivington

Cunliffe Farm, New Road, Anderton, Lancashire, PR6 9EY ☎ 07989 165370 ⊕ rivingtonbrewing.co.uk

☺Rivington Brewing Co was established in 2015, operating from a dairy farm. A new three-barrel plant has been installed to increase production with cask-conditioned ale accounting for about 30% of output. A number of local outlets are supplied direct from the brewery. RAIB

Proper Ace (ABV 3.7%)

Chillen (ABV 4%)

Sunset Strip (ABV 4.2%)

Bodacious (ABV 4.6%)

Never Known Fog Like It (ABV 5.2%)

Rye'n Gosling (ABV 5.5%)

That's Your Left Hand Sir (ABV 6.7%)

Roath (NEW)

32 Colchester Avenue, Cardiff, CF23 9BP

Brewing began in 2016. Only bottled beer is produced at present. No real ale.

Robin Hood SIBA

Unit 3, Northgate Place, High Church Street, New Basford, Nottingham, NG7 7JT ☎ 07804 499462
✉ brewery@robinhoodbrewery.com

THE BREWERIES

Robin Hood began brewing in 2012, originally using spare capacity at Wirksworth Brewery (qv). It moved to its own premises in 2013 using a 5.5-barrel plant. ♦V

Maiden's Pale (OG 1039, ABV 3.9%)
Lightly-hopped, pale-coloured session ale with fruity aroma and a hint of honey.

Sherwood Bitter (OG 1040, ABV 4%)
Traditional amber-coloured ale with malt flavours and a bitter finish.

Golden Archer (OG 1042, ABV 4.2%)
Golden ale with a subtle aroma and a moderate fruity hop taste. A mellow finish with orange notes.

Nottingham Pale Ale (OG 1042, ABV 4.2%)
A light gold-coloured ale, well-hopped with a ripe fruit nose and a complex citrus fruit flavour giving a zesty finish.

Red Knight (OG 1044, ABV 4.4%)
Red in colour and malty with an aroma of vine fruits and a smooth, complex berry taste.

Broadsword Porter (OG 1045, ABV 4.5%)
Rich ale with autumn fruit aromas. A sweet malt taste with a slight bitterness.

Little John IPA (OG 1050, ABV 5%)
Deep gold-coloured ale with classic IPA hops giving abundant aroma and a cordial bitter finish.

The Black Death (OG 1085, ABV 8.5%)
A liquorice aroma and flavours of dark chocolate, coffee and sweet, dark malt.

Robinsons SIBAIFBB 👁

Unicorn Brewery, Lower Hillgate, Stockport, Cheshire, SK1 1JJ
☎ (0161) 612 4061 ⊕ robinsonsbrewery.com

☺ Robinsons has been brewing since 1838 and the business is still owned and run by the family. It has an estate of around 290 pubs stretching from Cheshire to Cumbria and out to North Wales. In addition to the seasonal range a series of one-off 'White Label' beers are produced every 2-3 months. This year may also see more 'Trooper' beers brewed with Iron Maiden's Bruce Dickinson. In 2017 it took over production of Beacon Hill and Tiger for Everards (qv). ‼🍴♦

Wizard (OG 1037, ABV 3.7%)
Mid-brown-coloured session beer. Well-balanced, crisp and refreshing.

Dizzy Blonde (OG 1037, ABV 3.8%) ◕
A light-bodied beer, yellow in colour. It has malt and hops in the taste and a dry bitter finish.

Cumbria Way (OG 1040, ABV 4.1%) ◕
Pale brown in colour with a malty aroma, this beer has a balance of malt, some hops and a little fruit, with sweetness and bitterness throughout.

Cwrw'r Ddraig Aur (OG 1041, ABV 4.1%)

Unicorn (OG 1041, ABV 4.2%) ◕
Amber-coloured beer with a fruity aroma. Malt, hops and fruit in the taste with a bitter, malty finish.

Trooper (OG 1048, ABV 4.8%) ◕
Well-balanced, amber-coloured beer with malt and hops in aroma and taste.

Double Hop (OG 1050, ABV 5%) ◕

Pale brown-coloured beer with malt and fruit on the nose. Full hoppy taste with malt and fruit, leading to a hoppy, bitter finish.

Old Tom (OG 1079, ABV 8.5%) 🍷 🍴 ◕
A full-bodied, dark beer with malt, fruit and chocolate on the aroma. A complex range of flavours includes dark chocolate, full maltiness, port and fruits and lead to a long, bittersweet aftertaste.

Contract brewed for Everards Brewery:

Beacon Hill (OG 1036, ABV 3.8%)
Light, refreshing, well-balanced bitter in the Burton style.

Tiger (OG 1041, ABV 4.2%)
A well-balanced best bitter crafted for broad appeal, benefiting from a long, bittersweet finish.

Rock & Roll

Unit 2, 60 Regent Place, Hockley, Birmingham, B1 3NJ ☎ 07922 554181
✉ rnrbrewhouse@outlook.com

⊠ The Rock & Roll brewery started life as Birmingham's only rooftop pub brewery, set up by experienced brewer Mark Shepherd using a two-barrel plant. In 2014 brewster Lynn Crossland joined and now does most of the brewing. In 2016 the brewery moved and expanded to a six-barrel plant in Birmingham's historic Jewellery Quarter in order to increase capacity. A small bar has recently opened within the brewery. ‼♦RAIB V

Brew Springsteen (OG 1042, ABV 4.2%)
Pale ale with honey.

Instant Calmer (OG 1042, ABV 4.2%)

Mash City Rocker (OG 1045, ABV 4.5%)

Rock Mill

2a Rock Mill Lane, New Mills, Derbyshire, SK22 3BN
☎ 07971 747050

Office: 81-83 Bridge Street, New Mills, Derbyshire, SK22 4DN ✉ rbpine@Hotmail.co.uk

⊠ Rock Mills is a microbrewery established by Ray Barton in 2016, next door to his cabinet-making business.

Mermaids Pool (OG 1035, ABV 3.5%)

Strange Ways (OG 1038, ABV 3.8%)

Back to the Future (OG 1040, ABV 4%)

Cotton Spinner (OG 1040, ABV 4%)

Orangeytang (OG 1044, ABV 4.3%)
A golden-coloured bitter with a hint of orange.

Rock Solid (NEW)

Office: 25 Thornebank, Blackpool, FY3 8QE ☎ 07963 860080 ✉ rocksolidbrewingcompany@gmail.com

Brewing began in 2017, initially using spare capacity at Lytham Brewery (qv).

Blonde (ABV 3.9%)

Strawberry Blonde (ABV 3.9%)

Gold (ABV 4.2%)

Rock the Boat SIBA 👁

6 Little Crosby Village, Little Crosby, Merseyside, L23 4TS
☎ (0151) 924 7936 ☎ 07727 959356
⊕ rocktheboatbrewery.co.uk

Rock the Boat began brewing in 2015 in a converted 16th-century wheelwright's workshop in Little Crosby village. The beers can be found in a variety of pubs and clubs in the Crosby and Waterloo area, Liverpool city centre and as far as Chorley in Lancashire. RAIB V

Liverpool Light (OG 1037, ABV 3.4%)
A blonde session ale with subtle fruity hop flavours.

(Sittin' on) The Dock (OG 1042, ABV 3.5%)

Dazzle (OG 1039, ABV 3.6%)
Pale golden-coloured beer bursting with hop flavours, smooth in the mouth with a long bitter finish.

Bootle Bull (OG 1042, ABV 3.8%)
A smooth, malty ale balanced with a good hop character.

Mussel Wreck (OG 1041, ABV 3.9%)
A subtle blend of malt and hops creates an easy-drinking, smooth ale. Fruity hop flavours with a short bitter finish.

Faith Hope Charity (OG 1038, ABV 4%)
Deep golden-coloured bitter. A little malt flavour with a bitter edge.

Waterloo Sunset (OG 1047, ABV 4.2%)
Full-bodied beer with a subtle orange marmalade flavour.

Dragon's Teeth (OG 1046, ABV 4.3%)
A chocolate stout.

Fab Four IPA (OG 1043, ABV 4.4%)

Rocket (NEW)

Unit 10, Kingsmead, King's Cliffe, Northamptonshire, PE8 6YH
☎ (01733) 390828 ☎ 07747 617527
✉ mikeblakesley@virginmedia.com

Rocket Ales is a cuckoo brewery using spare capacity at King's Cliffe Brewery (qv).

Rocket Town

Unit 1, Cleveland Industrial Estate, Darlington, DL1 2PB
☎ (01325) 466720

Office: Hole in the Wall, 14-15 Horsemarket, Darlington, DL1 5PT
✉ rockettownbrewery@hotmail.com

Rocket Town began brewing in 2015.

Rockhopper (NEW)

1 Forrest Crescent, Luton, Bedfordshire, LU2 9AR
☎ 07879 810558 ⊕ rockhopperbrew.co

⊠ Rockhopper began brewing in 2016 using a 2-barrel plant. ◆ RAIB V

Rockin' Robin SIBA 👁

Campfield Farm, Haste Hill Road, Boughton Monchelsea, Kent, ME17 4LR
☎ (01622) 747106 ☎ 07787 416110
⊕ rockinrobinbrewery.co.uk

Brewing began in 2011 using a one-barrel plant in a garden shed. It moved to its current location in 2014. Outlets throughout Kent, Sussex and the South-east London borders are supplied, including several micropubs. ‼ ▤ ◆

Hoppin' Robin (OG 1036, ABV 3.7%)
A traditional English session bitter with full malt, fruit in the mouth and Kentish hops on the tongue.

Reliant Robin (OG 1036, ABV 3.7%)
An auburn-coloured classic session bitter. Rich with a fresh, spicy finish.

RPA (OG 1038, ABV 3.9%)
A light and refreshing pale ale.

Robin Redbest (OG 1041, ABV 4%)
Light amber in colour with initial good hop flavour moving to a pleasant malty finish.

Rocka Hula (OG 1039, ABV 4%)
A pale ale with a fruity and slightly spicy taste.

Blizzard of Oz (OG 1046, ABV 4.5%)
A rich, dark mahogany-coloured beer brewed using Kentish hops only.

Reckless Robin (OG 1044, ABV 4.5%)
A strong bitter that delivers a fresh, hoppy punch, well-balanced with soft fruit malt.

Stoutly Robin (OG 1046, ABV 4.5%)
A rich, creamy stout with a smooth, roasted character.

Crafty Robin (OG 1048, ABV 5%)
A dry-hopped, strong pale ale.

Portly Robin (OG 1049, ABV 5%)
Full-bodied, deep ruby-coloured porter. Rich fruits promote a vinous character with liquorice undertones.

Really Rockin (OG 1052, ABV 5%)
A classic, full-bodied pale ale with tropical fruity flavours.

Rockingham SIBA

Blatherwycke, Northamptonshire, PE8 6YN
☎ (01832) 280722

Office: 25 Wansford Road, Elton, PE8 6RZ
⊕ rockinghamales.co.uk

⊠ Rockingham is a small brewery established in 1997 that operates from a converted farm building near Blatherwycke, Northamptonshire, with a two-barrel plant producing a prolific range of beers. It supplies half a dozen local outlets. ◆

Forest Gold (OG 1039, ABV 3.9%)
A hoppy blonde ale with citrus flavours. Well-balanced and clean-finishing.

Hop Devil (OG 1040, ABV 3.9%)
Six hop varieties give this golden ale a bitter start and fruity finish.

White Rabbit (OG 1040, ABV 4%)
Light golden ale brewed with a bitter start and tropical fruit finish.

Saxon Cross (OG 1041, ABV 4.1%)

THE BREWERIES

A golden red-coloured ale with a nutty coffee aroma and fruit and blackcurrant undertones.

Fruits of the Forest (OG 1043, ABV 4.3%)
A multi-layered beer in which summer fruits and several spices compete with a big hop presence.

Dark Forest (OG 1050, ABV 5%)
A dark and complex beer with malty/smoky flavours that give way to a fruity bitter finish.

Rocky Head

Unit 16, Glenville Mews, Kimber Road, Southfields, London, SW18 4NJ
☎ (020) 8875 9917 ⊕ sites.google.com/site/rockyheadbrewery

Rocky Head is a microbrewery set up in 2012 by a group of friends inspired by the American craft brewing scene. A range of bottle-conditioned beers is brewed on a five-barrel plant. RAIB V

Romney Marsh

Unit 7, Jacks Park, Cinque Ports Road, New Romney, Kent, TN28 8AN
☎ (01797) 362333 ☎ 07796 176011
⊕ romneymarshbrewery.com

⊠ An award-winning 12-barrel, family-run brewery founded in 2015 by former Come Dine with Me executive producer Matt Calais. Beer is supplied to outlets throughout Kent and East Sussex. ‼ ⬚ RAIB

Mellow (OG 1036, ABV 3.6%)
American-style pale session ale with creamy hop flavours.

Romney Golden Ale (OG 1038, ABV 3.9%)
Honey, citrus and marmalade hop flavours.

Romney Best (OG 1039, ABV 4%)
Biscuit and chocolate malts with blackcurrant hop notes.

Gold (OG 1038, ABV 4.1%)
A refreshing ale with orange and lemon hop notes, a hint of strawberry and a smooth malt finish.

Romney Cinque Porter (OG 1040, ABV 4.2%)
Gentle citrus hop notes with roasted barley, crystal and chocolate malts.

Romney Amber Ale (OG 1042, ABV 4.4%)
Tropical hop flavours with a hint of caramel.

Rooster's SIBA ⊙

Unit 3, Grimbald Park, Wetherby Road, Knaresborough, North Yorkshire, HG5 8LJ
☎ (01423) 865959 ⊕ roosters.co.uk

☺Founded in 1993 by Sean and Alison Franklin, Rooster's is now owned and operated by Ian Fozard and his sons, Tom and Oliver. One-off experimental beers are also brewed under the Outlaw Brewing Co name. ♦

Buckeye (OG 1035.5, ABV 3.5%)
An easy-drinking pale ale with an orange, citrus fruit aroma and a refreshing level of bitterness.

Highway 51 (OG 1036.5, ABV 3.7%)
Juicy, tropical fruit flavours come to the fore in this dry-hopped session pale ale, backed by a hint of citrus and a grapefruit finish.

YPA (Yorkshire Pale Ale) (OG 1039.5, ABV 4.1%)

A pale, aromatic ale that offers up delicate peachy and berry fruit flavours.

Yankee (OG 1041, ABV 4.3%) ◣
A straw-coloured beer with a delicate, fruity aroma leading to a well-balanced taste of malt and hops with a slight evidence of sweetness, followed by a refreshing, fruity/bitter finish.

Baby-Faced Assassin (OG 1058, ABV 6.1%)
Aromas of mango, apricot, grapefruit and mandarin orange, along with a lasting, juicy, tropical fruit bitterness.

Roseland

▤ c/o Roseland Inn, Philleigh, St Mawes, Cornwall, TR2 5NB
☎ (01872) 580254 ☎ 07977 472484
⊕ roselandinn.co.uk

Established in 2009 by its owner/brewer at the Roseland Inn, St. Mawes. The beers are mostly named after local birds and are generally only available in the pub itself. Beers were contract brewed by Keltek Brewery (qv) but brewing is currently suspended.

Rossendale

▤ Griffin Inn, 84 Hud Rake, Haslingden, Lancashire, BB4 5AF
☎ (01706) 214021 ⊕ rossendalebrewery.co.uk

The brewery acquired the brew plant previously used by Porter Brewing Co in 2007 and is based in the cellar of the Griffin Inn in Haslingden. The Sportsman in Hyde and many other local outlets are also supplied.

Floral Dance (OG 1040, ABV 3.8%)
A pale and fruity session beer.

Hameldon Bitter (OG 1040, ABV 3.8%)
A dark-coloured, traditional bitter with a dry and assertive character that develops in the finish.

Ale (OG 1045, ABV 4%)
A malty aroma leads to a malt dominated flavour, supported by a dry, increasingly bitter finish.

Glen Top Bitter (OG 1040.5, ABV 4%)
A citrus, full-bodied, pale beer with a dry aftertaste.

Halo Pale (OG 1045, ABV 4.5%)
A citrus pale ale brewed with a slightly bitter aftertaste.

Pitch Porter (OG 1050, ABV 5%)
A full-bodied beer with a slightly sweet, malty start, balanced with sharp bitterness.

Sunshine (OG 1055, ABV 5.3%)
A hoppy, bitter beer with a citrus character. The lingering finish is dry and spicy.

Rother Valley SIBA

Gate Court Farm, Station Road, Northiam, East Sussex, TN31 6QT
☎ (01797) 252922 ☎ 07798 877551
⊕ rothervalleybrewery.co.uk

⊠ Rother Valley Brewing Co was established in Northiam in 1993, overlooking the Rother Levels and the Kent & East Sussex Railway. Established and new hop varieties are grown on the farm and also sourced locally. Brewing is split between cask and an ever-increasing range of filtered bottled beers. Around 100 outlets are supplied direct and through wholesalers. ‼◆

Honeyfuzz (OG 1038, ABV 3.8%)
A pale-coloured bitter flavoured with Sussex honey. Subtle but not sweet with a citrus twang on the finish.

Smild (OG 1038, ABV 3.8%)
A full-bodied, dark-coloured, creamy mild with hints of chocolate.

Level Best (OG 1040, ABV 4%) ◆
Full-bodied, tawny-coloured session bitter with a malt and fruit aroma, malty taste and a dry, hoppy finish.

Copper Ale (OG 1041, ABV 4.1%)
A copper-coloured ale with a good balance of malt and hops.

Hoppers Ale (OG 1044, ABV 4.4%)
A copper-coloured ale. The initial burst of hop is followed by a pleasant caramel taste.

Boadicea (OG 1045, ABV 4.5%)
A straw-coloured beer with a delicate, fruity flavour.

Blues (OG 1050, ABV 5%)

Rothes

77 New Street, Rothes, AB38 7BJ ☎ 07336 233634
✉ therothesbrewery@sky.com

⊠ Situated in the heart of the Spey Valley, Rothes began producing commercially in 2014. Initially producing only bottle-conditioned beers, cask ales are now also brewed. RAIB

Round Tower SIBA

Unit 11a, Robjohns House, Navigation Road, Chelmsford, Essex, CM2 6ND
☎ (01245) 807343 ☎ 07905 255909
⊕ roundtowerbrewery.co.uk

Round Tower began brewing in 2013, the first brewery in Chelmsford since Grays & Sons ceased brewing in 1974. Former home brewer Simon Tippler started on a small scale but has now expanded to a brew length of five barrels. Several local pubs are supplied and the beers can also be found in the Grays & Sons estate and other selected free houses. ◆RAIB

Stout (OG 1043, ABV 4.3%)

Slipstream (OG 1053, ABV 5.4%)

Roundhill (NEW) SIBA

Unit 1, Lagonda Court, Cowpen Lane Industrial Estate, Cowpen Bewley, TS23 4JF ☎ 07910 567847

Office: 9 Trevine Gardens, Ingleby Barwick, TS17 5HD
✉ roundhillbrewery@outlook.com

☺Brewing commenced in 2016 on a five-barrel plant.

Bitter (OG 1038, ABV 4.1%)
A refreshing, copper-coloured, traditional bitter.

Pale & Golden (OG 1040, ABV 4.2%)
A citrus burst with a pleasing bitterness.

Dark Ale (OG 1047, ABV 5.2%)
A dark ruby-coloured, rich ale with subtle fruit overtones.

Rowditch

⊟ Rowditch Inn, 246 Uttoxeter New Road, Derby, DE22 3LL
☎ (01332) 343123

The Rowditch Brewery was established in 2010 and is a 3.75-barrel plant situated on the premises of the Rowditch pub. One-off ales are periodically available.

Rowett

Storrs Cottage, The Square, North Thoresby, Lincolnshire, DN36 5QL
☎ (01472) 841080 ⊕ rowettbrewing.com

Founded in 2014 as a commercial 1.5-barrel nanobrewery, Rowett Brewing supplies its beers to pubs in Grimsby and the Lincolnshire Wolds. ◆RAIB

Six Hour Lunch (ABV 4.2%)

Oak Barrel Stout (OG 1056, ABV 5.2%)

Rowton SIBA ◉

Stone House, Rowton, Telford, Shropshire, TF6 6QX
☎ 07854 885870 ⊕ rowtonbrewery.com

Established in 2008, Rowton is run by a father and son team using a four-barrel plant in a Victorian cattle shed on a farm. The water is drawn from a borehole on site. The Pheasant Inn, Wellington, was recently acquired. ◆

Moonstruck Mild (OG 1033, ABV 3.3%)

Pure Gold (OG 1038, ABV 3.8%)

Bitter (OG 1040, ABV 3.9%)

Ironbridge Gold (ABV 4.4%)

Portly Stout (OG 1045, ABV 4.5%)

Area 51 (OG 1051, ABV 5.1%)

RPM

⊟ 118 High Street, Weston-super-Mare, BS23 1HP
☎ (01934) 632629

Office: 19 Orchard Street, Weston-super-Mare, BS23 1RG

Established in 2015 and operating on a 10-gallon system out of the Brit Bar in Weston-super-Mare.

RT (NEW)

6b/6c Alexandra Industrial Estate, Wentloog Road, Rumney, CF3 1EY
☎ (029) 2036 2213 ☎ 07738 659101 ⊕ rtales.co.uk

Brewing began in 2016. In addition to the core range of beers, a series of specials named the Mutation Range are available. ‼◆

Pale Ale (ABV 3.8%)

Ruddles

See Greene King

Rudgate SIBA ◉

2 Centre Park, Marston Moor Business Park, Tockwith, York, North Yorkshire, YO26 7QF
☎ (01423) 358382 ⊕ rudgatebrewery.co.uk

THE BREWERIES

⊕Established in 1992, the original brewery was a former ammunition building at RAF Marston Moor Airfield, which was home to Halifax Bombers in WWII, expanding to a modern facility in 2011. The old Roman road of Rudgate runs through the airfield and Vikings used it, defeating the Romans, so beer names are Viking themed. ◆

Jorvik (OG 1036, ABV 3.8%)
Blonde ale with a balanced hoppy bitterness and a crisp, fruity finish.

Viking (OG 1036, ABV 3.8%) ◣
An initially warming and malty, full-bodied beer, with hops and fruit lingering into the aftertaste.

Battle Axe (OG 1040, ABV 4.2%) ◣
A well-hopped bitter with slightly sweet initial taste and light bitterness. Complex fruit character gives a memorable aftertaste.

Ruby Mild (OG 1041, ABV 4.4%) ◳ ◣
Nutty, rich ruby-coloured ale, stronger than usual for a mild.

Valkyrie APA (ABV 5%)

York Chocolate Stout (OG 1049, ABV 5%)
Deep, rich stout with complex balanced flavours and a subtle chocolate finish.

Runaway

Unit 4, Millgate, Dantzic Street, Manchester, M4 4JW
☎ (0161) 832 2628 ☎ 07505 237078
⊕ therunawaybrewery.com

Runaway is located in a railway arch outside Manchester Victoria station. It began brewing in 2014 using a 5.5-barrel plant producing KeyCask and bottle-conditioned beers. Beers are increasingly distributed locally. ◆RAIB

Ryedale SIBA

Hardings House, Hardings Lane, Cross Hills, North Yorkshire, BD20 7AD
☎ (01535) 637026 ☎ 07850 510859
⊕ ryedalebrewing.co.uk

⊕Rydale began brewing in 2013 using a four-barrel plant. In 2016 it relocated to Cross Hills. Brewing is currently suspended. ‼

S&P

Homestead, Drayton Lane, Horsford, Norfolk, NR10 3AN ☎ 07552 300768 ⊕ spbrewery.co.uk

⊠ Production commenced in 2013 using a 10-barrel plant constructed upon land once owned by prominent Norfolk brewers Steward & Patteson (1800-1965), hence the name. Locally produced malts are used as is water from the brewery's own borehole. ‼

Topaz Blonde (OG 1038, ABV 3.7%)
A golden-coloured beer with a citrus aroma and grapefruit taste. A crisp, bitter finish.

Afterglow (OG 1041.6, ABV 3.9%)
An amber-coloured ale with full-bodied maltiness and subtle hop aromas and tastes.

Between the Posts (OG 1040.2, ABV 3.9%)

Barrack Street Bitter (OG 1041, ABV 4%) ◣
A refreshing amber-coloured ale. A gentle hop aroma sits comfortably with the malty biscuit flavour. An increasingly bitter finish.

First Light (OG 1042, ABV 4.1%) ◣
A light golden-coloured beer. A strong citrus aroma and deep hoppy flavour is complemented by a lingering bitter finish.

Dennis (OG 1042, ABV 4.2%)
A rich, amber-coloured bitter with a well-balanced malty sweetness.

Eve's Drop (OG 1046, ABV 4.3%) ◣
A well-balanced, golden brown-coloured ale. Hops and malts dominate with a peppery mouthfeel giving way to lingering sweetness.

Darkest Hour (OG 1047, ABV 4.4%)
Roasted barley gives a faint coffee aroma and taste to this full-bodied Irish stout.

Shady Sadie Mild (OG 1047, ABV 4.4%)
Full-bodied mild with roasted malt flavours.

NASHA IPA (OG 1050, ABV 5%)
A persistent head sits atop a rich amber-coloured ale with well-balanced malty sweetness.

Saddleworth

⬚ **Church Inn, Church Lane, Uppermill, Oldham, OL3 6LW**
☎ (01457) 820902 ⊕ churchinnsaddleworth.co.uk

Saddleworth started brewing in 1997 in a 120-year old brewhouse at the Church Inn. Brewery and inn are set above a valley overlooking Saddleworth Moor. Brewing capacity was significantly expanded in 2011 with a new 13-barrel plant. Brewing is currently suspended.

Sadler's SIBA ⊙

Unit 2, Conyers Trading Estate, Station Drive, Lye, West Midlands, DY9 8ER
☎ (01384) 895230 ⊕ sadlersales.co.uk

⊕Third and fourth generation brewers John and Chris Sadler re-opened this historic brewery in 2004. The brewery tap house was built and opened in 2006 next to the brewery. Around 250 outlets are supplied. A new 30-barrel plant, visitor centre, shop and tasting room opened in 2015. ‼ ▤

JPA (OG 1038, ABV 3.8%)
A pale, hoppy bitter with a crisp and zesty lemon undertone.

Mellow Yellow (OG 1041, ABV 4.1%)
A pale ale brewed with plenty of hop and honey.

Worcester Sorcerer (OG 1043, ABV 4.3%)
Brewed with English hops and barley with hints of mint and lemon, creating a floral aroma and crisp bitterness.

Thin Ice (OG 1045, ABV 4.5%)
A pale ale. Bitter but with an orange and lemon finish.

Peaky Blinder (OG 1046, ABV 4.6%) ◣
Black in colour with malt and fruit in the aroma. Smoky bitterness and toffee in the taste with powerful hops lingering.

Boris Citrov (OG 1047, ABV 4.7%)
A punchy orange marmalade ale leading to a sweet, crisp and fruity finish.

Hop Bomb (OG 1050, ABV 5%)
A powerful IPA with a balanced malt sweetness and big hop aroma and flavour explosion.

Red IPA (OG 1057, ABV 5.7%)

Mud City Stout (OG 1066, ABV 6.6%) ◆
Soft fruity aroma, malty taste with caramel and raisins, lingering sweet aftertaste with a hint of bitterness.

Saffron SIBA

The Cartshed, Parsonage Farm, Henham, Essex, CM22 6AN
☎ (01279) 850923 ☎ 07980 972067
⊕ saffronbrewery.co.uk

⊗ Founded in 2005, the brewery was upgraded to a 15-barrel plant in early 2008 and re-located to a converted barn at Parsonage Farm, with a purpose-built reed bed for environmentally-friendly disposal of waste products. 40 outlets are supplied direct.
‼ ☲ ◆ RAIB

IPA (OG 1036, ABV 3.6%)

Citra (ABV 3.8%)
Light golden ale brewed with grapefruit aromas and a crisp gooseberry finish.

Dawn Til Dusk (ABV 3.8%)
Traditional copper-coloured bitter with hints of citrus and biscuit maltiness.

Ramblers Tipple (OG 1040, ABV 3.9%)
A rich, copper-coloured bitter with toffee and caramel flavours.

Brewhouse Bell (OG 1041, ABV 4%)
Golden amber in colour with citrus and hop flavours balancing well for a clean, fresh finish.

Littlebury Lighthouse (OG 1043, ABV 4.2%)

Blonde (OG 1044, ABV 4.3%)
A light golden ale with a delicate balance of citrus and smooth, malty flavours and a crisp finish.

Squires Gamble (OG 1044, ABV 4.3%)
Traditional-style, copper-coloured ale; soft, mellow, full-flavoured and hoppy with citrus and biscuit hints.

Porter (ABV 5.2%)
Ruby-coloured porter with rich chocolate and coffee aromas. Ruby port and red grape juice create a soft fruit and spice finish.

St Andrews (Norwich) SIBA

☱ City Pub Co, 41 St Andrews Street, Norwich, NR2 4TP
☎ (01603) 305995 ☎ 07976 652410
⊕ standrewsbrewhouse.com

A city centre brewpub opened in 2015 in the premises formerly occupied by Delaney's Irish Bar.

St Andrews (St Andrews)

Unit 7, Bassaguard Business Park, St Andrews, KY16 8AL
☎ (01334) 208586
⊕ standrewsbrewingcompany.com

Established in 2012, bottle-conditioned beers are brewed in small batches of 1,200–1,800 bottles. Cask beers are supplied to a number of local outlets including the brewery tap in St Andrews, opened in 2013. ◆ RAIB V

Fife Gold (OG 1040, ABV 4.2%)
Straw-coloured with a fresh, floral aroma backed up with a citrus punch of lemon, lime and grapefruit.

Crail Ale (OG 1042, ABV 4.5%)
A bright golden ale with long-lasting citrus and floral flavours.

Oatmeal Stout (OG 1045, ABV 4.5%)
A full-bodied oatmeal stout. Strong coffee, chocolate and dark fruit flavours balanced against a blend of hops to create a rich, silky aftertaste.

Eighty Bob (OG 1047, ABV 4.8%)
A traditional Scottish 80/- ale. Complex malt flavours dominate.

India Pale Ale (OG 1050, ABV 5%)
Bold IPA with a big hop kick and a depth of orange and tropical fruit flavours.

St Austell SIBA ◉

63 Trevarthian Road, St Austell, Cornwall, PL25 4BY
☎ (01726) 74444 ⊕ staustellbrewery.co.uk

⊗ Founded in 1851, St Austell Brewery remains family owned. Its cask beers are available in all its pubs, and throughout the UK. The brewery hosts its own Celtic beer festival in November each year. A visitor centre with a 10-barrel small batch plant has recently opened. In 2016 it purchased Bath Ales (qv). ‼ ☲ ◆ RAIB

Cornish Best Bitter (OG 1035, ABV 3.5%) ◆
Light, refreshing copper-coloured bitter with malt aroma. Gentle biscuit malt and hops flavour with low bitterness. Bitter, dry finish.

Trelawny (OG 1039, ABV 3.8%) ◆
Tawny-coloured bitter with aroma of hops and stone fruits. Hop bitterness and some citrus develop into caramel malt sweetness. Refreshing, crisp finish.

Nicholson's Pale Ale (OG 1040, ABV 4.1%) ◆
Amber-coloured best bitter. Light roast malt and hops dominate the taste with sweet fruit tones. Dry bitterness rises in the finish.

Tribute (OG 1043, ABV 4.2%) ◆
Pale brown-coloured best bitter with malt and hop aroma. Dominant hop bitterness with biscuit malt, ending refreshingly bitter and dry.

Proper Job (OG 1046, ABV 4.5%) ☐ ◆
Golden ale with resinous hop aroma. Copious citrus fruits with bitterness and crisp hop bitter and grapefruit finish, becoming dry.

HSD (OG 1052, ABV 5%) ◆
Malt and stone fruit aroma leads into rich, balanced fruit, caramel, bitterness and malt which last into the long finish.

St George's

The Old Bakery, Bush Lane, Callow End, Worcestershire, WR2 4TF
☎ (01905) 831316 ⊕ stgeorgesbrewery.co.uk

The brewery was established in 1998 in old village bakery premises and acquired in 2006 by Duncan Ironmonger, who owns three nearby pubs. The brewery supplies local free houses and wholesalers for a wider distribution ‼ ◆

By George (OG 1036, ABV 3.6%)
Clean-drinking, pale golden ale with a strong floral aroma and citrus notes.

Friar Tuck (OG 1040, ABV 4%)
A golden-coloured bitter with a smooth, refreshing bitter and citrus character.

Lazy Days (OG 1042, ABV 4.1%)
A light golden-coloured ale with mellow floral hop aromas followed by a distinctive hoppy taste.

Worcester Sauce (OG 1043, ABV 4.3%)
A chestnut-coloured ale with a hoppy aroma and a strong bitter finish.

Dream Weaver (OG 1045, ABV 4.5%)
A light golden ale with citrus and pine notes.

Charger (OG 1046, ABV 4.6%)
A light golden-coloured beer with a citrus blast and a hint of grapefruit.

Dragons Blood (OG 1048, ABV 4.8%)
A ruby red-coloured porter with a hint of chocolate and an earthy and slightly spicy aroma.

St Ives

Trewidden Road, St Ives, Cornwall, TR26 2BX
☎ (01736) 793467 ☎ 07702 311595
⊕ stives-brewery.co.uk

Owner Marco Amura started the brewery in 2010, though all beers at the time were produced under licence by various local breweries. In 2015 a two-storey brewhouse was constructed with a 10-barrel plant, incorporating a visitor centre and gift shop plus a 60-seat café enjoying panoramic views of St Ives bay. Commercial brewing began in 2016.
‼ ⇋ ♦ RAIB

Harbourside Light Ale (OG 1038, ABV 3.8%)
A hoppy ale with a floral aroma.

Boilers Golden Ale (OG 1040, ABV 4%)
A light golden ale with a floral and citrus hop finish.

XPA (OG 1048, ABV 4.8%)
Hoppy with a lingering bitter finish.

Knill by Mouth (OG 1048, ABV 5%) ◥
Tawny-coloured, strong bitter with cherries, hops and malt aroma. Sweet cherry and damson flavours, bubblegum and balanced malt and hops.

**Brewhouse Belgian Golden Ale
(OG 1076, ABV 7.3%)**
Smooth on the palate with hints of elderflower and stoned fruits, and a slightly sweet finish.

St Judes

⚏ 2 Cardigan Street, Ipswich, Suffolk, IP1 3PF
☎ (01473) 413334 ☎ 07879 360879
⊕ stjudestavern.com

The brewery resumed brewing in 2015 on a newly installed 10-barrel plant. Run by Frank Walsh and Colleen Seymour, the beers are sold mainly through their Ipswich tavern, but can occasionally be found further afield through a distribution agreement with Nethergate Brewery (qv).

Devereaux Porter (OG 1043, ABV 4.2%)
An easy-drinking porter with a rounded flavour.

Gainsborough Bitter (OG 1044, ABV 4.4%)
An amber-coloured bitter with a good body and hoppy aftertaste.

John Orford Brown Ale (OG 1050, ABV 4.8%)
An old-fashioned brown-coloured ale. Rich, sweet and satisfying flavour.

Coachmans Whip (OG 1052, ABV 5.2%)
A strong, complex bitter with a powerful fruity flavour and a long bitter finish.

St Peter's SIBA ◉

St Peter's Hall, St Peter South Elmham, Suffolk, NR35 1NQ
☎ (01986) 782322 ⊕ stpetersbrewery.co.uk

⊠ St Peter's Brewery is based adjacent to a moated medieval hall near Bungay, Suffolk. Established in 1996 it concentrates in the main on bottled beer/keg (85% of capacity) but has a rapidly increasing cask market. Two pubs are owned. 50% of production is exported to 50 countries worldwide. ‼ ⇋ ♦

Best Bitter (OG 1037, ABV 3.7%) ◥
A complex but well-balanced hoppy brew. A gentle hop nose introduces a singular hoppiness with supporting malt notes and underlying bitterness. Other flavours fade to leave a long, dry, hoppy finish.

Mild (OG 1037, ABV 3.7%) ◥
Heady aroma of caramelised blackberries and black toffee. Complex flavours with caramel, blackberries, hops and an astringent bitterness. Long, sustained finish with a roast coffee bitterness; increasingly dry.

Golden Ale (OG 1040, ABV 4%) ◥
Amber-coloured, full-bodied, robust ale. A strong hop bouquet leads to a mix of malt and hops combined with a dry, fruity hoppiness. The malt quickly subsides, leaving creamy bitterness.

Organic Best (OG 1041, ABV 4.1%) ◥
A dry and bitter beer with a growing astringency. Pale brown in colour, it has a gentle hop aroma which makes the definitive bitterness surprising.

G-Free (OG 1048, ABV 4.2%)
A pale gold-coloured gluten-free ale with aromas of citrus and mandarin.

Ruby Red (OG 1043, ABV 4.3%)
A tawny red-coloured ale with subtle malt undertones and a distinctive spicy hop aroma.

Organic Ale (OG 1045, ABV 4.5%) ◥
A rich toffee apple aroma and a smooth, grainy feel. Malt and caramel initially match the dry hoppy bitterness. As the flavours mature, liquorice dryness develops. Full-bodied.

Grapefruit Beer (OG 1047, ABV 4.7%) ◥
Fudge as well as grapefruit on the nose. A refreshing fruit flavour with hints of grapefruit peel in the aftertaste.

IPA (OG 1055, ABV 5.5%)
A full-bodied, highly-hopped pale ale with a zesty character.

Salamander SIBA

22 Harry Street, Dudley Hill, Bradford, West Yorkshire, BD4 9PH
☎ (01274) 652323 ⊕ salamanderbrewing.co.uk

⊠ Salamander first brewed in 2000 in a former pork pie factory. An expansion in 2004 increased capacity to 40 barrels per week. Direct deliveries are made to around 100 outlets in Cumbria, Derbyshire, Lancashire, Leicestershire, Lincolnshire, Manchester and Yorkshire. ‼ ♦

Blondie (OG 1040, ABV 4%)
A refreshing pale ale, malty with a gently-hopped aroma.

Mudpuppy (OG 1042, ABV 4.2%) ◥

A well-balanced, copper-coloured best bitter with a fruity, hoppy nose and a bitter finish.

Golden Salamander (OG 1045, ABV 4.5%) ◆
Citrus hops characterise the aroma and taste of this golden premium bitter, which has malt undertones throughout. The aftertaste is dry, hoppy and bitter.

Spectre Stout (OG 1045, ABV 4.5%) ◆
Rich roast malts dominate the smooth coffee and chocolate flavour. Nicely balanced. A dry, roast, bitter finish develops over time.

Bright Black Porter (ABV 4.8%)
An intense porter with a hint of rum and caramel.

Salcombe SIBA

Estuary View, Ledstone, Devon, TQ7 4BL
☎ (01548) 854888 ⏺ salcombebrewery.com

⊠ Formerly known as Quercus, brewing began in 2007 using an eight-barrel plant, before being sold to local residents John Tiner and Mike George in 2012. A complete rebranding occurred in 2016, with the brewery relocating to a new purpose-built brewery and visitor centre in 2017. ‼️🛒◆

Devon Amber (OG 1038, ABV 3.8%)
A classic bitter. Amber in colour with a dry, hoppy aroma and flavour with a sweet malt backbone.

Gold (OG 1042, ABV 4.2%)
A light, refreshing, straw-coloured ale with a hoppy aroma and taste and a long, hoppy finish.

Shingle Bay (OG 1042, ABV 4.2%)
A light, easy-drinking ale with a fruity aroma and flavour. Smooth to the taste with a crisp finish.

Seahorse (OG 1044, ABV 4.4%)
A smooth-drinking ale, deep gold in colour with a spicy hop character.

Lifesaver (OG 1048, ABV 4.8%)
A refreshing ale, deep copper in colour with a smack of citrus and orange peel and malty flavour. A dry citrus finish with a taste of liquorice.

Salopian SIBA ◉

The Old Station Yard, Station Road, Hadnall, Shropshire, SY4 3DD
☎ (01743) 248414 ⏺ salopianbrewery.co.uk

☺The brewery was established in 1995 in an old dairy on the outskirts of Shrewsbury but moved in 2014 to its new location in an industrial unit in the village of Hadnall, where it now produces more than 150 barrels a week. ‼️🛒◆RAIB

Shropshire Gold (OG 1037, ABV 3.8%) 🍴
A light, copper-coloured ale with an unusual blend of body and dryness.

Oracle (OG 1040, ABV 4%) 🍴 ◆
Citrus aromas lead to an impressive dry and increasing citrus taste.

Darwins Origin (OG 1042, ABV 4.3%) 🍴 📦
A light copper-coloured ale with a striking hop profile, which is balanced by a refined malt finish.

Hop Twister (OG 1044, ABV 4.5%)
A premium bitter with a citrus flavour and complex hop finish. Refreshing and crisp.

Lemon Dream (OG 1043.5, ABV 4.5%) 📦
A light gold-coloured ale brewed with wheat malt and subtly flavoured with fresh lemons.

Golden Thread (OG 1048, ABV 5%)

A bright gold-coloured ale. Strong and quite bitter but well-balanced.

Kashmir (OG 1053.5, ABV 5.5%)

Automaton (OG 1068, ABV 7%) 📦

Saltaire SIBA ◉

Unit 6, County Works, Dockfield Road, Shipley, West Yorkshire, BD17 7AR
☎ (01274) 594959 ⏺ saltairebrewery.co.uk

☺Launched in 2006, Saltaire is an award-winning brewery based in a former Victorian power station. A brewery tap is open on site. More than 600 pubs are supplied across West Yorkshire and the north of England. 🛒◆

South Island Pale (OG 1035, ABV 3.5%) ◆
This low strength, golden-coloured bitter has an intensely hoppy aroma which follows through to a well-balanced fruity, citrus hop flavour and a long, hoppy finish.

Pride (OG 1039, ABV 3.9%)
A deep gold-coloured beer with toasty malt and rich, spicy hop flavours.

Blonde (OG 1040, ABV 4%) ◆
Thirst-quenching and quaffable, this straw-coloured beer is slightly sweet and well-rounded with fruit, malt and hops in the taste and a fruity, hoppy finish.

Citra Pale (ABV 4.2%)
A pale ale with mango and rich tropical fruit flavours balanced by sweet malt.

Cascade Pale Ale (OG 1046, ABV 4.8%) ◆
A well-balanced, golden-coloured bitter with smooth mouthfeel, floral hop aromas and pronounced bitterness, culminating in a long, dry finish and dry aftertaste.

Triple Chocoholic (OG 1048.5, ABV 4.8%) 🍴 📦 ◆
A creamy, dark brown-coloured, roast, chocolate stout with a dry bitter finish and a rich chocolate aroma.

New World Red (ABV 5.2%)
A deep red-coloured malty ale with firm bitterness and citrus notes.

Stateside IPA (ABV 6%)
American-style IPA with balanced bitterness and full fruity, citrus flavours.

Kala Black (ABV 6.2%)
A black IPA with smooth roast malt character and big American hop presence.

Sambrook's SIBA ◉

Units 1-3, Yelverton Road, Battersea, London, SW11 3QG
☎ (020) 7228 0598 ⏺ sambrooksbrewery.co.uk

⊠ Sambrook's was founded by Duncan Sambrook and David Welsh in 2008, supplying its award-winning ales throughout London. The brewery bar hosts regular events and is available for private booking. ‼️🛒◆RAIB

Wandle Ale (OG 1038.5, ABV 3.8%) 🍴 📦 ◆
Dryness balances the rounded, sweetish malt flavour of this fruity, quaffable pale brown-coloured bitter. Some peach and citrus notes.

Pumphouse Pale Ale (OG 1041.5, ABV 4.2%) ◆

THE BREWERIES

Refreshing golden-coloured beer with a hint of citrus aroma becoming more pronounced on the palate, lingering into the bitter finish.

Junction Ale (OG 1045.5, ABV 4.5%) 🖵 ◆
Smooth, full-bodied, brown-coloured best bitter. Fruit and spicy hoppy aroma and flavour, lingering in the dry, slightly bitter finish.

Powerhouse Porter (OG 1050, ABV 4.9%) ◆
Dark brown-coloured porter with a pleasant roasted malt nose with some sultana, blackcurrant and treacle character. Dry roasted finish.

Samphire (NEW)

118 Sandgate Road, Folkestone, Kent, CT20 2AL
☎ (01303) 250373

Small brewery established in 2015 in a converted back room of a home brew shop.

Sandiway

Blakemere Village, Chester Road, Sandiway, Cheshire, CW8 2EB
☎ (01606) 301000 ⊕ sandiwayales.co.uk

☺Sandiway began brewing in 2015 using a five-barrel plant in the premises of the former Blakemere Brewery at Blakemere Village Craft Centre. Aimed at local trade, outlets include the on-site shop called 'Wee Howff'. Beers are also available at the No. 4 Bar in Winsford and limited outlets throughout Cheshire and surrounding areas. ‼🍴

Hop Salvo (OG 1037, ABV 3.8%)
Light session bitter with citrus flavours.

Hop Schism (OG 1040, ABV 4.1%)
Golden ale with a hint of orange peel.

Hop Sepia (OG 1041, ABV 4.3%)
Copper-coloured ale with liquorice and caramel hints.

Hop Secret (OG 1043, ABV 4.5%)
Dark-coloured porter with coffee notes.

Chainbreaker (ABV 4.8%)
An American-hopped IPA.

Sandstone SIBA

Unit 5, Wrexham Enterprise Park, Preston Road, off Ash Road, North Wrexham Industrial Estate, Wrexham, LL13 9JT
☎ (01978) 664805 ☎ 07851 001118
⊕ sandstonebrewery.co.uk

☺ Sandstone Brewery was established as a four-barrel plant in 2008. It was taken over by the current owners in 2013. Beers are available at around 50 outlets in North-west England and North Wales. ‼🍴◆

Edge (OG 1039, ABV 3.8%) ◆
A satisfying session ale, this pale, dry, bitter beer has a full mouthfeel and a lingering hoppy finish that belies its modest strength.

Onyx Dragon (OG 1040, ABV 4%)
Coal black in colour with hints of chocolate, toffee and caramel.

Post Mistress (OG 1046, ABV 4.4%) ◆
A full-bodied, smooth premium bitter, ruby-red in colour, with a rich, mellow taste. Good

combination of malt, hops and fruit in aroma and initial taste leading to a lasting, satisfying finish.

Racing Dragon (OG 1044, ABV 4.4%)

Twisted Dragon (OG 1058, ABV 5.8%)

Savour

Office: 10 Stephenson Drive, Windsor, Berkshire, SL4 5LG ⊕ savourbeer.com

Inspired by the farmhouse beers of Belgium and Northern France, Savour was founded in 2013 and focuses mainly on bottle-conditioned beers. The company is based in Windsor and the beers are brewed in small batches using the kit at Firebrand Brewing (qv) in Cornwall. RAIB

Sawbridgeworth SIBA

🗏 81 London Road, Sawbridgeworth, Hertfordshire, CM21 9JJ
☎ (01279) 722313 ☎ 07446 960409
⊕ thegatepub.net

Set up in 2000 by owners Tom and Gary Barnett, the brewery is situated behind the Gate Inn. Tom is a former professional footballer whose clubs included Crystal Palace.

Scarborough SIBA

Unit 21b, Stadium Works, Barry's Lane, Scarborough, North Yorkshire, YO12 4HA
☎ (01723) 367506 ⊕ scarboroughbrewery.co.uk

Scarborough is a family-run brewery established in 2009 using a one-barrel plant., expanding to 10 barrels in 2011. Beers can be found at its brewery tap, the Valley Bar in Scarborough, and nationwide via wholesalers. ◆

Citra (OG 1040.7, ABV 4.2%)
Refreshing and light golden-coloured beer with citrus aromas.

Sealord (OG 1041.7, ABV 4.3%)
Golden ale brewed with a combination of hops that give subtle hints of lime, grapefruit and melon.

Ship of Fools (OG 1043.6, ABV 4.5%)
American-hopped, golden-coloured pale ale with flavours of pineapple and grapefruit.

Stout (OG 1044.6, ABV 4.6%)
Full-bodied, dark-coloured stout brewed using five malts giving depth of flavour and a bitter chocolate aroma.

Old Sailor (OG 1047.5, ABV 4.9%)
American-style, gold-coloured ale packed with hops for tropical flavours and a hoppy aroma.

Schoolhouse SIBA

Unit 1, Cleveland Industrial Estate, Darlington, DL1 2PB
☎ (01325) 461812
✉ gannaway@schoolhousebrewery.co.uk

☺ Schoolhouse began brewing in 2013 on a six-barrel plant, the first brewery to be based in Darlington for more than 70 years. The brewery does not artificially enhance the mineral or acidity content of its brewing water, ensuring its beer reflects the geology of the North East. ‼

100 Lines (ABV 3.8%)

Scribbler's

7 Lime Grove, Stapleford, Nottinghamshire, NG9 7GF
☎ (0115) 875 1759 ☎ 07780 662244
⊕ scribblers-ales.com

Scribbler's was established in 2014 by Richard Nettleton, an author (hence the name) and Roger Frost. The 4.5-barrel plant was constructed by the owners, the fermentation and mash tun converted from old ice cream vessels. Beer names are based on classic book titles.

Beerfest at Tiffanys (OG 1046, ABV 3.8%) ◆
Golden-coloured with a citrus fruit aroma and taste with a dry bitter finish.

Hoppy Potter and the Goblet of Ale (OG 1048, ABV 4.2%)
Light-coloured ale with with citrus hop aromas.

Masher in the Rye (OG 1053, ABV 4.8%) ◆
Golden-coloured, delicately-hopped beer, subtle malt, hint of fruit, soft bitterness.

Rubecca (OG 1053, ABV 4.8%) ◆
Dark ruby-coloured ale with a mixture of roast malt, raisin, fruit and chocolate, leading to a gentle bitter finish.

One Brew Over the Cuckoo's Nest (OG 1058, ABV 5.3%)
A premium ale with a distinctive mouthfeel and smooth, sweet traditional hop flavours.

Beyond Reasonable Stout (OG 1068, ABV 6%) ◆
Initial roast malt and coffee giving way to moderate bitterness and a dark fruit finish.

Seal Bay (NEW)

Parc-y-Pratt Farm, Fishguard Road, Cardigan, SA43 3DR ☎ 07966 593552
✉ colintmathew@yahoo.com

Seal Bay was established in 2016 in a farm outbuilding using a one-barrel plant. Beer is supplied to local pubs and parties.

Craig (OG 1042, ABV 4.2%)
Straw-coloured best bitter with distinctive malt and hop flavours.

Secret Herb Garden

See Top Out

Sentinel (NEW) SIBA

🏛 178 Shoreham Street, Sheffield, South Yorkshire, S1 4SQ ⊕ sentinelbrewing.co

Brewhouse and taproom established in 2016.

Seren SIBA

Syfnau House, Rosebush, SA66 7QY
☎ (01437) 532098 ⊕ serenbrewing.com

⊠ Seren Brewing Company is a nanobrewery on the edge of the Preseli Mountains in North Pembrokeshire producing bottle-conditioned beers. ⏎ RAIB

Serious

Unit C5, Fieldhouse Industrial Estate, Fieldhouse Road, Rochdale, OL12 0AA ☎ 07840 301797
✉ jenny@seriousbrewing.co.uk

Established in 2015 and run by a husband-and-wife team. The focus is on producing high quality beers drawing influences from traditional British ales, US craft beers and artisanal Belgian beers. Available nationwide through Direct Drinks. ◆ RAIB

Evergreen (ABV 4.5%)

Moonlight (ABV 4.5%)
Silky smooth stout with chocolate notes and a bitter hop finish.

Redsmith (ABV 4.5%)
A copper-coloured English-style IPA .

Settle SIBA

Unit 2b, The Sidings Industrial Estate, Settle, North Yorkshire, BD24 9RP
☎ (01729) 824936 ⊕ settlebrewery.co.uk

☺ Settle Brewery is located in a small industrial unit adjacent to Settle railway station. Brewing started in 2013 using a 12-barrel plant. More than 40 outlets across Cumbria, the Yorkshire Dales, West Yorkshire and North Lancashire are supplied. The beers are also available through wholesalers. ‼◆

Blonde (OG 1036, ABV 3.6%)
A straw-coloured beer with a subtle blend of fruit and spice flavours and citrus overtones.

Mainline (OG 1037.5, ABV 3.8%) ◆
Creamy traditional Yorkshire Bitter. Good balance of rich malt and bittering hops, giving a pronounced raspberry fruitiness and hints of nuts in both aroma and taste.

Attermire IPA (OG 1041, ABV 4.2%)

Contract brewed for Nine Standards Brewery:

No. 4 Amber Ale (OG 1037, ABV 3.7%)
A dark amber-coloured bitter with a fruity, spicy nose.

No. 1 Golden Ale (OG 1040, ABV 4.1%)
A golden ale with a hint of blackcurrant.

No. 2 Pale Ale (OG 1042, ABV 4.3%)
A classic pale ale with a strong hoppy aroma.

No. 3 Porter (OG 1048, ABV 4.7%) ◆
Roasty porter with coffee and dark fruits. Hints of liquorice and plums in the aroma. The finish is bitter and roasty.

Seven Bro7hers SIBA ◉

Unit 63, Waybridge Enterprise Centre, Daniel Adamson Road, Salford, M50 1DS
☎ (0161) 637 9929 ☎ 07968 538572
⊕ sevenbro7hers.com

Brewing began in 2014 using a 10-barrel plant. A new brewhouse and fermentation tanks doubled brewing capacity in 2017 and allowed for the brewing of speciality and one-off beers plus a brewery tap. The Seven Bro7hers Beerhouse in Ancoats opened in 2016. ◆

Session (ABV 3.8%)

A session ale with citrus aromas and tropical fruit flavours. A light malt base give strawberry and elderberry undertones on the palate.

Ruby (ABV 4%)
Sweet caramel notes and aromas of tropical fruit, grapefruit and champagne. A subtle combination of tangerine, spiced cherry and herbal vanilla flavours.

Water Melon (ABV 4.5%)
A wheat beer with a subtle infusion of fresh watermelon. Mellow strawberry and pineapple aromas.

EPA (ABV 4.8%)
An English pale ale with a tropical fruit aroma. The flavour is sweet with tropical fruit notes and a caramel finish.

IPA (ABV 5%)
An American-style IPA, bitter rather than sweet. Hoppy with grapefruit and floral undertones and a citrus aroma.

Stout (ABV 5.2%)
A silky stout with a hit of roasted coffee and chocolate and fruity hop undertones. Star anise is added to give a distinctive but subtle liquorice character.

Shalford SIBA 👁

Hyde Farm, Shalford, CM7 5WP ☎ 07749 658512

Correspondence: PO Box 10411, Braintree, Essex, CM7 5WP ☎ (01371) 850925
⊕ shalfordbrewery.co.uk

Shalford began brewing in 2007 on a five-barrel plant at Hyde Farm in the Pant Valley in Essex. More than 50 outlets are supplied direct. ♦ RAIB

1319 Mild (OG 1037, ABV 3.7%)
Roast malt and chocolate sweetness with a slight bitter finish.

Barnfield Pale Ale (OG 1038, ABV 3.8%) 🍂
Pale-coloured but full-flavoured, this is a traditional, hoppy bitter rather than a golden ale. Malt persists throughout, with bitterness becoming more dominant towards the end.

Braintree Market Ale (OG 1040, ABV 4%)
Traditional, easy-drinking session ale with a hoppy, lingering, dry finish.

Levelly Gold (OG 1040, ABV 4%)
Golden, summery bitter with a pleasant finish.

Stoneley Bitter (OG 1042, ABV 4.2%) 🍂
Dark amber-coloured session beer whose vivid hop character is supported by a juicy, malty body. A dry finish makes this beer very drinkable.

Hyde Bitter (OG 1047, ABV 4.7%) 🍂
Stronger version of Barnfield, with a similar but more assertive character.

Levelly Black (OG 1048, ABV 4.8%)
A dark-coloured, heavy, well-hopped ale with a grainy toffee taste topped with a thick creamy head.

Rotten End (OG 1065, ABV 6.5%)
Strong beer with slightly sweet, nutty undertones and a bitter edge to finish.

> Beer makes you feel the way you ought to feel without beer. **Henry Lawson**

Shardlow 👁

The Old Brewery Stables, British Waterways Yard, Cavendish Bridge, Leicestershire, DE72 2HL
☎ (01332) 799188 ✉ nev@shardlowbrewery.co.uk

☺On a site associated with brewing since 1819, Shardlow delivers to more than 100 outlets throughout the East Midlands and is also one of the largest UK cider distributors. Reverend Eaton is named after a scion of the Eaton brewing family, Rector of Shardlow for 40 years. The brewery tap is the Blue Bell Inn at Melbourne, Derbyshire. Prolific supplier of beers to local beer festivals. !! ♦ RAIB

Chancellors Revenge (OG 1036, ABV 3.6%)
A light-coloured, refreshing, full-flavoured and well-hopped session bitter.

Cavendish Dark (OG 1037, ABV 3.7%)
A mild, well-balanced beer with a hoppy aftertaste.

Golden Hop (OG 1041, ABV 4.1%)
Golden-coloured, sweet-tasting beer.

Kiln House (OG 1041, ABV 4.1%)
A refreshing golden ale with a lingering bitter finish.

Narrow Boat (OG 1043, ABV 4.3%)
A pale amber-coloured bitter with a short, crisp, hoppy aftertaste.

Cavendish Bridge (OG 1045, ABV 4.5%)
Pale amber-coloured premium bitter. Refreshing, clean and fruity with a pleasing bitter finish.

Cavendish Gold (OG 1045, ABV 4.5%)
Pale gold-coloured, bright and clean tasting. A full-bodied ale with pronounced bitterness and complexity.

Reverend Eaton (OG 1045, ABV 4.5%)
A smooth, medium-strong bitter, full of malt and hop flavours with a sweet aftertaste.

Mayfly (OG 1048, ABV 4.8%)
Fruit notes predominate together with a pronounced malty aroma. Easy drinking but strong.

Five Bells (OG 1050, ABV 5%)
Dark, rich, ruby-coloured ale, powerful and bittersweet to the palate. Coffee notes complete the profile.

Whistlestop (OG 1050, ABV 5%)
A smooth and surprisingly strong pale beer.

Sharp's 👁

Pityme Business Centre, Rock, Cornwall, PL27 6NU
☎ (01208) 862121 ⊕ sharpsbrewery.co.uk

⊗ Sharp's was bought for £20 million by Molson Coors in 2011. The brewery was founded in 1994 and within 15 years had grown from producing 1,500 barrels a year to 60,000. £7.5 million of investment from Molson Coors has brought the capacity up to 200,000 barrels a year. The company owns no pubs and delivers beer to more than 1,200 outlets across the south of England via temperature-controlled depots in Bristol and London. Molson Coors has stressed that it will maintain production in Cornwall. Part of Molson Coors PLC. ➤ ♦ RAIB

Cornish Coaster (OG 1035.2, ABV 3.6%) 🍂
Refreshing copper-coloured bitter. Gentle balance of biscuit malt, fruit and sweetness. Fruit in the finish with bitterness and faint dryness.

Doom Bar (OG 1038.5, ABV 4%) 🍂

Tawny brown-coloured bitter with gentle fruit aroma. Balanced taste of biscuit malt, resinous hops with apple, strawberry and plum fruits.

Atlantic (OG 1043, ABV 4.2%) ◆
Gold-coloured best bitter with fragrant hop aroma. Orange citrus with caramel sweetness balanced by malt and bitterness. Tropical fruit hints.

Original (OG 1042.5, ABV 4.4%) ◆
Brown-coloured best bitter with English hop and malt aroma. Fruity, hoppy taste with malt and bitter roasted biscuit, finishing dry.

Special/Sea Fury (OG 1048.5, ABV 5%) ◆
A tawny-coloured, strong bitter with hops and caramel aroma. Sweet malty taste, with fruit and light roast throughout, becoming dry.

Shed

Broadfields, Pewsey, Wiltshire, SN9 5DT
☎ (01672) 564533 ☎ 07769 812643
⊕ shedales.com

Shed Ales was launched in 2012 operating from a one-barrel plant in a converted garden shed. The brewery currently produces three core ales and several bespoke beers, available at selected local outlets including the brewery owned Shed Alehouse, a micropub in Pewsey. ◆

Dig It (OG 1037.5, ABV 3.7%)

Shed Some Light (OG 1041, ABV 3.8%)
A refreshing blonde-style beer made with a light, earthy hop aroma and flavour.

Dibber (OG 1042.5, ABV 4.2%)
Easy-drinking ale with a biscuit malt and citrus hop aroma, a good balance of malt and fruity hop notes and dry finish.

Sheelin

178 Derrylin Road, Bellanaleck, County Fermanagh, BT92 2BA ☎ 07730 432232 ⊕ sheelin.com

Sheelin was established by brewer and chemist Dr George Cathcart in 2013. Beer is mainly available in bottles.

Sheffield SIBA

Unit 111, JC Albyn Complex, Burton Road, Sheffield, South Yorkshire, S3 8BT
☎ (0114) 272 7256 ⊕ sheffieldbrewery.com

☺Established in 2006, Sheffield Brewery Company is situated in a rustic Victorian factory, originally known for making Blanco Polish. The 10-barrel plant operates on a gravity-fed tower based system. The brewery has its own on-site tap room. More than 50 outlets are supplied direct. ‼

Crucible Best (OG 1038, ABV 3.8%)
A well-balanced session best bitter.

Five Rivers (OG 1038, ABV 3.8%)
Easy-drinking, straw-coloured session ale. The hoppy aroma carries through to the finish.

Seven Hills (OG 1039, ABV 4.1%)
A dry, hoppy pale ale.

Blanco Blonde (OG 1042, ABV 4.2%)

Sheffield Porter (OG 1045, ABV 4.4%)
Rich chocolate, malty and caramel flavours.

Forgemasters (OG 1038, ABV 4.8%)

IPA (OG 1048, ABV 5%)

Shepherd Neame IFBB 👁

17 Court Street, Faversham, Kent, ME13 7AX
☎ (01795) 532206 ⊕ shepherdneame.co.uk

⊠ Shepherd Neame traces its history back to 1698, making it the oldest continuous brewer in the country, though brewing probably began even earlier. The company has 350 tied houses in the South-east, nearly all selling cask ale. More than 2,000 other outlets are also supplied. The cask beers are made with mostly Kentish hops, and water from the brewery's own artesian well. There is a microplant within the brewery to produce speciality ales for special occasions and product development. These beers may be available in selected pubs. The company also brews cask ales under the Faversham Steam Brewery and No. 18 Yard Brewhouse names. ‼ ➤ ◆RAIB

Master Brew (OG 1032, ABV 3.7%) ◆
A distinctive bitter, mid-brown in colour, with a hoppy aroma. Well-balanced, with a nicely aggressive bitter taste from its hops, it leaves a hoppy/bitter finish, tinged with sweetness.

Whitstable Bay (OG 1038, ABV 3.9%)
A full-bodied, fruity ale with a subtle bitterness and grapefruit and pine aromas.

Kent's Best (OG 1036, ABV 4.1%)
A robust bitter which merges the biscuity sweetness of English malt with the fruity, floral bitterness of locally-grown hops.

Spitfire Gold (OG 1039, ABV 4.1%)
Well-balanced with tropical fruit and pine aromas, and a subtle bitterness.

Spitfire (OG 1036, ABV 4.2%)
Hints of marmalade, red grapes and pepper, with warm, mellow malts. A fruity finish with hints of spice and raspberry.

Bishops Finger (OG 1046, ABV 5%)
Strong ale with a complex hop aroma reminiscent of lemons, oranges and bananas combined with malt, molasses and toffee. Refreshing with a good malt character tinged with a lingering bitterness.

Sherfield Village SIBA

Goddards Farm, Goddards Lane, Sherfield on Loddon, Hampshire, RG27 0EL ☎ 07906 060429
⊕ sherfieldvillagebrewery.co.uk

Sherfield Village started brewing in 2011, based in a converted barn on a working dairy farm. The brewery uses a five-barrel plant, supplying local pubs and regional festivals. Extensive use is made of New World hops (prefixed SOLO), particularly those from New Zealand. Dry-hopped versions of single-hop beers are usually available. ◆RAIB

Threesome (OG 1030, ABV 3%)
Copper-coloured session beer with a long, hoppy finish.

SOLO Southern Gold (OG 1040, ABV 4%)
A golden-coloured beer with a citrus flavour and a floral nose.

SOLO Green Bullet (OG 1042, ABV 4.3%) ◆
A strong lemony nose, with hops dominating the taste building to a strong aftertaste with a big astringent hit at the end.

SOLO Single Hop (OG 1042, ABV 4.3%)

THE BREWERIES

A golden-coloured ale which uses a single hop variety that changes every month.

Hoppy Harrington (OG 1046, ABV 4.7%)
A mid-brown-coloured strong bitter with a complex, sweetish flavour and a satisfying hoppy finish.

Pioneer Stout (OG 1048, ABV 5%)
A black-coloured stout, packed with chocolate malt and Pioneer hops, and a hint of vanilla.

Shilling (NEW)

📧 92 West George Street, Glasgow, G2 1PJ
☎ (0141) 353 1654 ⊕ shillingbrewingcompany.co.uk

Brewing began in 2016.

ShinDigger

Office: 170 Vie Building, 185 Water Street, Manchester, M3 4JU ⊕ shindiggerbrewing.co

Established in 2012, ShinDigger is the project of two former Manchester University students. Output is predominantly keg and cans. Contract brewed at Tractor Shed (qv).

Shiny SIBA

📧 Unit 10, Old Hall Mill Business Centre, Little Eaton, Derbyshire, DE21 5EJ
☎ (01332) 902809

Brewing commenced in 2012 using a six-barrel plant sited in the beer garden of the Furnace Inn. After initially brewing solely for the pub, 2014 saw an increase in scale and output, with beers distributed across most of the country. A second 12-barrel brew plant was built in 2015 to increase capacity and host a visitor centre and shop.

New World (OG 1039, ABV 3.7%)
Golden in colour with powerful citrus hop flavours.

Pail (OG 1041, ABV 4%)
Regular series showcasing a particular hop.

Wrench (OG 1045, ABV 4.4%)

4 Wood (OG 1045, ABV 4.5%)
Traditional, well-balanced, light chestnut-coloured ale with a delicate hop finish.

Affinity (OG 1046, ABV 4.6%)
Strong, golden-coloured bitter with lots of fruity hops.

Tomahawk (OG 1058, ABV 6%)
Refreshing American-style brown-coloured IPA with citrus flavour and aromas.

Ship & Mitre (NEW)

c/o Ship & Mitre, 133 Dale Street, Liverpool, L2 2JH
☎ (0151) 236 0859

Launched in 2016, the Ship & Mitre Brewing Co primarily supplies the iconic city centre pub, with some sales locally and nationally. Beers are brewed using spare capacity at other breweries.

Lupa (OG 1037, ABV 3.6%)
A blend of citrus peels and hops for a sweeter, balanced pale ale.

Sublime (OG 1038, ABV 3.7%)
A light session pale ale with a citrus hop tang.

Silhouette (OG 1045, ABV 4.5%)

A dry stout with plenty of roasted, toasted richness.

Radiant (OG 1049, ABV 5%)
Warming and robust with fruity hops and a little honeyed sweetness.

Ship Inn

📧 Ship Inn, Ship Inn Brewery, Low Newton-by-the-Sea, Northumberland, NE66 3EL
☎ (01665) 576262 ⊕ shipinnewton.co.uk

Brewing commenced in 2008 on a 2.5-barrel plant. The brewery now produces 7.5 barrels per week. All regular beers are brewed in constant rotation but are only available on the premises. A special beer (4.2% ABV) is brewed for every 100 brews.

Shipstone's SIBA

📧 Little Star Brewery, Fox & Crown, Church Street, Old Basford, Nottingham, NG6 0GA
☎ (0115) 871 6477 ☎ 07528 415695

Office: 27 Grace Drive, Nottingham, NG8 5AG
⊕ shipstones.com

Set up in 1996, originally as Fiddlers Ales. In 1999 it became Alcazar Brewery on change of ownership. A full mash brewery with a 10-barrel brew length, it is located behind the Fox & Crown. The brewery changed hands in early 2016, when the name of the brewery was changed again and a new portfolio of beers established but this was short lived and it soon reverted back to the name Alcazar. In late 2016 Shipstone's took over brewing, producing its range of beers that had previously been contract brewed at Belvoir Brewery (qv).

Original Bitter (OG 1036, ABV 3.8%)
Amber-coloured, dry, classic Nottingham-style bitter.

Nut Brown Ale (OG 1041, ABV 4%)
Full-bodied, brown-coloured ale with a malty finish. Hints of butterscotch and mild liquorice, caramel and roasted cacao flavours.

Gold Star Blonde (OG 1041, ABV 4.2%)
Smooth, well-balanced blonde ale, clean and crisp with a light, subtle hop finish.

IPA (ABV 5.5%)

Shortts SIBA

Shortts Farm, Thorndon, Suffolk, IP23 7LS ☎ 07900 268100 ⊕ shorttsfarmbrewery.com

An award-winning brewery established in 2012 by Matt Hammond on what has been the family farm for over a century. The beers are based around a mucial theme and can be found throughout East Anglia. RAIB

The Cure (ABV 3.6%)
A traditional, tawny-coloured bitter with rich, malty flavours.

Strummer (OG 1038, ABV 3.8%)
An amber-coloured ale. Easy-drinking, light and hoppy bitter with a malty character.

Two Tone (ABV 3.8%)
A dark mild with dark chocolate and caramel malt flavours.

Blondie (OG 1040, ABV 4%)

A blonde ale with refreshing fruity hops and biscuity malt flavours.

Rockabilly (ABV 4.3%)
A hoppy American-style pale ale. Refreshing, fruity and citrus.

Skiffle (OG 1047, ABV 4.5%)
A chestnut-coloured, rich and malty premium bitter.

Indie (OG 1048, ABV 4.8%)
Subtle but refreshing citrus fruit followed by a spicy, almost honey-like, lingering bitter finish.

Darkside (ABV 5%)
A traditional, rich and satisfying porter.

Shotover SIBA

Coopers Yard, Manor Farm Road, Horspath, Oxfordshire, OX33 1SD
☎ (01865) 604620 ☎ 07710 883273
⊕ shotoverbrewing.com

⊠ A family-owned and -run brewery four miles from Oxford city centre. It began brewing in 2009 and supplies outlets in the Oxford area. ‼ ☕ ◆ RAIB

Prospect (OG 1040, ABV 3.7%)
A flavoursome local bitter, packed with hops.

Trinity (OG 1040, ABV 4.2%)
Pale gold in colour with an intense grapefruit hop character.

Scholar (OG 1047, ABV 4.5%)
Deep copper-coloured premium bitter combining a silky malt base with a mixture of oranges, grapefruit and spiciness.

Shottle Farm

School House Farm, Lodge Lane, Shottle, Derbyshire, DE56 2DS
☎ (01773) 550056 ☎ 07877 723075
⊕ shottlefarmbrewery.co.uk

Located in the hills above Belper, the Grade II-listed farm is part of the Chatsworth Estate. Family-run, Shottle Farm Brewery has been in production since 2011 with a 10-barrel plant. It has an on-site bar, the Bull Shed. ◆ RAIB

Shottlecock (OG 1034.9, ABV 3.6%)
Single malt light ale made with local honey. In the summer the honey is replaced with homemade elderflower syrup.

Black Peggy (OG 1037.8, ABV 3.9%)
Smooth, easy-drinking stout with chocolate malt and oatmeal. Light-bodied with pleasing hints of liquorice.

Shottle Pale Ale (OG 1037.8, ABV 4%)
Pale ale with a hint of citrus, brewed with local honey.

BOB (Best of Both) (OG 1038.8, ABV 4.1%)
A full-flavoured real lager with a pronounced sparkle and zing.

Eight Shilling (OG 1038.8, ABV 4.1%)
A rich, dark-coloured beer, smooth and malty. Full-bodied, pleasant aftertaste with undertones of treacle and caramel.

Shottle Gold (OG 1041.7, ABV 4.3%)
Golden ale with a floral aroma and a fruity hint of citrus lemon. Crisp and easy on the palate.

Dilks (OG 1048.4, ABV 5%)

Smooth and well-balanced, amber-coloured ale with a slight sweetness and hint of citrus.

Shugborough

Shugborough Estate, Milford, Staffordshire, ST17 0XB
☎ (01782) 823447 ⊕ shugborough.org.uk

Brewing in the original brewhouse at Shugborough, home of the Earls of Lichfield, restarted in 1990, but a lack of expertise led to the brewery being a static museum piece until Titanic Brewery of Stoke-on-Trent (qv) began helping in 1996. ‼

Signal (NEW) SIBA

8 Stirling Way, Beddington Farm Road, Croydon, CR0 4XN
☎ (020) 8684 6111 ⊕ signallager.com

No real ale.

Signature Brew SIBA ⊙

Unit 25, Leyton Business Centre, Etloe Road, Leyton, London, E10 7BT
☎ (020) 7684 4664 ⊕ signaturebrew.co.uk

Signature Brew has been brewing beer inspired by music since 2011. Originally using spare capacity at a number of breweries, a successful crowd funding initiative has resulted in it owning its own brewery in Leyton. Special seasonal beers are brewed in collaboration with music artists. ☕ ◆ RAIB

Session (OG 1042, ABV 4%) ◗
Refreshing bitter with spicy hop on the nose and palate balanced by a malty sweetness and a lingering bitterness.

Signature Pale (OG 1033, ABV 4.1%) ◗
Golden-coloured beer using pale malts with a little wheat. The American hops give the beer its fruity character.

Black Vinyl Stout (OG 1046, ABV 4.2%) ◗
Rich cocoa roasted notes predominate on the palate balanced by some sweetness and American hops giving lightness to the flavour.

Red Wedge (OG 1047, ABV 4.7%) ◗
Reddish brown-coloured beer with hoppy fruity aroma. Flavour is dominated by hops with bitterness coming through later. Tangerine fruit notes.

Backstage IPA (OG 1054, ABV 5.6%) ◗
Amber-coloured, unfined IPA with fruity hops and a bitterness, overlaid with some banana and biscuity malty notes. Lingering, dry finish.

Silhill SIBA

Oak Farm, Hampton Lane, Solihull, West Midlands, B92 0JB
☎ (0845) 519 5101 ☎ 07977 444564

Office: PO Box 15739, Solihull, B93 3FW
⊕ silhillbrewery.co.uk

⊠ Established in 2010, Silhill is a small independent brewery based in premises just outside Solihull town centre using a 10-barrel plant. Bottling operations commenced in 2015. Beers are available in Solihull, Birmingham and Stratford-upon-Avon as well as in Malmaison restaurants. ‼ RAIB

Gold Star (OG 1039, ABV 3.9%)
An amber-coloured ale. Malty and smooth, finishing with a delicate honey note.

Blonde Star (OG 1041, ABV 4.1%)
A refreshing, sweet citrus pale ale.

Pure Star (OG 1043, ABV 4.3%)
A chestnut-coloured ale, warming and well-balanced, with a hint of chocolate.

Silks SIBA

Wash Farm, Queen Street, Sible Hedingham, Essex, CO9 3RH
☎ (01787) 275513 ☎ 07921 654910
⊕ silksbrewery@co.uk

Silks is a five-barrel microbrewery producing hand-crafted ales in small batches. Established in 2015, it is based on a North Essex farm in a converted grain store. ◆RAIB

Molly's Jolly Mild (OG 1036, ABV 3.6%)
A dark-coloured, mellow-flavoured mild with a hint of dark chocolate and roasted coffee.

Veteran Campaigner (OG 1037, ABV 3.8%)
An amber-coloured session ale.

Whacker Payne (OG 1037, ABV 3.8%)
A golden-coloured ale, crisp and refreshing with subtle fruity citrus hints.

Old Man Shirv (OG 1043, ABV 4.5%)
A smooth, full-bodied, copper-coloured premium ale with a rich malt flavour.

Silver Street

Britannia Mill, Cobden Street, Bury, BL9 6AW
☎ 07515 651874
⊕ silverstreetbrewingcompany.com

☺Brewing began in 2014 at the Clarence on Silver Street, Bury. The brewery has since expanded to a 15-barrel plant at Britannia Mill. ‼◆

Session (OG 1039, ABV 3.9%)

Fire Island (OG 1040, ABV 4%)

One (OG 1040, ABV 4%)

Ruby, Ruby, Ruby, Ruby (OG 1047, ABV 4.7%)
Deep ruby-coloured ale with a slight treacle undertone and a floral aroma.

Porter (OG 1053, ABV 5%)
An easy-drinking porter with a treacle toffee flavour.

Red (OG 1055, ABV 5.5%)
An IPA with biscuity flavours, floral hops and intense maltiness.

USA IPA (OG 1056, ABV 5.7%)
Malty caramel undertones and bold American hops.

Silverstone SIBA

Office: Shacks Barn Farm, Silverstone, Northamptonshire, NN12 8TB
☎ (01280) 860288 ☎ 07918 031464
⊕ silverstonerealale.com

This traditional tower brewery, which is located near the celebrated motor racing circuit, opened in 2008. With a change of hands in 2015 the brewery re-engineered its range of real ales. ‼◆

Ignition (OG 1036, ABV 3.4%)

Floral, hoppy blonde ale with a zesty, powerful taste for its strength.

Pitstop (OG 1040, ABV 3.9%)
Session bitter with a mellow bitter flavour and undertones of lime.

Polestar (OG 1042, ABV 4.1%)
Amber-coloured ale with hints of caramel toffee and a long, bittersweet finish.

Chequered Flag (OG 1043, ABV 4.3%)
Full-bodied, amber-coloured IPA with a complex taste and citrus finish.

Octane (OG 1047, ABV 4.8%)
A stronger ale, rich with hints of honey and toffee and a mellow, slightly coffee aroma.

Classic IPA (OG 1057, ABV 5.6%)
A mildly hoppy IPA with a touch of bitter honey.

Simpsons

▤ **White Swan, Eardisland, Herefordshire, HR6 9BD**
☎ (01544) 388635 ⊕ simpsonsfineales.co.uk

Tim Simpson acquired the White Swan in 2011 and set up the brewery at the rear of the pub in 2013. Beers are currently served in the White Swan, and locally to the free trade.

Golden Cock (OG 1037, ABV 3.7%)

Red Leg (OG 1043, ABV 4.3%)

Black Grouse (OG 1045, ABV 4.5%)

Old English (OG 1047, ABV 4.7%)

Siren Craft SIBA

Unit 1, Hogwood Industrial Estate, Weller Drive, Finchampstead, Berkshire, RG40 4QZ
☎ (0118) 973 0929 ⊕ sirencraftbrew.com

⊠ Established in 2013, Siren is a 40-barrel craft brewery. Rapid growth has necessitated continuous expansion with 800 hectolitres of fermentation capacity added. A state-of-the-art bottling facility and further major expansions to double production were completed in 2017. An extensive barrel-ageing programme commenced in 2013. ‼◆RAIB

Yu Lu (OG 1041, ABV 3.6%)
A pale ale made with lemon zest and loose leaf Earl Grey tea. It has a hoppy bitterness, bergamot orange and lemon notes and a peach and apricot finish.

Undercurrent Oatmeal Pale Ale (OG 1042, ABV 4.5%)
A pale ale with spicy, grassy aromas and a taste of grapefruit and apricot.

Soundwave IPA (OG 1056, ABV 5.6%)
An American-style West Coast IPA: golden-coloured and immensely hoppy with grapefruit, peach and mango flavours.

Liquid Mistress Red IPA (OG 1061, ABV 5.8%)
An American-style West Coast bright red-coloured ale: burnt raisins and crackers balanced by a citrus grapefruit and peach spark.

Broken Dream Breakfast Stout (OG 1072, ABV 6.5%)
A breakfast stout with a gentle touch of smoke, coffee and chocolate.

Six Bells

🏠 Church Street, Bishop's Castle, Shropshire, SY9 5AA
☎ (01588) 638930 🌐 sixbellsbrewery.co.uk

The Six Bells Brewery started in 1997 using a five-barrel plant. It supplies customers both within Shropshire and over the border in Wales. A new 12-barrel plant opened in 2010.

Noggin' (OG 1037, ABV 3.8%)
A pale, fairly hoppy bitter.

Ow Do! (OG 1040, ABV 4%)
Rich, amber-coloured ale full of spicy, fruity character.

Spikey Blonde (OG 1040, ABV 4%)

Cloud Nine (OG 1043, ABV 4.2%)
Golden ale, well-hopped with citrus notes throughout.

six°north

Reekie House, Aberdeen Road, Laurencekirk,
AB30 1AG
☎ (01561) 377047 ☎ 07840 678243
🌐 sixdnorth.co.uk

⊠ Established in 2013, the brewery brews beers in the Belgian tradition, using a purpose-built 470-hectolitre plant. Depending on beer style, the beers are supplied as cask or keg as appropriate. ‼

Six O'Clock

Gould Street, Manchester, M4 4RN
🌐 sixoclockbeer.co.uk

Six O'Clock began brewing in 2013 and has its own plant on the premises of BlackJack Brewery (qv). The plant is just over one barrel length and is in full production. There is direct distribution to pubs in Manchester city centre and further afield through Glassworks Distribution. ‼♦

Overtime (OG 1042, ABV 4.2%)
A light, hoppy pale ale.

Annuit Coeptis (OG 1048, ABV 4.8%)

Union (OG 1048, ABV 5%)

Bolt (OG 1054, ABV 5.6%)

Sixpenny SIBA

The Old Dairy, Holwell Farm, Cranborne, Dorset,
BH21 5QP
☎ (01725) 762006 🌐 sixpennybrewery.co.uk

⊠ Established in 2007 as Waylands Brewery in Addlestone, Surrey, using a 2.5-barrel plant. It relocated in 2009 to Sixpenny Handley in Dorset, changing its name and increasing its plant size to 20 barrels. The brewery moved again in 2016 to larger premises in renovated farm buildings near Cranborne. The onsite brewery bar and shop (the Sixpenny Tap) are located in the former stables building. More than 50 outlets are supplied including house beers to local Wetherspoon pubs. ‼🛒♦

6d Best Bitter (OG 1042, ABV 3.8%)
A well-balanced ale with a rounded malt flavour that leads to a pleasantly bitter and hoppy finish.

6d Gold (OG 1043, ABV 4%)
A golden ale, slightly citrus flavoured with a distinct hoppy, floral aroma.

6d IPA (OG 1053, ABV 5.2%)
Traditional IPA with a powerful hop character and a long, rounded malt finish.

Skinner's SIBA 👁

Riverside, Newham Road, Truro, Cornwall, TR1 2DP
☎ (01872) 271885 🌐 skinnersbrewery.com

⊠ Award-winning brewery established in 1997. The brewery moved to bigger premises in 2003, opening a shop and visitor centre. The 25-barrel plant produces 25,000 hectolitres a year, using local Cornish barley only. ‼🛒♦

Cornish Trawler (OG 1038, ABV 3.8%) 🍺
Refreshing gold-coloured ale with hop, malt and toffee aroma. Grassy, resinous hops with summer fruits. Long and gentle hop-bitter finish.

Betty Stogs (OG 1040, ABV 4%) 🍺
Copper-coloured bitter with gentle hop aroma. Balance of light citrus hops and apple, sweet malt and bitterness. Long finish.

Hops n Honey (OG 1040, ABV 4%) 🍺
Amber-coloured honey beer with delicate malt aroma. Citrus, apple and tropical fruit flavours with honey and grassy hops. Long finish.

River Cottage EPA (OG 1040, ABV 4%) 🍺
Gold-coloured bitter with floral hop aroma. Robust hops, sweet fruit, bitterness and malt flavours. Hoppy, rising bitter, dry finish.

Lushingtons (OG 1041, ABV 4.2%) 🍺
Smooth golden ale with citrus hop aroma. Lemon zest and marmalade citrus hop flavours with tropical fruits and faint malt.

Cornish Knocker (OG 1044, ABV 4.5%) 🍺
Refreshing ale with fragrant apple and hop aroma. Citrus hops, malt and summer fruit flavours. Bitter and dry finish.

PennyComeQuick (OG 1046, ABV 4.5%) 🍺
Creamy, smooth, dark brown-coloured stout with roast grain aroma. Heavy roast coffee, malt, fig and cherry flavours. Roast, dry finish.

Porthleven (OG 1048, ABV 4.8%) 🍺
Refreshing golden ale with citrus hop and pine nose. Assertive citrus hop, bitter and fruity flavour. Bitter citrus hop finish.

Skippool Creek (NEW)

15 Alexandra Road, Thornton-Cleveleys, Lancashire,
FY5 5DB
☎ (01253) 858904 ☎ 07446 219497
🌐 skippoolcreek.co.uk

☺A nanobrewery based in Thornton-Cleveleys on the Fylde coast with a 100-litre brewing capacity. Brewing began in 2016, supplying local pubs and clubs. ♦RAIB

Skipper's Dark Ale (OG 1032, ABV 3.2%)
A dark-coloured ale with a delicate, slightly floral aroma. The balanced malt flavour gives overtones of caramelised toffee with a hint of nuts.

Top Sail Pale Ale (OG 1042, ABV 4.2%)
A pale ale with a complex blackcurrant, loganberry and spice note to the aroma with a gentle grapefruit and lime flavour. A crisp, delicate finish.

Slater's SIBAIFBB ⊙

St Albans Road, Common Road Industrial Estate, Stafford, ST16 3DR
☎ (01785) 257976 ⊕ slatersales.co.uk

⊙The brewery was opened in 1995 and in 2006 moved to new, larger premises. It has won numerous awards from CAMRA and SIBA and supplies a large number of outlets. 2015 saw Slater's celebrate its 20th anniversary. ‼🍺

Ultra (OG 1036.5, ABV 3.7%)
Amber in colour with a hop and malt aroma. Hoppiness develops into a long, dry finish.

Top Totty (OG 1039, ABV 4%) ◆
Yellow-hued with a fruit and hop nose. Big malty start leads to citrus hints with mouth-watering edges. Dry finish with tangs of lingering lemon bitterness.

Premium (OG 1042.5, ABV 4.4%) ◆
Pale brown-coloured bitter with malt and caramel aroma. Malt and caramel taste supported by hops and some fruit provide a warming descent and satisfyingly bitter mouthfeel.

Haka (OG 1049, ABV 5.2%) ◆
Exotic aromas of tropical fruits lead to a sweet fruity start with background bitterness. This erupts into a mouthy bitterness with a long finish.

Slaughterhouse SIBA

Bridge Street, Warwick, CV34 5PD
☎ (01926) 490986 ☎ 07951 842690
⊕ slaughterhousebrewery.com

⊙Production began in 2003 on a four-barrel plant in a former slaughterhouse. Around 30 outlets are supplied. The brewery premises are licensed for off-sales direct to the public. In 2010 Slaughterhouse opened its first pub, the Wild Boar in Warwick, adding a two-barrel plant. ‼

Saddleback Best Bitter (OG 1038, ABV 3.8%)
Amber-coloured session bitter with a distinctive hop flavour.

Extra Stout Snout (OG 1044, ABV 4.4%)

Boar D'eau (OG 1045, ABV 4.5%)

Wild Boar (OG 1052, ABV 5.2%)

Slightly Foxed SIBA

2 Richmond House, Caldene Business Park, Mytholmroyd, West Yorkshire, HX7 5QL ☎ 07412 008221 ⊕ slightlyfoxedbrewery.co.uk

⊙ Launched in 2011 and originally using spare capacity at Brass Monkey Brewery, Slightly Foxed bought the brewery in 2012 when Brass Monkey closed. It moved to its present location in 2016 following extensive flood damage to its old premises. ◆

Howlin Fox (OG 1035, ABV 3.5%) ◆
Easy-drinking, crisp and refreshing session beer. Hoppy with a light, fruity, citrus palate followed by a mellow finish.

Slightly Foxed (OG 1038, ABV 3.8%) ◆
Session bitter with a good mix of malt, fruit and hops. Bitterness develops in the aftertaste.

Crafty Fox (OG 1041, ABV 4.1%)
A golden-coloured, hoppy ale with a citrus punch.

Flying Fox (OG 1043, ABV 4.3%)
Pale and hoppy bitter with a touch of apricot flavour.

Fox Glove (OG 1043, ABV 4.3%)
A golden-coloured premium best bitter with a full-bodied fruity flavour and fruit aromas.

Craic Fox (OG 1045, ABV 4.5%)
A velvety Irish-style stout.

Urban Fox (OG 1048, ABV 4.8%) ◆
Well-balanced, dark-coloured porter. Chocolate nose with a rich, fruity, roast flavour. A mild aftertaste makes it taste like velvet in a glass.

Bengal Fox (OG 1052, ABV 5.2%)
A golden-coloured beer with a complex combination of pine, citrus and vanilla flavours.

Prairie Fox (OG 1052, ABV 5.2%) ◆
An American-style pale ale. Plenty of hops on the nose. It has a mildly spicy and predominately citrus palate followed by a mellow and dry aftertaste.

Small Paul's

27 Briar Close, Gillingham, Dorset, SP8 4SS
☎ (01747) 823574 ✉ smallbrewer@btinternet.com

⊠ Launched in 2006, this half-barrel brewery is located in the owner's garage. There are usually two brews a month. A small number of local pubs, clubs and beer festivals are supplied direct and beers can be designed and brewed to order. ◆

Gylla's Gold (OG 1039, ABV 3.8%) ◆
Drinkable session ale. Mild fruit hop aromas lead to bitter hop flavours and a lingering dry hop aftertaste.

Amber Nectar (OG 1042, ABV 4.2%)
Best bitter with a slightly citrus aroma, balanced malt, spicy hop flavours and a bitter finish.

Invicta (OG 1042, ABV 4.2%)
Pale, aromatic and hoppy with a long bitter finish.

Challenger II (OG 1044, ABV 4.3%)
A copper-coloured, slightly sweet, malty bitter.

Wyvern (OG 1044, ABV 4.4%) ◆
Red-brown coloured, well-balanced best bitter with malt and caramel flavours and short, bittersweet finish.

Gillingham Pale (OG 1045, ABV 4.5%) ◆
Fruity, caramel aromas lead to complex bitter flavours and short, dry finish.

Small World SIBA

Unit 10, Barncliffe Business Park, Near Bank, Shelley, West Yorkshire, HD8 8LU
☎ (01484) 602805 ⊕ smallworldbeers.com

The brewery is situated in the picturesque Barncliffe valley in rural Shelley. The beers are brewed on a 20-barrel plant using spring water from an on-site bore hole. ‼◆

Barncliffe Bitter (OG 1037, ABV 3.7%)
Pleasant, light-drinking bitter with fruit and citrus notes and a lasting bitterness through the finish.

Long Moor Pale (OG 1039, ABV 3.9%)
Pale ale with grapefruit and citrus notes. A light bitter finish.

Spike's Gold (OG 1043, ABV 4.4%)
Smooth, well-balanced golden ale with fruit and hop flavours through to the finish.

Thunderbridge Stout (OG 1050, ABV 5.2%)
Traditional dry stout with roast flavours giving way to smooth coffee undertones and a sharp, dry finish.

Twin Falls (OG 1050, ABV 5.2%)
Full-bodied pale ale with fruity aroma, strong tropical fruit and hop taste.

Joseph Herbert Smith

🍺 Fox Inn, Hanley Broadheath, Worcestershire, WR15 8QS
☎ (01886) 853189 ☎ 07527 066474
🌐 jhstraditionalbrewery.com

The brewery was established in Staffordshire in 2007 by Jonathan Smith. In 2008 it relocated to barns adjacent to the Fox Inn. All equipment is gas fired and ingredients are sourced locally where possible.

Samuel Smith

High Street, Tadcaster, North Yorkshire, LS24 9SB
☎ (01937) 832225 🌐 samuelsmithsbrewery.co.uk

☺Fiercely independent, family-owned company. Tradition, quality and value are important, resulting in brewing without any artificial additives. All real ale is supplied in wooden casks. A bottle-conditioned beer (Yorkshire Stingo, ABV 8%) is only available in specialist off-licences. **RAIB**

Old Brewery Bitter (OG 1040, ABV 4%)
Malt dominates the aroma, with an initial burst of malt, hops and fruit in the taste, which is sustained in the aftertaste.

John Smith's

The Brewery, Tadcaster, North Yorkshire, LS24 9SA
☎ (01937) 832091 🌐 heineken.com

No real ale. The brewery was built in 1879 by a relative of Samuel Smith (qv). John Smith's became part of the Courage group in 1970 before being taken over by S&N and now Heineken UK. John Smith's cask Magnet has been discontinued. John Smith's Bitter in cask form is brewed by Caledonian Brewery (qv) in Edinburgh.

Snaggletooth

Rear of 11 Pole Lane, Darwen, Lancashire, BB3 3LD
☎ 07810 365701 🌐 snaggletoothbrewing.com

Snaggletooth was established in 2012 by three beer geeks with a passion for crafting ales. A 2.5-barrel plant is used at the Hopstar Brewery (qv) in Darwen, Lancashire. Beers are available throughout East Lancashire and Manchester.

Allotropic Pale Ale (ABV 3.8%)
A pale ale with floral and citrus notes.

Aint Afraid of Noh Ghost (ABV 3.9%)

Noh Ghost (ABV 3.9%)

Three Amigos (ABV 3.9%)

Deja Brewed (OG 1040, ABV 4%)
Refreshing ale with floral, spicy and citrus flavours.

Rolling Maul (ABV 4.1%)
Pale ale with floral notes and a citrus finish.

'Cos I'm a Lobster (OG 1044, ABV 4.2%)

Summery red-coloured ale with subtly roasted malts.

Snowdonia

🍺 Snowdonia Parc Brewpub & Campsite, Waunfawr, Caernarfon, LL55 4AQ
☎ (01286) 650409 🌐 snowdonia-park.co.uk

Snowdonia started brewing in 1998 in a two-barrel brewhouse. The brewing is now carried out by the owner, Carmen Pierce. The beer is brewed solely for the Snowdonia Park pub and campsite.

Snowhill

Snowhill Cottage, Snow Hill Lane, Scorton, Lancashire, PR3 1BA
☎ (01524) 791352

☺Snowhill was established in 2015 by Nigel Stokes following several years of small scale brewing. It uses a 1.5-barrel plant. A one-man operation, Nigel brews 3-4 times per month to supply pubs in North-west Lancashire. An environmentally-friendly plant sees the spent grain feeding local cattle and waste water treated through a small reed bed. ♦

Pale (OG 1037, ABV 3.7%)
A fruity, pale yellow-coloured beer with a fairly bitter aftertaste.

Blonded (ABV 3.9%)
A light, fruity, well-hopped blonde ale with a bitter, slightly astringent finish.

Gold (OG 1039, ABV 3.9%)
Fruit and malt dominate, with a bitter, dry finish.

Best Bitter (OG 1042, ABV 4.2%)
Smooth, rich and malty with caramel notes leading to a pronounced bitter finish.

Black Magic IPA (OG 1042, ABV 4.2%)
A complex black IPA with a hoppy aroma and taste and hints of roast.

Winter Porter (OG 1050, ABV 4.8%)
Rich and black in colour, the initial roast and malty taste leads to a bitter, fruity and hoppy aftertaste.

Sociable (NEW)

6 – 8 Britannia Road, Worcester, WR1 3BQ ☎ 07957 583984 🌐 thesociablebeercompany.com

Originally home brewers, Steve and Jason traded in their farmyard shed for city centre premises in Worcester in 2017 with a purpose-built brew plant from Slovenia and an on-site tap room.

Solvay Society

Cuckoo Hall Brewery, Unit 8, Aldborough Hall Farm, Aldborough Hatch, Essex, IG2 7TD

Solvay Society began brewing in 2014 in the cellar of a Walthamstow pub using a small 0.5-hectolitre kit. In 2015 it transferred the equipment to the Hops & Glory pub in North London. In 2016 the brewery moved again, taking over the old equipment from the Ha'penny Brewery in Aldborough Hatch. Production is mostly keg but bottle-conditioned beer is also available. **RAIB**

Son of Sid

🍴 Chequers, 71 Main Road, Little Gransden, Cambridgeshire, SG19 3DW
☎ (01767) 677348 ⊕ sonofsid.co.uk

Son of Sid was established in 2007. The three-barrel plant is situated in a separate room at the back of the pub and can be viewed from a window in the lounge bar. It is named after the father of the current landlord, who ran the pub for 42 years. His son has carried the business on as a family-run enterprise. Beer is sold in the pub and at local beer festivals.

Sonnet 43 SIBA ◉

Durham Road, Coxhoe, County Durham, DH6 4HX
☎ (0191) 377 3039 ⊕ sonnet43.com

☺Sonnet 43 began brewing in 2012. The name and brewing ethos is inspired by the most famous work of poet Elizabeth Barrett Browning, who was born nearby. A limited edition beer range is brewed comprising original recipes with experimental ingredients. The brewery has seven outlets in the North East and supplies extensively to the free trade. Expansion is planned.

Abolition (OG 1038, ABV 3.8%)
An amber-coloured ale, well-balanced with sourdough and nut aromas. Refreshing with a slightly bitter aftertaste.

Seraphim (OG 1041, ABV 4.1%)
A straw-coloured, wheat-style beer with a sweet, delicate, floral aroma.

The Raven (OG 1046, ABV 4.3%)
Bourbon, cocoa and oats give this dark-coloured beer a rich, full-bodied, chocolaty bitterness.

The Aurora (OG 1044, ABV 4.4%)
A strong pale ale with a complex hoppy aroma and delicate, fruity malt taste.

Impressment (OG 1055, ABV 5.4%)
A bronze-coloured beer with a spicy, peppery aroma and a fruity, malty and spicy flavour.

South Hams SIBA

Stokeley Barton, Stokenham, Devon, TQ7 2SE
☎ (01548) 581151 ⊕ southhamsbrewery.co.uk

⊠ The brewery moved to its present site, a milking parlour, in 2003, with a 10-barrel plant and plenty of room to expand. It supplies more than 60 outlets in Plymouth and South Devon. Wholesalers are used to distribute to other areas. The brewer, Mark Brooking, is now assisted by Sam, his youngest son. ‼🍴♦RAIB

Devon Pride (OG 1039, ABV 3.8%)
A dark amber-coloured beer, smooth to drink with a malty palate.

Wild Blonde (OG 1044, ABV 4.4%) 🍺
Subtle notes of malt, roast and caramel, dominated by fruity hops. These persist to a refreshing hint of lemon.

Hopnosis (OG 1046, ABV 4.5%)

Eddystone (OG 1050, ABV 4.8%) 🍺
Hops and fruit dominate nose and taste with hints of malt and roast and subtle caramel. Slightly dry aftertaste.

Pandemonium (OG 1054, ABV 5%)

South Lakes

Unit 30, Ulverston Auction Mart, North Lonsdale Road, Ulverston, Cumbria, LA12 0AU ☎ 07795 363523
✉ aaronpos1@hotmail.com

South Lakes began brewing on a 1.5-barrel plant in 2016, in a part of the Auction Mart in Ulverston.

Poison Dwarf (OG 1043, ABV 4.1%)

Rakau (OG 1048, ABV 4.7%)
A strong blonde ale bursting with hops and fruit.

American Pale Ale (OG 1050, ABV 4.8%)
A rich golden ale with lots of citrus.

Southbourne

45 Poole Hill, Bournemouth, Dorset, BH2 5PW
☎ (01202) 421190 ☎ 07845 795464
⊕ southbourneales.co.uk

⊠ Jennifer Tingay, former technologist and brewer for Ringwood, began brewing in 2013 using spare capacity at Town Mill brewery. Using crowdfunding she secured the lease of a former nightclub on Bournemouth's West Cliff and in 2017 transferred the brewery there and opened a bar. ‼🍴♦

Paddlers (OG 1037, ABV 3.6%)
A light but balanced session bitter with moderate hop characteristics.

Sunbather (OG 1040, ABV 4%)
A red-coloured ale with moderate hop bitterness, toffee notes and a distinctive malt character.

Headlander (OG 1043, ABV 4.2%)
Floral aroma and full hop bitterness balanced with malt.

Beachcomber (OG 1058, ABV 5.7%)
A full-flavoured, brown-coloured ale with a good malt and hop balance.

Southey (NEW)

21 Southey Street, Penge, London, SE20 7JD ☎ 07450 573577

⊠ The Southey Brewing Company has taken over the premises formerly used by the Late Knights Brewery. Brewing began in 2016 using a five-barrel plant. The brewery tap is open Fridays and Saturdays (3-9pm). The brewery also supplies two other outlets, the London Beer Dispensary, Brockley, and the Brighton Beer Dispensary. ♦

Southport SIBA

Unit 3, Enterprise Business Park, Russell Road, Southport, Merseyside, PR9 7RF ☎ 07748 387652
⊕ southportbrewery.co.uk

☺Southport Brewery was established in 2004 on a five-barrel plant. Outlets are supplied in Southport, North-west England and nationally. ♦

Sandgrounder Bitter (OG 1039.5, ABV 3.8%)
Pale, hoppy session bitter with a floral character.

Dark Night (OG 1040.5, ABV 3.9%)
A dark-coloured, traditional mild.

Carousel (OG 1041.5, ABV 4%)
A refreshing, floral, hoppy best bitter.

Golden Sands (OG 1041.5, ABV 4%)
A golden-coloured, triple-hopped bitter with citrus flavour.

Ruck & Maul (OG 1040, ABV 4%)
A copper-coloured ale with a subtle bitterness leading to a lemon grapefruit flavour.

Natterjack (OG 1043.5, ABV 4.3%)
A premium bitter with fruit notes and a hint of coffee.

Band Stand (OG 1046, ABV 4.5%)

Southsea

**Southsea Castle, Clarence Esplanade, Southsea, Hampshire, PO5 3PA ☎ 07939 063970
⊕ southseabrewing.co.uk**

⊗ Launched in 2016, Southsea Brewing is located in an old ammunition storage room within the walls of a coastal defence fort built by Henry VIII in 1544. All beers are unfined, unfiltered and unpasteurised and bottled on site. ‼⬛RAIB

Southwark SIBA ◉

**46 Druid Street, Bermondsey, London, SE1 2EZ
☎ (020) 3302 4190 ⊕ southwarkbrewing.co.uk**

⊗ A further addition to the burgeoning Bermondsey brewing scene, Southwark Brewing Company opened in 2014 focusing on cask ales. A tap room is open Thursday-Sunday. ⬛♦RAIB

London Pale Ale (OG 1038.5, ABV 4%) ◣
Pale golden-coloured, smooth beer. Sweet biscuity malt is balanced by pineapple and pithy citrus. Dry aftertaste with a building bitterness.

Potters' Fields Porter (OG 1040, ABV 4%) ◣
Dark brown-coloured porter. Raisins, prunes and cocoa in the flavour and aroma fading in the dry, roast bitter aftertaste.

Bermondsey Best (OG 1042, ABV 4.4%) ◣
A well-balanced best bitter with fruity notes developing in the finish, which is bitter. Some malty notes on the palate.

Gold (OG 1047, ABV 5.2%) ◣
Pleasant earthy hop on the nose and palate becoming peppery in the finish. Sweet pink grapefruit and orange pith flavour.

Harvard (OG 1049, ABV 5.5%) ◣
Honey with sweet orange and grapefruit marmalade character are present in this rich, smooth pale brown-coloured beer. Dry bitter finish.

Spa Town

See Harrogate

Sperrin

▤ **Lord Nelson Inn, Birmingham Road, Ansley, Warwickshire, CV10 9PQ
☎ (024) 7639 2305 ☎ 07917 772208
⊕ sperrinbrewery.co.uk**

Sperrin began brewing in 2012 and is situated by the side of the Lord Nelson Inn. A brewery was first established there in 1868. Beers are also available at its sister pub, the Blue Boar in Mancetter.

Spey Valley SIBA

Mains of Mulben, Mulben, Keith, AB55 6YH ☎ 07780 655199 ⊕ speyvalleybrewery.co.uk

⊗ Pilot brewery was established in 2007 at Mulben Mains Farm. Originally using a two-barrel plant from Loch Ness Brewery, it now brews on a 20-barrel plant at a site in Mulben. ♦

Sunshine on Keith (OG 1036, ABV 3.5%) ◣
Golden-coloured, light citrus, bitter hop.

David's Not So Bitter (OG 1046, ABV 4.4%) ◣
Light brown-coloured beer with a good mix of malts, hops and red fruits.

Stillman's IPA (OG 1047.6, ABV 4.6%) ◣
Amber-coloured, hoppy bitter with a whisky background.

1814 (OG 1050, ABV 5%)

Spey Stout (OG 1055, ABV 5.4%) ◣
A good thick, dark, malty stout with a smoky blackcurrant background.

Speyside Craft SIBA

**2 Greshop Road, Forres, IV36 2GU
☎ (01309) 358082 ☎ 07854 053277
⊕ speysidecraftbrewery.com**

Based in a traditional whisky-producing area, Speyside Brewery uses the same water that goes into the production of Scottish whiskies. A number of local outlets are supplied. A donation from sales of Bottlenose Bitter goes to help support the work of the Whale & Dolphin Conservation Society. ♦

Bow Fiddle Blonde (OG 1038, ABV 3.8%)

Bottlenose Bitter (OG 1041, ABV 4.1%) ◣
Slightly citrus, hoppy bitter.

Randolph's Leap (OG 1049, ABV 4.9%)

Moray IPA (OG 1055, ABV 5.5%)

Findhorn Killer Red IPA (OG 1056, ABV 5.6%)

Spire SIBA ◉

**Bull Paddock Farm, Sutton Lane, Sutton Scarsdale, Derbyshire, S44 5UW
☎ (01246) 807940 ⊕ spirebrewing.co.uk**

☺ Originally set up in 2006, the Spire brand came under the ownership of a long-standing CAMRA member in 2014 and relocated to Sutton Scarsdale. The old 10-barrel plant was replaced with a new 15-barrel one and a bottling line added. More than 100 outlets are supplied direct. An onsite brewery tap, the Snug, opened in 2016. ⬛♦RAIB

HoPink Mad (OG 1038, ABV 3.8%)
A dry, pale-coloured beer with plenty of hop characteristics, both in bitterness and aroma.

Whiter Shade (OG 1039, ABV 4%)
Pale straw-coloured session bitter with a subtle lemon hop finish.

Dark Side (OG 1043, ABV 4.3%) ◣
Complex and satisfying ruby-coloured mild with coffee aroma and toffee flavours. Dark and sweet but not too strong.

Chesterfield Best Bitter (OG 1044, ABV 4.5%) ◣
Classic brown-coloured strong bitter with malt and fruit flavours and a hint of caramel and chocolate in the finish. There is a little bitterness in the aftertaste.

Jail Break American IPA (ABV 5.9%)

A slight floral and assertive fruity nose. The distinct candy flavour accompanies a hint of malty sweetness followed by a pleasant bitterness.

Yaroslavna Stout (OG 1063, ABV 6%)
Filled with rich, complex coffee aromas mingled with light liquorice notes. The bitterness of the hops and roasted barley balance the slight sweetness in the finish.

Spitting Feathers SIBA ⊚

Common Farm, Waverton, Cheshire, CH3 7QT
☎ (01244) 332052 ☎ 07974 348325
⊕ spittingfeathers.org

☺Spitting Feathers was established in 2005. The brewery is located in a sandstone building set around a cobbled yard. Around 200 local outlets are supplied. ‼♦

Session Beer (OG 1035, ABV 3.6%)
A golden-coloured session bitter. Traditional English malts and hops combine to make this a well-balanced and satisfying beer.

Thirstquencher (OG 1038, ABV 3.9%) ◗
Powerful hop aroma leads into the taste. Bitterness and a fruity citrus hop flavour fight for attention. A sharp, clean, golden-coloured beer with a long, dry, bitter aftertaste.

Special Ale (OG 1041, ABV 4.2%) ◗
Complex tawny-coloured beer with a sharp, grainy mouthfeel. Malty with good hop coming through in the aroma and taste. Hints of nuttiness and a touch of acidity. Dry, astringent finish.

Old Wavertonian (OG 1043, ABV 4.4%) ◗
Creamy and smooth stout. Full-flavoured with coffee notes in aroma and taste. Roast and nut flavours throughout, leading to a hoppy, bitter finish.

Empire IPA (ABV 5.2%)
A highly-hopped IPA brewed specifically for export.

Springhead SIBA ⊚

Robin Hood Site, Main Street, Laneham, Nottinghamshire, DN22 0NA
☎ (01777) 228080 ☎ 07720 461655
⊕ springhead.co.uk

☺Springhead Brewery opened in 1990, expanding and moving to bigger premises three years later to meet increased demand. In 2011 the brewery relocated to its current address. Around 500 outlets are supplied direct and the brewery owns five pubs, one of which, the Bees Knees, is adjacent to the brewery. ‼🛒♦V

Outlawed (OG 1040, ABV 3.8%)
A triple-hopped, easy-drinking American-style pale ale with a citrus aroma.

Drop of the Black Stuff (OG 1041, ABV 4%)
A smooth, dark-coloured, easy-drinking porter.

Robin Hood (OG 1041, ABV 4%)
A chestnut-coloured traditional bitter with a good head and plenty of hops.

Maid Marian (OG 1045, ABV 4.5%)
A pale golden-coloured beer with a fruity orange aroma and dry finish.

Leveller (OG 1047, ABV 4.8%)
A dark, smoky intense flavour with a toffee finish. Brewed in the style of a Belgian Trappist ale.

Roaring Meg (OG 1052, ABV 5.5%)
A smooth, classic IPA. Golden in colour with a citrus honey aroma and dry finish.

Squawk

Unit 4, Tonge Street, Ardwick, Manchester, M12 6LY
☎ 07590 387559 ⊕ squawkbrewingco.com

Squawk initially cuckoo-brewed on the Hand Drawn Monkey plant in Huddersfield in 2013, with the first brew from the Manchester site being in 2014. The eight-barrel plant is located in a railway arch in Ardwick. Beers are widely available in the North West and Yorkshire. RAIB

Espresso Stout (OG 1060, ABV 6.5%)
A silky smooth, rich beer with an espresso flavour.

Stables

🍴 Beamish Hall Country House Hotel, Beamish, County Durham, DH9 0YB
☎ (01207) 288750 ⊕ beamish-hall.co.uk/stables

Stables was established as part of a £1 million development of an old stable block of Beamish Hall, converting a disused building to a restaurant and eight-barrel microbrewery. The hotel is supplied plus the Sun Inn at Beamish Museum. Beers are also brewed under the Bull Lane Brewery name.

Beamish Hall Best Bitter (OG 1038, ABV 3.8%)

Old Miner Tommy (OG 1037, ABV 3.8%)

Bobby Dazzler (OG 1042, ABV 4.2%)

Coppy Lane (OG 1043, ABV 4.2%)

Silver Buckles (OG 1044, ABV 4.4%)

Beamish Burn (OG 1045, ABV 4.5%)

Bell Tower (OG 1052, ABV 5%)

Staffordshire

12 Churnet Court, Cheddleton, Staffordshire, ST13 7EF
☎ (01538) 361919 ☎ 07971 808370
⊕ staffordshirebrewery.co.uk

No real ale. Brewing started in 2002. The brewery was renamed from Leek Brewery in 2013 at which time cask production ceased, being replaced by filtered, pasteurised bottled beers only. ‼

Stag (Cheshire) (NEW)

🍴 Stag at Walton, Chester Road, Walton, Cheshire, WA4 6EG
☎ (01925) 261680 ⊕ thestagatwalton.co.uk

Nanobrewery based at the Stag at Walton, near Warrington. Beers are available in the pub and occasionally at local beer festivals.

Stag (Kent) (NEW)

Little Engeham Farm, Woodchurch, Kent, TN26 3QY
☎ 07539 974068 ⊕ stagbrewery.co.uk

Brewing began in 2016. ♦RAIB

Staggeringly Good SIBA

Unit 3, St Georges Industrial Estate, Rodney Road, Southsea, Hampshire, PO4 8SS

☎ (023) 9229 7033 ⊕ staggeringlygood.com

⊗ Brewing began in 2014, originally using spare capacity at other breweries. In 2015 a 10-barrel plant at its own premises came on stream. There is an on-site shop and tap room with limited opening hours. ‼ ☛ ♦ RAIB V

Staggersaurus (OG 1039, ABV 4%)
A golden ale with summer fruit aromas and grapefruit on the palate. It has a light bitterness which quickly softens giving a refreshing finish.

ThaiRannoCitrus (ABV 4%)
A pale ale with distinct lime and peach flavours and aromas, balanced with hoppy bitterness.

Dawn Stealer (OG 1051, ABV 5.2%)

Post Impact Porter (OG 1057, ABV 5.4%)
An intensely rich porter with roasted malts and hints of dark chocolate.

VelociRapture (OG 1060, ABV 6.5%)
An American-style IPA with a strong fruit character and bitterness. A well-rounded, crisp and refreshing ale.

Stamps SIBA

The Basement, 17 Boundary Street, Everton, Liverpool, L5 9UB ☎ 07779 000094
⊕ stampsbrewery.co.uk

☺Brewing began in 2012 on an environmentally-friendly brew plant: power for brewing comes from 52 solar panels and a biomass boiler, used grain is sent to a local city farm for animal feed and rainwater is recycled and used for floor cleaning. The beers are named after famous world postage stamps. ‼ ☛

Blonde Moment (OG 1037, ABV 3.6%)
A pale-coloured beer with a smooth floral and citrus aroma and flavour. A good session beer.

Bondi Blonde (OG 1037, ABV 3.7%)
A full-flavoured blonde beer with floral and citrus notes.

Ahtanum (OG 1039, ABV 3.9%)

Mail Train (OG 1042, ABV 4.2%)
Traditional bitter, an abundance of hops leaves a noticeable bitterness with a delightful malt character.

The Russian (OG 1040, ABV 4.2%)
A copper-coloured ale with a hoppy finish.

Swedish Blonde (OG 1041, ABV 4.3%)
A session ale with a strong hint of citrus.

Inverted Jenny (OG 1046, ABV 4.6%)
Golden-coloured beer with a grassy and floral bouquet and a tinge of caramel.

Flying Cloud (OG 1052, ABV 5.2%)
Strong American-style lager beer.

Penny Black (OG 1055, ABV 5.5%)

Stancill SIBA ⊚

Unit 2, Oakham Drive, off Rutland Road, Sheffield, South Yorkshire, S3 9QX
☎ (0114) 275 2788 ☎ 07809 427716

☺Stancill began brewing in 2014 and is named after the first head brewer and co-founder. It is situated on the doorstep of the late Cannon

Brewery, taking advantage of the soft Yorkshire water. ‼

Barnsley Bitter (OG 1037.5, ABV 3.8%)

Blonde (OG 1038.5, ABV 3.9%)

India (ABV 4%)

No. 7 (OG 1042, ABV 4.3%)

Stainless (ABV 4.3%)

Porter (OG 1042.5, ABV 4.4%)

Black Gold (ABV 5%)

Stannary (NEW)

Unit 5a, Pixon Trading Centre, Tavistock, Devon, PL19 8DH
☎ (01822) 258130 ☎ 07971 238758
⊕ stannarybrewing.co.uk

Stannary was establsihed in 2016 by four keen home brewers using a 2.5-barrel plant. A brewery tap room is open on Thursday evenings (see social media for further opening times). ♦

Pale Ale (OG 1041, ABV 4.1%)
A refreshing beer with flavours and aromas of citrus and marmalade.

Stanway

Stanway House, Stanway, Gloucestershire, GL54 5PQ
☎ (01386) 584320 ⊕ stanwaybrewery.co.uk

☺Stanway is a small brewery founded in 1993 with a five-barrel plant that confines its sales to the Cotswolds area (15 to 20 outlets). The brewery is the only known plant in the country to use wood-fired coppers for all its production. ♦

Stanney Bitter (OG 1042, ABV 4.5%) ◣
A light, refreshing, amber-coloured beer, dominated by hops in the aroma, with a bitter taste and a hoppy, bitter finish.

Star Wing (NEW) SIBA

Unit 6, Hall Farm, Church Road, Redgrave, Suffolk, IP22 1RJ
☎ (01379) 890586 ⊕ starwingbrewery.com

⊗ Brewing began in 2017 after converting an old sawmill into a brewery. Half an acre of hops have been planted with plans to grow more and to convert part of the sawmill into a tap room. Around 30 outlets are supplied direct. ☛

Gospel Oak (OG 1038, ABV 3.8%)
A copper-coloured bitter, well-balanced with slight esters and biscuit undertones balancing the smooth bitterness and fruity aroma.

Spire Light (OG 1041, ABV 4.2%)
A light, refreshing pale ale with a floral aroma.

Four Acre Arcadia (OG 1048, ABV 5%)
A hoppy, crisp IPA with resin, citrus and slight pine undertones and a good mouthfeel.

Stain Glass Blue (OG 1055, ABV 5.4%)
A black-coloured porter. Although notably bitter the rounded malt profile creates a well-balanced beer.

THE BREWERIES

Stardust (NEW) SIBA

Unit 5, How Lane Farm Estate, Howe Lane, White Waltham, Berkshire, SL6 3JP
☎ (01628) 947325 ⊕ stardustbrewery.co.uk

⊠ An independent, family-owned and run brewery, Stardust was established in 2016. Tucked towards the back of a farm estate, brewing takes place on a six-barrel plant. 🍽

Easy Pale (OG 1038, ABV 3.8%)
Easy-drinking session pale ale with a subtle blend of hops and a pale malt body.

English Bitter (OG 1041, ABV 4%)
Notes of roasted caramel balanced by a clean bitter finish with a classic hop aroma.

American Pale (OG 1043, ABV 4.5%)
An American-style pale ale with citrus and pine hop aromas balanced by a light malt body.

PK3 (OG 1051, ABV 5.6%)
An American-style IPA with a complex tropical, spicy and fruity hop profile.

Station 119

Unit 4, Progress Way, Eye, Suffolk, IP23 7HU
☎ (01379) 882230 ⊕ station119.co.uk

Brewing started in 2014 using a two-barrel plant. The focus is firmly towards American craft style and all the beers have hop dominant flavours. Beers are available locally from Snape Maltings, Marlesford Farm Shop/cafe and the White Horse, Sweffling. RAIB

Station Works

Camlough Road, Newry, Northern Ireland, BT35 6JP

A sister brewery to Cumberland Breweries, Station Works was bought by the US firm Alltech in 2015.

The Foxes Rock (OG 1042, ABV 4.2%)

Finn (OG 1045, ABV 4.5%)

Steamin' Billy

See Belvoir

Steampunk (NEW)

29 Hillcrest Drive, Castleford, West Yorkshire, WF10 3QW ☎ 07789 988077

Brewing began in 2016.

Blacker Namba (ABV 4%)

Steel City

Sheffield ⊕ steelcitybrewing.co.uk

⊠ Steel City was established in 2009 and operates on a cuckoo basis. It is due to announce a new home and continues to collaborate with local breweries, brewing monthly at present. ♦

Stewart SIBA

26a Dryden Road, Bilston Glen Industrial Estate, Loanhead, EH20 9LZ
☎ (0131) 440 2442 ⊕ stewartbrewing.co.uk

☺Established in 2004 by Steve and Jo Stewart, the brewery moved to a larger, custom-built brewery in 2013 with a brand new 50-hectolitre plant. It also runs Natural Selection Brewing, a collaboration with Heriot Watt students. Beers are distributed throughout the UK, although they are mainly sold in South-east Scotland. ‼🍽♦RAIB

Jack Back (OG 1039, ABV 3.7%)
A pale, hoppy beer with strong citrus and tropical fruit aromas.

Pentland IPA (OG 1040, ABV 3.9%) ◆
A pleasing, hoppy, golden-coloured session ale. The dry bitter taste is well balanced by sweetness from the malt and fruit flavours. The aftertaste is dry with a lingering bitterness.

Crossfire (OG 1045, ABV 4.3%)
Pine and citrus aromas on the nose with a distinct malt profile and a crisp bitterness in its complex flavour.

80/- (OG 1044, ABV 4.4%) ◆
A traditional Scottish heavy. The complex profile is dominated by malt with fruit flavours giving the sweetish character typical of this beer style. Hops provide a gentle balancing bitterness that intensifies in the dry finish.

Edinburgh Gold (OG 1048, ABV 4.8%) ◆
A full-bodied but easy-drinking Continental-style golden ale. Bitterness from the hop character is strong in the finish and complemented in the taste by a little sweetness from malt and fruit flavours.

Sticklegs

Primrose Farm, Hall Road, Great Bromley, Essex, CO7 7TR ☎ 07971 138038 ⊕ sticklegs.co.uk

⊠ Sticklegs was established in 2008 at the Cross Inn, Great Bromley. The brewery expanded and relocated to Elmstead Market, where it continued to grow. In 2016 it moved to Primrose Farm. The brewery is owned and run by Phil Reeve and his wife Linda, the brewster. ♦

Stour Gold (OG 1040, ABV 3.8%)

Bar'King (ABV 4%)

Stocklinch

Unit 3, Manor Farm, Stocklinch, Somerset, TA19 9JG
☎ 07711 479917 ⊕ stocklinchales.co.uk

⊠ Established in 2012 in a converted farm building, Stocklinch uses a five-barrel plant supplying a number of local outlets. The brewery is licensed to open for a few days each month, mainly at weekends, which compensates for the lack of a village pub. ‼🍽♦

Ramblers Gold (OG 1038, ABV 3.8%)
Refreshing light golden-coloured beer with a slight aftertaste of grapefruit.

Jakes (OG 1040, ABV 4%)

Gunner Boyce (OG 1042, ABV 4.2%)

Jucy Lucy (OG 1042, ABV 4.2%)
A golden-coloured beer with hints of initial fruit and a lingering aftertaste.

Jakes Special (OG 1045, ABV 4.5%)

Ramblers Gold Extra (OG 1045, ABV 4.5%)

Rusty Boiler (OG 1045, ABV 4.5%)

Mid brown-coloured best bitter, strong fruity flavours with a lick of caramel.

Black Smock (OG 1050, ABV 5%)
Dark-coloured beer with strong, rich tastes of chocolate, liquorice and coffee and a hint of blackcurrant.

Stockport SIBA 👁

Arch 14, Heaton Lane, Stockport, SK4 1AQ
☎ (0161) 477 1084 ☎ 07442 530728
⊕ stockportbrewingcompany.com

😊 A former cuckoo brewery, Stockport Brewing installed its own eight-barrel plant in an arch of the iconic Stockport Viaduct in 2014. The beers are available at more than 100 pubs across the Northwest including its tap, the Crown on Heaton Lane. ‼🏪♦

Cascade (ABV 4%)
Light in colour and gently-hopped with a slight citrus flavour.

Bitter Lemon (ABV 4.2%)
A straw-coloured, hoppy beer with a bitter lemon finish.

Crown Best Bitter (ABV 4.2%)
Amber-coloured ale with a smooth, hoppy taste.

Stock Porter (ABV 4.8%)
A liquorice and malty nose with coffee and chocolate notes.

Heaton Rifles (ABV 6.6%)
A volley of hops burst through the malt base.

Stockton

28 Light Pipe Hall Road, Stockton on Tees, County Durham, TS18 4AH
☎ (01642) 678334
⊕ stocktonbrewingcompany.co.uk

Stockton Brewing Co started production in 2015 based in an industrial unit. It uses a 2.5-barrel plant. RAIB

Black Swann (ABV 5%)
An oatmeal stout with a creamy mouthfeel and chocolate notes, with a dry finish.

New World Order (ABV 6.2%)
An IPA with a light caramel body and a powerful hoppy aroma and character.

Stod Fold SIBA 👁

Stod Fold Farm, Hays Lane, Halifax, West Yorkshire, HX2 8UL
☎ (01224) 245951 ☎ 07870 498324
⊕ stodfoldbrewring.com

Stod Fold was founded by childhood friends Paul Harris and Angus Wood. They designed and built the brewery themselves and the result is a state of the art 10-barrel plant.

Gold (OG 1038, ABV 3.8%) 🍺
A refreshing, hoppy and fruity session ale. It has a crisp, bitter aftertaste.

Amber (OG 1042, ABV 4.2%) 🍺
Well-balanced best bitter. Overtones of fruit and hops. Easy-drinking with a mild bitter finish.

Blonde (OG 1045, ABV 4.5%) 🍺

Smooth-tasting, fruity beer with a lingering, dry finish.

Stokesley

See Wainstones

Stonehenge SIBA 👁

The Old Mill, Mill Road, Netheravon, Wiltshire, SP4 9QB
☎ (01980) 670631 ⊕ stonehengeales.co.uk

⊗ The brewery was founded in 1984 in what was originally a water-driven mill built in 1914. In 1993 the company was bought by Danish master brewer Stig Andersen and now supplies more than 300 outlets. From 2013 a new borehole, accessing the Salisbury Plain aquifer, has been supplying the brewery's water. ‼♦

Spire Ale (OG 1037, ABV 3.8%) 🍺
A pale golden-coloured session bitter with an initial bitterness giving way to a well-rounded bitter aftertaste with discernible fruit balance.

Pigswill (OG 1039, ABV 4%) 🍺
A tawny-coloured session bitter with an initial pleasant hop aroma and slight bitterness to the initial taste moving to a well-rounded bitter finish with slight malt and fruit.

Heel Stone (OG 1042, ABV 4.3%) 🍺
A copper-coloured best bitter with some malt and fruit in the aroma continuing into the initial taste along with pleasant hoppiness. Medium-bodied with plenty of flavour in the aftertaste with noticeable malt, fruit and hops.

Great Bustard (OG 1046, ABV 4.8%) 🍺
A copper-brown coloured strong bitter. Complex malt and fruit flavours at first with a long fruit and bitter aftertaste.

Danish Dynamite (OG 1048, ABV 5%) 🍺
Golden-coloured strong bitter with good hop and fruit aromas. Complex flavours in the initial taste with a beautifully balanced, full-bodied aftertaste with hops and fruit to the fore.

Stonehouse SIBA

Stonehouse, Weston, Oswestry, Shropshire, SY10 9ES
☎ (01691) 676457 ⊕ stonehousebrewery.co.uk

Stonehouse is a family-run brewery, established in 2007, and operates a 22-barrel plant. The purpose-built brewery is next to the preserved Cambrian railway line and includes a bar, visitor centre and large beer garden next to its cider orchard. Direct delivery is within 30 miles of the brewery. ‼🏪♦

Sunlander (OG 1037, ABV 3.7%)
Pale ale with a good balance of citrus and floral hops.

Station Bitter (OG 1041, ABV 3.9%)
A traditional, amber-coloured session bitter. Full-bodied with a good balance of fruity hops and roasted malt.

Zaffir (OG 1040, ABV 4%)
Pale and well-balanced with hints of tropical fruit hops.

Cambrian Gold (OG 1042, ABV 4.2%)
A deep golden-coloured, fruity beer with a subtle, dry finish.

THE BREWERIES

Tekau (OG 1047, ABV 4.3%)
A pale, easy-drinking beer with refreshing pine and citrus notes.

Witbier (OG 1043, ABV 4.5%)
A naturally cloudy, Belgian-style wheat beer with hints of orange peel, coriander and cloves.

Off the Rails (OG 1048, ABV 4.8%)
A rich and malty premium bitter with a classic British hop flavour.

Stoney Ford

Crown Lodge, Crown Street, Ryhall, Rutland, PE9 4HQ
☎ (01780) 753747 ☎ 07803 050108
⊕ stoneyfordbrewco.co.uk

⊠ Stoney Ford Brew Co was established in 2016 by Tim Nicol and Simon Watson, using a 2.5-barrel plant. Only English hops and malt are used. !! ♦

PE9 Paradise Pale (ABV 4%)
Soft, rounded pale ale with pronounced bitterness and a hoppy flavour.

All Saints Almighty Amber (ABV 4.2%)
A dark-coloured ale with gentle bitterness and a resinous, marmalade and orange aromatic and citrus bite.

Storm SIBA

2 Waterside, Macclesfield, Cheshire, SK11 7HJ
☎ (01625) 431234 ⊕ stormbrewing.co.uk

☺Storm Brewing was founded in 1998. In 2001 it moved to its current location, a old riverside pub building, which until 1937 was called the Mechanics Arms. More than 60 outlets are supplied. ♦ RAIB

Beauforts Ale (OG 1038, ABV 3.8%)
Golden brown-coloured, full-flavoured session bitter with a lingering hoppy taste.

Desert Storm (OG 1040, ABV 3.9%)
Amber-coloured beer with a smoky flavour of fruit and malt.

Bosley Cloud (OG 1041, ABV 4.1%) ◄
Dry, golden-coloured bitter with peppery hop notes throughout. Some initial sweetness and a mainly bitter aftertaste. Soft, well-balanced and quaffable.

Ale Force (OG 1042, ABV 4.2%) ◄
Amber-coloured, smooth-tasting, complex beer that balances malt, hop and fruit on the taste, leading to a roasty, slightly sweet aftertaste.

Dexter (OG 1040, ABV 4.2%)
A crisp, refreshing, light ale with a zesty finish.

Downpour (OG 1043, ABV 4.3%)
A pale ale with a full, fruity flavour, a hint of apple and a sightly hoppy aftertaste.

PGA (OG 1044, ABV 4.4%) ◄
Light, crisp, lager-style beer with a balance of malt, hops and fruit. Moderately bitter and slight dry aftertaste.

Hurricane Hubert (OG 1045, ABV 4.5%)
A dark-coloured beer with a refreshing full, fruity hop aroma and a subtle bitter aftertaste.

Silk of Amnesia (OG 1047, ABV 4.7%) ◄
Smooth, premium, easy-drinking bitter. Fruit and hops dominate throughout. Not too sweet, with a good, lasting finish.

Red Mist (OG 1049, ABV 4.8%)

A dark red/black-coloured porter with fruity notes and a hoppy finish.

Stowey

Old Cider House, 25 Castle Street, Nether Stowey, Somerset, TA5 1LN
☎ (01278) 732228 ⊕ stoweybrewery.co.uk

Somerset's smallest brewery was established in 2006, primarily to supply the owners' guesthouse and to provide beer to participants at events run from the accommodation. The small quantities of beer produced are also supplied to limited outlets in Nether Stowey and Watchet on a regular basis. !! ♦

Nether Ending (OG 1044, ABV 4.2%)

Strands

☗ Strands Inn, Nether Wasdale, Cumbria, CA20 1ET
☎ (01946) 726237 ⊕ strandshotel.com

Strands Brewery is a six-barrel plant with a 30-barrel fermentation capacity. The majority of beers are available bottle conditioned. Six of the beers are available on the bar of the Strands Inn at all times.

1492 (OG 1035, ABV 3.5%)
A session IPA with the hop profile of a stronger beer.

Green Bullet (OG 1035, ABV 3.5%)
A single hop beer with well-rounded bitterness.

Responsibly (OG 1037, ABV 3.7%)
A pale ale brewed with beech smoked barley, giving it a distinctive smoky flavour. A dry, hoppy finish.

Brown Bitter (OG 1038, ABV 3.8%) ◄
A complex-tasting, brown-coloured beer with a lingering bitter aftertaste.

Errmmm... (OG 1038, ABV 3.8%) ◄
A complex, traditional bitter.

Scafell Summit (OG 1040, ABV 4%)
A modern pale ale using American hops. Smooth grapefruit and tropical fruit flavours.

Low Flyer (OG 1042, ABV 4.3%)
A dark amber-coloured beer with satisfying biscuit and caramel flavours.

Red Screes (OG 1043, ABV 4.5%) ◄
A rich-tasting, smooth, strong bitter; full-flavoured with plenty of roast and malt tastes.

T'errmmm-inator (OG 1052, ABV 4.9%) ◄
A smooth, dark brown-coloured, roast-led beer. Full-bodied and well-balanced.

Brewed for Independent Lakeland Breweries:

Gold Wing (OG 1040, ABV 4%) ◄
A full-bodied, hoppy, bitter beer with a malty start.

Dark Knight (OG 1050, ABV 5%)
Dark-coloured, smooth ale with chocolate and coffee flavours.

Stratford Upon Avon SIBA ⊙

Warwick Road, Stratford-upon-Avon, Warwickshire, CV37 0NT ☎ 07866 495232 ⊕ sua-brewery.co.uk

Stratford Upon Avon is the first brewery in Stratford since Flowers in the 1960s. It was established by Richard Williams in 2014 on his family farm, which lies on the River Avon. The brewery has been developed around an environmentally-friendly approach, using the farm's own small solar farm, wind turbine and bore hole. One pub is owned, the Norman Knight, Whichford. ◆

Stratford Gold (OG 1038, ABV 3.8%)
A light golden-coloured, refreshing ale.

Louis's Pale Ale (OG 1040, ABV 4%)
A hoppy beer with powerful floral flavours.

Stratford Mosaic (OG 1042, ABV 4.2%)
A single hopped blonde ale.

Malty Pig Bitter (OG 1044, ABV 4.4%)
A malty but well-hopped ale with biscuity flavours.

Dark Star Porter (OG 1046, ABV 4.6%)
A full-bodied ale with hints of coffee and chocolate.

American Amarillo (OG 1050, ABV 5%)

Strathaven SIBA ◉

Craigmill Brewery, Sandford Road, Strathaven, ML10 6PB
☎ (01357) 520419 ⊕ strathavenales.com

Strathaven Ales is a 10-barrel brewery on the River Avon close to Strathaven and was converted from the remains of a 16th-century mill. The range is distributed throughout Scotland and the north of England. ‼ ⬛◆

Craigmill Mild (OG 1035, ABV 3.5%)

Clydesdale (OG 1038, ABV 3.8%)

Duchess Anne (ABV 3.9%)

Avondale (OG 1048, ABV 4%)

Old Mortality (OG 1046, ABV 4.2%)

Claverhouse (OG 1046, ABV 4.5%)

Strathbraan SIBA

Deanshaugh, Amulree, PH8 0EB
☎ (01350) 725264 ☎ 07747 857908
✉ strathbraan.bry@btinternet.com

Straathbraan began brewing in 2012 using a 10-barrel plant. RAIB

Due South (OG 1038, ABV 3.8%)

Head East (OG 1042, ABV 4.2%)

Strathcarron (NEW)

Arinackaig, Strathcarron, IV54 8YN
⊕ strathcarronbrewery.com

Brewing began in 2016 using a 2.5-barrel plant. Fresh West Highland water is used from an on-site spring. Beer is only available locally. RAIB

Golden Cow (OG 1038, ABV 3.8%)

Black Cow (OG 1042, ABV 4.2%)

Red Cow (OG 1042, ABV 4.2%)

Streatham (NEW)

The Old Stables, c/o Railway Pub, 2 Greyhound Lane, Streatham, London, SW16 5SD
⊕ streathambrew.co.uk

Streatham Brewing Co was established in 2016 on a tiny 200-litre kit in bijou accommodation behind the Railway pub in Streatham Common. The brewer, Phil, also teaches brewing workshops at the London Beer Lab in nearby Brixton (as well as being a trained opera singer). All beer is currently only available bottle conditioned. RAIB

Stringers SIBA

Unit 3, Low Mill Business Park, Ulverston, Cumbria, LA12 9EE
☎ (01229) 581387 ⊕ stringersbeer.co.uk

Stringers is a small, family-run brewery. Brewing started in 2008 on a five-barrel plant run on 100% renewable energy. ◆RAIB GF V

Plan B (OG 1036, ABV 3.7%) ◣
An easy-drinking, zingy, pale thirst quencher.

No. 2 Stout (OG 1042, ABV 4%) ◣
A robust, drying stout full of roast and hop bitterness.

Bauhaus (OG 1045, ABV 4.7%) ◣
Citrus and tropical fruits dominate this golden ale.

The North Will Rise Again (OG 1046, ABV 4.9%)

Turbine Porter (OG 1058, ABV 5.1%)

Brewed for Independent Lakeland Breweries:

Furness Gold (OG 1035, ABV 3.5%) ◣
A hoppy aroma and a fruity, full-bodied taste of hops, finishing with a drying bitterness.

Stripey Cat (NEW)

🛢 Tiger Inn, 14-16 Barrack Street, Bridport, Dorset, DT6 3LY
☎ (01308) 427543 ⊕ tigerinnbridport.co.uk

Brewing began in 2017 at the Tiger Inn.

Stroud SIBA ◉

Unit 11, Phoenix Works, London Road, Thrupp, Gloucestershire, GL5 2BU
☎ (01453) 887122 ⊕ stroudbrewery.co.uk

⊠ Established in 2006, Stroud Brewery supports the local economy and does not sell its bottled beers through supermarkets. The ales are sold in 40-50 pubs, independent retailers and the brewery shop. All beers have full organic status. A tap room is open Thursday-Saturday evenings. ‼ ⬛◆RAIB

Tom Long (OG 1039, ABV 3.8%)
Amber-coloured session beer with a spicy citrus aroma.

Organic Pale Ale (OG 1041, ABV 4%)
A refreshing, golden-coloured organic ale with a delicate apple aroma.

Budding (OG 1045, ABV 4.5%)
Pale ale with a grassy bitterness, sweet malt and floral aroma.

Stu Brew (NEW)

Newcastle University, Room 2.41, Merz Court, Newcastle upon Tyne, NE1 7RU ⊕ stubrew.com

☺Stu Brew is Europe's first student-run microbrewery based at Newcastle University. The brewery was set up as part of a research project aimed at reducing waste and costs in all parts of brewing. The university and local pubs are supplied. ◆RAIB V

Lab Session (OG 1043, ABV 4.3%)

Wheat Wanderer (OG 1044, ABV 4.5%)

Red Brick (OG 1047, ABV 4.8%)

Extended Overdraft (OG 1050, ABV 5.2%)

Into the Black (OG 1053, ABV 5.6%)

Stubborn Mule

Unit 2, Radium Works, Bridgewater Road, Altrincham, WA14 1LZ ☎ 07730 515251 ⊕ stubbornmulebrewery.com

Brewing began in 2015, producing mainly bottled beers to micro pubs, specialist beer shops and restaurants in the Manchester area. Cask-conditioned beer is supplied to festivals. The brewery relocated to an old iron foundry in 2016 using a 10-barrel plant. A tap room is now open. ‼ ⮞ ◆ RAIB V

Absolute Banker (OG 1047, ABV 4.7%)

Pre-Prohibition Cream Ale (OG 1050, ABV 5.5%)

Single Hop IPA (OG 1054, ABV 5.7%)

Chocolate Stout (OG 1052, ABV 5.8%)

WA15 Magnum Red IPA (OG 1066, ABV 7.2%)

Stumptail

North Street, Great Dunham, Norfolk, PE32 2LR ☎ (01328) 701042 ✉ stumptail@btinternet.com

⊠ Stumptail began commercial home-brewing in 2011 using a 100-litre plant. Bottle-conditioned beers are produced with cask-conditioned versions brewed to order. Only the West Norfolk area is supplied. RAIB

Suddaby's

See Leeds

Sulwath SIBA

The Brewery, 209 King Street, Castle Douglas, DG7 1DT
☎ (01556) 504525 ⊕ sulwathbrewers.co.uk

⊚Sulwath started brewing in 1995. The beers are supplied to markets as far away as Devon in the south and Aberdeen in the north. The brewery has a fully licensed brewery tap. Cask ales are sold to around 100 outlets and four wholesalers. Beers are also brewed for other breweries. ‼ ⮞ ◆ RAIB V

Cuil Hill (OG 1039, ABV 3.6%) ◕
Distinctively fruity session ale with malt and hop undertones. The taste is bittersweet with a long-lasting, dry finish.

Tri-ball (OG 1039, ABV 3.9%)
A fresh, crisp session blonde ale.

The Grace (OG 1044, ABV 4.3%)
A refreshing, rich ale with a full-bodied flavour that balances the caramel undertones.

Black Galloway (OG 1046, ABV 4.4%) ▮

Criffel (OG 1044, ABV 4.6%) ◕
Full-bodied beer with a distinctive bitterness. Fruit is to the fore of the taste with hops becoming increasingly dominant in the taste and finish.

Galloway Gold (OG 1049, ABV 5%) ◕

A cask-conditioned lager that will be too sweet for many despite being heavily hopped.

Knockendoch (OG 1047, ABV 5%) ◕
Dark copper-coloured, reflecting a roast malt content, with bitterness from Challenger hops.

Solway Mist (OG 1052, ABV 5.5%)
A naturally cloudy wheat beer. Sweetish and fruity.

Summer Wine

The Old Furnace, Unit 15, Crossley Mills, New Mill Road, Honley, West Yorkshire, HD9 6QB
☎ (01484) 665466 ⊕ summerwinebrewery.co.uk

⊚Brewing commenced in 2006 on a 10-gallon kit. A 2007 upgrade saw a 0.5-barrel plant installed and in 2008 the brewery expanded to a six-barrel plant. More than 500 outlets are supplied direct. ◆

Resistance (OG 1037, ABV 3.7%)
Dark ruby-coloured mild with a malty body and hints of caramel, cocoa and bitter roasted barley combined with a light, fruity hop character.

Zenith (OG 1040, ABV 4%)
Pale golden-coloured beer with floral aroma and a crisp bitter finish.

Barista (OG 1048, ABV 4.8%)
A rich coffee flavoured stout with ground arabica added at the end of the boil.

Teleporter (OG 1050, ABV 5%)
A porter with a creamy body and cocoa, caramel and vanilla flavours.

Oregon (OG 1055, ABV 5.5%)
American-style pale ale with a grapefruit, spicy and floral aroma, malty body and hoppy finish.

Rogue Red Hop Ale (OG 1058, ABV 5.8%)
Deep ruby red-coloured ale with good body and rich flavour and finish.

Diablo (OG 1060, ABV 6%)
A strong IPA with tropical fruit aroma and flavours.

Summerskills SIBA ⊙

15 Pomphlett Farm Industrial Estate, Broxton Drive, Billacombe, Plymouth, Devon, PL9 7BG
☎ (01752) 481283 ⊕ summerskills.co.uk

⊠ Established in a vineyard in 1983 at Bigbury-on-Sea, Summerskills moved to its present site in 1985 and is the oldest brewery in Plymouth. Wholesalers and pub companies perform national distribution and the beers regularly appear in a selection of local outlets. ◆ RAIB

Start Point (OG 1036, ABV 3.7%) ◕
Golden ale with a clean and fresh nose. Sweet upfront with a delicate bitter finish.

Westward Ho! (OG 1040, ABV 4.1%) ◕
Malt dominates a light nose. Gentle bitterness introduces its malty-fruit character. Malt and bitterness remain, with bitterness dominating the conversation.

Best Bitter (OG 1042, ABV 4.3%) ◕
A mid-brown-coloured beer, with plenty of malt and hops through the aroma, taste and finish. A good session beer.

Tamar (OG 1042, ABV 4.3%)
A tawny-coloured bitter with a fruity aroma and a hop taste and finish.

Devon Dew (OG 1044, ABV 4.5%)

Honey yellow in colour with a floral, clean, malty aroma. Sweet lemon up front with a long grapefruit finish. Mildly hopped.

Devon Frost (OG 1044, ABV 4.5%)
A lighter, slightly more hoppy version of Devon Dew.

Menacing Dennis (OG 1045, ABV 4.5%)
Golden amber-coloured ale with aromas of dark malt and hops and a slight hint of liquorice.

Bolt Head (OG 1046, ABV 4.7%) ◆
Fruit-hop nose has roast malt hints. Bitter flavours with sweet malt, roast and hoppiness. Lingering bitter finish with background malt and fruit.

Whistle Belly Vengeance (OG 1047, ABV 4.7%)
Russet brown-coloured beer with a smoky, caramel aroma and a rich, sharp chocolate taste.

Ninja (OG 1049, ABV 5%)

First Light (OG 1054, ABV 5.5%) ◆
Refreshing and strong, slightly flowery with a mix of malts, roast and hints of caramel. Strong and complex aftertaste.

Indiana's Bones (OG 1055, ABV 5.6%)
Russet brown in colour, with a smoky, fresh hop aroma. Full-bodied with a roasty and slightly sweet taste.

Sunbeam

52 Fernbank Road, Leeds, West Yorkshire, LS13 1BU
☎ 07772 002437 ⊕ sunbeamales.co.uk

☺Sunbeam Ales was established in a house in Leeds in 2009 with commercial brewing beginning in 2011. Since moving, capacity has increased to a two-barrel plant based in a garage. The core range of ales, available in West and North Yorkshire at present, are brewed on rotation once a week with occasional brews every six weeks or so. ◆

Surfing Monkey

31 Fairwater Grove West, Cardiff, CF5 2JN ☎ 07412 365789 ⊕ surfingmonkeybrewery.com

Brewing began in 2014 utilising a large garage at the rear of a private house. ◆V

Hang Ten Tamarin (OG 1040, ABV 4%)
An amber-coloured session ale, malty but ending with fruit, spice and bitterness.

Offshore Howler (OG 1040, ABV 4%)
Cloudy wheat beer with orange and coriander.

Messed up Macaque (ABV 5.2%)
An American-style pale ale with sweet and sour tastes.

Surrey Hills SIBA

Denbies Wine Estate, London Road, Dorking, Surrey, RH5 6AA
☎ (01306) 883603 ⊕ surreyhills.co.uk

⊠ Surrey Hills began brewing in 2005 near Shere, moving to Dorking in 2011. Nearly 95% of production is sold within 15 miles of the brewery. The beers have won several local and national awards. ‼🍴◆

Ranmore (OG 1039, ABV 3.8%) ◆

A light, flavoursome session beer. An earthy hoppy nose leads into a grapefruit and hoppy taste and a clean bitter finish.

Shere Drop (OG 1043, ABV 4.2%) 🍴 🍴 ◆
A hoppy ale with some balancing malt. A pleasant citrus aroma and a noticeable fruitiness in the taste, with some sweetness.

Gilt Complex (OG 1047, ABV 4.6%)

Greensand IPA (OG 1047, ABV 4.6%) 🍴 ◆
A strong-flavoured and easily drinkable IPA with intense grapefruit and hops in the aroma and taste and soft citrus finish.

Collusion (OG 1053, ABV 5.2%)

Suthwyk

See Bowman

Swan SIBA

Unit 17, Rural Enterprise Centre, Brunel Road, Leominster, Herefordshire, HR6 0LX
☎ (01568) 617709 ☎ 07508 207928
⊕ swanbrewery.co.uk

Swan Brewery was established in 2016 by Jimmy Swan and partner Gill Bullock using a 10-barrel plant in Leominster. Jimmy was previously head brewer at Wye Valley Brewery. A 1.3-barrel plant is used to brew bespoke beers for local pubs. ◆

Cygneture Ale (OG 1037, ABV 3.6%)

Ruffled Feathers (OG 1040.5, ABV 3.8%)

Gold (OG 1042, ABV 4.2%)
A golden ale with floral, herbal and zesty notes.

Amber (OG 1044, ABV 4.4%)

Brewed for the Balance Inn, Luston:

Balance Ale (ABV 3.8%)

Swan on the Green

▤ Swan on the Green, West Peckham, Kent, ME18 5JW
☎ (01622) 812271 ⊕ swan-on-the-green.co.uk

The brewery was established in 2000 in an old coal shed behind the Swan on the Green pub using a two-barrel plant.

Swannay

Swannay Brewery, Swannay by Evie, Orkney, KW17 2NP
☎ (01856) 721700 ⊕ swannaybrewery.com

☺Brewing began in 2006 at the redundant Swannay dairy on Orkney mainland's exposed north-western tip. Two brewing plants are utilised, a five and a twenty barrel. ‼▤◆

Orkney Best (OG 1038, ABV 3.6%) ◆
A refreshing, light-bodied, golden-coloured beer bursting with hop, peach and sweet malt flavours. The long, hoppy finish leaves a dry bitterness.

Island Hopping (OG 1039, ABV 3.9%) ◆
Fruity hoppiness with some caramel with a lasting bitter aftertaste.

Dark Munro (OG 1040, ABV 4%) ◆
The nose presents an intense roast hit which is followed by summer fruits in the mouth. The strong roast malt continues into the aftertaste.

Scapa Special (OG 1042, ABV 4.2%) 🍷 🍴 🥄
A good copy of a typical Lancashire bitter, full of bitterness and background hops, leaving your mouth tingling in the lingering aftertaste.

**Sneaky Wee Orkney Stout
(OG 1044, ABV 4.2%)** 🥄
Bags of malt and roast with a mixed fruit berry background. Dry bitter finish.

Pale Ale (OG 1047, ABV 4.7%)

Orkney IPA (OG 1048, ABV 4.8%) 🥄
A traditional bitter with light hop and fruit flavour throughout.

Duke IPA (OG 1053, ABV 5.2%)
Assertively-hopped, American-style IPA.

Orkney Blast (OG 1058, ABV 6%) 🥄
Plenty of alcohol in this warming strong bitter/ barley wine. A mushroom and woody aroma blossoms into a well-balanced smack of malt and hop in the taste.

Swansea SIBA

🍴 Joiners Arms, 50 Bishopston Road, Bishopston, Swansea, SA3 3EJ
☎ (01792) 232658

Opened in 1996, Swansea was the first commercial brewery in the area for almost 30 years. Two regular outlets are supplied along with other pubs in the South Wales area.

Taddington

Blackwell Hall, Blackwell, Buxton, Derbyshire, SK17 9TQ
☎ (01298) 85734

Taddington started brewing in 2007, and brews one Czech-style unpasteurised lager in two different strengths. No real ale.

Tally Ho! SIBA

🍴 14 Market Street, Hatherleigh, Devon, EX20 3JN
☎ (01837) 810306 ☎ 07532 105871
🌐 tallyhobrewery.co.uk

The Tally Ho! brewery was recommissioned in 2015 by four brewing enthusiasts after a number of years lying dormant. As well as the pub, local free houses and other establishments are supplied.

Tankleys (NEW)

Correspondence: 33 Beech Avenue, Sidcup, Kent, DA15 8NH ☎ 07901 333273 🌐 tankleysbrewery.com

⊠ Tankleys is a cuckoo brewery based in South-east London producing small batch beers. Its Australian brewer has been brewing for 17 years and enjoys producing a range of styles. ♦

Golden Ale (OG 1040, ABV 4.5%)

Tap East SIBA

🍴 7 International Square, The Great Eastern Market, Westfield Stratford City, Montfichet Road, Stratford, London, E20 1EE
☎ (020) 8555 4467 🌐 tapeast.co.uk

Tap East is located in Westfield Stratford City shopping centre opposite the main entrance to Stratford International Station. Brewing began in 2011. One-off and collaborative beers with other breweries are also produced.

Tap House

See Leatherbritches

Tap It (NEW)

Unit 6, Muira Industrial Estate, William Street, Southampton, Hampshire, SO14 5QH
🌐 tapitbrew.co.uk

Brewing began in 2017. Beer is mostly available in kegs, however small volumes of cask-conditioned beer are available, mainly for beer festivals.

Tap Social Movement (NEW)

27 Curtis Industrial Estate, North Hinksey Lane, Oxford, OX2 0LX
☎ (01865) 236330 🌐 tapsocialmovement.com

⊠ A 1,000-litre brewery, founded in 2016 to provide training and opportunities for effective rehabilitation for people serving prison sentences. The three co-founders all have a background in the criminal justice system. 🍴 RAIB V

TAP

Marsden Estate, Rendcomb, Gloucestershire, GL7 7EX
☎ 07931 920988 🌐 tapbrewerygloucestershire.com

⊠ TAP is a microbrewery established near Cirencester in 2015. It prides itself on sourcing materials and services locally, with malt from Warminster, hops from Worcester and the beer labels produced in Cirencester. Twelve local pubs are regularly supplied. 🍴🍴♦ RAIB

Old Dairy Mild (OG 1038, ABV 3.2%)

Old Dairy Gold (OG 1040, ABV 3.9%)
A golden ale with a zesty finish.

Old Dairy Bronze (OG 1043, ABV 4.2%)

Tapped SIBA 👁

🍴 Sheffield: Sheffield Tap, Platform 1b, Sheffield Station, Sheaf Street, Sheffield, S1 2BP
☎ (0114) 273 7558

Leeds: Leeds Tap, 51 Boar Lane, Leeds, LS1 5EL
☎ (0113) 244 1953 🌐 tappedbrewco.com

Brewing began in 2013 after the old Edwardian dining rooms were converted into an onsite brewery with a viewing gallery at the Sheffield Tap pub. The beer is supplied via the company's specialist beer wholesale business, Pivovar. A further on-site brewery opened at the Leeds Tap in 2014.

Ale (OG 1035, ABV 3.5%)

Mojo (OG 1036, ABV 3.6%)
A clear, crisp, light pale ale.

Rodeo (OG 1039, ABV 4%)
American-hopped session pale ale.

Stogie (OG 1041, ABV 4%)
English dry stout with a bitter, slightly sour finish.

Bramling (OG 1042, ABV 4.2%)

Golden-coloured best bitter taking its character from the classic hop variety.

Liberty (OG 1052, ABV 5.2%)
Rich, dark-coloured treacle stout with subtle bitterness and hop aroma.

Miami Weisse (OG 1055, ABV 5.5%)
Fresh-tasting Hefe Weiss-style beer with banana and clove aromas.

Bullet (OG 1059, ABV 5.9%)
Strong IPA with a fruit candy aroma.

Tapstone

11 Bartlett Park, Millfield, Chard, Somerset, TA20 2BB
☎ (01460) 929156 ☎ 07969 651998
⊕ tapstone.co.uk

⊠ Founded in 2015, the brewery was custom built around a unique brewing process that preserves delicate hop oils – making beers with a saturated hop flavour. It is growing Centennial hops about two miles from the brewery.

Zen Garden (OG 1036, ABV 3.6%)

Sea Monster (ABV 4.2%)
Fresh and fruity pale ale with tropical flavours of blueberry, mango and lime.

Kush Kingdom (OG 1050, ABV 5%)
Golden-coloured beer with fruity, citrus flavours and a complex, resiny mouthfeel.

Sledge Hammer (OG 1060, ABV 6%)
A double IPA with a powerful hop flavour.

Target

Roden Nurseries, Roden Lane, Roden, Shropshire, TF6 6BP ☎ 07474 066611
✉ mark@targetbrewery.com

Formally known as Dickensian, Target Brewery was renamed in 2015. Brewing takes place on a 15-barrel plant based in an old vehicle storage shed. The beers are named around Shropshire legends. ♦

Marmid Gold (OG 1039, ABV 3.9%)
Well-balanced traditional session bitter.

Wrekin Giant (OG 1042, ABV 4.2%)
A hoppy pale ale with a clean, dry finish and a distinctive fruity kick.

Equinox (OG 1045, ABV 4.5%)
An American-style pale ale with a clean, hoppy flavour and a dry, spicy finish.

Tarn Hows SIBA

Low Bield, Knipe Fold, Outgate, Cumbria, LA22 0PU
☎ (01539) 436409 ☎ 07935 789581
⊕ tarnhowsbrewery.com

A small micro-brewery near Hawkshead specialising in traditional British ales using oak casks that provide a further dimension to the beer flavour.

Pigling Blonde (OG 1039, ABV 3.8%)
Blonde ale with peach and caramel notes.

Grized Ale (OG 1038, ABV 3.9%)
Dark chestnut-coloured beer with spice and pine flavours.

Beertrix Porter (OG 1042, ABV 4%) ◥
The beer is sold in oak casks and this flavour is present throughout. A well-balanced fruity beer

with some liquorice aromas and a lasting finish of bitterness and roast.

Puddled Duck (OG 1048, ABV 4.9%)

Tatton SIBA

Unit 7, Longridge Trading Estate, Knutsford, Cheshire, WA16 8PR
☎ (01565) 750747 ☎ 07738 150898
⊕ tattonbrewery.co.uk

☺Tatton is a family-run business based in the heart of Cheshire. Brewing commenced in 2010 using a steam-fired, custom-built 15-barrel brewhouse. It supplies pubs throughout Cheshire and the North-west. ‼🍺♦

Ale (OG 1036, ABV 3.7%)
An easy-drinking session ale with a rich copper colour. It has a full malty/toffee flavour balanced by a soft bitterness and hoppy, fruity taste and aroma.

Blonde (OG 1039, ABV 4%)
A clean-tasting, smooth pale ale with a good hop aroma.

Best (OG 1040.5, ABV 4.2%)
A classic light amber-coloured best bitter with a clean malt flavour and fine hop character derived from a blend of aroma hops.

Gold (OG 1046, ABV 4.5%)
A golden-coloured special ale with a maltiness backed by a robust hop character.

Tavernale

⧩ Bridge Tavern, 7 Akenside Hill, Newcastle upon Tyne, NE1 3UF
☎ (0191) 232 1122 ⊕ thebridgetavern.com

A two-barrel plant supplying beers to the Bridge Tavern only. All beers brewed are one-offs.

Tavy SIBA

Unit 9, Porsham Close, Beliver Industrial Estate, Plymouth, Devon, PL6 7DB ☎ 07971 411727

Office: 15 Hawkmoor Parke, Bovey Tracey, TQ13 9NL
⊕ tavyales.co.uk

⊠ Committed to producing small batch beers using a combination of traditional and modern brewing techniques and local ingredients, Tavy Ales is a six-barrel microbrewery situated in Plymouth. With a focus on sustainability, spent grain is taken to a local farm for animal feed. ‼♦RAIB

Golden Ale (ABV 4%)
A balanced session beer with a hoppy flavour and aroma, backed up with malt.

Best Bitter (OG 1043, ABV 4.3%) ◥
Malt dominates the nose and taste with caramel, roast and hops overpowering a subtle hint of fruit. A complex aftertaste.

Ideal Pale Ale (OG 1048, ABV 4.8%)
A golden-coloured beer loaded with citrus flavour and a balanced bitterness. It has a strong floral and hoppy aroma.

Sound Bitter (OG 1048, ABV 4.8%)

Porter (OG 1052, ABV 5.2%) 🍺 ◥
Bursting with flavours from nose through taste to aftertaste. Heavy roasted malt dominates.

Lingering aftertaste infused with sweet, fruity hoppiness.

Timothy Taylor SIBAIFBB ◉

Knowle Spring Brewery, Keighley, West Yorkshire, BD21 1AW
☎ (01535) 603139 ⊕ timothy-taylor.co.uk

◎ An independent, family-owned company established in 1858, it has occupied the Knowle Spring site since 1863. Pennine spring water is used to brew its award-winning ales on both the established main plant and a 10-barrel plant introduced in 2017 to develop new beers, including occasional specials.

Dark Mild (OG 1034, ABV 3.5%) ◄
Malt and caramel dominate throughout in this sweetish beer with background hop and fruit notes.

Golden Best (OG 1033, ABV 3.5%) ◄
Refreshing, amber-coloured, traditional Pennine mild. A delicate fruity, hoppy aroma leads to a fruity taste with underlying hops and malt. Fruity finish.

Boltmaker (OG 1038, ABV 4%) 🗂 ◄
Tawny-coloured bitter combining hops, fruit and biscuity malt. Lingering, increasingly bitter aftertaste. Formerly and sometimes still sold as Best Bitter.

Knowle Spring (OG 1041, ABV 4.2%)
Blonde ale with a citrus and floral nose, zesty spiced orange flavour and clean bitterness.

Landlord (OG 1042, ABV 4.3%) 🔳 ◄
A tasty bitter combining citrus peel aromas, malt and grassy hops, marmalade sweetness and a long bitter finish.

Ram Tam (OG 1043, ABV 4.3%) 🗂 ◄
A black-coloured beer with red highlights topped by a coffee-coloured head. Burnt caramel on the nose, sweetish caramel taste leading to a light, sweet finish

Taylors

⊟ London Tavern, Church Street, Attleborough, Norfolk, NR17 2AH ☎ 07983 178799
✉ taylorsbrewery@gmail.com

Brewing began in 2014, primarily to supply the London Tavern but the beers are now supplied to beer festivals and the free trade.

Number One (ABV 3.9%)

Second Coming (ABV 3.9%)
The mix of hops and malts results in a well-balanced traditional English session bitter.

Dogtooth (ABV 4%)

English Pale Ale (OG 1040, ABV 4%)

Remember Me (OG 1044, ABV 4.4%)
Malty beer with a caramel note and dry finish.

Stitched Up (ABV 4.7%)

Teignworthy SIBA

The Maltings, Teign Road, Newton Abbot, Devon, TQ12 4AA
☎ (01626) 332066 ⊕ teignworthybrewery.com

⊗ Teignworthy Brewery opened in 1994 within Tuckers historic maltings building. The 20-barrel plant produces 50 barrels a week using malt from Tuckers and supplies around 300 outlets in Devon and Somerset. ‼ 🏭 ◆ RAIB

Neap Tide (OG 1038, ABV 3.8%)
A pale-coloured, fruity bitter.

Reel Ale (OG 1039.5, ABV 4%) ◄
Subtle aromas. The taste is also gentle with malt and fruit dominating the hops. The aftertaste is dry.

Gun Dog (OG 1043.5, ABV 4.3%) ◄
Easy-drinking session best bitter. Fruity throughout. Dry aftertaste lingers; sweetness and fruit over malt and caramel, progressing into hoppiness.

Spring Tide (OG 1043.5, ABV 4.3%) ◄
A full and well-rounded, mid-brown-coloured beer with a dry, bitter taste and aftertaste.

Old Moggie (OG 1044.5, ABV 4.4%)
A golden-coloured, hoppy and fruity ale.

Beachcomber (OG 1045.5, ABV 4.5%) ◄
A pale brown-coloured beer with a light, refreshing fruit and hop nose, grapefruit taste and a dry, hoppy finish.

Teme Valley SIBA ◉

⊟ Talbot, Bromyard Road, Knightwick, Worcestershire, WR6 5PH
☎ (01886) 821235 ☎ 07792 394151
⊕ temevalleybrewery.co.uk

Teme Valley was established in 1997 to brew beer for the Talbot, Knightwick. Only hops grown in Herefordshire and Worcestershire are used in brewing. Cask and bottle-conditioned beers are supplied throughout the West Midlands and Marches.

T'Other (OG 1035, ABV 3.5%) ◄
Refreshing, amber-coloured beer offering an abundance of flavour in the fruity aroma, followed by a short, dry bitterness.

This (OG 1037, ABV 3.7%) ◄
Dark gold-coloured brew with a mellow array of flavours in a malty balance.

That (OG 1041, ABV 4.1%) ◄
A rich, fruity nose and a wide range of hoppy and malty flavours in this copper-coloured best bitter.

Talbot Blond (OG 1042, ABV 4.4%)
A smooth, rich, pale-coloured beer.

Tempest SIBA

Block 11, Units 1 & 2, Tweedbank Industrial Estate, Tweedbank, TD1 3RS
☎ (01896) 759500 ⊕ tempestbrewingco.com

Based in a former dairy, Tempest was set up in 2010 by Gavin Meiklejohn, brewer and co-proprietor of the Cobbles Inn in Kelso, which is the brewery tap. In 2015 the brewery moved from Kelso to new premises at Tweedbank. ‼ 🏭 ◆ RAIB

Pemberton Pale (OG 1037, ABV 3.7%)
An American-style pale ale, straw-like colour with a refreshing hop character. Aromas of lemon and lime, some tropical notes and subtle spice.

Armadillo (OG 1039, ABV 3.8%)
Waves of zesty citrus amplified with hops.

Cascadian (OG 1039, ABV 3.9%)

Light, citrus, hoppy session ale.

White Light (OG 1047, ABV 4.7%)
American hop hitter with a smooth citrus finish.

Tenby SIBA

Unit 15, The Salterns, Tenby, SA70 8EQ
☎ (01834) 218090 ☎ 07410 169447
⊕ tenbybrewingco.com

Formerly known as Preseli, Tenby Brewing Co uses a six-barrel plant. Beer is supplied to outlets in Pembrokeshire, neighbouring counties and further afield. Spent grain is fed to animals at a local eco farm and through energy savings the brewery plans to become carbon neutral. RAIB

West Coast Rocks (OG 1040, ABV 3.8%)
A malty body with a hint of spiced blackberry.

Pembrokeshire Promise (OG 1046, ABV 4.5%)
An extra special bitter with hints of caramel, complex grain and mellow bitter hops.

Barefoot Blonde (OG 1041, ABV 4.6%)
A refreshing, clean, crisp blonde. Infused with Kafir lime leaves.

Black Flag Porter (OG 1055, ABV 5.6%)
Coffee and chocolate notes with a hint of vanilla spiced rum.

Thame

≣ East Street, Thame, Oxfordshire, OX9 3JS
☎ (01844) 218202
✉ thamebrewery@btinternet.com

This one-barrel brewery was set up in 2009 by Peter Lambert and Oak Taverns in the old stables at the Cross Keys. Beer is produced for the Cross Keys and beer festivals, and includes many one-off brews.

Thames Side SIBA

Unit 7, Tims Boatyard, Timsway, Staines-upon-Thames, Surrey, TW18 3JY
☎ (01784) 409887 ☎ 07749 204242
⊕ thamessidebrewery.co.uk

⊗ Thames Side was founded in 2015 by Andy Hayward using a four-barrel plant situated in an old boatyard on the banks of the river. Beer is supplied to the local area as well as into central London. Beers are named after birds found on or near the River Thames. ♦RAIB

Harrier Bitter (OG 1036, ABV 3.4%)
A hoppy English session bitter.

Heron Ale (OG 1038, ABV 3.7%)
A traditional English ale, malty but well balanced.

White Swan Pale Ale (OG 1041, ABV 4.5%)

Egyptian Goose India Pale Ale (ABV 4.8%)

Wryneck Rye IPA (OG 1055, ABV 5.6%)
A spicy but hoppy rye IPA.

Theakston 👁

The Brewery, Masham, North Yorkshire, HG4 4YD
☎ (01765) 680000 ⊕ theakstons.co.uk

☺After several years under the control of other companies Theakston is now owned by four brothers, grandsons of Thomas Theakston, the son

of the company's founder who built the brewery in 1875. A new fermentation room was built in 2004 to provide additional flexibility and capacity, and further capacity was added in 2006. All Theakston beers are now brewed in Masham. ‼♦

Best Bitter (OG 1038, ABV 3.8%)
A golden-coloured beer with a full flavour that lingers pleasantly on the palate. With a good bittersweet balance, this beer has a robust hop character, citrus and spicy.

Black Bull Bitter (OG 1037, ABV 3.9%) ◗
A distinctively hoppy aroma leads to a bitter, hoppy taste with some fruitiness and a short bitter finish.

Lightfoot (OG 1041, ABV 4.1%)

XB (OG 1044, ABV 4.5%)
A sweet-tasting bitter with background fruit and spicy hop. Some caramel character gives this ale a malty dominance.

Old Peculier (OG 1057, ABV 5.6%) ◗
A full-bodied, dark brown, strong ale. Slightly malty but with hints of roast coffee and liquorice. A smooth caramel overlay and a complex fruitiness leads to a bitter chocolate finish.

Third Eye

The Mill, Hurst House Farm Barn, Halfpenny Lane, Heskin, Lancashire, PR7 5PR ☎ 07871 870015
⊕ thirdeyebrewery.co.uk

☺ Third Eye began brewing in 2015 using a 1.5-barrel plant. Local specialist real ale outlets and beer festivals are supplied direct, mainly within a 20-mile radius of the brewery. ♦

Session Ale (OG 1041, ABV 3.9%)
A hoppy pale ale with some residual sweetness and body to balance the hops.

Thirst Class

Unit 16, Station Road Industrial Estate, Reddish, Stockport, SK5 6ND
☎ (0161) 431 3998 ⊕ thirstclassale.co.uk

☺ Thirst Class opened in 2014 in the centre of Stockport using a purpose-built two-barrel plant. In 2016 the brewery relocated to larger premises and installed a 10-barrel plant. ♦RAIB

High 5 (OG 1053, ABV 4.2%)
A session pale ale, light and hoppy with a citrus aroma and flavour.

Stocky Oatmeal Stout (ABV 4.7%)
Smooth, full-bodied oatmeal stout with notes of coffee and chocolate.

Green Bullet Pale Ale (ABV 4.8%)
A traditional-style English pale ale with floral flavours.

American Brown Ale (ABV 5.6%)
A hoppy ale with a pronounced roasted maltiness.

Hoppy Couple IPA (ABV 6.2%)
American-style IPA. Rich copper in colour with a big citrus hop aroma and flavour.

Thomas Guest

See Black Country

THE BREWERIES

John Thompson

🏠 Ingleby, Melbourne, Derbyshire, DE73 7HW
☎ (01332) 862469 ⊕ johnthompsoninn.com

Established by John Thompson in 1977 as an addition to the John Thompson Inn, which he converted from a 15th-century farmhouse in 1968, and is now run by his son Nick. John Thompson Special (formerly JTS XXX) is Derbyshire's longest continuously brewed ale.

Thorley & Sons

30 East Street, Ilkeston, Derbyshire, DE7 5JB ☎ 07899 067723 ✉ dylan.thorley1@yahoo.co.uk

Thorley & Sons began brewing commercially in 2016 on a 1.5-barrel plant located in an old coach house at the rear of brewer Dylan Thorley's house.

No. 1 Amber (ABV 3.9%)
A traditional session beer with a zesty taste.

Pale & Interesting (ABV 4.5%)
Easy-drinking pale ale with a subtle hint of citrus in the taste.

Dark & Mysterious (ABV 4.9%)
A dark-coloured stout, lively and easy drinking.

Thornbridge SIBA ⊚

Riverside Business Park, Buxton Road, Bakewell, Derbyshire, DE45 1GS
☎ (01629) 815999 ⊕ thornbridgebrewery.co.uk

⊚The first Thornbridge craft beers were produced in 2005 using a 10-barrel brewery, housed in the grounds of Thornbridge Hall. The beers have gained considerable success with over 300 consumer and industry awards won. A 30-barrel brewery opened in Bakewell in 2009. The original site continues to develop new, seasonal and speciality beers. 200 outlets are supplied direct. 12 pubs are managed and owned. ‼ ▀ ◆ RAIB

Wild Swan (OG 1035, ABV 3.5%) 🍺 ◣
Pale yet flavoursome and refreshing beer. Plenty of lemon citrus hop flavour, becoming increasingly dry and bitter in the finish and aftertaste.

Brother Rabbit (OG 1035, ABV 4%)
Yellow in colour with a clean, hoppy aroma. a resinous finish and some bitterness.

Lord Marples (OG 1041, ABV 4%) ◣
Smooth, traditional, easy-drinking bitter. Caramel, malt and coffee flavours fall away to leave a long, bitter finish.

Ashford (OG 1043, ABV 4.2%)
A brown-coloured ale with a floral hoppiness, a smooth, malty kick and a delicate coffee finish.

Kipling (OG 1050, ABV 5.2%) ◣
Golden-coloured bitter with aromas of grapefruit and passion fruit. Intense fruit flavours continue throughout, leading to a long bitter aftertaste.

Jaipur IPA (OG 1055, ABV 5.9%)
Flavoursome IPA packed with citrus hoppiness that's nicely counterbalanced by malt and underlying sweetness and robust fruit flavours.

Saint Petersburg Imperial Russian Stout (OG 1073, ABV 7.4%) 🍾 ◣
Good example of an imperial stout. Smooth and easy to drink with raisins, bitter chocolate and hops

throughout, leading to a lingering coffee and chocolate aftertaste.

Thousand Trades (NEW)

Unit 5, 270 Lakey Lane Hall Green, Birmingham, B28 8RA ☎ 07768 454741
⊕ thousandtradesbrewing.co.uk

⊠ Brewing began in 2016. Beers are only available locally at present. ◆

Difference Engineer (ABV 3.8%)

Arts of Teleforce (ABV 4.5%)

New Mechanic (ABV 4.6%)

Three B's SIBA ⊚

🏠 Black Bull, Brokenstone Road, Blackburn, Lancashire, BB3 0LL
☎ (01254) 581381 ⊕ threebsbrewery.co.uk

Robert Bell acquired the Black Bull in 2011 and the brew pub now supplies 50 outlets.

Bee Thrifty (OG 1036, ABV 3.4%)
A light and refreshing amber-coloured beer.

Stoker's Slake (OG 1038, ABV 3.6%) ◣
Lightly roasted coffee flavours are in the aroma and the initial taste. A well-rounded, dark brown-coloured mild with dried fruit flavours in the long finish.

Honey Bee (OG 1039, ABV 3.7%)
A golden honey-coloured beer with honey apparent in both aroma and taste.

Bobbin's Bitter (OG 1038, ABV 3.8%)
A golden-coloured bitter with warm aromas of nutty grain and a full, fruity flavour with a light, dry finish.

Bee Blonde (OG 1041, ABV 4%)
A distinctive, pale bitter with a light, dry balance of grain and hops and a delicate finish with citrus fruits.

Black Bull (OG 1042, ABV 4%)
Dark ruby-coloured bitter with a rich character and a hint of chocolate.

Tackler's Tipple (OG 1044, ABV 4.3%)
A dark-coloured best bitter with a full hop flavour, biscuit tones on the tongue and a deep, dry finish.

Doff Cocker (OG 1045, ABV 4.5%) ◣
Yellow in colour with a hoppy aroma and initial taste giving way to subtle malt notes and orchard fruit flavours. Crisp, dry finish.

Lager (ABV 4.5%)

Pinch Noggin (OG 1046, ABV 4.6%)
A dark-coloured, strong best bitter with full hop flavour and a long aftertaste.

Knocker Up (OG 1047, ABV 4.8%) ◣
A smooth, rich, creamy porter. The roast flavour is foremost without dominating and is balanced by fruit and hop notes.

Shuttle Ale (OG 1050, ABV 5.2%)
A traditional strong pale ale.

Three Blind Mice

Unit W10, Black Bank Business Park, Black Bank Road, Little Downham, Cambridgeshire, CB6 2UA
☎ 07912 875825 ✉ blindmice3@btinternet.com

Three Blind Mice began brewing in 2014 using a five-barrel plant. The name comes from the three owners/brewers, who reckoned they didn't have a clue what they were doing when they first started brewing. An ever-changing range of beers is available throughout the year. A tap room is planned. ◆

Table Liquor (ABV 2.8%)
A dry, light and bitter pale ale.

Lonely Snake (ABV 3.5%)

Dirty Goulash (ABV 8.2%)
Rum flavours balance nicely with the sweet, roasted malt backbone.

Three Brothers (NEW) SIBA

Unit 4, Clayton Court, Bowesfield Crescent, Stockton on Tees, TS18 3QX
☎ (01642) 678084 ☎ 07588 318075
⊕ threebrothersbrewing.co.uk

☺The brewery is the vision of Kit Dodd after brewing for five years with another local brewery. He established it in 2016, together with his brother Dave and brother-in-law Chris. ‼◆

The Ex Wife (OG 1037, ABV 3.7%)
A bitter beer brewed in a traditional way with a modern, slightly fruity twist.

Honeysuckle Smash (OG 1040, ABV 4%)
A delicate golden ale which packs a punch with North Yorkshire honey.

Au (OG 1042, ABV 4.2%)
A refreshingly crisp, lightly-hopped golden ale with light citrus notes.

Brew No. 1 (OG 1050, ABV 5%)
A golden-coloured beer with a light bitter flavour and a smooth mouthfeel.

Three Castles

Unit 12, Salisbury Road Business Park, Pewsey, Wiltshire, SN9 5PZ
☎ (01672) 564433 ☎ 07725 148671
⊕ threecastlesbrewery.co.uk

Three Castles is an independent, family-run brewery established in 2006. It delivers direct to around 80 pubs and independent retailers. Wholesalers and beer festivals are also supplied. ‼ ▬ ◆ RAIB

Barbury Castle (OG 1039, ABV 3.9%)
A balanced, easy-drinking pale ale with a hoppy, spicy palate.

Saxon Archer (OG 1040, ABV 4%)
A balanced, easy-drinking session ale with a wonderful aroma and a hoppy, fruity palate.

Heritage (OG 1042, ABV 4.2%)
A bronze-coloured best bitter with a smooth taste.

Uffington Castle (OG 1042, ABV 4.2%)
A dark brown-coloured ale with a malty and nutty palate and a pleasant bitterness. The hop comes through well with a big spicy aroma.

Vale Ale (OG 1043, ABV 4.3%)
Golden-coloured beer with a fruity palate and strong floral aroma.

Corn Dolly (OG 1047, ABV 4.7%)
Honey-coloured, easy-drinking ale with a delicate, slightly floral aroma.

Three Daggers SIBA ◉

Westbury Road, Edington, Westbury, Wiltshire, BA13 4PG
☎ (01380) 830940 ⊕ threedaggersbrewery.com

⊗ Three Daggers Brewery was established in 2013 using a 2.5-barrel brew plant in a farm shop next to a popular roadside pub. Malt is sourced locally from Warminster Maltings and hops from Charles Faram in Herefordshire. ‼◆RAIB

Daggers Blonde (OG 1037, ABV 3.6%)

Daggers Ale (OG 1041, ABV 4.1%)
A refreshingly malty ale with a dry, hoppy finish.

Daggers Edge (OG 1047, ABV 4.7%)
A full-bodied, well-balanced strong bitter.

Three Fiends SIBA

Brookfield Farm, 148 Mill Moor Road, Meltham, West Yorkshire, HD9 5LN ☎ 07810 370430
⊕ threefiends.co.uk

The brewery was set up by three friends in 2015 and is based in one of the outbuildings at Brookfield Farm. The current two-barrel plant is in the process of being upgraded. Beers are available around Huddersfield and at CAMRA beer festivals.

Two Face (OG 1041, ABV 4%)
An easy-drinking session ale with floral, citrus and honey-like tones.

Bad Uncle Barry (OG 1042, ABV 4.2%)

Boomer (OG 1043, ABV 4.3%)

Mok Titi (OG 1045, ABV 4.6%)

Dark Side (OG 1053, ABV 5.3%)
A black IPA with a smooth chocolate start, leading to an increasingly bitter finish.

Little Devil (OG 1051, ABV 5.3%)

Voodoo (OG 1061, ABV 6%)

Bukowski (OG 1065, ABV 7%)

Three Hills (NEW)

4 Thrapston Road, Woodford, Northamptonshire, NN14 4HY ☎ 07400 706884 ⊕ threehillsbrewing.com

Named after the ancient communal tombs that stand on the outskirts of the village of Woodford, Three Hills is a small batch brewery established in 2016. RAIB

Three Kings SIBA

14 Prospect Terrace, North Shields, Tyne & Wear, NE30 1DX ☎ 07580 004565
⊕ threekingsbrewery.co.uk

Three Kings started in 2012 using a 2.5-barrel plant, upgrading to a five-barrel one in 2013. Four house beers are brewed for local pubs. In 2016 the brewery upgraded to a 10-barrel plant and expanded into the adjacent unit. ◆RAIB

Billy Mill Ale (OG 1040, ABV 4%)

Darkside of the Toon (OG 1042, ABV 4.1%)
A dry, Irish-style stout.

Ring of Fire (OG 1045, ABV 4.5%)

Silver Darling (OG 1053, ABV 5.6%)

Three Legs

7 Burnt House Farm, Udimore Road, Brede, East
Sussex, TN31 6BX ☎ 07939 997622
⊕ thethreelegs.co.uk

⊠ Three Legs was started in 2015 by three friends
who met studying wine-making and viticulture at
university. Initially a nanobrewery, it has expanded
to a four-barrel plant, in a converted farm barn. 20
local pubs and several local bottle shops are
supplied. Beers are also available from the on-site
brewery tap. !! ➡ RAIB

Pale (OG 1033, ABV 3.7%)
An aromatic beer, light in body and crisp with low
bitterness.

Red (OG 1040, ABV 4.2%)
An aromatic yet malty beer that balances
bitterness with mouthfeel and aroma.

Dark (OG 1045, ABV 4.5%)
A stout with a huge roasted character, chocolate
and coffee flavours and a dry finish.

English IPA (OG 1050, ABV 5.5%)
Locally-grown hops give a citrus and orange punch
and assertive bitterness.

Three Peaks

Scar Top, Buck Haw Brow, Settle, North Yorkshire,
BD24 0DJ
☎ (01729) 822939 ☎ 07795 358932

Office: 7 Craven Terrace, Settle, BD24 9DB
⊕ threepeaksbrewery.co.uk

⊠ Formed in 2006 using a five-barrel plant, Three
Peaks is run by husband and wife team Colin and
Susan Ashwell assisted by Andrew Murphy. ♦

Pen-y-Ghent Bitter (OG 1040, ABV 3.8%) ◀
The malty character of this mid-brown-coloured
session bitter is balanced by fruit in the aroma and
taste. The finish is malty and hoppy.

Ingleborough Gold (OG 1041, ABV 4%) ◀
This golden-coloured best bitter is hoppy
throughout with fruit in the aroma and taste and a
hoppy bitter finish.

Whernside Pale Ale (OG 1042, ABV 4.2%)

Blea Moor Porter (OG 1045, ABV 4.5%) ◀
Dark brown-coloured porter with a predominantly
roast malt character, a background of dark fruit and
a woody note.

Three Shires SIBA

Unit 10, Park Boulevard, Worcester, WR2 4GD
☎ 07964 196194 ⊕ threeshiresbrewery.co.uk

Three Shires began brewing in 2014 on a hand-
built plant in Worcester. Local outlets are supplied.

Kenelm (OG 1041, ABV 3.8%) ◀
Golden in colour, a smoky aroma and initial
sweetness give way to a malt whisky flavour with
peat and fruit undertones. Dry hop and peaty
finish.

Hafren (OG 1043, ABV 4%) ◀
Tawny-coloured beer with a butterscotch aroma
and caramel flavours predominating, balanced by a
slightly hoppy finish.

Three Sods SIBA 👁

🏢 Bethnal Green Working Men's Club, 42 Pollard Row,
Bethnal Green, London, E2 6NB ☎ 07544 422236
⊕ threesodsbrewery.com

Based in a working men's club in East London,
Three Sods is run by head brewer David Jonsson
Buttery and specialises in small batch beers
produced using a range of malt and hops from
around the world. A brewery tap is now open, the
Workers Arms.

Trade Union Pale Ale (ABV 4.5%)
A light and fruity pale ale with a slight bitterness
and citrus notes.

Mud Puddler Black IPA (OG 1050, ABV 4.9%) ◀
Creamy beer with malty, slightly fruity aroma.
Flavour is of dry coffee, fruit, spicy hops and a
growing, lingering bitterness.

Belgian Bugger (OG 1051, ABV 5%)
An unfined beer with a hint of wheat and a
massive floral hop hit.

Leapyear Golden Ale (ABV 5%)
Sweet malts combined with tropical fruits. Subtle
tastes of pineapple and a dry, light bitter finish.

Three Tuns SIBA 👁

🏢 Salop Street, Bishop's Castle, Shropshire, SY9 5BN
☎ 07973 301099

Office: 16 Market Square, Bishops Castle, SY9 5BW
⊕ threetunsbrewery.co.uk

Brewing on this site started in the 16th century and
was licensed in 1642. A small-scale tower brewery
from late 19th century survives. Three Tuns was
one of only four pub breweries still running in the
1970s.

Mild (OG 1040, ABV 3.4%)
Tawny-coloured beer of rich maltiness with burnt
and roasted flavours.

Rantipole (OG 1036, ABV 3.7%)

1642 Bitter (OG 1042, ABV 3.8%)
A golden ale with a light, nutty maltiness and spicy
bitterness.

Solstice (OG 1037, ABV 3.9%)
Pale straw-coloured beer. Lightly malty with crisp,
fruity bitterness and citrus flavours.

XXX (OG 1046, ABV 4.3%) ◀
A pale-coloured, sweetish bitter with a light hop
aftertaste that has a honey finish.

Stout (OG 1048, ABV 4.4%)

Cleric's Cure (OG 1059, ABV 5%)
A light tan-coloured ale with a malty sweetness.
Strong and spicy with a floral bitterness.

Steampunk (OG 1065, ABV 6.5%)
Rich, dark and fiery barley wine with flavours of
liquorice, ginger, caramel and roasted malts lasting
through into a strong bitter finish.

**Three Tuns XXXXXXX Strong Ale
(OG 1095, ABV 9.5%)**
Spicy, strong old ale.

Thurstons (Horsell) SIBA 👁

The Courtyard, 102c High Street, Horsell, Surrey,
GU21 4ST

☎ (01483) 729555 ☎ 07789936784
⊕ thurstonsbrewery.co.uk

⊗ Originally based in the Crown, Horsell, Thurstons moved next door in 2014 when the brewery upgraded to a 4.5-barrel plant. The brewery supplies pubs across Surrey. ◆ RAIB

Horsell Best (OG 1040, ABV 3.8%) ◥
Traditional, well-balanced bitter, initially malty with strong caramel flavours throughout and balancing bitterness, becoming drier in the finish.

Horsell Gold (OG 1040, ABV 3.8%) ◥
Light fruit and slightly nutty aroma, lead to some bitterness and malt, which soon fades into a light bitter finish.

Stedmans Ale (OG 1042, ABV 4.1%) ◥
Golden in colour with citrus and caramel aroma, and malt and hops more pronounced in the taste.

Milk Stout (OG 1055, ABV 4.5%) ◥
Smooth, sweet stout, with a chocolaty flavour. A sweet malty flavour with a pleasant sharpness and a slightly dry finish.

Thwaites IFBB ◉

Star Brewery, Penny Street, Blackburn, Lancashire, BB1 6HL
☎ (01254) 686868 ⊕ thwaites.co.uk

⊛ Founded in 1807, Thwaites closed its bulk beer operation in 2014 and now brews on a 20-barrel plant on the original Blackburn site, having sold its Wainwright and Lancaster Bomber brands, free trade business, distribution depot and dray fleet to Marston's in 2015. The company's Original Bitter continues to be brewed by Marston's. Blackburn brewing is exclusively for the company's own pubs. All of these can sell Thwaites Best Cask (TBC), which may appear re-badged as a house beer, and Nutty Black. Additionally, members of the 1807 Cask Club are able to select from four or more monthly Blackburn-brewed beers from the 'Seasonal Ales' range. A new brewery on a greenfield site at Mellor Brook in the Ribble Valley, some four miles from Blackburn, is planned to become operational in 2018. Around 275 pubs are owned. See Banks's. ◆ RAIB

Nutty Black (OG 1036, ABV 3.3%)
Traditional, malty, dark mild with caramel notes and a slightly bitter finish.

TBC (Thwaites Best Cask) (OG 1038, ABV 3.8%)
Well-balanced, traditional, amber-coloured bitter.

Ticketybrew SIBA ◉

16 Waterloo Court, Stalybridge, SK15 2AU
☎ (0161) 258 8570 ☎ 07970 093665
⊕ ticketybrew.co.uk

⊛ Ticketybrew opened in 2013 using a five-barrel plant. In 2016 it expanded to a 10-barrel plant. ◆ RAIB

Session IPA (ABV 3.5%)

Golden Bitter (ABV 3.6%)

Jasmin Green Tea (OG 1038, ABV 3.8%)
A light and refreshing ale. Hop bitterness is complemented by fresh lemon rind.

Munchner (ABV 4.3%)

Mixing malty caramel sweetness with hops; a traditional beer is given a new lease of life with the spicy flavours of Belgian yeast.

Rose & Ginger Wheat Beer (OG 1044, ABV 4.5%)
A beer with the unique aroma of roses, balanced by a subtle kick of fresh ginger.

Coffee & Star Anise Porter (ABV 4.9%)

Pale Ale (OG 1050, ABV 5.3%)

Blonde (OG 1047, ABV 5.6%)
A blonde ale with soft floral and fruit on the nose, and a spicy, fruity and yeasty flavour.

Tigertops

22 Oakes Street, Flanshaw, Wakefield, West Yorkshire, WF2 9LN
☎ (01229) 716238 ☎ 07951 812986
✉ tigertopsbrewery@hotmail.com

⊛ Tigertops was established in 1995 by Stuart Johnson and his wife Lynda who, as well as owning the brewery, run the Foxfield brewpub in Cumbria (qv). The brewery is run on their behalf by Barry Smith, supplying five regular outlets. ◆

Tiley's

⊟ Salutation Inn, Ham, Gloucestershire, GL13 9QH
☎ (01453) 810284 ⊕ sallyatham.com

This 2.5-barrel microbrewery was established in an outbuilding of the award-winning Salutation Inn in 2015 by owner/brewer Peter Tiley. In 2017 experienced brewer Jonny Mills, from Bristol Beer Factory, took over brewing responsibilities. Collaboration brews with other local brewers are planned.

Tilford (NEW)

⊟ Duke of Cambridge, Tilford Road, Tilford, Surrey, GU10 2DD ☎ 07710 500967
✉ genesiscraftales@hotmail.com

Tilford Brewery was started in 2017 using a 2.5-barrel plant in an old coaching house on the site of the Duke of Cambridge pub. A shop, tasting room and mini maltings are planned for the upstairs of the building.

Tillingbourne SIBA

Old Scotland Farm, Staple Lane, Shere, Surrey, GU5 9TE
☎ (01483) 222228 ⊕ tillybeer.co.uk

⊗ Tillingbourne began in 2011 on a farm site previously used by Surrey Hills Brewery using its old 17-barrel plant. Around 25 local outlets are supplied. ‼ ⛟ ◆

The Source (OG 1033, ABV 3.3%) ◥
Light and crisp golden ale with strong grapefruit flavours. Packed full of hops and drinking well above its strength.

AONB (OG 1036, ABV 4%) ◥
Golden ale in which citrus hop dominates throughout. Some balancing malt in the aroma and taste, however.

Falls Gold (OG 1037, ABV 4.2%) ◥

While hops dominate, balancing malt is evident throughout. Hints of grapefruit in the aroma and taste lead to a dry finish.

Hop Troll (OG 1045, ABV 4.8%) ◀
Golden ale with big hop flavours together with peach and apricot. Sweet, fruity taste leads to a floral bitter finish.

Time and Tide

Statenborough Farm, Felderland Lane, Eastry, Kent, CT14 0BX ☎ 07739 868256

Office: 10 Herschell Road, East Walmer, Kent, CT14 7SQ ⊕ timeandtidebrewing.co.uk

Time and Tide began brewing in 2013 using spare capacity at Ripple Steam Brewery (qv). In 2015 it obtained its own 20-barrel brewhouse. No real ale. ◆

Tindall

Toad Lane, Seething, Norfolk, NR35 2EQ

Tindall Ales began brewing in 1998. It was originally based in Ditchingham but moved to its current location towards the end of 2001. ◆

Best Bitter (OG 1037, ABV 3.7%)

Fuggled Up (OG 1037, ABV 3.7%)

Mild (OG 1037, ABV 3.7%)

Liberator (OG 1038, ABV 3.8%)

Alltime (OG 1040, ABV 4%)

Mundham Mild (OG 1040, ABV 4%)

Ditchingham Dam (OG 1042, ABV 4.2%)

Seething Pint (OG 1043, ABV 4.3%)

Norwich Dragon (OG 1046, ABV 4.6%)

Honeydo (OG 1050, ABV 5%)

Tinpot

Allanwater Brewhouse, Queens Lane, Bridge of Allan, FK9 4NY
☎ (01786) 834555 ☎ 07831 224242
✉ tinpot@bridgeofallan.co.uk

☺Tinpot opened in 2009 using a one-barrel plant designed to brew speciality beers, expanding in 2014 to a 1.5-barrel one. The beer range varies depending on season and demand. ‼ ☛ ◆ RAIB GF

Tintagel SIBA

Condolden Farm, Tintagel, Cornwall, PL34 0HJ
☎ (01840) 213371 ⊕ tintagelbrewery.co.uk

☒ This 7.5-barrel brewery was established in 2009 in a redundant milking parlour on the highest farm in Cornwall. Around 80 outlets are supplied direct. A new brewery is being built adjacent to the existing building. ☛◆

Castle Gold (OG 1038, ABV 3.8%) ◀
Heavily-hopped golden ale. Citrus hops and noticeable malt taste. Bitterness throughout with citrus and stone fruits. Lingering, dry finish.

Cornwall's Pride (OG 1040, ABV 4%) ◀
Tawny-coloured best bitter with peaty malt aroma. Nutty malt then hop bitterness with complex flavours. Bitterness and rising dry finish.

Arthur's Ale (OG 1044, ABV 4.4%) ◀
Copper-coloured best bitter with malt aroma. Malt, stone fruit sweetness and citrus hop bitterness.

Pendragon (ABV 4.5%) ◀
Smooth golden ale with powerful citrus hop nose. Refreshing strong hop bitterness taste with moderate dryness. Citrus fruit and grape flavours.

Poldark Ale (OG 1045.8, ABV 4.5%) ◀
Tawny-coloured strong mild. Assertive malty flavour with light caramel, roast notes and sweetness balanced by fruity hop bitterness. Caramel malt finish.

Harbour Special (OG 1048.9, ABV 4.8%) ◀
Brown-coloured strong bitter with ripe fruity, malty aroma. Rich nutty malt, stone fruits and esters taste, finishing bitter and dry.

Merlins Muddle (OG 1052, ABV 5.2%) ◀
Tawny-coloured old ale with assertive sweetness but faint bitterness. Malt dominates aroma and taste with treacle, citrus and summer fruits.

Gwaf Tan (ABV 5.5%) ▤

Tiny Rebel SIBA

Wern Industrial Estate, Rogerstone, NP10 9FQ
☎ (01633) 547378 ☎ 07903 470175
⊕ tinyrebel.co.uk

☺Established in 2012, Tiny Rebel moved to new, bespoke premises in 2017. Originally using a 12-barrel plant, the brewery now operates a dual-stream 30-barrel plant, and consists of 18 fermentation tanks and four conditioning tanks. ◆

Hank (OG 1039, ABV 4%) ▣
A light golden ale combining tropical aromas with floral and biscuit flavours.

Fugg Life (OG 1040, ABV 4.2%)
Pale ale with a woody, earthy bitterness.

FUBAR (OG 1042, ABV 4.4%)
A floral, hoppy pale ale with a dry, spicy finish.

Beat Box (OG 1042, ABV 4.5%)
American-style pale ale with grassy, floral flavours and pithy fruits.

Cwtch (OG 1045, ABV 4.6%) ▣ ▤
A balanced red-coloured ale that combines caramel malt flavours with citrus hops.

Juicy (OG 1046, ABV 4.8%)
A tropical golden ale with pungent fruit aromas and a juicy flavour.

Tipples

Unit 3, The Mill, Wood Green, Salhouse, Norfolk, NR13 6NY
☎ (01603) 721310 ⊕ tipplesbrewery.com

☒ Tipples was established in 2004 on a six-barrel brew plant. In addition to a full range of cask ales, an extensive range of bottled beers is produced, which can be found in some farmers markets and supermarkets in Norfolk. ◆RAIB

Hanged Monk (OG 1038, ABV 3.8%) ◀
Strong roast and malt notes dominate the aroma and taste. A grainy mouthfeel with caramel and a growing vinous finish.

Sundown (OG 1040, ABV 3.9%) ◀

Berries and malt introduce this smooth creamy bitter. Bitterness gives depth to the fruity malt core as it slowly sweetens.

Redhead (OG 1042, ABV 4.2%) ◆
Malt and hops in both nose and palate. Toffee in the initial taste gives way to an increasing bitterness.

Brewers Progress (OG 1046, ABV 4.6%) ◆
Solid and malty with strong caramel and vanilla support. Smooth and creamy with added depth by a bitter blackcurrant fruitiness.

Moonrocket (OG 1050, ABV 5%) ◆
A complex golden brew. Malt, hop, bitterness and a fruity sweetness swirl round in an ever-changing kaleidoscope of flavours.

Tipsy Angel

Unit 20, Manor Industrial Estate, Lower Wash Lane, Latchford, Warrington, Cheshire, WA4 1PL
☎ (01925) 653326 ☎ 07909 893912
✉ andycharlie1@hotmail.co.uk

☺Relocated from the Lower Angel pub in Warrington to the nearby 4Ts Brewery (qv) using its original 0.5-barrel plant. Some recipes are based on those from the now defunct Walker's of Warrington brewery. RAIB

Angels Mild (OG 1038, ABV 3.8%)
A dark mild brewed from the old Walker's recipe.

George Shaws Premium (OG 1043, ABV 4.3%)
An old-fashioned, well-balanced, amber-coloured bitter.

Angels Folly (OG 1052, ABV 5.2%)
A complex beer, rich in texture with an aroma of malted barley. Brewed from the old Walker's recipe.

Taipur (OG 1059, ABV 5.9%)

Tír Dhá Ghlas

☰ **Cullins Yard, 11 Cambridge Road, Dover, Kent, CT17 9BY**
☎ (01304) 211666 ⊕ cullinsyard.co.uk

Brewing began in 2012 using a two-barrel plant. Beers only available in the bar/restaurant and occasionally at the nearby Royal Cinque Ports Yacht Club, particularly at beer festivals.

Tirril SIBA

Red House, Long Marton, Cumbria, CA16 6BN
☎ (01768) 361846 ⊕ tirrilbrewery.co.uk

☺Established in 1999, Tirril Brewery has twice outgrown its premises. It has more than 170 outlets, 100 of which regularly stock the beer. One pub is owned. Contract brewing is also carried out for Bitter End Brewery. ‼◆

Original Bitter (OG 1038.5, ABV 3.8%)
Lightly-hopped, golden brown-coloured session beer.

Ullswater Blonde (OG 1038.5, ABV 3.8%)
A golden-coloured, easy-drinking session beer.

Grasmere Gold (OG 1039, ABV 3.9%)

Kirkstone Gold (OG 1039, ABV 3.9%)

Old Faithful (OG 1040, ABV 4%) ◆

Initially bitter, gold-coloured ale with an astringent finish.

1823 (OG 1041, ABV 4.1%)
A full-bodied session bitter with a gentle bitterness.

Academy Ale (OG 1041.5, ABV 4.2%)
A dark, full-bodied, traditional rich and malty ale.

Borrowdale Bitter (OG 1041.5, ABV 4.2%)
An amber-coloured ale with a nice bite.

Windermere IPA (OG 1043, ABV 4.3%)

Red Barn Ale (OG 1043, ABV 4.4%)
A ruby red-coloured ale with a strong hop finish.

Titan

c/o Golden Eagle, 6 St Katherine's Court (off Agard Street), Derby, DE22 3AY
☎ (01332) 298465 ☎ 07749 556837
⊕ titanbrewery.co.uk

☒ Set-up by former Mr Grundy's brewers in 2014. A pub has been acquired, the Golden Eagle, Derby. The brewery is in the process of obtaining a commercial unit but at present the beers are brewed using spare capacity at Mr Grundy's Brewery (qv).

Bitter (OG 1036.8, ABV 3.8%)

Pale (OG 1038.7, ABV 4%)

Gold (OG 1043.5, ABV 4.5%)

Ruby (OG 1044.6, ABV 4.6%)
Ruby-coloured ale with malt and coffee notes and a slightly spicy aroma.

Stout (OG 1066, ABV 4.8%)

IPA (OG 1048.5, ABV 5%)

Titanic SIBA ◎

Callender Place, Burslem, Stoke-on-Trent, Staffordshire, ST6 1JL
☎ (01782) 823447 ⊕ titanicbrewery.co.uk

☺Founded in 1985 and named after Captain Smith, a Potteries man and the captain of the Titanic. One of the earliest microbreweries, Titanic has grown into a local brewer with a small, constantly expanding tied pub estate and supplies free trade customers across the Midlands and the North-west. 2014 saw a major investment in the brewery and brewhouse creating a brewery shop and sample room. ‼◆RAIB

Mild (OG 1036, ABV 3.5%) ◆
Fresh, fruity hop aroma leads to a caramel start then a rush of bitter hoppiness ending with a lingering, dry finish.

Steerage (OG 1039.5, ABV 3.8%) ◆
Pale yellow-coloured bitter. Flavours start with hops and fruit but become zesty and refreshing in this light session beer with a long, dry finish.

Lifeboat (OG 1040, ABV 4%) ◆
Dark brown-coloured beer with fruit, malt and caramel aromas. Sweet start, malty and caramel middle with hoppiness developing into a fruity and dry, lingering finish.

Anchor Bitter (OG 1042, ABV 4.1%) ◆
Amber-coloured beer with a spicy hint to the fruity start that develops in to the rush of hops for the dry bitter finish.

THE BREWERIES

Iceberg (OG 1042, ABV 4.1%) ◆
Yellow gold-coloured sparkling wheat beer with a flowery start leading to a great hop crescendo.

Cherry Dark (OG 1045, ABV 4.4%)

Cappuccino Stout (OG 1046, ABV 4.5%)

Chocolate & Vanilla Stout (OG 1047, ABV 4.5%) ◆
Chocoholic paradise with real coffee and vanilla support. Cocoa, sherry and almonds lend depth to this creamy, drinkable stout.

Stout (OG 1046, ABV 4.5%) 🍴 ◆
Roasty, toasty with tobacco, autumn bonfires, chocolate and hints of liquorice; perfectly balanced with a bitter, dry finish reminiscent of real coffee.

White Star (OG 1048, ABV 4.5%) ◆
Hints of cinnamon apple pie are found before the hops take over to give a bitter edge to this well-balanced, refreshing, fruity beer.

Plum Porter (OG 1051, ABV 4.9%) 🍴 ◆
Dark brown-coloured beer with a powerful fruity aroma. A sweet plum fruitiness gives way to a gentle bitter finish.

**Captain Smith's Strong Ale
(OG 1054, ABV 5.2%)** ◆
Red brown in colour and full bodied, lots of malt and roast with a hint of honey but a strong bittersweet finish.

Toll End

⊟ c/o Waggon & Horses, 131 Toll End Road, Tipton, West Midlands, DY4 0ET ☎ 07903 725574

The four-barrel brewery opened in 2004. With the exception of Phoebe's Ale, named after the brewer's daughter, all brews commemorate local landmarks, events and people.

Tollgate SIBA

Unit 1, Southwood House Farm, Staunton Lane, Calke, LE65 1RG
☎ (01283) 229194 ⊕ tollgatebrewery.co.uk

⊠ This six-barrel brewery was founded in 2005 on the site of the old Brunt & Bucknall Brewery in Woodville, but relocated to new premises on the National Trust's Calke Park estate in 2012. Around 180 outlets are supplied direct, mainly in the North Midlands. The brewery owns three micropubs: the tap at No. 76 in Ashby-de-la-Zouch, the Tollgate Tap in Derby, and the Town Street Tap in Duffield.
‼ 🍴 ♦ RAIB V

Stand & Deliver (OG 1036, ABV 3.8%)
Traditional session bitter; medium malts with a smooth finish.

Hackney Blonde (OG 1036, ABV 3.9%)
Crisp, pale-coloured, lager-style session ale, refreshing with a citrus finish.

Melbourne Bitter (OG 1038, ABV 4%)
A golden-coloured, mellow bitter with a hint of citrus in the finish.

California Steam (OG 1041, ABV 4.2%)
A US West Coast inspired lager-style beer.

Red Storm (OG 1040, ABV 4.2%)
Based on an Irish recipe for a red ale, with soft malts and complex hops.

Bitter (OG 1041, ABV 4.3%)

Golden-coloured English bitter with a light malt base and a fruity, hoppy finish.

Duffield Amber (OG 1042, ABV 4.4%)
A traditional, amber-coloured bitter with English hops and malts.

Ashby Pale (OG 1043, ABV 4.5%)
A light, refreshing traditional English pale ale with a citrus finish.

Kalika IPA (OG 1043, ABV 4.5%)
A well-hopped, dark gold-coloured IPA.

Old Rasputin (OG 1043, ABV 4.5%)
Dark in colour with a hint of sweet creaminess, balanced with a smooth, slightly bitter finish.

Red Star IPA (OG 1043, ABV 4.5%)
Traditional IPA with smooth, hoppy flavours.

Billy's Best Bitter (OG 1044, ABV 4.6%)
A smooth-drinking, dark amber-coloured best bitter with good malt flavours balanced with fruity hops.

High Street Bitter (OG 1045, ABV 4.7%)
A dark, strong, smooth English bitter, brewed with rich malts.

Tolly Cobbold

See Greene King

Tom Herrick's

See under H

Tombstone SIBA

⊟ 6 George Street, Great Yarmouth, Norfolk, NR30 1HR ☎ 07584 504444
⊕ tombstonebrewery.co.uk

Established in 2013, the brewery is run by former home brewer Paul Hodgson. The original brewery backed onto the town cemetery, inspiring the name, but it has now relocated to the rear of its brewery tap, the Tombstone Saloon. Around 30 outlets are supplied.

Ale (OG 1038, ABV 3.7%)
Light golden ale with subtle citrus tones of oranges and lemons.

Arizona (OG 1040, ABV 3.9%) ◆
Gentle butterscotch airs. Strong bitter backbone with hints of lemon and malt. Increasingly dry finish.

Texas Jack (OG 1040, ABV 4%) ◆
Toffee apple and vanilla aroma. Caramel leads the smooth complex mix of flavours. A bittersweet fruitiness continues to the end.

Regulators (OG 1040, ABV 4.1%)
Golden-coloured, hoppy ale with a bitter, dry finish.

Gunslinger (OG 1044, ABV 4.3%)
Golden in colour with a caramel, nutty finish.

Lone Rider (OG 1044, ABV 4.3%)
A deep ruby-coloured, hoppy ale.

Stagecoach (OG 1044, ABV 4.4%)
Smooth, dark and malty ale with a hint of liquorice.

Cherokee (OG 1045, ABV 4.5%)
Amber-coloured ale with fruity overtones and aroma.

Santa Fe (ABV 5%)
A sweet and fruity ale.

Big Nose Kate (OG 1054, ABV 5.3%)
Ruby-coloured ale, malty and fruity with a subtle passion fruit taste.

6 Shooter (ABV 6.6%)
Fresh orchard fruits, floral with citrus undertones.

Tomos A Lilford SIBA

Unit 11b, Vale Business Park, Llandow, CF71 7PF
☎ (01446) 796905 ☎ 07779 132647

Office: 117 Boverton Road, Llantwit Major, CF61 1YA
✉ tomos.lilford@gmail.com

⌧ Tomos A Lilford was launched in 2013 by home brewers Rolant Tomos and brothers Rob and James Lilford. The brewery supplies pubs and clubs across the Vale of Glamorgan and further afield. All point of sale material is bilingual. ◆

Cob (OG 1040, ABV 4%)
Malty session beer with creamy, nutty notes.

Annwyl (OG 1050, ABV 5%)
American-style session bitter using three different hops.

Gaucho (OG 1050, ABV 5%)
An IPA with a long, smooth finish.

OPA (OG 1050, ABV 5%)
American-style IPA; hoppy, refreshing and satisfying.

Rosemary Ale (ABV 5%)
Pale-coloured, refreshing ale, bursting with the flavours of honey and rosemary.

Hay (OG 1052, ABV 5.2%)
An English-style IPA with added hay for sweetness and aroma.

Tonbridge SIBA

Unit 19, Branbridges Industrial Estate, East Peckham, Kent, TN12 5HF
☎ (01622) 871239 ⊕ tonbridgebrewery.co.uk

⌧ Tonbridge Brewery was launched in 2010 using a four-barrel plant, expanding in 2013 to a 12-barrel plant. It is owned and run jointly by Paul Bournazian and Mark Gardner. Pubs, clubs and shops are supplied throughout Kent and also parts of Surrey, Sussex, Essex and South-east London. ‼

Golden Rule (OG 1037, ABV 3.5%)
Hoppy golden ale with a light, crisp body and delicate floral aroma.

Traditional Ale (OG 1038, ABV 3.6%)
Easy-drinking and refreshing ale with a light, fruity taste and aroma.

Coppernob (OG 1039.5, ABV 3.8%)
A fairly dry, rich copper-coloured ale with a robust, fruity flavour.

Countryman (OG 1041, ABV 4%)
Classic best bitter with a light, malty taste. A refreshing spice and fruit finish.

Rustic (OG 1041.5, ABV 4%)
Deep bronze-coloured, rich-tasting country ale with a delicate spicy taste and aroma.

Blonde Ambition (OG 1043.5, ABV 4.2%)
Crisp, refreshing blonde ale with spicy and citrus notes.

Old Chestnut (OG 1045, ABV 4.4%)
Full-bodied, chestnut-coloured ale with a malty base and a berry/honey finish.

American Pale (OG 1050, ABV 5%)
Classic, full-bodied American-style pale ale with a refreshing citrus finish.

Toolmakers SIBA

6-8 Botsford Street, Sheffield, South Yorkshire, S3 9PF
☎ 07956 235332 ⊕ toolmakersbrewery.com

Toolmakers is a family-run brewery established in 2013 in an old tool-making factory. Beers are brewed on a five-barrel plant and are available within a 40-50 mile radius of the brewery. The adjoining Forest pub is owned. ‼◆

Lynch Pin (OG 1040, ABV 4%)
A best bitter with caramel undertones.

G Philips Driver (OG 1042, ABV 4.2%)

Black Edge (OG 1052, ABV 5.2%)
A dark-coloured beer with chocolate notes.

Top-Notch

Haywards Heath, West Sussex, RH16 1UQ ☎ 07963 829368 ⊕ topnotchbrewing.co.uk

This 0.5-barrel brewery is situated in a converted residential outbuilding in Haywards Heath. RAIB

Hop Festival (OG 1039, ABV 3.9%)

Royal Fanfare (OG 1046, ABV 4.6%)

Top Out SIBA

Unit 3, 6b Dryden Road, Loanhead, EH20 9LZ
☎ (0131) 440 0270 ☎ 07742 234970
⊕ topoutbrewery.com

Brewing began in 2013 using a six-barrel plant. Initially focusing on bottle-conditioned beers, the brewery has expanded into brewing cask beer for the on-trade. Bottle-conditioned beers are also brewed on Secret Herb Garden, a visitor attraction in Edinburgh. ◆RAIB

Copperheid (ABV 3.4%)

Eldorado (ABV 3.6%)

Staple (OG 1037, ABV 4%)

Altbier (ABV 4.5%)

Smoked Porter (OG 1060, ABV 5.6%)

South Face IPA (ABV 5.9%)

The Cone (OG 1058, ABV 6.8%)

Topsham

⛫ Rear of Globe Hotel, Fore Street, Topsham, Devon, EX3 0DP
☎ (01392) 874818 ⊕ topsham-ales.co.uk

Topsham Ales has operated since 2010 in premises within the Globe Hotel. It is run solely by volunteers, one of only a handful of co-operatively owned breweries in the UK. Brewing is currently suspended.

Torrside

New Mills Marina, Hibbert Street, New Mills, Derbyshire, SK22 3JJ ☎ 07539 149175
⊕ torrside.co.uk

☺ Torrside was established by three home-brewing friends in 2015, using a ten-barrel plant in a warehouse at the refurbished New Mills marina. Pubs, bars and bottle shops are supplied within a 50-mile radius. All beers are unfined. ☞♦RAIB V

Mam Tor (OG 1039, ABV 4%)
Fruity American-style pale ale.

Euro-Hop (ABV 4.5%)

West Of The Sun (ABV 4.5%)

I'm Spartacus (ABV 6%)

Totally Brewed SIBA ⊚

Units 8 & 9, Meadow Lane Fruit & Veg Market, Clarke Road, Nottingham, NG2 3JJ ☎ 07702 800639
⊕ totallybrewed.com

⊗ Totally Brewed began brewing in 2014 using a seven-barrel plant previously used at White Dog Brewery. A diverse range of hop-forward beers are produced. ♦

Guardian of the Forest (OG 1037, ABV 3.8%)

Slap in the Face (OG 1040, ABV 4%) ☙
Golden-coloured ale with citrus fruit hop aroma and taste and a dry bitter finish.

Crazy Like a Fox (OG 1045, ABV 4.5%) ☙
Copper-coloured malty best bitter with a caramel aroma and a gentle bitter finish.

Papa Jangle's Voodoo Stout (OG 1046, ABV 4.5%) ☙
Full-bodied, dark-coloured stout oozing complex malt tastes throughout.

Punch in the Face (OG 1047, ABV 4.8%) ☙
Golden-coloured ale, assertive hop aroma leading to grapefruit and malt taste with a hoppy, bitter finish.

Four Hopmen of the Apocalypse (OG 1047, ABV 5.2%) ☙
Immensely hoppy, fruity golden ale, moderate bitterness with a lasting hoppy finish.

Captain Hopbeard (OG 1050, ABV 5.5%) ☙
Amber-coloured ale with citrus hops aplenty and a strong bitter finish.

Totem

11 Cleaveland Rise, Ogwell, Newton Abbot, Devon, TQ12 6FF
☎ (01626) 330358 ✉ totembrewing@gmail.com

⊗ Established in 2014. No real ale. Brewing is currently suspended.

Totnes

▤ 59a High Street, Totnes, Devon, TQ9 5PB
☎ (01803) 849290 ☎ 07974 828971
✉ richard.kidd@idnet.net.uk

Brewing began in 2014 at a family-run pub at the foot of Totnes Castle. The brewery is situated immediately behind the bar. Beers are available almost exclusively at the pub.

Towcester Mill SIBA

The Mill, Chantry Lane, Towcester, Northamptonshire, NN12 6AD
☎ (01327) 437060 ☎ 07812 366369
⊕ towcestermillbrewery.co.uk

⊗ A five-barrel brew plant situated at the Old Mill in Towcester. There is a brewery tap on site and a shop off site at the Bell Plantation in Towcester. ‼☞♦

Crooked Hooker (OG 1038, ABV 3.8%)
Amber-coloured session ale with a satisfying bitter finish.

Mill Race (OG 1040, ABV 3.9%)
Blonde beer with a herbal and grapefruit finish.

Bell Ringer (OG 1044, ABV 4.4%)
Golden ale with subtle malt tones and hoppy orange and citrus notes.

Watling Street (OG 1050, ABV 5%)
A golden-coloured, hoppy premium bitter.

Black Fire (OG 1050, ABV 5.2%)

Tower SIBA

Old Water Tower, Walsitch Maltings, Glensyl Way, Burton upon Trent, Staffordshire, DE14 1PZ
☎ (01283) 562888 ☎ 07771 926323
⊕ towerbrewery.co.uk

☺Tower was established in 2001 by John Mills, formerly a brewer at Burton Bridge, in a converted derelict 19th-century water tower, originally built for Thomas Salt's Brewery. The conversion was given a Civic Society award for the restoration of a historic building later that year. Tower has 20 regular outlets. ‼☞♦

Salt's Burton Ale (OG 1035, ABV 3.5%)

Bitter (OG 1042, ABV 4.2%) ☙
Gold-coloured ale with a malty, caramel and hoppy aroma. A full hop and fruit taste with the fruit lingering. A bitter and astringent finish.

Gone for a Burton (OG 1046, ABV 4.6%)

Imperial IPA (OG 1050, ABV 5%)

Townes

▤ Speedwell Inn, Lowgates, Staveley, Derbyshire, S43 3TT
☎ (01246) 472252

Townes Brewery, which started in 1994, has been situated at the rear of the Speedwell Inn at Staveley since 1997. After the retirement of brewer Alan Wood in 2013, Lawrie and Nicoleta Evans have continued brewing to the same recipes on the five-barrel plant.

Townhouse

Units 1-4, Townhouse Studios, Townhouse Farm, Alsager Road, Audley, Staffordshire, ST7 8JQ ☎ 07976 209437 ✉ j.nixon2@btinternet.com

Townhouse was set up in 2002 with a 2.5-barrel plant. In 2004 the brewery scaled up to five barrels. ♦

Enigma (OG 1035, ABV 3.5%)

Styrian Pale (OG 1035, ABV 3.5%)

Rye Pale Ale (OG 1035, ABV 3.6%)

Flowerdew (OG 1039, ABV 4%) ◆
Golden ale with a floral aroma. Flavour of flowery hops delivering a crisp, hoppy bite and presenting a lingering taste of flowery citrus waves.

Meridian Mild (OG 1039, ABV 4%)

Barney's Stout (OG 1043, ABV 4.5%) ◆
Roast chocolate and toffee nose atop this black-coloured stout. Sweet start becoming bitter at the end, with velvety roast throughout.

Armstrong Ale (OG 1045, ABV 4.8%)
A rich, fruity, ruby red-coloured beer with a hoppy, dry finish.

Gladstone Strong Ale (OG 1048, ABV 5%)

Track

5 Sheffield Street, Manchester, M1 2ND
☎ (0161) 273 4832 ☎ 07725 692096
⊕ trackbrewing.co

Track Brewing Co is a microbrewery based in the heart of Manchester. Brewing began in 2014 using a nine-barrel plant plant. A varied range of beers is produced. There are regular brewry tap events.
‼️🍴◆

Sonoma (OG 1040, ABV 3.8%)
A light, pale-coloured ale with citrus and juicy fruit aromas.

Ozark (OG 1044, ABV 4.4%)
An American-style pale ale with a malt backbone accentuated by juicy hops for a light, easy-drinking finish.

Mazama (OG 1052, ABV 5.5%)
An IPA with a spicy, citrus aroma.

Toba (OG 1054, ABV 5.6%)
Oatmeal stout with a complex malt bill delivering chocolate and coffee flavours.

Tractor Shed SIBA

The Tractor Shed, Calva Brow, Workington, Cumbria, CA14 1DB
☎ (01900) 68860 ⊕ tractor-shed.co.uk

☺ Renamed from Mitchell Krause in 2014 and having previously had its beers brewed under contract, brewing started in an old tractor shed on the family farm in 2013. After initially focusing on bottled and kegged continental-style beers, the first cask-conditioned beer was produced in 2014. The brewery contract brews various beers for Shindigger (qv), mostly for bottle and keg. ‼️RAIB

Mowdy Pale Ale (OG 1039, ABV 3.9%)
An American-style pale ale with a fruity aroma and an intense, refreshing bitterness.

Clocker Stout (OG 1043, ABV 4%)

Traffic Street Specials

See Castle Rock

Traquair House SIBA

Traquair House, Innerleithen, EH44 6PW
☎ (01896) 830323 ⊕ traquair.co.uk/ traquair-house-brewery

The 18th century brewhouse is based in one of the wings of the 1,000-year-old Traquair House,

Scotland's oldest inhabited house. All the beers are oak-fermented and 60% of production is exported. ‼️🍴◆

Bear Ale (OG 1050, ABV 5%)

Treboom SIBA 👁

Millstone Yard, Main Street, Shipton-by-Beningbrough, North Yorkshire, YO30 1AA
☎ (01904) 471569 ☎ 07761 608662
⊕ treboom.co.uk

Treboom began in 2011 using a 10-barrel plant with the output distributed around the Yorkshire region. ‼️🍴◆

Tambourine Man (OG 1038.5, ABV 3.9%)
A golden ale with a hint of maltiness complemented by fruit hop flavours.

Yorkshire Sparkle (OG 1039, ABV 4%)
A pale ale with a fresh citrus taste.

Kettle Drum (OG 1042, ABV 4.3%)
Copper-coloured ale with a distinct fruitiness and robust hop flavours, leading to a clean finish.

Hop Britannia (OG 1050, ABV 5%)
A hoppy, strong pale ale. Honey in colour with intense citrus fruit and spice notes.

Baron Saturday (OG 1049, ABV 5.2%)
A strong porter with flavours of coffee and liquorice.

Treen's (NEW) SIBA

Unit 3, Viaduct Works, Frog Hill, Ponsanooth, Cornwall, TR3 7JW ☎ 07552 218788

Office; 18 St Michaels Road, Ponsanooth, Cornwall, TR3 7EA ⊕ treensbrewery.co.uk

⊠ Treen's was founded in 2016. Currently using spare capacity at a brewery in Falmouth, its own 12-barrel plant is due to come on stream.

Cuckoo (ABV 4.3%)

Tremethick

Grampound, Cornwall, TR2 4QY ☎ 07726 427775
⊕ tremethick.co.uk

Tremethick began brewing in 2015. Having brewed in small batches in a garage or using spare capacity at other breweries, a new building was completed and 5.5-barrel plant commissioned in 2016. RAIB

Pale Ale (OG 1043, ABV 4.3%) ◆
Golden ale with aroma of apples. Refreshing grassy citrus hops, bitterness and apple fruit. Lemon, grainy aftertaste.

Dark Ale (ABV 4.6%) ◆
Red-coloured strong mild with coffee malt nose. Sweet taste with coffee, roast malt, liquorice, caramel and fruits. Not bitter or hoppy.

Tres Bien

See Market Harborough

Tring SIBA

Dunsley Farm, London Road, Tring, Hertfordshire, HP23 6HA
☎ (01442) 890721 ⊕ tringbrewery.co.uk

Founded in 1992, Tring Brewery moved to its present site in 2010. It brews more than 130 barrels a week, producing a core range of ten beers augmented by monthly and seasonal specials, most taking their names from local myths and legends. !! ➡ ♦ RAIB

Side Pocket for a Toad (OG 1035, ABV 3.6%)
A straw-coloured ale with citrus notes and floral aroma with a crisp, dry finish.

Brock Bitter (OG 1036, ABV 3.7%)
A mid-brown-coloured quaffing ale with a hint of sweetness and caramel.

Mansion Mild (OG 1036, ABV 3.7%)
Smooth and creamy dark ruby mild with a fruity palate and gentle late hop.

Drop Bar Pale Ale (OG 1039, ABV 4%)
A pale ale with a biscuit malt base and citrus aroma.

Ridgeway (OG 1039, ABV 4%)
Balanced malt and hop flavours with a dry, flowery hop aftertaste.

Moongazing (OG 1042, ABV 4.2%)
Red-hued beer with a rounded bitterness and hoppy aftertaste.

Pale Four (OG 1048, ABV 4.6%)
A blend of four hop varieties and an American yeast, a light and satisfying golden ale.

Tea Kettle Stout (OG 1047, ABV 4.7%)
Rich and complex traditional stout with a hint of liquorice and moderate bitterness.

Colley's Dog (OG 1051, ABV 5.2%)
A premium ale with a long, dry finish and overtones of malt and walnuts.

Death or Glory (OG 1074, ABV 7.2%) 🍷
A strong, dark-coloured, aromatic barley wine.

Trinity Ales

5 Church Road, Gisleham, Suffolk, NR33 8DS
☎ (01502) 743121 ⊕ trinity-ales.co.uk

⊠ Trinity Ales was launched in 2009 using a four-barrel plant. It uses pure spring water from its own ancient well along with locally-sourced ingredients. Pubs, restaurants, retail outlets and festivals are supplied throughout Suffolk and beyond. RAIB

Wishing Well (OG 1039, ABV 3.8%)

High Light (OG 1040, ABV 4%)

Church Key (OG 1045, ABV 4.5%)

Gisleham Gold (OG 1045, ABV 4.5%)

Trinity Gold (OG 1045, ABV 4.5%)

Trinity

Wakefield Wildcats Rugby League Ground, Doncaster Road, Wakefield, West Yorkshire, WF1 5EY

Office: 3 George Street, Outwood, Wakefield, WF1 2LR
⊕ trinitybrewing.co.uk

☺Trinity is housed at the rear of the Wakefield Wildcats Rugby League ground. Brewing began in 2015 and the beers are rugby themed.

Ruby League (ABV 3.6%)

Belle Vue Blonde (ABV 4.2%)

Hop & Under (ABV 4.2%)

Legend (ABV 4.2%)

Triple fff SIBA 👁

Magpie Works, Station Approach, Four Marks, Alton, Hampshire, GU34 5HN
☎ (01420) 561422 ⊕ triplefff.com

⊠ Established in 1997 close to a stop on the Watercress Line, the brewery and all the beers except Alton's Pride are named following a musical theme. The fff refers to fortissimo, meaning louder or stronger. Brewing on a 50-barrel plant since 2006, multiple CAMRA awards have been won. Two pubs are owned: the Railway Arms, Alton, and the White Lion, Aldershot. !! ➡ RAIB

Alton's Pride (OG 1039, ABV 3.8%) 🍴 🍂
Full-bodied session biter. An initially malty flavour fades as citrus notes and hoppiness take over, leading to a lasting hoppy/bitter finish.

**Pressed Rat & Warthog
(OG 1039, ABV 3.8%)** 🍷 🍂
Toffee aroma with hints of blackcurrant and chocolate lead to a well-balanced flavour with roast, fruit and malt vying with the hoppy bitterness.

Moondance (OG 1042, ABV 4.2%) 🍂
An aromatic citrus hop nose, balanced by bitterness and sweetness in the mouth. Bitterness increases in the finish as fruit declines.

True North (NEW)

Eldon Street, Sheffield, South Yorkshire, S1 4GY
☎ (0114) 272 0569

Office: 127-129 Devonshire Street, Sheffield, S3 7SB
⊕ truenorthbrewco.uk

☺True North began brewing in 2012 using spare capacity at Welbeck Abbey Brewery (qv). It opened its own plant in Sheffield in 2016. 10 pubs are owned. ♦

Session Pale (OG 1034, ABV 3.6%)

Best (OG 1038, ABV 3.8%)

Blonde (OG 1039, ABV 4%)

Pale (OG 1040, ABV 4.3%)

Stout (OG 1057, ABV 5%)

IPA (OG 1048, ABV 5.4%)

Truman's SIBA 👁

The Eyrie, 2 & 3 Stour Road, Hackney Wick, London, E3 2NT
☎ (020) 8533 3575 ⊕ trumansbeer.co.uk

The legendary East London brewery Truman's reborn in 2013, 24 years after the original Brick Lane brewery's closure in 1989. The new brewery is a 40-barrel plant in Hackney Wick, just a stroll down the Roman Road from the original site. The original Truman's yeast, recovered from the National Collection of Yeast Cultures, is used. ♦ RAIB

Swift (OG 1040.5, ABV 3.9%) 🍂
Well-balanced, golden-coloured bitter with hops and a trace of grapefruit on the nose and palate and a bitter finish.

Runner (OG 1040, ABV 4%) 🍂

Traditional brown-coloured best bitter with a spicy, hoppy aroma and flavour fading in the dry aftertaste. Some marmalade fruity notes.

Lazarus (OG 1043, ABV 4.2%) ◆
Well-balanced pale golden ale with peaches and straw aroma, refreshing grassy and citrus flavour, continuing into the short finish.

Zephyr (ABV 4.4%) ◆
Pale brown-coloured, smooth beer with a slightly dry roasted character on palate and bitter finish. Touch of orange and hops.

Tryst SIBA

Lorne Road, Larbert, FK5 4AT
☎ (01324) 554000 ∰ trystbrewery.co.uk

Tryst started production in 2003. A large range of beers is produced. ‼️ 🍽 ◆ RAIB

Brockville Dark (OG 1039, ABV 3.8%)
A full-tasting session ale with hints of liquorice and roasted grains.

Brockville Pale (OG 1039, ABV 3.9%)
A pale golden-coloured session ale, smooth on the palate.

Hop Trial (OG 1040, ABV 3.9%)
Lager malt with a variable hop profile.

Bla'than (OG 1041, ABV 4%)
A strong floral nose and refreshing taste enhanced with elderflower and pale malts.

Carronade Pale Ale (OG 1043, ABV 4.2%) 🍷
A pale ale bursting with citrus flavours.

Drovers 80/- (OG 1044, ABV 4.3%)

Sherpa Porter (OG 1044, ABV 4.4%)

German Hops Pils (OG 1045, ABV 4.5%)

V.I.P. (OG 1046, ABV 4.5%)
Best bitter with a deep hop taste and floral nose.

Zetland Wheatbier (OG 1046, ABV 4.5%)
A refreshing, cloudy wheat beer with a distinctive banana nose.

RAJ IPA (OG 1055, ABV 5.5%) 🍷
Exclusively English hops with balanced flavours and a hoppy aroma and palate.

Tudor SIBA 👁

Unit A, Llanhilleth Industrial Estate, Llanhilleth, Gwent, NP13 2RX
☎ (01495) 214808 ☎ 07971 015844
∰ tudorbrewery.co.uk

☺ Tudor is a family-run, four-barrel plant that began brewing in 2007 in Abergavenny before moving in 2012 to Llanilleth. Several local pubs are supplied, in addition to others further afield. RAIB

Blorenge (OG 1038, ABV 3.8%)
A light, pale ale with a fresh citrus undertone.

Black Mountain Stout (OG 1039, ABV 4%) 🍷

IPA (OG 1039, ABV 4%)
A classic IPA with a sharp, hoppy, grapefruit finish.

Skirrid (OG 1040, ABV 4.2%)
A full-flavoured, dark-coloured beer.

Sugarloaf (OG 1044, ABV 4.7%)
A rounded, full-bodied ale with smooth caramel undertones.

Winter Cheer (OG 1046, ABV 5%)

A dark-coloured ale infused with ground ginger, lemon rind, honey, cinnamon and nutmeg.

Black Rock (OG 1050, ABV 5.6%) 🍺
A dark-coloured ale with a rich aroma and a smooth chocolate-coffee aftertaste.

Tunnel 👁

Correspondence: Red House Farm, Nuneaton Road, Ansley, Nuneaton, Warwickshire, CV10 0QU ☎ 07765 223110 ∰ tunnelbrewery.co.uk

Beers are brewed at various local breweries for the Tunnel and Battlefield brands. Plans are underway to install a new brewery. ‼️ 🍽 ◆ RAIB

Percheron (OG 1037, ABV 3.7%)
A refreshing, citrus pale golden-coloured ale.

Light at The End Of The Tunnel (OG 1040, ABV 4%)
A golden amber-coloured session bitter. Fruity, citrus aroma with perfumed hops and a bitter finish.

Trade Winds (OG 1045, ABV 4.6%)
An IPA, bright gold in colour. Refreshing with a clean, crisp finish.

Shadow Weaver (OG 1046, ABV 4.7%)
Deep red-coloured stout/porter. Chocolate and coffee give way to a mellow fruit finish.

Nelson's Column (OG 1051, ABV 5.2%)
A ruby red-coloured ale with a complex blend of fruit, malt and hops.

East India Pale Ale (OG 1058, ABV 5.9%)
Copper/red-coloured, full-bodied ale with a robust hit of hops and a caramel, toffee finish.

Brewed under the Battlefield Brewery name:

Let Battle Commence (OG 1041, ABV 4%)
Amber-coloured bitter with well-balanced malt and hops.

Richard III (OG 1042, ABV 4%)
A pale ale with a sweet start and dry finish.

Henry Tudor (OG 1050, ABV 5%)
Chestnut red-coloured ale with a fruit and malt nose and a mellow hop finish.

Turnstone

20 West Cliff, Whitstable, Kent, CT5 1DN ☎ 07807 262662 ✉ turnstoneales@outlook.com

⊗ Turnstone Ales is a small, 0.5-barrel home-based brewery set up in 2014 by a part-time teacher. The beers are supplied to three local pubs. The brewery also has a regular stall at the Best of Faversham market. RAIB

Turpin

Turpins Lodge, Lodge Farm, Tadmarton Heath Road, Hook Norton, Oxfordshire, OX15 5DQ
☎ (01608) 737033
✉ turpinbrewery@btconnect.com

⊗ Brewing started in 2013. A number of local pubs are supplied regularly, as well as a few pubs further afield in Rugby and Birmingham. ◆

Golden Citrus (OG 1042, ABV 4.2%)
A golden-coloured beer with a pronounced citrus character and a lasting bitter hop finish.

Turpin's

Unit 13b, Sawston Trade Park, London Road,
Pampisford, Cambridgeshire, CB22 3EE
☎ (01223) 833883 ⊕ turpinsbrewery.co.uk

Turpin's opened in 2015 at the Med pub in
Cambridge, but due to increased demand brewing
has moved to Pampisford. ♦

Meditation (ABV 4.3%)

Cambridge Black (ABV 4.6%)

Tweed SIBA ◉

Unit D1C, Newton Business Park, Talbot Road,
Newton, Hyde, SK14 4UQ
☎ (0161) 368 8608 ⊕ tweedbrewing.com

Tweed began brewing in 2014 and expanded to
bottle production in 2015. Beers are available in
Manchester, particularly the Northern Quarter. ♦

Sorachi (ABV 3.7%)
Brewed with a generous amount of hops and a late
addition of dried lemon peel.

Pale Ale (ABV 3.8%)
A well-balanced English pale ale with delicate pine
and cedar notes washed down by a sweet honey
finish.

Hopster (ABV 3.9%)
A single-hopped, pineapple-infused pale ale with
citrus flavours and a rounded body.

Orange County IPA (ABV 4.3%)
A refreshing, well-balanced IPA with the addition
of Orange County oranges.

Twickenham SIBA ◉

Unit 6, 18 Mereway Road, Twickenham, TW2 6RG
☎ (020) 8241 1825 ⊕ twickenham-fine-ales.co.uk

⊗ Established in 2004, Twickenham Fine Ales is
London's oldest microbrewery. Operating a 25-
barrel plant, it is the first brewery in Twickenham
since the 1920s. !! ▤ ♦

Sundancer (OG 1037.5, ABV 3.7%) ◥
Light, zesty golden ale with citrus notes
dominating from beginning to end. Finish is bitter
but balanced by biscuity sweetness.

Grandstand Bitter (OG 1038, ABV 3.8%) ◥
Pale brown-coloured beer with peach, citrus and
malt on the palate, fading in the bitter, slightly dry
finish.

Redhead (OG 1041, ABV 4.1%) ◥
A tasty, creamy, chestnut brown-coloured best
bitter with interesting sweet caramel hints and a
mild, short, roasted bitter finish.

Naked Ladies (OG 1044, ABV 4.4%) ◥
Refreshing dark golden ale with a touch of spicy
hop in the flavour but fruit dominates with a lasting
bitterness.

Twisted Barrel

Unit 5, Fargo Village, Far Gosford Street, Coventry,
CV1 5ED
☎ (024) 7610 1701 ⊕ twistedbarrelale.co.uk

⊗ Commencing commercial production as a
picobrewery in 2013 using a brew length of 60
litres, Twisted Barrel expanded to a six-barrel
brewery and moved to its new location in 2015

with an on-site tap house open at weekends. Local
outlets are supplied but beers can occasionally be
found in Birmingham, Yorkshire, Manchester and in
the London area. !! ▤ ♦ RAIB V

Beast of a Midlands Mild (OG 1044, ABV 3.5%)

Gunderson (ABV 3.6%)

God's Twisted Sister (OG 1050, ABV 4.5%)

Inspired (OG 1046, ABV 4.5%)

Sine Qua Non (OG 1046, ABV 4.5%)

The Morgul Path (ABV 4.5%)

Saison From Another Place (ABV 5.5%)

Call of Korriban (OG 1056, ABV 5.7%)

In Amber Clad (OG 1059, ABV 6%)

Twisted Oak SIBA ◉

Yeowood Farm, Iwood Lane, Wrington, Bristol,
BS40 5NU ☎ 07917 457797
⊕ twistedoakbrewery.co.uk

⊗ Brewing began in 2012 using a five-barrel
plant. The brewery is situated in a former
agricultural building on a working farm in the north
Somerset countryside. The business is run by Keith
and Deb Hayles, who brew small batches of special
and unique ales. ♦ RAIB

Fallen Tree (OG 1039, ABV 3.8%) ◥
Bittersweet session bitter. Aroma and flavour of
hops and ripe fruit. Complex and satisfying bitter,
astringent finish.

Crack Gold (OG 1040, ABV 4%)

Wild Wood (OG 1040, ABV 4%) ◥
Little aroma. Smooth with flavours of hops and fruit
and a little malt. Minimal aftertaste.

Old Barn (OG 1045, ABV 4.5%) ◥
Fruity red-coloured ale. Well-balanced flavour with
a long bitter finish.

Spun Gold (OG 1045, ABV 4.5%) ⬓ ◥
Classic golden ale with a soft mouthfeel. Spicy
notes to the fruity malt aroma and flavour. Hops in
the aroma develop into a bitter finish.

Crack Amber (OG 1048, ABV 5%)

Twisted SIBA ◉

Unit 8, Commerce Business Centre, Commerce Close,
Westbury, Wiltshire, BA13 4LS
☎ (01373) 864441 ☎ 07512 261914
⊕ twisted-brewing.com

⊗ Twisted began brewing in 2014 using a new six-
barrel plant. Outlets in west Wiltshire and north
Somerset are supplied. ♦

Three & Sixpence (OG 1038, ABV 3.6%)
A light chestnut-coloured session ale with a hoppy
character.

WTF (OG 1040, ABV 3.8%)
A hoppy pale ale with a long finish.

Rider (OG 1041, ABV 4%)
A triple-hopped, amber-coloured ale with biscuit
malt flavours.

Conscript (OG 1043, ABV 4.2%)
A golden-coloured ale with a soft fruit aroma and
floral notes.

Pirate (OG 1043, ABV 4.2%)

A classic English best bitter, pale copper in colour with an aroma of roasted malt and coffee. Undertones of nutty fruit cake.

Gaucho (OG 1048, ABV 4.6%)
Ruby-coloured ale with aromas of soft fruits, coffee and a hint of chocolate.

Two Beach SIBA

Ness Cove, Shaldon, Devon, TQ14 0HP
☎ (01626) 873427 ⊕ odetruefood.com/brewery

⊠ Brewing began in 2013 using the plant previously used at Ringmore Craft Brewery. The brewery may relocate during the currency of this guide. ♦

Beer From Here (ABV 4.2%)
A bright golden-coloured session ale. Smooth, hoppy and well balanced.

ODE Ale (OG 1042, ABV 4.2%)
A light amber-coloured ale with a citrus twist. Hoppy with strong hints of elderflower.

Shaldon Shag Ale (OG 1042, ABV 4.2%)
An aroma of summer fruits with a hint of caramel. The taste is fruity, zesty hops with a well-balanced finish.

Oarsome Ale (OG 1047, ABV 4.6%)
Amber-coloured with hoppy tones. Aroma full of hops and barley with a hint of sweet fruit. Smooth on the palate with deep caramel flavours.

Two by Two

Unit 19, Point Pleasant Industrial Estate, Wallsend, NE28 6HA ☎ 07723 959168

Office: 14 Albany Gardens, Whitley Bay, NE26 2DY
✉ twobytwobrewing@gmail.com

Brewing began in 2014 using a five-barrel plant. ♦ RAIB

Two Cocks

Church Lane, Enborne, Berkshire, RG20 0HB
☎ (01635) 37777 ☎ 07831 201533
⊕ twococksbrewery.com

⊠ The brewery was established in 2011 after wild hops were found growing in the farm's hedgerows. A 180-feet deep borehole supplies water for the brewery. Most beer names refer to the 1st Battle of Newbury in the English Civil War.

Diamond Lil (OG 1035, ABV 3.2%)
A light and fruity golden ale.

1643 Cavalier (OG 1039, ABV 3.8%)
A light, refreshing golden ale with a combination of hops.

1643 Leveller (OG 1040, ABV 3.8%)
A malty session bitter brewed with a single variety of English hop.

1643 Roundhead (OG 1042, ABV 4.2%)
A full-bodied, smooth best bitter with a blend of hops.

1643 Puritan (OG 1049, ABV 4.5%)
A dark-coloured stout with notes of caramel and chocolate.

1643 Viscount (OG 1054, ABV 5.6%)
An unusually fruity strong beer.

Two Finches (NEW)

Finchley Cricket Club, 1 Arden Cottages, 33-45 East End Road, Finchley, London, N3 2TA
⊕ twofinchesbrewery.co.uk

Brewing began in 2015, originally brewing just for the cricket club. No real ale.

Two Rivers SIBA

2 Sluice Bank, Denver, Norfolk, PE38 0EQ
☎ (01366) 380131 ☎ 07518 099868
⊕ denverbrewery.co.uk

Two Rivers was established in 2012 by John Nash. Bottled-conditioned ale has been available since the establishment of the brewery and cask ales have been produced since 2013. ‼ ♦ RAIB V

Miners Mild (OG 1032, ABV 3.1%)
Tawny-coloured mild with good malt character, light finish and chocolate notes.

Hares Hopping (OG 1041, ABV 4.1%)
Clean-flavoured bitter with a distinctive late bitterness and dry finish.

Kiwi Kick (ABV 4.1%)
A golden-coloured bitter with a pleasant aroma and zesty hop finish.

Denver Diamond (OG 1047, ABV 4.4%)
A rounded bitter and malt taste with a grassy, slightly floral, aromatic character. A full-bodied malty finish.

Porters Pride (OG 1050, ABV 5%)
A full-bodied, well-balanced porter. Rich with a slight sweetness cutting through the smooth malt. Coffee and chocolate aromas and taste, with a liquorice/vanilla finish.

Norfolk Stoat (OG 1050, ABV 5.8%)
A full-bodied oatmeal stout. Silky with a subtle burnt edge.

Two Roses

Unit 9, Darton Business Park, Barnsley Road, Darton, South Yorkshire, S75 5QX ☎ 07780 701254
⊕ tworosesbrewery.co.uk

☺Two Roses started brewing in 2011 using an eight-barrel plant installed in a former carpet factory. Now only brewing occasionally for two local outlets. ‼ 🍺 ♦

Full Nelson (OG 1038, ABV 3.8%)

Chinook (OG 1040, ABV 4%)

Marynka (OG 1040, ABV 4%)

Heron Porter (OG 1041, ABV 4.2%)

Legacy (OG 1041, ABV 4.2%)

Two Thirsty Men (NEW) SIBA

74 High Street, Grantown-on-Spey, PH26 3EL
☎ (01479) 872246 ⊕ twothirstymen.com

Brewing began in 2016 in a garage at the back of a café bar.

Spey IPA (ABV 3.5%)

No. 74 (ABV 4.5%)

Two Towers SIBA

29 Shadwell Street, Birmingham, B4 6HB
☎ (0121) 439 3738 ☎ 07795 247059
⊕ twotowersbrewery.co.uk

⊠ Established in 2010, the 10-barrel brewery moved to its current location behind its tap house, the Gunmakers Arms, in 2016 and is visible from the beer garden. It undertakes bespoke brewing for special events, mainly local in nature. ‼️ ⟁ ♦ RAIB V

Baskerville Bitter (OG 1038, ABV 3.8%)
Full-bodied bitter, well-balanced and complex with a blend of four hops.

Hockley Gold (OG 1041, ABV 4.1%)
A bitter with a fruity aroma and distinctive English hop characteristics.

Complete Muppetry (OG 1043, ABV 4.3%)
An aromatic beer, well-balanced with powerful hop characteristics and citrus, fruity notes.

Chamberlain Pale Ale (OG 1042, ABV 4.5%)
A crisp, light ale loaded with grapefruit flavours and a long, hoppy finish.

Jewellery Porter (OG 1049, ABV 5%)
A full-bodied stout with a thick and slightly chocolate texture underlined with hops.

Birmingham Special Ale (OG 1053, ABV 5.4%)
Malty and full-bodied strong bitter.

Two Tribes

3-5 Jubilee Estate, Foundry Lane, Horsham, West Sussex, RH13 5UE
☎ (01403) 272102 ⊕ twotribesbrewing.com

Two Tribes began brewing in 2015. Beers are available in KeyKeg under its own label, and in collaboration with others, notably Island Records and Bison Beer. A range of cask-conditioned beer is also available under the Two Tribes Unbarred name.

Jago IPA (ABV 4.2%)

Twt Lol SIBA 👁

Unit B27, Trefforest Industrial Estate, Pontypridd, Glamorgan, CF37 5YB ☎ 07966 467295 ⊕ twtlol.com

Established in 2015 using a 10-barrel plant, the brewery has a capacity of 80 firkins a week, with the potential to expand to 160. All of its branding is produced in both Welsh and English. ‼️ ⟁ ♦

Glog (OG 1043, ABV 4%)
A bitter, caramel/toffee, malty beer.

Cwrw'r Afr Serchog / Horny Goat Ale (OG 1039, ABV 4.2%)
A golden ale with pine and citrus flavours. A hint of Horny Goat Weed is also used in the brew.

Pewin Ynfytyn / Crazy Peacock (OG 1045, ABV 4.8%)
Hoppy golden amber-coloured beer made with a hint of caramel malt.

Tydd Steam SIBA

Manor Barn, Kirkgate, Tydd Saint Giles, Cambridgeshire, PE13 5NE
☎ (01945) 871020 ☎ 07932 726552
⊕ tyddsteam.co.uk

⊠ Established in 2007 in a converted agricultural barn, the brewery is named after two farm steam engines. A 15-barrel plant was installed in 2011. Around 70 outlets are supplied direct. ‼️ ♦ RAIB

Barn Ale (OG 1038, ABV 3.9%) ◗
A golden-coloured bitter that has a good biscuity malt aroma and flavour, balanced by spicy hops. Long, dry, fairly astringent finish.

Piston Bob (OG 1044, ABV 4.6%) ◗
Malt and faint hops on the aroma progress through to a malty flavour complemented by a balance of hops and fruit. A long, dry finish rounds off this amber-coloured strong bitter.

Tydwals

Ty Newyth Farm, Llangorse, LD3 9LD ☎ 07851 958254

Tydwals began brewing in 2015, on the premises occupied by Redstone brewery, which closed in 2014. The brewery is named after a family ancestor.

Drysllwyn Bitter (OG 1043, ABV 4.5%)

Cennan Gold (OG 1049, ABV 5%)

Dinefer Porter (OG 1053, ABV 5.5%)

Tyne Bank SIBA

375 Walker Road, Newcastle upon Tyne, NE6 2AB
☎ (0191) 265 2828 ☎ 07989 426604
⊕ tynebankbrewery.co.uk

⊠ Tyne Bank began brewing in 2011. It moved and expanded in 2016 due to a successful crowd funding initiative. An on-site brewery tap is now open. ‼️ ⟁ ♦

Single Blonde (OG 1037, ABV 3.5%)
A light beer, slightly dry bitterness with hints of vanilla.

Summer Breeze (OG 1040, ABV 3.9%)

Pacifica (OG 1040, ABV 4%)

West Coast IPA (OG 1040, ABV 4%)

Monument Bitter (OG 1041, ABV 4.1%)
Smooth, balanced bitter with a berry fruit character.

Dark Brown Ale (OG 1042, ABV 4.2%)
A rich and malty ale. Slightly sweet and lightly hopped to give a berry fruit undertone.

Northern Porter (OG 1047, ABV 4.5%)
A subtle, smoky porter aged in oak.

Silver Dollar (OG 1050, ABV 4.9%)
Hoppy American-style pale ale with lasting bitterness and a citrus kick.

Ubrew (NEW)

29 Old Jamaica Business Estate, 24 Old Jamaica Road, Bermondsey, London, SE16 4AW ⊕ ubrew.cc

No real ale.

Uffa

▤ White Lion Inn, Lower Street, Lower Ufford, Suffolk, IP13 6DW
☎ (01394) 460770 ⊕ uffordwhitelion.co.uk/brewery

Uffa began brewing in 2011 using a 2.5-barrel plant. It is situated next to the White Lion pub in a converted coach house.

Uley

The Old Brewery, 31 The Street, Uley, Gloucestershire, GL11 5TB
☎ (01453) 860120 ⊕ uleybrewery.com

⊗ Uley started brewing in 1833 as Price's Brewery. After a long gap, the premises were restored and Uley Brewery opened in 1985. It has its own spring water, which is used to mash Tucker's Maris Otter malt, and boiled with Herefordshire hops. Uley delivers to 40-50 outlets in the Cotswold area while brewing to capacity. ♦

Hogshead Cotswold Pale Ale (OG 1035, ABV 3.5%) ◗
A pale-coloured, hoppy session bitter with a good hop aroma and a full flavour for its strength, ending in a bittersweet aftertaste.

Bitter (OG 1040, ABV 4%) ◗
A copper-coloured beer with hops and fruit in the aroma and a malty, fruity taste, underscored by a hoppy bitterness. The finish is dry with a balance of hops and malt.

Laurie Lee's Bitter (OG 1045, ABV 4.5%)
A copper-coloured, full-flavoured, hoppy bitter with some fruitiness and a smooth, long, balanced finish.

Old Spot Prize Strong Ale (OG 1050, ABV 5%) ◗
A ruby-coloured ale with an initial strong, malty sweetness that develops into a smooth, dry, malty finish. A beer that is deceptively easy to drink.

Pig's Ear Strong Beer (OG 1050, ABV 5%) ◗
A golden-coloured pale ale with an initial refreshing taste and a hint of fruitiness that develops into a light, malty finish. A smooth, quaffable strong ale.

Brewed for the Old Spot Inn, Dursley:

Old Ric (OG 1045, ABV 4.5%) ◗
A full-flavoured, hoppy bitter with some fruitiness and a smooth, balanced finish.

Ulverston

Lightburn Road, Ulverston, Cumbria, LA12 0AU
☎ (01229) 586870 ☎ 07840 192022
⊕ ulverstonbrewingcompany.co.uk

◉ The brewery occupies the octagonal bullring of the old livestock market. There is a bar that overlooks the brew-plant which opens by prior arrangement and during some local festivals. Some beers have a Laurel and Hardy theme: Stan Laurel was born in Ulverston. ‼ ⊨ ♦

Flying Elephants (OG 1037, ABV 3.7%) ◗
Clean, refreshing, yellow-coloured bitter, sweet and fruity with a dry citrus finish.

Celebration Ale (OG 1039, ABV 3.9%) ◗
Yellow-coloured, fruity bitter with hints of tangerine and a notably sustained dry finish.

Harvest Moon (OG 1039, ABV 3.9%) ◗
A well-balanced, pale, hoppy bitter.

Another Fine Mess (OG 1040, ABV 4%) ◗
A refreshing, gold-coloured bitter. Initially fruity but with a rising bitterness.

Laughing Gravy (OG 1040, ABV 4%) ◗

Smooth and grainy brown-coloured bitter with a good mix of flavours.

Lonesome Pine (OG 1042, ABV 4.2%) ◗
A fresh and fruity pale gold-coloured beer; honeyed, lemony and resiny with an increasingly bitter finish.

Fra Diavolo (OG 1043, ABV 4.3%)

Unbarred

33 Bolsover Road, Hove, East Sussex, BN3 5HQ
☎ 07850 070471 ⊕ unbarredbrewery.com

⊗ UnBarred uses a purpose-built brewery in the owner's garden. It produces beers in small batches, mainly in can and keg. Some cask-conditioned beer is produced for festivals and a small number of local pubs. ‼ RAIB

Benchmark (OG 1046, ABV 4.7%)

Under the Street

See One Mile End

Unity (NEW)

Unit 10, Belgrave Industrial Estate, Belgrave Road, Southampton, SO17 3EA
☎ (023) 8067 7070 ⊕ unitybrewingco.com

Founded in 2016, Unity Brewing Co is a six-barrel brewery. It produces beers influenced by Belgian and North-east American styles. ‼ ⊨ RAIB

Unity Brew House (NEW) SIBA

Old Chicken Shed, Stocks Farm, Suckley, Worcestershire, WR6 5EQ
☎ (01886) 884110 ☎ 07484 688026
⊕ unitybrewhouse.co.uk

Brewing began in 2016. It is the only brewery in the UK located on a commercial hop farm. Based in an old chicken shed, the beers are named after breeds of chicken. An on-site bar is open on Fridays and Saturdays. RAIB

Buckeye Session Bitter (ABV 3.4%)
Easy-drinking, copper-coloured beer with subtle fruity hop flavours.

Sebright Golden Ale (ABV 3.8%)
Straw-coloured ale with fruity hop aromas and flavours.

Silkie Amber Ale (ABV 4.2%)
Medium-bodied ale with a pleasant bitterness and gentle, citrus hop aroma.

Frizzle British IPA (ABV 4.5%)
Golden in colour with a fruity, floral hop aroma and a significant hoppy bitterness.

Unsworth's Yard SIBA

4 Unsworth's Yard, Ford Road, Cartmel, Cumbria, LA11 6PG ☎ 07810 461313 ⊕ unsworthsyard.co.uk

◉ Unsworth's Yard opened in 2011, brewing on a five-barrel plant. The brewery produces beers named after historic figures and legends associated with the Cartmel area. Beers are available in Cartmel pubs and other local outlets as well as the brewery's visitor centre. ‼ ⊨

**J.C.Dickinson's – The Land Of Cartmel
(OG 1038, ABV 3.7%)** ◥
Bitter pale ale, fruity and hoppy with some
grapefruit.

Cartmel Peninsula (OG 1039, ABV 3.8%)
A mellow and sweet English bitter.

Crusader Gold (OG 1041, ABV 4.1%)
A crisp and refreshing golden ale with a subtle
citrus finish.

**Cartmel Wharf Sandpiper Cask
(OG 1038, ABV 4.3%)**
A crisp, light blonde beer.

**Sir Edgar Harrington's Last Wolf
(OG 1045, ABV 4.5%)** ◥
Well-balanced, rich and fruity, tawny-coloured ale
with gentle bitterness.

The Flookburgh Cockler (OG 1057, ABV 5.5%)
Smooth, rich and dark-coloured with roasted grain
and mocha flavours.

Untapped SIBA 👁

**Unit 6, Little Castle Farm Business Park, Raglan,
NP15 2BX**
☎ (01291) 690074 ☎ 07988 197794
⊕ untappedbrew.com

Initially established in 2009, 2013 saw Untapped
move to its current premises, which have recently
been expanded. The 'Rare' range has been
developed consisting of experimental brews
primarily for the bottled market. It has obtained
organic certification. Beers are also contract
brewed for Whittingtons Brewery. ‼ ☟ ◆ RAIB

Border Bitter (OG 1036.8, ABV 3.8%)

Sundown (OG 1038.8, ABV 4%)

Monnow (OG 1038.3, ABV 4.2%)

UPA (OG 1043.6, ABV 4.5%)

Triple S (OG 1048.4, ABV 4.9%)

Crystal (OG 1052.3, ABV 6%)

Coldharbour (OG 1062, ABV 6.5%)

Contract brewed for Cold Black Label:

Bwlch Passage (ABV 4.5%)

Miner's Ale (ABV 4.6%)

Up Front (NEW)

Office: 1.1, 27 Skirving Street, Glasgow, G41 3AB
☎ 07526 088973 ⊕ upfrontbrewing.com

Established in 2016, Up Front is a gypsy brewery
producing canned beers. Cask-conditioned beers
are occasionally available.

Upham SIBA 👁

**Stakes Farm, Cross Lane, Upham, Hampshire,
SO32 1FL**
☎ (01489) 861383 ⊕ uphambrewery.co.uk

⊠ Upham began brewing in 2009 and expanded to
a 30-barrel plant in 2013. It manages 16 pubs and
supplies more than 250 outlets. ☟ ◆ RAIB

Tipster (OG 1036, ABV 3.6%) ◥
An easy-drinking and light golden ale. Initial
hoppiness and fruit is balanced by maltiness that
lasts into the finish.

Punter (OG 1039, ABV 4%)
Light amber-coloured ale with sweet and floral hop
aroma. A balanced flavour of refreshing bitterness
and maltiness with a dry, fruity finish. Also sold as
Sam FM Ale.

Stakes (OG 1045, ABV 4.8%)
A full-bodied ale with striking bitterness, tastes of
grapefruit and toffee, and a hoppy finish.

Urban Chicken (NEW)

**Ilkeston, Derbyshire ☎ 07976 913395
⊕ urbanchickenale.co.uk**

A nanobrewery producing small batches of beer for
local pubs, restaurants, bottle shops and beer
festivals. Registered as a commercial brewery in
2016. RAIB

Urban Island SIBA

**Unit 28, Limberline Industrial Estate, Limberline Spur,
Portsmouth, Hampshire, PO3 5DZ**
☎ (023) 9266 8726 ⊕ urbanislandbrewing.uk

⊠ Urban Island is a family-run brewery
which began production in 2015 on a bespoke five-
barrel purpose-built plant. The range is distributed
throughout Hampshire and the South East. ‼ ☟

Urban Pale (OG 1040, ABV 3.8%)
Hoppy pale ale with aromas of orange and pink
grapefruit.

DSB (Dolly's Special Beer) (OG 1045, ABV 4.6%)
A light, refreshing ale, slightly fruity with a bitter
hop finish.

Citra (OG 1050.6, ABV 5%)
A smooth, American-style ale with floral and
grapefruit aromas.

Porter 28 (OG 1056, ABV 5%)
A combination of seven malts giving gentle hints of
smokiness and chocolate with a roasted finish.

High & Dry (OG 1056, ABV 5.5%)
An American-hopped IPA with an earthy base and
citrus finish.

Uttoxeter (NEW) SIBA

**27 Demontfort Way, Uttoxeter, Staffordshire,
ST14 8XY ☎ 07734 392321
⊕ uttoxeterbrewingcompany.com**

A nanobrewery set up in 2016, exploiting the
famous Burton upon Trent hard water.

Full Gallop (ABV 4.4%)
Malty and spicy with slight sweetness and a toffee
note.

Dr Johnson's Contrafibularity (ABV 4.5%)
Hoppy IPA with an orange citrus flavour.

Earthmover (ABV 4.5%)
Traditional English bitter, hoppy with a good malty
flavour and a fruity finish.

Final Furlong (ABV 4.5%)
A smooth, spicy best bitter with floral notes.

Uxonian (ABV 4.5%)
An amber-coloured ale with white wine and
tangerine flavours.

Earthmover Gold (ABV 4.7%)
A bright, light-coloured, English-style golden ale.
Hoppy yet fruity.

Ground Breaker (ABV 4.7%)
A golden-coloured beer with a grassy, earthy aroma and tastes of pineapple.

Paddock Porter (ABV 4.8%)
A porter dominated by a distinctive dark roasted grain flavour with slight sweetness. Chocolaty.

American IPA (ABV 5.6%)
Powerful in strength, bitterness and fruitiness.

Vale SIBA ◎

Tramway Business Park, Ludgershall Road, Brill, Buckinghamshire, HP18 9TY
☎ (01844) 239237 ⊕ valebrewery.co.uk

⊠ Established in 1995 and initially based in Haddenham, Vale moved to Brill in 2007. In 2010 it expanded to a 20-barrel brew plant. Five pubs are owned, including the Hop Pole where sister brewery the Aylesbury Brewhouse (qv), opened in 2011. ‼ 🍺 ♦ RAIB

Brill Gold (OG 1035, ABV 3.5%)
Golden-coloured session ale with a full malt flavour, well balanced with fruity, slightly citrus hop aromas and a soft bitterness.

Best IPA (OG 1036, ABV 3.7%) ◄
This pale amber-coloured beer starts with a slight fruit aroma. This leads to a clean, bitter taste where hops and fruit dominate. The finish is long and bitter with a slight hop note.

Black Swan Mild (OG 1038, ABV 3.9%)
Dark and smooth with hints of chocolate and coffee on the nose and a malty, dry finish.

Wychert Ale (OG 1038, ABV 3.9%)
Woody flavours are notable in this malty beer with a finish of port and berries on the nose.

VPA (Vale Pale Ale) (OG 1042, ABV 4.2%)
An assertive, dry, hoppy ale with a citrus nose, combined with a pronounced malt background.

Red Kite (OG 1043, ABV 4.3%)
Refreshing, chestnut-coloured beer with a bitter finish.

Black Beauty Porter (OG 1044, ABV 4.4%) ◄
A dark-coloured ale, the initial aroma is malty. Roast malt dominates and is followed by a rich fruitiness, with some sweetness. The finish is increasingly hoppy and dry.

Gravitas (OG 1047, ABV 4.8%)
A strong pale ale packed with hop and citrus flavours, rounded off by a dry, malty, biscuit finish.

Valhalla

Haroldswick, Unst, Shetland, ZE2 9TJ
☎ (01957) 711658 ⊕ valhallabrewery.co.uk

Valhalla was set up by husband and wife team Sonny and Sylvia Priest in 1997. A bottling plant was installed in 1999. A new brewery building was officially opened in 2012, converted from part of the former RAF SaxaVoord camp at Haroldswick. ‼ ♦

Old Scatness (OG 1040, ABV 4%)
A light ale with a smoky peat and fruity finish. Honey is added to give a sweet taste.

Simmer Dim (OG 1040, ABV 4%) ◄
A light golden ale, named after the long Shetland twilight. The sulphur features do not mask the fruits and hops of this well-balanced beer.

Island Bere (OG 1052, ABV 4.2%) ◄
Original bere malt used with some citrus hops.

Auld Rock (OG 1052, ABV 4.5%) ◄
A full-bodied, dark-coloured, Scottish-style best bitter, it has a rich, malty nose but does not lack bitterness in the long, dry finish.

White Wife (OG 1045, ABV 4.5%) ◄
Predominantly hop and citrus fruit, which remain on the palate. The aftertaste is increasingly bitter.

Sjolmet Stout (OG 1049, ABV 5%) ◄
Full of malt and roast barley, especially in the taste. Smooth, creamy, fruity finish, not as dry as some stouts.

Spring I'da Air (OG 1050, ABV 5%)
Smooth, American-style IPA. Malty taste developing to hoppy bitterness with a slight sweetness.

Valve (NEW)

1 Hamilton Drive, Edinburgh, EH15 1NR

Office: 1 Burnside Way, Galashiels, TD1 2RS
✉ info@valvebrew.com

A picobrewery brewing small batch beers in Edinburgh.

Verdant (NEW)

Unit 6, Tressidder Close, Tregoniggie Industrial Estate, Falmouth, Cornwall, TR11 4SP
☎ (01326) 619117 ☎ 07970 503574
⊕ verdantbrewing.co

Brewery established in 2014 by keen home brewers using a 10-barrel plant. No real ale.

Vibrant Forest SIBA

Unit 3, Gordleton Business Park, Hannah Way, Bowling Green, Lymington, Hampshire, SO41 8JD
☎ (01590) 681094 ☎ 07921 753109
⊕ vibrantforest.co.uk

⊠ Located in the New Forest, Vibrant Forest began brewing commercially in 2011 using a one-barrel plant. This award-winning brewery has progressed to a 10-barrel capacity. ‼ 🍺 ♦ RAIB

Summerlands (OG 1036, ABV 3.5%)
An IPA-style bitter, well hopped with balanced malt flavours. An easy-drinking session beer.

Nova Foresta (OG 1038, ABV 3.8%)
A refreshing, well-hopped, light amber-coloured English bitter with a spicy fruitiness balanced by a pleasant maltiness.

Flying Saucer (OG 1041, ABV 4.3%)
A full-flavoured golden ale with fruity, floral and citrus-like flavours. Fresh and hoppy with a long bitter finish.

Cydonia (OG 1046, ABV 4.7%)
Grapefruit, citrus and pine flavours balanced with a sweet maltiness.

Black Forest (OG 1051, ABV 4.9%) 🍺

Farmhouse (OG 1043, ABV 5%)
A light golden ale with slightly peppery and spicy aromas, subtle bitter and fruity flavours and a dry finish.

Pale Ale (OG 1047, ABV 5%)

A golden ale brewed with a single rotating hop variety.

Kick Start (OG 1060, ABV 5.7%)
A rich, black-coloured and roasty stout made with freshly roasted Columbian coffee beans.

Metropolis (ABV 6%)
A hoppy black IPA with flavours of citrus and tropical fruits under a complex mix of chocolate and balanced bitterness.

Kaleidoscope (OG 1060, ABV 6.5%)
Massively-hopped, American-style IPA with intense citrus hops.

Umbral Abyss (ABV 8.8%)

Victoria Inn (NEW)

Roch, SA62 6AW
☎ (01437) 710426 ☎ 07814 684975
⊕ thevictoriainnroch.com

A four-barrel brewery in a separate building on the same site as the pub.

Village Brewer

See Hambleton

Village Brewer: Brew 22

⊟ Number Twenty 2, 22 Coniscliffe Road, Darlington, DL3 7RG
☎ (01325) 354590

One-barrel microbrewery, established in 2013, which has been brewing on a regular basis since 2015. The plant is also used to produce the malt wash for the distilling of gin and vodka on site. The beer strength and style varies from brew to brew and complement the Village Brewer beers produced by Hambleton Ales (qv) since 1992.

Villages (NEW)

21-22 Resolution Way, Deptford, London, SE8 4NT
☎ (020) 3489 1143 ⊕ villagesbrewery.com

Established in 2016 by brothers Archie and Louis Village. No real ale but cask-conditioned beers are planned. ▰♦

Vine Inn (NEW)

⊟ Vine Inn & Brewery, Sheep Fair, Rugeley, Staffordshire, WS15 2AT
☎ (01889) 574443 ⊠ oli@thevinebrewery.com

Brewery based within the Vine Inn public house, parts of which date back to the sixteenth century. Its beers can be found in a number of pubs in the Cannock Chase area.

EPA (OG 1045, ABV 4%)
A chestnut-coloured, well-balanced pale ale.

Vanilla Porter (OG 1046, ABV 4.5%)
A dark-coloured porter with coffee undertones and rising sweetness from the vanilla.

Grapefruit IPA (OG 1045, ABV 4.8%)
Well-hopped IPA with fresh grapefruit, giving it a balanced bitterness.

Violet Cottage

⊟ Gwaelod-y-Garth Inn, Main Road, Gwaelod y Garth, CF15 9HH
☎ (029) 2081 0408

The brewery was established in 2012 in a converted outbuilding at the rear of the Gwaelod-y-Garth Inn, within the grounds of the licensee's private house. Occasional collaborations with Swansea brewery take place. All brews are subject to availability as the brewer decides. Most of the production is sold within the pub.

VIP SIBA

Unit E, Hawkshill Business Park, Lesbury, Northumberland, NE66 3PG ☎ 07545 885352
⊕ thevillageinnpub.co.uk

Brewing began in 2012 using a five-barrel plant to serve the owner's pub, the Village Inn in Longframlington, and the local free trade. Around 150 outlets are supplied.

Village Bike (OG 1040, ABV 4%)

Village Copper (OG 1042, ABV 4.2%)

Village Ghost (OG 1045, ABV 4.5%)

Vocation SIBA ◉

Unit 8, Craggs Country Business Park, New Road, Cragg Vale, Hebden Bridge, West Yorkshire, HX7 5TT
☎ (01422) 410810 ⊕ vocationbrewery.com

☺Vocation began brewing in 2015 on a bespoke 20-barrel plant. The brewery is located high above Hebden Bridge. ▰♦

Bread & Butter (ABV 3.9%) ◀
A feast of floral hops with citrus aroma and taste. Robust bitter aftertaste.

Heart & Soul (ABV 4.5%) ◀
A golden ale with a strong citrus aroma. Hops dominate taste and aftertaste.

Pride & Joy (ABV 5.3%) ◀
IPA packed with citrus hoppiness. A hint of sweetness gives way to a mellow aftertaste.

Divine & Conquer (ABV 6.5%) ◀
Roast malt aroma and taste giving way to a hoppy and vinous mouthfeel. This black IPA has a smooth, slightly sweet finish.

Life & Death (OG 1061.3, ABV 6.5%)
An American-style IPA with flavours of tropical and citrus fruits with a lingering bitterness set against a smooth, malty backbone.

VOG SIBA

Unit 8a, Atlantic Trading Estate, Barry, CF63 3RF
☎ (01446) 730757 ⊕ vogbrewery.co.uk

☺Created in 2005, the founders handed over the reins to a new team in 2015 who have rebranded the brewery and added new beers. An experimental 'New Tricks' range of beers has also been introduced. ♦RAIB

Paradigm Shift (OG 1042, ABV 4.2%)

South Island (OG 1042, ABV 4.2%)
A pale ale, dry, bitter and refreshing with a big hop punch.

Dark Matter (OG 1044, ABV 4.4%) ⊓

A blackcurrant porter, rich and smooth with liquorice and chocolate notes.

Speak Easy IPA (OG 1046, ABV 4.6%)
An American-hopped IPA, underpinned by a big malt character with a bitter tropical citrus finish.

Volden

35a Neville Road, Croydon, CR0 2DS ⊕ volden.co.uk

⊠ Volden produce beer for the Antic pub group in South London. ◆

Session Ale (OG 1037, ABV 3.8%) ⬥
Amber-coloured bitter with a caramel and orange aroma. Lemon marmalade and sweetish malty biscuit that fades to a bitter, dryish finish.

Pale Ale (ABV 4.6%) ⬥
Dry, bitter floral hop flavour with a slight hint of fresh orange peel, becoming more bitter on drinking. A little malt.

Wadworth SIBAIFBB ◉

Northgate Brewery, Devizes, Wiltshire, SN10 1JW
☎ **(01380) 723361 ⊕ wadworth.co.uk**

⊠ Established in 1885 by Henry Wadworth, this impressive family-owned brewery has a modern brewhouse and a microbrewery, which enables it to create unique small batch beers. Its traditional horse-drawn drays deliver beer daily around Devizes. Wadworth has more than 200 pubs in the South-west of England. ‼ 🍺 ◆ RAIB

IPA (OG 1035, ABV 3.6%)
A classic session beer with malt-led flavours.

Horizon (OG 1039, ABV 4%)
A pale gold-coloured beer with zesty citrus and hop aromas and a crisp, tangy finish on the palate.

6X (OG 1040.5, ABV 4.1%) ⬥
Copper-coloured ale with a malty and fruity nose and some balancing hop character. The flavour is similar, with some bitterness and a lingering, malty but bitter finish.

Bishops Tipple (OG 1048, ABV 5%)
A golden-coloured brew giving well-balanced hop bitterness and a clean finish.

Swordfish (OG 1047.5, ABV 5%)
A full-bodied, deep copper-coloured ale flavoured with Pussers Rum.

Waen

See Pixie Spring

Wagtail

New Barn Farm, Wilby Warrens, Old Buckenham, Norfolk, NR17 1PF
☎ **(01953) 887133 ⊕ wagtailbrewery.com**

Wagtail Brewery went into full-time production in 2006. All beers are now only available bottle-conditioned. RAIB V

Wainstones SIBA ◉

1 North Side, Hutton Rudby, North Yorkshire, TS15 0DA ☎ 07885 240226
⊕ stokesleybrewing.co.uk

Wainstones began brewing in 2010 using a 2.5-barrel plant set up in an industrial unit in Stokesley, trading as the Stokesley Brewing Company. It moved to new premises in Hutton Rudby in 2017.

Amber (OG 1038, ABV 3.8%)
Light golden ale with moderate bitterness and a pleasant floral nose.

Sandstone (OG 1040, ABV 4%)
Traditional brown-coloured ale with moderate bitterness and a pleasant aftertaste.

Ironstone (OG 1042, ABV 4.2%)
A classic, rich, full-flavoured ale with a smooth aftertaste.

Copper (OG 1043, ABV 4.3%)

Steel River (OG 1043, ABV 4.3%)
Traditional chestnut-coloured, full-flavoured ale with medium bitterness.

Jet (OG 1045, ABV 4.5%)
An unusual black-coloured ale, full-flavoured with a hoppy aftertaste.

Transporter (OG 1045, ABV 4.5%)
A dark-coloured porter with a creamy head and deep, malty taste.

Walled City

🍴 70 Ebrington Square, Londonderry, BT47 6FA
☎ **(028) 7134 3336 ⊕ walledcitybrewery.com**

Restaurant-based brewery established in 2015. Beers are brewed on site.

Wantsum SIBA

Kent Barn, St Nicholas Court Farm, Court Road, St Nicholas at Wade, Kent, CT7 0PT
☎ **(01227) 910135 ⊕ wantsumbrewery.co.uk**

⊠ Wantsum Brewery was established by James Sandy in 2009 and takes its name from the nearby Wantsum Channel. Previously located in Hersden near Canterbury, the brewery relocated to a farm site in 2017 to allow for expansion. Outlets are supplied throughout Kent and the Home Counties. ‼ 🍺 ◆ RAIB

1381 (OG 1036, ABV 3.8%)
A light amber-coloured IPA with delicate citrus and herbal aromas.

Black Prince (OG 1036.5, ABV 3.9%)
A rich, full-bodied mild, smooth on the palate with subtle hop notes.

Imperium (OG 1037, ABV 4%)
A deep amber-coloured best bitter; smooth biscuit malts and rich, hoppy nose balance this beer perfectly.

Montgomery (OG 1037, ABV 4%)
Amber-coloured beer with spicy citrus aromas.

Fortitude (OG 1039, ABV 4.2%)
A full-bodied beer with a pronounced hop finish.

One Hop (OG 1040, ABV 4.2%)
A different hop is used in the brew every few months.

Dynamo (OG 1043, ABV 4.3%)
A crisp, light, golden ale, fruity and floral with an orange citrus twist.

Yellow Tail (OG 1043, ABV 4.5%)

A pale-coloured ale with a sweet, floral taste. Fruity with a hint of vanilla. Mild malt flavours.

Black Pig (OG 1044, ABV 4.8%)
A smooth beer with burnt chocolate and smoky malt notes mixed with delicate floral hop bitterness.

Hengist (OG 1045, ABV 5%)
A golden-coloured pale ale with flavours of biscuit malt balancing a deep, mellow, fruity nose.

Red Raddle (OG 1049, ABV 5%)
Ruby-coloured premium bitter, biscuit and toasted malt base supporting a broad, hoppy, smooth finish.

Golgotha (OG 1047, ABV 5.5%)
A rich, deep and broad malt base gives this stout a long, smooth finish. Hops are prominent on the nose with blackcurrant, liquorice and cedar.

Ravening Wolf (OG 1052, ABV 5.9%)
A light amber-coloured, strong pale ale; toasted biscuit and rye malt flavours support a pine and lemon hop crispness with a hint of vanilla.

Warwickshire SIBA 👁

Bakehouse Brewery, Queen Street, Cubbington, Warwickshire, CV32 7NA
☎ (01926) 450747 ⊕ warwickshirebeer.co.uk

A six-barrel brewery in a former village bakery which has been in operation since 1998. Bottled beers are available from local farm shops, garden centres, wine specialists, supermarkets, as well as from the brewery direct and its four pubs.
🍺♦RAIB

Shakespeare County (OG 1034, ABV 3.4%)
A refreshing, deep copper-coloured ale with fruity, spicy and floral aromas. Full-bodied, soft and hoppy to taste.

Fusilier (OG 1039, ABV 3.9%)
A traditional bitter with a fruity, hoppy, malty aroma and sharp, light and malty taste.

Darling Buds (OG 1041, ABV 4%)

Duck Soup (OG 1043, ABV 4.2%)
A copper-coloured beer with rich malty overtones.

Lady Godiva (OG 1042, ABV 4.2%)
A golden ale with honey and malt on the nose. A slightly sweet, biscuity maltiness to taste is balanced by the rounded bitterness of the hops.

Golden Bear (OG 1049, ABV 4.9%)
An assertive golden brown-coloured beer characterised by a long-lasting, slightly resiny bitterness. The finish is fruity and warming with hints of spice and orange.

Ball Stitcher (OG 1051, ABV 5%)

Kingmaker (OG 1055, ABV 5.5%)
A rich, fruity, amber-coloured beer with a malty, toffee aroma leading onto a palate with overtones of spice and caramel. A warming alcoholic, dry finish.

Watermill SIBA 👁

🍺 **Watermill Inn, Ings, Cumbria, LA8 9PY**
☎ (01539) 821309 ☎ 07831 873300
⊕ lakelandpub.co.uk

Watermill was established in 2006 in a purpose-built extension to the inn. The beers have a doggie

theme – dogs are allowed in the main bar. The brewery was extended in 2008 with a new brewery planned within the grounds. Also produces beers under the Windermere Brewery name.

Tomos Watkin SIBA

Unit 3, Alberto Road, Century Park, Valley Way, Swansea Enterprise Park, Swansea, SA6 8RP
☎ (01792) 797280 ⊕ tomoswatkin.com

⊛Brewing began in 1995, originally in Llandeilo behind the Castle Hotel. The brewery moved to Swansea in 2000 and was taken over by Hurns Water Mineral Company in 2002. More than 60% of production is bottled beers (not bottle conditioned). ‼🍺♦

Last Inch (ABV 4%)
A clean-drinking, amber-coloured ale with a light bitterness and gentle hop aroma.

OSB (Old Style Bitter) (ABV 4.5%) 🌾
Amber-coloured beer with an inviting aroma of hops and malt. Full-bodied; hops, fruit, malt and bitterness combine to give a balanced flavour continuing into the finish.

Pecker Wrecker (ABV 5%)
A rich, amber-coloured session ale.

Watling Street SIBA 👁

Radlett Brewery, Hilfield Farm, Hilfield Lane, Patchetts Green, Hertfordshire, WD25 8DD ☎ 07713 841936 ⊕ watlingstreetbeer.com

Brewing began in 2015 in Aldenham village and relocated to an old farm building on Hilfield Farm in 2016 to allow for expansion to a 10-barrel plant. There is an on-site bar and functions occur on a regular basis including comedy nights.

Golden Ale (ABV 3.8%)

Premium Ale (ABV 4.2%)

Pale Ale (ABV 4.3%)

Red Ale (ABV 4.6%)

Watson's (NEW)

Old Heath, Colchester, Essex, CO1 2HD ☎ 07804 641267 ⊕ watsonsbrewery.co.uk

Brewing began in 2017.

Watts Brewing?

🍺 **Magnet Freehouse, 51 Wellington Road North, Stockport, SK4 1HJ**
☎ (0161) 429 6287 ⊕ themagnetfreehouse.co.uk

Brewing began in 2014 on the premises of the Magnet freehouse. No regular beers. Speciality beers are brewed to suit the season, and are mostly sold in the pub.

Waveney

🍺 **Queen's Head, Station Road, Earsham, Norfolk, NR35 2TS**
☎ (01986) 892623 ✉ hampsoid@aol.com

Established at the Queen's Head in 2004, the five-barrel brewery produces three beers, regularly available at the pub along with other free trade outlets.

Way Outback (NEW)

Buchanan Avenue, Bournemouth, Dorset, BH7 7AA
⊕ thewayoutback.co.uk

Started in 2017 and born in a shed, the Way Outback is run by owner and head brewer Rich Brown with help from his able assistant Arthur.

Working like a Dog (ABV 3.6%)

Take Me to Valhalla (ABV 4%)
A pale ale with aromas of blueberry, citrus and tropical fruit.

Hopposites Attract (ABV 5.6%)
A double-hopped pale ale with aromas of passion fruit, grapefruit and gooseberry.

Monster Mash (ABV 6.7%)
A highly-hopped IPA with aromas of lemongrass, pine needles and grapefruit.

Weal SIBA

Unit 6, Newpark Business Park, London Road, Chesterton, Staffordshire, ST5 7HT
☎ (01782) 565635 ☎ 07980 606966
⊕ wealales.co.uk

☺ Weal Ales is an award-winning microbrewery established in 2014 on a one-barrel plant. It expanded to a six-barrel plant in 2015 and is now also bottling its beers. Its first pub, Wellers, opened in Newcastle under Lyme in 2016. ⚑RAIB

Sqweal (OG 1039, ABV 3.9%)
A refreshing golden ale, smooth and full-bodied with a slight hoppy flavour and a hint of caramel in the aftertaste.

Weally Hopper (OG 1042, ABV 4.2%)
A light and refreshing pale ale. It has a defining floral and citrus aroma with a dry, bitter finish.

Weller Weal (OG 1046, ABV 4.6%)
A hoppy pale ale with a citrus finish.

Robin Wealiant (ABV 4.7%)
A triple-hopped pale ale with a distinct fruit and floral aroma.

Noir (OG 1048, ABV 4.8%)
A rich and warming porter with a roast malt flavour throughout and a subtle hint of spice.

Centwealial Milk Stout (OG 1059, ABV 4.9%)
A sweet and creamy milk stout with a rich chocolate taste and a silky smooth finish.

Ginger Weal (ABV 5.5%)
A strong golden ale with a spicy kick.

Lemon & Ginger Weal (ABV 5.5%)
A strong golden ale. The addition of lemon and ginger gives it a distinctive citrus and spicy kick.

Potters Weal (OG 1055, ABV 5.5%)
A strong traditional bitter with a solid malty backbone and caramel hints.

Weard'ALE

⊟ **Hare & Hounds, 24 Front Street, Westgate, DL13 1RX**
☎ (01388) 517212

Brewing commenced in the Hare & Hounds in 2010. The beers are mainly sold on the premises

but some have found their way to nearby beer festivals and other local pubs.

Weatheroak Hill SIBA

⊟ **Coach & Horses, Weatheroak Hill, Alvechurch, Worcestershire, B48 7EA**
☎ (01564) 823386

Weatheroak Hill brews at the busy Coach & Horses pub and restaurant near Alvechurch.

Weatheroak

Unit 7, Victoria Works, Birmingham Road, Studley, Warwickshire, B80 7AP
☎ (0121) 445 4411 (eve) ☎ 07798 773894

Office: Victoria Works, 33 Redditch Road, Studley, B80 7AU ⊕ weatheroakbrewery.co.uk

⊠ The brewery was set up in 1997 at Weatheroak Hill. It is now in a spacious factory unit in Studley. Around 40 outlets are supplied direct. ‼♦

St Udley Mild (OG 1034, ABV 3.4%)

Ale (OG 1041, ABV 4.1%) ◆
The aroma is dominated by hops in this golden-coloured brew. Hops also feature in the mouth and there is a rapidly fading dry aftertaste.

Victoria Works (OG 1043, ABV 4.3%)
A pale, hoppy bitter with a citrus finish.

Redwood (OG 1047, ABV 4.7%)
A rich, tawny-coloured, strong but mellow beer with a short-lived sweet fruit and malt balance.

Keystone Hops (OG 1050, ABV 5%) ◆
A golden yellow-coloured beer that is surprisingly easy to quaff given the strength. Fruity hops are the dominant flavour without the commonly associated astringency.

Websters

⊟ **Graham's Place, 73 Bridgnorth Road, Wollaston, West Midlands, DY8 3PZ**
☎ (01384) 440315 ✉ info@grahams-place.co.uk

Microbrewery set up to the side of Graham's Place in 2014. Currently brewing with malt extract, full mash beers are planned. All beers are sold though the pub including some one-off specials.

Weetwood SIBA

The Brewery, Common Lane, Kelsall, Cheshire, CW6 0PY
☎ (01829) 752377 ⊕ weetwoodales.co.uk

☺Weetwood Ales began brewing in 1992 in a barn in the tiny hamlet of Weetwood. In 2011 it moved to a new 30-barrel plant. Under new ownership since 2014, there are plans to further increase capacity and broaden the beer range. Around 300 pubs are supplied throughout the North West and North Wales. ⚑

Southern Cross (ABV 3.6%)
A pale golden-coloured, hoppy session ale with a pine and lemon hop character.

Bitter (OG 1038.5, ABV 3.8%) ◆
Pale brown-coloured beer with an assertive bitterness and a lingering, dry finish. Despite initial sweetness, peppery hops dominate throughout.

Mad Hatter (OG 1038.5, ABV 3.9%)

A red-brown-coloured beer with fruity and malty flavours throughout. Brewed with American hops to give spicy and floral notes.

Cheshire Cat (OG 1040, ABV 4%) ◆
Pale, dry bitter with a spritzy lemon zest and grape aroma. Hoppy aroma leads through to the initial taste before fruitiness takes over. Smooth, creamy mouthfeel and a short, dry finish.

Eastgate (OG 1043.5, ABV 4.2%) ◆
Well-balanced and refreshing, clean, amber-coloured beer. Citrus fruit flavours predominate in the taste and there is a short, dry aftertaste.

Old Dog (OG 1045, ABV 4.5%) ◆
Robust, well-balanced, amber-coloured beer with a slightly fruity aroma. Rich malt and fruit flavours are balanced by bitterness. Some sweetness and a hint of sulphur on nose and taste.

Oregon Pale (ABV 4.5%)
Pale-coloured ale with big citrus and grapefruit hop flavours.

Oast House (OG 1050, ABV 5%) ◆
Straw-coloured, crisp, full-bodied and fruity golden ale with a good dry finish.

Weighbridge SIBA

▤ Penzance Drive, Swindon, Wiltshire, SN5 7JL
☎ (01793) 881500 ⊕ weighbridgebrewhouse.co.uk

A microbrewery established in 2011 and based within the Weighbridge Brewhouse Restaurant and Bar, in the building which was formerly the home of Archer's brewery and once part of Swindon Railway Works. It was acquired by Upham Brewery (qv) of Hampshire, but remains separate to that company.

Weird Beard SIBA

Unit 5, Boston Business Park, Trumpers Way, Hanwell, W7 2QA
☎ (020) 3645 2711 ⊕ weirdbeardbrewco.com

⊗ Brewing began in 2013 on an industrial estate in Hanwell. The plant has expanded again with two new 20-barrel fermenters in addition to six 10-barrel ones. Beer is mostly sold bottle-conditioned or in KeyKeg, but some is available cask conditioned. **RAIB**

Dark Hopfler (OG 1043, ABV 2.5%)
A hoppy, dark-coloured beer boasting pine and chocolate on the nose. Roasted malt and sweet cocoa flavours carry into the taste, which is balanced with resinous hop bitterness.

Little Things That Kill (OG 1044, ABV 3.9%) ◆
Hoppy, fruity golden ale which varies in flavour as the hops that are used can alter.

Black Perle (OG 1058.5, ABV 4.5%) ◆
Coffee milk stout with roast notes throughout in this full-flavoured, sweetish beer. Finish has some roast bitter dryness.

Hops Maiden England (OG 1046.7, ABV 4.5%)
An oatmeal pale ale with earthy hop aromas and flavours that change with different varietals.

Mariana Trench (OG 1048, ABV 5.3%) ◆
Passion fruit and citrus are noticeable throughout this malty, sweet, golden-coloured beer. Bitterness builds and lingers, overlaid by dryness.

Decadence Stout (OG 1062, ABV 5.5%) ◆

Orange with some black treacle sweetness balances the dry chocolate and coffee character that lingers pleasantly with the bitterness developing.

K*ntish Town Beard (OG 1054, ABV 5.5%)

Fade to Black (OG 1063, ABV 6.5%) ◆
Balanced black IPA with some fruitiness. The beer contains crystal rye and chocolate malt, which gives roast coffee notes throughout.

Five O'Clock Shadow (OG 1066.1, ABV 7%)

Welbeck Abbey SIBA 👁

Brewery Yard, Welbeck, Nottinghamshire, S80 3LT
☎ (01909) 512539 ☎ 07921 066274
⊕ welbeckabbeybrewery.co.uk

Welbeck Abbey opened in 2011. The microbrewery is housed in a listed barn at the centre of the traditional landed Welbeck estate. General Manager Claire Monk trained at the Kelham Island Brewery after studying microbiology at Sheffield University. !! ♦

Henrietta (OG 1035, ABV 3.6%)
Bitter hop notes are balanced by citrus and grassy aromas.

Red Feather (OG 1040, ABV 3.9%)
A traditional dark amber-coloured ale with subtle notes of caramel and toffee.

Harley (OG 1038, ABV 4.3%)
A lightly citrus pale ale.

Portland Black (OG 1043, ABV 4.5%) ◆
Black-coloured ale with a roast malt aroma and taste throughout and a well-balanced bitterness.

Cavendish (OG 1046, ABV 5%) ◆
Golden in colour with a smooth, hoppy and malt mouthfeel and a lingering, hoppy, bitter finish.

Weldon

Bencroft Grange, Bedford Road, Rushden, Northamptonshire, NN10 0SE
☎ (01536) 601016

Office: 12 Chapel Road, Weldon, NN17 3HP
⊕ weldonbrewery.co.uk

Weldon originally started brewing in 2014 on a two-barrel plant at the Shoulder of Mutton, after which the brewery was originally named. In 2016 the premises and 3.5-barrel kit of the former Copper Kettle brewery in Rushden were purchased and became the main production facility, with the brewery being renamed Weldon. The original plant at the Shoulder of Mutton has been retained and is used for small runs and test batches. ♦

Dragline (OG 1040, ABV 3.9%)
Golden ale, light and crisp with delicate fruit and floral notes.

Stahlstadt (OG 1040, ABV 4%)
A blonde ale, light and refreshing with delicate hints of lemon and fragrant garden herbs.

Galvy Stout (OG 1042, ABV 4.2%)
A classic stout with hints of coffee, chocolate and liquorice.

Rosie's Sweatbox (OG 1042, ABV 4.2%)
A deep ruby-coloured ale, fruity in character with hints of toffee and wood smoke.

Windmill (OG 1042, ABV 4.2%)

Oresome (ABV 4.3%)
An American-style pale ale, tawny-coloured and hoppy.

Well Drawn (NEW)

Unit 5, Greenway Workshops, Bedwas House Industrial Estate, Caerphilly, CF83 8HW ☎ 07376 556745 ⊕ welldrawnbrewing.co.uk

Brewing began in 2017 using a six-barrel plant.

WD Pale Ale (ABV 3.8%)
Session ale with a floral aroma with hints of elderflower.

Wells IFBB 👁

The Brewery, Havelock Street, Bedford, MK40 4LU ☎ (01234) 272766 ⊕ charleswells.co.uk

☺ Charles Wells was founded in Bedford in 1876 and remained in family hands until May 2017 when the brewery and its brands were sold to Marston's (qv) for £55 million. Wells itself had expanded rapidly, merging its brewing and brands with Young's of Wandsworth, London, in 2006: the brands became wholly owned by Wells in 2014 while Young's concentrated on its pub estate. In 2007 Wells bought the Courage brands from Scottish & Newcastle – now Heineken – and in 2011 added the former McEwan's brands, giving it a presence in the Scottish market. Marston's plans to maintain production at the Eagle Brewery in Bedford while Wells will build a new brewery with an output of 30,000 barrels a year in the Bedford area during the next two years. The new plant will supply Wells' estate of 200 pubs, which the company plans to extend: the pubs will also take beers from Marston's. The beer list below is liable to change. Tasting notes are for the beers currently brewed and may also change. Part of Marston's PLC. ‼ ⬛ ◆ RAIB

Bombardier Pale Ale (OG 1033, ABV 3.6%)
Golden-coloured pale ale with a hoppy aroma and notes of grapefruit and honey, balanced with a gentle, sweet maltiness and dry finish.

Eagle IPA (OG 1035, ABV 3.6%) ◆
A refreshing, amber-coloured session bitter with pronounced citrus hop aroma and palate, faint malt in the mouth, and a lasting, dry bitter finish.

Bombardier (OG 1041, ABV 4.1%) ◆
A heavy aroma of malt and raspberry jam. Traces of hops and bitterness are quickly submerged under a smooth, malty sweetness. A solid, rich finish.

Bombardier Burning Gold (OG 1037, ABV 4.1%)
Zesty aromas waken the senses, leading to a dry, crisp flavour with more than a hint of citrus on the palate and a smooth, lasting finish.

Brewed under the Courage brand name:

Best Bitter (OG 1038, ABV 4%)
Good fullness mixed with a bitter, fruity palate.

Director's (OG 1043, ABV 4.8%)
A rich, fruity and full-bodied, chestnut-coloured classic ale.

Brewed under the McEwan's brand name:

IPA (OG 1037, ABV 4%)
A classic full-bodied, hoppy ale that delivers a citrus fruit aroma and a dry, refreshing finish.

Signature (OG 1043, ABV 4.8%)

Chestnut brown in colour with an appealing aroma of citrus, biscuits and spice.

Brewed under the Young's brand name:

Bitter (OG 1034, ABV 3.7%) ◆
This light-drinking, amber-coloured bitter has citrus initially on the palate with sweet malt and a hint of hops that linger into a slightly dry and bitter finish.

London Gold (OG 1037, ABV 4%) ◆
A dark gold-coloured beer with a smooth mouthfeel. Citrus and malt in the low aroma, coming through more strongly on the palate and aftertaste with a little peach. Dry finish.

Special (OG 1043, ABV 4.5%) ◆
Pale brown in colour, this rounded best bitter has citrus throughout plus some slight creamy toffee, which balances the bitterness that grows in the aftertaste.

Weltons SIBA

1 Mulberry Trading Estate, Foundry Lane, Horsham, West Sussex, RH13 5PX ☎ (01403) 242901 ⊕ weltonsbeer.co.uk

⊠ Ray Welton moved the brewery into a factory unit in 2003. Over 70 different beers are brewed every year. Pubs throughout the South-east and London are supplied. ‼ ◆ RAIB

Pride 'n' Joy (OG 1028, ABV 2.8%) ◆
A light brown-coloured bitter with a slight malty and hoppy aroma. Fruity with a pleasant hoppiness and some sweetness in the flavour, leading to a short, malty finish.

Horsham Pale (OG 1037, ABV 3.7%)
Amber-coloured ale, bitter but with a huge aroma.

English Pride (OG 1038, ABV 3.8%)
A fruity, hoppy best bitter with caramel notes.

Sussex Pride (OG 1040, ABV 4%)

Old Cocky (OG 1043, ABV 4.3%)

American Graffiti (OG 1045, ABV 4.5%)
A pale ale with with citrus bitterness and a powerful, lingering aroma.

Old Harry (OG 1051, ABV 5.2%)

Churchillian Stout (OG 1066, ABV 6.6%)
Hints of burnt toast, balanced by good levels of hops with a long finish.

Wensleydale SIBA

Unit F, Manor Road, Bellerby, North Yorkshire, DL8 5QH ☎ (01969) 622463 ☎ 07765 596666 ⊕ wensleydalebrewery.co.uk

☺Wensleydale was set up in 2003 and currently operates on a 5-barrel plant. It was taken over by Geoff Southgate and Carl Gehrman in 2013. Around 100 outlets are supplied direct. ‼ ⬛ ◆ RAIB

Lidstone's Rowley Mild (OG 1032, ABV 3.2%) ◆
Chocolate and toffee aromas lead into what, for its strength, is an impressively rich and flavoursome taste. The finish is pleasantly bittersweet.

Bitter (OG 1036, ABV 3.7%) ◆
Intensely aromatic, straw-coloured ale offering a superb balance of malt and hops on the tongue.

Falconer Session Bitter (OG 1038, ABV 3.9%)

A fruity, malt-based session ale, copper in colour, with a long, bitter, dry finish.

Semerwater Summer Ale (OG 1040, ABV 4.1%)
A pale ale with citrus aromas. The clean, hoppy nose is balanced by a light, malty sweetness.

Coverdale Gamekeeper (OG 1042, ABV 4.3%)
A copper-coloured best bitter with huge spicy hop and juicy malt flavours.

Black Dub Oat Stout (OG 1043, ABV 4.4%)
Black-coloured, silky oat stout.

Gold (OG 1044, ABV 4.5%)
A light golden-coloured best bitter with aromatic and spicy hop flavours.

Coverdale Poacher IPA (OG 1048, ABV 5%) ◥
Citrus flavours dominate both aroma and taste in this pale, smooth, refreshing beer; the aftertaste is quite dry.

Wessex

Rye Hill Farm, Longbridge Deverill, Wiltshire, BA12 7DE
☎ (01985) 844532
✉ wessexbrewery@tinyworld.co.uk

⊠ Wessex was estabished in 2001 and moved to its current location in 2004. 15 local outlets are supplied as well as selected wholesalers. Beers are occasionally contract brewed when capacity permits. ◆

Stourton Pale Ale (OG 1038, ABV 3.5%)
A pale, hoppy session beer with plenty of character.

Potter's Ale (OG 1038, ABV 3.8%)

Longleat Pride (OG 1040, ABV 4%)

Kilmington Best (OG 1041, ABV 4.2%)
Slightly sweet, amber-coloured best bitter with balanced malt and hop characteristics.

Warminster Warrior (OG 1045, ABV 4.5%)

Golden Apostle (OG 1048, ABV 4.8%)

Russian Stoat (OG 1080, ABV 9%)

West Berkshire SIBA ◉

The Flour Barn, Frilsham Home Farm Units, Yattendon, Berkshire, RG18 0XT
☎ (01635) 202968 ⊕ wbbrew.com

⊠ West Berkshire was established in 1995. In 2017, following a £6m investment from new shareholders, capacity has been increased threefold. The new state-of-the-art brewery is located in a former dairy building. The site also includes a shop, café and brewery tap. ‼ ☛◆RAIB

Mr Chubb's Lunchtime Bitter (OG 1041, ABV 3.7%) ◥
Balanced session bitter. A malty caramel note dominates aroma and taste and is accompanied by a nutty bittersweetness and a hoppy aftertaste.

Maggs' Magnificent Mild (OG 1041, ABV 3.8%) 📦 ◥
Silky, full-bodied dark mild with a creamy head. Roast malt aroma is joined in the taste by caramel, sweetness and mild, fruity hoppiness. Aftertaste of roast malt with balancing bitterness.

Good Old Boy (OG 1043, ABV 4%) 📦 ◥

Well-rounded, tawny-coloured bitter with malt and hops dominating throughout. A balancing bitterness accompanies the taste and aftertaste.

Mr Swift's Pale Ale (OG 1043, ABV 4%)
A golden-coloured, fruity session bitter.

Dr Hexter's Healer (OG 1051, ABV 5%) ◥
An amber-coloured strong bitter with malt, caramel and hops in the aroma. Taste is a balance of malt, caramel, fruit, hops and bittersweetness. Caramel, fruit and bittersweetness dominate the aftertaste.

West by Three (NEW)

Unit 19, St Lukes Court, Swansea, SA1 7ER ☎ 07291 253227 ⊕ westbythree.com

West by Three was established in 2016 and brews small batch beers. No real ale.

West Coast

See Conwy

West End

🏠 68-70 Braunstone Gate, Leicester, LE3 5LG
☎ 07875 745302 ⊕ thewestendbrewery.co.uk

The West End Brewery is Leicester city centre's original brewpub, which opened in 2016.

WEST

🏠 Binnie Place, Glasgow Green, Glasgow, G40 1AW
☎ (0141) 550 0135 ⊕ westbeer.com

Brewery-bar and restaurant, producing German-style beer to the Bavarian Purity Law. Beers are usually served under pressure, but not pasteurised. In 2017 a bottle-conditioned beer was introduced to the range.

Westerham SIBA ◉

Beggars Lane, Westerham, Kent, TN16 1QP
☎ (01732) 864427 ⊕ westerhambrewery.co.uk

The brewery was established in 2004 at the National Trust's Grange Farm. More than 500 outlets are supplied in Kent, Surrey, Sussex and London. In 2017 more than £1.6m was invested in a new building, which houses the brewery, tap room, shop and the tasting room for the Squerryes Estate Winery. ◆RAIB GF

Finchcocks Original (OG 1036.2, ABV 3.5%)
Mid-gold-coloured session beer. Citrus notes on the palate with a hint of biscuit and resiny hoppiness.

Grasshopper Kentish Bitter (OG 1039, ABV 3.8%)
A dark-coloured, malty bitter with nutty, roasted notes.

Summer Perle (OG 1038.5, ABV 3.8%)
Golden ale with a spicy, refreshing finish.

Spirit of Kent (OG 1039.5, ABV 4%)
Crisp golden ale with floral and fruity notes. Complex tropical fruit and citrus flavours blend with the sweet malt. Assertive dry hop notes on the finish.

British Bulldog (OG 1040, ABV 4.1%)

A rich, full-bodied best bitter with a massive aroma and palate of jammy fruit, biscuity malt and bitter hop resins.

1965 Special Bitter Ale (OG 1047.5, ABV 4.8%)
A clean, refreshing bitter with a full-bodied flavour.

Hop Rocket India Pale Ale (OG 1052, ABV 5.5%)
Traditional IPA with plum jam and blackcurrant aroma and palate, balanced by sappy malt and a long, lingering bitter and fruity finish.

Audit Ale (OG 1061, ABV 6.2%)
Hoppy, strong and bitter.

Brewed for Hop Yard Brewery:

Golden Ale (OG 1050, ABV 5%)
A medium-bodied beer with predominant hop flavours.

Brewed for the Spirit Pub Company:

**Taylor Walker 1730 Special Pale Ale
(OG 1040, ABV 4%)**
Flavours of lemon balm, honey and blackcurrant, merged with grassy, earthy and botanical tones to create a perfectly balanced ale.

Westmorland

Kendal, Cumbria ☎ 07554 562662

Office: Mint Street, Kendal, Cumbria, LA9 6DS
✉ westmorlandbrewery@yahoo.com

Westmorland began brewing in 2016 using a one-barrel plant.

Westwood (NEW)

▤ Lowes Arms, 301 Hyde Road, Denton, M34 3FF
☎ (0161) 336 3064 ⊕ lowesarms.co.uk

A microbrewery based at the Lowes Arms, established in 2016. Beers are produced for the pub and the local free trade.

I Am Pilgrim (ABV 3.8%)

Sleeping Giant (ABV 4.2%)

The Hoff (ABV 4.3%)

Alpha (ABV 4.5%)

WH Buckley

See Evan Evans

Whaley Bridge

Unit 8, Furness Vale Business Centre, Furness Vale, Derbyshire, SK23 7SW ☎ 07890 455279
⊕ whaleybridgebrewery.co.uk

Whaley Bridge was set up by a former home brewer and launched commercially in 2012. The brewery moved to new premises in 2015, and a new six-barrel purpose-built plant was installed. RAIB

Dolly Pit DPA (OG 1040, ABV 4%)
A refreshing, lightly-hopped bitter.

Hockerley Hole Southern Red (OG 1040, ABV 4%)
A ruby-coloured ale, fruity with a hoppy aroma and a hint of treacle.

Roots Wharf (OG 1045, ABV 4.4%)
A heavily-hopped, American-style beer.

Mount Famine IPA (OG 1046, ABV 4.8%)

A pale-coloured ale with tropical notes.

Stoneheads West Coast Pale (OG 1047, ABV 4.8%)
A complex beer with tastes of citrus, a honey finish and hoppy aroma.

Wharfe Bank ◉

Unit 4, Pool Business Park, Pool Road, Pool-in-Wharfedale, West Yorkshire, LS21 1EG
☎ (0113) 284 2392 ⊕ wharfebankbrewery.co.uk

☺Wharfe Bank commenced brewing in 2010 using a 20-barrel plant in a converted paper mill on the banks of the River Wharfe. The regular range of beers is complemented by two distinct series of monthly specials often featuring unusual ingredients or rare beer styles. A separate range of beers is also brewed under the Firestorm Brewing Company brand name. Brewing is currently suspended. ‼◆

Wharfedale SIBA ◉

▤ Back Barn, 16 Church Street, Ilkley, West Yorkshire, LS29 9DS
☎ (01943) 609587 ⊕ wharfedalebrewery.com

Wharfedale began brewing in 2012 using spare capacity at Five Towns brewery in Wakefield. Brewing moved to Ilkley in 2013 using a 2.5-barrel plant located at the rear of the Flying Duck pub.

Whim SIBA

Whim Farm, Hartington, Derbyshire, SK17 0AX
☎ (01298) 84991 ⊕ whimales.co.uk

Whim opened in 1993 in outbuildings at Whim Farm. The beers are available in 50-70 outlets and the brewery's tied house, the Wilkes Head in Leek.
◆

Arbor Light (OG 1035, ABV 3.6%)
Light-coloured bitter, sharp and clean with lots of hop character and a delicate, light aroma.

Hartington Bitter (OG 1039, ABV 4%)
A light, golden-coloured, well-hopped session beer. A dry finish with a spicy, floral aroma.

Earl Grey Bitter (OG 1042, ABV 4.2%)
Traditional, full-bodied, deep golden brown-coloured ale.

Hartington IPA (OG 1045, ABV 4.5%)
Light-coloured ale, smooth on the palate allowing malt to predominate. Slightly sweet finish combined with distinctive light hop bitterness.

Flower Power (OG 1053, ABV 5.3%)
Light, golden-coloured beer with a flowery hop aroma, citrus with mild spice on the palate and a dry, bitter finish.

Whippet (NEW) SIBA ◉

Unit 9, Brown Place, Leeds, West Yorkshire, LS11 0EF
☎ (0113) 271 0299 ☎ 07928 101783
✉ sales@whippetbrewing.beer

☺Founded in 2015 by beer writer Sam Parker, beers were originally brewed at Burley Street Brewery (qv). In 2017 production moved to Bosun's Brewery (qv). Brewing should be taking place at its own Leeds-based premises during the currency of this guide. ◆

House Dogge (OG 1038, ABV 3.7%)

English Whippet (OG 1041, ABV 4.2%)

Rabbit Dog (OG 1044, ABV 4.7%)

Little Curre (OG 1049, ABV 5.2%)

Snap Dog (OG 1058, ABV 5.7%)

Whitby SIBA 👁

East Cliff, Whitby, North Yorkshire, YO22 4JR
☎ (01947) 228871 ⊕ whitby-brewery.com

Whitby brewery was established in 2012 under the Conquest name by a local team who built the brewery from scratch. It expanded in 2016 to a new site overlooking Whitby Bay with a 20-barrel capacity and an on-site tap room. ‼🍴

Abbey Blonde (OG 1038, ABV 3.8%)
A blonde ale with a zesty finish and strong notes of toffee.

Whaler (OG 1040, ABV 4%)
A fruity pale ale with a malty, citrus flavour and a mild bitter finish.

Saltwick Nab (OG 1042, ABV 4.2%)
A full-bodied, ruby-coloured ale with a pleasantly fruity finish.

Smugglers Gold (OG 1043, ABV 4.2%)
An easy-drinking, smooth golden ale.

Jet Black (OG 1046, ABV 4.5%)
A porter packed with liquorice, coffee and sweet toffee.

Black Death (OG 1050, ABV 5%)
A stout originally brewed for Whitby Goth Weekend.

IPA (OG 1048, ABV 5.2%)
A hoppy, bright and refreshing IPA.

Brewed for the Station Inn, Whitby:

Platform 3 (OG 1038, ABV 3.6%)
A nutty pale ale with a smooth citrus finish.

White Hart Tap (NEW)

🏠 4 Keyfield Terrace, St Albans, Hertfordshire, AL1 1QJ
☎ (01727) 860974 ⊕ whitetharttap.co.uk

Brewing began in 2015. Beers are only available in the pub.

White Hart (NEW)

🏠 White Hart Hotel & Restaurant, 15 High Street, Halstead, Essex, CO9 2AP
☎ (01787) 475657 ⊕ whitehartbrewery.co.uk

Brewing began in 2017 on the premises of the White Hart Hotel in Halstead.

White Horse SIBA 👁

3 Ware Road, White Horse Business Park, Stanford-in-the-Vale, Oxfordshire, SN7 8NY
☎ (01367) 718700 ⊕ breweryoxfordshire.co.uk

⊠ White Horse was founded in 2004. The brewery now has its own pub in Oxford, the Royal Blenheim, as well as supplying outlets nationally. 🍴♦

Bitter (OG 1038.7, ABV 3.7%)

Golden-coloured bitter, well-hopped with a clean, fruity finish.

Black Beauty (OG 1043.2, ABV 3.9%)
Rich, deep ruby mild.

Village Idiot (OG 1041.8, ABV 4.1%)
A blonde ale with a complex hop aroma and taste.

Wayland Smithy (OG 1047.1, ABV 4.4%)
A red-brown-coloured ale with a biscuit flavour balanced with a spicy hop finish.

White Park SIBA

Perry Hill Farm, Bourne End Road, Cranfield, Bedfordshire, MK43 0BA
☎ (01223) 911357 ⊕ whiteparkbrewery.co.uk

⊠ White Park is a family business established in 2007 on a five-barrel plant. Spent malt is recycled as feed for rare breed cattle. 60 outlets are supplied direct. In 2009 the brewery began bottling, and supplies direct to pubs and local stores. ♦

Park Light (ABV 3.6%)
A nutty IPA with a sweet hop aroma, balanced with a crisp, dry taste.

White Gold (OG 1037, ABV 3.8%)
Golden-coloured session ale. Gentle malt flavour giving rise to floral hoppiness.

Cranfield Best (ABV 4.2%)
A traditional best bitter with a complex biscuit malt flavour.

Oast House (ABV 4.8%)
Light yellow-coloured, zesty pale ale with four varieties of hop.

Malt Store (OG 1047, ABV 5%)
A malty and strong English ale.

Moonshine (OG 1050, ABV 5.2%)
Citrus, strong pale ale brewed in the Trappist style.

White Rock SIBA

Units 6 & 7, Dysons Complex, Southside, St Sampsons, Guernsey, GY2 4QJ
☎ (01481) 249920 ☎ 07911 760302
⊕ whiterockbrewery.gg

White Rock began brewing in 2013 in a modern industrial unit and supplies the limited free trade on the island as well as a small number of tied houses. There are plans for a bottling line. ‼

Pushang (OG 1038, ABV 3.8%)
Golden ale with a light floral aroma and subtle sweetness which provides for a generous length of flavour.

Wonky Donkey (OG 1047, ABV 4.7%)
A distinctive hoppy bitter with hints of citrus. Quite bitter on the tongue initially.

Lost Tourist (OG 1050, ABV 5.3%)
An IPA with a hoppy, citrus and slightly caramel flavour.

Whitewater

40 Tullyframe Road, Kilkeel, Co Down, Northern Ireland, BT34 4RZ
☎ (028) 4176 9449 ⊕ whitewaterbrewery.com

Established in 1996, Whitewater is now the biggest brewery in Northern Ireland. ‼♦

Copperhead (OG 1037, ABV 3.7%)

Crown & Glory (OG 1038, ABV 3.8%)

Belfast Black (OG 1042, ABV 4.2%)

Belfast Ale (OG 1046, ABV 4.5%)

Maggie's Leap IPA (OG 1047, ABV 4.7%)
Triple-hopped IPA with powerful hop and fruit aromas. Full-bodied, rich and complex.

Clotworthy Dobbin (OG 1050, ABV 5%)

Whitley Bay (NEW)

1 East Parade, Whitley Bay, NE26 1AW ☎ 07392 823480 ✉ gary.h11@hotmail.com

A five-barrel brewery at the rear of the King George pub in Whitley Bay. More than 40 outlets are supplied.

Slow Joe (ABV 3.9%)
A yellow-coloured Pilsner with a hint of magnolia.

Warrior (ABV 3.9%)
A well-balanced pale ale with a pleasant bitter aftertaste.

Spanish City Blonde (ABV 4.2%)
A light golden ale with moderate bitterness and a hint of grapefruit and citrus.

Ghost Ships (ABV 4.3%)
A session IPA.

A Dog Called Mouse (ABV 4.7%)
A dark-coloured, malty brew.

Whitstable SIBA

Little Telpits Farm, Woodcock Lane, Grafty Green, Kent, ME17 2AY
☎ (01622) 851007 ⊕ whitstablebrewery.co.uk

Whitstable Brewery was founded in 2003. It currently provides all the beer for the Whitstable Oyster Company's three restaurants, their hotel and a brewery tap as well as supplying cask ale to pubs all over Kent, London and Surrey. ♦

Native Bitter (OG 1036, ABV 3.7%)
A classic copper-coloured Kentish session bitter with hoppy aroma and a long, dry, bitter hop finish.

Renaissance Ruby Mild (OG 1038, ABV 3.7%)
Deep ruby in colour, this classic mild has a nutty taste with a gentle roast malt aroma.

East India Pale Ale (OG 1040, ABV 4.1%)
A well-hopped, golden-coloured IPA with good grapefruit aroma, hop character and lingering bitter finish.

Oyster Stout (OG 1045, ABV 4.5%)
Rich, dry, deep chocolate, coffee and roast malt flavours.

Pearl of Kent (OG 1043, ABV 4.5%)
A well-rounded premium golden ale with a subtle bitterness and hints of tropical fruit.

Winkle Picker (OG 1042, ABV 4.5%)
A well-balanced, amber-coloured best bitter. A pleasant maltiness is offset by a firm but not overpowering bitterness and hints of orange.

Kentish Reserve (OG 1047, ABV 5%)
Reddish-amber-coloured premium bitter. Malty notes with flavours of peaches and plums, ending on a note of rich ruby port.

Whittingtons

See Untapped

Why Not

27 Redfern Road, Norwich, NR7 9RB
☎ (01603) 300786 ⊕ thewhynotbrewery.co.uk

Why Not began brewing 2005 on a 1.5-barrel plant located to the rear of the house of proprietor Colin Emms. In 2006 the brewery was extensively upgraded, doubling in capacity. In 2011 the brewery was moved to a new location in Thorpe St Andrew. RAIB

Wally's Revenge (OG 1040, ABV 4%)
An overtly bitter beer with a hoppy background. The bitterness holds on to the end as an increasing astringent dryness develops.

Roundhead Porter (OG 1045, ABV 4.5%)
A traditional, old-style London porter.

Cavalier Red (OG 1047, ABV 4.7%)
Explosive fruity nose belies the gentleness of the taste. The summer fruit aroma dominates this red-gold-coloured brew. A sweet, fruity start disappears under a quick, bitter ending.

Norfolk Honey Ale (OG 1050, ABV 5%)
A golden-coloured beer with a honey nose. A definite hop edge leaves a honey aftertaste.

Chocolate Nutter (OG 1056, ABV 5.5%)

Wibblers SIBA

Goldsands Road, Southminster, Essex, CM0 7JW
☎ (01621) 772044 ⊕ wibblers.com

Wibblers was established in 2007 and expanded to a 20-barrel plant in 2009. In 2016 the brewery moved to new premises in Southminster with a tap room. Production is currently 70 barrels per week. More than 100 outlets are supplied including many Gray & Sons pubs. RAIB

Dengie IPA (OG 1037, ABV 3.6%)
Malty, full-flavoured ale with gentle bitterness and balanced sweetness.

Apprentice (OG 1039, ABV 3.9%)
Amber-coloured session beer with a hoppy aroma and light, malty taste.

Dengie Dark (OG 1039, ABV 4%)
Smooth, light malty beer with subtle bitterness and balancing sweetness.

Dengie Gold (OG 1040, ABV 4%)
Golden-coloured beer with a refreshing hop punch, a citrus aroma and balanced bitterness.

Hop Black (OG 1041, ABV 4%)
A dark-coloured bitter that tastes light and hoppy.

Dengie Best (OG 1041, ABV 4.1%)
A pale ale with a balance of malty mouthfeel and peppery bitterness.

Crafty Stoat (OG 1056, ABV 5.3%)

Wickwar SIBA

Old Brewery, Station Road, Wickwar, Gloucestershire, GL12 8NB
☎ (01454) 292000 ⊕ wickwarbrewing.co.uk

Wickwar was established as a 10-barrel brewery in 1990, expanding to 50 barrels in 2004. 350 outlets are supplied on a regular basis and the beers are available nationally through most distributors and SIBA. Wickwar purchased all Moles Brewery's beer brands in mid 2017. It is planned to relocate the Moles plant to the Wickwar site during the currency of this guide. ‼️🍺♦

BOB (OG 1040, ABV 4%) 🍺
Amber-coloured, this has a distinctive blend of hop, malt and apple/pear citrus fruits. The slightly sweet taste turns into a fine, dry bitterness, with a similar malty, lasting finish.

Cotswold Way (OG 1042, ABV 4.2%) 🍺
Amber-coloured, it has a pleasant aroma of pale malt, hop and fruit. Good dry bitterness in the taste with some sweetness. Similar though less sweet in the finish, with good hop content.

Falling Star (OG 1045, ABV 4.2%)
A golden-coloured premium beer with a floral aroma and light, malty finish.

Station Porter (OG 1061, ABV 6.1%)
Aromas of roasted malt, coffee, chocolate and rich fruits, and flavours of chocolate, liquorice, coffee and smoke. Smooth and warming roast and slightly sweet finish.

Wild Beer SIBA

Lower Westcombe Farm, Evercreech, Somerset, BA4 6ER
☎ (01749) 838742 ☎ 07968 721841
🌐 wildbeerco.com

Brewing began in 2012 using a 24-hectolitre plant. ♦ RAIB

Bibble (OG 1042, ABV 4.2%)

Scarlet Fever (OG 1048, ABV 4.8%)

Fresh (OG 1055, ABV 5.5%)

Madness IPA (OG 1068, ABV 6.8%)

Wild Boar

🛏 Wild Boar, Crook Road, Bowness-on-Windermere, Cumbria, LA23 3NF
☎ (08458) 504604 🌐 englishlakes.co.uk

Brewing began in 2013 on a microbrewery at the Wild Boar, a large, traditional Lakeland luxury hotel. The hotel is part of the English Lakes Hotels group and supplies beers to hotels within the group.

Wild Card SIBA

Unit 7, Ravenswood Industrial Estate, Shernhall Street, Walthamstow, E17 9HQ ☎ 07982 402650
🌐 wildcardbrewery.co.uk

⊗ Wild Card began brewing in 2013, initially using spare capacity at several breweries in and around London. It now has its own six-barrel plant in Walthamstow. 🍺

Pale (ABV 3.6%)

Jack of Clubs (ABV 4.5%) 🍺
Complex ruby-brown-coloured best bitter with a malty nose. Flavour has hints of chocolate, citrus and malt and a slightly bitter finish.

King of Hearts (ABV 4.5%) 🍺
Easy-drinking beer with a lager character in the lemony flavour, which is sweet and biscuity. Clean dry finish.

Ace of Spades (ABV 4.7%) 🍺
Black-coloured porter with a fruity nose overlaid with a little roast. Liquorice, caramelised fruit and roasted malt flavour. Lingering dryness.

Queen of Diamonds (ABV 5%) 🍺
Smooth golden ale with strong citrus aroma and flavour alongside biscuit notes. The finish is dry with a little bitterness.

Wild Horse SIBA

Unit 4, Cae Bach Builder Street, Llandudno, LL30 1DR
☎ (01492) 868292 🌐 wildhorsebrewing.co.uk

No real ale. Small brewery concentrating on supplying KeyKeg and bottled beers to local bars and off-licences.

Wild Weather SIBA 👁

Unit 19, Easter Park, Benyon Road, Aldermaston, Berkshire, RG7 2PQ
☎ (0118) 970 1837 🌐 wildweatherales.com

Wild Weather was established in 2013 on the Hampshire/Berkshire border. American and other New World hops are used to create distinctive ales. 🍺♦ RAIB

Big Muddy (OG 1038, ABV 3.8%)
Tawny-coloured session beer where smooth malty bitterness combines with floral, spicy and mild citrus hoppy overtones.

Black Night (OG 1039, ABV 3.9%)
A dark mild with a light taste that rapidly develops into a complex blend of rich malt and hop flavours and a hint of caramel. The aftertaste is long, dry, hoppy and toasty.

Serendipity (OG 1037, ABV 3.9%)
A fruity golden ale.

Betrayal (OG 1039, ABV 4%)
Golden ale with tropical fruit flavours and a long, hoppy finish.

Shepherd's Warning (OG 1056, ABV 5.6%)
A smooth, rich IPA with strong hoppy flavours of grapefruit, peach and mango.

Wildcraft (NEW)

Foragers' Rest, Buxton, Norfolk, NR10 5JD
☎ (01603) 278054 🌐 wildcraftbrewery.co.uk

⊗ Wildcraft was set up in 2016 through crowd funding and uses as much in the way of foraged and locally sourced ingredients as possible to produce its beers. RAIB V

Wild Eye P.A. (ABV 3.8%)

Wild Bill Hiccup (ABV 4.5%)

Wild Weather (ABV 4.5%)

Wild Awake (ABV 5%)

Wilde Child (NEW)

Vesper Walk, Leeds, West Yorkshire, LS5 3NQ
☎ 07908 419028 🌐 wildechildbrewing.co.uk

Microbrewery that initially produced strong keg and bottled beers but now brews three cask-conditioned ales on demand.

Wildside

See Brightside

Williams Bros SIBA 👁

New Alloa Brewery, Kelliebank, Alloa, FK10 1NT
☎ (01259) 725511 ⊕ williamsbrosbrew.com

☺A brotherhood of brewers, creating unique beers. Bruce and Scott Williams started brewing Heather Ale in 1988. A range of indigenous, historic ales have been added since. Hundreds of cask ale outlets are supplied worldwide. Contact the brewery for the latest cask beers available. ‼◆

Gold (OG 1040, ABV 3.9%)
Golden-coloured session beer with a crisp mouthfeel and lemony hop aromas.

Harvest Sun (OG 1041, ABV 3.9%)
A gold-coloured beer with a pleasant citrus aroma giving way to a balanced, bitter finish.

Fraoch Heather Ale (OG 1041, ABV 4.1%) ◆
The unique taste of heather flowers is noticeable in this beer. A fine floral aroma and spicy taste give character to this drinkable speciality beer.

Black (OG 1042, ABV 4.2%) 🍺
A light-bodied, rich, dark-coloured ale in the style of Czech dark lagers. Aromatic and full flavoured with coffee and chocolate undertones and a blackcurrant aroma.

Birds & Bees (OG 1044, ABV 4.3%)
A bright golden ale with a late infusion of elderflower and lemon zest. Fruity, aromatic and refreshing.

Kelpie (OG 1045, ABV 4.4%)
A rich, dark chocolate ale with the aroma of a fresh Scottish sea breeze and a distinctive malty texture.

Williams Red (OG 1045, ABV 4.5%)
Rich ruby red-coloured beer with toffee flavours and citrus hop aromas.

Joker IPA (OG 1050, ABV 5%)
A well-balanced IPA. Fruity on the nose with hints of cedar.

Seven Giraffes (OG 1051, ABV 5.1%)
Classic IPA with a late infusion of elderflower and lemon. Biscuity malts balanced by hop bitterness, lemon freshness and a lingering floral elderflower aftertaste.

Midnight Sun (OG 1058, ABV 5.6%)
A rich, black-coloured, smooth porter with an after bite of fresh root ginger.

Willy Good Ale

The Old Forge, Hartley Farm, Winsley, Wiltshire, BA15 2JB ☎ 07711 364202 ⊕ willygoodale.com

⊠ This award-winning brewery was set up by well-travelled Will Southward in 2010. While in North America, Will discovered a taste for well-hopped beers, and a flair for flavours. The brewery at Hartley Farm quickly out-grew demand and expanded to a six-barrel plant in 2011. Local pubs, shops and restaurants are supplied directly, with

beer festivals, parties and weddings also catered for. 🚌◆RAIB

Willy Hop (OG 1040, ABV 4%)
An amber-coloured ale with a medium body and rich toasted/caramel overtones.

Beerier Beer (OG 1042, ABV 4.2%)
An English amber-coloured ale with vanilla overtones.

High Fives (OG 1048, ABV 5%)
A light but hoppy pale ale with hints of grapefruit.

Hopadelic (OG 1048, ABV 5%)
An American-style IPA with a citrus taste and floral aroma.

Willy Brown (OG 1048, ABV 5%)
A rich, malty, nut brown-coloured ale.

Wheat a Second (OG 1050, ABV 5.2%)
Wheat ale with a hint of orange and coriander.

Willy's

🏠 **17 High Cliff Road, Cleethorpes, Lincolnshire, DN35 8RQ**
☎ (01472) 602145

The brewery opened in 1989 to provide beer mainly for its in-house pub in Cleethorpes, although some beer is sold in the free trade. It has a five-barrel plant with maximum capacity of 15 barrels a week. The brewery can be viewed at any time from pub or street.

Wily Fox (NEW) SIBA 👁

1 Kellet Close, Wigan, WN5 0LP
☎ (01942) 215525 ⊕ wilyfoxbrewery.co.uk

Brewing commenced in 2016 in Wigan. The head brewer was formerly from Thwaites (qv). ‼◆

Blonde Vixen (OG 1039.5, ABV 3.8%)
A blonde session ale, light and refreshing with spicy citrus character and grapefruit overtones.

Crafty Fox (OG 1042.5, ABV 4%)
A full-bodied bitter ale with a spicy, earthy aroma.

The Fox Hat (OG 1044, ABV 4.2%)
A hoppy golden ale, bitter and zesty with spicy citrus and grapefruit notes.

Mutiny IPA (ABV 5%)
A pale-coloured, hoppy IPA with a pronounced, lingering, dry finish.

Wimbledon SIBA 👁

8 College Fields, Prince George's Road, Colliers Wood, London, SW19 2PT
☎ (020) 3674 9786 ⊕ wimbledonbrewery.com

⊠ Set up by Mark Gordon after a 23 year career in the City, Wimbledon began production in 2015 with former Young's brewer Derek Prentice at the helm of a brand new 30-barrel plant. ‼◆RAIB

Common PA (ABV 3.7%) ◆
Well-balanced, gold-coloured bitter with mandarin and hoppy flavours and aroma. Floral note in the lingering finish with some dry bitterness.

Tower SPA (ABV 4.6%) ◆
Fruit and honey aroma. Flavour has a balanced malt and hoppy character with bittersweet finish and some fading orange notes.

Quartermaine IPA (ABV 5.8%) ◆

Amber-coloured beer with slight sweetness complementing citrus and summer fruits plus spicy hops. Fruit, spice and bittersweet finish. Hoppy nose.

Wincle SIBA

Tolls Farm Barn, Dane Bridge, Wincle, Cheshire, SK11 0QE
☎ (01260) 227777 ☎ 07701 075368
⊕ winclebeer.co.uk

☺Wincle Beer Company was set up in 2008 in a redundant milking parlour on a working farm located within the Peak District National Park. The brewery now operates a 15-barrel plant in Wincle using water from its own borehole. An adjacent storeroom was converted into a separate brewery shop. ‼ 🍺 ♦ RAIB

Waller (OG 1038, ABV 3.8%)
A pale and refreshing beer with a distinctive hop character.

Rambler (ABV 4%)
A beer with a subtle balance of malt and autumn fruit hoppiness.

Sir Philip (OG 1041, ABV 4.2%)
Amber in colour this premium bitter has a light malty overtone balanced with classic hops.

Wibbly Wallaby (OG 1043, ABV 4.4%)
A full-bodied, golden-coloured beer with fruity hop overtones and a dry, slightly biscuity finish.

Burke's Special (ABV 5%)
A chestnut-coloured English special bitter with a full malty and fruity taste.

Windermere

See Watermill

Windmill (NEW)

Standish Hall Farm, Beech Walk, Standish, WN6 0YQ
☎ (01257) 472482 ☎ 07831 225656
⊕ windmillbrewery.co.uk

☺Brewing began in 2016 in converted farm buidlings near Standish. Run by the owner of the Windmill pub in Parbold, beers are supplied to the Windmill and other local free trade outlets, mainly in Merseyside, West Lancashire and Wigan. ‼

Deckhand (OG 1038, ABV 3.8%)

Anderson Amber Bitter (OG 1046, ABV 4.4%)

Liverpool Porter (OG 1049, ABV 4.5%)

Windsor & Eton SIBA ◉

Unit 1, Vansittart Estate, Duke Street, Windsor, Berkshire, SL4 1SE
☎ (01753) 854075 ⊕ webrew.co.uk

⊗ Four friends, including two fully-qualified brewers, set up the brewery in 2010 though their brewing experience goes back to the original Courage Brewery. The purpose-built plant is 18 barrels, which supplies around 250 outlets in London and the Thames Valley area. ‼🍺♦

ParkLife (OG 1037, ABV 3.2%)
A full-flavoured, light ale with a citrus aroma and taste.

Knight of the Garter (OG 1036.5, ABV 3.8%) ◀
Hoppy golden ale with grapefruit notes. Dry, refreshing finish.

Windsor Knot (OG 1039, ABV 4%) 🍶
Amber-coloured ale with a grapefruit aroma. An initially sweet malt and fruit taste followed by a mild bitter finish.

Guardsman (OG 1041, ABV 4.2%)
A tangy best bitter, tawny in colour, with a fresh hoppy finish.

Conqueror (OG 1049, ABV 5%) ◀
A black IPA. Malty and hoppy with berry notes. A full, rounded, slightly dry finish.

Windswept SIBA ◉

Unit B, 13 Coulardbank Industrial Estate, Lossiemouth, IV31 6NG
☎ (01343) 814310 ☎ 07896 897944
⊕ windsweptbrewing.com

Windswept began brewing in 2012 using a 10-barrel plant installed by John Trow of Oban Ales. It is situated near the gates of RAF Lossiemouth and run by two former Tornado pilots who are CAMRA members. ‼🍺♦RAIB V

Blonde (OG 1039, ABV 4%) ◀
Smooth, golden, citrus hoppy brew with hints of grapefruit.

APA (OG 1046, ABV 5%) ◀
Amber, oranges and peachy, fully hopped brew.

Weizen (OG 1052, ABV 5.2%) ◀
Cloudy wheat beer full of bananas and pear drops with a hint of spice.

Wolf (OG 1064, ABV 6%) 🍶 ◀
Dark, strong-tasting, slightly sweet, roasted malty brew with chocolate and a vanilla coffee background.

Windy SIBA

🏠 **Volunteer Inn, New Road, Seavington St Michael, Somerset, TA19 0QE**
☎ (01460) 240126 ⊕ thevolly.co.uk

The brewery was established in 2011. The name stems from the time when alterations were carried out to the back of the pub and the workmen suffered extremes of varying weather conditions.

Winning Post

🏠 **Winning Post Pub, 6 Pope Iron Road, Worcester, WR1 3HB**
☎ (01905) 21178

A small pub brewery established in 2014.

Winster Valley

🏠 **Brown Horse Inn, Winster, Cumbria, LA23 3NR**
☎ (01539) 443443 ⊕ winstervalleybrewery.co.uk

Winster Valley was established in 2009 using a 2.5-barrel plant at the Brown Horse Inn in Winster. Brewing is currently suspended.

Winter's

8 Keelan Close, Norwich, NR6 6QZ
☎ (01603) 787820 ⊕ wintersbrewery.com

Winter's was established in 2001 by David Winter, who had previous award-winning success as a brewer for both Woodforde's and Chalk Hill breweries. Winter's ales have won many awards, with David now passing his brewing knowledge to his son, Mark, an award-winning brewer in his own right. ◆

Mild (OG 1036.5, ABV 3.6%) ▣ ◈
A long-lasting, biscuity roast backbone. Caramel notes give depth as a growing hoppy bitterness adds complexity to the finish.

Cloudburst (OG 1037.5, ABV 3.7%) ◈
Copper coloured with a malty nose. A bitter beginning with malt and hop notes ends in a long, dry finale.

Bitter (OG 1038.5, ABV 3.8%) ◈
A well-balanced, amber-coloured bitter. Hops and malt are balanced by a crisp citrus fruitiness. A pleasant hoppy nose with a hint of grapefruit. Long, sustained, dry, grapefruit finish.

Geniuss (OG 1041.5, ABV 4.1%) ◈
A dark brown-coloured stout that has a smooth mouthfeel with a grainy edge. Roast dominates throughout but is balanced by a mix of malt, a bittersweet fruitiness and an increasingly nutty finish.

Golden (OG 1041.9, ABV 4.1%) ◈
Just a hint of hops in the aroma. The initial taste combines a dry bitterness with a fruity apple buttress. The finish slowly subsides into a long, dry bitterness.

Revenge (OG 1047.9, ABV 4.7%) ◈
Blackcurrant notes give depth to the inherent maltiness of this pale brown-coloured beer. A bittersweet background becomes more pronounced as the fruitiness gently wanes.

Storm Force (OG 1053, ABV 5.3%) ◈
A well-defined, sweetish brew. Hops and vine fruit give depth to the malty backbone of this pale brown-coloured, strong beer. All flavours hold up well as the finish develops a warming softness.

Wiper and True SIBA

2 – 8 York Street, St Werburghs, Bristol, BS2 9XT
☎ (0117) 941 2501 ⊕ wiperandtrue.com

Originally launched in 2012 by Michael Wiper as a cuckoo brewery, Wiper and True has operated since 2015 using its own 20-barrel plant. It produces an ever-changing range of bottle-conditioned beers, with a small amount going into casks. The beers are available locally in Bristol/Bath, nationally and internationally. RAIB

Wishbone SIBA ◉

2a Worth Bridge Industrial Estate, Chesham Street, Keighley, West Yorkshire, BD21 4LG
☎ (01535) 600412 ⊕ wishbonebrewery.co.uk

Established in 2015 and run by a husband and wife team with many years previous experience in the brewing industry, beers are brewed on a modern 10-barrel brew plant. The on-site bar is open to the public two days each month.

Blonde (OG 1037, ABV 3.6%) ◈
A hoppy golden ale with with a strong citrus character. A bitter, hoppy and slightly astringent finish.

Bandit (OG 1038, ABV 3.8%) ◈
Lightly-hopped golden ale. Grapefruit on the tongue leads to a lingering citrus bitter finish in this quaffable ale.

Flux (OG 1041, ABV 4.1%)

Abyss (OG 1048, ABV 4.3%)

Gumption (OG 1046, ABV 4.5%) ◈
Well-balanced, amber-coloured best bitter. Look for hints of dried fruit, biscuit and nuts, underpinned by dry hoppiness, leading to a bitter finish.

Divination (OG 1057, ABV 5.6%) ◈
A pale-coloured American-style IPA. Heavily hopped with resinous pine notes and bitter orange peel. Orange fruitiness continues alongside the hop into a lingering bitter finish.

Witham

c/o The Chicken Sheds, Upp Hall Farm, Salmons Lane, Coggeshall, Essex, CO6 1RY
☎ (01376) 563123 ☎ 07824 698235
✉ glennackerman15@gmail.com

Brewing started in 2012, using a 0.5-barrel plant at the Woolpack Inn, Witham. In 2015 it began using spare capacity at the Red Fox Brewery (qv). The beer continues to be available at the Woolpack. One-off beers are occasionally made.

Scruffy (OG 1041, ABV 3.9%)

No Name (OG 1043, ABV 4.3%)

Withnell's (NEW) SIBA

Unit 35, The Old Mill Industrial Estate, School Lane, Bamber Bridge, PR5 6SY
☎ (01254) 830989

Office: Chapel House, 45a Bury Lane, Withnell, PR6 8SB ⊕ withnells.co.uk

☺Withnell's was established in 2016 using a five-barrel plant. Seasonal and limited run beers are planned as experiments continue with locally-sourced, sustainable and organic ingredients. Beers are supplied direct to pubs within a 20-mile radius of the brewery and occasionally beyond.

Hoppy Fettler (OG 1043, ABV 4.3%)
A refreshing pale ale with tropical hop flavours.

Push Iron (OG 1045, ABV 4.5%)
A golden ale with notes of caramel and pine.

Tin Basher (OG 1047, ABV 4.7%)
A ruby-coloured ale using vanilla, honey and spice.

Wobbly SIBA

Unit 22c, Beech Business Park, Tillington Road, Hereford, HR4 9QJ
☎ (01432) 355496 ☎ 07702 739357
⊕ wobblybrewing.co.uk

Wobbly began brewing in 2013 using a 2.5-barrel plant and is an off-shoot of AJP Process Pipework. There is an on-site bottling/canning plant in production, which undertakes contract work. A new 30-barrel plant is now operational and the brewery has recently taken on the tenancy of a local pub. ⑪⏰◆RAIB

Wabbit (ABV 4%)

Gold (OG 1036.5, ABV 4.2%)

American Amber (ABV 4.5%)

An amber-coloured ale with complex malt layers, hoppy tropical flavours and a big citrus aroma.

Backfire (ABV 4.5%)

Welder (OG 1046.5, ABV 4.8%)

Wold Top SIBA 👁

Hunmanby Grange, Wold Newton, East Yorkshire, YO25 3HS

☎ (01723) 892222 ⊕ woldtopbrewery.co.uk

An integral part of Hunmanby Grange Farm, Wold Top brewed its first ale in 2003 and uses home and Wolds-grown malting barley and chalk filtered water from the farm's own borehole. Now brewing on a 40-barrel plant, the range includes special edition cask and bottled beers plus three gluten-free beers. The brewery installed a bottling line in 2007 and contract bottles for other breweries. ♦ GF

Bitter (OG 1037, ABV 3.7%)
A crisp, clean, aromatic session bitter. Full-flavoured with a long, hoppy finish.

Anglers Reward (OG 1039, ABV 4%)
A refreshing, golden-coloured pale ale with a fruity bitterness and lingering aftertaste.

Wolds Way (OG 1039, ABV 4%)
A golden-coloured ale with a fruity bitterness.

Headland Red (OG 1042, ABV 4.3%)
A red-coloured ale with a mellow, malty flavour.

Against the Grain (OG 1044, ABV 4.5%)
A full-flavoured beer with refreshing bitterness and a citrus aftertaste.

Wold Gold (OG 1046, ABV 4.8%)
A light-coloured beer with a soft, fruity flavour and a hint of spice.

Scarborough Fair IPA (OG 1056, ABV 6%)
A strong, well-hopped ale.

Wolf SIBA 👁

Decoy Farm, Old Norwich Road, Besthorpe, Norfolk, NR17 2LA

☎ (01953) 457775 ⊕ wolfbrewery.com

The brewery was founded in 1996 on a 20-barrel plant, which was upgraded to a 25-barrel plant in 2006. It moved to its current site in 2013. In 2009 the brewery installed a Moravek bottling plant with an output capability of 2,000 bottles per hour. More than 300 outlets are supplied. 🛒♦

Edith Cavell (OG 1037, ABV 3.7%)
A hoppy, thirst-quenching beer with a fruity finish.

Golden Jackal (OG 1039, ABV 3.7%) 🍺
A hoppy, citrus nose and first taste. Increasingly dry bitter ending as citrus notes fade.

Wolf in Sheep's Clothing (OG 1039, ABV 3.7%) 🍺
Strong, fruity nose with roast. A strong caramel beginning with a bitter roast counterpoint. Gently tapering finish. Increasing raspberry sweetness.

Lavender Honey (OG 1038, ABV 3.8%)

Ale (OG 1039, ABV 3.9%)
A copper-coloured, full-bodied ale.

Battle of Britain (OG 1039, ABV 3.9%)
A complex brew with caramel, vine fruit and an initial sweetness. Dramatic, quick bitter finish.

Lupus Lupus (OG 1042, ABV 4.2%) 🍺
Hops, with a citrus edge, dominate both aroma and taste. A biscuity background disappears quickly in a short, sharp finish.

Sirius Dog Star (OG 1044, ABV 4.4%) 🍺
Roast, coffee and caramel aroma flows into a similar first taste. Big mouthfeel with a slightly sour caramel enhanced finale.

Sly Wolf (OG 1041, ABV 4.4%)
Pale, refreshing ale infused with lime.

Straw Dog (OG 1045, ABV 4.5%) 🍺
Delicately flavoured with a fruity character. A redcurrant aroma gives way to marmalade and hops. A strong, increasingly bitter finish.

Mad Wolf (OG 1048, ABV 4.7%)
Smooth, dark and malty ale.

Granny Wouldn't Like It (OG 1049, ABV 4.8%) 🍺
Complex, with a malty bouquet. Increasing bitterness is softened by malt as a gentle, fruity sweetness adds depth.

Woild Moild (OG 1048, ABV 4.8%) 🍺
Heavy and complex with malt, vine fruit, bitterness and roast notes vying for dominance. Increasingly dry finish.

Contract brewed for City of Cambridge Brewery:

Boathouse (OG 1037, ABV 3.7%)
A light, copper-coloured session bitter with a pleasant aroma.

Hobson's Choice (OG 1041, ABV 4.2%)
A pale-coloured ale with a refreshing hoppy aftertaste.

Atom Splitter (OG 1045, ABV 4.5%)
A golden ale bursting with hoppy flavours.

Parkers Piece (OG 1050, ABV 5%)
A chestnut-coloured, fruity beer with a long-lasting hop bitterness.

Tom Wood's SIBA 👁

Melton High Wood Farm, Melton High Wood, Melton Ross, Lincolnshire, DN38 6AA

☎ (01652) 680001 ⊕ tom-wood.com

The Tom Wood range of beers is brewed in the 60-barrel Highwood plant. ♦

Best Bitter (OG 1035.5, ABV 3.5%) 🍺
A good citrus, passion fruit hop dominates the nose and taste, with background malt. A lingering hoppy and bitter finish.

Lincoln Gold (OG 1041, ABV 4%)
Pale-coloured bitter with a fruity aroma and slightly zesty flavour but retaining malt characteristics.

Bomber County (OG 1046, ABV 4.8%) 🍺
An earthy malt aroma but with a complex underlying mix of coffee, hops, caramel and apple fruit. The beer starts bitter and intensifies to the end.

Wood SIBA 👁

Wistanstow, Shropshire, SY7 8DG

☎ (01588) 672523 ⊕ woodbrewery.co.uk

The brewery opened in 1980 in buildings next to the Plough Inn, still the brewery's only tied house. Steady growth over the years included the acquisition of the Sam Powell Brewery and its beers in 1991. Around 200 outlets are supplied. ‼♦

Parish Bitter (OG 1038, ABV 3.8%) ◈
A blend of malt and hops with a bitter aftertaste. Pale brown in colour.

Shropshire Lass (OG 1040, ABV 4%)
A golden ale with zesty bitterness.

Beauty (OG 1042, ABV 4.2%)
Mid amber colour. A fusion of fruity hops give a lingering bitter aftertaste together with a well-rounded maltiness.

Shropshire Lad (OG 1045, ABV 4.5%)
A strong, well-rounded bitter.

Woodbury (NEW) SIBA

Sandy Bottoms Brewery, Rydon Lane, Woodbury Salterton, Devon, EX5 1JZ ☎ 07985 769171

Woodbury Ales was established in 2016 by Paul Thomas and Chris Marriott. Brewing is currently suspended.

Woodcote Manor

Kidderminster Road, Dodford, Worcestershire, B61 9DY
☎ (01527) 558141 ☎ 07779 166174
⊕ woodcotemanor.com

⊗ Woodcote Manor opened in 2015 in former dairy outbuildings attached to the brewer's house. The 20-barrel plant came from Pembrokeshire Brewery, and is run by a keen home brewer who turned his hobby into a business. The regular beers use locally-sourced ingredients, including own grown hops, and are distributed to a number of local pubs. ♦RAIB

Supreme Pale Ale (OG 1041, ABV 4.1%)
Golden orange in colour with malty, soft citrus and fruity mango aromas. The taste has a malt biscuit character with a touch of tangy fruit suggesting passion fruit followed by a light bitter finish.

Oatmeal Stout (OG 1044, ABV 4.5%)
A rich, dark-coloured stout with a subtle roasted aroma, an initial burst of bitterness followed by a sweet, long-lasting taste.

Squire's Gold (OG 1045, ABV 4.5%)
Aromas of sweet grain, honey and dried fruit are followed by a taste that is smooth with light smoky malt, fresh hops and a hint of fruit.

Amber Ale (OG 1049, ABV 4.9%)
Mixture of toasted grain and light caramel notes and a range of floral, citrus and fruity hops with a light bitterness and a spicy finish.

IPA (OG 1049, ABV 4.9%)
A triple IPA with complex malt flavours balanced by tropical and fruity aromas and taste.

Stout (OG 1049, ABV 4.9%)
Easy-drinking stout with vanilla overtones.

Wooden Hand

Unit 3, Grampound Road Industrial Estate, Grampound Road, Cornwall, TR2 4TB
☎ (01726) 884596 ⊕ woodenhand.co.uk

⊗ Wooden Hand was founded in 2004. It changed hands in 2015 and again in 2017. The brewery is now part of the Cornish Brewing Company, along with Wooden Hand Wines. A bottling line was installed in 2005, which also contract-bottles for other breweries. ☛♦

Dab Hand (OG 1043, ABV 4.5%)
Pale gold in colour, zesty and tangy with a crisp, dry finish.

Woodforde's SIBA ◉

Woodbastwick, Norfolk, NR13 6SW
☎ (01603) 720353 ⊕ woodfordes.co.uk

⊗ Founded in 1981 by two members of the Homebrewers' Society, Woodforde's is named after Parson Woodforde, the 18th century Norfolk diarist with a penchant for real ale. In 1989 the brewery moved to its current home at Woodbastwick, where it has its own boreholes and brews using locally-grown Maris Otter. Investment in 2001 and 2008 more than doubled the production capacity. The brewery tap, the Fur & Feather, is located next door, and more than 600 outlets are supplied on a regular basis. ‼☛♦RAIB

Mardler's (OG 1036, ABV 3.5%) ◈
Chocolate and roast aromas introduce this well-balanced dark mild. Vanilla, caramel and malt boost the dominant roast and chocolate flavours.

Wherry (OG 1037.5, ABV 3.8%) ⊓ ◈
Biscuity bouquet with grassy nuances. Citrus notes, malt, and toffee with a growing bitterness in a long, dry finish.

Once Bittern (OG 1040, ABV 4%) ◈
A light malty nose. A dark marmalade tang gives an edge to the dominant malt character. Long bittersweet ending.

Sundew (OG 1039, ABV 4.1%) ◈
Hops emerge from a mix of malt, fruit and bitterness to provide a cutting edge to both taste and aroma.

Reedlighter (OG 1040, ABV 4.2%) ◈
A hop, lemon and biscuit nose. Well-balanced with citrus and hop softened by a biscuity background. Short lemony ending.

Bure Gold (OG 1043, ABV 4.3%) ◈
A bouncy orange and biscuit bouquet. A bittersweet hoppy beginning develops into a full-bodied marmalade ending.

Nelsons Revenge (OG 1045, ABV 4.5%) ◈
Rich dark and fruity. A complex and smooth-drinking bitter. Dundee cake in a glass.

Norfolk Nog (OG 1047, ABV 4.6%) ◈
Echoes of Pontefract cake dominate. A plummy sweetness is aided by a dry bitterness and a hint of caramel.

Woodman's (NEW)

Unit 5, Viaduct Works, Frog Lane, Ponsanooth, Cornwall, TR3 7JW ☎ 07941 069890
⊕ woodmanswildale.com

Stuart Woodman is well regarded as a forager. In 2016 he took over Verdant Brewery's former premises to start brewing beers in small batches featuring foraged ingredients. ‼♦RAIB

Wooha SIBA

Unit 8A1, Balmakeith Business Park, Nairn, IV12 5QR

☎ (01667) 459929 ☎ 07811 260732
⊕ woohabrewing.com

Wooha opened in 2015 using a 10-barrel plant. It specialises in producing bottle-conditioned ales. Cask-conditioned beers are brewed on demand for beer festivals. Pubs and retail outlets are supplied locally, in Nairn, and across Scotland. **RAIB**

Blonde (ABV 4.5%)

Lager (ABV 5%)

Porter (ABV 5%)

IPA (ABV 6.2%) ◆
Malty background but with a strong peachy hop character in this pale brown-coloured IPA.

Wheat (ABV 6.4%)

Worcester

Arch 49, Cherry Tree Walk, Worcester, WR1 3AU
☎ 07906 432049 ⊕ worcesterbrewingco.co.uk

A small brewery in the heart of Worcester. A range of beers is brewed in rotation using traditional British hops, with a loose association with the English Civil War.

Holy Ground (OG 1042, ABV 4.2%)

Powick Porter (ABV 4.5%)

1651 (ABV 5.1%)

Sabrina's Dark Ruby Ale (ABV 5.5%)

Worcestershire

Hartlebury Brewery, Station Road, Hartlebury, Worcestershire, DY11 7YJ
☎ (01299) 253617
⊕ worcestershirebrewingcompany.co.uk

☺Worcestershire Brewing Co was established in 2011 as Attwood Ales on a new 10- barrel plant to the rear of the Tap House, a conversion of the original Hartlebury station ticket office. It has five tied pubs. Beers are sold direct to free houses, clubs and pub companies in Worcestershire and the West Midlands. ◆

Gold (OG 1038, ABV 3.8%) ◆
Amber-coloured bitter, faintly grassy aroma, slightly sweet with malt, subtle hops and a little hops on the aftertaste.

APA (OG 1039, ABV 4%) ◆
Hops predominate in the aroma followed by clean hops, a little sweetness with background citrus taste and a bitter finish.

Nectar Bitter (OG 1043, ABV 4.2%) ◆
Amber best bitter. Faint aroma having just a hint of leather, sweetness and light hops on the palate, initially sweet then lingering bitter finish.

Copper Hopper (OG 1045, ABV 4.5%)
A triple-hopped, copper-coloured ale with a tropical fruit character.

Working Hand SIBA

⬛ **Three Horseshoes, Pit House Lane, Leamside, DH4 6QQ**
☎ (0191) 584 2394
⊕ threehorseshoesleamside.co.uk

Brewing began in 2012 using a 2.5-barrel plant. Beers are available at the Three Horseshoes as well as the four other pubs in the group.

World's End

⬛ **Crown Inn, 60 Wilcot Road, Pewsey, Wiltshire, SN9 5EL**
☎ (01672) 562653 ⊕ thecrowninnpewsey.com

World's End Ales was established in 2009 on a one-barrel plant at the rear of the Crown Inn in Pewsey. World's End is the 18th-century name for the area in which the brewery is located.

Worsthorne SIBA

Unit 11, Siberia Mill, Holgate Street, Briercliffe, Lancashire, BB10 2HQ
☎ (01282) 422588 ☎ 07815 708289
⊕ worsthornebrewingcompany.co.uk

Worsthorne began brewing in 2011 using a 5.5-barrel plant. The brewery moved to larger premises behind the original building in 2014. An expansion to a 10-barrel plant was carried out in 2016, including a licensed visitor centre. More than 150 outlets are supplied. ‼◆

Gold (OG 1036, ABV 3.6%)
Lightly bittered golden ale with a spicy aroma.

Packhorse (OG 1037, ABV 3.7%)
Pale amber-coloured ale with subtle, earthy bitterness and floral, spicy finish.

Foxstones (OG 1039, ABV 3.9%)
Amber-coloured bitter with well-balanced hoppy aroma and lingering floral aftertaste.

Some Like It Blond (OG 1039, ABV 3.9%)
A blonde beer brewed using German hops with a lingering, dry aftertaste.

Hop the Mayflower (OG 1040, ABV 4%)
A lightly-hopped beer with a tangerine finish.

Redman (OG 1042, ABV 4.2%)
Light bitter with overtones of honey and citrus, a satisfying aftertaste and a lingering bitterness.

Trust the Clarets (OG 1043, ABV 4.3%)

Old Trout (OG 1045, ABV 4.5%)

Blackthorn Stout (OG 1049, ABV 4.9%)
Rich, dark-coloured stout with distinct chocolate and liquorice flavours. A hint of ripe berries and a smooth, bitter aftertaste.

Colliers Clog (OG 1055, ABV 5.5%)
A strong pale ale lightly bittered with spicy overtones and citrus finish.

Worthington's

See Heritage

Wrexham Lager

42 St Georges Crescent, Wrexham, LL13 8DB
☎ (01978) 266222 ⊕ wrexhamlager.co.uk

Brewing began in 2011. No real ale.

Wriggle Valley SIBA

Unit 4, The Sidings, Station Road, Stalbridge, Dorset, DT10 2RQ ☎ 07952 198777
⊕ wrigglevalleybrewery.co.uk

⊗ Wriggle Valley began brewing in 2014 based in a converted garage at the owner's house but relocated in 2017 to an industrial unit using a three-barrel plant. Beers are mainly supplied within a 15-mile radius of the brewery. ◆RAIB

Dorset Pilgrim (ABV 3.8%)
Session bitter with a good level of bitterness and some fruit.

Ryme Rambler (OG 1040, ABV 4%)

Copper Hoppa (OG 1047, ABV 4.5%)
A full-bodied, dark copper-coloured ale with big fruit aromas and flavour.

Valley Gold (ABV 4.5%)

George Wright SIBA

Unit 11, Diamond Business Park, Sandwash Close, Rainford, Merseyside, WA11 8LY
☎ (01744) 886686 ⊕ georgewrightbrewing.co.uk

George Wright started production in 2003. The original 2.5-barrel plant was replaced by a five-barrel one, which has since been upgraded again to 25 barrels. ‼🍽◆

Drunken Duck (OG 1040, ABV 3.9%) ◆
Fruity, gold-coloured bitter beer with good hop and a dry aftertaste. Some acidity.

Longboat (OG 1040, ABV 3.9%) ◆
Good hoppy bitter with grapefruit and an almost tart bitterness throughout. Some astringency in the aftertaste. Well-balanced, light and refreshing with a good mouthfeel and long, dry finish.

Blonde Moment (OG 1040, ABV 4%)
A premium blonde beer. Light in colour with a herbal nose and sweet aftertaste.

Mild (OG 1042, ABV 4%)

Pipe Dream (OG 1044, ABV 4.3%) ◆
Hoppy best bitter with a fruity nose and grapefruit to the fore in the taste. Lasting dry, bitter finish.

Pure Blonde (OG 1045, ABV 4.6%)
A premium blonde ale, light and hoppy with an earthy hop flavour.

Cheeky Pheasant (OG 1047, ABV 4.7%)
Light amber in colour, distinctive fruit, malty taste with a sweet aftertaste.

Roman Black (OG 1047, ABV 4.8%)
A dark-coloured premium ale, smooth and creamy with a long, malty, sweet taste.

Blue Moon (OG 1048, ABV 5%) ◆
Easy-drinking, strong, gold-coloured beer. Good malt/bitter balance and well hopped.

Mocne Piwo (OG 1051, ABV 5%)
Strong ale with a hoppy aftertaste.

Northern Lights (OG 1049, ABV 5.1%)
Strong ale, amber in colour. A strong citrus taste balanced by the bitter hop.

Wychwood 👁

Eagle Maltings, The Crofts, Witney, Oxfordshire, OX28 4DP
☎ (01993) 890800 ⊕ wychwood.co.uk

Wychwood brewery is located in the Cotswold market town of Witney. The brewers take inspiration from the myths and legends associated with the ancient medieval Wychwood forest. Part of Marston's PLC. ‼🍽◆RAIB

Hobgoblin Gold (OG 1042, ABV 4.2%)
A golden-coloured beer full of malty flavours with a refreshing bitterness and zesty aroma.

Hobgoblin (OG 1045, ABV 4.5%)
A well-balanced blend of smooth, rich malt flavours combined with a crisp hop bitterness.

Wye Valley SIBA 👁

Stoke Lacy, Herefordshire, HR7 4HG
☎ (01885) 490505 ☎ 07970 597937
⊕ wyevalleybrewery.co.uk

☺Founded in 1985 at Canon Pyon, the award-winning brewery is now in Stoke Lacy. A new brewhouse was commissioned in 2013. ‼🍽RAIB

Bitter (OG 1037, ABV 3.7%) ◆
A beer whose aroma gives little hint of the bitter hoppiness that follows through to the aftertaste.

The Hopfather (OG 1039, ABV 3.9%)
A smooth-bodied ale featuring spicy honey, pine and grapefruit flavours.

HPA (OG 1040, ABV 4%) 🍷 ◆
A pale, hoppy, malty brew with a hint of sweetness before a dry finish.

Golden Ale (OG 1042, ABV 4.2%)
A light, gold-coloured ale with a good hop character throughout.

Butty Bach (OG 1046, ABV 4.5%)
A gold-coloured, full-bodied premium ale.

Wholesome Stout (OG 1046, ABV 4.6%) ◆
A smooth and satisfying stout with a bitter edge to its roast flavours. The finish combines roast grain and malt.

IPA (OG 1058, ABV 6%)
Strong ale with a pronounced hop character.

Wylam SIBA

Palace of Arts, Exhibition Park, Newcastle upon Tyne, NE2 4PZ
☎ (0191) 650 0651 ⊕ wylambrewery.co.uk

☺Wylam commenced brewing in 2000 on a 4.5-barrel plant. Originally brewing in Heddon-on-the-Wall in Northumberland, the brewery moved to Newcastle upon Tyne in 2016 with a new 30-barrel brew kit with an on-site brewery tap. ‼◆

Bitter (OG 1039, ABV 3.8%) ◆
A refreshing, copper-coloured, hoppy bitter with a clean, bitter finish.

Galatia (OG 1039, ABV 3.9%)
Light session pale ale with fresh orange pith, stone fruit and a clean, dry, fresh pine kick to the finish.

Gold Tankard (OG 1040, ABV 4%) ◆
Fresh, clean flavour, full of hops. This golden ale has a hint of citrus in the finish.

Cascade (OG 1040.5, ABV 4.1%)
A pale ale with huge notes of pink grapefruit and sherbet lemon.

Collingwood (OG 1041, ABV 4.1%)

THE BREWERIES

Honey-coloured beer with a tangerine aroma. Citrus zest and fresh pine flavours with a dry bitter finish.

Angel (OG 1044, ABV 4.3%)
A pale copper-coloured, well-balanced bitter with a citrus character.

Red Kite (OG 1046.5, ABV 4.5%)
A ruby-coloured ale with hops balanced by residual maltiness and a rich palate.

Puffing Billy (OG 1055, ABV 5.5%)
A smoked, black-coloured bitter with a mellow blend of malts. Notes of coffee, tobacco and dark chocolate with a bitter hop finish.

Jakehead IPA (OG 1058, ABV 6.3%)
IPA with lots of hop aroma. Bittersweet on the palate with a massive hop complexity.

Wyre Piddle

See Ambridge

XT SIBA

Notley Farm, Chearsley Road, Long Crendon, Buckinghamshire, HP18 9ER
☎ (01844) 208310 ⊕ xtbrewing.com

⊗ XT started brewing in 2011 with a British-built 18-barrel plant. It supplies direct to pubs in Buckinghamshire, Oxfordshire and the Midlands. The brewery shop sells its bottle-conditioned beers and locally-made cider. A range of limited edition, one-off brews is produced under the Animal Brewing Co name. ‼ ➤ ◆ RAIB

Four (OG 1037, ABV 3.8%)
A balanced, mellow session amber-coloured ale with pine and citrus hop notes.

One (OG 1041, ABV 4.2%)
Blonde beer with dry citrus, lemon and spice notes.

Three (OG 1041, ABV 4.2%)
An American-style pale ale with citrus and pine flavours and a light biscuit malt character.

Two (OG 1041, ABV 4.2%)
Golden ale with chewy juicy malts and mellow balanced hop character.

Eight (OG 1045, ABV 4.5%)
A full-bodied, dark-coloured porter with roast malt, coffee and bitter chocolate notes.

Fifteen (OG 1044, ABV 4.5%)
A pale amber-coloured IPA with caramel malt notes and a lasting floral, grassy hop character.

Six (OG 1045, ABV 4.5%)
A rich, ruby-coloured red beer with a strong malt character and soft citrus hop finish.

Thirteen (OG 1044, ABV 4.5%)
A red-coloured ale, brewed with a range of citrus aromatic hops selected from around the Pacific rim.

Five (OG 1052, ABV 5.5%)
An American-style, amber-coloured ale with intense hop character on a full-bodied malt base.

XPA (OG 1055, ABV 5.9%)
An American-style IPA. Clean malt character with an intense mix of aromatic fruity hops.

Xtreme

Unit 21, Alfric Square, Maxwell Road, Woodston, Peterborough, Cambridgeshire, PE2 7JP ☎ 07427 661839 ⊕ xtremeales.com

⊗ Founded in 2013, this independent, family-run brewery initially started brewing on a one-barrel plant in Turves. Demand has meant a move to bigger premises in Peterborough using a 2.5-barrel plant. A number of local pubs and beer festivals are supplied around the area. In addition to its regular range, the brewery specialises in developing one-off brews for festivals. ‼ ◆

Route 701 (OG 1040, ABV 4%)
A pale session ale with citrus flavours.

Pigeon Ale (OG 1043, ABV 4.3%)
A light hoppy beer with a citrus aftertaste.

Milk Stout (OG 1045, ABV 4.5%)
A traditional creamy milk stout with dry roast flavours to the fore.

Yankee Pigeon (OG 1045, ABV 4.5%)
A light beer with a good nose, plenty of flavour and a strong, dry finish.

Chocolate Stout (OG 1050, ABV 5%)
Rich, full-flavoured chocolate stout with a creamy taste.

Evil Pigeon (OG 1055, ABV 5.5%)
A strong, hoppy ale with a citrus, bitter taste and a long, dry finish.

Yaarbrew (NEW)

c/o Pleasure Boat, Staithe Road, Hickling, Norfolk, NR12 0YW ☎ 07708 430230 ⊕ yaarbrew.co.uk

Formed in 2016 by four work colleagues who had been keen home brewers and real ale enthusiasts for a number of years. The 1.5-barrel plant is located in the former Post Office next to the Pleasure Boat Inn at Hickling Broad. Beer is available around Norfolk and further afield.

Citrus Gold (OG 1044, ABV 4.2%)
A rich, golden-coloured session beer with hints of orange and grapefruit and pine aromas.

Ginger Porter (OG 1048, ABV 4.2%)
A rich, dark-coloured porter with root ginger added to give the beer some heat and sweetness.

Robust Porter (OG 1048, ABV 4.2%)
A rich, dark-coloured, full-bodied porter.

Smoked Chilli IPA (OG 1050, ABV 4.8%)
A smooth-flavoured, smoky IPA with a touch of heat due to the green chillies added to the brew.

Yard of Ale

▤ **Surtees Arms, Chilton Lane, Ferryhill, DL17 0DH**
☎ (01740) 655724 ☎ 07540 733513
⊕ thesurteesarms.co.uk

Established in 2008, the 2.5-barrel microbrewery supplies ales to its brewery tap, the Surtees Arms, beer festivals and to a growing number of pubs.

Reach for the Yard (ABV 3.8%)

Yard Dog Brown Ale (ABV 4%)

One Foot In The Yard (OG 1044, ABV 4.5%)
A premium golden ale, fruity on the nose and palate with a sweet finish.

Yates SIBA

Ghyll Farm, Westnewton, Cumbria, CA7 3NX
☎ (01697) 321081 ⊕ yatesbrewery.co.uk

⊛ Established in 1986 and owned by Graeme and Caroline Baxter, Yates brews using a 20-barrel plant and uses a limited number of site-grown hops. There is a reed bed effluent system. ‼◆

Bitter (OG 1036, ABV 3.7%) ◆
A well-balanced, full-bodied bitter, golden in colour with complex hop bitterness. Good aroma and distinctive flavour.

Golden Ale (OG 1038, ABV 3.9%) ▣ ◆
Skilful use of lager malt and hops results in a pale beer with a light bitterness; melon fruit and a clean, refreshing finish.

Sun Goddess (OG 1041, ABV 4.2%) ◆
A full-bodied beer packed with tropical fruit.

Solway 4 Hop (OG 1044, ABV 4.5%)

Yates' SIBA

Unit 4c, Langbridge Business Centre, Newchurch, Isle of Wight, PO36 0NP
☎ (01983) 867878 ⊕ yates-brewery.co.uk

Brewing started in 2000 on a five-barrel plant at the Inn at St Lawrence. In 2009 it moved to Newchurch and upgraded to a 10-barrel plant. In 2015 the brewery was moved on to the same site as the wholesale unit. ‼◆RAIB

Golden (OG 1040, ABV 4%)
A light ale with fruity tones, finished with a subtle bitter finish.

Islander (OG 1040, ABV 4%)

Beachcomber (OG 1043, ABV 4.3%)

Holy Joe (OG 1050, ABV 4.9%)
Golden-coloured ale with a citrus aroma. Plenty of bitterness along with slightly toasted, sweet malt flavours, citrus notes and spicy coriander.

Dark Side of the Wight (OG 1049, ABV 5%)
A malty milk chocolate and orange fruit aroma. Bitter, malty and toasted to taste with perfumed bitter orange notes. Bitter roasted finish.

Yelland Manor

Lower Yelland Farm, Yelland, Devon, EX31 3EN
☎ (01271) 860355 ☎ 07770 267592
✉ yellandmanor@gmail.com

⊠ Located on the Taw Estuary and close to the Tarka Trail, this is a five-barrel plant in a converted milking parlour. The brewery began production in 2013 and now supplies a small number of local pubs and hotels. ◆

Standard (OG 1043, ABV 4.2%)

Yeovil SIBA ⊙

Unit 5, Bofors Park, Artillery Road, Lufton Trading Estate, Yeovil, Somerset, BA22 8YH
☎ (01935) 414888 ⊕ yeovilales.com

⊠ Yeovil Ales was established in 2006 using an 18-barrel plant. More than 300 pubs are supplied in the South West. ‼�`▆◆RAIB V

Glory (OG 1039, ABV 3.8%)
A well-balanced bitter with citrus hop notes.

Star Gazer (OG 1042, ABV 4%)
Dark copper-coloured bitter with a floral bouquet.

Summerset (OG 1041, ABV 4.1%)
Blonde ale with a fruity hop finish.

Lynx Wildcat (OG 1044, ABV 4.3%)
Full-bodied hoppy bitter with grapefruit hop flavours.

Stout Hearted (OG 1045, ABV 4.3%)
A smooth, dark-coloured stout, full-bodied with rich roast flavours.

Ruby (OG 1047, ABV 4.5%)
Red-coloured bitter with rich malt depth.

POSH IPA (OG 1052, ABV 5.4%)
A strong IPA with a fruity body and hoppy finish.

Yetman's

Bayfield Farm Barns, Bayfield Brecks Farm, Bayfield, Norfolk, NR25 7DZ ☎ 07774 809016 ⊕ yetmans.net

A 2.5-barrel plant built by Moss Brew was installed in restored medieval barns near Holt in 2005. The brewery supplies local free trade outlets. Bottle-conditioned beers are available in many Waitrose stores throughout the East Anglian area. RAIB

Red (OG 1036, ABV 3.8%)

York SIBA ⊙

12 Toft Green, York, North Yorkshire, YO1 6JT
☎ (01904) 621162 ⊕ york-brewery.co.uk

York started production in 1996. It was the first brewery in the city for 40 years and was acquired by Mitchell's of Lancaster in 2008. Five pubs are owned in York and Leeds. The 20-barrel plant has a viewing platform overlooking the conditioning and fermenting rooms. ‼➁▆◆

Guzzler (OG 1036, ABV 3.6%) ▣ ◆
Refreshing golden ale with dominant hop and fruit flavours developing throughout.

Blonde (OG 1039, ABV 3.9%)
Fruity beer with light bitterness, hints of stone fruit and citrus on the aftertaste.

Yorkshire Terrier (OG 1041, ABV 4.2%) ◆
Refreshing and distinctive brew where fruit and hops dominate the aroma and taste. Hoppy bitterness remains assertive in the aftertaste.

Otherside IPA (OG 1044, ABV 4.5%)
A hoppy IPA packed with tropical fruit notes against a background of citrus and pine.

Centurion's Ghost Ale (OG 1051, ABV 5.4%) ◆
Dark ruby in colour, full-tasting with mellow roast malt character balanced by light bitterness and autumn fruit flavours that linger into the aftertaste.

Yorkshire Dales

Abbey Works, Askrigg, North Yorkshire, DL8 4LP
☎ (01969) 622027 ☎ 07818 035592
⊕ yorkshiredalesbrewery.com

⊛ Situated in the heart of the Yorkshire Dales, brewing started in a converted milking parlour in 2005. In 2016 the brewery moved to larger premises. More than 100 pubs are supplied throughout the north of England. A tap and bottle shop opened at the brewery in 2017. ◆RAIB

Butter Tubs (OG 1037, ABV 3.7%)

A pale golden beer with a dry bitterness complemented by strong citrus flavours and aroma.

Askrigg Bitter (OG 1038, ABV 3.8%)

Bainbridge Blonde (OG 1038, ABV 3.8%)

Buckden Pike (OG 1040, ABV 3.9%)
A refreshing blonde beer with a crisp, fruity finish.

Nappa Scarr (OG 1041, ABV 4%)
Golden ale with fruity flavours throughout.

Muker Silver (OG 1041, ABV 4.1%)
A Helles-style ale with a clean, refreshing flavour.

Askrigg Ale (OG 1043, ABV 4.3%)
A hoppy session IPA with an intense aroma, crisp flavour and a long, sharp finish.

Garsdale Smokebox (OG 1057, ABV 5.6%)
A complex ale with rich chocolate and coffee flavours to complement the smokiness.

Yorkshire Heart SIBA

The Vineyard, Pool Lane, Nun Monkton, YO26 8EL
☎ (01423) 330716 ☎ 07838 030067
⊕ yorkshireheart.com

☺Yorkshire Heart has been brewing since 2011 and is situated adjacent to the Yorkshire Heart vineyard and winery, not far from York. ‼◆

Lightheart (OG 1033, ABV 3.3%)
A pale ale with citrus and spice flavours.

Hearty Bitter (OG 1037, ABV 3.7%)
A chestnut-coloured bitter with toffee flavours.

Dark Heart (OG 1039, ABV 4%)
Coffee-coloured ale with a smooth treacle flavour.

SilverHeart IPA (OG 1039, ABV 4%)
Amber-coloured ale with a citrus and spice flavour.

JRT Golden Best Bitter (OG 1041, ABV 4.2%)
Golden ale with a caramel and citrus flavour.

Blackheart Stout (OG 1047, ABV 4.8%)
Stout with a roasted coffee flavour.

Platinum EPA (OG 1047, ABV 5%)
Extra pale ale with zest and spice flavours.

Yorkshire SIBA

Brewery Wharf, 70 Humber Street, Fruit Market, Hull, East Yorkshire, HU1 1TU
☎ (01482) 618000 ☎ 07850 494990
✉ info@yorkshirebrewing.co.uk

☺Brewing started in 2012 in the Fruit Market Arts Quarter of Hull using a six-barrel plant. Two of the beers are named in honour of the Holy Trinity Church in Hull. A bottling plant, tours and a retail outlet are established. Festivals and local outlets are supplied. ‼🍺◆RAIB

Mosaic (OG 1042, ABV 4.2%)
Easy-drinking session bitter with a mango, peach and tangerine finish.

Mutiny (OG 1042, ABV 4.2%)
A London porter with coffee and chocolate characteristics.

Blackjack (OG 1045, ABV 4.5%)
A complex stout fortified with fresh blackberries providing lasting fruit and chocolate characteristics.

Moondance (OG 1045, ABV 4.5%)
Wheat beer brewed with coriander and curacao oranges.

Oregon Gold (OG 1045, ABV 4.5%)
American-style pale ale with a melon aftertaste.

Passion (OG 1045, ABV 4.5%)
A refreshing golden ale infused with passion fruit.

Supernatural Blonde (OG 1045, ABV 4.5%)
Hoppy, thirst-quenching citrus pale ale.

Raspberry Tipple (OG 1048, ABV 4.8%)
Wheat beer infused with raspberries.

Strawberry Blonde (OG 1048, ABV 4.8%)
Wheat beer infused with strawberries.

Waverider (OG 1052, ABV 5.2%)
A complex West Coast-style IPA.

Shangri-la (OG 1067, ABV 6.7%)
A double IPA with a lingering grapefruit finish.

Young's

See Charles Wells (under W)

Yubberton

See North Cotswold

Zapato (NEW)

Correspondence: 2 Pollard Lane, Leeds, West Yorkshire, LS13 1EY ⊕ zapatobrewery.co.uk

Small company, established in 2016, that cuckoo brews in the Leeds area.

Zeitgeist

c/o Crown & Kettle, 2 Oldham Road, Manchester, M4 5FE ⊕ zeitgeistbrew.co.uk

Established in 2015, Zeitgeist is a small band of brewers cuckooing in breweries with spare capacity. Output is mainly bottled.

Zerodegrees SIBA

🏠 Blackheath: 29-31 Montpelier Vale, Blackheath, London, SE3 0TJ

Bristol: 53 Colston Street, Bristol, BS1 5BA ☎ (0117) 925 2706

Cardiff: 27 Westgate Street, Cardiff, CF10 1DD
☎ (029) 2022 9494

Reading: 9 Bridge Street, Reading, RG1 2LR ☎ (0118) 959 7959

Brewing started in 2000 in Blackheath, London and now four brewpubs are owned, each incorporating a state-of-the-art, computer-controlled, German plant producing unfiltered and unfined ales and lagers. All beers use natural ingredients, are suitable for vegetarians, and are served from tanks using air pressure (not CO2).

Zymurgorium

Unit 19, Irlam Business Centre, Soapstone Way, Irlam, M44 6RA ⊕ zymurgorium.com

The UK's first craft meadery and Manchester's first distillery. In combination with the brewery it was established in Irlam in 2013. Most of its output is in bottled form.

Closed breweries

The following breweries have closed, gone out of business or suspended operations since the 2017 Guide was published:

Acton, North Seaton, Northumberland
Adkin, Wantage, Oxfordshire
Ale House Rock, Peebles, Borders
Aleyard, Riddlesworth, Norfolk
Appleford, Brightwell-cum-Sotwell, Oxfordshire
Attwell's, St Nicholas at Wade, Kent
Baltic Fleet, Liverpool, Merseyside
Barkston, Barkston Ash, North Yorkshire
Beeches, Lochgelly, Kingdom of Fife
Bendigo, Nottinghamshire
Big Rabbit, Butterleigh, Devon
Big Shed, Shrewsbury, Shropshire
Bird Brain, Howden, East Yorkshire
Black Cat, Framfield, East Sussex
BlackBar, Harston, Cambridgeshire
Bloomsbury, WC1: Bloomsbury, Greater London
Blue Cow, South Witham, Lincolnshire
Blueball, Runcorn, Cheshire
Brandy Cask, Pershore, Worcestershire
Braunton, Braunton, Devon
Bryncelyn, Ystradgynlais, Mid Wales
Brythonic, St Briavels, Gloucestershire & Bristol
Bumpmill, Shirland, Derbyshire
Butcher's Dog, Driffield, East Yorkshire
Castle Combe, Preston, Wiltshire
Cathedral Heights, Bracebridge Heath, Lincolnshire
Collingham, Collingham, West Yorkshire
Combined Brewers, Falfield, Gloucestershire & Bristol
Compass, Carterton, Oxfordshire
Crane, Bristol, Gloucestershire & Bristol
Crooked Brook, Copthorne, West Sussex
Crystalbrew, Brough, East Yorkshire
Drink Up, Horwich, Greater Manchester
Erddig, Wrexham, North East Wales
Evesham, Evesham, Worcestershire
Fat Brewer, Crook, Durham
Fighting Cocks, Burnley, Lancashire
Freeminer, Cinderford, Gloucestershire & Bristol
Fulflood Arms, Winchester, Hampshire

Fulstow, Louth, Lincolnshire
Glenfinnan, Glenfinnan, Highlands & Western Isles
Glentworth, Skellow, South Yorkshire
Grafters, Willingham-by-Stow, Lincolnshire
Great Central, Leicester, Leicestershire
Hale's, Worksop, Nottinghamshire
Harthill Village, Harthill, South Yorkshire
Hedgedog, Virginia Water, Surrey
Hop Art, Liphook, Hampshire
Hop King, Reading, Berkshire
Hope Valley, Castleton, DerbyShire
Hops & Glory, N1: Islington, Greater London
Houston, Hillington, Greater Glasgow & Clyde Valley
Hunsbury Craft, East Hunsbury, Northamptonshire
Intrepid, Brough, Derbyshire
Isfield, Isfield, East Sussex
Jacobi, Pumsaint, West Wales
Jo C's, West Barsham, Norfolk
Kitchen Garden, Sheffield Park, East Sussex
Late Knights, SE20: Penge, Greater London
Lion's Tale, Cheswardine, Shropshire
Little Brew, York, North Yorkshire
Littlehampton, Littlehampton, West Sussex
Loch Ness, Drumnadrochit, Highlands & Western Isles
Long Lane, Appleby Magna, Leicestershire
Mulberry Duck, Burghill, Herefordshire
Naked Brewer, Westwood, Nottinghamshire
Ninety-Ninety, Kettleshulme, Cheshire
Norland, Blackshaw Head, West Yorkshire
North Curry, North Curry, Somerset
Oakleaf, Gosport, Hampshire
Otherton, Audley, Staffordshire
Pembrokeshire, Saundersfoot, West Wales

Pickled Pig, Staunton in the Vale, Nottinghamshire
Pocket, St Ouen: Jersey, Channel Islands
Porter, George N, Whitley Bay, Tyne & Wear
Quantum, Stockport, Greater Manchester
RCH, West Hewish, Somerset
Rotters, Talgarth, Mid Wales
Rtwo Dtoo, Urmston, Greater Manchester
Sacre Brew, Wolverhampton, West Midlands
Saxon City, Hereford, Herefordshire
Shoes, Norton Canon, Herefordshire
Sleaford, Sleaford, Lincolnshire
Tom Smith, Kettering, Northamptonshire
Songbird, Long Eaton, Derbyshire
Star, Market Deeping, Lincolnshire
Talke O' Th' Hill, Talke, Staffordshire
Tanners, Wiveliscombe, Somerset
Tap House, Smisby, Derbyshire
That Little, Harpenden, Hertfordshire
Tinshed, Kimbolton, Cambridgeshire
Towles', Bristol, Gloucestershire & Bristol
Tres Bien, Tur Langton, Leicestershire
Truefitt, Middlesbrough, North Yorkshire
Turners, Ringmer, East Sussex
Two Crowns, Sowerby Bridge, West Yorkshire
Usher's, Edinburgh, Edinburgh & the Lothians
Vagrant, Manchester, Greater Manchester
Verulam, St Albans, Hertfordshire
Waen, Llanidloes, Mid Wales
Wentwell, Derby, Derbyshire
Whistling Kite, Kettering, Northamptonshire
White Rose, Sheffield, South Yorkshire
Wilson Potter, Manchester, Greater Manchester
Wizard, Ilfracombe, Devon
Wollaton, Nottingham, Nottinghamshire
Wrekin, Telford, Shropshire

Future breweries

The following new breweries have been notified to the Guide and will start to produce beer during 2017/2018. In a few cases, they were in production during the summer of 2017 but were too late for a full listing:

3 Piers, Poulton-le-Fylde, Lancashire
71, Dundee, Tayside
Abyss, Lewes, East Sussex
Arbier, Jarrow, Tyne & Wear
Avid, Quernmore, Lancashire
Barrow Green, Oxted, Surrey
Bicester, Bicester, Oxfordshire
Black Mountain, Lisburn, Northern Ireland
Blimey!, Norwich, Norfolk
Bont, Bridgend, Glamorgan
Brew Toon, Peterhead, Aberdeen
BrewBoard, Cambridge, Cambridgeshire
Brewhouse & Kitchen, Lichfield, West Midlands
BrewIT, W1: Fitzrovia, Greater London
Campbells, Peebles, Edinburgh & the Lothians
Chicken Foot, Bonsall, Derbyshire
Crafty Little, Yorkshire
Derbyshire, Barlow, Derbyshire

Dronfield, Hollingwood, Derbyshire
Edinburgh Beer Factory, Edinburgh, Edinburgh & the Lothians
Ethical, Mauchline, Ayrshire & Arran
Fighting Cocks, St Albans, Hertfordshire
First & Last, Rochester, Northumberland
Five Arches, Darlington, Durham
Folkestone, Folkestone, Kent
Four Mice, Bolton-by-Bowland, Lancashire
Furnace, Derby, Derbyshire
Hop Forge, Lledrod, West Wales
Ignition, SE13: Lewisham, Greater London
Little Shed, Thorp Arch, West Yorkshire
Load of Hay, NW3: Haverstock Hill, Greater London
Loch Earn, St Fillans, Tayside
Margate, Margate, Kent
Mercian, Buxton, Derbyshire

Oxbrew, Enstone, Oxfordshire
Partridge, Chipping, Lancashire
Pit Top, Willimoteswick, Northumberland
Pitchfork, West Huish, Somerset
Prince of Ales, Broadlay, West Wales
Providence, Bamber Bridge, Lancashire
Ribble, Leyland, Lancashire
Roebuck, Draycott-in-the-Clay, Derbyshire
Saints Row, Darlington, Durham
Stow, Stow, Edinburgh & the Lothians
Three Legged Fox, Darlington, Durham
Tin Miner's, Philleigh, Cornwall
Vinyl Valley, Manchester, Greater Manchester
Winton, Pencaitland, Edinburgh & the Lothians
Woodbine, Waltham Abbey, Essex
Zepto, Caerphilly, Glamorgan

Places index

PLACES INDEX

Beers index

These beers refer to those in bold type in the breweries section (beers in regular production) and so therefore do not include seasonal, special or occasional beers that may be mentioned elsewhere in the text.

BEERS INDEX

Bluebird Premium XB Coniston *754*
Bluenette Church Hanbrewery *750*
Blues Rother Valley *905*
Boadicea Rother Valley *905*
Boar D'eau Slaughterhouse *918*
Boardwalk Kiln *835*
Boathouse City of Cambridge (Wolf) *966*
BOB (Best of Both) Shottle Farm *915*
BOB (Best Oxted Bitter) Oxted *881*
BOB Wickwar *962*
Bobbin's Bitter Three B's *934*
Bobby Dazzler Stables *922*
Bodacious Rivington *901*
Bodelwyddan Bitter North Wales *873*
Bodicacia Corinium *755*
Body Snatcher Beer Nouveau *710*
Bog Standard Bitter Big Bog *714*
Bog Super IPA Big Bog *714*
Bog Trotter Big Bog *714* Poachers *889*
Bohemian Hipster Mad Dog *852*
Boilers Golden Ale St Ives *908*
Boiling Well Ludlow *850*
Bollywood IPA Happy Valley *808*
Bolster's Blood Driftwood *771*
Bolt Head Summerskills *929*
Bolt Six O'Clock *917*
Boltmaker Timothy Taylor *932*
Bombardier Burning Gold Wells *957*
Bombardier Pale Ale Wells *957*
Bombardier Wells *957*
Bombay Honey Indian *827*
Bombay Social Angels & Demons *696*
Bomber Command Tom Herrick's *815*
Bomber County Tom Wood's *966*
Bomber's Blonde Martland Mill *856*
Bondi Blonde Stamps *923*
Bonneville Kelpaul *832*
Bonnie 'n' Clyde Loch Lomond *847*
Bonnie Hops LoveBeer *850*
Bonny's Gold Golden Triangle *795*
Bonum Mild Dow Bridge *769*
Boom! Holsworthy *819*
Boomer Three Fiends *935*
Boomslang Pale Recoil *896*
Boondoggle Ringwood *901*
Boosh Philsters *886*
Booskor Driftwood *771*
Bootle Bull Rock the Boat *903*
Booze Hound Gun Dog *804*
Border Bitter Untapped *950*
Border Steeans Beckstones *709*
Boris Citrov Sadler's *906*
Borrowdale Bitter Tirril *939*
Bosley Cloud Storm *926*
Botanic Kew *834*
Botany Bay Captain Cook *745*
Bottle Wreck Porter Hammerpot *807*
Bottlenose Bitter Speyside Craft *921*
Boudicea Kendricks *833*
Bourne Blonde FILO *783*
Bow Fiddle Blonde Speyside Craft *921*
Bowler Strong Ale Langton *839*
Boyo Cwm Rhondda *761*

BPM 4Four *690*
BQ Blonde Baa *702*
Bradford's Wrath Hedge Row *813*
Bradley's Finest Golden Black Country *717*
Braintree Market Ale Shalford *912*
Brake Neck Alechemy *693*
Brakspear Special Bell Street *711*
Bramber Downlands *769*
Bramling Cross Blackjack *720*
Bramling Tapped *930*
Brandeston Gold Earl Soham *773*
Brandy Snap Funfair *791*
Branoc Branscombe Vale *729*
Brass Hand Holler Boys *818*
Brathay Gold Barngates *706*
Brave Boss *725*
Braw Cross Borders *760*
Brawn Boss *725*
Brazilian Coffee & Vanilla Porter Colchester *754*
Bread & Butter Vocation *952*
Bread and Circuses Pale Chapter *748*
Breakfast Barum *706* Black Brook *717*
Brenin Enlli Llŷn *846*
Brenin Nant *867*
Brew 1 Gower *797*
Brew It Again Sam George Samuel *793*
Brew No. 1 Three Brothers *935*
Brew Springsteen Rock & Roll *902*
Brew.T Fish Key *784*
Brew York Brew York *730*
Brewards Droop IPA Dowr Kammel *770*
Brewed Awakening Cromarty *759*
Brewer's Dark Lees *841*
Brewer's Droop Brandon *728*
Brewer's Gold Broughton *736*
Brewers Gold Crouch Vale *760* Northallerton *873* Pictish *887*
Brewers Progress Tipples *939*
Brewers Reserve Kent *833*
Brewery Dug Arran *698*
Brewhouse Belgian Golden Ale St Ives *908*
Brewhouse Bell Saffron *907*
Brick Field Brown Five Points *785*
Bricks & Porter Kiln *835*
Brickworks Bitter Binghams *715*
Bridge Bitter Burton Bridge *739*
Bridge Street Bitter Green Dragon *801*
Bridgewater Blonde Lymm *851*
Bridgnorth Porter Hop & Stagger *820*
Bright Black Porter Salamander *909*
Bright Otter *880*
Brighton Belle Hammerpot *807*
Brighton Bier Brighton Bier *733*
Brill Gold Vale *951*
Brim Fell Hesket Newmarket *815*
Bristol Best Dawkins *764*
Bristol Blonde Dawkins *764*
Bristol Gold Dawkins *764*
Britannia Celebration Ale Evan Evans *778*
Britannia Navigation *868*
British Bulldog Westerham *958*
Broadland Sunrise Humpty Dumpty *824*

Broadside Adnams *692*
Broadsword Porter Robin Hood *902*
Broadsword George's *793*
Broadway Reel Ale Nottingham *874*
Brock Bitter Tring *944*
Brockville Dark Tryst *945*
Brockville Pale Tryst *945*
Brockwell IPA Canopy *744*
Brodie's Prime Hawkshead *812*
Broken Biscuit Broken Bridge *736*
Broken Dream Breakfast Stout Siren Craft *916*
Bronescombe's Vision Granite Rock *799*
Brooklyn Nights Hartshorns *810*
Broomsquire Patriot *884*
Brother Rabbit Thornbridge *934*
Brown Bitter Strands *926*
Brown Market Harborough *855*
Brownian Motion Hardknott *809*
Brown's Porter Church Farm *750*
Bruce Kennet & Avon *833*
Bruins Ruin Beartown *709*
The Bruiser Hogarths *818*
Brunette Baildon *703*
Buccaneer Mr Majolica *866*
Buckden Pike Yorkshire Dales *972*
Buckeye Session Bitter Unity Brew House *949*
Buckeye Rooster's *904*
Budding Stroud *927*
Buff Blindmans *721*
Buffalo Buffalo Dorking *768*
Built to Fall APA Marble *855*
Bukowski Three Fiends *935*
Bull Village Brewer (Hambleton) *807*
Bullet Tapped *931*
Bullion Bomb Hop Fuzz *820*
Bullion Nottingham *874* Old Mill *877*
Bullseye Langton *839*
Bumble's Honeyed Ale Ramsbottom Craft *894*
Bunny Chaser Longdog *848*
Bunny Hop Purity *892*
Bure Gold Woodforde's *967*
Burke's Special Wincle *964*
Burning Gull Ayr *702*
Burning House Madrigal *852*
Burrough Bitter Parish *883*
Burston's Cuckoo Elmtree *776*
Burton IPA Burton Town *740*
Burton Porter Burton Bridge *739*
Burton Snatch Fellows *782*
Business As Usual Derby *765*
Buster IPA Bowland *726*
Buster Muckle *866*
Butcher's Bitter Draycott (Derbyshire) *770*
Butchers Mitchell's Hop House *861*
Butter Tubs Yorkshire Dales *971*
Butts Pale Ale Ashover *700*
Butty Bach Wye Valley *969*
Buzzard Session Ale (BSA) Buzzard *741*
BVB Best Bitter Branscombe Vale *729*
Bwlch Passage Cold Black (Untapped) *950*
Bwncath Buzzard *741*
By George She's Got It George Samuel *793*

Cheshire Best Bitter Cheshire Brew Brothers 749
Cheshire Cat Weetwood 956
Cheshire Gap Cheshire Brewhouse 749
Cheshire Gold Coach House 752
Cheshire IPA Dunham Massey 772
Cheshire Set Cheshire Brewhouse 749
Chester Gold Cheshire Brew Brothers 749
Chesterfield Best Bitter Spire 921
Chestnut Burton Old Cottage 740
Chestnuts Roasting Landlord's Friend 839
Cheswold Doncaster 768
Chief Jester Farr Brew 781
Chief Green Mill 801
Chieftain Celt Experience (Evan Evans) 778
Chieftains Export Burnside 739
Chiffchaff Digfield 767
Chillen Rivington 901
Chilli Beer North Wales 873
Chilli Hopstar 822
Chinook Blonde Goose Eye 797
Chinook & Grapefruit Bollington 723
Chinook Pale Poynton 891
Chinook Two Roses 947
Chirk Castle Cold Black (Rhymney) 900
Chockwork Orange Brentwood 730
Chococino Dark Beer Pitfield (Dominion) 767
Chocolate Cherry Mild Dunham Massey 772
Chocolate Nutter Why Not 961
Chocolate Orange Delight Downton 770
Chocolate Orange Stout Amber 695
Moonshine 864
Chocolate Porter Beer Brothers 710
Ramsbottom Craft 894
Chocolate Stout MASH 856
Stubborn Mule 928
Xtreme 970
Chocolate & Vanilla Stout Titanic 940
Chonkin Feckle Martland Mill 856
Chopper Great Heck 799
Christies Golden Ale Mauldons 857
Christmas in July Draycott (Derbyshire) 770
Christopher Great Heck 799
Chronicle High Weald 816
Chuckle Muckle 866
Church Key Trinity Ales 944
Church Ledge Noss Beer Works 874
Churches Pale Ale FILO 783
Churchillian Stout Weltons 957
Churchyard Oatmeal Stout Hoxne 823
Chwaden Aur Nant 867
Circuit Bitter Castle Combe (Flying Monk) 786
Ciste Dhubh Plockton 889
Citadel Clun 752
Citra IPA Franklins 788
Citra Nova Durham 772

Citra Pale Ale North Riding (Brewery) 873
Citra Pale Poynton 891
Saltaire 909
Citra Plus Hopcraft (Pixie Spring/ Hopcraft) 888
Citra Star Anarchy 696
Citra Storm Deeply Vale 764
Citra Tip Double Top 768
Citra Ambridge 695
Brodie's 735
CITRA Dove Street 769
Citra Hart 810
Hop Back 820
Isca 828
Oakham 875
Saffron 907
Scarborough 910
Urban Island 950
Citropolis Golden Triangle 795
Citrus Gold Yaarbrew 970
Citrus Pale Ale Lakehouse 838
Citrus Snap Green Mill 801
City Gold Golden Triangle 795
Civitas Derventio 765
Clachertyfarlie Fintry 783
Clansman Ale Hebridean 813
Claridges Crystal Nobby's 872
Clash Porter Revolutions 899
Claspers Citra Blonde Great North Eastern 800
Classic Blonde Clark's 751
Classic Dark Mild Milestone 860
Classic English Ale 3 Brewers of St Albans 689
Classic Gold Great Western 801
Classic IPA Silverstone 916
Classic Old Ale Hepworth 814
Classic Porter Matlock Wolds Farm 857
Classic Kingstone 836
Claudia Moor 864
Claverhouse Strathaven 927
Cleadale 80/- Laig Bay 838
Clear Cut Geeves 792
Clearwater Pale Ale Axholme 701
Clearwater Pale Credence 759
Cleddau Gold Little Dragon 844
Cleethorpes Pale Ale Axholme 701
Cleopatra Derventio 765
Cleric's Cure Three Tuns 936
Clever Fellow Fellows 782
Clever Girl Errant 778
ClIPAty Hop Coach House 753
Clipper IPA Broughton 736
Clippings IPA Flipside 786
Clock Brew Eden St Andrews 774
Clocker Stout Tractor Shed 943
Clogmaker Martland Mill 856
Clogwyn Gold Conwy 755
Clotworthy Dobbin Whitewater 961
Cloud Nine Six Bells 917
Cloudburst Winter's 965
Cloudy Wheat Beer Beer Brothers 710
Clout Stout Clouded Minds 752
Club Bitter Concertina 754
Club Hammer Stout Pope's Yard 890
Cluckstar Mouselow Farm 866
Clun Pale Clun 752
Clwyd Gold Facer's 780
Clyde Puffer Arran 698

Clydesdale Strathaven 927
Coachman's Best Bitter Coach House 752
Coachmans Whip St Judes 908
Coal Aston Porter Drone Valley 771
Coalface Firebrick 783
Coaltown Coffee Stout Backyard 703
Coast to Coast Hadrian Border 805
The Coaster Platform 5 889
Cob Tomos A Lilford 941
Cobb Lyme Regis 850
Cobbett's Botley 725
Cobbler's Ale Phipps 886
Cobnut Kent 833
Cock 'n' Bull Story Concrete Cow 754
Cock-A-Snook Isla Vale 829
Cocker Hoop Jennings 831
Cocket Hat Brew Shed 730
Cockleboats George's 793
Cocky IPA Piddle 887
Coco le Ram Hooded Ram 819
Coco Loco Grafton 798
Coconut Porter Burning Soul 739
Coconut Shy PA Idle Valley 826
Code Black Hardknott 809
Coffee & Star Anise Porter Ticketybrew 937
Coffee Stout Binghams 715
Coffin Lane Stout Ashover 700
Coggeshall Gold Red Fox 897
Cold Bath Gold Harrogate 810
Coldharbour Hell Yeah Lager Clarkshaws 751
Coldharbour Untapped 950
Colin Brown Ale Hamelsworde 807
Collaborator Heavy Industry 813
Collapsed Front Row 789
Colley's Dog Tring 944
Colliers Clog Worsthorne 968
Collingwood Wylam 969
Collision ESB (Extra Special Belgian) Blackened Sun 720
Collision Pilsner Recoil 896
Collusion Surrey Hills 929
Columbus Brown Doghouse 767
Columbus IPA Durham 773
Columbus Bottle Brook 725
Comanche Errant 778
Comet Newby Wyke 871
Comfortably Numb BAD 703
Commando Hoofing Cotleigh 756
Common PA Wimbledon 963
Commonside Pale Ale Belleville 712
CommRed Edinbrew 774
Complete Muppetry Two Towers 948
Comrade Bill Bartram's Egalitarian Anti Imperialist Soviet Stout Bartrams 706
Conclusion Axiom 701
The Cone Top Out 941
Confidence Moor 864
Conger Tun Ale Cheshire Brewhouse 749
Congo Driftwood Dancing Man 762
Conkerwood Lord Conrad's 849
Conqueror Windsor & Eton 964
Conqueror's Premium Bitter Haresfoot 809
Conquest Battle 707
Conscript Twisted 946

Damson Porter 8 Sail 690
  Burton Bridge 739
Dancing Dragonfly Pheasantry 886
Dandelion & Burdock North
  Wales 873
Dane'ish Cheshire Brewhouse 749
Dangerously Dark Happy
  Valley 808
Danish Dynamite Stonehenge 925
Daracha Inveralmond 828
Dark 'n' Cloudy Broughton 736
Dark Alchemy Atom 701
Dark Ale Archerfield (Knops) 838
  Pheasantry 886
  Roundhill 905
  Tremethick 943
Dark Alliance Moor 864
Dark Arts Magic Rock 853
Dark Beacons Brecon 729
Dark & Bitter Gyle 59 804
Dark Bomb Holsworthy 819
Dark Brown Ale Tyne Bank 948
Dark Burton Ale Burton Town 740
Dark Delight Downton 770
Dark Denomination Flipside 786
Dark Destroyer CrackleRock 757
Dark Drake Dancing Duck 762
Dark Dunter Broughton 736
Dark Energy Hardknott 809
Dark Forest Rockingham 904
Dark Fox Hornes 823
Dark Heart Mantle 855
  Yorkshire Heart 972
Dark Hopfler Weird Beard 956
Dark Horse Milk Stout GT 804
Dark Horse Stout Elmtree 776
Dark Horse Barlow 705
  Belvoir 712
  Born in the Borders 724
  Hepworth 814
  Maldon 853
  Nene Valley 869
Dark Island Orkney 880
Dark Knight Hopstar 822
  Independent Lakeland
  (Strands) 926
Dark Lane Porter Castle Combe
  (Flying Monk) 786
Dark Magic Merlin 858
Dark Masquerade Half Moon 806
Dark Matter VOG 952
Dark Mild 3 Brewers of St
  Albans 689
  Bank Top 704
  Foxfield 788
  Golcar 795
  Highgate (Blue Bear) 721
  Timothy Taylor 932
Dark Moor Kelburn 832
Dark Munro Swannay 929
Dark & Mysterious Thorley &
  Sons 934
Dark Night Southport 920
Dark Nirvana Pokertree 890
Dark Peak Stout Raw 895
Dark Peak Howard Town 823
Dark Porter Fuddy Duck 790
Dark Raven Beowulf 712
Dark Ruby Mild Consall Forge 755
  Sarah Hughes 824
Dark Ruby Dhillon's 766
Dark Rum Blackedge 720
Dark Seam Black Paw 719
Dark Secret Monty's 863
Dark Side of the Wight Yates' 971

Dark Side Poynton 891
  Spire 921
  Three Fiends 935
Dark Spartan Stout Parker 883
Dark Star Porter Stratford Upon
  Avon 927
Dark Times Hafod 805
Dark Wheat Beer Beer
  Brothers 710
Dark Wing Olde Potting Shed 878
Dark Arran 698
  Brains 727
  Dow Bridge 769
  Ledbury 841
  Moles 862
  Northallerton 873
  Rhymney 900
  River Leven 901
  Three Legs 936
Darkest Devon Exe Valley 778
Darkest Hour S&P 906
Darkest Ennerdale 777
Darkness Exeter 779
DarkNESS Loch Ness
  (Cairngorm) 743
Darkroom Anstey 697
Darkside of the Toon Three
  Kings 935
Darkside Stout Brightside 733
Darkside Bartrams 706
  Shortts 915
Darling Buds Warwickshire 954
Dartford Wobbler Millis (Dartford
  Wobbler) 861
Darwins Origin Salopian 909
Dashingly Dark Derby 765
Dave Great Heck 799
David's Not So Bitter Spey
  Valley 921
Davy's Lamp Merry Miner 859
Dawlish Bitter Isca 828
Dawlish Pale Isca 829
Dawlish Summer Isca 828
Dawn Stealer Staggeringly
  Good 923
Dawn Til Dusk Saffron 907
Dawn's Autumn Gold Hay
  Rake 812
Dawn's Called Thyme Hay
  Rake 812
Dawn's Dark Side Hay Rake 812
Dawn's Hopping Mad Hay
  Rake 812
Daymer Extra Pale Harbour 808
Dazed & Confused BAD 703
Dazzle Rock the Boat 903
Dazzler IPA Littleover 845
DB One Dorking 768
DBA Cheshire Brewhouse 749
DCUK Dancing Duck 762
De La Creme Mad Squirrel 852
De Lovetot Dukeries 772
Dead Beard IPA Hairy Brewers 806
Dead Man's Fist Smoked Porter
  Chapter 748
Dead Pony BrewDog 731
Deadbeat Peerless 884
Death or Glory Tring 944
Death Valley Pentrich 885
Debonair Hophurst 822
Decadence Stout Weird Beard 956
Decadence Brewster's 732
Deception Abbeydale 691
Deckhand Windmill 964
Deep Porter New Plassey 870

Deep Black Rock 719
Deeply Blonde Deeply Vale 764
Deeply Red Deeply Vale 764
Deer Beer Dunham Massey 772
Deerstalker Ramsbury 894
Defender Oatmeal IPA Hoxne 823
Deja Brewed Snaggletooth 919
Delank Dynamite Dowr
  Kammel 770
Delapre Dark Great Oakley 800
Deliverance Cambrinus (Liverpool
  Organic) 846
  Neath 868
Dengie Best Wibblers 961
Dengie Dark Wibblers 961
Dengie Gold Wibblers 961
Dengie IPA Wibblers 961
Dennis Mitchell's Hop House 862
  S&P 906
Denver Diamond Two Rivers 947
Deputy Drop Merry Miner 859
Derbyshire Classic Marlpool 856
Dere Street Mithril 862
Desert Storm Storm 926
Detention Old School 878
Deuchars IPA Caledonian 743
Devereaux Porter St Judes 908
Deviant Dark Revolution 763
The Devil Made Me Brew It
  Arbor 697
Devil's Elbow Hexhamshire 816
Devil's Jump Dowr Kammel 770
Devil's Rest IPA Burning Sky 739
Devils Dyke Porter Downlands 769
Devils Dyke Salted Caramel
  Downlands 769
Devils Whiskers Hairy Brewers 806
Devil's Water Hexhamshire 816
Devon Amber Salcombe 909
Devon Darter Clearwater 751
Devon Dew Summerskills 928
Devon Dreamer Hunters 824
Devon Dumpling Bays 708
Devon Dympsy Clearwater 751
Devon Earth Devon Earth 766
Devon Frost Summerskills 929
Devon Glory Exe Valley 779
Devon Maid Forge 787
Devon Pale Isca 829
Devon Pride South Hams 920
Devonshire Pale Ale Black Tor 719
Dewhopper Cask Lager
  Norfolk 872
Dewi Sant Neath 868
Dexter Storm 926
DHB (Dave's Hoppy Beer)
  Facer's 780
Diablo Summer Wine 928
Diamond Ale Phipps 886
Diamond Black Stout Chantry 747
Diamond Geezer By The Horns 741
Diamond Lil Two Cocks 947
Diawl Bach Heavy Industry 813
Dibber Shed 913
Dick Turpin Coach House 753
Dick's Extraordinary Bitter Nene
  Valley 869
Dickie MiG Langwith 840
Difference Engineer Thousand
  Trades 934
Dig It Shed 913
Diggers Gold Grey Trees 803
Dilks Shottle Farm 915
Dinefer Porter Tydwals 948
Dinner Ale Bollington 723

Gladstone Strong Ale
Townhouse *943*
Glasney College Porter Granite
Rock *799*
Glass Blower Philsters *886*
Glen Top Bitter Rossendale *904*
Glencoe Black Wolf *719*
Glog Twt Lol *948*
Glorious Devon Isca *828*
Glory Yeovil *971*
Glott's Hop Howard Town *823*
Glyder Fawr Cold Black
(Rhymney) *900*
Goat's Leap Cheddar *749*
Goats Milk Church End *750*
Gobble Great Oakley *800*
Gobbolino By The Mile *742*
Goblin Tower Denbigh *764*
God's Twisted Sister Twisted
Barrel *946*
An Gof Lizard *846*
Going Off Half-Cocked
Bespoke *713*
Going Underground Merry
Miner *859*
Gold Beacons Brecon *729*
Gold Bullion Camerons *743*
Gold Digger Bank Top *704*
Gold Dust Born in the Borders *724*
Gold Hill Keystone *835*
Gold Muddler Andwells *696*
Gold Pale Ale Farmageddon *781*
Littleover *845*
Gold Rush CrackleRock *757*
Dynamite Valley *773*
Lenton Lane *842*
Pin-Up *888*
Prospect *892*
Gold Star Blonde Shipstone's *914*
Gold Star Strong Ale Goacher's *794*
Gold Star Phipps *886*
Silhill *916*
Gold Tankard Wylam *969*
Gold Top Old Dairy *877*
Gold Wing Independent Lakeland
(Strands) *926*
Gold Atlantic *700*
Backyard *703*
Batemans *707*
Bays *708*
Bowland *726*
Brentwood *730*
Brewsmith *732*
Butcombe *741*
Cader *742*
Chalk Hill *747*
Corinium *755*
Dancing Duck *762*
Derventio *765*
Donnington *768*
Eden *774*
Exmoor *779*
FILO *783*
Four Kings *787*
Gloucester *794*
Gower *797*
Great North Eastern *800*
Green Dragon *801*
Green Mill *801*
Hop Studio *821*
Horbury *822*
Isca *828*
Keswick *834*
Kingstone *836*
Ledbury *841*

Ludlow *850*
Lytham *851*
Mersea Island *859*
Moles *862*
Mumbles *867*
Naylor's *868*
Old Sawley *878*
Quirky *893*
Ramsbury *894*
Riviera *901*
Rock Solid *902*
Romney Marsh *904*
Salcombe *909*
Snowhill *919*
Southwark *921*
Stod Fold *925*
Swan *929*
Tatton *931*
Titan *939*
Wensleydale *958*
Williams Bros *963*
Wobbly *965*
Worcestershire *968*
Worsthorne *968*
Golden Acre Bexley *714*
Golden Ale Ampthill *695*
Anglesey *697*
Archerfield (Knops) *838*
Black Hole *717*
Britman *735*
Brockley *735*
Cellar Head *747*
Chadlington *747*
Hackney *805*
Hop Yard (Westerham) *959*
Isca *828*
Lister's *844*
Malt *854*
McColl's *851*
Ouseburn Valley *881*
St Peter's *908*
Tankleys *930*
Tavy *931*
Watling Street *954*
Wye Valley *969*
Yates *971*
Golden Amber Atlas (Orkney) *880*
Golden Anchor Navigation *868*
Golden Apostle Wessex *958*
Golden Archer Robin Hood *902*
Golden Arrow Double Top *768*
Golden Bear Warwickshire *954*
Golden Best Green Jack *801*
Jolly Boys *831*
Timothy Taylor *932*
Golden Bine Ballard's *703*
Golden Bitter Ale Gwaun
Valley *804*
Golden Bitter Gorgeous Beer *797*
Ticketybrew *937*
Golden Bolt Box Steam *727*
Golden Braid Hopdaemon *821*
Golden Bud Brampton *728*
Golden Buzzard Buzzard *741*
Golden Cascade Fuzzy Duck *791*
Golden Chalice Glastonbury *794*
Golden Citrus Turpin *945*
Golden Cock Simpsons *916*
Golden Cow Strathcarron *927*
Golden Crown Idle *826*
Golden Dawn Red Kite *897*
Golden Delicious Burton
Bridge *739*
Golden Duck Mallard *854*

Golden English Ale 3 Brewers of St
Albans *689*
Golden Fiddle Branscombe
Vale *729*
Golden Fleece Cotswold Lion *757*
Dent *765*
Golden Fox B&T *702*
Golden Gauntlet Castle *745*
Golden Glow Holden's *818*
Golden Goose Goose Eye *797*
Golden Gosling Mouselow
Farm *866*
Golden Gozzard Barn Owl *705*
Golden Grains Bournemouth *726*
Golden Hinde Coastal *753*
Golden Hop Shardlow *912*
Golden Hour Fisher's *784*
Golden IPA Mad Cat *852*
Golden Jackal Wolf *966*
Golden Lance Keltek *832*
Golden Newt Elgood's *775*
Golden Pale Ale Dhillon's *766*
Elmtree *776*
Golden Panther Panther *882*
Golden Pheasant Old
Chimneys *876*
Golden Pig Country Life *757*
Golden Pixie Pixie Spring/
Hopcraft *888*
Golden Plover Allendale *694*
Golden Poacher Longdog *848*
Golden Rule Bespoke *713*
Tonbridge *941*
Golden Salamander
Salamander *909*
Golden Sands Southport *920*
Golden Seahawk Cotleigh *756*
Golden Sheep Black Sheep *719*
Golden Shot Range *895*
Golden Sovereign Flipside *786*
Golden Spring Blindmans *721*
Golden State Black Brook *717*
Golden Thread Salopian *909*
Golden Torc Boudicca *725*
Golden Vale Deeply Vale *764*
Golden Venture Druid *771*
Golden Wander Hop & Stagger *820*
Golden Warrior Empire *776*
Golden Wellingtons George
Samuel *793*
Golden Wobbler Millis (Dartford
Wobbler) *861*
Golden X Burnside *739*
Golden XPA Caledonian *743*
Golden Bedlam *709*
Winter's *965*
Yates' *971*
Goldi-hops Bond Brews *723*
Goldie Hops Black Bear *716*
Goldie Yubberton (North
Cotswold) *872*
Goldihops Kelburn *832*
Golding Delicious Isla Vale *829*
Goldings Leatherbritches *841*
Goldy Locks Blonde Bingley *716*
Golgotha Wantsum *954*
Gollop With Zest Froth
Blowers *789*
Gone Fishing ESB Green Jack *801*
Gone for a Burton Tower *942*
Good Evening Goody *796*
Good Health Goody *796*
Good Heavens Goody *796*
Good Knight Felstar *782*
Good Life Goody *796*

Good Old Boy West Berkshire *958*
Good Ordinary Bitter
  Greyhound *803*
Good Sheppard Goody *796*
The Good Stuff Edinbrew *774*
Goodens Gold Flowerpots *786*
Goodhew's Dry Stout
  Barngates *706*
Goodness Gracious Me Goody *797*
Gordon Bennett Belvoir *712*
Gorge Best Cheddar *748*
Gorgon's Alive Clarkshaws *751*
Gorlovka Imperial Stout
  Acorn *691*
Gosforth Gold Drone Valley *771*
Goshawk Blackpit *721*
Gospel Oak Star Wing *923*
The Governor Lees *841*
Gozzard's Guzzler Barn Owl *705*
The Grace Sulwath *928*
Graffiti IPA Firebrand
  (Altarnun) *694*
Graham's McCanns (Angels &
  Demons) *696*
Grainger Ale Hadrian Border *805*
Grand Porter Brighton Bier *733*
Grand Prix Prescott *891*
Grandstand Bitter
  Twickenham *946*
Granny Wouldn't Like It Wolf *966*
Grantham Stout Oldershaw *879*
Grapefruit Beer St Peter's *908*
Grapefruit IPA Incredible *826*
  Vine Inn *952*
Grapeshot Cannon Royall *744*
Grapevine Fallen *780*
Grasmere Gold Tirril *939*
Grasmoor Dark Ale Cumbrian
  Legendary *761*
Grasshopper Kentish Bitter
  Westerham *958*
Gravediggers Ale Church End *750*
Graveyard Eyes Hopcraft (Pixie
  Spring/Hopcraft) *888*
Gravitas Vale *951*
Great Bustard Stonehenge *925*
Great Expectations Oldershaw *879*
Great Raft Bitter Old
  Chimneys *876*
Great Tom Mild One Mile End *879*
Great Tom Lincolnshire *843*
Great White Hawkshead *812*
Green Bullet Pale Ale Thirst
  Class *933*
Green Bullet Strands *926*
Green Daemon Hopdaemon *821*
Green Hop Holsworthy *819*
Green Hopped IPA Ripple
  Steam *901*
Greenfield Greenfield *802*
Greenmantle Broughton *736*
Greensand IPA Surrey Hills *929*
Greenstede High Weald *816*
Greet Ale Mallard *853*
Grey Ghost IPA Raw *895*
Grey Heart Hale's (Grafton) *798*
Greyfriars Stout Richmond *900*
Griffin IPA Reedley Hallows *899*
Griffin Brampton *728*
Griffin's Irish Stout Hill Island *817*
The Grifter Hopjacker *822*
Grip Yorkshire Ale Revolutions *899*
Grized Ale Tarn Hows *931*
Ground Breaker Uttoxeter *951*
Grounded Devon Earth *766*

Grumpy Bastard Brandon *728*
Guardian of the Forest Totally
  Brewed *942*
Guardian Cold Black
  (Rhymney) *900*
Guardsman Windsor & Eton *964*
Gubbins Lord Conrad's *849*
Guerrilla Blue Monkey *722*
Guid Ale Arran *698*
Guilsborough Gold Nobby's *872*
Guilsborough Guzzler Nobby's *872*
Guinea Guzzler Millis (Dartford
  Wobbler) *860*
Gulf Stream Golden Ale
  Portpatrick *890*
Gulp IPA Milk Street *860*
Gulping Fellow Fellows *782*
Gumption Wishbone *965*
Gun Dog Bitter Northallerton *873*
Gun Dog Teignworthy *932*
Gunderson Twisted Barrel *946*
Gunhild Fownes *787*
Gunner Boyce Stocklinch *924*
Gunner's Daughter Old
  Cannon *876*
Gunners Gold Loose Cannon *849*
Gunpowder Mild Coach House *752*
Gunslinger Tombstone *940*
Gunsmoke Dukeries *772*
Gurt Stout Cerne Abbas *747*
Guthlac's Porter Golcar *795*
Guzzler York *971*
Gwaf Tan Tintagel *938*
Gwydion Lleu *846*
Gylla's Gold Small Paul's *918*
Gypsy Queen Baltic Porter
  Moonchild *863*

H

H:E Hafod *805*
H!PA Helmsley *814*
Ha'Penny Mild Harwich Town *811*
Habit Flying Monk *786*
Hackney Blonde Tollgate *940*
Hackney Red IPA Brodie's *736*
Hades Epicurus *778*
Hafren Three Shires *936*
Hail Merri Merrimen *858*
Hair of the Dog Hairy Brewers *805*
  Pennine *885*
Hair of the Doug LoveBeer *850*
Hairy Helmet Leatherbritches *841*
Haka Slater's *918*
Halcyon Daze Burton Old
  Cottage *740*
  Gyle 59 *804*
Haley's Comet Hamelsworde *807*
Half Bore Hunters *824*
Half Centurion Kinver *836*
Half Nelson Papworth *882*
Halfway to Heaven Langham *839*
Halo Pale Rossendale *904*
Halo Cross Bay *759*
Halt Hilden *816*
Hameldon Bitter Rossendale *904*
Hammer Hafod *805*
Hammerstone IPA Bluestone
  (Pembrokeshire) *722*
Hampshire Bitter Botley *725*
Hampshire Rose Itchen Valley *830*
Hancock's HB Brains *728*
Handliner Coastal *753*
Handsome Forge *787*

Hang Ten Tamarin Surfing
  Monkey *929*
Hanged Man Madrigal *853*
Hanged Monk Tipples *938*
Hanging Stone Ilkley *826*
Hank Tiny Rebel *937*
Hansom Ale Elliswood *775*
Happy Chappy Cromarty *759*
Harbinger Branscombe Vale *729*
Harbour Special Tintagel *938*
Harbourside Light Ale St Ives *908*
Hares Hopping Two Rivers *947*
Harlech Castle Cold Black
  (Rhymney) *900*
Harley Welbeck Abbey *956*
Harlot Kendricks *833*
Harpers Great Oakley *800*
Harrier Bitter Thames Side *933*
Harrier Cotleigh *756*
Harry Hop McCanns (Angels &
  Demons) *696*
Harry's Heifer Church Farm *750*
Hartington Bitter Whim *959*
Hartington IPA Whim *959*
Hartland Blonde Forge *787*
Harts No. 1 Hart Family *810*
Harts No. 3 Hart Family *810*
Harts No. 8 Hart Family *810*
Harts No. 9 Hart Family *810*
Harvard Southwark *921*
Harvest Home Red Rye
  Moonchild *863*
Harvest Moon Mild
  Moonshine *864*
Harvest Moon Ulverston *949*
Harvest Pale Castle Rock *746*
Harvest Sun Williams Bros *963*
Haseley Gold Philsters *886*
Hat Trick IPA Muirhouse *867*
Havana Moon Red Star *897*
Havelock IPA Lord's *849*
Haven Bude *737*
Havok Big Hand *714*
Hay Tomos A Lilford *941*
Haystacks Hesket Newmarket *815*
Hazelnut Milk Stout Little
  Critters *844*
Hazelnutter Clouded Minds *752*
HBA Hattie Brown's *811*
HBB Hogs Back *818*
HCL Hillside *817*
Head East Strathbraan *927*
Head Otter *881*
Headland Red Wold Top *966*
Headlander Southbourne *920*
Headless RedWillow *898*
Headmaster Old School *878*
Heanor Pale Ale Bottle Brook *725*
Heart & Soul Vocation *952*
Heart Quartz *893*
Hearty Bitter Yorkshire Heart *972*
Heath Robinson Barlow *705*
Heather Honey Black Isle *718*
Heaton Rifles Stockport *925*
Heavenly Blonde Oldershaw *878*
Heavenly Matter Moonshine *864*
Heavy Lifting Holler Boys *818*
Heavy Cross Borders *759*
Hebden's Wheat Little Valley *845*
Hedge Hop Flack Manor *785*
Hedge Hopper RAN *895*
Hedge Monkey Glastonbury *794*
HedgeHopper Mobberley *862*
Hedgerow Hop Lord Conrad's *849*
Hedone Saison Blackened Sun *720*

Hedonism Potbelly *891*
Heel Stone Stonehenge *925*
Hefeweizen Geipel *793*
Heisenberg's Principle Draycott
   (Derbyshire) *770*
Helix Gene Pool *793*
Hellfire Corner Breakwater *729*
Hellhound IPA Clarkshaws *751*
Helvellyn Gold Hesket
   Newmarket *815*
Hen Harrier Bowland *726*
Henchman Broken Bridge *736*
Hengist Wantsum *954*
Henrietta Welbeck Abbey *956*
Henry Tudor Battlefield
   (Tunnel) *945*
Heresy Bishop Nick *716*
Heritage Trail Ale Lymm *851*
Heritage XX Firebird *783*
Heritage Three Castles *935*
Heroes Bitter Beowulf *713*
Heron Ale Thames Side *933*
Heron Porter Two Roses *947*
Herr Keith Keith *831*
Hetton Hare-raiser Hetton
   Law *815*
Hetton Harlot Hetton Law *815*
Hetton Harvest Hetton Law *815*
Hetton Howler Hetton Law *815*
Hetton Pale Ale Dark Horse *763*
Hex Six Hop IPA Revolutions *899*
Hey Blondie Cap House *744*
Hibiscus Market Harborough *855*
High 5 Thirst Class *933*
High & Dry Urban Island *950*
High Fives Willy Good Ale *963*
High Light Trinity Ales *944*
High Pike Hesket Newmarket *815*
High Rise London Brewing *847*
High Street Bitter Tollgate *940*
High Wire Magic Rock *853*
Highgate Hartshorns *810*
Highland IPA Cairngorm *743*
Highlander Fyne *791*
Highway 51 Rooster's *904*
Highwayman Buntingford *738*
Hill Climb Prescott *891*
Hillfoot Best Bitter Blue Bee *721*
Hindsight Hybrid *825*
Hinkypunk Big Bog *714*
Hip Hop Ards *698*
   Fish Key *784*
   Langham *839*
Hippy Chick Hybrid *825*
Hirondelle Coffee Milk Stout
   Arundel *699*
Hit the Lip Cromarty *759*
Hitched Plockton *893*
HMS Minnow Breakwater *729*
The Hoard Backyard *702*
Hob Bitter Hoskins Brothers
   (Belvoir) *712*
Hobby Horse Rhymney *900*
Hobgoblin Gold Wychwood *969*
Hobgoblin Wychwood *969*
Hobson's Choice City of Cambridge
   (Wolf) *966*
Hockerley Hole Southern Red
   Whaley Bridge *959*
Hockley Gold Two Towers *948*
Hockley Soul McCanns (Angels &
   Demons) *696*
The Hoff Westwood *959*
Hogget Cotswold Lion *757*
Hogsgate Austendyke *701*

Hogshead Cotswold Pale Ale
   Uley *949*
Holbeach High Street
   Austendyke *701*
Holcombe White Isca *829*
Holderness Dark Great
   Newsome *799*
Hole Hearted Fallen Acorn *780*
Holy Cow Born in the Borders *724*
   Bridgehouse *733*
Holy Grail Black Sheep *719*
Holy Ground Worcester *968*
Holy Joe Yates' *971*
Holy Smoke Beerblefish *710*
Honey Bee Three B's *934*
Honey Blond Liverpool Organic *846*
Honey Blonde Downton *770*
Honey Bunny Ambridge *695*
Honey Buzzard Cotleigh *756*
Honey Dragon Middle Earth *859*
Honey Fayre Conwy *755*
Honey Panther Panther *882*
Honey Heathen *813*
   Helmsley *814*
Honeydo Tindall *938*
Honeyfuggle Cornish Crown *756*
Honeyfuzz Rother Valley *905*
Honeypot Bitter Coach House *752*
Honeypot Pale Landlocked *839*
Honeysuckle Smash Three
   Brothers *935*
Hood Cannon Royall *744*
   Lincoln Green *843*
Hook Island Red Five Points *785*
Hooky Gold Hook Norton *820*
Hooky Mild Hook Norton *819*
Hooky Hook Norton *819*
Hop A Doodle Doo Brewster's *732*
Hop Black Wibblers *961*
Hop Bomb Sadler's *906*
Hop Britannia Treboom *943*
Hop Devil Rockingham *903*
Hop Festival Top-Notch *941*
Hop Fusion Maypole *857*
Hop Garden Gold Hogs Back *818*
Hop Gear Co Pilot *752*
Hop & Glory Brew Foundation *730*
   Craddock's *757*
   Hubsters *824*
Hop on the Good Foot
   Hubsters *824*
Hop Hop Hooray Opa Hay's *879*
Hop Kick Mumbles *867*
Hop Lobster Golden Triangle *795*
Hop Mama Hubsters *824*
Hop Market Pope's *890*
Hop the Mayflower
   Worsthorne *968*
Hop Monster Coastal *753*
   Exit 33 *779*
Hop Pocket 1648 *689*
Hop Rocket India Pale Ale
   Westerham *959*
Hop on the Run Holsworthy *819*
Hop Salvo Sandiway *910*
Hop Schism Sandiway *910*
Hop Secret Sandiway *910*
Hop Sepia Sandiway *910*
Hop Till You Drop Derby *765*
Hop Tipple Crafty Brewing *758*
Hop Token: Amarillo Adur *692*
Hop Token: Summit Adur *692*
Hop Trial Tryst *945*
Hop Troll Tillingbourne *938*
Hop Twister Salopian *909*

Hop & Under Trinity *944*
HoP Blackedge *720*
Hop On Kings Clipstone *835*
   Langton *839*
Hop-trotter Potbelly *890*
Hop2It Fish Key *784*
Hopadelic Willy Good Ale *963*
Hope & Glory Brentwood *730*
   Pope's *890*
HOPeration IPA Arkell's *698*
Hopfather Oxted *881*
The Hopfather Wye Valley *969*
Hopfest Mad Squirrel *852*
Hophead Brewster's *732*
   Dark Star *763*
HoPink Mad Spire *921*
Hopleaf Buffy's *738*
Hopler Effect Heathen *813*
Hoplite Derventio *765*
Hopnosis Hopshackle *822*
   South Hams *920*
Hopopotamus Broughton *736*
Hopper Hafod *805*
Hoppers Ale Rother Valley *905*
Hoppily Ever After Magpie *853*
Hoppin Buzzard Buzzard *741*
Hoppin' Robin Rockin' Robin *903*
Hoppiness Moor *864*
Hopping Mad Isla Vale *829*
Hopping Toad Castor *746*
Hopping Baa *702*
Hoppit Loddon *847*
Hopposites Attract Way
   Outback *955*
Hoppy as Funk Chapel-en-le-
   Frith *748*
Hoppy Birthday Ampthill *695*
Hoppy Couple IPA Thirst Class *933*
Hoppy Daze Kirrie *837*
   Poynton *891*
Hoppy Fettler Withnell's *965*
Hoppy Harrington Sherfield
   Village *914*
Hoppy Hen Felstar *782*
Hoppy Hilda Little London *845*
Hoppy Pale Market
   Harborough *855*
Hoppy Potter and the Goblet of
   Ale Scribbler's *911*
Hoppy Valley IPA Boothtown *724*
Hoppylicious Cap House *744*
HoppyNESS Loch Ness
   (Cairngorm) *743*
Hops & Dreams Brew
   Foundation *730*
Hops Maiden England Weird
   Beard *956*
Hops n Honey Skinner's *917*
Hopsack Phoenix *886*
Hopscotch Hubsters *824*
   Old School *878*
Hopspur Redemption Brew *898*
Hopster Tweed *946*
Hoptical Illusion Brass Castle *729*
Hopweaver Nethergate *869*
Horbury Blond Bosun's *725*
Horizon APA Lawman *840*
Horizon Wadworth *953*
Hornswoggle Froth Blowers *789*
Horse & Jockey Full Mash *790*
Horsell Best Thurstons
   (Horsell) *937*
Horsell Gold Thurstons
   (Horsell) *937*

GOOD BEER GUIDE 2018

London Glory Greene King 802
London Gold Young's (Wells) 957
London IPA Enfield 777
London Pale Ale Enfield 777
  Southwark 921
London Porter Britman 735
  Enfield 777
  Mad Squirrel 852
London Pride Fuller's 790
London Tap New River 870
Lone Rider Tombstone 940
Lone Star Nene Valley 869
Lonely Snake Three Blind Mice 935
Lonesome Pine Ulverston 949
Long Blonde Long Man 848
The Long Con Hopjacker 822
Long Drop Hardknott 809
Long Hop Bollington 723
  Quirky 893
Long Lane Austendyke 701
Long Moor Pale Small World 918
Longboat George Wright 969
Longbow Empire 776
Longdendale Lights Howard
  Town 823
Longleat Pride Wessex 958
Loophole Clun 752
Lord Barker Gun Dog 804
Lord Humungous Langwith 840
Lord Marples Thornbridge 934
Lord of the Glen Hart 810
Lost in the Woods Devon Earth 766
Lost Tourist White Rock 960
Lottie Dod Peerless 884
Lou's Brew Driftwood 771
Louhi Black Metal 718
Louis's Pale Ale Stratford Upon
  Avon 927
Love Monkey Glastonbury 794
Love Or Nothing Art Brew 699
Love Over Gold BAD 703
Lovelight Melwood 858
Lovely Nelly Cullercoats 761
Low Flyer Strands 926
Low Hanging Fruit Paradigm 883
Loweswater Gold Cumbrian
  Legendary 761
Lowrider Hippy Killer 817
Lowry Hydes 825
Loxhill Biscuit Crafty Brewing 758
Loxley Ale Milestone 860
LPA (Light Pale Ale) Enville 777
LSD (Langham Special Draught)
  Langham 839
Lucem Light Ale Connoisseur 755
Lucifer's Desire Horncastle 823
Lucky Penny Long Arm 848
Lucretius Derventio 765
Lucy Locket Langwith 840
Luddite Ale Mill Valley 860
Luddite Dark Mill Valley 860
Lumberjack Brentwood 730
Luminaire Pope's Yard 890
Lunar White Dorking 768
Lunar Half Moon 806
Lunnys No. 8 Golden Duck 795
Lupa Ship & Mitre 914
Luppol Clouded Minds 752
Lupus Lupus Wolf 966
Lurcher Stout Green Jack 801
Lush Hopstar 822
Lushingtons Skinner's 917
Lux Borealis Hardknott 809
Luxury IPA Edinbrew 774
Lyme Gold Lyme Regis 850

Lynch Pin Toolmakers 941
Lynx Wildcat Yeovil 971

M

M&B Brew XI Brains 728
MòR Ish! MòR 865
MòR Please! MòR 865
MòR Tea Vicar? MòR 865
M-PIRE Burnside 739
MaCavity Red Cat 896
Macbeth Deeside 764
Machlyd Mawddach Cader 742
Mad Carew Manchester 854
Mad Dogs & Englishmen Irwell
  Works 828
Mad Dogz Burnside 739
Mad Goose Purity 892
Mad Hatter Weetwood 955
Mad Jack Papworth 882
Mad Monk Digfield 767
Mad Trappiste Dominion 767
Mad Wolf Wolf 966
Madagascar Mild Kelpaul 832
Madarina Cornovia Atlantic 700
Madchester Cream Mighty
  Medicine 859
Madgwick Gold Hammerpot 807
Madhouse Double Top 769
Madness IPA Wild Beer 962
Madness Mitchell's Hop House 862
Maggie's Leap IPA Whitewater 961
Maggs' Magnificent Mild West
  Berkshire 958
Magic Number Carlisle 745
Magic Porridge Hybrid 825
Magic Potion Bakers Dozen 703
Magik Keltek 832
Magiovinum Bucks Star 737
Magnitude Monty's 863
Magnum IPA Green Dragon 801
Magnum Mild Muirhouse 867
Magus Durham 772
Mahseer IPA Green Jack 801
Maid Marian Springhead 922
Maiden Voyage Bosun's 725
  Great Western 800
  NauticAles 867
Maiden's Pale Robin Hood 902
The Maids Bute 741
Mail Train Stamps 923
Mainbrace Jollyboat 831
Mainline Settle 911
Mainsail Emsworth Brewhouse 777
Mainwarings Mild Firehouse 784
Major Oak Maypole 858
Make Me Hoppy Holsworthy 819
Maldon Gold Mighty Oak 859
Malt Dark Ale Malt 854
Malt Shovel Mild Fernandes 782
Malt Store White Park 960
Malthouse Bitter Brancaster
  (Beeston) 711
Maltravers Session IPA
  Arundel 699
Malty Pig Bitter Stratford Upon
  Avon 927
Malty Python Little Critters 844
Malvern Spring Malvern Hills 854
Mam Tor Torriside 942
Mama Knows Best Franklins 788
Man Overboard Cromarty 759
Man Up! Manning 854
Manchester Bitter Marble 855
Manchester Pale Ale Lees 841

Manchester Skyline Brightside 734
Mandalay Mobberley 862
Mandarina Red Kissingate 837
Mane Event New Lion 870
Mango Beach Ramsbottom
  Craft 894
Manhaton Pale?? Full Mash 790
Manifesto Stout Revolutions 899
Manky Blonde Dalrannoch 761
Mansion Mild Tring 944
Maori Mobberley 862
Marcus Aurelius Milton 861
Mardler's Woodforde's 967
Mariana Trench Weird Beard 956
Marianna Porter Moseley 865
Marilyn Mitchell's Hop House 862
Marion Lincoln Green 843
Maris the Otter Brew York 730
Marld Bartrams 706
Marmid Gold Target 931
Marmoset Blue Monkey 722
Marquis Brewster's 732
Marsh Mild Firehouse 784
Marshall Port Stout Derwent 766
Martello Hop Fuzz 820
Marvellous Maple Mild
  Brentwood 729
Mary Jane Ilkley 826
Marynka Two Roses 947
Mary's Ruby Mild Kissingate 837
Masala Chai PA Atlantic 700
Mash City Rocker Rock & Roll 902
Mash Tun Bitter Leadmill 840
Masher in the Rye Scribbler's 911
Masquerade Monty's 863
Master Brew Shepherd Neame 913
Masterpiece IPA Heritage 815
Mat Black Church Hanbrewery 750
Matchlock Musket 867
Mate, Spawn & Die Hopcraft (Pixie
  Spring/Hopcraft) 889
Matfen Magic High House
  Farm 816
Matilda's Revenge Opa Hay's 879
Maverick IPA Brightside 734
Maverick Fyne 791
Maximus Maxim 857
May Day Padstow 882
Maybug Kinver 836
Mayfly Shardlow 912
Mayor of Garratt By The Horns 741
Mazama Track 943
McConnells Irish Stout Great North
  Eastern 800
Meditation Turpin's 946
Meikle Bin Fintry 783
Melbourne Bitter Tollgate 940
Mellors Hophurst 822
Mellow Yellow Bottle Brook 725
  Sadler's 906
Mellow Romney Marsh 904
Melyn Big Hand 714
Men of Steel Consett Ale
  Works 755
Menacing Dennis
  Summerskills 929
Meon Valley Bitter Bowman 726
The Merchant's Ale Canterbury
  Ales 744
Mercia IPA Derby 765
Mercian Shine Beowulf 713
Mercy Great Heck 799
Meridian Mild Townhouse 943
Merlin's Ale Broughton 736
Merlin's Gold Merlin 858

Mr Cuddle Landlord's Friend *839*
Mr JK's Itish Landlord's Friend *839*
Mr M's Porter Red Cat *896*
Mr & Mrs Smith's Smooth Alcoholic Ginger Beer Fallen Angel *780*
Mr Sheppard's Crook Exe Valley *779*
Mr Swift's Pale Ale West Berkshire *958*
Mr Webster's Brown Ale Landlord's Friend *839*
Mrs Simpsons Thriller in Vanilla Brown Cow *737*
Muck 'n' Straw Holsworthy *819*
Mucky Duck Buffy's *738*
Fuzzy Duck *791*
Mud City Stout Sadler's *907*
Mud Puddler Black IPA Three Sods *936*
Mudpuppy Salamander *908*
Muker Silver Yorkshire Dales *972*
Munchner Ticketybrew *937*
Mundham Mild Tindall *938*
Mussel Wreck Rock the Boat *903*
Musselburgh Broke Knops *837*
Mutineer Derwent *765*
Mutiny on the Bounty Campervan *744*
Mutiny IPA Wily Fox *963*
Mutiny Yorkshire *972*
Muzzleloader Musket *867*
MV Enterprise Harbwr Tenby *809*
Mwnci Nel Nant *867*
My Name is Earl Tres Bien (Market Harborough) *855*
Mystery Tor Glastonbury *793*
Mystic Peg Langwith *840*

N
N1 Wheat Beer Pitfield (Dominion) *767*
N1 Hammerton *807*
N18 Clouded Minds *752*
N253 Clouded Minds *752*
N29 Clouded Minds *752*
N7 Hammerton *807*
Nailmaker Mild Enville *777*
Naked Ladies Twickenham *946*
Nanny Flyer Leyden *843*
Nappa Scarr Yorkshire Dales *972*
Narrow Boat Shardlow *912*
Narrow Gauge Leighton Buzzard *842*
NASHA IPA S&P *906*
Native Bitter Whitstable *961*
Natterjack Frog Island *789*
Southport *921*
Natural Blonde Isla Vale *829*
Natural Gold Pennine *885*
Naughty Pilchard Black Flag *717*
Navigator Great Heck *799*
Navvy Phoenix *886*
Neanderthal Caveman *746*
Neap Tide Teignworthy *932*
Nectar Bitter Worcestershire *968*
Nectar Fell *782*
Neet Bude *737*
Nektar Cronx *759*
Nel's Best High House Farm *816*
Nelson Mild Double Top *768*
Nelson's Column Tunnel *945*
Nelson's Delight Downton *770*
Nelson's Right Arm Elliswood *776*

Nelsons Blood Nelson *868*
Nelsons Eye Heavy Industry *813*
Nelsons Revenge Woodforde's *967*
Nemesis Peakstones Rock *884*
Neolithic Caveman *746*
Neptune's Gold Hill Island *817*
Nero Milton *861*
Nessies Monster Mash Cairngorm *742*
Nether Ending Stowey *926*
Nettlethrasher Elland *775*
Never Known Fog Like It Rivington *901*
Never Mind the Kent Hops London Brewing *848*
Nevermore Full Mash *790*
Nevis Black Wolf *719*
New Dawn Pale Navigation *868*
New Deck Blackjack *720*
New England Best Exit 33 *779*
New Forest Ale Downton *770*
New India IPA Plan B *889*
New Laund Dark Reedley Hallows *899*
New Mechanic Thousand Trades *934*
New World Order Stockton *925*
New World Pale Little Black Dog *844*
New Plassey *870*
New World Red Saltaire *909*
New World Shiny *914*
New York Pale Chantry *747*
New Zealand Gold Harbour *808*
New Zealand Pale Brewsmith *732*
Newton's Drop Oldershaw *878*
Nice Weather Dancing Duck *762*
Nicholas De Luda Black Horse *718*
Nicholson's Pale Ale St Austell *907*
Nicky Nacky Noo Axton *701*
Night Hops Stout Bluestone (Lancashire) *722*
Night Jar Dark Horse *763*
Night Watch Porter Moonshine *864*
Nightfall Pale Bitter Cross Bay *759*
Nighthawk Hillfire *817*
Nightlight Mild Elmtree *776*
Nightmare Porter Hambleton *806*
Nightshade Kew *834*
Nightwatchman East London *773*
Ninja Summerskills *929*
Ninkasi Pale Ale Isla Vale *829*
Nip Grainstore *798*
Nipper Bitter Island *829*
Nirvana Odyssey *875*
No. 1 Amber Thorley & Sons *934*
No. 1: East Coast Pale Ale Bullards *738*
No. 1 Golden Ale Nine Standards (Settle) *911*
No 1 Pale Ale Burnside *739*
No. 1 Bucks Star *737*
Colchester *753*
No. 10 King's Cliffe *835*
No. 2: India Pale Ale Bullards *738*
No. 2 Pale Ale Nine Standards (Settle) *911*
No. 2 Stout Stringers *927*
No. 3: Amber Ale Bullards *738*
No. 3 Porter Nine Standards (Settle) *911*
No. 4 Amber Ale Nine Standards (Settle) *911*
No. 4: Session IPA Bullards *738*

No. 5: Best Red Bitter Bullards *738*
No. 5 Porter Harrogate *810*
No. 6: Rye Pale Ale Bullards *738*
No. 7 Stancill *923*
No. 74 Two Thirsty Men *947*
No. 79 Firebird *783*
No. 84 India Pale Ale Isaac Poad *828*
No. 86 Golden Ale Isaac Poad *828*
No. 9 Barley Wine Coniston *754*
No Brakes IPA Fixed Wheel *785*
No Chaff Broken Bridge *736*
No Escape Reality *895*
No Name Stout Brighton Bier *733*
No Name Witham *965*
No Notion Porter All Hallows *693*
No Prisoners Gaol *792*
Noble Kinver *836*
Nobleman Redcastle *898*
Noggin' Six Bells *917*
Noh Ghost Snaggletooth *919*
Noir Weal *955*
Nook of Pendle Reedley Hallows *899*
Nor'Hop Moor *864*
Norfolk Honey Ale Why Not *961*
Norfolk Nog Woodforde's *967*
Norfolk Stoat Two Rivers *947*
Norfolk Terrier Buffy's *738*
Norfolk's 80 Shilling Ale Elmtree *776*
North Coast IPA GT *803*
North Coast Voodoo Madrigal *853*
North Shore IPA Franklins *788*
North Star Porter Facer's *780*
North Star Harbwr Tenby *809*
North Wall Hop Kettle *820*
The North Will Rise Again Stringers *927*
Northampton Red Nobby's *872*
Northamptonshire Bitter Hoggleys (Phipps) *886*
Northcote Blonde Belleville *711*
Northdown Bitter People's *885*
Northern Blonde Brass Castle *729*
Northern Light Orkney *880*
Northern Lights George Wright *969*
Green Mill *802*
Northern Porter Tyne Bank *948*
Northern Soul Briggs *733*
Northern Star Hop Fuzz *820*
Northfield Garage Pentrich *885*
Northumbrian Blonde Mordue *865*
Northumbrian Gold Hadrian Border *805*
Northway IPA Firehouse *784*
Norwegian Blue Buffy's *738*
Newark *871*
Norwich Dragon Tindall *938*
Nos Smoked Porter Heavy Industry *813*
Nosey Parker Indigenous *827*
Not Just For Mother Landlord's Friend *839*
Not So Black & White Godstone *795*
Notting Hill Amber Moncada *862*
Notting Hill Bitter Moncada *862*
Notting Hill Blonde Moncada *862*
Notting Hill Ruby Rye Moncada *863*
Notting Hill Stout Moncada *863*

Brunning & Price (Phoenix) 887
Butcombe 741
Dark Star 763
Holsworthy 818
Hydes 825
Sharp's 913
Thwaites (Banks's) 704
Orion G2 791
Orkney Best Swannay 929
Orkney Blast Swannay 930
Orkney IPA Swannay 930
Orme Great Orme 800
Orsino Newby Wyke 871
OSB (Old Style Bitter) Tomos
Watkin 954
OSB Old Spot 878
Oscar Wilde Mighty Oak 859
Ossian Inveralmond 828
Otherside IPA York 971
Otley Gold Briscoe's 734
Otters Pocket Marlpool 855
Our Auld Ale FILO 783
Our Greatest Golden Farr
Brew 781
Our Most Perfect Pale Farr
Brew 781
Our Most Potent Porter Farr
Brew 781
Our Town Brightside 733
Ouseburn Porter Hadrian
Border 805
Out of Step IPA Offbeat 876
Outlandish Pale Offbeat 876
Outlawed Springhead 922
Outline Kettlesmith 834
Outsider Ale Art Brew 699
Over a Barrel Bespoke 713
Over the Edge Kinver 836
Over the Hill Hillside 817
Over the Moon Gold Brown
Cow 737
Over & Stout Goose Eye 797
Overtime Six O'Clock 917
Overture 4Four 690
Ow Do! Six Bells 917
Owd Flya RAN 895
Owl Porter Rigg & Furrow 900
Own Gear Co Pilot 752
Owt L Do Five Towns 785
Oxford Blonde Chadlington 747
Oxford Gold Brakspear 728
Oyster Catcher Oatmeal Stout
Brimstage 734
Oyster Stout Leyden 843
London Brewing 848
Mersea Island 859
Whitstable 961
Oystermouth Stout Mumbles 867
Oz Bomb Arbor 697
Ozark Track 943

P _____

P'Ale Cocksure 753
Pacific Gold Dorking 768
Pacific Red Oxted 881
Pacifica Tyne Bank 948
Packhorse Bridge Anstey 697
Packhorse Worsthorne 968
Paddlers Southbourne 920
Paddock Porter Uttoxeter 951
Pagan Queen Firebrick 783
Pagoda Pale Kew 834
Pail Ale Concrete Cow 754
Pail Shiny 914

Palace Pale Kings Clipstone 835
Palaeolithic Caveman 746
Pale Ale 4Ts 690
Ashley Down 700
Atom 701
Battledown 707
Beardy Monkey 708
Black Brook 717
Black Rock 719
Brew Shack 730
Brockley 735
Chiltern 749
Church Farm 750
Dan's 762
Davenports (Blue Bear) 721
Doghouse 767
East London 773
Fuddy Duck 790
Hand 807
Hedge Row 813
Husk 825
Incredible 826
Joule's 831
Kirkstall 837
Market Bosworth 855
McColl's 851
Moseley 866
Padstow 882
Pershore 885
Pheasantry 886
Redemption Brew 898
The Pale Ale Rigg & Furrow 900
Pale Ale RT 905
Stannary 923
Swannay 930
Ticketybrew 937
Tremethick 943
Tweed 946
Vibrant Forest 951
Volden 953
Watling Street 954
Pale Amber Sarah Hughes 824
Pale & Bitter Gyle 59 804
Pale Brummie Birmingham
Brewing 716
Pale Eagle Eagles Crag 773
Pale Four Tring 944
Pale Gold Ossett 880
Pale & Golden Roundhill 905
Pale Ice Durham 772
Pale & Interesting Thorley &
Sons 934
Pale Keith Keith 831
Pale Moonlight Phoenix 886
Pale of Clwyd Buzzard 741
Pale Rider Kelham Island 832
Pale Tale Moody Fox 863
Pale 360° 689
Art Brew 699
Barngates 705
Borough (Lancaster) 724
Brewshed 731
Brewsmith 732
Cross Borders 759
Five Points 784
Harbour 809
Harrogate 810
Hart Family 810
Heathen 813
Hop Studio 821
Hop Stuff 821
Hopburst 821
Ilkley 826
Kent 833
Larkins 840

Leeds 841
Left Handed Giant 842
MASH 856
Nomadic 872
Peerless 884
Portobello 890
Snowhill 919
Three Legs 936
Titan 939
True North 944
Wild Card 962
Paleface APA Firebird 783
Paleface Anstey 697
Paler Shade of Ale Holsworthy 818
Palmers Poison Blythe 723
Palmerston's Folly Suthwyk
(Bowman) 726
Pamplemousse Waen (Pixie
Spring/Hopcraft) 889
Panama Jazz Angels &
Demons 696
Panda Frog Pandarillo
Mordue 865
Panda Frog Project Allelic Drift
Mordue 865
Panda Frog Project Pils
Mordue 865
Pandemonium South Hams 920
Pandit IPA New Lion 870
Panther Ale Mill Valley 860
The Panther Oatmeal Stout
Littleover 845
Papa Jangle's Voodoo Stout Totally
Brewed 942
Parabellum Milk Stout Gun 804
Parabolic Pale Ale Eight Arch 774
Paradigm Shift VOG 952
Parakeet Tres Bien (Market
Harborough) 855
The Pardoner's Ale Canterbury
Ales 744
Parish Bitter Wood 967
Park Light White Park 960
Park Your Thirst Keswick 834
Parkers Piece City of Cambridge
(Wolf) 966
Parkeston Porter Harwich
Town 811
ParkLife Windsor & Eton 964
Parsons Pledge Derwent 765
Partisan Red Star 898
Partridge Best Bitter Dark Star 763
Passion Yorkshire 972
Pastiche Burton Old Cottage 740
Pathfinder Red 897
Pause Front Row 789
Pavilion Pale Ale Bank Top 704
Paw's Gold Black Paw 719
Paxton Pale Ale London Beer
Factory 847
PE9 Paradise Pale Stoney Ford 926
Peacock Indian 827
Peaky Blinder Sadler's 906
Pearl of Kent Whitstable 961
Pecker Wrecker Tomos Watkin 954
Pecking Order Felstar 782
Peddlars Best Millis (Dartford
Wobbler) 861
Pedigree Marston's 856
Peg Fyfe Dark Mild All Hallows 693
Pegasus Milton 861
Pemberton Pale Tempest 932
Pembrokeshire Best Bitter Gwaun
Valley 804

Pre-Prohibition Cream Ale
  Stubborn Mule *928*
Premier Bitter Bartrams *706*
  Moorhouse's *865*
Premium Ale Watling Street *954*
Premium Stout Kingstone *836*
Premium Big Lamp *715*
  Hunters *824*
  Slater's *918*
Preservation Fine Ale Castle
  Rock *746*
Pressed Rat & Warthog Triple
  fff *944*
Pricky Back Otchan Great
  Newsome *799*
Pride 'n' Joy Weltons *957*
Pride & Joy Vocation *952*
Pride of Dartmoor Black Tor *719*
Pride of Fulstow Firehouse *784*
Pride of Pendle Moorhouse's *865*
Pride of Sheffield Kelham
  Island *832*
Pride Abstract Jungle *691*
  Devon *766*
  Front Row *789*
  Padstow *882*
  Saltaire *909*
Primordial Ooze Gene Pool *793*
Prince Bishop Ale Big Lamp *715*
Prior's Pale Prior's Well *892*
Priory Gold Prior's Well *892*
Priory Mild Nethergate *869*
Prism Red Clearsky (Hilden) *816*
Private Sector Betteridge's *713*
Profits of Doom Hopcraft (Pixie
  Spring/Hopcraft) *888*
Progress Pilgrim *888*
Prohibition Kent *833*
Project Babylon Pale Ale Gun *804*
Proper Ace Rivington *901*
Proper Ansome Clearwater *751*
Proper IPA Broughton *736*
Proper Job St Austell *907*
Proper Lager Holsworthy *819*
Prophecy Bath *707*
Propshaft Crankshaft *758*
Prospect Organic Hepworth *814*
Prospect Bexar County *714*
  Shotover *915*
Prospector Dynamite Valley *773*
Prototype North *872*
Proud Miner Boothtown *724*
Prowler Pale Red Cat *896*
Pryde Little London *845*
PSB Parish *883*
Pucks Folly Maldon *853*
Puddled Duck Tarn Hows *931*
Puddlers Peril Borough Arms *725*
Puffin Ale Orkney *880*
Puffing Billy Wylam *970*
Pugin's Gold Peakstones Rock *884*
Pullet Please High House Farm *816*
Pullman First Class Ale
  Hepworth *814*
Pulp Fiction Nene Valley *869*
Pump Fiction Hoggleys
  (Phipps) *886*
Pumphouse Pale Ale
  Sambrook's *909*
Punch in the Face Totally
  Brewed *942*
Punter Upham *950*
Purbeck Best Bitter Isle of
  Purbeck *829*
Purbeck IPA Isle of Purbeck *830*

Purdy Peculiar LoveBeer *850*
Pure Blonde George Wright *969*
Pure Gold Itchen Valley *830*
  Newark *871*
  Purity *892*
  Rowton *905*
Pure Star Silhill *916*
Pure UBU Purity *892*
Pursers Pussy Porter Nelson *868*
The Pursuit of Hoppiness Session
  Brinkburn Street *734*
Push Iron Withnell's *965*
Pushang White Rock *960*
Pyrites Hopjacker *822*
Python IPA Little Valley *845*

Q _____

QED Itchen Valley *830*
Quacker Jack Mallard *854*
Quadhop Downton *772*
Quadrant Oatmeal Stout East
  London *774*
Quagmire Big Bog *714*
Quarrymans Stout Bluestone
  (Lancashire) *722*
Quartermaine IPA Wimbledon *963*
Quartermaster Pope's Yard *890*
Quay Ale Caffle *742*
Queen Bee Kings Clipstone *835*
Queen of Diamonds Wild Card *962*
Queen of Hops Boudicca *725*
Queens Black Horse *718*
Quench Pilgrim *888*
Quest Pilgrim *888*
Quicker Than The Eye Hand *807*
Quiet Riot Anarchy *696*
Quintessential Derby *765*

R _____

R Harvey's *811*
Ra Milk Street *860*
Rabbie's Porter Ayr *702*
Rabbit Dog Whippet *960*
Rabbit Ear Origami *879*
Rabbit Hunt Blackjack *720*
Racing Dragon Sandstone *910*
Racing Tiger Angels & Demons *696*
Rack & Roll Fine Tuned *783*
Radgie Gadgie Mordue *865*
Radiance Moor *864*
Radiant Ship & Mitre *914*
Radical Red Kirkby Lonsdale *836*
Ragged Robyn All Hallows *693*
Raglan Sleeve Leyden *843*
On the Rails Ascot *699*
Railway Porter Bond Brews *723*
  Brunswick *737*
  Five Points *785*
RAJ IPA Tryst *945*
Rakau South Lakes *920*
Ram Tam Timothy Taylor *932*
Rambler Frensham *789*
  Wincle *964*
Ramblers Gold Extra
  Stocklinch *924*
Ramblers Gold Stocklinch *924*
Ramblers Tipple Saffron *907*
Ramblers' Gold By The Mile *742*
Rambrau Dent *765*
Ramification Lenton Lane *842*
Rammy Ale Ramsbottom Craft *894*
Rammy Rocket Leyden *843*
Rampart Conwy *755*

Rams Head Bitter Hooded
  Ram *819*
Ramsay Lane Brew Shed *730*
Ramsbottom Strong Ale Dent *765*
Randolph's Leap Speyside
  Craft *921*
Random Toss Flipside *786*
Ranmore Surrey Hills *929*
Rantipole Three Tuns *936*
Rapture Bottle Brook *725*
  Magic Rock *853*
Raspberry Porter Moonshine *864*
Raspberry Tipple Yorkshire *972*
Raspberry Wheat Beer
  Milestone *860*
  Moonshine *864*
Ratae'd Dow Bridge *769*
Ratliffe's Celebrated Stout
  Phipps *886*
RAUK Church Hanbrewery *750*
Raven Stout Magpie *853*
Raven Black Tor *719*
  Orkney *879*
The Raven Sonnet 43 *920*
Ravening Wolf Wantsum *954*
Raveningham Bitter People's *885*
Raver Beat Ales *709*
Raw Moor *864*
Razorback Ringwood *900*
RBC Best Riviera *901*
Reach for the Yard Yard of Ale *970*
Reading Best Loddon *847*
Real Blonde Pennine *885*
Real Mild Ale Goacher's *794*
Real Smiler Clearwater *751*
Reality Czech Reality *895*
Reality Shift Druid *771*
Really Dumb Blonde Nessie *869*
Really Rockin Rockin' Robin *903*
Reaper Derwent *765*
Rebel Porter O'Brien *875*
Rebel Yell Leighton Buzzard *842*
Rebel Lyme Regis *850*
Reckless Robin Rockin' Robin *903*
Rector's Light Relief Rectory *896*
The Rector's Revenge Rectory *896*
Red Ale Brockley *735*
  Lola Rose *847*
  Mad Cat *852*
  Pitfield (Dominion) *767*
  Watling Street *954*
Red Bandit Cader *742*
Red Barn Ale Tirril *939*
Red Baron Davenports (Blue
  Bear) *721*
Red Beacons Brecon *729*
Red Bear Electric Bear *775*
Red Beast Cold Black
  (Rhymney) *900*
Red Beetter Church
  Hanbrewery *750*
Red Boy Little London *845*
Red Brick Stu Brew *928*
Red Bull Terrier Barngates *706*
Red Cow Strathcarron *927*
Red Diesel Colchester *753*
Red Dragon Great Orme *800*
Red Dust Consett Ale Works *755*
Red Earl Ruby Ale Pokertree *890*
Red Ellen Great North Eastern *800*
Red Falcon Hawk Hill *811*
Red Feather Welbeck Abbey *956*
Red from the Shed Kirrie *837*
Red Herring Green Jack *801*
Red Hunter Hammerpot *807*

Rougham Ready Bartrams *706*
Roughtor Altarnun *694*
Roundhead Porter Why Not *961*
The Rouser Holler Boys *818*
Route 701 Xtreme *970*
Rowlock Clearsky (Hilden) *816*
Royal Fanfare Top-Notch *941*
Royal Ginger Brandon *728*
Royal Hunt Hunters *824*
Royal Standard 1485
    Elliswood *776*
Royal Standard Pale
    moogBREW *863*
Royal Lytham *851*
RPA Rockin' Robin *903*
Rubecca Scribbler's *911*
Ruby (1874) Mild Bushy's *740*
Ruby Duck Fuzzy Duck *791*
Ruby English Ale 3 Brewers of St
    Albans *689*
Ruby League Trinity *944*
Ruby Mild Rudgate *906*
Ruby Red Mild Red Fox *897*
Ruby Red Moorstone *865*
    St Peter's *908*
Ruby Ruby Ruby Ruby
    Connoisseur *755*
Ruby, Ruby, Ruby, Ruby Silver
    Street *916*
Ruby AJ's *693*
    Freewheelin' *788*
    MASH *856*
    Quirky *893*
    Seven Bro7hers *912*
    Titan *939*
    Yeovil *971*
Ruck & Maul Southport *921*
Rucking Mole Moles *862*
Ruddy Darter Andwells *696*
Ruddy Duck Goldstone *796*
Rudy English IPA Revolutions *899*
Ruffled Feathers Swan *929*
Rum 'n' Raisin Stout RAN *895*
Rum Porter Beer Nouveau *710*
Rumour Gower *797*
Run, Hop, Run Rigg & Furrow *900*
Runner Truman's *944*
Running the Gauntlet
    Bespoke *713*
Ruskins Bitter Kirkby Lonsdale *836*
Russian Rouble Flipside *786*
Russian Stoat Wessex *958*
The Russian Stamps *923*
Rustic Tonbridge *941*
Rusty Boiler Stocklinch *924*
Rusty Bucket Brandon *728*
Rusty Fang Lion's Lair *843*
Rusty Lane Kennet & Avon *833*
Rusty Nail Lion's Lair *843*
Rusty's Ale Godstone *795*
Rutland Beast Grainstore *798*
Rutland Bitter Grainstore *798*
Rutland Panther Grainstore *798*
Rwster Nant *867*
Rye Pale Ale Boutilliers *726*
    Townhouse *942*
Rye'n Gosling Rivington *901*
Ryejoice Emmanuales *776*
Ryme Rambler Wriggle Valley *969*

S
SA Gold Brains *728*
SA Brains *727*
Saaz Blonde Hopstar *822*

Saaz Enville *777*
SaaziNESS Loch Ness
    (Cairngorm) *743*
Sabrina's Dark Ruby Ale
    Worcester *968*
Sabut Jung Battlefield
    (Shrewsbury) *708*
Sacred Heart Hale's (Grafton) *798*
Sacrificed Soul Horncastle *823*
Saddle Tank Marston's *856*
Saddleback Best Bitter
    Slaughterhouse *918*
Sail Ale Golden Ale Rebel *896*
Sail G2 *791*
St Andrew's Ale Belhaven *711*
St Andrews Blonde Eden St
    Andrews *774*
St Davids Special Gwaun
    Valley *804*
St Georges Ale Boot Town *723*
St Michaels Cornish Crown *756*
St. Modwen Golden Ale
    Heritage *815*
St Nonna's Altarnun *694*
Saint Petersburg Imperial
    Russian Stout Thornbridge *934*
St Pirans Porter Coastal *753*
St Udley Mild Weatheroak *955*
Saison Citron Brodie's *736*
Saison From Another Place
    Twisted Barrel *946*
Saison Langham *839*
Salem Porter Batemans *707*
Salt's Burton Ale Tower *942*
Salters Tree Castor *746*
Saltwick Nab Whitby *960*
Salvation Pale Ale One Mile
    End *879*
Salvation Charnwood *748*
Samba Red Star *897*
Same Again Milk Street *860*
    Ramsbury *894*
Samson Maxim *857*
Sanctuary Applecross *697*
Sand House Doncaster *768*
Sand in the Wind Bottle Brook *725*
Sandbanks Export
    Bournemouth *726*
Sandbanks Extra Reserve
    Bournemouth *726*
Sandbanks Tempestatum
    Bournemouth *726*
Sandbanks Bournemouth *726*
Sandgrounder Bitter
    Southport *920*
Sandilands Brew Shed *730*
Sandpiper Light Ale Brimstage *734*
Sandstone Wainstones *953*
Sandstorm Brecon *729*
Sandycombe Gold Kew *834*
Santa Fe Tombstone *941*
Satan's Fury Horncastle *823*
Satsumo Stout Boat Lane *723*
Saturdays Blonde Black Horse *718*
Sauvignon Blonde Crafty
    Beers *758*
Saved by the Bell Bespoke *713*
Savernake Kennet & Avon *833*
Saxon Archer Three Castles *935*
Saxon Bronze Alfred's *693*
Saxon Cross Rockingham *903*
Saxon Gold Battlefield
    (Shrewsbury) *708*
    Brandon *728*

Craddock's *757*
    King Alfred *835*
Saxon Red Ale Parker *883*
Sayers Stout London Beer
    Factory *847*
SBA Donnington *768*
Scafell Blonde Hesket
    Newmarket *815*
Scafell Summit Strands *926*
Scalded Shoulder
    Hamelsworde *807*
Scalpsie Blonde Bute *741*
Scapa Special Swannay *930*
Scaramanga Extra Pale Gun *804*
Scarborough Fair IPA Wold Top *966*
Scarecrow Bitter Brimstage *734*
Scarlet Fever Wild Beer *962*
Scarlet Macaw Oakham *875*
Scary Hairy Export
    Leatherbritches *841*
Scary Hairy Leatherbritches *841*
Schafkopf Blackjack *720*
Schiehallion Harviestoun *811*
Scholar Shotover *915*
Schooner Black Dog
    (Hambleton) *807*
Schrodingers Cat Atom *701*
Scorned Woman Burton Town *740*
Scottish Maiden Morton *866*
Scoundrel Leatherbritches *841*
Scratch Red Cat *896*
Scratty Ratty Marlpool *855*
Screech Owl Castle Rock *746*
Scruffy Witham *965*
Scrum Dog Gun Dog *804*
Scrum Kendricks *833*
Scrumdiggity Goddards *794*
Scullion Irish Ale Hilden *816*
Scullion's Irish Hilden *816*
Scuttlebutt IPA Hawk Hill *811*
Sea Breeze Ale By The Mile *742*
Sea Dog Cliff Quay *751*
Sea Monster Tapstone *931*
Seafarers Ale Gale's (Fuller's) *790*
Seaforth Ale Hebridean *813*
Seahorse Salcombe *909*
Sealord Scarborough *910*
Seamless RedWillow *898*
Seance Full Mash *790*
Sebright Golden Ale Unity Brew
    House *949*
Second Coming Taylors *932*
Secret Citra Alechemy *693*
Secret Kingdom Hadrian
    Border *805*
Sedgley Surprise Sarah
    Hughes *824*
Seduction Dancing Duck *762*
Seek Medical Help Black
    Horse *718*
Seething Pint Tindall *938*
Seggie Porter Eden St
    Andrews *774*
Seithenyn Llŷn *846*
Self Rescuer Merry Miner *859*
Semerwater Summer Ale
    Wensleydale *958*
SEMP (Samuel Engels Meister
    Pils) Opa Hay's *879*
Senior Moment Appleby *697*
Seraphim Sonnet 43 *920*
Serendipity Plockton *889*
    Wild Weather *962*
Serious Black Betteridge's *713*

Smelter's Stout Kissingate *837*
Smild Rother Valley *905*
Smoke Bomb Anarchy *696*
The Smoke Padstow *882*
The Smoked Brown Anspach & Hobday *697*
Smoked Chilli IPA Yaarbrew *970*
Smoked Green Tea PA Atlantic *700*
Smoked Oatmeal Stout Boutilliers *726*
Smoked Porter Franklins *788* Top Out *941*
Smokehouse Arundel *699*
Smokeless RedWillow *899*
Smokestack Lightnin' Dorking *768*
Smokestack Lightning Porter New Lion *870*
Smokey Horyzon Moor *864*
Smokey Joe Stout Geeves *792*
Smokey Joe Ferry Ales *782*
Smokey Joe's Black Beer Hopstar *822*
Smooth Hoperator Calvors *743*
Smuggler Rebellion *896*
Smugglers Gold Whitby *960*
Snake Eyes Black Iris *718*
Snap Dog Whippet *960*
Sneaky Steamer Riverside *901*
Sneaky Wee Orkney Stout Swannay *930*
Sneck Lifter Jennings *831*
Snetterton Scary Tree Elmtree *776*
Snow Storm Northallerton *873*
Snow Top Old Dairy *877*
Snowdown Mild By The Mile *742*
So.LA Dark Revolution *763*
So'Hop Moor *864*
SOD B&T *702*
Sod Idle *826*
Solar Power Isle of Purbeck *830*
Solar Clun *752*
Solaris Big Hand *714* Newbridge *871*
Solitaire Blackjack *720*
Solitude Long Hop *848*
SOLO Green Bullet Sherfield Village *913*
SOLO Single Hop Sherfield Village *913*
SOLO Southern Gold Sherfield Village *913*
Solstice Stout Hoggleys (Phipps) *886*
Solstice Mobberley *862* Three Tuns *936*
Solway 4 Hop Yates *971*
Solway Mist Sulwath *928*
Soma Pentrich *885*
Sombrero Elephant School (Brentwood) *730*
Some Like It Blond Worsthorne *968*
Somerset Ale Abbey *691*
Somerset Blonde Patriot *884*
Son of a Bitch Bullmastiff *738*
Sonny Blonde Lion's Lair *843*
Sonoma Track *943*
Sorachi Pale Milltown *861*
Sorachi Tweed *946*
Sorley Boy's Stash Lacada *838*
SOS B&T *702*
Soul Frensham *789*
Sound Bitter Tavy *931*
Soundwave IPA Siren Craft *916*
The Source Tillingbourne *937*

South Eastern Bloc Stout Bullfinch *738*
South Face IPA Top Out *941*
South Island Pale Saltaire *909*
South Island VOG *952*
Southern Cross G2 *791* Weetwood *951*
Southern Pale Kiln *835*
Southern Summit Loch Lomond *847*
Southwold Bitter Adnams *692*
Sovereign Gold Burton Bridge *739*
Sovereign Ram Single Hop Hooded Ram *819*
SPA (Special Pale Ale) Buxton *741*
SPA AJ's *692* Cornish Crown *756*
Space Hoppy IPA Binghams *715*
Space is the Place Out There *881*
Spanish City Blonde Whitley Bay *961*
Spanish Stout Hamelsworde *807*
Spankers IPA Park Brewery *883*
Sparkling WIT Connoisseur *755*
Sparkplug 3 Potts *689*
Sparta Milton *861*
Spartan Derventio *765*
Speak Easy IPA VOG *953*
Speak Easy Transatlantic Pale Ale Powderkeg *891*
Specduckular Mallard *854*
Special Ale Lister's *844* Spitting Feathers *922*
Special English Ale 3 Brewers of St Albans *689*
Special Oatmeal Stout Coniston *754*
Special Pale Ale Bath *707*
Special Reserve Axholme *701* Bullmastiff *738* Chantry *747*
Special Holden's *818* Keswick *834* Young's (Wells) *957*
Special/House Ale Goacher's *794*
Special/Sea Fury Sharp's *913*
Speciale Brampton *728*
Spectre Stout Salamander *909*
Spectre Ghost *793*
Spellbound Merlin *858*
Spey IPA Two Thirsty Men *947*
Spey Stout Spey Valley *921*
Spicy Sausage Lincolnshire *843*
Spike's Gold Small World *918*
Spikey Blonde Six Bells *917*
Spilt Milk Electric Bear *775*
Spinner's Gold Martland Mill *856*
Spiral Stout Boudicca *725*
Spire Ale Stonehenge *925*
Spire Light Star Wing *923*
Spirit of Kent Westerham *958*
Spitfire Gold Shepherd Neame *913*
Spitfire Shepherd Neame *913*
Spodden Pilsner Bluestone (Lancashire) *722*
Spot Light Old Spot *878*
Spot O'Bother Old Spot *878*
Spotland Gold Phoenix *886*
Sprilly Maid Caffle *742*
Spring Gold Hart *810*
Spring I'da Air Valhalla *951*
Spring Tide Teignworthy *932*
Springfield Broughs *736*
Springwell Goose Eye *797*

Spun Gold Carlisle *745* Twisted Oak *946*
Sputnik North *872*
Square Rigger IPA Daleside *761*
Squire's Gold Woodcote Manor *967*
Squires Gamble Saffron *907*
The Squirrels Nuts Beeston *711*
Sqweal Weal *955*
Staffie Blythe *723*
Stag Cairngorm *742* Exmoor *779* Quantock *893*
Stagecoach Tombstone *940*
Staggersaurus Staggeringly Good *923*
Stahlstadt Weldon *956*
Stain Glass Blue Star Wing *923*
Stainless Stancill *923*
Stairway to Heaven Burton Bridge *739*
Stairway Ludlow *850*
Stakes Upham *950*
Stallion Amber Hambleton *806*
Stamford Bitter Dunham Massey *772*
Stamford Pale Bakers Dozen *703*
Stand & Deliver Tollgate *940*
Standard Cronx *759* Yelland Manor *971*
Stanley Gold Melwood *858*
Stanley's Pale Ale Kirkby Lonsdale *836*
Stanney Bitter Stanway *923*
Staple Top Out *941*
Star Bitter Belvoir *712*
Star Gazer Yeovil *971*
Star Portobello *890*
Starboard! Plockton *889*
Stardust Haresfoot *809*
Stargazer Ridgeside *900*
Starhopper Alechemy *693*
Stark Reality Reality *895*
Starry Nights Malt *854*
Starship Fleet Elusive *776*
Starstruck Gyle 59 *804*
Start Point Summerskills *928*
Stateless RedWillow *898*
Stateside IPA Saltaire *909*
Station Ale Richmond *900*
Station Bitter Stonehouse *925*
Station Porter Dent *765* Wickwar *962*
Staughton Bitter Red *897*
Steadfast Koln-ish Bier Lawman *840*
Steady State Bingley *716*
Stealth Burnside *739*
Steam Plate Irwell Works *828*
Steampunk Three Tuns *936*
Stedmans Ale Thurstons (Horsell) *937*
Steel River Wainstones *953*
Steel Town Bitter Consett Ale Works *755*
Steelback IPA Grainstore *798*
Steelos Chantry *747*
Steerage Titanic *939*
Stella Spark Firebrick *783*
Stellar IPA Ramsbottom Craft *894*
Sterling Gold Milltown *861*
Sterling Pale Flipside *786*
Steven Bang-On *704*
Steyning Stinker Riverside *901*
Sticky Dog Ambridge *695*
Stiff Upper Lip By The Horns *741*

Swedish Blonde Maxim *857*
  Stamps *923*
Sweeneys Bank Top *704*
Sweet Michael Hedge Row *813*
Swelkie John o'Groats *831*
Swift Best Bowness Bay *727*
Swift Nick Peak *884*
Swift One Bowman *726*
Swift Truman's *944*
Switch Revolutions *899*
Swordfish Wadworth *953*
Swordsman Beowulf *712*
Sworn Secret Happy Valley *808*
SX Dark Hope *821*
SX Gold Hope *821*
SX Pale Hope *821*
SYL First Chop *784*
Synergy Paradigm *883*
Syren Odyssey *875*
System of a Brown Bakers
  Dozen *703*

T _____

T'errmmm-inator Strands *926*
T'Other Teme Valley *932*
T'owd Tup Dent *765*
Tabaknakas Kings Clipstone *835*
Tabatha Partners *884*
Table Liquor Three Blind Mice *935*
Tackler's Tipple Three B's *934*
Tag Lag Barngates *706*
Tahkir Khing Pershore *886*
Tail Gunner Brass Castle *729*
Tailshaker Great Oakley *800*
Taiphoon Hop Back *820*
Taipur Tipsy Angel *939*
Take It Easy Gyle 59 *804*
Take Me to Valhalla Way
  Outback *955*
Talbot Blond Teme Valley *932*
Talisman IPA Pictish *887*
Talisman Green Mill *802*
Tally Ho! Palmers *882*
Tallyllyn Pale Ale Cader *742*
Talwar Reunion *899*
Tamar Black Holsworthy *819*
Tamar Summerskills *928*
Tambourine Man Treboom *943*
Tanglefoot Hall & Woodhouse
  (Badger) *806*
Tank 3 Pin-Up *888*
Tap Bitter Chalk Hill *747*
Tap House Tipple Draycott
  (Derbyshire) *770*
Tarasgeir Isle of Skye *830*
Tawny Owl Cotleigh *756*
Taylor Walker 1730 Special Pale
  Ale Westerham *959*
TBC (Thwaites Best Cask)
  Thwaites *937*
Tea Kettle Stout Tring *944*
TEA Hogs Back *818*
Teacups Funfair *791*
Tectonic Peerless *884*
Teddy Bear Cannon Royall *744*
Tekau Stonehouse *926*
Teleporter Summer Wine *928*
Temperance Session Ale One Mile
  End *879*
Tempest Stout Blue Bee *721*
Temple of Love Hopcraft (Pixie
  Spring/Hopcraft) *888*
Temptress Cap House *745*
Ten Fifty Grainstore *798*

Tequila Blonde Bridgehouse *733*
Term IPA Bowness Bay *727*
Tetley Bitter Carlsberg
  (Banks's) *705*
Tetley Gold Carlsberg (Banks's) *705*
Tetley Mild Carlsberg (Banks's) *705*
Tewdric's Tipple Kingstone *836*
Texas Jack Tombstone *940*
Textbook Old School *878*
ThaIPA Hill Island *817*
ThaiRannoCitrus Staggeringly
  Good *923*
Thames Surf IPA Belleville *712*
Thanks PA Black Horse *718*
That Teme Valley *932*
That's Your Left Hand Sir
  Rivington *901*
Theo's Brew Moorstone *865*
Theodore Pinchbeck's Spurious
  Stout Dominion *767*
Thieves & Fakirs Millis (Dartford
  Wobbler) *861*
Thieving Rogue Magpie *853*
Thin Ice Sadler's *906*
Third Eye Blind Mad Dog *852*
Thirst Aid Exit 33 *779*
Thirst Born Greenfield *802*
Thirst Celebration Keswick *834*
Thirst of Many GT *803*
Thirst Quencher Keswick *834*
Thirst Run Keswick *834*
Thirstquencher Spitting
  Feathers *922*
Thirsty Moon Phoenix *887*
Thirsty Walker Dove Street *769*
Thirteen XT *970*
Thirty Three Brighton Bier *733*
This Splendid Ale Facer's *780*
This Teme Valley *932*
Thomas Miller 1785 Ferry
  Brewery *783*
Thomas Sykes Burton Bridge *740*
Thomcat Burton Town *740*
Thoroughbred Bad Ram Haywood
  Bad Ram *812*
Three Amigos Snaggletooth *919*
Three Beacons Brecon *729*
Three Cs Gold Crossed Anchors *760*
Three Graves Pentrich *885*
Three Shires Bitter Millstone *861*
Three & Sixpence Twisted *946*
Three Swords Kirkstall *837*
Three Tails Boudicca *725*
Three Tuns XXXXXXX Strong Ale
  Three Tuns *936*
Three Valleys IPA Barlow *705*
Three XT *970*
ThreeOneSix Grain *798*
Threesome Sherfield Village *913*
Thriller Cappuccino Porter
  Glastonbury *794*
Through & Off Fixed Wheel *785*
Thrums Best Kirrie *837*
Thunderball Force *787*
Thunderbird Glamorgan *793*
Thunderbridge Stout Small
  World *919*
Thurlton Gold People's *885*
Thurstein Pilsner Coniston *754*
Thy Last Drop Bartrams *706*
Tickle Muckle *866*
Tidefall Clearsky (Hilden) *816*
Tie the Knot Happy Valley *808*
Tiffield Thunderbolt Great
  Oakley *800*

Tiffin Gold Kirkby Lonsdale *836*
Tiger Rut Millstone *861*
Tiger Everards (Robinsons) *902*
Timeline Kettlesmith *834*
Tin Basher Withnell's *965*
Tin Plate Irwell Works *828*
Tinderbox IPA Fell *782*
Tino Brinkburn Street *734*
Tip of the Tongue Cryptic *760*
Tipple Digfield *767*
Tipster Upham *950*
Tipsy Fisherman Steamin' Billy
  (Belvoir) *712*
Tiramisu Horbury *822*
Tithe House Bitter Lord's *849*
TNT IPA Dynamite Valley *773*
Toad Stabber Beer Bores *709*
Toba Track *943*
TOC (That Old Chestnut) Frog
  Island *789*
Tod's Blonde Little Valley *845*
Toff in a Shed Connoisseur *755*
Toffee Cog Kissingate *837*
Tollbridge Porter Old Sawley *878*
Tolly Roger Cliff Quay *751*
Tom Brown's Dorset *768*
Tom Long Stroud *927*
Tomahawk Chop Hand *807*
Tomahawk Hop Fuzz *820*
  Shiny *914*
TomCat Red Cat *896*
Tommy Box Cwm Rhondda *761*
Tongue Idle *826*
Toon Broon Firebrick *783*
Top Beer Bilbrough Top *715*
Top Dog Stout/Bramble Stout
  Burton Bridge *740*
Top Knot Handsome *808*
Top Notch Brightwater *734*
Top of the Hops Draycott
  (Derbyshire) *770*
Top Sail Pale Ale Skippool
  Creek *917*
Top Totty Slater's *918*
Topaz Blonde S&P *906*
Topaz Session Pale Geeves *792*
Topsail Bays *708*
Torbay Express Riviera *901*
Torpid Expression Idle Valley *826*
Totem American IPA
  Haresfoot *809*
Totnes Stout New Lion *870*
Totty Pot Cheddar *748*
Touch Point Paradigm *883*
Toujours Gyle 59 *804*
Tournament Goff's *795*
Tow'd Navigation Nobby's *872*
Tower IPA Redcastle *898*
Tower SPA Wimbledon *963*
Town Crier Hobsons *818*
Town End Bitter Golcar *795*
Town Mill Best Lyme Regis *850*
Towy Gold Castlegate *746*
TQ9 New Lion *870*
Track Record Prescott *891*
Trade Star Firebrick *783*
Trade Union Pale Ale Three
  Sods *936*
Trade Winds Cairngorm *742*
  Tunnel *945*
Traditional Ale Larkins *840*
  Tonbridge *941*
Traditional Bitter Old Mill *877*
Traditional IPA River Leven *901*
Traditional Mild Old Mill *877*

Award winning pubs

Local CAMRA Pubs of the Year

The Pub of the Year competition is judged by CAMRA members. Each of the CAMRA branches votes for its favourite pub: criteria include the quality and choice of real ale, atmosphere, customer service and value. The pubs listed below are current winners of the title; look out for the ♥ next to the entries in the Guide.

England

♥ Bedfordshire
Three Cups, Bedford
New Inn Ale House & Kitchen,
   Biggleswade
Black Lion, Leighton Buzzard

♥ Berkshire
Nag's Head, Reading
Queen's Head, Wokingham
Rowbarge, Woolhampton

♥ Buckinghamshire
White Horse, Hedgerley
Wetherspoons, Milton Keynes: Central

♥ Cambridgeshire
Drayman's Son, Ely
King of the Belgians, Hartford
Red Lion, Histon
Letter B, Whittlesey

♥ Cheshire
Bhurtpore, Aston
Telford's Warehouse, Chester
Tap & Bottle, Knutsford
Egerton Arms, Little Budworth

♥ Cornwall
Old Ale House, Truro

♥ Cumbria
King's Arms, Barrow-in-Furness
Gosforth Hall Inn, Gosforth
Factory Tap, Kendal
Drovers Rest, Monkhill

♥ Derbyshire
Artisan, Ashbourne
White Hart, Belper
Druid Inn, Birchover
Brunswick Inn, Derby
Queens Arms, Glossop
Miners Arms, Hundall
Burnt Pig, Ilkeston
Arkwright Arms,
   Sutton cum Duckmanton

♥ Devon
Foxhound Inn, Brixton
Red Lion, Exbourne
Tom Cobley Tavern, Spreyton
Rugglestone Inn,
   Widecombe-in-the-Moor

♥ Dorset
Drift, Poole
Saxon Arms, Stratton

♥ Durham
Smiths Arms, Chester-le-Street
Quakerhouse, Darlington
Victoria Inn, Durham
Golden Smog, Stockton-on-Tees

♥ Essex
Red Lion, Belchamp Otten
Hop Beer Shop, Chelmsford
New Inn, Colchester
White Hart, Grays
Compasses, Great Totham
Mawson's Micro Pub,
   Southend-on-Sea
White Hart, Weeley Heath

♥ Gloucestershire & Bristol
Drapers Arms, Bristol: Horfield
Bakers Arms, Broad Campden
Jolly Brewmaster, Cheltenham
Salutation Inn, Ham

♥ Hampshire
Bookshop Alehouse, Southampton
Wonston Arms, Wonston

♥ Herefordshire
Alma Inn, Linton

♥ Hertfordshire
Valiant Trooper, Aldbury
Land of Liberty, Peace & Plenty,
   Heronsgate
Rising Sun, High Wych
Red Lion, Preston
Mermaid, St Albans

♥ Isle of Wight
Castle Inn, Sandown

♥ Kent
New Inn, Canterbury
Lanes, Dover
Past & Present, Gillingham
Bowl Inn, Hastingleigh
Flower Pot, Maidstone
London Tavern, Margate
Paper Mill, Sittingbourne
Queen, South Darenth
Fuggles Beer Cafe, Tunbridge Wells

♥ Lancashire
Pump & Truncheon, Blackpool
Malt 'n' Hops, Chorley
New Inn, Clitheroe
Three Mariners, Lancaster
Cricketers, Ormskirk

♥ Leicestershire
Geese & Fountain, Croxton Kerrial

Queen's Head, Hinckley
Real Ale Classroom, Leicester
White Hart, Loughborough
Boat, Melton Mowbray

♥ Lincolnshire
White Swan, Barton-upon-Humber
Nottingham House, Cleethorpes
Willy's, Cleethorpes
Elm Cottage, Gainsborough
White Hart, Ludford
Green Man, Ropsley
Dambusters Inn, Scampton
Blacksmiths Arms, Skendleby
Jolly Brewer, Stamford

♥ London, Greater
Mirth, Marvel & Maud,
   E17: Walthamstow
Wenlock Arms, N1: Hoxton
Long Pond, SE9: Eltham
Star Tavern, SW1: Belgravia
Grosvenor, W7: Hanwell
Hope, Carshalton
Penny Farthing, Crayford
Castle, Harrow
Olde Mitre Inne, High Barnet
Greyhound, Keston
JJ Moon's, Ruislip Manor
Antelope, Surbiton
Masons Arms, Teddington
Upminster TapRoom, Upminster

♥ Manchester, Greater
Bank Top Brewery Tap, Bolton
Trackside Bar, Bury
Chiverton Tap, Cheadle Hulme
Samuel Oldknow, Marple
Flying Horse Hotel, Rochdale
New Oxford, Salford
Wigan Central, Wigan

♥ Merseyside
Lazy Landlord Ale House, Liscard
Cask, Liverpool: Stoneycroft
Cricketers Arms, St Helens
Tap & Bottles, Southport

♥ Norfolk
Old King's Head, Brockdish
King's Head, Norwich
King's Arms, Shouldham

♥ Northamptonshire
Towcester Mill Brewery Tap,
   Towcester

♥ Northumberland
Office, Morpeth

♥ Nottinghamshire
Horse & Plough, Bingham
Brown Cow, Mansfield
Just Beer Micropub, Newark
Poppy & Pint, West Bridgford
Mallard, Worksop

♥ Oxfordshire
Fleur de Lys, East Hagbourne
Red Lion, Horley
Seven Stars on the Green,
Marsh Baldon
Cross Keys, Thame
Royal Oak, Wantage

♥ Rutland
Fox, North Luffenham

♥ Shropshire
Railwayman's Arms, Bridgnorth
Red Lion, Market Drayton
White Hart, Shifnal
Prince of Wales, Shrewsbury

♥ Somerset
Bird in Hand, Henstridge
Crossways Inn, West Huntspill

♥ Staffordshire
Dog Inn, Burton upon Trent
Crown Joule's, Codsal
Cat Inn, Enville
George & the Dragon, Gnosall
Cross Keys Hotel, Hednesford
Earl Grey Inn, Leek
Horse & Jockey, Lichfield
Dog & Partridge, Marchington
Holy Inadequate,
Stoke-on-Trent: Etruria

♥ Suffolk
Dove, Bury St Edmunds
Stanford Arms, Lowestoft
White Horse, Sweffling

♥ Surrey
Thyme at the Tavern, Chertsey
Wheatsheaf, Esher
Jolly Sailor, Farnham
Garland, Redhill

♥ Sussex, East
Brighton Beer Dispensary,
Brighton
Tower, St Leonards on Sea

♥ Sussex, West
Anchor Tap, Horsham
Inglenook, Pagham
Anchored in Worthing, Worthing

♥ Tyne & Wear
Free Trade Inn, Newcastle upon
Tyne: Byker
Steamboat, South Shields

♥ Warwickshire
Old Bakery, Kenilworth
Lord Hop, Nuneaton
Rugby Tap, Rugby
Wild Boar, Warwick
Norman Knight, Whichford

♥ West Midlands
Inn on the Green, Birmingham:
Acocks Green
Waggon & Horses, Halesowen
Beacon Hotel, Sedgley
Pup & Duckling, Solihull
Fountain Inn, Walsall

♥ Wiltshire
Castle Inn, Bradford-on-Avon
Three Crowns, Chippenham
Red Lion, Cricklade
Wyndham Arms, Salisbury

♥ Worcestershire
Swan, Chaddesley Corbett
Coach & Horses, Harvington
Weavers Real Ale House,
Kidderminster
Plough, Worcester

♥ Yorkshire, East
Butcher's Dog, Driffield
Goodmanham Arms,
Goodmanham
Whalebone, Hull

♥ Yorkshire, North
Little Ale House, Harrogate
George & Dragon, Hudswell
Infant Hercules, Middlesbrough
Sun Inn, Pickering
Stumble Inn, Scarborough
Waggon & Horses, York

♥ Yorkshire, South
Arcade Alehouse, Barnsley
Corner Pin, Doncaster
Doncaster Brewery Tap, Doncaster
Baxter Arms, Fenwick
Kelham Island Tavern,
Sheffield: Kelham Island

♥ Yorkshire, West
Record Cafe, Bradford
West Riding Refreshment Rooms,
Dewsbury
Cross Keys, Halifax: Siddal
King's Head, Huddersfield
Kirkstall Bridge Inn,
Leeds: Kirkstall
King's Arms, Silsden
Black Rock, Wakefield

Wales

♥ Glamorgan
Hopbunker, Cardiff
Golden Lion, Penarth
Pontardawe Inn, Pontardawe
Queen's Hotel, Swansea
Pencelli Hotel, Treorchy

♥ Gwent
Queen's Head, Chepstow
Queen's Head, Cwmyoy

♥ Mid-Wales
New Inn, Bwlch
Arvon Ale House, Llandrindod Wells

♥ North-East Wales
Mold Alehouse, Mold
Bridge End Inn, Ruabon

♥ North-West Wales
Bay Hop, Colwyn Bay
Torrent Walk Hotel, Dolgellau

♥ West Wales
Friends Arms, Carmarthen
Druid Inn, Goginan
Bridge End Inn, Llanychaer

Scotland

♥ Aberdeen & Grampian
Redgarth, Oldmeldrum

♥ Ayrshire & Arran
Wellingtons Bar, Ayr

♥ Borders
Bridge Inn (Trust), Peebles

♥ Dumfries & Galloway
Cavens Arms, Dumfries

♥ Edinburgh & the Lothians
Volunteer Arms (Staggs),
Musselburgh

♥ Greater Glasgow & Clyde Valley
Crown Inn, Biggar
Callum's, Johnstone

♥ Highlands & Western Isles
Kinlochewe Hotel (Beinn Eighe Bar),
Kinlochewe

♥ Kingdom of Fife
Hillend Tavern, Hillend

♥ Loch Lomond, Stirling
& the Trossachs
Corbie Inn, Bo'ness
King's Seat, Dollar

♥ Tayside
Speedwell Bar (Mennie's), Dundee

Northern Ireland
Crown, Belfast

Channel Islands

♥ Guernsey
Mermaid Tavern, Herm Island

♥ Jersey
Lamplighter, St Helier

Isle of Man
White House Hotel, Peel

Readers' recommendations

Suggestions for pubs to be included or excluded

All pubs are regularly surveyed by local branches of the Campaign for Real Ale to ensure they meet the standards required by the *Good Beer Guide*. If you would like to comment on a pub already featured, or on any you think should be featured, please fill in the form below (or a copy of it), and send it to the address indicated. Alternatively, email **gbgeditor@camra.org.uk**. Your views will be passed on to the branch concerned. Please mark your envelope/email with the county where the pub is, which will help us to direct your comments efficiently.

Pub name:

Address:

Reason for recommendation/criticism:

Pub name:

Address:

Reason for recommendation/criticism:

Pub name:

Address:

Reason for recommendation/criticism:

Your name and address:

Please send to: [Name of county] Section, Good Beer Guide, 230 Hatfield Road, St Albans, Hertfordshire AL1 4LW

OUTSIDE INFLUENCES

Outside influences

Italy & Belgium add to the pleasures of beer

Thomas Hardy's Ale, a famous English bottled beer that was treated with the reverence given to vintage French wine, has been restored to ale's hall of fame. It's a barley wine, an historic English style, and the country lost part of its brewing heritage when Hardy's Ale disappeared in 2009.

It appears in this section of the Guide because, despite its English credentials, the brand is now owned by Italians. Interbrau, a beer import and export company based in Padova, is run by the brothers Sandro and Michele Vecchiato.

But Thomas Hardy's Ale is brewed for Interbrau in England, at Meantime Brewery in London, under the care of master brewer Alastair Hook. Alastair trained at both Heriot-Watt and Munich brewing schools. He loves traditional brewing styles, both ale and lager, and is experienced at producing bottle-conditioned beers.

How did a revered beer end up owned by Italians? Like a Thomas Hardy novel, it's a long story. Hardy was born, lived and died in the Dorchester area, at the heart of his ever-expanding, semi-fictional region of Wessex. He loved the area, its people and its beer. In *The Trumpet Major* he famously wrote of Dorchester ale: 'It was of the most beautiful colour that the eye of an artist in beer could desire; full in body, yet brisk as a volcano; piquant, yet without a twang; luminous as an autumn sunset; free from streakiness of taste, but, finally, rather heady. The masses worshipped it, the minor gentry loved it more than wine...'

Thomas Hardy's... classic English ale now owned by Italians but brewed in London

In 1968, the Dorchester brewer Eldridge Pope produced a beer for a literary festival that celebrated the writer's life and marked the 40th anniversary of his death. The beer was 12% alcohol and was aged in sherry casks for nine months before it was bottled. It was meant to be a one-off brew but it aroused such interest that it became an annual vintage.

Waiting for the release of the new vintage each year aroused enormous interest among beer lovers so, there was great anguish in the 1990s when Eldridge Pope made the calamitous decision to divide brewing from retailing. Its pubs were gobbled up by predators and the brewery eventually closed in 2003, with the last vintage of Thomas Hardy's Ale being produced in 1999. The loss of the beer caused distress not only to beer lovers in Britain but also to George Saxon, an American who had successfully imported the beer to the United States for several years.

Saxon's company, Phoenix Imports, acquired the brand and recipe and had the beer resurrected by O'Hanlon's Brewery in Devon. The beer reappeared in 2003 and was met with acclamation, underscored when it won the Supreme Champion award in the 2006 International Beer Challenge held in London.

But once again – and very Hardyesque – hubris was followed by nemesis. O'Hanlon's said it took so long to make a batch of Hardy's Ale that it held up its mainstream beers and it stopped production in 2009.

Another rescue bid followed, with Interbrau's Vecchiato brothers buying Thomas Hardy's from George Saxon in 2012. After several years of development, the first new vintage was produced in 2015. Tasted in Milan in September 2016 (after the last edition of this Guide was published) it was superb: smoky, with blackcurrant fruitiness, burnt grain and peppery hops.

The new Hardy's beer is brewed with pale and crystal malts and hopped with English Challenger, Goldings and Northdown, with Styrian Goldings. The finished beer has 75 units of bitterness. Primary fermentation lasts for 2½ weeks as the yeast grapples with such a large amount of malt sugar. The beer then enjoys three months' secondary fermentation and ageing, followed by one month of cold conditioning and nine months in bottle before it's released. And it will improve with age – for up to 25 years, it is claimed.

1025

Interbrau plans to launch the beer in London early in 2018. When you acquire a bottle, it should, perhaps, best be sipped and savoured while reading Hardy's novel *The Return of the Native*.

New taste for flavours of old

The first version of Thomas Hardy's Ale was aged in sherry casks, which gives it a powerful link to Belgian lambic beers that are now being replicated by several British brewers under the name of 'sour'. Lambic – and its blended version known as gueuze – is made by wild or spontaneous fermentation and is the oldest beer style in the world, dating from long before brewers and scientists were able to develop pure strains of yeast.

A mash of malted barley and wheat is boiled with hops and the liquid is left in large open vessels at the top of breweries where windows are left open to encourage wild yeasts to enter and gorge on the sugars in the liquid, starting the conversion to alcohol.

The liquid is then pumped to giant oak casks obtained from the port and wine industries and left to age for a year or more. During that time, the beer is attacked by other wild yeasts and bacteria trapped in the wood that create further fermentation, flavour and aroma. To add to the character of the beer, brewers also add fruits, such as cherries and raspberries, whose sugars create yet further fermentation and result in beers called kriek (cherry) and framboise (raspberry).

A number of British brewers are now making what Americans call sour beers, or sours for short – a term disliked by Belgian lambic brewers who say their beers are acidic, like Brut champagne, rather than sour. Wild Beer in Somerset specialises in sour beers, with links to not only lambic but to the Berliner Weisse style of 'sour dough' brewing. Wild Beer uses yeasts found in surrounding apple orchards and then brews and ages in wood. Co-founder Andrew Cooper says the production of sour beers is about 'trying to add layers of intrigue and complexity with time spent barrel-ageing – the beers are ready when they're ready.'

His Sourdough is brewed with a 58 year-old sour dough culture and the mash goes straight into oak fermenters. It receives five months of maturation and the beer that emerges has an acidic, lemon and toasted note not dissimilar to champagne.

Evin O'Riordan at the Kernel Brewery in London's Bermondsey, is renowned for his classy IPAs but he also produces a memorable London Sour based on the Berliner Weisse model: the beer is tart, fruity and quenching.

A beer style similar in many ways to both lambic and Berliner Weisse is Gose from Leipzig. Gose has only recently come to attention as its home city was lost from view during the time of the East German regime. Gose is also made by the sour dough principle but it has its own idiosyncratic character due to the addition of salt, which acts as both a preservative and a flavour enhancer. The beer is sour, acidic and naturally salty.

Magic Rock Brewing in Huddersfield make a number of sour dough and Gose beers, including one that has the addition of gooseberries for an additional tart and fruity note.

Martin Warren at Poppyland Brewery in Cromer, Norfolk, also brews sour sough and Gose-style beers. In his case, he forages on the beaches and cliffs of the seaside town to add herbs, plants and spices to his brews. He even makes a Crab Saison – 'Why not?' he asks. 'Cromer is famous for its crabs!'

Saison is yet another European style finding favour in both the UK and US. It comes from Wallonia, the French-speaking region of Belgium. It started life as a beer brewed by farmers to refresh their workers during the harvest period, using barley and hops from the surrounding fields. In an age of massively hopped pale ales and IPAs, the rich malty character of a Saison offers welcome balance and belief in the importance of grain as well as bitterness in beer

Further British interpretations of the Saison style are produced by Black Flag, Langham and Twisted Barrel.

Kernel's London Sour: a British take on Berliner Weisse

Poppyland's beers are influenced by traditional European styles

Books for beer lovers

CAMRA Books publishes a range of other titles on beer, pubs and brewing. Some of our latest titles are detailed below. You can buy our books – and a selection of beer-related titles from other publishers – from us direct, by visiting our online bookshop at **www.camra.org.uk/books** or calling **01727 867201**. Discounts are available for CAMRA members.

CAMRA'S Home-Brewing Problem Solver
Erik Lars Myers

Real ale and other craft beers have become increasingly popular over the past few years, and as a result more people have been compelled to try making their own home-brew. However, while the concept behind making beer is simple, the execution can at times seem complex and confusing. *CAMRA's Home-brewing Problem Solver* provides the information you need to nip problems in the bud – and, better still, to avoid them in the first place.

RRP £12.99 ISBN: 978-1-85249-347-9

Wild Pub Walks   Daniel Neilson

This book is aimed at hill walkers who enjoy long days out followed by some refreshing beer in a welcoming pub. Join the author on 22 walks in beautiful remote or mountain landscapes, each with one or more great pubs – often with historical significance – at journey's end. The areas covered are: Peak District; Lake District; Highlands/Islands; Scottish Borders; Snowdonia; Pembrokeshire/South Wales; North York Moors National Park; and Yorkshire Dales National Park. The walks vary in the level of challenge, from long walks in lower-lying areas to Grade 1 scrambles.

RRP £11.99 ISBN 978-1-85249-340-0

Historic Coaching Inns of the Great North Road   Roger Protz

The Great North Road is a UK icon, the Route 66 of Britain, but instead of gas stations and diners, we have magnificent coaching inns. Taking in the history of these buildings, as well as the literature that has celebrated them – from Charles Dickens through to JB Priestley – Roger Protz describes these coaching houses with an expert and discerning eye, producing not only a great pub guide but also a gazetteer of the history and culture that are draped along this iconic road.

RRP £12.99 ISBN: 978-1-85249-339-4

Britain's Best Real Heritage Pubs
(2nd edition)   Geoff Brandwood

This definitive listing is the result of 25 years' research by CAMRA to discover pubs that are either unaltered in 70 years or have features of truly national historic importance. Fully revised, this latest edition boasts updated information and a new set of evocative illustrations. Among the 260 pubs, there are unspoilt country locals, Victorian drinking palaces and mighty roadhouses. The book has features describing how the pub developed, what's distinctive about pubs in different parts of the country, and how pubs provided take-out sales in the pre-supermarket era.

RRP £9.99 ISBN: 978-1-85249-334-9

CAMRA'S Beer Anthology
Edited by Roger Protz

A highly quaffable anthology of excerpts from literature, television, film and music about beer, pubs and drinking. Roger Protz, in themed chapters, demonstrates how deeply beer and pubs are woven into the DNA of British culture. The book runs the gamut of culture, from *Eastenders* to Dickens, and is ideal for the casual reader looking for beer-based entertainment or for the more studious one who wants a sense of how Britain's national drink – and its consumption – have been represented in many media through history.

RRP £9.99 ISBN: 978-1-85249-333-2

So You Want to Be a Beer Expert
Jeff Evans

More people than ever are searching for an understanding of what makes a great beer. This book meets that demand by presenting a hands-on course in beer appreciation, leading to an understanding of world beer styles, beer flavours, how beer is made, the ingredients, buying and storing beer, and more. The novelty of this book is that it doesn't just relate the facts, but helps readers reach conclusions for themselves, with interactive tasting sessions that show readers – through their own tasting experiences – what beer is all about.

RRP £12.99 ISBN: 978-1-85249-322-6

CAMRA's 101 Beer Days Out
(Revised edition)   Tim Hampson

101 Beer Days Out is the perfect handbook for the beer tourist wanting to explore beer, pubs and brewing in the UK. From brewery tours to rail-ale trails, beer festivals to hop farms, brewing courses to historic pubs, Britain has a huge variety of beer experiences to explore and enjoy. *101 Beer Days Out* is ordered geographically, so you can easily find a beer day out wherever you are in Britain, and includes full visitor information, maps and colour photography, with detailed information on opening hours, local landmarks and public transport links to make planning easy.

RRP £12.99 ISBN 978-1-85249-328-8

London's Best Beer, Pubs & Bars
(2nd edition)   Des de Moor

The essential guide to London beer, *London's Best Beer, Pubs & Bars* is packed with detailed maps and easy-to-use listings to help you find the best places to enjoy perfect pints in the capital. Laid out by area, the book will be your companion in exploring the best pubs serving the best British and world beers. Additional features include descriptions of London's rich history of brewing and the city's vibrant modern brewing scene, where brewery numbers have more than doubled in the last three years. The venue listings are fully illustrated with colour photographs and include a variety of real ale pubs, bars and other outlets, with detailed information to make planning any excursion quick and easy.

'...meticulously researched and open-minded' Will Hawkes, *The Independent*

RRP £12.99 ISBN 978-1-85249-323-3

Good Beer Guide digital editions

The *Good Beer Guide* is also available in digital formats, including an all-new mobile app, an e-book and a sat-nav download. Together, these offer the perfect solution to pub-finding on the move. To discover more, visit **www.camra.org.uk/gbg**.

NEW! Good Beer Guide app

Launched in August 2017, the all-new Good Beer Guide mobile app provides detailed information on the latest *Good Beer Guide* pubs, breweries and beers wherever you are or wherever you are going. Social media integration lets you share your beer experiences with other users. Features include:†

- Search results with full pub descriptions and detailed visitor information for 4,500 pubs listed in the *Good Beer Guide* plus basic information for 31,000 other real ale pubs all over the UK, collated by CAMRA

- Detailed information on all UK real-ale breweries and their regular beers along with hundreds of CAMRA tasting notes

- Custom functions allow you to mark your favourite pubs, breweries and beers and write and share your own personal reviews

- Pump-clip recognition feature along with photo capture

- Social media functions and improved search functionality for non-subscribers

Download on the App Store

GET IT ON Google Play

For more information visit **www.camra.org.uk/gbg-mobile**

†App is free to download with an in-app subscription required for full features. NOTE: Standard network charges apply when using the app.

Good Beer Guide e-book

The *Good Beer Guide 2018* is available as an e-book in ePUB and Kindle formats from major online e-book retailers. Key features include:

- Portable, electronic version of the printed Guide

- Fully interactive, searchable content

- Full-colour* features and images from the printed edition, as well as complete pubs and breweries listings

- Active e-mail and web links within entries*

- Postcode links to Google maps to help you navigate*

*Where e-reader allows

ePUB   **amazon**kindle

Available on the iBookstore

Good Beer Guide POI files

Priced at just £2.99, the Good Beer Guide POI (Points of Interest) file allows users of TomTom, Garmin and Navman sat-nav systems to find the locations of all 4,500 current *Good Beer Guide* pubs and all the UK's real-ale breweries and plan routes to them.

For more information and to download visit **www.camra.org.uk/gbg-sat-nav**

Tap into Britain's best pubs

with our NEW Good Beer Guide app!

Our new app puts thousands of
pubs and beers at your fingertips
Download for FREE today

CAMPAIGN
FOR
REAL ALE